Collins German Dictionary

Collins
German
Dictionary

HarperCollins Publishers
Westerhill Road
Bishopbriggs
Glasgow
G64 2QT
Great Britain

First edition 2007

Reprint 10 9 8 7 6 5 4 3 2 1 0

ISBN 978-0-00-779341-9

www.collins.co.uk

A catalogue record for this book is available from the British Library

Designed by Mark Thomson

Typeset by Wordcraft Ltd, Glasgow

Printed in Great Britain by Clays Ltd, St Ives plc

Acknowledgements
We would like to thank those authors and publishers who kindly gave permission for copyright material to be used in the Collins Word Web. We would also like to thank Times Newspapers Ltd for providing valuable data.

Inhalt

Contents

GESAMTLEITUNG/PUBLISHING DIRECTOR
Lorna Sinclair Knight

PROJEKTLEITUNG/PROJECT MANAGEMENT
Maree Airlie

LEITENDE REDAKTEURE/SENIOR EDITORS
Horst Kopleck, Joyce Littlejohn

MITARBEITER/CONTRIBUTIONS FROM
Dagmar Förtsch, Hildegard Pesch, Veronika Schnorr, Gisela Moohan, Ulrike Seeberger, Elspeth Anderson, Val McNulty, Eva Vennebusch, Robin Sawers, Ilse MacLean, Beate Wengel

DATENVERARBEITUNG/COMPUTING STAFF
Thomas Callan

Einleitung

Sie möchten Englisch lernen oder vielleicht bereits vorhandene Kenntnisse vertiefen. Sie möchten sich auf Englisch ausdrücken, englische Texte lesen oder übersetzen, oder Sie möchten sich ganz einfach mit Englisch sprechenden Menschen unterhalten können. Ganz gleich ob Sie Englisch an der Schule oder an der Universität lernen, in einem Büro oder in einem Unternehmen tätig sind: Sie haben sich den richtigen Begleiter für Ihre Arbeit ausgesucht! Dieses Buch ist der ideale Helfer, wenn Sie sich in englischer Sprache ausdrücken und verständlich machen wollen, ob Sie nun sprechen oder schreiben. Unser Wörterbuch ist ganz bewusst praktisch und modern, es räumt vor allem der Alltagssprache und der Sprache, wie sie Ihnen in Zeitungen und Nachrichten, im Geschäftsleben, im Büro und im Urlaub begegnet, großen Raum ein. Wie in allen unseren Wörterbüchern haben wir das Hauptgewicht auf zeitgenössische Sprache und idiomatische Redewendungen gelegt.

Wie man dieses Buch benutzt
Im Folgenden geben wir einige Erklärungen darüber, wie die Einträge Ihres Wörterbuchs aufgebaut sind. Unser Ziel: Wir wollen Ihnen so viel Information wie möglich bieten, ohne dabei an Klarheit und Verständlichkeit einzubüßen.

Die Wörterbucheinträge
Ein typischer Eintrag in Ihres Wörterbuchs besteht aus folgenden Elementen:

Lautschrift
Wie die meisten modernen Wörterbücher geben wir die Aussprache mit Zeichen an, die zum „internationalen phonetischen Alphabet" gehören. Weiter unten (auf den Seiten xiv) finden Sie eine vollständige Liste der Zeichen, die in diesem System benutzt werden. Die Aussprache englischer Wörter geben wir auf der englisch-deutschen Seite unmittelbar hinter dem jeweiligen Wort in eckigen Klammern an. Die deutsche Aussprache erscheint im deutsch-englischen Teil ebenfalls auf diese Weise unmittelbar hinter den Worteinträgen. Allerdings wird sie nicht immer angegeben, zum Beispiel bei zusammengesetzten Wörtern wie „Liebesbrief", deren Bestandteile schon an anderer Stelle im Wörterbuch zu finden sind.

Grammatik-Information
Alle Wörter gehören zu einer der folgenden grammatischen Klassen: Substantiv, Verb, Adjektiv, Pronomen, Artikel, Konjunktion, Präposition, Interjektion, Abkürzung. Substantive können im Deutschen männlich, weiblich oder sächlich sein. Verben können transitiv, intransitiv, reflexiv oder auch unpersönlich sein. Die Wortart folgt auf die Lautschrift und ist in *Kursivschrift* angegeben. Wo bei Übersetzungen eine Geschlechtsangabe erforderlich ist, wird diese ebenfalls in *Kursivschrift* gegeben.

Oft gehören Wörter zu zwei oder mehr grammatischen Klassen. So kann das deutsche Wort **gut** ein Adjektiv („good") oder auch ein Adverb („well") sein, und das englische Wort **spell** ist sowohl ein Substantiv („Zauber") als auch ein Verb („schreiben, buchstabieren"). Das Verb **reden** ist manchmal transitiv, d. h. es hat ein Objekt („sie redet Unsinn"), manchmal intransitiv, d.h. es wird ohne Objekt gebraucht („er redet ständig vom Wetter"). Zur besseren Übersichtlichkeit sind verschiedene Wortarten durch das Symbol ▹ abgegrenzt; alle Beispielsätze werden dann unter den entsprechenden grammatischen Kategorien gegeben.

Bedeutungsunterschiede
Die meisten Wörter haben mehr als eine Bedeutung. So kann z.B. **Rad** einen Teil eines Autos oder Fahrrads bezeichnen, aber auch ein Wort für das Fahrrad selbst sein. Andere Wörter haben je nach Kontext verschiedene Übersetzungen; so bedeutet das Verb **to recede** abhängig vom Subjekt des Satzes entweder „zurückgehen" oder „verschwinden". Damit Sie in jedem Zusammenhang immer die richtige Übersetzung finden, haben wir die Einträge nach Bedeutungen eingeteilt: jede Kategorie wird durch einen „Verwendungshinweis" bestimmt, der *kursiv* gedruckt ist und in

Klammern steht. Die beiden Beispiele von oben sehen dann so aus:

Rad *nt* wheel; (*Fahrrad*) bike
recede *vi* (*tide*) zurückgehen; (*lights etc*) verschwinden

Andere Wörter haben in verschiedenen Sachzusammenhängen unterschiedliche Bedeutungen. Das Wort **Rezept** z. B. bezeichnet eine Koch- oder Backanleitung, bezieht sich in medizinischen Zusammenhängen jedoch auf ein ärztlich verordnetes Medikament. Wir zeigen Ihnen, welche Übersetzung Sie auswählen sollten, indem wir wieder in Klammern solche Fachgebiete in *kursiven* Buchstaben angeben, mit dem Anfangsbuchstaben großgeschrieben, im vorigen Fall *Koch* als Abkürzung für *Kochen* und *Med* als Abkürzung für *Medizin*:

Rezept *nt* (*Koch*) recipe; (*Med*) prescription

Sie finden eine Liste aller in diesem Wörterbuch benutzten Abkürzungen für solche Sachgebiete auf den Seiten x–xii.

Übersetzungen
Die meisten deutschen Wörter können mit einem einzigen englischen Wort übersetzt werden und umgekehrt. Aber manchmal gibt es eine solche genaue Entsprechung nicht. In diesen Fällen haben wir eine ungefähre Entsprechung angegeben, gekennzeichnet durch ≈. Dies ist z. B. der Fall bei **Gymnasium** mit den englischen bzw. amerikanischen Äquivalenten „grammar school" und „high school", die aufgrund der unterschiedlichen Ausbildungssysteme lediglich ungefähre Entsprechungen sein können.

Gymnasium *nt* ≈ grammar school (*Brit*), high school (US)

Manchmal kann man nicht einmal ein ungefähres Äquivalent finden. Besonders oft ist das der Fall beim Essen, insbesondere bei lokalen Spezialitäten wie dieser schottischen Speise:

haggis (*Scot*) *n Gericht aus gehackten Schafsinnereien und Haferschrot, im Schafsmagen gekocht*

Hier wird statt einer Übersetzung (die es einfach gar nicht gibt) eine Erklärung gegeben, die durch *Kursivschrift* als solche kenntlich gemacht ist.

Im Deutschen wissen Sie, in welcher Situation Sie den Ausdruck **ich bin pleite** verwenden würden, wann Sie **ich bin knapp bei Kasse** sagen und wann **ich bin in Geldschwierigkeiten.** Wenn Sie jedoch Englisch verstehen oder selbst sprechen wollen, ist es wichtig zu wissen, welcher Ausdruck etwa höflich ist und welcher nicht. Um Ihnen hierbei zu helfen, haben wir für umgangssprachliche Ausdrücke die Kennzeichnung (*umg*) bzw. (*inf*) verwendet. Besonders anstößige Ausdrücke sind zusätzlich mit einem Ausrufezeichen versehen, also (*umg!*) bzw. (*inf!*), um den Benutzer zu warnen, diese nur mit großer Vorsicht zu verwenden. Angaben wie (*umg*) oder (*inf*) werden bei Übersetzungen in der Regel nicht wiederholt, wenn das Sprachniveau der Zielsprache dem der Ausgangssprache entspricht.

Im Text werden einige Einträge, wie etwa **to be** und **to do** und ihre deutschen Entsprechungen **sein** und **machen**, als Grundelemente der Sprache besonders ausführlich behandelt.

Introduction

You may be starting to learn German, or you may wish to extend your knowledge of the language. Perhaps you want to read and study German books, newspapers and magazines, or perhaps simply have a conversation with German speakers. Whatever the reason, whether you're a student, a tourist or want to use German for business, this is the ideal book to help you understand and communicate. This modern, user-friendly dictionary gives priority to everyday vocabulary and the language of current affairs, business and tourism. As in all Collins dictionaries, the emphasis is firmly placed on contemporary language and expressions.

How To Use This Dictionary

You will find below an outline of the way in which information is presented in your dictionary. Our aim is to give you the maximum amount of information whilst still providing a text which is clear and user-friendly.

Entries

A typical entry in your dictionary will be made up of the following elements:

Phonetic transcription

Phonetics appear in square brackets immediately after the headword. They are shown using the International Phonetic Alphabet (IPA), and a complete list of the symbols used in this system can be found on pages xiv and xv.

Grammatical information

All words belong to one of the following parts of speech: noun, verb, adjective, adverb, pronoun, article, conjunction, preposition, exclamation, abbreviation. Nouns can be singular or plural and, in German, masculine, feminine or neuter. Verbs can be transitive, intransitive, reflexive or impersonal. Parts of speech appear in *italics* immediately after the phonetic spelling of the headword. The gender of the translation appears in *italics* immediately following the key element of the translation.

Often a word can have more than one part of speech. Just as the English word **next** can be an adjective or an adverb, the German word **gut** can be an adjective ("good") or an adverb ("well"). In the same way the verb **to walk** is sometimes transitive, i.e. it takes an object ("to walk the dog") and sometimes intransitive, i.e. it doesn't take an object ("to walk to school"). To help you find the meaning you are looking for quickly and for clarity of presentation, the different part of speech categories are separated by an open white triangle ▷.

Meaning divisions

Most words have more than one meaning. Take, for example, **punch** which can be, amongst other things, a blow with the fist or an object used for making holes. Other words are translated differently depending on the context in which they are used. The intransitive verb **to recede**, for example, can be translated by "zurückgehen" or "verschwinden" depending on *what* is receding. To help you select the most appropriate translation in every context, entries are divided according to meaning. Each different meaning is introduced by an "indicator" in *italics* and in brackets. Thus, the examples given above will be shown as follows:

> **punch** *n* (*blow*) Schlag *m*; (*tool*) Locher *m*
> **recede** *vi* (*tide*) zurückgehen; (*lights etc*) verschwinden

Likewise, some words can have a different meaning when used to talk about a specific subject area or field. For example, **bishop**, which in a religious context means a high-ranking clergyman, is also the name of a chess piece. To show English speakers which translation to use, we have added "subject field labels" in italics with initial capitals and in brackets, in this case (*Rel*) and (*Chess*):

bishop *n* (*Rel*) Bischof *m*; (*Chess*) Läufer *m*

Field labels are often shortened to save space. You will find a complete list of abbreviations used in the dictionary on pages x to xii

Translations
Most English words have a direct translation in German and vice versa, as shown in the examples given above. Sometimes, however, no exact equivalent exists in the target language. In such cases we have given an approximate equivalent, indicated by the sign ≈. Such is the case of **high school**, the German equivalent of which is "Oberschule *f*". This is not an exact translation since the systems of the two countries in question are quite different:

high school *n* ≈ Oberschule *f*

On occasion it is impossible to find even an approximate equivalent. This may be the case, for example, with the names of culinary specialities like this German cake:

Streuselkuchen *m cake with crumble topping*

Here the translation (which doesn't exist) is replaced by an explanation. For increased clarity the explanation, or "gloss", is shown in *italics*.

Register
In English you instinctively know when to say **I'm broke** *or* **I'm a bit short of cash** and when to say **I don't have any money**. When you are trying to understand someone who is speaking German, however, or when you yourself try to speak German, it is especially important to know what is polite and what is less so. To help you with this, we have added the register labels (*umg*) and (*inf*) to colloquial or offensive expressions. Those expressions which are particularly vulgar are also given an exclamation mark (*umg!*) or (*inf!*), warning you to use them with extreme care. Please note that the register labels (*umg*) and (*inf*) are not repeated in the target language when the register of the translation matches that of the word or phrase being translated.

Some words in the text, such as **be** and **do** or their German equivalents **sein** and **machen**, have been given special treatment because they form the basic elements of the language. This extra help will ensure that you know how to use these complex words with confidence.

Abkürzungen		Abbreviations
Abkürzung	*abk, abbr*	abbreviation
Adjektiv	*adj*	adjective
Verwaltung	*Admin*	administration
Adverb	*adv*	adverb
Landwirtschaft	*Agr*	agriculture
Akkusativ	*akk, acc*	accusative
Anatomie	*Anat*	anatomy
Architektur	*Archit*	architecture
Artikel	*art*	article
Kunst	*Art*	
Astrologie	*Astrol*	astrology
Astronomie	*Astron*	astronomy
attributiv	*attrib*	attributive
Kraftfahrzeuge	*Aut*	automobiles
Hilfsverb	*aux*	auxiliary
Luftfahrt	*Aviat*	aviation
Bergbau	*Bergb*	mining
besonders	*bes*	especially
Biologie	*Biol*	biology
Botanik	*Bot*	botany
britisch	*Brit*	British
Kartenspiel	*Cards*	
Chemie	*Chem*	chemistry
Film	*Cine*	cinema
Handel	*Comm*	commerce
Komparativ	*comp*	comparative
Computer	*Comput*	computers
Konjunktion	*conj*	conjunction
Bauwesen	*Constr*	building
zusammengesetztes Wort	*cpd*	compound
Kochen und Backen	*Culin*	cooking
Dativ	*dat*	dative
bestimmt	*def*	definite
diminutiv	*dimin*	diminutive
dekliniert	*dekl*	declined
kirchlich	*Eccl*	ecclesiastical
Volkswirtschaft	*Econ*	economics
Eisenbahn	*Eisenb*	railways
Elektrizität	*Elek, Elec*	electricity
besonders	*esp*	especially
und so weiter	*etc*	et cetera
etwas	*etw*	something
Euphemismus	*euph*	euphemism
Ausruf	*excl*	exclamation
Femininum	*f*	feminine
übertragen	*fig*	figurative
Film	*Film*	cinema
Finanzen	*Fin*	finance
formell	*form*	formal
'phrasal verb', bei dem Partikel und Verb nicht getrennt werden können	*fus*	fused: phrasal verb where the particle cannot be separated from the verb
gehoben	*geh*	elevated

Genitiv	*gen*	genitive
Geografie	*Geog*	geography
Geologie	*Geol*	geology
Geometrie	*Geom*	geometry
Grammatik	*Gram*	grammar
Geschichte	*Hist*	history
scherzhaft	*hum*	humorous
Imperfekt	*imperf*	imperfect
unpersönlich	*impers*	impersonal
unbestimmt	*indef*	indefinite
umgangssprachlich	*inf*	informal
untrennbares Verb	*insep*	inseparable
Interjektion	*interj*	interjection
Interrogativ	*interrog*	interrogative
unveränderlich	*inv*	invariable
unregelmäßig	*irreg*	irregular
jemand	*jd*	somebody
jemandem	*jdm*	(to) somebody
jemanden	*jdn*	somebody
jemandes	*jds*	somebody's
Rechtswesen	*Jur*	law
Kartenspiel	*Karten*	cards
Kochen und Backen	*Koch*	cooking
Komparativ	*komp*	comparative
Konjunktion	*konj*	conjunction
Rechtswesen	*Law*	law
Sprachwissenschaft	*Ling*	linguistics
wörtlich	*lit*	literal
literarisch	*liter*	literary
Literatur	*Liter*	literature
Maskulinum	*m*	masculine
Mathematik	*Math*	mathematics
Medizin	*Med*	medicine
Meteorologie	*Met*	meteorology
Militärwesen	*Mil*	military
Bergbau	*Min*	mining
Musik	*Mus*	music
Substantiv	*n*	noun
nautisch	*Naut*	nautical
Nominativ	*nom*	nominative
norddeutsch	*Nordd*	North Germany
Neutrum	*nt*	neuter
Zahlwort	*num*	numeral
Objekt	*obj*	object
oder	*od*	or
veraltet	*old*	
sich	*o.s.*	oneself
österreichisch	*Österr*	Austria
Parlament	*Parl*	parliament
pejorativ	*pej*	pejorative
Person/persönlich	*pers*	person/personal
Pharmazie	*Pharm*	pharmacy
Fotografie	*Phot*	photography
Physik	*Phys*	physics
Physiologie	*Physiol*	physiology

Plural	*pl*	plural
Politik	*Pol*	politics
possessiv	*poss*	possessive
Partizip Perfekt	*pp*	past participle
Präfix	*präf, pref*	prefix
Präposition	*präp, prep*	preposition
Präsens	*präs, pres*	present
Pronomen	*pron*	pronoun
Psychologie	*Psych*	psychology
Imperfekt	*pt*	past tense
Radio	*Radio*	radio
Eisenbahn	*Rail*	railways
Religion	*Rel*	religion
Relativ-	*rel*	relative
Rundfunk	*Rundf*	broadcasting
jemand (-en, -en)	*sb*	somebody
Schulwesen	*Sch*	school
Naturwissenschaft	*Sci*	science
Schulwesen	*Scol*	school
schottisch	*Scot*	Scottish
Singular	*sing*	singular
Skisport	*Ski*	skiing
etwas	*sth*	something
Süddeutschland	*Südd*	South German
Suffix	*suff*	suffix
Superlativ	*superl*	superlative
Technik	*Tech*	technology
Telekommunikation	*Tel*	telecommunications
Theater	*Theat*	theatre
Fernsehen	*TV*	television
Typografie	*Typ*	typography
umgangssprachlich	*umg*	colloquial
Universität	*Univ*	university
unpersönlich	*unpers*	impersonal
unregelmäßig	*unreg*	irregular
untrennbar	*untr*	inseparable
unveränderlich	*unver*	invariable
(nord)amerikanisch	*US*	(North)American
gewöhnlich	*usu*	usually
und so weiter	*usw*	et cetera
Verb	*vb*	verb
intransitives Verb	*vi*	intransitive verb
reflexives Verb	*vr*	reflexive verb
transitives Verb	*vt*	transitive verb
Wirtschaft	*Wirts*	economy
Zoologie	*Zool*	zoology
zusammengesetztes Wort	*zW*	compound
ungefähre Entsprechung	≈	cultural equivalent
eingetragenes Warenzeichen	®	registered trademark

German Noun Endings

After many noun entries on the German-English side of the dictionary, you will find two pieces of grammatical information, separated by commas, to help you with the declension of the noun, e.g. **-, -n** or **-(e)s, -e**. The first item shows you the genitive singular form, and the second gives the plural form. The hyphen stands for the word itself and the other letters are endings. Sometimes an umlaut is shown over the hyphen, which means an umlaut must be placed on the vowel of the word, e.g.:

DICTIONARY ENTRY	GENITIVE SINGULAR	PLURAL
Mann *m* **-(e)s, ¨-er**	**Mannes** *or* **Manns**	**Männer**
Jacht *f* **-, -en**	**Jacht**	**Jachten**

This information is not given when the noun has one of the regular German noun endings below, and you should refer to this table in such cases. Similarly, genitive and plural endings are not shown when the German entry is a compound consisting of two or more words which are to be found elsewhere in the dictionary, since the compound form takes the endings of the LAST word of which it is formed, e.g.:

for **Nebenstraße** *see* **Straße**
for **Schneeball** *see* **Ball**

Regular German Noun Endings

NOM	GEN	PL
-ant *m*	-anten	-anten
-anz *f*	-anz	-anzen
-ar *m*	-ar(e)s	-are
-chen *nt*	-chens	-chen
-ei *f*	-ei	-eien
-elle *f*	-elle	-ellen
-ent *m*	-enten	-enten
-enz *f*	-enz	-enzen
-ette *f*	-ette	-etten
-eur *m*	-eurs	-eure
-euse *f*	-euse	-eusen
-heit *f*	-heit	-heiten
-ie *f*	-ie	-ien
-ik *f*	-ik	-iken
-in *f*	-in	-innen
-ine *f*	-ine	-inen
-ion *f*	-ion	-ionen
-ist *m*	-isten	-isten
-ium *nt*	-iums	-ien
-ius *m*	-ius	-iusse
-ive *f*	-ive	-iven
-keit *f*	-keit	-keiten
-lein *nt*	-leins	-lein
-ling *m*	-lings	-linge
-ment *nt*	-ments	-mente
-mus *m*	-mus	-men
-schaft *f*	-schaft	-schaften
-tät *f*	-tät	-täten
-tor *m*	-tors	-toren
-ung *f*	-ung	-ungen
-ur *f*	-ur	-uren

Phonetic Symbols

Lautschrift

NB: All vowels sounds are approximate only.

NB: Alle Vokallaute sind nur ungefähre Entsprechungen.

Vowels		Vokale
m*a*tt	[a]	
F*ah*ne	[aː]	
Vat*er*	[ər]	
	[ɑː]	c*al*m, p*ar*t
	[æ]	s*a*t
R*en*dezvous	[ã]	
Ch*an*ce	[aː]	
	[ɑ̃ː]	cli*en*tele
*E*tage	[e]	
S*ee*le, M*eh*l	[eː]	
W*ä*sche, B*e*tt	[ɛ]	*e*gg
z*äh*len	[ɛː]	
T*ei*nt	[ɛ̃ː]	
mach*e*	[ə]	*a*bove
	[əː]	b*ur*n, *ear*n
K*i*ste	[ɪ]	p*i*t, awfull*y*
V*i*tamin	[i]	
Z*ie*l	[iː]	p*ea*t
*O*ase	[o]	
*o*ben	[oː]	
Champign*on*	[õ]	
Sal*on*	[õː]	
M*o*st	[ɔ]	c*o*t
	[ɔː]	b*or*n, j*aw*
*ö*konomisch	[ø]	
bl*ö*d	[øː]	
G*ö*ttin	[œ]	
	[ʌ]	h*u*t
z*u*letzt	[u]	p*u*t
M*u*t	[uː]	p*oo*l
M*u*tter	[ʊ]	
Ph*y*sik	[y]	
K*ü*bel	[yː]	
S*ü*nde	[ʏ]	

Diphthongs		Diphthonge
Styling	[ai]	
weit	[aɪ]	buy, die, my
umbauen	[au]	house, now
Haus	[aʊ]	
	[eɪ]	pay, mate
	[ɛə]	pair, mare
	[əu]	no, boat
	[ɪə]	mere, shear
Heu, Häuser	[ɔʏ]	
	[ɔɪ]	boy, coin
	[uə]	tour, poor

Consonants		Konsonanten
Ball	[b]	ball
mich	[ç]	
	[tʃ]	child
fern	[f]	field
gern	[g]	good
Hand	[h]	hand
ja	[j]	yet, million
	[dʒ]	just
Kind	[k]	kind, catch
links, Pult	[l]	left, little
matt	[m]	mat
Nest	[n]	nest
lang	[ŋ]	long
Paar	[p]	put
rennen	[r]	run
fast, fassen	[s]	sit
Chef, Stein, Schlag	[ʃ]	shall
Tafel	[t]	tab
	[θ]	thing
	[ð]	this
wer	[v]	very
	[w]	wet
Loch	[x]	loch
fix	[ks]	box
singen	[z]	pods, zip
Zahn	[ts]	
genieren	[ʒ]	measure

Other signs		Andere Zeichen
glottal stop	|	Knacklaut
main stress	[ˈ]	Hauptton
long vowel	[ː]	Längezeichen

German Irregular Verbs

* with "sein"

INFINITIV	PRÄSENS 2., 3. SINGULAR	PRÄTERITUM	PARTIZIP PERFEKT
abwägen	wägst ab, wägt ab	wog ab	abgewogen
ausbedingen	bedingst aus, bedingt aus	bedang *od* bedingte aus	ausbedungen
backen	bäckst, bäckt	backte *od* buk	gebacken
befehlen	befiehlst, befiehlt	befahl	befohlen
beginnen	beginnst, beginnt	begann	begonnen
beißen	beißt, beißt	biss	gebissen
bergen	birgst, birgt	barg	geborgen
bersten*	birst, birst	barst	geborsten
betrügen	betrügst, betrügt	betrog	betrogen
bewegen	bewegst, bewegt	bewog	bewogen
biegen	biegst, biegt	bog	gebogen
bieten	bietest, bietet	bot	geboten
binden	bindest, bindet	band	gebunden
bitten	bittest, bittet	bat	gebeten
blasen	bläst, bläst	blies	geblasen
bleiben*	bleibst, bleibt	blieb	geblieben
braten	brätst, brät	briet	gebraten
brechen*	brichst, bricht	brach	gebrochen
brennen	brennst, brennt	brannte	gebrannt
bringen	bringst, bringt	brachte	gebracht
denken	denkst, denkt	dachte	gedacht
dreschen	drischst, drischt	drosch	gedroschen
dringen*	dringst, dringt	drang	gedrungen
dürfen	darfst, darf	durfte	gedurft
empfangen	empfängst, empfängt	empfing	empfangen
empfehlen	empfiehlst, empfiehlt	empfahl	empfohlen
empfinden	empfindest, empfindet	empfand	empfunden
erbleichen*	erbleichst, erbleicht	erbleichte	erblichen
erloschen*	erlischst, erlischt	erlosch	erloschen
erschrecken*	erschrickst, erschrickt	erschrak	erschrocken
erwägen	erwägst, erwägt	erwog	erwogen
essen	isst, isst	aß	gegessen
fahren*	fährst, fährt	fuhr	gefahren
fallen*	fällst, fällt	fiel	gefallen
fangen	fängst, fängt	fing	gefangen
fechten	fichst, ficht	focht	gefochten
finden	findest, findet	fand	gefunden
flechten	flichtst, flicht	flocht	geflochten
fliegen*	fliegst, fliegt	flog	geflogen
fliehen*	fliehst, flieht	floh	geflohen
fließen*	fließt, fließt	floss	geflossen
fressen	frisst, frisst	fraß	gefressen
frieren	frierst, friert	fror	gefroren
gären*	gärst, gärt	gor	gegoren
gebären	gebierst, gebiert	gebar	geboren
geben	gibst, gibt	gab	gegeben
gedeihen*	gedeihst, gedeiht	gedieh	gediehen
gehen*	gehst, geht	ging	gegangen

* with "sein"

INFINITIV	PRÄSENS 2., 3. SINGULAR	PRÄTERITUM	PARTIZIP PERFEKT
gelingen*	–, gelingt	gelang	gelungen
gelten	giltst, gilt	galt	gegolten
genesen*	genest, genest	genas	genesen
genießen	genießt, genießt	genoss	genossen
geraten*	gerätst, gerät	geriet	geraten
geschehen*	–, geschieht	geschah	geschehen
gewinnen	gewinnst, gewinnt	gewann	gewonnen
gießen	gießt, gießt	goss	gegossen
gleichen	gleichst, gleicht	glich	geglichen
gleiten*	gleitest, gleitet	glitt	geglitten
glimmen	glimmst, glimmt	glomm	geglommen
graben	gräbst, gräbt	grub	gegraben
greifen	greifst, greift	griff	gegriffen
haben	hast, hat	hatte	gehabt
halten	hältst, hält	hielt	gehalten
hängen	hängst, hängt	hing	gehangen
hauen	haust, haut	haute	gehauen
heben	hebst, hebt	hob	gehoben
heißen	heißt, heißt	hieß	geheißen
helfen	hilfst, hilft	half	geholfen
kennen	kennst, kennt	kannte	gekannt
klimmen*	klimmst, klimmt	klomm	geklommen
klingen	klingst, klingt	klang	geklungen
kneifen	kneifst, kneift	kniff	gekniffen
kommen*	kommst, kommt	kam	gekommen
können	kannst, kann	konnte	gekonnt
kriechen*	kriechst, kriecht	kroch	gekrochen
laden	lädst, lädt	lud	geladen
lassen	lässt, lässt	ließ	gelassen
laufen*	läufst, läuft	lief	gelaufen
leiden	leidest, leidet	litt	gelitten
leihen	leihst, leiht	lieh	geliehen
lesen	liest, liest	las	gelesen
liegen	liegst, liegt	lag	gelegen
lügen	lügst, lügt	log	gelogen
mahlen	mahlst, mahlt	mahlte	gemahlen
meiden	meidest, meidet	mied	gemieden
melken	melkst, melkt	melkte *od* molk	gemolken
messen	misst, misst	maß	gemessen
misslingen*	–, misslingt	misslang	misslungen
mögen	magst, mag	mochte	gemocht
müssen	musst, muss	musste	gemusst
nehmen	nimmst, nimmt	nahm	genommen
nennen	nennst, nennt	nannte	genannt
pfeifen	pfeifst, pfeift	pfiff	gepfiffen
preisen	preist, preist	pries	gepriesen
quellen*	quillst, quillt	quoll	gequollen
raten	rätst, rät	riet	geraten
reiben	reibst, reibt	rieb	gerieben

* with "sein"

INFINITIV	PRÄSENS 2., 3. SINGULAR	PRÄTERITUM	PARTIZIP PERFEKT
reißen*	reißt, reißt	riss	gerissen
reiten*	reitest, reitet	ritt	geritten
rennen*	rennst, rennt	rannte	gerannt
riechen	riechst, riecht	roch	gerochen
ringen	ringst, ringt	rang	gerungen
rinnen*	rinnst, rinnt	rann	geronnen
rufen	rufst, ruft	rief	gerufen
salzen	salzt, salzt	salzte	gesalzen
saufen	säufst, säuft	soff	gesoffen
saugen	saugst, saugt	sog *od* saugte	-gesogen *od* gesaugt
schaffen	schaffst, schafft	schuf	geschaffen
schallen	schallst, schallt	scholl	geschollen
scheiden*	scheidest, scheidet	schied	geschieden
scheinen	scheinst, scheint	schien	geschienen
scheißen	scheißt, scheißt	schiss	geschissen
schelten	schiltst, schilt	schalt	gescholten
scheren	scherst, schert	schor	geschoren
schieben	schiebst, schiebt	schob	geschoben
schießen	schießt, schießt	schoss	geschossen
schinden	schindest, schindet	schindete	geschunden
schlafen	schläfst, schläft	schlief	geschlafen
schlagen	schlägst, schlägt	schlug	geschlagen
schleichen*	schleichst, schleicht	schlich	geschlichen
schleifen	schleifst, schleift	schliff	geschliffen
schließen	schließt, schließt	schloss	geschlossen
schlingen	schlingst, schlingt	schlang	geschlungen
schmeißen	schmeißt, schmeißt	schmiss	geschmissen
schmelzen*	schmilzt, schmilzt	schmolz	geschmolzen
schneiden	schneidest, schneidet	schnitt	geschnitten
schreiben	schreibst, schreibt	schrieb	geschrieben
schreien	schreist, schreit	schrie	geschrie(e)n
schreiten	schreitest, schreitet	schritt	geschritten
schweigen	schweigst, schweigt	schwieg	geschwiegen
schwellen*	schwillst, schwillt	schwoll	geschwollen
schwimmen*	schwimmst, schwimmt	schwamm	geschwommen
schwinden*	schwindest, schwindet	schwand	geschwunden
schwingen	schwingst, schwingt	schwang	geschwungen
schwören	schwörst, schwört	schwor	geschworen
sehen	siehst, sieht	sah	gesehen
sein*	bist, ist	war	gewesen
senden	sendest, sendet	sandte	gesandt
singen	singst, singt	sang	gesungen
sinken*	sinkst, sinkt	sank	gesunken
sinnen	sinnst, sinnt	sann	gesonnen
sitzen	sitzt, sitzt	saß	gesessen
sollen	sollst, soll	sollte	gesollt
speien	speist, speit	spie	gespie(e)n
spinnen	spinnst, spinnt	spann	gesponnen
sprechen	sprichst, spricht	sprach	gesprochen
sprießen*	sprießt, sprießt	spross	gesprossen
springen*	springst, springt	sprang	gesprungen

* with "sein"

INFINITIV	PRÄSENS 2., 3. SINGULAR	PRÄTERITUM	PARTIZIP PERFEKT
stechen	stichst, sticht	stach	gestochen
stecken	steckst, steckt	steckte *od* stack	gesteckt
stehen	stehst, steht	stand	gestanden
stehlen	stiehlst, stiehlt	stahl	gestohlen
steigen*	steigst, steigt	stieg	gestiegen
sterben*	stirbst, stirbt	starb	gestorben
stinken	stinkst, stinkt	stank	gestunken
stoßen	stößt, stößt	stieß	gestoßen
streichen	streichst, streicht	strich	gestrichen
streiten	streitest, streitet	stritt	gestritten
tragen	trägst, trägt	trug	getragen
treffen	triffst, trifft	traf	getroffen
treiben*	treibst, treibt	trieb	getrieben
treten*	trittst, tritt	trat	getreten
trinken	trinkst, trinkt	trank	getrunken
trügen	trügst, trügt	trog	getrogen
tun	tust, tut	tat	getan
verderben	verdirbst, verdirbt	verdarb	verdorben
verdrießen	verdrießt, verdrießt	verdross	verdrossen
vergessen	vergisst, vergisst	vergaß	vergessen
verlieren	verlierst, verliert	verlor	verloren
verschleißen	verschleißt, verschleißt	verschliss	verschlissen
verschwinden	verschwindest, verschwindet	verschwand	verschwunden
verzeihen	verzeihst, verzeiht	verzieh	verziehen
wachsen*	wächst, wächst	wuchs	gewachsen
wägen	wägst, wägt	wog	gewogen
waschen	wäschst, wäscht	wusch	gewaschen
weben	webst, webt	webte *od* wob	gewoben
weichen*	weichst, weicht	wich	gewichen
weisen	weist, weist	wies	gewiesen
wenden	wendest, wendet	wandte	gewandt
werben	wirbst, wirbt	warb	geworben
werden*	wirst, wird	wurde	geworden
werfen	wirfst, wirft	warf	geworfen
wiegen	wiegst, wiegt	wog	gewogen
winden	windest, windet	wand	gewunden
wissen	weißt, weiß	wusste	gewusst
wollen	willst, will	wollte	gewollt
wringen	wringst, wringt	wrang	gewrungen
zeihen	zeihst, zeiht	zieh	geziehen
ziehen*	ziehst, zieht	zog	gezogen
zwingen	zwingst, zwingt	zwang	gezwungen

A[1], **a** [a:] *nt* A, a; **A wie Anton** ≈ A for Andrew, ≈ A for Able (*US*); **das A und O** the be-all and end-all; (*eines Wissensgebietes*) the basics *pl*; **wer A sagt, muss auch B sagen** (*Sprichwort*) in for a penny, in for a pound (*Sprichwort*)
A[2] *f abk* (= *Autobahn*) ≈ M (*Brit*)
Aachen ['a:xən] (**-s**) *nt* Aachen
Aal [a:l] (**-(e)s, -e**) *m* eel
Aas [a:s] (**-es, -e** *od* **Äser**) *nt* carrion; **Aasgeier** *m* vulture
ab [ap] *präp +dat* from; **ab Werk** (*Comm*) ex works; **Kinder ab 12 Jahren** children from the age of 12; **ab morgen** from tomorrow; **ab sofort** as of now
▷ *adv* **1** off; **links ab** to the left; **der Knopf ist ab** the button has come off; **ab nach Hause!** off home with you!; **ab durch die Mitte!** (*umg*) beat it!
2 (*zeitlich*): **von da ab** from then on; **von heute ab** from today, as of today
3 (*auf Fahrplänen*): **München ab 12.20** leaving Munich 12.20
4: ab und zu *od* **an** now and then *od* again
Abänderung *f* alteration; amendment; revision
abarbeiten ['ap|arbaɪtən] *vr* to slave away
Abart ['ap|a:rt] *f* (*Biol*) variety
abartig *adj* abnormal
Abbau ['apbaʊ] (**-(e)s**) *m (+gen)* dismantling; (*Verminderung*) reduction (in); (*Verfall*) decline (in); (*Min*) mining; (*über Tage*) quarrying; (*Chem*) decomposition
abbaubar *adj*: **biologisch ~** biodegradable
abbauen *vt* to dismantle; (*verringern*) to reduce; (*Min*) to mine; to quarry; (*Chem*) to break down; **Arbeitsplätze ~** to make job cuts
abbeißen ['apbaɪsən] *unreg vt* to bite off
abbekommen ['apbəkɔmən] *unreg vt*: **etwas ~** to get some (of it); (*beschädigt werden*) to get damaged; (*verletzt werden*) to get hurt
abberufen ['apbəru:fən] *unreg vt* to recall
abbestellen ['apbəʃtɛlən] *vt* to cancel
abbezahlen ['apbətsa:lən] *vt* to pay off
abbiegen ['apbi:gən] *unreg vi* to turn off; (*Straße*) to bend ▷ *vt* to bend; (*verhindern*) to ward off
Abbiegespur *f* turning lane
Abbild ['apbɪlt] *nt* portrayal; (*einer Person*) image, likeness; **abbilden** ['apbɪldən] *vt* to portray; **Abbildung** *f* illustration; (*Schaubild*) diagram
abbinden ['apbɪndən] *unreg vt* (*Med: Arm, Bein etc*) to ligature
Abbitte ['apbɪtə] *f*: **~ leisten** *od* **tun (bei)** to make one's apologies (to)
abblasen ['apbla:zən] *unreg vt* to blow off; (*fig: umg*) to call off
abblenden ['apblɛndən] *vt* (*Aut*) to dip (*Brit*), dim (*US*) ▷ *vi* to dip (*Brit*) *od* dim (*US*) one's headlights
Abblendlicht ['apblɛntlɪçt] *nt* dipped (*Brit*) *od* dimmed (*US*) headlights *pl*
abbrechen ['apbrɛçən] *unreg vt* to break off; (*Gebäude*) to pull down; (*Zelt*) to take down; (*aufhören*) to stop; (*Comput*) to abort ▷ *vi* to break off; to stop; **sich** *dat* **einen ~** (*umg: sich sehr anstrengen*) to bust a gut
abbrennen ['apbrɛnən] *unreg vt* to burn off; (*Feuerwerk*) to let off ▷ *vi* (*Hilfsverb sein*) to burn down; **abgebrannt sein** (*umg*) to be broke
abbringen ['apbrɪŋən] *unreg vt*: **jdn von etw ~** to dissuade sb from sth; **jdn vom Weg ~** to divert sb; **ich bringe den Verschluss nicht ab** (*umg*) I can't get the top off
Abbruch ['apbrʊx] *m* (*von Verhandlungen etc*) breaking off; (*von Haus*) demolition; (*Comput*) abort; **jdm/etw ~ tun** to harm sb/sth; **abbruchreif** *adj* only fit for demolition
abbrühen ['apbry:ən] *vt* to scald
abbuchen ['apbu:xən] *vt* to debit; (*durch Dauerauftrag*): **~ (von)** to pay by standing order (from)
abbürsten ['apbʏrstən] *vt* to brush off
abdanken ['apdaŋkən] *vi* to resign; (*König*) to abdicate
abdecken ['apdɛkən] *vt* to uncover; (*Tisch*) to clear; (*Loch*) to cover
abdichten ['apdɪçtən] *vt* to seal; (*Naut*) to caulk
abdrängen ['apdrɛŋən] *vt* to push off
abdrehen ['apdre:ən] *vt* (*Gas*) to turn off; (*Licht*) to switch off; (*Film*) to shoot ▷ *vi* (*Schiff*) to change course; **jdm den Hals ~** to wring sb's neck
Abdruck ['apdrʊk] *m* (*Nachdrucken*) reprinting; (*Gedrucktes*) reprint; (*Gipsabdruck, Wachsabdruck*) impression; (*Fingerabdruck*) print; **abdrucken**

vt to print
abdrücken ['apdrʏkən] *vt* to make an impression of; (*Waffe*) to fire; (*umg: Person*) to hug, squeeze ▷ *vr* to leave imprints; (*abstoßen*) to push o.s. away; **jdm die Luft ~** to squeeze all the breath out of sb
abebben ['ap|ɛbən] *vi* to ebb away
Abend ['a:bənt] (**-s, -e**) *m* evening; **gegen ~** towards (the) evening; **den ganzen ~ (über)** the whole evening; **zu ~ essen** to have dinner *od* supper; **heute ~** this evening; **Abendbrot** *nt* supper; **abendfüllend** *adj* taking up the whole evening; **Abendkleid** *nt* evening gown; **Abendkurs** *m* evening classes *pl*; **Abendland** *nt* West; **abendlich** *adj* evening; **Abendmahl** *nt* Holy Communion; **Abendrot** *nt* sunset
abends *adv* in the evening
Abendzeitung *f* evening paper
Abenteuer ['a:bəntɔʏər] (**-s, -**) *nt* adventure; (*Liebesabenteuer*) affair; **abenteuerlich** *adj* adventurous; **Abenteuerspielplatz** *m* adventure playground
Abenteurer (**-s, -**) *m* adventurer
aber ['a:bər] *konj* but; (*jedoch*) however ▷ *adv*: **oder ~** or else; **bist du ~ braun!** aren't you brown!; **das ist ~ schön** that's really nice; **nun ist ~ Schluss!** now that's enough!; **Aber** *nt* but
Aberglaube ['a:bərglaʊbə] *m* superstition
abergläubisch ['a:bərglɔʏbɪʃ] *adj* superstitious
aberkennen ['ap|ɛrkɛnən] *unreg vt*: **jdm etw ~** to deprive sb of sth, take sth (away) from sb
abermalig *adj* repeated
abermals *adv* once again
Abf. *abk* (= *Abfahrt*) dep.
abfahren ['apfa:rən] *unreg vi* to leave, depart ▷ *vt* to take *od* cart away; (*Film*) to start; (*Film, TV: Kamera*) to roll; (*Strecke*) to drive; (*Reifen*) to wear; (*Fahrkarte*) to use; **der Zug ist abgefahren** (*lit*) the train has left; (*fig*) we've/you've *etc* missed the boat; **der Zug fährt um 8.00 von Bremen ab** the train leaves Bremen at 8 o'clock; **jdn ~ lassen** (*umg: abweisen*) to tell sb to get lost; **auf jdn ~** (*umg*) to really go for sb
Abfahrt ['apfa:rt] *f* departure; (*Autobahnabfahrt*) exit; (*Ski*) descent; (*Piste*) run; **Vorsicht bei der ~ des Zuges!** stand clear, the train is about to leave!
Abfahrts- *zW*: **Abfahrtslauf** *m* (*Ski*) downhill; **Abfahrtstag** *m* day of departure; **Abfahrtszeit** *f* departure time
Abfall ['apfal] *m* waste; (*von Speisen etc*) rubbish (*Brit*), garbage (*US*); (*Neigung*) slope; (*Verschlechterung*) decline; **Abfalleimer** *m* rubbish bin (*Brit*), garbage can (*US*)
abfallen *unreg vi* (*lit, fig*) to fall *od* drop off; (*Pol, vom Glauben*) to break away; (*sich neigen*) to fall *od* drop away; **wie viel fällt bei dem Geschäft für mich ab?** (*umg*) how much do I get out of the deal?
abfällig ['apfɛlɪç] *adj* disparaging, deprecatory
Abfallprodukt *nt* (*lit, fig*) waste product
abfangen ['apfaŋən] *unreg vt* to intercept; (*Person*) to catch; (*unter Kontrolle bringen*) to check; (*Aufprall*) to absorb; (*Kunden*) to lure away
abfärben ['apfɛrbən] *vi* (*lit*) to lose its colour; (*Wäsche*) to run; (*fig*) to rub off
abfassen ['apfasən] *vt* to write, draft
abfertigen ['apfɛrtɪgən] *vt* to prepare for dispatch, process; (*an der Grenze*) to clear; (*Kundschaft*) to attend to; **jdn kurz ~** to give sb short shrift
abfeuern ['apfɔʏərn] *vt* to fire
abfinden ['apfɪndən] *unreg vt* to pay off ▷ *vr* to come to terms; **sich mit jdm ~/nicht ~** to put up with/not to get on with sb; **er konnte sich nie damit ~, dass ...** he could never accept the fact that ...
Abfindung *f* (*von Gläubigern*) payment; (*Geld*) sum in settlement
abflauen ['apflaʊən] *vi* (*Wind, Erregung*) to die away, subside; (*Nachfrage, Geschäft*) to fall *od* drop off
abfliegen ['apfli:gən] *unreg vi* to take off ▷ *vt* (*Gebiet*) to fly over
abfließen ['apfli:sən] *unreg vi* to drain away; **ins Ausland ~** (*Geld*) to flow out of the country
Abflug ['apflu:k] *m* departure; (*Start*) take-off; **Abflugzeit** *f* departure time
Abfluss ['apflʊs] *m* draining away; (*Öffnung*) outlet
abfragen ['apfra:gən] *vt* to test; (*Comput*) to call up; **jdn etw ~** to question sb on sth
Abfuhr ['apfu:r] (**-, -en**) *f* removal; (*fig*) snub, rebuff; **sich** *dat* **eine ~ holen** to meet with a rebuff
abführen ['apfy:rən] *vt* to lead away; (*Gelder, Steuern*) to pay ▷ *vi* (*Med*) to have a laxative effect
Abführmittel *nt* laxative, purgative
abfüllen ['apfʏlən] *vt* to draw off; (*in Flaschen*) to bottle
Abgabe ['apga:bə] *f* handing in; (*von Ball*) pass; (*Steuer*) tax; (*einer Erklärung*) giving
abgabenfrei *adj* tax-free
abgabenpflichtig *adj* liable to tax
Abgang ['apgaŋ] *m* (*von Schule*) leaving; (*Theat*) exit; (*Med: Ausscheiden*) passing; (*: Fehlgeburt*) miscarriage; (*Abfahrt*) departure; (*der Post, von Waren*) dispatch
Abgas ['apga:s] *nt* waste gas; (*Aut*) exhaust
abgeben ['apge:bən] *unreg vt* (*Gegenstand*) to hand *od* give in; (*Ball*) to pass; (*Wärme*) to give off; (*Amt*) to hand over; (*Schuss*) to fire; (*Erklärung, Urteil*) to give; (*darstellen*) to make ▷ *vr*: **sich mit jdm/etw ~** to associate with sb/bother with sth; **„Kinderwagen abzugeben"** "pram for sale"; **jdm etw ~** (*überlassen*) to let sb have sth
abgedroschen ['apgədrɔʃən] *adj* trite; (*Witz*)

corny
abgefeimt ['apgəfaɪmt] *adj* cunning
abgegriffen ['apgəgrɪfən] *adj* (*Buch*) well-thumbed; (*Redensart*) trite
abgehen ['apge:ən] *unreg vi* to go away, leave; (*Theat*) to exit; (*Post*) to go; (*Med*) to be passed; (*sterben*) to die; (*Knopf etc*) to come off; (*abgezogen werden*) to be taken off; (*Straße*) to branch off; (*abweichen*): **von einer Forderung ~** to give up a demand ▷ *vt* (*Strecke*) to go *od* walk along; (*Mil: Gelände*) to patrol; **von seiner Meinung ~** to change one's opinion; **davon gehen 5% ab** 5% is taken off that; **etw geht jdm ab** (*fehlt*) sb lacks sth
abgelegen ['apgəle:gən] *adj* remote
abgemacht ['apgəmaxt] *adj* fixed; **~!** done!
abgeneigt ['apgənaɪkt] *adj* averse
Abgeordnete, r ['apgə|ɔrdnətə(r)] *f(m)* elected representative; (*von Parlament*) member of parliament
Abgesandte, r ['apgəzantə(r)] *f(m)* delegate; (*Pol*) envoy
abgeschmackt ['apgəʃmakt] *adj* tasteless; **Abgeschmacktheit** *f* lack of taste; (*Bemerkung*) tasteless remark
abgesehen ['apgəze:ən] *adj*: **es auf jdn/etw ~ haben** to be after sb/sth; **~ von ...** apart from ...
abgespannt ['apgəʃpant] *adj* tired out
abgestanden ['apgəʃtandən] *adj* stale; (*Bier*) flat
abgestorben ['apgəʃtɔrbən] *adj* numb; (*Biol, Med*) dead
abgetragen ['apgətra:gən] *adj* worn
abgewinnen ['apgəvɪnən] *unreg vt*: **jdm Geld ~** to win money from sb; **einer Sache etw/ Geschmack ~** to get sth/pleasure from sth
abgewogen ['apgəvo:gən] *adj* (*Urteil, Worte*) balanced
abgewöhnen ['apgəvø:nən] *vt*: **jdm/sich etw ~** to cure sb of sth/give sth up
abgießen ['apgi:sən] *unreg vt* (*Flüssigkeit*) to pour off
abgleiten ['apglaɪtən] *unreg vi* to slip, slide
Abgott ['apgɔt] *m* idol
abgöttisch ['apgœtɪʃ] *adj*: **~ lieben** to idolize
abgrenzen ['apgrɛntsən] *vt* (*lit, fig*) to mark off; (*Gelände*) to fence off ▷ *vr*: **sich ~ (gegen)** to dis(as)sociate o.s. (from)
Abgrund ['apgrʊnt] *m* (*lit, fig*) abyss
abgründig ['apgrʏndɪç] *adj* unfathomable; (*Lächeln*) cryptic
Abguss ['apgʊs] *m* (*Kunst, Metallurgie: Vorgang*) casting; (*: Form*) cast
abhaken ['apha:kən] *vt* to tick off (*Brit*), check off (*US*)
abhalten ['aphaltən] *unreg vt* (*Versammlung*) to hold; **jdn von etw ~** (*fernhalten*) to keep sb away from sth; (*hindern*) to keep sb from sth
abhandeln ['aphandəln] *vt* (*Thema*) to deal with; **jdm die Waren/10 Euro ~** to do a deal with sb for the goods/beat sb down 10 euros
Abhandlung ['aphandlʊŋ] *f* treatise, discourse
Abhang ['aphaŋ] *m* slope
abhängen ['aphɛŋən] *unreg vt* (*Bild*) to take down; (*Anhänger*) to uncouple; (*Verfolger*) to shake off ▷ *vi* (*Fleisch*) to hang; **von jdm/etw ~** to depend on sb/sth; **das hängt ganz davon ab** it all depends; **er hat abgehängt** (*Tel: umg*) he hung up (on me *etc*)
abhängig ['aphɛŋɪç] *adj*: **~ (von)** dependent (on); **Abhängigkeit** *f*: **Abhängigkeit (von)** dependence (on)
abhärten ['aphɛrtən] *vt* to toughen up ▷ *vr* to toughen (o.s.) up; **sich gegen etw ~** to harden o.s. to sth
abhauen ['aphaʊən] *unreg vt* to cut off; (*Baum*) to cut down ▷ *vi* (*umg*) to clear off *od* out; **hau ab!** beat it!
abheben ['aphe:bən] *unreg vt* to lift (up); (*Karten*) to cut; (*Masche*) to slip; (*Geld*) to withdraw, take out ▷ *vi* (*Flugzeug*) to take off; (*Rakete*) to lift off; (*Karten*) to cut ▷ *vr*: **sich ~ von** to stand out from, contrast with
abhelfen ['aphɛlfən] *unreg vi +dat* to remedy
abhetzen ['aphɛtsən] *vr* to wear *od* tire o.s. out
Abhilfe ['aphɪlfə] *f* remedy; **~ schaffen** to put things right
abholen ['apho:lən] *vt* (*Gegenstand*) to fetch, collect; (*Person*) to call for; (*am Bahnhof etc*) to pick up, meet
Abholmarkt *m* cash and carry
abholzen ['aphɔltsən] *vt* (*Wald*) to clear, deforest
abhorchen ['aphɔrçən] *vt* (*Med*) to listen to, sound
abhören ['aphø:rən] *vt* (*Vokabeln*) to test; (*Telefongespräch*) to tap; (*Tonband etc*) to listen to; **abgehört werden** (*umg*) to be bugged
Abhörgerät *nt* bug
Abitur [abi'tu:r] **(-s, -e)** *nt German school-leaving examination*, ≈ A-levels *pl* (*Brit*); **(das) ~ machen** to take one's school-leaving exam *od* A-levels
Abiturient, in [abitʊri'ɛnt(ɪn)] *m(f)* candidate for school-leaving certificate
abkämmen ['apkɛmən] *vt* (*Gegend*) to comb, scour
abkapseln ['apkapsəln] *vr* to shut *od* cut o.s. off
abkaufen ['apkaʊfən] *vt*: **jdm etw ~** to buy sth from sb
abkehren ['apke:rən] *vt* (*Blick*) to avert, turn away ▷ *vr* to turn away
abklären ['apklɛ:rən] *vt* (*klarstellen*) to clear up, clarify ▷ *vr* (*sich setzen*) to clarify
Abklatsch ['apklatʃ] **(-es, -e)** *m* (*fig*) (poor) copy
abklingen ['apklɪŋən] *unreg vi* to die away; (*Rundf*) to fade out
abknöpfen ['apknœpfən] *vt* to unbutton; **jdm etw ~** (*umg*) to get sth off sb
abkochen ['apkɔxən] *vt* to boil; (*keimfrei machen*) to sterilize (by boiling)

abkommen ['apkɔmən] *unreg vi* to get away; **(vom Thema) ~** to get off the subject, digress; **von der Straße/einem Plan ~** to leave the road/give up a plan
abkömmlich ['apkœmlıç] *adj* available, free
abkratzen ['apkratsən] *vt* to scrape off ▷ *vi* (*umg*) to kick the bucket
abkriegen ['apkri:gən] (*umg*) *vt* = **abbekommen**
abkühlen ['apky:lən] *vt* to cool down ▷ *vr* (*Mensch*) to cool down *od* off; (*Wetter*) to get cool; (*Zuneigung*) to cool
abkürzen ['apkʏrtsən] *vt* to shorten; (*Wort*) to abbreviate; **den Weg ~** to take a short cut
Abkürzung *f* abbreviation; short cut
abladen ['apla:dən] *unreg vi* to unload ▷ *vt* to unload; (*fig: umg*): **seinen Ärger (bei jdm) ~** to vent one's anger (on sb)
Ablage ['apla:gə] *f* place to keep/put sth; (*Aktenordnung*) filing; (*für Akten*) tray
ablagern ['apla:gərn] *vt* to deposit ▷ *vr* to be deposited ▷ *vi* to mature
ablassen ['aplasən] *unreg vt* (*Wasser, Dampf*) to let out *od* off; (*vom Preis*) to knock off ▷ *vi*: **von etw ~** to give sth up, abandon sth
Ablauf *m* (*Abfluss*) drain; (*von Ereignissen*) course; (*einer Frist, Zeit*) expiry (*Brit*), expiration (*US*); **nach ~ des Jahres/dieser Zeit** at the end of the year/this time
ablaufen ['aplaʊfən] *unreg vi* (*abfließen*) to drain away; (*Ereignisse*) to happen; (*Frist, Zeit, Pass*) to expire ▷ *vt* (*Sohlen*) to wear (down *od* out); **~ lassen** (*abspulen, abspielen: Platte, Tonband*) to play; (*Film*) to run; **sich** *dat* **die Beine** *od* **Hacken nach etw ~** (*umg*) to walk one's legs off looking for sth; **jdm den Rang ~** to steal a march on sb
ablegen ['aple:gən] *vt* to put *od* lay down; (*Kleider*) to take off; (*Gewohnheit*) to get rid of; (*Prüfung*) to take, sit (*Brit*); (*Zeugnis*) to give; (*Schriftwechsel*) to file (away); (*nicht mehr tragen: Kleidung*) to discard, cast off; (*Schwur, Eid*) to swear ▷ *vi* (*Schiff*) to cast off
Ableger (-s, -) *m* layer; (*fig*) branch, offshoot
ablehnen ['aple:nən] *vt* to reject; (*missbilligen*) to disapprove of; (*Einladung*) to decline, refuse ▷ *vi* to decline, refuse
ableiten ['aplaıtən] *vt* (*Wasser*) to divert; (*deduzieren*) to deduce; (*Wort*) to derive
Ableitung *f* diversion; deduction; derivation; (*Wort*) derivative
ablenken ['aplɛŋkən] *vt* to turn away, deflect; (*zerstreuen*) to distract ▷ *vi* to change the subject; **das lenkt ab** (*zerstreut*) it takes your mind off things; (*stört*) it's distracting
Ablenkung *f* deflection; distraction
Ablenkungsmanöver *nt* diversionary tactic; (*um vom Thema abzulenken*) red herring
ablesen ['aple:zən] *unreg vt* to read; **jdm jeden Wunsch von den Augen ~** to anticipate sb's every wish
ableugnen ['aplɔygnən] *vt* to deny
abliefern ['apli:fərn] *vt* to deliver; **etw bei jdm/einer Dienststelle ~** to hand sth over to sb/in at an office
abliegen ['apli:gən] *unreg vi* to be some distance away; (*fig*) to be far removed
ablisten ['aplıstən] *vt*: **jdm etw ~** to trick *od* con sb out of sth
ablösen ['aplø:zən] *vt* (*abtrennen*) to take off, remove; (*in Amt*) to take over from; (*Fin: Schuld, Hypothek*) to pay off, redeem; (*Methode, System*) to supersede ▷ *vr* (*auch*: **einander ablösen**) to take turns; (*Fahrer, Kollegen, Wachen*) to relieve each other
ABM *pl abk* (= *Arbeitsbeschaffungsmaßnahmen*) *job-creation scheme*
abmachen ['apmaxən] *vt* to take off; (*vereinbaren*) to agree; **etw mit sich allein ~** to sort sth out for o.s.
Abmachung *f* agreement
abmagern ['apma:gərn] *vi* to get thinner, become emaciated
Abmagerungskur *f* diet; **eine ~ machen** to go on a diet
Abmarsch ['apmarʃ] *m* departure; **abmarschbereit** *adj* ready to start
abmelden ['apmɛldən] *vt* (*Auto*) to take off the road; (*Telefon*) to have disconnected; (*Comput*) to log off ▷ *vr* to give notice of one's departure; (*im Hotel*) to check out; **ein Kind von einer Schule ~** to take a child away from a school; **er/sie ist bei mir abgemeldet** (*umg*) I don't want anything to do with him/her; **jdn bei der Polizei ~** to register sb's departure with the police
abmessen ['apmɛsən] *unreg vt* to measure
abmontieren ['apmɔnti:rən] *vt* to take off; (*Maschine*) to dismantle
abmühen ['apmy:ən] *vr* to wear o.s. out
abnabeln ['apna:bəln] *vt*: **jdn ~** (*auch fig*) to cut sb's umbilical cord
Abnäher ['apnɛ:ər] **(-s, -)** *m* dart
Abnahme ['apna:mə] *f* (*+gen*) removal; (*Comm*) buying; (*Verringerung*) decrease (in)
abnehmen ['apne:mən] *unreg vt* to take off, remove; (*Führerschein*) to take away; (*Prüfung*) to hold; (*Maschen*) to decrease; (*Hörer*) to lift, pick up; (*begutachten: Gebäude, Auto*) to inspect ▷ *vi* to decrease; (*schlanker werden*) to lose weight; **jdm etw ~** (*Geld*) to get sth out of sb; (*kaufen: auch umg: glauben*) to buy sth from sb; **kann ich dir etwas ~?** (*tragen*) can I take something for you?; **jdm Arbeit ~** to take work off sb's shoulders; **jdm ein Versprechen ~** to make sb promise sth
Abnehmer (-s, -) *m* purchaser, customer; **viele/wenige ~ finden** (*Comm*) to sell well/badly
Abneigung ['apnaıgʊŋ] *f* aversion, dislike
abnorm [ap'nɔrm] *adj* abnormal
abnutzen ['apnʊtsən] *vt* to wear out
Abo ['abo] **(-s, -s)** (*umg*) *nt* = **Abonnement**
Abonnement [abɔn(ə)'mã:] **(-s, -s** *od* **-e)** *nt* subscription; (*Theaterabonnement*) season ticket

Abonnent, in [abɔ'nɛnt(ɪn)] *m(f)* subscriber
abonnieren [abɔ'ni:rən] *vt* to subscribe to
abordnen ['ap|ordnən] *vt* to delegate
Abordnung *f* delegation
Abort [a'bɔrt] (**-(e)s, -e**) *m* (*veraltet*) lavatory
abpacken ['appakən] *vt* to pack
abpassen ['appasən] *vt* (*Person, Gelegenheit*) to wait for; (*warten auf*) to catch; (*jdm auflauern*) to waylay; **etw gut ~** to time sth well
abpfeifen ['appfaɪfən] *unreg vt, vi* (*Sport*): **(das Spiel) ~** to blow the whistle (for the end of the game)
Abpfiff ['appfɪf] *m* final whistle
abplagen ['appla:gən] *vr* to struggle (away)
Abprall ['appral] *m* rebound; (*von Kugel*) ricochet
abprallen ['appralən] *vi* to bounce off; to ricochet; **an jdm ~** (*fig*) to make no impression on sb
abputzen ['appʊtsən] *vt* to clean; (*Nase etc*) to wipe
abquälen ['apkvɛ:lən] *vr* to struggle (away)
abrackern ['aprakərn] (*umg*) *vr* to slave away
abraten ['apra:tən] *unreg vi*: **jdm von etw ~** to advise sb against sth, warn sb against sth
abräumen ['aprɔʏmən] *vt* to clear up *od* away; (*Tisch*) to clear ▷ *vi* to clear up *od* away
abreagieren ['apreagi:rən] *vt*: **seinen Zorn (an jdm/etw) ~** to work one's anger off (on sb/sth) ▷ *vr* to calm down; **seinen Ärger an anderen ~** to take it out on others
abrechnen ['aprɛçnən] *vt* to deduct, take off ▷ *vi* (*lit*) to settle up; (*fig*) to get even; **darf ich ~?** would you like your bill (*Brit*) *od* check (*US*) now?
Abrechnung *f* settlement; (*Rechnung*) bill; (*Aufstellung*) statement; (*Bilanz*) balancing; (*fig: Rache*) revenge; **in ~ stellen** (*form: Abzug*) to deduct; **~ über** *+akk* bill/statement for
abregen ['apre:gən] (*umg*) *vr* to calm *od* cool down
abreiben ['apraɪbən] *unreg vt* to rub off; (*säubern*) to wipe; **jdn mit einem Handtuch ~** to towel sb down
Abreise ['apraɪzə] *f* departure
abreisen *vi* to leave, set off
abreißen ['apraɪsən] *unreg vt* (*Haus*) to tear down; (*Blatt*) to tear off ▷ *vi*: **den Kontakt nicht ~ lassen** to stay in touch
abrichten ['aprɪ̣tən] *vt* to train
abriegeln ['apri:gəln] *vt* (*Tür*) to bolt; (*Straße, Gebiet*) to seal off
Abriss ['aprɪs] (**-es, -e**) *m* (*Übersicht*) outline; (*Abbruch*) demolition
Abruf ['apru:f] *m*: **auf ~** on call
abrufen *unreg vt* (*Mensch*) to call away; (*Comm: Ware*) to request delivery of; (*Comput*) to recall, retrieve
abrunden ['aprʊndən] *vt* to round off
abrüsten ['aprʏstən] *vi* to disarm
Abrüstung *f* disarmament
abrutschen ['aprʊtʃən] *vi* to slip; (*Aviat*) to sideslip

Abs. *abk* = **Absender**; (= *Absatz*) par., para
Absage ['apza:gə] (**-, -n**) *f* refusal; (*auf Einladung*) negative reply
absagen *vt* to cancel, call off; (*Einladung*) to turn down ▷ *vi* to cry off; (*ablehnen*) to decline; **jdm ~** to tell sb that one can't come
absägen ['apzɛ:gən] *vt* to saw off
absahnen ['apza:nən] *vt* (*lit*) to skim; **das Beste für sich ~** (*fig*) to take the cream
Absatz ['apzats] *m* (*Comm*) sales *pl*; (*Jur*) section; (*Bodensatz*) deposit; (*neuer Abschnitt*) paragraph; (*Treppenabsatz*) landing; (*Schuhabsatz*) heel; **Absatzgebiet** *nt* (*Comm*) market; sales territory
abschaffen ['apʃafən] *vt* to abolish, do away with
abschalten ['apʃaltən] *vt, vi* (*lit: umg*) to switch off
abschätzen ['apʃɛtsən] *vt* to estimate; (*Lage*) to assess; (*Person*) to size up
abschätzig ['apʃɛtsɪç] *adj* disparaging, derogatory
Abschaum ['apʃaʊm] (**-(e)s**) *m* scum
Abscheu ['apʃɔʏ] (**-(e)s**) *m* loathing, repugnance; **abscheulich** *adj* abominable
abschicken ['apʃɪkən] *vt* to send off
abschieben ['apʃi:bən] *unreg vt* to push away; (*Person*) to pack off; (*ausweisen: Ausländer*) to deport; (*fig: Verantwortung, Schuld*): **~ (auf** *+akk***)** to shift (onto)
Abschied ['apʃi:t] (**-(e)s, -e**) *m* parting; (*von Armee*) discharge; **(von jdm) ~ nehmen** to say goodbye (to sb), take one's leave (of sb); **seinen ~ nehmen** (*Mil*) to apply for discharge; **zum ~** on parting
Abschiedsbrief *m* farewell letter
Abschiedsfeier *f* farewell party
abschießen ['apʃi:sən] *unreg vt* (*Flugzeug*) to shoot down; (*Geschoss*) to fire; (*umg: Minister*) to get rid of
abschirmen ['apʃɪrmən] *vt* to screen; (*schützen*) to protect ▷ *vr* (*sich isolieren*): **sich ~ (gegen)** to cut o.s. off (from)
abschlagen ['apʃla:gən] *unreg vt* (*abhacken, Comm*) to knock off; (*ablehnen*) to refuse; (*Mil*) to repel
abschlägig ['apʃlɛ:gɪç] *adj* negative; **jdn/etw ~ bescheiden** (*form*) to turn sb/sth down
Abschlagszahlung *f* interim payment
abschleifen ['apʃlaɪfən] *unreg vt* to grind down; (*Holzboden*) to sand (down) ▷ *vr* to wear off
Abschleppdienst *m* (*Aut*) breakdown service (*Brit*), towing company (*US*)
abschleppen ['apʃlɛpən] *vt* to (take in) tow
Abschleppseil *nt* towrope
abschließen ['apʃli:sən] *unreg vt* (*Tür*) to lock; (*beenden*) to conclude, finish; (*Vertrag, Handel*) to conclude; (*Versicherung*) to take out; (*Wette*) to place ▷ *vr* (*sich isolieren*) to cut o.s. off; **mit abgeschlossenem Studium** with a degree; **mit der Vergangenheit ~** to break with the past

Abschluss ['apʃlʊs] *m* (*Beendigung*) close, conclusion; (*Comm: Bilanz*) balancing; (*von Vertrag, Handel*) conclusion; **zum ~** in conclusion; **Abschlussfeier** *f* (*Sch*) school-leavers' ceremony; **Abschlussrechnung** *f* final account

abschmieren ['apʃmi:rən] *vt* (*Aut*) to grease, lubricate

abschminken ['apʃmɪŋkən] *vt*: **sich ~** to remove one's make-up

abschnallen ['apʃnalən] *vr* to unfasten one's seat belt ▷ *vi* (*umg: nicht mehr folgen können*) to give up; (*: fassungslos sein*) to be staggered

abschneiden ['apʃnaɪdən] *unreg vt* to cut off ▷ *vi* to do, come off; **bei etw gut/schlecht ~** (*umg*) to come off well/badly in sth

Abschnitt ['apʃnɪt] *m* section; (*Mil*) sector; (*Kontrollabschnitt*) counterfoil (*Brit*), stub (*US*); (*Math*) segment; (*Zeitabschnitt*) period

abschrauben ['apʃraʊbən] *vt* to unscrew

abschrecken ['apʃrɛkən] *vt* to deter, put off; (*mit kaltem Wasser*) to plunge into cold water

abschreckend *adj* deterrent; **~es Beispiel** warning; **eine abschreckende Wirkung haben, ~ wirken** to act as a deterrent

abschreiben ['apʃraɪbən] *unreg vt* to copy; (*verloren geben*) to write off; (*Comm*) to deduct; **er ist bei mir abgeschrieben** I'm finished with him

Abschrift ['apʃrɪft] *f* copy

Abschuss ['apʃʊs] *m* (*eines Geschützes*) firing; (*Herunterschießen*) shooting down; (*Tötung*) shooting

abschüssig ['apʃʏsɪç] *adj* steep

abschütteln ['apʃʏtəln] *vt* to shake off

abschwächen ['apʃvɛçən] *vt* to lessen; (*Behauptung, Kritik*) to tone down ▷ *vr* to lessen

abschweifen ['apʃvaɪfən] *vi* to wander; (*Redner*) to digress

abschwellen ['apʃvɛlən] *unreg vi* (*Geschwulst*) to go down; (*Lärm*) to die down

abschwören ['apʃvø:rən] *unreg vi +dat* to renounce

absehbar ['apze:ba:r] *adj* foreseeable; **in ~er Zeit** in the foreseeable future; **das Ende ist ~** the end is in sight

absehen *unreg vt* (*Ende, Folgen*) to foresee ▷ *vi*: **von etw ~** to refrain from sth; (*nicht berücksichtigen*) to leave sth out of consideration; **jdm etw ~** (*erlernen*) to copy sth from sb

Abseits ['apzaɪts] *nt* (*Sport*) offside; **im ~ stehen** to be offside; **im ~ leben** (*fig*) to live in the shadows

abseits *adv* out of the way ▷ *präp +gen* away from

absenden ['apzɛndən] *unreg vt* to send off, dispatch

Absender *m* sender

absetzbar ['apzɛtsba:r] *adj* (*Beamter*) dismissible; (*Waren*) saleable; (*von Steuer*) deductible

absetzen ['apzɛtsən] *vt* (*niederstellen, aussteigen lassen*) to put down; (*abnehmen; auch Theaterstück*) to take off; (*Comm: verkaufen*) to sell; (*Fin: abziehen*) to deduct; (*entlassen*) to dismiss; (*König*) to depose; (*streichen*) to drop; (*Fußballspiel, Termin*) to cancel; (*hervorheben*) to pick out ▷ *vi*: **er trank das Glas aus, ohne abzusetzen** he emptied his glass in one ▷ *vr* (*sich entfernen*) to clear off; (*sich ablagern*) to be deposited; **das kann man ~** that is tax-deductible

absichern ['apzɪçərn] *vt* to make safe; (*schützen*) to safeguard ▷ *vr* to protect o.s.

Absicht ['apzɪçt] *f* intention; **mit ~** on purpose; **absichtlich** *adj* intentional, deliberate

absitzen ['apzɪtsən] *unreg vi* to dismount ▷ *vt* (*Strafe*) to serve

absolut [apzo'lu:t] *adj* absolute

Absolutismus [apzolu:'tɪsmʊs] *m* absolutism

absolvieren [apzɔl'vi:rən] *vt* (*Sch*) to complete

absonderlich [ap'zɔndərlɪç] *adj* odd, strange

absondern *vt* to separate; (*ausscheiden*) to give off, secrete ▷ *vr* to cut o.s. off

absparen ['apʃpa:rən] *vt*: **sich** *dat* **etw ~** to scrimp and save for sth

abspecken ['apʃpɛkən] (*umg*) *vt* to shed ▷ *vi* to lose weight

abspeisen ['apʃpaɪzən] *vt* (*fig*) to fob off

abspenstig ['apʃpɛnstɪç] *adj*: **(jdm) ~ machen** to lure away (from sb)

absperren ['apʃpɛrən] *vt* to block *od* close off; (*Tür*) to lock

Absperrung *f* (*Vorgang*) blocking *od* closing off; (*Sperre*) barricade

abspielen ['apʃpi:lən] *vt* (*Platte, Tonband*) to play; (*Sport: Ball*) to pass ▷ *vr* to happen; **vom Blatt ~** (*Mus*) to sight-read

Absprache ['apʃpra:xə] *f* arrangement; **ohne vorherige ~** without prior consultation

absprechen ['apʃprɛçən] *unreg vt* (*vereinbaren*) to arrange ▷ *vr*: **die beiden hatten sich vorher abgesprochen** they had agreed on what to do/say *etc* in advance; **jdm etw ~** to deny sb sth; (*in Abrede stellen: Begabung*) to dispute sb's sth

abspringen ['apʃprɪŋən] *unreg vi* to jump down/off; (*Farbe, Lack*) to flake off; (*Aviat*) to bale out; (*sich distanzieren*) to back out

Absprung ['apʃprʊŋ] *m* jump; **den ~ schaffen** (*fig*) to make the break (*umg*)

abspülen ['apʃpy:lən] *vt* to rinse; **Geschirr ~** to wash up (*Brit*), do the dishes

abstammen ['apʃtamən] *vi* to be descended; (*Wort*) to be derived

Abstammung *f* descent; derivation; **französischer ~** of French extraction *od* descent

Abstand ['apʃtant] *m* distance; (*zeitlich*) interval; **davon ~ nehmen, etw zu tun** to refrain from doing sth; **~ halten** (*Aut*) to keep one's distance; **~ von etw gewinnen** (*fig*) to distance o.s. from sth; **mit großem ~ führen** to lead by a wide margin; **mit ~ der**

Beste by far the best
Abstandssumme *f* compensation
abstatten ['apʃtatən] *vt* (*form*: *Dank*) to give; (: *Besuch*) to pay
abstauben ['apʃtaʊbən] *vt, vi* to dust; (*umg*: *mitgehen lassen*) to help oneself to, pinch; **(den Ball) ~** (*Sport*) to tuck the ball away
abstechen ['apʃtɛçən] *unreg vt* to cut; (*Tier*) to cut the throat of ▷ *vi*: **~ gegen** *od* **von** to contrast with
Abstecher (**-s, -**) *m* detour
abstecken ['apʃtɛkən] *vt* (*Fläche*) to mark out; (*Saum*) to pin
abstehen ['apʃte:ən] *unreg vi* (*Ohren, Haare*) to stick out; (*entfernt sein*) to stand away
absteigen ['apʃtaɪgən] *unreg vi* (*vom Rad etc*) to get off, dismount; **in einem Gasthof ~** to put up at an inn; **(in die Zweite Liga) ~** to be relegated (to the second division); **auf dem ~den Ast sein** (*umg*) to be going downhill, be on the decline
abstellen ['apʃtɛlən] *vt* (*niederstellen*) to put down; (*entfernt stellen*) to pull out; (*hinstellen*: *Auto*) to park; (*ausschalten*) to turn *od* switch off; (*Missstand, Unsitte*) to stop; (*abkommandieren*) to order off; (*ausrichten*): **~ auf** *+akk* to gear to; **das lässt sich nicht/ lässt sich ~** nothing/something can be done about that
Abstellgleis *nt* siding; **jdn aufs ~ schieben** (*fig*) to cast sb aside
abstempeln ['apʃtɛmpəln] *vt* to stamp; (*fig*): **~ zu** *od* **als** to brand as
absterben ['apʃtɛrbən] *unreg vi* to die; (*Körperteil*) to go numb
Abstieg ['apʃti:k] (**-(e)s, -e**) *m* descent; (*Sport*) relegation; (*fig*) decline
abstimmen ['apʃtɪmən] *vi* to vote ▷ *vt*: **~ (auf** *+akk***)** (*Instrument*) to tune (to); (*Interessen*) to match (with); (*Termine, Ziele*) to fit in (with) ▷ *vr* to agree
Abstimmung *f* vote; (*geheime Abstimmung*) ballot
abstinent [apsti'nɛnt] *adj* (*von Alkohol*) teetotal
Abstinenz [apsti'nɛnts] *f* teetotalism
Abstinenzler, in (**-s, -**) *m(f)* teetotaller
abstoßen ['apʃto:sən] *unreg vt* to push off *od* away; (*anekeln*) to repel; (*Comm*: *Ware, Aktien*) to sell off
abstoßend *adj* repulsive
abstrahieren [apstra'hi:rən] *vt, vi* to abstract
abstrakt [ap'strakt] *adj* abstract ▷ *adv* abstractly, in the abstract
Abstraktion [apstraktsi'o:n] *f* abstraction
abstreifen ['apʃtraɪfən] *vt* (*abtreten*: *Schuhe, Füße*) to wipe; (*abziehen*: *Schmuck*) to take off, slip off
abstreiten ['apʃtraɪtən] *unreg vt* to deny
Abstrich ['apʃtrɪç] *m* (*Abzug*) cut; (*Med*) smear; **~e machen** to lower one's sights
abstufen ['apʃtu:fən] *vt* (*Hang*) to terrace; (*Farben*) to shade; (*Gehälter*) to grade
abstumpfen ['apʃtʊmpfən] *vt* (*lit, fig*) to dull, blunt ▷ *vi* to become dulled
Absturz ['apʃtʊrts] *m* fall; (*Aviat*) crash
abstürzen ['apʃtʏrtsən] *vi* to fall; (*Aviat*) to crash
absuchen ['apzu:xən] *vt* to scour, search
absurd [ap'zʊrt] *adj* absurd
Abszess [aps'tsɛs] (**-es, -sse**) *m* abscess
Abt [apt] (**-(e)s, ¨-e**) *m* abbot
abtasten ['aptastən] *vt* to feel, probe; (*Elek*) to scan; (*bei Durchsuchung*): **~ (auf** *+akk***)** to frisk (for)
abtauen ['aptaʊən] *vt, vi* to thaw; (*Kühlschrank*) to defrost
Abtei [ap'taɪ] (**-, -en**) *f* abbey
Abteil [ap'taɪl] (**-(e)s, -e**) *nt* compartment
abteilen ['aptaɪlən] *vt* to divide up; (*abtrennen*) to divide off
Abteilung *f* (*in Firma, Kaufhaus*) department; (*Mil*) unit; (*in Krankenhaus, Jur*) section
Abteilungsleiter, in *m(f)* head of department; (*in Kaufhaus*) department manager(ess)
Äbtissin [ɛp'tɪsɪn] *f* abbess
abtragen ['aptra:gən] *unreg vt* (*Hügel, Erde*) to level down; (*Essen*) to clear away; (*Kleider*) to wear out; (*Schulden*) to pay off
abträglich ['aptrɛ:klɪç] *adj* (*+dat*) harmful (to)
abtransportieren ['aptranspɔrti:rən] *vt* to transport; to evacuate
abtreiben ['aptraɪbən] *unreg vt* (*Boot, Flugzeug*) to drive off course; (*Kind*) to abort ▷ *vi* to be driven off course; (*Frau*) to have an abortion
Abtreibung *f* abortion
Abtreibungsversuch *m* attempted abortion
abtrennen ['aptrɛnən] *vt* (*lostrennen*) to detach; (*entfernen*) to take off; (*abteilen*) to separate off
abtreten ['aptre:tən] *unreg vt* to wear out; (*überlassen*) to hand over, cede; (*Rechte, Ansprüche*) to transfer ▷ *vi* to go off; (*zurücktreten*) to step down; **sich** *dat* **die Füße ~** to wipe one's feet; **~!** (*Mil*) dismiss!
abtrocknen ['aptrɔknən] *vt* to dry ▷ *vi* to do the drying-up
abtrünnig ['aptrʏnɪç] *adj* renegade
abtun ['aptu:n] *unreg vt* to take off; (*fig*) to dismiss; **etw kurz ~** to brush sth aside
aburteilen ['ap|ʊrtaɪlən] *vt* to condemn
abverlangen ['apfɛrlaŋən] *vt*: **jdm etw ~** to demand sth from sb
abwägen ['apvɛ:gən] *unreg vt* to weigh up
abwählen ['apvɛ:lən] *vt* to vote out (of office); (*Sch*: *Fach*) to give up
abwandeln ['apvandəln] *vt* to adapt
abwandern ['apvandərn] *vi* to move away
Abwärme ['apvɛrmə] *f* waste heat
abwarten ['apvartən] *vt* to wait for ▷ *vi* to wait; **das Gewitter ~** to wait till the storm is over; **~ und Tee trinken** (*umg*) to wait and see; **eine ~de Haltung einnehmen** to play a waiting game
abwärts ['apvɛrts] *adv* down; **mit ihm/dem Land geht es ~** he/the country is going

downhill
Abwasch ['apvaʃ] (**-(e)s**) *m* washing-up; **du kannst das auch machen, das ist (dann) ein ~** (*umg*) you could do that as well and kill two birds with one stone
abwaschen *unreg vt* (*Schmutz*) to wash off; (*Geschirr*) to wash (up)
Abwasser ['apvasər] (**-s, -wässer**) *nt* sewage
abwechseln ['apvɛksəln] *vi, vr* to alternate; (*Personen*) to take turns
abwechselnd *adj* alternate
Abwechslung *f* change; (*Zerstreuung*) diversion; **für ~ sorgen** to provide entertainment
abwechslungsreich *adj* varied
Abweg ['apve:k] *m*: **auf ~e geraten/führen** to go/lead astray
abwegig ['apve:gɪç] *adj* wrong; (*Verdacht*) groundless
Abwehr ['apve:r] (**-**) *f* defence; (*Schutz*) protection; (*Abwehrdienst*) counter-intelligence (service); **auf ~ stoßen** to be repulsed; **abwehren** *vt* to ward off; (*Ball*) to stop; **abwehrende Geste** dismissive gesture
abweichen ['apvaɪçən] *unreg vi* to deviate; (*Meinung*) to differ; **vom rechten Weg ~** (*fig*) to wander off the straight and narrow
abweisen ['apvaɪzən] *unreg vt* to turn away; (*Antrag*) to turn down; **er lässt sich nicht ~** he won't take no for an answer
abweisend *adj* (*Haltung*) cold
abwenden ['apvɛndən] *unreg vt* to avert ▷ *vr* to turn away
abwerben ['apvɛrbən] *unreg vt*: **(jdm) ~** to woo away (from sb)
abwerfen ['apvɛrfən] *unreg vt* to throw off; (*Profit*) to yield; (*aus Flugzeug*) to drop; (*Spielkarte*) to discard
abwerten ['apvɛrtən] *vt* (*Fin*) to devalue
abwesend ['apve:zənt] *adj* absent; (*zerstreut*) far away
Abwesenheit ['apve:zənhaɪt] *f* absence; **durch ~ glänzen** (*ironisch*) to be conspicuous by one's absence
abwickeln ['apvɪkəln] *vt* to unwind; (*Geschäft*) to transact, conclude; (*fig: erledigen*) to deal with
abwiegen ['apvi:gən] *unreg vt* to weigh out
abwimmeln ['apvɪməln] (*umg*) *vt* (*Person*) to get rid of; (*: Auftrag*) to get out of
abwinken ['apvɪŋkən] *vi* to wave it/him *etc* aside; (*fig: ablehnen*) to say no
abwirtschaften ['apvɪrtʃaftən] *vi* to go downhill
abwischen ['apvɪʃən] *vt* to wipe off *od* away; (*putzen*) to wipe
Abwurf ['apvʊrf] *m* throwing off; (*von Bomben etc*) dropping; (*von Reiter, Sport*) throw
abwürgen ['apvʏrgən] (*umg*) *vt* to scotch; (*Motor*) to stall; **etw von vornherein ~** to nip sth in the bud
abzahlen ['aptsa:lən] *vt* to pay off
abzählen ['aptsɛ:lən] *vt* to count (up); **abgezähltes Fahrgeld** exact fare
Abzahlung *f* repayment; **auf ~ kaufen** to buy on hire purchase (*Brit*) *od* the installment plan (*US*)
abzapfen ['aptsapfən] *vt* to draw off; **jdm Blut ~** to take blood from sb
abzäunen ['aptsɔʏnən] *vt* to fence off
Abzeichen ['aptsaɪçən] *nt* badge; (*Orden*) decoration
abzeichnen ['aptsaɪçnən] *vt* to draw, copy; (*unterschreiben*) to initial ▷ *vr* to stand out; (*fig: bevorstehen*) to loom
Abziehbild *nt* transfer
abziehen ['aptsi:ən] *unreg vt* to take off; (*Tier*) to skin; (*Bett*) to strip; (*Truppen*) to withdraw; (*subtrahieren*) to take away, subtract; (*kopieren*) to run off; (*Schlüssel*) to take out, remove ▷ *vi* to go away; (*Truppen*) to withdraw; (*abdrücken*) to pull the trigger, fire
abzielen ['aptsi:lən] *vi*: **~ auf** *+akk* to be aimed at
Abzug ['aptsu:k] *m* departure; (*von Truppen*) withdrawal; (*Kopie*) copy; (*Subtraktion*) subtraction; (*Betrag*) deduction; (*Rauchabzug*) flue; (*von Waffen*) trigger; (*Rabatt*) discount; (*Korrekturfahne*) proof; (*Phot*) print; **jdm freien ~ gewähren** to grant sb safe passage
abzüglich ['aptsy:klɪç] *präp +gen* less
abzweigen ['aptsvaɪgən] *vi* to branch off ▷ *vt* to set aside
Abzweigung *f* junction
Accessoires [aksɛso'a:rs] *pl* accessories *pl*
ach [ax] *interj* oh; **~ so!** I see!; **mit A~ und Krach** by the skin of one's teeth; **~ was** *od* **wo, das ist doch nicht so schlimm!** come on now, it's not that bad!
Achse ['aksə] (**-, -n**) *f* axis; (*Aut*) axle; **auf ~ sein** (*umg*) to be on the move
Achsel ['aksəl] (**-, -n**) *f* shoulder; **Achselhöhle** *f* armpit; **Achselzucken** *nt* shrug (of one's shoulders)
Achsenbruch *m* (*Aut*) broken axle
Acht[1] [axt] (**-, -en**) *f* eight; (*beim Eislaufen etc*) figure (of) eight
Acht[2] (**-**) *f* attention; **hab ~** (*Mil*) attention!; **~ geben = achtgeben**; **sich in ~ nehmen (vor** *+dat***)** to be careful (of), watch out (for); **etw außer ~ lassen** to disregard sth
acht *num* eight; **~ Tage** a week
achtbar *adj* worthy
achte, r, s *adj* eighth
Achtel *nt* eighth
achten *vt* to respect ▷ *vi*: **~ (auf** *+akk***)** to pay attention (to); **darauf ~, dass ...** to be careful that ...
Achterbahn *f* roller coaster
Achterdeck *nt* (*Naut*) afterdeck
achtfach *adj* eightfold
achtgeben *unreg vi*: **~ (auf** *+akk***)** to take care (of); (*aufmerksam sein*) to pay attention (to)
achtlos *adj* careless; **viele gehen ~ daran vorbei** many people just pass by without noticing

achtmal *adv* eight times
achtsam *adj* attentive
Achtung ['axtʊŋ] *f* attention; (*Ehrfurcht*) respect ▷ *interj* look out!; (*Mil*) attention!; **alle ~!** good for you/him *etc*!; **~, fertig, los!** ready, steady, go!; **„~ Hochspannung!"** "danger, high voltage"; **„~ Lebensgefahr/ Stufe!"** "danger/mind the step!"
achtzehn *num* eighteen
achtzig *num* eighty
ächzen ['ɛçtsən] *vi*: **~ (vor** *+dat***)** to groan (with)
Acker ['akər] (**-s, ¨**) *m* field; **Ackerbau** *m* agriculture; **Ackerbau und Viehzucht** farming
ackern *vi* to plough; (*umg*) to slog away
ADAC (-) *m abk* (*= Allgemeiner Deutscher Automobil-Club*) *German motoring organization*, ≈ AA (*Brit*), ≈ AAA (*US*)
addieren [a'di:rən] *vt* to add (up)
Addition [aditsi'o:n] *f* addition
ade *interj* bye!
Adel ['a:dəl] (**-s**) *m* nobility; **~ verpflichtet** noblesse oblige
Ader ['a:dər] (**-, -n**) *f* vein; (*fig: Veranlagung*) bent
Adjektiv ['atjɛkti:f] (**-s, -e**) *nt* adjective
Adler ['a:dlər] (**-s, -**) *m* eagle
Admiral [atmi'ra:l] (**-s, -e**) *m* admiral
adoptieren [adɔp'ti:rən] *vt* to adopt
Adoption [adɔptsi'o:n] *f* adoption
Adoptiveltern *pl* adoptive parents *pl*
Adoptivkind *nt* adopted child
Adressant [adrɛ'sant] *m* sender
Adressat [adrɛ'sa:t] (**-en, -en**) *m* addressee
Adressbuch *nt* directory; (*privat*) address book
Adresse [a'drɛsə] (**-, -n**) *f* (*auch Comput*) address; **an der falschen ~ sein** (*umg*) to have gone/come to the wrong person; **absolute ~** absolute address; **relative ~** relative address
adressieren [adrɛ'si:rən] *vt*: **~ (an** *+akk***)** to address (to)
Advent [at'vɛnt] (**-(e)s, -e**) *m* Advent; **der erste/zweite ~** the first/second Sunday in Advent
Adventskranz *m* Advent wreath
Adverb [at'vɛrp] *nt* adverb
adverbial [atverbi'a:l] *adj* adverbial
aero- [aero] *präf* aero-
Aerobic [ae'ro:bik] (**-s**) *nt* aerobics *sing*
Affäre [a'fɛ:rə] (**-, -n**) *f* affair; **sich aus der ~ ziehen** (*umg*) to get (o.s.) out of it
Affe ['afə] (**-n, -n**) *m* monkey; (*umg: Kerl*) berk (*Brit*)
affektiert [afɛk'ti:rt] *adj* affected
Affen- *zW*: **affenartig** *adj* like a monkey; **mit affenartiger Geschwindigkeit** (*umg*) like a flash; **Affenhitze** (*umg*) *f* incredible heat; **Affenschande** (*umg*) *f* crying shame
affig ['afɪç] *adj* affected
Afghane [af'ga:nə] (**-n, -n**) *m* Afghan
Afghanin [af'ga:nɪn] *f* Afghan
afghanisch *adj* Afghan
Afghanistan [af'ga:nɪsta:n] (**-s**) *nt* Afghanistan
Afrika ['a:frika] (**-s**) *nt* Africa
Afrikaner, in [afri'ka:nər(ɪn)] (**-s, -**) *m(f)* African
afrikanisch *adj* African
After ['aftər] (**-s, -**) *m* anus
AG (-) *f abk* (*= Aktiengesellschaft*) ≈ plc (*Brit*), ≈ corp., inc. (*US*)
Ägäis [ɛ'gɛ:ɪs] (-) *f* Aegean (Sea)
Agent, in [a'gɛnt(ɪn)] *m(f)* agent
Agentur [agɛn'tu:r] *f* agency
Aggregat [agre'ga:t] (**-(e)s, -e**) *nt* aggregate; (*Tech*) unit; **Aggregatzustand** *m* (*Phys*) state
Aggression [agrɛsi'o:n] *f* aggression
aggressiv [agrɛ'si:f] *adj* aggressive
Aggressivität [agrɛsivi'tɛ:t] *f* aggressiveness
Agitation [agitatsi'o:n] *f* agitation
Agrarpolitik *f* agricultural policy
Agrarstaat *m* agrarian state
Ägypten [ɛ'gʏptən] (**-s**) *nt* Egypt
ägyptisch *adj* Egyptian
aha [a'ha:] *interj* aha!
Aha-Erlebnis *nt* sudden insight
ähneln ['ɛ:nəln] *vi +dat* to be like, resemble ▷ *vr* to be alike *od* similar
ahnen ['a:nən] *vt* to suspect; (*Tod, Gefahr*) to have a presentiment of; **nichts Böses ~** to be unsuspecting; **du ahnst es nicht!** you have no idea!; **davon habe ich nichts geahnt** I didn't have the slightest inkling of it
ähnlich ['ɛ:nlɪç] *adj (+dat)* similar (to); **das sieht ihm (ganz) ~!** (*umg*) that's just like him!, that's him all over!; **Ähnlichkeit** *f* similarity
Ahnung ['a:nʊŋ] *f* idea, suspicion; (*Vorgefühl*) presentiment
ahnungslos *adj* unsuspecting
Ahorn ['a:hɔrn] (**-s, -e**) *m* maple
Ähre ['ɛ:rə] (**-, -n**) *f* ear
Aids [e:dz] (-) *nt* Aids
Airbag ['ɛ: bɛ:g] (**-s, -s**) *m* (*Aut*) airbag
Akademie [akade'mi:] *f* academy
Akademiker, in [aka'de:mikər(ɪn)] (**-s, -**) *m(f)* university graduate
akademisch *adj* academic
akklimatisieren [aklimati'zi:rən] *vr* to become acclimatized
Akkord [a'kɔrt] (**-(e)s, -e**) *m* (*Mus*) chord; **im ~ arbeiten** to do piecework; **Akkordarbeit** *f* piecework
Akkordeon [a'kɔrdeɔn] (**-s, -s**) *nt* accordion
Akkusativ ['akuzati:f] (**-s, -e**) *m* accusative (case)
Akne ['aknə] (**-, -n**) *f* acne
Akrobat, in [akro'ba:t(ɪn)] (**-en, -en**) *m(f)* acrobat
Akt [akt] (**-(e)s, -e**) *m* act; (*Kunst*) nude
Akte ['aktə] (**-, -n**) *f* file; **etw zu den ~n legen** (*lit, fig*) to file sth away
Akten- *zW*: **Aktenkoffer** *m* attaché case; **aktenkundig** *adj* on record; **Aktenschrank** *m*

filing cabinet; **Aktentasche** *f* briefcase
Aktie ['aktsiə] (**-, -n**) *f* share; **wie stehen die ~n?** (*hum: umg*) how are things?
Aktien- *zW*: **Aktienemission** *f* share issue; **Aktiengesellschaft** *f* joint-stock company
Aktion [aktsi'o:n] *f* campaign; (*Polizeiaktion, Suchaktion*) action
Aktionär, in [aktsio'nɛ:r(ɪn)] (**-s, -e**) *m(f)* shareholder
aktiv [ak'ti:f] *adj* active; (*Mil*) regular; **Aktiv** (**-s**) *nt* (*Gram*) active (voice)
Aktiva [ak'ti:va] *pl* assets *pl*
aktivieren [akti'vi:rən] *vt* to activate; (*fig: Arbeit, Kampagne*) to step up; (*Mitarbeiter*) to get moving
Aktivität [aktivi'tɛ:t] *f* activity
Aktivsaldo *m* (*Comm*) credit balance
Aktivurlaub *m* activity holiday
aktualisieren [aktuali'zi:rən] *vt* (*Comput*) to update
Aktualität [aktuali'tɛ:t] *f* topicality; (*einer Mode*) up-to-dateness
aktuell [aktu'ɛl] *adj* topical; up-to-date; **eine ~e Sendung** (*Rundf, TV*) a current affairs programme
Akupunktur [akupuŋk'tu:ər] *f* acupuncture
Akustik [a'kʊstɪk] *f* acoustics *pl*
akut [a'ku:t] *adj* acute; (*Frage*) pressing, urgent
AKW *nt abk* = **Atomkraftwerk**
Akzent [ak'tsɛnt] (**-(e)s, -e**) *m* accent; (*Betonung*) stress; **~e setzen** (*fig*) to bring out *od* emphasize the main points
akzeptabel [aktsɛp'ta:bl] *adj* acceptable
akzeptieren [aktsɛp'ti:rən] *vt* to accept
Alarm [a'larm] (**-(e)s, -e**) *m* alarm; (*Zustand*) alert; **~ schlagen** to give *od* raise the alarm; **Alarmanlage** *f* alarm system; **Alarmbereitschaft** *f* stand-by
alarmieren [alar'mi:rən] *vt* to alarm
Alaska [a'laska] (**-s**) *nt* Alaska
Albaner, in [al'ba:nər(ɪn)] (**-s, -**) *m(f)* Albanian
Albanien [al'ba:niən] (**-s**) *nt* Albania
albanisch *adj* Albanian
albern ['albərn] *adj* silly
Albtraum ['alptraʊm] *m* nightmare
Album ['albʊm] (**-s, Alben**) *nt* album
Alge ['algə] (**-, -n**) *f* alga
Algebra ['algebra] (**-**) *f* algebra
Algerien [al'ge:riən] (**-s**) *nt* Algeria
Algerier, in (**-s, -**) *m(f)* Algerian
algerisch [al'ge:rɪʃ] *adj* Algerian
Algorithmus [algo'rɪtmʊs] *m* (*Comput*) algorithm
alias ['a:lias] *adv* alias
Alibi ['a:libi] (**-s, -s**) *nt* alibi
Alimente [ali'mɛntə] *pl* alimony *sing*
Alkohol ['alkohɔl] (**-s, -e**) *m* alcohol; **unter ~ stehen** to be under the influence (of alcohol); **alkoholfrei** *adj* non-alcoholic
Alkoholiker, in [alko'ho:likər(ɪn)] (**-s, -**) *m(f)* alcoholic
alkoholisch *adj* alcoholic
Alkoholverbot *nt* ban on alcohol
All [al] (**-s**) *nt* universe; (*Raumfahrt*) space; (*außerhalb unseres Sternsystems*) outer space
allabendlich *adj* every evening
alle *adj siehe* **alle(r, s)**
Allee [a'le:] (**-, -n**) *f* avenue
allein [a'laɪn] *adj, adv* alone; (*ohne Hilfe*) on one's own, by oneself ▷ *konj* (*geh*) but, only; **von ~** by oneself/itself; **nicht ~** (*nicht nur*) not only; **~ schon der Gedanke** the very *od* mere thought ..., the thought alone ...; **Alleinerziehende, r** *f(m)*, **Alleinerzieher, in** *m(f)* single parent; **Alleingang** *m*: **im Alleingang** on one's own; **Alleinherrscher, in** *m(f)* autocrat; **Alleinhersteller, in** *m(f)* sole manufacturer
alleinig [a'laɪnɪç] *adj* sole
alleinstehend *adj* single
allemal ['alə'ma:l] *adv* (*jedes Mal*) always; (*ohne Weiteres*) with no bother; *siehe auch* **Mal**
allenfalls ['alən'fals] *adv* at all events; (*höchstens*) at most
alle, r, s *adj* **1** (*sämtliche*) all; **wir alle** all of us; **alle Kinder waren da** all the children were there; **alle Kinder mögen ...** all children like ...; **alle beide** both of us/them; **sie kamen alle** they all came; **alles Gute** all the best; **alles in allem** all in all; **vor allem** above all; **das ist alles andere als ...** that's anything but ...; **es hat alles keinen Sinn mehr** nothing makes sense any more; **was habt ihr alles gemacht?** what did you get up to?
2 (*mit Zeit- oder Maßangaben*) every; **alle vier Jahre** every four years; **alle fünf Meter** every five metres
▷ *pron* everything; **alles was er sagt** everything he says, all that he says; **trotz allem** in spite of everything
▷ *adv* (*zu Ende, aufgebraucht*) finished; **die Milch ist alle** the milk's all gone, there's no milk left; **etw alle machen** to finish sth up
allerbeste, r, s ['alər'bɛstə(r, s)] *adj* very best
allerdings ['alər'dɪŋs] *adv* (*zwar*) admittedly; (*gewiss*) certainly
Allergie [aler'gi:] *f* allergy
allergisch [a'lɛrgɪʃ] *adj* allergic; **auf etw** *akk* **~ reagieren** to be allergic to sth
allerhand (*umg*) *adj inv* all sorts of; **das ist doch ~!** that's a bit much!; **~!** (*lobend*) good show!
Allerheiligen *nt* All Saints' Day
aller- *zW*: **allerhöchste, r, s** *adj* very highest; **es wird allerhöchste Zeit, dass ...** it's really high time that ...; **allerhöchstens** *adv* at the very most; **allerlei** *adj inv* all sorts of; **allerletzte, r, s** *adj* very last; **der/das ist das Allerletzte** (*umg*) he's/it's the absolute end!
Allerseelen (**-s**) *nt* All Soul's Day; *siehe auch* **Allerheiligen**; **allerseits** *adv* on all sides; **prost allerseits!** cheers everyone!
allerwenigste, r, s *adj* very least; **die ~n Menschen wissen das** very few people

know that
alles *pron* everything; *siehe auch* **alle(r; s)**
Alleskleber (**-s, -**) *m* all-purpose adhesive
allgegenwärtig *adj* omnipresent, ubiquitous
allgemein ['algəmaın] *adj* general ▷ *adv*: **es ist ~ üblich** it's the general rule; **~ verständlich** generally intelligible; **im A~** in general; **im ~en Interesse** in the common interest; **auf ~en Wunsch** by popular request; **Allgemeinbildung** *f* general *od* all-round education; **allgemeingültig** *adj* generally accepted; **Allgemeinheit** *f* (*Menschen*) general public; **Allgemeinheiten** *pl* (*Redensarten*) general remarks *pl*
Alliierte, r [ali'i:rtə(r)] *f(m)* ally
all- *zW*: **alljährlich** *adj* annual; **allmählich** *adv* gradually; **es wird allmählich Zeit** (*umg*) it's about time; **Allradantrieb** *m* all-wheel drive; **Alltag** *m* everyday life; **alltäglich** *adj* daily; (*gewöhnlich*) commonplace
all- *zW*: **allwissend** *adj* omniscient; **allzu** *adv* all too; **allzu gern** (*mögen*) only too much; (*bereitwillig*) only too willingly; **allzu oft** all too often; **allzu viel** too much
Alm [alm] (**-, -en**) *f* alpine pasture
Almosen ['almo:zən] (**-s, -**) *nt* alms *pl*
Alpen ['alpən] *pl* Alps *pl*
Alphabet [alfa'be:t] (**-(e)s, -e**) *nt* alphabet
alphabetisch *adj* alphabetical
alphanumerisch [alfanu'me:rıʃ] *adj* (*Comput*) alphanumeric
Alptraum ['alptraʊm] *m* = **Albtraum**
als [als] *konj* **1** (*zeitlich*) when; (*gleichzeitig*) as; **damals als ...** (in the days) when ...; **gerade als ...** just as ...
2 (*in der Eigenschaft*) than; **als Antwort** as an answer; **als Kind** as a child
3 (*bei Vergleichen*) than; **ich kam später als er** I came later than he (did) *od* later than him; **lieber ... als ...** rather ... than ...; **alles andere als** anything but; **nichts als Ärger** nothing but trouble; **so viel/so weit als möglich** (*bei Vergleichen*) as much/far as possible
4: als ob/wenn as if
also ['alzo:] *konj* so; (*folglich*) therefore; **~ wie ich schon sagte** well (then), as I said before; **ich komme ~ morgen** so I'll come tomorrow; **~ gut** *od* **schön!** okay then; **~, so was!** well really!; **na ~!** there you are then!
Alt [alt] (**-s, -e**) *m* (*Mus*) alto
alt *adj* old; **ich bin nicht mehr der A~e** I am not the man I was; **alles beim A~en lassen** to leave everything as it was; **ich werde heute nicht ~ (werden)** (*umg*) I won't last long today/tonight *etc*; **~ aussehen** (*fig: umg*) to be in a pickle
Altar [al'ta:r] (**-(e)s, -äre**) *m* altar
alt- *zW*: **Altbau** *m* old building; **altbekannt** *adj* well-known; **Altbier** *nt top-fermented German dark beer*; **Alteisen** *nt* scrap iron
Alter ['altər] (**-s, -**) *nt* age; (*hohes*) old age; **er ist in deinem ~** he's your age; **im ~ von** at the age of
altern ['altərn] *vi* to grow old, age
Alternativ- [altɛrna'ti:f] *in zW* alternative
alternativ *adj*: **A~e Liste** *electoral pact between the Greens and alternative parties*; **~ leben** to live an alternative way of life
Alternative [altɛrna'ti:və] *f* alternative; **Alternativmedizin** *f* alternative medicine
Alters- *zW*: **Altersgrenze** *f* age limit; **flexible Altersgrenze** flexible retirement age; **Altersheim** *nt* old people's home; **Altersrente** *f* old age pension; **altersschwach** *adj* (*Mensch*) old and infirm; (*Auto, Möbel*) decrepit; **Altersversorgung** *f* provision for old age
Altertum ['altərtu:m] *nt* antiquity
alt- *zW*: **Altglas** *nt* used glass (*for recycling*), scrap glass; **Altglascontainer** *m* bottle bank; **althergebracht** *adj* traditional; **altklug** *adj* precocious; **Altlasten** *pl* legacy *sing* of dangerous waste; **Altmaterial** *nt* scrap; **altmodisch** *adj* old-fashioned; **Altpapier** *nt* waste paper; **Altstadt** *f* old town
Altstimme *f* alto
Altweibersommer *m* Indian summer
Alufolie ['a:lufo:liə] *f* tinfoil
Aluminium [alu'mi:niʊm] (**-s**) *nt* aluminium, aluminum (*US*)
Alzheimerkrankheit ['altshaımər'kraŋkhaıt] *f* Alzheimer's disease
am [am] = **an dem**; **am Sterben** on the point of dying; **am 15. März** on March 15th; **am letzten Sonntag** last Sunday; **am Morgen/Abend** in the morning/evening; **am besten/schönsten** best/most beautiful
Amalgam [amal'ga:m] (**-s, -e**) *nt* amalgam
Amateur [ama'tø:r] *m* amateur
Amazonas [ama'tso:nas] (**-**) *m* Amazon (river)
Amboss ['ambɔs] (**-es, -e**) *m* anvil
ambulant [ambu'lant] *adj* outpatient
Ameise ['a:maızə] (**-, -n**) *f* ant
Amerika [a'me:rika] (**-s**) *nt* America
Amerikaner [ameri'ka:nər] (**-s, -**) *m* American; (*Gebäck*) *flat iced cake*
amerikanisch *adj* American
Ampel ['ampəl] (**-, -n**) *f* traffic lights *pl*
amphibisch [am'fi:bıʃ] *adj* amphibious
amputieren [ampu'ti:rən] *vt* to amputate
Amsel ['amzəl] (**-, -n**) *f* blackbird
Amt [amt] (**-(e)s, ¨-er**) *nt* office; (*Pflicht*) duty; (*Tel*) exchange; **zum zuständigen ~ gehen** to go to the relevant authority; **von ~s wegen** (*auf behördliche Anordnung hin*) officially
amtieren [am'ti:rən] *vi* to hold office; (*fungieren*): **als ...** ~ to act as ...
amtlich *adj* official; **~es Kennzeichen** registration (number), license number (*US*)
Amts- *zW*: **Amtsperson** *f* official; **Amtsrichter** *m* district judge; **Amtsstunden** *pl* office hours *pl*; **Amtszeit** *f* period of office
amüsant [amy'zant] *adj* amusing
Amüsement [amyzə'mã:] *nt* amusement
amüsieren [amy'zi:rən] *vt* to amuse ▷ *vr* to

enjoy o.s.; **sich über etw** *akk* ~ to find sth funny; (*unfreundlich*) to make fun of sth

an [an] *präp +dat* **1** (*räumlich: wo?*) at; (*auf, bei*) on; (*nahe bei*) near; **an diesem Ort** at this place; **an der Wand** on the wall; **zu nahe an etw** too near to sth; **unten am Fluss** down by the river; **Köln liegt am Rhein** Cologne is on the Rhine; **an der gleichen Stelle** at *od* on the same spot; **jdn an der Hand nehmen** to take sb by the hand; **sie wohnen Tür an Tür** they live next door to one another; **es an der Leber** *etc* **haben** (*umg*) to have liver *etc* trouble
2 (*zeitlich: wann?*) on; **an diesem Tag** on this day; **an Ostern** at Easter
3: arm an Fett low in fat; **jung an Jahren sein** to be young in years; **an der ganzen Sache ist nichts** there is nothing in it; **an etw sterben** to die of sth; **an (und für) sich** actually
▷ *präp +akk* **1** (*räumlich: wohin?*) to; **er ging ans Fenster** he went (over) to the window; **etw an die Wand hängen/schreiben** to hang/write sth on the wall; **an die Arbeit gehen** to get down to work
2 (*zeitlich: woran?*): **an etw denken** to think of sth
3 (*gerichtet an*) to; **ein Gruß/eine Frage an dich** greetings/a question to you
▷ *adv* **1** (*ungefähr*) about; **an die Hundert** about a hundred; **an die 10 Euro** around 10 euros
2 (*auf Fahrplänen*): **Frankfurt an 18.30** arriving Frankfurt 18.30
3 (*ab*): **von dort/heute an** from there/today onwards
4 (*angeschaltet, angezogen*) on; **an sein** (*umg*) to be on; **das Licht ist an** the light is on; **ohne etwas an** with nothing on; *siehe auch* **am**

analog [ana'lo:k] *adj* analogous

Analogie [analo'gi:] *f* analogy

Analogrechner [ana'lo:kreçnər] *m* analog computer

Analyse [ana'ly:zə] (**-, -n**) *f* analysis

analysieren [analy'zi:rən] *vt* to analyse (*Brit*), analyze (*US*)

Ananas ['ananas] (**-,** - *od* **-se**) *f* pineapple

Anarchie [anar'çi:] *f* anarchy

Anarchist, in [anar'çɪst(ɪn)] *m(f)* (**-en, -en**) anarchist

Anatomie [anato'mi:] *f* anatomy

anbahnen ['anba:nən] *vr* to open up; (*sich andeuten*) to be in the offing; (*Unangenehmes*) to be looming ▷ *vt* to initiate

Anbau ['anbaʊ] *m* (*Agr*) cultivation; (*Gebäude*) extension

anbauen *vt* (*Agr*) to cultivate; (*Gebäudeteil*) to build on

anbehalten ['anbəhaltən] *unreg vt* to keep on

anbei [an'baɪ] *adv* enclosed (*form*); **~ schicken wir Ihnen ...** please find enclosed ...

anbelangen ['anbəlaŋən] *vt* to concern; **was mich anbelangt** as far as I am concerned

anbeten ['anbe:tən] *vt* to worship

Anbetracht ['anbətraxt] *m*: **in ~** *+gen* in view of

anbiedern ['anbi:dərn] (*pej*) *vr*: **sich ~ (bei)** to curry favour (with)

anbieten ['anbi:tən] *unreg vt* to offer ▷ *vr* to volunteer; **das bietet sich als Lösung an** that would provide a solution

anbinden ['anbɪndən] *unreg vt* to tie up; (*verbinden*) to connect

Anblick ['anblɪk] *m* sight

anblicken *vt* to look at

anbraten ['anbra:tən] *unreg vt* (*Fleisch*) to brown

anbrechen ['anbreçən] *unreg vt* to start; (*Vorräte*) to break into ▷ *vi* to start; (*Tag*) to break; (*Nacht*) to fall

anbrennen ['anbrɛnən] *unreg vi* to catch fire; (*Koch*) to burn

anbringen ['anbrɪŋən] *unreg vt* to bring; (*Ware*) to sell; (*festmachen*) to fasten; (*Telefon etc*) to install

Anbruch ['anbrʊx] *m* beginning; **~ des Tages** dawn; **~ der Nacht** nightfall

anbrüllen ['anbrʏlən] *vt* to roar at

Andacht ['andaxt] (**-, -en**) *f* devotion; (*Versenkung*) rapt interest; (*Gottesdienst*) prayers *pl*; (*Ehrfurcht*) reverence

andächtig ['andɛçtɪç] *adj* devout

andauern ['andaʊərn] *vi* to last, go on

andauernd *adj* continual

Anden ['andən] *pl*: **die ~** the Andes *pl*

Andenken ['andɛŋkən] (**-s, -**) *nt* memory; (*Reiseandenken*) souvenir; (*Erinnerungsstück*): **ein ~ (an** *+akk*) a memento (of), a keepsake (from)

andere, r, s *adj* other; (*verschieden*) different; **am ~n Tage** the next day; **ein ~s Mal** another time; **kein ~r** nobody else; **alles ~ als zufrieden** anything but pleased, far from pleased; **von etwas ~m sprechen** to talk about something else; **es blieb mir nichts ~s übrig als selbst hinzugehen** I had no alternative but to go myself; **unter ~m** among other things; **von einem Tag zum ~n** overnight; **sie hat einen ~n** she has someone else

ändern ['ɛndərn] *vt* to alter, change ▷ *vr* to change

andernfalls *adv* otherwise

anders *adv*: **~ (als)** differently (from); **wer ~?** who else?; **niemand ~** no-one else; **wie nicht ~ zu erwarten** as was to be expected; **wie könnte es ~ sein?** how could it be otherwise?; **ich kann nicht ~** (*kann es nicht lassen*) I can't help it; (*muss leider*) I have no choice; **~ ausgedrückt** to put it another way; **jemand/irgendwo ~** somebody/somewhere else; **~ aussehen/klingen** to look/sound different; **~ lautend = anderslautend**

andersartig *adj* different

anders- *zW*: **andersfarbig** *adj* of a different colour; **andersgläubig** *adj* of a different faith; **andersherum** *adv* the other way round; **anderswo** *adv* elsewhere; **anderswoher** *adv* from elsewhere; **anderswohin** *adv* elsewhere

anderthalb ['andərt'halp] *adj* one and a half

Änderung ['ɛndərʊŋ] *f* alteration, change

anderweitig ['andər'vaɪtɪç] *adj* other ▷ *adv* otherwise; (*anderswo*) elsewhere

andeuten ['andɔʏtən] *vt* to indicate; (*Wink geben*) to hint at

Andeutung *f* indication; hint

andeutungsweise *adv* (*als Anspielung, Anzeichen*) by way of a hint; (*als flüchtiger Hinweis*) in passing

Andorra [an'dɔra] (**-s**) *nt* Andorra

Andrang ['andraŋ] *m* crush

andrehen ['andre:ən] *vt* to turn *od* switch on; **jdm etw ~** (*umg*) to unload sth onto sb

androhen ['andro:ən] *vt*: **jdm etw ~** to threaten sb with sth

aneignen ['an|aɪgnən] *vt*: **sich** *dat* **etw ~** to acquire sth; (*widerrechtlich*) to appropriate sth; (*sich mit etw vertraut machen*) to learn sth

aneinander [an|aɪ'nandər] *adv* at/on/to *etc* one another *od* each other

anekeln ['an|e:kəln] *vt* to disgust

Anemone [ane'mo:nə] (**-, -n**) *f* anemone

anerkannt ['an|ɛrkant] *adj* recognized, acknowledged

anerkennen ['an|ɛrkɛnən] *unreg vt* to recognize, acknowledge; (*würdigen*) to appreciate; **das muss man ~** (*zugeben*) you can't argue with that; (*würdigen*) one has to appreciate that

anerkennend *adj* appreciative

anerkennenswert *adj* praiseworthy

Anerkennung *f* recognition, acknowledgement; appreciation

anfahren ['anfa:rən] *unreg vt* to deliver; (*fahren gegen*) to hit; (*Hafen*) to put into; (*umg*) to bawl at ▷ *vi* to drive up; (*losfahren*) to drive off

Anfall ['anfal] *m* (*Med*) attack; **in einem ~ von** (*fig*) in a fit of

anfallen *unreg vt* to attack ▷ *vi* (*Arbeit*) to come up; (*Produkt, Nebenprodukte*) to be obtained; (*Zinsen*) to accrue; (*sich anhäufen*) to accumulate; **die ~den Kosten/ Reparaturen** the costs/repairs incurred

anfällig ['anfɛlɪç] *adj* delicate; **~ für etw** prone to sth

Anfang ['anfaŋ] (**-(e)s, -fänge**) *m* beginning, start; **von ~ an** right from the beginning; **zu ~** at the beginning; **~ fünfzig** in one's early fifties; **~ Mai/1994** at the beginning of May/1994

anfangen ['anfaŋən] *unreg vt* to begin, start; (*machen*) to do ▷ *vi* to begin, start; **damit kann ich nichts ~** (*nützt mir nichts*) that's no good to me; (*verstehe ich nicht*) it doesn't mean a thing to me; **mit dir ist heute (aber) gar nichts anzufangen!** you're no fun at all today!; **bei einer Firma ~** to start working for a firm

Anfänger, in ['anfɛŋər(ɪn)] (**-s, -**) *m(f)* beginner

anfänglich ['anfɛŋlɪç] *adj* initial

anfangs *adv* at first; **wie ich schon ~ erwähnte** as I mentioned at the beginning; **Anfangsbuchstabe** *m* initial *od* first letter; **Anfangsstadium** *nt* initial stages *pl*

anfassen ['anfasən] *vt* to handle; (*berühren*) to touch ▷ *vi* to lend a hand ▷ *vr* to feel

anfechten ['anfɛçtən] *unreg vt* to dispute; (*Meinung, Aussage*) to challenge; (*Urteil*) to appeal against; (*beunruhigen*) to trouble

anfertigen ['anfɛrtɪgən] *vt* to make

anfeuern ['anfɔʏərn] *vt* (*fig*) to spur on

anflehen ['anfle:ən] *vt* to implore

anfliegen ['anfli:gən] *unreg vt* to fly to ▷ *vi* to fly up

Anflug ['anflu:k] *m* (*Aviat*) approach; (*Spur*) trace

anfordern ['anfɔrdərn] *vt* to demand; (*Comm*) to requisition

Anforderung *f* (*+gen*) demand (for); (*Comm*) requisition

Anfrage ['anfra:gə] *f* inquiry; (*Parl*) question

anfragen ['anfra:gən] *vi* to inquire

anfreunden ['anfrɔʏndən] *vr* to make friends; **sich mit etw ~** (*fig*) to get to like sth

anfügen ['anfy:gən] *vt* to add; (*beifügen*) to enclose

anfühlen ['anfy:lən] *vt, vr* to feel

anführen ['anfy:rən] *vt* to lead; (*zitieren*) to quote; (*umg: betrügen*) to lead up the garden path

Anführer, in (**-s, -**) *m(f)* leader

Angabe ['anga:bə] *f* statement; (*Tech*) specification; (*umg: Prahlerei*) boasting; (*Sport*) service; **Angaben** *pl* (*Auskunft*) particulars *pl*; **ohne ~ von Gründen** without giving any reasons; **~n zur Person** (*form*) personal details *od* particulars

angeben ['ange:bən] *unreg vt* to give; (*anzeigen*) to inform on; (*bestimmen*) to set ▷ *vi* (*umg*) to boast; (*Sport*) to serve

Angeber, in (**-s, -**) (*umg*) *m(f)* show-off

Angeberei [ange:bə'raɪ] (*umg*) *f* showing off

angeblich ['ange:plɪç] *adj* alleged

angeboren ['angəbo:rən] *adj* (*+dat*) inborn, innate (in); (*Med, fig*): **~ (bei)** congenital (to)

Angebot ['angəbo:t] *nt* offer; (*Comm*): **~ (an** *+dat***)** supply (of); **im ~** (*umg*) on special offer

angebracht ['angəbraxt] *adj* appropriate

angegriffen ['angəgrɪfən] *adj*: **er wirkt ~** he looks as if he's under a lot of strain

angeheitert ['angəhaɪtərt] *adj* tipsy

angehen ['ange:ən] *unreg vt* to concern; (*angreifen*) to attack; (*bitten*): **jdn ~ (um)** to approach sb (for) ▷ *vi* (*Feuer*) to light; (*umg: beginnen*) to begin; **das geht ihn gar nichts an** that's none of his business; **gegen jdn ~** (*entgegentreten*) to fight sb; **gegen etw ~** (*entgegentreten*) to fight sth; (*Missstände, Zustände*) to take measures against sth

angehend *adj* prospective; (*Musiker, Künstler*) budding

angehören ['angəhø:rən] *vi +dat* to belong to
Angehörige, r *f(m)* relative
Angeklagte, r ['angəkla:ktə(r)] *f(m)* accused, defendant
Angel ['aŋəl] (**-, -n**) *f* fishing rod; (*Türangel*) hinge; **die Welt aus den ~n heben** (*fig*) to turn the world upside down
Angelegenheit ['angəle:gənhaɪt] *f* affair, matter
Angelhaken *m* fish hook
angeln ['aŋəln] *vt* to catch ▷*vi* to fish; **Angeln** (**-s**) *nt* angling, fishing
Angelrute *f* fishing rod
angemessen ['angəmɛsən] *adj* appropriate, suitable; **eine der Leistung ~e Bezahlung** payment commensurate with the input
angenehm ['angəne:m] *adj* pleasant; **~!** (*bei Vorstellung*) pleased to meet you; **das A~e mit dem Nützlichen verbinden** to combine business with pleasure
angenommen ['angənɔmən] *pp von* **annehmen** ▷*adj* assumed; (*Kind*) adopted; **~, wir ...** assuming we ...
angepasst ['angəpast] *adj* conformist
angesehen ['angəze:ən] *pp von* **ansehen** ▷*adj* respected
angesichts ['angəzɪçts] *präp +gen* in view of, considering
angespannt ['angəʃpant] *adj* (*Aufmerksamkeit*) close; (*Nerven, Lage*) tense, strained; (*Comm: Markt*) tight, overstretched; (*Arbeit*) hard
Angestellte, r ['angəʃtɛltə(r)] *f(m)* employee; (*Büroangestellte*) white-collar worker
angetan ['angəta:n] *adj*: **von jdm/etw ~ sein** to be taken with sb/sth; **es jdm ~ haben** to appeal to sb
angewiesen ['angəvi:zən] *adj*: **auf jdn/etw ~ sein** to be dependent on sb/sth; **auf sich selbst ~ sein** to be left to one's own devices
angewöhnen ['angəvø:nən] *vt*: **jdm/sich etw ~** to accustom sb/become accustomed to sth
Angewohnheit ['angəvo:nhaɪt] *f* habit
angleichen ['anglaɪçən] *unreg vt, vr* to adjust
Angler ['aŋlər] (**-s, -**) *m* angler
Angola [aŋ'go:la] (**-s**) *nt* Angola
angreifen ['angraɪfən] *unreg vt* to attack; (*anfassen*) to touch; (*Arbeit*) to tackle; (*beschädigen*) to damage
Angriff ['angrɪf] *m* attack; **etw in ~ nehmen** to make a start on sth
angriffslustig *adj* aggressive
Angst [aŋst] (**-, ¨e**) *f* fear; **~ haben (vor** *+dat***)** to be afraid *od* scared (of); **~ um jdn/etw haben** to be worried about sb/sth; **jdm ~ einflößen** *od* **einjagen** to frighten sb; **jdm ~ machen** to scare sb; **nur keine ~!** don't be scared; **angst** *adj*: **jdm ist angst** sb is afraid *od* scared; **Angsthase** (*umg*) *m* chicken, scaredy-cat
ängstigen ['ɛŋstɪgən] *vt* to frighten ▷*vr*: **sich ~ (vor** *+dat od* **um)** to worry (o.s.) (about)
ängstlich *adj* nervous; (*besorgt*) worried; (*schüchtern*) timid; **Ängstlichkeit** *f* nervousness
anhaben ['anha:bən] *unreg vt* to have on; **er kann mir nichts ~** he can't hurt me
anhalten ['anhaltən] *unreg vt* to stop ▷*vi* to stop; (*andauern*) to persist; (*werben*): **um die Hand eines Mädchens ~** to ask for a girl's hand in marriage; **(jdm) etw ~** to hold sth up (against sb); **jdn zur Arbeit/Höflichkeit ~** to get sb to work/teach sb to be polite
anhaltend *adj* persistent
Anhalter, in (**-s, -**) *m(f)* hitch-hiker; **per ~ fahren** to hitch-hike
Anhaltspunkt *m* clue
anhand [an'hant] *präp +gen* with; **~ eines Beispiels** by means of an example
Anhang ['anhaŋ] *m* appendix; (*Leute*) family; (*Anhängerschaft*) supporters *pl*
anhängen ['anhɛŋən] *unreg vt* to hang up; (*Wagen*) to couple up; (*Zusatz*) to add (on); (*Comput*) to append; **sich an jdn ~** to attach o.s. to sb; **jdm etw ~** (*umg: nachsagen, anlasten*) to blame sb for sth, blame sth on sb; (*: Verdacht, Schuld*) to pin sth on sb
Anhänger (**-s, -**) *m* supporter; (*Aut*) trailer; (*am Koffer*) tag; (*Schmuck*) pendant; **Anhängerschaft** *f* supporters *pl*
anhängig *adj* (*Jur*) sub judice; **etw ~ machen** to start legal proceedings over sth
anhänglich *adj* devoted; **Anhänglichkeit** *f* devotion
Anhäufung ['anhɔʏfʊŋ] *f* accumulation
anheben ['anhe:bən] *unreg vt* to lift up; (*Preise*) to raise
anheimelnd ['anhaɪməlnt] *adj* comfortable, cosy
anheuern ['anhɔʏərn] *vt, vi* (*Naut, fig*) to sign on *od* up
Anhieb ['anhi:b] *m*: **auf ~** straight off, first go; **es klappte auf ~** it was an immediate success
Anhöhe ['anhø:ə] *f* hill
anhören ['anhø:rən] *vt* to listen to; (*anmerken*) to hear ▷*vr* to sound
animieren [ani'mi:rən] *vt* to encourage, urge on
Anis [a'ni:s] (**-es, -e**) *m* aniseed
Ankauf ['ankaʊf] *m*: **~ und Verkauf von ...** we buy and sell ...; **ankaufen** *vt* to purchase, buy
Anker ['aŋkər] (**-s, -**) *m* anchor; **vor ~ gehen** to drop anchor
ankern *vt, vi* to anchor
Ankerplatz *m* anchorage
Anklage ['ankla:gə] *f* accusation; (*Jur*) charge; **gegen jdn ~ erheben** (*Jur*) to bring *od* prefer charges against sb; **Anklagebank** *f* dock
anklagen ['ankla:gən] *vt* to accuse; **jdn (eines Verbrechens) ~** (*Jur*) to charge sb (with a crime)
Ankläger, in ['anklɛ:gər(ɪn)] (**-s, -**) *m(f)* accuser

Anklang ['anklaŋ] *m*: **bei jdm ~ finden** to meet with sb's approval
Ankleidekabine *f* changing cubicle
ankleiden ['anklaɪdən] *vt, vr* to dress
anklopfen ['anklɔpfən] *vi* to knock
ankommen ['ankɔmən] *unreg vi* to arrive; (*näher kommen*) to approach; (*Anklang finden*): **bei jdm (gut) ~** to go down well with sb ▷ *vi unpers*: **er ließ es auf einen Streit/einen Versuch ~** he was prepared to argue about it/to give it a try; **es kommt darauf an** it depends; (*wichtig sein*) that is what matters; **es kommt auf ihn an** it depends on him; **es darauf ~ lassen** to let things take their course; **gegen jdn/etw ~** to cope with sb/sth; **damit kommst du bei ihm nicht an!** you won't get anywhere with him like that
ankreuzen ['ankrɔʏtsən] *vt* to mark with a cross
ankündigen ['ankʏndɪgən] *vt* to announce
Ankunft ['ankʊnft] (**-, -künfte**) *f* arrival
Ankunftszeit *f* time of arrival
Anlage ['anla:gə] *f* disposition; (*Begabung*) talent; (*Park*) gardens *pl*; (*Beilage*) enclosure; (*Tech*) plant; (*Einrichtung*: *Mil, Elek*) installation(s *pl*); (*Sportanlage etc*) facilities *pl*; (*umg*: *Stereoanlage*) (stereo) system; (*Fin*) investment; (*Entwurf*) layout; **als ~** *od* **in der ~ erhalten Sie ...** please find enclosed ...
Anlass ['anlas] (**-es, -lässe**) *m*: **~ (zu)** cause (for); (*Ereignis*) occasion; **aus ~** *+gen* on the occasion of; **~ zu etw geben** to give rise to sth; **beim geringsten/bei jedem ~** for the slightest reason/at every opportunity; **etw zum ~ nehmen** to take the opportunity of sth
anlassen *unreg vt* to leave on; (*Motor*) to start ▷ *vr* (*umg*) to start off
Anlasser (**-s, -**) *m* (*Aut*) starter
anlässlich ['anlɛslɪç] *präp +gen* on the occasion of
anlasten ['anlastən] *vt*: **jdm etw ~** to blame sb for sth
Anlauf ['anlaʊf] *m* run-up; (*fig*: *Versuch*) attempt, try
anlaufen *unreg vi* to begin; (*Film*) to be showing; (*Sport*) to run up; (*Fenster*) to mist up; (*Metall*) to tarnish ▷ *vt* to call at; **rot ~** to turn *od* go red; **gegen etw ~** to run into *od* up against sth; **angelaufen kommen** to come running up
Anlaufstelle *f* place to go (with one's problems)
anläuten ['anlɔʏtən] *vi* to ring
anlegen ['anle:gən] *vt* to put; (*anziehen*) to put on; (*gestalten*) to lay out; (*Kartei, Akte*) to start; (*Comput*: *Datei*) to create; (*Geld*) to invest ▷ *vi* to dock; (*Naut*) to berth; **etw an etw** *akk* **~** to put sth against *od* on sth; **ein Gewehr ~ (auf** *+akk***)** to aim a weapon (at); **es auf etw** *akk* **~** to be out for sth/to do sth; **strengere Maßstäbe ~ (bei)** to lay down *od* impose stricter standards (in); **sich mit jdm ~** (*umg*) to quarrel with sb
Anlegeplatz *m* landing place
anlehnen ['anle:nən] *vt* to lean; (*Tür*) to leave ajar; **(sich) an etw** *akk* **~** to lean on *od* against sth
anleiern ['anlaɪərn] (*umg*) *vt* to get going
anleiten ['anlaɪtən] *vt* to instruct
Anleitung *f* instructions *pl*
anlernen ['anlɛrnən] *vt* to teach, instruct
Anliegen ['anli:gən] (**-s, -**) *nt* matter; (*Wunsch*) wish
anliegen *unreg vi* (*Kleidung*) to cling
anliegend *adj* adjacent; (*beigefügt*) enclosed
Anlieger (**-s, -**) *m* resident; **~ frei** no thoroughfare – residents only
anlügen ['anly:gən] *unreg vt* to lie to
anmachen ['anmaxən] *vt* to attach; (*Elektrisches*) to put on; (*Salat*) to dress; **jdn ~** (*umg*) to try and pick sb up
anmaßen ['anma:sən] *vt*: **sich** *dat* **etw ~** to lay claim to sth
anmaßend *adj* arrogant
Anmaßung *f* presumption
Anmeldeformular ['anmɛldəfɔrmʊla:r] *nt* registration form
anmelden *vt* to announce; (*geltend machen*: *Recht, Ansprüche, zu Steuerzwecken*) to declare; (*Comput*) to log on ▷ *vr* (*sich ankündigen*) to make an appointment; (*polizeilich, für Kurs etc*) to register; **ein Gespräch nach Deutschland ~** (*Tel*) to book a call to Germany
Anmeldung *f* announcement; appointment; registration; **nur nach vorheriger ~** by appointment only
anmerken ['anmɛrkən] *vt* to observe; (*anstreichen*) to mark; **jdm seine Verlegenheit** *etc* **~** to notice sb's embarrassment *etc*; **sich** *dat* **nichts ~ lassen** not to give anything away
Anmerkung *f* note
Anmut ['anmu:t] (**-**) *f* grace
anmutig *adj* charming
annähen ['annɛ:ən] *vt* to sew on
annähernd *adj* approximate; **nicht ~ so viel** not nearly as much
Annäherung *f* approach
Annäherungsversuch *m* advances *pl*
Annahme ['anna:mə] (**-, -n**) *f* acceptance; (*Vermutung*) assumption
annehmbar ['anne:mba:r] *adj* acceptable
annehmen *unreg vt* to accept; (*Namen*) to take; (*Kind*) to adopt; (*vermuten*) to suppose, assume ▷ *vr* (*+gen*) to take care (of); **jdn an Kindes statt ~** to adopt sb; **angenommen, das ist so** assuming that is so
Annehmlichkeit *f* comfort
annektieren [anɛk'ti:rən] *vt* to annex
Annonce [a'nõ:sə] (**-, -n**) *f* advertisement
annoncieren [anõ'si:rən] *vt, vi* to advertise
annullieren [anʊ'li:rən] *vt* to annul
Anode [a'no:də] (**-, -n**) *f* anode

anöden ['an|ø:dən] *(umg) vt* to bore stiff
anonym [ano'ny:m] *adj* anonymous
Anorak ['anorak] **(-s, -s)** *m* anorak
anordnen ['an|ɔrdnən] *vt* to arrange; *(befehlen)* to order
Anordnung *f* arrangement; order; **~en treffen** to give orders
anorganisch ['an|ɔrga:nɪʃ] *adj (Chem)* inorganic
anpacken ['anpakən] *vt* to grasp; *(fig)* to tackle; **mit ~** to lend a hand
anpassen ['anpasən] *vt (Kleidung)* to fit; *(fig)* to adapt ▷ *vr* to adapt
Anpassung *f* fitting; adaptation
anpassungsfähig *adj* adaptable
Anpfiff ['anpfɪf] *m (Sport)* (starting) whistle; *(Spielbeginn: Fußball etc)* kick-off; **einen ~ bekommen** *(umg)* to get a rocket *(Brit)*
anpöbeln ['anpø:bəln] *vt* to abuse; *(umg)* to pester
anprangern ['anpraŋərn] *vt* to denounce
anpreisen ['anpraɪzən] *unreg vt* to extol; **sich ~ (als)** to sell o.s. (as); **etw ~** to extol (the virtues of) sth; **seine Waren ~** to cry one's wares
Anprobe ['anpro:bə] *f* trying on
anprobieren ['anprobi:rən] *vt* to try on
anrechnen ['anrɛçnən] *vt* to charge; *(fig)* to count; **jdm etw hoch ~** to think highly of sb for sth
Anrecht ['anrɛçt] *nt*: **~ auf** *+akk* right (to); **ein ~ auf etw haben** to be entitled to sth, have a right to sth
Anrede ['anre:də] *f* form of address
anreden *vt* to address
anregen ['anre:gən] *vt* to stimulate; **angeregte Unterhaltung** lively discussion
anregend *adj* stimulating
Anregung *f* stimulation; *(Vorschlag)* suggestion
anreichern ['anraɪçərn] *vt* to enrich
Anreise ['anraɪzə] *f* journey there/here
anreisen *vi* to arrive
Anreiz ['anraɪts] *m* incentive
Anrichte ['anrɪçtə] **(-, -n)** *f* sideboard
anrichten *vt* to serve up; **Unheil ~** to make mischief; **da hast du aber etwas angerichtet!** *(umg: verursacht)* you've started something there all right!; *(: angestellt)* you've really made a mess there!
anrüchig ['anrʏçɪç] *adj* dubious
anrücken ['anrʏkən] *vi* to approach; *(Mil)* to advance
Anruf ['anru:f] *m* call; **Anrufbeantworter** *m* (telephone) answering machine, answerphone
anrufen *unreg vt* to call out to; *(bitten)* to call on; *(Tel)* to ring up, phone, call
anrühren ['anry:rən] *vt* to touch; *(mischen)* to mix
ans [ans] = **an das**
Ansage ['anza:gə] *f* announcement
ansagen *vt* to announce ▷ *vr* to say one will come
Ansager, in **(-s, -)** *m(f)* announcer
ansammeln ['anzaməln] *vt* to collect ▷ *vr* to accumulate; *(fig: Wut, Druck)* to build up
Ansammlung *f* collection; *(Leute)* crowd
ansässig ['anzɛsɪç] *adj* resident
Ansatz ['anzats] *m* start; *(Haaransatz)* hairline; *(Halsansatz)* base; *(Verlängerungsstück)* extension; *(Veranschlagung)* estimate; **die ersten Ansätze zu etw** the beginnings of sth; **Ansatzpunkt** *m* starting point
anschaffen ['anʃafən] *vt* to buy, purchase ▷ *vi*: **~ gehen** *(umg: durch Prostitution)* to be on the game; **sich** *dat* **Kinder ~** *(umg)* to have children
Anschaffung *f* purchase
anschalten ['anʃaltən] *vt* to switch on
anschauen ['anʃaʊən] *vt* to look at
anschaulich *adj* illustrative
Anschauung *f (Meinung)* view; **aus eigener ~** from one's own experience
Anschauungsmaterial *nt* illustrative material
Anschein ['anʃaɪn] *m* appearance; **allem ~ nach** to all appearances; **den ~ haben** to seem, appear
anscheinend *adj* apparent
Anschlag ['anʃla:k] *m* notice; *(Attentat)* attack; *(Comm)* estimate; *(auf Klavier)* touch; *(auf Schreibmaschine)* keystroke; **einem ~ zum Opfer fallen** to be assassinated; **ein Gewehr im ~ haben** *(Mil)* to have a rifle at the ready
anschlagen ['anʃla:gən] *unreg vt* to put up; *(beschädigen)* to chip; *(Akkord)* to strike; *(Kosten)* to estimate ▷ *vi* to hit; *(wirken)* to have an effect; *(Glocke)* to ring; *(Hund)* to bark; **einen anderen Ton ~** *(fig)* to change one's tune; **an etw** *akk* **~** to hit against sth
Anschlagzettel *m* notice
anschließen ['anʃli:sən] *unreg vt* to connect up; *(Sender)* to link up; *(in Steckdose)* to plug in; *(fig: hinzufügen)* to add ▷ *vi*: **an etw** *akk* **~** *(zeitlich)* to follow sth ▷ *vr*: **sich jdm/etw ~** to join sb/sth; *(beipflichten)* to agree with sb/sth; **sich an etw** *akk* **~** *(angrenzen)* to adjoin sth
anschließend *adj* adjacent; *(zeitlich)* subsequent ▷ *adv* afterwards; **~ an** *+akk* following
Anschluss ['anʃlʊs] *m (Elek, Eisenb, Tel)* connection; *(weiterer Apparat)* extension; *(von Wasser etc)* supply; *(Comput)* port; **im ~ an** *+akk* following; **~ finden** to make friends; **~ bekommen** to get through; **kein ~ unter dieser Nummer** number unobtainable; **den ~ verpassen** *(Eisenb etc)* to miss one's connection; *(fig)* to miss the boat
anschmiegsam ['anʃmi:kza:m] *adj* affectionate
anschmieren ['anʃmi:rən] *vt* to smear; *(umg)* to take in
anschnallen ['anʃnalən] *vt* to buckle on ▷ *vr* to fasten one's seat belt
Anschnallpflicht *f*: **für Kinder besteht ~**

children must wear seat belts
anschneiden ['anʃnaɪdən] *unreg vt* to cut into; (*Thema*) to introduce
Anschnitt ['anʃnɪt] *m* first slice
anschreiben ['anʃraɪbən] *unreg vt* to write (up); (*Comm*) to charge up; (*benachrichtigen*) to write to; **bei jdm gut/schlecht angeschrieben sein** to be well/badly thought of by sb, be in sb's good/bad books
anschreien ['anʃraɪən] *unreg vt* to shout at
Anschrift ['anʃrɪft] *f* address
Anschuldigung ['anʃʊldɪgʊŋ] *f* accusation
anschwellen ['anʃvɛlən] *unreg vi* to swell (up)
anschwemmen ['anʃvɛmən] *vt* to wash ashore
anschwindeln ['anʃvɪndəln] (*umg*) *vt* to lie to
ansehen ['anze:ən] *unreg vt* to look at; **jdm etw ~** to see sth (from sb's face); **jdn/etw als etw ~** to look on sb/sth as sth; **~ für** to consider; **(sich *dat*) etw ~** to (have a) look at sth; (*Fernsehsendung*) to watch sth; (*Film, Stück, Sportveranstaltung*) to see sth; **etw (mit) ~** to watch sth, see sth happening
Ansehen (**-s**) *nt* respect; (*Ruf*) reputation; **ohne ~ der Person** (*Jur*) without respect of person
ansehnlich ['anze:nlɪç] *adj* fine-looking; (*beträchtlich*) considerable
an sein ['anzaɪn] *siehe* **an**
ansetzen ['anzɛtsən] *vt* (*festlegen*) to fix; (*entwickeln*) to develop; (*Fett*) to put on; (*Blätter*) to grow; (*zubereiten*) to prepare ▷ *vi* (*anfangen*) to start, begin; (*Entwicklung*) to set in; (*dick werden*) to put on weight ▷ *vr* (*Rost etc*) to start to develop; **~ an** *+akk* (*anfügen*) to fit on to; (*anlegen, an Mund etc*) to put to; **zu etw ~** to prepare to do sth; **jdn/etw auf jdn/etw ~** to set sb/sth on sb/sth
Ansicht ['anzɪçt] *f* (*Anblick*) sight; (*Meinung*) view, opinion; **zur ~** on approval; **meiner ~ nach** in my opinion
Ansichtskarte *f* picture postcard
Ansichtssache *f* matter of opinion
anspannen ['anʃpanən] *vt* to harness; (*Muskel*) to strain
Anspannung *f* strain
Anspiel ['anʃpi:l] *nt* (*Sport*) start of play
anspielen *vt* (*Sport*) to play the ball *etc* to ▷ *vi*: **auf etw** *akk* **~** to refer *od* allude to sth
Anspielung *f*: **~ (auf** *+akk***)** reference (to), allusion (to)
Ansporn ['anʃpɔrn] (**-(e)s**) *m* incentive
Ansprache ['anʃpra:xə] *f* (*Rede*) address
ansprechen ['anʃprɛçən] *unreg vt* to speak to; (*bitten, gefallen*) to appeal to; (*Eindruck machen auf*) to make an impression on ▷ *vi*: **~ auf** *+akk* (*Patient*) to respond (to); (*Messgerät*) to react (to); **jdn auf etw** *akk* **(hin) ~** to ask sb about sth
ansprechend *adj* attractive
Ansprechpartner *m* contact
anspringen ['anʃprɪŋən] *unreg vi* (*Aut*) to start ▷ *vt* (*anfallen*) to jump; (*Raubtier*) to pounce (up)on; (*Hund: hochspringen*) to jump up at
Anspruch ['anʃprʊx] (**-s, -sprüche**) *m* (*Recht*): **~ (auf** *+akk***)** claim (to); **den Ansprüchen gerecht werden** to meet the requirements; **hohe Ansprüche stellen/haben** to demand/expect a lot; **jdn/etw in ~ nehmen** to occupy sb/take up sth
anspruchslos *adj* undemanding
anspruchsvoll *adj* demanding; (*Comm*) upmarket
anspucken ['anʃpʊkən] *vt* to spit at
anstacheln ['anʃtaxəln] *vt* to spur on
Anstalt ['anʃtalt] (**-, -en**) *f* institution; **~en machen, etw zu tun** to prepare to do sth
Anstand ['anʃtant] *m* decency; (*Manieren*) (good) manners *pl*
anständig ['anʃtɛndɪç] *adj* decent; (*umg*) proper; (*groß*) considerable; **Anständigkeit** *f* propriety, decency
anstandslos *adv* without any ado
anstarren ['anʃtarən] *vt* to stare at
anstatt [an'ʃtat] *präp +gen* instead of ▷ *konj*: **~ etw zu tun** instead of doing sth
anstechen ['anʃtɛçən] *unreg vt* to prick; (*Fass*) to tap
anstecken ['anʃtɛkən] *vt* to pin on; (*Ring*) to put *od* slip on; (*Med*) to infect; (*Pfeife*) to light; (*Haus*) to set fire to ▷ *vr*: **ich habe mich bei ihm angesteckt** I caught it from him ▷ *vi* (*fig*) to be infectious
ansteckend *adj* infectious
Ansteckung *f* infection
anstehen ['anʃte:ən] *unreg vi* to queue (up) (*Brit*), line up (*US*); (*Verhandlungspunkt*) to be on the agenda
anstelle, **an Stelle** [an'ʃtɛlə] *präp +gen* in place of
anstellen ['anʃtɛlən] *vt* (*einschalten*) to turn on; (*Arbeit geben*) to employ; (*umg: Unfug treiben*) to get up to; (*: machen*) to do ▷ *vr* to queue (up) (*Brit*), line up (*US*); (*umg*) to act; (*: sich zieren*) to make a fuss, act up
Anstellung *f* employment; (*Posten*) post, position; **~ auf Lebenszeit** tenure
Anstieg ['anʃti:k] (**-(e)s, -e**) *m* climb; (*fig: von Preisen etc*) increase
anstiften ['anʃtɪftən] *vt* (*Unglück*) to cause; **jdn zu etw ~** to put sb up to sth
Anstifter (**-s, -**) *m* instigator
anstimmen ['anʃtɪmən] *vt* (*Lied*) to strike up (with); (*Geschrei*) to set up ▷ *vi* to strike up
Anstoß ['anʃto:s] *m* impetus; (*Ärgernis*) offence (*Brit*), offense (*US*); (*Sport*) kick-off; **der erste ~** the initiative; **ein Stein des ~es** (*umstrittene Sache*) a bone of contention; **~ nehmen an** *+dat* to take offence at
anstoßen *unreg vt* to push; (*mit Fuß*) to kick ▷ *vi* to knock, bump; (*mit der Zunge*) to lisp; (*mit Gläsern*) to drink a toast; **an etw** *akk* **~** (*angrenzen*) to adjoin sth; **~ auf** *+akk* to drink (a toast) to
anstößig ['anʃtø:sɪç] *adj* offensive, indecent; **Anstößigkeit** *f* indecency, offensiveness

anstreben ['anʃtre:bən] *vt* to strive for
anstreichen ['anʃtraɪçən] *unreg vt* to paint; **(jdm) etw als Fehler ~** to mark sth wrong
Anstreicher, in (**-s, -**) *m(f)* painter
anstrengen ['anʃtrɛŋən] *vt* to strain; (*strapazieren: jdn*) to tire out; (*: Patienten*) to fatigue; (*Jur*) to bring ▷ *vr* to make an effort; **eine Klage ~ (gegen)** (*Jur*) to initiate *od* institute proceedings (against)
anstrengend *adj* tiring
Anstrengung *f* effort
Anstrich ['anʃtrɪç] *m* coat of paint
Ansturm ['anʃtʊrm] *m* rush; (*Mil*) attack
Ansuchen ['anzu:xən] (**-s, -**) *nt* request
ansuchen ['anzu:xən] *vi*: **um etw ~** to apply for sth
Antagonismus [antago'nɪsmʊs] *m* antagonism
Antarktis [ant'|arktɪs] (**-**) *f* Antarctic
antarktisch *adj* Antarctic
antasten ['antastən] *vt* to touch; (*Recht*) to infringe upon; (*Ehre*) to question
Anteil ['antaɪl] (**-s, -e**) *m* share; (*Mitgefühl*) sympathy; **~ nehmen an** *+dat* to share in; (*sich interessieren*) to take an interest in; **~ an etw** *dat* **haben** (*beitragen*) to contribute to sth; (*teilnehmen*) to take part in sth
Anteilnahme (**-**) *f* sympathy
Antenne [an'tɛnə] (**-, -n**) *f* aerial; (*Zool*) antenna; **eine/keine ~ für etw haben** (*fig: umg*) to have a/no feeling for sth
Anthrazit [antra'tsi:t] (**-s, -e**) *m* anthracite
Anti- *zW*: **Antialkoholiker** *m* teetotaller; **antiautoritär** *adj* anti-authoritarian; **Antibiotikum** (**-s, -ka**) *nt* antibiotic
antik [an'ti:k] *adj* antique
Antike (**-, -n**) *f* (*Zeitalter*) ancient world; (*Kunstgegenstand*) antique
Antikörper *m* antibody
Antillen [an'tɪlən] *pl* Antilles *pl*
Antilope [anti'lo:pə] (**-, -n**) *f* antelope
Antipathie [antipa'ti:] *f* antipathy
Antiquariat [antikvari'a:t] (**-(e)s, -e**) *nt* secondhand bookshop; **modernes ~** remainder bookshop/department
Antiquitäten [antikvi'tɛ:tən] *pl* antiques *pl*; **Antiquitätenhandel** *m* antique business; **Antiquitätenhändler, in** *m(f)* antique dealer
Antisemitismus [antizemi'tɪsmʊs] *m* anti-semitism
antörnen ['antœrnən] (*umg*) *vt* (*Drogen, Musik*) to turn on ▷ *vi*: **... törnt an** ... turns you on
Antrag ['antra:k] (**-(e)s, -träge**) *m* proposal; (*Parl*) motion; (*Gesuch*) application; **einen ~ auf etw** *akk* **stellen** to make an application for sth; (*Jur etc*) to file a petition/claim for sth
antreffen ['antrɛfən] *unreg vt* to meet
antreiben ['antraɪbən] *unreg vt* to drive on; (*Motor*) to drive; (*anschwemmen*) to wash up ▷ *vi* to be washed up; **jdn zur Eile/Arbeit ~** to urge sb to hurry up/to work
antreten ['antre:tən] *unreg vt* (*Amt*) to take up; (*Erbschaft*) to come into; (*Beweis*) to offer; (*Reise*) to start, begin ▷ *vi* (*Mil*) to fall in; (*Sport*) to line up; (*zum Dienst*) to report; **gegen jdn ~** to play/fight against sb
Antrieb ['antri:p] *m* (*lit, fig*) drive; **aus eigenem ~** of one's own accord
Antritt ['antrɪt] *m* beginning, commencement; (*eines Amts*) taking up
antun ['antu:n] *unreg vt*: **jdm etw ~** to do sth to sb; **sich** *dat* **Zwang ~** to force o.s.
Antwort ['antvɔrt] (**-, -en**) *f* answer, reply; **um ~ wird gebeten** RSVP
antworten *vi* to answer, reply
anvertrauen ['anfertraʊən] *vt*: **jdm etw ~** to entrust sb with sth; **sich jdm ~** to confide in sb
anwachsen ['anvaksən] *unreg vi* to grow; (*Pflanze*) to take root
Anwalt ['anvalt] (**-(e)s, -wälte**) *m* solicitor; lawyer; (*fig: Fürsprecher*) advocate; (*: der Armen etc*) champion
Anwaltskosten *pl* legal expenses *pl*
Anwandlung ['anvandlʊŋ] *f* caprice; **eine ~ von etw** a fit of sth
Anwärter, in ['anvɛrtər(ɪn)] *m(f)* candidate
anweisen ['anvaɪzən] *unreg vt* to instruct; (*zuteilen*) to assign
Anweisung *f* instruction; (*Comm*) remittance; (*Postanweisung, Zahlungsanweisung*) money order
anwendbar ['anvɛntba:r] *adj* practicable, applicable
anwenden ['anvɛndən] *unreg vt* to use, employ; (*Gesetz, Regel*) to apply
Anwendersoftware *f* application package
Anwendung *f* use; application
anwesend ['anve:zənt] *adj* present; **die A~en** those present
Anwesenheit *f* presence
Anwesenheitsliste *f* attendance register
anwidern ['anvi:dərn] *vt* to disgust
Anzahl ['antsa:l] *f*: **~ (an** *+dat***)** number (of)
anzahlen *vt* to pay on account
Anzahlung *f* deposit, payment on account
anzapfen ['antsapfən] *vt* to tap
Anzeichen ['antsaɪçən] *nt* sign, indication; **alle ~ deuten darauf hin, dass ...** all the signs are that ...
Anzeige ['antsaɪgə] (**-, -n**) *f* (*Zeitungsanzeige*) announcement; (*Werbung*) advertisement; (*Comput*) display; (*bei Polizei*) report; **gegen jdn ~ erstatten** to report sb (to the police)
anzeigen *vt* (*zu erkennen geben*) to show; (*bekannt geben*) to announce; (*bei Polizei*) to report
Anzeigenteil *m* advertisements *pl*
Anzeiger *m* indicator
anzetteln ['antsɛtəln] (*umg*) *vt* to instigate
anziehen ['antsi:ən] *unreg vt* to attract; (*Kleidung*) to put on; (*Mensch*) to dress; (*Schraube, Seil*) to pull tight; (*Knie*) to draw up; (*Feuchtigkeit*) to absorb ▷ *vr* to get dressed
anziehend *adj* attractive
Anziehung *f* (*Reiz*) attraction

Anziehungskraft *f* power of attraction; (*Phys*) force of gravitation
Anzug ['antsu:k] *m* suit; **im ~ sein** to be approaching
anzüglich ['antsy:klıç] *adj* personal; (*anstößig*) offensive
anzünden ['antsʏndən] *vt* to light
Anzünder *m* lighter
anzweifeln ['antsvaıfəln] *vt* to doubt
apart [a'part] *adj* distinctive
Apartment [a'partmənt] (**-s, -s**) *nt* flat (*Brit*), apartment (*bes US*)
Apathie [apa'ti:] *f* apathy
apathisch [a'pa:tıʃ] *adj* apathetic
Apfel ['apfəl] (**-s, ⸚**) *m* apple; **in den sauren ~ beißen** (*fig: umg*) to swallow the bitter pill; **etw für einen ~ und ein Ei kaufen** (*umg*) to buy sth dirt cheap *od* for a song; **Apfelmus** *nt* apple purée; (*als Beilage*) apple sauce; **Apfelsaft** *m* apple juice
Apfelsine [apfəl'zi:nə] (**-, -n**) *f* orange
Apfelwein *m* strong cider
Apostel [a'pɔstəl] (**-s, -**) *m* apostle
Apostroph [apo'stro:f] (**-s, -e**) *m* apostrophe
Apotheke [apo'te:kə] (**-, -n**) *f* chemist's (shop) (*Brit*), drugstore (*US*)
Apotheker, in (**-s, -**) *m(f)* pharmacist, (dispensing) chemist (*Brit*), druggist (*US*)
Apparat [apa'ra:t] (**-(e)s, -e**) *m* piece of apparatus; (*Fotoapparat*) camera; (*Telefon*) telephone; (*Rundf, TV*) set; (*Verwaltungsapparat, Parteiapparat*) machinery, apparatus; **am ~** on the phone; (*als Antwort*) speaking; **am ~ bleiben** to hold the line
Apparatur [apara'tu:r] *f* apparatus
Appartement [apart(ə)'mã:] (**-s, -s**) *nt* flat (*Brit*), apartment (*bes US*)
Appell [a'pɛl] (**-s, -e**) *m* (*Mil*) muster, parade; (*fig*) appeal; **zum ~ antreten** to line up for roll call
appellieren [apɛ'li:rən] *vi*: **~ (an** *+akk*) to appeal (to)
Appetit [ape'ti:t] (**-(e)s, -e**) *m* appetite; **guten ~!** enjoy your meal; **appetitlich** *adj* appetizing; **Appetitlosigkeit** *f* lack of appetite
Applaus [ap'laʊs] (**-es, -e**) *m* applause
Appretur [apre'tu:r] *f* finish; (*Wasserundurchlässigkeit*) waterproofing
Aprikose [apri'ko:zə] (**-, -n**) *f* apricot
April [a'prıl] (**-(s), -e**) (*pl selten*) *m* April; **jdn in den ~ schicken** to make an April fool of sb; *siehe auch* **September**; **Aprilwetter** *nt* April showers *pl*
Aquaplaning [akva'pla:nıŋ] (**-(s)**) *nt* aquaplaning
Aquarell [akva'rɛl] (**-s, -e**) *nt* watercolour (*Brit*), watercolor (*US*)
Aquarium [a'kva:riʊm] *nt* aquarium
Äquator [ɛ'kva:tɔr] (**-s**) *m* equator
Araber, in ['a:rabər(ın)] (**-s, -**) *m(f)* Arab
Arabien [a'ra:biən] (**-s**) *nt* Arabia
arabisch *adj* Arab; (*Arabien betreffend*) Arabian; (*Sprache*) Arabic; **A~er Golf** Arabian Gulf; **A~es Meer** Arabian Sea; **A~e Wüste** Arabian Desert
Arbeit ['arbaıt] (**-, -en**) *f* work; (*Stelle*) job; (*Erzeugnis*) piece of work; (*wissenschaftliche*) dissertation; (*Klassenarbeit*) test; **Tag der ~** Labour (*Brit*) *od* Labor (*US*) Day; **sich an die ~ machen, an die ~ gehen** to get down to work, start working; **jdm ~ machen** (*Mühe*) to put sb to trouble; **das war eine ~** that was a hard job
arbeiten *vi* to work ▷ *vt* to make ▷ *vr*: **sich nach oben/an die Spitze ~** (*fig*) to work one's way up/to the top
Arbeiter, in (**-s, -**) *m(f)* worker; (*ungelernt*) labourer (*Brit*), laborer (*US*)
Arbeiterschaft *f* workers *pl*, labour (*Brit*) *od* labor (*US*) force
Arbeit- *zW*: **Arbeitgeber** (**-s, -**) *m* employer; **Arbeitnehmer** (**-s, -**) *m* employee; **arbeitsam** *adj* industrious
Arbeits- *zW*: **Arbeitsamt** *nt* employment exchange, Job Centre (*Brit*); **Arbeitserlaubnis** *f* work permit; **arbeitsfähig** *adj* fit for work, able-bodied; **Arbeitsgang** *m* operation; **Arbeitsgemeinschaft** *f* study group; **arbeitslos** *adj* unemployed, out-of-work; **Arbeitslosengeld** *nt* unemployment benefit; **Arbeitslosenhilfe** *f* supplementary benefit; **Arbeitslosigkeit** *f* unemployment; **Arbeitsmarkt** *m* job market; **Arbeitsplatz** *m* place of work; (*Stelle*) job; **arbeitsscheu** *adj* workshy; **Arbeitstag** *m* work(ing) day; **Arbeitsteilung** *f* division of labour (*Brit*) *od* labor (*US*); **arbeitsunfähig** *adj* unfit for work; **Arbeitszeit** *f* working hours *pl*; **Arbeitszeitkonto** *nt* record of hours worked; **Arbeitszeitverkürzung** *f* reduction in working hours
Archäologe [arçɛo'lo:gə] (**-n, -n**) *m* arch(a)eologist
Architekt, in [arçi'tɛkt(ın)] (**-en, -en**) *m(f)* architect
Architektur [arçitɛk'tu:r] *f* architecture
Archiv [ar'çi:f] (**-s, -e**) *nt* archive
arg [ark] *adj* bad, awful ▷ *adv* awfully, very; **es zu ~ treiben** to go too far
Argentinien [argɛn'ti:niən] (**-s**) *nt* Argentina, the Argentine
Argentinier, in (**-s, -**) *m(f)* Argentine, Argentinian (*Brit*), Argentinean (*US*)
argentinisch [argɛn'ti:nıʃ] *adj* Argentine, Argentinian (*Brit*), Argentinean (*US*)
Ärger ['ɛrgər] (**-s**) *m* (*Wut*) anger; (*Unannehmlichkeit*) trouble; **jdm ~ machen** *od* **bereiten** to cause sb a lot of trouble *od* bother; **ärgerlich** *adj* (*zornig*) angry; (*lästig*) annoying, aggravating
ärgern *vt* to annoy ▷ *vr* to get annoyed
Ärgernis (**-ses, -se**) *nt* annoyance; (*Anstoß*) offence (*Brit*), offense (*US*), outrage; **öffentliches ~ erregen** to be a public nuisance

arg- *zW*: **arglistig** *adj* cunning, insidious; **arglistige Täuschung** fraud; **arglos** *adj* guileless, innocent
Argument [argu'mɛnt] *nt* argument
Argwohn *m* suspicion
argwöhnisch *adj* suspicious
Arie ['a:riə] *f* aria
Aristokrat, in [arɪsto'kra:t(ɪn)] (**-en, -en**) *m(f)* aristocrat
Aristokratie [arɪstokra:'ti:] *f* aristocracy
aristokratisch *adj* aristocratic
arithmetisch [arɪt'me:tɪʃ] *adj* arithmetical; **~es Mittel** arithmetic mean
Arktis ['arktɪs] (-) *f* Arctic
arktisch *adj* Arctic
arm [arm] *adj* poor; **~ dran sein** (*umg*) to have a hard time of it
Arm (**-(e)s, -e**) *m* arm; (*Flussarm*) branch; **jdn auf den ~ nehmen** (*fig: umg*) to pull sb's leg; **jdm unter die ~e greifen** (*fig*) to help sb out; **einen langen/den längeren ~ haben** (*fig*) to have a lot of/more pull (*umg*) *od* influence
Armatur [arma'tu:r] *f* (*Elek*) armature
Armaturenbrett *nt* instrument panel; (*Aut*) dashboard
Armband *nt* bracelet; **Armbanduhr** *f* (wrist) watch
Arme, r *f(m)* poor man/woman; **die ~n** the poor
Armee [ar'me:] (**-, -n**) *f* army
Ärmel ['ɛrməl] (**-s, -**) *m* sleeve; **etw aus dem ~ schütteln** (*fig*) to produce sth just like that
Ärmelkanal *m* (English) Channel
Armenien [ar'me:niən] (**-s**) *nt* Armenia
armenisch [ar'me:nɪʃ] *adj* Armenian
ärmlich ['ɛrmlɪç] *adj* poor; **aus ~en Verhältnissen** from a poor family
armselig *adj* wretched, miserable; (*mitleiderregend*) pathetic, pitiful
Armut ['armu:t] (-) *f* poverty
Armutszeugnis *nt* (*fig*): **jdm/sich ein ~ ausstellen** to show sb's/one's shortcomings
Aroma [a'ro:ma] (**-s, Aromen**) *nt* aroma; **Aromatherapie** *f* aromatherapy
aromatisch [aro'ma:tɪʃ] *adj* aromatic
arrangieren [arã:'ʒi:rən] *vt* to arrange ▷ *vr* to come to an arrangement
Arrest [a'rɛst] (**-(e)s, -e**) *m* detention
arrogant [aro'gant] *adj* arrogant
Arroganz *f* arrogance
Arsch [arʃ] (**-es, ¨-e**) (*umg!*) *m* arse (*!*); **leck mich am ~!** (*lass mich in Ruhe*) get stuffed! (*!*), fuck off! (*!*); **am ~ der Welt** (*umg*) in the back of beyond; **Arschkriecher** (*umg!*) *m* arse licker (*!*), crawler
Art [a:rt] (**-, -en**) *f* (*Weise*) way; (*Sorte*) kind, sort; (*Biol*) species; **eine ~ (von) Frucht** a kind of fruit; **Häuser aller ~** houses of all kinds; **einzig in seiner ~ sein** to be the only one of its kind, be unique; **auf diese ~ und Weise** in this way; **das ist doch keine ~!** that's no way to behave!; **es ist nicht seine ~, das zu tun** it's not like him to do that; **ich mache das auf meine ~** I do that my (own) way; **Schnitzel nach ~ des Hauses** chef's special escalope
Artenschutz *m* protection of endangered species
Arterie [ar'te:riə] *f* artery
Arterienverkalkung *f* arteriosclerosis
artig ['a:rtɪç] *adj* good, well-behaved
Artikel [ar'ti:kəl] (**-s, -**) *m* article
Artillerie [artɪlə'ri:] *f* artillery
Artischocke [arti'ʃɔkə] (**-, -n**) *f* artichoke
Arznei [a:rts'naɪ] *f* medicine; **Arzneimittel** *nt* medicine, medicament
Arzt [a:rtst] (**-es, ¨-e**) *m* doctor; **praktischer ~** general practitioner, GP
Arzthelferin *f* doctor's assistant
ärztlich ['ɛ:rtstlɪç] *adj* medical
Asbest [as'bɛst] (**-(e)s, -e**) *m* asbestos
Asche ['aʃə] (**-, -n**) *f* ash
Aschen- *zW*: **Aschenbahn** *f* cinder track; **Aschenbecher** *m* ashtray; **Aschenbrödel** *nt* (*Liter, fig*) Cinderella
Aschermittwoch *m* Ash Wednesday
Aserbaidschan [azɛrbaɪ'dʒa:n] (**-s**) *nt* Azerbaijan
Asiat, in [azi'a:t(ɪn)] (**-en, -en**) *m(f)* Asian
asiatisch *adj* Asian, Asiatic
Asien ['a:ziən] (**-s**) *nt* Asia
asozial ['azotsia:l] *adj* antisocial; (*Familie*) asocial
Aspekt [as'pɛkt] (**-(e)s, -e**) *m* aspect
Asphalt [as'falt] (**-(e)s, -e**) *m* asphalt
asphaltieren [asfal'ti:rən] *vt* to asphalt
Asphaltstraße *f* asphalt road
aß *etc* [a:s] *vb siehe* **essen**
Ass [as] (**-es, -e**) *nt* ace
Assistent, in [asɪs'tɛnt(ɪn)] *m(f)* assistant
Assoziation [asotsiatsi'o:n] *f* association
Ast [ast] (**-(e)s, ¨-e**) *m* branch; **sich** *dat* **einen ~ lachen** (*umg*) to double up (with laughter)
Aster ['astər] (**-, -n**) *f* aster
ästhetisch [ɛs'te:tɪʃ] *adj* aesthetic (*Brit*), esthetic (*US*)
Asthma ['astma] (**-s**) *nt* asthma
Asthmatiker, in [ast'ma:tikər(ɪn)] (**-s, -**) *m(f)* asthmatic
Astrologe [astro'lo:gə] (**-n, -n**) *m* astrologer
Astrologie [astrolo'gi:] *f* astrology
Astronaut, in [astro'naʊt(ɪn)] (**-en, -en**) *m(f)* astronaut
Astronautik *f* astronautics
Astronom, in [astro'no:m(ɪn)] (**-en, -en**) *m(f)* astronomer
Astronomie [astrono'mi:] *f* astronomy
Asyl [a'zy:l] (**-s, -e**) *nt* asylum; (*Heim*) home; (*Obdachlosenasyl*) shelter
Asylant, in [azy'lant(ɪn)] (**-en, -en**) *m(f)* person seeking (political) asylum
Asylrecht *nt* (*Pol*) right of (political) asylum
Atelier [atəli'e:] (**-s, -s**) *nt* studio
Atem ['a:təm] (**-s**) *m* breath; **den ~ anhalten** to hold one's breath; **außer ~** out of breath; **jdn in ~ halten** to keep sb in suspense *od* on

tenterhooks; **das verschlug mir den ~** it took my breath away; **einen langen/den längeren ~ haben** to have a lot of staying power; **atemberaubend** *adj* breathtaking; **atemlos** *adj* breathless; **Atempause** *f* breather; **Atemzug** *m* breath

Atheismus [ate'ɪsmʊs] *m* atheism

Atheist, in *m(f)* atheist; **atheistisch** *adj* atheistic

Athen [a'te:n] (**-s**) *nt* Athens

Äther ['ɛ:tər] (**-s, -**) *m* ether

Äthiopien [ɛti'o:piən] (**-s**) *nt* Ethiopia

äthiopisch *adj* Ethiopian

Athlet, in [at'le:t(ɪn)] (**-en, -en**) *m(f)* athlete

Athletik *f* athletics *sing*

Atlantik [at'lantɪk] (**-s**) *m* Atlantic

atlantisch *adj* Atlantic; **der A~e Ozean** the Atlantic Ocean

Atlas ['atlas] (**-** *od* **-ses, -se** *od* **Atlanten**) *m* atlas

atmen ['a:tmən] *vt, vi* to breathe

Atmosphäre [atmo'sfɛ:rə] (**-, -n**) *f* atmosphere

atmosphärisch *adj* atmospheric

Atmung ['a:tmʊŋ] *f* respiration

Atom [a'to:m] (**-s, -e**) *nt* atom

atomar [ato'ma:r] *adj* atomic, nuclear; (*Drohung*) nuclear

Atom- *zW*: **Atombombe** *f* atom bomb; **Atomenergie** *f* nuclear *od* atomic energy; **Atomkern** *m* atomic nucleus; **Atomkraft** *f* nuclear power; **Atomkraftwerk** *nt* nuclear power station; **Atomkrieg** *m* nuclear *od* atomic war; **Atommacht** *f* nuclear *od* atomic power; **Atommüll** *m* nuclear waste; **Atomsperrvertrag** *m* (*Pol*) nuclear non-proliferation treaty; **Atomsprengkopf** *m* nuclear *od* atomic warhead; **Atomwaffen** *pl* nuclear *od* atomic weapons *pl*; **atomwaffenfrei** *adj* (*Zone*) nuclear-free; **Atomzeitalter** *nt* atomic age

Attentat [atɛn'ta:t] (**-(e)s, -e**) *nt*: **~ (auf** *+akk***)** (attempted) assassination (of)

Attentäter, in [atɛn'tɛ:tər(ɪn)] (**-s, -**) *m(f)* (would-be) assassin

Attest [a'tɛst] (**-(e)s, -e**) *nt* certificate

attraktiv [atrak'ti:f] *adj* attractive

Attrappe [a'trapə] (**-, -n**) *f* dummy; **bei ihr ist alles ~** everything about her is false

Attribut [atri'bu:t] (**-(e)s, -e**) *nt* (*Gram*) attribute

ätzen ['ɛtsən] *vi* to be caustic

ätzend *adj* (*lit: Säure*) corrosive; (*Geruch*) pungent; (*fig: umg: furchtbar*) dreadful, horrible; (*: toll*) magic

auch [aʊx] *adv* **1** (*ebenfalls*) also, too, as well; **das ist auch schön** that's nice too *od* as well; **er kommt — ich auch** he's coming — so am I *od* me too; **auch nicht** not ... either; **ich auch nicht** nor I, me neither; **oder auch** or; **auch das noch!** not that as well!; **nicht nur ..., sondern auch ...** not only ... but also ...

2 (*selbst, sogar*) even; **auch wenn das Wetter schlecht ist** even if the weather is bad; **ohne auch nur zu fragen** without even asking

3 (*wirklich*) really; **du siehst müde aus — bin ich auch** you look tired — (so) I am; **so sieht es auch aus** (and) that's what it looks like

4 (*auch immer*): **wer auch** whoever; **was auch** whatever; **wozu auch?** (*emphatisch*) whatever for?; **wie dem auch sei** be that as it may; **wie sehr er sich auch bemühte** however much he tried

audiovisuell [aʊdiovizu'ɛl] *adj* audiovisual

auf [aʊf] *präp +dat* (*wo?*) on; **auf dem Tisch** on the table; **auf der Reise** on the way; **auf der Post/dem Fest** at the post office/party; **auf der Straße** on the road; **auf dem Land/der ganzen Welt** in the country/the whole world; **was hat es damit auf sich?** what does it mean?

▷ *präp +akk* **1** (*wohin?*) on(to); **auf den Tisch** on(to) the table; **auf die Post gehen** to go to the post office; **auf das Land** into the country; **etw auf einen Zettel schreiben** to write sth on a piece of paper; **auf eine Tasse Kaffee/eine Zigarette(nlänge)** for a cup of coffee/a smoke; **die Nacht (von Montag) auf Dienstag** Monday night; **auf einen Polizisten kommen 1.000 Bürger** there is one policeman to every 1,000 citizens

2: auf Deutsch in German; **auf Lebenszeit** for my/his lifetime; **bis auf ihn** except for him; **auf einmal** at once; **auf seinen Vorschlag (hin)** at his suggestion

▷ *adv* **1** (*offen*) open; **auf sein** to be open; **das Fenster ist auf** the window is open

2 (*hinauf*) up; **auf und ab** up and down; **auf und davon** up and away; **auf!** (*los!*) come on!; **von klein auf** from childhood onwards

3 (*aufgestanden*) up; **auf sein** (*Person*) to be up; **ist er schon auf?** is he up yet?

▷ *konj*: **auf dass** (so) that

aufatmen ['aʊf|a:tmən] *vi* to heave a sigh of relief

aufbahren ['aʊfba:rən] *vt* to lay out

Aufbau ['aʊfbaʊ] *m* (*Bauen*) building, construction; (*Struktur*) structure; (*aufgebautes Teil*) superstructure

aufbauen ['aʊfbaʊən] *vt* to erect, build (up); (*Existenz*) to make; (*gestalten*) to construct; (*gründen*): **~ (auf** *+dat***)** to found (on), base (on) ▷ *vr*: **sich vor jdm ~** to draw o.s. up to one's full height in front of sb

aufbäumen ['aʊfbɔymən] *vr* to rear; (*fig*) to revolt, rebel

aufbauschen ['aʊfbaʊʃən] *vt* to puff out; (*fig*) to exaggerate

aufbehalten ['aʊfbəhaltən] *unreg vt* to keep on

aufbekommen ['aʊfbəkɔmən] *unreg* (*umg*) *vt* (*öffnen*) to get open; (*: Hausaufgaben*) to be given

aufbereiten ['aʊfbəraɪtən] *vt* to process; (*Trinkwasser*) to purify; (*Text etc*) to work up
aufbessern ['aʊfbɛsərn] *vt* (*Gehalt*) to increase
aufbewahren ['aʊfbəva:rən] *vt* to keep; (*Gepäck*) to put in the left-luggage office
Aufbewahrung *f* (safe)keeping; (*Gepäckaufbewahrung*) left-luggage office (*Brit*), baggage check (*US*); **jdm etw zur ~ geben** to give sb sth for safekeeping
Aufbewahrungsort *m* storage place
aufbieten ['aʊfbi:tən] *unreg vt* (*Kraft*) to summon (up); (*Armee, Polizei*) to mobilize
aufblasen ['aʊfbla:zən] *unreg vt* to blow up, inflate ▷ *vr* (*umg*) to become big-headed
aufbleiben ['aʊfblaɪbən] *unreg vi* (*Laden*) to remain open; (*Person*) to stay up
aufblenden ['aʊfblɛndən] *vt* (*Scheinwerfer*) to turn on full beam
aufblicken ['aʊfblɪkən] *vi* to look up; **~ zu** (*lit*) to look up at; (*fig*) to look up to
aufblühen ['aʊfbly:ən] *vi* to blossom; (*fig*) to blossom, flourish
aufbrauchen ['aʊfbraʊxən] *vt* to use up
aufbrausen ['aʊfbraʊzən] *vi* (*fig*) to flare up
aufbrausend *adj* hot-tempered
aufbrechen ['aʊfbrɛçən] *unreg vt* to break open, to prise (*Brit*) *od* pry (*US*) open ▷ *vi* to burst open; (*gehen*) to start, set off
aufbringen ['aʊfbrɪŋən] *unreg vt* (*öffnen*) to open; (*in Mode*) to bring into fashion; (*beschaffen*) to procure; (*Fin*) to raise; (*ärgern*) to irritate; **Verständnis für etw ~** to be able to understand sth
Aufbruch ['aʊfbrʊx] *m* departure
aufbrühen ['aʊfbry:ən] *vt* (*Tee*) to make
aufbürden ['aʊfbʏrdən] *vt*: **jdm etw ~** to burden sb with sth
aufdecken ['aʊfdɛkən] *vt* to uncover; (*Spielkarten*) to show
aufdrängen ['aʊfdrɛŋən] *vt*: **jdm etw ~** to force sth on sb ▷ *vr*: **sich jdm ~** to intrude on sb
aufdringlich ['aʊfdrɪŋlɪç] *adj* pushy; (*Benehmen*) obtrusive; (*Parfüm*) powerful
aufeinander [aʊf|aɪ'nandər] *adv* on top of one another; (*schießen*) at each other; (*warten*) for one another; (*vertrauen*) each other; **Aufeinanderfolge** *f* succession, series
Aufenthalt ['aʊf|ɛnthalt] *m* stay; (*Verzögerung*) delay; (*Eisenb: Halten*) stop; (*Ort*) haunt
auferlegen ['aʊf|ɛrle:gən] *vt*: **(jdm) ~** to impose (upon sb)
Auferstehung *f* resurrection
aufessen ['aʊf|ɛsən] *unreg vt* to eat up
auffahren ['aʊffa:rən] *unreg vi* (*herankommen*) to draw up; (*hochfahren*) to jump up; (*wütend werden*) to flare up; (*in den Himmel*) to ascend ▷ *vt* (*Kanonen, Geschütz*) to bring up; **~ auf** *+akk* (*Auto*) to run *od* crash into
auffahrend *adj* hot-tempered
Auffahrt *f* (*Hausauffahrt*) drive; (*Autobahnauffahrt*) slip road (*Brit*), entrance ramp (*US*)
Auffahrunfall *m* pile-up
auffallen ['aʊffalən] *unreg vi* to be noticeable; **angenehm/unangenehm ~** to make a good/bad impression; **jdm ~** (*bemerkt werden*) to strike sb
auffallend *adj* striking
auffällig ['aʊffɛlɪç] *adj* conspicuous, striking
auffangen ['aʊffaŋən] *unreg vt* to catch; (*Funkspruch*) to intercept; (*Preise*) to peg; (*abfangen: Aufprall etc*) to cushion, absorb
Auffanglager *nt* reception camp
auffassen ['aʊffasən] *vt* to understand, comprehend; (*auslegen*) to see, view
Auffassung *f* (*Meinung*) opinion; (*Auslegung*) view, conception; (*auch*: **Auffassungsgabe**) grasp
auffindbar ['aʊffɪntba:r] *adj* to be found
auffordern ['aʊffɔrdərn] *vt* to challenge; (*befehlen*) to call upon, order; (*bitten*) to ask
Aufforderung *f* (*Befehl*) order; (*Einladung*) invitation
auffrischen ['aʊffrɪʃən] *vt* to freshen up; (*Kenntnisse*) to brush up; (*Erinnerungen*) to reawaken ▷ *vi* (*Wind*) to freshen
aufführen ['aʊffy:rən] *vt* (*Theat*) to perform; (*in einem Verzeichnis*) to list, specify ▷ *vr* (*sich benehmen*) to behave; **einzeln ~** to itemize
Aufführung *f* (*Theat*) performance; (*Liste*) specification
Aufgabe ['aʊfga:bə] **(-, -n)** *f* task; (*Sch*) exercise; (*Hausaufgabe*) homework; (*Verzicht*) giving up; (*von Gepäck*) registration; (*von Post*) posting; (*von Inserat*) insertion; **sich** *dat* **etw zur ~ machen** to make sth one's job *od* business
Aufgabenbereich *m* area of responsibility
Aufgang ['aʊfgaŋ] *m* ascent; (*Sonnenaufgang*) rise; (*Treppe*) staircase
aufgeben ['aʊfge:bən] *unreg vt* (*verzichten auf*) to give up; (*Paket*) to send, post; (*Gepäck*) to register; (*Bestellung*) to give; (*Inserat*) to insert; (*Rätsel, Problem*) to set ▷ *vi* to give up
Aufgebot ['aʊfgəbo:t] *nt* supply; (*von Kräften*) utilization; (*Eheaufgebot*) banns *pl*
aufgedreht ['aʊfgədre:t] (*umg*) *adj* excited
aufgedunsen ['aʊfgedʊnzən] *adj* swollen, puffed up
aufgehen ['aʊfge:ən] *unreg vi* (*Sonne, Teig*) to rise; (*sich öffnen*) to open; (*Theat: Vorhang*) to go up; (*Knopf, Knoten etc*) to come undone; (*klar werden*) to become clear; (*Math*) to come out exactly; **~ (in** *+dat***)** (*sich widmen*) to be absorbed (in); **in Rauch/Flammen ~** to go up in smoke/flames
aufgeklärt ['aʊfgəklɛ:rt] *adj* enlightened; (*sexuell*) knowing the facts of life
aufgekratzt ['aʊfgəkratst] (*umg*) *adj* in high spirits, full of beans
aufgelegt ['aʊfgəle:kt] *adj*: **gut/schlecht ~ sein** to be in a good/bad mood; **zu etw ~ sein** to be in the mood for sth
aufgeregt ['aʊfgəre:kt] *adj* excited

aufgeschlossen ['aʊfgəʃlɔsən] *adj* open, open-minded
aufgeschmissen ['aʊfgəʃmɪsən] (*umg*) *adj* in a fix, stuck
aufgeweckt ['aʊfgəvɛkt] *adj* bright, intelligent
aufgießen ['aʊfgi:sən] *unreg vt* (*Wasser*) to pour over; (*Tee*) to infuse
aufgreifen ['aʊfgraɪfən] *unreg vt* (*Thema*) to take up; (*Verdächtige*) to pick up, seize
aufgrund, **auf Grund** [aʊf'grʊnt] *präp +gen*: **~ von** on the basis of; (*wegen*) because of
aufhaben ['aʊfha:bən] *unreg vt* (*Hut etc*) to have on; (*Arbeit*) to have to do
aufhalsen ['aʊfhalzən] (*umg*) *vt*: **jdm etw ~** to saddle *od* lumber sb with sth
aufhalten ['aʊfhaltən] *unreg vt* (*Person*) to detain; (*Entwicklung*) to check; (*Tür, Hand*) to hold open; (*Augen*) to keep open ▷ *vr* (*wohnen*) to live; (*bleiben*) to stay; **jdn (bei etw) ~** (*abhalten, stören*) to hold *od* keep sb back (from sth); **sich über etw/jdn ~** to go on about sth/sb; **sich mit etw ~** to waste time over sth; **sich bei etw ~** (*sich befassen*) to dwell on sth
aufhängen ['aʊfhɛŋən] *unreg vt* (*Wäsche*) to hang up; (*Menschen*) to hang ▷ *vr* to hang o.s.
Aufhänger (**-s, -**) *m* (*am Mantel*) hook; (*fig*) peg
aufheben ['aʊfhe:bən] *unreg vt* (*hochheben*) to raise, lift; (*Sitzung*) to wind up; (*Urteil*) to annul; (*Gesetz*) to repeal, abolish; (*aufbewahren*) to keep; (*ausgleichen*) to offset, make up for ▷ *vr* to cancel itself out; **viel A~(s) machen (von)** to make a fuss (about); **bei jdm gut aufgehoben sein** to be well looked after at sb's
aufheitern ['aʊfhaɪtərn] *vt, vr* (*Himmel, Miene*) to brighten; (*Mensch*) to cheer up
aufhellen ['aʊfhɛlən] *vt, vr* to clear up; (*Farbe, Haare*) to lighten
aufhetzen ['aʊfhɛtsən] *vt* to stir up
aufholen ['aʊfho:lən] *vt* to make up ▷ *vi* to catch up
aufhorchen ['aʊfhɔrçən] *vi* to prick up one's ears
aufhören ['aʊfhø:rən] *vi* to stop; **~, etw zu tun** to stop doing sth
aufklären ['aʊfklɛ:rən] *vt* (*Geheimnis etc*) to clear up; (*Person*) to enlighten; (*sexuell*) to tell the facts of life to; (*Mil*) to reconnoitre ▷ *vr* to clear up
Aufklärung *f* (*von Geheimnis*) clearing up; (*Unterrichtung, Zeitalter*) enlightenment; (*sexuell*) sex education; (*Mil, Aviat*) reconnaissance
aufkleben ['aʊfkle:bən] *vt* to stick on
Aufkleber (**-s, -**) *m* sticker
aufknöpfen ['aʊfknœpfən] *vt* to unbutton
aufkommen ['aʊfkɔmən] *unreg vi* (*Wind*) to come up; (*Zweifel, Gefühl*) to arise; (*Mode*) to start; **für jdn/etw ~** to be liable *od* responsible for sb/sth; **für den Schaden ~** to pay for the damage; **endlich kam Stimmung auf** at last things livened up
aufladen ['aʊfla:dən] *unreg vt* to load ▷ *vr* (*Batterie etc*) to be charged; (*neu aufladen*) to be recharged; **jdm/sich etw ~** (*fig*) to saddle sb/o.s. with sth
Auflage ['aʊfla:gə] *f* edition; (*Zeitung*) circulation; (*Bedingung*) condition; **jdm etw zur ~ machen** to make sth a condition for sb
auflassen ['aʊflasən] *unreg* (*umg*) *vt* (*offen*) to leave open; (*: aufgesetzt*) to leave on; **die Kinder länger ~** to let the children stay up (longer)
auflauern ['aʊflaʊərn] *vi*: **jdm ~** to lie in wait for sb
Auflauf ['aʊflaʊf] *m* (*Koch*) pudding; (*Menschenauflauf*) crowd
aufleben ['aʊfle:bən] *vi* to revive
auflegen ['aʊfle:gən] *vt* to put on; (*Hörer*) to put down; (*Typ*) to print ▷ *vi* (*Tel*) to hang up
auflehnen ['aʊfle:nən] *vt* to lean on ▷ *vr* to rebel
Auflehnung *f* rebellion
auflesen ['aʊfle:zən] *unreg vt* to pick up
aufleuchten ['aʊflɔʏçtən] *vi* to light up
aufliegen ['aʊfli:gən] *unreg vi* to lie on; (*Comm*) to be available
auflockern ['aʊflɔkərn] *vt* to loosen; (*fig: Eintönigkeit etc*) to liven up; (*entspannen, zwangloser machen*) to make relaxed; (*Atmosphäre*) to make more relaxed, ease
auflösen ['aʊflø:zən] *vt* to dissolve; (*Missverständnis*) to sort out; (*Konto*) to close; (*Firma*) to wind up; (*Haushalt*) to break up; **in Tränen aufgelöst sein** to be in tears
aufmachen ['aʊfmaxən] *vt* to open; (*Kleidung*) to undo; (*zurechtmachen*) to do up ▷ *vr* to set out
Aufmachung *f* (*Kleidung*) outfit, get-up; (*Gestaltung*) format
aufmerksam ['aʊfmɛrkza:m] *adj* attentive; **auf etw** *akk* **~ werden** to become aware of sth; **jdn auf etw** *akk* **~ machen** to point sth out to sb; **(das ist) sehr ~ von Ihnen** (*zuvorkommend*) (that's) most kind of you; **Aufmerksamkeit** *f* attention, attentiveness; (*Geschenk*) token (gift)
aufmuntern ['aʊfmʊntərn] *vt* (*ermutigen*) to encourage; (*erheitern*) to cheer up
Aufnahme ['aʊfna:mə] (**-, -n**) *f* reception; (*Beginn*) beginning; (*in Verein etc*) admission; (*in Liste etc*) inclusion; (*Notieren*) taking down; (*Phot*) shot; (*auf Tonband etc*) recording; **aufnahmefähig** *adj* receptive; **Aufnahmeprüfung** *f* entrance test
aufnehmen ['aʊfne:mən] *unreg vt* to receive; (*hochheben*) to pick up; (*beginnen*) to take up; (*in Verein etc*) to admit; (*in Liste etc*) to include; (*fassen*) to hold; (*begreifen*) to take in, grasp; (*beim Stricken: Maschen*) to increase, make; (*notieren*) to take down; (*fotografieren*) to photograph; (*auf Tonband, Platte*) to record; (*Fin: leihen*) to take out; **es mit jdm ~ können** to be able to compete with sb

aufopfern ['aʊf|ɔpfərn] *vt* to sacrifice ▷ *vr* to sacrifice o.s.
aufopfernd *adj* selfless
aufpassen ['aʊfpasən] *vi* (*aufmerksam sein*) to pay attention; **auf jdn/etw ~** to look after *od* watch sb/sth; **aufgepasst!** look out!
Aufprall ['aʊfpral] (**-(e)s, -e**) *m* impact
aufprallen *vi* to hit, strike
Aufpreis ['aʊfpraɪs] *m* extra charge
aufpumpen ['aʊfpʊmpən] *vt* to pump up
aufputschen ['aʊfpʊtʃən] *vt* (*aufhetzen*) to inflame; (*erregen*) to stimulate
Aufputschmittel *nt* stimulant
aufraffen ['aʊfrafən] *vr* to rouse o.s.
aufräumen ['aʊfrɔʏmən] *vt, vi* (*Dinge*) to clear away; (*Zimmer*) to tidy up
aufrecht ['aʊfrɛçt] *adj* (*lit, fig*) upright
aufrechterhalten *unreg vt* to maintain
aufregen ['aʊfre:gən] *vt* to excite; (*ärgerlich machen*) to irritate, annoy; (*nervös machen*) to make nervous; (*beunruhigen*) to disturb ▷ *vr* to get excited
aufregend *adj* exciting
Aufregung *f* excitement
aufreiben ['aʊfraɪbən] *unreg vt* (*Haut*) to rub raw; (*erschöpfen*) to exhaust; (*Mil: völlig vernichten*) to wipe out, annihilate
aufreibend *adj* strenuous
aufreißen ['aʊfraɪsən] *unreg vt* (*Umschlag*) to tear open; (*Augen*) to open wide; (*Tür*) to throw open; (*Straße*) to take up; (*umg: Mädchen*) to pick up
aufreizen ['aʊfraɪtsən] *vt* to incite, stir up
aufreizend *adj* exciting, stimulating
aufrichten ['aʊfrɪçtən] *vt* to put up, erect; (*moralisch*) to console ▷ *vr* to rise; (*moralisch*): **sich ~ (an** *+dat***)** to take heart (from); **sich im Bett ~** to sit up in bed
aufrichtig ['aʊfrɪçtɪç] *adj* sincere; honest; **Aufrichtigkeit** *f* sincerity
aufrücken ['aʊfrʏkən] *vi* to move up; (*beruflich*) to be promoted
Aufruf ['aʊfru:f] *m* summons; (*zur Hilfe*) call; (*des Namens*) calling out
aufrufen *unreg vt* (*Namen*) to call out; (*auffordern*): **jdn ~ (zu)** to call upon sb (for); **einen Schüler ~** to ask a pupil (to answer) a question
Aufruhr ['aʊfru:r] (**-(e)s, -e**) *m* uprising, revolt; **in ~ sein** to be in uproar
aufrührerisch ['aʊfry:rərɪʃ] *adj* rebellious
aufrunden ['aʊfrʊndən] *vt* (*Summe*) to round up
aufrüsten ['aʊfrʏstən] *vt, vi* to arm
Aufrüstung *f* rearmament
aufrütteln ['aʊfrʏtəln] *vt* (*lit, fig*) to shake up
aufs [aʊfs] = **auf das**
aufsagen ['aʊfza:gən] *vt* (*Gedicht*) to recite; (*geh: Freundschaft*) to put an end to
aufsammeln ['aʊfzaməln] *vt* to gather up
aufsässig ['aʊfzɛsɪç] *adj* rebellious
Aufsatz ['aʊfzats] *m* (*Geschriebenes*) essay, composition; (*auf Schrank etc*) top
aufsaugen ['aʊfzaʊgən] *unreg vt* to soak up
aufschauen ['aʊfʃaʊən] *vi* to look up
aufscheuchen ['aʊfʃɔʏçən] *vt* to scare, startle
aufschieben ['aʊfʃi:bən] *unreg vt* to push open; (*verzögern*) to put off, postpone
Aufschlag ['aʊfʃla:k] *m* (*Ärmelaufschlag*) cuff; (*Jackenaufschlag*) lapel; (*Hosenaufschlag*) turn-up (*Brit*), cuff (*US*); (*Aufprall*) impact; (*Preisaufschlag*) surcharge; (*Tennis*) service
aufschlagen ['aʊfʃla:gən] *unreg vt* (*öffnen*) to open; (*verwunden*) to cut; (*hochschlagen*) to turn up; (*aufbauen: Zelt, Lager*) to pitch, erect; (*Wohnsitz*) to take up ▷ *vi* (*aufprallen*) to hit; (*teurer werden*) to go up; (*Tennis*) to serve; **schlagt Seite 111 auf** open your books at page 111
aufschließen ['aʊfʃli:sən] *unreg vt* to open up, unlock ▷ *vi* (*aufrücken*) to close up
Aufschluss ['aʊfʃlʊs] *m* information
aufschlussreich *adj* informative, illuminating
aufschnappen ['aʊfʃnapən] *vt* (*umg*) to pick up ▷ *vi* to fly open
aufschneiden ['aʊfʃnaɪdən] *unreg vt* to cut open; (*Brot*) to cut up; (*Med: Geschwür*) to lance ▷ *vi* (*umg*) to brag
Aufschneider (**-s, -**) *m* boaster, braggart
Aufschnitt ['aʊfʃnɪt] *m* (slices of) cold meat
aufschnüren ['aʊfʃny:rən] *vt* to unlace; (*Paket*) to untie
aufschrauben ['aʊfʃraʊbən] *vt* (*festschrauben*) to screw on; (*lösen*) to unscrew
aufschrecken ['aʊfʃrɛkən] *vt* to startle ▷ *vi* (*unreg*) to start up
Aufschrei ['aʊfʃraɪ] *m* cry
aufschreiben ['aʊfʃraɪbən] *unreg vt* to write down
Aufschrift ['aʊfʃrɪft] *f* (*Inschrift*) inscription; (*Etikett*) label
Aufschub ['aʊfʃu:p] (**-(e)s, -schübe**) *m* delay, postponement; **jdm ~ gewähren** to grant sb an extension
aufschwatzen ['aʊfʃvatsən] (*umg*) *vt*: **jdm etw ~** to talk sb into (getting/having *etc*) sth
Aufschwung ['aʊfʃvʊŋ] *m* (*Elan*) boost; (*wirtschaftlich*) upturn, boom; (*Sport: an Gerät*) mount
aufsehen ['aʊfze:ən] *unreg vi* to look up; **~ zu** (*lit*) to look up at; (*fig*) to look up to; **Aufsehen** (**-s**) *nt* sensation, stir
Aufseher, in (**-s, -**) *m(f)* guard; (*im Betrieb*) supervisor; (*Museumsaufseher*) attendant; (*Parkaufseher*) keeper
auf sein ['aʊfzaɪn] *siehe* **auf**
aufsetzen ['aʊfzɛtsən] *vt* to put on; (*Flugzeug*) to put down; (*Dokument*) to draw up ▷ *vr* to sit upright ▷ *vi* (*Flugzeug*) to touch down
Aufsicht ['aʊfzɪçt] *f* supervision; **die ~ haben** to be in charge; **bei einer Prüfung ~ führen** to invigilate (*Brit*) *od* supervise an exam
Aufsichtsrat *m* board (of directors)
aufsitzen ['aʊfzɪtsən] *unreg vi* (*aufgerichtet sitzen*) to sit up; (*aufs Pferd, Motorrad*) to mount,

get on; (*Schiff*) to run aground; **jdn ~ lassen** (*umg*) to stand sb up; **jdm ~** (*umg*) to be taken in by sb
aufspalten ['aʊfʃpaltən] *vt* to split
aufsparen ['aʊfʃpa:rən] *vt* to save (up)
aufsperren ['aʊfʃpɛrən] *vt* to unlock; (*Mund*) to open wide; **die Ohren ~** (*umg*) to prick up one's ears
aufspielen ['aʊfʃpi:lən] *vr* to show off; **sich als etw ~** to try to come on as sth
aufspringen ['aʊfʃprɪŋgən] *unreg vi* (*hochspringen*) to jump up; (*sich öffnen*) to spring open; (*Hände, Lippen*) to become chapped; **~ auf** *+akk* to jump onto
aufspüren ['aʊfʃpy:rən] *vt* to track down, trace
aufstacheln ['aʊfʃtaxəln] *vt* to incite
Aufstand ['aʊfʃtant] *m* insurrection, rebellion
aufständisch ['aʊfʃtɛndɪʃ] *adj* rebellious, mutinous
aufstechen ['aʊfʃtɛçən] *unreg vt* to prick open, puncture
aufstehen ['aʊfʃte:ən] *unreg vi* to get up; (*Tür*) to be open; **da musst du früher** *od* **eher ~!** (*fig: umg*) you'll have to do better than that!
aufsteigen ['aʊfʃtaɪgən] *unreg vi* (*hochsteigen*) to climb; (*Rauch*) to rise; **~ auf** *+akk* to get onto; **in jdm ~** (*Hass, Verdacht, Erinnerung etc*) to well up in sb
aufstellen ['aʊfʃtɛlən] *vt* (*aufrecht stellen*) to put up; (*Maschine*) to install; (*aufreihen*) to line up; (*Kandidaten*) to nominate; (*Forderung, Behauptung*) to put forward; (*formulieren: Programm etc*) to draw up; (*leisten: Rekord*) to set up
Aufstellung *f* (*Sport*) line-up; (*Liste*) list
Aufstieg ['aʊfʃti:k] **(-(e)s, -e)** *m* (*auf Berg*) ascent; (*Fortschritt*) rise; (*beruflich, Sport*) promotion
aufstoßen ['aʊfʃto:sən] *unreg vt* to push open ▷ *vi* to belch
aufstrebend ['aʊfʃtre:bənd] *adj* ambitious; (*Land*) striving for progress
aufstützen ['aʊfʃtʏtsən] *vt* (*Körperteil*) to prop, lean; (*Person*) to prop up ▷ *vr*: **sich ~ auf** *+akk* to lean on
aufsuchen ['aʊfzu:xən] *vt* (*besuchen*) to visit; (*konsultieren*) to consult
auftakeln ['aʊfta:kəln] *vt* (*Naut*) to rig (out) ▷ *vr* (*pej: umg*) to deck o.s. out
Auftakt ['aʊftakt] *m* (*Mus*) upbeat; (*fig*) prelude
auftanken ['aʊftaŋkən] *vi* to get petrol (*Brit*) *od* gas (*US*) ▷ *vt* to refuel
auftauchen ['aʊftaʊxən] *vi* to appear; (*gefunden werden, kommen*) to turn up; (*aus Wasser etc*) to emerge; (*U-Boot*) to surface; (*Zweifel*) to arise
auftauen ['aʊftaʊən] *vt* to thaw ▷ *vi* to thaw; (*fig*) to relax
aufteilen ['aʊftaɪlən] *vt* to divide up; (*Raum*) to partition
auftischen ['aʊftɪʃən] *vt* to serve (up); (*fig*) to tell
Auftrag ['aʊftra:k] **(-(e)s, -träge)** *m* order; (*Anweisung*) commission; (*Aufgabe*) mission; **etw in ~ geben (bei)** to order/commission sth (from); **im ~ von** on behalf of; **im** *od* **i. ~ A. J. Burnett** pp J. Burnett
auftragen ['aʊftra:gən] *unreg vt* (*Essen*) to serve; (*Farbe*) to put on; (*Kleidung*) to wear out ▷ *vi* (*dick machen*): **die Jacke trägt auf** the jacket makes one look fat; **jdm etw ~** to tell sb sth; **dick ~** (*umg*) to exaggerate
Auftraggeber, in **(-s, -)** *m(f)* client; (*Comm*) customer
auftreiben ['aʊftraɪbən] *unreg* (*umg*) *vt* (*beschaffen*) to raise
auftreten ['aʊftre:tən] *unreg vt* to kick open ▷ *vi* to appear; (*mit Füßen*) to tread; (*sich verhalten*) to behave; (*fig: eintreten*) to occur; (*Schwierigkeiten etc*) to arise; **als Vermittler** *etc* **~** to act as intermediary *etc*; **geschlossen ~** to put up a united front
Auftreten **(-s)** *nt* (*Vorkommen*) appearance; (*Benehmen*) behaviour (*Brit*), behavior (*US*)
Auftrieb ['aʊftri:p] *m* (*Phys*) buoyancy, lift; (*fig*) impetus
Auftritt ['aʊftrɪt] *m* (*des Schauspielers*) entrance; (*lit, fig: Szene*) scene
auftun ['aʊftu:n] *unreg vt* to open ▷ *vr* to open up
aufwachen ['aʊfvaxən] *vi* to wake up
aufwachsen ['aʊfvaksən] *unreg vi* to grow up
Aufwand ['aʊfvant] **(-(e)s)** *m* expenditure; (*Kosten*) expense; (*Luxus*) show; **bitte, keinen ~!** please don't go out of your way
aufwändig ['aʊfvɛndɪç] *adj, adv* costly
aufwärmen ['aʊfvɛrmən] *vt* to warm up; (*alte Geschichten*) to rake up
aufwärts ['aʊfvɛrts] *adv* upwards; **es geht ~** things are looking up; **Aufwärtsentwicklung** *f* upward trend
aufwecken ['aʊfvɛkən] *vt* to wake(n) up
aufweisen ['aʊfvaɪzən] *unreg vt* to show
aufwenden ['aʊfvɛndən] *unreg vt* to expend; (*Geld*) to spend; (*Sorgfalt*) to devote
aufwendig ['aʊfvɛndɪç] *adj, adv* costly
aufwerfen ['aʊfvɛrfən] *unreg vt* (*Fenster etc*) to throw open; (*Probleme*) to throw up, raise ▷ *vr*: **sich zu etw ~** to make o.s. out to be sth
aufwerten ['aʊfvɛrtən] *vt* (*Fin*) to revalue; (*fig*) to raise in value
aufwiegeln ['aʊfvi:gəln] *vt* to stir up, incite
aufwiegen ['aʊfvi:gən] *unreg vt* to make up for
Aufwind ['aʊfvɪnt] *m* up-current; **neuen ~ bekommen** (*fig*) to get new impetus
aufzählen ['aʊftsɛ:lən] *vt* to count out
aufzeichnen ['aʊftsaɪçnən] *vt* to sketch; (*schriftlich*) to jot down; (*auf Band*) to record
Aufzeichnung *f* (*schriftlich*) note; (*Tonbandaufzeichnung, Filmaufzeichnung*) recording
aufzeigen ['aʊftsaɪgən] *vt* to show, demonstrate

aufziehen ['aʊftsi:ən] *unreg vt* (*hochziehen*) to raise, draw up; (*öffnen*) to pull open; (*: Reißverschluss*) to undo; (*Gardinen*) to draw (back); (*Uhr*) to wind; (*großziehen: Kinder*) to raise, bring up; (*Tiere*) to rear; (*umg: necken*) to tease; (*: veranstalten*) to set up; (*: Fest*) to arrange ▷ *vi* (*Gewitter, Wolken*) to gather
Aufzug ['aʊftsu:k] *m* (*Fahrstuhl*) lift (*Brit*), elevator (*US*); (*Aufmarsch*) procession, parade; (*Kleidung*) get-up; (*Theat*) act
aufzwingen ['aʊftsvɪngən] *unreg vt*: **jdm etw ~** to force sth upon sb
Augapfel ['aʊk|apfəl] *m* eyeball; (*fig*) apple of one's eye
Auge ['aʊgə] (**-s, -n**) *nt* eye; (*Fettauge*) globule of fat; **unter vier ~n** in private; **vor aller ~n** in front of everybody, for all to see; **jdn/etw mit anderen ~n (an)sehen** to see sb/sth in a different light; **ich habe kein ~ zugetan** I didn't sleep a wink; **ein ~/beide ~n zudrücken** (*umg*) to turn a blind eye; **jdn/etw aus den ~n verlieren** to lose sight of sb/sth; (*fig*) to lose touch with sb/sth; **etw ins ~ fassen** to contemplate sth; **das kann leicht ins ~ gehen** (*fig: umg*) it might easily go wrong
Augenarzt *m* eye specialist, ophthalmologist
Augenblick *m* moment; **im ~** at the moment; **im ersten ~** for a moment; **augenblicklich** *adj* (*sofort*) instantaneous; (*gegenwärtig*) present
Augen- *zW*: **Augenbraue** *f* eyebrow; **Augenschein** *m*: **jdn/etw in Augenschein nehmen** to have a close look at sb/sth; **augenscheinlich** *adj* obvious; **Augenweide** *f* sight for sore eyes; **Augenzeuge** *m* eye witness
August [aʊ'gʊst] (**-(e)s** *od* **-, -e**) (*pl selten*) *m* August; *siehe auch* **September**
Auktion [aʊktsi'o:n] *f* auction
Auktionator [aʊktsio'na:tɔr] *m* auctioneer
Aula ['aʊla] (**-, Aulen** *od* **-s**) *f* assembly hall
Aus [aʊs] (**-**) *nt* (*Sport*) outfield; **ins ~ gehen** to go out
aus [aʊs] *präp +dat* **1** (*räumlich*) out of; (*von ... her*) from; **er ist aus Berlin** he's from Berlin; **aus dem Fenster** out of the window
2 (*gemacht/hergestellt aus*) made of; **ein Herz aus Stein** a heart of stone
3 (*auf Ursache deutend*) out of; **aus Mitleid** out of sympathy; **aus Erfahrung** from experience; **aus Spaß** for fun
4: aus ihr wird nie etwas she'll never get anywhere
▷ *adv* **1** (*zu Ende*) finished, over; **aus sein** to be over; **es ist aus mit ihm** he is finished, he has had it; **aus und vorbei** over and done with
2 (*ausgeschaltet, ausgezogen*) off; **aus sein** to be out; **Licht aus!** lights out!
3 (*in Verbindung mit von*): **von Rom aus** from Rome; **vom Fenster aus** out of the window; **von sich aus** (*selbstständig*) of one's own accord; **von mir aus** as far as I'm concerned
4: aus und ein gehen to come and go; (*bei jdm*) to visit frequently; **weder aus noch ein wissen** to be at one's wits' end; **auf etw** *akk* **aus sein** to be after sth
ausarbeiten ['aʊs|arbaɪtən] *vt* to work out
ausarten ['aʊs|artən] *vi* to degenerate; (*Kind*) to become overexcited
ausatmen ['aʊs|a:tmən] *vi* to breathe out
ausbaden ['aʊsba:dən] (*umg*) *vt*: **etw ~ müssen** to carry the can for sth
Ausbau ['aʊsbaʊ] *m* extension, expansion; removal
ausbauen *vt* to extend, expand; (*herausnehmen*) to take out, remove
ausbaufähig *adj* (*fig*) worth developing
ausbedingen ['aʊsbədɪŋən] *unreg vt*: **sich** *dat* **etw ~** to insist on sth
ausbessern ['aʊsbɛsərn] *vt* to mend, repair
ausbeulen ['aʊsbɔylən] *vt* to beat out
Ausbeute ['aʊsbɔytə] *f* yield; (*Gewinn*) profit, gain; (*Fische*) catch
ausbeuten *vt* to exploit; (*Min*) to work
ausbilden ['aʊsbɪldən] *vt* to educate; (*Lehrling, Soldat*) to instruct, train; (*Fähigkeiten*) to develop; (*Geschmack*) to cultivate
Ausbilder, in (**-s, -**) *m(f)* instructor, instructress
Ausbildung *f* education; training, instruction; development; cultivation; **er ist noch in der ~** he's still a trainee; he hasn't finished his education; **Ausbildungsplatz** *m* (*Stelle*) training vacancy
ausbitten ['aʊsbɪtən] *unreg vt*: **sich** *dat* **etw ~** (*geh: erbitten*) to ask for sth; (*verlangen*) to insist on sth
ausbleiben ['aʊsblaɪbən] *unreg vi* (*Personen*) to stay away, not come; (*Ereignisse*) to fail to happen, not happen; **es konnte nicht ~, dass ...** it was inevitable that ...
Ausblick ['aʊsblɪk] *m* (*lit, fig*) prospect, outlook, view
ausbomben ['aʊsbɔmbən] *vt* to bomb out
ausbrechen ['aʊsbrɛçən] *unreg vi* to break out ▷ *vt* to break off; **in Tränen/Gelächter ~** to burst into tears/out laughing
ausbreiten ['aʊsbraɪtən] *vt* to spread (out); (*Arme*) to stretch out ▷ *vr* to spread; **sich über ein Thema ~** to expand *od* enlarge on a topic
ausbrennen ['aʊsbrɛnən] *unreg vt* to scorch; (*Wunde*) to cauterize ▷ *vi* to burn out
Ausbruch ['aʊsbrʊx] *m* outbreak; (*von Vulkan*) eruption; (*Gefühlsausbruch*) outburst; (*von Gefangenen*) escape
ausbrüten ['aʊsbry:tən] *vt* (*lit, fig*) to hatch
Ausbuchtung ['aʊsbʊxtʊŋ] *f* bulge; (*Küste*) cove
ausbuhen ['aʊsbu:ən] *vt* to boo
ausbürsten ['aʊsbʏrstən] *vt* to brush out
Ausdauer ['aʊsdaʊər] *f* stamina; (*Beharrlichkeit*) perseverance
ausdauernd *adj* persevering
ausdehnen ['aʊsde:nən] *vt, vr* (*räumlich*) to

expand; (*zeitlich, auch Gummi*) to stretch; (*Nebel, fig: Macht*) to extend

ausdenken ['aʊsdɛŋkən] *unreg vt* (*zu Ende denken*) to think through; **sich** *dat* **etw ~** to think sth up; **das ist nicht auszudenken** (*unvorstellbar*) it's inconceivable

ausdiskutieren ['aʊsdɪskuti:rən] *vt* to talk out

ausdrehen ['aʊsdre:ən] *vt* to turn *od* switch off

Ausdruck ['aʊsdrʊk] (**-s, -drücke**) *m* expression, phrase; (*Kundgabe, Gesichtsausdruck*) expression; (*Fachausdruck*) term; (*Comput*) hard copy; **mit dem ~ des Bedauerns** (*form*) expressing regret

ausdrucken *vt* (*Text*) to print out

ausdrücken ['aʊsdrʏkən] *vt* (*auch vr: formulieren, zeigen*) to express; (*Zigarette*) to put out; (*Zitrone*) to squeeze

ausdrücklich *adj* express, explicit

Ausdrucks- *zW*: **ausdruckslos** *adj* expressionless, blank; **ausdrucksvoll** *adj* expressive; **Ausdrucksweise** *f* mode of expression

auseinander [aʊs|aɪ'nandər] *adv* (*getrennt*) apart; **weit ~** far apart; **Auseinandersetzung** *f* argument

ausfahren ['aʊsfa:rən] *unreg vi* to drive out; (*Naut*) to put out (to sea) ▷ *vt* to take out; (*Aut*) to drive flat out; (*ausliefern: Waren*) to deliver; **ausgefahrene Wege** rutted roads

Ausfahrt *f* (*des Zuges etc*) leaving, departure; (*Autobahnausfahrt, Garagenausfahrt*) exit, way out; (*Spazierfahrt*) drive, excursion

Ausfall ['aʊsfal] *m* loss; (*Nichtstattfinden*) cancellation; (*das Versagen: Tech, Med*) failure; (*von Motor*) breakdown; (*Produktionsstörung*) stoppage; (*Mil*) sortie; (*Fechten*) lunge; (*radioaktiv*) fallout

ausfallen ['aʊsfalən] *unreg vi* (*Zähne, Haare*) to fall *od* come out; (*nicht stattfinden*) to be cancelled; (*wegbleiben*) to be omitted; (*Person*) to drop out; (*Lohn*) to be stopped; (*nicht funktionieren*) to break down; (*Resultat haben*) to turn out; **wie ist das Spiel ausgefallen?** what was the result of the game?; **die Schule fällt morgen aus** there's no school tomorrow

ausfallend *adj* impertinent

Ausfallstraße *f* arterial road

Ausfallzeit *f* (*Maschine*) downtime

ausfeilen ['aʊsfaɪlən] *vt* to file out; (*Stil*) to polish up

ausfertigen ['aʊsfɛrtɪgən] *vt* (*form*) to draw up; (*Rechnung*) to make out; **doppelt ~** to duplicate

Ausfertigung *f* (*form*) drawing up; making out; (*Exemplar*) copy; **in doppelter/dreifacher ~** in duplicate/triplicate

ausfindig ['aʊsfɪndɪç] *adj*: **~ machen** to discover

ausfliegen ['aʊsfli:gən] *unreg vi* to fly away ▷ *vt* to fly out; **sie sind ausgeflogen** (*umg*) they're out

ausflippen ['aʊsflɪpən] (*umg*) *vi* to freak out

Ausflucht ['aʊsflʊxt] (**-, -flüchte**) *f* excuse

Ausflug ['aʊsflu:k] *m* excursion, outing

Ausflügler, in ['aʊsfly:klər(ɪn)] (**-s, -**) *m(f)* tripper (*Brit*), excursionist (*US*)

Ausfluss ['aʊsflʊs] *m* outlet; (*Med*) discharge

ausfragen ['aʊsfra:gən] *vt* to interrogate, question

ausfransen ['aʊsfranzən] *vi* to fray

ausfressen ['aʊsfrɛsən] *unreg* (*umg*) *vt* (*anstellen*) to be up to

Ausfuhr ['aʊsfu:r] (**-, -en**) *f* export, exportation; (*Ware*) export ▷ *in zw* export

ausführbar ['aʊsfy:rba:r] *adj* feasible; (*Comm*) exportable

ausführen ['aʊsfy:rən] *vt* (*verwirklichen*) to carry out; (*Person*) to take out; (*Hund*) to take for a walk; (*Comm*) to export; (*erklären*) to give details of; **die ~de Gewalt** (*Pol*) the executive

ausführlich *adj* detailed ▷ *adv* in detail; **Ausführlichkeit** *f* detail

Ausführung *f* execution, performance; (*von Waren*) design; (*von Thema*) exposition; (*Durchführung*) completion; (*Herstellungsart*) version; (*Erklärung*) explanation

ausfüllen ['aʊsfʏlən] *vt* to fill up; (*Fragebogen etc*) to fill in; (*Beruf*) to be fulfilling for; **jdn (ganz) ~** (*Zeit in Anspruch nehmen*) to take (all) sb's time

Ausgabe ['aʊsga:bə] *f* (*Geld*) expenditure, outlay; (*Aushändigung*) giving out; (*Schalter*) counter; (*Ausführung*) version; (*Buch*) edition; (*Nummer*) issue

Ausgang ['aʊsgaŋ] *m* way out, exit; (*Ende*) end; (*Ausgangpunkt*) starting point; (*Ergebnis*) result; (*Ausgehtag*) free time, time off; **ein Unfall mit tödlichem ~** a fatal accident; **kein ~** no exit

Ausgangs- *zW*: **Ausgangsbasis** *f* starting point; **Ausgangspunkt** *m* starting point; **Ausgangssperre** *f* curfew

ausgeben ['aʊsge:bən] *unreg vt* (*Geld*) to spend; (*austeilen*) to issue, distribute; (*Comput*) to output ▷ *vr*: **sich für etw/jdn ~** to pass o.s. off as sth/sb; **ich gebe heute Abend einen aus** (*umg*) it's my treat this evening

ausgebucht ['aʊsgəbu:xt] *adj* fully booked

ausgedient ['aʊsgədi:nt] *adj* (*Soldat*) discharged; (*verbraucht*) no longer in use; **~ haben** to have come to the end of its useful life

ausgefallen ['aʊsgəfalən] *adj* (*ungewöhnlich*) exceptional

ausgeglichen ['aʊsgəglɪçən] *adj* (well-)balanced; **Ausgeglichenheit** *f* balance; (*von Mensch*) even-temperedness

ausgehen ['aʊsge:ən] *unreg vi* (*auch Feuer, Ofen, Licht*) to go out; (*zu Ende gehen*) to come to an end; (*Benzin*) to run out; (*Haare, Zähne*) to fall *od* come out; (*Strom*) to go off; (*Resultat haben*) to turn out; (*spazieren gehen*) to go (out) for a walk; (*abgeschickt werden: Post*) to be sent off;

mir ging das Benzin aus I ran out of petrol (*Brit*) *od* gas (*US*); **auf etw** *akk* **~** to aim at sth; **von etw ~** (*wegführen*) to lead away from sth; (*herrühren*) to come from sth; (*zugrunde legen*) to proceed from sth; **wir können davon ~, dass ...** we can proceed from the assumption that ..., we can take as our starting point that ...; **leer ~** to get nothing; **schlecht ~** to turn out badly

ausgelassen ['aʊsgəlasən] *adj* boisterous, high-spirited, exuberant; **Ausgelassenheit** *f* boisterousness, high spirits *pl*, exuberance

ausgelastet ['aʊsgəlastət] *adj* fully occupied

ausgelernt ['aʊsgəlɛrnt] *adj* trained, qualified

ausgemacht ['aʊsgəmaxt] *adj* settled; (*umg: Dummkopf etc*) out-and-out, downright; **es gilt als ~, dass ...** it is settled that ...; **es war eine ~e Sache, dass ...** it was a foregone conclusion that ...

ausgenommen ['aʊsgənɔmən] *konj* except; **Anwesende sind ~** present company excepted

ausgepowert ['aʊsgəpo:vərt] *adj*: **~ sein** (*umg*) to be tired, be exhausted

ausgeprägt ['aʊsgəprɛ:kt] *adj* prominent; (*Eigenschaft*) distinct

ausgerechnet ['aʊsgərɛçnət] *adv* just, precisely; **~ du** you of all people; **~ heute** today of all days

ausgeschlossen ['aʊsgəʃlɔsən] *pp von* **ausschließen** ▷ *adj* (*unmöglich*) impossible, out of the question; **es ist nicht ~, dass ...** it cannot be ruled out that ...

ausgeschnitten ['aʊsgəʃnɪtən] *adj* (*Kleid*) low-necked

ausgesprochen ['aʊsgəʃprɔxən] *adj* (*Faulheit, Lüge etc*) out-and-out; (*unverkennbar*) marked ▷ *adv* decidedly

ausgezeichnet ['aʊsgətsaɪçnət] *adj* excellent

ausgiebig ['aʊsgi:bɪç] *adj* (*Gebrauch*) full, good; (*Essen*) generous, lavish; **~ schlafen** to have a good sleep

Ausgleich ['aʊsglaɪç] (**-(e)s, -e**) *m* balance; (*von Fehler, Mangel*) compensation; (*Sport*): **den ~ erzielen** to equalize; **zum ~** *+gen* in order to offset sth; **das ist ein guter ~** (*entspannend*) that's very relaxing

ausgleichen ['aʊsglaɪçən] *unreg vt* to balance (out); (*Konflikte*) to reconcile; (*Höhe*) to even up ▷ *vi* (*Sport*) to equalize; **~de Gerechtigkeit** poetic justice

Ausgleichssport *m* keep-fit activity

ausgraben ['aʊsgra:bən] *unreg vt* to dig up; (*Leichen*) to exhume; (*fig*) to unearth

Ausgrabung *f* excavation

ausgrenzen ['aʊsgrɛntsən] *vt* to shut out, separate

Ausguss ['aʊsgʊs] *m* (*Spüle*) sink; (*Abfluss*) outlet; (*Tülle*) spout

aushaben ['aʊsha:bən] *unreg* (*umg*) *vt* (*Kleidung*) to have taken off; (*Buch*) to have finished

aushalten ['aʊshaltən] *unreg vt* to bear, stand; (*umg: Geliebte*) to keep ▷ *vi* to hold out; **das ist nicht zum A~** that is unbearable; **sich von jdm ~ lassen** to be kept by sb

aushandeln ['aʊshandəln] *vt* to negotiate

aushändigen ['aʊshɛndɪgən] *vt*: **jdm etw ~** to hand sth over to sb

Aushang ['aʊshaŋ] *m* notice

aushängen ['aʊshɛŋən] *unreg vt* (*Meldung*) to put up; (*Fenster*) to take off its hinges ▷ *vi* to be displayed ▷ *vr* to hang out

Aushängeschild *nt* (shop) sign; (*fig*): **als ~ für etw dienen** to promote sth

ausharren ['aʊsharən] *vi* to hold out

ausheben ['aʊshe:bən] *unreg vt* (*Erde*) to lift out; (*Grube*) to hollow out; (*Tür*) to take off its hinges; (*Diebesnest*) to clear out; (*Mil*) to enlist

aushecken ['aʊshɛkən] (*umg*) *vt* to concoct, think up

aushelfen ['aʊshɛlfən] *unreg vi*: **jdm ~** to help sb out

Aushilfe ['aʊshɪlfə] *f* help, assistance; (*Person*) (temporary) worker

Aushilfs- *zW*: **Aushilfskraft** *f* temporary worker; **aushilfsweise** *adv* temporarily, as a stopgap

ausholen ['aʊsho:lən] *vi* to swing one's arm back; (*zur Ohrfeige*) to raise one's hand; (*beim Gehen*) to take long strides; **zum Gegenschlag ~** (*lit, fig*) to prepare for a counter-attack

auskennen ['aʊskɛnən] *unreg vr* to know a lot; (*an einem Ort*) to know one's way about; (*in Fragen etc*) to be knowledgeable; **man kennt sich bei ihm nie aus** you never know where you are with him

auskippen ['aʊskɪpən] *vt* to empty

ausklammern ['aʊsklamərn] *vt* (*Thema*) to exclude, leave out

Ausklang ['aʊsklaŋ] *m* (*geh*) end

ausklingen ['aʊsklɪŋən] *unreg vi* to end; (*Ton, Lied*) to die away; (*Fest*) to come to an end

ausklopfen ['aʊsklɔpfən] *vt* (*Teppich*) to beat; (*Pfeife*) to knock out

auskochen ['aʊskɔxən] *vt* to boil; (*Med*) to sterilize

auskommen ['aʊskɔmən] *unreg vi*: **mit jdm ~** to get on with sb; **mit etw ~** to get by with sth; **Auskommen** (**-s**) *nt*: **sein Auskommen haben** to get by; **mit ihr ist kein Auskommen** she's impossible to get on with

auskosten ['aʊskɔstən] *vt* to enjoy to the full

auskugeln ['aʊsku:gəln] *vr*: **sich** *dat* **den Arm ~** to dislocate one's arm

auskundschaften ['aʊskʊntʃaftən] *vt* to spy out; (*Gebiet*) to reconnoitre (*Brit*), reconnoiter (*US*)

Auskunft ['aʊskʊnft] (**-, -künfte**) *f* information; (*nähere*) details *pl*, particulars *pl*; (*Stelle*) information office; (*Tel*) inquiries; **jdm ~ erteilen** to give sb information

auskurieren ['aʊskuri:rən] (*umg*) *vt* to cure

auslachen ['aʊslaxən] *vt* to laugh at, mock

ausladen ['aʊsla:dən] *unreg vt* to unload; (*umg: Gäste*) to cancel an invitation to ▷ *vi* (*Äste*) to spread
Auslage ['aʊsla:gə] *f* shop window (display)
Ausland ['aʊslant] *nt* foreign countries *pl*; **im ~** abroad; **ins ~** abroad
Ausländer, in ['aʊslɛndər(ɪn)] (**-s, -**) *m(f)* foreigner
Ausländerfeindlichkeit *f* hostility to foreigners, xenophobia
ausländisch *adj* foreign
Auslands- *zW*: **Auslandsgespräch** *nt* international call; **Auslandskorrespondent, in** *m(f)* foreign correspondent; **Auslandsreise** *f* trip abroad; **Auslandsschutzbrief** *m* international travel cover
auslassen ['aʊslasən] *unreg vt* to leave out; (*Wort etc*) to omit; (*Fett*) to melt; (*Kleidungsstück*) to let out ▷ *vr*: **sich über etw** *akk* **~** to speak one's mind about sth; **seine Wut** *etc* **an jdm ~** to vent one's rage *etc* on sb
Auslassung *f* omission
Auslassungszeichen *nt* apostrophe
Auslauf ['aʊslaʊf] *m* (*für Tiere*) run; (*Ausfluss*) outflow, outlet
auslaufen *unreg vi* to run out; (*Behälter*) to leak; (*Naut*) to put out (to sea); (*langsam aufhören*) to run down
Ausläufer ['aʊslɔyfər] *m* (*von Gebirge*) spur; (*Pflanze*) runner; (*Met: von Hoch*) ridge; (*: von Tief*) trough
ausleeren ['aʊsle:rən] *vt* to empty
auslegen ['aʊsle:gən] *vt* (*Waren*) to lay out; (*Köder*) to put down; (*Geld*) to lend; (*bedecken*) to cover; (*Text etc*) to interpret
Ausleihe ['aʊslaɪə] (**-, -n**) *f* issuing; (*Stelle*) issue desk
ausleihen ['aʊslaɪən] *unreg vt* (*verleihen*) to lend; **sich** *dat* **etw ~** to borrow sth
Auslese ['aʊsle:zə] (**-, -n**) *f* selection; (*Elite*) elite; (*Wein*) choice wine
auslesen ['aʊsle:zən] *unreg vt* to select; (*umg: zu Ende lesen*) to finish
ausliefern ['aʊsli:fərn] *vt* to hand over; (*Comm*) to deliver ▷ *vr*: **sich jdm ~** to give o.s. up to sb; **~ (an** *+akk***)** to deliver (up) (to), hand over (to); (*an anderen Staat*) to extradite (to); **jdm/etw ausgeliefert sein** to be at the mercy of sb/sth
ausliegen ['aʊsli:gən] *unreg vi* (*zur Ansicht*) to be displayed; (*Zeitschriften etc*) to be available (to the public); (*Liste*) to be up
auslöschen ['aʊslœʃən] *vt* to extinguish; (*fig*) to wipe out, obliterate
auslosen ['aʊslo:zən] *vt* to draw lots for
auslösen ['aʊsløːzən] *vt* (*Explosion, Schuss*) to set off; (*hervorrufen*) to cause, produce; (*Gefangene*) to ransom; (*Pfand*) to redeem
Auslöser (**-s, -**) *m* trigger; (*Phot*) release; (*Anlass*) cause
ausmachen ['aʊsmaxən] *vt* (*Licht, Radio*) to turn off; (*Feuer*) to put out; (*entdecken*) to make out; (*vereinbaren*) to agree; (*beilegen*) to settle; (*Anteil darstellen, betragen*) to represent; (*bedeuten*) to matter; **das macht ihm nichts aus** it doesn't matter to him; **macht es Ihnen etwas aus, wenn ...?** would you mind if ...?
ausmalen ['aʊsma:lən] *vt* to paint; (*fig*) to describe; **sich** *dat* **etw ~** to imagine sth
Ausmaß ['aʊsma:s] *nt* dimension; (*fig*) scale
ausmerzen ['aʊsmɛrtsən] *vt* to eliminate
ausmessen ['aʊsmɛsən] *unreg vt* to measure
Ausnahme ['aʊsna:mə] (**-, -n**) *f* exception; **eine ~ machen** to make an exception; **Ausnahmefall** *m* exceptional case; **Ausnahmezustand** *m* state of emergency
ausnahmslos *adv* without exception
ausnahmsweise *adv* by way of exception, for once
ausnehmen ['aʊsne:mən] *unreg vt* to take out, remove; (*Tier*) to gut; (*Nest*) to rob; (*umg: Geld abnehmen*) to clean out; (*ausschließen*) to make an exception of ▷ *vr* to look, appear
ausnehmend *adj* exceptional
ausnutzen ['aʊsnʊtsən] *vt* (*Zeit, Gelegenheit*) to use, turn to good account; (*Einfluss*) to use; (*Mensch, Gutmütigkeit*) to exploit
auspacken ['aʊspakən] *vt* to unpack ▷ *vi* (*umg: alles sagen*) to talk
auspfeifen ['aʊspfaɪfən] *unreg vt* to hiss/boo at
ausplaudern ['aʊsplaʊdərn] *vt* (*Geheimnis*) to blab
ausprobieren ['aʊsprobi:rən] *vt* to try (out)
Auspuff ['aʊspʊf] (**-(e)s, -e**) *m* (*Tech*) exhaust; **Auspuffrohr** *nt* exhaust (pipe); **Auspufftopf** *m* (*Aut*) silencer (*Brit*), muffler (*US*)
ausradieren ['aʊsradi:rən] *vt* to erase, rub out
ausrangieren ['aʊsrãʒi:rən] (*umg*) *vt* to chuck out; (*Maschine, Auto*) to scrap
ausrauben ['aʊsraʊbən] *vt* to rob
ausräumen ['aʊsrɔymən] *vt* (*Dinge*) to clear away; (*Schrank, Zimmer*) to empty; (*Bedenken*) to put aside
ausrechnen ['aʊsrɛçnən] *vt* to calculate, reckon
Ausrede ['aʊsre:də] *f* excuse
ausreden ['aʊsre:dən] *vi* to have one's say ▷ *vt*: **jdm etw ~** to talk sb out of sth; **er hat mich nicht mal ~ lassen** he didn't even let me finish (speaking)
ausreichen ['aʊsraɪçən] *vi* to suffice, be enough
ausreichend *adj* sufficient, adequate; (*Sch*) adequate
Ausreise ['aʊsraɪzə] *f* departure; **bei der ~** when leaving the country; **Ausreiseerlaubnis** *f* exit visa
ausreisen ['aʊsraɪzən] *vi* to leave the country
ausreißen ['aʊsraɪsən] *unreg vt* to tear *od* pull out ▷ *vi* (*Riss bekommen*) to tear; (*umg*) to make off, scram; **er hat sich** *dat* **kein Bein ausgerissen** (*umg*) he didn't exactly overstrain himself
ausrenken ['aʊsrɛŋkən] *vt* to dislocate

ausrichten ['aʊsrɪçtən] *vt* (*Botschaft*) to deliver; (*Gruß*) to pass on; (*Hochzeit etc*) to arrange; (*in gerade Linie bringen*) to get in a straight line; (*angleichen*) to bring into line; (*Typ etc*) to justify; **etwas/nichts bei jdm ~** to get somewhere/nowhere with sb; **jdm etw ~** to take a message for sb; **ich werde es ihm ~** I'll tell him

ausrotten ['aʊsrɔtən] *vt* to stamp out, exterminate

ausrücken ['aʊsrʏkən] *vi* (*Mil*) to move off; (*Feuerwehr, Polizei*) to be called out; (*umg: weglaufen*) to run away

Ausruf ['aʊsru:f] *m* (*Schrei*) cry, exclamation; (*Verkünden*) proclamation

ausrufen *unreg vt* to cry out, exclaim; to call out; **jdn ~ (lassen)** (*über Lautsprecher etc*) to page sb

Ausrufezeichen *nt* exclamation mark

ausruhen ['aʊsru:ən] *vt, vi, vr* to rest

ausrüsten ['aʊsrʏstən] *vt* to equip, fit out

Ausrüstung *f* equipment

ausrutschen ['aʊsrʊtʃən] *vi* to slip

Aussage ['aʊsza:gə] (**-, -n**) *f* (*Jur*) statement; **der Angeklagte/Zeuge verweigerte die ~** the accused/witness refused to give evidence

aussagen ['aʊsza:gən] *vt* to say, state ▷ *vi* (*Jur*) to give evidence

ausschalten ['aʊsʃaltən] *vt* to switch off; (*fig*) to eliminate

Ausschank ['aʊsʃaŋk] (**-(e)s, -schänke**) *m* dispensing, giving out; (*Comm*) selling; (*Theke*) bar

Ausschau ['aʊsʃaʊ] *f*: **~ halten (nach)** to look out (for), watch (for)

ausscheiden ['aʊsʃaɪdən] *unreg vt* (*aussondern*) to take out; (*Med*) to excrete ▷ *vi*: **~ (aus)** to leave; (*aus einem Amt*) to retire (from); (*Sport*) to be eliminated (from), be knocked out (of); **er scheidet für den Posten aus** he can't be considered for the job

ausschenken ['aʊsʃɛŋkən] *vt* to pour out; (*am Ausschank*) to serve

ausschimpfen ['aʊsʃɪmpfən] *vt* to scold, tell off

ausschlachten ['aʊsʃlaxtən] *vt* (*Auto*) to cannibalize; (*fig*) to make a meal of

ausschlafen ['aʊsʃla:fən] *unreg vi, vr* to sleep late ▷ *vt* to sleep off; **ich bin nicht ausgeschlafen** I didn't have *od* get enough sleep

Ausschlag ['aʊsʃla:k] *m* (*Med*) rash; (*Pendelausschlag*) swing; (*von Nadel*) deflection; **den ~ geben** (*fig*) to tip the balance

ausschlagen ['aʊsʃla:gən] *unreg vt* to knock out; (*auskleiden*) to deck out; (*verweigern*) to decline ▷ *vi* (*Pferd*) to kick out; (*Bot*) to sprout; (*Zeiger*) to be deflected

ausschlaggebend *adj* decisive

ausschließen ['aʊsʃli:sən] *unreg vt* to shut *od* lock out; (*Sport*) to disqualify; (*Fehler, Möglichkeit etc*) to rule out; (*fig*) to exclude; **ich will mich nicht ~** myself not excepted

ausschließlich *adj* exclusive ▷ *adv* exclusively ▷ *präp +gen* excluding, exclusive of

Ausschluss ['aʊsʃlʊs] *m* exclusion; **unter ~ der Öffentlichkeit stattfinden** to be closed to the public; (*Jur*) to be held in camera

ausschmücken ['aʊsʃmʏkən] *vt* to decorate; (*fig*) to embellish

ausschneiden ['aʊsʃnaɪdən] *unreg vt* to cut out; (*Büsche*) to trim

Ausschnitt ['aʊsʃnɪt] *m* (*Teil*) section; (*von Kleid*) neckline; (*Zeitungsausschnitt*) cutting (*Brit*), clipping (*US*); (*aus Film etc*) excerpt

ausschreiben ['aʊsʃraɪbən] *unreg vt* (*ganz schreiben*) to write out (in full); (*Scheck, Rechnung etc*) to write (out); (*Stelle, Wettbewerb etc*) to announce, advertise

Ausschuss ['aʊsʃʊs] *m* committee, board; (*Abfall*) waste, scraps *pl*; (*Comm: auch:* **Ausschussware**) reject

ausschütten ['aʊsʃʏtən] *vt* to pour out; (*Eimer*) to empty; (*Geld*) to pay ▷ *vr* to shake (with laughter)

ausschweifend ['aʊsʃvaɪfənt] *adj* (*Leben*) dissipated, debauched; (*Fantasie*) extravagant

Ausschweifung *f* excess

ausschweigen ['aʊsʃvaɪgən] *unreg vr* to keep silent

ausschwitzen ['aʊsʃvɪtsən] *vt* to sweat out

aussehen ['aʊsze:ən] *unreg vi* to look; **gut ~** to look good/well; **wie siehts aus?** (*umg: wie stehts?*) how's things?; **das sieht nach nichts aus** that doesn't look anything special; **es sieht nach Regen aus** it looks like rain; **es sieht schlecht aus** things look bad; **Aussehen** (**-s**) *nt* appearance

aus sein ['aussaɪn] *siehe* **aus**

außen ['aʊsən] *adv* outside; (*nach außen*) outwards; **~ ist es rot** it's red (on the) outside

Außen- *zW*: **Außenantenne** *f* outside aerial; **Außenbordmotor** *m* outboard motor

aussenden ['aʊszɛndən] *unreg vt* to send out, emit

Außen- *zW*: **Außendienst** *m* outside *od* field service; (*von Diplomat*) foreign service; **Außenhandel** *m* foreign trade; **Außenminister** *m* foreign minister; **Außenministerium** *nt* foreign office; **Außenpolitik** *f* foreign policy; **Außenseite** *f* outside; **Außenseiter, in** (**-s, -**) *m(f)* outsider; **Außenspiegel** *m* (*Aut*) outside mirror; **Außenstände** *pl* (*bes Comm*) outstanding debts *pl*, arrears *pl*; **Außenstehende, r** *f(m)* outsider

außer ['aʊsər] *präp +dat* (*räumlich*) out of; (*abgesehen von*) except ▷ *konj* (*ausgenommen*) except; **~ Gefahr sein** to be out of danger; **~ Zweifel** beyond any doubt; **~ Betrieb** out of order; **~ sich** *dat* **sein/geraten** to be beside o.s.; **~ Dienst** retired; **~ Landes** abroad; **~ wenn** unless; **~ dass** except

außerdem *konj* besides, in addition ▷ *adv* anyway

außerdienstlich *adj* private
äußere, r, s ['ɔʏsərə(r,s)] *adj* outer, external
außer- *zW*: **außerehelich** *adj* extramarital; **außergewöhnlich** *adj* unusual; **außerhalb** *präp +gen* outside ▷ *adv* outside; **Außerkraftsetzung** *f* repeal
äußerlich *adj* external; **rein ~ betrachtet** on the face of it; **Äußerlichkeit** *f* (*fig*) triviality; (*Oberflächlichkeit*) superficiality; (*Formalität*) formality
äußern *vt* to utter, express; (*zeigen*) to show ▷ *vr* to give one's opinion; (*sich zeigen*) to show itself
außer- *zW*: **außerordentlich** *adj* extraordinary; **außerplanmäßig** *adj* unscheduled
äußerst ['ɔʏsərst] *adv* extremely, most
außerstande, **außer Stande** [aʊsər'ʃtandə] *adv* (*nicht in der Lage*) not in a position; (*nicht fähig*) unable
äußerste, r, s *adj* utmost; (*räumlich*) farthest; (*Termin*) last possible; (*Preis*) highest; **mein ~s Angebot** my final offer
äußerstenfalls *adv* if the worst comes to the worst
Äußerung *f* (*Bemerkung*) remark, comment; (*Behauptung*) statement; (*Zeichen*) expression
aussetzen ['aʊszɛtsən] *vt* (*Kind, Tier*) to abandon; (*Boote*) to lower; (*Belohnung*) to offer; (*Urteil, Verfahren*) to postpone ▷ *vi* (*aufhören*) to stop; (*Pause machen*) to have a break; **jdn/sich einer Sache** *dat* **~** to lay sb/o.s. open to sth; **jdm/etw ausgesetzt sein** to be exposed to sb/sth; **was haben Sie daran auszusetzen?** what's your objection to it?; **an jdm/etw etwas ~** to find fault with sb/sth
Aussicht ['aʊszɪçt] *f* view; (*in Zukunft*) prospect; **in ~ sein** to be in view; **etw in ~ haben** to have sth in view; **jdm etw in ~ stellen** to promise sb sth
Aussichts- *zW*: **aussichtslos** *adj* hopeless; **Aussichtspunkt** *m* viewpoint; **aussichtsreich** *adj* promising; **Aussichtsturm** *m* observation tower
Aussiedler, in ['aʊszi:dlər(ɪn)] **(-s, -)** *m(f)* (*Auswanderer*) emigrant
aussöhnen ['aʊszø:nən] *vt* to reconcile ▷ *vr* (*einander*) to become reconciled; **sich mit jdm/etw ~** to reconcile o.s. with sb/to sth
aussondern ['aʊszɔndərn] *vt* to separate off, select
aussortieren ['aʊszɔrti:rən] *vt* to sort out
ausspannen ['aʊsʃpanən] *vt* to spread *od* stretch out; (*Pferd*) to unharness; (*umg*: *Mädchen*): **jdm jdn ~** to steal sb from sb ▷ *vi* to relax
aussparen ['aʊsʃpa:rən] *vt* to leave open
aussperren ['aʊsʃpɛrən] *vt* to lock out
Aussperrung *f* (*Industrie*) lock-out
ausspielen ['aʊsʃpi:lən] *vt* (*Karte*) to lead; (*Geldprämie*) to offer as a prize ▷ *vi* (*Karten*) to lead; **ausgespielt haben** to be finished; **jdn gegen jdn ~** to play sb off against sb
Aussprache ['aʊsʃpra:xə] *f* pronunciation; (*Unterredung*) (frank) discussion
aussprechen ['aʊsʃprɛçən] *unreg vt* to pronounce; (*zu Ende sprechen*) to speak; (*äußern*) to say, express ▷ *vr* (*sich äußern*): **sich ~ (über +akk)** to speak (about); (*sich anvertrauen*) to unburden o.s. (about *od* on); (*diskutieren*) to discuss ▷ *vi* (*zu Ende sprechen*) to finish speaking; **der Regierung das Vertrauen ~** to pass a vote of confidence in the government
Ausspruch ['aʊsʃprʊx] *m* remark; (*geflügeltes Wort*) saying
ausspülen ['aʊsʃpy:lən] *vt* to wash out; (*Mund*) to rinse
Ausstand ['aʊsʃtant] *m* strike; **in den ~ treten** to go on strike; **seinen ~ geben** to hold a leaving party
ausstatten ['aʊsʃtatən] *vt* (*Zimmer etc*) to furnish; **jdn mit etw ~** to equip sb *od* kit sb out with sth
Ausstattung *f* (*Ausstatten*) provision; (*Kleidung*) outfit; (*Aussteuer*) dowry; (*Aufmachung*) make-up; (*Einrichtung*) furnishing
ausstechen ['aʊsʃtɛçən] *unreg vt* (*Torf, Kekse*) to cut out; (*Augen*) to gouge out; (*übertreffen*) to outshine
ausstehen ['aʊsʃte:ən] *unreg vt* to stand, endure ▷ *vi* (*noch nicht da sein*) to be outstanding
aussteigen ['aʊsʃtaɪgən] *unreg vi* to get out, alight; **alles ~!** (*von Schaffner*) all change!; **aus der Gesellschaft ~** to drop out (of society)
Aussteiger, in (*umg*) *m(f)* dropout
ausstellen ['aʊsʃtɛlən] *vt* to exhibit, display; (*umg*: *ausschalten*) to switch off; (*Rechnung etc*) to make out; (*Pass, Zeugnis*) to issue
Ausstellung *f* exhibition; (*Fin*) drawing up; (*einer Rechnung*) making out; (*eines Passes etc*) issuing
aussterben ['aʊsʃtɛrbən] *unreg vi* to die out
Aussteuer ['aʊsʃtɔʏər] *f* dowry
Ausstieg ['aʊsʃti:k] **(-(e)s, -e)** *m* (*Ausgang*) exit; **~ aus der Atomenergie** abandonment of nuclear energy
ausstopfen ['aʊsʃtɔpfən] *vt* to stuff
ausstoßen ['aʊsʃto:sən] *unreg vt* (*Luft, Rauch*) to give off, emit; (*aus Verein etc*) to expel, exclude; (*herstellen*: *Teile, Stückzahl*) to turn out, produce
ausstrahlen ['aʊsʃtra:lən] *vt, vi* to radiate; (*Rundf*) to broadcast
Ausstrahlung *f* radiation; (*fig*) charisma
ausstrecken ['aʊsʃtrɛkən] *vt, vr* to stretch out
ausstreichen ['aʊsʃtraɪçən] *unreg vt* to cross out; (*glätten*) to smooth out
ausströmen ['aʊsʃtrø:mən] *vi* (*Gas*) to pour out, escape ▷ *vt* to give off; (*fig*) to radiate
aussuchen ['aʊszu:xən] *vt* to select, pick out
Austausch ['aʊstaʊʃ] *m* exchange; **austauschbar** *adj* exchangeable

austauschen *vt* to exchange, swop
Austauschmotor *m* replacement engine; (*gebraucht*) factory-reconditioned engine
austeilen ['aʊstaɪlən] *vt* to distribute, give out
Auster ['aʊstər] (**-, -n**) *f* oyster
austoben ['aʊsto:bən] *vr* (*Kind*) to run wild; (*Erwachsene*) to let off steam; (*sich müde machen*) to tire o.s. out
austragen ['aʊstra:gən] *unreg vt* (*Post*) to deliver; (*Streit etc*) to decide; (*Wettkämpfe*) to hold; **ein Kind ~** (*nicht abtreiben*) to have a child
Austräger ['aʊstrɛ:gər] *m* delivery boy; (*Zeitungsausträger*) newspaper boy
Australien [aʊs'tra:liən] (**-s**) *nt* Australia
Australier, in (**-s, -**) *m(f)* Australian
australisch *adj* Australian
austreiben ['aʊstraɪbən] *unreg vt* to drive out, expel; (*Teufel etc*) to exorcize; **jdm etw ~** to cure sb of sth; (*bes durch Schläge*) to knock sth out of sb
austreten ['aʊstre:tən] *unreg vi* (*zur Toilette*) to be excused ▷ *vt* (*Feuer*) to tread out, trample; (*Schuhe*) to wear out; (*Treppe*) to wear down; **aus etw ~** to leave sth
austrinken ['aʊstrɪŋkən] *unreg vt* (*Glas*) to drain; (*Getränk*) to drink up ▷ *vi* to finish one's drink, drink up
Austritt ['aʊstrɪt] *m* emission; (*aus Verein, Partei etc*) retirement, withdrawal
austrocknen ['aʊstrɔknən] *vt, vi* to dry up
ausüben ['aʊs|y:bən] *vt* (*Beruf*) to practise (*Brit*), practice (*US*), carry out; (*innehaben: Amt*) to hold; (*Funktion*) to perform; (*Einfluss*) to exert; **einen Reiz auf jdn ~** to hold an attraction for sb; **eine Wirkung auf jdn ~** to have an effect on sb
Ausverkauf ['aʊsfɛrkaʊf] *m* sale; (*fig: Verrat*) sell-out
ausverkauft *adj* (*Karten, Artikel*) sold out; (*Theat: Haus*) full
Auswahl ['aʊsva:l] *f*: **eine ~ (an** *+dat***)** a selection (of), a choice (of)
auswählen ['aʊsvɛ:lən] *vt* to select, choose
Auswanderer ['aʊsvandərər] (**-s, -**) *m* emigrant
auswandern *vi* to emigrate
Auswanderung *f* emigration
auswärtig ['aʊsvɛrtɪç] *adj* (*nicht am/vom Ort*) out-of-town; (*ausländisch*) foreign; **das A~e Amt** the Foreign Office (*Brit*), the State Department (*US*)
auswärts ['aʊsvɛrts] *adv* outside; (*nach außen*) outwards; **~ essen** to eat out; **Auswärtsspiel** *nt* away game
auswechseln ['aʊsvɛksəln] *vt* to change, substitute
Ausweg ['aʊsve:k] *m* way out; **der letzte ~** the last resort; **ausweglos** *adj* hopeless
ausweichen ['aʊsvaɪçən] *unreg vi*: **jdm/etw ~** (*lit*) to move aside *od* make way for sb/sth; (*fig*) to sidestep sb/sth; **jdm/einer Begegnung ~** to avoid sb/a meeting
ausweichend *adj* evasive
ausweinen ['aʊsvaɪnən] *vr* to have a (good) cry
Ausweis ['aʊsvaɪs] (**-es, -e**) *m* identity card; passport; (*Mitgliedsausweis, Bibliotheksausweis etc*) card; **~, bitte** your papers, please
ausweisen ['ausvaɪzən] *unreg vt* to expel, banish ▷ *vr* to prove one's identity
Ausweisung *f* expulsion
ausweiten ['aʊsvaɪtən] *vt* to stretch
auswendig ['aʊsvɛndɪç] *adv* by heart; **~ lernen** to learn by heart
auswerfen ['aʊsvɛrfən] *unreg vt* (*Anker, Netz*) to cast
auswerten ['aʊsvɛrtən] *vt* to evaluate
auswirken ['aʊsvɪrkən] *vr* to have an effect
auswischen ['aʊsvɪʃən] *vt* to wipe out; **jdm eins ~** (*umg*) to put one over on sb
Auswuchs ['aʊsvu:ks] *m* (out)growth; (*fig*) product; (*Missstand, Übersteigerung*) excess
auswuchten ['aʊsvʊxtən] *vt* (*Aut*) to balance
auszahlen ['aʊstsa:lən] *vt* (*Lohn, Summe*) to pay out; (*Arbeiter*) to pay off; (*Miterben*) to buy out ▷ *vr* (*sich lohnen*) to pay
auszählen ['aʊstsɛ:lən] *vt* (*Stimmen*) to count; (*Boxen*) to count out
auszeichnen ['aʊstsaɪçnən] *vt* to honour (*Brit*), honor (*US*); (*Mil*) to decorate; (*Comm*) to price ▷ *vr* to distinguish o.s.; **der Wagen zeichnet sich durch ... aus** one of the car's main features is ...
Auszeichnung *f* distinction; (*Comm*) pricing; (*Ehrung*) awarding of decoration; (*Ehre*) honour (*Brit*), honor (*US*); (*Orden*) decoration; **mit ~** with distinction
ausziehen ['aʊstsi:ən] *unreg vt* (*Kleidung*) to take off; (*Haare, Zähne, Tisch etc*) to pull out ▷ *vr* to undress ▷ *vi* (*aufbrechen*) to leave; (*aus Wohnung*) to move out
Auszubildende, r ['aʊstsʊbɪldəndə(r)] *f(m)* trainee; (*als Handwerker*) apprentice
Auszug ['aʊstsu:k] *m* (*aus Wohnung*) removal; (*aus Buch etc*) extract; (*Kontoauszug*) statement; (*Ausmarsch*) departure
Auto ['aʊto] (**-s, -s**) *nt* (motor-)car, automobile (*US*); **mit dem ~ fahren** to go by car; **~ fahren** to drive
Autobahn *f* motorway (*Brit*), expressway (*US*); *see cultture note*
Autobahndreieck *nt* motorway (*Brit*) *od* expressway (*US*) junction
Autobahnkreuz *nt* motorway (*Brit*) *od* expressway (*US*) intersection
Auto- *zW*: **Autobombe** *f* car bomb; **Autofahrer, in** *m(f)* motorist, driver; **Autofahrt** *f* drive
autogen [aʊto'ge:n] *adj* autogenous; **~es Training** (*Psych*) relaxation through self-hypnosis
Autogramm [aʊto'gram] *nt* autograph
Automat (**-en, -en**) *m* machine
automatisch *adj* automatic

autonom [aʊto'no:m] *adj* autonomous
Autopsie [aʊtɔ'psi:] *f* post-mortem, autopsy
Autor ['aʊtɔr] (**-s, -en**) *m* author
Auto- *zW*: **Autoradio** *nt* car radio; **Autoreifen** *m* car tyre (*Brit*) *od* tire (*US*); **Autoreisezug** *m* motorail train; **Autorennen** *nt* motor race; (*Sportart*) motor racing
autoritär [aʊtori'tɛ:r] *adj* authoritarian
Autorität *f* authority
Auto- *zW*: **Autotelefon** *nt* car phone; **Autounfall** *m* car *od* motor accident; **Autoverleih** *m*, **Autovermietung** *f* car hire (*Brit*) *od* rental (*US*)
Axt [akst] (**-, ⁼e**) *f* axe (*Brit*), ax (*US*)
Azteke [ats'te:kə] (**-n, -n**) *m* Aztec

Bb

B[1], **b** [beː] *nt* (*letter*) B, b; **B wie Bertha** ≈ B for Benjamin, ≈ B for Baker (*US*); **B-Dur/b-Moll** (the key of) B flat major/minor
B[2] [beː] *f abk* = **Bundesstraße**
Baby ['beːbi] (**-s, -s**) *nt* baby; **Babysitter** ['beːbisɪtər] (**-s, -**) *m* baby-sitter
Bach [bax] (**-(e)s, ¨-e**) *m* stream, brook
Backe (**-, -n**) *f* cheek
backen ['bakən] *unreg vt, vi* to bake; **frisch/knusprig ge~es Brot** fresh/crusty bread
Backenbart *m* sideboards *pl*
Backenzahn *m* molar
Bäcker, in ['bɛkər(ɪn)] (**-s, -**) *m(f)* baker
Bäckerei [bɛkə'raɪ] *f* bakery; (*Bäckerladen*) baker's (shop)
Back- *zW*: **Backform** *f* baking tin (*Brit*) *od* pan (*US*); **Backobst** *nt* dried fruit; **Backofen** *m* oven; **Backpulver** *nt* baking powder; **Backstein** *m* brick
Bad [baːt] (**-(e)s, ¨-er**) *nt* bath; (*Schwimmen*) bathing; (*Ort*) spa
Bade- *zW*: **Badeanstalt** *f* swimming pool; **Badeanzug** *m* bathing suit; **Badehose** *f* bathing *od* swimming trunks *pl*; **Badekappe** *f* bathing cap; **Bademantel** *m* bath(ing) robe; **Bademeister** *m* swimming pool attendant
baden ['baːdən] *vi* to bathe, have a bath ▷ *vt* to bath; **~ gehen** (*fig: umg*) to come a cropper
Baden-Württemberg ['baːdən'vʏrtəmbɛrk] *nt* Baden-Württemberg
Bade- *zW*: **Badeort** *m* spa; **Badetuch** *nt* bath towel; **Badewanne** *f* bath(tub); **Badezimmer** *nt* bathroom
Bagatelle [baga'tɛlə] (**-, -n**) *f* trifle
Bagger ['bagər] (**-s, -**) *m* excavator; (*Naut*) dredger
baggern *vt, vi* to excavate; (*Naut*) to dredge
Bahamas [ba'haːmas] *pl*: **die ~** the Bahamas *pl*
Bahn [baːn] (**-, -en**) *f* railway (*Brit*), railroad (*US*); (*Weg*) road, way; (*Spur*) lane; (*Rennbahn*) track; (*Astron*) orbit; (*Stoffbahn*) length; **mit der ~** by train *od* rail/tram; **frei ~** (*Comm*) carriage free to station of destination; **jdm/etw die ~ ebnen** (*fig*) to clear the way for sb/sth; **von der rechten ~ abkommen** to stray from the straight and narrow; **jdn aus der ~ werfen** (*fig*) to shatter sb; **bahnbrechend** *adj* pioneering; **Bahndamm** *m* railway embankment
Bahnfahrt *f* railway (*Brit*) *od* railroad (*US*) journey
Bahnhof *m* station; **auf dem ~** at the station; **ich verstehe nur ~** (*hum: umg*) it's all Greek to me
Bahnhofshalle *f* station concourse
Bahnhofsmission *f* *charitable organization for helping rail travellers*
Bahnhofswirtschaft *f* station restaurant
Bahn- *zW*: **Bahnlinie** *f* (railway (*Brit*) *od* railroad (*US*)) line; **Bahnsteig** *m* platform; **Bahnstrecke** *f* railway (*Brit*) *od* railroad (*US*) line; **Bahnübergang** *m* level (*Brit*) *od* grade (*US*) crossing; **beschrankter Bahnübergang** crossing with gates; **unbeschrankter Bahnübergang** unguarded crossing; **Bahnwärter** *m* signalman
Bahrain [ba'raɪn] (**-s**) *nt* Bahrain
Bahre ['baːrə] (**-, -n**) *f* stretcher
Balance [ba'lãːsə] (**-, -n**) *f* balance, equilibrium
balancieren *vt, vi* to balance
bald [balt] *adv* (*zeitlich*) soon; (*beinahe*) almost; **~ ... ~ ...** now ... now ...; **~ darauf** soon afterwards; **bis ~!** see you soon
baldig ['baldɪç] *adj* early, speedy
baldmöglichst *adv* as soon as possible
Baldrian ['baldriaːn] (**-s, -e**) *m* valerian
Balearen [bale'aːrən] *pl*: **die ~** the Balearics *pl*
Balkan ['balkaːn] *m*: **der ~** the Balkans *pl*
Balken ['balkən] (**-s, -**) *m* beam; (*Tragbalken*) girder; (*Stützbalken*) prop
Balkon [bal'kõː] (**-s, -s** *od* **-e**) *m* balcony; (*Theat*) (dress) circle
Ball [bal] (**-(e)s, ¨-e**) *m* ball; (*Tanz*) dance, ball
Ballast ['balast] (**-(e)s, -e**) *m* ballast; (*fig*) weight, burden; **Ballaststoffe** *pl* (*Med*) roughage *sing*
Ballen ['balən] (**-s, -**) *m* bale; (*Anat*) ball
Ballett [ba'lɛt] (**-(e)s, -e**) *nt* ballet; **Balletttänzer, in** *m(f)* ballet dancer
Balljunge *m* ball boy
Ballon [ba'lõː] (**-s, -s** *od* **-e**) *m* balloon
Ballspiel *nt* ball game
Ballung ['balʊŋ] *f* concentration; (*von Energie*) build-up
Ballungs- *zW*: **Ballungsgebiet** *nt*, **Ballungsraum** *m* conurbation;

Ballungszentrum *nt* centre (*Brit*) *od* center (*US*) (*of population, industry etc*)
Balsam ['balza:m] (**-s, -e**) *m* balsam; (*fig*) balm
Baltikum ['baltikʊm] (**-s**) *nt*: **das ~** the Baltic States *pl*
Bambus ['bambʊs] (**-ses, -se**) *m* bamboo; **Bambusrohr** *nt* bamboo cane
banal [ba'na:l] *adj* banal
Banalität [banali'tɛ:t] *f* banality
Banane [ba'na:nə] (**-, -n**) *f* banana
Banause [ba'naʊzə] (**-n, -n**) *m* philistine
Band[1] [bant] (**-(e)s, ¨-e**) *m* (*Buchband*) volume; **das spricht Bände** that speaks volumes
Band[2] (**-(e)s, ¨-er**) *nt* (*Stoffband*) ribbon, tape; (*Fließband*) production line; (*Fassband*) hoop; (*Zielband, Tonband*) tape; (*Anat*) ligament; **etw auf ~ aufnehmen** to tape sth; **am laufenden ~** (*umg*) non-stop
Band[3] (**-(e)s, -e**) *nt* (*Freundschaftsband etc*) bond
Band[4] [bɛnt] (**-, -s**) *f* band, group
band *etc* [bant] *vb siehe* **binden**
bandagieren *vt* to bandage
Bandbreite *f* (*von Meinungen etc*) range
Bande ['bandə] (**-, -n**) *f* band; (*Straßenbande*) gang
bändigen ['bɛndɪgən] *vt* (*Tier*) to tame; (*Trieb, Leidenschaft*) to control, restrain
Bandit [ban'di:t] (**-en, -en**) *m* bandit
Band- *zW*: **Bandmaß** *nt* tape measure; **Bandsäge** *f* band saw; **Bandscheibe** *f* (*Anat*) disc; **Bandwurm** *m* tapeworm
bange ['baŋə] *adj* scared; (*besorgt*) anxious; **jdm wird es ~** sb is becoming scared; **jdm B~ machen** to scare sb; **Bangemacher** (**-s, -**) *m* scaremonger
bangen *vi*: **um jdn/etw ~** to be anxious *od* worried about sb/sth
Bangladesch [baŋgla'dɛʃ] (**-s**) *nt* Bangladesh
Bank[1] [baŋk] (**-, ¨-e**) *f* (*Sitzbank*) bench; (*Sandbank etc*) (sand)bank, (sand)bar; **etw auf die lange ~ schieben** (*umg*) to put sth off
Bank[2] (**-, -en**) *f* (*Geldbank*) bank; **bei der ~** at the bank; **Geld auf der ~ haben** to have money in the bank; **Bankanweisung** *f* banker's order
Bankett [baŋ'kɛt] (**-(e)s, -e**) *nt* (*Essen*) banquet; (*Straßenrand*) verge (*Brit*), shoulder (*US*)
Bankier [baŋki'e:] (**-s, -s**) *m* banker
Bank- *zW*: **Bankkonto** *nt* bank account; **Bankleitzahl** *f* bank code number; **Banknote** *f* banknote; **Bankraub** *m* bank robbery
bankrott [baŋ'krɔt] *adj* bankrupt; **Bankrott** (**-(e)s, -e**) *m* bankruptcy; **Bankrott machen** to go bankrupt; **den Bankrott anmelden** *od* **erklären** to declare o.s. bankrupt
Banküberfall *m* bank raid
Bann [ban] (**-(e)s, -e**) *m* (*Hist*) ban; (*Kirchenbann*) excommunication; (*fig: Zauber*) spell; **bannen** *vt* (*Geister*) to exorcize; (*Gefahr*) to avert; (*bezaubern*) to enchant; (*Hist*) to banish
Banner (**-s, -**) *nt* banner, flag
Bar [ba:r] (**-, -s**) *f* bar
bar *adj* (*+gen*) (*unbedeckt*) bare; (*frei von*) lacking (in); (*offenkundig*) utter, sheer; **~e(s) Geld** cash; **etw (in) ~ bezahlen** to pay sth (in) cash; **etw für ~e Münze nehmen** (*fig*) to take sth at face value; **~ aller Hoffnung** (*liter*) devoid of hope, completely without hope
Bär [bɛ:r] (**-en, -en**) *m* bear; **jdm einen ~en aufbinden** (*umg*) to have sb on
Baracke [ba'rakə] (**-, -n**) *f* hut
barbarisch [bar'ba:rɪʃ] *adj* barbaric, barbarous
Barbestand *m* money in hand
Bardame *f* barmaid
barfuß *adj* barefoot
barg *etc* [bark] *vb siehe* **bergen**
Bargeld *nt* cash, ready money
bargeldlos *adj* non-cash; **~er Zahlungsverkehr** non-cash *od* credit transactions *pl*
Bariton ['ba:ritɔn] *m* baritone
Barkauf *m* cash purchase
Barkeeper ['ba:rki:pər] (**-s, -**) *m* barman, bartender
barmherzig [barm'hɛrtsɪç] *adj* merciful, compassionate; **Barmherzigkeit** *f* mercy, compassion
Barometer [baro'me:tər] (**-s, -**) *nt* barometer; **das ~ steht auf Sturm** (*fig*) there's a storm brewing
Baron [ba'ro:n] (**-s, -e**) *m* baron
Barren ['barən] (**-s, -**) *m* parallel bars *pl*; (*Goldbarren*) ingot
Barriere [bari'ɛ:rə] (**-, -n**) *f* barrier
Barrikade [bari'ka:də] (**-, -n**) *f* barricade
Barsch [barʃ] (**-(e)s, -e**) *m* perch
barsch [barʃ] *adj* brusque, gruff; **jdn ~ anfahren** to snap at sb
Barschaft *f* ready money
Barscheck *m* open *od* uncrossed cheque (*Brit*), open check (*US*)
barst *etc* [barst] *vb siehe* **bersten**
Bart [ba:rt] (**-(e)s, ¨-e**) *m* beard; (*Schlüsselbart*) bit
bärtig ['bɛ:rtɪç] *adj* bearded
Barzahlung *f* cash payment
Basar [ba'za:r] (**-s, -e**) *m* bazaar
Base ['ba:zə] (**-, -n**) *f* (*Chem*) base; (*Cousine*) cousin
Basel ['ba:zəl] (**-s**) *nt* Basle
basieren [ba'zi:rən] *vt* to base ▷ *vi* to be based
Basis ['ba:zɪs] (**-**, *pl* **Basen**) *f* basis; (*Archit, Mil, Math*) base; **~ und Überbau** (*Pol, Soziologie*) foundation and superstructure; **die ~** (*umg*) the grass roots
Baske ['baskə] (**-n, -n**) *m* Basque
Baskenland *nt* Basque region
Baskin *f* Basque
Bass [bas] (**-es, ¨-e**) *m* bass
Bassin [ba'sɛ̃:] (**-s, -s**) *nt* pool
Bassstimme *f* bass voice
Bast [bast] (**-(e)s, -e**) *m* raffia
basteln ['bastəln] *vt* to make ▷ *vi* to do

handicrafts; **an etw** *dat* ~ (*an etw herumbasteln*) to tinker with sth

Bastler ['bastlər] (**-s, -**) *m* do-it-yourselfer; (*handwerklich*) handicrafts enthusiast

bat *etc* [ba:t] *vb siehe* **bitten**

Bataillon [batal'jo:n] (**-s, -e**) *nt* battalion

Batist [ba'tɪst] (**-(e)s, -e**) *m* batiste

Batterie [batə'ri:] *f* battery

Bau [baʊ] (**-(e)s**) *m* (*Bauen*) building, construction; (*Aufbau*) structure; (*Körperbau*) frame; (*Baustelle*) building site; (*pl Baue: Tierbau*) hole, burrow; (*: Min*) working(s); (*pl Bauten: Gebäude*) building; **sich im ~ befinden** to be under construction; **Bauarbeiter** *m* building worker

Bauch [baʊx] (**-(e)s, Bäuche**) *m* belly; (*Anat*) stomach, abdomen; **sich** *dat* **(vor Lachen) den ~ halten** (*umg*) to split one's sides (laughing); **mit etw auf den ~ fallen** (*umg*) to come a cropper with sth; **Bauchfell** *nt* peritoneum

Bauch- *zW*: **Bauchmuskel** *m* abdominal muscle; **Bauchnabel** *m* navel, belly-button (*umg*); **Bauchredner** *m* ventriloquist; **Bauchschmerzen** *pl* stomachache *sing*; **Bauchtanz** *m* belly dance; belly dancing; **Bauchweh** *nt* stomachache

Baudrate [baʊt'ra:tə] *f* (*Comput*) baud rate

bauen ['baʊən] *vt* to build; (*Tech*) to construct; (*umg: verursachen: Unfall*) to cause ▷ *vi* to build; **auf jdn/etw ~** to depend *od* count upon sb/sth; **da hast du Mist gebaut** (*umg*) you really messed that up

Bauer[1] ['baʊər] (**-n** *od* **-s, -n**) *m* farmer; (*Schach*) pawn

Bauer[2] (**-s, -**) *nt od m* (*Vogelbauer*) cage

bäuerlich *adj* rustic

Bauern- *zW*: **Bauernfängerei** *f* deception, confidence trick(s); **Bauernhaus** *nt* farmhouse; **Bauernhof** *m* farm

Bau- *zW*: **baufällig** *adj* dilapidated; **Baufälligkeit** *f* dilapidation; **Baufirma** *f* construction firm; **Baugelände** *nt* building site; **Baugenehmigung** *f* building permit; **Bauherr** *m* client (*of construction firm*); **Baujahr** *nt* year of construction; (*von Auto*) year of manufacture; **Baukasten** *m* box of bricks; **Baukosten** *pl* construction costs *pl*; **baulich** *adj* structural

Baum [baʊm] (**-(e)s**, *pl* **Bäume**) *m* tree; **heute könnte ich Bäume ausreißen** I feel full of energy today

Baumarkt *m* DIY superstore

baumeln ['baʊməln] *vi* to dangle

Baum- *zW*: **Baumschule** *f* nursery; **Baumstamm** *m* tree trunk; **Baumstumpf** *m* tree stump; **Baumwolle** *f* cotton

Bau- *zW*: **Bauplan** *m* architect's plan; **Bauplatz** *m* building site; **bausparen** *vi untr* to save with a building society (*Brit*) *od* a building and loan association (*US*); **Bausparkasse** *f* building society (*Brit*), building and loan association (*US*); **Bausparvertrag** *m* savings contract with a building society (*Brit*) *od* building and loan association (*US*); **Baustein** *m* building stone, freestone; **Baustelle** *f* building site; **Bauteil** *nt* prefabricated part (of building); **Bauunternehmer** *m* contractor, builder; **Bauweise** *f* (method of) construction; **Bauwerk** *nt* building; **Bauzaun** *m* hoarding

Bayern *nt* Bavaria

Bazillus [ba'tsɪlʊs] (**-**, *pl* **Bazillen**) *m* bacillus

beabsichtigen [bə'|apzɪçtɪgən] *vt* to intend

beachten [bə'|axtən] *vt* to take note of; (*Vorschrift*) to obey; (*Vorfahrt*) to observe

beachtenswert *adj* noteworthy

beachtlich *adj* considerable

Beachtung *f* notice, attention, observation; **jdm keine ~ schenken** to take no notice of sb

Beamte, r [bə'|amtə(r)] (**-n, -n**) *m* official; (*Staatsbeamte*) civil servant; (*Bankbeamte etc*) employee

beängstigend [bə'|ɛŋstɪgənt] *adj* alarming

beanspruchen [bə'|anʃprʊxən] *vt* to claim; (*Zeit, Platz*) to take up, occupy; **jdn ~** to take up sb's time; **etw stark ~** to put sth under a lot of stress

beanstanden [bə'|anʃtandən] *vt* to complain about, object to; (*Rechnung*) to query

beantragen [bə'|antra:gən] *vt* to apply for, ask for

beantworten [bə'|antvɔrtən] *vt* to answer

bearbeiten [bə'|arbaɪtən] *vt* to work; (*Material*) to process; (*Thema*) to deal with; (*Land*) to cultivate; (*Chem*) to treat; (*Buch*) to revise; (*umg: beeinflussen wollen*) to work on

Beatmung [bə'|a:tmʊŋ] *f* respiration

beaufsichtigen [bə'|aʊfzɪçtɪgən] *vt* to supervise

beauftragen [bə'|aʊftra:gən] *vt* to instruct; **jdn mit etw ~** to entrust sb with sth

beben ['be:bən] *vi* to tremble, shake; **Beben** (**-s -**) *nt* earthquake

bebildern [bə'bɪldərn] *vt* to illustrate

Becher ['bɛçər] (**-s, -**) *m* mug; (*ohne Henkel*) tumbler

bechern ['bɛçərn] (*umg*) *vi* (*trinken*) to have a few (drinks)

Becken ['bɛkən] (**-s, -**) *nt* basin; (*Mus*) cymbal; (*Anat*) pelvis

bedächtig [bə'dɛçtɪç] *adj* (*umsichtig*) thoughtful, reflective; (*langsam*) slow, deliberate

bedanken [bə'daŋkən] *vr*: **sich (bei jdm) ~** to say thank you (to sb); **ich bedanke mich herzlich** thank you very much

Bedarf [bə'darf] (**-(e)s**) *m* need; (*Bedarfsmenge*) requirements *pl*; (*Comm*) demand; supply; **alles für den häuslichen ~** all household requirements; **je nach ~** according to demand; **bei ~** if necessary; **~ an etw** *dat* **haben** to be in need of sth

Bedarfs- *zW*: **Bedarfsartikel** *m* requisite; **Bedarfsfall** *m* case of need;

Bedarfshaltestelle *f* request stop
bedauerlich [bə'daʊərlɪç] *adj* regrettable
bedauern [bə'daʊərn] *vt* to be sorry for; (*bemitleiden*) to pity; **wir ~, Ihnen mitteilen zu müssen, ...** we regret to have to inform you ...; **Bedauern** (**-s**) *nt* regret
bedauernswert *adj* (*Zustände*) regrettable; (*Mensch*) pitiable, unfortunate
bedecken [bə'dɛkən] *vt* to cover
bedenken [bə'dɛŋkən] *unreg vt* to think over, consider; **ich gebe zu ~, dass ...** (*geh*) I would ask you to consider that ...; **Bedenken** (**-s, -**) *nt* (*Überlegen*) consideration; (*Zweifel*) doubt; (*Skrupel*) scruple; **mir kommen Bedenken** I am having second thoughts
bedenklich *adj* doubtful; (*bedrohlich*) dangerous, risky
Bedenkzeit *f* time to consider; **zwei Tage ~** two days to think about it
bedeuten [bə'dɔʏtən] *vt* to mean; to signify; (*wichtig sein*) to be of importance; **das bedeutet nichts Gutes** that means trouble
bedeutend *adj* important; (*beträchtlich*) considerable
Bedeutung *f* meaning; significance; (*Wichtigkeit*) importance
bedeutungslos *adj* insignificant, unimportant
bedeutungsvoll *adj* momentous, significant
bedienen [bə'di:nən] *vt* to serve; (*Maschine*) to work, operate ▷ *vr* (*beim Essen*) to help o.s.; (*gebrauchen*): **sich jds/einer Sache ~** to make use of sb/sth; **werden Sie schon bedient?** are you being served?; **damit sind Sie sehr gut bedient** that should serve you very well; **ich bin bedient!** (*umg*) I've had enough
Bedienung *f* service; (*Kellner etc*) waiter/ waitress; (*Zuschlag*) service (charge); (*von Maschinen*) operation
Bedienungsanleitung *f* operating instructions *pl*
bedingen [bə'dɪŋən] *vt* (*voraussetzen*) to demand, involve; (*verursachen*) to cause, occasion
bedingt *adj* limited; (*Straferlass*) conditional; (*Reflex*) conditioned; **(nur) ~ gelten** to be (only) partially valid; **~ geeignet** suitable up to a point
Bedingung *f* condition; (*Voraussetzung*) stipulation; **mit** *od* **unter der ~, dass ...** on condition that ...; **zu günstigen ~en** (*Comm*) on favourable (*Brit*) *od* favorable (*US*) terms
bedingungslos *adj* unconditional
bedrängen [bə'drɛŋən] *vt* to pester, harass
bedrohen [bə'dro:ən] *vt* to threaten
bedrohlich *adj* ominous, threatening
bedrücken [bədrʏkən] *vt* to oppress, trouble
Bedürfnis [bə'dʏrfnɪs] (**-ses, -se**) *nt* need; **das ~ nach etw haben** to need sth; **Bedürfnisanstalt** *f* (*form*) public convenience (*Brit*), comfort station (*US*)
bedürftig *adj* in need, poor, needy
beeilen [bə'|aɪlən] *vr* to hurry
beeindrucken [bə'|aɪndrʊkən] *vt* to impress, make an impression on
beeinflussen [bə'|aɪnflʊsən] *vt* to influence
beeinträchtigen [bə'|aɪntrɛçtɪgən] *vt* to affect adversely; (*Sehvermögen*) to impair; (*Freiheit*) to infringe upon
beenden [bə'|ɛndən], **beendigen** [bə'|ɛndɪgən] *vt* to end, finish, terminate
beerdigen [bə'|e:rdɪgən] *vt* to bury
Beerdigung *f* funeral, burial
Beere ['be:rə] (**-, -n**) *f* berry; (*Traubenbeere*) grape
Beet [be:t] (**-(e)s, -e**) *nt* (*Blumenbeet*) bed
Befähigung *f* capability; (*Begabung*) talent, aptitude; **die ~ zum Richteramt** the qualifications to become a judge
befahl *etc* [bə'fa:l] *vb siehe* **befehlen**
befahrbar [bə'fa:rba:r] *adj* passable; (*Naut*) navigable; **nicht ~ sein** (*Straße, Weg*) to be closed (to traffic); (*wegen Schnee etc*) to be impassable
befahren [bə'fa:rən] *unreg vt* to use, drive over; (*Naut*) to navigate ▷ *adj* used
befallen [bə'falən] *unreg vt* to come over
befangen [bə'faŋən] *adj* (*schüchtern*) shy, self-conscious; (*voreingenommen*) bias(s)ed
befassen [bə'fasən] *vr* to concern o.s.
Befehl [bə'fe:l] (**-(e)s, -e**) *m* command, order; (*Comput*) command; **auf ~ handeln** to act under orders; **zu ~, Herr Hauptmann!** (*Mil*) yes, sir; **den ~ haben** *od* **führen (über** *+akk***)** to be in command (of)
befehlen *unreg vt* to order ▷ *vi* to give orders; **jdm etw ~** to order sb to do sth; **du hast mir gar nichts zu ~** I won't take orders from you
Befehls- *zW*: **Befehlsempfänger** *m* subordinate; **Befehlshaber** (**-s, -**) *m* commanding officer; **Befehlsverweigerung** *f* insubordination
befestigen [bə'fɛstɪgən] *vt* to fasten; (*stärken*) to strengthen; (*Mil*) to fortify; **~ an** *+dat* to fasten to
Befestigung *f* fastening; strengthening; (*Mil*) fortification
befinden [bə'fɪndən] *unreg vr* to be; (*sich fühlen*) to feel ▷ *vt*: **jdn/etw für** *od* **als etw ~** to deem sb/sth to be sth ▷ *vi*: **~ (über** *+akk***)** to decide (on), adjudicate (on)
Befinden (**-s**) *nt* health, condition; (*Meinung*) view, opinion
befohlen [bə'fo:lən] *pp von* **befehlen**
befolgen [bə'fɔlgən] *vt* to comply with, follow
befördern [bə'fœrdərn] *vt* (*senden*) to transport, send; (*beruflich*) to promote; **etw mit der Post/per Bahn ~** to send sth by post/by rail
Beförderung *f* transport; promotion
Beförderungskosten *pl* transport costs *pl*
befragen [bə'fra:gən] *vt* to question; (*um Stellungnahme bitten*): **~ (über** *+akk***)** to consult (about)
befreien [bə'fraɪən] *vt* to set free; (*erlassen*) to exempt

Befreiung *f* liberation, release; (*Erlassen*) exemption
befreunden [bəˈfrɔyndən] *vr* to make friends; (*mit Idee etc*) to acquaint o.s.
befreundet *adj* friendly; **wir sind schon lange (miteinander) ~** we have been friends for a long time
befriedigen [bəˈfriːdɪgən] *vt* to satisfy
befriedigend *adj* satisfactory
Befriedigung *f* satisfaction, gratification
befristet [bəˈfrɪstət] *adj* limited; (*Arbeitsverhältnis, Anstellung*) temporary
befruchten [bəˈfrʊxtən] *vt* to fertilize; (*fig*) to stimulate
befugt *adj* authorized, entitled
Befund [bəˈfʊnt] (**-(e)s, -e**) *m* findings *pl*; (*Med*) diagnosis; **ohne ~** (*Med*) (results) negative
befürchten [bəˈfʏrçtən] *vt* to fear
Befürchtung *f* fear, apprehension
befürworten [bəˈfyːrvɔrtən] *vt* to support, speak in favour (*Brit*) *od* favor (*US*) of
Befürworter, in (**-s, -**) *m(f)* supporter, advocate
begabt [bəˈgaːpt] *adj* gifted
Begabung [bəˈgaːbʊŋ] *f* talent, gift
begann *etc* [bəˈgan] *vb siehe* **beginnen**
begeben [bəˈgeːbən] *unreg vr* (*gehen*) to proceed; (*geschehen*) to occur; **sich ~ nach** *od* **zu** to proceed to(wards); **sich in ärztliche Behandlung ~** to undergo medical treatment; **sich in Gefahr ~** to expose o.s. to danger; **Begebenheit** *f* occurrence
begegnen [bəˈgeːgnən] *vi*: **jdm ~** to meet sb; (*behandeln*) to treat; **Blicke ~ sich** eyes meet
Begegnung *f* meeting; (*Sport*) match
begehen [bəˈgeːən] *unreg vt* (*Straftat*) to commit; (*Weg etc*) to use, negotiate; (*geh: feiern*) to celebrate
begehren [bəˈgeːrən] *vt* to desire
begehrt *adj* in demand; (*Junggeselle*) eligible
begeistern [bəˈgaɪstərn] *vt* to fill with enthusiasm; (*inspirieren*) to inspire ▷ *vr*: **sich für etw ~** to get enthusiastic about sth; **er ist für nichts zu ~** he's not interested in doing anything
begeistert *adj* enthusiastic
Begeisterung *f* enthusiasm
begierig [bəˈgiːrɪç] *adj* eager, keen; (*voll Verlangen*) hungry, greedy
Beginn [bəˈgɪn] (**-(e)s**) *m* beginning; **zu ~** at the beginning
beginnen *unreg vt, vi* to start, begin
beglaubigen [bəˈglaʊbɪgən] *vt* to countersign; (*Abschrift*) to authenticate; (*Echtheit, Übersetzung*) to certify
Beglaubigung *f* countersignature
Beglaubigungsschreiben *nt* credentials *pl*
begleichen [bəˈglaɪçən] *unreg vt* to settle, pay; **mit Ihnen habe ich noch eine Rechnung zu ~** (*fig*) I've a score to settle with you
begleiten [bəˈglaɪtən] *vt* to accompany; (*Mil*) to escort
Begleiter, in (**-s, -**) *m(f)* companion; (*zum Schutz*) escort; (*Mus*) accompanist
Begleit- *zW*: **Begleiterscheinung** *f* side effect; **Begleitschreiben** *nt* covering letter
Begleitung *f* company; (*Mil*) escort; (*Mus*) accompaniment
beglückwünschen [bəˈglʏkvʏnʃən] *vt*: **~ (zu)** to congratulate (on)
begnadigen [bəˈgnaːdɪgən] *vt* to pardon
Begnadigung *f* pardon
begnügen [bəˈgnyːgən] *vr*: **sich ~ mit** to be satisfied with, content o.s. with
Begonie [bəˈgoːniə] *f* begonia
begonnen [bəˈgɔnən] *pp von* **beginnen**
begraben [bəˈgraːbən] *unreg vt* to bury; (*aufgeben: Hoffnung*) to abandon; (*beenden: Streit etc*) to end; **dort möchte ich nicht ~ sein** (*umg*) I wouldn't like to be stuck in that hole
begradigen [bəˈgraːdɪgən] *vt* to straighten (out)
begreifen [bəˈgraɪfən] *unreg vt* to understand, comprehend
begreiflich [bəˈgraɪflɪç] *adj* understandable; **ich kann mich ihm nicht ~ machen** I can't make myself clear to him
Begrenztheit [bəˈgrɛntsthaɪt] *f* limitation, restriction; (*fig*) narrowness
Begriff [bəˈgrɪf] (**-(e)s, -e**) *m* concept, idea; **im ~ sein, etw zu tun** to be about to do sth; **sein Name ist mir ein/kein ~** his name means something/doesn't mean anything to me; **du machst dir keinen ~ (davon)** you've no idea; **für meine ~e** in my opinion; **schwer von ~** (*umg*) slow on the uptake
begründen [bəˈgrʏndən] *vt* (*Gründe geben*) to justify; **etw näher ~** to give specific reasons for sth
begründet *adj* well-founded, justified; **sachlich ~** founded on fact
Begründung *f* justification, reason
begrüßen [bəˈgryːsən] *vt* to greet, welcome
begrüßenswert *adj* welcome
Begrüßung *f* greeting, welcome
begünstigen [bəˈgʏnstɪgən] *vt* (*Person*) to favour (*Brit*), favor (*US*); (*Sache*) to further, promote
begutachten [bəˈguːt|axtən] *vt* to assess; (*umg: ansehen*) to have a look at
begütert [bəˈgyːtərt] *adj* wealthy, well-to-do
behaart [bəˈhaːrt] *adj* hairy
behäbig [bəˈhɛːbɪç] *adj* (*dick*) portly, stout; (*geruhsam*) comfortable
behagen [bəˈhaːgən] *vi*: **das behagt ihm nicht** he does not like it; **Behagen** (**-s**) *nt* comfort, ease; **mit Behagen essen** to eat with relish
behaglich [bəˈhaːklɪç] *adj* comfortable, cosy; **Behaglichkeit** *f* comfort, cosiness
behalten [bəˈhaltən] *unreg vt* to keep, retain; (*im Gedächtnis*) to remember; **~ Sie (doch) Platz!** please don't get up!
Behälter [bəˈhɛltər] (**-s, -**) *m* container, receptacle

behandeln [bəˈhandəln] *vt* to treat; (*Thema*) to deal with; (*Maschine*) to handle; **der ~de Arzt** the doctor in attendance
Behandlung *f* treatment; (*von Maschine*) handling
beharren [bəˈharən] *vi*: **auf etw** *dat* **~** to stick *od* keep to sth
beharrlich [bəˈharlıç] *adj* (*ausdauernd*) steadfast, unwavering; (*hartnäckig*) tenacious, dogged; **Beharrlichkeit** *f* steadfastness; tenacity
behaupten [bəˈhaʊptən] *vt* to claim, assert, maintain; (*sein Recht*) to defend ▷ *vr* to assert o.s.; **von jdm ~, dass ...** to say (of sb) that ...; **sich auf dem Markt ~** to establish itself on the market
Behauptung *f* claim, assertion
Behausung [bəˈhaʊzʊŋ] *f* dwelling, abode; (*armselig*) hovel
beheizen [bəˈhaıtsən] *vt* to heat
Behelf [bəˈhɛlf] (**-(e)s, -e**) *m* expedient, makeshift; **behelfen** *unreg vr*: **sich mit etw behelfen** to make do with sth
behelfsmäßig *adj* improvised, makeshift; (*vorübergehend*) temporary
beherbergen [bəˈhɛrbɛrgən] *vt* (*lit, fig*) to house
beherrschen [bəˈhɛrʃən] *vt* (*Volk*) to rule, govern; (*Situation*) to control; (*Sprache, Gefühle*) to master ▷ *vr* to control o.s.
beherrscht *adj* controlled; **Beherrschtheit** *f* self-control
Beherrschung *f* rule; control; mastery; **die ~ verlieren** to lose one's temper
beherzigen [bəˈhɛrtsıgən] *vt* to take to heart
behilflich [bəˈhılflıç] *adj* helpful; **jdm ~ sein (bei)** to help sb (with)
behindern [bəˈhındərn] *vt* to hinder, impede
Behinderte, r *f(m)* disabled person
Behinderung *f* hindrance; (*Körperbehinderung*) handicap
Behörde [bəˈhøːrdə] (**-, -n**) *f* authorities *pl*; (*Amtsgebäude*) office(*s pl*)
behördlich [bəˈhøːrtlıç] *adj* official
behüten [bəˈhyːtən] *vt* to guard; **jdn vor etw** *dat* **~** to preserve sb from sth
behutsam [bəˈhuːtzaːm] *adj* cautious, careful; **man muss es ihr ~ beibringen** it will have to be broken to her gently
bei [baı] *präp +dat* **1** (*nahe bei*) near; (*zum Aufenthalt*) at, with; (*unter, zwischen*) among; **bei München** near Munich; **bei uns** at our place; **beim Friseur** at the hairdresser's; **bei seinen Eltern wohnen** to live with one's parents; **bei einer Firma arbeiten** to work for a firm; **etw bei sich haben** to have sth on one; **jdn bei sich haben** to have sb with one; **bei Goethe** in Goethe; **beim Militär** in the army
2 (*zeitlich*) at, on; (*während*) during; (*Zustand, Umstand*) in; **bei Nacht** at night; **bei Nebel** in fog; **bei Regen** if it rains; **bei solcher Hitze** in such heat; **bei meiner Ankunft** on my arrival; **bei der Arbeit** when I'm *etc* working; **beim Fahren** while driving; **bei offenem Fenster schlafen** to sleep with the window open; **bei Feuer Scheibe einschlagen** in case of fire break glass; **bei seinem Talent** with his talent
beibehalten [ˈbaıbəhaltən] *unreg vt* to keep, retain
Beiblatt [ˈbaıblat] *nt* supplement
beibringen [ˈbaıbrıŋən] *unreg vt* (*Beweis, Zeugen*) to bring forward; (*Gründe*) to adduce; **jdm etw ~** (*zufügen*) to inflict sth on sb; (*zu verstehen geben*) to make sb understand sth; (*lehren*) to teach sb sth
Beichte [ˈbaıçtə] *f* confession
beichten *vt* to confess ▷ *vi* to go to confession
Beichtgeheimnis *nt* secret of the confessional
Beichtstuhl *m* confessional
beide [ˈbaıdə] *pron, adj* both; **meine ~n Brüder** my two brothers, both my brothers; **die ersten ~n** the first two; **wir ~** we two; **einer von ~n** one of the two; **alles ~s** both (of them); **~ Mal** both times
beider- *zW*: **beiderlei** *adj inv* of both; **beiderseitig** *adj* mutual, reciprocal; **beiderseits** *adv* mutually ▷ *präp +gen* on both sides of
beieinander [baı|aıˈnandər] *adv* together; **gut ~ sein** (*umg: gesundheitlich*) to be in good shape; (*: geistig*) to be all there
Beifahrer, in [ˈbaıfaːrər(ın)] (**-s, -**) *m(f)* passenger; **Beifahrerairbag** *m* (*Aut*) passenger airbag; **Beifahrersitz** *m* passenger seat
Beifall [ˈbaıfal] (**-(e)s**) *m* applause; (*Zustimmung*) approval; **~ heischend** fishing for applause/approval
beifügen [ˈbaıfyːgən] *vt* to enclose
beige [ˈbeːʒ] *adj* beige
Beigeschmack [ˈbaıgeʃmak] *m* aftertaste
Beihilfe [ˈbaıhılfə] *f* aid, assistance; (*Studienbeihilfe*) grant; (*Jur*) aiding and abetting; **wegen ~ zum Mord** (*Jur*) because of being an accessory to the murder
Beil [baıl] (**-(e)s, -e**) *nt* axe (*Brit*), ax (*US*), hatchet
Beilage [ˈbaılaːgə] *f* (*Buchbeilage etc*) supplement; (*Koch*) accompanying vegetables; (*getrennt serviert*) side dish
beiläufig [ˈbaılɔyfıç] *adj* casual, incidental ▷ *adv* casually, by the way
beilegen [ˈbaıleːgən] *vt* (*hinzufügen*) to enclose, add; (*beimessen*) to attribute, ascribe; (*Streit*) to settle
Beileid [ˈbaılaıt] *nt* condolence, sympathy; **herzliches ~** deepest sympathy
beiliegend [ˈbaıliːgənt] *adj* (*Comm*) enclosed
beim [baım] = **bei dem**
beimessen [ˈbaımɛsən] *unreg vt* to attribute, ascribe
Bein [baın] (**-(e)s, -e**) *nt* leg; **jdm ein ~ stellen** (*lit, fig*) to trip sb up; **wir sollten**

uns auf die ~e machen (*umg*) we ought to be making tracks; **jdm ~e machen** (*umg: antreiben*) to make sb get a move on; **die ~e in die Hand nehmen** (*umg*) to take to one's heels; **sich** *dat* **die ~e in den Bauch stehen** (*umg*) to stand about until one is fit to drop; **etw auf die ~e stellen** (*fig*) to get sth off the ground

beinah [baɪˈnaː], **beinahe** [baɪˈnaːə] *adv* almost, nearly

Beinbruch *m* fracture of the leg; **das ist kein ~** (*fig: umg*) it could be worse

beipflichten [ˈbaɪpflɪçtən] *vi*: **jdm/etw ~** to agree with sb/sth

beisammen [baɪˈzamən] *adv* together; **Beisammensein** (**-s**) *nt* get-together

Beischlaf [ˈbaɪʃlaːf] *m* (*Jur*) sexual intercourse

Beisein [ˈbaɪzaɪn] (**-s**) *nt* presence

beiseite [baɪˈzaɪtə] *adv* to one side, aside; (*stehen*) on one side, aside; **Spaß ~!** joking apart!

Beisetzung *f* funeral

Beisitzer, in [ˈbaɪzɪtsər(ɪn)] (**-s, -**) *m(f)* (*Jur*) assessor; (*bei Prüfung*) observer

Beispiel [ˈbaɪʃpiːl] (**-(e)s, -e**) *nt* example; **mit gutem ~ vorangehen** to set a good example; **sich** *dat* **an jdm ein ~ nehmen** to take sb as an example; **zum ~** for example; **beispielhaft** *adj* exemplary; **beispiellos** *adj* unprecedented

beispielsweise *adv* for instance, for example

beißen [ˈbaɪsən] *unreg vt, vi* to bite; (*stechen: Rauch, Säure*) to burn ▷ *vr* (*Farben*) to clash

beißend *adj* biting, caustic; (*Geruch*) pungent, sharp; (*fig*) sarcastic

Beißzange [ˈbaɪstsaŋgə] *f* pliers *pl*

Beistand [ˈbaɪʃtant] (**-(e)s, ¨-e**) *m* support, help; (*Jur*) adviser; **jdm ~ leisten** to give sb assistance/one's support

beistehen [ˈbaɪʃteːən] *unreg vi*: **jdm ~** to stand by sb

beisteuern [ˈbaɪʃtɔʏərn] *vt* to contribute

Beistrich [ˈbaɪʃtrɪç] *m* comma

Beitrag [ˈbaɪtraːk] (**-(e)s, ¨-e**) *m* contribution; (*Zahlung*) fee, subscription; (*Versicherungsbeitrag*) premium; **einen ~ zu etw leisten** to make a contribution to sth

beitragen [ˈbaɪtraːgən] *unreg vt, vi*: **~ (zu)** to contribute (to); (*mithelfen*) to help (with)

beitreten [ˈbaɪtreːtən] *unreg vi +dat* to join

Beitritt [ˈbaɪtrɪt] *m* joining; membership

Beiwagen [ˈbaɪvaːgən] *m* (*Motorradbeiwagen*) sidecar; (*Straßenbahnbeiwagen*) extra carriage

Beize [ˈbaɪtsə] (**-, -n**) *f* (*Holzbeize*) stain; (*Koch*) marinade

beizeiten [baɪˈtsaɪtən] *adv* in time

bejahen [bəˈjaːən] *vt* (*Frage*) to say yes to, answer in the affirmative; (*gutheißen*) to agree with

bejammern [bəˈjamərn] *vt* to lament, bewail

bejammernswert *adj* lamentable

bekämpfen [bəˈkɛmpfən] *vt* (*Gegner*) to fight; (*Seuche*) to combat ▷ *vr* to fight

bekannt [bəˈkant] *adj* (well-)known; (*nicht fremd*) familiar; **~ geben** to announce publicly; **mit jdm ~ sein** to know sb; **~ machen** to announce; **jdn mit jdm ~ machen** to introduce sb to sb; **sich mit etw ~ machen** to familiarize o.s. with sth; **das ist mir ~** I know that; **es/sie kommt mir ~ vor** it/she seems familiar; **durch etw ~ werden** to become famous because of sth

Bekannte, r *f(m)* friend, acquaintance

bekannt- *zW*: **Bekanntgabe** *f* announcement; **Bekanntheitsgrad** *m* degree of fame; **bekanntlich** *adv* as is well known, as you know; **Bekanntmachung** *f* publication; (*Anschlag etc*) announcement; **Bekanntschaft** *f* acquaintance

bekehren [bəˈkeːrən] *vt* to convert ▷ *vr* to be *od* become converted

bekennen [bəˈkɛnən] *unreg vt* to confess; (*Glauben*) to profess ▷ *vr*: **sich zu jdm/etw ~** to declare one's support for sb/sth; **Farbe ~** (*umg*) to show where one stands

Bekenntnis [bəˈkɛntnɪs] (**-ses, -se**) *nt* admission, confession; (*Religion*) confession, denomination; **ein ~ zur Demokratie ablegen** to declare one's belief in democracy; **Bekenntnisschule** *f* denominational school

beklagen [bəˈklaːgən] *vt* to deplore, lament ▷ *vr* to complain

beklagenswert *adj* lamentable, pathetic; (*Mensch*) pitiful; (*Zustand*) deplorable; (*Unfall*) terrible

bekleiden [bəˈklaɪdən] *vt* to clothe; (*Amt*) to occupy, fill

Bekleidung *f* clothing; (*form: eines Amtes*) tenure

Bekleidungsindustrie *f* clothing industry, rag trade (*umg*)

beklommen [bəˈklɔmən] *adj* anxious, uneasy

bekommen [bəˈkɔmən] *unreg vt* to get, receive; (*Kind*) to have; (*Zug*) to catch, get ▷ *vi*: **jdm ~** to agree with sb; **es mit jdm zu tun ~** to get into trouble with sb; **wohl bekomms!** your health!

bekömmlich [bəˈkœmlɪç] *adj* easily digestible

bekräftigen [bəˈkrɛftɪgən] *vt* to confirm, corroborate

bekreuzigen [bəˈkrɔʏtsɪgən] *vr* to cross o.s.

bekümmern [bəˈkʏmərn] *vt* to worry, trouble

bekunden [bəˈkʊndən] *vt* (*sagen*) to state; (*zeigen*) to show

belächeln [bəˈlɛçəln] *vt* to laugh at

beladen [bəˈlaːdən] *unreg vt* to load

Belag [bəˈlaːk] (**-(e)s, ¨-e**) *m* covering, coating; (*Brotbelag*) spread; (*auf Pizza, Brot*) topping; (*auf Tortenboden, zwischen Brotscheiben*) filling; (*Zahnbelag*) tartar; (*auf Zunge*) fur; (*Bremsbelag*) lining

Belagerung *f* siege

Belagerungszustand *m* state of siege

Belang [bəˈlaŋ] (**-(e)s**) *m* importance

belangen *vt* (*Jur*) to take to court

belanglos *adj* trivial, unimportant

Belanglosigkeit *f* triviality
belassen [bə'lasən] *unreg vt* (*in Zustand, Glauben*) to leave; (*in Stellung*) to retain; **es dabei ~** to leave it at that
Belastbarkeit *f* (*von Brücke, Aufzug*) load-bearing capacity; (*von Menschen, Nerven*) ability to take stress
belasten [bə'lastən] *vt* (*lit*) to burden; (*fig: bedrücken*) to trouble, worry; (*Comm: Konto*) to debit; (*Jur*) to incriminate ▷ *vr* to weigh o.s. down; (*Jur*) to incriminate o.s.; **etw (mit einer Hypothek) ~** to mortgage sth
belästigen [bə'lɛstɪgən] *vt* to annoy, pester
Belästigung *f* annoyance, pestering; (*körperlich*) molesting
Belastung [bə'lastʊŋ] *f* (*lit*) load; (*fig: Sorge etc*) weight; (*Comm*) charge, debit(ing); (*mit Hypothek*): **~** (*+gen*) mortgage (on); (*Jur*) incriminating evidence
Belastungs- *zW*: **Belastungsprobe** *f* capacity test; (*fig*) test; **Belastungszeuge** *m* witness for the prosecution
belaufen [bə'laʊfən] *unreg vr*: **sich ~ auf** *+akk* to amount to
belauschen [bə'laʊʃən] *vt* to eavesdrop on
belebt [bə'le:pt] *adj* (*Straße*) crowded
Beleg [bə'le:k] (**-(e)s, -e**) *m* (*Comm*) receipt; (*Beweis*) documentary evidence, proof; (*Beispiel*) example
belegen [bə'le:gən] *vt* to cover; (*Kuchen, Brot*) to spread; (*Platz*) to reserve, book; (*Kurs, Vorlesung*) to register for; (*beweisen*) to verify, prove
Belegschaft *f* personnel, staff
belegt *adj* (*Zunge*) furred; (*Stimme*) hoarse; (*Zimmer*) occupied; **~e Brote** open sandwiches
belehren [bə'le:rən] *vt* to instruct, teach; **jdn eines Besseren ~** to teach sb better; **er ist nicht zu ~** he won't be told
beleidigen [bə'laɪdɪgən] *vt* to insult; to offend
Beleidigung *f* insult; (*Jur*) slander; (*: schriftlich*) libel
belesen [bə'le:zən] *adj* well-read
Beleuchtung *f* lighting, illumination
Belgien ['bɛlgiən] (**-s**) *nt* Belgium
Belgier, in (**-s, -**) *m(f)* Belgian
belgisch *adj* Belgian
belichten [bə'lɪçtən] *vt* to expose
Belichtung *f* exposure
Belichtungsmesser *m* exposure meter
Belieben [bə'li:bən] *nt*: **(ganz) nach ~** (just) as you wish
beliebig [bə'li:bɪç] *adj* any you like, as you like; **~ viel** as much as you like; **in ~er Reihenfolge** in any order whatever; **ein ~es Thema** any subject you like *od* want
beliebt [bə'li:pt] *adj* popular; **sich bei jdm ~ machen** to make o.s. popular with sb
beliefern [bə'li:fərn] *vt* to supply
bellen ['bɛlən] *vi* to bark
Belohnung *f* reward
belügen [bə'ly:gən] *unreg vt* to lie to, deceive
belustigen [bə'lʊstɪgən] *vt* to amuse
bemalen [bə'ma:lən] *vt* to paint ▷ *vr* (*pej: schminken*) to put on one's war paint (*umg*)
bemängeln [bə'mɛŋəln] *vt* to criticize
bemerkbar *adj* perceptible, noticeable; **sich ~ machen** (*Person*) to make *od* get o.s. noticed; (*Unruhe*) to become noticeable
bemerken [bə'mɛrkən] *vt* (*wahrnehmen*) to notice, observe; (*sagen*) to say, mention; **nebenbei bemerkt** by the way
bemerkenswert *adj* remarkable, noteworthy
Bemerkung *f* remark, comment; (*schriftlich*) comment, note
bemitleiden [bə'mɪtlaɪdən] *vt* to pity
bemühen [bə'my:ən] *vr* to take trouble; **sich um eine Stelle ~** to try to get a job
Bemühung *f* trouble, pains *pl*, effort
benachbart [bə'naxba:rt] *adj* neighbouring (*Brit*), neighboring (*US*)
benachrichtigen [bə'na:xrɪçtɪgən] *vt* to inform
benachteiligen [bə'na:xtaɪlɪgən] *vt* to (put at a) disadvantage, victimize
benehmen [bə'ne:mən] *unreg vr* to behave; **Benehmen** (**-s**) *nt* behaviour (*Brit*), behavior (*US*); **kein Benehmen haben** not to know how to behave
beneiden [bə'naɪdən] *vt* to envy
beneidenswert *adj* enviable
Beneluxländer ['be:nelʊkslɛndər] *pl* Benelux (countries *pl*)
Bengel ['bɛŋəl] (**-s, -**) *m* (little) rascal *od* rogue
Benin [be'ni:n] (**-s**) *nt* Benin
benommen [bə'nɔmən] *adj* dazed
benoten [bə'no:tən] *vt* to mark
benötigen [bə'nø:tɪgən] *vt* to need
benutzen [bə'nʊtsən] *vt* to use
Benutzer, in (**-s, -**) *m(f)* user; **benutzerdefiniert** *adj* (*Comput*) user-defined; **benutzerfreundlich** *adj* user-friendly; **Benutzername** *m* username
Benutzung *f* utilization, use; **jdm etw zur ~ überlassen** to put sth at sb's disposal
Benzin [bɛnt'si:n] (**-s, -e**) *nt* (*Aut*) petrol (*Brit*), gas(oline) (*US*); **Benzinkanister** *m* petrol (*Brit*) *od* gas (*US*) can; **Benzintank** *m* petrol (*Brit*) *od* gas (*US*) tank; **Benzinuhr** *f* petrol (*Brit*) *od* gas (*US*) gauge
beobachten [bə'|o:baxtən] *vt* to observe
Beobachter, in (**-s, -**) *m(f)* observer; (*eines Unfalls*) witness; (*Presse, TV*) correspondent
Beobachtung *f* observation
bepacken [bə'pakən] *vt* to load, pack
bequem [bə'kve:m] *adj* comfortable; (*Ausrede*) convenient; (*Person*) lazy, indolent
Bequemlichkeit *f* convenience, comfort; (*Faulheit*) laziness, indolence
beraten [bə'ra:tən] *unreg vt* to advise; (*besprechen*) to discuss, debate ▷ *vr* to consult; **gut/schlecht ~ sein** to be well/ill advised; **sich ~ lassen** to get advice
Berater, in (**-s, -**) *m(f)* adviser
beratschlagen [bə'ra:tʃla:gən] *vi* to

deliberate, confer ▷ *vt* to deliberate on, confer about
Beratung *f* advice; (*Besprechung*) consultation
Beratungsstelle *f* advice centre (*Brit*) *od* center (*US*)
berauben [bə'raʊbən] *vt* to rob
berechenbar [bə'rɛçənba:r] *adj* calculable; (*Verhalten*) predictable
berechnen [bə'rɛçnən] *vt* to calculate; (*Comm: anrechnen*) to charge
berechnend *adj* (*Mensch*) calculating, scheming
Berechnung *f* calculation; (*Comm*) charge
berechtigen [bə'rɛçtɪgən] *vt* to entitle; (*bevollmächtigen*) to authorize; (*fig*) to justify
berechtigt [bə'rɛçtɪçt] *adj* justifiable, justified
Berechtigung *f* authorization; (*fig*) justification
Bereich [bə'raɪç] (**-(e)s, -e**) *m* (*Bezirk*) area; (*Ressort, Gebiet*) sphere; **im ~ des Möglichen liegen** to be within the bounds of possibility
bereichern [bə'raɪçərn] *vt* to enrich ▷ *vr* to get rich; **sich auf Kosten anderer ~** to feather one's nest at the expense of other people
Bereifung [bə'raɪfʊŋ] *f* (set of) tyres (*Brit*) *od* tires (*US*) *pl*; (*Vorgang*) fitting with tyres (*Brit*) *od* tires (*US*)
bereinigen [bə'raɪnɪgən] *vt* to settle
bereisen [bə'raɪzən] *vt* to travel through; (*Comm: Gebiet*) to travel, cover
bereit [bə'raɪt] *adj* ready, prepared; **zu etw ~ sein** to be ready for sth; **sich ~ erklären** to declare o.s. willing; **(sich) ~ machen** to prepare, to get ready
bereiten *vt* to prepare, make ready; (*Kummer, Freude*) to cause; **einer Sache** *dat* **ein Ende ~** to put an end to sth
bereit- *zW*: **bereithalten** *unreg vt* to keep in readiness; **bereitlegen** *vt* to lay out; **bereitmachen** *vt, vr siehe* **bereit**
bereits *adv* already
bereit- *zW*: **Bereitschaft** *f* readiness; (*Polizei*) alert; **in Bereitschaft sein** to be on the alert *od* on stand-by; **Bereitschaftsdienst** *m* emergency service; **bereitstehen** *unreg vi* (*Person*) to be prepared; (*Ding*) to be ready; **bereitstellen** *vt* (*Kisten, Pakete etc*) to put ready; (*Geld etc*) to make available; (*Truppen, Maschinen*) to put at the ready
bereitwillig *adj* willing, ready; **Bereitwilligkeit** *f* willingness, readiness
bereuen [bə'rɔʏən] *vt* to regret
Berg [bɛrk] (**-(e)s, -e**) *m* mountain; (*kleiner*) hill; **mit etw hinterm ~ halten** (*fig*) to keep quiet about sth; **über alle ~e sein** to be miles away; **da stehen einem ja die Haare zu ~e** it's enough to make your hair stand on end; **bergab** *adv* downhill; **Bergarbeiter** *m* miner; **bergauf** *adv* uphill; **Bergbahn** *f* mountain railway (*Brit*) *od* railroad (*US*); **Bergbau** *m* mining
bergen ['bɛrgən] *unreg vt* (*retten*) to rescue; (*Ladung*) to salvage; (*enthalten*) to contain
Bergführer *m* mountain guide
Berggipfel *m* mountain top, peak, summit
bergig ['bɛrgɪç] *adj* mountainous, hilly
Berg- *zW*: **Bergkamm** *m* crest, ridge; **Bergkette** *f* mountain range; **Bergmann** (**-(e)s**, *pl* **Bergleute**) *m* miner; **Bergschuh** *m* walking boot; **Bergsteigen** *nt* mountaineering; **Bergsteiger, in** *m(f)* mountaineer, climber
Bergung ['bɛrgʊŋ] *f* (*von Menschen*) rescue; (*von Material*) recovery; (*Naut*) salvage
Bergwacht *f* mountain rescue service
Bergwerk *nt* mine
Bericht [bə'rɪçt] (**-(e)s, -e**) *m* report, account; **berichten** *vt, vi* to report; **Berichterstatter** (**-s, -**) *m* reporter, (newspaper) correspondent; **Berichterstattung** *f* reporting
berichtigen [bə'rɪçtɪgən] *vt* to correct
beritten [bə'rɪtən] *adj* mounted
Berlin [bɛr'li:n] (**-s**) *nt* Berlin
Berliner[1] *adj attrib* Berlin
Berliner[2] (**-s, -**) *m* (*Person*) Berliner; (*Koch*) jam doughnut
Bermudas [bɛr'mu:das] *pl*: **auf den ~** in Bermuda
Bern [bɛrn] (**-s**) *nt* Berne
Bernstein ['bɛrnʃtaɪn] *m* amber
bersten ['bɛrstən] *unreg vi* to burst, split
berüchtigt [bə'rʏçtɪçt] *adj* notorious, infamous
berücksichtigen [bə'rʏkzɪçtɪgən] *vt* to consider, bear in mind
Beruf [bə'ru:f] (**-(e)s, -e**) *m* occupation, profession; (*Gewerbe*) trade; **was sind Sie von ~?** what is your occupation *etc*?, what do you do for a living?; **seinen ~ verfehlt haben** to have missed one's vocation
berufen *unreg vt* (*in Amt*): **jdn in etw** *akk* **~** to appoint sb to sth ▷ *vr*: **sich auf jdn/etw ~** to refer *od* appeal to sb/sth ▷ *adj* competent, qualified; (*ausersehen*): **zu etw ~ sein** to have a vocation for sth
beruflich *adj* professional; **er ist ~ viel unterwegs** he is away a lot on business
Berufs- *zW*: **Berufsausbildung** *f* vocational *od* professional training; **Berufsberater** *m* careers adviser; **Berufsberatung** *f* vocational guidance; **Berufserfahrung** *f* (professional) experience; **Berufskrankheit** *f* occupational disease; **Berufsleben** *nt* professional life; **im Berufsleben stehen** to be working *od* in employment; **Berufsrisiko** *nt* occupational hazard; **Berufsschule** *f* vocational *od* trade school; **Berufssoldat** *m* professional soldier, regular; **Berufssportler** *m* professional (sportsman); **berufstätig** *adj* employed; **Berufsverkehr** *m* commuter traffic
Berufung *f* vocation, calling; (*Ernennung*) appointment; (*Jur*) appeal; **~ einlegen** to appeal; **unter ~ auf etw** *akk* (*form*) with reference to sth

beruhen [bə'ru:ən] *vi*: **auf etw** *dat* **~** to be based on sth; **etw auf sich ~ lassen** to leave sth at that; **das beruht auf Gegenseitigkeit** the feeling is mutual
beruhigen [bə'ru:ɪgən] *vt* to calm, pacify, soothe ▷ *vr* (*Mensch*) to calm (o.s.) down; (*Situation*) to calm down
beruhigend *adj* (*Gefühl, Wissen*) reassuring; (*Worte*) comforting; (*Mittel*) tranquillizing
Beruhigung *f* reassurance; (*der Nerven*) calming; **zu jds ~** to reassure sb
Beruhigungsmittel *nt* sedative
Beruhigungspille *f* tranquillizer
berühmt [bə'ry:mt] *adj* famous; **das war nicht ~** (*umg*) it was nothing to write home about; **Berühmtheit** *f* (*Ruf*) fame; (*Mensch*) celebrity
berühren [bə'ry:rən] *vt* to touch; (*gefühlsmäßig bewegen*) to affect; (*flüchtig erwähnen*) to mention, touch on ▷ *vr* to meet, touch; **von etw peinlich berührt sein** to be embarrassed by sth
Berührung *f* contact
Berührungspunkt *m* point of contact
besagt *adj* (*form: Tag etc*) in question
besänftigen [bə'zɛnftɪgən] *vt* to soothe, calm
besänftigend *adj* soothing
Besatz [bə'zats] (**-es, ⸚e**) *m* trimming, edging
Besatzung *f* garrison; (*Naut, Aviat*) crew
Besatzungsmacht *f* occupying power
besaufen [bə'zaʊfən] *unreg* (*umg*) *vr* to get drunk *od* stoned
beschädigen [bə'ʃɛ:dɪgən] *vt* to damage
Beschädigung *f* damage; (*Stelle*) damaged spot
beschaffen [bə'ʃafən] *vt* to get, acquire ▷ *adj* constituted; **so ~ sein wie ...** to be the same as ...; **Beschaffenheit** *f* constitution, nature; **je nach Beschaffenheit der Lage** according to the situation
Beschaffung *f* acquisition
beschäftigen [bə'ʃɛftɪgən] *vt* to occupy; (*beruflich*) to employ; (*innerlich*): **jdn ~** to be on sb's mind ▷ *vr* to occupy *od* concern o.s.
Beschäftigung *f* (*Beruf*) employment; (*Tätigkeit*) occupation; (*geistige Beschäftigung*) preoccupation; **einer ~ nachgehen** (*form*) to be employed
Beschäftigungstherapie *f* occupational therapy
beschämen [bə'ʃɛ:mən] *vt* to put to shame
beschämend *adj* shameful; (*Hilfsbereitschaft*) shaming
beschämt *adj* ashamed
beschatten [bə'ʃatən] *vt* to shade; (*Verdächtige*) to shadow
beschaulich [bə'ʃaʊlɪç] *adj* contemplative; (*Leben, Abend*) quiet, tranquil
Bescheid [bə'ʃaɪt] (**-(e)s, -e**) *m* information; (*Weisung*) directions *pl*; **~ wissen (über** *+akk***)** to be well-informed (about); **ich weiß ~** I know; **jdm ~ geben** *od* **sagen** to let sb know; **jdm ordentlich ~ sagen** (*umg*) to tell sb where to go
bescheiden [bə'ʃaɪdən] *unreg vr* to content o.s. ▷ *vt*: **etw abschlägig ~** (*form*) to turn sth down ▷ *adj* modest; **Bescheidenheit** *f* modesty
bescheinen [bə'ʃaɪnən] *unreg vt* to shine on
bescheinigen [bə'ʃaɪnɪgən] *vt* to certify; (*bestätigen*) to acknowledge; **hiermit wird bescheinigt, dass ...** this is to certify that ...
Bescheinigung *f* certificate; (*Quittung*) receipt
bescheißen [bə'ʃaɪsən] *unreg* (*umg!*) *vt* to cheat
beschenken [bə'ʃɛŋkən] *vt* to give presents to
Bescherung *f* giving of presents; (*umg*) mess; **da haben wir die ~!** (*umg*) what did I tell you!
beschildern [bə'ʃɪldərn] *vt* to signpost
beschimpfen [bə'ʃɪmpfən] *vt* to abuse
Beschiss [bə'ʃɪs] (**-es**) (*umg*) *m*: **das ist ~** that is a cheat
beschissen *pp von* **bescheißen** ▷ *adj* (*umg!*) bloody awful, lousy
Beschlag [bə'ʃla:k] (**-(e)s, ⸚e**) *m* (*Metallband*) fitting; (*auf Fenster*) condensation; (*auf Metall*) tarnish; finish; (*Hufeisen*) horseshoe; **jdn/etw in ~ nehmen** *od* **mit ~ belegen** to monopolize sb/sth
beschlagen [bə'ʃla:gən] *unreg vt* to cover; (*Pferd*) to shoe; (*Fenster, Metall*) to cover ▷ *vi, vr* (*Fenster etc*) to mist over; **~ sein (in** *od* **auf** *+dat***)** to be well versed (in)
beschlagnahmen *vt* to seize, confiscate
beschleunigen [bə'ʃlɔʏnɪgən] *vt* to accelerate, speed up ▷ *vi* (*Aut*) to accelerate
Beschleunigung *f* acceleration
beschließen [bə'ʃli:sən] *unreg vt* to decide on; (*beenden*) to end, close
Beschluss [bə'ʃlʊs] (**-es, ⸚e**) *m* decision, conclusion; (*Ende*) close, end; **einen ~ fassen** to pass a resolution
beschmutzen [bə'ʃmʊtsən] *vt* to dirty, soil
beschneiden [bə'ʃnaɪdən] *unreg vt* to cut; (*stutzen*) to trim; (*: Strauch*) to prune; (*Rel*) to circumcise
beschönigen [bə'ʃø:nɪgən] *vt* to gloss over; **~der Ausdruck** euphemism
beschränken [bə'ʃrɛŋkən] *vt, vr*: **(sich) ~ (auf** *+akk***)** to limit *od* restrict (o.s.) (to)
beschrankt [bə'ʃraŋkt] *adj* (*Bahnübergang*) with barrier
beschränkt [bə'ʃrɛŋkt] *adj* confined, narrow; (*Mensch*) limited, narrow-minded; (*pej: geistig*) dim; **Gesellschaft mit ~er Haftung** limited company (*Brit*), corporation (*US*)
beschreiben [bə'ʃraɪbən] *unreg vt* to describe; (*Papier*) to write on
Beschreibung *f* description
Beschriftung *f* lettering
beschuldigen [bə'ʃʊldɪgən] *vt* to accuse
Beschuldigung *f* accusation
beschützen [bə'ʃʏtsən] *vt*: **~ (vor** *+dat***)** to protect (from)
Beschützer, in (**-s, -**) *m(f)* protector
Beschwerde [bə'ʃve:rdə] (**-, -n**) *f* complaint;

(*Mühe*) hardship; (*Industrie*) grievance; **Beschwerden** *pl* (*Leiden*) trouble; **~ einlegen** (*form*) to lodge a complaint

beschweren [bəˈʃveːrən] *vt* to weight down; (*fig*) to burden ▷ *vr* to complain

beschwerlich *adj* tiring, exhausting

beschwichtigen [bəˈʃvɪçtɪɡən] *vt* to soothe, pacify

beschwingt [bəˈʃvɪŋt] *adj* cheery, in high spirits

beschwipst [bəˈʃvɪpst] *adj* tipsy

beschwören [bəˈʃvøːrən] *unreg vt* (*Aussage*) to swear to; (*anflehen*) to implore; (*Geister*) to conjure up

besehen [bəˈzeːən] *unreg vt* to look at; **genau ~** to examine closely

beseitigen [bəˈzaɪtɪɡən] *vt* to remove

Besen [ˈbeːzən] **(-s, -)** *m* broom; (*pej: umg: Frau*) old bag; **ich fresse einen ~, wenn das stimmt** (*umg*) if that's right, I'll eat my hat

besessen [bəˈzɛsən] *adj* possessed; (*von einer Idee etc*): **~ (von)** obsessed (with)

besetzen [bəˈzɛtsən] *vt* (*Haus, Land*) to occupy; (*Platz*) to take, fill; (*Posten*) to fill; (*Rolle*) to cast; (*mit Edelsteinen*) to set

besetzt *adj* full; (*Tel*) engaged, busy; (*Platz*) taken; (*WC*) engaged; **Besetztzeichen** *nt* engaged tone (*Brit*), busy signal (*US*)

Besetzung *f* occupation; (*von Stelle*) filling; (*von Rolle*) casting; (*die Schauspieler*) cast; **zweite ~** (*Theat*) understudy

besichtigen [bəˈzɪçtɪɡən] *vt* to visit, look at

Besichtigung *f* visit

besiegen [bəˈziːɡən] *vt* to defeat, overcome

Besiegte, r [bəˈziːktə(r)] *f(m)* loser

besinnlich *adj* contemplative

Besinnung *f* consciousness; **bei/ohne ~ sein** to be conscious/unconscious; **zur ~ kommen** to recover consciousness; (*fig*) to come to one's senses

Besitz [bəˈzɪts] **(-es)** *m* possession; (*Eigentum*) property; **besitzanzeigend** *adj* (*Gram*) possessive

besitzen *unreg vt* to possess, own; (*Eigenschaft*) to have

Besitzer, in **(-s, -)** *m(f)* owner, proprietor

besoffen [bəˈzɔfən] (*umg*) *adj* sozzled

besohlen [bəˈzoːlən] *vt* to sole

Besoldung [bəˈzɔldʊŋ] *f* salary, pay

besondere, r, s [bəˈzɔndərə(r, s)] *adj* special; (*eigen*) particular; (*gesondert*) separate; (*eigentümlich*) peculiar

Besonderheit *f* peculiarity

besonders *adv* especially, particularly; (*getrennt*) separately; **das Essen/der Film war nicht ~** the food/film was nothing special *od* out of the ordinary; **wie gehts dir? — nicht ~** how are you? — not too hot

besorgen [bəˈzɔrɡən] *vt* (*beschaffen*) to acquire; (*kaufen*) to purchase; (*erledigen: Geschäfte*) to deal with; (*sich kümmern um*) to take care of; **es jdm ~** (*umg*) to sort sb out

Besorgnis **(-, -se)** *f* anxiety, concern

besorgt [bəˈzɔrkt] *adj* anxious, worried

Besorgung *f* acquisition; (*Kauf*) purchase; (*Einkauf*): **~en machen** to do some shopping

besprechen [bəˈʃprɛçən] *unreg vt* to discuss; (*Tonband etc*) to record, speak onto; (*Buch*) to review ▷ *vr* to discuss, consult

Besprechung *f* meeting, discussion; (*von Buch*) review

besser [ˈbɛsər] *adj* better; **nur ein ~er ...** just a glorified ...; **~e Leute** a better class of people; **es geht ihm ~** he feels better; *siehe auch* **besserstehen**

bessern *vt* to make better, improve ▷ *vr* to improve; (*Mensch*) to reform

Besserung *f* improvement; **auf dem Weg(e) der ~ sein** to be getting better, be improving; **gute ~!** get well soon!

Besserwisser, in **(-s, -)** *m(f)* know-all (*Brit*), know-it-all (*US*)

Bestand [bəˈʃtant] **(-(e)s, ⸚e)** *m* (*Fortbestehen*) duration, continuance; (*Kassenbestand*) amount, balance; (*Vorrat*) stock; **eiserner ~** iron rations *pl*; **~ haben, von ~ sein** to last long, endure

beständig [bəˈʃtɛndɪç] *adj* (*ausdauernd*) constant (*auch fig*); (*Wetter*) settled; (*Stoffe*) resistant; (*Klagen etc*) continual

Bestandsaufnahme *f* stocktaking

Bestandteil *m* part, component; (*Zutat*) ingredient; **sich in seine ~e auflösen** to fall to pieces

bestärken [bəˈʃtɛrkən] *vt*: **jdn in etw** *dat* **~** to strengthen *od* confirm sb in sth

bestätigen [bəˈʃtɛːtɪɡən] *vt* to confirm; (*anerkennen, Comm*) to acknowledge; **jdn (im Amt) ~** to confirm sb's appointment

Bestätigung *f* confirmation; acknowledgement

bestatten [bəˈʃtatən] *vt* to bury

Bestattung *f* funeral

bestäuben [bəˈʃtɔʏbən] *vt* to powder, dust; (*Pflanze*) to pollinate

beste, r, s [ˈbɛstə(r, s)] *adj* best; **sie singt am ~n** she sings best; **so ist es am ~n** it's best that way; **am ~n gehst du gleich** you'd better go at once; **jdn zum B~n haben** to pull sb's leg; **einen Witz** *etc* **zum B~n geben** to tell a joke *etc*; **aufs B~** in the best possible way; **zu jds B~n** for the benefit of sb; **es steht nicht zum B~n** it does not look too promising

bestechen [bəˈʃtɛçən] *unreg vt* to bribe ▷ *vi* (*Eindruck machen*): **(durch etw) ~** to be impressive (because of sth)

bestechlich *adj* corruptible: **Bestechlichkeit** *f* corruptibility

Bestechung *f* bribery, corruption

Besteck [bəˈʃtɛk] **(-(e)s, -e)** *nt* knife, fork and spoon, cutlery; (*Med*) set of instruments

bestehen [bəˈʃteːən] *unreg vi* to exist; (*andauern*) to last ▷ *vt* (*Probe, Prüfung*) to pass; (*Kampf*) to win; **~ bleiben** to last, endure; (*Frage, Hoffnung*) to remain; **die**

Schwierigkeit/das Problem besteht darin, dass ... the difficulty/problem lies in the fact that ..., the difficulty/problem is that ...; **~ auf** *+dat* to insist on; **~ aus** to consist of

bestehlen [bəˈʃteːlən] *unreg vt* to rob

besteigen [bəˈʃtaɪgən] *unreg vt* to climb, ascend; (*Pferd*) to mount; (*Thron*) to ascend

Bestellbuch *nt* order book

bestellen [bəˈʃtɛlən] *vt* to order; (*kommen lassen*) to arrange to see; (*nominieren*) to name; (*Acker*) to cultivate; (*Grüße, Auftrag*) to pass on; **wie bestellt und nicht abgeholt** (*hum: umg*) like orphan Annie; **er hat nicht viel/nichts zu ~** he doesn't have much/any say here; **ich bin für 10 Uhr bestellt** I have an appointment for *od* at 10 o'clock; **es ist schlecht um ihn bestellt** (*fig*) he is in a bad way

Bestell- *zW*: **Bestellnummer** *f* order number; **Bestellschein** *m* order coupon

Bestellung *f* (*Comm*) order; (*Bestellen*) ordering; (*Ernennung*) nomination, appointment

bestenfalls [ˈbɛstənˈfals] *adv* at best

bestens [ˈbɛstəns] *adv* very well

besteuern [bəˈʃtɔʏərn] *vt* to tax

Bestie [ˈbɛstiə] *f* (*lit, fig*) beast

bestimmen [bəˈʃtɪmən] *vt* (*Regeln*) to lay down; (*Tag, Ort*) to fix; (*prägen*) to characterize; (*ausersehen*) to mean; (*ernennen*) to appoint; (*definieren*) to define; (*veranlassen*) to induce ▷ *vi*: **du hast hier nicht zu ~** you don't make the decisions here; **er kann über sein Geld allein ~** it is up to him what he does with his money

bestimmt *adj* (*entschlossen*) firm; (*gewiss*) certain, definite; (*Artikel*) definite ▷ *adv* (*gewiss*) definitely, for sure; **suchen Sie etwas B~es?** are you looking for anything in particular?; **Bestimmtheit** *f* certainty; **in** *od* **mit aller Bestimmtheit** quite categorically

Bestimmung *f* (*Verordnung*) regulation; (*Festsetzen*) determining; (*Verwendungszweck*) purpose; (*Schicksal*) fate; (*Definition*) definition

Bestimmungsort *m* destination

Bestleistung *f* best performance

bestmöglich *adj* best possible

Best.-Nr. *abk* = **Bestellnummer**

bestrafen [bəˈʃtraːfən] *vt* to punish

bestrahlen [bəˈʃtraːlən] *vt* to shine on; (*Med*) to treat with X-rays

Bestrahlung *f* (*Med*) X-ray treatment, radiotherapy

Bestreben [bəˈʃtreːbən] (**-s**) *nt* endeavour (*Brit*), endeavor (*US*), effort

bestreichen [bəˈʃtraiçən] *unreg vt* (*Brot*) to spread

bestreiken [bəˈʃtraɪkən] *vt* (*Industrie*) to black; **die Fabrik wird zur Zeit bestreikt** there's a strike on in the factory at the moment

bestreiten [bəˈʃtraɪtən] *unreg vt* (*abstreiten*) to dispute; (*finanzieren*) to pay for, finance; **er hat das ganze Gespräch allein bestritten** he did all the talking

bestreuen [bəˈʃtrɔʏən] *vt* to sprinkle, dust; (*Straße*) to (spread with) grit

Bestseller [ˈbɛstsɛlər] (**-s, -**) *m* best-seller

bestürmen [bəˈʃtʏrmən] *vt* (*mit Fragen, Bitten etc*) to overwhelm, swamp

bestürzen [bəˈʃtʏrtsən] *vt* to dismay

bestürzt *adj* dismayed

Besuch [bəˈzuːx] (**-(e)s, -e**) *m* visit; (*Person*) visitor; **einen ~ bei jdm machen** to pay sb a visit *od* call; **~ haben** to have visitors; **bei jdm auf** *od* **zu ~ sein** to be visiting sb

besuchen *vt* to visit; (*Sch etc*) to attend; **gut besucht** well-attended

Besucher, in (**-s, -**) *m(f)* visitor, guest

Besuchszeit *f* visiting hours *pl*

betagt [bəˈtaːkt] *adj* aged

betasten [bəˈtastən] *vt* to touch, feel

betätigen [bəˈtɛːtɪgən] *vt* (*bedienen*) to work, operate ▷ *vr* to involve o.s.; **sich politisch ~** to be involved in politics; **sich als etw ~** to work as sth

Betätigung *f* activity; (*beruflich*) occupation; (*Tech*) operation

betäuben [bəˈtɔʏbən] *vt* to stun; (*fig: Gewissen*) to still; (*Med*) to anaesthetize (*Brit*), anesthetize (*US*); **ein ~der Duft** an overpowering smell

Betäubungsmittel *nt* anaesthetic (*Brit*), anesthetic (*US*)

Bete [ˈbeːtə] (**-, -n**) *f*: **Rote ~** beetroot (*Brit*), beet (*US*)

beteiligen [bəˈtaɪlɪgən] *vr*: **sich (an etw** *dat***) ~** to take part (in sth), participate (in sth); (*an Geschäft: finanziell*) to have a share (in sth) ▷ *vt*: **jdn (an etw** *dat***) ~** to give sb a share *od* interest (in sth); **sich an den Unkosten ~** to contribute to the expenses

Beteiligung *f* participation; (*Anteil*) share, interest; (*Besucherzahl*) attendance

beten [ˈbeːtən] *vi* to pray ▷ *vt* (*Rosenkranz*) to say

Beton [beˈtõː] (**-s, -s**) *m* concrete

betonen [bəˈtoːnən] *vt* to stress

betonieren [betoˈniːrən] *vt* to concrete

Betonung *f* stress, emphasis

Betr. *abk* = **Betreff**

Betracht [bəˈtraxt] *m*: **in ~ kommen** to be concerned *od* relevant; **nicht in ~ kommen** to be out of the question; **etw in ~ ziehen** to consider sth; **außer ~ bleiben** not to be considered

betrachten *vt* to look at; (*fig*) to consider, look at

beträchtlich [bəˈtrɛçtlɪç] *adj* considerable

Betrachtung *f* (*Ansehen*) examination; (*Erwägung*) consideration; **über etw** *akk* **~en anstellen** to reflect on *od* contemplate sth

Betrag [bəˈtraːk] (**-(e)s, ¨-e**) *m* amount, sum; **~ erhalten** (*Comm*) sum received

betragen [bəˈtraːgən] *unreg vt* to amount to ▷ *vr* to behave

Betragen (**-s**) *nt* behaviour (*Brit*), behavior (*US*); (*bes in Zeugnis*) conduct
betreffen [bə'trɛfən] *unreg vt* to concern, affect; **was mich betrifft** as for me
betreffend *adj* relevant, in question
betreffs [bə'trɛfs] *präp +gen* concerning, regarding
betreiben [bə'traɪbən] *unreg vt* (*ausüben*) to practise (*Brit*), practice (*US*); (*Politik*) to follow; (*Studien*) to pursue; (*vorantreiben*) to push ahead; (*Tech: antreiben*) to drive; **auf jds B~** *akk* **hin** (*form*) at sb's instigation
betreten [bə'tre:tən] *unreg vt* to enter; (*Bühne etc*) to step onto ▷ *adj* embarrassed; **„B~ verboten"** "keep off/out"
betreuen [bə'trɔʏən] *vt* to look after
Betrieb (**-(e)s, -e**) *m* (*Firma*) firm, concern; (*Anlage*) plant; (*Tätigkeit*) operation; (*Treiben*) bustle; (*Verkehr*) traffic; **außer ~ sein** to be out of order; **in ~ sein** to be in operation; **eine Maschine in/außer ~ setzen** to start a machine up/stop a machine; **eine Maschine/Fabrik in ~ nehmen** to put a machine/factory into operation; **in den Geschäften herrscht großer ~** the shops are very busy; **er hält den ganzen ~ auf** (*umg*) he's holding everything up
Betriebs- *zW*: **Betriebsausflug** *m* firm's outing; **Betriebsferien** *pl* company holidays *pl* (*Brit*) *od* vacation *sing* (*US*); **Betriebsklima** *nt* (working) atmosphere; **Betriebskosten** *pl* running costs; **Betriebsrat** *m* workers' council; **Betriebssystem** *nt* (*Comput*) operating system; **Betriebsunfall** *m* industrial accident; **Betriebswirtschaft** *f* business management
betrinken [bə'trɪŋkən] *unreg vr* to get drunk
betroffen [bə'trɔfən] *pp von* **betreffen** ▷ *adj* (*bestürzt*) amazed, perplexed; **von etw ~ werden** *od* **sein** to be affected by sth
betrübt [bə'try:pt] *adj* sorrowful, grieved
Betrug (**-(e)s**) *m* deception; (*Jur*) fraud
betrügen [bə'try:gən] *unreg vt* to cheat; (*Jur*) to defraud; (*Ehepartner*) to be unfaithful to ▷ *vr* to deceive o.s.
Betrüger, in (**-s, -**) *m(f)* cheat, deceiver
betrügerisch *adj* deceitful; (*Jur*) fraudulent; **in ~er Absicht** with intent to defraud
betrunken [bə'trʊŋkən] *adj* drunk
Bett [bɛt] (**-(e)s, -en**) *nt* bed; **im ~** in bed; **ins** *od* **zu ~ gehen** to go to bed; **Bettdecke** *f* blanket; (*Daunenbettdecke*) quilt; (*Überwurf*) bedspread
betteln *vi* to beg
Bett- *zW*: **bettlägerig** *adj* bedridden; **Bettlaken** *nt* sheet
Bettler, in ['bɛtlər(ɪn)] (**-s, -**) *m(f)* beggar
Bett- *zW*: **Bettnässer** (**-s, -**) *m* bedwetter; **Bettvorleger** *m* bedside rug; **Bettwäsche** *f* bedclothes *pl*, bedding
beugen ['bɔʏgən] *vt* to bend; (*Gram*) to inflect ▷ *vr* (*+dat*) (*sich fügen*) to bow (to)
Beule ['bɔʏlə] (**-, -n**) *f* bump
beunruhigen [bə'|ʊnru:ɪgən] *vt* to disturb, alarm ▷ *vr* to become worried
beurkunden [bə'|u:rkʊndən] *vt* to attest, verify
beurlauben [bə'|u:rlaʊbən] *vt* to give leave *od* holiday to (*Brit*), grant vacation to (*US*); **beurlaubt sein** to have leave of absence; (*suspendiert sein*) to have been relieved of one's duties
beurteilen [bə'|ʊrtaɪlən] *vt* to judge; (*Buch etc*) to review
Beurteilung *f* judgement; (*von Buch etc*) review; (*Note*) mark
Beute ['bɔʏtə] (**-**) *f* booty, loot; (*von Raubtieren etc*) prey
Beutel (**-s, -**) *m* bag; (*Geldbeutel*) purse; (*Tabaksbeutel*) pouch
Bevölkerung *f* population; **Bevölkerungsexplosion** *f* population explosion
bevollmächtigen [bə'fɔlmɛçtɪgən] *vt* to authorize
Bevollmächtigte, r *f(m)* authorized agent
bevor [bə'fo:r] *konj* before; **bevormunden** *vt untr* to dominate; **bevorstehen** *unreg vi*: **(jdm) bevorstehen** to be in store (for sb); **bevorzugen** *vt untr* to prefer
bewachen [bə'vaxən] *vt* to watch, guard
Bewachung *f* (*Bewachen*) guarding; (*Leute*) guard, watch
bewaffnen [bə'vafnən] *vt* to arm
Bewaffnung *f* (*Vorgang*) arming; (*Ausrüstung*) armament, arms *pl*
bewahren [bə'va:rən] *vt* to keep; **jdn vor jdm/etw ~** to save sb from sb/sth; **(Gott) bewahre!** (*umg*) heaven *od* God forbid!
bewähren [bə'vɛ:rən] *vr* to prove o.s.; (*Maschine*) to prove its worth
bewahrheiten [bə'va:rhaɪtən] *vr* to come true
bewährt *adj* reliable
Bewährung *f* (*Jur*) probation; **ein Jahr Gefängnis mit ~** a suspended sentence of one year with probation
Bewährungsfrist *f* (period of) probation
bewältigen [bə'vɛltɪgən] *vt* to overcome; (*Arbeit*) to finish; (*Portion*) to manage; (*Schwierigkeiten*) to cope with
bewandert [bə'vandərt] *adj* expert, knowledgeable
bewässern [bə'vɛsərn] *vt* to irrigate
bewegen [bə've:gən] *vt, vr* to move; **der Preis bewegt sich um die 50 Euro** the price is about 50 euros; **jdn zu etw ~** to induce sb to do sth
Beweggrund *m* motive
beweglich *adj* movable, mobile; (*flink*) quick
bewegt [bə've:kt] *adj* (*Leben*) eventful; (*Meer*) rough; (*ergriffen*) touched
Bewegung *f* movement, motion; (*innere*) emotion; (*körperlich*) exercise; **sich** *dat* **~ machen** to take exercise
Bewegungsfreiheit *f* freedom of movement; (*fig*) freedom of action

bewegungslos *adj* motionless
Beweis [bə'vaɪs] **(-es, -e)** *m* proof; (*Zeichen*) sign; **beweisbar** *adj* provable
beweisen *unreg vt* to prove; (*zeigen*) to show; **was zu ~ war** QED
Beweis- *zW*: **Beweisführung** *f* reasoning; (*Jur*) presentation of one's case; **Beweiskraft** *f* weight, conclusiveness; **beweiskräftig** *adj* convincing, conclusive; **Beweismittel** *nt* evidence
bewerben [bə'vɛrbən] *unreg vr*: **sich ~ (um)** to apply (for)
Bewerber, in (**-s, -**) *m(f)* applicant
Bewerbung *f* application
bewerten [bə've:rtən] *vt* to assess
bewilligen [bə'vɪlɪgən] *vt* to grant, allow
bewirken [bə'vɪrkən] *vt* to cause, bring about
bewirten [bə'vɪrtən] *vt* to entertain
Bewirtung *f* hospitality; **die ~ so vieler Gäste** catering for so many guests
bewohnen [bə'vo:nən] *vt* to inhabit, live in
Bewohner, in (**-s, -**) *m(f)* inhabitant; (*von Haus*) resident
bewölkt [bə'vœlkt] *adj* cloudy, overcast
Bewölkung *f* clouds *pl*
Bewunderer, in (**-s, -**) *m(f)* admirer
bewundern [bə'vʊndərn] *vt* to admire
bewundernswert *adj* admirable, wonderful
Bewunderung *f* admiration
bewusst [bə'vʊst] *adj* conscious; (*absichtlich*) deliberate; **jdm etw ~ machen** to make sb conscious of sth; **sich** *dat* **etw ~ machen** to realize sth; **sich** *dat* **einer Sache** *gen* **~ sein** to be aware of sth; **bewusstlos** *adj* unconscious; **Bewusstlosigkeit** *f* unconsciousness; **bis zur Bewusstlosigkeit** (*umg*) ad nauseam; **Bewusstsein** *nt* consciousness; **bei Bewusstsein** conscious; **im Bewusstsein, dass ...** in the knowledge that ...
bezahlen [bə'tsa:lən] *vt* to pay (for); **es macht sich bezahlt** it will pay
Bezahlfernsehen *nt* pay TV
Bezahlung *f* payment; **ohne/gegen** *od* **für ~** without/for payment
bezaubern [bə'tsaʊbərn] *vt* to enchant, charm
bezeichnen [bə'tsaɪçnən] *vt* (*kennzeichnen*) to mark; (*nennen*) to call; (*beschreiben*) to describe; (*zeigen*) to show, indicate
bezeichnend *adj*: **~ (für)** characteristic (of), typical (of)
Bezeichnung *f* (*Zeichen*) mark, sign; (*Beschreibung*) description; (*Ausdruck*) expression, term
bezeugen [bə'tsɔʏgən] *vt* to testify to
bezichtigen [bə'tsɪçtɪgən] *vt (+gen)* to accuse (of)
beziehen [bə'tsi:ən] *unreg vt* (*mit Überzug*) to cover; (*Haus, Position*) to move into; (*Standpunkt*) to take up; (*erhalten*) to receive; (*Zeitung*) to subscribe to, take ▷ *vr* (*Himmel*) to cloud over; **die Betten frisch ~** to change the beds; **etw auf jdn/etw ~** to relate sth to sb/sth; **sich ~ auf** *+akk* to refer to
Beziehung *f* (*Verbindung*) connection; (*Zusammenhang*) relation; (*Verhältnis*) relationship; (*Hinsicht*) respect; **diplomatische ~en** diplomatic relations; **seine ~en spielen lassen** to pull strings; **in jeder ~** in every respect; **~en haben** (*vorteilhaft*) to have connections *od* contacts
Beziehungskiste (*umg*) *f* relationship
beziehungsweise *adv* or; (*genauer gesagt*) that is, or rather; (*im anderen Fall*) and ... respectively
Bezirk [bə'tsɪrk] **(-(e)s, -e)** *m* district
Bezug [bə'tsu:k] **(-(e)s, ¨-e)** *m* (*Hülle*) covering; (*Comm*) ordering; (*Gehalt*) income, salary; (*Beziehung*): **~ (zu)** relationship (to); **in ~ auf** *+akk* with reference to; **mit** *od* **unter ~ auf** *+akk* regarding; (*form*) with reference to; **~ nehmen auf** *+akk* to refer to
bezüglich [bə'tsy:klɪç] *präp +gen* concerning, referring to ▷ *adj* concerning; (*Gram*) relative
Bezugnahme *f*: **~ (auf** *+akk***)** reference (to):
Bezugspreis *m* retail price
bezwecken [bə'tsvɛkən] *vt* to aim at
bezweifeln [bə'tsvaɪfəln] *vt* to doubt
BH (**-s, -(s)**) *m abk* (*= Büstenhalter*) bra
Bhf. *abk* = **Bahnhof**
Bibel ['bi:bəl] (**-, -n**) *f* Bible
Biber ['bi:bər] (**-s, -**) *m* beaver
Bibliothek [biblio'te:k] (**-, -en**) *f* (*auch Comput*) library
Bibliothekar, in [bibliote'ka:r(ɪn)] (**-s, -e**) *m(f)* librarian
bieder ['bi:dər] *adj* upright, worthy; (*pej*) conventional; (*Kleid etc*) plain
biegen ['bi:gən] *unreg vt, vr* to bend ▷ *vi* to turn; **sich vor Lachen ~** (*fig*) to double up with laughter; **auf B~ oder Brechen** (*umg*) by hook or by crook
Biegung *f* bend, curve
Biene ['bi:nə] (**-, -n**) *f* bee; (*veraltet: umg: Mädchen*) bird (*Brit*), chick (*bes US*); **Bienenwachs** *nt* beeswax
Bier [bi:r] **(-(e)s, -e)** *nt* beer; **zwei ~, bitte!** two beers, please
Bier- *zW*: **Bierbrauer** *m* brewer; **Bierdeckel** *m* beer mat
Biest [bi:st] **(-(e)s, -er)** (*pej: umg*) *nt* (*Mensch*) (little) wretch; (*Frau*) bitch (*!*)
bieten ['bi:tən] *unreg vt* to offer; (*bei Versteigerung*) to bid ▷ *vr* (*Gelegenheit*): **sich jdm ~** to present itself to sb; **sich** *dat* **etw ~ lassen** to put up with sth
Bigamie [biga'mi:] *f* bigamy
Bikini [bi'ki:ni] (**-s, -s**) *m* bikini
Bilanz [bi'lants] *f* balance; (*fig*) outcome; **eine ~ aufstellen** to draw up a balance sheet; **~ ziehen (aus)** to take stock (of)
bilateral ['bi:latera:l] *adj* bilateral; **~er Handel** bilateral trade; **~es Abkommen** bilateral agreement
Bild [bɪlt] **(-(e)s, -er)** *nt* (*lit, fig*) picture; photo;

(*Spiegelbild*) reflection; (*fig: Vorstellung*) image, picture; **ein ~ machen** to take a photo *od* picture; **im ~e sein (über** *+akk***)** to be in the picture (about)
bilden ['bɪldən] *vt* to form; (*erziehen*) to educate; (*ausmachen*) to constitute ▷ *vr* to arise; (*durch Lesen etc*) to improve one's mind; (*erziehen*) to educate o.s.
Bild- *zW*: **Bildfläche** *f* screen; (*fig*) scene; **von der Bildfläche verschwinden** (*fig: umg*) to disappear (from the scene); **Bildhauer** *m* sculptor; **bildhübsch** *adj* lovely, pretty as a picture; **bildlich** *adj* figurative; pictorial; **sich** *dat* **etw bildlich vorstellen** to picture sth in one's mind's eye; **Bildplatte** *f* videodisc; **Bildschirm** *m* (*TV, Comput*) screen; **Bildschirmgerät** *nt* (*Comput*) visual display unit, VDU; **Bildschirmschoner** (**-s, -**) *m* (*Comput*) screen saver; **Bildschirmtext** *m* teletext; ≈ Ceefax®, Oracle®; **bildschön** *adj* lovely
Bildtelefon *nt* videophone
Bildung ['bɪldʊŋ] *f* formation; (*Wissen, Benehmen*) education
Bildungs- *zW*: **Bildungslücke** *f* gap in one's education; **Bildungspolitik** *f* educational policy; **Bildungsurlaub** *m* educational holiday; **Bildungswesen** *nt* education system
Bildweite *f* (*Phot*) distance
Billard ['bɪljart] (**-s, -e**) *nt* billiards; **Billardball** *m* billiard ball
billig ['bɪlɪç] *adj* cheap; (*gerecht*) fair, reasonable; **~e Handelsflagge** flag of convenience; **~es Geld** cheap/easy money
billigen ['bɪlɪgən] *vt* to approve of; **etw stillschweigend ~** to condone sth
Billigung *f* approval
Billion [bɪli'o:n] *f* billion (*Brit*), trillion (*US*)
Bimsstein ['bɪmsʃtaɪn] *m* pumice stone
binär [bi'nɛ:r] *adj* binary
Binde ['bɪndə] (**-, -n**) *f* bandage; (*Armbinde*) band; (*Med*) sanitary towel (*Brit*) *od* napkin (*US*); **sich** *dat* **einen hinter die ~ gießen** *od* **kippen** (*umg*) to put a few drinks away; **Bindeglied** *nt* connecting link
binden *unreg vt* to bind, tie ▷ *vr* (*sich verpflichten*): **sich ~ (an** *+akk***)** to commit o.s. (to)
Bindestrich *m* hyphen
Bindfaden *m* string; **es regnet Bindfäden** (*umg*) it's sheeting down
Bindung *f* bond, tie; (*Ski*) binding; **Binnenhafen** *m* inland harbour (*Brit*) *od* harbor (*US*); **Binnenhandel** *m* internal trade; **Binnenmarkt** *m* home market; **Europäischer Binnenmarkt** single European market
Binse ['bɪnzə] (**-, -n**) *f* rush, reed; **in die ~n gehen** (*fig: umg*) to be a wash-out
Binsenwahrheit *f* truism
Biografie [biogra'fi:] *f* biography
Biologe [bio'lo:gə] (**-n, -n**) *m* biologist
Biologie [biolo'gi:] *f* biology
biologisch [bio'lo:gɪʃ] *adj* biological; **~e Vielfalt** biodiversity; **~e Uhr** biological clock
Bio- [bio-] *zW*: **Biosphäre** *f* biosphere; **Biotechnik** [bio'tɛçnɪk] *f* biotechnology; **Biotreibstoff** ['bi:otraipʃtɔf] *m* biofuel
Birke ['bɪrkə] (**-, -n**) *f* birch
Birma ['bɪrma] (**-s**) *nt* Burma
Birnbaum *m* pear tree
Birne ['bɪrnə] (**-, -n**) *f* pear; (*Elek*) (light) bulb
bis [bɪs] *adv, präp +akk* **1** (*zeitlich*) till, until; (*bis spätestens*) by; **Sie haben bis Dienstag Zeit** you have until *od* till Tuesday; **bis zum Wochenende** up to *od* until the weekend; (*spätestens*) by the weekend; **bis Dienstag muss es fertig sein** it must be ready by Tuesday; **bis wann ist das fertig?** when will that be finished?; **bis auf Weiteres** until further notice; **bis in die Nacht** into the night; **bis bald!/gleich!** see you later/soon
2 (*räumlich*) (up) to; **ich fahre bis Köln** I'm going as far as Cologne; **bis an unser Grundstück** (right *od* up) to our plot; **bis hierher** this far; **bis zur Straße kommen** to get as far as the road
3 (*bei Zahlen, Angaben*) up to; **bis zu** up to; **Gefängnis bis zu 8 Jahren** a maximum of 8 years' imprisonment
4: bis auf etw *akk* (*außer*) except sth; (*einschließlich*) including sth
▷ *konj* **1** (*mit Zahlen*) to; **10 bis 20** 10 to 20
2 (*zeitlich*) till, until; **bis es dunkel wird** till *od* until it gets dark; **von ... bis ...** from ... to ...
Bischof ['bɪʃɔf] (**-s, ¨-e**) *m* bishop
bischöflich ['bɪʃø:flɪç] *adj* episcopal
bisexuell [bizɛksu'ɛl] *adj* bisexual
bisher [bɪs'he:r] *adv* till now, hitherto
bisherig [bɪs'he:rɪç] *adj* till now
Biskaya [bɪs'ka:ya] *f*: **Golf von ~** Bay of Biscay
Biskuit [bɪs'kvi:t] (**-(e)s, -s** *od* **-e**) *m od nt* biscuit; **Biskuitteig** *m* sponge mixture
bislang [bɪs'laŋ] *adv* hitherto
Biss (**-es, -e**) *m* bite
biss *etc* [bɪs] *vb siehe* **beißen**
bisschen ['bɪsçən] *adj, adv* bit
Bissen ['bɪsən] (**-s, -**) *m* bite, morsel; **sich** *dat* **jeden ~ vom** *od* **am Munde absparen** to watch every penny one spends
bissig ['bɪsɪç] *adj* (*Hund*) snappy; vicious; (*Bemerkung*) cutting, biting; **„Vorsicht, ~er Hund"** "beware of the dog"
Bistum ['bɪstu:m] *nt* bishopric
bisweilen [bɪs'vaɪlən] *adv* at times, occasionally
Bit [bɪt] (**-(s), -(s)**) *nt* (*Comput*) bit
Bitte ['bɪtə] (**-, -n**) *f* request; **auf seine ~ hin** at his request; **bitte** *interj* please; (*als Antwort auf Dank*) you're welcome; **wie bitte?** (I beg your) pardon?; **bitte schön!** it was a pleasure; **bitte schön?** (*in Geschäft*) can I help you?; **na bitte!** there you are!

bitten *unreg vt* to ask ▷ *vi* (*einladen*): **ich lasse ~** would you ask him/her *etc* to come in now?; **~ um** to ask for; **aber ich bitte dich!** not at all; **ich bitte darum** (*form*) if you wouldn't mind; **ich muss doch (sehr) ~!** well I must say!

bittend *adj* pleading, imploring

bitter ['bɪtər] *adj* bitter; (*Schokolade*) plain; **etw ~ nötig haben** to be in dire need of sth; **bitterböse** *adj* very angry; **Bitterkeit** *f* bitterness; **bitterlich** *adj* bitter ▷ *adv* bitterly

Blabla [bla:'bla:] (**-s**) (*umg*) *nt* waffle

Blähungen *pl* (*Med*) wind *sing*

blamabel [bla'ma:bəl] *adj* disgraceful

Blamage [bla'ma:ʒə] (**-, -n**) *f* disgrace

blamieren [bla'mi:rən] *vr* to make a fool of o.s., disgrace o.s. ▷ *vt* to let down, disgrace

blank [blaŋk] *adj* bright; (*unbedeckt*) bare; (*sauber*) clean, polished; (*umg: ohne Geld*) broke; (*offensichtlich*) blatant

blanko ['blaŋko] *adv* blank; **Blankoscheck** *m* blank cheque (*Brit*) *od* check (*US*)

Bläschen ['blɛːsçən] *nt* bubble; (*Med*) small blister

Blase ['bla:zə] (**-, -n**) *f* bubble; (*Med*) blister; (*Anat*) bladder

Blasebalg *m* bellows *pl*

blasen *unreg vt, vi* to blow; **zum Aufbruch ~** (*fig*) to say it's time to go

blasiert [bla'zi:rt] (*pej*) *adj* (*geh*) blasé

Blas- *zW*: **Blasinstrument** *nt* wind instrument; **Blaskapelle** *f* brass band

blass [blas] *adj* pale; (*Ausdruck*) weak, insipid; (*fig: Ahnung, Vorstellung*) faint, vague; **~ vor Neid werden** to go green with envy

Blässe ['blɛsə] (**-**) *f* paleness, pallor

Blatt [blat] (**-(e)s, ¨er**) *nt* leaf; (*von Papier*) sheet; (*Zeitung*) newspaper; (*Karten*) hand; **vom ~ singen/spielen** to sight-read; **kein ~ vor den Mund nehmen** not to mince one's words

blättern ['blɛtərn] *vi*: **in etw** *dat* **~** to leaf through sth

Blätterteig *m* flaky *od* puff pastry

blau [blaʊ] *adj* blue; (*umg*) drunk, stoned; (*Koch*) boiled; (*Auge*) black; **~er Fleck** bruise; **mit einem ~en Auge davonkommen** (*fig*) to get off lightly; **~er Brief** (*Sch*) *letter telling parents a child may have to repeat a year*; **er wird sein ~es Wunder erleben** (*umg*) he won't know what's hit him

blau- *zW*: **Blauhelm** (*umg*) *m* UN Soldier; **Blaukraut** *nt* red cabbage; **blaumachen** (*umg*) *vi* to skive off work; **Blaustrumpf** *m* (*fig*) bluestocking

Blech [blɛç] (**-(e)s, -e**) *nt* tin, sheet metal; (*Backblech*) baking tray; **~ reden** (*umg*) to talk rubbish *od* nonsense; **Blechbüchse** *f* tin, can

Blechschaden *m* (*Aut*) damage to bodywork

Blei [blaɪ] (**-(e)s, -e**) *nt* lead

Bleibe (**-, -n**) *f* roof over one's head

bleiben *unreg vi* to stay, remain; **bitte, ~ Sie doch sitzen** please don't get up; **wo bleibst du so lange?** (*umg*) what's keeping you?; **das bleibt unter uns** (*fig*) that's (just) between ourselves; **~ lassen** (*aufgeben*) to give up; **etw ~ lassen** (*unterlassen*) to give sth a miss

bleich [blaɪç] *adj* faded, pale; **bleichen** *vt* to bleach

Blei- *zW*: **bleifrei** *adj* lead-free; **bleihaltig** *adj*: **bleihaltig sein** to contain lead; **Bleistift** *m* pencil; **Bleistiftspitzer** *m* pencil sharpener

Blende ['blɛndə] (**-, -n**) *f* (*Phot*) aperture; (*: Einstellungsposition*) f-stop

blenden *vt* to blind, dazzle; (*fig*) to hoodwink

blendend (*umg*) *adj* grand; **~ aussehen** to look smashing

Blick [blɪk] (**-(e)s, -e**) *m* (*kurz*) glance, glimpse; (*Anschauen*) look, gaze; (*Aussicht*) view; **Liebe auf den ersten ~** love at first sight; **den ~ senken** to look down; **den bösen ~ haben** to have the evil eye; **einen (guten) ~ für etw haben** to have an eye for sth; **mit einem ~** at a glance

blicken *vi* to look; **das lässt tief ~** that's very revealing; **sich ~ lassen** to put in an appearance

Blick- *zW*: **Blickfang** *m* eye-catcher; **Blickfeld** *nt* range of vision (*auch fig*)

blieb *etc* [bli:p] *vb siehe* **bleiben**

blies *etc* [bli:s] *vb siehe* **blasen**

blind [blɪnt] *adj* blind; (*Glas etc*) dull; (*Alarm*) false; **~er Passagier** stowaway

Blinddarm *m* appendix; **Blinddarmentzündung** *f* appendicitis

Blindenschrift *f* braille

Blind- *zW*: **Blindheit** *f* blindness; **mit Blindheit geschlagen sein** (*fig*) to be blind; **blindlings** *adv* blindly; **Blindschleiche** *f* slow worm; **blindschreiben** *unreg vi* to touch-type

blinken ['blɪŋkən] *vi* to twinkle, sparkle; (*Licht*) to flash, signal; (*Aut*) to indicate ▷ *vt* to flash, signal

Blinker (**-s, -**) *m* (*Aut*) indicator

blinzeln ['blɪntsəln] *vi* to blink, wink

Blitz [blɪts] (**-es, -e**) *m* (flash of) lightning; **wie ein ~ aus heiterem Himmel** (*fig*) like a bolt from the blue; **Blitzableiter** *m* lightning conductor; (*fig*) vent *od* safety valve for feelings; **blitzen** *vi* (*aufleuchten*) to glint, shine; **es blitzt** (*Met*) there's a flash of lightning; **Blitzlicht** *nt* flashlight; **blitzschnell** *adj, adv* as quick as a flash

Block [blɔk] (**-(e)s, ¨e**) *m* (*lit, fig*) block; (*von Papier*) pad; (*Pol: Staatenblock*) bloc; (*Fraktion*) faction

Blockade [blɔ'ka:də] (**-, -n**) *f* blockade

Block- *zW*: **Blockflöte** *f* recorder; **blockfrei** *adj* (*Pol*) non-aligned

blockieren [blɔ'ki:rən] *vt* to block ▷ *vi* (*Räder*) to jam

Blockschrift *f* block letters *pl*

blöd [blø:t] *adj* silly, stupid

blödeln ['blø:dəln] (*umg*) *vi* to fool around

Blödsinn *m* nonsense

blond [blɔnt] *adj* blond(e), fair-haired

bloß [blo:s] *adj* **1** (*unbedeckt*) bare; (*nackt*) naked; **mit der bloßen Hand** with one's bare hand; **mit bloßem Auge** with the naked eye
2 (*alleinig: nur*) mere; **der bloße Gedanke** the very thought; **bloßer Neid** sheer envy ▷ *adv* only, merely; **lass das bloß!** just don't do that!; **wie ist das bloß passiert?** how on earth did that happen?

blühen ['bly:ən] *vi* (*lit*) to bloom, be in bloom; (*fig*) to flourish; (*umg: bevorstehen*): **(jdm) ~** to be in store (for sb)

blühend *adj*: **wie das ~e Leben aussehen** to look the very picture of health

Blume ['blu:mə] (**-, -n**) *f* flower; (*von Wein*) bouquet; **jdm etw durch die ~ sagen** to say sth in a roundabout way to sb

Blumen- *zW*: **Blumenkohl** *m* cauliflower; **Blumentopf** *m* flowerpot; **Blumenzwiebel** *f* bulb

Bluse ['blu:zə] (**-, -n**) *f* blouse

Blut [blu:t] (**-(e)s**) *nt* (*lit, fig*) blood; **(nur) ruhig ~** keep your shirt on (*umg*); **jdn/sich bis aufs ~ bekämpfen** to fight sb/fight bitterly; **~ stillend** styptic; **blutbefleckt** *adj* bloodstained; **Blutbuche** *f* copper beech; **Blutdruck** *m* blood pressure

Blüte ['bly:tə] (**-, -n**) *f* blossom; (*fig*) prime

Blutegel ['blu:t|e:gəl] *m* leech

bluten *vi* to bleed

Blütenstaub *m* pollen

Bluter (**-s, -**) *m* (*Med*) haemophiliac (*Brit*), hemophiliac (*US*)

Bluterguss *m* haemorrhage (*Brit*), hemorrhage (*US*); (*auf Haut*) bruise

Blütezeit *f* flowering period; (*fig*) prime

Blutgruppe *f* blood group

blutig *adj* bloody; (*umg: Anfänger*) absolute; (*: Ernst*) deadly

Blut- *zW*: **blutjung** *adj* very young; **Blutkonserve** *f* unit *od* pint of stored blood; **Blutprobe** *f* blood test; **Blutspender** *m* blood donor

Blutung *f* bleeding, haemorrhage (*Brit*), hemorrhage (*US*)

Blut- *zW*: **Blutvergiftung** *f* blood poisoning; **Blutwurst** *f* black pudding; **Blutzuckerspiegel** *m* blood sugar level

BLZ *abk* = **Bankleitzahl**

Bock [bɔk] (**-(e)s, ¨-e**) *m* buck, ram; (*Gestell*) trestle, support; (*Sport*) buck; **alter ~** (*umg*) old goat; **den ~ zum Gärtner machen** (*fig*) to choose the worst possible person for the job; **einen ~ schießen** (*fig: umg*) to (make a) boob; **~ haben, etw zu tun** (*umg: Lust*) to fancy doing sth

Boden ['bo:dən] (**-s, ¨-**) *m* ground; (*Fußboden*) floor; (*Meeresboden, Fassboden*) bottom; (*Speicher*) attic; **den ~ unter den Füßen verlieren** (*lit*) to lose one's footing; (*fig: in Diskussion*) to get out of one's depth; **ich hätte (vor Scham) im ~ versinken können** (*fig*) I was so ashamed, I wished the ground would swallow me up; **am ~ zerstört sein** (*umg*) to be shattered; **etw aus dem ~ stampfen** (*fig*) to conjure sth up out of nothing; (*Häuser*) to build overnight; **auf dem ~ der Tatsachen bleiben** (*fig: Grundlage*) to stick to the facts; **zu ~ fallen** to fall to the ground; **festen ~ unter den Füßen haben** to be on firm ground, be on terra firma; **Bodenpersonal** *nt* (*Aviat*) ground personnel *pl*, ground staff; **Bodensatz** *m* dregs *pl*, sediment; **Bodenschätze** *pl* mineral wealth *sing*

Bodenturnen *nt* floor exercises *pl*

Böe (**-, -n**) *f* squall

bog *etc* [bo:k] *vb siehe* **biegen**

Bogen ['bo:gən] (**-s, -**) *m* (*Biegung*) curve; (*Archit*) arch; (*Waffe, Mus*) bow; (*Papier*) sheet; **den ~ heraushaben** (*umg*) to have got the hang of it; **einen großen ~ um jdn/etw machen** (*meiden*) to give sb/sth a wide berth; **jdn in hohem ~ hinauswerfen** (*umg*) to fling sb out; **Bogengang** *m* arcade

Böhmen (**-s**) *nt* Bohemia

Bohne ['bo:nə] (**-, -n**) *f* bean; **blaue ~** (*umg*) bullet; **nicht die ~** not one little bit

Bohnenkaffee *m* real coffee

bohren ['bo:rən] *vt* to bore; (*Loch*) to drill ▷ *vi* to drill; (*fig: drängen*) to keep on; (*peinigen: Schmerz, Zweifel etc*) to gnaw; **nach Öl/Wasser ~** drill for oil/water; **in der Nase ~** to pick one's nose

Bohrer (**-s, -**) *m* drill

Bohr- *zW*: **Bohrinsel** *f* oil rig; **Bohrmaschine** *f* drill; **Bohrturm** *m* derrick

Boiler ['bɔʏlər] (**-s, -**) *m* water heater

Boje ['bo:jə] (**-, -n**) *f* buoy

Bolivien [bo'li:viən] *nt* Bolivia

Bolzen ['bɔltsən] (**-s, -**) *m* bolt

bombardieren [bɔmbar'di:rən] *vt* to bombard; (*aus der Luft*) to bomb

Bombe ['bɔmbə] (**-, -n**) *f* bomb; **wie eine ~ einschlagen** to come as a (real) bombshell

Bomben- *zW*: **Bombenangriff** *m* bombing raid; **Bombenanschlag** *m* bomb attack; **Bombenerfolg** (*umg*) *m* huge success

Bonbon [bõ'bõ:] (**-s, -s**) *nt od m* sweet

Bonus ['bo:nʊs] (**-, -se**) *m* bonus

Boot [bo:t] (**-(e)s, -e**) *nt* boat

Bord [bɔrt] (**-(e)s, -e**) *m* (*Aviat, Naut*) board ▷ *nt* (*Brett*) shelf; **über ~ gehen** to go overboard; (*fig*) to go by the board; **an ~** on board

Bordell [bɔr'dɛl] (**-s, -e**) *nt* brothel

borgen ['bɔrgən] *vt* to borrow; **jdm etw ~** to lend sb sth

borniert [bɔr'ni:rt] *adj* narrow-minded

Börse ['bœ:rzə] (**-, -n**) *f* stock exchange; (*Geldbörse*) purse

Borste ['bɔrstə] (**-, -n**) *f* bristle

bös [bø:s] *adj* = **böse**; **bösartig** *adj* malicious; (*Med*) malignant

Böschung ['bœʃʊŋ] *f* slope; (*Uferböschung etc*) embankment

böse ['bø:zə] *adj* bad, evil; (*zornig*) angry; **das war nicht ~ gemeint** I/he *etc* didn't mean

it nastily
boshaft ['bo:shaft] *adj* malicious, spiteful
Bosheit *f* malice, spite
Bosnien ['bɔsniən] (**-s**) *nt* Bosnia
Bosnien-Herzegowina ['bɔsniənhɛrtsə'go:vi:na] (**-s**) *nt* Bosnia-Herzegovina
Bosnier, in (**-s, -**) *m(f)* Bosnian
bosnisch *adj* Bosnian
böswillig ['bø:svılıç] *adj* malicious
bot *etc* [bo:t] *vb siehe* **bieten**
Botanik [bo'ta:nık] *f* botany
botanisch [bo'ta:nıʃ] *adj* botanical
Bote ['bo:tə] (**-n, -n**) *m* messenger
Botenjunge *m* errand boy
Botin ['bo:tın] *f* messenger
Botschaft *f* message, news; (*Pol*) embassy; **die Frohe ~** the Gospel; **Botschafter** (**-s, -**) *m* ambassador
Bowle ['bo:lə] (**-, -n**) *f* punch
boxen *vi* to box
Boxer (**-s, -**) *m* boxer
Boxhandschuh *m* boxing glove
Boxkampf *m* boxing match
Boykott [bɔʏ'kɔt] (**-(e)s, -s**) *m* boycott
boykottieren [bɔʏkɔ'ti:rən] *vt* to boycott
brach *etc* [bra:x] *vb siehe* **brechen**
brachte *etc* ['braxtə] *vb siehe* **bringen**
Branche ['brɑ̃:ʃə] (**-, -n**) *f* line of business
Branchenverzeichnis *nt* trade directory
Brand [brant] (**-(e)s, ⸚e**) *m* fire; (*Med*) gangrene
branden ['brandən] *vi* to surge; (*Meer*) to break
Brandenburg ['brandənbʊrk] (**-s**) *nt* Brandenburg
brandmarken *vt* to brand; (*fig*) to stigmatize
Brand- *zW*: **Brandsalbe** *f* ointment for burns; **Brandstifter** *m* arsonist, fire-raiser; **Brandstiftung** *f* arson
Brandung *f* surf
Brandwunde *f* burn
brannte *etc* ['brantə] *vb siehe* **brennen**
Branntwein ['brantvaın] *m* brandy
Brasilianer, in [brazili'a:nər(ın)] (**-s, -**) *m(f)* Brazilian
brasilianisch *adj* Brazilian
Brasilien [bra'zi:liən] *nt* Brazil
Bratapfel *m* baked apple
braten ['bra:tən] *unreg vt* to roast; (*in Pfanne*) to fry; **Braten** (**-s, -**) *m* roast, joint; **den Braten riechen** (*umg*) to smell a rat, suss something
Brat- *zW*: **Brathähnchen** *nt* (*Südd, Österr*) roast chicken; **Bratkartoffeln** *pl* fried/roast potatoes *pl*
Bratsche ['bra:tʃə] (**-, -n**) *f* viola
Bratspieß *m* spit
Bratwurst *f* grilled sausage
Brauch [braʊx] (**-(e)s**, *pl* **Bräuche**) *m* custom
brauchbar *adj* usable, serviceable; (*Person*) capable
brauchen *vt* (*bedürfen*) to need; (*müssen*) to have to; (*verwenden*) to use; **wie lange braucht man, um ...?** how long does it take to ...?
Braue ['braʊə] (**-, -n**) *f* brow
brauen ['braʊən] *vt* to brew
Brauerei [braʊə'raı] *f* brewery
braun [braʊn] *adj* brown; (*von Sonne*) tanned; **~ gebrannt** tanned; (*pej*) Nazi
Bräune ['brɔʏnə] (**-, -n**) *f* brownness; (*Sonnenbräune*) tan
Brause ['braʊzə] (**-, -n**) *f* shower; (*von Gießkanne*) rose; (*Getränk*) lemonade
brausen *vi* to roar; (*auch vr: duschen*) to take a shower
Brausepulver *nt* lemonade powder
Braut [braʊt] (**-**, *pl* **Bräute**) *f* bride; (*Verlobte*) fiancée
Bräutigam ['brɔʏtıgam] (**-s, -e**) *m* bridegroom; (*Verlobter*) fiancé
Brautpaar *nt* bride and bridegroom, bridal pair
brav [bra:f] *adj* (*artig*) good; (*ehrenhaft*) worthy, honest; (*bieder: Frisur, Kleid*) plain; **sei schön ~!** be a good boy/girl
BRD (**-**) *f abk* (= *Bundesrepublik Deutschland*) FRG; **die alte ~** former West Germany
Brecheisen *nt* crowbar
brechen *unreg vt, vi* to break; (*Licht*) to refract; (*speien*) to vomit; **die Ehe ~** to commit adultery; **mir bricht das Herz** it breaks my heart; **~d voll sein** to be full to bursting
Brechreiz *m* nausea
Brei [braı] (**-(e)s, -e**) *m* (*Masse*) pulp; (*Koch*) gruel; (*Haferbrei*) porridge (*Brit*), oatmeal (*US*); (*für Kinder, Kranke*) mash; **um den heißen ~ herumreden** (*umg*) to beat about the bush
breit [braıt] *adj* broad; (*bei Maßangabe*) wide; **die ~e Masse** the masses *pl* ▷ *adv*: **ein ~ gefächertes Angebot** a wide range
Breite (**-, -n**) *f* breadth; (*bei Maßangabe*) width; (*Geog*) latitude
Breitengrad *m* degree of latitude
breit- *zW*: **breitmachen** *unreg* (*umg*) *vr* to spread o.s. out; **breittreten** *unreg* (*umg*) *vt* to go on about; **Breitwandfilm** *m* wide-screen film
Bremen ['bre:mən] (**-s**) *nt* Bremen
Bremsbelag *m* brake lining
Bremse ['brɛmzə] (**-, -n**) *f* brake; (*Zool*) horsefly
bremsen *vi* to brake, apply the brakes ▷ *vt* (*Auto*) to brake; (*fig*) to slow down ▷ *vr*: **ich kann mich ~** (*umg*) not likely!
Brems- *zW*: **Bremsflüssigkeit** *f* brake fluid; **Bremslicht** *nt* brake light; **Bremspedal** *nt* brake pedal; **Bremsschuh** *m* brake shoe; **Bremsspur** *f* tyre (*Brit*) *od* tire (*US*) marks *pl*; **Bremsweg** *m* braking distance
brennbar *adj* inflammable; **leicht ~** highly inflammable
Brennelement *nt* fuel element
brennen ['brɛnən] *unreg vi* to burn, be on fire; (*Licht, Kerze etc*) to burn ▷ *vt* (*Holz etc*) to burn; (*Ziegel, Ton*) to fire; (*Kaffee*) to roast;

(*Branntwein*) to distil; **wo brennts denn?** (*fig: umg*) what's the panic?; **darauf ~, etw zu tun** to be dying to do sth
Brenn- *zW*: **Brennmaterial** *nt* fuel; **Brennnessel** *f* nettle; **Brennpunkt** *m* (*Math, Optik*) focus; **Brennspiritus** *m* methylated spirits *pl*; **Brennstoff** *m* liquid fuel
Brett [brɛt] (**-(e)s, -er**) *nt* board, plank; (*Bord*) shelf; (*Spielbrett*) board; **Bretter** *pl* (*Ski*) skis *pl*; (*Theat*) boards *pl*; **Schwarzes ~** notice board; **er hat ein ~ vor dem Kopf** (*umg*) he's really thick
Bretterzaun *m* wooden fence
Brezel ['bre:tsəl] (**-, -n**) *f* pretzel
Brief [bri:f] (**-(e)s, -e**) *m* letter; **Brieffreund, in** *m(f)* pen friend, pen-pal; **Briefkasten** *m* letter box; (*Comput*) mailbox; **brieflich** *adj, adv* by letter; **Briefmarke** *f* postage stamp; **Briefpapier** *nt* notepaper; **Brieftasche** *f* wallet; **Briefträger** *m* postman; **Briefumschlag** *m* envelope; **Briefwechsel** *m* correspondence
briet *etc* [bri:t] *vb siehe* **braten**
Brikett [bri'kɛt] (**-s, -s**) *nt* briquette
brillant [brɪl'jant] *adj* (*fig*) sparkling, brilliant; **Brillant** (**-en, -en**) *m* brilliant, diamond
Brille ['brɪlə] (**-, -n**) *f* spectacles *pl*; (*Schutzbrille*) goggles *pl*; (*Toilettenbrille*) (toilet) seat
bringen ['brɪŋən] *unreg vt* to bring; (*mitnehmen, begleiten*) to take; (*einbringen: Profit*) to bring in; (*veröffentlichen*) to publish; (*Theat, Film*) to show; (*Rundf, TV*) to broadcast; (*in einen Zustand versetzen*) to get; (*umg: tun können*) to manage; **jdn dazu ~, etw zu tun** to make sb do sth; **jdn zum Lachen/Weinen ~** to make sb laugh/cry; **es weit ~** to do very well, get far; **jdn nach Hause ~** to take sb home; **jdn um etw ~** to make sb lose sth; **jdn auf eine Idee ~** to give sb an idea
Brise ['bri:zə] (**-, -n**) *f* breeze
Brite ['bri:tə] (**-n, -n**) *m* Briton, Britisher (*US*); **die ~n** the British
britisch ['bri:tɪʃ] *adj* British; **die B~en Inseln** the British Isles
Brocken ['brɔkən] (**-s, -**) *m* piece, bit; (*Felsbrocken*) lump of rock; **ein paar ~ Spanisch** a smattering of Spanish; **ein harter ~** (*umg*) a tough nut to crack
Brokat [bro'ka:t] (**-(e)s, -e**) *m* brocade
Brokkoli ['brɔkoli] *pl* broccoli
Brombeere ['brɔmbe:rə] *f* blackberry, bramble (*Brit*)
Bronchien ['brɔnçiən] *pl* bronchial tubes *pl*
Bronchitis [brɔn'çi:tɪs] (**-, -tiden**) *f* bronchitis
Bronze ['brõ:sə] (**-, -n**) *f* bronze
Brosame ['bro:za:mə] (**-, -n**) *f* crumb
Brosche ['brɔʃə] (**-, -n**) *f* brooch
Broschüre [brɔ'ʃy:rə] (**-, -n**) *f* pamphlet
Brot [bro:t] (**-(e)s, -e**) *nt* bread; (*Brotlaib*) loaf; **das ist ein hartes ~** (*fig*) that's a hard way to earn one's living
Brötchen ['brø:tçən] *nt* roll; **kleine ~ backen** (*fig*) to set one's sights lower
browsen ['brauzən] *vi* (*Comput*) to browse
Bruch [brʊx] (**-(e)s, ¨-e**) *m* breakage; (*zerbrochene Stelle*) break; (*fig*) split, breach; (*Med: Eingeweidebruch*) rupture, hernia; (*Beinbruch etc*) fracture; (*Math*) fraction; **zu ~ gehen** to get broken; **sich einen ~ heben** to rupture o.s.
brüchig ['brʏçɪç] *adj* brittle, fragile
Bruch- *zW*: **Bruchlandung** *f* crash landing; **Bruchstrich** *m* (*Math*) line; **Bruchstück** *nt* fragment; **Bruchteil** *m* fraction
Brücke ['brʏkə] (**-, -n**) *f* bridge; (*Teppich*) rug; (*Turnen*) crab
Bruder ['bru:dər] (**-s, ¨-**) *m* brother; **unter Brüdern** (*umg*) between friends
Brüderschaft *f* brotherhood, fellowship; **~ trinken** to agree to use the familiar "du" (*over a drink*)
Brühe ['bry:ə] (**-, -n**) *f* broth, stock; (*pej*) muck
Brühwürfel *m* stock cube (*Brit*), bouillon cube (*US*)
brüllen ['brʏlən] *vi* to bellow, roar
brummen *vi* (*Bär, Mensch etc*) to growl; (*Insekt, Radio*) to buzz; (*Motor*) to roar; (*murren*) to grumble ▷ *vt* to growl; **jdm brummt der Kopf** sb's head is buzzing
brünett [brʏ'nɛt] *adj* brunette, brown-haired
Brunnen ['brʊnən] (**-s, -**) *m* fountain; (*tief*) well; (*natürlich*) spring
brüsk [brʏsk] *adj* abrupt, brusque
Brüssel ['brʏsəl] (**-s**) *nt* Brussels
Brust [brʊst] (**-, ¨-e**) *f* breast; (*Männerbrust*) chest; **einem Kind die ~ geben** to breast-feed (*Brit*) *od* nurse (*US*) a baby
brüsten ['brʏstən] *vr* to boast
Brust- *zW*: **Brustfellentzündung** *f* pleurisy; **Brustkasten** *m* chest; **Brustschwimmen** *nt* breast-stroke
Brüstung ['brʏstʊŋ] *f* parapet
Brustwarze *f* nipple
brutal [bru'ta:l] *adj* brutal; **Brutalität** *f* brutality
Brutapparat *m* incubator
brüten ['bry:tən] *vi* (*auch fig*) to brood; **~de Hitze** oppressive *od* stifling heat
Brüter (**-s, -**) *m* (*Tech*): **Schneller ~** fast-breeder (reactor)
Brutkasten *m* incubator
brutto ['brʊto] *adv* gross; **Bruttoeinkommen** *nt* gross salary; **Bruttogewicht** *nt* gross weight; **Bruttoinlandsprodukt** *nt* gross domestic product; **Bruttolohn** *m* gross wages *pl*; **Bruttosozialprodukt** *nt* gross national product
Btx *abk* = **Bildschirmtext**
Buch [bu:x] (**-(e)s, ¨-er**) *nt* book; (*Comm*) account book; **er redet wie ein ~** (*umg*) he never stops talking; **ein ~ mit sieben Siegeln** (*fig*) a closed book; **über etw** *akk* **~ führen** to keep a record of sth; **zu ~(e) schlagen** to make a significant difference, tip the balance; **Buchbinder** *m* bookbinder; **Buchdrucker** *m* printer

Buche (**-, -n**) *f* beech tree
buchen *vt* to book; (*Betrag*) to enter; **etw als Erfolg ~** to put sth down as a success
Bücherbrett *nt* bookshelf
Bücherei [by:çə'raɪ] *f* library
Bücherregal *nt* bookshelves *pl*, bookcase
Bücherschrank *m* bookcase
Bücherwurm (*umg*) *m* bookworm
Buchfink ['bu:xfɪŋk] *m* chaffinch
Buch- *zW*: **Buchführung** *f* book-keeping, accounting; **Buchhalter, in** (**-s, -**) *m(f)* book-keeper; **Buchhandel** *m* book trade; **im Buchhandel erhältlich** available in bookshops; **Buchhändler, in** *m(f)* bookseller; **Buchhandlung** *f* bookshop
Büchse ['bʏksə] (**-, -n**) *f* tin, can; (*Holzbüchse*) box; (*Gewehr*) rifle
Büchsenfleisch *nt* tinned meat
Büchsenöffner *m* tin *od* can opener
Buchstabe (**-ns, -n**) *m* letter (of the alphabet)
buchstabieren [bu:xʃta'bi:rən] *vt* to spell
buchstäblich ['bu:xʃtɛ:plɪç] *adj* literal
Bucht ['bʊxt] (**-, -en**) *f* bay
Buchung ['bu:xʊŋ] *f* booking; (*Comm*) entry
Buckel ['bʊkəl] (**-s, -**) *m* hump; **er kann mir den ~ runterrutschen** (*umg*) he can (go and) take a running jump
bücken ['bʏkən] *vr* to bend; **sich nach etw ~** to bend down *od* stoop to pick sth up
Budget [bʏ'dʒe:] (**-s, -s**) *nt* budget
Büfett [bʏ'fɛt] (**-s, -s**) *nt* (*Anrichte*) sideboard; (*Geschirrschrank*) dresser; **kaltes ~** cold buffet
Büffel ['bʏfəl] (**-s, -**) *m* buffalo
Bügel ['by:gəl] (**-s, -**) *m* (*Kleiderbügel*) hanger; (*Steigbügel*) stirrup; (*Brillenbügel*) arm; **Bügelbrett** *nt* ironing board; **Bügeleisen** *nt* iron; **Bügelfalte** *f* crease
bügeln *vt, vi* to iron
Bühne ['by:nə] (**-, -n**) *f* stage
Bühnenbild *nt* set, scenery
Buhruf ['bu:ru:f] *m* boo
Bulette [bu'lɛtə] *f* meatball
Bulgare [bʊl'ga:rə] (**-n, -n**) *m* Bulgarian
Bulgarien (**-s**) *nt* Bulgaria
Bulgarin *f* Bulgarian
bulgarisch *adj* Bulgarian
Bulimie [bʊli'mi:] *f* (*Med*) bulimia
Bull- *zW*: **Bulldogge** *f* bulldog; **Bulldozer** ['bʊldo:zər] (**-s, -**) *m* bulldozer
Bulle (**-n, -n**) *m* b ıll; **die ~n** (*pej: umg*) the fuzz *sing*, the cops
Bummel ['bʊməl] (**-s, -**) *m* stroll; (*Schaufensterbummel*) window-shopping (expedition)
Bummelant [bʊmə'lant] *m* slowcoach
Bummelei [bʊmə'laɪ] *f* wandering; dawdling; skiving
bummeln *vi* to wander, stroll; (*trödeln*) to dawdle; (*faulenzen*) to skive (*Brit*), loaf around
Bummelstreik *m* go-slow (*Brit*), slowdown (*US*)
Bummelzug *m* slow train
bumsen ['bʊmzən] *vi* (*schlagen*) to thump; (*prallen, stoßen*) to bump, bang; (*umg: koitieren*) to bonk, have it off (*Brit*)
Bund[1] [bʊnt] (**-(e)s, ¨-e**) *m* (*Freundschaftsbund etc*) bond; (*Organisation*) union; (*Pol*) confederacy; (*Hosenbund, Rockbund*) waistband; **den ~ fürs Leben schließen** to take the marriage vows
Bund[2] [bʊnt] (**-(e)s, -e**) *nt* bunch; (*Strohbund*) bundle
Bündchen ['bʏntçən] *nt* ribbing; (*Ärmelbündchen*) cuff
Bündel (**-s, -**) *nt* bundle, bale
Bundes- ['bʊndəs] *in zw* Federal; **Bundesbürger** *m* German citizen; (*vor 1990*) West German citizen; **Bundeshauptstadt** *f* Federal capital; **Bundeskanzler** *m* Federal Chancellor
Bundes- *zW*: **Bundesland** *nt* state, Land; **Bundesliga** *f* (*Sport*) national league; **Bundesnachrichtendienst** *m* Federal Intelligence Service ▷ *m*; **Bundesregierung** *f* Federal Government; **Bundesrepublik** *f* Federal Republic (of Germany); **Bundesstaat** *m* Federal state; **Bundesstraße** *f* Federal Highway, main road ▷ *m*; **Bundestagswahl** *f* (Federal) parliamentary elections *pl*; **Bundesverfassungsgericht** *nt* Federal Constitutional Court; **Bundeswehr** *f* German *od* (*vor 1990*) West German Armed Forces *pl*
Bundfaltenhose *f* pleated trousers *pl*
bündig ['bʏndɪç] *adj* (*kurz*) concise
Bündnis ['bʏntnɪs] (**-ses, -se**) *nt* alliance
Bunker ['bʊŋkər] (**-s, -**) *m* bunker; (*Luftschutzbunker*) air-raid shelter
bunt [bʊnt] *adj* coloured (*Brit*), colored (*US*); (*gemischt*) mixed; **jdm wird es zu ~** it's getting too much for sb; **Buntstift** *m* coloured (*Brit*) *od* colored (*US*) pencil, crayon
Burg [bʊrk] (**-, -en**) *f* castle, fort
Bürge ['bʏrgə] (**-n, -n**) *m* guarantor
bürgen *vi* to vouch; **für jdn ~** (*fig*) to vouch for sb; (*Fin*) to stand surety for sb
Bürger, in (**-s, -**) *m(f)* citizen; member of the middle class; **Bürgerinitiative** *f* citizen's initiative; **Bürgerkrieg** *m* civil war; **bürgerlich** *adj* (*Rechte*) civil; (*Klasse*) middle-class; (*pej*) bourgeois; **bürgerliches Gesetzbuch** Civil Code; **Bürgermeister** *m* mayor; **Bürgerrecht** *nt* civil rights *pl*; **Bürgerschaft** *f* population, citizens *pl*; **Bürgerschaftswahl** *f* metropolitan council election; **Bürgersteig** *m* pavement (*Brit*), sidewalk (*US*); **Bürgertum** *nt* citizens *pl*
Bürgin *f* guarantor
Bürgschaft *f* surety; **~ leisten** to give security
Büro [by'ro:] (**-s, -s**) *nt* office; **Büroangestellte, r** *f(m)* office worker; **Büroklammer** *f* paper clip
Bürokrat [byro'kra:t] (**-en, -en**) *m* bureaucrat
Bürokratie [byrokra'ti:] *f* bureaucracy
bürokratisch *adj* bureaucratic
Büroschluss *m* office closing time

Bursche (**-n, -n**) *m* lad, fellow; (*Diener*) servant
burschikos [bʊrʃi'ko:s] *adj* (*jungenhaft*) (tom)boyish; (*unbekümmert*) casual
Bürste ['bʏrstə] (**-, -n**) *f* brush
bürsten *vt* to brush
Bus [bʊs] (**-ses, -se**) *m* bus
Busch [bʊʃ] (**-(e)s, ¨-e**) *m* bush, shrub; **bei jdm auf den ~ klopfen** (*umg*) to sound sb out
Büschel ['bʏʃəl] (**-s, -**) *nt* tuft
Busen ['bu:zən] (**-s, -**) *m* bosom; (*Meerbusen*) inlet, bay
Bussard ['bʊsart] (**-s, -e**) *m* buzzard
Buße ['bu:sə] (**-, -n**) *f* atonement, penance; (*Geld*) fine
büßen ['by:sən] *vi* to do penance, atone ▷ *vt* to atone for
Bußgeld *nt* fine
Büste ['bʏstə] (**-, -n**) *f* bust
Büstenhalter *m* bra
Butan [bu'ta:n] (**-s**) *nt* butane
Butter ['bʊtər] (**-**) *f* butter; **alles (ist) in ~** (*umg*) everything is fine *od* hunky-dory; **Butterberg** (*umg*) *m* butter mountain; **Butterblume** *f* buttercup; **Butterbrot** *nt* (piece of) bread and butter; **Butterbrotpapier** *nt* greaseproof paper; **Butterdose** *f* butter dish; **Buttermilch** *f* buttermilk; **butterweich** *adj* soft as butter; (*fig: umg*) soft
b. w. *abk* (= *bitte wenden*) p.t.o.
Byte [baɪt] (**-s, -s**) *nt* (*Comput*) byte
bzgl. *abk* (= *bezüglich*) re.
bzw. *abk* = **beziehungsweise**

Cc

C[1], **c** [tseː] *nt* C, c; **C wie Cäsar** ≈ C for Charlie
C[2] [tseː] *abk* (= *Celsius*) C
Café [ka'feː] (**-s, -s**) *nt* café
Cafeteria [kafete'riːa] (**-, -s**) *f* cafeteria
Callcenter ['kɔːlsɛntər] *nt* call centre (*Brit*), call center (*US*)
Camcorder (**-s, -**) *m* camcorder
Camper, in (**-s, -**) *m(f)* camper
Camping ['kɛmpɪŋ] (**-s**) *nt* camping; **Campingbus** *m* camper; **Campingplatz** *m* camp(ing) site
Caravan ['karavan] (**-s, -s**) *m* caravan
Cäsium ['tsɛːziʊm] *nt* caesium (*Brit*), cesium (*US*)
CD *f abk* (= *Compact Disc*) CD; **CD-Brenner** *m* CD burner; **CD-ROM** (**-, -s**) *f* CD-ROM; **CD-Spieler** *m* CD player
CDU [tseːdeː'|uː] (**-**) *f abk* (= *Christlich-Demokratische Union (Deutschlands)*) Christian Democratic Union
Cellist, in [tʃɛ'lɪst(ɪn)] *m(f)* cellist
Cello ['tʃɛlo] (**-s, -s** *od* **Celli**) *nt* cello
Celsius ['tsɛlziʊs] *m* Celsius
Cent [(t)sɛnt] (**-(s), -(s)**) *m* cent
Chamäleon [ka'mɛːleɔn] (**-s, -s**) *nt* chameleon
Champagner [ʃam'panjər] (**-s, -**) *m* champagne
Champignon ['ʃampɪnjõ] (**-s, -s**) *m* button mushroom
Chance ['ʃãːs(ə)] (**-, -n**) *f* chance, opportunity
Chaos ['kaːɔs] (**-**) *nt* chaos
Chaot, in [ka'oːt(ɪn)] (**-en, -en**) *m(f)* (*Pol: pej*) anarchist (*pej*)
chaotisch [ka'oːtɪʃ] *adj* chaotic
Charakter [ka'raktər] (**-s, -e**) *m* character; **charakterfest** *adj* of firm character
charakterisieren [karakteri'ziːrən] *vt* to characterize
Charakteristik [karakte'rɪstɪk] *f* characterization
charakteristisch [karakte'rɪstɪʃ] *adj*: **~ (für)** characteristic (of), typical (of)
Charakter- *zW*: **charakterlos** *adj* unprincipled; **Charakterschwäche** *f* weakness of character; **Charakterstärke** *f* strength of character; **Charakterzug** *m* characteristic, trait
charmant [ʃar'mant] *adj* charming
Charme [ʃarm] (**-s**) *m* charm
Charterflug ['tʃartərfluːk] *m* charter flight
Chassis [ʃa'siː] (**-, -**) *nt* chassis
Chatroom ['tʃɛtruːm] *m* (*Comput*) chatroom
Chauffeur [ʃɔ'føːr] *m* chauffeur
Chauvi ['ʃovi] (**-s, -s**) (*umg*) *m* male chauvinist
Chauvinismus [ʃovi'nɪsmʊs] *m* chauvinism
Chauvinist [ʃovi'nɪst] *m* chauvinist
checken ['tʃɛkən] *vt* (*überprüfen*) to check; (*umg: verstehen*) to get
Chef, in [ʃɛf(ɪn)] (**-s, -s**) *m(f)* head; (*umg*) boss; **Chefarzt** *m* senior consultant; **Chefredakteur** *m* editor-in-chief
Chemie [çe'miː] (**-**) *f* chemistry; **Chemiefaser** *f* man-made fibre (*Brit*) *od* fiber (*US*)
Chemikalie [çemi'kaːliə] *f* chemical
Chemiker, in ['çeːmikər(ɪn)] (**-s, -**) *m(f)* (industrial) chemist
chemisch ['çeːmɪʃ] *adj* chemical; **~e Reinigung** dry cleaning
Chemotherapie [çemotera'piː] *f* chemotherapy
Chicorée [ʃiko'reː] (**-s**) *f od m* chicory
Chiffre ['ʃɪfrə] (**-, -n**) *f* (*Geheimzeichen*) cipher; (*in Zeitung*) box number
Chiffriermaschine [ʃɪ'friːrmaʃiːnə] *f* cipher machine
Chile ['tʃiːle] (**-s**) *nt* Chile
Chilene [tʃi'leːnə] (**-n, -n**) *m* Chilean
chilenisch *adj* Chilean
China ['çiːna] (**-s**) *nt* China
Chinese [çi'neːzə] (**-n, -n**) *m* Chinaman, Chinese
chinesisch *adj* Chinese
Chinin [çi'niːn] (**-s**) *nt* quinine
Chipkarte ['tʃɪpkartə] *f* smart card
Chips [tʃɪps] *pl* crisps *pl* (*Brit*), chips *pl* (*US*)
Chirurg, in [çi'rʊrg(ɪn)] (**-en, -en**) *m(f)* surgeon
Chirurgie [çirʊr'giː] *f* surgery
chirurgisch *adj* surgical; **ein ~er Eingriff** surgery
Chlor [kloːr] (**-s**) *nt* chlorine
Chloroform [kloro'fɔrm] (**-s**) *nt* chloroform
Chlorophyll [kloro'fʏl] (**-s**) *nt* chlorophyll
Cholera ['koːlera] (**-**) *f* cholera
cholerisch [ko'leːrɪʃ] *adj* choleric
Cholesterin [kolɛste'riːn] (**-s**) *nt* cholesterol
Chor [koːr] (**-(e)s, ⸚e**) *m* choir; (*Musikstück,*

Theat) chorus
Choreograf, in [koreo'gra:f(ɪn)] (**-en, -en**) *m(f)* choreographer
Choreografie [koreogra'fi:] *f* choreography
Chorgestühl *nt* choir stalls *pl*
Chorknabe *m* choirboy
Christ [krɪst] (**-en, -en**) *m* Christian
Christenheit *f* Christendom
Christentum (**-s**) *nt* Christianity
Christkind *nt* ≈ Father Christmas; (*Jesus*) baby Jesus
christlich *adj* Christian; **C~er Verein Junger Männer** Young Men's Christian Association
Christus (**Christi**) *m* Christ; **Christi Himmelfahrt** Ascension Day
Chrom [kro:m] (**-s**) *nt* (*Chem*) chromium; chrome
Chromosom [kromo'zo:m] (**-s, -en**) *nt* (*Biol*) chromosome
Chronik ['kro:nɪk] *f* chronicle
chronisch *adj* chronic
Chronologie [kronolo'gi:] *f* chronology
chronologisch *adj* chronological
Chrysantheme [kryzan'te:mə] (**-, -n**) *f* chrysanthemum
circa ['tsɪrka] *adv* (round) about
clever ['klɛvər] *adj* clever; (*gerissen*) crafty
Clique ['klɪkə] (**-, -n**) *f* set, crowd
Clou [klu:] (**-s, -s**) *m* (*von Geschichte*) (whole) point; (*von Show*) highlight, high spot
Clown [klaʊn] (**-s, -s**) *m* clown
Cocktail ['kɔkte:l] (**-s, -s**) *m* cocktail
Code [ko:t] (**-s, -s**) *m* code
Cola ['ko:la] (**-(s), -s**) *nt od f* Coke®
Computer [kɔm'pju:tər] (**-s, -**) *m* computer; **computergestützt** *adj* computer-based; **computergestütztes Design** computer-aided design; **Computerspiel** *nt* computer game
Conférencier [kõferãsi'e:] (**-s, -s**) *m* compère
Container [kɔn'te:nər] (**-s, -**) *m* container
cool [ku:l] (*umg*) *adj* (*gefasst*) cool
Couch [kaʊtʃ] (**-, -es** *od* **-en**) *f* couch
Coupé [ku'pe:] (**-s, -s**) *nt* (*Aut*) coupé, sports version
Coupon [ku'põ:, ku'pɔŋ] (**-s, -s**) *m* coupon, voucher; (*Stoffcoupon*) length of cloth
Cousin [ku'zɛ̃:] (**-s, -s**) *m* cousin
Crack [krɛk] (**-**) *nt* (*Droge*) crack
Creme [krɛ:m] (**-, -s**) *f* (*lit, fig*) cream; (*Schuhcreme*) polish; (*Koch*) mousse; **cremefarben** *adj* cream(-coloured (*Brit*) *od* -colored (*US*))
CSU [tse:|ɛs'|u:] (**-**) *f abk* (= *Christlich-Soziale Union*) Christian Social Union
Currywurst *f* curried sausage
Cursor ['kø:rsər] (**-s**) *m* (*Comput*) cursor; **Cursortaste** *f* cursor key
Cutter, in ['katər(ɪn)] (**-s, -**) *m(f)* (*Film*) editor

Dd

D, d [deː] *nt* D, d; **D wie Dora** ≈ D for David, ≈ D for Dog (*US*)

da [daː] *adv* **1** (*örtlich*) there; (*hier*) here; **da draußen** out there; **da sein** to be there; **ein Arzt, der immer für seine Patienten da ist** a doctor who always has time for his patients; **da bin ich** here I am; **da hast du dein Geld** (there you are,) there's your money; **da, wo** where; **ist noch Milch da?** is there any milk left?
2 (*zeitlich*) then; (*folglich*) so; **es war niemand im Zimmer, da habe ich ...** there was nobody in the room, so I ...
3: **da haben wir Glück gehabt** we were lucky there; **was gibts denn da zu lachen?** what's so funny about that?; **da kann man nichts machen** there's nothing one can do (in a case like that)
▷ *konj* (*weil*) as, since

dabehalten *unreg vt* to keep

dabei [da'baɪ] *adv* (*räumlich*) close to it; (*noch dazu*) besides; (*zusammen mit*) with them/it *etc*; (*zeitlich*) during this; (*obwohl doch*) but, however; **~ sein** (*anwesend*) to be present; (*beteiligt*) to be involved; **ich bin ~!** count me in!; **was ist schon ~?** what of it?; **es ist doch nichts ~, wenn ...** it doesn't matter if ...; **bleiben wir ~** let's leave it at that; **es soll nicht ~ bleiben** this isn't the end of it; **es bleibt ~** that's settled; **das Dumme/Schwierige ~** the stupid/difficult part of it; **er war gerade ~ zu gehen** he was just leaving; **hast du ~ etwas gelernt?** did you learn anything from it?; **~ darf man nicht vergessen, dass ...** it shouldn't be forgotten that ...; **die ~ entstehenden Kosten** the expenses arising from this; **es kommt doch nichts ~ heraus** nothing will come of it; **ich finde gar nichts ~** I don't see any harm in it; **dabeistehen** *unreg vi* to stand around

Dach [dax] **(-(e)s, ¨-er)** *nt* roof; **unter ~ und Fach sein** (*abgeschlossen*) to be in the bag (*umg*); (*Vertrag, Geschäft*) to be signed and sealed; (*in Sicherheit*) to be safe; **jdm eins aufs ~ geben** (*umg*: *ausschimpfen*) to give sb a (good) talking to; **Dachboden** *m* attic, loft; **Dachdecker** **(-s, -)** *m* slater, tiler; **Dachfenster** *nt* skylight; (*ausgestellt*) dormer window; **Dachluke** *f* skylight; **Dachpappe** *f* roofing felt; **Dachrinne** *f* gutter

Dachs [daks] **(-es, -e)** *m* badger

Dachziegel *m* roof tile

Dackel ['dakəl] **(-s, -)** *m* dachshund

dadurch [da'dʊrç] *adv* (*räumlich*) through it; (*durch diesen Umstand*) thereby, in that way; (*deshalb*) because of that, for that reason
▷ *konj*: **~, dass** because

dafür [da'fyːr] *adv* for it; (*anstatt*) instead; (*zum Ausgleich*): **in Latein ist er schlecht, ~ kann er gut Fußball spielen** he's bad at Latin but he makes up for it at football; **er ist bekannt ~** he is well-known for that; **was bekomme ich ~?** what will I get for it?; **~ ist er immer zu haben** he never says no to that; **~ bin ich ja hier** that's what I'm here for; **er kann nichts ~ (, dass ...)** he can't help it (that ...)

dagegen [da'geːgən] *adv* against it; (*im Vergleich damit*) in comparison with it; (*bei Tausch*) for it ▷ *konj* however; **haben Sie etwas ~, wenn ich rauche?** do you mind if I smoke?; **ich habe nichts ~** I don't mind; **ich war ~** I was against it; **ich hätte nichts ~ (einzuwenden)** that's okay by me; **~ kann man nichts tun** one can't do anything about it; **dagegenhalten** *unreg vt* (*vergleichen*) to compare with it; (*entgegnen*) to put forward as an objection

daheim [da'haɪm] *adv* at home; **bei uns ~** back home; **Daheim** **(-s)** *nt* home

daher [da'heːr] *adv* (*räumlich*) from there; (*Ursache*) from that ▷ *konj* (*deshalb*) that's why; **das kommt ~, dass ...** that is because ...; **~ kommt er auch** that's where he comes from too; **~ die Schwierigkeiten** that's what is causing the difficulties

dahin [da'hɪn] *adv* (*räumlich*) there; (*zeitlich*) then; (*vergangen*) gone; **ist es noch weit bis ~?** is there still far to go?; **~ gehend** on this matter; **das tendiert ~** it is tending towards that; **er bringt es noch ~, dass ich ...** he'll make me ...; **dahingegen** *konj* on the other hand; **dahingestellt** *adv*: **dahingestellt bleiben** to remain to be seen; **etw dahingestellt sein lassen** to leave sth open *od* undecided

dahinten [da'hɪntən] *adv* over there

dahinter [da'hɪntər] *adv* behind it; **sich ~**

klemmen *od* **knien** (*umg*) to put one's back into it; **~ kommen** (*umg*) to find out

Dahlie ['da:liə] (**-, -n**) *f* dahlia

dalassen ['da:lasən] *unreg vt* to leave (behind)

damals ['da:ma:ls] *adv* at that time, then

Dame ['da:mə] (**-, -n**) *f* lady; (*Schach, Karten*) queen; (*Spiel*) draughts (*Brit*), checkers (*US*)

Damenbinde *f* sanitary towel (*Brit*) *od* napkin (*US*)

Damespiel *nt* draughts (*Brit*), checkers (*US*)

damit [da'mɪt] *adv* with it; (*begründend*) by that ▷ *konj* in order that *od* to; **was meint er ~?** what does he mean by that?; **was soll ich ~?** what am I meant to do with that?; **muss er denn immer wieder ~ ankommen?** must he keep on about it?; **was ist ~?** what about it?; **genug ~!** that's enough!; **~ basta!** and that's that!; **~ eilt es nicht** there's no hurry

Damm [dam] (**-(e)s, ⸚e**) *m* dyke (*Brit*), dike (*US*); (*Staudamm*) dam; (*Hafendamm*) mole; (*Bahndamm, Straßendamm*) embankment

dämmerig *adj* dim, faint

Dämmerung *f* twilight; (*Morgendämmerung*) dawn; (*Abenddämmerung*) dusk

dämonisch [dɛ'mo:nɪʃ] *adj* demonic

Dampf [dampf] (**-(e)s, ⸚e**) *m* steam; (*Dunst*) vapour (*Brit*), vapor (*US*); **jdm ~ machen** (*umg*) to make sb get a move on; **~ ablassen** (*lit, fig*) to let off steam; **dampfen** *vi* to steam

dämpfen ['dɛmpfən] *vt* (*Koch*) to steam; (*bügeln*) to iron with a damp cloth; (*mit Dampfbügeleisen*) to steam iron; (*fig*) to dampen, subdue

Dampfer ['dampfər] (**-s, -**) *m* steamer; **auf dem falschen ~ sein** (*fig*) to have got the wrong idea

Dampf- *zW*: **Dampfkochtopf** *m* pressure cooker; **Dampfschiff** *nt* steamship; **Dampfwalze** *f* steamroller

danach [da'na:x] *adv* after that; (*zeitlich*) afterwards; (*gemäß*) accordingly; (*laut diesem*) according to which *od* that; **mir war nicht ~ (zumute)** I didn't feel like it; **er griff schnell ~** he grabbed at it; **~ kann man nicht gehen** you can't go by that; **er sieht ~ aus** he looks it

Däne ['dɛ:nə] (**-n, -n**) *m* Dane, Danish man/boy

daneben [da'ne:bən] *adv* beside it; (*im Vergleich*) in comparison; **~ sein** (*umg: verwirrt sein*) to be completely confused; **danebengehen** *unreg vi* to miss; (*Plan*) to fail

Dänemark ['dɛ:nəmark] (**-s**) *nt* Denmark

Dänin ['dɛ:nɪn] *f* Dane, Danish woman *od* girl

dänisch *adj* Danish

Dank [daŋk] (**-(e)s**) *m* thanks *pl*; **vielen** *od* **schönen ~** many thanks; **jdm ~ sagen** to thank sb; **mit (bestem) ~ zurück!** many thanks for the loan; **dank** *präp* (*+dat od gen*) thanks to; **dankbar** *adj* grateful; (*Aufgabe*) rewarding; (*haltbar*) hard-wearing; **Dankbarkeit** *f* gratitude

danke *interj* thank you, thanks

danken *vi +dat* to thank; **nichts zu ~!** don't mention it; **~d erhalten/ablehnen** to receive/decline with thanks

dann [dan] *adv* then; **~ und wann** now and then; **~ eben nicht** well, in that case (there's no more to be said); **erst ~, wenn ...** only when ...; **~ erst recht nicht!** in that case no way (*umg*)

daran [da'ran] *adv* on it; (*stoßen*) against it; **es liegt ~, dass ...** the cause of it is that ...; **gut/schlecht ~ sein** to be well/badly off; **das Beste/Dümmste ~** the best/stupidest thing about it; **ich war nahe ~, zu ...** I was on the point of ...; **im Anschluss ~** (*zeitlich: danach anschließend*) following that *od* this; **wir können nichts ~ machen** we can't do anything about it; **es ist nichts ~** (*ist nicht fundiert*) there's nothing in it; (*ist nichts Besonderes*) it's nothing special; **er ist ~ gestorben** he died from *od* of it: **darangehen** *unreg vi* to start; **daransetzen** *vt* to stake; **er hat alles darangesetzt, von Glasgow wegzukommen** he has done his utmost to get away from Glasgow

darauf [da'raʊf] *adv* (*räumlich*) on it; (*zielgerichtet*) towards it; (*danach*) afterwards; **~ folgend** following; **es kommt ganz ~ an, ob ...** it depends whether ...; **seine Behauptungen stützen sich ~, dass ...** his claims are based on the supposition that ...; **wie kommst du ~?** what makes you think that?; **die Tage ~** the days following *od* thereafter; **am Tag ~** the next day

daraus [da'raʊs] *adv* from it; **was ist ~ geworden?** what became of it?; **~ geht hervor, dass ...** this means that ...

Darbietung *f* performance

darin [da'rɪn] *adv* in (there), in it; **der Unterschied liegt ~, dass ...** the difference is that ...

darlegen ['da:rle:gən] *vt* to explain, expound, set forth

Darm [darm] (**-(e)s, ⸚e**) *m* intestine; (*Wurstdarm*) skin; **Darmsaite** *f* gut string

darstellen ['da:rʃtɛlən] *vt* (*abbilden, bedeuten*) to represent; (*Theat*) to act; (*beschreiben*) to describe ▷ *vr* to appear to be

Darsteller, in (**-s, -**) *m(f)* actor, actress

Darstellung *f* portrayal, depiction

darüber [da'ry:bər] *adv* (*räumlich*) over/above it; (*fahren*) over it; (*mehr*) more; (*währenddessen*) meanwhile; (*sprechen, streiten*) about it; **~ hinweg sein** (*fig*) to have got over it; **~ hinaus** over and above that; **~ geht nichts** there's nothing like it; **seine Gedanken ~** his thoughts about *od* on it; **~ liegen** (*fig*) to be higher

darum [da'rʊm] *adv* (*räumlich*) round it ▷ *konj* that's why; **~ herum** round about (it); **er bittet ~** he is pleading for it; **es geht ~, dass ...** the thing is that ...; **~ geht es mir/geht es mir nicht** that's my point/that's not the point for me; **er würde viel ~ geben, wenn ...** he would give a lot to ...; *siehe auch* **drum**

darunter [da'rʊntər] *adv (räumlich)* under it; *(dazwischen)* among them; *(weniger)* less; **ein Stockwerk ~** one floor below (it); **was verstehen Sie ~?** what do you understand by that?; **~ kann ich mir nichts vorstellen** that doesn't mean anything to me; **~ fallen** to be included; **~ mischen** *(Mehl)* to mix in; **sich ~ mischen** to mingle; **~ setzen** *(Unterschrift)* to put to it

das [das] *pron* that ▷ *def art* the; *siehe auch* **der**; **~ heißt** that is; **~ und das** such and such

Dasein ['da:zaɪn] **(-s)** *nt (Leben)* life; *(Anwesenheit)* presence; *(Bestehen)* existence

da sein *unreg vi siehe* **da**

dass [das] *konj* that

dasselbe [das'zɛlbə] *nt pron* the same

dastehen ['da:ʃte:ən] *unreg vi* to stand there; *(fig)*: **gut/schlecht ~** to be in a good/bad position; **allein ~** to be on one's own

Datei [da'taɪ] *f (Comput)* file; **Dateimanager** *m* file manager; **Dateiname** *m* file name

Daten ['da:tən] *pl (Comput)* data; *(Angaben)* data *pl*, particulars; *siehe auch* **Datum**; **Datenautobahn** *f* information (super)highway; **Datenbank** *f* database; **Datenerfassung** *f* data capture; **Datenschutz** *m* data protection; **Datenträger** *m* data carrier; **Datenübertragung** *f* data transmission; **Datenverarbeitung** *f* data processing

datieren [da'ti:rən] *vt* to date

Dativ ['da:ti:f] **(-s, -e)** *m* dative

Dattel ['datəl] **(-, -n)** *f* date

Datum ['da:tʊm] **(-s, Daten)** *nt* date; **das heutige ~** today's date

Dauer ['daʊər] **(-, -n)** *f* duration; *(gewisse Zeitspanne)* length; *(Bestand, Fortbestehen)* permanence; **es war nur von kurzer ~** it didn't last long; **auf die ~** in the long run; *(auf längere Zeit)* indefinitely; **Dauerauftrag** *m* standing order; **dauerhaft** *adj* lasting, durable; **Dauerkarte** *f* season ticket

dauern *vi* to last; **es hat sehr lang gedauert, bis er ...** it took him a long time to ...

dauernd *adj* constant

Dauer- *zW*: **Dauerwelle** *f* perm, permanent wave; **Dauerwurst** *f* German salami; **Dauerzustand** *m* permanent condition

Daumen ['daʊmən] **(-s, -)** *m* thumb; **jdm die ~ drücken** *od* **halten** to keep one's fingers crossed for sb; **über den ~ peilen** to guess roughly

Daune ['daʊnə] **(-, -n)** *f* down

Daunendecke *f* down duvet

davon [da'fɔn] *adv* of it; *(räumlich)* away; *(weg von)* away from it; *(Grund)* because of it; *(mit Passiv)* by it; **das kommt ~!** that's what you get; **~ abgesehen** apart from that; **wenn wir einmal ~ absehen, dass ...** if for once we overlook the fact that ...; **~ sprechen/wissen** to talk/know of *od* about it; **was habe ich ~?** what's the point?; **~ betroffen werden** to be affected by it; **davonlaufen** *unreg vi* to run away

davor [da'fo:r] *adv (räumlich)* in front of it; *(zeitlich)* before (that); **~ warnen** to warn about it

dazu [da'tsu:] *adv (legen, stellen)* by it; *(essen)* with it; **und ~ noch** and in addition; **ein Beispiel/seine Gedanken ~** one example for/his thoughts on this; **wie komme ich denn ~?** why should I?; **... aber ich bin nicht ~ gekommen** ... but I didn't get around to it; **das Recht ~** the right to do it; **~ bereit sein, etw zu tun** to be prepared to do sth; **~ fähig sein** to be capable of it; **sich ~ äußern** to say something on it; **dazugehören** *vi* to belong to it; **das gehört dazu** *(versteht sich von selbst)* it's all part of it; **es gehört schon einiges dazu, das zu tun** it takes a lot to do that; **dazukommen** *unreg vi (Ereignisse)* to happen too; *(an einen Ort)* to come along; **kommt noch etwas dazu?** will there be anything else?

dazwischen [da'tsvɪʃən] *adv* in between; *(zusammen mit)* among them; **der Unterschied ~** the difference between them; **dazwischenkommen** *unreg vi (hineingeraten)* to get caught in it; **es ist etwas dazwischengekommen** something (has) cropped up; **dazwischenreden** *vi (unterbrechen)* to interrupt; *(sich einmischen)* to interfere; **dazwischentreten** *unreg vi* to intervene

DDR (-) *f abk (früher: = Deutsche Demokratische Republik)* GDR

Dealer, in ['di:lər(ɪn)] **(-s, -)** *(umg) m(f)* pusher

Debatte [de'batə] **(-, -n)** *f* debate; **das steht hier nicht zur ~** that's not the issue

Deck [dɛk] **(-(e)s, -s** *od* **-e)** *nt* deck; **an ~ gehen** to go on deck

Deckblatt *nt (Schutzblatt)* cover

Decke **(-, -n)** *f* cover; *(Bettdecke)* blanket; *(Tischdecke)* tablecloth; *(Zimmerdecke)* ceiling; **unter einer ~ stecken** to be hand in glove; **an die ~ gehen** to hit the roof; **mir fällt die ~ auf den Kopf** *(fig)* I feel really claustrophobic

Deckel **(-s, -)** *m* lid; **du kriegst gleich eins auf den ~** *(umg)* you're going to catch it

decken *vt* to cover ▷ *vr* to coincide ▷ *vi* to lay the table; **mein Bedarf ist gedeckt** I have all I need; *(fig)* I've had enough; **sich an einen gedeckten Tisch setzen** *(fig)* to be handed everything on a plate

Deckung *f (das Schützen)* covering; *(Schutz)* cover; *(Sport)* defence *(Brit)*, defense *(US)*; *(Übereinstimmen)* agreement; **zur ~ seiner Schulden** to meet his debts

deckungsgleich *adj* congruent

Decoder *m (TV)* decoder

Defekt [de'fɛkt] **(-(e)s, -e)** *m* fault, defect; **defekt** *adj* faulty

defensiv [defɛn'si:f] *adj* defensive
Definition [definitsi'o:n] *f* definition
Defizit ['de:fitsɪt] (**-s, -e**) *nt* deficit
Degen ['de:gən] (**-s, -**) *m* sword
degenerieren [degene'ri:rən] *vi* to degenerate
dehnbar ['de:nba:r] *adj* elastic; (*fig: Begriff*) loose
dehnen *vt, vr* to stretch
Deich [daɪç] (**-(e)s, -e**) *m* dyke (*Brit*), dike (*US*)
deichseln *vt* (*fig: umg*) to wangle
dein [daɪn] *pron* your; (*adjektivisch*): **herzliche Grüße, D~e Elke** with best wishes, yours *od* (*herzlicher*) love, Elke
deine, r, s *poss pron* yours
deiner *gen von* **du** *pron* of you
deinerseits *adv* on your part
deinesgleichen *pron* people like you
deinetwegen ['daɪnət've:gən] *adv* (*für dich*) for your sake; (*wegen dir*) on your account
dekadent [deka'dɛnt] *adj* decadent
Dekadenz *f* decadence
deklinieren [dekli'ni:rən] *vt* to decline
Dekolleté, Dekolletee [dekɔl'te:] (**-s, -s**) *nt* low neckline
dekomprimieren *vt* (*Comput*) to decompress
Dekorateur, in [dekora'tø:r(ɪn)] *m(f)* window dresser
Dekoration [dekoratsi'o:n] *f* decoration; (*in Laden*) window dressing
dekorativ [dekora'ti:f] *adj* decorative
dekorieren [deko'ri:rən] *vt* to decorate; (*Schaufenster*) to dress
Delegation [delegatsi'o:n] *f* delegation
Delfin [dɛl'fi:n] (**-s, -e**) *m* dolphin
delikat [deli'ka:t] *adj* (*zart, heikel*) delicate; (*köstlich*) delicious
Delikatesse [delika'tɛsə] (**-, -n**) *f* delicacy
Delikatessengeschäft *nt* delicatessen (shop)
Delikt [de'lɪkt] (**-(e)s, -e**) *nt* (*Jur*) offence (*Brit*), offense (*US*)
Delle ['dɛlə] (**-, -n**) (*umg*) *f* dent
Delta ['dɛlta] (**-s, -s**) *nt* delta
dem [de(:)m] *art dat von* **der; das**; **wie ~ auch sei** be that as it may
Demagoge [dema'go:gə] (**-n, -n**) *m* demagogue
dementieren [demɛn'ti:rən] *vt* to deny
dem- *zW*: **demgemäß** *adv* accordingly; **demnach** *adv* accordingly; **demnächst** *adv* shortly
Demo ['de:mo] (**-s, -s**) (*umg*) *f* demo
Demokrat, in [demo'kra:t(ɪn)] (**-en, -en**) *m(f)* democrat
Demokratie [demokra'ti:] *f* democracy
demokratisch *adj* democratic
demokratisieren [demokrati'zi:rən] *vt* to democratize
demolieren [demo'li:rən] *vt* to demolish
Demonstrant, in [demɔn'strant(ɪn)] *m(f)* demonstrator
Demonstration [demɔnstratsi'o:n] *f* demonstration
demonstrieren [demɔn'stri:rən] *vt, vi* to demonstrate
Demoskopie [demosko'pi:] *f* public opinion research
Demut ['de:mu:t] (**-**) *f* humility
demütig ['de:my:tɪç] *adj* humble
demütigen ['de:my:tɪgən] *vt* to humiliate
Demütigung *f* humiliation
demzufolge ['de:mtsu'fɔlgə] *adv* accordingly
den [de(:)n] *art akk von* **der**
denen ['de:nən] *pron dat pl von* **der; die; das**
denken ['dɛŋkən] *unreg vi* to think ▷ *vt*: **für jdn/etw gedacht sein** to be intended *od* meant for sb/sth ▷ *vr* (*vorstellen*): **das kann ich mir ~** I can imagine; (*beabsichtigen*): **sich** *dat* **etw bei etw ~** to mean sth by sth; **wo ~ Sie hin!** what an idea!; **ich denke schon** I think so; **an jdn/etw ~** to think of sb/sth; **daran ist gar nicht zu ~** that's (quite) out of the question; **ich denke nicht daran, das zu tun** there's no way I'm going to do that (*umg*)
Denken (**-s**) *nt* thinking
Denk- *zW*: **Denkfähigkeit** *f* intelligence; **denkfaul** *adj* mentally lazy; **Denkfehler** *m* logical error
Denkmal (**-s, ¨er**) *nt* monument; **Denkmalschutz** *m*: **etw unter Denkmalschutz stellen** to classify sth as a historical monument
denkwürdig *adj* memorable
denn [dɛn] *konj* for; (*konzessiv*): **es sei ~, (dass)** unless ▷ *adv* then; (*nach Komparativ*) than
dennoch ['dɛnnɔx] *konj* nevertheless ▷ *adv*: **und ~, ...** and yet ...
Denunziant, in [denʊntsi'ant(ɪn)] *m(f)* informer
Deospray ['de:oʃpreɪ] *nt od m* deodorant spray
Deponie *f* dump, disposal site
deponieren [depo'ni:rən] *vt* (*Comm*) to deposit
Depot [de'po:] (**-s, -s**) *nt* warehouse; (*Busdepot, Eisenb*) depot; (*Bankdepot*) strongroom (*Brit*), safe (*US*)
Depression [deprɛsi'o:n] *f* depression
deprimieren [depri'mi:rən] *vt* to depress
der [de(:)r] (*f* **die**, *nt* **das**, *gen* **des, der, des**, *dat* **dem, der, dem**, *akk* **den**) *def art* the; **der Rhein** the Rhine; **der Klaus** (*umg*) Klaus; **die Frau** (*im Allgemeinen*) women; **der Tod/das Leben** death/life; **der Fuß des Berges** the foot of the hill; **gib es der Frau** give it to the woman; **er hat sich** *dat* **die Hand verletzt** he has hurt his hand
▷ *rel pron* (*bei Menschen*) who, that; (*bei Tieren, Sachen*) which, that; **der Mann, den ich gesehen habe** the man who *od* whom *od* that I saw
▷ *demon pron* he/she/it; (*jener, dieser*) that; (*pl*) those; **der/die war es** it was him/her; **der mit der Brille** the one with the glasses; **ich will den (da)** I want that one
derart ['de:r'a:rt] *adv* (*Art und Weise*) in such a way; (*Ausmaß: vor adj*) so; (*: vor vb*) so much
derartig *adj* such, this sort of

derb [dɛrp] *adj* sturdy; (*Kost*) solid; (*grob*) coarse
der- *zW*: **derjenige** *pron* he; she; it; (*rel*) the one (who); that (which); **dermaßen** *adv* to such an extent, so; **derselbe** *m pron* the same; **derzeitig** *adj* present, current; (*damalig*) then
des [dɛs] *art gen von* **der**
desertieren [dezɛr'ti:rən] *vi* to desert
deshalb ['dɛs'halp] *adv, konj* therefore, that's why
Design [di'zaɪn] (**-s, -s**) *nt* design
Desinfektion [dezɪnfɛktsi'o:n] *f* disinfection
Desinfektionsmittel *nt* disinfectant
desinfizieren [dezɪnfi'tsi:rən] *vt* to disinfect
Desinteresse [dɛs|ɪntə'rɛsə] (**-s**) *nt*: **~ (an** *+dat*) lack of interest (in)
dessen ['dɛsən] *pron gen von* **der; das**; **~ ungeachtet** nevertheless, regardless
Dessert [dɛ'sɛ:r] (**-s, -s**) *nt* dessert
destillieren [dɛstɪ'li:rən] *vt* to distil
desto ['dɛsto] *adv* all *od* so much the; **~ besser** all the better
deswegen ['dɛs've:gən] *konj* therefore, hence
Detail [de'taɪ] (**-s, -s**) *nt* detail
Detektiv [detɛk'ti:f] (**-s, -e**) *m* detective
deuten ['dɔʏtən] *vt* to interpret; (*Zukunft*) to read ▷ *vi*: **~ (auf** *+akk*) to point (to *od* at)
deutlich *adj* clear; (*Unterschied*) distinct; **jdm etw ~ zu verstehen geben** to make sth perfectly clear *od* plain to sb; **Deutlichkeit** *f* clarity; distinctness
deutsch [dɔʏtʃ] *adj* German; **~e Schrift** Gothic script; **auf D~** in German; **auf gut D~ (gesagt)** (*fig: umg*) ≈ in plain English; **D~e Demokratische Republik** (*Hist*) German Democratic Republic
Deutsche, r *f(m)*: **er ist ~r** he is (a) German
Deutschland *nt* Germany
Devise [de'vi:zə] (**-, -n**) *f* motto, device; **Devisen** *pl* (*Fin*) foreign currency *od* exchange
Dezember [de'tsɛmbər] (**-(s), -**) *m* December; *siehe auch* **September**
dezent [de'tsɛnt] *adj* discreet
dezimal [detsi'ma:l] *adj* decimal; **Dezimalbruch** *m* decimal (fraction); **Dezimalsystem** *nt* decimal system
DGB *m abk* (*= Deutscher Gewerkschaftsbund*) ≈ TUC
d. h. *abk* (*= das heißt*) i.e.
Dia ['di:a] (**-s, -s**) *nt* = **Diapositiv**
Diabetes [dia'be:tɛs] (**-, -**) *m* (*Med*) diabetes
Diabetiker, in [dia'be:tikər(ɪn)] (**-s, -**) *m(f)* diabetic
Diagnose [dia'gno:zə] (**-, -n**) *f* diagnosis
diagonal [diago'na:l] *adj* diagonal
Diagonale (**-, -n**) *f* diagonal
Diagramm [dia'gram] *nt* diagram
Dialekt [dia'lɛkt] (**-(e)s, -e**) *m* dialect
Dialog [dia'lo:k] (**-(e)s, -e**) *m* dialogue
Diamant [dia'mant] *m* diamond
Diapositiv [diapozi'ti:f] (**-s, -e**) *nt* (*Phot*) slide, transparency
Diät [di'ɛ:t] (**-**) *f* diet; **Diäten** *pl* (*Pol*) allowance *sing*; **~ essen** to eat according to a diet; **(nach einer) ~ leben** to be on a special diet
dich [dɪç] *akk von* **du** ▷ *pron* you ▷ *refl pron* yourself
dicht [dɪçt] *adj* dense; (*Nebel*) thick; (*Gewebe*) close; (*undurchlässig*) (water)tight; (*fig*) concise; (*umg: zu*) shut, closed ▷ *adv*: **~ an/bei** close to; **er ist nicht ganz ~** (*umg*) he's crackers; **~ machen** to make watertight/airtight; **~ hintereinander** right behind one another; **~ bevölkert** densely *od* heavily populated; *siehe auch* **dichtmachen**
Dichte (**-, -n**) *f* density; thickness; closeness; (water)tightness; (*fig*) conciseness
dichten *vt* (*dicht machen*) to make watertight; to seal; (*Naut*) to caulk; (*Liter*) to compose, write ▷ *vi* (*Liter*) to compose, write
Dichter, in (**-s, -**) *m(f)* poet; (*Autor*) writer; **dichterisch** *adj* poetical; **dichterische Freiheit** poetic licence (*Brit*) *od* license (*US*)
dichthalten *unreg* (*umg*) *vi* to keep one's mouth shut
Dichtung *f* (*Tech*) washer; (*Aut*) gasket; (*Gedichte*) poetry; (*Prosa*) (piece of) writing; **~ und Wahrheit** (*fig*) fact and fantasy
dick [dɪk] *adj* thick; (*fett*) fat; **durch ~ und dünn** through thick and thin
Dicke (**-, -n**) *f* thickness; fatness
dickflüssig *adj* viscous
Dickicht (**-s, -e**) *nt* thicket
dick- *zW*: **Dickkopf** *m* mule; **Dickmilch** *f* soured milk
die [di:] *def art* the; *siehe auch* **der**
Dieb, in [di:p, 'di:bɪn] (**-(e)s, -e**) *m(f)* thief; **haltet den ~!** stop thief!; **diebisch** *adj* thieving; (*umg*) immense; **Diebstahl** *m* theft
diejenige ['di:je:nɪgə] *pron siehe* **derjenige**
dienen ['di:nən] *vi*: **(jdm) ~** to serve (sb); **womit kann ich Ihnen ~?** what can I do for you?; (*in Geschäft*) can I help you?
Diener (**-s, -**) *m* servant; (*umg: Verbeugung*) bow
Dienerschaft *f* servants *pl*
Dienst [di:nst] (**-(e)s, -e**) *m* service; (*Arbeit, Arbeitszeit*) work; **~ am Kunden** customer service; **jdm zu ~en stehen** to be at sb's disposal; **außer ~** retired; **~ haben** to be on duty; **~ habend** = **diensthabend**; **~ tuend** = **diensttuend**; **der öffentliche ~** the civil service
Dienstag *m* Tuesday; **am ~** on Tuesday; **~ in acht Tagen** *od* **in einer Woche** a week on Tuesday, Tuesday week; **~ vor einer Woche** *od* **acht Tagen** a week (ago) last Tuesday
dienstags *adv* on Tuesdays
Dienst- *zW*: **diensthabend** *adj* (*Arzt, Offizier*) on duty; **Dienstleistung** *f* service; **dienstlich** *adj* official; (*Angelegenheiten*) business *attrib*; **Dienstmädchen** *nt* domestic servant; **Dienststelle** *f* office; **Dienstvorschrift** *f* service regulations *pl*; **Dienstweg** *m* official channels *pl*
diesbezüglich *adj* (*Frage*) on this matter

diese, r, s *pron* this (one) ▷ *adj* this; **~ Nacht** tonight
Diesel ['di:zəl] (**-s**) *m* (*Kraftstoff*) diesel fuel
dieselbe [di:'zɛlbə] *f pron* the same
Dieselöl ['di:zəlø:l] *nt* diesel oil
diesig *adj* drizzly
dies- *zW*: **diesjährig** *adj* this year's; **diesmal** *adv* this time; **Diesseits** (-) *nt* this life; **diesseits** *präp +gen* on this side
Dietrich ['di:trɪç] (**-s, -e**) *m* picklock
Differenz [dɪfe'rɛnts] *f* difference
Differenzialgetriebe *nt* differential gear; **Differenzialrechnung** *f* differential calculus
differenzieren [dɪferɛn'tsi:rən] *vt* to make distinctions in ▷ *vi*: **~ (bei)** to make distinctions (in)
Digital- [digi'ta:l-] *zW*: **Digitalanzeige** *f* digital display; **Digitalfernsehen** *nt* digital TV; **Digitalrechner** *m* digital computer; **Digitaluhr** *f* digital watch
Diktafon, **Diktaphon** [dɪkta'fo:n] *nt* dictaphone®
Diktat [dɪk'ta:t] (**-(e)s, -e**) *nt* dictation; (*fig*: *Gebot*) dictate; (*Pol*) diktat, dictate
Diktator [dɪk'ta:tɔr] *m* dictator; **diktatorisch** [-a'to:rɪʃ] *adj* dictatorial
Diktatur [dɪkta'tu:r] *f* dictatorship
diktieren [dɪk'ti:rən] *vt* to dictate
Dimension [dimɛnzi'o:n] *f* dimension
Ding [dɪŋ] (**-(e)s, -e**) *nt* thing; object; **das ist ein ~ der Unmöglichkeit** that is totally impossible; **guter ~e sein** to be in good spirits; **so wie die ~e liegen, nach Lage der ~e** as things are; **es müsste nicht mit rechten ~en zugehen, wenn ...** it would be more than a little strange if ...; **ein krummes ~ drehen** to commit a crime; to do something wrong; **dinglich** *adj* real, concrete
Dingsbums ['dɪŋsbʊms] (-) (*umg*) *nt* thingummybob (*Brit*)
Dinosaurier [dino'zaʊriər] *m* dinosaur
Diözese [diø'tse:zə] (**-, -n**) *f* diocese
Diphtherie [dɪfte'ri:] *f* diphtheria
Diplom [di'plo:m] (**-(e)s, -e**) *nt* diploma; (*Hochschulabschluss*) degree
Diplomat [diplo'ma:t] (**-en, -en**) *m* diplomat
Diplomatie [diploma'ti:] *f* diplomacy
diplomatisch [diplo'ma:tɪʃ] *adj* diplomatic
dir [di:r] *dat von* **du** ▷ *pron* (to) you
direkt [di'rɛkt] *adj* direct; **~ fragen** to ask outright *od* straight out
Direktor, in *m(f)* director; (*von Hochschule*) principal; (*von Schule*) principal, head (teacher) (*Brit*)
Direktübertragung *f* live broadcast
Dirigent, in [diri'gɛnt(ɪn)] *m(f)* conductor
dirigieren [diri'gi:rən] *vt* to direct; (*Mus*) to conduct
Dirne ['dɪrnə] (**-, -n**) *f* prostitute
Diskette [dɪs'kɛtə] *f* disk, diskette
Diskettenlaufwerk *nt* disk drive
Disko ['dɪsko] (**-, -s**) *f* disco
Diskont [dɪs'kɔnt] (**-s, -e**) *m* discount; **Diskontsatz** *m* rate of discount
Diskothek [dɪsko'te:k] (**-, -en**) *f* disco(theque)
diskret [dɪs'kre:t] *adj* discreet
Diskretion [dɪskretsi'o:n] *f* discretion; **strengste ~ wahren** to preserve the strictest confidence
diskriminieren [dɪskrimi'ni:rən] *vt* to discriminate against
Diskussion [dɪskʊsi'o:n] *f* discussion; **zur ~ stehen** to be under discussion
diskutabel [dɪsku'ta:bəl] *adj* debatable
diskutieren [dɪsku'ti:rən] *vt, vi* to discuss; **darüber lässt sich ~** that sounds like something we could talk about
disqualifizieren [dɪskvalifi'tsi:rən] *vt* to disqualify
Distanz [dɪs'tants] *f* distance; (*fig*: *Abstand, Entfernung*) detachment; (*Zurückhaltung*) reserve
distanzieren [dɪstan'tsi:rən] *vr*: **sich von jdm/etw ~** to dissociate o.s. from sb/sth
Distel ['dɪstəl] (**-, -n**) *f* thistle
Disziplin [dɪstsi'pli:n] (**-, -en**) *f* discipline
Dividende [divi'dɛndə] (**-, -n**) *f* dividend
dividieren [divi'di:rən] *vt*: **~ (durch)** to divide (by)
DM *f abk* (*Hist*: *= Deutsche Mark*) DM
D-Mark ['de:mark] (**-, -**) *f* (*Hist*) deutschmark
DNS *f abk* (*= Desoxyribo(se)nukleinsäure*) DNA
doch [dɔx] *adv* **1** (*dennoch*) after all; (*sowieso*) anyway; **er kam doch noch** he came after all; **du weißt es ja doch besser** you know more about it (than I do) anyway; **es war doch ganz interessant** it was actually quite interesting; **und doch, ...** and yet ...
2 (*als bejahende Antwort*) yes I do/it does *etc*; **das ist nicht wahr — doch!** that's not true — yes it is!
3 (*auffordernd*): **komm doch** do come; **lass ihn doch** just leave him; **nicht doch!** oh no!
4: **sie ist doch noch so jung** but she's still so young; **Sie wissen doch, wie das ist** you know how it is(, don't you?); **wenn doch** if only
▷ *konj* (*aber*) but; (*trotzdem*) all the same; **und doch hat er es getan** but still he did it
Docht [dɔxt] (**-(e)s, -e**) *m* wick
Dogge ['dɔgə] (**-, -n**) *f* bulldog; **Deutsche ~** Great Dane
Dogma ['dɔgma] (**-s, -men**) *nt* dogma
dogmatisch [dɔ'gma:tɪʃ] *adj* dogmatic
Doktor ['dɔktɔr] (**-s, -en**) *m* doctor; **den ~ machen** (*umg*) to do a doctorate *od* Ph.D.
Doktor- *zW*: **Doktorarbeit** *f* doctoral thesis
Dokument [doku'mɛnt] *nt* document
Dokumentar- *zW*: **Dokumentarbericht** *m* documentary; **Dokumentarfilm** *m* documentary (film); **dokumentarisch** *adj* documentary
dokumentieren [dokumɛn'ti:rən] *vt* to document; (*fig*: *zu erkennen geben*) to reveal, show
Dolch [dɔlç] (**-(e)s, -e**) *m* dagger

dolmetschen ['dɔlmɛtʃən] *vt, vi* to interpret
Dolmetscher, in (**-s, -**) *m(f)* interpreter
Dolomiten [dolo'mi:tən] *pl* (*Geog*): **die ~** the Dolomites *pl*
Dom [do:m] (**-(e)s, -e**) *m* cathedral
Domäne [do'mɛ:nə] (**-, -n**) *f* (*fig*) domain, province
dominieren [domi'ni:rən] *vt* to dominate ▷ *vi* to predominate
Dominikanische Republik [domini'ka:nɪʃərepu'bli:k] *f* Dominican Republic
Dompfaff ['do:mpfaf] (**-en, -en**) *m* bullfinch
Donau ['do:naʊ] *f*: **die ~** the Danube
Donner ['dɔnər] (**-s, -**) *m* thunder; **wie vom ~ gerührt** (*fig*) thunderstruck
donnern *vi unpers* to thunder ▷ *vt* (*umg*) to slam, crash
Donnerstag *m* Thursday; *siehe auch* **Dienstag**
doof [do:f] (*umg*) *adj* daft, stupid
Dopingkontrolle ['dɔpɪŋkɔntrɔlə] *f* (*Sport*) dope check
Doppel ['dɔpəl] (**-s, -**) *nt* duplicate; (*Sport*) doubles; **Doppelbett** *nt* double bed; **Doppelfenster** *nt* double glazing; **Doppelgänger, in** (**-s, -**) *m(f)* double; **Doppelpunkt** *m* colon; **Doppelstecker** *m* two-way adaptor
doppelt *adj* double; (*Comm: Buchführung*) double-entry; (*Staatsbürgerschaft*) dual ▷ *adv*: **die Karte habe ich ~** I have two of these cards; **~ gemoppelt** (*umg*) saying the same thing twice over; **in ~er Ausführung** in duplicate
Doppel- *zW*: **Doppelzentner** *m* 100 kilograms; **Doppelzimmer** *nt* double room
Dorf [dɔrf] (**-(e)s, ¨-er**) *nt* village
Dorn[1] [dɔrn] (**-(e)s, -en**) *m* (*Bot*) thorn; **das ist mir ein ~ im Auge** (*fig*) it's a thorn in my flesh
Dorn[2] [dɔrn] (**-(e)s, -e**) *m* (*Schnallendorn*) tongue, pin
dornig *adj* thorny
dörren ['dœrən] *vt* to dry
Dörrobst ['dœro:pst] *nt* dried fruit
dort [dɔrt] *adv* there; **~ drüben** over there; **dorther** *adv* from there; **dorthin** *adv* (to) there
dortig *adj* of that place; in that town
Dose ['do:zə] (**-, -n**) *f* box; (*Blechdose*) tin, can; **in ~n** (*Konserven*) canned, tinned (*Brit*)
Dosenöffner *m* tin (*Brit*) *od* can opener
Dosis ['do:zɪs] (**-, Dosen**) *f* dose
Dotter ['dɔtər] (**-s, -**) *m* egg yolk
Download ['daunlo:d] *m* (*Comput*) download
downloaden ['daunlo:dən] *vti* (*Comput*) to download
Downsyndrom *nt no pl* (*Med*) Down's Syndrome
Dozent, in [do'tsɛnt(ɪn)] (**-en, -en**) *m(f)*: **~ (für)** lecturer (in), professor (of) (*US*)
Dr. *abk* = **Doktor**
Drache ['draxə] (**-n, -n**) *m* (*Tier*) dragon
Drachen (**-s, -**) *m* kite; **einen ~ steigen lassen** to fly a kite; **Drachenfliegen** *nt* (*Sport*) hang-gliding
Draht [dra:t] (**-(e)s, ¨-e**) *m* wire; **auf ~ sein** to be on the ball; **Drahtseil** *nt* cable; **Nerven wie Drahtseile** (*umg*) nerves of steel; **Drahtseilbahn** *f* cable railway; **Drahtzange** *f* pliers *pl*
Drama ['dra:ma] (**-s, Dramen**) *nt* drama
Dramatiker, in [dra'ma:tikər(ɪn)] (**-s, -**) *m(f)* dramatist
dramatisch [dra'ma:tɪʃ] *adj* dramatic
dran [dran] (*umg*) *adv* (*an der Reihe*): **jetzt bist du ~** it's your turn now; **früh/spät ~ sein** to be early/late; **ich weiß nicht, wie ich (bei ihm) ~ bin** I don't know where I stand (with him); *siehe auch* **daran**
Drang (**-(e)s, ¨-e**) *m* (*Trieb*) urge, yearning; (*Druck*) pressure; **~ nach** urge *od* yearning for
drängen ['drɛŋən] *vt* (*schieben*) to push, press; (*antreiben*) to urge ▷ *vi* (*eilig sein*) to be urgent; (*Zeit*) to press; **auf etw** *akk* **~** to press for sth
drastisch ['drastɪʃ] *adj* drastic
drauf [draʊf] (*umg*) *adv*: **~ und dran sein, etw zu tun** to be on the point of doing sth; *siehe auch* **darauf**; **Draufgänger** (**-s, -**) *m* daredevil
draußen ['draʊsən] *adv* outside, out-of-doors
Dreck [drɛk] (**-(e)s**) *m* mud, dirt; **~ am Stecken haben** (*fig*) to have a skeleton in the cupboard; **das geht ihn einen ~ an** (*umg*) that's none of his business
dreckig *adj* dirty, filthy; **es geht mir ~** (*umg*) I'm in a bad way
Dreharbeiten *pl* (*Film*) shooting *sing*
drehen *vt* to turn, rotate; (*Zigaretten*) to roll; (*Film*) to shoot ▷ *vi* to turn, rotate ▷ *vr* to turn; (*handeln von*): **sich um etw ~** to be about sth; **ein Ding ~** (*umg*) to play a prank
Dreh- *zW*: **Drehorgel** *f* barrel organ; **Drehtür** *f* revolving door; **Drehzahl** *f* rate of revolution; **Drehzahlmesser** *m* rev(olution) counter
drei [draɪ] *num* three; **~ viertel** three quarters; **aller guten Dinge sind ~!** (*Sprichwort*) all good things come in threes!; (*nach zwei missglückten Versuchen*) third time lucky!; **Dreieck** *nt* triangle; **dreieckig** *adj* triangular; **dreieinhalb** *num* three and a half; **Dreieinigkeit** [-'|aɪnɪçkaɪt] *f* Trinity
dreierlei *adj inv* of three kinds
drei- *zW*: **dreifach** *adj* triple, treble ▷ *adv* three times; **die dreifache Menge** three times the amount; **dreihundert** *num* three hundred; **Dreikönigsfest** *nt* Epiphany; **dreimal** *adv* three times, thrice
dreißig ['draɪsɪç] *num* thirty
drei- *zW*: **Dreiviertelstunde** *f* three-quarters of an hour; **dreizehn** *num* thirteen; **jetzt schlägts dreizehn!** (*umg*) that's a bit much
Dresden ['dre:sdən] (**-s**) *nt* Dresden
dressieren [drɛ'si:rən] *vt* to train
Drillbohrer *m* light drill
drin [drɪn] (*umg*) *adv*: **bis jetzt ist noch alles**

~ everything is still quite open; *siehe auch* **darin**

dringen ['drɪŋən] *unreg vi* (*Wasser, Licht, Kälte*): ~ **(durch/in** *+akk***)** to penetrate (through/into); **auf etw** *akk* **~** to insist on sth; **in jdn ~** (*geh*) to entreat sb

dringend ['drɪŋənt] *adj* urgent; **~ empfehlen** to recommend strongly

drinnen ['drɪnən] *adv* inside, indoors

dritt *adv*: **wir kommen zu ~** three of us are coming together

dritte, r, s *adj* third; **D~ Welt** Third World; **im Beisein D~r** in the presence of a third party

Drittel (-s, -) *nt* third

drittens *adv* thirdly

droben ['dro:bən] *adv* above, up there

Droge ['dro:gə] **(-, -n)** *f* drug; **drogenabhängig** *adj* addicted to drugs

Drogerie [drogə'ri:] *f* chemist's shop (*Brit*), drugstore (*US*)

drohen ['dro:ən] *vi*: **(jdm) ~** to threaten (sb)

dröhnen ['drø:nən] *vi* (*Motor*) to roar; (*Stimme, Musik*) to ring, resound

Drohung ['dro:ʊŋ] *f* threat

drollig ['drɔlɪç] *adj* droll

Drossel ['drɔsəl] **(-, -n)** *f* thrush

drüben ['dry:bən] *adv* over there, on the other side

drüber ['dry:bər] (*umg*) *adv* = **darüber**

Druck [drʊk] **(-(e)s, -e)** *m* (*Zwang, Phys*) pressure; (*Typ: Vorgang*) printing; (*: Produkt*) print; (*fig: Belastung*) burden, weight; **~ hinter etw** *akk* **machen** to put some pressure on sth; **Druckbuchstabe** *m* block letter; **in Druckbuchstaben schreiben** to print

drucken ['drʊkən] *vt, vi* (*Typ, Comput*) to print

drücken ['drʏkən] *vt* (*Knopf, Hand*) to press; (*zu eng sein*) to pinch; (*fig: Preise*) to keep down; (*: belasten*) to oppress, weigh down ▷ *vi* to press; to pinch ▷ *vr*: **sich vor etw** *dat* **~** to get out of (doing) sth; **jdm etw in die Hand ~** to press sth into sb's hand

drückend *adj* oppressive; (*Last, Steuern*) heavy; (*Armut*) grinding; (*Wetter, Hitze*) oppressive, close

Drucker (-s, -) *m* printer

Druckerei [drʊkə'raɪ] *f* printing works, press

Druckerschwärze *f* printer's ink

Druck- *zW*: **Druckfehler** *m* misprint; **Druckknopf** *m* press stud (*Brit*), snap fastener; **Drucksache** *f* printed matter; **Druckschrift** *f* printing; (*gedrucktes Werk*) pamphlet

drunten ['drʊntən] *adv* below, down there

Drüse ['dry:zə] **(-, -n)** *f* gland

Dschungel ['dʒʊŋəl] **(-s, -)** *m* jungle

DTP (-) *nt abk* (*= Desktop publishing*) DTP

du [du:] *pron* you; **mit jdm per du sein** to be on familiar terms with sb

ducken ['dʊkən] *vt* (*Kopf*) to duck; (*fig*) to take down a peg or two ▷ *vr* to duck

Duckmäuser ['dʊkmɔʏzər] **(-s, -)** *m* yes-man

Duell [du'ɛl] **(-s, -e)** *nt* duel

Duett [du'ɛt] **(-(e)s, -e)** *nt* duet

Duft [dʊft] **(-(e)s, ⸚e)** *m* scent, odour (*Brit*), odor (*US*); **duften** *vi* to smell, be fragrant

duftig *adj* (*Stoff, Kleid*) delicate, diaphanous; (*Muster*) fine

Duftnote *f* (*von Parfüm*) scent

dulden ['dʊldən] *vt* to suffer; (*zulassen*) to tolerate ▷ *vi* to suffer

duldsam *adj* tolerant

dumm [dʊm] *adj* stupid; **das wird mir zu ~** that's just too much; **der D~e sein** to be the loser; **der ~e August** (*umg*) the clown; **du willst mich wohl für ~ verkaufen** you must think I'm stupid; **sich ~ und dämlich reden** (*umg*) to talk till one is blue in the face; **so etwas D~es** how stupid; what a nuisance

dummerweise *adv* stupidly

Dummheit *f* stupidity; (*Tat*) blunder, stupid mistake

Dummkopf *m* blockhead

dumpf [dʊmpf] *adj* (*Ton*) hollow, dull; (*Luft*) close; (*Erinnerung, Schmerz*) vague

Düne ['dy:nə] **(-, -n)** *f* dune

düngen ['dʏŋən] *vt* to fertilize

Dünger (-s, -) *m* fertilizer; (*Dung*) manure

dunkel ['dʊŋkəl] *adj* dark; (*Stimme*) deep; (*Ahnung*) vague; (*rätselhaft*) obscure; (*verdächtig*) dubious, shady; **im D~n tappen** (*fig*) to grope in the dark

Dunkelheit *f* darkness; (*fig*) obscurity; **bei Einbruch der ~** at nightfall

Dunkelkammer *f* (*Phot*) dark room

Dunkelziffer *f* estimated number of unnotified cases

dünn [dʏn] *adj* thin ▷ *adv*: **~ gesät** scarce; **dünnflüssig** *adj* watery, thin

Dunst [dʊnst] **(-es, ⸚e)** *m* vapour (*Brit*), vapor (*US*); (*Wetter*) haze

dünsten ['dʏnstən] *vt* to steam

Duplikat [dupli'ka:t] **(-(e)s, -e)** *nt* duplicate

Dur [du:r] **(-, -)** *nt* (*Mus*) major

durch [dʊrç] *präp +akk* **1** (*hindurch*) through; **durch den Urwald** through the jungle; **durch die ganze Welt reisen** to travel all over the world
2 (*mittels*) through, by (means of); (*aufgrund*) due to, owing to; **Tod durch Herzschlag/den Strang** death from a heart attack/by hanging; **durch die Post** by post; **durch seine Bemühungen** through his efforts
▷ *adj* **1** (*hindurch*) through; **die ganze Nacht durch** all through the night; **den Sommer durch** during the summer; **8 Uhr durch** past 8 o'clock; **durch und durch** completely; **das geht mir durch und durch** that goes right through me
2 (*Koch: umg: durchgebraten*) done; **(gut) durch** well-done

durcharbeiten *vt, vi* to work through ▷ *vr*: **sich durch etw ~** to work one's way through sth

durchaus [dʊrç'aʊs] *adv* completely; (*unbedingt*) definitely; **~ nicht** (*in verneinten Sätzen: als Verstärkung*) by no means; (*: als Antwort*) not at all; **das lässt sich ~ machen** that sounds feasible; **ich bin ~ Ihrer Meinung** I quite *od* absolutely agree with you
durchblättern *vt* to leaf through
Durchblick ['dʊrçblɪk] *m* view; (*fig*) comprehension; **den ~ haben** (*fig: umg*) to know what's what
durchblicken *vi* to look through; (*umg: verstehen*): **(bei etw) ~** to understand (sth); **etw ~ lassen** (*fig*) to hint at sth
durchbrechen[1] ['dʊrçbrɛçən] *unreg vt, vi* to break
durchbrechen[2] [dʊrç'brɛçən] *unreg vt untr* (*Schranken*) to break through
durchbrennen *unreg vi* (*Draht, Sicherung*) to burn through; (*umg*) to run away
Durchbruch ['dʊrçbrʊx] *m* (*Öffnung*) opening; (*Mil*) breach; (*von Gefühlen etc*) eruption; (*der Zähne*) cutting; (*fig*) breakthrough; **zum ~ kommen** to break through
durchdacht [dʊrç'daxt] *adj* well thought-out
durchdenken *unreg vt untr* to think out
durchdrehen *vt* (*Fleisch*) to mince ▷ *vi* (*umg*) to crack up
durchdringen[1] ['dʊrçdrɪŋən] *unreg vi* to penetrate, get through
durchdringen[2] [dʊrç'drɪŋən] *unreg vt untr* to penetrate
durcheinander [dʊrç|aɪ'nandər] *adv* in a mess, in confusion; (*verwirrt*) confused; **Durcheinander** (**-s**) *nt* (*Verwirrung*) confusion; (*Unordnung*) mess
durch- *zW*: **durchfahren** *unreg vi*: **er ist bei Rot durchgefahren** he jumped the lights ▷ *vt*: **die Nacht durchfahren** to travel through the night; **Durchfahrt** *f* transit; (*Verkehr*) thoroughfare; **Durchfahrt bitte freihalten!** please keep access free; **Durchfahrt verboten!** no through road; **Durchfall** *m* (*Med*) diarrhoea (*Brit*), diarrhea (*US*); **durchfallen** *unreg vi* to fall through; (*in Prüfung*) to fail
durchfragen *vr* to find one's way by asking
durchführbar *adj* feasible, practicable
durchführen ['dʊrçfy:rən] *vt* to carry out; (*Gesetz*) to implement; (*Kursus*) to run
Durchführung *f* execution, performance
Durchgang ['dʊrçgaŋ] *m* passage(way); (*bei Produktion, Versuch*) run; (*Sport*) round; (*bei Wahl*) ballot; **~ verboten** no thoroughfare
Durchgangs- *zW*: **Durchgangslager** *nt* transit camp; **Durchgangsverkehr** *m* through traffic
durchgefroren ['dʊrçgəfro:rən] *adj* (*See*) completely frozen; (*Mensch*) frozen stiff
durchgehen ['dʊrçge:ən] *unreg vt* (*behandeln*) to go over *od* through ▷ *vi* to go through; (*ausreißen: Pferd*) to break loose; (*Mensch*) to run away; **mein Temperament ging mit mir durch** my temper got the better of me; **jdm etw ~ lassen** to let sb get away with sth
durchgehend *adj* (*Zug*) through; (*Öffnungszeiten*) continuous
durch- *zW*: **durchgreifen** *unreg vi* to take strong action; **durchhalten** *unreg vi* to last out ▷ *vt* to keep up; **durchkommen** *unreg vi* to get through; (*überleben*) to pull through
durchkreuzen *vt untr* to thwart, frustrate
durchlassen *unreg vt* (*Person*) to let through; (*Wasser*) to let in
durchlässig *adj* leaky
Durchlauf ['dʊrçlaʊf] *m* (*Comput*) run
Durchlaufzeit *f* (*Comput*) length of the run
durch- *zW*: **durchleben** *vt untr* (*Zeit*) to live *od* go through; (*Jugend, Gefühl*) to experience; **durchlesen** *unreg vt* to read through; **durchleuchten** *vt untr* to X-ray; **durchmachen** *vt* to go through; **die Nacht durchmachen** to make a night of it
Durchmesser (**-s, -**) *m* diameter
durch- *zW*: **durchnehmen** *unreg vt* to go over; **durchnummerieren** *vt* to number consecutively
durchqueren [dʊrç'kve:rən] *vt untr* to cross
durch- *zW*: **Durchreiche** (**-, -n**) *f* (serving) hatch, pass-through (*US*); **Durchreise** *f* transit; **auf der Durchreise** passing through; (*Güter*) in transit; **durchringen** *unreg vr* to make up one's mind finally; **durchrosten** *vi* to rust through
durchs [dʊrçs] = **durch das**
Durchsage ['dʊrçza:gə] *f* intercom *od* radio announcement
durchschauen[1] ['dʊrçʃaʊən] *vt, vi* (*lit*) to look *od* see through
durchschauen[2] [dʊrç'ʃaʊən] *vt untr* (*Person, Lüge*) to see through
durchscheinen ['dʊrçʃaɪnən] *unreg vi* to shine through
Durchschlag ['dʊrçʃla:k] *m* (*Doppel*) carbon copy; (*Sieb*) strainer
durchschlagen *unreg vt* (*entzweischlagen*) to split (in two); (*sieben*) to sieve ▷ *vi* (*zum Vorschein kommen*) to emerge, come out ▷ *vr* to get by
durchschlagend *adj* resounding; **(eine) ~e Wirkung haben** to be totally effective; **durchschneiden** *unreg vt* to cut through
Durchschnitt ['dʊrçʃnɪt] *m* (*Mittelwert*) average; **über/unter dem ~** above/below average; **im ~** on average; **durchschnittlich** *adj* average ▷ *adv* on average; **durchschnittlich begabt/groß** *etc* of average ability/height *etc*
Durchschnitts- *zW*: **Durchschnittsgeschwindigkeit** *f* average speed; **Durchschnittsmensch** *m* average man, man in the street; **Durchschnittswert** *m* average
durch- *zW*: **Durchschrift** *f* copy; **durchsehen** *unreg vt* to look through
durchsetzen[1] ['dʊrçzɛtsən] *vt* to enforce ▷ *vr* (*Erfolg haben*) to succeed; (*sich behaupten*) to get

one's way; **seinen Kopf ~** to get one's own way
durchsetzen² [dʊrç'zɛtsən] *vt untr* to mix
Durchsicht ['dʊrçzıçt] *f* looking through, checking
durchsichtig *adj* transparent; **Durchsichtigkeit** *f* transparency
durch- *zW*: **durchsprechen** *unreg vt* to talk over; **durchstehen** *unreg vt* to live through; **durchstreichen** *unreg vt* to cross out; **durchsuchen** *vt untr* to search; **Durchsuchung** *f* search; **Durchsuchungsbefehl** *m* search warrant; **durchtrieben** *adj* cunning, wily
Durchwahl ['dʊrçva:l] *f* (*Tel*) direct dialling; (*bei Firma*) extension
durch- *zW*: **durchweg** *adv* throughout, completely; **Durchzug** *m* (*Luft*) draught (*Brit*), draft (*US*); (*von Truppen, Vögeln*) passage
dürfen ['dʏrfən] *unreg vi* **1** (*Erlaubnis haben*) to be allowed to; **ich darf das** I'm allowed to (do that); **darf ich?** may I?; **darf ich ins Kino?** can *od* may I go to the cinema?; **es darf geraucht werden** you may smoke
2 (*in Verneinungen*): **er darf das nicht** he's not allowed to (do that); **das darf nicht geschehen** that must not happen; **da darf sie sich nicht wundern** that shouldn't surprise her; **das darf doch nicht wahr sein!** that can't be true!
3 (*in Höflichkeitsformeln*): **darf ich Sie bitten, das zu tun?** may *od* could I ask you to do that?; **wir freuen uns, Ihnen mitteilen zu dürfen** we are pleased to be able to tell you; **was darf es sein?** what can I get for you?
4 (*können*): **das dürfen Sie mir glauben** you can believe me
5 (*Möglichkeit*): **das dürfte genug sein** that should be enough; **es dürfte Ihnen bekannte sein, dass ...** as you will probably know ...
dürftig ['dʏrftıç] *adj* (*ärmlich*) needy, poor; (*unzulänglich*) inadequate
dürr [dʏr] *adj* dried-up; (*Land*) arid; (*mager*) skinny
Dürre (**-, -n**) *f* aridity; (*Zeit*) drought
Durst [dʊrst] (**-(e)s**) *m* thirst; **~ haben** to be thirsty; **einen über den ~ getrunken haben** (*umg*) to have had one too many
durstig *adj* thirsty
Dusche ['dʊʃə] (**-, -n**) *f* shower; **das war eine kalte ~** (*fig*) that really brought him/her *etc* down with a bump
duschen *vi, vr* to have a shower
Düse ['dy:zə] (**-, -n**) *f* nozzle; (*Flugzeugdüse*) jet
Düsen- *zW*: **Düsenantrieb** *m* jet propulsion; **Düsenflugzeug** *nt* jet (plane); **Düsenjäger** *m* jet fighter
Dussel ['dʊsəl] (**-s, -**) (*umg*) *m* twit, berk
düster ['dy:stər] *adj* dark; (*Gedanken, Zukunft*) gloomy
Dutzend ['dʊtsənt] (**-s, -e**) *nt* dozen; **~(e) Mal** a dozen times; **dutzendweise** *adv* by the dozen
duzen ['du:tsən] *vt* to address with the familiar "du" form ▷ *vr* to address each other with the familiar "du" form; *siehe auch* **siezen**
DVD (**-, -s**) *f abk* (*= Digital Versatile Disc*) DVD
Dynamik [dy'na:mık] *f* (*Phys*) dynamics; (*fig: Schwung*) momentum; (*von Mensch*) dynamism
dynamisch [dy'na:mıʃ] *adj* (*lit, fig*) dynamic; (*rentendynamisch*) index-linked
Dynamit [dyna'mi:t] (**-s**) *nt* dynamite
Dynamo [dy'na:mo] (**-s, -s**) *m* dynamo
D-Zug ['de:tsu:k] *m* through train; **ein alter Mann ist doch kein ~** (*umg*) I am going as fast as I can

Ee

E[1], e [eː] *nt* E, e; **E wie Emil** ≈ E for Edward, ≈ E for Easy (*US*)
E[2] [eː] *abk* = **Eilzug; Europastraße**
Ebbe [ˈɛbə] (**-, -n**) *f* low tide; **~ und Flut** ebb and flow
eben [ˈeːbən] *adj* level; (*glatt*) smooth ▷ *adv* just; (*bestätigend*) exactly; **das ist ~ so** that's just the way it is; **mein Bleistift war doch ~ noch da** my pencil was there (just) a minute ago; **~ deswegen** just because of that
ebenbürtig *adj*: **jdm ~ sein** to be sb's peer
Ebene (**-, -n**) *f* plain; (*Math, Phys*) plane; (*fig*) level
eben- *zW*: **ebenfalls** *adv* likewise; **ebenso** *adv* just as; **ebenso gut** just as well; **ebenso oft** just as often; **ebenso viel** just as much; **ebenso weit** just as far; **ebenso wenig** just as little
Eber [ˈeːbər] (**-s, -**) *m* boar
Eberesche *f* mountain ash, rowan
ebnen [ˈeːbnən] *vt* to level; **jdm den Weg ~** (*fig*) to smooth the way for sb
Echo [ˈɛço] (**-s, -s**) *nt* echo; **(bei jdm) ein lebhaftes ~ finden** (*fig*) to meet with a lively response (from sb)
echt [ɛçt] *adj* genuine; (*typisch*) typical; **ich hab ~ keine Zeit** (*umg*) I really don't have any time; **Echtheit** *f* genuineness
Eckball [ˈɛkbal] *m* corner (kick)
Ecke [ˈɛkə] (**-, -n**) *f* corner; (*Math*) angle; **gleich um die ~** just around the corner; **an allen ~n und Enden sparen** (*umg*) to pinch and scrape; **jdn um die ~ bringen** (*umg*) to bump sb off; **mit jdm um ein paar ~n herum verwandt sein** (*umg*) to be distantly related to sb, be sb's second cousin twice removed (*hum*)
Ecstasy [ˈɛkstəsɪ] *nt* (*Droge*) ecstasy
Ecuador [ekuaˈdoːr] (**-s**) *nt* Ecuador
edel [ˈeːdəl] *adj* noble; **Edelgas** *nt* rare gas; **Edelmetall** *nt* rare metal; **Edelstein** *m* precious stone
EDV (**-**) *f abk* (= *elektronische Datenverarbeitung*) EDP
EEG (**-**) *nt abk* (= *Elektroenzephalogramm*) EEG
Efeu [ˈeːfɔʏ] (**-s**) *m* ivy
Effekt [ɛˈfɛkt] (**-(e)s, -e**) *m* effect
effektiv [ɛfɛkˈtiːf] *adj* effective, actual
EG (**-**) *f abk* (= *Europäische Gemeinschaft*) EC
egal [eˈgaːl] *adj* all the same; **das ist mir ganz ~** it's all the same to me
Egoismus [egoˈɪsmʊs] *m* selfishness, egoism
Egoist, in *m(f)* egoist; **egoistisch** *adj* selfish, egoistic
Ehe [ˈeːə] (**-, -n**) *f* marriage; **die ~ eingehen** (*form*) to enter into matrimony; **sie leben in wilder ~** (*veraltet*) they are living in sin
ehe *konj* before
Ehe- *zW*: **Ehebrecher** (**-s, -**) *m* adulterer; **Ehebruch** *m* adultery; **Ehefrau** *f* wife; **Eheleute** *pl* married couple *pl*; **ehelich** *adj* matrimonial; (*Kind*) legitimate
ehemalig *adj* former
ehemals *adv* formerly
Ehe- *zW*: **Ehemann** *m* married man; (*Partner*) husband; **Ehepaar** *nt* married couple
eher [ˈeːər] *adv* (*früher*) sooner; (*lieber*) rather, sooner; (*mehr*) more; **nicht ~ als** not before; **umso ~, als** the more so because
eheste, r, s [ˈeːəstə(r, s)] *adj* (*früheste*) first, earliest; **am ~n** (*am liebsten*) soonest; (*meist*) most; (*am wahrscheinlichsten*) most probably
ehrbar [ˈeːrbaːr] *adj* honourable (*Brit*), honorable (*US*), respectable
Ehre (**-, -n**) *f* honour (*Brit*), honor (*US*); **etw in ~n halten** to treasure *od* cherish sth
ehren *vt* to honour (*Brit*), honor (*US*)
Ehren- *zW*: **ehrenhaft** *adj* honourable (*Brit*), honorable (*US*); **Ehrenrunde** *f* lap of honour (*Brit*) *od* honor (*US*); **Ehrensache** *f* point of honour (*Brit*) *od* honor (*US*); **Ehrensache!** (*umg*) you can count on me; **ehrenvoll** *adj* honourable (*Brit*), honorable (*US*); **Ehrenwort** *nt* word of honour (*Brit*) *od* honor (*US*); **Urlaub auf Ehrenwort** parole
Ehr- *zW*: **Ehrfurcht** *f* awe, deep respect; **Ehrfurcht gebietend** awesome; (*Stimme*) authoritative; **Ehrgefühl** *nt* sense of honour (*Brit*) *od* honor (*US*); **Ehrgeiz** *m* ambition; **ehrgeizig** *adj* ambitious; **ehrlich** *adj* honest; **ehrlich verdientes Geld** hard-earned money; **ehrlich gesagt ...** quite frankly *od* honestly ...; **Ehrlichkeit** *f* honesty; **ehrlos** *adj* dishonourable (*Brit*), dishonorable (*US*)
Ehrung *f* honour(ing) (*Brit*), honor(ing) (*US*)
Ei [aɪ] (**-(e)s, -er**) *nt* egg; **Eier** *pl* (*umg!*: *Hoden*) balls *pl* (*!*); **jdn wie ein rohes Ei behandeln** (*fig*) to handle sb with kid gloves; **wie aus**

dem Ei gepellt aussehen (*umg*) to look spruce

ei *interj* well, well; (*beschwichtigend*) now, now

Eichamt ['aɪç|amt] *nt* Office of Weights and Measures

Eiche (**-, -n**) *f* oak (tree)

Eichel (**-, -n**) *f* acorn; (*Karten*) club; (*Anat*) glans

eichen *vt* to calibrate

Eichhörnchen *nt* squirrel

Eichmaß *nt* standard

Eid ['aɪt] (**-(e)s, -e**) *m* oath; **eine Erklärung an ~es statt abgeben** (*Jur*) to make a solemn declaration

Eidechse ['aɪdɛksə] (**-, -n**) *f* lizard

eidesstattlich *adj*: **~e Erklärung** affidavit

Eidgenosse *m* Swiss

Eidotter *nt* egg yolk

Eier- *zW*: **Eierbecher** *m* egg cup; **Eierkuchen** *m* pancake; (*Omelett*) omelette (*Brit*), omelet (*US*); **Eierlikör** *m* advocaat; **Eierschale** *f* eggshell; **Eierstock** *m* ovary; **Eieruhr** *f* egg timer

Eifer ['aɪfər] (**-s**) *m* zeal, enthusiasm; **mit großem ~ bei der Sache sein** to put one's heart into it; **im ~ des Gefechts** (*fig*) in the heat of the moment; **Eifersucht** *f* jealousy; **eifersüchtig** *adj*: **eifersüchtig (auf** *+akk***)** jealous (of)

eifrig ['aɪfrɪç] *adj* zealous, enthusiastic

Eigelb ['aɪgɛlp] (**-(e)s, -e** *od* **-**) *nt* egg yolk

eigen ['aɪgən] *adj* own; (*eigenartig*) peculiar; (*ordentlich*) particular; (*übergenau*) fussy; **ich möchte kurz in ~er Sache sprechen** I would like to say something on my own account; **mit dem ihm ~en Lächeln** with that smile peculiar to him; **sich** *dat* **etw zu ~ machen** to make sth one's own; **Eigenart** *f* (*Besonderheit*) peculiarity; (*Eigenschaft*) characteristic; **eigenartig** *adj* peculiar; **eigenhändig** *adj* with one's own hand; **Eigenheit** *f* peculiarity; **eigenmächtig** *adj* high-handed; (*eigenverantwortlich*) taken/done *etc* on one's own authority; (*unbefugt*) unauthorized; **Eigenname** *m* proper name

eigens *adv* expressly, on purpose

eigen- *zW*: **Eigenschaft** *f* quality, property, attribute; **Eigensinn** *m* obstinacy; **eigensinnig** *adj* obstinate

eigentlich *adj* actual, real ▷*adv* actually, really; **was willst du ~ hier?** what do you want here anyway?

eigen- *zW*: **Eigentor** *nt* own goal; **Eigentum** *nt* property; **eigentümlich** *adj* peculiar; **Eigentümlichkeit** *f* peculiarity

Eigentumswohnung *f* freehold flat

eignen ['aɪgnən] *vr* to be suited

Eignung *f* suitability

Eilbote *m* courier; **per** *od* **durch ~n** express

Eilbrief *m* express letter

Eile (**-**) *f* haste; **es hat keine ~** there's no hurry

eilen *vi* (*Mensch*) to hurry; (*dringend sein*) to be urgent

Eilgut *nt* express goods *pl*, fast freight (*US*)

eilig *adj* hasty, hurried; (*dringlich*) urgent; **es ~ haben** to be in a hurry; **Eilzug** *m* fast stopping train

Eimer ['aɪmər] (**-s, -**) *m* bucket, pail; **im ~ sein** (*umg*) to be up the spout

ein, e ['aɪn(ə)] *num* one ▷*indef art* a, an ▷*adv*: **nicht ~ noch aus wissen** not to know what to do; **E~/Aus** (*an Geräten*) on/off; **er ist ihr E~ und Alles** he means everything to her; **er geht bei uns ~ und aus** he is always round at our place

einander [aɪ'nandər] *pron* one another, each other

einarbeiten ['aɪn|arbaɪtən] *vr*: **sich (in etw** *akk***) ~** to familiarize o.s. (with sth)

einatmen ['aɪn|a:tmən] *vt, vi* to inhale, breathe in

Einbahnstraße ['aɪnba:nʃtrasə] *f* one-way street

Einband ['aɪnbant] *m* binding, cover

einbauen ['aɪnbaʊən] *vt* to build in; (*Motor*) to install, fit; **Einbaumöbel** *pl* built-in furniture *sing*

einberufen *unreg vt* to convene; (*Mil*) to call up (*Brit*), draft (*US*)

Einbettzimmer *nt* single room

einbilden ['aɪnbɪldən] *vr*: **sich** *dat* **etw ~** to imagine sth; **sich** *dat* **viel auf etw** *akk* **~**: *stolz sein*) to be conceited about sth

Einbildung *f* imagination; (*Dünkel*) conceit

Einbildungskraft *f* imagination

einbinden ['aɪnbɪndən] *unreg vt* to bind (up)

Einblick ['aɪnblɪk] *m* insight; **~ in die Akten nehmen** to examine the files; **jdm ~ in etw** *akk* **gewähren** to allow sb to look at sth

einbrechen ['aɪnbrɛçən] *unreg vi* (*einstürzen*) to fall in; (*Einbruch verüben*) to break in; **bei ~der Dunkelheit** at nightfall

Einbrecher (**-s, -**) *m* burglar

einbringen ['aɪnbrɪŋən] *unreg vt* to bring in; (*Geld, Vorteil*) to yield; (*mitbringen*) to contribute; **das bringt nichts ein** (*fig*) it's not worth it

Einbruch ['aɪnbrʊx] *m* (*Hauseinbruch*) break-in, burglary; (*des Winters*) onset; (*Einsturz, Fin*) collapse; (*Mil: in Front*) breakthrough; **bei ~ der Nacht** at nightfall

einbürgern ['aɪnbʏrgərn] *vt* to naturalize ▷*vr* to become adopted; **das hat sich so eingebürgert** that's become a custom

Einbuße ['aɪnbu:sə] *f* loss, forfeiture

einbüßen ['aɪnby:sən] *vt* to lose, forfeit

eindeutig ['aɪndɔʏtɪç] *adj* unequivocal

eindringen ['aɪndrɪŋən] *unreg vi*: **~ (in** *+akk***)** to force one's way in(to); (*in Haus*) to break in(to); (*in Land*) to invade; (*Gas, Wasser*) to penetrate; **auf jdn ~** (*mit Bitten*) to pester sb

eindringlich *adj* forcible, urgent; **ich habe ihn ~ gebeten ...** I urged him ...

Eindruck ['aɪndrʊk] *m* impression

eindrucksvoll *adj* impressive

eine, r, s *pron* one; (*jemand*) someone; **wie**

kann ~r nur so dumm sein! how could anybody be so stupid!; **es kam ~s zum anderen** it was (just) one thing after another; **sich** *dat* **~n genehmigen** (*umg*) to have a quick one

eineiig ['aɪn|aɪɪç] *adj* (*Zwillinge*) identical

eineinhalb ['aɪn|aɪn'halp] *num* one and a half

Einerlei ['aɪnər'laɪ] **(-s)** *nt* monotony; **einerlei** *adj* (*gleichartig*) the same kind of; **es ist mir einerlei** it is all the same to me

einerseits *adv* on the one hand

einfach ['aɪnfax] *adj* simple; (*nicht mehrfach*) single ▷ *adv* simply; **Einfachheit** *f* simplicity

einfahren ['aɪnfa:rən] *unreg vt* to bring in; (*Barriere*) to knock down; (*Auto*) to run in ▷ *vi* to drive in; (*Zug*) to pull in; (*Min*) to go down

Einfahrt *f* (*Vorgang*) driving in; pulling in; (*Min*) descent; (*Ort*) entrance; (*von Autobahn*) slip road (*Brit*), entrance ramp (*US*)

Einfall ['aɪnfal] *m* (*Idee*) idea, notion; (*Lichteinfall*) incidence; (*Mil*) raid

einfallen *unreg vi* (*einstürzen*) to fall in, collapse; (*Licht*) to fall; (*Mil*) to raid; (*einstimmen*): **~ (in** *+akk***)** to join in (with); **etw fällt jdm ein** sth occurs to sb; **das fällt mir gar nicht ein!** I wouldn't dream of it; **sich** *dat* **etwas ~ lassen** to have a good idea; **dabei fällt mir mein Onkel ein, der ...** that reminds me of my uncle who ...; **es fällt mir jetzt nicht ein** I can't think of it *od* it won't come to me at the moment

Einfamilienhaus [aɪnfa'mi:liənhaʊs] *nt* detached house

einfarbig ['aɪnfarbɪç] *adj* all one colour (*Brit*) *od* color (*US*); (*Stoff etc*) self-coloured (*Brit*), self-colored (*US*)

einfinden ['aɪnfɪndən] *unreg vr* to come, turn up

einfließen ['aɪnfli:sən] *unreg vi* to flow in

einflößen ['aɪnflø:sən] *vt*: **jdm etw ~** (*lit*) to give sb sth; (*fig*) to instil sth into sb

Einfluss ['aɪnflʊs] *m* influence; **~ nehmen** to bring an influence to bear; **Einflussbereich** *m* sphere of influence; **einflussreich** *adj* influential

einförmig ['aɪnfœrmɪç] *adj* uniform; (*eintönig*) monotonous; **Einförmigkeit** *f* uniformity; monotony

einfrieren ['aɪnfri:rən] *unreg vi* to freeze (in) ▷ *vt* to freeze; (*Pol: Beziehungen*) to suspend

einfügen ['aɪnfy:gən] *vt* to fit in; (*zusätzlich*) to add; (*Comput*) to insert

Einfühlungsvermögen *nt* empathy; **mit großem ~** with a great deal of sensitivity

Einfuhr ['aɪnfu:r] **(-)** *f* import; **Einfuhrartikel** *m* imported article

einführen ['aɪnfy:rən] *vt* to bring in; (*Mensch, Sitten*) to introduce; (*Ware*) to import; **jdn in sein Amt ~** to install sb (in office)

Einführung *f* introduction

Einführungspreis *m* introductory price

Eingabe ['aɪnga:bə] *f* petition; (*Dateneingabe*) input; **~/Ausgabe** (*Comput*) input/output

Eingang ['aɪngaŋ] *m* entrance; (*Comm: Ankunft*) arrival; (*Sendung*) post; **wir bestätigen den ~ Ihres Schreibens vom ...** we acknowledge receipt of your letter of the ...

eingangs *adv* at the outset ▷ *präp +gen* at the outset of

eingeben ['aɪnge:bən] *unreg vt* (*Arznei*) to give; (*Daten etc*) to enter; (*Gedanken*) to inspire

eingebildet ['aɪngəbɪldət] *adj* imaginary; (*eitel*) conceited; **~er Kranker** hypochondriac

Eingebung *f* inspiration

eingehen ['aɪnge:ən] *unreg vi* (*Aufnahme finden*) to come in; (*Sendung, Geld*) to be received; (*Tier, Pflanze*) to die; (*Firma*) to fold; (*schrumpfen*) to shrink ▷ *vt* (*abmachen*) to enter into; (*Wette*) to make; **auf etw** *akk* **~** to go into sth; **auf jdn ~** to respond to sb; **jdm ~** (*verständlich sein*) to be comprehensible to sb; **auf einen Vorschlag/Plan ~** (*zustimmen*) to go along with a suggestion/plan; **bei dieser Hitze/ Kälte geht man ja ein!** (*umg*) this heat/cold is just too much!

Eingemachte, s ['aɪngəma:xtə(s)] *nt* preserves *pl*

eingenommen ['aɪngənɔmən] *adj*: **~ (von)** fond (of), partial (to); **~ (gegen)** prejudiced (against)

eingeschrieben ['aɪngəʃri:bən] *adj* registered

eingespielt ['aɪngəʃpi:lt] *adj*: **aufeinander ~ sein** to be in tune with each other

eingetragen ['aɪngətra:gən] *adj* (*Comm*) registered; **~er Gesellschaftssitz** registered office; **~es Warenzeichen** registered trademark

Eingeweide ['aɪngəvaɪdə] **(-s, -)** *nt* innards *pl*, intestines *pl*

Eingeweihte, r ['aɪngəvaɪtə(r)] *f(m)* initiate

eingleisig ['aɪnglaɪzɪç] *adj* single-track; **er denkt sehr ~** (*fig*) he's completely single-minded

eingreifen ['aɪngraɪfən] *unreg vi* to intervene, interfere; (*Zahnrad*) to mesh

Eingreiftruppe *f* (*Mil*) strike force

Eingriff ['aɪngrɪf] *m* intervention, interference; (*Operation*) operation

einhaken ['aɪnha:kən] *vt* to hook in ▷ *vr*: **sich bei jdm ~** to link arms with sb ▷ *vi* (*sich einmischen*) to intervene

Einhalt ['aɪnhalt] *m*: **~ gebieten** *+dat* to put a stop to

einhalten *unreg vt* (*Regel*) to keep ▷ *vi* to stop

einhändig ['aɪnhɛndɪç] *adj* one-handed

einhängen ['aɪnhɛŋən] *vt* to hang; (*Telefon: auch vi*) to hang up; **sich bei jdm ~** to link arms with sb

einheimisch ['aɪnhaɪmɪʃ] *adj* native

Einheimische, r *f(m)* local

Einheit ['aɪnhaɪt] *f* unity; (*Maß, Mil*) unit; **eine geschlossene ~ bilden** to form an integrated whole: **einheitlich** *adj* uniform

Einheitspreis *m* uniform price

einholen ['aɪnho:lən] *vt* (*Tau*) to haul in;

(*Fahne, Segel*) to lower; (*Vorsprung aufholen*) to catch up with; (*Verspätung*) to make up; (*Rat, Erlaubnis*) to ask ▷ *vi* (*einkaufen*) to buy, shop
Einhorn ['aɪnhɔrn] *nt* unicorn
einhundert ['aɪn'hʊndərt] *num* one hundred
einig ['aɪnɪç] *adj* (*vereint*) united; **sich** *dat* **~ sein** to be in agreement; **~ werden** to agree
einige, r, s *adj, pron* some ▷ *pl* some; (*mehrere*) several; **mit Ausnahme ~r weniger** with a few exceptions; **vor ~n Tagen** the other day, a few days ago; **dazu ist noch ~s zu sagen** there are still one or two things to say about that; **~ Mal** a few times
einigen *vt* to unite ▷ *vr*: **sich (auf etw** *akk***) ~** to agree (on sth)
einigermaßen *adv* somewhat; (*leidlich*) reasonably
einiges *pron siehe* **einige(r, s)**
einiggehen *unreg vi* to agree
Einigkeit *f* unity; (*Übereinstimmung*) agreement
Einigung *f* agreement; (*Vereinigung*) unification
einjährig ['aɪnjɛːrɪç] *adj* of *od* for one year; (*Alter*) one-year-old; (*Pflanze*) annual
einkalkulieren ['aɪnkalkuliːrən] *vt* to take into account, allow for
Einkauf ['aɪnkaʊf] *m* purchase; (*Comm: Abteilung*) purchasing (department)
einkaufen *vt* to buy ▷ *vi* to shop; **~ gehen** to go shopping
Einkaufs- *zW*: **Einkaufsbummel** *m*: **einen Einkaufsbummel machen** to go on a shopping spree; **Einkaufsnetz** *nt* string bag; **Einkaufspreis** *m* cost price, wholesale price; **Einkaufswagen** *m* trolley (*Brit*), cart (*US*); **Einkaufszentrum** *nt* shopping centre
einklammern ['aɪnklamərn] *vt* to put in brackets, bracket
Einklang ['aɪnklaŋ] *m* harmony
einklemmen ['aɪnklɛmən] *vt* to jam
Einkommen ['aɪnkɔmən] **(-s, -)** *nt* income
einkommensschwach *adj* low-income *attrib*
einkommensstark *adj* high-income *attrib*
Einkünfte ['aɪnkʏnftə] *pl* income *sing*, revenue *sing*
einladen ['aɪnlaːdən] *unreg vt* (*Person*) to invite; (*Gegenstände*) to load; **jdn ins Kino ~** to take sb to the cinema
Einladung *f* invitation
Einlage ['aɪnlaːgə] *f* (*Programmeinlage*) interlude; (*Spareinlage*) deposit; (*Fin: Kapitaleinlage*) investment; (*Schuheinlage*) insole; (*Fußstütze*) support; (*Zahneinlage*) temporary filling; (*Koch*) *noodles, vegetables etc (in clear soup)*
einlassen *unreg vt* to let in; (*einsetzen*) to set in ▷ *vr*: **sich mit jdm/auf etw** *akk* **~** to get involved with sb/sth; **sich auf einen Kompromiss ~** to agree to a compromise; **ich lasse mich auf keine Diskussion ein** I'm not having any discussion about it
Einlauf ['aɪnlaʊf] *m* arrival; (*von Pferden*) finish; (*Med*) enema
einlaufen *unreg vi* to arrive, come in; (*Sport*) to finish; (*Wasser*) to run in; (*Stoff*) to shrink ▷ *vt* (*Schuhe*) to break in ▷ *vr* (*Sport*) to warm up; (*Motor, Maschine*) to run in; **jdm das Haus ~** to invade sb's house; **in den Hafen ~** to enter the harbour
einleben ['aɪnleːbən] *vr* to settle down
einlegen ['aɪnleːgən] *vt* (*einfügen: Blatt, Sohle*) to insert; (*Koch*) to pickle; (*in Holz etc*) to inlay; (*Geld*) to deposit; (*Pause*) to have; (*Protest*) to make; (*Veto*) to use; (*Berufung*) to lodge; **ein gutes Wort bei jdm ~** to put in a good word with sb
einleiten ['aɪnlaɪtən] *vt* to introduce, start; (*Geburt*) to induce
Einleitung *f* introduction; induction
einleuchten ['aɪnlɔʏçtən] *vi*: **(jdm) ~** to be clear *od* evident (to sb)
einleuchtend *adj* clear
einlösen ['aɪnløːzən] *vt* (*Scheck*) to cash; (*Schuldschein, Pfand*) to redeem; (*Versprechen*) to keep
einmachen ['aɪnmaxən] *vt* to preserve
einmal ['aɪnmaːl] *adv* once; (*erstens*) first of all, firstly; (*später*) one day; **nehmen wir ~ an** just let's suppose; **noch ~** once more; **nicht ~** not even; **auf ~** all at once; **es war ~** once upon a time there was/were; **~ ist keinmal** (*Sprichwort*) once doesn't count; **waren Sie schon ~ in Rom?** have you ever been to Rome?
Einmaleins *nt* multiplication tables *pl*; (*fig*) ABC, basics *pl*
einmalig *adj* unique; (*einmal geschehend*) single; (*prima*) fantastic
Einmannbetrieb *m* one-man business
Einmannbus *m* one-man-operated bus
Einmarsch ['aɪnmarʃ] *m* entry; (*Mil*) invasion
einmütig ['aɪnmyːtɪç] *adj* unanimous
Einnahme ['aɪnnaːmə] **(-, -n)** *f* (*Geld*) takings *pl*, revenue; (*von Medizin*) taking; (*Mil*) capture, taking; **~n und Ausgaben** income and expenditure; **Einnahmequelle** *f* source of income
einnehmen ['aɪnneːmən] *unreg vt* to take; (*Stellung, Raum*) to take up; **~ für/gegen** to persuade in favour of/against
einnehmend *adj* charming
Einöde ['aɪn|øːdə] **(-, -n)** *f* desert, wilderness
einordnen ['aɪn|ɔrdnən] *vt* to arrange, fit in ▷ *vr* to adapt; (*Aut*) to get in(to) lane
einpacken ['aɪnpakən] *vt* to pack (up)
einparken ['aɪnparkən] *vt, vi* to park
einpendeln ['aɪnpɛndəln] *vr* to even out
einpflanzen ['aɪnpflantsən] *vt* to plant; (*Med*) to implant
einplanen ['aɪnplaːnən] *vt* to plan for
einprägen ['aɪnprɛːgən] *vt* to impress, imprint; (*beibringen*): **jdm etw ~** to impress sth on sb; **sich** *dat* **etw ~** to memorize sth
einrahmen ['aɪnraːmən] *vt* to frame
einräumen ['aɪnrɔʏmən] *vt* (*ordnend*) to put

away; (*überlassen*: *Platz*) to give up; (*zugestehen*) to admit, concede

einreden ['aɪnre:dən] *vt*: **jdm/sich etw ~** to talk sb/o.s. into believing sth ▷ *vi*: **auf jdn ~** to keep on and on at sb

einreiben ['aɪnraɪbən] *unreg vt* to rub in

einreichen ['aɪnraɪçən] *vt* to hand in; (*Antrag*) to submit

Einreise ['aɪnraɪzə] *f* entry; **Einreisebestimmungen** *pl* entry regulations *pl*; **Einreiseerlaubnis** *f* entry permit

einreisen ['aɪnraɪzən] *vi*: **in ein Land ~** to enter a country

einrichten ['aɪnrɪçtən] *vt* (*Haus*) to furnish; (*schaffen*) to establish, set up; (*arrangieren*) to arrange; (*möglich machen*) to manage ▷ *vr* (*in Haus*) to furnish one's house; **sich ~ (auf +akk)** (*sich vorbereiten*) to prepare o.s. (for); (*sich anpassen*) to adapt (to)

Einrichtung *f* (*Wohnungseinrichtung*) furnishings *pl*; (*öffentliche Anstalt*) organization; (*Dienste*) service; (*Laboreinrichtung etc*) equipment; (*Gewohnheit*): **zur ständigen ~ werden** to become an institution

einrosten ['aɪnrɔstən] *vi* to get rusty

Eins [aɪns] **(-, -en)** *f* one; **eins** *num* one; **es ist mir alles eins** it's all one to me; **eins zu eins** (*Sport*) one all; **eins a** (*umg*) first-rate

einsam ['aɪnza:m] *adj* lonely, solitary; **~e Klasse/Spitze** (*umg*: *hervorragend*) absolutely fantastic; **Einsamkeit** *f* loneliness, solitude

Einsatz ['aɪnzats] *m* (*Teil*) insert; (*an Kleid*) insertion; (*Tischeinsatz*) leaf; (*Verwendung*) use, employment; (*Spieleinsatz*) stake; (*Risiko*) risk; (*Mil*) operation; (*Mus*) entry; **im ~** in action; **etw unter ~ seines Lebens tun** to risk one's life to do sth; **einsatzbereit** *adj* ready for action

einschalten ['aɪnʃaltən] *vt* (*Elek*) to switch on; (*einfügen*) to insert; (*Pause*) to make; (*Aut*: *Gang*) to engage; (*Anwalt*) to bring in ▷ *vr* (*dazwischentreten*) to intervene

einschätzen ['aɪnʃɛtsən] *vt* to estimate, assess ▷ *vr* to rate o.s.

einschenken ['aɪnʃɛŋkən] *vt* to pour out

einschicken ['aɪnʃɪkən] *vt* to send in

einschl. *abk* (= *einschließlich*) inc.

einschlafen ['aɪnʃla:fən] *unreg vi* to fall asleep, go to sleep; (*fig*: *Freundschaft*) to peter out

einschläfernd *adj* (*Med*) soporific; (*langweilig*) boring; (*Stimme*) lulling

einschlagen ['aɪnʃla:gən] *unreg vt* to knock in; (*Fenster*) to smash, break; (*Zähne, Schädel*) to smash in; (*Steuer*) to turn; (*kürzer machen*) to take up; (*Ware*) to pack, wrap up; (*Weg, Richtung*) to take ▷ *vi* to hit; (*sich einigen*) to agree; (*Anklang finden*) to work, succeed; **es muss irgendwo eingeschlagen haben** something must have been struck by lightning; **gut ~** (*umg*) to go down well, be a big hit; **auf jdn ~** to hit sb

einschlägig ['aɪnʃlɛ:gɪç] *adj* relevant; **er ist ~ vorbestraft** (*Jur*) he has a previous conviction for a similar offence

einschließen ['aɪnʃli:sən] *unreg vt* (*Kind*) to lock in; (*Häftling*) to lock up; (*Gegenstand*) to lock away; (*Bergleute*) to cut off; (*umgeben*) to surround; (*Mil*) to encircle; (*fig*) to include, comprise ▷ *vr* to lock o.s. in

einschließlich *adv* inclusive ▷ *präp +gen* inclusive of, including

einschmeicheln ['aɪnʃmaɪçəln] *vr*: **sich (bei jdm) ~** to ingratiate o.s. (with sb)

einschnappen ['aɪnʃnapən] *vi* (*Tür*) to click to; (*fig*) to be touchy; **eingeschnappt sein** to be in a huff

einschneidend ['aɪnʃnaɪdənt] *adj* incisive

Einschnitt ['aɪnʃnɪt] *m* (*Med*) incision; (*im Tal, Gebirge*) cleft; (*im Leben*) decisive point

einschränken ['aɪnʃrɛŋkən] *vt* to limit, restrict; (*Kosten*) to cut down, reduce ▷ *vr* to cut down (on expenditure); **~d möchte ich sagen, dass ...** I'd like to qualify that by saying ...

Einschränkung *f* restriction, limitation; reduction; (*von Behauptung*) qualification

einschreiben ['aɪnʃraɪbən] *unreg vt* to write in; (*Post*) to send by registered (*Brit*) *od* certified (*US*) mail ▷ *vr* to register; (*Univ*) to enrol; **Einschreiben** *nt* registered (*Brit*) *od* certified (*US*) letter

einschreiten ['aɪnʃraɪtən] *unreg vi* to step in, intervene; **~ gegen** to take action against

einschüchtern ['aɪnʃʏçtərn] *vt* to intimidate

einschweißen ['aɪnʃvaɪsən] *vt* (*in Plastik*) to shrink-wrap; (*Tech*): **etw in etw** *akk* **~** to weld sth into sth

einsehen ['aɪnze:ən] *unreg vt* (*prüfen*) to inspect; (*Fehler etc*) to recognize; (*verstehen*) to see; **das sehe ich nicht ein** I don't see why; **Einsehen (-s)** *nt* understanding; **ein Einsehen haben** to show understanding

einseitig ['aɪnzaɪtɪç] *adj* one-sided; (*Pol*) unilateral; (*Ernährung*) unbalanced; (*Diskette*) single-sided

einsenden ['aɪnzɛndən] *unreg vt* to send in

Einsender, in (-s, -) *m(f)* sender, contributor

einsetzen ['aɪnzɛtsən] *vt* to put (in); (*in Amt*) to appoint, install; (*Geld*) to stake; (*verwenden*) to use; (*Mil*) to employ ▷ *vi* (*beginnen*) to set in; (*Mus*) to enter, come in ▷ *vr* to work hard; **sich für jdn/etw ~** to support sb/sth; **ich werde mich dafür ~, dass ...** I will do what I can to see that ...

Einsicht ['aɪnzɪçt] *f* insight; (*in Akten*) look, inspection; **zu der ~ kommen, dass ...** to come to the conclusion that ...

einsichtig *adj* (*Mensch*) judicious; **jdm etw ~ machen** to make sb understand *od* see sth

Einsichtnahme (-, -n) *f* (*form*) perusal; **„zur ~"** "for attention"

einsichtslos *adj* unreasonable

einsichtsvoll *adj* understanding

Einsiedler ['aɪnzi:dlər] **(-s, -)** *m* hermit

einsilbig ['aɪnzɪlbɪç] *adj* (*lit, fig*) monosyllabic

einspeichern ['aɪnʃpaɪçərn] *vt*: **etw (in etw** *+akk*) **~**: *Comput*) to feed sth in(to sth)
einsperren ['aɪnʃpɛrən] *vt* to lock up
einspielen ['aɪnʃpi:lən] *vr* (*Sport*) to warm up ▷ *vt* (*Film: Geld*) to bring in; (*Instrument*) to play in; **sich aufeinander ~** to become attuned to each other; **gut eingespielt** running smoothly
einsprachig ['aɪnʃpra:xɪç] *adj* monolingual
einspringen ['aɪnʃprɪŋən] *unreg vi* (*aushelfen*) to stand in; (*mit Geld*) to help out
Einspritzmotor *m* (*Aut*) injection engine
Einspruch ['aɪnʃprʊx] *m* protest, objection; **~ einlegen** (*Jur*) to file an objection
Einspruchsrecht *nt* veto
einspurig ['aɪnʃpu:rɪç] *adj* single-lane; (*Eisenb*) single-track
einst [aɪnst] *adv* once; (*zukünftig*) one *od* some day
einstecken ['aɪnʃtɛkən] *vt* to stick in, insert; (*Brief*) to post, mail (*US*); (*Elek: Stecker*) to plug in; (*Geld*) to pocket; (*mitnehmen*) to take; (*überlegen sein*) to put in the shade; (*hinnehmen*) to swallow
einstehen ['aɪnʃte:ən] *unreg vi*: **für jdn ~** to vouch for sb; **für etw ~** to guarantee sth, vouch for sth; (*Ersatz leisten*) to make good sth
einsteigen ['aɪnʃtaɪgən] *unreg vi* to get in *od* on; (*in Schiff*) to go on board; (*sich beteiligen*) to come in; (*hineinklettern*) to climb in; **~!** (*Eisenb etc*) all aboard!
einstellen ['aɪnʃtɛlən] *vt* (*in Firma*) to employ, take on; (*aufhören*) to stop; (*Geräte*) to adjust; (*Kamera etc*) to focus; (*Sender, Radio*) to tune in to; (*unterstellen*) to put ▷ *vi* to take on staff/ workers ▷ *vr* (*anfangen*) to set in; (*kommen*) to arrive; **Zahlungen ~** to suspend payment; **etw auf etw** *akk* **~** to adjust sth to sth; to focus sth on sth; **sich auf jdn/etw ~** to adapt to sb/prepare o.s. for sth
Einstellung *f* (*Aufhören*) suspension, cessation; (*von Gerät*) adjustment; (*von Kamera etc*) focusing; (*von Arbeiter etc*) appointment; (*Haltung*) attitude
Einstieg ['aɪnʃti:k] (**-(e)s, -e**) *m* entry; (*fig*) approach; (*von Bus, Bahn*) door; **kein ~** exit only
einstig ['aɪnstɪç] *adj* former
einstimmig *adj* unanimous; (*Mus*) for one voice
einstmalig *adj* former
einstmals *adv* once, formerly
einstöckig ['aɪnʃtœkɪç] *adj* two-storeyed (*Brit*), two-storied (*US*)
Einsturz ['aɪnʃtʊrts] *m* collapse
einstürzen ['aɪnʃtʏrtsən] *vi* to fall in, collapse; **auf jdn ~** (*fig*) to overwhelm sb
Einsturzgefahr *f* danger of collapse
einstweilen *adv* meanwhile; (*vorläufig*) temporarily, for the time being
einstweilig *adj* temporary; **~e Verfügung** (*Jur*) temporary *od* interim injunction
eintägig ['aɪntɛ:gɪç] *adj* one-day
eintauschen ['aɪntaʊʃən] *vt* to exchange
eintausend ['aɪn'taʊzənt] *num* one thousand
einteilen ['aɪntaɪlən] *vt* (*in Teile*) to divide (up); (*Menschen*) to assign
einteilig *adj* one-piece
eintönig ['aɪntø:nɪç] *adj* monotonous; **Eintönigkeit** *f* monotony
Eintopf ['aɪntɔpf] *m* stew
Eintracht ['aɪntraxt] (-) *f* concord, harmony
einträchtig ['aɪntrɛçtɪç] *adj* harmonious
Eintrag ['aɪntra:k] (**-(e)s, ¨-e**) *m* entry; **amtlicher ~** entry in the register
eintragen ['aɪntra:gən] *unreg vt* (*in Buch*) to enter; (*Profit*) to yield ▷ *vr* to put one's name down; **jdm etw ~** to bring sb sth
einträglich ['aɪntrɛ:klɪç] *adj* profitable
eintreffen ['aɪntrɛfən] *unreg vi* to happen; (*ankommen*) to arrive; (*fig: wahr werden*) to come true
eintreten ['aɪntre:tən] *unreg vi* (*hineingehen*) to enter; (*sich ereignen*) to occur ▷ *vt* (*Tür*) to kick open; **in etw** *akk* **~** to enter sth; (*in Klub, Partei*) to join sth; **für jdn/etw ~** to stand up for sb/sth
Eintritt ['aɪntrɪt] *m* (*Betreten*) entrance; (*in Klub etc*) joining; **~ frei** admission free; **„~ verboten"** "no admittance"; **bei ~ der Dunkelheit** at nightfall
Eintritts- *zW*: **Eintrittsgeld** *nt* admission charge; **Eintrittspreis** *m* admission charge
einüben ['aɪn|y:bən] *vt* to practise (*Brit*), practice (*US*), drill
Einvernehmen ['aɪnfɛrne:mən] (**-s, -**) *nt* agreement, understanding
einverstanden ['aɪnfɛrʃtandən] *interj* agreed ▷ *adj*: **~ sein** to agree, be agreed; **sich mit etw ~ erklären** to give one's agreement to sth
Einverständnis ['aɪnfɛrʃtɛntnɪs] (**-ses**) *nt* understanding; (*gleiche Meinung*) agreement; **im ~ mit jdm handeln** to act with sb's consent
Einwand ['aɪnvant] (**-(e)s, ¨-e**) *m* objection; **einen ~ erheben** to raise an objection
Einwanderer ['aɪnvandərər] *m* immigrant
einwandern *vi* to immigrate
Einwanderung *f* immigration
einwandfrei *adj* perfect; **etw ~ beweisen** to prove sth beyond doubt
Einwegflasche ['aɪnve:gflaʃə] *f* non-returnable bottle
Einwegspritze *f* disposable (hypodermic) syringe
einweihen ['aɪnvaɪən] *vt* (*Kirche*) to consecrate; (*Brücke*) to open; (*Gebäude*) to inaugurate; (*Person*): **in etw** *akk* **~** to initiate in sth; **er ist eingeweiht** (*fig*) he knows all about it
Einweihung *f* consecration; opening; inauguration; initiation
einweisen ['aɪnvaɪzən] *unreg vt* (*in Amt*) to install; (*in Arbeit*) to introduce; (*in Anstalt*) to send; (*in Krankenhaus*): **~ (in** *+akk*) to admit (to)

einwenden ['aɪnvɛndən] *unreg vt*: **etwas ~ gegen** to object to, oppose
einwerfen ['aɪnvɛrfən] *unreg vt* to throw in; (*Brief*) to post; (*Geld*) to put in, insert; (*Fenster*) to smash; (*äußern*) to interpose
einwilligen ['aɪnvɪlɪgən] *vi*: **(in etw** *akk***) ~** to consent (to sth), agree (to sth)
Einwilligung *f* consent
einwirken ['aɪnvɪrkən] *vi*: **auf jdn/etw ~** to influence sb/sth
Einwohner, in ['aɪnvo:nər(ɪn)] **(-s, -)** *m(f)* inhabitant; **Einwohnermeldeamt** *nt* registration office; **sich beim Einwohnermeldeamt (an)melden** ≈ to register with the police; **Einwohnerschaft** *f* population, inhabitants *pl*
Einwurf ['aɪnvʊrf] *m* (*Öffnung*) slot; (*Einwand*) objection; (*Sport*) throw-in
einzahlen *vt* to pay in
Einzahlung *f* payment; (*auf Sparkonto*) deposit
Einzel ['aɪntsəl] **(-s, -)** *nt* (*Tennis*) singles *pl*
Einzel- *zW*: **Einzelfall** *m* single instance, individual case; **Einzelgänger**, **in** *m(f)* loner; **Einzelhaft** *f* solitary confinement; **Einzelheit** *f* particular, detail; **Einzelkind** *nt* only child
einzeln *adj* single; (*von Paar*) odd ▷ *adv* singly; **~ angeben** to specify; **E~e** some (people), a few (people); **der/die E~e** the individual; **das E~e** the particular; **ins E~e gehen** to go into detail(s); **etw im E~en besprechen** to discuss sth in detail; **~ aufführen** to list separately *od* individually; **bitte ~ eintreten** please come in one (person) at a time
Einzelteil *nt* individual part; (*Ersatzteil*) spare part; **etw in seine ~e zerlegen** to take sth to pieces, dismantle sth
Einzelzimmer *nt* single room
einziehen ['aɪntsi:ən] *unreg vt* to draw in, take in; (*Kopf*) to duck; (*Fühler, Antenne, Fahrgestell*) to retract; (*Steuern, Erkundigungen*) to collect; (*Mil*) to call up, draft (*US*); (*aus dem Verkehr ziehen*) to withdraw; (*konfiszieren*) to confiscate ▷ *vi* to move in; (*Friede, Ruhe*) to come; (*Flüssigkeit*): **~ (in** *+akk***)** to soak in(to)
einzig ['aɪntsɪç] *adj* only; (*ohnegleichen*) unique ▷ *adv*: **~ und allein** solely; **das E~e** the only thing; **der/die E~e** the only one; **kein ~es Mal** not once, not one single time; **kein E~er** nobody, not a single person; **einzigartig** *adj* unique
Einzug ['aɪntsu:k] *m* entry, moving in
Eis [aɪs] **(-es, -)** *nt* ice; (*Speiseeis*) ice cream; **~ am Stiel** ice lolly (*Brit*), popsicle® (*US*); **Eisbahn** *f* ice *od* skating rink; **Eisbär** *m* polar bear; **Eisbecher** *m* sundae; **Eisbein** *nt* pig's trotters *pl*; **Eisberg** *m* iceberg
Eisdecke *f* sheet of ice
Eisdiele *f* ice-cream parlour (*Brit*) *od* parlor (*US*)
Eisen ['aɪzən] **(-s, -)** *nt* iron; **zum alten ~ gehören** (*fig*) to be on the scrap heap
Eisenbahn *f* railway, railroad (*US*); **es ist (aller)höchste ~** (*umg*) it's high time; **Eisenbahner (-s, -)** *m* railwayman, railway employee, railroader (*US*); **Eisenbahnschaffner** *m* railway guard, (railroad) conductor (*US*); **Eisenbahnübergang** *m* level crossing, grade crossing (*US*); **Eisenbahnwagen** *m* railway *od* railroad (*US*) carriage
Eisen- *zW*: **Eisenerz** *nt* iron ore; **eisenhaltig** *adj* containing iron
eisern ['aɪzərn] *adj* iron; (*Gesundheit*) robust; (*Energie*) unrelenting; (*Reserve*) emergency; **der E~e Vorhang** the Iron Curtain; **in etw** *dat* **~ sein** to be adamant about sth; **er ist ~ bei seinem Entschluss geblieben** he stuck firmly to his decision
Eis- *zW*: **Eisfach** *nt* freezer compartment, icebox; **eisfrei** *adj* clear of ice; **Eishockey** *nt* ice hockey
eisig ['aɪzɪç] *adj* icy
Eis- *zW*: **eiskalt** *adj* icy cold; **Eiskunstlauf** *m* figure skating; **Eisläufer** *m* ice-skater; **Eispickel** *m* ice-axe (*Brit*), ice-ax (*US*); **Eisschießen** *nt* ≈ curling; **Eisschrank** *m* fridge, icebox (*US*); **Eiswürfel** *m* ice cube; **Eiszapfen** *m* icicle; **Eiszeit** *f* Ice Age
eitel ['aɪtəl] *adj* vain; **Eitelkeit** *f* vanity
Eiter ['aɪtər] **(-s)** *m* pus
eitern *vi* to suppurate
Ei- *zW*: **Eiweiß (-es, -e)** *nt* white of an egg; (*Chem*) protein; **Eizelle** *f* ovum
Ekel[1] ['e:kəl] **(-s)** *m* nausea, disgust; **vor jdm/etw einen ~ haben** to loathe sb/sth
Ekel[2] ['e:kəl] **(-s, -)** (*umg*) *nt* (*Mensch*) nauseating person
ekelhaft *adj*, **ekelig** *adj* nauseating, disgusting
ekeln *vt* to disgust ▷ *vr*: **sich vor etw** *dat* **~** to be disgusted at sth; **es ekelt ihn** he is disgusted
EKG (-) *nt abk* (= *Elektrokardiogramm*) ECG
Ekstase [ɛk'sta:zə] **(-, -n)** *f* ecstasy; **jdn in ~ versetzen** to send sb into ecstasies
Ekzem [ɛk'tse:m] **(-s, -e)** *nt* (*Med*) eczema
Elan [e'lã:] **(-s)** *m* élan
elastisch [e'lastɪʃ] *adj* elastic
Elastizität [elastitsi'tɛ:t] *f* elasticity
Elbe ['ɛlbə] *f* (*Fluss*) Elbe
Elch [ɛlç] **(-(e)s, -e)** *m* elk
Elefant [ele'fant] *m* elephant; **wie ein ~ im Porzellanladen** (*umg*) like a bull in a china shop
elegant [ele'gant] *adj* elegant
Eleganz [ele'gants] *f* elegance
Elektriker [e'lɛktrikər] **(-s, -)** *m* electrician
elektrisch [e'lɛktrɪʃ] *adj* electric
elektrisieren [elɛktri'zi:rən] *vt* (*lit, fig*) to electrify; (*Mensch*) to give an electric shock to ▷ *vr* to get an electric shock
Elektrizität [elɛktritsi'tɛ:t] *f* electricity
Elektrizitätswerk *nt* electric power station
Elektrode [elɛk'tro:də] **(-, -n)** *f* electrode
Elektro- *zW*: **Elektrogerät** *nt* electrical appliance; **Elektroherd** *m* electric

cooker; **Elektrokardiogramm** *nt* (*Med*) electrocardiogram
Elektrolyse [elektro'ly:zə] (**-, -n**) *f* electrolysis
Elektromotor *m* electric motor
Elektron [e'lɛktrɔn] (**-s, -en**) *nt* electron
Elektronenrechner *m* computer
Elektronik [elɛk'tro:nɪk] *f* electronics *sing*; (*Teile*) electronics *pl*
elektronisch *adj* electronic; **~e Post** electronic mail
Elektrorasierer (**-s, -**) *m* electric razor
Element [ele'mɛnt] (**-s, -e**) *nt* element; (*Elek*) cell, battery
elementar [elemɛn'ta:r] *adj* elementary; (*naturhaft*) elemental
Elend ['e:lɛnt] (**-(e)s**) *nt* misery; **da kann man das heulende ~ kriegen** (*umg*) it's enough to make you scream; **elend** *adj* miserable; **mir ist ganz elend** I feel really awful
Elendsviertel *nt* slum
elf [ɛlf] *num* eleven; **Elf** (**-, en**) *f* (*Sport*) eleven
Elfenbein *nt* ivory; **Elfenbeinküste** *f* Ivory Coast
Elfmeter *m* (*Sport*) penalty (kick)
Elfmeterschießen *nt* (*Sport*) penalty shoot-out
Elite [e'li:tə] (**-, -n**) *f* elite
Elixier [elɪ'ksi:r] (**-s, -e**) *nt* elixir
Ellipse [ɛ'lɪpsə] (**-, -n**) *f* ellipse
Elsass ['ɛlzas] *nt*: **das ~** Alsace
Elster ['ɛlstər] (**-, -n**) *f* magpie
elterlich *adj* parental
Eltern ['ɛltərn] *pl* parents *pl*; **nicht von schlechten ~ sein** (*umg*) to be quite something; **Elternhaus** *nt* home; **elternlos** *adj* orphaned
Email [e'ma:j] (**-s, -s**) *nt* enamel
E-Mail ['i:me:l] (**-, -s**) *f* E-mail, e-mail; **E-Mail-Adresse** *f* E-mail address
emaillieren [ema'ji:rən] *vt* to enamel
Emanze (**-, -n**) (*pej*) *f* women's libber (*umg*)
Emanzipation [emantsipatsi'o:n] *f* emancipation
emanzipieren [emantsi'pi:rən] *vt* to emancipate
Embargo [ɛm'bargo] (**-s, -s**) *nt* embargo
Embryo ['ɛmbryo] (**-s, -s** *od* **-nen**) *m* embryo
Emigration [emigratsi'o:n] *f* emigration
emigrieren [emi'gri:rən] *vi* to emigrate
emotional [emotsio'na:l] *adj* emotional; (*Ausdrucksweise*) emotive
Empfang [ɛm'pfaŋ] (**-(e)s, ⸚e**) *m* reception; (*Erhalten*) receipt; **in ~ nehmen** to receive; **(zahlbar) nach** *od* **bei ~** *+gen* (payable) on receipt (of)
empfangen *unreg vt* to receive ▷ *vi* (*schwanger werden*) to conceive
Empfänger, in [ɛm'pfɛŋər(ɪn)] (**-s, -**) *m(f)* receiver; (*Comm*) addressee, consignee; **~ unbekannt** (*auf Briefen*) not known at this address
empfänglich *adj* receptive, susceptible
Empfängnis (**-, -se**) *f* conception; **Empfängnisverhütung** *f* contraception
Empfangs- *zW*: **Empfangsbestätigung** *f* (acknowledgement of) receipt; **Empfangsdame** *f* receptionist; **Empfangsschein** *m* receipt; **Empfangszimmer** *nt* reception room
empfehlen [ɛm'pfe:lən] *unreg vt* to recommend ▷ *vr* to take one's leave
empfehlenswert *adj* recommendable
Empfehlung *f* recommendation; **auf ~ von** on the recommendation of
empfinden [ɛm'pfɪndən] *unreg vt* to feel; **etw als Beleidigung ~** to find sth insulting
empfindlich *adj* sensitive; (*Stelle*) sore; (*reizbar*) touchy; **deine Kritik hat ihn ~ getroffen** your criticism cut him to the quick
Empfindung *f* feeling, sentiment
empfohlen [ɛm'pfo:lən] *pp von* **empfehlen** ▷ *adj*: **~er Einzelhandelspreis** recommended retail price
empfunden [ɛm'pfʊndən] *pp von* **empfinden**
empor [ɛm'po:r] *adv* up, upwards
empören [ɛm'pø:rən] *vt* to make indignant; to shock ▷ *vr* to become indignant
empörend *adj* outrageous
Emporkömmling *m* upstart, parvenu
Empörung *f* indignation
emsig ['ɛmzɪç] *adj* diligent, busy
Ende ['ɛndə] (**-s, -n**) *nt* end; **am ~** at the end; (*schließlich*) in the end; **am ~ sein** to be at the end of one's tether; **~ Dezember** at the end of December; **zu ~ sein** to be finished; **zu ~ gehen** to come to an end; **zu ~ führen** to finish (off); **letzten ~s** in the end, at the end of the day; **ein böses ~ nehmen** to come to a bad end; **ich bin mit meiner Weisheit am ~** I'm at my wits' end; **er wohnt am ~ der Welt** (*umg*) he lives at the back of beyond
enden *vi* to end
endgültig *adj* final, definite
Endivie [ɛn'di:viə] *f* endive
End- *zW*: **Endlager** *nt* permanent waste disposal site; **Endlagerung** *f* permanent disposal; **endlich** *adj* final; (*Math*) finite ▷ *adv* finally; **endlich!** at last!; **hör endlich damit auf!** will you stop that!; **endlos** *adj* endless; **Endlospapier** *nt* continuous paper; **Endspiel** *nt* final(s); **Endspurt** *m* (*Sport*) final spurt; **Endstation** *f* terminus
Endung *f* ending
Energie [enɛr'gi:] *f* energy; **energielos** *adj* lacking in energy, weak; **Energiewirtschaft** *f* energy industry
energisch [e'nɛrgɪʃ] *adj* energetic; **~ durchgreifen** to take vigorous *od* firm action
eng [ɛŋ] *adj* narrow; (*Kleidung*) tight; (*fig: Horizont*) narrow, limited; (*Freundschaft, Verhältnis*) close; **~ an etw** *dat* close to sth; **in die ~ere Wahl kommen** to be short-listed (*Brit*)
Engagement [ãgaʒə'mã:] (**-s, -s**) *nt* engagement; (*Verpflichtung*) commitment

engagieren [ãga'ʒiːrən] *vt* to engage ▷*vr* to commit o.s.; **ein engagierter Schriftsteller** a committed writer
Enge ['ɛŋə] **(-, -n)** *f (lit, fig)* narrowness; *(Landenge)* defile; *(Meerenge)* straits *pl*; **jdn in die ~ treiben** to drive sb into a corner
Engel ['ɛŋəl] **(-s, -)** *m* angel; **engelhaft** *adj* angelic; **Engelmacher, in (-s, -)** *(umg) m(f)* backstreet abortionist
engherzig *adj* petty
England ['ɛŋlant] *nt* England
Engländer ['ɛŋlɛndər] **(-s, -)** *m* Englishman; English boy; **die Engländer** *pl* the English, the Britishers *(US)*
englisch ['ɛŋlɪʃ] *adj* English
Engpass *m* defile, pass; *(fig: Verkehr)* bottleneck
en gros [ã'gro] *adv* wholesale
engstirnig ['ɛŋʃtɪrnɪç] *adj* narrow-minded
Enkel ['ɛŋkəl] **(-s, -)** *m* grandson
en masse [ã'mas] *adv* en masse
enorm [e'nɔrm] *adj* enormous; *(umg: herrlich, kolossal)* tremendous
Ensemble [ã'sãbəl] **(-s, -s)** *nt* ensemble
entbehrlich *adj* superfluous
entbinden [ɛnt'bɪndən] *unreg vt (+gen)* to release (from); *(Med)* to deliver ▷*vi (Med)* to give birth
Entbindung *f* release; *(Med)* delivery, birth
Entbindungsheim *nt* maternity hospital
entdecken [ɛnt'dɛkən] *vt* to discover; **jdm etw ~** to disclose sth to sb
Entdecker, in (-s, -) *m(f)* discoverer
Entdeckung *f* discovery
Ente ['ɛntə] **(-, -n)** *f* duck; *(fig)* canard, false report; *(Aut)* Citroën 2CV, deux-chevaux
enteignen [ɛnt'|aɪgnən] *vt* to expropriate; *(Besitzer)* to dispossess
enteisen [ɛnt'|aɪzən] *vt* to de-ice; *(Kühlschrank)* to defrost
enterben [ɛnt'|ɛrbən] *vt* to disinherit
entfallen [ɛnt'falən] *unreg vi* to drop, fall; *(wegfallen)* to be dropped; **jdm ~** *(vergessen)* to slip sb's memory; **auf jdn ~** to be allotted to sb
Entfaltung *f* unfolding; *(von Talenten)* development
entfernen [ɛnt'fɛrnən] *vt* to remove; *(hinauswerfen)* to expel ▷*vr* to go away, retire, withdraw
entfernt *adj* distant ▷*adv*: **nicht im E~esten!** not in the slightest!; **weit davon ~ sein, etw zu tun** to be far from doing sth
Entfernung *f* distance; *(Wegschaffen)* removal; **unerlaubte ~ von der Truppe** absence without leave
Entfernungsmesser *m (Phot)* rangefinder
entfremden [ɛnt'frɛmdən] *vt* to estrange, alienate
entfrosten [ɛnt'frɔstən] *vt* to defrost
Entfroster (-s, -) *m (Aut)* defroster
entführen [ɛnt'fyːrən] *vt* to abduct, kidnap; *(Flugzeug)* to hijack
Entführer (-s, -) *m* kidnapper *(Brit)*, kidnaper *(US)*; hijacker
Entführung *f* abduction, kidnapping *(Brit)*, kidnaping *(US)*; hijacking
entgegen [ɛnt'geːgən] *präp +dat* contrary to, against ▷*adv* towards; **entgegenbringen** *unreg vt* to bring; *(fig)*: **jdm etw entgegenbringen** to show sb sth; **entgegengesetzt** *adj* opposite; *(widersprechend)* opposed; **entgegenhalten** *unreg vt (fig)*: **einer Sache** *dat* **entgegenhalten, dass ...** to object to sth that ...; **Entgegenkommen** *nt* obligingness; **entgegenkommen** *unreg vi +dat* to come towards, approach; *(fig)*: **jdm entgegenkommen** to accommodate sb; **das kommt unseren Plänen sehr entgegen** that fits in very well with our plans; **entgegenkommend** *adj* obliging; **entgegennehmen** *unreg vt* to receive, accept; **entgegensehen** *unreg vi +dat* to await; **entgegensetzen** *vt* to oppose; **dem habe ich entgegenzusetzen, dass ...** against that I'd like to say that ...; **jdm/etw Widerstand entgegensetzen** to put up resistance to sb/sth
entgegnen [ɛnt'geːgnən] *vt* to reply, retort
entgehen [ɛnt'geːən] *unreg vi (fig)*: **jdm ~** to escape sb's notice; **sich** *dat* **etw ~ lassen** to miss sth
entgeistert [ɛnt'gaɪstərt] *adj* thunderstruck
Entgelt [ɛnt'gɛlt] **(-(e)s, -e)** *nt* remuneration
entgleisen [ɛnt'glaɪzən] *vi (Eisenb)* to be derailed; *(fig: Person)* to misbehave; **~ lassen** to derail
entgräten [ɛnt'grɛːtən] *vt* to fillet, bone
Enthaarungsmittel [ɛnt'haːrʊŋsmɪtəl] *nt* depilatory
enthalten [ɛnt'haltən] *unreg vt* to contain ▷*vr +gen* to abstain from, refrain from; **sich (der Stimme) ~** to abstain
enthaltsam [ɛnt'haltzaːm] *adj* abstinent, abstemious; **Enthaltsamkeit** *f* abstinence
enthemmen [ɛnt'hɛmən] *vt*: **jdn ~** to free sb from his/her inhibitions
entkommen [ɛnt'kɔmən] *unreg vi* to get away, escape; **jdm/etw** *od* **aus etw ~** to get away *od* escape from sb/sth
entkräften [ɛnt'krɛftən] *vt* to weaken, exhaust; *(Argument)* to refute
entladen [ɛnt'laːdən] *unreg vt* to unload; *(Elek)* to discharge ▷*vr (Gewehr, Elek)* to discharge; *(Ärger etc)* to vent itself
entlang [ɛnt'laŋ] *präp (+akk od dat)* along ▷*adv* along; **~ dem Fluss, den Fluss ~** along the river; **hier ~** this way; **entlanggehen** *unreg vi* to walk along
entlarven [ɛnt'larfən] *vt* to unmask, expose
entlassen [ɛnt'lasən] *unreg vt* to discharge; *(Arbeiter)* to dismiss; *(nach Stellenabbau)* to make redundant
Entlassung *f* discharge; dismissal; **es gab 20 ~en** there were 20 redundancies

entlasten [ɛnt'lastən] *vt* to relieve; (*Arbeit abnehmen*) to take some of the load off; (*Angeklagte*) to exonerate; (*Konto*) to clear
Entlastung *f* relief; (*Comm*) crediting
entlegen [ɛnt'le:gən] *adj* remote
entlocken [ɛnt'lɔkən] *vt*: **jdm etw ~** to elicit sth from sb
entmachten [ɛnt'maxtən] *vt* to deprive of power
entmilitarisiert [ɛntmilitari'zi:rt] *adj* demilitarized
entmündigen [ɛnt'mʏndɪgən] *vt* to certify; (*Jur*) to (legally) incapacitate, declare incapable of managing one's own affairs
entmutigen [ɛnt'mu:tɪgən] *vt* to discourage
entnehmen [ɛnt'ne:mən] *unreg vt +dat* to take out of, take from; (*folgern*) to infer from; **wie ich Ihren Worten entnehme, ...** I gather from what you say that ...
entrahmen [ɛnt'ra:mən] *vt* to skim
entrichten [ɛnt'rɪçtən] *vt* (*form*) to pay
entrosten [ɛnt'rɔstən] *vt* to derust
entrüsten [ɛnt'rʏstən] *vt* to incense, outrage ▷ *vr* to be filled with indignation
entrüstet *adj* indignant, outraged
Entrüstung *f* indignation
entschädigen [ɛnt'ʃɛ:dɪgən] *vt* to compensate
Entschädigung *f* compensation
entschärfen [ɛnt'ʃɛrfən] *vt* to defuse; (*Kritik*) to tone down
Entscheid [ɛnt'ʃaɪt] (**-(e)s, -e**) *m* (*form*) decision
entscheiden *unreg vt, vi, vr* to decide; **darüber habe ich nicht zu ~** that is not for me to decide; **sich für jdn/etw ~** to decide in favour of sb/sth; to decide on sb/sth
entscheidend *adj* decisive; (*Stimme*) casting; **das E~e** the decisive *od* deciding factor
Entscheidung *f* decision; **wie ist die ~ ausgefallen?** which way did the decision go?
Entscheidungsträger *m* decision-maker
entschieden [ɛnt'ʃi:dən] *pp von* **entscheiden** ▷ *adj* decided; (*entschlossen*) resolute; **das geht ~ zu weit** that's definitely going too far; **Entschiedenheit** *f* firmness, determination
entschlacken [ɛnt'ʃlakən] *vt* (*Med: Körper*) to purify
entschließen [ɛnt'ʃli:sən] *unreg vr* to decide; **sich zu nichts ~ können** to be unable to make up one's mind; **kurz entschlossen** straight away
entschlossen [ɛnt'ʃlɔsən] *pp von* **entschließen** ▷ *adj* determined, resolute; **Entschlossenheit** *f* determination
Entschluss [ɛnt'ʃlʊs] *m* decision; **aus eigenem ~ handeln** to act on one's own initiative; **es ist mein fester ~** it is my firm intention
entschlüsseln [ɛnt'ʃlʏsəln] *vt* to decipher; (*Funkspruch*) to decode
entschlussfreudig *adj* decisive
Entschlusskraft *f* determination, decisiveness
entschuldigen [ɛnt'ʃʊldɪgən] *vt* to excuse ▷ *vr* to apologize ▷ *vi*: **~ Sie (bitte)!** excuse me; (*Verzeihung*) sorry; **jdn bei jdm ~** to make sb's excuses *od* apologies to sb; **sich ~ lassen** to send one's apologies
Entschuldigung *f* apology; (*Grund*) excuse; **jdn um ~ bitten** to apologize to sb; **~!** excuse me; (*Verzeihung*) sorry
Entschwefelungsanlage *f* desulphurization plant
entsetzen [ɛnt'zɛtsən] *vt* to horrify ▷ *vr* to be horrified *od* appalled; **Entsetzen** (**-s**) *nt* horror, dismay
entsetzlich *adj* dreadful, appalling
entsorgen [ɛnt'zɔrgən] *vt*: **eine Stadt ~** to dispose of a town's refuse and sewage
Entsorgung *f* waste disposal; (*von Chemikalien*) disposal
entspannen [ɛnt'ʃpanən] *vt, vr* (*Körper*) to relax; (*Pol: Lage*) to ease
Entspannung *f* relaxation, rest; (*Pol*) détente
Entspannungspolitik *f* policy of détente
Entspannungsübungen *pl* relaxation exercises *pl*
entsprechen [ɛnt'ʃprɛçən] *unreg vi +dat* to correspond to; (*Anforderungen, Wünschen*) to meet, comply with
entsprechend *adj* appropriate ▷ *adv* accordingly ▷ *präp +dat*: **er wird seiner Leistung ~ bezahlt** he is paid according to output
entspringen [ɛnt'ʃprɪŋən] *unreg vi (+dat)* to spring (from)
entstehen [ɛnt'ʃte:ən] *unreg vi*: **~ (aus** *od* **durch)** to arise (from), result (from); **wir wollen nicht den Eindruck ~ lassen, ...** we don't want to give rise to the impression that ...; **für ~den** *od* **entstandenen Schaden** for damages incurred
Entstehung *f* genesis, origin
entstellen [ɛnt'ʃtɛlən] *vt* to disfigure; (*Wahrheit*) to distort
entstören [ɛnt'ʃtø:rən] *vt* (*Rundf*) to eliminate interference from; (*Aut*) to suppress
enttäuschen [ɛnt'tɔʏʃən] *vt* to disappoint
Enttäuschung *f* disappointment
entwässern [ɛnt'vɛsərn] *vt* to drain
entweder [ɛnt've:dər] *konj* either; **~ ... oder ...** either ... or ...
entwenden [ɛnt'vɛndən] *unreg vt* to purloin, steal
entwerfen [ɛnt'vɛrfən] *unreg vt* (*Zeichnung*) to sketch; (*Modell*) to design; (*Vortrag, Gesetz etc*) to draft
entwerten [ɛnt've:rtən] *vt* to devalue; (*stempeln*) to cancel
Entwerter (**-s, -**) *m* (ticket-)cancelling (*Brit*) *od* canceling (*US*) machine
entwickeln [ɛnt'vɪkəln] *vt* to develop (*auch* PHOT); (*Mut, Energie*) to show, display ▷ *vr* to develop
Entwickler (**-s, -**) *m* developer

Entwicklung [ɛnt'vɪklʊŋ] *f* development; (*Phot*) developing; **in der ~** at the development stage; (*Jugendliche etc*) still developing

Entwicklungs- *zW*: **Entwicklungshelfer, in** *m(f)* VSO worker (*Brit*), Peace Corps worker (*US*); **Entwicklungshilfe** *f* aid for developing countries; **Entwicklungsjahre** *pl* adolescence *sing*; **Entwicklungsland** *nt* developing country

entwöhnen [ɛnt'vøːnən] *vt* to wean; (*Süchtige*): **(einer Sache** *dat od* **von etw) ~** to cure (of sth)

Entwöhnung *f* weaning; cure, curing

entwürdigend [ɛnt'vʏrdɪgənt] *adj* degrading

Entwurf [ɛnt'vʊrf] *m* outline, design; (*Vertragsentwurf, Konzept*) draft

entziehen [ɛnt'tsiːən] *unreg vt (+dat)* to withdraw (from), take away (from); (*Flüssigkeit*) to draw (from), extract (from) ▷ *vr (+dat)* to escape (from); (*jds Kenntnis*) to be outside *od* beyond; (*der Pflicht*) to shirk (from); **sich jds Blicken ~** to be hidden from sight

Entziehung *f* withdrawal

Entziehungskur *f* treatment for drug addiction/alcoholism

entziffern [ɛnt'tsɪfərn] *vt* to decipher; (*Funkspruch*) to decode

entzücken [ɛnt'tsʏkən] *vt* to delight; **Entzücken (-s)** *nt* delight

entzückend *adj* delightful, charming

Entzugserscheinung *f* withdrawal symptom

entzünden [ɛnt'tsʏndən] *vt* to light, set light to; (*fig, Med*) to inflame; (*Streit*) to spark off ▷ *vr* (*lit, fig*) to catch fire; (*Streit*) to start; (*Med*) to become inflamed

Entzündung *f* (*Med*) inflammation

entzwei [ɛnt'tsvaɪ] *adv* in two; broken; **entzweibrechen** *unreg vt, vi* to break in two

entzweien *vt* to set at odds ▷ *vr* to fall out

entzweigehen *unreg vi* to break (in two)

Enzian ['ɛntsiaːn] **(-s, -e)** *m* gentian

Enzyklopädie [ɛntsyklopɛ'diː] *f* encyclop(a)edia

Enzym [ɛn'tsyːm] **(-s, -e)** *nt* enzyme

Epidemie [epide'miː] *f* epidemic

Epilepsie [epile'psiː] *f* epilepsy

Episode [epi'zoːdə] **(-, -n)** *f* episode

Epoche [e'pɔxə] **(-, -n)** *f* epoch

Epos ['eːpɔs] **(-, Epen)** *nt* epic (poem)

er [eːr] *pron* he; it

erachten [ɛr'|axtən] *vt* (*geh*): **~ für** *od* **als** to consider (to be); **meines E~s** in my opinion

erarbeiten [ɛr'|arbaɪtən] *vt* to work for, acquire; (*Theorie*) to work out

erbarmen [ɛr'barmən] *vr (+gen)* to have pity *od* mercy (on) ▷ *vt*: **er sieht zum E~ aus** he's a pitiful sight; **Herr, erbarme dich (unser)!** Lord, have mercy (upon us)!; **Erbarmen (-s)** *nt* pity

erbärmlich [ɛr'bɛrmlɪç] *adj* wretched, pitiful; **Erbärmlichkeit** *f* wretchedness

Erbauer (-s, -) *m* builder

erbaulich *adj* edifying

Erbauung *f* construction; (*fig*) edification

Erbe[1] ['ɛrbə] **(-n, -n)** *m* heir; **jdn zum** *od* **als ~n einsetzen** to make sb one's/sb's heir

Erbe[2] ['ɛrbə] **(-s)** *nt* inheritance; (*fig*) heritage

erben *vt* to inherit; (*umg: geschenkt bekommen*) to get, be given

erbeuten [ɛr'bɔʏtən] *vt* to carry off; (*Mil*) to capture

Erbfaktor *m* gene

Erbfehler *m* hereditary defect

Erbin *f* heiress

erbittern [ɛr'bɪtərn] *vt* to embitter; (*erzürnen*) to incense

erbittert [ɛr'bɪtərt] *adj* (*Kampf*) fierce, bitter

erblassen [ɛr'blasən] *vi* to (turn) pale

erblich ['ɛrplɪç] *adj* hereditary; **er/sie ist ~ (vor)belastet** it runs in the family

Erbmasse ['ɛrpmasə] *f* estate; (*Biol*) genotype

erbosen [ɛr'boːzən] *vt* (*geh*) to anger ▷ *vr* to grow angry

erbrechen [ɛr'brɛçən] *unreg vt, vr* to vomit

Erbrecht *nt* hereditary right; (*Gesetze*) law of inheritance

Erbschaft *f* inheritance, legacy

Erbse ['ɛrpsə] **(-, -n)** *f* pea

Erb- *zW*

Erd- *zW*: **Erdachse** *f* earth's axis; **Erdapfel** (*Österr*) *m* potato; **Erdatmosphäre** *f* earth's atmosphere; **Erdbeben** *nt* earthquake; **Erdbeere** *f* strawberry; **Erdboden** *m* ground; **etw dem Erdboden gleichmachen** to level sth, raze sth to the ground

Erde (-, -n) *f* earth; **zu ebener ~** at ground level; **auf der ganzen ~** all over the world; **du wirst mich noch unter die ~ bringen** (*umg*) you'll be the death of me yet

erden *vt* (*Elek*) to earth

erdenklich [ɛr'dɛŋklɪç] *adj* = **erdenkbar**

Erd- *zW*: **Erdgas** *nt* natural gas; **Erdgeschoss** *nt* ground floor (*Brit*), first floor (*US*); **Erdkunde** *f* geography; **Erdnuss** *f* peanut; **Erdoberfläche** *f* surface of the earth; **Erdöl** *nt* (mineral) oil

erdreisten [ɛr'draɪstən] *vr* to dare, have the audacity (*to do sth*)

erdrosseln [ɛr'drɔsəln] *vt* to strangle, throttle

erdrücken [ɛr'drʏkən] *vt* to crush; **~de Übermacht/~des Beweismaterial** overwhelming superiority/evidence

Erd- *zW*: **Erdrutsch** *m* landslide; **Erdteil** *m* continent

erdulden [ɛr'dʊldən] *vt* to endure, suffer

ereifern [ɛr'|aɪfərn] *vr* to get excited

ereignen [ɛr'|aɪgnən] *vr* to happen

Ereignis [ɛr'|aɪgnɪs] **(-ses, -se)** *nt* event; **ereignisreich** *adj* eventful

erfahren [ɛr'faːrən] *unreg vt* to learn, find out; (*erleben*) to experience ▷ *adj* experienced

Erfahrung *f* experience; **~en sammeln** to gain experience; **etw in ~ bringen** to learn *od* find out sth

erfahrungsgemäß *adv* according to experience
erfassen [ɛr'fasən] *vt* to seize; (*fig: einbeziehen*) to include, register; (*verstehen*) to grasp
erfinden [ɛr'fɪndən] *unreg vt* to invent; **frei erfunden** completely fictitious
Erfinder, in (**-s, -**) *m(f)* inventor; **erfinderisch** *adj* inventive
Erfindung *f* invention
Erfindungsgabe *f* inventiveness
Erfolg [ɛr'fɔlk] (**-(e)s, -e**) *m* success; (*Folge*) result; **~ versprechend** promising; **viel ~!** good luck!
erfolgen [ɛr'fɔlgən] *vi* to follow; (*sich ergeben*) to result; (*stattfinden*) to take place; (*Zahlung*) to be effected; **nach erfolgter Zahlung** when payment has been made
Erfolg- *zW*: **erfolglos** *adj* unsuccessful; **Erfolglosigkeit** *f* lack of success; **erfolgreich** *adj* successful
Erfolgserlebnis *nt* feeling of success, sense of achievement
erfolgversprechend *adj siehe* **Erfolg**
erforderlich *adj* requisite, necessary
erfordern [ɛr'fɔrdərn] *vt* to require, demand
erforschen [ɛr'fɔrʃən] *vt* (*Land*) to explore; (*Problem*) to investigate; (*Gewissen*) to search
Erforschung *f* exploration; investigation; searching
erfreuen [ɛr'frɔʏən] *vr*: **sich ~ an** *+dat* to enjoy ▷ *vt* to delight; **sich einer Sache** *gen* **~** (*geh*) to enjoy sth; **sehr erfreut!** (*form: bei Vorstellung*) pleased to meet you!
erfreulich [ɛr'frɔʏlɪç] *adj* pleasing, gratifying
erfreulicherweise *adv* happily, luckily
erfrieren [ɛr'fri:rən] *unreg vi* to freeze (to death); (*Glieder*) to get frostbitten; (*Pflanzen*) to be killed by frost
erfrischen [ɛr'frɪʃən] *vt* to refresh
Erfrischung *f* refreshment
Erfrischungsraum *m* snack bar, cafeteria
erfüllen [ɛr'fʏlən] *vt* (*Raum etc*) to fill; (*fig: Bitte etc*) to fulfil (*Brit*), fulfill (*US*) ▷ *vr* to come true; **ein erfülltes Leben** a full life
ergänzen [ɛr'gɛntsən] *vt* to supplement, complete ▷ *vr* to complement one another
Ergänzung *f* completion; (*Zusatz*) supplement
ergeben [ɛr'ge:bən] *unreg vt* to yield, produce ▷ *vr* to surrender; (*folgen*) to result ▷ *adj* devoted; (*demütig*) humble; **sich einer Sache** *dat* **~** (*sich hingeben*) to give o.s. up to sth, yield to sth; **es ergab sich, dass unsere Befürchtungen ...** it turned out that our fears ...; **dem Trunk ~** addicted to drink; **Ergebenheit** *f* devotion; humility
Ergebnis [ɛr'ge:pnɪs] (**-ses, -se**) *nt* result; **zu einem ~ kommen** to come to *od* reach a conclusion; **ergebnislos** *adj* without result, fruitless; **ergebnislos bleiben** *od* **verlaufen** to come to nothing
ergehen [ɛr'ge:ən] *unreg vi* (*form*) to be issued, go out ▷ *vi unpers*: **es ergeht ihm gut/schlecht** he's faring *od* getting on well/badly ▷ *vr*: **sich in etw** *dat* **~** to indulge in sth; **etw über sich** *akk* **~ lassen** to put up with sth; **sich (in langen Reden) über ein Thema ~** (*fig*) to hold forth at length on sth
ergiebig [ɛr'gi:bɪç] *adj* productive
Ergonomie [ɛrgono'mi:] *f* ergonomics *pl*
ergötzen [ɛr'gœtsən] *vt* to amuse, delight
ergreifen [ɛr'graɪfən] *unreg vt* (*lit, fig*) to seize; (*Beruf*) to take up; (*Maßnahmen*) to resort to; (*rühren*) to move; **er ergriff das Wort** he began to speak
ergriffen *pp von* **ergreifen** ▷ *adj* deeply moved
Erguss [ɛr'gʊs] (**-es, ¨-e**) *m* discharge; (*fig*) outpouring, effusion
erhaben [ɛr'ha:bən] *adj* (*lit*) raised, embossed; (*fig*) exalted, lofty; **über etw** *akk* **~ sein** to be above sth
erhalten [ɛr'haltən] *unreg vt* to receive; (*bewahren*) to preserve, maintain; **das Wort ~** to receive permission to speak; **jdn am Leben ~** to keep sb alive; **gut ~** in good condition
erhältlich [ɛr'hɛltlɪç] *adj* obtainable, available
Erhaltung *f* maintenance, preservation
erhärten [ɛr'hɛrtən] *vt* to harden; (*These*) to substantiate, corroborate
erheben [ɛr'he:bən] *unreg vt* to raise; (*Protest, Forderungen*) to make; (*Fakten*) to ascertain ▷ *vr* to rise (up); **sich über etw** *akk* **~** to rise above sth
erheblich [ɛr'he:plɪç] *adj* considerable
erheitern [ɛr'haɪtərn] *vt* to amuse, cheer (up)
Erheiterung *f* exhilaration; **zur allgemeinen ~** to everybody's amusement
erhitzen [ɛr'hɪtsən] *vt* to heat ▷ *vr* to heat up; (*fig*) to become heated *od* aroused
erhöhen [ɛr'hø:ən] *vt* to raise; (*verstärken*) to increase; **erhöhte Temperatur haben** to have a temperature
erholen [ɛr'ho:lən] *vr* to recover; (*entspannen*) to have a rest; (*fig: Preise, Aktien*) to rally, pick up
erholsam *adj* restful
Erholung *f* recovery; relaxation, rest
erholungsbedürftig *adj* in need of a rest, run-down
Erholungsheim *nt* convalescent home
erhören [ɛr'hø:rən] *vt* (*Gebet etc*) to hear; (*Bitte etc*) to yield to
erinnern [ɛr'|ɪnərn] *vt*: **~ (an** *+akk***)** to remind (of) ▷ *vr*: **sich (an etw** *akk***) ~** to remember (sth)
Erinnerung *f* memory; (*Andenken*) reminder; **Erinnerungen** *pl* (*Lebenserinnerung*) reminiscences *pl*; (*Liter*) memoirs *pl*; **jdn/etw in guter ~ behalten** to have pleasant memories of sb/sth
Eritrea [eri'tre:a] (**-s**) *nt* Eritrea
erkälten [ɛr'kɛltən] *vr* to catch cold; **sich** *dat* **die Blase ~** to catch a chill in one's bladder
Erkältung *f* cold

erkennbar *adj* recognizable
erkennen [ɛr'kɛnən] *unreg vt* to recognize; (*sehen, verstehen*) to see; **jdm zu ~ geben, dass ...** to give sb to understand that ...
erkenntlich *adj*: **sich ~ zeigen** to show one's appreciation; **Erkenntlichkeit** *f* gratitude; (*Geschenk*) token of one's gratitude
Erkenntnis (**-, -se**) *f* knowledge; (*das Erkennen*) recognition; (*Einsicht*) insight; **zur ~ kommen** to realize
Erkennung *f* recognition
Erkennungsmarke *f* identity disc
Erker ['ɛrkər] (**-s, -**) *m* bay; **Erkerfenster** *nt* bay window
erklären [ɛr'klɛ:rən] *vt* to explain; (*Rücktritt*) to announce; (*Politiker, Pressesprecher etc*) to say; **ich kann mir nicht ~, warum ...** I can't understand why ...
Erklärung *f* explanation; (*Aussage*) declaration
erkranken [ɛr'kraŋkən] *vi*: **~ (an** *+dat***)** to be taken ill (with); (*Organ, Pflanze, Tier*) to become diseased (with)
Erkrankung *f* illness
erkunden [ɛr'kʊndən] *vt* to find out, ascertain; (*bes Mil*) to reconnoitre (*Brit*), reconnoiter (*US*)
erkundigen *vr*: **sich ~ (nach)** to inquire (about); **ich werde mich ~** I'll find out
Erkundigung *f* inquiry; **~en einholen** to make inquiries
erlahmen [ɛr'la:mən] *vi* to tire; (*nachlassen*) to flag, wane
erlangen [ɛr'laŋən] *vt* to attain, achieve
Erlass [ɛr'las] (**-es, ¨-e**) *m* decree; (*Aufhebung*) remission
erlassen *unreg vt* (*Verfügung*) to issue; (*Gesetz*) to enact; (*Strafe*) to remit; **jdm etw ~** to release sb from sth
erlauben [ɛr'laʊbən] *vt* to allow, permit ▷ *vr*: **sich** *dat* **etw ~** (*Zigarette, Pause*) to permit o.s. sth; (*Bemerkung, Verschlag*) to venture sth; (*sich leisten*) to afford sth; **jdm etw ~** to allow *od* permit sb (to do) sth; **~ Sie?** may I?; **~ Sie mal!** do you mind!; **was ~ Sie sich (eigentlich)!** how dare you!
Erlaubnis [ɛr'laʊpnɪs] (**-, -se**) *f* permission
erläutern [ɛr'lɔʏtərn] *vt* to explain
Erläuterung *f* explanation; **zur ~** in explanation
Erle ['ɛrlə] (**-, -n**) *f* alder
erleben [ɛr'le:bən] *vt* to experience; (*Zeit*) to live through; (*miterleben*) to witness; (*noch miterleben*) to live to see; **so wütend habe ich ihn noch nie erlebt** I've never seen *od* known him so furious
Erlebnis [ɛr'le:pnɪs] (**-ses, -se**) *nt* experience
erledigen [ɛr'le:dɪgən] *vt* to take care of, deal with; (*Antrag etc*) to process; (*umg: erschöpfen*) to wear out; (*ruinieren*) to finish; (*umbringen*) to do in ▷ *vr*: **das hat sich erledigt** that's all settled; **das ist erledigt** that's taken care of, that's been done; **ich habe noch einiges in der Stadt zu ~** I've still got a few things to do in town
erleichtern [ɛr'laɪçtərn] *vt* to make easier; (*fig: Last*) to lighten; (*lindern, beruhigen*) to relieve
erleichtert *adj* relieved; **~ aufatmen** to breathe a sigh of relief
Erleichterung *f* facilitation; lightening; relief
erleiden [ɛr'laɪdən] *unreg vt* to suffer, endure
erlernbar *adj* learnable
erlernen [ɛr'lɛrnən] *vt* to learn, acquire
erlesen [ɛr'le:zən] *adj* select, choice
erleuchten [ɛr'lɔʏçtən] *vt* to illuminate; (*fig*) to inspire
Erleuchtung *f* (*Einfall*) inspiration
Erlös [ɛr'lø:s] (**-es, -e**) *m* proceeds *pl*
erlösen [ɛr'lø:zən] *vt* to redeem, save
Erlösung *f* release; (*Rel*) redemption
ermächtigen [ɛr'mɛçtɪgən] *vt* to authorize, empower
Ermächtigung *f* authorization
ermahnen [ɛr'ma:nən] *vt* to admonish, exhort
Ermahnung *f* admonition, exhortation
ermäßigen [ɛr'mɛsɪgən] *vt* to reduce
Ermäßigung *f* reduction
Ermessen (**-s**) *nt* estimation; discretion; **in jds Ermessen** *dat* **liegen** to lie within sb's discretion; **nach meinem Ermessen** in my judgement
ermitteln [ɛr'mɪtəln] *vt* to determine; (*Täter*) to trace ▷ *vi*: **gegen jdn ~** to investigate sb
Ermittlung [ɛr'mɪtlʊŋ] *f* determination; (*Polizeiermittlung*) investigation; **~en anstellen (über** *+akk***)** to make inquiries (about)
ermöglichen [ɛr'mø:klɪçən] *vt (+dat)* to make possible (for)
ermorden [ɛr'mɔrdən] *vt* to murder
Ermordung *f* murder
ermüden [ɛr'my:dən] *vt* to tire; (*Tech*) to fatigue ▷ *vi* to tire
ermüdend *adj* tiring; (*fig*) wearisome
Ermüdung *f* fatigue
Ermüdungserscheinung *f* sign of fatigue
ermutigen [ɛr'mu:tɪgən] *vt* to encourage
ernähren [ɛr'nɛ:rən] *vt* to feed, nourish; (*Familie*) to support ▷ *vr* to support o.s., earn a living; **sich ~ von** to live on
Ernährer, in (**-s, -**) *m(f)* breadwinner
Ernährung *f* nourishment; (*Med*) nutrition; (*Unterhalt*) maintenance
ernennen [ɛr'nɛnən] *unreg vt* to appoint
Ernennung *f* appointment
erneuern [ɛr'nɔʏərn] *vt* to renew; (*restaurieren*) to restore; (*renovieren*) to renovate
Erneuerung *f* renewal; restoration; renovation
erneut *adj* renewed, fresh ▷ *adv* once more
Ernst [ɛrnst] (**-es**) *m* seriousness; **das ist mein ~** I'm quite serious; **im ~** in earnest; **~ machen mit etw** to put sth into practice;

ernst *adj* serious ▷ *adv*: **es steht ernst um ihn** things don't look too good for him; **ernst gemeint** meant in earnest, serious; **Ernstfall** *m* emergency; **ernsthaft** *adj* serious; **Ernsthaftigkeit** *f* seriousness; **ernstlich** *adj* serious
Ernte ['ɛrntə] (**-, -n**) *f* harvest
ernten *vt* to harvest; (*Lob etc*) to earn
ernüchtern [ɛr'nʏçtərn] *vt* to sober up; (*fig*) to bring down to earth
Ernüchterung *f* sobering up; (*fig*) disillusionment
erobern *vt* to conquer
Eroberung *f* conquest
eröffnen [ɛr'|œfnən] *vt* to open ▷ *vr* to present itself; **jdm etw ~** (*geh*) to disclose sth to sb
Eröffnung *f* opening
Eröffnungsfeier *f* opening ceremony
erogen [ɛro'ge:n] *adj* erogenous
erörtern [ɛr'|œrtərn] *vt* to discuss (in detail)
Erotik [e'ro:tɪk] *f* eroticism
erotisch *adj* erotic
erpicht [ɛr'pɪçt] *adj*: **~ (auf** *+akk***)** keen (on)
erpressen [ɛr'prɛsən] *vt* (*Geld etc*) to extort; (*jdn*) to blackmail
Erpresser (**-s, -**) *m* blackmailer
Erpressung *f* blackmail; extortion
erraten [ɛr'ra:tən] *unreg vt* to guess
erregen [ɛr're:gən] *vt* to excite; (*sexuell*) to arouse; (*ärgern*) to infuriate; (*hervorrufen*) to arouse, provoke ▷ *vr* to get excited *od* worked up
Erreger (**-s, -**) *m* causative agent
Erregung *f* excitement; (*sexuell*) arousal
erreichbar *adj* accessible, within reach
erreichen [ɛr'raɪçən] *vt* to reach; (*Zweck*) to achieve; (*Zug*) to catch; **wann kann ich Sie morgen ~?** when can I get in touch with you tomorrow?; **vom Bahnhof leicht zu ~** within easy reach of the station
erringen [ɛr'rɪŋən] *unreg vt* to gain, win
erröten [ɛr'rø:tən] *vi* to blush, flush
Errungenschaft [ɛr'rʊŋənʃaft] *f* achievement; (*umg: Anschaffung*) acquisition
Ersatz [ɛr'zats] (**-es**) *m* substitute; replacement; (*Schadenersatz*) compensation; (*Mil*) reinforcements *pl*; **als ~ für jdn einspringen** to stand in for sb; **Ersatzbefriedigung** *f* vicarious satisfaction; **Ersatzdienst** *m* (*Mil*) alternative service; **Ersatzteil** *nt* spare (part)
erschaffen [ɛr'ʃafən] *unreg vt* to create
erscheinen [ɛr'ʃaɪnən] *unreg vi* to appear
Erscheinung *f* appearance; (*Geist*) apparition; (*Gegebenheit*) phenomenon; (*Gestalt*) figure; **in ~ treten** (*Merkmale*) to appear; (*Gefühle*) to show themselves
erschießen [ɛr'ʃi:sən] *unreg vt* to shoot (dead)
erschlagen [ɛr'ʃla:gən] *unreg vt* to strike dead ▷ *adj* (*umg: todmüde*) worn out, dead beat (*umg*)
erschöpfen [ɛr'ʃœpfən] *vt* to exhaust
erschöpfend *adj* exhaustive, thorough
erschöpft *adj* exhausted
Erschöpfung *f* exhaustion
erschrecken[1] [ɛr'ʃrɛkən] *vt* to startle, frighten
erschrecken[2] [ɛr'ʃrɛkən] *unreg vi* to be frightened *od* startled
erschreckend *adj* alarming, frightening
erschrocken [ɛr'ʃrɔkən] *pp von* **erschrecken**[2] ▷ *adj* frightened, startled
erschüttern [ɛr'ʃʏtərn] *vt* to shake; (*ergreifen*) to move deeply; **ihn kann nichts ~** he always keeps his cool (*umg*)
Erschütterung *f* (*des Bodens*) tremor; (*tiefe Ergriffenheit*) shock
erschweren [ɛr'ʃve:rən] *vt* to complicate; **~de Umstände** (*Jur*) aggravating circumstances; **es kommt noch ~d hinzu, dass ...** to compound matters ...
erschwinglich *adj* affordable
ersehen [ɛr'ze:ən] *unreg vt*: **aus etw ~, dass ...** to gather from sth that ...
ersetzbar *adj* replaceable
ersetzen [ɛr'zɛtsən] *vt* to replace; **jdm Unkosten** *etc* **~** to pay sb's expenses *etc*
ersichtlich [ɛr'zɪçtlɪç] *adj* evident, obvious
ersparen [ɛr'ʃpa:rən] *vt* (*Ärger etc*) to spare; (*Geld*) to save; **ihr blieb auch nichts erspart** she was spared nothing
Ersparnis (**-, -se**) *f* saving
erst [e:rst] *adv* **1** first; **mach erst (ein)mal die Arbeit fertig** finish your work first; **wenn du das erst (ein)mal hinter dir hast** once you've got that behind you
2 (*nicht früher als, nur*) only; (*nicht bis*) not till; **erst gestern** only yesterday; **erst morgen** not until tomorrow; **erst als** only when, not until; **wir fahren erst später** we're not going until later; **er ist (gerade) erst angekommen** he's only just arrived
3: wäre er doch erst zurück! if only he were back!; **da fange ich erst gar nicht an** I simply won't bother to begin; **jetzt erst recht!** that just makes me all the more determined; **da gings erst richtig los** then things really got going
erstatten [ɛr'ʃtatən] *vt* (*Unkosten*) to refund; **Anzeige gegen jdn ~** to report sb; **Bericht ~** to make a report
Erstaufführung ['e:rst|aʊffy:rʊŋ] *f* first performance
erstaunen [ɛr'ʃtaʊnən] *vt* to astonish ▷ *vi* to be astonished; **Erstaunen** (**-s**) *nt* astonishment
erstaunlich *adj* astonishing
Erstausgabe *f* first edition
erstbeste, r, s *adj* first that comes along
erste, r, s *adj* first; **als E~s** first of all; **in ~r Linie** first and foremost; **fürs E~** for the time being; **E~ Hilfe** first aid; **das ~ Mal** the first time
erstechen [ɛr'ʃtɛçən] *unreg vt* to stab (to death)
erstens *adv* firstly, in the first place
ersticken [ɛr'ʃtɪkən] *vt* (*lit, fig*) to stifle; (*Mensch*) to suffocate; (*Flammen*) to smother

▷ *vi* (*Mensch*) to suffocate; (*Feuer*) to be smothered; **mit erstickter Stimme** in a choked voice; **in Arbeit ~** to be snowed under with work
erst- *zW*: **erstklassig** *adj* first-class; **Erstkommunion** *f* first communion; **erstmalig** *adj* first; **erstmals** *adv* for the first time
erstrebenswert [ɛrˈʃtre:bənsve:rt] *adj* desirable, worthwhile
erstrecken [ɛrˈʃtrɛkən] *vr* to extend, stretch
Ersttagsstempel *m* first-day (date) stamp
ersuchen [ɛrˈzu:xən] *vt* to request
ertappen [ɛrˈtapən] *vt* to catch, detect
erteilen [ɛrˈtaɪlən] *vt* to give
Ertrag [ɛrˈtra:k] (**-(e)s, ¨-e**) *m* yield; (*Gewinn*) proceeds *pl*
ertragen *unreg vt* to bear, stand
erträglich [ɛrˈtrɛ:klɪç] *adj* tolerable, bearable
ertrinken [ɛrˈtrɪŋkən] *unreg vi* to drown; **Ertrinken** (**-s**) *nt* drowning
erübrigen [ɛrˈ|y:brɪgən] *vt* to spare ▷ *vr* to be unnecessary
erwachsen [ɛrˈvaksən] *adj* grown-up *unreg* ▷ *vi*: **daraus erwuchsen ihm Unannehmlichkeiten** that caused him some trouble
Erwachsene, r *f(m)* adult
Erwachsenenbildung *f* adult education
erwägen [ɛrˈvɛ:gən] *unreg vt* to consider
Erwägung *f* consideration; **etw in ~ ziehen** to take sth into consideration
erwähnen [ɛrˈvɛ:nən] *vt* to mention
erwähnenswert *adj* worth mentioning
Erwähnung *f* mention
erwarten [ɛrˈvartən] *vt* to expect; (*warten auf*) to wait for; **etw kaum ~ können** to hardly be able to wait for sth
Erwartung *f* expectation; **in ~ Ihrer baldigen Antwort** (*form*) in anticipation of your early reply
erwartungsgemäß *adv* as expected
erwartungsvoll *adj* expectant
erwecken [ɛrˈvɛkən] *vt* to rouse, awake; **den Anschein ~** to give the impression; **etw zu neuem Leben ~** to resurrect sth
erweisen [ɛrˈvaɪzən] *unreg vt* to prove ▷ *vr*: **sich ~ als** to prove to be; **jdm einen Gefallen/Dienst ~** to do sb a favour/service; **sich jdm gegenüber dankbar ~** to show one's gratitude to sb
Erwerb [ɛrˈvɛrp] (**-(e)s, -e**) *m* acquisition; (*Beruf*) trade
erwerben [ɛrˈvɛrbən] *unreg vt* to acquire; **er hat sich** *dat* **große Verdienste um die Firma erworben** he has done great service for the firm
Erwerbs- *zW*: **erwerbslos** *adj* unemployed; **Erwerbsquelle** *f* source of income; **erwerbstätig** *adj* (gainfully) employed; **erwerbsunfähig** *adj* unable to work
erwidern [ɛrˈvi:dərn] *vt* to reply; (*vergelten*) to return
erwiesen [ɛrˈvi:zən] *adj* proven
erwischen [ɛrˈvɪʃən] (*umg*) *vt* to catch, get; **ihn hats erwischt!** (*umg: verliebt*) he's got it bad; (*: krank*) he's got it; **kalt ~** (*umg*) to catch off-balance
erwünscht [ɛrˈvʏnʃt] *adj* desired
erwürgen [ɛrˈvʏrgən] *vt* to strangle
Erz [e:rts] (**-es, -e**) *nt* ore
erzählen [ɛrˈtsɛ:lən] *vt, vi* to tell; **dem werd ich was ~!** (*umg*) I'll have something to say to him; **~de Dichtung** narrative fiction
Erzähler, in (**-s, -**) *m(f)* narrator
Erzählung *f* story, tale
Erzbischof *m* archbishop
Erzengel *m* archangel
erzeugen [ɛrˈtsɔʏgən] *vt* to produce; (*Strom*) to generate
Erzeugnis (**-ses, -se**) *nt* product, produce
Erzeugung *f* production; generation
erziehen [ɛrˈtsi:ən] *unreg vt* to bring up; (*bilden*) to educate, train
Erzieher, in (**-s, -**) *m(f)* educator; (*in Kindergarten*) nursery school teacher
Erziehung *f* bringing up; (*Bildung*) education
Erziehungs- *zW*: **Erziehungsberechtigte, r** *f(m)* parent, legal guardian; **Erziehungsheim** *nt* community home; **Erziehungsurlaub** *m* leave for a new parent
erzielen [ɛrˈtsi:lən] *vt* to achieve, obtain; (*Tor*) to score
es [ɛs] *nom, akk pron* it
Esche [ˈɛʃə] (**-, -n**) *f* ash
Esel [ˈe:zəl] (**-s, -**) *m* donkey, ass; **ich ~!** (*umg*) silly me!
Eselsbrücke *f* (*Gedächtnishilfe*) mnemonic, aide-mémoire
Eskalation [ɛskalatsiˈo:n] *f* escalation
Eskimo [ˈɛskimo] (**-s, -s**) *m* eskimo
essbar [ˈɛsba:r] *adj* eatable, edible
essen [ˈɛsən] *unreg vt, vi* to eat; **~ gehen** (*auswärts*) to eat out; **~ Sie gern Äpfel?** do you like apples?; **Essen** (**-s, -**) *nt* (*Mahlzeit*) meal; (*Nahrung*) food; **Essen auf Rädern** meals on wheels
Essens- *zW*: **Essensmarke** *f* meal voucher; **Essenszeit** *f* mealtime
Essig [ˈɛsɪç] (**-s, -e**) *m* vinegar; **damit ist es ~** (*umg*) it's all off; **Essiggurke** *f* gherkin
Esskastanie *f* sweet chestnut
Ess- *zW*: **Esslöffel** *m* tablespoon; **Esstisch** *m* dining table; **Esswaren** *pl* foodstuffs *pl*; **Esszimmer** *nt* dining room
Estland [ˈe:stlant] *nt* Estonia
estnisch [ˈe:stnɪʃ] *adj* Estonian
etablieren [etaˈbli:rən] *vr* to establish o.s.; (*Comm*) to set up
Etage [eˈta:ʒə] (**-, -n**) *f* floor, storey (*Brit*), story (*US*)
Etagenwohnung *f* flat (*Brit*), apartment (*US*)
Etappe [eˈtapə] (**-, -n**) *f* stage
Etat [eˈta:] (**-s, -s**) *m* budget
etepetete [e:təpeˈte:tə] (*umg*) *adj* fussy
Ethik [ˈe:tɪk] *f* ethics *sing*

ethisch ['e:tɪʃ] *adj* ethical
ethnisch ['ɛtnɪʃ] *adj* ethnic; **~e Säuberung** ethnic cleansing
Etikett [eti'kɛt] (**-(e)s, -e**) *nt* (*lit, fig*) label
Etikette *f* etiquette, manners *pl*
etikettieren [etikɛ'ti:rən] *vt* to label
etliche, r, s ['ɛtlɪçə(r, s)] *adj* quite a lot of ▷ *pron pl* some, quite a few; **~s** quite a lot
Etui [ɛt'vi:] (**-s, -s**) *nt* case
etwa ['ɛtva] *adv* (*ungefähr*) about; (*vielleicht*) perhaps; (*beispielsweise*) for instance; (*entrüstet, erstaunt*): **hast du ~ schon wieder kein Geld dabei?** don't tell me you haven't got any money again! ▷ *adv* (*zur Bestätigung*): **Sie kommen doch, oder ~ nicht?** you are coming, aren't you?; **nicht ~** by no means; **willst du ~ schon gehen?** (surely) you don't want to go already?
etwaig ['ɛtvaɪç] *adj* possible
etwas *pron* something; (*fragend, verneinend*) anything; (*ein wenig*) a little ▷ *adv* a little; **er kann ~** he's good
Etymologie [etymolo'gi:] *f* etymology
EU [e:'|u:] (-) *f abk* (= *Europäische Union*) EU
euch [ɔʏç] *pron* (*akk von ihr*) you; yourselves; (*dat von ihr*) (to/for) you ▷ *refl pron* yourselves
euer ['ɔʏər] *pron gen von* **ihr** of you ▷ *adj* your
EU-Erweiterung [e:'|u:-] *f* enlargement of the EU
Eule ['ɔʏlə] (**-, -n**) *f* owl
eure, r, s ['ɔʏrə(r, s)] *pron* yours
eurerseits *adv* on your part
euresgleichen *pron* people like you
euretwegen ['ɔʏrət'vegən] *adv* (*für euch*) for your sakes; (*wegen euch*) on your account
Euro ['ɔʏro] (**-, -s**) *m* (*Fin*) euro
Eurocheque [ɔʏro'ʃɛk] (**-s, -s**) *m* Eurocheque
Europa [ɔʏ'ro:pa] (**-s**) *nt* Europe
Europäer, in [ɔʏro'pɛ:ər(ɪn)] (**-s, -**) *m(f)* European
europäisch *adj* European; **das E~e Parlament** the European Parliament; **E~e Union** European Union; **E~e (Wirtschafts)gemeinschaft** European (Economic) Community, Common Market; **Europameister** *m* European champion
Euter ['ɔʏtər] (**-s, -**) *nt* udder
Euthanasie [ɔʏtana'zi:] *f* euthanasia
ev. *abk* = **evangelisch**
evakuieren [evaku'i:rən] *vt* to evacuate
evangelisch [evaŋ'ge:lɪʃ] *adj* Protestant
Evangelium [evaŋ'ge:liʊm] *nt* Gospel
eventuell [evɛntu'ɛl] *adj* possible ▷ *adv* possibly, perhaps
EWG [e:ve:'ge:] (-) *f abk* (*früher*: = *Europäische Wirtschaftsgemeinschaft*) EEC
ewig ['e:vɪç] *adj* eternal ▷ *adv*: **auf ~** forever; **ich habe Sie ~ lange nicht gesehen** (*umg*) I haven't seen you for ages; **Ewigkeit** *f* eternity; **bis in alle Ewigkeit** forever
EWS (-) *nt abk* (= *Europäisches Währungssystem*) EMS
EWU (-) *f abk* (= *Europäische Währungsunion*) EMU
exakt [ɛ'ksakt] *adj* exact
Examen [ɛ'ksa:mən] (**-s, -** *od* **Examina**) *nt* examination
Exemplar [ɛksɛm'pla:r] (**-s, -e**) *nt* specimen; (*Buchexemplar*) copy; **exemplarisch** *adj* exemplary
exerzieren [ɛksɛr'tsi:rən] *vi* to drill
Exil [ɛ'ksi:l] (**-s, -e**) *nt* exile
Existenz [ɛksɪs'tɛnts] *f* existence; (*Unterhalt*) livelihood, living; (*pej: Mensch*) character
Existenzkampf *m* struggle for existence
Existenzminimum (**-s, -ma**) *nt* subsistence level
existieren [ɛksɪs'ti:rən] *vi* to exist
exklusiv [ɛksklu'zi:f] *adj* exclusive
exklusive [ɛksklu'zi:və] *präp +gen* exclusive of, not including ▷ *adv* exclusive of, excluding
exorzieren [ɛksɔr'tsi:rən] *vt* to exorcize
exotisch [ɛ'kso:tɪʃ] *adj* exotic
Expedition [ɛkspeditsi'o:n] *f* expedition; (*Comm*) forwarding department
Experiment [ɛksperi'mɛnt] *nt* experiment
experimentell [ɛksperimɛn'tɛl] *adj* experimental
experimentieren [ɛksperimɛn'ti:rən] *vi* to experiment
Experte [ɛks'pɛrtə] (**-n, -n**) *m* expert, specialist
explodieren [ɛksplo'di:rən] *vi* to explode
Explosion [ɛksplozi'o:n] *f* explosion
explosiv [ɛksplo'zi:f] *adj* explosive
Exponent [ɛkspo'nɛnt] *m* exponent
Export [ɛks'pɔrt] (**-(e)s, -e**) *m* export
Exportartikel *m* export
Exporthandel *m* export trade
exportieren [ɛkspɔr'ti:rən] *vt* to export
Exportland *nt* exporting country
Expressgut [ɛks'prɛsgut] *nt* express goods *pl od* freight
extra ['ɛkstra] *adj inv* (*umg: gesondert*) separate; (*besondere*) extra ▷ *adv* (*gesondert*) separately; (*speziell*) specially; (*absichtlich*) on purpose; (*vor Adjektiven, zusätzlich*) extra; **Extra** (**-s, -s**) *nt* extra; **Extraausgabe** *f* special edition
Extrakt [ɛks'trakt] (**-(e)s, -e**) *m* extract
Extrawurst (*umg*) *f* (*Sonderwunsch*): **er will immer eine ~ (gebraten haben)** he always wants something different
Extrem [ɛks'tre:m] (**-s, -e**) *nt* extreme; **extrem** *adj* extreme
extremistisch [ɛkstre'mɪstɪʃ] *adj* (*Pol*) extremist
Extremitäten [ɛkstremi'tɛ:tən] *pl* extremities *pl*
Exzellenz [ɛkstsɛ'lɛnts] *f* excellency
exzentrisch [ɛks'tsɛntrɪʃ] *adj* eccentric
Exzess [ɛks'tsɛs] (**-es, -e**) *m* excess

F, **f**[1] [ef] (**-, -**) *nt* F, f; **F wie Friedrich** ≈ F for Frederick, ≈ F for Fox (*US*); **nach Schema F** (*umg*) in the usual old way
f[2] *abk* (= *feminin*) fem.
Fabel ['fa:bəl] (**-, -n**) *f* fable; **fabelhaft** *adj* fabulous, marvellous (*Brit*), marvelous (*US*)
Fabrik [fa'bri:k] *f* factory
Fabrikant [fabri:'kant] *m* (*Hersteller*) manufacturer; (*Besitzer*) industrialist
Fabrikarbeiter, in *m(f)* factory worker
Fabrikat [fabri:'ka:t] (**-(e)s, -e**) *nt* product; (*Marke*) make
Fabrikation [fabri:katsi'o:n] *f* manufacture, production
Fabrikgelände *nt* factory site
Fach [fax] (**-(e)s, ¨-er**) *nt* compartment; (*in Schrank, Regal etc*) shelf; (*Sachgebiet*) subject; **ein Mann/eine Frau vom ~** an expert; **Facharbeiter** *m* skilled worker; **Facharzt** *m* (medical) specialist; **Fachausdruck** *m* technical term
Fächer ['fɛçər] (**-s, -**) *m* fan
Fach- *zW*: **Fachfrau** *f* expert; **Fachgeschäft** *nt* specialist shop (*Brit*) *od* store (*US*); **Fachhochschule** *f* college; **fachlich** *adj* technical; (*beruflich*) professional; **Fachmann** (**-(e)s**, *pl* **Fachleute**) *m* expert; **fachmännisch** *adj* professional; **Fachschule** *f* technical college; **fachsimpeln** *vi* to talk shop; **Fachwerk** *nt* timber frame; **Fachwerkhaus** *nt* half-timbered house
Fackel ['fakəl] (**-, -n**) *f* torch
fad, fade *adj* insipid; (*langweilig*) dull; (*Essen*) tasteless
Faden ['fa:dən] (**-s, ¨-**) *m* thread; **der rote ~** (*fig*) the central theme; **alle Fäden laufen hier zusammen** this is the nerve centre (*Brit*) *od* center (*US*) of the whole thing; **Fadennudeln** *pl* vermicelli *sing*; **fadenscheinig** *adj* (*lit, fig*) threadbare
fähig ['fɛ:ɪç] *adj*: **~ (zu** *od* **+*gen*)** capable (of); able (to); **zu allem ~ sein** to be capable of anything; **Fähigkeit** *f* ability
fahnden ['fa:ndən] *vi*: **~ nach** to search for
Fahndung *f* search
Fahndungsliste *f* list of wanted criminals, wanted list
Fahne ['fa:nə] (**-, -n**) *f* flag; standard; **mit fliegenden ~n zu jdm/etw überlaufen** to go over to sb/sth; **eine ~ haben** (*umg*) to smell of drink
Fahrausweis *m* (*form*) ticket
Fahrbahn *f* carriageway (*Brit*), roadway
Fähre ['fɛ:rə] (**-, -n**) *f* ferry
fahren ['fa:rən] *unreg vt* to drive; (*Rad*) to ride; (*befördern*) to drive, take; (*Rennen*) to drive in ▷ *vi* (*sich bewegen*) to go; (*Schiff*) to sail; (*abfahren*) to leave; **mit dem Auto/Zug ~** to go *od* travel by car/train; **mit dem Aufzug ~** to take the lift, ride the elevator (*US*); **links/rechts ~** to drive on the left/right; **gegen einen Baum ~** to drive *od* go into a tree; **die U-Bahn fährt alle fünf Minuten** the underground goes *od* runs every five minutes; **mit der Hand ~ über** *+akk* to pass one's hand over; **(bei etw) gut/schlecht ~** (*zurechtkommen*) to do well/badly (with sth); **was ist (denn) in dich ge~?** what's got (*Brit*) *od* gotten (*US*) into you?; **einen ~ lassen** (*umg*) to fart (*!*)
Fahrer, in ['fa:rər(ɪn)] (**-s, -**) *m(f)* driver; **Fahrerflucht** *f* hit-and-run driving
Fahr- *zW*: **Fahrgast** *m* passenger; **Fahrgeld** *nt* fare; **Fahrgestell** *nt* chassis; (*Aviat*) undercarriage; **Fahrkarte** *f* ticket; **Fahrkartenausgabe** *f* ticket office; **Fahrkartenautomat** *m* ticket machine; **Fahrkartenschalter** *m* ticket office
fahrlässig *adj* negligent; **~e Tötung** manslaughter; **Fahrlässigkeit** *f* negligence
Fahr- *zW*: **Fahrlehrer** *m* driving instructor; **Fahrplan** *m* timetable; **fahrplanmäßig** *adj* (*Eisenb*) scheduled; **Fahrpreis** *m* fare; **Fahrprüfung** *f* driving test; **Fahrrad** *nt* bicycle; **Fahrradweg** *m* cycle path; **Fahrschein** *m* ticket; **Fahrschule** *f* driving school; **Fahrstuhl** *m* lift (*Brit*), elevator (*US*); **Fahrstunde** *f* driving lesson
Fahrt [fa:rt] (**-, -en**) *f* journey; (*kurz*) trip; (*Aut*) drive; (*Geschwindigkeit*) speed; **gute ~!** safe journey!; **volle ~ voraus!** (*Naut*) full speed ahead!
Fährte ['fɛ:rtə] (**-, -n**) *f* track, trail; **jdn auf eine falsche ~ locken** (*fig*) to put sb off the scent
Fahrtkosten *pl* travelling expenses *pl*
Fahrtrichtung *f* course, direction
Fahr- *zW*: **Fahrzeug** *nt* vehicle;

Fahrzeughalter (**-s, -**) *m* owner of a vehicle
fair [fɛːr] *adj* fair
Faktor *m* factor
Faktum (**-s, -ten**) *nt* fact
Fakultät [fakʊl'tɛːt] *f* faculty
Falke ['falkə] (**-n, -n**) *m* falcon
Falklandinseln ['falklant'ɪnzəln] *pl* Falkland Islands, Falklands
Fall [fal] (**-(e)s, ⸚e**) *m* (*Sturz*) fall; (*Sachverhalt, Jur, Gram*) case; **auf jeden ~, auf alle Fälle** in any case; (*bestimmt*) definitely; **gesetzt den ~** assuming (that); **jds ~ sein** (*umg*) to be sb's cup of tea; **klarer ~!** (*umg*) sure thing!, you bet!; **das mache ich auf keinen ~** there's no way I'm going to do that
Falle (**-, -n**) *f* trap; (*umg: Bett*) bed; **jdm eine ~ stellen** to set a trap for sb
fallen *unreg vi* to fall; (*im Krieg*) to fall, be killed; **etw ~ lassen** to drop sth; (*Bemerkung*) to make sth; (*Plan*) to abandon sth, to drop sth
fällen ['fɛlən] *vt* (*Baum*) to fell; (*Urteil*) to pass
fällig ['fɛlɪç] *adj* due; (*Wechsel*) mature(d); **längst ~** long overdue
falls *adv* in case, if
Fall- *zW*: **Fallschirm** *m* parachute; **Fallschirmjäger** *m* paratrooper; **Fallschirmspringer, in** *m(f)* parachutist
falsch [falʃ] *adj* false; (*unrichtig*) wrong; **ein ~es Spiel (mit jdm) treiben** to play (sb) false; **etw ~ verstehen** to misunderstand sth, get sth wrong; *siehe auch* **falschliegen**
fälschen ['fɛlʃən] *vt* to forge
Falschgeld *nt* counterfeit money
fälschlich *adj* false
fälschlicherweise *adv* mistakenly
Fälschung *f* forgery
fälschungssicher *adj* forgery-proof
Faltblatt *nt* leaflet; (*in Zeitschrift etc*) insert
Falte ['faltə] (**-, -n**) *f* (*Knick*) fold, crease; (*Hautfalte*) wrinkle; (*Rockfalte*) pleat
falten *vt* to fold; (*Stirn*) to wrinkle
Falter ['faltər] (**-s, -**) *m* (*Tagfalter*) butterfly; (*Nachtfalter*) moth
faltig ['faltɪç] *adj* (*Haut*) wrinkled; (*Rock usw*) creased
familiär [famili'ɛːr] *adj* familiar
Familie [fa'miːliə] *f* family; **~ Otto Francke** (*als Anschrift*) Mr. & Mrs. Otto Francke and family; **zur ~ gehören** to be one of the family
Familien- *zW*: **Familienkreis** *m* family circle; **Familienmitglied** *nt* member of the family; **Familienname** *m* surname; **Familienplanung** *f* family planning; **Familienstand** *m* marital status
Fanatiker, in [fa'naːtikər(ɪn)] (**-s, -**) *m(f)* fanatic
fanatisch *adj* fanatical
Fanatismus [fana'tɪsmʊs] *m* fanaticism
Fang [faŋ] (**-(e)s, ⸚e**) *m* catch; (*Jagen*) hunting; (*Kralle*) talon, claw
fangen *unreg vt* to catch ▷ *vr* to get caught; (*Flugzeug*) to level out; (*Mensch: nicht fallen*) to steady o.s.; (*fig*) to compose o.s.; (*in Leistung*) to get back on form
Fantasie [fanta'ziː] *f* imagination; **in seiner ~** in his mind; **fantasielos** *adj* unimaginative
fantasieren [fanta'ziːren] *vi* to fantasize; (*Med*) to be delirious
fantasievoll *adj* imaginative
fantastisch *adj* fantastic
Farb- *zW*: **Farbaufnahme** *f* colour (*Brit*) *od* color (*US*) photograph; **Farbband** *nt* typewriter ribbon
Farbe ['faːrbə] (**-, -n**) *f* colour (*Brit*), color (*US*); (*zum Malen etc*) paint; (*Stofffarbe*) dye; (*Karten*) suit
farbecht ['farp|ɛçt] *adj* colourfast (*Brit*), colorfast (*US*)
färben ['fɛrbən] *vt* to colour (*Brit*), color (*US*); (*Stoff, Haar*) to dye
Farbfernsehen *nt* colour (*Brit*) *od* color (*US*) television
Farbfilm *m* colour (*Brit*) *od* color (*US*) film
farbig *adj* coloured (*Brit*), colored (*US*)
Farbige, r *f(m)* coloured (*Brit*) *od* colored (*US*) person
Farb- *zW*: **Farbkasten** *m* paintbox; **farblos** *adj* colourless (*Brit*), colorless (*US*); **Farbstift** *m* coloured (*Brit*) *od* colored (*US*) pencil; **Farbstoff** *m* dye; (*Lebensmittelfarb*) (artificial) colouring (*Brit*) *od* coloring (*US*); **Farbton** *m* hue, tone
Färbung ['fɛrbʊŋ] *f* colouring (*Brit*), coloring (*US*); (*Tendenz*) bias
Farn [farn] (**-(e)s, -e**) *m* fern; (*Adlerfarn*) bracken
Fasan [fa'zaːn] (**-(e)s, -e(n)**) *m* pheasant
Fasching ['faʃɪŋ] (**-s, -e** *od* **-s**) *m* carnival
Faschismus [fa'ʃɪsmʊs] *m* fascism
Faschist, in *m(f)* fascist
faschistisch [fa'ʃɪstɪʃ] *adj* fascist
Faser ['faːzər] (**-, -n**) *f* fibre
Fass [fas] (**-es, ⸚er**) *nt* vat, barrel; (*für Öl*) drum; **Bier vom ~** draught beer; **ein ~ ohne Boden** (*fig*) a bottomless pit
Fassade [fa'saːdə] *f* (*lit, fig*) façade
fassbar *adj* comprehensible
Fassbier *nt* draught beer
fassen ['fasən] *vt* (*ergreifen*) to grasp, take; (*inhaltlich*) to hold; (*Entschluss etc*) to take; (*verstehen*) to understand; (*Ring etc*) to set; (*formulieren*) to formulate, phrase ▷ *vr* to calm down; **nicht zu ~** unbelievable; *siehe auch* **kurzfassen**
Fassung ['fasʊŋ] *f* (*Umrahmung*) mounting; (*Lampenfassung*) socket; (*Wortlaut*) version; (*Beherrschung*) composure; **jdn aus der ~ bringen** to upset sb; **völlig außer ~ geraten** to lose all self-control
fassungslos *adj* speechless
fast [fast] *adv* almost, nearly; **~ nie** hardly ever
fasten ['fastən] *vi* to fast; **Fastenzeit** *f* Lent
Fastnacht *f* Shrovetide carnival
faszinieren [fastsi'niːrən] *vt* to fascinate

fatal [fa'ta:l] *adj* fatal; (*peinlich*) embarrassing
faul [faʊl] *adj* rotten; (*Person*) lazy; (*Ausreden*) lame; **daran ist etwas ~** there's something fishy about it
faulen *vi* to rot
faulenzen ['faulɛntsən] *vi* to idle
Faulenzer, in (**-s, -**) *m(f)* idler, loafer
Faulheit *f* laziness
faulig *adj* putrid
Fäulnis ['fɔʏlnɪs] (**-**) *f* decay, putrefaction
Faust ['faʊst] (**-, Fäuste**) *f* fist; **das passt wie die ~ aufs Auge** (*passt nicht*) it's all wrong; **auf eigene ~** (*fig*) on one's own initiative
Fausthandschuh *m* mitten
Favorit, in [favo'ri:t(ɪn)] (**-en, -en**) *m(f)* favourite (*Brit*), favorite (*US*)
Fax [faks] (**-, -e**) *nt* fax; **faxen** *vt* to fax
Fazit ['fa:tsɪt] (**-s, -s** *od* **-e**) *nt*: **wenn wir aus diesen vier Jahren das ~ ziehen** if we take stock of these four years
FCKW (**-s, -s**) *m abk* (*= Fluorchlorkohlenwasserstoff*) CFC
FDP, F.D.P. *f abk* (*= Freie Demokratische Partei*) Free Democratic Party
Februar ['fe:brua:r] (**-(s), -e**) (*pl selten*) *m* February; *siehe auch* **September**
fechten ['fɛçtən] *unreg vi* to fence
Feder ['fe:dər] (**-, -n**) *f* feather; (*Schreibfeder*) pen nib; (*Tech*) spring; **in den ~n liegen** (*umg*) to be/stay in bed; **Federball** *m* shuttlecock; **Federbett** *nt* continental quilt; **Federhalter** *m* pen; **federleicht** *adj* light as a feather
federn *vi* (*nachgeben*) to be springy; (*sich bewegen*) to bounce ▷ *vt* to spring
Federung *f* suspension
Fegefeuer ['fe:gəfɔʏər] *nt* purgatory
fegen ['fe:gən] *vt* to sweep
fehl [fe:l] *adj*: **~ am Platz** *od* **Ort** out of place
fehlen *vi* to be wanting *od* missing; (*abwesend sein*) to be absent ▷ *vi unpers*: **es fehlte nicht viel und ich hätte ihn verprügelt** I almost hit him; **etw fehlt jdm** sb lacks sth; **du fehlst mir** I miss you; **was fehlt ihm?** what's wrong with him?; **der/das hat mir gerade noch gefehlt!** (*ironisch*) he/that was all I needed; **weit gefehlt!** (*fig*) you're way out! (*umg*); (*ganz im Gegenteil*) far from it!; **mir ~ die Worte** words fail me; **wo fehlt es?** what's the trouble?, what's up? (*umg*)
Fehler (**-s, -**) *m* mistake, error; (*Mangel, Schwäche*) fault; **ihr ist ein ~ unterlaufen** she's made a mistake; **fehlerfrei** *adj* faultless; without any mistakes; **fehlerhaft** *adj* incorrect; faulty; **Fehlermeldung** *f* (*Comput*) error message
fehl- *zW*: **Fehlgeburt** *f* miscarriage; **Fehlgriff** *m* blunder; **Fehlkonstruktion** *f*: **eine Fehlkonstruktion sein** to be badly designed; **Fehlschlag** *m* failure; **fehlschlagen** *unreg vi* to fail; **Fehlstart** *m* (*Sport*) false start; **Fehlzündung** *f* (*Aut*) misfire, backfire
Feier ['faɪər] (**-, -n**) *f* celebration; **Feierabend** *m* time to stop work; **Feierabend machen** to stop, knock off; **was machst du am Feierabend?** what are you doing after work?; **jetzt ist Feierabend!** that's enough!
feierlich *adj* solemn; **das ist ja nicht mehr ~** (*umg*) that's beyond a joke; **Feierlichkeit** *f* solemnity; **Feierlichkeiten** *pl* festivities *pl*
feiern *vt, vi* to celebrate
Feiertag *m* holiday
feig *adj* cowardly
Feige ['faɪgə] (**-, -n**) *f* fig
Feigheit *f* cowardice
Feigling *m* coward
Feile ['faɪlə] (**-, -n**) *f* file
feilschen ['faɪlʃən] *vi* to haggle
fein [faɪn] *adj* fine; (*vornehm*) refined; (*Gehör etc*) keen; **~!** great!; **er ist ~ raus** (*umg*) he's sitting pretty; **sich ~ machen** to get all dressed up
Feind, in [faɪnt, 'faɪndɪn] (**-(e)s, -e**) *m(f)* enemy; **Feindbild** *nt* concept of an/the enemy; **feindlich** *adj* hostile; **Feindschaft** *f* enmity; **feindselig** *adj* hostile; **Feindseligkeit** *f* hostility
Fein- *zW*: **feinfühlend** *adj* sensitive; **Feingefühl** *nt* delicacy, tact; **Feinheit** *f* fineness; refinement; keenness; **Feinkostgeschäft** *nt* delicatessen (shop), deli; **Feinschmecker** (**-s, -**) *m* gourmet
Feld [fɛlt] (**-(e)s, -er**) *nt* field; (*Schach*) square; (*Sport*) pitch; **Argumente ins ~ führen** to bring arguments to bear; **das ~ räumen** (*fig*) to bow out; **Feldherr** *m* commander; **Feldsalat** *m* lamb's lettuce; **Feldstecher** *m* (pair of) binoculars *pl od* field glasses *pl*; **Feldwebel** (**-s, -**) *m* sergeant; **Feldweg** *m* path
Felge ['fɛlgə] (**-, -n**) *f* (wheel) rim
Fell [fɛl] (**-(e)s, -e**) *nt* fur; coat; (*von Schaf*) fleece; (*von toten Tieren*) skin; **ein dickes ~ haben** to be thick-skinned, have a thick skin; **ihm sind die ~e weggeschwommen** (*fig*) all his hopes were dashed
Fels [fɛls] (**-en, -en**) *m* = **Felsen**; **felsenfest** *adj* firm
felsig *adj* rocky
Felsspalte *f* crevice
Felsvorsprung *m* ledge
feminin [femi'ni:n] *adj* feminine; (*pej*) effeminate
Fenchel ['fɛnçəl] (**-s**) *m* fennel
Fenster ['fɛnstər] (**-s, -**) *nt* window; **weg vom ~** (*umg*) out of the game, finished; **Fensterplatz** *m* window seat; **Fensterscheibe** *f* windowpane; **Fenstersims** *m* windowsill
Ferien ['fe:riən] *pl* holidays *pl*, vacation (*US*); **die großen ~** the summer holidays (*Brit*), the long vacation (*US Univ*); **~ haben** to be on holiday; **Ferienkurs** *m* holiday course; **Ferienreise** *f* holiday; **Ferienwohnung** *f* holiday flat (*Brit*), vacation apartment (*US*);

Ferienzeit *f* holiday period
Ferkel ['fɛrkəl] (**-s, -**) *nt* piglet
fern [fern] *adj, adv* far-off, distant; **~ von hier** a long way (away) from here; *siehe auch* **fernhalten; fernliegen**; **Fernamt** *nt* (*Tel*) exchange; **Fernbedienung** *f* remote control
Ferne (**-, -n**) *f* distance
ferner *adj, adv* further; (*weiterhin*) in future; **unter „~ liefen" rangieren** (*umg*) to be an also-ran
fern- *zW*: **Fernflug** *m* long-distance flight; **Ferngespräch** *nt* long-distance call (*Brit*), toll call (*US*); **ferngesteuert** *adj* remote-controlled; (*Rakete*) guided; **Fernglas** *nt* binoculars *pl*; **fernhalten** *unreg vt* to keep away; **Fernlenkung** *f* remote control; **Fernrohr** *nt* telescope; **Fernschreiber** *m* teleprinter
Fernsehapparat *m* television (set)
fernsehen ['fernze:ən] *unreg vi* to watch television; **Fernsehen** (**-s**) *nt* television; **im Fernsehen** on television
Fernseher (**-s, -**) *m* television (set)
Fernseh- *zW*: **Fernsehgebühr** *f* television licence (*Brit*) *od* license (*US*) fee; **Fernsehgerät** *nt* television set
Fern- *zW*: **Fernsprecher** *m* telephone; **Fernsprechzelle** *f* telephone box (*Brit*) *od* booth (*US*); **Fernsteuerung** *f* remote control
Fernverkehr *m* long-distance traffic
Ferse ['fɛrzə] (**-, -n**) *f* heel
fertig ['fɛrtɪç] *adj* (*bereit*) ready; (*beendet*) finished; (*gebrauchsfertig*) ready-made; **~ ausgebildet** fully qualified; **mit jdm/etw ~ werden** to cope with sb/sth; **mit den Nerven ~ sein** to be at the end of one's tether; **~ bringen** *od* **machen** (*beenden*) to finish; **sich ~ machen** to get ready; **~ essen/lesen** to finish eating/reading; **~ stellen** to complete; **Fertigbau** *m* prefab(ricated house)
Fertig- *zW*: **Fertiggericht** *nt* ready-to-serve meal; **Fertigkeit** *f* skill; **fertigmachen** (*umg*) *vt* (*Person*) to finish; (*körperlich*) to exhaust; (*moralisch*) to get down; *siehe auch* **fertig**; **fertigstellen** *vt* to complete
Fessel ['fɛsəl] (**-, -n**) *f* fetter
fesseln *vt* to bind; (*mit Fesseln*) to fetter; (*fig*) to grip; **ans Bett gefesselt** (*fig*) confined to bed
fesselnd *adj* gripping
Fest [fɛst] (**-(e)s, -e**) *nt* (*Feier*) celebration; (*Party*) party; **man soll die ~e feiern wie sie fallen** (*Sprichwort*) make hay while the sun shines
fest *adj* firm; (*Nahrung*) solid; (*Gehalt*) regular; (*Gewebe, Schuhe*) strong, sturdy; (*Freund(in)*) steady ▷ *adv* (*schlafen*) soundly; **~ angestellt** employed on a permanent basis; **~ entschlossen sein** to be absolutely determined; **~ umrissen** clearcut; **~e Kosten** (*Comm*) fixed costs *pl*
festbinden *unreg vt* to tie, fasten
Festessen *nt* banquet
festhalten *unreg vt* to seize, hold fast; (*Ereignis*) to record ▷ *vr*: **sich ~ (an** *+dat***)** to hold on (to)
festigen *vt* to strengthen
Festigkeit *f* strength
fest- *zW*: **Festland** *nt* mainland; **festlegen** *vt* to fix ▷ *vr* to commit o.s.; **jdn auf etw** *akk* **festlegen** (*festnageln*) to tie sb (down) to sth; (*verpflichten*) to commit sb to sth
festlich *adj* festive
fest- *zW*: **festmachen** *vt* to fasten; (*Termin etc*) to fix; **Festnahme** (**-, -n**) *f* capture; **festnehmen** *unreg vt* to capture, arrest; **Festplatte** *f* (*Comput*) hard disk
Festrede *f* speech, address
festsetzen *vt* to fix, settle
Festspiel *nt* festival
fest- *zW*: **feststehen** *unreg vi* to be certain; **feststellen** *vt* to establish; (*sagen*) to remark; (*Tech*) to lock (fast)
Festung *f* fortress
Fett [fɛt] (**-(e)s, -e**) *nt* fat, grease; **fett** *adj* fat; (*Essen etc*) greasy; **fett gedruckt** bold-type; **fettarm** *adj* low fat; **fetten** *vt* to grease; **fettig** *adj* greasy, fatty; **Fettnäpfchen** *nt*: **ins Fettnäpfchen treten** to put one's foot in it
feucht [fɔʏçt] *adj* damp; (*Luft*) humid
Feuchtigkeit *f* dampness; humidity
Feuchtigkeitscreme *f* moisturizer
Feuer ['fɔʏər] (**-s, -**) *nt* fire; (*zum Rauchen*) a light; (*fig: Schwung*) spirit; **für jdn durchs ~ gehen** to go through fire and water for sb; **~ und Flamme (für etw) sein** (*umg*) to be dead keen (on sth); **~ für etw/jdn fangen** (*fig*) to develop a great interest in sth/sb; **Feueralarm** *m* fire alarm; **feuerfest** *adj* fireproof; **Feuergefahr** *f* danger of fire; **bei Feuergefahr** in the event of fire; **feuergefährlich** *adj* inflammable; **Feuerleiter** *f* fire escape ladder; **Feuerlöscher** (**-s, -**) *m* fire extinguisher; **Feuermelder** (**-s, -**) *m* fire alarm
feuern *vt, vi* (*lit, fig*) to fire
Feuer- *zW*: **Feuerstein** *m* flint; **Feuerwehr** *f* fire brigade; **Feuerwehrauto** *nt* fire engine; **Feuerwerk** *nt* fireworks *pl*; **Feuerzeug** *nt* (cigarette) lighter
feurig ['fɔʏrɪç] *adj* fiery
Fichte ['fɪçtə] (**-, -n**) *f* spruce
ficken ['fɪkən] (*umg!*) *vt, vi* to fuck (*!*)
Fieber ['fi:bər] (**-s, -**) *nt* fever, temperature; (*Krankheit*) fever; **~ haben** to have a temperature; **fieberhaft** *adj* feverish; **Fiebermesser** *m* thermometer
fies [fi:s] (*umg*) *adj* nasty
Figur [fi'gu:r] (**-, -en**) *f* figure; (*Schachfigur*) chessman, chess piece; **eine gute/schlechte/traurige ~ abgeben** to cut a good/poor/sorry figure
Filiale [fili'a:lə] (**-, -n**) *f* (*Comm*) branch
Film [fɪlm] (**-(e)s, -e**) *m* film, movie (*bes US*); **da ist bei mir der ~ gerissen** (*umg*) I had a mental blackout
filmen *vt, vi* to film
Film- *zW*: **Filmkamera** *f* cine-camera;

Filmvorführgerät *nt* cine-projector
Filter ['fɪltər] (**-s, -**) *m* filter
filtern *vt* to filter
Filterpapier *nt* filter paper
Filterzigarette *f* tipped cigarette
Filz [fɪlts] (**-es, -e**) *m* felt
filzen *vt* (*umg*) to frisk ▷ *vi* (*Wolle*) to mat
Finale [fi'na:lə] (**-s, -(s)**) *nt* finale; (*Sport*) final(s *pl*)
Finanzamt *nt* ≈ Inland Revenue Office (*Brit*), ≈ Internal Revenue Office (*US*); **Finanzbeamte, r** *f(m)* revenue officer
finanziell [finantsi'ɛl] *adj* financial
finanzieren [finan'tsi:rən] *vt* to finance, to fund
Finanzminister *m* ≈ Chancellor of the Exchequer (*Brit*), Minister of Finance
finden ['fɪndən] *unreg vt* to find; (*meinen*) to think ▷ *vr* to be (found); (*sich fassen*) to compose o.s. ▷ *vi*: **ich finde schon allein hinaus** I can see myself out; **ich finde nichts dabei, wenn ...** I don't see what's wrong if ...; **das wird sich ~** things will work out
Finder, in (**-s, -**) *m(f)* finder
findig *adj* resourceful
Finger ['fɪŋər] (**-s, -**) *m* finger; **mit ~n auf jdn zeigen** (*fig*) to look askance at sb; **das kann sich jeder an den (fünf) ~n abzählen** (*umg*) it sticks out a mile; **sich** *dat* **etw aus den ~n saugen** to conjure sth up; **lange ~ machen** (*umg*) to be light-fingered; **Fingerabdruck** *m* fingerprint; **Fingerhut** *m* thimble; (*Bot*) foxglove; **Fingernagel** *m* fingernail; **Fingerspitze** *f* fingertip; **Fingerspitzengefühl** *nt* sensitivity
fingieren [fɪŋ'gi:rən] *vt* to feign
Fink ['fɪŋk] (**-en, -en**) *m* finch
Finne ['fɪnə] (**-n, -n**) *m* Finn
finnisch *adj* Finnish
Finnland *nt* Finland
finster ['fɪnstər] *adj* dark, gloomy; (*verdächtig*) dubious; (*verdrossen*) grim; (*Gedanke*) dark; **jdn ~ ansehen** to give sb a black look; **Finsternis** (-) *f* darkness, gloom
Finte ['fɪntə] (**-, -n**) *f* feint, trick
Firma (**-, -men**) *f* firm; **die ~ dankt** (*hum*) much obliged (to you)
Firmen- *zW*: **Firmeninhaber** *m* proprietor (*of firm*); **Firmenschild** *nt* (shop) sign; **Firmenzeichen** *nt* trademark
Firnis ['fɪrnɪs] (**-ses, -se**) *m* varnish
Fis [fɪs] (**-, -**) *nt* (*Mus*) F sharp
Fisch [fɪʃ] (**-(e)s, -e**) *m* fish; **Fische** *pl* (*Astrol*) Pisces *sing*; **das sind kleine ~e** (*fig: umg*) that's child's play
fischen *vt, vi* to fish
Fischer (**-s, -**) *m* fisherman
Fisch- *zW*: **Fischfang** *m* fishing; **Fischgeschäft** *nt* fishmonger's (shop); **Fischgräte** *f* fishbone; **Fischstäbchen** *nt* fish finger (*Brit*), fish stick (*US*)
fit [fɪt] *adj* fit
Fitness ['fɪtnəs] *nt* fitness
fix [fɪks] *adj* (*flink*) quick; (*Person*) alert, smart; **~e Idee** obsession, idée fixe; **~ und fertig** finished; (*erschöpft*) done in; **jdn ~ und fertig machen** (*nervös machen*) to drive sb mad
fixen (*umg*) *vi* (*Drogen spritzen*) to fix
Fixer, in ['fɪksər(ɪn)] (*umg*) *m(f)* junkie (*inf*); **Fixerstube** (*umg*) *f* junkies' centre (*inf*)
fixieren [fɪ'ksi:rən] *vt* to fix; (*anstarren*) to stare at; **er ist zu stark auf seine Mutter fixiert** (*Psych*) he has a mother fixation
flach [flax] *adj* flat; (*Gefäß*) shallow; **auf dem ~en Land** in the middle of the country
Fläche ['flɛçə] (**-, -n**) *f* area; (*Oberfläche*) surface
Flächeninhalt *m* surface area
Flachland *nt* lowland
flackern ['flakərn] *vi* to flare, flicker
Flagge ['flagə] (**-, -n**) *f* flag; **~ zeigen** (*fig*) to nail one's colours to the mast
Flamme ['flamə] (**-, -n**) *f* flame; **in ~n stehen/aufgehen** to be in/go up in flames
Flanell [fla'nɛl] (**-s, -e**) *m* flannel
Flanke ['flaŋkə] (**-, -n**) *f* flank; (*Sport: Seite*) wing
Flasche ['flaʃə] (**-, -n**) *f* bottle; (*umg: Versager*) wash-out; **zur ~ greifen** (*fig*) to hit the bottle
Flaschen- *zW*: **Flaschenbier** *nt* bottled beer; **Flaschenöffner** *m* bottle opener; **Flaschenzug** *m* pulley
flatterhaft *adj* flighty, fickle
flattern ['flatərn] *vi* to flutter
flau [flaʊ] *adj* (*Brise, Comm*) slack; **jdm ist ~ (im Magen)** sb feels queasy
Flaum [flaʊm] (**-(e)s**) *m* (*Feder*) down
flauschig ['flaʊʃɪç] *adj* fluffy
Flausen ['flaʊzən] *pl* silly ideas *pl*; (*Ausflüchte*) weak excuses *pl*
Flaute ['flaʊtə] (**-, -n**) *f* calm; (*Comm*) recession
Flechte ['flɛçtə] (**-, -n**) *f* (*Med*) dry scab; (*Bot*) lichen
flechten *unreg vt* to plait; (*Kranz*) to twine
Fleck [flɛk] (**-(e)s, -e**) *m* (*Schmutzfleck*) stain; (*Farbfleck*) patch; (*Stelle*) spot; **nicht vom ~ kommen** (*lit, fig*) not to get any further; **sich nicht vom ~ rühren** not to budge; **vom ~ weg** straight away; **Fleckenmittel** *nt* stain remover
fleckig *adj* marked; (*schmutzig*) stained
Fledermaus ['fle:dərmaʊs] *f* bat
Flegel ['fle:gəl] (**-s, -**) *m* flail; (*Person*) lout; **flegelhaft** *adj* loutish, unmannerly; **Flegeljahre** *pl* adolescence *sing*
flehen ['fle:ən] *vi* (*geh*) to implore
flehentlich *adj* imploring
Fleisch ['flaɪʃ] (**-(e)s**) *nt* flesh; (*Essen*) meat; **sich** *dat od akk* **ins eigene ~ schneiden** to cut off one's nose to spite one's face (*Sprichwort*); **es ist mir in ~ und Blut übergegangen** it has become second nature to me; **Fleischbrühe** *f* meat stock
Fleischer (**-s, -**) *m* butcher
Fleischerei [flaɪʃə'raɪ] *f* butcher's (shop)
Fleischwolf *m* mincer

Fleiß ['flaɪs] (**-es**) *m* diligence, industry; **ohne ~ kein Preis** (*Sprichwort*) success never comes easily
fleißig *adj* diligent, industrious; **~ studieren/arbeiten** to study/work hard
fletschen ['flɛtʃən] *vt* (*Zähne*) to show
flexibel [flɛ'ksi:bəl] *adj* flexible
Flicken ['flɪkən] (**-s, -**) *m* patch
flicken *vt* to mend
Flieder ['fli:dər] (**-s, -**) *m* lilac
Fliege ['fli:gə] (**-, -n**) *f* fly; (*Schlips*) bow tie; **zwei ~n mit einer Klappe schlagen** (*Sprichwort*) to kill two birds with one stone; **ihn stört die ~ an der Wand** every little thing irritates him
fliegen *unreg vt, vi* to fly; **auf jdn/etw ~** (*umg*) to be mad about sb/sth; **aus der Kurve ~** to skid off the bend; **aus der Firma ~** (*umg*) to get the sack
Fliegengewicht *nt* (*Sport, fig*) flyweight
Fliegenpilz *m* fly agaric
Flieger (**-s, -**) *m* flier, airman
fliehen ['fli:ən] *unreg vi* to flee
Fliese ['fli:zə] (**-, -n**) *f* tile
Fließband ['fli:sbant] *nt* assembly *od* production line; **am ~ arbeiten** to work on the assembly *od* production line; **Fließbandarbeit** *f* production-line work
fließen *unreg vi* to flow
fließend *adj* flowing; (*Rede, Deutsch*) fluent; (*Übergang*) smooth
flimmern ['flɪmərn] *vi* to glimmer; **es flimmert mir vor den Augen** my head's swimming
flink [flɪŋk] *adj* nimble, lively; **mit etw ~ bei der Hand sein** to be quick (off the mark) with sth
Flinte ['flɪntə] (**-, -n**) *f* shotgun; **die ~ ins Korn werfen** to throw in the sponge
Flirt [flœrt] (**-s, -s**) *m* flirtation; **einen ~ (mit jdm) haben** flirt (with sb)
flirten ['flɪrtən] *vi* to flirt
Flitterwochen *pl* honeymoon *sing*
flitzen ['flɪtsən] *vi* to flit
Flocke ['flɔkə] (**-, -n**) *f* flake
Floh [flo:] (**-(e)s, ¨-e**) *m* flea; **jdm einen ~ ins Ohr setzen** (*umg*) to put an idea into sb's head
Flohmarkt *m* flea market
florieren [flo'rierən] *vi* to flourish
Floskel ['flɔskəl] (**-, -n**) *f* set phrase
Flosse ['flɔsə] (**-, -n**) *f* fin; (*Taucherflosse*) flipper; (*umg: Hand*) paw
Flöte ['flø:tə] (**-, -n**) *f* flute; (*Blockflöte*) recorder
Flötist, in [flø'tɪst(ɪn)] *m(f)* flautist, flutist (*bes US*)
flott [flɔt] *adj* lively; (*elegant*) smart; (*Naut*) afloat
Flotte (**-, -n**) *f* fleet
flottmachen *vt* (*Schiff*) to float off; (*Auto, Fahrrad etc*) to put back on the road
Fluch [flu:x] (**-(e)s, ¨-e**) *m* curse; **fluchen** *vi* to curse, swear
Flucht [flʊxt] (**-, -en**) *f* flight; (*Fensterflucht*) row; (*Reihe*) range; (*Zimmerflucht*) suite; (*geglückt*) flight, escape; **jdn/etw in die ~ schlagen** to put sb/sth to flight
fluchtartig *adj* hasty
flüchten ['flʏçtən] *vi* to flee ▷ *vr* to take refuge
flüchtig *adj* fugitive; (*Chem*) volatile; (*oberflächlich*) cursory; (*eilig*) fleeting; **~er Speicher** (*Comput*) volatile memory; **jdn ~ kennen** to have met sb briefly; **Flüchtigkeit** *f* transitoriness; volatility; cursoriness; **Flüchtigkeitsfehler** *m* careless slip
Flüchtling *m* refugee
Flüchtlingslager *nt* refugee camp
Flug [flu:k] (**-(e)s, ¨-e**) *m* flight; **im ~** airborne, in flight; **wie im ~(e)** (*fig*) in a flash: **Flugbahn** *f* flight path; (*Kreisbahn*) orbit; **Flugbegleiter, in** *m(f)* (*Aviat*) flight attendant; **Flugblatt** *nt* pamphlet
Flügel ['fly:gəl] (**-s, -**) *m* wing; (*Mus*) grand piano
Fluggast *m* airline passenger
Flug- *zW*: **Fluggeschwindigkeit** *f* flying *od* air speed; **Fluggesellschaft** *f* airline (company); **Flughafen** *m* airport; **Flughöhe** *f* altitude (of flight); **Fluglotse** *m* air traffic *od* flight controller; **Flugplan** *m* flight schedule; **Flugplatz** *m* airport; (*klein*) airfield; **Flugschein** *m* pilot's licence (*Brit*) *od* license (*US*); **Flugschreiber** *m* flight recorder; **Flugsteig** *m* gate; **Flugverkehr** *m* air traffic
Flugzeug (**-(e)s, -e**) *nt* plane, aeroplane (*Brit*), airplane (*US*); **Flugzeugentführung** *f* hijacking of a plane; **Flugzeughalle** *f* hangar; **Flugzeugträger** *m* aircraft carrier
Flunder ['flʊndər] (**-, -n**) *f* flounder
flunkern ['flʊŋkərn] *vi* to fib, tell stories
Fluor ['flu:ɔr] (**-s**) *nt* fluorine
Flur[1] [flu:r] (**-(e)s, -e**) *m* hall; (*Treppenflur*) staircase
Flur[2] [flu:r] (**-, -en**) *f* (*geh*) open fields *pl*; **allein auf weiter ~ stehen** (*fig*) to be out on a limb
Fluss [flʊs] (**-es, ¨-e**) *m* river; (*Fließen*) flow; **im ~ sein** (*fig*) to be in a state of flux; **etw in ~** *akk* **bringen** to get sth moving; **Flussdiagramm** *nt* flow chart
flüssig ['flʏsɪç] *adj* liquid; (*Stil*) flowing; **~es Vermögen** (*Comm*) liquid assets *pl*; **Flüssigkeit** *f* liquid; (*Zustand*) liquidity; **flüssigmachen** *vt* (*Geld*) to make available
flüstern ['flʏstərn] *vt, vi* to whisper
Flut [flu:t] (**-, -en**) *f* (*lit, fig*) flood; (*Gezeiten*) high tide; **Flutlicht** *nt* floodlight
focht *etc* [fɔxt] *vb siehe* **fechten**
Fohlen ['fo:lən] (**-s, -**) *nt* foal
Föhn [fø:n] (**-(e)s, -e**) *m* foehn, *warm dry alpine wind*; (*Haartrockner*) hairdryer
föhnen *vt* to blow-dry
Föhre ['fø:rə] (**-, -n**) *f* Scots pine
Folge ['fɔlgə] (**-, -n**) *f* series, sequence; (*Fortsetzung*) instalment (*Brit*), installment (*US*); (*TV, Rundf*) episode; (*Auswirkung*) result; **in rascher ~** in quick succession; **etw zur**

~ haben to result in sth; **~n haben** to have consequences; **einer Sache** *dat* **~ leisten** to comply with sth
folgen *vi+dat* to follow ▷ *vi* (*gehorchen*) to obey; **jdm ~ können** (*fig*) to follow *od* understand sb; **daraus folgt, dass ...** it follows from this that ...
folgend *adj* following; **im F~en** in the following; (*schriftlich*) below
folgendermaßen ['fɔlgəndər'ma:sən] *adv* as follows, in the following way
folgern *vt*: **~ (aus)** to conclude (from)
Folgerung *f* conclusion
folglich ['fɔlklıç] *adv* consequently
folgsam ['fɔlkza:m] *adj* obedient
Folie ['fo:liə] (**-, -n**) *f* foil
Folter ['fɔltər] (**-, -n**) *f* torture; (*Gerät*) rack; **jdn auf die ~ spannen** (*fig*) to keep sb on tenterhooks
foltern *vt* to torture
fönen *vt siehe* **föhnen**
Fontäne [fɔn'tɛ:nə] (**-, -n**) *f* fountain
fordern ['fɔrdərn] *vt* to demand; (*fig: kosten: Opfer*) to claim; (*: herausfordern*) to challenge
fördern ['fœrdərn] *vt* to promote; (*unterstützen*) to help; (*Kohle*) to extract; (*finanziell: Projekt*) to sponsor; (*jds Talent, Neigung*) to encourage, foster
Forderung ['fɔrdərʊŋ] *f* demand
Förderung ['fœrdərʊŋ] *f* promotion; help; extraction
Forelle [fo'rɛlə] *f* trout
Form [fɔrm] (**-, -en**) *f* shape; (*Gestaltung*) form; (*Gussform*) mould; (*Backform*) baking tin; **in ~ von** in the shape of; **in ~ sein** to be in good form *od* shape; **die ~ wahren** to observe the proprieties; **in aller ~** formally
formalisieren [fɔrmali'zi:rən] *vt* to formalize
Formalität [fɔrmalı'tɛ:t] *f* formality; **alle ~en erledigen** to go through all the formalities
Format [fɔr'ma:t] (**-(e)s, -e**) *nt* format; (*fig*) quality
formatieren [fɔrma'ti:rən] *vt* (*Text, Diskette*) to format
formbar *adj* malleable
Formel (**-, -n**) *f* formula; (*von Eid etc*) wording; (*Floskel*) set phrase
formell [fɔr'mɛl] *adj* formal
formen *vt* to form, shape
Formfehler *m* faux pas, gaffe; (*Jur*) irregularity
förmlich ['fœrmlıç] *adj* formal; (*umg*) real; **Förmlichkeit** *f* formality
formlos *adj* shapeless; (*Benehmen etc*) informal; (*Antrag*) unaccompanied by a form *od* any forms
Formular [fɔrmu'la:r] (**-s, -e**) *nt* form
formulieren [fɔrmu'li:rən] *vt* to formulate
Formulierung *f* wording
forschen [fɔrʃən] *vi* to search; (*wissenschaftlich*) to (do) research; **~ nach** to search for
forschend *adj* searching
Forscher (**-s, -**) *m* research scientist; (*Naturforscher*) explorer
Forschung ['fɔrʃʊŋ] *f* research; **~ und Lehre** research and teaching; **~ und Entwicklung** research and development
Forschungsreise *f* scientific expedition
Förster ['fœrstər] (**-s, -**) *m* forester; (*für Wild*) gamekeeper
fort [fɔrt] *adv* away; (*verschwunden*) gone; (*vorwärts*) on; **und so ~** and so on; **in einem ~** incessantly; **fortbestehen** *unreg vi* to continue to exist; **fortbewegen** *vt, vr* to move away; **fortbilden** *vr* to continue one's education; **Fortbildung** *f* further education; **fortbleiben** *unreg vi* to stay away; **Fortdauer** *f* continuance; **fortfahren** *unreg vi* to depart; (*fortsetzen*) to go on, continue; **fortführen** *vt* to continue, carry on; **fortgehen** *unreg vi* to go away; **fortgeschritten** *adj* advanced; **fortmüssen** *unreg vi* to have to go; **fortpflanzen** *vr* to reproduce; **Fortpflanzung** *f* reproduction
Forts. *abk* = **Fortsetzung**
fortschaffen *vt* to remove
Fortschritt ['fɔrtʃrıt] *m* advance; **~e machen** to make progress; **dem ~ dienen** to further progress; **fortschrittlich** *adj* progressive
fort- *zW*: **fortsetzen** *vt* to continue; **Fortsetzung** *f* continuation; (*folgender Teil*) instalment (*Brit*), installment (*US*); **Fortsetzung folgt** to be continued
Foto ['fo:to] (**-s, -s**) *nt* photo(graph); **ein ~ machen** to take a photo(graph); **Fotoalbum** *nt* photograph album; **Fotoapparat** *m* camera; **Fotograf, in** (**-en, -en**) *m(f)* photographer; **Fotografie** *f* photography; (*Bild*) photograph; **fotografieren** *vt* to photograph ▷ *vi* to take photographs; **Fotokopie** *f* photocopy; **fotokopieren** *vt* to photocopy; **Fotokopierer** *m* photocopier
Foul [faʊl] (**-s, -s**) *nt* foul
Fr. *abk* (= *Frau*) Mrs, Ms
Fracht [fraxt] (**-, -en**) *f* freight; (*Naut*) cargo; (*Preis*) carriage; **~ zahlt Empfänger** (*Comm*) carriage forward
Frachter (**-s, -**) *m* freighter
Frachtgut *nt* freight
Frack [frak] (**-(e)s, ¨-e**) *m* tails *pl*, tail coat
Frage ['fra:gə] (**-, -n**) *f* question; **jdm eine ~ stellen** to ask sb a question, put a question to sb; **das ist gar keine ~, das steht außer ~** there's no question about it; *siehe auch* **infrage**; **Fragebogen** *m* questionnaire
fragen *vt, vi* to ask ▷ *vr* to wonder; **nach Arbeit/Post ~** to ask whether there is/was any work/mail; **da fragst du mich zu viel** (*umg*) I really couldn't say; **nach** *od* **wegen** (*umg*) **jdm ~** to ask for sb; (*nach jds Befinden*) to ask after sb; **ohne lange zu ~** without asking a lot of questions
Fragezeichen *nt* question mark
fraglich *adj* questionable, doubtful;

(*betreffend*) in question
fraglos *adv* unquestionably
Fragment [fra'gmɛnt] *nt* fragment
fragwürdig ['fra:kvʏrdɪç] *adj* questionable, dubious
Fraktion [fraktsi'o:n] *f* parliamentary party
Franken[1] ['fraŋkən] *nt* Franconia
Franken[2] ['fraŋkən] (**-, -**) *m*: **(Schweizer) ~** (Swiss) Franc
frankieren [fraŋ'ki:rən] *vt* to stamp, frank
franko *adv* carriage paid; (*Post*) post-paid
Frankreich ['fraŋkraɪç] (**-s**) *nt* France
Franzose [fran'tso:zə] (**-n, -n**) *m* Frenchman; French boy
französisch *adj* French; **~es Bett** double bed
fraß *etc* [fra:s] *vb siehe* **fressen**
Frau [fraʊ] (**-, -en**) *f* woman; (*Ehefrau*) wife; (*Anrede*) Mrs, Ms; **~ Doktor** Doctor
Frauen- *zW*: **Frauenarzt** *m* gynaecologist (*Brit*), gynecologist (*US*); **Frauenbewegung** *f* feminist movement; **frauenfeindlich** *adj* anti-women, misogynous; **Frauenhaus** *nt* women's refuge; **Frauenquote** *f* recommended proportion of women (employed)
Fräulein ['frɔʏlaɪn] *nt* young lady; (*Anrede*) Miss; (*Verkäuferin*) assistant (*Brit*), sales clerk (*US*); (*Kellnerin*) waitress
fraulich ['fraʊlɪç] *adj* womanly
frech [frɛç] *adj* cheeky, impudent; **~ wie Oskar sein** (*umg*) to be a little monkey; **Frechdachs** *m* cheeky monkey; **Frechheit** *f* cheek, impudence; **sich** *dat* **(einige) Frechheiten erlauben** to be a bit cheeky (*bes Brit*) *od* fresh (*bes US*)
Fregatte [fre'gatə] (**-, -n**) *f* frigate
frei [fraɪ] *adj* free; (*Stelle*) vacant; (*Mitarbeiter*) freelance; (*Geld*) available; (*unbekleidet*) bare; **aus ~en Stücken** *od* **~em Willen** of one's own free will; **~ nach ...** based on ...; **für etw ~e Fahrt geben** (*fig*) to give sth the go-ahead; **der Film ist ~ ab 16 (Jahren)** the film may be seen by people of 16 years (of age) and over; **unter ~em Himmel** in the open (air); **morgen/Mittwoch ist ~** tomorrow/ Wednesday is a holiday; **„Zimmer ~"** "vacancies"; **auf ~er Strecke** (*Eisenb*) between stations; (*Aut*) on the road; **~er Wettbewerb** fair/open competition; **~ Haus** (*Comm*) carriage paid; **~ Schiff** (*Comm*) free on board; **~e Marktwirtschaft** free market economy; **von etw ~ sein** to be free of sth; **im F~en** in the open air; **~ halten** (*Ausfahrt etc*) to keep free; **~ sprechen** to talk without notes; **Freibad** *nt* open-air swimming pool; **freibekommen** *unreg vt*: **jdn/einen Tag freibekommen** to get sb freed/get a day off; **freiberuflich** *adj* self-employed; **Freibetrag** *m* tax allowance
Frei- *zW*: **freigebig** *adj* generous; **freihalten** *unreg vt* (*bezahlen*) to pay for; *siehe auch* **frei**; **freihändig** *adv* (*fahren*) with no hands
Freiheit *f* freedom; **sich** *dat* **die ~ nehmen, etw zu tun** to take the liberty of doing sth; **freiheitlich** *adj* liberal; (*Verfassung*) based on the principle of liberty; (*Demokratie*) free
Freiheitsstrafe *f* prison sentence
frei- *zW*: **Freikarte** *f* free ticket; **freilassen** *unreg vt* to (set) free; **freilegen** *vt* to expose; **freilich** *adv* certainly, admittedly; **ja freilich!** yes of course; **Freilichtbühne** *f* open-air theatre; **freimachen** *vt* (*Post*) to frank ▷ *vr* to arrange to be free; **Tage freimachen** to take days off; **sich freimachen** (*beim Arzt*) to take one's clothes off, strip
freimütig ['fraɪmy:tɪç] *adj* frank, honest
Frei- *zW*: **freinehmen** *vt*: **sich** *dat* **einen Tag freinehmen** to take a day off; **freisprechen** *unreg vt*: **freisprechen (von)** to acquit (of); **Freispruch** *m* acquittal; **freistellen** *vt*: **jdm etw freistellen** to leave sth (up) to sb; **Freistoß** *m* free kick
Freitag *m* Friday; *siehe auch* **Dienstag**
freitags *adv* on Fridays
Frei- *zW*: **freiwillig** *adj* voluntary; **Freizeichen** *nt* (*Tel*) ringing tone; **Freizeit** *f* spare *od* free time
fremd [frɛmt] *adj* (*unvertraut*) strange; (*ausländisch*) foreign; (*nicht eigen*) someone else's; **etw ist jdm ~** sth is foreign to sb; **ich bin hier ~** I'm a stranger here; **sich ~ fühlen** to feel like a stranger; **fremdartig** *adj* strange
Fremde (-) *f* (*liter*): **die ~** foreign parts *pl*
Fremden- *zW*: **Fremdenführer** *m* (tourist) guide; (*Buch*) guide (book); **Fremdenlegion** *f* foreign legion; **Fremdenverkehr** *m* tourism; **Fremdenzimmer** *nt* guest room
fremd- *zW*: **fremdgehen** *unreg* (*umg*) *vi* to be unfaithful; **Fremdkörper** *m* foreign body; **fremdländisch** *adj* foreign; **Fremdsprache** *f* foreign language
Frequenz [fre'kvɛnts] *f* (*Rundf*) frequency
fressen ['frɛsən] *unreg vt, vi* to eat ▷ *vr*: **sich satt ~** to gorge o.s.; **einen Narren an jdm/ etw ge~ haben** to dote on sb/sth
Freude ['frɔʏdə] (**-, -n**) *f* joy, delight; **~ an etw** *dat* **haben** to get *od* derive pleasure from sth; **jdm eine ~ machen** *od* **bereiten** to make sb happy
freuen ['frɔʏən] *vt unpers* to make happy *od* pleased ▷ *vr* to be glad *od* happy; **sich auf etw** *akk* **~** to look forward to sth; **sich über etw** *akk* **~** to be pleased about sth; **sich zu früh ~** to get one's hopes up too soon
Freund ['frɔʏnt] (**-(e)s, -e**) *m* friend; (*Liebhaber*) boyfriend; **ich bin kein ~ von so etwas** I'm not one for that sort of thing; **freundlich** *adj* kind, friendly; **bitte recht freundlich!** smile please!; **würden Sie bitte so freundlich sein und das tun?** would you be so kind as to do that?; **freundlicherweise** *adv* kindly; **Freundlichkeit** *f* friendliness, kindness; **Freundschaft** *f* friendship; **freundschaftlich** *adj* friendly
Frieden ['fri:dən] (**-s, -**) *m* peace; **im ~** in

peacetime; **~ schließen** to make one's peace; (*Pol*) to make peace; **um des lieben ~s willen** (*umg*) for the sake of peace and quiet; **ich traue dem ~ nicht** (*umg*) something (fishy) is going on

Friedens- *zW*: **Friedensbewegung** *f* peace movement; **Friedensschluss** *m* peace agreement; **Friedenstruppe** *f* peace-keeping force; **Friedensvertrag** *m* peace treaty; **Friedenszeit** *f* peacetime

fried- *zW*: **Friedhof** *m* cemetery; **friedlich** *adj* peaceful; **etw auf friedlichem Wege lösen** to solve sth by peaceful means

frieren ['fri:rən] *unreg vi* to freeze ▷ *vt unpers* to freeze ▷ *vi unpers*: **heute Nacht hat es gefroren** it was below freezing last night; **ich friere, es friert mich** I am freezing, I'm cold; **wie ein Schneider ~** (*umg*) to be *od* get frozen to the marrow

Fries [fri:s] (**-es, -e**) *m* (*Archit*) frieze

frigid, **frigide** *adj* frigid

Frikadelle [frika'dɛlə] *f* meatball

frisch [frɪʃ] *adj* fresh; (*lebhaft*) lively; **~ gestrichen!** wet paint!; **sich ~ machen** to freshen (o.s.) up; **jdn auf ~er Tat ertappen** to catch sb red-handed *od* in the act

Frischhaltefolie *f* clingfilm

Friseur [fri'zø:r] *m* hairdresser

frisieren [fri'zi:rən] *vt* (*Haar*) to do; (*fig*: *Abrechnung*) to fiddle, doctor ▷ *vr* to do one's hair; **jdn ~, jdm das Haar ~** to do sb's hair

Frisiersalon *m* hairdressing salon

Frisiertisch *m* dressing table

Frist [frɪst] (**-, -en**) *f* period; (*Termin*) deadline; **eine ~ einhalten/verstreichen lassen** to meet a deadline/let a deadline pass; (*bei Rechnung*) to pay/not to pay within the period stipulated; **jdm eine ~ von vier Tagen geben** to give sb four days' grace

fristlos *adj* (*Entlassung*) instant

Frisur [fri'zu:r] *f* hairdo, hairstyle

frittieren [fri'ti:rən] *vt* to deep fry

frivol [fri'vo:l] *adj* frivolous

Frl. *abk* (= *Fräulein*) Miss

froh [fro:] *adj* happy, cheerful; **ich bin ~, dass ...** I'm glad that ...

fröhlich ['frø:lɪç] *adj* merry, happy; **Fröhlichkeit** *f* merriment, gaiety

Frohsinn *m* cheerfulness

fromm [frɔm] *adj* pious, good; (*Wunsch*) idle

Frömmigkeit *f* piety

Fronleichnam [fro:n'laɪçna:m] (**-(e)s**) *m* Corpus Christi

Front [frɔnt] (**-, -en**) *f* front; **klare ~en schaffen** (*fig*) to clarify the position

frontal [frɔn'ta:l] *adj* frontal

Frosch [frɔʃ] (**-(e)s, ⸚e**) *m* frog; (*Feuerwerk*) squib; **sei kein ~!** (*umg*) be a sport!; **Froschmann** *m* frogman; **Froschschenkel** *m* frog's leg

Frost [frɔst] (**-(e)s, ⸚e**) *m* frost; **Frostbeule** *f* chilblain

frostig *adj* frosty

Frostschutzmittel *nt* anti-freeze

Frottee, **Frotté** [frɔ'te:] (**-(s), -s**) *nt od m* towelling

Frucht [frʊxt] (**-, ⸚e**) *f* (*lit, fig*) fruit; (*Getreide*) corn; (*Embryo*) foetus; **fruchtbar** *adj* fruitful, fertile; **Fruchtbarkeit** *f* fertility

fruchten *vi* to be of use

fruchtlos *adj* fruitless

Fruchtsaft *m* fruit juice

früh [fry:] *adj, adv* early; **heute ~** this morning; **von ~ auf** from an early age

Frühe (**-**) *f* early morning; **in aller ~** at the crack of dawn

früher *adj* earlier; (*ehemalig*) former ▷ *adv* formerly; **~ war das anders** that used to be different; **~ oder später** sooner or later

frühestens *adv* at the earliest

Frühgeburt *f* premature birth; (*Kind*) premature baby

Frühjahr *nt* spring

Frühjahrsmüdigkeit *f* springtime lethargy

Frühling *m* spring; **im ~** in spring

früh- *zW*: **frühreif** *adj* precocious; **Frührentner** *m person who has retired early*; **Frühstück** *nt* breakfast; **frühstücken** *vi* to (have) breakfast; **frühzeitig** *adj* early; (*vorzeitig*) premature

Frust (**-(e)s**) (*umg*) *m* frustration

frustrieren [frʊs'tri:rən] *vt* to frustrate

Fuchs [fʊks] (**-es, ⸚e**) *m* fox

fuchsen (*umg*) *vt* to rile, annoy ▷ *vr* to be annoyed

Füchsin ['fʏksɪn] *f* vixen

fuchsteufelswild *adj* hopping mad

fuchteln ['fʊxtəln] *vi* to gesticulate wildly

fügen ['fy:gən] *vt* to place, join ▷ *vr unpers* to happen ▷ *vr*: **sich ~ (in** *+akk***)** to be obedient (to); (*anpassen*) to adapt o.s. (to)

fügsam ['fy:kza:m] *adj* obedient

fühlbar *adj* perceptible, noticeable

fühlen ['fy:lən] *vt, vi, vr* to feel

Fühler (**-s, -**) *m* feeler

führen ['fy:rən] *vt* to lead; (*Geschäft*) to run; (*Name*) to bear; (*Buch*) to keep; (*im Angebot haben*) to stock ▷ *vi* to lead ▷ *vr* to behave; **was führt Sie zu mir?** (*form*) what brings you to me?; **Geld/seine Papiere bei sich ~** (*form*) to carry money/one's papers on one's person; **das führt zu nichts** that will come to nothing

Führer, in ['fy:rər(ɪn)] (**-s, -**) *m(f)* leader; (*Fremdenführer*) guide; **Führerschein** *m* driving licence (*Brit*), driver's license (*US*); **den Führerschein machen** (*Aut*) to learn to drive; (*die Prüfung ablegen*) to take one's (driving) test

Führung ['fy:rʊŋ] *f* leadership; (*eines Unternehmens*) management; (*Mil*) command; (*Benehmen*) conduct; (*Museumsführung*) conducted tour

Führungs- *zW*: **Führungskraft** *f* executive; **Führungszeugnis** *nt* certificate of good

conduct
Fülle ['fʏlə] **(-)** *f* wealth, abundance
füllen *vt* to fill; (*Koch*) to stuff ▷ *vr* to fill (up)
Füller **(-s, -)** *m* fountain pen
füllig ['fʏlɪç] *adj* (*Mensch*) corpulent, portly; (*Figur*) ample
Füllung *f* filling; (*Holzfüllung*) panel
fummeln ['fʊməln] (*umg*) *vi* to fumble
Fund [fʊnt] **(-(e)s, -e)** *m* find
Fundament [fʊnda'mɛnt] *nt* foundation
Fundamentalismus *m* fundamentalism
Fundbüro *nt* lost property office, lost and found (*US*)
Fundgrube *f* (*fig*) treasure trove
fundieren [fʊn'di:rən] *vt* to back up
fundiert *adj* sound
fünf [fʏnf] *num* five; **seine ~ Sinne beisammen haben** to have all one's wits about one; **~(e) gerade sein lassen** (*umg*) to turn a blind eye; **fünfhundert** *num* five hundred; **fünfjährig** *adj* (*Frist, Plan*) five-year; (*Kind*) five-year-old; **Fünfkampf** *m* pentathlon
Fünfprozentklausel *f* (*Parl*) *clause debarring parties with less than 5% of the vote from Parliament*
Fünftagewoche *f* five-day week
fünfte, r, s *adj* fifth
Fünftel **(-s, -)** *nt* fifth
fünfzehn *num* fifteen
fünfzig *num* fifty
Funk [fʊŋk] **(-s)** *m* radio, wireless (*Brit old*)
Funke **(-ns, -n)** *m* (*lit, fig*) spark
funkeln *vi* to sparkle
Funken **(-s, -)** *m* = **Funke**
Funker **(-s, -)** *m* radio operator
Funk- *zW*: **Funkgerät** *nt* radio set; **Funkspruch** *m* radio signal; **Funkstation** *f* radio station; **Funkstreife** *f* police radio patrol; **Funktaxi** *nt* radio taxi; **Funktelefon** *nt* cell phone
Funktion [fʊŋktsi'o:n] *f* function; **in ~ treten/sein** to come into/be in operation
Funktionär, in [fʊŋktsio'nɛ:r(ɪn)] **(-s, -e)** *m(f)* functionary, official
funktionieren [fʊŋktsio'ni:rən] *vi* to work, function
Funktions- *zW*: **funktionsfähig** *adj* working; **Funktionstaste** *f* (*Comput*) function key
für [fy:r] *präp +akk* for; **was ~** what kind *od* sort of; **~s Erste** for the moment; **was Sie da sagen, hat etwas ~ sich** there's something in what you're saying; **Tag ~ Tag** day after day; **Schritt ~ Schritt** step by step; **das F~ und Wider** the pros and cons *pl*; **Fürbitte** *f* intercession
Furche ['fʊrçə] **(-, -n)** *f* furrow
Furcht [fʊrçt] **(-)** *f* fear; **furchtbar** *adj* terrible, awful
fürchten ['fʏrçtən] *vt* to be afraid of, fear ▷ *vr*: **sich ~ (vor** *+dat***)** to be afraid (of)
fürchterlich *adj* awful
furchtlos *adj* fearless
furchtsam *adj* timorous
füreinander [fy:r|aɪ'nandər] *adv* for each other
Furnier [fʊr'ni:r] **(-s, -e)** *nt* veneer
fürs [fy:rs] = **für das**
Fürsorge ['fy:rzɔrgə] *f* care; (*Sozialfürsorge*) welfare; **von der ~ leben** to live on social security (*Brit*) *od* welfare (*US*)
Fürsorger, in **(-s, -)** *m(f)* welfare worker
Fürsorgeunterstützung *f* social security (*Brit*), welfare benefit (*US*)
fürsorglich *adj* caring
Fürsprache *f* recommendation; (*um Gnade*) intercession
Fürsprecher *m* advocate
Fürst [fʏrst] **(-en, -en)** *m* prince
Fürstentum *nt* principality
fürstlich *adj* princely
Furt [fʊrt] **(-, -en)** *f* ford
Furunkel [fu'rʊŋkəl] **(-s, -)** *nt od m* boil
Fürwort ['fy:rvɔrt] *nt* pronoun
furzen ['fʊrtsən] (*umg!*) *vi* to fart (*!*)
Fusion [fuzi'o:n] *f* amalgamation; (*von Unternehmen*) merger; (*von Atomkernen, Zellen*) fusion
Fuß [fu:s] **(-es, ¨-e)** *m* foot; (*von Glas, Säule etc*) base; (*von Möbel*) leg; **zu ~** on foot; **bei ~!** heel!; **jdm etw vor die Füße werfen** (*lit*) to throw sth at sb; (*fig*) to tell sb to keep sth; **(festen) ~ fassen** (*lit, fig*) to gain a foothold; (*sich niederlassen*) to settle down; **mit jdm auf gutem ~ stehen** to be on good terms with sb; **auf großem ~ leben** to live the high life
Fußball *m* football; **Fußballplatz** *m* football pitch; **Fußballspiel** *nt* football match; **Fußballspieler** *m* footballer (*Brit*), football player (*US*)
Fußboden *m* floor
Fußbremse *f* (*Aut*) foot brake
Fuß- *zW*: **Fußgänger, in** **(-s, -)** *m(f)* pedestrian; **Fußgängerzone** *f* pedestrian precinct; **Fußnote** *f* footnote; **Fußspur** *f* footprint; **Fußtritt** *m* kick; (*Spur*) footstep; **Fußweg** *m* footpath
Futter ['fʊtər] **(-s, -)** *nt* fodder, feed; (*Stoff*) lining
Futteral [fʊtə'ra:l] **(-s, -e)** *nt* case
futtern ['fʊtərn] *vi* (*hum: umg*) to stuff o.s. ▷ *vt* to scoff
füttern ['fʏtərn] *vt* to feed; (*Kleidung*) to line; **„F~ verboten"** "do not feed the animals"
Futur [fu'tu:r] **(-s, -e)** *nt* future

Gg

G, g[1] [geː] *nt* G, g; **G wie Gustav** ≈ G for George
g[2] *abk* (*Österr*) = **Groschen**; (= *Gramm*) g
gab *etc* [gaːp] *vb siehe* **geben**
Gabe ['gaːbə] (**-, -n**) *f* gift
Gabel ['gaːbəl] (**-, -n**) *f* fork; (*Tel*) rest, cradle; **gabeln** *vr* to fork; **Gabelung** *f* fork
Gabun [ga'buːn] *nt* Gabon
gackern ['gakərn] *vi* to cackle
gaffen ['gafən] *vi* to gape
Gag [gɛk] (**-s, -s**) *m* (*Filmgag*) gag; (*Werbegag*) gimmick
Gage ['gaːʒə] (**-, -n**) *f* fee
gähnen ['gɛːnən] *vi* to yawn; **~de Leere** total emptiness
galant [ga'lant] *adj* gallant, courteous
Galerie [galə'riː] *f* gallery
Galgen ['galgən] (**-s, -**) *m* gallows *pl*; **Galgenhumor** *m* macabre humour (*Brit*) *od* humor (*US*)
Galle ['galə] (**-, -n**) *f* gall; (*Organ*) gall bladder; **jdm kommt die ~ hoch** sb's blood begins to boil
Galopp [ga'lɔp] (**-s, -s** *od* **-e**) *m* gallop; **im ~** (*lit*) at a gallop; (*fig*) at top speed
galoppieren [galɔ'piːrən] *vi* to gallop
galt *etc* [galt] *vb siehe* **gelten**
Gamasche [ga'maʃə] (**-, -n**) *f* gaiter; (*kurz*) spat
gammeln ['gaməln] (*umg*) *vi* to loaf about
Gammler, in ['gamlər(ɪn)] (**-s, -**) *m(f)* dropout
Gämse ['gɛmzə] (**-, -n**) *f* chamois
Gang[1] [gaŋ] (**-(e)s, ¨-e**) *m* walk; (*Botengang*) errand; (*Gangart*) gait; (*Abschnitt eines Vorgangs*) operation; (*Essensgang, Ablauf*) course; (*Flur etc*) corridor; (*Durchgang*) passage; (*Aut, Tech*) gear; (*in Kirche, Theat, Aviat*) aisle; **den ersten ~ einlegen** to engage first (gear); **einen ~ machen/tun** to go on an errand/for a walk; **den ~ nach Canossa antreten** (*fig*) to eat humble pie; **seinen gewohnten ~ gehen** (*fig*) to run its usual course; **in ~ bringen** to start up; (*fig*) to get off the ground; **in ~ sein** to be in operation; (*fig*) to be under way
Gang[2] [gɛŋ] (**-, -s**) *f* gang
Gangart *f* way of walking, walk, gait; (*von Pferd*) gait; **eine härtere ~ einschlagen** (*fig*) to apply harder tactics
gängig ['gɛŋɪç] *adj* common, current; (*Ware*) in demand, selling well
Gangschaltung *f* gears *pl*
Gangway ['gæŋweɪ] *f* (*Naut*) gangway; (*Aviat*) steps *pl*
Ganove [ga'noːvə] (**-n, -n**) (*umg*) *m* crook
Gans [gans] (**-, ¨-e**) *f* goose
Gänse- *zW*: **Gänseblümchen** *nt* daisy; **Gänsefüßchen** (*umg*) *pl* inverted commas *pl* (*Brit*), quotes *pl*; **Gänsehaut** *f* goose pimples *pl*; **Gänsemarsch** *m*: **im Gänsemarsch** in single file
Gänserich (**-s, -e**) *m* gander
ganz [gants] *adj* whole; (*vollständig*) complete ▷ *adv* quite; (*völlig*) completely; (*sehr*) really; (*genau*) exactly; **~ Europa** all Europe; **im (Großen und) G~en genommen** on the whole, all in all; **etw wieder ~ machen** to mend sth; **sein ~es Geld** all his money; **~ gewiss!** absolutely!; **ein ~ klein wenig** just a tiny bit; **das mag ich ~ besonders gern(e)** I'm particularly fond of that; **sie ist ~ die Mutter** she's just *od* exactly like her mother; **~ und gar nicht** not at all
gänzlich ['gɛntslɪç] *adj* complete, entire ▷ *adv* completely, entirely
gar [gaːr] *adj* cooked, done ▷ *adv* quite; **~ nicht/nichts/keiner** not/nothing/nobody at all; **~ nicht schlecht** not bad at all; **~ kein Grund** no reason whatsoever *od* at all; **er wäre ~ zu gern noch länger geblieben** he would really have liked to stay longer
Garage [ga'raːʒə] (**-, -n**) *f* garage
Garantie [garan'tiː] *f* guarantee; **das fällt noch unter die ~** that's covered by the guarantee
garantieren *vt* to guarantee
Garbe ['garbə] (**-, -n**) *f* sheaf; (*Mil*) burst of fire
Garderobe [gardə'roːbə] (**-, -n**) *f* wardrobe; (*Abgabe*) cloakroom (*Brit*), checkroom (*US*); (*Kleiderablage*) hall stand; (*Theat: Umkleideraum*) dressing room
Garderobenfrau *f* cloakroom attendant
Garderobenständer *m* hall stand
Gardine [gar'diːnə] (**-, -n**) *f* curtain
gären ['gɛːrən] *unreg vi* to ferment
Garn [garn] (**-(e)s, -e**) *nt* thread; (*Häkelgarn, fig*) yarn
Garnele [gar'neːlə] (**-, -n**) *f* shrimp, prawn
garnieren [gar'niːrən] *vt* to decorate; (*Speisen*) to garnish
Garnitur [garni'tuːr] *f* (*Satz*) set; (*Unterwäsche*)

set of (matching) underwear; **erste ~** (*fig*) top rank; **zweite ~** second rate
garstig ['garstɪç] *adj* nasty, horrid
Garten ['gartən] (**-s, ¨**) *m* garden; **Gartenarbeit** *f* gardening; **Gartenlokal** *nt* beer garden; **Gartenschere** *f* pruning shears *pl*
Gärtner, in ['gɛrtnər(ɪn)] (**-s, -**) *m(f)* gardener
Gärtnerei [gɛrtnə'raɪ] *f* nursery; (*Gemüsegärtnerei*) market garden (*Brit*), truck farm (*US*)
Gärung ['gɛ:rʊŋ] *f* fermentation
Gas [ga:s] (**-es, -e**) *nt* gas; **~ geben** (*Aut*) to accelerate, step on the gas
Gas- *zW*: **Gasherd** *m* gas cooker; **Gasleitung** *f* gas pipeline; **Gasmaske** *f* gas mask; **Gaspedal** *nt* accelerator, gas pedal (*US*)
Gasse ['gasə] (**-, -n**) *f* lane, alley
Gassenjunge *m* street urchin
Gast [gast] (**-es, ¨e**) *m* guest; **bei jdm zu ~ sein** to be sb's guest(s); **Gastarbeiter** *m* foreign worker
Gäste- *zW*: **Gästebuch** *nt* visitors' book; **Gästezimmer** *nt* guest room
Gast- *zW*: **gastfreundlich** *adj* hospitable; **Gastgeber, in** (**-s, -**) *m(f)* host(ess); **Gasthaus** *nt* hotel, inn
gastieren [gas'ti:rən] *vi* (*Theat*) to (appear as a) guest
Gast- *zW*: **gastlich** *adj* hospitable; **Gastrolle** *f* (*Theat*) guest role; **eine Gastrolle spielen** to make a guest appearance
Gastronomie [gastrono'mi:] *f* (*form: Gaststättengewerbe*) catering trade
gastronomisch [gastro'no:mɪʃ] *adj* gastronomic(al)
Gast- *zW*: **Gastspiel** *nt* (*Sport*) away game; **ein Gastspiel geben** (*Theat*) to give a guest performance; (*fig*) to put in a brief appearance; **Gaststätte** *f* restaurant; (*Trinklokal*) pub; **Gastwirtschaft** *f* hotel, inn; **Gastzimmer** *nt* guest room
Gas- *zW*: **Gasvergiftung** *f* gas poisoning; **Gaswerk** *nt* gasworks *sing od pl*; **Gaszähler** *m* gas meter
Gatte ['gatə] (**-n, -n**) *m* (*form*) husband, spouse; **die ~n** husband and wife
Gatter ['gatər] (**-s, -**) *nt* grating; (*Tür*) gate
Gattin *f* (*form*) wife, spouse
Gattung ['gatʊŋ] *f* (*Biol*) genus; (*Sorte*) kind
Gaul [gaʊl] (**-(e)s, Gäule**) (*pej*) *m* nag
Gaumen ['gaʊmən] (**-s, -**) *m* palate
Gauner ['gaʊnər] (**-s, -**) *m* rogue
geb. *abk* = **geboren**
Gebäck [gə'bɛk] (**-(e)s, -e**) *nt* (*Kekse*) biscuits *pl* (*Brit*), cookies *pl* (*US*); (*Teilchen*) pastries *pl*
gebacken [gə'bakən] *pp von* **backen**
Gebälk [gə'bɛlk] (**-(e)s**) *nt* timberwork
gebar *etc* [gə'ba:r] *vb siehe* **gebären**
Gebärde [gə'bɛ:rdə] (**-, -n**) *f* gesture
gebärden *vr* to behave
Gebaren [gə'ba:rən] (**-s**) *nt* behaviour (*Brit*), behavior (*US*); (*Geschäftsgebaren*) conduct
gebären [gə'bɛ:rən] *unreg vt* to give birth to
Gebärmutter *f* uterus, womb
Gebäude [gə'bɔʏdə] (**-s, -**) *nt* building; **Gebäudekomplex** *m* (building) complex
Gebell [gə'bɛl] (**-(e)s**) *nt* barking
geben ['ge:bən] *unreg vt, vi* to give; (*Karten*) to deal ▷ *vt unpers*: **es gibt** there is/are; there will be ▷ *vr* (*sich verhalten*) to behave, act; (*aufhören*) to abate; **jdm etw ~** to give sb sth *od* sth to sb; **in die Post ~** to post; **das gibt keinen Sinn** that doesn't make sense; **er gibt Englisch** he teaches English; **viel/nicht viel auf etw** *akk* **~** to set great store/not much store by sth; **etw von sich ~** (*Laute etc*) to utter; **ein Wort gab das andere** one angry word led to another; **ein gutes Beispiel ~** to set a good example; **~ Sie mir bitte Herrn Braun** (*Tel*) can I speak to Mr Braun please?; **ein Auto in Reparatur ~** to have a car repaired; **was gibts?** what's the matter?, what's up?; **was gibts zum Mittagessen?** what's for lunch?; **das gibts doch nicht!** that's impossible!; **sich geschlagen ~** to admit defeat; **das wird sich schon ~** that'll soon sort itself out
Gebet [gə'be:t] (**-(e)s, -e**) *nt* prayer; **jdn ins ~ nehmen** (*fig*) to take sb to task
gebeten [gə'be:tən] *pp von* **bitten**
Gebiet [gə'bi:t] (**-(e)s, -e**) *nt* area; (*Hoheitsgebiet*) territory; (*fig*) field
gebieten *unreg vt* to command, demand; **gebieterisch** *adj* imperious
Gebilde [gə'bɪldə] (**-s, -**) *nt* object, structure
gebildet *adj* cultured, educated
Gebirge [gə'bɪrgə] (**-s, -**) *nt* mountains *pl*
Gebiss [gə'bɪs] (**-es, -e**) *nt* teeth *pl*; (*künstlich*) dentures *pl*
gebissen *pp von* **beißen**
Gebläse [gə'blɛ:zə] (**-s, -**) *nt* fan, blower
geblasen [gə'bla:zən] *pp von* **blasen**
geblieben [gə'bli:bən] *pp von* **bleiben**
gebogen [gə'bo:gən] *pp von* **biegen**
geboren [gə'bo:rən] *pp von* **gebären** ▷ *adj* born; (*Frau*) née; **wo sind Sie ~?** where were you born?
geborgen [gə'bɔrgən] *pp von* **bergen** ▷ *adj* secure, safe
geborsten [gə'bɔrstən] *pp von* **bersten**
Gebot (**-(e)s, -e**) *nt* (*Gesetz*) law; (*Rel*) commandment; (*bei Auktion*) bid; **das ~ der Stunde** the needs of the moment
geboten [gə'bo:tən] *pp von* **bieten; gebieten** ▷ *adj* (*geh: ratsam*) advisable; (*: notwendig*) necessary; (*: dringend geboten*) imperative
gebracht [gə'braxt] *pp von* **bringen**
gebrannt [gə'brant] *pp von* **brennen** ▷ *adj*: **ein ~es Kind scheut das Feuer** (*Sprichwort*) once bitten twice shy (*Sprichwort*)
gebraten [gə'bra:tən] *pp von* **braten**
Gebrauch [gə'braʊx] (**-(e)s, Gebräuche**) *m* use; (*Sitte*) custom; **zum äußerlichen/ innerlichen ~** for external use/to be taken internally

gebrauchen *vt* to use; **er/das ist zu nichts zu ~** he's/that's (of) no use to anybody
gebräuchlich [gəˈbrɔʏçlɪç] *adj* usual, customary
Gebrauchs- *zW*: **Gebrauchsanweisung** *f* directions *pl* for use; **Gebrauchsartikel** *m* article of everyday use; **gebrauchsfertig** *adj* ready for use; **Gebrauchsgegenstand** *m* commodity
gebraucht [gəˈbraʊxt] *adj* used; **Gebrauchtwagen** *m* second-hand *od* used car
gebrechlich [gəˈbrɛçlɪç] *adj* frail
gebrochen [gəˈbrɔxən] *pp von* **brechen**
Gebrüder [gəˈbry:dər] *pl* brothers *pl*
Gebrüll [gəˈbrʏl] (**-(e)s**) *nt* (*von Mensch*) yelling; (*von Löwe*) roar
Gebühr [gəˈby:r] (**-, -en**) *f* charge; (*Postgebühr*) postage *no pl*; (*Honorar*) fee; **zu ermäßigter ~** at a reduced rate; **~ (be)zahlt Empfänger** postage to be paid by addressee; **nach ~** suitably; **über ~** excessively
gebühren *vi* (*geh*): **jdm ~** to be sb's due *od* due to sb ▷ *vr* to be fitting
gebührend *adj* (*verdient*) due; (*angemessen*) suitable
Gebühren- *zW*: **Gebühreneinheit** *f* (*Tel*) tariff unit; **Gebührenermäßigung** *f* reduction of fees; **gebührenfrei** *adj* free of charge; **gebührenpflichtig** *adj* subject to charges; **gebührenpflichtige Verwarnung** (*Jur*) fine
gebunden [gəˈbʊndən] *pp von* **binden** ▷ *adj*: **vertraglich ~ sein** to be bound by contract
Geburt [gəˈbu:rt] (**-, -en**) *f* birth; **das war eine schwere ~!** (*fig: umg*) that took some doing
Geburten- *zW*: **Geburtenkontrolle** *f* birth control; **Geburtenregelung** *f* birth control; **Geburtenrückgang** *m* drop in the birth rate; **geburtenschwach** *adj* (*Jahrgang*) with a low birth rate
gebürtig [gəˈbʏrtɪç] *adj* born in, native of; **~e Schweizerin** native of Switzerland, Swiss-born woman
Geburts- *zW*: **Geburtsanzeige** *f* birth notice; **Geburtsdatum** *nt* date of birth; **Geburtshelfer** *m* (*Arzt*) obstetrician; **Geburtsjahr** *nt* year of birth; **Geburtsort** *m* birthplace; **Geburtstag** *m* birthday; **herzlichen Glückwunsch zum Geburtstag!** happy birthday!, many happy returns (of the day)!; **Geburtsurkunde** *f* birth certificate
Gebüsch [gəˈbʏʃ] (**-(e)s, -e**) *nt* bushes *pl*
gedacht [gəˈdaxt] *pp von* **denken; gedenken**
Gedächtnis [gəˈdɛçtnɪs] (**-ses, -se**) *nt* memory; **wenn mich mein ~ nicht trügt** if my memory serves me right
Gedanke [gəˈdaŋkə] (**-ns, -n**) *m* thought; (*Idee, Plan, Einfall*) idea; (*Konzept*) concept; **sich über etw** *akk* **~n machen** to think about sth; **jdn auf andere ~n bringen** to make sb think about other things; **etw ganz in ~n** *dat* **tun** to do sth without thinking; **auf einen ~n kommen** to have *od* get an idea
Gedanken- *zW*: **gedankenlos** *adj* thoughtless; **Gedankenlosigkeit** *f* thoughtlessness; **Gedankenstrich** *m* dash; **Gedankenübertragung** *f* thought transference, telepathy; **gedankenvoll** *adj* thoughtful
Gedeck [gəˈdɛk] (**-(e)s, -e**) *nt* cover(ing); (*Menü*) set meal; **ein ~ auflegen** to lay a place
gedeihen [gəˈdaɪən] *unreg vi* to thrive, prosper; **die Sache ist so weit gediehen, dass ...** the matter has reached the point *od* stage where ...
gedenken [gəˈdɛŋkən] *unreg vi +gen* (*geh: denken an*) to remember; (*beabsichtigen*) to intend
Gedenk- *zW*: **Gedenkminute** *f* minute's silence; **Gedenktag** *m* remembrance day
Gedicht [gəˈdɪçt] (**-(e)s, -e**) *nt* poem
gediegen [gəˈdi:gən] *adj* (good) quality; (*Mensch*) reliable; (*rechtschaffen*) honest
gedieh *etc* [gəˈdi:] *vb siehe* **gedeihen**
gediehen *pp von* **gedeihen**
Gedränge [gəˈdrɛŋə] (**-s**) *nt* crush, crowd; **ins ~ kommen** (*fig*) to get into difficulties
gedrängt *adj* compressed; **~ voll** packed
gedrungen [gəˈdrʊŋən] *pp von* **dringen** ▷ *adj* thickset, stocky
Geduld [gəˈdʊlt] (**-**) *f* patience; **mir reißt die ~, ich verliere die ~** my patience is wearing thin, I'm losing my patience
geduldig *adj* patient
gedurft [gəˈdʊrft] *pp von* **dürfen**
geehrt [gəˈ|e:rt] *adj*: **Sehr ~e Damen und Herren!** Ladies and Gentlemen!; (*in Briefen*) Dear Sir or Madam
geeignet [gəˈ|aɪgnət] *adj* suitable; **im ~en Augenblick** at the right moment
Gefahr [gəˈfa:r] (**-, -en**) *f* danger; **~ laufen, etw zu tun** to run the risk of doing sth; **auf eigene ~** at one's own risk; **außer ~** (*nicht gefährdet*) not in danger; (*nicht mehr gefährdet*) out of danger; (*Patienten*) off the danger list
gefährden [gəˈfɛ:rdən] *vt* to endanger
gefahren [gəˈfa:rən] *pp von* **fahren**
Gefahren- *zW*: **Gefahrenquelle** *f* source of danger; **Gefahrenzulage** *f* danger money
gefährlich [gəˈfɛ:rlɪç] *adj* dangerous
Gefälle [gəˈfɛlə] (**-s, -**) *nt* (*von Land, Straße*) slope; (*Neigungsgrad*) gradient; **starkes ~!** steep hill
Gefallen¹ [gəˈfalən] (**-s, -**) *m* favour; **jdm etw zu ~ tun** to do sth to please sb
Gefallen² [gəˈfalən] (**-s**) *nt* pleasure; **an etw** *dat* **~ finden** to derive pleasure from sth; **an jdm ~ finden** to take to sb
gefallen *pp von* **fallen; gefallen** ▷ *vi* (*unreg*): **jdm ~** to please sb; **er/es gefällt mir** I like him/it; **das gefällt mir an ihm** that's one thing I like about him; **sich** *dat* **etw ~ lassen** to put up with sth
gefällig [gəˈfɛlɪç] *adj* (*hilfsbereit*) obliging; (*erfreulich*) pleasant; **sonst noch etwas ~?** (*veraltet, ironisch*) will there be anything

else?; **Gefälligkeit** *f* favour (*Brit*), favor (*US*); helpfulness; **etw aus Gefälligkeit tun** to do sth as a favour (*Brit*) *od* favor (*US*)
gefälligst (*umg*) *adv* kindly; **sei ~ still!** will you kindly keep your mouth shut!
gefangen [gə'faŋən] *pp von* **fangen** ▷ *adj* captured; (*fig*) captivated; **~ halten** to keep prisoner; **~ nehmen** to capture
Gefangene, r *f(m)* prisoner, captive
Gefangen- *zW*: **Gefangennahme** (**-, -n**) *f* capture; **Gefangenschaft** *f* captivity
Gefängnis [gə'fɛŋnɪs] (**-ses, -se**) *nt* prison; **zwei Jahre ~ bekommen** to get two years' imprisonment; **Gefängnisstrafe** *f* prison sentence; **Gefängniswärter** *m* prison warder (*Brit*) *od* guard
Gefäß [gə'fɛ:s] (**-es, -e**) *nt* vessel (*auch ANAT*), container
gefasst [gə'fast] *adj* composed, calm; **auf etw** *akk* **~ sein** to be prepared *od* ready for sth; **er kann sich auf etwas ~ machen** (*umg*) I'll give him something to think about
Gefecht [gə'fɛçt] (**-(e)s, -e**) *nt* fight; (*Mil*) engagement; **jdn/etw außer ~ setzen** (*lit, fig*) to put sb/sth out of action
Gefieder [gə'fi:dər] (**-s, -**) *nt* plumage, feathers *pl*
gefiel *etc* [gə'fi:l] *vb siehe* **gefallen**
gefleckt [gə'flɛkt] *adj* spotted; (*Blume, Vogel*) speckled
geflochten [gə'flɔxtən] *pp von* **flechten**
geflogen [gə'flo:gən] *pp von* **fliegen**
geflohen [gə'flo:ən] *pp von* **fliehen**
geflossen [gə'flɔsən] *pp von* **fließen**
Geflügel [gə'fly:gəl] (**-s**) *nt* poultry
gefochten [gə'fɔxtən] *pp von* **fechten**
Gefolgschaft [gə'fɔlkʃaft] *f* following
gefragt [ge'fra:kt] *adj* in demand
gefräßig [gə'frɛ:sɪç] *adj* voracious
Gefreite, r [gə'fraɪtə(r)] *m* (*Mil*) lance corporal (*Brit*), private first class (*US*); (*Naut*) able seaman (*Brit*), seaman apprentice (*US*); (*Aviat*) aircraftman (*Brit*), airman first class (*US*)
gefressen [gə'frɛsən] *pp von* **fressen** ▷ *adj*: **den hab(e) ich ~** (*umg*) I'm sick of him
gefrieren [gə'fri:rən] *unreg vi* to freeze
Gefrier- *zW*: **Gefrierfach** *nt* freezer compartment; **Gefrierfleisch** *nt* frozen meat; **gefriergetrocknet** *adj* freeze-dried; **Gefrierpunkt** *m* freezing point; **Gefriertruhe** *f* deep-freeze
gefroren *pp von* **frieren, gefrieren**
gefügig *adj* submissive; (*gehorsam*) obedient
Gefühl [gə'fy:l] (**-(e)s, -e**) *nt* feeling; **etw im ~ haben** to have a feel for sth; **gefühllos** *adj* unfeeling; (*Glieder*) numb
Gefühls- *zW*: **gefühlsbetont** *adj* emotional; **Gefühlsduselei** [-du:zə'laɪ] (*pej*) *f* mawkishness; **gefühlsmäßig** *adj* instinctive
gefunden [gə'fʊndən] *pp von* **finden** ▷ *adj*: **das war ein ~es Fressen für ihn** that was handing it to him on a plate
gegangen [gə'gaŋən] *pp von* **gehen**
gegeben [gə'ge:bən] *pp von* **geben** ▷ *adj* given; **zu ~er Zeit** in due course
gegebenenfalls [gə'ge:bənənfals] *adv* if need be
gegen ['ge:gən] *präp +akk* **1** against; **nichts gegen jdn haben** to have nothing against sb; **X gegen Y** (*Sport, Jur*) X versus Y; **ein Mittel gegen Schnupfen** something for colds
2 (*in Richtung auf*) towards; **gegen Osten** to(wards) the east; **gegen Abend** towards evening; **gegen einen Baum fahren** to drive into a tree
3 (*ungefähr*) round about; **gegen 3 Uhr** around 3 o'clock
4 (*gegenüber*) towards; (*ungefähr*) around; **gerecht gegen alle** fair to all
5 (*im Austausch für*) for; **gegen bar** for cash; **gegen Quittung** against a receipt
6 (*verglichen mit*) compared with
Gegen- *zW*: **Gegenangriff** *m* counter-attack; **Gegenbeweis** *m* counter-evidence
Gegend ['ge:gənt] (**-, -en**) *f* area, district
Gegen- *zW*: **Gegendarstellung** *f* (*Presse*) reply; **gegeneinander** *adv* against one another; **Gegenfahrbahn** *f* opposite carriageway; **Gegenfrage** *f* counterquestion; **Gegengewicht** *nt* counterbalance; **Gegengift** *nt* antidote; **Gegenleistung** *f* service in return; **Gegenmaßnahme** *f* countermeasure; **Gegenmittel** *nt*: **Gegenmittel (gegen)** (*Med*) antidote (to)
Gegensatz (**-es, ¨-e**) *m* contrast; **Gegensätze überbrücken** to overcome differences
gegensätzlich *adj* contrary, opposite; (*widersprüchlich*) contradictory
Gegen- *zW*: **gegenseitig** *adj* mutual, reciprocal; **sich gegenseitig helfen** to help each other; **in gegenseitigem Einverständnis** by mutual agreement; **Gegenspieler** *m* opponent; **Gegenstand** *m* object; **gegenständlich** *adj* objective, concrete; (*Kunst*) representational; **gegenstandslos** *adj* (*überflüssig*) irrelevant; (*grundlos*) groundless; **Gegenstimme** *f* vote against; **Gegenstück** *nt* counterpart; **Gegenteil** *nt* opposite; **im Gegenteil** on the contrary; **das Gegenteil bewirken** to have the opposite effect; (*Mensch*) to achieve the exact opposite; **ganz im Gegenteil** quite the reverse; **ins Gegenteil umschlagen** to swing to the other extreme; **gegenteilig** *adj* opposite, contrary; **ich habe nichts Gegenteiliges gehört** I've heard nothing to the contrary
gegenüber [ge:gən'|y:bər] *präp +dat* opposite; (*zu*) to(wards); (*in Bezug auf*) with regard to; (*im Vergleich zu*) in comparison with; (*angesichts*) in the face of ▷ *adv* opposite; **mir ~ hat er das nicht geäußert** he didn't say that to me; **Gegenüber** (**-s, -**) *nt* person opposite; (*bei Kampf*) opponent; (*bei Diskussion*) opposite number; **gegenüberliegen** *unreg*

vr to face each other; **gegenüberstehen** *unreg vr* to be opposed (to each other); **gegenüberstellen** *vt* to confront; (*fig*) to contrast; **Gegenüberstellung** *f* confrontation; (*fig*) contrast; (: *Vergleich*) comparison

Gegen- *zW*: **Gegenverkehr** *m* oncoming traffic; **Gegenvorschlag** *m* counterproposal

Gegenwart ['ge:gənvart] *f* present; **in ~ von** in the presence of

gegenwärtig *adj* present ▷ *adv* at present; **das ist mir nicht mehr ~** that has slipped my mind

Gegen- *zW*: **Gegenwert** *m* equivalent; **Gegenwind** *m* headwind; **gegenzeichnen** *vt* to countersign

gegessen [gə'gɛsən] *pp von* **essen**

geglichen [gə'glıçən] *pp von* **gleichen**

geglitten [gə'glıtən] *pp von* **gleiten**

geglommen [gə'glɔmən] *pp von* **glimmen**

Gegner, in ['ge:gnər(ın)] (**-s, -**) *m(f)* opponent; **gegnerisch** *adj* opposing; **Gegnerschaft** *f* opposition

gegolten [gə'gɔltən] *pp von* **gelten**

gegoren [gə'go:rən] *pp von* **gären**

gegossen [gə'gɔsən] *pp von* **gießen**

gegraben [gə'gra:bən] *pp von* **graben**

gegriffen [gə'grıfən] *pp von* **greifen**

Gehabe [gə'ha:bə] (**-s**) (*umg*) *nt* affected behaviour (*Brit*) *od* behavior (*US*)

gehabt [gə'ha:pt] *pp von* **haben**

Gehackte, s [ge'haktə(s)] *nt* mince(d meat) (*Brit*), ground meat (*US*)

Gehalt[1] [gə'halt] (**-(e)s, -e**) *m* content

Gehalt[2] [gə'halt] (**-(e)s, ¨er**) *nt* salary

gehalten [gə'haltən] *pp von* **halten** ▷ *adj*: **~ sein, etw zu tun** (*form*) to be required to do sth

Gehalts- *zW*: **Gehaltsabrechnung** *f* salary statement; **Gehaltsempfänger** *m* salary earner; **Gehaltserhöhung** *f* salary increase; **Gehaltszulage** *f* salary increment

gehaltvoll [gə'haltfɔl] *adj* (*Speise, Buch*) substantial

gehangen [gə'haŋən] *pp von* **hängen**

gehässig [gə'hɛsıç] *adj* spiteful, nasty; **Gehässigkeit** *f* spite(fulness)

Gehäuse [gə'hɔʏzə] (**-s, -**) *nt* case; (*Radiogehäuse, Uhrgehäuse*) casing; (*von Apfel etc*) core

geheim [gə'haım] *adj* secret; (*Dokumente*) classified; **streng ~** top secret; **~ halten** to keep secret; **Geheimdienst** *m* secret service, intelligence service

Geheimnis (**-ses, -se**) *nt* secret; (*rätselhaftes Geheimnis*) mystery; **geheimnisvoll** *adj* mysterious

Geheim- *zW*: **Geheimnummer** *f* (*Tel*) secret number; **Geheimpolizei** *f* secret police; **Geheimtipp** *m* (personal) tip

geheißen [gə'haısən] *pp von* **heißen**

gehemmt [gə'hɛmt] *adj* inhibited

gehen ['ge:ən] *unreg vi* (*auch Auto, Uhr*) to go; (*zu Fuß gehen*) to walk; (*funktionieren*) to work; (*Teig*) to rise ▷ *vt* to go; to walk ▷ *vi unpers*: **wie geht es dir?** how are you *od* things?; **~ nach** (*Fenster*) to face; **in sich** *akk* **~** to think things over; **nach etw ~** (*urteilen*) to go by sth; **sich ~ lassen** to lose one's self-control; (*nachlässig sein*) to let o.s. go; **wie viele Leute ~ in deinen Wagen?** how many people can you get in your car?; **nichts geht über** *+akk* **...** there's nothing to beat ..., there's nothing better than ...; **schwimmen/schlafen ~** to go swimming/to bed; **in die Tausende ~** to run into (the) thousands; **mir/ihm geht es gut** I'm/he's (doing) fine; **geht das?** is that possible?; **gehts noch?** can you manage?; **es geht** not too bad, O.K.; **das geht nicht** that's not on; **es geht um etw** it concerns sth, it's about sth; **lass es dir gut ~** look after yourself, take care of yourself; **so geht das, das geht so** that/this is how it's done; **darum geht es (mir) nicht** that's not the point; (*spielt keine Rolle*) that's not important to me; **morgen geht es nicht** tomorrow's no good; **wenn es nach mir ginge ...** if it were *od* was up to me ...

geheuer [gə'hɔʏər] *adj*: **nicht ~** eerie; (*fragwürdig*) dubious

Gehilfe [gə'hılfə] (**-n, -n**) *m* assistant

Gehirn [gə'hırn] (**-(e)s, -e**) *nt* brain; **Gehirnerschütterung** *f* concussion; **Gehirnwäsche** *f* brainwashing

gehoben [gə'ho:bən] *pp von* **heben** ▷ *adj*: **~er Dienst** *professional and executive levels of the civil service*

geholfen [gə'hɔlfən] *pp von* **helfen**

Gehör [gə'hø:r] (**-(e)s**) *nt* hearing; **musikalisches ~** ear; **absolutes ~** perfect pitch; **~ finden** to gain a hearing; **jdm ~ schenken** to give sb a hearing

gehorchen [gə'hɔrçən] *vi +dat* to obey

gehören [gə'hø:rən] *vi* to belong ▷ *vr unpers* to be right *od* proper; **das gehört nicht zur Sache** that's irrelevant; **dazu gehört (schon) einiges** *od* **etwas** that takes some doing (*umg*); **er gehört ins Bett** he should be in bed

gehörig *adj* proper; **~ zu** *od +dat* (*geh*) belonging to

gehorsam [gə'ho:rza:m] *adj* obedient; **Gehorsam** (**-s**) *m* obedience

Gehsteig ['ge:ʃtaık] *m*, **Gehweg** ['ge:vɛk] *m* pavement (*Brit*), sidewalk (*US*)

Geier ['gaıər] (**-s, -**) *m* vulture; **weiß der ~!** (*umg*) God knows

Geige ['gaıgə] (**-, -n**) *f* violin; **die erste/zweite ~ spielen** (*lit*) to play first/second violin; (*fig*) to call the tune/play second fiddle

Geiger, in (**-s, -**) *m(f)* violinist

Geigerzähler *m* geiger counter

geil [gaıl] *adj* randy (*Brit*), horny (*US*); (*pej*: *lüstern*) lecherous; (*umg*: *gut*) fantastic

Geisel ['gaızəl] (**-, -n**) *f* hostage; **Geiselnahme**

(-) *f* taking of hostages

Geist [gaɪst] (**-(e)s, -er**) *m* spirit; (*Gespenst*) ghost; (*Verstand*) mind; **von allen guten ~ern verlassen sein** (*umg*) to have taken leave of one's senses; **hier scheiden sich die ~er** this is the parting of the ways; **den** *od* **seinen ~ aufgeben** to give up the ghost

Geister- *zW*: **Geisterfahrer** (*umg*) *m* ghost-driver (US), *person driving in the wrong direction*; **geisterhaft** *adj* ghostly

Geistes- *zW*: **geistesabwesend** *adj* absent-minded; **Geistesblitz** *m* brain wave; **Geistesgegenwart** *f* presence of mind; **geistesgegenwärtig** *adj* quick-witted; **geisteskrank** *adj* mentally ill; **Geisteskranke, r** *f(m)* mentally ill person; **Geisteskrankheit** *f* mental illness; **Geisteswissenschaften** *pl* arts (subjects) *pl*; **Geisteszustand** *m* state of mind; **jdn auf seinen Geisteszustand untersuchen** to give sb a psychiatric examination

geistig *adj* intellectual; (*Psych*) mental; (*Getränke*) alcoholic; **~ behindert** mentally handicapped; **~-seelisch** mental and spiritual

geistlich *adj* spiritual; (*religiös*) religious; **Geistliche, r** *m* clergyman; **Geistlichkeit** *f* clergy

geist- *zW*: **geistlos** *adj* uninspired, dull; **geistreich** *adj* intelligent; (*witzig*) witty; **geisttötend** *adj* soul-destroying

Geiz [gaɪts] (**-es**) *m* miserliness, meanness; **geizen** *vi* to be miserly; **Geizhals** *m* miser

geizig *adj* miserly, mean

Geizkragen *m* miser

gekannt [gəˈkant] *pp von* **kennen**

geklungen [gəˈklʊŋən] *pp von* **klingen**

geknickt [gəˈknɪkt] *adj* (*fig*) dejected

gekniffen [gəˈknɪfən] *pp von* **kneifen**

gekommen [gəˈkɔmən] *pp von* **kommen**

gekonnt [gəˈkɔnt] *pp von* **können** ▷ *adj* skilful (Brit), skillful (US)

Gekritzel [gəˈkrɪtsəl] (**-s**) *nt* scrawl, scribble

gekrochen [gəˈkrɔxən] *pp von* **kriechen**

gekünstelt [geˈkʏnstəlt] *adj* artificial; (*Sprache, Benehmen*) affected

Gel [geːl] (**-s, -e**) *nt* gel

Gelächter [gəˈlɛçtər] (**-s, -**) *nt* laughter; **in ~ ausbrechen** to burst out laughing

geladen [geˈlaːdən] *pp von* **laden** ▷ *adj* loaded; (*Elek*) live; (*fig*) furious

gelähmt [gəˈlɛːmt] *adj* paralysed

Gelände [gəˈlɛndə] (**-s, -**) *nt* land, terrain; (*von Fabrik, Sportgelände*) grounds *pl*; (*Baugelände*) site; **Geländefahrzeug** *nt* cross-country vehicle; **geländegängig** *adj* able to go cross-country; **Geländelauf** *m* cross-country race

Geländer [gəˈlɛndər] (**-s, -**) *nt* railing; (*Treppengeländer*) banister(s)

gelang *etc vb siehe* **gelingen**

gelangen [gəˈlaŋən] *vi*: **~ an** *+akk od* **zu** to reach; (*erwerben*) to attain; **in jds Besitz** *akk* **~** to come into sb's possession; **in die richtigen/falschen Hände ~** to fall into the right/wrong hands

gelangweilt *adj* bored

gelassen [gəˈlasən] *pp von* **lassen** ▷ *adj* calm; (*gefasst*) composed; **Gelassenheit** *f* calmness; composure

Gelatine [ʒelaˈtiːnə] *f* gelatine

gelaufen [gəˈlaʊfən] *pp von* **laufen**

geläufig [gəˈlɔʏfɪç] *adj* (*üblich*) common; **das ist mir nicht ~** I'm not familiar with that

gelaunt [gəˈlaʊnt] *adj*: **schlecht/gut ~** in a bad/good mood; **wie ist er ~?** what sort of mood is he in?

gelb [gɛlp] *adj* yellow; (*Ampellicht*) amber (*Brit*), yellow (US); **~e Seiten** Yellow Pages; **gelblich** *adj* yellowish

Gelbsucht *f* jaundice

Geld [gɛlt] (**-(e)s, -er**) *nt* money; **etw zu ~ machen** to sell sth off; **er hat ~ wie Heu** (*umg*) he's stinking rich; **am ~ hängen** *od* **kleben** to be tight with money; **staatliche/öffentliche ~er** state/public funds *pl od* money; **Geldanlage** *f* investment; **Geldautomat** *m* cash dispenser; **Geldbeutel** *m* purse; **Geldgeber** (**-s, -**) *m* financial backer; **geldgierig** *adj* avaricious; **Geldschein** *m* banknote; **Geldstrafe** *f* fine; **Geldstück** *nt* coin; **Geldwechsel** *m* exchange (of money); **„Geldwechsel"** "bureau de change"; **Geldwert** *m* cash value; (*Fin: Kaufkraft*) currency value

Gelee [ʒeˈleː] (**-s, -s**) *nt od m* jelly

gelegen [gəˈleːgən] *pp von* **liegen** ▷ *adj* situated; (*passend*) convenient, opportune; **etw kommt jdm ~** sth is convenient for sb; **mir ist viel/nichts daran ~** (*wichtig*) it matters a great deal/doesn't matter to me

Gelegenheit [gəˈleːgənhaɪt] *f* opportunity; (*Anlass*) occasion; **bei ~** some time (or other); **bei jeder ~** at every opportunity

Gelegenheits- *zW*: **Gelegenheitsarbeit** *f* casual work; **Gelegenheitsarbeiter** *m* casual worker; **Gelegenheitskauf** *m* bargain

gelegentlich [gəˈleːgəntlɪç] *adj* occasional ▷ *adv* occasionally; (*bei Gelegenheit*) some time (or other) ▷ *präp +gen* on the occasion of

gelehrt *adj* learned; **Gelehrte, r** *f(m)* scholar; **Gelehrtheit** *f* scholarliness

Geleit [gəˈlaɪt] (**-(e)s, -e**) *nt* escort; **freies** *od* **sicheres ~** safe conduct; **geleiten** *vt* to escort; **Geleitschutz** *m* escort

Gelenk [gəˈlɛŋk] (**-(e)s, -e**) *nt* joint

gelenkig *adj* supple

gelernt [gəˈlɛrnt] *adj* skilled

gelesen [gəˈleːzən] *pp von* **lesen**

Geliebte *f* sweetheart; (*Liebhaberin*) mistress

geliehen [gəˈliːən] *pp von* **leihen**

gelingen [gəˈlɪŋən] *unreg vi* to succeed; **die Arbeit gelingt mir nicht** I'm not doing very well with this work; **es ist mir gelungen, etw zu tun** I succeeded in doing sth

gelitten [gəˈlɪtən] *pp von* **leiden**

geloben [gəˈloːbən] *vt, vi* to vow, swear; **das**

Gelobte Land (*Rel*) the Promised Land
gelogen [gəˈlo:gən] *pp von* **lügen**
gelten [ˈgɛltən] *unreg vt* (*wert sein*) to be worth ▷ *vi* (*gültig sein*) to be valid; (*erlaubt sein*) to be allowed ▷ *vb unpers* (*geh*): **es gilt, etw zu tun** it is necessary to do sth; **was gilt die Wette?** do you want a bet?; **das gilt nicht!** that doesn't count!; (*nicht erlaubt*) that's not allowed; **etw gilt bei jdm viel/wenig** sb values sth highly/doesn't value sth very highly; **jdm viel/wenig ~** to mean a lot/not mean much to sb; **jdm ~** (*gemünzt sein auf*) to be meant for *od* aimed at sb; **etw ~ lassen** to accept sth; **für diesmal lasse ichs ~** I'll let it go this time; **als** *od* **für etw ~** to be considered to be sth; **jdm** *od* **für jdn ~** (*betreffen*) to apply to sb
Geltung [ˈgɛltʊŋ] *f*: **~ haben** to have validity; **sich/etw** *dat* **~ verschaffen** to establish o.s./sth; **etw zur ~ bringen** to show sth to its best advantage; **zur ~ kommen** to be seen/heard *etc* to its best advantage
Geltungsbedürfnis *nt* desire for admiration
Gelübde [gəˈlʏpdə] (**-s, -**) *nt* vow
gelungen [gəˈlʊŋən] *pp von* **gelingen** ▷ *adj* successful
gemächlich [gəˈmɛ:çlɪç] *adj* leisurely
Gemahl [gəˈma:l] (**-(e)s, -e**) *m* (*geh, form*) spouse, husband
gemahlen [gəˈma:lən] *pp von* **mahlen**
Gemälde [gəˈmɛ:ldə] (**-s, -**) *nt* picture, painting
gemäß [gəˈmɛ:s] *präp +dat* in accordance with ▷ *adj +dat* appropriate to
gemäßigt *adj* moderate; (*Klima*) temperate
gemein [gəˈmaɪn] *adj* common; (*niederträchtig*) mean; **etw ~ haben (mit)** to have sth in common (with)
Gemeinde [gəˈmaɪndə] (**-, -n**) *f* district; (*Bewohner*) community; (*Pfarrgemeinde*) parish; (*Kirchengemeinde*) congregation; **Gemeindesteuer** *f* local rates *pl*; **Gemeindeverwaltung** *f* local administration; **Gemeindewahl** *f* local election
Gemein- *zW*: **gemeingefährlich** *adj* dangerous to the public; **Gemeinheit** *f* (*Niedertracht*) meanness; **das war eine Gemeinheit** that was a mean thing to do/to say; **gemeinsam** *adj* joint, common (*auch MATH*) ▷ *adv* together; **gemeinsame Sache mit jdm machen** to be in cahoots with sb; **der Gemeinsame Markt** the Common Market; **gemeinsames Konto** joint account; **etw gemeinsam haben** to have sth in common; **Gemeinsamkeit** *f* common ground; **Gemeinschaft** *f* community; **in Gemeinschaft mit** jointly *od* together with; **eheliche Gemeinschaft** (*Jur*) matrimony; **Gemeinschaft Unabhängiger Staaten** Commonwealth of Independent States; **gemeinschaftlich** *adj* = **gemeinsam**; **Gemeinschaftsarbeit** *f* teamwork; **Gemeinwohl** *nt* common good
Gemenge [gəˈmɛŋə] (**-s, -**) *nt* mixture; (*Handgemenge*) scuffle
gemessen [gəˈmɛsən] *pp von* **messen** ▷ *adj* measured
Gemetzel [gəˈmɛtsəl] (**-s, -**) *nt* slaughter, carnage
gemieden [gəˈmi:dən] *pp von* **meiden**
Gemisch [gəˈmɪʃ] (**-es, -e**) *nt* mixture
gemischt *adj* mixed
gemocht [gəˈmɔxt] *pp von* **mögen**
gemolken [gəˈmɔlkən] *pp von* **melken**
Gemse [ˈgɛmzə] (**-, -n**) *f siehe* **Gämse**
Gemunkel [gəˈmʊŋkəl] (**-s**) *nt* gossip
Gemurmel [gəˈmʊrməl] (**-s**) *nt* murmur(ing)
Gemüse [gəˈmy:zə] (**-s, -**) *nt* vegetables *pl*; **Gemüsegarten** *m* vegetable garden; **Gemüsehändler** *m* greengrocer (*Brit*), vegetable dealer (*US*)
gemusst [gəˈmʊst] *pp von* **müssen**
gemustert [gəˈmʊstərt] *adj* patterned
Gemüt [gəˈmy:t] (**-(e)s, -er**) *nt* disposition, nature; (*fig: Mensch*) person; **sich** *dat* **etw zu ~e führen** (*umg*) to indulge in sth; **die ~er erregen** to arouse strong feelings; **wir müssen warten, bis sich die ~er beruhigt haben** we must wait until feelings have cooled down
gemütlich *adj* comfortable, cosy; (*Person*) good-natured; **wir verbrachten einen ~en Abend** we spent a very pleasant evening; **Gemütlichkeit** *f* comfortableness, cosiness; amiability
Gemüts- *zW*: **Gemütsmensch** *m* sentimental person; **Gemütsruhe** *f* composure; **in aller Gemütsruhe** (*umg*) (as) cool as a cucumber; (*gemächlich*) at a leisurely pace; **Gemütszustand** *m* state of mind
gemütvoll *adj* warm, tender
Gen [ge:n] (**-s, -e**) *nt* gene
genannt [gəˈnant] *pp von* **nennen**
genas *etc* [gəˈna:s] *vb siehe* **genesen**
genau [gəˈnaʊ] *adj* exact, precise ▷ *adv* exactly, precisely; **etw ~ nehmen** to take sth seriously; **~ genommen** strictly speaking; **G~eres** further details *pl*; **etw ~ wissen** to know sth for certain; **~ auf die Minute, auf die Minute genau** exactly on time
Genauigkeit *f* exactness, accuracy
genauso [gəˈnaʊzo:] *adv* (*vor Adjektiv*) just as; (*allein stehend*) just *od* exactly the same
genehm [gəˈne:m] *adj* agreeable, acceptable
genehmigen *vt* to approve, authorize; **sich** *dat* **etw ~** to indulge in sth
Genehmigung *f* approval, authorization
General [geneˈra:l] (**-s, -e** *od* **¨-e**) *m* general; **Generaldirektor** *m* chairman (*Brit*), president (*US*); **Generalkonsulat** *nt* consulate general; **Generalprobe** *f* dress rehearsal; **Generalstreik** *m* general strike; **generalüberholen** *vt* to overhaul thoroughly
Generation [generatsiˈo:n] *f* generation
Generator [geneˈra:tɔr] *m* generator, dynamo

generell [genəˈrɛl] *adj* general
genesen [geˈne:zən] *unreg vi* (*geh*) to convalesce, recover
Genesung *f* recovery, convalescence
genetisch [geˈne:tɪʃ] *adj* genetic
Genf [ˈgɛnf] (**-s**) *nt* Geneva
genial [geniˈa:l] *adj* brilliant
Genialität [genialiˈtɛ:t] *f* brilliance, genius
Genick [gəˈnɪk] (**-(e)s, -e**) *nt* (back of the) neck; **jdm/etw das ~ brechen** (*fig*) to finish sb/sth; **Genickstarre** *f* stiff neck
Genie [ʒeˈni:] (**-s, -s**) *nt* genius
genieren [ʒeˈni:rən] *vr* to be embarrassed ▷ *vt* to bother; **geniert es Sie, wenn ...?** do you mind if ...?
genießbar *adj* edible; (*trinkbar*) drinkable
genießen [gəˈni:sən] *unreg vt* to enjoy; (*essen*) to eat; (*trinken*) to drink; **er ist heute nicht zu ~** (*umg*) he is unbearable today
Genießer, in (**-s, -**) *m(f)* connoisseur; (*des Lebens*) pleasure-lover; **genießerisch** *adj* appreciative ▷ *adv* with relish
Genitiv [ˈge:niti:f] *m* genitive
Genmais *m* GM maize
genmanipuliert *adj* genetically modified
genommen [gəˈnɔmən] *pp von* **nehmen**
genoss *etc* [gəˈnɔs] *vb siehe* **genießen**
Genosse [gəˈnɔsə] (**-n, -n**) *m* comrade (*bes* POL), companion
genossen *pp von* **genießen**
Genossenschaft *f* cooperative (association)
Genossin [gəˈnɔsɪn] *f* comrade (*bes* POL), companion
Gentechnik *f*, **Gentechnologie** *f* gene technology
genug [gəˈnu:k] *adv* enough; **jetzt ist(s) aber ~!** that's enough!
Genüge [gəˈny:gə] *f*: **jdm/etw ~ tun** *od* **leisten** to satisfy sb/sth; **etw zur ~ kennen** to know sth well enough; (*abwertender*) to know sth only too well
genügen *vi* to be enough; (*den Anforderungen etc*) to satisfy; **jdm ~** to be enough for sb
genügsam [gəˈny:kza:m] *adj* modest, easily satisfied
Genugtuung [gəˈnu:ktu:ʊŋ] *f* satisfaction
Genuss [gəˈnʊs] (**-es, ¨-e**) *m* pleasure; (*Zusichnehmen*) consumption; **etw mit ~ essen** to eat sth with relish; **in den ~ von etw kommen** to receive the benefit of sth
genüsslich [gəˈnʏslɪç] *adv* with relish
Genussmittel *pl* (semi-)luxury items *pl*
geöffnet [gəˈœfnət] *adj* open
Geograf [geoˈgra:f] (**-en, -en**) *m* geographer
Geografie [geograˈfi:] *f* geography
geografisch *adj* geographical
Geologe [geoˈlo:gə] (**-n, -n**) *m* geologist
Geologie [geolo:ˈgi:] *f* geology
Geometrie [geomeˈtri:] *f* geometry
Georgien [geˈɔrgiən] (**-s**) *nt* Georgia
Gepäck [gəˈpɛk] (**-(e)s**) *nt* luggage, baggage; **mit leichtem ~ reisen** to travel light; **Gepäckabfertigung** *f* luggage desk/office; **Gepäckannahme** *f* (*Bahnhof*) baggage office; (*Flughafen*) baggage check-in; **Gepäckaufbewahrung** *f* left-luggage office (*Brit*), baggage check (*US*); **Gepäckausgabe** *f* (*Bahnhof*) baggage office; (*Flughafen*) baggage reclaim; **Gepäcknetz** *nt* luggage rack; **Gepäckschein** *m* luggage *od* baggage ticket; **Gepäckstück** *nt* piece of baggage; **Gepäckträger** *m* porter; (*Fahrrad*) carrier; **Gepäckwagen** *m* luggage van (*Brit*), baggage car (*US*)
gepfiffen [gəˈpfɪfən] *pp von* **pfeifen**
gepflegt [gəˈpfle:kt] *adj* well-groomed; (*Park etc*) well looked after; (*Atmosphäre*) sophisticated; (*Ausdrucksweise, Sprache*) cultured
gepriesen [gəˈpri:zən] *pp von* **preisen**
gequollen [gəˈkvɔlən] *pp von* **quellen**
Gerade [gəˈra:də] (**-n, -n**) *f* straight line
gerade [gəˈra:də] *adj* straight; (*aufrecht*) upright; **eine gerade Zahl** an even number ▷ *adv* **1** (*genau*) just, exactly; (*speziell*) especially; **gerade deshalb** that's just *od* exactly why; **das ist es ja gerade!** that's just it; **gerade du** you especially; **warum gerade ich?** why me (of all people)?; **jetzt gerade nicht!** not now!; **gerade neben** right next to; **nicht gerade schön** not exactly beautiful; **gerade biegen** to straighten out; **gerade stehen** (*aufrecht*) to stand up straight **2** (*eben, soeben*) just; **er wollte gerade aufstehen** he was just about to get up; **da wir gerade von Geld sprechen ...** talking of money ...; **gerade erst** only just; **gerade noch** (only) just
gerade- *zW*: **geradeaus** *adv* straight ahead; **geradeheraus** *adv* straight out, bluntly
geradeso *adv* just so; **~ dumm** *etc* just as stupid *etc*; **~ wie** just as
geradezu *adv* (*beinahe*) virtually, almost
gerannt [gəˈrant] *pp von* **rennen**
Gerät [gəˈrɛ:t] (**-(e)s, -e**) *nt* device; (*Apparat*) gadget; (*elektrisches Gerät*) appliance; (*Werkzeug*) tool; (*Sport*) apparatus; (*Zubehör*) equipment *no pl*
geraten [gəˈra:tən] *unreg pp von* **raten; geraten** ▷ *vi* (*gedeihen*) to thrive; (*gelingen*): **(jdm) ~** to turn out well (for sb); (*zufällig gelangen*): **~ in** *+akk* to get into; **gut/schlecht ~** to turn out well/badly; **an jdn ~** to come across sb; **an den Richtigen/Falschen ~** to come to the right/wrong person; **in Angst ~** to get frightened; **nach jdm ~** to take after sb
Geratewohl [gəra:təˈvo:l] *nt*: **aufs ~** on the off chance; (*bei Wahl*) at random
geräumig [gəˈrɔʏmɪç] *adj* roomy
Geräusch [gəˈrɔʏʃ] (**-(e)s, -e**) *nt* sound; (*unangenehm*) noise; **geräuschlos** *adj* silent
gerben [ˈgɛrbən] *vt* to tan
gerecht [gəˈrɛçt] *adj* just, fair; **jdm/etw ~ werden** to do justice to sb/sth
Gerechtigkeit *f* justice, fairness
Gerede [gəˈre:də] (**-s**) *nt* talk; (*Klatsch*) gossip

geregelt [gə're:gəlt] *adj* (*Arbeit, Mahlzeiten*) regular; (*Leben*) well-ordered

gereizt [gə'raɪtst] *adj* irritable; **Gereiztheit** *f* irritation

Gericht [gə'rɪçt] (**-(e)s, -e**) *nt* court; (*Essen*) dish; **jdn/einen Fall vor ~ bringen** to take sb/a case to court; **mit jdm ins ~ gehen** (*fig*) to judge sb harshly; **über jdn zu ~ sitzen** to sit in judgement on sb; **das Jüngste ~** the Last Judgement; **gerichtlich** *adj* judicial, legal ▷ *adv* judicially, legally; **ein gerichtliches Nachspiel haben** to finish up in court; **gerichtlich gegen jdn vorgehen** to take legal proceedings against sb

Gerichts- *zW*: **Gerichtsbarkeit** *f* jurisdiction; **Gerichtshof** *m* court (of law); **Gerichtskosten** *pl* (legal) costs *pl*; **Gerichtssaal** *m* courtroom; **Gerichtsverfahren** *nt* legal proceedings *pl*; **Gerichtsverhandlung** *f* court proceedings *pl*; **Gerichtsvollzieher** *m* bailiff

gerieben [gə'ri:bən] *pp von* **reiben** ▷ *adj* grated; (*umg: schlau*) smart, wily

geriet *etc* [gə'ri:t] *vb siehe* **geraten**

gering [gə'rɪŋ] *adj* slight, small; (*niedrig*) low; (*Zeit*) short ▷ *adv*: **~ achten** to think little of; **geringfügig** *adj* slight, trivial; **geringfügig Beschäftigte** ≈ part-time workers *pl*; **geringschätzig** *adj* disparaging

geringste, r, s *adj* slightest, least; **nicht im G~n** not in the least *od* slightest

gerinnen [gə'rɪnən] *unreg vi* to congeal; (*Blut*) to clot; (*Milch*) to curdle

Gerippe [gə'rɪpə] (**-s, -**) *nt* skeleton

gerissen [gə'rɪsən] *pp von* **reißen** ▷ *adj* wily, smart

geritten [gə'rɪtən] *pp von* **reiten**

Germanistik *f* German (studies *pl*)

gern [gɛrn] *adv* willingly, gladly; **(aber) ~!** of course!; **~ mögen** to like; **etw ~ tun** to like doing sth; **~ geschehen!** you're welcome!, not at all!; **ein ~ gesehener Gast** a welcome visitor; **ich hätte** *od* **möchte ~ ...** I would like ...; *siehe auch* **gernhaben**

gerochen [gə'rɔxən] *pp von* **riechen**

Geröll [gə'rœl] (**-(e)s, -e**) *nt* scree

geronnen [gə'rɔnən] *pp von* **rinnen; gerinnen**

Gerste ['gɛrstə] (**-, -n**) *f* barley

Gerstenkorn *nt* (*im Auge*) stye

Geruch [gə'rʊx] (**-(e)s, ¨-e**) *m* smell, odour (*Brit*), odor (*US*); **geruchlos** *adj* odourless (*Brit*), odorless (*US*)

Geruchssinn *m* sense of smell

Gerücht [gə'rʏçt] (**-(e)s, -e**) *nt* rumour (*Brit*), rumor (*US*)

geruchtilgend *adj* deodorant

gerufen [gə'ru:fən] *pp von* **rufen**

geruhsam [gə'ru:za:m] *adj* peaceful; (*Spaziergang etc*) leisurely

Gerümpel [gə'rʏmpəl] (**-s**) *nt* junk

gerungen [gə'rʊŋən] *pp von* **ringen**

Gerüst [gə'rʏst] (**-(e)s, -e**) *nt* (*Baugerüst*) scaffold(ing); (*fig*) framework

gesalzen [gə'zaltsən] *pp von* **salzen** ▷ *adj* (*fig: umg: Preis, Rechnung*) steep, stiff

gesamt [gə'zamt] *adj* whole, entire; (*Kosten*) total; (*Werke*) complete; **im G~en** all in all; **gesamtdeutsch** *adj* all-German; **Gesamteindruck** *m* general impression; **Gesamtheit** *f* totality, whole; **Gesamtschule** *f* ≈ comprehensive school

gesandt *pp von* **senden**

Gesandte, r [gə'zantə(r)] *f(m)* envoy

Gesandtschaft [gə'zantʃaft] *f* legation

Gesang [gə'zaŋ] (**-(e)s, ¨-e**) *m* song; (*Singen*) singing

Gesäß [gə'zɛ:s] (**-es, -e**) *nt* seat, bottom

geschaffen [gə'ʃafən] *pp von* **schaffen**

Geschäft [gə'ʃɛft] (**-(e)s, -e**) *nt* business; (*Laden*) shop; (*Geschäftsabschluss*) deal; **mit jdm ins ~ kommen** to do business with sb; **dabei hat er ein ~ gemacht** he made a profit by it; **im ~** at work; (*im Laden*) in the shop; **sein ~ verrichten** to do one's business (*euph*)

geschäftig *adj* active, busy; (*pej*) officious

geschäftlich *adj* commercial ▷ *adv* on business; **~ unterwegs** away on business

Geschäfts- *zW*: **Geschäftsbericht** *m* financial report; **Geschäftsessen** *nt* business lunch; **Geschäftsführer** *m* manager; (*Klub*) secretary; **Geschäftsjahr** *nt* financial year; **Geschäftslage** *f* business conditions *pl*; **Geschäftsleitung** *f* management; **Geschäftsmann** (**-(e)s,** *pl* **-leute**) *m* businessman; **Geschäftspartner** *m* partner; **Geschäftsreise** *f* business trip; **Geschäftsschluss** *m* closing time; **Geschäftsstelle** *f* office(s *pl*), place of business; **geschäftstüchtig** *adj* business-minded

geschehen [gə'ʃe:ən] *unreg vi* to happen; **das geschieht ihm (ganz) recht** it serves him (jolly well (*umg*)) right; **was soll mit ihm/damit ~?** what is to be done with him/it?; **es war um ihn ~** that was the end of him

gescheit [gə'ʃaɪt] *adj* clever; (*vernünftig*) sensible

Geschenk [gə'ʃɛŋk] (**-(e)s, -e**) *nt* present, gift; **Geschenkgutschein** *m* gift voucher

Geschichte [gə'ʃɪçtə] (**-, -n**) *f* story; (*Sache*) affair; (*Historie*) history

geschichtlich *adj* historical; (*bedeutungsvoll*) historic

Geschick [gə'ʃɪk] (**-(e)s, -e**) *nt* skill; (*geh: Schicksal*) fate

Geschicklichkeit *f* skill, dexterity

geschickt *adj* skilful (*Brit*), skillful (*US*); (*taktisch*) clever; (*beweglich*) agile

geschieden [gə'ʃi:dən] *pp von* **scheiden** ▷ *adj* divorced

geschienen [gə'ʃi:nən] *pp von* **scheinen**

Geschirr [gə'ʃɪr] (**-(e)s, -e**) *nt* crockery; (*Küchengeschirr*) pots and pans *pl*; (*Pferdegeschirr*) harness; **Geschirrspülmaschine** *f* dishwasher; **Geschirrtuch** *nt* tea towel (*Brit*), dishtowel (*US*)

geschlafen [gəˈʃlaːfən] *pp von* **schlafen**
geschlagen [gəˈʃlaːgən] *pp von* **schlagen**
Geschlecht [gəˈʃlɛçt] **(-(e)s, -er)** *nt* sex; (*Gram*) gender; (*Gattung*) race; (*Abstammung*) lineage; **geschlechtlich** *adj* sexual
Geschlechts- *zW*: **Geschlechtskrankheit** *f* sexually-transmitted disease; **Geschlechtsteil** *nt od m* genitals *pl*; **Geschlechtsverkehr** *m* sexual intercourse; **Geschlechtswort** *nt* (*Gram*) article
geschlichen [gəˈʃlɪçən] *pp von* **schleichen**
geschliffen [gəˈʃlɪfən] *pp von* **schleifen**
geschlossen [gəˈʃlɔsən] *pp von* **schließen** ▷ *adj*: **~e Gesellschaft** (*Fest*) private party ▷ *adv*: **~ hinter jdm stehen** to stand solidly behind sb; **~e Ortschaft** built-up area
geschlungen [gəˈʃlʊŋən] *pp von* **schlingen**
Geschmack [gəˈʃmak] **(-(e)s, ⸚e)** *m* taste; **nach jds ~** to sb's taste; **~ an etw** *dat* **finden** to (come to) like sth; **je nach ~** to one's own taste; **er hat einen guten ~** (*fig*) he has good taste; **geschmacklos** *adj* tasteless; (*fig*) in bad taste
geschmackvoll *adj* tasteful
geschmeidig *adj* supple; (*formbar*) malleable
geschmissen [gəˈʃmɪsən] *pp von* **schmeißen**
geschmolzen [gəˈʃmɔltsən] *pp von* **schmelzen**
geschnitten [gəˈʃnɪtən] *pp von* **schneiden**
geschoben [gəˈʃoːbən] *pp von* **schieben**
gescholten [gəˈʃɔltən] *pp von* **schelten**
Geschöpf [gəˈʃœpf] **(-(e)s, -e)** *nt* creature
geschoren [gəˈʃoːrən] *pp von* **scheren**
Geschoss [gəˈʃɔs] **(-es, -e)** *nt*, **Geschoß** [gəˈʃoːs] **(-sses, -sse)** (*Österr*) *nt* (*Mil*) projectile; (*Rakete*) missile; (*Stockwerk*) floor
geschossen [gəˈʃɔsən] *pp von* **schießen**
Geschrei [gəˈʃraɪ] **(-s)** *nt* cries *pl*, shouting; (*fig: Aufheben*) noise, fuss
geschrieben [gəˈʃriːbən] *pp von* **schreiben**
geschritten [gəˈʃrɪtən] *pp von* **schreiten**
geschunden [gəˈʃʊndən] *pp von* **schinden**
Geschütz [gəˈʃʏts] **(-es, -e)** *nt* gun, piece of artillery; **ein schweres ~ auffahren** (*fig*) to bring out the big guns
geschützt *adj* protected; (*Winkel, Ecke*) sheltered
Geschwafel [gəˈʃvaːfəl] **(-s)** *nt* silly talk
Geschwätz [gəˈʃvɛts] **(-es)** *nt* chatter; (*Klatsch*) gossip
geschwätzig *adj* talkative
geschweige [gəˈʃvaɪgə] *adv*: **~ (denn)** let alone, not to mention
geschwiegen [gəˈʃviːgən] *pp von* **schweigen**
geschwind [gəˈʃvɪnt] *adj* quick, swift
Geschwindigkeit [gəˈʃvɪndɪçkaɪt] *f* speed, velocity
Geschwindigkeits- *zW*: **Geschwindigkeitsbegrenzung** *f*, **Geschwindigkeitsbeschränkung** *f* speed limit; **Geschwindigkeitsüberschreitung** *f* speeding
Geschwister [gəˈʃvɪstər] *pl* brothers and sisters *pl*
geschwollen [gəˈʃvɔlən] *pp von* **schwellen** ▷ *adj* pompous
geschwommen [gəˈʃvɔmən] *pp von* **schwimmen**
geschworen [gəˈʃvoːrən] *pp von* **schwören**
Geschworene, r *f(m)* juror; **die Geschworenen** *pl* the jury
Geschwulst [gəˈʃvʊlst] **(-, ⸚e)** *f* growth, tumour
geschwunden [gəˈʃvʊndən] *pp von* **schwinden**
geschwungen [gəˈʃvʊŋən] *pp von* **schwingen** ▷ *adj* curved
Geschwür [gəˈʃvyːr] **(-(e)s, -e)** *nt* ulcer; (*Furunkel*) boil
gesehen [gəˈzeːən] *pp von* **sehen**
Geselle [gəˈzɛlə] **(-n, -n)** *m* fellow; (*Handwerksgeselle*) journeyman
gesellig *adj* sociable; **~es Beisammensein** get-together; **Geselligkeit** *f* sociability
Gesellschaft *f* society; (*Begleitung, Comm*) company; (*Abendgesellschaft etc*) party; (*pej*) crowd (*umg*); (*Kreis von Menschen*) group of people; **in schlechte ~ geraten** to get into bad company; **geschlossene ~** private party; **jdm ~ leisten** to keep sb company
gesellschaftlich *adj* social
Gesellschafts- *zW*: **Gesellschaftsordnung** *f* social structure; **Gesellschaftsschicht** *f* social stratum
gesessen [gəˈzɛsən] *pp von* **sitzen**
Gesetz [gəˈzɛts] **(-es, -e)** *nt* law; (*Parl*) act; (*Satzung, Regel*) rule; **vor dem ~** in (the eyes of the) law; **nach dem ~** under the law; **das oberste ~ (der Wirtschaft** *etc***)** the golden rule (of industry *etc*); **Gesetzbuch** *nt* statute book; **Gesetzentwurf** *m* bill
Gesetz- *zW*: **gesetzgebend** *adj* legislative; **gesetzlich** *adj* legal, lawful; **Gesetzlichkeit** *f* legality, lawfulness; **gesetzlos** *adj* lawless; **gesetzmäßig** *adj* lawful
gesetzt *adj* (*Mensch*) sedate ▷ *konj*: **~ den Fall ...** assuming (that) ...
gesetzwidrig *adj* illegal; (*unrechtmäßig*) unlawful
ges. gesch. *abk* (*= gesetzlich geschützt*) reg.
Gesicht [gəˈzɪçt] **(-(e)s, -er)** *nt* face; **das Zweite ~** second sight; **das ist mir nie zu ~ gekommen** I've never laid eyes on that; **jdn zu ~ bekommen** to clap eyes on sb; **jdm etw ins ~ sagen** to tell sb sth to his face; **sein wahres ~ zeigen** to show (o.s. in) one's true colours; **jdm wie aus dem ~ geschnitten sein** to be the spitting image of sb
Gesichts- *zW*: **Gesichtsausdruck** *m* (facial) expression; **Gesichtsfarbe** *f* complexion; **Gesichtspunkt** *m* point of view; **Gesichtswasser** *nt* face lotion
Gesindel [gəˈzɪndəl] **(-s)** *nt* rabble
gesinnt [gəˈzɪnt] *adj* disposed, minded
Gesinnung [gəˈzɪnʊŋ] *f* disposition; (*Ansicht*) views *pl*
Gesinnungswandel *m* change of opinion
gesittet [gəˈzɪtət] *adj* well-mannered

gesoffen [gəˈzɔfən] *pp von* **saufen**
gesogen [gəˈzoːgən] *pp von* **saugen**
gesonnen [gəˈzɔnən] *pp von* **sinnen**
Gespann [gəˈʃpan] (**-(e)s, -e**) *nt* team; (*umg*) couple
gespannt *adj* tense, strained; (*neugierig*) curious; (*begierig*) eager; **ich bin ~, ob** I wonder if *od* whether; **auf etw/jdn ~ sein** to look forward to sth/to meeting sb; **ich bin ~ wie ein Flitzebogen** (*hum: umg*) I'm on tenterhooks
Gespenst [gəˈʃpɛnst] (**-(e)s, -er**) *nt* ghost; (*fig: Gefahr*) spectre (*Brit*), specter (*US*); **~er sehen** (*fig: umg*) to imagine things
gespensterhaft, **gespenstisch** *adj* ghostly
gesponnen [gəʃpɔnən] *pp von* **spinnen**
Gespött [gəˈʃpœt] (**-(e)s**) *nt* mockery; **zum ~ werden** to become a laughing stock
Gespräch [gəˈʃprɛːç] (**-(e)s, -e**) *nt* conversation; (*Diskussion*) discussion; (*Anruf*) call; **zum ~ werden** to become a topic of conversation; **ein ~ unter vier Augen** a confidential *od* private talk; **mit jdm ins ~ kommen** to get into conversation with sb; (*fig*) to establish a dialogue with sb
gesprächig *adj* talkative; **Gesprächigkeit** *f* talkativeness
Gesprächs- *zW*: **Gesprächsstoff** *m* topics *pl*; **Gesprächsthema** *nt* subject *od* topic (of conversation)
gesprochen [gəˈʃprɔxən] *pp von* **sprechen**
gesprungen [gəˈʃprʊŋən] *pp von* **springen**
Gespür [gəˈʃpyːr] (**-s**) *nt* feeling
gest. *abk* (= *gestorben*) dec.
Gestalt [gəˈʃtalt] (**-, -en**) *f* form, shape; (*Person*) figure; (*Liter: pej: Mensch*) character; **in ~ von** in the form of; **~ annehmen** to take shape
gestalten *vt* (*formen*) to shape, form; (*organisieren*) to arrange, organize ▷ *vr*: **sich ~ (zu)** to turn out (to be); **etw interessanter** *etc* **~** to make sth more interesting *etc*
Gestaltung *f* formation; organization
gestanden [gəʃtandən] *pp von* **stehen; gestehen**
Geständnis [gəˈʃtɛntnɪs] (**-ses, -se**) *nt* confession
Gestank [gəˈʃtaŋk] (**-(e)s**) *m* stench
gestatten [gəˈʃtatən] *vt* to permit, allow; **~ Sie?** may I?; **sich** *dat* **~, etw zu tun** to take the liberty of doing sth
Geste [ˈgɛstə] (**-, -n**) *f* gesture
gestehen [gəˈʃteːən] *unreg vt* to confess; **offen gestanden** quite frankly
Gestein [gəˈʃtaɪn] (**-(e)s, -e**) *nt* rock
Gestell [gəˈʃtɛl] (**-(e)s, -e**) *nt* stand; (*Regal*) shelf; (*Bettgestell, Brillengestell*) frame
gestern [ˈgɛstərn] *adv* yesterday; **~ Abend/ Morgen** yesterday evening/morning; **er ist nicht von ~** (*umg*) he wasn't born yesterday
gestiegen [gəˈʃtiːgən] *pp von* **steigen**
Gestirn [gəˈʃtɪrn] (**-(e)s, -e**) *nt* star
gestochen [gəˈʃtɔxən] *pp von* **stechen** ▷ *adj* (*Handschrift*) clear, neat
gestohlen [gəˈʃtoːlən] *pp von* **stehlen** ▷ *adj*: **der/das kann mir ~ bleiben** (*umg*) he/it can go hang
gestorben [gəˈʃtɔrbən] *pp von* **sterben**
gestört [gəˈʃtøːrt] *adj* disturbed; (*Rundfunkempfang*) poor, with a lot of interference
gestoßen [gəˈʃtoːsən] *pp von* **stoßen**
gestreift [gəˈʃtraɪft] *adj* striped
gestrichen [gəˈʃtrɪçən] *pp von* **streichen** ▷ *adj*: **~ voll** (*genau voll*) level; (*sehr voll*) full to the brim; **ein ~er Teelöffel voll** a level teaspoon(ful)
gestrig [ˈgɛstrɪç] *adj* yesterday's
gestritten [gəˈʃtrɪtən] *pp von* **streiten**
Gestrüpp [gəˈʃtrʏp] (**-(e)s, -e**) *nt* undergrowth
gestunken [gəˈʃtʊŋkən] *pp von* **stinken**
Gestüt [gəˈʃtyːt] (**-(e)s, -e**) *nt* stud farm
Gesuch [gəˈzuːx] (**-(e)s, -e**) *nt* petition; (*Antrag*) application
gesucht *adj* (*begehrt*) sought after
gesund [gəˈzʊnt] *adj* healthy; **wieder ~ werden** to get better; **~ und munter** hale and hearty; **Gesundheit** *f* health; (*Sportlichkeit, fig*) healthiness; **Gesundheit!** bless you!; **bei guter Gesundheit** in good health; **gesundheitlich** *adj* health *attrib*, physical ▷ *adv* physically; **wie geht es Ihnen gesundheitlich?** how's your health?
Gesundheits- *zW*: **Gesundheitsamt** *nt* public health department; **Gesundheitsfarm** *f* health farm; **gesundheitsschädlich** *adj* unhealthy; **Gesundheitswesen** *nt* health service; **Gesundheitszustand** *m* state of health
gesundschreiben *unreg vt*: **jdn ~** to certify sb (as) fit
gesungen [gəˈzʊŋən] *pp von* **singen**
gesunken [gəˈzʊŋkən] *pp von* **sinken**
getan [gəˈtaːn] *pp von* **tun** ▷ *adj*: **nach ~er Arbeit** when the day's work is done
Getöse [gəˈtøːzə] (**-s**) *nt* din, racket
getragen [gəˈtraːgən] *pp von* **tragen**
Getränk [gəˈtrɛŋk] (**-(e)s, -e**) *nt* drink
Getränkeautomat *m* drinks machine *od* dispenser
Getränkekarte *f* (*in Café*) list of beverages; (*in Restaurant*) wine list
getrauen [gəˈtraʊən] *vr* to dare
Getreide [gəˈtraɪdə] (**-s, -**) *nt* cereal, grain
getrennt [gəˈtrɛnt] *adj* separate; **~ leben** to be separated, live apart
getreten [gəˈtreːtən] *pp von* **treten**
Getriebe [gəˈtriːbə] (**-s, -**) *nt* (*Leute*) bustle; (*Aut*) gearbox
getrieben *pp von* **treiben**
Getriebeöl *nt* transmission oil
getroffen [gəˈtrɔfən] *pp von* **treffen**
getrogen [gəˈtroːgən] *pp von* **trügen**
getrost [gəˈtroːst] *adv* confidently; **~ sterben** to die in peace; **du kannst dich ~ auf ihn verlassen** you need have no fears about relying on him

getrunken [gəˈtrʊŋkən] *pp von* **trinken**
Getue [gəˈtuːə] (**-s**) *nt* fuss
geübt [gəˈyːpt] *adj* experienced
Gewächs [gəˈvɛks] (**-es, -e**) *nt* growth; (*Pflanze*) plant
gewachsen [gəˈvaksən] *pp von* **wachsen** ▷ *adj*: **jdm/etw ~ sein** to be sb's equal/equal to sth
Gewächshaus *nt* greenhouse
gewagt [gəˈvaːkt] *adj* daring, risky
Gewähr [gəˈvɛːr] (-) *f* guarantee; **keine ~ übernehmen für** to accept no responsibility for; **die Angabe erfolgt ohne ~** this information is supplied without liability
gewähren *vt* to grant; (*geben*) to provide; **jdn ~ lassen** not to stop sb
gewährleisten *vt* to guarantee
Gewahrsam [gəˈvaːrzaːm] (**-s, -e**) *m* safekeeping; (*Polizeigewahrsam*) custody
Gewährung *f* granting
Gewalt [gəˈvalt] (**-, -en**) *f* power; (*große Kraft*) force; (*Gewalttaten*) violence; **mit aller ~** with all one's might; **die ausübende/ gesetzgebende/richterliche ~** the executive/legislature/judiciary; **elterliche ~** parental authority; **höhere ~** acts/an act of God; **Gewaltanwendung** *f* use of force
gewaltig *adj* tremendous; (*Irrtum*) huge; **sich ~ irren** to be very much mistaken
Gewalt- *zW*: **Gewaltmarsch** *m* forced march; **Gewaltmonopol** *nt* monopoly on the use of force; **gewaltsam** *adj* forcible; **gewalttätig** *adj* violent; **Gewaltverbrechen** *nt* crime of violence; **Gewaltverzicht** *m* non-aggression
gewandt [gəˈvant] *pp von* **wenden** ▷ *adj* deft, skilful (*Brit*), skillful (*US*); (*erfahren*) experienced; **Gewandtheit** *f* dexterity, skill
gewann *etc* [gəˈvan] *vb siehe* **gewinnen**
gewaschen [gəˈvaʃən] *pp von* **waschen**
Gewässer [gəˈvɛsər] (**-s, -**) *nt* waters *pl*
Gewebe [gəˈveːbə] (**-s, -**) *nt* (*Stoff*) fabric; (*Biol*) tissue
Gewehr [gəˈveːr] (**-(e)s, -e**) *nt* (*Flinte*) rifle; (*Schrotbüchse*) shotgun; **Gewehrlauf** *m* rifle barrel; barrel of a shotgun
Geweih [gəˈvaɪ] (**-(e)s, -e**) *nt* antlers *pl*
Gewerbe [gəˈvɛrbə] (**-s, -**) *nt* trade, occupation; **Handel und ~** trade and industry; **fahrendes ~** mobile trade; *siehe auch* **gewerbetreibend**; **Gewerbeschule** *f* technical school
gewerblich *adj* industrial
gewerbsmäßig *adj* professional
Gewerbszweig *m* line of trade
Gewerkschaft [gəˈvɛrkʃaft] *f* trade *od* labor (*US*) union
Gewerkschaftsbund *m* federation of trade *od* labor (*US*) unions, ≈ Trades Union Congress (*Brit*), ≈ Federation of Labor (*US*)
gewesen [gəˈveːzən] *pp von* **sein**
gewichen [gəˈvɪçən] *pp von* **weichen**
Gewicht [gəˈvɪçt] (**-(e)s, -e**) *nt* weight; (*fig*) importance
gewieft [gəˈviːft] (*umg*) *adj* shrewd, cunning
gewiesen [gəˈviːzən] *pp von* **weisen**
Gewimmel [gəˈvɪməl] (**-s**) *nt* swarm; (*Menge*) crush
Gewinde [gəˈvɪndə] (**-s, -**) *nt* (*Kranz*) wreath; (*von Schraube*) thread
Gewinn [gəˈvɪn] (**-(e)s, -e**) *m* profit; (*bei Spiel*) winnings *pl*; **~ bringend** profitable; **etw mit ~ verkaufen** to sell sth at a profit; **aus etw ~ schlagen** (*umg*) to make a profit out of sth; **Gewinnbeteiligung** *f* profit-sharing; **gewinnbringend** *adj* profitable
gewinnen *unreg vt* to win; (*erwerben*) to gain; (*Kohle, Öl*) to extract ▷ *vi* to win; (*profitieren*) to gain; **jdn (für etw) ~** to win sb over (to sth); **an etw** *dat* **~** to gain in sth
Gewinner, in (**-s, -**) *m(f)* winner
Gewinn- *zW*: **Gewinnnummer** *f* winning number; **Gewinnspanne** *f* profit margin
Gewinnung *f* (*von Kohle etc*) mining; (*von Zucker etc*) extraction
Gewirr [gəˈvɪr] (**-(e)s, -e**) *nt* tangle; (*von Straßen*) maze
gewiss [gəˈvɪs] *adj* certain ▷ *adv* certainly; **in ~em Maße** to a certain extent
Gewissen [gəˈvɪsən] (**-s, -**) *nt* conscience; **jdm ins ~ reden** to have a serious talk with sb; **gewissenhaft** *adj* conscientious; **Gewissenhaftigkeit** *f* conscientiousness; **gewissenlos** *adj* unscrupulous
Gewissens- *zW*: **Gewissensbisse** *pl* pangs of conscience *pl*, qualms *pl*; **Gewissensfreiheit** *f* freedom of conscience; **Gewissenskonflikt** *m* moral conflict
gewissermaßen [gəvɪsərˈmaːsən] *adv* more or less, in a way
Gewissheit *f* certainty; **sich** *dat* **~ verschaffen** to find out for certain
gewisslich *adv* surely
Gewitter [gəˈvɪtər] (**-s, -**) *nt* thunderstorm
gewittern *vi unpers*: **es gewittert** there's a thunderstorm
gewitzt [gəˈvɪtst] *adj* shrewd, cunning
gewoben [gəˈvoːbən] *pp von* **weben**
gewogen [gəˈvoːgən] *pp von* **wiegen** ▷ *adj (+dat)* well-disposed (towards)
gewöhnen [gəˈvøːnən] *vt*: **jdn an etw** *akk* **~** to accustom sb to sth; (*erziehen zu*) to teach sb sth ▷ *vr*: **sich an etw** *akk* **~** to get used *od* accustomed to sth
Gewohnheit [gəˈvoːnhaɪt] *f* habit; (*Brauch*) custom; **aus ~** from habit; **zur ~ werden** to become a habit; **sich** *dat* **etw zur ~ machen** to make a habit of sth; **Gewohnheitsmensch** *m* creature of habit
gewöhnlich [gəˈvøːnlɪç] *adj* usual; (*durchschnittlich*) ordinary; (*pej*) common; **wie ~** as usual
gewohnt [gəˈvoːnt] *adj* usual; **etw ~ sein** to be used to sth
Gewöhnung *f*: **~ (an** *+akk***)** getting accustomed (to); (*das Angewöhnen*) training (in)

Gewölbe [gə'vœlbə] (**-s, -**) *nt* vault
gewonnen [gə'vɔnən] *pp von* **gewinnen**
geworben [gə'vɔrbən] *pp von* **werben**
geworden [gə'vɔrdən] *pp von* **werden**
geworfen [gə'vɔrfən] *pp von* **werfen**
gewrungen [gə'vrʊŋən] *pp von* **wringen**
Gewühl [gə'vy:l] (**-(e)s**) *nt* throng
gewunden [gə'vʊndən] *pp von* **winden**
Gewürz [gə'vʏrts] (**-es, -e**) *nt* spice; (*Pfeffer, Salz*) seasoning; **Gewürzgurke** *f* pickled gherkin; **Gewürznelke** *f* clove
gewusst [gə'vʊst] *pp von* **wissen**
Gezeiten [gə'tsaɪtən] *pl* tides *pl*
gezielt [gə'tsi:lt] *adj* (*Frage, Maßnahme*) specific; (*Hilfe*) well-directed; (*Kritik*) pointed
geziert [gə'tsi:rt] *adj* affected
gezogen [gə'tso:gən] *pp von* **ziehen**
gezwungen [gə'tsvʊŋən] *pp von* **zwingen** ▷ *adj* forced; (*Atmosphäre*) strained
ggf. *abk* = **gegebenenfalls**
Gibraltar [gi'braltar] (**-s**) *nt* Gibraltar
Gicht [gɪçt] (**-**) *f* gout
Giebel ['gi:bəl] (**-s, -**) *m* gable; **Giebeldach** *nt* gable(d) roof; **Giebelfenster** *nt* gable window
Gier [gi:r] (**-**) *f* greed
gierig *adj* greedy
gießen ['gi:sən] *unreg vt* to pour; (*Blumen*) to water; (*Metall*) to cast; (*Wachs*) to mould ▷ *vi unpers*: **es gießt in Strömen** it's pouring down
Gießkanne *f* watering can
Gift [gɪft] (**-(e)s, -e**) *nt* poison; **das ist ~ für ihn** (*umg*) that is very bad for him; **darauf kannst du ~ nehmen** (*umg*) you can bet your life on it
giftig *adj* poisonous; (*fig: boshaft*) venomous
Gift- *zW*: **Giftmüll** *m* toxic waste; **Giftstoff** *m* toxic substance; **Giftzahn** *m* fang
Gigabyte ['gɪgabaɪt] *nt* (*Comput*) gigabyte
Ginster ['gɪnstər] (**-s, -**) *m* broom
Gipfel ['gɪpfəl] (**-s, -**) *m* summit, peak; (*fig*) height; **das ist der ~!** (*umg*) that's the limit!
gipfeln *vi* to culminate
Gipfeltreffen *nt* summit (meeting)
Gips [gɪps] (**-es, -e**) *m* plaster; (*Med*) plaster (of Paris); **Gipsabdruck** *m* plaster cast; **gipsen** *vt* to plaster; **Gipsverband** *m* plaster (cast)
Giraffe [gi'rafə] (**-, -n**) *f* giraffe
Girlande [gɪr'landə] (**-, -n**) *f* garland
Giro ['ʒi:ro] (**-s, -s**) *nt* giro; **Girokonto** *nt* current account (*Brit*), checking account (*US*)
Gitarre [gi'tarə] (**-, -n**) *f* guitar
Gitter ['gɪtər] (**-s, -**) *nt* grating, bars *pl*; (*für Pflanzen*) trellis; (*Zaun*) railing(s); **Gitterbett** *nt* cot (*Brit*), crib (*US*); **Gitterfenster** *nt* barred window; **Gitterzaun** *m* railing(s)
Glacéhandschuh, Glaceehandschuh [gla'se:hantʃu:] *m* kid glove
Gladiole [gladi'o:lə] (**-, -n**) *f* gladiolus
Glanz [glants] (**-es**) *m* shine, lustre (*Brit*), luster (*US*); (*fig*) splendour (*Brit*), splendor (*US*)
glänzen ['glɛntsən] *vi* to shine (*also fig*), gleam
glänzend *adj* shining; (*fig*) brilliant; **wir haben uns ~ amüsiert** we had a marvellous *od* great time
Glanz- *zW*: **Glanzleistung** *f* brilliant achievement; **glanzlos** *adj* dull; **Glanzzeit** *f* heyday
Glas [gla:s] (**-es, ⁼er**) *nt* glass; (*Brillenglas*) lens *sing*; **zwei ~ Wein** two glasses of wine; **Glasbläser** *m* glass blower; **Glaser** (**-s, -**) *m* glazier; **Glasfaserkabel** *nt* optical fibre (*Brit*) *od* fiber (*US*) cable
glasieren [gla'zi:rən] *vt* to glaze
glasig *adj* glassy; (*Zwiebeln*) transparent
Glasscheibe *f* pane
Glasur [gla'zu:r] *f* glaze; (*Koch*) icing, frosting (*bes US*)
glatt [glat] *adj* smooth; (*rutschig*) slippery; (*Absage*) flat; (*Lüge*) downright; (*Haar*) straight; (*Med: Bruch*) clean; (*pej: allzu gewandt*) smooth, slick ▷ *adv*: **~ rasiert** (*Mann, Kinn*) clean-shaven; **~ streichen** to smooth out; *siehe auch* **glattgehen**
Glätte ['glɛtə] (**-, -n**) *f* smoothness; slipperiness
Glatteis *nt* (black) ice; **„Vorsicht ~!"** "danger, black ice!"; **jdn aufs ~ führen** (*fig*) to take sb for a ride
glätten *vt* to smooth out
Glatze ['glatsə] (**-, -n**) *f* bald head; **eine ~ bekommen** to go bald
Glaube ['glaʊbə] (**-ns, -n**) *m*: **~ (an** *+akk***)** faith (in); (*Überzeugung*) belief (in); **den ~n an jdn/etw verlieren** to lose faith in sb/sth
glauben *vt, vi* to believe; (*meinen*) to think; **jdm ~** to believe sb; **~ an** *+akk* to believe in; **jdm (etw) aufs Wort ~** to take sb's word (for sth); **wers glaubt, wird selig** (*ironisch*) a likely story
Glaubensbekenntnis *nt* creed
glaubhaft ['glaʊbhaft] *adj* credible; **jdm etw ~ machen** to satisfy sb of sth
gläubig ['glɔʏbɪç] *adj* (*Rel*) devout; (*vertrauensvoll*) trustful; **Gläubige, r** *f(m)* believer; **die Gläubigen** *pl* the faithful
Gläubiger, in (**-s, -**) *m(f)* creditor
glaubwürdig ['glaʊbvʏrdɪç] *adj* credible; (*Mensch*) trustworthy; **Glaubwürdigkeit** *f* credibility; trustworthiness
gleich [glaɪç] *adj* equal; (*identisch*) (the) same, identical ▷ *adv* equally; (*sofort*) straight away; (*bald*) in a minute; (*räumlich*): **~ hinter dem Haus** just behind the house; (*zeitlich*): **~ am Anfang** at the very beginning; **es ist mir ~** it's all the same to me; **zu ~en Teilen** in equal parts; **das ~e, aber nicht dasselbe Auto** a similar car, but not the same one; **ganz ~ wer/was** *etc* no matter who/what *etc*; **2 mal 2 ~ 4** 2 times 2 is *od* equals 4; **bis ~!** see you soon!; **wie war doch ~ Ihr Name?** what was your name again?; **es ist ~ drei Uhr** it's very nearly three o'clock; **~ gesinnt** like-minded; **~ lautend** identical; **sie sind ~ groß** they are the same size; **~ nach/an** right

after/at; **gleichaltrig** *adj* of the same age; **gleichartig** *adj* similar; **gleichbedeutend** *adj* synonymous; **gleichberechtigt** *adj* with equal rights; **Gleichberechtigung** *f* equal rights *pl*; **gleichbleibend** *adj* constant; **bei gleichbleibendem Gehalt** when one's salary stays the same

gleichen *unreg vi*: **jdm/etw ~** to be like sb/sth ▷ *vr* to be alike

gleich- *zW*: **gleichfalls** *adv* likewise; **danke gleichfalls!** the same to you; **Gleichförmigkeit** *f* uniformity; **Gleichgewicht** *nt* equilibrium, balance; **jdm aus dem Gleichgewicht bringen** to throw sb off balance; **gleichgültig** *adj* indifferent; (*unbedeutend*) unimportant; **Gleichgültigkeit** *f* indifference; **Gleichheit** *f* equality; (*Identität*) identity; (*Industrie*) parity; **gleichkommen** *unreg vi +dat* to be equal to; **gleichmäßig** *adj* even, equal; **Gleichmut** *m* equanimity

Gleichnis (**-ses, -se**) *nt* parable

gleich- *zW*: **gleichsam** *adv* as it were; **gleichstellen** *vt* (*rechtlich etc*) to treat as equal; **Gleichstrom** *m* (*Elek*) direct current; **gleichtun** *unreg vi*: **es jdm gleichtun** to match sb

Gleichung *f* equation

gleich- *zW*: **gleichwertig** *adj* of the same value; (*Leistung, Qualität*) equal; (*Gegner*) evenly matched; **gleichzeitig** *adj* simultaneous

Gleis [glaɪs] (**-es, -e**) *nt* track, rails *pl*; (*am Bahnhof*) platform (*Brit*), track (*US*)

gleiten *unreg vi* to glide; (*rutschen*) to slide

Gleitzeit *f* flex(i)time

Gletscher ['glɛtʃər] (**-s, -**) *m* glacier; **Gletscherspalte** *f* crevasse

glich *etc* [glɪç] *vb siehe* **gleichen**

Glied [gli:t] (**-(e)s, -er**) *nt* member; (*Arm, Bein*) limb; (*Penis*) penis; (*von Kette*) link; (*Mil*) rank(s); **der Schreck steckt ihr noch in den ~ern** she is still shaking with the shock

gliedern *vt* to organize, structure

Gliederung *f* structure, organization

Gliedmaßen *pl* limbs *pl*

glimmen ['glɪmən] *unreg vi* to glow

glimpflich ['glɪmpflɪç] *adj* mild, lenient; **~ davonkommen** to get off lightly

glitt *etc* [glɪt] *vb siehe* **gleiten**

glitzern ['glɪtsərn] *vi* to glitter; (*Stern*) to twinkle

global [glo'ba:l] *adj* (*weltweit*) global, worldwide; (*ungefähr, pauschal*) general

Globalisierung [globalɪ'zi:rʊŋ] *f* globalization

Globus ['glo:bʊs] (**-** *od* **-ses, Globen** *od* **-se**) *m* globe

Glocke ['glɔkə] (**-, -n**) *f* bell; **etw an die große ~ hängen** (*fig*) to shout sth from the rooftops

Glocken- *zW*: **Glockengeläut** *nt* peal of bells; **Glockenspiel** *nt* chime(s); (*Mus*) glockenspiel; **Glockenturm** *m* belfry, bell-tower

Glotze (**-, -n**) (*umg*) *f* gogglebox (*Brit*), TV set

glotzen ['glɔtsən] (*umg*) *vi* to stare

Glück [glʏk] (**-(e)s**) *nt* luck, fortune; (*Freude*) happiness; **~ haben** to be lucky; **viel ~** good luck; **zum ~** fortunately; **ein ~!** how lucky!, what a stroke of luck!; **auf gut ~** (*aufs Geratewohl*) on the off-chance; (*unvorbereitet*) trusting to luck; (*wahllos*) at random; **sie weiß noch nichts von ihrem ~** (*ironisch*) she doesn't know anything about it yet; **er kann von ~ sagen, dass ...** he can count himself lucky that ...

glücken *vi* to succeed; **es glückte ihm, es zu bekommen** he succeeded in getting it

gluckern ['glʊkərn] *vi* to glug

glücklich *adj* fortunate; (*froh*) happy ▷ *adv* happily; (*umg: endlich, zu guter Letzt*) finally, eventually

glücklicherweise *adv* fortunately

Glücksbringer (**-s, -**) *m* lucky charm

glückselig [glʏk'ze:lɪç] *adj* blissful

Glücks- *zW*: **Glücksfall** *m* stroke of luck; **Glückskind** *nt* lucky person; **Glückssache** *f* matter of luck; **Glücksspiel** *nt* game of chance

Glückwunsch *m*: **~ (zu)** congratulations *pl* (on), best wishes *pl* (on)

Glühbirne *f* light bulb

glühen ['gly:ən] *vi* to glow

glühend *adj* glowing; (*heiß glühend: Metall*) red-hot; (*Hitze*) blazing; (*fig: leidenschaftlich*) ardent; (*: Hass*) burning; (*Wangen*) flushed, burning

Glüh- *zW*: **Glühwein** *m* mulled wine; **Glühwürmchen** *nt* glow-worm

Glut [glu:t] (**-, -en**) *f* (*Röte*) glow; (*Feuersglut*) fire; (*Hitze*) heat; (*fig*) ardour (*Brit*), ardor (*US*)

GmbH (**-, -s**) *f abk* (*= Gesellschaft mit beschränkter Haftung*) ≈ Ltd. (*Brit*), plc (*Brit*), Inc. (*US*)

Gnade ['gna:də] (**-, -n**) *f* (*Gunst*) favour (*Brit*), favor (*US*); (*Erbarmen*) mercy; (*Milde*) clemency; **~ vor Recht ergehen lassen** to temper justice with mercy

gnadenlos *adj* merciless

gnädig ['gnɛ:dɪç] *adj* gracious; (*voll Erbarmen*) merciful; **~e Frau** (*form*) madam, ma'am

Gold [gɔlt] (**-(e)s**) *nt* gold; **nicht mit ~ zu bezahlen** *od* **aufzuwiegen sein** to be worth one's weight in gold; **golden** *adj* golden; **goldene Worte** words of wisdom; **der Tanz ums Goldene Kalb** (*fig*) the worship of Mammon; **Goldfisch** *m* goldfish

goldig ['gɔldɪç] *adj* (*fig: umg*) sweet, cute

Gold- *zW*: **Goldregen** *m* laburnum; (*fig*) riches *pl*; **Goldschmied** *m* goldsmith

Golf[1] [gɔlf] (**-(e)s, -e**) *m* gulf; **der (Persische) ~** the Gulf

Golf[2] [gɔlf] (**-s**) *nt* golf; **Golfplatz** *m* golf course; **Golfschläger** *m* golf club; **Golfspieler** *m* golfer

Golfstrom *m* (*Geog*) Gulf Stream

Gondel ['gɔndəl] (**-, -n**) *f* gondola; (*von Seilbahn*) cable car

gondeln (*umg*) *vi*: **durch die Welt ~** to go globetrotting
gönnen ['gœnən] *vt*: **jdm etw ~** not to begrudge sb sth; **sich** *dat* **etw ~** to allow o.s. sth
goss *etc* [gɔs] *vb siehe* **gießen**
Gosse ['gɔsə] (**-, -n**) *f* gutter
Gott [gɔt] (**-es, ¨-er**) *m* god; (*als Name*) God; **um ~es Willen!** for heaven's sake!; **~ sei Dank!** thank God!; **grüß ~!** (*bes Südd, Österr*) hello, good morning/afternoon/evening; **den lieben ~ einen guten Mann sein lassen** (*umg*) to take things as they come; **ein Bild für die Götter** (*hum: umg*) a sight for sore eyes; **das wissen die Götter** (*umg*) God (only) knows; **über ~ und die Welt reden** (*fig*) to talk about everything under the sun; **wie ~ in Frankreich leben** (*umg*) to be in clover
Gottes- *zW*: **Gottesdienst** *m* service; **Gotteslästerung** *f* blasphemy
Gottheit *f* deity
Göttin ['gœtɪn] *f* goddess
göttlich *adj* divine
gottlos *adj* godless
Götze ['gœtsə] (**-n, -n**) *m* idol
Grab [gra:p] (**-(e)s, ¨-er**) *nt* grave
Graben ['gra:bən] (**-s, ¨-**) *m* ditch; (*Mil*) trench
graben *unreg vt* to dig
Grabstein *m* gravestone
Grad [gra:t] (**-(e)s, -e**) *m* degree; **im höchsten ~(e)** extremely; **Verbrennungen ersten ~es** (*Med*) first-degree burns; **Gradeinteilung** *f* graduation
Graf [gra:f] (**-en, -en**) *m* count, earl (*Brit*)
Grafik ['gra:fɪk] (**-, -en**) *f* (*Comput, Tech*) graphics; (*Art*) graphic arts *pl*
Grafiker, in ['gra:fɪkər(ɪn)] (**-s, -**) *m(f)* graphic artist; (*Illustrator*) illustrator
Gräfin ['grɛ:fɪn] *f* countess
grafisch *adj* ['gra:fɪʃ] ▷ *adj* graphic; **~e Darstellung** graph
Gram [gra:m] (**-(e)s**) *m* (*geh*) grief, sorrow
grämen ['grɛ:mən] *vr* to grieve; **sich zu Tode ~** to die of grief *od* sorrow
Gramm [gram] (**-s, -e**) *nt* gram(me)
Grammatik [gra'matɪk] *f* grammar
grammatisch *adj* grammatical
Grammofon, Grammophon [gramo'fo:n] (**-s, -e**) *nt* gramophone
Granat [gra'na:t] (**-(e)s, -e**) *m* (*Stein*) garnet; **Granatapfel** *m* pomegranate
Granate (**-, -n**) *f* (*Mil*) shell; (*Handgranate*) grenade
Granit [gra'ni:t] (**-s, -e**) *m* granite; **auf ~ beißen (bei ...)** to bang one's head against a brick wall (with ...)
Gras [gra:s] (**-es, ¨-er**) *nt* grass; (*auch umg: Marihuana*) grass; **über etw** *akk* **~ wachsen lassen** (*fig*) to let the dust settle on sth; **grasen** *vi* to graze; **Grashalm** *m* blade of grass
grassieren [gra'si:rən] *vi* to be rampant, rage
grässlich ['grɛslɪç] *adj* horrible
Grat [gra:t] (**-(e)s, -e**) *m* ridge
Gräte ['grɛ:tə] (**-, -n**) *f* fish-bone
gratis ['gra:tɪs] *adj, adv* free (of charge); **Gratisprobe** *f* free sample
Gratulation [gratulatsi'o:n] *f* congratulation(s)
gratulieren [gratu'li:rən] *vi*: **jdm (zu etw) ~** to congratulate sb (on sth); **(ich) gratuliere!** congratulations!
grau [graʊ] *adj* grey (*Brit*), gray (*US*); **der ~e Alltag** drab reality; **~ meliert** grey-flecked (*Brit*), gray-flecked (*US*)
Gräuel ['grɔʏəl] (**-s, -**) *m* horror; (*Gräueltat*) atrocity; **etw ist jdm ein ~** sb loathes sth; **Gräueltat** *f* atrocity
Grauen (**-s**) *nt* horror
grauen *vi* (*Tag*) to dawn ▷ *vi unpers*: **es graut jdm vor etw** sb dreads sth, sb is afraid of sth ▷ *vr*: **sich ~ vor** to dread
grauenhaft, grauenvoll *adj* horrible
grauhaarig *adj* grey-haired (*Brit*), gray-haired (*US*)
grausam ['graʊza:m] *adj* cruel; **Grausamkeit** *f* cruelty
Grausen ['graʊzən] (**-s**) *nt* horror; **da kann man das kalte ~ kriegen** (*umg*) it's enough to give you the creeps
grausen *vb* = **grauen**
gravieren [gra'vi:rən] *vt* to engrave
gravierend *adj* grave
Grazie ['gra:tsiə] *f* grace
graziös [gratsi'ø:s] *adj* graceful
Greencard, Green Card ['gri:nka:əd] (**-, -s**) *f* green card
greifbar *adj* tangible, concrete; **in ~er Nähe** within reach
greifen ['graɪfən] *unreg vt* (*nehmen*) to grasp; (*grapschen*) to seize, grab ▷ *vi* (*nicht rutschen, einrasten*) to grip; **nach etw ~** to reach for sth; **um sich ~** (*fig*) to spread; **zu etw ~** (*fig*) to turn to sth; **diese Zahl ist zu niedrig gegriffen** (*fig*) this figure is too low; **aus dem Leben gegriffen** taken from life
Greis [graɪs] (**-es, -e**) *m* old man
Greisenalter *nt* old age
greisenhaft *adj* very old
grell [grɛl] *adj* harsh
Gremium ['gre:miʊm] *nt* body; (*Ausschuss*) committee
Grenzbeamte, r *m* frontier official
Grenze (**-, -n**) *f* border; (*zwischen Grundstücken, fig*) boundary; (*Staatsgrenze*) frontier; (*Schranke*) limit; **über die ~ gehen/fahren** to cross the border; **hart an der ~ des Erlaubten** bordering on the limits of what is permitted
grenzen *vi*: **~ an** *+akk* to border on
grenzenlos *adj* boundless
Grenz- *zW*: **Grenzfall** *m* borderline case; **Grenzübergang** *m* frontier crossing; **Grenzwert** *m* limit
Greuel *etc* ['grɔʏəl] *siehe* **Gräuel**

Grieche ['gri:çə] (**-n, -n**) *m* Greek
Griechenland *nt* Greece
Griechin ['gri:çɪn] *f* Greek
griechisch *adj* Greek
griesgrämig ['gri:sgrɛ:mɪç] *adj* grumpy
Grieß [gri:s] (**-es, -e**) *m* (*Koch*) semolina
Griff [grɪf] (**-(e)s, -e**) *m* grip; (*Vorrichtung*) handle; (*das Greifen*): **der ~ nach etw** reaching for sth; **jdn/etw in den ~ bekommen** (*fig*) to gain control of sb/sth; **etw in den ~ bekommen** (*geistig*) to get a grasp of sth
griff *etc vb siehe* **greifen**
griffbereit *adj* handy
Grill [grɪl] (**-s, -s**) *m* grill; (*Aut*) grille
Grille ['grɪlə] (**-, -n**) *f* cricket; (*fig*) whim
grillen *vt* to grill
Grimasse [gri'masə] (**-, -n**) *f* grimace; **~n schneiden** to make faces
grimmig *adj* furious; (*heftig*) fierce, severe
grinsen ['grɪnzən] *vi* to grin; (*höhnisch*) to smirk
Grippe ['grɪpə] (**-, -n**) *f* influenza, flu
grob [gro:p] *adj* coarse, gross; (*Fehler, Verstoß*) gross; (*brutal, derb*) rough; (*unhöflich*) ill-mannered; **~ geschätzt** at a rough estimate; **Grobheit** *f* coarseness; (*Beschimpfung*) coarse expression
grölen ['grø:lən] (*pej*) *vt, vi* to bawl
Groll [grɔl] (**-(e)s**) *m* resentment; **grollen** *vi* (*Donner*) to rumble; **grollen (mit** *od* **+dat)** to bear ill will (towards)
Grönland ['grø:nlant] (**-s**) *nt* Greenland
Groschen ['grɔʃən] (**-s, -**) (*umg*) *m* 10-pfennig piece; (*Österr*) groschen; (*fig*) penny, cent (*US*)
groß [gro:s] *adj* big, large; (*hoch*) tall; (*Freude, Werk*) great ▷ *adv* greatly; **im G~en und Ganzen** on the whole; **wie ~ bist du?** how tall are you?; **die G~en** (*Erwachsene*) the grown-ups; **mit etw ~ geworden sein** to have grown up with sth; **die G~en Seen** the Great Lakes *pl*; **~en Hunger haben** to be very hungry; **~e Mode sein** to be all the fashion; **~ angelegt** large-scale, on a large scale; **~ und breit** (*fig: umg*) at great *od* enormous length; *siehe auch* **großschreiben**; **großartig** *adj* great, splendid; **Großaufnahme** *f* (*Film*) close-up; **Großbritannien** (**-s**) *nt* (Great) Britain
Größe ['grø:sə] (**-, -n**) *f* size; (*Länge*) height; (*fig*) greatness; **eine unbekannte ~** (*lit, fig*) an unknown quantity
Groß- *zW*: **Großeinkauf** *m* bulk purchase; **Großeltern** *pl* grandparents *pl*
Größenordnung *f* scale; (*Größe*) magnitude; (*Math*) order (of magnitude)
großenteils *adv* for the most part
Größenwahn *m*, **Größenwahnsinn** *m* megalomania, delusions *pl* of grandeur
Groß- *zW*: **Großformat** *nt* large size; **Großhandel** *m* wholesale trade; **Großhändler** *m* wholesaler; **Großmacht** *f* great power; **Großmaul** *m* braggart; **großmütig** *adj* magnanimous; **Großmutter** *f* grandmother; **Großraumbüro** *nt* open-plan office; **Großrechner** *m* mainframe; **großspurig** *adj* pompous; **Großstadt** *f* city
größte, r, s [grø:stə(r, s)] *adj superl von* **groß**
größtenteils *adv* for the most part
Groß- *zW*: **großtun** *unreg vi* to boast; **Großvater** *m* grandfather; **großzügig** *adj* generous; (*Planung*) on a large scale
grotesk [gro'tɛsk] *adj* grotesque
Grotte ['grɔtə] (**-, -n**) *f* grotto
Grübchen ['gry:pçən] *nt* dimple
Grube ['gru:bə] (**-, -n**) *f* pit; (*Bergwerk*) mine
grübeln ['gry:bəln] *vi* to brood
Gruft [gruft] (**-, ⸚e**) *f* tomb, vault
grün [gry:n] *adj* green; (*ökologisch*) green; (*Pol*): **die G~en** the Greens; **~e Minna** (*umg*) Black Maria (*Brit*), paddy wagon (*US*); **~e Welle** phased traffic lights; **~e Versicherungskarte** (*Aut*) green card; **sich ~ und blau** *od* **gelb ärgern** (*umg*) to be furious; **auf keinen ~en Zweig kommen** (*fig: umg*) to get nowhere; **jdm ~es Licht geben** to give sb the green light; **Grünanlage** *f* park
Grund [grʊnt] (**-(e)s, ⸚e**) *m* ground; (*von See, Gefäß*) bottom; (*fig*) reason; **von ~ auf** entirely, completely; **aus gesundheitlichen** *etc* **Gründen** for health *etc* reasons; **im ~e genommen** basically; **ich habe ~ zu der Annahme, dass ...** I have reason to believe that ...; **einer Sache** *dat* **auf den ~ gehen** (*fig*) to get to the bottom of sth; **in ~ und Boden** (*fig*) utterly, thoroughly; *siehe auch* **aufgrund; zugrunde**; **Grundbesitz** *m* land(ed property), real estate
gründen [grʏndən] *vt* to found ▷ *vr*: **sich ~ auf** *+akk* to be based on; **~ auf** *+akk* to base on
Gründer, in (**-s, -**) *m(f)* founder
Grund- *zW*: **Grundgebühr** *f* basic charge; **Grundgesetz** *nt* constitution; **Grundkurs** *m* basic course; **Grundlage** *f* foundation; **jeder Grundlage** *gen* **entbehren** to be completely unfounded; **grundlegend** *adj* fundamental
gründlich *adj* thorough; **jdm ~ die Meinung sagen** to give sb a piece of one's mind
Grund- *zW*: **grundlos** *adj* (*fig*) groundless; **Grundriss** *m* plan; (*fig*) outline; **Grundsatz** *m* principle; **grundsätzlich** *adj* fundamental; (*Frage*) of principle ▷ *adv* fundamentally; (*prinzipiell*) on principle; **das ist grundsätzlich verboten** it is absolutely forbidden
Grundschule *f* primary (*Brit*) *od* elementary school
Grundstück *nt* plot (of land); (*Anwesen*) estate
Gründung *f* foundation
Grund- *zW*: **grundverschieden** *adj* utterly different; **Grundwasser** *nt* ground water
Grüne (**-n**) *nt*: **im ~n** in the open air; **ins ~ fahren** to go to the country
Grün- *zW*: **Grünkohl** *m* kale; **Grünschnabel**

m greenhorn; **Grünspan** *m* verdigris; **Grünstreifen** *m* central reservation

grunzen ['grʊntsən] *vi* to grunt

Gruppe ['grʊpə] (**-, -n**) *f* group

Gruppen- *zW*: **Gruppenarbeit** *f* teamwork; **gruppenweise** *adv* in groups

gruppieren [grʊ'pi:rən] *vt, vr* to group

gruselig *adj* creepy

gruseln ['gru:zəln] *vi unpers*: **es gruselt jdm vor etw** sth gives sb the creeps ▷ *vr* to have the creeps

Gruß [gru:s] (**-es, ¨-e**) *m* greeting; (*Mil*) salute; **viele Grüße** best wishes; **Grüße an** *+akk* regards to; **einen (schönen) ~ an Ihre Frau!** (*geh*) my regards to your wife; **mit freundlichen Grüßen** (*als Briefformel*) Yours sincerely

grüßen ['gry:sən] *vt* to greet; (*Mil*) to salute; **jdn von jdm ~** to give sb sb's regards; **jdn ~ lassen** to send sb one's regards

Guatemala [guate'ma:la] (**-s**) *nt* Guatemala

gucken ['gʊkən] *vi* to look

Guinea [gi'ne:a] (**-s**) *nt* Guinea

Gulasch ['gu:laʃ] (**-(e)s, -e**) *nt* goulash

gültig ['gʏltɪç] *adj* valid; **~ werden** to become valid; (*Gesetz, Vertrag*) to come into effect; (*Münze*) to become legal tender; **Gültigkeit** *f* validity

Gummi ['gʊmi] (**-s, -s**) *nt od m* rubber; (*Gummiharze*) gum; (*umg: Kondom*) rubber, Durex®; (*Gummiband*) rubber *od* elastic band; (*Hosengummi*) elastic; **Gummiband** *nt* rubber *od* elastic band; **Gummibärchen** *nt* jelly baby; **Gummiknüppel** *m* rubber truncheon; **Gummistiefel** *m* rubber boot, wellington (boot) (*Brit*); **Gummistrumpf** *m* elastic stocking

günstig ['gʏnstɪç] *adj* favourable (*Brit*), favorable (*US*); (*Angebot, Preis etc*) reasonable, good; **bei ~er Witterung** weather permitting; **im ~sten Fall(e)** with luck

gurgeln *vi* to gurgle; (*im Rachen*) to gargle

Gurke ['gʊrkə] (**-, -n**) *f* cucumber; **saure ~** pickled cucumber, gherkin

Gurt [gʊrt] (**-(e)s, -e**) *m* belt

Gürtel ['gʏrtəl] (**-s, -**) *m* belt; (*Geog*) zone; **Gürtelreifen** *m* radial tyre

GUS [ge:|u:'|ɛs] *f abk* (= *Gemeinschaft Unabhängiger Staaten*) CIS

Guss [gʊs] (**-es, ¨-e**) *m* casting; (*Regenguss*) downpour; (*Koch*) glazing; **Gusseisen** *nt* cast iron

Gut [gu:t] (**-(e)s, ¨-er**) *nt* (*Besitz*) possession; (*Landgut*) estate; **Güter** *pl* (*Waren*) goods *pl*

gut *adj* good; **das ist gut gegen** *od* **für** (*umg*) **Husten** it's good for coughs; **sei so gut (und) gib mir das** would you mind giving me that; **dafür ist er sich zu gut** he wouldn't stoop to that sort of thing; **das ist ja alles gut und schön, aber ...** that's all very well but ...; **du bist gut!** (*umg*) you're a fine one!; **alles Gute** all the best; **also gut** all right then
▷ *adv* well; **gut gehen** to work, come off; **es geht jdm gut** sb's doing fine; **das ist noch einmal gut gegangen** it turned out all right; **gut gehend** thriving; **gut gelaunt** cheerful, in a good mood; **gut gemeint** well meant; **du hast es gut!** you've got it made!; **gut situiert** well-off; **gut unterrichtet** well-informed; **gut, aber ...** OK, but ...; **(na) gut, ich komme** all right, I'll come; **gut drei Stunden** a good three hours; **das kann gut sein** that may well be; **gut und gern** easily; **lass es gut sein** that'll do; *siehe auch* **guttun**

Gut- *zW*: **Gutachten** (**-s, -**) *nt* report; **Gutachter** (**-s, -**) *m* expert; **gutartig** *adj* good-natured; (*Med*) benign; **gutbürgerlich** *adj* (*Küche*) (good) plain; **Gutdünken** *nt*: **nach Gutdünken** at one's discretion

Güte ['gy:tə] (**-**) *f* goodness, kindness; (*Qualität*) quality; **ach du liebe** *od* **meine ~!** (*umg*) goodness me!

Güter- *zW*: **Güterabfertigung** *f* (*Eisenb*) goods office; **Güterbahnhof** *m* goods station; **Güterwagen** *m* goods waggon (*Brit*), freight car (*US*); **Güterzug** *m* goods train (*Brit*), freight train (*US*)

gut- *zW*: **gutgläubig** *adj* trusting; **Guthaben** (**-s**) *nt* credit; **gutheißen** *unreg vt* to approve (of)

gütig ['gy:tɪç] *adj* kind

gütlich ['gy:tlɪç] *adj* amicable

gut- *zW*: **gutmütig** *adj* good-natured; **Gutmütigkeit** *f* good nature; **Gutschein** *m* voucher; **gutschreiben** *unreg vt* to credit; **Gutschrift** *f* credit

guttun *unreg vi*: **jdm ~** to do sb good

gutwillig *adj* willing

Gymnasium [gʏm'na:ziʊm] *nt* ≈ grammar school (*Brit*), high school (*US*)

Gymnastik [gʏm'nastɪk] *f* exercises *pl*, keep-fit; **~ machen** to do keep-fit (exercises)/gymnastics

Gynäkologe [gynɛko'lo:gə] (**-n, -n**) *m* gynaecologist (*Brit*), gynecologist (*US*)

H, h [haː] *nt* H, h; **H wie Heinrich** ≈ H for Harry, ≈ H for How (*US*); (*Mus*) B

Haar [haːr] **(-(e)s, -e)** *nt* hair; **um ein ~** nearly; **~e auf den Zähnen haben** to be a tough customer; **sich die ~e raufen** (*umg*) to tear one's hair; **sich** *dat* **in die ~e kriegen** (*umg*) to quarrel; **das ist an den ~en herbeigezogen** that's rather far-fetched; **Haarbürste** *f* hairbrush

haaren *vi, vr* to lose hair

Haaresbreite *f*: **um ~** by a hair's-breadth

Haarfestiger (-s, -) *m* setting lotion

haargenau *adv* precisely

haarig *adj* hairy; (*fig*) nasty

Haar- *zW*: **Haarnadel** *f* hairpin; **haarscharf** *adv* (*beobachten*) very sharply; (*verfehlen*) by a hair's breadth; **Haarschnitt** *m* haircut; **Haarspange** *f* hair slide; **haarsträubend** *adj* hair-raising; **Haarteil** *nt* hairpiece; **Haarwaschmittel** *nt* shampoo

Habe ['haːbə] **(-)** *f* property

haben ['haːbən] *unreg vt, hilfsverb* to have ▷ *vr unpers*: **und damit hat es sich** (*umg*) and that's that; **Hunger/Angst ~** to be hungry/afraid; **da hast du 10 Mark** there's 10 Marks; **die ~s (ja)** (*umg*) they can afford it; **Ferien ~** to be on holiday; **es am Herzen ~** (*umg*) to have heart trouble; **sie ist noch zu ~** (*umg: nicht verheiratet*) she's still single; **für etw zu ~ sein** to be keen on sth; **sie werden schon merken, was sie an ihm ~** they'll see how valuable he is; **haste was, biste was** (*Sprichwort*) money brings status; **wie gehabt!** some things don't change; **das hast du jetzt davon** now see what's happened; **woher hast du das?** where did you get that from?; **was hast du denn?** what's the matter (with you)?; **ich habe zu tun** I'm busy

Haben (-s, -) *nt* (*Comm*) credit

Habgier *f* avarice

habgierig *adj* avaricious

Habicht ['haːbɪçt] **(-(e)s, -e)** *m* hawk

Habseligkeiten ['haːpzeːlɪçkaɪtən] *pl* belongings *pl*

Hachse ['haksə] **(-, -n)** *f* (*Koch*) knuckle

Hacke ['hakə] **(-, -n)** *f* hoe; (*Ferse*) heel

hacken *vt* to hack, chop; (*Erde*) to hoe

Hacker ['hakər] **(-s, -)** *m* (*Comput*) hacker

Hackfleisch *nt* mince, minced meat, ground meat (*US*)

Hafen ['haːfən] **(-s, ⸚)** *m* harbour, harbor (*US*), port; (*fig*) haven; **Hafenarbeiter** *m* docker; **Hafendamm** *m* jetty, mole; **Hafenstadt** *f* port

Hafer ['haːfər] **(-s, -)** *m* oats *pl*; **ihn sticht der ~** (*umg*) he is feeling his oats; **Haferflocken** *pl* rolled oats *pl* (*Brit*), oatmeal (*US*); **Haferschleim** *m* gruel

Haft [haft] **(-)** *f* custody; **haftbar** *adj* liable, responsible; **Haftbefehl** *m* warrant (for arrest); **einen Haftbefehl gegen jdn ausstellen** to issue a warrant for sb's arrest

haften *vi* to stick, cling; **~ für** to be liable *od* responsible for; **für Garderobe kann nicht gehaftet werden** all articles are left at owner's risk; **~ bleiben (an** *+dat***)** to stick (to)

Häftling ['hɛftlɪŋ] *m* prisoner

Haft- *zW*: **Haftpflicht** *f* liability; **Haftpflichtversicherung** *f* third party insurance

Haftschalen *pl* contact lenses *pl*

Haftung *f* liability

Hagebutte ['haːgəbʊtə] **(-, -n)** *f* rose hip

Hagedorn *m* hawthorn

Hagel ['haːgəl] **(-s)** *m* hail

hageln *vi unpers* to hail

hager ['haːgər] *adj* gaunt

Häher ['hɛːər] **(-s, -)** *m* jay

Hahn [haːn] **(-(e)s, ⸚e)** *m* cock; (*Wasserhahn*) tap, faucet (*US*); (*Abzug*) trigger; **~ im Korb sein** (*umg*) to be cock of the walk; **danach kräht kein ~ mehr** (*umg*) no one cares two hoots about that any more

Hähnchen ['hɛːnçən] *nt* cockerel; (*Koch*) chicken

Haiti [ha'iːti] **(-s)** *nt* Haiti

Häkchen ['hɛːkçən] *nt* small hook

Häkelarbeit *f* crochet work

häkeln ['hɛːkəln] *vt* to crochet

Häkelnadel *f* crochet hook

Haken ['haːkən] **(-s, -)** *m* hook; (*fig*) catch; **einen ~ schlagen** to dart sideways; **Hakenkreuz** *nt* swastika; **Hakennase** *f* hooked nose

halb [halp] *adj* half ▷ *adv* (*beinahe*) almost; **~ eins** half past twelve; **~ offen** half-open; **ein ~es Dutzend** half a dozen; **nichts H~es**

und nichts Ganzes neither one thing nor the other; **(noch) ein ~es Kind sein** to be scarcely more than a child; **das ist ~ so schlimm** it's not as bad as all that; **mit jdm ~e-halbe machen** (*umg*) to go halves with sb

halb- *zW*: **Halbbruder** *m* half-brother; **Halbdunkel** *nt* semi-darkness

halber ['halbər] *präp +gen* (*wegen*) on account of; (*für*) for the sake of

Halbheit *f* half-measure

halbieren [hal'bi:rən] *vt* to halve

Halb- *zW*: **Halbinsel** *f* peninsula; **halbjährlich** *adj* half-yearly; **Halbkreis** *m* semicircle; **Halbkugel** *f* hemisphere; **Halbleiter** *m* (*Phys*) semiconductor; **halbmast** *adv* at half-mast; **Halbmond** *m* half-moon; (*fig*) crescent; **Halbpension** *f* half-board (*Brit*), European plan (*US*); **Halbschuh** *m* shoe; **Halbschwester** *f* half-sister; **halbtags** *adv*: **halbtags arbeiten** to work part-time; **Halbtagsarbeit** *f* part-time work; **Halbton** *m* half-tone; (*Mus*) semitone; **Halbwaise** *f* *child/person who has lost one parent*; **halbwegs** *adv* half-way; **halbwegs besser** more or less better; **Halbwertzeit** *f* half-life; **Halbwüchsige, r** *f(m)* adolescent; **Halbzeit** *f* (*Sport*) half; (*Pause*) half-time

Hälfte ['hɛlftə] **(-, -n)** *f* half; **um die ~ steigen** to increase by half

Halfter[1] ['halftər] **(-s, -)** *m od nt* (*für Tiere*) halter

Halfter[2] ['halftər] **(-, -n** *od* **-s, -)** *f od nt* (*Pistolenhalfter*) holster

Halle ['halə] **(-, -n)** *f* hall; (*Aviat*) hangar

hallen *vi* to echo, resound; **Hallenbad** *nt* indoor swimming pool

hallo [ha'lo:] *interj* hallo

Halluzination [halutsinatsi'o:n] *f* hallucination

Halm ['halm] **(-(e)s, -e)** *m* blade, stalk

Hals [hals] **(-es, ¨-e)** *m* neck; (*Kehle*) throat; **sich** *dat* **nach jdm/etw den ~ verrenken** (*umg*) to crane one's neck to see sb/sth; **jdm um den ~ fallen** to fling one's arms around sb's neck; **aus vollem ~(e)** at the top of one's voice; **~ über Kopf** in a rush; **jdn auf dem** *od* **am ~ haben** (*umg*) to be lumbered *od* saddled with sb; **das hängt mir zum ~ raus** (*umg*) I'm sick and tired of it; **sie hat es in den falschen ~ bekommen** (*falsch verstehen*) she took it wrongly; **Halsband** *nt* (*Hundehalsband*) collar; **Halskette** *f* necklace; **Hals-Nasen-Ohren-Arzt** *m* ear, nose and throat specialist; **Halsschlagader** *f* carotid artery; **Halsschmerzen** *pl* sore throat *sing*; **Halstuch** *nt* scarf; **Halswirbel** *m* cervical vertebra

Halt [halt] **(-(e)s, -e)** *m* stop; (*fester Halt*) hold; (*innerer Halt*) stability; **~!, halt!** stop!, halt!; **~ machen** to stop

Halt- *zW*: **haltbar** *adj* durable; (*Lebensmittel*) non-perishable; (*Mil, fig*) tenable; **haltbar bis 6.11.** use by 6 Nov.; **Haltbarkeitsdatum** *nt* best-before date

halten ['haltən] *unreg vt* to keep; (*festhalten*) to hold ▷ *vi* to hold; (*frisch bleiben*) to keep; (*stoppen*) to stop ▷ *vr* (*frisch bleiben*) to keep; (*sich behaupten*) to hold out; **den Mund ~** (*umg*) to keep one's mouth shut; **~ für** to regard as; **~ von** to think of; **das kannst du ~ wie du willst** that's completely up to you; **der Film hält nicht, was er verspricht** the film doesn't live up to expectations; **davon halt(e) ich nichts** I don't think much of it; **zu jdm ~** to stand *od* stick by sb; **an sich** *akk* **~** to restrain o.s.; **auf sich** *akk* **~** (*auf Äußeres achten*) to take a pride in o.s.; **er hat sich gut ge~** (*umg*) he's well-preserved; **sich an ein Versprechen ~** to keep a promise; **sich rechts/links ~** to keep to the right/left

Haltestelle *f* stop

Halteverbot *nt*: **absolutes ~** no stopping; **eingeschränktes ~** no waiting; **hier ist ~** you cannot stop here

haltlos *adj* unstable

haltmachen *vi* to stop

Haltung *f* posture; (*fig*) attitude; (*Selbstbeherrschung*) composure; **~ bewahren** to keep one's composure

Halunke [ha'lʊŋkə] **(-n, -n)** *m* rascal

Hamburg ['hambʊrk] **(-s)** *nt* Hamburg

Hamburger (-s, -) *m* (*Koch*) burger, hamburger

hämisch ['hɛ:mɪʃ] *adj* malicious

Hammel ['haməl] **(-s, ¨-** *od* **-)** *m* wether

Hammelsprung *m* (*Parl*) division

Hammer ['hamər] **(-s, ¨-)** *m* hammer; **das ist ein ~!** (*umg: unerhört*) that's absurd!

hämmern ['hɛmərn] *vt, vi* to hammer

Hampelmann ['hampəlman] *m* (*lit, fig*) puppet

Hamster ['hamstər] **(-s, -)** *m* hamster

Hamsterei [hamstə'raɪ] *f* hoarding

hamstern *vi* to hoard

Hand [hant] **(-, ¨-e)** *f* hand; **etw zur ~ haben** to have sth to hand; (*Ausrede, Erklärung*) to have sth ready; **jdm zur ~ gehen** to lend sb a helping hand; **zu Händen von jdm** for the attention of sb; **in festen Händen sein** to be spoken for; **die ~ für jdn ins Feuer legen** to vouch for sb; **hinter vorgehaltener ~** on the quiet; **~ aufs Herz** cross your heart; **jdn auf Händen tragen** to cherish sb; **bei etw die** *od* **seine ~ im Spiel haben** to have a hand in sth; **eine ~ wäscht die andere** (*Sprichwort*) if you scratch my back I'll scratch yours; **das hat weder ~ noch Fuß** that doesn't make sense; **das liegt auf der ~** (*umg*) that's obvious; **unter der ~** secretly; (*verkaufen*) privately; *siehe auch* **anhand**; **Handarbeit** *f* manual work; (*Nadelarbeit*) needlework; **Handball** *m* handball; **Handbremse** *f* handbrake; **Handbuch** *nt* handbook, manual

Handel[1] ['handəl] **(-s)** *m* trade; (*Geschäft*) transaction; **im ~ sein** to be on the market; **(mit jdm) ~ treiben** to trade (with sb); **etw in den ~ bringen/aus dem ~ ziehen** to put sth on/take sth off the market

Handel² (**-s, ⸚**) *m* quarrel
handeln ['handəln] *vi* to trade; (*tätig werden*) to act ▷ *vr unpers*: **sich ~ um** to be a question of, be about; **~ von** to be about; **ich lasse mit mir ~** I'm open to persuasion; (*in Bezug auf Preis*) I'm open to offers
Handeln (**-s**) *nt* action
Handels- *zW*: **Handelsbilanz** *f* balance of trade; **aktive/passive Handelsbilanz** balance of trade surplus/deficit; **Handelsgesellschaft** *f* commercial company; **Handelskammer** *f* chamber of commerce; **Handelsreisende**, **r** *f(m)* = **Handlungsreisende(r)** commercial traveller; **Handelsschule** *f* business school; **handelsüblich** *adj* customary; **Handelsvertreter** *m* sales representative
Hand- *zW*: **Handfeger** (**-s, -**) *m* brush; **handfest** *adj* hefty; **handgearbeitet** *adj* handmade; **Handgelenk** *nt* wrist; **aus dem Handgelenk** (*umg: ohne Mühe*) effortlessly; (*: improvisiert*) off the cuff; **Handgemenge** *nt* scuffle; **Handgepäck** *nt* hand baggage *od* luggage; **Handgranate** *f* hand grenade; **Handgriff** *m* flick of the wrist; **handhaben** *unreg vt untr* to handle; **Handkuss** *m* kiss on the hand
Händler ['hɛndlər] (**-s, -**) *m* trader, dealer
handlich ['hantlıç] *adj* handy
Handlung ['handlʊŋ] *f* action; (*Tat*) act; (*in Buch*) plot; (*Geschäft*) shop
Handlungsweise *f* manner of dealing
Hand- *zW*: **Handpflege** *f* manicure; **Handschelle** *f* handcuff; **Handschlag** *m* handshake; **keinen Handschlag tun** not to do a stroke (of work); **Handschrift** *f* handwriting; (*Text*) manuscript; **Handschuh** *m* glove; **Handschuhfach** *nt* (*Aut*) glove compartment; **Handtasche** *f* handbag (*Brit*), pocket book (*US*), purse (*US*); **Handtuch** *nt* towel
Handwerk *nt* trade, craft; **jdm das ~ legen** (*fig*) to put a stop to sb's game
Handwerker (**-s, -**) *m* craftsman, artisan; **wir haben seit Wochen die ~ im Haus** we've had workmen in the house for weeks
Handwerkszeug *nt* tools *pl*
Handy ['hɛndi] (**-s, -s**) *nt* (*Tel*) mobile (phone)
Hanf [hanf] (**-(e)s**) *m* hemp
Hang [haŋ] (**-(e)s, ⸚e**) *m* inclination; (*Abhang*) slope
Hängebrücke *f* suspension bridge; **Hängematte** *f* hammock
hängen *unreg vi* to hang ▷ *vt*: **~ (an** *+akk*) to hang (on(to)); **an jdm ~** (*fig*) to be attached to sb; **~ bleiben** to be caught; (*fig*) to remain, stick; **~ bleiben an** *+dat* to catch *od* get caught on; **es bleibt ja doch alles an mir ~** (*fig: umg*) in the end it's all down to me anyhow; **~ lassen** (*vergessen*) to leave behind; **sich ~ lassen** to let o.s. go; **den Kopf ~ lassen** (*fig*) to be downcast; **die ganze Sache hängt an ihm** it all depends on him; **sich ~ an** *+akk* to hang on to, cling to
Hannover [ha'no:fər] (**-s**) *nt* Hanover
Hansestadt ['hanzəʃtat] *f* Hanseatic *od* Hanse town
Hantel ['hantəl] (**-, -n**) *f* (*Sport*) dumb-bell
hantieren [han'ti:rən] *vi* to work, be busy; **mit etw ~** to handle sth
hapern ['ha:pərn] *vi unpers*: **es hapert an etw** *dat* there is a lack of sth
Happen ['hapən] (**-s, -**) *m* mouthful
Hardware ['ha:dwɛə] (**-, -s**) *f* hardware
Harfe ['harfə] (**-, -n**) *f* harp
Harke ['harkə] (**-, -n**) *f* rake
harken *vt, vi* to rake
harmlos ['harmlo:s] *adj* harmless
Harmlosigkeit *f* harmlessness
Harmonie [harmo'ni:] *f* harmony
harmonieren *vi* to harmonize
Harmonika [har'mo:nika] (**-, -s**) *f* (*Ziehharmonika*) concertina
harmonisch [har'mo:nıʃ] *adj* harmonious
Harmonium [har'mo:niʊm] (**-s, -nien** *od* **-s**) *nt* harmonium
Harn ['harn] (**-(e)s, -e**) *m* urine; **Harnblase** *f* bladder
Harpune [har'pu:nə] (**-, -n**) *f* harpoon
harren ['harən] *vi*: **~ auf** *+akk* to wait for
hart [hart] *adj* hard; (*fig*) harsh ▷ *adv*: **das ist ~ an der Grenze** that's almost going too far; **~e Währung** hard currency; **~ bleiben** to stand firm; **~ gekocht** hard-boiled; **~ gesotten** (*Ei*) hard-boiled; **es geht ~ auf hart** it's a tough fight
Härte ['hɛrtə] (**-, -n**) *f* hardness; (*fig*) harshness; **soziale ~n** social hardships
hart- *zW*: **hartherzig** *adj* hard-hearted; **hartnäckig** *adj* stubborn
Harz¹ [ha:rts] (**-es, -e**) *nt* resin
Harz² (**-es**) *m* (*Geog*) Harz Mountains *pl*
Haschee [ha'ʃe:] (**-s, -s**) *nt* hash
Haschisch ['haʃıʃ] (**-**) *nt* hashish
Hase ['ha:zə] (**-n, -n**) *m* hare; **falscher ~** (*Koch*) meat loaf; **wissen, wie der ~ läuft** (*fig: umg*) to know which way the wind blows; **mein Name ist ~(, ich weiß von nichts)** I don't know anything about anything
Haselnuss ['ha:zəlnʊs] *f* hazelnut
Hasenfuß *m* coward
Hasenscharte *f* harelip
Hass [has] (**-es**) *m* hate, hatred; **einen ~ (auf jdn) haben** (*umg: Wut*) to be really mad (with sb)
hassen ['hasən] *vt* to hate; **etw ~ wie die Pest** (*umg*) to detest sth
hässlich ['hɛslıç] *adj* ugly; (*gemein*) nasty; **Hässlichkeit** *f* ugliness; nastiness
Hast [hast] (**-**) *f* haste
hasten *vi, vr* to rush
hastig *adj* hasty
hatte *etc* ['hatə] *vb siehe* **haben**
Haube ['haʊbə] (**-, -n**) *f* hood; (*Mütze*) cap; (*Aut*) bonnet (*Brit*), hood (*US*); **unter der ~ sein/unter die ~ kommen** (*hum*) to be/get

married

Hauch [haʊx] (**-(e)s, -e**) *m* breath; (*Lufthauch*) breeze; (*fig*) trace; **hauchdünn** *adj* extremely thin; (*Scheiben*) wafer-thin; (*fig: Mehrheit*) extremely narrow; **hauchen** *vi* to breathe; **hauchfein** *adj* very fine

Haue ['haʊə] (**-, -n**) *f* hoe; (*Pickel*) pick; (*umg*) hiding

hauen *unreg vt* to hew, cut; (*umg*) to thrash

Haufen ['haʊfən] (**-s, -**) *m* heap; (*Leute*) crowd; **ein ~ (Bücher)** (*umg*) loads *od* a lot (of books); **auf einem ~** in one heap; **etw über den ~ werfen** (*umg: verwerfen*) to chuck sth out; **jdn über den ~ rennen** *od* **fahren** *etc* (*umg*) to knock sb down

häufen ['hɔʏfən] *vt* to pile up ▷ *vr* to accumulate

haufenweise *adv* in heaps; in droves; **etw ~ haben** to have piles of sth

häufig ['hɔʏfɪç] *adj* frequent ▷ *adv* frequently; **Häufigkeit** *f* frequency

Haupt [haʊpt] (**-(e)s, Häupter**) *nt* head; (*Oberhaupt*) chief ▷ *in zw* main; **Hauptbahnhof** *m* central station; **hauptberuflich** *adv* as one's main occupation; **Hauptdarsteller, in** *m(f)* leading actor, leading actress; **Haupteingang** *m* main entrance; **Hauptfach** *nt* (*Sch, Univ*) main subject, major (*US*); **etw im Hauptfach studieren** to study sth as one's main subject, major in sth (*US*); **Hauptgeschäftszeit** *f* peak (shopping) period; **Hauptgewinn** *m* first prize; **einer der Hauptgewinne** one of the main prizes

Häuptling ['hɔʏptlɪŋ] *m* chief(tain)

Haupt- *zW*: **Hauptmann** (**-(e)s**, *pl* **-leute**) *m* (*Mil*) captain; **Hauptperson** *f* (*im Roman usw*) main character; (*fig*) central figure; **Hauptpostamt** *nt* main post office; **Hauptrolle** *f* leading part; **Hauptsache** *f* main thing; **in der Hauptsache** in the main, mainly; **hauptsächlich** *adj* chief ▷ *adv* chiefly; **Hauptsaison** *f* peak *od* high season; **Hauptsatz** *m* main clause; **Hauptschlagader** *f* aorta

Hauptschule *f* ≈ secondary modern (school) (*Brit*), junior high (school) (*US*)

Haupt- *zW*: **Hauptstadt** *f* capital; **Hauptstraße** *f* main street; **Hauptverkehrszeit** *f* rush hour; **Hauptversammlung** *f* general meeting; **Hauptwort** *nt* noun

Haus [haʊs] (**-es, Häuser**) *nt* house; **nach ~e** home; **zu ~e** at home; **fühl dich wie zu ~e!** make yourself at home!; **ein Freund des ~es** a friend of the family; **~ halten** (*sparen*) to economize; **wir liefern frei ~** (*Comm*) we offer free delivery; **das erste ~ am Platze** (*Hotel*) the best hotel in town; **Hausangestellte** *f* domestic servant; **Hausarbeit** *f* housework; (*Sch*) homework; **Hausarzt** *m* family doctor; **Hausaufgabe** *f* (*Sch*) homework; **Hausbesetzung** *f* squat; **Hausbesitzer** *m* house-owner

Haus- *zW*: **Hausfrau** *f* housewife; **Hausfreund** *m* family friend; (*umg*) lover; **Hausfriedensbruch** *m* (*Jur*) trespass (*in sb's house*); **hausgemacht** *adj* home-made; **Haushalt** *m* household; (*Pol*) budget

Haushalts- *zW*: **Haushaltsgeld** *nt* housekeeping (money); **Haushaltsgerät** *nt* domestic appliance; **Haushaltsjahr** *nt* (*Pol, Wirts*) financial *od* fiscal year

Haus- *zW*: **Hausherr** *m* host; (*Vermieter*) landlord; **haushoch** *adv*: **haushoch verlieren** to lose by a mile

hausieren [haʊ'zi:rən] *vi* to peddle

Hausierer (**-s, -**) *m* pedlar (*Brit*), peddler (*US*)

häuslich ['hɔʏslɪç] *adj* domestic; **sich irgendwo ~ einrichten** *od* **niederlassen** to settle in somewhere

Haus- *zW*: **Hausmann** (**-(e)s**, *pl* **-männer**) *m* (*den Haushalt versorgender Mann*) househusband; **Hausmeister** *m* caretaker, janitor; **Hausnummer** *f* house number; **Hausordnung** *f* house rules *pl*; **Hausputz** *m* house cleaning; **Hausratversicherung** *f* (household) contents insurance; **Hausschlüssel** *m* front-door key; **Haustier** *nt* domestic animal; **Haustür** *f* front door; **Hauswirt** *m* landlord; **Hauswirtschaft** *f* domestic science

Haut [haʊt] (**-, Häute**) *f* skin; (*Tierhaut*) hide; **mit ~ und Haar(en)** (*umg*) completely; **aus der ~ fahren** (*umg*) to go through the roof; **Hautarzt** *m* skin specialist, dermatologist

hauteng *adj* skintight

Hautfarbe *f* complexion

Haxe ['haksə] (**-, -n**) *f* = **Hachse**

Hbf. *abk* = **Hauptbahnhof**

Hebamme ['he:p|amə] *f* midwife

Hebel ['he:bəl] (**-s, -**) *m* lever; **alle ~ in Bewegung setzen** (*umg*) to move heaven and earth; **am längeren ~ sitzen** (*umg*) to have the whip hand

heben ['he:bən] *unreg vt* to raise, lift; (*steigern*) to increase; **einen ~ gehen** (*umg*) to go for a drink

Hecht [hɛçt] (**-(e)s, -e**) *m* pike

Heck [hɛk] (**-(e)s, -e**) *nt* stern; (*von Auto*) rear

Hecke ['hɛkə] (**-, -n**) *f* hedge

Heckenrose *f* dog rose

Heckenschütze *m* sniper

Heck- *zW*: **Heckklappe** *f* tailgate; **Heckmotor** *m* rear engine

Heer [he:r] (**-(e)s, -e**) *nt* army

Hefe ['he:fə] (**-, -n**) *f* yeast

Heft ['hɛft] (**-(e)s, -e**) *nt* exercise book; (*Zeitschrift*) number; (*von Messer*) haft; **jdm das ~ aus der Hand nehmen** (*fig*) to seize control *od* power from sb

heften *vt*: **~ (an +akk)** to fasten (to); (*nähen*) to tack (on (to)); (*mit Heftmaschine*) to staple *od* fasten (to) ▷ *vr*: **sich an jds Fersen** *od* **Sohlen ~** (*fig*) to dog sb's heels

Hefter (**-s, -**) *m* folder

heftig *adj* fierce, violent; **Heftigkeit** *f*

fierceness, violence
Heft- *zW*: **Heftklammer** *f* staple; **Heftmaschine** *f* stapling machine; **Heftpflaster** *nt* sticking plaster; **Heftzwecke** *f* drawing pin (*Brit*), thumb tack (*US*)
Hehl [he:l] *m od nt*: **kein(en) ~ aus etw machen** to make no secret of sth
Hehler (**-s, -**) *m* receiver (of stolen goods), fence
Heide[1] ['haɪdə] (**-, -n**) *f* heath, moor; (*Heidekraut*) heather
Heide[2] ['haɪdə] (**-n, -n**) *m* heathen, pagan
Heidekraut *nt* heather
Heidelbeere *f* bilberry
Heidentum *nt* paganism
Heidin *f* heathen, pagan
heikel ['haɪkəl] *adj* awkward, thorny; (*wählerisch*) fussy
Heil [haɪl] (**-(e)s**) *nt* well-being; (*Seelenheil*) salvation ▷ *interj* hail; **Ski/Petri ~!** good skiing/fishing!
heil *adj* in one piece, intact; **mit ~er Haut davonkommen** to escape unscathed; **die ~e Welt** an ideal world (*without problems etc*)
Heiland (**-(e)s, -e**) *m* saviour (*Brit*), savior (*US*)
heilbar *adj* curable
heilen *vt* to cure ▷ *vi* to heal; **als geheilt entlassen werden** to be discharged with a clean bill of health
heilfroh *adj* very relieved
heilig ['haɪlɪç] *adj* holy; **jdm ~ sein** (*lit, fig*) to be sacred to sb; **die H~e Schrift** the Holy Scriptures *pl*; **es ist mein ~er Ernst** I am deadly serious; *siehe auch* **heiligsprechen**; **Heiligabend** *m* Christmas Eve
Heilige, r *f(m)* saint
Heiligenschein *m* halo
Heiligkeit *f* holiness
heiligsprechen *unreg vt* to canonize
Heiligtum *nt* shrine; (*Gegenstand*) relic
heillos *adj* unholy; (*Schreck*) terrible
Heil- *zW*: **Heilmittel** *nt* remedy; **Heilpraktiker, in** (**-s, -**) *m(f)* non-medical practitioner; **heilsam** *adj* (*fig*) salutary
Heilsarmee *f* Salvation Army
Heilung *f* cure
heim [haɪm] *adv* home
Heim (**-(e)s, -e**) *nt* home; (*Wohnheim*) hostel
Heimat ['haɪma:t] (**-, -en**) *f* home (town/country *etc*); **Heimatland** *nt* homeland; **heimatlich** *adj* native, home *attrib*; (*Gefühle*) nostalgic; **heimatlos** *adj* homeless; **Heimatort** *m* home town *od* area; **Heimatvertriebene, r** *f(m)* displaced person
heimbegleiten *vt* to accompany home
heimelig ['haɪməlɪç] *adj* homely
Heim- *zW*: **heimfahren** *unreg vi* to drive *od* go home; **Heimfahrt** *f* journey home; **heimgehen** *unreg vi* to go home; (*sterben*) to pass away; **heimisch** *adj* (*gebürtig*) native; **sich heimisch fühlen** to feel at home; **Heimkehr** (**-, -en**) *f* homecoming
heimlich *adj* secret ▷ *adv*: **~, still und leise** (*umg*) quietly, on the quiet; **Heimlichkeit** *f* secrecy
Heim- *zW*: **Heimreise** *f* journey home; **Heimspiel** *nt* home game; **heimsuchen** *vt* to afflict; (*Geist*) to haunt; **heimtückisch** *adj* malicious; **Heimweg** *m* way home; **Heimweh** *nt* homesickness; **Heimweh haben** to be homesick; **Heimwerker** *m* handyman; **heimzahlen** *vt*: **jdm etw heimzahlen** to pay back sb for sth
Heirat ['haɪra:t] (**-, -en**) *f* marriage; **heiraten** *vt, vi* to marry
Heiratsantrag *m* proposal (of marriage)
heiser ['haɪzər] *adj* hoarse; **Heiserkeit** *f* hoarseness
heiß [haɪs] *adj* hot; (*Thema*) hotly disputed; (*Diskussion, Kampf*) heated, fierce; (*Begierde, Liebe, Wunsch*) burning; **es wird nichts so ~ gegessen, wie es gekocht wird** (*Sprichwort*) things are never as bad as they seem; **~er Draht** hot line; **~es Eisen** (*fig: umg*) hot potato; **~es Geld** hot money; **~ ersehnt** longed for; **~ umstritten** hotly debated; **jdn/etw ~ und innig lieben** to love sb/sth madly; **heißblütig** *adj* hot-blooded
heißen ['haɪsən] *unreg vi* to be called; (*bedeuten*) to mean ▷ *vt* to command; (*nennen*) to name ▷ *vi unpers*: **es heißt hier ...** it says here ...; **es heißt, dass ...** they say that ...; **wie ~ Sie?** what's your name?; **... und wie sie alle ~ ...** and the rest of them; **das will schon etwas ~** that's quite something; **jdn willkommen ~** to bid sb welcome; **das heißt** that is; (*mit anderen Worten*) that is to say
Heiß- *zW*: **Heißhunger** *m* ravenous hunger; **Heißwasserbereiter** *m* water heater
heiter ['haɪtər] *adj* cheerful; (*Wetter*) bright; **aus ~em Himmel** (*fig*) out of the blue; **Heiterkeit** *f* cheerfulness; (*Belustigung*) amusement
heizbar *adj* heated; (*Raum*) with heating; **leicht ~** easily heated
Heizdecke *f* electric blanket
heizen *vt* to heat
Heizer (**-s, -**) *m* stoker
Heiz- *zW*: **Heizkörper** *m* radiator; **Heizöl** *nt* fuel oil; **Heizsonne** *f* electric fire
Heizung *f* heating
Heizungsanlage *f* heating system
hektisch ['hɛktɪʃ] *adj* hectic
Held [hɛlt] (**-en, -en**) *m* hero
helfen ['hɛlfən] *unreg vi* to help; (*nützen*) to be of use ▷ *vb unpers*: **es hilft nichts, du musst ...** it's no use, you'll have to ...; **jdm (bei etw) ~** to help sb (with sth); **sich** *dat* **zu ~ wissen** to be resourceful; **er weiß sich** *dat* **nicht mehr zu ~** he's at his wits' end
Helfer, in (**-s, -**) *m(f)* helper, assistant
Helfershelfer *m* accomplice
Helgoland ['helgolant] (**-s**) *nt* Heligoland
hell [hɛl] *adj* clear; (*Licht, Himmel*) bright; (*Farbe*) light; **~es Bier** ≈ lager; **von etw ~ begeistert sein** to be very enthusiastic

about sth; **es wird ~** it's getting light; **hellblau** *adj* light blue; **hellblond** *adj* ash-blond

Helle (-) *f* clearness; brightness

hell- *zW*: **Hellseher, in** *m(f)* clairvoyant; **hellwach** *adj* wide-awake

Helm ['hɛlm] (**-(e)s, -e**) *m* helmet

Hemd [hɛmt] (**-(e)s, -en**) *nt* shirt; (*Unterhemd*) vest; **Hemdbluse** *f* blouse

Hemisphäre [hemi'sfɛːrə] *f* hemisphere

hemmen ['hɛmən] *vt* to check, hold up; **gehemmt sein** to be inhibited

Hemmung *f* check; (*Psych*) inhibition; (*Bedenken*) scruple

hemmungslos *adj* unrestrained, without restraint

Hengst [hɛŋst] (**-es, -e**) *m* stallion

Henkel ['hɛŋkəl] (**-s, -**) *m* handle

Henker (**-s, -**) *m* hangman

Henne ['hɛnə] (**-, -n**) *f* hen

Hepatitis [hepa'tiːtɪs] *f* (**-, Hepatitiden**) hepatitis

her [heːr] *adv* **1** (*Richtung*): **komm her zu mir** come here (to me); **von England her** from England; **von weit her** from a long way away; **her damit!** hand it over!; **wo bist du her?** where do you come from?; **wo hat er das her?** where did he get that from?; **hinter jdm/etw her sein** to be after sb/sth
2 (*Blickpunkt*): **von der Form her** as far as the form is concerned
3 (*zeitlich*): **das ist 5 Jahre her** that was 5 years ago; **ich kenne ihn von früher her** I know him from before

herab [hɛ'rap] *adv* down, downward(s); **herabhängen** *unreg vi* to hang down; **herablassen** *unreg vt* to let down ▷ *vr* to condescend; **herablassend** *adj* condescending; **herabsetzen** *vt* to lower, reduce; (*fig*) to belittle, disparage; **zu stark herabgesetzten Preisen** at greatly reduced prices

heran [hɛ'ran] *adv*: **näher ~!** come closer!; **~ zu mir!** come up to me!; **heranbringen** *unreg vt*: **heranbringen (an** *+akk***)** to bring up (to); **heranfahren** *unreg vi*: **heranfahren (an** *+akk***)** to drive up (to); **herankommen** *unreg vi*: **(an jdn/etw) herankommen** to approach (sb/sth), come near ((to) sb/sth); **er lässt alle Probleme an sich herankommen** he always adopts a wait-and-see attitude; **heranmachen** *vr*: **sich an jdn heranmachen** to make up to sb; (*umg*) to approach sb; **heranziehen** *unreg vt* to pull nearer; (*aufziehen*) to raise; (*ausbilden*) to train; (*zu Hilfe holen*) to call in; (*Literatur*) to consult; **etw zum Vergleich heranziehen** to use sth by way of comparison; **jdn zu etw heranziehen** to call upon sb to help in sth

herauf [hɛ'raʊf] *adv* up, upward(s), up here; **heraufbeschwören** *unreg vt* to conjure up, evoke; **heraufbringen** *unreg vt* to bring up

heraus [hɛ'raʊs] *adv* out; **nach vorn ~ wohnen** to live at the front (of the house); **aus dem Gröbsten ~ sein** to be over the worst; **~ mit der Sprache!** out with it!; **herausbekommen** *unreg vt* to get out; (*fig*) to find *od* figure out; (*Wechselgeld*) to get back; **herausbringen** *unreg vt* to bring out; (*Geheimnis*) to elicit; **jdn/etw ganz groß herausbringen** (*umg*) to give sb/sth a big build-up; **aus ihm war kein Wort herauszubringen** they couldn't get a single word out of him; **herausfinden** *unreg vt* to find out; **herausfordern** *vt* to challenge; (*provozieren*) to provoke; **Herausforderung** *f* challenge; provocation; **herausgeben** *unreg vt* to give up, surrender; (*Geld*) to give back; (*Buch*) to edit; (*veröffentlichen*) to publish ▷ *vi* (*Wechselgeld geben*): **können Sie (mir) herausgeben?** can you give me change?; **Herausgeber** (**-s, -**) *m* editor; (*Verleger*) publisher; **heraushalten** *unreg vr*: **sich aus etw heraushalten** to keep out of sth; **heraushängen** *unreg vt, vi* to hang out; **herausholen** *vt*: **herausholen (aus)** to get out (of); **herauskommen** *unreg vi* to come out; **dabei kommt nichts heraus** nothing will come of it; **er kam aus dem Staunen nicht heraus** he couldn't get over his astonishment; **es kommt auf dasselbe heraus** it comes (down) to the same thing; **herausreißen** *unreg vt* to tear out; (*Zahn, Baum*) to pull out; **herausrücken** *vt* (*Geld*) to fork out, hand over; **mit etw herausrücken** (*fig*) to come out with sth; **herausstellen** *vr*: **sich herausstellen (als)** to turn out (to be); **das muss sich erst herausstellen** that remains to be seen; **heraussuchen** *vt*: **sich** *dat* **jdn/etw heraussuchen** to pick out sb/sth; **herausziehen** *unreg vt* to pull out, extract

herb [hɛrp] *adj* (slightly) bitter, acid; (*Wein*) dry; (*fig: schmerzlich*) bitter; (*: streng*) stern, austere

herbei [hɛr'baɪ] *adv* (over) here; **herbeiführen** *vt* to bring about; **herbeischaffen** *vt* to procure

herbemühen ['heːrbəmyːən] *vr* to take the trouble to come

Herberge ['hɛrbɛrgə] (**-, -n**) *f* (*Jugendherberge etc*) hostel

Herbergsmutter *f* warden

herbitten *unreg vt* to ask to come (here)

herbringen *unreg vt* to bring here

Herbst [hɛrpst] (**-(e)s, -e**) *m* autumn, fall (*US*); **im ~** in autumn, in the fall (*US*); **herbstlich** *adj* autumnal

Herd [heːrt] (**-(e)s, -e**) *m* cooker; (*fig, Med*) focus, centre (*Brit*), center (*US*)

Herde ['heːrdə] (**-, -n**) *f* herd; (*Schafherde*) flock

herein [hɛ'raɪn] *adv* in (here), here; **~!** come in!; **hereinbitten** *unreg vt* to ask in; **hereinbrechen** *unreg vi* to set in; **hereinbringen** *unreg vt* to bring in; **hereindürfen** *unreg vi* to have permission to enter; **hereinfallen** *unreg vi* to be caught, be taken in; **hereinfallen auf** *+akk* to fall for; **hereinkommen** *unreg vi* to come in; **hereinlassen** *unreg vt* to admit

her- *zW*: **Herfahrt** *f* journey here; **herfallen** *unreg vi*: **herfallen über** *+akk* to fall upon; **Hergang** *m* course of events, circumstances *pl*; **hergeben** *unreg vt* to give, hand (over); **sich zu etw hergeben** to lend one's name to sth; **das Thema gibt viel/nichts her** there's a lot/nothing to this topic; **hergehen** *unreg vi*: **hinter jdm hergehen** to follow sb; **es geht hoch her** there are a lot of goings-on; **herhören** *vi* to listen; **hör mal her!** listen here!

Hering ['he:rɪŋ] (**-s, -e**) *m* herring; (*Zeltpflock*) (tent) peg

herkommen *unreg vi* to come; **komm mal her!** come here!

herkömmlich *adj* traditional

Herkunft (**-, -künfte**) *f* origin

herlaufen *unreg vi*: **herlaufen hinter** *+dat* to run after

Hermelin [hɛrmə'li:n] (**-s, -e**) *m od nt* ermine

hermetisch [hɛr'me:tɪʃ] *adj* hermetic; **~ abgeriegelt** completely sealed off

Heroin [hero'i:n] (**-s**) *nt* heroin

Herpes [['hɛrpɛs]] *m* (-) (*Med*) herpes

Herr [hɛr] (**-(e)n, -en**) *m* master; (*Mann*) gentleman; (*adliger, Rel*) Lord; (*vor Namen*) Mr; **mein ~!** sir!; **meine ~en!** gentlemen!; **Lieber ~ A, Sehr geehrter ~ A** (*in Brief*) Dear Mr A; **„~en"** (*Toilette*) "gentlemen" (*Brit*), "men's room" (*US*); **die ~en der Schöpfung** (*hum: Männer*) the gentlemen

Herren- *zW*: **Herrendoppel** *nt* men's doubles; **Herreneinzel** *nt* men's singles; **Herrenhaus** *nt* mansion; **herrenlos** *adj* ownerless

Herrgott *m*: **~ noch mal!** (*umg*) damn it all!

herrichten ['he:rrɪçtən] *vt* to prepare

Herrin *f* mistress

herrisch *adj* domineering

herrlich *adj* marvellous (*Brit*), marvelous (*US*), splendid; **Herrlichkeit** *f* splendour (*Brit*), splendor (*US*), magnificence

Herrschaft *f* power, rule; (*Herr und Herrin*) master and mistress; **meine ~en!** ladies and gentlemen!

herrschen ['hɛrʃən] *vi* to rule; (*bestehen*) to prevail, be; **hier ~ ja Zustände!** things are in a pretty state round here!

Herrscher, in (**-s, -**) *m(f)* ruler

her- *zW*: **herrühren** *vi* to arise, originate; **herstellen** *vt* to make, manufacture; (*zustande bringen*) to establish; **Hersteller** (**-s, -**) *m* manufacturer; **Herstellung** *f* manufacture

herüber [hɛ'ry:bər] *adv* over (here), across

herum [hɛ'rʊm] *adv* about, (a)round; **um etw ~** around sth; **herumführen** *vt* to show around; **herumgehen** *unreg vi* (*herumspazieren*) to walk about; **um etw herumgehen** to walk *od* go round sth; **etw herumgehen lassen** to circulate sth; **herumirren** *vi* to wander about; **herumkommen** *unreg* (*umg*) *vi*: **um etw herumkommen** to get out of sth; **er ist viel herumgekommen** he has been around a lot; **herumkriegen** *vt* to bring *od* talk round; **herumsprechen** *unreg vr* to get around, be spread; **herumtreiben** *unreg vi, vr* to drift about; **herumziehen** *unreg vi, vr* to wander about

herunter [hɛ'rʊntər] *adv* downward(s), down (there); **mit den Nerven/der Gesundheit ~ sein** (*umg*) to be at the end of one's tether/be run-down; **herunterfahren** *unreg vti* (*Comput, Tech*) to shut down; **heruntergekommen** *adj* run-down; **herunterhängen** *unreg vi* to hang down; **herunterholen** *vt* to bring down; **herunterkommen** *unreg vi* to come down; (*fig*) to come down in the world; **heruntermachen** *vt* to take down; (*schlechtmachen*) to run down, knock

hervor [hɛr'fo:r] *adv* out, forth; **hervorbringen** *unreg vt* to produce; (*Wort*) to utter; **hervorheben** *unreg vt* to stress; (*als Kontrast*) to set off; **hervorragend** *adj* excellent; (*lit*) projecting; **hervorrufen** *unreg vt* to cause, give rise to; **hervortun** *unreg vr* to distinguish o.s.; (*umg: sich wichtigtun*) to show off; **sich mit etw hervortun** to show off sth

Herz [hɛrts] (**-ens, -en**) *nt* heart; (*Karten: Farbe*) hearts *pl*; **mit ganzem ~en** wholeheartedly; **etw auf dem ~en haben** to have sth on one's mind; **sich** *dat* **etw zu ~en nehmen** to take sth to heart; **du sprichst mir aus dem ~en** that's just what I feel; **es liegt mir am ~en** I am very concerned about it; **seinem ~en Luft machen** to give vent to one's feelings; **sein ~ an jdn/etw hängen** to commit o.s. heart and soul to sb/sth; **ein ~ und eine Seele sein** to be the best of friends; **jdn/etw auf ~ und Nieren prüfen** to examine sb/sth very thoroughly

Herzenslust *f*: **nach ~** to one's heart's content

Herz- *zW*: **Herzfehler** *m* heart defect; **herzhaft** *adj* hearty; **Herzinfarkt** *m* heart attack; **Herzklopfen** *nt* palpitation; **herzkrank** *adj* suffering from a heart condition

herzlich *adj* cordial ▷ *adv* (*sehr*): **~ gern!** with the greatest of pleasure!; **~en Glückwunsch** congratulations *pl*; **~e Grüße** best wishes; **Herzlichkeit** *f* cordiality

herzlos *adj* heartless

Herzog ['hɛrtso:k] (**-(e)s, ¨-e**) *m* duke; **herzoglich** *adj* ducal; **Herzogtum** *nt* duchy

Herz- *zW*: **Herzschlag** *m* heartbeat; (*Med*) heart attack; **Herzschrittmacher** *m* pacemaker; **herzzerreißend** *adj* heartrending

Hessen ['hɛsən] (**-s**) *nt* Hesse

heterogen [hetero'ge:n] *adj* heterogeneous

heterosexuell [heterozɛksu'ɛl] *adj* heterosexual

Hetze ['hɛtsə] *f* (*Eile*) rush
hetzen *vt* to hunt; (*verfolgen*) to chase ▷ *vi* (*eilen*) to rush; **jdn/etw auf jdn/etw ~** to set sb/sth on sb/sth; **~ gegen** to stir up feeling against; **~ zu** to agitate for
Heu [hɔʏ] (**-(e)s**) *nt* hay
Heuchelei [hɔʏçə'laɪ] *f* hypocrisy
heucheln ['hɔʏçəln] *vt* to pretend, feign ▷ *vi* to be hypocritical
Heuchler, in [hɔʏçlər(ɪn)] (**-s, -**) *m(f)* hypocrite; **heuchlerisch** *adj* hypocritical
heuer *adv* this year
heulen ['hɔʏlən] *vi* to howl; (*weinen*) to cry; **das ~de Elend bekommen** to get the blues
heurig ['hɔʏrɪç] *adj* this year's
Heuschnupfen *m* hay fever
Heuschrecke *f* grasshopper; (*in heißen Ländern*) locust
heute ['hɔʏtə] *adv* today; **~ Abend/früh** this evening/morning; **~ Morgen** this morning; **~ in einer Woche** a week today, today week; **von ~ auf morgen** (*fig: plötzlich*) overnight, from one day to the next; **das H~** today
heutig ['hɔʏtɪç] *adj* today's; **unser ~es Schreiben** (*Comm*) our letter of today('s date)
heutzutage ['hɔʏttsuta:gə] *adv* nowadays
Hexe ['hɛksə] (**-, -n**) *f* witch
hexen *vi* to practise witchcraft; **ich kann doch nicht ~** I can't work miracles
Hexen- *zW*: **Hexenkessel** *m* (*lit, fig*) cauldron; **Hexenschuss** *m* lumbago
Hieb (**-(e)s, -e**) *m* blow; (*Wunde*) cut, gash; (*Stichelei*) cutting remark; **~e bekommen** to get a thrashing
hier [hi:r] *adv* here; **~ spricht Dr. Müller** (*Tel*) this is Dr Müller (speaking); **er ist von ~** he's a local (man); *siehe auch* **hierbehalten; hierbleiben; hierlassen**
hier- *zW*: **hierauf** *adv* thereupon; (*danach*) after that; **hierbei** *adv* (*bei dieser Gelegenheit*) on this occasion; **hierbleiben** *unreg vi* to stay here; **hierdurch** *adv* by this means; (*örtlich*) through here; **hierher** *adv* this way, here; **hierher gehören** to belong here; (*fig: relevant sein*) to be relevant; **hierlassen** *unreg vt* to leave here; **hiermit** *adv* hereby; **hiermit erkläre ich ...** (*form*) I hereby declare ...; **hiernach** *adv* hereafter; **hierzulande**, **hier zu Lande** *adv* in this country
hiesig ['hi:zɪç] *adj* of this place, local
hieß *etc* [hi:s] *vb siehe* **heißen**
Hi-Fi-Anlage ['haɪfianla:gə] *f* hi-fi set *od* system
Hilfe ['hɪlfə] (**-, -n**) *f* help; (*für Notleidende*) aid; **Erste ~** first aid; **jdm ~ leisten** to help sb; **~!** help!
Hilf- *zW*: **hilflos** *adj* helpless; **Hilflosigkeit** *f* helplessness; **hilfreich** *adj* helpful
Hilfs- *zW*: **Hilfsarbeiter** *m* labourer (*Brit*), laborer (*US*); **hilfsbereit** *adj* ready to help; **Hilfskraft** *f* assistant, helper
Himbeere ['hɪmbe:rə] (**-, -n**) *f* raspberry
Himmel ['hɪməl] (**-s, -**) *m* sky; (*Rel*) heaven; **um ~s willen** (*umg*) for Heaven's sake; **zwischen ~ und Erde** in midair; **himmelblau** *adj* sky-blue
Himmelfahrt *f* Ascension
himmelschreiend *adj* outrageous
Himmelsrichtung *f* direction; **die vier ~en** the four points of the compass
himmlisch ['hɪmlɪʃ] *adj* heavenly
hin [hɪn] *adv* **1** (*Richtung*): **hin und zurück** there and back; **einmal London hin und zurück** a return to London (*Brit*), a roundtrip ticket to London (*US*); **hin und her** to and fro; **etw hin und her überlegen** to turn sth over and over in one's mind; **bis zur Mauer hin** up to the wall; **wo ist er hin?** where has he gone?; **nichts wie hin!** (*umg*) let's go then!; **nach außen hin** (*fig*) outwardly; **Geld hin, Geld her** money or no money
2 (*auf ... hin*): **auf meine Bitte hin** at my request; **auf seinen Rat hin** on the basis of his advice; **auf meinen Brief hin** on the strength of my letter
3: **hin sein** (*umg: kaputt sein*) to have had it; (*Ruhe*) to be gone; **mein Glück ist hin** my happiness has gone; **hin und wieder** (every) now and again
hinab [hɪ'nap] *adv* down; **hinabgehen** *unreg vi* to go down; **hinabsehen** *unreg vi* to look down
hinauf [hɪ'naʊf] *adv* up; **hinaufarbeiten** *vr* to work one's way up; **hinaufsteigen** *unreg vi* to climb
hinaus [hɪ'naʊs] *adv* out; **hinten/vorn ~** at the back/front; **darüber ~** over and above this; **auf Jahre ~** for years to come; **hinausgehen** *unreg vi* to go out; **hinausgehen über** *+akk* to exceed; **hinauslaufen** *unreg vi* to run out; **hinauslaufen auf** *+akk* to come to, amount to; **hinausschieben** *unreg vt* to put off, postpone; **hinauswollen** *vi* to want to go out; **hoch hinauswollen** to aim high; **hinauswollen auf** *+akk* to drive at, get at
Hinblick ['hɪnblɪk] *m*: **in** *od* **im ~ auf** *+akk* in view of
hinderlich ['hɪndərlɪç] *adj* awkward; **jds Karriere** *dat* **~ sein** to be a hindrance to sb's career
hindern *vt* to hinder, hamper; **jdn an etw** *dat* **~** to prevent sb from doing sth
Hindernis (**-ses, -se**) *nt* obstacle
Hinduismus [hɪndu'ɪsmʊs] *m* Hinduism
hindurch [hɪn'dʊrç] *adv* through; across; (*zeitlich*) over
hinein [hɪ'naɪn] *adv* in; **bis tief in die Nacht ~** well into the night; **hineinfallen** *unreg vi* to fall in; **hineinfallen in** *+akk* to fall into; **hineingehen** *unreg vi* to go in; **hineingehen in** *+akk* to go into, enter; **hineingeraten** *unreg vi*: **hineingeraten in** *+akk* to get into; **hineinpassen** *vi* to fit in; **hineinpassen in** *+akk* to fit into; **hineinstecken** *vt*: **Geld/Arbeit in etw** *akk* **hineinstecken** to put money/some work into sth; **hineinsteigern**

vr to get worked up; **hineinversetzen** *vr*: **sich in jdn hineinversetzen** to put o.s. in sb's position

hin- *zW*: **hinfahren** *unreg vi* to go; to drive ▷ *vt* to take; to drive; **Hinfahrt** *f* journey there; **hinfallen** *unreg vi* to fall down; **hinfällig** *adj* frail, decrepit; (*Regel etc*) unnecessary; **Hinflug** *m* outward flight; **hingeben** *unreg vr +dat* to give o.s. up to, devote o.s. to; **hingehen** *unreg vi* to go; (*Zeit*) to pass; **gehst du auch hin?** are you going too?; **hinhalten** *unreg vt* to hold out; (*warten lassen*) to put off, stall

hinken ['hɪŋkən] *vi* to limp; (*Vergleich*) to be unconvincing

hin- *zW*: **hinkommen** *unreg* (*umg*) *vi* (*auskommen*) to manage; (*: ausreichen, stimmen*) to be right; **hinlänglich** *adj* adequate ▷ *adv* adequately; **hinlegen** *vt* to put down ▷ *vr* to lie down; **sich der Länge nach hinlegen** (*umg*) to fall flat; **hinnehmen** *unreg vt* (*fig*) to put up with, take; **Hinreise** *f* journey out; **hinreißen** *unreg vt* to carry away, enrapture; **sich hinreißen lassen, etw zu tun** to get carried away and do sth; **hinsichtlich** *präp +gen* with regard to; **Hinspiel** *nt* (*Sport*) first leg; **hinstellen** *vt* to put (down) ▷ *vr* to place o.s.

hintanstellen [hɪnt'|anʃtɛlən] *vt* (*fig*) to ignore

hinten ['hɪntən] *adv* behind; (*rückwärtig*) at the back; **~ und vorn** (*fig: betrügen*) left, right and centre; **das reicht ~ und vorn nicht** that's nowhere near enough; **hintenherum** *adv* round the back; (*fig*) secretly

hinter ['hɪntər] *präp* (*+dat od akk*) behind; (*: nach*) after; **~ jdm her sein** to be after sb; **~ die Wahrheit kommen** to get to the truth; **sich ~ jdn stellen** (*fig*) to support sb; **etw ~ sich** *dat* **haben** (*zurückgelegt haben*) to have got through sth; **sie hat viel ~ sich** she has been through a lot; **Hinterachse** *f* rear axle; **Hinterbliebene, r** *f(m)* surviving relative

hintere, r, s *adj* rear, back

hinter- *zW*: **hintereinander** *adv* one after the other; **zwei Tage hintereinander** two days running; **Hintergedanke** *m* ulterior motive; **Hintergrund** *m* background; **hinterhältig** *adj* underhand, sneaky; **hinterher** *adv* afterwards, after; **er ist hinterher, dass ...** (*fig*) he sees to it that ...; **Hinterhof** *m* back yard; **Hinterkopf** *m* back of one's head; **hinterlassen** *unreg vt untr* to leave; **hinterlegen** *vt untr* to deposit; **Hinterlist** *f* cunning, trickery; (*Handlung*) trick, dodge; **hinterlistig** *adj* cunning, crafty; **Hintermann** (**-(e)s**, *pl* **-männer**) *m* person behind; **die Hintermänner des Skandals** the men behind the scandal

Hintern ['hɪntərn] (**-s, -**) (*umg*) *m* bottom, backside; **jdm den ~ versohlen** to smack sb's bottom

hinter- *zW*: **Hinterrad** *nt* back wheel; **Hinterradantrieb** *m* (*Aut*) rear-wheel drive; **hinterrücks** *adv* from behind; **Hintertür** *f* back door; (*fig: Ausweg*) escape, loophole; **hinterziehen** *unreg vt untr* (*Steuern*) to evade (paying)

hinüber [hɪ'ny:bər] *adv* across, over; **hinübergehen** *unreg vi* to go over *od* across

hinunter [hɪ'nʊntər] *adv* down; **hinunterbringen** *unreg vt* to take down; **hinunterschlucken** *vt* (*lit, fig*) to swallow; **hinuntersteigen** *unreg vi* to descend

Hinweg ['hɪnve:k] *m* journey out

hinweg- [hɪn'vɛk] *zW*: **hinweghelfen** *unreg vi*: **jdm über etw** *akk* **hinweghelfen** to help sb to get over sth; **hinwegsetzen** *vr*: **sich hinwegsetzen über** *+akk* to disregard

Hinweis ['hɪnvaɪs] (**-es, -e**) *m* (*Andeutung*) hint; (*Anweisung*) instruction; (*Verweis*) reference; **sachdienliche ~e** relevant information

hinweisen *unreg vi*: **~ auf** *+akk* to point to; (*verweisen*) to refer to; **darauf ~, dass ...** to point out that ...; (*anzeigen*) to indicate that ...

hinwerfen *unreg vt* to throw down; **eine hingeworfene Bemerkung** a casual remark

hinziehen *unreg vr* (*fig*) to drag on

hinzu [hɪn'tsu:] *adv* in addition; **hinzufügen** *vt* to add; **hinzukommen** *unreg vi*: **es kommt noch hinzu, dass ...** there is also the fact that ...; **hinzuziehen** *unreg vt* to consult

Hirn [hɪrn] (**-(e)s, -e**) *nt* brain(s); **Hirngespinst** (**-(e)s, -e**) *nt* fantasy; **hirnverbrannt** *adj* (*umg*) harebrained

Hirsch [hɪrʃ] (**-(e)s, -e**) *m* stag

Hirse ['hɪrzə] (**-, -n**) *f* millet

Hirt ['hɪrt] (**-en, -en**) *m*, **Hirte** (**-n, -n**) *m* herdsman; (*Schafhirt, fig*) shepherd

hissen ['hɪsən] *vt* to hoist

Historiker [hɪs'to:rikər] (**-s, -**) *m* historian

historisch [hɪs'to:rɪʃ] *adj* historical

Hit [hɪt] (**-s, -s**) (*umg*) *m* (*Mus, fig*) hit; **Hitparade** *f* hit parade

Hitze ['hɪtsə] (**-**) *f* heat; **hitzebeständig** *adj* heat-resistant; **Hitzewelle** *f* heat wave

hitzig *adj* hot-tempered; (*Debatte*) heated

Hitz- *zW*: **Hitzkopf** *m* hothead; **hitzköpfig** *adj* fiery, hot-headed; **Hitzschlag** *m* heatstroke

HIV-negativ *adj* HIV-negative

HIV-positiv *adj* HIV-positive

H-Milch ['ha:mɪlç] *f* long-life milk, UHT milk

Hobby ['hɔbi] (**-s, -s**) *nt* hobby

Hobel ['ho:bəl] (**-s, -**) *m* plane; **Hobelbank** *f* carpenter's bench

hobeln *vt, vi* to plane

Hobelspäne *pl* wood shavings *pl*

hoch [ho:x] (*attrib* **hohe(r, s)**) *adj* high ▷ *adv*: **~ achten** to respect; **~ begabt** = **hochbegabt**; **~ dotiert** highly paid; **~ entwickelt** (*Kultur, Land*) highly developed; (*Geräte, Methoden*) sophisticated; **wenn es ~ kommt** (*umg*) at (the) most, at the outside; **das ist mir zu ~** (*umg*) that's above my head; **ein hohes Tier** (*umg*) a big fish; **es ging ~ her** (*umg*) we/they *etc* had a whale of a time; **~ und heilig versprechen** to promise faithfully; *siehe auch*

hochempfindlich; hochgestellt

Hoch (**-s, -s**) *nt* (*Ruf*) cheer; (*Met, fig*) high

hoch- *zW*: **Hochachtung** *f* respect, esteem; **mit vorzüglicher Hochachtung** (*form: Briefschluss*) yours faithfully; **hochachtungsvoll** *adv* yours faithfully; **Hochamt** *nt* high mass; **hochbegabt** *adj* extremely gifted, aged; **Hochbetrieb** *m* intense activity; (*Comm*) peak time; **Hochbetrieb haben** to be at one's *od* its busiest; **Hochburg** *f* stronghold; **Hochdeutsch** *nt* High German; **Hochdruck** *m* high pressure; **Hochebene** *f* plateau; **hochempfindlich** *adj* highly sensitive; (*Film*) high-speed; **hocherfreut** *adj* highly delighted; **hochfahren** *unreg vi* (*erschreckt*) to jump; (*Comput, Tech*) to start up; **Hochform** *f* top form; **Hochgebirge** *nt* high mountains *pl*; **hochhalten** *unreg vt* to hold up; (*fig*) to uphold, cherish; **Hochhaus** *nt* multi-storey building; **hochheben** *unreg vt* to lift (up); **Hochkonjunktur** *f* boom; **Hochland** *nt* highlands *pl*; **hochleben** *vi*: **jdn hochleben lassen** to give sb three cheers; **Hochleistungssport** *m* competitive sport; **Hochmut** *m* pride; **hochmütig** *adj* proud, haughty; **hochnäsig** *adj* stuck-up, snooty; **Hochofen** *m* blast furnace; **hochprozentig** *adj* (*Alkohol*) strong; **Hochrechnung** *f* projected result; **Hochsaison** *f* high season; **Hochschätzung** *f* high esteem

Hochschulabschluss *m* degree

Hochschule *f* college; (*Universität*) university

hoch- *zW*: **hochschwanger** *adj* heavily pregnant, well advanced in pregnancy; **Hochsommer** *m* middle of summer; **Hochspannung** *f* high tension; **Hochsprung** *m* high jump

höchst [hø:çst] *adv* highly, extremely

Hochstapler ['ho:xsta:plər] (**-s, -**) *m* swindler

höchste, r, s *adj* highest; (*äußerste*) extreme; **die ~ Instanz** (*Jur*) the supreme court of appeal

höchstens *adv* at the most

Höchstgeschwindigkeit *f* maximum speed

Höchst- *zW*: **höchstpersönlich** *adv* personally, in person; **Höchstpreis** *m* maximum price; **höchstwahrscheinlich** *adv* most probably

Hoch- *zW*: **Hochwasser** *nt* high water; (*Überschwemmung*) floods *pl*; **hochwertig** *adj* high-class, first-rate; **Hochwürden** *m* Reverend; **Hochzahl** *f* (*Math*) exponent

Hochzeit ['hɔxtsaɪt] (**-, -en**) *f* wedding; **man kann nicht auf zwei ~en tanzen** (*Sprichwort*) you can't have your cake and eat it

Hochzeitsreise *f* honeymoon

Höcker ['hœkər] (**-s, -**) *m* hump

Hockey ['hɔki] (**-s**) *nt* hockey

Hoden [['ho:dən]] (**-s, -**) *m* testicle

Hof [ho:f] (**-(e)s, ⸚e**) *m* (*Hinterhof*) yard; (*Bauernhof*) farm; (*Königshof*) court; **einem Mädchen den ~ machen** (*veraltet*) to court a girl

hoffen ['hɔfən] *vi*: **~ (auf** *+akk***)** to hope (for)

hoffentlich *adv* I hope, hopefully

Hoffnung ['hɔfnʊŋ] *f* hope; **jdm ~en machen** to raise sb's hopes; **sich** *dat* **~en machen** to have hopes; **sich** *dat* **keine ~en machen** not to hold out any hope(s)

Hoffnungs- *zW*: **hoffnungslos** *adj* hopeless; **Hoffnungslosigkeit** *f* hopelessness; **Hoffnungsschimmer** *m* glimmer of hope; **hoffnungsvoll** *adj* hopeful

höflich ['hø:flɪç] *adj* courteous, polite; **Höflichkeit** *f* courtesy, politeness

hohe, r, s ['ho:ə(r, s)] *adj siehe* **hoch**

Höhe ['hø:ə] (**-, -n**) *f* height; (*Anhöhe*) hill; **nicht auf der ~ sein** (*fig: umg*) to feel below par; **ein Scheck in ~ von ...** a cheque (*Brit*) *od* check (*US*) for the amount of ...; **das ist doch die ~** (*fig: umg*) that's the limit; **er geht immer gleich in die ~** (*umg*) he always flares up; **auf der ~ der Zeit sein** to be up-to-date

Hoheit ['ho:haɪt] *f* (*Pol*) sovereignty; (*Titel*) Highness

Hoheits- *zW*: **Hoheitsgebiet** *nt* sovereign territory; **Hoheitsgewässer** *nt* territorial waters *pl*

Höhen- *zW*: **Höhenangabe** *f* altitude reading; (*auf Karte*) height marking; **Höhenmesser** *m* altimeter; **Höhensonne** *f* sun lamp; **Höhenunterschied** *m* difference in altitude

Höhepunkt *m* climax; (*des Lebens*) high point

höher *adj, adv* higher

hohl [ho:l] *adj* hollow; (*umg: dumm*) hollow(-headed)

Höhle ['hø:lə] (**-, -n**) *f* cave; hole; (*Mundhöhle*) cavity; (*fig, Zool*) den

Hohl- *zW*: **Hohlheit** *f* hollowness; **Hohlmaß** *nt* measure of volume

Hohn [ho:n] (**-(e)s**) *m* scorn; **das ist der reinste ~** it's sheer mockery

höhnisch *adj* scornful, taunting

holen ['ho:lən] *vt* to get, fetch; (*Atem*) to take; **jdn/etw ~ lassen** to send for sb/sth; **sich** *dat* **eine Erkältung ~** to catch a cold

Holland ['hɔlant] (**-s**) *nt* Holland

Holländer ['hɔlɛndər] (**-s, -**) *m* Dutchman

holländisch *adj* Dutch

Hölle ['hœlə] (**-, -n**) *f* hell; **ich werde ihm die ~ heißmachen** (*umg*) I'll give him hell

höllisch ['hœlɪʃ] *adj* hellish, infernal

Hologramm [holo'gram] (**-s, -e**) *nt* hologram

Holunder [ho'lʊndər] (**-s, -**) *m* elder

Holz [hɔlts] (**-es, ⸚er**) *nt* wood; **aus ~** made of wood, wooden; **aus einem anderen/demselben ~ geschnitzt sein** (*fig*) to be cast in a different/the same mould; **gut ~!** (*Kegeln*) have a good game!

hölzern ['hœltsərn] *adj* (*lit, fig*) wooden

Holzfäller (**-s, -**) *m* lumberjack, woodcutter

holzig *adj* woody

Holz- *zW*: **Holzkohle** *f* charcoal; **Holzscheit** *nt* log; **Holzschuh** *m* clog; **Holzweg** *m* (*fig*)

wrong track; **Holzwolle** *f* fine wood shavings *pl*; **Holzwurm** *m* woodworm
Homepage ['hoʊm'pa:ɡə] *nt* (*Comput*) home page
Homöopathie [homøopa'ti:] *f* homeopathy, homeopathic medicine
homosexuell [homozɛksu'ɛl] *adj* homosexual
Honduras [hɔn'du:ras] (-) *nt* Honduras
Honig ['ho:nɪç] (**-s, -e**) *m* honey; **Honigmelone** *f* honeydew melon; **Honigwabe** *f* honeycomb
Honorar [hono'ra:r] (**-s, -e**) *nt* fee
honorieren [hono'ri:rən] *vt* to remunerate; (*Scheck*) to honour (*Brit*), honor (*US*)
Hopfen ['hɔpfən] (**-s, -**) *m* hops *pl*; **bei ihm ist ~ und Malz verloren** (*umg*) he's a dead loss
hopsen ['hɔpsən] *vi* to hop
hörbar *adj* audible
horch [hɔrç] *interj* listen
horchen *vi* to listen; (*pej*) to eavesdrop
hören ['hø:rən] *vt, vi* to hear; **auf jdn/etw ~** to listen to sb/sth; **ich lasse von mir ~** I'll be in touch; **etwas/nichts von sich ~ lassen** to get/not to get in touch
Hörer (**-s, -**) *m* (*Rundf*) listener; (*Univ*) student; (*Telefonhörer*) receiver
Hörgerät *nt* hearing aid
Horizont [hori'tsɔnt] (**-(e)s, -e**) *m* horizon; **das geht über meinen ~** (*fig*) that is beyond me
horizontal [horitsɔ'ta:l] *adj* horizontal
Hormon [hɔr'mo:n] (**-s, -e**) *nt* hormone
Hörmuschel *f* (*Tel*) earpiece
Horn [hɔrn] (**-(e)s, ¨-er**) *nt* horn; **ins gleiche** *od* **in jds ~ blasen** to chime in; **sich** *dat* **die Hörner abstoßen** (*umg*) to sow one's wild oats
Hornhaut *f* horny skin; (*des Auges*) cornea
Hornisse [hɔr'nɪsə] (**-, -n**) *f* hornet
Horoskop [horo'sko:p] (**-s, -e**) *nt* horoscope
Hörsaal *m* lecture room
Hose ['ho:ze] (**-, -n**) *f* trousers *pl*, pants *pl* (*US*); **in die ~ gehen** (*umg*) to be a complete flop
Hosen- *zW*: **Hosenanzug** *m* trouser suit, pantsuit (*US*); **Hosenträger** *pl* braces *pl* (*Brit*), suspenders *pl* (*US*)
Hostie ['hɔstiə] *f* (*Rel*) host
Hotel [ho'tɛl] (**-s, -s**) *nt* hotel
Hotelier [hotɛli'e:] (**-s, -s**) *m* hotelier
HTML *abk* (*= Hyper Text Markup Language*) HTML
Hubraum *m* (*Aut*) cubic capacity
hübsch [hypʃ] *adj* pretty, nice; **immer ~ langsam!** (*umg*) nice and easy
Hubschrauber (**-s, -**) *m* helicopter
Huf ['hu:f] (**-(e)s, -e**) *m* hoof; **Hufeisen** *nt* horseshoe
Hüfte ['hyftə] (**-, -n**) *f* hip
Hüftgürtel *m* girdle
Hügel ['hy:ɡəl] (**-s, -**) *m* hill
hügelig, **hüglig** *adj* hilly
Huhn [hu:n] (**-(e)s, ¨-er**) *nt* hen; (*Koch*) chicken; **da lachen ja die Hühner** (*umg*) it's enough to make a cat laugh; **er sah aus wie ein gerupftes ~** (*umg*) he looked as if he'd been dragged through a hedge backwards
Hühner- *zW*: **Hühnerauge** *nt* corn; **Hühnerbrühe** *f* chicken broth
Hülle ['hʏlə] (**-, -n**) *f* cover(ing); (*Zellophanhülle*) wrapping; **in ~ und Fülle** galore; **die ~n fallen lassen** (*fig*) to strip off
hüllen *vt*: **~ (in** *+akk***)** to cover (with); to wrap (in)
Hülse ['hʏlzə] (**-, -n**) *f* husk, shell
Hülsenfrucht *f* pulse
human [hu'ma:n] *adj* humane
humanitär [humani'tɛ:r] *adj* humanitarian
Humanität *f* humanity
Hummel ['hʊməl] (**-, -n**) *f* bumblebee
Hummer ['hʊmər] (**-s, -**) *m* lobster
Humor [hu'mo:r] (**-s, -e**) *m* humour (*Brit*), humor (*US*); **~ haben** to have a sense of humo(u)r; **Humorist, in** *m(f)* humorist; **humoristisch** *adj* humorous
humpeln ['hʊmpəln] *vi* to hobble
Hund [hʊnt] (**-(e)s, -e**) *m* dog; **auf den ~ kommen, vor die Hunde gehen** (*fig: umg*) to go to the dogs; **~e, die bellen, beißen nicht** (*Sprichwort*) empty vessels make most noise (*Sprichwort*); **er ist bekannt wie ein bunter ~** (*umg*) everybody knows him
Hunde- *zW*: **Hundehütte** *f* (dog) kennel; **hundemüde** (*umg*) *adj* dog-tired
hundert ['hʊndərt] *num* hundred
hundert- *zW*: **Hundertjahrfeier** *f* centenary; **hundertprozentig** *adj, adv* one hundred per cent
Hündin ['hʏndɪn] *f* bitch
Hunger ['hʊŋər] (**-s**) *m* hunger; **~ haben** to be hungry; **ich sterbe vor ~** (*umg*) I'm starving
hungern *vi* to starve
Hungersnot *f* famine
Hungerstreik *m* hunger strike
hungrig ['hʊŋrɪç] *adj* hungry
Hupe ['hu:pə] (**-, -n**) *f* horn
hupen *vi* to hoot, sound one's horn
hüpfen ['hʏpfən] *vi* = **hupfen**
Hürde ['hʏrdə] (**-, -n**) *f* hurdle; (*für Schafe*) pen
Hürdenlauf *m* hurdling
Hure ['hu:rə] (**-, -n**) *f* whore
hurra [hʊ'ra:] *interj* hurray, hurrah
huschen ['hʊʃən] *vi* to flit, scurry
Husten ['hu:stən] (**-s**) *m* cough; **husten** *vi* to cough; **auf etw** *akk* **husten** (*umg*) not to give a damn for sth; **Hustenanfall** *m* coughing fit; **Hustenbonbon** *m od nt* cough drop; **Hustensaft** *m* cough mixture
Hut[1] [hu:t] (**-(e)s, ¨-e**) *m* hat; **unter einen ~ bringen** (*umg*) to reconcile; (*Termine etc*) to fit in
Hut[2] [hu:t] (-) *f* care; **auf der ~ sein** to be on one's guard
hüten ['hy:tən] *vt* to guard ▷ *vr* to watch out; **das Bett/Haus ~** to stay in bed/indoors; **sich ~ zu** to take care not to; **sich ~ vor** *+dat* to beware of; **ich werde mich ~!** not likely!
Hütte ['hʏtə] (**-, -n**) *f* hut; (*Holzhütte, Blockhütte*)

cabin; (*Eisenhütte*) forge; (*umg*: *Wohnung*) pad; (*Tech*: *Hüttenwerk*) iron and steel works
Hüttenwerk *nt* iron and steel works
Hyäne [hy'ɛ:nə] (**-, -n**) *f* hyena
Hyazinthe [hya'tsɪntə] (**-, -n**) *f* hyacinth
Hydrant [hy'drant] *m* hydrant
hydraulisch [hy'draʊlɪʃ] *adj* hydraulic
Hygiene [hygi'e:nə] (**-**) *f* hygiene
hygienisch [hygi'e:nɪʃ] *adj* hygienic
Hymne ['hʏmnə] (**-, -n**) *f* hymn, anthem
hyper- ['hypɛr] *präf* hyper-
Hypnose [hʏp'no:zə] (**-, -n**) *f* hypnosis
hypnotisch *adj* hypnotic
Hypnotiseur [hʏpnoti'zø:r] *m* hypnotist
hypnotisieren [hʏpnoti|zi:rən] *vt* to hypnotize
Hypothek [hypo'te:k] (**-, -en**) *f* mortgage; **eine ~ aufnehmen** to raise a mortgage; **etw mit einer ~ belasten** to mortgage sth
Hypothese [hypo'te:zə] (**-, -n**) *f* hypothesis
hypothetisch [hypo'te:tɪʃ] *adj* hypothetical
Hysterie [hyste'ri:] *f* hysteria
hysterisch [hʏs'te:riʃ] *adj* hysterical; **einen ~en Anfall bekommen** (*fig*) to have hysterics

I, i [iː] *nt* I, i; **I wie Ida** ≈ I for Isaac, ≈ I for Item (*US*); **das Tüpfelchen auf dem i** (*fig*) the final touch
i. A. *abk* (= *im Auftrag*) p.p.
IC (-) *m abk* = **Intercityzug**
ICE *m abk* (= *Intercity-Expresszug*) inter-city train
ich [ɪç] *pron* I; **~ bins!** it's me!; **Ich** (**-(s), -(s)**) *nt* self; (*Psych*) ego
Ideal [ide'aːl] (**-s, -e**) *nt* ideal; **ideal** *adj* ideal
Idealismus [idea'lɪsmʊs] *m* idealism
Idealist, in *m(f)* idealist
idealistisch *adj* idealistic
Idee [i'deː] (**-, -n**) *f* idea; (*ein wenig*) shade, trifle; **jdn auf die ~ bringen, etw zu tun** to give sb the idea of doing sth
identifizieren [idɛntifi'tsiːrən] *vt* to identify
identisch [i'dɛntɪʃ] *adj* identical
Identität [idɛnti'tɛːt] *f* identity
Ideologe [ideo'loːgə] (**-n, -n**) *m* ideologist
Ideologie [ideolo'giː] *f* ideology
ideologisch [ideo'loːgɪʃ] *adj* ideological
Idiot [idi'oːt] (**-en, -en**) *m* idiot
idiotisch *adj* idiotic
idyllisch [i'dʏlɪʃ] *adj* idyllic
IG *abk* (= *Industriegewerkschaft*) *industrial trade union*
Igel ['iːgəl] (**-s, -**) *m* hedgehog
ignorieren [ɪgno'riːrən] *vt* to ignore
ihm [iːm] *pron dat von* **er, es** (to) him, (to) it; **es ist ~ nicht gut** he doesn't feel well
ihn [iːn] *pron akk von* **er** him; (*bei Tieren, Dingen*) it
ihnen ['iːnən] *pron dat pl von* **sie** (to) them; (*nach Präpositionen*) them
Ihnen *pron dat von* **Sie** (to) you; (*nach Präpositionen*) you
ihr [iːr] *pron* **1** (*nom pl*) you; **ihr seid es** it's you **2** (*dat von sie*) (to) her; (*bei Tieren, Dingen*) (to) it; **gib es ihr** give it to her; **er steht neben ihr** he is standing beside her
▷ *poss pron* **1** (*sing*) her; (*: bei Tieren, Dingen*) its; **ihr Mann** her husband
2 (*pl*) their; **die Bäume und ihre Blätter** the trees and their leaves
Ihr *poss pron* your
Ihre, r, s *poss pron* yours; **tun Sie das ~** (*geh*) you do your bit
ihre, r, s *poss pron* hers; (*eines Tieres*) its; (*von mehreren*) theirs; **sie taten das I~** (*geh*) they did their bit
ihrer ['iːrər] *pron gen sing von* **sie** of her; (*pl*) of them
Ihrer *pron gen von* **Sie** of you
Ihrerseits *adv* for your part
ihrerseits *adv* for her/their part
ihresgleichen *pron* people like her/them; (*von Dingen*) others like it; **eine Frechheit, die ~ sucht!** an incredible cheek!
ihretwegen *adv* (*für sie*) for her/its/their sake; (*wegen ihr, ihnen*) on her/its/their account; **sie sagte, ~ könnten wir gehen** she said that, as far as she was concerned, we could go
illegal ['ɪlegaːl] *adj* illegal
Illusion [ɪluzi'oːn] *f* illusion; **sich** *dat* **~en machen** to delude o.s.
illusorisch [ɪlu'zoːrɪʃ] *adj* illusory
illustrieren [ɪlʊs'triːrən] *vt* to illustrate
Illustrierte (**-n, -n**) *f* picture magazine
Iltis ['ɪltɪs] (**-ses, -se**) *m* polecat
im [ɪm] = **in dem** *präp*: **etw im Liegen/Stehen tun** do sth lying down/standing up
Image ['ɪmɪtʃ] (**-(s), -s**) *nt* image
Imbiss ['ɪmbɪs] (**-es, -e**) *m* snack; **Imbisshalle** *f* snack bar
imitieren [imi'tiːrən] *vt* to imitate
immatrikulieren [ɪmatriku'liːrən] *vi, vr* to register
immer ['ɪmər] *adv* always; **~ wieder** again and again; **etw ~ wieder tun** to keep on doing sth; **~ noch** still; **~ noch nicht** still not; **für ~** forever; **~ wenn ich ...** every time I ...; **~ schöner** more and more beautiful; **~ trauriger** sadder and sadder; **was/wer (auch) ~** whatever/whoever; **immerhin** *adv* all the same; **immerzu** *adv* all the time
Immobilien [ɪmo'biːliən] *pl* real property (*Brit*), real estate (*US*); (*in Zeitungsannoncen*) property *sing*
immun [ɪ'muːn] *adj* immune
Immunität [ɪmuːni'tɛːt] *f* immunity
Immunschwäche *f* immunodeficiency
Immunsystem *nt* immune system
Imperfekt ['ɪmpɛrfɛkt] (**-s, -e**) *nt* imperfect (tense)
impfen ['ɪmpfən] *vt* to vaccinate
Impf- *zW*: **Impfpass** *m* vaccination card; **Impfstoff** *m* vaccine; **Impfung** *f* vaccination; **Impfzwang** *m* compulsory vaccination

imponieren [ɪmpo'ni:rən] *vi +dat* to impress
Import [ɪm'pɔrt] (**-(e)s, -e**) *m* import
importieren [ɪmpɔr'ti:rən] *vt* to import
impotent ['ɪmpotɛnt] *adj* impotent
Impotenz ['ɪmpotɛnts] *f* impotence
imprägnieren [ɪmprɛ'gni:rən] *vt* to (water)proof
improvisieren [ɪmprovi'zi:rən] *vt, vi* to improvise
Impuls [ɪm'pʊls] (**-es, -e**) *m* impulse; **etw aus einem ~ heraus tun** to do sth on impulse
impulsiv [ɪmpʊl'zi:f] *adj* impulsive
imstande, im Stande [ɪm'ʃtandə] *adj*: **~ sein** to be in a position; (*fähig*) to be able; **er ist zu allem ~** he's capable of anything
in [ɪn] *präp +akk* **1** (*räumlich: wohin*) in, into; **in die Stadt** into town; **in die Schule gehen** to go to school; **in die Hunderte gehen** to run into (the) hundreds
2 (*zeitlich*): **bis ins 20. Jahrhundert** into *od* up to the 20th century
▷ *präp +dat* **1** (*räumlich: wo*) in; **in der Stadt** in town; **in der Schule sein** to be at school; **es in sich haben** (*umg: Text*) to be tough; (*: Drink*) to have quite a kick
2 (*zeitlich: wann*): **in diesem Jahr** this year; (*in jenem Jahr*) in that year; **heute in zwei Wochen** two weeks today
Inanspruchnahme [ɪn'|anʃprʊxna:mə] (**-, -n**) *f*: **~ (+gen)** demands *pl* (on); **im Falle einer ~ der Arbeitslosenunterstützung** (*form*) where unemployment benefit has been sought
Inbegriff ['ɪnbəgrɪf] *m* embodiment, personification
inbegriffen *adv* included
indem [ɪn'de:m] *konj* while; **~ man etw macht** (*dadurch*) by doing sth
Inder, in ['ɪndər(ɪn)] (**-s, -**) *m(f)* Indian
Indianer, in [ɪndi'a:nər(ɪn)] (**-s, -**) *m(f)* (Red *od* American) Indian
indianisch *adj* (Red *od* American) Indian
Indien ['ɪndiən] (**-s**) *nt* India
indirekt ['ɪndirɛkt] *adj* indirect; **~e Steuer** indirect tax
indisch ['ɪndɪʃ] *adj* Indian; **I~er Ozean** Indian Ocean
indiskret ['ɪndɪskre:t] *adj* indiscreet
indiskutabel ['ɪndɪskuta:bəl] *adj* out of the question
Individualist [ɪndividua'lɪst] *m* individualist
Individualität [ɪndividuali'tɛt] *f* individuality
individuell [ɪndividu'ɛl] *adj* individual; **etw ~ gestalten** to give sth a personal note
Individuum [ɪndi'vi:duʊm] (**-s, -duen**) *nt* individual
Indiz [ɪn'di:ts] (**-es, -ien**) *nt* (*Jur*) clue; **~ (für)** sign (of)
Indochina ['ɪndo'çi:na] (**-s**) *nt* Indochina
Indonesien [ɪndo'ne:ziən] (**-s**) *nt* Indonesia
indonesisch [ɪndo'ne:zɪʃ] *adj* Indonesian
industrialisieren [ɪndʊstriali'zɪ:rən] *vt* to industrialize
Industrie [ɪndʊs'tri:] *f* industry; **in der ~ arbeiten** to be in industry; **Industriegebiet** *nt* industrial area
industriell [ɪndʊstri'ɛl] *adj* industrial; **~e Revolution** industrial revolution
Industriezweig *m* branch of industry
ineinander [ɪn|aɪ'nandər] *adv* in(to) one another *od* each other; **~ übergehen** to merge (into each other)
Infarkt [ɪn'farkt] (**-(e)s, -e**) *m* coronary (thrombosis)
Infektion [ɪnfɛktsi'o:n] *f* infection
Infektionskrankheit *f* infectious disease
Infinitiv ['ɪnfiniti:f] (**-s, -e**) *m* infinitive
in flagranti [ɪn fla'granti] *adv* in the act, red-handed
Inflation [ɪnflatsi'o:n] *f* inflation
inflationär [ɪnflatsio'nɛ:r] *adj* inflationary
Inflationsrate *f* rate of inflation
Info ['ɪnfo] (**-s, -s**) (*umg*) *nt* (information) leaflet
infolge [ɪn'fɔlgə] *präp +gen* as a result of, owing to; **infolgedessen** *adv* consequently
Informatik [ɪnfɔr'ma:tɪk] *f* information studies *pl*
Informatiker, in (**-s, -**) *m(f)* computer scientist
Information [ɪnfɔrmatsi'o:n] *f* information *no pl*; **Informationen** *pl* (*Comput*) data; **zu Ihrer ~** for your information
informieren [ɪnfɔr'mi:rən] *vt*: **~ (über +akk)** to inform (about) ▷ *vr*: **sich ~ (über +akk)** to find out (about)
Infrastruktur ['ɪnfraʃtrʊktu:r] *f* infrastructure
Infusion [ɪnfuzi'o:n] *f* infusion
Ing. *abk* = **Ingenieur**
Ingenieur [ɪnʒeni'ø:r] *m* engineer; **Ingenieurschule** *f* school of engineering
Ingwer ['ɪŋvər] (**-s**) *m* ginger
Inhaber, in ['ɪnha:bər(ɪn)] (**-s, -**) *m(f)* owner; (*Comm*) proprietor; (*Hausinhaber*) occupier; (*Lizenzinhaber*) licensee, holder; (*Fin*) bearer
inhalieren [ɪnha'li:rən] *vt, vi* to inhale
Inhalt ['ɪnhalt] (**-(e)s, -e**) *m* contents *pl*; (*eines Buchs etc*) content; (*Math: Flächen*) area; (*: Rauminhalt*) volume; **inhaltlich** *adj* as regards content
Inhalts- *zW*: **Inhaltsangabe** *f* summary; **Inhaltsverzeichnis** *nt* table of contents; (*Comput*) directory
inhuman ['ɪnhuma:n] *adj* inhuman
Initiative [initsia'ti:və] *f* initiative; **die ~ ergreifen** to take the initiative
Injektion [ɪnjɛktsi'o:n] *f* injection
inklusive [ɪnklu'zi:və] *präp +gen* inclusive of ▷ *adv* inclusive
inkognito [ɪn'kɔgnito] *adv* incognito
Inkubationszeit [ɪnkubatsi'o:nstsaɪt] *f* (*Med*) incubation period
Inland ['ɪnlant] (**-(e)s**) *nt* (*Geog*) inland; (*Pol, Comm*) home (country); **im ~ und Ausland** at

home and abroad
Inlandsporto *nt* inland postage
innehaben ['ɪnəha:bən] *unreg vt* to hold
innen ['ɪnən] *adv* inside; **nach ~** inwards; **von ~** from the inside; **Innenarchitekt** *m* interior designer; **Inneneinrichtung** *f* (interior) furnishings *pl*; **Innenleben** *nt* (*seelisch*) emotional life; (*umg: körperlich*) insides *pl*; **Innenminister** *m* minister of the interior, Home Secretary (*Brit*); **Innenpolitik** *f* domestic policy; **Innenstadt** *f* town *od* city centre (*Brit*) *od* center (*US*)
Innere, s *nt* inside; (*Mitte*) centre (*Brit*), center (*US*); (*fig*) heart
innere, r, s *adj* inner; (*im Körper, inländisch*) internal
Innereien [ɪnə'raɪən] *pl* innards *pl*
inner- *zW*: **innerhalb** *adv* within; (*räumlich*) inside ▷ *prep +dat* within; inside; **innerlich** *adj* internal; (*geistig*) inward
Innerste, s *nt* heart; **bis ins ~ getroffen** hurt to the quick
innerste, r, s *adj* innermost
Innovation [ɪnovatsi'o:n] *f* innovation
inoffiziell ['ɪn|ofitsiɛl] *adj* unofficial
ins [ɪns] = **in das**
Insasse ['ɪnzasə] (**-n, -n**) *m*, **Insassin** *f* (*einer Anstalt*) inmate; (*Aut*) passenger
insbesondere [ɪnsbə'zɔndərə] *adv* (e)specially
Inschrift ['ɪnʃrɪft] *f* inscription
Insekt [ɪn'zɛkt] (**-(e)s, -en**) *nt* insect
Insel ['ɪnzəl] (**-, -n**) *f* island
Inserat [ɪnze'ra:t] (**-(e)s, -e**) *nt* advertisement
Inserent [ɪnze'rɛnt] *m* advertiser
inserieren [ɪnze'ri:rən] *vt, vi* to advertise
insgesamt [ɪnsgə'zamt] *adv* altogether, all in all
insofern [ɪnzo'fɛrn] *adv* in this respect ▷ *konj* if; (*deshalb*) (and) so; **~ als** in so far as
Installateur [ɪnstala'tø:r] *m* plumber; (*Elektroinstallateur*) electrician
installieren [ɪnsta'li:rən] *vt* to install (*auch fig, COMPUT*)
Instandhaltung [ɪn'ʃtanthaltʊŋ] *f* maintenance
Instandsetzung *f* overhaul; (*eines Gebäudes*) restoration
Instanz [ɪn'stants] *f* authority; (*Jur*) court; **Verhandlung in erster/zweiter ~** first/second court case
Instinkt [ɪn'stɪŋkt] (**-(e)s, -e**) *m* instinct
instinktiv [ɪnstɪŋk'ti:f] *adj* instinctive
Institut [ɪnsti'tu:t] (**-(e)s, -e**) *nt* institute
Institution [ɪnstitutsi'o:n] *f* institution
Instrument [ɪnstru'mɛnt] *nt* instrument
Insulin [ɪnzu'li:n] (**-s**) *nt* insulin
Integration [ɪntegratsi'o:n] *f* integration
intellektuell [ɪntɛlɛktu'ɛl] *adj* intellectual
intelligent [ɪnteli'gɛnt] *adj* intelligent
Intelligenz [ɪntɛli'gɛnts] *f* intelligence; (*Leute*) intelligentsia *pl*
Intendant [ɪntɛn'dant] *m* director
Intensität [ɪntɛnzi'tɛ:t] *f* intensity
intensiv [ɪntɛn'zi:f] *adj* intensive
Intensivkurs *m* intensive course
Intensivstation *f* intensive care unit
interaktiv *adj* (*Comput*) interactive
interessant [ɪnterɛ'sant] *adj* interesting; **sich ~ machen** to attract attention
interessanterweise *adv* interestingly enough
Interesse [ɪnte'rɛsə] (**-s, -n**) *nt* interest; **~ haben an** *+dat* to be interested in
Interessent, in [ɪnterɛ'sɛnt(ɪn)] *m(f)* interested party; **es haben sich mehrere ~en gemeldet** several people have shown interest
interessieren [ɪnterɛ'si:rən] *vt*: **jdn (für etw** *od* **an etw** *dat*) **~** to interest sb (in sth) ▷ *vr*: **sich ~ für** to be interested in
intern [ɪn'tɛrn] *adj* internal
Internat [ɪntɛr'na:t] (**-(e)s, -e**) *nt* boarding school
international [ɪntɛrnatsio'na:l] *adj* international
Internet ['ɪntɛrnɛt] (**-s**) *nt*: **das ~** the internet; **Internetcafé** *nt* internet café; **Internetseite** *f* web page
Internist, in *m(f)* internist
Interpretation [ɪntərpretatsi'o:n] *f* interpretation
interpretieren [ɪntɛrpre'ti:rən] *vt* to interpret
Intervall [ɪntɛr'val] (**-s, -e**) *nt* interval
intervenieren [ɪntɛrve'ni:rən] *vi* to intervene
Interview [ɪntər'vju:] (**-s, -s**) *nt* interview; **interviewen** [-'vju:ən] *vt* to interview
intim [ɪn'ti:m] *adj* intimate
Intimität [ɪntimi'tɛ:t] *f* intimacy
intolerant ['ɪntolerant] *adj* intolerant
intransitiv ['ɪntranziti:f] *adj* (*Gram*) intransitive
Intrige [ɪn'tri:gə] (**-, -n**) *f* intrigue, plot
introvertiert [ɪntrovɛr'ti:rt] *adj*: **~ sein** to be an introvert
intuitiv [ɪntui'ti:f] *adj* intuitive
intus ['ɪntʊs] *adj*: **etw ~ haben** (*umg: Wissen*) to have got sth into one's head; (*Essen, Trinken*) to have got sth down one (*umg*)
Invalide [ɪnva'li:də] (**-n, -n**) *m* disabled person, invalid
Inventar [ɪnvɛn'ta:r] (**-s, -e**) *nt* inventory; (*Comm*) assets and liabilities *pl*
Inventur [ɪnvɛn'tu:r] *f* stocktaking; **~ machen** to stocktake
investieren [ɪnvɛs'ti:rən] *vt* to invest
Investition [ɪnvɛstitsi'o:n] *f* investment
inwiefern [ɪnvi'fɛrn] *adv* how far, to what extent
inzwischen [ɪn'tsvɪʃən] *adv* meanwhile
Ion [i'o:n] (**-s, -en**) *nt* ion
Irak [i'ra:k] (**-s**) *m*: **(der) ~** Iraq
irakisch *adj* Iraqi
Iran [i'ra:n] (**-s**) *m*: **(der) ~** Iran
iranisch *adj* Iranian
irdisch ['ɪrdɪʃ] *adj* earthly; **den Weg alles**

I~en gehen to go the way of all flesh
Ire ['i:rə] (**-n, -n**) *m* Irishman; **die ~n** the Irish
irgend ['ɪrgənt] *adv* at all; **wann/was/wer ~** whenever/whatever/whoever; **irgendein, e, s** *adj* some, any; **haben Sie (sonst) noch irgendeinen Wunsch?** is there anything else you would like?; **irgendeine, r, s** *pron* (*Person*) somebody; (*Ding*) something; (*fragend, verneinend*) anybody/anything; **ich will nicht bloß irgendein(e)s** I don't want any old one; **irgendeinmal** *adv* sometime or other; (*fragend*) ever; **irgendetwas** *pron* something; (*fragend, verneinend*) anything; **irgendjemand** *pron* somebody; (*fragend, verneinend*) anybody; **irgendwann** *adv* sometime; **irgendwer** (*umg*) *pron* somebody; (*fragend, verneinend*) anybody; **irgendwie** *adv* somehow; **irgendwo** *adv* somewhere (*Brit*), someplace (*US*); (*fragend, verneinend, bedingend*) anywhere (*Brit*), any place (*US*); **irgendwohin** *adv* somewhere (*Brit*), someplace (*US*); (*fragend, verneinend, bedingend*) anywhere (*Brit*), any place (*US*)
Irin ['i:rɪn] *f* Irishwoman; Irish girl
irisch *adj* Irish; **I~e See** Irish Sea
Irland ['ɪrlant] (**-s**) *nt* Ireland; (*Republik Irland*) Eire
Ironie [iro'ni:] *f* irony
ironisch [i'ro:nɪʃ] *adj* ironic(al)
irre ['ɪrə] *adj* crazy, mad; **~ gut** (*umg*) way out (*umg*); **Irre, r** *f(m)* lunatic; **irreführen** *vt* to mislead
irremachen *vt* to confuse
irren *vi* to be mistaken; (*umherirren*) to wander, stray ▷ *vr* to be mistaken; **jeder kann sich mal ~** anyone can make a mistake;
Irrenanstalt *f* (*veraltet*) lunatic asylum
Irr- *zW*: **Irrsinn** *m* madness; **so ein Irrsinn, das zu tun!** what a crazy thing to do!; **irrsinnig** *adj* mad, crazy; (*umg*) terrific; **irrsinnig komisch** incredibly funny; **Irrtum** (**-s, -tümer**) *m* mistake, error; **im Irrtum sein** to be wrong *od* mistaken; **Irrtum!** wrong!; **irrtümlich** *adj* mistaken
ISBN *f abk* (= *Internationale Standardbuchnummer*) ISBN
Ischias ['ɪʃias] (**-**) *m od nt* sciatica
Islam ['ɪslam] (**-s**) *m* Islam
islamisch [ɪs'la:mɪʃ] *adj* Islamic
Island ['i:slant] (**-s**) *nt* Iceland
Isländer, in ['i:slɛndər(ɪn)] (**-s, -**) *m(f)* Icelander
isländisch *adj* Icelandic
Isolation [izolatsi'o:n] *f* isolation; (*Elek*) insulation; (*von Häftlingen*) solitary confinement
Isolierband *nt* insulating tape
isolieren [ɪzo'li:rən] *vt* to isolate; (*Elek*) to insulate
Isolierstation *f* (*Med*) isolation ward
Isolierung *f* isolation; (*Elek*) insulation
Israel ['ɪsrae:l] (**-s**) *nt* Israel
Israeli[1] [ɪsra'e:li] (**-(s), -s**) *m* Israeli
Israeli[2] [ɪsra'e:li] (**-, -(s)**) *f* Israeli
israelisch *adj* Israeli
Istanbul ['ɪstambu:l] (**-s**) *nt* Istanbul
Italien [i'ta:liən] (**-s**) *nt* Italy
Italiener, in [itali'e:nər(ɪn)] (**-s, -**) *m(f)* Italian
italienisch *adj* Italian; **die ~e Schweiz** Italian-speaking Switzerland
IWF *m abk* (= *Internationaler Währungsfonds*) IMF

J, j [jɔt] *nt* J, j; **J wie Julius** ≈ J for Jack, ≈ J for Jig (*US*)

ja [ja:] *adv* **1** yes; **haben Sie das gesehen? — ja** did you see it? — yes(, I did); **ich glaube ja** (yes) I think so; **zu allem Ja und Amen sagen** (*umg*) to accept everything without question
2 (*fragend*) really; **ich habe gekündigt — ja?** I've quit — have you?; **du kommst, ja?** you're coming, aren't you?
3: sei ja vorsichtig do be careful; **Sie wissen ja, dass ...** as you know, ...; **tu das ja nicht!** don't do that!; **sie ist ja erst fünf** (after all) she's only five; **Sie wissen ja, wie das so ist** you know how it is; **ich habe es ja gewusst** I just knew it; **ja, also ...** well you see ...

Jacht [jaxt] (**-, -en**) *f* yacht

Jacke ['jakə] (**-, -n**) *f* jacket; (*Wolljacke*) cardigan

Jackett [ʒa'kɛt] (**-s, -s** *od* **-e**) *nt* jacket

Jagd [ja:kt] (**-, -en**) *f* hunt; (*Jagen*) hunting; **Jagdgewehr** *nt* sporting gun

jagen ['ja:gən] *vi* to hunt; (*eilen*) to race ▷ *vt* to hunt; (*wegjagen*) to drive (off); (*verfolgen*) to chase; **mit diesem Essen kannst du mich ~** (*umg*) I wouldn't touch that food with a barge pole (*Brit*) *od* ten-foot pole (*US*)

Jäger ['jɛ:gər] (**-s, -**) *m* hunter

jäh [jɛ:] *adj* abrupt, sudden; (*steil*) steep, precipitous

Jahr [ja:r] (**-(e)s, -e**) *nt* year; **im ~(e) 1066** in (the year) 1066; **die Sechzigerjahre** *od* **sechziger ~e** the sixties *pl*; **mit dreißig ~en** at the age of thirty; **in den besten ~en sein** to be in the prime of (one's) life; **nach ~ und Tag** after (many) years; **zwischen den ~en** (*umg*) between Christmas and New Year

jahrelang *adv* for years

Jahres- *zW*: **Jahresabonnement** *nt* annual subscription; **Jahresabschluss** *m* end of the year; (*Comm*) annual statement of account; **Jahresbericht** *m* annual report; **Jahreswechsel** *m* turn of the year; **Jahreszahl** *f* date, year; **Jahreszeit** *f* season

Jahr- *zW*: **Jahrgang** *m* age group; (*von Wein*) vintage; **er ist Jahrgang 1950** he was born in 1950; **Jahrhundert** *nt* century

jährlich ['jɛ:rlɪç] *adj, adv* yearly; **zweimal ~** twice a year

Jahr- *zW*: **Jahrmarkt** *m* fair; **Jahrzehnt** *nt* decade

Jähzorn ['jɛ:tsɔrn] *m* hot temper

jähzornig *adj* hot-tempered

Jalousie [ʒalu'zi:] *f* venetian blind

Jamaika [ja'maɪka] (**-s**) *nt* Jamaica

Jammer ['jamər] (**-s**) *m* misery; **es ist ein ~, dass ...** it is a crying shame that ...

jämmerlich ['jɛmərlɪç] *adj* wretched, pathetic

jammern *vi* to wail ▷ *vt unpers*: **es jammert mich** it makes me feel sorry

jammerschade *adj*: **es ist ~** it is a crying shame

Januar ['janua:r] (**-s, -e**) (*pl selten*) *m* January; *siehe auch* **September**

Japan ['ja:pan] (**-s**) *nt* Japan

Japaner, in [ja'pa:nər(ɪn)] (**-s, -**) *m(f)* Japanese

japanisch *adj* Japanese

Jargon [ʒar'gõ:] (**-s, -s**) *m* jargon

jäten ['jɛ:tən] *vt, vi* to weed

jauchzen ['jaʊxtsən] *vi* to rejoice, shout (with joy)

Jauchzer (**-s, -**) *m* shout of joy

jaulen ['jaʊlən] *vi* to howl

Jause ['jaʊzə] (*Österr*) *f* snack

jawohl *adv* yes (of course)

Jawort *nt* consent; **jdm das ~ geben** to consent to marry sb; (*bei Trauung*) to say "I do"

Jazz [dʒæz] (**-**) *m* jazz

je [je:] *adv* **1** (*jemals*) ever; **hast du so was je gesehen?** did you ever see anything like it?
2 (*jeweils*) every, each; **sie zahlten je 15 Euro** they paid 15 euros each
▷ *konj* **1: je nach** depending on; **je nachdem** it depends; **je nachdem, ob ...** depending on whether ...
2: je eher, desto *od* **umso besser** the sooner the better; **je länger, je lieber** the longer the better

Jeans [dʒi:nz] *pl* jeans *pl*

jede, r, s ['je:də(r, s)] *adj* (*einzeln*) each; (*von zweien*) either; (*jede von allen*) every ▷ *indef pron* (*einzeln*) each (one); (*jede von allen*) everyone, everybody; **ohne ~ Anstrengung** without any effort; **~r Zweite** every other (one); **~s Mal** every time, each time

jedenfalls *adv* in any case

jedermann *pron* everyone; **das ist nicht ~s Sache** it's not everyone's cup of tea

jederzeit *adv* at any time
jedoch [je'dɔx] *adv* however
jemals ['je:ma:ls] *adv* ever
jemand ['je:mant] *indef pron* someone, somebody; (*bei Fragen, bedingenden Sätzen, Negation*) anyone, anybody
Jemen ['je:mən] (**-s**) *m* Yemen
jene, r, s ['je:nə(r, s)] *adj* that; (*pl*) those ▷ *pron* that one; (*pl*) those; (*der Vorherige, die Vorherigen*) the former
jenseits ['je:nzaɪts] *adv* on the other side ▷ *präp +gen* on the other side of, beyond
jetzig ['jɛtsɪç] *adj* present
jetzt [jɛtst] *adv* now; **~ gleich** right now
jeweilig *adj* respective; **die ~e Regierung** the government of the day
jeweils *adv*: **~ zwei zusammen** two at a time; **zu ~ 10 Euro** at 10 euros each; **~ das Erste** the first each time; **~ am Monatsletzten** on the last day of each month
Jh. *abk* (= *Jahrhundert*) cent.
Job [dʒɔp] (**-s, -s**) (*umg*) *m* job
Jod [jo:t] (**-(e)s**) *nt* iodine
jodeln ['jo:dəln] *vi* to yodel
joggen ['dʒɔgən] *vi* to jog
Johannisbeere [jo'hanɪsbe:rə] *f*: **Rote ~** redcurrant; **Schwarze ~** blackcurrant
johlen ['jo:lən] *vi* to yell
Joint [dʒɔɪnt] (**-s, -s**) (*umg*) *m* joint
Jolle ['jɔlə] (**-, -n**) *f* dinghy
jonglieren [ʒõ'gli:rən] *vi* to juggle
Jordanien [jɔr'da:niən] (**-s**) *nt* Jordan
jordanisch *adj* Jordanian
Journalismus [ʒʊrna'lɪsmʊs] *m* journalism
Journalist, in [ʒʊrna'lɪst(ɪn)] *m(f)* journalist; **journalistisch** *adj* journalistic
Jubel ['ju:bəl] (**-s**) *m* rejoicing; **~, Trubel, Heiterkeit** laughter and merriment
jubeln *vi* to rejoice
Jubiläum [jubi'lɛ:ʊm] (**-s, Jubiläen**) *nt* jubilee; (*Jahrestag*) anniversary
jucken ['jʊkən] *vi* to itch ▷ *vt*: **es juckt mich am Arm** my arm is itching; **das juckt mich** that's itchy; **das juckt mich doch nicht** (*umg*) I don't care
Juckreiz *m* itch
Jude ['ju:də] (**-n, -n**) *m* Jew
Juden- *zW*: **Judentum** (**-s**) *nt* (*die Juden*) Jewry; **Judenverfolgung** *f* persecution of the Jews
Jüdin ['jy:dɪn] *f* Jewess
jüdisch *adj* Jewish
Judo ['ju:do] (**-(s)**) *nt* judo
Jugend ['ju:gənt] (-) *f* youth; **Jugendherberge** *f* youth hostel; **Jugendkriminalität** *f* juvenile crime; **jugendlich** *adj* youthful; **Jugendliche, r** *f(m)* teenager, young person
Jugoslawien [jugo'sla:viən] (**-s**) *nt* Yugoslavia
jugoslawisch *adj* Yugoslav(ian)
Juli ['ju:li] (**-(s), -s**) (*pl selten*) *m* July; *siehe auch* **September**
jung [jʊŋ] *adj* young
Junge (**-n, -n**) *m* boy, lad ▷ *nt* young animal; (*pl*) young *pl*
Jünger ['jʏŋər] (**-s, -**) *m* disciple
Jungfer (**-, -n**) *f*: **alte ~** old maid
Jungfernfahrt *f* maiden voyage
Jung- *zW*: **Jungfrau** *f* virgin; (*Astrol*) Virgo; **Junggeselle** *m* bachelor
jüngst [jʏŋst] *adv* lately, recently
jüngste, r, s *adj* youngest; (*neueste*) latest; **das J~ Gericht** the Last Judgement; **der J~ Tag** Doomsday, the Day of Judgement
Juni ['ju:ni] (**-(s), -s**) (*pl selten*) *m* June; *siehe auch* **September**
Junior ['ju:niɔr] (**-s, -en**) *m* junior
Jura ['ju:ra] *no art* (*Univ*) law
Jurist, in [ju'rɪst(ɪn)] *m(f)* jurist, lawyer; (*Student*) law student; **juristisch** *adj* legal
Justiz [jʊs'ti:ts] (-) *f* justice; **Justizbeamte, r** *m* judicial officer; **Justizirrtum** *m* miscarriage of justice; **Justizminister** *m* minister of justice
Juwel [ju've:l] (**-s, -en**) *m od nt* jewel
Juwelier [juve'li:r] (**-s, -e**) *m* jeweller (*Brit*), jeweler (*US*); **Juweliergeschäft** *nt* jeweller's (*Brit*) *od* jeweler's (*US*) (shop)
Jux [jʊks] (**-es, -e**) *m* joke, lark; **etw aus ~ tun/sagen** (*umg*) to do/say sth in fun

Kk

K, k [ka:] *nt* K, k; **K wie Kaufmann** ≈ K for King

Kabarett [kaba'rɛt] (**-s, -e** *od* **-s**) *nt* cabaret; **Kabarettist, in** [kabarɛ'tɪst(ɪn)] *m(f)* cabaret artiste

Kabel ['ka:bəl] (**-s, -**) *nt* (*Elek*) wire; (*stark*) cable; **Kabelfernsehen** *nt* cable television

Kabeljau ['ka:bəljaʊ] (**-s, -e** *od* **-s**) *m* cod

Kabine [ka'bi:nə] *f* cabin; (*Zelle*) cubicle

Kabinett [kabi'nɛt] (**-s, -e**) *nt* (*Pol*) cabinet; (*kleines Zimmer*) small room ▷ *m high-quality German white wine*

Kachel ['kaxəl] (**-, -n**) *f* tile

kacheln *vt* to tile

Kachelofen *m* tiled stove

Käfer ['kɛ:fər] (**-s, -**) *m* beetle

Kaff [kaf] (**-s, -s**) (*umg*) *nt* dump, hole

Kaffee ['kafe] (**-s, -s**) *m* coffee; **zwei ~, bitte!** two coffees, please; **das ist kalter ~** (*umg*) that's old hat; **Kaffeekanne** *f* coffeepot; **Kaffeeklatsch** *m*, **Kaffeekränzchen** *nt* coffee circle; **Kaffeelöffel** *m* coffee spoon; **Kaffeemaschine** *f* coffee maker; **Kaffeemühle** *f* coffee grinder; **Kaffeesatz** *m* coffee grounds *pl*

Käfig ['kɛ:fɪç] (**-s, -e**) *m* cage

kahl [ka:l] *adj* bald; **~ fressen** to strip bare; **~ geschoren** shaven, shorn; **Kahlheit** *f* baldness; **kahlköpfig** *adj* bald-headed

Kahn [ka:n] (**-(e)s, ¨-e**) *m* boat, barge

Kai [kaɪ] (**-s, -e** *od* **-s**) *m* quay

Kaiser ['kaɪzər] (**-s, -**) *m* emperor; **kaiserlich** *adj* imperial; **Kaiserreich** *nt* empire; **Kaiserschnitt** *m* (*Med*) Caesarean (*Brit*) *od* Cesarean (*US*) (section)

Kakao [ka'ka:o] (**-s, -s**) *m* cocoa; **jdn durch den ~ ziehen** (*umg: veralbern*) to make fun of sb; (*: boshaft reden*) to run sb down

Kaktee [kak'te:ə] (**-, -n**) *f* cactus

Kalb [kalp] (**-(e)s, ¨-er**) *nt* calf; **Kalbfleisch** *nt* veal

Kalbsleder *nt* calf(skin)

Kalender [ka'lɛndər] (**-s, -**) *m* calendar; (*Taschenkalender*) diary

Kaliber [ka'li:bər] (**-s, -**) *nt* (*lit, fig*) calibre (*Brit*), caliber (*US*)

Kalk [kalk] (**-(e)s, -e**) *m* lime; (*Biol*) calcium; **Kalkstein** *m* limestone

kalkulieren [kalku'li:rən] *vt* to calculate

Kalorie [kalo'ri:] (**-, -n**) *f* calorie

kalorienarm *adj* low-calorie

kalt [kalt] *adj* cold; **mir ist (es) ~** I am cold; **~e Platte** cold meat; **der K~e Krieg** the Cold War; **etw ~ stellen** to chill, to put sth to chill; **die Wohnung kostet ~ 500 Euro** the flat costs 500 euros without heating; **~ bleiben** to be unmoved; **~ lächelnd** (*ironisch*) cool as you please; **kaltblütig** *adj* cold-blooded; (*ruhig*) cool

Kälte ['kɛltə] (**-**) *f* coldness; (*Wetter*) cold; **Kälteeinbruch** *m* cold spell; **Kältegrad** *m* degree of frost *od* below zero; **Kältewelle** *f* cold spell

kalt- *zW*: **kaltherzig** *adj* cold-hearted; **kaltschnäuzig** *adj* cold, unfeeling; **kaltstellen** *vt* (*fig*) to leave out in the cold

Kalzium ['kaltsiʊm] (**-s**) *nt* calcium

kam *etc* [ka:m] *vb siehe* **kommen**

Kambodscha [kam'bɔdʒa] *nt* Cambodia

Kamel [ka'me:l] (**-(e)s, -e**) *nt* camel

Kamera ['kamera] (**-, -s**) *f* camera

Kamerad, in [kamə'ra:t, -'ra:dɪn] (**-en, -en**) *m(f)* comrade, friend; **Kameradschaft** *f* comradeship; **kameradschaftlich** *adj* comradely

Kamerun ['kaməru:n] (**-s**) *nt* Cameroon

Kamille [ka'mɪlə] (**-, -n**) *f* camomile

Kamillentee *m* camomile tea

Kamin [ka'mi:n] (**-s, -e**) *m* (*außen*) chimney; (*innen*) fireside; (*Feuerstelle*) fireplace: **Kaminfeger** (**-s, -**) *m* chimney sweep

Kamm [kam] (**-(e)s,¨-e**) *m* comb; (*Bergkamm*) ridge; (*Hahnenkamm*) crest; **alle/alles über einen ~ scheren** (*fig*) to lump everyone/everything together

kämmen ['kɛmən] *vt* to comb

Kammer ['kamər] (**-, -n**) *f* chamber; (*Zimmer*) small bedroom

Kampagne [kam'panjə] (**-, -n**) *f* campaign

Kampf [kampf] (**-(e)s, ¨-e**) *m* fight, battle; (*Wettbewerb*) contest; (*fig: Anstrengung*) struggle; **jdm/etw den ~ ansagen** (*fig*) to declare war on sb/sth; **kampfbereit** *adj* ready for action

kämpfen ['kɛmpfən] *vi* to fight; **ich habe lange mit mir ~ müssen, ehe ...** I had a long battle with myself before ...

Kämpfer, in (**-s, -**) *m(f)* fighter, combatant

Kampf- *zW*: **Kampfhandlung** *f* action; **Kampfrichter** *m* (*Sport*) referee
Kanada ['kanada] (**-s**) *nt* Canada
Kanadier, in [ka'na:diər(ɪn)] (**-s, -**) *m(f)* Canadian
kanadisch [ka'na:dɪʃ] *adj* Canadian
Kanal [ka'na:l] (**-s, Kanäle**) *m* (*Fluss*) canal; (*Rinne*) channel; (*für Abfluss*) drain; **der ~** (*auch*: **der Ärmelkanal**) the (English) Channel
Kanalisation [kanalizatsi'o:n] *f* sewage system
kanalisieren [kanali'zi:rən] *vt* to provide with a sewage system; (*fig*: *Energie etc*) to channel
Kanaltunnel *m* Channel Tunnel
Kanarienvogel [ka'na:riənfo:gəl] *m* canary
Kandidat, in [kandi'da:t(ɪn)] (**-en, -en**) *m(f)* candidate; **jdn als ~en aufstellen** to nominate sb
Kandidatur [kandida'tu:r] *f* candidature, candidacy
kandidieren [kandi'di:rən] *vi* (*Pol*) to stand, run
Känguru ['kɛŋguru] (**-s, -s**) *nt* kangaroo
Kaninchen [ka'ni:nçən] *nt* rabbit
Kanister [ka'nɪstər] (**-s, -**) *m* can, canister
Kännchen ['kɛnçən] *nt* pot; (*für Milch*) jug
Kanne ['kanə] (**-, -n**) *f* (*Krug*) jug; (*Kaffeekanne*) pot; (*Milchkanne*) churn; (*Gießkanne*) watering can
Kannibale [kani'ba:lə] (**-n, -n**) *m* cannibal
kannte *etc* ['kantə] *vb siehe* **kennen**
Kanon ['ka:nɔn] (**-s, -s**) *m* canon
Kanone [ka'no:nə] (**-, -n**) *f* gun; (*Hist*) cannon; (*fig*: *Mensch*) ace; **das ist unter aller ~** (*umg*) that defies description
Kantate [kan'ta:tə] (**-, -n**) *f* cantata
Kante ['kantə] (**-, -n**) *f* edge; **Geld auf die hohe ~ legen** (*umg*) to put money by
Kantine [kan'ti:nə] *f* canteen
Kanton [kan'to:n] (**-s, -e**) *m* canton
Kanu ['ka:nu] (**-s, -s**) *nt* canoe
Kanzel ['kantsəl] (**-, -n**) *f* pulpit; (*Aviat*) cockpit
Kanzler, in ['kantslər] (**-s, -**) *m(f)* chancellor
Kap [kap] (**-s, -s**) *nt* cape; **das ~ der guten Hoffnung** the Cape of Good Hope
Kapazität [kapatsi'tɛ:t] *f* capacity; (*Fachmann*) authority
Kapelle [ka'pɛlə] *f* (*Gebäude*) chapel; (*Mus*) band
Kaper ['ka:pər] (**-, -n**) *f* caper
kapieren [ka'pi:rən] (*umg*) *vt, vi* to understand
Kapital [kapi'ta:l] (**-s, -e** *od* **-ien**) *nt* capital; **aus etw ~ schlagen** (*pej*: *lit, fig*) to make capital out of sth; **Kapitalanlage** *f* investment
Kapitalismus [kapita'lɪsmʊs] *m* capitalism
Kapitalist [kapita'lɪst] *m* capitalist
kapitalistisch *adj* capitalist
Kapitän [kapi'tɛ:n] (**-s, -e**) *m* captain
Kapitel [ka'pɪtəl] (**-s, -**) *nt* chapter; **ein trauriges ~** (*Angelegenheit*) a sad story
Kapitulation [kapitulatsi'o:n] *f* capitulation
kapitulieren [kapitu'li:rən] *vi* to capitulate
Kaplan [ka'pla:n] (**-s, Kapläne**) *m* chaplain
Kappe ['kapə] (**-, -n**) *f* cap; (*Kapuze*) hood; **das nehme ich auf meine ~** (*fig*: *umg*) I'll take the responsibility for that
kappen *vt* to cut
Kapsel ['kapsəl] (**-, -n**) *f* capsule
kaputt [ka'pʊt] (*umg*) *adj* smashed, broken; (*Person*) exhausted, knackered; **etw ~ machen/schlagen** to break/smash sth; **der Fernseher ist ~** the TV's not working; **ein ~er Typ** a bum; *siehe auch* **kaputtmachen**: **kaputtgehen** *unreg vi* to break; (*Schuhe*) to fall apart; (*Firma*) to go bust; (*Stoff*) to wear out; (*sterben*) to cop it (*umg*); **kaputtlachen** *vr* to laugh o.s. silly; **kaputtmachen** *vt* to break; (*Mensch*) to exhaust, wear out
Kapuze [ka'pu:tsə] (**-, -n**) *f* hood
Karabiner [kara'bi:nər] (**-s, -**) *m* (*Gewehr*) carbine
Karaffe [ka'rafə] (**-, -n**) *f* carafe; (*geschliffen*) decanter
Karamell [kara'mɛl] (**-s**) *m* caramel; **Karamellbonbon** *m od nt* toffee
Karat [ka'ra:t] (**-(e)s, -e**) *nt* carat
Karate (**-s**) *nt* karate
Kardinal [kardi'na:l] (**-s, Kardinäle**) *m* cardinal; **Kardinalzahl** *f* cardinal number
Karfreitag [ka:r'fraɪta:k] *m* Good Friday
kärglich ['kɛrklɪç] *adj* poor, scanty
Karibik [ka'ri:bɪk] (**-**) *f*: **die ~** the Caribbean
karibisch *adj* Caribbean; **das K~e Meer** the Caribbean Sea
kariert [ka'ri:rt] *adj* (*Stoff*) checked (*Brit*), checkered (*US*); (*Papier*) squared; **~ reden** (*umg*) to talk rubbish *od* nonsense
Karies ['ka:riɛs] (**-**) *f* caries
Karikatur [karika'tu:r] *f* caricature; **Karikaturist, in** [karikatu:'rɪst(ɪn)] *m(f)* cartoonist
Karneval ['karnəval] (**-s, -e** *od* **-s**) *m* carnival
Kärnten ['kɛrntən] (**-s**) *nt* Carinthia
Karo ['ka:ro] (**-s, -s**) *nt* square; (*Karten*) diamonds
Karosserie [karɔsə'ri:] *f* (*Aut*) body(work)
Karotte [ka'rɔtə] (**-, -n**) *f* carrot
Karpfen ['karpfən] (**-s, -**) *m* carp
Karriere [kari'ɛ:rə] (**-, -n**) *f* career; **~ machen** to get on, get to the top; **Karrieremacher, in** *m(f)* careerist
Karte ['kartə] (**-, -n**) *f* card; (*Landkarte*) map; (*Speisekarte*) menu; (*Eintrittskarte, Fahrkarte*) ticket; **mit offenen ~n spielen** (*fig*) to put one's cards on the table; **alles auf eine ~ setzen** to put all one's eggs in one basket
Kartei [kar'taɪ] *f* card index; **Karteikarte** *f* index card
Kartell [kar'tɛl] (**-s, -e**) *nt* cartel
Karten- *zW*: **Kartenspiel** *nt* card game; (*Karten*) pack (*Brit*) *od* deck (*US*) of cards; **Kartentelefon** *nt* cardphone; **Kartenvorverkauf** *m* advance sale of tickets

Kartoffel [kar'tɔfəl] (**-, -n**) *f* potato; **Kartoffelbrei** *m* mashed potatoes *pl*; **Kartoffelpüree** *nt* mashed potatoes *pl*; **Kartoffelsalat** *m* potato salad
Karton [kar'tõ:] (**-s, -s**) *m* cardboard; (*Schachtel*) cardboard box
kartoniert [karto'ni:rt] *adj* hardback
Karussell [karʊ'sɛl] (**-s, -s**) *nt* roundabout (*Brit*), merry-go-round
Karwoche ['ka:rvɔxə] *f* Holy Week
Karzinom [kartsi'no:m] (**-s, -e**) *nt* (*Med*) carcinoma
Kasachstan [kazaxs'ta:n] (**-s**) *nt* (*Geog*) Kazakhstan
Käse ['kɛ:zə] (**-s, -**) *m* cheese; (*umg: Unsinn*) rubbish, twaddle; **Käseblatt** (*umg*) *nt* (local) rag; **Käsekuchen** *m* cheesecake
Kaserne [ka'zɛrnə] (**-, -n**) *f* barracks *pl*
Kasernenhof *m* parade ground
Kasino [ka'zi:no] (**-s, -s**) *nt* club; (*Mil*) officers' mess; (*Spielkasino*) casino
Kasse ['kasə] (**-, -n**) *f* (*Geldkasten*) cashbox; (*in Geschäft*) till, cash register; (*Kinokasse, Theaterkasse etc*) box office; (*Krankenkasse*) health insurance; (*Sparkasse*) savings bank; **die ~ führen** to be in charge of the money; **jdn zur ~ bitten** to ask sb to pay up; **~ machen** to count the money; **getrennte ~ führen** to pay separately; **an der ~** (*in Geschäft*) at the (cash) desk; **gut bei ~ sein** to be in the money
Kassen- *zW*: **Kassenarzt** *m* ≈ National Health doctor (*Brit*), ≈ panel doctor (*US*); **Kassenpatient** *m* ≈ National Health patient (*Brit*); **Kassenzettel** *m* sales slip
Kassette [ka'sɛtə] *f* small box; (*Tonband, Phot*) cassette; (*Comput*) cartridge, cassette; (*Bücherkassette*) case
Kassettenrekorder (**-s, -**) *m* cassette recorder
kassieren [ka'si:rən] *vt* (*Gelder etc*) to collect; (*umg: wegnehmen*) to take (away) ▷ *vi*: **darf ich ~?** would you like to pay now?
Kassierer, in [ka'si:rər(ɪn)] (**-s, -**) *m(f)* cashier; (*von Klub*) treasurer
Kastanie [kas'ta:niə] *f* chestnut
Kasten ['kastən] (**-s, ¨**) *m* box (*auch* SPORT), case; (*Truhe*) chest; **er hat was auf dem ~** (*umg*) he's brainy; **Kastenwagen** *m* van
kastrieren [kas'tri:rən] *vt* to castrate
katalanisch [kata'la:nɪʃ] *adj* Catalan
Katalog [kata'lo:k] (**-(e)s, -e**) *m* catalogue (*Brit*), catalog (*US*)
katalogisieren [katalogi'zi:rən] *vt* to catalogue (*Brit*), catalog (*US*)
Katalysator [kataly'za:tɔr] *m* (*lit, fig*) catalyst; (*Aut*) catalytic converter; **~-Auto** vehicle fitted with a catalytic converter
Katar ['ka:tar] *nt* Qatar
katastrophal [katastro'fa:l] *adj* catastrophic
Katastrophe [kata'stro:fə] (**-, -n**) *f* catastrophe, disaster
Katastrophenschutz *m* disaster control
Kategorie [katego'ri:] *f* category
kategorisch [kate'go:rɪʃ] *adj* categorical
Kater ['ka:tər] (**-s, -**) *m* tomcat; (*umg*) hangover
kath. *abk* = **katholisch**
Kathedrale [kate'dra:lə] (**-, -n**) *f* cathedral
Kathode [ka'to:də] (**-, -n**) *f* cathode
Katholik, in [kato'li:k(ɪn)] (**-en, -en**) *m(f)* Catholic
katholisch [ka'to:lɪʃ] *adj* Catholic
Katholizismus [katoli'tsɪsmʊs] *m* Catholicism
Kätzchen ['kɛtsçən] *nt* kitten
Katze ['katsə] (**-, -n**) *f* cat; **die ~ im Sack kaufen** to buy a pig in a poke; **für die Katz** (*umg*) in vain, for nothing
Katzensprung (*umg*) *m* stone's throw, short distance
Kauderwelsch ['kaʊdərvɛlʃ] (**-(s)**) *nt* jargon; (*umg*) double Dutch (*Brit*)
kauen ['kaʊən] *vt, vi* to chew
Kauf [kaʊf] (**-(e)s, Käufe**) *m* purchase, buy; (*Kaufen*) buying; **ein guter ~** a bargain; **etw in ~ nehmen** to put up with sth
kaufen *vt* to buy; **dafür kann ich mir nichts ~** (*ironisch*) what use is that to me!
Käufer, in ['kɔʏfər(ɪn)] (**-s, -**) *m(f)* buyer
Kauf- *zW*: **Kauffrau** *f* businesswoman; (*Einzelhandelskauffrau*) shopkeeper; **Kaufhaus** *nt* department store; **Kaufkraft** *f* purchasing power
käuflich ['kɔʏflɪç] *adj* purchasable, for sale; (*pej*) venal ▷ *adv*: **~ erwerben** to purchase
Kauf- *zW*: **kauflustig** *adj* interested in buying; **Kaufmann** (**-(e)s**, *pl* **-leute**) *m* businessman; (*Einzelhandelskaufmann*) shopkeeper; **kaufmännisch** *adj* commercial; **kaufmännischer Angestellter** clerk; **Kaufvertrag** *m* bill of sale
Kaugummi ['kaʊgʊmi] *m* chewing gum
Kaukasus ['kaʊkazʊs] *m*: **der ~** the Caucasus
Kaulquappe ['kaʊlkvapə] (**-, -n**) *f* tadpole
kaum [kaʊm] *adv* hardly, scarcely; **wohl ~, ich glaube ~** I hardly think so
Kaution [kaʊtsi'o:n] *f* deposit; (*Jur*) bail
Kauz [kaʊts] (**-es, Käuze**) *m* owl; (*fig*) queer fellow
Kavalier [kava'li:r] (**-s, -e**) *m* gentleman
Kavaliersdelikt *nt* peccadillo
Kaviar ['ka:viar] *m* caviar
KB *nt abk* (= *Kilobyte*) KB, kbyte
keck [kɛk] *adj* daring, bold
Kegel ['ke:gəl] (**-s, -**) *m* skittle; (*Math*) cone; **Kegelbahn** *f* skittle alley, bowling alley
kegeln *vi* to play skittles
Kehle ['ke:lə] (**-, -n**) *f* throat; **er hat das in die falsche ~ bekommen** (*lit*) it went down the wrong way; (*fig*) he took it the wrong way; **aus voller ~** at the top of one's voice
Kehl- *zW*: **Kehlkopf** *m* larynx; **Kehllaut** *m* guttural
Kehre ['ke:rə] (**-, -n**) *f* turn(ing), bend
kehren *vt, vi* (*wenden*) to turn; (*mit Besen*) to sweep; **sich an etw** *dat* **nicht ~** not to heed

sth; **in sich** *akk* **gekehrt** (*versunken*) pensive; (*verschlossen*) introspective, introverted
Kehricht (**-s**) *m* sweepings *pl*
Kehr- *zW*: **Kehrmaschine** *f* sweeper; **Kehrseite** *f* reverse, other side; (*ungünstig*) wrong *od* bad side; **die Kehrseite der Medaille** the other side of the coin
kehrtmachen *vi* to turn about, about-turn
keifen ['kaɪfən] *vi* to scold, nag
Keil [kaɪl] (**-(e)s, -e**) *m* wedge; (*Mil*) arrowhead
Keilriemen *m* (*Aut*) fan belt
Keim [kaɪm] (**-(e)s, -e**) *m* bud; (*Med, fig*) germ; **etw im ~ ersticken** to nip sth in the bud
keimen *vi* to germinate
Keim- *zW*: **keimfrei** *adj* sterile; **Keimzelle** *f* (*fig*) nucleus
kein ['kaɪn], **keine** ['kaɪnə] *pron* none ▷ *adj* no, not any; **~e schlechte Idee** not a bad idea; **~e Stunde/drei Monate** (*nicht einmal*) less than an hour/three months
keine, r, s *indef pron* no one, nobody; (*von Gegenstand*) none
keinerlei ['kaɪnər'laɪ] *adj attrib* no ... whatever
keinesfalls *adv* on no account
keineswegs *adv* by no means
keinmal *adv* not once
Keks [ke:ks] (**-es, -e**) *m od nt* biscuit (*Brit*), cookie (*US*)
Kelch [kɛlç] (**-(e)s, -e**) *m* cup, goblet, chalice
Kelle ['kɛlə] (**-, -n**) *f* ladle; (*Maurerkelle*) trowel
Keller ['kɛlər] (**-s, -**) *m* cellar; **Kellerassel** (**-, -n**) *f* woodlouse
Kellerwohnung *f* basement flat (*Brit*) *od* apartment (*US*)
Kellner, in ['kɛlnər(ɪn)] (**-s, -**) *m(f)* waiter, waitress
keltern ['kɛltərn] *vt* to press
Kenia ['ke:nia] (**-s**) *nt* Kenya
kennen ['kɛnən] *unreg vt* to know; **~ Sie sich schon?** do you know each other (already)?; **kennst du mich noch?** do you remember me?
Kenner, in (**-s, -**) *m(f)*: **~ (von** *od* **+***gen***)** connoisseur (of); expert (on)
kenntlich *adj* distinguishable, discernible; **etw ~ machen** to mark sth
Kenntnis (**-, -se**) *f* knowledge *no pl*; **etw zur ~ nehmen** to note sth; **von etw ~ nehmen** to take notice of sth; **jdn in ~ setzen** to inform sb; **über ~se von etw verfügen** to be knowledgeable about sth
Kenn- *zW*: **Kennwort** *nt* (*Chiffre*) code name; (*Losungswort*) password, code word; **Kennzeichen** *nt* mark, characteristic; **(amtliches/polizeiliches) Kennzeichen** (*Aut*) number plate (*Brit*), license plate (*US*); **kennzeichnen** *vt untr* to characterize; **Kennziffer** *f* (code) number; (*Comm*) reference number
kentern ['kɛntərn] *vi* to capsize
Keramik [ke'ra:mɪk] (**-, -en**) *f* ceramics *pl*, pottery; (*Gegenstand*) piece of ceramic work *od* pottery
Kerbe ['kɛrbə] (**-, -n**) *f* notch, groove
Kerbel (**-s, -**) *m* chervil
Kerbholz *nt*: **etw auf dem ~ haben** to have done sth wrong
Kerker ['kɛrkər] (**-s, -**) *m* prison
Kerl [kɛrl] (**-s, -e**) (*umg*) *m* chap, bloke (*Brit*), guy; **du gemeiner ~!** you swine!
Kern [kɛrn] (**-(e)s, -e**) *m* (*Obstkern*) pip, stone; (*Nusskern*) kernel; (*Atomkern*) nucleus; (*fig*) heart, core; **Kernenergie** *f* nuclear energy; **Kernforschung** *f* nuclear research; **Kernfrage** *f* central issue; **Kernfusion** *f* nuclear fusion; **kerngesund** *adj* thoroughly healthy, fit as a fiddle
kernig *adj* robust; (*Ausspruch*) pithy
Kern- *zW*: **Kernkraftwerk** *nt* nuclear power station; **kernlos** *adj* seedless, pipless; **Kernphysik** *f* nuclear physics *sing*; **Kernreaktion** *f* nuclear reaction; **Kernschmelze** *f* meltdown; **Kernseife** *f* washing soap; **Kernspaltung** *f* nuclear fission; **Kernwaffen** *pl* nuclear weapons *pl*
Kerze ['kɛrtsə] (**-, -n**) *f* candle; (*Zündkerze*) plug
Kerzen- *zW*: **kerzengerade** *adj* straight as a die; **Kerzenhalter** *m* candlestick
kess [kɛs] *adj* saucy
Kessel ['kɛsəl] (**-s, -**) *m* kettle; (*von Lokomotive etc*) boiler; (*Mulde*) basin; (*Geog*) depression; (*Mil*) encirclement
Kette ['kɛtə] (**-, -n**) *f* chain; **jdn an die ~ legen** (*fig*) to tie sb down
ketten *vt* to chain
Kettenreaktion *f* chain reaction
Ketzer, in ['kɛtsər(ɪn)] (**-s, -**) *m(f)* heretic
keuchen ['kɔʏçən] *vi* to pant, gasp
Keuchhusten *m* whooping cough
Keule ['kɔʏlə] (**-, -n**) *f* club; (*Koch*) leg
keusch [kɔʏʃ] *adj* chaste; **Keuschheit** *f* chastity
kfm. *abk* = **kaufmännisch**
Kfz (**-(s), -(s)**) *f abk* = **Kraftfahrzeug**
kichern ['kɪçərn] *vi* to giggle
kidnappen ['kɪtnɛpən] *vt* to kidnap
Kiefer[1] ['ki:fər] (**-s, -**) *m* jaw
Kiefer[2] ['ki:fər] (**-, -n**) *f* pine
Kiefernzapfen *m* pine cone
Kieferorthopäde *m* orthodontist
Kiel [ki:l] (**-(e)s, -e**) *m* (*Federkiel*) quill; (*Naut*) keel
Kieme ['ki:mə] (**-, -n**) *f* gill
Kies [ki:s] (**-es, -e**) *m* gravel; (*umg: Geld*) money, dough
kiffen ['kɪfən] (*umg*) *vt* to smoke pot *od* grass
Kilo ['ki:lo] (**-s, -(s)**) *nt* kilo; **Kilobyte** [kilo'baɪt] *nt* (*Comput*) kilobyte; **Kilogramm** [kilo'gram] *nt* kilogram
Kilometer [kilo'me:tər] *m* kilometre (*Brit*), kilometer (*US*); **Kilometerzähler** *m* ≈ mileometer
Kilowatt [kilo'vat] *nt* kilowatt
Kind [kɪnt] (**-(e)s, -er**) *nt* child; **sich freuen wie ein ~** to be as pleased as Punch; **mit ~ und Kegel** (*hum: umg*) with the whole family;

von ~ auf from childhood
Kinderarzt *m* paediatrician (*Brit*), pediatrician (*US*)
Kinderbett *nt* cot (*Brit*), crib (*US*)
Kinderei [kɪndəˈraɪ] *f* childishness
Kindergarten *m* nursery school
Kinder- *zW*: **Kindergärtner, in** *m(f)* nursery-school teacher; **Kindergeld** *nt* child benefit (*Brit*); **Kinderkrankheit** *f* childhood illness; **Kinderlähmung** *f* polio(myelitis); **kinderleicht** *adj* childishly easy; **kinderlos** *adj* childless; **Kindermädchen** *nt* nursemaid; **kinderreich** *adj* with a lot of children; **Kindertagesstätte** *f* day-nursery; **Kinderzimmer** *nt* child's/children's room; (*für Kleinkinder*) nursery
Kind- *zW*: **Kindheit** *f* childhood; **kindisch** *adj* childish; **kindlich** *adj* childlike
Kinn [kɪn] (**-(e)s, -e**) *nt* chin; **Kinnhaken** *m* (*Boxen*) uppercut; **Kinnlade** *f* jaw
Kino [ˈkiːno] (**-s, -s**) *nt* cinema (*Brit*), movies (*US*); **Kinobesucher** *m*, **Kinogänger** *m* cinema-goer (*Brit*), movie-goer (*US*); **Kinoprogramm** *nt* film programme (*Brit*), movie program (*US*)
Kiosk [kiˈɔsk] (**-(e)s, -e**) *m* kiosk
Kippe [ˈkɪpə] (**-, -n**) *f* (*umg*) cigarette end; **auf der ~ stehen** (*fig*) to be touch and go
kippen *vi* to topple over, overturn ▷ *vt* to tilt
Kippschalter *m* rocker switch
Kirche [ˈkɪrçə] (**-, -n**) *f* church
Kirchen- *zW*: **Kirchenlied** *nt* hymn; **Kirchensteuer** *f* church tax
Kirch- *zW*: **Kirchgänger, in** (**-s, -**) *m(f)* churchgoer; **Kirchhof** *m* churchyard; **kirchlich** *adj* ecclesiastical; **Kirchturm** *m* church tower, steeple
Kirschbaum [ˈkɪrʃbaʊm] *m* cherry tree; (*Holz*) cherry (wood)
Kirsche [ˈkɪrʃə] (**-, -n**) *f* cherry; **mit ihm ist nicht gut ~n essen** (*fig*) it's best not to tangle with him
Kirschwasser *nt* kirsch
Kissen [ˈkɪsən] (**-s, -**) *nt* cushion; (*Kopfkissen*) pillow; **Kissenbezug** *m* pillow case
Kiste [ˈkɪstə] (**-, -n**) *f* box; (*Truhe*) chest; (*umg: Bett*) sack; (*: Fernsehen*) box (*Brit*), tube (*US*)
Kitsch [kɪtʃ] (**-(e)s**) *m* trash
kitschig *adj* trashy
Kitt [kɪt] (**-(e)s, -e**) *m* putty
Kittel (**-s, -**) *m* overall; (*von Arzt, Laborant etc*) (white) coat
kitten *vt* to putty; (*fig*) to patch up
Kitz [kɪts] (**-es, -e**) *nt* kid; (*Rehkitz*) fawn
kitzelig [ˈkɪtsəlɪç] *adj* (*lit, fig*) ticklish
kitzeln *vt, vi* to tickle
Kiwi [ˈkiːvi] (**-, -s**) *f* kiwi fruit
KKW (**-, -s**) *nt abk* = **Kernkraftwerk**
kläffen [ˈklɛfən] *vi* to yelp
Klage [ˈklaːgə] (**-, -n**) *f* complaint; (*Jur*) action; **eine ~ gegen jdn einreichen** *od* **erheben** to institute proceedings against sb
klagen *vi* (*wehklagen*) to lament, wail; (*sich beschweren*) to complain; (*Jur*) to take legal action; **jdm sein Leid/seine Not ~** to pour out one's sorrow/distress to sb
Kläger, in [ˈklɛːgər(ɪn)] (**-s, -**) *m(f)* (*Jur: im Zivilrecht*) plaintiff; (*: im Strafrecht*) prosecuting party; (*: in Scheidung*) petitioner
kläglich [ˈklɛːklɪç] *adj* wretched
klamm *adj* (*Finger*) numb; (*feucht*) damp
Klammer [ˈklamər] (**-, -n**) *f* clamp; (*in Text*) bracket; (*Büroklammer*) clip; (*Wäscheklammer*) peg (*Brit*), pin (*US*); (*Zahnklammer*) brace; **~ auf/zu** open/close brackets
klammern *vr*: **sich ~ an** *+akk* to cling to
klang *etc* [klaŋ] *vb siehe* **klingen**
Klang (**-(e)s, ¨-e**) *m* sound
Klappe [ˈklapə] (**-, -n**) *f* valve; (*an Oboe etc*) key; (*Film*) clapperboard; (*Ofenklappe*) damper; (*umg: Mund*) trap; **die ~ halten** to shut one's trap
klappen *vi* (*Geräusch*) to click; (*Sitz etc*) to tip ▷ *vt* to tip ▷ *vi unpers* to work; **hat es mit den Karten/dem Job geklappt?** did you get the tickets/job O.K.?
Klapper [ˈklapər] (**-, -n**) *f* rattle
klapperig *adj* run-down, worn-out
klappern *vi* to clatter, rattle
Klapperschlange *f* rattlesnake
Klapperstorch *m* stork; **er glaubt noch an den ~** he still thinks babies are found under the gooseberry bush
Klapp- *zW*: **Klappmesser** *nt* jackknife; **Klapprad** *nt* collapsible *od* folding bicycle; **Klappstuhl** *m* folding chair
klar [klaːr] *adj* clear; (*Naut*) ready to sail; (*Mil*) ready for action; **bei ~em Verstand sein** to be in full possession of one's faculties; **sich** *dat* **im K~en sein über** *+akk* to be clear about; **ins K~e kommen** to get clear; **~ sehen** to see clearly; **sich** *dat* **über etw** *akk* **~ werden** to get sth clear in one's mind
Kläranlage *f* sewage plant; (*von Fabrik*) purification plant
klären *vt* (*Flüssigkeit*) to purify; (*Probleme*) to clarify ▷ *vr* to clear (itself) up
Klarheit *f* clarity; **sich** *dat* **~ über etw** *akk* **verschaffen** to get sth straight
Klarinette [klariˈnɛtə] *f* clarinet
klar- *zW*: **klarkommen** *unreg* (*umg*) *vi*: **mit jdm/etw klarkommen** to be able to cope with sb/sth; **klarmachen** *vt* (*Schiff*) to get ready for sea; **jdm etw klarmachen** to make sth clear to sb; **Klarsichtfolie** *f* transparent film; **klarstellen** *vt* to clarify
Klärung [ˈklɛːrʊŋ] *f* purification; clarification
Klasse [ˈklasə] (**-, -n**) *f* class; (*Sch*) class, form; (*auch*: **Steuerklasse**) bracket; (*Güterklasse*) grade
klasse (*umg*) *adj* smashing
Klassen- *zW*: **Klassenarbeit** *f* test; **Klassenbewusstsein** *nt* class-consciousness; **Klassengesellschaft** *f* class society; **Klassenkampf** *m* class conflict;

Klassenlehrer, in *m(f)* class teacher; **klassenlos** *adj* classless; **Klassensprecher, in** *m(f)* class spokesperson; **Klassenzimmer** *nt* classroom

klassifizieren [klasifi'tsi:rən] *vt* to classify

Klassik ['klasɪk] *f* (*Zeit*) classical period; (*Stil*) classicism; **Klassiker** (**-s, -**) *m* classic

klassisch *adj* (*lit, fig*) classical

Klassizismus [klasi'tsɪsmʊs] *m* classicism

Klatsch [klatʃ] (**-(e)s, -e**) *m* smack, crack; (*Gerede*) gossip; **Klatschbase** *f* gossip(monger)

klatschen *vi* (*tratschen*) to gossip; (*Beifall spenden*) to applaud, to clap ▷ *vt*: **(jdm) Beifall ~** to applaud *od* clap (sb)

Klatsch- *zW*: **Klatschmohn** *m* (corn) poppy; **klatschnass** *adj* soaking wet

Klaue ['klaʊə] (**-, -n**) *f* claw; (*umg: Schrift*) scrawl

klauen *vt* to claw; (*umg*) to pinch

Klausel ['klaʊzəl] (**-, -n**) *f* clause; (*Vorbehalt*) proviso

Klausur [klaʊ'zu:r] *f* seclusion; **Klausurarbeit** *f* examination paper

Klaviatur [klavia'tu:r] *f* keyboard

Klavier [kla'vi:r] (**-s, -e**) *nt* piano

kleben ['kle:bən] *vt, vi*: **~ (an** *+akk***)** to stick (to); **jdm eine ~** (*umg*) to belt sb one

klebrig *adj* sticky

Klebstoff *m* glue

Klecks [klɛks] (**-es, -e**) *m* blot, stain; **klecksen** *vi* to blot; (*pej*) to daub

Klee [kle:] (**-s**) *m* clover; **jdn/etw über den grünen ~ loben** (*fig*) to praise sb/sth to the skies; **Kleeblatt** *nt* cloverleaf; (*fig*) trio

Kleid [klaɪt] (**-(e)s, -er**) *nt* garment; (*Frauenkleid*) dress; **Kleider** *pl* clothes *pl*

kleiden ['klaɪdən] *vt* to clothe, dress ▷ *vr* to dress; **jdn ~** to suit sb

Kleider- *zW*: **Kleiderbügel** *m* coat hanger; **Kleiderbürste** *f* clothes brush; **Kleiderschrank** *m* wardrobe

Kleidung *f* clothing

Kleidungsstück *nt* garment

Kleie ['klaɪə] (**-, -n**) *f* bran

klein [klaɪn] *adj* little, small; **haben Sie es nicht ~er?** haven't you got anything smaller?; **ein ~es Bier, ein K~es** (*umg*) ≈ half a pint, ≈ a half; **von ~ an** *od* **auf** (*von Kindheit an*) from childhood; (*von Anfang an*) from the very beginning; **das ~ere Übel** the lesser evil; **sein Vater war (ein) ~er Beamter** his father was a minor civil servant; **~ anfangen** to start off in a small way; **~ geschrieben werden** (*umg*) to count for (very) little; **~ hacken** to chop up; **~ schneiden** to chop up; **Kleinanzeige** *f* small ad (*Brit*), want ad (*US*); **Kleinanzeigen** *pl* classified advertising *sing*; **Kleinasien** *nt* Asia Minor; **Kleinbürgertum** *nt* petite bourgeoisie

klein- *zW*: **Kleinformat** *nt* small size; **im Kleinformat** small-scale; **Kleingedruckte, s** *nt* small print; **Kleingeld** *nt* small change; **das nötige Kleingeld haben** (*fig*) to have the wherewithal (*umg*); **kleinhacken** *vt* to chop up

Kleinigkeit *f* trifle; **wegen** *od* **bei jeder ~** for the slightest reason; **eine ~ essen** to have a bite to eat

klein- *zW*: **Kleinkind** *nt* infant; **Kleinkram** *m* details *pl*; **kleinlaut** *adj* dejected, quiet; **kleinlich** *adj* petty, paltry

Kleinod ['klaɪno:t] (**-s, -odien**) *nt* gem; (*fig*) treasure

klein- *zW*: **kleinschneiden** *unreg vt* to chop up; **Kleinstadt** *f* small town; **kleinstädtisch** *adj* provincial

kleinstmöglich *adj* smallest possible

Kleister ['klaɪstər] (**-s, -**) *m* paste

kleistern *vt* to paste

Klemme ['klɛmə] (**-, -n**) *f* clip; (*Med*) clamp; (*fig*) jam; **in der ~ sitzen** *od* **sein** (*fig: umg*) to be in a fix

klemmen *vt* (*festhalten*) to jam; (*quetschen*) to pinch, nip ▷ *vr* to catch o.s.; (*sich hineinzwängen*) to squeeze o.s. ▷ *vi* (*Tür*) to stick, jam; **sich hinter jdn/etw ~** to get on to sb/get down to sth

Klempner ['klɛmpnər] (**-s, -**) *m* plumber

Kleptomanie [klɛptoma'ni:] *f* kleptomania

Klerus ['kle:rʊs] (**-**) *m* clergy

Klette ['klɛtə] (**-, -n**) *f* burr; **sich wie eine ~ an jdn hängen** to cling to sb like a limpet

Kletterer ['klɛtərər] (**-s, -**) *m* climber

klettern *vi* to climb

Kletterpflanze *f* creeper

Klettverschluss *m* Velcro® fastener

klicken ['klɪkən] *vi* to click

Klient, in [kli'ɛnt(ɪn)] *m(f)* client

Klima ['kli:ma] (**-s, -s** *od* **-te**) *nt* climate; **Klimaanlage** *f* air conditioning

Klimaschutz *m* climate protection

klimatisieren [kli:mati'zi:rən] *vt* to air-condition

Klimawechsel *m* change of air

Klinge ['klɪŋə] (**-, -n**) *f* blade, sword; **jdn über die ~ springen lassen** (*fig: umg*) to allow sb to run into trouble

Klingel ['klɪŋəl] (**-, -n**) *f* bell; **Klingelbeutel** *m* collection bag

klingeln *vi* to ring; **es hat geklingelt** (*an Tür*) somebody just rang the doorbell, the doorbell just rang

klingen ['klɪŋən] *unreg vi* to sound; (*Gläser*) to clink

Klinik ['kli:nɪk] *f* clinic

Klinke ['klɪŋkə] (**-, -n**) *f* handle

Klippe ['klɪpə] (**-, -n**) *f* cliff; (*im Meer*) reef; (*fig*) hurdle

klipp und klar ['klɪp|ʊntkla:r] *adj* clear and concise

Klips [klɪps] (**-es, -e**) *m* clip; (*Ohrklips*) earring

klirren ['klɪrən] *vi* to clank, jangle; (*Gläser*) to clink; **~de Kälte** biting cold

Klischee [klɪ'ʃe:] (**-s, -s**) *nt* (*Druckplatte*) plate, block; (*fig*) cliché; **Klischeevorstellung** *f*

stereotyped idea

Klo [klo:] (**-s, -s**) (*umg*) *nt* loo (*Brit*), john (*US*)

Kloake [klo'a:kə] (**-, -n**) *f* sewer

Klon [klo:n] (**-s, -e**) *m* clone

klopfen ['klɔpfən] *vi* to knock; (*Herz*) to thump ▷*vt* to beat; **es klopft** somebody's knocking; **jdm auf die Finger ~** (*lit, fig*) to give sb a rap on the knuckles; **jdm auf die Schulter ~** to tap sb on the shoulder

Klopfer (**-s, -**) *m* (*Teppichklopfer*) beater; (*Türklopfer*) knocker

Klops [klɔps] (**-es, -e**) *m* meatball

Klosett [klo'zɛt] (**-s, -e** *od* **-s**) *nt* lavatory, toilet; **Klosettpapier** *nt* toilet paper

Kloß [klo:s] (**-es, ⸚e**) *m* (*Erdkloß*) clod; (*im Hals*) lump; (*Koch*) dumpling

Kloster ['klo:stər] (**-s, ⸚**) *nt* (*Männerkloster*) monastery; (*Frauenkloster*) convent; **ins ~ gehen** to become a monk/nun

klösterlich ['klø:stərlıç] *adj* monastic; convent

Klotz [klɔts] (**-es, ⸚e**) *m* log; (*Hackklotz*) block; **jdm ein ~ am Bein sein** (*fig*) to be a millstone round sb's neck

Klub [klʊp] (**-s, -s**) *m* club; **Klubsessel** *m* easy chair

Kluft [klʊft] (**-, ⸚e**) *f* cleft, gap; (*Geog*) chasm; (*Uniform*) uniform; (*umg: Kleidung*) gear

klug [klu:k] *adj* clever, intelligent; **ich werde daraus nicht ~** I can't make head or tail of it; **Klugheit** *f* cleverness, intelligence

klumpen ['klʊmpən] *vi* to go lumpy, clot

Klumpen (**-s, -**) *m* (*Koch*) lump; (*Erdklumpen*) clod; (*Blutklumpen*) clot; (*Goldklumpen*) nugget

knabbern ['knabərn] *vt, vi* to nibble; **an etw** *dat* **~** (*fig: umg*) to puzzle over sth

Knabe ['kna:bə] (**-n, -n**) *m* boy

knabenhaft *adj* boyish

Knäckebrot ['knɛkəbro:t] *nt* crispbread

knacken ['knakən] *vi* (*lit, fig*) to crack ▷*vt* (*umg: Auto*) to break into

Knacks [knaks] (**-es, -e**) *m*: **einen ~ weghaben** (*umg*) to be uptight about sth

Knall [knal] (**-(e)s, -e**) *m* bang; (*Peitschenknall*) crack; **~ auf Fall** (*umg*) just like that; **einen ~ haben** (*umg*) to be crazy *od* crackers; **Knallbonbon** *nt* cracker; **knallen** *vi* to bang; to crack ▷*vt*: **jdm eine knallen** (*umg*) to clout sb; **knallhart** (*umg*) *adj* really hard; (*: Worte*) hard-hitting; (*: Film*) brutal; (*: Porno*) hard-core; **knallrot** *adj* bright red

knapp [knap] *adj* tight; (*Geld*) scarce; (*kurz*) short; (*Mehrheit, Sieg*) narrow; (*Sprache*) concise; **meine Zeit ist ~ bemessen** I am short of time; **mit ~er Not** only just; *siehe auch* **knapphalten**

Knappheit *f* tightness; scarcity; conciseness

knarren *vi* to creak

knattern ['knatərn] *vi* to rattle; (*Maschinengewehr*) to chatter

Knäuel ['knɔʏəl] (**-s, -**) *m od nt* (*Wollknäuel*) ball; (*Menschenknäuel*) knot

Knauf [knaʊf] (**-(e)s, Knäufe**) *m* knob; (*Schwertknauf*) pommel

knautschen ['knaʊtʃən] *vt, vi* to crumple

kneifen ['knaıfən] *unreg vt* to pinch ▷*vi* to pinch; (*sich drücken*) to back out; **vor etw** *dat* **~** to dodge sth

Kneipe ['knaıpə] (**-, -n**) (*umg*) *f* pub (*Brit*), bar, saloon (*US*)

Knete ['kne:tə] (*umg*) *f* (*Geld*) dough

kneten *vt* to knead; (*Wachs*) to mould (*Brit*), mold (*US*)

Knetmasse *f* Plasticine®

Knick [knık] (**-(e)s, -e**) *m* (*Sprung*) crack; (*Kurve*) bend; (*Falte*) fold

knicken *vt, vi* (*springen*) to crack; (*brechen*) to break; (*Papier*) to fold; **„nicht ~!"** "do not bend"; **geknickt sein** to be downcast

Knicks [knıks] (**-es, -e**) *m* curts(e)y; **knicksen** *vi* to curts(e)y

Knie [kni:] (**-s, -**) *nt* knee; **in die ~ gehen** to kneel; (*fig*) to be brought to one's knees; **Kniebeuge** (**-, -n**) *f* knee bend; **Kniefall** *m* genuflection; **Kniegelenk** *nt* knee joint; **Kniekehle** *f* back of the knee

knien *vi* to kneel ▷*vr*: **sich in die Arbeit ~** (*fig*) to get down to (one's) work

Kniescheibe *f* kneecap

Kniestrumpf *m* knee-length sock

kniff *etc* [knıf] *vb siehe* **kneifen**

knipsen ['knıpsən] *vt* (*Fahrkarte*) to punch; (*Phot*) to take a snap of, snap ▷*vi* (*Phot*) to take snaps/a snap

Knirps [knırps] (**-es, -e**) *m* little chap; **Er hat einen neuen ~® gekauft** He has bought a new Knirps® (*folding umbrella*)

knirschen ['knırʃən] *vi* to crunch; **mit den Zähnen ~** to grind one's teeth

knistern ['knıstərn] *vi* to crackle; (*Papier, Seide*) to rustle

Knitterfalte *f* crease

knitterfrei *adj* non-crease

knittern *vi* to crease

Knoblauch ['kno:plaʊx] (**-(e)s**) *m* garlic

Knöchel ['knœçəl] (**-s, -**) *m* knuckle; (*Fußknöchel*) ankle

Knochen ['knɔxən] (**-s, -**) *m* bone; **Knochenbau** *m* bone structure; **Knochenbruch** *m* fracture; **Knochengerüst** *nt* skeleton; **Knochenmark** *nt* bone marrow

knöchern ['knœçərn] *adj* bone

knochig ['knɔxıç] *adj* bony

Knödel ['knø:dəl] (**-s, -**) *m* dumpling

Knopf [knɔpf] (**-(e)s, ⸚e**) *m* button

knöpfen ['knœpfən] *vt* to button

Knopfloch *nt* buttonhole

Knorpel ['knɔrpəl] (**-s, -**) *m* cartilage, gristle

knorpelig *adj* gristly

Knospe ['knɔspə] (**-, -n**) *f* bud

knoten ['kno:tən] *vt* to knot; **Knoten** (**-s, -**) *m* knot; (*Haar*) bun; (*Bot*) node; (*Med*) lump

Knotenpunkt *m* junction

Knüller ['knʏlər] (**-s, -**) (*umg*) *m* hit; (*Reportage*) scoop

knüpfen ['knʏpfən] *vt* to tie; (*Teppich*) to knot;

(*Freundschaft*) to form
Knüppel ['knʏpəl] (**-s, -**) *m* cudgel; (*Polizeiknüppel*) baton, truncheon; (*Aviat*) (joy)stick; **jdm ~ zwischen die Beine werfen** (*fig*) to put a spoke in sb's wheel; **Knüppelschaltung** *f* (*Aut*) floor-mounted gear change
knurren ['knʊrən] *vi* (*Hund*) to snarl, growl; (*Magen*) to rumble; (*Mensch*) to mutter
knutschen ['knu:tʃən] (*umg*) *vt* to snog with ▷ *vi, vr* to snog
k. o. *adj* (*Sport*) knocked out; (*fig: umg*) whacked
Koalition [koalitsi'o:n] *f* coalition
Kobalt ['ko:balt] (**-s**) *nt* cobalt
Kobold ['ko:bɔlt] (**-(e)s, -e**) *m* imp
Kobra ['ko:bra] (**-, -s**) *f* cobra
Koch [kɔx] (**-(e)s, ¨-e**) *m* cook; **Kochbuch** *nt* cookery book, cookbook
kochen *vi* to cook; (*Wasser*) to boil ▷ *vt* (*Essen*) to cook; **er kochte vor Wut** (*umg*) he was seething; **etw auf kleiner Flamme ~** to simmer sth over a low heat
Kocher (**-s, -**) *m* stove, cooker
Köcher ['kœçər] (**-s, -**) *m* quiver
Kochgelegenheit *f* cooking facilities *pl*
Köchin ['kœçɪn] *f* cook
Koch- *zW*: **Kochlöffel** *m* kitchen spoon; **Kochnische** *f* kitchenette; **Kochplatte** *f* hotplate; **Kochsalz** *nt* cooking salt; **Kochtopf** *m* saucepan, pot; **Kochwäsche** *f* washing that can be boiled
Köder ['kø:dər] (**-s, -**) *m* bait, lure
Koexistenz [koɛksɪs'tɛnts] *f* coexistence
Koffein [kɔfe'i:n] (**-s**) *nt* caffeine; **koffeinfrei** *adj* decaffeinated
Koffer ['kɔfər] (**-s, -**) *m* suitcase; (*Schrankkoffer*) trunk; **die ~ packen** (*lit, fig*) to pack one's bags; **Kofferkuli** *m* (luggage) trolley (*Brit*), cart (*US*); **Kofferradio** *nt* portable radio; **Kofferraum** *m* (*Aut*) boot (*Brit*), trunk (*US*)
Kognak ['kɔnjak] (**-s, -s**) *m* brandy, cognac
Kohl [ko:l] (**-(e)s, -e**) *m* cabbage
Kohle ['ko:lə] (**-, -n**) *f* coal; (*Holzkohle*) charcoal; (*Chem*) carbon; (*umg: Geld*): **die ~n stimmen** the money's right; **Kohlehydrat** (**-(e)s, -e**) *nt* carbohydrate; **Kohlekraftwerk** *nt* coal-fired power station
Kohlen- *zW*: **Kohlendioxid** (**-(e)s, -e**) *nt* carbon dioxide; **Kohlenhändler** *m* coal merchant, coalman; **Kohlensäure** *f* carbon dioxide; **ein Getränk ohne Kohlensäure** a non-fizzy *od* still drink; **Kohlenstoff** *m* carbon
Kohlepapier *nt* carbon paper
Kohlestift *m* charcoal pencil
Kohlrübe *f* turnip
Koje ['ko:jə] (**-, -n**) *f* cabin; (*Bett*) bunk
Kokain [koka'i:n] (**-s**) *nt* cocaine
kokett [ko'kɛt] *adj* coquettish, flirtatious
Kokosnuss ['ko:kɔsnʊs] *f* coconut
Koks [ko:ks] (**-es, -e**) *m* coke
Kolben ['kɔlbən] (**-s, -**) *m* (*Gewehrkolben*) butt; (*Keule*) club; (*Chem*) flask; (*Tech*) piston; (*Maiskolben*) cob
Kolik ['ko:lɪk] *f* colic, gripe
Kollaps [kɔ'laps] (**-es, -e**) *m* collapse
Kolleg [kɔl'e:k] (**-s, -s** *od* **-ien**) *nt* lecture course
Kollege [kɔ'le:gə] (**-n, -n**) *m* colleague
Kollegium *nt* board; (*Sch*) staff
Kollekte [kɔ'lɛktə] (**-, -n**) *f* (*Rel*) collection
kollektiv [kɔlɛk'ti:f] *adj* collective
Kollision [kɔlizi'o:n] *f* collision; (*zeitlich*) clash
Köln [kœln] (**-s**) *nt* Cologne
Kölnischwasser *nt* eau de Cologne
Kolonie [kolo'ni:] *f* colony
kolonisieren [koloni'zi:rən] *vt* to colonize
Kolonne [ko'lɔnə] (**-, -n**) *f* column; (*von Fahrzeugen*) convoy
Koloss [ko'lɔs] (**-es, -e**) *m* colossus
kolossal [kolɔ'sa:l] *adj* colossal
Kolumbianer, in [kolʊmbi'a:nər(ɪn)] *m(f)* Columbian
kolumbianisch *adj* Columbian
Kolumbien [ko'lʊmbiən] (**-s**) *nt* Columbia
Koma ['ko:ma] (**-s, -s** *od* **-ta**) *nt* (*Med*) coma
Kombi ['kɔmbi] (**-s, -s**) *m* (*Aut*) estate (car) (*Brit*), station wagon (*US*)
Kombination [kɔmbinatsi'o:n] *f* combination; (*Vermutung*) conjecture; (*Hemdhose*) combinations *pl*; (*Aviat*) flying suit
kombinieren [kɔmbi'ni:rən] *vt* to combine ▷ *vi* to deduce, work out; (*vermuten*) to guess
Kombiwagen *m* (*Aut*) estate (car) (*Brit*), station wagon (*US*)
Kombizange *f* (pair of) pliers
Komet [ko'me:t] (**-en, -en**) *m* comet
Komfort [kɔm'fo:r] (**-s**) *m* luxury; (*von Möbel etc*) comfort; (*von Wohnung*) amenities *pl*; (*von Auto*) luxury features *pl*; (*von Gerät*) extras *pl*
Komik ['ko:mɪk] *f* humour (*Brit*), humor (*US*), comedy; **Komiker** (**-s, -**) *m* comedian
komisch ['ko:mɪʃ] *adj* funny; **mir ist so ~** (*umg*) I feel funny *od* strange *od* odd
Komitee [komi'te:] (**-s, -s**) *nt* committee
Komma ['kɔma] (**-s, -s** *od* **-ta**) *nt* comma; (*Math*) decimal point; **fünf ~ drei** five point three
Kommandant [kɔman'dant] *m* commander, commanding officer
kommandieren [kɔman'di:rən] *vt* to command ▷ *vi* to command; (*Befehle geben*) to give orders
Kommando [kɔ'mando] (**-s, -s**) *nt* command, order; (*Truppe*) detachment, squad; **auf ~** to order
kommen ['kɔmən] *unreg vi* to come; (*näher kommen*) to approach; (*passieren*) to happen; (*gelangen, geraten*) to get; (*Blumen, Zähne, Tränen etc*) to appear; (*in die Schule, ins Gefängnis etc*) to go; **was kommt diese Woche im Kino?** what's on at the cinema this week? ▷ *vi unpers*: **es kam eins zum anderen** one thing led to another; **~ lassen** to send for; **in Bewegung ~** to start moving; **jdn besuchen ~** to come and visit sb; **das kommt davon!** see what happens?; **du kommst mir**

gerade recht (*ironisch*) you're just what I need; **das kommt in den Schrank** that goes in the cupboard; **an etw** *akk* ~ (*berühren*) to touch sth; (*sich verschaffen*) to get hold of sth; **auf etw** *akk* ~ (*sich erinnern*) to think of sth; (*sprechen über*) to get onto sth; **das kommt auf die Rechnung** that goes onto the bill; **hinter etw** *akk* ~ (*herausfinden*) to find sth out; **zu sich** ~ to come round *od* to; **zu etw** ~ to acquire sth; **um etw** ~ to lose sth; **nichts auf jdn/etw ~ lassen** to have nothing said against sb/sth; **jdm frech** ~ to get cheeky with sb; **auf jeden vierten kommt ein Platz** there's one place to every fourth person; **mit einem Anliegen** ~ to have a request (to make); **wer kommt zuerst?** who's first?; **wer zuerst kommt, mahlt zuerst** (*Sprichwort*) first come first served; **unter ein Auto** ~ to be run over by a car; **das kommt zusammen auf 20 Euro** that comes to 20 euros altogether; **und so kam es, dass ...** and that is how it happened that ...; **daher kommt es, dass ...** that's why ...

Kommen (**-s**) *nt* coming

kommend *adj* (*Jahr, Woche, Generation*) coming; (*Ereignisse, Mode*) future; (*Trend*) upcoming; **(am) ~en Montag** next Monday

Kommentar [kɔmɛn'ta:r] *m* commentary; **kein** ~ no comment; **kommentarlos** *adj* without comment

Kommentator [kɔmɛn'ta:tɔr] *m* (*TV*) commentator

kommentieren [kɔmɛn'ti:rən] *vt* to comment on; **kommentierte Ausgabe** annotated edition

kommerziell [kɔmɛrtsi'ɛl] *adj* commercial

Kommissar [kɔmɪ'sa:r] *m* police inspector

Kommission [kɔmɪsi'o:n] *f* (*Comm*) commission; (*Ausschuss*) committee; **in ~ geben** to give (to a dealer) for sale on commission

Kommode [kɔ'mo:də] (**-, -n**) *f* (chest of) drawers

Kommunalwahlen *pl* local (government) elections *pl*

Kommune [kɔ'mu:nə] (**-, -n**) *f* commune

Kommunikation [kɔmunɪkatsi'o:n] *f* communication

Kommunion [kɔmuni'o:n] *f* communion

Kommuniqué [kɔmyni'ke:] (**-s, -s**) *nt* communiqué

Kommunismus [kɔmu'nɪsmʊs] *m* communism

Kommunist, in [kɔmu'nɪst(ɪn)] *m(f)* communist; **kommunistisch** *adj* communist

kommunizieren [kɔmuni'tsi:rən] *vi* to communicate; (*Eccl*) to receive communion

Komödie [ko'mø:diə] *f* comedy; **~ spielen** (*fig*) to put on an act

Kompagnon [kɔmpan'jõ:] (**-s, -s**) *m* (*Comm*) partner

kompakt [kɔm'pakt] *adj* compact

Kompanie [kɔmpa'ni:] *f* company

Kompass ['kɔmpas] (**-es, -e**) *m* compass

kompatibel [kɔmpa'ti:bəl] *adj* (*auch Comput*) compatible

Kompatibilität [kɔmpatibili'tɛ:t] *f* (*auch Comput*) compatibility

kompetent [kɔmpe'tɛnt] *adj* competent

Kompetenz *f* competence, authority

komplett [kɔm'plɛt] *adj* complete

Komplex (**-es, -e**) *m* complex

Komplikation [kɔmplikatsi'o:n] *f* complication

Kompliment [kɔmpli'mɛnt] *nt* compliment

Komplize [kɔm'pli:tsə] (**-n, -n**) *m* accomplice

komplizieren [kɔmpli'tsi:rən] *vt* to complicate

kompliziert *adj* complicated; (*Med: Bruch*) compound

Komplizin [kɔm'pli:tsɪn] *f* accomplice

komponieren [kɔmpo'ni:rən] *vt* to compose

Komponist, in [kɔmpo'nɪst(ɪn)] *m(f)* composer

Komposition [kɔmpozitsi'o:n] *f* composition

Kompost [kɔm'pɔst] (**-(e)s, -e**) *m* compost; **Komposthaufen** *m* compost heap

Kompott [kɔm'pɔt] (**-(e)s, -e**) *nt* stewed fruit

Kompresse [kɔm'prɛsə] (**-, -n**) *f* compress

Kompromiss [kɔmpro'mɪs] (**-es, -e**) *m* compromise; **einen ~ schließen** to compromise; **kompromissbereit** *adj* willing to compromise; **Kompromisslösung** *f* compromise solution

Kondensation [kɔndɛnzatsi'o:n] *f* condensation

Kondensator [kɔndɛn'za:tɔr] *m* condenser

kondensieren [kɔndɛn'zi:rən] *vt* to condense

Kondensmilch *f* condensed milk

Kondensstreifen *m* vapour (*Brit*) *od* vapor (*US*) trail

Kondition [kɔnditsi'o:n] *f* condition, shape; (*Durchhaltevermögen*) stamina

Konditionstraining *nt* fitness training

Konditor [kɔn'di:tɔr] *m* pastry-cook

Konditorei [kɔndito'raɪ] *f* cake shop; (*mit Café*) café

Kondom [kɔn'do:m] (**-s, -e**) *m or nt* condom

Konfektionskleidung *f* ready-to-wear *od* off-the-peg clothing

Konferenz [kɔnfe'rɛnts] *f* conference; (*Besprechung*) meeting; **Konferenzschaltung** *f* (*Tel*) conference circuit; (*Rundf, TV*) television *od* radio link-up

Konfession [kɔnfɛsi'o:n] *f* religion; (*christlich*) denomination; **konfessionell** [-'nɛl] *adj* denominational

konfessionslos *adj* non-denominational

Konfetti [kɔn'fɛti] (**-(s)**) *nt* confetti

Konfiguration [kɔnfiguratsi'o:n] *f* (*Comput*) configuration

Konfirmand, in [kɔnfɪr'mant, -'mandɪn] *m(f)* candidate for confirmation

Konfirmation [kɔnfɪrmatsi'o:n] *f* (*Eccl*) confirmation

konfirmieren [kɔnfɪr'mi:rən] *vt* to confirm

konfiszieren [kɔnfɪs'tsiːrən] *vt* to confiscate
Konfitüre [kɔnfi'tyːrə] (**-, -n**) *f* jam
Konflikt [kɔn'flɪkt] (**-(e)s, -e**) *m* conflict
Konfrontation [kɔnfrɔntatsi'oːn] *f* confrontation
konfrontieren [kɔnfrɔn'tiːrən] *vt* to confront
konfus [kɔn'fuːs] *adj* confused
Kongo ['kɔŋgo] (**-(s)**) *m* Congo
Kongress [kɔn'grɛs] (**-es, -e**) *m* congress
König ['køːnɪç] (**-(e)s, -e**) *m* king
Königin ['køːnɪgɪn] *f* queen
königlich *adj* royal ▷ *adv*: **sich ~ amüsieren** (*umg*) to have the time of one's life
Königreich *nt* kingdom
Königtum ['køːnɪçtuːm] (**-(e)s, -tümer**) *nt* kingship; (*Reich*) kingdom
Konjugation [kɔnjugatsi'oːn] *f* conjugation
konjugieren [kɔnju'giːrən] *vt* to conjugate
Konjunktion [kɔnjʊŋktsi'oːn] *f* conjunction
Konjunktiv ['kɔnjʊŋktiːf] (**-s, -e**) *m* subjunctive
Konjunktur [kɔnjʊŋk'tuːr] *f* economic situation; (*Hochkonjunktur*) boom; **steigende/ fallende ~** upward/downward economic trend
konkav [kɔn'kaːf] *adj* concave
konkret [kɔn'kreːt] *adj* concrete
Konkurrent, in [kɔnkʊ'rɛnt(ɪn)] *m(f)* competitor
Konkurrenz [kɔnkʊ'rɛnts] *f* competition; **jdm ~ machen** (*Comm, fig*) to compete with sb; **konkurrenzfähig** *adj* competitive; **Konkurrenzkampf** *m* competition; (*umg*) rat race
konkurrieren [kɔnkʊ'riːrən] *vi* to compete
Konkurs [kɔn'kʊrs] (**-es, -e**) *m* bankruptcy; **in ~ gehen** to go into receivership; **~ machen** (*umg*) to go bankrupt
können ['kœnən] (*pt* **konnte**, *pp* **gekonnt** *od* (*als Hilfsverb*) **können**) *vt, vi* **1** to be able to; **ich kann es machen** I can do it, I am able to do it; **ich kann es nicht machen** I can't do it, I'm not able to do it; **ich kann nicht ...** I can't ..., I cannot ...; **was können Sie?** what can you do?; **ich kann nicht mehr** I can't go on; **ich kann nichts dafür** I can't help it; **du kannst mich (mal)!** (*umg*) get lost!
2 (*wissen, beherrschen*) to know; **können Sie Deutsch?** can you speak German?; **er kann gut Englisch** he speaks English well; **sie kann keine Mathematik** she can't do mathematics
3 (*dürfen*) to be allowed to; **kann ich gehen?** can I go?; **könnte ich ...?** could I ...?; **kann ich mit?** (*umg*) can I come with you?
4 (*möglich sein*): **Sie könnten recht haben** you may be right; **das kann sein** that's possible; **kann sein** maybe
Können (**-s**) *nt* ability
konsequent [kɔnze'kvɛnt] *adj* consistent; **ein Ziel ~ verfolgen** to pursue an objective single-mindedly
Konsequenz [kɔnze'kvɛnts] *f* consistency; (*Folgerung*) conclusion; **die ~en tragen** to take the consequences; **(aus etw) die ~en ziehen** to take the appropriate steps
konservativ [kɔnzɛrva'tiːf] *adj* conservative
Konserve [kɔn'zɛrvə] (**-, -n**) *f* tinned (*Brit*) *od* canned food
Konservenbüchse *f*, **Konservendose** *f* tin (*Brit*), can
konservieren [kɔnzɛr'viːrən] *vt* to preserve
Konservierung *f* preservation
Konsonant [kɔnzo'nant] *m* consonant
konstant [kɔn'stant] *adj* constant
Konstellation [kɔnstɛlatsi'oːn] *f* constellation; (*fig*) line-up; (*von Faktoren etc*) combination
konstruieren [kɔnstru'iːrən] *vt* to construct
Konstrukteur, in [kɔnstrʊk'tøːr(ɪn)] *m(f)* designer
Konstruktion [kɔnstrʊktsi'on] *f* construction
konstruktiv [kɔnstrʊk'tiːf] *adj* constructive
Konsul ['kɔnzʊl] (**-s, -n**) *m* consul
Konsulat [kɔnzʊ'laːt] (**-(e)s, -e**) *nt* consulate
konsultieren [kɔnzʊl'tiːrən] *vt* to consult
Konsum[1] [kɔn'zuːm] (**-s**) *m* consumption
Konsum[2] ['kɔnzuːm] (**-s, -s**) *m* (*Genossenschaft*) cooperative society; (*Laden*) cooperative store, co-op (*umg*)
Konsumartikel *m* consumer article
Konsument [kɔnzu'mɛnt] *m* consumer
Konsumgesellschaft *f* consumer society
konsumieren [kɔnzu'miːrən] *vt* to consume
Kontakt [kɔn'takt] (**-(e)s, -e**) *m* contact; **mit jdm ~ aufnehmen** to get in touch with sb; **kontaktarm** *adj* unsociable; **kontaktfreudig** *adj* sociable; **Kontaktlinsen** *pl* contact lenses *pl*
kontern ['kɔntərn] *vt, vi* to counter
Kontinent [kɔnti'nɛnt] *m* continent
kontinuierlich [kɔntinu'iːrlɪç] *adj* continuous
Konto ['kɔnto] (**-s, Konten**) *nt* account; **das geht auf mein ~** (*umg: ich bin schuldig*) I am to blame for this; (*ich zahle*) this is on me (*umg*); **Kontoauszug** *m* statement (of account); **Kontoinhaber, in** *m(f)* account holder; **Kontostand** *m* bank balance
Kontra (**-s, -s**) *nt* (*Karten*) double; **jdm ~ geben** (*fig*) to contradict sb
Kontrabass *m* double bass
Kontrahent [-'hɛnt] *m* contracting party; (*Gegner*) opponent
Kontrapunkt *m* counterpoint
Kontrast [kɔn'trast] (**-(e)s, -e**) *m* contrast
Kontrolle [kɔn'trɔlə] (**-, -n**) *f* control, supervision; (*Passkontrolle*) passport control
Kontrolleur [kɔntrɔ'løːr] *m* inspector
kontrollieren [kɔntrɔ'liːrən] *vt* to control, supervise; (*nachprüfen*) to check
Kontroverse [kɔntro'vɛrzə] (**-, -n**) *f* controversy
Kontur [kɔn'tuːr] *f* contour
Konvention [kɔnvɛntsi'oːn] *f* convention
konventionell [kɔnvɛntsio'nɛl] *adj* conventional

Konversation [kɔnvɛrzatsi'o:n] *f* conversation
Konversationslexikon *nt* encyclopaedia
konvex [kɔn'vɛks] *adj* convex
Konvoi ['kɔnvɔʏ] (**-s, -s**) *m* convoy
Konzentrat [kɔntsɛn'tra:t] (**-s, -e**) *nt* concentrate
Konzentration [kɔntsɛntratsi'o:n] *f* concentration
Konzentrationslager *nt* concentration camp
konzentrieren [kɔntsɛn'tri:rən] *vt, vr* to concentrate
Konzern [kɔn'tsɛrn] (**-s, -e**) *m* combine
Konzert [kɔn'tsɛrt] (**-(e)s, -e**) *nt* concert; (*Stück*) concerto; **Konzertsaal** *m* concert hall
Konzession [kɔntsɛsi'o:n] *f* licence (*Brit*), license (*US*); (*Zugeständnis*) concession; **die ~ entziehen** *+dat: Comm*) to disenfranchise
Konzil [kɔn'tsi:l] (**-s, -e** *od* **-ien**) *nt* council
koordinieren [ko|ɔrdi'ni:rən] *vt* to coordinate
Kopf [kɔpf] (**-(e)s, ⸚e**) *m* head; **~ hoch!** chin up!; **~ an Kopf** shoulder to shoulder; (*Sport*) neck and neck; **pro ~** per person *od* head; **~ oder Zahl?** heads or tails?; **jdm den ~ waschen** (*fig: umg*) to give sb a piece of one's mind; **jdm über den ~ wachsen** (*lit*) to outgrow sb; (*fig: Sorgen etc*) to be more than sb can cope with; **jdn vor den ~ stoßen** to antagonize sb; **sich** *dat* **an den ~ fassen** (*fig*) to be speechless; **sich** *dat* **über etw** *akk* **den ~ zerbrechen** to rack one's brains over sth; **sich** *dat* **etw durch den ~ gehen lassen** to think about sth; **sich** *dat* **etw aus dem ~ schlagen** to put sth out of one's mind; **... und wenn du dich auf den ~ stellst!** (*umg*) ... no matter what you say/do!; **er ist nicht auf den ~ gefallen** he's no fool; **Kopfbedeckung** *f* headgear
Kopf- *zW*: **Kopfhaut** *f* scalp; **Kopfhörer** *m* headphone; **Kopfkissen** *nt* pillow; **kopflos** *adj* panic-stricken; **kopfrechnen** *vi* to do mental arithmetic; **Kopfsalat** *m* lettuce; **Kopfschmerzen** *pl* headache *sing*; **Kopfsprung** *m* header, dive; **Kopfstand** *m* headstand; **Kopftuch** *nt* headscarf; **Kopfweh** *nt* headache; **Kopfzerbrechen** *nt*: **jdm Kopfzerbrechen machen** to give sb a lot of headaches
Kopie [ko'pi:] *f* copy
kopieren [ko'pi:rən] *vt* to copy
Kopierer (**-s, -**) *m* (photo)copier
Koppel[1] ['kɔpəl] (**-, -n**) *f* (*Weide*) enclosure
Koppel[2] ['kɔpəl] (**-s, -**) *nt* (*Gürtel*) belt
koppeln *vt* to couple
Koppelung *f* coupling
Koppelungsmanöver *nt* docking manoeuvre (*Brit*) *od* maneuver (*US*)
Koralle [ko'ralə] (**-, -n**) *f* coral
Korallenriff *nt* coral reef
Korb [kɔrp] (**-(e)s,⸚e**) *m* basket; **jdm einen ~ geben** (*fig*) to turn sb down
Kord [kɔrt] (**-(e)s, -e** *od* **-s**) *m* = **Cord**
Kordel ['kɔrdəl] (**-, -n**) *f* cord, string
Korea [ko're:a] (**-s**) *nt* Korea
Korfu ['kɔrfu] (**-s**) *nt* Corfu
Kork [kɔrk] (**-(e)s, -e**) *m* cork
Korken (**-s, -**) *m* stopper, cork; **Korkenzieher** (**-s, -**) *m* corkscrew
Korn[1] [kɔrn] (**-(e)s, ⸚er**) *nt* corn, grain
Korn[2] [kɔrn] (**-(e)s, -e**) *nt* (*Gewehr*) sight; **etw aufs ~ nehmen** (*fig: umg*) to hit out at sth
Korn[3] [kɔrn] (**-, -s**) *m* (*Kornbranntwein*) corn schnapps
Kornblume *f* cornflower
Körper ['kœrper] (**-s, -**) *m* body; **Körperbau** *m* build; **körperbehindert** *adj* disabled; **Körpergeruch** *m* body odour (*Brit*) *od* odor (*US*); **Körpergewicht** *nt* weight; **Körpergröße** *f* height; **körperlich** *adj* physical; **körperliche Arbeit** manual work; **Körperpflege** *f* personal hygiene; **Körperschaft** *f* corporation; **Körperschaft des öffentlichen Rechts** public corporation *od* body; **Körperteil** *m* part of the body
korpulent [kɔrpu'lɛnt] *adj* corpulent
korrekt [kɔ'rɛkt] *adj* correct
Korrektor, in [kɔ'rɛktɔr, -'to:rɪn] (**-s, -**) *m(f)* proofreader
Korrektur [kɔrɛk'tu:r] *f* (*eines Textes*) proofreading; (*Text*) proof; (*Sch*) marking, correction; **(bei etw) ~ lesen** to proofread (sth)
Korrespondent, in [kɔrɛspɔn'dɛnt(ɪn)] *m(f)* correspondent
Korrespondenz [kɔrɛspɔn'dɛnts] *f* correspondence
Korridor ['kɔrido:r] (**-s, -e**) *m* corridor
korrigieren [kɔri'gi:rən] *vt* to correct; (*Meinung, Einstellung*) to change
Korrosion [kɔrozi'o:n] *f* corrosion
Korruption [kɔrʊptsi'o:n] *f* corruption
Korsett [kɔr'zɛt] (**-(e)s, -e**) *nt* corset
Korsika ['kɔrzika] (**-s**) *nt* Corsica
Koseform ['ko:zəfɔrm] *f* pet form
Kosename *m* pet name
Kosewort *nt* term of endearment
Kosmetik [kɔs'me:tɪk] *f* cosmetics *pl*
kosmetisch *adj* cosmetic; (*Chirurgie*) plastic
kosmisch ['kɔsmɪʃ] *adj* cosmic
Kosmonaut [kɔsmo'naʊt] (**-en, -en**) *m* cosmonaut
Kosmopolit [kɔsmopo'li:t] (**-en, -en**) *m* cosmopolitan; **kosmopolitisch** [-po'li:tiʃ] *adj* cosmopolitan
Kosmos ['kɔsmɔs] (**-**) *m* cosmos
Kost [kɔst] (**-**) *f* (*Nahrung*) food; (*Verpflegung*) board; **~ und Logis** board and lodging
kostbar *adj* precious; (*teuer*) costly, expensive; **Kostbarkeit** *f* preciousness; costliness, expensiveness; (*Wertstück*) treasure
Kosten *pl* cost(s); (*Ausgaben*) expenses *pl*; **auf ~ von** at the expense of; **auf seine ~ kommen** (*fig*) to get one's money's worth
kosten *vt* to cost; (*versuchen*) to taste ▷ *vi* to taste; **koste es, was es wolle** whatever the

cost
Kosten- *zW*: **kostenlos** *adj* free (of charge); **Kostenvoranschlag** *m* (costs) estimate
köstlich ['kœstlɪç] *adj* precious; (*Einfall*) delightful; (*Essen*) delicious; **sich ~ amüsieren** to have a marvellous time
Kostprobe *f* taste; (*fig*) sample
kostspielig *adj* expensive
Kostüm [kɔs'ty:m] (**-s, -e**) *nt* costume; (*Damenkostüm*) suit; **Kostümfest** *nt* fancy-dress party; **Kostümverleih** *m* costume agency
Kot [ko:t] (**-(e)s**) *m* excrement
Kotelett [kotə'lɛt] (**-(e)s, -e** *od* **-s**) *nt* cutlet, chop
Koteletten *pl* sideboards *pl* (*Brit*), sideburns *pl* (*US*)
Köter ['kø:tər] (**-s, -**) *m* cur
Kotflügel *m* (*Aut*) wing
kotzen ['kɔtsən] (*umg!*) *vi* to puke (*!*), throw up; **das ist zum K~** it makes you sick
Krabbe ['krabə] (**-, -n**) *f* shrimp
krabbeln *vi* to crawl
Krach [krax] (**-(e)s, -s** *od* **-e**) *m* crash; (*andauernd*) noise; (*umg*: *Streit*) quarrel, argument; **~ schlagen** to make a fuss; **krachen** *vi* to crash; (*beim Brechen*) to crack ▷ *vr* (*umg*) to argue, quarrel
krächzen ['krɛçtsən] *vi* to croak
kraft [kraft] *präp +gen* by virtue of
Kraft (**-, ¨-e**) *f* strength; (*von Stimme, fig*) power, force; (*Arbeitskraft*) worker; **mit vereinten Kräften werden wir ...** if we combine our efforts we will ...; **nach (besten) Kräften** to the best of one's abilities; **außer ~ sein** (*Jur*: *Geltung*) to be no longer in force; **in ~ treten** to come into effect
Kraftfahrer *m* motor driver
Kraftfahrzeug *nt* motor vehicle: **Kraftfahrzeugbrief** *m* (*Aut*) logbook (*Brit*), motor-vehicle registration certificate (*US*); **Kraftfahrzeugschein** *m* (*Aut*) car licence (*Brit*) *od* license (*US*); **Kraftfahrzeugsteuer** *f* ≈ road tax
kräftig ['krɛftɪç] *adj* strong; (*Suppe, Essen*) nourishing
Kraft- *zW*: **kraftlos** *adj* weak; powerless; (*Jur*) invalid; **Kraftprobe** *f* trial of strength; **Kraftrad** *nt* motorcycle; **kraftvoll** *adj* vigorous; **Kraftwagen** *m* motor vehicle; **Kraftwerk** *nt* power station
Kragen ['kra:gən] (**-s, -**) *m* collar; **da ist mir der ~ geplatzt** (*umg*) I blew my top; **es geht ihm an den ~** (*umg*) he's in for it; **Kragenweite** *f* collar size; **das ist nicht meine Kragenweite** (*fig*: *umg*) that's not my cup of tea
Krähe ['krɛ:ə] (**-, -n**) *f* crow
krähen *vi* to crow
krakeelen [kra'ke:lən] (*umg*) *vi* to make a din
Kralle ['kralə] (**-, -n**) *f* claw; (*Vogelkralle*) talon
Kram [kra:m] (**-(e)s**) *m* stuff, rubbish; **den ~ hinschmeißen** (*umg*) to chuck the whole thing; **kramen** *vi* to rummage; **Kramladen** (*pej*) *m* small shop
Krampf [krampf] (**-(e)s, ¨-e**) *m* cramp; (*zuckend*) spasm; (*Unsinn*) rubbish; **krampfhaft** *adj* convulsive; (*fig*: *Versuche*) desperate
Kran [kra:n] (**-(e)s, ¨-e**) *m* crane; (*Wasserkran*) tap (*Brit*), faucet (*US*)
Kranich ['kra:nɪç] (**-s, -e**) *m* (*Zool*) crane
krank [kraŋk] *adj* ill, sick; **das macht mich ~!** (*umg*) it gets on my nerves!, it drives me round the bend!; **sich ~ stellen** to pretend to be ill, malinger
Kranke, r *f*(*m*) sick person, invalid; (*Patient*) patient
kränkeln ['krɛŋkəln] *vi* to be in bad health
kränken ['krɛŋkən] *vt* to hurt
Kranken- *zW*: **Krankenbericht** *m* medical report; **Krankengeld** *nt* sick pay; **Krankengeschichte** *f* medical history; **Krankengymnastik** *f* physiotherapy; **Krankenhaus** *nt* hospital; **Krankenkasse** *f* health insurance; **Krankenpfleger** *m* orderly; (*mit Schwesternausbildung*) male nurse; **Krankenschein** *m* medical insurance certificate; **Krankenschwester** *f* nurse; **Krankenversicherung** *f* health insurance; **Krankenwagen** *m* ambulance
krankfeiern (*umg*) *vi* to be off sick; (*vortäuschend*) to skive (*Brit*)
krankhaft *adj* diseased; (*Angst etc*) morbid; **sein Geiz ist schon ~** his meanness is almost pathological
Krankheit *f* illness; disease; **nach langer schwerer ~** after a long serious illness
Krankheitserreger *m* disease-causing agent
kränklich ['krɛŋklɪç] *adj* sickly
krankmelden *vr* to let one's boss *etc* know that one is ill; (*telefonisch*) to phone in sick; (*bes Mil*) to report sick
krankschreiben *unreg vt* to give sb a medical certificate; (*bes Mil*) to put sb on the sick list
Kränkung *f* insult, offence (*Brit*), offense (*US*)
Kranz [krants] (**-es, ¨-e**) *m* wreath, garland
krass [kras] *adj* crass; (*Unterschied*) extreme
Krater ['kra:tər] (**-s, -**) *m* crater
Kratzbürste ['kratsbʏrstə] *f* (*fig*) crosspatch
kratzen ['kratsən] *vt, vi* to scratch; (*abkratzen*): **etw von etw ~** to scrape sth off sth
Kratzer (**-s, -**) *m* scratch; (*Werkzeug*) scraper; **kraulen** *vi* (*schwimmen*) to do the crawl ▷ *vt* (*streicheln*) to tickle
kraus [kraʊs] *adj* crinkly; (*Haar*) frizzy; (*Stirn*) wrinkled
Krause ['kraʊzə] (**-, -n**) *f* frill, ruffle
Kraut [kraʊt] (**-(e)s, Kräuter**) *nt* plant; (*Gewürz*) herb; (*Gemüse*) cabbage; **dagegen ist kein ~ gewachsen** (*fig*) there's nothing anyone can do about that; **ins ~ schießen** (*lit*) to run to seed; (*fig*) to get out of control; **wie ~ und Rüben** (*umg*) extremely untidy
Krawall [kra'val] (**-s, -e**) *m* row, uproar

Krawatte [kra'vatə] (**-, -n**) *f* tie
kreativ [krea'ti:f] *adj* creative
Kreativität [kreativi'tɛ:t] *f* creativity
Krebs [kre:ps] (**-es, -e**) *m* crab; (*Med*) cancer; (*Astrol*) Cancer
Kredit [kre'di:t] (**-(e)s, -e**) *m* credit; (*Darlehen*) loan; (*fig*) standing; **Kreditkarte** *f* credit card; **kreditwürdig** *adj* creditworthy
Kreide ['kraɪdə] (**-, -n**) *f* chalk; **bei jdm (tief) in der ~ stehen** to be (deep) in debt to sb; **kreidebleich** *adj* as white as a sheet
Kreis [kraɪs] (**-es, -e**) *m* circle; (*Stadtkreis etc*) district; **im ~ gehen** (*lit, fig*) to go round in circles; **(weite) ~e ziehen** (*fig*) to have (wide) repercussions; **weite ~e der Bevölkerung** wide sections of the population; **eine Feier im kleinen ~e** a celebration for a few close friends and relatives
kreischen ['kraɪʃən] *vi* to shriek, screech
Kreisel ['kraɪzəl] (**-s, -**) *m* top; (*Verkehrskreisel*) roundabout (*Brit*), traffic circle (*US*)
kreisen ['kraɪzən] *vi* to spin; (*fig: Gedanken, Gespräch*): **~ um** to revolve around
Kreislauf *m* (*Med*) circulation; (*fig: der Natur etc*) cycle; **Kreislaufstörungen** *pl* circulation trouble *sing*
Kreißsaal ['kraɪsza:l] *m* delivery room
Kreisstadt *f* ≈ county town
Kreisverkehr *m* roundabout (*Brit*), traffic circle (*US*)
Krematorium [krema'to:riʊm] *nt* crematorium
Kreml ['kre:ml] (**-s**) *m*: **der ~** the Kremlin
krepieren [kre'pi:rən] (*umg*) *vi* (*sterben*) to die, kick the bucket
Krepp [krɛp] (**-s, -s** *od* **-e**) *m* crêpe
Krepppapier *nt* crêpe paper
Kreppsohle *f* crêpe sole
Kresse ['krɛsə] (**-, -n**) *f* cress
Kreta ['kre:ta] (**-s**) *nt* Crete
Kreuz (**-es, -e**) *nt* cross; (*Anat*) small of the back; (*Karten*) clubs; (*Mus*) sharp; (*Autobahnkreuz*) intersection; **zu ~e kriechen** (*fig*) to eat humble pie, eat crow (*US*); **jdn aufs ~ legen** to throw sb on his back; (*fig: umg*) to take sb for a ride
kreuzen *vt* to cross ▷ *vr* to cross; (*Meinungen etc*) to clash ▷ *vi* (*Naut*) to cruise; **die Arme ~** to fold one's arms
Kreuzer (**-s, -**) *m* (*Schiff*) cruiser
Kreuz- *zW*: **Kreuzfahrt** *f* cruise; **Kreuzgang** *m* cloisters *pl*
kreuzigen *vt* to crucify
Kreuzigung *f* crucifixion
Kreuzotter *f* adder
Kreuzung *f* (*Verkehrskreuzung*) crossing, junction; (*Züchtung*) cross
Kreuz- *zW*: **Kreuzverhör** *nt* cross-examination; **ins Kreuzverhör nehmen** to cross-examine; **Kreuzworträtsel** *nt* crossword puzzle; **Kreuzzeichen** *nt* sign of the cross; **Kreuzzug** *m* crusade
kriechen ['kri:çən] *unreg vi* to crawl, creep; (*pej*) to grovel, crawl
Kriecher (**-s, -**) *m* crawler
Kriechspur *f* crawler lane (*Brit*)
Kriechtier *nt* reptile
Krieg [kri:k] (**-(e)s, -e**) *m* war; **~ führen (mit *od* gegen)** to wage war (on)
kriegen ['kri:gən] (*umg*) *vt* to get; **kriegerisch** *adj* warlike
Kriegs- *zW*: **Kriegsdienstverweigerer** *m* conscientious objector; **Kriegserklärung** *f* declaration of war; **Kriegsfuß** *m*: **mit jdm/etw auf Kriegsfuß stehen** to be at loggerheads with sb/not to get on with sth; **Kriegsgefangene, r** *f(m)* prisoner of war; **Kriegsgefangenschaft** *f* captivity; **Kriegsgericht** *nt* court-martial; **Kriegsschiff** *nt* warship; **Kriegsschuld** *f* war guilt; **Kriegsverbrecher** *m* war criminal; **Kriegsversehrte, r** *f(m)* person disabled in the war; **Kriegszustand** *m* state of war
Krim [krɪm] *f*: **die ~** the Crimea
Krimi ['kri:mi] (**-s, -s**) (*umg*) *m* thriller; **Kriminalbeamte, r** *m* detective
Kriminalität [kriminali'tɛ:t] *f* criminality
Kriminalpolizei *f* ≈ Criminal Investigation Department (*Brit*), ≈ Federal Bureau of Investigation (*US*)
Kriminalroman *m* detective story
kriminell [kri:mi'nɛl] *adj* criminal
Kriminelle, r *f(m)* criminal
Krimskrams ['krɪmskrams] (**-es**) (*umg*) *m* odds and ends *pl*
Kripo ['kri:po] (**-, -s**) *f abk* (= *Kriminalpolizei*) ≈ CID (*Brit*), ≈ FBI (*US*)
Krippe ['krɪpə] (**-, -n**) *f* manger, crib; (*Kinderkrippe*) crèche
Krise ['kri:zə] (**-, -n**) *f* crisis
kriseln *vi*: **es kriselt** there's a crisis looming, there is trouble brewing
Krisenstab *m* action *od* crisis committee
Kristall[1] [krɪs'tal] (**-s, -e**) *m* crystal
Kristall[2] (**-s**) *nt* (*Glas*) crystal
Kriterium [kri'te:riʊm] *nt* criterion
Kritik [kri'ti:k] *f* criticism; (*Zeitungskritik*) review, write-up; **an jdm/etw ~ üben** to criticize sb/sth; **unter aller ~ sein** (*umg*) to be beneath contempt
Kritiker, in ['kri:tikər(ɪn)] (**-s, -**) *m(f)* critic
kritiklos *adj* uncritical
kritisch ['kri:tɪʃ] *adj* critical
kritisieren [kriti'zi:rən] *vt, vi* to criticize
kritzeln ['krɪtsəln] *vt, vi* to scribble, scrawl
Kroatien [kro'a:tsiən] (**-s**) *nt* Croatia
kroatisch *adj* Croatian
kroch *etc* [krɔx] *vb siehe* **kriechen**
Krokodil [kroko'di:l] (**-s, -e**) *nt* crocodile
Krokus ['kro:kʊs] (**-, -** *od* **-se**) *m* crocus
Krone ['kro:nə] (**-, -n**) *f* crown; (*Baumkrone*) top; **einen in der ~ haben** (*umg*) to be tipsy
krönen ['krø:nən] *vt* to crown
Kron- *zW*: **Kronkorken** *m* bottle top; **Kronleuchter** *m* chandelier; **Kronprinz** *m* crown prince

Krönung ['krø:nʊŋ] *f* coronation
Kropf [krɔpf] (**-(e)s, ⸚e**) *m* (*Med*) goitre (*Brit*), goiter (*US*); (*von Vogel*) crop
Kröte ['krø:tə] (**-, -n**) *f* toad; **Kröten** *pl* (*umg: Geld*) pennies *pl*
Krücke ['krʏkə] (**-, -n**) *f* crutch
Krug [kru:k] (**-(e)s, ⸚e**) *m* jug; (*Bierkrug*) mug
Krümel ['kry:məl] (**-s, -**) *m* crumb
krümeln *vt, vi* to crumble
krumm [krʊm] *adj* (*lit, fig*) crooked; (*kurvig*) curved; **keinen Finger ~ machen** (*umg*) not to lift a finger; **ein ~es Ding drehen** (*umg*) to do something crooked; *siehe auch* **krummnehmen**; **krummbeinig** *adj* bandy-legged
krummlachen (*umg*) *vr* to laugh o.s. silly; **sich krumm- und schieflachen** to fall about laughing
krummnehmen *unreg* (*umg*) *vt*: **jdm etw ~** (*umg*) to take sth amiss
Krümmung *f* bend, curve
Krüppel ['krʏpəl] (**-s, -**) *m* cripple
Kruste ['krʊstə] (**-, -n**) *f* crust
Kruzifix [krutsi'fɪks] (**-es, -e**) *nt* crucifix
Kuba ['ku:ba] (**-s**) *nt* Cuba
Kubaner, in [ku'ba:nər(ɪn)] (**-s, -**) *m(f)* Cuban
kubanisch [ku'ba:nɪʃ] *adj* Cuban
Kübel ['ky:bəl] (**-s, -**) *m* tub; (*Eimer*) pail; **Kubikmeter** *m* cubic metre (*Brit*) *od* meter (*US*)
Küche ['kʏçə] (**-, -n**) *f* kitchen; (*Kochen*) cooking, cuisine
Kuchen ['ku:xən] (**-s, -**) *m* cake; **Kuchenblech** *nt* baking tray; **Kuchenform** *f* baking tin (*Brit*) *od* pan (*US*); **Kuchengabel** *f* pastry fork
Küchen- *zW*: **Küchenherd** *m* cooker, stove; **Küchenmaschine** *f* food processor; **Küchenschabe** *f* cockroach; **Küchenschrank** *m* kitchen cabinet
Kuckuck ['kʊkʊk] (**-s, -e**) *m* cuckoo; (*umg: Siegel des Gerichtsvollziehers*) bailiff's seal (*for distraint of goods*); **das weiß der ~** heaven (only) knows
Kuddelmuddel ['kʊdəlmʊdəl] (**-s**) (*umg*) *m od nt* mess
Kufe ['ku:fə] (**-, -n**) *f* (*Fasskufe*) vat; (*Schlittenkufe*) runner; (*Aviat*) skid
Kugel ['ku:gəl] (**-, -n**) *f* ball; (*Math*) sphere; (*Mil*) bullet; (*Erdkugel*) globe; (*Sport*) shot; **eine ruhige ~ schieben** (*umg*) to have a cushy number; **kugelförmig** *adj* spherical; **Kugelkopfschreibmaschine** *f* golf-ball typewriter; **Kugellager** *nt* ball bearing; **kugelrund** *adj* (*Gegenstand*) round; (*umg: Person*) tubby; **Kugelschreiber** *m* ball-point (pen), Biro®; **kugelsicher** *adj* bulletproof; **Kugelstoßen** (**-s**) *nt* shot put
Kuh [ku:] (**-, ⸚e**) *f* cow
kühl [ky:l] *adj* (*lit, fig*) cool; **Kühlanlage** *f* refrigeration plant
Kühle (-) *f* coolness
kühlen *vt* to cool
Kühler (**-s, -**) *m* (*Aut*) radiator; **Kühlerhaube** *f* (*Aut*) bonnet (*Brit*), hood (*US*)
Kühl- *zW*: **Kühlhaus** *nt* cold-storage depot; **Kühlraum** *m* cold-storage chamber; **Kühlschrank** *m* refrigerator; **Kühltruhe** *f* freezer
Kühlung *f* cooling
Kühlwagen *m* (*Lastwagen, Eisenb*) refrigerator van
Kühlwasser *nt* coolant
kühn [ky:n] *adj* bold, daring; **Kühnheit** *f* boldness
Küken ['ky:kən] (**-s, -**) *nt* chicken; (*umg: Nesthäkchen*) baby of the family
kulant [ku'lant] *adj* obliging
Kuli ['ku:li] (**-s, -s**) *m* coolie; (*umg: Kugelschreiber*) Biro®
Kulisse [ku'lɪsə] (**-, -n**) *f* scene
kullern ['kʊlərn] *vi* to roll
Kult [kʊlt] (**-(e)s, -e**) *m* worship, cult; **mit etw ~ treiben** to make a cult out of sth
kultivieren [kʊlti'vi:rən] *vt* to cultivate
kultiviert *adj* cultivated, refined
Kultur [kʊl'tu:r] *f* culture; (*Lebensform*) civilization; (*des Bodens*) cultivation; **Kulturbeutel** *m* toilet bag (*Brit*), washbag
kulturell [kʊltu'rɛl] *adj* cultural
Kulturfilm *m* documentary film
Kultusminister ['kʊltʊsminɪstər] *m* minister of education and the arts
Kümmel ['kʏməl] (**-s, -**) *m* caraway seed; (*Branntwein*) kümmel
Kummer ['kʊmər] (**-s**) *m* grief, sorrow
kümmerlich ['kʏmərlɪç] *adj* miserable, wretched
kümmern *vr*: **sich um jdn ~** to look after sb ▷ *vt* to concern; **sich um etw ~** to see to sth; **das kümmert mich nicht** that doesn't worry me
Kumpel ['kʊmpəl] (**-s, -**) (*umg*) *m* mate
Kunde[1] ['kʊndə] (**-n, -n**) *m* customer
Kunde[2] ['kʊndə] (**-, -n**) *f* (*Botschaft*) news
Kundendienst *m* after-sales service
Kund- *zW*: **kundgeben** *unreg vt* to announce; **Kundgebung** *f* announcement; (*Versammlung*) rally
kündigen ['kʏndɪgən] *vi* to give in one's notice ▷ *vt* to cancel; **jdm ~** to give sb his notice; **zum 1. April ~** to give one's notice for April 1st; (*Mieter*) to give notice for April 1st; (*bei Mitgliedschaft*) to cancel one's membership as of April 1st; **(jdm) die Stellung ~** to give (sb) notice; **sie hat ihm die Freundschaft gekündigt** she has broken off their friendship
Kündigung *f* notice
Kündigungsfrist *f* period of notice
Kundin *f* customer
Kundschaft *f* customers *pl*, clientele
künftig ['kʏnftɪç] *adj* future ▷ *adv* in future
Kunst [kʊnst] (**-, ⸚e**) *f* (*auch Sch*) art; (*Können*) skill; **das ist doch keine ~** it's easy; **mit seiner ~ am Ende sein** to be at one's wits' end; **das ist eine**

brotlose ~ there's no money in that; **Kunstdruck** *m* art print; **Kunstdünger** *m* artificial manure; **Kunstfaser** *f* synthetic fibre (*Brit*) *od* fiber (*US*); **Kunstfehler** *m* professional error; (*weniger ernst*) slip; **Kunstfertigkeit** *f* skilfulness (*Brit*), skillfulness (*US*); **Kunstgeschichte** *f* history of art; **Kunstgewerbe** *nt* arts and crafts *pl*; **Kunsthändler** *m* art dealer; **Kunstharz** *nt* artificial resin

Künstler, in ['kʏnstlər(ɪn)] (**-s, -**) *m(f)* artist; **künstlerisch** *adj* artistic; **Künstlername** *m* pseudonym; (*von Schauspieler*) stage name

künstlich ['kʏnstlɪç] *adj* artificial; **~e Intelligenz** (*Comput*) artificial intelligence; **sich ~ aufregen** (*umg*) to get all worked up about nothing

Kunst- *zW*: **Kunstsammler** *m* art collector; **Kunstseide** *f* artificial silk; **Kunststoff** *m* synthetic material; **Kunststopfen** (**-s**) *nt* invisible mending; **Kunststück** *nt* trick; **das ist kein Kunststück** (*fig*) there's nothing to it; **Kunstturnen** *nt* gymnastics *sing*; **kunstvoll** *adj* artistic; **Kunstwerk** *nt* work of art

kunterbunt ['kʊntərbʊnt] *adj* higgledy-piggledy

Kupfer ['kʊpfər] (**-s, -**) *nt* copper; **Kupfergeld** *nt* coppers *pl*

kupfern *adj* copper ▷ *vt* (*fig: umg*) to plagiarize, copy, imitate

Kuppe ['kʊpə] (**-, -n**) *f* (*Bergkuppe*) top; (*Fingerkuppe*) tip

Kuppel (**-, -n**) *f* cupola, dome

Kuppelei [kʊpə'laɪ] *f* (*Jur*) procuring

kuppeln *vi* (*Jur*) to procure; (*Aut*) to operate *od* use the clutch ▷ *vt* to join

Kupplung *f* (*auch Tech*) coupling; (*Aut etc*) clutch; **die ~ (durch)treten** to disengage the clutch

Kur [kuːr] (**-, -en**) *f* (*im Kurort*) (health) cure, (course of) treatment; (*Schlankheitskur*) diet; **eine ~ machen** to take a cure (in a health resort)

Kür [kyːr] (**-, -en**) *f* (*Sport*) free exercises *pl*

Kurbel ['kʊrbəl] (**-, -n**) *f* crank, winder; (*Aut*) starting handle; **Kurbelwelle** *f* crankshaft

Kürbis ['kʏrbɪs] (**-ses, -se**) *m* pumpkin; (*exotisch*) gourd

Kurde ['kʊrdə] (**-n, -n**) *m*, **Kurdin** *f* Kurd

Kurgast *m* visitor (to a health resort)

Kurier [ku'riːr] (**-s, -e**) *m* courier, messenger

kurieren [ku'riːrən] *vt* to cure

kurios [kuri'oːs] *adj* curious, odd

Kuriosität [kuriozi'tɛːt] *f* curiosity

Kur- *zW*: **Kurort** *m* health resort; **Kurpfuscher** *m* quack

Kurs [kʊrs] (**-es, -e**) *m* course; (*Fin*) rate; **hoch im ~ stehen** (*fig*) to be highly thought of; **einen ~ besuchen** *od* **mitmachen** to attend a class; **harter/weicher ~** (*Pol*) hard/soft line; **Kursbuch** *nt* timetable

kursiv *adv* in italics

Kurswagen *m* (*Eisenb*) through carriage

Kurtaxe *f* spa tax (*paid by visitors*)

Kurve ['kʊrvə] (**-, -n**) *f* curve; (*Straßenkurve*) bend; (*statistisch, Fieberkurve etc*) graph; **die ~ nicht kriegen** (*umg*) not to get around to it

kurvenreich *adj*: **„~e Strecke"** "bends"

kurz [kʊrts] *adj* short ▷ *adv*: **~ und bündig** concisely; **zu ~ kommen** to come off badly; **den Kürzeren ziehen** to get the worst of it; **~ und gut** in short; **über ~ oder lang** sooner or later; **eine Sache ~ abtun** to dismiss sth out of hand; **~ gefasst** concise; **darf ich mal ~ stören?** could I just interrupt for a moment?; *siehe auch* **kurzfassen; kurzhalten; kurztreten**

Kurzarbeit *f* short-time work

Kürze ['kʏrtsə] (**-, -n**) *f* shortness, brevity

kürzen *vt* to cut short; (*in der Länge*) to shorten; (*Gehalt*) to reduce

kurzerhand ['kʊrtsər'hant] *adv* without further ado; (*entlassen*) on the spot

kurz- *zW*: **kurzfristig** *adj* short-term; **kurzfristige Verbindlichkeiten** current liabilities *pl*; **Kurzgeschichte** *f* short story; **kurzhalten** *unreg vt* to keep short; **kurzlebig** *adj* short-lived

kürzlich ['kʏrtslɪc] *adv* lately, recently

Kurz- *zW*: **Kurzschluss** *m* (*Elek*) short circuit; **Kurzschrift** *f* shorthand; **kurzsichtig** *adj* short-sighted

Kurzwaren *pl* haberdashery (*Brit*), notions *pl* (*US*)

Kurzwelle *f* short wave

kuscheln ['kʊʃəln] *vr* to snuggle up

Kusine [ku'ziːnə] *f* cousin

Kuss [kʊs] (**-es, ¨-e**) *m* kiss

küssen ['kʏsən] *vt, vr* to kiss

Küste ['kʏstə] (**-, -n**) *f* coast, shore

Küstenwache *f* coastguard (station)

Küster ['kʏstər] (**-s, -**) *m* sexton, verger

Kutsche ['kʊtʃə] (**-, -n**) *f* coach, carriage

Kutscher (**-s, -**) *m* coachman

Kutte ['kʊtə] (**-, -n**) *f* cowl

Kuvert [ku'vɛrt] (**-s, -e** *od* **-s**) *nt* envelope; (*Gedeck*) cover

Kuwait [ku'vaɪt] (**-s**) *nt* Kuwait

Kybernetik [kybɛr'neːtɪk] *f* cybernetics *sing*

kybernetisch [kybɛr'neːtɪʃ] *adj* cybernetic

KZ (**-s, -s**) *nt abk* = **Konzentrationslager**

L l

L, l¹ [ɛl] *nt* L, l; **L wie Ludwig** ≈ L for Lucy, ≈ L for Love (*US*)
l² [ɛl] *abk* (= *Liter*) l
labil [la'bi:l] *adj* (*physisch: Gesundheit*) delicate; (*: Kreislauf*) poor; (*psychisch*) unstable
Labor [la'bo:r] (**-s, -e** *od* **-s**) *nt* lab(oratory)
Laborant, in [labo'rant(ɪn)] *m(f)* lab(oratory) assistant
Labyrinth [laby'rɪnt] (**-s, -e**) *nt* labyrinth
lächeln ['lɛçəln] *vi* to smile; **Lächeln** (**-s**) *nt* smile
lachen ['laxən] *vi* to laugh; **mir ist nicht zum L~ (zumute)** I'm in no laughing mood; **dass ich nicht lache!** (*umg*) don't make me laugh!; **das wäre doch gelacht** it would be ridiculous; **Lachen** *nt*: **dir wird das Lachen schon noch vergehen!** you'll soon be laughing on the other side of your face
lächerlich ['lɛçərlɪç] *adj* ridiculous
Lach- *zW*: **Lachgas** *nt* laughing gas; **lachhaft** *adj* laughable
Lachs [laks] (**-es, -e**) *m* salmon
Lack [lak] (**-(e)s, -e**) *m* lacquer, varnish; (*von Auto*) paint
lackieren [la'ki:rən] *vt* to varnish; (*Auto*) to spray
Lackierer [la'ki:rər] (**-s, -**) *m* varnisher
Lackleder *nt* patent leather
Lackmus ['lakmʊs] (**-**) *m od nt* litmus
Laden ['la:dən] (**-s, ¨**) *m* shop; (*Fensterladen*) shutter; (*umg: Betrieb*) outfit; **der ~ läuft** (*umg*) business is good
laden ['la:dən] *unreg vt* (*Lasten, Comput*) to load; (*Jur*) to summon; (*einladen*) to invite; **eine schwere Schuld auf sich** *akk* **~** to place o.s. under a heavy burden of guilt
Laden- *zW*: **Ladendieb** *m* shoplifter; **Ladendiebstahl** *m* shoplifting; **Ladenschluss** *m*, **Ladenschlusszeit** *f* closing time; **Ladentisch** *m* counter
lädieren [lɛ'di:rən] *vt* to damage
Ladung ['la:dʊŋ] *f* (*Last*) cargo, load; (*Beladen*) loading; (*Jur*) summons; (*Einladung*) invitation; (*Sprengladung*) charge
lag *etc* [la:k] *vb siehe* **liegen**
Lage ['la:gə] (**-, -n**) *f* position, situation; (*Schicht*) layer; **in der ~ sein** to be in a position; **eine gute/ruhige ~ haben** to be in a good/peaceful location; **Herr der ~ sein** to be in control of the situation
Lager ['la:gər] (**-s, -**) *nt* camp; (*Comm*) warehouse; (*Schlaflager*) bed; (*von Tier*) lair; (*Tech*) bearing; **etw auf ~ haben** to have sth in stock; **Lagerhaus** *nt* warehouse, store
lagern ['la:gərn] *vi* (*Dinge*) to be stored; (*Menschen*) to camp; (*auch vr: rasten*) to lie down ▷ *vt* to store; (*betten*) to lay down; (*Maschine*) to bed
Lagune [la'gu:nə] (**-, -n**) *f* lagoon
lahm [la:m] *adj* lame; (*umg: langsam, langweilig*) dreary, dull; (*Geschäftsgang*) slow, sluggish; **eine ~e Ente sein** (*umg*) to have no zip; *siehe auch* **lahmlegen**
lahmen *vi* to be lame, limp
lähmen ['lɛ:mən], **lahmlegen** *vt* to paralyse (*Brit*), paralyze (*US*)
Lähmung *f* paralysis
Laib [laɪp] (**-s, -e**) *m* loaf
Laie ['laɪə] (**-n, -n**) *m* layman; (*fig, Theat*) amateur
laienhaft *adj* amateurish
Laken ['la:kən] (**-s, -**) *nt* sheet
Lakritze [la'krɪtsə] (**-, -n**) *f* liquorice
lallen ['lalən] *vt, vi* to slur; (*Baby*) to babble
Lama ['la:ma] (**-s, -s**) *nt* llama
Lamelle [la'mɛlə] *f* lamella; (*Elek*) lamina; (*Tech*) plate
Lamm [lam] (**-(e)s, ¨er**) *nt* lamb
Lampe ['lampə] (**-, -n**) *f* lamp
Lampenfieber *nt* stage fright
Lampenschirm *m* lampshade
Lampion [lampi'õ:] (**-s, -s**) *m* Chinese lantern
Land [lant] (**-(e)s, ¨er**) *nt* land; (*Nation, nicht Stadt*) country; (*Bundesland*) state; **auf dem ~(e)** in the country; **an ~ gehen** to go ashore; **endlich sehe ich ~** (*fig*) at last I can see the light at the end of the tunnel; **einen Auftrag an ~ ziehen** (*umg*) to land an order; **aus aller Herren Länder** from all over the world; *siehe auch* **hierzulande**
Landbesitz *m* landed property
Landebahn *f* runway
landen ['landən] *vt, vi* to land; **mit deinen Komplimenten kannst du bei mir nicht ~** your compliments won't get you anywhere with me
Landes- *zW*: **Landesfarben** *pl* national colours *pl* (*Brit*) *od* colors *pl* (*US*); **Landesinnere,**

s *nt* inland region; **Landesverweisung** *f* banishment; **Landeswährung** *f* national currency
Land- *zW*: **Landhaus** *nt* country house; **Landkarte** *f* map; **Landkreis** *m* administrative region
ländlich ['lɛntlɪç] *adj* rural
Land- *zW*: **Landschaft** *f* countryside; (*Kunst*) landscape; **die politische Landschaft** the political scene; **landschaftlich** *adj* scenic; (*Besonderheiten*) regional
Landsmann (**-(e)s**, *pl* **-leute**) *m* compatriot, fellow countryman
Land- *zW*: **Landstraße** *f* country road; **Landstreicher** (**-s, -**) *m* tramp; **Landstrich** *m* region; **Landtag** *m* (*Pol*) regional parliament
Landung ['landʊŋ] *f* landing
Landungs- *zW*: **Landungsbrücke** *f* jetty, pier; **Landungsstelle** *f* landing place
Land- *zW*: **Landwirt** *m* farmer; **Landwirtschaft** *f* agriculture; **Landwirtschaft betreiben** to farm; **Landzunge** *f* spit
lang [laŋ] *adj* long; (*umg*: *Mensch*) tall ▷ *adv*: **~ anhaltender Beifall** prolonged applause; **~ ersehnt** longed-for; **hier wird mir die Zeit nicht ~** I won't get bored here; **er machte ein ~es Gesicht** his face fell; **~ und breit** at great length; **langatmig** *adj* long-winded
lange *adv* for a long time; (*dauern, brauchen*) a long time; **~ nicht so ...** not nearly as ...; **wenn der das schafft, kannst du das schon ~** if he can do it, you can do it easily
Länge ['lɛŋə] (**-, -n**) *f* length; (*Geog*) longitude; **etw der ~ nach falten** to fold sth lengthways; **etw in die ~ ziehen** to drag sth out (*umg*); **der ~ nach hinfallen** to fall flat (on one's face)
langen ['laŋən] *vi* (*ausreichen*) to do, suffice; (*fassen*): **~ nach** to reach for; **es langt mir** I've had enough; **jdm eine ~** (*umg*) to give sb a clip on the ear
Längengrad *m* longitude
Längenmaß *nt* linear measure
Langeweile *f* boredom
lang- *zW*: **langfristig** *adj* long-term ▷ *adv* in the long term; (*planen*) for the long term; **langfristige Verbindlichkeiten** long-term liabilities *pl*; **Langlauf** *m* (*Ski*) cross-country skiing; **langlebig** *adj* long-lived; **langlebige Gebrauchsgüter** consumer durables *pl*
länglich *adj* longish
längs [lɛŋs] *präp* (*+gen od dat*) along ▷ *adv* lengthways
langsam *adj* slow; **immer schön ~!** (*umg*) easy does it!; **ich muss jetzt ~ gehen** I must be getting on my way; **~ (aber sicher) reicht es mir** I've just about had enough; **Langsamkeit** *f* slowness
Langschläfer *m* late riser
Langspielplatte *f* long-playing record
längst [lɛŋst] *adv*: **das ist ~ fertig** that was finished a long time ago, that has been finished for a long time
längste, r, s *adj* longest
Languste [laŋ'gʊstə] (**-, -n**) *f* crayfish, crawfish (*US*)
lang- *zW*: **langweilen** *vt untr* to bore ▷ *vr untr* to be *od* get bored; **langweilig** *adj* boring, tedious; **Langwelle** *f* long wave; **langwierig** *adj* lengthy, long-drawn-out
Lanze ['lantsə] (**-, -n**) *f* lance
Laos ['la:ɔs] (**-**) *nt* Laos
laotisch [la'o:tɪʃ] *adj* Laotian
Lappalie [la'pa:liə] *f* trifle
Lappen (**-s, -**) *m* cloth, rag; (*Anat*) lobe; **jdm durch die ~ gehen** (*umg*) to slip through sb's fingers
läppisch ['lɛpɪʃ] *adj* foolish
Lappland ['laplant] (**-s**) *nt* Lapland
Lapsus ['lapsʊs] (**-, -**) *m* slip
Laptop ['lɛptɔp] (**-s, -s**) *m* laptop
Lärche ['lɛrçə] (**-, -n**) *f* larch
Lärm [lɛrm] (**-(e)s**) *m* noise; **lärmen** *vi* to be noisy, make a noise
Larve ['larfə] (**-, -n**) *f* mask; (*Biol*) larva
Laser ['le:zər] (**-s, -**) *m* laser; **Laserdrucker** *m* laser printer
lassen ['lasən] (*pt* **ließ**, *pp* **gelassen** *od* (*als Hilfsverb*) **lassen**) *vt* **1** (*unterlassen*) to stop; (*momentan*) to leave; **lass das (sein)!** don't (do it)!; (*hör auf*) stop it!; **lass mich!** leave me alone!; **lassen wir das!** let's leave it; **er kann das Trinken nicht lassen** he can't stop drinking; **tu, was du nicht lassen kannst!** if you must, you must!
2 (*zurücklassen*) to leave; **etw lassen, wie es ist** to leave sth (just) as it is
3 (*erlauben*) to let, allow; **lass ihn doch** let him; **jdn ins Haus lassen** to let sb into the house; **das muss man ihr lassen** (*zugestehen*) you've got to grant her that
▷ *vi*: **lass mal, ich mache das schon** leave it, I'll do it
▷ *hilfsverb* **1** (*veranlassen*): **etw machen lassen** to have *od* get sth done; **jdn etw machen lassen** to get sb to do sth; (*durch Befehl usw*) to make sb do sth; **er ließ mich warten** he kept me waiting; **mein Vater wollte mich studieren lassen** my father wanted me to study; **sich** *dat* **etw schicken lassen** to have sth sent (to one)
2 (*zulassen*): **jdn etw wissen lassen** to let sb know sth; **das Licht brennen lassen** to leave the light on; **einen Bart wachsen lassen** to grow a beard; **lass es dir gut gehen!** take care of yourself!
3: lass uns gehen let's go
▷ *vr*: **das lässt sich machen** that can be done; **es lässt sich schwer sagen** it's difficult to say
lässig ['lɛsɪç] *adj* casual; **Lässigkeit** *f* casualness
Last [last] (**-, -en**) *f* load; (*Traglast*) burden; (*Naut, Aviat*) cargo; (*meist pl*: *Gebühr*) charge; **jdm zur ~ fallen** to be a burden to sb

lasten *vi*: **~ auf** *+dat* to weigh on
Laster ['lastər] (**-s, -**) *nt* vice ▷ *m* (*umg*) lorry (*Brit*), truck
lästern ['lɛstərn] *vt, vi* (*Gott*) to blaspheme; (*schlecht sprechen*) to mock
lästig ['lɛstɪç] *adj* troublesome, tiresome; **(jdm) ~ werden** to become a nuisance (to sb); (*zum Ärgernis werden*) to get annoying (to sb)
Last- *zW*: **Lastkahn** *m* barge; **Lastkraftwagen** *m* heavy goods vehicle; **Lastschrift** *f* debiting; (*Eintrag*) debit item; **Lastwagen** *m* lorry (*Brit*), truck
Latein [la'taɪn] (**-s**) *nt* Latin; **mit seinem ~ am Ende sein** (*fig*) to be stumped (*umg*); **Lateinamerika** *nt* Latin America; **lateinisch** *adj* Latin
Laterne [la'tɛrnə] (**-, -n**) *f* lantern; (*Straßenlaterne*) lamp, light
Laternenpfahl *m* lamppost
latschen (*umg*) *vi* (*gehen*) to wander, go; (*lässig*) to slouch
Latte ['latə] (**-, -n**) *f* lath; (*Sport*) goalpost; (*quer*) crossbar
Latz [lats] (**-es, ¨-e**) *m* bib; (*Hosenlatz*) front flap
Lätzchen ['lɛtsçən] *nt* bib
Latzhose *f* dungarees *pl*
lau [laʊ] *adj* (*Nacht*) balmy; (*Wasser*) lukewarm; (*fig: Haltung*) half-hearted
Laub [laʊp] (**-(e)s**) *nt* foliage; **Laubbaum** *m* deciduous tree; **Laubfrosch** *m* tree frog; **Laubsäge** *f* fretsaw
Lauch [laʊx] (**-(e)s, -e**) *m* leek
Lauer ['laʊər] *f*: **auf der ~ sein** *od* **liegen** to lie in wait
lauern *vi* to lie in wait; (*Gefahr*) to lurk
Lauf [laʊf] (**-(e)s, Läufe**) *m* run; (*Wettlauf*) race; (*Entwicklung, Astron*) course; (*Gewehrlauf*) barrel; **im ~e des Gesprächs** during the conversation; **sie ließ ihren Gefühlen freien ~** she gave way to her feelings; **einer Sache** *dat* **ihren ~ lassen** to let sth take its course; **Laufbahn** *f* career; **eine Laufbahn einschlagen** to embark on a career
laufen ['laʊfən] *unreg vi* to run; (*umg: gehen*) to walk; (*Uhr*) to go; (*funktionieren*) to work; (*Elektrogerät: eingeschaltet sein*) to be on; (*gezeigt werden: Film, Stück*) to be on; (*Bewerbung, Antrag*) to be under consideration ▷ *vt* to run; **es lief mir eiskalt über den Rücken** a chill ran up my spine; **ihm läuft die Nase** he's got a runny nose; **~ lassen** (*Person*) to let go; **die Dinge ~ lassen** to let things slide; **die Sache ist ge~** (*umg*) it's in the bag; **das Auto läuft auf meinen Namen** the car is in my name; **Ski/Schlittschuh/Rollschuh** *etc* **~** to ski/skate/rollerskate *etc*
laufend *adj* running; (*Monat, Ausgaben*) current; **auf dem L~en sein/halten** to be/keep up to date; **am ~en Band** (*fig*) continuously; **~e Nummer** serial number; (*von Konto*) number; **~e Kosten** running costs *pl*
Läufer ['lɔʏfər] (**-s, -**) *m* (*Teppich, Sport*) runner; (*Fußball*) half-back; (*Schach*) bishop
Lauf- *zW*: **Laufmasche** *f* run, ladder (*Brit*); **Laufpass** *m*: **jdm den Laufpass geben** (*umg*) to give sb his/her marching orders; **Laufsteg** *m* catwalk; **Laufwerk** *nt* running gear; (*Comput*) drive
Lauge ['laʊgə] (**-, -n**) *f* soapy water; (*Chem*) alkaline solution
Laune ['laʊnə] (**-, -n**) *f* mood, humour (*Brit*), humor (*US*); (*Einfall*) caprice; (*schlechte Laune*) temper
launenhaft *adj* capricious, changeable
launisch *adj* moody
Laus [laʊs] (**-, Läuse**) *f* louse; **ihm ist (wohl) eine ~ über die Leber gelaufen** (*umg*) something's biting him; **Lausbub** *m* rascal, imp
lauschen ['laʊʃən] *vi* to eavesdrop, listen in
lausig ['laʊzɪç] (*umg*) *adj* lousy; (*Kälte*) perishing ▷ *adv* awfully
laut [laʊt] *adj* loud ▷ *adv* loudly; (*lesen*) aloud ▷ *präp* (*+gen od dat*) according to
Laut (**-(e)s, -e**) *m* sound
lauten ['laʊtən] *vi* to say; (*Urteil*) to be
läuten ['lɔʏtən] *vt, vi* to ring, sound; **er hat davon (etwas) ~ hören** (*umg*) he has heard something about it
lauter ['laʊtər] *adj* (*Wasser*) clear, pure; (*Wahrheit, Charakter*) honest ▷ *adj inv* (*Freude, Dummheit etc*) sheer ▷ *adv* (*nur*) nothing but, only
laut- *zW*: **lauthals** *adv* at the top of one's voice; **lautlos** *adj* noiseless, silent; **Lautschrift** *f* phonetics *pl*; **Lautsprecher** *m* loudspeaker; **Lautsprecherwagen** *m* loudspeaker van; **lautstark** *adj* vociferous; **Lautstärke** *f* (*Rundf*) volume
lauwarm ['laʊvarm] *adj* (*lit, fig*) lukewarm
Lava ['la:va] (**-, Laven**) *f* lava
Lavendel [la'vɛndəl] (**-s, -**) *m* lavender
Lawine [la'vi:nə] *f* avalanche
Lawinengefahr *f* danger of avalanches
lax [laks] *adj* lax
Lazarett [latsa'rɛt] (**-(e)s, -e**) *nt* (*Mil*) hospital, infirmary
leasen ['li:zən] *vt* to lease
Leasing ['li:zɪŋ] (**-s, -s**) *nt* (*Comm*) leasing
Leben ['le:bən] (**-s, -**) *nt* life; **am ~ sein/bleiben** to be/stay alive; **ums ~ kommen** to die; **etw ins ~ rufen** to bring sth into being; **seines ~s nicht mehr sicher sein** to fear for one's life; **etw für sein ~ gern tun** to love doing sth
leben *vt, vi* to live
lebend *adj* living; **~es Inventar** livestock
lebendig [le'bɛndɪç] *adj* living, alive; (*lebhaft*) lively; **Lebendigkeit** *f* liveliness
Lebens- *zW*: **Lebensart** *f* way of life; **Lebenserfahrung** *f* experience of life; **Lebenserwartung** *f* life expectancy; **lebensfähig** *adj* able to live; **Lebensgefahr** *f*: **Lebensgefahr!** danger!; **in Lebensgefahr** critically *od* dangerously ill; **lebensgefährlich**

adj dangerous; (*Krankheit, Verletzung*) critical; **Lebenshaltungskosten** *pl* cost of living *sing*; **Lebensjahr** *nt* year of life; **Lebenslage** *f* situation in life; **lebenslänglich** *adj* (*Strafe*) for life; **Lebenslauf** *m* curriculum vitae, CV; **lebenslustig** *adj* cheerful, lively; **Lebensmittel** *pl* food *sing*; **Lebensmittelgeschäft** *nt* grocer's; **lebensmüde** *adj* tired of life; **Lebensqualität** *f* quality of life; **Lebensretter** *m* lifesaver; **Lebensstandard** *m* standard of living; **Lebensunterhalt** *m* livelihood; **Lebensversicherung** *f* life insurance; **Lebenswandel** *m* way of life; **Lebenszeichen** *nt* sign of life; **Lebenszeit** *f* lifetime; **Beamter auf Lebenszeit** permanent civil servant

Leber ['le:bər] (**-, -n**) *f* liver; **frei** *od* **frisch von der ~ weg reden** (*umg*) to speak out frankly; **Leberfleck** *m* mole; **Lebertran** *m* cod-liver oil; **Leberwurst** *f* liver sausage

Lebewesen *nt* creature

leb- *zW*: **lebhaft** *adj* lively, vivacious; **Lebkuchen** *m* gingerbread; **leblos** *adj* lifeless

leck [lɛk] *adj* leaky, leaking; **Leck** (**-(e)s, -e**) *nt* leak

lecken[1] *vi* (*Loch haben*) to leak

lecken[2] *vt, vi* (*schlecken*) to lick

lecker ['lɛkər] *adj* delicious, tasty; **Leckerbissen** *m* dainty morsel

led. *abk* = **ledig**

Leder ['le:dər] (**-s, -**) *nt* leather; (*umg: Fußball*) ball; **Lederhose** *f* leather trousers *pl*; (*von Tracht*) leather shorts *pl*

ledern *adj* leather

Lederwaren *pl* leather goods *pl*

ledig ['le:dɪç] *adj* single; **einer Sache** *gen* **~ sein** to be free of sth; **lediglich** *adv* merely, solely

leer [le:r] *adj* empty; (*Blick*) vacant; **~ gefegt** (*Straße*) deserted; **~ stehend** empty

Leere (**-**) *f* emptiness; **(eine) gähnende ~** a gaping void

leeren *vt* to empty ▷ *vr* to (become) empty

Leer- *zW*: **Leergewicht** *nt* unladen weight; **Leergut** *nt* empties *pl*; **Leerlauf** *m* (*Aut*) neutral; **Leertaste** *f* (*Schreibmaschine*) space-bar

Leerung *f* emptying; (*Post*) collection

legal [le'ga:l] *adj* legal, lawful

legalisieren [legali'zi:rən] *vt* to legalize

Legalität [legali'tɛ:t] *f* legality; **(etwas) außerhalb der ~** (*euph*) (slightly) outside the law

Legasthenie [legaste'ni:] *f* dyslexia

Legebatterie *f* laying battery

legen ['le:gən] *vt* to lay, put, place; (*Ei*) to lay ▷ *vr* to lie down; (*fig*) to subside; **sich ins Bett ~** to go to bed

Legende [le'gɛndə] (**-, -n**) *f* legend

leger [le'ʒɛ:r] *adj* casual

legieren [le'gi:rən] *vt* to alloy

Legierung *f* alloy

Legislative [legɪsla'ti:və] *f* legislature

Legislaturperiode [legɪsla'tu:rperio:də] *f* parliamentary (*Brit*) *od* congressional (*US*) term

legitim [legi'ti:m] *adj* legitimate

Legitimation [legiti:matsi'o:n] *f* legitimation

Lehm [le:m] (**-(e)s, -e**) *m* loam

lehmig *adj* loamy

Lehne ['le:nə] (**-, -n**) *f* arm; (*Rückenlehne*) back

lehnen *vt, vr* to lean

Lehr- *zW*: **Lehramt** *nt* teaching profession; **Lehrbuch** *nt* textbook

Lehre ['le:rə] (**-, -n**) *f* teaching, doctrine; (*beruflich*) apprenticeship; (*moralisch*) lesson; (*Tech*) gauge; **bei jdm in die ~ gehen** to serve one's apprenticeship with sb

lehren *vt* to teach

Lehrer, in (**-s, -**) *m(f)* teacher; **Lehrerzimmer** *nt* staff room

Lehr- *zW*: **Lehrgang** *m* course; **Lehrjahre** *pl* apprenticeship *sing*; **Lehrkraft** *f* (*form*) teacher; **Lehrling** *m* apprentice; trainee; **Lehrplan** *m* syllabus; **lehrreich** *adj* instructive; **Lehrstelle** *f* apprenticeship; **Lehrstuhl** *m* chair

Leib [laɪp] (**-(e)s, -er**) *m* body; **halt ihn mir vom ~!** keep him away from me!; **etw am eigenen ~(e) spüren** to experience sth for o.s.

Leiche ['laɪçə] (**-, -n**) *f* corpse; **er geht über ~n** (*umg*) he'd stick at nothing

Leichen- *zW*: **Leichenhalle** *f* mortuary; **Leichenwagen** *m* hearse

Leichnam ['laɪçna:m] (**-(e)s, -e**) *m* corpse

leicht [laɪçt] *adj* light; (*einfach*) easy ▷ *adv*: **~ zerbrechlich** very fragile; **es sich** *dat* **~ machen** to make things easy for o.s.; (*nicht gewissenhaft sein*) to take the easy way out; **~ verletzt** slightly injured; **nichts ~er als das!** nothing (could be) simpler!; *siehe auch* **leichtfallen; leichtnehmen**; **Leichtathletik** *f* athletics *sing*; **leichtfallen** *unreg vi*: **jdm leichtfallen** to be easy for sb; **leichtgläubig** *adj* gullible, credulous; **Leichtgläubigkeit** *f* gullibility, credulity; **leichthin** *adv* lightly

Leichtigkeit *f* easiness; **mit ~** with ease

leicht- *zW*: **Leichtmetall** *nt* light alloy; **leichtsinnig** *adj* careless

Leid [laɪt] (**-(e)s**) *nt* grief, sorrow; **jdm sein ~ klagen** to tell sb one's troubles

leid *adj*: **etw ~ haben** *od* **sein** to be tired of sth; *siehe auch* **leidtun**

leiden ['laɪdən] *unreg vt* to suffer; (*erlauben*) to permit ▷ *vi* to suffer; **jdn/etw nicht ~ können** not to be able to stand sb/sth; **Leiden** (**-s, -**) *nt* suffering; (*Krankheit*) complaint

Leidenschaft *f* passion; **leidenschaftlich** *adj* passionate

leider ['laɪdər] *adv* unfortunately; **ja, ~** yes, I'm afraid so; **~ nicht** I'm afraid not

Leidtragende, r *f(m)* bereaved;

(*Benachteiligter*) one who suffers
Leidwesen *nt*: **zu jds ~** to sb's dismay
Leier ['laɪər] (**-, -n**) *f* lyre; (*fig*) old story
Leierkasten *m* barrel organ
Leih- *zW*: **Leiharbeit** *f* subcontracted labour; **Leihbibliothek** *f*, **Leihbücherei** *f* lending library
leihen ['laɪən] *unreg vt* to lend; **sich** *dat* **etw ~** to borrow sth
Leih- *zW*: **Leihgabe** *f* loan; **Leihgebühr** *f* hire charge; **Leihhaus** *nt* pawnshop; **Leihmutter** *f* surrogate mother; **Leihschein** *m* pawn ticket; (*in der Bibliothek*) borrowing slip; **Leihwagen** *m* hired car (*Brit*), rental car (*US*)
Leim [laɪm] (**-(e)s, -e**) *m* glue; **jdm auf den ~ gehen** to be taken in by sb; **leimen** *vt* to glue
Leine ['laɪnə] (**-, -n**) *f* line, cord; (*Hundeleine*) leash, lead; **~ ziehen** (*umg*) to clear out
Leinen (**-s, -**) *nt* linen; (*grob, segeltuchartig*) canvas; (*als Bucheinband*) cloth
Lein- *zW*: **Leintuch** *nt* linen cloth; (*Bettuch*) sheet; **Leinwand** *f* (*Kunst*) canvas; (*Film*) screen
leise ['laɪzə] *adj* quiet; (*sanft*) soft, gentle; **mit ~r Stimme** in a low voice; **nicht die ~ste Ahnung haben** not to have the slightest (idea)
Leiste ['laɪstə] (**-, -n**) *f* ledge; (*Zierleiste*) strip; (*Anat*) groin
leisten ['laɪstən] *vt* (*Arbeit*) to do; (*Gesellschaft*) to keep; (*Ersatz*) to supply; (*vollbringen*) to achieve; **sich** *dat* **etw ~** to allow o.s. sth; (*sich gönnen*) to treat o.s. to sth; **sich** *dat* **etw ~ können** to be able to afford sth
Leistenbruch *m* (*Med*) hernia, rupture
Leistung *f* performance; (*gute*) achievement; (*eines Motors*) power; (*von Krankenkasse etc*) benefit; (*Zahlung*) payment
Leistungs- *zW*: **Leistungsdruck** *m* pressure; **leistungsfähig** *adj* efficient; **Leistungsgesellschaft** *f* meritocracy; **Leistungskurs** *m* (*Sch*) set; **Leistungssport** *m* competitive sport; **Leistungszulage** *f* productivity bonus
Leitartikel *m* leader
Leitbild *nt* model
leiten ['laɪtən] *vt* to lead; (*Firma*) to manage; (*in eine Richtung*) to direct; (*Elek*) to conduct; **sich von jdm/etw ~ lassen** (*lit, fig*) to (let o.s.) be guided by sb/sth
leitend *adj* leading; (*Gedanke, Idee*) dominant; (*Stellung, Position*) managerial; (*Ingenieur, Beamter*) in charge; (*Phys*) conductive; **~er Angestellter** executive
Leiter[1] ['laɪtər] (**-s, -**) *m* leader, head; (*Elek*) conductor
Leiter[2] ['laɪtər] (**-, -n**) *f* ladder
Leit- *zW*: **Leitmotiv** *nt* leitmotiv; **Leitplanke** *f* crash barrier
Leitung *f* (*Führung*) direction; (*Film, Theat etc*) production; (*von Firma*) management; directors *pl*; (*Wasserleitung*) pipe; (*Kabel*) cable; **eine lange ~ haben** to be slow on the uptake; **da ist jemand in der ~** (*umg*) there's somebody else on the line
Leitungs- *zW*: **Leitungsdraht** *m* wire; **Leitungswasser** *nt* tap water
Leitwerk *nt* (*Aviat*) tail unit
Lektion [lɛktsi'o:n] *f* lesson; **jdm eine ~ erteilen** (*fig*) to teach sb a lesson
Lektüre [lɛk'ty:rə] (**-, -n**) *f* (*Lesen*) reading; (*Lesestoff*) reading matter
Lende ['lɛndə] (**-, -n**) *f* loin
Lendenstück *nt* fillet
lenkbar ['lɛŋkba:r] *adj* (*Fahrzeug*) steerable; (*Kind*) manageable
lenken *vt* to steer; (*Kind*) to guide; (*Gespräch*) to lead; **~ auf** *+akk* (*Blick, Aufmerksamkeit*) to direct at; (*Verdacht*) to throw on(to); (*: auf sich*) to draw onto
Lenkrad *nt* steering wheel
Lenkstange *f* handlebars *pl*
Leopard [leo'part] (**-en, -en**) *m* leopard
Lepra ['le:pra] (**-**) *f* leprosy
Lerche ['lɛrçə] (**-, -n**) *f* lark
lernbegierig *adj* eager to learn
lernbehindert *adj* educationally handicapped (*Brit*) *od* handicaped (*US*)
lernen *vt* to learn ▷ *vi*: **er lernt bei der Firma Braun** he's training at Braun's
lesbar ['le:sba:r] *adj* legible
Lesbierin ['lɛsbiərɪn] *f* lesbian
lesbisch *adj* lesbian
Lese ['le:zə] (**-, -n**) *f* (*Weinlese*) harvest
lesen *unreg vt* to read; (*ernten*) to gather, pick ▷ *vi* to read; **~/schreiben** (*Comput*) to read/write
Leser, in (**-s, -**) *m(f)* reader
Leser- *zW*: **Leserbrief** *m* reader's letter; **„Leserbriefe"** "letters to the editor"; **leserlich** *adj* legible
Lesotho [le'zo:to] (**-s**) *nt* Lesotho
Lesung ['le:zʊŋ] *f* (*Parl*) reading; (*Eccl*) lesson
lettisch *adj* Latvian
Lettland ['lɛtlant] (**-s**) *nt* Latvia
letzte, r, s ['lɛtstə(r, s)] *adj* last; (*neueste*) latest; **der L~ Wille** the last will and testament; **bis zum L~n** to the utmost; **zum ~n Mal** for the last time; **in ~r Zeit** recently
letztens *adv* lately
letztere, r, s *adj* the latter
Leuchte ['lɔʏçtə] (**-, -n**) *f* lamp, light; (*umg: Mensch*) genius
leuchten *vi* to shine, gleam
Leuchter (**-s, -**) *m* candlestick
Leucht- *zW*: **Leuchtfarbe** *f* fluorescent colour (*Brit*) *od* color (*US*); **Leuchtkugel** *f* flare; **Leuchtreklame** *f* neon sign; **Leuchtröhre** *f* strip light; **Leuchtturm** *m* lighthouse; **Leuchtzifferblatt** *nt* luminous dial
leugnen ['lɔʏgnən] *vt, vi* to deny
Leukämie [lɔʏkɛ'mi:] *f* leukaemia (*Brit*), leukemia (*US*)
Leumund ['lɔʏmʊnt] (**-(e)s, -e**) *m* reputation
Leumundszeugnis *nt* character reference
Leute ['lɔʏtə] *pl* people *pl*; **kleine ~** (*fig*)

ordinary people; **etw unter die ~ bringen** (*umg*: *Gerücht etc*) to spread sth around
Leutnant ['lɔʏtnant] (**-s, -s** *od* **-e**) *m* lieutenant
Lexikon ['lɛksikɔn] (**-s, Lexiken** *od* **Lexika**) *nt* encyclopedia
libanesisch *adj* Lebanese
Libanon ['li:banɔn] (**-s**) *m*: **der ~** the Lebanon
Libelle [li'bɛlə] (**-, -n**) *f* dragonfly; (*Tech*) spirit level
liberal [libe'ra:l] *adj* liberal
Liberalismus [libera'lɪsmʊs] *m* liberalism
Liberia [li'be:ria] (**-s**) *nt* Liberia
Libero ['li:bero] (**-s, -s**) *m* (*Fussball*) sweeper
Libyen ['li:byən] (**-s**) *nt* Libya
libysch *adj* Libyan
Licht [lɪçt] (**-(e)s, -er**) *nt* light; **~ machen** (*anschalten*) to turn on a light; (*anzünden*) to light a candle *etc*; **mir geht ein ~ auf** it's dawned on me; **jdn hinters ~ führen** (*fig*) to lead sb up the garden path
Licht- *zW*: **Lichtbild** *nt* photograph; (*Dia*) slide; **Lichtblick** *m* cheering prospect; **lichtempfindlich** *adj* sensitive to light
lichten ['lɪçtən] *vt* to clear; (*Anker*) to weigh ▷ *vr* (*Nebel*) to clear; (*Haar*) to thin
Licht- *zW*: **Lichtgriffel** *m* (*Comput*) light pen; **Lichthupe** *f* flashing of headlights; **Lichtjahr** *nt* light year; **Lichtmaschine** *f* dynamo; **Lichtmess** (**-**) *f* Candlemas; **Lichtschalter** *m* light switch
Lichtung *f* clearing, glade
Lid [li:t] (**-(e)s, -er**) *nt* eyelid; **Lidschatten** *m* eyeshadow
lieb [li:p] *adj* dear; **(viele) ~e Grüße, Deine Silvia** love, Silvia; **Liebe Anna, ~er Klaus! ...** Dear Anna and Klaus, ...; **am ~sten lese ich Kriminalromane** best of all I like detective novels; **den ~en langen Tag** (*umg*) all the livelong day; **sich bei jdm ~ Kind machen** (*pej*) to suck up to sb (*umg*); **~ gewinnen** to get fond of; **~ haben** to love; (*weniger stark*) to be (very) fond of
liebäugeln ['li:p|ɔʏgəln] *vi untr*: **mit dem Gedanken ~, etw zu tun** to toy with the idea of doing sth
Liebe ['li:bə] (**-, -n**) *f* love; **liebebedürftig** *adj*: **liebebedürftig sein** to need love
Liebelei *f* flirtation
lieben ['li:bən] *vt* to love; (*weniger stark*) to like; **etw ~d gern tun** to love to do sth
liebens- *zW*: **liebenswert** *adj* loveable; **liebenswürdig** *adj* kind; **liebenswürdigerweise** *adv* kindly; **Liebenswürdigkeit** *f* kindness
lieber ['li:bər] *adv* rather, preferably; **ich gehe ~ nicht** I'd rather not go; **ich trinke ~ Wein als Bier** I prefer wine to beer; **bleib ~ im Bett** you'd better stay in bed
Liebes- *zW*: **Liebesbrief** *m* love letter; **Liebeskummer** *m*: **Liebeskummer haben** to be lovesick; **Liebespaar** *nt* courting couple, lovers *pl*
liebevoll *adj* loving
lieb- *zW*: **Liebhaber, in** (**-s, -**) *m(f)* lover; (*Sammler*) collector; **Liebhaberei** *f* hobby; **liebkosen** *vt untr* to caress; **lieblich** *adj* lovely, charming; (*Duft, Wein*) sweet
Liebling *m* darling
Lieblings- *in zW* favourite (*Brit*), favorite (*US*)
lieblos *adj* unloving
Liebschaft *f* love affair
Liechtenstein ['lɪçtənʃtaɪn] (**-s**) *nt* Liechtenstein
Lied [li:t] (**-(e)s, -er**) *nt* song; (*Eccl*) hymn; **davon kann ich ein ~ singen** (*fig*) I could tell you a thing or two about that (*umg*)
Liederbuch *nt* songbook; (*Rel*) hymn book
liederlich ['li:dərlɪç] *adj* slovenly; (*Lebenswandel*) loose, immoral; **Liederlichkeit** *f* slovenliness; immorality
lief *etc* [li:f] *vb siehe* **laufen**
Lieferant [li:fə'rant] *m* supplier
liefern ['li:fərn] *vt* to deliver; (*versorgen mit*) to supply; (*Beweis*) to produce
Lieferschein *m* delivery note
Liefertermin *m* delivery date
Lieferung *f* delivery; (*Versorgung*) supply
Lieferwagen *m* (delivery) van, panel truck (*US*)
Liege ['li:gə] (**-, -n**) *f* bed; (*Campingliege*) camp bed (*Brit*), cot (*US*)
liegen ['li:gən] *unreg vi* to lie; (*sich befinden*) to be (situated); **mir liegt nichts/viel daran** it doesn't matter to me/it matters a lot to me; **es liegt bei Ihnen, ob ...** it rests with you whether ...; **Sprachen ~ mir nicht** languages are not my line; **woran liegt es?** what's the cause?; **so, wie die Dinge jetzt ~** as things stand at the moment; **an mir soll es nicht ~, wenn die Sache schiefgeht** it won't be my fault if things go wrong; **~ bleiben** (*Person*) to stay in bed; (*nicht aufstehen*) to stay lying down; (*Ding*) to be left (behind); (*nicht ausgeführt werden*) to be left (undone); **~ lassen** (*vergessen*) to leave behind
Liege- *zW*: **Liegesitz** *m* (*Aut*) reclining seat; **Liegestuhl** *m* deck chair; **Liegewagen** *m* (*Eisenb*) couchette car
lieh *etc* [li:] *vb siehe* **leihen**
ließ *etc* [li:s] *vb siehe* **lassen**
Lift [lɪft] (**-(e)s, -e** *od* **-s**) *m* lift
Likör [li'kø:r] (**-s, -e**) *m* liqueur
lila ['li:la] *adj inv* purple
Lilie ['li:liə] *f* lily
Liliputaner, in [lilipu'ta:nər(ɪn)] (**-s, -**) *m(f)* midget
Limonade [limo'na:də] (**-, -n**) *f* lemonade
Linde ['lɪndə] (**-, -n**) *f* lime tree, linden
lindern ['lɪndərn] *vt* to alleviate, soothe
Linderung *f* alleviation
Lineal [line'a:l] (**-s, -e**) *nt* ruler
Linguistik *f* linguistics *sing*
Linie ['li:niə] *f* line; **in erster ~** first and foremost; **auf die ~ achten** to watch one's figure; **fahren Sie mit der ~ 2** take the number 2 (bus *etc*)

Linien- *zW*: **Linienblatt** *nt* ruled sheet; **Linienflug** *m* scheduled flight; **Linienrichter** *m* (*Sport*) linesman
Link [lɪŋk] (**-s, -s**) *m* (*Comput*) link
Linke ['lɪŋkə] (**-, -n**) *f* left side; left hand; (*Pol*) left
linke, r, s *adj* left; **~ Masche** purl
linkisch *adj* awkward, gauche
links *adv* left; to *od* on the left; **~ von mir** on *od* to my left; **~ von der Mitte** left of centre; **jdn ~ liegen lassen** (*fig: umg*) to ignore sb; **das mache ich mit ~** (*umg*) I can do that with my eyes shut; **Linksaußen** (**-s, -**) *m* (*Sport*) outside left; **Linkshänder, in** (**-s, -**) *m(f)* left-handed person; **Linkskurve** *f* left-hand bend; **Linksverkehr** *m* driving on the left
Linse ['lɪnzə] (**-, -n**) *f* lentil; (*optisch*) lens
Lippe ['lɪpə] (**-, -n**) *f* lip
Lippenstift *m* lipstick
lispeln ['lɪspəln] *vi* to lisp
Lissabon ['lɪsabɔn] *nt* Lisbon
List [lɪst] (**-, -en**) *f* cunning; (*Plan*) trick, ruse; **mit ~ und Tücke** (*umg*) with a lot of coaxing
Liste ['lɪstə] (**-, -n**) *f* list
listig *adj* cunning, sly
Litanei [lita'naɪ] *f* litany
Litauen ['li:taʊən] (**-s**) *nt* Lithuania
litauisch *adj* Lithuanian
Liter ['li:tər] (**-s, -**) *m od nt* litre (*Brit*), liter (*US*)
literarisch [lɪte'ra:rɪʃ] *adj* literary
Literatur [lɪtera'tu:r] *f* literature
Litfaßsäule ['lɪtfaszɔʏlə] *f* advertising (*Brit*) *od* advertizing (*US*) pillar
Lithografie [litogra'fi:] *f* lithography
litt *etc* [lɪt] *vb siehe* **leiden**
Liturgie [litʊr'gi:] *f* liturgy
liturgisch [li'tʊrgɪʃ] *adj* liturgical
Litze ['lɪtsə] (**-, -n**) *f* braid; (*Elek*) flex
live [laɪf] *adj, adv* (*Rundf, TV*) live
Lizenz [li'tsɛnts] *f* licence (*Brit*), license (*US*)
Lkw, LKW (**-(s), -(s)**) *m abk* = **Lastkraftwagen**
Lob [lo:p] (**-(e)s**) *nt* praise
loben ['lo:bən] *vt* to praise; **das lob ich mir** that's what I like (to see/hear *etc*)
lobenswert *adj* praiseworthy
löblich ['lø:plɪç] *adj* praiseworthy, laudable
Loch [lɔx] (**-(e)s, ¨-er**) *nt* hole; **lochen** *vt* to punch holes in; **Locher** (**-s, -**) *m* punch
löcherig ['lœçərɪç] *adj* full of holes
Locke ['lɔkə] (**-, -n**) *f* lock, curl
locken *vt* to entice; (*Haare*) to curl
Lockenwickler (**-s, -**) *m* curler
locker ['lɔkər] *adj* loose; (*Kuchen, Schaum*) light; (*umg*) cool: **lockerlassen** *unreg vi*: **nicht lockerlassen** not to let up
lockern *vt* to loosen ▷ *vr* (*Atmosphäre*) to get more relaxed
lockig ['lɔkɪç] *adj* curly
Lodenmantel ['lo:dənmantəl] *m* thick woollen coat
lodern ['lo:dərn] *vi* to blaze
Löffel ['lœfəl] (**-s, -**) *m* spoon
log *etc* [lo:k] *vb siehe* **lügen**
Logarithmus [loga'rɪtmʊs] *m* logarithm
Loge ['lo:ʒə] (**-, -n**) *f* (*Theat*) box; (*Freimaurerloge*) (masonic) lodge; (*Pförtnerloge*) office
Logik ['lo:gɪk] *f* logic
logisch ['lo:gɪʃ] *adj* logical; (*umg: selbstverständlich*): **gehst du auch hin? — ~** are you going too? — of course
Lohn [lo:n] (**-(e)s, ¨-e**) *m* reward; (*Arbeitslohn*) pay, wages *pl*; **Lohnbüro** *nt* wages office; **Lohnempfänger** *m* wage earner
lohnen ['lo:nən] *vt* (*liter*): **jdm etw ~** to reward sb for sth ▷ *vr unpers* to be worth it
Lohn- *zW*: **Lohnfortzahlung** *f* continued payment of wages; **Lohngefälle** *nt* wage differential; **Lohnsteuer** *f* income tax; **Lohnsteuerjahresausgleich** *m* income tax return; **Lohnsteuerkarte** *f* (income) tax card; **Lohnstreifen** *m* pay slip; **Lohntüte** *f* pay packet
lokal [lo'ka:l] *adj* local
Lokal (**-(e)s, -e**) *nt* pub(lic house) (*Brit*)
lokalisieren [loka:li'zi:rən] *vt* to localize
Lokomotive [lokomo'ti:və] (**-, -n**) *f* locomotive
Lokomotivführer *m* engine driver (*Brit*), engineer (*US*)
London ['lɔndɔn] (**-s**) *nt* London
Lorbeer ['lɔrbe:r] (**-s, -en**) *m* (*lit, fig*) laurel; **Lorbeerblatt** *nt* (*Koch*) bay leaf
Lore ['lo:rə] (**-, -n**) *f* (*Min*) truck
Los [lo:s] (**-es, -e**) *nt* (*Schicksal*) lot, fate; (*in der Lotterie*) lottery ticket; **das große ~ ziehen** (*lit, fig*) to hit the jackpot; **etw durch das ~ entscheiden** to decide sth by drawing lots
los *adj* loose ▷ *adv*: **~!** go on!; **etw ~ sein** to be rid of sth; **was ist ~?** what's the matter?; **dort ist nichts/viel ~** there's nothing/a lot going on there; **ich bin mein ganzes Geld ~** (*umg*) I'm cleaned out; **irgendwas ist mit ihm ~** there's something wrong with him; **wir wollen früh ~** we want to be off early; **nichts wie ~!** let's get going; **losbinden** *unreg vt* to untie
löschen ['lœʃən] *vt* (*Feuer, Licht*) to put out, extinguish; (*Durst*) to quench; (*Comm*) to cancel; (*Tonband*) to erase; (*Fracht*) to unload; (*Comput*) to delete; (*Tinte*) to blot ▷ *vi* (*Feuerwehr*) to put out a fire; (*Papier*) to blot
Lösch- *zW*: **Löschfahrzeug** *nt* fire engine; **Löschgerät** *nt* fire extinguisher; **Löschpapier** *nt* blotting paper; **Löschtaste** *f* (*Comput*) delete key
lose ['lo:zə] *adj* loose
Lösegeld *nt* ransom
losen ['lo:zən] *vi* to draw lots
lösen ['lø:zən] *vt* to loosen; (*Handbremse*) to release; (*Husten, Krampf*) to ease; (*Rätsel etc*) to solve; (*Verlobung*) to call off; (*Chem*) to dissolve; (*Partnerschaft*) to break up; (*Fahrkarte*) to buy ▷ *vr* (*aufgehen*) to come loose; (*Schuss*) to go off; (*Zucker etc*) to dissolve; (*Problem, Schwierigkeit*) to (re)solve itself
los- *zW*: **losfahren** *unreg vi* to leave; **losgehen**

unreg vi to set out; (*anfangen*) to start; (*Bombe*) to go off; **jetzt gehts los!** here we go!; **nach hinten losgehen** (*umg*) to backfire; **auf jdn losgehen** to go for sb; **loskaufen** *vt* (*Gefangene, Geiseln*) to pay ransom for; **loskommen** *unreg vi* (*sich befreien*) to free o.s.; **von etw loskommen** to get away from sth; **loslassen** *unreg vt* (*Seil etc*) to let go of; **der Gedanke lässt mich nicht mehr los** the thought haunts me; **loslaufen** *unreg vi* to run off; **loslegen** (*umg*) *vi*: **nun leg mal los und erzähl(e) ...** now come on and tell me/us ...

löslich ['lø:slɪç] *adj* soluble

loslösen *vt* to free ▷ *vr*: **sich (von etw) ~** to detach o.s. (from sth)

losmachen *vt* to loosen; (*Boot*) to unmoor ▷ *vr* to get free; **losschrauben** *vt* to unscrew

Losung ['lo:zʊŋ] *f* watchword, slogan

Lösung ['lø:zʊŋ] *f* (*Lockermachen*) loosening; (*eines Rätsels, Chem*) solution

Lösungsmittel *nt* solvent

loswerden *unreg vt* to get rid of

Lot [lo:t] (**-(e)s, -e**) *nt* plumbline; (*Math*) perpendicular; **im ~** vertical; (*fig*) on an even keel; **die Sache ist wieder im ~** things have been straightened out

löten ['lø:tən] *vt* to solder

Lötkolben *m* soldering iron

Lotse ['lo:tsə] (**-n, -n**) *m* pilot; (*Aviat*) air traffic controller

lotsen *vt* to pilot; (*umg*) to lure

Lotterie [lɔtə'ri:] *f* lottery

Lotto ['lɔto] (**-s, -s**) *nt* ≈ National Lottery

Lottozahlen *pl* winning Lotto numbers *pl*

Löwe ['lø:və] (**-n, -n**) *m* lion; (*Astrol*) Leo

Löwen- *zW*: **Löwenanteil** *m* lion's share; **Löwenmaul** *nt*, **Löwenmäulchen** *nt* antirrhinum, snapdragon; **Löwenzahn** *m* dandelion

Löwin ['lø:vɪn] *f* lioness

loyal [loa'ja:l] *adj* loyal

Loyalität [loajali'tɛ:t] *f* loyalty

LP (**-, -s**) *f abk* (= *Langspielplatte*) LP

Luchs [lʊks] (**-es, -e**) *m* lynx

Lücke ['lʏkə] (**-, -n**) *f* gap; (*Gesetzeslücke*) loophole; (*in Versorgung*) break

Lücken- *zW*: **Lückenbüßer** (**-s, -**) *m* stopgap; **lückenlos** *adj* complete

lud *etc* [lu:t] *vb siehe* **laden**

Luder ['lu:dər] (**-s, -**) (*pej*) *nt* (*Frau*) hussy; (*bedauernswert*) poor wretch

Luft [lʊft] (**-, ¨e**) *f* air; (*Atem*) breath; **die ~ anhalten** (*lit*) to hold one's breath; **seinem Herzen ~ machen** to get everything off one's chest; **in der ~ liegen** to be in the air; **dicke ~** (*umg*) a bad atmosphere; **(frische) ~ schnappen** (*umg*) to get some fresh air; **in die ~ fliegen** (*umg*) to explode; **diese Behauptung ist aus der ~ gegriffen** this statement is (a) pure invention; **die ~ ist rein** (*umg*) the coast is clear; **jdn an die (frische) ~ setzen** (*umg*) to show sb the door; **er ist ~ für mich** I'm not speaking to him; **jdn wie ~ behandeln** to ignore sb; **Luftangriff** *m* air raid; **Luftballon** *m* balloon; **Luftblase** *f* air bubble; **Luftbrücke** *f* airlift; **luftdicht** *adj* airtight; **Luftdruck** *m* atmospheric pressure

lüften ['lʏftən] *vt* to air; (*Hut*) to lift, raise ▷ *vi* to let some air in

Luft- *zW*: **Luftfahrt** *f* aviation; **luftgekühlt** *adj* air-cooled

luftig *adj* (*Ort*) breezy; (*Raum*) airy; (*Kleider*) summery

Luft- *zW*: **Luftkissenfahrzeug** *nt* hovercraft; **Luftkurort** *m* health resort; **luftleer** *adj*: **luftleerer Raum** vacuum; **Luftlinie** *f*: **in der Luftlinie** as the crow flies; **Luftloch** *nt* air hole; (*Aviat*) air pocket; **Luftmatratze** *f* Lilo® (*Brit*), air mattress; **Luftpirat** *m* hijacker; **Luftpost** *f* airmail; **Luftröhre** *f* (*Anat*) windpipe; **Luftschlange** *f* streamer

Lüftung ['lʏftʊŋ] *f* ventilation

Luft- *zW*: **Luftverkehr** *m* air traffic; **Luftverschmutzung** *f* air pollution; **Luftwaffe** *f* air force; **Luftzug** *m* draught (*Brit*), draft (*US*)

Lüge ['ly:gə] (**-, -n**) *f* lie; **jdn/etw ~n strafen** to give the lie to sb/sth

lügen ['ly:gən] *unreg vi* to lie; **wie gedruckt ~** (*umg*) to lie like mad

Lügner, in (**-s, -**) *m(f)* liar

Luke ['lu:kə] (**-, -n**) *f* hatch; (*Dachluke*) skylight

Lümmel ['lʏməl] (**-s, -**) *m* lout

lümmeln *vr* to lounge (about)

Lump [lʊmp] (**-en, -en**) *m* scamp, rascal

lumpen ['lʊmpən] *vt*: **sich nicht ~ lassen** not to be mean

Lumpen (**-s, -**) *m* rag

lumpig ['lʊmpɪç] *adj* shabby; **~e 10 Euro** (*umg*) 10 measly euros

Lunge ['lʊŋə] (**-, -n**) *f* lung

Lungen- *zW*: **Lungenentzündung** *f* pneumonia; **lungenkrank** *adj* suffering from a lung disease

lungern ['lʊŋərn] *vi* to hang about

Lupe ['lu:pə] (**-, -n**) *f* magnifying glass; **unter die ~ nehmen** (*fig*) to scrutinize

Lupine [lu'pi:nə] *f* lupin

Lurch [lʊrç] (**-(e)s, -e**) *m* amphibian

Lust [lʊst] (**-, ¨e**) *f* joy, delight; (*Neigung*) desire; (*sexuell*) lust (*pej*); **~ haben zu** *od* **auf etw** *akk***/etw zu tun** to feel like sth/doing sth; **hast du ~?** how about it?; **er hat die ~ daran verloren** he has lost all interest in it; **je nach ~ und Laune** just depending on how I *od* you *etc* feel

lüstern ['lʏstərn] *adj* lustful, lecherous

Lustgefühl *nt* pleasurable feeling

lustig ['lʊstɪç] *adj* (*komisch*) amusing, funny; (*fröhlich*) cheerful; **sich über jdn/etw ~ machen** to make fun of sb/sth

Lüstling *m* lecher

Lust- *zW*: **lustlos** *adj* unenthusiastic; **Lustmord** *m* sex(ual) murder; **Lustspiel** *nt* comedy

lutherisch ['lʊtərɪʃ] *adj* Lutheran
lutschen ['lʊtʃən] *vt, vi* to suck; **am Daumen** ~ to suck one's thumb
Lutscher (**-s, -**) *m* lollipop
Luxemburg ['lʊksəmbʊrk] (**-s**) *nt* Luxembourg
luxemburgisch *adj* Luxembourgian
luxuriös [lʊksuri'øːs] *adj* luxurious
Luxus ['lʊksʊs] (**-**) *m* luxury; **Luxusartikel** *pl* luxury goods *pl*; **Luxushotel** *nt* luxury hotel
Lymphe ['lʏmfə] (**-, -n**) *f* lymph
lynchen ['lʏnçən] *vt* to lynch
Lyrik ['lyːrɪk] *f* lyric poetry; **Lyriker, in** (**-s, -**) *m(f)* lyric poet
lyrisch ['lyːrɪʃ] *adj* lyrical

Mm

M, m¹ [ɛm] *nt* M, m; **M wie Martha** ≈ M for Mary, ≈ M for Mike (*US*)
m² *abk* (= *Meter*) m; (= *männlich*) m.
Machart *f* make
machbar *adj* feasible
Mache (-) (*umg*) *f* show, sham; **jdn in der ~ haben** to be having a go at sb
machen ['maxən] *vt* **1** to do; **was machst du da?** what are you doing there?; **das ist nicht zu machen** that can't be done; **was machen Sie (beruflich)?** what do you do for a living?; **mach, dass du hier verschwindest!** (you just) get out of here!; **mit mir kann mans ja machen!** (*umg*) the things I put up with!; **das lässt er nicht mit sich machen** he won't stand for that; **eine Prüfung machen** to take an exam
2 (*herstellen*) to make; **das Radio leiser machen** to turn the radio down; **aus Holz gemacht** made of wood; **das Essen machen** to get the meal; **Schluss machen** to finish (off)
3 (*verursachen, bewirken*) to make; **jdm Angst machen** to make sb afraid; **das macht die Kälte** it's the cold that does that
4 (*ausmachen*) to matter; **das macht nichts** that doesn't matter; **die Kälte macht mir nichts** I don't mind the cold
5 (*kosten: ergeben*) to be; **3 und 5 macht 8** 3 and 5 is *od* are 8; **was** *od* **wie viel macht das?** how much does that come to?
6: was macht die Arbeit? how's the work going?; **was macht dein Bruder?** how is your brother doing?; **das Auto machen lassen** to have the car done; **machs gut!** take care!; (*viel Glück*) good luck!
▷ *vi*: **mach schnell!** hurry up!; **mach schon!** come on!; **jetzt macht sie auf große Dame** (*umg*) she's playing the lady now; **lass mich mal machen** (*umg*) let me do it; (*ich bringe das in Ordnung*) I'll deal with it; **groß/klein machen** (*umg: Notdurft*) to do a big/little job; **sich** *dat* **in die Hose machen** to wet o.s.; **ins Bett machen** to wet one's bed; **das macht müde** it makes you tired; **in etw** *dat* **machen** to be *od* deal in sth
▷ *vr* to come along (nicely); **sich an etw** *akk* **machen** to set about sth; **sich verständlich machen** to make o.s. understood; **sich** *dat* **viel aus jdm/etw machen** to like sb/sth; **mach dir nichts daraus** don't let it bother you; **sich auf den Weg machen** to get going; **sich an etw** *akk* **machen** to set about sth
Macho ['matʃo] (*umg*) *adj* macho
Macht [maxt] (**-, ̈-e**) *f* power; **mit aller ~** with all one's might; **an der ~ sein** to be in power; **alles in unserer ~ Stehende** everything in our power; **Machthaber** (**-s, -**) *m* ruler
mächtig ['mɛçtɪç] *adj* powerful, mighty; (*umg: ungeheuer*) enormous
Macht- *zW*: **machtlos** *adj* powerless; **Machtprobe** *f* trial of strength; **Machtstellung** *f* position of power; **Machtwort** *nt*: **ein Machtwort sprechen** to lay down the law
Machwerk *nt* work; (*schlechte Arbeit*) botched job
Madagaskar [mada'gaskar] (**-s**) *nt* Madagascar
Mädchen ['mɛːtçən] *nt* girl; **ein ~ für alles** (*umg*) a dogsbody; (*im Büro etc*) a girl Friday; **mädchenhaft** *adj* girlish; **Mädchenname** *m* maiden name
Made ['maːdə] (**-, -n**) *f* maggot
Madeira¹ [ma'deːra] (**-s**) *nt* (*Geog*) Madeira
Madeira² (**-s, -s**) *m* (*Wein*) Madeira
madig ['maːdɪç] *adj* maggoty
Magazin [maga'tsiːn] (**-s, -e**) *nt* (*Zeitschrift, am Gewehr*) magazine; (*Lager*) storeroom; (*Bibliotheksmagazin*) stockroom
Magen ['maːgən] (**-s, -** *od* **̈-**) *m* stomach; **jdm auf den ~ schlagen** (*umg*) to upset sb's stomach; (*fig*) to upset sb; **sich** *dat* **den ~ verderben** to upset one's stomach; **Magengeschwür** *nt* stomach ulcer; **Magenschmerzen** *pl* stomach-ache *sing*
mager ['maːgər] *adj* lean; (*dünn*) thin; **Magerkeit** *f* leanness; thinness; **Magersucht** *f* (*Med*) anorexia; **magersüchtig** *adj* anorexic
Magie [ma'giː] *f* magic
Magier ['maːgiər] (**-s, -**) *m* magician
magisch ['maːgɪʃ] *adj* magical
Magnet [ma'gneːt] (**-s** *od* **-en, -en**) *m* magnet; **Magnetband** *nt* (*Comput*) magnetic tape; **magnetisch** *adj* magnetic
magnetisieren [magneti'ziːrən] *vt* to

magnetize
Magnetnadel *f* magnetic needle
Mahagoni [maha'go:ni] (**-s**) *nt* mahogany
mähen ['mɛ:ən] *vt, vi* to mow
Mahl [ma:l] (**-(e)s, -e**) *nt* meal
mahlen *unreg vt* to grind
Mahlstein *m* grindstone
Mahlzeit *f* meal ▷ *interj* enjoy your meal!
Mahnbrief *m* reminder
Mähne ['mɛ:nə] (**-, -n**) *f* mane
mahnen ['ma:nən] *vt* to remind; (*warnend*) to warn; (*wegen Schuld*) to demand payment from; **jdn zur Eile/Geduld** *etc* **~** (*auffordern*) to urge sb to hurry/be patient *etc*
Mahnung *f* admonition, warning; (*Mahnbrief*) reminder
Mai [maɪ] (**-(e)s, -e**) (*pl selten*) *m* May; *siehe auch* **September**: **Maiglöckchen** *nt* lily of the valley; **Maikäfer** *m* cockchafer
Mail [me:l] (**-, -s**) *f* (*Comput*) e-mail
Main [maɪn] (**-(e)s**) *m* (*Fluss*) Main
Mais [maɪs] (**-es, -e**) *m* maize, corn (*US*); **Maiskolben** *m* corncob
Majestät [majɛs'tɛ:t] *f* majesty
majestätisch *adj* majestic
Majonäse [majɔ'nɛ:zə] (**-, -n**) *f* mayonnaise
Major [ma'jo:r] (**-s, -e**) *m* (*Mil*) major; (*Aviat*) squadron leader
Majoran [majo'ra:n] (**-s, -e**) *m* marjoram
makaber [ma'ka:bər] *adj* macabre
Makel ['ma:kəl] (**-s, -**) *m* blemish; (*moralisch*) stain; **ohne ~** flawless; **makellos** *adj* immaculate, spotless
mäkeln ['mɛ:kəln] *vi* to find fault
Make-up [me:k'|ap] (**-s, -s**) *nt* make-up; (*flüssig*) foundation
Makkaroni [maka'ro:ni] *pl* macaroni *sing*
Makler ['ma:klər] (**-s, -**) *m* broker; (*Grundstücksmakler*) estate agent (*Brit*), realtor (*US*)
Makrele [ma'kre:lə] (**-, -n**) *f* mackerel
Makrone [ma'kro:nə] (**-, -n**) *f* macaroon
Mal [ma:l] (**-(e)s, -e**) *nt* mark, sign; (*Zeitpunkt*) time; **ein für alle ~** once and for all; **mit einem ~(e)** all of a sudden; **das erste ~** the first time; **jedes ~** every time, each time; **zum letzten ~** for the last time; **ein paar ~** a few times
mal *adv* times
Malawi [ma'la:vi] (**-s**) *nt* Malawi
Malaysia [ma'laɪzia] (**-s**) *nt* Malaysia
Malediven [male'di:vən] *pl*: **die ~** the Maldive Islands
malen *vt, vi* to paint
Maler (**-s, -**) *m* painter
Malerei [ma:lə'raɪ] *f* painting
malerisch *adj* picturesque
Malkasten *m* paintbox
Mallorca [ma'jɔrka, ma'lɔrka] (**-s**) *nt* Majorca
Malta ['malta] (**-s**) *nt* Malta
maltesisch *adj* Maltese
Malz [malts] (**-es**) *nt* malt; **Malzbonbon** *nt or m* cough drop; **Malzkaffee** *m coffee substitute made from malt barley*
Mama ['mama:] (**-, -s**) (*umg*) *f* mum(my) (*Brit*), mom(my) (*US*)
Mammut ['mamʊt] (**-s, -e** *od* **-s**) *nt* mammoth ▷ *in zW* mammoth, giant
man [man] *pron* one, you, people *pl*; **~ hat mir gesagt ...** I was told ...
managen ['mɛnɪdʒən] *vt* to manage; **ich manage das schon!** (*umg*) I'll fix it somehow!
Manager, in (**-s, -**) *m(f)* manager
manche, r, s *adj* many a; (*pl*) a number of ▷ *pron* some
mancherlei [mançər'laɪ] *adj inv* various ▷ *pron* a variety of things
manchmal *adv* sometimes
Mandant, in [man'dant(ɪn)] *m(f)* (*Jur*) client
Mandarine [manda'ri:nə] *f* mandarin, tangerine
Mandat [man'da:t] (**-(e)s, -e**) *nt* mandate; **sein ~ niederlegen** (*Parl*) to resign one's seat
Mandel ['mandəl] (**-, -n**) *f* almond; (*Anat*) tonsil; **Mandelentzündung** *f* tonsillitis
Manege [ma'nɛ:ʒə] (**-, -n**) *f* ring, arena
Mangel[1] ['maŋəl] (**-, -n**) *f* mangle; **durch die ~ drehen** (*fig: umg*) to put through it; (*Prüfling etc*) to put through the mill
Mangel[2] ['maŋəl] (**-s, ¨-**) *m* lack; (*Knappheit*) shortage; (*Fehler*) defect, fault; **~ an** *+dat* shortage of
Mangelerscheinung *f* deficiency symptom
mangelhaft *adj* poor; (*fehlerhaft*) defective, faulty; (*Schulnote*) unsatisfactory
mangeln *vi unpers*: **es mangelt jdm an etw** *dat* sb lacks sth ▷ *vt* (*Wäsche*) to mangle
mangels *präp +gen* for lack of
Manie [ma'ni:] *f* mania
Manier [ma'ni:r] (**-**) *f* manner; (*Stil*) style; (*pej*) mannerism
Manifest [mani'fɛst] (**-es, -e**) *nt* manifesto
Maniküre [mani'ky:rə] (**-, -n**) *f* manicure
maniküren *vt* to manicure
manipulieren [manipu'li:rən] *vt* to manipulate
Manko ['maŋko] (**-s, -s**) *nt* deficiency; (*Comm*) deficit
Mann [man] (**-(e)s, ¨-er** *od* (*Naut*) **Leute**) *m* man; (*Ehemann*) husband; (*Naut*) hand; **pro ~** per head; **mit ~ und Maus untergehen** to go down with all hands; (*Passagierschiff*) to go down with no survivors; **seinen ~ stehen** to hold one's own; **etw an den ~ bringen** (*umg*) to get rid of sth; **einen kleinen ~ im Ohr haben** (*hum: umg*) to be crazy
Männchen ['mɛnçən] *nt* little man; (*Tier*) male; **~ machen** (*Hund*) to (sit up and) beg
Mannequin [manə'kɛ̃:] (**-s, -s**) *nt* fashion model
männlich ['mɛnlɪç] *adj* (*Biol*) male; (*fig, Gram*) masculine
Mannschaft *f* (*Sport, fig*) team; (*Naut, Aviat*) crew; (*Mil*) other ranks *pl*
Mannweib (*pej*) *nt* mannish woman

Manöver [ma'nø:vər] (**-s, -**) *nt* manoeuvre (*Brit*), maneuver (*US*)
manövrieren [manø'vri:rən] *vt, vi* to manoeuvre (*Brit*), maneuver (*US*)
Mansarde [man'zardə] (**-, -n**) *f* attic
Manschette [man'ʃɛtə] *f* cuff; (*Papiermanschette*) paper frill; (*Tech*) sleeve
Manschettenknopf *m* cufflink
Mantel ['mantəl] (**-s, ¨**) *m* coat; (*Tech*) casing, jacket
Manuskript [manu'skrɪpt] (**-(e)s, -e**) *nt* manuscript
Mappe ['mapə] (**-, -n**) *f* briefcase; (*Aktenmappe*) folder
Märchen ['mɛ:rçən] *nt* fairy tale; **märchenhaft** *adj* fabulous; **Märchenprinz** *m* prince charming
Marder ['mardər] (**-s, -**) *m* marten
Margarine [marga'ri:nə] *f* margarine
Marienkäfer *m* ladybird
Marihuana [marihu'a:na] (**-s**) *nt* marijuana
Marine [ma'ri:nə] *f* navy; **marineblau** *adj* navy-blue
marinieren [mari'ni:rən] *vt* to marinate
Marionette [mario'nɛtə] *f* puppet
Mark¹ [mark] (**-, -**) *f* (*Hist: Geld*) mark
Mark² [mark] (**-(e)s**) *nt* (*Knochenmark*) marrow; **jdn bis ins ~ treffen** (*fig*) to cut sb to the quick; **jdm durch ~ und Bein gehen** to go right through sb
markant [mar'kant] *adj* striking
Marke ['markə] (**-, -n**) *f* mark; (*Warensorte*) brand; (*Fabrikat*) make; (*Rabattmarke, Briefmarke*) stamp; (*Essen(s)marke*) luncheon voucher; (*aus Metall etc*) token, disc
Marketing ['markətɪŋ] (**-s**) *nt* marketing
markieren [mar'ki:rən] *vt* to mark; (*umg*) to act ▷ *vi* (*umg*) to act it
Markierung *f* marking
Markise [mar'ki:zə] (**-, -n**) *f* awning
Markstück *nt* (*Hist*) one-mark piece
Markt [markt] (**-(e)s, ¨e**) *m* market: **Marktanteil** *m* market share; **Marktforschung** *f* market research; **Marktplatz** *m* market place; **Marktwirtschaft** *f* market economy
Marmelade [marmə'la:də] (**-, -n**) *f* jam
Marmor ['marmɔr] (**-s, -e**) *m* marble
marmorieren [marmo'ri:rən] *vt* to marble
marmorn *adj* marble
Marokkaner, in [marɔ'ka:nər(ɪn)] (**-s, -**) *m(f)* Moroccan
marokkanisch *adj* Moroccan
Marokko [ma'rɔko] (**-s**) *nt* Morocco
Marone [ma'ro:nə] (**-, -n**) *f* chestnut
Marotte [ma'rɔtə] (**-, -n**) *f* fad, quirk
Marsch¹ [marʃ] (**-, -en**) *f* marsh
Marsch² (**-(e)s, ¨e**) *m* march; **jdm den ~ blasen** (*umg*) to give sb a rocket; **marsch** *interj* march; **marsch ins Bett!** off to bed with you!
Marschbefehl *m* marching orders *pl*
marschbereit *adj* ready to move
marschieren [mar'ʃi:rən] *vi* to march
Märtyrer, in ['mɛrtyrər(ɪn)] (**-s, -**) *m(f)* martyr
März [mɛrts] (**-(es), -e**) (*pl selten*) *m* March; *siehe auch* **September**
Marzipan [martsi'pa:n] (**-s, -e**) *nt* marzipan
Masche ['maʃə] (**-, -n**) *f* mesh; (*Strickmasche*) stitch; **das ist die neueste ~** that's the latest dodge; **durch die ~n schlüpfen** to slip through the net
Maschendraht *m* wire mesh
Maschine [ma'ʃi:nə] *f* machine; (*Motor*) engine; **~ schreiben** to type
maschinell [maʃi'nɛl] *adj* machine(-), mechanical
Maschinen- *zW*: **Maschinenbauer** *m* mechanical engineer; **Maschinengewehr** *nt* machine gun; **maschinenlesbar** *adj* (*Comput*) machine-readable; **Maschinenpistole** *f* submachine gun; **Maschinenschaden** *m* mechanical fault; **Maschinenschlosser** *m* fitter; **Maschinenschrift** *f* typescript
Maschinist, in [maʃi'nɪst(ɪn)] *m(f)* engineer
Maser ['ma:zər] (**-, -n**) *f* grain
Masern *pl* (*Med*) measles *sing*
Maserung *f* grain(ing)
Maske ['maskə] (**-, -n**) *f* mask
Maskenball *m* fancy-dress ball
Maskerade [maskə'ra:də] *f* masquerade
maskieren [mas'ki:rən] *vt* to mask; (*verkleiden*) to dress up ▷ *vr* to disguise o.s., dress up
Maskulinum [masku'li:nʊm] (**-s, Maskulina**) *nt* (*Gram*) masculine noun
Maß¹ [ma:s] (**-es, -e**) *nt* measure; (*Mäßigung*) moderation; (*Grad*) degree, extent; **über alle ~en** (*liter*) extremely, beyond measure; **~ halten** = **maßhalten**; **mit zweierlei ~ messen** (*fig*) to operate a double standard; **sich** *dat* **etw nach ~ anfertigen lassen** to have sth made to measure *od* order (*US*); **in besonderem ~e** especially; **das ~ ist voll** (*fig*) that's enough (of that)
Maß² (**-, -(e)**) *f* litre (*Brit*) *od* liter (*US*) of beer
maß *etc vb siehe* **messen**
Massage [ma'sa:ʒə] (**-, -n**) *f* massage
Maßanzug *m* made-to-measure suit
Maßarbeit *f* (*fig*) neat piece of work
Masse ['masə] (**-, -n**) *f* mass; **eine ganze ~** (*umg*) a great deal
Massen- *zW*: **Massenartikel** *m* mass-produced article; **Massengrab** *nt* mass grave; **massenhaft** *adj* masses of; **Massenmedien** *pl* mass media *pl*
Masseur [ma'sø:r] *m* masseur
Maß- *zW*: **maßgebend** *adj* authoritative; **maßgebende Kreise** influential circles; **maßhalten** *unreg vi* to exercise moderation
massieren [ma'si:rən] *vt* to massage; (*Mil*) to mass
massig ['masɪç] *adj* massive; (*umg*) a massive amount of
mäßig ['mɛ:sɪç] *adj* moderate; **mäßigen** ['mɛ:sɪgən] *vt* to restrain, moderate; **sein**

Tempo mäßigen to slacken one's pace; **Mäßigkeit** *f* moderation
massiv [ma'si:f] *adj* solid; (*fig*) heavy, rough; **~ werden** (*umg*) to turn nasty; **Massiv** (**-s, -e**) *nt* massif
Maß- *zW*: **Maßkrug** *m* tankard; **maßlos** *adj* (*Verschwendung, Essen, Trinken*) excessive, immoderate; (*Enttäuschung, Ärger etc*) extreme; **Maßnahme** (**-, -n**) *f* measure, step
Maßstab *m* rule, measure; (*fig*) standard; (*Geog*) scale; **als ~ dienen** to serve as a model
maßvoll *adj* moderate
Mast [mast] (**-(e)s, -e(n)**) *m* mast; (*Elek*) pylon
mästen ['mɛstən] *vt* to fatten
Material [materi'a:l] (**-s, -ien**) *nt* material(s); **Materialfehler** *m* material defect
Materialismus [materia'lismus] *m* materialism
Materialist, in *m(f)* materialist; **materialistisch** *adj* materialistic
Materie [ma'te:riə] *f* matter, substance
materiell [materi'ɛl] *adj* material
Mathematik [matema'ti:k] *f* mathematics *sing*; **Mathematiker, in** [mate'ma:tıkər(ın)] (**-s, -**) *m(f)* mathematician
mathematisch [mate'ma:tıʃ] *adj* mathematical
Matjeshering ['matjəshe:rıŋ] (*umg*) *m* salted young herring
Matratze [ma'tratsə] (**-, -n**) *f* mattress
Matrixdrucker *m* dot-matrix printer
Matrose [ma'tro:zə] (**-n, -n**) *m* sailor
Matsch [matʃ] (**-(e)s**) *m* mud; (*Schneematsch*) slush
matschig *adj* muddy; slushy
matt [mat] *adj* weak; (*glanzlos*) dull; (*Phot*) matt; (*Schach*) mate; **jdn ~ setzen** (*lit*) to checkmate sb; *siehe auch* **mattsetzen**
Matte ['matə] (**-, -n**) *f* mat; **auf der ~ stehen** (*am Arbeitsplatz etc*) to be in
Mattscheibe *f* (*TV*) screen; **~ haben** (*umg*) to be not quite with it
Matura [ma'tu:ra] (**-**) (*Österr, Schweiz*) *f* = **Abitur**
Mauer ['mauər] (**-, -n**) *f* wall
mauern *vi* to build, lay bricks ▷ *vt* to build
Maul [maul] (**-(e)s, Mäuler**) *nt* mouth; **ein loses** *od* **lockeres ~ haben** (*umg: frech sein*) to be an impudent so-and-so; (*: indiskret sein*) to be a blabbermouth; **halts ~!** (*umg*) shut your face! (*!*); **darüber werden sich die Leute das ~ zerreißen** (*umg*) that will start people's tongues wagging; **dem Volk** *od* **den Leuten aufs ~ schauen** (*umg*) to listen to what ordinary people say: **maulen** (*umg*) *vi* to grumble; **Maulesel** *m* mule; **Maulkorb** *m* muzzle; **Maulsperre** *f* lockjaw; **Maultier** *nt* mule
Maulwurf *m* mole
Maurer ['maurər] (**-s, -**) *m* bricklayer; **pünktlich wie die ~** (*hum*) super-punctual
Mauretanien [maurə'ta:niən] (**-s**) *nt* Mauritania
Maus [maus] (**-, Mäuse**) *f* (*auch Comput*) mouse; **Mäuse** *pl* (*umg: Geld*) bread *sing*, dough *sing*
Mausefalle *f* mousetrap
mausen *vt* (*umg*) to pinch ▷ *vi* to catch mice
mausern *vr* to moult (*Brit*), molt (*US*)
mausetot *adj* stone dead
Mausklick [mausklık] *nt* (*Comput*) (mouse) click
Maut [maut] (**-, -en**) *f* toll
maximal [maksi'ma:l] *adj* maximum
Maxime [ma'ksi:mə] (**-, -n**) *f* maxim
maximieren [maksi'mi:rən] *vt* to maximize
Mayonnaise [majɔ'nɛ:zə] (**-, -n**) *f* mayonnaise
Mazedonien [matse'do:niən] (**-s**) *nt* Macedonia
Mechanik [me'ça:nık] *f* mechanics *sing*; (*Getriebe*) mechanics *pl*; **Mechaniker** (**-s, -**) *m* mechanic, engineer
mechanisch *adj* mechanical
Mechanismus [meça'nısmus] *m* mechanism
meckern ['mɛkərn] *vi* to bleat; (*umg*) to moan
Mecklenburg-Vorpommern (**-s**) *nt* (state of) Mecklenburg-Vorpommern
Medaille [me'daljə] (**-, -n**) *f* medal
Medaillon [medal'jõ:] (**-s, -s**) *nt* (*Schmuck*) locket
Medien ['me:diən] *pl* media *pl*; **Mediengesellschaft** *f* media society
Medikament [medika'mɛnt] *nt* medicine
Meditation [meditatsi'o:n] *f* meditation
meditieren [medi'ti:rən] *vi* to meditate
Medizin [medi'tsi:n] (**-, -en**) *f* medicine
medizinisch *adj* medical; **~-technische Assistentin** medical assistant
Meer [me:r] (**-(e)s, -e**) *nt* sea; **am ~(e)** by the sea; **ans ~ fahren** to go to the sea(side); **Meerbusen** *m* bay, gulf; **Meerenge** *f* straits *pl*
Meeresspiegel *m* sea level
Meer- *zW*: **Meerrettich** *m* horseradish; **Meerschweinchen** *nt* guinea pig
Mega-, mega- [mɛga-] *in zw* mega-; **Megabyte** [mega'baıt] *nt* megabyte; **Megafon**, **Megaphon** [mega'fo:n] (**-s, -e**) *nt* megaphone
Mehl [m'e:l] (**-(e)s, -e**) *nt* flour
mehlig *adj* floury
mehr [me:r] *adv* more; **nie ~** never again, nevermore (*liter*); **es war niemand ~ da** there was no one left; **nicht ~ lange** not much longer; **Mehraufwand** *m* additional expenditure; **mehrdeutig** *adj* ambiguous
mehrere *indef pron* several; (*verschiedene*) various; **~s** several things
mehrfach *adj* multiple; (*wiederholt*) repeated
Mehrheit *f* majority
mehr- *zW*: **mehrmalig** *adj* repeated; **mehrmals** *adv* repeatedly; **Mehrprogrammbetrieb** *m* (*Comput*) multiprogramming; **mehrsprachig** *adj* multilingual; **mehrstimmig** *adj* for several

voices; **mehrstimmig singen** to harmonize; **Mehrwegflasche** *f* returnable bottle; **Mehrwertsteuer** *f* value added tax, VAT; **Mehrzahl** *f* majority; (*Gram*) plural

Mehrzweck- *in zw* multipurpose

meiden ['maɪdən] *unreg vt* to avoid

Meile ['maɪlə] (**-, -n**) *f* mile; **das riecht man drei ~n gegen den Wind** (*umg*) you can smell that a mile off

Meilenstein *m* milestone

meilenweit *adj* for miles

mein [maɪn] *pron* my

meine, r, s *poss pron* mine

Meineid ['maɪn|aɪt] *m* perjury

meinen ['maɪnən] *vt* to think; (*sagen*) to say; (*sagen wollen*) to mean ▷*vi* to think; **wie Sie ~!** as you wish; **damit bin ich gemeint** that refers to me; **das will ich ~** I should think so

meiner *gen von* **ich** ▷*pron* of me

meinerseits *adv* for my part

meinesgleichen ['maɪnəs'glaɪçən] *pron* people like me

meinetwegen ['maɪnət've:gən] *adv* (*für mich*) for my sake; (*wegen mir*) on my account; (*von mir aus*) as far as I'm concerned; (*ich habe nichts dagegen*) I don't care *od* mind

Meinung ['maɪnʊŋ] *f* opinion; **meiner ~ nach** in my opinion; **einer ~ sein** to think the same; **jdm die ~ sagen** to give sb a piece of one's mind

Meinungs- *zW*: **Meinungsaustausch** *m* exchange of views; **Meinungsumfrage** *f* opinion poll; **Meinungsverschiedenheit** *f* difference of opinion

Meise ['maɪzə] (**-, -n**) *f* tit(mouse); **eine ~ haben** (*umg*) to be crackers

Meißel ['maɪsəl] (**-s, -**) *m* chisel

meißeln *vt* to chisel

meist [maɪst] *adj* most ▷*adv* mostly

meiste, r, s *superl von* **viel**

meistens *adv* mostly

Meister ['maɪstər] (**-s, -**) *m* master; (*Sport*) champion; **seinen ~ machen** to take one's master craftsman's diploma; **es ist noch kein ~ vom Himmel gefallen** (*Sprichwort*) no one is born an expert; **meisterhaft** *adj* masterly

Meister- *zW*: **Meisterschaft** *f* mastery; (*Sport*) championship; **Meisterstück** *nt* masterpiece

Melancholie [melaŋko'li:] *f* melancholy

melancholisch [melaŋ'ko:lɪʃ] *adj* melancholy

Meldefrist *f* registration period

melden *vt* to report; (*registrieren*) to register ▷*vr* to report; to register; (*Sch*) to put one's hand up; (*freiwillig*) to volunteer; (*auf etw, am Telefon*) to answer; **nichts zu ~ haben** (*umg*) to have no say; **wen darf ich ~?** who shall I say (is here)?; **sich ~ bei** to report to; to register with; **sich auf eine Anzeige ~** to answer an advertisement; **es meldet sich niemand** there's no answer; **sich zu Wort ~** to ask to speak

Meldepflicht *f* obligation to register with the police

Meldestelle *f* registration office

Meldung ['mɛldʊŋ] *f* announcement; (*Bericht*) report

meliert [me'li:rt] *adj* mottled, speckled

melken ['mɛlkən] *unreg vt* to milk

Melodie [melo'di:] *f* melody, tune

melodisch [me'lo:dɪʃ] *adj* melodious, tuneful

Melone [me'lo:nə] (**-, -n**) *f* melon; (*Hut*) bowler (hat)

Membran [mem'bra:n] (**-, -en**) *f* (*Tech*) diaphragm; (*Anat*) membrane

Memoiren [memo'a:rən] *pl* memoirs *pl*

Menge ['mɛŋə] (**-, -n**) *f* quantity; (*Menschenmenge*) crowd; (*große Anzahl*) lot (of); **jede ~** (*umg*) masses *pl*, loads *pl*

mengen *vt* to mix ▷*vr*: **sich ~ in** *+akk* to meddle with

Mengen- *zW*: **Mengenlehre** *f* (*Math*) set theory; **Mengenrabatt** *m* bulk discount

Menorca [me'nɔrka] (**-s**) *nt* Menorca

Mensa ['mɛnza] (**-, -s** *od* **Mensen**) *f* (*Univ*) refectory (*Brit*), commons (*US*)

Mensch [mɛnʃ] (**-en, -en**) *m* human being, man; (*Person*) person; **kein ~** nobody; **ich bin auch nur ein ~!** I'm only human; **~ ärgere dich nicht** *nt* (*Spiel*) ludo

Menschen- *zW*: **Menschenfeind** *m* misanthrope; **menschenfreundlich** *adj* philanthropical; **Menschenkenner** *m* judge of human nature; **menschenmöglich** *adj* humanly possible; **Menschenrechte** *pl* human rights *pl*; **menschenunwürdig** *adj* degrading; **Menschenverstand** *m*: **gesunder Menschenverstand** common sense

Mensch- *zW*: **Menschheit** *f* humanity, mankind; **menschlich** *adj* human; (*human*) humane; **Menschlichkeit** *f* humanity

Menstruation [mɛnstruatsi'o:n] *f* menstruation

Mentalität [mɛntali'tɛ:t] *f* mentality

Menü [me'ny:] (**-s, -s**) *nt* (*auch Comput*) menu; **menügesteuert** *adj* (*Comput*) menu-driven

Merkblatt *nt* instruction sheet *od* leaflet

merken ['mɛrkən] *vt* to notice; **sich** *dat* **etw ~** to remember sth; **sich** *dat* **eine Autonummer ~** to make a (mental) note of a licence (*Brit*) *od* license (*US*) number

merklich *adj* noticeable

Merkmal *nt* sign, characteristic

merkwürdig *adj* odd

Mess- *zW*: **messbar** *adj* measurable; **Messbecher** *m* measuring cup

Messbuch *nt* missal

Messe ['mɛsə] (**-, -n**) *f* fair; (*Eccl*) mass; (*Mil*) mess; **auf der ~** at the fair; **Messegelände** *nt* exhibition centre (*Brit*) *od* center (*US*)

messen *unreg vt* to measure ▷*vr* to compete

Messer (**-s, -**) *nt* knife; **auf des ~s Schneide stehen** (*fig*) to hang in the balance; **jdm ins offene ~ laufen** (*fig*) to walk into a trap; **Messerspitze** *f* knife point; (*in Rezept*) pinch

Messestand *m* exhibition stand

Messgerät *nt* measuring device, gauge
Messgewand *nt* chasuble
Messing ['mɛsɪŋ] (**-s**) *nt* brass
Metall [me'tal] (**-s, -e**) *nt* metal; **die ~ verarbeitende Industrie** the metal-processing industry; **metallen** *adj* metallic
Metastase [meta'sta:zə] (**-, -n**) *f* (*Med*) secondary growth
Meteor [mete'o:r] (**-s, -e**) *m* meteor
Meter ['me:tər] (**-s, -**) *m od nt* metre (*Brit*), meter (*US*); **in 500 ~ Höhe** at a height of 500 metres; **Metermaß** *nt* tape measure
Methode [me'to:də] (**-, -n**) *f* method
methodisch [me'to:dɪʃ] *adj* methodical
Metropole [metro'po:lə] (**-, -n**) *f* metropolis
Metzger ['mɛtsgər] (**-s, -**) *m* butcher
Metzgerei [mɛtsgə'raɪ] *f* butcher's (shop)
Meute ['mɔʏtə] (**-, -n**) *f* pack
Meuterei [mɔʏtə'raɪ] *f* mutiny
meutern *vi* to mutiny
Mexikaner, in [mɛksi'ka:nər(ɪn)] (**-s, -**) *m(f)* Mexican
mexikanisch *adj* Mexican
Mexiko ['mɛksiko] (**-s**) *nt* Mexico
MfG *abk* (= *mit freundlichen Grüßen*) (with) best wishes
MHz *abk* (= *Megahertz*) MHz
miauen [mi'aʊən] *vi* to miaow
mich [mɪç] *akk von* **ich** ▷ *pron* me; (*reflexiv*) myself
mied *etc* [mi:t] *vb siehe* **meiden**
Miene ['mi:nə] (**-, -n**) *f* look, expression; **gute ~ zum bösen Spiel machen** to grin and bear it
mies [mi:s] (*umg*) *adj* lousy
Mietauto *nt* hired car (*Brit*), rental car (*US*)
Miete ['mi:tə] (**-, -n**) *f* rent; **zur ~ wohnen** to live in rented accommodation *od* accommodations (*US*)
mieten *vt* to rent; (*Auto*) to hire (*Brit*), rent
Mieter, in (**-s, -**) *m(f)* tenant
Mietshaus *nt* tenement, block of flats (*Brit*) *od* apartments (*US*)
Miet- *zW*: **Mietvertrag** *m* tenancy agreement; **Mietwagen** *m* = **Mietauto**
Migräne [mi'grɛ:nə] (**-, -n**) *f* migraine
Mikrobe [mi'kro:bə] (**-, -n**) *f* microbe
Mikrochip *m* microchip
Mikrofon [mikro'fo:n] (**-s, e**) *nt* microphone
Mikroprozessor (**-s, -oren**) *m* microprocessor
Mikroskop [mikro'sko:p] (**-s, -e**) *nt* microscope; **mikroskopisch** *adj* microscopic
Mikrowelle ['mi:krovɛlə] *f* microwave
Mikrowellenherd *m* microwave (oven)
Milch [mɪlç] (**-**) *f* milk; (*Fischmilch*) milt, roe; **Milchglas** *nt* frosted glass
milchig *adj* milky
Milch- *zW*: **Milchkaffee** *m* white coffee; **Milchmixgetränk** *nt* milk shake; **Milchpulver** *nt* powdered milk; **Milchstraße** *f* Milky Way; **Milchzahn** *m* milk tooth
mild [mɪlt] *adj* mild; (*Richter*) lenient; (*freundlich*) kind, charitable
Milde ['mɪldə] (**-, -n**) *f* mildness; leniency
mildern *vt* to mitigate, soften; (*Schmerz*) to alleviate; **~de Umstände** extenuating circumstances
Milieu [mili'ø:] (**-s, -s**) *nt* background, environment; **milieugeschädigt** *adj* maladjusted
militant [mili'tant] *adj* militant
Militär [mili'tɛ:r] (**-s**) *nt* military, army; **Militärgericht** *nt* military court; **militärisch** *adj* military
Militarismus [milita'rɪsmʊs] *m* militarism
militaristisch *adj* militaristic
Militärpflicht *f* (compulsory) military service
Milliardär, in [mɪliar'dɛ:r(ɪn)] (**-s, -e**) *m(f)* multimillionaire
Milliarde [mɪli'ardə] (**-, -n**) *f* milliard, billion (*bes US*)
Millimeter *m* millimetre (*Brit*), millimeter (*US*)
Million [mɪli'o:n] (**-, -en**) *f* million
Millionär, in [mɪlio'nɛ:r(ɪn)] (**-s, -e**) *m(f)* millionaire
Milz [mɪlts] (**-, -en**) *f* spleen
Mimik ['mi:mɪk] *f* mime
Mimose [mi'mo:zə] (**-, -n**) *f* mimosa; (*fig*) sensitive person
minder ['mɪndər] *adj* inferior ▷ *adv* less
Minderheit *f* minority
minderjährig *adj* minor; **Minderjährigkeit** *f* minority
mindern *vt, vr* to decrease, diminish
Minderung *f* decrease
minder- *zW*: **minderwertig** *adj* inferior; **Minderwertigkeitskomplex** (**-es, -e**) *m* inferiority complex
Mindestalter *nt* minimum age
Mindestbetrag *m* minimum amount
mindeste, r, s *adj* least
mindestens *adv* at least
Mindest- *zW*: **Mindestlohn** *m* minimum wage; **Mindestmaß** *nt* minimum
Mine ['mi:nə] (**-, -n**) *f* mine; (*Bleistiftmine*) lead; (*Kugelschreibermine*) refill
Minenfeld *nt* minefield
Mineral [mine'ra:l] (**-s, -e** *od* **-ien**) *nt* mineral; **mineralisch** *adj* mineral; **Mineralölsteuer** *f* tax on oil and petrol (*Brit*) *od* gasoline (*US*); **Mineralwasser** *nt* mineral water
Miniatur [minia'tu:r] *f* miniature
minimal [mini'ma:l] *adj* minimal
Minimum ['mi:nimʊm] (**-s, Minima**) *nt* minimum
Minirock ['mɪnirɔk] *m* miniskirt
Minister, in [mi'nɪstər(ɪn)] (**-s, -**) *m(f)* (*Pol*) minister
ministeriell [minɪsteri'ɛl] *adj* ministerial
Ministerium [minɪs'te:riʊm] *nt* ministry
Ministerpräsident, in *m(f)* prime minister
minus ['mi:nʊs] *adv* minus; **Minus** (**-, -**) *nt* deficit; **Minuspol** *m* negative pole; **Minuszeichen** *nt* minus sign
Minute [mi'nu:tə] (**-, -n**) *f* minute; **auf die ~**

(genau *od* **pünktlich)** (right) on the dot
Minutenzeiger *m* minute hand
mir [mi:r] *dat von* **ich** ▷ *pron* (to) me; **von ~ aus!** I don't mind; **wie du ~, so ich dir** (*Sprichwort*) tit for tat (*umg*); (*als Drohung*) I'll get my own back; **~ nichts, dir nichts** just like that
Mischehe *f* mixed marriage
mischen *vt* to mix; (*Comput: Datei, Text*) to merge; (*Karten*) to shuffle ▷ *vi* (*Karten*) to shuffle
Misch- *zW*: **Mischling** *m* half-caste; **Mischpult** *nt* (*Rundf, TV*) mixing panel
Mischung *f* mixture
miserabel [mizə'ra:bəl] (*umg*) *adj* lousy; (*Gesundheit*) wretched; (*Benehmen*) dreadful
Miss- *zW*: **missachten** *vt untr* to disregard; **Missachtung** *f* disregard; **Missbehagen** *nt* uneasiness; (*Missfallen*) discontent; **Missbildung** *f* deformity; **missbilligen** *vt untr* to disapprove of; **Missbilligung** *f* disapproval; **Missbrauch** *m* abuse; (*falscher Gebrauch*) misuse; **missbrauchen** *vt untr* to abuse; to misuse; (*vergewaltigen*) to assault; **jdn zu** *od* **für etw missbrauchen** to use sb for *od* to do sth
Misserfolg *m* failure
Missetat ['mɪsəta:t] *f* misdeed
Missetäter *m* criminal; (*umg*) scoundrel
Miss- *zW*: **missfallen** *unreg vi untr*: **jdm missfallen** to displease sb; **Missfallen** (**-s**) *nt* displeasure; **Missgeburt** *f* freak; (*fig*) failure; **Missgeschick** *nt* misfortune; **missglücken** *vi untr* to fail; **jdm missglückt etw** sb does not succeed with sth; **Missgriff** *m* mistake; **Missgunst** *f* envy; **missgünstig** *adj* envious; **misshandeln** *vt untr* to ill-treat; **Misshandlung** *f* ill-treatment
Mission [mɪsi'o:n] *f* mission
Missionar, in [mɪsio'na:r(ɪn)] *m(f)* missionary
Missklang *m* discord
Misskredit *m* discredit
misslingen [mɪs'lɪŋən] *unreg vi untr* to fail
Miss- *zW*: **Missmut** *m* bad temper; **missmutig** *adj* cross; **missraten** *unreg vi untr* to turn out badly ▷ *adj* ill-bred; **Missstand** *m* deplorable state of affairs; **Missstimmung** *f* discord; (*Missmut*) ill feeling; **misstrauen** *vi untr* to mistrust; **Misstrauen** (**-s**) *nt*: **Misstrauen (gegenüber)** distrust (of), suspicion (of); **Misstrauensantrag** *m* (*Pol*) motion of no confidence; **Misstrauensvotum** *nt* (*Pol*) vote of no confidence; **misstrauisch** *adj* distrustful, suspicious; **Missverhältnis** *nt* disproportion; **Missverständnis** *nt* misunderstanding; **missverstehen** *unreg vt untr* to misunderstand
Mist [mɪst] (**-(e)s**) *m* dung; (*umg*) rubbish; **~!** (*umg*) blast!; **das ist nicht auf seinem ~ gewachsen** (*umg*) he didn't think that up himself
Mistel (**-, -n**) *f* mistletoe
Misthaufen *m* dungheap
mit [mɪt] *präp +dat* with; (*mittels*) by ▷ *adv* along, too; **~ der Bahn** by train; **~ dem nächsten Flugzeug/Bus kommen** to come on the next plane/bus; **~ Bleistift schreiben** to write in pencil; **~ Verlust** at a loss; **er ist ~ der Beste in der Gruppe** he is among the best in the group; **wie wärs ~ einem Bier?** (*umg*) how about a beer?; **~ 10 Jahren** at the age of 10; **wollen Sie ~?** do you want to come along?
Mitarbeit ['mit|arbaɪt] *f* cooperation; **mitarbeiten** *vi*: **mitarbeiten (an** *+dat***)** to cooperate (on), collaborate (on)
Mitarbeiter, in *m(f)* (*an Projekt*) collaborator; (*Kollege*) colleague; (*Angestellter*) member of staff ▷ *pl* staff
mit- *zW*: **Mitbestimmung** *f* participation in decision-making; (*Pol*) determination; **mitbringen** *unreg vt* to bring along; **Mitbringsel** ['mɪtbrɪŋzəl] (**-s, -**) *nt* (*Geschenk*) small present; (*Andenken*) souvenir; **Mitbürger, in** *m(f)* fellow citizen
miteinander [mɪt|aɪ'nandər] *adv* together, with one another
miterleben *vt* to see, witness
Mitesser ['mɪt|ɛsər] (**-s, -**) *m* blackhead
mit- *zW*: **mitfahren** *unreg vi*: **(mit jdm) mitfahren** to go (with sb); (*auf Reise auch*) to go *od* travel (with sb); **Mitfahrgelegenheit** *f* lift; **mitgeben** *unreg vt* to give; **Mitgefühl** *nt* sympathy; **mitgehen** *unreg vi* to go *od* come along; **etw mitgehen lassen** (*umg*) to pinch sth; **mitgenommen** *adj* done in, in a bad way; **Mitgift** *f* dowry
Mitglied ['mɪtgli:t] *nt* member
Mitgliedsbeitrag *m* membership fee, subscription
Mitgliedschaft *f* membership
mit- *zW*: **mithalten** *unreg vi* to keep up; **mithelfen** *vi unreg* to help, lend a hand; **bei etw mithelfen** to help with sth; **Mithilfe** *f* help, assistance; **mithören** *vt* to listen in to; **mitkommen** *unreg vi* to come along; (*verstehen*) to keep up, follow; **Mitläufer** *m* hanger-on; (*Pol*) fellow traveller
Mitleid *nt* sympathy; (*Erbarmen*) compassion
Mitleidenschaft *f*: **in ~ ziehen** to affect
mitleidig *adj* sympathetic
mitleidslos *adj* pitiless, merciless
mit- *zW*: **mitmachen** *vt* to join in, take part in; (*umg: einverstanden sein*): **da macht mein Chef nicht mit** my boss won't go along with that; **Mitmensch** *m* fellow man; **mitnehmen** *unreg vt* to take along *od* away; (*anstrengen*) to wear out, exhaust; **mitgenommen aussehen** to look the worse for wear
mitsamt [mɪt'zamt] *präp +dat* together with
Mitschuld *f* complicity
mitschuldig *adj*: **~ (an** *+dat***)** implicated (in); (*an Unfall*) partly responsible (for)
Mitschuldige, r *f(m)* accomplice
mit- *zW*: **Mitschüler, in** *m(f)* schoolmate;

mitspielen *vi* to join in, take part; **er hat ihr übel** *od* **hart mitgespielt** (*Schaden zufügen*) he has treated her badly; **Mitspieler, in** *m(f)* partner; **Mitspracherecht** *nt* voice, say
Mittag ['mɪta:k] (**-(e)s, -e**) *m* midday, noon, lunchtime; **morgen ~** tomorrow at lunchtime *od* noon; **~ machen** to take one's lunch hour; **(zu) ~ essen** to have lunch; **Mittagessen** *nt* lunch, dinner
mittags *adv* at lunchtime *od* noon
Mittags- *zW*: **Mittagspause** *f* lunch break; **Mittagsschlaf** *m* early afternoon nap, siesta; **Mittagszeit** *f*: **während** *od* **in der Mittagszeit** at lunchtime
Mittäter, in ['mɪttɛ:tər(ɪn)] *m(f)* accomplice
Mitte ['mɪtə] (**-, -n**) *f* middle; **aus unserer ~** from our midst
mitteilen ['mɪttaɪlən] *vt*: **jdm etw ~** to inform sb of sth, communicate sth to sb ▷ *vr*: **sich (jdm) ~** to communicate (with sb)
Mitteilung *f* communication; **jdm (eine) ~ von etw machen** (*form*) to inform sb of sth; (*bekannt geben*) to announce sth to sb
Mittel ['mɪtəl] (**-s, -**) *nt* means; (*Methode*) method; (*Math*) average; (*Med*) medicine; **kein ~ unversucht lassen** to try everything; **als letztes ~** as a last resort; **ein ~ zum Zweck** a means to an end; **Mittelalter** *nt* Middle Ages *pl*; **mittelalterlich** *adj* medieval; **Mittelamerika** *nt* Central America (and the Caribbean); **Mittelding** *nt* (*Mischung*) cross; **Mitteleuropa** *nt* Central Europe; **mittellos** *adj* without means; **mittelmäßig** *adj* mediocre, middling; **Mittelmäßigkeit** *f* mediocrity; **Mittelmeer** *nt* Mediterranean (Sea); **Mittelpunkt** *m* centre (*Brit*), center (*US*); **im Mittelpunkt stehen** to be centre-stage
mittels *präp +gen* by means of
Mittel- *zW*: **Mittelstand** *m* middle class; **Mittelstreckenrakete** *f* medium-range missile; **Mittelstreifen** *m* central reservation (*Brit*), median strip (*US*); **Mittelstürmer** *m* centre forward; **Mittelweg** *m* middle course; **Mittelwelle** *f* (*Rundf*) medium wave
mitten ['mɪtən] *adv* in the middle; **~ auf der Straße/in der Nacht** in the middle of the street/night
Mitternacht ['mɪtərnaxt] *f* midnight
mittlere, r, s ['mɪtlərə(r, s)] *adj* middle; (*durchschnittlich*) medium, average; **der M~ Osten** the Middle East; **~s Management** middle management; **~ Reife**
mittlerweile ['mɪtlər'vaɪlə] *adv* meanwhile
Mittwoch ['mɪtvɔx] (**-(e)s, -e**) *m* Wednesday; *siehe auch* **Dienstag**
mittwochs *adv* on Wednesdays
mitunter [mɪt'|ʊntər] *adv* occasionally, sometimes
mit- *zW*: **mitverantwortlich** *adj* also responsible; **Mitverschulden** *nt* contributory negligence; **mitwirken** *vi*: **(bei etw) mitwirken** to contribute (to sth); (*Theat*) to take part (in sth); **Mitwirkung** *f* contribution; participation; **unter Mitwirkung von** with the help of
Mixer ['mɪksər] (**-s, -**) *m* (*Barmixer*) cocktail waiter; (*Küchenmixer*) blender; (*Rührmaschine, Rundf, TV*) mixer
mobben ['mɔbən] *vt* to bully (at work)
Mobbing ['mɔbɪŋ] (**-s**) *nt* workplace bullying
Möbel ['mø:bəl] (**-s, -**) *nt* (piece of) furniture; **Möbelwagen** *m* furniture *od* removal van (*Brit*), moving van (*US*)
mobil [mo'bi:l] *adj* mobile; (*Mil*) mobilized
Mobilfunk *m* cellular telephone service
Mobiliar [mobili'a:r] (**-s, -e**) *nt* movable assets *pl*
Mobilmachung *f* mobilization
Mobiltelefon *nt* (*Telec*) mobile phone
möblieren [mø'bli:rən] *vt* to furnish; **möbliert wohnen** to live in furnished accommodation
mochte *etc* ['mɔxtə] *vb siehe* **mögen**
Mode ['mo:də] (**-, -n**) *f* fashion
Modell [mo'dɛl] (**-s, -e**) *nt* model
modellieren [modɛ'li:rən] *vt* to model
Modem ['mo:dɛm] (**-s, -s**) *nt* (*Comput*) modem
modern [mo'dɛrn] *adj* modern; (*modisch*) fashionable
modernisieren [modɛrni'zi:rən] *vt* to modernize
Mode- *zW*: **Modeschmuck** *m* fashion jewellery (*Brit*) *od* jewelry (*US*); **Modewort** *nt* fashionable word
modisch ['mo:dɪʃ] *adj* fashionable
Modul ['mo:dʊl] (**-s, -n**) *nt* (*Comput*) module
Modus ['mo:dʊs] (**-, Modi**) *m* way; (*Gram*) mood; (*Comput*) mode
Mofa ['mo:fa] (**-s, -s**) *nt* (*= Motorfahrrad*) small moped
mogeln ['mo:gəln] (*umg*) *vi* to cheat
mögen ['mø:gən] (*pt* **mochte**, *pp* **gemocht** *od (als Hilfsverb)* **mögen**) *vt, vi* to like; **magst du/mögen Sie ihn?** do you like him?; **ich möchte ...** I would like ..., I'd like ...; **er möchte in die Stadt** he'd like to go into town; **ich möchte nicht, dass du ...** I wouldn't like you to ...; **ich mag nicht mehr** I've had enough; (*bin am Ende*) I can't take any more; **man möchte meinen, dass ...** you would think that ...
▷ *hilfsverb* to like to; (*wollen*) to want; **möchtest du etwas essen?** would you like something to eat?; **sie mag nicht bleiben** she doesn't want to stay; **das mag wohl sein** that may very well be; **was mag das heißen?** what might that mean?; **Sie möchten zu Hause anrufen** could you please call home?
möglich ['mø:klɪç] *adj* possible; **er tat sein M~stes** he did his utmost
möglicherweise *adv* possibly
Möglichkeit *f* possibility; **nach ~** if possible
möglichst *adv* as ... as possible
Mohn [mo:n] (**-(e)s, -e**) *m* (*Mohnblume*) poppy;

(*Mohnsamen*) poppy seed
Möhre ['mø:rə] (**-, -n**) *f* carrot
mokieren [mo'ki:rən] *vr*: **sich über etw** *akk* **~** to make fun of sth
Moldawien [mɔl'da:viən] (**-s**) *nt* Moldavia
Mole ['mo:lə] (**-, -n**) *f* (*Naut*) mole
Molekül [mole'ky:l] (**-s, -e**) *nt* molecule
molk *etc* [mɔlk] *vb siehe* **melken**
Molkerei [mɔlkə'raɪ] *f* dairy
Moll [mɔl] (**-, -**) *nt* (*Mus*) minor (key)
mollig *adj* cosy; (*dicklich*) plump
Moment [mo'mɛnt] (**-(e)s, -e**) *m* moment ▷ *nt* factor, element; **im ~** at the moment; **~ mal!** just a minute!; **im ersten ~** for a moment
momentan [momɛn'ta:n] *adj* momentary ▷ *adv* at the moment
Monaco [mo'nako, 'mo:nako] (**-s**) *nt* Monaco
Monarch [mo'narç] (**-en, -en**) *m* monarch
Monarchie [monar'çi:] *f* monarchy
Monat ['mo:nat] (**-(e)s, -e**) *m* month; **sie ist im sechsten ~ (schwanger)** she's five months pregnant; **was verdient er im ~?** how much does he earn a month?
monatelang *adv* for months
monatlich *adj* monthly; **Monatskarte** *f* monthly ticket
Mönch [mœnç] (**-(e)s, -e**) *m* monk
Mond [mo:nt] (**-(e)s, -e**) *m* moon; **auf** *od* **hinter dem ~ leben** (*umg*) to be behind the times; **Mondfähre** *f* lunar (excursion) module; **Mondfinsternis** *f* eclipse of the moon; **Mondlandung** *f* moon landing; **Mondschein** *m* moonlight; **Mondsonde** *f* moon probe
monegassisch *adj* Monegasque
Mongole [mɔŋ'go:lə] (**-n, -n**) *m* Mongolian, Mongol
Mongolei [mɔŋgo'laɪ] *f*: **die ~** Mongolia
Mongolin *f* Mongolian, Mongol
mongolisch [mɔŋ'go:lɪʃ] *adj* Mongolian
mongoloid [mɔŋgolo'i:t] *adj* (*Med*) mongoloid
Monitor ['mo:nitɔr] *m* (*Bildschirm*) monitor
Monolog [mono'lo:k] (**-s, -e**) *m* monologue
Monopol (**-s, -e**) *nt* monopoly
monopolisieren [monopoli'zi:rən] *vt* to monopolize
monoton [mono'to:n] *adj* monotonous
Monotonie [monoto'ni:] *f* monotony
Monsun [mɔn'zu:n] (**-s, -e**) *m* monsoon
Montag ['mo:nta:k] (**-(e)s, -e**) *m* Monday; *siehe auch* **Dienstag**
Montage [mɔn'ta:ʒə] (**-, -n**) *f* (*Phot etc*) montage; (*Tech*) assembly; (*Einbauen*) fitting
montags *adv* on Mondays
Monteur [mɔn'tø:r] *m* fitter, assembly man
montieren [mɔn'ti:rən] *vt* to assemble, set up
Monument [monu'mɛnt] *nt* monument
monumental [monumɛn'ta:l] *adj* monumental
Moor [mo:r] (**-(e)s, -e**) *nt* moor
Moos [mo:s] (**-es, -e**) *nt* moss
Moped ['mo:pɛt] (**-s, -s**) *nt* moped
Mops [mɔps] (**-es, ¨-e**) *m* (*Hund*) pug
Moral [mo'ra:l] (**-, -en**) *f* morality; (*einer Geschichte*) moral; (*Disziplin: von Volk, Soldaten*) morale; **moralisch** *adj* moral; **einen** *od* **den moralischen haben** (*umg*) to have (a fit of) the blues
Moräne [mo'rɛ:nə] (**-, -n**) *f* moraine
Morast [mo'rast] (**-(e)s, -e**) *m* morass, mire
morastig *adj* boggy
Mord [mɔrt] (**-(e)s, -e**) *m* murder; **dann gibt es ~ und Totschlag** (*umg*) there'll be hell to pay; **Mordanschlag** *m* murder attempt
Mörder ['mœrdər] (**-s, -**) *m* murderer
Mordkommission *f* murder squad
Mords- *zW*: **Mordsglück** (*umg*) *nt* amazing luck; **mordsmäßig** (*umg*) *adj* terrific, enormous; **Mordsschreck** (*umg*) *m* terrible fright
Mord- *zW*: **Mordverdacht** *m* suspicion of murder; **Mordwaffe** *f* murder weapon
morgen ['mɔrgən] *adv* tomorrow; **bis ~!** see you tomorrow!; **~ in acht Tagen** a week (from) tomorrow; **~ um diese Zeit** this time tomorrow; **~ früh** tomorrow morning; **Morgen** (**-s, -**) *m* morning; (*Maß*) ≈ acre; **am Morgen** in the morning; **guten Morgen!** good morning!
Morgenmantel *m* dressing gown
morgens *adv* in the morning; **von ~ bis abends** from morning to night
morgig ['mɔrgɪç] *adj* tomorrow's; **der ~e Tag** tomorrow
Morphium ['mɔrfiʊm] *nt* morphine
morsch [mɔrʃ] *adj* rotten
Morsealphabet ['mɔrzə|alfabe:t] *nt* Morse code
morsen *vi* to send a message by Morse code
Mörtel ['mœrtəl] (**-s, -**) *m* mortar
Mosaik [moza'i:k] (**-s, -en** *od* **-e**) *nt* mosaic
Mosambik [mosam'bi:k] (**-s**) *nt* Mozambique
Moschee [mɔ'ʃe:] (**-, -n**) *f* mosque
Mosel[1] ['mo:zəl] *f* (*Geog*) Moselle
Mosel[2] (**-s, -**) *m* (*auch*: **Moselwein**) Moselle (wine)
Moskau ['mɔskaʊ] (**-s**) *nt* Moscow
Moskito [mɔs'ki:to] (**-s, -s**) *m* mosquito
Moslem ['mɔslɛm] (**-s, -s**) *m* Muslim
moslemisch [mɔs'le:mɪʃ] *adj* Muslim
Most [mɔst] (**-(e)s, -e**) *m* (unfermented) fruit juice; (*Apfelwein*) cider
Motel [mo'tɛl] (**-s, -s**) *nt* motel
Motiv [mo'ti:f] (**-s, -e**) *nt* motive; (*Mus*) theme
Motivation [motivatsi'o:n] *f* motivation
motivieren [moti'vi:rən] *vt* to motivate
Motivierung *f* motivation
Motor ['mo:tɔr] (**-s, -en**) *m* engine; (*bes Elek*) motor; **Motorboot** *nt* motorboat
Motorenöl *nt* engine oil
Motorhaube *f* (*Aut*) bonnet (*Brit*), hood (*US*)
motorisieren [motori'zi:rən] *vt* to motorize
Motor- *zW*: **Motorrad** *nt* motorcycle; **Motorradfahrer** *m* motorcyclist; **Motorroller** *m* motor scooter; **Motorschaden** *m* engine trouble *od* failure; **Motorsport** *m* motor sport

Motte ['mɔtə] (**-, -n**) *f* moth; **Mottenkugel** *f* mothball
Motto ['mɔto] (**-s, -s**) *nt* motto
Mountainbike *nt* mountain bike
Möwe ['mø:və] (**-, -n**) *f* seagull
MP3 *abk* (*Comput*) MP3
MS *abk* (= *Motorschiff*) motor vessel, MV; (= *multiple Sklerose*) MS
Mucke ['mʊkə] (**-, -n**) *f* (*meist pl*) caprice; (*von Ding*) snag, bug; **seine ~n haben** to be temperamental
Mücke ['mʏkə] (**-, -n**) *f* midge, gnat; **aus einer ~ einen Elefanten machen** (*umg*) to make a mountain out of a molehill
Mückenstich *m* midge *od* gnat bite
müde ['my:də] *adj* tired; **nicht ~ werden, etw zu tun** never to tire of doing something
Müdigkeit ['my:dɪçkait] *f* tiredness; **nur keine ~ vorschützen!** (*umg*) don't (you) tell me you're tired!
Muff [mʊf] (**-(e)s, -e**) *m* (*Handwärmer*) muff
Muffel (**-s, -**) (*umg*) *m* killjoy, sourpuss
muffig *adj* (*Luft*) musty
Mühe ['my:ə] (**-, -n**) *f* trouble, pains *pl*; **mit Müh(e) und Not** with great difficulty; **sich** *dat* **~ geben** to go to a lot of trouble; **mühelos** *adj* effortless, easy
muhen ['mu:ən] *vi* to low, moo
mühevoll *adj* laborious, arduous
Mühle ['my:lə] (**-, -n**) *f* mill; (*Kaffeemühle*) grinder; (*Mühlespiel*) nine men's morris
Mühsal (**-, -e**) *f* tribulation
mühsam *adj* arduous, troublesome ▷ *adv* with difficulty
mühselig *adj* arduous, laborious
Mulde ['mʊldə] (**-, -n**) *f* hollow, depression
Mull [mʊl] (**-(e)s, -e**) *m* thin muslin
Müll [mʏl] (**-(e)s**) *m* refuse, rubbish, garbage (*US*); **Müllabfuhr** *f* refuse *od* garbage (*US*) collection; (*Leute*) dustmen *pl* (*Brit*), garbage collectors *pl* (*US*); **Müllabladeplatz** *m* rubbish dump
Mullbinde *f* gauze bandage
Mülldeponie *f* waste disposal site, rubbish tip
Mülleimer *m* rubbish bin (*Brit*), garbage can (*US*)
Müller (**-s, -**) *m* miller
Müll- *zW*: **Müllschlucker** *m* waste (*Brit*) *od* garbage (*US*) disposal unit; **Mülltonne** *f* dustbin (*Brit*), trashcan (*US*); **Müllverbrennung** *f* rubbish *od* garbage (*US*) incineration; **Müllverbrennungsanlage** *f* incinerator, incinerating plant; **Müllwagen** *m* dustcart (*Brit*), garbage truck (*US*)
mulmig ['mʊlmɪç] *adj* rotten; (*umg*) uncomfortable; **jdm ist ~** sb feels funny
Multi ['mʊlti] (**-s, -s**) (*umg*) *m* multinational (organization)
multiple Sklerose [mʊl'ti:plə skle'ro:zə] *f* multiple sclerosis
multiplizieren [mʊltipli'tsi:rən] *vt* to multiply
Mumie ['mu:miə] *f* (*Leiche*) mummy
Mumm [mʊm] (**-s**) (*umg*) *m* gumption, nerve
Mumps [mʊmps] (**-**) *m od f* mumps *sing*
München ['mʏnçən] *nt* Munich
Mund [mʊnt] (**-(e)s, ¨er**) *m* mouth; **den ~ aufmachen** (*fig: seine Meinung sagen*) to speak up; **sie ist nicht auf den ~ gefallen** (*umg*) she's never at a loss for words; **Mundart** *f* dialect
Mündel ['mʏndəl] (**-s, -**) *nt* (*Jur*) ward
münden ['mʏndən] *vi*: **in etw** *akk* **~** to flow into sth
Mund- *zW*: **mundfaul** *adj* uncommunicative; **Mundgeruch** *m* bad breath; **Mundharmonika** *f* mouth organ
mündig ['mʏndɪç] *adj* of age; **Mündigkeit** *f* majority
mündlich ['mʏntlɪç] *adj* oral; **~e Prüfung** oral (exam); **~e Verhandlung** (*Jur*) hearing; **alles Weitere ~!** let's talk about it more when I see you
Mundstück *nt* mouthpiece; (*von Zigarette*) tip
Mündung ['mʏndʊŋ] *f* estuary; (*von Fluss, Rohr etc*) mouth; (*Gewehrmündung*) muzzle
Mund- *zW*: **Mundwasser** *nt* mouthwash; **Mundwerk** *nt*: **ein großes Mundwerk haben** to have a big mouth; **Mundwinkel** *m* corner of the mouth
Munition [munitsi'o:n] *f* ammunition
Munitionslager *nt* ammunition dump
munkeln ['mʊŋkəln] *vi* to whisper, mutter; **man munkelt, dass ...** there's a rumour (*Brit*) *od* rumor (*US*) that ...
Münster ['mʏnstər] (**-s, -**) *nt* minster
munter ['mʊntər] *adj* lively; (*wach*) awake; (*aufgestanden*) up and about; **Munterkeit** *f* liveliness
Münze ['mʏntsə] (**-, -n**) *f* coin
münzen *vt* to coin, mint; **auf jdn gemünzt sein** to be aimed at sb
Münzfernsprecher ['mʏntsfɛrnʃprɛçər] *m* callbox (*Brit*), pay phone (*US*)
mürb ['mʏrb], **mürbe** ['mʏrbə] *adj* (*Gestein*) crumbly; (*Holz*) rotten; (*Gebäck*) crisp; **jdn ~(e) machen** to wear sb down
murmeln *vt, vi* to murmur, mutter
Murmeltier ['mʊrməlti:r] *nt* marmot; **schlafen wie ein ~** to sleep like a log
murren ['mʊrən] *vi* to grumble, grouse
mürrisch ['mʏrɪʃ] *adj* sullen
Mus [mu:s] (**-es, -e**) *nt* purée
Muschel ['mʊʃəl] (**-, -n**) *f* mussel; (*Muschelschale*) shell; (*Telefonmuschel*) receiver
Muse ['mu:zə] (**-, -n**) *f* muse
Museum [mu'ze:ʊm] (**-s, Museen**) *nt* museum
Musik [mu'zi:k] *f* music; (*Kapelle*) band
musikalisch [muzi:'ka:lɪʃ] *adj* musical
Musikbox *f* jukebox
Musiker, in ['mu:zikər(ɪn)] (**-s, -**) *m(f)* musician
Musik- *zW*: **Musikhochschule** *f* music school; **Musikinstrument** *nt* musical instrument

musizieren [muzi'tsi:rən] *vi* to make music
Muskat [mʊs'ka:t] (**-(e)s, -e**) *m* nutmeg
Muskel ['mʊskəl] (**-s, -n**) *m* muscle; **Muskelkater** *m*: **einen Muskelkater haben** to be stiff
Muskulatur [mʊskula'tu:r] *f* muscular system
muskulös [mʊsku'lø:s] *adj* muscular
Müsli ['my:sli] (**-s, -**) *nt* muesli
Muss [mʊs] (**-**) *nt* necessity, must
Muße ['mu:sə] (**-**) *f* leisure
müßig ['my:sɪç] *adj* idle; **Müßiggang** *m* idleness
müssen ['mʏsən] (*pt* **musste**, *pp* **gemusst** *od (als Hilfsverb)* **müssen**) *vi* **1** (*Zwang*) must (*nur im Präsens*), to have to; **ich muss es tun** I must do it, I have to do it; **ich musste es tun** I had to do it; **er muss es nicht tun** he doesn't have to do it; **muss ich?** must I?, do I have to?; **wann müsst ihr zur Schule?** when do you have to go to school?; **der Brief muss heute noch zur Post** the letter must be posted (*Brit*) *od* mailed (*US*) today; **er hat gehen müssen** he (has) had to go; **muss das sein?** is that really necessary?; **wenn es (unbedingt) sein muss** if it's absolutely necessary; **ich muss mal** (*umg*) I need to go to the loo (*Brit*) *od* bathroom (*US*)
2 (*sollen*): **das musst du nicht tun!** you oughtn't to *od* shouldn't do that; **das müsstest du eigentlich wissen** you ought to *od* you should know that; **Sie hätten ihn fragen müssen** you should have asked him
3: **es muss geregnet haben** it must have rained; **es muss nicht wahr sein** it needn't be true
musste *etc* ['mʊstə] *vb siehe* **müssen**
Muster ['mʊstər] (**-s, -**) *nt* model; (*Dessin*) pattern; (*Probe*) sample; **~ ohne Wert** free sample; **mustergültig** *adj* exemplary
mustern *vt* (*betrachten, Mil*) to examine; (*Truppen*) to inspect
Musterung *f* (*von Stoff*) pattern; (*Mil*) inspection
Mut [mu:t] *m* courage; **nur ~!** cheer up!; **jdm ~ machen** to encourage sb; **~ fassen** to pluck up courage
mutig *adj* courageous
mutlos *adj* discouraged, despondent
mutmaßlich ['mu:tma:slɪç] *adj* presumed ▷ *adv* probably
Mutprobe *f* test of courage
Mutter[1] ['mʊtər] (**-, -n**) *f* (*Schraubenmutter*) nut
Mutter[2] ['mʊtər] (**-, ¨**) *f* mother
mütterlich ['mʏtərlɪç] *adj* motherly
mütterlicherseits *adv* on the mother's side
Mutter- *zW*: **Mutterliebe** *f* motherly love; **Muttermal** *nt* birthmark
Mutterschaft *f* motherhood
Mutterschaftsurlaub *m* maternity leave
Mutter- *zW*: **Mutterschutz** *m* maternity regulations *pl*; **mutterseelenallein** *adj* all alone; **Muttersprache** *f* native language; **Muttertag** *m* Mother's Day
Mutti (**-, -s**) (*umg*) *f* mum(my) (*Brit*), mom(my) (*US*)
mutwillig ['mu:tvɪlɪç] *adj* deliberate
Mütze ['mʏtsə] (**-, -n**) *f* cap
mysteriös [mʏsteri'ø:s] *adj* mysterious
Mythos ['my:tɔs] (**-, Mythen**) *m* myth

Nn

N¹, n [ɛn] *nt* N, n; **N wie Nordpol** ≈ N for Nellie, ≈ N for Nan (*US*)
N² [ɛn] *abk* (= *Norden*) N
na [na] *interj* well; **na gut** (*umg*) all right, OK; **na also!** (well,) there you are (then)!; **na so was!** well, I never!; **na und?** so what?
Nabel ['na:bəl] **(-s, -)** *m* navel; **der ~ der Welt** (*fig*) the hub of the universe; **Nabelschnur** *f* umbilical cord
nach [na:x] *präp +dat* **1** (*örtlich*) to; **nach Berlin** to Berlin; **nach links/rechts** (to the) left/right; **nach oben/hinten** up/back; **er ist schon nach London abgefahren** he has already left for London
2 (*zeitlich*) after; **einer nach dem anderen** one after the other; **nach Ihnen!** after you!; **zehn (Minuten) nach drei** ten (minutes) past *od* after (*US*) three
3 (*gemäß*) according to; **nach dem Gesetz** according to the law; **die Uhr nach dem Radio stellen** to put a clock right by the radio; **ihrer Sprache nach (zu urteilen)** judging by her language; **dem Namen nach** judging by his/her name; **nach allem, was ich weiß** as far as I know
▷ *adv*: **ihm nach!** after him!; **nach und nach** gradually, little by little; **nach wie vor** still
nachahmen ['na:x|a:mən] *vt* to imitate
Nachahmung *f* imitation; **etw zur ~ empfehlen** to recommend sth as an example
Nachbar, in ['naxba:r(ɪn)] **(-s, -n)** *m(f)* neighbour (*Brit*), neighbor (*US*); **Nachbarhaus** *nt*: **im Nachbarhaus** next door; **nachbarlich** *adj* neighbourly (*Brit*), neighborly (*US*); **Nachbarschaft** *f* neighbourhood (*Brit*), neighborhood (*US*); **Nachbarstaat** *m* neighbouring (*Brit*) *od* neighboring (*US*) state
nach- *zW*: **nachbestellen** *vt* to order again; **Nachbestellung** *f* (*Comm*) repeat order; **nachbilden** *vt* to copy; **Nachbildung** *f* imitation, copy; **nachblicken** *vi* to look *od* gaze after; **nachdatieren** *vt* to postdate
nachdem [na:x'de:m] *konj* after; (*weil*) since; **je ~ (ob)** it depends (whether)
nach- *zW*: **nachdenken** *unreg vi*: **über etw** *akk* **nachdenken** to think about sth; **darüber darf man gar nicht nachdenken** it doesn't bear thinking about; **Nachdenken** *nt* reflection, meditation; **nachdenklich** *adj* thoughtful, pensive; **nachdenklich gestimmt sein** to be in a thoughtful mood
Nachdruck ['na:xdrʊk] *m* emphasis; (*Typ*) reprint, reproduction; **besonderen ~ darauf legen, dass ...** to stress *od* emphasize particularly that ...
nachdrücklich ['na:xdrʏklɪç] *adj* emphatic; **~ auf etw** *dat* **bestehen** to insist firmly (up)on sth
nacheinander [na:x|aɪ'nandər] *adv* one after the other; **kurz ~** shortly after each other; **drei Tage ~** three days running, three days on the trot (*umg*)
nachempfinden ['na:x|ɛmpfɪndən] *unreg vt*: **jdm etw ~** to feel sth with sb
Nacherzählung *f* reproduction (of a story)
Nachfahr ['na:xfa:r] **(-en, -en)** *m* descendant
Nachfolge ['na:xfɔlgə] *f* succession; **die/jds ~ antreten** to succeed/succeed sb
nachfolgen *vi* (*lit*): **jdm/etw ~** to follow sb/sth
Nachfolger, in **(-s, -)** *m(f)* successor
nachforschen *vt, vi* to investigate
Nachforschung *f* investigation; **~en anstellen** to make enquiries
Nachfrage ['na:xfra:gə] *f* inquiry; (*Comm*) demand; **es besteht eine rege ~** (*Comm*) there is a great demand; **danke der ~** (*form*) thank you for your concern; (*umg*) nice of you to ask
nachfragen *vi* to inquire
nach- *zW*: **nachfühlen** *vt* = **nachempfinden**; **nachfüllen** *vt* to refill; **nachgeben** *unreg vi* to give way, yield
Nachgebühr *f* surcharge; (*Post*) excess postage
Nachgeburt *f* afterbirth
nachgehen ['na:xge:ən] *unreg vi* (*+dat*) to follow; (*erforschen*) to inquire (into); (*Uhr*) to be slow; **einer geregelten Arbeit ~** to have a steady job
Nachgeschmack ['na:xgəʃmak] *m* aftertaste
nachgiebig ['na:xgi:bɪç] *adj* soft, accommodating; **Nachgiebigkeit** *f* softness
nachhaltig ['na:xhaltɪç] *adj* lasting; (*Widerstand*) persistent
nachhelfen ['na:xhɛlfən] *unreg vi*: **jdm ~** to help *od* assist sb; **er hat dem Glück ein**

bisschen nachgeholfen he engineered himself a little luck
nachher [na:x'he:r] *adv* afterwards; **bis ~** see you later!
Nachholbedarf *m*: **einen ~ an etw** *dat* **haben** to have a lot of sth to catch up on
nachholen ['na:xho:lən] *vt* to catch up with; (*Versäumtes*) to make up for
Nachkomme ['na:xkɔmə] (**-n, -n**) *m* descendant
nachkommen *unreg vi* to follow; (*einer Verpflichtung*) to fulfil; **Sie können Ihr Gepäck ~ lassen** you can have your luggage sent on (after)
Nachkommenschaft *f* descendants *pl*
Nachkriegszeit *f* postwar period
Nach- *zW*: **Nachlass** (**-es, -lässe**) *m* (*Comm*) discount, rebate; (*Erbe*) estate; **nachlassen** *unreg vt* (*Strafe*) to remit; (*Summe*) to take off; (*Schulden*) to cancel ▷ *vi* to decrease, ease off; (*Sturm*) to die down; (*schlechter werden*) to deteriorate; **er hat nachgelassen** he has got worse; **nachlässig** *adj* negligent, careless; **Nachlässigkeit** *f* negligence, carelessness
nachlaufen ['na:xlaʊfən] *unreg vi*: **jdm ~** to run after *od* chase sb
nachlösen ['na:xlø:zən] *vi* to pay on the train/when one gets off; (*zur Weiterfahrt*) to pay the extra
nachmachen ['na:xmaxən] *vt* to imitate, copy; (*fälschen*) to counterfeit; **jdm etw ~** to copy sth from sb; **das soll erst mal einer ~!** I'd like to see anyone else do that!
Nachmittag ['na:xmɪta:k] *m* afternoon; **am ~** in the afternoon; **gestern/heute ~** yesterday/this afternoon
nachmittags *adv* in the afternoon
Nachnahme (**-, -n**) *f* cash on delivery (*Brit*), collect on delivery (*US*); **per ~** C.O.D.
Nachname *m* surname
Nachporto *nt* excess postage
nachprüfen ['na:xpry:fən] *vt* to check, verify
nachrechnen ['na:xrɛçnən] *vt* to check
Nachrede ['na:xre:də] *f*: **üble ~** (*Jur*) defamation of character
Nachricht ['na:xrɪçt] (**-, -en**) *f* (piece of) news *sing*; (*Mitteilung*) message; **Nachrichtenagentur** *f* news agency; **Nachrichtendienst** *m* (*Mil*) intelligence service; **Nachrichtensprecher, in** *m(f)* newsreader; **Nachrichtentechnik** *f* telecommunications *sing*
Nachruf ['na:xru:f] *m* obituary (notice)
nachrüsten ['na:xrʏstən] *vt* (*Kraftwerk etc*) to modernize; (*Auto etc*) to refit; (*Waffen*) to keep up to date ▷ *vi* (*Mil*) to deploy new arms
nachsagen ['na:xza:gən] *vt* to repeat; **jdm etw ~** to say sth of sb; **das lasse ich mir nicht ~!** I'm not having that said of me!
nachschicken ['na:xʃɪkən] *vt* to forward
nachschlagen ['na:xʃla:gən] *unreg vt* to look up ▷ *vi*: **jdm ~** to take after sb
Nachschlagewerk *nt* reference book
Nachschlüssel *m* master key
Nachschub ['na:xʃu:p] *m* supplies *pl*; (*Truppen*) reinforcements *pl*
nachsehen ['na:xze:ən] *unreg vt* (*prüfen*) to check ▷ *vi* (*erforschen*) to look and see; **jdm etw ~** to forgive sb sth; **jdm ~** to gaze after sb
nachsenden ['na:xzɛndən] *unreg vt* to send on, forward
Nachsicht ['na:xzɪçt] (**-**) *f* indulgence, leniency
nachsichtig *adj* indulgent, lenient
Nachspeise ['na:xʃpaɪzə] *f* dessert, sweet (*Brit*)
Nachspiel ['na:xʃpi:l] *nt* epilogue; (*fig*) sequel
nachsprechen ['na:xʃprɛçən] *unreg vt*: **(jdm) ~** to repeat (after sb)
nächstbeste, r, s *adj* first that comes along; (*zweitbeste*) next-best
Nächste, r, s *f(m)* neighbour (*Brit*), neighbor (*US*)
nächste, r, s *adj* next; (*nächstgelegen*) nearest; **aus ~r Nähe** from close by; (*betrachten*) at close quarters; **Ende ~n Monats** at the end of next month; **am ~n Tag** (the) next day; **bei ~r Gelegenheit** at the earliest opportunity; **in ~r Zeit** some time soon; **der ~ Angehörige** the next of kin
Nächstenliebe *f* love for one's fellow men
nächstens *adv* shortly, soon
nächstmöglich *adj* next possible
Nacht [naxt] (**-, ¨e**) *f* night; **gute ~!** good night!; **heute ~** tonight; **in der ~** at night; **in der ~ auf Dienstag** during Monday night; **in der ~ vom 12. zum 13. April** during the night of April 12th to 13th; **über ~** (*auch fig*) overnight; **bei ~ und Nebel** (*umg*) at dead of night; **sich** *dat* **die ~ um die Ohren schlagen** (*umg*) to stay up all night; (*mit Feiern, arbeiten*) to make a night of it
Nachteil ['na:xtaɪl] *m* disadvantage; **im ~ sein** to be at a disadvantage
nachteilig *adj* disadvantageous
Nachthemd *nt* (*Herrennachthemd*) nightshirt; nightdress (*Brit*), nightgown
Nachtigall ['naxtɪgal] (**-, -en**) *f* nightingale
Nachtisch ['na:xtɪʃ] *m* = **Nachspeise**
Nachtleben *nt* night life
nächtlich ['nɛçtlɪç] *adj* nightly
nach- *zW*: **Nachtrag** ['na:xtra:k] (**-(e)s, -träge**) *m* supplement; **nachtragen** *unreg vt* (*zufügen*) to add; **jdm etw nachtragen** to carry sth after sb; (*fig*) to hold sth against sb; **nachträglich** *adj* later, subsequent; (*zusätzlich*) additional ▷ *adv* later, subsequently; (*zusätzlich*) additionally; **nachtrauern** *vi*: **jdm/etw nachtrauern** to mourn the loss of sb/sth
Nachtruhe ['naxtru:ə] *f* sleep
nachts *adv* by night
Nachtschicht *f* night shift
Nacht- *zW*: **Nachttarif** *m* off-peak tariff; **Nachttisch** *m* bedside table; **Nachttopf** *m* chamber pot; **Nachtwächter** *m* night

watchman

Nach- *zW*: **Nachuntersuchung** *f* checkup; **nachwachsen** *unreg vi* to grow again; **Nachwehen** *pl* afterpains *pl*; (*fig*) aftereffects *pl*

Nachweis ['na:xvaɪs] (**-es, -e**) *m* proof; **den ~ für etw erbringen** *od* **liefern** to furnish proof of sth; **nachweisbar** *adj* provable, demonstrable; **nachweisen** ['na:xvaɪzən] *unreg vt* to prove; **jdm etw nachweisen** to point sth out to sb; **nachweislich** *adj* evident, demonstrable

nach- *zW*: **nachwirken** *vi* to have aftereffects; **Nachwirkung** *f* aftereffect; **Nachwort** *nt* appendix; **Nachwuchs** *m* offspring; (*beruflich etc*) new recruits *pl*; **nachzahlen** *vt, vi* to pay extra; **nachzählen** *vt* to count again

Nachzügler (**-s, -**) *m* straggler

Nacken ['nakən] (**-s, -**) *m* nape of the neck; **jdm im ~ sitzen** (*umg*) to breathe down sb's neck

nackt [nakt] *adj* naked; (*Tatsachen*) plain, bare; **Nacktheit** *f* nakedness; **Nacktkultur** *f* nudism

Nadel ['na:dəl] (**-, -n**) *f* needle; (*Stecknadel*) pin; **Nadelkissen** *nt* pincushion; **Nadelöhr** *nt* eye of a needle; **Nadelwald** *m* coniferous forest

Nagel ['na:gəl] (**-s, ¨-**) *m* nail; **sich** *dat* **etw unter den ~ reißen** (*umg*) to pinch sth; **etw an den ~ hängen** (*fig*) to chuck sth in (*umg*); **Nägel mit Köpfen machen** (*umg*) to do the job properly; **Nagelbürste** *f* nailbrush; **Nagelfeile** *f* nailfile; **Nagelhaut** *f* cuticle; **Nagellack** *m* nail varnish (*Brit*) *od* polish; **Nagellackentferner** (**-s, -**) *m* nail polish remover

nageln *vt, vi* to nail

nagelneu *adj* brand-new

Nagelschere *f* nail scissors *pl*

nagen ['na:gən] *vt, vi* to gnaw

Nagetier ['na:gəti:r] *nt* rodent

Nahaufnahme *f* close-up

nahe *adj* (*räumlich*) near(by); (*Verwandte*) near, close; (*Freunde*) close; (*zeitlich*) near, close ▷ *adv*: **von nah und fern** from near and far ▷ *präp +dat* near (to), close to; **von N~m** at close quarters; **der N~ Osten** the Middle East; **jdm ~ kommen** to get close to sb; **~ stehend** close; **jdm zu ~ treten** (*fig*) to offend sb; **mit jdm ~ verwandt sein** to be closely related to sb; *siehe auch* **naheliegen; nahestehen** *etc*

Nähe ['nɛ:ə] (**-**) *f* nearness, proximity; (*Umgebung*) vicinity; **in der ~** close by; at hand; **aus der ~** from close to

nahebei *adv* nearby

nahegehen *unreg vi* (*fig*): **jdm ~** to grieve sb

nahelegen *vi* (*fig*): **jdm etw ~** to suggest sth to sb

naheliegen *unreg vi* (*fig*) to be obvious; **der Verdacht liegt nahe, dass ...** it seems reasonable to suspect that ...; **~d** obvious

nahen *vi, vr* to approach, draw near

nähen ['nɛ:ən] *vt, vi* to sew

näher *adj* nearer; (*Erklärung, Erkundigung*) more detailed ▷ *adv* nearer; in greater detail; **~ kommen** to get closer; **ich kenne ihn nicht ~** I don't know him well

Näherei [nɛ:ə'raɪ] *f* sewing, needlework

Naherholungsgebiet *nt* recreational area (*close to a centre of population*)

Näherin *f* seamstress

nähern *vr* to approach

Näherungswert *m* approximate value

nahestehen *unreg vi* (*fig*): **jdm ~** to be close to sb; **einer Sache ~** to sympathize with sth

nahezu *adv* nearly

Nähgarn *nt* thread

nahm *etc* [na:m] *vb siehe* **nehmen**

Nähmaschine *f* sewing machine

Nähnadel *f* (sewing) needle

nähren ['nɛ:rən] *vt* to feed ▷ *vr* (*Person*) to feed o.s.; (*Tier*) to feed; **er sieht gut genährt aus** he looks well fed

nahrhaft ['na:rhaft] *adj* (*Essen*) nourishing

Nahrung ['na:rʊŋ] *f* food; (*fig*) sustenance

Nahrungs- *zW*: **Nahrungskette** *f* food chain; **Nahrungsmittel** *nt* food(stuff); **Nahrungsmittelindustrie** *f* food industry; **Nahrungssuche** *f* search for food

Nährwert *m* nutritional value

Naht [na:t] (**-, ¨-e**) *f* seam; (*Med*) suture; (*Tech*) join; **aus allen Nähten platzen** (*umg*) to be bursting at the seams; **nahtlos** *adj* seamless; **nahtlos ineinander übergehen** to follow without a gap

Nahverkehr *m* local traffic

Nahverkehrszug *m* local train

Nahziel *nt* immediate objective

naiv [na'i:f] *adj* naïve

Naivität [naivi'tɛ:t] *f* naïveté, naïvety

Name ['na:mə] (**-ns, -n**) *m* name; **im ~n von** on behalf of; **dem ~n nach müsste sie Deutsche sein** judging by her name she must be German; **die Dinge beim ~n nennen** (*fig*) to call a spade a spade; **ich kenne das Stück nur dem ~n nach** I've heard of the play but that's all

namens *adv* by the name of

Namenstag *m* name day, saint's day

namentlich ['na:məntlɪç] *adj* by name ▷ *adv* particularly, especially

namhaft ['na:mhaft] *adj* (*berühmt*) famed, renowned; (*beträchtlich*) considerable; **~ machen** to name, identify

Namibia [na'mi:bia] (**-s**) *nt* Namibia

nämlich ['nɛ:mlɪç] *adv* that is to say, namely; (*denn*) since; **der/die/das N~e** the same

nannte *etc* ['nantə] *vb siehe* **nennen**

Napf [napf] (**-(e)s, ¨-e**) *m* bowl, dish

Narbe ['narbə] (**-, -n**) *f* scar

narbig ['narbɪç] *adj* scarred

Narkose [nar'ko:ze] (**-, -n**) *f* anaesthetic (*Brit*), anesthetic (*US*)

Narr [nar] (**-en, -en**) *m* fool; **jdn zum ~en halten** to make a fool of sb; **narren** *vt* to fool

Narrheit *f* foolishness
Närrin ['nɛrɪn] *f* fool
närrisch *adj* foolish, crazy; **die ~en Tage** *Fasching and the period leading up to it*
Narzisse [nar'tsɪsə] (**-, -n**) *f* narcissus
naschen ['naʃən] *vt* to nibble; (*heimlich*) to eat secretly ▷ *vi* to nibble sweet things; **~ von** *od* **an** *+dat* to nibble at
naschhaft *adj* sweet-toothed
Nase ['na:zə] (**-, -n**) *f* nose; **sich** *dat* **die ~ putzen** to wipe one's nose; (*sich schnäuzen*) to blow one's nose; **jdm auf der ~ herumtanzen** (*umg*) to play sb up; **jdm etw vor der ~ wegschnappen** (*umg*) to just beat sb to sth; **die ~ vollhaben** (*umg*) to have had enough; **jdm etw auf die ~ binden** (*umg*) to tell sb all about sth; **(immer) der ~ nachgehen** (*umg*) to follow one's nose; **jdn an der ~ herumführen** (*als Täuschung*) to lead sb by the nose; (*als Scherz*) to pull sb's leg
Nasen- *zW*: **Nasenbluten** (**-s**) *nt* nosebleed; **Nasenloch** *nt* nostril; **Nasentropfen** *pl* nose drops *pl*
naseweis *adj* pert, cheeky; (*neugierig*) nosey
Nashorn ['na:shɔrn] *nt* rhinoceros
nass [nas] *adj* wet
Nässe ['nɛsə] (**-**) *f* wetness
nässen *vt* to wet
nasskalt *adj* wet and cold
Nassrasur *f* wet shave
Nation [natsi'o:n] *f* nation
national [natsio'na:l] *adj* national; **Nationalfeiertag** *m* national holiday; **Nationalhymne** *f* national anthem
nationalisieren [natsiona:li'zi:rən] *vt* to nationalize
Nationalisierung *f* nationalization
Nationalismus [natsiona:'lɪsmʊs] *m* nationalism
nationalistisch [natsiona:'lɪstɪʃ] *adj* nationalistic
Nationalität [natsionali'tɛ:t] *f* nationality
National- *zW*: **Nationalmannschaft** *f* international team; **Nationalsozialismus** *m* National Socialism
Natrium ['na:triʊm] (**-s**) *nt* sodium
Natron ['na:trɔn] (**-s**) *nt* soda
Natter ['natər] (**-, -n**) *f* adder
Natur [na'tu:r] *f* nature; (*körperlich*) constitution; (*freies Land*) countryside; **das geht gegen meine ~** it goes against the grain
Naturalien [natu'ra:liən] *pl* natural produce *sing*; **in ~** in kind
Naturalismus [natu:ra'lɪsmʊs] *m* naturalism
Natur- *zW*: **Naturerscheinung** *f* natural phenomenon *od* event; **naturfarben** *adj* natural-coloured (*Brit*) *od* -colored (*US*); **naturgemäß** *adj* natural; **Naturgesetz** *nt* law of nature; **Naturkatastrophe** *f* natural disaster
natürlich [na'ty:rlɪç] *adj* natural ▷ *adv* naturally; **eines ~en Todes sterben** to die of natural causes
Natürlichkeit *f* naturalness
Natur- *zW*: **Naturprodukt** *nt* natural product; **naturrein** *adj* natural, pure; **Naturschutz** *m*: **unter Naturschutz stehen** to be legally protected; **Naturschutzgebiet** *nt* nature reserve (*BRIT*), national park (*US*); **Naturwissenschaft** *f* natural science; **Naturwissenschaftler** *m* scientist; **Naturzustand** *m* natural state
nautisch ['naʊtɪʃ] *adj* nautical
Navigation [navigatsi'o:n] *f* navigation
Navigationsfehler *m* navigational error
Navigationsinstrumente *pl* navigation instruments *pl*
Nazi ['na:tsi] (**-s, -s**) *m* Nazi
n. Chr. *abk* (*= nach Christus*) A.D.
Nebel ['ne:bəl] (**-s, -**) *m* fog, mist
nebelig *adj* foggy, misty
Nebel- *zW*: **Nebelscheinwerfer** *m* fog-lamp; **Nebelschlussleuchte** *f* (*Aut*) rear fog-light
neben ['ne:bən] *präp +akk* next to ▷ *präp +dat* next to; (*außer*) apart from, besides; **nebenan** [ne:bən|'an] *adv* next door; **Nebenanschluss** *m* (*Tel*) extension; **nebenbei** [ne:bən'baɪ] *adv* at the same time; (*außerdem*) additionally; (*beiläufig*) incidentally; **nebenbei bemerkt** *od* **gesagt** by the way, incidentally; **Nebenbeschäftigung** *f* sideline; (*Zweitberuf*) extra job; **Nebenbuhler, in** (**-s, -**) *m(f)* rival; **nebeneinander** [ne:bənaɪ'nandər] *adv* side by side; **Nebeneingang** *m* side entrance; **Nebenerscheinung** *f* side effect; **Nebenfach** *nt* subsidiary subject; **Nebenfluss** *m* tributary; **Nebengeräusch** *nt* (*Rundf*) atmospherics *pl*, interference; **nebenher** [ne:bən'he:r] *adv* (*zusätzlich*) besides; (*gleichzeitig*) at the same time; (*daneben*) alongside; **nebenherfahren** *unreg vi* to drive alongside; **Nebenkosten** *pl* extra charges *pl*, extras *pl*; **Nebenprodukt** *nt* by-product; **Nebensache** *f* trifle, side issue; **nebensächlich** *adj* minor, peripheral; **Nebensaison** *f* low season; **Nebensatz** *m* (*Gram*) subordinate clause; **Nebenstraße** *f* side street
Necessaire [nesɛ'sɛ:r] (**-s, -s**) *nt* (*Nähnecessaire*) needlework box; (*Nagelnecessaire*) manicure case
necken ['nɛkən] *vt* to tease
Neckerei [nɛkə'raɪ] *f* teasing
neckisch *adj* coy; (*Einfall, Lied*) amusing
Neffe ['nɛfə] (**-n, -n**) *m* nephew
negativ ['ne:gati:f] *adj* negative; **Negativ** (**-s, -e**) *nt* (*Phot*) negative
nehmen ['ne:mən] *unreg vt, vi* to take; **etw zu sich ~** to take sth, partake of sth (*liter*); **jdm etw ~** to take sth (away) from sb; **sich ernst ~** to take o.s. seriously; **~ Sie sich doch bitte** help yourself; **man nehme ...** (*Koch*) take ...; **wie mans nimmt** depending on your point of view; **die Mauer nimmt einem die ganze Sicht** the wall blocks the whole view;

er ließ es sich *dat* **nicht ~, es persönlich zu tun** he insisted on doing it himself
Neid [naɪt] (**-(e)s**) *m* envy
Neider ['naɪdər] (**-s, -**) *m* envier
neidisch *adj* envious, jealous
neigen ['naɪgən] *vt* to incline, lean; (*Kopf*) to bow ▷ *vi*: **zu etw ~** to tend to sth
Neigung *f* (*des Geländes*) slope; (*Tendenz*) tendency, inclination; (*Vorliebe*) liking; (*Zuneigung*) affection
Neigungswinkel *m* angle of inclination
nein [naɪn] *adv* no
Nelke ['nɛlkə] (**-, -n**) *f* carnation, pink; (*Gewürznelke*) clove
nennen ['nɛnən] *unreg vt* to name; (*mit Namen*) to call; **das nenne ich Mut!** that's what I call courage!
nennenswert *adj* worth mentioning
Nenner (**-s, -**) *m* denominator; **etw auf einen ~ bringen** (*lit, fig*) to reduce sth to a common denominator
Nennwert *m* nominal value; (*Comm*) par
Neon ['neːɔn] (**-s**) *nt* neon
Neonazi [neo'naːtsi] *m* Neonazi
Neon- *zW*: **Neonlicht** *nt* neon light; **Neonröhre** *f* neon tube
Nepal ['neːpal] (**-s**) *nt* Nepal
Nerv [nɛrf] (**-s, -en**) *m* nerve; **die ~en sind mit ihm durchgegangen** he lost control, he snapped (*umg*); **jdm auf die ~en gehen** to get on sb's nerves
nerven (*umg*) *vt*: **jdn ~** to get on sb's nerves
Nerven- *zW*: **Nervenbündel** *nt* bundle of nerves; **Nervenheilanstalt** *f* mental hospital; **Nervenklinik** *f* psychiatric clinic; **nervenkrank** *adj* mentally ill; **Nervensäge** (*umg*) *f* pain (in the neck); **Nervenschwäche** *f* neurasthenia; **Nervensystem** *nt* nervous system; **Nervenzusammenbruch** *m* nervous breakdown
nervig ['nɛrvɪç] (*umg*) *adj* exasperating, annoying
nervös [nɛr'vøːs] *adj* nervous
Nervosität [nɛrvozi'tɛːt] *f* nervousness
nervtötend *adj* nerve-racking; (*Arbeit*) soul-destroying
Nerz [nɛrts] (**-es, -e**) *m* mink
Nessel ['nɛsəl] (**-, -n**) *f* nettle; **sich in die ~n setzen** (*fig: umg*) to put o.s. in a spot
Nessessär [nesɛ'sɛːr] (**-s, -s**) *nt* = **Necessaire**
Nest [nɛst] (**-(e)s, -er**) *nt* nest; (*umg: Ort*) dump; (*fig: Bett*) bed; (*: Schlupfwinkel*) hide-out, lair; **da hat er sich ins warme ~ gesetzt** (*umg*) he's got it made
nett [nɛt] *adj* nice; **sei so ~ und räum auf!** would you mind clearing up?
netterweise ['nɛtər'vaɪzə] *adv* kindly
netto *adv* net
Netz [nɛts] (**-es, -e**) *nt* net; (*Gepäcknetz*) rack; (*Einkaufsnetz*) string bag; (*Spinnennetz*) web; (*System, Comput*) network; (*Stromnetz*) mains *sing od pl*; **das soziale ~** the social security network; **jdm ins ~ gehen** (*fig*) to fall into sb's trap; **Netzanschluss** *m* mains connection; **Netzbetreiber** *m* (*Comput*) Internet provider; **Netzhaut** *f* retina
neu [nɔʏ] *adj* new; (*Sprache, Geschichte*) modern; **der/die N~e** the new person, the newcomer; **seit N~estem** (since) recently; **~ schreiben** to rewrite, write again; **auf ein N~es!** (*Aufmunterung*) let's try again; **was gibts N~es?** (*umg*) what's the latest?; **von N~em** (*von vorn*) from the beginning; (*wieder*) again; **sich ~ einkleiden** to buy o.s. a new set of clothes; **~ eröffnet** newly-opened; (*wieder geöffnet*) reopened; **Neuanschaffung** *f* new purchase *od* acquisition; **neuartig** *adj* new kind of; **Neuauflage** *f* new edition; **Neubau** (**-(e)s, -ten**) *m* new building
neuerdings *adv* (*kürzlich*) (since) recently; (*von Neuem*) again
Neuerung *f* innovation, new departure
Neufundland [nɔʏ'fʊntlant] *nt* Newfoundland
Neugier *f* curiosity
neugierig *adj* curious
Neuguinea [nɔʏgi'neːa] (**-s**) *nt* New Guinea
Neuheit *f* novelty; (*neuartige Ware*) new thing
Neuigkeit *f* news *sing*
neu- *zW*: **Neujahr** *nt* New Year; **neulich** *adv* recently, the other day; **Neuling** *m* novice; **Neumond** *m* new moon
neun [nɔʏn] *num* nine
neunzehn *num* nineteen
neunzig *num* ninety
neureich *adj* nouveau riche; **Neureiche, r** *f(m)* nouveau riche
Neurose [nɔʏ'roːzə] (**-, -n**) *f* neurosis
Neurotiker, in [nɔʏ'roːtikər(ɪn)] (**-s, -**) *m(f)* neurotic
neurotisch *adj* neurotic
Neuseeland [nɔʏ'zeːlant] *nt* New Zealand; **neuseeländisch** *adj* New Zealand *attrib*
neutral [nɔʏ'traːl] *adj* neutral
neutralisieren [nɔʏtrali'ziːrən] *vt* to neutralize
Neutralität [nɔʏtrali'tɛːt] *f* neutrality
Neutron ['nɔʏtrɔn] (**-s, -en**) *nt* neutron
Neutrum ['nɔʏtrʊm] (**-s, Neutra** *od* **Neutren**) *nt* neuter
Neu- *zW*: **Neuwert** *m* purchase price; **neuwertig** *adj* as new; **Neuzeit** *f* modern age; **neuzeitlich** *adj* modern, recent
Nicaragua [nika'raːgua] (**-s**) *nt* Nicaragua; **Nicaraguaner, in** [nikaragu'aːnər(ɪn)] (**-s, -**) *m(f)* Nicaraguan; **nicaraguanisch** [nikaragu'aːnɪʃ] *adj* Nicaraguan
nicht [nɪçt] *adv* **1** (*Verneinung*) not; **er ist es nicht** it's not him, it isn't him; **nicht rostend** stainless; **er raucht nicht** (*gerade*) he isn't smoking; (*gewöhnlich*) he doesn't smoke; **ich kann das nicht — ich auch nicht** I can't do it — neither *od* nor can I; **es regnet nicht mehr** it's not raining any more; **nicht mehr als** no more than
2 (*Bitte, Verbot*): **nicht!** don't!, no!; **nicht**

berühren! do not touch!; **nicht doch!** don't! **3** (*rhetorisch*): **du bist müde, nicht (wahr)?** you're tired, aren't you?; **das ist schön, nicht (wahr)?** it's nice, isn't it? **4: was du nicht sagst!** the things you say! ▷ *präf* non-

Nicht- *zW*: **Nichtachtung** *f* disregard; **Nichtangriffspakt** *m* non-aggression pact

Nichte ['nɪçtə] (**-, -n**) *f* niece

nichtig ['nɪçtɪç] *adj* (*ungültig*) null, void; (*wertlos*) futile; **Nichtigkeit** *f* nullity, invalidity; (*Sinnlosigkeit*) futility

Nichtraucher *m* nonsmoker; **ich bin ~** I don't smoke

nichts [nɪçts] *pron* nothing; **~ ahnend** unsuspecting; **~ sagend** meaningless; **~ als** nothing but; **~ da!** (*ausgeschlossen*) nothing doing (*umg*); **~ wie raus/hin** *etc* (*umg*) let's get out/over there *etc* (on the double); **für ~ und wieder nichts** for nothing at all; **Nichts** (**-s**) *nt* nothingness; (*pej: Person*) nonentity

Nichtschwimmer (**-s, -**) *m* nonswimmer

nichts- *zW*: **nichtsdestoweniger** *adv* nevertheless; **Nichtsnutz** (**-es, -e**) *m* good-for-nothing; **nichtsnutzig** *adj* worthless, useless; **nichtssagend** *adj* meaningless; **Nichtstun** (**-s**) *nt* idleness

Nichtzutreffende, s *nt*: **~s (bitte) streichen** (please) delete as applicable

Nickel ['nɪkəl] (**-s**) *nt* nickel

nicken ['nɪkən] *vi* to nod

Nickerchen ['nɪkərçən] *nt* nap; **ein ~ machen** (*umg*) to have forty winks

nie [ni:] *adv* never; **~ wieder** *od* **mehr** never again; **~ und nimmer** never ever; **fast ~** hardly ever

nieder ['ni:dər] *adj* low; (*gering*) inferior ▷ *adv* down; **Niedergang** *m* decline; **niedergehen** *unreg vi* to descend; (*Aviat*) to come down; (*Regen*) to fall; (*Boxer*) to go down; **niedergeschlagen** *adj* depressed, dejected; **Niedergeschlagenheit** *f* depression, dejection; **Niederlage** *f* defeat

Niederlande ['ni:dərlandə] *pl*: **die ~** the Netherlands *pl*

Niederländer, in ['ni:dərlɛndər(ɪn)] (**-s, -**) *m(f)* Dutchman, Dutchwoman

niederländisch *adj* Dutch, Netherlands *attrib*

nieder- *zW*: **niederlassen** *unreg vr* (*sich setzen*) to sit down; (*an Ort*) to settle (down); (*Arzt, Rechtsanwalt*) to set up in practice; **Niederlassung** *f* settlement; (*Comm*) branch; **niederlegen** *vt* to lay down; (*Arbeit*) to stop; (*Amt*) to resign; **Niederösterreich** *nt* Lower Austria; **Niedersachsen** *nt* Lower Saxony; **Niederschlag** *m* (*Chem*) precipitate; (*Bodensatz*) sediment; (*Met*) precipitation (*form*), rainfall; (*Boxen*) knockdown; **radioaktiver Niederschlag** (radioactive) fallout; **niederschlagen** *unreg vt* (*Gegner*) to beat down; (*Gegenstand*) to knock down; (*Augen*) to lower; (*Jur: Prozess*) to dismiss; (*Aufstand*) to put down ▷ *vr* (*Chem*) to precipitate; **sich in etw** *dat* **niederschlagen** (*Erfahrungen etc*) to find expression in sth; **Niederschrift** *f* transcription; **niederträchtig** *adj* base, mean; **Niederträchtigkeit** *f* despicable *od* malicious behaviour

Niederung *f* (*Geog*) depression

niedlich ['ni:tlɪç] *adj* sweet, nice, cute

niedrig ['ni:drɪç] *adj* low; (*Stand*) lowly, humble; (*Gesinnung*) mean

niemals ['ni:ma:ls] *adv* never

niemand ['ni:mant] *pron* nobody, no-one

Niemandsland ['ni:mantslant] *nt* no-man's-land

Niere ['ni:rə] (**-, -n**) *f* kidney; **künstliche ~** kidney machine

Nierenentzündung *f* kidney infection

nieseln ['ni:zəln] *vi* to drizzle

niesen ['ni:zən] *vi* to sneeze

Niete ['ni:tə] (**-, -n**) *f* (*Tech*) rivet; (*Los*) blank; (*Reinfall*) flop; (*Mensch*) failure

nieten *vt* to rivet

Niger[1] ['ni:gər] (**-s**) *nt* (*Staat*) Niger

Niger[2] ['ni:gər] (**-s**) *m* (*Fluss*) Niger

Nigeria [ni'ge:ria] (**-s**) *nt* Nigeria

Nihilismus [nihi'lɪsmʊs] *m* nihilism

Nihilist [nihi'lɪst] *m* nihilist; **nihilistisch** *adj* nihilistic

Nikolaus ['ni:kolaʊs] (**-, -e** *od* (*hum: umg*) **-läuse**) *m* ≈ Santa Claus, ≈ Father Christmas

Nikotin [niko'ti:n] (**-s**) *nt* nicotine; **nikotinarm** *adj* low-nicotine

Nil [ni:l] (**-s**) *m* Nile; **Nilpferd** *nt* hippopotamus

Nimmersatt (**-(e)s, -e**) *m* glutton

nippen ['nɪpən] *vt, vi* to sip

nirgends ['nɪrgənts] *adv* nowhere; **überall und ~** here, there and everywhere

nirgendwohin *adv* nowhere

Nische ['ni:ʃə] (**-, -n**) *f* niche

nisten ['nɪstən] *vi* to nest

Nitrat [ni'tra:t] (**-(e)s, -e**) *nt* nitrate

Niveau [ni'vo:] (**-s, -s**) *nt* level; **diese Schule hat ein hohes ~** this school has high standards; **unter meinem ~** beneath me

Nixe ['nɪksə] (**-, -n**) *f* water nymph

noch [nɔx] *adv* **1** (*weiterhin*) still; **noch nicht** not yet; **noch nie** never (yet); **noch immer** *od* **immer noch** still; **bleiben Sie doch noch** stay a bit longer; **ich gehe kaum noch aus** I hardly go out any more
2 (*in Zukunft*) still, yet; (*irgendwann einmal*) one day; **das kann noch passieren** that might still happen; **er wird noch kommen** he'll come (yet); **das wirst du noch bereuen** you'll come to regret it (one day)
3 (*nicht später als*): **noch vor einer Woche** only a week ago; **noch am selben Tag** the very same day; **noch im 19. Jahrhundert** as late as the 19th century; **noch heute** today
4 (*zusätzlich*): **wer war noch da?** who else was there?; **noch (ein)mal** once more, again; **noch dreimal** three more times; **noch einer** another one; **und es regnete auch noch**

and on top of that it was raining
5 (*bei Vergleichen*): **noch größer** even bigger; **das ist noch besser** that's better still; **und wenn es noch so schwer ist** however hard it is
6: **Geld noch und noch** heaps (and heaps) of money; **sie hat noch und noch versucht, ...** she tried again and again to ...
▷ *konj*: **weder A noch B** neither A nor B
nochmal, nochmals *adv siehe* **noch**
nochmalig *adj* repeated
Nockenwelle ['nɔkənvɛlə] *f* camshaft
Nominalwert [nomi'na:lve:rt] *m* (*Fin*) nominal *od* par value
Nominativ ['no:minati:f] (**-s, -e**) *m* nominative
nominell [nomi'nɛl] *adj* nominal
Nonne ['nɔnə] (**-, -n**) *f* nun
Nordamerika *nt* North America
norddeutsch *adj* North German
Norddeutschland *nt* North(ern) Germany
Norden ['nɔrdən] *m* north
Nord- *zW*: **Nordirland** *nt* Northern Ireland, Ulster; **nordisch** *adj* northern; **nordische Kombination** (*Ski*) nordic combination; **Nordkorea** ['nɔrtko're:a] *nt* North Korea
nördlich ['nœrtlɪç] *adj* northerly, northern ▷ *präp +gen* (to the) north of; **der ~e Polarkreis** the Arctic Circle; **N~es Eismeer** Arctic Ocean; **~ von** north of
Nordpol *m* North Pole
Nordrhein-Westfalen ['nɔrtraɪnvɛst'fa:lən] (**-s**) *nt* North Rhine-Westphalia
Nordsee *f* North Sea
Nörgelei [nœrgə'laɪ] *f* grumbling
nörgeln *vi* to grumble
Nörgler, in (**-s, -**) *m(f)* grumbler
Norm [nɔrm] (**-, -en**) *f* norm; (*Leistungssoll*) quota; (*Größenvorschrift*) standard (specification)
normal [nɔr'ma:l] *adj* normal; **bist du noch ~?** (*umg*) have you gone mad?; **Normalbenzin** *nt* two-star petrol (*Brit veraltet*), regular gas (*US*)
normalerweise *adv* normally
normalisieren [nɔrmali'zi:rən] *vt* to normalize ▷ *vr* to return to normal
normen *vt* to standardize
Norwegen ['nɔrve:gən] (**-s**) *nt* Norway
Norweger, in (**-s, -**) *m(f)* Norwegian
norwegisch *adj* Norwegian
Not [no:t] (**-, ¨-e**) *f* need; (*Mangel*) want; (*Mühe*) trouble; (*Zwang*) necessity; **~ leidend** needy; **zur ~** if necessary; (*gerade noch*) just about; **wenn ~ am Mann ist** if you/they *etc* are short (*umg*); (*im Notfall*) in an emergency; **er hat seine liebe ~ mit ihr/damit** he really has problems with her/it; **in seiner ~** in his hour of need
Notar, in [no'ta:r(ɪn)] (**-s, -e**) *m(f)* notary; **notariell** *adj* notarial; **notariell beglaubigt** attested by a notary
Not- *zW*: **Notarzt** *m* doctor on emergency call; **Notausgang** *m* emergency exit; **Notbehelf** *m* stopgap; **Notbremse** *f* emergency brake; **Notdienst** *m*: **Notdienst haben** (*Apotheke*) to be open 24 hours; (*Arzt*) to be on call; **notdürftig** *adj* scanty; (*behelfsmäßig*) makeshift; **sich notdürftig verständigen können** to be able to communicate to some extent
Note ['no:tə] (**-, -n**) *f* note; (*Sch*) mark (*Brit*), grade (*US*); **Noten** *pl* (*Mus*) music *sing*; **eine persönliche ~** a personal touch
Noten- *zW*: **Notenblatt** *nt* sheet of music; **Notenschlüssel** *m* clef; **Notenständer** *m* music stand
Not- *zW*: **Notfall** *m* (case of) emergency; **notfalls** *adv* if need be; **notgedrungen** *adj* necessary, unavoidable; **etw notgedrungen machen** to be forced to do sth
notieren [no'ti:rən] *vt* to note; (*Comm*) to quote
Notierung *f* (*Comm*) quotation
nötig ['nø:tɪç] *adj* necessary ▷ *adv* (*dringend*): **etw ~ brauchen** to need sth urgently; **etw ~ haben** to need sth; **das habe ich nicht ~!** I can do without that!
nötigen *vt* to compel, force; **nötigenfalls** *adv* if necessary
Notiz [no'ti:ts] (**-, -en**) *f* note; (*Zeitungsnotiz*) item; **~ nehmen** to take notice; **Notizbuch** *nt* notebook; **Notizzettel** *m* piece of paper
Not- *zW*: **Notlage** *f* crisis, emergency; **notlanden** *vi* to make a forced *od* emergency landing; **Notlandung** *f* forced *od* emergency landing; **Notlösung** *f* temporary solution; **Notlüge** *f* white lie
notorisch [no'to:rɪʃ] *adj* notorious
Not- *zW*: **Notruf** *m* emergency call; **Notrufsäule** *f* emergency telephone; **Notstand** *m* state of emergency; **Notstandsgesetz** *nt* emergency law; **Notunterkunft** *f* emergency accommodation; **Notverband** *m* emergency dressing; **Notwehr** (-) *f* self-defence; **notwendig** *adj* necessary; **Notzucht** *f* rape
Novelle [no'vɛlə] (**-, -n**) *f* novella; (*Jur*) amendment
November [no'vɛmbər] (**-(s), -**) *m* November; *siehe auch* **September**
Nr. *abk* (*= Nummer*) no.
Nu [nu:] *m*: **im Nu** in an instant
Nuance [ny'ã:sə] (**-, -n**) *f* nuance; (*Kleinigkeit*) shade
nüchtern ['nʏçtərn] *adj* sober; (*Magen*) empty; (*Urteil*) prudent; **Nüchternheit** *f* sobriety
null [nʊl] *num* zero; (*Fehler*) no; **~ Uhr** midnight; **in ~ Komma nichts** (*umg*) in less than no time; **die Stunde ~** the new starting point; **gleich ~ sein** to be absolutely nil; **~ und nichtig** null and void; **Nullpunkt** *m* zero; **auf dem Nullpunkt** at zero; **Nulltarif** *m* (*für Verkehrsmittel*) free travel; **zum Nulltarif** free of charge
numerieren [nume'ri:rən] *vt siehe*

nummerieren
numerisch [nu'meːrɪʃ] *adj* numerical; **~es Tastenfeld** (*Comput*) numeric pad
Nummer ['nʊmər] (**-, -n**) *f* number; **auf ~ sicher gehen** (*umg*) to play (it) safe
nummerieren [nume'riːrən] *vt* to number
Nummern- *zW*: **Nummernkonto** *nt* numbered bank account; **Nummernschild** *nt* (*Aut*) number *od* license (*US*) plate
nun [nuːn] *adv* now ▹ *interj* well
nur [nuːr] *adv* just, only; **nicht ~ ..., sondern auch ...** not only ... but also ...; **alle, ~ ich nicht** everyone but me; **ich hab das ~ so gesagt** I was just talking
Nuss [nʊs] (**-, ¨-e**) *f* nut; **eine doofe ~** (*umg*) a stupid twit; **eine harte ~** a hard nut (to crack); **Nussbaum** *m* walnut tree; **Nussknacker** (**-s, -**) *m* nutcracker
Nüster ['nyːstər] (**-, -n**) *f* nostril
Nutte ['nʊtə] (**-, -n**) *f* tart (*Brit*), hooker (*US*)
nutz [nʊts] *adj* = **nütze**
nutzen *vi* to be of use ▹ *vt*: **(zu etw) ~** to use (for sth); **was nutzt es?** what's the use?, what use is it?; **Nutzen** (**-s**) *m* usefulness; (*Gewinn*) profit; **von Nutzen** useful
nützlich ['nʏtslɪç] *adj* useful: **Nützlichkeit** *f* usefulness
Nutz- *zW*: **nutzlos** *adj* useless; (*unnötig*) needless; **Nutzlosigkeit** *f* uselessness; **Nutznießer** (**-s, -**) *m* beneficiary
Nylon ['naɪlɔn] (**-s**) *nt* nylon
Nymphe ['nʏmfə] (**-, -n**) *f* nymph

Oo

O[1], **o** [oː] *nt* O, o; **O wie Otto** ≈ O for Olive, ≈ O for Oboe (*US*)
O[2] [oː] *abk* (= *Osten*) E
Oase [o'aːzə] (**-, -n**) *f* oasis
OB (**-s, -s**) *m abk* = **Oberbürgermeister**
ob [ɔp] *konj* if, whether; **ob das wohl wahr ist?** can that be true?; **ob ich (nicht) lieber gehe?** maybe I'd better go; **(so) tun als ob** (*umg*) to pretend; **und ob!** you bet!
Obdach ['ɔpdax] (**-(e)s**) *nt* shelter, lodging; **obdachlos** *adj* homeless; **Obdachlose, r** *f(m)* homeless person
Obduktion [ɔpdʊktsi'oːn] *f* postmortem
obduzieren [ɔpdu'tsiːrən] *vt* to do a postmortem on
O-Beine ['oːbaɪnə] *pl* bow *od* bandy legs *pl*
oben ['oːbən] *adv* above; (*in Haus*) upstairs; (*am oberen Ende*) at the top; **~ erwähnt, ~ genannt** above-mentioned; **nach ~** up; **von ~** down; **siehe ~** see above; **ganz ~** right at the top; **~ ohne** topless; **die Abbildung ~ links** *od* **links oben** the illustration in the top left-hand corner; **jdn von ~ herab behandeln** to treat sb condescendingly; **jdn von ~ bis unten ansehen** to look sb up and down; **Befehl von ~** orders from above; **die da ~** (*umg: die Vorgesetzten*) the powers that be
Ober ['oːbər] (**-s, -**) *m* waiter
Ober- *zW*: **Oberarm** *m* upper arm; **Oberarzt** *m* senior physician; **Oberaufsicht** *f* supervision; **Oberbefehl** *m* supreme command; **Oberbefehlshaber** *m* commander-in-chief; **Oberbekleidung** *f* outer clothing; **Oberbürgermeister** *m* lord mayor; **Oberdeck** *nt* upper *od* top deck
obere, r, s *adj* upper; **die O~n** the bosses; (*Eccl*) the superiors; **die ~n Zehntausend** (*umg*) high society
Ober- *zW*: **Oberfläche** *f* surface; **oberflächlich** *adj* superficial; **bei oberflächlicher Betrachtung** at a quick glance; **jdn (nur) oberflächlich kennen** to know sb (only) slightly; **Obergeschoss** *nt* upper storey *od* story (*US*); **im zweiten Obergeschoss** on the second floor (*Brit*), on the third floor (*US*); **oberhalb** *adv* above ▷ *präp +gen* above; **Oberhaupt** *nt* head, chief; **Oberhaus** *nt* (*in Großbritannien*) upper house, House of Lords; **Oberhemd** *nt* shirt; **Oberherrschaft** *f* supremacy, sovereignty
Oberin *f* matron; (*Eccl*) Mother Superior
Ober- *zW*: **Oberkellner** *m* head waiter; **Oberkiefer** *m* upper jaw; **Oberkörper** *m* upper part of body; **Oberleitung** *f* (*Elek*) overhead cable; **Oberlicht** *nt* skylight; **Oberlippe** *f* upper lip; **Oberösterreich** *nt* Upper Austria; **Oberschenkel** *m* thigh; **Oberschicht** *f* upper classes *pl*; **Oberschule** *f* grammar school (*Brit*), high school (*US*); **Oberschwester** *f* (*Med*) matron
Oberst ['oːbərst] (**-en** *od* **-s, -en** *od* **-e**) *m* colonel
oberste, r, s *adj* very top, topmost
Ober- *zW*: **Oberstufe** *f* upper school; **Oberteil** *nt* upper part; **Oberweite** *f* bust *od* chest measurement
obgleich [ɔp'glaɪç] *konj* although
Obhut ['ɔphuːt] (**-**) *f* care, protection; **in jds ~** *dat* **sein** to be in sb's care
obig ['oːbɪç] *adj* above
Objekt [ɔp'jɛkt] (**-(e)s, -e**) *nt* object
objektiv [ɔpjɛk'tiːf] *adj* objective
Objektiv (**-s, -e**) *nt* lens *sing*
Objektivität [ɔpjɛktivi'tɛːt] *f* objectivity
Oblate [o'blaːtə] (**-, -n**) *f* (*Gebäck*) wafer; (*Eccl*) host
obligatorisch [obliga'toːrɪʃ] *adj* compulsory, obligatory
Oboe [o'boːə] (**-, -n**) *f* oboe
obschon [ɔp'ʃoːn] *konj* although
Observatorium [ɔpzɛrva'toːriʊm] *nt* observatory
obskur [ɔps'kuːr] *adj* obscure; (*verdächtig*) dubious
Obst [oːpst] (**-(e)s**) *nt* fruit; **Obstbaum** *m* fruit tree; **Obstgarten** *m* orchard; **Obsthändler** *m* fruiterer (*Brit*), fruit merchant; **Obstkuchen** *m* fruit tart; **Obstsalat** *m* fruit salad
obszön [ɔps'tsøːn] *adj* obscene
Obszönität [ɔpstøni'tɛːt] *f* obscenity
obwohl [ɔp'voːl] *konj* although
Ochse ['ɔksə] (**-n, -n**) *m* ox; (*umg: Dummkopf*) twit; **er stand da wie der ~ vorm Berg** (*umg*) he stood there utterly bewildered
Ochsenschwanzsuppe *f* oxtail soup
Ochsenzunge *f* ox tongue
öd [øːt(ə)] *adj* = **öde**
Öde (**-, -n**) *f* desert, waste(land); (*fig*) tedium
oder ['oːdər] *konj* or; **entweder ... ~** either ...

or; **du kommst doch, ~?** you're coming, aren't you?
Ofen ['o:fən] (**-s, ⸚**) *m* oven; (*Heizofen*) fire, heater; (*Kohleofen*) stove; (*Hochofen*) furnace; (*Herd*) cooker, stove; **jetzt ist der ~ aus** (*umg*) that does it!; **Ofenrohr** *nt* stovepipe
offen ['ɔfən] *adj* open; (*aufrichtig*) frank; (*Stelle*) vacant; (*Bein*) ulcerated; (*Haare*) loose; **~er Wein** wine by the carafe *od* glass; **auf ~er Strecke** (*Straße*) on the open road; (*Eisenb*) between stations; **Tag der ~en Tür** open day (*Brit*), open house (*US*); **~e Handelsgesellschaft** (*Comm*) general *od* ordinary (*US*) partnership; **~ bleiben** (*Fenster*) to stay open; **~ halten** to keep open; **~ lassen** to leave open; **~ stehen** to be open; **seine Meinung ~ sagen** to speak one's mind; **ein ~es Wort mit jdm reden** to have a frank talk with sb; **~ gesagt** to be honest; *siehe auch* **offenbleiben; offenstehen**
offenbar *adj* obvious; (*vermutlich*) apparently
offenbaren [ɔfən'ba:rən] *vt* to reveal, manifest
Offenbarung *f* (*Rel*) revelation
Offen- *zW*: **offenbleiben** *unreg vi* (*fig*: *Frage, Entscheidung*) to remain open; *siehe auch* **offen**; **Offenheit** *f* candour (*Brit*), candor (*US*), frankness; **offenherzig** *adj* candid, frank; (*hum*: *Kleid*) revealing; **offenkundig** *adj* well-known; (*klar*) evident; **offensichtlich** *adj* evident, obvious
offensiv [ɔfɛn'zi:f] *adj* offensive
Offensive (**-, -n**) *f* offensive
offenstehen *unreg vi* (*fig*: *Rechnung*) to be unpaid; **es steht Ihnen offen, es zu tun** you are at liberty to do it; **die (ganze) Welt steht ihm offen** he has the (whole) world at his feet; *siehe auch* **offen**
öffentlich ['œfəntlıç] *adj* public; **die ~e Hand** (central/local) government; **Anstalt des ~en Rechts** public institution; **Ausgaben der ~en Hand** public spending *sing*
Öffentlichkeit *f* (*Leute*) public; (*einer Versammlung etc*) public nature; **in aller ~** in public; **an die ~ dringen** to reach the public ear; **unter Ausschluss der ~** in secret; (*Jur*) in camera
offerieren [ɔfe'ri:rən] *vt* to offer
Offerte [ɔ'fɛrtə] (**-, -n**) *f* offer
offiziell [ɔfitsi'ɛl] *adj* official
Offizier [ɔfi'tsi:r] (**-s, -e**) *m* officer
Offizierskasino *nt* officers' mess
öffnen ['œfnən] *vt, vr* to open; **jdm die Tür ~** to open the door for sb
Öffner ['œfnər] (**-s, -**) *m* opener
Öffnung ['œfnʊŋ] *f* opening
Öffnungszeiten *pl* opening times *pl*
oft [ɔft] *adv* often
öfter ['œftər] *adv* more often *od* frequently; **des Öfteren** quite frequently; **~ mal was Neues** (*umg*) variety is the spice of life (*Sprichwort*)
oftmals *adv* often, frequently
OHG *f abk* (= *offene Handelsgesellschaft*) *siehe* **offen**
ohne ['o:nə] *präp +akk, konj* without; **das Darlehen ist ~ Weiteres bewilligt worden** the loan was granted without any problem; **das kann man nicht ~ Weiteres voraussetzen** you can't just assume that automatically; **das ist nicht ~** (*umg*) it's not bad; **~ Weiteres** without a second thought; (*sofort*) immediately; **ohnedies** *adv* anyway; **ohneeinander** [o:nə|aı'nandər] *adv* without each other; **ohnegleichen** *adj* unsurpassed, without equal; **ohnehin** *adv* anyway, in any case; **es ist ohnehin schon spät** it's late enough already
Ohnmacht ['o:nmaxt] *f* faint; (*fig*) impotence; **in ~ fallen** to faint
ohnmächtig ['o:nmɛçtıç] *adj* in a faint, unconscious; (*fig*) weak, impotent; **sie ist ~** she has fainted; **ohnmächtige Wut, ~er Zorn** helpless rage; **einer Sache** *dat* **~ gegenüberstehen** to be helpless in the face of sth
Ohr [o:r] (**-(e)s, -en**) *nt* ear; (*Gehör*) hearing; **sich aufs ~ legen** *od* **hauen** (*umg*) to kip down; **jdm die ~en lang ziehen** (*umg*) to tweak sb's ear(s); **jdm in den ~en liegen** to keep on at sb; **jdn übers ~ hauen** (*umg*) to pull a fast one on sb; **auf dem ~ bin ich taub** (*fig*) nothing doing (*umg*); **schreib es dir hinter die ~en** (*umg*) will you (finally) get that into your (thick) head!; **bis über die** *od* **beide ~en verliebt sein** to be head over heels in love; **viel um die ~en haben** (*umg*) to have a lot on (one's plate); **halt die ~en steif!** keep a stiff upper lip!
Öhr [ø:r] (**-(e)s, -e**) *nt* eye
Ohren- *zW*: **Ohrenarzt** *m* ear specialist; **ohrenbetäubend** *adj* deafening; **Ohrenschmalz** *nt* earwax; **Ohrenschmerzen** *pl* earache *sing*; **Ohrenschützer** (**-s, -**) *m* earmuff
Ohr- *zW*: **Ohrfeige** *f* slap on the face; (*als Strafe*) box on the ears; **ohrfeigen** *vt untr*: **jdn ohrfeigen** to slap sb's face; to box sb's ears; **ich könnte mich selbst ohrfeigen, dass ich das gemacht habe** I could kick myself for doing that; **Ohrläppchen** *nt* ear lobe; **Ohrwurm** *m* earwig; (*Mus*) catchy tune
okkupieren [ɔku'pi:rən] *vt* to occupy
Ökologie [økolo'gi:] *f* ecology
ökologisch [øko'lo:gıʃ] *adj* ecological, environmental
ökonomisch [øko'no:mıʃ] *adj* economical
Ökopax [øko'paks] (**-en, -e**) (*umg*) *m* environmentalist
Ökosystem ['ø:kozʏste:m] *nt* ecosystem
Oktanzahl *f* octane rating
Oktave [ɔk'ta:və] (**-, -n**) *f* octave
Oktober [ɔk'to:bər] (**-(s), -**) *m* October; *siehe auch* **September**
Oktoberfest *nt*
ökumenisch [øku'me:nıʃ] *adj* ecumenical

Öl [øːl] (**-(e)s, -e**) *nt* oil; **auf Öl stoßen** to strike oil
Öl- *zW*: **Ölbaum** *m* olive tree; **ölen** *vt* to oil; (*Tech*) to lubricate; **wie ein geölter Blitz** (*umg*) like greased lightning; **Ölfarbe** *f* oil paint; **Ölfeld** *nt* oilfield; **Ölfilm** *m* film of oil; **Ölheizung** *f* oil-fired central heating
ölig *adj* oily
Olive [o'liːvə] (**-, -n**) *f* olive
Öl- *zW*: **Ölmessstab** *m* dipstick; **Ölpest** *f* oil pollution; **Ölsardine** *f* sardine; **Ölscheich** *m* oil sheik; **Ölstandanzeiger** *m* (*Aut*) oil level indicator; **Ölteppich** *m* oil slick
Ölung *f* oiling; (*Eccl*) anointment; **die Letzte ~** Extreme Unction
Ölwechsel *m* oil change
Olympiade [olympi'aːdə] (**-, -n**) *f* Olympic Games *pl*
Olympiasieger, in [o'lympiaziːgər(ɪn)] *m(f)* Olympic champion
olympisch [o'lympɪʃ] *adj* Olympic
Ölzeug *nt* oilskins *pl*
Oma ['oːma] (**-, -s**) (*umg*) *f* granny
Oman [o'maːn] (**-s**) *nt* Oman
Omelett [ɔm(ə)'lɛt] (**-(e)s, -s**) *nt* omelette (*Brit*), omelet (*US*)
Omen ['oːmɛn] (**-s, -** *od* **Omina**) *nt* omen
Omnibus ['ɔmnibʊs] *m* (omni)bus
onanieren *vi* to masturbate
Onkel ['ɔŋkəl] (**-s, -**) *m* uncle
online ['ɔnlaɪn] *adj* (*Comput*) on-line
Onlinedienst *m* (*Comput*) on-line service
Opa ['oːpa] (**-s, -s**) (*umg*) *m* grandpa
Opal [o'paːl] (**-s, -e**) *m* opal
Oper ['oːpər] (**-, -n**) *f* opera; (*Opernhaus*) opera house
Operation [operatsi'oːn] *f* operation
Operationssaal *m* operating theatre (*Brit*) *od* theater (*US*)
Operette [ope'rɛtə] *f* operetta
operieren [ope'riːrən] *vt, vi* to operate; **sich ~ lassen** to have an operation
Opern- *zW*: **Opernglas** *nt* opera glasses *pl*; **Opernhaus** *nt* opera house; **Opernsänger, in** *m(f)* opera singer
Opfer ['ɔpfər] (**-s, -**) *nt* sacrifice; (*Mensch*) victim
opfern *vt* to sacrifice
Opferstock *m* (*Eccl*) offertory box
Opferung *f* sacrifice; (*Eccl*) offertory
Opium ['oːpiʊm] (**-s**) *nt* opium
opponieren [ɔpo'niːrən] *vi*: **gegen jdn/etw ~** to oppose sb/sth
opportun [ɔpɔr'tuːn] *adj* opportune; **Opportunismus** [-'nɪsmʊs] *m* opportunism; **Opportunist, in** [-'nɪst(ɪn)] *m(f)* opportunist
Opposition [ɔpozitsi'oːn] *f* opposition
oppositionell [ɔpozitsio:'nɛl] *adj* opposing
Optik ['ɔptɪk] *f* optics *sing*
Optiker, in (**-s, -**) *m(f)* optician
optimal [ɔpti'maːl] *adj* optimal, optimum
Optimismus [ɔpti'mɪsmʊs] *m* optimism
Optimist, in [ɔpti'mɪst(ɪn)] *m(f)* optimist; **optimistisch** *adj* optimistic
optisch ['ɔptɪʃ] *adj* optical; **~e Täuschung** optical illusion
Orakel [o'raːkəl] (**-s, -**) *nt* oracle
Orange [o'rãːʒə] (**-, -n**) *f* orange; **orange** *adj* orange
Orangeade [orã'ʒaːdə] (**-, -n**) *f* orangeade
Orangeat [orã'ʒaːt] (**-s, -e**) *nt* candied peel
Orangensaft *m* orange juice
Orchester [ɔr'kɛstər] (**-s, -**) *nt* orchestra
Orchidee [ɔrçi'deːə] (**-, -n**) *f* orchid
Orden ['ɔrdən] (**-s, -**) *m* (*Eccl*) order; (*Mil*) decoration
Ordensschwester *f* nun
ordentlich ['ɔrdəntlɪç] *adj* (*anständig*) decent, respectable; (*geordnet*) tidy, neat; (*umg: annehmbar*) not bad; (*: tüchtig*) real, proper; (*Leistung*) reasonable; **~es Mitglied** full member; **~er Professor** (full) professor; **eine ~e Tracht Prügel** a proper hiding; **~ arbeiten** to be a thorough and precise worker; **Ordentlichkeit** *f* respectability; tidiness
Ordinalzahl [ɔrdi'naːltsaːl] *f* ordinal number
ordinär [ɔrdi'nɛːr] *adj* common, vulgar
ordnen ['ɔrdnən] *vt* to order, put in order
Ordner (**-s, -**) *m* steward; (*Comm*) file
Ordnung *f* order; (*Ordnen*) ordering; (*Geordnetsein*) tidiness; **geht in ~** (*umg*) that's all right *od* OK (*umg*); **~ schaffen, für ~ sorgen** to put things in order, tidy things up; **jdn zur ~ rufen** to call sb to order; **bei ihm muss alles seine ~ haben** (*räumlich*) he has to have everything in its proper place; (*zeitlich*) he has to do everything according to a fixed schedule; **das Kind braucht seine ~** the child needs a routine
Ordnungs- *zW*: **ordnungsgemäß** *adj* proper, according to the rules; **ordnungshalber** *adv* as a matter of form; **Ordnungsstrafe** *f* fine; **ordnungswidrig** *adj* contrary to the rules, irregular; **Ordnungszahl** *f* ordinal number
Organ [ɔr'gaːn] (**-s, -e**) *nt* organ; (*Stimme*) voice
Organisation [ɔrganizatsi'oːn] *f* organization
Organisationstalent *nt* organizing ability; (*Person*) good organizer
Organisator [ɔrgani'zaːtɔr] *m* organizer
organisch [ɔr'gaːnɪʃ] *adj* organic; (*Erkrankung, Leiden*) physical
organisieren [ɔrgani'ziːrən] *vt* to organize, arrange; (*umg: beschaffen*) to acquire ▷ *vr* to organize
Organismus [ɔrga'nɪsmʊs] *m* organism
Organist [ɔrga'nɪst] *m* organist
Organspender *m* donor (of an organ)
Orgasmus [ɔr'gasmʊs] *m* orgasm
Orgel ['ɔrgəl] (**-, -n**) *f* organ; **Orgelpfeife** *f* organ pipe; **wie die Orgelpfeifen stehen** to stand in order of height
Orgie ['ɔrgiə] *f* orgy
Orient ['oːriɛnt] (**-s**) *m* Orient, east; **der Vordere ~** the Near East

Orientale [oːriɛn'taːlə] (**-n, -n**) *m* Oriental
orientalisch *adj* oriental
orientieren [oːriɛn'tiːrən] *vt* (*örtlich*) to locate; (*fig*) to inform ▷ *vr* to find one's way *od* bearings; (*fig*) to inform o.s.
Orientierung [oːriɛn'tiːrʊŋ] *f* orientation; (*fig*) information; **die ~ verlieren** to lose one's bearings
Orientierungssinn *m* sense of direction
original [origi'naːl] *adj* original; **~ Meißener Porzellan** genuine Meissen porcelain; **Original** (**-s, -e**) *nt* original; (*Mensch*) character; **Originalfassung** *f* original version
Originalität [originali'tɛːt] *f* originality
originell [origi'nɛl] *adj* original
Orkan [ɔr'kaːn] (**-(e)s, -e**) *m* hurricane
Ornament [ɔrna'mɛnt] *nt* decoration, ornament
ornamental [ɔrnamɛn'taːl] *adj* decorative, ornamental
Ort[1] [ɔrt] (**-(e)s, -e**) *m* place; **an ~ und Stelle** on the spot; **am ~** in the place; **am angegebenen ~** in the place quoted, loc. cit.; **~ der Handlung** (*Theat*) scene of the action; **das ist höheren ~(e)s entschieden worden** (*hum: form*) the decision came from above
Ort[2] [ɔrt] (**-(e)s, ¨-er**) *m*: **vor ~** at the (coal) face; (*auch fig*) on the spot
orten *vt* to locate
orthodox [ɔrto'dɔks] *adj* orthodox
Orthografie [ɔrtogra'fiː] *f* spelling, orthography
orthografisch [ɔrto'graːfɪʃ] *adj* orthographic
Orthopäde [ɔrto'pɛːdə] (**-n, -n**) *m* orthopaedic (*Brit*) *od* orthopedic (*US*) specialist, orthopaedist (*Brit*), orthopedist (*US*)
Orthopädie [ɔrtopɛ'diː] *f* orthopaedics *sing* (*Brit*), orthopedics *sing* (*US*)
orthopädisch *adj* orthopaedic (*Brit*), orthopedic (*US*)
örtlich ['œrtlɪç] *adj* local; **jdn ~ betäuben** to give sb a local anaesthetic (*Brit*) *od* anesthetic (*US*); **Örtlichkeit** *f* locality; **sich mit den Örtlichkeiten vertraut machen** to get to know the place
Ortsangabe *f* (name of the) town; **ohne ~** (*Buch*) no place of publication indicated
ortsansässig *adj* local
Ortschaft *f* village, small town; **geschlossene ~** built-up area
Orts- *zW*: **ortsfremd** *adj* nonlocal; **Ortsfremde, r** *f(m)* stranger; **Ortsgespräch** *nt* local (phone) call; **Ortsname** *m* place name; **Ortsnetz** *nt* (*Tel*) local telephone exchange area; **Ortssinn** *m* sense of direction; **Ortszeit** *f* local time
Ortung *f* locating
Öse ['øːzə] (**-, -n**) *f* loop; (*an Kleidung*) eye
Ossi ['ɔsi] (**-s, -s**) (*umg*) *m* East German
Ostdeutschland *nt* (*Pol: früher*) East Germany; (*Geog*) Eastern Germany
Osten (**-s**) *m* east; **der Ferne ~** the Far East; **der Nahe ~** the Middle East, the Near East
ostentativ [ɔstɛnta'tiːf] *adj* pointed, ostentatious
Oster- *zW*: **Osterei** *nt* Easter egg; **Osterfest** *nt* Easter; **Osterglocke** *f* daffodil; **Osterhase** *m* Easter bunny; **Osterinsel** *f* Easter Island; **Ostermontag** *m* Easter Monday
Ostern (**-s, -**) *nt* Easter; **frohe** *od* **fröhliche ~!** Happy Easter!; **zu ~** at Easter
Österreich ['øːstəraɪç] (**-s**) *nt* Austria
Österreicher, in (**-s, -**) *m(f)* Austrian
österreichisch *adj* Austrian
Ostersonntag *m* Easter Day *od* Sunday
östlich ['œstlɪç] *adj* eastern, easterly; **Ostsee** *f* Baltic Sea
oszillieren [ɔstsɪ'liːrən] *vi* to oscillate
Otter[1] ['ɔtər] (**-s, -**) *m* otter
Otter[2] ['ɔtər] (**-, -n**) *f* (*Schlange*) adder
Ouvertüre [uvɛr'tyːrə] (**-, -n**) *f* overture
oval [o'vaːl] *adj* oval
Ovation [ovatsi'oːn] *f* ovation
Overall ['oʊvərɔːl] (**-s, -s**) *m* (*Schutzanzug*) overalls *pl*
ÖVP (**-**) *f abk* (= *Österreichische Volkspartei*) Austrian People's Party
Ovulation [ovulatsi'oːn] *f* ovulation
Oxid, Oxyd [ɔ'ksyːt] (**-(e)s, -e**) *nt* oxide
oxidieren, oxydieren [ɔksy'diːrən] *vt, vi* to oxidize
Ozean ['oːtseaːn] (**-s, -e**) *m* ocean; **Ozeandampfer** *m* (ocean-going) liner
Ozon [o'tsoːn] (**-s**) *nt* ozone; **Ozonloch** *nt* hole in the ozone layer; **Ozonschicht** *f* ozone layer

Pp

P, p [peː] *nt* P, p; **P wie Peter** ≈ P for Peter
Paar [paːr] (**-(e)s, -e**) *nt* pair; (*Liebespaar*) couple
paar *adj inv*: **ein ~** a few; (*zwei oder drei*) a couple of; *siehe auch* **paarmal**
paaren *vt, vr* (*Tiere*) to mate, pair
Paar- *zW*: **Paarlauf** *m* pair skating; **paarmal** *adv*: **ein paarmal** a few times
Paarung *f* combination; (*von Tieren*) mating
paarweise *adv* in pairs; in couples
Pacht [paxt] (**-, -en**) *f* lease; (*Entgelt*) rent; **pachten** *vt* to lease; **du hast das Sofa doch nicht für dich gepachtet** (*umg*) don't hog the sofa
Pächter, in ['pɛçtər(ɪn)] (**-s, -**) *m(f)* leaseholder; tenant
Pack[1] [pak] (**-(e)s, -e** *od* **¨-e**) *m* bundle, pack
Pack[2] [pak] (**-(e)s**) (*pej*) *nt* mob, rabble
Päckchen ['pɛkçən] *nt* small package; (*Zigaretten*) packet; (*Postpäckchen*) small parcel
Packen (**-s, -**) *m* bundle; (*fig: Menge*) heaps (of); **packen** *vt, vi* (*auch Comput*) to pack; (*fassen*) to grasp, seize; (*umg: schaffen*) to manage; (*fig: fesseln*) to grip; **packen wirs!** (*umg: gehen*) let's go
Packer, in (**-s, -**) *m(f)* packer
Packesel *m* pack mule; (*fig*) packhorse
Packpapier *nt* brown paper, wrapping paper
Packung *f* packet; (*Pralinenpackung*) box; (*Med*) compress
Pädagoge [pɛda'goːgə] (**-n, -n**) *m* educationalist
Pädagogik *f* education
pädagogisch *adj* educational, pedagogical; **~e Hochschule** college of education
Paddel ['padəl] (**-s, -**) *nt* paddle; **Paddelboot** *nt* canoe
paddeln *vi* to paddle
Page ['paːʒə] (**-n, -n**) *m* page(boy)
Pagenkopf *m* pageboy cut
Paket [pa'keːt] (**-(e)s, -e**) *nt* packet; (*Postpaket*) parcel; **Paketkarte** *f* dispatch note; **Paketpost** *f* parcel post; **Paketschalter** *m* parcels counter
Pakistan ['paːkɪstaːn] (**-s**) *nt* Pakistan
pakistanisch *adj* Pakistani
Pakt [pakt] (**-(e)s, -e**) *m* pact
Palast [pa'last] (**-es, Paläste**) *m* palace
Palästina [palɛ'stiːna] (**-s**) *nt* Palestine
Palästinenser, in [palɛsti'nɛnzər(ɪn)] (**-s, -**) *m(f)* Palestinian
palästinensisch *adj* Palestinian
Palette [pa'lɛtə] *f* palette; (*fig*) range; (*Ladepalette*) pallet
Palme ['palmə] (**-, -n**) *f* palm (tree); **jdn auf die ~ bringen** (*umg*) to make sb see red
Palmsonntag *m* Palm Sunday
Pampelmuse ['pampəlmuːzə] (**-, -n**) *f* grapefruit
pampig ['pampɪç] (*umg*) *adj* (*frech*) fresh
Panama ['panama] (**-s**) *nt* Panama; **Panamakanal** *m* Panama Canal
panieren [pa'niːrən] *vt* (*Koch*) to coat with egg and breadcrumbs
Paniermehl [pa'niːrmeːl] *nt* breadcrumbs *pl*
Panik ['paːnɪk] *f* panic; **nur keine ~!** don't panic!; **in ~ ausbrechen** to panic
panisch ['paːnɪʃ] *adj* panic-stricken
Panne ['panə] (**-, -n**) *f* (*Aut etc*) breakdown; (*Missgeschick*) slip; **uns ist eine ~ passiert** we've boobed (*Brit*) (*umg*) *od* goofed (*US*) (*umg*)
Pannendienst *m* breakdown service
panschen ['panʃən] *vi* to splash about ▷ *vt* to water down
Pantoffel [pan'tɔfəl] (**-s, -n**) *m* slipper; **Pantoffelheld** (*umg*) *m* henpecked husband
Pantomime [panto'miːmə] (**-, -n**) *f* mime
Panzer ['pantsər] (**-s, -**) *m* armour (*Brit*), armor (*US*); (*fig*) shield; (*Platte*) armo(u)r plate; (*Fahrzeug*) tank; **Panzerglas** *nt* bulletproof glass
panzern *vt* to armour (*Brit*) *od* armor (*US*) plate ▷ *vr* (*fig*) to arm o.s.
Papa [pa'paː] (**-s, -s**) (*umg*) *m* dad(dy), pa
Papagei [papaː'gaɪ] (**-s, -en**) *m* parrot
Papier [pa'piːr] (**-s, -e**) *nt* paper; (*Wertpapier*) share; **Papiere** *pl* (identity) papers *pl*; (*Urkunden*) documents *pl*; **seine ~e bekommen** (*entlassen werden*) to get one's cards; **Papierfabrik** *f* paper mill; **Papiergeld** *nt* paper money; **Papierkorb** *m* wastepaper basket; **Papiertüte** *f* paper bag; **Papiervorschub** *m* (*Drucker*) paper advance
Pappbecher *m* paper cup
Pappdeckel (**-, -n**) *m* cardboard
Pappe ['papə] *f* cardboard; **das ist nicht von ~** (*umg*) that is really something
Pappeinband *m* pasteboard

Pappel (-, **-n**) *f* poplar
pappig *adj* sticky
Pappteller *m* paper plate
Paprika ['paprika] (**-s, -s**) *m* (*Gewürz*) paprika; (*Paprikaschote*) pepper
Papst [pa:pst] (**-(e)s, ¨-e**) *m* pope
päpstlich ['pɛ:pstlıç] *adj* papal; **~er als der Papst sein** to be more Catholic than the Pope
Parabel [pa'ra:bəl] (**-, -n**) *f* parable; (*Math*) parabola
Parabolantenne [para'bo:l|antɛnə] *f* (*TV*) satellite dish
Parade [pa'ra:də] (**-, -n**) *f* (*Mil*) parade, review; (*Sport*) parry; **Parademarsch** *m* march past
Paradies [para'di:s] (**-es, -e**) *nt* paradise; **paradiesisch** *adj* heavenly
Paradox [para'dɔks] (**-es, -e**) *nt* paradox; **paradox** *adj* paradoxical
Paraguay [paragu'a:i] (**-s**) *nt* Paraguay
Paraguayer, in [para'gua:jər(ın)] (**-s, -**) *m(f)* Paraguayan
paraguayisch *adj* Paraguayan
parallel [para'le:l] *adj* parallel; **~ schalten** (*Elek*) to connect in parallel
Parallele (**-, -n**) *f* parallel
Parameter [pa'ra:metər] *m* parameter
Paranuss ['pa:ranʊs] *f* Brazil nut
paraphieren [para'fi:rən] *vt* (*Vertrag*) to initial
Parasit [para'zi:t] (**-en, -en**) *m* (*lit, fig*) parasite
parat [pa'ra:t] *adj* ready
Pärchen ['pɛ:rçən] *nt* couple
Parfüm [par'fy:m] (**-s, -s** *od* **-e**) *nt* perfume
Parfümerie [parfymə'ri:] *f* perfumery
Parfümflasche *f* scent bottle
parfümieren [parfy'mi:rən] *vt* to scent, perfume
parieren [pa'ri:rən] *vt* to parry ▷ *vi* (*umg*) to obey
Paris [pa'ri:s] (**-**) *nt* Paris
Pariser [pa'ri:zər] (**-s, -**) *m* Parisian; (*umg: Kondom*) rubber ▷ *adj attrib* Parisian, Paris *attrib*
Parität [pari'tɛ:t] *f* parity
Park [park] (**-s, -s**) *m* park
Parka ['parka] (**-(s), -s**) *m* parka
Parkanlage *f* park; (*um Gebäude*) grounds *pl*
parken *vt, vi* to park; **„P~ verboten!"** "No Parking"
Parkett [par'kɛt] (**-(e)s, -e**) *nt* parquet (floor); (*Theat*) stalls *pl* (*Brit*), orchestra (*US*)
Park- *zW*: **Parkhaus** *nt* multistorey car park; **Parklücke** *f* parking space; **Parkplatz** *m* car park, parking lot (*US*); parking place; **Parkscheibe** *f* parking disc; **Parkuhr** *f* parking meter; **Parkverbot** *nt* parking ban
Parlament [parla'mɛnt] *nt* parliament
Parlamentarier [parlamɛn'ta:riər] (**-s, -**) *m* parliamentarian
parlamentarisch *adj* parliamentary
Parlaments- *zW*: **Parlamentsbeschluss** *m* vote of parliament; **Parlamentsmitglied** *nt* Member of Parliament (*Brit*), Congressman (*US*); **Parlamentssitzung** *f* sitting (of parliament)
Parodie [paro'di:] *f* parody
parodieren *vt* to parody
Parodontose [parodɔn'to:zə] (**-, -n**) *f* shrinking gums *pl*
Parole [pa'ro:lə] (**-, -n**) *f* password; (*Wahlspruch*) motto
Partei [par'taı] *f* party; (*im Mietshaus*) tenant, party (*form*); **für jdn ~ ergreifen** to take sb's side; **parteiisch** *adj* partial, bias(s)ed; **Parteinahme** (**-, -n**) *f* partisanship; **Parteitag** *m* party conference; **Parteivorsitzende, r** *f(m)* party leader
Parterre [par'tɛr] (**-s, -s**) *nt* ground floor; (*Theat*) stalls *pl* (*Brit*), orchestra (*US*)
Partie [par'ti:] *f* part; (*Spiel*) game; (*Ausflug*) outing; (*Mann, Frau*) catch; (*Comm*) lot; **mit von der ~ sein** to join in
Partisan, in [parti'za:n(ın)] (**-s** *od* **-en, -en**) *m(f)* partisan
Partitur [parti'tu:r] *f* (*Mus*) score
Partizip [parti'tsi:p] (**-s, -ien**) *nt* participle; **~ Präsens/Perfekt** (*Gram*) present/past participle
Partner, in ['partnər(ın)] (**-s, -**) *m(f)* partner; **partnerschaftlich** *adj* as partners; **Partnerstadt** *f* twin town (*Brit*)
Party ['pa:rti] (**-, -s**) *f* party
Pass [pas] (**-es, ¨-e**) *m* pass; (*Ausweis*) passport
passabel [pa'sa:bəl] *adj* passable, reasonable
Passage [pa'sa:ʒə] (**-, -n**) *f* passage; (*Ladenstraße*) arcade
Passagier [pasa'ʒi:r] (**-s, -e**) *m* passenger; **Passagierdampfer** *m* passenger steamer; **Passagierflugzeug** *nt* airliner
Passamt *nt* passport office
Passant, in [pa'sant(ın)] *m(f)* passer-by
Passbild *nt* passport photo(graph)
passen ['pasən] *vi* to fit; (*auf Frage, Karten*) to pass; **~ zu** (*Farbe etc*) to go with; **Sonntag passt uns nicht** Sunday is no good for us; **die Schuhe ~ (mir) gut** the shoes are a good fit (for me); **zu jdm ~** (*Mensch*) to suit sb; **das passt mir nicht** that doesn't suit me; **er passt nicht zu dir** he's not right for you; **das könnte dir so ~!** (*umg*) you'd like that, wouldn't you?
passend *adj* suitable; (*zusammenpassend*) matching; (*angebracht*) fitting; (*Zeit*) convenient; **haben Sie es ~?** (*Geld*) have you got the right money?
passierbar [pa'si:rba:r] *adj* passable; (*Fluss, Kanal*) negotiable
passieren *vt* to pass; (*durch Sieb*) to strain ▷ *vi* (*Hilfsverb sein*) to happen; **es ist ein Unfall passiert** there has been an accident
Passierschein *m* pass, permit
Passion [pasi'o:n] *f* passion
passioniert [pasio:'ni:rt] *adj* enthusiastic, passionate
Passionsfrucht *f* passion fruit
Passionsspiel *nt* Passion Play

passiv ['pasi:f] *adj* passive; **~es Rauchen** passive smoking; **Passiv** (**-s, -e**) *nt* passive
Passiva [pa'si:va] *pl* (*Comm*) liabilities *pl*
Passivität [pasivi'tɛ:t] *f* passiveness
Pass- *zW*: **Passkontrolle** *f* passport control; **Passstelle** *f* passport office; **Passstraße** *f* (mountain) pass
Paste ['pastə] (**-, -n**) *f* paste
Pastell [pas'tɛl] (**-(e)s, -e**) *nt* pastel
Pastete [pas'te:tə] (**-, -n**) *f* pie; (*Pastetchen*) vol-au-vent; (: *ungefüllt*) vol-au-vent case
pasteurisieren [pastøri'zi:rən] *vt* to pasteurize
Pastor ['pastɔr] *m* vicar; pastor, minister
Pate ['pa:tə] (**-n, -n**) *m* godfather; **bei etw ~ gestanden haben** (*fig*) to be the force behind sth
Patenkind *nt* godchild
patent [pa'tɛnt] *adj* clever
Patent (**-(e)s, -e**) *nt* patent; (*Mil*) commission; **etw als** *od* **zum ~ anmelden** to apply for a patent on sth
Patentamt *nt* patent office
patentieren [patɛn'ti:rən] *vt* to patent
Patentinhaber *m* patentee
Pater ['pa:tər] (**-s, -** *od* **Patres**) *m* Father
pathetisch [pa'te:tɪʃ] *adj* emotional
Pathologe [pato'lo:gə] (**-n, -n**) *m* pathologist
pathologisch *adj* pathological
Pathos ['pa:tɔs] (**-**) *nt* pathos
Patient, in [patsi'ɛnt(ɪn)] *m(f)* patient
Patin ['pa:tɪn] *f* godmother
Patriarch [patri'arç] (**-en, -en**) *m* patriarch
Patriot, in [patri'o:t(ɪn)] (**-en, -en**) *m(f)* patriot; **patriotisch** *adj* patriotic
Patriotismus [patrio:'tɪsmʊs] *m* patriotism
Patron [pa'tro:n] (**-s, -e**) *m* patron; (*Eccl*) patron saint
Patrone (**-, -n**) *f* cartridge
Patronenhülse *f* cartridge case
Patsche (**-, -n**) (*umg*) *f* (*Händchen*) paw; (*Fliegenpatsche*) swat; (*Feuerpatsche*) beater; (*Bedrängnis*) mess, jam
patschen *vi* to smack, slap; (*im Wasser*) to splash
patschnass *adj* soaking wet
patzig ['patsɪç] (*umg*) *adj* cheeky, saucy
Pauke ['paʊkə] (**-, -n**) *f* kettledrum; **auf die ~ hauen** to live it up; **mit ~n und Trompeten durchfallen** (*umg*) to fail dismally
pausbäckig ['paʊsbɛkɪç] *adj* chubby-cheeked
pauschal [paʊ'ʃa:l] *adj* (*Kosten*) inclusive; (*einheitlich*) flat-rate *attrib*; (*Urteil*) sweeping; **die Werkstatt berechnet ~ pro Inspektion 130 Euro** the garage has a flat rate of 130 euros per service
Pauschale (**-, -n**) *f* flat rate; (*vorläufig geschätzter Betrag*) estimated amount
Pauschal- *zW*: **Pauschalgebühr** *f* flat rate; **Pauschalpreis** *m* all-in price; **Pauschalreise** *f* package tour; **Pauschalsumme** *f* lump sum
Pause ['paʊzə] (**-, -n**) *f* break; (*Theat*) interval; (*das Innehalten*) pause; (*Mus*) rest; (*Kopie*) tracing
pausen *vt* to trace
Pausen- *zW*: **pausenlos** *adj* nonstop; **Pausenzeichen** *nt* (*Rundf*) call sign; (*Mus*) rest
Pauspapier ['paʊspapi:r] *nt* tracing paper
Pavian ['pa:via:n] (**-s, -e**) *m* baboon
Pazifik [pa'tsi:fɪk] (**-s**) *m* Pacific
Pazifist, in [patsi'fɪst(ɪn)] *m(f)* pacifist; **pazifistisch** *adj* pacifist
PC *m abk* (*= Personal Computer*) PC
PDS *f abk* (*= Partei des Demokratischen Sozialismus*) *German Socialist Party*
Pech [pɛç] (**-s, -e**) *nt* pitch; (*fig*) bad luck; **~ haben** to be unlucky; **die beiden halten zusammen wie ~ und Schwefel** (*umg*) the two are inseparable; **~ gehabt!** tough! (*umg*); **pechschwarz** *adj* pitch-black; **Pechsträhne** (*umg*) *f* unlucky patch; **Pechvogel** (*umg*) *m* unlucky person
Pedal [pe'da:l] (**-s, -e**) *nt* pedal; **in die ~e treten** to pedal (hard)
Pedant [pe'dant] *m* pedant
Pedanterie [pedantə'ri:] *f* pedantry
pedantisch *adj* pedantic
Peddigrohr ['pɛdɪçro:r] *nt* cane
Pegel ['pe:gəl] (**-s, -**) *m* water gauge; (*Geräuschpegel*) noise level; **Pegelstand** *m* water level
peilen ['paɪlən] *vt* to get a fix on; **die Lage ~** (*umg*) to see how the land lies
peinigen *vt* to torture; (*plagen*) to torment
peinlich *adj* (*unangenehm*) embarrassing, awkward, painful; (*genau*) painstaking; **in seinem Zimmer herrschte ~e Ordnung** his room was meticulously tidy; **er vermied es ~st, davon zu sprechen** he was at pains not to talk about it; **Peinlichkeit** *f* painfulness, awkwardness; (*Genauigkeit*) scrupulousness
Peitsche ['paɪtʃə] (**-, -n**) *f* whip
peitschen *vt* to whip; (*Regen*) to lash
Peking ['pe:kɪŋ] (**-s**) *nt* Peking
Pelikan ['pe:lika:n] (**-s, -e**) *m* pelican
Pelle ['pɛlə] (**-, -n**) *f* skin; **der Chef sitzt mir auf der ~** (*umg*) I've got the boss on my back
pellen *vt* to skin, peel
Pellkartoffeln *pl* jacket potatoes *pl*
Pelz [pɛlts] (**-es, -e**) *m* fur
Pendel ['pɛndəl] (**-s, -**) *nt* pendulum
pendeln *vi* (*schwingen*) to swing (to and fro); (*Zug, Fähre etc*) to shuttle; (*Mensch*) to commute; (*fig*) to fluctuate
Pendelverkehr *m* shuttle service; (*Berufsverkehr*) commuter traffic
Pendler, in ['pɛndlər(ɪn)] (**-s, -**) *m(f)* commuter
penetrant [pene'trant] *adj* sharp; (*Person*) pushing; **das schmeckt/riecht ~ nach Knoblauch** it has a very strong taste/smell of garlic
Penis ['pe:nɪs] (**-, -se**) *m* penis
pennen (*umg*) *vi* to kip
Penner (**-s, -**) (*pej: umg*) *m* tramp (*Brit*), hobo

(US)

Pension [pɛnzi'o:n] *f* (*Geld*) pension; (*Ruhestand*) retirement; (*für Gäste*) boarding house, guesthouse; **halbe/volle ~** half/full board; **in ~ gehen** to retire

Pensionär, in [pɛnzio'nɛ:r(ɪn)] (**-s, -e**) *m(f)* pensioner

pensionieren [pɛnzio'ni:rən] *vt* to pension (off); **sich ~ lassen** to retire

pensioniert *adj* retired

Pensionierung *f* retirement

Pensionsgast *m* boarder, paying guest

Pensum ['pɛnzʊm] (**-s, Pensen**) *nt* quota; (*Sch*) curriculum

Peperoni [pepe'ro:ni] *pl* chillies *pl*

per [pɛr] *präp +akk* by, per; (*pro*) per; (*bis*) by; **~ Adresse** (*Comm*) care of, c/o; **mit jdm ~ du sein** (*umg*) to be on first-name terms with sb

Perfekt ['pɛrfɛkt] (**-(e)s, -e**) *nt* perfect

perfekt [pɛr'fɛkt] *adj* perfect; (*abgemacht*) settled; **die Sache ~ machen** to clinch the deal; **der Vertrag ist ~** the contract is all settled

Perfektionismus [pɛrfɛktsio'nɪsmʊs] *m* perfectionism

perforieren [pɛrfo'ri:rən] *vt* to perforate

Pergament [pɛrga'mɛnt] *nt* parchment; **Pergamentpapier** *nt* greaseproof paper (*Brit*), wax(ed) paper (*US*)

Periode [peri'o:də] (**-, -n**) *f* period; **0,33 ~** 0.33 recurring

periodisch [peri'o:dɪʃ] *adj* periodic; (*dezimal*) recurring

Peripheriegerät *nt* (*Comput*) peripheral

Perle ['pɛrlə] (**-, -n**) *f* (*lit, fig*) pearl; (*Glasperle, Holzperle, Tropfen*) bead; (*veraltet: umg: Hausgehilfin*) maid

perlen *vi* to sparkle; (*Tropfen*) to trickle

Perlhuhn *nt* guinea fowl

Perlmutt ['pɛrlmʊt] (**-s**) *nt* mother-of-pearl

perplex [pɛr'plɛks] *adj* dumbfounded

Perser ['pɛrzər] (**-s, -**) *m* (*Person*) Persian; (*umg: Teppich*) Persian carpet

Persianer [pɛrzi'a:nər] (**-s, -**) *m* Persian lamb (coat)

Persien ['pɛrziən] (**-s**) *nt* Persia

persisch *adj* Persian; **P~er Golf** Persian Gulf

Person [pɛr'zo:n] (**-, -en**) *f* person; (*pej: Frau*) female; **sie ist Köchin und Haushälterin in einer ~** she is cook and housekeeper rolled into one; **ich für meine ~** personally I

Personal [pɛrzo'na:l] (**-s**) *nt* personnel; (*Bedienung*) servants *pl*; **Personalausweis** *m* identity card

Personalien [pɛrzo'na:liən] *pl* particulars *pl*

Personalpronomen *nt* personal pronoun

Personenaufzug *m* lift, elevator (*US*); **Personenkraftwagen** *m* private motorcar, automobile (*US*); **Personenschaden** *m* injury to persons; **Personenwaage** *f* scales *pl*; **Personenzug** *m* stopping train; passenger train

personifizieren [pɛrzonifi'tsi:rən] *vt* to personify

persönlich [pɛr'zø:nlɪç] *adj* personal ▷ *adv* in person; personally; (*auf Briefen*) private (and confidential); **~ haften** (*Comm*) to be personally liable; **Persönlichkeit** *f* personality; **Persönlichkeiten des öffentlichen Lebens** public figures

Peru [pe'ru:] (**-s**) *nt* Peru

Peruaner, in [peru'a:nər(ɪn)] (**-s, -**) *m(f)* Peruvian

peruanisch *adj* Peruvian

Perücke [pe'rʏkə] (**-, -n**) *f* wig

pervers [pɛr'vɛrs] *adj* perverse

Perversität [pɛrvɛrzi'tɛ:t] *f* perversity

Pessimismus [pɛsi'mɪsmʊs] *m* pessimism

Pessimist, in [pɛsi'mɪst(ɪn)] *m(f)* pessimist; **pessimistisch** *adj* pessimistic

Pest [pɛst] (**-**) *f* plague; **jdn/etw wie die ~ hassen** (*umg*) to loathe (and detest) sb/sth

Petersilie [petər'zi:liə] *f* parsley

Petrodollar [petro'dɔlar] *m* petrodollar

Petroleum [pe'tro:leʊm] (**-s**) *nt* paraffin (*Brit*), kerosene (*US*)

petzen ['pɛtsən] (*umg*) *vi* to tell tales; **er petzt immer** he always tells

Pfad [pfa:t] (**-(e)s, -e**) *m* path; **Pfadfinder** *m* Boy Scout; **er ist bei den Pfadfindern** he's in the (Boy) Scouts

Pfahl [pfa:l] (**-(e)s, ¨-e**) *m* post, stake; **Pfahlbau** *m* pile dwelling

Pfand [pfant] (**-(e)s, ¨-er**) *nt* pledge, security; (*Flaschenpfand*) deposit; (*im Spiel*) forfeit; (*fig: der Liebe etc*) pledge; **Pfandbrief** *m* bond

pfänden ['pfɛndən] *vt* to seize, impound

Pfänderspiel *nt* game of forfeits

Pfand- *zW*: **Pfandhaus** *nt* pawnshop; **Pfandschein** *m* pawn ticket

Pfändung ['pfɛndʊŋ] *f* seizure, distraint (*form*)

Pfanne ['pfanə] (**-, -n**) *f* (frying) pan; **jdn in die ~ hauen** (*umg*) to tear a strip off sb

Pfannkuchen *m* pancake; (*Berliner*) doughnut (*Brit*), donut (*US*)

Pfarrei [pfar'raɪ] *f* parish

Pfarrer (**-s, -**) *m* priest; (*evangelisch*) vicar; (*von Freikirchen*) minister

Pfarrhaus *nt* vicarage

Pfau [pfaʊ] (**-(e)s, -en**) *m* peacock

Pfauenauge *nt* peacock butterfly

Pfeffer ['pfɛfər] (**-s, -**) *m* pepper; **er soll bleiben, wo der ~ wächst!** (*umg*) he can take a running jump; **Pfefferkorn** *nt* peppercorn; **Pfefferkuchen** *m* gingerbread; **Pfefferminze** *f* peppermint (plant); **Pfeffermühle** *f* pepper mill

pfeffern *vt* to pepper; (*umg: werfen*) to fling; **gepfefferte Preise/Witze** steep prices/spicy jokes

Pfeife ['pfaɪfə] (**-, -n**) *f* whistle; (*Tabakpfeife, Orgelpfeife*) pipe; **nach jds ~ tanzen** to dance to sb's tune

pfeifen *unreg vt, vi* to whistle; **auf dem letzten Loch ~** (*umg: erschöpft sein*) to be on

one's last legs; (: *finanziell*) to be on one's beam ends; **ich pfeif(e) drauf!** (*umg*) I don't give a damn!
Pfeifer (**-s, -**) *m* piper
Pfeil [pfaıl] (**-(e)s, -e**) *m* arrow
Pfeiler ['pfaılər] (**-s, -**) *m* pillar, prop; (*Brückenpfeiler*) pier
Pfennig ['pfɛnıç] (**-(e)s, -e**) *m* (*Hist*) pfennig (*one hundredth of a mark*)
Pferd [pfe:rt] (**-(e)s, -e**) *nt* horse; **wie ein ~ arbeiten** (*umg*) to work like a Trojan; **mit ihm kann man ~e stehlen** (*umg*) he's a great sport; **auf das falsche/richtige ~ setzen** (*lit, fig*) to back the wrong/right horse
Pferde- *zW*: **Pferderennen** *nt* horse-race; (*Sportart*) horse-racing; **Pferdeschwanz** *m* (*Frisur*) ponytail
Pfiff (**-(e)s, -e**) *m* whistle; (*Kniff*) trick
Pfifferling ['pfıfərlıŋ] *m* yellow chanterelle; **keinen ~ wert** not worth a thing
pfiffig *adj* smart
Pfingsten ['pfıŋstən] (**-, -**) *nt* Whitsun
Pfingstrose *f* peony
Pfirsich ['pfırzıç] (**-s, -e**) *m* peach
Pflanze ['pflantsə] (**-, -n**) *f* plant
pflanzen *vt* to plant ▷ *vr* (*umg*) to plonk o.s.
Pflanzenfett *nt* vegetable fat
pflanzlich *adj* vegetable
Pflanzung *f* plantation
Pflaster ['pflastər] (**-s, -**) *nt* plaster; (*Straßenpflaster*) pavement (*Brit*), sidewalk (*US*); **ein teures ~** (*umg*) a pricey place; **ein heißes ~** a dangerous *od* unsafe place; **pflastermüde** *adj* dead on one's feet
Pflasterstein *m* paving stone
Pflaume ['pflaʊmə] (**-, -n**) *f* plum; (*umg: Mensch*) twit (*Brit*)
Pflege ['pfle:gə] (**-, -n**) *f* care; (*von Idee*) cultivation; (*Krankenpflege*) nursing; **jdn/etw in ~ nehmen** to look after sb/sth; **in ~ sein** (*Kind*) to be fostered out; **pflegebedürftig** *adj* needing care; **Pflegeeltern** *pl* foster parents *pl*; **Pflegekind** *nt* foster child; **pflegeleicht** *adj* easy-care; **Pflegemutter** *f* foster mother
pflegen *vt* to look after; (*Kranke*) to nurse; (*Beziehungen*) to foster ▷ *vi* (*gewöhnlich tun*): **sie pflegte zu sagen** she used to say
Pfleger (**-s, -**) *m* (*im Krankenhaus*) orderly; (*voll qualifiziert*) male nurse
Pflegevater *m* foster father
Pflegeversicherung *f* geriatric care insurance
Pflicht [pflıçt] (**-, -en**) *f* duty; (*Sport*) compulsory section; **Rechte und ~en** rights and responsibilities; **pflichtbewusst** *adj* conscientious; **Pflichtfach** *nt* (*Sch*) compulsory subject; **Pflichtgefühl** *nt* sense of duty; **pflichtgemäß** *adj* dutiful; **Pflichtversicherung** *f* compulsory insurance
pflücken ['pflʏkən] *vt* to pick
Pflug [pflu:k] (**-(e)s, ¨-e**) *m* plough (*Brit*), plow (*US*)
pflügen ['pfly:gən] *vt* to plough (*Brit*), plow (*US*)
Pforte ['pfɔrtə] (**-, -n**) *f* (*Tor*) gate
Pförtner ['pfœrtnər] (**-s, -**) *m* porter, doorkeeper, doorman
Pfosten ['pfɔstən] (**-s, -**) *m* post; (*senkrechter Balken*) upright
Pfote ['pfo:tə] (**-, -n**) *f* paw; (*umg: Schrift*) scrawl
Pfropf [pfrɔpf] (**-(e)s, -e**) *m* (*Flaschenpfropf*) stopper; (*Blutpfropf*) clot
Pfropfen (**-s, -**) *m* = **Pfropf**
pfui [pfʊı] *interj* ugh!; (*na na*) tut tut!; (*Buhruf*) boo!; **~ Teufel!** (*umg*) ugh!, yuck!
Pfund [pfʊnt] (**-(e)s, -e**) *nt* (*Gewicht, Fin*) pound; **das ~ sinkt** sterling *od* the pound is falling
pfundig (*umg*) *adj* great
pfuschen ['pfʊʃən] *vi* to bungle; (*einen Fehler machen*) to slip up
Pfuscher, in ['pfʊʃər(ın)] (**-s, -**) (*umg*) *m(f)* sloppy worker; (*Kurpfuscher*) quack
Pfuscherei [pfʊʃə'raı] (*umg*) *f* sloppy work; (*Kurpfuscherei*) quackery
Pfütze ['pfʏtsə] (**-, -n**) *f* puddle
Phänomen [fɛno'me:n] (**-s, -e**) *nt* phenomenon
Phantombild *nt* Identikit® picture
Pharisäer [fari'zɛ:ər] (**-s, -**) *m* (*lit, fig*) pharisee
Pharmazeut, in [farma'tsɔʏt(ın)] (**-en, -en**) *m(f)* pharmacist
Phase ['fa:zə] (**-, -n**) *f* phase
Philippinen *pl* Philippines *pl*, Philippine Islands *pl*
philippinisch *adj* Filipino
Philologe [filo'lo:gə] (**-n, -n**) *m* philologist
Philologie [filolo'gi:] *f* philology
Philosoph, in [filo'zo:f(ın)] (**-en, -en**) *m(f)* philosopher
Philosophie [filozo'fi:] *f* philosophy
philosophisch *adj* philosophical
Phlegma ['flɛgma] (**-s**) *nt* lethargy
phlegmatisch [flɛ'gma:tıʃ] *adj* lethargic
Phonetik [fo'ne:tık] *f* phonetics *sing*
phonetisch *adj* phonetic
Phosphat [fɔs'fa:t] (**-(e)s, -e**) *nt* phosphate
Phosphor ['fɔsfɔr] (**-s**) *m* phosphorus
phosphoreszieren [fɔsforɛs'tsi:rən] *vt* to phosphoresce
Photo *etc* ['fo:to] = **Foto** *etc*
Phrase ['fra:zə] (**-, -n**) *f* phrase; (*pej*) hollow phrase; **~n dreschen** (*umg*) to churn out one cliché after another
pH-Wert [pe:'ha:ve:rt] *m* pH value
Physik [fy'zi:k] *f* physics *sing*
physikalisch [fyzi'ka:lıʃ] *adj* of physics
Physiker, in ['fy:zikər(ın)] (**-s, -**) *m(f)* physicist
Physiologe [fyzio'lo:gə] (**-n, -n**) *m* physiologist
Physiologie [fyziolo'gi:] *f* physiology
physisch ['fy:zıʃ] *adj* physical
Pianist, in [pia'nıst(ın)] *m(f)* pianist
picheln ['pıçəln] (*umg*) *vi* to booze
Pickel ['pıkəl] (**-s, -**) *m* pimple; (*Werkzeug*) pickaxe; (*Bergpickel*) ice axe

pickelig, **picklig** *adj* pimply
picken ['pɪkən] *vt* to peck ▷*vi*: ~ **(nach)** to peck (at)
Picknick ['pɪknɪk] (**-s, -e** *od* **-s**) *nt* picnic; ~ **machen** to have a picnic
piepen ['pi:pən] *vi* to chirp; (*Funkgerät etc*) to bleep; **bei dir piepts wohl!** (*umg*) are you off your head?; **es war zum P~!** (*umg*) it was a scream!
Pietät [pie'tɛ:t] *f* piety; reverence; **pietätlos** *adj* impious, irreverent
Pigment [pɪg'mɛnt] (**-(e)s, -e**) *nt* pigment
Pik [pi:k] (**-s, -s**) *nt* (*Karten*) spades; **einen ~ auf jdn haben** (*umg*) to have it in for sb
pikant [pi'kant] *adj* spicy, piquant; (*anzüglich*) suggestive
Piktogramm [pɪkto'gram] *nt* pictogram
Pilger, in ['pɪlgər(ɪn)] (**-s, -**) *m(f)* pilgrim; **Pilgerfahrt** *f* pilgrimage
Pille ['pɪlə] (**-, -n**) *f* pill
Pilot, in [pi'lo:t(ɪn)] (**-en, -en**) *m(f)* pilot
Pils [pɪls] (**-, -**) *nt* Pilsner (lager)
Pilz [pɪlts] (**-es, -e**) *m* fungus; (*essbar*) mushroom; (*giftig*) toadstool; **wie ~e aus dem Boden schießen** (*fig*) to mushroom; **Pilzkrankheit** *f* fungal disease
pingelig ['pɪŋəlɪç] (*umg*) *adj* fussy
Pinguin ['pɪŋgui:n] (**-s, -e**) *m* penguin
Pinie ['pi:niə] *f* pine
pinkeln ['pɪŋkəln] (*umg*) *vi* to pee
Pinnwand ['pɪnvant] *f* pinboard
Pinsel ['pɪnzəl] (**-s, -**) *m* paintbrush
Pinzette [pɪn'tsɛtə] *f* tweezers *pl*
Pionier [pio'ni:r] (**-s, -e**) *m* pioneer; (*Mil*) sapper, engineer
Pirat [pi'ra:t] (**-en, -en**) *m* pirate
Piratensender *m* pirate radio station
Piste ['pɪstə] (**-, -n**) *f* (*Ski*) run, piste; (*Aviat*) runway
Pistole [pɪs'to:lə] (**-, -n**) *f* pistol; **wie aus der ~ geschossen** (*fig*) like a shot; **jdm die ~ auf die Brust setzen** (*fig*) to hold a pistol to sb's head
Plackerei [plakə'raɪ] *f* drudgery
plädieren [plɛ'di:rən] *vi* to plead
Plädoyer [plɛdoa'je:] (**-s, -s**) *nt* speech for the defence; (*fig*) plea
Plage ['pla:gə] (**-, -n**) *f* plague; (*Mühe*) nuisance; **Plagegeist** *m* pest, nuisance
plagen *vt* to torment ▷*vr* to toil, slave
Plakat [pla'ka:t] (**-(e)s, -e**) *nt* poster; (*aus Pappe*) placard
Plakette [pla'kɛtə] (**-, -n**) *f* (*Abzeichen*) badge; (*Münze*) commemorative coin; (*an Wänden*) plaque
Plan [pla:n] (**-(e)s, ⸚e**) *m* plan; (*Karte*) map; **Pläne schmieden** to make plans; **nach ~ verlaufen** to go according to plan; **jdn auf den ~ rufen** (*fig*) to bring sb into the arena
Plane (**-, -n**) *f* tarpaulin
planen *vt* to plan; (*Mord etc*) to plot
Planer, in (**-s, -**) *m(f)* planner
Planet [pla'ne:t] (**-en, -en**) *m* planet
Planetenbahn *f* orbit (of a planet)
planieren [pla'ni:rən] *vt* to level off
Planierraupe *f* bulldozer
Planke ['plaŋkə] (**-, -n**) *f* plank
Plänkelei [plɛŋkə'laɪ] *f* skirmish(ing)
plänkeln ['plɛŋkəln] *vi* to skirmish
Plankton ['plaŋktɔn] (**-s**) *nt* plankton
planlos *adj* (*Vorgehen*) unsystematic; (*Umherlaufen*) aimless
planmäßig *adj* according to plan; (*methodisch*) systematic; (*Eisenb*) scheduled
Planschbecken, **Plantschbecken** ['planʃbɛkən] *nt* paddling pool
planschen, **plantschen** *vi* to splash
Plansoll *nt* output target
Planstelle *f* post
Plantage [plan'ta:ʒə] (**-, -n**) *f* plantation
Planung *f* planning
Planwirtschaft *f* planned economy
plappern ['plapərn] *vi* to chatter
plärren ['plɛrən] *vi* (*Mensch*) to cry, whine; (*Radio*) to blare
Plasma ['plasma] (**-s, Plasmen**) *nt* plasma
Plastik[1] ['plastɪk] *f* sculpture
Plastik[2] ['plastɪk] (**-s**) *nt* (*Kunststoff*) plastic; **Plastikfolie** *f* plastic film; **Plastiktüte** *f* plastic bag
Plastilin [plasti'li:n] (**-s**) *nt* Plasticine®
plastisch ['plastɪʃ] *adj* plastic; **stell dir das ~ vor!** just picture it!
Platane [pla'ta:nə] (**-, -n**) *f* plane (tree)
Platin ['pla:ti:n] (**-s**) *nt* platinum
platonisch [pla'to:nɪʃ] *adj* platonic
platsch [platʃ] *interj* splash!
platschen *vi* to splash
plätschern ['plɛtʃərn] *vi* to babble
platschnass *adj* drenched
platt [plat] *adj* flat; (*umg: überrascht*) flabbergasted; (*fig: geistlos*) flat, boring; **einen P~en haben** to have a flat (*umg*), have a flat tyre (*Brit*) *od* tire (*US*)
plattdeutsch *adj* Low German
Platte (**-, -n**) *f* (*Speisenplatte, Phot, Tech*) plate; (*Steinplatte*) flag; (*Kachel*) tile; (*Schallplatte*) record; **kalte ~** cold dish; **die ~ kenne ich schon** (*umg*) I've heard all that before
Platten- *zW*: **Plattenspieler** *m* record player; **Plattenteller** *m* turntable
Plattfuß *m* flat foot; (*Reifen*) flat tyre (*Brit*) *od* tire (*US*)
Platz [plats] (**-es, ⸚e**) *m* place; (*Sitzplatz*) seat; (*Raum*) space, room; (*in Stadt*) square; (*Sportplatz*) playing field; **~ machen** to get out of the way; **~ nehmen** to take a seat; **jdm ~ machen** to make room for sb; **~ sparend** space-saving; **auf ~ zwei** in second place; **fehl am ~e sein** to be out of place; **seinen ~ behaupten** to stand one's ground; **das erste Hotel am ~** the best hotel in town; **auf die Plätze, fertig, los!** (*beim Sport*) on your marks, get set, go!; **einen Spieler vom ~ stellen** *od* **verweisen** (*Sport*) to send a player off; **Platzangst** *f* (*Med*) agoraphobia;

(*umg*) claustrophobia; **Platzangst haben/ bekommen** (*umg*) to feel/get claustrophobic; **Platzanweiser, in** (**-s, -**) *m(f)* usher(ette)
Plätzchen ['plɛtsçən] *nt* spot; (*Gebäck*) biscuit
platzen *vi* (*Hilfsverb sein*) to burst; (*Bombe*) to explode; (*Naht, Hose, Haut*) to split; (*umg: scheitern: Geschäft*) to fall through; (*: Freundschaft*) to break up; (*: Theorie, Verschwörung*) to collapse; (*: Wechsel*) to bounce; **vor Wut ~** (*umg*) to be bursting with anger
platzieren [pla'tsi:rən] *vt* to place ▷ *vr* (*Sport*) to be placed; (*Tennis*) to be seeded; (*umg: sich setzen, stellen*) to plant o.s.
Platz- *zW*: **Platzkarte** *f* seat reservation; **Platzmangel** *m* lack of space; **Platzpatrone** *f* blank cartridge; **Platzregen** *m* downpour; **Platzwunde** *f* cut
Plauderei [plaʊdə'raɪ] *f* chat, conversation
plaudern ['plaʊdərn] *vi* to chat, talk
plausibel [plaʊ'zi:bəl] *adj* plausible
Play-back, Playback ['pleɪbæk] (**-s, -s**) *nt* (*Verfahren: Schallplatte*) double-tracking; (*TV*) miming
plazieren [pla'tsi:rən] *vt siehe* **platzieren**
Plebejer, in [ple'be:jər(ɪn)] (**-s, -**) *m(f)* plebeian
plebejisch [ple'be:jɪʃ] *adj* plebeian
pleite ['plaɪtə] (*umg*) *adj* broke; **Pleite** (**-, -n**) *f* bankruptcy; (*umg: Reinfall*) flop; **Pleite machen** to go bust
Plenum ['ple:nʊm] (**-s, Plenen**) *nt* plenum
Plissee [plɪ'se:] (**-s, -s**) *nt* pleat
Plombe ['plɔmbə] (**-, -n**) *f* lead seal; (*Zahnplombe*) filling
plombieren [plɔm'bi:rən] *vt* to seal; (*Zahn*) to fill
Plotter ['plɔtər] (**-s, -s**) *m* (*Comput*) plotter
plötzlich ['plœtslɪç] *adj* sudden ▷ *adv* suddenly; **~er Kindstod** SIDS (= sudden infant death syndrome)
plump [plʊmp] *adj* clumsy; (*Hände*) coarse; (*Körper*) shapeless; **~e Annäherungsversuche** very obvious advances
plumpsen (*umg*) *vi* to plump down, fall
Plunder ['plʊndər] (**-s**) *m* junk, rubbish
plündern ['plʏndərn] *vt* to plunder; (*Stadt*) to sack ▷ *vi* to plunder
Plünderung ['plʏndərʊŋ] *f* plundering, sack, pillage
Plural ['plu:ra:l] (**-s, -e**) *m* plural; **im ~ stehen** to be (in the) plural
pluralistisch [plura'lɪstɪʃ] *adj* pluralistic
plus [plʊs] *adv* plus; **mit ~ minus null abschließen** (*Comm*) to break even; **Plus** (**-, -**) *nt* plus; (*Fin*) profit; (*Vorteil*) advantage
Plüsch [ply:ʃ] (**-(e)s, -e**) *m* plush; **Plüschtier** *nt* ≈ soft toy
Plus- *zW*: **Pluspol** *m* (*Elek*) positive pole; **Pluspunkt** *m* (*Sport*) point; (*fig*) point in sb's favour
Plutonium [plu'to:niʊm] (**-s**) *nt* plutonium
PLZ *abk* = **Postleitzahl**
Pneu [pnɔʏ] (**-s, -s**) *m abk* (= *Pneumatik*) tyre (*Brit*), tire (*US*)
Po [po:] (**-s, -s**) (*umg*) *m* bum (*Brit*), fanny (*US*)
Pöbel ['pø:bəl] (**-s**) *m* mob, rabble
Pöbelei [pø:bə'laɪ] *f* vulgarity
pöbelhaft *adj* low, vulgar
pochen ['pɔxən] *vi* to knock; (*Herz*) to pound; **auf etw** *akk* **~** (*fig*) to insist on sth
Pocken ['pɔkən] *pl* smallpox *sing*
Podium ['po:diʊm] *nt* podium
Podiumsdiskussion *f* panel discussion
Poesie [poe'zi:] *f* poetry
Poet [po'e:t] (**-en, -en**) *m* poet; **poetisch** *adj* poetic
Pointe [po'ɛ̃:tə] (**-, -n**) *f* point; (*eines Witzes*) punch line
Pokal [po'ka:l] (**-s, -e**) *m* goblet; (*Sport*) cup; **Pokalspiel** *nt* cup tie
Pökelfleisch ['pø:kəlflaɪʃ] *nt* salt meat
pökeln *vt* (*Fleisch, Fisch*) to pickle, salt
Pol [po:l] (**-s, -e**) *m* pole; **der ruhende ~** (*fig*) the calming influence
polar [po'la:r] *adj* polar
Polarkreis *m* polar circle; **nördlicher/ südlicher ~** Arctic/Antarctic Circle
Pole ['po:lə] (**-n, -n**) *m* Pole
Polemik [po'le:mɪk] *f* polemics *sing*
polemisch *adj* polemical
polemisieren [polemi'zi:rən] *vi* to polemicize
Polen ['po:lən] (**-s**) *nt* Poland
Police [po'li:s(ə)] (**-, -n**) *f* insurance policy
Polier [po'li:r] (**-s, -e**) *m* foreman
polieren *vt* to polish
Poliklinik [poli'kli:nɪk] *f* outpatients (department) *sing*
Polin *f* Pole, Polish woman
Politik [poli'ti:k] *f* politics *sing*; (*eine bestimmte*) policy; **in die ~ gehen** to go into politics; **eine ~ verfolgen** to pursue a policy
Politiker, in [po'li:tikər(ɪn)] (**-s, -**) *m(f)* politician
politisch [po'li:tɪʃ] *adj* political
politisieren [politi'zi:rən] *vi* to talk politics ▷ *vt* to politicize; **jdn ~** to make sb politically aware
Politur [poli'tu:r] *f* polish
Polizei [poli'tsaɪ] *f* police; **Polizeibeamte, r** *m* police officer; **polizeilich** *adj* police *attrib*; **sich polizeilich melden** to register with the police; **polizeiliches Führungszeugnis** *certificate of "no criminal record" issued by the police*; **Polizeirevier** *nt* police station; **Polizeistaat** *m* police state; **Polizeistreife** *f* police patrol; **Polizeistunde** *f* closing time; **polizeiwidrig** *adj* illegal
Polizist, in [poli'tsɪst(ɪn)] (**-en, -en**) *m(f)* policeman/-woman
Pollen ['pɔlən] (**-s, -**) *m* pollen
polnisch ['pɔlnɪʃ] *adj* Polish
Polohemd ['po:lohɛmt] *nt* polo shirt
Polster ['pɔlstər] (**-s, -**) *nt* cushion; (*Polsterung*) upholstery; (*in Kleidung*) padding; (*fig: Geld*) reserves *pl*; **Polsterer** (**-s, -**) *m* upholsterer;

Polstermöbel *pl* upholstered furniture *sing*
polstern *vt* to upholster; (*Kleidung*) to pad; **sie ist gut gepolstert** (*umg*) she's well padded; (: *finanziell*) she's not short of the odd penny
Polsterung *f* upholstery
Polterabend ['pɔltəra:bənt] *m party on the eve of a wedding*
poltern *vi* (*Krach machen*) to crash; (*schimpfen*) to rant
Polygamie [polyga'mi:] *f* polygamy
Polynesien [poly'ne:ziən] (**-s**) *nt* Polynesia
Polyp [po'ly:p] (**-en, -en**) *m* polyp; (*umg*) cop; **Polypen** *pl* (*Med*) adenoids *pl*
Pomade [po'ma:də] *f* pomade
Pommern ['pɔmərn] (**-s**) *nt* Pomerania
Pommes frites [pɔm'frɪt] *pl* chips *pl* (*Brit*), French fried potatoes *pl* (*Brit*), French fries *pl* (*US*)
Pomp [pɔmp] (**-(e)s**) *m* pomp
pompös [pɔm'pø:s] *adj* grandiose
Pony ['pɔni] (**-s, -s**) *m* (*Frisur*) fringe (*Brit*), bangs *pl* (*US*) ▷ *nt* (*Pferd*) pony
Popmusik *f* pop music
Popo [po'po:] (**-s, -s**) (*umg*) *m* bottom, bum (*Brit*)
populär [popu'lɛ:r] *adj* popular
Popularität [populari'tɛ:t] *f* popularity
populärwissenschaftlich *adj* popular science
Pore ['po:rə] (**-, -n**) *f* pore
Pornografie [pɔrnogra'fi:] *f* pornography
porös [po'rø:s] *adj* porous
Porree ['pɔre] (**-s, -s**) *m* leek
Portal [pɔr'ta:l] (**-s, -e**) *nt* portal
Portemonnaie [pɔrtmɔ'nɛ:] (**-s, -s**) *nt* purse
Portier [pɔrti'e:] (**-s, -s**) *m* porter; (*Pförtner*) porter, doorkeeper, doorman
Portion [pɔrtsi'o:n] *f* portion, helping; (*umg: Anteil*) amount; **eine halbe ~** (*fig: umg: Person*) a half-pint; **eine ~ Kaffee** a pot of coffee
Portmonee [pɔrtmɔ'nɛ:] (**-s, -s**) *nt* purse
Porto ['pɔrto] (**-s, -s** *od* **Porti**) *nt* postage; **~ zahlt Empfänger** postage paid; **portofrei** *adj* post-free, (postage) prepaid
Porträt [pɔr'trɛ:] (**-s, -s**) *nt* portrait
porträtieren [pɔrtrɛ'ti:rən] *vt* to paint (a portrait of); (*fig*) to portray
Portugal ['pɔrtugal] (**-s**) *nt* Portugal
Portugiese [pɔrtu'gi:zə] (**-n, -n**) *m* Portuguese
portugiesisch *adj* Portuguese
Porzellan [pɔrtsɛ'la:n] (**-s, -e**) *nt* china, porcelain; (*Geschirr*) china
Posaune [po'zaʊnə] (**-, -n**) *f* trombone
Pose ['po:zə] (**-, -n**) *f* pose
posieren [po'zi:rən] *vi* to pose
Position [pozitsi'o:n] *f* position; (*Comm: auf Liste*) item
Positionslichter *pl* navigation lights *pl*
positiv ['po:ziti:f] *adj* positive; **~ zu etw stehen** to be in favour (*Brit*) *od* favor (*US*) of sth; **Positiv** (**-s, -e**) *nt* (*Phot*) positive
possessiv ['pɔsɛsi:f] *adj* possessive; **Possessivpronomen** (**-s, -e**) *nt* possessive pronoun
possierlich [pɔ'si:rlɪç] *adj* funny
Post [pɔst] (**-, -en**) *f* post (office); (*Briefe*) post, mail; **ist ~ für mich da?** are there any letters for me?; **mit getrennter ~** under separate cover; **etw auf die ~ geben** to post (*Brit*) *od* mail sth; **auf die** *od* **zur ~ gehen** to go to the post office; **Postamt** *nt* post office; **Postanweisung** *f* postal order (*Brit*), money order; **Postbote** *m* postman (*Brit*), mailman (*US*)
Posten (**-s, -**) *m* post, position; (*Comm*) item; (: *Warenmenge*) quantity, lot; (*auf Liste*) entry; (*Mil*) sentry; (*Streikposten*) picket; **~ beziehen** to take up one's post; **nicht ganz auf dem ~ sein** (*nicht gesund sein*) to be off-colour (*Brit*) *od* off-color (*US*)
Poster ['pɔstər] (**-s, -(s)**) *nt* poster
Postf. *abk* (= *Postfach*) PO Box
Post- *zW*: **Postfach** *nt* post office box; **Postkarte** *f* postcard; **postlagernd** *adv* poste restante; **Postleitzahl** *f* postal code
postmodern [pɔstmo'dɛrn] *adj* postmodern
Post- *zW*: **Postscheckkonto** *nt* Post Office Giro account (*Brit*); **Postsparkasse** *f* post office savings bank; **Poststempel** *m* postmark; **postwendend** *adv* by return (of post)
potent [po'tɛnt] *adj* potent; (*fig*) high-powered
Potential [potɛntsi'a:l] (**-s, -e**) *nt* = **Potenzial**
potentiell [potɛntsi'ɛl] *adj* = **potenziell**
Potenz [po'tɛnts] *f* power; (*eines Mannes*) potency
Potenzial [potɛntsi'a:l] (**-s, -e**) *nt* potential
potenziell [potɛntsi'ɛl] *adj* potential
Pracht [praxt] (**-**) *f* splendour (*Brit*), splendor (*US*), magnificence; **es ist eine wahre ~** it's (really) marvellous
prächtig ['prɛçtɪç] *adj* splendid
Prachtstück *nt* showpiece
prachtvoll *adj* splendid, magnificent
Prädikat [prɛdi'ka:t] (**-(e)s, -e**) *nt* title; (*Gram*) predicate; (*Zensur*) distinction; **Wein mit ~** special quality wine
Prag [pra:k] (**-s**) *nt* Prague
prägen ['prɛ:gən] *vt* to stamp; (*Münze*) to mint; (*Ausdruck*) to coin; (*Charakter*) to form; (*kennzeichnen: Stadtbild*) to characterize; **das Erlebnis prägte ihn** the experience left its mark on him
prägnant [prɛ'gnant] *adj* concise, terse
Prägnanz *f* conciseness, terseness
Prägung ['prɛ:gʊŋ] *f* minting; forming; (*Eigenart*) character, stamp
prahlen ['pra:lən] *vi* to boast, brag
Prahlerei [pra:lə'raɪ] *f* boasting
prahlerisch *adj* boastful
praktikabel [praktɪ'ka:bəl] *adj* practicable
Praktikant, in [praktɪ'kant(ɪn)] *m(f)* trainee
Praktikum (**-s, Praktika** *od* **Praktiken**) *nt* practical training

praktisch ['praktɪʃ] *adj* practical, handy; **~er Arzt** general practitioner; **~es Beispiel** concrete example
praktizieren [prakti'tsi:rən] *vt, vi* to practise (*Brit*), practice (*US*)
Praline [pra'li:nə] *f* chocolate
prall [pral] *adj* firmly rounded; (*Segel*) taut; (*Arme*) plump; (*Sonne*) blazing
prallen *vi* to bounce, rebound; (*Sonne*) to blaze
Prämie ['prɛ:miə] *f* premium; (*Belohnung*) award, prize
prämieren [prɛ'mi:rən] *vt* to give an award to
Pranger ['praŋər] (**-s, -**) *m* (*Hist*) pillory; **jdn an den ~ stellen** (*fig*) to pillory sb
Pranke ['praŋkə] (**-, -n**) *f* (*Tierpranke: umg: Hand*) paw
Präparat [prɛpa'ra:t] (**-(e)s, -e**) *nt* (*Biol*) preparation; (*Med*) medicine
Präposition [prɛpozitsi'o:n] *f* preposition
Prärie [prɛ'ri:] *f* prairie
Präsens ['prɛ:zɛns] (**-**) *nt* present tense
präsentieren [prɛzɛn'ti:rən] *vt* to present
Präservativ [prɛzɛrva'ti:f] (**-s, -e**) *nt* condom, sheath
Präsident, in [prɛzi'dɛnt(ɪn)] *m(f)* president; **Präsidentschaft** *f* presidency; **Präsidentschaftskandidat** *m* presidential candidate
Präsidium [prɛ'zi:diʊm] *nt* presidency, chairmanship; (*Polizeipräsidium*) police headquarters *pl*
prasseln ['prasəln] *vi* (*Feuer*) to crackle; (*Hagel*) to drum; (*Wörter*) to rain down
prassen ['prasən] *vi* to live it up
Präteritum [prɛ'te:ritʊm] (**-s, Präterita**) *nt* preterite
Praxis ['praksɪs] (**-, Praxen**) *f* practice; (*Erfahrung*) experience; (*Behandlungsraum*) surgery; (*von Anwalt*) office; **die ~ sieht anders aus** the reality is different; **ein Beispiel aus der ~** an example from real life
Präzedenzfall [prɛtse:'dɛntsfal] *m* precedent
präzis [prɛ'tsi:s] *adj* precise
Präzision [prɛtsizi'o:n] *f* precision
predigen ['pre:dɪgən] *vt, vi* to preach
Prediger (**-s, -**) *m* preacher
Predigt ['pre:dɪçt] (**-, -en**) *f* sermon
Preis [praɪs] (**-es, -e**) *m* price; (*Siegespreis*) prize; (*Auszeichnung*) award; **um keinen ~** not at any price; **um jeden ~** at all costs; **Preisausschreiben** *nt* competition
Preiselbeere *f* cranberry
preisen [praɪzən] *unreg vt* to praise; **sich glücklich ~** (*geh*) to count o.s. lucky
Preis- *zW*
preisgeben *unreg vt* to abandon; (*opfern*) to sacrifice; (*zeigen*) to expose
Preis- *zW*: **preisgekrönt** *adj* prizewinning; **Preisgericht** *nt* jury; **preisgünstig** *adj* inexpensive; **Preislage** *f* price range; **preislich** *adj* price *attr*, in price; **Preisschild** *nt* price tag; **Preissturz** *m* slump; **Preisträger** *m* prizewinner; **preiswert** *adj* inexpensive
prekär [pre'kɛ:r] *adj* precarious
Prellbock [prɛlbɔk] *m* buffers *pl*
prellen *vt* to bruise; (*fig*) to cheat, swindle
Prellung *f* bruise
Premiere [prəmi'ɛ:rə] (**-, -n**) *f* premiere
Premierminister, in [prəmɪ'e:mɪnɪstər(ɪn)] *m(f)* prime minister, premier
Presse ['prɛsə] (**-, -n**) *f* press; **Pressefreiheit** *f* freedom of the press; **Pressekonferenz** *f* press conference; **Pressemeldung** *f* press report
pressen *vt* to press
Presse- *zW*
Pressluft ['prɛslʊft] *f* compressed air: **Pressluftbohrer** *m* pneumatic drill
Prestige [prɛs'ti:ʒə] (**-s**) *nt* prestige
Preußen (**-s**) *nt* Prussia
preußisch *adj* Prussian
prickeln ['prɪkəln] *vi* to tingle; (*kitzeln*) to tickle; (*Bläschen bilden*) to sparkle, bubble ▷*vt* to tickle
pries *etc* [pri:s] *vb siehe* **preisen**
Priester ['pri:stər] (**-s, -**) *m* priest
prima *adj inv* first-class, excellent
primär [pri'mɛ:r] *adj* primary
Primel ['pri:məl] (**-, -n**) *f* primrose
primitiv [primi'ti:f] *adj* primitive
Prinz [prɪnts] (**-en, -en**) *m* prince
Prinzessin [prɪn'tsɛsɪn] *f* princess
Prinzip [prɪn'tsi:p] (**-s, -ien**) *nt* principle; **aus ~** on principle; **im ~** in principle
prinzipiell [prɪntsi'piɛl] *adj* on principle
prinzipienlos *adj* unprincipled
Priorität [priori'tɛ:t] *f* priority; **Prioritäten** *pl* (*Comm*) preference shares *pl*, preferred stock *sing* (*US*); **~en setzen** to establish one's priorities
Prise ['pri:zə] (**-, -n**) *f* pinch
Prisma ['prɪsma] (**-s, Prismen**) *nt* prism
privat [pri'va:t] *adj* private; **jdn ~ sprechen** to speak to sb in private; **Privatfernsehen** *nt* commercial television
Privatschule *f* private school
Privileg [privi'le:k] (**-(e)s, -ien**) *nt* privilege
Pro [pro:] (**-**) *nt* pro
pro *präp +akk* per; **~ Stück** each, apiece
Probe ['pro:bə] (**-, -n**) *f* test; (*Teststück*) sample; (*Theat*) rehearsal; **jdn auf die ~ stellen** to put sb to the test; **er ist auf ~ angestellt** he's employed for a probationary period; **zur ~** to try out; **Probeexemplar** *nt* specimen copy; **Probefahrt** *f* test drive
proben *vt* to try; (*Theat*) to rehearse
Probe- *zW*: **probeweise** *adv* on approval; **Probezeit** *f* probation period
probieren [pro'bi:rən] *vt* to try; (*Wein, Speise*) to taste, sample ▷*vi* to try; to taste
Problem [pro'ble:m] (**-s, -e**) *nt* problem; **vor einem ~ stehen** to be faced with a problem
Problematik [proble:'ma:tɪk] *f* problem
problematisch [proble:'ma:tɪʃ] *adj* problematic
problemlos *adj* problem-free

Produkt [pro'dʊkt] (**-(e)s, -e**) *nt* product; (*Agr*) produce *no pl*
Produktion [prodʊktsi'o:n] *f* production
produktiv [prodʊk'ti:f] *adj* productive
Produktivität [prodʊktivi'tɛ:t] *f* productivity
Produzent [produ'tsɛnt] *m* manufacturer; (*Film*) producer
produzieren [produ'tsi:rən] *vt* to produce ▷ *vr* to show off
Professor, in [pro'fɛsɔr, profɛ'so:rɪn] *m(f)* professor; (*Österr: Gymnasiallehrer*) grammar school teacher (*Brit*), high school teacher (*US*)
Professur [profɛ'su:r] *f*: **~ (für)** chair (of)
Profi ['pro:fi] (**-s, -s**) *m abk* (*= Professional*) pro
Profil [pro'fi:l] (**-s, -e**) *nt* profile; (*fig*) image; (*Querschnitt*) cross section; (*Längsschnitt*) vertical section; (*von Reifen, Schuhsohle*) tread
profilieren [profi'li:rən] *vr* to create an image for o.s.
Profit [pro'fi:t] (**-(e)s, -e**) *m* profit
profitieren [profi'ti:rən] *vi*: **~ (von)** to profit (from)
Prognose [pro'gno:zə] (**-, -n**) *f* prediction, prognosis
Programm [pro'gram] (**-s, -e**) *nt* programme (*Brit*), program (*US*); (*Comput*) program; (*TV: Sender*) channel; (*Kollektion*) range; **nach ~** as planned
programmieren [progra'mi:rən] *vt* to programme (*Brit*), program (*US*); (*Comput*) to program; **auf etw** *akk* **programmiert sein** (*fig*) to be geared to sth
Programmierer, in (**-s, -**) *m(f)* programmer
Programmiersprache *f* (*Comput*) programming language
progressiv [progrɛ'si:f] *adj* progressive
Projekt [pro'jɛkt] (**-(e)s, -e**) *nt* project
Projektor [pro'jɛktɔr] *m* projector
projizieren [proji'tsi:rən] *vt* to project
proklamieren [prokla'mi:rən] *vt* to proclaim
Prolet [pro'le:t] (**-en, -en**) *m* prole, pleb
Proletariat [proletari'a:t] (**-(e)s, -e**) *nt* proletariat
Proletarier [prole'ta:riər] (**-s, -**) *m* proletarian
Prolog [pro'lo:k] (**-(e)s, -e**) *m* prologue
Promenade [promə'na:də] (**-, -n**) *f* promenade
Promille [pro'mɪle] (**-(s), -**) (*umg*) *nt* alcohol level; **Promillegrenze** *f* legal (alcohol) limit
Prominenz [promi'nɛnts] *f* VIPs *pl*
Promotion [promotsi'o:n] *f* doctorate, Ph.D.
promovieren [promo'vi:rən] *vi* to receive a doctorate *etc*
prompt [prɔmpt] *adj* prompt
Pronomen [pro'no:mɛn] (**-s, -**) *nt* pronoun
Propaganda [propa'ganda] (**-**) *f* propaganda
Propeller [pro'pɛlər] (**-s, -**) *m* propeller
Prophet, in [pro'fe:t(ɪn)] (**-en, -en**) *m(f)* prophet(ess)
prophezeien [profe'tsaɪən] *vt* to prophesy
Prophezeiung *f* prophecy
Proportion [propɔrtsi'o:n] *f* proportion
proportional [propɔrtsio'na:l] *adj* proportional; **Proportionalschrift** *f* (*Comput*) proportional printing
Prosa ['pro:za] (**-**) *f* prose
prosaisch [pro'za:ɪʃ] *adj* prosaic
prosit ['pro:zɪt] *interj* cheers!; **~ Neujahr!** happy New Year!
Prospekt [pro'spɛkt] (**-(e)s, -e**) *m* leaflet, brochure
prost [pro:st] *interj* cheers!
Prostituierte [prostitu'i:rtə] (**-n, -n**) *f* prostitute
Prostitution [prostitutsi'o:n] *f* prostitution
Protest [pro'tɛst] (**-(e)s, -e**) *m* protest
Protestant, in [protɛs'tant(ɪn)] *m(f)* Protestant; **protestantisch** *adj* Protestant
protestieren [protɛs'ti:rən] *vi* to protest
Protestkundgebung *f* (protest) rally
Prothese [pro'te:zə] (**-, -n**) *f* artificial limb; (*Zahnprothese*) dentures *pl*
Protokoll [proto'kɔl] (**-s, -e**) *nt* register; (*Niederschrift*) record; (*von Sitzung*) minutes *pl*; (*diplomatisch*) protocol; (*Polizeiprotokoll*) statement; (*Strafzettel*) ticket; **(das) ~ führen** (*bei Sitzung*) to take the minutes; (*bei Gericht*) to make a transcript of the proceedings; **etw zu ~ geben** to have sth put on record; (*bei Polizei*) to say sth in one's statement
protokollieren [protokɔ'li:rən] *vt* to take down; (*Bemerkung*) to enter in the minutes
Proton ['pro:tɔn] (**-s, -en**) *nt* proton
Prototyp *m* prototype
Protz ['prɔts] (**-es, -e**) *m* swank; **protzen** *vi* to show off
protzig *adj* ostentatious
Proviant [provi'ant] (**-s, -e**) *m* provisions *pl*, supplies *pl*
Provinz [pro'vɪnts] (**-, -en**) *f* province; **das ist finsterste ~** (*pej*) it's a cultural backwater
provinziell [provɪn'tsiɛl] *adj* provincial
Provision [provizi'o:n] *f* (*Comm*) commission
provisorisch [provi'zo:rɪʃ] *adj* provisional
Provokation [provokatsi'o:n] *f* provocation
provozieren [provo'tsi:rən] *vt* to provoke
Prozedur [protse'du:r] *f* procedure; (*pej*) carry-on; **die ~ beim Zahnarzt** the ordeal at the dentist's
Prozent [pro'tsɛnt] (**-(e)s, -e**) *nt* per cent, percentage; **Prozentrechnung** *f* percentage calculation; **Prozentsatz** *m* percentage
prozentual [protsɛntu'a:l] *adj* percentage *attrib*
Prozess [pro'tsɛs] (**-es, -e**) *m* trial, case; (*Vorgang*) process; **es zum ~ kommen lassen** to go to court; **mit jdm/etw kurzen ~ machen** (*fig: umg*) to make short work of sb/sth
prozessieren [protsɛ'si:rən] *vi*: **~ (mit)** to bring an action (against), go to law (with *od* against)
Prozession [protsɛsi'o:n] *f* procession
prüde ['pry:də] *adj* prudish
Prüderie [pry:də'ri:] *f* prudery
prüfen ['pry:fən] *vt* to examine, test;

(*nachprüfen*) to check; (*erwägen*) to consider; (*Geschäftsbücher*) to audit; (*mustern*) to scrutinize

Prüfer, in (**-s, -**) *m(f)* examiner

Prüfling *m* examinee

Prüfung *f* (*Sch, Univ*) examination, exam; (*Überprüfung*) checking; **eine ~ machen** to take *od* sit (*Brit*) an exam(ination); **durch eine ~ fallen** to fail an exam(ination)

Prüfungs- *zW*: **Prüfungsausschuss** *m* examining board; **Prüfungsordnung** *f* exam(ination) regulations *pl*

Prügel ['pry:gəl] (**-s, -**) *m* cudgel ▷ *pl* beating *sing*

Prügelei [pry:gə'laɪ] *f* fight

Prügelknabe *m* scapegoat

prügeln *vt* to beat ▷ *vr* to fight

Prügelstrafe *f* corporal punishment

Prunk [prʊŋk] (**-(e)s**) *m* pomp, show; **prunkvoll** *adj* splendid, magnificent

PS *abk* (= *Pferdestärke*) hp; (= *Postskript(um)*) PS

Psalm [psalm] (**-s, -en**) *m* psalm

Psychiater [psy'çia:tər] (**-s, -**) *m* psychiatrist

psychisch ['psy:çɪʃ] *adj* psychological; **~ gestört** emotionally *od* psychologically disturbed

Psychoanalyse [psyçoana'ly:zə] *f* psychoanalysis

Psychologe [psyço'lo:gə] (**-n, -n**) *m* psychologist

Psychologie *f* psychology

psychologisch *adj* psychological

Psychotherapie *f* psychotherapy

Pubertät [pubɛr'tɛ:t] *f* puberty

Publikum ['pu:blikʊm] (**-s**) *nt* audience; (*Sport*) crowd; **das ~ in dieser Bar ist sehr gemischt** you get a very mixed group of people using this bar

publizieren [publi'tsi:rən] *vt* to publish

Pudding ['pʊdɪŋ] (**-s, -e** *od* **-s**) *m* blancmange

Pudel ['pu:dəl] (**-s, -**) *m* poodle; **das also ist des ~s Kern** (*fig*) that's what it's really all about

Puder ['pu:dər] (**-s, -**) *m* powder; **Puderdose** *f* powder compact

pudern *vt* to powder

Puderzucker *m* icing sugar (*Brit*), confectioner's sugar (*US*)

Puff[1] [pʊf] (**-(e)s, -e**) *m* (*Wäschepuff*) linen basket; (*Sitzpuff*) pouf

Puff[2] (**-(e)s, ¨-e**) (*umg*) *m* (*Stoß*) push

Puff[3] (**-s, -s**) (*umg*) *m od nt* (*Bordell*) brothel

Puffer (**-s, -**) *m* (*auch Comput*) buffer; **Pufferspeicher** *m* (*Comput*) cache; **Pufferstaat** *m* buffer state

Pulli ['pʊli] (**-s, -s**) (*umg*) *m* sweater, jumper (*Brit*)

Puls [pʊls] (**-es, -e**) *m* pulse; **Pulsader** *f* artery; **sich** *dat* **die Pulsader(n) aufschneiden** to slash one's wrists

pulsieren [pʊl'zi:rən] *vi* to throb, pulsate

Pult [pʊlt] (**-(e)s, -e**) *nt* desk

Pulver ['pʊlfər] (**-s, -**) *nt* powder

pulverig *adj* powdery

pulverisieren [pʊlveri'zi:rən] *vt* to pulverize

Pulverschnee *m* powdery snow

pummelig ['pʊməlɪç] *adj* chubby

Pumpe ['pʊmpə] (**-, -n**) *f* pump; (*umg: Herz*) ticker

pumpen *vt* to pump; (*umg*) to lend; (*: entleihen*) to borrow

Punkt [pʊŋkt] (**-(e)s, -e**) *m* point; (*bei Muster*) dot; (*Satzzeichen*) full stop, period (*bes US*); **~ 12 Uhr** at 12 o'clock on the dot; **nun mach aber mal einen ~!** (*umg*) come off it!

punktieren [pʊŋk'ti:rən] *vt* to dot; (*Med*) to aspirate

pünktlich ['pʏŋktlɪç] *adj* punctual; **Pünktlichkeit** *f* punctuality

Punkt- *zW*: **Punktsieg** *m* victory on points; **Punktzahl** *f* score

Punsch [pʊnʃ] (**-(e)s, -e**) *m* (hot) punch

Pupille [pu'pɪlə] (**-, -n**) *f* (*im Auge*) pupil

Puppe ['pʊpə] (**-, -n**) *f* doll; (*Marionette*) puppet; (*Insektenpuppe*) pupa, chrysalis; (*Schaufensterpuppe, Übungspuppe*) dummy; (*umg: Mädchen*) doll, bird (*bes Brit*)

Puppen- *zW*: **Puppenspieler** *m* puppeteer; **Puppenstube** *f* (single-room) doll's house *od* dollhouse (*US*); **Puppenwagen** *m* doll's pram

pur [pu:r] *adj* pure; (*völlig*) sheer; (*Whisky*) neat

Püree [py're:] (**-s, -s**) *nt* purée; (*Kartoffelpüree*) mashed potatoes *pl*

Purzelbaum ['pʊrtsəlbaʊm] *m* somersault

purzeln *vi* to tumble

Puste ['pu:stə] (**-**) (*umg*) *f* puff; (*fig*) steam

Pustel ['pʊstəl] (**-, -n**) *f* pustule

pusten ['pu:stən] (*umg*) *vi* to puff

Pute ['pu:tə] (**-, -n**) *f* turkey hen

Puter (**-s, -**) *m* turkey cock

Putsch [pʊtʃ] (**-(e)s, -e**) *m* revolt, putsch; **putschen** *vi* to revolt; **Putschist** *m* rebel

Putz [pʊts] (**-es**) *m* (*Mörtel*) plaster, roughcast; **eine Mauer mit ~ verkleiden** to roughcast a wall

putzen *vt* to clean; (*Nase*) to wipe, blow ▷ *vr* to clean o.s.; (*veraltet: sich schmücken*) to dress o.s. up

Putzfrau *f* cleaning lady, charwoman (*Brit*)

putzig *adj* quaint, funny

Putzlappen *m* cloth

Putzzeug *nt* cleaning things *pl*

Puzzle ['pasəl] (**-s, -s**) *nt* jigsaw (puzzle)

Pyjama [pi'dʒa:ma] (**-s, -s**) *m* pyjamas *pl* (*Brit*), pajamas *pl* (*US*)

Pyramide [pyra'mi:də] (**-, -n**) *f* pyramid

Pyrenäen [pyre'nɛ:ən] *pl*: **die ~** the Pyrenees *pl*

Python ['py:tɔn] (**-s, -s**) *m* python

Qq

Q, **q** [ku:] *nt* Q, q; **Q wie Quelle** ≈ Q for Queen
Quacksalber ['kvakzalbər] (**-s, -**) *m* quack (doctor)
Quader ['kva:dər] (**-s, -**) *m* square stone block; (*Math*) cuboid
Quadrat [kva'dra:t] (**-(e)s, -e**) *nt* square; **quadratisch** *adj* square; **Quadratmeter** *m* square metre (*Brit*) *od* meter (*US*)
quaken ['kva:kən] *vi* to croak; (*Ente*) to quack
quäken ['kvɛ:kən] *vi* to screech
quäkend *adj* screeching
Qual [kva:l] (**-, -en**) *f* pain, agony; (*seelisch*) anguish; **er machte ihr das Leben zur ~** he made her life a misery
quälen ['kvɛ:lən] *vt* to torment ▷ *vr* (*sich abmühen*) to struggle; (*geistig*) to torment o.s.; **~de Ungewissheit** agonizing uncertainty
Quälerei [kvɛ:lə'raɪ] *f* torture, torment
Quälgeist (*umg*) *m* pest
qualifizieren [kvalifi'tsi:rən] *vt* to qualify; (*einstufen*) to label ▷ *vr* to qualify
Qualität [kvali'tɛ:t] *f* quality; **von ausgezeichneter ~** (of) top quality
Qualitätsware *f* article of high quality
Qualle ['kvalə] (**-, -n**) *f* jellyfish
Qualm [kvalm] (**-(e)s**) *m* thick smoke
qualmen *vt, vi* to smoke
qualvoll ['kva:lfɔl] *adj* painful; (*Schmerzen*) excruciating, agonizing
Quantentheorie ['kvantənteori:] *f* quantum theory
Quantität [kvanti'tɛ:t] *f* quantity
quantitativ [kvantita'ti:f] *adj* quantitative
Quantum ['kvantʊm] (**-s, Quanten**) *nt* quantity, amount
Quarantäne [karan'tɛ:nə] (**-, -n**) *f* quarantine
Quark[1] [kvark] (**-s**) *m* curd cheese, quark; (*umg*) rubbish
Quark[2] [kvark] (**-s, -s**) *nt* (*Phys*) quark
Quartal [kvar'ta:l] (**-s, -e**) *nt* quarter (year); **Kündigung zum ~** quarterly notice date
Quartier [kvar'ti:r] (**-s, -e**) *nt* accommodation (*Brit*), accommodations *pl* (*US*); (*Mil*) quarters *pl*; (*Stadtquartier*) district
Quarz [kva:rts] (**-es, -e**) *m* quartz
quasi ['kva:zi] *adv* virtually ▷ *präf* quasi
quasseln ['kvasəln] (*umg*) *vi* to natter
Quatsch [kvatʃ] (**-es**) (*umg*) *m* rubbish, hogwash; **hört doch endlich auf mit dem ~!** stop being so stupid!; **~ machen** to mess about
quatschen *vi* to chat, natter
Quatschkopf (*umg*) *m* (*pej: Schwätzer*) windbag; (*Dummkopf*) twit (*Brit*)
Quecksilber ['kvɛkzɪlbər] *nt* mercury
Quelle ['kvɛlə] (**-, -n**) *f* spring; (*eines Flusses, Comput*) source; **an der ~ sitzen** (*fig*) to be well placed; **aus zuverlässiger ~** from a reliable source
quellen *vi* (*hervorquellen*) to pour *od* gush forth; (*schwellen*) to swell
quengeln (*umg*) *vi* to whine
quer [kve:r] *adv* crossways, diagonally; (*rechtwinklig*) at right angles; **~ gestreift** horizontally striped; **~ auf dem Bett** across the bed; *siehe auch* **querlegen**; **Querbalken** *m* crossbeam; **Querdenker** *m* maverick; **querfeldein** *adv* across country; **Querflöte** *f* flute; **Querformat** *nt* oblong format; **Querschiff** *nt* transept; **Querschnitt** *m* cross section; **querschnittsgelähmt** *adj* paraplegic, paralysed below the waist; **Querstraße** *f* intersecting road
quetschen ['kvɛtʃən] *vt* to squash, crush; (*Med*) to bruise ▷ *vr* (*sich klemmen*) to be caught; (*sich zwängen*) to squeeze (o.s.)
Quetschung *f* bruise, contusion (*form*)
quieken ['kvi:kən] *vi* to squeak
quietschen ['kvi:tʃən] *vi* to squeak
Quintessenz ['kvɪntɛsɛnts] *f* quintessence
Quirl [kvɪrl] (**-(e)s, -e**) *m* whisk
quitt [kvɪt] *adj* quits, even
Quitte (**-, -n**) *f* quince
quittieren [kvɪ'ti:rən] *vt* to give a receipt for; (*Dienst*) to leave
Quittung *f* receipt; **er hat seine ~ bekommen** he's paid the penalty *od* price
Quiz [kvɪs] (**-, -**) *nt* quiz
quoll *etc* [kvɔl] *vb siehe* **quellen**
Quote ['kvo:tə] (**-, -n**) *f* proportion; (*Rate*) rate
Quotenregelung *f* quota system (*for ensuring adequate representation of women*)

Rr

R¹, r *nt* R, r; **R wie Richard** ≈ R for Robert, ≈ R for Roger (*US*)
R², r *abk* (= *Radius*) r.
Rabatt [ra'bat] (**-(e)s, -e**) *m* discount
Rabatte (**-, -n**) *f* flower bed, border
Rabattmarke *f* trading stamp
Rabe ['ra:bə] (**-n, -n**) *m* raven
rabiat [rabi'a:t] *adj* furious
Rache ['raxə] (**-**) *f* revenge, vengeance
Rachen (**-s, -**) *m* throat
rächen ['rɛçən] *vt* to avenge, revenge ▷ *vr* to take (one's) revenge; **das wird sich ~** you'll pay for that
Rachitis [ra'xi:tɪs] (**-**) *f* rickets *sing*
Rad [ra:t] (**-(e)s, ¨-er**) *nt* wheel; (*Fahrrad*) bike; **~ fahren** to cycle; **unter die Räder kommen** (*umg*) to fall into bad ways; **das fünfte ~ am Wagen sein** (*umg*) to be in the way
Radar ['ra:da:r] (**-s**) *m od nt* radar; **Radarfalle** *f* speed trap; **Radarkontrolle** *f* radar-controlled speed check
Radau [ra'daʊ] (**-s**) (*umg*) *m* row; **~ machen** to kick up a row; (*Unruhe stiften*) to cause trouble
radebrechen ['ra:dəbrɛçən] *vi untr*: **Deutsch** *etc* **~** to speak broken German *etc*
radeln *vi* (*Hilfsverb sein*) to cycle
Rädelsführer ['rɛ:dəlsfy:rər] (**-s, -**) *m* ringleader
Rad- *zW*: **Radfahrer** *m* cyclist; (*pej: umg*) crawler; **Radfahrweg** *m* cycle track *od* path
radieren [ra'di:rən] *vt* to rub out, erase; (*Art*) to etch
Radiergummi *m* rubber (*Brit*), eraser (*bes US*)
Radierung *f* etching
Radieschen [ra'di:sçən] *nt* radish
radikal [radi'ka:l] *adj* radical; **~ gegen etw vorgehen** to take radical steps against sth
Radikale, r *f(m)* radical
Radio ['ra:dio] (**-s, -s**) *nt* radio, wireless (*bes Brit*); **im ~** on the radio; **radioaktiv** *adj* radioactive; **radioaktiver Niederschlag** (radioactive) fallout; **Radioaktivität** *f* radioactivity; **Radioapparat** *m* radio (set); **Radiorekorder** *m* radio-cassette recorder
Radium ['ra:diʊm] (**-s**) *nt* radium
Radius ['ra:diʊs] (**-, Radien**) *m* radius
Radkappe *f* (*Aut*) hub cap
Rad- *zW*: **Radrennen** *nt* cycle race; (*Sportart*) cycle racing; **Radsport** *m* cycling
RAF (**-**) *f abk* (= *Rote Armee Fraktion*) Red Army Faction
raffen ['rafən] *vt* to snatch, pick up; (*Stoff*) to gather (up); (*Geld*) to pile up, rake in; (*umg: verstehen*) to catch on to
Raffinade [rafi'na:də] *f* refined sugar
raffinieren [rafi'ni:rən] *vt* to refine
raffiniert *adj* crafty, cunning; (*Zucker*) refined
ragen ['ra:gən] *vi* to tower, rise
Rahm [ra:m] (**-s**) *m* cream
Rahmen (**-s, -**) *m* frame(work); **aus dem ~ fallen** to go too far; **im ~ des Möglichen** within the bounds of possibility; **rahmen** *vt* to frame
Rakete [ra'ke:tə] (**-, -n**) *f* rocket; **ferngelenkte ~** guided missile
rammen ['ramən] *vt* to ram
Rampe ['rampə] (**-, -n**) *f* ramp
Rampenlicht *nt* (*Theat*) footlights *pl*; **sie möchte immer im ~ stehen** (*fig*) she always wants to be in the limelight
ramponieren [rampo'ni:rən] (*umg*) *vt* to damage
Ramsch [ramʃ] (**-(e)s, -e**) *m* junk
ran [ran] (*umg*) *adv* = **heran**
Rand [rant] (**-(e)s, ¨-er**) *m* edge; (*von Brille, Tasse etc*) rim; (*Hutrand*) brim; (*auf Papier*) margin; (*Schmutzrand, unter Augen*) ring; (*fig*) verge, brink; **außer ~ und Band** wild; **am ~e bemerkt** mentioned in passing; **am ~e der Stadt** on the outskirts of the town; **etw am ~e miterleben** to experience sth from the sidelines
randalieren [randa'li:rən] *vi* to (go on the) rampage
rang *etc* [raŋ] *vb siehe* **ringen**
Rang (**-(e)s, ¨-e**) *m* rank; (*Stand*) standing; (*Wert*) quality; (*Theat*) circle; **ein Mann ohne ~ und Namen** a man without any standing; **erster/zweiter ~** dress/upper circle
Rangierbahnhof [rã'ʒi:rba:nho:f] *m* marshalling yard
rangieren *vt* (*Eisenb*) to shunt, switch (*US*) ▷ *vi* to rank, be classed
Rangiergleis *nt* siding
Ranke ['raŋkə] (**-, -n**) *f* tendril, shoot
rann *etc* [ran] *vb siehe* **rinnen**
rannte *etc* ['rantə] *vb siehe* **rennen**

ranzig ['rantsɪç] *adj* rancid
Rappe ['rapə] (**-n, -n**) *m* black horse
Rappen ['rapən] (**-s, -**) (*Schweiz*) *m* (*Geld*) centime, rappen
Raps [raps] (**-es, -e**) *m* (*Bot*) rape
rar [ra:r] *adj* rare; *siehe auch* **rarmachen**
Rarität [rari'tɛ:t] *f* rarity; (*Sammelobjekt*) curio
rasant [ra'zant] *adj* quick, rapid
rasch [raʃ] *adj* quick
rasen ['ra:zən] *vi* to rave; (*sich schnell bewegen*) to race
Rasen (**-s, -**) *m* grass; (*gepflegt*) lawn
rasend *adj* furious; **~e Kopfschmerzen** a splitting headache
Rasen- *zW*: **Rasenmäher** (**-s, -**) *m* lawnmower; **Rasenplatz** *m* lawn
Rasier- *zW*: **Rasierapparat** *m* shaver; **Rasiercreme** *f* shaving cream; **rasieren** *vt, vr* to shave; **Rasierklinge** *f* razor blade; **Rasiermesser** *nt* razor; **Rasierpinsel** *m* shaving brush; **Rasierseife** *f* shaving soap *od* stick; **Rasierwasser** *nt* aftershave
Rasse ['rasə] (**-, -n**) *f* race; (*Tierrasse*) breed
Rassenhass *m* race *od* racial hatred
Rassentrennung *f* racial segregation
Rassismus [ra'sɪsmʊs] (**-**) *m* racialism, racism
rassistisch [ra'sɪstɪʃ] *adj* racialist, racist
Rast [rast] (**-, -en**) *f* rest; **rasten** *vi* to rest
Rast- *zW*: **Rasthof** *m* (motorway) motel; (*mit Tankstelle*) service area (*with a motel*); **rastlos** *adj* tireless; (*unruhig*) restless; **Rastplatz** *m* (*Aut*) lay-by (*Brit*); **Raststätte** *f* service area, services *pl*
Rasur [ra'zu:r] *f* shave; (*das Rasieren*) shaving
Rat [ra:t] (**-(e)s, -schläge**) *m* (piece of) advice; **jdm mit ~ und Tat zur Seite stehen** to support sb in (both) word and deed; **sich ~ suchend an jdn wenden** to turn to sb for advice; **(sich** *dat***) keinen ~ wissen** not to know what to do; *siehe auch* **zurate**
Rate (**-, -n**) *f* instalment (*Brit*), installment (*US*); **auf ~n kaufen** to buy on hire purchase (*Brit*) *od* on the installment plan (*US*); **in ~n zahlen** to pay in instalments (*Brit*) *od* installments (*US*)
raten *unreg vt, vi* to guess; (*empfehlen*): **jdm ~** to advise sb; **dreimal darfst du ~** I'll give you three guesses (*auch ironisch*)
ratenweise *adv* by instalments (*Brit*) *od* installments (*US*)
Ratenzahlung *f* hire purchase (*Brit*), installment plan (*US*)
Ratgeber (**-s, -**) *m* adviser
Rathaus *nt* town hall; (*einer Großstadt*) city hall (*bes US*)
ratifizieren [ratifi'tsi:rən] *vt* to ratify
Ration [ratsi'o:n] *f* ration
rational [ratsio'na:l] *adj* rational
rationalisieren [ratsionali'zi:rən] *vt* to rationalize
rationell [ratsio'nɛl] *adj* efficient
rationieren [ratsio'ni:rən] *vt* to ration
ratlos *adj* at a loss, helpless
rätoromanisch [rɛtoro'ma:nɪʃ] *adj* Rhaetian
ratsam *adj* advisable
Ratschlag *m* (piece of) advice
Rätsel ['rɛ:tsəl] (**-s, -**) *nt* puzzle; (*Worträtsel*) riddle; **vor einem ~ stehen** to be baffled; **rätselhaft** *adj* mysterious; **es ist mir rätselhaft** it's a mystery to me
Ratte ['ratə] (**-, -n**) *f* rat
Rattenfänger (**-s, -**) *m* rat-catcher
rattern ['ratərn] *vi* to rattle, clatter
rau [raʊ] *adj* rough, coarse; (*Wetter*) harsh; **in ~en Mengen** (*umg*) by the ton, galore
Raub [raʊp] (**-(e)s**) *m* robbery; (*Beute*) loot, booty; **Raubbau** *m* overexploitation
rauben ['raʊbən] *vt* to rob; (*jdn*) to kidnap, abduct
Räuber ['rɔʏbər] (**-s, -**) *m* robber
Raub- *zW*: **Raubmord** *m* robbery with murder; **Raubtier** *nt* predator; **Raubüberfall** *m* robbery with violence; **Raubvogel** *m* bird of prey
Rauch [raʊx] (**-(e)s**) *m* smoke
rauchen *vt, vi* to smoke; **mir raucht der Kopf** (*fig*) my head's spinning; **„R~ verboten"** "no smoking"
Raucher, in (**-s, -**) *m(f)* smoker; **Raucherabteil** *nt* (*Eisenb*) smoker
räuchern ['rɔʏçərn] *vt* to smoke, cure
Rauchfleisch *nt* smoked meat
rauchig *adj* smoky
rauf [raʊf] (*umg*) *adv* = **herauf; hinauf**
raufen *vt* (*Haare*) to pull out ▷ *vi, vr* to fight
Rauferei [raʊfə'raɪ] *f* brawl, fight
rauh *etc siehe* **rau** *etc*
Raum [raʊm] (**-(e)s, Räume**) *m* space; (*Zimmer, Platz*) room; (*Gebiet*) area; **~ sparend** space-saving; **eine Frage im ~ stehen lassen** to leave a question unresolved
räumen ['rɔʏmən] *vt* to clear; (*Wohnung, Platz*) to vacate, move out of; (*verlassen: Gebäude, Gebiet*) to evacuate; (*wegbringen*) to shift, move; (*in Schrank etc*) to put away
Raum- *zW*: **Raumfähre** *f* space shuttle; **Raumfahrt** *f* space travel
Rauminhalt *m* cubic capacity, volume
räumlich ['rɔʏmlɪç] *adj* spatial; **Räumlichkeiten** *pl* premises *pl*
Raum- *zW*: **Raummeter** *m* cubic metre (*Brit*) *od* meter (*US*); **Raumschiff** *nt* spaceship; **Raumschifffahrt** *f* space travel; **Raumstation** *f* space station
Räumung ['rɔʏmʊŋ] *f* clearing (away); (*von Haus etc*) vacating; (*wegen Gefahr*) evacuation; (*unter Zwang*) eviction; **Räumungsverkauf** *m* clearance sale
Raupe ['raʊpə] (**-, -n**) *f* caterpillar; (*Raupenkette*) (caterpillar) track
Raupenschlepper *m* caterpillar tractor
Raureif ['raʊraɪf] *m* hoarfrost
raus [raʊs] (*umg*) *adv* = **heraus; hinaus**
Rausch [raʊʃ] (**-(e)**, *pl* **Räusche**) *m* intoxication; **einen ~ haben** to be drunk
rauschen *vi* (*Wasser*) to rush; (*Baum*) to rustle;

(*Radio etc*) to hiss; (*Mensch*) to sweep, sail
rauschend *adj* (*Beifall*) thunderous; (*Fest*) sumptuous
Rauschgift *nt* drug; **Rauschgiftsüchtige, r** *f(m)* drug addict
räuspern ['rɔʏspərn] *vr* to clear one's throat
Razzia ['ratsia] (**-, Razzien**) *f* raid
Reagenzglas [rea'gɛntsgla:s] *nt* test tube
reagieren [rea'gi:rən] *vi*: **~ (auf** *+akk***)** to react (to)
Reaktion [reaktsi'o:n] *f* reaction
reaktionär [reaktsio'nɛ:r] *adj* reactionary
Reaktionsgeschwindigkeit *f* speed of reaction
Reaktor [re'aktɔr] *m* reactor; **Reaktorkern** *m* reactor core
real [re'a:l] *adj* real, material
Realismus [rea'lɪsmʊs] *m* realism
Realist, in [rea'lɪst(ɪn)] *m(f)* realist; **realistisch** *adj* realistic
Realität [reali'tɛ:t] *f* reality; **Realitäten** *pl* (*Gegebenheiten*) facts *pl*
Realschule *f* ≈ middle school (*Brit*), junior high school (*US*)
Rebe ['re:bə] (**-, -n**) *f* vine
Rebell, in [re'bɛl(ɪn)] (**-en, -en**) *m(f)* rebel
Rebellion [rebɛli'o:n] *f* rebellion
rebellisch [re'bɛlɪʃ] *adj* rebellious
Reb- [rɛp] *zW*
Rechen ['rɛçən] (**-s, -**) *m* rake: **rechen** *vt, vi* to rake
Rechen- *zW*: **Rechenfehler** *m* miscalculation; **Rechenmaschine** *f* adding machine
Rechenschaft *f* account; **jdm über etw** *akk* **~ ablegen** to account to sb for sth; **jdn zur ~ ziehen (für)** to call sb to account (for *od* over); **jdm ~ schulden** to be accountable to sb
Rechenschieber *m* slide rule
Rechenzentrum *nt* computer centre (*Brit*) *od* center (*US*)
rechnen ['rɛçnən] *vt, vi* to calculate; (*veranschlagen*) to estimate, reckon; **jdn/etw zu etw ~** to count sb/sth among sth; **~ mit** to reckon with; **~ auf** *+akk* to count on
Rechnen *nt* arithmetic; (*bes Sch*) sums *pl*
Rechner (**-s, -**) *m* calculator; (*Comput*) computer
Rechnung *f* calculation(s); (*Comm*) bill (*Brit*), check (*US*); **auf eigene ~** on one's own account; **(jdm) etw in ~ stellen** to charge (sb) for sth; **jdm/etw ~ tragen** to take sb/sth into account
Rechnungs- *zW*: **Rechnungsjahr** *nt* financial year; **Rechnungsprüfer** *m* auditor
recht [rɛçt] *adj* right ▷ *adv* (*vor Adjektiv*) really, quite; **das ist mir ~** that suits me; **jetzt erst ~** now more than ever; **alles, was ~ ist** (*empört*) fair's fair; (*anerkennend*) you can't deny it; **nach dem R~en sehen** to see that everything's O.K.; **~ haben** to be right; **jdm ~ geben** to agree with sb, admit that sb is right; **du kommst gerade ~, um ...** you're just in time to ...; **gehe ich ~ in der Annahme, dass ...?** am I correct in assuming that ...?; **~ herzlichen Dank** thank you very much indeed
Recht (**-(e)s, -e**) *nt* right; (*Jur*) law; **~ sprechen** to administer justice; **mit** *od* **zu ~** rightly, justly; **von ~s wegen** by rights; **zu seinem ~ kommen** (*lit*) to gain one's rights; (*fig*) to come into one's own; **gleiches ~ für alle!** equal rights for all!
Rechte *f* right (hand); (*Pol*) Right
rechte, r, s *adj* right; (*Pol*) right-wing
recht- *zW*: **Rechteck** (**-(e)s, -e**) *nt* rectangle; **rechteckig** *adj* rectangular; **rechtfertigen** *vt untr* to justify ▷ *vr untr* to justify o.s.; **rechtlich** *adj* legal, lawful; **rechtlich nicht zulässig** not permissible in law, illegal
rechts [rɛçts] *adv* on *od* to the right; **~ stehen** *od* **sein** (*Pol*) to be right-wing; **~ stricken** to knit (plain); **Rechtsanwalt** *m*, **Rechtsanwältin** *f* lawyer, barrister; **Rechtsaußen** (**-, -**) *m* (*Sport*) outside right
rechtschaffen *adj* upright
Rechtschreibung *f* spelling
Rechts- *zW*: **Rechtsextremismus** *m* right-wing extremism; **Rechtsextremist** *m* right-wing extremist; **Rechtsfall** *m* (law) case; **Rechtshänder, in** (**-s, -**) *m(f)* right-handed person; **rechtskräftig** *adj* valid, legal; **Rechtskurve** *f* right-hand bend
Rechts- *zW*: **rechtsradikal** *adj* (*Pol*) extreme right-wing; **Rechtsstreit** *m* lawsuit; **Rechtsverkehr** *m* driving on the right; **Rechtsweg** *m*: **der Rechtsweg ist ausgeschlossen** ≈ the judges' decision is final; **rechtswidrig** *adj* illegal
rechtwinklig *adj* right-angled
rechtzeitig *adj* timely ▷ *adv* in time
Reck [rɛk] (**-(e)s, -e**) *nt* horizontal bar
recken *vt, vr* to stretch
recyceln [ri:'saɪkəln] *vt* to recycle
Recycling [ri'saɪklɪŋ] (**-s**) *nt* recycling
Redakteur, in [redak'tø:r(ɪn)] *m(f)* editor
Redaktion [redaktsi'o:n] *f* editing; (*Leute*) editorial staff; (*Büro*) editorial office(s *pl*)
Rede ['re:də] (**-, -n**) *f* speech; (*Gespräch*) talk; **jdn zur ~ stellen** to take sb to task; **eine ~ halten** to make a speech; **das ist nicht der ~ wert** it's not worth mentioning; **davon kann keine ~ sein** it's out of the question; **redegewandt** *adj* eloquent
Reden (**-s**) *nt* talking, speech
reden *vi* to talk, speak ▷ *vt* to say; (*Unsinn etc*) to talk; **(viel) von sich ~ machen** to become (very much) a talking point; **darüber lässt sich ~** that's a possibility; (*über Preis, Bedingungen*) I think we could discuss that; **er lässt mit sich ~** he could be persuaded; (*in Bezug auf Preis*) he's open to offers; (*gesprächsbereit*) he's open to discussion
Redensart *f* set phrase
Redewendung *f* expression, idiom
redlich ['re:tlɪç] *adj* honest

Redner, in (**-s, -**) *m(f)* speaker, orator
reduzieren [redu'tsi:rən] *vt* to reduce
Reede ['re:də] (**-, -n**) *f* protected anchorage
Reeder (**-s, -**) *m* shipowner
Reederei [re:də'raı] *f* shipping line *od* firm
reell [re'ɛl] *adj* fair, honest; (*Preis*) fair; (*Comm: Geschäft*) sound; (*Math*) real
Referat [refe'ra:t] (**-(e)s, -e**) *nt* report; (*Vortrag*) paper; (*Gebiet*) section; (*Verwaltung: Ressort*) department; **ein ~ halten** to present a seminar paper
Referent, in [refe'rɛnt(ın)] *m(f)* speaker; (*Berichterstatter*) reporter; (*Sachbearbeiter*) expert
Referenz [refe'rɛnts] *f* reference
referieren [refe'ri:rən] *vi*: **~ über** *+akk* to speak *od* talk on
Reflex [re'flɛks] (**-es, -e**) *m* reflex; **Reflexbewegung** *f* reflex action
reflexiv [reflɛ'ksi:f] *adj* (*Gram*) reflexive
Reform [re'fɔrm] (**-, -en**) *f* reform
Reformation [refɔrmatsi'o:n] *f* reformation; **reformatorisch** *adj* reformatory, reforming
Reformhaus *nt* health food shop
reformieren [refɔr'mi:rən] *vt* to reform
Regal [re'ga:l] (**-s, -e**) *nt* (book)shelves *pl*, bookcase; (*Typ*) stand, rack
Regel ['re:gəl] (**-, -n**) *f* rule; (*Med*) period; **in der ~** as a rule; **nach allen ~n der Kunst** (*fig*) thoroughly; **sich** *dat* **etw zur ~ machen** to make a habit of sth; **regelmäßig** *adj* regular; **Regelmäßigkeit** *f* regularity
regeln *vt* to regulate, control; (*Angelegenheit*) to settle ▷ *vr*: **sich von selbst ~** to take care of itself; **gesetzlich geregelt sein** to be laid down by law
regelrecht *adj* proper, thorough
Regelung *f* regulation; settlement
regelwidrig *adj* irregular, against the rules
Regen (**-s, -**) *m* rain; **vom ~ in die Traufe kommen** (*Sprichwort*) to jump out of the frying pan into the fire (*Sprichwort*)
Regenbogen *m* rainbow; **Regenbogenpresse** *f* trashy magazines *pl*
Regen- *zW*: **Regenmantel** *m* raincoat, mac(kintosh); **Regenschauer** *m* shower (of rain); **Regenschirm** *m* umbrella; **Regenwald** *m* (*Geog*) rain forest; **Regenwurm** *m* earthworm
Regie [re'ʒi:] *f* (*Film etc*) direction; (*Theat*) production; **unter der ~ von** directed *od* produced by
regieren [re'gi:rən] *vt, vi* to govern, rule
Regierung *f* government; (*Monarchie*) reign; **an die ~ kommen** to come to power
Regierungs- *zW*: **Regierungswechsel** *m* change of government; **Regierungszeit** *f* period in government; (*von König*) reign
Regiment [regi'mɛnt] (**-s, -er**) *nt* regiment
Region [regi'o:n] *f* region
Regisseur, in [reʒı'sø:r(ın)] *m(f)* director; (*Theat*) (stage) producer
Register [re'gıstər] (**-s, -**) *nt* register; (*in Buch*) table of contents, index; **alle ~ ziehen** (*fig*) to pull out all the stops
registrieren [regıs'tri:rən] *vt* to register; (*umg: zur Kenntnis nehmen*) to note
Regler ['re:glər] (**-s, -**) *m* regulator, governor
reglos ['re:klo:s] *adj* motionless
regnen ['re:gnən] *vi unpers* to rain ▷ *vt unpers*: **es regnet Glückwünsche** congratulations are pouring in; **es regnet in Strömen** it's pouring (with rain)
regnerisch *adj* rainy
regulär [regu'lɛ:r] *adj* regular
regulieren [regu'li:rən] *vt* to regulate; (*Comm*) to settle; **sich von selbst ~** to be self-regulating
Regung ['re:gʊŋ] *f* motion; (*Gefühl*) feeling, impulse
Reh [re:] (**-(e)s, -e**) *nt* deer; (*weiblich*) roe deer
Reh- *zW*: **Rehbock** *m* roebuck; **Rehkalb** *nt* fawn
Reibe ['raıbə] (**-, -n**) *f* grater
Reibekuchen *m* (*Koch*) ≈ potato waffle
reiben *unreg vt* to rub; (*Koch*) to grate
Reiberei [raıbə'raı] *f* friction *no pl*
Reibfläche *f* rough surface
Reibung *f* friction
reibungslos *adj* smooth; **~ verlaufen** to go off smoothly
Reich [raıç] (**-(e)s, -e**) *nt* empire, kingdom; (*fig*) realm; **das Dritte ~** the Third Reich
reich *adj* rich ▷ *adv*: **eine ~ ausgestattete Bibliothek** a well-stocked library
reichen *vi* to reach; (*genügen*) to be enough *od* sufficient ▷ *vt* to hold out; (*geben*) to pass, hand; (*anbieten*) to offer; **so weit das Auge reicht** as far as the eye can see; **jdm ~** (*genügen*) to be enough *od* sufficient for sb; **mir reichts!** I've had enough!
reich- *zW*: **reichhaltig** *adj* ample, rich; **reichlich** *adj* ample, plenty of; **Reichtum** (**-s, -tümer**) *m* wealth
reif [raıf] *adj* ripe; (*Mensch, Urteil*) mature; **für etw ~ sein** (*umg*) to be ready for sth
Reif[1] (**-(e)s**) *m* hoarfrost
Reif[2] (**-(e)s, -e**) *m* (*Ring*) ring, hoop
Reife (**-**) *f* ripeness; maturity; **mittlere ~** (*Sch*) *first public examination in secondary school*, ≈ O-Levels *pl* (*Brit*)
Reifen (**-s, -**) *m* ring, hoop; (*Fahrzeugreifen*) tyre (*Brit*), tire (*US*)
reifen *vi* to mature; (*Obst*) to ripen
Reifen- *zW*: **Reifenpanne** *f* puncture, flat; **Reifenschaden** *m* puncture, flat
Reihe ['raıə] (**-, -n**) *f* row; (*von Tagen etc: umg: Anzahl*) series *sing*; **eine ganze ~ (von)** (*unbestimmte Anzahl*) a whole lot (of); **der ~ nach** in turn; **er ist an der ~** it's his turn; **an die ~ kommen** to have one's turn; **außer der ~** out of turn; (*ausnahmsweise*) out of the usual way of things; **aus der ~ tanzen** (*fig: umg*) to be different; (*gegen Konventionen verstoßen*) to step out of line; **ich kriege heute nichts auf die ~** I can't get my act

together today; **Reihenfolge** *f* sequence; **alphabetische Reihenfolge** alphabetical order

Reiher (**-s, -**) *m* heron

Reim [raɪm] (**-(e)s, -e**) *m* rhyme; **sich** *dat* **einen ~ auf etw** *akk* **machen** (*umg*) to make sense of sth; **reimen** *vt* to rhyme

rein[1] [raɪn] (*umg*) *adv* = **herein; hinein**

rein[2] [raɪn] *adj* pure; (*sauber*) clean ▷ *adv* purely; **~ waschen** to clear o.s.; **das ist die ~ste Freude/der ~ste Hohn** *etc* it's pure *od* sheer joy/mockery *etc*; **etw ins R~e schreiben** to make a fair copy of sth; **etw ins R~e bringen** to clear sth up; **~en Tisch machen** (*fig*) to get things straight; **~ unmöglich** (*umg: ganz, völlig*) absolutely impossible

rein- *zW*: **Reinfall** (*umg*) *m* let-down; (*Misserfolg*) flop; **Reingewinn** *m* net profit; **Reinheit** *f* purity; cleanness

reinigen ['raɪnɪgən] *vt* to clean; (*Wasser*) to purify

Reinigung *f* cleaning; purification; (*Geschäft*) cleaner's; **chemische ~** dry-cleaning; (*Geschäft*) dry-cleaner's

rein- *zW*: **reinlich** *adj* clean; **reinrassig** *adj* pedigree; **Reinschrift** *f* fair copy

Reis[1] [raɪs] (**-es, -e**) *m* rice

Reis[2] [raɪs] (**-es, -er**) *nt* twig, sprig

Reise ['raɪzə] (**-, -n**) *f* journey; (*Schiffsreise*) voyage; **Reisen** *pl* travels *pl*; **gute ~!** bon voyage!, have a good journey!; **auf ~n sein** to be away (travelling (*Brit*) *od* traveling (*US*)); **er ist viel auf ~n** he does a lot of travelling (*Brit*) *od* traveling (*US*); **Reiseandenken** *nt* souvenir; **Reisebüro** *nt* travel agency; **reisefertig** *adj* ready to start; **Reiseführer** *m* guide(book); (*Mensch*) (travel) guide; **Reisegepäck** *nt* luggage; **Reisegesellschaft** *f* party of travellers (*Brit*) *od* travelers (*US*); **Reisekosten** *pl* travelling (*Brit*) *od* traveling (*US*) expenses *pl*; **Reiseleiter** *m* courier; **Reiselektüre** *f* reading for the journey

reisen *vi* to travel; **~ nach** to go to

Reisende, r *f(m)* traveller (*Brit*), traveler (*US*)

Reise- *zW*: **Reisepass** *m* passport; **Reiseproviant** *m* provisions *pl* for the journey; **Reisescheck** *m* traveller's cheque (*Brit*), traveler's check (*US*); **Reisetasche** *f* travelling (*Brit*) *od* traveling (*US*) bag *od* case; **Reiseveranstalter** *m* tour operator; **Reiseverkehr** *m* tourist *od* holiday traffic; **Reiseziel** *nt* destination

reißen ['raɪsən] *unreg vt* to tear; (*ziehen*) to pull, drag; (*Witz*) to crack ▷ *vi* to tear; to pull, drag; **etw an sich ~** to snatch sth up; (*fig*) to take sth over; **sich um etw ~** to scramble for sth; **wenn alle Stricke ~** (*fig: umg*) if the worst comes to the worst; *siehe auch* **hingerissen**

Reiß- *zW*: **Reißnagel** *m* drawing pin (*Brit*), thumbtack (*US*); **Reißverschluss** *m* zip (fastener) (*Brit*), zipper (*US*); **Reißzeug** *nt* geometry set; **Reißzwecke** *f* = **Reißnagel**

reiten ['raɪtən] *unreg vt, vi* to ride

Reiter (**-s, -**) *m* rider; (*Mil*) cavalryman, trooper

Reit- *zW*: **Reithose** *f* riding breeches *pl*; **Reitpferd** *nt* saddle horse; **Reitstiefel** *m* riding boot; **Reitzeug** *nt* riding outfit

Reiz [raɪts] (**-es, -e**) *m* stimulus; (*angenehm*) charm; (*Verlockung*) attraction

reizbar *adj* irritable

reizen *vt* to stimulate; (*unangenehm*) to irritate; (*verlocken*) to appeal to, attract; (*Karten*) to bid ▷ *vi*: **zum Widerspruch ~** to invite contradiction

reizend *adj* charming

Reiz- *zW*: **Reizgas** *nt* tear gas, CS gas; **Reizwäsche** *f* sexy underwear

rekeln ['re:kəln] *vr* to stretch out; (*lümmeln*) to lounge *od* loll about

Reklamation [reklamatsi'o:n] *f* complaint

Reklame [re'kla:mə] (**-, -n**) *f* advertising; (*Anzeige*) advertisement; **mit etw ~ machen** (*pej*) to show off about sth; **für etw ~ machen** to advertise sth

rekonstruieren [rekɔnstru'i:rən] *vt* to reconstruct

Rekonvaleszenz [rekɔnvalɛs'tsɛnts] *f* convalescence

Rekord [re'kɔrt] (**-(e)s, -e**) *m* record; **Rekordleistung** *f* record performance

Rektor ['rɛktɔr] *m* (*Univ*) rector, vice-chancellor; (*Sch*) head teacher (*Brit*), principal (*US*)

Rektorat [rɛktɔ'rat] (**-(e)s, -e**) *nt* rectorate, vice-chancellorship; headship (*Brit*), principalship (*US*); (*Zimmer*) rector's *etc* office

Relais [rə'lɛ:] (**-, -**) *nt* relay

relativ [rela'ti:f] *adj* relative

Relativität [relativi'tɛ:t] *f* relativity

relevant [rele'vant] *adj* relevant

Relief [reli'ɛf] (**-s, -s**) *nt* relief

Religion [religi'o:n] *f* religion

religiös [religi'ø:s] *adj* religious

Reling ['re:lɪŋ] (**-, -s**) *f* (*Naut*) rail

Reliquie [re'li:kviə] *f* relic

Remoulade [remu'la:də] (**-, -n**) *f* remoulade

Rendezvous [rãde'vu:] (**-, -**) *nt* rendezvous

Rendite [rɛn'di:tə] (**-, -n**) *f* (*Fin*) yield, return on capital

Rennbahn *f* racecourse; (*Aut*) circuit, racetrack

rennen ['rɛnən] *unreg vt, vi* to run, race; **um die Wette ~** to have a race; **Rennen** (**-s, -**) *nt* running; (*Wettbewerb*) race; **das Rennen machen** (*lit, fig*) to win (the race)

Renner (**-s, -**) (*umg*) *m* winner, worldbeater

Renn- *zW*: **Rennfahrer** *m* racing driver (*Brit*), race car driver (*US*); **Rennpferd** *nt* racehorse; **Rennrad** *nt* racing cycle; **Rennwagen** *m* racing car (*Brit*), race car (*US*)

renovieren [reno'vi:rən] *vt* to renovate

Renovierung *f* renovation

rentabel [rɛn'ta:bəl] *adj* profitable, lucrative

Rentabilität [rɛntabili'tɛ:t] *f* profitability

Rente ['rɛntə] (**-, -n**) *f* pension; **Rentenversicherung** *f* pension scheme
Rentier ['rɛnti:r] *nt* reindeer
rentieren [rɛn'ti:rən] *vi, vr* to pay, be profitable; **das rentiert (sich) nicht** it's not worth it
Rentner, in ['rɛntnər(ɪn)] (**-s, -**) *m(f)* pensioner
Reparatur [repara'tu:r] *f* repairing; repair; **etw in ~ geben** to have sth repaired; **Reparaturwerkstatt** *f* repair shop; (*Aut*) garage
reparieren [repa'ri:rən] *vt* to repair
Reportage [repɔr'ta:ʒə] (**-, -n**) *f* report
Reporter, in [re'pɔrtər(ɪn)] (**-s, -**) *m(f)* reporter, commentator
Repressalien [reprɛ'sa:liən] *pl* reprisals *pl*
Reproduktion [reprodʊktsi'o:n] *f* reproduction
reproduzieren [reprodu'tsi:rən] *vt* to reproduce
Reptil [rɛp'ti:l] (**-s, -ien**) *nt* reptile
Republik [repu'bli:k] *f* republic
Republikaner [republi'ka:nər] (**-s, -**) *m* republican
republikanisch *adj* republican
Reservat [rezɛr'va:t] (**-(e)s, -e**) *nt* reservation
Reserve [re'zɛrvə] (**-, -n**) *f* reserve; **jdn aus der ~ locken** to bring sb out of his/her shell; **Reserverad** *nt* (*Aut*) spare wheel; **Reservespieler** *m* reserve; **Reservetank** *m* reserve tank
reservieren [rezɛr'vi:rən] *vt* to reserve
Reservoir [rezɛrvo'a:r] (**-s, -e**) *nt* reservoir
Residenz [rezi'dɛnts] *f* residence, seat
resignieren [rezɪ'gni:rən] *vi* to resign
resolut [rezo'lu:t] *adj* resolute
Resonanz [rezo'nants] *f* (*lit, fig*) resonance
Resozialisierung *f* rehabilitation
Respekt [rɛ'spɛkt] (**-(e)s**) *m* respect; (*Angst*) fear; **bei allem ~ (vor jdm/etw)** with all due respect (to sb/for sth)
respektieren [rɛspɛk'ti:rən] *vt* to respect
respektlos *adj* disrespectful
respektvoll *adj* respectful
Ressort [rɛ'so:r] (**-s, -s**) *nt* department; **in das ~ von jdm fallen** (*lit, fig*) to be sb's department
Rest [rɛst] (**-(e)s, -e**) *m* remainder, rest; (*Überrest*) remains *pl*; **Reste** *pl* (*Comm*) remnants *pl*; **das hat mir den ~ gegeben** (*umg*) that finished me off
Restaurant [rɛsto'rã:] (**-s, -s**) *nt* restaurant
restaurieren [restaʊ'ri:rən] *vt* to restore
Rest- *zW*: **Restbetrag** *m* remainder, outstanding sum; **restlich** *adj* remaining; **restlos** *adj* complete
Resultat [rezʊl'ta:t] (**-(e)s, -e**) *nt* result
Retorte [re'tɔrtə] (**-, -n**) *f* retort; **aus der ~** (*umg*) synthetic
Retortenbaby *nt* test-tube baby
retten ['rɛtən] *vt* to save, rescue ▷ *vr* to escape; **bist du noch zu ~?** (*umg*) are you out of your mind?; **sich vor etw** *dat* **nicht mehr ~ können** (*fig*) to be swamped with sth
Rettich ['rɛtɪç] (**-s, -e**) *m* radish
Rettung *f* rescue; (*Hilfe*) help; **seine letzte ~** his last hope
Rettungs- *zW*: **Rettungsboot** *nt* lifeboat; **rettungslos** *adj* hopeless; **Rettungsring** *m* = **Rettungsgürtel**; **Rettungswagen** *m* ambulance
Return-Taste [ri'tø:rntastə] *f* (*Comput*) return key
retuschieren [retʊ'ʃi:rən] *vt* (*Phot*) to retouch
Reue ['rɔʏə] (**-**) *f* remorse; (*Bedauern*) regret
reuen *vt*: **es reut ihn** he regrets it, he is sorry about it
reuig ['rɔʏɪç] *adj* penitent
Revanche [re'vã:ʃə] (**-, -n**) *f* revenge; (*Sport*) return match
revanchieren [revã'ʃi:rən] *vr* (*sich rächen*) to get one's own back, have one's revenge; (*erwidern*) to reciprocate, return the compliment
Revier [re'vi:r] (**-s, -e**) *nt* district; (*Min: Kohlenrevier*) (coal)mine; (*Jagdrevier*) preserve; (*Polizeirevier*) police station, station house (*US*); (*Dienstbereich*) beat (*Brit*), precinct (*US*); (*Mil*) sick bay
Revolution [revolutsi'o:n] *f* revolution
revolutionär [revolutsio'nɛ:r] *adj* revolutionary
Revolutionär, in [revolutsio'nɛ:r(ɪn)] (**-s, -e**) *m(f)* revolutionary
revolutionieren [revolutsio'ni:rən] *vt* to revolutionize
Rezept [re'tsɛpt] (**-(e)s, -e**) *nt* (*Koch*) recipe; (*Med*) prescription
Rezeption [retsɛptsi'o:n] *f* (*von Hotel: Empfang*) reception
rezeptpflichtig *adj* available only on prescription
Rezession [retsɛsi'o:n] *f* (*Fin*) recession
rezitieren [retsi'ti:rən] *vt* to recite
Rhabarber [ra'barbər] (**-s**) *m* rhubarb
Rhein [raɪn] (**-(e)s**) *m* Rhine
Rheinland-Pfalz *nt* Rhineland-Palatinate
Rhesusfaktor ['re:zusfaktɔr] *m* rhesus factor
rhetorisch [re'to:rɪʃ] *adj* rhetorical
Rheuma ['rɔʏma] (**-s**) *nt* rheumatism
Rhinozeros [ri'no:tserɔs] (**-** *od* **-ses, -se**) *nt* rhinoceros; (*umg: Dummkopf*) fool
Rhodos ['ro:dɔs] (**-**) *nt* Rhodes
rhythmisch ['rytmɪʃ] *adj* rhythmical
Rhythmus *m* rhythm
richten ['rɪçtən] *vt* to direct; (*Waffe*) to aim; (*einstellen*) to adjust; (*instand setzen*) to repair; (*zurechtmachen*) to prepare, get ready; (*adressieren: Briefe, Anfragen*) to address; (*Bitten, Forderungen*) to make; (*in Ordnung bringen*) to do, fix; (*bestrafen*) to pass judgement on ▷ *vr*: **sich ~ nach** to go by; **~ an** *+akk* to direct at; (*fig*) to direct to; (*Briefe etc*) to address to; (*Bitten etc*) to make to; **~ auf** *+akk* to aim at; **wir ~ uns ganz nach unseren Kunden** we are guided

entirely by our customers' wishes
Richter, in (**-s, -**) *m(f)* judge; **sich zum ~ machen** *(fig)* to set (o.s.) up in judgement; **richterlich** *adj* judicial
richtig *adj* right, correct; *(echt)* proper ▷ *adv* correctly, right; *(umg: sehr)* really; **der/die R~e** the right one *od* person; **das R~e** the right thing; **die Uhr geht ~** the clock is right; **Richtigkeit** *f* correctness; **das hat schon seine Richtigkeit** it's right enough
Richt- *zW*: **Richtlinie** *f* guideline; **Richtpreis** *m* recommended price
Richtung *f* direction; *(Tendenz)* tendency, orientation; **in jeder ~** each way
rieb *etc* [ri:p] *vb siehe* **reiben**
riechen ['ri:çən] *unreg vt, vi* to smell; **an etw** *dat* **~** to smell sth; **es riecht nach Gas** there's a smell of gas; **ich kann das/ihn nicht ~** *(umg)* I can't stand it/him; **das konnte ich doch nicht ~!** *(umg)* how was I (supposed) to know?
rief *etc* [ri:f] *vb siehe* **rufen**
Riegel ['ri:gəl] (**-s, -**) *m* bolt, bar; **einer Sache** *dat* **einen ~ vorschieben** *(fig)* to clamp down on sth
Riemen ['ri:mən] (**-s, -**) *m* strap; *(Gürtel, Tech)* belt; *(Naut)* oar; **sich am ~ reißen** *(fig: umg)* to get a grip on o.s.
Riese ['ri:zə] (**-n, -n**) *m* giant
rieseln *vi* to trickle; *(Schnee)* to fall gently
Riesen- *zW*: **Riesenerfolg** *m* enormous success; **riesengroß** *adj*, **riesenhaft** *adj* colossal, gigantic, huge; **Riesenrad** *nt* big *od* Ferris wheel
riesig ['ri:zıç] *adj* enormous, huge, vast
Riesin *f* giantess
riet *etc* [ri:t] *vb siehe* **raten**
Riff [rıf] (**-(e)s, -e**) *nt* reef
Rille ['rılə] (**-, -n**) *f* groove
Rind [rınt] (**-(e)s, -er**) *nt* ox; *(Kuh)* cow; *(Koch)* beef; **Rinder** *pl* cattle *pl*; **vom ~** beef
Rinde ['rındə] (**-, -n**) *f* rind; *(Baumrinde)* bark; *(Brotrinde)* crust
Rindfleisch *nt* beef
Rindvieh *nt* cattle *pl*; *(umg)* blockhead, stupid oaf
Ring [rıŋ] (**-(e)s, -e**) *m* ring; **Ringbuch** *nt* ring binder
Ringelnatter *f* grass snake
ringen *unreg vi* to wrestle; **nach** *od* **um etw ~** *(streben)* to struggle for sth; **Ringen** (**-s**) *nt* wrestling
Ring- *zW*: **Ringfinger** *m* ring finger; **Ringkampf** *m* wrestling bout; **Ringrichter** *m* referee
rings *adv*: **~ um** round; **ringsherum** *adv* round about
Ringstraße *f* ring road
Rinne ['rınə] (**-, -n**) *f* gutter, drain
rinnen *unreg vi* to run, trickle
Rinnstein *m* gutter
Rippchen ['rıpçən] *nt* small rib; cutlet
Rippe ['rıpə] (**-, -n**) *f* rib
Rippen- *zW*: **Rippenfellentzündung** *f* pleurisy
Risiko ['ri:ziko] (**-s, -s** *od* **Risiken**) *nt* risk
riskant [rıs'kant] *adj* risky, hazardous
riskieren [rıs'ki:rən] *vt* to risk
riss *etc* [rıs] *vb siehe* **reißen**
Riss (**-es, -e**) *m* tear; *(in Mauer, Tasse etc)* crack; *(in Haut)* scratch; *(Tech)* design
rissig ['rısıç] *adj* torn; cracked; scratched
ritt *etc* [rıt] *vb siehe* **reiten**
Ritt (**-(e)s, -e**) *m* ride
Ritter (**-s, -**) *m* knight; **jdn zum ~ schlagen** to knight sb; **arme ~** *sweet French toast, made with bread soaked in milk*; **ritterlich** *adj* chivalrous
Ritze ['rıtsə] (**-, -n**) *f* crack, chink
Rivale [ri'va:lə] (**-n, -n**) *m*, **Rivalin** *f* rival
Rivalität [rivali'tɛ:t] *f* rivalry
Rizinusöl ['ri:tsinʊs|ø:l] *nt* castor oil
Robbe ['rɔbə] (**-, -n**) *f* seal
Roboter ['rɔbɔtər] (**-s, -**) *m* robot
roch *etc* [rɔx] *vb siehe* **riechen**
Rock[1] [rɔk] (**-(e)s, ¨-e**) *m* skirt; *(Jackett)* jacket; *(Uniformrock)* tunic
Rock[2] [rɔk] (**-(s), -(s)**) *m* *(Mus)* rock
Rodel ['ro:dəl] (**-s, -**) *m* toboggan; **Rodelbahn** *f* toboggan run
rodeln *vi* to toboggan
Rogen ['ro:gən] (**-s, -**) *m* roe
Roggen ['rɔgən] (**-s, -**) *m* rye
roh [ro:] *adj* raw; *(Mensch)* coarse, crude; **~e Gewalt** brute force; **Rohbau** *m* shell of a building; **Rohmaterial** *nt* raw material; **Rohöl** *nt* crude oil
Rohr [ro:r] (**-(e)s, -e**) *nt* pipe, tube; *(Bot)* cane; *(Schilf)* reed; *(Gewehrrohr)* barrel; **Rohrbruch** *m* burst pipe
Röhre ['rø:rə] (**-, -n**) *f* tube, pipe; *(Rundf etc)* valve; *(Backröhre)* oven
Rohr- *zW*
Rohseide *f* raw silk
Rohstoff *m* raw material
Rokoko ['rɔkoko] (**-s**) *nt* rococo
Rolle ['rɔlə] (**-, -n**) *f* roll; *(Theat, Soziologie)* role; *(Garnrolle etc)* reel, spool; *(Walze)* roller; *(Wäscherolle)* mangle, wringer; **bei** *od* **in etw** *dat* **eine ~ spielen** to play a part in sth; **aus der ~ fallen** *(fig)* to forget o.s.; **keine ~ spielen** not to matter
rollen *vi* to roll; *(Aviat)* to taxi ▷ *vt* to roll; *(Wäsche)* to mangle, put through the wringer; **den Stein ins R~ bringen** *(fig)* to start the ball rolling
Rollen- *zW*: **Rollenspiel** *nt* role-play; **Rollentausch** *m* exchange of roles; *(Soziologie)* role reversal
Roller (**-s, -**) *m* scooter; *(Welle)* roller
Roll- *zW*: **Rollfeld** *nt* runway; **Rollladen** *m* shutter; **Rollmops** *m* pickled herring; **Rollschuh** *m* roller skate; **Rollstuhl** *m* wheelchair; **Rolltreppe** *f* escalator
Rom [ro:m] (**-s**) *nt* Rome; **das sind Zustände wie im alten ~** *(umg: unmoralisch)* it's disgraceful; *(: primitiv)* it's medieval *(umg)*

Roman [ro'ma:n] (**-s, -e**) *m* novel; **(jdm) einen ganzen ~ erzählen** (*umg*) to give (sb) a long rigmarole
Romantik [ro'mantɪk] *f* romanticism
Romantiker, in (**-s, -**) *m(f)* romanticist
romantisch *adj* romantic
Romanze [ro'mantsə] (**-, -n**) *f* romance
Römer ['rø:mər] (**-s, -**) *m* wineglass; (*Mensch*) Roman
römisch ['rø:mɪʃ] *adj* Roman; **römisch-katholisch** *adj* Roman Catholic
röntgen ['rœntgən] *vt* to X-ray; **Röntgenaufnahme** *f* X-ray; **Röntgenstrahlen** *pl* X-rays *pl*
rosa ['ro:za] *adj inv* pink, rose(-coloured)
Rose ['ro:zə] (**-, -n**) *f* rose
Rosé [ro'ze:] (**-s, -s**) *m* rosé
Rosenkohl *m* Brussels sprouts *pl*
Rosenkranz *m* rosary
rosig ['ro:zɪç] *adj* rosy
Rosine [ro'zi:nə] *f* raisin; **(große) ~n im Kopf haben** (*umg*) to have big ideas
Rosmarin ['ro:smari:n] (**-s**) *m* rosemary
Ross [rɔs] (**-es, -e**) *nt* horse, steed; **auf dem hohen ~ sitzen** (*fig*) to be on one's high horse; **Rosskastanie** *f* horse chestnut
Rost [rɔst] (**-(e)s, -e**) *m* rust; (*Gitter*) grill, gridiron; (*Bettrost*) springs *pl*; **Rostbraten** *m* roast(ed) meat, roast
rosten *vi* to rust
rösten ['rø:stən] *vt* to roast; (*Brot*) to toast
rostfrei *adj* (*Stahl*) stainless
rostig *adj* rusty
Rostschutz *m* rustproofing
rot [ro:t] *adj* red; **~ werden, einen roten Kopf bekommen** to blush, go red; **die R~e Armee** the Red Army; **das R~e Kreuz** the Red Cross; **das R~e Meer** the Red Sea
Rotation [rotatsi'o:n] *f* rotation
Röte ['rø:tə] (**-**) *f* redness
Röteln *pl* German measles *sing*
röten *vt, vr* to redden
rothaarig *adj* red-haired
rotieren [ro'ti:rən] *vi* to rotate
Rot- *zW*: **Rotkehlchen** *nt* robin; **Rotkraut** *nt* red cabbage; **Rotstift** *m* red pencil; **Rotwein** *m* red wine
Roulade [ru'la:də] (**-, -n**) *f* (*Koch*) beef olive
Route ['ru:tə] (**-, -n**) *f* route
Routine [ru'ti:nə] *f* experience; (*Gewohnheit*) routine
Rowdy ['raʊdɪ] (**-s, -s**) *m* hooligan; (*zerstörerisch*) vandal; (*lärmend*) rowdy (type)
Ruanda [ru'anda] *nt* Rwanda
rubbeln ['rʊbəln] (*umg*) *vt, vi* to rub
Rübe ['ry:bə] (**-, -n**) *f* turnip; **Gelbe ~** carrot; **Rote ~** beetroot (*Brit*), beet (*US*)
Rübenzucker *m* beet sugar
Rubin [ru'bi:n] (**-s, -e**) *m* ruby
Rubrik [ru'bri:k] *f* heading; (*Spalte*) column
Rückantwort *f* reply, answer; **um ~ wird gebeten** please reply
Rück- *zW*: **rückbezüglich** *adj* reflexive; **rückblickend** *adj* retrospective ▷ *adv* in retrospect
Rücken (**-s, -**) *m* back; (*Bergrücken*) ridge; **jdm in den ~ fallen** (*fig*) to stab sb in the back
rücken *vt, vi* to move
Rücken- *zW*: **Rückenmark** *nt* spinal cord; **Rückenschwimmen** *nt* backstroke
Rück- *zW*: **Rückerstattung** *f* return, restitution; **Rückfahrkarte** *f* return ticket (*Brit*), round-trip ticket (*US*); **Rückfahrt** *f* return journey; **Rückfall** *m* relapse; **rückfällig** *adj* relapsed; **rückfällig werden** to relapse; **Rückflug** *m* return flight; **Rückfrage** *f* question; **nach Rückfrage bei der zuständigen Behörde ...** after checking this with the appropriate authority ...; **Rückgabe** *f* return; **gegen Rückgabe (+gen)** on return (of); **Rückgang** *m* decline, fall; **rückgängig** *adj*: **etw rückgängig machen** (*widerrufen*) to undo sth; (*Bestellung*) to cancel sth
Rückgrat *nt* spine, backbone
Rück- *zW*: **Rückkehr** (**-, -en**) *f* return; **Rücklicht** *nt* rear light; **rücklings** *adv* from behind; (*rückwärts*) backwards; **Rücknahme** (**-, -n**) *f* taking back; **Rückporto** *nt* return postage; **Rückreise** *f* return journey; (*Naut*) home voyage; **Rückruf** *m* recall
Rucksack ['rʊkzak] *m* rucksack
Rück- *zW*: **Rückschau** *f* reflection; **Rückschluss** *m* conclusion; **Rückschritt** *m* retrogression; **rückschrittlich** *adj* reactionary; (*Entwicklung*) retrograde; **Rückseite** *f* back; (*von Münze etc*) reverse; **siehe Rückseite** see over(leaf)
Rücksicht *f* consideration; **~ nehmen auf** *+akk* to show consideration for
rücksichtslos *adj* inconsiderate; (*Fahren*) reckless; (*unbarmherzig*) ruthless
rücksichtsvoll *adj* considerate
Rück- *zW*: **Rücksitz** *m* back seat; **Rückspiegel** *m* (*Aut*) rear-view mirror; **Rückspiel** *nt* return match; **Rückstand** *m* arrears *pl*; (*Verzug*) delay; **rückständig** *adj* backward, out-of-date; (*Zahlungen*) in arrears; **Rückstrahler** (**-s, -**) *m* rear reflector; **Rücktaste** *f* (*an Schreibmaschine*) backspace key; **Rücktritt** *m* resignation; **Rücktrittbremse** *f* backpedal brake; **Rückvergütung** *f* repayment; (*Comm*) refund; **rückwärtig** *adj* rear; **rückwärts** *adv* backward(s), back; **Rückwärtsgang** *m* (*Aut*) reverse gear; **im Rückwärtsgang fahren** to reverse; **Rückweg** *m* return journey, way back; **rückwirkend** *adj* retroactive; **Rückzahlung** *f* repayment; **Rückzieher** (*umg*) *m*: **einen Rückzieher machen** to back out
Rudel ['ru:dəl] (**-s, -**) *nt* pack; (*von Hirschen*) herd
Ruder ['ru:dər] (**-s, -**) *nt* oar; (*Steuer*) rudder; **das ~ fest in der Hand haben** (*fig*) to be in control of the situation; **Ruderboot** *nt* rowing boat

rudern *vt, vi* to row; **mit den Armen ~** (*fig*) to flail one's arms about
Ruf [ru:f] (**-(e)s, -e**) *m* call, cry; (*Ansehen*) reputation; (*Univ: Berufung*) offer of a chair
rufen *unreg vt, vi* to call; (*ausrufen*) to cry; **um Hilfe ~** to call for help; **das kommt mir wie ge~** that's just what I needed
Ruf- *zW*: **Rufname** *m* usual (first) name; **Rufnummer** *f* (tele)phone number; **Rufzeichen** *nt* (*Rundf*) call sign; (*Tel*) ringing tone
Ruhe ['ru:ə] (**-**) *f* rest; (*Ungestörtheit*) peace, quiet; (*Gelassenheit, Stille*) calm; (*Schweigen*) silence; **~!** be quiet!, silence!; **angenehme ~!** sleep well!; **~ bewahren** to stay cool *od* calm; **das lässt ihm keine ~** he can't stop thinking about it; **sich zur ~ setzen** to retire; **die ~ weghaben** (*umg*) to be unflappable; **immer mit der ~** (*umg*) don't panic; **die letzte ~ finden** (*liter*) to be laid to rest
ruhen *vi* to rest; (*Verkehr*) to cease; (*Arbeit*) to stop, cease; (*Waffen*) to be laid down; (*begraben sein*) to lie, be buried
Ruhe- *zW*: **Ruhepause** *f* break; **Ruhestand** *m* retirement; **Ruhestätte** *f*: **letzte Ruhestätte** final resting place; **Ruhestörung** *f* breach of the peace; **Ruhetag** *m* closing day
ruhig ['ru:ɪç] *adj* quiet; (*bewegungslos*) still; (*Hand*) steady; (*gelassen, friedlich*) calm; (*Gewissen*) clear; **tu das ~** feel free to do that; **etw ~ mit ansehen** (*gleichgültig*) to stand by and watch sth; **du könntest ~ mal etwas für mich tun!** it's about time you did something for me!
Ruhm [ru:m] (**-(e)s**) *m* fame, glory
rühmen ['ry:mən] *vt* to praise ▷ *vr* to boast
Ruhr [ru:r] (**-**) *f* dysentery
Rührei ['ry:r|aɪ] *nt* scrambled egg
rühren *vt* (*lit, fig*) to move, stir (*auch* KOCH) ▷ *vr* (*lit, fig*) to move, stir ▷ *vi*: **~ von** to come *od* stem from; **~ an** *+akk* to touch; (*fig*) to touch on
rührend *adj* touching, moving; **das ist ~ von Ihnen** that is sweet of you
Ruhrgebiet *nt* Ruhr (area)
rührig *adj* active, lively
rührselig *adj* sentimental, emotional
Rührung *f* emotion
Ruin [ru'i:n] (**-s**) *m* ruin; **vor dem ~ stehen** to be on the brink *od* verge of ruin
Ruine (**-, -n**) *f* (*lit, fig*) ruin
ruinieren [rui'ni:rən] *vt* to ruin
rülpsen ['rʏlpsən] *vi* to burp, belch
Rum [rʊm] (**-s, -s**) *m* rum
Rumäne [ru'mɛ:nə] (**-n, -n**) *m* Romanian
Rumänien (**-s**) *nt* Romania
rumänisch *adj* Romanian
Rumpf [rʊmpf] (**-(e)s, ⸚e**) *m* trunk, torso; (*Aviat*) fuselage; (*Naut*) hull
rümpfen ['rʏmpfən] *vt* (*Nase*) to turn up
rund [rʊnt] *adj* round ▷ *adv* (*etwa*) around; **~ um etw** round sth; **jetzt gehts ~** (*umg*) this is where the fun starts; **wenn er das erfährt, gehts ~** (*umg*) there'll be a to-do when he finds out; **Rundbrief** *m* circular
Runde ['rʊndə] (**-, -n**) *f* round; (*in Rennen*) lap; (*Gesellschaft*) circle; **die ~ machen** to do the rounds; (*herumgegeben werden*) to be passed round; **über die ~n kommen** (*Sport, fig*) to pull through; **eine ~ spendieren** *od* **schmeißen** (*umg: Getränke*) to stand a round
Rundfahrt *f* (round) trip
Rundfunk ['rʊntfʊŋk] (**-(e)s**) *m* broadcasting; (*bes Hörfunk*) radio; (*Rundfunkanstalt*) broadcasting corporation; **im ~** on the radio; **Rundfunkgerät** *nt* radio set; **Rundfunksendung** *f* broadcast, radio programme (*Brit*) *od* program (*US*)
Rund- *zW*: **rundlich** *adj* plump, rounded; **Rundreise** *f* round trip; **Rundschreiben** *nt* (*Comm*) circular
runter ['rʊntər] (*umg*) *adv* = **herunter; hinunter**
Runzel ['rʊntsəl] (**-, -n**) *f* wrinkle
runzelig, runzlig *adj* wrinkled
runzeln *vt* to wrinkle; **die Stirn ~** to frown
rupfen ['rʊpfən] *vt* to pluck
ruppig ['rʊpɪç] *adj* rough, gruff
Rüsche ['ry:ʃə] (**-, -n**) *f* frill
Ruß [ru:s] (**-es**) *m* soot
Russe ['rʊsə] (**-n, -n**) *m* Russian
Rüssel ['rʏsəl] (**-s, -**) *m* snout; (*Elefantenrüssel*) trunk
rußig *adj* sooty
Russin *f* Russian
russisch *adj* Russian; **~e Eier** (*Koch*) egg(s) mayonnaise
Russland (**-s**) *nt* Russia
rustikal [rʊsti'ka:l] *adj*: **sich ~ einrichten** to furnish one's home in a rustic style
Rüstung ['rʏstʊŋ] *f* preparation; (*Mil*) arming; (*Ritterrüstung*) armour (*Brit*), armor (*US*); (*Waffen etc*) armaments *pl*; **Rüstungswettlauf** *m* arms race
Rute ['ru:tə] (**-, -n**) *f* rod, switch
Rutsch [rʊtʃ] (**-(e)s, -e**) *m* slide; (*Erdrutsch*) landslide; **guten ~!** (*umg*) have a good New Year!; **Rutschbahn** *f* slide
rutschen *vi* to slide; (*ausrutschen*) to slip; **auf dem Stuhl hin und her ~** to fidget around on one's chair
rutschfest *adj* non-slip
rutschig *adj* slippery
rütteln ['rʏtəln] *vt, vi* to shake, jolt; **daran ist nicht zu ~** (*fig: umg: an Grundsätzen*) there's no doubt about that

Ss

S[1], **s**[1] [ɛs] *nt* S, s; **S wie Samuel** ≈ S for Sugar
S[2] [ɛs] *abk* (= *Süden*) S; (= *Seite*) p; (= *Schilling*) S
s[2] *abk* (= *Sekunde*) sec.; (= *siehe*) v., vid.
Saal [za:l] (**-(e)s, Säle**) *m* hall; (*für Sitzungen etc*) room
Saarland ['za:rlant] (**-s**) *nt* Saarland
Saat [za:t] (**-, -en**) *f* seed; (*Pflanzen*) crop; (*Säen*) sowing
Säbel ['zɛ:bəl] (**-s, -**) *m* sabre (*Brit*), saber (*US*)
Sabotage [zabo'ta:ʒə] (**-, -n**) *f* sabotage
sabotieren [zabo'ti:rən] *vt* to sabotage
Sachbearbeiter, in *m(f)*: **~ (für)** (*Beamter*) official in charge (of)
sachdienlich *adj* relevant, helpful
Sache ['zaxə] (**-, -n**) *f* thing; (*Angelegenheit*) affair, business; (*Frage*) matter; (*Pflicht*) task; (*Thema*) subject; (*Jur*) case; (*Aufgabe*) job; (*Ideal*) cause; (*umg: km/h*): **mit 60/100 ~n** ≈ at 40/60 (mph); **ich habe mir die ~ anders vorgestellt** I had imagined things differently; **er versteht seine ~** he knows what he's doing; **das ist so eine ~** (*umg*) it's a bit tricky; **mach keine ~n!** (*umg*) don't be daft!; **bei der ~ bleiben** (*bei Diskussion*) to keep to the point; **bei der ~ sein** to be with it (*umg*); **das ist ~ der Polizei** this is a matter for the police; **zur ~** to the point; **das ist eine runde ~** that is well-balanced *od* rounded-off
Sach- *zW*: **sachkundig** *adj* (well-)informed; **sich sachkundig machen** to inform oneself; **sachlich** *adj* matter-of-fact; (*Kritik etc*) objective; (*Irrtum, Angabe*) factual; **bleiben Sie bitte sachlich** don't get carried away (*umg*); (*nicht persönlich werden*) please stay objective
sächlich ['zɛxlɪç] *adj* neuter
Sachschaden *m* material damage
Sachsen (**-s**) *nt* Saxony; **Sachsen-Anhalt** (**-s**) *nt* Saxony Anhalt
sächsisch ['zɛksɪʃ] *adj* Saxon
sacht, **sachte** *adv* softly, gently
Sach- *zW*: **Sachverständige, r** *f(m)* expert; **Sachzwang** *m* force of circumstances
Sack [zak] (**-(e)s, ¨-e**) *m* sack; (*aus Papier, Plastik*) bag; (*Anat, Zool*) sac; (*umg!: Hoden*) balls *pl* (!); (*: Kerl, Bursche*) bastard (!); **mit ~ und Pack** (*umg*) with bag and baggage
Sackgasse *f* cul-de-sac, dead-end street (*US*)
Sadismus [za'dɪsmʊs] *m* sadism
Sadist, in [za'dɪst(ɪn)] *m(f)* sadist; **sadistisch** *adj* sadistic
säen ['zɛ:ən] *vt, vi* to sow; **dünn gesät** (*fig*) thin on the ground, few and far between
Safe [ze:f] (**-s, -s**) *m od nt* safe
Saft [zaft] (**-(e)s, ¨-e**) *m* juice; (*Bot*) sap; **ohne ~ und Kraft** (*fig*) wishy-washy (*umg*), effete
saftig *adj* juicy; (*Grün*) lush; (*umg: Rechnung, Ohrfeige*) hefty; (*Brief, Antwort*) hard-hitting
Sage ['za:gə] (**-, -n**) *f* saga
Säge ['zɛ:gə] (**-, -n**) *f* saw; **Sägemehl** *nt* sawdust
sagen ['za:gən] *vt, vi*: **(jdm etw) ~** to say (sth to sb), tell (sb sth); **unter uns gesagt** between you and me (and the gatepost (*hum umg*)); **lass dir das gesagt sein** take it from me; **das hat nichts zu ~** that doesn't mean anything; **sagt dir der Name etwas?** does the name mean anything to you?; **das ist nicht gesagt** that's by no means certain; **sage und schreibe** (whether you) believe it or not
sägen *vt, vi* to saw; (*hum: umg: schnarchen*) to snore, saw wood (*US*)
sagenhaft *adj* legendary; (*umg*) great, smashing
sah *etc* [za:] *vb siehe* **sehen**
Sahara [za'ha:ra] *f* Sahara (Desert)
Sahne ['za:nə] (**-**) *f* cream
Saison [zɛ'zõ:] (**-, -s**) *f* season
Saisonarbeiter *m* seasonal worker
Saite ['zaɪtə] (**-, -n**) *f* string; **andere ~n aufziehen** (*umg*) to get tough
Saiteninstrument *nt* string(ed) instrument
Sakko ['zako] (**-s, -s**) *m od nt* jacket
Sakrament [zakra'mɛnt] *nt* sacrament
Sakristei [zakrɪs'taɪ] *f* sacristy
Salat [za'la:t] (**-(e)s, -e**) *m* salad; (*Kopfsalat*) lettuce; **da haben wir den ~!** (*umg*) now we're in a fine mess!; **Salatsoße** *f* salad dressing
Salbe ['zalbə] (**-, -n**) *f* ointment
Salbei ['zalbaɪ] (**-s**) *m* sage
salben *vt* to anoint
salbungsvoll *adj* unctuous
Saldo ['zaldo] (**-s, Salden**) *m* balance
Salmiak [zalmi'ak] (**-s**) *m* sal ammoniac; **Salmiakgeist** *m* liquid ammonia

salopp [za'lɔp] *adj* casual; (*Manieren*) slovenly; (*Sprache*) slangy
Salpeter [zal'pe:tər] (**-s**) *m* saltpetre (*Brit*), saltpeter (*US*); **Salpetersäure** *f* nitric acid
Salz [zalts] (**-es, -e**) *nt* salt
salzen *unreg vt* to salt
salzig *adj* salty
Salz- *zW*: **Salzkartoffeln** *pl* boiled potatoes *pl*; **Salzsäure** *f* hydrochloric acid; **Salzstange** *f* pretzel stick; **Salzstreuer** *m* salt cellar; **Salzwasser** *nt* salt water
Sambia ['zambia] (**-s**) *nt* Zambia
Samen ['za:mən] (**-s, -**) *m* seed; (*Anat*) sperm
Sammel- *zW*: **Sammelband** *m* anthology; **Sammelbegriff** *m* collective term; **Sammelbestellung** *f* collective order
sammeln *vt* to collect ▷ *vr* to assemble, gather; (*sich konzentrieren*) to collect one's thoughts
Sammlung ['zamlʊŋ] *f* collection; (*Konzentration*) composure
Samstag ['zamsta:k] *m* Saturday; *siehe auch* **Dienstag**
samstags *adv* (on) Saturdays
samt [zamt] *präp +dat* (along) with, together with; **~ und sonders** each and every one (of them); **Samt** (**-(e)s, -e**) *m* velvet; **in Samt und Seide** (*liter*) in silks and satins
Sand [zant] (**-(e)s, -e**) *m* sand; **das/die gibts wie ~ am Meer** (*umg*) there are piles of it/heaps of them; **im ~e verlaufen** to peter out
Sandale [zan'da:lə] (**-, -n**) *f* sandal
Sandbank *f* sandbank
sandig ['zandıç] *adj* sandy
Sand- *zW*: **Sandkasten** *m* sandpit; **Sandkuchen** *m* Madeira cake; **Sandpapier** *nt* sandpaper; **Sandstein** *m* sandstone; **sandstrahlen** *vt, vi untr* to sandblast
sandte *etc* ['zantə] *vb siehe* **senden**
Sanduhr *f* hourglass; (*Eieruhr*) egg timer
sanft [zanft] *adj* soft, gentle; **sanftmütig** *adj* gentle, meek
sang *etc* [zaŋ] *vb siehe* **singen**
Sänger, in ['zɛŋər(ın)] (**-s, -**) *m(f)* singer
sanieren [za'ni:rən] *vt* to redevelop; (*Betrieb*) to make financially sound; (*Haus*) to renovate ▷ *vr* to line one's pockets; (*Unternehmen*) to become financially sound
sanitär [zani'tɛ:r] *adj* sanitary; **~e Anlagen** sanitation *sing*
Sanitäter [zani'tɛ:tər] (**-s, -**) *m* first-aid attendant; (*in Krankenwagen*) ambulance man; (*Mil*) (medical) orderly
sank *etc* [zaŋk] *vb siehe* **sinken**
Sanktion [zaŋktsi'o:n] *f* sanction
sanktionieren [zaŋktsio'ni:rən] *vt* to sanction
sann *etc* [zan] *vb siehe* **sinnen**
Saphir ['za:fi:r] (**-s, -e**) *m* sapphire
Sardelle [zar'dɛlə] *f* anchovy
Sardine [zar'di:nə] *f* sardine
Sardinien [zar'di:niən] (**-s**) *nt* Sardinia
Sarg [zark] (**-(e)s, ⸚e**) *m* coffin
Sarkasmus [zar'kasmʊs] *m* sarcasm
sarkastisch [zar'kastıʃ] *adj* sarcastic
saß *etc* [zas] *vb siehe* **sitzen**
Satan ['za:tan] (**-s, -e**) *m* Satan; (*fig*) devil
Satellit [zatɛ'li:t] (**-en, -en**) *m* satellite
Satelliten- *zW*: **Satellitenfernsehen** *nt* satellite television; **Satellitenfoto** *nt* satellite picture; **Satellitenschüssel** *f* satellite dish
Satire [za'ti:rə] (**-, -n**) *f*: **~ (auf** *+akk***)** satire (on)
satirisch [za'ti:rıʃ] *adj* satirical
satt [zat] *adj* full; (*Farbe*) rich, deep; (*blasiert, übersättigt*) well-fed; (*selbstgefällig*) smug; **jdn/etw ~ sein** to be fed-up with sb/sth; **sich ~ essen** to eat one's fill; **~ machen** to be filling; *siehe auch* **satthaben; satthören; sattsehen**
Sattel ['zatəl] (**-s, ⸚**) *m* saddle; (*Berg*) ridge
satteln *vt* to saddle
sättigen ['zɛtıgən] *vt* to satisfy; (*Chem*) to saturate
Satz [zats] (**-es, ⸚e**) *m* (*Gram*) sentence; (*Nebensatz, Adverbialsatz*) clause; (*Theorem*) theorem; (*der gesetzte Text*) type; (*Mus*) movement; (*Comput*) record; (*Briefmarken, Zusammengehöriges, Tennis*) set; (*Kaffeesatz*) grounds *pl*; (*Bodensatz*) dregs *pl*; (*Spesensatz*) allowance; (*Comm*) rate; (*Sprung*) jump
Satzung *f* statute, rule; (*Firma*) (memorandum and) articles of association
Satzzeichen *nt* punctuation mark
Sau [zaʊ] (**-, Säue**) *f* sow; (*umg*) dirty pig; **die ~ rauslassen** (*fig: umg*) to let it all hang out
sauber ['zaʊbər] *adj* clean; (*anständig*) honest, upstanding; (*umg: großartig*) fantastic, great; (*: ironisch*) fine; **~ sein** (*Kind*) to be (potty-)trained; (*Hund etc*) to be house-trained; **~ halten** to keep clean; **~ machen** to clean; **Sauberkeit** *f* cleanness; (*einer Person*) cleanliness
säuberlich ['zɔʏbərlıç] *adv* neatly
säubern *vt* to clean; (*Pol etc*) to purge
Säuberung *f* cleaning; purge
Sauce ['zo:sə] (**-, -n**) *f* = **Soße**
Saudi- [zaʊdi-] *zW*: **Saudi-Arabien** (**-s**) *nt* Saudi Arabia
sauer ['zaʊər] *adj* sour; (*Chem*) acid; (*umg*) cross; **saurer Regen** acid rain; **~ werden** (*Milch, Sahne*) to go sour, turn; **jdm das Leben ~ machen** to make sb's life a misery
Sauerei [zaʊə'raı] (*umg*) *f* rotten state of affairs, scandal; (*Schmutz etc*) mess; (*Unanständigkeit*) obscenity
Sauerkraut (**-(e)s**) *nt* sauerkraut, pickled cabbage
Sauer- *zW*: **Sauermilch** *f* sour milk; **Sauerstoff** *m* oxygen; **Sauerstoffgerät** *nt* breathing apparatus
saufen ['zaʊfən] *unreg* (*umg*) *vt, vi* to drink, booze; **wie ein Loch ~** (*umg*) to drink like a fish
Säufer, in ['zɔʏfər(ın)] (**-s, -**) (*umg*) *m(f)* boozer, drunkard

saugen ['zaʊgən] *unreg vt, vi* to suck
Sauger ['zaʊgər] (**-s, -**) *m* dummy (*Brit*), pacifier (*US*); (*auf Flasche*) teat; (*Staubsauger*) vacuum cleaner, hoover® (*Brit*)
Säugetier *nt* mammal
Säugling *m* infant, baby
Säule ['zɔʏlə] (**-, -n**) *f* column, pillar
Säulengang *m* arcade
Saum [zaʊm] (**-(e)s, Säume**) *m* hem; (*Naht*) seam
säumen ['zɔʏmən] *vt* to hem; to seam ▷ *vi* to delay, hesitate
Sauna ['zaʊna] (**-, -s**) *f* sauna
Säure ['zɔʏrə] (**-, -n**) *f* acid; (*Geschmack*) sourness, acidity
sausen ['zaʊzən] *vi* to blow; (*umg: eilen*) to rush; (*Ohren*) to buzz; **etw ~ lassen** (*umg*) not to bother with sth; **Saustall** (*umg*) *m* pigsty
Saxofon, Saxophon [zakso'fo:n] (**-s, -e**) *nt* saxophone
S-Bahn *f abk* (= *Schnellbahn*) *high-speed suburban railway or railroad* (*US*)
schäbig ['ʃɛ:bɪç] *adj* shabby; (*Mensch*) mean; **Schäbigkeit** *f* shabbiness
Schablone [ʃa'blo:nə] (**-, -n**) *f* stencil; (*Muster*) pattern; (*fig*) convention
Schach [ʃax] (**-s, -s**) *nt* chess; (*Stellung*) check; **im ~ stehen** to be in check; **jdn in ~ halten** (*fig*) to stall sb; **Schachbrett** *nt* chessboard
Schach- *zW*: **Schachfigur** *f* chessman; **schachmatt** *adj* checkmate; **jdn schachmatt setzen** (*lit*) to (check)mate sb; (*fig*) to snooker sb (*umg*)
Schacht [ʃaxt] (**-(e)s, ¨-e**) *m* shaft
Schachtel (**-, -n**) *f* box; (*pej: Frau*) bag, cow (*Brit*)
schade ['ʃa:də] *adj* a pity *od* shame ▷ *interj* (what a) pity *od* shame; **sich** *dat* **für etw zu ~ sein** to consider o.s. too good for sth; **um sie ist es nicht ~** she's no great loss
Schädel ['ʃɛ:dəl] (**-s, -**) *m* skull; **einen dicken ~ haben** (*fig: umg*) to be stubborn; **Schädelbruch** *m* fractured skull
Schaden (**-s, ¨**) *m* damage; (*Verletzung*) injury; (*Nachteil*) disadvantage; **zu ~ kommen** to suffer; (*physisch*) to be injured; **jdm ~ zufügen** to harm sb
schaden ['ʃa:dən] *vi +dat* to hurt; **einer Sache ~** to damage sth
Schaden- *zW*: **Schadenersatz** *m* compensation, damages *pl*; **Schadenersatz leisten** to pay compensation; **Schadenfreude** *f* malicious delight
schadhaft ['ʃa:thaft] *adj* faulty, damaged
schädigen ['ʃɛdɪgən] *vt* to damage; (*Person*) to do harm to, harm
schädlich *adj*: **~ (für)** harmful (to); **Schädlichkeit** *f* harmfulness
Schädlingsbekämpfungsmittel *nt* pesticide
Schadstoff (**-(e)s, -e**) *m* pollutant; **schadstoffarm** *adj* low in pollutants
Schaf [ʃa:f] (**-(e)s, -e**) *nt* sheep; (*umg: Dummkopf*) twit (*Brit*), dope; **Schafbock** *m* ram
Schäfchen ['ʃɛ:fçən] *nt* lamb; **sein ~ ins Trockene bringen** (*Sprichwort*) to see o.s. all right (*umg*); **Schäfchenwolken** *pl* cirrus clouds *pl*
Schäfer ['ʃɛ:fər] (**-s, -**) *m* shepherd; **Schäferhund** *m* Alsatian (dog) (*Brit*), German shepherd (dog) (*US*)
Schaffen ['ʃafən] (**-s**) *nt* (creative) activity
schaffen[1] *unreg vt* to create; (*Platz*) to make; **sich** *dat* **etw ~** to get o.s. sth; **dafür ist er wie ge~** he's just made for it
schaffen[2] ['ʃafən] *vt* (*erreichen*) to manage, do; (*erledigen*) to finish; (*Prüfung*) to pass; (*transportieren*) to take ▷ *vi* (*tun*) to do; (*umg: arbeiten*) to work; **das ist nicht zu ~** that can't be done; **das hat mich geschafft** it took it out of me; (*nervlich*) it got on top of me; **ich habe damit nichts zu ~** that has nothing to do with me; **jdm (schwer) zu ~ machen** (*zusetzen*) to cause sb (a lot of) trouble; (*bekümmern*) to worry sb (a lot); **sich** *dat* **an etw** *dat* **zu ~ machen** to busy o.s. with sth
Schaffner, in ['ʃafnər(ɪn)] (**-s, -**) *m(f)* (*Busschaffner*) conductor, conductress; (*Eisenb*) guard (*Brit*), conductor (*US*)
Schakal [ʃa'ka:l] (**-s, -e**) *m* jackal
Schäker, in ['ʃɛ:kər(ɪn)] (**-s, -**) *m(f)* flirt; (*Witzbold*) joker
schäkern *vi* to flirt; to joke
Schal [ʃa:l] (**-s, -s** *od* **-e**) *m* scarf
schal *adj* flat; (*fig*) insipid
Schälchen ['ʃɛ:lçən] *nt* bowl
Schale ['ʃa:lə] (**-, -n**) *f* skin; (*abgeschält*) peel; (*Nussschale, Muschelschale, Eierschale*) shell; (*Geschirr*) dish, bowl; **sich in ~ werfen** (*umg*) to get dressed up
schälen ['ʃɛ:lən] *vt* to peel; to shell ▷ *vr* to peel
Schall [ʃal] (**-(e)s, -e**) *m* sound; **Name ist ~ und Rauch** what's in a name?; **Schalldämpfer** *m* (*Aut*) silencer (*Brit*), muffler (*US*); **schalldicht** *adj* soundproof
schallen *vi* to (re)sound
schallend *adj* resounding, loud
Schallplatte *f* record
schalt *etc* [ʃalt] *vb siehe* **schelten**
Schaltbild *nt* circuit diagram
Schaltbrett *nt* switchboard
schalten ['ʃaltən] *vt* to switch, turn ▷ *vi* (*Aut*) to change (gear); (*umg: begreifen*) to catch on; (*reagieren*) to react; **in Reihe/parallel ~** (*Elek*) to connect in series/in parallel; **~ und walten** to do as one pleases
Schalter (**-s, -**) *m* counter; (*an Gerät*) switch; **Schalterbeamte, r** *m* counter clerk; **Schalterstunden** *pl* hours of business *pl*
Schalt- *zW*: **Schalthebel** *m* switch; (*Aut*) gear lever (*Brit*), gearshift (*US*); **Schaltjahr** *nt* leap year; **Schaltkreis** *m* (switching) circuit
Schaltung *f* switching; (*Elek*) circuit; (*Aut*) gear change
Scham [ʃa:m] (**-**) *f* shame; (*Schamgefühl*)

modesty; (*Organe*) private parts *pl*
schämen ['ʃɛ:mən] *vr* to be ashamed;
schamlos *adj* shameless; (*unanständig*) indecent; (*Lüge*) brazen, barefaced
Schande ['ʃandə] (-) *f* disgrace; **zu meiner ~ muss ich gestehen, dass ...** to my shame I have to admit that ...
schänden ['ʃɛndən] *vt* to violate
schändlich ['ʃɛntlıç] *adj* disgraceful, shameful
Schändung *f* violation, defilement
Schanktisch *m* bar
Schanze ['ʃantsə] (**-, -n**) *f* (*Mil*) fieldwork, earthworks *pl*; (*Sprungschanze*) ski jump
Schar [ʃa:r] (**-, -en**) *f* band, company; (*Vögel*) flock; (*Menge*) crowd; **in ~en** in droves
scharf [ʃarf] *adj* sharp; (*Verstand, Augen*) keen; (*Kälte, Wind*) biting; (*Protest*) fierce; (*Ton*) piercing, shrill; (*Essen*) hot, spicy; (*Munition*) live; (*Maßnahmen*) severe; (*Bewachung*) close, tight; (*Geruch, Geschmack*) pungent, acrid; (*umg: geil*) randy (*Brit*), horny; (*Film*) sexy, blue *attrib*; **~ nachdenken** to think hard; **~ aufpassen/zuhören** to pay close attention/listen closely; **etw ~ einstellen** (*Bild, Diaprojektor etc*) to bring sth into focus; **mit ~em Blick** (*fig*) with penetrating insight; **auf etw** *akk* **~ sein** (*umg*) to be keen on sth; **~e Sachen** (*umg*) hard stuff
Schärfe ['ʃɛrfə] (**-, -n**) *f* sharpness; (*Strenge*) rigour (*Brit*), rigor (*US*); (*an Kamera, Fernsehen*) focus
schärfen *vt* to sharpen
Scharf- *zW*: **scharfmachen** (*umg*) *vt* to stir up; **Scharfrichter** *m* executioner; **Scharfschütze** *m* marksman, sharpshooter; **Scharfsinn** *m* astuteness, shrewdness; **scharfsinnig** *adj* astute, shrewd
Scharnier [ʃar'ni:r] (**-s, -e**) *nt* hinge
Schärpe ['ʃɛrpə] (**-, -n**) *f* sash
scharren ['ʃarən] *vt, vi* to scrape, scratch
Schaschlik ['ʃaʃlık] (**-s, -s**) *m od nt* (shish) kebab
Schatten ['ʃatən] (**-s, -**) *m* shadow; (*schattige Stelle*) shade; **jdn/etw in den ~ stellen** (*fig*) to put sb/sth in the shade
Schatten- *zW*: **Schattenriss** *m* silhouette; **Schattenseite** *f* shady side; (*von Planeten*) dark side; (*fig: Nachteil*) drawback
schattieren [ʃa'ti:rən] *vt, vi* to shade
schattig ['ʃatıç] *adj* shady
Schatulle [ʃa'tʊlə] (**-, -n**) *f* casket; (*Geldschatulle*) coffer
Schatz [ʃats] (**-es, ⸚e**) *m* treasure; (*Person*) darling
schätzbar ['ʃɛtsba:r] *adj* assessable
Schätzchen *nt* darling, love
schätzen *vt* (*abschätzen*) to estimate; (*Gegenstand*) to value; (*würdigen*) to value, esteem; (*vermuten*) to reckon; **etw zu ~ wissen** to appreciate sth; **sich glücklich ~** to consider o.s. lucky; **~ lernen** to learn to appreciate
Schätzung *f* estimate; estimation; valuation; **nach meiner ~ ...** I reckon that ...
schätzungsweise *adv* (*ungefähr*) approximately; (*so vermutet man*) it is thought
Schau [ʃaʊ] (-) *f* show; (*Ausstellung*) display, exhibition; **etw zur ~ stellen** to make a show of sth, show sth off; **eine ~ abziehen** (*umg*) to put on a show; **Schaubild** *nt* diagram
Schauder ['ʃaʊdər] (**-s, -**) *m* shudder; (*wegen Kälte*) shiver; **schauderhaft** *adj* horrible
schaudern *vi* to shudder; (*wegen Kälte*) to shiver
schauen ['ʃaʊən] *vi* to look; **da schau her!** well, well!
Schauer ['ʃaʊər] (**-s, -**) *m* (*Regenschauer*) shower; (*Schreck*) shudder; **schauerlich** *adj* horrific, spine-chilling
Schaufel ['ʃaʊfəl] (**-, -n**) *f* shovel; (*Kehrichtschaufel*) dustpan; (*von Turbine*) vane; (*Naut*) paddle; (*Tech*) scoop
schaufeln *vt* to shovel; (*Grab, Grube*) to dig ▷ *vi* to shovel
Schaufenster *nt* shop window; **Schaufensterauslage** *f* window display; **Schaufensterbummel** *m* window-shopping (expedition)
Schaukel ['ʃaʊkəl] (**-, -n**) *f* swing
schaukeln *vi* to swing, rock ▷ *vt* to rock; **wir werden das Kind** *od* **das schon ~** (*fig: umg*) we'll manage it
Schaukelpferd *nt* rocking horse
Schaukelstuhl *m* rocking chair
Schaum [ʃaʊm] (**-(e)s, Schäume**) *m* foam; (*Seifenschaum*) lather; (*von Getränken*) froth; (*von Bier*) head
schäumen ['ʃɔʏmən] *vi* to foam
Schaumgummi *m* foam (rubber)
schaumig *adj* frothy, foamy
Schaum- *zW*: **Schaumschlägerei** *f* (*fig: umg*) hot air; **Schaumwein** *m* sparkling wine
Schauplatz *m* scene
schaurig *adj* horrific, dreadful
Schauspiel *nt* spectacle; (*Theat*) play
Schauspieler, in *m(f)* actor, actress
schauspielern *vi untr* to act
Scheck [ʃɛk] (**-s, -s**) *m* cheque (*Brit*), check (*US*); **Scheckbuch** *nt*, **Scheckheft** *nt* cheque book (*Brit*), check book (*US*)
Scheckkarte *f* cheque (*Brit*) *od* check (*US*) card, banker's card
scheel [ʃe:l] (*umg*) *adj* dirty; **jdn ~ ansehen** to give sb a dirty look
scheffeln ['ʃɛfəln] *vt* to amass
Scheibe ['ʃaıbə] (**-, -n**) *f* disc (*Brit*), disk (*US*); (*Brot etc*) slice; (*Glasscheibe*) pane; (*Mil*) target; (*Eishockey*) puck; (*Töpferscheibe*) wheel; (*umg: Schallplatte*) disc (*Brit*), disk (*US*); **von ihm könntest du dir eine ~ abschneiden** (*fig: umg*) you could take a leaf out of his book
Scheiben- *zW*: **Scheibenbremse** *f* (*Aut*) disc brake; **Scheibenwaschanlage** *f* (*Aut*) windscreen (*Brit*) *od* windshield (*US*) washers *pl*; **Scheibenwischer** *m* (*Aut*) windscreen (*Brit*)

od windshield (*US*) wiper

Scheich [ʃaɪç] (**-s, -e** *od* **-s**) *m* sheik(h)

Scheide ['ʃaɪdə] (**-, -n**) *f* sheath; (*Anat*) vagina

scheiden *unreg vt* to separate; (*Ehe*) to dissolve ▷ *vi* to depart; (*sich trennen*) to part ▷ *vr* (*Wege*) to divide; (*Meinungen*) to diverge; **sich ~ lassen** to get a divorce; **von dem Moment an waren wir (zwei) geschiedene Leute** (*umg*) after that it was the parting of the ways for us; **aus dem Leben ~** to depart this life

Scheidung *f* (*Ehescheidung*) divorce; **die ~ einreichen** to file a petition for divorce

Schein [ʃaɪn] (**-(e)s, -e**) *m* light; (*Anschein*) appearance; (*Geldschein*) (bank)note; (*Bescheinigung*) certificate; **den ~ wahren** to keep up appearances; **etw zum ~ tun** to pretend to do sth, make a pretence (*Brit*) *od* pretense (*US*) of doing sth

scheinen *unreg vi* to shine; (*Anschein haben*) to seem

Schein- *zW*: **scheinheilig** *adj* hypocritical; **Scheinwerfer** (**-s, -**) *m* floodlight; (*Theat*) spotlight; (*Suchscheinwerfer*) searchlight; (*Aut*) headlight

Scheiße ['ʃaɪsə] (**-**) (*umg!*) *f* shit (!)

Scheit [ʃaɪt] (**-(e)s, -e** *od* **-er**) *nt* log

Scheitel ['ʃaɪtəl] (**-s, -**) *m* top; (*Haar*) parting (*Brit*), part (*US*)

scheiteln *vt* to part

Scheitelpunkt *m* zenith, apex

scheitern ['ʃaɪtərn] *vi* to fail

Schellfisch ['ʃɛlfɪʃ] *m* haddock

Schelm [ʃɛlm] (**-(e)s, -e**) *m* rogue

schelmisch *adj* mischievous, roguish

Schelte ['ʃɛltə] (**-, -n**) *f* scolding

schelten *unreg vt* to scold

Schema ['ʃe:ma] (**-s, -s** *od* **-ta**) *nt* scheme, plan; (*Darstellung*) schema; **nach ~ F** quite mechanically

schematisch [ʃe'ma:tɪʃ] *adj* schematic; (*pej*) mechanical

Schemel ['ʃe:məl] (**-s, -**) *m* (foot)stool

Schenkel ['ʃɛŋkəl] (**-s, -**) *m* thigh; (*Math: von Winkel*) side

schenken ['ʃɛŋkən] *vt* (*lit, fig*) to give; (*Getränk*) to pour; **ich möchte nichts geschenkt haben!** (*lit*) I don't want any presents!; (*fig: bevorzugt werden*) I don't want any special treatment!; **sich** *dat* **etw ~** (*umg*) to skip sth; **jdm etw ~** (*erlassen*) to let sb off sth; **ihm ist nie etwas geschenkt worden** (*fig*) he never had it easy; **das ist geschenkt!** (*billig*) that's a giveaway!; (*nichts wert*) that's worthless!

Schenkung *f* gift

Scherbe ['ʃɛrbə] (**-, -n**) *f* broken piece, fragment; (*archäologisch*) potsherd

Schere ['ʃe:rə] (**-, -n**) *f* scissors *pl*; (*groß*) shears *pl*; (*Zool*) pincer; (*von Hummer, Krebs etc*) pincer, claw; **eine ~** a pair of scissors

scheren *unreg vt* to cut; (*Schaf*) to shear; (*stören*) to bother ▷ *vr* (*sich kümmern*) to care; **scher dich (zum Teufel)!** get lost!

Schererei [ʃe:rə'raɪ] (*umg*) *f* bother, trouble

Scherz [ʃɛrts] (**-es, -e**) *m* joke; fun; **scherzen** *vi* to joke; (*albern*) to banter; **Scherzfrage** *f* conundrum; **scherzhaft** *adj* joking, jocular

Scheu [ʃɔʏ] (**-**) *f* shyness; (*Ehrfurcht*) awe; (*Angst*): **~ (vor** *+dat*) fear (of)

scheu [ʃɔʏ] *adj* shy

scheuen *vr*: **sich ~ vor** *+dat* to be afraid of, shrink from ▷ *vt* to shun ▷ *vi* (*Pferd*) to shy; **weder Mühe noch Kosten ~** to spare neither trouble nor expense

scheuern *vt* to scour; (*mit Bürste*) to scrub ▷ *vr*: **sich** *akk* **(wund) ~** to chafe o.s.; **jdm eine ~** (*umg*) to clout sb one

Scheuklappe *f* blinker

Scheune ['ʃɔʏnə] (**-, -n**) *f* barn

Scheusal ['ʃɔʏza:l] (**-s, -e**) *nt* monster

scheußlich ['ʃɔʏslɪç] *adj* dreadful, frightful: **Scheußlichkeit** *f* dreadfulness

Schi [ʃi:] *m* = **Ski**

Schicht [ʃɪçt] (**-, -en**) *f* layer; (*Klasse*) class, level; (*in Fabrik etc*) shift; **Schichtarbeit** *f* shift work

schichten *vt* to layer, stack

schick [ʃɪk] *adj* = **chic**

schicken *vt* to send ▷ *vr*: **sich ~ (in** *+akk*) to resign o.s. (to) ▷ *vb unpers* (*anständig sein*) to be fitting

schicklich *adj* proper, fitting

Schicksal (**-s, -e**) *nt* fate

Schicksalsschlag *m* great misfortune, blow

Schiebedach *nt* (*Aut*) sunroof, sunshine roof

schieben ['ʃi:bən] *unreg vt* (*auch Drogen*) to push; (*Schuld*) to put; (*umg: handeln mit*) to traffic in; **die Schuld auf jdn ~** to put the blame on (to) sb; **etw vor sich** *dat* **her ~** (*fig*) to put sth off

Schiebetür *f* sliding door

Schiebung *f* fiddle; **das war doch ~** (*umg*) that was rigged *od* a fix

schied *etc* [ʃi:t] *vb siehe* **scheiden**

Schieds- *zW*: **Schiedsgericht** *nt* court of arbitration; **Schiedsrichter** *m* referee, umpire; (*Schlichter*) arbitrator

schief [ʃi:f] *adj* crooked; (*Ebene*) sloping; (*Turm*) leaning; (*Winkel*) oblique; (*Blick*) wry; (*Vergleich*) distorted ▷ *adv* crookedly; (*ansehen*) askance; **auf die ~e Bahn geraten** (*fig*) to leave the straight and narrow; **etw ~ stellen** to slope sth; *siehe auch* **schiefgehen; schiefliegen**

Schiefer ['ʃi:fər] (**-s, -**) *m* slate; **Schieferdach** *nt* slate roof; **Schiefertafel** *f* (child's) slate

schiefgehen (*umg: unreg*) *vi* to go wrong; **es wird schon ~!** (*hum*) it'll be OK

schieflachen (*umg*) *vr* to kill o.s. laughing

schielen ['ʃi:lən] *vi* to squint; **nach etw ~** (*fig*) to eye sth up

schien *etc* [ʃi:n] *vb siehe* **scheinen**

Schienbein *nt* shinbone

Schiene ['ʃi:nə] *f* rail; (*Med*) splint

schienen *vt* to put in splints

schier [ʃi:r] *adj* pure; (*fig*) sheer ▷ *adv* nearly, almost

Schießbude *f* shooting gallery
schießen ['ʃiːsən] *unreg vi* to shoot; (*Salat etc*) to run to seed ▷*vt* to shoot; (*Ball*) to kick; (*Geschoss*) to fire; **~ auf** *+akk* to shoot at; **aus dem Boden ~** (*lit, fig*) to spring *od* sprout up; **jdm durch den Kopf ~** (*fig*) to flash through sb's mind
Schießerei [ʃiːsə'raɪ] *f* shoot-out, gun battle
Schieß- *zW*: **Schießpulver** *nt* gunpowder; **Schießscharte** *f* embrasure
Schiff [ʃɪf] (**-(e)s, -e**) *nt* ship, vessel; (*Kirchenschiff*) nave
Schiff- *zW*: **Schiffbau** *m* shipbuilding; **Schiffbruch** *m* shipwreck; **Schiffbruch erleiden** (*lit*) to be shipwrecked; (*fig*) to fail; (*Unternehmen*) to founder
Schiffchen *nt* small boat; (*Weben*) shuttle; (*Mütze*) forage cap
Schiff- *zW*: **Schifffahrt** *f* shipping; (*Reise*) voyage; **Schifffahrtslinie** *f* shipping route
schiitisch *adj* Shiite
Schikane [ʃi'kaːnə] (**-, -n**) *f* harassment; dirty trick; **mit allen ~n** with all the trimmings; **das hat er aus reiner ~ gemacht** he did it out of sheer bloody-mindedness
schikanieren [ʃika'niːrən] *vt* to harass; (*Ehepartner*) to mess around; (*Mitschüler*) to bully
Schild[1] [ʃɪlt] (**-(e)s, -e**) *m* shield; (*Mützenschild*) peak, visor; **etwas im ~e führen** to be up to something
Schild[2] [ʃɪlt] (**-(e)s, -er**) *nt* sign; (*Namensschild*) nameplate; (*an Monument, Haus, Grab*) plaque; (*Etikett*) label
Schilddrüse *f* thyroid gland
schildern ['ʃɪldərn] *vt* to describe; (*Menschen etc*) to portray; (*skizzieren*) to outline
Schilderung *f* description; portrayal
Schildkröte *f* tortoise; (*Wasserschildkröte*) turtle
Schilf [ʃɪlf] (**-(e)s, -e**) *nt*, **Schilfrohr** *nt* (*Pflanze*) reed; (*Material*) reeds *pl*, rushes *pl*
schillern ['ʃɪlərn] *vi* to shimmer
schillernd *adj* iridescent; (*fig: Charakter*) enigmatic
Schilling ['ʃɪlɪŋ] (**-s, -** *od* **(Schillingstücke) -e**) (*Österr*) *m* schilling
Schimmel ['ʃɪməl] (**-s, -**) *m* mould (*Brit*), mold (*US*); (*Pferd*) white horse
schimmelig *adj* mouldy (*Brit*), moldy (*US*)
schimmeln *vi* to go mouldy (*Brit*) *od* moldy (*US*)
Schimpanse [ʃɪm'panzə] (**-n, -n**) *m* chimpanzee
schimpfen *vi* (*sich beklagen*) to grumble; (*fluchen*) to curse
Schimpfwort *nt* term of abuse
Schindel ['ʃɪndəl] (**-, -n**) *f* shingle
schinden ['ʃɪndən] *unreg vt* to maltreat, drive too hard ▷*vr*: **sich ~ (mit)** to sweat and strain (at), toil away (at); **Eindruck ~** (*umg*) to create an impression
Schinderei [ʃɪndə'raɪ] *f* grind, drudgery
Schinken ['ʃɪŋkən] (**-s, -**) *m* ham; (*gekocht und geräuchert*) gammon; (*pej: umg: Theaterstück etc*) hackneyed and clichéd play *etc*
Schippe ['ʃɪpə] (**-, -n**) *f* shovel; **jdn auf die ~ nehmen** (*fig: umg*) to pull sb's leg
schippen *vt* to shovel
Schirm [ʃɪrm] (**-(e)s, -e**) *m* (*Regenschirm*) umbrella; (*Sonnenschirm*) parasol, sunshade; (*Wandschirm, Bildschirm*) screen; (*Lampenschirm*) (lamp)shade; (*Mützenschirm*) peak; (*Pilzschirm*) cap; **Schirmbildaufnahme** *f* X-ray; **Schirmherr, in** *m(f)* patron(ess); **Schirmherrschaft** *f* patronage; **Schirmmütze** *f* peaked cap
schizophren [ʃitso'freːn] *adj* schizophrenic
Schlacht [ʃlaxt] (**-, -en**) *f* battle
schlachten *vt* to slaughter, kill
Schlachtenbummler (*umg*) *m* visiting football fan
Schlachter (**-s, -**) *m* butcher
Schlacht- *zW*: **Schlachtfeld** *nt* battlefield; **Schlachthaus** *nt*, **Schlachthof** *m* slaughterhouse, abattoir (*Brit*); **Schlachtvieh** *nt* animals *pl* kept for meat
Schlacke ['ʃlakə] (**-, -n**) *f* slag
Schlaf [ʃlaːf] (**-(e)s**) *m* sleep; **um seinen ~ kommen** *od* **gebracht werden** to lose sleep; **Schlafanzug** *m* pyjamas *pl* (*Brit*), pajamas *pl* (*US*)
Schläfe (**-, -n**) *f* (*Anat*) temple
schlafen *unreg vi* to sleep; (*umg: nicht aufpassen*) to be asleep; **~ gehen** to go to bed; **bei jdm ~** to stay overnight with sb
Schlafenszeit *f* bedtime
schlaff [ʃlaf] *adj* slack; (*Haut*) loose; (*Muskeln*) flabby; (*energielos*) limp; (*erschöpft*) exhausted
Schlafgelegenheit *f* place to sleep
Schlaf- *zW*: **Schlaflied** *nt* lullaby; **schlaflos** *adj* sleepless; **Schlaflosigkeit** *f* sleeplessness, insomnia; **Schlafmittel** *nt* sleeping drug; (*fig, ironisch*) soporific
schläfrig ['ʃlɛːfrɪç] *adj* sleepy
Schlaf- *zW*: **Schlafsaal** *m* dormitory; **Schlafsack** *m* sleeping bag
Schlaf- *zW*: **Schlaftablette** *f* sleeping pill; **Schlafwagen** *m* sleeping car, sleeper; **schlafwandeln** *vi untr* to sleepwalk; **Schlafzimmer** *nt* bedroom
Schlag [ʃlaːk] (**-(e)s, ¨-e**) *m* (*lit, fig*) blow; (*auch Med*) stroke; (*Pulsschlag, Herzschlag*) beat; (*Elek*) shock; (*Blitzschlag*) bolt, stroke; (*Glockenschlag*) chime; (*Autotür*) car door; (*umg: Portion*) helping; (*: Art*) kind, type; **Schläge** *pl* (*Tracht Prügel*) beating *sing*; **~ acht Uhr** (*umg*) on the stroke of eight; **mit einem ~** all at once; **~ auf Schlag** in rapid succession; **die haben keinen ~ getan** (*umg*) they haven't done a stroke (of work); **ich dachte, mich trifft der ~** (*umg*) I was thunderstruck; **vom gleichen ~ sein** to be cast in the same mould (*Brit*) *od* mold (*US*); (*pej*) to be tarred with the same brush; **ein ~ ins Wasser** (*umg*) a washout; **Schlagabtausch** *m* (*Boxen*) exchange of

blows; (*fig*) (verbal) exchange; **Schlagader** *f* artery; **Schlaganfall** *m* stroke; **schlagartig** *adj* sudden, without warning; **Schlagbaum** *m* barrier

Schlägel ['ʃlɛ:gl] (**-s, -**) *m* drumstick; (*Hammer*) hammer

schlagen ['ʃla:gən] *unreg vt* to strike, hit; (*wiederholt schlagen, besiegen*) to beat; (*Glocke*) to ring; (*Stunde*) to strike; (*Kreis, Bogen*) to describe; (*Purzelbaum*) to do; (*Sahne*) to whip; (*Schlacht*) to fight; (*einwickeln*) to wrap ▷ *vi* to strike, hit; to beat; to ring; to strike ▷ *vr* to fight; **um sich ~** to lash out; **ein Ei in die Pfanne ~** to crack an egg into the pan; **eine ge~e Stunde** a full hour; **na ja, ehe ich mich ~ lasse!** (*hum: umg*) I suppose you could twist my arm; **nach jdm ~** (*fig*) to take after sb; **sich gut ~** (*fig*) to do well; **sich nach links/Norden ~** to strike out to the left/(for the) north; **sich auf jds Seite** *akk* **~** to side with sb; (*die Fronten wechseln*) to go over to sb

Schlager ['ʃla:gər] (**-s, -**) *m* (*Mus, fig*) hit

Schläger ['ʃlɛ:gər] (**-s, -**) *m* brawler; (*Sport*) bat; (*Tennis etc*) racket; (*Golf*) club; (*Hockeyschläger*) hockey stick

Schlägerei [ʃlɛ:gə'raɪ] *f* fight, punch-up

Schlagersänger *m* pop singer

Schlag- *zW*: **schlagfertig** *adj* quick-witted; **Schlagfertigkeit** *f* ready wit, quickness of repartee; **Schlagloch** *nt* pothole; **Schlagobers** (**-, -**) (*Österr*) *nt*, **Schlagrahm** *m*, **Schlagsahne** *f* (whipped) cream; **Schlagseite** *f* (*Naut*) list

Schlag- *zW*: **Schlagwort** *nt* slogan, catch phrase; **Schlagzeile** *f* headline; **Schlagzeilen machen** (*umg*) to hit the headlines; **Schlagzeug** *nt* drums *pl*; (*in Orchester*) percussion; **Schlagzeuger** (**-s, -**) *m* drummer; percussionist

Schlamassel [ʃla'masəl] (**-s, -**) (*umg*) *m* mess

Schlamm [ʃlam] (**-(e)s, -e**) *m* mud

schlammig *adj* muddy

Schlampe ['ʃlampə] (**-, -n**) (*umg*) *f* slattern, slut

schlampen (*umg*) *vi* to be sloppy

Schlamperei [ʃlampə'raɪ] (*umg*) *f* disorder, untidiness; (*schlechte Arbeit*) sloppy work

schlampig (*umg*) *adj* slovenly, sloppy

schlang *etc* [ʃlaŋ] *vb siehe* **schlingen**

Schlange ['ʃlaŋə] (**-, -n**) *f* snake; (*Menschenschlange*) queue (*Brit*), line (*US*); **~ stehen** to (form a) queue (*Brit*), stand in line (*US*); **eine falsche ~** a snake in the grass

Schlangen- *zW*: **Schlangenbiss** *m* snake bite; **Schlangengift** *nt* snake venom; **Schlangenlinie** *f* wavy line

schlank [ʃlaŋk] *adj* slim, slender; **Schlankheit** *f* slimness, slenderness; **Schlankheitskur** *f* diet

schlapp [ʃlap] *adj* limp; (*locker*) slack; (*umg: energielos*) listless; (*nach Krankheit etc*) run-down

Schlappe (**-, -n**) (*umg*) *f* setback

Schlapphut *m* slouch hat

Schlaraffenland [ʃla'rafənlant] *nt* land of milk and honey

schlau [ʃlaʊ] *adj* crafty, cunning; **ich werde nicht ~ aus ihm** I don't know what to make of him

Schlauch [ʃlaʊx] (**-(e)s, Schläuche**) *m* hose; (*in Reifen*) inner tube; (*umg: Anstrengung*) grind; **auf dem ~ stehen** (*umg*) to be in a jam *od* fix; **Schlauchboot** *nt* rubber dinghy

schlauchen (*umg*) *vt* to tell on, exhaust

schlauchlos *adj* (*Reifen*) tubeless

Schläue ['ʃlɔʏə] (**-**) *f* cunning

Schlaukopf *m* clever Dick

schlecht [ʃlɛçt] *adj* bad; (*ungenießbar*) bad, off (*Brit*) ▷ *adv*: **jdm geht es ~** sb is in a bad way; **heute geht es ~** today is not very convenient; **er kann ~ Nein sagen** he finds it hard to say no, he can't say no; **jdm ist ~** sb feels sick *od* ill; **~ und recht** after a fashion; **auf jdn ~ zu sprechen sein** not to have a good word to say for sb; **er hat nicht ~ gestaunt** (*umg*) he wasn't half surprised; *siehe auch* **schlechtmachen**

Schlechtigkeit *f* badness; (*Tat*) bad deed

schlechtmachen *vt* to run down, denigrate

schlecken ['ʃlɛkən] *vt, vi* to lick

Schlegel ['ʃle:gəl] (**-s, -**) *m* (*Koch*) leg; *siehe auch* **Schlägel**

schleichen ['ʃlaɪçən] *unreg vi* to creep, crawl

schleichend *adj* creeping; (*Krankheit, Gift*) insidious

Schleichwerbung *f*: **eine ~** a plug

Schleie ['ʃlaɪə] (**-, -n**) *f* tench

Schleier ['ʃlaɪər] (**-s, -**) *m* veil; **schleierhaft** (*umg*) *adj*: **jdm schleierhaft sein** to be a mystery to sb

Schleife ['ʃlaɪfə] (**-, -n**) *f* (*auch Comput*) loop; (*Band*) bow; (*Kranzschleife*) ribbon

schleifen[1] *vt* to drag; (*Mil: Festung*) to raze ▷ *vi* to drag; **die Kupplung ~ lassen** (*Aut*) to slip the clutch

schleifen[2] *unreg vt* to grind; (*Edelstein*) to cut; (*Mil: Soldaten*) to drill

Schleim [ʃlaɪm] (**-(e)s, -e**) *m* slime; (*Med*) mucus; (*Koch*) gruel; **Schleimhaut** *f* mucous membrane

schleimig *adj* slimy

schlemmen ['ʃlɛmən] *vi* to feast

Schlemmer, in (**-s, -**) *m(f)* gourmet, bon vivant

Schlemmerei [ʃlɛmə'raɪ] *f* feasting

schlendern ['ʃlɛndərn] *vi* to stroll

Schlendrian ['ʃlɛndria:n] (**-(e)s**) *m* sloppy way of working

schlenkern *vt, vi* to swing, dangle

Schleppe ['ʃlɛpə] (**-, -n**) *f* train

schleppen *vt* to drag; (*Auto, Schiff*) to tow; (*tragen*) to lug

schleppend *adj* dragging; (*Bedienung, Abfertigung*) sluggish, slow

Schlepper (**-s, -**) *m* tractor; (*Schiff*) tug

Schlesien ['ʃle:ziən] (**-s**) *nt* Silesia

Schleswig-Holstein ['ʃle:svɪç'hɔlʃtaɪn] (**-s**) *nt* Schleswig-Holstein

Schleuder ['ʃlɔʏdər] (**-, -n**) *f* catapult; (*Wäscheschleuder*) spin-dryer; (*Zentrifuge*) centrifuge

schleudern *vt* to hurl; (*Wäsche*) to spin-dry ▷ *vi* (*Aut*) to skid; **ins S~ kommen** (*Aut*) to go into a skid; (*fig: umg*) to run into trouble

Schleuder- *zW*: **Schleuderpreis** *m* give-away price; **Schleudersitz** *m* (*Aviat*) ejector seat; (*fig*) hot seat; **Schleuderware** *f* cut-price (*Brit*) *od* cut-rate (*US*) goods *pl*

schleunigst *adv* straight away

Schleuse ['ʃlɔʏzə] (**-, -n**) *f* lock; (*Schleusentor*) sluice

schlich *etc* [ʃlɪç] *vb siehe* **schleichen**

schlicht [ʃlɪçt] *adj* simple, plain

schlichten *vt* to smooth; (*beilegen*) to settle; (*Streit: vermitteln*) to mediate, arbitrate

Schlichter, in (**-s, -**) *m(f)* mediator, arbitrator

Schlichtung *f* settlement; arbitration

Schlick [ʃlɪk] (**-(e)s, -e**) *m* mud; (*Ölschlick*) slick

schlief *etc* [ʃli:f] *vb siehe* **schlafen**

Schließe ['ʃli:sə] (**-, -n**) *f* fastener

schließen ['ʃli:sən] *unreg vt* to close, shut; (*beenden*) to close; (*Freundschaft, Bündnis, Ehe*) to enter into; (*Comput: Datei*) to close; (*folgern*): **~ (aus)** to infer (from) ▷ *vi, vr* to close, shut; **auf etw** *akk* **~ lassen** to suggest sth; **jdn/etw in sein Herz ~** to take sb/sth to one's heart; **etw in sich ~** to include sth; **„geschlossen"** "closed"

Schließfach *nt* locker

schließlich *adv* finally; (*schließlich doch*) after all

Schliff (**-(e)s, -e**) *m* cut(ting); (*fig*) polish; **einer Sache den letzten ~ geben** (*fig*) to put the finishing touch(es) to sth

schliff *etc* [ʃlɪf] *vb siehe* **schleifen**

schlimm [ʃlɪm] *adj* bad; **das war ~** that was terrible; **das ist halb so ~!** that's not so bad!; **schlimmer** *adj* worse; **schlimmste, r, s** *adj* worst

schlimmstenfalls *adv* at (the) worst

Schlinge ['ʃlɪŋə] (**-, -n**) *f* loop; (*an Galgen*) noose; (*Falle*) snare; (*Med*) sling

Schlingel (**-s, -**) *m* rascal

schlingen *unreg vt* to wind ▷ *vi* (*essen*) to bolt one's food, gobble

schlingern *vi* to roll

Schlips [ʃlɪps] (**-es, -e**) *m* tie, necktie (*US*); **sich auf den ~ getreten fühlen** (*fig: umg*) to feel offended

Schlitten ['ʃlɪtən] (**-s, -**) *m* sledge, sled; (*Pferdeschlitten*) sleigh; **mit jdm ~ fahren** (*umg*) to give sb a rough time; **Schlittenbahn** *f* toboggan run

schlittern ['ʃlɪtərn] *vi* to slide; (*Wagen*) to skid

Schlittschuh ['ʃlɪtʃu:] *m* skate; **~ laufen** to skate; **Schlittschuhläufer** *m* skater

Schlitz [ʃlɪts] (**-es, -e**) *m* slit; (*für Münze*) slot; (*Hosenschlitz*) flies *pl*; **schlitzäugig** *adj* slant-eyed; **schlitzen** *vt* to slit; **Schlitzohr** *nt* (*fig*) sly fox

Schloss (**-es, ¨-er**) *nt* lock, padlock; (*an Schmuck etc*) clasp; (*Bau*) castle; (*Palast*) palace; **ins ~ fallen** to lock (itself)

schloss *etc* [ʃlɔs] *vb siehe* **schließen**

Schlosser ['ʃlɔsər] (**-s, -**) *m* (*Autoschlosser*) fitter; (*für Schlüssel etc*) locksmith

Schlosserei [slɔsə'raɪ] *f* metal(working) shop

Schlot [ʃlo:t] (**-(e)s, -e**) *m* chimney; (*Naut*) funnel

schlottern ['ʃlɔtərn] *vi* to shake; (*vor Angst*) to tremble; (*Kleidung*) to be baggy

Schlucht [ʃlʊxt] (**-, -en**) *f* gorge, ravine

schluchzen ['ʃlʊxtsən] *vi* to sob

Schluck [ʃlʊk] (**-(e)s, -e**) *m* swallow; (*größer*) gulp; (*kleiner*) sip; (*ein bisschen*) drop

Schluckauf (**-s**) *m* hiccups *pl*

schlucken *vt* to swallow; (*umg: Alkohol, Benzin*) to guzzle; (*: verschlingen*) to swallow up ▷ *vi* to swallow

schludern ['ʃlu:dərn] (*umg*) *vi* to do slipshod work

schlug *etc* [ʃlu:k] *vb siehe* **schlagen**

Schlummer ['ʃlʊmər] (**-s**) *m* slumber

schlummern *vi* to slumber

Schlund [ʃlʊnt] (**-(e)s, ¨-e**) *m* gullet; (*fig*) jaw

schlüpfen ['ʃlʏpfən] *vi* to slip; (*Vogel etc*) to hatch (out)

Schlüpfer ['ʃlʏpfər] (**-s, -**) *m* panties *pl*, knickers *pl*

schlüpfrig ['ʃlʏpfrɪç] *adj* slippery; (*fig*) lewd; **Schlüpfrigkeit** *f* slipperiness; lewdness

schlurfen ['ʃlʊrfən] *vi* to shuffle

schlürfen ['ʃlʏrfən] *vt, vi* to slurp

Schluss [ʃlʊs] (**-es, ¨-e**) *m* end; (*Schlussfolgerung*) conclusion; **am ~** at the end; **~ für heute!** that'll do for today; **~ jetzt!** that's enough now!; **~ machen mit** to finish with

Schlüssel ['ʃlʏsəl] (**-s, -**) *m* (*lit, fig*) key; (*Schraubschlüssel*) spanner, wrench; (*Mus*) clef; **Schlüsselbein** *nt* collarbone; **Schlüsselblume** *f* cowslip, primrose; **Schlüsselbund** *m* bunch of keys; **Schlüsselloch** *nt* keyhole; **Schlüsselposition** *f* key position

schlüssig ['ʃlʏsɪç] *adj* conclusive; **sich** *dat* **(über etw** *akk***) ~ sein** to have made up one's mind (about sth)

Schluss- *zW*: **Schlusslicht** *nt* rear light (*Brit*), taillight (*US*); (*fig*) tail ender; **Schlussstrich** *m* (*fig*) final stroke; **einen Schlussstrich unter etw** *akk* **ziehen** to consider sth finished; **Schlussverkauf** *m* clearance sale

schmächtig ['ʃmɛçtɪç] *adj* slight

schmackhaft ['ʃmakhaft] *adj* tasty; **jdm etw ~ machen** (*fig*) to make sth palatable to sb

schmal [ʃma:l] *adj* narrow; (*Person, Buch etc*) slender, slim; (*karg*) meagre (*Brit*), meager (*US*)

schmälern ['ʃmɛ:lərn] *vt* to diminish; (*fig*) to belittle

Schmalz [ʃmalts] (**-es, -e**) *nt* dripping; (*Schweineschmalz*) lard; (*fig*) sentiment, schmaltz

schmalzig *adj* (*fig*) schmaltzy, slushy
schmarotzen [ʃma'rɔtsən] *vi* (*Biol*) to be parasitic; (*fig*) to sponge
Schmarotzer (**-s, -**) *m* (*auch fig*) parasite
Schmarren ['ʃmarən] (**-s, -**) *m* (*Österr*) small pieces of pancake; (*fig*) rubbish, tripe
schmatzen ['ʃmatsən] *vi* to eat noisily
schmecken ['ʃmɛkən] *vt, vi* to taste; **es schmeckt ihm** he likes it; **schmeckt es Ihnen?** is it good?, are you enjoying your food *od* meal?; **das schmeckt nach mehr!** (*umg*) it's very moreish (*hum*); **es sich ~ lassen** to tuck in
Schmeichelei [ʃmaɪçə'laɪ] *f* flattery
schmeichelhaft ['ʃmaɪçəlhaft] *adj* flattering
schmeicheln *vi* to flatter
schmeißen ['ʃmaɪsən] *unreg* (*umg*) *vt* to throw, chuck; (*spendieren*): **eine Runde** *od* **Lage ~** to stand a round
Schmeißfliege *f* bluebottle
Schmelz [ʃmɛlts] (**-es, -e**) *m* enamel; (*Glasur*) glaze; (*von Stimme*) melodiousness; **schmelzbar** *adj* fusible
schmelzen *unreg vt* to melt; (*Erz*) to smelt ▷ *vi* to melt
Schmelz- *zW*: **Schmelzpunkt** *m* melting point; **Schmelzwasser** *nt* melted snow
Schmerz [ʃmɛrts] (**-es, -en**) *m* pain; (*Trauer*) grief *no pl*; **~en haben** to be in pain; **schmerzempfindlich** *adj* sensitive to pain
schmerzen *vt, vi* to hurt
Schmerzensgeld *nt* compensation
Schmerz- *zW*: **schmerzhaft** *adj* painful; **schmerzlich** *adj* painful; **schmerzlindernd** *adj* pain-relieving; **Schmerzmittel** *nt* painkiller, analgesic; **schmerzstillend** *adj* pain-killing, analgesic; **Schmerztablette** *f* pain-killing tablet
Schmetterling ['ʃmɛtərlɪŋ] *m* butterfly
Schmied [ʃmi:t] (**-(e)s, -e**) *m* blacksmith
Schmiede ['ʃmi:də] (**-, -n**) *f* smithy, forge; **Schmiedeeisen** *nt* wrought iron
schmieden *vt* to forge; (*Pläne*) to devise, concoct
schmiegen ['ʃmi:gən] *vt* to press, nestle ▷ *vr*: **sich ~ an** *+akk* to cuddle up to, nestle up to
Schmiere ['ʃmi:rə] *f* grease; (*Theat*) greasepaint, make-up; (*pej: schlechtes Theater*) fleapit; **~ stehen** (*umg*) to be the look-out
schmieren *vt* to smear; (*ölen*) to lubricate, grease; (*bestechen*) to bribe ▷ *vi* (*schreiben*) to scrawl; **es läuft wie geschmiert** it's going like clockwork; **jdm eine ~** (*umg*) to clout sb one
Schmier- *zW*: **Schmierfett** *nt* grease; **Schmierfink** *m* messy person; **Schmiergeld** *nt* bribe
schmierig *adj* greasy
Schminke ['ʃmɪŋkə] (**-, -n**) *f* make-up
schminken *vt, vr* to make up
schmirgeln ['ʃmɪrgəln] *vt* to sand (down)
Schmirgelpapier (**-s**) *nt* emery paper
schmiss *etc* [ʃmɪs] *vb siehe* **schmeißen**
schmollen ['ʃmɔlən] *vi* to pout; (*gekränkt*) to sulk
schmolz *etc* [ʃmɔlts] *vb siehe* **schmelzen**
Schmorbraten *m* stewed *od* braised meat
schmoren ['ʃmo:rən] *vt* to braise
Schmuck [ʃmʊk] (**-(e)s, -e**) *m* jewellery (*Brit*), jewelry (*US*); (*Verzierung*) decoration
schmücken ['ʃmʏkən] *vt* to decorate
Schmuck- *zW*: **schmucklos** *adj* unadorned, plain; **Schmucklosigkeit** *f* simplicity; **Schmucksachen** *pl* jewels *pl*, jewellery *sing* (*Brit*), jewelry *sing* (*US*)
Schmuggel ['ʃmʊgəl] (**-s**) *m* smuggling
schmuggeln *vt, vi* to smuggle
Schmuggler, in (**-s, -**) *m(f)* smuggler
schmunzeln ['ʃmʊntsəln] *vi* to smile benignly
schmusen ['ʃmu:zən] (*umg*) *vi* (*zärtlich sein*) to cuddle; **mit jdm ~** to cuddle sb
Schmutz [ʃmʊts] (**-es**) *m* dirt; (*fig*) filth; **Schmutzfink** *m* filthy creature; **Schmutzfleck** *m* stain
schmutzig *adj* dirty; **~e Wäsche waschen** (*fig*) to wash one's dirty linen in public
Schnabel ['ʃna:bəl] (**-s, ¨-**) *m* beak, bill; (*Ausguss*) spout; (*umg: Mund*) mouth; **reden, wie einem der ~ gewachsen ist** to say exactly what comes into one's head; (*unaffektiert*) to talk naturally
Schnake ['ʃna:kə] (**-, -n**) *f* crane fly; (*Stechmücke*) gnat
Schnalle ['ʃnalə] (**-, -n**) *f* buckle; (*an Handtasche, Buch*) clasp
schnallen *vt* to buckle
Schnäppchen ['ʃnɛpçən] (*umg*) *nt* bargain, snip
schnappen ['ʃnapən] *vt* to grab, catch; (*umg: ergreifen*) to snatch ▷ *vi* to snap
Schnappschloss *nt* spring lock
Schnappschuss *m* (*Phot*) snapshot
Schnaps [ʃnaps] (**-es, ¨-e**) *m* schnapps; (*umg: Branntwein*) spirits *pl*
schnarchen ['ʃnarçən] *vi* to snore
schnaufen ['ʃnaʊfən] *vi* to puff, pant
Schnauzbart ['ʃnaʊtsba:rt] *m* moustache (*Brit*), mustache (*US*)
Schnauze (**-, -n**) *f* snout, muzzle; (*Ausguss*) spout; (*umg*) gob; **auf die ~ fallen** (*fig*) to come a cropper (*umg*); **etw frei nach ~ machen** to do sth any old how
schnäuzen ['ʃnɔʏtsn] *vr* to blow one's nose
Schnecke ['ʃnɛkə] (**-, -n**) *f* snail; (*Nacktschnecke*) slug; (*Koch: Gebäck*) ≈ Chelsea bun; **jdn zur ~ machen** (*umg*) to give sb a real bawling out
Schneckenhaus *nt* snail's shell
Schneckentempo (*umg*) *nt*: **im ~** at a snail's pace
Schnee [ʃne:] (**-s**) *m* snow; (*Eischnee*) beaten egg white; **~ von gestern** old hat; water under the bridge; **Schneeball** *m* snowball; **Schneeflocke** *f* snowflake; **Schneegestöber**

nt snowstorm; **Schneeglöckchen** *nt* snowdrop; **Schneekette** *f* (*Aut*) snow chain; **Schneemann** *m* snowman; **Schneepflug** *m* snowplough (*Brit*), snowplow (*US*); **Schneeschmelze** *f* thaw; **Schneewehe** *f* snowdrift

Schneid [ʃnaɪt] (**-(e)s**) (*umg*) *m* pluck

Schneide [ˈʃnaɪdə] (**-, -n**) *f* edge; (*Klinge*) blade

schneiden *unreg vt* to cut; (*Film, Tonband*) to edit; (*kreuzen*) to cross, intersect ▷ *vr* to cut o.s.; (*umg: sich täuschen*): **da hat er sich aber geschnitten!** he's very much mistaken; **die Luft ist zum S~** (*fig: umg*) the air is very bad

Schneider (**-s, -**) *m* tailor; **frieren wie ein ~** (*umg*) to be frozen to the marrow; **aus dem ~ sein** (*fig*) to be out of the woods

schneidern *vt* to make ▷ *vi* to be a tailor

Schneidezahn *m* incisor

schneien [ˈʃnaɪən] *vi* to snow; **jdm ins Haus ~** (*umg: Besuch*) to drop in on sb; (*: Rechnung, Brief*) to come in the post (*Brit*) *od* mail (*US*)

Schneise [ˈʃnaɪzə] (**-, -n**) *f* (*Waldschneise*) clearing

schnell [ʃnɛl] *adj* quick, fast ▷ *adv* quick(ly), fast; **das ging ~** that was quick

Schnellhefter *m* loose-leaf binder

Schnelligkeit *f* speed

Schnellimbiss *m* (*Essen*) (quick) snack; (*Raum*) snack bar

schnellstens *adv* as quickly as possible

Schnellstraße *f* expressway

Schnellzug *m* fast *od* express train

schneuzen [ˈʃnɔʏtsən] *vr siehe* **schnäuzen**

Schnickschnack [ˈʃnɪkʃnak] (**-(e)s**) (*umg*) *m* twaddle

schnippisch [ˈʃnɪpɪʃ] *adj* sharp-tongued

Schnitt (**-(e)s, -e**) *m* cut(ting); (*Schnittpunkt*) intersection; (*Querschnitt*) (cross) section; (*Durchschnitt*) average; (*Schnittmuster*) pattern; (*Ernte*) crop; (*an Buch*) edge; (*umg: Gewinn*) profit; **~: L. Schwarz** (*Film*) editor – L. Schwarz; **im ~** on average

schnitt *etc* [ʃnɪt] *vb siehe* **schneiden**

Schnittblumen *pl* cut flowers *pl*

Schnitte (**-, -n**) *f* slice; (*belegt*) sandwich

Schnittfläche *f* section

Schnitt- *zW*: **Schnittlauch** *m* chive; **Schnittmuster** *nt* pattern; **Schnittpunkt** *m* (point of) intersection; **Schnittstelle** *f* (*Comput*) interface; **Schnittwunde** *f* cut

Schnitzarbeit *f* wood carving

Schnitzel (**-s, -**) *nt* scrap; (*Koch*) escalope

schnitzen [ˈʃnɪtsən] *vt* to carve

Schnitzer (**-s, -**) *m* carver; (*umg*) blunder

Schnitzerei [ʃnɪtsəˈraɪ] *f* wood carving

schnodderig [ˈʃnɔdərɪç] (*umg*) *adj* snotty

Schnorchel [ˈʃnɔrçəl] (**-s, -**) *m* snorkel

schnorcheln *vi* to go snorkelling

Schnörkel [ˈʃnœrkəl] (**-s, -**) *m* flourish; (*Archit*) scroll

schnorren [ˈʃnɔrən] *vt, vi* to cadge (*Brit*)

schnüffeln [ˈʃnʏfəln] *vi* to sniff; (*fig: umg: spionieren*) to snoop around

Schnuller [ˈʃnʊlər] (**-s, -**) *m* dummy (*Brit*), pacifier (*US*)

Schnupfen [ˈʃnʊpfən] (**-s, -**) *m* cold

schnuppern [ˈʃnʊpərn] *vi* to sniff

Schnur [ʃnuːr] (**-, ¨-e**) *f* string; (*Kordel*) cord; (*Elek*) flex

schnüren [ˈʃnyːrən] *vt* to tie

schnurgerade *adj* straight (as a die *od* an arrow)

Schnurrbart [ˈʃnʊrbaːrt] *m* moustache (*Brit*), mustache (*US*)

schnurren [ˈʃnʊrən] *vi* to purr; (*Kreisel*) to hum

Schnürschuh *m* lace-up (shoe)

Schnürsenkel *m* shoelace

schnurstracks *adv* straight (away); **~ auf jdn/etw zugehen** to make a beeline for sb/sth (*umg*)

schob *etc* [ʃoːp] *vb siehe* **schieben**

Schock [ʃɔk] (**-(e)s, -e**) *m* shock; **unter ~ stehen** to be in (a state of) shock

schockieren *vt* to shock, outrage

Schokolade [ʃokoˈlaːdə] (**-, -n**) *f* chocolate

Scholle [ˈʃɔlə] (**-, -n**) *f* clod; (*Eisscholle*) ice floe; (*Fisch*) plaice

schon [ʃoːn] *adv* **1** (*bereits*) already; **er ist schon da** he's there/here already, he's already there/here; **ist er schon da?** is he there/here yet?; **warst du schon einmal dort?** have you ever been there?; **ich war schon einmal dort** I've been there before; **das war schon immer so** that has always been the case; **hast du schon gehört?** have you heard?; **schon 1920** as early as 1920; **schon vor 100 Jahren** as far back as 100 years ago; **er wollte schon die Hoffnung aufgeben, als ...** he was just about to give up hope when ...; **wartest du schon lange?** have you been waiting (for) long?; **wie schon so oft** as so often (before); **was, schon wieder?** what – again?

2 (*bestimmt*) all right; **du wirst schon sehen** you'll see (all right); **das wird schon noch gut gehen** that should turn out OK (in the end)

3 (*bloß*) just; **allein schon das Gefühl ...** just the very feeling ...; **schon der Gedanke** the mere *od* very thought; **wenn ich das schon höre** I only have to hear that

4 (*einschränkend*): **ja schon, aber ...** yes (well), but ...

5: **das ist schon möglich** that's quite possible; **schon gut** OK; **du weißt schon** you know; **komm schon** come on; **hör schon auf damit!** will you stop that!; **was macht das schon, wenn ...?** what does it matter if ...?; **und wenn schon!** (*umg*) so what?

schön [ʃøːn] *adj* beautiful; (*Mann*) handsome; (*nett*) nice ▷ *adv*: **sich ganz ~ ärgern** to be very angry; **da hast du etwas S~es angerichtet** you've made a fine *od* nice mess; **sich ~ machen** to make o.s. look nice; **~e Grüße** best wishes; **~en Dank** (many)

thanks; **~ weich/warm** nice and soft/warm
schonen ['ʃo:nən] *vt* to look after; (*jds Nerven*) to spare; (*Gegner, Kind*) to be easy on; (*Teppich, Füße*) to save ▷ *vr* to take it easy
schonend *adj* careful, gentle; **jdm etw ~ beibringen** to break sth to sb gently
Schönheit *f* beauty
Schönheits- *zW*: **Schönheitsfehler** *m* blemish, flaw; **Schönheitsoperation** *f* cosmetic surgery
Schonung *f* good care; (*Nachsicht*) consideration; (*Forst*) plantation of young trees
schonungslos *adj* ruthless, harsh
Schonzeit *f* close season
schöpfen ['ʃœpfən] *vt* to scoop; (*Suppe*) to ladle; (*Mut*) to summon up; (*Luft*) to breathe in; (*Hoffnung*) to find
Schöpfer (**-s, -**) *m* creator; (*Gott*) Creator; (*umg*: *Schöpfkelle*) ladle; **schöpferisch** *adj* creative
Schöpfkelle *f* ladle
Schöpfung *f* creation
schor *etc* [ʃo:r] *vb siehe* **scheren**
Schorf [ʃɔrf] (**-(e)s, -e**) *m* scab
Schornstein ['ʃɔrnʃtaɪn] *m* chimney; (*Naut*) funnel; **Schornsteinfeger** (**-s, -**) *m* chimney sweep
Schoß (**-es, ̈-e**) *m* lap; (*Rockschoß*) coat tail; **im ~e der Familie** in the bosom of one's family
schoss *etc* [ʃɔs] *vb siehe* **schießen**
Schoßhund *m* lapdog
Schote ['ʃo:tə] (**-, -n**) *f* pod
Schotte ['ʃɔtə] (**-n, -n**) *m* Scot, Scotsman
Schotter ['ʃɔtər] (**-s**) *m* gravel; (*im Straßenbau*) road metal; (*Eisenb*) ballast
Schottin ['ʃɔtɪn] *f* Scot, Scotswoman
schottisch ['ʃɔtɪʃ] *adj* Scottish, Scots; **das ~e Hochland** the Scottish Highlands *pl*
Schottland (**-s**) *nt* Scotland
schraffieren [ʃra'fi:rən] *vt* to hatch
schräg [ʃrɛ:k] *adj* slanting; (*schief, geneigt*) sloping; (*nicht gerade od parallel*) oblique ▷ *adv*: **~ gedruckt** in italics; **etw ~ stellen** to put sth at an angle; **~ gegenüber** diagonally opposite
Schräge ['ʃrɛ:gə] (**-, -n**) *f* slant
Schräg- *zW*: **Schrägstreifen** *m* bias binding; **Schrägstrich** *m* oblique stroke
Schramme ['ʃramə] (**-, -n**) *f* scratch
schrammen *vt* to scratch
Schrank [ʃraŋk] (**-(e)s, ̈-e**) *m* cupboard (*Brit*), closet (*US*); (*Kleiderschrank*) wardrobe
Schranke (**-, -n**) *f* barrier; (*fig*: *Grenze*) limit; (: *Hindernis*) barrier; **jdn in seine ~n (ver)weisen** (*fig*) to put sb in his place
Schrankenwärter *m* (*Eisenb*) level-crossing (*Brit*) *od* grade-crossing (*US*) attendant
Schrankkoffer *m* wardrobe trunk
Schraube ['ʃraʊbə] (**-, -n**) *f* screw
schrauben *vt* to screw; **etw in die Höhe ~** (*fig*: *Preise, Rekorde*) to push sth up; (: *Ansprüche*) to raise sth
Schraubenschlüssel *m* spanner (*Brit*), wrench (*US*)
Schraubenzieher (**-s, -**) *m* screwdriver
Schraubstock ['ʃraʊpʃtɔk] *m* (*Tech*) vice (*Brit*), vise (*US*)
Schreck [ʃrɛk] (**-(e)s, -e**) *m* fright; **o ~ lass nach!** (*hum*: *umg*) for goodness' sake!; **schrecken** *vt* to frighten, scare ▷ *vi*: **aus dem Schlaf schrecken** to be startled out of one's sleep
Schreck- *zW*: **Schreckgespenst** *nt* nightmare; **schreckhaft** *adj* jumpy, easily frightened; **schrecklich** *adj* terrible, dreadful; **schrecklich gerne!** (*umg*) I'd absolutely love to; **Schreckschuss** *m* shot fired in the air
Schrei [ʃraɪ] (**-(e)s, -e**) *m* scream; (*Ruf*) shout; **der letzte ~** (*umg*) the latest thing, all the rage
Schreibblock *m* writing pad
schreiben ['ʃraɪbən] *unreg vt* to write; (*mit Schreibmaschine*) to type out; (*berichten*: *Zeitung etc*) to say; (*buchstabieren*) to spell ▷ *vi* to write; to type; to say; to spell ▷ *vr*: **wie schreibt sich das?** how is that spelt?; **Schreiben** (**-s, -**) *nt* letter, communication
Schreiber, in (**-s, -**) *m(f)* writer; (*Büroschreiber*) clerk
Schreib- *zW*: **schreibfaul** *adj* lazy about writing letters; **Schreibfehler** *m* spelling mistake; **Schreibkraft** *f* typist; **Schreibmaschine** *f* typewriter; **Schreibschutz** *m* (*Comput*) write-protect; **Schreibtisch** *m* desk
Schreibung *f* spelling
Schreib- *zW*: **Schreibwaren** *pl* stationery *sing*; **Schreibweise** *f* spelling; (*Stil*) style; **Schreibzeug** *nt* writing materials *pl*
schreien ['ʃraɪən] *unreg vt, vi* to scream; (*rufen*) to shout; **es war zum S~** (*umg*) it was a scream *od* a hoot; **nach etw ~** (*fig*) to cry out for sth
schreiend *adj* (*fig*) glaring; (: *Farbe*) loud
Schreiner ['ʃraɪnər] (**-s, -**) *m* joiner; (*Zimmermann*) carpenter; (*Möbelschreiner*) cabinetmaker
Schreinerei [ʃraɪnə'raɪ] *f* joiner's workshop
schreiten ['ʃraɪtən] *unreg vi* to stride
schrie *etc* [ʃri:] *vb siehe* **schreien**
schrieb *etc* [ʃri:p] *vb siehe* **schreiben**
Schrift [ʃrɪft] (**-, -en**) *f* writing; (*Handschrift*) handwriting; (*Schriftart*) script; (*Typ*) typeface; (*Buch*) work; **Schriftart** *f* (*Handschrift*) script; (*Typ*) typeface; **Schriftdeutsch** *nt* written German; **Schriftführer** *m* secretary; **schriftlich** *adj* written ▷ *adv* in writing; **das kann ich Ihnen schriftlich geben** (*fig*: *umg*) I can tell you that for free
Schriftsteller, in (**-s, -**) *m(f)* writer
Schriftstück *nt* document
schrill [ʃrɪl] *adj* shrill
Schritt (**-(e)s, -e**) *m* step; (*Gangart*) walk;

(*Tempo*) pace; (*von Hose*) crotch, crutch (*Brit*); **auf ~ und Tritt** (*lit, fig*) wherever *od* everywhere one goes; **„~ fahren"** "dead slow"; **mit zehn ~en Abstand** at a distance of ten paces; **den ersten ~ tun** (*fig*) to make the first move; (: *etw beginnen*) to take the first step

schritt *etc* [ʃrɪt] *vb siehe* **schreiten**

Schritt- *zW*: **Schrittmacher** *m* pacemaker; **Schritttempo** *nt*: **im Schritttempo** at a walking pace

schroff [ʃrɔf] *adj* steep; (*zackig*) jagged; (*fig*) brusque; (*ungeduldig*) abrupt

schröpfen ['ʃrœpfən] *vt* (*fig*) to fleece

Schrot [ʃro:t] (**-(e)s, -e**) *m od nt* (*Blei*) (small) shot; (*Getreide*) coarsely ground grain, groats *pl*; **Schrotflinte** *f* shotgun

Schrott [ʃrɔt] (**-(e)s, -e**) *m* scrap metal; **ein Auto zu ~ fahren** to write off a car; **Schrotthaufen** *m* scrap heap; **schrottreif** *adj* ready for the scrap heap

schrubben ['ʃrʊbən] *vt* to scrub

Schrulle ['ʃrʊlə] (**-, -n**) *f* eccentricity, quirk

schrumpfen ['ʃrʊmpfən] *vi* (*Hilfsverb sein*) to shrink; (*Apfel*) to shrivel; (*Leber, Niere*) to atrophy; **Schubfach** *nt* drawer; **Schubkarren** *m* wheelbarrow; **Schublade** *f* drawer

schüchtern ['ʃʏçtərn] *adj* shy; **Schüchternheit** *f* shyness

schuf *etc* [ʃu:f] *vb siehe* **schaffen**

Schuft [ʃʊft] (**-(e)s, -e**) *m* scoundrel

schuften (*umg*) *vi* to graft, slave away

Schuh [ʃu:] (**-(e)s, -e**) *m* shoe; **jdm etw in die ~e schieben** (*fig: umg*) to put the blame for sth on sb; **wo drückt der ~?** (*fig*) what's troubling you?; **Schuhband** *nt* shoelace; **Schuhcreme** *f* shoe polish; **Schuhgröße** *f* shoe size; **Schuhlöffel** *m* shoehorn; **Schuhmacher** *m* shoemaker; **Schuhwerk** *nt* footwear

Schul- *zW*: **Schulaufgaben** *pl* homework *sing*; **Schulbesuch** *m* school attendance; **Schulbuch** *nt* schoolbook

Schuld [ʃʊlt] (**-, -en**) *f* guilt; (*Fin*) debt; (*Verschulden*) fault; **~ haben (an** *+dat***)** to be to blame (for); **jdm (die) ~ geben, jdm die ~ zuschieben** to blame sb; **ich bin mir keiner ~ bewusst** I'm not aware of having done anything wrong; **~ und Sühne** crime and punishment; **ich stehe tief in seiner ~** (*fig*) I'm deeply indebted to him; **~en machen** to run up debts; *siehe auch* **zuschulden**; **schuld** *adj*: **schuld sein (an** *+dat***)** to be to blame (for); **er ist schuld** it's his fault

schuldenfrei *adj* free from debt

Schuldgefühl *nt* feeling of guilt

schuldig *adj* guilty; (*gebührend*) due; **an etw** *dat* **~ sein** to be guilty of sth; **jdm etw ~ sein** *od* **bleiben** to owe sb sth; **jdn ~ sprechen** to find sb guilty; **~ geschieden sein** to be the guilty party in a divorce

schuldlos *adj* innocent, blameless

Schuldner, in (**-s, -**) *m(f)* debtor

Schuld- *zW*: **Schuldschein** *m* promissory note, IOU; **Schuldspruch** *m* verdict of guilty

Schule ['ʃu:lə] (**-, -n**) *f* school; **auf** *od* **in der ~** at school; **in die ~ kommen/gehen** to start school/go to school; **~ machen** (*fig*) to become the accepted thing

schulen *vt* to train, school

Schüler, in ['ʃy:lər(ɪn)] (**-s, -**) *m(f)* pupil; **Schülerausweis** *m* (school) student card

Schul- *zW*: **Schulferien** *pl* school holidays *pl* (*Brit*) *od* vacation *sing* (*US*); **schulfrei** *adj*: **die Kinder haben morgen schulfrei** the children don't have to go to school tomorrow; **Schulhof** *m* playground, schoolyard

Schul- *zW*: **Schuljahr** *nt* school year; **Schuljunge** *m* schoolboy; **Schulmedizin** *f* orthodox medicine; **schulpflichtig** *adj* of school age; **Schulstunde** *f* period, lesson; **Schultasche** *f* school bag

Schulter ['ʃʊltər] (**-, -n**) *f* shoulder; **auf die leichte ~ nehmen** to take lightly; **Schulterblatt** *nt* shoulder blade

schultern *vt* to shoulder

Schulung *f* education, schooling

Schulzeugnis *nt* school report

Schund (**-(e)s**) *m* trash, garbage

Schundroman *m* trashy novel

Schuppe ['ʃʊpə] (**-, -n**) *f* scale; **Schuppen** *pl* (*Haarschuppen*) dandruff

Schuppen (**-s, -**) *m* shed; (*umg: übles Lokal*) dive; *siehe auch* **Schuppe**

schuppen *vt* to scale ▷ *vr* to peel

schuppig ['ʃʊpɪç] *adj* scaly

Schur [ʃu:r] (**-, -en**) *f* shearing

schüren ['ʃy:rən] *vt* to rake; (*fig*) to stir up

schürfen ['ʃʏrfən] *vt, vi* to scrape, scratch; (*Min*) to prospect; to dig

Schürfung *f* abrasion; (*Min*) prospecting

Schurke ['ʃʊrkə] (**-n, -n**) *m* rogue

Schürze ['ʃʏrtsə] (**-, -n**) *f* apron

Schuss [ʃʊs] (**-es, ⸚e**) *m* shot; (*Fussball*) kick; (*Spritzer: von Wein, Essig etc*) dash; (*Weben*) weft; **(gut) in ~ sein** (*umg*) to be in good shape *od* nick; (*Mensch*) to be in form; **etw in ~ halten** to keep sth in good shape; **weitab vom ~ sein** (*fig: umg*) to be miles from where the action is; **der goldene ~** ≈ a lethal dose of a drug; **ein ~ in den Ofen** (*umg*) a complete waste of time, a failure; **Schussbereich** *m* effective range

Schüssel ['ʃʏsəl] (**-, -n**) *f* bowl, basin; (*Servierschüssel, umg: Satellitenschüssel*) dish; (*Waschschüssel*) basin

schusselig ['ʃʊsəlɪç] (*umg*) *adj* (*zerstreut*) scatterbrained, muddle-headed (*umg*)

Schuss- *zW*: **Schusslinie** *f* line of fire; **Schussverletzung** *f* bullet wound; **Schusswaffe** *f* firearm; **Schussweite** *f* range (of fire)

Schuster ['ʃu:stər] (**-s, -**) *m* cobbler, shoemaker

Schutt [ʃʊt] (**-(e)s**) *m* rubbish; (*Bauschutt*)

rubble; **„~ abladen verboten"** "no tipping"; **Schuttabladeplatz** *m* refuse dump
Schüttelfrost *m* shivering
schütteln ['ʃʏtəln] *vt* to shake ▷ *vr* to shake o.s.; **sich vor Kälte ~** to shiver with cold; **sich vor Ekel ~** to shudder with *od* in disgust
schütten ['ʃʏtən] *vt* to pour; (*Zucker, Kies etc*) to tip; (*verschütten*) to spill ▷ *vi unpers* to pour (down)
Schutthalde *f* dump
Schutthaufen *m* heap of rubble
Schutz [ʃʊts] (**-es**) *m* protection; (*Unterschlupf*) shelter; **jdn in ~ nehmen** to stand up for sb; **Schutzanzug** *m* overalls *pl*; **Schutzblech** *nt* mudguard; **Schutzbrille** *f* goggles *pl*
Schütze ['ʃʏtsə] (**-n, -n**) *m* gunman; (*Gewehrschütze*) rifleman; (*Scharfschütze, Sportschütze*) marksman; (*Astrol*) Sagittarius
schützen ['ʃʏtsən] *vt* to protect ▷ *vr* to protect o.s.; **(sich) ~ vor** *+dat od* **gegen** to protect (o.s.) from *od* against; **gesetzlich geschützt** registered; **urheberrechtlich geschützt** protected by copyright; **vor Nässe ~!** keep dry
Schützenfest *nt fair featuring shooting matches*
Schutzengel *m* guardian angel
Schutz- *zW*: **Schutzgebiet** *nt* protectorate; (*Naturschutzgebiet*) reserve; **Schutzhelm** *m* safety helmet; **Schutzimpfung** *f* immunization
Schutz- *zW*: **schutzlos** *adj* defenceless (*Brit*), defenseless (*US*); **Schutzmann** (**-(e)s**, *pl* **-leute** *od* **-männer**) *m* policeman; **Schutzmaßnahme** *f* precaution; **Schutzpatron** *m* patron saint; **Schutzvorrichtung** *f* safety device
Schwabe ['ʃvaːbə] (**-n, -n**) *m* Swabian
Schwaben (**-s**) *nt* Swabia
Schwäbin ['ʃvɛːbɪn] *f* Swabian
schwäbisch ['ʃvɛːbɪʃ] *adj* Swabian
schwach [ʃvax] *adj* weak, feeble; (*Gedächtnis, Gesundheit*) poor; (*Hoffnung*) faint; **~ werden** to weaken; **das ist ein ~es Bild** (*umg*) *od* **eine ~e Leistung** (*umg*) that's a poor show; **ein ~er Trost** cold *od* small comfort; **mach mich nicht ~!** (*umg*) don't say that!; **auf ~en Beinen** *od* **Füßen stehen** (*fig*) to be on shaky ground; (*: Theorie*) to be shaky
Schwäche ['ʃvɛçə] (**-, -n**) *f* weakness
schwächen *vt* to weaken; **Schwachkopf** (*umg*) *m* dimwit, idiot
schwächlich *adj* weakly, delicate
Schwächling *m* weakling
Schwach- *zW*: **Schwachsinn** *m* (*Med*) mental deficiency, feeble-mindedness (*veraltet*); (*umg: Quatsch*) rubbish; (*fig: umg: unsinnige Tat*) idiocy; **schwachsinnig** *adj* mentally deficient; (*Idee*) idiotic; **Schwachstelle** *f* weak point; **Schwachstrom** *m* weak current
Schwächung ['ʃvɛçʊŋ] *f* weakening
schwafeln ['ʃvaːfəln] (*umg*) *vi* to blather, drivel; (*in einer Prüfung*) to waffle
Schwager ['ʃvaːgər] (**-s, ¨**) *m* brother-in-law
Schwalbe ['ʃvalbə] (**-, -n**) *f* swallow
Schwall [ʃval] (**-(e)s, -e**) *m* surge; (*Worte*) flood, torrent
Schwamm (**-(e)s, ¨e**) *m* sponge; (*Pilz*) fungus; **~ drüber!** (*umg*) (let's) forget it!
schwamm *etc* [ʃvam] *vb siehe* **schwimmen**
schwammig *adj* spongy; (*Gesicht*) puffy; (*vage: Begriff*) woolly (*Brit*), wooly (*US*)
Schwan [ʃvaːn] (**-(e)s, ¨e**) *m* swan
schwand *etc* [ʃvant] *vb siehe* **schwinden**
schwanen *vi unpers*: **jdm schwant es** sb has a foreboding *od* forebodings; **jdm schwant etwas** sb senses something might happen
schwang *etc* [ʃvaŋ] *vb siehe* **schwingen**
schwanger ['ʃvangər] *adj* pregnant
schwängern ['ʃvɛŋərn] *vt* to make pregnant
Schwangerschaft *f* pregnancy
Schwangerschaftsabbruch *m* termination of pregnancy, abortion
Schwank [ʃvaŋk] (**-(e)s, ¨e**) *m* funny story; (*Liter*) merry *od* comical tale; (*Theat*) farce
schwanken *vi* to sway; (*taumeln*) to stagger, reel; (*Preise, Zahlen*) to fluctuate; (*zögern*) to hesitate; (*Überzeugung etc*) to begin to waver; **ins S~ kommen** (*Baum, Gebäude etc*) to start to sway; (*Preise, Kurs etc*) to start to fluctuate *od* vary
Schwankung *f* fluctuation
Schwanz [ʃvants] (**-es, ¨e**) *m* tail; (*umg!: Penis*) prick (*!*); **kein ~** (*umg*) not a (blessed) soul
schwänzen ['ʃvɛntsən] (*umg*) *vt* (*Stunde, Vorlesung*) to skip ▷ *vi* to play truant
Schwarm [ʃvarm] (**-(e)s, ¨e**) *m* swarm; (*umg*) heart-throb, idol
schwärmen ['ʃvɛrmən] *vi* to swarm; **~ für** to be mad *od* wild about
Schwärmerei [ʃvɛrmə'raɪ] *f* enthusiasm
schwärmerisch *adj* impassioned, effusive
Schwarte ['ʃvartə] (**-, -n**) *f* hard skin; (*Speckschwarte*) rind; (*umg: Buch*) tome (*hum*)
schwarz [ʃvarts] *adj* black; (*umg: ungesetzlich*) illicit; (*: katholisch*) Catholic, Papist (*pej*); (*Pol*) Christian Democrat; **ins S~e treffen** (*lit, fig*) to hit the bull's-eye; **das S~e Brett** the notice (*Brit*) *od* bulletin (*US*) board; **~e Liste** blacklist; **~es Loch** black hole; **das S~e Meer** the Black Sea; **S~er Peter** (*Karten*) *children's card game*; **jdm den ~en Peter zuschieben** (*fig: die Verantwortung abschieben*) to pass the buck to sb (*umg*); **dort wählen alle ~** they all vote conservative there; **in den ~en Zahlen** in the black; *siehe auch* **schwarzärgern; schwarzmalen; schwarzsehen**; **Schwarzarbeit** *f* illicit work, moonlighting; **Schwarzbrot** *nt* (*Pumpernickel*) black bread, pumpernickel; (*braun*) brown rye bread
Schwärze ['ʃvɛrtsə] (**-, -n**) *f* blackness; (*Farbe*) blacking; (*Druckerschwärze*) printer's ink
Schwarze, r *f(m)* (*Neger*) black; (*umg: Katholik*) Papist; (*Pol: umg*) Christian Democrat
schwärzen *vt* to blacken
Schwarz- *zW*: **schwarzfahren** *unreg vi* to travel without paying; (*ohne Führerschein*) to

drive without a licence (*Brit*) *od* license (*US*); **Schwarzfahrer** *m* (*Bus etc*) fare dodger (*umg*); **Schwarzhandel** *m* black market (trade); **schwarzhören** *vi* to listen to the radio without a licence (*Brit*) *od* license (*US*)

Schwarz- *zW*: **Schwarzmarkt** *m* black market; **schwarzsehen** *vi unreg* (*TV*) to watch TV without a licence (*Brit*) *od* license (*US*); (*umg*) to see the gloomy side of things; **Schwarzseher** *m* pessimist; (*TV*) viewer without a licence (*Brit*) *od* license (*US*); **Schwarzwald** *m* Black Forest

schwatzen ['ʃvatsən] *vi* to chat; (*schnell, unaufhörlich*) to chatter; (*über belanglose Dinge*) to prattle; (*Unsinn reden*) to blether (*umg*)

Schwätzer, in ['ʃvɛtsər(ɪn)] (**-s, -**) *m(f)* chatterbox; (*Schwafler*) gasbag (*umg*); (*Klatschbase*) gossip

schwatzhaft *adj* talkative, gossipy

Schwebe ['ʃve:bə] *f*: **in der ~** (*fig*) in abeyance; (*Jur, Comm*) pending

Schwebebahn *f* overhead railway (*Brit*) *od* railroad (*US*)

Schwebebalken *m* (*Sport*) beam

schweben *vi* to drift, float; (*hoch*) to soar; (*unentschieden sein*) to be in the balance; **es schwebte mir vor Augen** (*Bild*) I saw it in my mind's eye

Schwede ['ʃve:də] (**-n, -n**) *m* Swede

Schweden (**-s**) *nt* Sweden

Schwedin ['ʃve:dɪn] *f* Swede

schwedisch *adj* Swedish

Schwefel ['ʃve:fəl] (**-s**) *m* sulphur (*Brit*), sulfur (*US*)

schwefelig *adj* sulphurous (*Brit*), sulfurous (*US*)

Schwefelsäure *f* sulphuric (*Brit*) *od* sulfuric (*US*) acid

Schweigegeld *nt* hush money

schweigen ['ʃvaɪgən] *unreg vi* to be silent; (*still sein*) to keep quiet; **kannst du ~?** can you keep a secret?; **ganz zu ~ von ...** to say nothing of ...; **Schweigen** (**-s**) *nt* silence

schweigsam ['ʃvaɪkza:m] *adj* silent; (*als Charaktereigenschaft*) taciturn; **Schweigsamkeit** *f* silence; taciturnity

Schwein [ʃvaɪn] (**-(e)s, -e**) *nt* pig; (*fig: umg*) (good) luck; **kein ~** (*umg*) nobody, not a single person

Schweine- *zW*: **Schweinefleisch** *nt* pork; **Schweinehund** (*umg*) *m* stinker, swine

Schweinerei [ʃvaɪnə'raɪ] *f* mess; (*Gemeinheit*) dirty trick; **so eine ~!** (*umg*) how disgusting!

Schweinestall *m* pigsty

schweinisch *adj* filthy

Schweinsleder *nt* pigskin

Schweiß [ʃvaɪs] (**-es**) *m* sweat, perspiration

schweißen *vt, vi* to weld

Schweißer (**-s, -**) *m* welder

Schweiß- *zW*: **Schweißfüße** *pl* sweaty feet *pl*; **Schweißnaht** *f* weld

Schweiz [ʃvaɪts] *f*: **die ~** Switzerland

Schweizer ['ʃvaɪtsər] (**-s, -**) *m* Swiss ▷ *adj attrib* Swiss; **Schweizerdeutsch** *nt* Swiss German; **schweizerisch** *adj* Swiss

schwelgen ['ʃvɛlgən] *vi* to indulge o.s.; **~ in** *+dat* to indulge in

Schwelle ['ʃvɛlə] (**-, -n**) *f* (*auch fig*) threshold; (*Eisenb*) sleeper (*Brit*), tie (*US*)

schwellen *unreg vi* to swell

Schwellenland *nt* threshold country

Schwellung *f* swelling

schwenkbar *adj* swivel-mounted

schwenken *vt* to swing; (*Kamera*) to pan; (*Fahne*) to wave; (*Kartoffeln*) to toss; (*abspülen*) to rinse ▷ *vi* to turn, swivel; (*Mil*) to wheel

Schwenkung *f* turn; (*Mil*) wheel

schwer [ʃve:r] *adj* heavy; (*schwierig*) difficult, hard; (*schlimm*) serious, bad ▷ *adv* (*sehr*) very (much); (*verletzt etc*) seriously, badly; **~ erziehbar** maladjusted; **jdm/sich etw ~ machen** to make sth difficult for sb/o.s.; **~ verdaulich** indigestible; (*fig*) heavy; **~ verdient** (*Geld*) hard-earned; **~ verletzt** seriously *od* badly injured; **~ verwundet** seriously wounded; **~ erkältet sein** to have a heavy cold; **er lernt ~** he's a slow learner; **er ist ~ in Ordnung** (*umg*) he's a good bloke (*Brit*) *od* guy; **~ hören** to be hard of hearing; *siehe auch* **schwerfallen; schwernehmen; schwertun; schwerwiegend**; **Schwerarbeiter** *m* labourer (*Brit*), laborer (*US*)

Schwere (**-, -n**) *f* weight; heaviness; (*Phys*) gravity; **schwerelos** *adj* weightless; **Schwerelosigkeit** *f* weightlessness

schwer- *zW*: **schwerfallen** *unreg vi*: **jdm schwerfallen** to be difficult for sb; **schwerfällig** *adj* (*auch Stil*) ponderous; (*Gang*) clumsy, awkward; (*Verstand*) slow; **Schwergewicht** *nt* heavyweight; (*fig*) emphasis; **schwerhörig** *adj* hard of hearing; **Schwerindustrie** *f* heavy industry; **Schwerkraft** *f* gravity; **Schwerkranke, r** *f(m)* person who is seriously ill; **schwerlich** *adv* hardly; **Schwermetall** *nt* heavy metal; **schwermütig** *adj* melancholy; **schwernehmen** *unreg vt* to take to heart; **Schwerpunkt** *m* centre (*Brit*) *od* center (*US*) of gravity; (*fig*) emphasis, crucial point

Schwert [ʃve:rt] (**-(e)s, -er**) *nt* sword; **Schwertlilie** *f* iris

schwer- *zW*: **schwertun** *unreg vr*: **sich** *dat od akk* **schwertun** to have difficulties; **Schwerverbrecher** *m* criminal; **schwerwiegend** *adj* weighty, important

Schwester ['ʃvɛstər] (**-, -n**) *f* sister; (*Med*) nurse; **schwesterlich** *adj* sisterly

schwieg *etc* [ʃvi:k] *vb siehe* **schweigen**

Schwieger- *zW*: **Schwiegereltern** *pl* parents-in-law *pl*; **Schwiegermutter** *f* mother-in-law; **Schwiegersohn** *m* son-in-law; **Schwiegertochter** *f* daughter-in-law; **Schwiegervater** *m* father-in-law

Schwiele ['ʃvi:lə] (**-, -n**) *f* callus

schwierig ['ʃvi:rɪç] *adj* difficult, hard;

Schwierigkeit *f* difficulty
Schwimmbad *nt* swimming baths *pl*
schwimmen *unreg vi* to swim; (*treiben, nicht sinken*) to float; (*fig: unsicher sein*) to be all at sea; **im Geld ~** (*umg*) to be rolling in money; **mir schwimmt es vor den Augen** I feel dizzy
Schwimmer (**-s, -**) *m* swimmer; (*Angeln*) float
Schwimm- *zW*: **Schwimmflosse** *f* (*von Taucher*) flipper; **Schwimmlehrer** *m* swimming instructor; **Schwimmsport** *m* swimming; **Schwimmweste** *f* life jacket
Schwindel ['ʃvɪndəl] (**-s**) *m* dizziness; (*Betrug*) swindle, fraud; (*Zeug*) stuff; **in ~ erregender Höhe** at a dizzy height; **schwindelfrei** *adj* free from giddiness
schwindeln *vi* (*umg: lügen*) to fib; **mir schwindelt** I feel dizzy; **jdm schwindelt es** sb feels dizzy
schwinden ['ʃvɪndən] *unreg vi* to disappear; (*Kräfte*) to fade, fail; (*sich verringern*) to decrease
Schwindler (**-s, -**) *m* swindler; (*Hochstapler*) con man, fraud; (*Lügner*) liar
schwindlig *adj* dizzy; **mir ist ~** I feel dizzy
schwingen ['ʃvɪŋən] *unreg vt* to swing; (*Waffe etc*) to brandish ▷ *vi* to swing; (*vibrieren*) to vibrate; (*klingen*) to sound
Schwinger (**-s, -**) *m* (*Boxen*) swing
Schwingtür *f* swing door(s *pl*) (*Brit*), swinging door(s *pl*) (*US*)
Schwingung *f* vibration; (*Phys*) oscillation
Schwips [ʃvɪps] (**-es, -e**) *m*: **einen ~ haben** to be tipsy
schwirren ['ʃvɪrən] *vi* to buzz
schwitzen *vi* to sweat, perspire
schwoll *etc* [ʃvɔl] *vb siehe* **schwellen**
schwören ['ʃvø:rən] *unreg vt, vi* to swear; **auf jdn/etw ~** (*fig*) to swear by sb/sth
schwul [ʃvu:l] (*umg*) *adj* gay, queer (*pej*)
schwül [ʃvy:l] *adj* sultry, close
Schwule, r (*umg*) *m* gay, queer (*pej*), fag (*US pej*)
Schwüle (**-**) *f* sultriness, closeness
schwülstig ['ʃvʏlstɪç] *adj* pompous
Schwung [ʃvʊŋ] (**-(e)s, ¨-e**) *m* swing; (*Triebkraft*) momentum; (*fig: Energie*) verve, energy; (*umg: Menge*) batch; **in ~ sein** (*fig*) to be in full swing; **~ in die Sache bringen** (*umg*) to liven things up; **schwunghaft** *adj* brisk, lively; **schwungvoll** *adj* vigorous
Schwur (**-(e)s, ¨-e**) *m* oath
Schwurgericht *nt* court with a jury
sechs [zɛks] *num* six; **Sechseck** *nt* hexagon; **sechshundert** *num* six hundred
sechste, r, s *adj* sixth
Sechstel ['zɛkstəl] (**-s, -**) *nt* sixth
sechzehn ['zɛçtse:n] *num* sixteen
sechzig ['zɛçtsɪç] *num* sixty
See[1] [ze:] (**-, -n**) *f* sea; **an der ~** by the sea, at the seaside; **in ~ stechen** to put to sea; **auf hoher ~** on the high seas
See[2] [ze:] (**-s, -n**) *m* lake
See- *zW*: **Seebad** *nt* seaside resort; **Seefahrt** *f* seafaring; (*Reise*) voyage; **Seegang** *m* (motion of the) sea; **Seegras** *nt* seaweed; **Seehund** *m* seal; **Seeigel** *m* sea urchin; **seekrank** *adj* seasick; **Seekrankheit** *f* seasickness; **Seelachs** *m* rock salmon
Seele ['ze:lə] (**-, -n**) *f* soul; (*Mittelpunkt*) life and soul; **jdm aus der ~ sprechen** to express exactly what sb feels; **das liegt mir auf der ~** it weighs heavily on my mind; **eine ~ von Mensch** an absolute dear; **seelenruhig** *adv* calmly
Seeleute ['ze:lɔʏtə] *pl* seamen *pl*
Seel- *zW*: **seelisch** *adj* mental; (*Rel*) spiritual; (*Belastung*) emotional; **Seelsorge** *f* pastoral duties *pl*; **Seelsorger** (**-s, -**) *m* clergyman
See- *zW*: **Seemacht** *f* naval power; **Seemann** (**-(e)s**, *pl* **-leute**) *m* seaman, sailor; **Seemeile** *f* nautical mile
See- *zW*: **Seenot** *f*: **in Seenot** (*Schiff etc*) in distress; **Seeräuber** *m* pirate; **Seerose** *f* waterlily; **Seestern** *m* starfish; **seetüchtig** *adj* seaworthy; **Seeweg** *m* sea route; **auf dem Seeweg** by sea; **Seezunge** *f* sole
Segel ['ze:gəl] (**-s, -**) *nt* sail; **mit vollen ~n** under full sail *od* canvas; (*fig*) with gusto; **die ~ streichen** (*fig*) to give in; **Segelboot** *nt* yacht; **Segelfliegen** (**-s**) *nt* gliding; **Segelflieger** *m* glider pilot; **Segelflugzeug** *nt* glider
segeln *vt, vi* to sail; **durch eine Prüfung ~** (*umg*) to flop in an exam, fail (in) an exam
Segel- *zW*: **Segelschiff** *nt* sailing vessel; **Segelsport** *m* sailing; **Segeltuch** *nt* canvas
Segen ['ze:gən] (**-s, -**) *m* blessing
segensreich *adj* beneficial
Segler ['ze:glər] (**-s, -**) *m* sailor, yachtsman; (*Boot*) sailing boat
segnen ['ze:gnən] *vt* to bless
sehen ['ze:ən] *unreg vt, vi* to see; (*in bestimmte Richtung*) to look; (*Fernsehsendung*) to watch; **sieht man das?** does it show?; **da sieht man(s) mal wieder!** that's typical!; **du siehst das nicht richtig** you've got it wrong; **so ge~** looked at in this way; **sich ~ lassen** to put in an appearance, appear; **das neue Rathaus kann sich ~ lassen** the new town hall is certainly something to be proud of; **siehe oben/unten** see above/below; **da kann man mal ~** that just shows (you) *od* just goes to show (*umg*); **mal ~!** we'll see!; **darauf ~, dass ...** to make sure (that) ...; **jdn kommen ~** to see sb coming
sehenswert *adj* worth seeing
Sehenswürdigkeiten *pl* sights *pl* (of a town)
Seher (**-s, -**) *m* seer
Sehfehler *m* sight defect
Sehne ['ze:nə] (**-, -n**) *f* sinew; (*an Bogen*) string
sehnen *vr*: **sich ~ nach** to long *od* yearn for
sehnig *adj* sinewy
sehnlich *adj* ardent
Sehnsucht *f* longing
sehnsüchtig *adj* longing; (*Erwartung*) eager
sehr [ze:r] *adv* (*vor adj, adv*) very; (*mit Verben*) a lot, (very) much; **zu ~** too much; **er ist ~ dafür/dagegen** he is all for it/very much

against it; **wie ~ er sich auch bemühte ...** however much he tried ...
seicht [zaɪçt] *adj* (*lit, fig*) shallow
Seide ['zaɪdə] (**-, -n**) *f* silk
seiden *adj* silk; **Seidenpapier** *nt* tissue paper
seidig ['zaɪdɪç] *adj* silky
Seife ['zaɪfə] (**-, -n**) *f* soap
Seifen- *zW*: **Seifenlauge** *f* soapsuds *pl*; **Seifenschale** *f* soap dish; **Seifenschaum** *m* lather
seihen ['zaɪən] *vt* to strain, filter
Seil [zaɪl] (**-(e)s, -e**) *nt* rope; (*Kabel*) cable; **Seilbahn** *f* cable railway; **Seiltänzer, in** *m(f)* tightrope walker; **Seilzug** *m* tackle
sein [zaɪn] (*pt* **war**, *pp* **gewesen**) *vi* **1** to be; **ich bin** I am; **du bist** you are; **er/sie/es ist** he/she/it is; **wir sind/ihr seid/sie sind** we/you/they are; **wir waren** we were; **wir sind gewesen** we have been
2: **seien Sie nicht böse** don't be angry; **sei so gut und ...** be so kind as to ...; **das wäre gut** that would *od* that'd be a good thing; **wenn ich Sie wäre** if I were *od* was you; **das wärs** that's all, that's it; **morgen bin ich in Rom** tomorrow I'll *od* I will *od* I shall be in Rome; **waren Sie mal in Rom?** have you ever been to Rome?
3: **wie ist das zu verstehen?** how is that to be understood?; **er ist nicht zu ersetzen** he cannot be replaced; **mit ihr ist nicht zu reden** you can't talk to her
4: **mir ist kalt** I'm cold; **mir ist, als hätte ich ihn früher schon einmal gesehen** I've a feeling I've seen him before; **was ist?** what's the matter?, what is it?; **ist was?** is something the matter?; **es sei denn(, dass ...)** unless ...; **wie dem auch sei** be that as it may; **wie wäre es mit ...?** how *od* what about ...?; **etw sein lassen** (*aufhören*) to stop (doing) sth; (*nicht tun*) to drop sth, leave sth; **lass das sein!** stop that!; **es ist an dir, zu ...** it's up to you to ...; **was sind Sie (beruflich)?** what do you do?; **das kann schon sein** that may well be
▷ *pron* his; (*bei Dingen*) its
seine, r, s *poss pron* his; its; **er ist gut ~ zwei Meter** (*umg*) he's a good two metres (*Brit*) *od* meters (*US*); **die S~n** (*geh*) his family, his people; **jedem das S~** to each his own
seiner *gen von* **er; es** ▷ *pron* of him; of it
seinerseits *adv* for his part
seinerzeit *adv* in those days, formerly
seinesgleichen *pron* people like him
seinetwegen *adv* (*für ihn*) for his sake; (*wegen ihm*) on his account; (*von ihm aus*) as far as he is concerned
Seismograf [zaɪsmo'gra:f] (**-en, -en**) *m* seismograph
seit [zaɪt] *präp +dat* since; (*Zeitdauer*) for, in (*bes US*) ▷ *konj* since; **er ist ~ einer Woche hier** he has been here for a week; **~ Langem** for a long time; **seitdem** *adv, konj* since
Seite ['zaɪtə] (**-, -n**) *f* side; (*Buchseite*) page; (*Mil*) flank; **~ an Seite** side by side; **jdm zur ~ stehen** (*fig*) to stand by sb's side; **jdn zur ~ nehmen** to take sb aside *od* on one side; **auf der einen ~ ..., auf der anderen (seite) ...** on the one hand ..., on the other (hand) ...; **einer Sache** *dat* **die beste ~ abgewinnen** to make the best *od* most of sth; *siehe auch* **aufseiten; vonseiten**
Seiten- *zW*: **Seitenairbag** *m* (*Aut*) side-impact airbag; **Seitenansicht** *f* side view; **Seitenhieb** *m* (*fig*) passing shot, dig; **Seitenruder** *nt* (*Aviat*) rudder
seitens *präp +gen* on the part of
Seiten- *zW*: **Seitenschiff** *nt* aisle; **Seitensprung** *m* extramarital escapade; **Seitenstechen** *nt* (a) stitch; **Seitenstraße** *f* side road; **Seitenstreifen** *m* (*der Straße*) verge (*Brit*), berm (*US*); (*der Autobahn*) hard shoulder (*Brit*), shoulder (*US*)
seit- *zW*: **seither** [zaɪt'he:r] *adv, konj* since (then); **seitlich** *adv* on one/the side ▷ *adj* side *attrib*; **seitwärts** *adv* sideways
Sekretär [zekre'tɛ:r] *m* secretary; (*Möbel*) bureau
Sekretariat [zekretari'a:t] (**-(e)s, -e**) *nt* secretary's office, secretariat
Sekt [zɛkt] (**-(e)s, -e**) *m* sparkling wine
Sekte (**-, -n**) *f* sect
Sektor ['zɛktɔr] *m* sector; (*Sachgebiet*) field
Sekunde [ze'kʊndə] (**-, -n**) *f* second; **Sekundenkleber** *m* superglue
selber ['zɛlbər] *demon pron* = **selbst**
Selbst [zɛlpst] (**-**) *nt* self
selbst [zɛlpst] *pron* **1**: **ich/er/wir selbst** I myself/he himself/we ourselves; **sie ist die Tugend selbst** she's virtue itself; **er braut sein Bier selbst** he brews his own beer; **das muss er selbst wissen** it's up to him; **wie gehts? — gut, und selbst?** how are things? — fine, and yourself?
2 (*ohne Hilfe*) alone, on my/his/one's *etc* own; **von selbst** by itself; **er kam von selbst** he came of his own accord; **selbst ist der Mann/die Frau!** self-reliance is the name of the game (*umg*); **selbst gemacht** home-made; **selbst gestrickt** hand-knitted; (*umg: Methode etc*) homespun, amateurish; **selbst verdientes Geld** money one has earned o.s.
▷ *adv* even; **selbst wenn** even if; **selbst Gott** even God (himself)
Selbstachtung *f* self-respect
selbständig *etc* ['zɛlpʃtɛndɪç] *adj* = **selbstständig** *etc*
Selbst- *zW*: **Selbstauslöser** *m* (*Phot*) delayed-action shutter release; **Selbstbedienung** *f* self-service; **Selbstbefriedigung** *f* masturbation; (*fig*) self-gratification; **Selbstbeherrschung** *f* self-control; **selbstbewusst** *adj* self-confident; (*selbstsicher*) self-assured; **Selbstbewusstsein** *nt* self-confidence; **Selbsterhaltung** *f* self-preservation; **Selbsterkenntnis** *f* self-

knowledge; **selbstgefällig** *adj* smug, self-satisfied; **Selbstgespräch** *nt* conversation with o.s.; **selbstklebend** *adj* self-adhesive; **Selbstkostenpreis** *m* cost price; **selbstlos** *adj* unselfish, selfless; **Selbstmord** *m* suicide; **Selbstmörder, in** *m(f)* (*Person*) suicide; **selbstmörderisch** *adj* suicidal; **selbstsicher** *adj* self-assured; **selbstständig** ['zɛlpstʃtɛndɪç] *adj* independent; **sich Selbst machen** (*beruflich*) to set up on one's own, start one's own business; **Selbstständigkeit** *f* independence; **selbsttätig** *adj* automatic; **Selbstversorger** *m*: **Selbstversorger sein** to be self-sufficient *od* self-reliant; **Urlaub für Selbstversorger** self-catering holiday

selbstverständlich *adj* obvious ▷ *adv* naturally; **ich halte das für ~** I take that for granted

Selbstverständlichkeit *f* (*Unbefangenheit*) naturalness; (*natürliche Voraussetzung*) matter of course

Selbst- *zW*: **Selbstverteidigung** *f* self-defence (*Brit*), self-defense (*US*); **Selbstvertrauen** *nt* self-confidence; **Selbstverwaltung** *f* autonomy, self-government

selig ['ze:lɪç] *adj* happy, blissful; (*Rel*) blessed; (*tot*) late; **Seligkeit** *f* bliss

Sellerie ['zɛləri:] (**-s, -(s)** *od* **-, -n**) *m od f* celery

selten ['zɛltən] *adj* rare ▷ *adv* seldom, rarely; **Seltenheit** *f* rarity

Selterswasser ['zɛltərsvasər] *nt* soda water

seltsam ['zɛltza:m] *adj* curious, strange

seltsamerweise *adv* curiously, strangely

Seltsamkeit *f* strangeness

Semester [ze'mɛstər] (**-s, -**) *nt* semester; **ein älteres ~** a senior student

Semikolon [-'ko:lɔn] (**-s, -s**) *nt* semicolon

Seminar [zemi'na:r] (**-s, -e**) *nt* seminary; (*Kurs*) seminar; (*Univ: Ort*) department building

Semmel ['zɛməl] (**-, -n**) *f* roll

sen. *abk* (= *senior*) sen.

Senat [ze'na:t] (**-(e)s, -e**) *m* senate

Sendebereich *m* transmission range

Sendefolge *f* (*Serie*) series

senden[1] *unreg vt* to send

senden[2] *vt, vi* (*Rundf, TV*) to transmit, broadcast

Sender (**-s, -**) *m* station; (*Anlage*) transmitter

Sendestation *f* transmitting station

Sendung ['zɛndʊŋ] *f* consignment; (*Aufgabe*) mission; (*Rundf, TV*) transmission; (*Programm*) programme (*Brit*), program (*US*)

Senegal ['ze:negal] (**-s**) *nt* Senegal

Senf [zɛnf] (**-(e)s, -e**) *m* mustard; **seinen ~ dazugeben** (*umg*) to put one's oar in

Senior ['ze:niɔr] (**-s, -en**) *m* (*Rentner*) senior citizen; (*Geschäftspartner*) senior partner

Seniorenpass [zeni'o:rənpas] *m* senior citizen's travel pass (*Brit*)

Senkblei ['zɛŋkblaɪ] *nt* plumb

Senke (**-, -n**) *f* depression

Senkel (**-s, -**) *m* (shoe)lace

senken *vt* to lower; (*Kopf*) to bow; (*Tech*) to sink ▷ *vr* to sink; (*Stimme*) to drop

Senk- *zW*: **Senkfuß** *m* flat foot; **senkrecht** *adj* vertical, perpendicular; **Senkrechte** *f* perpendicular

Sensation [zɛnzatsi'o:n] *f* sensation

sensationell [zɛnzatsio'nɛl] *adj* sensational

Sense ['zɛnzə] (**-, -n**) *f* scythe; **dann ist ~!** (*umg*) that's the end!

sensibel [zɛn'zi:bəl] *adj* sensitive

sensibilisieren [zɛnzibili'zi:rən] *vt* to sensitize

sentimental [zɛntimɛn'ta:l] *adj* sentimental

Sentimentalität [zɛntimɛntali'tɛ:t] *f* sentimentality

separat [zepa'ra:t] *adj* separate; (*Wohnung, Zimmer*) self-contained

September [zɛp'tɛmbər] (**-(s), -**) *m* September; **im ~** in September; **im Monat ~** in the month of September; **heute ist der zweite ~** today is the second of September *od* September second (*US*); (*geschrieben*) today is 2nd September; **in diesem ~** this September; **Anfang/Ende/Mitte ~** at the beginning/end/in the middle of September

sequentiell [zekvɛntsi'ɛl] *adj* = **sequenziell**

Serbe ['zɛrbə] (**-n, -n**) *m* Serbian

Serbien (**-s**) *nt* Serbia; **~ und Montenegro** Serbia and Montenegro

Serbin *f* Serbian

serbisch *adj* Serbian

Serie ['ze:riə] *f* series

seriell [zeri'ɛl] *adj* (*Comput*) serial; **~e Daten** serial data *pl*; **~er Anschluss** serial port; **~er Drucker** serial printer; **serienweise** *adv* in series

seriös [zeri'ø:s] *adj* serious; (*anständig*) respectable

Serpentine [zɛrpɛn'ti:nə] *f* hairpin (bend)

Serum ['ze:rʊm] (**-s, Seren**) *nt* serum

Service[1] [zɛr'vi:s] (**-(s), -**) *nt* (*Gläserservice*) set; (*Geschirr*) service

Service[2] ['sə:vɪs] (**-, -s**) *m* (*Comm, Sport*) service

servieren [zɛr'vi:rən] *vt, vi* to serve

Serviette [zɛrvi'ɛtə] *f* napkin, serviette

Servolenkung *f* power steering

Sessel ['zɛsəl] (**-s, -**) *m* armchair; **Sessellift** *m* chairlift

sesshaft ['zɛshaft] *adj* settled; (*ansässig*) resident

Set [zɛt] (**-s, -s**) *nt od m* set; (*Deckchen*) tablemat

setzen ['zɛtsən] *vt* to put, place, set; (*Baum etc*) to plant; (*Segel, Typ*) to set ▷ *vr* (*Platz nehmen*) to sit down; (*Kaffee, Tee*) to settle ▷ *vi* to leap; (*wetten*) to bet; (*Typ*) to set; **jdm ein Denkmal ~** to build a monument to sb; **sich zu jdm ~** to sit with sb

Setzer ['zɛtsər] (**-s, -**) *m* (*Typ*) typesetter

Setzerei [zɛtsə'raɪ] *f* caseroom; (*Firma*) typesetting firm

Setzling *m* young plant

Seuche ['zɔʏçə] (**-, -n**) *f* epidemic

Seuchengebiet *nt* infected area

seufzen ['zɔʏftsən] *vt, vi* to sigh
Seufzer ['zɔʏftsər] (**-s, -**) *m* sigh
Sex [zɛks] (**-(es)**) *m* sex
Sexualität [zɛksuali'tɛ:t] *f* sex, sexuality
Sexualobjekt *nt* sex object
sexuell [zɛksu'ɛl] *adj* sexual
Seychellen [ze'ʃɛlən] *pl* Seychelles *pl*
sezieren [ze'tsi:rən] *vt* to dissect
Shampoo [ʃam'pu:] (**-s, -s**) *nt* shampoo
Shorts [ʃo:rts] *pl* shorts *pl*
Sibirien [zi'bi:riən] (**-s**) *nt* Siberia
sibirisch *adj* Siberian
sich [zɪç] *pron* **1** (*akk*): **er/sie/es ... sich** he/she/it ... himself/herself/itself; **sie** *pl*/ **man ... sich** they/one ...themselves/oneself; **Sie ... sich** you ... yourself/yourselves *pl*; **sich wiederholen** to repeat oneself/itself
2 (*dat*): **er/sie/es ... sich** he/she/it ... to himself/herself/itself; **sie** *pl*/**man ... sich** they/one ... to themselves/oneself; **Sie ... sich** you ... to yourself/yourselves *pl*; **sie hat sich einen Pullover gekauft** she bought herself a jumper; **sich die Haare waschen** to wash one's hair
3 (*mit Präposition*): **haben Sie Ihren Ausweis bei sich?** do you have your pass on you?; **er hat nichts bei sich** he's got nothing on him; **sie bleiben gern unter sich** they keep themselves to themselves
4 (*einander*) each other, one another; **sie bekämpfen sich** they fight each other *od* one another
5: dieses Auto fährt sich gut this car drives well; **hier sitzt es sich gut** it's good to sit here
Sichel ['zɪçəl] (**-, -n**) *f* sickle; (*Mondsichel*) crescent
sicher ['zɪçər] *adj* safe; (*gewiss*) certain; (*Hand, Job*) steady; (*zuverlässig*) secure, reliable; (*selbstsicher*) confident; (*Stellung*) secure ▷ *adv* (*natürlich*): **du hast dich ~ verrechnet** you must have counted wrongly; **vor jdm/etw ~ sein** to be safe from sb/sth; **sich** *dat* **einer Sache/jds ~ sein** to be sure of sth/sb; **~ ist sicher** you can't be too sure
Sicherheit ['zɪçərhaɪt] *f* safety; (*auch Fin*) security; (*Gewissheit*) certainty; (*Selbstsicherheit*) confidence; **die öffentliche ~** public security; **~ im Straßenverkehr** road safety; **~ leisten** (*Comm*) to offer security
Sicherheits- *zW*: **Sicherheitsabstand** *m* safe distance; **Sicherheitsglas** *nt* safety glass; **Sicherheitsgurt** *m* seat belt; **sicherheitshalber** *adv* to be on the safe side; **Sicherheitsnadel** *f* safety pin; **Sicherheitsvorkehrung** *f* safety precaution
sicherlich *adv* certainly, surely
sichern *vt* to secure; (*schützen*) to protect; (*Bergsteiger etc*) to belay; (*Waffe*) to put the safety catch on; (*Comput: Daten*) to back up; **jdm/sich etw ~** to secure sth for sb/for o.s.
sicherstellen *vt* to impound; (*garantieren*) to guarantee
Sicherung *f* (*Sichern*) securing; (*Vorrichtung*) safety device; (*an Waffen*) safety catch; (*Elek*) fuse; **da ist (bei) ihm die ~ durchgebrannt** (*fig: umg*) he blew a fuse
Sicherungskopie *f* backup copy
Sicht [zɪçt] (**-**) *f* sight; (*Aussicht*) view; (*Sehweite*) visibility; **auf** *od* **nach ~** (*Fin*) at sight; **auf lange ~** on a long-term basis; **sichtbar** *adj* visible
sichten *vt* to sight; (*auswählen*) to sort out; (*ordnen*) to sift through
Sicht- *zW*: **sichtlich** *adj* evident, obvious; **Sichtverhältnisse** *pl* visibility *sing*; **Sichtvermerk** *m* visa; **Sichtweite** *f* visibility; **außer Sichtweite** out of sight
sickern ['zɪkərn] *vi* (*Hilfsverb sein*) to seep; (*in Tropfen*) to drip
Sie [zi:] *nom, akk pron* you
sie *pron* (*sing: nom*) she; (*: akk*) her; (*pl: nom*) they; (*: akk*) them
Sieb [zi:p] (**-(e)s, -e**) *nt* sieve; (*Koch*) strainer; (*Gemüsesieb*) colander
sieben[1] ['zi:bən] *vt* to sieve, sift; (*Flüssigkeit*) to strain ▷ *vi*: **bei der Prüfung wird stark gesiebt** (*fig: umg*) the exam will weed a lot of people out
sieben[2] ['zi:bən] *num* seven; **siebenhundert** *num* seven hundred; **Siebensachen** *pl* belongings *pl*
siebte, r, s ['zi:ptə(r, s)] *adj* seventh
Siebtel (**-s, -**) *nt* seventh
siebzehn ['zi:ptse:n] *num* seventeen
siebzig ['zi:ptsɪç] *num* seventy
sieden ['zi:dən] *vt, vi* to boil
Siedepunkt *m* boiling point
Siedlung *f* settlement; (*Häusersiedlung*) housing estate (*Brit*) *od* development (*US*)
Sieg [zi:k] (**-(e)s, -e**) *m* victory
Siegel ['zi:gəl] (**-s, -**) *nt* seal; **Siegellack** *m* sealing wax; **Siegelring** *m* signet ring
siegen ['zi:gən] *vi* to be victorious; (*Sport*) to win; **über jdn/etw ~** (*fig*) to triumph over sb/sth; (*in Wettkampf*) to beat sb/sth
Sieger, in (**-s, -**) *m(f)* victor; (*Sport etc*) winner
siegessicher *adj* sure of victory
siehe ['zi:ə] *imperativ* see; (*siehe da*) behold
siezen ['zi:tsən] *vt* to address as "Sie"; *siehe auch* **duzen**
Signal [zɪ'gna:l] (**-s, -e**) *nt* signal
signalisieren [zɪgnali'zi:rən] *vt* (*lit, fig*) to signal
Silbe ['zɪlbə] (**-, -n**) *f* syllable; **er hat es mit keiner ~ erwähnt** he didn't say a word about it
Silber ['zɪlbər] (**-s**) *nt* silver; **Silberblick** *m*: **einen Silberblick haben** to have a slight squint
silbern *adj* silver
Silberpapier *nt* silver paper
Silhouette [zilu'ɛtə] *f* silhouette
Silo ['zi:lo] (**-s, -s**) *nt od m* silo
Silvester [zɪl'vɛstər] (**-s, -**) *m or nt* New Year's Eve, Hogmanay (*Scot*)

Simbabwe [zɪm'ba:bvə] (**-s**) *nt* Zimbabwe
simpel ['zɪmpəl] *adj* simple
Sims [zɪms] (**-es, -e**) *nt od m* (*Kaminsims*) mantelpiece; (*Fenstersims*) (window)sill
Simulant, in [zimu'lant(ɪn)] (**-en, -en**) *m(f)* malingerer
simulieren [zimu'li:rən] *vt* to simulate; (*vortäuschen*) to feign ▷ *vi* to feign illness
simultan [zimʊl'ta:n] *adj* simultaneous
Sinfonie [zɪnfo'ni:] *f* symphony
Singapur ['zɪŋgapu:r] (**-s**) *nt* Singapore
singen ['zɪŋən] *unreg vt, vi* to sing
Single[1] ['sɪŋgəl] (**-s, -s**) *m* (*Alleinlebender*) single person
Single[2] ['sɪŋgəl] (**-, -s**) *f* (*Mus*) single
Singular ['zɪŋgula:r] *m* singular
Singvogel ['zɪŋfo:gəl] *m* songbird
sinken ['zɪŋkən] *unreg vi* to sink; (*Boden, Gebäude*) to subside; (*Fundament*) to settle; (*Preise etc*) to fall, go down; **den Mut/die Hoffnung ~ lassen** to lose courage/hope
Sinn [zɪn] (**-(e)s, -e**) *m* mind; (*Wahrnehmungssinn*) sense; (*Bedeutung*) sense, meaning; **im ~e des Gesetzes** according to the spirit of the law; **~ für etw** sense of sth; **im ~e des Verstorbenen** in accordance with the wishes of the deceased; **von ~en sein** to be out of one's mind; **das ist nicht der ~ der Sache** that is not the point; **das hat keinen ~** there is no point in that; **Sinnbild** *nt* symbol
sinnen *unreg vi* to ponder; **auf etw** *akk* **~** to contemplate sth; **über etw** *akk* **~** to reflect on sth
Sinnenmensch *m* sensualist
Sinnestäuschung *f* illusion
sinngemäß *adj* faithful; (*Wiedergabe*) in one's own words
sinnig *adj* apt; (*ironisch*) clever
Sinn- *zW*: **sinnlich** *adj* sensual, sensuous; (*Wahrnehmung*) sensory; **Sinnlichkeit** *f* sensuality; **sinnlos** *adj* senseless, meaningless; **sinnlos betrunken** blind drunk; **Sinnlosigkeit** *f* senselessness, meaninglessness; **sinnvoll** *adj* meaningful; (*vernünftig*) sensible
Sintflut ['zɪntflu:t] *f* Flood; **nach uns die ~** (*umg*) it doesn't matter what happens after we've gone
Siphon [zi'fõ:] (**-s, -s**) *m* siphon
Sippe ['zɪpə] (**-, -n**) *f* (extended) family; (*umg*: *Verwandtschaft*) clan
Sippschaft ['zɪpʃaft] (*pej*) *f* tribe; (*Bande*) gang
Sirene [zi're:nə] (**-, -n**) *f* siren
Sirup ['zi:rʊp] (**-s, -e**) *m* syrup
Sitte ['zɪtə] (**-, -n**) *f* custom; **Sitten** *pl* morals *pl*; **was sind denn das für ~n?** what sort of way is that to behave?; **Sittenpolizei** *f* vice squad
Sitt- *zW*: **sittlich** *adj* moral; **Sittlichkeit** *f* morality; **Sittlichkeitsverbrechen** *nt* sex offence (*Brit*) *od* offense (*US*)
Situation [zituatsi'o:n] *f* situation
Sitz [zɪts] (**-es, -e**) *m* seat; (*von Firma, Verwaltung*) headquarters *pl*; **der Anzug hat einen guten ~** the suit sits well
sitzen *unreg vi* to sit; (*Bemerkung, Schlag*) to strike home; (*Gelerntes*) to have sunk in; (*umg*: *im Gefängnis sitzen*) to be inside; **locker ~** to be loose; **einen ~ haben** (*umg*) to have had one too many; **er sitzt im Kultusministerium** (*umg*: *sein*) he's in the Ministry of Education; **~ bleiben** to remain seated; (*Sch*) to have to repeat a year; **auf etw** *dat* **~ bleiben** to be lumbered with sth; **~ lassen** (*Sch*) to keep down a year; (*Mädchen*) to jilt; (*Wartenden*) to stand up; **etw auf sich** *dat* **~ lassen** to take sth lying down
sitzend *adj* (*Tätigkeit*) sedentary
Sitz- *zW*: **Sitzgelegenheit** *f* seats *pl*; **Sitzplatz** *m* seat; **Sitzstreik** *m* sit-down strike
Sitzung *f* meeting
sizilianisch *adj* Sicilian
Sizilien [zi'tsi:liən] (**-s**) *nt* Sicily
Skala ['ska:la] (**-, Skalen**) *f* scale; (*fig*) range
Skalpell [skal'pɛl] (**-s, -e**) *nt* scalpel
Skandal [skan'da:l] (**-s, -e**) *m* scandal
skandalös [skanda'lø:s] *adj* scandalous
Skandinavien [skandi'na:viən] (**-s**) *nt* Scandinavia
Skandinavier, in (**-s, -**) *m(f)* Scandinavian
skandinavisch *adj* Scandinavian
Skelett [ske'lɛt] (**-(e)s, -e**) *nt* skeleton
Skepsis ['skɛpsɪs] (**-**) *f* scepticism (*Brit*), skepticism (*US*)
skeptisch ['skɛptɪʃ] *adj* sceptical (*Brit*), skeptical (*US*)
Ski [ʃi:] (**-s, -er**) *m* ski; **~ laufen** *od* **fahren** to ski; **Skifahrer** *m* skier; **Skilehrer** *m* ski instructor; **Skilift** *m* ski lift; **Skispringen** *nt* ski jumping; **Skistiefel** *m* ski boot; **Skistock** *m* ski pole
Skizze ['skɪtsə] (**-, -n**) *f* sketch
skizzieren [skɪ'tsi:rən] *vt* to sketch; (*fig*: *Plan etc*) to outline ▷ *vi* to sketch
Sklave ['skla:və] (**-n, -n**) *m* slave
Skonto ['skɔnto] (**-s, -s**) *nt od m* discount
Skorpion [skɔrpi'o:n] (**-s, -e**) *m* scorpion; (*Astrol*) Scorpio
Skrupel ['skru:pəl] (**-s, -**) *m* scruple; **skrupellos** *adj* unscrupulous
Skulptur [skʊlp'tu:r] *f* sculpture
Slalom ['sla:lɔm] (**-s, -s**) *m* slalom
Slip [slɪp] (**-s, -s**) *m* (pair of) briefs *pl*
Slowake [slo'va:kə] (**-n, -n**) *m* Slovak
Slowakei [slova'kaɪ] *f* Slovakia; **slowakisch** *adj* Slovak
Slowenien [slo've:niən] (**-s**) *nt* Slovenia
slowenisch *adj* Slovene
Smaragd [sma'rakt] (**-(e)s, -e**) *m* emerald
Smoking ['smo:kɪŋ] (**-s, -s**) *m* dinner jacket (*Brit*), tuxedo (*US*)
SMS (**-, -**) *f abk* (= *Short Message Service*) SMS; **jdm eine ~ schicken** to send sb a text
so [zo:] *adv* **1** (*so sehr*) so; **so groß/schön** *etc* so big/nice *etc*; **so groß/schön wie ...** as big/nice as ...; **das hat ihn so geärgert, dass ...**

that annoyed him so much that ...
2 (*auf diese Weise*) like this; **so genannt** so-called; **mach es nicht so** don't do it like that; **so oder so** (in) one way or the other; **... oder so** something (like that); **und so weiter** and so on; **so viel (wie)** as much as; **rede nicht so viel** don't talk so much; **so weit sein** to be ready; **so weit wie** *od* **als möglich** as far as possible; **ich bin so weit zufrieden** by and large I'm quite satisfied; **es ist bald so weit** it's nearly time; **so wenig (wie)** no more (than), not any more (than); **so wenig wie möglich** as little as possible; **so ein ...** such a ...; **so einer wie ich** somebody like me; **so (et)was** something like this/that; **na so was!** well I never!; **das ist gut so** that's fine; **sie ist nun einmal so** that's just the way she is; **das habe ich nur so gesagt** I didn't really mean it
3 (*umg: umsonst*): **ich habe es so bekommen** I got it for nothing
4 (*als Füllwort: nicht übersetzt*): **so mancher** a number of people *pl*
▷ *konj*: **so wie es jetzt ist** as things are at the moment; *siehe auch* **sodass**
▷ *interj*: **so?** really?; **so, das wärs** right, that's it then

Söckchen [zœkçən] *nt* ankle sock
Socke ['zɔkə] (**-, -n**) *f* sock; **sich auf die ~n machen** (*umg*) to get going
sodass [zo'das] *konj* so that
Sodawasser ['zo:davasər] *nt* soda water
Sodbrennen ['zo:tbrɛnən] (**-s**) *nt* heartburn
soeben [zo'|e:bən] *adv* just (now)
Sofa ['zo:fa] (**-s, -s**) *nt* sofa
sofern [zo'fɛrn] *konj* if, provided (that)
soff *etc* [zɔf] *vb siehe* **saufen**
sofort [zo'fɔrt] *adv* immediately, at once; **(ich) komme ~!** (I'm) just coming!
sofortig *adj* immediate
Softeis ['sɔft|aɪs] (**-es**) *nt* soft ice-cream
Softie ['zɔfti:] (**-s, -s**) (*umg*) *m* softy
Software ['zɔftwɛ:ər] (**-, -s**) *f* software; **Softwarepaket** *nt* software package
sog *etc* [zo:k] *vb siehe* **saugen**
sogar [zo'ga:r] *adv* even
sogenannt ['zo:gənant] *adj attrib* so-called
sogleich [zo'glaɪç] *adv* straight away, at once
Sohle ['zo:lə] (**-, -n**) *f* (*Fußsohle*) sole; (*Talsohle etc*) bottom; (*Min*) level; **auf leisen ~n** (*fig*) softly, noiselessly
Sohn [zo:n] (**-(e)s, ¨-e**) *m* son
Sojasoße ['zo:jazo:sə] *f* soy *od* soya sauce
solang, solange *konj* as *od* so long as
Solarium [zo'la:riʊm] *nt* solarium
Solbad ['zo:lba:t] *nt* saltwater bath
solch [zɔlç] *adj inv* such
Soldat [zɔl'da:t] (**-en, -en**) *m* soldier
Söldner ['zœldnər] (**-s, -**) *m* mercenary
solidarisch [zoli'da:rɪʃ] *adj* in *od* with solidarity; **sich ~ erklären** to declare one's solidarity
solidarisieren [zolidari'zi:rən] *vr*: **sich ~ mit** to show (one's) solidarity with
Solidarität [zolidari'tɛ:t] *f* solidarity
Solist, in [zo'lɪst(ɪn)] *m(f)* (*Mus*) soloist
Soll [zɔl] (**-(s), -(s)**) *nt* (*Fin*) debit (side); (*Arbeitsmenge*) quota, target; **~ und Haben** debit and credit
sollen ['zɔlən] (*pt* **sollte**, *pp* **gesollt** *od* (*als Hilfsverb*) **sollen**) *hilfsverb* **1** (*Pflicht, Befehl*) be supposed to; **du hättest nicht gehen sollen** you shouldn't have gone, you oughtn't to have gone; **er sollte eigentlich morgen kommen** he was supposed to come tomorrow; **soll ich?** shall I?; **soll ich dir helfen?** shall I help you?; **sag ihm, er soll warten** tell him he's to wait; **was soll ich machen?** what should I do?; **mir soll es gleich sein** it's all the same to me; **er sollte sie nie wiedersehen** he was never to see her again
2 (*Vermutung*): **sie soll verheiratet sein** she's said to be married; **was soll das heißen?** what's that supposed to mean?; **man sollte glauben, dass ...** you would think that ...; **sollte das passieren, ...** if that should happen ...
▷ *vt, vi*: **was soll das?** what's all this about *od* in aid of?; **das sollst du nicht** you shouldn't do that; **was solls?** what the hell!

Solo ['zo:lo] (**-s, -s** *od* **Soli**) *nt* solo
Somalia [zo'ma:lia] (**-s**) *nt* Somalia
somit [zo'mɪt] *konj* and so, therefore
Sommer ['zɔmər] (**-s, -**) *m* summer; **~ wie Winter** all year round; **sommerlich** *adj* summer *attrib*; (*sommerartig*) summery; **Sommerloch** *nt* silly season; **Sommerschlussverkauf** *m* summer sale; **Sommersprossen** *pl* freckles *pl*; **Sommerzeit** *f* summertime
Sonate [zo'na:tə] (**-, -n**) *f* sonata
Sonde ['zɔndə] (**-, -n**) *f* probe
Sonder- ['zɔndər] *in zw* special; **Sonderangebot** *nt* special offer; **sonderbar** *adj* strange, odd; **Sonderfahrt** *f* special trip; **Sonderfall** *m* special case; **sondergleichen** *adj inv* without parallel, unparalleled; **eine Frechheit sondergleichen** the height of cheek; **sonderlich** *adj* particular; (*außergewöhnlich*) remarkable; (*eigenartig*) peculiar; **Sondermüll** *m* dangerous waste
sondern *konj* but ▷ *vt* to separate; **nicht nur ..., ~ auch** not only ..., but also
Sonder- *zW*: **Sonderschule** *f* special school; **Sonderzug** *m* special train
Sonett [zo'nɛt] (**-(e)s, -e**) *nt* sonnet
Sonnabend ['zɔn|a:bənt] *m* Saturday; *siehe auch* **Dienstag**
Sonne ['zɔnə] (**-, -n**) *f* sun; **an die ~ gehen** to go out in the sun
sonnen *vr* to sun o.s.; **sich in etw** *dat* **~** (*fig*) to bask in sth
Sonnen- *zW*: **Sonnenaufgang** *m* sunrise; **sonnenbaden** *vi* to sunbathe; **Sonnenblume** *f* sunflower; **Sonnenbrand** *m* sunburn;

Sonnenbrille *f* sunglasses *pl*; **Sonnencreme** *f* suntan lotion; **Sonnenenergie** *f* solar energy; **Sonnenfinsternis** *f* solar eclipse; **Sonnenkollektor** *m* solar panel; **Sonnenöl** *nt* suntan oil; **Sonnenschein** *m* sunshine; **Sonnenschirm** *m* sunshade; **Sonnenschutzmittel** *nt* sunscreen; **Sonnenstich** *m* sunstroke; **du hast wohl einen Sonnenstich!** (*hum: umg*) you must have been out in the sun too long!; **Sonnenuhr** *f* sundial; **Sonnenuntergang** *m* sunset; **Sonnenwende** *f* solstice

sonnig ['zɔnɪç] *adj* sunny

Sonntag ['zɔnta:k] *m* Sunday; *siehe auch* **Dienstag**

sonntags *adv* (on) Sundays

Sonntagsfahrer (*pej*) *m* Sunday driver

sonst [zɔnst] *adv* otherwise; (*mit pron, in Fragen*) else; (*zu anderer Zeit*) at other times; (*gewöhnlich*) usually, normally ▷ *konj* otherwise; **er denkt, er ist ~ wer** (*umg*) he thinks he's somebody special; **~ gehts dir gut?** (*ironisch: umg*) are you feeling okay?; **wenn ich Ihnen ~ noch behilflich sein kann** if I can help you in any other way; **~ noch etwas?** anything else?; **~ nichts** nothing else; **~ jemand** (*umg*) anybody (at all); **da kann ja ~ was passieren** (*umg*) anything could happen; **~ wo** (*umg*) somewhere else; **~ woher** (*umg*) from somewhere else; **~ wohin** (*umg*) somewhere else

sonstig *adj* other; **„S~es"** "other"

sooft [zo'|ɔft] *konj* whenever

Sopran [zo'pra:n] (**-s, -e**) *m* soprano (voice)

Sorge ['zɔrgə] (**-, -n**) *f* care, worry; **dafür ~ tragen, dass ...** (*geh*) to see to it that ...

sorgen *vi*: **für jdn ~** to look after sb ▷ *vr*: **sich ~ (um)** to worry (about); **für etw ~** to take care of *od* see to sth; **dafür ~, dass ...** to see to it that ...; **dafür ist gesorgt** that's taken care of

Sorgen- *zW*: **sorgenfrei** *adj* carefree; **Sorgenkind** *nt* problem child; **sorgenvoll** *adj* troubled, worried

Sorgerecht (**-(e)s**) *nt* custody (of a child)

Sorgfalt ['zɔrkfalt] (**-**) *f* care(fulness); **viel ~ auf etw** *akk* **verwenden** to take a lot of care over sth

sorgfältig *adj* careful

sorglos *adj* careless; (*ohne Sorgen*) carefree

sorgsam *adj* careful

Sorte ['zɔrtə] (**-, -n**) *f* sort; (*Warensorte*) brand; **Sorten** *pl* (*Fin*) foreign currency *sing*

sortieren [zɔr'ti:rən] *vt* to sort (out); (*Comput*) to sort

Sortiment [zɔrti'mɛnt] *nt* assortment

sosehr [zo'ze:r] *konj* as much as

Soße ['zo:sə] (**-, -n**) *f* sauce; (*Bratensoße*) gravy

Souffleur [zu'flø:r] *m* prompter

soufflieren [zu'fli:rən] *vt, vi* to prompt

souverän [zuvə'rɛ:n] *adj* sovereign; (*überlegen*) superior; (*fig*) supremely good

soviel [zo'fi:l] *konj* as far as

sowenig [zo've:nɪç] *konj* however little

sowie [zo'vi:] *konj* (*sobald*) as soon as; (*ebenso*) as well as

sowieso [zovi'zo:] *adv* anyway

sowjetisch [zɔ'vjɛtɪʃ] *adj* (*früher*) Soviet; **Sowjetunion** *f* Soviet Union

sowohl [zo'vo:l] *konj*: **~ ... als** *od* **wie auch ...** both ... and ...

sozial [zotsi'a:l] *adj* social; **~ eingestellt** public-spirited; **~ verträglich** socially acceptable; **~er Wohnungsbau** public-sector housing (programme); **Sozialabgaben** *pl* National Insurance contributions *pl* (*Brit*), Social Security contributions *pl* (*US*); **Sozialarbeiter** *m* social worker; **Sozialdemokrat** *m* social democrat; **Sozialhilfe** *f* welfare (aid)

Sozialismus [zotsia'lɪsmʊs] *m* socialism

Sozialist, in [zotsia'lɪst(ɪn)] *m(f)* socialist

Sozial- *zW*: **Sozialplan** *m* redundancy payments scheme; **Sozialpolitik** *f* social welfare policy; **Sozialprodukt** *nt* (gross *od* net) national product; **Sozialstaat** *m* welfare state; **Sozialversicherung** *f* national insurance (*Brit*), social security (*US*); **Sozialwohnung** *f* ≈ council flat (*Brit*), state-subsidized apartment

Soziologe [zotsio'lo:gə] (**-n, -n**) *m* sociologist

Soziologie [zotsiolo'gi:] *f* sociology

soziologisch [zotsio'lo:gɪʃ] *adj* sociological

sozusagen [zotsu'za:gən] *adv* so to speak

Spachtel ['ʃpaxtəl] (**-s, -**) *m* spatula

spähen ['ʃpɛ:ən] *vi* to peep, peek

Spalier [ʃpa'li:r] (**-s, -e**) *nt* (*Gerüst*) trellis; (*Leute*) guard of honour (*Brit*) *od* honor (*US*); **~ stehen, ein ~ bilden** to form a guard of honour (*Brit*) *od* honor (*US*)

Spalt [ʃpalt] (**-(e)s, -e**) *m* crack; (*Türspalt*) chink; (*fig: Kluft*) split

Spalte (**-, -n**) *f* crack, fissure; (*Gletscherspalte*) crevasse; (*in Text*) column

spalten *vt, vr* (*lit, fig*) to split

Spaltung *f* splitting

Span [ʃpa:n] (**-(e)s, ¨-e**) *m* shaving

Spanferkel *nt* sucking pig

Spange ['ʃpaŋə] (**-, -n**) *f* clasp; (*Haarspange*) hair slide; (*Schnalle*) buckle; (*Armspange*) bangle

Spanien ['ʃpa:niən] (**-s**) *nt* Spain

Spanier, in (**-s, -**) *m(f)* Spaniard

spanisch *adj* Spanish; **das kommt mir ~ vor** (*umg*) that seems odd to me; **~e Wand** (folding) screen

spann *etc* [ʃpan] *vb siehe* **spinnen**

Spanne (**-, -n**) *f* (*Zeitspanne*) space; (*Differenz*) gap; *siehe auch* **Spann**

spannen *vt* (*straffen*) to tighten, tauten; (*befestigen*) to brace ▷ *vi* to be tight

spannend *adj* exciting, gripping; **machs nicht so ~!** (*umg*) don't keep me *etc* in suspense!

Spannung *f* tension; (*Elek*) voltage; (*fig*)

suspense; *(unangenehm)* tension
Spannungsprüfer *m* voltage detector
Sparbuch *nt* savings book
Sparbüchse *f* moneybox
sparen ['ʃpa:rən] *vt, vi* to save; **sich** *dat* **etw ~** to save o.s. sth; *(Bemerkung)* to keep sth to o.s.; **mit etw ~** to be sparing with sth; **an etw** *dat* **~** to economize on sth
Sparer, in (**-s, -**) *m(f)* *(bei Bank etc)* saver
Spargel ['ʃpargəl] (**-s, -**) *m* asparagus
Spar- *zW*: **Sparkasse** *f* savings bank; **Sparkonto** *nt* savings account
spärlich ['ʃpɛ:rlɪç] *adj* meagre *(Brit)*, meager *(US)*; *(Bekleidung)* scanty; *(Beleuchtung)* poor
Spar- *zW*: **Sparmaßnahme** *f* economy measure; **sparsam** *adj* economical, thrifty; **sparsam im Verbrauch** economical; **Sparsamkeit** *f* thrift, economizing; **Sparschwein** *nt* piggy bank
Sparte ['ʃpartə] (**-, -n**) *f* field; *(Comm)* line of business; *(Presse)* column
Spaß [ʃpa:s] (**-es, ¨-e**) *m* joke; *(Freude)* fun; **~ muss sein** there's no harm in a joke; **jdm ~ machen** to be fun (for sb); **spaßen** *vi* to joke; **mit ihm ist nicht zu spaßen** you can't take liberties with him
spaßeshalber *adv* for the fun of it
spaßig *adj* funny, droll
Spaßverderber (**-s, -**) *m* spoilsport
spät [ʃpɛ:t] *adj, adv* late; **heute Abend wird es ~** it'll be a late night tonight
Spaten ['ʃpa:tən] (**-s, -**) *m* spade
später *adj, adv* later; **an ~ denken** to think of the future; **bis ~!** see you later!
spätestens *adv* at the latest
Spätlese *f* late vintage
Spatz [ʃpats] (**-en, -en**) *m* sparrow
spazieren [ʃpa'tsi:rən] *vi* *(Hilfsverb sein)* to stroll; **~ fahren** to go for a drive; **~ gehen** to go for a walk
Spazier- *zW*: **Spaziergang** *m* walk; **einen Spaziergang machen** to go for a walk; **Spazierstock** *m* walking stick; **Spazierweg** *m* path, walk
SPD (**-**) *f abk* (= *Sozialdemokratische Partei Deutschlands*) German Social Democratic Party
Specht [ʃpɛçt] (**-(e)s, -e**) *m* woodpecker
Speck [ʃpɛk] (**-(e)s, -e**) *m* bacon; **mit ~ fängt man Mäuse** *(Sprichwort)* you need a sprat to catch a mackerel; **ran an den ~** *(umg)* let's get stuck in
Spediteur [ʃpedi'tø:r] *m* carrier; *(Möbelspediteur)* furniture remover
Spedition [ʃpeditsi'o:n] *f* carriage; *(Speditionsfirma)* road haulage contractor; *(Umzugsfirma)* removal *(Brit)* *od* moving *(US)* firm
Speer [ʃpe:r] (**-(e)s, -e**) *m* spear; *(Sport)* javelin
Speiche ['ʃpaɪçə] (**-, -n**) *f* spoke
Speichel ['ʃpaɪçəl] (**-s**) *m* saliva, spit(tle)
Speicher ['ʃpaɪçər] (**-s, -**) *m* storehouse; *(Dachspeicher)* attic, loft; *(Kornspeicher)* granary; *(Wasserspeicher)* tank; *(Tech)* store; *(Comput)* memory; **Speicherauszug** *m* *(Comput)* dump
speichern *vt* *(auch Comput)* to store
speien ['ʃpaɪən] *unreg vt, vi* to spit; *(erbrechen)* to vomit; *(Vulkan)* to spew
Speise ['ʃpaɪzə] (**-, -n**) *f* food; **kalte und warme ~n** hot and cold meals; **Speiseeis** *nt* ice-cream; **Speisekammer** *f* larder, pantry; **Speisekarte** *f* menu
speisen *vt* to feed; to eat ▷ *vi* to dine
Speise- *zW*: **Speiseröhre** *f* *(Anat)* gullet, oesophagus *(Brit)*, esophagus *(US)*; **Speisesaal** *m* dining room; **Speisewagen** *m* dining car
Spekulant, in [ʃpeku'lant(ɪn)] *m(f)* speculator
Spekulation [ʃpekulatsi'o:n] *f* speculation
spekulieren [ʃpeku'li:rən] *vi* *(fig)* to speculate; **auf etw** *akk* **~** to have hopes of sth
Spelunke [ʃpe'lʊŋkə] (**-, -n**) *f* dive
Spende ['ʃpɛndə] (**-, -n**) *f* donation
spenden *vt* to donate, give
Spender, in (**-s, -**) *m(f)* donator; *(Med)* donor
spendieren [ʃpɛn'di:rən] *vt* to pay for, buy; **jdm etw ~** to treat sb to sth, stand sb sth
Sperling ['ʃpɛrlɪŋ] *m* sparrow
Sperma ['spɛrma] (**-s, Spermen**) *nt* sperm
Sperre (**-, -n**) *f* barrier; *(Verbot)* ban; *(Polizeisperre)* roadblock
sperren ['ʃpɛrən] *vt* to block; *(Comm: Konto)* to freeze; *(Comput: Daten)* to disable; *(Sport)* to suspend, bar; *(: vom Ball)* to obstruct; *(einschließen)* to lock; *(verbieten)* to ban ▷ *vr* to baulk, jibe, jib
Sperr- *zW*: **Sperrgebiet** *nt* prohibited area; **Sperrholz** *nt* plywood
sperrig *adj* bulky
Sperr- *zW*: **Sperrmüll** *m* bulky refuse; **Sperrsitz** *m* *(Theat)* stalls *pl* *(Brit)*, orchestra *(US)*; **Sperrstunde** *f* closing time
Spesen ['ʃpe:zən] *pl* expenses *pl*
spezialisieren [ʃpetsiali'zi:rən] *vr* to specialize
Spezialist, in [ʃpetsia'lɪst(ɪn)] *m(f)*: **~ (für)** specialist (in)
Spezialität [ʃpetsiali'tɛ:t] *f* speciality *(Brit)*, specialty *(US)*
speziell [ʃpetsi'ɛl] *adj* special
spezifisch [ʃpe'tsi:fɪʃ] *adj* specific
Sphäre ['sfɛ:rə] (**-, -n**) *f* sphere
spie *etc* [ʃpi:] *vb siehe* **speien**
Spiegel ['ʃpi:gəl] (**-s, -**) *m* mirror; *(Wasserspiegel)* level; *(Mil)* tab; **Spiegelbild** *nt* reflection; **spiegelbildlich** *adj* reversed
Spiegelei ['ʃpi:gəl|aɪ] *nt* fried egg
spiegeln *vt* to mirror, reflect ▷ *vr* to be reflected ▷ *vi* to gleam; *(widerspiegeln)* to be reflective
Spiegelreflexkamera *f* reflex camera
Spiegelschrift *f* mirror writing
Spiegelung *f* reflection
Spiel [ʃpi:l] (**-(e)s, -e**) *nt* game; *(Schauspiel)* play; *(Tätigkeit)* play(ing); *(Karten)* pack *(Brit)*, deck *(US)*; *(Tech)* (free) play; **leichtes ~ (bei** *od* **mit jdm) haben** to have an easy job of it (with sb); **die Hand** *od* **Finger im ~ haben** to

have a hand in affairs; **jdn/etw aus dem ~ lassen** to leave sb/sth out of it; **auf dem ~(e) stehen** to be at stake; **Spieldose** *f* musical box (*Brit*), music box (*US*)
spielen *vt, vi* to play; (*um Geld*) to gamble; (*Theat*) to perform, act; **was wird hier gespielt?** (*umg*) what's going on here?
spielend *adv* easily
Spieler, in (**-s, -**) *m(f)* player; (*um Geld*) gambler
Spielerei [ʃpiːlə'raɪ] *f* (*Kinderspiel*) child's play
Spiel- *zW*: **Spielfeld** *nt* pitch, field; **Spielfilm** *m* feature film; **Spielplan** *m* (*Theat*) programme (*Brit*), program (*US*); **Spielplatz** *m* playground; **Spielraum** *m* room to manoeuvre (*Brit*) *od* maneuver (*US*), scope; **Spielsachen** *pl* toys *pl*; **Spielverderber** (**-s, -**) *m* spoilsport; **Spielwaren** *pl* toys *pl*; **Spielzeug** *nt* toy; (*Spielsachen*) toys *pl*
Spieß [ʃpiːs] (**-es, -e**) *m* spear; (*Bratspieß*) spit; (*Mil: umg*) sarge; **den ~ umdrehen** (*fig*) to turn the tables; **wie am ~(e) schreien** (*umg*) to squeal like a stuck pig
Spießbürger (**-s, -**) *m* bourgeois
Spikes [spaɪks] *pl* (*Sport*) spikes *pl*; (*Aut*) studs *pl*
Spinat [ʃpi'naːt] (**-(e)s, -e**) *m* spinach
Spind [ʃpɪnt] (**-(e)s, -e**) *m od nt* locker
Spinne ['ʃpɪnə] (**-, -n**) *f* spider
spinnen *unreg vt* to spin ▷ *vi* (*umg*) to talk rubbish; (*verrückt*) to be crazy *od* mad; **ich denk ich spinne** (*umg*) I don't believe it
Spinner, in (**-s, -**) *m(f)* (*fig: umg*) screwball, crackpot
Spinnerei [ʃpɪnə'raɪ] *f* spinning mill; **Spinnrad** *nt* spinning wheel
Spion [ʃpi'oːn] (**-s, -e**) *m* spy; (*in Tür*) spyhole
Spionage [ʃpio'naːʒə] (**-**) *f* espionage
spionieren [ʃpio'niːrən] *vi* to spy
Spirale [ʃpi'raːlə] (**-, -n**) *f* spiral; (*Med*) coil
Spirituosen [ʃpiritu'oːzən] *pl* spirits *pl*
Spiritus ['ʃpiːritʊs] (**-, -se**) *m* (methylated) spirits *pl*
spitz *adj* pointed; (*Winkel*) acute; (*fig: Zunge*) sharp; (*: Bemerkung*) caustic
Spitz- *zW*: **Spitzbogen** *m* pointed arch; **Spitzbube** *m* rogue
Spitze (**-, -n**) *f* point, tip; (*Bergspitze*) peak; (*Bemerkung*) taunt; (*fig: Stichelei*) dig; (*erster Platz*) lead, top; (*meist pl: Gewebe*) lace; **etw auf die ~ treiben** to carry sth too far
Spitzel (**-s, -**) *m* police informer
spitzen *vt* to sharpen; (*Lippen, Mund*) to purse; (*lit, fig: Ohren*) to prick up
Spitzen- *in zw* top; **Spitzenleistung** *f* top performance; **Spitzenlohn** *m* top wages *pl*; **Spitzensportler** *m* top-class sportsman
spitzfindig *adj* (over)subtle
Spitzname *m* nickname
Splitter (**-s, -**) *m* splinter; **splitternackt** *adj* stark naked
SPÖ (**-**) *f abk* (*= Sozialistische Partei Österreichs*) Austrian Socialist Party
sponsern ['ʃpɔnzərn] *vt* to sponsor
Sponsor ['ʃpɔnzɔr] (**-s, -en**) *m* sponsor
spontan [ʃpɔn'taːn] *adj* spontaneous
Sport [ʃpɔrt] (**-(e)s, -e**) *m* sport; (*fig*) hobby; **treiben Sie ~?** do you do any sport?; **Sportlehrer** *m* games *od* P.E. teacher
Sportler, in (**-s, -**) *m(f)* sportsman, sportswoman
Sport- *zW*: **sportlich** *adj* sporting; (*Mensch*) sporty; (*durchtrainiert*) athletic; (*Kleidung*) smart but casual; **Sportplatz** *m* playing *od* sports field; **Sportschuh** *m* sports shoe; (*sportlicher Schuh*) casual shoe
Sport- *zW*: **Sportverein** *m* sports club; **Sportwagen** *m* sports car; **Sportzeug** *nt* sports gear
Spott [ʃpɔt] (**-(e)s**) *m* mockery, ridicule; **spottbillig** *adj* dirt-cheap; **spotten** *vi* to mock; **spotten über** *+akk* to mock (at), ridicule; **das spottet jeder Beschreibung** that simply defies description
spöttisch ['ʃpœtɪʃ] *adj* mocking
sprach *etc* [ʃpraːx] *vb siehe* **sprechen**
sprachbegabt *adj* good at languages
Sprache (**-, -n**) *f* language; **heraus mit der ~!** (*umg*) come on, out with it!; **zur ~ kommen** to be mentioned; **in französischer ~** in French
Sprach- *zW*: **Sprachfehler** *m* speech defect; **Sprachführer** *m* phrase book; **Sprachgefühl** *nt* feeling for language; **Sprachkenntnisse** *pl*: **mit englischen Sprachkenntnissen** with a knowledge of English; **Sprachkurs** *m* language course; **Sprachlabor** *nt* language laboratory; **sprachlich** *adj* linguistic; **sprachlos** *adj* speechless; **Sprachrohr** *nt* megaphone; (*fig*) mouthpiece; **Sprachwissenschaft** *f* linguistics *sing*
sprang *etc* [ʃpraŋ] *vb siehe* **springen**
Spray [spreː] (**-s, -s**) *m od nt* spray; **Spraydose** *f* aerosol (can), spray
Sprechanlage *f* intercom
sprechen ['ʃprɛçən] *unreg vi* to speak, talk ▷ *vt* to say; (*Sprache*) to speak; (*Person*) to speak to; **mit jdm ~** to speak *od* talk to sb; **das spricht für ihn** that's a point in his favour; **frei ~** to extemporize; **nicht gut auf jdn zu ~ sein** to be on bad terms with sb; **es spricht vieles dafür, dass ...** there is every reason to believe that ...; **hier spricht man Spanisch** Spanish spoken; **wir ~ uns noch!** you haven't heard the last of this!
Sprecher, in (**-s, -**) *m(f)* speaker; (*für Gruppe*) spokesman, spokeswoman; (*Rundf, TV*) announcer
Sprech- *zW*: **Sprechstunde** *f* consultation (hour); (*von Arzt*) (doctor's) surgery (*Brit*); **Sprechstundenhilfe** *f* (doctor's) receptionist; **Sprechzimmer** *nt* consulting room, surgery (*Brit*)
Sprengarbeiten *pl* blasting operations *pl*
sprengen ['ʃprɛŋən] *vt* to sprinkle; (*mit Sprengstoff*) to blow up; (*Gestein*) to blast; (*Versammlung*) to break up

Spreng- *zW*: **Sprengladung** *f* explosive charge; **Sprengstoff** *m* explosive(s *pl*)
Spreu [ʃprɔʏ] (-) *f* chaff
Sprichwort *nt* proverb
sprichwörtlich *adj* proverbial
Springbrunnen *m* fountain
springen [ˈʃprɪŋən] *unreg vi* to jump, leap; (*Glas*) to crack; (*mit Kopfsprung*) to dive; **etw ~ lassen** (*umg*) to fork out sth
Springer (**-s, -**) *m* jumper; (*Schach*) knight
Spritze [ˈʃprɪtsə] (**-, -n**) *f* syringe; (*Injektion*) injection; (*an Schlauch*) nozzle
spritzen *vt* to spray; (*Wein*) to dilute with soda water/lemonade; (*Med*) to inject ▷ *vi* to splash; (*heißes Fett*) to spit; (*herausspritzen*) to spurt; (*aus einer Tube etc*) to squirt; (*Med*) to give injections
Spritzpistole *f* spray gun
spröde [ˈʃprøːdə] *adj* brittle; (*Person*) reserved; (*Haut*) rough
Spruch [ʃprʊx] (**-(e)s, ¨-e**) *m* saying, maxim; (*Jur*) judgement; **Sprüche klopfen** (*umg*) to talk fancy
Sprudel [ˈʃpruːdəl] (**-s, -**) *m* mineral water; (*süß*) lemonade
sprudeln *vi* to bubble
Sprüh- *zW*: **Sprühdose** *f* aerosol (can); **sprühen** *vi* to spray; (*fig*) to sparkle ▷ *vt* to spray
Sprung [ʃprʊŋ] (**-(e)s, ¨-e**) *m* jump; (*schwungvoll, fig*: *Gedankensprung*) leap; (*Riss*) crack; **immer auf dem ~ sein** (*umg*) to be always on the go; **jdm auf die Sprünge helfen** (*wohlwollend*) to give sb a (helping) hand; **auf einen ~ bei jdm vorbeikommen** (*umg*) to drop in to see sb; **damit kann man keine großen Sprünge machen** (*umg*) you can't exactly live it up on that; **Sprungbrett** *nt* springboard; **sprunghaft** *adj* erratic; (*Aufstieg*) rapid; **Sprungschanze** *f* ski jump
Spucke [ˈʃpʊkə] (-) *f* spit
spucken *vt, vi* to spit; **in die Hände ~** (*fig*) to roll up one's sleeves
Spuk [ʃpuːk] (**-(e)s, -e**) *m* haunting; (*fig*) nightmare; **spuken** *vi* to haunt; **hier spukt es** this place is haunted
Spule [ˈʃpuːlə] (**-, -n**) *f* spool; (*Elek*) coil
Spüle [ˈʃpyːlə] (**-, -n**) *f* (kitchen) sink
spülen *vt* to rinse; (*Geschirr*) to wash, do; (*Toilette*) to flush ▷ *vi* to rinse; to wash up (*Brit*), do the dishes; to flush; **etw an Land ~** to wash sth ashore
Spül- *zW*: **Spülmaschine** *f* dishwasher; **Spülmittel** *nt* washing-up liquid (*Brit*), dish-washing liquid
Spülung *f* rinsing; (*Wasserspülung*) flush; (*Med*) irrigation
Spur [ʃpuːr] (**-, -en**) *f* trace; (*Fußspur, Radspur, Tonbandspur*) track; (*Fährte*) trail; (*Fahrspur*) lane; **jdm auf die ~ kommen** to get onto sb; **(seine) ~en hinterlassen** (*fig*) to leave its mark; **keine ~** (*umg*) not/nothing at all
spürbar *adj* noticeable, perceptible
spüren [ˈʃpyːrən] *vt* to feel; **etw zu ~ bekommen** (*lit*) to feel sth; (*fig*) to feel the (full) force of sth
Spurenelement *nt* trace element
spurlos *adv* without (a) trace; **~ an jdm vorübergehen** to have no effect on sb
Spurt [ʃpʊrt] (**-(e)s, -s** *od* **-e**) *m* spurt
sputen [ˈʃpuːtən] *vr* to make haste
Squash [skvɔʃ] (-) *nt* (*Sport*) squash
Staat [ʃtaːt] (**-(e)s, -en**) *m* state; (*Prunk*) show; (*Kleidung*) finery; **mit etw ~ machen** to show off *od* parade sth
staatenlos *adj* stateless
staatlich *adj* state *attrib*; state-run ▷ *adv*: **~ geprüft** state-certified
Staats- *zW*: **Staatsangehörigkeit** *f* nationality; **Staatsanwalt** *m* public prosecutor; **Staatsbürger** *m* citizen; **Staatsbürgerschaft** *f* nationality; **doppelte Staatsbürgerschaft** dual nationality; **Staatsdienst** *m* civil service; **staatseigen** *adj* state-owned; **Staatsexamen** *nt* (*Univ*) degree; **staatsfeindlich** *adj* subversive; **Staatsmann** (**-(e)s**, *pl* **-männer**) *m* statesman; **Staatsoberhaupt** *nt* head of state; **Staatssekretär** *m* secretary of state; **Staatsverschuldung** *f* national debt
Stab [ʃtaːp] (**-(e)s, ¨-e**) *m* rod; (*für Stabhochsprung*) pole; (*für Staffellauf*) baton; (*Gitterstab*) bar; (*Menschen*) staff; (*von Experten*) panel
Stäbchen [ˈʃtɛːpçən] *nt* (*Essstäbchen*) chopstick
Stabhochsprung *m* pole vault
stabil [ʃtaˈbiːl] *adj* stable; (*Möbel*) sturdy
stabilisieren [ʃtabiliˈziːrən] *vt* to stabilize
Stabreim *m* alliteration
stach *etc* [ʃtaːx] *vb siehe* **stechen**
Stachel [ˈʃtaxəl] (**-s, -n**) *m* spike; (*von Tier*) spine; (*von Insekten*) sting; **Stachelbeere** *f* gooseberry; **Stacheldraht** *m* barbed wire
stachelig, stachlig *adj* prickly
Stachelschwein *nt* porcupine
Stadion [ˈʃtaːdiɔn] (**-s, Stadien**) *nt* stadium
Stadium [ˈʃtaːdiʊm] *nt* stage, phase
Stadt [ʃtat] (**-, ¨-e**) *f* town; (*Großstadt*) city; (*Stadtverwaltung*) (town/city) council
Städtchen [ˈʃtɛːtçən] *nt* small town
Städtebau (**-(e)s**) *m* town planning
Städter, in (**-s, -**) *m(f)* town/city dweller, townie
städtisch *adj* municipal; (*nicht ländlich*) urban
Stadt- *zW*: **Stadtmauer** *f* city wall(s *pl*); **Stadtmitte** *f* town/city centre (*Brit*) *od* center (*US*); **Stadtplan** *m* street map; **Stadtrand** *m* outskirts *pl*; **Stadtteil** *m* district, part of town
Staffel [ˈʃtafəl] (**-, -n**) *f* rung; (*Sport*) relay (team); (*Aviat*) squadron
staffeln *vt* to graduate
Stahl (**-(e)s, ¨-e**) *m* steel
stahl *etc* [ʃtaːl] *vb siehe* **stehlen**
Stahlhelm *m* steel helmet
Stall [ʃtal] (**-(e)s, ¨-e**) *m* stable; (*Kaninchenstall*) hutch; (*Schweinestall*) sty; (*Hühnerstall*)

henhouse
Stamm [ʃtam] (**-(e)s, ⸚e**) *m* (*Baumstamm*) trunk; (*Menschenstamm*) tribe; (*Gram*) stem; (*Bakterienstamm*) strain; **Stammbaum** *m* family tree; (*von Tier*) pedigree
stammeln *vt, vi* to stammer
stammen *vi*: **~ von** *od* **aus** to come from
Stammgast *m* regular (customer)
stämmig [ˈʃtɛmɪç] *adj* sturdy; (*Mensch*) stocky
Stammtisch *m* (*Tisch in Gasthaus*) *table reserved for the regulars*
stampfen [ˈʃtampfən] *vi* to stamp; (*stapfen*) to tramp ▷ *vt* (*mit Stampfer*) to mash
Stand (**-(e)s, ⸚e**) *m* position; (*Wasserstand, Benzinstand etc*) level; (*Zählerstand etc*) reading; (*Stehen*) standing position; (*Zustand*) state; (*Spielstand*) score; (*Messestand etc*) stand; (*Klasse*) class; (*Beruf*) profession; **bei jdm** *od* **gegen jdn einen schweren ~ haben** (*fig*) to have a hard time of it with sb; **etw auf den neuesten ~ bringen** to bring sth up to date; *siehe auch* **außerstande; imstande; zustande**
stand *etc* [ʃtant] *vb siehe* **stehen**
Standard [ˈʃtandart] (**-s, -s**) *m* standard
Ständchen [ˈʃtɛntçən] *nt* serenade
Ständer (**-s, -**) *m* stand
Standes- *zW*: **Standesamt** *nt* registry office (*Brit*), city/county clerk's office (*US*); **Standesbeamte, r** *m* registrar; **standesgemäß** *adj, adv* according to one's social position; **Standesunterschied** *m* social difference
Stand- *zW*: **standhaft** *adj* steadfast; **Standhaftigkeit** *f* steadfastness; **standhalten** *unreg vi*: **(jdm/etw) standhalten** to stand firm (against sb/sth), resist (sb/sth)
ständig [ˈʃtɛndɪç] *adj* permanent; (*ununterbrochen*) constant, continual
Stand- *zW*: **Standlicht** *nt* sidelights *pl* (*Brit*), parking lights *pl* (*US*); **Standort** *m* location; (*Mil*) garrison; **Standpunkt** *m* standpoint; **Standspur** *f* (*Aut*) hard shoulder (*Brit*), berm (*US*)
Stange [ˈʃtaŋə] (**-, -n**) *f* stick; (*Stab*) pole; (*Querstange*) bar; (*Zigaretten*) carton; **von der ~** (*Comm*) off the peg (*Brit*) *od* rack (*US*); **eine ~ Geld** quite a packet; **jdm die ~ halten** (*umg*) to stick up for sb; **bei der ~ bleiben** (*umg*) to stick at *od* to sth
Stängel [ˈʃtɛŋl] (**-s, -**) *m* stalk; **vom ~ fallen** (*umg: überrascht sein*) to be staggered
Stangenbrot *nt* French bread; (*Laib*) French stick (loaf)
stank *etc* [ʃtaŋk] *vb siehe* **stinken**
Stanniol [ʃtaniˈoːl] (**-s, -e**) *nt* tinfoil
Stapel [ˈʃtaːpəl] (**-s, -**) *m* pile; (*Naut*) stocks *pl*; **Stapellauf** *m* launch
stapeln *vt* to pile (up)
Stapelverarbeitung *f* (*Comput*) batch processing
Star[1] [ʃtaːr] (**-(e)s, -e**) *m* starling; **grauer/grüner ~** (*Med*) cataract/glaucoma
Star[2] [ʃtaːr] (**-s, -s**) *m* (*Filmstar etc*) star
starb *etc* [ʃtarp] *vb siehe* **sterben**
stark [ʃtark] *adj* strong; (*heftig, groß*) heavy; (*Maßangabe*) thick; (*umg: hervorragend*) great ▷ *adv* very; (*beschädigt etc*) badly; (*vergrößert, verkleinert*) greatly; **das ist ein ~es Stück!** (*umg*) that's a bit much!; **er ist ~ erkältet** he has a bad cold; *siehe auch* **starkmachen**
Stärke [ˈʃtɛrkə] (**-, -n**) *f* strength (*auch fig*); heaviness; thickness; (*von Mannschaft*) size; (*Wäschestärke, Koch*) starch
stärken *vt* (*lit, fig*) to strengthen; (*Wäsche*) to starch; (*Selbstbewusstsein*) to boost; (*Gesundheit*) to improve; (*erfrischen*) to fortify ▷ *vi* to be fortifying; **~des Mittel** tonic
Starkstrom *m* heavy current
Stärkung [ˈʃtɛrkʊŋ] *f* strengthening; (*Essen*) refreshment
starr [ʃtar] *adj* stiff; (*unnachgiebig*) rigid; (*Blick*) staring
starren *vi* to stare; **~ vor** *+dat od* **von** (*voll von*) to be covered in; (*Waffen*) to be bristling with; **vor sich** *akk* **hin ~** to stare straight ahead
starr- *zW*: **Starrheit** *f* rigidity; **starrköpfig** *adj* stubborn; **Starrsinn** *m* obstinacy
Start [ʃtart] (**-(e)s, -e**) *m* start; (*Aviat*) takeoff; **Startautomatik** *f* (*Aut*) automatic choke; **Startbahn** *f* runway; **starten** *vi* to start; (*Aviat*) to take off ▷ *vt* to start; **Starter** (**-s, -**) *m* starter; **Starterlaubnis** *f* takeoff clearance; **Starthilfekabel** *nt* jump leads *pl* (*Brit*), jumper cables *pl* (*US*)
Station [ʃtatsiˈoːn] *f* station; (*Krankenstation*) hospital ward; (*Haltestelle*) stop; **~ machen** to stop off
stationieren [ʃtatsioˈniːrən] *vt* to station; (*Atomwaffen etc*) to deploy
Statist, in [ʃtaˈtɪst(ɪn)] *m(f)* (*Film*) extra; (*Theat*) supernumerary
Statistik *f* statistic; (*Wissenschaft*) statistics *sing*
Statistiker, in (**-s, -**) *m(f)* statistician
statistisch *adj* statistical
Stativ [ʃtaˈtiːf] (**-s, -e**) *nt* tripod
statt *konj* instead of ▷ *präp* (*+dat od gen*) instead of
Stätte [ˈʃtɛtə] (**-, -n**) *f* place
statt- *zW*: **stattfinden** *unreg vi* to take place; **statthaft** *adj* admissible; **stattlich** *adj* imposing, handsome; (*Bursche*) strapping; (*Sammlung*) impressive; (*Familie*) large; (*Summe*) handsome
Statue [ˈʃtaːtuə] (**-, -n**) *f* statue
Stau [ʃtaʊ] (**-(e)s, -e**) *m* blockage; (*Verkehrsstau*) (traffic) jam
Staub [ʃtaʊp] (**-(e)s**) *m* dust; **~ saugen** to vacuum; **~ wischen** to dust; **sich aus dem ~ machen** (*umg*) to clear off
stauben [ˈʃtaʊbən] *vi* to be dusty
staubig [ˈstaʊbɪç] *adj* dusty
Staub- *zW*: **staubsaugen** (*pp* **staubgesaugt**) *vi untr* to vacuum; **Staubsauger** *m* vacuum cleaner

Staudamm *m* dam
Staude [ˈʃtaʊdə] (**-, -n**) *f* shrub
stauen [ˈʃtaʊən] *vt* (*Wasser*) to dam up; (*Blut*) to stop the flow of ▷ *vr* (*Wasser*) to become dammed up; (*Verkehr, Med*) to become congested; (*Menschen*) to collect together; (*Gefühle*) to build up
staunen [ˈʃtaʊnən] *vi* to be astonished; **da kann man nur noch ~** it's just amazing; **Staunen** (**-s**) *nt* amazement
Stausee [ˈʃtaʊzeː] *m* reservoir; artificial lake
Stauung [ˈʃtaʊʊŋ] *f* (*von Wasser*) damming-up; (*von Blut, Verkehr*) congestion
Steak [ʃteːk] (**-s, -s**) *nt* steak
Stechen [ˈʃtɛçən] (**-s, -**) *nt* (*Sport*) play-off; (*Springreiten*) jump-off; (*Schmerz*) sharp pain
stechen *unreg vt* (*mit Nadel etc*) to prick; (*mit Messer*) to stab; (*mit Finger*) to poke; (*Biene etc*) to sting; (*Mücke*) to bite; (*Karten*) to take; (*Kunst*) to engrave; (*Torf, Spargel*) to cut ▷ *vi* (*Sonne*) to beat down; (*mit Stechkarte*) to clock in ▷ *vr*: **sich** *akk od dat* **in den Finger ~** to prick one's finger; **es sticht** it is prickly; **in See ~** to put to sea
stechend *adj* piercing, stabbing; (*Geruch*) pungent
Stech- *zW*: **Stechginster** *m* gorse; **Stechpalme** *f* holly; **Stechuhr** *f* time clock
Steck- *zW*: **Steckbrief** *m* "wanted" poster; **Steckdose** *f* (wall) socket
stecken [ˈʃtɛkən] *vt* to put; (*einführen*) to insert; (*Nadel*) to stick; (*Pflanzen*) to plant; (*beim Nähen*) to pin ▷ *vi* (*auch unreg*) to be; (*festsitzen*) to be stuck; (*Nadeln*) to stick; **etw in etw** *akk* **~** (*umg: Geld, Mühe*) to put sth into sth; (*: Zeit*) to devote sth to sth; **der Schlüssel steckt** the key is in the lock; **wo steckt er?** where has he got to?; **zeigen, was in einem steckt** to show what one is made of; **~ bleiben** to get stuck; **~ lassen** to leave in
Steckenpferd *nt* hobbyhorse
Stecker (**-s, -**) *m* (*Elek*) plug
Steck- *zW*: **Stecknadel** *f* pin; **Steckrübe** *f* swede, turnip
Steg [ʃteːk] (**-(e)s, -e**) *m* small bridge; (*Anlegesteg*) landing stage
Stegreif *m*: **aus dem ~** just like that
stehen [ˈʃteːən] *unreg vi* to stand; (*sich befinden*) to be; (*in Zeitung*) to say; (*angehalten haben*) to have stopped ▷ *vi unpers*: **es steht schlecht um ...** things are bad for ... ▷ *vr*: **sich gut/schlecht ~** to be well-off/badly off; **zu jdm/etw ~** to stand by sb/sth; **jdm ~** to suit sb; **ich tue, was in meinen Kräften steht** I'll do everything I can; **es steht 2:1 für München** the score is 2-1 to Munich; **mit dem Dativ ~** (*Gram*) to take the dative; **auf Betrug steht eine Gefängnisstrafe** the penalty for fraud is imprisonment; **wie ~ Sie dazu?** what are your views on that?; **wie stehts?** how are things?; (*Sport*) what's the score?; **wie steht es damit?** how about it?; **~ bleiben** (*Uhr*) to stop; (*Zeit*) to stand still; (*Auto, Zug*) to stand; (*Fehler*) to stay as it is; (*Verkehr, Produktion etc*) to come to a standstill *od* stop; **~ lassen** to leave; (*Bart*) to grow; **alles ~ und liegen lassen** to drop everything
stehlen [ˈʃteːlən] *unreg vt* to steal
Steiermark [ˈʃtaɪrmark] *f*: **die ~** Styria
steif [ʃtaɪf] *adj* stiff; **~ und fest auf etw** *dat* **beharren** to insist stubbornly on sth
Steifheit *f* stiffness
Steigbügel [ˈʃtaɪkbyːgəl] *m* stirrup
Steigeisen *nt* crampon
steigen *unreg vi* to rise; (*klettern*) to climb ▷ *vt* (*Treppen, Stufen*) to climb (up); **das Blut stieg ihm in den Kopf** the blood rushed to his head; **~ in** *+akk***/auf** *+akk* to get in/on
steigern *vt* to raise; (*Gram*) to compare ▷ *vi* (*Auktion*) to bid ▷ *vr* to increase
Steigerung *f* raising; (*Gram*) comparison
Steigung *f* incline, gradient, rise
steil [ʃtaɪl] *adj* steep
Stein [ʃtaɪn] (**-(e)s, -e**) *m* stone; (*in Uhr*) jewel; **mir fällt ein ~ vom Herzen!** (*fig*) that's a load off my mind!; **bei jdm einen ~ im Brett haben** (*fig: umg*) to be well in with sb; **jdm ~e in den Weg legen** to make things difficult for sb; **Steinbock** *m* (*Astrol*) Capricorn; **Steinbruch** *m* quarry
steinern *adj* (made of) stone; (*fig*) stony
Stein- *zW*: **Steingut** *nt* stoneware; **steinhart** *adj* hard as stone
steinig *adj* stony
steinigen *vt* to stone
Stein- *zW*: **Steinkohle** *f* mineral coal; **Steinmetz** (**-es, -e**) *m* stonemason
Stelle [ˈʃtɛlə] (**-, -n**) *f* place; (*Arbeit*) post, job; (*Amt*) office; (*Abschnitt*) passage; (*Textstelle, bes beim Zitieren*) reference; **drei ~n hinter dem Komma** (*Math*) three decimal places; **eine freie** *od* **offene ~** a vacancy; **an dieser ~** in this place, here; **an anderer ~** elsewhere; **nicht von der ~ kommen** not to make any progress; **auf der ~** (*fig: sofort*) on the spot; *siehe auch* **anstelle**
stellen *vt* to put; (*Uhr etc*) to set; (*zur Verfügung stellen*) to supply; (*fassen: Dieb*) to apprehend; (*Antrag, Forderung*) to make; (*Aufnahme*) to pose; (*arrangieren: Szene*) to arrange ▷ *vr* (*sich aufstellen*) to stand; (*sich einfinden*) to present o.s.; (*bei Polizei*) to give o.s. up; (*vorgeben*) to pretend (to be); **das Radio lauter/leiser ~** to turn the radio up/down; **auf sich** *akk* **selbst gestellt sein** (*fig*) to have to fend for o.s.; **sich hinter jdn/etw ~** (*fig*) to support sb/sth; **sich einer Herausforderung ~** to take up a challenge; **sich zu etw ~** to have an opinion of sth
Stellen- *zW*: **Stellenangebot** *nt* offer of a post; (*in Zeitung*): **„Stellenangebote"** "vacancies"; **Stellenanzeige** *f* job advertisement *od* ad (*umg*); **Stellengesuch** *nt* application for a post; **„Stellengesuche"** "situations wanted"; **Stellennachweis** *m* employment

agency; **Stellenwert** *m* (*fig*) status
Stellung *f* position; (*Mil*) line; **~ nehmen zu** to comment on
Stellungnahme *f* comment
Stell- *zW*: **stellvertretend** *adj* deputy *attrib*, acting *attrib*; **Stellvertreter** *m* (*von Amts wegen*) deputy, representative
Stelze ['ʃtɛltsə] (**-, -n**) *f* stilt
Stemmbogen *m* (*Ski*) stem turn
stemmen ['ʃtɛmən] *vt* to lift (up); (*drücken*) to press; **sich ~ gegen** (*fig*) to resist, oppose
Stempel ['ʃtɛmpəl] (**-s, -**) *m* stamp; (*Poststempel*) postmark; (*Tech: Prägestempel*) die; (*Bot*) pistil; **Stempelkissen** *nt* inkpad
stempeln *vt* to stamp; (*Briefmarke*) to cancel ▷ *vi* (*umg: Stempeluhr betätigen*) to clock in/out; **~ gehen** (*umg*) to be *od* go on the dole (*Brit*) *od* on welfare (*US*)
Stengel ['ʃtɛŋəl] (**-s, -**) *m siehe* **Stängel**; **Stenografie** [-gra'fi:] *f* shorthand; **stenografieren** [-gra'fi:rən] *vt, vi* to write (in) shorthand; **Stenogramm** [-'gram] *nt* text in shorthand; **Stenotypist, in** [-ty'pɪst(ɪn)] *m(f)* shorthand typist (*Brit*), stenographer (*US*)
Steppdecke *f* quilt
Steppe (**-, -n**) *f* steppe
steppen ['ʃtɛpən] *vt* to stitch ▷ *vi* to tap-dance
Sterbe- *zW*: **Sterbefall** *m* death; **Sterbehilfe** *f* euthanasia
sterben ['ʃtɛrbən] *unreg vi* to die; **an einer Krankheit/Verletzung ~** to die of an illness/from an injury; **er ist für mich gestorben** (*fig: umg*) he might as well be dead
sterblich ['ʃtɛrplɪç] *adj* mortal; **Sterblichkeit** *f* mortality; **Sterblichkeitsziffer** *f* death rate; **Stereoanlage** *f* stereo unit; **stereotyp** *adj* stereotyped
steril [ʃte'ri:l] *adj* sterile
sterilisieren [ʃterili'zi:rən] *vt* to sterilize
Stern [ʃtɛrn] (**-(e)s, -e**) *m* star; **das steht (noch) in den ~en** (*fig*) it's in the lap of the gods; **Sternbild** *nt* constellation; **Sternschnuppe** (**-, -n**) *f* meteor, falling star; **Sternstunde** *f* historic moment
stet [ʃte:t] *adj* steady
stetig *adj* constant, continual; (*Math: Funktion*) continuous
stets *adv* continually, always
Steuer[1] ['ʃtɔʏər] (**-s, -**) *nt* (*Naut*) helm; (*Steuerruder*) rudder; (*Aut*) steering wheel; **am ~ sitzen** (*Aut*) to be at the wheel; (*Aviat*) to be at the controls
Steuer[2] (**-, -n**) *f* tax
Steuer- *zW*: **Steuerberater, in** *m(f)* tax consultant; **Steuererklärung** *f* tax return; **Steuerhinterziehung** *f* tax evasion; **Steuerklasse** *f* tax group; **Steuerknüppel** *m* control column; (*Aviat, Comput*) joystick; **Steuermann** (**-(e)s**, *pl* **-männer** *od* **-leute**) *m* helmsman
steuern *vt* to steer; (*Flugzeug*) to pilot; (*Entwicklung, Tonstärke*) to control ▷ *vi* to steer; (*in Flugzeug etc*) to be at the controls; (*bei Entwicklung etc*) to be in control
Steuer- *zW*: **Steuernummer** *f* ≈ National Insurance Number (*Brit*), ≈ Social Security Number (*US*); **steuerpflichtig** *adj* taxable; (*Person*) liable to pay tax; **Steuerrad** *nt* steering wheel
Steuerung *f* steering (*auch Aut*), piloting; control; (*Vorrichtung*) controls *pl*; **automatische ~** (*Aviat*) autopilot; (*Tech*) automatic steering (device)
Steuerzahler *m* taxpayer
Steward ['stju:ərt] (**-s, -s**) *m* steward
Stewardess ['stju:ərdɛs] (**-, -en**) *f* stewardess
Stich [ʃtɪç] (**-(e)s, -e**) *m* (*Insektenstich*) sting; (*Messerstich*) stab; (*beim Nähen*) stitch; (*Färbung*) tinge; (*Karten*) trick; (*Art*) engraving; (*fig*) pang; **ein ~ ins Rote** a tinge of red; **einen ~ haben** (*umg: Esswaren*) to be bad *od* off (*Brit*); (*: Mensch: verrückt sein*) to be nuts; **jdn im ~ lassen** to leave sb in the lurch
sticheln *vi* (*fig*) to jibe; (*pej: umg*) to make snide remarks
Stich- *zW*: **stichhaltig** *adj* valid; (*Beweis*) conclusive; **Stichprobe** *f* spot check
Stichtag *m* qualifying date
Stichwahl *f* final ballot
Stichwort *nt* (*pl* **-worte**) cue; (*: für Vortrag*) note (*pl* **-wörter**) (*in Wörterbuch*) headword
sticken ['ʃtɪkən] *vt, vi* to embroider
Stickerei [ʃtɪkə'raɪ] *f* embroidery
stickig *adj* stuffy, close
Stickstoff (**-(e)s**) *m* nitrogen
Stiefel ['ʃti:fəl] (**-s, -**) *m* boot; (*Trinkgefäß*) *large boot-shaped beer glass*
Stief- *zW*: **Stiefkind** *nt* stepchild; (*fig*) Cinderella; **Stiefmutter** *f* stepmother; **Stiefmütterchen** *nt* pansy; **Stiefvater** *m* stepfather
stieg *etc* [ʃti:k] *vb siehe* **steigen**
Stiege ['ʃti:gə] (**-, -n**) *f* staircase
Stiel [ʃti:l] (**-(e)s, -e**) *m* handle; (*Bot*) stalk
Stier (**-(e)s, -e**) *m* bull; (*Astrol*) Taurus
stier [ʃti:r] *adj* staring, fixed
stieren *vi* to stare
stieß *etc* [ʃti:s] *vb siehe* **stoßen**
Stift [ʃtɪft] (**-(e)s, -e**) *m* peg; (*Nagel*) tack; (*Buntstift*) crayon; (*Bleistift*) pencil; (*umg: Lehrling*) apprentice (boy)
stiften *vt* to found; (*Unruhe*) to cause; (*spenden*) to contribute; **~ gehen** to hop it
Stifter, in (**-s, -**) *m(f)* founder
Stiftung *f* donation; (*Organisation*) foundation
Stiftzahn *m* post crown
Stil [ʃti:l] (**-(e)s, -e**) *m* style; (*Eigenart*) way, manner
still [ʃtɪl] *adj* quiet; (*unbewegt*) still; (*heimlich*) secret; **ich dachte mir im S~en** I thought to myself; **er ist ein ~es Wasser** he's a deep one; **~er Teilhaber** (*Comm*) sleeping (*Brit*) *od* silent (*US*) partner; **der S~e Ozean** the Pacific (Ocean); **~ stehen** (*unbewegt*) to stand still
Stille (**-, -n**) *f* quietness; stillness; **in aller ~**

quietly
stillen *vt* to stop; (*befriedigen*) to satisfy; (*Säugling*) to breast-feed
still- *zW*: **stillhalten** *unreg vi* to keep still; **stilllegen** *vt* to close down; **Stillschweigen** *nt* silence; **stillschweigend** *adj* silent; (*Einverständnis*) tacit ▷ *adv* silently; tacitly; **Stillstand** *m* standstill; **stillstehen** *unreg vi* to stand still
stimmberechtigt *adj* entitled to vote
Stimme ['ʃtɪmə] (**-, -n**) *f* voice; (*Wahlstimme*) vote; (*Mus: Rolle*) part; **mit leiser/lauter ~** in a soft/loud voice; **seine ~ abgeben** to vote
stimmen *vi* (*richtig sein*) to be right; (*wählen*) to vote ▷ *vt* (*Instrument*) to tune; **stimmt so!** that's all right; **für/gegen etw ~** to vote for/against sth; **jdn traurig ~** to make sb feel sad
Stimmenmehrheit *f* majority (of votes)
Stimm- *zW*: **Stimmenthaltung** *f* abstention; **Stimmgabel** *f* tuning fork; **stimmhaft** *adj* voiced
Stimm- *zW*: **stimmlos** *adj* (*Ling*) unvoiced; **Stimmrecht** *nt* right to vote
Stimmung *f* mood; (*Atmosphäre*) atmosphere; (*Moral*) morale; **in ~ kommen** to liven up; **~ gegen/für jdn/etw machen** to stir up (public) opinion against/in favour of sb/sth
stimmungsvoll *adj* (*Atmosphäre*) enjoyable; (*Gedicht*) full of atmosphere
Stimmzettel *m* ballot paper
stinken ['ʃtɪŋkən] *unreg vi* to stink; **die Sache stinkt mir** (*umg*) I'm fed-up to the back teeth (with it)
Stipendium [ʃti'pɛndiʊm] *nt* grant; (*als Auszeichnung*) scholarship
Stirn [ʃtɪrn] (**-, -en**) *f* forehead, brow; (*Frechheit*) impudence; **die ~ haben zu ...** to have the nerve to ...; **Stirnhöhle** *f* sinus; **Stirnrunzeln** (**-s**) *nt* frown
stöbern ['ʃtøbərn] *vi* to rummage
stochern ['stɔxərn] *vi* to poke (about)
Stock[1] [ʃtɔk] (**-(e)s, ¨-e**) *m* stick; (*Rohrstock*) cane; (*Zeigestock*) pointer; (*Bot*) stock; **über ~ und Stein** up hill and down dale
Stock[2] [ʃtɔk] (**-(e)s, -** *od* **-werke**) *m* storey (*Brit*), story (*US*); **im ersten ~** on the first (*Brit*) *od* second (*US*) floor
stock- *in zw* (*vor adj: umg*) completely
stocken *vi* to stop, pause; (*Arbeit, Entwicklung*) to make no progress; (*im Satz*) to break off; (*Verkehr*) to be held up
stockend *adj* halting
Stockung *f* stoppage
Stockwerk *nt* storey (*Brit*), story (*US*), floor
Stoff [ʃtɔf] (**-(e)s, -e**) *m* (*Gewebe*) material, cloth; (*Materie*) matter; (*von Buch etc*) subject (matter); (*umg: Rauschgift*) dope
Stoff- *zW*: **stofflich** *adj* with regard to subject matter; **Stofftier** *nt* soft toy; **Stoffwechsel** *m* metabolism
stöhnen ['ʃtøːnən] *vi* to groan
stoisch ['ʃtoːɪʃ] *adj* stoical
Stollen ['ʃtɔlən] (**-s, -**) *m* (*Min*) gallery; (*Koch*) stollen, *cake eaten at Christmas*; (*von Schuhen*) stud
stolpern ['ʃtɔlpərn] *vi* to stumble, trip; (*fig: zu Fall kommen*) to come a cropper (*umg*)
stolz [ʃtɔlts] *adj* proud; (*imposant: Bauwerk*) majestic; (*ironisch: Preis*) princely; **Stolz** (**-es**) *m* pride
stolzieren [ʃtɔl'tsiːrən] *vi* to strut
stopfen ['ʃtɔpfən] *vt* (*hineinstopfen*) to stuff; (*nähen*) to darn ▷ *vi* (*Med*) to cause constipation; **jdm das Maul ~** (*umg*) to silence sb
Stopfgarn *nt* darning thread
Stoppel ['ʃtɔpəl] (**-, -n**) *f* stubble
stoppen *vt* to stop; (*mit Uhr*) to time ▷ *vi* to stop
Stoppschild *nt* stop sign
Stoppuhr *f* stopwatch
Stöpsel ['ʃtœpsəl] (**-s, -**) *m* plug; (*für Flaschen*) stopper
Storch [ʃtɔrç] (**-(e)s, ¨-e**) *m* stork
stören ['ʃtøːrən] *vt* to disturb; (*behindern, Rundf*) to interfere with ▷ *vr*: **sich an etw** *dat* **~** to let sth bother one ▷ *vi* to get in the way; **was mich an ihm/daran stört** what I don't like about him/it; **stört es Sie, wenn ich rauche?** do you mind if I smoke?; **ich möchte nicht ~** I don't want to be in the way
störend *adj* disturbing, annoying
Störenfried (**-(e)s, -e**) *m* troublemaker
Störfall *m* (*in Kraftwerk etc*) malfunction, accident
stornieren [ʃtɔr'niːrən] *vt* (*Comm: Auftrag*) to cancel; (*: Buchungsfehler*) to reverse
störrisch ['ʃtœrɪʃ] *adj* stubborn, perverse
Störsender *m* jammer, jamming transmitter
Störung *f* disturbance; interference; (*Tech*) fault; (*Med*) disorder
Stoß [ʃtoːs] (**-es, ¨-e**) *m* (*Schub*) push; (*leicht*) poke; (*Schlag*) blow; (*mit Schwert*) thrust; (*mit Ellbogen*) nudge; (*mit Fuß*) kick; (*Erdstoß*) shock; (*Haufen*) pile; **seinem Herzen einen ~ geben** to pluck up courage; **Stoßdämpfer** *m* shock absorber
stoßen *unreg vt* (*mit Druck*) to shove, push; (*mit Schlag*) to knock, bump; (*mit Ellbogen*) to nudge; (*mit Fuß*) to kick; (*mit Schwert*) to thrust; (*anstoßen: Kopf etc*) to bump; (*zerkleinern*) to pulverize ▷ *vr* to get a knock ▷ *vi*: **~ an** *od* **auf** *+akk* to bump into; (*finden*) to come across; (*angrenzen*) to be next to; **sich ~ an** *+dat* (*fig*) to take exception to; **zu jdm ~** to meet up with sb
Stoßstange *f* (*Aut*) bumper
Stoß- *zW*
stottern ['ʃtɔtərn] *vt, vi* to stutter
Stövchen ['ʃtøːfçən] *nt* (*teapot- etc*) warmer
Str. *abk* (*= Straße*) St.
stracks [ʃtraks] *adv* straight
Straf- *zW*: **Strafanstalt** *f* penal institution; **strafbar** *adj* punishable; **sich strafbar machen** to commit an offence (*Brit*) *od*

offense (*US*); **Strafbarkeit** *f* criminal nature
Strafe ['ʃtra:fə] (**-, -n**) *f* punishment; (*Jur*) penalty; (*Gefängnisstrafe*) sentence; (*Geldstrafe*) fine; **... bei ~ verboten** ... forbidden; **100 Dollar ~ zahlen** to pay a $100 fine; **er hat seine ~ weg** (*umg*) he's had his punishment
strafen *vt, vi* to punish; **mit etw gestraft sein** to be cursed with sth
straff [ʃtraf] *adj* tight; (*streng*) strict; (*Stil etc*) concise; (*Haltung*) erect
straffen *vt* to tighten
Straf- *zW*: **Strafgefangene, r** *f(m)* prisoner, convict; **Strafgesetzbuch** *nt* penal code
sträflich ['ʃtrɛ:flɪç] *adj* criminal ▷ *adv* (*vernachlässigen etc*) criminally
Sträfling *m* convict
Straf- *zW*: **Strafporto** *nt* excess postage (charge); **Strafpredigt** *f* severe lecture; **Strafraum** *m* (*Sport*) penalty area; **Strafrecht** *nt* criminal law; **Strafstoß** *m* (*Sport*) penalty (kick); **Straftat** *f* punishable act; **Strafzettel** (*umg*) *m* ticket
Strahl [ʃtra:l] (**-(e)s, -en**) *m* ray, beam; (*Wasserstrahl*) jet
strahlen *vi* (*Kernreaktor*) to radiate; (*Sonne, Licht*) to shine; (*fig*) to beam
Strahlenbehandlung *f* radiotherapy
Strahlenbelastung *f* (effects of) radiation
Strahlen- *zW*: **Strahlendosis** *f* radiation dose; **Strahlentherapie** *f* radiotherapy
Strahlung *f* radiation
Strähne ['strɛ:nə] (**-, -n**) *f* strand
stramm [ʃtram] *adj* tight; (*Haltung*) erect; (*Mensch*) robust
strampeln ['ʃtrampəln] *vi* to kick (about), fidget
Strand [ʃtrant] (**-(e)s, ¨-e**) *m* shore; (*Meeresstrand*) beach; **am ~** on the beach; **Strandbad** *nt* open-air swimming pool; (*Badeort*) bathing resort
stranden ['ʃtrandən] *vi* to run aground; (*fig: Mensch*) to fail
Strandgut *nt* flotsam and jetsam
Strandkorb *m* beach chair
Strapaze [ʃtra'pa:tsə] (**-, -n**) *f* strain
strapazieren [ʃtrapa'tsi:rən] *vt* (*Material*) to be hard on, punish; (*jdn*) to be a strain on; (*erschöpfen*) to wear out, exhaust
strapazierfähig *adj* hard-wearing
strapaziös [ʃtrapatsi'ø:s] *adj* exhausting, tough
Straßburg ['ʃtra:sbʊrk] (**-s**) *nt* Strasbourg
Straße ['ʃtra:sə] (**-, -n**) *f* road; (*in Stadt, Dorf*) street; **auf der ~** in the street; **auf der ~ liegen** (*fig: umg*) to be out of work; **auf die ~ gesetzt werden** (*umg*) to be turned out (onto the streets)
Straßen- *zW*: **Straßenbahn** *f* tram (*Brit*), streetcar (*US*); **Straßenbeleuchtung** *f* street lighting; **Straßenfeger** (**-s, -**) *m* roadsweeper; **Straßenkehrer** (**-s, -**) *m* roadsweeper; **Straßensperre** *f* roadblock; **Straßenverkehr** *m* road traffic; **Straßenverkehrsordnung** *f* Highway Code (*Brit*)
Stratege [ʃtra'te:gə] (**-n, -n**) *m* strategist
Strategie [ʃtrate'gi:] *f* strategy
strategisch *adj* strategic
Stratosphäre [ʃtrato'sfɛ:rə] (**-**) *f* stratosphere
sträuben ['ʃtrɔʏbən] *vt* to ruffle ▷ *vr* to bristle; (*Mensch*): **sich (gegen etw) ~** to resist (sth)
Strauch [ʃtraʊx] (**-(e)s, Sträucher**) *m* bush, shrub
Strauß[1] [ʃtraʊs] (**-es, Sträuße**) *m* (*Blumenstrauß*) bouquet, bunch
Strauß[2] [ʃtraʊs] (**-es, -e**) *m* ostrich
Streber (**-s, -**) *m* (*pej*) pushy person; (*Sch*) swot (*Brit*)
Strecke ['ʃtrɛkə] (**-, -n**) *f* stretch; (*Entfernung*) distance; (*Eisenb, Math*) line; **auf der ~ Paris-Brüssel** on the way from Paris to Brussels; **auf der ~ bleiben** (*fig*) to fall by the wayside; **zur ~ bringen** (*Jagd*) to bag
strecken *vt* to stretch; (*Waffen*) to lay down; (*Koch*) to eke out ▷ *vr* to stretch (o.s.)
Streich [ʃtraɪç] (**-(e)s, -e**) *m* trick, prank; (*Hieb*) blow; **jdm einen ~ spielen** (*Person*) to play a trick on sb
streicheln *vt* to stroke
streichen *unreg vt* (*berühren*) to stroke; (*auftragen*) to spread; (*anmalen*) to paint; (*durchstreichen*) to delete; (*nicht genehmigen*) to cancel; (*Schulden*) to write off; (*Zuschuss etc*) to cut ▷ *vi* (*berühren*) to brush past; (*schleichen*) to prowl; **etw glatt ~** to smooth sth (out)
Streich- *zW*: **Streichholz** *nt* match; **Streichinstrument** *nt* string(ed) instrument
Streife (**-, -n**) *f* patrol
streifen ['ʃtraɪfən] *vt* (*leicht berühren*) to brush against, graze; (*Blick*) to skim over; (*Thema, Problem*) to touch on; (*abstreifen*) to take off ▷ *vi* (*gehen*) to roam
Streifen (**-s, -**) *m* (*Linie*) stripe; (*Stück*) strip; (*Film*) film
Streifendienst *m* patrol duty
Streifenwagen *m* patrol car
Streifschuss *m* graze, grazing shot
Streifzug *m* scouting trip; (*Bummel*) expedition; (*fig: kurzer Überblick*): **~ (durch)** brief survey (of)
Streik [ʃtraɪk] (**-(e)s, -s**) *m* strike; **in den ~ treten** to come out on strike, strike; **Streikbrecher** *m* blackleg (*Brit*), strikebreaker; **streiken** *vi* to strike; **der Computer streikt** the computer's packed up (*umg*), the computer's on the blink (*umg*); **da streike ich** (*umg*) I refuse!; **Streikkasse** *f* strike fund; **Streikposten** *m* (peaceful) picket
Streit [ʃtraɪt] (**-(e)s, -e**) *m* argument; (*Auseinandersetzung*) dispute
streiten *unreg vi, vr* to argue; to dispute; **darüber lässt sich ~** that's debatable
streitig *adj*: **jdm etw ~ machen** to dispute sb's right to sth; **Streitigkeiten** *pl* quarrel *sing*, dispute *sing*
Streitkräfte *pl* (*Mil*) armed forces *pl*

streng [ʃtrɛŋ] *adj* severe; (*Lehrer, Maßnahme*) strict; (*Geruch etc*) sharp; **~ geheim** top-secret; **~ genommen** strictly speaking; **~ verboten!** strictly prohibited
Strenge (-) *f* severity; strictness; sharpness
strenggläubig *adj* strict
Stress [ʃtrɛs] (**-es, -e**) *m* stress
stressen *vt* to put under stress
stressfrei *adj* without stress
stressig *adj* stressful
Streu [ʃtrɔʏ] (**-, -en**) *f* litter, bed of straw
streuen *vt* to strew, scatter, spread ▷ *vi* (*mit Streupulver*) to grit; (*mit Salz*) to put down salt
Streuung *f* dispersion; (*Statistik*) mean variation; (*Phys*) scattering
Strich (**-(e)s, -e**) *m* (*Linie*) line; (*Federstrich, Pinselstrich*) stroke; (*von Geweben*) nap; (*von Fell*) pile; (*Querstrich*) dash; (*Schrägstrich*) oblique, slash (*bes US*); **einen ~ machen durch** (*lit*) to cross out; (*fig*) to foil; **jdm einen ~ durch die Rechnung machen** to thwart *od* foil sb's plans; **einen ~ unter etw** *akk* **machen** (*fig*) to forget sth; **nach ~ und Faden** (*umg*) good and proper; **auf den ~ gehen** (*umg*) to walk the streets; **jdm gegen den ~ gehen** to rub sb up the wrong way
strich *etc* [ʃtrɪç] *vb siehe* **streichen**
Strich- *zW*: **Strichjunge** (*umg*) *m* male prostitute; **Strichkode** *m* = **Strichcode**; **Strichmädchen** *nt* streetwalker; **Strichpunkt** *m* semicolon; **strichweise** *adv* here and there; **strichweise Regen** (*Met*) rain in places
Strick [ʃtrɪk] (**-(e)s, -e**) *m* rope; **jdm aus etw einen ~ drehen** to use sth against sb
stricken *vt, vi* to knit
Strick- *zW*: **Strickjacke** *f* cardigan; **Strickleiter** *f* rope ladder; **Stricknadel** *f* knitting needle; **Strickwaren** *pl* knitwear *sing*
strikt [strɪkt] *adj* strict
stritt *etc* [ʃtrɪt] *vb siehe* **streiten**
strittig [ˈʃtrɪtɪç] *adj* disputed, in dispute
Stroh [ʃtroː] (**-(e)s**) *nt* straw; **Strohblume** *f* everlasting flower; **Strohdach** *nt* thatched roof; **Strohhalm** *m* (drinking) straw
Strom [ʃtroːm] (**-(e)s, ¨-e**) *m* river; (*fig*) stream; (*Elek*) current; **unter ~ stehen** (*Elek*) to be live; (*fig*) to be excited; **der Wein floss in Strömen** the wine flowed like water; **in Strömen regnen** to be pouring with rain; **stromabwärts** *adv* downstream; **stromaufwärts** *adv* upstream
strömen [ˈʃtrøːmən] *vi* to stream, pour
Strom- *zW*: **Stromkreis** *m* (electrical) circuit; **stromlinienförmig** *adj* streamlined; **Stromrechnung** *f* electricity bill; **Stromsperre** *f* power cut; **Stromstärke** *f* amperage
Strömung [ˈʃtrøːmʊŋ] *f* current
Strophe [ˈʃtroːfə] (**-, -n**) *f* verse
strotzen [ˈʃtrɔtsən] *vi*: **~ vor** *+dat od* **von** to abound in, be full of
Strudel [ˈʃtruːdəl] (**-s, -**) *m* whirlpool, vortex; (*Koch*) strudel
Struktur [ʃtrʊkˈtuːr] *f* structure
Strumpf [ʃtrʊmpf] (**-(e)s, ¨-e**) *m* stocking; **Strumpfband** *nt* garter; **Strumpfhose** *f* (pair of) tights *pl* (*Brit*) *od* pantihose *pl* (*US*)
Stube [ˈʃtuːbə] (**-, -n**) *f* room; **die gute ~** (*veraltet*) the parlour (*Brit*) *od* parlor (*US*)
Stuben- *zW*: **Stubenarrest** *m* confinement to one's room; (*Mil*) confinement to quarters; **Stubenhocker** (*umg*) *m* stay-at-home; **stubenrein** *adj* house-trained
Stuck [ʃtʊk] (**-(e)s**) *m* stucco
Stück [ʃtʏk] (**-(e)s, -e**) *nt* piece; (*etwas*) bit; (*Theat*) play; **am ~** in one piece; **das ist ein starkes ~!** (*umg*) that's a bit much!; **große ~e auf jdn halten** to think highly of sb
Stück- *zW*: **Stückgut** *nt* (*Eisenb*) parcel service; **Stücklohn** *m* piecework rates *pl*; **stückweise** *adv* bit by bit, piecemeal; (*Comm*) individually; **Stückwerk** *nt* bits and pieces *pl*
Student, in [ʃtuˈdɛnt(ɪn)] *m(f)* student
Studenten- *zW*: **Studentenausweis** *m* student card; **Studentenwohnheim** *nt* hall of residence (*Brit*), dormitory (*US*)
studentisch *adj* student *attrib*
Studie [ˈʃtuːdiə] *f* study
Studienplatz *m* university place
studieren [ʃtuˈdiːrən] *vt, vi* to study; **bei jdm ~** to study under sb
Studio [ˈʃtuːdio] (**-s, -s**) *nt* studio
Studium [ˈʃtuːdiʊm] *nt* studies *pl*
Stufe [ˈʃtuːfə] (**-, -n**) *f* step; (*Entwicklungsstufe*) stage; (*Niveau*) level
Stufen- *zW*: **Stufenplan** *m* graduated plan; **stufenweise** *adv* gradually
Stuhl [ʃtuːl] (**-(e)s, ¨-e**) *m* chair; **zwischen zwei Stühlen sitzen** (*fig*) to fall between two stools
Stuhlgang *m* bowel movement
stülpen [ˈʃtʏlpən] *vt* (*bedecken*) to put; **etw über etw** *akk* **~** to put sth over sth; **den Kragen nach oben ~** to turn up one's collar
stumm [ʃtʊm] *adj* silent; (*Med*) dumb
Stummel (**-s, -**) *m* stump; (*Zigarettenstummel*) stub
Stummfilm *m* silent film (*Brit*) *od* movie (*US*)
Stümper, in [ˈʃtʏmpər(ɪn)] (**-s, -**) *m(f)* incompetent, duffer; **stümperhaft** *adj* bungling, incompetent
stümpern (*umg*) *vi* to bungle
Stumpf [ʃtʊmpf] (**-(e)s, ¨-e**) *m* stump; **etw mit ~ und Stiel ausrotten** to eradicate sth root and branch
stumpf *adj* blunt; (*teilnahmslos, glanzlos*) dull; (*Winkel*) obtuse
Stumpfsinn (**-(e)s**) *m* tediousness
stumpfsinnig *adj* dull
Stunde [ˈʃtʊndə] (**-, -n**) *f* hour; (*Augenblick, Zeitpunkt*) time; (*Sch*) lesson, period (*Brit*); **~ um Stunde** hour after hour; **80 Kilometer in der ~** ≈ 50 miles per hour
stunden *vt*: **jdm etw ~** to give sb time to pay

sth
Stunden- *zW*: **Stundengeschwindigkeit** *f* average speed (per hour); **Stundenkilometer** *pl* kilometres (*Brit*) *od* kilometers (*US*) per hour; **stundenlang** *adj* for hours; **Stundenlohn** *m* hourly wage; **Stundenplan** *m* timetable; **stundenweise** *adv* by the hour; (*stündlich*) every hour
stündlich ['ʃtʏntlɪç] *adj* hourly
Stups [ʃtʊps] (**-es, -e**) (*umg*) *m* push
Stupsnase *f* snub nose
stur [ʃtu:r] *adj* obstinate, stubborn; (*Nein, Arbeiten*) dogged; **er fuhr ~ geradeaus** he just carried straight on; **sich ~ stellen, auf ~ stellen** (*umg*) to dig one's heels in; **ein ~er Bock** (*umg*) a pig-headed fellow
Sturm [ʃtʊrm] (**-(e)s, ¨-e**) *m* storm; (*Wind*) gale; (*Mil etc*) attack, assault; **~ läuten** to keep one's finger on the doorbell; **gegen etw ~ laufen** (*fig*) to be up in arms against sth
stürmen ['ʃtʏrmən] *vi* (*Wind*) to blow hard, to rage; (*rennen*) to storm ▷ *vt* (*Mil, fig*) to storm ▷ *vi unpers*: **es stürmt** there's a gale blowing
Stürmer (**-s, -**) *m* (*Sport*) forward
stürmisch *adj* stormy; (*fig*) tempestuous; (*Entwicklung*) rapid; (*Liebhaber*) passionate; (*Beifall*) tumultuous; **nicht so ~** take it easy
Sturm- *zW*: **Sturmwarnung** *f* gale warning; **Sturmwind** *m* gale
Sturz [ʃtʊrts] (**-es, ¨-e**) *m* fall; (*Pol*) overthrow; (*in Temperatur, Preis*) drop
stürzen ['ʃtʏrtsən] *vt* (*werfen*) to hurl; (*Pol*) to overthrow; (*umkehren*) to overturn ▷ *vr* to rush; (*hineinstürzen*) to plunge ▷ *vi* to fall; (*Aviat*) to dive; (*rennen*) to dash; **jdn ins Unglück ~** to bring disaster upon sb; **„nicht ~"** "this side up"; **sich auf jdn/etw ~** to pounce on sb/sth; **sich in Unkosten ~** to go to great expense
Sturzflug *m* nose dive
Sturzhelm *m* crash helmet
Stute ['ʃtu:tə] (**-, -n**) *f* mare
Stütze ['ʃtʏtsə] (**-, -n**) *f* support; (*Hilfe*) help; **die ~n der Gesellschaft** the pillars of society
stutzen ['ʃtʊtsən] *vt* to trim; (*Ohr, Schwanz*) to dock; (*Flügel*) to clip ▷ *vi* to hesitate; (*argwöhnisch werden*) to become suspicious
stützen *vt* (*lit, fig*) to support; (*Ellbogen etc*) to prop up ▷ *vr*: **sich auf jdn/etw ~** (*lit*) to lean on sb/sth; (*Beweise, Theorie*) to be based on sb/sth
stutzig *adj* perplexed, puzzled; (*misstrauisch*) suspicious
Stützmauer *f* supporting wall
Stützpunkt *m* point of support; (*von Hebel*) fulcrum; (*Mil, fig*) base
Subjekt [zʊp'jɛkt] (**-(e)s, -e**) *nt* subject; (*pej: Mensch*) character (*umg*)
subjektiv [zʊpjɛk'ti:f] *adj* subjective
Subjektivität [zʊpjɛktivi'tɛ:t] *f* subjectivity
Substantiv ['zʊpstanti:f] (**-s, -e**) *nt* noun
Substanz [zʊp'stants] *f* substance; **von der ~ zehren** to live on one's capital
subtil [zʊp'ti:l] *adj* subtle
subtrahieren [zʊptra'hi:rən] *vt* to subtract
Subvention [zʊpvɛntsi'o:n] *f* subsidy
subventionieren [zʊpvɛntsio'ni:rən] *vt* to subsidize
Suchaktion *f* search
Suche (**-, -n**) *f* search
suchen ['zu:xən] *vt* to look for, seek; (*versuchen*) to try ▷ *vi* to seek, search; **du hast hier nichts zu ~** you have no business being here; **nach Worten ~** to search for words; (*sprachlos sein*) to be at a loss for words; **such!** (*zu Hund*) seek!, find!; **~ und ersetzen** (*Comput*) search and replace
Sucher (**-s, -**) *m* seeker, searcher; (*Phot*) viewfinder
Suchmaschine *f* (*Comput*) search engine
Sucht [zʊxt] (**-, ¨-e**) *f* mania; (*Med*) addiction
süchtig ['zʏçtɪç] *adj* addicted
Süchtige, r *f(m)* addict; **Südafrika** *nt* South Africa; **Südamerika** *nt* South America
Sudan [zu'da:n] (**-s**) *m*: **der ~** the Sudan
süddeutsch *adj* South German
Süddeutschland *nt* South(ern) Germany
Süden ['zy:dən] (**-s**) *m* south
Süd- *zW*: **Südfrüchte** *pl* Mediterranean fruit; **Südkorea** *nt* South Korea; **südlich** *adj* southern; **südlich von** (to the) south of; **Südpol** *m* South Pole; **Südsee** *f* South Seas *pl*, South Pacific; **Südtirol** *nt* South Tyrol
Sueskanal ['zu:ɛskana:l] (**-s**) *m* Suez Canal
süffig ['zʏfɪç] *adj* (*Wein*) very drinkable
süffisant [zʏfi'zant] *adj* smug
suggerieren [zʊge'ri:rən] *vt* to suggest
Sultan ['zʊltan] (**-s, -e**) *m* sultan
Sultanine [zʊlta'ni:nə] *f* sultana
Sülze ['zʏltsə] (**-, -n**) *f* brawn (*Brit*), headcheese (*US*); (*Aspik*) aspic
Summe (**-, -n**) *f* sum, total
summen *vi* to buzz ▷ *vt* (*Lied*) to hum
Sumpf [zʊmpf] (**-(e)s, ¨-e**) *m* swamp, marsh
sumpfig *adj* marshy
Sünde ['zʏndə] (**-, -n**) *f* sin
Sünden- *zW*: **Sündenbock** *m* (*fig*) scapegoat; **Sündenfall** *m* (*Rel*) Fall
Sünder, in (**-s, -**) *m(f)* sinner
Super ['zu:pər] (**-s**) *nt* (*Benzin*) four-star (petrol) (*Brit*), premium (*US*)
super (*umg*) *adj* super ▷ *adv* incredibly well
Superlativ ['zu:pərlati:f] (**-s, -e**) *m* superlative
Supermarkt *m* supermarket
Suppe ['zʊpə] (**-, -n**) *f* soup; (*mit Einlage*) broth; (*klare Brühe*) bouillon; (*fig: umg: Nebel*) peasouper (*Brit*), pea soup (*US*); **jdm die ~ versalzen** (*umg*) to put a spoke in sb's wheel
Surfbrett ['zø:rfbrɛt] *nt* surfboard
surfen ['zø:rfən] *vi* to surf
Surfer, in *m(f)* surfer
suspekt [zʊs'pɛkt] *adj* suspect
süß [zy:s] *adj* sweet
Süße (**-**) *f* sweetness
süßen *vt* to sweeten
Süßigkeit *f* sweetness; (*Bonbon etc*) sweet

(*Brit*), candy (*US*)
süß- *zW*: **süßlich** *adj* sweetish; (*fig*) sugary; **Süßspeise** *f* pudding, sweet (*Brit*); **Süßstoff** *m* sweetener; **Süßwasser** *nt* fresh water
Swasiland ['sva:zilant] (**-s**) *nt* Swaziland
Sylvester [zyl'vɛstər] (**-s, -**) *nt* = **Silvester**
Symbol [zym'bo:l] (**-s, -e**) *nt* symbol
symbolisch *adj* symbolic(al)
Symmetrie [zyme'tri:] *f* symmetry; **Symmetrieachse** *f* symmetric axis
symmetrisch [zy'me:trɪʃ] *adj* symmetrical
Sympathie [zympa'ti:] *f* liking; sympathy; **er hat sich** *dat* **alle ~(n) verscherzt** he has turned everyone against him
Sympathisant, in *m(f)* sympathizer
sympathisch [zym'pa:tɪʃ] *adj* likeable, congenial; **er ist mir ~** I like him
sympathisieren [zympati'zi:rən] *vi* to sympathize
Symptom [zymp'to:m] (**-s, -e**) *nt* symptom
symptomatisch [zympto'ma:tɪʃ] *adj* symptomatic
Synagoge [zyna'go:gə] (**-, -n**) *f* synagogue
synchron [zyn'kro:n] *adj* synchronous; **Synchrongetriebe** *nt* synchromesh gearbox (*Brit*) *od* transmission (*US*)
synchronisieren [zynkroni'zi:rən] *vt* to synchronize; (*Film*) to dub
Syndrom [zyn'dro:m] (**-s, -e**) *nt* syndrome
Synonym [zyno'ny:m] (**-s, -e**) *nt* synonym
Syntax ['zyntaks] (**-, -en**) *f* syntax
Synthese [zyn'te:zə] (**-, -n**) *f* synthesis
synthetisch *adj* synthetic
Syphilis ['zy:filɪs] (-) *f* syphilis
Syrien (**-s**) *nt* Syria
syrisch *adj* Syrian
System [zys'te:m] (**-s, -e**) *nt* system; **Systemanalyse** *f* systems analysis; **Systemanalytiker, in** *m(f)* systems analyst
systematisch [zyste'ma:tɪʃ] *adj* systematic
systematisieren [zystemati'zi:rən] *vt* to systematize
Systemkritiker *m* critic of the system
Szene ['stse:nə] (**-, -n**) *f* scene; **sich in der ~ auskennen** (*umg*) to know the scene; **sich in ~ setzen** to play to the gallery
Szenerie [stsenə'ri:] *f* scenery

Tt

T, t[1] [teː] *nt* T, t; **T wie Theodor** ≈ T for Tommy
t[2] *abk* (= *Tonne*) t
Tabak ['taːbak] (**-s, -e**) *m* tobacco
tabellarisch [tabɛ'laːrɪʃ] *adj* tabular
Tabelle (**-, -n**) *f* table
Tabellenführer *m* (*Sport*) top of the table, league leader
Tabernakel [tabɛr'naːkəl] (**-s, -**) *nt* tabernacle
Tablett (**-(e)s, -s** *od* **-e**) *nt* tray
Tablette [ta'blɛtə] (**-, -n**) *f* tablet, pill
Tabu [ta'buː] (**-s, -s**) *nt* taboo
Tabulator [tabu'laːtɔr] *m* tabulator, tab (*umg*)
Tachometer [taxo'meːtər] (**-s, -**) *m* (*Aut*) speedometer
Tadel ['taːdəl] (**-s, -**) *m* censure, scolding; (*Fehler*) fault; (*Makel*) blemish; **tadellos** *adj* faultless, irreproachable
tadeln *vt* to scold
Tadschikistan [ta'dʒiːkistaːn] (**-s**) *nt* Tajikistan
Tafel ['taːfəl] (**-, -n**) *f* (*form: festlicher Speisetisch, Math*) table; (*Festmahl*) meal; (*Anschlagtafel*) board; (*Wandtafel*) blackboard; (*Schiefertafel*) slate; (*Gedenktafel*) plaque; (*Illustration*) plate; (*Schalttafel*) panel; (*Schokoladentafel etc*) bar
Taft [taft] (**-(e)s, -e**) *m* taffeta
Tag [taːk] (**-(e)s, -e**) *m* day; (*Tageslicht*) daylight; **am ~** during the day; **für** *od* **auf ein paar ~e** for a few days; **in den ~ hinein leben** to take each day as it comes; **bei ~(e)** (*ankommen*) while it's light; (*arbeiten, reisen*) during the day; **unter ~e** (*Min*) underground; **über ~e** (*Min*) on the surface; **an den ~ kommen** to come to light; **er legte großes Interesse an den ~** he showed great interest; **auf den ~ (genau)** to the day; **auf seine alten ~e** at his age; **guten ~!** good morning/afternoon!; *siehe auch* **zutage**; **Tagdienst** *m* day duty
Tage- *zW*: **Tagebuch** *nt* diary; **Tagegeld** *nt* daily allowance; **tagelang** *adv* for days
tagen *vi* to sit, meet ▷ *vi unpers*: **es tagt** dawn is breaking
Tages- *zW*: **Tagesablauf** *m* daily routine; **Tagesanbruch** *m* dawn; **Tageskarte** *f* (*Eintrittskarte*) day ticket; (*Speisekarte*) menu of the day; **Tageslicht** *nt* daylight; **Tagesordnung** *f* agenda; **an der Tagesordnung sein** (*fig*) to be the order of the day; **Tagesschau** *f* (*TV*) television news (programme (*Brit*) *od* program (*US*)); **Tageszeit** *f* time of day; **zu jeder Tages- und Nachtzeit** at all hours of the day and night; **Tageszeitung** *f* daily (paper)
täglich ['tɛːklɪç] *adj, adv* daily; **einmal ~** once a day; **tagsüber** *adv* during the day
Tagung *f* conference
Taille ['taljə] (**-, -n**) *f* waist
tailliert [ta'jiːrt] *adj* waisted, gathered at the waist
Taiwan ['taɪvan] (**-s**) *nt* Taiwan
Takt [takt] (**-(e)s, -e**) *m* tact; (*Mus*) time; **Taktgefühl** *nt* tact
Taktik *f* tactics *pl*
taktisch *adj* tactical
Takt- *zW*: **taktlos** *adj* tactless; **Taktlosigkeit** *f* tactlessness; **Taktstock** *m* (conductor's) baton; **Taktstrich** *m* (*Mus*) bar (line); **taktvoll** *adj* tactful
Tal [taːl] (**-(e)s, ¨-er**) *nt* valley
Talent [ta'lɛnt] (**-(e)s, -e**) *nt* talent
talentiert [talɛn'tiːrt] *adj* talented, gifted
Talisman ['taːlɪsman] (**-s, -e**) *m* talisman
Tal- *zW*: **Talsohle** *f* bottom of a valley; **Talsperre** *f* dam
Tamburin [tambu'riːn] (**-s, -e**) *nt* tambourine
Tampon ['tampɔn] (**-s, -s**) *m* tampon
Tang [taŋ] (**-(e)s, -e**) *m* seaweed
Tangente [taŋ'gɛntə] (**-, -n**) *f* tangent
tangieren [taŋ'giːrən] *vt* (*Problem*) to touch on; (*fig*) to affect
Tank [taŋk] (**-s, -s**) *m* tank
tanken *vt* (*Wagen etc*) to fill up with petrol (*Brit*) *od* gas (*US*); (*Benzin etc*) to fill up with; (*Aviat*) to (re)fuel; (*umg: frische Luft, neue Kräfte*) to get ▷ *vi* to fill up (with petrol *od* gas); to (re)fuel
Tanker (**-s, -**) *m* tanker
Tank- *zW*: **Tankstelle** *f* petrol (*Brit*) *od* gas (*US*) station; **Tankwart** *m* petrol pump (*Brit*) *od* gas station (*US*) attendant
Tanne ['tanə] (**-, -n**) *f* fir
Tannenbaum *m* fir tree
Tannenzapfen *m* fir cone
Tansania [tan'zaːnia] (**-s**) *nt* Tanzania
Tante ['tantə] (**-, -n**) *f* aunt
Tanz [tants] (**-es, ¨-e**) *m* dance

tanzen *vt, vi* to dance
Tänzer, in (**-s, -**) *m(f)* dancer
Tanzfläche *f* (dance) floor
Tapete [ta'pe:tə] (**-, -n**) *f* wallpaper
Tapetenwechsel *m* (*fig*) change of scenery
tapezieren [tape'tsi:rən] *vt* to (wall)paper
Tapezierer (**-s, -**) *m* (interior) decorator
tapfer ['tapfər] *adj* brave; **sich ~ schlagen** (*umg*) to put on a brave show; **Tapferkeit** *f* courage, bravery
Tarif [ta'ri:f] (**-s, -e**) *m* tariff, (scale of) fares/ charges; **nach/über/unter ~ bezahlen** to pay according to/above/below the (union) rate(s); **Tariflohn** *m* standard wage rate; **Tarifpartner** *m*: **die Tarifpartner** union and management; **Tarifvertrag** *m* pay agreement
tarnen ['tarnən] *vt* to camouflage; (*Person, Absicht*) to disguise
Tarnfarbe *f* camouflage paint
Tarnung *f* camouflaging; disguising
Tasche ['taʃə] (**-, -n**) *f* pocket; (*Handtasche*) handbag; **in die eigene ~ wirtschaften** to line one's own pockets; **jdm auf der ~ liegen** (*umg*) to live off sb
Taschen- *zW*: **Taschenbuch** *nt* paperback; **Taschendieb** *m* pickpocket; **Taschengeld** *nt* pocket money; **Taschenlampe** *f* (electric) torch, flashlight (*US*); **Taschenmesser** *nt* penknife; **Taschenrechner** *m* pocket calculator; **Taschentuch** *nt* handkerchief
Tasse ['tasə] (**-, -n**) *f* cup; **er hat nicht alle ~n im Schrank** (*umg*) he's not all there
Tastatur [tasta'tu:r] *f* keyboard
Taste ['tastə] (**-, -n**) *f* push-button control; (*an Schreibmaschine*) key
tasten *vt* to feel, touch; (*drücken*) to press ▷ *vi* to feel, grope ▷ *vr* to feel one's way
Tastentelefon *nt* push-button telephone
Tastsinn *m* sense of touch
Tat (**-, -en**) *f* act, deed, action; **in der ~** indeed, as a matter of fact; **etw in die ~ umsetzen** to put sth into action
tat *etc* [ta:t] *vb siehe* **tun**
Tatbestand *m* facts *pl* of the case
tatenlos *adj* inactive
Täter, in ['tɛ:tər(ɪn)] (**-s, -**) *m(f)* perpetrator, culprit; **Täterschaft** *f* guilt
tätig *adj* active; **~er Teilhaber** active partner; **in einer Firma ~ sein** to work for a firm
Tätigkeit *f* activity; (*Beruf*) occupation
tätlich *adj* violent
tätowieren [tɛto'vi:rən] *vt* to tattoo
Tätowierung *f* tattooing; (*Ergebnis*) tattoo
Tatsache *f* fact; **jdn vor vollendete ~n stellen** to present sb with a fait accompli
tatsächlich *adj* actual ▷ *adv* really
Tau[1] [taʊ] (**-(e)s, -e**) *nt* rope
Tau[2] (**-(e)s**) *m* dew
taub [taʊp] *adj* deaf; (*Nuss*) hollow; **sich ~ stellen** to pretend not to hear
Taube ['taʊbə] (**-, -n**) *f* (*Zool*) pigeon; (*fig*) dove
Taubenschlag *m* dovecote; **hier geht es zu wie im ~** (*fig: umg*) it's like Waterloo Station here (*Brit*), it's like Grand Central Station here (*US*)
Taubheit *f* deafness
taubstumm *adj* deaf-mute
tauchen ['taʊxən] *vt* to dip ▷ *vi* to dive; (*Naut*) to submerge
Taucher (**-s, -**) *m* diver; **Taucheranzug** *m* diving suit
Tauchsieder (**-s, -**) *m* portable immersion heater
tauen ['taʊən] *vt, vi* to thaw ▷ *vi unpers*: **es taut** it's thawing
Taufbecken *nt* font
Taufe ['taʊfə] (**-, -n**) *f* baptism
taufen *vt* to baptize; (*nennen*) to christen
Tauf- *zW*: **Taufname** *m* Christian name; **Taufpate** *m* godfather; **Taufpatin** *f* godmother; **Taufschein** *m* certificate of baptism
taugen ['taʊgən] *vi* to be of use; **~ für** to do *od* be good for; **nicht ~** to be no good *od* useless
Taugenichts (**-es, -e**) *m* good-for-nothing
tauglich ['taʊklɪç] *adj* suitable; (*Mil*) fit (for service)
Tausch [taʊʃ] (**-(e)s, -e**) *m* exchange; **einen guten/schlechten ~ machen** to get a good/bad deal
tauschen *vt* to exchange, swap ▷ *vi*: **ich möchte nicht mit ihm ~** I wouldn't like to be in his place
täuschen ['tɔʏʃən] *vt* to deceive ▷ *vi* to be deceptive ▷ *vr* to be wrong; **wenn mich nicht alles täuscht** unless I'm completely wrong
täuschend *adj* deceptive
Tauschhandel *m* barter
Täuschung *f* deception; (*optisch*) illusion
tausend ['taʊzənt] *num* a *od* one thousand
Tausendfüßler (**-s, -**) *m* centipede
Taxi ['taksi] (**-(s), -(s)**) *nt* taxi, cab
Taxi- *zW*: **Taxifahrer** *m* taxi driver; **Taxistand** *m* taxi rank (*Brit*) *od* stand (*US*)
Teamarbeit ['ti:m|arbaɪt] *f* teamwork
Technik ['tɛçnɪk] *f* technology; (*Methode, Kunstfertigkeit*) technique
Techniker, in (**-s -**) *m(f)* technician
technisch *adj* technical; **~e Hochschule** ≈ polytechnic
Technologie [tɛçnolo'gi:] *f* technology
technologisch [tɛçno'lo:gɪʃ] *adj* technological
Tee [te:] (**-s, -s**) *m* tea; **Teebeutel** *m* tea bag; **Teekanne** *f* teapot; **Teelöffel** *m* teaspoon
Teer [te:r] (**-(e)s, -e**) *m* tar; **teeren** *vt* to tar
Teesieb *nt* tea strainer
Teewagen *m* tea trolley
Teich [taɪç] (**-(e)s, -e**) *m* pond
Teig [taɪk] (**-(e)s, -e**) *m* dough
teigig ['taɪgɪç] *adj* doughy
Teigwaren *pl* pasta *sing*
Teil [taɪl] (**-(e)s, -e**) *m od nt* part; (*Anteil*) share ▷ *nt* (*Bestandteil*) component, part; (*Ersatzteil*) spare (part); **zum ~** partly; **ich für mein(en)**

~ ... I, for my part ...; **sich** *dat* **sein ~ denken** (*umg*) to draw one's own conclusions; **er hat sein(en) ~ dazu beigetragen** he did his bit *od* share; **teilbar** *adj* divisible; **Teilbetrag** *m* instalment (*Brit*), installment (*US*); **Teilchen** *nt* (atomic) particle

teilen *vt* to divide; (*mit jdm*) to share ▷ *vr* to divide; (*in Gruppen*) to split up

Teil- *zW*: **teilhaben** *unreg vi*: **an etw** *dat* **teilhaben** to share in sth; **Teilhaber** (**-s, -**) *m* partner; **Teilkaskoversicherung** *f* third party, fire and theft insurance

Teilnahme (**-, -n**) *f* participation; (*Mitleid*) sympathy; **jdm seine herzliche ~ aussprechen** to offer sb one's heartfelt sympathy

teilnahmslos *adj* disinterested, apathetic

teilnehmen *unreg vi*: **an etw** *dat* **~** to take part in sth

Teilnehmer, in (**-s, -**) *m(f)* participant

teils *adv* partly

Teilung *f* division

Teil- *zW*: **teilweise** *adv* partially, in part; **Teilzahlung** *f* payment by instalments (*Brit*) *od* installments (*US*)

Teint [tɛ̃:] (**-s, -s**) *m* complexion

Telearbeit ['te:learbaɪt] *f* teleworking

Telebanking ['te:lebɛŋkɪŋ] (**-s**) *nt* telebanking

Telefax ['te:lefaks] (**-**) *nt* telefax

Telefon [tele'fo:n] (**-s, -e**) *nt* (tele)phone; **ans ~ gehen** to answer the phone; **Telefonanruf** *m* (tele)phone call

Telefon- *zW*: **Telefonbuch** *nt* (tele)phone directory; **Telefongespräch** *nt* (tele)phone call

telefonieren [telefo'ni:rən] *vi* to (tele)phone; **bei jdm ~** to use sb's phone; **mit jdm ~** to speak to sb on the phone

telefonisch [tele'fo:nɪʃ] *adj* telephone; (*Benachrichtigung*) by telephone; **ich bin ~ zu erreichen** I can be reached by phone

Telefonist, in [telefo'nɪst(ɪn)] *m(f)* telephonist

Telefon- *zW*: **Telefonkarte** *f* phone card; **Telefonnummer** *f* (tele)phone number; **Telefonverbindung** *f* telephone connection; **Telefonzelle** *f* telephone box (*Brit*) *od* booth (*US*), callbox (*Brit*); **Telefonzentrale** *f* telephone exchange

Telegrafenmast *m* telegraph pole

Telegrafie [telegra'fi:] *f* telegraphy

telegrafieren [telegra'fi:rən] *vt, vi* to telegraph, cable, wire

telegrafisch [tele'gra:fɪʃ] *adj* telegraphic; **jdm ~ Geld überweisen** to cable sb money

Telegramm [tele'gram] (**-s, -e**) *nt* telegram, cable; **Telegrammadresse** *f* telegraphic address; **Telegrammformular** *nt* telegram form

Telekolleg ['te:ləkɔle:k] *nt* ≈ Open University (*Brit*)

Teleobjektiv ['te:lə|ɔpjɛkti:f] *nt* telephoto lens

Telepathie [telepa'ti:] *f* telepathy

telepathisch [tele'pa:tɪʃ] *adj* telepathic

Teleskop [tele'sko:p] (**-s, -e**) *nt* telescope

Telespiel *nt* video game

Telex ['te:lɛks] (**-, -(e)**) *nt* telex

Teller ['tɛlər] (**-s, -**) *m* plate

Tempel ['tɛmpəl] (**-s, -**) *m* temple

Temperament [tɛmpera'mɛnt] *nt* temperament; (*Schwung*) vivacity, vitality; **sein ~ ist mit ihm durchgegangen** he went over the top; **temperamentlos** *adj* spiritless; **temperamentvoll** *adj* high-spirited, lively

Temperatur [tɛmpera'tu:r] *f* temperature; **erhöhte ~ haben** to have a temperature

Tempo[1] ['tɛmpo] (**-s, -s**) *nt* speed, pace; **~!** get a move on!

Tempo[2] ['tɛmpo] (**-s, Tempi**) *nt* (*Mus*) tempo; **das ~ angeben** (*fig*) to set the pace; **Tempolimit** *nt* speed limit

Tendenz [tɛn'dɛnts] *f* tendency; (*Absicht*) intention

tendieren [tɛn'di:rən] *vi*: **zu etw ~** to show a tendency to(wards) sth, incline to(wards) sth

Tennis ['tɛnɪs] (**-**) *nt* tennis; **Tennisplatz** *m* tennis court; **Tennisschläger** *m* tennis racket; **Tennisspieler** *m* tennis player

Tenor [te'no:r] (**-s, ¨-e**) *m* tenor

Teppich ['tɛpɪç] (**-s, -e**) *m* carpet; **Teppichboden** *m* wall-to-wall carpeting

Termin [tɛr'mi:n] (**-s, -e**) *m* (*Zeitpunkt*) date; (*Frist*) deadline; (*Arzttermin etc*) appointment; (*Jur: Verhandlung*) hearing; **sich** *dat* **einen ~ geben lassen** to make an appointment

Terminkalender *m* diary, appointments book

Termite [tɛr'mi:tə] (**-, -n**) *f* termite

Terpentin [tɛrpɛn'ti:n] (**-s, -e**) *nt* turpentine, turps *sing*

Terrasse [tɛ'rasə] (**-, -n**) *f* terrace

Terrine [tɛ'ri:nə] *f* tureen

Territorium [tɛri'to:riʊm] *nt* territory

Terror ['tɛrɔr] (**-s**) *m* terror; (*Terrorherrschaft*) reign of terror; **blanker ~** sheer terror; **Terroranschlag** *m* terrorist attack

terrorisieren [tɛrori'zi:rən] *vt* to terrorize

Terrorismus [tɛro'rɪsmʊs] *m* terrorism

Terrorist, in *m(f)* terrorist

Test [tɛst] (**-s, -s**) *m* test

Testament [tɛsta'mɛnt] *nt* will, testament; (*Rel*) Testament; **Altes/Neues ~** Old/New Testament

Testamentsvollstrecker, in (**-s, -**) *m(f)* executor (of a will)

Test- *zW*: **Testbild** *nt* (*TV*) test card; **testen** *vt* to test

Tetanus ['te:tanʊs] (**-**) *m* tetanus; **Tetanusimpfung** *f* (anti-)tetanus injection

teuer ['tɔʏər] *adj* dear, expensive; **teures Geld** good money; **das wird ihn ~ zu stehen kommen** (*fig*) that will cost him dear

Teuerung *f* increase in prices

Teuerungszulage *f* cost-of-living bonus

Teufel ['tɔʏfəl] (**-s, -**) *m* devil; **den ~ an die**

Wand malen (*schwarzmalen*) to imagine the worst; (*Unheil heraufbeschwören*) to tempt fate *od* providence; **in ~s Küche kommen** to get into a mess; **jdn zum ~ jagen** (*umg*) to send sb packing
Teufelei [tɔʏfə'laɪ] *f* devilment
Teufels- *zW*: **Teufelsaustreibung** *f* exorcism; **Teufelskreis** *m* vicious circle
teuflisch ['tɔʏflɪʃ] *adj* fiendish, diabolic
Text [tɛkst] (**-(e)s, -e**) *m* text; (*Liedertext*) words *pl*; (: *von Schlager*) lyrics *pl*; **texten** *vi* to write the words
textil [tɛks'ti:l] *adj* textile
Textilien *pl* textiles *pl*
Textilindustrie *f* textile industry
Textilwaren *pl* textiles *pl*
TH (**-, -s**) *f abk* (= *technische Hochschule*) *siehe* **technisch**
Thailand ['taɪlant] (**-s**) *nt* Thailand
Theater [te'a:tər] (**-s, -**) *nt* theatre (*Brit*), theater (*US*); (*umg*) fuss; **(ein) ~ machen** to make a (big) fuss; **~ spielen** to act; (*fig*) to put on an act; **Theaterbesucher** *m* playgoer; **Theaterkasse** *f* box office; **Theaterstück** *nt* (stage) play
theatralisch [tea'tra:lɪʃ] *adj* theatrical
Theke ['te:kə] (**-, -n**) *f* (*Schanktisch*) bar; (*Ladentisch*) counter
Thema ['te:ma] (**-s, Themen** *od* **-ta**) *nt* (*Leitgedanke, Mus*) theme; topic, subject; **beim ~ bleiben/vom ~ abschweifen** to stick to/wander off the subject
Themenpark *m* theme park
Theologe [teo'lo:gə] (**-n, -n**) *m* theologian
Theologie [teolo'gi:] *f* theology
theologisch [teo'lo:gɪʃ] *adj* theological
Theoretiker, in [teo're:tikər(ɪn)] (**-s, -**) *m(f)* theorist
theoretisch *adj* theoretical; **~ gesehen** in theory, theoretically
Theorie [teo'ri:] *f* theory
Therapeut [tera'pɔʏt] (**-en, -en**) *m* therapist
therapeutisch *adj* therapeutic
Therapie [tera'pi:] *f* therapy
Thermalbad [tɛr'ma:lba:t] *nt* thermal bath; (*Badeort*) thermal spa
Thermometer [tɛrmo'me:tər] (**-s, -**) *nt* thermometer
Thermostat [tɛrmo'sta:t] (**-(e)s** *od* **-en, -e(n)**) *m* thermostat
These ['te:zə] (**-, -n**) *f* thesis
Thrombose [trɔm'bo:sə] (**-, -n**) *f* thrombosis
Thron [tro:n] (**-(e)s, -e**) *m* throne
Thronfolge *f* succession (to the throne)
Thunfisch ['tu:nfɪʃ] *m* tuna (fish)
Thüringen ['ty:rɪŋən] (**-s**) *nt* Thuringia
Thymian ['ty:mia:n] (**-s, -e**) *m* thyme
Tibet ['ti:bɛt] (**-s**) *nt* Tibet
Tick [tɪk] (**-(e)s, -s**) *m* tic; (*Eigenart*) quirk; (*Fimmel*) craze
ticken *vi* to tick; **nicht richtig ~** (*umg*) to be off one's rocker
Ticket ['tɪkət] (**-s, -s**) *nt* ticket
tief [ti:f] *adj* deep; (*tiefsinnig*) profound; (*Ausschnitt, Ton*) low; **~er Teller** soup plate; **~ greifend** far-reaching; **~ schürfend** profound; **bis ~ in die Nacht hinein** late into the night; **Tief** (**-s, -s**) *nt* (*Met*) depression; (*fig*) low; **Tiefdruck** *m* (*Met*) low pressure
Tiefe (**-, -n**) *f* depth
Tiefebene ['ti:f|e:bənə] *f* plain
Tiefenpsychologie *f* depth psychology
Tiefenschärfe *f* (*Phot*) depth of focus
tief- *zW*: **tiefernst** *adj* very grave *od* solemn; **Tiefgarage** *f* underground car park (*Brit*) *od* parking lot (*US*); **tiefgekühlt** *adj* frozen; **Tiefkühlfach** *nt* freezer compartment; **Tiefkühlkost** *f* frozen food; **Tiefkühltruhe** *f* freezer, deep freeze (*US*); **Tiefland** *nt* lowlands *pl*; **Tiefpunkt** *m* low point; (*fig*) low ebb; **Tiefschlag** *m* (*Boxen, fig*) blow below the belt; **Tiefsee** *f* deep parts of the sea; **Tiefstand** *m* low level; **tiefstapeln** *vi* to be overmodest; **Tiefstart** *m* (*Sport*) crouch start
Tiefstwert *m* minimum *od* lowest value
Tier [ti:r] (**-(e)s, -e**) *nt* animal; **Tierarzt** *m*, **Tierärztin** *f* vet(erinary surgeon) (*Brit*), veterinarian (*US*); **Tiergarten** *m* zoo, zoological gardens *pl*; **tierisch** *adj* animal *attrib*; (*lit, fig*) brutish; (*fig*: *Ernst etc*) deadly; **Tierkreis** *m* zodiac; **Tierkunde** *f* zoology; **Tierquälerei** *f* cruelty to animals; **Tierschutzverein** *m* society for the prevention of cruelty to animals; **Tierversuch** *m* animal experiment
Tiger ['ti:gər] (**-s, -**) *m* tiger
tilgen ['tɪlgən] *vt* to erase; (*Sünden*) to expiate; (*Schulden*) to pay off
Tinktur [tɪŋk'tu:r] *f* tincture
Tinte ['tɪntə] (**-, -n**) *f* ink
Tinten- *zW*: **Tintenfisch** *m* cuttlefish; (*achtarmig*) octopus; **Tintenstift** *m* indelible pencil; **Tintenstrahldrucker** *m* ink-jet printer
Tipp [tɪp] (**-s, -s**) *m* (*Sport, Börse*) tip; (*Andeutung*) hint; (*an Polizei*) tip-off
tippen ['tɪpən] *vi* to tap, touch; (*umg*: *schreiben*) to type; (*im Lotto etc*) to bet ▷ *vt* to type; to bet; **auf jdn ~** (*umg*: *raten*) to tip sb, put one's money on sb (*fig*)
Tippfehler (*umg*) *m* typing error
Tippse (**-, -n**) (*umg*) *f* typist
tipptopp ['tɪp'tɔp] (*umg*) *adj* tiptop
Tippzettel *m* (pools) coupon
Tirol [ti'ro:l] (**-s**) *nt* the Tyrol
Tiroler, in (**-s, -**) *m(f)* Tyrolese, Tyrolean
Tisch [tɪʃ] (**-(e)s, -e**) *m* table; **bitte zu ~!** lunch *od* dinner is served; **bei ~** at table; **vor/nach ~** before/after eating; **unter den ~ fallen** (*fig*) to be dropped; **Tischdecke** *f* tablecloth
Tischler (**-s, -**) *m* carpenter, joiner
Tischlerei [tɪʃlə'raɪ] *f* joiner's workshop; (*Arbeit*) carpentry, joinery
tischlern *vi* to do carpentry *etc*
Tisch- *zW*: **Tischrechner** *m* desk calculator;

Tischrede *f* after-dinner speech; **Tischtennis** *nt* table tennis; **Tischtuch** *nt* tablecloth
Titel ['ti:təl] (**-s, -**) *m* title; **Titelanwärter** *m* (*Sport*) challenger; **Titelbild** *nt* cover (picture); (*von Buch*) frontispiece; **Titelrolle** *f* title role; **Titelseite** *f* cover; (*Buchtitel*) title page; **Titelverteidiger** *m* defending champion, title holder
Toast [to:st] (**-(e)s, -s** *od* **-e**) *m* toast
toasten *vi* to drink a toast ▷ *vt* (*Brot*) to toast; **auf jdn ~** to toast sb, drink a toast to sb
Toaster (**-s, -**) *m* toaster
toben ['to:bən] *vi* to rage; (*Kinder*) to romp about
tob- *zW*: **Tobsucht** *f* raving madness; **tobsüchtig** *adj* maniacal; **Tobsuchtsanfall** *m* maniacal fit
Tochter ['tɔxtər] (**-, ⸚**) *f* daughter; **Tochtergesellschaft** *f* subsidiary (company)
Tod [to:t] (**-(e)s, -e**) *m* death; **zu ~e betrübt sein** to be in the depths of despair; **eines natürlichen/gewaltsamen ~es sterben** to die of natural causes/die a violent death; **todernst** (*umg*) *adj* deadly serious ▷ *adv* in dead earnest
Todes- *zW*: **Todesangst** *f* mortal fear; **Todesängste ausstehen** (*umg*) to be scared to death; **Todesanzeige** *f* obituary (notice); **Todesfall** *m* death; **Todesopfer** *nt* death, casualty, fatality; **Todesstrafe** *f* death penalty; **Todesursache** *f* cause of death; **Todesurteil** *nt* death sentence; **Todesverachtung** *f* utter disgust
todkrank *adj* dangerously ill
tödlich ['tø:tlıç] *adj* fatal; (*Gift*) deadly, lethal
tod- *zW*: **todmüde** *adj* dead tired; **todschick** (*umg*) *adj* smart, classy; **todsicher** (*umg*) *adj* absolutely *od* dead certain; **Todsünde** *f* deadly sin
Tofu ['to:fu] (**-(s)**) *m* tofu
Toilette [toa'lɛtə] *f* toilet, lavatory (*Brit*), john (*US*); (*Frisiertisch*) dressing table; (*Kleidung*) outfit; **auf die ~ gehen/auf der ~ sein** to go to/be in the toilet
Toiletten- *zW*: **Toilettenartikel** *pl* toiletries *pl*, toilet articles *pl*; **Toilettenpapier** *nt* toilet paper; **Toilettentisch** *m* dressing table
toi, toi, toi ['tɔy'tɔy'tɔy] (*umg*) *interj* good luck; (*unberufen*) touch wood
tolerant [tole'rant] *adj* tolerant
Toleranz *f* tolerance
tolerieren [tole'ri:rən] *vt* to tolerate
toll [tɔl] *adj* mad; (*Treiben*) wild; (*umg*) terrific
tollen *vi* to romp
toll- *zW*: **Tollkirsche** *f* deadly nightshade; **tollkühn** *adj* daring; **Tollwut** *f* rabies
Tomate [to'ma:tə] (**-, -n**) *f* tomato; **du treulose ~!** (*umg*) you're a fine friend!
Tomatenmark (**-(e)s**) *nt* tomato purée
Ton¹ [to:n] (**-(e)s, -e**) *m* (*Erde*) clay
Ton² [to:n] (**-(e)s, ⸚e**) *m* (*Laut*) sound; (*Mus*) note; (*Redeweise*) tone; (*Farbton, Nuance*) shade; (*Betonung*) stress; **keinen ~ herausbringen** not to be able to say a word; **den ~ angeben** (*Mus*) to give an A; (*fig: Mensch*) to set the tone; **Tonabnehmer** *m* pick-up; **tonangebend** *adj* leading; **Tonart** *f* (musical) key; **Tonband** *nt* tape; **Tonbandgerät** *nt* tape recorder
tönen ['tø:nən] *vi* to sound ▷ *vt* to shade; (*Haare*) to tint
tönern ['tø:nərn] *adj* clay
Ton- *zW*: **Tonfall** *m* intonation; **Tonfilm** *m* sound film
Tonika ['to:nika] (**-, -iken**) *f* (*Mus*) tonic
Tonleiter *f* (*Mus*) scale
Tonne ['tɔnə] (**-, -n**) *f* barrel; (*Maß*) ton
Ton- *zW*: **Tonspur** *f* soundtrack; **Tontaube** *f* clay pigeon; **Tonwaren** *pl* pottery *sing*, earthenware *sing*
Topf [tɔpf] (**-(e)s, ⸚e**) *m* pot; **alles in einen ~ werfen** (*fig*) to lump everything together; **Topfblume** *f* pot plant
Töpfer, in ['tœpfər(ın)] (**-s, -**) *m(f)* potter
Töpferei [tœpfə'raı] *f* (*Töpferware*) pottery; (*Werkstatt*) pottery, potter's workshop
Töpferscheibe *f* potter's wheel
Topflappen *m* ovencloth
topografisch [topo'gra:fıʃ] *adj* topographic
topp [tɔp] *interj* O.K.
Tor¹ [to:r] (**-en, -en**) *m* fool
Tor² (**-(e)s, -e**) *nt* gate; (*Sport*) goal; **Torbogen** *m* archway
Torf [tɔrf] (**-(e)s**) *m* peat
töricht ['tørıçt] *adj* foolish
torkeln ['tɔrkəln] *vi* to stagger, reel
Torpedo [tɔr'pe:do] (**-s, -s**) *m* torpedo
Torte ['tɔrtə] (**-, -n**) *f* cake; (*Obsttorte*) flan, tart
Tortur [tɔr'tu:r] *f* ordeal
Torverhältnis *nt* goal average
Torwart (**-(e)s, -e**) *m* goalkeeper
tosen ['to:zən] *vi* to roar
tot [to:t] *adj* dead; **er war auf der Stelle ~** he died instantly; **~ geboren** stillborn; **sich ~ stellen** to pretend to be dead; **der ~e Winkel** the blind spot; **einen ~en Punkt haben** to be at one's lowest; **das T~e Meer** the Dead Sea
total [to'ta:l] *adj* total
totalitär [tɔtali'tɛ:r] *adj* totalitarian
Totalschaden *m* (*Aut*) complete write-off
Tote, r *f(m)* dead person
töten ['tøtən] *vt, vi* to kill
Toten- *zW*: **Totenbett** *nt* deathbed; **totenblass** *adj* deathly pale, white as a sheet; **Totenkopf** *m* skull; **Totenmesse** *f* requiem mass; **Totenschein** *m* death certificate; **Totenstille** *f* deathly silence
tot- *zW*: **totfahren** *unreg vt* to run over; **totlachen** (*umg*) *vr* to laugh one's head off
Toto ['to:to] (**-s, -s**) *m od nt* ≈ pools *pl*; **Totoschein** *m* ≈ pools coupon
tot- *zW*: **Totschlag** *m* (*Jur*) manslaughter, second degree murder (*US*); **totschlagen** *unreg vt* (*lit, fig*) to kill; **Totschläger** *m* (*Waffe*) cosh (*Brit*), blackjack (*US*); **totschweigen** *unreg vt* to hush up

Tötung ['tø:tʊŋ] *f* killing
Toupet [tu'pe:] (**-s, -s**) *nt* toupee
toupieren [tu'pi:rən] *vt* to backcomb
Tour [tu:r] (**-, -en**) *f* tour, trip; (*Umdrehung*) revolution; (*Verhaltensart*) way; **auf ~en kommen** (*Aut*) to reach top speed; (*fig*) to get into top gear; **auf vollen ~en laufen** (*lit*) to run at full speed; (*fig*) to be in full swing; **auf die krumme ~** by dishonest means; **in einer ~** incessantly
Tourenzahl *f* number of revolutions
Tourenzähler *m* rev counter
Tourismus [tu'rɪsmʊs] *m* tourism
Tourist, in *m(f)* tourist
Touristenklasse *f* tourist class
Tournee [tʊr'ne:] (**-, -s** *od* **-n**) *f* (*Theat etc*) tour; **auf ~ gehen** to go on tour
Trab [tra:p] (**-(e)s**) *m* trot; **auf ~ sein** (*umg*) to be on the go
Trabant [tra'bant] *m* satellite
Trabantenstadt *f* satellite town
traben ['tra:bən] *vi* to trot
Tracht [traxt] (**-, -en**) *f* (*Kleidung*) costume, dress; **eine ~ Prügel** a sound thrashing
trachten *vi* to strive, endeavour (*Brit*), endeavor (*US*); **danach ~, etw zu tun** to strive to do sth; **jdm nach dem Leben ~** to seek to kill sb
trächtig ['trɛçtɪç] *adj* (*Tier*) pregnant
Tradition [traditsi'o:n] *f* tradition
traditionell [traditsio:'nɛl] *adj* traditional
traf *etc* [tra:f] *vb siehe* **treffen**
Tragbahre *f* stretcher
tragbar *adj* (*Gerät*) portable; (*Kleidung*) wearable; (*erträglich*) bearable
träge ['trɛ:gə] *adj* sluggish, slow; (*Phys*) inert
tragen ['tra:gən] *unreg vt* to carry; (*Kleidung, Brille*) to wear; (*Namen, Früchte*) to bear; (*erdulden*) to endure ▷ *vi* (*schwanger sein*) to be pregnant; (*Eis*) to hold; **schwer an etw** *dat* **~** (*lit*) to have a job carrying sth; (*fig*) to find sth hard to bear; **zum T~ kommen** to come to fruition; (*nützlich werden*) to come in useful
Träger ['trɛ:gər] (**-s, -**) *m* carrier; wearer; bearer; (*Ordensträger*) holder; (*an Kleidung*) (shoulder) strap; (*Körperschaft etc*) sponsor; (*Holzträger, Betonträger*) (supporting) beam; (*Stahlträger, Eisenträger*) girder; (*Tech: Stütze von Brücken etc*) support
Träger- *zW*: **Trägerrakete** *f* launch vehicle; **Trägerrock** *m* skirt with shoulder straps
Tragetasche *f* carrier bag (*Brit*), carry-all (*US*)
Trag- *zW*: **Tragfläche** *f* (*Aviat*) wing; **Tragflügelboot** *nt* hydrofoil
Trägheit ['trɛ:khaɪt] *f* laziness; (*Phys*) inertia
Tragik ['tra:gɪk] *f* tragedy
tragisch *adj* tragic; **etw ~ nehmen** (*umg*) to take sth to heart
Tragödie [tra'gø:diə] *f* tragedy
Tragweite *f* range; (*fig*) scope; **von großer ~ sein** to have far-reaching consequences
Tragwerk *nt* wing assembly
Trainer, in ['trɛ:nər(ɪn)] (**-s, -**) *m(f)* (*Sport*) trainer, coach; (*Fussball*) manager
trainieren [trɛ'ni:rən] *vt* to train; (*Übung*) to practise (*Brit*), practice (*US*) ▷ *vi* to train; **Fußball ~** to do football practice
Training (**-s, -s**) *nt* training
Trainingsanzug *m* track suit
Traktor ['traktɔr] *m* tractor; (*von Drucker*) tractor feed
trällern ['trɛlərn] *vt, vi* to warble; (*Vogel*) to trill, warble
trampeln ['trampəln] *vt* to trample; (*abschütteln*) to stamp ▷ *vi* to stamp
trampen ['trɛmpən] *vi* to hitchhike
Tramper, in [trɛmpər(ɪn)] (**-s, -**) *m(f)* hitchhiker
Trampolin [trampo'li:n] (**-s, -e**) *nt* trampoline
Tranchierbesteck *nt* pair of carvers, carvers *pl*
tranchieren [trã'ʃi:rən] *vt* to carve
Träne ['trɛ:nə] (**-, -n**) *f* tear
tränen *vi* to water
Tränengas *nt* tear gas
trank *etc* [traŋk] *vb siehe* **trinken**
Transformator [transfɔr'ma:tɔr] *m* transformer
Transfusion [transfuzi'o:n] *f* transfusion
Transistor [tran'zistɔr] *m* transistor
transitiv ['tranziti:f] *adj* transitive
transparent [transpa'rɛnt] *adj* transparent; **Transparent** (**-(e)s, -e**) *nt* (*Bild*) transparency; (*Spruchband*) banner
transpirieren [transpi'ri:rən] *vi* to perspire
Transplantation [transplantatsi'o:n] *f* transplantation; (*Hauttransplantation*) graft(ing)
Transport [trans'pɔrt] (**-(e)s, -e**) *m* transport; (*Fracht*) consignment, shipment
transportieren [transpɔr'ti:rən] *vt* to transport
Transport- *zW*: **Transportkosten** *pl* transport charges *pl*, carriage *sing*; **Transportmittel** *nt* means *sing* of transport; **Transportunternehmen** *nt* carrier
Transvestit [transvɛs'ti:t] (**-en, -en**) *m* transvestite
Trapez [tra'pe:ts] (**-es, -e**) *nt* trapeze; (*Math*) trapezium
trat *etc* [tra:t] *vb siehe* **treten**
Traube ['traʊbə] (**-, -n**) *f* grape; (*ganze Frucht*) bunch (of grapes)
Traubenlese *f* grape harvest
Traubenzucker *m* glucose
trauen ['traʊən] *vi +dat* to trust ▷ *vr* to dare ▷ *vt* to marry; **jdm/etw ~** to trust sb/sth
Trauer ['traʊər] (**-**) *f* sorrow; (*für Verstorbenen*) mourning; **Trauerfall** *m* death, bereavement; **Trauermarsch** *m* funeral march
trauern *vi* to mourn; **um jdn ~** to mourn (for) sb
Trauer- *zW*: **Trauerrand** *m* black border; **Trauerspiel** *nt* tragedy; **Trauerweide** *f* weeping willow

traulich ['traʊlıç] *adj* cosy, intimate
Traum [traʊm] (**-(e)s, Träume**) *m* dream; **aus der ~!** it's all over!
Trauma (**-s, -men**) *nt* trauma
träumen ['trɔʏmən] *vt, vi* to dream; **das hätte ich mir nicht ~ lassen** I'd never have thought it possible
Träumerei [trɔʏmə'raı] *f* dreaming
träumerisch *adj* dreamy
traumhaft *adj* dreamlike; (*fig*) wonderful
traurig ['traʊrıç] *adj* sad; **Traurigkeit** *f* sadness
Trauring *m* wedding ring
Trauschein *m* marriage certificate
Trauung *f* wedding ceremony
Trauzeuge *m* witness (to a marriage)
treffen ['trɛfən] *unreg vt* to strike, hit; (*Bemerkung*) to hurt; (*begegnen*) to meet; (*Entscheidung etc*) to make; (*Maßnahmen*) to take ▷ *vi* to hit ▷ *vr* to meet; **er hat es gut getroffen** he did well; **er fühlte sich getroffen** he took it personally; **~ auf** *+akk* to come across, meet; **es traf sich, dass ...** it so happened that ...; **es trifft sich gut** it's convenient
Treffen (**-s, -**) *nt* meeting
treffend *adj* pertinent, apposite
Treffer (**-s, -**) *m* hit; (*Tor*) goal; (*Los*) winner
Treffpunkt *m* meeting place
Treibeis *nt* drift ice
treiben ['traıbən] *unreg vt* to drive; (*Studien etc*) to pursue; (*Sport*) to do, go in for ▷ *vi* (*Schiff etc*) to drift; (*Pflanzen*) to sprout; (*Koch: aufgehen*) to rise; (*Medikamente*) to be diuretic; **die ~de Kraft** (*fig*) the driving force; **Handel mit etw/jdm ~** to trade in sth/with sb; **es zu weit ~** to go too far; **Unsinn ~** to fool around
Treib- *zW*: **Treibhaus** *nt* greenhouse; **Treibhauseffekt** *m* greenhouse effect; **Treibhausgas** *nt* greenhouse gas; **Treibjagd** *f* shoot (*in which game is sent up*); (*fig*) witchhunt; **Treibstoff** *m* fuel
trennbar *adj* separable
trennen ['trɛnən] *vt* to separate; (*teilen*) to divide ▷ *vr* to separate; **sich ~ von** to part with
Trennschärfe *f* (*Rundf*) selectivity
Trennung *f* separation
Trennwand *f* partition (wall)
Treppe ['trɛpə] (**-, -n**) *f* stairs *pl*, staircase; (*im Freien*) steps *pl*; **eine ~** a staircase, a flight of stairs *od* steps; **sie wohnt zwei ~n hoch/höher** she lives two flights up/higher up
Treppengeländer *nt* banister
Treppenhaus *nt* staircase
Tresor [tre'zo:r] (**-s, -e**) *m* safe
Tretboot *nt* pedal boat, pedalo
treten ['tre:tən] *unreg vi* to step; (*Tränen, Schweiß*) to appear ▷ *vt* (*mit Fußtritt*) to kick; (*niedertreten*) to tread, trample; **~ nach** to kick at; **~ in** *+akk* to step in(to); **in Verbindung ~** to get in contact; **in Erscheinung ~** to appear; **der Fluss trat über die Ufer** the river overflowed its banks; **in Streik ~** to go on strike
treu [trɔʏ] *adj* faithful, true
Treue (-) *f* loyalty, faithfulness
Treuhänder (**-s, -**) *m* trustee
Treuhandgesellschaft *f* trust company
treu- *zW*: **treuherzig** *adj* innocent; **treulos** *adj* faithless; **treulos an jdm handeln** to fail sb
Tribüne [tri'by:nə] (**-, -n**) *f* grandstand; (*Rednertribüne*) platform
Trichter ['trıçtər] (**-s, -**) *m* funnel; (*Bombentrichter*) crater
Trick [trık] (**-s, -e** *od* **-s**) *m* trick; **Trickfilm** *m* cartoon
Trieb (**-(e)s, -e**) *m* urge, drive; (*Neigung*) inclination; (*Bot*) shoot
trieb *etc* [tri:p] *vb siehe* **treiben**
Trieb- *zW*: **Triebfeder** *f* (*fig*) motivating force; **Triebkraft** *f* (*fig*) drive; **Triebtäter** *m* sex offender; **Triebwagen** *m* (*Eisenb*) railcar; **Triebwerk** *nt* engine
triefen ['tri:fən] *vi* to drip
triftig ['trıftıç] *adj* convincing; (*Grund etc*) good
Trikot [tri'ko:] (**-s, -s**) *nt* vest; (*Sport*) shirt ▷ *m* (*Gewebe*) tricot
Trimm-dich-Pfad *m* keep-fit trail
trinkbar *adj* drinkable
trinken ['trıŋkən] *unreg vt, vi* to drink
Trinker, in (**-s, -**) *m(f)* drinker
Trink- *zW*: **Trinkgeld** *nt* tip; **Trinkhalm** *m* (drinking) straw; **Trinkspruch** *m* toast; **Trinkwasser** *nt* drinking water
trippeln ['trıpəln] *vi* to toddle
Tripper ['trıpər] (**-s, -**) *m* gonorrhoea (*Brit*), gonorrhea (*US*)
Tritt (**-(e)s, -e**) *m* step; (*Fußtritt*) kick
Trittbrett *nt* (*Eisenb*) step; (*Aut*) running board
Triumph [tri'ʊmf] (**-(e)s, -e**) *m* triumph; **Triumphbogen** *m* triumphal arch
triumphieren [triʊm'fi:rən] *vi* to triumph; (*jubeln*) to exult
trocken ['trɔkən] *adj* dry; **sich ~ rasieren** to use an electric razor; **Trockendock** *nt* dry dock; **Trockenelement** *nt* dry cell; **Trockenhaube** *f* hair-dryer; **Trockenheit** *f* dryness; **trockenlegen** *vt* (*Sumpf*) to drain; (*Kind*) to put a clean nappy (*Brit*) *od* diaper (*US*) on; **Trockenmilch** *f* dried milk
trocknen *vt, vi* to dry
Trockner (**-s, -**) *m* dryer
Trödel ['trø:dəl] (**-s**) (*umg*) *m* junk; **Trödelmarkt** *m* flea market
trödeln (*umg*) *vi* to dawdle
trog *etc* [tro:k] *vb siehe* **trügen**
Trommel ['trɔməl] (**-, -n**) *f* drum; **die ~ rühren** (*fig: umg*) to drum up support; **Trommelfell** *nt* eardrum
trommeln *vt, vi* to drum
Trommler, in ['trɔmlər(ın)] (**-s, -**) *m(f)* drummer
Trompete [trɔm'pe:tə] (**-, -n**) *f* trumpet
Trompeter (**-s, -**) *m* trumpeter
Tropen ['tro:pən] *pl* tropics *pl*; **Tropenhelm** *m*

topee, sun helmet
Tropf¹ [trɔpf] (**-(e)s, ⸚e**) (*umg*) *m* rogue; **armer ~** poor devil
Tropf² (**-(e)s**) (*umg*) *m* (*Med: Infusion*) drip (*umg*); **am ~ hängen** to be on a drip
tröpfeln ['trœpfəln] *vi* to drip, trickle
Tropfen (**-s, -**) *m* drop; **ein guter** *od* **edler ~** a good wine; **ein ~ auf den heißen Stein** (*fig: umg*) a drop in the ocean
tropfen *vt, vi* to drip ▷ *vi unpers*: **es tropft** a few raindrops are falling
tropfenweise *adv* in drops
Tropfsteinhöhle *f* stalactite cave
tropisch ['tro:pɪʃ] *adj* tropical
Trost [tro:st] (**-es**) *m* consolation, comfort; **trostbedürftig** *adj* in need of consolation
trösten ['trø:stən] *vt* to console, comfort
Tröster, in (**-s, -**) *m(f)* comfort(er)
tröstlich *adj* comforting
trost- *zW*: **trostlos** *adj* bleak; (*Verhältnisse*) wretched; **Trostpflaster** *nt* (*fig*) consolation; **Trostpreis** *m* consolation prize
Trott [trɔt] (**-(e)s, -e**) *m* trot; (*Routine*) routine
Trottel (**-s, -**) (*umg*) *m* fool, dope
trotten *vi* to trot
Trottoir [trɔto'a:r] (**-s, -s** *od* **-e**) *nt* (*veraltet*) pavement (*Brit*), sidewalk (*US*)
trotz [trɔts] *präp* (*+gen od dat*) in spite of
Trotz (**-es**) *m* pig-headedness; **etw aus ~ tun** to do sth just to show them; **jdm zum ~** in defiance of sb
trotzdem *adv* nevertheless ▷ *konj* although
trotzig *adj* defiant; (*Kind*) difficult, awkward
Trotzkopf *m* obstinate child
Trotzreaktion *f* fit of pique
trüb [try:p] *adj* dull; (*Flüssigkeit, Glas*) cloudy; (*fig*) gloomy; **~e Tasse** (*umg*) drip
Trubel ['tru:bəl] (**-s**) *m* hurly-burly
trüben ['try:bən] *vt* to cloud ▷ *vr* to become clouded
Trübsal (**-, -e**) *f* distress; **~ blasen** (*umg*) to mope
trüb- *zW*: **trübselig** *adj* sad, melancholy; **Trübsinn** *m* depression; **trübsinnig** *adj* depressed, gloomy
Trüffel ['trʏfəl] (**-, -n**) *f* truffle
trug *etc* [tru:k] *vb siehe* **tragen**
trügen ['try:gən] *unreg vt* to deceive ▷ *vi* to be deceptive; **wenn mich nicht alles trügt** unless I am very much mistaken
trügerisch *adj* deceptive
Trugschluss ['tru:gʃlʊs] *m* false conclusion
Truhe ['tru:ə] (**-, -n**) *f* chest
Trümmer ['trʏmər] *pl* wreckage *sing*; (*Bautrümmer*) ruins *pl*; **Trümmerhaufen** *m* heap of rubble
Trumpf [trʊmpf] (**-(e)s, ⸚e**) *m* (*lit, fig*) trump
Trunk [trʊŋk] (**-(e)s, ⸚e**) *m* drink; **Trunkenheit** *f* intoxication; **Trunkenheit am Steuer** drink-driving
Trunksucht *f* alcoholism
Trupp [trʊp] (**-s, -s**) *m* troop
Truppe (**-, -n**) *f* troop; (*Waffengattung*) force; (*Schauspieltruppe*) troupe; **nicht von der schnellen ~ sein** (*umg*) to be slow; **Truppenübungsplatz** *m* training area
Truthahn ['tru:tha:n] *m* turkey
Tschad [tʃat] (**-s**) *m*: **der ~** Chad
Tscheche ['tʃɛçə] (**-n, -n**) *m*, **Tschechin** *f* Czech
tschechisch *adj* Czech; **die T~e Republik** the Czech Republic
Tschechoslowakei [tʃɛçoslova:'kai] *f* (*früher*): **die ~** Czechoslovakia
T-Shirt ['ti:ʃø:t] (**-s, -s**) *nt* T-shirt
TU (**-**) *f abk* (= *technische Universität*) ≈ polytechnic
Tube ['tu:bə] (**-, -n**) *f* tube
Tuberkulose [tubɛrku'lo:zə] (**-, -n**) *f* tuberculosis
Tuch [tu:x] (**-(e)s, ⸚er**) *nt* cloth; (*Halstuch*) scarf; (*Kopftuch*) (head)scarf; (*Handtuch*) towel; **Tuchfühlung** *f* physical contact
tüchtig ['tʏçtɪç] *adj* efficient; (*fähig*) able, capable; (*umg: kräftig*) good, sound; **etwas T~es lernen/werden** (*umg*) to get a proper training/job; **Tüchtigkeit** *f* efficiency; ability
Tücke ['tʏkə] (**-, -n**) *f* (*Arglist*) malice; (*Trick*) trick; (*Schwierigkeit*) difficulty, problem; **seine ~n haben** to be temperamental
tückisch *adj* treacherous; (*böswillig*) malicious
Tugend ['tu:gənt] (**-, -en**) *f* virtue; **tugendhaft** *adj* virtuous
Tüll [tʏl] (**-s, -e**) *m* tulle
Tulpe ['tʊlpə] (**-, -n**) *f* tulip
Tumor ['tu:mɔr] (**-s, -e**) *m* tumour (*Brit*), tumor (*US*)
Tümpel ['tʏmpəl] (**-s, -**) *m* pond
Tumult [tu'mʊlt] (**-(e)s, -e**) *m* tumult
tun [tu:n] *unreg vt* (*machen*) to do; (*legen*) to put ▷ *vi* to act ▷ *vr*: **es tut sich etwas/viel** something/a lot is happening; **jdm etw ~** to do sth to sb; **etw tut es auch** sth will do; **das tut nichts** that doesn't matter; **das tut nichts zur Sache** that's neither here nor there; **du kannst ~ und lassen, was du willst** you can do as you please; **so ~, als ob** to act as if; **zu ~ haben** (*beschäftigt sein*) to be busy, have things *od* something to do
Tunesien [tu'ne:ziən] (**-s**) *nt* Tunisia
Tunesier, in (**-s, -**) *m(f)* Tunisian
tunesisch *adj* Tunisian
Tunfisch *m* = **Thunfisch**
Tunke ['tʊŋkə] (**-, -n**) *f* sauce
tunken *vt* to dip, dunk
tunlichst ['tu:nlɪçst] *adv* if at all possible; **~ bald** as soon as possible
Tunnel ['tʊnəl] (**-s, -s** *od* **-**) *m* tunnel
tupfen ['tʊpfən] *vt* to dab; (*mit Farbe*) to dot; **Tupfen** (**-s, -**) *m* dot, spot
Tür [ty:r] (**-, -en**) *f* door; **an die ~ gehen** to answer the door; **zwischen ~ und Angel** in passing; **Weihnachten steht vor der ~** (*fig*) Christmas is just around the corner; **mit der ~ ins Haus fallen** (*umg*) to blurt it *od* things

out

Turbine [tʊr'bi:nə] *f* turbine

turbulent [tʊrbu'lɛnt] *adj* turbulent

Türke ['tʏrkə] (**-n, -n**) *m* Turk

Türkei [tʏr'kaɪ] *f*: **die ~** Turkey

Türkin *f* Turk

Türkis [tʏr'ki:s] (**-es, -e**) *m* turquoise; **türkis** *adj* turquoise

türkisch *adj* Turkish

Turm [tʊrm] (**-(e)s, ¨-e**) *m* tower; (*Kirchturm*) steeple; (*Sprungturm*) diving platform; (*Schach*) castle, rook

türmen ['tʏrmən] *vr* to tower up ▷ *vt* to heap up ▷ *vi* (*umg*) to scarper, bolt

turnen ['tʊrnən] *vi* to do gymnastic exercises; (*herumklettern*) to climb about; (*Kind*) to romp ▷ *vt* to perform; **Turnen** (**-s**) *nt* gymnastics *sing*; (*Sch*) physical education, P.E.

Turner, in (**-s, -**) *m(f)* gymnast

Turnhalle *f* gym(nasium)

Turnhose *f* gym shorts *pl*

Turnier [tʊr'ni:r] (**-s, -e**) *nt* tournament

Turn- *zW*: **Turnlehrer, in** *m(f)* gym *od* PE teacher; **Turnschuh** *m* gym shoe

Turnverein *m* gymnastics club

Türöffner *m* buzzer

Tusche ['tʊʃə] (**-, -n**) *f* Indian ink

tuscheln ['tʊʃəln] *vt, vi* to whisper

Tuschkasten *m* paintbox

Tussi ['tʊsɪ] (**-, -s**) (*umg*) *f* (*Frau, Freundin*) bird (*Brit*), chick (*US*)

Tüte ['ty:tə] (**-, -n**) *f* bag; **in die ~ blasen** (*umg*) to be breathalyzed; **das kommt nicht in die ~!** (*umg*) no way!

Typ [ty:p] (**-s, -en**) *m* type

Type (**-, -n**) *f* (*Typ*) type

Typenrad *nt* (*Drucker*) daisywheel; **Typenraddrucker** *m* daisywheel printer

Typhus ['ty:fʊs] (-) *m* typhoid (fever)

typisch ['ty:pɪʃ] *adj*: **~ (für)** typical (of)

Tyrann [ty'ran] (**-en, -en**) *m(f)* tyrant

tyrannisch *adj* tyrannical

tyrannisieren [tyrani'zi:rən] *vt* to tyrannize

Uu

U, **u** [u:] *nt* U, u; **U wie Ulrich** ≈ U for Uncle
u. a. *abk* (= *und andere(s)*) and others; (= *unter anderem*) amongst other things
u. A. w. g. *abk* (= *um Antwort wird gebeten*) R.S.V.P.
U-Bahn ['u:ba:n] *f abk* (= *Untergrundbahn*) underground (*Brit*), subway (*US*)
übel ['y:bəl] *adj* bad; **jdm ist ~** sb feels sick; **~ gelaunt** bad-tempered, sullen; **jdm eine Bemerkung** *etc* **~ nehmen** to be offended at sb's remark *etc*; *siehe auch* **übelwollend**; **Übel** (**-s, -**) *nt* evil; (*Krankheit*) disease; **zu allem Übel ...** to make matters worse ...; **Übelkeit** *f* nausea; **übelwollend** *adj* malevolent
üben ['y:bən] *vt, vi, vr* to practise (*Brit*), practice (*US*); (*Gedächtnis, Muskeln*) to exercise; **Kritik an etw** *dat* **~** to criticize sth
über ['y:bər] *präp +dat* **1** (*räumlich*) over, above; **zwei Grad über null** two degrees above zero
2 (*zeitlich*) over; **über der Arbeit einschlafen** to fall asleep over one's work
▷ *präp +akk* **1** (*räumlich*) over; (*hoch über*) above; (*quer über*) across; **er lachte über das ganze Gesicht** he was beaming all over his face; **Macht über jdn haben** to have power over sb
2 (*zeitlich*) over; **über Weihnachten** over Christmas; **über kurz oder lang** sooner or later
3 (*auf dem Wege*) via; **nach Köln über Aachen** to Cologne via Aachen; **ich habe es über die Auskunft erfahren** I found out from information
4 (*betreffend*) about; **ein Buch über ...** a book about *od* on ...; **über jdn/etw lachen** to laugh about *od* at sb/sth; **ein Scheck über 200 Euro** a cheque for 200 euros
5: Fehler über Fehler mistake after mistake
▷ *adv* **1** (*mehr als*) over, more than; **Kinder über 12 Jahren** children over *od* above 12 years of age; **sie liebt ihn über alles** she loves him more than anything
2: über und über over and over; **den ganzen Tag/die ganze Zeit über** all day long/all the time; **jdm in etw** *dat* **über sein** to be superior to sb in sth
überall [y:bər'|al] *adv* everywhere
überanstrengen [y:bər'|anʃtrɛŋən] *vt untr* to overexert ▷ *vr untr* to overexert o.s.
überarbeiten [y:bər'|arbaıtən] *vt untr* to revise, rework ▷ *vr untr* to overwork (o.s.)
überaus ['y:bər|aʊs] *adv* exceedingly
überbelichten ['y:bərbəlıçtən] *vt untr* (*Phot*) to overexpose
überbieten [y:bər'bi:tən] *unreg vt untr* to outbid; (*übertreffen*) to surpass; (*Rekord*) to break ▷ *vr untr*: **sich in etw** *dat* **(gegenseitig) ~** to vie with each other in sth
Überbleibsel ['y:bərblaıpsəl] (**-s, -**) *nt* residue, remainder
Überblick ['y:bərblık] *m* view; (*fig: Darstellung*) survey, overview; (*Fähigkeit*): **~ (über** *+akk***)** overall view (of), grasp (of); **den ~ verlieren** to lose track (of things); **sich** *dat* **einen ~ verschaffen** to get a general idea
überblicken [y:bər'blıkən] *vt untr* to survey; (*fig*) to see; (*: Lage etc*) to grasp
überbringen [y:bər'brıŋən] *unreg vt untr* to deliver, hand over
Überbringer (**-s, -**) *m* bearer
Überbringung *f* delivery
überbrücken [y:bər'brʏkən] *vt untr* to bridge
überdauern [y:bər'daʊərn] *vt untr* to outlast
überdenken [y:bər'dɛŋkən] *unreg vt untr* to think over
überdies [y:bər'di:s] *adv* besides
überdimensional ['y:bərdimɛnziona:l] *adj* oversize
Überdosis ['y:bərdo:zıs] *f* overdose, OD (*umg*); (*zu große Zumessung*) excessive amount
Überdruss ['y:bərdrʊs] (**-es**) *m* weariness; **bis zum ~** ad nauseam
überdrüssig ['y:bərdrʏsıç] *adj +gen* tired of, sick of
übereifrig ['y:bər|aıfrıç] *adj* overzealous
übereilen [y:bər'|aılən] *vt untr* to hurry
übereinander [y:bər|aı'nandər] *adv* one upon the other; (*sprechen*) about each other
übereinkommen [y:bər'|aınkɔmən] *unreg vi* to agree
Übereinkunft [y:bər'|aınkʊnft] (**-, -künfte**) *f* agreement
übereinstimmen [y:bər'|aınʃtımən] *vi* to agree; (*Angaben, Messwerte etc*) to tally; (*mit Tatsachen*) to fit
Übereinstimmung *f* agreement
überempfindlich ['y:bər|ɛmpfıntlıç] *adj* hypersensitive

überfahren[1] ['y:bərfa:rən] *unreg vt* to take across ▷ *vi* to cross, go across
überfahren[2] [y:bər'fa:rən] *unreg vt untr* (*Aut*) to run over; (*fig*) to walk all over
Überfahrt ['y:bərfa:rt] *f* crossing
Überfall ['y:bərfal] *m* (*Banküberfall, Mil*) raid; (*auf jdn*) assault
überfallen [y:bər'falən] *unreg vt untr* to attack; (*Bank*) to raid; (*besuchen*) to drop in on, descend (up)on
überfällig ['y:bərfɛlıç] *adj* overdue
überfliegen [y:bər'fli:gən] *unreg vt untr* to fly over, overfly; (*Buch*) to skim through
Überfluss ['y:bərflʊs] *m*: **~ (an** *+dat***)** (super)abundance (of), excess (of); **zu allem** *od* **zum ~** (*unnötigerweise*) superfluously; (*obendrein*) to crown it all (*umg*); **Überflussgesellschaft** *f* affluent society
überflüssig ['y:bərflʏsıç] *adj* superfluous
überfordern [y:bər'fɔrdərn] *vt untr* to demand too much of; (*Kräfte etc*) to overtax
überführen[1] ['y:bərfy:rən] *vt* to transfer; (*Leiche etc*) to transport
überführen[2] [y:bər'fy:rən] *vt untr* (*Täter*) to have convicted
Überführung *f* (*siehe vbs*) transfer; transport; conviction; (*Brücke*) bridge, overpass
überfüllt [y:bər'fʏlt] *adj* overcrowded; (*Kurs*) oversubscribed
Übergabe ['y:bərga:bə] *f* handing over; (*Mil*) surrender
Übergang ['y:bərgaŋ] *m* crossing; (*Wandel, Überleitung*) transition
Übergangs- *zW*: **Übergangserscheinung** *f* transitory phenomenon; **Übergangslösung** *f* provisional solution, stopgap; **Übergangsstadium** *nt* state of transition; **Übergangszeit** *f* transitional period
übergeben [y:bər'ge:bən] *unreg vt untr* to hand over; (*Mil*) to surrender ▷ *vr untr* to be sick; **dem Verkehr ~** to open to traffic
übergehen[1] ['y:bərge:ən] *unreg vi* (*Besitz*) to pass; (*zum Feind etc*) to go over, defect; (*überwechseln*): **(zu etw) ~** to go on (to sth); **~ in** *+akk* to turn into
übergehen[2] [y:bər'ge:ən] *unreg vt untr* to pass over, omit
Übergewicht ['y:bərgəvıçt] *nt* excess weight; (*fig*) preponderance
überglücklich ['y:bərglʏklıç] *adj* overjoyed
übergroß ['y:bərgro:s] *adj* outsize, huge
überhaben ['y:bərha:bən] *unreg* (*umg*) *vt* to be fed up with
überhaupt [y:bər'haʊpt] *adv* at all; (*im Allgemeinen*) in general; (*besonders*) especially; **~ nicht** not at all; **wer sind Sie ~?** who do you think you are?
überheblich [y:bər'he:plıç] *adj* arrogant; **Überheblichkeit** *f* arrogance
überholen [y:bər'ho:lən] *vt untr* to overtake; (*Tech*) to overhaul
Überholspur *f* overtaking lane
überholt *adj* out-of-date, obsolete
Überholverbot [y:bər'ho:lfɛrbo:t] *nt* overtaking (*Brit*) *od* passing ban
überhören [y:bər'hø:rən] *vt untr* to not hear; (*absichtlich*) to ignore; **das möchte ich überhört haben!** (I'll pretend) I didn't hear that!
überirdisch ['y:bər|ırdıʃ] *adj* supernatural, unearthly
überladen [y:bər'ladən] *unreg vt untr* to overload ▷ *adj* (*fig*) cluttered
überlassen [y:bər'lasən] *unreg vt untr*: **jdm etw ~** to leave sth to sb ▷ *vr untr*: **sich einer Sache** *dat* **~** to give o.s. over to sth; **das bleibt Ihnen ~** that's up to you; **jdn sich** *dat* **selbst ~** to leave sb to his/her own devices
überlasten [y:bər'lastən] *vt untr* to overload; (*jdn*) to overtax
überlaufen[1] ['y:bərlaʊfən] *unreg vi* (*Flüssigkeit*) to flow over; (*zum Feind etc*) to go over, defect
überlaufen[2] [y:bər'laʊfən] *unreg vt untr* (*Schauer etc*) to come over ▷ *adj* overcrowded; **~ sein** to be inundated *od* besieged
Überläufer ['y:bərlɔʏfər] *m* deserter
überleben [y:bər'le:bən] *vt untr* to survive
Überlebende, r *f(m)* survivor
überlegen [y:bər'le:gən] *vt untr* to consider ▷ *adj* superior; **ich habe es mir anders** *od* **noch einmal überlegt** I've changed my mind; **Überlegenheit** *f* superiority
Überlegung *f* consideration, deliberation
überliefern [y:bər'li:fərn] *vt untr* to hand down, transmit
Überlieferung *f* tradition; **schriftliche ~en** (written) records
überlisten [y:bər'lıstən] *vt untr* to outwit
überm ['y:bərm] = **über dem**
Übermacht ['y:bərmaxt] *f* superior force, superiority
übermächtig ['y:bərmɛçtıç] *adj* superior (in strength); (*Gefühl etc*) overwhelming
übermannen [y:bər'manən] *vt untr* to overcome
Übermaß ['ybərma:s] *nt*: **~ (an** *+dat***)** excess (of)
übermäßig ['y:bərmɛ:sıç] *adj* excessive
Übermensch ['y:bərmɛnʃ] *m* superman; **übermenschlich** *adj* superhuman
übermitteln [y:bər'mıtəln] *vt untr* to convey
übermorgen ['y:bərmɔrgən] *adv* the day after tomorrow
Übermüdung [y:bər'my:dʊŋ] *f* overtiredness
Übermut ['y:bərmu:t] *m* exuberance
übermütig ['y:bərmy:tıç] *adj* exuberant, high-spirited; **~ werden** to get overconfident
übernächste, r, s ['y:bərnɛ:çstə(r, s)] *adj* next ... but one; (*Woche, Jahr etc*) after next
übernachten [y:bər'naxtən] *vi untr*: **(bei jdm) ~** to spend the night (at sb's place)
übernächtigt [y:bər'nɛçtıçt] *adj* sleepy, tired
Übernachtung *f*: **~ mit Frühstück** bed and breakfast
Übernahme ['y:bərna:mə] **(-, -n)** *f* taking over *od* on; (*von Verantwortung*) acceptance

übernehmen [y:bər'ne:mən] *unreg vt untr* to take on, accept; (*Amt, Geschäft*) to take over ▹ *vr untr* to take on too much; (*sich überanstrengen*) to overdo it
überprüfen [y:bər'pry:fən] *vt untr* to examine, check; (*Pol: jdn*) to screen
Überprüfung *f* examination
überqueren [y:bər'kve:rən] *vt untr* to cross
überragen [y:bər'ra:gən] *vt untr* to tower above; (*fig*) to surpass
überraschen [y:bər'raʃən] *vt untr* to surprise
Überraschung *f* surprise
überreden [y:bər're:dən] *vt untr* to persuade; **jdn zu etw ~** to talk sb into sth
überreichen [y:bər'raıçən] *vt untr* to hand over; (*feierlich*) to present
überreizt [y:bər'raıtst] *adj* overwrought
Überreste ['y:bərrɛstə] *pl* remains *pl*, remnants *pl*
überrumpeln [y:bər'rʊmpəln] *vt untr* to take by surprise; (*umg: überwältigen*) to overpower
überrunden [y:bər'rʊndən] *vt untr* (*Sport*) to lap
übers ['y:bərs] = **über das**
übersättigen [y:bər'zɛtıgən] *vt untr* to satiate; **Überschallflugzeug** *nt* supersonic jet; **Überschallgeschwindigkeit** *f* supersonic speed
überschätzen [y:bər'ʃɛtsən] *vt untr, vr untr* to overestimate
überschäumen ['y:bərʃɔymən] *vi* to froth over; (*fig*) to bubble over
Überschlag ['y:bərʃla:k] *m* (*Fin*) estimate; (*Sport*) somersault
überschlagen[1] [y:bər'ʃla:gən] *unreg vt untr* (*berechnen*) to estimate; (*auslassen: Seite*) to omit ▹ *vr untr* to somersault; (*Stimme*) to crack; (*Aviat*) to loop the loop ▹ *adj* lukewarm, tepid
überschlagen[2] ['y:bərʃla:gən] *unreg vt* (*Beine*) to cross; (*Arme*) to fold ▹ *vi* (*Hilfsverb sein: Wellen*) to break; (*: Funken*) to flash over; **in etw** *akk* **~** (*Stimmung etc*) to turn into sth
überschnappen ['y:bərʃnapən] *vi* (*Stimme*) to crack; (*umg: Mensch*) to flip one's lid
überschneiden [y:bər'ʃnaıdən] *unreg vr untr* (*lit, fig*) to overlap; (*Linien*) to intersect
überschreiben [y:bər'ʃraıbən] *unreg vt untr* to provide with a heading; (*Comput*) to overwrite; **jdm etw ~** to transfer *od* make over sth to sb
überschreiten [y:bər'ʃraıtən] *unreg vt untr* to cross over; (*fig*) to exceed; (*verletzen*) to transgress
Überschrift ['y:bərʃrıft] *f* heading, title
Überschuss ['y:bərʃʊs] *m*: **~ (an** *+dat***)** surplus (of)
überschüssig ['y:bərʃʏsıç] *adj* surplus, excess
überschütten [y:bər'ʃʏtən] *vt untr*: **jdn/etw mit etw ~** (*lit*) to pour sth over sb/sth; **jdn mit etw ~** (*fig*) to shower sb with sth
Überschwang ['y:bərʃvaŋ] *m* exuberance
überschwänglich ['y:bərʃvɛŋlıç] *adj* effusive; **Überschwänglichkeit** *f* effusion
überschwemmen [y:bər'ʃvɛmən] *vt untr* to flood
Überschwemmung *f* flood
überschwenglich ['y:bərʃvɛŋlıç] *adj siehe* **überschwänglich**
Übersee ['y:bərze:] *f*: **nach/in ~** overseas
überseeisch *adj* overseas
übersehen [y:bər'ze:ən] *unreg vt untr* to look (out) over; (*fig: Folgen*) to see, get an overall view of; (*: nicht beachten*) to overlook
übersenden [y:bər'zɛndən] *unreg vt untr* to send, forward
übersetzen[1] [y:bər'zɛtsən] *vt untr, vi untr* to translate
übersetzen[2] ['y:bərzɛtsən] *vi* (*Hilfsverb sein*) to cross
Übersetzer, in [y:bər'zɛtsər(ın)] **(-s, -)** *m(f)* translator
Übersetzung [y:bər'zɛtsʊŋ] *f* translation; (*Tech*) gear ratio
Übersicht ['y:bərzıçt] *f* overall view; (*Darstellung*) survey; **die ~ verlieren** to lose track; **übersichtlich** *adj* clear; (*Gelände*) open; **Übersichtlichkeit** *f* clarity, lucidity
übersiedeln[1] ['y:bərzi:dəln] *vi* to move
übersiedeln[2] [y:bər'zi:dəln] *vi untr* to move
überspannt *adj* eccentric; (*Idee*) wild, crazy; **Überspanntheit** *f* eccentricity
überspitzt [y:bər'ʃpıtst] *adj* exaggerated
überspringen [y:bər'ʃprıŋən] *unreg vt untr* to jump over; (*fig*) to skip
überstehen[1] [y:bər'ʃte:ən] *unreg vt untr* to overcome, get over; (*Winter etc*) to survive, get through
überstehen[2] ['y:bərʃte:ən] *unreg vi* to project
übersteigen [y:bər'ʃtaıgən] *unreg vt untr* to climb over; (*fig*) to exceed
überstimmen [y:ber'ʃtımən] *vt untr* to outvote
überströmen[1] [y:bər'ʃtrø:mən] *vt untr*: **von Blut überströmt sein** to be streaming with blood
überströmen[2] ['y:bərʃtrø:mən] *vi* (*lit, fig*): **~ (vor** *+dat***)** to overflow (with)
Überstunden ['y:bərʃtʊndən] *pl* overtime *sing*
überstürzen [y:bər'ʃtʏrtsən] *vt untr* to rush ▹ *vr untr* to follow (one another) in rapid succession
überstürzt *adj* (over)hasty
übertölpeln [y:bər'tœlpln] *vt untr* to dupe
übertönen [y:bər'tø:nən] *vt untr* to drown (out)
Übertrag ['y:bərtra:k] **(-(e)s, -träge)** *m* (*Comm*) amount brought forward
übertragbar [y:bər'tra:kba:r] *adj* transferable; (*Med*) infectious
übertragen [y:bər'tra:gən] *unreg vt untr* to transfer; (*Rundf*) to broadcast; (*anwenden: Methode*) to apply; (*übersetzen*) to render; (*Krankheit*) to transmit ▹ *vr untr* to spread ▹ *adj* figurative; **~ auf** *+akk* to transfer to; to apply to; **sich ~ auf** *+akk* to spread to; **jdm etw ~** to assign sth to sb; (*Verantwortung*

etc) to give sb sth *od* sth to sb
Übertragung *f* (*siehe vb*) transference; broadcast; rendering; transmission
übertreffen [y:bər'trɛfən] *unreg vt untr* to surpass
übertreiben [y:bər'traɪbən] *unreg vt untr* to exaggerate; **man kann es auch ~** you can overdo things
Übertreibung *f* exaggeration
übertreten[1] [y:bər'tre:tən] *unreg vt untr* to cross; (*Gebot etc*) to break
übertreten[2] ['y:bərtre:tən] *unreg vi* (*über Linie, Gebiet*) to step (over); (*Sport*) to overstep; (*zu anderem Glauben*) to be converted; **~ (in** *+akk***)**: *Pol*) to go over (to)
Übertretung [y:bər'tre:tʊŋ] *f* violation, transgression
übertrieben [y:bər'tri:bən] *adj* exaggerated, excessive
übertrumpfen [y:bər'trʊmpfən] *vt untr* to outdo; (*Karten*) to overtrump
übervorteilen [y:bər'fɔrtaɪlən] *vt untr* to dupe, cheat
überwachen [y:bər'vaxən] *vt untr* to supervise; (*Verdächtigen*) to keep under surveillance
Überwachung *f* supervision; surveillance
überwältigen [y:bər'vɛltɪgən] *vt untr* to overpower
überwältigend *adj* overwhelming
überweisen [y:bər'vaɪzən] *unreg vt untr* to transfer; (*Patienten*) to refer
Überweisung *f* transfer; (*von Patient*) referral
überwerfen[1] ['y:bərvɛrfən] *unreg vt* (*Kleidungsstück*) to put on; (*sehr rasch*) to throw on
überwerfen[2] [y:bər'vɛrfən] *unreg vr untr*: **sich (mit jdm) ~** to fall out (with sb)
überwiegen [y:bər'vi:gən] *unreg vi untr* to predominate
überwiegend *adj* predominant
überwinden [y:bər'vɪndən] *unreg vt untr* to overcome ▷ *vr untr*: **sich ~, etw zu tun** to make an effort to do sth, bring o.s. to do sth
Überwindung *f* overcoming; (*Selbstüberwindung*) effort of will
Überzahl ['y:bərtsa:l] *f* superior numbers *pl*, superiority; **in der ~ sein** to be numerically superior
überzählig ['y:bərtsɛ:lɪç] *adj* surplus
überzeugen [y:bər'tsɔʏgən] *vt untr* to convince
überzeugend *adj* convincing
Überzeugung *f* conviction; **zu der ~ gelangen, dass ...** to become convinced that ...
Überzeugungskraft *f* power of persuasion
überziehen[1] ['y:bərtsi:ən] *unreg vt* to put on
überziehen[2] [y:bər'tsi:ən] *unreg vt untr* to cover; (*Konto*) to overdraw; (*Redezeit etc*) to overrun ▷ *vr untr* (*Himmel*) to cloud over; **ein Bett frisch ~** to change a bed, change the sheets (on a bed)
Überzug ['y:bərtsu:k] *m* cover; (*Belag*) coating
üblich ['y:plɪç] *adj* usual; **allgemein ~ sein** to be common practice
U-Boot ['u:bo:t] *nt* U-boat, submarine
übrig ['y:brɪç] *adj* remaining; **die Übrigen** the others; **das Übrige** the rest; **im Übrigen** besides; **~ bleiben** to remain, be left (over); **~ lassen** to leave (over); **einiges/viel zu wünschen ~ lassen** (*umg*) to leave something/a lot to be desired; *siehe auch* **übrighaben**
übrigens ['y:brɪgəns] *adv* besides; (*nebenbei bemerkt*) by the way
Übung ['y:bʊŋ] *f* practice; (*Turnübung, Aufgabe etc*) exercise; **~ macht den Meister** (*Sprichwort*) practice makes perfect
Ufer ['u:fər] **(-s, -)** *nt* bank; (*Meeresufer*) shore
Uganda [u'ganda] **(-s)** *nt* Uganda
Uhr [u:r] **(-, -en)** *f* clock; (*Armbanduhr*) watch; **wie viel ~ ist es?** what time is it?; **um wie viel ~?** at what time?; **1 ~** 1 o'clock; **20 ~** 8 o'clock, 20.00 (twenty hundred) hours; **Uhrkette** *f* watch chain; **Uhrmacher** *m* watchmaker; **Uhrwerk** *nt* (*auch fig*) clockwork mechanism; **Uhrzeiger** *m* hand; **Uhrzeigersinn** *m*: **im Uhrzeigersinn** clockwise; **entgegen dem Uhrzeigersinn** anticlockwise; **Uhrzeit** *f* time (of day)
Uhu ['u:hu] **(-s, -s)** *m* eagle owl
Ukraine [ukra'i:nə] *f* Ukraine
UKW *abk* (= *Ultrakurzwelle*) VHF
Ulk [ʊlk] **(-s, -e)** *m* lark
ulkig ['ʊlkɪç] *adj* funny
Ulme ['ʊlmə] **(-, -n)** *f* elm
Ultimatum [ʊlti'ma:tʊm] **(-s, Ultimaten)** *nt* ultimatum; **jdm ein ~ stellen** to give sb an ultimatum
Ultra- *zW*: **Ultrakurzwelle** *f* very high frequency; **Ultraschall** *m* (*Phys*) ultrasound; **ultraviolett** *adj* ultraviolet
um [ʊm] *präp +akk* **1** (*um herum*) (a)round; **um Weihnachten** around Christmas; **er schlug um sich** he hit about him
2 (*mit Zeitangabe*) at; **um acht (Uhr)** at eight (o'clock)
3 (*mit Größenangabe*) by; **etw um 4 cm kürzen** to shorten sth by 4 cm; **um 10% teurer** 10% more expensive; **um vieles besser** better by far; **um nichts besser** not in the least bit better; *siehe auch* **umso**
4: der Kampf um den Titel the battle for the title; **um Geld spielen** to play for money; **es geht um das Prinzip** it's a question of principle; **Stunde um Stunde** hour after hour; **Auge um Auge** an eye for an eye
▷ *präp +gen*: **um ... willen** for the sake of ...; **um Gottes willen** for goodness *od* (*stärker*) God's sake
▷ *konj*: **um ... zu** (in order) to ...; **zu klug, um zu ...** too clever to ...; *siehe auch* **umso**
▷ *adv* **1** (*ungefähr*) about; **um (die) 30 Leute** about *od* around 30 people

2 (*vorbei*): **die zwei Stunden sind um** the two hours are up

umadressieren ['ʊm|adrɛsi:rən] *vt untr* to readdress

umändern ['ʊm|ɛndərn] *vt* to alter

Umänderung *f* alteration

umarbeiten ['ʊm|arbaɪtən] *vt* to remodel; (*Buch etc*) to revise, rework

umarmen [ʊm'|armən] *vt untr* to embrace

Umbau ['ʊmbaʊ] (**-(e)s, -e** *od* **-ten**) *m* reconstruction, alteration(s *pl*)

umbauen ['ʊmbauən] *vt* to rebuild, reconstruct

umbenennen ['ʊmbənɛnən] *unreg vt untr* to rename

umbilden ['ʊmbɪldən] *vt* to reorganize; (*Pol: Kabinett*) to reshuffle

umbinden[1] ['ʊmbɪndən] *unreg vt* (*Krawatte etc*) to put on

umbinden[2] [ʊm'bɪndən] *unreg vt untr*: **etw mit etw ~** to tie sth round sth

umblättern ['ʊmblɛtərn] *vt* to turn over

umblicken ['ʊmblɪkən] *vr* to look around

umbringen ['ʊmbrɪŋən] *unreg vt* to kill

Umbruch ['ʊmbrʊx] *m* radical change; (*Typ*) make-up (into page)

umbuchen ['ʊmbu:xən] *vi* to change one's reservation *od* flight *etc* ▷ *vt* to change

umdenken ['ʊmdɛŋkən] *unreg vi* to adjust one's views

umdrehen ['ʊmdre:ən] *vt* to turn (round); (*Hals*) to wring ▷ *vr* to turn (round); **jdm den Arm ~** to twist sb's arm

Umdrehung *f* turn; (*Phys*) revolution, rotation

umeinander [ʊm|aɪ'nandər] *adv* round one another; (*füreinander*) for one another

umfahren[1] ['ʊmfa:rən] *unreg vt* to run over

umfahren[2] [ʊm'fa:rən] *unreg vt untr* to drive round; (*die Welt*) to sail round

umfallen ['ʊmfalən] *unreg vi* to fall down *od* over; (*fig: umg: nachgeben*) to give in

Umfang ['ʊmfaŋ] *m* extent; (*von Buch*) size; (*Reichweite*) range; (*Fläche*) area; (*Math*) circumference; **in großem ~** on a large scale; **umfangreich** *adj* extensive; (*Buch etc*) voluminous

umfassen [ʊm'fasən] *vt untr* to embrace; (*umgeben*) to surround; (*enthalten*) to include

umfassend *adj* comprehensive; (*umfangreich*) extensive

Umfeld ['ʊmfɛlt] *nt*: **zum ~ von etw gehören** to be associated with sth

umformen ['ʊmfɔrmən] *vi* to transform

Umfrage ['ʊmfra:gə] *f* poll; **~ halten** to ask around

umfüllen ['ʊmfʏlən] *vt* to transfer; (*Wein*) to decant

umfunktionieren ['ʊmfʊŋktsioni:rən] *vt untr* to convert

Umgang ['ʊmgaŋ] *m* company; (*mit jdm*) dealings *pl*; (*Behandlung*) dealing

umgänglich ['ʊmgɛŋlɪç] *adj* sociable

Umgangs- *zW*: **Umgangsformen** *pl* manners *pl*; **Umgangssprache** *f* colloquial language

umgeben [ʊm'ge:bən] *unreg vt untr* to surround

Umgebung *f* surroundings *pl*; (*Milieu*) environment; (*Personen*) people in one's circle; **in der näheren/weiteren ~ Münchens** on the outskirts/in the environs of Munich

umgehen[1] ['ʊmge:ən] *unreg vi* to go (a)round; **im Schlosse ~** to haunt the castle; **mit jdm/etw ~ können** to know how to handle sb/sth; **mit jdm grob** *etc* **~** to treat sb roughly *etc*; **mit Geld sparsam ~** to be careful with one's money

umgehen[2] [ʊm'ge:ən] *unreg vt untr* to bypass; (*Mil*) to outflank; (*Gesetz, Vorschrift etc*) to circumvent; (*vermeiden*) to avoid

umgehend *adj* immediate

Umgehung *f* (*siehe vb*) bypassing; outflanking; circumvention; avoidance

Umgehungsstraße *f* bypass

umgekehrt ['ʊmgəke:rt] *adj* reverse(d); (*gegenteilig*) opposite ▷ *adv* the other way around; **und ~** and vice versa

umgraben ['ʊmgra:bən] *unreg vt* to dig up

umgruppieren ['ʊmgrʊpi:rən] *vt untr* to regroup

Umhang ['ʊmhaŋ] *m* wrap, cape

umhängen ['ʊmhɛŋən] *vt* (*Bild*) to hang somewhere else; **jdm etw ~** to put sth on sb

Umhängetasche *f* shoulder bag

umhauen ['ʊmhaʊən] *vt* to fell; (*fig*) to bowl over

umher [ʊm'he:r] *adv* about, around; **umhergehen** *unreg vi* to walk about; **umherreisen** *vi* to travel about; **umherziehen** *unreg vi* to wander from place to place

umhinkönnen [ʊm'hɪnkœnən] *unreg vi*: **ich kann nicht umhin, das zu tun** I can't help doing it

umhören ['ʊmhø:rən] *vr* to ask around

Umkehr ['ʊmke:r] **(-)** *f* turning back; (*Änderung*) change

umkehren *vi* to turn back; (*fig*) to change one's ways ▷ *vt* to turn round, reverse; (*Tasche etc*) to turn inside out; (*Gefäß etc*) to turn upside down

umkippen ['ʊmkɪpən] *vt* to tip over ▷ *vi* to overturn; (*umg: ohnmächtig werden*) to keel over; (*fig: Meinung ändern*) to change one's mind

Umkleidekabine ['ʊmklaɪdəkabi:nə] *f* changing cubicle (*Brit*), dressing room (*US*)

Umkleideraum ['ʊmklaɪdəraʊm] *m* changing room; (*US: Theat*) dressing room

umkommen ['ʊmkɔmən] *unreg vi* to die, perish; (*Lebensmittel*) to go bad

Umkreis ['ʊmkraɪs] *m* neighbourhood (*Brit*), neighborhood (*US*); **im ~ von** within a radius of

umkrempeln ['ʊmkrɛmpəln] *vt* to turn up; (*mehrmals*) to roll up; (*umg: Betrieb*) to shake up

umladen ['ʊmla:dən] *unreg vt* to transfer, reload
Umlage ['ʊmla:gə] *f* share of the costs
Umlauf *m* (*Geldumlauf*) circulation; (*von Gestirn*) revolution; (*Schreiben*) circular; **in ~ bringen** to circulate; **Umlaufbahn** *f* orbit
Umlaut ['ʊmlaʊt] *m* umlaut
umlegen ['ʊmle:gən] *vt* to put on; (*verlegen*) to move, shift; (*Kosten*) to share out; (*umkippen*) to tip over; (*umg: töten*) to bump off
umleiten ['ʊmlaɪtən] *vt* to divert
Umleitung *f* diversion
umlernen ['ʊmlɛrnən] *vi* to learn something new; (*fig*) to adjust one's views
umliegend ['ʊmli:gənt] *adj* surrounding
Umnachtung [ʊm'naxtʊŋ] *f* mental derangement
umranden [ʊm'randən] *vt untr* to border, edge
umrechnen ['ʊmrɛçnən] *vt* to convert
Umrechnung *f* conversion
Umrechnungskurs *m* rate of exchange
umreißen [ʊm'raɪsən] *unreg vt untr* to outline
umringen [ʊm'rɪŋən] *vt untr* to surround
Umriss ['ʊmrɪs] *m* outline
umrühren ['ʊmry:rən] *vt, vi* to stir
ums [ʊms] = **um das**
umsatteln ['ʊmzatəln] (*umg*) *vi* to change one's occupation, switch jobs
Umsatz ['ʊmzats] *m* turnover
umschalten ['ʊmʃaltən] *vt* to switch ▷ *vi* to push/pull a lever; (*auf anderen Sender*): **~ (auf** *+akk*) to change over (to); (*Aut*): **~ in** *+akk* to change (*Brit*) *od* shift into; **„wir schalten jetzt um nach Hamburg"** "and now we go over to Hamburg"
Umschalttaste *f* shift key
Umschau *f* look(ing) round; **~ halten nach** to look around for
umschauen ['ʊmʃaʊən] *vr* to look round
Umschlag ['ʊmʃla:k] *m* cover; (*Buchumschlag*) jacket, cover; (*Med*) compress; (*Briefumschlag*) envelope; (*Gütermenge*) volume of traffic; (*Wechsel*) change; (*von Hose*) turn-up (*Brit*), cuff (*US*)
umschlagen ['ʊmʃla:gən] *unreg vi* to change; (*Naut*) to capsize ▷ *vt* to knock over; (*Ärmel*) to turn up; (*Seite*) to turn over; (*Waren*) to transfer
Umschlagplatz *m* (*Comm*) distribution centre (*Brit*) *od* center (*US*)
umschreiben¹ ['ʊmʃraɪbən] *unreg vt* (*neu umschreiben*) to rewrite; (*übertragen*) to transfer; **~ auf** *+akk* to transfer to
umschreiben² [ʊm'ʃraɪbən] *unreg vt untr* to paraphrase; (*abgrenzen*) to circumscribe, define
umschulen ['ʊmʃu:lən] *vt* to retrain; (*Kind*) to send to another school
umschwärmen [ʊm'ʃvɛrmən] *vt untr* to swarm round; (*fig*) to surround, idolize
Umschweife ['ʊmʃvaɪfə] *pl*: **ohne ~** without beating about the bush, straight out
Umschwung ['ʊmʃvʊŋ] *m* (*Gymnastik*) circle; (*fig: ins Gegenteil*) change (around)
umsehen ['ʊmze:ən] *unreg vr* to look around *od* about; (*suchen*): **sich ~ (nach)** to look out (for); **ich möchte mich nur mal ~** (*in Geschäft*) I'm just looking
umseitig ['ʊmzaɪtɪç] *adv* overleaf
Umsicht ['ʊmzɪçt] *f* prudence, caution
umsichtig *adj* prudent, cautious
umso ['ʊmzo] *konj*: **~ besser/schlimmer** so much the better/worse; **~ mehr, als ...** all the more considering ...
umsonst [ʊm'zɔnst] *adv* in vain; (*gratis*) for nothing
umspringen ['ʊmʃprɪŋən] *unreg vi* to change; **mit jdm ~** to treat sb badly
Umstand ['ʊmʃtant] *m* circumstance; **Umstände** *pl* (*fig: Schwierigkeiten*) fuss *sing*; **in anderen Umständen sein** to be pregnant; **Umstände machen** to go to a lot of trouble; **den Umständen entsprechend** much as one would expect (under the circumstances); **die näheren Umstände** further details; **unter Umständen** possibly; **mildernde Umstände** (*Jur*) extenuating circumstances
umständlich ['ʊmʃtɛntlɪç] *adj* (*Methode*) cumbersome, complicated; (*Ausdrucksweise, Erklärung*) long-winded; (*ungeschickt*) ponderous; **etw ~ machen** to make heavy weather of (doing) sth
Umstandskleid *nt* maternity dress
Umstandswort *nt* adverb
umsteigen ['ʊmʃtaɪgən] *unreg vi* (*Eisenb*) to change; (*fig: umg*): **~ (auf** *+akk*) to change over (to), switch (over) (to)
umstellen¹ ['ʊmʃtɛlən] *vt* (*an anderen Ort*) to change round, rearrange; (*Tech*) to convert ▷ *vr*: **sich ~ (auf** *+akk*) to adapt o.s. (to)
umstellen² [ʊm'ʃtɛlən] *vt untr* to surround
Umstellung *f* change; (*Umgewöhnung*) adjustment; (*Tech*) conversion
umstimmen ['ʊmʃtɪmən] *vt* (*Mus*) to retune; **jdn ~** to make sb change his mind
umstoßen ['ʊmʃto:sən] *unreg vt* (*lit*) to overturn; (*Plan etc*) to change, upset
umstritten [ʊm'ʃtrɪtən] *adj* disputed; (*fraglich*) controversial
Umsturz ['ʊmʃtʊrts] *m* overthrow
umstürzen ['ʊmʃtʏrtsən] *vt* (*umwerfen*) to overturn ▷ *vi* to collapse, fall down; (*Wagen*) to overturn
umstürzlerisch *adj* revolutionary
Umtausch ['ʊmtaʊʃ] *m* exchange; **diese Waren sind vom ~ ausgeschlossen** these goods cannot be exchanged
umtauschen *vt* to exchange
Umtriebe ['ʊmtri:bə] *pl* machinations *pl*, intrigues *pl*
umtun ['ʊmtu:n] *unreg vr*: **sich nach etw ~** to look for sth
umwandeln ['ʊmvandəln] *vt* to change, convert; (*Elek*) to transform
umwechseln ['ʊmvɛksəln] *vt* to change
Umweg ['ʊmve:k] *m* detour; (*fig*) roundabout

way

Umwelt ['ʊmvɛlt] *f* environment; **Umweltbelastung** *f* environmental pollution; **umweltfreundlich** *adj* environment-friendly; **Umweltkriminalität** *f* crimes *pl* against the environment; **umweltschädlich** *adj* harmful to the environment; **Umweltschutz** *m* environmental protection; **Umweltschützer** (**-s, -**) *m* environmentalist; **Umweltverschmutzung** *f* pollution (of the environment); **umweltverträglich** *adj* not harmful to the environment

umwerben [ʊm'vɛrbən] *unreg vt untr* to court, woo

umwerfen ['ʊmvɛrfən] *unreg vt* (*lit*) to upset, overturn; (*Mantel*) to throw on; (*fig: erschüttern*) to upset, throw

umwerfend (*umg*) *adj* fantastic

umziehen ['ʊmtsi:ən] *unreg vt, vr* to change ▷ *vi* to move

Umzug ['ʊmtsu:k] *m* procession; (*Wohnungsumzug*) move, removal

un- *zW*: **unabänderlich** *adj* irreversible, unalterable; **unabänderlich feststehen** to be absolutely certain; **unabhängig** *adj* independent; **Unabhängigkeit** *f* independence; **unabkömmlich** *adj* indispensable; **zur Zeit unabkömmlich** not free at the moment; **unablässig** *adj* incessant, constant; **unabsehbar** *adj* immeasurable; (*Folgen*) unforeseeable; (*Kosten*) incalculable; **unabsichtlich** *adj* unintentional; **unabwendbar** *adj* inevitable

unachtsam ['ʊn|axtza:m] *adj* careless; **Unachtsamkeit** *f* carelessness

un- *zW*: **unanfechtbar** *adj* indisputable; **unangebracht** *adj* uncalled-for; **unangemessen** *adj* inadequate; **unangenehm** *adj* unpleasant; (*peinlich*) embarrassing; **Unannehmlichkeit** *f* inconvenience; **Unannehmlichkeiten** *pl* trouble *sing*; **unansehnlich** *adj* unsightly; **unanständig** *adj* indecent, improper; **Unanständigkeit** *f* indecency, impropriety

unappetitlich ['ʊn|apeti:tlɪç] *adj* unsavoury (*Brit*), unsavory (*US*)

Unart ['ʊn|a:rt] *f* bad manners *pl*; (*Angewohnheit*) bad habit

unartig *adj* naughty, badly behaved

un- *zW*: **unauffällig** *adj* unobtrusive; (*Kleidung*) inconspicuous; **unauffindbar** *adj* not to be found; **unaufgefordert** *adj* unsolicited ▷ *adv* unasked, spontaneously; **unaufgefordert zugesandte Manuskripte** unsolicited manuscripts; **unaufhaltsam** *adj* irresistible; **unaufhörlich** *adj* incessant, continuous; **unaufmerksam** *adj* inattentive; **unaufrichtig** *adj* insincere

un- *zW*: **unausgeglichen** *adj* volatile; **unaussprechlich** *adj* inexpressible; **unausstehlich** *adj* intolerable

unbändig ['ʊnbɛndɪç] *adj* extreme, excessive

unbarmherzig ['ʊnbarmhɛrtsɪç] *adj* pitiless, merciless

unbeabsichtigt ['ʊnbə|apzɪçtɪçt] *adj* unintentional

unbeachtet ['ʊnbə|axtət] *adj* unnoticed; (*Warnung*) ignored

unbedenklich ['ʊnbədɛŋklɪç] *adj* unhesitating; (*Plan*) unobjectionable ▷ *adv* without hesitation

unbedeutend ['ʊnbədɔʏtənt] *adj* insignificant, unimportant; (*Fehler*) slight

unbedingt ['ʊnbədɪŋt] *adj* unconditional ▷ *adv* absolutely; **musst du ~ gehen?** do you really have to go?; **nicht ~** not necessarily

unbefangen ['ʊnbəfaŋən] *adj* impartial, unprejudiced; (*ohne Hemmungen*) uninhibited; **Unbefangenheit** *f* impartiality; uninhibitedness

unbefriedigend ['ʊnbəfri:dɪgənd] *adj* unsatisfactory

unbefriedigt ['ʊnbəfri:dɪçt] *adj* unsatisfied; (*unzufrieden*) dissatisfied; (*unerfüllt*) unfulfilled

unbefugt ['ʊnbəfʊ:kt] *adj* unauthorized; **U~en ist der Eintritt verboten** no admittance to unauthorized persons

unbegabt ['ʊnbəga:pt] *adj* untalented

unbegreiflich [ʊnbə'graɪflɪç] *adj* inconceivable

unbegrenzt ['ʊnbəgrɛntst] *adj* unlimited

unbegründet ['ʊnbəgrʏndət] *adj* unfounded

Unbehagen ['ʊnbəha:gən] *nt* discomfort

unbehaglich ['ʊnbəha:klɪç] *adj* uncomfortable; (*Gefühl*) uneasy

unbeholfen ['ʊnbəhɔlfən] *adj* awkward, clumsy; **Unbeholfenheit** *f* awkwardness, clumsiness

unbeirrt ['ʊnbə|ɪrt] *adj* imperturbable

unbekannt ['ʊnbəkant] *adj* unknown; **~e Größe** (*Math, fig*) unknown quantity

unbekümmert ['ʊnbəkʏmərt] *adj* unconcerned

unbeliebt ['ʊnbəli:pt] *adj* unpopular; **Unbeliebtheit** *f* unpopularity

unbequem ['ʊnbəkve:m] *adj* (*Stuhl*) uncomfortable; (*Mensch*) bothersome; (*Regelung*) inconvenient

unberechenbar [ʊnbə'rɛçənba:r] *adj* incalculable; (*Mensch, Verhalten*) unpredictable

unberechtigt ['ʊnbərɛçtɪçt] *adj* unjustified; (*nicht erlaubt*) unauthorized

unberufen [ʊnbə'ru:fən] *interj* touch wood!

unberührt ['ʊnbəry:rt] *adj* untouched; (*Natur*) unspoiled; **sie ist noch ~** she is still a virgin

unbescheiden ['ʊnbəʃaɪdən] *adj* presumptuous

unbeschreiblich [ʊnbə'ʃraɪplɪç] *adj* indescribable

unbesonnen ['ʊnbəzɔnən] *adj* unwise, rash, imprudent

unbeständig ['ʊnbəʃtɛndɪç] *adj* (*Mensch*) inconstant; (*Wetter*) unsettled; (*Lage*) unstable

unbestechlich [ʊnbəˈʃtɛçlɪç] *adj* incorruptible
unbestimmt [ˈʊnbəʃtɪmt] *adj* indefinite; (*Zukunft*) uncertain; **Unbestimmtheit** *f* vagueness
unbeteiligt [ʊnbəˈtaɪlɪçt] *adj* unconcerned; (*uninteressiert*) indifferent
unbeugsam [ˈʊnbɔʏkza:m] *adj* stubborn, inflexible; (*Wille*) unbending
unbewacht [ˈʊnbəvaxt] *adj* unguarded, unwatched
unbeweglich [ˈʊnbəve:klɪç] *adj* immovable
unbewusst [ˈʊnbəvʊst] *adj* unconscious
unbrauchbar [ˈʊnbraʊxba:r] *adj* (*nutzlos*) useless; (*Gerät*) unusable; **Unbrauchbarkeit** *f* uselessness
unbürokratisch [ˈʊnbyrokratɪʃ] *adj* without any red tape
und [ʊnt] *konj* and; **~ so weiter** and so on
Undank [ˈʊndaŋk] *m* ingratitude; **undankbar** *adj* ungrateful; **Undankbarkeit** *f* ingratitude
undefinierbar [ʊndefiˈni:rba:r] *adj* indefinable
undenkbar [ʊnˈdɛŋkba:r] *adj* inconceivable
undeutlich [ˈʊndɔʏtlɪç] *adj* indistinct; (*Schrift*) illegible; (*Ausdrucksweise*) unclear
undicht [ˈʊndɪçt] *adj* leaky
Unding [ˈʊndɪŋ] *nt* absurdity
unduldsam [ˈʊnduldsa:m] *adj* intolerant
un- *zW*: **undurchführbar** *adj* impracticable; **undurchlässig** *adj* impervious; (*wasserundurchlässig*) waterproof, impermeable; **undurchsichtig** *adj* opaque; (*Motive*) obscure; (*fig: pej: Mensch, Methoden*) devious
uneben [ˈʊn|e:bən] *adj* uneven
unecht [ˈʊn|ɛçt] *adj* artificial, fake; (*pej: Freundschaft, Lächeln*) false
unehelich [ˈʊn|e:əlɪç] *adj* illegitimate
uneigennützig [ˈʊn|aɪgənnʏtsɪç] *adj* unselfish
uneinig [ˈʊn|aɪnɪç] *adj* divided; **~ sein** to disagree; **Uneinigkeit** *f* discord, dissension
uneins [ˈʊn|aɪns] *adj* at variance, at odds
unempfindlich [ˈʊn|ɛmpfɪntlɪç] *adj* insensitive; **Unempfindlichkeit** *f* insensitivity
unendlich [ʊnˈ|ɛntlɪç] *adj* infinite ▷ *adv* endlessly; (*fig: sehr*) terribly; **Unendlichkeit** *f* infinity
un- *zW*: **unentbehrlich** *adj* indispensable; **unentgeltlich** *adj* free (of charge); **unentschieden** *adj* undecided; **unentschieden enden** (*Sport*) to end in a draw; **unentschlossen** *adj* undecided; (*entschlusslos*) irresolute; **unentwegt** *adj* unswerving; (*unaufhörlich*) incessant
un- *zW*: **unerbittlich** *adj* unyielding, inexorable; **unerfahren** *adj* inexperienced; **unerfreulich** *adj* unpleasant; **Unerfreuliches** (*schlechte Nachrichten*) bad news *sing*; (*Übles*) bad things *pl*; **unergründlich** *adj* unfathomable; **unerheblich** *adj* unimportant; **unerhört** *adj* unheard-of; (*unverschämt*) outrageous; (*Bitte*) unanswered; **unerlässlich** *adj* indispensable; **unerlaubt** *adj* unauthorized; **unermesslich** *adj* immeasurable, immense; **unermüdlich** *adj* indefatigable; **unersättlich** *adj* insatiable; **unerschöpflich** *adj* inexhaustible; **unerschütterlich** *adj* unshakeable; **unerschwinglich** *adj* (*Preis*) prohibitive; **unerträglich** *adj* unbearable; (*Frechheit*) insufferable; **unerwartet** *adj* unexpected; **unerwünscht** *adj* undesirable, unwelcome
unfähig [ˈʊnfɛ:ɪç] *adj* incapable; (*attrib*) incompetent; **zu etw ~ sein** to be incapable of sth; **Unfähigkeit** *f* inability; incompetence
unfair [ˈʊnfɛ:r] *adj* unfair
Unfall [ˈʊnfal] *m* accident; **Unfallflucht** *f* hit-and-run (driving); **Unfallstelle** *f* scene of the accident; **Unfallversicherung** *f* accident insurance
unfassbar [ʊnˈfasba:r] *adj* inconceivable
unfehlbar [ʊnˈfe:lba:r] *adj* infallible ▷ *adv* without fail; **Unfehlbarkeit** *f* infallibility
unfolgsam [ˈʊnfɔlkza:m] *adj* disobedient
unfrankiert [ˈʊnfraŋki:rt] *adj* unfranked
unfrei [ˈʊnfraɪ] *adj* not free
unfreiwillig *adj* involuntary
unfreundlich [ˈʊnfrɔʏntlɪç] *adj* unfriendly; **Unfreundlichkeit** *f* unfriendliness
unfruchtbar [ˈʊnfrʊxtba:r] *adj* infertile; (*Gespräche*) fruitless; **Unfruchtbarkeit** *f* infertility; fruitlessness
Unfug [ˈʊnfu:k] (**-s**) *m* (*Benehmen*) mischief; (*Unsinn*) nonsense; **grober ~** (*Jur*) gross misconduct
Ungar, in [ˈʊŋgar(ɪn)] (**-n, -n**) *m(f)* Hungarian; **ungarisch** *adj* Hungarian
Ungarn (**-s**) *nt* Hungary
ungeachtet [ˈʊngə|axtət] *präp +gen* notwithstanding
ungeahnt [ˈʊngə|a:nt] *adj* unsuspected, undreamt-of
ungebeten [ˈʊngəbe:tən] *adj* uninvited
ungebildet [ˈʊngəbɪldət] *adj* uncultured; (*ohne Bildung*) uneducated
ungebräuchlich [ˈʊngəbrɔʏçlɪç] *adj* unusual, uncommon
ungedeckt [ˈʊngədɛkt] *adj* (*schutzlos*) unprotected; (*Scheck*) uncovered
Ungeduld [ˈʊngədʊlt] *f* impatience
ungeduldig [ˈʊngədʊldɪç] *adj* impatient
ungeeignet [ˈʊngə|aɪgnət] *adj* unsuitable
ungefähr [ˈʊngəfɛ:r] *adj* rough, approximate ▷ *adv* roughly, approximately; **so ~!** more or less!; **das kommt nicht von ~** that's hardly surprising
ungefährlich [ˈʊngəfɛ:rlɪç] *adj* not dangerous, harmless
ungehalten [ˈʊngəhaltən] *adj* indignant
ungeheuer [ˈʊngəhɔʏər] *adj* huge ▷ *adv* (*umg*) enormously; **Ungeheuer** (**-s, -**) *nt* monster; **ungeheuerlich** [ʊngəˈhɔʏərlɪç] *adj*

monstrous
ungehobelt ['ʊngəho:bəlt] *adj* (*fig*) uncouth
ungehörig ['ʊngəhø:rɪç] *adj* impertinent, improper; **Ungehörigkeit** *f* impertinence
ungehorsam ['ʊngəho:rza:m] *adj* disobedient; **Ungehorsam** *m* disobedience
ungeklärt ['ʊngəklɛ:rt] *adj* not cleared up; (*Rätsel*) unsolved; (*Abwasser*) untreated
ungeladen ['ʊngəla:dən] *adj* not loaded; (*Elek*) uncharged; (*Gast*) uninvited
ungelegen ['ʊngəle:gən] *adj* inconvenient; **komme ich (Ihnen) ~?** is this an inconvenient time for you?
ungelernt ['ʊngəlɛrnt] *adj* unskilled
ungelogen ['ʊngəlo:gən] *adv* really, honestly
ungemein ['ʊngəmaɪn] *adj* immense
ungemütlich ['ʊngəmy:tlɪç] *adj* uncomfortable; (*Person*) disagreeable; **er kann ~ werden** he can get nasty
ungenau ['ʊngənaʊ] *adj* inaccurate
Ungenauigkeit *f* inaccuracy
ungeniert ['ʊnʒeni:rt] *adj* free and easy; (*bedenkenlos, taktlos*) uninhibited ▷ *adv* without embarrassment, freely
ungenießbar ['ʊngəni:sba:r] *adj* inedible; (*nicht zu trinken*) undrinkable; (*umg*) unbearable
ungenügend ['ʊngəny:gənt] *adj* insufficient, inadequate; (*Sch*) unsatisfactory
ungepflegt ['ʊngəpfle:kt] *adj* (*Garten etc*) untended; (*Person*) unkempt; (*Hände*) neglected
ungerade ['ʊngəra:də] *adj* odd, uneven (*US*)
ungerecht ['ʊngərɛçt] *adj* unjust
ungerechtfertigt *adj* unjustified
Ungerechtigkeit *f* unfairness, injustice
ungern ['ʊngɛrn] *adv* unwillingly, reluctantly
ungeschehen ['ʊngəʃe:ən] *adj*: **~ machen** to undo
Ungeschicklichkeit ['ʊngəʃɪklɪçkaɪt] *f* clumsiness
ungeschickt *adj* awkward, clumsy
ungeschminkt ['ʊngəʃmɪŋkt] *adj* without make-up; (*fig*) unvarnished
ungesetzlich ['ʊngəzɛtslɪç] *adj* illegal
ungestempelt ['ʊngəʃtɛmpəlt] *adj* (*Briefmarke*) unfranked, mint
ungestört ['ʊngəʃtø:rt] *adj* undisturbed
ungestraft ['ʊngəʃtra:ft] *adv* with impunity
ungestüm ['ʊngəʃty:m] *adj* impetuous; **Ungestüm** (**-(e)s**) *nt* impetuosity
ungesund ['ʊngəzʊnt] *adj* unhealthy
ungetrübt ['ʊngətry:pt] *adj* clear; (*fig*) untroubled; (*Freude*) unalloyed
Ungetüm ['ʊngəty:m] (**-(e)s, -e**) *nt* monster
ungewiss ['ʊngəvɪs] *adj* uncertain; **Ungewissheit** *f* uncertainty
ungewöhnlich ['ʊngəvø:nlɪç] *adj* unusual
ungewohnt ['ʊngəvo:nt] *adj* unusual
Ungeziefer ['ʊngətsi:fər] (**-s**) *nt* vermin *pl*
ungezogen ['ʊngətso:gən] *adj* rude, impertinent; **Ungezogenheit** *f* rudeness, impertinence
ungezwungen ['ʊngətsvʊŋən] *adj* natural, unconstrained
ungläubig ['ʊnglɔʏbɪç] *adj* unbelieving; **ein ~er Thomas** a doubting Thomas; **die U~en** the infidel(s *pl*)
unglaublich [ʊn'glaʊplɪç] *adj* incredible
ungleich ['ʊnglaɪç] *adj* dissimilar; (*Mittel, Waffen*) unequal ▷ *adv* incomparably; **ungleichartig** *adj* different; **Ungleichheit** *f* dissimilarity; inequality
Unglück ['ʊnglʏk] *nt* misfortune; (*Pech*) bad luck; (*Unglücksfall*) calamity, disaster; (*Verkehrsunglück*) accident; **zu allem ~** to make matters worse; **unglücklich** *adj* unhappy; (*erfolglos*) unlucky; (*unerfreulich*) unfortunate; **unglücklicherweise** *adv* unfortunately; **unglückselig** *adj* calamitous; (*Person*) unfortunate
Unglücksfall *m* accident, mishap
ungültig ['ʊngʏltɪç] *adj* invalid; **etw für ~ erklären** to declare sth null and void; **Ungültigkeit** *f* invalidity
ungünstig ['ʊngʏnstɪç] *adj* unfavourable (*Brit*), unfavorable (*US*); (*Termin*) inconvenient; (*Augenblick, Wetter*) bad; (*nicht preiswert*) expensive
unhaltbar ['ʊnhaltba:r] *adj* untenable
Unheil ['ʊnhaɪl] *nt* evil; (*Unglück*) misfortune; **~ anrichten** to cause mischief; **~ bringend** fatal, fateful
unheilbar [un'haɪlbar] *adj* incurable
unheilvoll *adj* disastrous
unheimlich ['ʊnhaɪmlɪç] *adj* weird, uncanny ▷ *adv* (*umg*) tremendously; **das/er ist mir ~** it/he gives me the creeps (*umg*)
unhöflich ['ʊnhø:flɪç] *adj* impolite; **Unhöflichkeit** *f* impoliteness
unhygienisch ['ʊnhygie:nɪʃ] *adj* unhygienic
Uni ['ʊni] (**-, -s**) (*umg*) *f* university
Uniform [uni'fɔrm] (**-, -en**) *f* uniform
uniformiert [unifɔr'mi:rt] *adj* uniformed
uninteressant ['ʊn|ɪntərɛsant] *adj* uninteresting
Universität [univɛrzi'tɛ:t] *f* university; **auf die ~ gehen, die ~ besuchen** to go to university
Universum [uni'vɛrzʊm] (**-s**) *nt* universe
unkenntlich ['ʊnkɛntlɪç] *adj* unrecognizable
Unkenntnis ['ʊnkɛntnɪs] *f* ignorance
unklar ['ʊnkla:r] *adj* unclear; **im U~en sein über** *+akk* to be in the dark about; **Unklarheit** *f* unclarity; (*Unentschiedenheit*) uncertainty
unklug ['ʊnklu:k] *adj* unwise
Unkosten ['ʊnkɔstən] *pl* expense(s *pl*); **sich in ~ stürzen** (*umg*) to go to a lot of expense
Unkraut ['ʊnkraʊt] *nt* weed; weeds *pl*; **~ vergeht nicht** (*Sprichwort*) it would take more than that to finish me/him *etc* off
unlängst ['ʊnlɛŋst] *adv* not long ago
unlauter ['ʊnlaʊtər] *adj* unfair
unleserlich ['ʊnle:zərlɪç] *adj* illegible
unlogisch ['ʊnlo:gɪʃ] *adj* illogical
unlösbar [ʊn'lø:sbar] *adj* insoluble

Unlust ['ʊnlʊst] *f* lack of enthusiasm
unlustig *adj* unenthusiastic ▷ *adv* without enthusiasm
unmäßig ['ʊnmɛːsɪç] *adj* immoderate
Unmenge ['ʊnmɛŋə] *f* tremendous number, vast number
Unmensch ['ʊnmɛnʃ] *m* ogre, brute; **unmenschlich** *adj* inhuman, brutal; (*ungeheuer*) awful
unmerklich [ʊn'mɛrklɪç] *adj* imperceptible
unmissverständlich ['ʊnmɪsfɛrʃtɛntlɪç] *adj* unmistakable
unmittelbar ['ʊnmɪtəlbaːr] *adj* immediate; **~er Kostenaufwand** direct expense
unmöbliert ['ʊnmøbliːrt] *adj* unfurnished
unmöglich ['ʊnmøːklɪç] *adj* impossible; **ich kann es ~ tun** I can't possibly do it; **~ aussehen** (*umg*) to look ridiculous; **Unmöglichkeit** *f* impossibility
unmoralisch ['ʊnmoraːlɪʃ] *adj* immoral
Unmut ['ʊnmuːt] *m* ill humour (*Brit*) *od* humor (*US*)
unnachgiebig ['ʊnnaːxgiːbɪç] *adj* unyielding
unnahbar [ʊn'naːbaːr] *adj* unapproachable
unnötig ['ʊnnøːtɪç] *adj* unnecessary
unnütz ['ʊnnʏts] *adj* useless
unordentlich ['ʊn|ɔrdəntlɪç] *adj* untidy
Unordnung ['ʊn|ɔrdnʊŋ] *f* disorder; (*Durcheinander*) mess
unparteiisch ['ʊnpartaɪɪʃ] *adj* impartial
Unparteiische, r *f(m)* umpire; (*Fussball*) referee
unpassend ['ʊnpasənt] *adj* inappropriate; (*Zeit*) inopportune
unpässlich ['ʊnpɛslɪç] *adj* unwell
unpersönlich ['ʊnpɛrzøːnlɪç] *adj* impersonal
unpolitisch ['ʊnpoliːtɪʃ] *adj* apolitical
unpraktisch ['ʊnpraktɪʃ] *adj* impractical, unpractical
unproduktiv ['ʊnprodʊktiːf] *adj* unproductive
unproportioniert ['ʊnpropɔrtsioniːrt] *adj* out of proportion
unpünktlich ['ʊnpʏŋktlɪç] *adj* unpunctual
unrationell ['ʊnratsionɛl] *adj* inefficient
unrecht ['ʊnrɛçt] *adj* wrong; **das ist mir gar nicht so ~** I don't really mind; **~ haben** to be wrong; **Unrecht** *nt* wrong; **zu Unrecht** wrongly; **nicht zu Unrecht** not without good reason; **im Unrecht sein** to be wrong
unrechtmäßig *adj* unlawful, illegal
unregelmäßig ['ʊnreːgəlmɛːsɪç] *adj* irregular; **Unregelmäßigkeit** *f* irregularity
unreif ['ʊnraɪf] *adj* (*Obst*) unripe; (*fig*) immature
unrentabel ['ʊnrɛntaːbəl] *adj* unprofitable
unrichtig ['ʊnrɪçtɪç] *adj* incorrect, wrong
Unruh ['ʊnruː] (**-, -en**) *f* (*von Uhr*) balance
Unruhe (**-, -n**) *f* unrest; **Unruhestifter** *m* troublemaker
unruhig *adj* restless; (*nervös*) fidgety; (*belebt*) noisy; (*Schlaf*) fitful; (*Zeit etc, Meer*) troubled
uns [ʊns] *pron akk, dat von* **wir** us; (*reflexiv*) ourselves
unsachlich ['ʊnzaxlɪç] *adj* not to the point, irrelevant; (*persönlich*) personal
unsagbar [ʊn'zaːkbaːr] *adj* indescribable
unsanft ['ʊnzanft] *adj* rough
unsauber ['ʊnzaʊbər] *adj* (*schmutzig*) dirty; (*fig*) crooked; (*: Klang*) impure
unschädlich ['ʊnʃɛːtlɪç] *adj* harmless; **jdn/etw ~ machen** to render sb/sth harmless
unscharf ['ʊnʃarf] *adj* indistinct; (*Bild etc*) out of focus, blurred
unscheinbar ['ʊnʃaɪnbaːr] *adj* insignificant; (*Aussehen, Haus etc*) unprepossessing
unschlagbar [ʊn'ʃlaːkbaːr] *adj* invincible
unschlüssig ['ʊnʃlʏsɪç] *adj* undecided
Unschuld ['ʊnʃʊlt] *f* innocence
unschuldig ['ʊnʃʊldɪç] *adj* innocent
unser ['ʊnzər] *poss pron* our ▷ *pron gen von* **wir** of us
unsere, r, s *poss pron* ours; **wir tun das U~** (*geh*) we are doing our bit
unsererseits ['ʊnzərər'zaɪts] *adv* on our part
unseresgleichen *pron* the likes of us
unsicher ['ʊnzɪçər] *adj* uncertain; (*Mensch*) insecure; **die Gegend ~ machen** (*fig: umg*) to knock about the district; **Unsicherheit** *f* uncertainty; insecurity
unsichtbar ['ʊnzɪçtbaːr] *adj* invisible; **Unsichtbarkeit** *f* invisibility
Unsinn ['ʊnzɪn] *m* nonsense
unsinnig *adj* nonsensical
Unsitte ['ʊnzɪtə] *f* deplorable habit
unsittlich ['ʊnzɪtlɪç] *adj* indecent; **Unsittlichkeit** *f* indecency
unsportlich ['ʊnʃpɔrtlɪç] *adj* not sporty; (*Verhalten*) unsporting
unsre *etc* ['ʊnzrə] *poss pron* = **unsere** *etc*; *siehe auch* **unser**
unsterblich ['ʊnʃtɛrplɪç] *adj* immortal; **Unsterblichkeit** *f* immortality
Unstimmigkeit ['ʊnʃtɪmɪçkaɪt] *f* inconsistency; (*Streit*) disagreement
unsympathisch ['ʊnzʏmpaːtɪʃ] *adj* unpleasant; **er ist mir ~** I don't like him
untätig ['ʊntɛːtɪç] *adj* idle
untauglich ['ʊntaʊklɪç] *adj* unsuitable; (*Mil*) unfit; **Untauglichkeit** *f* unsuitability; unfitness
unteilbar [ʊn'taɪlbaːr] *adj* indivisible
unten ['ʊntən] *adv* below; (*im Haus*) downstairs; (*an der Treppe etc*) at the bottom; **~ genannt** undermentioned; **siehe ~** see below; **nach ~** down; **~ am Berg** *etc* at the bottom of the mountain *etc*; **er ist bei mir ~ durch** (*umg*) I'm through with him
unter ['ʊntər] *präp +dat* **1** (*räumlich*) under; (*drunter*) underneath, below
2 (*zwischen*) among(st); **sie waren unter sich** they were by themselves; **einer unter ihnen** one of them; **unter anderem** among other things; **unter der Hand** secretly; (*verkaufen*) privately
▷ *präp +akk* under, below

▷ *adv* (*weniger als*) under; **Mädchen unter 18 Jahren** girls under *od* less than 18 (years of age)

Unter- *zW*: **Unterabteilung** *f* subdivision; **Unterarm** *m* forearm

unterbelichten [ˈʊntərbəlɪçtən] *vt untr* (*Phot*) to underexpose

Unterbewusstsein [ˈʊntərbəvʊstzaɪn] *nt* subconscious

unterbezahlt [ˈʊntərbətsa:lt] *adj* underpaid

unterbieten [ʊntərˈbi:tən] *unreg vt untr* (*Comm*) to undercut; (*fig*) to surpass

unterbinden [ʊntərˈbɪndən] *unreg vt untr* to stop, call a halt to

Unterbodenschutz [ʊntərˈbo:dənʃʊts] *m* (*Aut*) underseal

unterbrechen [ʊntərˈbrɛçən] *unreg vt untr* to interrupt

Unterbrechung *f* interruption

unterbringen [ˈʊntərbrɪŋən] *unreg vt* (*in Koffer*) to stow; (*in Zeitung*) to place; (*Person: in Hotel etc*) to accommodate, put up; (*: beruflich*): ~ **(bei)** to fix up (with)

unterdessen [ʊntərˈdɛsən] *adv* meanwhile

Unterdruck [ˈʊntərdrʊk] *m* (*Tech*) below atmospheric pressure

unterdrücken [ʊntərˈdrʏkən] *vt untr* to suppress; (*Leute*) to oppress

untere, r, s [ˈʊntərə(r, s)] *adj* lower

untereinander [ʊntər|aɪˈnandər] *adv* (*gegenseitig*) each other; (*miteinander*) among themselves *etc*

unterentwickelt [ˈʊntər|ɛntvɪkəlt] *adj* underdeveloped

unterernährt [ˈʊntər|ɛrnɛ:rt] *adj* undernourished

Unterernährung *f* malnutrition

Unterführung [ʊntər|fy:rʊŋ] *f* subway, underpass

Untergang [ˈʊntərgaŋ] *m* (down)fall, decline; (*Naut*) sinking; (*von Gestirn*) setting; **dem ~ geweiht sein** to be doomed

untergeben [ʊntərˈge:bən] *adj* subordinate

untergehen [ˈʊntərge:ən] *unreg vi* to go down; (*Sonne*) to set, go down; (*Staat*) to fall; (*Volk*) to perish; (*Welt*) to come to an end; (*im Lärm*) to be drowned

Untergeschoss [ˈʊntərgəʃɔs] *nt* basement

untergliedern [ʊntərˈgli:dərn] *vt untr* to subdivide

Untergrund [ˈʊntərgrʊnt] *m* foundation; (*Pol*) underground; **Untergrundbahn** *f* underground (*Brit*), subway (*US*); **Untergrundbewegung** *f* underground (movement)

unterhalb [ˈʊntərhalp] *präp +gen* below ▷ *adv* below; **~ von** below

Unterhalt [ˈʊntərhalt] *m* maintenance; **seinen ~ verdienen** to earn one's living

unterhalten [ʊntərˈhaltən] *unreg vt untr* to maintain; (*belustigen*) to entertain; (*versorgen*) to support; (*Geschäft, Kfz*) to run; (*Konto*) to have ▷ *vr untr* to talk; (*sich belustigen*) to enjoy o.s.

unterhaltend, unterhaltsam [ʊntərˈhaltza:m] *adj* entertaining

Unterhaltszahlung *f* maintenance payment

Unterhaltung *f* maintenance; (*Belustigung*) entertainment, amusement; (*Gespräch*) talk

Unterhändler [ˈʊntərhɛntlər] *m* negotiator

Unterhemd [ˈʊntərhɛmt] *nt* vest (*Brit*), undershirt (*US*)

Unterhose [ˈʊntərho:zə] *f* underpants *pl*

unterirdisch [ˈʊntər|ɪrdɪʃ] *adj* underground

Unterkiefer [ˈʊntərki:fər] *m* lower jaw

unterkommen [ˈʊntərkɔmən] *unreg vi* to find shelter; (*Stelle finden*) to find work; **das ist mir noch nie untergekommen** I've never met with that; **bei jdm ~** to stay at sb's (place)

Unterkunft [ˈʊntərkʊnft] (**-, -künfte**) *f* accommodation (*Brit*), accommodations *pl* (*US*); **~ und Verpflegung** board and lodging

Unterlage [ˈʊntərla:gə] *f* foundation; (*Beleg*) document; (*Schreibunterlage etc*) pad

unterlassen [ʊntərˈlasən] *unreg vt untr* (*versäumen*) to fail to do; (*sich enthalten*) to refrain from

unterlaufen [ʊntərˈlaʊfən] *unreg vi untr* to happen ▷ *adj*: **mit Blut ~** suffused with blood; (*Augen*) bloodshot; **mir ist ein Fehler ~** I made a mistake

unterlegen[1] [ˈʊntərle:gən] *vt* to lay *od* put under

unterlegen[2] [ʊntərˈle:gən] *adj* inferior; (*besiegt*) defeated

Unterleib [ˈʊntərlaɪp] *m* abdomen

unterliegen [ʊntərˈli:gən] *unreg vi untr +dat* to be defeated *od* overcome (by); (*unterworfen sein*) to be subject (to)

Untermiete [ˈʊntərmi:tə] *f* subtenancy; **bei jdm zur ~ wohnen** to rent a room from sb

Untermieter, in *m(f)* lodger

unternehmen [ʊntərˈne:mən] *unreg vt untr* to do; (*durchführen*) to undertake; (*Versuch, Reise*) to make; **Unternehmen** (**-s, -**) *nt* undertaking, enterprise (*auch Comm*); (*Firma*) business

unternehmend *adj* enterprising, daring

Unternehmensberater *m* management consultant

Unternehmer, in [ʊntərˈne:mər(ɪn)] (**-s, -**) *m(f)* (business) employer; (*alten Stils*) entrepreneur

unternehmungslustig *adj* enterprising

Unterredung [ʊntərˈre:dʊŋ] *f* discussion, talk

Unterricht [ˈʊntərrɪçt] (**-(e)s**) *m* teaching; (*Stunden*) lessons *pl*; **jdm ~ (in etw *dat*) geben** to teach sb (sth)

unterrichten [ʊntərˈrɪçtən] *vt untr* to instruct; (*Sch*) to teach ▷ *vr untr*: **sich ~ (über *+akk*)** to inform o.s. (about), obtain information (about)

Unterrock [ˈʊntərrɔk] *m* petticoat, slip

untersagen [ʊntərˈza:gən] *vt untr* to forbid;

jdm etw ~ to forbid sb to do sth
unterschätzen [ʊntərˈʃɛtsən] *vt untr* to underestimate
unterscheiden [ʊntərˈʃaɪdən] *unreg vt untr* to distinguish ▷ *vr untr* to differ
Unterscheidung *f* (*Unterschied*) distinction; (*Unterscheiden*) differentiation
Unterschied [ˈʊntərʃiːt] (**-(e)s, -e**) *m* difference, distinction; **im ~ zu** as distinct from: **unterschiedlich** *adj* varying, differing; (*diskriminierend*) discriminatory
unterschiedslos *adv* indiscriminately
unterschlagen [ʊntərˈʃlagən] *unreg vt untr* to embezzle; (*verheimlichen*) to suppress
Unterschlagung *f* embezzlement; (*von Briefen, Beweis*) withholding
Unterschlupf [ˈʊntərʃlʊpf] (**-(e)s, -schlüpfe**) *m* refuge
unterschreiben [ʊntərˈʃraɪbən] *unreg vt untr* to sign
Unterschrift [ˈʊntərʃrɪft] *f* signature; (*Bildunterschrift*) caption
Unterseeboot [ˈʊntərzeːboːt] *nt* submarine
Untersetzer [ˈʊntərzɛtsər] *m* tablemat; (*für Gläser*) coaster
untersetzt [ʊntərˈzɛtst] *adj* stocky
unterste, r, s [ˈʊntərstə(r, s)] *adj* lowest, bottom
unterstehen[1] [ʊntərˈʃteːən] *unreg vi untr +dat* to be under ▷ *vr untr* to dare
unterstehen[2] [ˈʊntərʃteːən] *unreg vi* to shelter
unterstellen[1] [ʊntərˈʃtɛlən] *vt untr* to subordinate; (*fig*) to impute; **jdm/etw unterstellt sein** to be under sb/sth; (*in Firma*) to report to sb/sth
unterstellen[2] [ˈʊntərʃtɛlən] *vt* (*Auto*) to garage, park ▷ *vr* to take shelter
unterstreichen [ʊntərˈʃtraɪçən] *unreg vt untr* (*lit, fig*) to underline
Unterstufe [ˈʊntərʃtuːfə] *f* lower grade
unterstützen [ʊntərˈʃtʏtsən] *vt untr* to support
Unterstützung *f* support, assistance
untersuchen [ʊntərˈzuːxən] *vt untr* (*Med*) to examine; (*Polizei*) to investigate; **sich ärztlich ~ lassen** to have a medical (*Brit*) *od* physical (*US*) (examination), have a check-up
Untersuchung *f* examination; investigation, inquiry
Untersuchungs- *zW*: **Untersuchungsausschuss** *m* committee of inquiry; **Untersuchungshaft** *f* custody; **in Untersuchungshaft sein** to be remanded in custody
untertänig [ˈʊntərtɛːnɪç] *adj* submissive, humble
Untertasse [ˈʊntərtasə] *f* saucer
untertauchen [ˈʊntərtaʊxən] *vi* to dive; (*fig*) to disappear, go underground
Unterteil [ˈʊntərtaɪl] *nt od m* lower part, bottom
unterteilen [ʊntərˈtaɪlən] *vt untr* to divide up
Untertitel [ˈʊntərtiːtəl] *m* subtitle; (*für Bild*) caption
unterwandern [ʊntərˈvandərn] *vt untr* to infiltrate
Unterwäsche [ˈʊntərvɛʃə] *f* underwear
unterwegs [ʊntərˈveːks] *adv* on the way; (*auf Reisen*) away
unterweisen [ʊntərˈvaɪzən] *unreg vt untr* to instruct
Unterwelt [ˈʊntərvɛlt] *f* (*lit, fig*) underworld
unterwerfen [ʊntərˈvɛrfən] *unreg vt untr* to subject; (*Volk*) to subjugate ▷ *vr untr* to submit
unterwürfig [ʊntərˈvʏrfɪç] *adj* obsequious
unterzeichnen [ʊntərˈtsaɪçnən] *vt untr* to sign
untreu [ˈʊntrɔʏ] *adj* unfaithful; **sich** *dat* **selbst ~ werden** to be untrue to o.s.
Untreue *f* unfaithfulness
untröstlich [ʊnˈtrøːstlɪç] *adj* inconsolable
un- *zW*: **unüberlegt** *adj* ill-considered ▷ *adv* without thinking; **unübersehbar** *adj* (*Schaden etc*) incalculable; (*Menge*) vast, immense; (*auffällig: Fehler etc*) obvious; **unübersichtlich** *adj* (*Gelände*) broken; (*Kurve*) blind; (*System, Plan*) confused
unumgänglich *adj* indispensable, vital
ununterbrochen [ˈʊn|ʊntərbrɔxən] *adj* uninterrupted
un- *zW*: **unveränderlich** *adj* unchangeable; **unverantwortlich** *adj* irresponsible; (*unentschuldbar*) inexcusable; **unverbesserlich** *adj* incorrigible; **unverbindlich** *adj* not binding; (*Antwort*) curt ▷ *adv* (*Comm*) without obligation; **unverbleit** [-fɛrblaɪt] *adj* (*Benzin*) unleaded; **unverblümt** [-fɛrˈblyːmt] *adj* plain, blunt ▷ *adv* plainly, bluntly; **unverdaulich** *adj* indigestible; **unverdorben** *adj* unspoilt; **unvereinbar** *adj* incompatible; **unverfänglich** *adj* harmless; **unverfroren** *adj* impudent; **unvergesslich** *adj* unforgettable; **unverhofft** *adj* unexpected; **unverkennbar** *adj* unmistakable; **unvermeidlich** *adj* unavoidable; **unvermutet** *adj* unexpected; **unvernünftig** *adj* foolish; **unverschämt** *adj* impudent; **Unverschämtheit** *f* impudence, insolence; **unversehens** *adv* all of a sudden; **unversehrt** [-fɛrzeːrt] *adj* uninjured; **unversöhnlich** *adj* irreconcilable; **unverständlich** *adj* unintelligible; **unverträglich** *adj* quarrelsome; (*Meinungen, Med*) incompatible; **unverwüstlich** *adj* indestructible; (*Mensch*) irrepressible; **unverzeihlich** *adj* unpardonable; **unverzüglich** [-fɛrˈtsyːklɪç] *adj* immediate; **unvollkommen** *adj* imperfect; **unvollständig** *adj* incomplete; **unvorbereitet** *adj* unprepared; **unvoreingenommen** *adj* unbiased; **unvorhergesehen** *adj* unforeseen; **unvorsichtig** *adj* careless, imprudent; **unvorstellbar** *adj* inconceivable; **unvorteilhaft** *adj* disadvantageous
unwahr [ˈʊnvaːr] *adj* untrue;

unwahrscheinlich *adj* improbable, unlikely ▷ *adv* (*umg*) incredibly
unweigerlich [ʊn'vaɪgərlɪç] *adj* unquestioning ▷ *adv* without fail
Unwesen ['ʊnveːzən] *nt* nuisance; (*Unfug*) mischief; **sein ~ treiben** to wreak havoc; (*Mörder etc*) to be at large
unwesentlich *adj* inessential, unimportant; **~ besser** marginally better
Unwetter ['ʊnvɛtər] *nt* thunderstorm
unwichtig ['ʊnvɪçtɪç] *adj* unimportant
un- *zW*: **unwiderlegbar** *adj* irrefutable; **unwiderruflich** *adj* irrevocable; **unwiderstehlich** [-viːdər'ʃteːlɪç] *adj* irresistible
unwillig *adj* indignant; (*widerwillig*) reluctant
unwillkürlich ['ʊnvɪlkyːrlɪç] *adj* involuntary ▷ *adv* instinctively; (*lachen*) involuntarily
unwirklich ['ʊnvɪrklɪç] *adj* unreal
unwirksam ['ʊnvɪrkzaːm] *adj* ineffective
unwirsch ['ʊnvɪrʃ] *adj* cross, surly
unwirtlich ['ʊnvɪrtlɪç] *adj* inhospitable
unwirtschaftlich ['ʊnvɪrtʃaftlɪç] *adj* uneconomical
unwissend ['ʊnvɪsənt] *adj* ignorant
Unwissenheit *f* ignorance
unwissenschaftlich *adj* unscientific
unwohl ['ʊnvoːl] *adj* unwell, ill; **Unwohlsein** (**-s**) *nt* indisposition
unwürdig ['ʊnvʏrdɪç] *adj* unworthy
unzählig [ʊn'tsɛːlɪç] *adj* innumerable, countless
un- *zW*: **unzerbrechlich** *adj* unbreakable; **unzerreißbar** *adj* untearable; **unzerstörbar** *adj* indestructible; **unzertrennlich** *adj* inseparable
Unzucht ['ʊntsʊxt] *f* sexual offence
unzüchtig ['ʊntsʏçtɪç] *adj* immoral
un- *zW*: **unzufrieden** *adj* dissatisfied; **Unzufriedenheit** *f* discontent; **unzulänglich** *adj* inadequate; **unzulässig** *adj* inadmissible; **unzurechnungsfähig** *adj* irresponsible; **jdn für unzurechnungsfähig erklären lassen** (*Jur*) to have sb certified (insane); **unzusammenhängend** *adj* disconnected; (*Äußerung*) incoherent; **unzutreffend** *adj* incorrect; **„Unzutreffendes bitte streichen"** "delete as applicable"; **unzuverlässig** *adj* unreliable
unzweideutig ['ʊntsvaɪdɔʏtɪç] *adj* unambiguous
üppig ['ʏpɪç] *adj* (*Frau*) curvaceous; (*Essen*) sumptuous, lavish; (*Vegetation*) luxuriant, lush; (*Haar*) thick
Urabstimmung ['uːr|apʃtɪmʊŋ] *f* ballot
Ural [u'raːl] (**-s**) *m*: **der ~** the Ural mountains *pl*, the Urals *pl*
uralt ['uːr|alt] *adj* ancient, very old
Uran [u'raːn] (**-s**) *nt* uranium
Uraufführung *f* first performance
Ur- *zW*: **Ureinwohner** *m* original inhabitant; **Ureltern** *pl* ancestors *pl*; **Urenkel, in** *m(f)* great-grandchild; **Urgroßmutter** *f* great-grandmother; **Urgroßvater** *m* great-grandfather
Urheber (**-s, -**) *m* originator; (*Autor*) author
urig ['uːrɪç] (*umg*) *adj* (*Mensch, Atmosphäre*) earthy
Urin [u'riːn] (**-s, -e**) *m* urine
urkomisch *adj* incredibly funny
Urkunde *f* document; (*Kaufurkunde*) deed
Urlaub ['uːrlaʊp] (**-(e)s, -e**) *m* holiday(s *pl*) (*Brit*), vacation (*US*); (*Mil etc*) leave; **Urlauber** (**-s, -**) *m* holiday-maker (*Brit*), vacationer (*US*)
Urmensch *m* primitive man
Urne ['ʊrnə] (**-, -n**) *f* urn; **zur ~ gehen** to go to the polls
Ursache ['uːrzaxə] *f* cause; **keine ~!** (*auf Dank*) don't mention it, you're welcome; (*auf Entschuldigung*) that's all right
Ursprung ['uːrʃprʊŋ] *m* origin, source; (*von Fluss*) source
ursprünglich ['uːrʃprʏŋlɪç] *adj* original ▷ *adv* originally
Urteil ['ʊrtaɪl] (**-s, -e**) *nt* opinion; (*Jur*) sentence, judgement; **sich** *dat* **ein ~ über etw** *akk* **erlauben** to pass judgement on sth; **ein ~ über etw** *akk* **fällen** to pass judgement on sth; **urteilen** *vi* to judge
Urteilsspruch *m* sentence; verdict
Uruguay [uru'guaːi] (**-s**) *nt* Uruguay
Uruguayer, in (**-s, -**) *m(f)* Uruguayan
uruguayisch *adj* Uruguayan
Ur- *zW*: **Urwald** *m* jungle; **Urzeit** *f* prehistoric times *pl*
USA [uː'ɛs'|aː] *pl abk*: **die ~** the USA *sing*
Usbekistan [ʊs'beːkistaːn] (**-s**) *nt* Uzbekistan
usw. *abk* (= *und so weiter*) etc.
Utensilien [utɛn'ziːliən] *pl* utensils *pl*
Utopie [uto'piː] *f* pipe dream
utopisch [u'toːpɪʃ] *adj* utopian

V¹, v [faʊ] *nt* V, v; **V wie Viktor** ≈ V for Victor
V² [faʊ] *abk* (= *Volt*) v
Vagina [va'gi:na] (**-, Vaginen**) *f* vagina
Vakuum ['va:kuʊm] (**-s, Vakua** *od* **Vakuen**) *nt* vacuum; **vakuumverpackt** *adj* vacuum-packed
Vandalismus [vanda'lɪsmʊs] *m* vandalism
Vanille [va'nɪljə] (-) *f* vanilla
Variation [variatsi'o:n] *f* variation
variieren [vari'i:rən] *vt, vi* to vary
Vase ['va:zə] (**-, -n**) *f* vase
Vater ['fa:tər] (**-s, ¨-**) *m* father; **~ Staat** (*umg*) the State; **Vaterland** *nt* native country; (*bes Deutschland*) Fatherland; **Vaterlandsliebe** *f* patriotism
väterlich ['fɛ:tərlɪç] *adj* fatherly
väterlicherseits *adv* on the father's side
Vaterschaft *f* paternity
Vaterunser (**-s, -**) *nt* Lord's Prayer
Vatikan [vati'ka:n] (**-s**) *m* Vatican
v. Chr. *abk* (= *vor Christus*) B.C.
Vegetarier, in [vege'ta:riər(ɪn)] (**-s, -**) *m(f)* vegetarian
vegetarisch *adj* vegetarian
Vegetation [vegetatsi'o:n] *f* vegetation
vegetieren [vege'ti:rən] *vi* to vegetate; (*kärglich leben*) to eke out a bare existence
Veilchen ['faɪlçən] *nt* violet; (*umg: blaues Auge*) shiner, black eye
Vene ['ve:nə] (**-, -n**) *f* vein
Venezolaner, in [venetso'la:nər(ɪn)] (**-s, -**) *m(f)* Venezuelan
venezolanisch *adj* Venezuelan
Venezuela [venetsu'e:la] (**-s**) *nt* Venezuela
Ventil [vɛn'ti:l] (**-s, -e**) *nt* valve
Ventilator [vɛnti'la:tɔr] *m* ventilator
verabreden [fɛr'|apre:dən] *vt* to arrange; (*Termin*) to agree upon ▷ *vr* to arrange to meet; **sich (mit jdm) ~** to arrange to meet (sb); **schon verabredet sein** to have a prior engagement (*form*), have something else on
Verabredung *f* arrangement; (*Treffen*) appointment; **ich habe eine ~** I'm meeting somebody
verabscheuen [fɛr'|apʃɔyən] *vt* to detest, abhor
verabschieden [fɛr'|apʃi:dən] *vt* (*Gäste*) to say goodbye to; (*entlassen*) to discharge; (*Gesetz*) to pass ▷ *vr*: **sich ~ (von)** to take one's leave (of)
Verabschiedung *f* (*von Beamten etc*) discharge; (*von Gesetz*) passing
verachten [fɛr'|axtən] *vt* to despise; **nicht zu ~** (*umg*) not to be scoffed at
verächtlich [fɛr'|ɛçtlɪç] *adj* contemptuous; (*verachtenswert*) contemptible; **jdn ~ machen** to run sb down
Verachtung *f* contempt; **jdn mit ~ strafen** to treat sb with contempt
verallgemeinern [fɛr|algə'maɪnərn] *vt* to generalize
Verallgemeinerung *f* generalization
veralten [fɛr'|altən] *vi* to become obsolete *od* out-of-date
Veranda [ve'randa] (**-, Veranden**) *f* veranda
veränderlich [fɛr'|ɛndərlɪç] *adj* variable; (*Wetter*) changeable
verändern *vt, vr* to change
Veränderung *f* change; **eine berufliche ~** a change of job
veranlagt *adj*: **praktisch ~ sein** to be practically-minded; **zu** *od* **für etw ~ sein** to be cut out for sth
Veranlagung *f* disposition, aptitude
veranlassen [fɛr'|anlasən] *vt* to cause; **Maßnahmen ~** to take measures; **sich veranlasst sehen** to feel prompted; **etw ~** to arrange for sth; (*befehlen*) to order sth
veranschaulichen [fɛr'|anʃaʊlɪçən] *vt* to illustrate
veranschlagen [fɛr'|anʃla:gən] *vt* to estimate
veranstalten [fɛr'|anʃtaltən] *vt* to organize, arrange
Veranstalter, in (**-s, -**) *m(f)* organizer; (*Comm: von Konzerten etc*) promoter
Veranstaltung *f* (*Veranstalten*) organizing; (*Veranstaltetes*) event; (*feierlich, öffentlich*) function
verantworten [fɛr'|antvɔrtən] *vt* to accept responsibility for; (*Folgen etc*) to answer for ▷ *vr* to justify o.s.; **etw vor jdm ~** to answer to sb for sth
verantwortlich *adj* responsible
Verantwortung *f* responsibility; **jdn zur ~ ziehen** to call sb to account
verantwortungs- *zW*: **verantwortungsbewusst** *adj* responsible; **Verantwortungsgefühl** *nt* sense of responsibility; **verantwortungslos** *adj*

irresponsible

verarbeiten [fɛr'|arbaɪtən] *vt* to process; (*geistig*) to assimilate; (*Erlebnis etc*) to digest; **etw zu etw ~** to make sth into sth; **~de Industrie** processing industries *pl*

Verarbeitung *f* processing; assimilation

verärgern [fɛr'|ɛrgərn] *vt* to annoy

verarzten [fɛr'|a:rtstən] *vt* to fix up (*umg*)

verausgaben [fɛr'|aʊsga:bən] *vr* to run out of money; (*fig*) to exhaust o.s.

veräußern [fɛr'|ɔʏsərn] *vt* (*form: verkaufen*) to dispose of

Verb [vɛrp] (**-s, -en**) *nt* verb

Verband [fɛr'bant] (**-(e)s, ⸚e**) *m* (*Med*) bandage, dressing; (*Bund*) association, society; (*Mil*) unit

Verbandzeug *nt* bandage, dressing material

verbarrikadieren [fɛrbarika'di:rən] *vt* to barricade ▷ *vr* to barricade o.s. in

verbergen [fɛr'bɛrgən] *unreg vt, vr*: **(sich) ~ (vor** *+dat*) to hide (from)

verbessern [fɛr'bɛsərn] *vt* to improve; (*berichtigen*) to correct ▷ *vr* to improve; to correct o.s.

Verbesserung *f* improvement; correction

verbeugen [fɛr'bɔʏgən] *vr* to bow

Verbeugung *f* bow

verbiegen [fɛr'bi:gən] *unreg vi* to bend

verbieten [fɛr'bi:tən] *unreg vt* to forbid; (*amtlich*) to prohibit; (*Zeitung, Partei*) to ban; **jdm etw ~** to forbid sb to do sth

verbinden [fɛr'bɪndən] *unreg vt* to connect; (*kombinieren*) to combine; (*Med*) to bandage ▷ *vr* to combine (*auch Chem*), join (together); **jdm die Augen ~** to blindfold sb

verbindlich [fɛr'bɪntlɪç] *adj* binding; (*freundlich*) obliging; **~ zusagen** to accept definitely; **Verbindlichkeit** *f* obligation; (*Höflichkeit*) civility; **Verbindlichkeiten** *pl* (*Jur*) obligations *pl*; (*Comm*) liabilities *pl*

Verbindung *f* connection; (*Zusammensetzung*) combination; (*Chem*) compound; (*Univ*) club; (*Tel: Anschluss*) line; **mit jdm in ~ stehen** to be in touch *od* contact with sb; **~ mit jdm aufnehmen** to contact sb

verbitten [fɛr'bɪtən] *unreg vt*: **sich** *dat* **etw ~** not to tolerate sth, not to stand for sth

verblassen [fɛr'blasən] *vi* to fade

Verbleib [fɛr'blaɪp] (**-(e)s**) *m* whereabouts

verbleiben [fɛr'blaɪbən] *unreg vi* to remain; **wir sind so verblieben, dass wir ...** we agreed to ...

verbleit [fɛr'blaɪt] *adj* leaded

verblöden [fɛr'blø:dən] *vi* (*Hilfsverb sein*) to get stupid

verblüffen [fɛr'blʏfən] *vt* to amaze; (*verwirren*) to baffle

Verblüffung *f* stupefaction

verblühen [fɛr'bly:ən] *vi* to wither, fade

verbluten [fɛr'blu:tən] *vi* to bleed to death

verbohrt *adj* (*Haltung*) stubborn, obstinate

verborgen [fɛr'bɔrgən] *adj* hidden; **~e Mängel** latent defects *pl*

Verbot [fɛr'bo:t] (**-(e)s, -e**) *nt* prohibition, ban

verboten *adj* forbidden; **Rauchen ~!** no smoking; **er sah ~ aus** (*umg*) he looked a real sight

verbotenerweise *adv* though it is forbidden

Verbotsschild *nt* prohibitory sign

Verbrauch [fɛr'braʊx] (**-(e)s**) *m* consumption

verbrauchen *vt* to use up; **der Wagen verbraucht 10 Liter Benzin auf 100 km** the car does 10 kms to the litre (*Brit*) *od* liter (*US*)

Verbraucher, in (**-s, -**) *m(f)* consumer; **Verbrauchermarkt** *m* hypermarket

verbraucht *adj* used up, finished; (*Luft*) stale; (*Mensch*) worn-out

Verbrechen (**-s, -**) *nt* crime

Verbrecher, in (**-s, -**) *m(f)* criminal; **verbrecherisch** *adj* criminal

verbreiten [fɛr'braɪtən] *vt* to spread; (*Licht*) to shed; (*Wärme, Ruhe*) to radiate ▷ *vr* to spread; **eine (weit) verbreitete Ansicht** a widely held opinion; **sich über etw** *akk* **~** to expound on sth

verbreitern [fɛr'braɪtərn] *vt* to broaden

Verbreitung *f* spread(ing); shedding; radiation

verbrennen [fɛr'brɛnən] *unreg vt* to burn; (*Leiche*) to cremate; (*versengen*) to scorch; (*Haar*) to singe; (*verbrühen*) to scald

Verbrennung *f* burning; (*in Motor*) combustion; (*von Leiche*) cremation

Verbrennungsmotor *m* internal-combustion engine

verbringen [fɛr'brɪŋən] *unreg vt* to spend

verbrühen [fɛr'bry:ən] *vt* to scald

verbuchen [fɛr'bu:xən] *vt* (*Fin*) to register; (*Erfolg*) to enjoy; (*Misserfolg*) to suffer

verbunden [fɛr'bʊndən] *adj* connected; **jdm ~ sein** to be obliged *od* indebted to sb; **ich/er** *etc* **war falsch ~** (*Tel*) it was a wrong number

verbünden [fɛr'bʏndən] *vr* to form an alliance

Verbundenheit *f* bond, relationship

Verbündete, r *f(m)* ally

verbürgen [fɛr'bʏrgən] *vr*: **sich ~ für** to vouch for; **ein verbürgtes Recht** an established right

verbüßen [fɛr'by:sən] *vt*: **eine Strafe ~** to serve a sentence

verchromt [fɛr'kro:mt] *adj* chromium-plated

Verdacht [fɛr'daxt] (**-(e)s**) *m* suspicion; **~ schöpfen (gegen jdn)** to become suspicious (of sb); **jdn in ~ haben** to suspect sb; **es besteht ~ auf Krebs** *akk* cancer is suspected

verdächtig *adj* suspicious

verdächtigen [fɛr'dɛçtɪgən] *vt* to suspect

Verdächtigung *f* suspicion

verdammen [fɛr'damən] *vt* to damn, condemn

verdammt (*umg*) *adj, adv* damned; **~ noch mal!** bloody hell (!), damn (!)

verdampfen [fɛr'dampfən] *vt, vi* (*vi Hilfsverb sein*) to vaporize; (*Koch*) to boil away

verdanken [fɛr'daŋkən] *vt*: **jdm etw ~** to owe sb sth
verdauen [fɛr'daʊən] *vt* (*lit, fig*) to digest ▷ *vi* (*lit*) to digest
verdaulich [fɛr'daʊlɪç] *adj* digestible; **das ist schwer ~** that is hard to digest
Verdauung *f* digestion
Verdeck [fɛr'dɛk] (**-(e)s, -e**) *nt* (*Aut*) soft top; (*Naut*) deck
verdecken *vt* to cover (up); (*verbergen*) to hide
verdenken [fɛr'dɛŋkən] *unreg vt*: **jdm etw ~** to blame sb for sth, hold sth against sb
verderben [fɛr'dɛrbən] *unreg vt* to spoil; (*schädigen*) to ruin; (*moralisch*) to corrupt ▷ *vi* (*Essen*) to spoil, rot; (*Mensch*) to go to the bad; **es mit jdm ~** to get into sb's bad books
Verderben (**-s**) *nt* ruin
verderblich *adj* (*Einfluss*) pernicious; (*Lebensmittel*) perishable
verdeutlichen [fɛr'dɔʏtlɪçən] *vt* to make clear
verdichten [fɛr'dɪçtən] *vt* (*Phys, fig*) to compress ▷ *vr* to thicken; (*Verdacht, Eindruck*) to deepen
verdienen [fɛr'di:nən] *vt* to earn; (*moralisch*) to deserve ▷ *vi* (*Gewinn machen*): **~ (an** *+dat*) to make (a profit) (on)
Verdienst [fɛr'di:nst] (**-(e)s, -e**) *m* earnings *pl* ▷ *nt* merit; (*Dank*) credit; (*Leistung*): **~ (um)** service (to), contribution (to)
verdient [fɛr'di:nt] *adj* well-earned; (*Person*) of outstanding merit; (*Lohn, Strafe*) rightful; **sich um etw ~ machen** to do a lot for sth
verdoppeln [fɛr'dɔpəln] *vt* to double
verdorben [fɛr'dɔrbən] *pp von* **verderben** ▷ *adj* spoilt; (*geschädigt*) ruined; (*moralisch*) corrupt
verdrängen [fɛr'drɛŋən] *vt* to oust; (*auch Phys*) to displace; (*Psych*) to repress
verdrehen [fɛr'dre:ən] *vt* (*lit, fig*) to twist; (*Augen*) to roll; **jdm den Kopf ~** (*fig*) to turn sb's head
verdreifachen [fɛr'draɪfaxən] *vt* to treble
verdrießlich [fɛr'dri:slɪç] *adj* peevish, annoyed
verdrossen [fɛr'drɔsən] *pp von* **verdrießen** ▷ *adj* cross, sulky
Verdruss [fɛr'drʊs] (**-es, -e**) *m* frustration; **zu jds ~** to sb's annoyance
verdummen [fɛr'dʊmən] *vt* to make stupid ▷ *vi* to grow stupid
verdunkeln [fɛr'dʊŋkəln] *vt* to darken; (*fig*) to obscure ▷ *vr* to darken
verdünnen [fɛr'dʏnən] *vt* to dilute
verdunsten [fɛr'dʊnstən] *vi* to evaporate
verdursten [fɛr'dʊrstən] *vi* to die of thirst
verdutzt [fɛr'dʊtst] *adj* nonplussed (*Brit*), nonplused (*US*), taken aback
verehren [fɛr'|e:rən] *vt* to venerate, worship (*auch REL*); **jdm etw ~** to present sb with sth
Verehrer, in (**-s, -**) *m(f)* admirer, worshipper (*Brit*), worshiper (*US*)
verehrt *adj* esteemed; **(sehr) ~e Anwesende/ verehrtes Publikum** Ladies and Gentlemen
Verehrung *f* respect; (*Rel*) worship
vereidigen [fɛr'|aɪdɪgən] *vt* to put on oath; **jdn auf etw** *akk* **~** to make sb swear on sth
Vereidigung *f* swearing in
Verein [fɛr'|aɪn] (**-(e)s, -e**) *m* club, association; **ein wohltätiger ~** a charity
vereinbar *adj* compatible
vereinbaren [fɛr'|aɪnba:rən] *vt* to agree upon
Vereinbarung *f* agreement
vereinfachen [fɛr'|aɪnfaxən] *vt* to simplify
vereinigen [fɛr'|aɪnɪgən] *vt, vr* to unite; **Vereinigte Arabische Emirate** *pl* United Arab Emirates
Vereinigung *f* union; (*Verein*) association
vereint [fɛr'|aɪnt] *adj* united
vereinzelt [fɛr'|aɪntsəlt] *adj* isolated
vereisen [fɛr'|aɪzən] *vi* to freeze, ice over ▷ *vt* (*Med*) to freeze
vereiteln [fɛr'|aɪtəln] *vt* to frustrate
vereitern [fɛr'|aɪtərn] *vi* to suppurate, fester
verengen [fɛr'|ɛŋən] *vr* to narrow
vererben [fɛr'|ɛrbən] *vt* to bequeath; (*Biol*) to transmit ▷ *vr* to be hereditary
vererblich [fɛr'|ɛrplɪç] *adj* hereditary
Vererbung *f* bequeathing; (*Biol*) transmission; **das ist ~** (*umg*) it's hereditary
verewigen [fɛr'|e:vɪgən] *vt* to immortalize ▷ *vr* (*umg*) to leave one's name
verfahren [fɛr'fa:rən] *unreg vi* to act ▷ *vr* to get lost ▷ *adj* tangled; **~ mit** to deal with
Verfahren (**-s, -**) *nt* procedure; (*Tech*) process; (*Jur*) proceedings *pl*
Verfall [fɛr'fal] (**-(e)s**) *m* decline; (*von Haus*) dilapidation; (*Fin*) expiry
verfallen *unreg vi* to decline; (*Haus*) to be falling down; (*Fin*) to lapse ▷ *adj* (*Gebäude*) dilapidated, ruined; (*Karten, Briefmarken*) invalid; (*Strafe*) lapsed; (*Pass*) expired; **~ in** *+akk* to lapse into; **~ auf** *+akk* to hit upon; **einem Laster ~ sein** to be addicted to a vice; **jdm völlig ~ sein** to be completely under sb's spell
Verfallsdatum *nt* expiry date; (*der Haltbarkeit*) best-before date
verfänglich [fɛr'fɛŋlɪç] *adj* awkward, tricky; (*Aussage, Beweismaterial etc*) incriminating; (*gefährlich*) dangerous
verfärben [fɛr'fɛrbən] *vr* to change colour (*Brit*) *od* color (*US*)
verfassen [fɛr'fasən] *vt* to write; (*Gesetz, Urkunde*) to draw up
Verfasser, in (**-s, -**) *m(f)* author, writer
Verfassung *f* constitution (*auch Pol*); (*körperlich*) state of health; (*seelisch*) state of mind; **sie ist in guter/schlechter ~** she is in good/bad shape
Verfassungs- *zW*: **Verfassungsgericht** *nt* constitutional court; **verfassungsmäßig** *adj* constitutional; **verfassungswidrig** *adj* unconstitutional
verfaulen [fɛr'faʊlən] *vi* to rot
verfehlen [fɛr'fe:lən] *vt* to miss; **das Thema ~** to be completely off the subject
verfilmen [fɛr'fɪlmən] *vt* to film, make a

film of
verfliegen [fɛr'fli:gən] *unreg vi* to evaporate; (*Zeit*) to pass, fly ▷ *vr* to stray (past)
verflixt [fɛr'flɪkst] (*umg*) *adj, adv* darned
verflossen [fɛr'flɔsən] *adj* past, former
verfluchen [fɛr'flu:xən] *vt* to curse
verflüchtigen [fɛr'flʏçtɪgən] *vr* to evaporate; (*Geruch*) to fade
verfolgen [fɛr'fɔlgən] *vt* to pursue; (*gerichtlich*) to prosecute; (*grausam, bes Pol*) to persecute
Verfolger, in (**-s, -**) *m(f)* pursuer
Verfolgung *f* pursuit; persecution; **strafrechtliche ~** prosecution
Verfolgungswahn *m* persecution mania
verfremden [fɛr'frɛmdən] *vt* to alienate, distance
verfrüht [fɛr'fry:t] *adj* premature
verfügbar *adj* available
verfügen [fɛr'fy:gən] *vt* to direct, order ▷ *vr* to proceed ▷ *vi*: **~ über** *+akk* to have at one's disposal; **über etw** *akk* **frei ~ können** to be able to do as one wants with sth
Verfügung *f* direction, order; (*Jur*) writ; **zur ~** at one's disposal; **jdm zur ~ stehen** to be available to sb
verführen [fɛr'fy:rən] *vt* to tempt; (*sexuell*) to seduce; (*die Jugend, das Volk etc*) to lead astray
verführerisch *adj* seductive
Verführung *f* seduction; (*Versuchung*) temptation
vergammeln [fɛr'gaməln] (*umg*) *vi* to go to seed; (*Nahrung*) to go off; (*Zeit*) to waste
vergangen [fɛr'gaŋən] *adj* past; **Vergangenheit** *f* past; **Vergangenheitsbewältigung** *f* coming to terms with the past
vergänglich [fɛr'gɛŋlɪç] *adj* transitory; **Vergänglichkeit** *f* transitoriness, impermanence
vergasen [fɛr'ga:zən] *vt* to gasify; (*töten*) to gas
Vergaser (**-s, -**) *m* (*Aut*) carburettor (*Brit*), carburetor (*US*)
vergaß *etc* [fɛr'ga:s] *vb siehe* **vergessen**
vergeben [fɛr'ge:bən] *unreg vt* to forgive; (*weggeben*) to give away; (*fig: Chance*) to throw away; (*Auftrag, Preis*) to award; (*Studienplätze, Stellen*) to allocate; **jdm (etw) ~** to forgive sb (sth); **~ an** *+akk* to award to; to allocate to; **~ sein** to be occupied; (*umg: Mädchen*) to be spoken for
vergebens *adv* in vain
vergeblich [fɛr'ge:plɪç] *adv* in vain ▷ *adj* vain, futile
Vergebung *f* forgiveness
vergehen [fɛr'ge:ən] *unreg vi* to pass by *od* away ▷ *vr* to commit an offence (*Brit*) *od* offense (*US*); **vor Angst ~** to be scared to death; **jdm vergeht etw** sb loses sth; **sich an jdm ~** to (sexually) assault sb; **Vergehen** (**-s, -**) *nt* offence (*Brit*), offense (*US*)
vergelten [fɛr'gɛltən] *unreg vt*: **jdm etw ~** to pay sb back for sth, repay sb for sth
Vergeltung *f* retaliation, reprisal
Vergeltungsschlag *m* (*Mil*) reprisal
vergessen [fɛr'gɛsən] *unreg vt* to forget; **Vergessenheit** *f* oblivion; **in Vergessenheit geraten** to fall into oblivion
vergesslich [fɛr'gɛslɪç] *adj* forgetful; **Vergesslichkeit** *f* forgetfulness
vergeuden [fɛr'gɔʏdən] *vt* to squander, waste
vergewaltigen [fɛrgə'valtɪgən] *vt* to rape; (*fig*) to violate
Vergewaltigung *f* rape
vergewissern [fɛrgə'vɪsərn] *vr* to make sure; **sich einer Sache** *gen od* **über etw** *akk* **~** to make sure of sth
vergießen [fɛr'gi:sən] *unreg vt* to shed
vergiften [fɛr'gɪftən] *vt* to poison
Vergiftung *f* poisoning
Vergissmeinnicht [fɛr'gɪsmaɪnnɪçt] (**-(e)s, -e**) *nt* forget-me-not
verglasen [fɛr'gla:zən] *vt* to glaze
Vergleich [fɛr'glaɪç] (**-(e)s, -e**) *m* comparison; (*Jur*) settlement; **einen ~ schließen** (*Jur*) to reach a settlement; **in keinem ~ zu etw stehen** to be out of all proportion to sth; **im ~ mit** *od* **zu** compared with *od* to; **vergleichbar** *adj* comparable
vergleichen *unreg vt* to compare ▷ *vr* (*Jur*) to reach a settlement
vergnügen [fɛr'gny:gən] *vr* to enjoy *od* amuse o.s.; **Vergnügen** (**-s, -**) *nt* pleasure; **das war ein teures Vergnügen** (*umg*) that was an expensive bit of fun; **viel Vergnügen!** enjoy yourself!
vergnügt [fɛr'gny:kt] *adj* cheerful
Vergnügung *f* pleasure, amusement
Vergnügungs- *zW*: **Vergnügungspark** *m* amusement park; **vergnügungssüchtig** *adj* pleasure-loving
vergolden [fɛr'gɔldən] *vt* to gild
vergöttern [fɛr'gœtərn] *vt* to idolize
vergraben [fɛr'gra:bən] *unreg vt* to bury
vergreifen [fɛr'graɪfən] *unreg vr*: **sich an jdm ~** to lay hands on sb; **sich an etw** *dat* **~** to misappropriate sth; **sich im Ton ~** to say the wrong thing
vergriffen [fɛr'grɪfən] *adj* (*Buch*) out of print; (*Ware*) out of stock
vergrößern [fɛr'grø:sərn] *vt* to enlarge; (*mengenmäßig*) to increase; (*Lupe*) to magnify
Vergrößerung *f* enlargement; increase; magnification
Vergrößerungsglas *nt* magnifying glass
Vergünstigung [fɛr'gʏnstɪgʊŋ] *f* concession; (*Vorteil*) privilege
vergüten [fɛr'gy:tən] *vt*: **jdm etw ~** to compensate sb for sth; (*Arbeit, Leistung*) to pay sb for sth
Vergütung *f* compensation; payment
verhaften [fɛr'haftən] *vt* to arrest
Verhaftung *f* arrest
verhallen [fɛr'halən] *vi* to die away
verhalten [fɛr'haltən] *unreg vr* (*Sache*) to be, stand; (*sich benehmen*) to behave; (*Math*) to be

in proportion to ▷ *vr unpers*: **wie verhält es sich damit?** (*wie ist die Lage?*) how do things stand?; (*wie wird das gehandhabt?*) how do you go about it? ▷ *adj* restrained; **sich ruhig ~** to keep quiet; (*sich nicht bewegen*) to keep still; **wenn sich das so verhält ...** if that is the case ...; **Verhalten** (**-s**) *nt* behaviour (*Brit*), behavior (*US*)

Verhaltensforschung *f* behavioural (*Brit*) *od* behavioral (*US*) science; **verhaltensgestört** *adj* disturbed

Verhältnis [fɛrˈhɛltnɪs] (**-ses, -se**) *nt* relationship; (*Liebesverhältnis*) affair; (*Math*) proportion, ratio; (*Einstellung*): **~ (zu)** attitude (to); **Verhältnisse** *pl* (*Umstände*) conditions *pl*; **aus was für ~sen kommt er?** what sort of background does he come from?; **für klare ~se sorgen, klare ~se schaffen** to get things straight; **über seine ~se leben** to live beyond one's means; **verhältnismäßig** *adj* relative, comparative ▷ *adv* relatively, comparatively; **Verhältniswahl** *f* proportional representation

verhandeln [fɛrˈhandəln] *vi* to negotiate; (*Jur*) to hold proceedings ▷ *vt* to discuss; (*Jur*) to hear; **über etw** *akk* **~** to negotiate sth *od* about sth

Verhandlung *f* negotiation; (*Jur*) proceedings *pl*; **~en führen** to negotiate

verhängen [fɛrˈhɛŋən] *vt* (*fig*) to impose, inflict

Verhängnis [fɛrˈhɛŋnɪs] (**-ses, -se**) *nt* fate; **jdm zum ~ werden** to be sb's undoing; **verhängnisvoll** *adj* fatal, disastrous

verharmlosen [fɛrˈharmlo:zən] *vt* to make light of, play down

verhasst [fɛrˈhast] *adj* odious, hateful

verheerend [fɛrˈhe:rənt] *adj* disastrous, devastating

verheilen [fɛrˈhaɪlən] *vi* to heal

verheimlichen [fɛrˈhaɪmlɪçən] *vt*: **(jdm) etw ~** to keep sth secret (from sb)

verheiratet [fɛrˈhaɪra:tət] *adj* married

verheißungsvoll *adj* promising

verhelfen [fɛrˈhɛlfən] *unreg vi*: **jdm zu etw ~** to help sb to get sth

verherrlichen [fɛrˈhɛrlɪçən] *vt* to glorify

verhexen [fɛrˈhɛksən] *vt* to bewitch; **es ist wie verhext** it's jinxed

verhindern [fɛrˈhɪndərn] *vt* to prevent; **verhindert sein** to be unable to make it; **das lässt sich leider nicht ~** it can't be helped, unfortunately; **ein verhinderter Politiker** (*umg*) a would-be politician

Verhinderung *f* prevention

verhöhnen [fɛrˈhø:nən] *vt* to mock, sneer at

Verhör [fɛrˈhø:r] (**-(e)s, -e**) *nt* interrogation; (*gerichtlich*) (cross-)examination

verhören *vt* to interrogate; to (cross-)examine ▷ *vr* to mishear

verhungern [fɛrˈhʊŋərn] *vi* to starve, die of hunger

verhüten [fɛrˈhy:tən] *vt* to prevent, avert

Verhütung *f* prevention

Verhütungsmittel *nt* contraceptive

verirren [fɛrˈ|ɪrən] *vr* to get lost, lose one's way; (*fig*) to go astray; (*Tier, Kugel*) to stray

verjagen [fɛrˈja:gən] *vt* to drive away *od* out

Verjährungsfrist *f* limitation period

verkabeln [fɛrˈka:bəln] *vt* (*TV*) to link up to the cable network

Verkabelung *f* (*TV*) linking up to the cable network

verkalken [fɛrˈkalkən] *vi* to calcify; (*umg*) to become senile

verkalkulieren [fɛrkalkuˈli:rən] *vr* to miscalculate

verkannt [fɛrˈkant] *adj* unappreciated

Verkauf [fɛrˈkaʊf] *m* sale; **zum ~ stehen** to be up for sale

verkaufen *vt, vi* to sell; **„zu ~"** "for sale"

Verkäufer, in [fɛrˈkɔʏfər(ɪn)] (**-s, -**) *m(f)* seller; (*im Außendienst*) salesman, saleswoman; (*in Laden*) shop assistant (*Brit*), sales clerk (*US*)

verkäuflich [fɛrˈkɔʏflɪç] *adj* saleable

Verkaufs- *zW*: **verkaufsoffen** *adj*: **verkaufsoffener Samstag** *Saturday on which the shops are open all day*; **Verkaufsschlager** *m* big seller

Verkehr [fɛrˈke:r] (**-s, -e**) *m* traffic; (*Umgang, bes sexuell*) intercourse; (*Umlauf*) circulation; **aus dem ~ ziehen** to withdraw from service; **für den ~ freigeben** (*Straße etc*) to open to traffic; (*Transportmittel*) to bring into service

verkehren *vi* (*Fahrzeug*) to ply, run ▷ *vt, vr* to turn, transform; **~ mit** to associate with; **mit jdm brieflich** *od* **schriftlich ~** (*form*) to correspond with sb; **bei jdm ~** to visit sb regularly

Verkehrs- *zW*: **Verkehrsampel** *f* traffic lights *pl*; **Verkehrsamt** *nt* tourist (information) office; **Verkehrsaufkommen** *nt* volume of traffic; **verkehrsberuhigt** *adj* traffic-calmed; **Verkehrsberuhigung** *f* traffic-calming; **Verkehrsdelikt** *nt* traffic offence (*Brit*) *od* violation (*US*); **Verkehrsinsel** *f* traffic island; **Verkehrsmittel** *nt*: **öffentliche/private Verkehrsmittel** public/private transport *sing*; **Verkehrsschild** *nt* road sign; **verkehrssicher** *adj* (*Fahrzeug*) roadworthy; **Verkehrsstockung** *f* traffic jam, stoppage; **Verkehrssünder** (*umg*) *m* traffic offender; **Verkehrsteilnehmer** *m* road user; **Verkehrsunfall** *m* traffic accident; **verkehrswidrig** *adj* contrary to traffic regulations; **Verkehrszeichen** *nt* road sign

verkehrt *adj* wrong; (*umgekehrt*) the wrong way round

verkennen [fɛrˈkɛnən] *unreg vt* to misjudge; (*unterschätzen*) to underestimate

verklagen [fɛrˈkla:gən] *vt* to take to court

verklappen [fɛrˈklapən] *vt* to dump (at sea)

verkleben [fɛrˈkle:bən] *vt* to glue up, stick ▷ *vi* to stick together

verkleiden [fɛrˈklaɪdən] *vt* to disguise; (*kostümieren*) to dress up; (*Schacht, Tunnel*) to

line; (*vertäfeln*) to panel; (*Heizkörper*) to cover in ▷*vr* to disguise o.s.; to dress up
Verkleidung *f* disguise; (*Archit*) panelling (*Brit*), paneling (*US*)
verkleinern [fɛrˈklaɪnərn] *vt* to make smaller, reduce in size
verklemmt [fɛrˈklɛmt] *adj* (*fig*) inhibited
verklingen [fɛrˈklɪŋən] *unreg vi* to die away
verkneifen [fɛrˈknaɪfən] (*umg*) *vt*: **sich** *dat* **etw ~** to stop o.s. from doing sth; **ich konnte mir das Lachen nicht ~** I couldn't help laughing
verknüpfen [fɛrˈknʏpfən] *vt* to tie (up), knot; (*fig*) to connect
Verknüpfung *f* connection
verkommen [fɛrˈkɔmən] *unreg vi* to deteriorate, decay; (*Mensch*) to go downhill, come down in the world ▷*adj* (*moralisch*) dissolute, depraved; **Verkommenheit** *f* depravity
verkörpern [fɛrˈkœrpərn] *vt* to embody, personify
verkrachen [fɛrˈkraxən] (*umg*) *vr*: **sich (mit jdm) ~** to fall out (with sb)
verkraften [fɛrˈkraftən] *vt* to cope with
verkriechen [fɛrˈkriːçən] *unreg vr* to creep away, creep into a corner
Verkrümmung *f* bend, warp; (*Anat*) curvature
verkrüppelt [fɛrˈkrʏpəlt] *adj* crippled
verkrustet [fɛrˈkrʊstət] *adj* encrusted
verkühlen [fɛrˈkyːlən] *vr* to get a chill
verkümmern [fɛrˈkʏmərn] *vi* to waste away; **emotionell/geistig ~** to become emotionally/intellectually stunted
verkünden [fɛrˈkʏndən] *vt* to proclaim; (*Urteil*) to pronounce
verkürzen [fɛrˈkʏrtsən] *vt* to shorten; (*Wort*) to abbreviate; **sich** *dat* **die Zeit ~** to while away the time; **verkürzte Arbeitszeit** shorter working hours *pl*
Verkürzung *f* shortening; abbreviation
verladen [fɛrˈlaːdən] *unreg vt* to load
Verlag [fɛrˈlaːk] (**-(e)s, -e**) *m* publishing firm
verlangen [fɛrˈlaŋən] *vt* to demand; (*wollen*) to want ▷*vi*: **~ nach** to ask for; **Sie werden am Telefon verlangt** you are wanted on the phone; **~ Sie Herrn X** ask for Mr X; **Verlangen** (**-s, -**) *nt*: **Verlangen (nach)** desire (for); **auf jds Verlangen** *akk* **(hin)** at sb's request
verlängern [fɛrˈlɛŋərn] *vt* to extend; (*länger machen*) to lengthen; (*zeitlich*) to prolong; (*Pass, Abonnement etc*) to renew; **ein verlängertes Wochenende** a long weekend
Verlängerung *f* extension; (*Sport*) extra time
Verlängerungsschnur *f* extension cable
verlangsamen [fɛrˈlaŋzaːmən] *vt, vr* to decelerate, slow down
Verlass [fɛrˈlas] *m*: **auf ihn/das ist kein ~** he/it cannot be relied upon
verlassen [fɛrˈlasən] *unreg vt* to leave ▷*vr*: **sich ~ auf** *+akk* to depend on ▷*adj* desolate; (*Mensch*) abandoned; **einsam und ~** so all alone; **Verlassenheit** *f* loneliness (*Brit*), lonesomeness (*US*)
verlässlich [fɛrˈlɛslɪç] *adj* reliable
Verlauf [fɛrˈlaʊf] *m* course; **einen guten/schlechten ~ nehmen** to go well/badly
verlaufen *unreg vi* (*zeitlich*) to pass; (*Farben*) to run ▷*vr* to get lost; (*Menschenmenge*) to disperse
verlauten [fɛrˈlaʊtən] *vi*: **etw ~ lassen** to disclose sth; **wie verlautet** as reported
verleben [fɛrˈleːbən] *vt* to spend
verlebt [fɛrˈleːpt] *adj* dissipated, worn-out
verlegen [fɛrˈleːgən] *vt* to move; (*verlieren*) to mislay; (*Kabel, Fliesen etc*) to lay; (*Buch*) to publish; (*verschieben*): **~ (auf** *+akk***)** to postpone (until) ▷*vr*: **sich auf etw** *akk* **~** to resort to sth ▷*adj* embarrassed; **nicht ~ um** never at a loss for; **Verlegenheit** *f* embarrassment; (*Situation*) difficulty, scrape
Verleih [fɛrˈlaɪ] (**-(e)s, -e**) *m* hire service; (*das Verleihen*) renting (out), hiring (out) (*Brit*); (*Filmverleih*) distribution
verleihen *unreg vt*: **etw (an jdn) ~** to lend sth (to sb), lend (sb) sth; (*gegen Gebühr*) to rent sth (out) (to sb), hire sth (out) (to sb) (*Brit*); (*Kraft, Anschein*) to confer sth (on sb), bestow sth (on sb); (*Preis, Medaille*) to award sth (to sb), award (sb) sth
Verleihung *f* lending; (*von Kraft etc*) bestowal; (*von Preis*) award
verleiten [fɛrˈlaɪtən] *vt* to lead astray; **~ zu** to talk into, tempt into
verlernen [fɛrˈlɛrnən] *vt* to forget, unlearn
verlesen [fɛrˈleːzən] *unreg vt* to read out; (*aussondern*) to sort out ▷*vr* to make a mistake in reading
verletzen [fɛrˈlɛtsən] *vt* (*lit, fig*) to injure, hurt; (*Gesetz etc*) to violate
verletzend *adj* (*fig: Worte*) hurtful
verletzlich *adj* vulnerable
Verletzte, r *f(m)* injured person
Verletzung *f* injury; (*Verstoß*) violation, infringement
verleumden [fɛrˈlɔʏmdən] *vt* to slander; (*schriftlich*) to libel
Verleumdung *f* slander; libel
verlieben *vr*: **sich ~ (in** *+akk***)** to fall in love (with)
verliebt [fɛrˈliːpt] *adj* in love; **Verliebtheit** *f* being in love
verlieren [fɛrˈliːrən] *unreg vt, vi* to lose ▷*vr* to get lost; (*verschwinden*) to disappear; **das/er hat hier nichts verloren** (*umg*) that/he has no business to be here
Verlierer, in (**-s, -**) *m(f)* loser
verloben [fɛrˈloːbən] *vr*: **sich ~ (mit)** to get engaged (to); **verlobt sein** to be engaged
Verlobte, r [fɛrˈloːptə(r)] *f(m)*: **mein ~r** my fiancé; **meine ~** my fiancée
Verlobung *f* engagement
verlocken [fɛrˈlɔkən] *vt* to entice, lure
verlockend *adj* (*Angebot, Idee*) tempting

Verlockung *f* temptation, attraction
verlogen [fɛr'lo:gən] *adj* untruthful; (*Komplimente, Versprechungen*) false; (*Moral, Gesellschaft*) hypocritical; **Verlogenheit** *f* untruthfulness
verlor *etc* [fɛr'lo:r] *vb siehe* **verlieren**
verloren *pp von* **verlieren** ▷ *adj* lost; (*Eier*) poached; **der ~e Sohn** the prodigal son; **auf ~em Posten kämpfen** *od* **stehen** to be fighting a losing battle; **etw ~ geben** to give sth up for lost; **~ gehen** to get lost; **an ihm ist ein Sänger ~ gegangen** he would have made a (good) singer
verlöschen [fɛr'lœʃən] *vi* (*Hilfsverb sein*) to go out; (*Inschrift, Farbe, Erinnerung*) to fade
verlosen [fɛr'lo:zən] *vt* to raffle (off), draw lots for
Verlosung *f* raffle, lottery
Verlust [fɛr'lʊst] (**-(e)s, -e**) *m* loss; (*Mil*) casualty; **mit ~ verkaufen** to sell at a loss
vermachen [fɛr'maxən] *vt* to bequeath, leave
Vermächtnis [fɛr'mɛçtnɪs] (**-ses, -se**) *nt* legacy
Vermählung *f* wedding, marriage
vermasseln [fɛr'masəln] (*umg*) *vt* to mess up
vermehren [fɛr'me:rən] *vt, vr* to multiply; (*Menge*) to increase
Vermehrung *f* multiplying; increase
vermeiden [fɛr'maɪdən] *unreg vt* to avoid
vermeintlich [fɛr'maɪntlɪç] *adj* supposed
Vermerk [fɛr'mɛrk] (**-(e)s, -e**) *m* note; (*in Ausweis*) endorsement
vermerken *vt* to note
vermessen [fɛr'mɛsən] *unreg vt* to survey ▷ *vr* (*falsch messen*) to measure incorrectly ▷ *adj* presumptuous, bold; **Vermessenheit** *f* presumptuousness
Vermessung *f* survey(ing)
vermieten [fɛr'mi:tən] *vt* to let (*Brit*), rent (out); (*Auto*) to hire out, rent
Vermieter, in (**-s, -**) *m(f)* landlord, landlady
Vermietung *f* letting, renting (out); (*von Autos*) hiring (out), rental
vermindern [fɛr'mɪndərn] *vt, vr* to lessen, decrease
Verminderung *f* reduction
vermischen [fɛr'mɪʃən] *vt, vr* to mix; (*Teesorten etc*) to blend; **vermischte Schriften** miscellaneous writings
vermissen [fɛr'mɪsən] *vt* to miss; **vermisst sein, als vermisst gemeldet sein** to be reported missing; **wir haben dich bei der Party vermisst** we didn't see you at the party
Vermisste, r *f(m)* missing person
vermitteln [fɛr'mɪtəln] *vi* to mediate ▷ *vt* to arrange; (*Gespräch*) to connect; (*Stelle*) to find; (*Gefühl, Bild, Idee etc*) to convey; (*Wissen*) to impart; **~de Worte** conciliatory words; **jdm etw ~** to help sb to obtain sth; (*Stelle*) to find sth for sb
Vermittler, in [fɛr'mɪtlər(ɪn)] (**-s, -**) *m(f)* (*Comm*) agent; (*Schlichter*) mediator
Vermittlung *f* procurement; (*Stellenvermittlung*) agency; (*Tel*) exchange; (*Schlichtung*) mediation; **Vermögen** (**-s, -**) *nt* wealth; (*Fähigkeit*) ability; **mein ganzes Vermögen besteht aus ...** my entire assets consist of ...; **ein Vermögen kosten** to cost a fortune
vermögend *adj* wealthy
vermummen [fɛr'mʊmən] *vr* to wrap up (warm); (*sich verkleiden*) to disguise
vermuten [fɛr'mu:tən] *vt* to suppose; (*argwöhnen*) to suspect
vermutlich *adj* supposed, presumed ▷ *adv* probably
Vermutung *f* supposition; suspicion; **die ~ liegt nahe, dass ...** there are grounds for assuming that ...
vernachlässigen [fɛr'na:xlɛsɪgən] *vt* to neglect ▷ *vr* to neglect o.s. *od* one's appearance
Vernachlässigung *f* neglect
vernehmen [fɛr'ne:mən] *unreg vt* to hear, perceive; (*erfahren*) to learn; (*Jur*) to (cross-)examine; (*Polizei*) to question
vernehmlich *adj* audible
Vernehmung *f* (cross-)examination
verneigen [fɛr'naɪgən] *vr* to bow
verneinen [fɛr'naɪnən] *vt* (*Frage*) to answer in the negative; (*ablehnen*) to deny; (*Gram*) to negate
verneinend *adj* negative
Verneinung *f* negation
vernichten [fɛr'nɪçtən] *vt* to destroy, annihilate
vernichtend *adj* (*fig*) crushing; (*Blick*) withering; (*Kritik*) scathing
Vernichtung *f* destruction, annihilation
verniedlichen [fɛr'ni:tlɪçən] *vt* to play down
Vernunft [fɛr'nʊnft] (**-**) *f* reason; **~ annehmen** to see reason
vernünftig [fɛr'nʏnftɪç] *adj* sensible, reasonable
veröden [fɛr'|ø:dən] *vi* to become desolate ▷ *vt* (*Med*) to remove
veröffentlichen [fɛr'|œfəntlɪçən] *vt* to publish
Veröffentlichung *f* publication
verordnen [fɛr'|ɔrdnən] *vt* (*Med*) to prescribe
Verordnung *f* order, decree; (*Med*) prescription
verpachten [fɛr'paxtən] *vt* to lease (out)
verpacken [fɛr'pakən] *vt* to pack; (*verbrauchergerecht*) to package; (*einwickeln*) to wrap
Verpackung *f* packing; packaging; wrapping
verpassen [fɛr'pasən] *vt* to miss; **jdm eine Ohrfeige ~** (*umg*) to give sb a clip round the ear
verpesten [fɛr'pɛstən] *vt* to pollute
verpflegen [fɛr'pfle:gən] *vt* to feed, cater for (*Brit*)
Verpflegung *f* catering; (*Kost*) food; (*in Hotel*) board

verpflichten [fɛr'pflıçtən] *vt* to oblige, bind; (*anstellen*) to engage ▹ *vr* to undertake; (*Mil*) to sign on ▹ *vi* to carry obligations; **jdm verpflichtet sein** to be under an obligation to sb; **sich zu etw ~** to commit o.s. to doing sth; **jdm zu Dank verpflichtet sein** to be obliged to sb

Verpflichtung *f* obligation; (*Aufgabe*) duty

verpfuschen [fɛr'pfʊʃən] (*umg*) *vt* to bungle, make a mess of

verplempern [fɛr'plɛmpərn] (*umg*) *vt* to waste

verpönt [fɛr'pø:nt] *adj*: **~ (bei)** frowned upon (by)

verprügeln [fɛr'pry:gəln] (*umg*) *vt* to beat up

Verputz [fɛr'pʊts] *m* plaster; (*Rauputz*) roughcast: **verputzen** *vt* to plaster; (*umg: Essen*) to put away

verquollen [fɛr'kvɔlən] *adj* swollen; (*Holz*) warped

Verrat [fɛr'ra:t] **(-(e)s)** *m* treachery; (*Pol*) treason; **~ an jdm üben** to betray sb

verraten *unreg vt* to betray; (*fig: erkennen lassen*) to show; (*Geheimnis*) to divulge ▹ *vr* to give o.s. away

Verräter, in [fɛr'rɛ:tər(ın)] **(-s, -)** *m(f)* traitor, traitress; **verräterisch** *adj* treacherous

verrechnen [fɛr'rɛçnən] *vt*: **~ mit** to set off against ▹ *vr* to miscalculate

Verrechnungsscheck *m* crossed cheque (*Brit*)

verregnet [fɛr're:gnət] *adj* rainy, spoilt by rain

verreisen [fɛr'raızən] *vi* to go away (on a journey); **er ist geschäftlich verreist** he's away on business

verreißen [fɛr'raısən] *unreg vt* to pull to pieces

verrenken [fɛr'rɛŋkən] *vt* to contort; (*Med*) to dislocate; **sich** *dat* **den Knöchel ~** to sprain one's ankle

verrichten [fɛr'rıçtən] *vt* (*Arbeit*) to do, perform

verringern [fɛr'rıŋərn] *vt* to reduce ▹ *vr* to decrease

verrinnen [fɛr'rınən] *unreg vi* to run out *od* away; (*Zeit*) to elapse

verrosten [fɛr'rɔstən] *vi* to rust

verrotten [fɛr'rɔtən] *vi* to rot

verrücken [fɛr'rʏkən] *vt* to move, shift

verrückt *adj* crazy, mad; **Verrückte, r** *f(m)* lunatic; **Verrücktheit** *f* madness, lunacy

Verruf [fɛr'ru:f] *m*: **in ~ geraten/bringen** to fall/bring into disrepute

verrufen *adj* disreputable

Vers [fɛrs] **(-es, -e)** *m* verse

versagen [fɛr'za:gən] *vt*: **jdm/sich etw ~** to deny sb/o.s. sth ▹ *vi* to fail

Versager (-s, -) *m* failure

versalzen [fɛr'zaltsən] *vt* to put too much salt in; (*fig*) to spoil

versammeln [fɛr'zaməln] *vt, vr* to assemble, gather

Versammlung *f* meeting, gathering

Versand [fɛr'zant] **(-(e)s)** *m* dispatch; (*Versandabteilung*) dispatch department; **Versandhaus** *nt* mail-order firm

versäumen [fɛr'zɔʏmən] *vt* to miss; (*Pflicht*) to neglect; (*Zeit*) to lose

Versäumnis (-ses, -se) *nt* neglect; (*Unterlassung*) omission

verschaffen [fɛr'ʃafən] *vt*: **jdm/sich etw ~** to get *od* procure sth for sb/o.s.

verschämt [fɛr'ʃɛ:mt] *adj* bashful

verschandeln [fɛr'ʃandəln] (*umg*) *vt* to spoil

verschärfen [fɛr'ʃɛrfən] *vt* to intensify; (*Lage*) to aggravate; (*strenger machen: Kontrollen, Gesetze*) to tighten up ▹ *vr* to intensify; to become aggravated; to become tighter

verschätzen [fɛr'ʃɛtsən] *vr* to miscalculate

verschenken [fɛr'ʃɛŋkən] *vt* to give away

verscherzen [fɛr'ʃɛrtsən] *vt*: **sich** *dat* **etw ~** to lose sth, throw sth away

verscheuchen [fɛr'ʃɔʏçən] *vt* to frighten away

verschicken [fɛr'ʃıkən] *vt* to send off; (*Sträfling*) to transport

verschieben [fɛr'ʃi:bən] *unreg vt* to shift; (*Eisenb*) to shunt; (*Termin*) to postpone; (*umg: Waren, Devisen*) to traffic in

verschieden [fɛr'ʃi:dən] *adj* different; **das ist ganz ~** (*wird verschieden gehandhabt*) that varies, that just depends; **sie sind ~ groß** they are of different sizes; **Verschiedene** *pron pl* various people; various things *pl*; **Verschiedenes** *pron* various things *pl*; **etwas Verschiedenes** something different; **Verschiedenheit** *f* difference

verschiedentlich *adv* several times

verschimmeln [fɛr'ʃıməln] *vi* (*Nahrungsmittel*) to go mouldy (*Brit*) *od* moldy (*US*); (*Leder, Papier etc*) to become mildewed

verschlafen [fɛr'ʃla:fən] *unreg vt* to sleep through; (*fig: versäumen*) to miss ▹ *vi, vr* to oversleep ▹ *adj* sleepy

Verschlag [fɛr'ʃla:k] *m* shed

verschlagen [fɛr'ʃla:gən] *unreg vt* to board up; (*Tennis*) to hit out of play; (*Buchseite*) to lose ▹ *adj* cunning; **jdm den Atem ~** to take sb's breath away; **an einen Ort ~ werden** to wind up in a place

verschlechtern [fɛr'ʃlɛçtərn] *vt* to make worse ▹ *vr* to deteriorate, get worse; (*gehaltlich*) to take a lower-paid job

Verschlechterung *f* deterioration

Verschleiß [fɛr'ʃlaıs] **(-es, -e)** *m* wear and tear

verschleißen *unreg vt, vi, vr* to wear out

verschleppen [fɛr'ʃlɛpən] *vt* to carry off, abduct; (*zeitlich*) to drag out, delay; (*verbreiten: Seuche*) to spread

verschleudern [fɛr'ʃlɔʏdərn] *vt* to squander; (*Comm*) to sell dirt-cheap

verschließbar *adj* lockable

verschließen [fɛr'ʃli:sən] *unreg vt* to lock ▹ *vr*: **sich einer Sache** *dat* **~** to close one's mind to sth

verschlimmern [fɛr'ʃlımərn] *vt* to make worse, aggravate ▹ *vr* to get worse,

deteriorate
Verschlimmerung *f* deterioration
verschlingen [fɛrˈʃlɪŋən] *unreg vt* to devour, swallow up; (*Fäden*) to twist
verschliss *etc* [fɛrˈʃlɪs] *vb siehe* **verschleißen**
verschlissen [fɛrˈʃlɪsən] *pp von* **verschleißen** ▷ *adj* worn(-out)
verschlossen [fɛrˈʃlɔsən] *adj* locked; (*fig*) reserved; (*schweigsam*) tight-lipped; **Verschlossenheit** *f* reserve
verschlucken [fɛrˈʃlʊkən] *vt* to swallow ▷ *vr* to choke
Verschluss [fɛrˈʃlʊs] *m* lock; (*von Kleid etc*) fastener; (*Phot*) shutter; (*Stöpsel*) plug; **unter ~ halten** to keep under lock and key
verschlüsseln [fɛrˈʃlʏsəln] *vt* to encode
verschmähen [fɛrˈʃmɛːən] *vt* to scorn
verschmerzen [fɛrˈʃmɛrtsən] *vt* to get over
verschmitzt [fɛrˈʃmɪtst] *adj* mischievous
verschmutzen [fɛrˈʃmʊtsən] *vt* to soil; (*Umwelt*) to pollute
verschneit [fɛrˈʃnaɪt] *adj* covered in snow, snowed up
verschnüren [fɛrˈʃnyːrən] *vt* to tie up
verschollen [fɛrˈʃɔlən] *adj* lost, missing
verschonen [fɛrˈʃoːnən] *vt*: **jdn mit etw ~** to spare sb sth; **von etw verschont bleiben** to escape sth
verschönern [fɛrˈʃøːnərn] *vt* to decorate; (*verbessern*) to improve
verschreiben [fɛrˈʃraɪbən] *unreg vt* (*Papier*) to use up; (*Med*) to prescribe ▷ *vr* to make a mistake (in writing); **sich einer Sache** *dat* **~** to devote o.s. to sth
verschroben [fɛrˈʃroːbən] *adj* eccentric, odd
verschrotten [fɛrˈʃrɔtən] *vt* to scrap
verschüchtert [fɛrˈʃʏçtərt] *adj* subdued, intimidated
verschulden [fɛrˈʃʊldən] *vt* to be guilty of ▷ *vi* (*in Schulden geraten*) to get into debt; **Verschulden** (**-s**) *nt* fault
verschuldet *adj* in debt
Verschuldung *f* debts *pl*
verschütten [fɛrˈʃʏtən] *vt* to spill; (*zuschütten*) to fill; (*unter Trümmer*) to bury
verschweigen [fɛrˈʃvaɪgən] *unreg vt* to keep secret; **jdm etw ~** to keep sth from sb
verschwenden [fɛrˈʃvɛndən] *vt* to squander
Verschwender, in (**-s, -**) *m(f)* spendthrift; **verschwenderisch** *adj* wasteful; (*Leben*) extravagant
Verschwendung *f* waste
verschwiegen [fɛrˈʃviːgən] *adj* discreet; (*Ort*) secluded; **Verschwiegenheit** *f* discretion; seclusion; **zur Verschwiegenheit verpflichtet** bound to secrecy
verschwimmen [fɛrˈʃvɪmən] *unreg vi* to grow hazy, become blurred
verschwinden [fɛrˈʃvɪndən] *unreg vi* to disappear, vanish; **verschwinde!** clear off! (*umg*); **Verschwinden** (**-s**) *nt* disappearance
verschwitzen [fɛrˈʃvɪtsən] *vt* to stain with sweat; (*umg*) to forget
verschwitzt *adj* (*Kleidung*) sweat-stained; (*Mensch*) sweaty
verschwommen [fɛrˈʃvɔmən] *adj* hazy, vague
verschwören [fɛrˈʃvøːrən] *unreg vr* to conspire, plot
Verschwörer, in (**-s, -**) *m(f)* conspirator
Verschwörung *f* conspiracy, plot
versehen [fɛrˈzeːən] *unreg vt* to supply, provide; (*Pflicht*) to carry out; (*Amt*) to fill; (*Haushalt*) to keep ▷ *vr* (*fig*) to make a mistake; **ehe er (es) sich ~ hatte ...** before he knew it ...; **Versehen** (**-s, -**) *nt* oversight; **aus Versehen** by mistake
versehentlich *adv* by mistake
Versehrte, r [fɛrˈzeːrtə(r)] *f(m)* disabled person
versenden [fɛrˈzɛndən] *unreg vt* to send; (*Comm*) to forward
versenken [fɛrˈzɛŋkən] *vt* to sink ▷ *vr*: **sich ~ in** *+akk* to become engrossed in
versessen [fɛrˈzɛsən] *adj*: **~ auf** *+akk* mad about, hellbent on
versetzen [fɛrˈzɛtsən] *vt* to transfer; (*verpfänden*) to pawn; (*umg: vergeblich warten lassen*) to stand up; (*nicht geradlinig anordnen*) to stagger; (*Sch: in höhere Klasse*) to move up ▷ *vr*: **sich in jdn** *od* **in jds Lage ~** to put o.s. in sb's place; **jdm einen Tritt/Schlag ~** to kick/hit sb; **etw mit etw ~** to mix sth with sth; **jdm einen Stich ~** (*fig*) to cut sb to the quick, wound sb (deeply); **jdn in gute Laune ~** to put sb in a good mood
Versetzung *f* transfer; **seine ~ ist gefährdet** (*Sch*) he's in danger of having to repeat a year
verseuchen [fɛrˈzɔʏçən] *vt* to contaminate
versichern [fɛrˈzɪçərn] *vt* to assure; (*mit Geld*) to insure ▷ *vr*: **sich ~** *+gen* to make sure of
Versicherung *f* assurance; insurance
Versicherungs- *zW*: **Versicherungsnehmer** (**-s, -**) *m* (*form*) insured, policy holder; **Versicherungspolice** *f* insurance policy
versinken [fɛrˈzɪŋkən] *unreg vi* to sink; **ich hätte im Boden** *od* **vor Scham ~ mögen** I wished the ground would swallow me up
Version [vɛrziˈoːn] *f* version
versöhnen [fɛrˈzøːnən] *vt* to reconcile ▷ *vr* to become reconciled
Versöhnung *f* reconciliation
versorgen [fɛrˈzɔrgən] *vt* to provide, supply; (*Familie etc*) to look after ▷ *vr* to look after o.s.
Versorgung *f* provision; (*Unterhalt*) maintenance; (*Altersversorgung etc*) benefit, assistance
verspäten [fɛrˈʃpɛːtən] *vr* to be late
verspätet *adj* late
Verspätung *f* delay; **~ haben** to be late; **mit zwanzig Minuten ~** twenty minutes late
versperren [fɛrˈʃpɛrən] *vt* to bar, obstruct
verspotten [fɛrˈʃpɔtən] *vt* to ridicule, scoff at
versprechen [fɛrˈʃprɛçən] *unreg vt* to promise ▷ *vr* (*etwas Nichtgemeintes sagen*) to make a slip of the tongue; **sich** *dat* **etw von etw ~** to expect sth from sth; **Versprechen** (**-s, -**) *nt*

promise
verstaatlichen [fɛrˈʃtaːtlɪçən] *vt* to nationalize
Verstand [fɛrˈʃtant] *m* intelligence; (*Intellekt*) mind; (*Fähigkeit zu denken*) reason; **den ~ verlieren** to go out of one's mind; **über jds ~** *akk* **gehen** to be beyond sb
verständig [fɛrˈʃtɛndɪç] *adj* sensible
verständigen [fɛrˈʃtɛndɪgən] *vt* to inform ▷*vr* to communicate; (*sich einigen*) to come to an understanding
Verständigung *f* communication; (*Benachrichtigung*) informing; (*Einigung*) agreement
verständlich [fɛrˈʃtɛntlɪç] *adj* understandable, comprehensible; (*hörbar*) audible; **sich ~ machen** to make o.s. understood; (*sich klar ausdrücken*) to make o.s. clear
Verständlichkeit *f* clarity, intelligibility
Verständnis (**-ses, -se**) *nt* understanding; **für etw kein ~ haben** to have no understanding *od* sympathy for sth; (*für Kunst etc*) to have no appreciation of sth; **verständnislos** *adj* uncomprehending; **verständnisvoll** *adj* understanding, sympathetic
verstärken [fɛrˈʃtɛrkən] *vt* to strengthen; (*Ton*) to amplify; (*erhöhen*) to intensify ▷*vr* to intensify
Verstärker (**-s, -**) *m* amplifier
Verstärkung *f* strengthening; (*Hilfe*) reinforcements *pl*; (*von Ton*) amplification
verstauchen [fɛrˈʃtaʊxən] *vt* to sprain
verstauen [fɛrˈʃtaʊən] *vt* to stow away
Versteck [fɛrˈʃtɛk] (**-(e)s, -e**) *nt* hiding (place)
verstecken *vt, vr* to hide
versteckt *adj* hidden; (*Tür*) concealed; (*fig: Lächeln, Blick*) furtive; (*Andeutung*) veiled
verstehen [fɛrˈʃteːən] *unreg vt, vi* to understand; (*können, beherrschen*) to know ▷*vr* (*auskommen*) to get on; **das ist nicht wörtlich zu ~** that isn't to be taken literally; **das versteht sich von selbst** that goes without saying; **die Preise ~ sich einschließlich Lieferung** prices are inclusive of delivery; **sich auf etw** *akk* **~** to be an expert at sth
versteigern [fɛrˈʃtaɪgərn] *vt* to auction
Versteigerung *f* auction
verstellbar *adj* adjustable, variable
verstellen [fɛrˈʃtɛlən] *vt* to move, shift; (*Uhr*) to adjust; (*versperren*) to block; (*fig*) to disguise ▷*vr* to pretend, put on an act
verstiegen [fɛrˈʃtiːgən] *adj* exaggerated
verstohlen [fɛrˈʃtoːlən] *adj* stealthy
verstopfen [fɛrˈʃtɔpfən] *vt* to block, stop up; (*Med*) to constipate
Verstopfung *f* obstruction; (*Med*) constipation
verstorben [fɛrˈʃtɔrbən] *adj* deceased, late
verstört [fɛrˈʃtøːrt] *adj* (*Mensch*) distraught
Verstoß [fɛrˈʃtoːs] *m*: **~ (gegen)** infringement (of), violation (of)
verstoßen *unreg vt* to disown, reject ▷*vi*: **~ gegen** to offend against
verstreichen [fɛrˈʃtraɪçən] *unreg vt* to spread ▷*vi* to elapse; (*Zeit*) to pass (by); (*Frist*) to expire
verstreuen [fɛrˈʃtrɔʏən] *vt* to scatter (about)
verstümmeln [fɛrˈʃtʏməln] *vt* to maim, mutilate (*auch fig*)
verstummen [fɛrˈʃtʊmən] *vi* to go silent; (*Lärm*) to die away
Versuch [fɛrˈzuːx] (**-(e)s, -e**) *m* attempt; (*Chem etc*) experiment; **das käme auf einen ~ an** we'll have to have a try
versuchen *vt* to try; (*verlocken*) to tempt ▷*vr*: **sich an etw** *dat* **~** to try one's hand at sth
Versuchs- *zW*: **Versuchskaninchen** *nt* guinea pig; **versuchsweise** *adv* tentatively
Versuchung *f* temptation
versunken [fɛrˈzʊŋkən] *adj* sunken; **~ sein in** *+akk* to be absorbed *od* engrossed in
Vertagung *f* adjournment
vertauschen [fɛrˈtaʊʃən] *vt* to exchange; (*versehentlich*) to mix up; **vertauschte Rollen** reversed roles
verteidigen [fɛrˈtaɪdɪgən] *vt* to defend ▷*vr* to defend o.s.; (*vor Gericht*) to conduct one's own defence (*Brit*) *od* defense (*US*)
Verteidiger, in (**-s, -**) *m(f)* defender; (*Anwalt*) defence (*Brit*) *od* defense (*US*) lawyer
Verteidigung *f* defence (*Brit*), defense (*US*)
verteilen [fɛrˈtaɪlən] *vt* to distribute; (*Rollen*) to assign; (*Salbe*) to spread
Verteilung *f* distribution
vertiefen [fɛrˈtiːfən] *vt* to deepen; (*Sch*) to consolidate ▷*vr*: **sich in etw** *akk* **~** to become engrossed *od* absorbed in sth
Vertiefung *f* depression
vertikal [vɛrtiˈkaːl] *adj* vertical
vertilgen [fɛrˈtɪlgən] *vt* to exterminate; (*umg*) to eat up, consume
vertippen [fɛrˈtɪpən] *vr* to make a typing mistake
vertonen [fɛrˈtoːnən] *vt* to set to music; (*Film etc*) to add a soundtrack to
Vertrag [fɛrˈtraːk] (**-(e)s, ¨-e**) *m* contract, agreement; (*Pol*) treaty
vertragen [fɛrˈtraːgən] *unreg vt* to tolerate, stand ▷*vr* to get along; (*sich aussöhnen*) to become reconciled; **viel ~ können** (*umg: Alkohol*) to be able to hold one's drink; **sich mit etw ~** (*Nahrungsmittel, Farbe*) to go with sth; (*Aussage, Verhalten*) to be consistent with sth
vertraglich *adj* contractual
verträglich [fɛrˈtrɛːklɪç] *adj* good-natured; (*Speisen*) easily digested; (*Med*) easily tolerated; **Verträglichkeit** *f* good nature; digestibility
Vertrags- *zW*: **Vertragsbruch** *m* breach of contract; **Vertragspartner** *m* party to a contract; **Vertragsspieler** *m* (*Sport*) player

under contract; **vertragswidrig** *adj, adv* contrary to contract
vertrauen [fɛr'traʊən] *vi*: **jdm ~** to trust sb; **~ auf** *+akk* to rely on; **Vertrauen** (**-s**) *nt* confidence; **jdn ins Vertrauen ziehen** to take sb into one's confidence; **Vertrauen zu jdm fassen** to gain confidence in sb
Vertrauens- *zW*: **Vertrauenssache** *f* (*vertrauliche Angelegenheit*) confidential matter; (*Frage des Vertrauens*) question of trust; **vertrauensvoll** *adj* trustful; **vertrauenswürdig** *adj* trustworthy
vertraulich [fɛr'traʊlɪç] *adj* familiar; (*geheim*) confidential
verträumt [fɛr'trɔʏmt] *adj* dreamy; (*Städtchen etc*) sleepy
vertraut [fɛr'traʊt] *adj* familiar; **sich mit dem Gedanken ~ machen, dass ...** to get used to the idea that ...
vertreiben [fɛr'traɪbən] *unreg vt* to drive away; (*aus Land*) to expel; (*Comm*) to sell; (*Zeit*) to pass
vertretbar *adj* justifiable; (*Theorie, Argument*) tenable
vertreten [fɛr'tre:tən] *unreg vt* to represent; (*Ansicht*) to hold, advocate; (*ersetzen*) to replace; (*Kollegen*) to cover for; (*Comm*) to be the agent for; **sich** *dat* **die Beine ~** to stretch one's legs
Vertreter, in (**-s, -**) *m(f)* representative; (*Verfechter*) advocate; (*Comm: Firma*) agent
Vertretung *f* representation; advocacy; **die ~ übernehmen (für)** to stand in (for)
Vertrieb [fɛr'tri:p] (**-(e)s, -e**) *m* marketing; **den ~ für eine Firma haben** to have the (selling) agency for a firm
Vertriebene, r [fɛr'tri:bənə(r)] *f(m)* exile
vertrocknen [fɛr'trɔknən] *vi* to dry up
vertrödeln [fɛr'trø:dəln] (*umg*) *vt* to fritter away
vertrösten [fɛr'trø:stən] *vt* to put off
vertun [fɛr'tu:n] *unreg vt* to waste ▷ *vr* (*umg*) to make a mistake
vertuschen [fɛr'tʊʃən] *vt* to hush *od* cover up
verübeln [fɛr'|y:bəln] *vt*: **jdm etw ~** to be cross *od* offended with sb on account of sth
verüben [fɛr'|y:bən] *vt* to commit
verunglimpfen [fɛr'|ʊnglɪmpfən] *vt* to disparage
verunglücken [fɛr'|ʊnglʏkən] *vi* to have an accident; (*fig: umg: misslingen*) to go wrong; **tödlich ~** to be killed in an accident
verunsichern [fɛr'|ʊnzɪçərn] *vt* to rattle (*fig*)
verunstalten [fɛr'|ʊnʃtaltən] *vt* to disfigure; (*Gebäude etc*) to deface
veruntreuen [fɛr'|ʊntrɔʏən] *vt* to embezzle
verursachen [fɛr'|u:rzaxən] *vt* to cause
verurteilen [fɛr'|u:rtaɪlən] *vt* to condemn; (*zu Strafe*) to sentence; (*für schuldig befinden*): **jdn ~ (für)** to convict sb (of)
Verurteilung *f* condemnation; (*Jur*) sentence; conviction
vervielfachen [fɛr'fi:lfaxən] *vt* to multiply
vervielfältigen [fɛr'fi:lfɛltɪgən] *vt* to duplicate, copy
Vervielfältigung *f* duplication, copying
vervollkommnen [fɛr'fɔlkɔmnən] *vt* to perfect
vervollständigen [fɛr'fɔlʃtɛndɪgən] *vt* to complete
verwackeln [fɛr'vakəln] *vt* (*Foto*) to blur
verwählen [fɛr'vɛ:lən] *vr* (*Tel*) to dial the wrong number
verwahren [fɛr'va:rən] *vt* to keep (safe) ▷ *vr* to protest
verwahrlosen *vi* to become neglected; (*moralisch*) to go to the bad
verwalten [fɛr'valtən] *vt* to manage; (*Behörde*) to administer
Verwalter, in (**-s, -**) *m(f)* administrator; (*Vermögensverwalter*) trustee
Verwaltung *f* management; administration
Verwaltungsbezirk *m* administrative district
verwandeln [fɛr'vandəln] *vt* to change, transform ▷ *vr* to change
Verwandlung *f* change, transformation
verwandt [fɛr'vant] *adj*: **~ (mit)** related (to); **geistig ~ sein** (*fig*) to be kindred spirits
Verwandte, r *f(m)* relative, relation
Verwandtschaft *f* relationship; (*Menschen*) relatives *pl*, relations *pl*; (*fig*) affinity
verwarnen [fɛr'varnən] *vt* to caution
Verwarnung *f* caution
verwechseln [fɛr'vɛksəln] *vt*: **~ mit** to confuse with; **zum V~ ähnlich** as like as two peas
Verwechslung *f* confusion, mixing up; **das muss eine ~ sein** there must be some mistake
verwegen [fɛr've:gən] *adj* daring, bold
Verwehung [fɛr've:ʊŋ] *f* (*Schneeverwehung*) snowdrift; (*Sandverwehung*) sanddrift
verweichlicht *adj* effeminate, soft
verweigern [fɛr'vaɪgərn] *vt*: **jdm etw ~** to refuse sb sth; **den Gehorsam/die Aussage ~** to refuse to obey/testify
Verweigerung *f* refusal
Verweis [fɛr'vaɪs] (**-es, -e**) *m* reprimand, rebuke; (*Hinweis*) reference
verweisen [fɛr'vaɪzən] *unreg vt* to refer; **jdn auf etw** *akk***/an jdn ~** (*hinweisen*) to refer sb to sth/sb; **jdn vom Platz** *od* **des Spielfeldes ~** (*Sport*) to send sb off; **jdn von der Schule ~** to expel sb (from school); **jdn des Landes ~** to deport sb
verwelken [fɛr'vɛlkən] *vi* to fade; (*Blumen*) to wilt
verwenden [fɛr'vɛndən] *unreg vt* to use; (*Mühe, Zeit, Arbeit*) to spend ▷ *vr* to intercede
Verwendung *f* use
verwerfen [fɛr'vɛrfən] *unreg vt* to reject; (*Urteil*) to quash; (*kritisieren: Handlungsweise*) to condemn
verwerflich [fɛr'vɛrflɪç] *adj* reprehensible
verwerten [fɛr've:rtən] *vt* to utilize
Verwertung *f* utilization

verwesen [fɛrˈveːzən] *vi* to decay
verwickeln [fɛrˈvɪkəln] *vt* to tangle (up); (*fig*) to involve ▷ *vr* to get tangled (up); **jdn ~ in** *+akk* to involve sb in, get sb involved in; **sich ~ in** *+akk* to get involved in
verwickelt *adj* involved
verwildern [fɛrˈvɪldərn] *vi* to run wild
verwinden [fɛrˈvɪndən] *unreg vt* to get over
verwirklichen [fɛrˈvɪrklɪçən] *vt* to realize, put into effect
Verwirklichung *f* realization
verwirren [fɛrˈvɪrən] *vt* to tangle (up); (*fig*) to confuse
Verwirrung *f* confusion
verwittern [fɛrˈvɪtərn] *vi* to weather
verwitwet [fɛrˈvɪtvət] *adj* widowed
verwöhnen [fɛrˈvøːnən] *vt* to spoil, pamper
verworfen [fɛrˈvɔrfən] *adj* depraved
verworren [fɛrˈvɔrən] *adj* confused
verwundbar [fɛrˈvʊntbaːr] *adj* vulnerable
verwunden [fɛrˈvʊndən] *vt* to wound
verwunderlich [fɛrˈvʊndərlɪç] *adj* surprising; (*stärker*) astonishing
Verwunderung *f* astonishment
Verwundete, r *f(m)* injured person; **die ~n** the injured; (*Mil*) the wounded
Verwundung *f* wound, injury
verwünschen [fɛrˈvʏnʃən] *vt* to curse
verwüsten [fɛrˈvyːstən] *vt* to devastate
Verwüstung *f* devastation
verzagen [fɛrˈtsaːgən] *vi* to despair
verzählen [fɛrˈtsɛːlən] *vr* to miscount
verzaubern [fɛrˈtsaʊbərn] *vt* (*lit*) to cast a spell on; (*fig: jdn*) to enchant
verzehren [fɛrˈtseːrən] *vt* to consume
verzeichnen [fɛrˈtsaɪçnən] *vt* to list; (*Niederlage, Verlust*) to register
Verzeichnis (**-ses, -se**) *nt* list, catalogue (*Brit*), catalog (*US*); (*in Buch*) index; (*Comput*) directory
verzeihen [fɛrˈtsaɪən] *unreg vt, vi* to forgive; **jdm etw ~** to forgive sb (for) sth; **~ Sie!** excuse me!
verzeihlich *adj* pardonable
Verzeihung *f* forgiveness, pardon; **~!** sorry!, excuse me!; **(jdn) um ~ bitten** to apologize (to sb)
Verzicht [fɛrˈtsɪçt] (**-(e)s, -e**) *m*: **~ (auf** *+akk*) renunciation (of); **verzichten** *vi*: **verzichten auf** *+akk* to forego, give up
verziehen [fɛrˈtsiːən] *unreg vi* (*Hilfsverb sein*) to move ▷ *vt* to put out of shape; (*Kind*) to spoil; (*Pflanzen*) to thin out ▷ *vr* to go out of shape; (*Gesicht*) to contort; (*verschwinden*) to disappear; **verzogen** (*Vermerk*) no longer at this address; **keine Miene ~** not to turn a hair; **das Gesicht ~** to pull a face
verzieren [fɛrˈtsiːrən] *vt* to decorate
Verzierung *f* decoration
verzinsen [fɛrˈtsɪnzən] *vt* to pay interest on
verzögern [fɛrˈtsøːgərn] *vt* to delay
Verzögerung *f* delay
Verzögerungstaktik *f* delaying tactics *pl*
verzollen [fɛrˈtsɔlən] *vt* to pay duty on; **haben Sie etwas zu ~?** have you anything to declare?
verzweifeln [fɛrˈtsvaɪfəln] *vi* to despair
verzweifelt *adj* desperate
Verzweiflung *f* despair
verzweigen [fɛrˈtsvaɪgən] *vr* to branch out
verzwickt [fɛrˈtsvɪkt] (*umg*) *adj* awkward, complicated
Veto [ˈveːto] (**-s, -s**) *nt* veto
Vetter [ˈfɛtər] (**-s, -n**) *m* cousin
vgl. *abk* (= *vergleiche*) cf
VHS (-) *f abk* = **Volkshochschule**
vibrieren [viˈbriːrən] *vi* to vibrate
Video [ˈviːdeo] (**-s, -s**) *nt* video; **Videokamera** *f* video camera; **Videorekorder** *m* video recorder; **Videospiel** *nt* video game
Vieh [fiː] (**-(e)s**) *nt* cattle *pl*; (*Nutztiere*) livestock; (*umg: Tier*) animal; **viehisch** *adj* bestial
viel [fiːl] *adj* a lot of, much ▷ *adv* a lot, much; **in ~em** in many respects; **noch (ein)mal so ~** (*Zeit etc*) as much (time *etc*) again; **einer zu ~** one too many; **~ zu wenig** much too little; **~ beschäftigt** very busy; **~ geprüft** (*hum*) sorely tried; **~ sagend** significant; **~ versprechend** promising; **viele** *pl* a lot of, many; **gleich viele (Angestellte/Anteile** *etc*) the same number (of employees/shares *etc*)
vielerlei *adj* a great variety of
viel- *zW*: **vielfach** *adj, adv* many times; **auf vielfachen Wunsch** at the request of many people; **Vielfalt** (-) *f* variety; **vielfältig** *adj* varied, many-sided
vielleicht [fiˈlaɪçt] *adv* perhaps; (*in Bitten*) by any chance; **du bist ~ ein Idiot!** (*umg*) you really are an idiot!
viel- *zW*: **vielmal, vielmals** *adv* many times; **danke vielmals** many thanks; **ich bitte vielmals um Entschuldigung!** I do apologize!; **vielmehr** *adv* rather, on the contrary; **vielsagend** *adj* significant; **vielseitig** *adj* many-sided; (*Ausbildung*) all-round *attr*; (*Interessen*) varied; (*Mensch, Gerät*) versatile; **vielversprechend** *adj* promising
vier [fiːr] *num* four; **alle ~e von sich strecken** (*umg*) to stretch out; **Viereck** (**-(e)s, -e**) *nt* four-sided figure; (*gleichseitig*) square; **viereckig** *adj* four-sided; square; **vierhundert** *num* four hundred
viert *adj*: **wir gingen zu ~** four of us went
Viertaktmotor *m* four-stroke engine
vierte, r, s [ˈfiːrtə(r, s)] *adj* fourth
Viertel [ˈfɪrtəl] (**-s, -**) *nt* quarter; **ein ~ Leberwurst** a quarter of liver sausage; **Vierteljahr** *nt* three months *pl*, quarter (*Comm, Fin*); **vierteljährlich** *adj* quarterly; **Viertelnote** *f* crotchet (*Brit*), quarter note (*US*); **Viertelstunde** *f* quarter of an hour
vier- *zW*: **vierzehn** [ˈfɪrtseːn] *num* fourteen; **in vierzehn Tagen** in a fortnight (*Brit*), in two weeks (*US*); **vierzehntägig** *adj* fortnightly

vierzig ['fɪrtsɪç] *num* forty
Vietnam [viɛt'nam] (**-s**) *nt* Vietnam
vietnamesisch *adj* Vietnamese
Vikar [vi'ka:r] (**-s, -e**) *m* curate
Villa ['vɪla] (**-, Villen**) *f* villa
Villenviertel *nt* (prosperous) residential area
violett [vio'lɛt] *adj* violet
Violinbogen *m* violin bow
Violine [vio'li:nə] (**-, -n**) *f* violin
Violinschlüssel *m* treble clef
virtuell [vɪrtu'ɛl] *adj* (*Comput*) virtual; **~e Realität** virtual reality
Virus ['vi:rʊs] (**-, Viren**) *m od nt* (*also Comput*) virus
Virusinfektion *f* virus infection
Visier [vi'zi:r] (**-s, -e**) *nt* gunsight; (*am Helm*) visor
Visite [vi'zi:tə] (**-, -n**) *f* (*Med*) visit
Visitenkarte *f* visiting card
visuell [vizu'ɛl] *adj* visual
Visum ['vi:zʊm] (**-s, Visa** *od* **Visen**) *nt* visa
vital [vi'ta:l] *adj* lively, full of life; (*lebenswichtig*) vital
Vitamin [vita'mi:n] (**-s, -e**) *nt* vitamin; **Vitaminmangel** *m* vitamin deficiency
Vogel ['fo:gəl] (**-s, ¨-**) *m* bird; **einen ~ haben** (*umg*) to have bats in the belfry; **den ~ abschießen** (*umg*) to surpass everyone (*ironisch*); **Vogelbauer** *nt* birdcage; **Vogelscheuche** *f* scarecrow
Vogesen [vo'ge:zən] *pl* Vosges *pl*
Vokabel [vo'ka:bəl] (**-, -n**) *f* word
Vokabular [vokabu'la:r] (**-s, -e**) *nt* vocabulary
Vokal [vo'ka:l] (**-s, -e**) *m* vowel
Volk [fɔlk] (**-(e)s, ¨-er**) *nt* people; (*Nation*) nation; **etw unters ~ bringen** (*Nachricht*) to spread sth
Völker- *zW*: **Völkerbund** *m* League of Nations; **Völkerrecht** *nt* international law; **völkerrechtlich** *adj* according to international law; **Völkerverständigung** *f* international understanding; **Völkerwanderung** *f* migration
Volks- *zW*: **Volksabstimmung** *f* referendum; **Volksbegehren** *nt* petition for a referendum; **volkseigen** *adj* (*DDR*) nationally-owned; **Volksfest** *nt* popular festival; (*Jahrmarkt*) fair
Volkshochschule *f* adult education classes *pl*
Volks- *zW*: **Volkslied** *nt* folk song; **Volksmund** *m* vernacular; **Volksrepublik** *f* people's republic; **Volkstanz** *m* folk dance; **volkstümlich** *adj* popular; **Volkswirtschaft** *f* national economy; (*Fach*) economics *sing*, political economy; **Volkszählung** *f* (national) census
voll [fɔl] *adj* full ▷ *adv* fully; (*Tafel*) to cover (with writing); **jdn für ~ nehmen** (*umg*) to take sb seriously; **aus dem V~en schöpfen** to draw on unlimited resources; **in ~er Größe** (*Bild*) life-size(d); (*bei plötzlicher Erscheinung etc*) large as life; **~ sein** (*umg*: *satt*) to be full (up); (*: betrunken*) to be plastered; **~ und ganz** completely; *siehe auch* **vollmachen; vollschreiben; volltanken**
vollauf [fɔl'|aʊf] *adv* amply; **~ zu tun haben** to have quite enough to do
voll- *zW*: **Vollbart** *m* full beard; **Vollbeschäftigung** *f* full employment; **Vollbremsung** *f* emergency stop; **vollbringen** *unreg vt untr* to accomplish; **vollenden** *vt untr* to finish, complete; **vollendet** *adj* (*vollkommen*) perfect; (*Tänzer etc*) accomplished; **vollends** *adv* completely; **Vollendung** *f* completion
voller *adj* fuller; **~ Flecken/Ideen** full of stains/ideas
Volleyball ['vɔlibal] (**-(e)s**) *m* volleyball
Vollgas *nt*: **mit** ~ at full throttle; **~ geben** to step on it
völlig ['fœlɪç] *adj* complete ▷ *adv* completely
voll- *zW*: **volljährig** *adj* of age; **Vollkaskoversicherung** *f* fully comprehensive insurance; **vollkommen** *adj* perfect; (*völlig*) complete, absolute; **Vollkommenheit** *f* perfection; **Vollkornbrot** *nt* wholemeal (*Brit*) *od* whole-wheat (*US*) bread; **vollmachen** *vt* to fill (up); **Vollmacht** *f* authority, power of attorney; **Vollmilch** *f* full-cream milk; **Vollmond** *m* full moon; **Vollpension** *f* full board; **vollschlank** *adj* plump, stout; **vollständig** *adj* complete; **vollstrecken** *vt untr* to execute; **volltanken** *vt, vi* to fill up; **Volltreffer** *m* (*lit, fig*) bull's-eye; **Vollversammlung** *f* general meeting; **vollzählig** *adj* complete; (*anwesend*) in full number; **vollziehen** *unreg vt untr* to carry out ▷ *vr untr* to happen; **Vollzug** *m* execution
Volt [vɔlt] (**-** *od* **-(e)s, -**) *nt* volt
Volumen [vo'lu:mən] (**-s, -** *od* **Volumina**) *nt* volume
vom [fɔm] = **von dem**
von [fɔn] *präp +dat* **1** (*Ausgangspunkt*) from; **von ... bis** from ... to; **von morgens bis abends** from morning till night; **von ... nach ...** from ... to ...; **von ... an** from ...; **von ... aus** from ...; **von dort aus** from there; **etw von sich aus tun** to do sth of one's own accord; **von mir aus** (*umg*) if you like, I don't mind; **von wo/wann ...?** where/when ... from?
2 (*Ursache, im Passiv*) by; **ein Gedicht von Schiller** a poem by Schiller; **von etw müde** tired from sth
3 (*als Genitiv*) of; **ein Freund von mir** a friend of mine; **nett von dir** nice of you; **jeweils zwei von zehn** two out of every ten
4 (*über*) about; **er erzählte vom Urlaub** he talked about his holiday
5: von wegen! (*umg*) no way!
voneinander *adv* from each other
vor [fo:r] *präp +dat* **1** (*räumlich*) in front of
2 (*zeitlich, Reihenfolge*) before; **ich war vor ihm da** I was there before him; **X kommt vor Y** X comes before Y; **vor zwei Tagen** two days ago; **5 (Minuten) vor 4** 5 (minutes) to 4; **vor Kurzem** a little while ago

3 (*Ursache*) with; **vor Wut/Liebe** with rage/love; **vor Hunger sterben** to die of hunger; **vor lauter Arbeit** because of work
4: vor allem, vor allen Dingen above all
▷ *präp +akk* (*räumlich*) in front of; **vor sich hin summen** to hum to oneself
▷ *adv*: **vor und zurück** backwards and forwards

Vorabend *m* evening before, eve

voran [fo'ran] *adv* before, ahead; **vorangehen** *unreg vi* to go ahead; **einer Sache** *dat* **vorangehen** to precede sth; **vorangehend** *adj* previous; **vorankommen** *unreg vi* to make progress, come along

Voranschlag ['fo:r|anʃla:k] *m* estimate

Vorarbeiter ['fo:r|arbaɪtər] *m* foreman

voraus [fo'raʊs] *adv* ahead; (*zeitlich*) in advance; **jdm ~ sein** to be ahead of sb; **im V~** in advance; **vorausgehen** *unreg vi* to go (on) ahead; (*fig*) to precede; **voraushaben** *unreg vt*: **jdm etw voraushaben** to have the edge on sb in sth; **Voraussage** *f* prediction; **voraussagen** *vt* to predict; **voraussehen** *unreg vt* to foresee; **voraussetzen** *vt* to assume; (*sicher annehmen*) to take for granted; (*erfordern: Kenntnisse, Geduld*) to require, demand; **vorausgesetzt, dass ...** provided that ...; **Voraussetzung** *f* requirement, prerequisite; **unter der Voraussetzung, dass ...** on condition that ...; **Voraussicht** *f* foresight; **aller Voraussicht nach** in all probability; **in der Voraussicht, dass ...** anticipating that ...; **voraussichtlich** *adv* probably

vorbauen ['fo:rbaʊən] *vt* to build up in front
▷ *vi +dat* to take precautions (against)

Vorbehalt ['fo:rbəhalt] *m* reservation, proviso; **unter dem ~, dass ...** with the reservation that ...

vorbehalten *unreg vt*: **sich/jdm etw ~** to reserve sth (for o.s.)/for sb; **alle Rechte ~** all rights reserved

vorbei [fɔr'baɪ] *adv* by, past; **aus und ~** over and done with; **damit ist es nun ~** that's all over now; **vorbeigehen** *unreg vi* to pass by, go past; **vorbeikommen** *unreg vi*: **bei jdm vorbeikommen** to drop *od* call in on sb

vorbelastet ['fo:rbəlastət] *adj* (*fig*) handicapped (*Brit*), handicaped (*US*)

vorbereiten ['fo:rbəraɪtən] *vt* to prepare

Vorbereitung *f* preparation

vorbestellen ['fo:rbəʃtɛlən] *vt* to book (in advance), reserve

vorbestraft ['fo:rbəʃtraft] *adj* previously convicted, with a record

vorbeugen ['fo:rbɔʏgən] *vt, vr* to lean forward
▷ *vi +dat* to prevent

vorbeugend *adj* preventive

Vorbeugung *f* prevention; **zur ~ gegen** for the prevention of

Vorbild ['fo:rbɪlt] *nt* model; **sich** *dat* **jdn zum ~ nehmen** to model o.s. on sb; **vorbildlich** *adj* model, ideal

vorbringen ['fo:rbrɪŋən] *unreg vt* to voice; (*Meinung etc*) to advance, state; (*umg: nach vorne*) to bring to the front

Vorder- *zW*: **Vorderachse** *f* front axle; **Vorderasien** *nt* Near East

vordere, r, s *adj* front

Vorder- *zW*: **Vordergrund** *m* foreground; **im Vordergrund stehen** (*fig*) to be to the fore; **Vordermann** (**-(e)s**, *pl* **-männer**) *m* man in front; **jdn auf Vordermann bringen** (*umg*) to get sb to shape up; **Vorderseite** *f* front (side)

vorderste, r, s *adj* front

vorehelich ['fo:r|e:əlɪç] *adj* premarital

voreilig ['fo:r|aɪlɪç] *adj* hasty, rash; **~e Schlüsse ziehen** to jump to conclusions

voreinander [fo:r|aɪ'nandər] *adv* (*räumlich*) in front of each other; (*einander gegenüber*) face to face

voreingenommen ['fo:r|aɪngənɔmən] *adj* bias(s)ed; **Voreingenommenheit** *f* bias

vorenthalten ['fo:r|ɛnthaltən] *unreg vt*: **jdm etw ~** to withhold sth from sb

vorerst ['fo:r|e:rst] *adv* for the moment *od* present

Vorfahr ['fo:rfa:r] (**-en, -en**) *m* ancestor

vorfahren *unreg vi* to drive (on) ahead; (*vors Haus etc*) to drive up

Vorfahrt *f* (*Aut*) right of way; **„~ (be)achten“** “give way” (*Brit*), “yield” (*US*)

Vorfahrts- *zW*: **Vorfahrtsregel** *f* rule of right of way; **Vorfahrtsschild** *nt* “give way” (*Brit*) *od* “yield” (*US*) sign

Vorfall ['fo:rfal] *m* incident

vorfallen *unreg vi* to occur

Vorfeld ['fo:rfɛlt] *nt* (*fig*): **im ~ (+gen)** in the run-up (to)

vorfinden ['fo:rfɪndən] *unreg vt* to find

Vorfreude ['fo:rfrɔʏdə] *f* anticipation

vorführen ['fo:rfy:rən] *vt* to show, display; (*Theaterstück, Kunststücke*): **(jdm) etw ~** to perform sth (to *od* in front of sb); **dem Gericht ~** to bring before the court

Vorgang ['fo:rgaŋ] *m* (*Ereignis*) event; (*Ablauf*) course of events; (*Chem etc*) process

Vorgänger, in ['fo:rgɛŋər(ɪn)] (**-s, -**) *m(f)* predecessor

vorgeben ['fo:rge:bən] *unreg vt* to pretend, use as a pretext; (*Sport*) to give an advantage *od* a start of

vorgefasst ['fo:rgəfast] *adj* preconceived

vorgefertigt ['fo:rgəfɛrtɪçt] *adj* prefabricated

vorgehen ['fo:rge:ən] *unreg vi* (*voraus*) to go (on) ahead; (*nach vorn*) to go forward; (*handeln*) to act, proceed; (*Uhr*) to be fast; (*Vorrang haben*) to take precedence; (*passieren*) to go on

Vorgehen (**-s**) *nt* action

Vorgeschmack ['fo:rgəʃmak] *m* foretaste

Vorgesetzte, r ['fo:rgəzɛtstə(r)] *f(m)* superior

vorgestern ['fo:rgɛstərn] *adv* the day before yesterday; **von ~** (*fig*) antiquated

vorhaben ['fo:rha:bən] *unreg vt* to intend; **hast du schon was vor?** have you got

anything on?
Vorhaben (**-s, -**) *nt* intention
vorhalten ['fo:rhaltən] *unreg vt* to hold *od* put up ▷ *vi* to last; **jdm etw ~** to reproach sb for sth
Vorhaltung *f* reproach
vorhanden [fo:r'handən] *adj* existing; (*erhältlich*) available
Vorhang ['fo:rhaŋ] *m* curtain
Vorhängeschloss ['fo:rhɛŋəʃlɔs] *nt* padlock
Vorhaut ['fo:rhaʊt] *f* (*Anat*) foreskin
vorher [fo:r'he:r] *adv* before(hand); **vorherbestimmen** *vt* (*Schicksal*) to preordain; **vorhergehen** *unreg vi* to precede
vorherig [fo:r'he:rıç] *adj* previous
Vorherrschaft ['fo:rhɛrʃaft] *f* predominance, supremacy
vorherrschen *vi* to predominate
vorher- *zW*: **Vorhersage** *f* forecast; **vorhersagen** *vt* to forecast, predict; **vorhersehbar** *adj* predictable; **vorhersehen** *unreg vt* to foresee
vorhin [fo:r'hın] *adv* not long ago, just now
Vorhinein ['fo:rhınaın] *adv*: **im ~** beforehand
vorig ['fo:rıç] *adj* previous, last
Vorkehrung ['fo:rke:rʊŋ] *f* precaution
vorkommen ['fo:rkɔmən] *unreg vi* to come forward; (*geschehen, sich finden*) to occur; (*scheinen*) to seem (to be); **so was soll ~!** that's life!; **sich** *dat* **dumm** *etc* **~** to feel stupid *etc*
Vorkommen *nt* occurrence; (*Min*) deposit
Vorkommnis ['fo:rkɔmnıs] (**-ses, -se**) *nt* occurrence
Vorkriegs- ['fo:rkri:ks] *in zW* pre-war
Vorladung *f* summons
Vorlage ['fo:rla:gə] *f* model, pattern; (*das Vorlegen*) presentation; (*von Beweismaterial*) submission; (*Gesetzesvorlage*) bill; (*Sport*) pass
vorlassen ['fo:rlasən] *unreg vt* to admit; (*überholen lassen*) to let pass; (*vorgehen lassen*) to allow to go in front
vorläufig ['fo:rlɔyfıç] *adj* temporary; (*provisorisch*) provisional
vorlaut ['fo:rlaʊt] *adj* impertinent, cheeky
vorlesen ['fo:rle:zən] *unreg vt* to read (out)
Vorlesung *f* (*Univ*) lecture
Vorlesungsverzeichnis *nt* lecture timetable
vorletzte, r, s ['fo:rlɛtstə(r, s)] *adj* last but one, penultimate
Vorliebe ['fo:rli:bə] *f* preference, special liking; **etw mit ~ tun** to particularly like doing sth
vorliegen ['fo:rli:gən] *unreg vi* to be (here); **etw liegt jdm vor** sb has sth; **etw liegt gegen jdn vor** sb is charged with sth
vorliegend *adj* present, at issue
vormachen ['fo:rmaxən] *vt*: **jdm etw ~** to show sb how to do sth; **jdm etwas ~** (*fig*) to fool sb; **mach mir doch nichts vor** don't try and fool me
Vormachtstellung ['fo:rmaxtʃtɛlʊŋ] *f* supremacy
Vormarsch ['fo:rmarʃ] *m* advance
vormerken ['fo:rmɛrkən] *vt* to book; (*notieren*) to make note of; (*bei Bestellung*) to take an order for
Vormittag ['fo:rmıta:k] *m* morning; **am ~** in the morning
vormittags *adv* in the morning, before noon
Vormund ['fo:rmʊnt] (**-(e)s, -e** *od* **-münder**) *m* guardian
vorn [fɔrn] *adv* in front; **von ~ anfangen** to start at the beginning; **nach ~** to the front; **er betrügt sie von ~ bis hinten** he deceives her right, left and centre
Vorname ['fo:rna:mə] *m* first *od* Christian name
vorne ['fɔrnə] = **vorn**
vornehm ['fo:rne:m] *adj* distinguished; (*Manieren etc*) refined; (*Kleid*) elegant; **in ~en Kreisen** in polite society
vornehmen *unreg vt* (*fig*) to carry out; **sich** *dat* **etw ~** to start on sth; (*beschließen*) to decide to do sth; **sich** *dat* **zu viel ~** to take on too much; **sich** *dat* **jdn ~** to tell sb off
vornehmlich *adv* chiefly, specially
vornherein ['fɔrnhɛraın] *adv*: **von ~** from the start
Vorort ['fo:r|ɔrt] *m* suburb; **Vorortzug** *m* commuter train
Vorrang ['fo:rraŋ] *m* precedence, priority
vorrangig *adj* of prime importance, primary
Vorrat ['fo:rra:t] *m* stock, supply; **solange der ~ reicht** (*Comm*) while stocks last
vorrätig ['fo:rrɛ:tıç] *adj* in stock
Vorratskammer *f* store cupboard; (*für Lebensmittel*) larder
Vorrecht ['fo:rrɛçt] *nt* privilege
Vorrichtung ['fo:rrıçtʊŋ] *f* device, gadget
vorrücken ['fo:rrʏkən] *vi* to advance ▷ *vt* to move forward
Vorruhestand ['fo:rru:əʃtant] *m* early retirement
Vorsaison ['fo:rzɛzõ:] *f* early season, low season
Vorsatz ['fo:rzats] *m* intention; (*Jur*) intent; **einen ~ fassen** to make a resolution
vorsätzlich ['fo:rzɛtslıç] *adj* intentional; (*Jur*) premeditated ▷ *adv* intentionally
Vorschau ['fo:rʃaʊ] *f* (*Rundf, TV*) (programme (*Brit*) *od* program (*US*)) preview; (*Film*) trailer
vorschießen ['fo:rʃi:sən] *unreg* (*umg*) *vt*: **jdm Geld ~** to advance sb money
Vorschlag ['fo:rʃla:k] *m* suggestion, proposal
vorschlagen ['fo:rʃla:gən] *unreg vt* to suggest, propose
vorschnell ['fo:rʃnɛl] *adj* hasty, too quick
vorschreiben ['fo:rʃraıbən] *unreg vt* (*Dosis*) to prescribe; (*befehlen*) to specify; **(jdm) etw ~** (*lit*) to write sth out (for sb); **ich lasse mir nichts ~** I won't be dictated to
Vorschrift ['fo:rʃrıft] *f* regulation(s *pl*), rule(s *pl*); (*Anweisungen*) instruction(s *pl*); **jdm ~en machen** to give sb orders; **Dienst nach ~** work-to-rule (*Brit*), slowdown (*US*)
vorschriftsmäßig *adv* as per regulations/

instructions
Vorschule ['fo:rʃu:lə] *f* nursery school
Vorschuss ['fo:rʃʊs] *m* advance
vorschweben ['fo:rʃve:bən] *vi*: **jdm schwebt etw vor** sb has sth in mind
vorsehen ['fo:rze:ən] *unreg vt* to provide for; (*planen*) to plan ▷ *vr* to take care, be careful
Vorsehung *f* providence
vorsetzen ['fo:rzɛtsən] *vt* to move forward; (*davor setzen*): **~ vor** *+akk* to put in front of; (*anbieten*): **jdm etw ~** to offer sb sth
Vorsicht ['fo:rzɪçt] *f* caution, care; **~!** look out!, take care!; (*auf Schildern*) caution!, danger!; **~ Stufe!** mind the step!; **etw mit ~ genießen** (*umg*) to take sth with a pinch of salt
vorsichtig *adj* cautious, careful
vorsichtshalber *adv* just in case
Vorsichtsmaßnahme *f* precaution
Vorsilbe ['fo:rzɪlbə] *f* prefix
Vorsitz ['fo:rzɪts] *m* chair(manship); **den ~ führen** to chair the meeting
Vorsitzende, r *f(m)* chairman/-woman, chair(person)
Vorsorge ['fo:rzɔrgə] *f* precaution(s *pl*); (*Fürsorge*) provision(s *pl*)
vorsorgen *vi*: **~ für** to make provision(s *pl*) for
Vorsorgeuntersuchung ['fo:rzɔrgə-|ʊntərzu:xʊŋ] *f* medical check-up
vorsorglich ['fo:rzɔrklɪç] *adv* as a precaution
Vorspeise ['fo:rʃpaɪzə] *f* hors d'(oe)uvre, starter
Vorspiel ['fo:rʃpi:l] *nt* prelude; (*bei Geschlechtsverkehr*) foreplay
vorsprechen ['fo:rʃprɛçən] *unreg vt* to say out loud; (*vortragen*) to recite ▷ *vi* (*Theat*) to audition; **bei jdm ~** to call on sb
Vorsprung ['fo:rʃprʊŋ] *m* projection; (*Felsvorsprung*) ledge; (*fig*) advantage, start
Vorstadt ['fo:rʃtat] *f* suburbs *pl*
Vorstand ['fo:rʃtant] *m* executive committee; (*Comm*) board (of directors); (*Person*) director; (*Leiter*) head
vorstehen ['fo:rʃte:ən] *unreg vi* to project; **einer Sache** *dat* **~** (*fig*) to be the head of sth
vorstellbar *adj* conceivable
vorstellen ['fo:rʃtɛlən] *vt* to put forward; (*vor etw*) to put in front; (*bekannt machen*) to introduce; (*darstellen*) to represent ▷ *vr* to introduce o.s.; (*bei Bewerbung*) to go for an interview; **sich** *dat* **etw ~** to imagine sth; **stell dir das nicht so einfach vor** don't think it's so easy
Vorstellung *f* (*Bekanntmachen*) introduction; (*Theat etc*) performance; (*Gedanke*) idea
Vorstellungsgespräch *nt* interview
Vorstrafe ['fo:rʃtra:fə] *f* previous conviction
vorstrecken ['fo:rʃtrɛkən] *vt* to stretch out; (*Geld*) to advance
vortäuschen ['fo:rtɔʏʃən] *vt* to pretend, feign
Vorteil ['fo:rtaɪl] (**-s, -e**) *m*: **~ (gegenüber)** advantage (over); **im ~ sein** to have the advantage; **die Vor- und Nachteile** the pros and cons; **vorteilhaft** *adj* advantageous; (*Kleider*) flattering; (*Geschäft*) lucrative
Vortrag ['fo:rtra:k] (**-(e)s, Vorträge**) *m* talk, lecture; (*Vortragsart*) delivery; (*von Gedicht*) rendering; (*Comm*) balance carried forward; **einen ~ halten** to give a lecture *od* talk
vortragen ['fo:rtra:gən] *unreg vt* to carry forward (*auch Comm*); (*fig*) to recite; (*Rede*) to deliver; (*Lied*) to perform; (*Meinung etc*) to express
vortrefflich [fo:r'trɛflɪç] *adj* excellent
vortreten ['fo:rtre:tən] *unreg vi* to step forward; (*Augen etc*) to protrude
Vortritt ['fo:rtrɪt] *m*: **jdm den ~ lassen** (*lit, fig*) to let sb go first
vorüber [fo'ry:bər] *adv* past, over; **vorübergehen** *unreg vi* to pass (by); **vorübergehen an** *+dat* (*fig*) to pass over; **vorübergehend** *adj* temporary, passing
Vorurteil ['fo:r|ʊrtaɪl] *nt* prejudice
Vorverkauf ['fo:rfɛrkaʊf] *m* advance booking
Vorwahl ['fo:rva:l] *f* preliminary election; (*Tel*) dialling (*Brit*) *od* area (*US*) code
Vorwand ['fo:rvant] (**-(e)s, Vorwände**) *m* pretext
vorwärts ['fo:rvɛrts] *adv* forward; **~!** (*umg*) let's go!; (*Mil*) forward march!; *siehe auch* **vorwärtsgehen; vorwärtskommen**; **Vorwärtsgang** *m* (*Aut etc*) forward gear; **vorwärtsgehen** *unreg vi* to progress; **vorwärtskommen** *unreg vi* to get on, make progress
vorweg [fo:r'vɛk] *adv* in advance; **Vorwegnahme** (**-, -n**) *f* anticipation; **vorwegnehmen** *unreg vt* to anticipate
vorweisen ['fo:rvaɪzən] *unreg vt* to show, produce
vorwerfen ['fo:rvɛrfən] *unreg vt*: **jdm etw ~** to reproach sb for sth, accuse sb of sth; **sich** *dat* **nichts vorzuwerfen haben** to have nothing to reproach o.s. with; **das wirft er mir heute noch vor** he still holds it against me; **Tieren/Gefangenen etw ~** (*lit*) to throw sth down for the animals/prisoners
vorwiegend ['fo:rvi:gənt] *adj* predominant ▷ *adv* predominantly
vorwitzig *adj* saucy, cheeky
Vorwort ['fo:rvɔrt] (**-(e)s, -e**) *nt* preface
Vorwurf ['fo:rvʊrf] (**-(e)s, ¨-e**) *m* reproach; **jdm/sich Vorwürfe machen** to reproach sb/o.s.
vorwurfsvoll *adj* reproachful
Vorzeichen ['fo:rtsaɪçən] *nt* (*Omen*) omen; (*Med*) early symptom; (*Math*) sign
vorzeigen ['fo:rtsaɪgən] *vt* to show, produce
vorzeitig *adj* premature
vorziehen ['fo:rtsi:ən] *unreg vt* to pull forward; (*Gardinen*) to draw; (*zuerst behandeln, abfertigen*) to give priority to; (*lieber haben*) to prefer
Vorzug ['fo:rtsu:k] *m* preference; (*gute Eigenschaft*) merit, good quality; (*Vorteil*) advantage; (*Eisenb*) relief train; **einer Sache** *dat* **den ~ geben** (*form*) to prefer sth; (*Vorrang*

geben) to give sth precedence
vulgär [vʊl'gɛːr] *adj* vulgar

Vulkan [vʊl'kaːn] (**-s, -e**) *m* volcano
vulkanisieren [vʊlkani'ziːrən] *vt* to vulcanize

W, w [ve:] *nt* W, w; **W wie Wilhelm** ≈ W for William
Waage ['va:gə] (**-, -n**) *f* scales *pl*; (*Astrol*) Libra; **sich** *dat* **die ~ halten** (*fig*) to balance one another
Wabe ['va:bə] (**-, -n**) *f* honeycomb
wach [vax] *adj* awake; (*fig*) alert; **~ werden** to wake up
Wache (**-, -n**) *f* guard, watch; **~ halten** to keep watch; **~ stehen** *od* **schieben** (*umg*) to be on guard (duty)
wachen *vi* to be awake; (*Wache halten*) to keep watch; **bei jdm ~** to sit up with sb
Wacholder [va'xɔldər] (**-s, -**) *m* juniper
Wachs [vaks] (**-es, -e**) *nt* wax
wachsam ['vaxza:m] *adj* watchful, vigilant, alert; **Wachsamkeit** *f* vigilance
wachsen[1] *unreg vi* to grow
wachsen[2] *vt* (*Skier*) to wax
Wachstuch ['vakstu:x] *nt* oilcloth
Wachstum ['vakstu:m] (**-s**) *nt* growth
Wachstumsrate *f* growth rate
Wächter ['vɛçtər] (**-s, -**) *m* guard; (*Parkwächter*) warden, keeper; (*Museumswächter, Parkplatzwächter*) attendant
wackelig *adj* shaky, wobbly; **auf ~en Beinen stehen** to be wobbly on one's legs; (*fig*) to be unsteady
Wackelkontakt *m* loose connection
wackeln *vi* to shake; (*fig: Position*) to be shaky; **mit den Hüften/dem Schwanz ~** to wiggle one's hips/wag its tail
wacker ['vakər] *adj* valiant, stout; **sich ~ schlagen** (*umg*) to put up a brave fight
Wade ['va:də] (**-, -n**) *f* (*Anat*) calf
Waffe ['vafə] (**-, -n**) *f* weapon; **jdn mit seinen eigenen ~n schlagen** (*fig*) to beat sb at his own game
Waffel ['vafəl] (**-, -n**) *f* waffle; (*Eiswaffel*) wafer
Waffen- *zW*: **Waffenschein** *m* firearms *od* gun licence (*Brit*), firearms license (*US*); **Waffenstillstand** *m* armistice, truce
Wagemut ['va:gəmu:t] *m* daring
Wagen ['va:gən] (**-s, -**) *m* vehicle; (*Auto*) car, automobile (*US*); (*Eisenb*) car, carriage (*Brit*); (*Pferdewagen*) wag(g)on, cart
wagen *vt* to venture, dare
Wagenheber (**-s, -**) *m* jack
Waggon [va'gõ:] (**-s, -s**) *m* wag(g)on; (*Güterwaggon*) goods van (*Brit*), freight truck (*US*)
waghalsig ['va:khalzıç] *adj* foolhardy
Wagnis ['va:knıs] (**-ses, -se**) *nt* risk
Wagon (**-s, -s**) *m* = **Waggon**
Wahl [va:l] (**-, -en**) *f* choice; (*Pol*) election; **erste ~** (*Qualität*) top quality; (*Gemüse, Eier*) grade one; **zweite ~** (*Comm*) seconds *pl*; **aus freier ~** of one's own free choice; **wer die ~ hat, hat die Qual** (*Sprichwort*) he is *od* you are *etc* spoilt for choice; **die ~ fiel auf ihn** he was chosen; **sich zur ~ stellen** (*Pol etc*) to stand (*Brit*) *od* run (for parliament *etc*)
wählbar *adj* eligible
Wahl- *zW*: **wahlberechtigt** *adj* entitled to vote; **Wahlbeteiligung** *f* poll, turnout
wählen ['vɛ:lən] *vt* to choose; (*Pol*) to elect, vote for; (*Tel*) to dial ▷ *vi* to choose; (*Pol*) to vote; (*Tel*) to dial
Wähler, in (**-s, -**) *m(f)* voter; **wählerisch** *adj* fastidious, particular; **Wählerschaft** *f* electorate
Wahl- *zW*: **Wahlfach** *nt* optional subject; **Wahlgang** *m* ballot; **Wahlkabine** *f* polling booth; **Wahlkampf** *m* election campaign; **Wahlkreis** *m* constituency; **Wahllokal** *nt* polling station; **wahllos** *adv* at random; (*nicht wählerisch*) indiscriminately; **Wahlrecht** *nt* franchise; **allgemeines Wahlrecht** universal franchise; **das aktive Wahlrecht** the right to vote; **das passive Wahlrecht** eligibility (for political office); **Wahlspruch** *m* motto; **wahlweise** *adv* alternatively
Wahn [va:n] (**-(e)s**) *m* delusion; **Wahnsinn** *m* madness; **wahnsinnig** *adj* insane, mad ▷ *adv* (*umg*) incredibly
wahr [va:r] *adj* true; **da ist (et)was W~es dran** there's some truth in that
wahren *vt* to maintain, keep
währen ['vɛ:rən] *vi* to last
während *präp +gen* during ▷ *konj* while; **währenddessen** *adv* meanwhile
wahr- *zW*: **wahrhaben** *unreg vt*: **etw nicht wahrhaben wollen** to refuse to admit sth; **wahrhaft** *adv* (*tatsächlich*) truly; **wahrhaftig** *adj* true, real ▷ *adv* really
Wahrheit *f* truth; **die ~ sagen** to tell the truth
wahrnehmen *unreg vt* to perceive; (*Frist*) to observe; (*Veränderungen etc*) to be aware of;

(*Gelegenheit*) to take; (*Interessen, Rechte*) to look after
Wahrnehmung *f* perception; observing; awareness; taking; looking after
wahrsagen *vi* to predict the future, tell fortunes
Wahrsager *m* fortune-teller
wahrscheinlich [vaːrˈʃaɪnlɪç] *adj* probable ▷ *adv* probably; **Wahrscheinlichkeit** *f* probability; **aller Wahrscheinlichkeit nach** in all probability
Währung [ˈvɛːrʊŋ] *f* currency
Währungs- *zW*: **Währungseinheit** *f* monetary unit; **Währungspolitik** *f* monetary policy; **Währungsraum** *m* currency area; **Währungsunion** *f* monetary union
Wahrzeichen *nt* (*Gebäude, Turm etc*) symbol; (*von Stadt, Verein*) emblem
Waise [ˈvaɪzə] (**-, -n**) *f* orphan
Waisen- *zW*: **Waisenhaus** *nt* orphanage; **Waisenkind** *nt* orphan
Wal [vaːl] (**-(e)s, -e**) *m* whale
Wald [valt] (**-(e)s, ¨er**) *m* wood(s *pl*); (*groß*) forest; **Waldsterben** *nt* *loss of trees due to pollution*
Walfisch [ˈvalfɪʃ] *m* whale
Wall [val] (**-(e)s, ¨e**) *m* embankment; (*Bollwerk*) rampart
Wallfahrer, in *m(f)* pilgrim
Wallfahrt *f* pilgrimage
Wallis [ˈvalɪs] (-) *nt*: **das ~** Valais
Walnuss [ˈvalnʊs] *f* walnut
Walross [ˈvalrɔs] *nt* walrus
Walze [ˈvaltsə] (**-, -n**) *f* (*Gerät*) cylinder; (*Fahrzeug*) roller
walzen *vt* to roll (out)
wälzen [ˈvɛltsən] *vt* to roll (over); (*Bücher*) to hunt through; (*Probleme*) to deliberate on ▷ *vr* to wallow; (*vor Schmerzen*) to roll about; (*im Bett*) to toss and turn
Walzer [ˈvaltsər] (**-s, -**) *m* waltz
Wand (**-, ¨e**) *f* wall; (*Trennwand*) partition; (*Bergwand*) precipice; (*Felswand*) (rock) face; (*fig*) barrier; **weiß wie die ~** as white as a sheet; **jdn an die ~ spielen** to put sb in the shade; (*Sport*) to outplay sb
wand *etc* [vant] *vb siehe* **winden**
Wandel [ˈvandəl] (**-s**) *m* change; **wandelbar** *adj* changeable, variable
wandeln *vt, vr* to change ▷ *vi* (*gehen*) to walk
Wanderausstellung *f* touring exhibition
Wanderbühne *f* touring theatre (*Brit*) *od* theater (*US*)
Wanderer (**-s, -**) *m* hiker, rambler
wandern *vi* to hike; (*Blick*) to wander; (*Gedanken*) to stray; (*umg: in den Papierkorb etc*) to land
Wanderschaft *f* travelling (*Brit*), traveling (*US*)
Wanderung *f* walk, hike; (*von Tieren, Völkern*) migration
Wandlung *f* change; (*völlige Umwandlung*) transformation; (*Rel*) transubstantiation
wandte *etc* [ˈvantə] *vb siehe* **wenden**
Wange [ˈvaŋə] (**-, -n**) *f* cheek
wankelmütig [ˈvaŋkəlmyːtɪç] *adj* fickle, inconstant
wanken [ˈvankən] *vi* to stagger; (*fig*) to waver
wann [van] *adv* when; **seit ~ bist/hast du ...?** how long have you been/have you had ...?
Wanne [ˈvanə] (**-, -n**) *f* tub
Wanze [ˈvantsə] (**-, -n**) *f* (*Abhörgerät, Zool*) bug
WAP-Handy *nt* WAP phone
Wappen [ˈvapən] (**-s, -**) *nt* coat of arms, crest; **Wappenkunde** *f* heraldry
war *etc* [vaːr] *vb siehe* **sein**
warb *etc* [varp] *vb siehe* **werben**
Ware [ˈvaːrə] (**-, -n**) *f* ware; **Waren** *pl* goods *pl*
Waren- *zW*: **Warenhaus** *nt* department store; **Warenlager** *nt* stock, store; **Warenprobe** *f* sample; **Warenzeichen** *nt* trademark
warf *etc* [varf] *vb siehe* **werfen**
warm [varm] *adj* warm; (*Essen*) hot; (*umg: homosexuell*) queer; **mir ist ~** I'm warm; **mit jdm ~ werden** (*umg*) to get close to sb; **~ laufen** (*Aut*) to warm up; *siehe auch* **warmhalten**
Wärme [ˈvɛrmə] (**-, -n**) *f* warmth; **10 Grad ~** 10 degrees above zero
wärmen *vt, vr* to warm (up), heat (up)
Wärmflasche *f* hot-water bottle
warm- *zW*: **Warmfront** *f* (*Met*) warm front; **warmherzig** *adj* warm-hearted
Warndreieck *nt* warning triangle
warnen [ˈvarnən] *vt* to warn
Warnstreik *m* token strike
Warnung *f* warning
warten [ˈvartən] *vi* to wait ▷ *vt* (*Auto, Maschine*) to service; **~ auf** *+akk* to wait for; **auf sich ~ lassen** to take a long time; **warte mal!** wait a minute!; (*überlegend*) let me see; **mit dem Essen auf jdn ~** to wait for sb before eating
Wärter, in [ˈvɛrtər(ɪn)] (**-s, -**) *m(f)* attendant
Wartesaal *m* (*Eisenb*) waiting room
Wartezimmer *nt* waiting room
Wartung *f* (*von Auto, Maschine*) servicing; **~ und Instandhaltung** maintenance
warum [vaˈrʊm] *adv* why; **~ nicht gleich so!** that's better
Warze [ˈvartsə] (**-, -n**) *f* wart
was [vas] *pron* what; (*umg: etwas*) something; **das, ~ ...** that which ...; **~ für ...?** what sort *od* kind of ...?
Wasch- *zW*: **waschbar** *adj* washable; **Waschbecken** *nt* washbasin
Wäsche [ˈvɛʃə] (**-, -n**) *f* wash(ing); (*Bettwäsche*) linen; (*Unterwäsche*) underwear; **dumm aus der ~ gucken** (*umg*) to look stupid
waschecht *adj* (*Farbe*) fast; (*fig*) genuine
Wäsche- *zW*: **Wäscheklammer** *f* clothes peg (*Brit*), clothespin (*US*); **Wäscheleine** *f* washing line (*Brit*), clothes line (*US*)
waschen [ˈvaʃən] *unreg vt, vi* to wash ▷ *vr* to (have a) wash; **sich** *dat* **die Hände ~** to wash one's hands; **~ und legen** (*Haare*) to

shampoo and set
Wäscherei [vɛʃə'raɪ] *f* laundry
Wäscheschleuder *f* spin-dryer
Wasch- *zW*: **Waschküche** *f* laundry room; **Waschlappen** *m* face cloth *od* flannel (*Brit*), washcloth (*US*); (*umg*) softy; **Waschmaschine** *f* washing machine; **Waschmittel** *nt* detergent; **Waschsalon** *m* Launderette® (*Brit*), Laundromat® (*US*)
Wasser[1] ['vasər] (**-s, -**) *nt* water; **~ abstoßend** water-repellent; **dort wird auch nur mit ~ gekocht** (*fig*) they're no different from anybody else (there); **ins ~ fallen** (*fig*) to fall through; **mit allen ~n gewaschen sein** (*umg*) to be a shrewd customer; **~ lassen** (*euph*) to pass water; **jdm das ~ abgraben** (*fig*) to take the bread from sb's mouth, take away sb's livelihood
Wasser[2] (**-s, ¨-**) *nt* (*Flüssigkeit*) water; (*Med*) lotion; (*Parfüm*) cologne; (*Mineralwasser*) mineral water
Wasser- *zW*: **wasserdicht** *adj* watertight; (*Stoff, Uhr*) waterproof; **Wasserfall** *m* waterfall; **Wasserfarbe** *f* watercolour (*Brit*), watercolor (*US*); **wassergekühlt** *adj* (*Aut*) water-cooled; **Wasserhahn** *m* tap, faucet (*US*)
Wasser- *zW*: **Wasserkraftwerk** *nt* hydroelectric power station; **Wasserleitung** *f* water pipe; (*Anlagen*) plumbing; **Wassermann** *m* (*Astrol*) Aquarius
wassern *vi* to land on the water
wässern ['vɛsərn] *vt, vi* to water
Wasser- *zW*: **wasserscheu** *adj* afraid of water; **Wasserski** *nt* water-skiing; **Wasserstoff** *m* hydrogen; **Wasserstoffbombe** *f* hydrogen bomb; **Wasserwaage** *f* spirit level; **Wasserwelle** *f* shampoo and set; **Wasserzeichen** *nt* watermark
waten ['va:tən] *vi* to wade
watscheln ['va:tʃəln] *vi* to waddle
Watt[1] [vat] (**-(e)s, -en**) *nt* mud flats *pl*
Watt[2] (**-s, -**) *nt* (*Elek*) watt
Watte (**-, -n**) *f* cotton wool (*Brit*), absorbent cotton (*US*)
Wattestäbchen *nt* cotton(-wool) swab
wattieren [va'ti:rən] *vt* to pad
WC [ve:'tse:] (**-s, -s**) *nt abk* (= *Wasserklosett*) WC
Web [wɛb] *nt* (*Comput*): **das ~** the Web; **im ~** on the Web
weben ['ve:bən] *unreg vt* to weave
Weberei [ve:bə'raɪ] *f* (*Betrieb*) weaving mill
Webseite ['wɛbzaɪtə] *f* Web page, web site
Webstuhl ['ve:pʃtu:l] *m* loom
Wechsel ['vɛksəl] (**-s, -**) *m* change; (*Geldwechsel*) exchange; (*Comm*) bill of exchange; **Wechselbeziehung** *f* correlation; **Wechselgeld** *nt* change; **wechselhaft** *adj* (*Wetter*) variable; **Wechseljahre** *pl* change of life, menopause; **in die Wechseljahre kommen** to start the change; **Wechselkurs** *m* rate of exchange
wechseln *vt* to change; (*Blicke*) to exchange ▷ *vi* to change; (*einander ablösen*) to alternate
Wechsel- *zW*: **Wechselstrom** *m* alternating current; **Wechselwirkung** *f* interaction
wecken ['vɛkən] *vt* to wake (up); (*fig*) to arouse; (*Bedarf*) to create; (*Erinnerungen*) to revive
Wecker (**-s, -**) *m* alarm clock; **jdm auf den ~ fallen** (*umg*) to get on sb's nerves
Weckruf *m* (*Tel*) alarm call
wedeln ['ve:dəln] *vi* (*mit Schwanz*) to wag; (*mit Fächer*) to fan; (*Ski*) to wedel
weder ['ve:dər] *konj* neither; **~ ... noch ...** neither ... nor ...
Weg [ve:k] (**-(e)s, -e**) *m* way; (*Pfad*) path; (*Route*) route; **sich auf den ~ machen** to be on one's way; **jdm aus dem ~ gehen** to keep out of sb's way; **jdm nicht über den ~ trauen** (*fig*) not to trust sb an inch; **den ~ des geringsten Widerstandes gehen** to follow the line of least resistance; **etw in die ~e leiten** to arrange sth; **jdm Steine in den ~ legen** (*fig*) to put obstacles in sb's way; *siehe auch* **zuwege**
weg [vɛk] *adv* away, off; **über etw** *akk* **~ sein** to be over sth; **er war schon ~** he had already left; **nichts wie** *od* **nur ~ von hier!** let's get out of here!; **~ damit!** (*mit Schere etc*) put it/them away!; **Finger ~!** hands off!
Wegbereiter (**-s, -**) *m* pioneer
wegblasen *unreg vt* to blow away; **wie weggeblasen sein** (*fig*) to have vanished
wegbleiben *unreg vi* to stay away; **mir bleibt die Spucke weg!** (*umg*) I am absolutely flabbergasted!
wegen ['ve:gən] (*umg*) *präp +gen od +dat* because of; **von ~!** you must be joking!
weg- *zW*: **wegfahren** *unreg vi* to drive away; (*abfahren*) to leave; **Wegfahrsperre** *f* (*Aut*): **(elektronische) Wegfahrsperre** (electronic) immobilizer; **wegfallen** *unreg vi* to be left out; (*Ferien, Bezahlung*) to be cancelled; (*aufhören*) to cease; **weggehen** *unreg vi* to go away, leave; (*umg: Ware*) to sell; **weglassen** *unreg vt* to leave out; **weglaufen** *unreg vi* to run away *od* off; **das läuft (dir) nicht weg!** (*fig hum*) that can wait; **weglegen** *vt* to put aside; **wegmachen** (*umg*) *vt* to get rid of; **wegmüssen** *unreg* (*umg*) *vi* to have to go; **wegnehmen** *unreg vt* to take away
weg- *zW*: **wegschaffen** *vt* to clear away; **wegtun** *unreg vt* to put away
Wegweiser ['ve:gvaɪzər] (**-s, -**) *m* road sign, signpost; (*fig: Buch etc*) guide
weg- *zW*: **wegwerfen** *unreg vt* to throw away; **wegziehen** *unreg vi* to move away
weh [ve:] *adj* sore
wehe *interj*: **~, wenn du ...** you'll regret it if you ...; **~ dir!** you dare!
Wehen *pl* (*Med*) contractions *pl*; **in den ~ liegen** to be in labour (*Brit*) *od* labor (*US*)
wehen *vt, vi* to blow; (*Fahnen*) to flutter
weh- *zW*: **wehleidig** *adj* oversensitive to pain; (*jammernd*) whiny, whining; **Wehmut** *f*

melancholy; **wehmütig** *adj* melancholy
Wehr[1] [veːr] (**-(e)s, -e**) *nt* weir
Wehr[2] [veːr] (**-, -en**) *f* (*Feuerwehr*) fire brigade (*Brit*) *od* department (*US*) ▷ *in zw* defence (*Brit*), defense (*US*); **sich zur ~ setzen** to defend o.s.
Wehrdienst *m* military service
Wehrdienstverweigerer *m* ≈ conscientious objector
wehren *vr* to defend o.s.
Wehr- *zW*: **wehrlos** *adj* defenceless (*Brit*), defenseless (*US*); **jdm wehrlos ausgeliefert sein** to be at sb's mercy; **Wehrpflicht** *f* conscription; **wehrpflichtig** *adj* liable for military service
wehtun ['veːtuːn] *unreg vt*: **jdm/sich ~** to hurt sb/o.s.
Weib [vaɪp] (**-(e)s, -er**) *nt* woman, female (*pej*)
Weibchen *nt* (*Ehefrau*) little woman; (*Zool*) female
weibisch ['vaɪbɪʃ] *adj* effeminate
weiblich *adj* feminine
weich [vaɪç] *adj* soft; (*Ei*) soft-boiled; **~e Währung** soft currency
Weiche (**-, -n**) *f* (*Eisenb*) points *pl*; **die ~n stellen** (*lit*) to switch the points; (*fig*) to set the course
weichen *unreg vi* to yield, give way; **(nicht) von jdm** *od* **von jds Seite ~** (not) to leave sb's side
weich- *zW*: **Weichheit** *f* softness; **weichlich** *adj* soft, namby-pamby; **Weichling** *m* wimp; **Weichspüler** (**-s, -**) *m* fabric conditioner
Weide ['vaɪdə] (**-, -n**) *f* (*Baum*) willow; (*Gras*) pasture
weiden *vi* to graze ▷ *vr*: **sich an etw** *dat* **~** to delight in sth
weidlich ['vaɪtlɪç] *adv* thoroughly
weigern ['vaɪgərn] *vr* to refuse
Weigerung ['vaɪgərʊŋ] *f* refusal
Weihe ['vaɪə] (**-, -n**) *f* consecration; (*Priesterweihe*) ordination
weihen *vt* to consecrate; (*widmen*) to dedicate; **dem Untergang geweiht** (*liter*) doomed
Weiher (**-s, -**) *m* pond
Weihnachten (**-**) *nt* Christmas; **fröhliche ~!** happy *od* merry Christmas!
weihnachtlich *adj* Christmas(sy)
Weihnachts- *zW*: **Weihnachtsabend** *m* Christmas Eve; **Weihnachtsbaum** *m* Christmas tree; **Weihnachtslied** *nt* Christmas carol; **Weihnachtsmann** *m* Father Christmas (*Brit*), Santa Claus
Weihnachtsmarkt *m* Christmas fair
Weihnachtstag *m*: **(erster) ~** Christmas day; **zweiter ~** Boxing Day (*Brit*)
Weihrauch *m* incense
Weihwasser *nt* holy water
weil [vaɪl] *konj* because
Weile ['vaɪlə] (**-**) *f* while, short time
Wein [vaɪn] (**-(e)s, -e**) *m* wine; (*Pflanze*) vine; **jdm reinen ~ einschenken** (*fig*) to tell sb the truth; **Weinbau** *m* cultivation of vines; **Weinbeere** *f* grape; **Weinberg** *m* vineyard; **Weinbergschnecke** *f* snail; **Weinbrand** *m* brandy
weinen *vt, vi* to cry; **das ist zum W~** it's enough to make you cry *od* weep
Wein- *zW*: **Weingeist** *m* (ethyl) alcohol; **Weinglas** *nt* wine glass
Wein- *zW*: **Weinlese** *f* vintage; **Weinprobe** *f* wine tasting; **Weinrebe** *f* vine; **Weinstein** *m* tartar; **Weinstock** *m* vine; **Weintraube** *f* grape
weise ['vaɪzə] *adj* wise
Weise (**-, -n**) *f* manner, way; (*Lied*) tune; **auf diese ~** in this way
weisen *unreg vt* to show; **etw (weit) von sich ~** (*fig*) to reject sth (emphatically)
Weisheit ['vaɪshaɪt] *f* wisdom
Weisheitszahn *m* wisdom tooth
weiß[1] [vaɪs] *vb siehe* **wissen**
weiß[2] *adj* white; **Weißblech** *nt* tin plate; **Weißbrot** *nt* white bread; **Weißglut** *f* (*Tech*) incandescence; **jdn zur Weißglut bringen** (*fig*) to make sb see red; **Weißkohl** *m* (white) cabbage
Weißrussland *nt* B(y)elorussia
Weißwein *m* white wine
Weisung ['vaɪzʊŋ] *f* instruction
weit [vaɪt] *adj* wide; (*Begriff*) broad; (*Reise, Wurf*) long ▷ *adv* far; **~ blickend** far-seeing; **~ hergeholt** far-fetched; **~ reichend** (*fig*) far-reaching; **~ verbreitet** widespread; **~ verzweigt** = **weitverzweigt**; **in ~er Ferne** in the far distance; **wie ~ ist es ...?** how far is it ...?; **das geht zu ~** that's going too far; **~ und breit** for miles around; **~ gefehlt!** far from it!; **es so ~ bringen, dass ...** to bring it about that ...; **~ zurückliegen** to be far behind; **von W~em** from a long way off; **weitaus** *adv* by far; **Weitblick** *m* (*fig*) far-sightedness; **weitblickend** *adj* far-seeing
Weite (**-, -n**) *f* width; (*Raum*) space; (*von Entfernung*) distance
weiter ['vaɪtər] *adj* wider; (*zusätzlich*) further ▷ *adv* further; **wenn es ~ nichts ist, ...** well, if that's all (it is), ...; **das hat ~ nichts zu sagen** that doesn't really matter; **immer ~** on and on; (*Anweisung*) keep on (going); **~ nichts/niemand** nothing/nobody else; **weiterarbeiten** *vi* to go on working; **weiterbilden** *vr* to continue one's studies; **Weiterbildung** *f* further education
weiter- *zW*: **weiterempfehlen** *unreg vt* to recommend (to others); **Weiterfahrt** *f* continuation of the journey; **weitergehen** *unreg vi* to go on; **weiterhin** *adv*: **etw weiterhin tun** to go on doing sth; **weiterleiten** *vt* to pass on; **weitermachen** *vt, vi* to continue; **weiterreisen** *vi* to continue one's journey
weit- *zW*: **weitgehend** *adj* considerable ▷ *adv* largely; **weitläufig** *adj* (*Gebäude*) spacious; (*Erklärung*) lengthy; (*Verwandter*) distant; **weitschweifig** *adj* long-winded; **weitsichtig** *adj* (*lit*) long-sighted (*Brit*), far-sighted

(US); (fig) far-sighted; **Weitsprung** *m* long jump; **weitverbreitet** *adj* widespread; **Weitwinkelobjektiv** *nt* (Phot) wide-angle lens

Weizen ['vaɪtzən] (**-s, -**) *m* wheat; **Weizenbier** *nt light, fizzy wheat beer*

welch [vɛlç] *pron*: **~ ein(e) ...** what a ...

welche, r, s *interrog pron* which; **welcher von beiden?** which (one) of the two?; **welchen hast du genommen?** which (one) did you take?; **welche Freude!** what joy! ▷ *indef pron* some; (*in Fragen*) any; **ich habe welche** I have some; **haben Sie welche?** do you have any? ▷ *rel pron* (*bei Menschen*) who; (*bei Sachen*) which, that; **welche(r, s) auch immer** whoever/whichever/whatever

welk [vɛlk] *adj* withered; **welken** *vi* to wither

Wellblech *nt* corrugated iron

Welle ['vɛlə] (**-, -n**) *f* wave; (*Tech*) shaft; **(hohe) ~n schlagen** (*fig*) to create (quite) a stir

Wellen- *zW*: **Wellenlänge** *f* (*lit, fig*) wavelength; **mit jdm auf einer Wellenlänge sein** (*fig*) to be on the same wavelength as sb

Wellensittich *m* budgerigar

Wellpappe *f* corrugated cardboard

Welt [vɛlt] (**-, -en**) *f* world; **aus der ~ schaffen** to eliminate; **in aller ~** all over the world; **vor aller ~** in front of everybody; **auf die ~ kommen** to be born; **Weltall** *nt* universe; **Weltanschauung** *f* philosophy of life; **weltberühmt** *adj* world-famous

weltfremd *adj* unworldly

Welt- *zW*: **Weltkrieg** *m* world war; **weltlich** *adj* worldly; (*nicht kirchlich*) secular; **Weltmacht** *f* world power; **weltmännisch** *adj* sophisticated; **Weltmeister** *m* world champion; **Weltmeisterschaft** *f* world *od* world's (US) championship; (*Fussball etc*) World Cup; **Weltraum** *m* space; **Weltraumstation** *f* space station; **Weltreise** *f* trip round the world; **Weltstadt** *f* metropolis; **weltweit** *adj* world-wide; **Weltwunder** *nt* wonder of the world

wem [ve:m] *dat von* **wer** ▷ *pron* to whom

wen [ve:n] *akk von* **wer** ▷ *pron* whom

Wende ['vɛndə] (**-, -n**) *f* turn; (*Veränderung*) change; **die ~** (*Pol*) (the) reunification (of Germany); **Wendekreis** *m* (*Geog*) tropic; (*Aut*) turning circle

Wendeltreppe *f* spiral staircase

wenden *unreg vt, vi, vr* to turn; **bitte ~!** please turn over; **sich an jdn ~** to go/come to sb

Wendepunkt *m* turning point

Wendung *f* turn; (*Redewendung*) idiom

wenig ['ve:nɪç] *adj, adv* little; **ein ~** a little; **er hat zu ~ Geld** he doesn't have enough money; **ein Exemplar zu ~** one copy too few

wenige ['ve:nɪgə] *pl* few *pl*; **in ~n Tagen** in (just) a few days

wenigste, r, s *adj* least

wenigstens *adv* at least

wenn [vɛn] *konj* if; (*zeitlich*) when; **~ auch ...** even if ...; **~ ich doch ...** if only I ...; **~ wir erst die neue Wohnung haben** once we get the new flat

wennschon *adv*: **na ~!** so what?; **~, dennschon!** in for a penny, in for a pound!

wer [ve:r] *pron* who

Werbe- *zW*: **Werbebanner** *nt* banner; **Werbefernsehen** *nt* commercial television; **Werbegeschenk** *nt* promotional gift, freebie (*umg*); (*zu Gekauftem*) free gift; **Werbekampagne** *f* advertising campaign

werben ['vɛrbən] *unreg vt* to win; (*Mitglied*) to recruit ▷ *vi* to advertise; **um jdn/etw ~** to try to win sb/sth; **für jdn/etw ~** to promote sb/sth

Werbe- *zW*: **Werbespot** *m* commercial; **werbewirksam** *adj*: **werbewirksam sein** to be good publicity

Werbung *f* advertising; (*von Mitgliedern*) recruitment; (*TV etc: Werbeblock*) commercial break; **~ um jdn/etw** promotion of sb/sth

Werdegang ['ve:rdəgaŋ] *m* development; (*beruflich*) career

werden ['ve:rdən] *unreg* (*pt* **wurde**, *pp* **geworden** *od* **(bei Passiv) worden**) *vi* to become; **was ist aus ihm/aus der Sache geworden?** what became of him/it?; **es ist nichts/gut geworden** it came to nothing/ turned out well; **es wird Nacht/Tage** it's getting dark/light; **es wird bald ein Jahr, dass ...** it's almost a year since ...; **er wird am 8. Mai 36** he will be 36 on the 8th May; **mir wird kalt** I'm getting cold; **mir wird schlecht** I feel ill; **Erster werden** to come *od* be first; **das muss anders werden** that will have to change; **rot/zu Eis werden** to turn red/to ice; **was willst du (mal) werden?** what do you want to be?; **die Fotos sind gut geworden** the photos turned out well
▷ *hilfsverb* **1** (*bei Futur*): **er wird es tun** he will *od* he'll do it; **er wird das nicht tun** he will not *od* he won't do it; **es wird gleich regnen** it's going to rain any moment
2 (*bei Konjunktiv*): **ich würde ...** I would ...; **er würde gern ...** he would *od* he'd like to ...; **ich würde lieber ...** I would *od* I'd rather ...
3 (*bei Vermutung*): **sie wird in der Küche sein** she will be in the kitchen
4 (*bei Passiv*): **gebraucht werden** to be used; **er ist erschossen worden** he has *od* he's been shot; **mir wurde gesagt, dass ...** I was told that ...

werfen ['vɛrfən] *unreg vt* to throw ▷ *vi* (*Tier*) to have its young; **„nicht ~"** "handle with care"

Werft [vɛrft] (**-, -en**) *f* shipyard; (*für Flugzeuge*) hangar

Werk [vɛrk] (**-(e)s, -e**) *nt* work; (*Tätigkeit*) job; (*Fabrik, Mechanismus*) works *pl*; **ans ~ gehen** to set to work; **das ist sein ~** this is his doing; **ab ~** (*Comm*) ex works

Werk- *zW*: **Werkstatt** (**-, -stätten**) *f*

workshop; (*Aut*) garage; **Werkstoff** *m* material; **Werktag** *m* working day; **werktags** *adv* on working days; **werktätig** *adj* working; **Werkzeug** *nt* tool; **Werkzeugkasten** *m* toolbox

Wermut ['ve:rmu:t] (**-(e)s, -s**) *m* wormwood; (*Wein*) vermouth

Wert [ve:rt] (**-(e)s, -e**) *m* worth; (*Fin*) value; **~ legen auf** *+akk* to attach importance to; **es hat doch keinen ~** it's useless; **im ~e von** to the value of

wert [ve:rt] *adj* worth; (*geschätzt*) dear; (*würdig*) worthy; **das ist nichts/viel ~** it's not worth anything/it's worth a lot; **das ist es/er mir ~** it's/he's worth that to me; **ein Auto ist viel ~** (*nützlich*) a car is very useful

Wertangabe *f* declaration of value

werten *vt* to rate; (*beurteilen*) to judge; (*Sport: als gültig werten*) to allow; **~ als** to rate as; to judge to be

Wert- *zW*: **Wertgegenstand** *m* article of value; **wertlos** *adj* worthless; **Wertpapier** *nt* security

wertvoll *adj* valuable

Wesen ['ve:zən] (**-s, -**) *nt* (*Geschöpf*) being; (*Natur, Character*) nature

wesentlich *adj* significant; (*beträchtlich*) considerable; **im W~en** essentially; (*im Großen*) in the main

weshalb [vɛs'halp] *adv* why

Wespe ['vɛspə] (**-, -n**) *f* wasp

wessen ['vɛsən] *gen von* **wer** ▷ *pron* whose

Wessi ['vɛsɪ] (**-s, -s**) (*umg*) *m* West German

Westdeutschland *nt* (*Pol: früher*) West Germany; (*Geog*) Western Germany

Weste ['vɛstə] (**-, -n**) *f* waistcoat, vest (*US*); **eine reine ~ haben** (*fig*) to have a clean slate

Westen (**-s**) *m* west

Westeuropa *nt* Western Europe

westlich *adj* western ▷ *adv* to the west

weswegen [vɛs've:gən] *adv* why

wett [vɛt] *adj* even; **~ sein** to be quits

Wettbewerb *m* competition

wettbewerbsfähig *adj* competitive

Wette (**-, -n**) *f* bet, wager; **um die ~ laufen** to run a race (with each other)

wetten ['vɛtən] *vt, vi* to bet; **so haben wir nicht gewettet!** that's not part of the bargain!

Wetter ['vɛtər] (**-s, -**) *nt* weather; (*Min*) air; **Wetterbericht** *m* weather report; **Wetterdienst** *m* meteorological service; **wetterfühlig** *adj* sensitive to changes in the weather; **Wetterlage** *f* (weather) situation

Wetter- *zW*: **Wettervorhersage** *f* weather forecast; **Wetterwarte** *f* weather station

Wett- *zW*: **Wettkampf** *m* contest; **Wettlauf** *m* race; **ein Wettlauf mit der Zeit** a race against time

wettmachen *vt* to make good

Wett- *zW*: **Wettspiel** *nt* match; **Wettstreit** *m* contest

WEZ *abk* (= *westeuropäische Zeit*) GMT

WG *abk* = **Wohngemeinschaft**

Whisky ['vɪski] (**-s, -s**) *m* whisky (*Brit*), whiskey (*US, Ireland*)

wich *etc* [vɪç] *vb siehe* **weichen**

Wicht [vɪçt] (**-(e)s, -e**) *m* titch; (*pej*) worthless creature

wichtig *adj* important; **sich selbst/etw (zu) ~ nehmen** to take o.s./sth (too) seriously; **Wichtigkeit** *f* importance

wickeln ['vɪkəln] *vt* to wind; (*Haare*) to set; (*Kind*) to change; **da bist du schief gewickelt!** (*fig: umg*) you're very much mistaken; **jdn/etw in etw** *akk* **~** to wrap sb/sth in sth

Widder ['vɪdər] (**-s, -**) *m* ram; (*Astrol*) Aries

wider ['vi:dər] *präp +akk* against

widerfahren *unreg vi untr*: **jdm ~** to happen to sb

widerlegen *vt untr* to refute

widerlich ['vi:dərlɪç] *adj* disgusting, repulsive; **Widerlichkeit** *f* repulsiveness

widerrechtlich *adj* unlawful

Widerrede *f* contradiction; **keine ~!** don't argue!

Widerruf ['vi:dərru:f] *m* retraction; countermanding; **bis auf ~** until revoked

widerrufen *unreg vt untr* to retract; (*Anordnung*) to revoke; (*Befehl*) to countermand

widersetzen *vr untr*: **sich jdm ~** to oppose sb; (*der Polizei*) to resist sb; **sich einer Sache ~** to oppose sth; (*einem Befehl*) to refuse to comply with sth

widerspenstig ['vi:dərʃpɛnstɪç] *adj* wilful (*Brit*), willful (*US*); **Widerspenstigkeit** *f* wilfulness (*Brit*), willfulness (*US*)

widersprechen *unreg vi untr*: **jdm ~** to contradict sb

Widerspruch ['vi:dərʃprʊx] *m* contradiction; **ein ~ in sich** a contradiction in terms

widersprüchlich ['vi:dərʃprʏçlɪç] *adj* contradictory, inconsistent

widerspruchslos *adv* without arguing

Widerstand ['vi:dərʃtant] *m* resistance; **der Weg des geringsten ~es** the line of least resistance; **jdm/etw ~ leisten** to resist sb/sth

Widerstands- *zW*: **Widerstandsbewegung** *f* resistance (movement); **widerstandsfähig** *adj* resistant, tough; **widerstandslos** *adj* unresisting

widerstehen *unreg vi untr*: **jdm/etw ~** to withstand sb/sth

Wider- *zW*: **widerwärtig** *adj* nasty, horrid; **Widerwille** *m*: **Widerwille (gegen)** aversion (to); (*Abneigung*) distaste (for); (*Widerstreben*) reluctance; **widerwillig** *adj* unwilling, reluctant

widmen ['vɪtmən] *vt* to dedicate ▷ *vr* to devote o.s.

Widmung *f* dedication

widrig ['vi:drɪç] *adj* (*Umstände*) adverse; (*Mensch*) repulsive

wie [vi:] *adv* how; **wie groß/schnell?** how big/fast?; **wie viel** how much; **wie viel Menschen** how many people; **wie wärs?**

how about it?; **wie wärs mit einem Whisky?** (*umg*) how about a whisky?; **wie nennt man das?** what is that called?; **wie ist er?** what's he like?; **wie gut du das kannst!** you're very good at it; **wie bitte?** pardon? (*Brit*), pardon me? (*US*); (*entrüstet*) I beg your pardon!; **und wie!** and how! ▷ *konj* **1** (*bei Vergleichen*): **so schön wie ...** as beautiful as ...; **wie ich schon sagte** as I said; **wie noch nie** as never before; **wie du** like you; **singen wie ein ...** to sing like a ...; **wie (zum Beispiel)** such as (for example) **2** (*zeitlich*): **wie er das hörte, ging er** when he heard that he left; **er hörte, wie der Regen fiel** he heard the rain falling

wieder ['vi:dər] *adv* again; **~ da sein** to be back (again); **gehst du schon ~?** are you off again?; **~ ein(e) ...** another ...; **das ist auch ~ wahr** that's true enough; **da sieht man mal ~ ...** it just shows ...; **~ finden, ~ gutmachen** *etc* = **wiederfinden, wiedergutmachen** *etc*

wieder- *zW*: **Wiederaufbau** [-'|aʊfbaʊ] *m* rebuilding; **wiederaufbereiten** *vt* to recycle; (*Atommüll*) to reprocess; **wiederbekommen** *unreg vt* to get back; **wiederbringen** *unreg vt* to bring back; **wiedererkennen** *unreg vt* to recognize; **Wiedererstattung** *f* reimbursement

Wiedergabe *f* (*von Rede, Ereignis*) account; (*Wiederholung*) repetition; (*Darbietung*) performance; (*Reproduktion*) reproduction

wieder- *zW*: **wiedergeben** *unreg vt* (*zurückgeben*) to return; (*Erzählung etc*) to repeat; (*Gefühle etc*) to convey; **wiedergutmachen** *vt* to make up for; (*Fehler*) to put right; **Wiedergutmachung** *f* reparation; **wiederherstellen** *vt* (*Gesundheit, Gebäude, Ruhe*) to restore

wiederholen *vt untr* to repeat

Wiederholung *f* repetition

wieder- *zW*: **Wiederhören** *nt*: **auf Wiederhören** (*Tel*) goodbye; **Wiederkehr (-)** *f* return; (*von Vorfall*) repetition, recurrence; **wiedersehen** *unreg vt* to see again; **auf Wiedersehen** goodbye; **wiederum** *adv* again; (*seinerseits etc*) in turn; (*andererseits*) on the other hand; **wiedervereinigen** *vt* to reunite; **Wiedervereinigung** *f* reunification; **Wiederwahl** *f* re-election

Wiege ['vi:ge] **(-, -n)** *f* cradle

wiegen[1] *vt* (*schaukeln*) to rock; (*Kopf*) to shake

wiegen[2] *unreg vt, vi* to weigh; **schwer ~** (*fig*) to carry a lot of weight; (*Irrtum*) to be serious

wiehern ['vi:ərn] *vi* to neigh, whinny

Wien [vi:n] **(-s)** *nt* Vienna

wies *etc* [vi:s] *vb siehe* **weisen**

Wiese ['vi:zə] **(-, -n)** *f* meadow

Wiesel ['vi:zəl] **(-s, -)** *nt* weasel; **schnell** *od* **flink wie ein ~** quick as a flash

wieso [vi:'zo:] *adv* why

wievielmal [vi:'fi:lma:l] *adv* how often

wievielte, r, s *adj*: **zum ~n Mal?** how many times?; **den W~n haben wir?** what's the date?; **an ~r Stelle?** in what place?; **der ~ Besucher war er?** how many visitors were there before him?

wieweit [vi:'vaɪt] *adv* to what extent

wild [vɪlt] *adj* wild; **~er Streik** unofficial strike; **in ~er Ehe leben** (*veraltet, hum*) to live in sin; **~ entschlossen** (*umg*) dead set

Wild **(-(e)s)** *nt* game

wildern ['vɪldərn] *vi* to poach

wild- *zW*: **wildfremd** ['vɪlt'frɛmt] (*umg*) *adj* quite strange *od* unknown; **Wildheit** *f* wildness; **Wildleder** *nt* suede

Wildnis **(-, -se)** *f* wilderness

Wildschwein *nt* (wild) boar

Wille ['vɪlə] **(-ns, -n)** *m* will; **jdm seinen ~n lassen** to let sb have his own way; **seinen eigenen ~n haben** to be self-willed

willen *präp +gen*: **um ... ~** for the sake of ...

willenlos *adj* weak-willed

willensstark *adj* strong-willed

willig *adj* willing

willkommen [vɪl'kɔmən] *adj* welcome; **jdn ~ heißen** to welcome sb; **herzlich ~ (in** *+dat***)** welcome (to); **Willkommen (-s, -)** *nt* welcome

willkürlich *adj* arbitrary; (*Bewegung*) voluntary

wimmeln ['vɪməln] *vi*: **~ (von)** to swarm (with)

wimmern ['vɪmərn] *vi* to whimper

Wimper ['vɪmpər] **(-, -n)** *f* eyelash; **ohne mit der ~ zu zucken** (*fig*) without batting an eyelid

Wimperntusche *f* mascara

Wind [vɪnt] **(-(e)s, -e)** *m* wind; **den Mantel** *od* **das Fähnchen nach dem ~ hängen** to trim one's sails to the wind; **etw in den ~ schlagen** to turn a deaf ear to sth

Windbeutel *m* cream puff; (*fig*) windbag

Winde ['vɪndə] **(-, -n)** *f* (*Tech*) winch, windlass; (*Bot*) bindweed

Windel ['vɪndəl] **(-, -n)** *f* nappy (*Brit*), diaper (*US*)

winden[1] ['vɪndən] *vi unpers* to be windy

winden[2] *unreg vt* to wind; (*Kranz*) to weave; (*entwinden*) to twist ▷ *vr* to wind; (*Person*) to writhe; (*fig: ausweichen*) to try to wriggle out

Windenergie *f* wind power

Windhose *f* whirlwind

Windhund *m* greyhound; (*Mensch*) fly-by-night

windig ['vɪndɪç] *adj* windy; (*fig*) dubious

Wind- *zW*: **Windkraftanlage** *f* wind power station; **Windmühle** *f* windmill; **gegen Windmühlen (an)kämpfen** (*fig*) to tilt at windmills; **Windpark** *m* wind farm

Windpocken *pl* chickenpox *sing*

Wind- *zW*: **Windschutzscheibe** *f* (*Aut*) windscreen (*Brit*), windshield (*US*); **Windstärke** *f* wind force; **Windstille** *f* calm; **Windsurfen** *nt* windsurfing

Wink [vɪŋk] **(-(e)s, -e)** *m* (*mit Kopf*) nod; (*mit Hand*) wave; (*Tipp, Hinweis*) hint; **ein ~ mit dem Zaunpfahl** a broad hint

Winkel ['vɪŋkəl] **(-s, -)** *m* (*Math*) angle; (*Gerät*)

set square; (*in Raum*) corner
winken ['vɪŋkən] *vt, vi* to wave; **dem Sieger winkt eine Reise nach Italien** the (lucky) winner will receive a trip to Italy
winseln ['vɪnzəln] *vi* to whine
Winter ['vɪntər] (**-s, -**) *m* winter; **winterlich** *adj* wintry; **Winterreifen** *m* winter tyre (*Brit*) *od* tire (*US*); **Winterschlussverkauf** *m* winter sale; **Wintersport** *m* winter sports *pl*
Winzer, in ['vɪntsər(ɪn)] (**-s, -**) *m(f)* wine-grower
winzig ['vɪntsɪç] *adj* tiny
Wipfel ['vɪpfəl] (**-s, -**) *m* treetop
wir [vi:r] *pron* we; **~ alle** all of us, we all
Wirbel ['vɪrbəl] (**-s, -**) *m* whirl, swirl; (*Trubel*) hurly-burly; (*Aufsehen*) fuss; (*Anat*) vertebra; **~ um jdn/etw machen** to make a fuss about sb/sth
Wirbelsäule *f* spine
wirken ['vɪrkən] *vi* to have an effect; (*erfolgreich sein*) to work; (*scheinen*) to seem ▷ *vt* (*Wunder*) to work; **etw auf sich** *akk* **~ lassen** to take sth in
wirklich ['vɪrklɪç] *adj* real; **Wirklichkeit** *f* reality
wirksam ['vɪrkza:m] *adj* effective; **Wirksamkeit** *f* effectiveness
Wirkung ['vɪrkʊŋ] *f* effect
Wirkungs- *zW*: **wirkungslos** *adj* ineffective; **wirkungslos bleiben** to have no effect; **wirkungsvoll** *adj* effective
wirr [vɪr] *adj* confused; (*unrealistisch*) wild; (*Haare etc*) tangled
Wirren *pl* disturbances *pl*
Wirrwarr ['vɪrvar] (**-s**) *m* disorder, chaos; (*von Stimmen*) hubbub; (*von Fäden, Haaren etc*) tangle
Wirt, in [vɪrt(ɪn)] (**-(e)s, -e**) *m(f)* landlord, landlady
Wirtschaft ['vɪrtʃaft] *f* (*Gaststätte*) pub; (*Haushalt*) housekeeping; (*eines Landes*) economy; (*Geschäftsleben*) industry and commerce; (*umg: Durcheinander*) mess; **wirtschaftlich** *adj* economical; (*Pol*) economic; **Wirtschaftlichkeit** *f* economy; (*von Betrieb*) viability
Wirtschafts- *zW*: **Wirtschaftskrise** *f* economic crisis; **Wirtschaftspolitik** *f* economic policy; **Wirtschaftsprüfer** *m* chartered accountant (*Brit*), certified public accountant (*US*); **Wirtschaftswunder** *nt* economic miracle
Wirtshaus *nt* inn
Wisch [vɪʃ] (**-(e)s, -e**) *m* scrap of paper
wischen *vt* to wipe
Wischer (**-s, -**) *m* (*Aut*) wiper
wispern ['vɪspərn] *vt, vi* to whisper
wissbegierig *adj* eager for knowledge
wissen ['vɪsən] *unreg vt, vi* to know; **von jdm/etw nichts ~ wollen** not to be interested in sb/sth; **sie hält sich für wer weiß wie klug** (*umg*) she doesn't half think she's clever; **gewusst wie/wo!** *etc* sheer brilliance!; **ich weiß seine Adresse nicht mehr** (*sich erinnern*) I can't remember his address; **Wissen** (**-s**) *nt* knowledge; **etw gegen (sein) besseres Wissen tun** to do sth against one's better judgement; **nach bestem Wissen und Gewissen** to the best of one's knowledge and belief
Wissenschaft ['vɪsənʃaft] *f* science
Wissenschaftler, in (**-s, -**) *m(f)* scientist; (*Geisteswissenschaftler*) academic
wissenschaftlich *adj* scientific; **W~er Assistent** assistant lecturer
wissenswert *adj* worth knowing
wissentlich *adj* knowing
wittern ['vɪtərn] *vt* to scent; (*fig*) to suspect
Witterung *f* weather; (*Geruch*) scent
Witwe ['vɪtvə] (**-, -n**) *f* widow
Witwer (**-s, -**) *m* widower
Witz [vɪts] (**-es, -e**) *m* joke; **der ~ an der Sache ist, dass ...** the great thing about it is that ...; **Witzbold** (**-(e)s, -e**) *m* joker
witzeln *vi* to joke
witzig *adj* funny
wo [vo:] *adv* where; (*umg: irgendwo*) somewhere ▷ *konj* (*wenn*) if; **im Augenblick, wo ...** the moment (that) ...; **die Zeit, wo ...** the time when ...
woanders [vo:'|andərs] *adv* elsewhere
wob *etc* [vo:p] *vb siehe* **weben**
wobei [vo:'baɪ] *adv* (*rel*) ... in/by/with which; (*interrog*) how; what ... in/by/with; **~ mir gerade einfällt ...** which reminds me ...
Woche ['vɔxə] (**-, -n**) *f* week
Wochen- *zW*: **Wochenende** *nt* weekend; **wochenlang** *adj* lasting weeks ▷ *adv* for weeks; **Wochentag** *m* weekday
wöchentlich ['vœçəntlɪç] *adj, adv* weekly
Wodka ['vɔtka] (**-s, -s**) *m* vodka
wodurch [vo'dʊrç] *adv* (*rel*) through which; (*interrog*) what ... through
wofür [vo'fy:r] *adv* (*rel*) for which; (*interrog*) what ... for
wog *etc* [vo:k] *vb siehe* **wiegen²**
Woge ['vo:gə] (**-, -n**) *f* wave
wogegen [vo'ge:gən] *adv* (*rel*) against which; (*interrog*) what ... against
wogen *vi* to heave, surge
woher [vo'he:r] *adv* where ... from; **~ kommt es eigentlich, dass ...?** how is it that ...?
wohin [vo'hɪn] *adv* where ... to; **~ man auch schaut** wherever you look
Wohl (**-(e)s**) *nt* welfare; **zum ~!** cheers!
wohl [vo:l] *adv* **1** well; (*behaglich*) at ease, comfortable; **sich wohl fühlen** *siehe* **wohlfühlen**; **wohl gemeint** = **wohlgemeint**; **bei dem Gedanken ist mir nicht wohl** I'm not very happy at the thought; **wohl oder übel** whether one likes it or not; **er weiß das sehr wohl** he knows that perfectly well **2** (*wahrscheinlich*) probably; (*vermutlich*) I suppose; (*gewiss*) certainly; (*vielleicht*) perhaps; **sie ist wohl zu Hause** she's probably at home; **sie wird wohl das Haus verkaufen** I suppose *od* presumably she's

going to sell the house; **das ist doch wohl nicht dein Ernst!** surely you're not serious!; **das mag wohl sein** that may well be; **ob das wohl stimmt?** I wonder if that's true; *siehe auch* **wohltun**

wohl- *zW*: **wohlauf** [vo:l'|aʊf] *adj* well, in good health; **Wohlbehagen** *nt* comfort; **wohlbehalten** *adj* safe and sound; **Wohlfahrt** *f* welfare; **Wohlfahrtsstaat** *m* welfare state; **wohlhabend** *adj* wealthy

wohlig *adj* contented; *(gemütlich)* comfortable

wohl- *zW*: **Wohlklang** *m* melodious sound; **wohlschmeckend** *adj* delicious; **Wohlstand** *m* prosperity; **Wohlstandsgesellschaft** *f* affluent society; **Wohltat** *f (Gefallen)* favour *(Brit)*, favor *(US)*; *(gute Tat)* good deed; *(Erleichterung)* relief; **Wohltäter** *m* benefactor; **wohltätig** *adj* charitable; **wohltun** *unreg vi*: **jdm wohltun** to do sb good; **wohlweislich** *adv* prudently; **Wohlwollen** (**-s**) *nt* good will; **wohlwollend** *adj* benevolent

wohnen ['vo:nən] *vi* to live

wohn- *zW*: **Wohngemeinschaft** *f* people sharing a flat *(Brit) od* apartment *(US)*; *(von Hippies)* commune; **wohnhaft** *adj* resident; **Wohnheim** *nt (für Studenten)* hall (of residence), dormitory *(US)*; *(für Senioren)* home; *(bes für Arbeiter)* hostel; **wohnlich** *adj* comfortable; **Wohnmobil** *nt* motor caravan *(Brit)*, motor home *(US)*; **Wohnort** *m* domicile; **Wohnsitz** *m* place of residence; **ohne festen Wohnsitz** of no fixed abode

Wohnung *f* house; *(Etagenwohnung)* flat *(Brit)*, apartment *(US)*

Wohnungsbau *m* house-building

wohn- *zW*: **Wohnwagen** *m* caravan *(Brit)*, trailer *(US)*; **Wohnzimmer** *nt* living room

wölben ['vœlbən] *vt, vr* to curve

Wölbung *f* curve

Wolf [vɔlf] (**-(e)s, ¨-e**) *m* wolf; *(Tech)* shredder; *(Fleischwolf)* mincer *(Brit)*, grinder *(US)*

Wolke ['vɔlkə] (**-, -n**) *f* cloud; **aus allen ~n fallen** *(fig)* to be flabbergasted *(umg)*

Wolkenkratzer *m* skyscraper

wolkig ['vɔlkɪç] *adj* cloudy

Wolle ['vɔlə] (**-, -n**) *f* wool; **sich mit jdm in die ~ kriegen** *(fig: umg)* to start squabbling with sb

wollen¹ ['vɔlən] *unreg (pt* **wollte**, *pp* **gewollt** *od (als Hilfsverb)* **wollen**) *vt, vi* to want; **ich will nach Hause** I want to go home; **er will nicht** he doesn't want to; **sie wollte das nicht** she didn't want it; **wenn du willst** if you like; **ich will, dass du mir zuhörst** I want you to listen to me; **oh, das hab ich nicht gewollt** oh, I didn't mean to do that; **ich weiß nicht, was er will** *(verstehe ihn nicht)* I don't know what he's on about ▷ *Hilfsverb*: **er will ein Haus kaufen** he wants to buy a house; **ich wollte, ich wäre ...** I wish I w ere ...; **etw gerade tun wollen** to be just about to *od* going to do sth; **und so jemand** *od* **etwas will Lehrer sein!** *(umg)* and he calls himself a teacher!; **das will alles gut überlegt sein** that needs a lot of thought

wollen² *adj* woollen *(Brit)*, woolen *(US)*

wollüstig ['vɔlʏstɪç] *adj* lusty, sensual

wo- *zW*: **womit** [vo'mɪt] *adv (rel)* with which; *(interrog)* what ... with; **womit kann ich dienen?** what can I do for you?; **womöglich** [vo'mø:klɪç] *adv* probably, I suppose; **wonach** [vo'na:x] *adv (rel)* after/for which; *(interrog)* what ... after

Wonne ['vɔnə] (**-, -n**) *f* joy, bliss

woran [vo'ran] *adv (rel)* on/at which; *(interrog)* what ... on/at; **~ liegt das?** what's the reason for it?

worauf [vo'raʊf] *adv (rel)* on which; *(interrog)* what ... on; *(zeitlich)* whereupon; **~ du dich verlassen kannst** of that you can be sure

woraus [vo'raʊs] *adv (rel)* from/out of which; *(interrog)* what ... from/out of

worin [vo'rɪn] *adv (rel)* in which; *(interrog)* what ... in

Wort [vɔrt] (**-(e)s, ¨-er** *od* **-e**) *nt* word; **jdn beim ~ nehmen** to take sb at his word; **ein ernstes ~ mit jdm reden** to have a serious talk with sb; **man kann sein eigenes ~ nicht (mehr) verstehen** you can't hear yourself speak; **jdm aufs ~ gehorchen** to obey sb's every word; **zu ~ kommen** to get a chance to speak; **jdm das ~ erteilen** to allow sb to speak; **wortbrüchig** *adj* not true to one's word

Wörterbuch ['vœrtərbu:x] *nt* dictionary

Wort- *zW*: **wortkarg** *adj* taciturn; **Wortlaut** *m* wording; **im Wortlaut** verbatim

wörtlich ['vœrtlɪç] *adj* literal

Wort- *zW*: **wortlos** *adj* mute; **wortreich** *adj* wordy, verbose; **Wortschatz** *m* vocabulary; **Wortspiel** *nt* play on words, pun

worüber [vo'ry:bər] *adv (rel)* over/about which; *(interrog)* what ... over/about

worum [vo'rʊm] *adv (rel)* about/round which; *(interrog)* what ... about/round; **~ handelt es sich?** what's it about?

worunter [vo'rʊntər] *adv (rel)* under which; *(interrog)* what ... under

wo- *zW*: **wovon** [vo'fɔn] *adv (rel)* from which; *(interrog)* what ... from; **wovor** [vo'fɔr] *adv (rel)* in front of/before which; *(interrog)* in front of/before what; **wozu** [vo'tsu] *adv (rel)* to/for which; *(interrog)* what ... for/to; *(warum)* why; **wozu soll das gut sein?** what's the point of that?

Wrack [vrak] (**-(e)s, -s**) *nt* wreck

wringen ['vrɪŋən] *unreg vt* to wring

Wucher ['vu:xər] (**-s**) *m* profiteering; **Wucherer** (**-s, -**) *m*, **Wucherin** *f* profiteer; **wucherisch** *adj* profiteering

wuchern *vi (Pflanzen)* to grow wild

Wucherung *f (Med)* growth

Wuchs [vu:ks] (**-es**) *m (Wachstum)* growth; *(Statur)* build

wuchs *etc vb siehe* **wachsen**[1]
Wucht [vʊxt] (-) *f* force
wuchtig *adj* massive, solid
wühlen ['vy:lən] *vi* to scrabble; (*Tier*) to root; (*Maulwurf*) to burrow; (*umg: arbeiten*) to slave away ▷ *vt* to dig
Wulst [vʊlst] (**-es, ¨-e**) *m* bulge; (*an Wunde*) swelling
Wunder (**-s, -**) *nt* miracle; **es ist kein ~** it's no wonder; **meine Eltern denken ~ was passiert ist** my parents think goodness knows what has happened; **wunderbar** *adj* wonderful, marvellous (*Brit*), marvelous (*US*); **Wunderkind** *nt* child prodigy; **wunderlich** *adj* odd, peculiar
wundern *vt* to surprise ▷ *vr*: **sich ~ über** *+akk* to be surprised at
Wunder- *zW*: **wunderschön** *adj* beautiful; **wundervoll** *adj* wonderful
Wundstarrkrampf ['vʊntʃtarkrampf] *m* tetanus, lockjaw
Wunsch [vʊnʃ] (**-(e)s, ¨-e**) *m* wish; **haben Sie (sonst) noch einen ~?** (*beim Einkauf etc*) is there anything else you'd like?; **auf jds (besonderen/ausdrücklichen) ~ hin** at sb's (special/express) request
wünschen ['vʏnʃən] *vt* to wish ▷ *vi*: **zu wünschen/viel zu ~ übrig lassen** to leave something/a great deal to be desired; **sich** *dat* **etw ~** to want sth, wish for sth; **was ~ Sie?** (*in Geschäft*) what can I do for you?; (*in Restaurant*) what would you like?
wünschenswert *adj* desirable
Würde ['vʏrdə] (**-, -n**) *f* dignity; (*Stellung*) honour (*Brit*), honor (*US*); **unter aller ~ sein** to be beneath contempt
Würdenträger *m* dignitary
würdevoll *adj* dignified
würdig ['vʏrdɪç] *adj* worthy; (*würdevoll*) dignified
würdigen ['vʏrdɪgən] *vt* to appreciate; **etw zu ~ wissen** to appreciate sth; **jdn keines Blickes ~** not to so much as look at sb
Wurf [vʊrf] (**-(e)s, ¨-e**) *m* throw; (*Junge*) litter
Würfel ['vʏrfəl] (**-s, -**) *m* dice; (*Math*) cube; **die ~ sind gefallen** the die is cast; **Würfelbecher** *m* (dice) cup
würfeln *vi* to play dice ▷ *vt* to dice
Würfelzucker *m* lump sugar
würgen ['vʏrgən] *vt, vi* to choke; **mit Hängen und W~** by the skin of one's teeth
Wurm [vʊrm] (**-(e)s, ¨-er**) *m* worm; **da steckt der ~ drin** (*fig: umg*) there's something wrong somewhere; (*verdächtig*) there's something fishy about it (*umg*)
wurmen (*umg*) *vt* to rile, nettle
Wurmfortsatz *m* (*Med*) appendix
wurmig *adj* worm-eaten
wurmstichig *adj* worm-ridden
Wurst [vʊrst] (**-, ¨-e**) *f* sausage; **das ist mir ~** (*umg*) I don't care, I don't give a damn; **jetzt geht es um die ~** (*fig: umg*) the moment of truth has come
Würstchen ['vʏrstçən] *nt* frankfurter, hot dog sausage
Würze ['vʏrtsə] (**-, -n**) *f* seasoning
Wurzel ['vʊrtsəl] (**-, -n**) *f* root; **~n schlagen** (*lit*) to root; (*fig*) to put down roots; **die ~ aus 4 ist 2** (*Math*) the square root of 4 is 2
würzen *vt* to season; (*würzig machen*) to spice
würzig *adj* spicy
wusch *etc* [vu:ʃ] *vb siehe* **waschen**
wusste *etc* ['vʊstə] *vb siehe* **wissen**
wüst [vy:st] *adj* untidy, messy; (*ausschweifend*) wild; (*öde*) waste; (*umg: heftig*) terrible; **jdn ~ beschimpfen** to use vile language to sb
Wüste (**-, -n**) *f* desert; **die ~ Gobi** the Gobi Desert; **jdn in die ~ schicken** (*fig*) to send sb packing
Wut [vu:t] (**-**) *f* rage, fury; **eine ~ (auf jdn/etw) haben** to be furious (with sb/sth); **Wutanfall** *m* fit of rage
wüten ['vy:tən] *vi* to rage
wütend *adj* furious, enraged

X, **x** [ɪks] *nt* X, x; **X wie Xanthippe** ≈ X for Xmas; **jdm ein X für ein U vormachen** to put one over on sb (*umg*)

X-Beine [ˈɪksbaɪnə] *pl* knock-knees *pl*

x-beliebig [ɪksbəˈliːbɪç] *adj* any (... whatever)

x-mal [ˈɪksmaːl] *adv* any number of times, n times

Y, y ['ʏpsilɔn] *nt* Y, y; **Y wie Ypsilon** ≈ Y for Yellow, ≈ Y for Yoke (*US*)
Yen [jɛn] (**-(s), -(s)**) *m* yen
Yoga ['jo:ga] (**-(s)**) *m od nt* yoga
Ypsilon ['ʏpsilɔn] (**-(s), -s**) *nt* the letter Y

Zz

Z, **z** [tsɛt] *nt* Z, z; **Z wie Zacharias** ≈ Z for Zebra
Zacke ['tsakə] (**-, -n**) *f* point; (*Bergzacke*) jagged peak; (*Gabelzacke*) prong; (*Kammzacke*) tooth
zackig ['tsakıç] *adj* jagged; (*umg*) smart; (: *Tempo*) brisk
zaghaft ['tsa:khaft] *adj* timid
Zaghaftigkeit *f* timidity
zäh [tsɛ:] *adj* tough; (*Mensch*) tenacious; (*Flüssigkeit*) thick; (*schleppend*) sluggish; **zähflüssig** *adj* viscous; (*Verkehr*) slow-moving
Zähigkeit *f* toughness; tenacity
Zahl [tsa:l] (**-, -en**) *f* number
zahlbar *adj* payable
zahlen *vt, vi* to pay; **~ bitte!** the bill *od* check (*US*) please!
zählen ['tsɛ:lən] *vt* to count ▷ *vi* (*sich verlassen*): **~ auf** *+akk* to count on; **seine Tage sind gezählt** his days are numbered; **~ zu** to be numbered among
zahlenmäßig *adj* numerical
Zähler (**-s, -**) *m* (*Tech*) meter; (*Math*) numerator
Zahl- *zW*: **zahllos** *adj* countless; **zahlreich** *adj* numerous; **Zahltag** *m* payday
Zahlung *f* payment; **in ~ geben/nehmen** to give/take in part exchange
Zahlungs- *zW*: **zahlungsfähig** *adj* solvent; **zahlungsunfähig** *adj* insolvent
Zahlwort *nt* numeral
zahm [tsa:m] *adj* tame
zähmen ['tsɛ:mən] *vt* to tame; (*fig*) to curb
Zahn [tsa:n] (**-(e)s, ¨-e**) *m* tooth; **die dritten Zähne** (*umg*) false teeth *pl*; **einen ~ draufhaben** (*umg*: *Geschwindigkeit*) to be going like the clappers (*Brit*) *od* like crazy (*US*); **jdm auf den ~ fühlen** (*fig*) to sound sb out; **einen ~ zulegen** (*fig*) to get a move on; **Zahnarzt** *m*, **Zahnärztin** *f* dentist; **Zahnbürste** *f* toothbrush; **Zahncreme** *f* toothpaste; **Zahnersatz** *m* denture; **Zahnfleisch** *nt* gums *pl*; **auf dem Zahnfleisch gehen** (*fig*: *umg*) to be all in, be at the end of one's tether; **Zahnpasta** *f*, **Zahnpaste** *f* toothpaste; **Zahnrad** *nt* cog(wheel); **Zahnradbahn** *f* rack railway; **Zahnschmerzen** *pl* toothache *sing*; **Zahnseide** *f* dental floss; **Zahnspange** *f* brace; **Zahnstein** *m* tartar; **Zahnstocher** (**-s, -**) *m* toothpick
Zaire [za'i:r] (**-s**) *nt* Zaire
Zange ['tsaŋə] (**-, -n**) *f* pliers *pl*; (*Zuckerzange etc*) tongs *pl*; (*Beißzange, Zool*) pincers *pl*; (*Med*) forceps *pl*; **jdn in die ~ nehmen** (*fig*) to put the screws on sb (*umg*)
zanken ['tsaŋkən] *vi, vr* to quarrel
Zäpfchen ['tsɛpfçən] *nt* (*Anat*) uvula; (*Med*) suppository
Zapfen ['tsapfən] (**-s, -**) *m* plug; (*Bot*) cone; (*Eiszapfen*) icicle
zapfen *vt* to tap
Zapfenstreich *m* (*Mil*) tattoo
Zapfsäule *f* petrol (*Brit*) *od* gas (*US*) pump
zappelig ['tsapəlıç] *adj* wriggly; (*unruhig*) fidgety
zappeln ['tsapəln] *vi* to wriggle; to fidget; **jdn ~ lassen** (*fig*: *umg*) to keep sb in suspense
Zar [tsa:r] (**-en, -en**) *m* tzar, czar
zart [tsa:rt] *adj* (*weich, leise*) soft; (*Braten etc*) tender; (*fein, schwächlich*) delicate; **Zartgefühl** *nt* tact; **Zartheit** *f* softness; tenderness; delicacy
zärtlich ['tsɛ:rtlıç] *adj* tender, affectionate; **Zärtlichkeit** *f* tenderness; **Zärtlichkeiten** *pl* caresses *pl*
Zauber ['tsaʊbər] (**-s, -**) *m* magic; (*Zauberbann*) spell; **fauler ~** (*umg*) humbug
Zauberei [tsaʊbə'raı] *f* magic
Zauberer (**-s, -**) *m* magician; (*Zauberkünstler*) conjurer
Zauber- *zW*: **zauberhaft** *adj* magical, enchanting; **Zauberin** *f* magician; conjurer; **Zauberkünstler** *m* conjurer
zaubern *vi* to conjure, do magic
zaudern ['tsaʊdərn] *vi* to hesitate
Zaum [tsaʊm] (**-(e)s, Zäume**) *m* bridle; **etw im ~ halten** to keep sth in check
Zaun [tsaʊn] (**-(e)s, Zäune**) *m* fence; **vom ~(e) brechen** (*fig*) to start; **Zaunkönig** *m* wren
z. B. *abk* (= *zum Beispiel*) e.g.
Zebra ['tse:bra] (**-s, -s**) *nt* zebra; **Zebrastreifen** *m* pedestrian crossing (*Brit*), crosswalk (*US*)
Zeche ['tsɛçə] (**-, -n**) *f* (*Rechnung*) bill, check (*US*); (*Bergbau*) mine
Zecke ['tsɛkə] (**-, -n**) *f* tick
Zehe ['tse:ə] (**-, -n**) *f* toe; (*Knoblauchzehe*) clove
zehn [tse:n] *num* ten
Zehnkampf *m* (*Sport*) decathlon
zehnte, r, s *adj* tenth
Zehntel (**-s, -**) *nt* tenth (part)

Zeichen ['tsaɪçən] (**-s, -**) *nt* sign; (*Comput*) character; **jdm ein ~ geben** to give sb a signal; **unser/Ihr ~** (*Comm*) our/your reference; **Zeichensatz** *m* (*Comput*) character set; **Zeichentrickfilm** *m* (animated) cartoon
zeichnen *vt* to draw; (*kennzeichnen*) to mark; (*unterzeichnen*) to sign ▷ *vi* to draw; to sign
Zeichner, in (**-s, -**) *m(f)* artist; **technischer ~** draughtsman (*Brit*), draftsman (*US*)
Zeichnung *f* drawing; (*Markierung*) markings *pl*
Zeigefinger *m* index finger
zeigen ['tsaɪgən] *vt* to show ▷ *vi* to point ▷ *vr* to show o.s.; **~ auf** *+akk* to point to; **es wird sich ~** time will tell; **es zeigte sich, dass …** it turned out that …
Zeiger (**-s, -**) *m* pointer; (*Uhrzeiger*) hand
Zeile ['tsaɪlə] (**-, -n**) *f* line; (*Häuserzeile*) row
Zeilen- *zW*: **Zeilenabstand** *m* line spacing; **Zeilenumbruch** *m* (*Comput*) wraparound
Zeit (**-, -en**) *f* time; (*Gram*) tense; **sich** *dat* **~ lassen** to take one's time; **eine Stunde ~ haben** to have an hour (to spare); **sich** *dat* **für jdn/etw ~ nehmen** to devote time to sb/sth; **eine ~ lang** a while, a time; **von ~ zu Zeit** from time to time; **~ raubend** = **zeitraubend**; **in letzter ~** recently; **nach ~ bezahlt werden** to be paid by the hour; **zu der ~, als …** (at the time) when …; *siehe auch* **zurzeit**
Zeit- *zW*: **Zeitalter** *nt* age; **Zeitarbeit** *f* temporary work; **Zeitgeist** *m* spirit of the times; **zeitgemäß** *adj* in keeping with the times; **Zeitgenosse** *m* contemporary
zeitig *adj, adv* early
Zeit- *zW*: **zeitlich** *adj* temporal ▷ *adv*: **das kann sie zeitlich nicht einrichten** she can't find (the) time for that; **das Zeitliche segnen** (*euph*) to depart this life; **Zeitlupe** *f* slow motion; **Zeitpunkt** *m* moment, point in time; **Zeitraffer** (**-s**) *m* time-lapse photography; **zeitraubend** *adj* time-consuming; **Zeitraum** *m* period; **Zeitrechnung** *f* time, era; **nach/vor unserer Zeitrechnung** A.D./B.C.; **Zeitschrift** *f* periodical
Zeitung *f* newspaper
Zeit- *zW*: **Zeitverschwendung** *f* waste of time; **Zeitvertreib** *m* pastime, diversion; **zeitweilig** *adj* temporary; **zeitweise** *adv* for a time; **Zeitwort** *nt* verb; **Zeitzeichen** *nt* (*Rundf*) time signal; **Zeitzone** *f* time zone; **Zeitzünder** *m* time fuse
Zelle ['tsɛlə] (**-, -n**) *f* cell; (*Telefonzelle*) callbox (*Brit*), booth
Zellstoff *m* cellulose
Zelt [tsɛlt] (**-(e)s, -e**) *nt* tent; **seine ~e aufschlagen/abbrechen** to settle down/pack one's bags; **zelten** *vi* to camp; **Zeltplatz** *m* camp site
Zement [tse'mɛnt] (**-(e)s, -e**) *m* cement
zementieren [tsemɛn'ti:rən] *vt* to cement
zensieren [tsɛn'zi:rən] *vt* to censor; (*Sch*) to mark
Zensur [tsɛn'zu:r] *f* censorship; (*Sch*) mark
Zentimeter [tsɛnti'me:tər] *m od nt* centimetre (*Brit*), centimeter (*US*)
Zentner ['tsɛntnər] (**-s, -**) *m* hundredweight
zentral [tsɛn'tra:l] *adj* central
Zentrale (**-, -n**) *f* central office; (*Tel*) exchange
Zentraleinheit *f* (*Comput*) central processing unit
Zentralheizung *f* central heating
zentralisieren [tsɛntrali'zi:rən] *vt* to centralize
Zentralverriegelung *f* (*Aut*) central locking
Zentrifugalkraft [tsɛntrifu'ga:lkraft] *f* centrifugal force
Zentrifuge [tsɛntri'fu:gə] (**-, -n**) *f* centrifuge; (*für Wäsche*) spin-dryer
Zentrum ['tsɛntrʊm] (**-s, Zentren**) *nt* centre (*Brit*), center (*US*)
Zepter ['tsɛptər] (**-s, -**) *nt* sceptre (*Brit*), scepter (*US*)
zerbrechen *unreg vt, vi* to break
zerbrechlich *adj* fragile
zerdrücken *vt* to squash; to crush; (*Kartoffeln*) to mash
Zeremonie [tseremo'ni:] *f* ceremony
Zerfall *m* decay, disintegration; (*von Kultur, Gesundheit*) decline; **zerfallen** *unreg vi* to disintegrate, decay; (*sich gliedern*): **zerfallen in** *+akk* to fall into
zerfetzen [tsɛr'fɛtsən] *vt* to tear to pieces
zergehen *unreg vi* to melt, dissolve
zerkleinern [tsɛr'klaɪnərn] *vt* to reduce to small pieces
zerlegbar [tsɛr'le:kba:r] *adj* able to be dismantled
zerlegen *vt* to take to pieces; (*Fleisch*) to carve; (*Satz*) to analyse
zerlumpt [tsɛr'lʊmpt] *adj* ragged
zermürben [tsɛr'mʏrbən] *vt* to wear down
zerquetschen *vt* to squash
Zerrbild ['tsɛrbɪlt] *nt* (*fig*) caricature, distorted picture
zerreiben *unreg vt* to grind down
zerreißen *unreg vt* to tear to pieces ▷ *vi* to tear, rip
zerren ['tsɛrən] *vt* to drag ▷ *vi*: **~ (an** *+dat***)** to tug (at)
zerrinnen *unreg vi* to melt away; (*Geld*) to disappear
zerrissen [tsɛr'rɪsən] *pp von* **zerreißen** ▷ *adj* torn, tattered; **Zerrissenheit** *f* tattered state; (*Pol*) disunion, discord; (*innere*) disintegration
Zerrung *f*: **eine ~** a pulled ligament/muscle
zerrütten [tsɛr'rʏtən] *vt* to wreck, destroy
zerrüttet *adj* wrecked, shattered
zerschlagen *unreg vt* to shatter, smash; (*fig: Opposition*) to crush; (*: Vereinigung*) to break up ▷ *vr* to fall through
zerschneiden *unreg vt* to cut up
zerspringen *unreg vi* to shatter ▷ *vi* (*fig*) to burst
Zerstäuber (**-s, -**) *m* atomizer

zerstören *vt* to destroy
Zerstörung *f* destruction
zerstreiten *unreg vr* to fall out, break up
zerstreuen *vt* to disperse, scatter; (*Zweifel etc*) to dispel ▷ *vr* (*sich verteilen*) to scatter; (*fig*) to be dispelled; (*sich ablenken*) to take one's mind off things
zerstreut *adj* scattered; (*Mensch*) absent-minded; **Zerstreutheit** *f* absent-mindedness
Zerstreuung *f* dispersion; (*Ablenkung*) diversion
zerstückeln [tsɛr'ʃtʏkəln] *vt* to cut into pieces
zerteilen *vt* to divide into parts
zertreten *unreg vt* to crush underfoot
Zerwürfnis [tsɛr'vʏrfnɪs] (**-ses, -se**) *nt* dissension, quarrel
zerzausen [tsɛr'tsaʊzən] *vt* (*Haare*) to ruffle up, tousle
Zettel ['tsɛtəl] (**-s, -**) *m* piece *od* slip of paper; (*Notizzettel*) note; (*Formular*) form; **„~ ankleben verboten"** "stick no bills"
Zeug [tsɔʏk] (**-(e)s, -e**) (*umg*) *nt* stuff; (*Ausrüstung*) gear; **dummes ~** (stupid) nonsense; **das ~ haben zu** to have the makings of; **sich ins ~ legen** to put one's shoulder to the wheel; **was das ~ hält** for all one is worth; **jdm am ~ flicken** to find fault with sb
Zeuge ['tsɔʏgə] (**-n, -n**) *m* witness
zeugen *vi* to bear witness, testify ▷ *vt* (*Kind*) to father; **es zeugt von ...** it testifies to ...
Zeugenaussage *f* evidence
Zeugin *f* witness
Zeugnis ['tsɔʏgnɪs] (**-ses, -se**) *nt* certificate; (*Sch*) report; (*Referenz*) reference; (*Aussage*) evidence, testimony; **~ geben von** to be evidence of, testify to
Zeugung ['tsɔʏgʊŋ] *f* procreation
zeugungsunfähig *adj* sterile
z. H., z. Hd. *abk* (= *zu Händen*) att., attn.
zickig *adj* (*albern*) silly; (*prüde*) prudish
Zickzack ['tsɪktsak] (**-(e)s, -e**) *m* zigzag
Ziege ['tsi:gə] (**-, -n**) *f* goat; (*pej*: *umg*: *Frau*) cow (!)
Ziegel ['tsi:gəl] (**-s, -**) *m* brick; (*Dachziegel*) tile
Ziegelei [tsi:gə'laɪ] *f* brickworks
Ziegelstein *m* brick
Ziegenleder *nt* kid
ziehen ['tsi:ən] *unreg vt* to draw; (*zerren*) to pull; (*Schach etc*) to move; (*züchten*) to rear ▷ *vi* to draw; (*umziehen, wandern*) to move; (*Rauch, Wolke etc*) to drift; (*reißen*) to pull ▷ *vb unpers*: **es zieht** there is a draught (*Brit*) *od* draft (*US*), it's draughty (*Brit*) *od* drafty (*US*) ▷ *vr* (*Gummi*) to stretch; (*Grenze etc*) to run; (*Gespräche*) to be drawn out; **etw nach sich ~** to lead to sth, entail sth; **etw ins Lächerliche ~** to ridicule sth; **so was zieht bei mir nicht** I don't like that sort of thing; **zu jdm ~** to move in with sb; **mir ziehts im Rücken** my back hurts
Ziehharmonika ['tsi:harmo:nika] *f* concertina
Ziehung ['tsi:ʊŋ] *f* (*Losziehung*) drawing

Ziel [tsi:l] (**-(e)s, -e**) *nt* (*einer Reise*) destination; (*Sport*) finish; (*Mil*) target; (*Absicht*) goal, aim; **jdm/sich ein ~ stecken** to set sb/o.s. a goal; **am ~ sein** to be at one's destination; (*fig*) to have reached one's goal; **über das ~ hinausschießen** (*fig*) to overshoot the mark; **zielen** *vi*: **zielen (auf** *+akk***)** to aim (at); **Zielgruppe** *f* target group; **Ziellinie** *f* (*Sport*) finishing line; **ziellos** *adj* aimless; **Zielscheibe** *f* target; **zielstrebig** *adj* purposeful
ziemlich ['tsi:mlɪç] *adj attrib* (*Anzahl*) fair ▷ *adv* quite, pretty (*umg*); (*beinahe*) almost, nearly; **eine ~e Anstrengung** quite an effort; **~ lange** quite a long time; **~ fertig** almost *od* nearly ready
Zierde ['tsi:rdə] (**-, -n**) *f* ornament, decoration; (*Schmuckstück*) adornment
zieren ['tsi:rən] *vr* to act coy
zierlich *adj* dainty; **Zierlichkeit** *f* daintiness
Zierstrauch *m* flowering shrub
Ziffer ['tsɪfər] (**-, -n**) *f* figure, digit; **römische/arabische ~n** roman/arabic numerals; **Zifferblatt** *nt* dial, (clock *od* watch) face
zig [tsɪk] (*umg*) *adj* umpteen
Zigarette [tsiga'rɛtə] *f* cigarette
Zigaretten- *zW*: **Zigarettenautomat** *m* cigarette machine; **Zigarettenschachtel** *f* cigarette packet *od* pack (*US*); **Zigarettenspitze** *f* cigarette holder
Zigarillo [tsiga'rɪlo] (**-s, -s**) *nt od m* cigarillo
Zigarre [tsi'garə] (**-, -n**) *f* cigar
Zigeuner, in [tsi'gɔʏnər(ɪn)] (**-s, -**) *m(f)* gipsy
Zimmer ['tsɪmər] (**-s, -**) *nt* room; **Zimmerantenne** *f* indoor aerial; **Zimmerlautstärke** *f* reasonable volume; **Zimmermädchen** *nt* chambermaid; **Zimmermann** (**-(e)s,** *pl* **-leute**) *m* carpenter
zimmern *vt* to make from wood
Zimmer- *zW*: **Zimmerpflanze** *f* indoor plant; **Zimmervermittlung** *f* accommodation (*Brit*) *od* accommodations (*US*) service
zimperlich ['tsɪmpərlɪç] *adj* squeamish; (*pingelig*) fussy, finicky
Zimt [tsɪmt] (**-(e)s, -e**) *m* cinnamon; **Zimtstange** *f* cinnamon stick
Zink [tsɪŋk] (**-(e)s**) *nt* zinc
Zinn [tsɪn] (**-(e)s**) *nt* (*Element*) tin; (*in Zinnwaren*) pewter
Zinnwaren *pl* pewter *sing*
Zins [tsɪns] (**-es, -en**) *m* interest
Zinseszins *m* compound interest
Zins- *zW*: **Zinsfuß** *m* rate of interest; **zinslos** *adj* interest-free; **Zinssatz** *m* rate of interest
Zipfel ['tsɪpfəl] (**-s, -**) *m* corner; (*von Land*) tip; (*Hemdzipfel*) tail; (*Wurstzipfel*) end; **Zipfelmütze** *f* pointed cap
zirka ['tsɪrka] *adv* = **circa**
Zirkel ['tsɪrkəl] (**-s, -**) *m* circle; (*Math*) pair of compasses
Zirkus ['tsɪrkʊs] (**-, -se**) *m* circus; (*umg*: *Getue*) fuss, to-do
Zirrhose [tsɪ'ro:zə] (**-, -n**) *f* cirrhosis

zischen ['tsɪʃən] *vi* to hiss; (*Limonade*) to fizz; (*Fett*) to sizzle
Zitat [tsi'ta:t] (**-(e)s, -e**) *nt* quotation, quote
zitieren [tsi'ti:rən] *vt* to quote; (*vorladen, rufen*): **~ (vor** *+akk***)** to summon (before)
Zitronat [tsitro'na:t] (**-(e)s, -e**) *nt* candied lemon peel
Zitrone [tsi'tro:nə] (**-, -n**) *f* lemon
Zitronen- *zW*: **Zitronenlimonade** *f* lemonade; **Zitronensaft** *m* lemon juice
zittern ['tsɪtərn] *vi* to tremble; **vor jdm ~** to be terrified of sb
zivil [tsi'vi:l] *adj* civilian; (*anständig*) civil; (*Preis*) moderate; **~er Ungehorsam** civil disobedience; **Zivil** (**-s**) *nt* plain clothes *pl*; (*Mil*) civilian clothing; **Zivilbevölkerung** *f* civilian population; **Zivilcourage** *f* courage of one's convictions
Zivildienst *m alternative service (for conscientious objectors)*
Zivilisation [tsivilizatsi'o:n] *f* civilization
Zivilisationserscheinung *f* phenomenon of civilization
Zivilisationskrankheit *f* disease of civilized man
zivilisieren [tsivili'zi:rən] *vt* to civilize
Zivilist [tsivi'lɪst] *m* civilian
zog *etc* [tso:k] *vb siehe* **ziehen**
zögern ['tsø:gərn] *vi* to hesitate
Zölibat [tsøli'ba:t] (**-(e)s**) *nt od m* celibacy
Zoll[1] [tsɔl] (**-(e)s, -**) *m* (*Maß*) inch
Zoll[2] (**-(e)s, ¨-e**) *m* customs *pl*; (*Abgabe*) duty; **Zollabfertigung** *f* customs clearance; **Zollamt** *nt* customs office; **Zollbeamte, r** *m* customs official; **Zollerklärung** *f* customs declaration; **zollfrei** *adj* duty-free; **zollpflichtig** *adj* liable to duty, dutiable
Zone ['tso:nə] (**-, -n**) *f* zone; (*von Fahrkarte*) fare stage
Zoo [tso:] (**-s, -s**) *m* zoo
Zoologe [tsoo'lo:gə] (**-n, -n**) *m* zoologist
Zoologie *f* zoology
zoologisch *adj* zoological
Zoom [zu:m] (**-s, -s**) *nt* zoom shot; (*Objektiv*) zoom lens
Zopf [tsɔpf] (**-(e)s, ¨-e**) *m* plait; pigtail; **alter ~** antiquated custom
Zorn [tsɔrn] (**-(e)s**) *m* anger
zornig *adj* angry
Zote ['tso:tə] (**-, -n**) *f* smutty joke/remark
zottig ['tsɔtɪç] *adj* shaggy
zu [tsu:] *präp +dat* **1** (*örtlich*) to; **zum Bahnhof/Arzt gehen** to go to the station/doctor; **zur Schule/Kirche gehen** to go to school/church; **sollen wir zu Euch gehen?** shall we go to your place?; **sie sah zu ihm hin** she looked towards him; **zum Fenster herein** through the window; **zu meiner Linken** to *od* on my left
2 (*zeitlich*) at; **zu Ostern** at Easter; **bis zum 1. Mai** until May 1st; (*nicht später als*) by May 1st; **zu meiner Zeit** in my time
3 (*Zusatz*) with; **Wein zum Essen trinken** to drink wine with one's meal; **sich zu jdm setzen** to sit down beside sb; **setz dich doch zu uns** (come and) sit with us; **Anmerkungen zu etw** notes on sth
4 (*Zweck*) for; **Wasser zum Waschen** water for washing; **Papier zum Schreiben** paper to write on; **etw zum Geburtstag bekommen** to get sth for one's birthday; **es ist zu seinem Besten** it's for his own good
5 (*Veränderung*) into; **zu etw werden** to turn into sth; **jdn zu etw machen** to make sb (into) sth; **zu Asche verbrennen** to burn to ashes
6 (*mit Zahlen*): **3 zu 2** (*Sport*) 3-2; **das Stück zu 5 Euro** at 5 euros each; **zum ersten Mal** for the first time
7: **zu meiner Freude** *etc* to my joy *etc*; **zum Glück** luckily; **zu Fuß** on foot; **es ist zum Weinen** it's enough to make you cry
▷ *konj* to; **etw zu essen** sth to eat; **um besser sehen zu können** in order to see better; **ohne es zu wissen** without knowing it; **noch zu bezahlende Rechnungen** outstanding bills
▷ *adv* **1** (*allzu*) too; **zu sehr** too much; **zu viel** too much; (*umg: zu viele*) too many; **er kriegt zu viel** (*umg*) he gets annoyed; **zu wenig** too little; (*umg: zu wenige*) too few
2 (*örtlich*) toward(s); **er kam auf mich zu** he came towards *od* up to me
3 (*geschlossen*) shut; closed; **die Geschäfte haben zu** the shops are closed; **zu sein** to be closed; **auf/zu** (*Wasserhahn etc*) on/off
4 (*umg: los*): **nur zu!** just keep at it!; **mach zu!** hurry up!
zuallererst *adv* first of all
zuallerletzt *adv* last of all
Zubehör ['tsu:bəhø:r] (**-(e)s, -e**) *nt* accessories *pl*
zubereiten ['tsu:bəraɪtən] *vt* to prepare
zubinden ['tsu:bɪndən] *unreg vt* to tie up; **jdm die Augen ~** to blindfold sb
zubringen ['tsu:brɪŋən] *unreg vt* to spend; (*herbeibringen*) to bring, take; (*umg: Tür*) to get shut
Zubringer (**-s, -**) *m* (*Tech*) feeder, conveyor; (*Verkehrsmittel*) shuttle; (*zum Flughafen*) airport bus
Zucchini [tsʊ'ki:ni:] *pl* courgettes *pl* (*Brit*), zucchini(s) *pl* (*US*)
Zucht [tsʊxt] (**-, -en**) *f* (*von Tieren*) breeding; (*von Pflanzen*) cultivation; (*Rasse*) breed; (*Erziehung*) raising; (*Disziplin*) discipline
züchten ['tsʏçtən] *vt* (*Tiere*) to breed; (*Pflanzen*) to cultivate, grow
Züchter, in (**-s, -**) *m(f)* breeder; grower
Zuchthaus *nt* prison, penitentiary (*US*)
Zuchthengst *m* stallion, stud
zucken ['tsʊkən] *vi* to jerk, twitch; (*Strahl etc*) to flicker ▷ *vt* to shrug; **der Schmerz zuckte (mir) durch den ganzen Körper** the pain shot right through my body
Zucker ['tsʊkər] (**-s, -**) *m* sugar; (*Med*)

diabetes; **~ haben** (*umg*) to be a diabetic; **Zuckerdose** *f* sugar bowl; **Zuckerguss** *m* icing; **zuckerkrank** *adj* diabetic

zuckern *vt* to sugar

Zucker- *zW*: **Zuckerrohr** *nt* sugar cane; **Zuckerrübe** *f* sugar beet; **Zuckerwatte** *f* candy floss (*Brit*), cotton candy (*US*)

Zuckung *f* convulsion, spasm; (*leicht*) twitch

zudecken ['tsu:dɛkən] *vt* to cover (up); (*im Bett*) to tuck up *od* in

zudem [tsu'de:m] *adv* in addition (to this)

zudrehen ['tsu:dre:ən] *vt* to turn off

zueinander [tsu|aɪ'nandər] *adv* to one other; (*in Verbverbindung*) together

zuerkennen ['tsu:|ɛrkɛnən] *unreg vt*: **jdm etw ~** to award sth to sb, award sb sth

zuerst [tsu'|e:rst] *adv* first; (*zu Anfang*) at first; **~ einmal** first of all

Zufahrt ['tsu:fa:rt] *f* approach; **„keine ~ zum Krankenhaus"** "no access to hospital"

Zufahrtsstraße *f* approach road; (*von Autobahn etc*) slip road (*Brit*), entrance ramp (*US*)

Zufall ['tsu:fal] *m* chance; (*Ereignis*) coincidence; **durch ~** by accident; **so ein ~!** what a coincidence!

zufallen *unreg vi* to close, shut; (*Anteil, Aufgabe*): **jdm ~** to fall to sb

zufällig ['tsu:fɛlɪç] *adj* chance ▷ *adv* by chance; (*in Frage*) by any chance

Zuflucht ['tsu:flʊxt] *f* recourse; (*Ort*) refuge; **zu etw ~ nehmen** (*fig*) to resort to sth

zufolge [tsu'fɔlgə] *präp +dat od +gen* (*laut*) according to; (*aufgrund*) as a result of

zufrieden [tsu'fri:dən] *adj* content(ed); **er ist mit nichts ~** nothing pleases him; **Zufriedenheit** *f* contentedness; (*Befriedigtsein*) satisfaction; **zufriedenstellen** *vt* to satisfy

zufrieren ['tsu:fri:rən] *unreg vi* to freeze up *od* over

zufügen ['tsu:fy:gən] *vt* to add; (*Leid etc*): **jdm etw ~** to cause sb sth

Zug [tsu:k] **(-(e)s, ⸚e)** *m* (*Eisenbahnzug*) train; (*Luftzug*) draught (*Brit*), draft (*US*); (*Ziehen*) pull(ing); (*Gesichtszug*) feature; (*Schach etc*) move; (*Klingelzug*) pull; (*Schriftzug, beim Schwimmen*) stroke; (*Atemzug*) breath; (*Charakterzug*) trait; (*an Zigarette*) puff, pull, drag; (*Schluck*) gulp; (*Menschengruppe*) procession; (*von Vögeln*) migration; (*Mil*) platoon; **etw in vollen Zügen genießen** to enjoy sth to the full; **in den letzten Zügen liegen** (*umg*) to be at one's last gasp; **im ~(e)** *+gen* (*im Verlauf*) in the course of; **~ um Zug** (*fig*) step by step; **zum ~(e) kommen** (*umg*) to get a look-in; **etw in groben Zügen darstellen** *od* **umreißen** to outline sth; **das war kein schöner ~ von dir** that wasn't nice of you

Zugabe ['tsu:ga:bə] *f* extra; (*in Konzert etc*) encore

Zugang ['tsu:gaŋ] *m* entrance; (*Zutritt, fig*) access

Zugbrücke *f* drawbridge

zugeben ['tsu:ge:bən] *unreg vt* (*beifügen*) to add, throw in; (*zugestehen*) to admit; (*erlauben*) to permit; **zugegeben ...** granted ...

zugehen ['tsu:ge:ən] *unreg vi* (*schließen*) to shut ▷ *vi unpers* (*sich ereignen*) to go on, happen; **auf jdn/etw ~** to walk towards sb/sth; **dem Ende ~** to be finishing; **er geht schon auf die siebzig zu** he's getting on for seventy; **hier geht es nicht mit rechten Dingen zu** there's something odd going on here; **dort geht es ... zu** things are ... there

Zugehörigkeit ['tsu:gəhø:rɪçkaɪt] *f*: **~ (zu)** membership (of), belonging (to)

Zugehörigkeitsgefühl *nt* feeling of belonging

Zügel ['tsy:gəl] **(-s, -)** *m* rein, reins *pl*; (*fig*) rein, curb; **die ~ locker lassen** to slacken one's hold on the reins; **die ~ locker lassen bei** (*fig*) to give free rein to

zügeln *vt* to curb; (*Pferd*) to rein in

Zugeständnis ['tsu:gəʃtɛntnɪs] **(-ses, -se)** *nt* concession; **~se machen** to make allowances

zugestehen *unreg vt* to admit; (*Rechte*) to concede

zügig ['tsy:gɪç] *adj* speedy, swift

zugleich [tsu'glaɪç] *adv* (*zur gleichen Zeit*) at the same time; (*ebenso*) both

zugreifen ['tsu:graɪfən] *unreg vi* to seize *od* grab it/them; (*helfen*) to help; (*beim Essen*) to help o.s.

Zugriff ['tsu:grɪf] *m* (*Comput*) access; **sich dem ~ der Polizei entziehen** (*fig*) to evade justice

zugrunde, zu Grunde [tsu'grʊndə] *adv*: **~ gehen** to collapse; (*Mensch*) to perish; **er wird daran nicht ~ gehen** he'll survive; (*finanziell*) it won't ruin him; **einer Sache** *dat* **etw ~ legen** to base sth on sth; **einer Sache** *dat* **~ liegen** to be based on sth; **~ richten** to ruin, destroy

zugunsten, zu Gunsten [tsu'gʊnstən] *präp +gen od +dat* in favour (*Brit*) *od* favor (*US*) of

Zugverbindung *f* train connection; **Zugvogel** *m* migratory bird

Zuhälter ['tsu:hɛltər] **(-s, -)** *m* pimp

Zuhause **(-s)** *nt* home

zuhören ['tsu:hø:rən] *vi* to listen

Zuhörer **(-s, -)** *m* listener; **Zuhörerschaft** *f* audience

zukleben ['tsu:kle:bən] *vt* to paste up

zukommen ['tsu:kɔmən] *unreg vi* to come up; **auf jdn ~** to come up to sb; **jdm ~** (*sich gehören*) to be fitting for sb; **diesem Treffen kommt große Bedeutung zu** this meeting is of the utmost importance; **jdm etw ~ lassen** to give sb sth; **die Dinge auf sich** *akk* **~ lassen** to take things as they come

Zukunft ['tsu:kʊnft] **(-,** *no pl***)** *f* future

zukünftig ['tsu:kʏnftɪç] *adj* future ▷ *adv* in future; **mein ~er Mann** my husband-to-be

Zulage ['tsu:la:gə] *f* bonus

zulassen ['tsu:lasən] *unreg vt* (*hereinlassen*) to admit; (*erlauben*) to permit; (*Auto*) to license;

(*umg: nicht öffnen*) to keep shut
zulässig ['tsu:lɛsɪç] *adj* permissible, permitted; **~e Höchstgeschwindigkeit** (upper) speed limit
zuleide [tsu'laɪdə] *adj*: **jdm etw ~ tun** to harm sb
zuletzt [tsu'lɛtst] *adv* finally, at last; **wir blieben bis ~** we stayed to the very end; **nicht ~ wegen** not least because of
zuliebe [tsu'li:bə] *adv*: **jdm ~** (in order) to please sb
zum [tsʊm] = **zu dem**; **~ dritten Mal** for the third time; **~ Scherz** as a joke; **~ Trinken** for drinking; **bis ~ 15. April** until 15th April; (*nicht später als*) by 15th April; **~ ersten Mal(e)** for the first time; **es ist ~ Weinen** it's enough to make you (want to) weep; **~ Glück** luckily
zumachen ['tsu:maxən] *vt* to shut; (*Kleidung*) to do up, fasten ▷ *vi* to shut; (*umg*) to hurry up
zumal [tsu'ma:l] *konj* especially (as)
zumeist [tsu'maɪst] *adv* mostly
zumindest [tsu'mɪndəst] *adv* at least
zumutbar ['tsu:mu:tba:r] *adj* reasonable
zumute [tsu'mu:tə] *adv*: **wie ist ihm ~?** how does he feel?
zumuten ['tsu:mu:tən] *vt*: **(jdm) etw ~** to expect *od* ask sth (of sb); **sich** *dat* **zu viel ~** to take on too much
Zumutung *f* unreasonable expectation *od* demand; (*Unverschämtheit*) impertinence; **das ist eine ~!** that's a bit much!
zunächst [tsu'nɛ:çst] *adv* first of all; **~ einmal** to start with
Zunahme ['tsu:na:mə] **(-, -n)** *f* increase
Zuname ['tsu:na:mə] *m* surname
zünden ['tsʏndən] *vi* (*Feuer*) to light, ignite; (*Motor*) to fire; (*fig*) to kindle enthusiasm ▷ *vt* to ignite; (*Rakete*) to fire
zündend *adj* fiery
Zünder (-s, -) *m* fuse; (*Mil*) detonator
Zünd- *zW*: **Zündkerze** *f* (*Aut*) spark(ing) plug; **Zündschlüssel** *m* ignition key; **Zündschnur** *f* fuse wire
Zündung *f* ignition
zunehmen ['tsu:ne:mən] *unreg vi* to increase, grow; (*Mensch*) to put on weight
Zuneigung *f* affection
Zunft [tsʊnft] **(-, ¨e)** *f* guild
zünftig ['tsʏnftɪç] *adj* (*Arbeit*) professional; (*umg: ordentlich*) proper, real
Zunge ['tsʊŋə] *f* tongue; (*Fisch*) sole; **böse ~n behaupten, ...** malicious gossip has it ...
Zungenbrecher *m* tongue-twister
zunutze [tsu'nʊtsə] *adv*: **sich** *dat* **etw ~ machen** to make use of sth
zuoberst [tsu'|o:bərst] *adv* at the top
zupacken ['tsu:pakən] (*umg*) *vi* (*zugreifen*) to make a grab for it; (*bei der Arbeit*) to get down to it; **mit ~** (*helfen*) to give me/them *etc* a hand
zupfen ['tsʊpfən] *vt* to pull, pick, pluck; (*Gitarre*) to pluck
zur [tsu:r] = **zu der**
zurechnungsfähig ['tsu:rɛçnʊŋsfɛ:ɪç] *adj* (*Jur*) responsible, of sound mind; **Zurechnungsfähigkeit** *f* responsibility, accountability
zurecht- *zW*: **zurechtfinden** *unreg vr* to find one's way (about); **zurechtkommen** *unreg vi* (*rechtzeitig kommen*) to come in time; (*schaffen*) to cope; (*finanziell*) to manage; **zurechtlegen** *vt* to get ready; (*Ausrede etc*) to have ready; **zurechtmachen** *vt* to prepare ▷ *vr* to get ready; (*sich schminken*) to put on one's make-up; **zurechtweisen** *unreg vt* to reprimand; **Zurechtweisung** *f* reprimand, rebuff
zureden ['tsu:re:dən] *vi*: **jdm ~** to persuade sb, urge sb
zurück [tsu'rʏk] *adv* back; (*mit Zahlungen*) behind; (*fig: zurückgeblieben: von Kind*) backward; **~!** get back!; **zurückbehalten** *unreg vt* to keep back; **er hat Schäden zurückbehalten** he suffered lasting damage; **zurückbekommen** *unreg vt* to get back; **zurückbleiben** *unreg vi* (*Mensch*) to remain behind; (*nicht nachkommen*) to fall behind, lag; (*Schaden*) to remain; **zurückbringen** *unreg vt* to bring back; **zurückfahren** *unreg vi* to travel back; (*vor Schreck*) to recoil ▷ *vt* to drive back; **zurückfinden** *unreg vi* to find one's way back; **zurückfordern** *vt* to demand back; **zurückführen** *vt* to lead back; **etw auf etw** *akk* **zurückführen** to trace sth back to sth; **zurückgeben** *unreg vt* to give back; (*antworten*) to retort with; **zurückgeblieben** *adj* retarded; **zurückgehen** *unreg vi* to go back; (*fallen*) to go down, fall; (*zeitlich*): **zurückgehen (auf** *+akk***)** to date back (to); **Waren zurückgehen lassen** to send back goods; **zurückgezogen** *adj* retired, withdrawn; **zurückhalten** *unreg vt* to hold back; (*Mensch*) to restrain; (*hindern*) to prevent ▷ *vr* (*reserviert sein*) to be reserved; (*im Essen*) to hold back; (*im Hintergrund bleiben*) to keep in the background; (*bei Verhandlung*) to keep a low profile; **zurückhaltend** *adj* reserved; **Zurückhaltung** *f* reserve; **zurückkommen** *unreg vi* to come back; **auf etw** *akk* **zurückkommen** to return to sth; **zurücklassen** *unreg vt* to leave behind; **zurücklegen** *vt* to put back; (*Geld*) to put by; (*reservieren*) to keep back; (*Strecke*) to cover ▷ *vr* to lie back; **zurücknehmen** *unreg vt* to take back; **zurückrufen** *unreg vt, vi* to call back; **etw ins Gedächtnis zurückrufen** to recall sth; **zurückschrecken** *vi*: **zurückschrecken vor** *+dat* to shrink from; **vor nichts zurückschrecken** to stop at nothing; **zurückstellen** *vt* to put back, replace; (*aufschieben*) to put off, postpone; (*Mil*) to turn down; (*Interessen*) to defer; (*Ware*) to keep; **persönliche Interessen hinter etw** *dat* **zurückstellen** to put sth before one's personal interests; **zurücktreten** *unreg vi* to step back; (*vom Amt*) to retire; (*von einem*

Vertrag etc): **zurücktreten (von)** to withdraw (from); **gegenüber** *od* **hinter etw** *dat* **zurücktreten** to diminish in importance in view of sth; **bitte zurücktreten!** stand back, please!; **zurückweichen** *unreg vi*: **zurückweichen (vor** *+dat***)** to shrink back (from); **zurückweisen** *unreg vt* to turn down; (*Mensch*) to reject; **zurückzahlen** *vt* to pay back, repay

Zuruf ['tsu:ru:f] *m* shout, cry

zurzeit [tsʊr'tsaɪt] *adv* at the moment

Zusage ['tsu:za:gə] *f* promise; (*Annahme*) consent

zusagen *vt* to promise ▷ *vi* to accept; **jdm etw auf den Kopf ~** (*umg*) to tell sb sth outright; **jdm ~** (*gefallen*) to appeal to *od* please sb

zusammen [tsu'zamən] *adv* together; **Zusammenarbeit** *f* cooperation; **zusammenarbeiten** *vi* to cooperate; **zusammenbeißen** *unreg vt* (*Zähne*) to clench; **zusammenbleiben** *unreg vi* to stay together; **zusammenbrechen** *unreg vi* (*Hilfsverb sein*) to collapse; (*Mensch*) to break down, collapse; (*Verkehr etc*) to come to a standstill; **zusammenbringen** *unreg vt* to bring *od* get together; (*Geld*) to get; (*Sätze*) to put together; **Zusammenbruch** *m* collapse; (*Comput*) crash; **zusammenfahren** *unreg vi* to collide; (*erschrecken*) to start; **zusammenfassen** *vt* to summarize; (*vereinigen*) to unite; **zusammenfassend** *adj* summarizing ▷ *adv* to summarize; **Zusammenfassung** *f* summary, résumé; **zusammengehören** *vi* to belong together; (*Paar*) to match; **zusammengesetzt** *adj* compound, composite; **zusammenhalten** *unreg vt* to hold together ▷ *vi* to hold together; (*Freunde, fig*) to stick together; **Zusammenhang** *m* connection; **im/aus dem Zusammenhang** in/out of context; **etw aus dem Zusammenhang reißen** to take sth out of its context; **zusammenhängen** *unreg vi* to be connected *od* linked; **zusammenkommen** *unreg vi* to meet, assemble; (*sich ereignen*) to occur at once *od* together; **zusammenlegen** *vt* to put together; (*stapeln*) to pile up; (*falten*) to fold; (*verbinden*) to combine, unite; (*Termine, Feste*) to combine; (*Geld*) to collect; **zusammennehmen** *unreg vt* to summon up ▷ *vr* to pull o.s. together; **alles zusammengenommen** all in all; **zusammenpassen** *vi* to go well together, match; **zusammenreißen** *unreg vr* to pull o.s. together; **zusammenschließen** *unreg vt, vr* to join (together); **Zusammenschluss** *m* amalgamation; **zusammenschreiben** *unreg vt* to write together; (*Bericht*) to put together; **Zusammensein** (**-s**) *nt* get-together; **zusammensetzen** *vt* to put together ▷ *vr*: **sich zusammensetzen aus** to consist of; **Zusammensetzung** *f* composition; **zusammenstellen** *vt* to put together; **Zusammenstoß** *m* collision; **zusammenstoßen** *unreg vi* (*Hilfsverb sein*) to collide; **Zusammentreffen** *nt* meeting; (*Zufall*) coincidence; **zusammentreffen** *unreg vi* (*Hilfsverb sein*) to coincide; (*Menschen*) to meet; **zusammenwachsen** *unreg vi* to grow together; **zusammenzählen** *vt* to add up; **zusammenziehen** *unreg vt* (*verengern*) to draw together; (*vereinigen*) to bring together; (*addieren*) to add up ▷ *vr* to shrink; (*sich bilden*) to form, develop; **zusammenzucken** *vi* (*Hilfsverb sein*) to start; **Zusatzgerät** *nt* attachment

zusätzlich ['tsu:zɛtslɪç] *adj* additional

zuschauen ['tsu:ʃaʊən] *vi* to watch, look on

Zuschauer (**-s, -**) *m* spectator ▷ *pl* (*Theat*) audience *sing*

zuschicken ['tsu:ʃɪkən] *vt*: **jdm etw ~** to send *od* forward sth to sb

Zuschlag ['tsu:ʃla:k] *m* extra charge; (*Erhöhung*) surcharge; (*Eisenb*) supplement

zuschlagen ['tsu:ʃla:gən] *unreg vt* (*Tür*) to slam; (*Ball*) to hit; (*bei Auktion*) to knock down; (*Steine etc*) to knock into shape ▷ *vi* (*Fenster, Tür*) to shut; (*Mensch*) to hit, punch

zuschneiden ['tsu:ʃnaɪdən] *unreg vt* to cut to size; (*Nähen*) to cut out; **auf etw** *akk* **zugeschnitten sein** (*fig*) to be geared to sth

zuschrauben ['tsu:ʃraʊbən] *vt* to screw shut

zuschreiben ['tsu:ʃraɪbən] *unreg vt* (*fig*) to ascribe, attribute; (*Comm*) to credit; **das hast du dir selbst zu~** you've only got yourself to blame

Zuschrift ['tsu:ʃrɪft] *f* letter, reply

zuschulden, **zu Schulden** [tsu'ʃʊldən] *adv*: **sich** *dat* **etw ~ kommen lassen** to make o.s. guilty of sth

Zuschuss ['tsu:ʃʊs] *m* subsidy

zusehen ['tsu:zɛːən] *unreg vi* to watch; (*dafür sorgen*) to take care; (*etw dulden*) to sit back (and watch); **jdm/etw ~** to watch sb/sth

zusehends *adv* visibly

zusenden ['tsu:zɛndən] *unreg vt* to forward, send on

zusichern ['tsu:zɪçərn] *vt*: **jdm etw ~** to assure sb of sth

zuspielen ['tsu:ʃpi:lən] *vt, vi* to pass; **jdm etw ~** to pass sth to sb; (*fig*) to pass sth on to sb; **etw der Presse ~** to leak sth to the press

zuspitzen ['tsu:ʃpɪtsən] *vt* to sharpen ▷ *vr* (*Lage*) to become critical

zusprechen ['tsu:ʃprɛçən] *unreg vt* (*zuerkennen*): **jdm etw ~** to award sb sth, award sth to sb ▷ *vi*: **jdm ~** to speak to sb; **jdm Trost ~** to comfort sb; **dem Essen/Alkohol ~** to eat/drink a lot

Zustand ['tsu:ʃtant] *m* state, condition; **in gutem/schlechtem ~** in good/poor condition; (*Haus*) in good/bad repair; **Zustände bekommen** *od* **kriegen** (*umg*) to have a fit

zustande, **zu Stande** [tsu'ʃtandə] *adv*: **~ bringen** to bring about; **~ kommen** to come about

zuständig ['tsu:ʃtɛndɪç] *adj* competent, responsible; **Zuständigkeit** *f* competence, responsibility
zustehen ['tsu:ʃte:ən] *unreg vi*: **jdm ~** to be sb's right
zustellen ['tsu:ʃtɛlən] *vt* (*verstellen*) to block; (*Post etc*) to send
zustimmen ['tsu:ʃtɪmən] *vi* to agree
Zustimmung *f* agreement; (*Einwilligung*) consent; **allgemeine ~ finden** to meet with general approval
zustoßen ['tsu:ʃto:sən] *unreg vi* (*fig*): **jdm ~** to happen to sb
Zustrom ['tsu:ʃtro:m] *m* (*fig: Menschenmenge*) stream (of visitors *etc*); (*hineinströmend*) influx; (*Met*) inflow
zutage, zu Tage [tsu'ta:gə] *adv*: **~ bringen** to bring to light; **~ treten** to come to light
Zutaten ['tsu:ta:tən] *pl* ingredients *pl*; (*fig*) accessories *pl*
zutiefst [tsu'ti:fst] *adv* deeply
zutragen ['tsu:tra:gən] *unreg vt*: **jdm etw ~** to bring sb sth, bring sth to sb ▷ *vt* (*Klatsch*) to tell sb sth ▷ *vr* to happen
zutrauen ['tsu:traʊən] *vt*: **jdm etw ~** to credit sb with sth; **sich** *dat* **nichts ~** to have no confidence in o.s.; **jdm viel ~** to think a lot of sb; **jdm wenig ~** not to think much of sb; **Zutrauen** (**-s**) *nt*: **Zutrauen (zu)** trust (in); **zu jdm Zutrauen fassen** to begin to trust sb
zutraulich *adj* trusting; (*Tier*) friendly; **Zutraulichkeit** *f* trust
zutreffen ['tsu:trɛfən] *unreg vi* to be correct; (*gelten*) to apply
zutreffend *adj* (*richtig*) accurate; **Z~es bitte unterstreichen** please underline where applicable
zutrinken ['tsu:trɪŋkən] *unreg vi*: **jdm ~** to drink to sb
Zutritt ['tsu:trɪt] *m* access; (*Einlass*) admittance; **kein Zutritt, ~ verboten** no admittance
Zutun (**-s**) *nt* assistance
zuverlässig ['tsu:fɛrlɛsɪç] *adj* reliable; **Zuverlässigkeit** *f* reliability
Zuversicht ['tsu:fɛrzɪçt] (**-**) *f* confidence; **zuversichtlich** *adj* confident; **Zuversichtlichkeit** *f* confidence
zu viel [tsu'fi:l] *siehe* **zu**
zuvor [tsu'fo:r] *adv* before, previously
zuvorkommen *unreg vi +dat* to anticipate; (*Gefahr etc*) to forestall; **jdm ~** to beat sb to it
zuvorkommend *adj* courteous; (*gefällig*) obliging
Zuwachs ['tsu:vaks] (**-es**) *m* increase, growth; (*umg*) addition
zuwachsen *unreg vi* to become overgrown; (*Wunde*) to heal (up)
Zuwachsrate *f* rate of increase
zuwege, zu Wege [tsu've:gə] *adv*: **etw ~ bringen** to accomplish sth; **mit etw ~ kommen** to manage sth; **gut ~ sein** to be (doing) well
zuweilen [tsu'vaɪlən] *adv* at times, now and then
zuweisen ['tsu:vaɪzən] *unreg vt* to assign, allocate
zuwenden ['tsu:vɛndən] *unreg vt +dat* to turn towards ▷ *vr +dat* to turn to; (*sich widmen*) to devote o.s. to; **jdm seine Aufmerksamkeit ~** to give sb one's attention
Zuwendung *f* (*Geld*) financial contribution; (*Liebe*) love and care
zu wenig [tsu've:nɪç] *siehe* **zu**
zuwider [tsu'vi:dər] *adv*: **etw ist jdm ~** sb loathes sth, sb finds sth repugnant ▷ *präp +dat* contrary to; **zuwiderhandeln** *vi +dat* to act contrary to; **einem Gesetz zuwiderhandeln** to contravene a law
zuziehen ['tsu:tsi:ən] *unreg vt* (*schließen: Vorhang*) to draw, close; (*herbeirufen: Experten*) to call in ▷ *vi* to move in, come; **sich** *dat* **etw ~** (*Krankheit*) to catch sth; (*Zorn*) to incur sth; **sich** *dat* **eine Verletzung ~** (*form*) to sustain an injury
zuzüglich ['tsu:tsy:klɪç] *präp +gen* plus, with the addition of
zuzwinkern ['tsu:tsvɪnkərn] *vi*: **jdm ~** to wink at sb
ZVS *f abk* (*= Zentralstelle für die Vergabe von Studienplätzen*) *central body organizing the granting of places at university*
Zwang (**-(e)s, ¨-e**) *m* compulsion; (*Gewalt*) coercion; **gesellschaftliche Zwänge** social constraints; **tu dir keinen ~ an** don't feel you have to be polite
zwang *etc* [tsvaŋ] *vb siehe* **zwingen**
zwängen ['tsvɛŋən] *vt, vr* to squeeze
Zwang- *zW*: **zwanghaft** *adj* compulsive; **zwanglos** *adj* informal
Zwangs- *zW*: **Zwangsarbeit** *f* forced labour (*Brit*) *od* labor (*US*); **Zwangsernährung** *f* force-feeding; **Zwangsjacke** *f* straitjacket; **Zwangslage** *f* predicament, tight corner; **zwangsläufig** *adj* inevitable
zwanzig ['tsvantsɪç] *num* twenty
zwar [tsva:r] *adv* to be sure, indeed; **das ist ~ ..., aber ...** that may be ... but ...; **und ~** in fact, actually; **und ~ am Sonntag** on Sunday to be precise; **und ~ so schnell, dass ...** in fact so quickly that ...
Zweck [tsvɛk] (**-(e)s, -e**) *m* purpose, aim; **es hat keinen ~, darüber zu reden** there is no point (in) talking about it; **zweckdienlich** *adj* practical; (*nützlich*) useful; **zweckdienliche Hinweise** (any) relevant information
Zwecke (**-, -n**) *f* hobnail; (*Heftzwecke*) drawing pin (*Brit*), thumbtack (*US*)
Zweck- *zW*: **zwecklos** *adj* pointless; **zweckmäßig** *adj* suitable, appropriate
zwecks *präp +gen* (*form*) for (the purpose of)
zwei [tsvaɪ] *num* two; **Zweibettzimmer** *nt* twin-bedded room; **zweideutig** *adj* ambiguous; (*unanständig*) suggestive
zweierlei ['tsvaɪər'laɪ] *adj* two kinds *od* sorts of; **~ Stoff** two different kinds of material; ~

zu tun haben to have two different things to do

zweifach *adj* double

Zweifel ['tsvaɪfəl] (**-s, -**) *m* doubt; **ich bin mir darüber im ~** I'm in two minds about it; **zweifelhaft** *adj* doubtful, dubious; **zweifellos** *adj* doubtless

zweifeln *vi*: **(an etw** *dat***) ~** to doubt (sth)

Zweifelsfall *m*: **im ~** in case of doubt

Zweig [tsvaɪk] (**-(e)s, -e**) *m* branch; **Zweiggeschäft** *nt* (*Comm*) branch

zwei- *zW*: **zweihundert** *num* two hundred; **Zweikampf** *m* duel; **zweimal** *adv* twice; **das lasse ich mir nicht zweimal sagen** I don't have to be told twice; **zweisprachig** *adj* bilingual; **zweispurig** *adj* (*Aut*) two-lane; **zweistimmig** *adj* for two voices

zweit [tsvaɪt] *adv*: **zu ~** (*in Paaren*) in twos

Zweitaktmotor *m* two-stroke engine

zweitbeste, r, s *adj* second best

zweite, r, s *adj* second; **Bürger ~r Klasse** second-class citizen(s *pl*)

zweitens *adv* secondly

zweit- *zW*: **zweitgrößte, r, s** *adj* second largest; **zweitklassig** *adj* second-class; **zweitletzte, r, s** *adj* last but one, penultimate; **zweitrangig** *adj* second-rate

Zwerchfell ['tsvɛrçfel] *nt* diaphragm

Zwerg, in [tsvɛrk, 'tsvɛrgɪn] (**-(e)s, -e**) *m(f)* dwarf; (*fig*: *Knirps*) midget

Zwickel ['tsvɪkəl] (**-s, -**) *m* gusset

zwicken ['tsvɪkən] *vt* to pinch, nip

Zwieback ['tsvi:bak] (**-(e)s, -e** *od* **-bäcke**) *m* rusk

Zwiebel ['tsvi:bəl] (**-, -n**) *f* onion; (*Blumenzwiebel*) bulb

Zwilling ['tsvɪlɪŋ] (**-s, -e**) *m* twin; **Zwillinge** *pl* (*Astrol*) Gemini

zwingen ['tsvɪŋən] *unreg vt* to force

zwingend *adj* (*Grund etc*) compelling; (*logisch notwendig*) necessary; (*Schluss, Beweis*) conclusive

zwinkern ['tsvɪŋkərn] *vi* to blink; (*absichtlich*) to wink

Zwirn [tsvɪrn] (**-(e)s, -e**) *m* thread

zwischen ['tsvɪʃən] *präp* (*+akk od dat*) between; (*bei mehreren*) among; **Zwischenbemerkung** *f* (incidental) remark; **Zwischenbilanz** *f* (*Comm*) interim balance; **zwischenblenden** *vt* (*Film, Rundf, TV*) to insert; **Zwischending** *nt* cross; **zwischendurch** *adv* in between; (*räumlich*) here and there; **Zwischenergebnis** *nt* intermediate result; **Zwischenfall** *m* incident; **Zwischenfrage** *f* question; **Zwischenhandel** *m* wholesaling; **Zwischenhändler** *m* middleman, agent; **Zwischenlagerung** *f* temporary storage; **Zwischenlandung** *f* (*Aviat*) stopover; **zwischenmenschlich** *adj* interpersonal; **Zwischenraum** *m* gap, space; **Zwischenstation** *f* intermediate station; **Zwischenstecker** *m* (*Elek*) adapter; **Zwischenzeit** *f* interval; **in der Zwischenzeit** in the interim, meanwhile

Zwist [tsvɪst] (**-es, -e**) *m* dispute

zwitschern ['tsvɪtʃərn] *vt, vi* to twitter, chirp; **einen ~** (*umg*) to have a drink

Zwitter ['tsvɪtər] (**-s, -**) *m* hermaphrodite

zwölf [tsvœlf] *num* twelve; **fünf Minuten vor ~** (*fig*) at the eleventh hour

Zyklus ['tsy:klʊs] (**-, Zyklen**) *m* cycle

Zylinder [tsi'lɪndər] (**-s, -**) *m* cylinder; (*Hut*) top hat; **zylinderförmig** *adj* cylindrical

Zyniker, in ['tsy:nikər(ɪn)] (**-s, -**) *m(f)* cynic

zynisch ['tsy:nɪʃ] *adj* cynical

Zynismus [tsy'nɪsmʊs] *m* cynicism

Zypern ['tsy:pərn] (**-s**) *nt* Cyprus

Zypresse [tsy'prɛsə] (**-, -n**) *f* (*Bot*) cypress

zypriotisch *adj* Cypriot, Cyprian

Zyste ['tsʏstə] (**-, -n**) *f* yst

Aa

A¹, a [eɪ] *n (letter)* A *nt*, a *nt*; *(Scol)* ≈ Eins *f*, sehr gut *nt*; **A for Andrew, A for Able** *(US)* ≈ A wie Anton; **A road** *(Brit: Aut)* Hauptverkehrsstraße *f*; **A shares** *(Brit: Stock Exchange)* stimmrechtslose Aktien *pl*
A² [eɪ] *n (Mus)* A *nt*, a *nt*
a [ə] *(before vowel and silent h:* **an***) indef art* **1** ein; *(before feminine noun)* eine; **a book** ein Buch; **a lamp** eine Lampe; **she's a doctor** sie ist Ärztin; **I haven't got a car** ich habe kein Auto; **a hundred/thousand** *etc* **pounds** einhundert/eintausend *etc* Pfund
2 *(in expressing ratios, prices etc)* pro; **3 a day/ week** 3 pro Tag/Woche, 3 am Tag/in der Woche; **10 km an hour** 10 km pro Stunde
A2 *(Brit) n (Scol) Mit "A2" wird das zweite Jahr der britischen Sekundarstufe II bezeichnet, in dem die übrigen drei Wahlpflichtfächer unterrichtet und am Ende des Schuljahres geprüft werden. Die Note für den "A level" setzt sich aus den Noten der Jahre "AS" und "A2" zusammen*
aback [ə'bæk] *adv*: **to be taken ~** verblüfft sein
abandon [ə'bændən] *vt* verlassen; *(child)* aussetzen; *(give up)* aufgeben ▷ *n (wild behaviour)*: **with ~** selbstvergessen; **to ~ ship** das Schiff verlassen
abate [ə'beɪt] *vi* nachlassen, sich legen
abattoir ['æbətwɑːʳ] *(Brit) n* Schlachthof *m*
abbey ['æbɪ] *n* Abtei *f*
abbot ['æbət] *n* Abt *m*
abbreviation [əbriːvɪ'eɪʃən] *n* Abkürzung *f*
abdicate ['æbdɪkeɪt] *vt* verzichten auf *+acc* ▷ *vi (monarch)* abdanken
abdomen ['æbdəmɛn] *n* Unterleib *m*
abduct [æb'dʌkt] *vt* entführen
aberration [æbə'reɪʃən] *n* Anomalie *f*; **in a moment of mental ~** in einem Augenblick geistiger Verwirrung
abide [ə'baɪd] *vt*: **I can't ~ it/him** ich kann es/ihn nicht ausstehen
▸ **abide by** *vt fus* sich halten an *+acc*
ability [ə'bɪlɪtɪ] *n* Fähigkeit *f*; **to the best of my ~** so gut ich es kann
abject ['æbdʒɛkt] *adj (poverty)* bitter; *(apology)* demütig; *(coward)* erbärmlich
ablaze [ə'bleɪz] *adj* in Flammen; **~ with light** hell erleuchtet
able ['eɪbl] *adj* fähig; **to be ~ to do sth** etw tun können
able-bodied ['eɪbl'bɔdɪd] *adj* kräftig; **~ seaman** *(Brit)* Vollmatrose *m*
ably ['eɪblɪ] *adv* gekonnt
abnormal [æb'nɔːməl] *adj* abnorm; *(child)* anormal
aboard [ə'bɔːd] *adv (Naut, Aviat)* an Bord ▷ *prep* an Bord *+gen*; **~ the train/bus** im Zug/Bus
abode [ə'bəud] *n (Law)*: **of no fixed ~** ohne festen Wohnsitz
abolish [ə'bɔlɪʃ] *vt* abschaffen
abolition [æbə'lɪʃən] *n* Abschaffung *f*
abort [ə'bɔːt] *vt* abtreiben; *(Med: miscarry)* fehlgebären; *(Comput)* abbrechen
abortion [ə'bɔːʃən] *n* Abtreibung *f*; *(miscarriage)* Fehlgeburt *f*; **to have an ~** abtreiben lassen
abortive [ə'bɔːtɪv] *adj* misslungen
about [ə'baut] *adv* **1** *(approximately)* etwa, ungefähr; **about a hundred/thousand** *etc* etwa hundert/tausend *etc*; **at about two o'clock** etwa um zwei Uhr; **I've just about finished** ich bin gerade fertig
2 *(referring to place)* herum; **to run/walk** *etc* **about** herumlaufen/-gehen *etc*; **is Paul about?** ist Paul da?
3: to be about to do sth im Begriff sein, etw zu tun; **he was about to cry** er fing fast an zu weinen; **she was about to leave/wash the dishes** sie wollte gerade gehen/das Geschirr spülen
▷ *prep* **1** *(relating to)* über *+acc*; **what is it about?** worum geht es?; *(book etc)* wovon handelt es?; **we talked about it** wir haben darüber geredet; **what** *or* **how about going to the cinema?** wollen wir ins Kino gehen?
2 *(referring to place)* um ... herum; **to walk about the town** durch die Stadt gehen; **her clothes were scattered about the room** ihre Kleider waren über das ganze Zimmer verstreut
above [ə'bʌv] *adv* oben; *(greater, more)* darüber ▷ *prep* über *+dat*; **to cost ~ £10** mehr als £10 kosten; **mentioned ~** oben genannt; **he's not ~ a bit of blackmail** er ist sich *dat* nicht zu gut für eine kleine Erpressung; **~ all** vor allem
abrasive [ə'breɪzɪv] *adj (substance)* Scheuer-; *(person, manner)* aggressiv

abreast [əˈbrɛst] *adv* nebeneinander; **three ~** zu dritt nebeneinander; **to keep ~ of** (*fig*) auf dem Laufenden bleiben mit
abroad [əˈbrɔːd] *adv* (*be*) im Ausland; (*go*) ins Ausland; **there is a rumour ~ that ...** (*fig*) ein Gerücht geht um *or* kursiert, dass ...
abrupt [əˈbrʌpt] *adj* abrupt; (*person, behaviour*) schroff
abruptly [əˈbrʌptlɪ] *adv* abrupt
abscess [ˈæbsɪs] *n* Abszess *m*
absence [ˈæbsəns] *n* Abwesenheit *f*; **in the ~ of** (*person*) in Abwesenheit *+gen*; (*thing*) in Ermangelung *+gen*
absent [ˈæbsənt] *adj* abwesend, nicht da ▷ *vt*: **to ~ o.s. from** fernbleiben *+dat*; **to be ~** fehlen; **to be ~ without leave** (*Mil*) sich unerlaubt von der Truppe entfernen
absentee [æbsənˈtiː] *n* Abwesende(r) *f(m)*
absent-minded [ˈæbsəntˈmaɪndɪd] *adj* zerstreut
absolute [ˈæbsəluːt] *adj* absolut; (*power*) uneingeschränkt
absolutely [æbsəˈluːtlɪ] *adv* absolut; (*agree*) vollkommen; **~!** genau!
absolve [əbˈzɔlv] *vt*: **to ~ sb (from)** jdn lossprechen (von); (*responsibility*) jdn entbinden (von)
absorb [əbˈzɔːb] *vt* aufnehmen (*also fig*); (*light, heat*) absorbieren; (*group, business*) übernehmen; **to be ~ed in a book** in ein Buch vertieft sein
absorbent cotton (*US*) *n* Watte *f*
absorbing [əbˈzɔːbɪŋ] *adj* saugfähig; (*book, film, work etc*) fesselnd
abstain [əbˈsteɪn] *vi* (*voting*) sich (der Stimme) enthalten; **to ~ (from)** (*eating, drinking etc*) sich enthalten (*+gen*)
abstract [ˈæbstrækt] *adj* abstrakt ▷ *n* (*summary*) Zusammenfassung *f* ▷ *vt*: **to ~ sth (from)** (*summarize*) etw entnehmen (aus); (*remove*) etw entfernen (aus)
absurd [əbˈsəːd] *adj* absurd
abundance [əˈbʌndəns] *n* Reichtum *m*; **an ~ of** eine Fülle von; **in ~** in Hülle und Fülle
abundant [əˈbʌndənt] *adj* reichlich
abuse [əˈbjuːs] *n* (*insults*) Beschimpfungen *pl*; (*ill-treatment*) Misshandlung *f*; (*misuse*) Missbrauch *m* ▷ *vt* (*see n*) beschimpfen; misshandeln; missbrauchen; **to be open to ~** sich leicht missbrauchen lassen
abusive [əˈbjuːsɪv] *adj* beleidigend
abysmal [əˈbɪzməl] *adj* entsetzlich; (*ignorance etc*) grenzenlos
abyss [əˈbɪs] *n* Abgrund *m*
AC *abbr* = **alternating current**; (*US*: = *athletic club*) ≈ SV *m*
academic [ækəˈdɛmɪk] *adj* akademisch (*also pej*); (*work*) wissenschaftlich; (*person*) intellektuell ▷ *n* Akademiker(in) *m(f)*
academic year *n* (*university year*) Universitätsjahr *nt*; (*school year*) Schuljahr *nt*
academy [əˈkædəmɪ] *n* Akademie *f*; (*school*) Hochschule *f*; **~ of music** Musikhochschule *f*; **military/naval ~** Militär-/Marineakademie *f*
accelerate [ækˈsɛləreɪt] *vt* beschleunigen ▷ *vi* (*Aut*) Gas geben
acceleration [æksɛləˈreɪʃən] *n* Beschleunigung *f*
accelerator [ækˈsɛləreɪtə^r^] *n* Gaspedal *nt*
accent [ˈæksɛnt] *n* Akzent *m*; (*fig: emphasis, stress*) Betonung *f*; **to speak with an Irish ~** mit einem irischen Akzent sprechen; **to have a strong ~** einen starken Akzent haben
accept [əkˈsɛpt] *vt* annehmen; (*fact, situation*) sich abfinden mit; (*risk*) in Kauf nehmen; (*responsibility*) übernehmen; (*blame*) auf sich *acc* nehmen
acceptable [əkˈsɛptəbl] *adj* annehmbar
acceptance [əkˈsɛptəns] *n* Annahme *f*; **to meet with general ~** allgemeine Anerkennung finden
access [ˈæksɛs] *n* Zugang *m* ▷ *vt* (*Comput*) zugreifen auf *+dat*; **the burglars gained ~ through a window** die Einbrecher gelangten durch ein Fenster hinein
accessible [ækˈsɛsəbl] *adj* erreichbar; (*knowledge, art etc*) zugänglich
accessory [ækˈsɛsərɪ] *n* Zubehörteil *nt*; (*Dress*) Accessoire *nt*; (*Law*): **~ to** Mitschuldige(r) *f(m)* an *+dat*; **accessories** *npl* Zubehör *nt*; **toilet accessories** (*Brit*) Toilettenartikel *pl*
accident [ˈæksɪdənt] *n* Zufall *m*; (*mishap, disaster*) Unfall *m*; **to meet with** *or* **to have an ~** einen Unfall haben, verunglücken; **~s at work** Arbeitsunfälle *pl*; **by ~** zufällig
accidental [æksɪˈdɛntl] *adj* zufällig; (*death, damage*) Unfall-
accidentally [æksɪˈdɛntəlɪ] *adv* zufällig
accident insurance *n* Unfallversicherung *f*
accident-prone [ˈæksɪdəntˈprəun] *adj* vom Pech verfolgt
acclaim [əˈkleɪm] *n* Beifall *m* ▷ *vt*: **to be ~ed for one's achievements** für seine Leistungen gefeiert werden
accommodate [əˈkɔmədeɪt] *vt* unterbringen; (*subj: car, hotel etc*) Platz bieten *+dat*; (*oblige, help*) entgegenkommen *+dat*; **to ~ one's plans to** seine Pläne anpassen an *+acc*
accommodating [əˈkɔmədeɪtɪŋ] *adj* entgegenkommend
accommodation [əkɔməˈdeɪʃən] *n* Unterkunft *f*; **accommodations** (*US*) *npl* Unterkunft *f*; **have you any ~?** haben Sie eine Unterkunft?; **"~ to let"** "Zimmer zu vermieten"; **they have ~ for 500** sie können 500 Personen unterbringen; **the hall has seating ~ for 600** (*Brit*) in dem Saal können 600 Personen sitzen
accompaniment [əˈkʌmpənɪmənt] *n* Begleitung *f*
accompany [əˈkʌmpənɪ] *vt* begleiten
accomplice [əˈkʌmplɪs] *n* Komplize *m*, Komplizin *f*
accomplish [əˈkʌmplɪʃ] *vt* vollenden; (*achieve*) erreichen

accomplishment [ə'kʌmplɪʃmənt] *n* Vollendung *f*; (*achievement*) Leistung *f*; (*skill: gen pl*) Fähigkeit *f*

accord [ə'kɔ:d] *n* Übereinstimmung *f*; (*treaty*) Vertrag *m* ▷ *vt* gewähren; **of his own ~** freiwillig; **with one ~** geschlossen; **to be in ~** übereinstimmen

accordance [ə'kɔ:dəns] *n*: **in ~ with** in Übereinstimmung mit

according [ə'kɔ:dɪŋ] *prep*: **~ to** zufolge *+dat*; **~ to plan** wie geplant

accordingly [ə'kɔ:dɪŋlɪ] *adv* entsprechend; (*as a result*) folglich

accordion [ə'kɔ:dɪən] *n* Akkordeon *nt*

account [ə'kaunt] *n* (*Comm: bill*) Rechnung *f*; (*in bank, department store*) Konto *nt*; (*report*) Bericht *m*; **accounts** *npl* (*Comm*) Buchhaltung *f*; (*Bookkeeping*) (Geschäfts)bücher *pl*; **"~ payee only"** (*Brit*) "nur zur Verrechnung"; **to keep an ~ of** Buch führen über *+acc*; **to bring sb to ~ for sth/for having embezzled £50,000** jdn für etw/für die Unterschlagung von £50.000 zur Rechenschaft ziehen; **by all ~s** nach allem, was man hört; **of no ~** ohne Bedeutung; **on ~** auf Kredit; **to pay £5 on ~** eine Anzahlung von £5 leisten; **on no ~** auf keinen Fall; **on ~ of** wegen *+gen*; **to take into account, take ~ of** berücksichtigen

▸ **account for** *vt fus* erklären; (*expenditure*) Rechenschaft ablegen für; (*represent*) ausmachen; **all the children were ~ed for** man wusste, wo alle Kinder waren; **four people are still not ~ed for** vier Personen werden immer noch vermisst

accountable [ə'kauntəbl] *adj*: **~ (to)** verantwortlich (gegenüber *+dat*); **to be held ~ for sth** für etw verantwortlich gemacht werden

accountancy [ə'kauntənsɪ] *n* Buchhaltung *f*

accountant [ə'kauntənt] *n* Buchhalter(in) *m(f)*

account number *n* Kontonummer *f*

accrue [ə'kru:] *vi* sich ansammeln; **to ~ to** zufließen *+dat*

accumulate [ə'kju:mjuleɪt] *vt* ansammeln ▷ *vi* sich ansammeln

accuracy ['ækjurəsɪ] *n* Genauigkeit *f*

accurate ['ækjurɪt] *adj* genau

accurately ['ækjurɪtlɪ] *adv* genau; (*answer*) richtig

accusation [ækju'zeɪʃən] *n* Vorwurf *m*; (*instance*) Beschuldigung *f*; (*Law*) Anklage *f*

accuse [ə'kju:z] *vt*: **to ~ sb (of sth)** jdn (einer Sache *gen*) beschuldigen; (*Law*) jdn (wegen etw *dat*) anklagen

accused [ə'kju:zd] *n* (*Law*): **the ~** der/die Angeklagte

accustom [ə'kʌstəm] *vt* gewöhnen; **to ~ o.s. to sth** sich an etw *acc* gewöhnen

accustomed [ə'kʌstəmd] *adj* gewohnt; (*in the habit*): **~ to** gewohnt an *+acc*

ace [eɪs] *n* As *nt*

ache [eɪk] *n* Schmerz *m* ▷ *vi* schmerzen, wehtun; (*yearn*): **to ~ to do sth** sich danach sehnen, etw zu tun; **I've got (a) stomach ~** ich habe Magenschmerzen; **I'm aching all over** mir tut alles weh; **my head ~s** mir tut der Kopf weh

achieve [ə'tʃi:v] *vt* (*aim, result*) erreichen; (*success*) erzielen; (*victory*) erringen

achievement [ə'tʃi:vmənt] *n* (*act of achieving*) Erreichen *nt*; (*success, feat*) Leistung *f*

acid ['æsɪd] *adj* sauer ▷ *n* (*Chem*) Säure *f*; (*inf: LSD*) Acid *nt*

acid rain *n* saurer Regen *m*

acknowledge [ək'nɔlɪdʒ] *vt* (*also*: **acknowledge receipt of**) den Empfang *+gen* bestätigen; (*fact*) zugeben; (*situation*) zur Kenntnis nehmen; (*person*) grüßen

acknowledgement [ək'nɔlɪdʒmənt] *n* Empfangsbestätigung *f*; **acknowledgements** *npl* (*in book*) ≈ Danksagung *f*

acne ['æknɪ] *n* Akne *f*

acorn ['eɪkɔ:n] *n* Eichel *f*

acoustic [ə'ku:stɪk] *adj* akustisch

acoustics [ə'ku:stɪks] *n* Akustik *f*

acquaint [ə'kweɪnt] *vt*: **to ~ sb with sth** jdn mit etw vertraut machen; **to be ~ed with** (*person*) bekannt sein mit; (*fact*) vertraut sein mit

acquaintance [ə'kweɪntəns] *n* Bekannte(r) *f(m)*; (*with person*) Bekanntschaft *f*; (*with subject*) Kenntnis *f*; **to make sb's ~** jds Bekanntschaft machen

acquire [ə'kwaɪə^r] *vt* erwerben; (*interest*) entwickeln; (*habit*) annehmen

acquisition [ækwɪ'zɪʃən] *n* (*see vb*) Erwerb *m*, Entwicklung *f*, Annahme *f*; (*thing acquired*) Errungenschaft *f*

acquit [ə'kwɪt] *vt* freisprechen; **to ~ o.s. well** seine Sache gut machen

acre ['eɪkə^r] *n* Morgen *m*

acrid ['ækrɪd] *adj* bitter; (*smoke, fig*) beißend

acrobat ['ækrəbæt] *n* Akrobat(in) *m(f)*

acronym ['ækrənɪm] *n* Akronym *nt*

across [ə'krɔs] *prep* über *+acc*; (*on the other side of*) auf der anderen Seite *+gen* ▷ *adv* (*direction*) hinüber, herüber; (*measurement*) breit; **to take sb ~ the road** jdn über die Straße bringen; **a road ~ the wood** eine Straße durch den Wald; **the lake is 12 km ~** der See ist 12 km breit; **~ from** gegenüber *+dat*; **to get sth ~ (to sb)** (jdm) etw klarmachen

acrylic [ə'krɪlɪk] *adj* (*acid, paint, blanket*) Acryl- ▷ *n* Acryl *nt*; **acrylics** *npl*: **he paints in ~s** er malt mit Acrylfarbe

act [ækt] *n* Tat *f*; (*of play*) Akt *m*; (*in a show etc*) Nummer *f*; (*Law*) Gesetz *nt* ▷ *vi* handeln; (*behave*) sich verhalten; (*have effect*) wirken; (*Theat*) spielen ▷ *vt* spielen; **it's only an ~** es ist nur Schau; **~ of God** (*Law*) höhere Gewalt *f*; **to be in the ~ of doing sth** dabei sein, etw zu tun; **to catch sb in the ~** jdn auf frischer Tat ertappen; **to ~ the fool** (*Brit*)

herumalbern; **he is only ~ing** er tut (doch) nur so; **to ~ as** fungieren als; **it ~s as a deterrent** es dient zur Abschreckung
▸ **act on** *vt*: **to ~ on sth** (*take action*) auf etw *+acc* hin handeln
▸ **act out** *vt* (*event*) durchspielen; (*fantasies*) zum Ausdruck bringen
acting ['æktɪŋ] *adj* stellvertretend ▹ *n* (*profession*) Schauspielkunst *f*; (*activity*) Spielen *nt*; **~ in my capacity as chairman ...** in meiner Eigenschaft als Vorsitzender ...
action ['ækʃən] *n* Tat *f*; (*motion*) Bewegung *f*; (*Mil*) Kampf *m*, Gefecht *nt*; (*Law*) Klage *f*; **to bring an ~ against sb** (*Law*) eine Klage gegen jdn anstrengen; **killed in ~** (*Mil*) gefallen; **out of ~** (*person*) nicht einsatzfähig; (*thing*) außer Betrieb; **to take ~** etwas unternehmen; **to put a plan into ~** einen Plan in die Tat umsetzen
action replay *n* (*TV*) Wiederholung *f*
activate ['æktɪveɪt] *vt* in Betrieb setzen; (*Chem, Phys*) aktivieren
active ['æktɪv] *adj* aktiv; (*volcano*) tätig; **to play an ~ part in sth** sich aktiv an etw *dat* beteiligen
actively ['æktɪvlɪ] *adv* aktiv; (*dislike*) offen
activist ['æktɪvɪst] *n* Aktivist(in) *m(f)*
activity [æk'tɪvɪtɪ] *n* Aktivität *f*; (*pastime, pursuit*) Betätigung *f*
activity holiday *n* Aktivurlaub *m*
actor ['æktər] *n* Schauspieler *m*
actress ['æktrɪs] *n* Schauspielerin *f*
actual ['æktjuəl] *adj* wirklich; (*emphatic use*) eigentlich
actually ['æktjuəlɪ] *adv* wirklich; (*in fact*) tatsächlich; (*even*) sogar
acupuncture ['ækjupʌŋktʃər] *n* Akupunktur *f*
acute [ə'kju:t] *adj* akut; (*anxiety*) heftig; (*mind*) scharf; (*person*) scharfsinnig; (*Math*: *angle*) spitz; (*Ling*): **~ accent** Akut *m*
ad [æd] (*inf*) *n* = **advertisement**
adamant ['ædəmənt] *adj*: **to be ~ that ...** darauf bestehen, dass ...; **to be ~ about sth** auf etw *dat* bestehen
adapt [ə'dæpt] *vt* anpassen; (*novel etc*) bearbeiten ▹ *vi*: **to ~ (to)** sich anpassen (an *+acc*)
adaptable [ə'dæptəbl] *adj* anpassungsfähig; (*device*) vielseitig
adapter [ə'dæptər] *n* (*Elec*) Adapter *m*; (: *for several plugs*) Mehrfachsteckdose *f*
add [æd] *vt* hinzufügen; (*figures*: *also*: **add up**) zusammenzählen ▹ *vi*: **to ~ to** (*increase*) beitragen zu
▸ **add on** *vt* (*amount*) dazurechnen; (*room*) anbauen
▸ **add up** *vt* (*figures*) zusammenzählen ▹ *vi* (*fig*): **it doesn't ~ up** es ergibt keinen Sinn; **it doesn't ~ up to much** (*fig*) das ist nicht berühmt (*inf*)
adder ['ædər] *n* Kreuzotter *f*, Viper *f*
addict ['ædɪkt] *n* Süchtige(r) *f(m)*; (*enthusiast*) Anhänger(in) *m(f)*
addicted [ə'dɪktɪd] *adj*: **to be ~ to drugs/drink** drogensüchtig/alkoholsüchtig sein; **to be ~ to football** (*fig*) ohne Fußball nicht mehr leben können
addiction [ə'dɪkʃən] *n* Sucht *f*
addictive [ə'dɪktɪv] *adj*: **to be ~** (*drug*) süchtig machen; (*activity*) zur Sucht werden können
addition [ə'dɪʃən] *n* (*adding up*) Zusammenzählen *nt*; (*thing added*) Zusatz *m*; (: *to payment, bill*) Zuschlag *m*; (: *to building*) Anbau *m*; **in ~ (to)** zusätzlich (zu)
additional [ə'dɪʃənl] *adj* zusätzlich
additive ['ædɪtɪv] *n* Zusatz *m*
address [ə'drɛs] *n* Adresse *f*; (*speech*) Ansprache *f* ▹ *vt* adressieren; (*speak to*: *person*) ansprechen; (: *audience*) sprechen zu; **form of ~** (Form *f* der) Anrede *f*; **what form of ~ do you use for ...?** wie redet man ... an?; **absolute/relative ~** (*Comput*) absolute/relative Adresse; **to ~ (o.s. to)** (*problem*) sich befassen mit
address book *n* Adressbuch *nt*
adept ['ædɛpt] *adj*: **to be ~ at** gut sein in *+dat*
adequate ['ædɪkwɪt] *adj* ausreichend, adäquat; (*satisfactory*) angemessen
adhere [əd'hɪər] *vi*: **to ~ to** haften an *+dat*; (*fig*: *abide by*) sich halten an *+acc*; (: *hold to*) festhalten an *+dat*
adhesive [əd'hi:zɪvr] *adj* klebend, Klebe- ▹ *n* Klebstoff *m*
adhesive tape *n* (*Brit*) Klebstreifen *m*; (*US*: *Med*) Heftpflaster *nt*
ad hoc [æd'hɔk] *adj* (*committee, decision*) Ad-hoc- ▹ *adv* ad hoc
adjacent [ə'dʒeɪsənt] *adj*: **~ to** neben *+dat*
adjective ['ædʒɛktɪv] *n* Adjektiv *nt*, Eigenschaftswort *nt*
adjoining [ə'dʒɔɪnɪŋ] *adj* benachbart, Neben-
adjourn [ə'dʒə:n] *vt* vertagen ▹ *vi* sich vertagen; **to ~ a meeting till the following week** eine Besprechung auf die nächste Woche vertagen; **they ~ed to the pub** (*Brit*: *inf*) sie begaben sich in die Kneipe
adjust [ə'dʒʌst] *vt* anpassen; (*change*) ändern; (*clothing*) zurechtrücken; (*machine etc*) einstellen; (*Insurance*) regulieren ▹ *vi*: **to ~ (to)** sich anpassen (an *+acc*)
adjustable [ə'dʒʌstəbl] *adj* verstellbar
adjustment [ə'dʒʌstmənt] *n* Anpassung *f*; (*to machine*) Einstellung *f*
ad-lib [æd'lɪb] *vi, vt* improvisieren ▹ *adv*: **ad lib** aus dem Stegreif
administer [əd'mɪnɪstər] *vt* (*country, department*) verwalten; (*justice*) sprechen; (*oath*) abnehmen; (*Med*: *drug*) verabreichen
administration [ədmɪnɪs'treɪʃən] *n* (*management*) Verwaltung *f*; (*government*) Regierung *f*; **the A~** (US) die Regierung
administrative [əd'mɪnɪstrətɪv] *adj* (*department, reform etc*) Verwaltungs-
administrator [əd'mɪnɪstreɪtər] *n* Verwaltungsbeamte(r) *f(m)*
admiral ['ædmərəl] *n* Admiral *m*

Admiralty [ˈædmərəltɪ] (*Brit*) *n*: **the ~** (*also*: **the Admiralty Board**) das Marineministerium

admiration [ædməˈreɪʃən] *n* Bewunderung *f*; **to have great ~ for sb/sth** jdn/etw sehr bewundern

admire [ədˈmaɪəʳ] *vt* bewundern

admirer [ədˈmaɪərəʳ] *n* (*suitor*) Verehrer *m*; (*fan*) Bewunderer *m*, Bewunderin *f*

admission [ədˈmɪʃən] *n* (*admittance*) Zutritt *m*; (*to exhibition, night club etc*) Einlass *m*; (*to club, hospital*) Aufnahme *f*; (*entry fee*) Eintritt(spreis) *m*; (*confession*) Geständnis *nt*; **"~ free", "free admission"** "Eintritt frei"; **by his own ~** nach eigenem Eingeständnis

admit [ədˈmɪt] *vt* (*confess*) gestehen; (*permit to enter*) einlassen; (*to club, hospital*) aufnehmen; (*responsibility etc*) anerkennen; **"children not ~ted"** "kein Zutritt für Kinder"; **this ticket ~s two** diese Karte ist für zwei Personen; **I must ~ that ...** ich muss zugeben, dass ...; **to ~ defeat** sich geschlagen geben
▸ **admit of** *vt fus* (*interpretation etc*) erlauben
▸ **admit to** *vt fus* (*murder etc*) gestehen

admittance [ədˈmɪtəns] *n* Zutritt *m*; **"no ~"** "kein Zutritt"

admittedly [ədˈmɪtɪdlɪ] *adv* zugegebenermaßen

ado [əˈduː] *n*: **without (any) more ~** ohne weitere Umstände

adolescence [ædəuˈlɛsns] *n* Jugend *f*

adolescent [ædəuˈlɛsnt] *adj* heranwachsend; (*remark, behaviour*) pubertär ▹ *n* Jugendliche(r) *f(m)*

adopt [əˈdɔpt] *vt* adoptieren; (*Pol*: *candidate*) aufstellen; (*policy, attitude, accent*) annehmen

adopted [əˈdɔptɪd] *adj* (*child*) adoptiert

adoption [əˈdɔpʃən] *n* (*see vb*) Adoption *f*; Aufstellung *f*; Annahme *f*

adore [əˈdɔːʳ] *vt* (*person*) verehren; (*film, activity etc*) schwärmen für

adorn [əˈdɔːn] *vt* schmücken

Adriatic [eɪdrɪˈætɪk] *n*: **the ~ (Sea)** (*Geog*) die Adria, das Adriatische Meer

adrift [əˈdrɪft] *adv* (*Naut*) treibend; (*fig*) ziellos; **to be ~** (*Naut*) treiben; **to come ~** (*boat*) sich losmachen; (*fastening etc*) sich lösen

adult [ˈædʌlt] *n* Erwachsene(r) *f(m)* ▹ *adj* erwachsen; (*animal*) ausgewachsen; (*literature etc*) für Erwachsene

adult education *n* Erwachsenenbildung *f*

adultery [əˈdʌltərɪ] *n* Ehebruch *m*

advance [ədˈvɑːns] *n* (*movement*) Vorrücken *nt*; (*progress*) Fortschritt *m*; (*money*) Vorschuss *m* ▹ *vt* (*money*) vorschießen; (*theory, idea*) vorbringen ▹ *vi* (*move forward*) vorrücken; (*make progress*) Fortschritte machen ▹ *adj*: **~ booking** Vorverkauf *m*; **to make ~s (to sb)** Annäherungsversuche (bei jdm) machen; **in ~** im Voraus; **to give sb ~ notice** jdm frühzeitig Bescheid sagen; **to give sb ~ warning** jdn vorwarnen

advanced [ədˈvɑːnst] *adj* (*Scol*: *studies*) für Fortgeschrittene; (*country*) fortgeschritten; (*child*) weit entwickelt; (*ideas*) fortschrittlich; **~ in years** in fortgeschrittenem Alter

advantage [ədˈvɑːntɪdʒ] *n* Vorteil *m*; **to take ~ of** ausnutzen; (*opportunity*) nutzen; **it's to our ~ (to)** es ist für uns von Vorteil(, wenn wir)

advent [ˈædvənt] *n* (*of innovation*) Aufkommen *nt*; (*Rel*): **A~** Advent *m*

adventure [ədˈvɛntʃəʳ] *n* Abenteuer *nt*

adventurous [ədˈvɛntʃərəs] *adj* abenteuerlustig; (*bold*) mutig

adverb [ˈædvəːb] *n* Adverb *nt*

adversary [ˈædvəsərɪ] *n* Widersacher(in) *m(f)*

adverse [ˈædvəːs] *adj* ungünstig; **in ~ circumstances** unter widrigen Umständen; **~ to** ablehnend gegenüber *+dat*

advert [ˈædvəːt] (*Brit*) *n* = **advertisement**

advertise [ˈædvətaɪz] *vi* (*Comm*) werben; (*in newspaper*) annoncieren, inserieren ▹ *vt* (*product, event*) werben für; (*job*) ausschreiben; **to ~ for** (*staff, accommodation etc*) (per Anzeige) suchen

advertisement [ədˈvəːtɪsmənt] *n* (*Comm*) Werbung *f*, Reklame *f*; (*in classified ads*) Anzeige *f*, Inserat *nt*

advertiser [ˈædvətaɪzəʳ] *n* (*in newspaper*) Inserent(in) *m(f)*; (*on television etc*) Firma, die im Fernsehen *etc* wirbt

advertising [ˈædvətaɪzɪŋ] *n* Werbung *f*

advice [ədˈvaɪs] *n* Rat *m*; (*notification*) Benachrichtigung *f*, Avis *m or nt* (*Comm*); **a piece of ~** ein Rat(schlag); **to ask sb for ~** jdn um Rat fragen; **to take legal ~** einen Rechtsanwalt zurate ziehen

advisable [ədˈvaɪzəbl] *adj* ratsam

advise [ədˈvaɪz] *vt* (*person*) raten *+dat*; (*company etc*) beraten; **to ~ sb of sth** jdn von etw in Kenntnis setzen; **to ~ against sth** von etw abraten; **to ~ against doing sth** davon abraten, etw zu tun; **you would be well-/ill--d to go** Sie wären gut/schlecht beraten, wenn Sie gingen

adviser [ədˈvaɪzəʳ] *n* Berater(in) *m(f)*

advisory [ədˈvaɪzərɪ] *adj* beratend, Beratungs-; **in an ~ capacity** in beratender Funktion

advocate [ˈædvəkɪt] *vt* befürworten ▹ *n* (*Law*) (Rechts)anwalt *m*, (Rechts)anwältin *f*; (*supporter, upholder*): **~ of** Befürworter(in) *m(f)* *+gen*; **to be an ~ of sth** etw befürworten

Aegean [iːˈdʒiːən] *n*: **the ~ (Sea)** (*Geog*) die Ägäis, das Ägäische Meer

aerial [ˈɛərɪəl] *n* Antenne *f* ▹ *adj* (*view, bombardment etc*) Luft-

aerobics [ɛəˈrəubɪks] *n* Aerobic *nt*

aeroplane [ˈɛərəpleɪn] (*Brit*) *n* Flugzeug *nt*

aerosol [ˈɛərəsɔl] *n* Sprühdose *f*

aesthetic [iːsˈθɛtɪk] *adj* ästhetisch

afar [əˈfɑːʳ] *adv*: **from ~** aus der Ferne

affair [əˈfɛəʳ] *n* Angelegenheit *f*; (*romance*: *also*: **love affair**) Verhältnis *nt*; **affairs** *npl* Geschäfte *pl*

affect [əˈfɛkt] *vt* (*influence*) sich auswirken auf *+acc*; (*subj: disease*) befallen; (*move deeply*) bewegen; (*concern*) betreffen; (*feign*) vortäuschen; **to be ~ed by sth** von etw beeinflusst werden
affected [əˈfɛktɪd] *adj* affektiert
affection [əˈfɛkʃən] *n* Zuneigung *f*
affectionate [əˈfɛkʃənɪt] *adj* liebevoll, zärtlich; (*animal*) anhänglich
affinity [əˈfɪnɪtɪ] *n*: **to have an ~ with** *or* **for** sich verbunden fühlen mit; (*resemblance*): **to have an ~ with** verwandt sein mit
afflict [əˈflɪkt] *vt* quälen; (*misfortune*) heimsuchen
affluence [ˈæfluəns] *n* Wohlstand *m*
affluent [ˈæfluənt] *adj* wohlhabend; **the ~ society** die Wohlstandsgesellschaft
afford [əˈfɔːd] *vt* sich *dat* leisten; (*time*) aufbringen; (*provide*) bieten; **can we ~ a car?** können wir uns ein Auto leisten?; **I can't ~ the time** ich habe einfach nicht die Zeit
affordable [əˈfɔːdəbl] *adj* erschwinglich
Afghanistan [æfˈgænɪstæn] *n* Afghanistan *nt*
afloat [əˈfləut] *adv* auf dem Wasser ▷ *adj*: **to be ~** schwimmen; **to stay ~** sich über Wasser halten; **to keep/get a business ~** ein Geschäft über Wasser halten/auf die Beine stellen
afoot [əˈfut] *adv*: **there is something ~** da ist etwas im Gang
afraid [əˈfreɪd] *adj* ängstlich; **to be ~ of** Angst haben vor *+dat*; **to be ~ of doing sth** *or* **to do sth** Angst davor haben, etw zu tun; **to be ~ to** sich scheuen, ...; **I am ~ that ...** leider ...; **I am ~ so/not** leider ja/nein
Africa [ˈæfrɪkə] *n* Afrika *nt*
African [ˈæfrɪkən] *adj* afrikanisch ▷ *n* Afrikaner(in) *m(f)*
after [ˈɑːftəʳ] *prep* nach *+dat*; (*of place*) hinter *+dat* ▷ *adv* danach ▷ *conj* nachdem; **~ dinner** nach dem Essen; **the day ~ tomorrow** übermorgen; **what are you ~?** was willst du; **who are you ~?** wen suchst du?; **the police are ~ him** die Polizei ist hinter ihm her; **to name sb ~ sb** jdn nach jdm nennen; **it's twenty ~ eight** (US) es ist zwanzig nach acht; **to ask ~ sb** nach jdm fragen; **~ all** schließlich; **~ you!** nach Ihnen!; **~ he left** nachdem er gegangen war; **~ having shaved** nachdem er sich rasiert hatte
aftermath [ˈɑːftəmɑːθ] *n* Auswirkungen *pl*; **in the ~ of** nach *+dat*
afternoon [ˈɑːftəˈnuːn] *n* Nachmittag *m*
afters [ˈɑːftəz] (*Brit: inf*) *n* Nachtisch *m*
after-sales service [ɑːftəˈseɪlz-] (*Brit*) *n* Kundendienst *m*
aftersun [ˈɑːftəsʌn] *n* After-Sun-Lotion *f*
afterthought [ˈɑːftəθɔːt] *n*: **as an ~** nachträglich; **I had an ~** mir ist noch etwas eingefallen
afterwards, (US) **afterward** [ˈɑːftəwəd(z)] *adv* danach
again [əˈgɛn] *adv* (*once more*) noch einmal; (*repeatedly*) wieder; **not him ~!** nicht schon wieder er!; **to do sth ~** etw noch einmal tun; **to begin ~** noch einmal anfangen; **to see ~** wiedersehen; **he's opened it ~** er hat er schon wieder geöffnet; **~ and again** immer wieder; **now and ~** ab und zu, hin und wieder
against [əˈgɛnst] *prep* gegen *+acc*; (*leaning on*) an *+acc*; (*compared to*) gegenüber *+dat*; **~ a blue background** vor einem blauen Hintergrund; **(as) ~** gegenüber *+dat*
age [eɪdʒ] *n* Alter *nt*; (*period*) Zeitalter *nt* ▷ *vi* altern, alt werden ▷ *vt* alt machen; **what ~ is he?** wie alt ist er?; **20 years of ~** 20 Jahre alt; **under ~** minderjährig; **to come of ~** mündig werden; **it's been ~s since ...** es ist ewig her, seit ...
aged[1] [eɪdʒd] *adj*: **~ ten** zehn Jahre alt, zehnjährig
aged[2] [ˈeɪdʒɪd] *npl*: **the ~** die Alten *pl*
age group *n* Altersgruppe *f*; **the 40 to 50 ~** die Gruppe der Vierzig- bis Fünfzigjährigen
age limit *n* Altersgrenze *f*
agency [ˈeɪdʒənsɪ] *n* Agentur *f*; (*government body*) Behörde *f*; **through** *or* **by the ~ of** durch die Vermittlung von
agenda [əˈdʒɛndə] *n* Tagesordnung *f*
agent [ˈeɪdʒənt] *n* (*Comm*) Vertreter(in) *m(f)*; (*representative, spy*) Agent(in) *m(f)*; (*Chem*) Mittel *nt*; (*fig*) Kraft *f*
aggravate [ˈægrəveɪt] *vt* verschlimmern; (*inf: annoy*) ärgern
aggression [əˈgrɛʃən] *n* Aggression *f*
aggressive [əˈgrɛsɪv] *adj* aggressiv
agile [ˈædʒaɪl] *adj* beweglich, wendig
agitate [ˈædʒɪteɪt] *vt* aufregen; (*liquid: stir*) aufrühren; (*: shake*) schütteln ▷ *vi*: **to ~ for/against sth** für/gegen etw agitieren
AGM *n abbr* (*= annual general meeting*) JHV *f*
ago [əˈgəu] *adv*: **two days ~** vor zwei Tagen; **not long ~** vor Kurzem; **as long ~ as 1980** schon 1980; **how long ~?** wie lange ist das her?
agony [ˈægənɪ] *n* (*pain*) Schmerz *m*; (*torment*) Qual *f*; **to be in ~** Qualen leiden
agree [əˈgriː] *vt* (*price, date*) vereinbaren ▷ *vi* übereinstimmen; (*consent*) zustimmen; **to ~ with sb** (*subj: person*) jdm zustimmen; (*: food*) jdm bekommen; **to ~ to sth** einer Sache *dat* zustimmen; **to ~ to do sth** sich bereit erklären, etw zu tun; **to ~ on sth** sich auf etw *acc* einigen; **to ~ that** (*admit*) zugeben, dass; **garlic doesn't ~ with me** Knoblauch vertrage ich nicht; **it was ~d that ...** es wurde beschlossen, dass ...; **they ~d on this** sie haben sich in diesem Punkt geeinigt; **they ~d on going** sie einigten sich darauf, zu gehen; **they ~d on a price** sie vereinbarten einen Preis
agreeable [əˈgriːəbl] *adj* angenehm; (*willing*) einverstanden; **are you ~ to this?** sind Sie hiermit einverstanden?
agreed [əˈgriːd] *adj* vereinbart; **to be ~** sich

dat einig sein

agreement [ə'gri:mənt] *n* (*concurrence*) Übereinstimmung *f*; (*consent*) Zustimmung *f*; (*arrangement*) Abmachung *f*; (*contract*) Vertrag *m*; **to be in ~ (with sb)** (mit jdm) einer Meinung sein; **by mutual ~** in gegenseitigem Einverständnis

agricultural [ægrɪ'kʌltʃərəl] *adj* landwirtschaftlich; (*show*) Landwirtschafts-

agriculture ['ægrɪkʌltʃəʳ] *n* Landwirtschaft *f*

aground [ə'graund] *adv*: **to run ~** auf Grund laufen

ahead [ə'hɛd] *adv* vor uns/ihnen *etc*; **~ of** (*in advance of*) vor *+dat*; **to be ~ of sb** (*in progress, ranking*) vor jdm liegen; **to be ~ of schedule** schneller als geplant vorankommen; **~ of time** zeitlich voraus; **to arrive ~ of time** zu früh ankommen; **go right** *or* **straight ~** gehen/fahren Sie geradeaus; **go ~!** (*fig*) machen Sie nur!, nur zu!; **they were (right) ~ of us** sie waren (genau) vor uns

aid [eɪd] *n* Hilfe *f*; (*to less developed country*) Entwicklungshilfe *f*; (*device*) Hilfsmittel *nt* ▷ *vt* (*help*) helfen, unterstützen; **with the ~ of** mithilfe von; **in ~ of** zugunsten *+gen*; **to ~ and abet** Beihilfe leisten; *see also* **hearing aid**

aide [eɪd] *n* Berater(in) *m(f)*; (*Mil*) Adjutant *m*

AIDS [eɪdz] *n abbr* (= *acquired immune deficiency syndrome*) AIDS *nt*

ailing ['eɪlɪŋ] *adj* kränklich; (*economy, industry etc*) krank

ailment ['eɪlmənt] *n* Leiden *nt*

aim [eɪm] *vt*: **to ~ at** (*gun, missile, camera*) richten auf *+acc*; (*blow*) zielen auf *+acc*; (*remark*) richten an *+acc* ▷ *vi* (*also*: **take aim**) zielen ▷ *n* (*objective*) Ziel *nt*; (*in shooting*) Zielsicherheit *f*; **to ~ at** zielen auf *+acc*; (*objective*) anstreben *+acc*; **to ~ to do sth** vorhaben, etw zu tun

aimless ['eɪmlɪs] *adj* ziellos

ain't [eɪnt] (*inf*) = **am not; aren't; isn't**

air [ɛəʳ] *n* Luft *f*; (*tune*) Melodie *f*; (*appearance*) Auftreten *nt*; (*demeanour*) Haltung *f*; (*of house etc*) Atmosphäre *f* ▷ *vt* lüften; (*grievances, views*) Luft machen *+dat*; (*knowledge*) zur Schau stellen; (*ideas*) darlegen ▷ *cpd* Luft-; **into the ~** in die Luft; **by ~** mit dem Flugzeug; **to be on the ~** (*Radio, TV*: *programme*) gesendet werden; (*: station*) senden; (*: person*) auf Sendung sein

airborne ['ɛəbɔ:n] *adj* in der Luft; (*plane, particles*) in der Luft befindlich; (*troops*) Luftlande-

air-conditioned ['ɛəkən'dɪʃənd] *adj* klimatisiert

air conditioning *n* Klimaanlage *f*

aircraft ['ɛəkrɑ:ft] *n inv* Flugzeug *nt*

aircraft carrier *n* Flugzeugträger *m*

airfield ['ɛəfi:ld] *n* Flugplatz *m*

Air Force *n* Luftwaffe *f*

air freshener *n* Raumspray *nt*

air hostess (*Brit*) *n* Stewardess *f*

air letter (*Brit*) *n* Luftpostbrief *m*

airlift ['ɛəlɪft] *n* Luftbrücke *f*

airline ['ɛəlaɪn] *n* Fluggesellschaft *f*

airliner ['ɛəlaɪnəʳ] *n* Verkehrsflugzeug *nt*

airplane ['ɛəpleɪn] (*US*) *n* Flugzeug *nt*

airport ['ɛəpɔ:t] *n* Flughafen *m*

air raid *n* Luftangriff *m*

airsick ['ɛəsɪk] *adj* luftkrank

airspace ['ɛəspeɪs] *n* Luftraum *m*

airstrip ['ɛəstrɪp] *n* Start-und-Lande-Bahn *f*

air terminal *n* Terminal *m or nt*

airtight ['ɛətaɪt] *adj* luftdicht

air-traffic controller ['ɛətræfɪk-] *n* Fluglotse *m*

airy ['ɛərɪ] *adj* luftig; (*casual*) lässig

aisle [aɪl] *n* Gang *m*; (*section of church*) Seitenschiff *nt*

aisle seat *n* Sitz *m* am Gang

ajar [ə'dʒɑ:ʳ] *adj* angelehnt

akin [ə'kɪn] *adj*: **~ to** ähnlich *+dat*

à la carte *adv* à la carte

alarm [ə'lɑ:m] *n* (*anxiety*) Besorgnis *f*; (*in shop, bank*) Alarmanlage *f* ▷ *vt* (*worry*) beunruhigen; (*frighten*) erschrecken

alarm call *n* Weckruf *m*

alarm clock *n* Wecker *m*

alarmed [ə'lɑ:md] *adj* beunruhigt; **don't be ~** erschrecken Sie nicht

alarming [ə'lɑ:mɪŋ] *adj* (*worrying*) beunruhigend; (*frightening*) erschreckend

alas [ə'læs] *excl* leider

Albania [æl'beɪnɪə] *n* Albanien *nt*

albeit [ɔ:l'bi:ɪt] *conj* wenn auch

album ['ælbəm] *n* Album *nt*

alcohol ['ælkəhɔl] *n* Alkohol *m*

alcoholic [ælkə'hɔlɪk] *adj* alkoholisch ▷ *n* Alkoholiker(in) *m(f)*

alcove ['ælkəuv] *n* Alkoven *m*, Nische *f*

ale [eɪl] *n* Ale *nt*

alert [ə'lə:t] *adj* aufmerksam ▷ *n* Alarm *m* ▷ *vt* alarmieren; **to be ~ to** (*danger, opportunity*) sich *dat* bewusst sein *+gen*; **to be on the ~** wachsam sein; **to ~ sb (to sth)** jdn (vor etw *dat*) warnen

algebra ['ældʒɪbrə] *n* Algebra *f*

Algeria [æl'dʒɪərɪə] *n* Algerien *nt*

Algerian [æl'dʒɪərɪən] *adj* algerisch ▷ *n* Algerier(in) *m(f)*

Algiers [æl'dʒɪəz] *n* Algier *nt*

alias ['eɪlɪəs] *adv* alias ▷ *n* Deckname *m*

alibi ['ælɪbaɪ] *n* Alibi *nt*

alien ['eɪlɪən] *n* Ausländer(in) *m(f)*; (*extraterrestrial*) außerirdisches Wesen *nt* ▷ *adj*: **~ (to)** fremd (*+dat*)

alienate ['eɪlɪəneɪt] *vt* entfremden; (*antagonize*) befremden

alight [ə'laɪt] *adj* brennend; (*eyes, expression*) leuchtend ▷ *vi* (*bird*) sich niederlassen; (*passenger*) aussteigen

align [ə'laɪn] *vt* ausrichten

alike [ə'laɪk] *adj* ähnlich ▷ *adv* (*similarly*) ähnlich; (*equally*) gleich; **to look ~** sich *dat* ähnlich sehen; **winter and summer ~** Sommer wie Winter

alimony ['ælɪmənɪ] *n* Unterhalt *m*
alive [ə'laɪv] *adj* (*living*) lebend; (*lively*) lebendig; (*active*) lebhaft; **~ with** erfüllt von; **to be ~ to sth** sich *dat* einer Sache *gen* bewusst sein
all [ɔ:l] *adj* alle(r, s); **all day/night** den ganzen Tag/die ganze Nacht (über); **all men are equal** alle Menschen sind gleich; **all five came** alle fünf kamen; **all the books** die ganzen Bücher, alle Bücher; **all the food** das ganze Essen; **all the time** die ganze Zeit (über); **all his life** sein ganzes Leben (lang) ▷ *pron* **1** alles; **I ate it all, I ate all of it** ich habe alles gegessen; **all of us/the boys went** wir alle/alle Jungen gingen; **we all sat down** wir setzten uns alle; **is that all?** ist das alles?; (*in shop*) sonst noch etwas? **2** (*in phrases*): **above all** vor allem; **after all** schließlich; **all in all** alles in allem ▷ *adv* ganz; **all alone** ganz allein; **it's not as hard as all that** so schwer ist es nun auch wieder nicht; **all the more/the better** um so mehr/besser; **all but** (*all except for*) alle außer; (*almost*) fast; **the score is 2 all** der Spielstand ist 2 zu 2
allegation [ælɪ'geɪʃən] *n* Behauptung *f*
allege [ə'lɛdʒ] *vt* behaupten; **he is ~d to have said that ...** er soll angeblich gesagt haben, dass ...
alleged [ə'lɛdʒd] *adj* angeblich
allegedly [ə'lɛdʒɪdlɪ] *adv* angeblich
allegiance [ə'li:dʒəns] *n* Treue *f*
allergic [ə'lə:dʒɪk] *adj* (*rash, reaction*) allergisch; (*person*): **~ to** allergisch gegen
allergy ['ælədʒɪ] *n* Allergie *f*
alleviate [ə'li:vɪeɪt] *vt* lindern
alley ['ælɪ] *n* Gasse *f*
alliance [ə'laɪəns] *n* Bündnis *nt*
allied ['ælaɪd] *adj* verbündet, alliiert; (*products, industries*) verwandt
alligator ['ælɪgeɪtə^r] *n* Alligator *m*
all-in ['ɔ:lɪn] (*Brit*) *adj* (*price*) Inklusiv-
all-night ['ɔ:l'naɪt] *adj* (*café, cinema*) die ganze Nacht geöffnet; (*party*) die ganze Nacht dauernd
allocate ['æləkeɪt] *vt* zuteilen
allot [ə'lɔt] *vt*: **to ~ (to)** zuteilen (*+dat*); **in the ~ted time** in der vorgesehenen Zeit
allotment [ə'lɔtmənt] *n* (*share*) Anteil *m*; (*garden*) Schrebergarten *m*
all-out ['ɔ:laut] *adj* (*effort, dedication etc*) äußerste(r, s); (*strike*) total ▷ *adv*: **all out** mit aller Kraft; **to go all out for** sein Letztes *or* Äußerstes geben für
allow [ə'lau] *vt* erlauben; (*behaviour*) zulassen; (*sum, time*) einplanen; (*claim, goal*) anerkennen; (*concede*): **to ~ that** annehmen, dass; **to ~ sb to do sth** jdm erlauben, etw zu tun; **he is ~ed to ...** er darf ...; **smoking is not ~ed** Rauchen ist nicht gestattet; **we must ~ three days for the journey** wir müssen für die Reise drei Tage einplanen ▸ **allow for** *vt fus* einplanen, berücksichtigen
allowance [ə'lauəns] *n* finanzielle Unterstützung *f*; (*welfare payment*) Beihilfe *f*; (*pocket money*) Taschengeld *nt*; (*tax allowance*) Freibetrag *m*; **to make ~s for** (*person*) Zugeständnisse machen für; (*thing*) berücksichtigen
alloy ['ælɔɪ] *n* Legierung *f*
all right *adv* (*well*) gut; (*correctly*) richtig; (*as answer*) okay, in Ordnung
all-rounder [ɔ:l'raundə^r] *n* Allrounder *m*; (*athlete etc*) Allroundsportler(in) *m(f)*
all-time ['ɔ:l'taɪm] *adj* aller Zeiten
ally ['ælaɪ] *n* Verbündete(r) *f(m)*; (*during wars*) Alliierte(r) *f(m)* ▷ *vt*: **to ~ o.s. with** sich verbünden mit
almighty [ɔ:l'maɪtɪ] *adj* allmächtig; (*tremendous*) mächtig
almond ['ɑ:mənd] *n* Mandel *f*; (*tree*) Mandelbaum *m*
almost ['ɔ:lməust] *adv* fast, beinahe; **he ~ fell** er wäre beinahe gefallen
alone [ə'ləun] *adj, adv* allein; **to leave sb ~** jdn in Ruhe lassen; **to leave sth ~** die Finger von etw lassen; **let ~ ...** geschweige denn ...
along [ə'lɔŋ] *prep* entlang *+acc* ▷ *adv*: **is he coming ~ with us?** kommt er mit?; **he was hopping/limping ~** er hüpfte/humpelte daher; **~ with** (*together with*) zusammen mit; **all ~** (*all the time*) die ganze Zeit
alongside [ə'lɔŋ'saɪd] *prep* neben *+dat*; (*ship*) längsseits *+gen* ▷ *adv* (*come*) nebendran; (*be*) daneben; **we brought our boat ~** wir brachten unser Boot heran; **a car drew up ~** ein Auto fuhr neben mich/ihn *etc* heran
aloof [ə'lu:f] *adj* unnahbar ▷ *adv*: **to stand ~** abseitsstehen
aloud [ə'laud] *adv* laut
alphabet ['ælfəbɛt] *n* Alphabet *nt*
alphabetical [ælfə'bɛtɪkl] *adj* alphabetisch; **in ~ order** in alphabetischer Reihenfolge
alpine ['ælpaɪn] *adj* alpin, Alpen-
Alps [ælps] *npl*: **the ~** die Alpen
already [ɔ:l'rɛdɪ] *adv* schon
alright ['ɔ:l'raɪt] (*Brit*) *adv* = **all right**
Alsatian [æl'seɪʃən] (*Brit*) *n* (*dog*) Schäferhund *m*
also ['ɔ:lsəu] *adv* (*too*) auch; (*moreover*) außerdem
altar ['ɔltə^r] *n* Altar *m*
alter ['ɔltə^r] *vt* ändern; (*clothes*) umändern ▷ *vi* sich (ver)ändern
alteration [ɔltə'reɪʃən] *n* Änderung *f*; (*to clothes*) Umänderung *f*; (*to building*) Umbau *m*; **alterations** *npl* (*Sewing*) Änderungen *pl*; (*Archit*) Umbau *m*
alternate [*adj* ɔl'tə:nɪt, *vi* 'ɔltəneɪt] *adj* abwechselnd; (*US: alternative: plans etc*) Alternativ- ▷ *vi*: **to ~ (with)** sich abwechseln (mit); **on ~ days** jeden zweiten Tag
alternative [ɔl'tə:nətɪv] *adj* alternativ; (*solution etc*) Alternativ- ▷ *n* Alternative *f*
alternatively [ɔl'tə:nətɪvlɪ] *adv*: **~ one could ...** oder man könnte ...

alternator ['ɔltə:neɪtəʳ] *n* (*Aut*) Lichtmaschine *f*
although [ɔ:l'ðəu] *conj* obwohl
altitude ['æltɪtju:d] *n* Höhe *f*
alto ['æltəu] *n* Alt *m*
altogether [ɔ:ltə'gɛðəʳ] *adv* ganz; (*on the whole, in all*) im Ganzen, insgesamt; **how much is that ~?** was macht das zusammen?
aluminium [ælju'mɪnɪəm], (*US*) **aluminum** [ə'lu:mɪnəm] *n* Aluminium *nt*
always ['ɔ:lweɪz] *adv* immer; **we can ~ ...** (*if all else fails*) wir können ja auch ...
Alzheimer's ['æltshaɪməz], **Alzheimer's disease** *n* (*Med*) Alzheimerkrankheit *f*
AM *abbr* (*= amplitude modulation*) AM, ≈ MW ▷ *n abbr* (*Brit: in Wales: Pol: = Assembly Member*) Mitglied *nt* der walisischen Versammlung
am [æm] *vb see* **be**
a.m. *adv abbr* (*= ante meridiem*) morgens; (*later*) vormittags
amalgamate [ə'mælgəmeɪt] *vi, vt* fusionieren
amass [ə'mæs] *vt* anhäufen; (*evidence*) zusammentragen
amateur ['æmətəʳ] *n* Amateur *m* ▷ *adj* (*Sport*) Amateur-; **~ dramatics** Laientheater *nt*
amateurish ['æmətərɪʃ] *adj* laienhaft; (*pej*) dilettantisch, stümperhaft
amaze [ə'meɪz] *vt* erstaunen; **to be ~d (at)** erstaunt sein (über *+acc*)
amazement [ə'meɪzmənt] *n* Erstaunen *nt*
amazing [ə'meɪzɪŋ] *adj* erstaunlich; (*bargain, offer*) sensationell
Amazon ['æməzən] *n* (*river*) Amazonas *m*; **the ~ basin** das Amazonastiefland; **the ~ jungle** der Amazonas-Regenwald
ambassador [æm'bæsədəʳ] *n* Botschafter(in) *m(f)*
amber ['æmbəʳ] *n* Bernstein *m*; **at ~** (*Brit: traffic lights*) auf Gelb; (*: move off*) bei Gelb
ambiguous [æm'bɪgjuəs] *adj* zweideutig; (*not clear*) unklar
ambition [æm'bɪʃən] *n* Ehrgeiz *m*; (*desire*) Ambition *f*; **to achieve one's ~** seine Ambitionen erfüllen
ambitious [æm'bɪʃəs] *adj* ehrgeizig
ambulance ['æmbjuləns] *n* Krankenwagen *m*
ambush ['æmbuʃ] *n* Hinterhalt *m*; (*attack*) Überfall *m* aus dem Hinterhalt ▷ *vt* (aus dem Hinterhalt) überfallen
amen ['ɑ:'mɛn] *excl* amen
amenable [ə'mi:nəbl] *adj*: **~ to** zugänglich *+dat*; (*to flattery etc*) empfänglich für; **~ to the law** dem Gesetz verantwortlich
amend [ə'mɛnd] *vt* ändern; (*habits, behaviour*) bessern
amendment [ə'mɛndmənt] *n* Änderung *f*; (*to law*) Amendement *nt*
amenities [ə'mi:nɪtɪz] *npl Einkaufs-, Unterhaltungs- und Transportmöglichkeiten*
America [ə'mɛrɪkə] *n* Amerika *nt*
American [ə'mɛrɪkən] *adj* amerikanisch ▷ *n* Amerikaner(in) *m(f)*
amiable ['eɪmɪəbl] *adj* liebenswürdig
amicable ['æmɪkəbl] *adj* freundschaftlich; (*settlement*) gütlich
amid [ə'mɪd], **amidst** [ə'mɪdst] *prep* inmitten *+gen*
amiss [ə'mɪs] *adj, adv*: **to take sth ~** etw übel nehmen; **there's something ~** da stimmt irgendetwas nicht
ammonia [ə'məunɪə] *n* Ammoniak *nt*
ammunition [æmju'nɪʃən] *n* Munition *f*
amnesty ['æmnɪstɪ] *n* Amnestie *f*; **to grant an ~ to** amnestieren
amok [ə'mɔk] *adv*: **to run ~** Amok laufen
among [ə'mʌŋ], **amongst** [ə'mʌŋst] *prep* unter *+dat*
amorous ['æmərəs] *adj* amourös
amount [ə'maunt] *n* (*quantity*) Menge *f*; (*sum of money*) Betrag *m*; (*total*) Summe *f*; (*of bill etc*) Höhe *f* ▷ *vi*: **to ~ to** (*total*) sich belaufen auf *+acc*; (*be same as*) gleichkommen *+dat*; **the total ~** (*of money*) die Gesamtsumme
amp ['æmp], **ampère** ['æmpɛəʳ] *n* Ampere *nt*; **a 3 ~(ère) fuse** eine Sicherung von 3 Ampere; **a 13 ~(ère) plug** ein Stecker mit einer Sicherung von 13 Ampere
ample ['æmpl] *adj* (*large*) üppig; (*abundant*) reichlich; (*enough*) genügend; **this is ~** das ist reichlich; **to have ~ time/room** genügend Zeit/Platz haben
amplifier ['æmplɪfaɪəʳ] *n* Verstärker *m*
amputate ['æmpjuteɪt] *vt* amputieren
amuse [ə'mju:z] *vt* (*entertain*) unterhalten; (*make smile*) amüsieren, belustigen; **to ~ o.s. with sth/by doing sth** sich die Zeit mit etw vertreiben/damit vertreiben, etw zu tun; **to be ~d at** sich amüsieren über *+acc*; **he was not ~d** er fand das gar nicht komisch *or* zum Lachen
amusement [ə'mju:zmənt] *n* (*mirth*) Vergnügen *nt*; (*pleasure*) Unterhaltung *f*; (*pastime*) Zeitvertreib *m*; **much to my ~** zu meiner großen Belustigung
amusement arcade *n* Spielhalle *f*
amusement park *n* Vergnügungspark *m*
amusing [ə'mju:zɪŋ] *adj* amüsant, unterhaltsam
an [æn, ən] *indef art see* **a**
anaemia, (*US*) **anemia** [ə'ni:mɪə] *n* Anämie *f*
anaemic, (*US*) **anemic** [ə'ni:mɪk] *adj* blutarm
anaesthetic, (*US*) **anesthetic** [ænɪs'θɛtɪk] *n* Betäubungsmittel *nt*; **under (the) ~** unter Narkose; **local ~** örtliche Betäubung *f*; **general ~** Vollnarkose *f*
analogue, (*US*) **analog** ['ænəlɔg] *adj* (*watch, computer*) Analog-
analogy [ə'nælədʒɪ] *n* Analogie *f*; **to draw an ~ between** eine Analogie herstellen zwischen *+dat*; **by ~** durch einen Analogieschluss
analyse, (*US*) **analyze** ['ænəlaɪz] *vt* analysieren; (*Chem, Med*) untersuchen; (*person*) psychoanalytisch behandeln
analysis [ə'næləsɪs] (*pl* **analyses**) *n* (*see vb*)

Analyse *f*; Untersuchung *f*; Psychoanalyse *f*; **in the last ~** letzten Endes
analyst ['ænəlɪst] *n* Analytiker(in) *m(f)*; (US) Psychoanalytiker(in) *m(f)*
analyze ['ænəlaɪz] (US) *vt* = **analyse**
anarchist ['ænəkɪstʳ] *adj* anarchistisch ▷ *n* Anarchist(in) *m(f)*
anarchy ['ænəkɪ] *n* Anarchie *f*
anatomy [ə'nætəmɪ] *n* Anatomie *f*; (*body*) Körper *m*
ancestor ['ænsɪstəʳ] *n* Vorfahr(in) *m(f)*
anchor ['æŋkəʳ] *n* Anker *m* ▷ *vi* (*also*: **to drop anchor**) ankern, vor Anker gehen ▷ *vt* (*fig*) verankern; **to ~ sth to** etw verankern in *+dat*; **to weigh ~** den Anker lichten
anchovy ['æntʃəvɪ] *n* Sardelle *f*, An(s)chovis *f*
ancient ['eɪnʃənt] *adj* alt; (*person, car*) uralt
ancillary [æn'sɪlərɪ] *adj* Hilfs-
and [ænd] *conj* und; **~ so on** und so weiter; **try ~ come please** bitte versuche zu kommen; **better ~ better** immer besser
Andorra [æn'dɔːrə] *n* Andorra *nt*
anesthetic *etc* [ænɪs'θɛtɪk] (US) = **anaesthetic** *etc*
anew [ə'njuː] *adv* von Neuem
angel ['eɪndʒəl] *n* Engel *m*
anger ['æŋgəʳ] *n* Zorn *m* ▷ *vt* ärgern; (*enrage*) erzürnen; **red with ~** rot vor Wut
angina [æn'dʒaɪnə] *n* Angina pectoris *f*
angle ['æŋgl] *n* Winkel *m*; (*viewpoint*): **from their ~** von ihrem Standpunkt aus ▷ *vi*: **to ~ for** (*invitation*) aus sein auf *+acc*; (*compliments*) fischen nach ▷ *vt*: **to ~ sth towards** *or* **to** etw ausrichten auf *+acc*
angler ['æŋgləʳ] *n* Angler(in) *m(f)*
Anglican ['æŋglɪkən] *adj* anglikanisch ▷ *n* Anglikaner(in) *m(f)*
angling ['æŋglɪŋ] *n* Angeln *nt*
Anglo- ['æŋgləu] *pref* Anglo-, anglo-
angrily ['æŋgrɪlɪ] *adv* verärgert
angry ['æŋgrɪ] *adj* verärgert; (*wound*) entzündet; **to be ~ with sb** auf jdn böse sein; **to be ~ at sth** über etw *acc* verärgert sein; **to get ~** wütend werden; **to make sb ~** jdn wütend machen
anguish ['æŋgwɪʃ] *n* Qual *f*
animal ['ænɪməl] *n* Tier *nt*; (*living creature*) Lebewesen *nt*; (*pej: person*) Bestie *f* ▷ *adj* tierhaft; (*attraction etc*) animalisch
animate [*vt* 'ænɪmeɪt, *adj* 'ænɪmɪt] *vt* beleben ▷ *adj* lebend
animated ['ænɪmeɪtɪd] *adj* lebhaft; (*film*) Zeichentrick-
animation [ænɪ'meɪʃən] *n* (*liveliness*) Lebhaftigkeit *f*; (*film*) Animation *f*
aniseed ['ænɪsiːd] *n* Anis *m*
ankle ['æŋkl] *n* Knöchel *m*
annex ['ænɛks] *n* (*also*: **annexe**: *Brit*) Anhang *m*; (*building*) Nebengebäude *nt*; (*extension*) Anbau *m* ▷ *vt* (*take over*) annektieren
anniversary [ænɪ'vəːsərɪ] *n* Jahrestag *m*
announce [ə'nauns] *vt* ankündigen; (*birth, death etc*) anzeigen; **he ~d that he wasn't going** er verkündete, dass er nicht gehen würde
announcement [ə'naunsmənt] *n* Ankündigung *f*; (*official*) Bekanntmachung *f*; (*of birth, death etc*) Anzeige *f*; **I'd like to make an ~** ich möchte etwas bekannt geben
announcer [ə'naunsəʳ] *n* Ansager(in) *m(f)*
annoy [ə'nɔɪ] *vt* ärgern; **to be ~ed (at sth/ with sb)** sich (über etw/jdn) ärgern; **don't get ~ed!** reg dich nicht auf!
annoyance [ə'nɔɪəns] *n* Ärger *m*
annoying [ə'nɔɪɪŋ] *adj* ärgerlich; (*person, habit*) lästig
annual ['ænjuəl] *adj* jährlich; (*income*) Jahres- ▷ *n* (*Bot*) einjährige Pflanze *f*; (*book*) Jahresband *m*
annually ['ænjuəlɪ] *adv* jährlich
annul [ə'nʌl] *vt* annullieren; (*law*) aufheben
annum ['ænəm] *n see* **per**
anonymous [ə'nɔnɪməs] *adj* anonym
anorak ['ænəræk] *n* Anorak *m*
anorexia [ænə'rɛksɪə] *n* Magersucht *f*, Anorexie *f*
anorexic [ænə'rɛksɪk] *adj* magersüchtig
another [ə'nʌðəʳ] *pron* (*additional*) noch eine(r, s); (*different*) ein(e) andere(r, s) ▷ *adj*: **~ book** (*one more*) noch ein Buch; (*a different one*) ein anderes Buch; **~ drink?** noch etwas zu trinken?; **in ~ five years** in weiteren fünf Jahren; *see also* **one**
answer ['ɑːnsəʳ] *n* Antwort *f*; (*to problem*) Lösung *f* ▷ *vi* antworten; (*Tel*) sich melden ▷ *vt* (*reply to: person*) antworten *+dat*; (*: letter, question*) beantworten; (*problem*) lösen; (*prayer*) erhören; **in ~ to your letter** in Beantwortung Ihres Schreibens; **to ~ the phone** ans Telefon gehen; **to ~ the bell** *or* **the door** die Tür aufmachen
▸ **answer back** *vi* widersprechen; (*child*) frech sein
▸ **answer for** *vt fus* (*person*) verantwortlich sein für, sich verbürgen für
▸ **answer to** *vt fus* (*description*) entsprechen *+dat*
answerable ['ɑːnsərəbl] *adj*: **to be ~ to sb for sth** jdm gegenüber für etw verantwortlich sein; **I am ~ to no-one** ich brauche mich vor niemandem zu verantworten
answering machine ['ɑːnsərɪŋ-] *n* Anrufbeantworter *m*
ant [ænt] *n* Ameise *f*
antagonism [æn'tægənɪzəm] *n* Feindseligkeit *f*, Antagonismus *m*
antagonize [æn'tægənaɪz] *vt* gegen sich aufbringen
Antarctic [ænt'ɑːktɪk] *n*: **the ~** die Antarktis
antelope ['æntɪləup] *n* Antilope *f*
antenatal ['æntɪ'neɪtl] *adj* vor der Geburt, Schwangerschafts-
antenatal clinic *n* Sprechstunde *f* für werdende Mütter
antenna [æn'tɛnə] (*pl* **~e**) *n* (*of insect*) Fühler *m*; (*Radio, TV*) Antenne *f*

anthem ['ænθəm] *n*: **national ~** Nationalhymne *f*
anthology [æn'θɔlədʒɪ] *n* Anthologie *f*
anthropology [ænθrə'pɔlədʒɪ] *n* Anthropologie *f*
anti-aircraft ['æntɪ'ɛəkrɑːft] *adj* (*gun, rocket*) Flugabwehr-
antibiotic ['æntɪbaɪ'ɔtɪk] *n* Antibiotikum *nt*
antibody ['æntɪbɔdɪ] *n* Antikörper *m*
anticipate [æn'tɪsɪpeɪt] *vt* erwarten; (*foresee*) vorhersehen; (*look forward to*) sich freuen auf +*acc*; (*forestall*) vorwegnehmen; **this is worse than I ~d** es ist schlimmer, als ich erwartet hatte; **as ~d** wie erwartet
anticipation [æntɪsɪ'peɪʃən] *n* Erwartung *f*; (*eagerness*) Vorfreude *f*; **thanking you in ~** vielen Dank im Voraus
anticlimax ['æntɪ'klaɪmæks] *n* Enttäuschung *f*
anticlockwise ['æntɪ'klɔkwaɪz] (*Brit*) *adv* gegen den Uhrzeigersinn
antics ['æntɪks] *npl* Mätzchen *pl*; (*of politicians etc*) Gehabe *nt*
antidote ['æntɪdəut] *n* Gegenmittel *nt*
antifreeze ['æntɪfriːz] *n* Frostschutzmittel *nt*
antihistamine ['æntɪ'hɪstəmɪn] *n* Antihistamin *nt*
antiperspirant ['æntɪ'pəːspɪrənt] *n* Antitranspirant *nt*
antiquated ['æntɪkweɪtɪd] *adj* antiquiert
antique [æn'tiːk] *n* Antiquität *f* ▷ *adj* antik
antique dealer *n* Antiquitätenhändler(in) *m(f)*
antique shop *n* Antiquitätenladen *m*
anti-Semitism ['æntɪ'sɛmɪtɪzəm] *n* Antisemitismus *m*
antiseptic [æntɪ'sɛptɪk] *n* Antiseptikum *nt* ▷ *adj* antiseptisch
antisocial ['æntɪ'səuʃəl] *adj* unsozial; (*person*) ungesellig
antlers ['æntləz] *npl* Geweih *nt*
anvil ['ænvɪl] *n* Amboss *m*
anxiety [æŋ'zaɪətɪ] *n* (*worry*) Sorge *f*; (*Med*) Angstzustand *m*; (*eagerness*): **~ to do sth** Verlangen (danach), etw zu tun
anxious ['æŋkʃəs] *adj* (*worried*) besorgt; (*situation*) Angst einflößend; (*question, moments*) bang(e); (*keen*): **to be ~ to do sth** etw unbedingt tun wollen; **I'm very ~ about you** ich mache mir große Sorgen um dich
any ['ɛnɪ] *adj* **1** (*in questions etc*): **have you any butter/children?** haben Sie Butter/Kinder?; **if there are any tickets left** falls noch Karten da sind
2 (*with negative*) kein(e); **I haven't any money/books** ich habe kein Geld/keine Bücher
3 (*no matter which*) irgendein(e); **choose any book you like** nehmen Sie irgendein Buch *or* ein beliebiges Buch
4 (*in phrases*): **in any case** in jedem Fall; **any day now** jeden Tag; **at any moment** jeden Moment; **at any rate** auf jeden Fall; **any time** (*at any moment*) jeden Moment; (*whenever*) jederzeit
▷ *pron* **1** (*in questions etc*): **have you got any?** haben Sie welche?; **can any of you sing?** kann (irgend)einer von euch singen?
2 (*with negative*): **I haven't any (of them)** ich habe keine (davon)
3 (*no matter which one(s)*) egal welche; **take any of those books (you like)** nehmen Sie irgendwelche von diesen Büchern
▷ *adv* **1** (*in questions etc*): **do you want any more soup/sandwiches?** möchtest du noch Suppe/Butterbrote?; **are you feeling any better?** geht es Ihnen etwas besser?
2 (*with negative*): **I can't hear him any more** ich kann ihn nicht mehr hören; **don't wait any longer** warte nicht noch länger
anybody ['ɛnɪbɔdɪ] *pron* = **anyone**
anyhow ['ɛnɪhau] *adv* **1** (*at any rate*) sowieso, ohnehin; **I shall go anyhow** ich gehe auf jeden Fall
2 (*haphazard*): **do it anyhow you like** machen Sie es, wie Sie wollen
anyone ['ɛnɪwʌn] *pron* **1** (*in questions etc*) (irgend)jemand; **can you see anyone?** siehst du jemanden?
2 (*with negative*) keine(r); **I can't see anyone** ich kann keinen *or* niemanden sehen
3 (*no matter who*) jede(r); **anyone could do it** das kann jeder
anything ['ɛnɪθɪŋ] *pron* **1** (*in questions etc*) (irgend)etwas; **can you see anything?** kannst du etwas sehen?
2 (*with negative*) nichts; **I can't see anything** ich kann nichts sehen
3 (*no matter what*) irgendetwas; **you can say anything you like** du kannst sagen, was du willst; **anything between 15 and 20 pounds** (ungefähr) zwischen 15 und 20 Pfund
anyway ['ɛnɪweɪ] *adv* **1** (*at any rate*) sowieso, ohnehin; **I shall go anyway** ich gehe auf jeden Fall
2 (*besides*): **anyway, I can't come** jedenfalls kann ich nicht kommen; **why are you phoning, anyway?** warum rufst du überhaupt *or* eigentlich an?
anywhere ['ɛnɪwɛəʳ] *adv* **1** (*in questions etc*) irgendwo; **can you see him anywhere?** kannst du ihn irgendwo sehen?
2 (*with negative*) nirgendwo, nirgends; **I can't see him anywhere** ich kann ihn nirgendwo *or* nirgends sehen
3 (*no matter where*) irgendwo; **put the books down anywhere** legen Sie die Bücher irgendwohin
apart [ə'pɑːt] *adv* (*be*) entfernt; (*move*) auseinander; (*aside*) beiseite; (*separately*) getrennt; **10 miles ~** 10 Meilen voneinander entfernt; **a long way ~** weit auseinander; **they are living ~** sie leben getrennt; **with one's legs ~** mit gespreizten Beinen; **to take ~** auseinandernehmen; **~ from** (*excepting*)

abgesehen von; (*in addition*) außerdem
apartheid [ə'pɑ:teɪt] *n* Apartheid *f*
apartment [ə'pɑ:tmənt] *n* (*US: flat*) Wohnung *f*; (*room*) Raum *m*, Zimmer *nt*
apartment building (*US*) *n* Wohnblock *m*
apathy ['æpəθɪ] *n* Apathie *f*, Teilnahmslosigkeit *f*
ape [eɪp] *n* (Menschen)affe *m* ▷ *vt* nachahmen
aperture ['æpətʃjuəʳ] *n* Öffnung *f*; (*Phot*) Blende *f*
APEX ['eɪpɛks] *n abbr* (*Aviat, Rail: = advance purchase excursion*) APEX
apex ['eɪpɛks] *n* Spitze *f*
apologetic [əpɔlə'dʒɛtɪk] *adj* entschuldigend; **to be very ~ (about sth)** sich (wegen etw *gen*) sehr entschuldigen
apologize [ə'pɔlədʒaɪz] *vi*: **to ~ (for sth to sb)** sich (für etw bei jdm) entschuldigen
apology [ə'pɔlədʒɪ] *n* Entschuldigung *f*; **to send one's apologies** sich entschuldigen lassen; **please accept my apologies** ich bitte um Verzeihung
apostle [ə'pɔsl] *n* Apostel *m*
apostrophe [ə'pɔstrəfɪ] *n* Apostroph *m*, Auslassungszeichen *nt*
appal [ə'pɔ:l] *vt* entsetzen; **to be ~led by** entsetzt sein über *+acc*
appalling [ə'pɔ:lɪŋ] *adj* entsetzlich; **she's an ~ cook** sie kann überhaupt nicht kochen
apparatus [æpə'reɪtəs] *n* Gerät *nt*; (*in gymnasium*) Geräte *pl*; (*of organization*) Apparat *m*; **a piece of ~** ein Gerät *nt*
apparel [ə'pærəl] (*US*) *n* Kleidung *f*
apparent [ə'pærənt] *adj* (*seeming*) scheinbar; (*obvious*) offensichtlich; **it is ~ that ...** es ist klar, dass ...
apparently [ə'pærəntlɪ] *adv* anscheinend
appeal [ə'pi:l] *vi* (*Law*) Berufung einlegen ▷ *n* (*Law*) Berufung *f*; (*plea*) Aufruf *m*; (*charm*) Reiz *m*; **to ~ (to sb) for** (jdn) bitten um; **to ~ to** (*be attractive to*) gefallen *+dat*; **it doesn't ~ to me** es reizt mich nicht; **right of ~** (*Law*) Berufungsrecht *nt*; **on ~** (*Law*) in der Berufung
appealing [ə'pi:lɪŋ] *adj* ansprechend; (*touching*) rührend
appear [ə'pɪəʳ] *vi* erscheinen; (*seem*) scheinen; **to ~ on TV/in "Hamlet"** im Fernsehen/in "Hamlet" auftreten; **it would ~ that ...** anscheinend ...
appearance [ə'pɪərəns] *n* Erscheinen *nt*; (*look*) Aussehen *nt*; (*in public, on TV*) Auftritt *m*; **to put in** *or* **make an ~** sich sehen lassen; **in** *or* **by order of ~** (*Theat etc*) in der Reihenfolge ihres Auftritts; **to keep up ~s** den (äußeren) Schein wahren; **to all ~s** allem Anschein nach
appease [ə'pi:z] *vt* beschwichtigen
appendices [ə'pɛndɪsi:z] *npl of* **appendix**
appendicitis [əpɛndɪ'saɪtɪs] *n* Blinddarmentzündung *f*
appendix [ə'pɛndɪks] (*pl* **appendices**) *n* (*Anat*) Blinddarm *m*; (*to publication*) Anhang *m*; **to have one's ~ out** sich *dat* den Blinddarm herausnehmen lassen
appetite ['æpɪtaɪt] *n* Appetit *m*; (*fig*) Lust *f*; **that walk has given me an ~** von dem Spaziergang habe ich Appetit bekommen
appetizer ['æpɪtaɪzəʳ] *n* (*food*) Appetithappen *m*; (*drink*) appetitanregendes Getränk *nt*
applaud [ə'plɔ:d] *vi* applaudieren, klatschen ▷ *vt* (*actor etc*) applaudieren *+dat*, Beifall spenden *or* klatschen *+dat*; (*action, attitude*) loben; (*decision*) begrüßen
applause [ə'plɔ:z] *n* Applaus *m*, Beifall *m*
apple ['æpl] *n* Apfel *m*; **he's the ~ of her eye** er ist ihr Ein und Alles
appliance [ə'plaɪəns] *n* Gerät *nt*
applicable [ə'plɪkəbl] *adj*: **~ (to)** anwendbar (auf *+acc*); (*on official forms*) zutreffend (auf *+acc*); **the law is ~ from January** das Gesetz gilt ab Januar
applicant ['æplɪkənt] *n* Bewerber(in) *m(f)*
application [æplɪ'keɪʃən] *n* (*for job*) Bewerbung *f*; (*for grant etc*) Antrag *m*; (*hard work*) Fleiß *m*; (*applying: of paint etc*) Auftragen *nt*; **on ~** auf Antrag
application form *n* (*for a job*) Bewerbungsformular *nt*; (*for a grant etc*) Antragsformular *nt*
applied [ə'plaɪd] *adj* angewandt
apply [ə'plaɪ] *vt* anwenden; (*paint etc*) auftragen ▷ *vi*: **to ~ (to)** (*be applicable*) gelten (für); **to ~ the brakes** die Bremse betätigen, bremsen; **to ~ o.s. to sth** sich bei etw anstrengen; **to ~ to** (*ask*) sich wenden an *+acc*; **to ~ for** (*permit, grant*) beantragen; (*job*) sich bewerben um
appoint [ə'pɔɪnt] *vt* ernennen; (*date, place*) festlegen, festsetzen
appointment [ə'pɔɪntmənt] *n* Ernennung *f*; (*post*) Stelle *f*; (*arranged meeting*) Termin *m*; **to make an ~ (with sb)** einen Termin (mit jdm) vereinbaren; **by ~** nach Anmeldung, mit Voranmeldung
appraisal [ə'preɪzl] *n* Beurteilung *f*
appreciate [ə'pri:ʃɪeɪt] *vt* (*like*) schätzen; (*be grateful for*) zu schätzen wissen; (*understand*) verstehen; (*be aware of*) sich *dat* bewusst sein *+gen* ▷ *vi* (*Comm: currency, shares*) im Wert steigen; **I ~ your help** ich weiß Ihre Hilfe zu schätzen
appreciation [əpri:ʃɪ'eɪʃən] *n* (*enjoyment*) Wertschätzung *f*; (*understanding*) Verständnis *nt*; (*gratitude*) Dankbarkeit *f*; (*Comm: in value*) (Wert)steigerung *f*
appreciative [ə'pri:ʃɪətɪv] *adj* dankbar; (*comment*) anerkennend
apprehension [æprɪ'hɛnʃən] *n* (*fear*) Besorgnis *f*; (*arrest*) Festnahme *f*
apprehensive [æprɪ'hɛnsɪv] *adj* ängstlich; **to be ~ about sth** sich *dat* Gedanken *or* Sorgen um etw machen
apprentice [ə'prɛntɪs] *n* Lehrling *m*, Auszubildende(r) *f(m)* ▷ *vt*: **to be ~d to sb** bei

jdm in der Lehre sein
apprenticeship [ə'prɛntɪsʃɪp] *n* Lehre *f*, Lehrzeit *f*; **to serve one's ~** seine Lehre machen
approach [ə'prəutʃ] *vi* sich nähern; (*event*) nahen ▷ *vt* (*come to*) sich nähern +*dat*; (*ask, apply to: person*) herantreten an +*acc*, ansprechen; (*situation, problem*) herangehen an +*acc*, angehen ▷ *n* (*advance*) (Heran)nahen *nt*; (*access*) Zugang *m*; (*: for vehicles*) Zufahrt *f*; (*to problem etc*) Ansatz *m*; **to ~ sb about sth** jdn wegen etw ansprechen
approachable [ə'prəutʃəbl] *adj* (*person*) umgänglich; (*place*) zugänglich
appropriate [*adj* ə'prəuprɪɪt, *vt* ə'prəuprɪeɪt] *adj* (*apt*) angebracht; (*relevant*) entsprechend ▷ *vt* sich *dat* aneignen; **it would not be ~ for me to comment** es wäre nicht angebracht, wenn ich mich dazu äußern würde
approval [ə'pru:vəl] *n* (*approbation*) Zustimmung *f*, Billigung *f*; (*permission*) Einverständnis *f*; **to meet with sb's ~** jds Zustimmung *or* Beifall finden; **on ~** (*Comm*) zur Probe
approve [ə'pru:v] *vt* billigen; (*motion, decision*) annehmen
▸ **approve of** *vt fus* etwas halten von; **I don't ~ of it/him** ich halte nichts davon/von ihm
approximate [*adj* ə'prɔksɪmɪt, *vb* ə'prɔksɪmeɪt] *adj* ungefähr ▷ *vt, vi*: **to ~ (to)** nahe kommen +*dat*
approximately [ə'prɔksɪmɪtlɪ] *adv* ungefähr
Apr. *abbr* = **April**
apricot ['eɪprɪkɔt] *n* Aprikose *f*
April ['eɪprəl] *n* April *m*; **~ fool!** April, April!; *see also* **July**
apron ['eɪprən] *n* Schürze *f*; (*Aviat*) Vorfeld *nt*
apt [æpt] *adj* (*suitable*) passend, treffend; (*likely*): **to be ~ to do sth** dazu neigen, etw zu tun
aquarium [ə'kwɛərɪəm] *n* Aquarium *nt*
Aquarius [ə'kwɛərɪəs] *n* Wassermann *m*; **to be ~** (ein) Wassermann sein
Arab ['ærəb] *adj* arabisch ▷ *n* Araber(in) *m(f)*
Arabia [ə'reɪbɪə] *n* Arabien *nt*
Arabian [ə'reɪbɪən] *adj* arabisch
Arabic ['ærəbɪk] *adj* arabisch ▷ *n* (*Ling*) Arabisch *nt*
arbitrary ['ɑ:bɪtrərɪ] *adj* willkürlich
arbitration [ɑ:bɪ'treɪʃən] *n* Schlichtung *f*; **the dispute went to ~** der Streit wurde vor eine Schlichtungskommission gebracht
arc [ɑ:k] *n* Bogen *m*
arcade [ɑ:'keɪd] *n* Arkade *f*; (*shopping mall*) Passage *f*
arch [ɑ:tʃ] *n* Bogen *m*; (*of foot*) Gewölbe *nt* ▷ *vt* (*back*) krümmen ▷ *adj* schelmisch ▷ *pref* Erz-
archaeologist [ɑ:kɪ'ɔlədʒɪst] *n* Archäologe *m*, Archäologin *f*
archaeology, (US) **archeology** [ɑ:kɪ'ɔlədʒɪ] *n* Archäologie *f*
archbishop [ɑ:tʃ'bɪʃəp] *n* Erzbischof *m*
archeology *etc* [ɑ:kɪ'ɔlədʒɪ] (US) = **archaeology** *etc*
archery ['ɑ:tʃərɪ] *n* Bogenschießen *nt*
architect ['ɑ:kɪtɛkt] *n* Architekt(in) *m(f)*
architectural [ɑ:kɪ'tɛktʃərəl] *adj* architektonisch
architecture ['ɑ:kɪtɛktʃə[r]] *n* Architektur *f*
archives ['ɑ:kaɪvz] *npl* Archiv *nt*
Arctic ['ɑ:ktɪk] *adj* arktisch ▷ *n*: **the ~** die Arktis
ardent ['ɑ:dənt] *adj* leidenschaftlich; (*admirer*) glühend
are [ɑ:[r]] *vb see* **be**
area ['ɛərɪə] *n* Gebiet *nt*; (*Geom etc*) Fläche *f*; (*dining area etc*) Bereich *m*; **in the London ~** im Raum London
area code (US) *n* Vorwahl(nummer) *f*
arena [ə'ri:nə] *n* Arena *f*
aren't [ɑ:nt] = **are not**
Argentina [ɑ:dʒən'ti:nə] *n* Argentinien *nt*
Argentinian [ɑ:dʒən'tɪnɪən] *adj* argentinisch ▷ *n* Argentinier(in) *m(f)*
arguably ['ɑ:gjuəblɪ] *adv* wohl; **it is ~ ...** es dürfte wohl ... sein
argue ['ɑ:gju:] *vi* (*quarrel*) sich streiten; (*reason*) diskutieren ▷ *vt* (*debate*) diskutieren, erörtern; **to ~ that ...** den Standpunkt vertreten, dass ...; **to ~ about sth** sich über etw *acc* streiten; **to ~ for/against sth** sich für/gegen etw aussprechen
argument ['ɑ:gjumənt] *n* (*reasons*) Argument *nt*; (*quarrel*) Streit *m*, Auseinandersetzung *f*; (*debate*) Diskussion *f*; **~ for/against** Argument für/gegen; **to have an ~** sich streiten
argumentative [ɑ:gju'mɛntətɪv] *adj* streitlustig
Aries ['ɛərɪz] *n* Widder *m*; **to be ~** (ein) Widder sein
arise [ə'raɪz] (*pt* **arose**, *pp* **~n**) *vi* (*difficulty etc*) sich ergeben; (*question*) sich stellen; **to ~ from** sich ergeben aus, herrühren von; **should the need ~** falls es nötig wird
aristocrat ['ærɪstəkræt] *n* Aristokrat(in) *m(f)*, Ad(e)lige(r) *f(m)*
arithmetic [ə'rɪθmətɪk] *n* Rechnen *nt*; (*calculation*) Rechnung *f*
ark [ɑ:k] *n*: **Noah's A~** die Arche Noah
arm [ɑ:m] *n* Arm *m*; (*of clothing*) Ärmel *m*; (*of chair*) Armlehne *f*; (*of organization etc*) Zweig *m* ▷ *vt* bewaffnen; **arms** *npl* (*weapons*) Waffen *pl*; (*Heraldry*) Wappen *nt*
armaments ['ɑ:məmənts] *npl* (*weapons*) (Aus)rüstung *f*
armchair ['ɑ:mtʃɛə[r]] *n* Sessel *m*, Lehnstuhl *m*
armed [ɑ:md] *adj* bewaffnet; **the ~ forces** die Streitkräfte *pl*
armed robbery *n* bewaffneter Raubüberfall *m*
armour, (US) **armor** ['ɑ:mə[r]] *n* (*Hist*) Rüstung *f*; (*also*: **armour-plating**) Panzerplatte *f*; (*Mil: tanks*) Panzerfahrzeuge *pl*
armoured car ['ɑ:məd-] *n* Panzerwagen *m*
armpit ['ɑ:mpɪt] *n* Achselhöhle *f*

armrest ['ɑːmrɛst] *n* Armlehne *f*
army ['ɑːmɪ] *n* Armee *f*, Heer *nt*; (*fig: host*) Heer
aroma [ə'rəumə] *n* Aroma *nt*, Duft *m*
aromatherapy [ərəumə'θɛrəpɪ] *n* Aromatherapie *f*
arose [ə'rəuz] *pt of* **arise**
around [ə'raund] *adv* (*about*) herum; (*in the area*) in der Nähe ▷ *prep* (*encircling*) um ... herum; (*near*) in der Nähe von; (*fig: about: dimensions*) etwa; (*: time*) gegen; (*: date*) um; **is he ~?** ist er da?; **~ £5** um die £5, etwa £5; **~ 3 o'clock** gegen 3 Uhr
arouse [ə'rauz] *vt* (*feelings, interest*) wecken
arrange [ə'reɪndʒ] *vt* (*meeting etc*) vereinbaren; (*tour etc*) planen; (*books etc*) anordnen; (*flowers*) arrangieren; (*Mus*) arrangieren, bearbeiten ▷ *vi*: **we have ~d for a car to pick you up** wir haben veranlasst, dass Sie mit dem Auto abgeholt werden; **it was ~d that ...** es wurde vereinbart, dass ...; **to ~ to do sth** vereinbaren *or* ausmachen, etw zu tun
arrangement [ə'reɪndʒmənt] *n* (*agreement*) Vereinbarung *f*; (*layout*) Anordnung *f*; (*Mus*) Arrangement *nt*, Bearbeitung *f*; **arrangements** *npl* Pläne *pl*; (*preparations*) Vorbereitungen *pl*; **to come to an ~ with sb** eine Regelung mit jdm treffen; **home deliveries by ~** nach Vereinbarung Lieferung ins Haus; **I'll make ~s for you to be met** ich werde veranlassen, dass Sie abgeholt werden
array [ə'reɪ] *n*: **an ~ of** (*things*) eine Reihe von; (*people*) Aufgebot an +*dat*; (*Math, Comput*) (Daten)feld *nt*
arrears [ə'rɪəz] *npl* Rückstand *m*; **to be in ~ with one's rent** mit seiner Miete im Rückstand sein
arrest [ə'rɛst] *vt* (*person*) verhaften; (*sb's attention*) erregen ▷ *n* Verhaftung *f*; **under ~** verhaftet
arrival [ə'raɪvl] *n* Ankunft *f*; (*Comm: of goods*) Sendung *f*; **new ~** (*person*) Neuankömmling *m*; (*baby*) Neugeborene(s) *nt*
arrive [ə'raɪv] *vi* ankommen
▸ **arrive at** *vt fus* (*fig: conclusion*) kommen zu; (*: situation*) es bringen zu
arrogance ['ærəgəns] *n* Arroganz *f*, Überheblichkeit *f*
arrogant ['ærəgənt] *adj* arrogant, überheblich
arrow ['ærəu] *n* Pfeil *m*
arse [ɑːs] (*Brit: inf!*) *n* Arsch *m* (*!*)
arson ['ɑːsn] *n* Brandstiftung *f*
art [ɑːt] *n* Kunst *f*; **Arts** *npl* (*Scol*) Geisteswissenschaften *pl*; **work of ~** Kunstwerk *nt*
artery ['ɑːtərɪ] *n* Arterie *f*, Schlagader *f*; (*fig*) Verkehrsader *f*
art gallery *n* Kunstgalerie *f*
arthritis [ɑː'θraɪtɪs] *n* Arthritis *f*
artichoke ['ɑːtɪtʃəuk] *n* (*also*: **globe artichoke**) Artischocke *f*; (*also*: **Jerusalem artichoke**) Topinambur *m*
article ['ɑːtɪkl] *n* Artikel *m*; (*object, item*) Gegenstand *m*; **articles** (*Brit*) *npl* (*Law*) (Rechts)referendarzeit *f*; **~ of clothing** Kleidungsstück *nt*
articulate [*adj* ɑː'tɪkjulɪt, *vt, vi* ɑː'tɪkjuleɪt] *adj* (*speech, writing*) klar; (*speaker*) redegewandt ▷ *vt* darlegen ▷ *vi* artikulieren; **to be ~** (*person*) sich gut ausdrücken können
articulated lorry (*Brit*) *n* Sattelschlepper *m*
artificial [ɑːtɪ'fɪʃəl] *adj* künstlich; (*manner*) gekünstelt; **to be ~** (*person*) gekünstelt *or* unnatürlich wirken
artificial respiration *n* künstliche Beatmung *f*
artist ['ɑːtɪst] *n* Künstler(in) *m(f)*
artistic [ɑː'tɪstɪk] *adj* künstlerisch
artistry ['ɑːtɪstrɪ] *n* künstlerisches Geschick *nt*
art school *n* Kunstakademie *f*, Kunsthochschule *f*
as [æz] *conj* **1** (*referring to time*) als; **as the years went by** mit den Jahren; **he came in as I was leaving** als er hereinkam, ging ich gerade; **as from tomorrow** ab morgen
2 (*in comparisons*): **as big as** so groß wie; **twice as big as** zweimal so groß wie; **as much/many as** so viel/so viele wie; **as soon as** sobald; **much as I admire her ...** sosehr ich sie auch bewundere ...
3 (*since, because*) da, weil; **as you can't come I'll go without you** da du nicht mitkommen kannst, gehe ich ohne dich
4 (*referring to manner, way*) wie; **do as you wish** mach, was du willst; **as she said** wie sie sagte; **he gave it to me as a present** er gab es mir als Geschenk; **as it were** sozusagen
5 (*in the capacity of*) als; **he works as a driver** er arbeitet als Fahrer
6 (*concerning*): **as for** *or* **to that** was das betrifft *or* angeht
7: as if *or* **though** als ob; *see also* **long; such; well**
a.s.a.p. *adv abbr* (*= as soon as possible*) baldmöglichst
asbestos [æz'bɛstəs] *n* Asbest *m*
ascend [ə'sɛnd] *vt* hinaufsteigen; (*throne*) besteigen
ascent [ə'sɛnt] *n* Aufstieg *m*
ascertain [æsə'teɪn] *vt* feststellen
ash [æʃ] *n* Asche *f*; (*wood, tree*) Esche *f*
ashamed [ə'ʃeɪmd] *adj* beschämt; **to be ~ of** sich schämen für; **to be ~ of o.s. for having done sth** sich schämen, dass man etw getan hat
ashore [ə'ʃɔːʳ] *adv* an Land
ashtray ['æʃtreɪ] *n* Aschenbecher *m*
Ash Wednesday *n* Aschermittwoch *m*
Asia ['eɪʃə] *n* Asien *nt*
Asian ['eɪʃən] *adj* asiatisch ▷ *n* Asiat(in) *m(f)*
aside [ə'saɪd] *adv* zur Seite; (*take*) beiseite ▷ *n* beiseite gesprochene Worte *pl*; **to brush objections ~** Einwände beiseiteschieben
ask [ɑːsk] *vt* fragen; (*invite*) einladen; **to ~ sb**

to do sth jdn bitten, etw zu tun; **to ~ (sb) sth** (jdn) etw fragen; **to ~ sb a question** jdm eine Frage stellen; **to ~ sb the time** jdn nach der Uhrzeit fragen; **to ~ sb about sth** jdn nach etw fragen; **to ~ sb out to dinner** jdn zum Essen einladen
▸ **ask after** *vt fus* fragen nach
▸ **ask for** *vt fus* bitten um; (*trouble*) haben wollen; **it's just ~ing for trouble/it** das kann ja nicht gut gehen

asking price [ˈɑːskɪŋ-] *n*: **the ~** der geforderte Preis

asleep [əˈsliːp] *adj* schlafend; **to be ~** schlafen; **to fall ~** einschlafen

AS level *n abbr* (*= Advanced Subsidiary level*) *Mit "AS level" wird das erste Jahr der Sekundarstufe II bezeichnet, nach dessen Abschluss Prüfungen in drei der insgesamt sechs für den "A level" benötigten Wahlpflichtfächern abgehalten werden*

asparagus [əsˈpærəgəs] *n* Spargel *m*

aspect [ˈæspɛkt] *n* (*of subject*) Aspekt *m*; (*of building etc*) Lage *f*; (*quality, air*) Erscheinung *f*; **to have a south-westerly ~** nach Südwesten liegen

aspire [əsˈpaɪəʳ] *vi*: **to ~ to** streben nach

aspirin [ˈæsprɪn] *n* Kopfschmerztablette *f*, Aspirin® *nt*

ass [æs] *n* (*also fig*) Esel *m*; (*US: inf!*) Arsch! *m*

assailant [əˈseɪlənt] *n* Angreifer(in) *m(f)*

assassin [əˈsæsɪn] *n* Attentäter(in) *m(f)*

assassinate [əˈsæsɪneɪt] *vt* ermorden, ein Attentat verüben auf *+acc*

assassination [əsæsɪˈneɪʃən] *n* Ermordung *f*, (geglücktes) Attentat *nt*

assault [əˈsɔːlt] *n* Angriff *m* ▹ *vt* angreifen; (*sexually*) vergewaltigen; **~ and battery** (*Law*) Körperverletzung *f*

assemble [əˈsɛmbl] *vt* versammeln; (*car, machine*) montieren; (*furniture etc*) zusammenbauen ▹ *vi* sich versammeln

assembly [əˈsɛmblɪ] *n* Versammlung *f*; (*of car, machine*) Montage *f*; (*of furniture*) Zusammenbau *m*

assembly line *n* Fließband *nt*

assent [əˈsɛnt] *n* Zustimmung *f* ▹ *vi*: **to ~ (to)** zustimmen (*+dat*)

assert [əˈsəːt] *vt* behaupten; (*innocence*) beteuern; (*authority*) geltend machen; **to ~ o.s.** sich durchsetzen

assertion [əˈsəːʃən] *n* Behauptung *f*

assess [əˈsɛs] *vt* (*situation*) einschätzen; (*abilities etc*) beurteilen; (*tax*) festsetzen; (*damages, property etc*) schätzen

assessment [əˈsɛsmənt] *n* (*see vt*) Einschätzung *f*; Beurteilung *f*; Festsetzung *f*; Schätzung *f*

assessor [əˈsɛsəʳ] *n* (*Law*) Gutachter(in) *m(f)*

asset [ˈæsɛt] *n* Vorteil *m*; (*person*) Stütze *f*; **assets** *npl* (*property, funds*) Vermögen *nt*; (*Comm*) Aktiva *pl*

assign [əˈsaɪn] *vt*: **to ~ (to)** (*date*) zuweisen (*+dat*); (*task*) übertragen (*+dat*); (*person*) einteilen (für); (*cause*) zuschreiben (*+dat*); (*meaning*) zuordnen (*+dat*); **to ~ sb to do sth** jdn damit beauftragen, etw zu tun

assignment [əˈsaɪnmənt] *n* Aufgabe *f*

assist [əˈsɪst] *vt* helfen; (*with money etc*) unterstützen

assistance [əˈsɪstəns] *n* Hilfe *f*; (*with money etc*) Unterstützung *f*

assistant [əˈsɪstənt] *n* Assistent(in) *m(f)*; (*Brit: also*: **shop assistant**) Verkäufer(in) *m(f)*

associate [*adj, n* əˈsəuʃɪɪt, *vt, vi* əˈsəuʃɪeɪt] *adj* (*director*) assoziiert; (*member, professor*) außerordentlich ▹ *n* (*at work*) Kollege *m*, Kollegin *f* ▹ *vt* in Verbindung bringen ▹ *vi*: **to ~ with sb** mit jdm verkehren

association [əsəusɪˈeɪʃən] *n* (*group*) Verband *m*; (*involvement*) Verbindung *f*; (*Psych*) Assoziation *f*; **in ~ with** in Zusammenarbeit mit

assorted [əˈsɔːtɪd] *adj* gemischt; (*various*) diverse(r, s); **in ~ sizes** in verschiedenen Größen

assortment [əˈsɔːtmənt] *n* Mischung *f*; (*of books, people etc*) Ansammlung *f*

assume [əˈsjuːm] *vt* annehmen; (*responsibilities etc*) übernehmen

assumption [əˈsʌmpʃən] *n* Annahme *f*; (*of power etc*) Übernahme *f*; **on the ~ that ...** vorausgesetzt, dass ...

assurance [əˈʃuərəns] *n* Versicherung *f*; (*promise*) Zusicherung *f*; (*confidence*) Zuversicht *f*; **I can give you no ~s** ich kann Ihnen nichts versprechen

assure [əˈʃuəʳ] *vt* versichern; (*guarantee*) sichern

asterisk [ˈæstərɪsk] *n* Sternchen *nt*

asthma [ˈæsmə] *n* Asthma *nt*

astonish [əˈstɔnɪʃ] *vt* erstaunen

astonishing [əˈstɔnɪʃɪŋ] *adj* erstaunlich; **I find it ~ that ...** es überrascht mich, dass ...

astonishment [əˈstɔnɪʃmənt] *n* Erstaunen *nt*

astound [əˈstaund] *vt* verblüffen, sehr erstaunen

astray [əˈstreɪ] *adv*: **to go ~** (*letter*) verloren gehen; (*fig*) auf Abwege geraten; **to lead ~** auf Abwege bringen; **to go ~ in one's calculations** sich verrechnen

astride [əˈstraɪd] *adv* (*sit, ride*) rittlings; (*stand*) breitbeinig ▹ *prep* rittlings auf *+dat*; breitbeinig über *+dat*

astrology [əsˈtrɔlədʒɪ] *n* Astrologie *f*

astronaut [ˈæstrənɔːt] *n* Astronaut(in) *m(f)*

astronomer [əsˈtrɔnəməʳ] *n* Astronom(in) *m(f)*

astronomical [æstrəˈnɔmɪkl] *adj* (*also fig*) astronomisch

astronomy [əsˈtrɔnəmɪ] *n* Astronomie *f*

astute [əsˈtjuːt] *adj* scharfsinnig; (*operator, behaviour*) geschickt

asylum [əˈsaɪləm] *n* Asyl *nt*; (*mental hospital*) psychiatrische Klinik *f*; **to seek political ~** um (politisches) Asyl bitten

at [æt] *prep* **1** (*referring to position, direction*) an *+dat*, in *+dat*; **at the top** an der Spitze; **at**

home zu Hause; **at school** in der Schule; **at the baker's** beim Bäcker; **to look at sth** auf etw *acc* blicken
2 (*referring to time*): **at four o'clock** um vier Uhr; **at night/dawn** bei Nacht/ Tagesanbruch; **at Christmas** zu Weihnachten; **at times** zuweilen
3 (*referring to rates, speed etc*): **at £2 a kilo** zu £2 pro Kilo; **two at a time** zwei auf einmal; **at 50 km/h** mit 50 km/h
4 (*referring to activity*): **to be at work** (*in office etc*) auf der Arbeit sein; **to play at cowboys** Cowboy spielen; **to be good at sth** gut in etw *dat* sein
5 (*referring to cause*): **shocked/surprised/ annoyed at sth** schockiert/überrascht/ verärgert über etw *acc*; **I went at his suggestion** ich ging auf seinen Vorschlag hin
6: not at all (*in answer to question*) überhaupt nicht, ganz und gar nicht; (*in answer to thanks*) nichts zu danken, keine Ursache; **I'm not at all tired** ich bin überhaupt nicht müde; **anything at all** irgendetwas

ate [eɪt] *pt of* **eat**
atheist ['eɪθɪɪst] *n* Atheist(in) *m(f)*
Athens ['æθɪnz] *n* Athen *nt*
athlete ['æθliːt] *n* Athlet(in) *m(f)*
athletic [æθ'lɛtɪk] *adj* sportlich; (*muscular*) athletisch
athletics [æθ'lɛtɪks] *n* Leichtathletik *f*
Atlantic [ət'læntɪk] *adj* atlantisch; (*coast etc*) Atlantik- ▷ *n*: **the ~ (Ocean)** der Atlantik
atlas ['ætləs] *n* Atlas *m*
atmosphere ['ætməsfɪəʳ] *n* Atmosphäre *f*; (*air*) Luft *f*
atom ['ætəm] *n* Atom *nt*
atom bomb *n* Atombombe *f*
atomic [ə'tɔmɪk] *adj* atomar; (*energy, weapons*) Atom-
atomic bomb *n* Atombombe *f*
atomizer ['ætəmaɪzəʳ] *n* Zerstäuber *m*
atone [ə'təun] *vi*: **to ~ for** büßen für
atrocious [ə'trəuʃəs] *adj* grauenhaft
atrocity [ə'trɔsɪtɪ] *n* Gräueltat *f*
attach [ə'tætʃ] *vt* befestigen; (*document, letter*) anheften, beiheften; (*employee, troops*) zuteilen; (*importance etc*) beimessen; **to be ~ed to sb/sth** (*like*) an jdm/etw hängen; (*be connected with*) mit jdm/etw zu tun haben; **the ~ed letter** der beiliegende Brief
attaché case *n* Aktenkoffer *m*
attachment [ə'tætʃmənt] *n* (*tool*) Zubehörteil *nt*; (*love*): **~ (to sb)** Zuneigung *f* (zu jdm)
attack [ə'tæk] *vt* angreifen; (*subj: criminal*) überfallen; (*task, problem etc*) in Angriff nehmen ▷ *n* (*also fig*) Angriff *m*; (*on sb's life*) Anschlag *m*; (*of illness*) Anfall *m*; **heart ~** Herzanfall *m*, Herzinfarkt *m*
attacker [ə'tækəʳ] *n* Angreifer(in) *m(f)*
attain [ə'teɪn] *vt* (*also*: **attain to**) erreichen; (*knowledge*) erlangen
attempt [ə'tɛmpt] *n* Versuch *m* ▷ *vt* versuchen; **to make an ~ on sb's life** einen Anschlag auf jdn verüben
attempted [ə'tɛmptɪd] *adj* versucht; **~ murder/suicide** Mord-/Selbstmordversuch *m*; **~ theft** versuchter Diebstahl
attend [ə'tɛnd] *vt* besuchen; (*patient*) behandeln
▸ **attend to** *vt fus* sich kümmern um; (*needs*) nachkommen *+dat*; (*customer*) bedienen
attendance [ə'tɛndəns] *n* Anwesenheit *f*; (*people present*) Besucherzahl *f*; (*Sport*) Zuschauerzahl *f*
attendant [ə'tɛndənt] *n* (*helper*) Begleiter(in) *m(f)*; (*in garage*) Tankwart *m*; (*in museum*) Aufseher(in) *m(f)* ▷ *adj* damit verbunden
attention [ə'tɛnʃən] *n* Aufmerksamkeit *f*; (*care*) Fürsorge *f* ▷ *excl* (*Mil*) Achtung!; **attentions** *npl* (*acts of courtesy*) Aufmerksamkeiten *pl*; **for the ~ of ...** zu Händen von ...; **it has come to my ~ that ...** ich bin darauf aufmerksam geworden, dass ...; **to stand to** *or* **at ~** (*Mil*) stillstehen
attentive [ə'tɛntɪv] *adj* aufmerksam
attest [ə'tɛst] *vt, vi*: **to ~ (to)** bezeugen
attic ['ætɪk] *n* Dachboden *m*
attitude ['ætɪtjuːd] *n* (*posture, manner*) Haltung *f*; (*mental*): **~ to** *or* **towards** Einstellung *f* zu
attorney [ə'təːnɪ] *n* (*US: lawyer*) (Rechts)anwalt *m*, (Rechts)anwältin *f*; (*having proxy*) Bevollmächtigte(r) *f(m)*; **power of ~** Vollmacht *f*
Attorney General *n* (*Brit*) ≈ Justizminister(in) *m(f)*; (*US*) ≈ Generalbundesanwalt *m*, ≈ Generalbundesanwältin *f*
attract [ə'trækt] *vt* (*draw*) anziehen; (*interest*) auf sich *acc* lenken; (*attention*) erregen
attraction [ə'trækʃən] *n* Anziehungskraft *f*; (*of house, city*) Reiz *m*; (*gen pl: amusements*) Attraktion *f*; (*fig*): **to feel an ~ towards sb/ sth** sich von jdm/etw angezogen fühlen
attractive [ə'træktɪv] *adj* attraktiv; (*price, idea, offer*) verlockend, reizvoll
attribute [*n* 'ætrɪbjuːt, *vt* ə'trɪbjuːt] *n* Eigenschaft *f* ▷ *vt*: **to ~ sth to** (*cause*) etw zurückführen auf *+acc*; (*poem, painting*) etw zuschreiben *+dat*; (*quality*) etw beimessen *+dat*
attrition [ə'trɪʃən] *n*: **war of ~** Zermürbungskrieg *m*
aubergine ['əubəʒiːn] *n* Aubergine *f*; (*colour*) Aubergine *nt*
auburn ['ɔːbən] *adj* rotbraun
auction ['ɔːkʃən] *n* (*also*: **sale by auction**) Versteigerung *f*, Auktion *f* ▷ *vt* versteigern
auctioneer [ɔːkʃə'nɪəʳ] *n* Versteigerer *m*
audible ['ɔːdɪbl] *adj* hörbar
audience ['ɔːdɪəns] *n* Publikum *nt*; (*Radio*) Zuhörer *pl*; (*TV*) Zuschauer *pl*; (*with queen etc*) Audienz *f*
audiovisual ['ɔːdɪəu'vɪzjuəl] *adj* audiovisuell
audit ['ɔːdɪt] *vt* (*Comm*) prüfen ▷ *n* Buchprüfung *f*, Rechnungsprüfung *f*
audition [ɔː'dɪʃən] *n* Vorsprechprobe *f* ▷ *vi*: **to**

~ **(for)** vorsprechen (für)
auditor ['ɔːdɪtəʳ] *n* Buchprüfer(in) *m(f)*, Rechnungsprüfer(in) *m(f)*
auditorium [ɔːdɪ'tɔːrɪəm] *n* (*building*) Auditorium *nt*; (*audience area*) Zuschauerraum *m*
Aug. *abbr* = **August**
augur ['ɔːgəʳ] *vi*: **it ~s well** das ist ein gutes Zeichen *or* Omen
August ['ɔːgəst] *n* August *m*; *see also* **July**
august [ɔː'gʌst] *adj* erhaben
aunt [ɑːnt] *n* Tante *f*
auntie ['ɑːntɪ] *n dimin of* **aunt**
au pair ['əu'pɛəʳ] *n* (*also*: **au pair girl**) Aupair(mädchen) *nt*, Au-pair(-Mädchen) *nt*
aura ['ɔːrə] *n* Aura *f*
auspicious [ɔːs'pɪʃəs] *adj* verheißungsvoll; (*opening, start*) vielversprechend
austerity [ɔs'tɛrɪtɪ] *n* Strenge *f*; (*of room etc*) Schmucklosigkeit *f*; (*hardship*) Entbehrung *f*
Australia [ɔs'treɪlɪə] *n* Australien *nt*
Australian [ɔs'treɪlɪən] *adj* australisch ▷ *n* Australier(in) *m(f)*
Austria ['ɔstrɪə] *n* Österreich *nt*
Austrian ['ɔstrɪən] *adj* österreichisch ▷ *n* Österreicher(in) *m(f)*
authentic [ɔː'θɛntɪk] *adj* authentisch
author ['ɔːθəʳ] *n* (*of text*) Verfasser(in) *m(f)*; (*profession*) Autor(in) *m(f)*, Schriftsteller(in) *m(f)*; (*creator*) Urheber(in) *m(f)*; (*: of plan*) Initiator(in) *m(f)*
authoritarian [ɔːθɔrɪ'tɛərɪən] *adj* autoritär
authoritative [ɔː'θɔrɪtətɪv] *adj* (*person, manner*) bestimmt, entschieden; (*source, account*) zuverlässig; (*study, treatise*) maßgeblich, maßgebend
authority [ɔː'θɔrɪtɪ] *n* Autorität *f*; (*government body*) Behörde *f*, Amt *nt*; (*official permission*) Genehmigung *f*; **the authorities** *npl* (*ruling body*) die Behörden *pl*; **to have the ~ to do sth** befugt sein, etw zu tun
authorize ['ɔːθəraɪz] *vt* genehmigen; **to ~ sb to do sth** jdn ermächtigen, etw zu tun
auto ['ɔːtəu] (*US*) *n* Auto *nt*, Wagen *m*
autobiography [ɔːtəbaɪ'ɔgrəfɪ] *n* Autobiografie *f*
autograph ['ɔːtəgrɑːf] *n* Autogramm *nt* ▷ *vt* signieren
automatic [ɔːtə'mætɪk] *adj* automatisch ▷ *n* (*gun*) automatische Waffe; (*washing machine*) Waschautomat *m*; (*car*) Automatikwagen *m*
automatically [ɔːtə'mætɪklɪ] *adv* automatisch
automation [ɔːtə'meɪʃən] *n* Automatisierung *f*
automobile ['ɔːtəməbiːl] (*US*) *n* Auto(mobil) *nt*
autonomous [ɔː'tɔnəməs] *adj* autonom
autonomy [ɔː'tɔnəmɪ] *n* Autonomie *f*
autumn ['ɔːtəm] *n* Herbst *m*; **in ~** im Herbst
auxiliary [ɔːg'zɪlɪərɪ] *adj* (*tool, verb*) Hilfs- ▷ *n* (*assistant*) Hilfskraft *f*
avail [ə'veɪl] *vt*: **to ~ o.s. of** Gebrauch machen von ▷ *n*: **to no ~** vergeblich, erfolglos
availability [əveɪlə'bɪlɪtɪ] *n* Erhältlichkeit *f*; (*of staff*) Vorhandensein *nt*
available [ə'veɪləbl] *adj* erhältlich; (*person: unoccupied*) frei, abkömmlich; (*: unattached*) zu haben; (*time*) frei, verfügbar; **every ~ means** alle verfügbaren Mittel; **is the manager ~?** ist der Geschäftsführer zu sprechen?; **to make sth ~ to sb** jdm etw zur Verfügung stellen
avalanche ['ævəlɑːnʃ] *n* (*also fig*) Lawine *f*
avenge [ə'vɛndʒ] *vt* rächen
avenue ['ævənjuː] *n* Straße *f*; (*drive*) Auffahrt *f*; (*means*) Weg *m*
average ['ævərɪdʒ] *n* Durchschnitt *m* ▷ *adj* durchschnittlich, Durchschnitts- ▷ *vt* (*reach an average of*) einen Durchschnitt erreichen von; **on ~** im Durchschnitt, durchschnittlich; **above/below (the) ~** über/unter dem Durchschnitt
▸ **average out** *vi*: **to ~ out at** durchschnittlich ausmachen
averse [ə'vəːs] *adj*: **to be ~ to sth/doing sth** eine Abneigung gegen etw haben/dagegen haben, etw zu tun; **I wouldn't be ~ to a drink** ich hätte nichts gegen einen Drink
avert [ə'vəːt] *vt* (*prevent*) verhindern; (*ward off*) abwehren; (*turn away*) abwenden
aviary ['eɪvɪərɪ] *n* Vogelhaus *nt*
avid ['ævɪd] *adj* begeistert, eifrig
avocado [ævə'kɑːdəu] (*Brit*) *n* (*also*: **avocado pear**) Avocado *f*
avoid [ə'vɔɪd] *vt* (*person, obstacle*) ausweichen *+dat*; (*trouble*) vermeiden; (*danger*) meiden
await [ə'weɪt] *vt* warten auf *+acc*; **~ing attention/delivery** zur Bearbeitung/Lieferung bestimmt; **long ~ed** lang ersehnt
awake [ə'weɪk] (*pt* **awoke**, *pp* **awoken** *or* **~d**) *adj* wach ▷ *vt* wecken ▷ *vi* erwachen, aufwachen; **~ to** sich *dat* bewusst werden *+gen*
awakening [ə'weɪknɪŋ] *n* (*also fig*) Erwachen *nt*
award [ə'wɔːd] *n* Preis *m*; (*for bravery*) Auszeichnung *f*; (*damages*) Entschädigung(ssumme) *f* ▷ *vt* (*prize*) verleihen; (*damages*) zusprechen
aware [ə'wɛəʳ] *adj*: **~ (of)** bewusst (*+gen*); **to become ~ of** sich *dat* bewusst werden *+gen*; **to become ~ that ...** sich *dat* bewusst werden, dass ...; **politically/socially ~** politik-/sozialbewusst; **I am fully ~ that** es ist mir völlig klar *or* bewusst, dass
awareness [ə'wɛənɪs] *n* Bewusstsein *nt*; **to develop people's ~ of sth** den Menschen etw zu Bewusstsein bringen
away [ə'weɪ] *adv* weg, fort; (*position*) entfernt; **two kilometres ~** zwei Kilometer entfernt; **two hours ~ by car** zwei Autostunden entfernt; **the holiday was two weeks ~** es war noch zwei Wochen bis zum Urlaub; **he's ~ for a week** er ist eine Woche nicht da; **he's ~ in Milan** er ist in Mailand; **to**

take ~ (from) (*remove*) entfernen (von); (*subtract*) abziehen (von); **to work/pedal** *etc* ~ unablässig arbeiten/strampeln *etc*; **to fade** ~ (*colour, light*) verblassen; (*sound*) verhallen; (*enthusiasm*) schwinden

away game *n* Auswärtsspiel *nt*

awe [ɔː] *n* Ehrfurcht *f*

awe-inspiring ['ɔːɪnspaɪərɪŋ] *adj* Ehrfurcht gebietend

awesome ['ɔːsəm] *adj* Ehrfurcht gebietend; (*fig: inf*) überwältigend

awful ['ɔːfəl] *adj* furchtbar, schrecklich; **an ~ lot (of)** furchtbar viel(e)

awfully ['ɔːfəlɪ] *adv* furchtbar, schrecklich

awkward ['ɔːkwəd] *adj* (*clumsy*) unbeholfen; (*inconvenient, difficult*) ungünstig; (*embarrassing*) peinlich

awning ['ɔːnɪŋ] *n* (*of tent, caravan*) Vordach *nt*; (*of shop etc*) Markise *f*

awoke [ə'wəuk] *pt of* **awake**

awoken [ə'wəukən] *pp of* **awake**

axe, (US) **ax** [æks] *n* Axt *f*, Beil *nt* ▷ *vt* (*employee*) entlassen; (*project, jobs etc*) streichen; **to have an ~ to grind** (*fig*) ein persönliches Interesse haben

axes[1] ['æksɪz] *npl of* **axe**

axes[2] ['æksiːz] *npl of* **axis**

axis ['æksɪs] (*pl* **axes[2]**) *n* Achse *f*

axle ['æksl] *n* (*also*: **axletree**) Achse *f*

azalea [ə'zeɪlɪə] *n* Azalee *f*

Bb

B¹, b [biː] *n* (*letter*) B *nt*, b *nt*; (*Scol*) ≈ Zwei *f*, ≈ Gut *nt*; **B for Benjamin, B for Baker** (*US*) ≈ B wie Bertha; **B road** (*Brit*) Landstraße *f*
B² [biː] *n* (*Mus*) H *nt*, h *nt*
babble ['bæbl] *vi* schwatzen; (*baby*) plappern; (*brook*) plätschern ▷ *n*: **a ~ of voices** ein Stimmengewirr *nt*
baby ['beɪbɪ] *n* Baby *nt*; (*US*: *inf*: *darling*) Schatz *m*, Schätzchen *nt*
baby carriage (*US*) *n* Kinderwagen *m*
baby-sit ['beɪbɪsɪt] *vi* babysitten
baby-sitter ['beɪbɪsɪtəʳ] *n* Babysitter(in) *m(f)*
baby wipe *n* Ölpflegetuch *nt*
bachelor ['bætʃələʳ] *n* Junggeselle *m*; **B~ of Arts/Science (degree)** ≈ Magister *m* der philosophischen Fakultät/der Naturwissenschaften
back [bæk] *n* Rücken *m*; (*of house, page*) Rückseite *f*; (*of chair*) (Rücken)lehne *f*; (*of train*) Ende *nt*; (*Football*) Verteidiger *m* ▷ *vt* (*candidate*: *also*: **back up**) unterstützen; (*horse*) setzen *or* wetten auf +*acc*; (*car*) zurücksetzen, zurückfahren ▷ *vi* (*also*: **back up**: *person*) rückwärtsgehen; (*car etc*) zurücksetzen, zurückfahren ▷ *cpd* (*payment, rent*) ausstehend ▷ *adv* hinten; **in the ~ (of the car)** hinten (im Auto); **at the ~ of the book/crowd/audience** hinten im Buch/in der Menge/im Publikum; **~ to front** verkehrt herum; **to break the ~ of a job** (*Brit*) mit einer Arbeit über den Berg sein; **to have one's ~ to the wall** (*fig*) in die Enge getrieben sein; **~ room** Hinterzimmer *nt*; **~ garden** Garten *m* (hinter dem Haus); **~ seat** (*Aut*) Rücksitz *m*; **to take a ~ seat** (*fig*) sich zurückhalten; **~ wheels** Hinterräder *pl*; **he's ~** er ist zurück *or* wieder da; **throw the ball ~** wirf den Ball zurück; **he called ~** er rief zurück; **he ran ~** er rannte zurück; **when will you be ~?** wann kommen Sie wieder?; **can I have it ~?** kann ich es zurückhaben *or* wiederhaben?
▸ **back down** *vi* nachgeben
▸ **back on to** *vt fus*: **the house ~s on to the golf course** das Haus grenzt hinten an den Golfplatz an
▸ **back out** *vi* (*of promise*) einen Rückzieher machen
▸ **back up** *vt* (*support*) unterstützen; (*Comput*) sichern
backache ['bækeɪk] *n* Rückenschmerzen *pl*
backbencher ['bæk'bɛntʃəʳ] (*Brit*) *n* Abgeordnete(r) *f(m)* (*in den hinteren Reihen im britischen Parlament*), Hinterbänkler(in) *m(f)* (*pej*); *see also* **back bench**
backbone ['bækbəun] *n* (*also fig*) Rückgrat *nt*
backdate [bæk'deɪt] *vt* (zu)rückdatieren; **~d pay rise** rückwirkend geltende Gehaltserhöhung *f*
backfire [bæk'faɪəʳ] *vi* (*Aut*) Fehlzündungen haben; (*plans*) ins Auge gehen
backgammon ['bækgæmən] *n* Backgammon *nt*
background ['bækgraund] *n* Hintergrund *m*; (*basic knowledge*) Grundkenntnisse *pl*; (*experience*) Erfahrung *f* ▷ *cpd* (*music*) Hintergrund-; **family ~** Herkunft *f*; **~ noise** Geräuschkulisse *f*; **~ reading** vertiefende Lektüre *f*
backhand ['bækhænd] *n* (*Tennis*: *also*: **backhand stroke**) Rückhand *f*
backhander ['bæk'hændəʳ] (*Brit*) *n* Schmiergeld *nt*
backing ['bækɪŋ] *n* (*Comm, fig*) Unterstützung *f*; (*Mus*) Begleitung *f*
backlash ['bæklæʃ] *n* (*fig*) Gegenreaktion *f*
backlog ['bæklɔg] *n*: **to have a ~ of work** mit der Arbeit im Rückstand sein
back number *n* alte Ausgabe *f or* Nummer *f*
backpack ['bækpæk] *n* Rucksack *m*
backpacker ['bækpækəʳ] *n* Rucksacktourist(in) *m(f)*
back pay *n* Nachzahlung *f*
backside ['bæksaɪd] (*inf*) *n* Hintern *m*
backslash ['bækslæʃ] *n* Backslash *m*
backstage [bæk'steɪdʒ] *adv* (*Theat*) hinter den Kulissen; (*: in dressing-room area*) in der Garderobe
backstroke ['bækstrəuk] *n* Rückenschwimmen *nt*
backup ['bækʌp] *adj* (*train, plane*) Entlastungs-; (*Comput*: *copy etc*) Sicherungs- ▷ *n* (*support*) Unterstützung *f*; (*Comput*: *also*: **backup disk, backup file**) Sicherungskopie *f*, Back-up *nt*
backward ['bækwəd] *adj* (*movement*)

Rückwärts-; (*person*) zurückgeblieben; (*country*) rückständig; **~ and forward movement** Vor- und Zurückbewegung *f*; **~ step/glance** Blick *m*/Schritt *m* zurück

backwards ['bækwədz] *adv* rückwärts; (*read*) von hinten nach vorne; (*fall*) nach hinten; (*in time*) zurück; **to know sth ~, to know sth ~ and forwards** (*US*) etw in- und auswendig kennen

backwater ['bækwɔ:təʳ] *n* (*fig*) Kaff *nt*

bacon ['beɪkən] *n* (Frühstücks)speck *m*, (Schinken)speck *m*

bacteria [bæk'tɪərɪə] *npl* Bakterien *pl*

bad [bæd] *adj* schlecht; (*naughty*) unartig, ungezogen; (*mistake, accident, injury*) schwer; **his ~ leg** sein schlimmes Bein; **to go ~** verderben, schlecht werden; **to have a ~ time of it** es schwer haben; **I feel ~ about it** es tut mir leid; **in ~ faith** mit böser Absicht

bade [bæd] *pt of* **bid**

badge [bædʒ] *n* Plakette *f*; (*stick-on*) Aufkleber *m*; (*fig*) Merkmal *nt*

badger ['bædʒəʳ] *n* Dachs *m* ▷ *vt* zusetzen *+dat*

badly ['bædlɪ] *adv* schlecht; **~ wounded** schwer verletzt; **he needs it ~** er braucht es dringend; **things are going ~** es sieht schlecht *or* nicht gut aus; **to be ~ off (for money)** wenig Geld haben

bad-mannered ['bæd'mænəd] *adj* ungezogen, unhöflich

badminton ['bædmɪntən] *n* Federball *m*

bad-tempered ['bæd'tɛmpəd] *adj* schlecht gelaunt; (*by nature*) übellaunig

baffle ['bæfl] *vt* verblüffen

bag [bæg] *n* Tasche *f*; (*made of paper, plastic*) Tüte *f*; (*handbag*) (Hand)tasche *f*; (*satchel*) Schultasche *f*; (*case*) Reisetasche *f*; (*of hunter*) Jagdbeute *f*; (*pej: woman*) Schachtel *f*; **~s of** (*inf: lots of*) jede Menge; **to pack one's ~s** die Koffer packen; **~s under the eyes** Ringe *pl* unter den Augen

baggage ['bægɪdʒ] *n* Gepäck *nt*

baggage allowance *n* Freigepäck *nt*

baggy ['bægɪ] *adj* weit; (*out of shape*) ausgebeult

bagpipes ['bægpaɪps] *npl* Dudelsack *m*

bail [beɪl] *n* (*Law: payment*) Kaution *f*; (*: release*) Freilassung *f* gegen Kaution ▷ *vt* (*prisoner*) gegen Kaution freilassen; (*boat: also:* **bail out**) ausschöpfen; **to be on ~** gegen Kaution freigelassen sein; **to be released on ~** gegen Kaution freigelassen werden; *see also* **bale**

▸ **bail out** *vt* (*prisoner*) gegen Kaution freibekommen; (*firm, friend*) aus der Patsche helfen *+dat*

bailiff ['beɪlɪf] *n* (*Law: Brit*) Gerichtsvollzieher(in) *m(f)*; (*: US*) Gerichtsdiener(in) *m(f)*; (*Brit: factor*) (Guts)verwalter(in) *m(f)*

bait [beɪt] *n* Köder *m* ▷ *vt* (*hook, trap*) mit einem Köder versehen; (*tease*) necken

bake [beɪk] *vt* backen; (*clay etc*) brennen ▷ *vi* backen

baked beans [beɪkt-] *npl* gebackene Bohnen *pl* (in Tomatensoße)

baked potato *n* in der Schale gebackene Kartoffel *f*

baker ['beɪkəʳ] *n* Bäcker(in) *m(f)*

bakery ['beɪkərɪ] *n* Bäckerei *f*

baking ['beɪkɪŋ] *n* Backen *nt*; (*batch*) Ofenladung *f* ▷ *adj* (*inf: hot*) wie im Backofen

baking powder *n* Backpulver *nt*

balance ['bæləns] *n* (*equilibrium*) Gleichgewicht *nt*; (*Comm: sum*) Saldo *m*; (*remainder*) Restbetrag *m*; (*scales*) Waage *f* ▷ *vt* ausgleichen; (*Aut: wheels*) auswuchten; (*pros and cons*) (gegeneinander) abwägen; **on ~** alles in allem; **~ of trade/payments** Handels-/Zahlungsbilanz *f*; **~ carried forward** *or* **brought forward** (*Comm*) Saldovortrag *m*, Saldoübertrag *m*; **to ~ the books** (*Comm*) die Bilanz ziehen *or* machen

balanced ['bælənst] *adj* ausgeglichen; (*report*) ausgewogen

balance sheet *n* Bilanz *f*

balcony ['bælkənɪ] *n* Balkon *m*; (*in theatre*) oberster Rang *m*

bald [bɔ:ld] *adj* kahl; (*tyre*) abgefahren; (*statement*) knapp

bale [beɪl] *n* (*Agr*) Bündel *nt*; (*of papers etc*) Packen *m*

▸ **bale out** *vi* (*of a plane*) abspringen ▷ *vt* (*water*) schöpfen; (*boat*) ausschöpfen

ball [bɔ:l] *n* Ball *m*; (*of wool, string*) Knäuel *m or nt*; **to set the ~ rolling** (*fig*) den Stein ins Rollen bringen; **to play ~ (with sb)** (*fig*) (mit jdm) mitspielen; **to be on the ~** (*fig: competent*) am Ball sein; (*: alert*) auf Draht *or* Zack sein; **the ~ is in their court** (*fig*) sie sind am Ball

ballast ['bæləst] *n* Ballast *m*

ballerina [bælə'ri:nə] *n* Ballerina *f*

ballet ['bæleɪ] *n* Ballett *nt*

ballet dancer *n* Balletttänzer(in) *m(f)*

balloon [bə'lu:n] *n* (Luft)ballon *m*; (*hot air balloon*) Heißluftballon *m*; (*in comic strip*) Sprechblase *f*

ballot ['bælət] *n* (geheime) Abstimmung *f*

ballot paper *n* Stimmzettel *m*

ballpoint ['bɔ:lpɔɪnt], **ballpoint pen** *n* Kugelschreiber *m*

ballroom ['bɔ:lrum] *n* Tanzsaal *m*

Baltic ['bɔ:ltɪk] *n*: **the ~ (Sea)** die Ostsee

bamboo [bæm'bu:] *n* Bambus *m*

ban [bæn] *n* Verbot *nt* ▷ *vt* verbieten; **he was ~ned from driving** (*Brit*) ihm wurde Fahrverbot erteilt

banana [bə'nɑ:nə] *n* Banane *f*

band [bænd] *n* (*group*) Gruppe *f*, Schar *f*; (*Mus: jazz, rock etc*) Band *f*; (*: military etc*) (Musik)kapelle *f*; (*strip, range*) Band *nt*; (*stripe*) Streifen *m*

▸ **band together** *vi* sich zusammenschließen

bandage ['bændɪdʒ] *n* Verband *m* ▷ *vt* verbinden

Band-Aid® ['bændeɪd] (*US*) *n* Heftpflaster *nt*

bandit ['bændɪt] *n* Bandit *m*
bandy-legged ['bændɪ'lɛgɪd] *adj* o-beinig
bang [bæŋ] *n* (*of door*) Knallen *nt*; (*of gun, exhaust*) Knall *m*; (*blow*) Schlag *m* ▷ *excl* peng ▷ *vt* (*door*) zuschlagen, zuknallen; (*one's head etc*) sich *dat* stoßen *+acc* ▷ *vi* knallen ▷ *adv*: **to be ~ on time** (*Brit: inf*) auf die Sekunde pünktlich sein; **to ~ at the door** gegen die Tür hämmern; **to ~ into sth** sich an etw *dat* stoßen
Bangladesh [bæŋglə'dɛʃ] *n* Bangladesch *nt*
bangle ['bæŋgl] *n* Armreif(en) *m*
bangs [bæŋz] (US) *npl* (*fringe*) Pony *m*
banish ['bænɪʃ] *vt* verbannen
banister ['bænɪstə^r] *n*, **banisters** ['bænɪstəz] *npl* Geländer *nt*
banjo ['bændʒəu] (*pl* **banjoes** *or* **~s**) *n* Banjo *nt*
bank [bæŋk] *n* Bank *f*; (*of river, lake*) Ufer *nt*; (*of earth*) Wall *m*; (*of switches*) Reihe *f* ▷ *vi* (*Aviat*) sich in die Kurve legen; (*Comm*): **they ~ with Pitt's** sie haben ihr Konto bei Pitt's
▸ **bank on** *vt fus* sich verlassen auf *+acc*
bank account *n* Bankkonto *nt*
bank balance *n* Kontostand *m*
bank card *n* Scheckkarte *f*
bank charges (*Brit*) *npl* Kontoführungsgebühren *pl*
banker ['bæŋkə^r] *n* Bankier *m*
bank holiday (*Brit*) *n* (öffentlicher) Feiertag *m*
banking ['bæŋkɪŋ] *n* Bankwesen *nt*
bank manager *n* Filialleiter(in) *m(f)* (einer Bank)
banknote ['bæŋknəut] *n* Geldschein *m*, Banknote *f*
bank rate *n* Diskontsatz *m*
bankrupt ['bæŋkrʌpt] *adj* bankrott ▷ *n* Bankrotteur(in) *m(f)*; **to go ~** Bankrott machen
bankruptcy ['bæŋkrʌptsɪ] *n* (*Comm, fig*) Bankrott *m*
bank statement *n* Kontoauszug *m*
banner ['bænə^r] *n* Banner *nt*; (*in demonstration*) Spruchband *nt*
bannister ['bænɪstə^r] *n*, **bannisters** ['bænɪstəz] *n(pl)* = **banister; banisters**
banquet ['bæŋkwɪt] *n* Bankett *nt*
baptism ['bæptɪzəm] *n* Taufe *f*
baptize [bæp'taɪz] *vt* taufen
bar [bɑː^r] *n* (*for drinking*) Lokal *nt*; (*counter*) Theke *f*; (*rod*) Stange *f*; (*on window etc*) (Gitter)stab *m*; (*slab: of chocolate*) Tafel *f*; (*fig: obstacle*) Hindernis *nt*; (*prohibition*) Verbot *nt*; (*Mus*) Takt *m* ▷ *vt* (*road*) blockieren, versperren; (*window*) verriegeln; (*person*) ausschließen; (*activity*) verbieten; **~ of soap** Stück *nt* Seife; **behind ~s** hinter Gittern; **the B~** (*Law*) die Anwaltschaft; **~ none** ohne Ausnahme
barbaric [bɑː'bærɪk] *adj* barbarisch
barbecue ['bɑːbɪkjuː] *n* Grill *m*; (*meal, party*) Barbecue *nt*
barbed wire ['bɑːbd-] *n* Stacheldraht *m*
barber ['bɑːbə^r] *n* (Herren)friseur *m*
bar code *n* Strichcode *m*
bare [bɛə^r] *adj* nackt; (*trees, countryside*) kahl; (*minimum*) absolut ▷ *vt* entblößen; (*teeth*) blecken; **the ~ essentials, the ~ necessities** das Allernotwendigste; **to ~ one's soul** sein Innerstes entblößen
bareback ['bɛəbæk] *adv* ohne Sattel
barefaced ['bɛəfeɪst] *adj* (*fig*) unverfroren, schamlos
barefoot ['bɛəfut] *adj* barfüßig ▷ *adv* barfuß
barely ['bɛəlɪ] *adv* kaum
bargain ['bɑːgɪn] *n* (*deal*) Geschäft *nt*; (*transaction*) Handel *m*; (*good offer*) Sonderangebot *nt*; (*good buy*) guter Kauf *m* ▷ *vi*: **to ~ (with sb)** (mit jdm) verhandeln; (*haggle*) (mit jdm) handeln; **into the ~** obendrein
▸ **bargain for** *vt fus*: **he got more than he ~ed for** er bekam mehr, als er erwartet hatte
barge [bɑːdʒ] *n* Lastkahn *m*, Frachtkahn *m*
▸ **barge in** *vi* (*enter*) hereinplatzen; (*interrupt*) unterbrechen
▸ **barge into** *vt fus* (*place*) hereinplatzen; (*person*) anrempeln
bark [bɑːk] *n* (*of tree*) Rinde *f*; (*of dog*) Bellen *nt* ▷ *vi* bellen; **she's ~ing up the wrong tree** (*fig*) sie ist auf dem Holzweg
barley ['bɑːlɪ] *n* Gerste *f*
barley sugar *n* Malzbonbon *nt or m*
barmaid ['bɑːmeɪd] *n* Bardame *f*
barman ['bɑːmən] (*irreg: like* **man**) *n* Barmann *m*
barn [bɑːn] *n* Scheune *f*
barometer [bə'rɔmɪtə^r] *n* Barometer *nt*
baron ['bærən] *n* Baron *m*; **industrial ~** Industriemagnat *m*; **press ~** Pressezar *m*
baroness ['bærənɪs] *n* (*baron's wife*) Baronin *f*; (*baron's daughter*) Baroness *f*, Baronesse *f*
barracks ['bærəks] *npl* Kaserne *f*
barrage ['bærɑːʒ] *n* (*Mil*) Sperrfeuer *nt*; (*dam*) Staustufe *f*; (*fig: of criticism, questions etc*) Hagel *m*
barrel ['bærəl] *n* FaSS *nt*; (*of oil*) Barrel *nt*; (*of gun*) Lauf *m*
barren ['bærən] *adj* unfruchtbar
barricade [bærɪ'keɪd] *n* Barrikade *f* ▷ *vt* (*road, entrance*) verbarrikadieren; **to ~ o.s. (in)** sich verbarrikadieren
barrier ['bærɪə^r] *n* (*at frontier, entrance*) Schranke *f*; (*Brit: also:* **crash barrier**) Leitplanke *f*; (*fig*) Barriere *f*; (*: to progress etc*) Hindernis *nt*
barring ['bɑːrɪŋ] *prep* außer im Falle *+gen*
barrister ['bærɪstə^r] (*Brit*) *n* Rechtsanwalt *m*, Rechtsanwältin *f*
barrow ['bærəu] *n* Schubkarre *f*, Schubkarren *m*; (*cart*) Karren *m*
bartender ['bɑːtɛndə^r] (*US*) *n* Barmann *m*
barter ['bɑːtə^r] *n* Tauschhandel *m* ▷ *vt*: **to ~ sth for sth** etw gegen etw tauschen
base [beɪs] *n* (*of tree etc*) Fuß *m*; (*of cup, box etc*) Boden *m*; (*foundation*) Grundlage *f*; (*centre*) Stützpunkt *m*, Standort *m*; (*for organization*)

Sitz *m* ▷ *adj* gemein, niederträchtig ▷ *vt*: **to ~ sth on** etw gründen *or* basieren auf *+acc*; **to be ~d at** (*troops*) stationiert sein in *+dat*; (*employee*) arbeiten in *+dat*; **I'm ~d in London** ich wohne in London; **a Paris-~d firm** eine Firma mit Sitz in Paris; **coffee-~d** auf Kaffeebasis

baseball ['beɪsbɔːl] *n* Baseball *m*

Basel [bɑːl] *n* = **Basle**

basement ['beɪsmənt] *n* Keller *m*

bases¹ ['beɪsɪz] *npl of* **base**

bases² ['beɪsiːz] *npl of* **basis**

bash [bæʃ] (*inf*) *vt* schlagen, hauen ▷ *n*: **I'll have a ~ (at it)** (*Brit*) ich probier's mal
▸ **bash up** *vt* (*car*) demolieren; (*Brit: person*) vermöbeln

bashful ['bæʃful] *adj* schüchtern

basic ['beɪsɪk] *adj* (*method, needs etc*) Grund-; (*principles*) grundlegend; (*problem*) grundsätzlich; (*knowledge*) elementar; (*facilities*) primitiv

basically ['beɪsɪklɪ] *adv* im Grunde

basics ['beɪsɪks] *npl*: **the ~** das Wesentliche

basil ['bæzl] *n* Basilikum *nt*

basin ['beɪsn] *n* Gefäß *nt*; (*Brit: for food*) Schüssel *f*; (*also*: **wash basin**) (Wasch)becken *nt*; (*of river, lake*) Becken *nt*

basis ['beɪsɪs] (*pl* **bases**) *n* Basis *f*, Grundlage *f*; **on a part-time ~** stundenweise; **on a trial ~** zur Probe; **on the ~ of what you've said** aufgrund dessen, was Sie gesagt haben

bask [bɑːsk] *vi*: **to ~ in the sun** sich sonnen

basket ['bɑːskɪt] *n* Korb *m*; (*smaller*) Körbchen *nt*

basketball ['bɑːskɪtbɔːl] *n* Basketball *m*

Basle [bɑːl] *n* Basel *nt*

Basque [bæsk] *adj* baskisch ▷ *n* Baske *m*, Baskin *f*

bass [beɪs] *n* Bass *m*

bassoon [bə'suːn] *n* Fagott *nt*

bastard ['bɑːstəd] *n* uneheliches Kind *nt*; (*inf!*) Arschloch *nt* (*!*)

bat [bæt] *n* (*Zool*) Fledermaus *f*; (*for cricket, baseball etc*) Schlagholz *nt*; (*Brit: for table tennis*) Schläger *m* ▷ *vt*: **he didn't ~ an eyelid** er hat nicht mit der Wimper gezuckt; **off one's own ~** auf eigene Faust

batch [bætʃ] *n* (*of bread*) Schub *m*; (*of letters, papers*) Stoß *m*, Stapel *m*; (*of applicants*) Gruppe *f*; (*of work*) Schwung *m*; (*of goods*) Ladung *f*, Sendung *f*

bated ['beɪtɪd] *adj*: **with ~ breath** mit angehaltenem Atem

bath [bɑːθ] *n* Bad *nt*; (*bathtub*) (Bade)wanne *f* ▷ *vt* baden; **to have a ~** baden, ein Bad nehmen; *see also* **baths**

bathe [beɪð] *vi, vt* (*also fig*) baden

bathing ['beɪðɪŋ] *n* Baden *nt*

bathing costume, (US) **bathing suit** *n* Badeanzug *m*

bathrobe ['bɑːθrəub] *n* Bademantel *m*

bathroom ['bɑːθrum] *n* Bad(ezimmer) *nt*

baths [bɑːðz] *npl* (*also*: **swimming baths**) (Schwimm)bad *nt*

bath towel *n* Badetuch *nt*

bathtub ['bɑːθtʌb] *n* (Bade)wanne *f*

baton ['bætən] *n* (*Mus*) Taktstock *m*; (*Athletics*) Staffelholz *nt*; (*policeman's*) Schlagstock *m*

batter ['bætəʳ] *vt* schlagen, misshandeln; (*subj: rain*) schlagen; (*wind*) rütteln ▷ *n* (*Culin*) Teig *m*; (*for frying*) (Ausback)teig *m*

battered ['bætəd] *adj* (*hat, pan*) verbeult; **~ wife** misshandelte Ehefrau; **~ child** misshandeltes Kind

battery ['bætərɪ] *n* Batterie *f*; (*of tests, reporters*) Reihe *f*

battery farming *n* Batteriehaltung *f*

battle ['bætl] *n* (*Mil*) Schlacht *f*; (*fig*) Kampf *m* ▷ *vi* kämpfen; **that's half the ~** damit ist schon viel gewonnen; **it's a losing ~, we're fighting a losing ~** (*fig*) es ist ein aussichtsloser Kampf

battlefield ['bætlfiːld] *n* Schlachtfeld *nt*

battleship ['bætlʃɪp] *n* Schlachtschiff *nt*

Bavaria [bə'vɛərɪə] *n* Bayern *nt*

bawl [bɔːl] *vi* brüllen, schreien

bay [beɪ] *n* Bucht *f*; (*Brit: for parking*) Parkbucht *f*; (*: for loading*) Ladeplatz *m*; (*horse*) Braune(r) *m*; **to hold sb at ~** jdn in Schach halten

bay leaf *n* Lorbeerblatt *nt*

bazaar [bə'zɑːʳ] *n* Basar *m*

BBC *n abbr* BBC *f*

be [biː] (*pt* **was, were**, *pp* **been**) *aux vb* **1** (*with present participle: forming continuous tenses*): **what are you doing?** was machst du?; **it is raining** es regnet; **have you been to Rome?** waren Sie schon einmal in Rom?

2 (*with pp: forming passives*) werden; **to be killed** getötet werden; **the box had been opened** die Kiste war geöffnet worden

3 (*in tag questions*): **he's good-looking, isn't he?** er sieht gut aus, nicht (wahr)?; **she's back again, is she?** sie ist wieder da, oder?

4 (*+ to + infinitive*): **the house is to be sold** das Haus soll verkauft werden; **he's not to open it** er darf es nicht öffnen

▷ *vb + complement* **1** sein; **I'm tired/English** ich bin müde/Engländer(in); **I'm hot/cold** mir ist heiß/kalt; **2 and 2 are 4** 2 und 2 ist *or* macht 4; **she's tall/pretty** sie ist groß/hübsch; **be careful/quiet** sei vorsichtig/ruhig

2 (*of health*): **how are you?** wie geht es Ihnen?

3 (*of age*): **how old are you?** wie alt bist du?; **I'm sixteen (years old)** ich bin sechzehn (Jahre alt)

4 (*cost*) kosten; **how much was the meal?** was hat das Essen gekostet?; **that'll be 5 pounds please** das macht 5 Pfund, bitte

▷ *vi* **1** (*exist, occur etc*) sein; **there is/are** es gibt; **is there a God?** gibt es einen Gott?; **be that as it may** wie dem auch sei; **so be it** gut (und schön)

2 (*referring to place*) sein, liegen; **Edinburgh is in Scotland** Edinburgh liegt *or* ist in Schottland; **I won't be here tomorrow**

morgen bin ich nicht da
3 (*referring to movement*) sein; **where have you been?** wo warst du?
▷ *impers vb* **1** (*referring to time, distance, weather*) sein; **it's 5 o'clock** es ist 5 Uhr; **it's 10 km to the village** es sind 10 km bis zum Dorf; **it's too hot/cold** es ist zu heiß/kalt
2 (*emphatic*): **it's only me** ich bins nur; **it's only the postman** es ist nur der Briefträger
beach [bi:tʃ] *n* Strand *m* ▷ *vt* (*boat*) auf (den) Strand setzen
beacon ['bi:kən] *n* Leuchtfeuer *nt*; (*marker*) Bake *f*; (*also*: **radio beacon**) Funkfeuer *nt*
bead [bi:d] *n* Perle *f*; **beads** *npl* (*necklace*) Perlenkette *f*
beak [bi:k] *n* Schnabel *m*
beaker ['bi:kəʳ] *n* Becher *m*
beam [bi:m] *n* (*Archit*) Balken *m*; (*of light*) Strahl *m*; (*Radio*) Leitstrahl *m* ▷ *vi* (*smile*) strahlen ▷ *vt* ausstrahlen, senden; **to ~ at sb** jdn anstrahlen; **to drive on full** *or* **main** *or* **high ~** mit Fernlicht fahren
bean [bi:n] *n* Bohne *f*; **runner ~** Stangenbohne *f*; **broad ~** dicke Bohne; **coffee ~** Kaffeebohne *f*
beansprouts ['bi:nsprauts] *npl* = **beanshoots**
bear [bɛəʳ] (*pt* **bore**, *pp* **borne**) *n* Bär *m*; (*Stock Exchange*) Baissier *m* ▷ *vt* tragen; (*tolerate, endure*) ertragen; (*examination*) standhalten *+dat*; (*traces, signs*) aufweisen, zeigen; (*Comm*: *interest*) tragen, bringen; (*produce*: *children*) gebären; (: *fruit*) tragen ▷ *vi*: **to ~ right/left** (*Aut*) sich rechts/links halten; **to ~ the responsibility of** die Verantwortung tragen für; **to ~ comparison with** einem Vergleich standhalten mit; **I can't ~ him** ich kann ihn nicht ausstehen; **to bring pressure to ~ on sb** Druck auf jdn ausüben
▸ **bear out** *vt* (*person, suspicions etc*) bestätigen
▸ **bear up** *vi* Haltung bewahren; **he bore up well** er hat sich gut gehalten
▸ **bear with** *vt fus* Nachsicht haben mit; **~ with me a minute** bitte gedulden Sie sich einen Moment
beard [bɪəd] *n* Bart *m*
bearded ['bɪədɪd] *adj* bärtig
bearer ['bɛərəʳ] *n* (*of letter, news*) Überbringer(in) *m(f)*; (*of cheque, passport, title etc*) Inhaber(in) *m(f)*
bearing ['bɛərɪŋ] *n* (*posture*) Haltung *f*; (*air*) Auftreten *nt*; (*connection*) Bezug *m*; (*Tech*) Lager *nt*; **bearings** *npl* (*also*: **ball bearings**) Kugellager *nt*; **to take a ~ with a compass** den Kompasskurs feststellen; **to get one's ~s** sich zurechtfinden
beast [bi:st] *n* (*animal*) Tier *nt*; (*inf*: *person*) Biest *nt*
beastly ['bi:stlɪ] *adj* scheußlich
beat [bi:t] (*pt* **~**, *pp* **~en**) *n* (*of heart*) Schlag *m*; (*Mus*) Takt *m*; (*of policeman*) Revier *nt* ▷ *vt* schlagen; (*record*) brechen ▷ *vi* schlagen; **to ~ time** den Takt schlagen; **to ~ it** (*inf*) abhauen, verschwinden; **that ~s everything** das ist doch wirklich der Gipfel *or* die Höhe; **to ~ about the bush** um den heißen Brei herumreden; **off the ~en track** abgelegen
▸ **beat down** *vt* (*door*) einschlagen; (*price*) herunterhandeln; (*seller*) einen niedrigeren Preis aushandeln mit ▷ *vi* (*rain*) herunterprasseln; (*sun*) herunterbrennen
▸ **beat off** *vt* (*attack, attacker*) abwehren
▸ **beat up** *vt* (*person*) zusammenschlagen; (*mixture, eggs*) schlagen
beating ['bi:tɪŋ] *n* Schläge *pl*, Prügel *pl*; **to take a ~** (*fig*) eine Schlappe einstecken
beautiful ['bju:tɪful] *adj* schön
beautifully ['bju:tɪflɪ] *adv* (*play, sing, drive etc*) hervorragend; (*quiet, empty etc*) schön
beauty ['bju:tɪ] *n* Schönheit *f*; (*fig*: *attraction*) Schöne *nt*; **the ~ of it is that ...** das Schöne daran ist, dass ...
beauty salon *n* Kosmetiksalon *m*
beauty spot (*Brit*) *n* besonders schöner Ort *m*
beaver ['bi:vəʳ] *n* Biber *m*
became [bɪ'keɪm] *pt of* **become**
because [bɪ'kɔz] *conj* weil; **~ of** wegen *+gen or* (*inf*) *+dat*
beck [bɛk] *n*: **to be at sb's ~ and call** nach jds Pfeife tanzen
beckon ['bɛkən] *vt* (*also*: **beckon to**) winken ▷ *vi* locken
become [bɪ'kʌm] (*irreg*: *like* **come**) *vi* werden; **it became known that** es wurde bekannt, dass; **what has ~ of him?** was ist aus ihm geworden?
becoming [bɪ'kʌmɪŋ] *adj* (*behaviour*) schicklich; (*clothes*) kleidsam
bed [bɛd] *n* Bett *nt*; (*of coal*) Flöz *nt*; (*of clay*) Schicht *f*; (*of river*) (Fluss)bett *nt*; (*of sea*) (Meeres)boden *m*, (Meeres)grund *m*; (*of flowers*) Beet *nt*; **to go to ~** ins *or* zu Bett gehen
▸ **bed down** *vi* sein Lager aufschlagen
bed and breakfast *n* (*place*) (Frühstücks)pension *f*; (*terms*) Übernachtung *f* mit Frühstück
bedclothes ['bɛdkləuðz] *npl* Bettzeug *nt*
bedding ['bɛdɪŋ] *n* Bettzeug *nt*
bedraggled [bɪ'drægld] *adj* (*wet*) triefnass, tropfnass; (*dirty*) verdreckt
bedridden ['bɛdrɪdn] *adj* bettlägerig
bedroom ['bɛdrum] *n* Schlafzimmer *nt*
bedside ['bɛdsaɪd] *n*: **at sb's ~** an jds Bett; **~ lamp** Nachttischlampe *f*; **~ book** Bettlektüre *f*
bedsit ['bɛdsɪt], **bedsitter** ['bɛdsɪtəʳ] (*Brit*) *n* möbliertes Zimmer *nt*
bedspread ['bɛdsprɛd] *n* Tagesdecke *f*
bedtime ['bɛdtaɪm] *n* Schlafenszeit *f*; **it's ~** es ist Zeit, ins Bett zu gehen
bee [bi:] *n* Biene *f*; **to have a ~ in one's bonnet about cleanliness** einen Sauberkeitsfimmel *or* Sauberkeitstick haben
beech [bi:tʃ] *n* Buche *f*
beef [bi:f] *n* Rind(fleisch) *nt*; **roast ~**

Rinderbraten *m*
▶ **beef up** (*inf*) *vt* aufmotzen; (*essay*) auswalzen
beefburger ['bi:fbə:gər] *n* Hamburger *m*
beehive ['bi:haɪv] *n* Bienenstock *m*
beeline ['bi:laɪn] *n*: **to make a ~ for** schnurstracks zugehen auf *+acc*
been [bi:n] *pp of* **be**
beer [bɪər] *n* Bier *nt*
beet [bi:t] *n* Rübe *f*; (*US*: *also*: **red beet**) Rote Bete *f*
beetle ['bi:tl] *n* Käfer *m*
beetroot ['bi:tru:t] (*Brit*) *n* Rote Bete *f*
before [bɪ'fɔ:r] *prep* vor *+dat*; (*with movement*) vor *+acc* ▷ *conj* bevor ▷ *adv* (*time*) vorher; (*space*) davor; **~ going** bevor er/sie *etc* geht/ging; **~ she goes** bevor sie geht; **the week ~** die Woche davor; **I've never seen it ~** ich habe es noch nie gesehen
beforehand [bɪ'fɔ:hænd] *adv* vorher
beg [bɛg] *vi* betteln ▷ *vt* (*food, money*) betteln um; (*favour, forgiveness etc*) bitten um; **to ~ for** (*food etc*) betteln um; (*forgiveness, mercy etc*) bitten um; **to ~ sb to do sth** jdn bitten, etw zu tun; **I ~ your pardon** (*apologizing*) entschuldigen Sie bitte; (*: not hearing*) (wie) bitte?; **to ~ the question** der Frage ausweichen; *see also* **pardon**
began [bɪ'gæn] *pt of* **begin**
beggar ['bɛgər] *n* Bettler(in) *m(f)*
begin [bɪ'gɪn] (*pt* **began**, *pp* **begun**) *vt, vi* beginnen, anfangen; **to ~ doing** *or* **to do sth** anfangen, etw zu tun; **~ning (from) Monday** ab Montag; **I can't ~ to thank you** ich kann Ihnen gar nicht genug danken; **we'll have soup to ~ with** als Vorspeise hätten wir gern Suppe; **to ~ with, I'd like to know ...** zunächst einmal möchte ich wissen, ...
beginner [bɪ'gɪnər] *n* Anfänger(in) *m(f)*
beginning [bɪ'gɪnɪŋ] *n* Anfang *m*; **right from the ~** von Anfang an
begun [bɪ'gʌn] *pp of* **begin**
behalf [bɪ'hɑ:f] *n*: **on ~ of, in ~ of** (*US*: *as representative of*) im Namen von; (*for benefit of*) zugunsten von; **on my/his ~** in meinem/seinem Namen; zu meinen/seinen Gunsten
behave [bɪ'heɪv] *vi* (*person*) sich verhalten, sich benehmen; (*thing*) funktionieren; (*also*: **behave o.s.**) sich benehmen
behaviour, (*US*) **behavior** [bɪ'heɪvjər] *n* Verhalten *nt*; (*manner*) Benehmen *nt*
behead [bɪ'hɛd] *vt* enthaupten
behind [bɪ'haɪnd] *prep* hinter ▷ *adv* (*at/towards the back*) hinten ▷ *n* (*buttocks*) Hintern *m*, Hinterteil *nt*; **~ the scenes** (*fig*) hinter den Kulissen; **we're ~ them in technology** auf dem Gebiet der Technologie liegen wir hinter ihnen zurück; **to be ~** (*schedule*) im Rückstand *or* Verzug sein; **to leave/stay ~** zurücklassen/-bleiben
behold [bɪ'həuld] (*irreg*: *like* **hold**) *vt* sehen, erblicken
beige [beɪʒ] *adj* beige
Beijing ['beɪ'dʒɪŋ] *n* Peking *nt*
being ['bi:ɪŋ] *n* (*creature*) (Lebe)wesen *nt*; (*existence*) Leben *nt*, (Da)sein *nt*; **to come into ~** entstehen
Beirut [beɪ'ru:t] *n* Beirut *nt*
Belarus [bɛlə'rus] *n* Weißrussland *nt*
belated [bɪ'leɪtɪd] *adj* verspätet
belch [bɛltʃ] *vi* rülpsen ▷ *vt* (*also*: **belch out**: *smoke etc*) ausstoßen
Belgian ['bɛldʒən] *adj* belgisch ▷ *n* Belgier(in) *m(f)*
Belgium ['bɛldʒəm] *n* Belgien *nt*
belie [bɪ'laɪ] *vt* (*contradict*) im Widerspruch stehen zu; (*give false impression of*) hinwegtäuschen über *+acc*; (*disprove*) widerlegen, Lügen strafen
belief [bɪ'li:f] *n* Glaube *m*; (*opinion*) Überzeugung *f*; **it's beyond ~** es ist unglaublich *or* nicht zu glauben; **in the ~ that** im Glauben, dass
believe [bɪ'li:v] *vt* glauben ▷ *vi* (an Gott) glauben; **he is ~d to be abroad** es heißt, dass er im Ausland ist; **to ~ in** (*God, ghosts*) glauben an *+acc*; (*method etc*) Vertrauen haben zu; **I don't ~ in corporal punishment** ich halte nicht viel von der Prügelstrafe
believer [bɪ'li:vər] *n* (*in idea, activity*) Anhänger(in) *m(f)*; (*Rel*) Gläubige(r) *f(m)*; **she's a great ~ in healthy eating** sie ist sehr für eine gesunde Ernährung
belittle [bɪ'lɪtl] *vt* herabsetzen
bell [bɛl] *n* Glocke *f*; (*small*) Glöckchen *nt*, Schelle *f*; (*on door*) Klingel *f*; **that rings a ~** (*fig*) das kommt mir bekannt vor
bellboy ['bɛlbɔɪ] (*Brit*) *n* Page *m*, Hoteljunge *m*
belligerent [bɪ'lɪdʒərənt] *adj* angriffslustig
bellow ['bɛləu] *vi, vt* brüllen
belly ['bɛlɪ] *n* Bauch *m*
belong [bɪ'lɔŋ] *vi*: **to ~ to** (*person*) gehören *+dat*; (*club etc*) angehören *+dat*; **this book ~s here** dieses Buch gehört hierher
belongings [bɪ'lɔŋɪŋz] *npl* Sachen *pl*, Habe *f*; **personal ~** persönlicher Besitz *m*, persönliches Eigentum *nt*
beloved [bɪ'lʌvɪd] *adj* geliebt ▷ *n* Geliebte(r) *f(m)*
below [bɪ'ləu] *prep* (*beneath*) unterhalb *+gen*; (*less than*) unter *+dat* ▷ *adv* (*beneath*) unten; **see ~** siehe unten; **temperatures ~ normal** Temperaturen unter dem Durchschnitt
belt [bɛlt] *n* Gürtel *m*; (*Tech*) (Treib)riemen *m* ▷ *vt* schlagen ▷ *vi* (*Brit*: *inf*): **to ~ along** rasen; **to ~ down/into** hinunter-/hineinrasen; **industrial ~** Industriegebiet *nt*
▶ **belt out** *vt* (*song*) schmettern
▶ **belt up** (*Brit*: *inf*) *vi* den Mund *or* die Klappe halten
beltway ['bɛltweɪ] (*US*) *n* Umgehungsstraße *f*, Ringstraße *f*; (*motorway*) Umgehungsautobahn *f*
bemused [bɪ'mju:zd] *adj* verwirrt
bench [bɛntʃ] *n* Bank *f*; (*work bench*) Werkbank

f; **the B~** (*Law: judges*) die Richter *pl*, der Richterstand

bend [bɛnd] (*pt, pp* **bent**) *vt* (*leg, arm*) beugen; (*pipe*) biegen ▷ *vi* (*person*) sich beugen ▷ *n* (*Brit: in road*) Kurve *f*; (*in pipe, river*) Biegung *f*; **bends** *npl* (*Med*): **the ~s** die Taucherkrankheit
▶ **bend down** *vi* sich bücken
▶ **bend over** *vi* sich bücken

beneath [bɪ'ni:θ] *prep* unter *+dat* ▷ *adv* darunter

benefactor ['bɛnɪfæktəʳ] *n* Wohltäter *m*

beneficial [bɛnɪ'fɪʃəl] *adj* (*effect*) nützlich; (*influence*) vorteilhaft; **~ (to)** gut (für)

benefit ['bɛnɪfɪt] *n* (*advantage*) Vorteil *m*; (*money*) Beihilfe *f*; (*also*: **benefit concert, benefit match**) Benefizveranstaltung *f* ▷ *vt* nützen *+dat*, zugutekommen *+dat* ▷ *vi*: **he'll ~ from it** er wird davon profitieren

Benelux ['bɛnɪlʌks] *n* die Beneluxstaaten *pl*

benevolent [bɪ'nɛvələnt] *adj* wohlwollend; (*organization*) Wohltätigkeits-

benign [bɪ'naɪn] *adj* gütig; (*Med*) gutartig

bent [bɛnt] *pt, pp of* **bend** ▷ *n* Neigung *f* ▷ *adj* (*wire, pipe*) gebogen; (*inf: dishonest*) korrupt; (*: pej: homosexual*) andersrum; **to be ~ on** entschlossen sein zu

bequest [bɪ'kwɛst] *n* Vermächtnis *nt*, Legat *nt*

bereaved [bɪ'ri:vdʳ] *adj* leidtragend ▷ *npl*: **the ~** die Hinterbliebenen *pl*

beret ['bɛreɪ] *n* Baskenmütze *f*

Berlin [bə:'lɪn] *n* Berlin *nt*; **East/West ~** (*formerly*) Ost-/Westberlin *nt*

berm [bə:m] (*US*) *n* Seitenstreifen *m*

Bermuda [bə:'mju:də] *n* Bermuda *nt*, die Bermudinseln *pl*

Bern [bə:n] *n* Bern *nt*

berry ['bɛrɪ] *n* Beere *f*

berserk [bə'sə:k] *adj*: **to go ~** wild werden

berth [bə:θ] *n* (*bed*) Bett *nt*; (*on ship*) Koje *f*; (*on train*) Schlafwagenbett *nt*; (*for ship*) Liegeplatz *m* ▷ *vi* anlegen; **to give sb a wide ~** (*fig*) einen großen Bogen um jdn machen

beseech [bɪ'si:tʃ] (*pt, pp* **besought**) *vt* anflehen

beset [bɪ'sɛt] (*pt, pp* **~**) *vt* (*subj: difficulties*) bedrängen; (*: fears, doubts*) befallen; **~ with** (*problems, dangers etc*) voller *+dat*

beside [bɪ'saɪd] *prep* neben *+dat*; (*with movement*) neben *+acc*; **to be ~ o.s.** außer sich sein; **that's ~ the point** das hat damit nichts zu tun

besides [bɪ'saɪdz] *adv* außerdem ▷ *prep* außer *+dat*

besiege [bɪ'si:dʒ] *vt* belagern; (*fig*) belagern, bedrängen

best [bɛst] *adj* beste(r, s) ▷ *adv* am besten ▷ *n*: **at ~** bestenfalls; **the ~ thing to do is ...** das Beste ist ...; **the ~ part of** der größte Teil *+gen*; **to make the ~ of sth** das Beste aus etw machen; **to do one's ~** sein Bestes tun; **to the ~ of my knowledge** meines Wissens; **to the ~ of my ability** so gut ich kann; **he's not exactly patient at the ~ of times** er ist schon normalerweise ziemlich ungeduldig

best-before date *n* Mindesthaltbarkeitsdatum *nt*

best man *n* Trauzeuge *m* (*des Bräutigams*)

bestow [bɪ'stəu] *vt* schenken; **to ~ sth on sb** (*honour, praise*) jdm etw zuteilwerden lassen; (*title*) jdm etw verleihen

bet [bɛt] (*pt, pp* **~** *or* **betted**) *n* Wette *f* ▷ *vi* wetten ▷ *vt*: **to ~ sb sth** mit jdm um etw wetten; **it's a safe ~** (*fig*) es ist so gut wie sicher; **to ~ money on sth** Geld auf etw *acc* setzen

betray [bɪ'treɪ] *vt* verraten; (*trust, confidence*) missbrauchen

better ['bɛtəʳ] *adj, adv* besser ▷ *vt* verbessern ▷ *n*: **to get the ~ of sb** jdn unterkriegen; (*curiosity*) über jdn siegen; **I had ~ go** ich gehe jetzt (wohl) besser; **you had ~ do it** tun Sie es lieber; **he thought ~ of it** er überlegte es sich *dat* anders; **to get ~** gesund werden; **that's ~!** so ist es besser!; **a change for the ~** eine Wendung zum Guten

betting ['bɛtɪŋ] *n* Wetten *nt*

betting shop (*Brit*) *n* Wettbüro *nt*

between [bɪ'twi:n] *prep* zwischen *+dat*; (*with movement*) zwischen *+acc*; (*amongst*) unter *+acc or dat* ▷ *adv* dazwischen; **the road ~ here and London** die Straße zwischen hier und London; **we only had £5 ~ us** wir hatten zusammen nur £5

beverage ['bɛvərɪdʒ] *n* Getränk *nt*

beware [bɪ'wɛəʳ] *vi*: **to ~ (of)** sich in Acht nehmen (vor *+dat*); **"~ of the dog"** "Vorsicht, bissiger Hund"

bewildered [bɪ'wɪldəd] *adj* verwirrt

beyond [bɪ'jɔnd] *prep* (*in space*) jenseits *+gen*; (*exceeding*) über *+acc* ... hinaus; (*after*) nach; (*above*) über *+dat* ▷ *adv* (*in space*) dahinter; (*in time*) darüber hinaus; **it is ~ doubt** es steht außer Zweifel; **~ repair** nicht mehr zu reparieren; **it is ~ my understanding** es übersteigt mein Begriffsvermögen; **it's ~ me** das geht über meinen Verstand

bias ['baɪəs] *n* (*prejudice*) Vorurteil *nt*; (*preference*) Vorliebe *f*

biased, biassed ['baɪəst] *adj* voreingenommen; **to be bias(s)ed against** voreingenommen sein gegen

bib [bɪb] *n* Latz *m*

Bible ['baɪbl] *n* Bibel *f*

bicarbonate of soda [baɪ'kɑ:bənɪt-] *n* Natron *nt*

biceps ['baɪsɛps] *n* Bizeps *m*

bicker ['bɪkəʳ] *vi* sich zanken

bicycle ['baɪsɪkl] *n* Fahrrad *nt*

bicycle pump *n* Luftpumpe *f*

bid [bɪd] (*pt* **bade** *or* **~**, *pp* **bidden** *or* **~**) *n* (*at auction*) Gebot *nt*; (*in tender*) Angebot *nt*; (*attempt*) Versuch *m* ▷ *vi* bieten; (*Cards*) bieten, reizen ▷ *vt* bieten; **to ~ sb good day** jdm einen Guten Tag wünschen

bidder ['bɪdəʳ] *n*: **the highest ~** der/die Höchstbietende *or* Meistbietende

bidding ['bɪdɪŋ] *n* Steigern *nt*, Bieten *nt*; (*order,* *command*): **to do sb's ~** tun, was jd einem sagt

bide [baɪd] *vt*: **to ~ one's time** den rechten Augenblick abwarten

bidet [ˈbiːdeɪ] *n* Bidet *nt*

bifocals [baɪˈfəuklz] *npl* Bifokalbrille *f*

big [bɪg] *adj* groß; **to do things in a ~ way** alles im großen Stil tun

bigheaded [ˈbɪgˈhɛdɪd] *adj* eingebildet

bigot [ˈbɪgət] *n* Eiferer *m*; (*about religion*) bigotter Mensch *m*

bigoted [ˈbɪgətɪd] *adj* (*see n*) eifernd; bigott

bigotry [ˈbɪgətrɪ] *n* (*see n*) eifernde Borniertheit *f*; Bigotterie *f*

big toe *n* große Zehe *f*

big top *n* Zirkuszelt *nt*

bike [baɪk] *n* (Fahr)rad *nt*; (*motorcycle*) Motorrad *nt*

bike lane *n* Fahrradspur *f*

bikini [bɪˈkiːnɪ] *n* Bikini *m*

bilateral [baɪˈlætərəl] *adj* bilateral

bilingual [baɪˈlɪŋgwəl] *adj* zweisprachig

bill [bɪl] *n* Rechnung *f*; (*Pol*) (Gesetz)entwurf *m*, (Gesetzes)vorlage *f*; (*US*: *banknote*) Banknote *f*, (Geld)schein *m*; (*of bird*) Schnabel *m* ▷ *vt* (*item*) in Rechnung stellen, berechnen; (*customer*) eine Rechnung ausstellen *+dat*; **"post no ~s"** "Plakate ankleben verboten"; **on the ~** (*Theat*) auf dem Programm; **to fit** *or* **fill the ~** (*fig*) der/die/das Richtige sein; **~ of exchange** Wechsel *m*, Tratte *f*; **~ of fare** Speisekarte *f*; **~ of lading** Seefrachtbrief *m*, Konnossement *nt*; **~ of sale** Verkaufsurkunde *f*

billboard [ˈbɪlbɔːd] *n* Reklametafel *f*

billet [ˈbɪlɪt] (*Mil*) *n* Quartier *nt* ▷ *vt* einquartieren

billfold [ˈbɪlfəuld] (*US*) *n* Brieftasche *f*

billiards [ˈbɪljədz] *n* Billard *nt*

billion [ˈbɪljən] *n* (*Brit*) Billion *f*; (*US*) Milliarde *f*

bimbo [ˈbɪmbəu] (*inf*: *pej*) *n* (*woman*) Puppe *f*, Häschen *nt*

bin [bɪn] *n* (*Brit*) Mülleimer *m*; (*container*) Behälter *m*

bind [baɪnd] (*pt, pp* **bound**) *vt* binden; (*tie together*: *hands and feet*) fesseln; (*constrain, oblige*) verpflichten ▷ *n* (*inf*: *nuisance*) Last *f*
▸ **bind over** *vt* rechtlich verpflichten
▸ **bind up** *vt* (*wound*) verbinden; **to be bound up in** sehr beschäftigt sein mit; **to be bound up with** verbunden *or* verknüpft sein mit

binding [ˈbaɪndɪŋ] *adj* bindend, verbindlich ▷ *n* (*of book*) Einband *m*

binge [bɪndʒ] (*inf*) *n*: **to go on a ~** auf eine Sauftour gehen

bingo [ˈbɪŋgəu] *n* Bingo *nt*

binoculars [bɪˈnɔkjuləz] *npl* Fernglas *nt*

biochemistry [baɪəˈkɛmɪstrɪ] *n* Biochemie *f*

biodegradable [ˈbaɪəudɪˈgreɪdəbl] *adj* biologisch abbaubar

biography [baɪˈɔgrəfɪ] *n* Biografie *f*

biological [baɪəˈlɔdʒɪkl] *adj* biologisch

biology [baɪˈɔlədʒɪ] *n* Biologie *f*

birch [bəːtʃ] *n* Birke *f*

bird [bəːd] *n* Vogel *m*; (*Brit*: *inf*: *girl*) Biene *f*

bird of prey *n* Raubvogel *m*

bird's-eye view [ˈbəːdzaɪ-] *n* Vogelperspektive *f*; (*overview*) Überblick *m*

Biro® [ˈbaɪərəu] *n* Kugelschreiber *m*, Kuli *m* (*inf*)

birth [bəːθ] *n* Geburt *f*; **to give ~ to** (*subj*: *woman*) gebären, entbunden werden von; (: *animal*) werfen

birth certificate *n* Geburtsurkunde *f*

birth control *n* Geburtenkontrolle *f*, Geburtenregelung *f*

birthday [ˈbəːθdeɪ] *n* Geburtstag *m* ▷ *cpd* Geburtstags-; *see also* **happy**

birthmark [ˈbəːθmɑːk] *n* Muttermal *nt*

birthplace [ˈbəːθpleɪs] *n* Geburtsort *m*; (*house*) Geburtshaus *nt*; (*fig*) Entstehungsort *m*

birth rate [ˈbəːθreɪt] *n* Geburtenrate *f*, Geburtenziffer *f*

biscuit [ˈbɪskɪt] *n* (*Brit*) Keks *m or nt*; (*US*) Brötchen *nt*

bisect [baɪˈsɛkt] *vt* halbieren

bishop [ˈbɪʃəp] *n* (*Rel*) Bischof *m*; (*Chess*) Läufer *m*

bistro [ˈbiːstrəu] *n* Bistro *nt*

bit [bɪt] *pt of* **bite** ▷ *n* (*piece*) Stück *nt*; (*of drill*) (Bohr)einsatz *m*, Bohrer *m*; (*of plane*) (Hobel)messer *nt*; (*Comput*) Bit *nt*; (*of horse*) Gebiss *nt*; (*US*): **two/four/six ~s** 25/50/75 Cent(s); **a ~ of** ein bisschen; **a ~ mad** ein bisschen verrückt; **a ~ dangerous** etwas gefährlich; **~ by bit** nach und nach; **to come to ~s** kaputtgehen; **bring all your ~s and pieces** bringen Sie Ihre (Sieben)sachen mit; **to do one's ~** sein(en) Teil tun *or* beitragen

bitch [bɪtʃ] *n* (*dog*) Hündin *f*; (*inf!*: *woman*) Miststück *nt*

bite [baɪt] (*pt* **bit**, *pp* **bitten**) *vt, vi* beißen; (*subj*: *insect etc*) stechen ▷ *n* (*insect bite*) Stich *m*; (*mouthful*) Bissen *m*; **to ~ one's nails** an seinen Nägeln kauen; **let's have a ~ (to eat)** (*inf*) lasst uns eine Kleinigkeit essen

bitten [ˈbɪtn] *pp of* **bite**

bitter [ˈbɪtəʳ] *adj* bitter; (*person*) verbittert; (*wind, weather*) bitterkalt, eisig; (*criticism*) scharf ▷ *n* (*Brit*: *beer*) *halbdunkles obergäriges Bier*; **to the ~ end** bis zum bitteren Ende

bitterness [ˈbɪtənɪs] *n* Bitterkeit *f*

bizarre [bɪˈzɑːʳ] *adj* bizarr

black [blæk] *adj* schwarz ▷ *vt* (*Brit*: *Industry*) boykottieren ▷ *n* Schwarz *nt*; (*person*): **B~** Schwarze(r) *f(m)*; **to give sb a ~ eye** jdm ein blaues Auge schlagen; **~ and blue** grün und blau; **there it is in ~ and white** (*fig*) da steht es schwarz auf weiß; **to be in the ~** in den schwarzen Zahlen sein
▸ **black out** *vi* (*faint*) ohnmächtig werden

blackberry [ˈblækbərɪ] *n* Brombeere *f*

blackbird [ˈblækbəːd] *n* Amsel *f*

blackboard [ˈblækbɔːd] *n* Tafel *f*

black coffee *n* schwarzer Kaffee *m*
blackcurrant ['blæk'kʌrənt] *n* Johannisbeere *f*
blacken ['blækn] *vt*: **to ~ sb's name/ reputation** (*fig*) jdn verunglimpfen
black ice *n* Glatteis *nt*
blackleg ['blæklɛg] (*Brit*) *n* Streikbrecher(in) *m(f)*
blacklist ['blæklɪst] *n* schwarze Liste *f* ▷ *vt* auf die schwarze Liste setzen
blackmail ['blækmeɪl] *n* Erpressung *f* ▷ *vt* erpressen
black market *n* Schwarzmarkt *m*
blackout ['blækaut] *n* (*in wartime*) Verdunkelung *f*; (*power cut*) Stromausfall *m*; (TV, *Radio*) Ausfall *m*; (*faint*) Ohnmachtsanfall *m*
black pepper *n* schwarzer Pfeffer *m*
Black Sea *n*: **the ~** das Schwarze Meer
black sheep *n* (*fig*) schwarzes Schaf *nt*
blacksmith ['blæksmɪθ] *n* Schmied *m*
black spot *n* (*Aut*) Gefahrenstelle *f*; (*for unemployment etc*) *Gebiet, in dem ein Problem besonders ausgeprägt ist*
bladder ['blædəʳ] *n* Blase *f*
blade [bleɪd] *n* (*of knife etc*) Klinge *f*; (*of oar, propeller*) Blatt *nt*; **a ~ of grass** ein Grashalm *m*
blame [bleɪm] *n* Schuld *f* ▷ *vt*: **to ~ sb for sth** jdm die Schuld an etw *dat* geben; **to be to ~** Schuld daran haben, schuld sein; **who's to ~?** wer hat Schuld *or* ist schuld?; **I'm not to ~** es ist nicht meine Schuld
bland [blænd] *adj* (*taste, food*) fade
blank [blæŋk] *adj* (*paper*) leer, unbeschrieben; (*look*) ausdruckslos ▷ *n* (*on form*) Lücke *f*; (*cartridge*) Platzpatrone *f*; **my mind was a ~** ich hatte ein Brett vor dem Kopf; **we drew a ~** (*fig*) wir hatten kein Glück
blanket ['blæŋkɪt] *n* Decke *f* ▷ *adj* (*statement*) pauschal; (*agreement*) Pauschal-
blare [blɛəʳ] *vi* (*brass band*) schmettern; (*horn*) tuten; (*radio*) plärren
▶ **blare out** *vi* (*radio, stereo*) plärren
blast [blɑ:st] *n* (*of wind*) Windstoß *m*; (*of whistle*) Trillern *nt*; (*shock wave*) Druckwelle *f*; (*of air, steam*) Schwall *m*; (*of explosive*) Explosion *f* ▷ *vt* (*blow up*) sprengen ▷ *excl* (*Brit: inf*) verdammt!, so ein Mist!; **at full ~** (*play music*) mit voller Lautstärke; (*move, work*) auf Hochtouren
▶ **blast off** *vi* (*Space*) abheben, starten
blatant ['bleɪtənt] *adj* offensichtlich
blaze [bleɪz] *n* (*fire*) Feuer *nt*, Brand *m*; (*fig: of colour*) Farbenpracht *f*; (*: of glory*) Glanz *m* ▷ *vi* (*fire*) lodern; (*guns*) feuern; (*fig: eyes*) glühen ▷ *vt*: **to ~ a trail** (*fig*) den Weg bahnen; **in a ~ of publicity** mit viel Publicity
blazer ['bleɪzəʳ] *n* Blazer *m*
bleach [bli:tʃ] *n* (*also*: **household bleach**) ≈ Reinigungsmittel *nt* ▷ *vt* bleichen
bleached [bli:tʃt] *adj* gebleicht
bleachers ['bli:tʃəz] (*US*) *npl* unüberdachte Zuschauertribüne *f*
bleak [bli:k] *adj* (*countryside*) öde; (*weather, situation*) trostlos; (*prospect*) trüb; (*expression, voice*) deprimiert
bleat [bli:t] *vi* (*goat*) meckern; (*sheep*) blöken ▷ *n* Meckern *nt*; Blöken *nt*
bled [blɛd] *pt, pp of* **bleed**
bleed [bli:d] (*pt, pp* **bled**) *vi* bluten; (*colour*) auslaufen ▷ *vt* (*brakes, radiator*) entlüften; **my nose is ~ing** ich habe Nasenbluten
bleeper ['bli:pəʳ] *n* Piepser *m* (*inf*), Funkrufempfänger *m*
blemish ['blɛmɪʃ] *n* Makel *m*
blend [blɛnd] *n* Mischung *f* ▷ *vt* (*Culin*) mischen, mixen; (*colours, styles, flavours etc*) vermischen ▷ *vi* (*colours etc*: *also*: **blend in**) harmonieren
blender ['blɛndəʳ] *n* (*Culin*) Mixer *m*
bless [blɛs] (*pt, pp* **~ed** *or* **blest**) *vt* segnen; **to be ~ed with** gesegnet sein mit; **~ you!** (*after sneeze*) Gesundheit!
blessing ['blɛsɪŋ] *n* (*approval*) Zustimmung *f*; (*Rel, fig*) Segen *m*; **to count one's ~s** von Glück sagen können; **it was a ~ in disguise** es war schließlich doch ein Segen
blew [blu:] *pt of* **blow**
blight [blaɪt] *vt* zerstören; (*hopes*) vereiteln; (*life*) verderben ▷ *n* (*of plants*) Brand *m*
blimey ['blaɪmɪ] (*Brit: inf*) *excl* Mensch!
blind [blaɪnd] *adj* blind ▷ *n* (*for window*) Rollo *nt*, Rouleau *nt*; (*also*: **Venetian blind**) Jalousie *f* ▷ *vt* blind machen; (*dazzle*) blenden; (*deceive: with facts etc*) verblenden; **the blind** *npl* (*blind people*) die Blinden *pl*; **to turn a ~ eye (on** *or* **to)** ein Auge zudrücken (bei); **to be ~ to sth** (*fig*) blind für etw sein
blind alley *n* (*fig*) Sackgasse *f*
blind corner (*Brit*) *n* unübersichtliche Ecke *f*
blindfold ['blaɪndfəuld] *n* Augenbinde *f* ▷ *adj, adv* mit verbundenen Augen ▷ *vt* die Augen verbinden *+dat*
blindly ['blaɪndlɪ] *adv* (*without seeing*) wie blind; (*without thinking*) blindlings
blindness ['blaɪndnɪs] *n* Blindheit *f*
blind spot *n* (*Aut*) toter Winkel *m*; (*fig: weak spot*) schwacher Punkt *m*
blink [blɪŋk] *vi* blinzeln; (*light*) blinken ▷ *n*: **the TV's on the ~** (*inf*) der Fernseher ist kaputt
blinkers ['blɪŋkəz] *npl* Scheuklappen *pl*
bliss [blɪs] *n* Glück *nt*, Seligkeit *f*
blister ['blɪstəʳ] *n* Blase *f* ▷ *vi* (*paint*) Blasen werfen
blizzard ['blɪzəd] *n* Schneesturm *m*
bloated ['bləutɪd] *adj* aufgedunsen; (*full*) (über)satt
blob [blɔb] *n* Tropfen *m*; (*sth indistinct*) verschwommener Fleck *m*
block [blɔk] *n* Block *m*; (*toy*) Bauklotz *m*; (*in pipes*) Verstopfung *f* ▷ *vt* blockieren; (*progress*) aufhalten; (*Comput*) blocken; **~ of flats** (*Brit*) Wohnblock *m*; **3 ~s from here** 3 Blocks *or* Straßen weiter; **mental ~** geistige Sperre *f*, Mattscheibe *f* (*inf*); **~ and tackle** Flaschenzug

m
▸ **block up** *vt, vi* verstopfen
blockade [blɔˈkeɪd] *n* Blockade *f* ▷ *vt* blockieren
blockage [ˈblɔkɪdʒ] *n* Verstopfung *f*
blockbuster [ˈblɔkbʌstəʳ] *n* Knüller *m*
block capitals *npl* Blockschrift *f*
block letters *npl* Blockschrift *f*
bloke [bləuk] (*Brit: inf*) *n* Typ *m*
blond, **blonde** [blɔnd] *adj* blond ▷ *n*: **~(e)** (*woman*) Blondine *f*
blood [blʌd] *n* Blut *nt*; **new ~** (*fig*) frisches Blut *nt*
blood donor *n* Blutspender(in) *m(f)*
blood group *n* Blutgruppe *f*
bloodhound [ˈblʌdhaund] *n* Bluthund *m*
blood poisoning *n* Blutvergiftung *f*
blood pressure *n* Blutdruck *m*; **to have high/low ~** hohen/niedrigen Blutdruck haben
bloodshed [ˈblʌdʃɛd] *n* Blutvergießen *nt*
bloodshot [ˈblʌdʃɔt] *adj* (*eyes*) blutunterlaufen
bloodstream [ˈblʌdstri:m] *n* Blut *nt*, Blutkreislauf *m*
blood test *n* Blutprobe *f*
bloodthirsty [ˈblʌdθə:stɪ] *adj* blutrünstig
blood transfusion *n* Blutübertragung *f*, (Blut)transfusion *f*
blood type *n* Blutgruppe *f*
blood vessel *n* Blutgefäß *nt*
bloody [ˈblʌdɪ] *adj* blutig; (*Brit: inf!*): **this ~ ...** diese(r, s) verdammte ...; **~ strong** (*inf!*) verdammt stark; **~ good** (*inf!*) echt gut
bloody-minded [ˈblʌdɪˈmaɪndɪd] (*Brit: inf*) *adj* stur
bloom [blu:m] *n* Blüte *f* ▷ *vi* blühen; **to be in ~** in Blüte stehen
blossom [ˈblɔsəm] *n* Blüte *f* ▷ *vi* blühen; (*fig*): **to ~ into** erblühen *or* aufblühen zu
blot [blɔt] *n* Klecks *m*; (*fig: on name etc*) Makel *m* ▷ *vt* (*liquid*) aufsaugen; (*make blot on*) beklecksen; **to be a ~ on the landscape** ein Schandfleck in der Landschaft sein; **to ~ one's copy book** (*fig*) sich unmöglich machen
▸ **blot out** *vt* (*view*) verdecken; (*memory*) auslöschen
blotchy [ˈblɔtʃɪ] *adj* fleckig
blotting paper [ˈblɔtɪŋ-] *n* Löschpapier *nt*
blouse [blauz] *n* Bluse *f*
blow [bləu] (*pt* **blew**, *pp* **~n**) *n* (*also fig*) Schlag *m* ▷ *vi* (*wind*) wehen; (*person*) blasen ▷ *vt* (*subj: wind*) wehen; (*instrument, whistle*) blasen; (*fuse*) durchbrennen lassen; **to come to ~s** handgreiflich werden; **to ~ off course** (*ship*) vom Kurs abgetrieben werden; **to ~ one's nose** sich *dat* die Nase putzen; **to ~ a whistle** pfeifen
▸ **blow away** *vt* wegblasen ▷ *vi* wegfliegen
▸ **blow down** *vt* umwehen
▸ **blow off** *vt* wegwehen ▷ *vi* wegfliegen
▸ **blow out** *vi* ausgehen
▸ **blow over** *vi* sich legen
▸ **blow up** *vi* ausbrechen ▷ *vt* (*bridge*) in die Luft jagen; (*tyre*) aufblasen; (*Phot*) vergrößern
blow-dry [ˈbləudraɪʳ] *vt* föhnen ▷ *n*: **to have a ~** sich föhnen lassen
blowlamp [ˈbləulæmp] (*Brit*) *n* Lötlampe *f*
blown [bləun] *pp of* **blow**
blowtorch [ˈbləutɔ:tʃ] *n* = **blowlamp**
blue [blu:] *adj* blau; (*depressed*) deprimiert, niedergeschlagen ▷ *n*: **out of the ~** (*fig*) aus heiterem Himmel; **blues** *n* (*Mus*): **the ~s** der Blues; **~ film** Pornofilm *m*; **~ joke** schlüpfriger Witz *m*; **(only) once in a ~ moon** (nur) alle Jubeljahre einmal; **to have the ~s** deprimiert *or* niedergeschlagen sein
bluebell [ˈblu:bɛl] *n* Glockenblume *f*
bluebottle [ˈblu:bɔtl] *n* Schmeißfliege *f*
blue cheese *n* Blauschimmelkäse *m*
blueprint [ˈblu:prɪnt] *n* (*fig*): **a ~ (for)** ein Plan *m or* Entwurf *m* (für)
bluff [blʌf] *vi* bluffen ▷ *n* Bluff *m*; (*cliff*) Klippe *f*; (*promontory*) Felsvorsprung *m*; **to call sb's ~** es darauf ankommen lassen
blunder [ˈblʌndəʳ] *n* (dummer) Fehler *m* ▷ *vi* einen (dummen) Fehler machen; **to ~ into sb** mit jdm zusammenstoßen; **to ~ into sth** in etw *acc* (hinein)tappen
blunt [blʌnt] *adj* stumpf; (*person*) direkt; (*talk*) unverblümt ▷ *vt* stumpf machen; **~ instrument** (*Law*) stumpfer Gegenstand *m*
blur [blə:ʳ] *n* (*shape*) verschwommener Fleck *m*; (*scene etc*) verschwommenes Bild *nt*; (*memory*) verschwommene Erinnerung *f* ▷ *vt* (*vision*) trüben; (*distinction*) verwischen
blurred [blə:d] *adj* (*photograph, TV picture etc*) verschwommen; (*distinction*) verwischt
blush [blʌʃ] *vi* erröten ▷ *n* Röte *f*
blusher [ˈblʌʃəʳ] *n* Rouge *nt*
blustery [ˈblʌstərɪ] *adj* stürmisch
boar [bɔ:ʳ] *n* (*male pig*) Eber *m*; (*wild pig*) Keiler *m*
board [bɔ:d] *n* Brett *nt*; (*cardboard*) Pappe *f*; (*committee*) Ausschuss *m*; (*in firm*) Vorstand *m* ▷ *vt* (*ship*) an Bord *+gen* gehen; (*train*) einsteigen in *+acc*; **on ~** (*Naut, Aviat*) an Bord; **full/half ~** (*Brit*) Voll-/Halbpension *f*; **~ and lodging** Unterkunft und Verpflegung *f*; **to go by the ~** (*fig*) unter den Tisch fallen; **above ~** (*fig*) korrekt; **across the ~** (*fig*) allgemein; (*: criticize, reject*) pauschal
▸ **board up** *vt* mit Brettern vernageln
boarder [ˈbɔ:dəʳ] *n* Internatsschüler(in) *m(f)*
board game *n* Brettspiel *nt*
boarding card [ˈbɔ:dɪŋ-] *n* (*Aviat, Naut*) = **boarding pass**
boarding house [ˈbɔ:dɪŋ-] *n* Pension *f*
boarding pass [ˈbɔ:dɪŋ-] *n* Bordkarte *f*
boarding school [ˈbɔ:dɪŋ-] *n* Internat *nt*
boast [bəust] *vi* prahlen ▷ *vt* (*fig: possess*) sich rühmen *+gen*, besitzen; **to ~ about** *or* **of** prahlen mit
boat [bəut] *n* Boot *nt*; (*ship*) Schiff *nt*; **to go by ~** mit dem Schiff fahren; **to be in the same ~** (*fig*) in einem Boot *or* im gleichen

Boot sitzen

bob [bɔb] *vi* (*also*: **bob up and down**) sich auf und ab bewegen ▷ *n* (*Brit*: *inf*) = **shilling**

▶ **bob up** *vi* auftauchen

bobby [ˈbɔbɪ] (*Brit*: *inf*) *n* Bobby *m*, Polizist *m*

bobsleigh [ˈbɔbsleɪ] *n* Bob *m*

bode [bəud] *vi*: **to ~ well/ill (for)** ein gutes/ schlechtes Zeichen sein (für)

bodily [ˈbɔdɪlɪ] *adj* körperlich; (*needs*) leiblich ▷ *adv* (*lift, carry*) mit aller Kraft

body [ˈbɔdɪ] *n* Körper *m*; (*corpse*) Leiche *f*; (*main part*) Hauptteil *m*; (*of car*) Karosserie *f*; (*of plane*) Rumpf *m*; (*group*) Gruppe *f*; (*organization*) Organ *nt*; **ruling ~** amtierendes Organ; **in a ~** geschlossen; **a ~ of facts** Tatsachenmaterial *nt*

bodyguard [ˈbɔdɪgɑːd] *n* (*group*) Leibwache *f*; (*one person*) Leibwächter *m*

bodywork [ˈbɔdɪwəːk] *n* Karosserie *f*

bog [bɔg] *n* Sumpf *m* ▷ *vt*: **to get ~ged down** (*fig*) sich verzetteln

bogus [ˈbəugəs] *adj* (*workman etc*) falsch; (*claim*) erfunden

boil [bɔɪl] *vt, vi* kochen ▷ *n* (*Med*) Furunkel *nt* *or m*; **to come to the ~** (*Brit*): **to come to a ~** (*US*) zu kochen anfangen

▶ **boil down to** *vt fus* (*fig*) hinauslaufen auf *+acc*

▶ **boil over** *vi* überkochen

boiled egg [bɔɪld-] *n* gekochtes Ei *nt*

boiler [ˈbɔɪləʳ] *n* Boiler *m*

boiling [ˈbɔɪlɪŋ] *adj*: **I'm ~ (hot)** (*inf*) mir ist fürchterlich heiß; **it's ~** es ist eine Affenhitze (*inf*)

boiling point *n* Siedepunkt *m*

boisterous [ˈbɔɪstərəs] *adj* ausgelassen

bold [bəuld] *adj* (*brave*) mutig; (*pej*: *cheeky*) dreist; (*pattern, colours*) kräftig

bollard [ˈbɔləd] (*Brit*) *n* Poller *m*

bolt [bəult] *n* Riegel *m*; (*with nut*) Schraube *f*; (*of lightning*) Blitz(strahl) *m* ▷ *vt* (*door*) verriegeln; (*also*: **bolt together**) verschrauben; (*food*) hinunterschlingen ▷ *vi* (*run away*: *person*) weglaufen; (: *horse*) durchgehen ▷ *adv*: **~ upright** kerzengerade; **a ~ from the blue** (*fig*) ein Blitz *m* aus heiterem Himmel

bomb [bɔm] *n* Bombe *f* ▷ *vt* bombardieren; (*plant bomb in or near*) einen Bombenanschlag verüben auf *+acc*

bombard [bɔmˈbɑːd] *vt* (*also fig*) bombardieren

bomb disposal *n*: **~ unit** Bombenräumkommando *nt*; **~ expert** Bombenräumexperte *m*, Bombenräumexpertin *f*

bomber [ˈbɔməʳ] *n* Bomber *m*; (*terrorist*) Bombenattentäter(in) *m(f)*

bombing [ˈbɔmɪŋ] *n* Bombenangriff *m*

bomb scare *n* Bombenalarm *m*

bombshell [ˈbɔmʃɛl] *n* (*fig*: *revelation*) Bombe *f*

bond [bɔnd] *n* Band *nt*, Bindung *f*; (*Fin*) festverzinsliches Wertpapier *nt*, Bond *m*

bondage [ˈbɔndɪdʒ] *n* Sklaverei *f*

bone [bəun] *n* Knochen *m*; (*of fish*) Gräte *f* ▷ *vt* (*meat*) die Knochen herauslösen aus; (*fish*) entgräten; **I've got a ~ to pick with you** ich habe mit Ihnen (noch) ein Hühnchen zu rupfen

bone-dry [ˈbəunˈdraɪ] *adj* knochentrocken

bone idle *adj* stinkfaul

bone marrow *n* Knochenmark *nt*

bonfire [ˈbɔnfaɪəʳ] *n* Feuer *nt*

bonnet [ˈbɔnɪt] *n* Haube *f*; (*for baby*) Häubchen *nt*; (*Brit*: *of car*) Motorhaube *f*

bonus [ˈbəunəs] *n* Prämie *f*; (*on wages*) Zulage *f*; (*at Christmas*) Gratifikation *f*; (*fig*: *additional benefit*) Plus *nt*

bony [ˈbəunɪ] *adj* knochig; (*Med*) knöchern; (*tissue*) knochenartig; (*meat*) mit viel Knochen; (*fish*) mit viel Gräten

boo [buː] *excl* buh ▷ *vt* auspfeifen, ausbuhen

booby trap [ˈbuːbɪ-] *n* versteckte Bombe *f*; (*fig*: *joke etc*) *als Schabernack versteckt angebrachte Falle*

book [buk] *n* Buch *nt*; (*of stamps, tickets*) Heftchen *nt* ▷ *vt* bestellen; (*seat, room*) buchen, reservieren lassen; (*subj*: *traffic warden, policeman*) aufschreiben; (: *referee*) verwarnen; **books** *npl* (*Comm*: *accounts*) Bücher *pl*; **to keep the ~s** die Bücher führen; **by the ~** nach Vorschrift; **to throw the ~ at sb** jdn nach allen Regeln der Kunst fertig machen

▶ **book in** (*Brit*) *vi* sich eintragen

▶ **book up** *vt*: **all seats are ~ed up** es ist bis auf den letzten Platz ausverkauft; **the hotel is ~ed up** das Hotel ist ausgebucht

bookcase [ˈbukkeɪs] *n* Bücherregal *nt*

booking [ˈbukɪŋ] (*Brit*) *n* Bestellung *f*; (*of seat, room*) Buchung *f*, Reservierung *f*

booking office (*Brit*) *n* (*Rail*) Fahrkartenschalter *m*; (*Theat*) Vorverkaufsstelle *f*, Vorverkaufskasse *f*

book-keeping [ˈbukˈkiːpɪŋ] *n* Buchhaltung *f*, Buchführung *f*

booklet [ˈbuklɪt] *n* Broschüre *f*

bookmaker [ˈbukmeɪkəʳ] *n* Buchmacher *m*

bookmark [ˈbukmɑːk] *n* Lesezeichen *nt*; (*Comput*) Bookmark *nt* ▷ *vt* (*Comput*) ein Bookmark einrichten für, bookmarken

bookseller [ˈbuksɛləʳ] *n* Buchhändler(in) *m(f)*

bookshelf [ˈbukʃɛlf] *n* Bücherbord *nt*; **bookshelves** *npl* Bücherregal *nt*

bookshop [ˈbukʃɔp] *n* Buchhandlung *f*

book store *n* = **bookshop**

boom [buːm] *n* Donnern *nt*, Dröhnen *nt*; (*in prices, population etc*) rapider Anstieg *m*; (*Econ*) Hochkonjunktur *f*; (*busy period*) Boom *m* ▷ *vi* (*guns*) donnern; (*thunder*) hallen; (*voice*) dröhnen; (*business*) florieren

boon [buːn] *n* Segen *m*

boost [buːst] *n* Auftrieb *m* ▷ *vt* (*confidence*) stärken; (*sales, economy etc*) ankurbeln; **to give a ~ to sb/sb's spirits** jdm Auftrieb geben

booster [ˈbuːstəʳ] *n* (*Med*)

Wiederholungsimpfung *f*; (*TV*) Zusatzgleichrichter *m*; (*Elec*) Puffersatz *m*; (*also*: **booster rocket**) Booster *m*, Startrakete *f*

boot [bu:t] *n* Stiefel *m*; (*ankle boot*) hoher Schuh *m*; (*Brit*: *of car*) Kofferraum *m* ▷ *vt* (*Comput*) laden; **... to ~** (*in addition*) obendrein ...; **to give sb the ~** (*inf*) jdn rauswerfen *or* rausschmeißen

booth [bu:ð] *n* (*at fair*) Bude *f*, Stand *m*; (*telephone booth*) Zelle *f*; (*voting booth*) Kabine *f*

booze [bu:z] (*inf*) *n* Alkohol *m* ▷ *vi* saufen

border ['bɔ:dəʳ] *n* Grenze *f*; (*for flowers*) Rabatte *f*; (*on cloth etc*) Bordüre *f* ▷ *vt* (*road*) säumen; (*another country*: *also*: **border on**) grenzen an +*acc*; **Borders** *n*: **the B~s** *das Grenzgebiet zwischen England und Schottland*

▸ **border on** *vt fus* (*fig*) grenzen an +*acc*

borderline ['bɔ:dəlaɪn] *n* (*fig*): **on the ~** an der Grenze

bore [bɔ:ʳ] *pt of* **bear** ▷ *vt* bohren; (*person*) langweilen ▷ *n* Langweiler *m*; (*of gun*) Kaliber *nt*; **to be ~d** sich langweilen; **he's ~d to tears** *or* **~d to death** *or* **~d stiff** er langweilt sich zu Tode

boredom ['bɔ:dəm] *n* Langeweile *f*; (*boring quality*) Langweiligkeit *f*

boring ['bɔ:rɪŋ] *adj* langweilig

born [bɔ:n] *adj*: **to be ~** geboren werden; **I was ~ in 1960** ich bin *or* wurde 1960 geboren; **~ blind** blind geboren, von Geburt (an) blind; **a ~ comedian** ein geborener Komiker

borne [bɔ:n] *pp of* **bear**

borough ['bʌrə] *n* Bezirk *m*, Stadtgemeinde *f*

borrow ['bɔrəu] *vt*: **to ~ sth** etw borgen, sich *dat* etw leihen; (*from library*) sich *dat* etw ausleihen; **may I ~ your car?** kann ich deinen Wagen leihen?

Bosnian ['bɔznɪən] *adj* bosnisch ▷ *n* Bosnier(in) *m(f)*

bosom ['buzəm] *n* Busen *m*; (*fig*: *of family*) Schoß *m*

boss [bɔs] *n* Chef(in) *m(f)*; (*leader*) Boss *m* ▷ *vt* (*also*: **boss around, boss about**) herumkommandieren; **stop ~ing everyone about!** hör auf mit dem ständigen Herumkommandieren!

bossy ['bɔsɪ] *adj* herrisch

bosun ['bəusn] *n* Bootsmann *m*

botany ['bɔtənɪ] *n* Botanik *f*

botch [bɔtʃ] *vt* (*also*: **botch up**) verpfuschen

both [bəuθ] *adj* beide ▷ *pron* beide; (*two different things*) beides ▷ *adv*: **~ A and B** sowohl A als auch B; **~ (of them)** (alle) beide; **~ of us went, we ~ went** wir gingen beide; **they sell ~ the fabric and the finished curtains** sie verkaufen sowohl den Stoff als auch die fertigen Vorhänge

bother ['bɔðəʳ] *vt* Sorgen machen +*dat*; (*disturb*) stören ▷ *vi* (*also*: **bother o.s.**) sich *dat* Sorgen *or* Gedanken machen ▷ *n* (*trouble*) Mühe *f*; (*nuisance*) Plage *f* ▷ *excl* Mist! (*inf*); **don't ~ phoning** du brauchst nicht anzurufen; **I'm sorry to ~ you** es tut mir leid, dass ich Sie belästigen muss; **I can't be ~ed** ich habe keine Lust; **please don't ~** bitte machen Sie sich keine Umstände; **don't ~!** lass es!; **it is a ~ to have to shave every morning** es ist wirklich lästig, sich jeden Morgen rasieren zu müssen; **it's no ~** es ist kein Problem

bottle ['bɔtl] *n* Flasche *f*; (*Brit*: *inf*: *courage*) Mumm *m* ▷ *vt* in Flaschen abfüllen; (*fruit*) einmachen; **a ~ of wine/milk** eine Flasche Wein/Milch; **wine/milk ~** Wein-/Milchflasche *f*

▸ **bottle up** *vt* in sich *dat* aufstauen

bottle bank *n* Altglascontainer *m*

bottleneck ['bɔtlnɛk] *n* (*also fig*) Engpass *m*

bottle-opener ['bɔtləupnəʳ] *n* Flaschenöffner *m*

bottom ['bɔtəm] *n* Boden *m*; (*buttocks*) Hintern *m*; (*of page, list*) Ende *nt*; (*of chair*) Sitz *m*; (*of mountain, tree*) Fuß *m* ▷ *adj* (*lower*) untere(r, s); (*last*) unterste(r, s); **at the ~ of** unten an/in +*dat*; **at the ~ of the page/list** unten auf der Seite/Liste; **to be at the ~ of the class** der/die Letzte in der Klasse sein; **to get to the ~ of sth** (*fig*) einer Sache *dat* auf den Grund kommen

bough [bau] *n* Ast *m*

bought [bɔ:t] *pt, pp of* **buy**

boulder ['bəuldəʳ] *n* Felsblock *m*

bounce [bauns] *vi* (auf)springen; (*cheque*) platzen ▷ *vt* (*ball*) (auf)springen lassen; (*signal*) reflektieren ▷ *n* Aufprall *m*; **he's got plenty of ~** (*fig*) er hat viel Schwung

bouncer ['baunsəʳ] (*inf*) *n* Rausschmeißer *m*

bound [baund] *pt, pp of* **bind** ▷ *n* Sprung *m*; (*gen pl*: *limit*) Grenze *f* ▷ *vi* springen ▷ *vt* begrenzen ▷ *adj*: **~ by** gebunden durch; **to be ~ to do sth** (*obliged*) verpflichtet sein, etw zu tun; (*very likely*) etw bestimmt tun; **he's ~ to fail** es kann ihm ja gar nicht gelingen; **~ for** nach; **the area is out of ~s** das Betreten des Gebiets ist verboten

boundary ['baundrɪ] *n* Grenze *f*

bouquet ['bukeɪ] *n* (Blumen)strauß *m*; (*of wine*) Bukett *nt*, Blume *f*

bourbon ['buəbən] (*US*) *n* (*also*: **bourbon whiskey**) Bourbon *m*

bout [baut] *n* Anfall *m*; (*Boxing etc*) Kampf *m*

boutique [bu:'ti:k] *n* Boutique *f*

bow¹ [bəu] *n* Schleife *f*; (*weapon, Mus*) Bogen *m*

bow² [bau] *n* Verbeugung *f*; (*Naut*: *also*: **bows**) Bug *m* ▷ *vi* sich verbeugen; (*yield*): **to ~ to** *or* **before** sich beugen +*dat*; **to ~ to the inevitable** sich in das Unvermeidliche fügen

bowels ['bauəlz] *npl* Darm *m*; (*of the earth etc*) Innere *nt*

bowl [bəul] *n* Schüssel *f*; (*shallower*) Schale *f*; (*ball*) Kugel *f*; (*of pipe*) Kopf *m*; (*US*: *stadium*) Stadion *nt* ▷ *vi* werfen

▸ **bowl over** *vt* (*fig*) überwältigen

bow-legged ['bəu'lɛgɪd] *adj* o-beinig

bowler ['bəuləʳ] *n* Werfer(in) *m(f)*; (*Brit*: *also*: **bowler hat**) Melone *f*

bowling ['bəulɪŋ] *n* Kegeln *nt*; (*on grass*) Bowling *nt*
bowling alley *n* Kegelbahn *f*
bowling green *n* Bowlingrasen *m*
bowls [bəulz] *n* Bowling *nt*
bow tie [bəu-] *n* Fliege *f*
box [bɔks] *n* Schachtel *f*; (*cardboard box*) Karton *m*; (*crate*) Kiste *f*; (*Theat*) Loge *f*; (*Brit: Aut*) *gelb schraffierter Kreuzungsbereich*; (*on form*) Feld *nt* ▷ *vt* (in eine Schachtel *etc*) verpacken; (*fighter*) boxen ▷ *vi* boxen; **to ~ sb's ears** jdm eine Ohrfeige geben
▸ **box in** *vt* einkeilen
▸ **box off** *vt* abtrennen
boxer ['bɔksəʳ] *n* (*person, dog*) Boxer *m*
boxing ['bɔksɪŋ] *n* Boxen *nt*
Boxing Day (*Brit*) *n* zweiter Weihnachts(feier)tag *m*
boxing gloves *npl* Boxhandschuhe *pl*
boxing ring *n* Boxring *m*
box office *n* Kasse *f*
boy [bɔɪ] *n* Junge *m*
boycott ['bɔɪkɔt] *n* Boykott *m* ▷ *vt* boykottieren
boyfriend ['bɔɪfrɛnd] *n* Freund *m*
boyish ['bɔɪɪʃ] *adj* jungenhaft; (*woman*) knabenhaft
bra [brɑː] *n* BH *m*
brace [breɪs] *n* (*on teeth*) (Zahn)klammer *f*, (Zahn)spange *f*; (*tool*) (Hand)bohrer *m*; (*also*: **brace bracket**) geschweifte Klammer *f* ▷ *vt* spannen; **braces** *npl* (*Brit*) Hosenträger *pl*; **to ~ o.s.** (*for weight*) sich stützen; (*for shock*) sich innerlich vorbereiten
bracelet ['breɪslɪt] *n* Armband *nt*
bracing ['breɪsɪŋ] *adj* belebend
bracket ['brækɪt] *n* Träger *m*; (*group, range*) Gruppe *f*; (*also*: **round bracket**) (runde) Klammer *f*; (*also*: **brace bracket**) geschweifte Klammer *f*; (*also*: **square bracket**) eckige Klammer *f* ▷ *vt* (*also*: **bracket together**) zusammenfassen; (*word, phrase*) einklammern; **income ~** Einkommensgruppe *f*; **in ~s** in Klammern
brag [bræg] *vi* prahlen
braid [breɪd] *n* Borte *f*; (*of hair*) Zopf *m*
brain [breɪn] *n* Gehirn *nt*; **brains** *npl* (*Culin*) Hirn *nt*; (*intelligence*) Intelligenz *f*; **he's got ~s** er hat Köpfchen *or* Grips
brainwash ['breɪnwɔʃ] *vt* einer Gehirnwäsche *dat* unterziehen
brainy ['breɪnɪ] *adj* intelligent
braise [breɪz] *vt* schmoren
brake [breɪk] *n* Bremse *f* ▷ *vi* bremsen
brake light *n* Bremslicht *nt*
bran [bræn] *n* Kleie *f*
branch [brɑːntʃ] *n* Ast *m*; (*of family, organization*) Zweig *m*; (*Comm*) Filiale *f*, Zweigstelle *f*; (*: bank, company etc*) Geschäftsstelle *f* ▷ *vi* sich gabeln
▸ **branch out** *vi* (*fig*): **to ~ out into** seinen (Geschäfts)bereich erweitern auf *+acc*
brand [brænd] *n* (*also*: **brand name**) Marke *f*; (*fig: type*) Art *f* ▷ *vt* mit einem Brandzeichen kennzeichnen; (*fig: pej*): **to ~ sb a communist** jdn als Kommunist brandmarken
brand name *n* Markenname *m*
brand-new ['brænd'njuː] *adj* nagelneu, brandneu
brandy ['brændɪ] *n* Weinbrand *m*
brash [bræʃ] *adj* dreist
brass [brɑːs] *n* Messing *nt*; **the ~** (*Mus*) die Blechbläser *pl*
brass band *n* Blaskapelle *f*
brat [bræt] (*pej*) *n* Balg *m or nt*, Gör *nt*
brave [breɪv] *adj* mutig; (*attempt, smile*) tapfer ▷ *n* (indianischer) Krieger *m* ▷ *vt* trotzen *+dat*
bravery ['breɪvərɪ] *n* (*see adj*) Mut *m*; Tapferkeit *f*
brawl [brɔːl] *n* Schlägerei *f* ▷ *vi* sich schlagen
brazen ['breɪzn] *adj* unverschämt, dreist; (*lie*) schamlos ▷ *vt*: **to ~ it out** durchhalten
brazier ['breɪzɪəʳ] *n* (*container*) Kohlenbecken *nt*
Brazil [brə'zɪl] *n* Brasilien *nt*
Brazilian [brə'zɪljən] *adj* brasilianisch ▷ *n* Brasilianer(in) *m(f)*
breach [briːtʃ] *vt* (*defence*) durchbrechen; (*wall*) eine Bresche schlagen in *+acc* ▷ *n* (*gap*) Bresche *f*; (*estrangement*) Bruch *m*; (*breaking*): **~ of contract** Vertragsbruch *m*; **~ of the peace** öffentliche Ruhestörung *f*; **~ of trust** Vertrauensbruch *m*
bread [brɛd] *n* Brot *nt*; (*inf: money*) Moos *nt*, Kies *m*; **to earn one's daily ~** sein Brot verdienen; **to know which side one's ~ is buttered (on)** wissen, wo etwas zu holen ist
breadcrumbs ['brɛdkrʌmz] *npl* Brotkrumen *pl*; (*Culin*) Paniermehl *nt*
breadline ['brɛdlaɪn] *n*: **to be on the ~** nur das Allernotwendigste zum Leben haben
breadth [brɛtθ] *n* (*also fig*) Breite *f*
breadwinner ['brɛdwɪnəʳ] *n* Ernährer(in) *m(f)*
break [breɪk] (*pt* **broke**, *pp* **broken**) *vt* zerbrechen; (*leg, arm*) sich *dat* brechen; (*promise, record*) brechen; (*law*) verstoßen gegen ▷ *vi* zerbrechen, kaputtgehen; (*storm*) losbrechen; (*weather*) umschlagen; (*dawn*) anbrechen; (*story, news*) bekannt werden ▷ *n* Pause *f*; (*gap*) Lücke *f*; (*fracture*) Bruch *m*; (*chance*) Chance *f*, Gelegenheit *f*; (*holiday*) Urlaub *m*; **to ~ the news to sb** es jdm sagen; **to ~ even** seine (Un)kosten decken; **to ~ with sb** mit jdm brechen, sich von jdm trennen; **to ~ free** *or* **loose** sich losreißen; **to take a ~** (eine) Pause machen; (*holiday*) Urlaub machen; **without a ~** ohne Unterbrechung *or* Pause, ununterbrochen; **a lucky ~** ein Durchbruch *m*
▸ **break down** *vt* (*figures, data*) aufschlüsseln; (*door etc*) einrennen ▷ *vi* (*car*) eine Panne haben; (*machine*) kaputtgehen; (*person, resistance*) zusammenbrechen; (*talks*) scheitern
▸ **break in** *vt* (*horse*) zureiten ▷ *vi* einbrechen;

(*interrupt*) unterbrechen
▸ **break into** *vt fus* einbrechen in +*acc*
▸ **break off** *vi* abbrechen ▹ *vt* (*talks*) abbrechen; (*engagement*) lösen
▸ **break open** *vt, vi* aufbrechen
▸ **break out** *vi* ausbrechen; **to ~ out in spots/a rash** Pickel/einen Ausschlag bekommen
▸ **break through** *vi*: **the sun broke through** die Sonne kam durch ▹ *vt fus* durchbrechen
▸ **break up** *vi* (*ship*) zerbersten; (*crowd, meeting, partnership*) sich auflösen; (*marriage*) scheitern; (*friends*) sich trennen; (*Scol*) in die Ferien gehen ▹ *vt* zerbrechen; (*journey, fight etc*) unterbrechen; (*meeting*) auflösen; (*marriage*) zerstören

breakage [ˈbreɪkɪdʒ] *n* Bruch *m*; **to pay for ~s** für zerbrochene Ware *or* für Bruch bezahlen
breakdown [ˈbreɪkdaun] *n* (*Aut*) Panne *f*; (*in communications*) Zusammenbruch *m*; (*of marriage*) Scheitern *nt*; (*also*: **nervous breakdown**) (Nerven)zusammenbruch *m*; (*of statistics*) Aufschlüsselung *f*
breaker [ˈbreɪkə^r] *n* (*wave*) Brecher *m*
breakfast [ˈbrɛkfəst] *n* Frühstück *nt* ▹ *vi* frühstücken
break-in [ˈbreɪkɪn] *n* Einbruch *m*
breaking and entering [ˈbreɪkɪŋənˈɛntrɪŋ] *n* (*Law*) Einbruch *m*
breakthrough [ˈbreɪkθruː] *n* Durchbruch *m*
breakwater [ˈbreɪkwɔːtə^r] *n* Wellenbrecher *m*
breast [brɛst] *n* Brust *f*; (*of meat*) Brust *f*, Bruststück *nt*
breast-feed [ˈbrɛstfiːd] (*irreg: like* **feed**) *vt, vi* stillen
breath [brɛθ] *n* Atem *m*; (*a breath*) Atemzug *m*; **to go out for a ~ of air** an die frische Luft gehen, frische Luft schnappen gehen; **out of ~** außer Atem, atemlos; **to get one's ~ back** wieder zu Atem kommen
Breathalyser® [ˈbrɛθəlaɪzə^r] *n* Promillemesser *m*
breathe [briːð] *vt, vi* atmen; **I won't ~ a word about it** ich werde kein Sterbenswörtchen darüber sagen
▸ **breathe in** *vt, vi* einatmen
▸ **breathe out** *vt, vi* ausatmen
breather [ˈbriːðə^r] *n* Atempause *f*, Verschnaufpause *f*
breathing [ˈbriːðɪŋ] *n* Atmung *f*
breathless [ˈbrɛθlɪs] *adj* atemlos, außer Atem; (*Med*) an Atemnot leidend; **I was ~ with excitement** die Aufregung verschlug mir den Atem
breathtaking [ˈbrɛθteɪkɪŋ] *adj* atemberaubend
breath test *n* Atemalkoholtest *m*
bred [brɛd] *pt, pp of* **breed**
breed [briːd] (*pt, pp* **bred**) *vt* züchten; (*fig: give rise to*) erzeugen; (*: hate, suspicion*) hervorrufen ▹ *vi* Junge *pl* haben ▹ *n* Rasse *f*; (*type, class*) Art *f*
breeding [ˈbriːdɪŋ] *n* Erziehung *f*
breeze [briːz] *n* Brise *f*
breezy [ˈbriːzɪ] *adj* (*manner, tone*) munter; (*weather*) windig
brevity [ˈbrɛvɪtɪ] *n* Kürze *f*
brew [bruː] *vt* (*tea*) aufbrühen, kochen; (*beer*) brauen ▹ *vi* (*tea*) ziehen; (*beer*) gären; (*storm, fig*) sich zusammenbrauen
brewery [ˈbruːərɪ] *n* Brauerei *f*
bribe [braɪb] *n* Bestechungsgeld *nt* ▹ *vt* bestechen; **to ~ sb to do sth** jdn bestechen, damit er etw tut
bribery [ˈbraɪbərɪ] *n* Bestechung *f*
bric-a-brac [ˈbrɪkəbræk] *n* Nippes *pl*, Nippsachen *pl*
brick [brɪk] *n* Ziegelstein *m*, Backstein *m*; (*of ice cream*) Block *m*
bricklayer [ˈbrɪkleɪə^r] *n* Maurer(in) *m(f)*
bridal [ˈbraɪdl] *adj* (*gown, veil etc*) Braut-
bride [braɪd] *n* Braut *f*
bridegroom [ˈbraɪdgruːm] *n* Bräutigam *m*
bridesmaid [ˈbraɪdzmeɪd] *n* Brautjungfer *f*
bridge [brɪdʒ] *n* Brücke *f*; (*Naut*) (Kommando)brücke *f*; (*of nose*) Sattel *m*; (*Cards*) Bridge *nt* ▹ *vt* (*river*) eine Brücke schlagen *or* bauen über +*acc*; (*fig*) überbrücken
bridle [ˈbraɪdl] *n* Zaum *m* ▹ *vt* aufzäumen ▹ *vi*: **to ~ (at)** sich entrüstet wehren (gegen)
bridle path *n* Reitweg *m*
brief [briːf] *adj* kurz ▹ *n* (*Law*) Auftrag *m*; (*task*) Aufgabe *f* ▹ *vt* instruieren; (*Mil etc*): **to ~ sb (about)** jdn instruieren (über +*acc*); **briefs** *npl* Slip *m*; **in ~ ...** kurz (gesagt) ...
briefcase [ˈbriːfkeɪs] *n* Aktentasche *f*
briefing [ˈbriːfɪŋ] *n* Briefing *nt*, Lagebespechung *f*
briefly [ˈbriːflɪ] *adv* kurz; **to glimpse sth ~** einen flüchtigen Blick von etw erhaschen
brigadier [brɪgəˈdɪə^r] *n* Brigadegeneral *m*
bright [braɪt] *adj* (*light, room*) hell; (*weather*) heiter; (*clever*) intelligent; (*lively*) heiter, fröhlich; (*colour*) leuchtend; (*outlook, future*) glänzend; **to look on the ~ side** die Dinge von der positiven Seite betrachten
brighten [ˈbraɪtn] (*also*: **brighten up**) *vt* aufheitern; (*event*) beleben ▹ *vi* (*weather, face*) sich aufheitern; (*person*) fröhlicher werden; (*prospects*) sich verbessern
brilliance [ˈbrɪljəns] *n* Strahlen *nt*; (*of person*) Genialität *f*, Brillanz *f*; (*of talent, skill*) Großartigkeit *f*
brilliant [ˈbrɪljənt] *adj* strahlend; (*person, idea*) genial, brillant; (*career*) großartig; (*inf: holiday etc*) fantastisch
brim [brɪm] *n* Rand *m*; (*of hat*) Krempe *f*
brine [braɪn] *n* Lake *f*
bring [brɪŋ] (*pt, pp* **brought**) *vt* bringen; (*with you*) mitbringen; **to ~ sth to an end** etw zu Ende bringen; **I can't ~ myself to fire him** ich kann es nicht über mich bringen, ihn zu entlassen
▸ **bring about** *vt* herbeiführen
▸ **bring back** *vt* (*restore*) wiedereinführen;

(*return*) zurückbringen
▸ **bring down** *vt* (*government*) zu Fall bringen; (*plane*) herunterholen; (*price*) senken
▸ **bring forward** *vt* (*meeting*) vorverlegen; (*proposal*) vorbringen; (*Bookkeeping*) übertragen
▸ **bring in** *vt* (*money*) (ein)bringen; (*include*) einbeziehen; (*person*) einschalten; (*legislation*) einbringen; (*verdict*) fällen
▸ **bring off** *vt* (*plan*) durchführen; (*deal*) zustande bringen
▸ **bring out** *vt* herausholen; (*meaning, book, album*) herausbringen
▸ **bring round** *vt* (*after faint*) wieder zu Bewusstsein bringen
▸ **bring up** *vt* heraufbringen; (*educate*) erziehen; (*question, subject*) zur Sprache bringen; (*food*) erbrechen

brink [brɪŋk] *n* Rand *m*; **on the ~ of doing sth** nahe daran, etw zu tun; **she was on the ~ of tears** sie war den Tränen nahe

brisk [brɪsk] *adj* (*abrupt: person, tone*) forsch; (*pace*) flott; (*trade*) lebhaft, rege; **to go for a ~ walk** einen ordentlichen Spaziergang machen; **business is ~** das Geschäft ist rege

bristle ['brɪsl] *n* Borste *f*; (*of beard*) Stoppel *f* ▹ *vi* zornig werden; **bristling with** strotzend von

Brit [brɪt] (*inf*) *n* (*= British person*) Brite *m*, Britin *f*

Britain ['brɪtən] *n* (*also*: **Great Britain**) Großbritannien *nt*

British ['brɪtɪʃ] *adj* britisch ▹ *npl*: **the ~** die Briten *pl*

British Isles *npl*: **the ~** die Britischen Inseln

British Rail *n* *britische Eisenbahngesellschaft*

Briton ['brɪtən] *n* Brite *m*, Britin *f*

Brittany ['brɪtənɪ] *n* die Bretagne

brittle ['brɪtl] *adj* spröde; (*glass*) zerbrechlich; (*bones*) schwach

broach [brəutʃ] *vt* (*subject*) anschneiden

broad [brɔːd] *adj* breit; (*general*) allgemein; (*accent*) stark ▹ *n* (*US: inf*) Frau *f*; **in ~ daylight** am helllichten Tag; **~ hint** deutlicher Wink *m*

broadband ['brɔːdbænd] (*Comput*) *adj* Breitband- ▹ *n* Breitband *nt*

broad bean *n* dicke Bohne *f*, Saubohne *f*

broadcast ['brɔːdkɑːst] (*pt, pp* **~**) *n* Sendung *f* ▹ *vt, vi* senden

broaden ['brɔːdn] *vt* erweitern ▹ *vi* breiter werden, sich verbreitern; **to ~ one's mind** seinen Horizont erweitern

broadly ['brɔːdlɪ] *adv* (*in general terms*) in großen Zügen; **~ speaking** allgemein *or* generell gesagt

broad-minded ['brɔːd'maɪndɪd] *adj* tolerant

broccoli ['brɔkəlɪ] *n* Brokkoli *pl*, Spargelkohl *m*

brochure ['brəuʃjuər] *n* Broschüre *f*

broil [brɔɪl] (*US*) *vt* grillen

broke [brəuk] *pt of* **break** ▹ *adj* (*inf*) pleite; **to go ~** pleitegehen

broken ['brəukn] *pp of* **break** ▹ *adj* zerbrochen; (*machine: also*: **broken down**) kaputt; (*promise, vow*) gebrochen; **a ~ leg** ein gebrochenes Bein; **a ~ marriage** eine gescheiterte Ehe; **a ~ home** zerrüttete Familienverhältnisse *pl*; **in ~ English/German** in gebrochenem Englisch/Deutsch

broker ['brəukər] *n* Makler(in) *m(f)*

brolly ['brɔlɪ] (*Brit: inf*) *n* (Regen)schirm *m*

bronchitis [brɔŋ'kaɪtɪs] *n* Bronchitis *f*

bronze [brɔnz] *n* Bronze *f*

brooch [brəutʃ] *n* Brosche *f*

brood [bruːd] *n* Brut *f* ▹ *vi* (*hen*) brüten; (*person*) grübeln
▸ **brood on** *vt fus* nachgrübeln über *+acc*
▸ **brood over** *vt fus* = **brood on**

broom [brum] *n* Besen *m*; (*Bot*) Ginster *m*

broomstick ['brumstɪk] *n* Besenstiel *m*

broth [brɔθ] *n* Suppe *f*, Fleischbrühe *f*

brothel ['brɔθl] *n* Bordell *nt*

brother ['brʌðər] *n* Bruder *m*; (*in trade union, society etc*) Kollege *m*

brother-in-law ['brʌðərɪn'lɔː] *n* Schwager *m*

brought [brɔːt] *pt, pp of* **bring**

brow [brau] *n* Stirn *f*; (*eyebrow*) (Augen)braue *f*; (*of hill*) (Berg)kuppe *f*

brown [braun] *adj* braun ▹ *n* Braun *nt* ▹ *vt* (*Culin*) (an)bräunen; **to go ~** braun werden

brown bread *n* Graubrot *nt*, Mischbrot *nt*

Brownie ['braunɪ] *n* (*also*: **Brownie Guide**) Wichtel *m*

brown paper *n* Packpapier *nt*

brown rice *n* Naturreis *m*

brown sugar *n* brauner Zucker *m*

browse [brauz] *vi* (*in shop*) sich umsehen; (*animal*) weiden; (*: deer*) äsen ▹ *vti* (*Comput*) browsen ▹ *n*: **to have a ~ (around)** sich umsehen; **to ~ through a book** in einem Buch schmökern

browser ['brauzər] *n* (*Comput*) Browser *m*

bruise [bruːz] *n* blauer Fleck *m*, Bluterguss *m*; (*on fruit*) Druckstelle *f* ▹ *vt* (*arm, leg etc*) sich *dat* stoßen; (*person*) einen blauen Fleck schlagen; (*fruit*) beschädigen ▹ *vi* (*fruit*) eine Druckstelle bekommen; **to ~ one's arm** sich *dat* den Arm stoßen, sich *dat* einen blauen Fleck am Arm holen

brunette [bruː'nɛt] *n* Brünette *f*

brunt [brʌnt] *n*: **to bear the ~ of** die volle Wucht *+gen* tragen

brush [brʌʃ] *n* Bürste *f*; (*for painting, shaving etc*) Pinsel *m*; (*quarrel*) Auseinandersetzung *f* ▹ *vt* fegen; (*groom*) bürsten; (*teeth*) putzen; (*also*: **brush against**) streifen; **to have a ~ with sb** (*verbally*) sich mit jdm streiten; (*physically*) mit jdm aneinandergeraten; **to have a ~ with the police** mit der Polizei aneinandergeraten
▸ **brush aside** *vt* abtun
▸ **brush past** *vt* streifen
▸ **brush up** *vt* auffrischen

brushwood ['brʌʃwud] *n* Reisig *nt*

Brussels ['brʌslz] *n* Brüssel *nt*

brutal ['bruːtl] *adj* brutal

brute [bru:t] *n* brutaler Kerl *m*; (*animal*) Tier *nt* ▷ *adj*: **by ~ force** mit roher Gewalt
BSE *n abbr* (= *bovine spongiform encephalopathy*) BSE *f*
bubble ['bʌbl] *n* Blase *f* ▷ *vi* sprudeln; (*sparkle*) perlen; (*fig: person*) übersprudeln
bubble bath *n* Schaumbad *nt*
bubble gum *n* Bubblegum *m*
buck [bʌk] *n* (*rabbit*) Rammler *m*; (*deer*) Bock *m*; (*US: inf*) Dollar *m* ▷ *vi* bocken; **to pass the ~** die Verantwortung abschieben; **to pass the ~ to sb** jdm die Verantwortung zuschieben
▸ **buck up** *vi* (*cheer up*) aufleben ▷ *vt*: **to ~ one's ideas up** sich zusammenreißen
bucket ['bʌkɪt] *n* Eimer *m* ▷ *vi* (*Brit: inf*): **the rain is ~ing (down)** es gießt *or* schüttet (wie aus Kübeln)
buckle ['bʌkl] *n* Schnalle *f* ▷ *vt* zuschnallen; (*wheel*) verbiegen ▷ *vi* sich verbiegen
▸ **buckle down** *vi* sich dahinter klemmen; **to ~ down to sth** sich hinter etw *acc* klemmen
bud [bʌd] *n* Knospe *f* ▷ *vi* knospen, Knospen treiben
Buddhism ['budɪzəm] *n* Buddhismus *m*
Buddhist ['budɪst] *adj* buddhistisch ▷ *n* Buddhist(in) *m(f)*
budding ['bʌdɪŋ] *adj* angehend
buddy ['bʌdɪ] (*US*) *n* Kumpel *m*
budge [bʌdʒ] *vt* (von der Stelle) bewegen; (*fig*) zum Nachgeben bewegen ▷ *vi* sich von der Stelle rühren; (*fig*) nachgeben
budgerigar ['bʌdʒərɪgɑːʳ] *n* Wellensittich *m*
budget ['bʌdʒɪt] *n* Budget *nt*, Etat *m*, Haushalt *m* ▷ *vi* Haus halten, haushalten, wirtschaften; **I'm on a tight ~** ich habe nicht viel Geld zur Verfügung; **she works out her ~ every month** sie macht (sich *dat*) jeden Monat einen Haushaltsplan; **to ~ for sth** etw kostenmäßig einplanen
budgie ['bʌdʒɪ] *n* = **budgerigar**
buff [bʌf] *adj* gelbbraun ▷ *n* (*inf*) Fan *m*
buffalo ['bʌfələu] (*pl* **~** *or* **buffaloes**) *n* (*Brit*) Büffel *m*; (*US*) Bison *m*
buffer ['bʌfəʳ] *n* (*Comput*) Puffer *m*, Pufferspeicher *m*; (*Rail*) Prellbock *m*; (*fig*) Polster *nt*
buffet[1] ['bufeɪ] (*Brit*) *n* Büfett *nt*, Bahnhofsrestaurant *nt*; (*food*) kaltes Buffet *nt*
buffet[2] ['bʌfɪt] *vt* (*subj: sea*) hin und her werfen; (*: wind*) schütteln
buffet car (*Brit*) *n* Speisewagen *m*
bug [bʌg] *n* (*esp US*) Insekt *nt*; (*Comput: of program*) Programmfehler *m*; (*: of equipment*) Fehler *m*; (*fig: germ*) Bazillus *m*; (*hidden microphone*) Wanze *f* ▷ *vt* (*inf*) nerven; (*telephone etc*) abhören; (*room*) verwanzen; **I've got the travel ~** (*fig*) mich hat die Reiselust gepackt
buggy ['bʌgɪ] *n* (*for baby*) Sportwagen *m*
bugle ['bju:gl] *n* Bügelhorn *nt*
build [bɪld] (*pt, pp* **built**) *n* Körperbau *m* ▷ *vt* bauen
▸ **build on** *vt fus* (*fig*) aufbauen auf *+dat*
▸ **build up** *vt* aufbauen; (*production*) steigern; (*morale*) stärken; (*stocks*) anlegen; **don't ~ your hopes up too soon** mach dir nicht zu früh Hoffnungen
builder ['bɪldəʳ] *n* Bauunternehmer *m*
building ['bɪldɪŋ] *n* (*industry*) Bauindustrie *f*; (*construction*) Bau *m*; (*structure*) Gebäude *nt*, Bau
building site *n* Baustelle *f*
building society (*Brit*) *n* Bausparkasse *f*
built [bɪlt] *pt, pp of* **build** ▷ *adj*: **~-in** eingebaut, Einbau-; (*safeguards*) eingebaut; **well-~** gut gebaut
bulb [bʌlb] *n* (Blumen)zwiebel *f*; (*Elec*) (Glüh)birne *f*
Bulgaria [bʌl'gɛərɪə] *n* Bulgarien *nt*
Bulgarian [bʌl'gɛərɪən] *adj* bulgarisch ▷ *n* Bulgare *m*, Bulgarin *f*; (*Ling*) Bulgarisch *nt*
bulge [bʌldʒ] *n* Wölbung *f*; (*in birth rate, sales*) Zunahme *f* ▷ *vi* (*pocket*) prall gefüllt sein; (*cheeks*) voll sein; (*file*) (zum Bersten) voll sein; **to be bulging with** prall gefüllt sein mit
bulimia [bə'lɪmɪə] *n* Bulimie *f*
bulk [bʌlk] *n* (*of thing*) massige Form *f*; (*of person*) massige Gestalt *f*; **in ~** im Großen, en gros; **the ~ of** der Großteil *+gen*
bulky ['bʌlkɪ] *adj* sperrig
bull [bul] *n* Stier *m*; (*male elephant or whale*) Bulle *m*; (*Stock Exchange*) Haussier *m*, Haussespekulant *m*; (*Rel*) Bulle *f*
bulldog ['buldɔg] *n* Bulldogge *f*
bulldozer ['buldəuzəʳ] *n* Bulldozer *m*, Planierraupe *f*
bullet ['bulɪt] *n* Kugel *f*
bulletin ['bulɪtɪn] *n* (*TV etc*) Kurznachrichten *pl*; (*journal*) Bulletin *nt*
bulletin board *n* (*Comput*) Schwarzes Brett *nt*
bulletproof ['bulɪtpru:f] *adj* kugelsicher
bullfight ['bulfaɪt] *n* Stierkampf *m*
bullfighter ['bulfaɪtəʳ] *n* Stierkämpfer *m*
bullfighting ['bulfaɪtɪŋ] *n* Stierkampf *m*
bullion ['buljən] *n*: **gold/silver ~** Barrengold *nt*/-silber *nt*
bullock ['bulək] *n* Ochse *m*
bullring ['bulrɪŋ] *n* Stierkampfarena *f*
bull's-eye ['bulzaɪ] *n* (*on a target*): **the ~** der Scheibenmittelpunkt, das Schwarze
bully ['bulɪ] *n* Tyrann *m* ▷ *vt* tyrannisieren; (*frighten*) einschüchtern
bum [bʌm] (*inf*) *n* Hintern *m*; (*esp US: good-for-nothing*) Rumtreiber *m*; (*tramp*) Penner *m*
▸ **bum around** (*inf*) *vi* herumgammeln
bumblebee ['bʌmblbi:] *n* Hummel *f*
bump [bʌmp] *n* Zusammenstoß *m*; (*jolt*) Erschütterung *f*; (*swelling*) Beule *f*; (*on road*) Unebenheit *f* ▷ *vt* stoßen; (*car*) eine Delle fahren in *+acc*
▸ **bump along** *vi* entlangholpern
▸ **bump into** *vt fus* (*obstacle*) stoßen gegen; (*inf: person*) treffen
bumper ['bʌmpəʳ] *n* Stoßstange *f* ▷ *adj*: **~ crop, ~ harvest** Rekordernte *f*
bumper cars *npl* Autoskooter *pl*
bumpy ['bʌmpɪ] *adj* holperig; **it was a ~**

flight/ride während des Fluges/auf der Fahrt wurden wir tüchtig durchgerüttelt

bun [bʌn] *n* Brötchen *nt*; (*of hair*) Knoten *m*

bunch [bʌntʃ] *n* Strauß *m*; (*of keys*) Bund *m*; (*of bananas*) Büschel *nt*; (*of people*) Haufen *m*; **bunches** *npl* (*in hair*) Zöpfe *pl*; **~ of grapes** Weintraube *f*

bundle ['bʌndl] *n* Bündel *nt* ▷ *vt* (*also*: **bundle up**) bündeln; (*put*): **to ~ sth into** etw stopfen *or* packen in *+acc*; **to ~ sb into** jdn schaffen in *+acc*

▶ **bundle off** *vt* schaffen

▶ **bundle out** *vt* herausschaffen

bungalow ['bʌŋgələu] *n* Bungalow *m*

bungee jumping ['bʌndʒi:'dʒʌmpɪŋ] *n* Bungeespringen *nt*

bungle ['bʌŋgl] *vt* verpfuschen

bunion ['bʌnjən] *n* entzündeter Ballen *m*

bunk [bʌŋk] *n* Bett *nt*, Koje *f*; **to do a ~** (*inf*) abhauen

▶ **bunk off** (*inf*) *vi* abhauen

bunk beds *npl* Etagenbett *nt*

bunker ['bʌŋkə^r] *n* Kohlenbunker *m*; (*Mil, Golf*) Bunker *m*

bunny ['bʌnɪ] *n* (*also*: **bunny rabbit**) Hase *m*, Häschen *nt*

bunting ['bʌntɪŋ] *n* (*flags*) Wimpel *pl*, Fähnchen *pl*

buoy [bɔɪ] *n* Boje *f*

▶ **buoy up** *vt* (*fig*) Auftrieb geben *+dat*

buoyant ['bɔɪənt] *adj* (*ship, object*) schwimmfähig; (*market*) fest; (*economy*) stabil; (*prices, currency*) fest, stabil; (*person, nature*) heiter

burden ['bə:dn] *n* Belastung *f*; (*load*) Last *f* ▷ *vt*: **to ~ sb with sth** jdn mit etw belasten; **to be a ~ to sb** jdm zur Last fallen

bureau ['bjuərəu] (*pl* **~x**) *n* (*Brit: writing desk*) Sekretär *m*; (*US: chest of drawers*) Kommode *f*; (*office*) Büro *nt*

bureaucracy [bjuə'rɔkrəsɪ] *n* Bürokratie *f*

bureaucrat ['bjuərəkræt] *n* Bürokrat(in) *m(f)*

bureaux ['bjuərəuz] *npl of* **bureau**

burger ['bə:gə^r] (*inf*) *n* Hamburger *m*

burglar ['bə:glə^r] *n* Einbrecher(in) *m(f)*

burglar alarm *n* Alarmanlage *f*

burglary ['bə:glərɪ] *n* Einbruch *m*

Burgundy ['bə:gəndɪ] *n* Burgund *nt*

burial ['bɛrɪəl] *n* Beerdigung *f*

burly ['bə:lɪ] *adj* kräftig, stämmig

Burma ['bə:mə] *n* Birma *nt*, Burma *nt*

burn [bə:n] (*pt, pp* **burned** *or* **~t**) *vt* verbrennen; (*fuel*) als Brennstoff verwenden; (*food*) anbrennen lassen; (*house etc*) niederbrennen ▷ *vi* brennen; (*food*) anbrennen ▷ *n* Verbrennung *f*; **the cigarette ~t a hole in her dress** die Zigarette brannte ein Loch in ihr Kleid; **I've ~t myself!** ich habe mich verbrannt!

▶ **burn down** *vt* abbrennen

▶ **burn out** *vt*: **to ~ o.s. out** (*writer etc*) sich völlig verausgaben; **the fire ~t itself out** das Feuer brannte aus

burner ['bə:nə^r] *n* Brenner *m*

burning ['bə:nɪŋ] *adj* brennend; (*sand, desert*) glühend heiß

burnt [bə:nt] *pt, pp of* **burn**

burp [bə:p] (*inf*) *n* Rülpser *m* ▷ *vt* (*baby*) aufstoßen lassen ▷ *vi* rülpsen

burrow ['bʌrəu] *n* Bau *m* ▷ *vi* graben; (*rummage*) wühlen

bursary ['bə:sərɪ] (*Brit*) *n* Stipendium *nt*

burst [bə:st] (*pt, pp* **~**) *vt* zum Platzen bringen, platzen lassen ▷ *vi* platzen ▷ *n* Salve *f*; (*also*: **burst pipe**) (Rohr)bruch *m*; **the river has ~ its banks** der Fluss ist über die Ufer getreten; **to ~ into flames** in Flammen aufgehen; **to ~ into tears** in Tränen ausbrechen; **to ~ out laughing** in Lachen ausbrechen; **~ blood vessel** geplatzte Ader *f*; **to be ~ing with** zum Bersten voll sein mit; (*pride*) fast platzen vor *+dat*; **to ~ open** aufspringen; **a ~ of energy** ein Ausbruch *m* von Energie; **a ~ of enthusiasm** ein Begeisterungsausbruch *m*; **a ~ of speed** ein Spurt *m*; **~ of laughter** Lachsalve *f*; **~ of applause** Beifallssturm *m*

▶ **burst in on** *vt fus*: **to ~ in on sb** bei jdm hereinplatzen

▶ **burst into** *vt fus* (*into room*) platzen in *+acc*

▶ **burst out of** *vt fus* (*of room*) stürmen *or* stürzen aus

bury ['bɛrɪ] *vt* begraben; (*at funeral*) beerdigen; **to ~ one's face in one's hands** das Gesicht in den Händen vergraben; **to ~ one's head in the sand** (*fig*) den Kopf in den Sand stecken; **to ~ the hatchet** (*fig*) das Kriegsbeil begraben

bus [bʌs] *n* (Auto)bus *m*, (Omni)bus *m*; (*double decker*) Doppeldecker *m* (*inf*)

bush [buʃ] *n* Busch *m*, Strauch *m*; (*scrubland*) Busch; **to beat about the ~** um den heißen Brei herumreden

bushy ['buʃɪ] *adj* buschig

busily ['bɪzɪlɪ] *adv* eifrig; **to be ~ doing sth** eifrig etw tun

business ['bɪznɪs] *n* (*matter*) Angelegenheit *f*; (*trading*) Geschäft *nt*; (*firm*) Firma *f*, Betrieb *m*; (*occupation*) Beruf *m*; **to be away on ~** geschäftlich unterwegs sein; **I'm here on ~** ich bin geschäftlich hier; **he's in the insurance/transport ~** er arbeitet in der Versicherungs-/Transportbranche; **to do ~ with sb** Geschäfte *pl* mit jdm machen; **it's my ~ to ...** es ist meine Aufgabe, zu ...; **it's none of my ~** es geht mich nichts an; **he means ~** er meint es ernst

businesslike ['bɪznɪslaɪk] *adj* geschäftsmäßig

businessman ['bɪznɪsmən] (*irreg: like* **man**) *n* Geschäftsmann *m*

business trip *n* Geschäftsreise *f*

businesswoman ['bɪznɪswumən] (*irreg: like* **woman**) *n* Geschäftsfrau *f*

busker ['bʌskə^r] (*Brit*) *n* Straßenmusikant(in) *m(f)*

bus shelter *n* Wartehäuschen *nt*

bus station *n* Busbahnhof *m*
bus stop *n* Bushaltestelle *f*
bust [bʌst] *n* Busen *m*; (*measurement*) Oberweite *f*; (*sculpture*) Büste *f* ▷ *adj* (*inf*) kaputt ▷ *vt* (*inf*) verhaften; **to go ~** pleitegehen
bustle ['bʌsl] *n* Betrieb *m* ▷ *vi* eilig herumlaufen
bustling ['bʌslɪŋ] *adj* belebt
busy ['bɪzɪ] *adj* (*person*) beschäftigt; (*shop, street*) belebt; (*Tel: esp US*) besetzt ▷ *vt*: **to ~ o.s. with** sich beschäftigen mit; **he's a ~ man** er ist ein viel beschäftigter Mann; **he's ~** er hat (zurzeit) viel zu tun
busybody ['bɪzɪbɔdɪ] *n*: **to be a ~** sich ständig einmischen
busy signal (*US*) *n* (*Tel*) Besetztzeichen *nt*
but [bʌt] *conj* **1** (*yet*) aber; **not blue but red** nicht blau, sondern rot; **he's not very bright, but he's hard-working** er ist nicht sehr intelligent, aber er ist fleißig
2 (*however*): **I'd love to come, but I'm busy** ich würde gern kommen, bin aber beschäftigt
3 (*showing disagreement, surprise etc*): **but that's far too expensive!** aber das ist viel zu teuer!; **but that's fantastic!** das ist doch toll!
▷ *prep* (*apart from, except*) außer *+dat*; **nothing but trouble** nichts als Ärger; **no-one but him can do it** keiner außer ihm kann es machen; **but for you** wenn Sie nicht gewesen wären; **but for your help** ohne Ihre Hilfe; **I'll do anything but that** ich mache alles, nur nicht das; **the last house but one** das vorletzte Haus; **the next street but one** die übernächste Straße
▷ *adv* (*just, only*) nur; **she's but a child** sie ist doch noch ein Kind; **I can but try** ich kann es ja versuchen
butcher ['butʃəʳ] *n* Fleischer *m*, Metzger *m*; (*pej: murderer*) Schlächter *m* ▷ *vt* schlachten; (*prisoners etc*) abschlachten
butcher's ['butʃəz], **butcher's shop** *n* Fleischerei *f*, Metzgerei *f*
butler ['bʌtləʳ] *n* Butler *m*
butt [bʌt] *n* großes Fass *nt*, Tonne *f*; (*thick end*) dickes Ende *nt*; (*of gun*) Kolben *m*; (*of cigarette*) Kippe *f*; (*Brit: fig: target*) Zielscheibe *f*; (*US: inf!*) Arsch *m* ▷ *vt* (*goat*) mit den Hörnern stoßen; (*person*) mit dem Kopf stoßen
▸ **butt in** *vi* sich einmischen, dazwischenfunken (*inf*)
butter ['bʌtəʳ] *n* Butter *f* ▷ *vt* buttern
buttercup ['bʌtəkʌp] *n* Butterblume *f*
butterfly ['bʌtəflaɪ] *n* Schmetterling *m*; (*Swimming: also:* **butterfly stroke**) Schmetterlingsstil *m*, Butterfly *m*
buttocks ['bʌtəks] *npl* Gesäß *nt*
button ['bʌtn] *n* Knopf *m*; (*US: badge*) Plakette *f* ▷ *vt* (*also:* **button up**) zuknöpfen ▷ *vi* geknöpft werden
buttress ['bʌtrɪs] *n* Strebepfeiler *m*
buy [baɪ] (*pt, pp* **bought**) *vt* kaufen; (*company*) aufkaufen ▷ *n* Kauf *m*; **that was a good/bad ~** das war ein guter/schlechter Kauf; **to ~ sb sth** jdm etw kaufen; **to ~ sth from sb** etw bei jdm kaufen; (*from individual*) jdm etw abkaufen; **to ~ sb a drink** jdm einen ausgeben (*inf*)
▸ **buy back** *vt* zurückkaufen
▸ **buy in** (*Brit*) *vt* einkaufen
▸ **buy into** (*Brit*) *vt fus* sich einkaufen in *+acc*
▸ **buy off** *vt* kaufen
▸ **buy out** *vt* (*partner*) auszahlen; (*business*) aufkaufen
▸ **buy up** *vt* aufkaufen
buyer ['baɪəʳ] *n* Käufer(in) *m(f)*; (*Comm*) Einkäufer(in) *m(f)*
buzz [bʌz] *vi* summen, brummen; (*saw*) kreischen ▷ *vt* rufen; (*with buzzer*) (mit dem Summer) rufen; (*Aviat: plane, building*) dicht vorbeifliegen an *+dat* ▷ *n* Summen *nt*, Brummen *nt*; (*inf*): **to give sb a ~** jdn anrufen; **my head is ~ing** mir schwirrt der Kopf
▸ **buzz off** (*inf*) *vi* abhauen
buzzer ['bʌzəʳ] *n* Summer *m*
buzz word (*inf*) *n* Modewort *nt*
by [baɪ] *prep* **1** (*referring to cause, agent*) von *+dat*, durch *+acc*; **killed by lightning** vom Blitz *or* durch einen Blitz getötet; **a painting by Picasso** ein Bild von Picasso
2 (*referring to method, manner, means*): **by bus/car/train** mit dem Bus/Auto/Zug; **to pay by cheque** mit *or* per Scheck bezahlen; **by saving hard, he was able to ...** indem er eisern sparte, konnte er ...
3 (*via, through*) über *+acc*; **we came by Dover** wir sind über Dover gekommen
4 (*close to*) bei *+dat*, an *+dat*; **the house by the river** das Haus am Fluss
5 (*past*) an ... *dat* vorbei; **she rushed by me** sie eilte an mir vorbei
6 (*not later than*) bis *+acc*; **by 4 o'clock** bis 4 Uhr; **by this time tomorrow** morgen um diese Zeit
7 (*amount*): **by the kilo/metre** kilo-/meterweise; **to be paid by the hour** stundenweise bezahlt werden
8 (*Math, measure*): **to divide by 3** durch 3 teilen; **to multiply by 3** mit 3 malnehmen; **it missed me by inches** es hat mich um Zentimeter verfehlt
9 (*according to*): **to play by the rules** sich an die Regeln halten; **it's all right by me** von mir aus ist es in Ordnung
10: (all) by myself/himself *etc* (ganz) allein
11: by the way übrigens
▷ *adv* **1** *see* **go, pass** *etc*
2: by and by irgendwann
3: by and large im Großen und Ganzen
bye ['baɪ], **bye-bye** ['baɪ'baɪ] *excl* (auf) Wiedersehen, tschüss (*inf*)
bye-law ['baɪlɔ:] *n see* **by-law**
by-election ['baɪɪlɛkʃən] (*Brit*) *n* Nachwahl *f*
bygone ['baɪgɔn] *adj* (längst) vergangen

▷ *n*: **let ~s be ~s** wir sollten die Vergangenheit ruhen lassen

by-law ['baɪlɔː] *n* Verordnung *f*

bypass ['baɪpɑːs] *n* Umgehungsstraße *f*; (*Med*) Bypassoperation *f* ▷ *vt* (*also fig*) umgehen

by-product ['baɪprɔdʌkt] *n* Nebenprodukt *nt*

bystander ['baɪstændəʳ] *n* Zuschauer(in) *m(f)*

byte [baɪt] *n* (*Comput*) Byte *nt*

byword ['baɪwəːd] *n*: **to be a ~ for** der Inbegriff *+gen* sein, gleichbedeutend sein mit

Cc

C¹, **c¹** [siː] *n* (*letter*) C *nt*, c *nt*; (*Scol*) ≈ Drei *f*, ≈ Befriedigend *nt*; **C for Charlie** ≈ C wie Cäsar
C² [siː] *n* (*Mus*) C *nt*, c *nt*
C³ [siː] *abbr* = **Celsius; centigrade**
c² *abbr* = **century**; (= *circa*) ca.; (*US etc*: = *cent(s)*) Cent
CA *n abbr* (*Brit*) = **chartered accountant** ▷ *abbr* = **Central America**; (*US*: *Post*: = *California*)
cab [kæb] *n* Taxi *nt*; (*of truck, train etc*) Führerhaus *nt*; (*horse-drawn*) Droschke *f*
cabaret ['kæbəreɪ] *n* Kabarett *nt*
cabbage ['kæbɪdʒ] *n* Kohl *m*
cabin ['kæbɪn] *n* Kabine *f*; (*house*) Hütte *f*
cabin cruiser *n* Kajütboot *nt*
cabinet ['kæbɪnɪt] *n* kleiner Schrank *m*; (*also*: **display cabinet**) Vitrine *f*; (*Pol*) Kabinett *nt*
cabinet minister *n* Mitglied *nt* des Kabinetts, Minister(in) *m(f)*
cable ['keɪbl] *n* Kabel *nt* ▷ *vt* kabeln
cable car *n* (Draht)seilbahn *f*
cable television *n* Kabelfernsehen *nt*
cache [kæʃ] *n* Versteck *nt*, geheimes Lager *nt*; **a ~ of food** ein geheimes Proviantlager
cackle ['kækl] *vi* (*person*: *laugh*) meckernd lachen; (*hen*) gackern
cactus ['kæktəs] (*pl* **cacti**) *n* Kaktus *m*
cadet [kə'dɛt] *n* Kadett *m*; **police ~** Polizeianwärter(in) *m(f)*
cadge [kædʒ] (*inf*) *vt*: **to ~ (from** *or* **off)** schnorren (bei *or* von +*dat*); **to ~ a lift with sb** von jdm mitgenommen werden
Caesarean [siː'zɛərɪən] *n*: **~ (section)** Kaiserschnitt *m*
café ['kæfeɪ] *n* Café *nt*
cafeteria [kæfɪ'tɪərɪə] *n* Cafeteria *f*
caffeine, **caffein** ['kæfiːn] *n* Koffein *nt*
cage [keɪdʒ] *n* Käfig *m*; (*of lift*) Fahrkorb *m* ▷ *vt* einsperren
cagey ['keɪdʒɪ] (*inf*) *adj* vorsichtig; (*evasive*) ausweichend
cagoule [kə'guːl] *n* Regenjacke *f*
Cairo ['kaɪərəu] *n* Kairo *nt*
cajole [kə'dʒəul] *vt*: **to ~ sb into doing sth** jdn bereden, etw zu tun
cake [keɪk] *n* Kuchen *m*; (*small*) Gebäckstück *nt*; (*of soap*) Stück *nt*; **it's a piece of ~** (*inf*) das ist ein Kinderspiel *or* ein Klacks; **he wants to have his ~ and eat it (too)** (*fig*) er will das eine, ohne das andere zu lassen
caked [keɪkt] *adj*: **~ with** (*mud, blood*) verkrustet mit
calcium ['kælsɪəm] *n* Kalzium *nt*
calculate ['kælkjuleɪt] *vt* (*work out*) berechnen; (*estimate*) abschätzen
▸ **calculate on** *vt fus*: **to ~ on sth** mit etw rechnen; **to ~ on doing sth** damit rechnen, etw zu tun
calculation [kælkju'leɪʃən] *n* (*see vt*) Berechnung *f*; Abschätzung *f*; (*sum*) Rechnung *f*
calculator ['kælkjuleɪtəʳ] *n* Rechner *m*
calendar ['kæləndəʳ] *n* Kalender *m*; (*timetable, schedule*) (Termin)kalender *m*
calendar year *n* Kalenderjahr *nt*
calf [kɑːf] (*pl* **calves**) *n* Kalb *nt*; (*of elephant, seal etc*) Junge(s) *nt*; (*also*: **calfskin**) Kalb(s)leder *nt*; (*Anat*) Wade *f*
calibre, (*US*) **caliber** ['kælɪbəʳ] *n* Kaliber *nt*; (*of person*) Format *nt*
call [kɔːl] *vt* (*name, consider*) nennen; (*shout out, summon*) rufen; (*Tel*) anrufen; (*witness, flight*) aufrufen; (*meeting*) einberufen; (*strike*) ausrufen ▷ *vi* rufen; (*Tel*) anrufen; (*visit*: *also*: **call in, call round**) vorbeigehen, vorbeikommen ▷ *n* Ruf *m*; (*Tel*) Anruf *m*; (*visit*) Besuch *m*; (*for a service etc*) Nachfrage *f*; (*for flight etc*) Aufruf *m*; (*fig*: *lure*) Ruf *m*, Verlockung *f*; **to be ~ed** (*named*) heißen; **who is ~ing?** (*Tel*) wer spricht da bitte?; **London ~ing** (*Radio*) hier ist London; **please give me a ~ at 7** rufen Sie mich bitte um 7 an; **to make a ~** ein (Telefon)gespräch führen; **to pay a ~ on sb** jdn besuchen; **on ~** dienstbereit; **to be on ~** einsatzbereit sein; (*doctor etc*) Bereitschaftsdienst haben; **there's not much ~ for these items** es besteht keine große Nachfrage nach diesen Dingen
▸ **call at** *vt fus* (*subj*: *ship*) anlaufen; (: *train*) halten in +*dat*
▸ **call back** *vi* (*return*) wiederkommen; (*Tel*) zurückrufen ▷ *vt* (*Tel*) zurückrufen
▸ **call for** *vt fus* (*demand*) fordern; (*fetch*) abholen
▸ **call in** *vt* (*doctor, expert, police*) zurate ziehen; (*books, cars, stock etc*) aus dem Verkehr ziehen ▷ *vi* vorbeigehen, vorbeikommen

▸ **call off** *vt* absagen
▸ **call on** *vt fus* besuchen; (*appeal to*) appellieren an *+acc*; **to ~ on sb to do sth** jdn bitten *or* auffordern, etw zu tun
▸ **call out** *vi* rufen ▹ *vt* rufen; (*police, troops*) alarmieren
▸ **call up** *vt* (*Mil*) einberufen; (*Tel*) anrufen
call box (*Brit*) *n* Telefonzelle *f*
call centre *n* Telefoncenter *nt*, Callcenter *nt*
caller ['kɔːlə^r] *n* Besucher(in) *m(f)*; (*Tel*) Anrufer(in) *m(f)*; **hold the line, ~!** (*Tel*) bitte bleiben Sie am Apparat!
call girl *n* Callgirl *nt*
call-in ['kɔːlɪn] (*US*) *n* (*Radio, TV*) Phone-in *nt*
calling ['kɔːlɪŋ] *n* (*trade*) Beruf *m*; (*vocation*) Berufung *f*
calling card (*US*) *n* Visitenkarte *f*
callous ['kæləs] *adj* herzlos
calm [kɑːm] *adj* ruhig; (*unworried*) gelassen ▹ *n* Ruhe *f* ▹ *vt* beruhigen; (*fears*) zerstreuen; (*grief*) lindern
▸ **calm down** *vt* beruhigen ▹ *vi* sich beruhigen
calmly ['kɑːmlɪ] *adv* (*see adj*) ruhig; gelassen
Calor gas® ['kælə^r-] *n* Butangas *nt*
calorie ['kælərɪ] *n* Kalorie *f*; **low-~ product** kalorienarmes Produkt *nt*
calves [kɑːvz] *npl of* **calf**
camber ['kæmbə^r] *n* Wölbung *f*
Cambodia [kæm'bəudɪə] *n* Kambodscha *nt*
camcorder ['kæmkɔːdə^r] *n* Camcorder *m*, Kamerarekorder *m*
came [keɪm] *pt of* **come**
camel ['kæməl] *n* Kamel *nt*
camera ['kæmərə] *n* (*Cine, Phot*) Kamera *f*; (*also*: **cine camera, movie camera**) Filmkamera *f*; **35 mm ~** Kleinbildkamera *f*; **in ~** (*Law*) unter Ausschluss der Öffentlichkeit
cameraman ['kæmərəmæn] (*irreg: like* **man**) *n* Kameramann *m*
camera phone *n* Kameratelefon *nt*
camouflage ['kæməflɑːʒ] *n* Tarnung *f* ▹ *vt* tarnen
camp [kæmp] *n* Lager *nt*; (*barracks*) Kaserne *f* ▹ *vi* zelten ▹ *adj* (*effeminate*) tuntenhaft (*inf*)
campaign [kæm'peɪn] *n* (*Mil*) Feldzug *m*; (*Pol etc*) Kampagne *f* ▹ *vi* kämpfen; **to ~ for/against** sich einsetzen für/gegen
campaigner [kæm'peɪnə^r] *n*: **~ for** Befürworter(in) *m(f) +gen*; **~ against** Gegner(in) *m(f) +gen*
camp bed (*Brit*) *n* Campingliege *f*
camper ['kæmpə^r] *n* (*person*) Camper *m*; (*vehicle*) Wohnmobil *nt*
camping ['kæmpɪŋ] *n* Camping *nt*; **to go ~** zelten gehen, campen
campus ['kæmpəs] *n* (*Univ*) Universitätsgelände *nt*, Campus *m*
can¹ [kæn] *n* Büchse *f*, Dose *f*; (*for oil, water*) Kanister *m* ▹ *vt* eindosen, in Büchsen *or* Dosen einmachen; **a ~ of beer** eine Dose Bier; **he had to carry the ~** (*Brit: inf*) er musste die Sache ausbaden
can² (*negative* **cannot, can't**, *conditional and pt* **could**) *aux vb* **1** (*be able to, know how to*) können; **you can do it if you try** du kannst es, wenn du es nur versuchst; **I can't see you** ich kann dich nicht sehen; **I can swim/drive** ich kann schwimmen/Auto fahren; **can you speak English?** sprechen Sie Englisch?
2 (*may*) können, dürfen; **can I use your phone?** kann *or* darf ich Ihr Telefon benutzen?; **could I have a word with you?** könnte ich Sie mal sprechen?
3 (*expressing disbelief, puzzlement*): **it can't be true!** das darf doch nicht wahr sein!
4 (*expressing possibility, suggestion, etc*): **he could be in the library** er könnte in der Bibliothek sein
Canada ['kænədə] *n* Kanada *nt*
Canadian [kə'neɪdɪən] *adj* kanadisch ▹ *n* Kanadier(in) *m(f)*
canal [kə'næl] *n* (*also Anat*) Kanal *m*
canary [kə'nɛərɪ] *n* Kanarienvogel *m*
cancel ['kænsəl] *vt* absagen; (*reservation*) abbestellen; (*train, flight*) ausfallen lassen; (*contract*) annullieren; (*order*) stornieren; (*cross out*) durchstreichen; (*stamp*) entwerten; (*cheque*) ungültig machen
▸ **cancel out** *vt* aufheben; **they ~ each other out** sie heben sich gegenseitig auf
cancellation [kænsə'leɪʃən] *n* Absage *f*; (*of reservation*) Abbestellung *f*; (*of train, flight*) Ausfall *m*; (*Tourism*) Rücktritt *m*
cancer ['kænsə^r] *n* (*also*: **Cancer**: *Astrol*) Krebs *m*; **to be C~** (ein) Krebs sein
candid ['kændɪd] *adj* offen, ehrlich
candidate ['kændɪdeɪt] *n* Kandidat(in) *m(f)*; (*for job*) Bewerber(in) *m(f)*
candle ['kændl] *n* Kerze *f*; (*of tallow*) Talglicht *nt*
candlelight ['kændllaɪt] *n*: **by ~** bei Kerzenlicht
candlestick ['kændlstɪk] *n* (*also, candleholder*) Kerzenhalter *m*; (*bigger, ornate*) Kerzenleuchter *m*
candour, (*US*) **candor** ['kændə^r] *n* Offenheit *f*
candy ['kændɪ] *n* (*also*: **sugar-candy**) Kandis(zucker) *m*; (*US*) Bonbon *nt or m*
candyfloss ['kændɪflɔs] (*Brit*) *n* Zuckerwatte *f*
cane [keɪn] *n* Rohr *nt*; (*stick*) Stock *m*; (*: for walking*) (Spazier)stock *m* ▹ *vt* (*Brit: Scol*) mit dem Stock schlagen
canister ['kænɪstə^r] *n* Dose *f*; (*pressurized container*) Sprühdose *f*; (*of gas, chemicals etc*) Kanister *m*
cannabis ['kænəbɪs] *n* Haschisch *nt*; (*also*: **cannabis plant**) Hanf *m*, Cannabis *m*
canned [kænd] *adj* Dosen-; (*inf: music*) aus der Konserve; (*US: inf: worker*) entlassen, rausgeschmissen (*inf*)
cannon ['kænən] (*pl* **~** *or* **cannons**) *n* Kanone *f*
cannot ['kænɔt] = **can not**
canoe [kə'nuː] *n* Kanu *nt*
canoeing [kə'nuːɪŋ] *n* Kanusport *m*

canon ['kænən] *n* Kanon *m*; (*clergyman*) Kanoniker *m*, Kanonikus *m*
can-opener ['kænəupnəʳ] *n* Dosenöffner *m*, Büchsenöffner *m*
canopy ['kænəpɪ] *n* (*also fig*) Baldachin *m*
can't [kænt] = **can not**
canteen [kæn'ti:n] *n* (*in school, workplace*) Kantine *f*; (: *mobile*) Feldküche *f*; (*Brit: of cutlery*) Besteckkasten *m*
canter ['kæntəʳ] *vi* leicht galoppieren, kantern ▷ *n* leichter Galopp *m*, Kanter *m*
canvas ['kænvəs] *n* Leinwand *f*; (*painting*) Gemälde *nt*; (*Naut*) Segeltuch *nt*; **under ~** im Zelt
canvass ['kænvəs] *vt* (*opinions, views*) erforschen; (*person*) für seine Partei zu gewinnen suchen; (*place*) Wahlwerbung machen in *+dat* ▷ *vi*: **to ~ for ...** (*Pol*) um Stimmen für ... werben
canyon ['kænjən] *n* Cañon *m*
cap [kæp] *n* Mütze *f*, Kappe *f*; (*of pen*) (Verschluss)kappe *f*; (*of bottle*) Verschluss *m*, Deckel *m*; (*contraceptive: also*: **Dutch cap**) Pessar *nt*; (*for toy gun*) Zündplättchen *nt*; (*for swimming*) Bademütze *f*, Badekappe *f*; (*Sport*) *Ehrenkappe, die Nationalspielern verliehen wird* ▷ *vt* (*outdo*) überbieten; (*Sport*) für die Nationalmannschaft aufstellen; **~ped with ...** mit ... obendrauf; **and to ~ it all, ...** und obendrein ...
capability [keɪpə'bɪlɪtɪ] *n* Fähigkeit *f*; (*Mil*) Potenzial *nt*
capable ['keɪpəbl] *adj* fähig; **to be ~ of doing sth** etw tun können, fähig sein, etw zu tun; **to be ~ of sth** (*interpretation etc*) etw zulassen
capacity [kə'pæsɪtɪ] *n* Fassungsvermögen *nt*; (*of lift etc*) Höchstlast *f*; (*capability*) Fähigkeit *f*; (*position, role*) Eigenschaft *f*; (*of factory*) Kapazität *f*; **filled to ~** randvoll; (*stadium etc*) bis auf den letzten Platz besetzt; **in his ~ as ...** in seiner Eigenschaft als ...; **this work is beyond my ~** zu dieser Arbeit bin ich nicht fähig; **in an advisory ~** in beratender Funktion; **to work at full ~** voll ausgelastet sein
cape [keɪp] *n* Kap *nt*; (*cloak*) Cape *nt*, Umhang *m*
caper ['keɪpəʳ] *n* (*Culin: usu pl*) Kaper *f*; (*prank*) Eskapade *f*, Kapriole *f*
capital ['kæpɪtl] *n* (*also*: **capital city**) Hauptstadt *f*; (*money*) Kapital *nt*; (*also*: **capital letter**) Großbuchstabe *m*
capital gains tax *n* Kapitalertragssteuer *f*
capitalism ['kæpɪtəlɪzəm] *n* Kapitalismus *m*
capitalist ['kæpɪtəlɪst] *adj* kapitalistisch ▷ *n* Kapitalist(in) *m(f)*
capitalize ['kæpɪtəlaɪz] *vt* (*Comm*) kapitalisieren ▷ *vi*: **to ~ on** Kapital schlagen aus
capital punishment *n* Todesstrafe *f*
Capitol ['kæpɪtl] *n*: **the ~** das Kapitol
Capricorn ['kæprɪkɔ:n] *n* (*Astrol*) Steinbock *m*; **to be ~** (ein) Steinbock sein
capsize [kæp'saɪz] *vt* zum Kentern bringen ▷ *vi* kentern
capsule ['kæpsju:l] *n* Kapsel *f*
captain ['kæptɪn] *n* Kapitän *m*; (*of plane*) (Flug)kapitän *m*; (*in army*) Hauptmann *m* ▷ *vt* (*ship*) befehligen; (*team*) anführen
caption ['kæpʃən] *n* Bildunterschrift *f*
captive ['kæptɪv] *adj* gefangen ▷ *n* Gefangene(r) *f(m)*
captivity [kæp'tɪvɪtɪ] *n* Gefangenschaft *f*
capture ['kæptʃəʳ] *vt* (*animal*) (ein)fangen; (*person*) gefangen nehmen; (*town, country, share of market*) erobern; (*attention*) erregen; (*Comput*) erfassen ▷ *n* (*of animal*) Einfangen *nt*; (*of person*) Gefangennahme *f*; (*of town etc*) Eroberung *f*; (*also*: **data capture**) Erfassung *f*
car [kɑ:ʳ] *n* Auto *nt*, Wagen *m*; (*Rail*) Wagen *m*; **by ~** mit dem Auto *or* Wagen
carafe [kə'ræf] *n* Karaffe *f*
caramel ['kærəməl] *n* Karamelle *f*, Karamellbonbon *m or nt*; (*burnt sugar*) Karamell *m*
carat ['kærət] *n* Karat *nt*; **18 ~ gold** achtzehnkarätiges Gold
caravan ['kærəvæn] *n* (*Brit*) Wohnwagen *m*; (*in desert*) Karawane *f*
caravan site (*Brit*) *n* Campingplatz *m* für Wohnwagen
carbohydrate [kɑ:bəu'haɪdreɪt] *n* Kohle(n)hydrat *nt*
carbon ['kɑ:bən] *n* Kohlenstoff *m*
carbon dioxide *n* Kohlendioxid *nt*
carbon monoxide [mɔ'nɔksaɪd] *n* Kohlenmonoxid *nt*
carbon paper *n* Kohlepapier *nt*
carburettor, (*US*) **carburetor** [kɑ:bju'rɛtəʳ] *n* Vergaser *m*
card [kɑ:d] *n* Karte *f*; (*material*) (dünne) Pappe *f*, Karton *m*; (*also*: **record card, index card etc**) (Kartei)karte *f*; (*also*: **membership card**) (Mitglieds)ausweis *m*; (*also*: **playing card**) (Spiel)karte *f*; (*also*: **visiting card**) (Visiten)karte *f*; **to play ~s** Karten spielen
cardboard ['kɑ:dbɔ:d] *n* Pappe *f*
card game *n* Kartenspiel *nt*
cardiac ['kɑ:dɪæk] *adj* (*failure, patient*) Herz-
cardigan ['kɑ:dɪgən] *n* Strickjacke *f*
cardinal ['kɑ:dɪnl] *adj* (*principle, importance*) Haupt- ▷ *n* Kardinal *m*; **~ number** Kardinalzahl *f*; **~ sin** Todsünde *f*
card index *n* Kartei *f*
cardphone *n* Kartentelefon *nt*
care [kɛəʳ] *n* (*attention*) Versorgung *f*; (*worry*) Sorge *f*; (*charge*) Obhut *f*, Fürsorge *f* ▷ *vi*: **to ~ about** sich kümmern um; **~ of** bei; **"handle with ~"** "Vorsicht, zerbrechlich"; **in sb's ~** in jds *dat* Obhut; **to take ~** aufpassen; **to take ~ to do sth** sich bemühen, etw zu tun; **to take ~ of** sich kümmern um; **the child has been taken into ~** das Kind ist in Pflege genommen worden; **would you ~ to/for ...?** möchten Sie gerne ...?; **I wouldn't ~ to do it** ich möchte es nicht gern tun; **I don't ~** es ist

mir egal *or* gleichgültig; **I couldn't ~ less** es ist mir völlig egal *or* gleichgültig

▸ **care for** *vt fus* (*look after*) sich kümmern um; (*like*) mögen

career [kəˈrɪəʳ] *n* Karriere *f*; (*job, profession*) Beruf *m*; (*life*) Laufbahn *f* ▹ *vi* (*also*: **career along**) rasen

career woman *n* Karrierefrau *f*

carefree [ˈkɛəfriː] *adj* sorglos

careful [ˈkɛəful] *adj* vorsichtig; (*thorough*) sorgfältig; **(be) ~!** Vorsicht!, pass auf!; **to be ~ with one's money** sein Geld gut zusammenhalten

carefully [ˈkɛəfəlɪ] *adv* vorsichtig; (*methodically*) sorgfältig

careless [ˈkɛəlɪs] *adj* leichtsinnig; (*negligent*) nachlässig; (*remark*) gedankenlos

carelessness [ˈkɛəlɪsnɪs] *n* (*see adj*) Leichtsinn *m*; Nachlässigkeit *f*; Gedankenlosigkeit *f*

caress [kəˈrɛs] *n* Streicheln *nt* ▹ *vt* streicheln

caretaker [ˈkɛəteɪkəʳ] *n* Hausmeister(in) *m(f)*

cargo [ˈkɑːgəu] (*pl* **~es**) *n* Fracht *f*, Ladung *f*

car hire (*Brit*) *n* Autovermietung *f*

Caribbean [kærɪˈbiːənʳ] *adj* karibisch ▹ *n*: **the ~ (Sea)** die Karibik, das Karibische Meer

caring [ˈkɛərɪŋ] *adj* liebevoll; (*society, organization*) sozial; (*behaviour*) fürsorglich

carnation [kɑːˈneɪʃən] *n* Nelke *f*

carnival [ˈkɑːnɪvl] *n* Karneval *m*; (*US: funfair*) Kirmes *f*

carol [ˈkærəl] *n*: **(Christmas) ~** Weihnachtslied *nt*

carousel [kærəˈsɛl] (*US*) *n* Karussell *nt*

carp [kɑːp] *n* Karpfen *m*

▸ **carp at** *vt fus* herumnörgeln an *+dat*

car park *n* Parkplatz *m*; (*building*) Parkhaus *nt*

carpenter [ˈkɑːpɪntəʳ] *n* Zimmermann *m*

carpentry [ˈkɑːpɪntrɪ] *n* Zimmerhandwerk *nt*; (*school subject, hobby*) Tischlern *nt*

carpet [ˈkɑːpɪt] *n* (*also fig*) Teppich *m* ▹ *vt* (mit Teppichen/Teppichboden) auslegen; **fitted ~** (*Brit*) Teppichboden *m*

car phone *n* (*Telec*) Autotelefon *nt*

car rental *n* Autovermietung *f*

carriage [ˈkærɪdʒ] *n* (*Rail, of typewriter*) Wagen *m*; (*horse-drawn vehicle*) Kutsche *f*; (*of goods*) Beförderung *f*; (*transport costs*) Beförderungskosten *pl*; **~ forward** Fracht zahlt Empfänger; **~ free** frachtfrei; **~ paid** frei Haus

carriageway [ˈkærɪdʒweɪ] (*Brit*) *n* Fahrbahn *f*

carrier [ˈkærɪəʳ] *n* Spediteur *m*, Transportunternehmer *m*; (*Med*) Überträger *m*

carrier bag (*Brit*) *n* Tragetasche *f*, Tragetüte *f*

carrot [ˈkærət] *n* Möhre *f*, Mohrrübe *f*, Karotte *f*; (*fig*) Köder *m*

carry [ˈkærɪ] *vt* tragen; (*transport*) transportieren; (*a motion, bill*) annehmen; (*responsibilities etc*) mit sich bringen; (*disease, virus*) übertragen ▹ *vi* (*sound*) tragen; **to get carried away** (*fig*) sich hinreißen lassen; **this loan carries 10% interest** dieses Darlehen wird mit 10% verzinst

▸ **carry forward** *vt* übertragen, vortragen

▸ **carry on** *vi* weitermachen; (*inf: make a fuss*) (ein) Theater machen ▹ *vt* fortführen; **to ~ on with sth** mit etw weitermachen; **to ~ on singing/eating** weitersingen/-essen

▸ **carry out** *vt* (*orders*) ausführen; (*investigation*) durchführen; (*idea*) in die Tat umsetzen; (*threat*) wahr machen

carrycot [ˈkærɪkɔt] (*Brit*) *n* Babytragetasche *f*

carry-on [ˈkærɪˈɔn] (*inf*) *n* Theater *nt*

cart [kɑːt] *n* Wagen *m*, Karren *m*; (*for passengers*) Wagen *m*; (*handcart*) (Hand)wagen *m* ▹ *vt* (*inf*) mit sich herumschleppen

carton [ˈkɑːtən] *n* (Papp)karton *m*; (*of yogurt*) Becher *m*; (*of milk*) Tüte *f*; (*of cigarettes*) Stange *f*

cartoon [kɑːˈtuːn] *n* (*drawing*) Karikatur *f*; (*Brit: comic strip*) Cartoon *m*; (*Cine*) Zeichentrickfilm *m*

cartridge [ˈkɑːtrɪdʒ] *n* (*for gun, pen*) Patrone *f*; (*music tape, for camera*) Kassette *f*; (*of record-player*) Tonabnehmer *m*

carve [kɑːv] *vt* (*meat*) (ab)schneiden; (*wood*) schnitzen; (*stone*) meißeln; (*initials, design*) einritzen

▸ **carve up** *vt* (*land etc*) aufteilen; (*meat*) aufschneiden

carving [ˈkɑːvɪŋ] *n* Skulptur *f*; (*in wood etc*) Schnitzerei *f*

carving knife *n* Tran(s)chiermesser *nt*

car wash *n* Autowaschanlage *f*

case [keɪs] *n* Fall *m*; (*for spectacles etc*) Etui *nt*; (*Brit*: *also*: **suitcase**) Koffer *m*; (*of wine, whisky etc*) Kiste *f*; (*Typ*): **lower/upper ~** klein-/großgeschrieben; **to have a good ~** gute Chancen haben, durchzukommen; **there's a strong ~ for reform** es spricht viel für eine Reform; **in ~ ...** falls ...; **in ~ of fire** bei Feuer; **in ~ of emergency** im Notfall; **in ~ he comes** falls er kommt; **in any ~** sowieso; **just in ~** für alle Fälle

cash [kæʃ] *n* (Bar)geld *nt* ▹ *vt* (*cheque etc*) einlösen; **to pay (in) ~** bar bezahlen; **~ on delivery** per Nachnahme; **~ with order** zahlbar bei Bestellung

▸ **cash in** *vt* einlösen

▸ **cash in on** *vt fus* Kapital schlagen aus

cash card (*Brit*) *n* (Geld)automatenkarte *f*

cash desk (*Brit*) *n* Kasse *f*

cash dispenser (*Brit*) *n* Geldautomat *m*

cashew [kæˈʃuː] *n* (*also*: **cashew nut**) Cashewnuss *f*

cashier [kæˈʃɪəʳ] *n* Kassierer(in) *m(f)*

cashmere [ˈkæʃmɪəʳ] *n* Kaschmir *m*

cash point *n* Geldautomat *m*

cash register *n* Registrierkasse *f*

casing [ˈkeɪsɪŋ] *n* Gehäuse *nt*

casino [kəˈsiːnəu] *n* Kasino *nt*

casket [ˈkɑːskɪt] *n* Schatulle *f*; (*US: coffin*) Sarg *m*

casserole [ˈkæsərəul] *n* Auflauf *m*; (*pot, container*) Kasserolle *f*

cassette [kæˈsɛt] *n* Kassette *f*

cassette player *n* Kassettenrekorder *m*
cassette recorder *n* Kassettenrekorder *m*
cast [kɑːst] (*pt, pp* **~**) *vt* werfen; (*net, fishing-line*) auswerfen; (*metal, statue*) gießen ▷ *vi* die Angel auswerfen ▷ *n* (*Theat*) Besetzung *f*; (*mould*) (Guss)form *f*; (*also*: **plaster cast**) Gipsverband *m*; **to ~ sb as Hamlet** (*Theat*) die Rolle des Hamlet mit jdm besetzen; **to ~ one's vote** seine Stimme abgeben; **to ~ one's eyes over sth** einen Blick auf etw *acc* werfen; **to ~ aspersions on sb/sth** abfällige Bemerkungen über jdn/etw machen; **to ~ doubts on sth** etw in Zweifel ziehen; **to ~ a spell on sb/sth** jdn/etw verzaubern; **to ~ its skin** sich häuten
▸ **cast aside** *vt* fallen lassen
▸ **cast off** *vi* (*Naut*) losmachen; (*Knitting*) abketten ▷ *vt* abketten
▸ **cast on** *vi, vt* (*Knitting*) anschlagen, aufschlagen
castaway ['kɑːstəweɪ] *n* Schiffbrüchige(r) *f(m)*
caster sugar ['kɑːstə-] (*Brit*) *n* Raffinade *f*
casting vote ['kɑːstɪŋ-] (*Brit*) *n* ausschlaggebende Stimme *f*
cast iron *n* Gusseisen *nt* ▷ *adj*: **cast-iron** (*fig*: *will*) eisern; (: *alibi, excuse etc*) hieb- und stichfest
castle ['kɑːsl] *n* Schloss *nt*; (*manor*) Herrenhaus *nt*; (*fortified*) Burg *f*; (*Chess*) Turm *m*
castor ['kɑːstə^r] *n* Rolle *f*
castor oil *n* Rizinusöl *nt*
castrate [kæs'treɪt] *vt* kastrieren
casual ['kæʒjul] *adj* (*by chance*) zufällig; (*work etc*) Gelegenheits-; (*unconcerned*) lässig, gleichgültig; (*clothes*) leger; **~ wear** Freizeitkleidung *f*
casually ['kæʒjulɪ] *adv* lässig; (*glance*) beiläufig; (*dress*) leger; (*by chance*) zufällig
casualty ['kæʒjultɪ] *n* (*of war etc*) Opfer *nt*; (*someone injured*) Verletzte(r) *f(m)*; (*someone killed*) Tote(r) *f(m)*; (*Med*) Unfallstation *f*; **heavy casualties** (*Mil*) schwere Verluste *pl*
cat [kæt] *n* Katze *f*; (*lion etc*) (Raub)katze *f*
catalogue, (US) **catalog** ['kætəlɔg] *n* Katalog *m* ▷ *vt* katalogisieren
catalyst ['kætəlɪst] *n* Katalysator *m*
catalytic converter [kætə'lɪtɪk kən'vəːtə^r] *n* (*Aut*) Katalysator *m*
catapult ['kætəpʌlt] (*Brit*) *n* Schleuder *f*; (*Mil*) Katapult *nt or m* ▷ *vi* geschleudert *or* katapultiert werden ▷ *vt* schleudern, katapultieren
cataract ['kætərækt] *n* (*Med*) grauer Star *m*
catarrh [kə'tɑː^r] *n* Katarrh *m*
catastrophe [kə'tæstrəfɪ] *n* Katastrophe *f*
catch [kætʃ] (*pt, pp* **caught**) *vt* fangen; (*take*: *bus, train etc*) nehmen; (*arrest*) festnehmen; (*surprise*) erwischen, ertappen; (*breath*) holen; (*attention*) erregen; (*hit*) treffen; (*hear*) mitbekommen; (*illness*) sich *dat* zuziehen *or* holen; (*person*: *also*: **catch up**) einholen ▷ *vi* (*fire*) (anfangen zu) brennen; (*become trapped*) hängen bleiben ▷ *n* Fang *m*; (*trick, hidden problem*) Haken *m*; (*of lock*) Riegel *m*; (*game*) Fangen *nt*; **to ~ sb's attention/eye** jdn auf sich *acc* aufmerksam machen; **to ~ fire** Feuer fangen; **to ~ sight of** erblicken
▸ **catch on** *vi* (*grow popular*) sich durchsetzen; **to ~ on (to sth)** (etw) kapieren
▸ **catch out** (*Brit*) *vt* (*fig*) hereinlegen
▸ **catch up** *vi* (*fig*: *with person*) mitkommen; (: *on work*) aufholen ▷ *vt*: **to ~ sb up, to ~ up with sb** jdn einholen
catching ['kætʃɪŋ] *adj* ansteckend
catchment area ['kætʃmənt-] (*Brit*) *n* Einzugsgebiet *nt*
catch phrase *n* Schlagwort *nt*, Slogan *m*
catchy ['kætʃɪ] *adj* (*tune*) eingängig
category ['kætɪgərɪ] *n* Kategorie *f*
cater ['keɪtə^r] *vi*: **to ~ (for)** die Speisen und Getränke liefern (für)
▸ **cater for** (*Brit*) *vt fus* (*needs, tastes*) gerecht werden *+dat*; (*readers, consumers*) eingestellt *or* ausgerichtet sein auf *+acc*
caterer ['keɪtərə^r] *n* Lieferant(in) *m(f)* von Speisen und Getränken; (*company*) Lieferfirma *f* für Speisen und Getränke
catering ['keɪtərɪŋ] *n* Gastronomie *f*
caterpillar ['kætəpɪlə^r] *n* Raupe *f* ▷ *cpd* (*vehicle*) Raupen-
cathedral [kə'θiːdrəl] *n* Kathedrale *f*, Dom *m*
Catholic ['kæθəlɪk] *adj* katholisch ▷ *n* Katholik(in) *m(f)*
catholic ['kæθəlɪk] *adj* vielseitig
cattle ['kætl] *npl* Vieh *nt*
catty ['kætɪ] *adj* gehässig
catwalk ['kætwɔːk] *n* Steg *m*; (*for models*) Laufsteg *m*
caucus ['kɔːkəs] *n* (*group*) Gremium *nt*, Ausschuss *m*; (US) Parteiversammlung *f*
caught [kɔːt] *pt, pp of* **catch**
cauliflower ['kɔlɪflauə^r] *n* Blumenkohl *m*
cause [kɔːz] *n* Ursache *f*; (*reason*) Grund *m*; (*aim*) Sache *f* ▷ *vt* verursachen; **there is no ~ for concern** es besteht kein Grund zur Sorge; **to ~ sth to be done** veranlassen, dass etw getan wird; **to ~ sb to do sth** jdn veranlassen, etw zu tun
caution ['kɔːʃən] *n* Vorsicht *f*; (*warning*) Warnung *f*; (: *Law*) Verwarnung *f* ▷ *vt* warnen; (*Law*) verwarnen
cautious ['kɔːʃəs] *adj* vorsichtig
cavalry ['kævəlrɪ] *n* Kavallerie *f*
cave [keɪv] *n* Höhle *f* ▷ *vi*: **to go caving** auf Höhlenexpedition(en) gehen
▸ **cave in** *vi* einstürzen; (*to demands*) nachgeben
caveman ['keɪvmæn] (*irreg*: *like* **man**) *n* Höhlenmensch *m*
caviar, **caviare** ['kævɪɑː^r] *n* Kaviar *m*
cavity ['kævɪtɪ] *n* Hohlraum *m*; (*in tooth*) Loch *nt*
CB *n abbr* (= *Citizens' Band (Radio)*) CB-Funk *m*
CBI *n abbr* (= *Confederation of British Industry*)

britischer Unternehmerverband, ≈ BDI *m*
cc *abbr* (= *cubic centimetre*) ccm; = **carbon copy**
CCTV *n abbr* = **closed-circuit television**
CD *abbr* (*Brit*: = *Corps Diplomatique*) CD ▷ *n abbr* (*Mil*: *Brit*: = *Civil Defence (Corps)*) Zivilschutz *m*; (: *US*: = *Civil Defense*) Zivilschutz *m*; (= *compact disc*) CD *f*; **CD player** CD-Spieler *m*
CD-ROM *n abbr* (= *compact disc read-only memory*) CD-ROM *f*
cease [si:s] *vt* beenden ▷ *vi* aufhören
ceasefire ['si:sfaɪəʳ] *n* Waffenruhe *f*
ceaseless ['si:slɪs] *adj* endlos, unaufhörlich
cedar ['si:dəʳ] *n* Zeder *f*; (*wood*) Zedernholz *nt*
ceilidh ['keɪlɪ] (*Scott*) *n* *Fest mit Volksmusik, Gesang und Tanz*
ceiling ['si:lɪŋ] *n* Decke *f*; (*upper limit*) Obergrenze *f*, Höchstgrenze *f*
celebrate ['sɛlɪbreɪt] *vt* feiern; (*mass*) zelebrieren ▷ *vi* feiern
celebrated ['sɛlɪbreɪtɪd] *adj* gefeiert
celebration [sɛlɪ'breɪʃən] *n* Feier *f*
celebrity [sɪ'lɛbrɪtɪ] *n* berühmte Persönlichkeit *f*
celery ['sɛlərɪ] *n* (Stangen)sellerie *f*
cell [sɛl] *n* Zelle *f*
cellar ['sɛləʳ] *n* Keller *m*; (*for wine*) (Wein)keller *m*
cello ['tʃɛləu] *n* Cello *nt*
cellphone ['sɛlfəun] *n* Funktelefon *nt*
Celsius ['sɛlsɪəs] *adj* (*scale*) Celsius-
Celt [kɛlt] *n* Kelte *m*, Keltin *f*
Celtic ['kɛltɪk] *adj* keltisch ▷ *n* (*Ling*) Keltisch *nt*
cement [sə'mɛnt] *n* Zement *m*; (*concrete*) Beton *m*; (*glue*) Klebstoff *m* ▷ *vt* zementieren; (*stick, glue*) kleben; (*fig*) festigen
cement mixer *n* Betonmischmaschine *f*
cemetery ['sɛmɪtrɪ] *n* Friedhof *m*
censor ['sɛnsəʳ] *n* Zensor(in) *m(f)* ▷ *vt* zensieren
censorship ['sɛnsəʃɪp] *n* Zensur *f*
censure ['sɛnʃəʳ] *vt* tadeln ▷ *n* Tadel *m*
census ['sɛnsəs] *n* Volkszählung *f*
cent [sɛnt] *n* Cent *m*; *see also* **per cent**
centenary [sɛn'ti:nərɪ] *n* hundertster Jahrestag *m*
center *etc* ['sɛntəʳ] (*US*) = **centre** *etc*
centigrade ['sɛntɪgreɪd] *adj* (*scale*) Celsius-
centimetre, (*US*) **centimeter** ['sɛntɪmi:təʳ] *n* Zentimeter *m or nt*
centipede ['sɛntɪpi:d] *n* Tausendfüßler *m*
central ['sɛntrəl] *adj* zentral; (*committee, government*) Zentral-; (*idea*) wesentlich
Central America *n* Mittelamerika *nt*
central heating *n* Zentralheizung *f*
central reservation (*Brit*) *n* Mittelstreifen *m*
centre, (*US*) **center** ['sɛntəʳ] *n* Mitte *f*; (*health centre etc, town centre*) Zentrum *nt*; (*of attention, interest*) Mittelpunkt *m*; (*of action, belief etc*) Kern *m* ▷ *vt* zentrieren; (*ball*) zur Mitte spielen ▷ *vi* (*concentrate*): **to ~ on** sich konzentrieren auf *+acc*
century ['sɛntjurɪ] *n* Jahrhundert *nt*; (*Cricket*) Hundert *f*; **in the twentieth ~** im zwanzigsten Jahrhundert
CEO *n abbr* = **chief executive officer**
ceramic [sɪ'ræmɪk] *adj* keramisch; (*tiles*) Keramik-
cereal ['si:rɪəl] *n* Getreide *nt*; (*food*) Getreideflocken *pl* (*Cornflakes etc*)
ceremony ['sɛrɪmənɪ] *n* Zeremonie *f*; (*behaviour*) Förmlichkeit *f*; **to stand on ~** förmlich sein
certain ['sə:tən] *adj* sicher; **a ~ Mr Smith** ein gewisser Herr Smith; **~ days/places** bestimmte Tage/Orte; **a ~ coldness** eine gewisse Kälte; **to make ~ of** sich vergewissern *+gen*; **for ~** ganz sicher, ganz genau
certainly ['sə:tənlɪ] *adv* bestimmt; (*of course*) sicherlich; **~!** (aber) sicher!
certainty ['sə:təntɪ] *n* Sicherheit *f*; (*inevitability*) Gewissheit *f*
certificate [sə'tɪfɪkɪt] *n* Urkunde *f*; (*diploma*) Zeugnis *nt*
certify ['sə:tɪfaɪ] *vt* bescheinigen; (*award a diploma to*) ein Zeugnis verleihen *+dat*; (*declare insane*) für unzurechnungsfähig erklären ▷ *vi*: **to ~ to** sich verbürgen für
cervical ['sə:vɪkl] *adj*: **~ cancer** Gebärmutterhalskrebs *m*; **~ smear** Abstrich *m*
cervix ['sə:vɪks] *n* Gebärmutterhals *m*
cf. *abbr* (= *compare*) vgl.
CFC *n abbr* (= *chlorofluorocarbon*) FCKW *m*
ch. *abbr* (= *chapter*) Kap.
chafe [tʃeɪf] *vt* (wund) reiben ▷ *vi* (*fig*): **to ~ against** sich ärgern über *+acc*
chain [tʃeɪn] *n* Kette *f* ▷ *vt* (*also*: **chain up**: *prisoner*) anketten; (: *dog*) an die Kette legen
chain reaction *n* Kettenreaktion *f*
chain-smoke ['tʃeɪnsməuk] *vi* eine Zigarette nach der anderen rauchen
chain store *n* Kettenladen *m*
chair [tʃɛəʳ] *n* Stuhl *m*; (*armchair*) Sessel *m*; (*of university*) Lehrstuhl *m*; (*of meeting, committee*) Vorsitz *m* ▷ *vt* den Vorsitz führen bei; **the ~** (*US*) der elektrische Stuhl
chairman ['tʃɛəmən] (*irreg*: *like* **man**) *n* Vorsitzende(r) *f(m)*; (*Brit*: *of company*) Präsident *m*
chairperson ['tʃɛəpə:sn] *n* Vorsitzende(r) *f(m)*
chairwoman ['tʃɛəwumən] (*irreg*: *like* **woman**) *n* Vorsitzende *f*
chalet ['ʃæleɪ] *n* Chalet *nt*
chalk [tʃɔ:k] *n* Kalkstein *m*, Kreide *f*; (*for writing*) Kreide *f*
▸ **chalk up** *vt* aufschreiben, notieren; (*fig*: *success etc*) verbuchen
challenge ['tʃælɪndʒ] *n* (*of new job*) Anforderungen *pl*; (*of unknown etc*) Reiz *m*; (*to authority etc*) Infragestellung *f*; (*dare*) Herausforderung *f* ▷ *vt* herausfordern; (*authority, right, idea etc*) infrage stellen; **to ~ sb to do sth** jdn dazu auffordern, etw zu

tun; **to ~ sb to a fight/game** jdn zu einem Kampf/Spiel herausfordern

challenging ['tʃælɪndʒɪŋ] *adj* (*career, task*) anspruchsvoll; (*tone, look etc*) herausfordernd

chamber ['tʃeɪmbəʳ] *n* Kammer *f*; (*Brit: Law: gen pl: of barristers*) Kanzlei *f*; (*: of judge*) Amtszimmer *nt*; **~ of commerce** Handelskammer *f*

chambermaid ['tʃeɪmbəmeɪd] *n* Zimmermädchen *nt*

chamber music *n* Kammermusik *f*

champagne [ʃæm'peɪn] *n* Champagner *m*

champion ['tʃæmpɪən] *n* Meister(in) *m(f)*; (*of cause, principle*) Verfechter(in) *m(f)*; (*of person*) Fürsprecher(in) *m(f)* ▷ *vt* eintreten für, sich engagieren für

championship ['tʃæmpɪənʃɪp] *n* Meisterschaft *f*; (*title*) Titel *m*

chance [tʃɑːns] *n* (*hope*) Aussicht *f*; (*likelihood, possibility*) Möglichkeit *f*; (*opportunity*) Gelegenheit *f*; (*risk*) Risiko *nt* ▷ *vt* riskieren ▷ *adj* zufällig; **the ~s are that ...** aller Wahrscheinlichkeit nach ..., wahrscheinlich ...; **there is little ~ of his coming** es ist unwahrscheinlich, dass er kommt; **to take a ~** es darauf ankommen lassen; **by ~** durch Zufall, zufällig; **it's the ~ of a lifetime** es ist eine einmalige Chance; **to ~ to do sth** zufällig etw tun; **to ~ it** es riskieren

▸ **chance (up)on** *vt fus* (*person*) zufällig begegnen *+dat*, zufällig treffen; (*thing*) zufällig stoßen auf *+acc*

chancellor ['tʃɑːnsələʳ] *n* Kanzler *m*

Chancellor of the Exchequer (*Brit*) *n* Schatzkanzler *m*, Finanzminister *m*

chandelier [ʃændə'lɪəʳ] *n* Kronleuchter *m*

change [tʃeɪndʒ] *vt* ändern; (*wheel, job, money, baby's nappy*) wechseln; (*bulb*) auswechseln; (*baby*) wickeln ▷ *vi* sich verändern; (*traffic lights*) umspringen ▷ *n* Veränderung *f*; (*difference*) Abwechslung *f*; (*of government, climate, job*) Wechsel *m*; (*coins*) Kleingeld *nt*; (*money returned*) Wechselgeld *nt*; **to ~ sb into** jdn verwandeln in *+acc*; **to ~ gear** (*Aut*) schalten; **to ~ one's mind** seine Meinung ändern, es sich *dat* anders überlegen; **to ~ hands** den Besitzer wechseln; **to ~ (trains/buses/planes** *etc*) umsteigen; **to ~ (one's clothes)** sich umziehen; **to ~ into** (*be transformed*) sich verwandeln in *+acc*; **she ~d into an old skirt** sie zog einen alten Rock an; **a ~ of clothes** Kleidung *f* zum Wechseln; **~ of government/climate/job** Regierungs-/Klima-/Berufswechsel *m*; **small ~** Kleingeld *nt*; **to give sb ~ for** *or* **of £10** jdm £10 wechseln; **keep the ~** das stimmt so, der Rest ist für Sie; **for a ~** zur Abwechslung

changeable ['tʃeɪndʒəbl] *adj* (*weather*) wechselhaft, veränderlich; (*mood*) wechselnd; (*person*) unbeständig

change machine *n* (Geld)wechselautomat *m*

changeover ['tʃeɪndʒəuvəʳ] *n* Umstellung *f*

changing ['tʃeɪndʒɪŋ] *adj* sich verändernd

changing room (*Brit*) *n* (Umkleide)kabine *f*; (*Sport*) Umkleideraum *m*

channel ['tʃænl] *n* (TV) Kanal *m*; (*of river, waterway*) (Fluss)bett *nt*; (*for boats*) Fahrrinne *f*; (*groove*) Rille *f*; (*fig: means*) Weg *m* ▷ *vt* leiten; (*fig*): **to ~ into** lenken auf *+acc*; **through the usual ~s** auf dem üblichen Wege; **green ~** (*Customs*) "nichts zu verzollen"; **red ~** (*Customs*) "Waren zu verzollen"; **the (English) C~** der Ärmelkanal; **the C~ Islands** die Kanalinseln *pl*

channel-hopping ['tʃænlhɔpɪŋ] *n* (TV) ständiges Umschalten

Channel Tunnel *n*: **the ~** der Kanaltunnel

chant [tʃɑːnt] *n* Sprechchor *m*; (*Rel*) Gesang *m* ▷ *vt* im (Sprech)chor rufen; (*Rel*) singen ▷ *vi* Sprechchöre anstimmen; (*Rel*) singen; **the demonstrators ~ed their disapproval** die Demonstranten machten ihrem Unmut in Sprechchören Luft

chaos ['keɪɔs] *n* Chaos *nt*, Durcheinander *nt*

chaotic [keɪ'ɔtɪk] *adj* chaotisch

chap [tʃæp] (*Brit: inf*) *n* Kerl *m*, Typ *m*; **old ~** alter Knabe *or* Junge

chapel ['tʃæpl] *n* Kapelle *f*; (*Brit: non-conformist chapel*) Sektenkirche *f*; (*: of union*) *Betriebsgruppe innerhalb der Gewerkschaft der Drucker und Journalisten*

chaplain ['tʃæplɪn] *n* Pfarrer(in) *m(f)*; (*Roman Catholic*) Kaplan *m*

chapped [tʃæpt] *adj* aufgesprungen, rau

chapter ['tʃæptəʳ] *n* Kapitel *nt*; **a ~ of accidents** eine Serie von Unfällen

char [tʃɑːʳ] *vt* verkohlen ▷ *vi* (*Brit*) putzen gehen ▷ *n* (*Brit*) = **charlady**

character ['kærɪktəʳ] *n* Charakter *m*; (*personality*) Persönlichkeit *f*; (*in novel, film*) Figur *f*, Gestalt *f*; (*eccentric*) Original *nt*; (*letter: also Comput*) Zeichen *nt*; **a person of good ~** ein guter Mensch

characteristic [kærɪktə'rɪstɪk] *n* Merkmal *nt* ▷ *adj*: **~ (of)** charakteristisch (für), typisch (für)

characterize ['kærɪktəraɪz] *vt* kennzeichnen, charakterisieren; (*describe the character of*): **to ~ (as)** beschreiben (als)

charcoal ['tʃɑːkəul] *n* Holzkohle *f*; (*for drawing*) Kohle *f*, Kohlestift *m*

charge [tʃɑːdʒ] *n* (*fee*) Gebühr *f*; (*accusation*) Anklage *f*; (*responsibility*) Verantwortung *f*; (*attack*) Angriff *m* ▷ *vt* (*customer*) berechnen *+dat*; (*sum*) berechnen; (*battery*) (auf)laden; (*gun*) laden; (*enemy*) angreifen; (*sb with task*) beauftragen ▷ *vi* angreifen; (*usu with: up, along etc*) stürmen; **charges** *npl* Gebühren *pl*; **labour ~s** Arbeitskosten *pl*; **to reverse the ~s** (*Brit: Tel*) ein R-Gespräch führen; **is there a ~?** kostet das etwas?; **there's no ~** es ist umsonst, es kostet nichts; **at no extra ~** ohne Aufpreis; **free of ~** kostenlos, gratis; **to take ~ of** (*child*) sich kümmern um; (*company*) übernehmen; **to be in ~ of**

die Verantwortung haben für; (*business*) leiten; **they ~d us £10 for the meal** das Essen kostete £10; **how much do you ~?** was verlangen Sie?; **to ~ an expense (up) to sb's account** eine Ausgabe auf jds Rechnung *acc* setzen; **to ~ sb (with)** (*Law*) jdn anklagen (wegen)

charge card *n* Kundenkreditkarte *f*

charger ['tʃɑ:dʒəʳ] *n* (*also*: **battery charger**) Ladegerät *nt*; (*warhorse*) (Schlacht)ross *nt*

charity ['tʃærɪtɪ] *n* (*organization*) karitative Organisation *f*, Wohltätigkeitsverein *m*; (*kindness, generosity*) Menschenfreundlichkeit *f*; (*money, gifts*) Almosen *nt*

charm [tʃɑ:m] *n* Charme *m*; (*to bring good luck*) Talisman *m*; (*on bracelet etc*) Anhänger *m* ▷ *vt* bezaubern

charming ['tʃɑ:mɪŋ] *adj* reizend, charmant; (*place*) bezaubernd

chart [tʃɑ:t] *n* Schaubild *nt*, Diagramm *nt*; (*map*) Karte *f*; (*also*: **weather chart**) Wetterkarte *f* ▷ *vt* (*course*) planen; (*progress*) aufzeichnen; **charts** *npl* (*hit parade*) Hitliste *f*

charter ['tʃɑ:təʳ] *vt* chartern ▷ *n* Charta *f*; (*of university, company*) Gründungsurkunde *f*; **on ~** gechartert

chartered accountant ['tʃɑ:təd-] (*Brit*) *n* Wirtschaftsprüfer(in) *m(f)*

charter flight *n* Charterflug *m*

chase [tʃeɪs] *vt* jagen, verfolgen; (*also*: **chase away**) wegjagen, vertreiben; (*business, job etc*) her sein hinter *+dat* (*inf*) ▷ *n* Verfolgungsjagd *f*

▸ **chase down** (*US*) *vt* = **chase up**

▸ **chase up** (*Brit*) *vt* (*person*) rankriegen (*inf*); (*information*) ranschaffen (*inf*)

chasm ['kæzəm] *n* Kluft *f*

chat [tʃæt] *vi* (*also*: **have a chat**) plaudern, sich unterhalten ▷ *n* Plauderei *f*, Unterhaltung *f*

▸ **chat up** (*Brit: inf*) *vt* anmachen

chat show (*Brit*) *n* Talkshow *f*

chatter ['tʃætəʳ] *vi* schwatzen; (*monkey*) schnattern; (*teeth*) klappern ▷ *n* (*see vi*) Schwatzen *nt*; Schnattern *nt*; Klappern *nt*; **my teeth are ~ing** mir klappern die Zähne

chatterbox ['tʃætəbɔks] (*inf*) *n* Quasselstrippe *f*

chatty ['tʃætɪ] *adj* geschwätzig; (*letter*) im Plauderton

chauffeur ['ʃəufəʳ] *n* Chauffeur *m*, Fahrer *m*

chauvinist ['ʃəuvɪnɪst] *n* Chauvinist *m*

cheap [tʃi:p] *adj* billig; (*reduced*) ermäßigt; (*poor quality*) billig, minderwertig; (*behaviour, joke*) ordinär ▷ *adv*: **to buy/sell sth ~** etw billig kaufen/verkaufen

cheap day return *n* Tagesrückfahrkarte *f* (*zu einem günstigeren Tarif*)

cheaply ['tʃi:plɪ] *adv* billig

cheat [tʃi:t] *vi* mogeln (*inf*), schummeln (*inf*) ▷ *n* Betrüger(in) *m(f)* ▷ *vt*: **to ~ sb (out of sth)** jdn (um etw) betrügen; **to ~ on sb** (*inf*) jdn betrügen

check [tʃɛk] *vt* überprüfen; (*passport, ticket*) kontrollieren; (*facts*) nachprüfen; (*enemy, disease*) aufhalten; (*impulse*) unterdrücken; (*person*) zurückhalten ▷ *vi* nachprüfen ▷ *n* Kontrolle *f*; (*curb*) Beschränkung *f*; (*US*) = **cheque**; (*: bill*) Rechnung *f*; (*pattern: gen pl*) Karo(muster) *nt* ▷ *adj* kariert; **to ~ o.s.** sich beherrschen; **to ~ with sb** bei jdm nachfragen; **to keep a ~ on sb/sth** jdn/etw kontrollieren

▸ **check in** *vi* (*at hotel*) sich anmelden; (*at airport*) einchecken ▷ *vt* (*luggage*) abfertigen lassen

▸ **check off** *vt* abhaken

▸ **check out** *vi* (*of hotel*) abreisen ▷ *vt* (*luggage*) abfertigen; (*investigate*) überprüfen

▸ **check up** *vi*: **to ~ up on sth** etw überprüfen; **to ~ up on sb** Nachforschungen über jdn anstellen

checkered ['tʃɛkəd] (*US*) *adj* = **chequered**

checkers ['tʃɛkəz] (*US*) *npl* Damespiel *nt*

check-in ['tʃɛkɪn], **check-in desk** *n* (*at airport*) Abfertigung *f*, Abfertigungsschalter *m*

checking account ['tʃɛkɪŋ-] (*US*) *n* Girokonto *nt*

checkmate ['tʃɛkmeɪt] *n* Schachmatt *nt*

checkout ['tʃɛkaut] *n* Kasse *f*

checkpoint ['tʃɛkpɔɪnt] *n* Kontrollpunkt *m*

checkroom ['tʃɛkrum] (*US*) *n* (*left-luggage office*) Gepäckaufbewahrung *f*

checkup ['tʃɛkʌp] *n* Untersuchung *f*

cheek [tʃi:k] *n* Backe *f*; (*impudence*) Frechheit *f*; (*nerve*) Unverschämtheit *f*

cheekbone ['tʃi:kbəun] *n* Backenknochen *m*

cheeky ['tʃi:kɪ] *adj* frech

cheep [tʃi:p] *vi* (*bird*) piep(s)en ▷ *n* Piep(s) *m*, Piepser *m*

cheer [tʃɪəʳ] *vt* zujubeln *+dat*; (*gladden*) aufmuntern, aufheitern ▷ *vi* jubeln, Hurra rufen ▷ *n* (*gen pl*) Hurraruf *m*, Beifallsruf *m*; **cheers** *npl* Hurrageschrei *nt*, Jubel *m*; **~s!** prost!

▸ **cheer on** *vt* anspornen, anfeuern

▸ **cheer up** *vi* vergnügter *or* fröhlicher werden ▷ *vt* aufmuntern, aufheitern

cheerful ['tʃɪəful] *adj* fröhlich

cheerio [tʃɪərɪ'əu] (*Brit*) *excl* tschüss (*inf*)

cheerleader ['tʃɪəli:dəʳ] *n jd, der bei Sportveranstaltungen etc die Zuschauer zu Beifallsrufen anfeuert*

cheese [tʃi:z] *n* Käse *m*

cheeseboard ['tʃi:zbɔ:d] *n* Käsebrett *nt*; (*with cheese on it*) Käseplatte *f*

cheeseburger ['tʃi:zbə:gəʳ] *n* Cheeseburger *m*

cheesecake ['tʃi:zkeɪk] *n* Käsekuchen *m*

cheetah ['tʃi:tə] *n* Gepard *m*

chef [ʃɛf] *n* Küchenchef(in) *m(f)*

chemical ['kɛmɪkl] *adj* chemisch ▷ *n* Chemikalie *f*

chemist ['kɛmɪst] *n* (*Brit: pharmacist*) Apotheker(in) *m(f)*; (*scientist*) Chemiker(in) *m(f)*

chemistry ['kɛmɪstrɪ] *n* Chemie *f*

chemist's ['kɛmɪsts], **chemist's shop** (*Brit*)

n Drogerie *f*; (*also*: **dispensing chemist's**) Apotheke *f*
cheque [tʃɛk] (*Brit*) *n* Scheck *m*; **to pay by ~** mit (einem) Scheck bezahlen
chequebook ['tʃɛkbuk] *n* Scheckbuch *nt*
cheque card (*Brit*) *n* Scheckkarte *f*
chequered, (*US*) **checkered** ['tʃɛkəd] *adj* (*fig*) bewegt
cherish ['tʃɛrɪʃ] *vt* (*person*) liebevoll sorgen für; (*memory*) in Ehren halten; (*dream*) sich hingeben *+dat*; (*hope*) hegen
cherry ['tʃɛrɪ] *n* Kirsche *f*; (*also*: **cherry tree**) Kirschbaum *m*
chess [tʃɛs] *n* Schach(spiel) *nt*
chessboard ['tʃɛsbɔːd] *n* Schachbrett *nt*
chest [tʃɛst] *n* Brust *f*, Brustkorb *m*; (*box*) Kiste *f*, Truhe *f*; **to get sth off one's ~** (*inf*) sich *dat* etw von der Seele reden
chestnut ['tʃɛsnʌt] *n* Kastanie *f* ▷ *adj* kastanienbraun
chest of drawers *n* Kommode *f*
chew [tʃuː] *vt* kauen
chewing gum ['tʃuːɪŋ-] *n* Kaugummi *m*
chic [ʃiːk] *adj* chic *inv*, schick
chick [tʃɪk] *n* Küken *nt*; (*inf*: *girl*) Mieze *f*
chicken ['tʃɪkɪn] *n* Huhn *nt*; (*meat*) Hähnchen *nt*; (*inf*: *coward*) Feigling *m*
▸ **chicken out** (*inf*) *vi*: **to ~ out of doing sth** davor kneifen, etw zu tun
chickenpox ['tʃɪkɪnpɔks] *n* Windpocken *pl*
chickpea ['tʃɪkpiː] *n* Kichererbse *f*
chicory ['tʃɪkərɪ] *n* (*in coffee*) Zichorie *f*; (*salad vegetable*) Chicorée *f or m*
chief [tʃiːf] *n* Häuptling *m*; (*of organization, department*) Leiter(in) *m(f)*, Chef(in) *m(f)* ▷ *adj* Haupt-, wichtigste(r, s)
chief executive, (*US*) **chief executive officer** *n* Generaldirektor(in) *m(f)*
chiefly ['tʃiːflɪ] *adv* hauptsächlich
chiffon ['ʃɪfɔn] *n* Chiffon *m*
chilblain ['tʃɪlbleɪn] *n* Frostbeule *f*
child [tʃaɪld] (*pl* **~ren**) *n* Kind *nt*; **do you have any ~ren?** haben Sie Kinder?
child benefit (*Brit*) *n* Kindergeld *nt*
childbirth ['tʃaɪldbəːθ] *n* Geburt *f*, Entbindung *f*
childhood ['tʃaɪldhud] *n* Kindheit *f*
childish ['tʃaɪldɪʃ] *adj* kindisch
childlike ['tʃaɪldlaɪk] *adj* kindlich
child minder (*Brit*) *n* Tagesmutter *f*
children ['tʃɪldrən] *npl of* **child**
Chile ['tʃɪlɪ] *n* Chile *nt*
chill [tʃɪl] *n* Kühle *f*; (*illness*) Erkältung *f* ▷ *adj* kühl; (*fig*: *reminder*) erschreckend ▷ *vt* kühlen; (*person*) frösteln *or* frieren lassen; **"serve ~ed"** "gekühlt servieren"
chilli, (*US*) **chili** ['tʃɪlɪ] *n* Peperoni *pl*
chilly ['tʃɪlɪ] *adj* kühl; (*person, response, look*) kühl, frostig; **to feel ~** frösteln, frieren
chime [tʃaɪm] *n* Glockenspiel *nt* ▷ *vi* läuten
chimney ['tʃɪmnɪ] *n* Schornstein *m*
chimney sweep *n* Schornsteinfeger(in) *m(f)*
chimpanzee [tʃɪmpæn'ziː] *n* Schimpanse *m*
chin [tʃɪn] *n* Kinn *nt*
China ['tʃaɪnə] *n* China *nt*
china ['tʃaɪnə] *n* Porzellan *nt*
Chinese [tʃaɪ'niːz] *adj* chinesisch ▷ *n inv* Chinese *m*, Chinesin *f*; (*Ling*) Chinesisch *nt*
chink [tʃɪŋk] *n* (*in door, wall etc*) Ritze *f*, Spalt *m*; (*of bottles etc*) Klirren *nt*
chip [tʃɪp] *n* (*gen pl*) Pommes frites *pl*; (*US*: *also*: **potato chip**) Chip *m*; (*of wood*) Span *m*; (*of glass, stone*) Splitter *m*; (*in glass, cup etc*) abgestoßene Stelle *f*; (*in gambling*) Chip *m*, Spielmarke *f*; (*Comput*: *also*: **microchip**) Chip *m* ▷ *vt* (*cup, plate*) anschlagen; **when the ~s are down** (*fig*) wenn es drauf ankommt
▸ **chip in** (*inf*) *vi* (*contribute*) etwas beisteuern; (*interrupt*) sich einschalten
chiropodist [kɪ'rɔpədɪst] (*Brit*) *n* Fußpfleger(in) *m(f)*
chirp [tʃəːp] *vi* (*bird*) zwitschern; (*crickets*) zirpen
chisel ['tʃɪzl] *n* (*for stone*) Meißel *m*; (*for wood*) Beitel *m*
chit [tʃɪt] *n* Zettel *m*
chitchat ['tʃɪttʃæt] *n* Plauderei *f*
chivalry ['ʃɪvəlrɪ] *n* Ritterlichkeit *f*
chives [tʃaɪvz] *npl* Schnittlauch *m*
chlorine ['klɔːriːn] *n* Chlor *nt*
chock-a-block ['tʃɔkə'blɔk] *adj* gerammelt voll
chocolate ['tʃɔklɪt] *n* Schokolade *f*; (*drink*) Kakao *m*, Schokolade *f*; (*sweet*) Praline *f* ▷ *cpd* Schokoladen-
choice [tʃɔɪs] *n* Auswahl *f*; (*option*) Möglichkeit *f*; (*preference*) Wahl *f* ▷ *adj* Qualitäts-, erstklassig; **I did it by** *or* **from ~** ich habe es mir so ausgesucht; **a wide ~** eine große Auswahl
choir ['kwaɪəʳ] *n* Chor *m*
choirboy ['kwaɪə'bɔɪ] *n* Chorknabe *m*
choke [tʃəuk] *vi* ersticken; (*with smoke, dust, anger etc*) keine Luft mehr bekommen ▷ *vt* erwürgen, erdrosseln ▷ *n* (*Aut*) Choke *m*, Starterklappe *f*; **to be ~d (with)** verstopft sein (mit)
cholesterol [kə'lɛstərɔl] *n* Cholesterin *nt*
choose [tʃuːz] (*pt* **chose**, *pp* **chosen**) *vt* (aus)wählen; (*profession, friend*) sich *dat* aussuchen ▷ *vi*: **to ~ between** wählen zwischen *+dat*, eine Wahl treffen zwischen *+dat*; **to ~ from** wählen aus *or* unter *+dat*, eine Wahl treffen aus *or* unter *+dat*; **to ~ to do sth** beschließen, etw zu tun
choosy ['tʃuːzɪ] *adj* wählerisch
chop [tʃɔp] *vt* (*wood*) hacken; (*also*: **chop up**: *vegetables, fruit, meat*) klein schneiden ▷ *n* Kotelett *nt*; **chops** (*inf*) *npl* (*of animal*) Maul *nt*; (*of person*) Mund *m*; **to get the ~** (*Brit*: *inf*: *project*) dem Rotstift zum Opfer fallen; (: *be sacked*) rausgeschmissen werden
▸ **chop down** *vt* (*tree*) fällen
chopper ['tʃɔpəʳ] (*inf*) *n* Hubschrauber *m*
choppy ['tʃɔpɪ] *adj* (*sea*) kabbelig, bewegt
chopsticks ['tʃɔpstɪks] *npl* Stäbchen *pl*

chord [kɔːd] *n* Akkord *m*; (*Math*) Sehne *f*
chore [tʃɔːʳ] *n* Hausarbeit *f*; (*routine task*) lästige Routinearbeit *f*; **household ~s** Hausarbeit
chortle ['tʃɔːtl] *vi* glucksen
chorus ['kɔːrəs] *n* Chor *m*; (*refrain*) Refrain *m*; (*of complaints*) Flut *f*
chose [tʃəuz] *pt of* **choose**
chosen ['tʃəuzn] *pp of* **choose**
chowder ['tʃaudəʳ] *n* (sämige) Fischsuppe *f*
Christ [kraɪst] *n* Christus *m*
christen ['krɪsn] *vt* taufen
christening ['krɪsnɪŋ] *n* Taufe *f*
Christian ['krɪstɪən] *adj* christlich ▷ *n* Christ(in) *m(f)*
Christianity [krɪstɪ'ænɪtɪ] *n* Christentum *nt*
Christian name *n* Vorname *m*
Christmas ['krɪsməs] *n* Weihnachten *nt*; **Happy** *or* **Merry ~!** frohe *or* fröhliche Weihnachten!
Christmas card *n* Weihnachtskarte *f*
Christmas Day *n* der erste Weihnachtstag
Christmas Eve *n* Heiligabend *m*
Christmas tree *n* Weihnachtsbaum *m*, Christbaum *m*
chrome [krəum] *n* = **chromium**
chromium ['krəumɪəm] *n* Chrom *nt*; (*also*: **chromium plating**) Verchromung *f*
chronic ['krɔnɪk] *adj* (*also fig*) chronisch; (*severe*) schlimm
chronicle ['krɔnɪkl] *n* Chronik *f*
chronological [krɔnə'lɔdʒɪkl] *adj* chronologisch
chrysanthemum [krɪ'sænθəməm] *n* Chrysantheme *f*
chubby ['tʃʌbɪ] *adj* pummelig; **~ cheeks** Pausbacken *pl*
chuck [tʃʌk] (*inf*) *vt* werfen, schmeißen; (*Brit*: *also*: **chuck up, chuck in**: *job*) hinschmeißen; (: *person*) Schluss machen mit
▸ **chuck out** *vt* (*person*) rausschmeißen; (*rubbish etc*) wegschmeißen
chuckle ['tʃʌkl] *vi* leise in sich *acc* hineinlachen
chug [tʃʌg] *vi* (*also*: **chug along**) tuckern
chum [tʃʌm] *n* Kumpel *m*
chunk [tʃʌŋk] *n* großes Stück *nt*
church [tʃəːtʃ] *n* Kirche *f*; **the C~ of England** die anglikanische Kirche
churchyard ['tʃəːtʃjɑːd] *n* Friedhof *m*
churn [tʃəːn] *n* Butterfass *nt*; (*also*: **milk churn**) Milchkanne *f*
▸ **churn out** *vt* am laufenden Band produzieren
chute [ʃuːt] *n* (*also*: **rubbish chute**) Müllschlucker *m*; (*for coal, parcels etc*) Rutsche *f*; (*Brit*: *slide*) Rutschbahn *f*, Rutsche *f*
chutney ['tʃʌtnɪ] *n* Chutney *nt*
CIA (*US*) *n abbr* (= *Central Intelligence Agency*) CIA *f or m*
CID (*Brit*) *n abbr* = **Criminal Investigation Department**
cider ['saɪdəʳ] *n* Apfelwein *m*
cigar [sɪ'gɑːʳ] *n* Zigarre *f*
cigarette [sɪgə'rɛt] *n* Zigarette *f*
cigarette case *n* Zigarettenetui *nt*
cigarette end *n* Zigarettenstummel *m*
Cinderella [sɪndə'rɛlə] *n* Aschenputtel *nt*, Aschenbrödel *nt*
cinema ['sɪnəmə] *n* Kino *nt*; (*film-making*) Film *m*
cinnamon ['sɪnəmən] *n* Zimt *m*
circle ['səːkl] *n* Kreis *m*; (*in cinema, theatre*) Rang *m* ▷ *vi* kreisen ▷ *vt* kreisen um; (*surround*) umgeben
circuit ['səːkɪt] *n* Runde *f*; (*Elec*) Stromkreis *m*; (*track*) Rennbahn *f*
circuitous [səː'kjuɪtəs] *adj* umständlich
circular ['səːkjuləʳ] *adj* rund; (*route*) Rund- ▷ *n* (*letter*) Rundschreiben *nt*, Rundbrief *m*; (*as advertisement*) Wurfsendung *f*; **~ argument** Zirkelschluss *m*
circulate ['səːkjuleɪt] *vi* (*traffic*) fließen; (*blood, report*) zirkulieren; (*news, rumour*) kursieren, in Umlauf sein; (*person*) die Runde machen ▷ *vt* herumgehen *or* zirkulieren lassen
circulation [səːkju'leɪʃən] *n* (*of traffic*) Fluss *m*; (*of air etc*) Zirkulation *f*; (*of newspaper*) Auflage *f*; (*Med*: *of blood*) Kreislauf *m*
circumflex ['səːkəmflɛks] *n* (*also*: **circumflex accent**) Zirkumflex *m*
circumstances ['səːkəmstənsɪz] *npl* Umstände *pl*; (*financial condition*) (finanzielle) Verhältnisse *pl*; **in the ~** unter diesen Umständen; **under no ~** unter (gar) keinen Umständen, auf keinen Fall
circus ['səːkəs] *n* Zirkus *m*; (*also*: **Circus**: *in place names*) Platz *m*
CIS *n abbr* (= *Commonwealth of Independent States*) GUS *f*
cistern ['sɪstən] *n* Zisterne *f*; (*of toilet*) Spülkasten *m*
cite [saɪt] *vt* zitieren; (*example*) anführen; (*Law*) vorladen
citizen ['sɪtɪzn] *n* Staatsbürger(in) *m(f)*; (*of town*) Bürger(in) *m(f)*
citizenship ['sɪtɪznʃɪp] *n* Staatsbürgerschaft *f*; (*Brit*: *Scol*) Gesellschaftskunde *f*
city ['sɪtɪ] *n* (Groß)stadt *f*; **the C~** (*Fin*) die City, das Londoner Banken- und Börsenviertel
city centre *n* Stadtzentrum *nt*, Innenstadt *f*
civic ['sɪvɪk] *adj* (*authorities etc*) Stadt-, städtisch; (*duties, pride*) Bürger-, bürgerlich
civic centre (*Brit*) *n* Stadtverwaltung *f*
civil ['sɪvɪl] *adj* (*disturbances, rights*) Bürger-; (*liberties, law*) bürgerlich; (*polite*) höflich
civil engineer *n* Bauingenieur(in) *m(f)*
civilian [sɪ'vɪlɪən] *adj* (*population*) Zivil- ▷ *n* Zivilist *m*; **~ casualties** Verluste *pl* unter der Zivilbevölkerung
civilization [sɪvɪlaɪ'zeɪʃən] *n* Zivilisation *f*; (*a society*) Kultur *f*
civilized ['sɪvɪlaɪzd] *adj* zivilisiert; (*person*) kultiviert; (*place, experience*) gepflegt
civil law *n* Zivilrecht *nt*, bürgerliches Recht *nt*

civil rights *npl* Bürgerrechte *pl*
civil servant *n* (Staats)beamter *m*, (Staats)beamtin *f*
Civil Service *n* Beamtenschaft *f*
civil war *n* Bürgerkrieg *m*
clad [klæd] *adj*: **~ (in)** gekleidet (in *+acc*)
claim [kleɪm] *vt* (*assert*) behaupten; (*responsibility*) übernehmen; (*credit*) in Anspruch nehmen; (*rights, inheritance*) Anspruch erheben auf *+acc*; (*expenses*) sich *dat* zurückerstatten lassen; (*compensation, damages*) verlangen ▷ *vi* (*for insurance*) Ansprüche geltend machen ▷ *n* (*assertion*) Behauptung *f*; (*for pension, wage rise, compensation*) Forderung *f*; (*right: to inheritance, land*) Anspruch *m*; (*for expenses*) Spesenabrechnung *f*; **(insurance) ~** (Versicherungs)anspruch *m*; **to put in a ~ for** beantragen
claimant ['kleɪmənt] *n* Antragsteller(in) *m(f)*
claim form *n* Antragsformular *nt*
clairvoyant [klɛə'vɔɪənt] *n* Hellseher(in) *m(f)*
clam [klæm] *n* Venusmuschel *f*
▸ **clam up** (*inf*) *vi* keinen Piep (mehr) sagen
clamber ['klæmbə^r] *vi* klettern
clammy ['klæmɪ] *adj* feucht
clamour, (*US*) **clamor** ['klæmə^r] *n* Lärm *m*; (*protest*) Protest *m*, Aufschrei *m* ▷ *vi*: **to ~ for** schreien nach
clamp [klæmp] *n* Schraubzwinge *f*, Klemme *f* ▷ *vt* (*two things*) zusammenklemmen; (*one thing on another*) klemmen; (*wheel*) krallen
▸ **clamp down on** *vt fus* rigoros vorgehen gegen
clan [klæn] *n* Clan *m*
clang [klæŋ] *vi* klappern; (*bell*) läuten ▷ *n* (*see vi*) Klappern *nt*; Läuten *nt*
clap [klæp] *vi* (Beifall) klatschen ▷ *vt*: **to ~ (one's hands)** (in die Hände) klatschen ▷ *n*: **a ~ of thunder** ein Donnerschlag *m*
clapping ['klæpɪŋ] *n* Beifall *m*
claret ['klærət] *n* roter Bordeaux(wein) *m*
clarify ['klærɪfaɪ] *vt* klären
clarinet [klærɪ'nɛt] *n* Klarinette *f*
clarity ['klærɪtɪ] *n* Klarheit *f*
clash [klæʃ] *n* (*fight*) Zusammenstoß *m*; (*disagreement*) Streit *m*, Auseinandersetzung *f*; (*of beliefs, ideas, views*) Konflikt *m*; (*of colours, styles, personalities*) Unverträglichkeit *f*; (*of events, dates, appointments*) Überschneidung *f*; (*noise*) Klirren *nt* ▷ *vi* (*fight*) zusammenstoßen; (*disagree*) sich streiten, eine Auseinandersetzung haben; (*beliefs, ideas, views*) aufeinanderprallen; (*colours*) sich beißen; (*styles, personalities*) nicht zusammenpassen; (*two events, dates, appointments*) sich überschneiden; (*make noise*) klirrend aneinanderschlagen
clasp [klɑːsp] *n* Griff *m*; (*embrace*) Umklammerung *f*; (*of necklace, bag*) Verschluss *m* ▷ *vt* (er)greifen; (*embrace*) umklammern
class [klɑːs] *n* Klasse *f*; (*lesson*) (Unterrichts)stunde *f* ▷ *adj* (*struggle, distinction*) Klassen- ▷ *vt* einordnen, einstufen
classic ['klæsɪk] *adj* klassisch ▷ *n* Klassiker *m*; (*race*) *bedeutendes Pferderennen für dreijährige Pferde*; **classics** *npl* (*Scol*) Altphilologie *f*
classical ['klæsɪkl] *adj* klassisch
classification [klæsɪfɪ'keɪʃən] *n* Klassifikation *f*; (*category*) Klasse *f*; (*system*) Einteilung *f*
classified ['klæsɪfaɪd] *adj* geheim
classify ['klæsɪfaɪ] *vt* klassifizieren, (ein)ordnen
classmate ['klɑːsmeɪt] *n* Klassenkamerad(in) *m(f)*
classroom ['klɑːsrum] *n* Klassenzimmer *nt*
classroom assistant *n* Assistenzlehrkraft *f*
classy ['klɑːsɪ] (*inf*) *adj* nobel, exklusiv; (*person*) todschick
clatter ['klætə^r] *n* Klappern *nt*; (*of hooves*) Trappeln *nt* ▷ *vi* (*see n*) klappern; trappeln
clause [klɔːz] *n* (*Law*) Klausel *f*; (*Ling*) Satz *m*
claustrophobic [klɔːstrə'fəubɪk] *adj* (*place, situation*) beengend; (*person*): **to be/feel ~** Platzangst haben/bekommen
claw [klɔː] *n* Kralle *f*; (*of lobster*) Schere *f*, Zange *f*
▸ **claw at** *vt fus* sich krallen an *+acc*
clay [kleɪ] *n* Ton *m*; (*soil*) Lehm *m*
clean [kliːn] *adj* sauber; (*fight*) fair; (*record, reputation*) einwandfrei; (*joke, story*) stubenrein, anständig; (*edge, fracture*) glatt ▷ *vt* sauber machen; (*car, hands, face etc*) waschen ▷ *adv*: **he ~ forgot** er hat es glatt(weg) vergessen; **to have a ~ driving licence, to have a ~ driving record** (*US*) keine Strafpunkte haben; **to ~ one's teeth** (*Brit*) sich *dat* die Zähne putzen; **the thief got ~ away** der Dieb konnte entkommen; **to come ~** (*inf*) auspacken
▸ **clean off** *vt* abwaschen, abwischen
▸ **clean out** *vt* gründlich sauber machen; (*inf: person*) ausnehmen
▸ **clean up** *vt* aufräumen; (*child*) sauber machen; (*fig*) für Ordnung sorgen in *+dat* ▷ *vi* aufräumen, sauber machen; (*inf: make profit*) absahnen
clean-cut ['kliːn'kʌt] *adj* gepflegt; (*situation*) klar
cleaner ['kliːnə^r] *n* Raumpfleger(in) *m(f)*; (*woman*) Putzfrau *f*; (*substance*) Reinigungsmittel *nt*, Putzmittel *nt*
cleaner's ['kliːnəz] *n* (*also*: **dry cleaner's**) Reinigung *f*
cleaning ['kliːnɪŋ] *n* Putzen *nt*
cleanliness ['klɛnlɪnɪs] *n* Sauberkeit *f*, Reinlichkeit *f*
cleanse [klɛnz] *vt* (*purify*) läutern; (*face, cut*) reinigen
cleanser ['klɛnzə^r] *n* (*for face*) Reinigungscreme *f*, Reinigungsmilch *f*
clean-shaven ['kliːn'ʃeɪvn] *adj* glatt rasiert
cleansing department ['klɛnzɪŋ-] (*Brit*) *n* ≈ Stadtreinigung *f*

clear [klɪəʳ] *adj* klar; (*footprint*) deutlich; (*photograph*) scharf; (*commitment*) eindeutig; (*glass, plastic*) durchsichtig; (*road, way, floor etc*) frei; (*conscience, skin*) rein ▷ *vt* (*room*) ausräumen; (*trees*) abholzen; (*weeds etc*) entfernen; (*slums etc, stock*) räumen; (*Law*) freisprechen; (*fence, wall*) überspringen; (*cheque*) verrechnen ▷ *vi* (*weather, sky*) aufklaren; (*fog, smoke*) sich auflösen; (*room etc*) sich leeren ▷ *adv*: **to be ~ of the ground** den Boden nicht berühren ▷ *n*: **to be in the ~** (*out of debt*) schuldenfrei sein; (*free of suspicion*) von jedem Verdacht frei sein; (*out of danger*) außer Gefahr sein; **~ profit** Reingewinn *m*; **I have a ~ day tomorrow** (*Brit*) ich habe morgen nichts vor; **to make o.s. ~** sich klar ausdrücken; **to make it ~ to sb that ...** es jdm (unmissverständlich) klarmachen, dass ...; **to ~ the table** den Tisch abräumen; **to ~ a space (for sth)** (für etw) Platz schaffen; **to ~ one's throat** sich räuspern; **to ~ a profit** einen Gewinn machen; **to keep ~ of sb** jdm aus dem Weg gehen; **to keep ~ of sth** etw meiden; **to keep ~ of trouble** allem Ärger aus dem Weg gehen
▸ **clear off** (*inf*) *vi* abhauen, verschwinden
▸ **clear up** *vt* aufräumen; (*mystery*) aufklären; (*problem*) lösen ▷ *vi* (*bad weather*) sich aufklären; (*illness*) sich bessern

clearance ['klɪərəns] *n* (*of slums*) Räumung *f*; (*of trees*) Abholzung *f*; (*permission*) Genehmigung *f*; (*free space*) lichte Höhe *f*

clear-cut ['klɪə'kʌt] *adj* klar

clearing ['klɪərɪŋ] *n* Lichtung *f*; (*Brit: Banking*) Clearing *nt*

clearing bank (*Brit*) *n* Clearingbank *f*

clearly ['klɪəlɪ] *adv* klar; (*obviously*) eindeutig

clearway ['klɪəweɪ] (*Brit*) *n* Straße *f* mit Halteverbot

clef [klɛf] *n* (Noten)schlüssel *m*

cleft [klɛft] *n* Spalte *f*

clench [klɛntʃ] *vt* (*fist*) ballen; (*teeth*) zusammenbeißen

clergy ['klə:dʒɪ] *n* Klerus *m*, Geistlichkeit *f*

clergyman ['klə:dʒɪmən] (*irreg: like* **man**) *n* Geistliche(r) *m*

clerical ['klɛrɪkl] *adj* (*job, worker*) Büro-; (*error*) Schreib-; (*Rel*) geistlich

clerk [klɑ:k, (US) klə:rk] *n* (*Brit*) Büroangestellte(r) *f(m)*; (*US: sales person*) Verkäufer(in) *m(f)*

clever ['klɛvəʳ] *adj* klug; (*deft, crafty*) schlau, clever (*inf*); (*device, arrangement*) raffiniert

cliché ['kli:ʃeɪ] *n* Klischee *nt*

click [klɪk] *vi* klicken ▷ *vt*: **to ~ one's tongue** mit der Zunge schnalzen; **to ~ one's heels** die Hacken zusammenschlagen

client ['klaɪənt] *n* Kunde *m*, Kundin *f*; (*of bank, lawyer*) Klient(in) *m(f)*; (*of restaurant*) Gast *m*

cliff [klɪf] *n* Kliff *nt*

climate ['klaɪmɪt] *n* Klima *nt*

climax ['klaɪmæks] *n* (*sexual*) Höhepunkt *m*

climb [klaɪm] *vi* klettern; (*plane, sun, prices, shares*) steigen ▷ *vt* (*stairs, ladder*) hochsteigen, hinaufsteigen; (*tree*) klettern auf *+acc*; (*hill*) steigen auf *+acc* ▷ *n* Aufstieg *m*; (*of prices etc*) Anstieg *m*; **to ~ over a wall/into a car** über eine Mauer/in ein Auto steigen *or* klettern
▸ **climb down** (*Brit*) *vi* (*fig*) nachgeben

climb-down ['klaɪmdaun] *n* Nachgeben *nt*, Rückzieher *m* (*inf*)

climber ['klaɪməʳ] *n* Bergsteiger(in) *m(f)*; (*plant*) Kletterpflanze *f*

climbing ['klaɪmɪŋ] *n* Bergsteigen *nt*

clinch [klɪntʃ] *vt* (*deal*) perfekt machen; (*argument*) zum Abschluss bringen

cling [klɪŋ] (*pt, pp* **clung**) *vi*: **to ~ to** (*mother, support*) sich festklammern an *+dat*; (*idea, belief*) festhalten an *+dat*; (*subj: clothes, dress*) sich anschmiegen *+dat*

clinic ['klɪnɪk] *n* Klinik *f*; (*session*) Sprechstunde *f*; (*: Sport*) Trainingstunde *f*

clinical ['klɪnɪkl] *adj* klinisch; (*fig*) nüchtern, kühl; (*: building, room*) steril

clink [klɪŋk] *vi* klirren

clip [klɪp] *n* (*also*: **paper clip**) Büroklammer *f*; (*Brit: also*: **bulldog clip**) Klammer *f*; (*holding wire, hose etc*) Klemme *f*; (*for hair*) Spange *f*; (*TV, Cine*) Ausschnitt *m* ▷ *vt* festklemmen; (*also*: **clip together**) zusammenheften; (*cut*) schneiden

clippers ['klɪpəz] *npl* (*for gardening*) Schere *f*; (*also*: **nail clippers**) Nagelzange *f*

clipping ['klɪpɪŋ] *n* (*from newspaper*) Ausschnitt *m*

cloak [kləuk] *n* Umhang *m* ▷ *vt* (*fig*) hüllen

cloakroom ['kləukrum] *n* Garderobe *f*; (*Brit: WC*) Toilette *f*

clock [klɔk] *n* Uhr *f*; **round the ~** rund um die Uhr; **30,000 on the ~** (*Brit: Aut*) ein Tachostand von 30.000; **to work against the ~** gegen die Uhr arbeiten
▸ **clock in** (*Brit*) *vi* (den Arbeitsbeginn) stempeln *or* stechen
▸ **clock off** (*Brit*) *vi* (das Arbeitsende) stempeln *or* stechen
▸ **clock on** (*Brit*) *vi* = **clock in**
▸ **clock out** (*Brit*) *vi* = **clock off**
▸ **clock up** *vt* (*miles*) fahren; (*hours*) arbeiten

clockwise ['klɔkwaɪz] *adv* im Uhrzeigersinn

clockwork ['klɔkwə:k] *n* Uhrwerk *nt* ▷ *adj* aufziehbar, zum Aufziehen; **like ~** wie am Schnürchen

clog [klɔg] *n* Clog *m*; (*wooden*) Holzschuh *m* ▷ *vt* verstopfen ▷ *vi* (*also*: **clog up**) verstopfen

cloister ['klɔɪstəʳ] *n* Kreuzgang *m*

clone [kləun] *n* Klon *m*

close¹ [kləus] *adj* (*writing, friend, contact*) eng; (*texture*) dicht, fest; (*relative*) nahe; (*examination*) genau, gründlich; (*watch*) streng, scharf; (*contest*) knapp; (*weather*) schwül; (*room*) stickig ▷ *adv* nahe; **~ (to)** nahe (*+gen*); **~ to** in der Nähe *+gen*; **~ by, ~ at hand** in der Nähe; **how ~ is Edinburgh to Glasgow?** wie weit ist Edinburgh von

Glasgow entfernt?; **a ~ friend** ein guter *or* enger Freund; **to have a ~ shave** (*fig*) gerade noch davonkommen; **at ~ quarters** aus der Nähe

close² [kləuz] *vt* schließen, zumachen; (*sale, deal, case*) abschließen; (*speech*) schließen, beenden ▷ *vi* schließen, zumachen; (*door, lid*) sich schließen, zugehen; (*end*) aufhören ▷ *n* Ende *nt*, Schlus *m*; **to bring sth to a ~** etw beenden

▸ **close down** *vi* (*factory*) stillgelegt werden; (*magazine etc*) eingestellt werden

▸ **close in** *vi* (*night*) hereinbrechen; (*fog*) sich verdichten; **to ~ in on sb/sth** jdm/etw auf den Leib rücken; **the days are closing in** die Tage werden kürzer

▸ **close off** *vt* (*area*) abriegeln; (*road*) sperren

closed [kləuzd] *adj* geschlossen; (*road*) gesperrt

closed shop *n* Betrieb *m* mit Gewerkschaftszwang

close-knit ['kləus'nɪt] *adj* eng zusammengewachsen

closely ['kləuslɪ] *adv* (*examine, watch*) genau; (*connected*) eng; (*related*) nah(e); (*resemble*) sehr; **we are ~ related** wir sind nah verwandt; **a ~ guarded secret** ein streng gehütetes Geheimnis

closet ['klɔzɪt] *n* Wandschrank *m*

close-up ['kləusʌp] *n* Nahaufnahme *f*

closing time (*Brit*) *n* (*in pub*) Polizeistunde *f*, Sperrstunde *f*

closure ['kləuʒəʳ] *n* (*of factory*) Stilllegung *f*; (*of magazine*) Einstellung *f*; (*of road*) Sperrung *f*; (*of border*) Schließung *f*

clot [klɔt] *n* (*blood clot*) (Blut)gerinnsel *nt*; (*inf*: *idiot*) Trottel *m* ▷ *vi* gerinnen; (*external bleeding*) zum Stillstand kommen

cloth [klɔθ] *n* (*material*) Stoff *m*, Tuch *nt*; (*rag*) Lappen *m*; (*Brit*: *also*: **teacloth**) (Spül)tuch *nt*; (*also*: **tablecloth**) Tischtuch *nt*, Tischdecke *f*

clothe [kləuð] *vt* anziehen, kleiden

clothes [kləuðz] *npl* Kleidung *f*, Kleider *pl*; **to put one's ~ on** sich anziehen; **to take one's ~ off** sich ausziehen

clothes brush *n* Kleiderbürste *f*

clothes peg, (*US*) **clothes pin** *n* Wäscheklammer *f*

clothing ['kləuðɪŋ] *n* = **clothes**

cloud [klaud] *n* Wolke *f* ▷ *vt* trüben; **every ~ has a silver lining** (*proverb*) auf Regen folgt Sonnenschein; **to ~ the issue** es unnötig kompliziert machen; (*deliberately*) die Angelegenheit verschleiern

▸ **cloud over** *vi* (*sky*) sich bewölken, sich bedecken; (*face, eyes*) sich verfinstern

cloudburst ['klaudbə:st] *n* Wolkenbruch *m*

cloudy ['klaudɪ] *adj* wolkig, bewölkt; (*liquid*) trüb

clout [klaut] *vt* schlagen, hauen ▷ *n* (*fig*) Schlagkraft *f*

clove [kləuv] *n* Gewürznelke *f*; **~ of garlic** Knoblauchzehe *f*

clover ['kləuvəʳ] *n* Klee *m*

clown [klaun] *n* Clown *m* ▷ *vi* (*also*: **clown about, clown around**) herumblödeln, herumkaspern

cloying ['klɔɪɪŋ] *adj* süßlich

club [klʌb] *n* Klub *m*, Verein *m*; (*weapon*) Keule *f*, Knüppel *m*; (*also*: **golf club**: *object*) Golfschläger *m* ▷ *vt* knüppeln ▷ *vi*: **to ~ together** zusammenlegen; **clubs** *npl* (*Cards*) Kreuz *nt*

club class *n* Klubklasse *f*, Businessklasse *f*

clubhouse ['klʌbhaus] *n* Klubhaus *nt*

cluck [klʌk] *vi* glucken

clue [klu:] *n* Hinweis *m*, Anhaltspunkt *m*; (*in crossword*) Frage *f*; **I haven't a ~** ich habe keine Ahnung

clump [klʌmp] *n* Gruppe *f*

clumsy ['klʌmzɪ] *adj* ungeschickt; (*object*) unförmig; (*effort, attempt*) plump

clung [klʌŋ] *pt, pp of* **cling**

cluster ['klʌstəʳ] *n* Gruppe *f* ▷ *vi* (*people*) sich scharen; (*houses*) sich drängen

clutch [klʌtʃ] *n* Griff *m*; (*Aut*) Kupplung *f* ▷ *vt* (*purse, hand*) umklammern; (*stick*) sich festklammern an +*dat* ▷ *vi*: **to ~ at** sich klammern an +*acc*

clutter ['klʌtəʳ] *vt* (*also*: **clutter up**: *room*) vollstopfen; (: *table*) vollstellen ▷ *n* Kram *m* (*inf*)

cm *abbr* (= *centimetre*) cm

CND (*Brit*) *n abbr* (= *Campaign for Nuclear Disarmament*) *Organisation für atomare Abrüstung*

Co. *abbr* = **company; county**

c/o *abbr* (= *care of*) bei, c/o

coach [kəutʃ] *n* (Reise)bus *m*; (*horse-drawn*) Kutsche *f*; (*of train*) Wagen *m*; (*Sport*) Trainer *m*; (*Scol*) Nachhilfelehrer(in) *m(f)* ▷ *vt* trainieren; (*student*) Nachhilfeunterricht geben +*dat*

coach trip *n* Busfahrt *f*

coal [kəul] *n* Kohle *f*

coalfield ['kəulfi:ld] *n* Kohlenrevier *nt*

coalition [kəuə'lɪʃən] *n* (*Pol*) Koalition *f*; (*of pressure groups etc*) Zusammenschluss *m*

coalman ['kəulmən] (*irreg*: *like* **man**) *n* Kohlenhändler *m*

coal mine *n* Kohlenbergwerk *nt*, Zeche *f*

coarse [kɔ:s] *adj* (*texture*) grob; (*vulgar*) gewöhnlich, derb; (*salt, sand etc*) grobkörnig

coast [kəust] *n* Küste *f* ▷ *vi* (im Leerlauf) fahren

coastal ['kəustl] *adj* Küsten-

coastguard ['kəustgɑ:d] *n* (*officer*) Küstenwächter *m*; (*service*) Küstenwacht *f*

coastline ['kəustlaɪn] *n* Küste *f*

coat [kəut] *n* Mantel *m*; (*of animal*) Fell *nt*; (*layer*) Schicht *f*; (: *of paint*) Anstrich *m* ▷ *vt* überziehen

coat hanger *n* Kleiderbügel *m*

coating ['kəutɪŋ] *n* (*of chocolate etc*) Überzug *m*; (*of dust etc*) Schicht *f*

coax [kəuks] *vt* (*person*) überreden

cob [kɔb] *n see* **corn**

cobbler ['kɔbləʳ] *n* Schuster *m*
cobbles ['kɔblz] *npl* Kopfsteinpflaster *nt*
cobweb ['kɔbwɛb] *n* Spinnennetz *nt*
cocaine [kə'keɪn] *n* Kokain *nt*
cock [kɔk] *n* Hahn *m*; (*male bird*) Männchen *nt* ▷ *vt* (*gun*) entsichern; **to ~ one's ears** (*fig*) die Ohren spitzen
cockerel ['kɔkərl] *n* junger Hahn *m*
cockle ['kɔkl] *n* Herzmuschel *f*
cockney ['kɔknɪ] *n* Cockney *m*, echter Londoner *m*; (*Ling*) Cockney *nt*
cockpit ['kɔkpɪt] *n* Cockpit *nt*
cockroach ['kɔkrəutʃ] *n* Küchenschabe *f*, Kakerlak *m*
cocktail ['kɔkteɪl] *n* Cocktail *m*; **fruit ~** Obstsalat *m*; **prawn ~** Krabbencocktail *m*
cocktail cabinet *n* Hausbar *f*
cocktail party *n* Cocktailparty *f*
cocoa ['kəukəu] *n* Kakao *m*
coconut ['kəukənʌt] *n* Kokosnuss *f*
cod [kɔd] *n* Kabeljau *m*
code [kəud] *n* (*cipher*) Chiffre *f*; (*also*: **dialling code**) Vorwahl *f*; (*also*: **post code**) Postleitzahl *f*; **~ of behaviour** Sittenkodex *m*; **~ of practice** Verfahrensregeln *pl*
cod-liver oil ['kɔdlɪvə-] *n* Lebertran *m*
coeducational ['kəuɛdju'keɪʃənl] *adj* (*school*) Koedukations-, gemischt
coercion [kəu'ə:ʃən] *n* Zwang *m*
coffee ['kɔfɪ] *n* Kaffee *m*; **black ~** schwarzer Kaffee *m*; **white ~** Kaffee mit Milch; **~ with cream** Kaffee mit Sahne
coffee bar (*Brit*) *n* Café *nt*
coffee bean *n* Kaffeebohne *f*
coffee break *n* Kaffeepause *f*
coffeepot ['kɔfɪpɔt] *n* Kaffeekanne *f*
coffee table *n* Couchtisch *m*
coffin ['kɔfɪn] *n* Sarg *m*
cog [kɔg] *n* (*wheel*) Zahnrad *nt*; (*tooth*) Zahn *m*
cogent ['kəudʒənt] *adj* stichhaltig, zwingend
cognac ['kɔnjæk] *n* Kognak *m*
coherent [kəu'hɪərənt] *adj* (*speech*) zusammenhängend; (*answer, theory*) schlüssig; (*person*) bei klarem Verstand
coil [kɔɪl] *n* Rolle *f*; (*one loop*) Windung *f*; (*of smoke*) Kringel *m*; (*Aut, Elec*) Spule *f*; (*contraceptive*) Spirale *f* ▷ *vt* aufrollen, aufwickeln
coin [kɔɪn] *n* Münze *f* ▷ *vt* prägen
coinage ['kɔɪnɪdʒ] *n* Münzen *pl*; (*Ling*) Prägung *f*
coincide [kəuɪn'saɪd] *vi* (*events*) zusammenfallen; (*ideas, views*) übereinstimmen
coincidence [kəu'ɪnsɪdəns] *n* Zufall *m*
Coke® [kəuk] *n* Coca-Cola® *nt or f*, Coke® *nt*
coke [kəuk] *n* Koks *m*
colander ['kɔləndəʳ] *n* Durchschlag *m*
cold [kəuld] *adj* kalt; (*unemotional*) kalt, kühl ▷ *n* Kälte *f*; (*Med*) Erkältung *f*; **it's ~** es ist kalt; **to be/feel ~** (*person*) frieren; (*object*) kalt sein; **in ~ blood** kaltblütig; **to have ~ feet** (*fig*) kalte Füße bekommen; **to give sb the ~ shoulder** jdm die kalte Schulter zeigen; **to catch ~, to catch a ~** sich erkälten
cold sore *n* Bläschenausschlag *m*
coleslaw ['kəulslɔ:] *n* Krautsalat *m*
colic ['kɔlɪk] *n* Kolik *f*
collaborate [kə'læbəreɪt] *vi* zusammenarbeiten; (*with enemy*) kollaborieren
collapse [kə'læps] *vi* zusammenbrechen; (*building*) einstürzen; (*plans*) scheitern; (*government*) stürzen ▷ *n* (*see vb*) Zusammenbruch *m*; Einsturz *m*; Scheitern *nt*; Sturz *m*
collapsible [kə'læpsəbl] *adj* Klapp-, zusammenklappbar
collar ['kɔləʳ] *n* Kragen *m*; (*of dog, cat*) Halsband *nt*; (*Tech*) Bund *m* ▷ *vt* (*inf*) schnappen
collarbone ['kɔləbəun] *n* Schlüsselbein *nt*
collateral [kə'lætərl] *n* (*Comm*) (zusätzliche) Sicherheit *f*
colleague ['kɔli:g] *n* Kollege *m*, Kollegin *f*
collect [kə'lɛkt] *vt* sammeln; (*mail*: *Brit*: *fetch*) abholen; (*debts*) eintreiben; (*taxes*) einziehen ▷ *vi* sich ansammeln ▷ *adv* (*US*: *Tel*): **to call ~** ein R-Gespräch führen; **to ~ one's thoughts** seine Gedanken ordnen, sich sammeln; **~ on delivery** (*US*: *Comm*) per Nachnahme
collection [kə'lɛkʃən] *n* Sammlung *f*; (*from place, person, of mail*) Abholung *f*; (*in church*) Kollekte *f*
collective [kə'lɛktɪv] *adj* kollektiv, gemeinsam ▷ *n* Kollektiv *nt*; **~ farm** landwirtschaftliche Produktionsgenossenschaft *f*
collector [kə'lɛktəʳ] *n* Sammler(in) *m(f)*; (*of taxes etc*) Einnehmer(in) *m(f)*; (*of rent, cash*) Kassierer(in) *m(f)*; **~'s item** *or* **piece** Sammlerstück *nt*, Liebhaberstück *nt*
college ['kɔlɪdʒ] *n* College *nt*; (*of agriculture, technology*) Fachhochschule *f*; **to go to ~** studieren; **~ of education** pädagogische Hochschule *f*
collide [kə'laɪd] *vi*: **to ~ (with)** zusammenstoßen (mit); (*fig*: *clash*) eine heftige Auseinandersetzung haben (mit)
colliery ['kɔlɪərɪ] (*Brit*) *n* (Kohlen)bergwerk *nt*, Zeche *f*
collision [kə'lɪʒən] *n* Zusammenstoß *m*; **to be on a ~ course** (*also fig*) auf Kollisionskurs sein
colloquial [kə'ləukwɪəl] *adj* umgangssprachlich
cologne [kə'ləun] *n* (*also*: **eau de cologne**) Kölnischwasser *nt*, Eau de Cologne *nt*
colon ['kəulən] *n* Doppelpunkt *m*; (*Anat*) Dickdarm *m*
colonel ['kə:nl] *n* Oberst *m*
colonial [kə'ləunɪəl] *adj* Kolonial-
colony ['kɔlənɪ] *n* Kolonie *f*
colour, (*US*) **color** ['kʌləʳ] *n* Farbe *f*; (*skin colour*) Hautfarbe *f*; (*of spectacle etc*) Atmosphäre *f* ▷ *vt* bemalen; (*with crayons*) ausmalen; (*dye*)

färben; (*fig*) beeinflussen ▷ *vi* (*blush*) erröten, rot werden ▷ *cpd* Farb-; **colours** *npl* (*of party, club etc*) Farben *pl*; **in ~** (*film*) in Farbe; (*illustrations*) bunt
▸ **colour in** *vt* ausmalen
colour bar *n* Rassenschranke *f*
colour-blind ['kʌləblaɪnd] *adj* farbenblind
coloured ['kʌləd] *adj* farbig; (*photo*) Farb-; (*illustration etc*) bunt
colour film *n* Farbfilm *m*
colourful ['kʌləful] *adj* bunt; (*account, story*) farbig, anschaulich; (*personality*) schillernd
colouring ['kʌlərɪŋ] *n* Gesichtsfarbe *f*, Teint *m*; (*in food*) Farbstoff *m*
colour scheme *n* Farbzusammenstellung *f*
colour television *n* Farbfernsehen *nt*; (*set*) Farbfernseher *m*
colt [kəult] *n* Hengstfohlen *nt*
column ['kɔləm] *n* Säule *f*; (*of people*) Kolonne *f*; (*of print*) Spalte *f*; (*gossip/sports column*) Kolumne *f*; **the editorial ~** der Leitartikel
columnist ['kɔləmnɪst] *n* Kolumnist(in) *m(f)*
coma ['kəumə] *n* Koma *nt*; **to be in a ~** im Koma liegen
comb [kəum] *n* Kamm *m* ▷ *vt* kämmen; (*area*) durchkämmen
combat ['kɔmbæt] *n* Kampf *m* ▷ *vt* bekämpfen
combination [kɔmbɪ'neɪʃən] *n* Kombination *f*
combine [*vti* kəm'baɪn, *n* 'kɔmbaɪn] *vt* verbinden ▷ *vi* sich zusammenschließen; (*Chem*) sich verbinden ▷ *n* Konzern *m*; (*Agr*) = **combine harvester**; **~d effort** vereintes Unternehmen
combine harvester *n* Mähdrescher *m*
come [kʌm] (*pt* **came**, *pp* **come**) *vi* **1** (*movement towards*) kommen; **come with me** kommen Sie mit mir; **to come running** angelaufen kommen; **coming!** ich komme!
2 (*arrive*) kommen; **they came to a river** sie kamen an einen Fluss; **to come home** nach Hause kommen
3 (*reach*): **to come to** kommen an *+acc*; **her hair came to her waist** ihr Haar reichte ihr bis zur Hüfte; **to come to a decision** zu einer Entscheidung kommen
4 (*occur*): **an idea came to me** mir kam eine Idee
5 (*be, become*) werden; **I've come to like him** mittlerweile mag ich ihn; **if it comes to it** wenn es darauf ankommt
▸ **come about** *vi* geschehen
▸ **come across** *vt fus* (*find: person, thing*) stoßen auf *+acc*
▷ *vi*: **to come across well/badly** (*idea etc*) gut/schlecht ankommen; (*meaning*) gut/schlecht verstanden werden
▸ **come along** *vi* (*arrive*) daherkommen; (*make progress*) vorankommen; **come along!** komm schon!
▸ **come apart** *vi* (*break in pieces*) auseinandergehen
▸ **come away** *vi* (*leave*) weggehen; (*become detached*) abgehen
▸ **come back** *vi* (*return*) zurückkommen; **to come back into fashion** wieder in Mode kommen
▸ **come by** *vt fus* (*acquire*) kommen zu
▸ **come down** *vi* (*price*) sinken, fallen; (*building: be demolished*) abgerissen werden; (*tree: during storm*) umstürzen
▸ **come forward** *vi* (*volunteer*) sich melden
▸ **come from** *vt fus* kommen von, stammen aus; (*person*) kommen aus
▸ **come in** *vi* (*enter*) hereinkommen; (*report, news*) eintreffen; (*on deal etc*) sich beteiligen; **come in!** herein!
▸ **come in for** *vt fus* (*criticism etc*) einstecken müssen
▸ **come into** *vt fus* (*inherit: money*) erben; **to come into fashion** in Mode kommen; **money doesn't come into it** Geld hat nichts damit zu tun
▸ **come off** *vi* (*become detached: button, handle*) sich lösen; (*succeed: attempt, plan*) klappen ▷ *vt fus* (*inf*): **come off it!** mach mal halblang!
▸ **come on** *vi* (*pupil, work, project*) vorankommen; (*lights etc*) angehen; **come on!** (*hurry up*) mach schon!; (*encouragement*) los!
▸ **come out** *vi* herauskommen; (*stain*) herausgehen; **to come out (on strike)** in den Streik treten
▸ **come over** *vt fus*: **I don't know what's come over him!** ich weiß nicht, was in ihn gefahren ist
▸ **come round** *vi* (*after faint, operation*) wieder zu sich kommen; (*visit*) vorbeikommen; (*agree*) zustimmen
▸ **come through** *vi* (*survive*) durchkommen; (*telephone call*) (durch)kommen
▷ *vt fus* (*illness etc*) überstehen
▸ **come to** *vi* (*regain consciousness*) wieder zu sich kommen
▷ *vt fus* (*add up to*): **how much does it come to?** was macht das zusammen?
▸ **come under** *vt fus* (*heading*) kommen unter *+acc*; (*criticism, pressure, attack*) geraten unter *+acc*
▸ **come up** *vi* (*approach*) herankommen; (*sun*) aufgehen; (*problem*) auftauchen; (*event*) bevorstehen; (*in conversation*) genannt werden; **something's come up** etwas ist dazwischengekommen
▸ **come up against** *vt fus* (*resistance, difficulties*) stoßen auf *+acc*
▸ **come upon** *vt fus* (*find*) stoßen auf *+acc*
▸ **come up to** *vt fus*: **the film didn't come up to our expectations** der Film entsprach nicht unseren Erwartungen; **it's coming up to 10 o'clock** es ist gleich 10 Uhr
▸ **come up with** *vt fus* (*idea*) aufwarten mit; (*money*) aufbringen
comeback ['kʌmbæk] *n* (*of film star etc*) Comeback *nt*; (*reaction, response*) Reaktion *f*
comedian [kə'mi:dɪən] *n* Komiker *m*

comedy ['kɔmɪdɪ] *n* Komödie *f*; (*humour*) Witz *m*
comet ['kɔmɪt] *n* Komet *m*
comeuppance [kʌm'ʌpəns] *n*: **to get one's ~** die Quittung bekommen
comfort ['kʌmfət] *n* (*physical*) Behaglichkeit *f*; (*material*) Komfort *m*; (*solace, relief*) Trost *m* ▷ *vt* trösten; **comforts** *npl* (*of home etc*) Komfort *m*, Annehmlichkeiten *pl*
comfortable ['kʌmfətəbl] *adj* bequem; (*room*) komfortabel; (*walk, climb etc*) geruhsam; (*income*) ausreichend; (*majority*) sicher; **to be ~** (*physically*) sich wohlfühlen; (*financially*) sehr angenehm leben; **the patient is ~** dem Patienten geht es den Umständen entsprechend gut; **I don't feel very ~ about it** mir ist nicht ganz wohl bei der Sache
comfortably ['kʌmfətəblɪ] *adv* (*sit*) bequem; (*live*) angenehm
comfort station (*US*) *n* öffentliche Toilette *f*
comic ['kɔmɪk] *adj* (*also*: **comical**) komisch ▷ *n* Komiker(in) *m(f)*; (*Brit: magazine*) Comicheft *nt*
comic strip *n* Comicstrip *m*
coming ['kʌmɪŋ] *n* Ankunft *f*, Kommen *nt* ▷ *adj* kommend; (*next*) nächste(r, s); **in the ~ weeks** in den nächsten Wochen
comma ['kɔmə] *n* Komma *nt*
command [kə'mɑ:nd] *n* (*also Comput*) Befehl *m*; (*control, charge*) Führung *f*; (*Mil: authority*) Kommando *nt*, Befehlsgewalt *f*; (*mastery*) Beherrschung *f* ▷ *vt* (*troops*) befehligen, kommandieren; (*be able to get*) verfügen über *+acc*; (*deserve: respect, admiration etc*) verdient haben; **to be in ~ of** das Kommando *or* den (Ober)befehl haben über *+acc*; **to have ~ of** das Kommando haben über *+acc*; **to take ~ of** das Kommando übernehmen *+gen*; **to have at one's ~** verfügen über *+acc*; **to ~ sb to do sth** jdm befehlen, etw zu tun
commandeer [kɔmən'dɪə^r] *vt* requirieren, beschlagnahmen; (*fig*) sich aneignen
commander [kə'mɑ:ndə^r] *n* Befehlshaber *m*, Kommandant *m*
commando [kə'mɑ:ndəu] *n* Kommando *nt*, Kommandotrupp *m*; (*soldier*) Angehörige(r) *m* eines Kommando(trupp)s
commemorate [kə'mɛməreɪt] *vt* gedenken *+gen*
commence [kə'mɛns] *vt, vi* beginnen
commend [kə'mɛnd] *vt* loben; **to ~ sth to sb** jdm etw empfehlen
commensurate [kə'mɛnʃərɪt] *adj*: **~ with** *or* **to** entsprechend *+dat*
comment ['kɔmɛnt] *n* Bemerkung *f*; (*on situation etc*) Kommentar *m* ▷ *vi*: **to ~ (on)** sich äußern (über *+acc or* zu); (*on situation etc*) einen Kommentar abgeben (zu); **"no ~"** "kein Kommentar!"; **to ~ that ...** bemerken, dass ...
commentary ['kɔməntərɪ] *n* Kommentar *m*; (*Sport*) Reportage *f*
commentator ['kɔmənteɪtə^r] *n* Kommentator(in) *m(f)*; (*Sport*) Reporter(in) *m(f)*
commerce ['kɔmə:s] *n* Handel *m*
commercial [kə'mə:ʃəl] *adj* kommerziell; (*organization*) Wirtschafts- ▷ *n* (*advertisement*) Werbespot *m*
commercial break *n* Werbung *f*
commiserate [kə'mɪzəreɪt] *vi*: **to ~ with sb** jdm sein Mitgefühl zeigen
commission [kə'mɪʃən] *n* (*order for work*) Auftrag *m*; (*Comm*) Provision *f*; (*committee*) Kommission *f*; (*Mil*) Offizierspatent *nt* ▷ *vt* (*work of art*) in Auftrag geben; (*Mil*) (zum Offizier) ernennen; **out of ~** außer Betrieb; (*Naut*) nicht im Dienst; **I get 10% ~** ich bekomme 10% Provision; **~ of inquiry** Untersuchungsausschuss *m*, Untersuchungskommission *f*; **to ~ sb to do sth** jdn damit beauftragen, etw zu tun; **to ~ sth from sb** jdm etw in Auftrag geben
commissionaire [kəmɪʃə'nɛə^r] (*Brit*) *n* Portier *m*
commissioner [kə'mɪʃənə^r] *n* Polizeipräsident *m*
commit [kə'mɪt] *vt* (*crime*) begehen; (*money, resources*) einsetzen; (*to sb's care*) anvertrauen; **to ~ o.s.** sich festlegen; **to ~ o.s. to do sth** sich (dazu) verpflichten, etw zu tun; **to ~ suicide** Selbstmord begehen; **to ~ to writing** zu Papier bringen; **to ~ sb for trial** jdn einem Gericht überstellen
commitment [kə'mɪtmənt] *n* Verpflichtung *f*; (*to ideology, system*) Engagement *nt*
committee [kə'mɪtɪ] *n* Ausschuss *m*, Komitee *nt*; **to be on a ~** in einem Ausschuss *or* Komitee sein *or* sitzen
commodity [kə'mɔdɪtɪ] *n* Ware *f*; (*food*) Nahrungsmittel *nt*
common ['kɔmən] *adj* (*shared by all*) gemeinsam; (*good*) Gemein-; (*property*) Gemeinschafts-; (*usual, ordinary*) häufig; (*vulgar*) gewöhnlich ▷ *n* Gemeindeland *nt*; **the Commons** (*Brit: Pol*) *npl* das Unterhaus; **in ~ use** allgemein gebräuchlich; **it's ~ knowledge that** es ist allgemein bekannt, dass; **to the ~ good** für das Gemeinwohl; **to have sth in ~ (with sb)** etw (mit jdm) gemein haben
commoner ['kɔmənə^r] *n* Bürgerliche(r) *f(m)*
common law *n* Gewohnheitsrecht *nt*
commonly ['kɔmənlɪ] *adv* häufig
Common Market *n*: **the ~** der Gemeinsame Markt
commonplace ['kɔmənpleɪs] *adj* alltäglich
common sense *n* gesunder Menschenverstand *m*
Commonwealth ['kɔmənwɛlθ] (*Brit*) *n*: **the ~** das Commonwealth
commotion [kə'məuʃən] *n* Tumult *m*
communal ['kɔmju:nl] *adj* gemeinsam, Gemeinschafts-; (*life*) Gemeinschafts-
commune [*n* 'kɔmju:n, *vi* kə'mju:n] *n* Kommune *f* ▷ *vi*: **to ~ with** Zwiesprache

halten mit
communicate [kə'mju:nɪkeɪt] *vt* mitteilen; (*idea, feeling*) vermitteln ▷ *vi*: **to ~ (with)** (*by speech, gesture*) sich verständigen (mit); (*in writing*) in Verbindung *or* Kontakt stehen (mit)
communication [kəmju:nɪ'keɪʃən] *n* Kommunikation *f*; (*letter, call*) Mitteilung *f*
communication cord (*Brit*) *n* Notbremse *f*
communion [kə'mju:nɪən] *n* (*also*: **Holy Communion**: *Catholic*) Kommunion *f*; (: *Protestant*) Abendmahl *nt*
communism ['kɔmjunɪzəm] *n* Kommunismus *m*
communist ['kɔmjunɪst] *adj* kommunistisch ▷ *n* Kommunist(in) *m(f)*
community [kə'mju:nɪtɪ] *n* Gemeinschaft *f*; (*within larger group*) Bevölkerungsgruppe *f*
community centre *n* Gemeindezentrum *nt*
community chest (*US*) *n* Wohltätigkeitsfonds *m*, Hilfsfonds *m*
community service *n* Sozialdienst *m*
commutation ticket [kɔmju'teɪʃən-] (*US*) *n* Zeitkarte *f*
commute [kə'mju:t] *vi* pendeln ▷ *vt* (*Law, Math*) umwandeln
commuter [kə'mju:tə^r] *n* Pendler(in) *m(f)*
compact [*adj* kəm'pækt, *n* 'kɔmpækt] *adj* kompakt ▷ *n* (*also*: **powder compact**) Puderdose *f*
compact disc *n* Compact Disc *f*, CD *f*
compact disc player *n* CD-Spieler *m*
companion [kəm'pænjən] *n* Begleiter(in) *m(f)*
companionship [kəm'pænjənʃɪp] *n* Gesellschaft *f*
company ['kʌmpənɪ] *n* Firma *f*; (*Theat*) (Schauspiel)truppe *f*; (*Mil*) Kompanie *f*; (*companionship*) Gesellschaft *f*; **he's good ~** seine Gesellschaft ist angenehm; **to keep sb ~** jdm Gesellschaft leisten; **to part ~ with** sich trennen von; **Smith and C~** Smith & Co
company car *n* Firmenwagen *m*
company director *n* Direktor(in) *m(f)*, Firmenchef(in) *m(f)*
company secretary (*Brit*) *n* ≈ Prokurist(in) *m(f)*
comparable ['kɔmpərəbl] *adj* vergleichbar
comparative [kəm'pærətɪv] *adj* relativ; (*study, literature*) vergleichend; (*Ling*) komparativ
comparatively [kəm'pærətɪvlɪ] *adv* relativ
compare [kəm'pɛə^r] *vt*: **to ~ (with** *or* **to)** vergleichen (mit) ▷ *vi*: **to ~ (with)** sich vergleichen lassen (mit); **how do the prices ~?** wie lassen sich die Preise vergleichen?; **~d with** *or* **to** im Vergleich zu, verglichen mit
comparison [kəm'pærɪsn] *n* Vergleich *m*; **in ~ (with)** im Vergleich (zu)
compartment [kəm'pɑ:tmənt] *n* (*Rail*) Abteil *nt*; (*section*) Fach *nt*
compass ['kʌmpəs] *n* Kompass *m*; (*fig: scope*) Bereich *m*; **compasses** *npl* (*also*: **pair of compasses**) Zirkel *m*; **within the ~ of** im Rahmen *or* Bereich *+gen*; **beyond the ~ of** über den Rahmen *or* Bereich *+gen* hinaus
compassion [kəm'pæʃən] *n* Mitgefühl *nt*
compassionate [kəm'pæʃənɪt] *adj* mitfühlend; **on ~ grounds** aus familiären Gründen
compatible [kəm'pætɪbl] *adj* (*ideas etc*) vereinbar; (*people*) zueinanderpassend; (*Comput*) kompatibel
compel [kəm'pɛl] *vt* zwingen
compelling [kəm'pɛlɪŋ] *adj* zwingend
compensate ['kɔmpənseɪt] *vt* entschädigen ▷ *vi*: **to ~ for** (*loss*) ersetzen; (*disappointment, change etc*) (wieder) ausgleichen
compensation [kɔmpən'seɪʃən] *n* (*see vb*) Entschädigung *f*; Ersatz *m*; Ausgleich *m*; (*money*) Schaden(s)ersatz *m*
compete [kəm'pi:t] *vi* (*in contest, game*) teilnehmen; (*two theories, statements*) unvereinbar sein; **to ~ (with)** (*companies, rivals*) konkurrieren (mit)
competent ['kɔmpɪtənt] *adj* fähig
competition [kɔmpɪ'tɪʃən] *n* Konkurrenz *f*; (*contest*) Wettbewerb *m*; **in ~ with** im Wettbewerb mit
competitive [kəm'pɛtɪtɪv] *adj* (*industry, society*) wettbewerbsbetont, wettbewerbsorientiert; (*person*) vom Konkurrenzdenken geprägt; (*price, product*) wettbewerbsfähig, konkurrenzfähig; (*sport*) (Wett)kampf-
competitor [kəm'pɛtɪtə^r] *n* Konkurrent(in) *m(f)*; (*participant*) Teilnehmer(in) *m(f)*
complacency [kəm'pleɪsnsɪ] *n* Selbstzufriedenheit *f*, Selbstgefälligkeit *f*
complacent [kəm'pleɪsnt] *adj* selbstzufrieden, selbstgefällig
complain [kəm'pleɪn] *vi* (*protest*) sich beschweren; **to ~ (about)** sich beklagen (über *+acc*); **to ~ of** (*headache etc*) klagen über *+acc*
complaint [kəm'pleɪnt] *n* Klage *f*; (*in shop etc*) Beschwerde *f*; (*illness*) Beschwerden *pl*
complement ['kɔmplɪmənt] *n* Ergänzung *f*; (*esp ship's crew*) Besatzung *f* ▷ *vt* ergänzen; **to have a full ~ of ...** (*people*) die volle Stärke an ... *dat* haben; (*items*) die volle Zahl an ... *dat* haben
complementary [kɔmplɪ'mɛntərɪ] *adj* komplementär, einander ergänzend
complete [kəm'pli:t] *adj* (*total: silence*) vollkommen; (: *change*) völlig; (: *success*) voll; (*whole*) ganz; (: *set*) vollständig; (: *edition*) Gesamt-; (*finished*) fertig ▷ *vt* fertigstellen; (*task*) beenden; (*set, group etc*) vervollständigen; (*fill in*) ausfüllen; **it's a ~ disaster** es ist eine totale Katastrophe
completely [kəm'pli:tlɪ] *adv* völlig, vollkommen
completion [kəm'pli:ʃən] *n* Fertigstellung *f*; (*of contract*) Abschluss *m*; **to be nearing ~** kurz vor dem Abschluss sein *or* stehen; **on ~ of the contract** bei Vertragsabschluss

complex ['kɔmplɛks] *adj* kompliziert ▷ *n* Komplex *m*
complexion [kəm'plɛkʃən] *n* Teint *m*, Gesichtsfarbe *f*; (*of event etc*) Charakter *m*; (*political, religious*) Anschauung *f*; **to put a different ~ on sth** etw in einem anderen Licht erscheinen lassen
compliance [kəm'plaɪəns] *n* Fügsamkeit *f*; (*agreement*) Einverständnis *nt*; **~ with** Einverständnis mit, Zustimmung *f* zu; **in ~ with** gemäß *+dat*
complicate ['kɔmplɪkeɪt] *vt* komplizieren
complicated ['kɔmplɪkeɪtɪd] *adj* kompliziert
complication [kɔmplɪ'keɪʃən] *n* Komplikation *f*
compliment [*n* 'kɔmplɪmənt, *vt* 'kɔmplɪmɛnt] *n* Kompliment *nt* ▷ *vt* ein Kompliment/ Komplimente machen; **compliments** *npl* (*regards*) Grüße *pl*; **to pay sb a ~** jdm ein Kompliment machen; **to ~ sb (on sth)** jdm Komplimente (wegen etw) machen; **to ~ sb on doing sth** jdm Komplimente machen, dass er/sie etw getan hat
complimentary [kɔmplɪ'mɛntərɪ] *adj* schmeichelhaft; (*ticket, copy of book etc*) Frei-
comply [kəm'plaɪ] *vi*: **to ~ with** (*law*) einhalten *+acc*; (*ruling*) sich richten nach
component [kəm'pəunənt] *adj* einzeln ▷ *n* Bestandteil *m*
compose [kəm'pəuz] *vt* (*music*) komponieren; (*poem*) verfassen; (*letter*) abfassen; **to be ~d of** bestehen aus; **to ~ o.s.** sich sammeln
composed [kəm'pəuzd] *adj* ruhig, gelassen
composer [kəm'pəuzə^r] *n* Komponist(in) *m(f)*
composition [kɔmpə'zɪʃən] *n* Zusammensetzung *f*; (*essay*) Aufsatz *m*; (*Mus*) Komposition *f*
composure [kəm'pəuʒə^r] *n* Fassung *f*, Beherrschung *f*
compound [*n, adj* 'kɔmpaund, *vt* kəm'paund] *n* (*Chem*) Verbindung *f*; (*enclosure*) umzäuntes Gebiet *or* Gelände *nt*; (*Ling*) Kompositum *nt* ▷ *adj* zusammengesetzt; (*eye*) Facetten- ▷ *vt* verschlimmern, vergrößern
compound fracture *n* komplizierter Bruch *m*
compound interest *n* Zinseszins *m*
comprehend [kɔmprɪ'hɛnd] *vt* begreifen, verstehen
comprehension [kɔmprɪ'hɛnʃən] *n* Verständnis *nt*
comprehensive [kɔmprɪ'hɛnsɪv] *adj* umfassend; (*insurance*) Vollkasko- ▷ *n* = **comprehensive school**
compress [*vt* kəm'prɛs, *n* 'kɔmprɛs] *vt* (*information etc*) verdichten; (*air*) komprimieren; (*cotton, paper etc*) zusammenpressen ▷ *n* (*Med*) Kompresse *f*
comprise [kəm'praɪz] *vt* (*also*: **be comprised of**) bestehen aus; (*constitute*) bilden, ausmachen
compromise ['kɔmprəmaɪz] *n* Kompromiss *m* ▷ *vt* (*beliefs, principles*) verraten; (*person*) kompromittieren ▷ *vi* Kompromisse schließen ▷ *cpd* (*solution etc*) Kompromiss-
compulsion [kəm'pʌlʃən] *n* Zwang *m*; (*force*) Druck *m*, Zwang *m*; **under ~** unter Druck *or* Zwang
compulsive [kəm'pʌlsɪv] *adj* zwanghaft; **it makes ~ viewing/reading** das muss man einfach sehen/lesen; **he's a ~ smoker** das Rauchen ist bei ihm zur Sucht geworden
compulsory [kəm'pʌlsərɪ] *adj* obligatorisch; (*retirement*) Zwangs-
computer [kəm'pju:tə^r] *n* Computer *m*, Rechner *m* ▷ *cpd* Computer-; **the process is done by ~** das Verfahren wird per Computer durchgeführt
computer game *n* Computerspiel *nt*
computerize [kəm'pju:təraɪz] *vt* auf Computer umstellen; (*information*) computerisieren
computer programmer *n* Programmierer(in) *m(f)*
computer programming *n* Programmieren *nt*
computer science *n* Informatik *f*
computing [kəm'pju:tɪŋ] *n* Informatik *f*; (*activity*) Computerarbeit *f*
comrade ['kɔmrɪd] *n* Genosse *m*, Genossin *f*; (*friend*) Kamerad(in) *m(f)*
con [kɔn] *vt* betrügen; (*cheat*) hereinlegen ▷ *n* Schwindel *m*; **to ~ sb into doing sth** jdn durch einen Trick dazu bringen, dass er/sie etw tut
conceal [kən'si:l] *vt* verbergen; (*information*) verheimlichen
concede [kən'si:d] *vt* zugeben ▷ *vi* nachgeben; (*admit defeat*) sich geschlagen geben; **to ~ defeat** sich geschlagen geben; **to ~ a point to sb** jdm in einem Punkt recht geben
conceit [kən'si:t] *n* Einbildung *f*
conceited [kən'si:tɪd] *adj* eingebildet
conceive [kən'si:v] *vt* (*child*) empfangen; (*plan*) kommen auf *+acc*; (*policy*) konzipieren ▷ *vi* empfangen; **to ~ of sth** sich *dat* etw vorstellen; **to ~ of doing sth** sich *dat* vorstellen, etw zu tun
concentrate ['kɔnsəntreɪt] *vi* sich konzentrieren ▷ *vt* konzentrieren
concentration [kɔnsən'treɪʃən] *n* Konzentration *f*
concentration camp *n* Konzentrationslager *nt*, KZ *nt*
concept ['kɔnsɛpt] *n* Vorstellung *f*; (*principle*) Begriff *m*
concern [kən'sə:n] *n* Angelegenheit *f*; (*anxiety, worry*) Sorge *f*; (*Comm*) Konzern *m* ▷ *vt* Sorgen machen *+dat*; (*involve*) angehen; (*relate to*) betreffen; **to be ~ed (about)** sich *dat* Sorgen machen (um); **"to whom it may ~"** (*on certificate*) "Bestätigung"; (*on reference*) "Zeugnis"; **as far as I am ~ed** was mich betrifft; **to be ~ed with** sich interessieren für; **the department ~ed** (*under discussion*) die betreffende Abteilung; (*involved*) die

zuständige Abteilung
concerning [kən'sə:nɪŋ] *prep* bezüglich *+gen*, hinsichtlich *+gen*
concert ['kɔnsət] *n* Konzert *nt*; **in ~** (*Mus*) live; (*activities, actions etc*) gemeinsam
concerted [kən'sə:tɪd] *adj* gemeinsam
concert hall *n* Konzerthalle *f*, Konzertsaal *m*
concerto [kən'tʃə:təu] *n* Konzert *nt*
concession [kən'sɛʃən] *n* Zugeständnis *nt*, Konzession *f*; (*Comm*) Konzession; **tax ~** Steuervergünstigung *f*
concise [kən'saɪs] *adj* kurz gefasst, prägnant
conclude [kən'klu:d] *vt* beenden, schließen; (*treaty, deal etc*) abschließen; (*decide*) schließen, folgern ▷ *vi* schließen; (*events*): **to ~ (with)** enden (mit); **"That," he ~d, "is why we did it."** "Darum", schloss er, "haben wir es getan"; **I ~ that ...** ich komme zu dem Schluss, dass ...
conclusion [kən'klu:ʒən] *n* (*see vb*) Ende *nt*; Schluss *m*; Abschluss *m*; Folgerung *f*; **to come to the ~ that ...** zu dem Schluss kommen, dass ...
conclusive [kən'klu:sɪv] *adj* (*evidence*) schlüssig; (*defeat*) endgültig
concoct [kən'kɔkt] *vt* (*excuse etc*) sich *dat* ausdenken; (*meal, sauce*) improvisieren
concoction [kən'kɔkʃən] *n* Zusammenstellung *f*; (*drink*) Gebräu *nt*
concourse ['kɔŋkɔ:s] *n* (Eingangs)halle *f*; (*crowd*) Menge *f*
concrete ['kɔŋkri:t] *n* Beton *m* ▷ *adj* (*ceiling, block*) Beton-; (*proposal, idea*) konkret
concur [kən'kə:r] *vi* übereinstimmen; **to ~ with** beipflichten *+dat*
concurrently [kən'kʌrntlɪ] *adv* gleichzeitig
concussion [kən'kʌʃən] *n* Gehirnerschütterung *f*
condemn [kən'dɛm] *vt* verurteilen; (*building*) für abbruchreif erklären
condensation [kɔndɛn'seɪʃən] *n* Kondenswasser *nt*
condense [kən'dɛns] *vi* kondensieren, sich niederschlagen ▷ *vt* zusammenfassen
condensed milk [kən'dɛnst-] *n* Kondensmilch *f*, Büchsenmilch *f*
condition [kən'dɪʃən] *n* Zustand *m*; (*requirement*) Bedingung *f*; (*illness*) Leiden *nt* ▷ *vt* konditionieren; (*hair*) in Form bringen; **conditions** *npl* (*circumstances*) Verhältnisse *pl*; **in good/poor ~** (*person*) in guter/schlechter Verfassung; (*thing*) in gutem/schlechtem Zustand; **a heart ~** ein Herzleiden *nt*; **weather ~s** die Wetterlage; **on ~ that ...** unter der Bedingung, dass ...
conditional [kən'dɪʃənl] *adj* bedingt; **to be ~ upon** abhängen von
conditioner [kən'dɪʃənər] *n* (*for hair*) Pflegespülung *f*; (*for fabrics*) Weichspüler *m*
condo ['kɔndəu] (*US: inf*) *n abbr* = **condominium**
condolences [kən'dəulənsɪz] *npl* Beileid *nt*
condom ['kɔndəm] *n* Kondom *m or nt*
condominium [kɔndə'mɪnɪəm] (*US*) *n* Haus *nt* mit Eigentumswohnungen; (*rooms*) Eigentumswohnung *f*
condone [kən'dəun] *vt* gutheißen
conducive [kən'dju:sɪv] *adj*: **~ to** förderlich *+dat*
conduct [*n* 'kɔndʌkt, *vt* kən'dʌkt] *n* Verhalten *nt* ▷ *vt* (*investigation etc*) durchführen; (*manage*) führen; (*orchestra, choir etc*) dirigieren; (*heat, electricity*) leiten; **to ~ o.s.** sich verhalten
conductor [kən'dʌktər] *n* (*of orchestra*) Dirigent(in) *m(f)*; (*on bus*) Schaffner *m*; (*US: on train*) Zugführer(in) *m(f)*; (*Elec*) Leiter *m*
conductress [kən'dʌktrɪs] *n* (*on bus*) Schaffnerin *f*
cone [kəun] *n* Kegel *m*; (*on road*) Leitkegel *m*; (*Bot*) Zapfen *m*; (*ice cream cornet*) (Eis)tüte *f*
confectioner [kən'fɛkʃənər] *n* (*maker*) Süßwarenhersteller(in) *m(f)*; (*seller*) Süßwarenhändler(in) *m(f)*; (*of cakes*) Konditor(in) *m(f)*
confectionery [kən'fɛkʃənrɪ] *n* Süßwaren *pl*, Süßigkeiten *pl*; (*cakes*) Konditorwaren *pl*
confer [kən'fə:r] *vt*: **to ~ sth (on sb)** (jdm) etw verleihen ▷ *vi* sich beraten; **to ~ with sb about sth** sich mit jdm über etw *acc* beraten, etw mit jdm besprechen
conference ['kɔnfərəns] *n* Konferenz *f*; (*more informal*) Besprechung *f*; **to be in ~** in *or* bei einer Konferenz/Besprechung sein
confess [kən'fɛs] *vt* bekennen; (*sin*) beichten; (*crime*) zugeben, gestehen ▷ *vi* (*admit*) gestehen; **to ~ to sth** (*crime*) etw gestehen; (*weakness etc*) sich zu etw bekennen; **I must ~ that I didn't enjoy it at all** ich muss sagen, dass es mir überhaupt keinen Spaß gemacht hat
confession [kən'fɛʃən] *n* Geständnis *nt*; (*Rel*) Beichte *f*; **to make a ~** ein Geständnis ablegen
confetti [kən'fɛtɪ] *n* Konfetti *nt*
confide [kən'faɪd] *vi*: **to ~ in** sich anvertrauen *+dat*
confidence ['kɔnfɪdns] *n* Vertrauen *nt*; (*self-assurance*) Selbstvertrauen *nt*; (*secret*) vertrauliche Mitteilung *f*, Geheimnis *nt*; **to have ~ in sb/sth** Vertrauen zu jdm/etw haben; **to have (every) ~ that ...** ganz zuversichtlich sein, dass ...; **motion of no ~** Misstrauensantrag *m*; **to tell sb sth in strict ~** jdm etw ganz im Vertrauen sagen; **in ~** vertraulich
confidence trick *n* Schwindel *m*
confident ['kɔnfɪdənt] *adj* (selbst)sicher; (*positive*) zuversichtlich
confidential [kɔnfɪ'dɛnʃəl] *adj* vertraulich; (*secretary*) Privat-
confine [kən'faɪn] *vt* (*shut up*) einsperren; **to ~ (to)** beschränken (auf *+acc*); **to ~ o.s. to sth** sich auf etw *acc* beschränken; **to ~ o.s. to doing sth** sich darauf beschränken, etw zu tun
confined [kən'faɪnd] *adj* begrenzt

confinement [kən'faınmənt] *n* Haft *f*
confines ['kɔnfaınz] *npl* Grenzen *pl*; (*of situation*) Rahmen *m*
confirm [kən'fə:m] *vt* bestätigen; **to be ~ed** (*Rel*) konfirmiert werden
confirmation [kɔnfə'meıʃən] *n* Bestätigung *f*; (*Rel*) Konfirmation *f*
confirmed [kən'fə:md] *adj* (*bachelor*) eingefleischt; (*teetotaller*) überzeugt
confiscate ['kɔnfıskeıt] *vt* beschlagnahmen, konfiszieren
conflict ['kɔnflıkt] *n* Konflikt *m*; (*fighting*) Zusammenstoß *m*, Kampf *m* ▷ *vi*: **to ~ (with)** im Widerspruch stehen (zu)
conflicting [kən'flıktıŋ] *adj* widersprüchlich
conform [kən'fɔ:m] *vi* sich anpassen; **to ~ to** entsprechen *+dat*
confound [kən'faund] *vt* verwirren; (*amaze*) verblüffen
confront [kən'frʌnt] *vt* (*problems, task*) sich stellen *+dat*; (*enemy, danger*) gegenübertreten *+dat*
confrontation [kɔnfrən'teıʃən] *n* Konfrontation *f*
confuse [kən'fju:z] *vt* verwirren; (*mix up*) verwechseln; (*complicate*) durcheinanderbringen
confused [kən'fju:zd] *adj* (*person*) verwirrt; (*situation*) verworren, konfus; **to get ~** konfus werden
confusing [kən'fju:zıŋ] *adj* verwirrend
confusion [kən'fju:ʒən] *n* (*mix-up*) Verwechslung *f*; (*perplexity*) Verwirrung *f*; (*disorder*) Durcheinander *nt*
congeal [kən'dʒi:l] *vi* (*blood*) gerinnen; (*sauce, oil*) erstarren
congenial [kən'dʒi:nıəl] *adj* ansprechend, sympathisch; (*atmosphere, place, work, company*) angenehm
congested [kən'dʒɛstıd] *adj* (*road*) verstopft; (*area*) überfüllt; (*nose*) verstopft; **his lungs are ~** in seiner Lunge hat sich Blut angestaut
congestion [kən'dʒɛstʃən] *n* (*Med*) Blutstau *m*; (*of road*) Verstopfung *f*; (*of area*) Überfüllung *f*
congratulate [kən'grætjuleıt] *vt* gratulieren; **to ~ sb (on sth)** jdm (zu etw) gratulieren
congratulations [kəngrætju'leıʃənz] *npl* Glückwunsch *m*, Glückwünsche *pl*; **~!** herzlichen Glückwunsch!; **~ on** Glückwünsche zu
congregate ['kɔŋgrıgeıt] *vi* sich versammeln
congregation [kɔŋgrı'geıʃən] *n* Gemeinde *f*
congress ['kɔŋgrɛs] *n* Kongress *m*; (*US*): **C~** der Kongress
congressman ['kɔŋgrɛsmən] (*US*) *n* (*irreg: like* **man**) Kongressabgeordnete(r) *m*
congresswoman ['kɔŋgrɛswumən] (*US irreg: like* **woman**) *n* Kongressabgeordnete *f*
conifer ['kɔnıfə^r] *n* Nadelbaum *m*
conjugate ['kɔndʒugeıt] *vt* konjugieren
conjugation [kɔndʒə'geıʃən] *n* Konjugation *f*
conjunction [kən'dʒʌŋkʃən] *n* Konjunktion *f*; **in ~ with** zusammen mit, in Verbindung mit
conjunctivitis [kəndʒʌŋktı'vaıtıs] *n* Bindehautentzündung *f*
conjure ['kʌndʒə^r] *vi* zaubern ▷ *vt* (*also fig*) hervorzaubern
▶ **conjure up** *vt* (*ghost, spirit*) beschwören; (*memories*) heraufbeschwören
conjurer ['kʌndʒərə^r] *n* Zauberer *m*, Zauberkünstler(in) *m(f)*
connect [kə'nɛkt] *vt* verbinden; (*Elec*) anschließen; (*Tel: caller*) verbinden; (*: subscriber*) anschließen; (*fig: associate*) in Zusammenhang bringen ▷ *vi*: **to ~ with** (*train, plane etc*) Anschluss haben an *+acc*; **to ~ sth to sth** etw mit einer Sache verbinden; **to be ~ed with** (*associated*) in einer Beziehung *or* in Verbindung stehen zu; (*have dealings with*) zu tun haben mit; **I am trying to ~ you** (*Tel*) ich versuche, Sie zu verbinden
connection [kə'nɛkʃən] *n* Verbindung *f*; (*Elec*) Kontakt *m*; (*train, plane etc, Tel: subscriber*) Anschluss *m*; (*fig: association*) Beziehung *f*, Zusammenhang *m*; **in ~ with** in Zusammenhang mit; **what is the ~ between them?** welche Verbindung besteht zwischen ihnen?; **business ~s** Geschäftsbeziehungen *pl*; **to get/miss one's ~** seinen Anschluss erreichen/ verpassen
connive [kə'naıv] *vi*: **to ~ at** stillschweigend dulden
conquer ['kɔŋkə^r] *vt* erobern; (*enemy, fear, feelings*) besiegen
conquest ['kɔŋkwɛst] *n* Eroberung *f*
cons [kɔnz] *npl see* **convenience** *see* **pro**
conscience ['kɔnʃəns] *n* Gewissen *nt*; **to have a guilty/clear ~** ein schlechtes/gutes Gewissen haben; **in all ~** allen Ernstes
conscientious [kɔnʃı'ɛnʃəs] *adj* gewissenhaft
conscious ['kɔnʃəs] *adj* bewusst; (*awake*) bei Bewusstsein; **to become ~ of sth** sich *dat* einer Sache *gen* bewusst werden; **to become ~ that ...** sich *dat* bewusst werden, dass ...
consciousness ['kɔnʃəsnıs] *n* Bewusstsein *nt*; **to lose ~** bewusstlos werden; **to regain ~** wieder zu sich kommen
conscript ['kɔnskrıpt] *n* Wehrpflichtige(r) *m*
consecutive [kən'sɛkjutıv] *adj* aufeinanderfolgend; **on three ~ occasions** dreimal hintereinander
consensus [kən'sɛnsəs] *n* Übereinstimmung *f*; **the ~ (of opinion)** die allgemeine Meinung
consent [kən'sɛnt] *n* Zustimmung *f* ▷ *vi*: **to ~ to** zustimmen *+dat*; **age of ~** Ehemündigkeitsalter *nt*; **by common ~** auf allgemeinen Wunsch
consequence ['kɔnsıkwəns] *n* Folge *f*; **of ~** bedeutend, wichtig; **it's of little ~** es spielt kaum eine Rolle; **in ~** folglich
consequently ['kɔnsıkwəntlı] *adv* folglich
conservation [kɔnsə'veıʃən] *n* Erhaltung *f*, Schutz *m*; (*of energy*) Sparen *nt*; (*also:* **nature conservation**) Umweltschutz *m*; (*of paintings,*

books) Erhaltung *f*, Konservierung *f*; **energy ~** Energieeinsparung *f*
conservative [kən'sə:vətɪv] *adj* konservativ; (*cautious*) vorsichtig; (*Brit: Pol*): **C~** konservativ ▷ *n* (*Brit: Pol*): **C~** Konservative(r) *f(m)*
conservatory [kən'sə:vətrɪ] *n* Wintergarten *m*; (*Mus*) Konservatorium *nt*
conserve [kən'sə:v] *vt* erhalten; (*supplies, energy*) sparen ▷ *n* Konfitüre *f*
consider [kən'sɪdəʳ] *vt* (*study*) sich *dat* überlegen; (*take into account*) in Betracht ziehen; **to ~ that ...** der Meinung sein, dass ...; **to ~ sb/sth as ...** jdn/etw für ... halten; **to ~ doing sth** in Erwägung ziehen, etw zu tun; **they ~ themselves to be superior** sie halten sich für etwas Besseres; **she ~ed it a disaster** sie betrachtete es als eine Katastrophe; **~ yourself lucky** Sie können sich glücklich schätzen; **all things ~ed** alles in allem
considerable [kən'sɪdərəbl] *adj* beträchtlich
considerably [kən'sɪdərəblɪ] *adv* beträchtlich; (*bigger, smaller etc*) um einiges
considerate [kən'sɪdərɪt] *adj* rücksichtsvoll
consideration [kənsɪdə'reɪʃən] *n* Überlegung *f*; (*factor*) Gesichtspunkt *m*, Faktor *m*; (*thoughtfulness*) Rücksicht *f*; (*reward*) Entgelt *nt*; **out of ~ for** aus Rücksicht auf *+acc*; **to be under ~** geprüft werden; **my first ~ is my family** ich denke zuerst an meine Familie
considering [kən'sɪdərɪŋ] *prep* in Anbetracht *+gen*; **~ (that)** wenn man bedenkt(, dass)
consign [kən'saɪn] *vt*: **to ~ to** (*object: to place*) verbannen in *+acc*; (*person: to sb's care*) anvertrauen *+dat*; (*: to poverty*) verurteilen zu; (*send*) versenden an *+acc*
consignment [kən'saɪnmənt] *n* Sendung *f*, Lieferung *f*
consist [kən'sɪst] *vi*: **to ~ of** bestehen aus
consistency [kən'sɪstənsɪ] *n* (*of actions etc*) Konsequenz *f*; (*of cream etc*) Konsistenz *f*, Dicke *f*
consistent [kən'sɪstənt] *adj* konsequent; (*argument, idea*) logisch, folgerichtig; **to be ~ with** entsprechen *+dat*
consolation [kɔnsə'leɪʃən] *n* Trost *m*
console [kən'səul] *vt* trösten ▷ *n* (*panel*) Schalttafel *f*
consonant ['kɔnsənənt] *n* Konsonant *m*, Mitlaut *m*
conspicuous [kən'spɪkjuəs] *adj* auffallend; **to make o.s. ~** auffallen
conspiracy [kən'spɪrəsɪ] *n* Verschwörung *f*, Komplott *nt*
constable ['kʌnstəbl] (*Brit*) *n* Polizist *m*; **chief ~** Polizeipräsident *m*, Polizeichef *m*
constabulary [kən'stæbjulərɪ] (*Brit*) *n* Polizei *f*
constant ['kɔnstənt] *adj* dauernd, ständig; (*fixed*) konstant, gleichbleibend
constantly ['kɔnstəntlɪ] *adv* (an)dauernd, ständig
constipated ['kɔnstɪpeɪtɪd] *adj*: **to be ~** Verstopfung haben, verstopft sein
constipation [kɔnstɪ'peɪʃən] *n* Verstopfung *f*
constituency [kən'stɪtjuənsɪ] *n* (*Pol*) Wahlkreis *m*; (*electors*) Wähler *pl* (*eines Wahlkreises*)
constituent [kən'stɪtjuənt] *n* (*Pol*) Wähler(in) *m(f)*; (*component*) Bestandteil *m*
constitute ['kɔnstɪtju:t] *vt* (*represent*) darstellen; (*make up*) bilden, ausmachen
constitution [kɔnstɪ'tju:ʃən] *n* (*Pol*) Verfassung *f*; (*of club etc*) Satzung *f*; (*health*) Konstitution *f*, Gesundheit *f*; (*make-up*) Zusammensetzung *f*
constitutional [kɔnstɪ'tju:ʃənl] *adj* (*government*) verfassungsmäßig; (*reform etc*) Verfassungs-
constraint [kən'streɪnt] *n* Beschränkung *f*, Einschränkung *f*; (*compulsion*) Zwang *m*; (*embarrassment*) Befangenheit *f*
construct [kən'strʌkt] *vt* bauen; (*machine*) konstruieren; (*theory, argument*) entwickeln
construction [kən'strʌkʃən] *n* Bau *m*; (*structure*) Konstruktion *f*; (*fig: interpretation*) Deutung *f*; **under ~** in *or* im Bau
constructive [kən'strʌktɪv] *adj* konstruktiv
consul ['kɔnsl] *n* Konsul(in) *m(f)*
consulate ['kɔnsjulɪt] *n* Konsulat *nt*
consult [kən'sʌlt] *vt* (*doctor, lawyer*) konsultieren; (*friend*) sich beraten *or* besprechen mit; (*reference book*) nachschlagen in *+dat*; **to ~ sb (about sth)** jdn (wegen etw) fragen
consultant [kən'sʌltənt] *n* (*Med*) Facharzt *m*, Fachärztin *f*; (*other specialist*) Berater(in) *m(f)* ▷ *cpd*: **~ engineer** beratender Ingenieur *m*; **~ paediatrician** Facharzt/-ärztin *m/f* für Pädiatrie *or* Kinderheilkunde; **legal/management ~** Rechts-/ Unternehmensberater(in) *m(f)*; **consultants** *npl* Beratungsbüro *nt or* -firma *f*
consultation [kɔnsəl'teɪʃən] *n* (*Med, Law*) Konsultation *f*; (*discussion*) Beratung *f*, Besprechung *f*; **in ~ with** in gemeinsamer Beratung mit
consulting room [kən'sʌltɪŋ-] (*Brit*) *n* Sprechzimmer *nt*
consume [kən'sju:m] *vt* (*food, drink*) zu sich nehmen, konsumieren; (*fuel, energy*) verbrauchen; (*time*) in Anspruch nehmen; (*subj: emotion*) verzehren; (*: fire*) vernichten
consumer [kən'sju:məʳ] *n* Verbraucher(in) *m(f)*
consumer goods *npl* Konsumgüter *pl*
consumer society *n* Konsumgesellschaft *f*
consummate ['kɔnsʌmeɪt] *vt* (*marriage*) vollziehen; (*ambition etc*) erfüllen
consumption [kən'sʌmpʃən] *n* Verbrauch *m*; (*of food*) Verzehr *m*; (*of drinks, buying*) Konsum *m*; (*Med*) Schwindsucht *f*; **not fit for human ~** zum Verzehr ungeeignet
cont. *abbr* (*= continued*) Forts.
contact ['kɔntækt] *n* Kontakt *m*; (*touch*) Berührung *f*; (*person*) Kontaktperson *f* ▷ *vt*

sich in Verbindung setzen mit; **to be in ~ with sb/sth** mit jdm/etw in Verbindung *or* Kontakt stehen; (*touch*) jdn/etw berühren; **business ~s** Geschäftsverbindungen *pl*

contact lenses *npl* Kontaktlinsen *pl*

contagious [kən'teɪdʒəs] *adj* ansteckend

contain [kən'teɪn] *vt* enthalten; (*growth, spread*) in Grenzen halten; (*feeling*) beherrschen; **to ~ o.s.** an sich *acc* halten

container [kən'teɪnəʳ] *n* Behälter *m*; (*for shipping etc*) Container *m* ▷ *cpd* Container-

contaminate [kən'tæmɪneɪt] *vt* (*water, food*) verunreinigen; (*soil etc*) verseuchen

cont'd *abbr* (= *continued*) Forts.

contemplate ['kɔntəmpleɪt] *vt* nachdenken über +*acc*; (*course of action*) in Erwägung ziehen; (*person, painting etc*) betrachten

contemporary [kən'tɛmpərərɪ] *adj* zeitgenössisch; (*present-day*) modern ▷ *n* Altersgenosse *m*, Altersgenossin *f*; **Samuel Pepys and his contemporaries** Samuel Pepys und seine Zeitgenossen

contempt [kən'tɛmpt] *n* Verachtung *f*; **~ of court** (*Law*) Missachtung *f* (der Würde) des Gerichts, Ungebühr *f* vor Gericht; **to have ~ for sb/sth** jdn/etw verachten; **to hold sb in ~** jdn verachten

contemptuous [kən'tɛmptjuəs] *adj* verächtlich, geringschätzig

contend [kən'tɛnd] *vt*: **to ~ that ...** behaupten, dass ...; **to ~ with** fertig werden mit; **to ~ for** kämpfen um; **to have to ~ with** es zu tun haben mit; **he has a lot to ~ with** er hat viel um die Ohren

contender [kən'tɛndəʳ] *n* (*Sport*) Wettkämpfer(in) *m(f)*; (*for title*) Anwärter(in) *m(f)*; (*Pol*) Kandidat(in) *m(f)*

content [*adj, vt* kən'tɛnt, *n* 'kɔntɛnt] *adj* zufrieden ▷ *vt* zufriedenstellen ▷ *n* Inhalt *m*; (*fat content, moisture content etc*) Gehalt *m*; **contents** *npl* Inhalt; **(table of) ~s** Inhaltsverzeichnis *nt*; **to be ~ with** zufrieden sein mit; **to ~ o.s. with sth** sich mit etw zufriedengeben *or* begnügen; **to ~ o.s. with doing sth** sich damit zufriedengeben *or* begnügen, etw zu tun

contented [kən'tɛntɪd] *adj* zufrieden

contention [kən'tɛnʃən] *n* Behauptung *f*; (*disagreement, argument*) Streit *m*; **bone of ~** Zankapfel *m*

contest [*n* 'kɔntɛst, *vt* kən'tɛst] *n* (*competition*) Wettkampf *m*; (*for control, power etc*) Kampf *m* ▷ *vt* (*election, competition*) teilnehmen an +*dat*; (*compete for*) kämpfen um; (*statement*) bestreiten; (*decision*) angreifen; (*Law*) anfechten

contestant [kən'tɛstənt] *n* (*in quiz*) Kandidat(in) *m(f)*; (*in competition*) Teilnehmer(in) *m(f)*; (*in fight*) Kämpfer(in) *m(f)*

context ['kɔntɛkst] *n* Zusammenhang *m*, Kontext *m*; **in ~** im Zusammenhang; **out of ~** aus dem Zusammenhang gerissen

continent ['kɔntɪnənt] *n* Kontinent *m*, Erdteil *m*; **the C~** (*Brit*) (Kontinental)europa *nt*; **on the C~** in (Kontinental)europa, auf dem Kontinent

continental [kɔntɪ'nɛntl] *adj* kontinental; (*European*) europäisch ▷ *n* (*Brit*) (Festlands)europäer(in) *m(f)*

continental breakfast *n* kleines Frühstück *nt*

continental quilt (*Brit*) *n* Steppdecke *f*

contingency [kən'tɪndʒənsɪ] *n* möglicher Fall *m*, Eventualität *f*

continual [kən'tɪnjuəl] *adj* ständig; (*process*) ununterbrochen

continually [kən'tɪnjuəlɪ] *adv* (*see adj*) ständig; ununterbrochen

continuation [kəntɪnju'eɪʃən] *n* Fortsetzung *f*; (*extension*) Weiterführung *f*

continue [kən'tɪnju:] *vi* weitermachen, andauern; (*performance, road*) weitergehen; (*person: talking*) fortfahren ▷ *vt* fortsetzen; **to ~ to do sth/doing sth** etw weiter tun; **"to be ~d"** "Fortsetzung folgt"; **"~d on page 10"** "Fortsetzung auf Seite 10"

continuity [kɔntɪ'nju:ɪtɪ] *n* Kontinuität *f*; (*TV, Cine*) Anschluß *m* ▷ *cpd* (*TV*): **~ announcer** Ansager(in) *m(f)*; **~ studio** Ansagestudio *nt*

continuous [kən'tɪnjuəs] *adj* ununterbrochen; (*growth etc*) kontinuierlich; **~ form** (*Ling*) Verlaufsform *f*; **~ performance** (*Cine*) durchgehende Vorstellung *f*

continuously [kən'tɪnjuəslɪ] *adv* dauernd, ständig; (*uninterruptedly*) ununterbrochen

contort [kən'tɔ:t] *vt* (*body*) verrenken, verdrehen; (*face*) verziehen

contour ['kɔntuəʳ] *n* (*also*: **contour line**) Höhenlinie *f*; (*shape, outline*: *gen pl*) Kontur *f*, Umriss *m*

contraband ['kɔntrəbænd] *n* Schmuggelware *f* ▷ *adj* Schmuggel-

contraception [kɔntrə'sɛpʃən] *n* Empfängnisverhütung *f*

contraceptive [kɔntrə'sɛptɪv] *adj* empfängnisverhütend ▷ *n* Verhütungsmittel *nt*

contract [*n, cpd* 'kɔntrækt, *vb* kən'trækt] *n* Vertrag *m* ▷ *vi* schrumpfen; (*metal, muscle*) sich zusammenziehen ▷ *vt* (*illness*) erkranken an +*dat* ▷ *cpd* vertraglich festgelegt; (*work*) Auftrags-; **~ of employment/service** Arbeitsvertrag *m*; **to ~ to do sth** (*Comm*) sich vertraglich verpflichten, etw zu tun

▸ **contract in** (*Brit*) *vi* beitreten

▸ **contract out** (*Brit*) *vi* austreten

contraction [kən'trækʃən] *n* Zusammenziehen *nt*; (*Ling*) Kontraktion *f*; (*Med*) Wehe *f*

contractor [kən'træktəʳ] *n* Auftragnehmer *m*; (*also*: **building contractor**) Bauunternehmer *m*

contradict [kɔntrə'dɪkt] *vt* widersprechen +*dat*

contradiction [kɔntrəˈdɪkʃən] *n* Widerspruch *m*; **to be in ~ with** im Widerspruch stehen zu; **a ~ in terms** ein Widerspruch in sich

contraption [kənˈtræpʃən] *(pej) n (device)* Vorrichtung *f*; *(machine)* Gerät *nt*, Apparat *m*

contrary[1] [ˈkɔntrərɪ] *adj* entgegengesetzt; *(ideas, opinions)* gegensätzlich; *(unfavourable)* widrig ▷ *n* Gegenteil *nt*; **~ to what we thought** im Gegensatz zu dem, was wir dachten; **on the ~** im Gegenteil; **unless you hear to the ~** sofern Sie nichts Gegenteiliges hören

contrary[2] [kənˈtrɛərɪ] *adj* widerspenstig

contrast [ˈkɔntrɑːst] *n* Gegensatz *m*, Kontrast *m* ▷ *vt* vergleichen, gegenüberstellen; **in ~ to** *or* **with** im Gegensatz zu

contravene [kɔntrəˈviːn] *vt* verstoßen gegen

contribute [kənˈtrɪbjuːt] *vi* beitragen ▷ *vt*: **to ~ £10/an article to** £10/einen Artikel beisteuern zu; **to ~ to** *(charity)* spenden für; *(newspaper)* schreiben für; *(discussion, problem etc)* beitragen zu

contribution [kɔntrɪˈbjuːʃən] *n* Beitrag *m*; *(donation)* Spende *f*

contributor [kənˈtrɪbjutə[r]] *n (to appeal)* Spender(in) *m(f)*; *(to newspaper)* Mitarbeiter(in) *m(f)*

contrive [kənˈtraɪv[r]] *vt (meeting)* arrangieren ▷ *vi*: **to ~ to do sth** es fertigbringen, etw zu tun

control [kənˈtrəul] *vt (country)* regieren; *(organization)* leiten; *(machinery, process)* steuern; *(wages, prices)* kontrollieren; *(temper)* zügeln; *(disease, fire)* unter Kontrolle bringen ▷ *n (of country)* Kontrolle *f*; *(of organization)* Leitung *f*; *(of oneself, emotions)* Beherrschung *f*; *(Sci: also:* **control group***)* Kontrollgruppe *f*; **controls** *npl (of vehicle)* Steuerung *f*; *(on radio, television etc)* Bedienungsfeld *nt*; *(governmental)* Kontrolle *f*; **to ~ o.s.** sich beherrschen; **to take ~ of** die Kontrolle übernehmen über *+acc*; *(Comm)* übernehmen; **to be in ~ of** unter Kontrolle haben; *(in charge of)* unter sich *dat* haben; **out of/under ~** außer/unter Kontrolle; **everything is under ~** ich habe/wir haben *etc* die Sache im Griff *(inf)*; **the car went out of ~** der Fahrer verlor die Kontrolle über den Wagen; **circumstances beyond our ~** unvorhersehbare Umstände

control panel *n* Schalttafel *f*; *(on television)* Bedienungsfeld *nt*

control room *n (Naut)* Kommandoraum *m*; *(Mil)* (Operations)zentrale *f*; *(Radio, TV)* Regieraum *m*

control tower *n* Kontrollturm *m*

controversial [kɔntrəˈvəːʃl] *adj* umstritten, kontrovers

controversy [ˈkɔntrəvəːsɪ] *n* Streit *m*, Kontroverse *f*

convalesce [kɔnvəˈlɛs] *vi* genesen

convector [kənˈvɛktə[r]] *n* Heizlüfter *m*

convene [kənˈviːn] *vt* einberufen ▷ *vi* zusammentreten

convenience [kənˈviːnɪəns] *n* Annehmlichkeit *f*; *(suitability)*: **the ~ of this arrangement/location** diese günstige Vereinbarung/Lage; **I like the ~ of having a shower** mir gefällt, wie angenehm es ist, eine Dusche zu haben; **I like the ~ of living in the city** mir gefällt, wie praktisch es ist, in der Stadt zu wohnen; **at your ~** wann es Ihnen passt; **at your earliest ~** möglichst bald, baldmöglichst; **with all modern ~s, with all mod cons** *(Brit)* mit allem modernen Komfort; *see also* **public convenience**

convenient [kənˈviːnɪənt] *adj* günstig; *(handy)* praktisch; *(house etc)* günstig gelegen; **if it is ~ to you** wenn es Ihnen (so) passt, wenn es Ihnen keine Umstände macht

convent [ˈkɔnvənt] *n* Kloster *nt*

convention [kənˈvɛnʃən] *n* Konvention *f*; *(conference)* Tagung *f*, Konferenz *f*; *(agreement)* Abkommen *nt*

conventional [kənˈvɛnʃənl] *adj* konventionell

convent school *n* Klosterschule *f*

conversant [kənˈvəːsnt] *adj*: **to be ~ with** vertraut sein mit

conversation [kɔnvəˈseɪʃən] *n* Gespräch *nt*, Unterhaltung *f*

converse [*n* ˈkɔnvəːs, *vi* kənˈvəːs] *n* Gegenteil *nt* ▷ *vi*: **to ~ (with sb) (about sth)** sich (mit jdm) (über etw) unterhalten

conversely [kɔnˈvəːslɪ] *adv* umgekehrt

conversion [kənˈvəːʃən] *n* Umwandlung *f*; *(of weights etc)* Umrechnung *f*; *(Rel)* Bekehrung *f*; *(Brit: of house)* Umbau *m*

convert [*vt* kənˈvəːt, *n* ˈkɔnvəːt] *vt* umwandeln; *(person)* bekehren; *(building)* umbauen; *(vehicle)* umrüsten; *(Comm)* konvertieren; *(Rugby)* verwandeln ▷ *n* Bekehrte(r) *f(m)*

convertible [kənˈvəːtəbl] *adj (currency)* konvertierbar ▷ *n (Aut)* Kabriolett *nt*

convey [kənˈveɪ] *vt (information etc)* vermitteln; *(cargo, traveller)* befördern; *(thanks)* übermitteln

conveyor belt *n* Fließband *nt*

convict [*vt* kənˈvɪkt, *n* ˈkɔnvɪkt] *vt* verurteilen ▷ *n* Sträfling *m*

conviction [kənˈvɪkʃən] *n* Überzeugung *f*; *(Law)* Verurteilung *f*

convince [kənˈvɪns] *vt* überzeugen; **to ~ sb (of sth)** jdn (von etw) überzeugen; **to ~ sb that ...** jdn davon überzeugen, dass ...

convinced [kənˈvɪnst] *adj*: **~ (of)** überzeugt (von); **~ that ...** überzeugt davon, dass ...

convincing [kənˈvɪnsɪŋ] *adj* überzeugend

convoluted [ˈkɔnvəluːtɪd] *adj* verwickelt, kompliziert; *(shape)* gewunden

convoy [ˈkɔnvɔɪ] *n* Konvoi *m*

convulse [kənˈvʌls] *vt*: **to be ~d with laughter/pain** sich vor Lachen schütteln/Schmerzen krümmen

cook [kuk] *vt* kochen, zubereiten ▷ *vi (person,*

food) kochen; (*fry, roast*) braten; (*pie*) backen ▷ *n* Koch *m*, Köchin *f*
▸ **cook up** (*inf*) *vt* sich *dat* einfallen lassen, zurechtbasteln
cookbook ['kukbuk] *n* Kochbuch *nt*
cooker ['kukəʳ] *n* Herd *m*
cookery ['kukərɪ] *n* Kochen *nt*, Kochkunst *f*
cookery book (*Brit*) *n* = **cookbook**
cookie ['kukɪ] (*US*) *n* Keks *m or nt*, Plätzchen *nt*
cooking ['kukɪŋ] *n* Kochen *nt*; (*food*) Essen *nt* ▷ *cpd* Koch-; (*chocolate*) Block-
cool [ku:l] *adj* kühl; (*dress, clothes*) leicht, luftig; (*person: calm*) besonnen; (*: unfriendly*) kühl ▷ *vt* kühlen ▷ *vi* abkühlen; **it's ~** es ist kühl; **to keep sth ~** *or* **in a ~ place** etw kühl aufbewahren; **to keep one's ~** die Ruhe bewahren
▸ **cool down** *vi* abkühlen; (*fig*) sich beruhigen
coop [ku:p] *n* (*for rabbits*) Kaninchenstall *m*; (*for poultry*) Hühnerstall *m* ▷ *vt*: **to ~ up** (*fig*) einsperren
cooperate [kəu'ɔpəreɪt] *vi* zusammenarbeiten; (*assist*) mitmachen, kooperieren; **to ~ with sb** mit jdm zusammenarbeiten
cooperation [kəuɔpə'reɪʃən] *n* (*see vb*) Zusammenarbeit *f*; Mitarbeit *f*, Kooperation *f*
cooperative [kəu'ɔpərətɪv] *adj* (*farm, business*) auf Genossenschaftsbasis; (*person*) kooperativ; (*: helpful*) hilfsbereit ▷ *n* Genossenschaft *f*, Kooperative *f*
coordinate [kəu'ɔ:dɪneɪt] *vt* koordinieren ▷ *n* (*Math*) Koordinate *f*; **coordinates** *npl* (*clothes*) Kleidung *f* zum Kombinieren
cop [kɔp] (*inf*) *n* Polizist(in) *m(f)*, Bulle *m* (*pej*)
cope [kəup] *vi* zurechtkommen; **to ~ with** fertig werden mit
copper ['kɔpəʳ] *n* Kupfer *nt*; (*Brit: inf*) Polizist(in) *m(f)*, Bulle *m* (*pej*); **coppers** *npl* (*small change, coins*) Kleingeld *nt*
copy ['kɔpɪ] *n* Kopie *f*; (*of book, record, newspaper*) Exemplar *nt*; (*for printing*) Artikel *m* ▷ *vt* (*person*) nachahmen; (*idea etc*) nachmachen; (*something written*) abschreiben; **this murder story will make good ~** (*Press*) aus diesem Mord kann man etwas machen
▸ **copy out** *vt* abschreiben
copyright ['kɔpɪraɪt] *n* Copyright *nt*, Urheberrecht *nt*; **~ reserved** urheberrechtlich geschützt
coral ['kɔrəl] *n* Koralle *f*
cord [kɔ:d] *n* Schnur *f*; (*string*) Kordel *f*; (*Elec*) Kabel *nt*, Schnur *f*; (*fabric*) Cord(samt) *m*; **cords** *npl* (*trousers*) Cordhosen *pl*
cordial ['kɔ:dɪəl] *adj* herzlich ▷ *n* (*Brit*) Fruchtsaftkonzentrat *nt*
cordless ['kɔ:dlɪs] *adj* schnurlos
cordon ['kɔ:dn] *n* Kordon *m*, Absperrkette *f*
▸ **cordon off** *vt* (*area*) absperren, abriegeln; (*crowd*) mit einer Absperrkette zurückhalten
corduroy ['kɔ:dərɔɪ] *n* Cord(samt) *m*
core [kɔ:ʳ] *n* Kern *m*; (*of fruit*) Kerngehäuse *nt* ▷ *vt* das Kerngehäuse ausschneiden aus; **rotten to the ~** durch und durch schlecht
coriander [kɔrɪ'ændəʳ] *n* Koriander *m*
cork [kɔ:k] *n* (*stopper*) Korken *m*; (*substance*) Kork *m*
corkscrew ['kɔ:kskru:] *n* Korkenzieher *m*
corn [kɔ:n] *n* (*Brit*) Getreide *nt*, Korn *nt*; (*US*) Mais *m*; (*on foot*) Hühnerauge *nt*; **~ on the cob** Maiskolben *m*
corned beef ['kɔ:nd-] *n* Corned Beef *nt*
corner ['kɔ:nəʳ] *n* Ecke *f*; (*bend*) Kurve *f* ▷ *vt* in die Enge treiben; (*Comm: market*) monopolisieren ▷ *vi* (*in car*) die Kurve nehmen; **to cut ~s** (*fig*) das Verfahren abkürzen
cornerstone ['kɔ:nəstəun] *n* (*fig*) Grundstein *m*, Eckstein *m*
cornet ['kɔ:nɪt] *n* (*Mus*) Kornett *nt*; (*Brit: for ice cream*) Eistüte *f*
cornflakes ['kɔ:nfleɪks] *npl* Cornflakes *pl*
cornflour ['kɔ:nflauəʳ] (*Brit*) *n* Stärkemehl *nt*
cornstarch ['kɔ:nstɑ:tʃ] (*US*) *n* = **cornflour**
Cornwall ['kɔ:nwəl] *n* Cornwall *nt*
corny ['kɔ:nɪ] (*inf*) *adj* (*joke*) blöd
coronary ['kɔrənərɪ] *n* (*also*: **coronary thrombosis**) Herzinfarkt *m*
coronation [kɔrə'neɪʃən] *n* Krönung *f*
coroner ['kɔrənəʳ] *n* *Beamter, der Todesfälle untersucht, die nicht eindeutig eine natürliche Ursache haben*
corporal ['kɔ:pərl] *n* Stabsunteroffizier *m*
corporate ['kɔ:pərɪt] *adj* (*organization*) körperschaftlich; (*action, effort, ownership*) gemeinschaftlich; (*finance*) Unternehmens-; (*image, identity*) Firmen-
corporation [kɔ:pə'reɪʃən] *n* (*Comm*) Körperschaft *f*; (*of town*) Gemeinde *f*, Stadt *f*
corps [kɔ:ʳ] (*pl* **~**) *n* Korps *nt*; **the press ~** die Presse
corpse [kɔ:ps] *n* Leiche *f*
correct [kə'rɛkt] *adj* richtig; (*proper*) korrekt ▷ *vt* korrigieren; (*mistake*) berichtigen, verbessern; **you are ~** Sie haben recht
correction [kə'rɛkʃən] *n* (*see vb*) Korrektur *f*; Berichtigung *f*, Verbesserung *f*
correspond [kɔrɪs'pɔnd] *vi*: **to ~ (with)** (*write*) korrespondieren (mit); (*be in accordance*) übereinstimmen (mit); **to ~ to** (*be equivalent*) entsprechen +*dat*
correspondence [kɔrɪs'pɔndəns] *n* Korrespondenz *f*, Briefwechsel *m*; (*relationship*) Beziehung *f*
correspondence course *n* Fernkurs *m*
correspondent [kɔrɪs'pɔndənt] *n* Korrespondent(in) *m(f)*
corresponding [kɔrɪs'pɔndɪŋ] *adj* entsprechend
corridor ['kɔrɪdɔ:ʳ] *n* Korridor *m*; (*in train*) Gang *m*
corrode [kə'rəud] *vt* zerfressen ▷ *vi* korrodieren
corrugated ['kɔrəgeɪtɪd] *adj* (*roof*) gewellt; (*cardboard*) Well-

corrugated iron *n* Wellblech *nt*
corrupt [kəˈrʌpt] *adj* korrupt; (*depraved*) verdorben ▷ *vt* korrumpieren; (*morally*) verderben; ~ **practices** Korruption *f*
corruption [kəˈrʌpʃən] *n* Korruption *f*
Corsica [ˈkɔːsɪkə] *n* Korsika *nt*
cosmetic [kɔzˈmɛtɪk] *n* Kosmetikum *nt* ▷ *adj* kosmetisch; ~ **surgery** (*Med*) kosmetische Chirurgie *f*
cosmopolitan [kɔzməˈpɔlɪtn] *adj* kosmopolitisch
cost [kɔst] (*pt, pp* ~) *n* Kosten *pl*; (*fig: loss, damage etc*) Preis *m* ▷ *vt* kosten; (*find out cost of*) (*pt, pp* **~ed**) veranschlagen; **costs** *npl* (*Comm, Law*) Kosten *pl*; **the ~ of living** die Lebenshaltungskosten *pl*; **at all ~s** um jeden Preis; **how much does it ~?** wie viel *or* was kostet es?; **it ~s £5/too much** es kostet £5/ist zu teuer; **what will it ~ to have it repaired?** wie viel kostet die Reparatur?; **to ~ sb time/effort** jdn Zeit/Mühe kosten; **it ~ him his life/job** es kostete ihn das Leben/ seine Stelle
co-star [ˈkəustɑːʳ] *n* einer der Hauptdarsteller *m*, eine der Hauptdarstellerinnen *f*; **she was Sean Connery's ~ in ...** sie spielte neben Sean Connery in ...
cost-effective [ˈkɔstɪˈfɛktɪv] *adj* rentabel; (*Comm*) kostengünstig
costly [ˈkɔstlɪ] *adj* teuer, kostspielig; (*in time, effort*) aufwendig
cost price (*Brit*) *n* Selbstkostenpreis *m*; **to sell/buy at ~** zum Selbstkostenpreis verkaufen/kaufen
costume [ˈkɔstjuːm] *n* Kostüm *nt*; (*Brit: also:* **swimming costume**) Badeanzug *m*
costume jewellery *n* Modeschmuck *m*
cosy, (*US*) **cozy** [ˈkəuzɪ] *adj* gemütlich, behaglich; (*bed, scarf, gloves*) warm; (*chat, evening*) gemütlich; **I'm very ~ here** ich fühle mich hier sehr wohl, ich finde es hier sehr gemütlich
cot [kɔt] *n* (*Brit*) Kinderbett *nt*; (*US: campbed*) Feldbett *nt*
cottage [ˈkɔtɪdʒ] *n* Cottage *nt*, Häuschen *nt*
cottage cheese *n* Hüttenkäse *m*
cotton [ˈkɔtn] *n* (*fabric*) Baumwollstoff *m*; (*plant*) Baumwollstrauch *m*; (*thread*) (Baumwoll)garn *nt* ▷ *cpd* (*dress etc*) Baumwoll-
▸ **cotton on** (*inf*) *vi*: **to ~ on** es kapieren *or* schnallen; **to ~ on to sth** etw kapieren *or* schnallen
cotton candy (*US*) *n* Zuckerwatte *f*
cotton wool (*Brit*) *n* Watte *f*
couch [kautʃ] *n* Couch *f* ▷ *vt* formulieren
couchette [kuːˈʃɛt] *n* Liegewagen(platz) *m*
cough [kɔf] *vi* husten; (*engine*) stottern ▷ *n* Husten *m*
cough mixture *n* Hustensaft *m*
could [kud] *pt of* **can²**
couldn't [ˈkudnt] = **could not**
council [ˈkaunsl] *n* Rat *m*; **city/town ~** Stadtrat *m*; **C~ of Europe** Europarat *m*
council estate (*Brit*) *n* Siedlung *f* mit Sozialwohnungen
council house (*Brit*) *n* Sozialwohnung *f*
councillor [ˈkaunsləʳ] *n* Stadtrat *m*, Stadträtin *f*
council tax (*Brit*) *n* Gemeindesteuer *f*
counsel [ˈkaunsl] *n* Rat(schlag) *m*; (*lawyer*) Rechtsanwalt *m*, Rechtsanwältin *f* ▷ *vt* beraten; **to ~ sth** etw raten *or* empfehlen; **to ~ sb to do sth** jdm raten *or* empfehlen, etw zu tun; **~ for the defence** Verteidiger(in) *m(f)*; **~ for the prosecution** Vertreter(in) *m(f)* der Anklage
counsellor [ˈkaunsləʳ] *n* Berater(in) *m(f)*; (*US: lawyer*) Rechtsanwalt *m*, Rechtsanwältin *f*
count [kaunt] *vt* zählen; (*include*) mitrechnen, mitzählen ▷ *vi* zählen; (*be considered*) betrachtet *or* angesehen werden ▷ *n* Zählung *f*; (*level*) Zahl *f*; (*nobleman*) Graf *m*; **to ~ (up) to 10** bis 10 zählen; **not ~ing the children** die Kinder nicht mitgerechnet; **10 ~ing him** 10, wenn man ihn mitrechnet; **to ~ the cost of sth** die Folgen von etw abschätzen; **it ~s for very little** es zählt nicht viel; **~ yourself lucky** Sie können sich glücklich schätzen; **to keep ~ of sth** die Übersicht über etw *acc* behalten; **blood ~** Blutbild *nt*; **cholesterol/ alcohol ~** Cholesterin-/Alkoholspiegel *m*
▸ **count on** *vt fus* rechnen mit; (*depend on*) sich verlassen auf *+acc*; **to ~ on doing sth** die feste Absicht haben, etw zu tun
▸ **count up** *vt* zusammenzählen, zusammenrechnen
countdown [ˈkauntdaun] *n* Countdown *m*
countenance [ˈkauntɪnəns] *n* Gesicht *nt* ▷ *vt* gutheißen
counter [ˈkauntəʳ] *n* (*in shop*) Ladentisch *m*; (*in café*) Theke *f*; (*in bank, post office*) Schalter *m*; (*in game*) Spielmarke *f*; (*Tech*) Zähler *m* ▷ *vt* (*oppose: sth said, sth done*) begegnen *+dat*; (*blow*) kontern ▷ *adv*: **~ to** gegen *+acc*; **to buy sth under the ~** (*fig*) etw unter dem Ladentisch bekommen; **to ~ sth with sth** auf etw *acc* mit etw antworten; **to ~ sth by doing sth** einer Sache damit begegnen, dass man etw tut
counteract [ˈkauntərˈækt] *vt* entgegenwirken *+dat*; (*effect*) neutralisieren
counterclockwise [ˈkauntəˈklɔkwaɪz] *adv* gegen den Uhrzeigersinn
counterfeit [ˈkauntəfɪt] *n* Fälschung *f* ▷ *vt* fälschen ▷ *adj* (*coin*) Falsch-
counterfoil [ˈkauntəfɔɪl] *n* Kontrollabschnitt *m*
counterpart [ˈkauntəpɑːt] *n* Gegenüber *nt*; (*of document etc*) Gegenstück *nt*, Pendant *nt*
countess [ˈkauntɪs] *n* Gräfin *f*
countless [ˈkauntlɪs] *adj* unzählig, zahllos
country [ˈkʌntrɪ] *n* Land *nt*; (*native land*) Heimatland *nt*; **in the ~** auf dem Land; **mountainous ~** gebirgige Landschaft *f*
country and western, **country and**

western music *n* Country-und-Western-Musik *f*
country dancing (*Brit*) *n* Volkstanz *m*
country house *n* Landhaus *nt*
countryman ['kʌntrɪmən] (*irreg: like* **man**) *n* (*compatriot*) Landsmann *m*; (*country dweller*) Landmann *m*
countryside ['kʌntrɪsaɪd] *n* Land *nt*; (*scenery*) Landschaft *f*, Gegend *f*
county ['kauntɪ] *n* (*Brit*) Grafschaft *f*; (*US*) (Verwaltungs)bezirk *m*
coup [ku:] (*pl* **~s**) *n* (*also*: **coup d'état**) Staatsstreich *m*, Coup d'Etat *m*; (*achievement*) Coup *m*
couple ['kʌpl] *n* Paar *nt*; (*also*: **married couple**) Ehepaar *nt* ▷ *vt* verbinden; (*vehicles*) koppeln; **a ~ of** (*two*) zwei; (*a few*) ein paar
coupon ['ku:pɔn] *n* Gutschein *m*; (*detachable form*) Abschnitt *m*; (*Comm*) Coupon *m*
courage ['kʌrɪdʒ] *n* Mut *m*
courageous [kə'reɪdʒəs] *adj* mutig
courgette [kuə'ʒɛt] (*Brit*) *n* Zucchino *m*
courier ['kurɪəʳ] *n* (*messenger*) Kurier(in) *m(f)*; (*for tourists*) Reiseleiter(in) *m(f)*
course [kɔ:s] *n* (*Scol*) Kurs(us) *m*; (*of ship*) Kurs *m*; (*of life, events, time etc, of river*) Lauf *m*; (*of argument*) Richtung *f*; (*part of meal*) Gang *m*; (*for golf*) Platz *m*; **of ~** natürlich; **of ~!** (aber) natürlich!, (aber) selbstverständlich!; **(no) of ~ not!** natürlich nicht!; **in the ~ of the next few days** während *or* im Laufe der nächsten paar Tage; **in due ~** zu gegebener Zeit; **~ (of action)** Vorgehensweise *f*; **the best ~ would be to ...** das Beste wäre es, zu ...; **we have no other ~ but to ...** es bleibt uns nichts anderes übrig, als zu ...; **~ of lectures** Vorlesungsreihe *f*; **~ of treatment** (*Med*) Behandlung *f*; **first/last ~** erster/letzter Gang, Vor-/Nachspeise *f*
court [kɔ:t] *n* Hof *m*; (*Law*) Gericht *nt*; (*for tennis, badminton etc*) Platz *m* ▷ *vt* den Hof machen *+dat*; (*favour, popularity*) werben um; (*death, disaster*) herausfordern; **out of ~** (*Law*) außergerichtlich; **to take to ~** (*Law*) verklagen, vor Gericht bringen
courteous ['kə:tɪəs] *adj* höflich
courtesy ['kə:təsɪ] *n* Höflichkeit *f*; **(by) ~ of** freundlicherweise zur Verfügung gestellt von
courtesy bus, **courtesy coach** *n* gebührenfreier Bus *m*
courtier ['kɔ:tɪəʳ] *n* Höfling *m*
court martial (*pl* **courts martial**) *n* Militärgericht *nt*
courtroom ['kɔ:trum] *n* Gerichtssaal *m*
courtyard ['kɔ:tjɑ:d] *n* Hof *m*
cousin ['kʌzn] *n* (*male*) Cousin *m*, Vetter *m*; (*female*) Cousine *f*; **first ~** Cousin(e) ersten Grades
cove [kəuv] *n* (kleine) Bucht *f*
covenant ['kʌvənənt] *n* Schwur *m* ▷ *vt*: **to ~ £200 per year to a charity** sich vertraglich verpflichten, £200 im Jahr für wohltätige Zwecke zu spenden
cover ['kʌvəʳ] *vt* bedecken; (*distance*) zurücklegen; (*Insurance*) versichern; (*topic*) behandeln; (*include*) erfassen; (*Press: report on*) berichten über *+acc* ▷ *n* (*for furniture*) Bezug *m*; (*for typewriter, PC etc*) Hülle *f*; (*of book, magazine*) Umschlag *m*; (*shelter*) Schutz *m*; (*Insurance*) Versicherung *f*; (*fig: for illegal activities*) Tarnung *f*; **to be ~ed in** *or* **with** bedeckt sein mit; **£10 will ~ my expenses** £10 decken meine Unkosten; **to take ~** (*from rain*) sich unterstellen; **under ~** geschützt; **under ~ of darkness** im Schutz(e) der Dunkelheit; **under separate ~** getrennt
▸ **cover up** *vt* zudecken; (*fig: facts, feelings*) verheimlichen; (*: mistakes*) vertuschen ▷ *vi* (*fig*): **to ~ up for sb** jdn decken
coverage ['kʌvərɪdʒ] *n* Berichterstattung *f*; **television ~ of the conference** Fernsehberichte *pl* über die Konferenz; **to give full ~ to** ausführlich berichten über *+acc*
cover charge *n* Kosten *pl* für ein Gedeck
covering ['kʌvərɪŋ] *n* Schicht *f*; (*of snow, dust etc*) Decke *f*
covering letter, (*US*) **cover letter** *n* Begleitbrief *m*
cover note *n* (*Insurance*) Deckungszusage *f*
covert ['kʌvət] *adj* versteckt; (*glance*) verstohlen
cover-up ['kʌvərʌp] *n* Vertuschung *f*, Verschleierung *f*
covet ['kʌvɪt] *vt* begehren
cow [kau] *n* (*animal, inf!: woman*) Kuh *f* ▷ *cpd* Kuh- ▷ *vt* einschüchtern
coward ['kauəd] *n* Feigling *m*
cowardice ['kauədɪs] *n* Feigheit *f*
cowardly ['kauədlɪ] *adj* feige
cowboy ['kaubɔɪ] *n* (*in US*) Cowboy *m*; (*pej: tradesman*) Pfuscher *m*
cower ['kauəʳ] *vi* sich ducken; (*squatting*) kauern
coy [kɔɪ] *adj* verschämt
cozy ['kəuzɪ] (*US*) *adj* = **cosy**
CPA (*US*) *n abbr* = **certified public accountant**
crab [kræb] *n* Krabbe *f*, Krebs *m*; (*meat*) Krabbe *f*
crab apple *n* Holzapfel *m*
crack [kræk] *n* (*noise*) Knall *m*; (*of wood breaking*) Knacks *m*; (*gap*) Spalte *f*; (*in bone, dish, glass*) Sprung *m*; (*in wall*) Riss *m*; (*joke*) Witz *m*; (*Drugs*) Crack *nt* ▷ *vt* (*whip*) knallen mit; (*twig*) knacken mit; (*dish, glass*) einen Sprung machen in *+acc*; (*bone*) anbrechen; (*nut, code*) knacken; (*wall*) rissig machen; (*problem*) lösen; (*joke*) reißen ▷ *adj* erstklassig; **to have a ~ at sth** (*inf*) etw mal probieren; **to ~ jokes** (*inf*) Witze reißen; **to get ~ing** (*inf*) loslegen
▸ **crack down on** *vt fus* hart durchgreifen gegen
▸ **crack up** *vi* durchdrehen, zusammenbrechen
cracked [krækt] (*inf*) *adj* übergeschnappt

cracker ['krækəʳ] *n* (*biscuit*) Cracker *m*; (*also*: **Christmas cracker**) Knallbonbon *nt*; (*firework*) Knallkörper *m*, Kracher *m*; **a ~ of a ...** (*Brit*: *inf*) ein(e) tolle(r, s) ...; **he's ~s** (*Brit*: *inf*) er ist übergeschnappt

crackle ['krækl] *vi* (*fire*) knistern, prasseln; (*twig*) knacken

cradle ['kreɪdl] *n* Wiege *f* ▷ *vt* fest in den Armen halten

craft [krɑ:ft] *n* (*skill*) Geschicklichkeit *f*; (*art*) Kunsthandwerk *nt*; (*trade*) Handwerk *nt*; (*pl inv*: *boat*) Boot *nt*; (*pl inv*: *plane*) Flugzeug *nt*

craftsman ['krɑ:ftsmən] (*irreg*: *like* **man**) *n* Handwerker *m*

craftsmanship ['krɑ:ftsmənʃɪp] *n* handwerkliche Ausführung *f*

crafty ['krɑ:ftɪ] *adj* schlau, clever

crag [kræg] *n* Fels *m*

cram [kræm] *vt* vollstopfen ▷ *vi* pauken (*inf*), büffeln (*inf*); **to ~ with** vollstopfen mit; **to ~ sth into** etw hineinstopfen in *+acc*

cramp [kræmp] *n* Krampf *m* ▷ *vt* hemmen

cramped [kræmpt] *adj* eng

cranberry ['krænbərɪ] *n* Preiselbeere *f*

crane [kreɪn] *n* Kran *m*; (*bird*) Kranich *m* ▷ *vt*: **to ~ one's neck** den Hals recken ▷ *vi*: **to ~ forward** den Hals recken

crank [kræŋk] *n* Spinner(in) *m(f)*; (*handle*) Kurbel *f*

cranny ['krænɪ] *n see* **nook**

crap [kræp] (*inf!*) *n* Scheiße *f* (*!*) ▷ *vi* scheißen (*!*); **to have a ~** scheißen (*!*)

crash [kræʃ] *n* (*noise*) Krachen *nt*; (*of car*) Unfall *m*; (*of plane etc*) Unglück *nt*; (*collision*) Zusammenstoß *m*; (*of stock market, business etc*) Zusammenbruch *m* ▷ *vt* (*car*) einen Unfall haben mit; (*plane etc*) abstürzen mit ▷ *vi* (*plane*) abstürzen; (*car*) einen Unfall haben; (*two cars*) zusammenstoßen; (*market*) zusammenbrechen; (*firm*) Pleite machen; **to ~ into** krachen *or* knallen gegen; **he ~ed the car into a wall** er fuhr mit dem Auto gegen eine Mauer

crash course *n* Schnellkurs *m*, Intensivkurs *m*

crash helmet *n* Sturzhelm *m*

crate [kreɪt] *n* (*also inf*) Kiste *f*; (*for bottles*) Kasten *m*

cravat [krə'væt] *n* Halstuch *nt*

crave [kreɪv] *vt, vi*: **to ~ (for)** sich sehnen nach

crawl [krɔ:l] *vi* kriechen; (*child*) krabbeln ▷ *n* (*Swimming*) Kraulstil *m*, Kraul(en) *nt*; **to ~ to sb** (*inf*) vor jdm kriechen; **to drive along at a ~** im Schneckentempo *or* Kriechtempo vorankommen

crayfish ['kreɪfɪʃ] *n inv* (*freshwater*) Flusskrebs *m*; (*saltwater*) Languste *f*

crayon ['kreɪən] *n* Buntstift *m*

craze [kreɪz] *n* Fimmel *m*; **to be all the ~** große Mode sein

crazy ['kreɪzɪ] *adj* wahnsinnig, verrückt; **~ about sb/sth** (*inf*) verrückt *or* wild auf jdn/etw; **to go ~** wahnsinnig *or* verrückt werden

creak [kri:k] *vi* knarren

cream [kri:m] *n* Sahne *f*, Rahm *m* (*Südd*); (*artificial cream, cosmetic*) Creme *f*; (*élite*) Creme *f*, Elite *f* ▷ *adj* cremefarben; **whipped ~** Schlagsahne *f*

▶ **cream off** *vt* absahnen (*inf*)

cream cake *n* Sahnetorte *f*; (*small*) Sahnetörtchen *nt*

cream cheese *n* (Doppelrahm)frischkäse *m*

creamy ['kri:mɪ] *adj* (*colour*) cremefarben; (*taste*) sahnig

crease [kri:s] *n* Falte *f*; (*in trousers*) Bügelfalte *f* ▷ *vt* zerknittern; (*forehead*) runzeln ▷ *vi* knittern; (*forehead*) sich runzeln

create [kri:'eɪt] *vt* schaffen; (*interest*) hervorrufen; (*problems*) verursachen; (*produce*) herstellen; (*design*) entwerfen, kreieren; (*impression, fuss*) machen

creation [kri:'eɪʃən] *n* (*see vb*) Schaffung *f*; Hervorrufen *nt*; Verursachung *f*; Herstellung *f*; Entwurf *m*, Kreation *f*; (*Rel*) Schöpfung *f*

creative [kri:'eɪtɪv] *adj* kreativ, schöpferisch

creator [kri:'eɪtəʳ] *n* Schöpfer(in) *m(f)*

creature ['kri:tʃəʳ] *n* Geschöpf *nt*; (*living animal*) Lebewesen *nt*

crèche [krɛʃ] *n* (Kinder)krippe *f*; (*all day*) (Kinder)tagesstätte *f*

credence ['kri:dns] *n*: **to lend** *or* **give ~ to sth** etw glaubwürdig erscheinen lassen *or* machen

credentials [krɪ'dɛnʃlz] *npl* Referenzen *pl*, Zeugnisse *pl*; (*papers of identity*) (Ausweis)papiere *pl*

credibility [krɛdɪ'bɪlɪtɪ] *n* Glaubwürdigkeit *f*

credible ['krɛdɪbl] *adj* glaubwürdig

credit ['krɛdɪt] *n* (*loan*) Kredit *m*; (*recognition*) Anerkennung *f*; (*Scol*) Schein *m* ▷ *adj* (*Comm*: *terms etc*) Kredit- ▷ *vt* (*Comm*) gutschreiben; (*believe*: *also*: **give credit to**) glauben; **credits** *npl* (*Cine, TV*: *at beginning*) Vorspann *m*; (*: at end*) Nachspann *m*; **to be in ~** (*person*) Geld auf dem Konto haben; (*bank account*) im Haben sein; **on ~** auf Kredit; **it is to his ~ that ...** es ehrt ihn, dass ...; **to take the ~ for** das Verdienst in Anspruch nehmen für; **it does him ~** es spricht für ihn; **he's a ~ to his family** er macht seiner Familie Ehre; **to ~ sb with sth** (*fig*) jdm etw zuschreiben; **to ~ £5 to sb** jdm £5 gutschreiben

credit card *n* Kreditkarte *f*

creditor ['krɛdɪtəʳ] *n* Gläubiger *m*

creed [kri:d] *n* Glaubensbekenntnis *nt*

creek [kri:k] *n* (kleine) Bucht *f*; (*US*: *stream*) Bach *m*; **to be up the ~** (*inf*) in der Tinte sitzen

creep [kri:p] (*pt, pp* **crept**) *vi* schleichen; (*plant*: *horizontally*) kriechen; (*: vertically*) klettern ▷ *n* (*inf*) Kriecher *m*; **to ~ up on sb** sich an jdn heranschleichen; (*time etc*) langsam auf jdn zukommen; **he's a ~** er ist ein widerlicher *or* fieser Typ; **it gives me the ~s** davon kriege ich das kalte Grausen

creeper ['kri:pəʳ] *n* Kletterpflanze *f*

creepy ['kri:pɪ] *adj* gruselig; (*experience*)

unheimlich, gruselig
cremate [krɪ'meɪt] *vt* einäschern
crematorium [krɛmə'tɔ:rɪəm] (*pl* **crematoria**) *n* Krematorium *nt*
crepe [kreɪp] *n* Krepp *m*; (*rubber*) Krepp(gummi) *m*
crepe bandage (*Brit*) *n* elastische Binde *f*
crept [krɛpt] *pt, pp of* **creep**
crescent ['krɛsnt] *n* Halbmond *m*; (*street*) *halbkreisförmig verlaufende Straße*
cress [krɛs] *n* Kresse *f*
crest [krɛst] *n* (*of hill*) Kamm *m*; (*of bird*) Haube *f*; (*coat of arms*) Wappen *nt*
crestfallen ['krɛstfɔ:lən] *adj* niedergeschlagen
Crete [kri:t] *n* Kreta *nt*
crevice ['krɛvɪs] *n* Spalte *f*
crew [kru:] *n* Besatzung *f*; (TV, *Cine*) Crew *f*; (*gang*) Bande *f*
crib [krɪb] *n* Kinderbett *nt*; (*Rel*) Krippe *f* ▷ *vt* (*inf: copy*) abschreiben
crick [krɪk] *n* Krampf *m*
cricket ['krɪkɪt] *n* Kricket *nt*; (*insect*) Grille *f*
cricketer ['krɪkɪtə^r] *n* Kricketspieler(in) *m(f)*
crime [kraɪm] *n* (*no pl: illegal activities*) Verbrechen *pl*; (*illegal action, fig*) Verbrechen *nt*; **minor ~** kleinere Vergehen *pl*
criminal ['krɪmɪnl] *n* Kriminelle(r) *f(m)*, Verbrecher(in) *m(f)* ▷ *adj* kriminell; **C~ Investigation Department** Kriminalpolizei *f*
crimson ['krɪmzn] *adj* purpurrot
cringe [krɪndʒ] *vi* (*in fear*) zurückweichen; (*in embarrassment*) zusammenzucken
crinkle ['krɪŋkl] *vt* (zer)knittern
cripple ['krɪpl] *n* Krüppel *m* ▷ *vt* zum Krüppel machen; (*ship, plane*) aktionsunfähig machen; (*production, exports*) lahmlegen, lähmen; **~d with rheumatism** von Rheuma praktisch gelähmt
crisis ['kraɪsɪs] (*pl* **crises**) *n* Krise *f*
crisp [krɪsp] *adj* (*vegetables etc*) knackig; (*bacon etc*) knusprig; (*weather*) frisch; (*manner, tone, reply*) knapp
crisps [krɪsps] (*Brit*) *npl* Chips *pl*
crisscross ['krɪskrɔs] *adj* (*pattern*) Kreuz- ▷ *vt* kreuz und quer durchziehen
criterion [kraɪ'tɪərɪən] (*pl* **criteria**) *n* Kriterium *nt*
critic ['krɪtɪk] *n* Kritiker(in) *m(f)*
critical ['krɪtɪkl] *adj* kritisch; **to be ~ of sb/sth** jdn/etw kritisieren; **he is in a ~ condition** sein Zustand ist kritisch
critically ['krɪtɪklɪ] *adv* kritisch; (*ill*) schwer
criticism ['krɪtɪsɪzəm] *n* Kritik *f*
criticize ['krɪtɪsaɪz] *vt* kritisieren
croak [krəuk] *vi* (*frog*) quaken; (*bird, person*) krächzen
Croat *n* Kroate *m*, Kroatin *f*; (*Ling*) Kroatisch *nt*
Croatia [krəu'eɪʃə] *n* Kroatien *nt*
Croatian [krəu'eɪʃən] *adj* kroatisch
crochet ['krəuʃeɪ] *n* (*activity*) Häkeln *nt*; (*result*) Häkelei *f*
crockery ['krɔkərɪ] *n* Geschirr *nt*
crocodile ['krɔkədaɪl] *n* Krokodil *nt*
crocus ['krəukəs] *n* Krokus *m*
croft [krɔft] (*Brit*) *n* kleines Pachtgut *nt*
crony ['krəunɪ] (*inf: pej*) *n* Kumpan(in) *m(f)*
crook [kruk] *n* (*criminal*) Gauner *m*; (*of shepherd*) Hirtenstab *m*; (*of arm*) Beuge *f*
crooked ['krukɪd] *adj* krumm; (*dishonest*) unehrlich
crop [krɔp] *n* (Feld)frucht *f*; (*amount produced*) Ernte *f*; (*riding crop*) Reitpeitsche *f*; (*of bird*) Kropf *m* ▷ *vt* (*hair*) stutzen; (*subj: animal: grass*) abfressen
▸ **crop up** *vi* aufkommen
cross [krɔs] *n* Kreuz *nt*; (*Biol, Bot*) Kreuzung *f* ▷ *vt* (*street*) überqueren; (*room etc*) durchqueren; (*cheque*) zur Verrechnung ausstellen; (*arms*) verschränken; (*legs*) übereinanderschlagen; (*animal, plant*) kreuzen; (*thwart: person*) verärgern; (*: plan*) durchkreuzen ▷ *adj* ärgerlich, böse ▷ *vi*: **the boat ~es from ... to ...** das Schiff fährt von ... nach ...; **to ~ o.s.** sich bekreuzigen; **we have a ~ed line** (*Brit*) es ist jemand in der Leitung; **they've got their lines** *or* **wires ~ed** (*fig*) sie reden aneinander vorbei; **to be/get ~ with sb (about sth)** mit jdm *or* auf jdn (wegen etw) böse sein/werden
▸ **cross out** *vt* streichen
▸ **cross over** *vi* hinübergehen
crossbar ['krɔsbɑ:^{r}] *n* (*Sport*) Querlatte *f*; (*of bicycle*) Stange *f*
cross-Channel ferry ['krɔs'tʃænl-] *n* Kanalfähre *f*
cross-country ['krɔs'kʌntrɪ], **cross-country race** *n* Querfeldeinrennen *nt*
cross-examine ['krɔsɪg'zæmɪn] *vt* ins Kreuzverhör nehmen
cross-eyed ['krɔsaɪd] *adj* schielend; **to be ~** schielen
crossfire ['krɔsfaɪə^r] *n* Kreuzfeuer *nt*; **to get caught in the ~** (*also fig*) ins Kreuzfeuer geraten
crossing ['krɔsɪŋ] *n* Überfahrt *f*; (*also:* **pedestrian crossing**) Fußgängerüberweg *m*
crossing guard (US) *n* ≈ Schülerlotse *m*
cross-purposes ['krɔs'pə:pəsɪz] *npl*: **to be at ~ with sb** jdn missverstehen; **we're (talking) at ~** wir reden aneinander vorbei
cross-reference ['krɔs'rɛfrəns] *n* (Quer)verweis *m*
crossroads ['krɔsrəudz] *n* Kreuzung *f*
cross section *n* Querschnitt *m*
crosswalk ['krɔswɔ:k] (US) *n* Fußgängerüberweg *m*
crosswind ['krɔswɪnd] *n* Seitenwind *m*
crossword ['krɔswə:d] *n* (*also:* **crossword puzzle**) Kreuzworträtsel *nt*
crotch [krɔtʃ] *n* Unterleib *m*; (*of garment*) Schritt *m*
crouch [krautʃ] *vi* kauern
crouton ['kru:tɔn] *n* Crouton *m*

crow [krəu] *n* (*bird*) Krähe *f*; (*of cock*) Krähen *nt* ▷ *vi* krähen; (*fig*) sich brüsten, angeben
crowbar ['krəubɑ:ʳ] *n* Brechstange *f*
crowd [kraud] *n* (Menschen)menge *f* ▷ *vt* (*room, stadium*) füllen ▷ *vi*: **to ~ round** sich herumdrängen; **~s of people** Menschenmassen *pl*; **the/our ~** (*of friends*) die/unsere Clique *f*; **to ~ sb/sth in** jdn/etw hineinstopfen; **to ~ sb/sth into** jdn pferchen/etw stopfen in *+acc*; **to ~ in** sich hineindrängen
crowded ['kraudɪd] *adj* überfüllt; (*densely populated*) dicht besiedelt; **~ with** voll von
crown [kraun] *n* (*also of tooth*) Krone *f*; (*of head*) Wirbel *m*; (*of hill*) Kuppe *f*; (*of hat*) Kopf *m* ▷ *vt* krönen; (*tooth*) überkronen; **the C~** die Krone; **and to ~ it all ...** (*fig*) und zur Krönung des Ganzen ...
crown jewels *npl* Kronjuwelen *pl*
crow's-feet ['krəuzfi:t] *npl* Krähenfüße *pl*
crucial ['kru:ʃl] *adj* (*decision*) äußerst wichtig; (*vote*) entscheidend; **~ to** äußerst wichtig für
crucifix ['kru:sɪfɪks] *n* Kruzifix *nt*
crucifixion [kru:sɪ'fɪkʃən] *n* Kreuzigung *f*
crude [kru:d] *adj* (*oil, fibre*) Roh-; (*fig: basic*) primitiv; (*: vulgar*) ordinär ▷ *n* = **crude oil**
cruel ['kruəl] *adj* grausam
cruelty ['kruəltɪ] *n* Grausamkeit *f*
cruise [kru:z] *n* Kreuzfahrt *f* ▷ *vi* (*ship*) kreuzen; (*car*) (mit Dauergeschwindigkeit) fahren; (*aircraft*) (mit Reisegeschwindigkeit) fliegen; (*taxi*) gemächlich fahren
cruiser ['kru:zəʳ] *n* Motorboot *nt*; (*warship*) Kreuzer *m*
crumb [krʌm] *n* Krümel *m*; (*fig: of information*) Brocken *m*; **a ~ of comfort** ein winziger Trost
crumble ['krʌmbl] *vt* (*bread*) zerbröckeln; (*biscuit etc*) zerkrümeln ▷ *vi* (*building, earth etc*) zerbröckeln; (*plaster*) abbröckeln; (*fig: opposition*) sich auflösen; (*: belief*) ins Wanken geraten
crumbly ['krʌmblɪ] *adj* krümelig
crumpet ['krʌmpɪt] *n* Teekuchen *m* (*zum Toasten*)
crumple ['krʌmpl] *vt* zerknittern
crunch [krʌntʃ] *vt* (*biscuit, apple etc*) knabbern; (*underfoot*) zertreten ▷ *n*: **the ~** der große Krach; **if it comes to the ~** wenn es wirklich dahin kommt; **when the ~ comes** wenn es hart auf hart geht
crunchy ['krʌntʃɪ] *adj* knusprig; (*apple etc*) knackig; (*gravel, snow etc*) knirschend
crusade [kru:'seɪd] *n* Feldzug *m* ▷ *vi*: **to ~ for/against sth** für/gegen etw zu Felde ziehen
crush [krʌʃ] *n* (*crowd*) Gedränge *nt* ▷ *vt* quetschen; (*grapes*) zerquetschen; (*paper, clothes*) zerknittern; (*garlic, ice*) (zer)stoßen; (*defeat*) niederschlagen; (*devastate*) vernichten; **to have a ~ on sb** (*love*) für jdn schwärmen; **lemon ~** Zitronensaftgetränk *nt*
crust [krʌst] *n* Kruste *f*
crusty ['krʌstɪ] *adj* knusprig
crutch [krʌtʃ] *n* Krücke *f*; (*support*) Stütze *f*; *see also* **crotch**
crux [krʌks] *n* Kern *m*
cry [kraɪ] *vi* weinen; (*also*: **cry out**) aufschreien ▷ *n* Schrei *m*; (*shout*) Ruf *m*; **what are you ~ing about?** warum weinst du?; **to ~ for help** um Hilfe rufen; **she had a good ~** sie hat sich (mal richtig) ausgeweint; **it's a far ~ from ...** (*fig*) das ist etwas ganz anderes als ...
▶ **cry off** (*inf*) *vi* absagen
cryptic ['krɪptɪk] *adj* hintergründig, rätselhaft; (*clue*) verschlüsselt
crystal ['krɪstl] *n* Kristall *m*; (*glass*) Kristall(glas) *nt*
CSA *n abbr* (*= Child Support Agency*) *Amt zur Regelung von Unterhaltszahlungen für Kinder*
CTC (*Brit*) *n abbr* = **city technology college**
cub [kʌb] *n* Junge(s) *nt*; (*also*: **cub scout**) Wölfling *m*
Cuba ['kju:bə] *n* Kuba *nt*
cube [kju:b] *n* Würfel *m*; (*Math: of number*) dritte Potenz *f* ▷ *vt* (*Math*) in die dritte Potenz erheben, hoch drei nehmen
cubic ['kju:bɪk] *adj* (*volume*) Kubik-; **~ metre** *etc* Kubikmeter *m etc*
cubicle ['kju:bɪkl] *n* Kabine *f*; (*in hospital*) Bettnische *f*
cuckoo ['kuku:] *n* Kuckuck *m*
cuckoo clock *n* Kuckucksuhr *f*
cucumber ['kju:kʌmbəʳ] *n* Gurke *f*
cuddle ['kʌdl] *vt* in den Arm nehmen, drücken ▷ *vi* schmusen
cue [kju:] *n* (*Sport*) Billardstock *m*, Queue *nt*; (*Theat: word*) Stichwort *nt*; (*: action*) (Einsatz)zeichen *nt*; (*Mus*) Einsatz *m*
cuff [kʌf] *n* (*of sleeve*) Manschette *f*; (*US: of trousers*) Aufschlag *m*; (*blow*) Klaps *m* ▷ *vt* einen Klaps geben *+dat*; **off the ~** aus dem Stegreif
cuisine [kwɪ'zi:n] *n* Küche *f*
cul-de-sac ['kʌldəsæk] *n* Sackgasse *f*
cull [kʌl] *vt* (zusammen)sammeln; (*animals*) ausmerzen ▷ *n* *Erlegen überschüssiger Tierbestände*
culminate ['kʌlmɪneɪt] *vi*: **to ~ in** gipfeln in *+dat*
culmination [kʌlmɪ'neɪʃən] *n* Höhepunkt *m*
culottes [kju:'lɔts] *npl* Hosenrock *m*
culprit ['kʌlprɪt] *n* Täter(in) *m(f)*
cult [kʌlt] *n* Kult *m*
cultivate ['kʌltɪveɪt] *vt* (*land*) bebauen, landwirtschaftlich nutzen; (*crop*) anbauen; (*feeling*) entwickeln; (*person*) sich *dat* warm halten (*inf*), die Beziehung pflegen zu
cultivation [kʌltɪ'veɪʃən] *n* (*of land*) Bebauung *f*, landwirtschaftliche Nutzung *f*; (*of crop*) Anbau *m*
cultural ['kʌltʃərəl] *adj* kulturell
culture ['kʌltʃəʳ] *n* Kultur *f*
cultured ['kʌltʃəd] *adj* kultiviert; (*pearl*) Zucht-

cumbersome ['kʌmbəsəm] *adj* (*suitcase etc*) sperrig, unhandlich; (*piece of machinery*) schwer zu handhaben; (*clothing*) hinderlich; (*process*) umständlich

cumin ['kʌmɪn] *n* Kreuzkümmel *m*

cunning ['kʌnɪŋ] *n* Gerissenheit *f* ▷ *adj* gerissen; (*device, idea*) schlau

cup [kʌp] *n* Tasse *f*; (*as prize*) Pokal *m*; (*of bra*) Körbchen *nt*; **a ~ of tea** eine Tasse Tee

cupboard ['kʌbəd] *n* Schrank *m*

cup final (*Brit*) *n* Pokalendspiel *nt*

cup tie (*Brit*) *n* Pokalspiel *nt*

curate ['kjuərɪt] *n* Vikar *m*

curator [kjuə'reɪtəʳ] *n* Kustos *m*

curb [kəːb] *vt* einschränken; (*person*) an die Kandare nehmen ▷ *n* Einschränkung *f*; (*US: kerb*) Bordstein *m*

curdle ['kəːdl] *vi* gerinnen

cure [kjuəʳ] *vt* heilen; (*Culin: salt*) pökeln; (*: smoke*) räuchern; (*: dry*) trocknen; (*problem*) abhelfen *+dat* ▷ *n* (*remedy*) (Heil)mittel *nt*; (*treatment*) Heilverfahren *nt*; (*solution*) Abhilfe *f*; **to be ~d of sth** von etw geheilt sein

curfew ['kəːfjuː] *n* Ausgangssperre *f*; (*time*) Sperrstunde *f*

curiosity [kjuərɪ'ɔsɪtɪ] *n* (*see adj*) Wissbegier(de) *f*; Neugier *f*; Merkwürdigkeit *f*

curious ['kjuərɪəs] *adj* (*interested*) wissbegierig; (*nosy*) neugierig; (*strange, unusual*) sonderbar, merkwürdig; **I'm ~ about him** ich bin gespannt auf ihn

curl [kəːl] *n* Locke *f*; (*of smoke etc*) Kringel *m* ▷ *vt* (*hair: loosely*) locken; (*: tightly*) kräuseln ▷ *vi* sich locken; sich kräuseln; (*smoke*) sich kringeln

▸ **curl up** *vi* sich zusammenrollen

curler ['kəːləʳ] *n* Lockenwickler *m*; (*Sport*) Curlingspieler(in) *m(f)*

curly ['kəːlɪ] *adj* lockig; (*tightly curled*) kraus

currant ['kʌrnt] *n* Korinthe *f*; (*blackcurrant, redcurrant*) Johannisbeere *f*

currency ['kʌrnsɪ] *n* (*system*) Währung *f*; (*money*) Geld *nt*; **foreign ~** Devisen *pl*; **to gain ~** (*fig*) sich verbreiten, um sich greifen

current ['kʌrnt] *n* Strömung *f*; (*Elec*) Strom *m*; (*of opinion*) Tendenz *f*, Trend *m* ▷ *adj* gegenwärtig; (*expression*) gebräuchlich; (*idea, custom*) verbreitet; **direct/alternating ~** (*Elec*) Gleich-/Wechselstrom *m*; **the ~ issue of a magazine** die neueste *or* letzte Nummer einer Zeitschrift; **in ~ use** allgemein gebräuchlich

current account (*Brit*) *n* Girokonto *nt*

current affairs *npl* Tagespolitik *f*

currently ['kʌrntlɪ] *adv* zurzeit

curriculum [kə'rɪkjuləm] (*pl* **~s** *or* **curricula**) *n* Lehrplan *m*

curriculum vitae [-'viːtaɪ] *n* Lebenslauf *m*

curry ['kʌrɪ] *n* (*dish*) Currygericht *nt* ▷ *vt*: **to ~ favour with** sich einschmeicheln bei

curry powder *n* Curry *m or nt*, Currypulver *nt*

curse [kəːs] *vi* fluchen ▷ *vt* verfluchen ▷ *n* Fluch *m*

cursor ['kəːsəʳ] *n* (*Comput*) Cursor *m*

cursory ['kəːsərɪ] *adj* flüchtig; (*examination*) oberflächlich

curt [kəːt] *adj* knapp, kurz angebunden

curtail [kəː'teɪl] *vt* einschränken; (*visit etc*) abkürzen

curtain ['kəːtn] *n* Vorhang *m*; (*net*) Gardine *f*; **to draw the ~s** (*together*) die Vorhänge zuziehen; (*apart*) die Vorhänge aufmachen

curtsey, curtsy ['kəːtsɪ] *vi* knicksen ▷ *n* Knicks *m*

curve [kəːv] *n* Bogen *m*; (*in the road*) Kurve *f* ▷ *vi* einen Bogen machen; (*surface, arch*) sich wölben ▷ *vt* biegen

curved [kəːvd] *adj* (*line*) gebogen; (*table legs etc*) geschwungen; (*surface, arch, sides of ship*) gewölbt

cushion ['kuʃən] *n* Kissen *nt* ▷ *vt* dämpfen; (*seat*) polstern

custard ['kʌstəd] *n* (*for pouring*) Vanillesoße *f*

custody ['kʌstədɪ] *n* (*of child*) Vormundschaft *f*; (*for offenders*) (polizeilicher) Gewahrsam *m*, Haft *f*; **to take into ~** verhaften; **in the ~ of** unter der Obhut *+gen*; **the mother has ~ of the children** die Kinder sind der Mutter zugesprochen worden

custom ['kʌstəm] *n* Brauch *m*; (*habit*) (An)gewohnheit *f*; (*Law*) Gewohnheitsrecht *nt*; (*Comm*) Kundschaft *f*

customary ['kʌstəmərɪ] *adj* (*conventional*) üblich; (*habitual*) gewohnt; **it is ~ to do it** es ist üblich, es zu tun

customer ['kʌstəməʳ] *n* Kunde *m*, Kundin *f*; **he's an awkward ~** (*inf*) er ist ein schwieriger Typ

customized ['kʌstəmaɪzd] *adj* individuell aufgemacht

custom-made ['kʌstəm'meɪd] *adj* (*shirt etc*) maßgefertigt, nach Maß; (*car etc*) speziell angefertigt

customs ['kʌstəmz] *npl* Zoll *m*; **to go through (the) ~** durch den Zoll gehen

customs officer *n* Zollbeamte(r) *m*, Zollbeamtin *f*

cut [kʌt] (*pt, pp* **~**) *vt* schneiden; (*text, programme, spending*) kürzen; (*prices*) senken, heruntersetzen, herabsetzen; (*supply*) einschränken; (*cloth*) zuschneiden; (*road*) schlagen, hauen; (*inf: lecture, appointment*) schwänzen ▷ *vi* schneiden; (*lines*) sich schneiden ▷ *n* Schnitt *m*; (*in skin*) Schnittwunde *f*; (*in salary, spending etc*) Kürzung *f*; (*of meat*) Stück *nt*; (*of jewel*) Schnitt *m*, Schliff *m*; **to ~ a tooth** zahnen, einen Zahn bekommen; **to ~ one's finger/hand/knee** sich in den Finger/in die Hand/am Knie schneiden; **to get one's hair ~** sich *dat* die Haare schneiden lassen; **to ~ sth short** etw vorzeitig abbrechen; **to ~ sb dead** jdn wie Luft behandeln; **cold ~s** (*US*) Aufschnitt *m*; **power ~** Stromausfall *m*

▸ **cut back** *vt* (*plants*) zurückschneiden;

(*production*) zurückschrauben; (*expenditure*) einschränken
▸ **cut down** *vt* (*tree*) fällen; (*consumption*) einschränken; **to ~ sb down to size** (*fig*) jdn auf seinen Platz verweisen
▸ **cut down on** *vt fus* einschränken
▸ **cut in** *vi* (*Aut*) sich direkt vor ein anderes Auto setzen; **to ~ in (on)** (*conversation*) sich einschalten (in *+acc*)
▸ **cut off** *vt* abschneiden; (*supply*) sperren; (*Tel*) unterbrechen; **we've been ~ off** (*Tel*) wir sind unterbrochen worden
▸ **cut out** *vt* ausschneiden; (*an activity etc*) aufhören mit; (*remove*) herausschneiden
▸ **cut up** *vt* klein schneiden; **it really ~ me up** (*inf*) es hat mich ziemlich mitgenommen; **to feel ~ up about sth** (*inf*) betroffen über etw *acc* sein

cutback ['kʌtbæk] *n* Kürzung *f*

cute [kju:t] *adj* süß, niedlich; (*clever*) schlau

cutlery ['kʌtlərı] *n* Besteck *nt*

cutlet ['kʌtlıt] *n* Schnitzel *nt*; (*also*: **vegetable cutlet, nut cutlet**) Bratling *m*

cutout ['kʌtaut] *n* (*switch*) Unterbrecher *m*; (*shape*) Ausschneidemodell *nt*; (*paper figure*) Ausschneidepuppe *f*

cut-price ['kʌt'praıs] *adj* (*goods*) heruntergesetzt; (*offer*) Billig-

cutting ['kʌtıŋ] *adj* (*edge, remark*) scharf ▹ *n* (*Brit: from newspaper*) Ausschnitt *m*; (: *Rail*) Durchstich *m*; (*from plant*) Ableger *m*

CV *n abbr* = **curriculum vitae**

cwt *abbr* = **hundredweight**

cyanide ['saıənaıd] *n* Zyanid *nt*

cycle ['saıkl] *n* (*bicycle*) (Fahr)rad *nt*; (*series: of seasons, songs etc*) Zyklus *m*; (: *of events*) Gang *m*; (: *Tech*) Periode *f* ▹ *vi* Rad fahren

cycle lane, **cycle path** *n* (Fahr)radweg *m*

cycling ['saıklıŋ] *n* Radfahren *nt*; **to go on a ~ holiday** (*Brit*) Urlaub mit dem Fahrrad machen

cyclist ['saıklıst] *n* (Fahr)radfahrer(in) *m(f)*

cyclone ['saıkləun] *n* Zyklon *m*

cygnet ['sıgnıt] *n* Schwanjunge(s) *nt*

cylinder ['sılındə[r]] *n* Zylinder *m*; (*of gas*) Gasflasche *f*

cymbals ['sımblz] *npl* (*Mus*) Becken *nt*

cynic ['sınık] *n* Zyniker(in) *m(f)*

cynical ['sınıkl] *adj* zynisch

cynicism ['sınısızəm] *n* Zynismus *m*

Cypriot ['sıprıət] *adj* zypriotisch, zyprisch ▹ *n* Zypriot(in) *m(f)*

Cyprus ['saıprəs] *n* Zypern *nt*

cyst [sıst] *n* Zyste *f*

cystitis [sıs'taıtıs] *n* Blasenentzündung *f*, Zystitis *f*

czar [zɑ:[r]] *n* = **tsar**

Czech [tʃɛk] *adj* tschechisch ▹ *n* Tscheche *m*, Tschechin *f*; (*language*) Tschechisch *nt*; **the ~ Republic** die Tschechische Republik *f*

Czechoslovak [tʃɛkə'sləuvæk] *adj, n* = **Czechoslovakian**

Czechoslovakia [tʃɛkəslə'vækıə] *n* (*formerly*) die Tschechoslowakei *f*

Czechoslovakian [tʃɛkəslə'vækıən] (*formerly*) *adj* tschechoslowakisch ▹ *n* Tschechoslowake *m*, Tschechoslowakin *f*

Dd

D¹, d¹ [diː] *n (letter)* D *nt*, d *nt*; **D for David, D for Dog** *(US)* ≈ D wie Dora
D² [diː] *n (Mus)* D *nt*, d *nt*
D³ [diː] *(US) abbr (Pol)* = **Democrat; Democratic**
d² *(Brit: formerly) abbr* = **penny**
dab [dæb] *vt* betupfen; *(paint, cream)* tupfen ▷ *n* Tupfer *m*; **to be a ~ hand at sth** gut in etw *dat* sein; **to be a ~ hand at doing sth** sich darauf verstehen, etw zu tun
▶ **dab at** *vt* betupfen
dabble ['dæbl] *vi*: **to ~ in** sich (nebenbei) beschäftigen mit
dad [dæd] *(inf) n* Papa *m*, Vati *m*
daffodil ['dæfədɪl] *n* Osterglocke *f*, Narzisse *f*
daft [dɑːft] *(inf) adj* doof *(inf)*, blöd *(inf)*; **to be ~ about sb/sth** verrückt nach jdm/etw sein
dagger ['dægəʳ] *n* Dolch *m*; **to be at ~s drawn with sb** mit jdm auf Kriegsfuß stehen; **to look ~s at sb** jdn mit Blicken durchbohren
daily ['deɪlɪ] *adj* täglich; *(wages)* Tages- ▷ *n (paper)* Tageszeitung *f*; *(Brit: also:* **daily help***)* Putzfrau *f* ▷ *adv* täglich; **twice ~** zweimal täglich *or* am Tag
dainty ['deɪntɪ] *adj* zierlich
dairy ['dɛərɪ] *n (Brit: shop)* Milchgeschäft *nt*; *(company)* Molkerei *f*; *(on farm)* Milchkammer *f* ▷ *cpd* Milch-; *(herd, industry, farming)* Milchvieh-
dairy products *npl* Milchprodukte *pl*, Molkereiprodukte *pl*
daisy ['deɪzɪ] *n* Gänseblümchen *nt*
dale [deɪl] *(Brit) n* Tal *nt*
dam [dæm] *n* (Stau)damm *m*; *(reservoir)* Stausee *m* ▷ *vt* stauen
damage ['dæmɪdʒ] *n* Schaden *m* ▷ *vt* schaden *+dat*; *(spoil, break)* beschädigen; **damages** *npl (Law)* Schaden(s)ersatz *m*; **~ to property** Sachbeschädigung *f*; **to pay £5,000 in ~s** 5000 Pfund Schaden(s)ersatz (be)zahlen
damn [dæm] *vt* verfluchen; *(condemn)* verurteilen ▷ *adj (inf: also:* **damned***)* verdammt ▷ *n (inf)*: **I don't give a ~** das ist mir scheißegal *(!)*; **~ (it)!** verdammt (noch mal)!
damning ['dæmɪŋ] *adj* belastend
damp [dæmp] *adj* feucht ▷ *n* Feuchtigkeit *f* ▷ *vt (also:* **dampen***)* befeuchten, anfeuchten; *(enthusiasm etc)* dämpfen
damson ['dæmzən] *n* Damaszenerpflaume *f*
dance [dɑːns] *n* Tanz *m*; *(social event)* Tanz(abend) *m* ▷ *vi* tanzen; **to ~ about** (herum)tänzeln
dance hall *n* Tanzsaal *m*
dancer ['dɑːnsəʳ] *n* Tänzer(in) *m(f)*
dancing ['dɑːnsɪŋ] *n* Tanzen *nt* ▷ *cpd (teacher, school, class etc)* Tanz-
dandelion ['dændɪlaɪən] *n* Löwenzahn *m*
dandruff ['dændrəf] *n* Schuppen *pl*
Dane [deɪn] *n* Däne *m*, Dänin *f*
danger ['deɪndʒəʳ] *n* Gefahr *f*; **there is ~ of fire/poisoning** es besteht Feuer-/Vergiftungsgefahr; **there is a ~ of sth happening** es besteht die Gefahr, dass etw geschieht; **"~!"** "Achtung!"; **in ~** in Gefahr; **to be in ~ of doing sth** Gefahr laufen, etw zu tun; **out of ~** außer Gefahr
dangerous ['deɪndʒrəs] *adj* gefährlich
dangle ['dæŋgl] *vt* baumeln lassen ▷ *vi* baumeln
Danish ['deɪnɪʃ] *adj* dänisch ▷ *n (Ling)* Dänisch *nt*
dare [dɛəʳ] *vt*: **to ~ sb to do sth** jdn dazu herausfordern, etw zu tun ▷ *vi*: **to ~ (to) do sth** es wagen, etw zu tun; **I ~n't tell him** *(Brit)* ich wage nicht, es ihm zu sagen; **I ~ say** ich nehme an
daring ['dɛərɪŋ] *adj* kühn, verwegen; *(bold)* gewagt ▷ *n* Kühnheit *f*
dark [dɑːk] *adj* dunkel; *(look)* finster ▷ *n*: **in the ~** im Dunkeln; **to be in the ~ about** *(fig)* keine Ahnung haben von; **after ~** nach Einbruch der Dunkelheit; **it is/is getting ~** es ist/wird dunkel; **~ chocolate** Zartbitterschokolade *f*
darken [dɑːkn] *vt* dunkel machen ▷ *vi* sich verdunkeln
dark glasses *npl* Sonnenbrille *f*
darkness ['dɑːknɪs] *n* Dunkelheit *f*, Finsternis *f*
darkroom ['dɑːkrum] *n* Dunkelkammer *f*
darling ['dɑːlɪŋ] *adj* lieb ▷ *n* Liebling *m*; **to be the ~ of** der Liebling *+gen* sein; **she is a ~** sie ist ein Schatz
darn [dɑːn] *vt* stopfen
dart [dɑːt] *n (in game)* (Wurf)pfeil *m*; *(in sewing)* Abnäher *m* ▷ *vi*: **to ~ towards** *(also:* **make a dart towards***)* zustürzen auf *+acc*; **to ~ away/**

along davon-/entlangflitzen
dartboard ['dɑ:tbɔ:d] *n* Dartscheibe *f*
darts [dɑ:ts] *n* Darts *nt*, Pfeilwurfspiel *nt*
dash [dæʃ] *n* (*sign*) Gedankenstrich *m*; (*rush*) Jagd *f* ▷ *vt* (*throw*) schleudern; (*hopes*) zunichtemachen ▷ *vi*: **to ~ towards** zustürzen auf *+acc*; **a ~ of ...** (*small quantity*) etwas ..., ein Schuss *m* ...; **to make a ~ for sth** auf etw *acc* zustürzen; **we'll have to make a ~ for it** wir müssen rennen, so schnell wir können
▸ **dash away** *vi* losstürzen
▸ **dash off** *vi* = **dash away**
dashboard ['dæʃbɔ:d] *n* Armaturenbrett *nt*
dashing ['dæʃɪŋ] *adj* flott
data ['deɪtə] *npl* Daten *pl*
database ['deɪtəbeɪs] *n* Datenbank *f*
data processing *n* Datenverarbeitung *f*
date [deɪt] *n* Datum *nt*; (*with friend*) Verabredung *f*; (*fruit*) Dattel *f* ▷ *vt* datieren; (*person*) ausgehen mit; **what's the ~ today?** der Wievielte ist heute?; **~ of birth** Geburtsdatum *nt*; **closing ~** Einsendeschluss *m*; **to ~** bis heute; **out of ~** altmodisch; (*expired*) abgelaufen; **up to ~** auf dem neuesten Stand; **to bring up to ~** auf den neuesten Stand bringen; (*person*) über den neuesten Stand der Dinge informieren; **a letter ~d 5 July** ein vom 5. Juli datierter Brief
dated ['deɪtɪd] *adj* altmodisch
date rape *n* Vergewaltigung *f* einer Bekannten (*mit der der Täter eine Verabredung hatte*)
daub [dɔ:b] *vt* schmieren; **to ~ with** beschmieren mit
daughter ['dɔ:tə^r] *n* Tochter *f*
daughter-in-law ['dɔ:tərɪnlɔ:] *n* Schwiegertochter *f*
daunting ['dɔ:ntɪŋ] *adj* entmutigend
dawdle ['dɔ:dl] *vi* trödeln; **to ~ over one's work** bei der Arbeit bummeln *or* trödeln
dawn [dɔ:n] *n* Tagesanbruch *m*, Morgengrauen *nt*; (*of period*) Anbruch *m* ▷ *vi* dämmern; (*fig*): **it ~ed on him that ...** es dämmerte ihm, dass ...; **from ~ to dusk** von morgens bis abends
day [deɪ] *n* Tag *m*; (*heyday*) Zeit *f*; **the ~ before/after** am Tag zuvor/danach; **the ~ after tomorrow** übermorgen; **the ~ before yesterday** vorgestern; **(on) the following ~** am Tag danach; **the ~ that ...** (am Tag,) als ...; **~ by day** jeden Tag, täglich; **by ~** tagsüber; **paid by the ~** tageweise bezahlt; **to work an eight hour ~** einen Achtstundentag haben; **these ~s, in the present ~** heute, heutzutage
daybreak ['deɪbreɪk] *n* Tagesanbruch *m*
day-care centre ['deɪkɛə-] *n* (*for children*) (Kinder)tagesstätte *f*; (*for old people*) Altentagesstätte *f*
daydream ['deɪdri:m] *vi* (mit offenen Augen) träumen ▷ *n* Tagtraum *m*, Träumerei *f*
daylight ['deɪlaɪt] *n* Tageslicht *nt*
day return (*Brit*) *n* Tagesrückfahrkarte *f*
daytime ['deɪtaɪm] *n* Tag *m*; **in the ~** tagsüber, bei Tage
day-to-day ['deɪtə'deɪ] *adj* täglich, Alltags-; **on a ~ basis** tageweise
day trip *n* Tagesausflug *m*
daze [deɪz] *vt* benommen machen ▷ *n*: **in a ~** ganz benommen
dazed [deɪzd] *adj* benommen
dazzle ['dæzl] *vt* blenden
dazzling ['dæzlɪŋ] *adj* (*light*) blendend; (*smile*) strahlend; (*career, achievements*) glänzend
DC *abbr* = **direct current**
D-day ['di:deɪ] *n* der Tag X
dead [dɛd] *adj* tot; (*flowers*) verwelkt; (*numb*) abgestorben, taub; (*battery*) leer; (*place*) wie ausgestorben ▷ *adv* total, völlig; (*directly, exactly*) genau ▷ *npl*: **the ~** die Toten *pl*; **to shoot sb ~** jdn erschießen; **~ silence** Totenstille *f*; **in the ~ centre (of)** genau in der Mitte *+gen*; **the line has gone ~** (*Tel*) die Leitung ist tot; **~ on time** auf die Minute pünktlich; **~ tired** todmüde; **to stop ~** abrupt stehen bleiben
deaden [dɛdn] *vt* (*blow*) abschwächen; (*pain*) mildern; (*sound*) dämpfen
dead end *n* Sackgasse *f*
dead heat *n*: **to finish in a ~** unentschieden ausgehen
deadline ['dɛdlaɪn] *n* (letzter) Termin *m*; **to work to a ~** auf einen Termin hinarbeiten
deadlock ['dɛdlɔk] *n* Stillstand *m*; **the meeting ended in ~** die Verhandlung war festgefahren
dead loss (*inf*) *n*: **to be a ~** ein hoffnungsloser Fall sein
deadly ['dɛdlɪ] *adj* tödlich ▷ *adv*: **~ dull** todlangweilig
deadpan ['dɛdpæn] *adj* (*look*) unbewegt; (*tone*) trocken
Dead Sea *n*: **the ~** das Tote Meer
deaf [dɛf] *adj* taub; (*partially*) schwerhörig; **to turn a ~ ear to sth** sich einer Sache *dat* gegenüber taub stellen
deafen ['dɛfn] *vt* taub machen
deafening ['dɛfnɪŋ] *adj* ohrenbetäubend
deaf-mute ['dɛfmju:t] *n* Taubstumme(r) *f(m)*
deafness ['dɛfnɪs] *n* Taubheit *f*
deal [di:l] (*pt, pp* **~t**) *n* Geschäft *nt*, Handel *m* ▷ *vt* (*blow*) versetzen; (*card*) geben, austeilen; **to strike a ~ with sb** ein Geschäft mit jdm abschließen; **it's a ~!** (*inf*) abgemacht!; **he got a fair/bad ~ from them** er ist von ihnen anständig/schlecht behandelt worden; **a good ~** (*a lot*) ziemlich viel; **a great ~ (of)** ziemlich viel
▸ **deal in** *vt fus* handeln mit
▸ **deal with** *vt fus* (*person*) sich kümmern um; (*problem*) sich befassen mit; (*successfully*) fertig werden mit; (*subject*) behandeln
dealer ['di:lə^r] *n* Händler(in) *m(f)*; (*in drugs*) Dealer *m*; (*Cards*) Kartengeber(in) *m(f)*
dealings ['di:lɪŋz] *npl* Geschäfte *pl*; (*relations*)

Beziehungen *pl*
dealt [dɛlt] *pt, pp of* **deal**
dean [di:n] *n* Dekan *m*; (*US: Scol: administrator*) *Schul- oder Collegeverwalter mit Beratungs- und Disziplinarfunktion*
dear [dɪəʳ] *adj* lieb; (*expensive*) teuer ▷ *n*: **(my) ~** (mein) Liebling *m* ▷ *excl*: **~ me!** (ach) du liebe Zeit!; **D~ Sir/Madam** Sehr geehrte Damen und Herren; **D~ Mr/Mrs X** Sehr geehrter Herr/geehrte Frau X; (*less formal*) Lieber Herr/Liebe Frau X
dearly ['dɪəlɪ] *adv* (*love*) von ganzem Herzen; (*pay*) teuer
death [dɛθ] *n* Tod *m*; (*fatality*) Tote(r) *f(m)*, Todesfall *m*
death certificate *n* Sterbeurkunde *f*, Totenschein *m*
deathly ['dɛθlɪ] *adj* (*silence*) eisig ▷ *adv* (*pale etc*) toten-
death penalty *n* Todesstrafe *f*
death rate *n* Sterbeziffer *f*
death sentence *n* Todesurteil *nt*
death toll *n* Zahl *f* der Todesopfer *or* Toten
debase [dɪ'beɪs] *vt* (*value, quality*) mindern, herabsetzen; (*person*) erniedrigen, entwürdigen
debatable [dɪ'beɪtəbl] *adj* fraglich
debate [dɪ'beɪt] *n* Debatte *f* ▷ *vt* debattieren über *+acc*; (*course of action*) überlegen ▷ *vi*: **to ~ whether** hin und her überlegen, ob
debit ['dɛbɪt] *n* Schuldposten *m* ▷ *vt*: **to ~ a sum to sb/sb's account** jdn/jds Konto mit einer Summe belasten; *see also* **direct**
debris ['dɛbri:] *n* Trümmer *pl*, Schutt *m*
debt [dɛt] *n* Schuld *f*; (*state of owing money*) Schulden *pl*, Verschuldung *f*; **to be in ~** Schulden haben, verschuldet sein; **bad ~** uneinbringliche Forderung *f*
debtor ['dɛtəʳ] *n* Schuldner(in) *m(f)*
debut ['deɪbju:] *n* Debüt *nt*
Dec. *abbr* = **December**
decade ['dɛkeɪd] *n* Jahrzehnt *nt*
decadence ['dɛkədəns] *n* Dekadenz *f*
decaffeinated [dɪ'kæfɪneɪtɪd] *adj* koffeinfrei
decanter [dɪ'kæntəʳ] *n* Karaffe *f*
decay [dɪ'keɪ] *n* Verfall *m*; (*of tooth*) Fäule *f* ▷ *vi* (*body*) verwesen; (*teeth*) faulen; (*leaves*) verrotten; (*fig: society etc*) verfallen
deceased [dɪ'si:st] *n*: **the ~** der/die Tote *or* Verstorbene
deceit [dɪ'si:t] *n* Betrug *m*
deceitful [dɪ'si:tful] *adj* betrügerisch
deceive [dɪ'si:v] *vt* täuschen; (*husband, wife etc*) betrügen; **to ~ o.s.** sich *dat* etwas vormachen
December [dɪ'sɛmbəʳ] *n* Dezember *m*; *see also* **July**
decency ['di:sənsɪ] *n* (*propriety*) Anstand *m*; (*kindness*) Anständigkeit *f*
decent ['di:sənt] *adj* anständig; **we expect you to do the ~ thing** wir erwarten, dass Sie die Konsequenzen ziehen; **they were very ~ about it** sie haben sich sehr anständig verhalten; **that was very ~ of him** das war sehr anständig von ihm; **are you ~?** (*dressed*) hast du etwas an?
deception [dɪ'sɛpʃən] *n* Täuschung *f*, Betrug *m*
deceptive [dɪ'sɛptɪv] *adj* irreführend, täuschend
decide [dɪ'saɪd] *vt* entscheiden; (*persuade*) veranlassen ▷ *vi* sich entscheiden; **to ~ to do sth/that** beschließen, etw zu tun/dass; **to ~ on sth** sich für etw entscheiden; **to ~ on/against doing sth** sich dafür/dagegen entscheiden, etw zu tun
decided [dɪ'saɪdɪd] *adj* entschieden; (*character*) entschlossen; (*difference*) deutlich
decidedly [dɪ'saɪdɪdlɪ] *adv* entschieden; (*emphatically*) entschlossen
deciduous [dɪ'sɪdjuəs] *adj* (*tree, woods*) Laub-
decimal ['dɛsɪməl] *adj* (*system, number*) Dezimal- ▷ *n* Dezimalzahl *f*; **to three ~ places** auf drei Dezimalstellen
decimal point *n* Komma *nt*
decipher [dɪ'saɪfəʳ] *vt* entziffern
decision [dɪ'sɪʒən] *n* Entscheidung *f*; (*decisiveness*) Bestimmtheit *f*, Entschlossenheit *f*; **to make a ~** eine Entscheidung treffen
decisive [dɪ'saɪsɪv] *adj* (*action etc*) entscheidend; (*person*) entschlussfreudig; (*manner, reply*) bestimmt, entschlossen
deck [dɛk] *n* Deck *nt*; (*also*: **record deck**) Plattenspieler *m*; (*of cards*) Spiel *nt*; **to go up on ~** an Deck gehen; **below ~** unter Deck; **top ~** (*of bus*) Oberdeck *nt*; **cassette ~** Tapedeck *nt*
declaration [dɛklə'reɪʃən] *n* Erklärung *f*
declare [dɪ'klɛəʳ] *vt* erklären; (*result*) bekannt geben, veröffentlichen; (*income etc*) angeben; (*goods at customs*) verzollen
decline [dɪ'klaɪn] *n* Rückgang *m*; (*decay*) Verfall *m* ▷ *vt* ablehnen ▷ *vi* (*strength*) nachlassen; (*business*) zurückgehen; (*old person*) abbauen; **~ in/of** Rückgang *m* *+gen*; **~ in living standards** Sinken *nt* des Lebensstandards
decoder [di:'kəudəʳ] *n* Decoder *m*
decorate ['dɛkəreɪt] *vt*: **to ~ (with)** verzieren (mit); (*tree, building*) schmücken (mit) ▷ *vt* (*room, house: from bare walls*) anstreichen und tapezieren; (*: redecorate*) renovieren
decoration [dɛkə'reɪʃən] *n* Verzierung *f*; (*on tree, building*) Schmuck *m*; (*act: see verb*) Verzieren *nt*; Schmücken *nt*; (An)streichen *nt*; Tapezieren *nt*; (*medal*) Auszeichnung *f*
decorator ['dɛkəreɪtəʳ] *n* Maler(in) *m(f)*, Anstreicher(in) *m(f)*
decoy ['di:kɔɪ] *n* Lockvogel *m*; (*object*) Köder *m*; **they used him as a ~ for the enemy** sie benutzten ihn dazu, den Feind anzulocken
decrease ['di:kri:s] *vt* verringern, reduzieren ▷ *vi* abnehmen, zurückgehen ▷ *n*: **~ (in)** Abnahme *f* (*+gen*), Rückgang *m* (*+gen*); **to be on the ~** abnehmen, zurückgehen
decree [dɪ'kri:] *n* (*Admin, Law*) Verfügung *f*;

(*Pol*) Erlass *m*; (*Rel*) Dekret *nt* ▷ *vt*: **to ~ (that)** verfügen(, dass), verordnen(, dass)

dedicate ['dɛdɪkeɪt] *vt*: **to ~ to** widmen *+dat*

dedicated ['dɛdɪkeɪtɪd] *adj* hingebungsvoll, engagiert; (*Comput*) dediziert; **~ word processor** dediziertes Textverarbeitungssystem *nt*

dedication [dɛdɪ'keɪʃən] *n* Hingabe *f*; (*in book, on radio*) Widmung *f*

deduce [dɪ'dju:s] *vt*: **to ~ (that)** schließen(, dass), folgern(, dass)

deduct [dɪ'dʌkt] *vt* abziehen; **to ~ sth (from)** etw abziehen (von); (*esp from wage etc*) etw einbehalten (von)

deduction [dɪ'dʌkʃən] *n* (*act of deducting*) Abzug *m*; (*act of deducing*) Folgerung *f*

deed [di:d] *n* Tat *f*; (*Law*) Urkunde *f*; **~ of covenant** Vertragsurkunde *f*

deem [di:m] *vt* (*formal*) erachten für, halten für; **to ~ it wise/helpful to do sth** es für klug/hilfreich halten, etw zu tun

deep [di:p] *adj* tief ▷ *adv*: **the spectators stood 20 ~** die Zuschauer standen in 20 Reihen hintereinander; **to be 4 metres ~** 4 Meter tief sein; **knee-~ in water** bis zu den Knien im Wasser; **he took a ~ breath** er holte tief Luft

deepen ['di:pn] *vt* vertiefen ▷ *vi* (*crisis*) sich verschärfen; (*mystery*) größer werden

deepfreeze ['di:p'fri:z] *n* Tiefkühltruhe *f*

deep-fry ['di:p'fraɪ] *vt* frittieren

deeply ['di:plɪ] *adv* (*breathe*) tief; (*interested*) höchst; (*moved, grateful*) zutiefst

deep-sea ['di:p'si:] *cpd* Tiefsee-; (*fishing*) Hochsee-

deep-seated ['di:p'si:tɪd] *adj* tief sitzend

deer [dɪə[r]] *n inv* Reh *nt*; (*male*) Hirsch *m*; **(red) ~** Rotwild *nt*; **(roe) ~** Reh *nt*; **(fallow) ~** Damwild *nt*

deerskin ['dɪəskɪn] *n* Hirschleder *nt*, Rehleder *nt*

deface [dɪ'feɪs] *vt* (*with paint etc*) beschmieren; (*slash, tear*) zerstören

default [dɪ'fɔ:lt] *n* (*also*: **default value**) Voreinstellung *f* ▷ *vi*: **to ~ on a debt** einer Zahlungsverpflichtung nicht nachkommen; **to win by ~** kampflos gewinnen

defeat [dɪ'fi:t] *vt* besiegen, schlagen ▷ *n* (*failure*) Niederlage *f*; (*of enemy*): **~ (of)** Sieg *m* (über *+acc*)

defect [*n* 'di:fɛkt, *vi* dɪ'fɛkt] *n* Fehler *m* ▷ *vi*: **to ~ to the enemy** zum Feind überlaufen; **physical/mental ~** körperlicher/geistiger Schaden *m or* Defekt *m*; **to ~ to the West** sich in den Westen absetzen

defective [dɪ'fɛktɪv] *adj* fehlerhaft

defence, (*US*) **defense** [dɪ'fɛns] *n* Verteidigung *f*; (*justification*) Rechtfertigung *f*; **in ~ of** zur Verteidigung *+gen*; **witness for the ~** Zeuge *m*/Zeugin *f* der Verteidigung; **the Ministry of D~, the Department of Defense** (*US*) das Verteidigungsministerium

defenceless [dɪ'fɛnslɪs] *adj* schutzlos

defend [dɪ'fɛnd] *vt* verteidigen

defendant [dɪ'fɛndənt] *n* Angeklagte(r) *f(m)*; (*in civil case*) Beklagte(r) *f(m)*

defender [dɪ'fɛndə[r]] *n* Verteidiger(in) *m(f)*

defense [dɪ'fɛns] (*US*) *n* = **defence**

defensive [dɪ'fɛnsɪv] *adj* defensiv ▷ *n*: **on the ~** in der Defensive

defer [dɪ'fə:[r]] *vt* verschieben

defiance [dɪ'faɪəns] *n* Trotz *m*; **in ~ of sth** einer Sache *dat* zum Trotz, unter Missachtung einer Sache *gen*

defiant [dɪ'faɪənt] *adj* trotzig; (*challenging*) herausfordernd

deficiency [dɪ'fɪʃənsɪ] *n* Mangel *m*; (*defect*) Unzulänglichkeit *f*; (*deficit*) Defizit *nt*

deficient [dɪ'fɪʃənt] *adj*: **sb/sth is ~ in sth** jdm/etw fehlt es an etw *dat*

deficit ['dɛfɪsɪt] *n* Defizit *nt*

define [dɪ'faɪn] *vt* (*limits, boundaries*) bestimmen, festlegen; (*word*) definieren

definite ['dɛfɪnɪt] *adj* definitiv; (*date etc*) fest; (*clear, obvious*) klar, eindeutig; (*certain*) bestimmt; **he was ~ about it** er war sich *dat* sehr sicher

definitely ['dɛfɪnɪtlɪ] *adv* bestimmt; (*decide*) fest, definitiv

definition [dɛfɪ'nɪʃən] *n* (*of word*) Definition *f*; (*of photograph etc*) Schärfe *f*

deflate [di:'fleɪt] *vt* (*tyre, balloon*) die Luft ablassen aus; (*person*) einen Dämpfer versetzen *+dat*; (*Econ*) deflationieren

deflect [dɪ'flɛkt] *vt* (*attention*) ablenken; (*criticism*) abwehren; (*shot*) abfälschen; (*light*) brechen, beugen

deformed [dɪ'fɔ:md] *adj* deformiert, missgebildet

defraud [dɪ'frɔ:d] *vt*: **to ~ sb (of sth)** jdn (um etw) betrügen

defrost [di:'frɔst] *vt* (*fridge*) abtauen; (*windscreen*) entfrosten; (*food*) auftauen

deft [dɛft] *adj* geschickt

defunct [dɪ'fʌŋkt] *adj* (*industry*) stillgelegt; (*organization*) nicht mehr bestehend

defuse [di:'fju:z] *vt* entschärfen

defy [dɪ'faɪ] *vt* sich widersetzen *+dat*; (*challenge*) auffordern; **it defies description** es spottet jeder Beschreibung

degenerate [dɪ'dʒɛnəreɪt] *vi* degenerieren ▷ *adj* degeneriert

degree [dɪ'gri:] *n* Grad *m*; (*Scol*) akademischer Grad *m*; **10 ~s below (zero)** 10 Grad unter null; **6 ~s of frost** 6 Grad Kälte *or* unter null; **a considerable ~ of risk** ein gewisses Risiko; **a ~ in maths** ein Hochschulabschluss *m* in Mathematik; **by ~s** nach und nach; **to some ~, to a certain ~** einigermaßen, in gewissem Maße

dehydrated [di:haɪ'dreɪtɪd] *adj* ausgetrocknet, dehydriert; (*milk, eggs*) pulverisiert, Trocken-

de-ice ['di:'aɪs] *vt* enteisen

de-icer ['di:'aɪsə[r]] *n* Defroster *m*

deign [deɪn] *vi*: **to ~ to do sth** sich

herablassen, etw zu tun

dejected [dɪ'dʒɛktɪd] *adj* niedergeschlagen, deprimiert

delay [dɪ'leɪ] *vt* (*decision, ceremony*) verschieben, aufschieben; (*person, plane, train*) aufhalten ▷ *vi* zögern ▷ *n* Verzögerung *f*; (*postponement*) Aufschub *m*; **to be ~ed** (*person*) sich verspäten; (*departure etc*) verspätet sein; (*flight etc*) Verspätung haben; **without ~** unverzüglich

delectable [dɪ'lɛktəbl] *adj* (*person*) reizend; (*food*) köstlich

delegate ['dɛlɪgɪt] *n* Delegierte(r) *f(m)* ▷ *vt* delegieren; **to ~ sth to sb** jdm mit etw beauftragen; **to ~ sb to do sth** jdn damit beauftragen, etw zu tun

delete [dɪ'liːt] *vt* streichen; (*Comput*) löschen

deli ['dɛlɪ] *n* Feinkostgeschäft *nt*

deliberate [*adj* dɪ'lɪbərɪt, *vi* dɪ'lɪbəreɪt] *adj* absichtlich; (*action, insult*) bewusst; (*slow*) bedächtig ▷ *vi* überlegen

deliberately [dɪ'lɪbərɪtlɪ] *adv* absichtlich, bewusst; (*slowly*) bedächtig

delicacy ['dɛlɪkəsɪ] *n* Feinheit *f*, Zartheit *f*; (*of problem*) Delikatheit *f*; (*choice food*) Delikatesse *f*

delicate ['dɛlɪkɪt] *adj* fein; (*colour, health*) zart; (*approach*) feinfühlig; (*problem*) delikat, heikel

delicatessen [dɛlɪkə'tɛsn] *n* Feinkostgeschäft *nt*

delicious [dɪ'lɪʃəs] *adj* köstlich; (*feeling, person*) herrlich

delight [dɪ'laɪt] *n* Freude *f* ▷ *vt* erfreuen; **sb takes (a) ~ in sth** etw bereitet jdm große Freude; **sb takes (a) ~ in doing sth** es bereitet jdm große Freude, etw zu tun; **to be the ~ of** die Freude *+gen* sein; **she was a ~ to interview** es war eine Freude, sie zu interviewen; **the ~s of country life** die Freuden des Landlebens

delighted [dɪ'laɪtɪd] *adj*: **~ (at** *or* **with)** erfreut (über *+acc*), entzückt (über *+acc*); **to be ~ to do sth** etw gern tun; **I'd be ~** ich würde mich sehr freuen

delightful [dɪ'laɪtful] *adj* reizend, wunderbar

delinquent [dɪ'lɪŋkwənt] *adj* straffällig ▷ *n* Delinquent(in) *m(f)*

delirious [dɪ'lɪrɪəs] *adj*: **to be ~** (*with fever*) im Delirium sein; (*with excitement*) im Taumel sein

deliver [dɪ'lɪvəʳ] *vt* liefern; (*letters, papers*) zustellen; (*hand over*) übergeben; (*message*) überbringen; (*speech*) halten; (*blow*) versetzen; (*Med: baby*) zur Welt bringen; (*warning*) geben; (*ultimatum*) stellen; (*free*): **to ~ (from)** befreien (von); **to ~ the goods** (*fig*) halten, was man versprochen hat

delivery [dɪ'lɪvərɪ] *n* Lieferung *f*; (*of letters, papers*) Zustellung *f*; (*of speaker*) Vortrag *m*; (*Med*) Entbindung *f*; **to take ~ of sth** etw in Empfang nehmen

delude [dɪ'luːd] *vt* täuschen; **to ~ o.s.** sich *dat* etwas vormachen

delusion [dɪ'luːʒən] *n* Irrglaube *m*; **to have ~s of grandeur** größenwahnsinnig sein

de luxe [də'lʌks] *adj* (*hotel, model*) Luxus-

delve [dɛlv] *vi*: **to ~ into** (*subject*) sich eingehend befassen mit; (*cupboard, handbag*) tief greifen in *+acc*

demand [dɪ'mɑːnd] *vt* verlangen; (*rights*) fordern; (*need*) erfordern, verlangen ▷ *n* Verlangen *nt*; (*claim*) Forderung *f*; (*Econ*) Nachfrage *f*; **to ~ sth (from** *or* **of sb)** etw (von jdm) verlangen *or* fordern; **to be in ~** gefragt sein; **on ~** (*available*) auf Verlangen; (*payable*) bei Vorlage *or* Sicht

demanding [dɪ'mɑːndɪŋ] *adj* anspruchsvoll; (*work, child*) anstrengend

demean [dɪ'miːn] *vt*: **to ~ o.s.** sich erniedrigen

demeanour, (*US*) **demeanor** [dɪ'miːnəʳ] *n* Benehmen *nt*, Auftreten *nt*

demented [dɪ'mɛntɪd] *adj* wahnsinnig

demise [dɪ'maɪz] *n* Ende *nt*; (*death*) Tod *m*

demister [diː'mɪstəʳ] (*Brit*) *n* (*Aut*) Gebläse *nt*

demo ['dɛməu] (*inf*) *n abbr* = **demonstration**

democracy [dɪ'mɔkrəsɪ] *n* Demokratie *f*

democrat ['dɛməkræt] *n* Demokrat(in) *m(f)*

democratic [dɛmə'krætɪk] *adj* demokratisch

demolish [dɪ'mɔlɪʃ] *vt* abreißen, abbrechen; (*fig: argument*) widerlegen

demolition [dɛmə'lɪʃən] *n* Abriss *m*, Abbruch *m*; (*of argument*) Widerlegung *f*

demon ['diːmən] *n* Dämon *m* ▷ *adj* teuflisch gut

demonstrate ['dɛmənstreɪt] *vt* (*theory*) demonstrieren; (*skill*) zeigen, beweisen; (*appliance*) vorführen ▷ *vi*: **to ~ (for/against)** demonstrieren (für/gegen)

demonstration [dɛmən'streɪʃən] *n* Demonstration *f*; (*of gadget, machine etc*) Vorführung *f*; **to hold a ~** eine Demonstration veranstalten *or* durchführen

demonstrator ['dɛmənstreɪtəʳ] *n* Demonstrant(in) *m(f)*; (*sales person*) Vorführer(in) *m(f)*; (*car*) Vorführwagen *m*; (*computer etc*) Vorführgerät *nt*

demote [dɪ'məut] *vt* zurückstufen; (*Mil*) degradieren

demure [dɪ'mjuəʳ] *adj* zurückhaltend; (*smile*) höflich; (*dress*) schlicht

den [dɛn] *n* Höhle *f*; (*of fox*) Bau *m*; (*room*) Bude *f*

denial [dɪ'naɪəl] *n* Leugnen *nt*; (*of rights*) Verweigerung *f*

denim ['dɛnɪm] *n* Jeansstoff *m*; **denims** *npl* (Blue) Jeans *pl*

Denmark ['dɛnmɑːk] *n* Dänemark *nt*

denomination [dɪnɔmɪ'neɪʃən] *n* (*of money*) Nennwert *m*; (*Rel*) Konfession *f*

denounce [dɪ'nauns] *vt* (*person*) anprangern; (*action*) verurteilen

dense [dɛns] *adj* dicht; (*inf: person*) beschränkt

densely ['dɛnslɪ] *adv* dicht

density ['dɛnsɪtɪ] *n* Dichte *f*; **single/double-~ disk** (*Comput*) Diskette *f* mit einfacher/

doppelter Dichte
dent [dɛnt] *n* Beule *f*; (*in pride, ego*) Knacks *m* ▷ *vt* (*also*: **make a dent in**) einbeulen; (*pride, ego*) anknacksen
dental ['dɛntl] *adj* (*filling, hygiene etc*) Zahn-; (*treatment*) zahnärztlich
dental floss [-flɔs] *n* Zahnseide *f*
dental surgeon *n* Zahnarzt *m*, Zahnärztin *f*
dentist ['dɛntɪst] *n* Zahnarzt *m*, Zahnärztin *f*; (*also*: **dentist's (surgery)**) Zahnarzt *m*, Zahnarztpraxis *f*
dentures ['dɛntʃəz] *npl* Zahnprothese *f*; (*full*) Gebiss *nt*
deny [dɪ'naɪ] *vt* leugnen; (*involvement*) abstreiten; (*permission, chance*) verweigern; (*country, religion etc*) verleugnen; **he denies having said it** er leugnet *or* bestreitet, das gesagt zu haben
deodorant [di:'əudərənt] *n* Deodorant *nt*
depart [dɪ'pɑ:t] *vi* (*visitor*) abreisen; (*: on foot*) weggehen; (*bus, train*) abfahren; (*plane*) abfliegen; **to ~ from** (*fig*) abweichen von
department [dɪ'pɑ:tmənt] *n* Abteilung *f*; (*Scol*) Fachbereich *m*; (*Pol*) Ministerium *nt*; **that's not my ~** (*fig*) dafür bin ich nicht zuständig; **D~ of State** (*US*) Außenministerium *nt*
department store *n* Warenhaus *nt*
departure [dɪ'pɑ:tʃə^r] *n* (*of visitor*) Abreise *f*; (*on foot, of employee etc*) Weggang *m*; (*of bus, train*) Abfahrt *f*; (*of plane*) Abflug *m*; (*fig*): **~ from** Abweichen *nt* von; **a new ~** ein neuer Weg *m*
departure lounge *n* Abflughalle *f*
depend [dɪ'pɛnd] *vi*: **to ~ on** abhängen von; (*rely on, trust*) sich verlassen auf *+acc*; (*financially*) abhängig sein von, angewiesen sein auf *+acc*; **it ~s** es kommt darauf an; **~ing on the result ...** je nachdem, wie das Ergebnis ausfällt, ...
dependable [dɪ'pɛndəbl] *adj* zuverlässig
dependant [dɪ'pɛndənt] *n* abhängige(r) (Familien)angehörige(r) *f(m)*
dependent [dɪ'pɛndənt] *adj*: **to be ~ on** (*person*) abhängig sein von, angewiesen sein auf *+acc*; (*decision*) abhängen von ▷ *n* = **dependant**
depict [dɪ'pɪkt] *vt* (*in picture*) darstellen; (*describe*) beschreiben
depleted [dɪ'pli:tɪd] *adj* (*reserves*) aufgebraucht; (*stocks*) erschöpft
deport [dɪ'pɔ:t] *vt* (*criminal*) deportieren; (*illegal immigrant*) abschieben
deposit [dɪ'pɔzɪt] *n* (*in account*) Guthaben *nt*; (*down payment*) Anzahlung *f*; (*for hired goods etc*) Sicherheit *f*, Kaution *f*; (*on bottle etc*) Pfand *nt*; (*Chem*) Ablagerung *f*; (*of ore, oil*) Lagerstätte *f* ▷ *vt* deponieren; (*subj: river: sand etc*) ablagern; **to put down a ~ of £50** eine Anzahlung von £50 machen
deposit account *n* Sparkonto *nt*
depot ['dɛpəu] *n* Lager(haus) *nt*; (*for vehicles*) Depot *nt*; (*US: station*) Bahnhof *m*; (*: bus station*) Busbahnhof *m*
depreciate [dɪ'pri:ʃɪeɪt] *vi* an Wert verlieren; (*currency*) an Kaufkraft verlieren; (*value*) sinken
depress [dɪ'prɛs] *vt* deprimieren; (*price, wages*) drücken; (*press down*) herunterdrücken
depressed [dɪ'prɛst] *adj* deprimiert, niedergeschlagen; (*price*) gesunken; (*industry*) geschwächt; (*area*) Notstands-; **to get ~** deprimiert werden
depressing [dɪ'prɛsɪŋ] *adj* deprimierend
depression [dɪ'prɛʃən] *n* (*Psych*) Depressionen *pl*; (*Econ*) Wirtschaftskrise *f*; (*Met*) Tief(druckgebiet) *nt*; (*hollow*) Vertiefung *f*
deprivation [dɛprɪ'veɪʃən] *n* Entbehrung *f*, Not *f*; (*of freedom, rights etc*) Entzug *m*
deprive [dɪ'praɪv] *vt*: **to ~ sb of sth** (*liberty*) jdm etw entziehen; (*life*) jdm etw nehmen
deprived [dɪ'praɪvd] *adj* benachteiligt; (*area*) Not leidend
depth [dɛpθ] *n* Tiefe *f*; **in the ~s of** in den Tiefen *+gen*; **in the ~s of despair** in tiefster Verzweiflung; **in the ~s of winter** im tiefsten Winter; **at a ~ of 3 metres** in 3 Meter Tiefe; **to be out of one's ~** (*in water*) nicht mehr stehen können; (*fig*) überfordert sein; **to study sth in ~** etw gründlich *or* eingehend studieren
deputize ['dɛpjutaɪz] *vi*: **to ~ for sb** jdn vertreten
deputy ['dɛpjutɪ] *cpd* stellvertretend ▷ *n* (Stell)vertreter(in) *m(f)*; (*Pol*) Abgeordnete(r) *f(m)*; (*US: also*: **deputy sheriff**) Hilfssheriff *m*; **~ head** (*Brit: Scol*) Konrektor(in) *m(f)*
derail [dɪ'reɪl] *vt*: **to be ~ed** entgleisen
deranged [dɪ'reɪndʒd] *adj*: **to be mentally ~** geistesgestört sein
derby ['də:rbɪ] *n* Derby *nt*; (*US: hat*) Melone *f*
derelict ['dɛrɪlɪkt] *adj* verfallen
derisory [dɪ'raɪsərɪ] *adj* spöttisch; (*sum*) lächerlich
derive [dɪ'raɪv] *vt*: **to ~ (from)** gewinnen (aus); (*benefit*) ziehen (aus) ▷ *vi*: **to ~ from** (*originate in*) sich herleiten *or* ableiten von; **to ~ pleasure from** Freude haben an *+dat*
derogatory [dɪ'rɔgətərɪ] *adj* abfällig
descend [dɪ'sɛnd] *vt* hinuntergehen, hinuntersteigen; (*lift, vehicle*) hinunterfahren; (*road*) hinunterführen ▷ *vi* hinuntergehen; (*lift*) nach unten fahren; **to ~ from** abstammen von; **to ~ to** sich erniedrigen zu; **in ~ing order of importance** nach Wichtigkeit geordnet
▸ **descend on** *vt fus* überfallen; (*subj: misfortune*) hereinbrechen über *+acc*; (*: gloom*) befallen; (*: silence*) sich senken auf *+acc*; **visitors ~ed (up)on us** der Besuch hat uns überfallen
descendant [dɪ'sɛndənt] *n* Nachkomme *m*
descent [dɪ'sɛnt] *n* Abstieg *m*; (*origin*) Abstammung *f*
describe [dɪs'kraɪb] *vt* beschreiben
description [dɪs'krɪpʃən] *n* Beschreibung *f*; (*sort*): **of every ~** aller Art

desecrate ['dɛsɪkreɪt] *vt* schänden
desert [*n* 'dɛzət, *vb* dɪ'zə:t] *n* Wüste *f* ▷ *vt* verlassen ▷ *vi* desertieren; *see also* **deserts**
deserter [dɪ'zə:təʳ] *n* Deserteur *m*
desertion [dɪ'zə:ʃən] *n* Desertion *f*, Fahnenflucht *f*; (*Law*) böswilliges Verlassen *nt*
desert island *n* einsame *or* verlassene Insel *f*
deserve [dɪ'zə:v] *vt* verdienen
deserving [dɪ'zə:vɪŋ] *adj* verdienstvoll
design [dɪ'zaɪn] *n* Design *nt*; (*process*) Entwurf *m*, Gestaltung *f*; (*sketch*) Entwurf *m*; (*layout, shape*) Form *f*; (*pattern*) Muster *nt*; (*of car*) Konstruktion *f*; (*intention*) Plan *m*, Absicht *f* ▷ *vt* entwerfen; **to have ~s on** es abgesehen haben auf *+acc*; **well-~ed** mit gutem Design
design and technology (*Brit*) *n* (*Scol*) ≈ Design und Technologie
designate [*vt* 'dɛzɪgneɪt, *adj* 'dɛzɪgnɪt] *vt* bestimmen, ernennen ▷ *adj* designiert
designer [dɪ'zaɪnəʳ] *n* Designer(in) *m(f)*; (*Tech*) Konstrukteur(in) *m(f)*; (*also*: **fashion designer**) Modeschöpfer(in) *m(f)* ▷ *adj* (*clothes etc*) Designer-
desirable [dɪ'zaɪərəbl] *adj* (*proper*) wünschenswert; (*attractive*) reizvoll, attraktiv
desire [dɪ'zaɪəʳ] *n* Wunsch *m*; (*sexual*) Verlangen *nt*, Begehren *nt* ▷ *vt* wünschen; (*lust after*) begehren; **to ~ to do sth/that** wünschen, etw zu tun/dass
desk [dɛsk] *n* Schreibtisch *m*; (*for pupil*) Pult *nt*; (*in hotel*) Empfang *m*; (*at airport*) Schalter *m*; (*Brit: in shop, restaurant*) Kasse *f*
desolate ['dɛsəlɪt] *adj* trostlos
despair [dɪs'pɛəʳ] *n* Verzweiflung *f* ▷ *vi*: **to ~ of** alle Hoffnung aufgeben auf *+acc*; **to be in ~** verzweifelt sein
despatch [dɪs'pætʃ] *n*, *vt* = **dispatch**
desperate ['dɛspərɪt] *adj* verzweifelt; (*shortage*) akut; (*criminal*) zum Äußersten entschlossen; **to be ~ for sth/to do sth** etw dringend brauchen/unbedingt tun wollen
desperately ['dɛspərɪtlɪ] *adv* (*shout, struggle etc*) verzweifelt; (*ill*) schwer; (*unhappy etc*) äußerst
desperation [dɛspə'reɪʃən] *n* Verzweiflung *f*; **in (sheer) ~** aus (reiner) Verzweiflung
despicable [dɪs'pɪkəbl] *adj* (*action*) verabscheuungswürdig; (*person*) widerwärtig
despise [dɪs'paɪz] *vt* verachten
despite [dɪs'paɪt] *prep* trotz *+gen*
despondent [dɪs'pɔndənt] *adj* niedergeschlagen, mutlos
dessert [dɪ'zə:t] *n* Nachtisch *m*, Dessert *nt*
dessertspoon [dɪ'zə:tspu:n] *n* Dessertlöffel *m*
destination [dɛstɪ'neɪʃən] *n* (Reise)ziel *nt*; (*of mail*) Bestimmungsort *m*
destined ['dɛstɪnd] *adj*: **to be ~ to do sth** dazu bestimmt *or* ausersehen sein, etw zu tun; **to be ~ for** bestimmt *or* ausersehen sein für
destiny ['dɛstɪnɪ] *n* Schicksal *nt*
destitute ['dɛstɪtju:t] *adj* mittellos
destroy [dɪs'trɔɪ] *vt* zerstören; (*animal*) töten
destroyer [dɪs'trɔɪəʳ] *n* Zerstörer *m*
destruction [dɪs'trʌkʃən] *n* Zerstörung *f*
destructive [dɪs'trʌktɪv] *adj* zerstörerisch; (*child, criticism etc*) destruktiv
detach [dɪ'tætʃ] *vt* (*remove*) entfernen; (*unclip*) abnehmen; (*unstick*) ablösen
detached [dɪ'tætʃt] *adj* distanziert; (*house*) frei stehend, Einzel-
detachment [dɪ'tætʃmənt] *n* Distanz *f*; (*Mil*) Sonderkommando *nt*
detail ['di:teɪl] *n* Einzelheit *f*; (*no pl: in picture, one's work etc*) Detail *nt*; (*trifle*) unwichtige Einzelheit ▷ *vt* (einzeln) aufführen; **in ~** in Einzelheiten; **to go into ~s** auf Einzelheiten eingehen, ins Detail gehen
detailed ['di:teɪld] *adj* detailliert, genau
detain [dɪ'teɪn] *vt* aufhalten; (*in captivity*) in Haft halten; (*in hospital*) festhalten
detect [dɪ'tɛkt] *vt* wahrnehmen; (*Med, Tech*) feststellen; (*Mil*) ausfindig machen
detection [dɪ'tɛkʃən] *n* Entdeckung *f*, Feststellung *f*; **crime ~** Ermittlungsarbeit *f*; **to escape ~** (*criminal*) nicht gefasst werden; (*mistake*) der Aufmerksamkeit *dat* entgehen
detective [dɪ'tɛktɪv] *n* Kriminalbeamte(r) *m*; **private ~** Privatdetektiv *m*
detective story *n* Kriminalgeschichte *f*, Detektivgeschichte *f*
detention [dɪ'tɛnʃən] *n* (*arrest*) Festnahme *f*; (*captivity*) Haft *f*; (*Scol*) Nachsitzen *nt*
deter [dɪ'tə:ʳ] *vt* (*discourage*) abschrecken; (*dissuade*) abhalten
detergent [dɪ'tə:dʒənt] *n* Reinigungsmittel *nt*; (*for clothes*) Waschmittel *nt*; (*for dishes*) Spülmittel *nt*
deteriorate [dɪ'tɪərɪəreɪt] *vi* sich verschlechtern
determination [dɪtə:mɪ'neɪʃən] *n* Entschlossenheit *f*; (*establishment*) Festsetzung *f*
determine [dɪ'tə:mɪn] *vt* (*facts*) feststellen; (*limits etc*) festlegen; **to ~ that** beschließen, dass; **to ~ to do sth** sich entschließen, etw zu tun
determined [dɪ'tə:mɪnd] *adj* entschlossen; (*quantity*) bestimmt; **to be ~ to do sth** (fest) entschlossen sein, etw zu tun
deterrent [dɪ'tɛrənt] *n* Abschreckungsmittel *nt*; **to act as a ~** als Abschreckung(smittel) dienen
detest [dɪ'tɛst] *vt* verabscheuen
detonate ['dɛtəneɪt] *vi* detonieren ▷ *vt* zur Explosion bringen
detour ['di:tuəʳ] *n* Umweg *m*; (*US: Aut*) Umleitung *f*
detract [dɪ'trækt] *vi*: **to ~ from** schmälern; (*effect*) beeinträchtigen
detriment ['dɛtrɪmənt] *n*: **to the ~ of** zum Schaden *+gen*; **without ~ to** ohne Schaden für
detrimental [dɛtrɪ'mɛntl] *adj*: **to be ~ to** schaden *+dat*

devaluation [dɪvælju'eɪʃən] *n* Abwertung *f*
devastate ['dɛvəsteɪt] *vt* verwüsten; (*fig: shock*): **to be ~d by** niedergeschmettert sein von
devastating ['dɛvəsteɪtɪŋ] *adj* verheerend; (*announcement, news*) niederschmetternd
develop [dɪ'vɛləp] *vt* entwickeln; (*business*) erweitern, ausbauen; (*land, resource*) erschließen; (*disease*) bekommen ▷ *vi* sich entwickeln; (*facts*) an den Tag kommen; (*symptoms*) auftreten; **to ~ a taste for sth** Geschmack an etw finden; **the machine/car ~ed a fault/engine trouble** an dem Gerät/dem Wagen trat ein Defekt/ein Motorschaden auf; **to ~ into** sich entwickeln zu, werden
developer [dɪ'vɛləpə^r] *n* (*also*: **property developer**) *Bauunternehmer und Immobilienmakler*
developing country [dɪ'vɛləpɪŋ-] *n* Entwicklungsland *nt*
development [dɪ'vɛləpmənt] *n* Entwicklung *f*; (*of land*) Erschließung *f*
device [dɪ'vaɪs] *n* Gerät *nt*; (*ploy, stratagem*) Trick *m*; **explosive ~** Sprengkörper *m*
devil ['dɛvl] *n* Teufel *m*; **go on, be a ~!** nur zu, riskier mal was!; **talk of the ~!** wenn man vom Teufel spricht!
devious ['di:vɪəs] *adj* (*person*) verschlagen; (*route, path*) gewunden
devise [dɪ'vaɪz] *vt* sich *dat* ausdenken; (*machine*) entwerfen
devoid [dɪ'vɔɪd] *adj*: **~ of** bar *+gen*, ohne *+acc*
devolution [di:və'lu:ʃən] *n* Dezentralisierung *f*
devote [dɪ'vəut] *vt*: **to ~ sth/o.s. to** etw/sich widmen *+dat*
devoted [dɪ'vəutɪd] *adj* treu; (*admirer*) eifrig; **to be ~ to sb** jdn innig lieben; **the book is ~ to politics** das Buch widmet sich ganz der Politik *dat*
devotee [dɛvəu'ti:] *n* (*fan*) Liebhaber(in) *m(f)*; (*Rel*) Anhänger(in) *m(f)*
devotion [dɪ'vəuʃən] *n* (*affection*) Ergebenheit *f*; (*dedication*) Hingabe *f*; (*Rel*) Andacht *f*
devour [dɪ'vauə^r] *vt* verschlingen
devout [dɪ'vaut] *adj* fromm
dew [dju:] *n* Tau *m*
diabetes [daɪə'bi:ti:z] *n* Zuckerkrankheit *f*
diabetic [daɪə'bɛtɪk] *adj* zuckerkrank; (*chocolate, jam*) Diabetiker- ▷ *n* Diabetiker(in) *m(f)*
diabolical [daɪə'bɔlɪkl] (*inf*) *adj* schrecklich, fürchterlich
diagnose [daɪəg'nəuz] *vt* diagnostizieren
diagnosis [daɪəg'nəusɪs] (*pl* **diagnoses**) *n* Diagnose *f*
diagonal [daɪ'ægənl] *adj* diagonal ▷ *n* Diagonale *f*
diagram ['daɪəgræm] *n* Diagramm *nt*, Schaubild *nt*
dial ['daɪəl] *n* Zifferblatt *nt*; (*on radio set*) Einstellskala *f*; (*of phone*) Wählscheibe *f* ▷ *vt* wählen; **to ~ a wrong number** sich verwählen; **can I ~ London direct?** kann ich nach London durchwählen?
dialect ['daɪəlɛkt] *n* Dialekt *m*
dialling code ['daɪəlɪŋ-], (*US*) **dial code** *n* Vorwahl *f*
dialling tone, (*US*) **dial tone** *n* Amtszeichen *nt*
dialogue, (*US*) **dialog** ['daɪəlɔg] *n* Dialog *m*; (*conversation*) Gespräch *nt*, Dialog *m*
diameter [daɪ'æmɪtə^r] *n* Durchmesser *m*
diamond ['daɪəmənd] *n* Diamant *m*; (*shape*) Raute *f*; **diamonds** *npl* (*Cards*) Karo *nt*
diaper ['daɪəpə^r] (*US*) *n* Windel *f*
diaphragm ['daɪəfræm] *n* Zwerchfell *nt*; (*contraceptive*) Pessar *nt*
diarrhoea, (*US*) **diarrhea** [daɪə'ri:ə] *n* Durchfall *m*
diary ['daɪərɪ] *n* (Termin)kalender *m*; (*daily account*) Tagebuch *nt*; **to keep a ~** Tagebuch führen
dice [daɪs] *n inv* Würfel *m* ▷ *vt* in Würfel schneiden
dictate [dɪk'teɪt] *vt* diktieren ▷ *n* Diktat *nt*; (*principle*): **the ~s of** die Gebote *+gen* ▷ *vi*: **to ~ to** diktieren *+dat*; **I won't be ~d to** ich lasse mir keine Vorschriften machen
dictation [dɪk'teɪʃən] *n* Diktat *nt*; **at ~ speed** im Diktiertempo
dictator [dɪk'teɪtə^r] *n* Diktator *m*
dictatorship [dɪk'teɪtəʃɪp] *n* Diktatur *f*
dictionary ['dɪkʃənrɪ] *n* Wörterbuch *nt*
did [dɪd] *pt of* **do**
didn't ['dɪdnt] = **did not**
die [daɪ] *n* (*pl*: *dice*) Würfel *m*; (*: dies*) Gussform *f* ▷ *vi* sterben; (*plant*) eingehen; (*fig: noise*) aufhören; (*: smile*) vergehen; (*engine*) stehen bleiben; **to ~ of** *or* **from** sterben an *+dat*; **to be dying** im Sterben liegen; **to be dying for sth** etw unbedingt brauchen; **to be dying to do sth** darauf brennen, etw zu tun
▸ **die away** *vi* (*sound*) schwächer werden; (*light*) nachlassen
▸ **die down** *vi* (*wind*) sich legen; (*fire*) herunterbrennen; (*excitement, noise*) nachlassen
▸ **die out** *vi* aussterben
diesel ['di:zl] *n* (*vehicle*) Diesel *m*; (*also*: **diesel oil**) Diesel(kraftstoff) *m*
diesel engine *n* Dieselmotor *m*
diet ['daɪət] *n* Ernährung *f*; (*Med*) Diät *f*; (*when slimming*) Schlankheitskur *f* ▷ *vi* (*also*: **be on a diet**) eine Schlankheitskur machen; **to live on a ~ of** sich ernähren von, leben von
differ ['dɪfə^r] *vi* (*be different*): **to ~ (from)** sich unterscheiden (von); (*disagree*): **to ~ (about)** anderer Meinung sein (über *+acc*); **to agree to ~** sich *dat* verschiedene Meinungen zugestehen
difference ['dɪfrəns] *n* Unterschied *m*; (*disagreement*) Differenz *f*, Auseinandersetzung *f*; **it makes no ~ to me** das ist mir egal *or* einerlei; **to settle one's ~s** die Differenzen *or*

Meinungsverschiedenheiten beilegen
different ['dɪfrənt] *adj* (*various people, things*) verschieden, unterschiedlich; **to be ~ (from)** anders sein (als)
differentiate [dɪfə'rɛnʃɪeɪt] *vi*: **to ~ (between)** unterscheiden (zwischen) ▷ *vt*: **to ~ A from B** A von B unterscheiden
differently ['dɪfrəntlɪ] *adv* anders; (*shaped, designed*) verschieden, unterschiedlich
difficult ['dɪfɪkəlt] *adj* schwierig; (*task, problem*) schwer, schwierig; **~ to understand** schwer zu verstehen
difficulty ['dɪfɪkəltɪ] *n* Schwierigkeit *f*; **to be in/get into difficulties** in Schwierigkeiten sein/geraten
diffident ['dɪfɪdənt] *adj* bescheiden, zurückhaltend
dig [dɪg] (*pt, pp* **dug**) *vt* graben; (*garden*) umgraben ▷ *n* (*prod*) Stoß *m*; (*archaeological*) (Aus)grabung *f*; (*remark*) Seitenhieb *m*, spitze Bemerkung *f*; **to ~ one's nails into sth** seine Nägel in etw *acc* krallen
▶ **dig in** *vi* (*fig: inf: eat*) reinhauen ▷ *vt* (*compost*) untergraben, eingraben; (*knife*) hineinstoßen; (*claw*) festkrallen; **to ~ one's heels in** (*fig*) sich auf die Hinterbeine stellen (*inf*)
▶ **dig into** *vt fus* (*savings*) angreifen; (*snow, soil*) ein Loch graben in *+acc*; **to ~ into one's pockets for sth** in seinen Taschen nach etw suchen *or* wühlen
▶ **dig out** *vt* ausgraben
▶ **dig up** *vt* ausgraben
digest [daɪ'dʒɛst] *vt* verdauen ▷ *n* Digest *m or nt*, Auswahl *f*
digestion [dɪ'dʒɛstʃən] *n* Verdauung *f*
digit ['dɪdʒɪt] *n* (*number*) Ziffer *f*; (*finger*) Finger *m*
digital ['dɪdʒɪtl] *adj* (*watch, display etc*) Digital-
digital TV *n* Digitalfernsehen *nt*
dignified ['dɪgnɪfaɪd] *adj* würdevoll
dignity ['dɪgnɪtɪ] *n* Würde *f*
digress [daɪ'grɛs] *vi*: **to ~ (from)** abschweifen (von)
digs [dɪgz] (*Brit: inf*) *npl* Bude *f*
dilapidated [dɪ'læpɪdeɪtɪd] *adj* verfallen
dilemma [daɪ'lɛmə] *n* Dilemma *nt*; **to be in a ~** sich in einem Dilemma befinden, in der Klemme sitzen (*inf*)
diligent ['dɪlɪdʒənt] *adj* fleißig; (*research*) sorgfältig, genau
dill [dɪl] *n* Dill *m*
dilute [daɪ'lu:t] *vt* verdünnen; (*belief, principle*) schwächen ▷ *adj* verdünnt
dim [dɪm] *adj* schwach; (*outline, figure*) undeutlich, verschwommen; (*room*) dämmerig; (*future*) düster; (*prospects*) schlecht; (*inf: person*) schwer von Begriff ▷ *vt* (*light*) dämpfen; (*US: Aut*) abblenden; **to take a ~ view of sth** wenig *or* nicht viel von etw halten
dime [daɪm] (*US*) *n* Zehncentstück *nt*
dimension [daɪ'mɛnʃən] *n* (*aspect*) Dimension *f*; (*measurement*) Abmessung *f*, Maß *nt*; (*also pl: scale, size*) Ausmaß *nt*
diminish [dɪ'mɪnɪʃ] *vi* sich verringern ▷ *vt* verringern
diminutive [dɪ'mɪnjutɪv] *adj* winzig ▷ *n* Verkleinerungsform *f*
dimmer ['dɪmə^r] *n* (*also*: **dimmer switch**) Dimmer *m*; (*US: Aut*) Abblendschalter *m*
dimple ['dɪmpl] *n* Grübchen *nt*
din [dɪn] *n* Lärm *m*, Getöse *nt* ▷ *vt* (*inf*): **to ~ sth into sb** jdm etw einbläuen
dine [daɪn] *vi* speisen
diner ['daɪnə^r] *n* Gast *m*; (*US: restaurant*) Esslokal *nt*
dinghy ['dɪŋgɪ] *n* (*also*: **rubber dinghy**) Schlauchboot *nt*; (*also*: **sailing dinghy**) Dingi *nt*
dingy ['dɪndʒɪ] *adj* schäbig; (*clothes, curtains etc*) schmuddelig
dining car ['daɪnɪŋ-] (*Brit*) *n* Speisewagen *m*
dining room *n* Esszimmer *nt*; (*in hotel*) Speiseraum *m*
dinner ['dɪnə^r] *n* (*evening meal*) Abendessen *nt*; (*lunch*) Mittagessen *nt*; (*banquet*) (Fest)essen *nt*
dinner jacket *n* Smokingjackett *nt*
dinner party *n* Abendgesellschaft *f* (mit Essen)
dinner time *n* Essenszeit *f*
dinosaur ['daɪnəsɔ:^r] *n* Dinosaurier *m*
dip [dɪp] *n* Senke *f*; (*in sea*) kurzes Bad *nt*; (*Culin*) Dip *m*; (*for sheep*) Desinfektionslösung *f* ▷ *vt* eintauchen; (*Brit: Aut*) abblenden ▷ *vi* abfallen
diploma [dɪ'pləumə] *n* Diplom *nt*
diplomacy [dɪ'pləuməsɪ] *n* Diplomatie *f*
diplomat ['dɪpləmæt] *n* Diplomat(in) *m(f)*
diplomatic [dɪplə'mætɪk] *adj* diplomatisch; **to break off ~ relations (with)** die diplomatischen Beziehungen abbrechen (mit)
dipstick ['dɪpstɪk] (*Brit*) *n* Ölmessstab *m*
dire [daɪə^r] *adj* schrecklich
direct [daɪ'rɛkt] *adj, adv* direkt ▷ *vt* richten; (*company, project, programme etc*) leiten; (*play, film*) Regie führen bei; **to ~ sb to do sth** jdn anweisen, etw zu tun; **can you ~ me to ...?** können Sie mir den Weg nach ... sagen?
direct debit (*Brit*) *n* Einzugsauftrag *m*; (*transaction*) automatische Abbuchung *f*
direction [dɪ'rɛkʃən] *n* Richtung *f*; (*TV, Radio*) Leitung *f*; (*Cine*) Regie *f*; **directions** *npl* (*instructions*) Anweisungen *pl*; **sense of ~** Orientierungssinn *m*; **~s for use** Gebrauchsanweisung *f*, Gebrauchsanleitung *f*; **to ask for ~s** nach dem Weg fragen; **in the ~ of** in Richtung
directly [dɪ'rɛktlɪ] *adv* direkt; (*at once*) sofort, gleich
director [dɪ'rɛktə^r] *n* Direktor(in) *m(f)*; (*of project, TV, Radio*) Leiter(in) *m(f)*; (*Cine*) Regisseur(in) *m(f)*
directory [dɪ'rɛktərɪ] *n* (*also*: **telephone directory**) Telefonbuch *nt*; (*also*: **street**

directory) Einwohnerverzeichnis *nt*; (*Comput*) Verzeichnis *nt*; (*Comm*) Branchenverzeichnis *nt*

directory enquiries, (*US*) **directory assistance** *n* (Fernsprech)auskunft *f*

dirt [dəːt] *n* Schmutz *m*; (*earth*) Erde *f*; **to treat sb like ~** jdn wie (den letzten) Dreck behandeln

dirt-cheap ['dəːt'tʃiːp] *adj* spottbillig

dirty ['dəːtɪ] *adj* schmutzig; (*story*) unanständig ▷ *vt* beschmutzen

disability [dɪsə'bɪlɪtɪ] *n* Behinderung *f*

disabled [dɪs'eɪbld] *adj* behindert ▷ *npl*: **the ~** die Behinderten *pl*

disadvantage [dɪsəd'vɑːntɪdʒ] *n* Nachteil *m*; (*detriment*) Schaden *m*; **to be at a ~** benachteiligt *or* im Nachteil sein

disagree [dɪsə'griː] *vi* nicht übereinstimmen; (*to be against, think differently*): **to ~ (with)** nicht einverstanden sein (mit); **I ~ with you** ich bin anderer Meinung; **garlic ~s with me** ich vertrage keinen Knoblauch, Knoblauch bekommt mir nicht

disagreeable [dɪsə'griːəbl] *adj* unangenehm; (*person*) unsympathisch

disagreement [dɪsə'griːmənt] *n* Uneinigkeit *f*; (*argument*) Meinungsverschiedenheit *f*; **to have a ~ with sb** sich mit jdm nicht einig sein

disallow ['dɪsə'lau] *vt* (*appeal*) abweisen; (*goal*) nicht anerkennen, nicht geben

disappear [dɪsə'pɪəʳ] *vi* verschwinden; (*custom etc*) aussterben

disappearance [dɪsə'pɪərəns] *n* (*see vi*) Verschwinden *nt*; Aussterben *nt*

disappoint [dɪsə'pɔɪnt] *vt* enttäuschen

disappointed [dɪsə'pɔɪntɪd] *adj* enttäuscht

disappointing [dɪsə'pɔɪntɪŋ] *adj* enttäuschend

disappointment [dɪsə'pɔɪntmənt] *n* Enttäuschung *f*

disapproval [dɪsə'pruːvəl] *n* Missbilligung *f*

disapprove [dɪsə'pruːv] *vi* dagegen sein; **to ~ of** missbilligen *+acc*

disarm [dɪs'ɑːm] *vt* entwaffnen; (*criticism*) zum Verstummen bringen ▷ *vi* abrüsten

disarmament [dɪs'ɑːməmənt] *n* Abrüstung *f*

disarray [dɪsə'reɪ] *n*: **in ~** (*army, organization*) in Auflösung (begriffen); (*hair, clothes*) unordentlich; (*thoughts*) durcheinander; **to throw into ~** durcheinanderbringen

disaster [dɪ'zɑːstəʳ] *n* Katastrophe *f*; (*Aviat etc*) Unglück *nt*; (*fig: mess*) Fiasko *nt*

disastrous [dɪ'zɑːstrəs] *adj* katastrophal

disband [dɪs'bænd] *vt* auflösen ▷ *vi* sich auflösen

disbelief ['dɪsbə'liːf] *n* Ungläubigkeit *f*; **in ~** ungläubig

disc [dɪsk] *n* (*Anat*) Bandscheibe *f*; (*record*) Platte *f*; (*Comput*) = **disk**

discard [dɪs'kɑːd] *vt* ausrangieren; (*fig: idea, plan*) verwerfen

discern [dɪ'səːn] *vt* wahrnehmen; (*identify*) erkennen

discerning [dɪ'səːnɪŋ] *adj* (*judgement*) scharfsinnig; (*look*) kritisch; (*listeners etc*) anspruchsvoll

discharge [dɪs'tʃɑːdʒ] *vt* (*duties*) nachkommen *+dat*; (*debt*) begleichen; (*waste*) ablassen; (*Elec*) entladen; (*Med*) ausscheiden, absondern; (*patient, employee, soldier*) entlassen; (*defendant*) freisprechen ▷ *n* (*of gas*) Ausströmen *nt*; (*of liquid*) Ausfließen *nt*; (*Elec*) Entladung *f*; (*Med*) Ausfluss *m*; (*of patient, employee, soldier*) Entlassung *f*; (*of defendant*) Freispruch *m*; **to ~ a gun** ein Gewehr abfeuern

discipline ['dɪsɪplɪn] *n* Disziplin *f* ▷ *vt* disziplinieren; (*punish*) bestrafen; **to ~ o.s. to do sth** sich dazu anhalten *or* zwingen, etw zu tun

disc jockey *n* Discjockey *m*

disclaim [dɪs'kleɪm] *vt* (*knowledge*) abstreiten; (*responsibility*) von sich weisen

disclose [dɪs'kləuz] *vt* enthüllen, bekannt geben

disclosure [dɪs'kləuʒəʳ] *n* Enthüllung *f*

disco ['dɪskəu] *n* = **discotheque**

discoloured [dɪs'kʌləd] *adj* verfärbt

discomfort [dɪs'kʌmfət] *n* (*unease*) Unbehagen *nt*; (*physical*) Beschwerden *pl*

disconcert [dɪskən'səːt] *vt* beunruhigen, irritieren

disconnect [dɪskə'nɛkt] *vt* abtrennen; (*Elec, Radio*) abstellen; **I've been ~ed** (*Tel*) das Gespräch ist unterbrochen worden; (*supply, connection*) man hat mir das Telefon/den Strom/das Gas *etc* abgestellt

discontent [dɪskən'tɛnt] *n* Unzufriedenheit *f*

discontented [dɪskən'tɛntɪd] *adj* unzufrieden

discontinue [dɪskən'tɪnjuː] *vt* einstellen; **"~d"** (*Comm*) "ausgelaufene Serie"

discord ['dɪskɔːd] *n* Zwietracht *f*; (*Mus*) Dissonanz *f*

discount [*n* 'dɪskaunt, *vt* dɪs'kaunt] *n* Rabatt *m* ▷ *vt* nachlassen; (*idea, fact*) unberücksichtigt lassen; **to give sb a ~ on sth** jdm auf etw *acc* Rabatt geben; **~ for cash** Skonto *nt or m* (bei Barzahlung); **at a ~** mit Rabatt

discourage [dɪs'kʌrɪdʒ] *vt* entmutigen; **to ~ sb from doing sth** jdm davon abraten, etw zu tun

discover [dɪs'kʌvəʳ] *vt* entdecken; (*missing person*) finden; **to ~ that ...** herausfinden, dass ...

discovery [dɪs'kʌvərɪ] *n* Entdeckung *f*

discredit [dɪs'krɛdɪt] *vt* in Misskredit bringen ▷ *n*: **to sb's ~** zu jds Schande

discreet [dɪs'kriːt] *adj* diskret; (*unremarkable*) dezent

discrepancy [dɪs'krɛpənsɪ] *n* Diskrepanz *f*

discretion [dɪs'krɛʃən] *n* Diskretion *f*; **at the ~ of** im Ermessen *+gen*; **use your own ~** Sie müssen nach eigenem Ermessen handeln

discriminate [dɪsˈkrɪmɪneɪt] *vi*: **to ~ between** unterscheiden zwischen *+dat*; **to ~ against** diskriminieren *+acc*
discriminating [dɪsˈkrɪmɪneɪtɪŋ] *adj* anspruchsvoll, kritisch; (*tax, duty*) Differenzial-
discrimination [dɪskrɪmɪˈneɪʃən] *n* Diskriminierung *f*; (*discernment*) Urteilsvermögen *nt*; **racial ~** Rassendiskriminierung *f*; **sexual ~** Diskriminierung aufgrund des Geschlechts
discuss [dɪsˈkʌs] *vt* besprechen; (*debate*) diskutieren; (*analyse*) erörtern, behandeln
discussion [dɪsˈkʌʃən] *n* Besprechung *f*; (*debate*) Diskussion *f*; **under ~** in der Diskussion
disdain [dɪsˈdeɪn] *n* Verachtung *f* ▷ *vt* verachten ▷ *vi*: **to ~ to do sth** es für unter seiner Würde halten, etw zu tun
disease [dɪˈziːz] *n* Krankheit *f*
disembark [dɪsɪmˈbɑːk] *vt* ausschiffen ▷ *vi* (*passengers*) von Bord gehen
disentangle [dɪsɪnˈtæŋgl] *vt* befreien; (*wool, wire*) entwirren
disfigure [dɪsˈfɪgəʳ] *vt* entstellen; (*object, place*) verunstalten
disgrace [dɪsˈgreɪs] *n* Schande *f*; (*scandal*) Skandal *m* ▷ *vt* Schande bringen über *+acc*
disgraceful [dɪsˈgreɪsful] *adj* skandalös
disgruntled [dɪsˈgrʌntld] *adj* verärgert
disguise [dɪsˈgaɪz] *n* Verkleidung *f* ▷ *vt*: **to ~ (as)** (*person*) verkleiden (als); (*object*) tarnen (als); **in ~** (*person*) verkleidet; **there's no disguising the fact that ...** es kann nicht geleugnet werden, dass ...; **to ~ o.s. as** sich verkleiden als
disgust [dɪsˈgʌst] *n* Abscheu *m* ▷ *vt* anwidern; **she walked off in ~** sie ging voller Empörung weg
disgusting [dɪsˈgʌstɪŋ] *adj* widerlich
dish [dɪʃ] *n* Schüssel *f*; (*flat*) Schale *f*; (*recipe, food*) Gericht *nt*; (*also*: **satellite dish**) Parabolantenne *f*, Schüssel (*inf*); **to do** *or* **wash the ~es** Geschirr spülen, abwaschen
▸ **dish out** *vt* verteilen; (*food, money*) austeilen; (*advice*) erteilen
▸ **dish up** *vt* (*food*) auftragen, servieren; (*facts, statistics*) auftischen (*inf*)
dishcloth [ˈdɪʃklɔθ] *n* Spültuch *nt*, Spüllappen *m*
dishearten [dɪsˈhɑːtn] *vt* entmutigen
dishevelled, (*US*) **disheveled** [dɪˈʃɛvəld] *adj* unordentlich; (*hair*) zerzaust
dishonest [dɪsˈɔnɪst] *adj* unehrlich; (*means*) unlauter
dishonour [dɪsˈɔnəʳ] *n* Schande *f*
dishonourable [dɪsˈɔnərəbl] *adj* unehrenhaft
dishtowel [ˈdɪʃtauəl] (*US*) *n* Geschirrtuch *nt*
dishwasher [ˈdɪʃwɔʃəʳ] *n* (*machine*) (Geschirr)spülmaschine *f*
disillusion [dɪsɪˈluːʒən] *vt* desillusionieren ▷ *n* = **disillusionment**; **to become ~ed (with)** seine Illusionen (über *+acc*) verlieren
disinfect [dɪsɪnˈfɛkt] *vt* desinfizieren
disinfectant [dɪsɪnˈfɛktənt] *n* Desinfektionsmittel *nt*
disintegrate [dɪsˈɪntɪgreɪt] *vi* zerfallen; (*marriage, partnership*) scheitern; (*organization*) sich auflösen
disinterested [dɪsˈɪntrəstɪd] *adj* (*advice*) unparteiisch, unvoreingenommen; (*help*) uneigennützig
disjointed [dɪsˈdʒɔɪntɪd] *adj* unzusammenhängend
disk [dɪsk] *n* Diskette *f*; **single-/double-sided ~** einseitige/zweiseitige Diskette
disk drive *n* Diskettenlaufwerk *nt*
diskette [dɪsˈkɛt] (*US*) *n* = **disk**
dislike [dɪsˈlaɪk] *n* Abneigung *f* ▷ *vt* nicht mögen; **to take a ~ to sb/sth** eine Abneigung gegen jdn/etw entwickeln; **I ~ the idea** die Idee gefällt mir nicht; **he ~s it** er kann es nicht leiden, er mag es nicht
dislocate [ˈdɪsləkeɪt] *vt* verrenken, ausrenken; **he has ~d his shoulder** er hat sich *dat* den Arm ausgekugelt
dislodge [dɪsˈlɔdʒ] *vt* verschieben
disloyal [dɪsˈlɔɪəl] *adj* illoyal
dismal [ˈdɪzml] *adj* trübe, trostlos; (*song, person, mood*) trübsinnig; (*failure*) kläglich
dismantle [dɪsˈmæntl] *vt* (*machine*) demontieren
dismay [dɪsˈmeɪ] *n* Bestürzung *f* ▷ *vt* bestürzen; **much to my ~** zu meiner Bestürzung; **in ~** bestürzt
dismiss [dɪsˈmɪs] *vt* entlassen; (*case*) abweisen; (*possibility, idea*) abtun
dismissal [dɪsˈmɪsl] *n* Entlassung *f*
dismount [dɪsˈmaunt] *vi* absteigen
disobedient [dɪsəˈbiːdɪənt] *adj* ungehorsam
disobey [dɪsəˈbeɪ] *vt* nicht gehorchen *+dat*; (*order*) nicht befolgen
disorder [dɪsˈɔːdəʳ] *n* Unordnung *f*; (*rioting*) Unruhen *pl*; (*Med*) (Funktions)störung *f*; **civil ~** öffentliche Unruhen *pl*
disorderly [dɪsˈɔːdəlɪ] *adj* unordentlich; (*meeting*) undiszipliniert; (*behaviour*) ungehörig
disorganized [dɪsˈɔːgənaɪzd] *adj* chaotisch
disorientated [dɪsˈɔːrɪɛnteɪtɪd] *adj* desorientiert, verwirrt
disown [dɪsˈəun] *vt* (*action*) verleugnen; (*child*) verstoßen
disparaging [dɪsˈpærɪdʒɪŋ] *adj* (*remarks*) abschätzig, geringschätzig; **to be ~ about sb/sth** (*person*) abschätzig *or* geringschätzig über jdn/etw urteilen
dispassionate [dɪsˈpæʃənət] *adj* nüchtern
dispatch [dɪsˈpætʃ] *vt* senden, schicken; (*deal with*) erledigen; (*kill*) töten ▷ *n* Senden *nt*, Schicken *nt*; (*Press*) Bericht *m*; (*Mil*) Depesche *f*
dispel [dɪsˈpɛl] *vt* (*myths*) zerstören; (*fears*) zerstreuen
dispense [dɪsˈpɛns] *vt* (*medicines*) abgeben; (*charity*) austeilen; (*advice*) erteilen

▸ **dispense with** *vt fus* verzichten auf *+acc*
dispenser [dɪs'pɛnsəʳ] *n* (*machine*) Automat *m*
dispensing chemist [dɪs'pɛnsɪŋ-] (*Brit*) *n* (*shop*) Apotheke *f*
disperse [dɪs'pə:s] *vt* (*objects*) verstreuen; (*crowd etc*) auflösen, zerstreuen; (*knowledge, information*) verbreiten ▹ *vi* (*crowd*) sich auflösen *or* zerstreuen
dispirited [dɪs'pɪrɪtɪd] *adj* entmutigt
displace [dɪs'pleɪs] *vt* ablösen
display [dɪs'pleɪ] *n* (*in shop*) Auslage *f*; (*exhibition*) Ausstellung *f*; (*of feeling*) Zeigen *nt*; (*pej*) Zurschaustellung *f*; (*Comput, Tech*) Anzeige *f* ▹ *vt* zeigen; (*ostentatiously*) zur Schau stellen; (*results, departure times*) aushängen; **on ~** ausgestellt
displease [dɪs'pli:z] *vt* verstimmen, verärgern
displeasure [dɪs'plɛʒəʳ] *n* Missfallen *nt*
disposable [dɪs'pəuzəbl] *adj* (*lighter*) Wegwerf-; (*bottle*) Einweg-; (*income*) verfügbar
disposal [dɪs'pəuzl] *n* (*of goods for sale*) Loswerden *nt*; (*of property, belongings: by selling*) Verkauf *m*; (*: by giving away*) Abgeben *nt*; (*of rubbish*) Beseitigung *f*; **at one's ~** zur Verfügung; **to put sth at sb's ~** jdm etw zur Verfügung stellen
dispose [dɪs'pəuz]: **~ of** *vt fus* (*body*) aus dem Weg schaffen; (*unwanted goods*) loswerden; (*problem, task*) erledigen; (*stock*) verkaufen
disposed [dɪs'pəuzd] *adj*: **to be ~ to do sth** (*inclined*) geneigt sein, etw zu tun; (*willing*) bereit sein, etw zu tun; **to be well ~ towards sb** jdm wohlwollen
disposition [dɪspə'zɪʃən] *n* (*nature*) Veranlagung *f*; (*inclination*) Neigung *f*
disproportionate [dɪsprə'pɔ:ʃənət] *adj* unverhältnismäßig; (*amount*) unverhältnismäßig hoch/niedrig
disprove [dɪs'pru:v] *vt* widerlegen
dispute [dɪs'pju:t] *n* Streit *m*; (*also*: **industrial dispute**) Auseinandersetzung *f* zwischen Arbeitgebern und Arbeitnehmern; (*Pol, Mil*) Streitigkeiten *pl* ▹ *vt* bestreiten; (*ownership etc*) anfechten; **to be in** *or* **under ~** umstritten sein
disqualify [dɪs'kwɔlɪfaɪ] *vt* disqualifizieren; **to ~ sb for sth** jdn für etw ungeeignet machen; **to ~ sb from doing sth** jdn ungeeignet machen, etw zu tun; **to ~ sb from driving** (*Brit*) jdm den Führerschein entziehen
disquiet [dɪs'kwaɪət] *n* Unruhe *f*
disregard [dɪsrɪ'gɑ:d] *vt* nicht beachten, ignorieren ▹ *n*: **~ (for)** Missachtung *f* (*+gen*); (*for danger, money*) Geringschätzung *f* (*+gen*)
disrepair ['dɪsrɪ'pɛəʳ] *n*: **to fall into ~** (*machine*) vernachlässigt werden; (*building*) verfallen
disreputable [dɪs'rɛpjutəbl] *adj* (*person*) unehrenhaft; (*behaviour*) unfein
disrespectful [dɪsrɪ'spɛktful] *adj* respektlos
disrupt [dɪs'rʌpt] *vt* (*plans*) durcheinanderbringen; (*conversation, proceedings*) unterbrechen
disruption [dɪs'rʌpʃən] *n* Unterbrechung *f*; (*disturbance*) Störung *f*
dissatisfaction [dɪssætɪs'fækʃən] *n* Unzufriedenheit *f*
dissatisfied [dɪs'sætɪsfaɪd] *adj*: **~ (with)** unzufrieden (mit)
dissect [dɪ'sɛkt] *vt* sezieren
dissent [dɪ'sɛnt] *n* abweichende Meinungen *pl*
dissertation [dɪsə'teɪʃən] *n* (*speech*) Vortrag *m*; (*piece of writing*) Abhandlung *f*; (*for PhD*) Dissertation *f*
disservice [dɪs'sə:vɪs] *n*: **to do sb a ~** jdm einen schlechten Dienst erweisen
dissimilar [dɪ'sɪmɪləʳ] *adj*: **~ (to)** anders (als)
dissipate ['dɪsɪpeɪt] *vt* (*heat*) neutralisieren; (*clouds*) auflösen; (*money, effort*) verschwenden
dissolute ['dɪsəlu:t] *adj* zügellos, ausschweifend
dissolve [dɪ'zɔlv] *vt* auflösen ▹ *vi* sich auflösen; **to ~ in(to) tears** in Tränen zerfließen
distance ['dɪstns] *n* Entfernung *f*; (*in time*) Abstand *m*; (*reserve*) Abstand, Distanz *f* ▹ *vt*: **to ~ o.s. (from)** sich distanzieren (von); **in the ~** in der Ferne; **what's the ~ to London?** wie weit ist es nach London?; **it's within walking ~** es ist zu Fuß erreichbar; **at a ~ of 2 metres** in 2 Meter(n) Entfernung; **keep your ~!** halten Sie Abstand!
distant ['dɪstnt] *adj* (*place*) weit entfernt, fern; (*time*) weit zurückliegend; (*relative*) entfernt; (*manner*) distanziert, kühl
distaste [dɪs'teɪst] *n* Widerwille *m*
distasteful [dɪs'teɪstful] *adj* widerlich; **to be ~ to sb** jdm zuwider sein
distended [dɪs'tɛndɪd] *adj* aufgebläht
distil, (US) **distill** [dɪs'tɪl] *vt* destillieren; (*fig*) (heraus)destillieren
distillery [dɪs'tɪlərɪ] *n* Brennerei *f*
distinct [dɪs'tɪŋkt] *adj* deutlich, klar; (*possibility*) eindeutig; (*different*) verschieden; **as ~ from** im Unterschied zu
distinction [dɪs'tɪŋkʃən] *n* Unterschied *m*; (*honour*) Ehre *f*; (*in exam*) Auszeichnung *f*; **to draw a ~ between** einen Unterschied machen zwischen *+dat*; **a writer of ~** ein Schriftsteller von Rang
distinctive [dɪs'tɪŋktɪv] *adj* unverwechselbar
distinguish [dɪs'tɪŋgwɪʃ] *vt* unterscheiden; (*details etc*) erkennen, ausmachen; **to ~ (between)** unterscheiden (zwischen *+dat*); **to ~ o.s.** sich hervortun
distinguished [dɪs'tɪŋgwɪʃt] *adj* von hohem Rang; (*career*) hervorragend; (*in appearance*) distinguiert
distinguishing [dɪs'tɪŋgwɪʃɪŋ] *adj* charakteristisch
distort [dɪs'tɔ:t] *vt* verzerren; (*argument*) verdrehen
distract [dɪs'trækt] *vt* ablenken

distracted [dɪs'træktɪd] *adj* unaufmerksam; (*anxious*) besorgt, beunruhigt
distraction [dɪs'trækʃən] *n* Unaufmerksamkeit *f*; (*confusion*) Verstörtheit *f*; (*sth which distracts*) Ablenkung *f*; (*amusement*) Zerstreuung *f*; **to drive sb to ~** jdn zur Verzweiflung treiben
distraught [dɪs'trɔːt] *adj* verzweifelt
distress [dɪs'trɛs] *n* Verzweiflung *f* ▷ *vt* Kummer machen *+dat*; **in ~** (*ship*) in Seenot; (*person*) verzweifelt; **~ed area** (*Brit*) Notstandsgebiet *nt*
distressing [dɪs'trɛsɪŋ] *adj* beunruhigend
distribute [dɪs'trɪbjuːt] *vt* verteilen; (*profits*) aufteilen
distribution [dɪstrɪ'bjuːʃən] *n* Vertrieb *m*; (*of profits*) Aufteilung *f*
distributor [dɪs'trɪbjutəʳ] *n* (*Comm*) Vertreiber(in) *m(f)*; (*Aut, Tech*) Verteiler *m*
district ['dɪstrɪkt] *n* Gebiet *nt*; (*of town*) Stadtteil *m*; (*Admin*) (Verwaltungs)bezirk *m*
district attorney (*US*) *n* Bezirksstaatsanwalt *m*, Bezirksstaatsanwältin *f*
district nurse (*Brit*) *n* Gemeindeschwester *f*
distrust [dɪs'trʌst] *n* Misstrauen *nt* ▷ *vt* misstrauen *+dat*
disturb [dɪs'təːb] *vt* stören; (*upset*) beunruhigen; (*disorganize*) durcheinanderbringen; **sorry to ~ you** entschuldigen Sie bitte die Störung
disturbance [dɪs'təːbəns] *n* Störung *f*; (*political etc*) Unruhe *f*; (*violent event*) Unruhen *pl*; (*by drunks etc*) (Ruhe)störung *f*; **to cause a ~** Unruhe/eine Ruhestörung verursachen; **~ of the peace** Ruhestörung
disturbed [dɪs'təːbd] *adj* beunruhigt; (*childhood*) unglücklich; **mentally/ emotionally ~** geistig/seelisch gestört
disturbing [dɪs'təːbɪŋ] *adj* beunruhigend
disuse [dɪs'juːs] *n*: **to fall into ~** nicht mehr benutzt werden
disused [dɪs'juːzd] *adj* (*building*) leer stehend; (*airfield*) stillgelegt
ditch [dɪtʃ] *n* Graben *m* ▷ *vt* (*inf*: *partner*) sitzen lassen; (: *plan*) sausen lassen; (: *car etc*) loswerden
dither ['dɪðəʳ] (*pej*) *vi* zaudern
ditto ['dɪtəu] *adv* dito, ebenfalls
dive [daɪv] *n* Sprung *m*; (*underwater*) Tauchen *nt*; (*of submarine*) Untertauchen *nt*; (*pej*: *place*) Spelunke *f* (*inf*) ▷ *vi* springen; (*under water*) tauchen; (*bird*) einen Sturzflug machen; (*submarine*) untertauchen; **to ~ into** (*bag, drawer etc*) greifen in *+acc*; (*shop, car etc*) sich stürzen in *+acc*
diver ['daɪvəʳ] *n* Taucher(in) *m(f)*; (*also*: **deep-sea diver**) Tiefseetaucher(in) *m(f)*
diverse [daɪ'vəːs] *adj* verschiedenartig
diversion [daɪ'vəːʃən] *n* (*Brit*: *Aut*) Umleitung *f*; (*distraction*) Ablenkung *f*; (*of funds*) Umlenkung *f*
diversity [daɪ'vəːsɪtɪ] *n* Vielfalt *f*
divert [daɪ'vəːt] *vt* (*sb's attention*) ablenken; (*funds*) umlenken; (*re-route*) umleiten
divide [dɪ'vaɪd] *vt* trennen; (*Math*) dividieren, teilen; (*share out*) verteilen ▷ *vi* sich teilen; (*road*) sich gabeln; (*people, groups*) sich aufteilen ▷ *n* Kluft *f*; **to ~ (between** *or* **among)** aufteilen (unter *+dat*); **40 ~d by 5** 40 geteilt *or* dividiert durch 5
▸ **divide out** *vt*: **to ~ out (between** *or* **among)** aufteilen (unter *+dat*)
divided highway (*US*) *n* ≈ Schnellstraße *f*
dividend ['dɪvɪdɛnd] *n* Dividende *f*; (*fig*): **to pay ~s** sich bezahlt machen
divine [dɪ'vaɪn] *adj* göttlich ▷ *vt* (*future*) weissagen, prophezeien; (*truth*) erahnen; (*water, metal*) aufspüren
diving ['daɪvɪŋ] *n* Tauchen *nt*; (*Sport*) Kunstspringen *nt*
diving board *n* Sprungbrett *nt*
divinity [dɪ'vɪnɪtɪ] *n* Göttlichkeit *f*; (*god or goddess*) Gottheit *f*; (*Scol*) Theologie *f*
division [dɪ'vɪʒən] *n* Teilung *f*; (*Math*) Teilen *nt*, Division *f*; (*sharing out*) Verteilung *f*; (*disagreement*) Uneinigkeit *f*; (*Brit*: *Pol*) Abstimmung *f* durch Hammelsprung; (*Comm*) Abteilung *f*; (*Mil*) Division *f*; (*esp Football*) Liga *f*; **~ of labour** Arbeitsteilung *f*
divorce [dɪ'vɔːs] *n* Scheidung *f* ▷ *vt* sich scheiden lassen von; (*dissociate*) trennen
divorced [dɪ'vɔːst] *adj* geschieden
divorcee [dɪvɔː'siː] *n* Geschiedene(r) *f(m)*
DIY (*Brit*) *n abbr* = **do-it-yourself**
dizzy ['dɪzɪ] *adj* schwind(e)lig; (*turn, spell*) Schwindel-; (*height*) schwindelerregend; **I feel ~** mir ist *or* ich bin schwind(e)lig
DJ *n abbr* = **disc jockey**
DNA *n abbr* (= *deoxyribonucleic acid*) DNS *f*
do [duː] (*pt* **did**, *pp* **done**) *aux vb* **1** (*in negative constructions*): **I don't understand** ich verstehe nicht
2 (*to form questions*): **didn't you know?** wusstest du das nicht?; **what do you think?** was meinst du?
3 (*for emphasis*): **she does seem rather upset** sie scheint wirklich recht aufgeregt zu sein; **do sit down/help yourself** bitte nehmen Sie Platz/bedienen Sie sich; **oh do shut up!** halte endlich den Mund!
4 (*to avoid repeating vb*): **she swims better than I do** sie schwimmt besser als ich; **she lives in Glasgow — so do I** sie wohnt in Glasgow — ich auch; **who made this mess? — I did** wer hat dieses Durcheinander gemacht? — ich
5 (*in question tags*): **you like him, don't you?** du magst ihn, nicht wahr?; **I don't know him, do I?** ich kenne ihn nicht, oder?
▷ *vt* **1** (*carry out, perform*) tun, machen; **what are you doing tonight?** was machen Sie heute Abend?; **what do you do (for a living)?** was machen Sie beruflich?; **to do one's teeth/nails** sich *dat* die Zähne putzen/die Nägel schneiden
2 (*Aut etc*) fahren; **the car was doing 100** das

Auto fuhr 100
▷ *vi* 1 (*act, behave*): **do as I do** mach es wie ich 2 (*get on, fare*): **he's doing well/badly at school** er ist gut/schlecht in der Schule; **the company is doing well** der Firma geht es gut; **how do you do?** guten Tag/Morgen/ Abend!
3 (*suit, be sufficient*) reichen; **will that do?** reicht das?; **will this dress do for the party?** ist dieses Kleid gut genug für die Party?; **will £10 do?** reichen £10?; **that'll do** das reicht; (*in annoyance*) jetzt reichts aber!; **to make do with** auskommen mit
▷ *n* (*inf: party etc*) Party *f*, Fete *f*; **it was quite a do** es war ganz schön was los
▶ **do away with** *vt fus* (*get rid of*) abschaffen
▶ **do for** (*inf*) *vt fus*: **to be done for** erledigt sein
▶ **do in** (*inf*) *vt* (*kill*) umbringen
▶ **do out of** (*inf*) *vt* (*deprive*) bringen um
▶ **do up** *vt fus* (*laces, dress, buttons*) zumachen; (*renovate: room, house*) renovieren
▶ **do with** *vt fus* 1 (*need*) brauchen; **I could do with some help/a drink** ich könnte Hilfe/ einen Drink gebrauchen
2: **it has to do with money** es hat mit Geld zu tun
▶ **do without** *vt fus* auskommen ohne

dock [dɔk] *n* Dock *nt*; (*Law*) Anklagebank *f*; (*Bot*) Ampfer *m* ▷ *vi* anlegen; (*Space*) docken ▷ *vt*: **they ~ed a third of his wages** sie kürzten seinen Lohn um ein Drittel; **docks** *npl* (*Naut*) Hafen *m*

docker ['dɔkəʳ] *n* Hafenarbeiter *m*, Docker *m*

dockyard ['dɔkjɑːd] *n* Werft *f*

doctor ['dɔktəʳ] *n* Arzt *m*, Ärztin *f*; (*PhD etc*) Doktor *m* ▷ *vt*: **to ~ a drink** *etc* einem Getränk *etc* etwas beimischen; **~'s office** (*US*) Sprechzimmer *nt*

Doctor of Philosophy *n* Doktor *m* der Philosophie

document ['dɔkjumənt] *n* Dokument *nt* ▷ *vt* dokumentieren

documentary [dɔkju'mɛntərɪ] *adj* dokumentarisch ▷ *n* Dokumentarfilm *m*

documentation [dɔkjumən'teɪʃən] *n* Dokumentation *f*

dodge [dɔdʒ] *n* Trick *m* ▷ *vt* ausweichen +*dat*; (*tax*) umgehen ▷ *vi* ausweichen; **to ~ out of the way** zur Seite springen; **to ~ through the traffic** sich durch den Verkehr schlängeln

dodgems ['dɔdʒəmz] (*Brit*) *npl* Autoskooter *pl*

dodgy ['dɔdʒɪ] (*inf*) *adj* (*person*) zweifelhaft; (*plan etc*) gewagt

doe [dəu] *n* Reh *nt*, Ricke *f*; (*rabbit*) (Kaninchen)weibchen *nt*

does [dʌz] *vb see* **do**

doesn't ['dʌznt] = **does not**

dog [dɔg] *n* Hund *m* ▷ *vt* (*subj: person*) auf den Fersen bleiben +*dat*; (*: bad luck, memory etc*) verfolgen; **to go to the ~s** (*inf*) vor die Hunde gehen

dog collar *n* Hundehalsband *nt*; (*Rel*) Kragen *m* des Geistlichen

dog-eared ['dɔgɪəd] *adj* mit Eselsohren

dogged ['dɔgɪd] *adj* beharrlich

doggy bag ['dɔgɪ-] *n Tüte für Essensreste, die man nach Hause mitnehmen möchte*

dogsbody ['dɔgzbɔdɪ] (*Brit: inf*) *n* Mädchen *nt* für alles

doings ['duɪŋz] *npl* Treiben *nt*

do-it-yourself ['duːɪtjɔː'sɛlf] *n* Heimwerken *nt*, Do-it-yourself *nt*

doldrums ['dɔldrəmz] *npl*: **to be in the ~** (*person*) niedergeschlagen sein; (*business*) in einer Flaute stecken

dole [dəul] (*Brit*) *n* Arbeitslosenunterstützung *f*; **on the ~** arbeitslos
▶ **dole out** *vt* austeilen, verteilen

doll [dɔl] *n* (*toy, also US: inf: woman*) Puppe *f*

dollar ['dɔləʳ] (*US etc*) *n* Dollar *m*

dolphin ['dɔlfɪn] *n* Delfin *m*

dome [dəum] *n* Kuppel *f*

domestic [də'mɛstɪk] *adj* (*trade*) Innen-; (*situation*) innenpolitisch; (*news*) Inland-, aus dem Inland; (*tasks, appliances*) Haushalts-; (*animal*) Haus-; (*duty, happiness*) häuslich

domesticated [də'mɛstɪkeɪtɪd] *adj* (*animal*) zahm; (*person*) häuslich

dominant ['dɔmɪnənt] *adj* dominierend; (*share*) größte(r, s)

dominate ['dɔmɪneɪt] *vt* dominieren, beherrschen

domineering [dɔmɪ'nɪərɪŋ] *adj* herrschsüchtig

dominion [də'mɪnɪən] *n* (*territory*) Herrschaftsgebiet *nt*; (*authority*): **to have ~ over** Macht haben über +*acc*

domino ['dɔmɪnəu] (*pl* **~es**) *n* (*block*) Domino(stein) *m*

dominoes ['dɔmɪnəuz] *n* (*game*) Domino(spiel) *nt*

don [dɔn] *n* (*Brit*) (Universitäts)dozent *m* (*besonders in Oxford und Cambridge*) ▷ *vt* anziehen

donate [də'neɪt] *vt*: **to ~ (to)** (*organization, cause*) spenden (für)

donation [də'neɪʃən] *n* (*act of donating*) Spenden *nt*; (*contribution*) Spende *f*

done [dʌn] *pp of* **do**

donkey ['dɔŋkɪ] *n* Esel *m*

donor ['dəunəʳ] *n* Spender(in) *m(f)*

donor card *n* Organspenderausweis *m*

don't [dəunt] = **do not**

donut ['dəunʌt] (*US*) *n* = **doughnut**

doodle ['duːdl] *vi* Männchen malen ▷ *n* Kritzelei *f*

doom [duːm] *n* Unheil *nt* ▷ *vt*: **to be ~ed to failure** zum Scheitern verurteilt sein

door [dɔːʳ] *n* Tür *f*; **to go from ~ to door** von Tür zu Tür gehen

door handle *n* Türklinke *f*; (*of car*) Türgriff *m*

doorman ['dɔːmən] (*irreg: like* **man**) *n* Portier *m*

doormat ['dɔːmæt] *n* Fußmatte *f*; (*fig*) Fußabtreter *m*

doorstep ['dɔːstɛp] *n* Eingangsstufe *f*,

Türstufe *f*; **on the ~** vor der Haustür
doorway ['dɔ:weɪ] *n* Eingang *m*
dope [dəup] *n* (*inf*) Stoff *m*, Drogen *pl*; (*: person*) Esel *m*, Trottel *m*; (*: information*) Informationen *pl* ▷ *vt* dopen
dormant ['dɔ:mənt] *adj* (*plant*) ruhend; (*volcano*) untätig; (*idea, report etc*): **to lie ~** schlummern
dormitory ['dɔ:mɪtrɪ] *n* Schlafsaal *m*; (*US: building*) Wohnheim *nt*
dormouse ['dɔ:maus] (*pl* **dormice**) *n* Haselmaus *f*
DOS [dɔs] *n abbr* (*Comput: = disk operating system*) DOS
dosage ['dəusɪdʒ] *n* Dosis *f*; (*on label*) Dosierung *f*
dose [dəus] *n* Dosis *f*; (*Brit: bout*) Ration *f* ▷ *vt*: **to ~ o.s.** Medikamente nehmen; **a ~ of flu** eine Grippe
dot [dɔt] *n* Punkt *m* ▷ *vt*: **~ted with** übersät mit; **on the ~** (auf die Minute) pünktlich
dotted line ['dɔtɪd-] *n* punktierte Linie *f*; **to sign on the ~** (*fig*) seine formelle Zustimmung geben
double ['dʌbl] *adj* doppelt; (*chin*) Doppel- ▷ *adv* (*cost*) doppelt so viel ▷ *n* Doppelgänger(in) *m(f)* ▷ *vt* verdoppeln; (*paper, blanket*) (einmal) falten ▷ *vi* sich verdoppeln; **~ five two six (5526)** (*Brit: Tel*) fünfundfünfzig sechsundzwanzig; **it's spelt with a ~ "l"** es wird mit zwei l geschrieben; **an egg with a ~ yolk** ein Ei mit zwei Dottern; **on the ~, at the ~** (*Brit: quickly*) schnell; (*immediately*) unverzüglich; **to ~ as ...** (*person*) auch als ... fungieren; (*thing*) auch als ... dienen
▸ **double back** *vi* kehrtmachen, zurückgehen/-fahren
▸ **double up** *vi* sich krümmen; (*share room*) sich ein Zimmer teilen
double bass *n* Kontrabass *m*
double bed *n* Doppelbett *nt*
double-breasted ['dʌbl'brɛstɪd] *adj* (*jacket, coat*) zweireihig
double-check ['dʌbl'tʃɛk] *vt* noch einmal (über)prüfen ▷ *vi* es noch einmal (über)prüfen
double-cross [dʌbl'krɔs] *vt* ein Doppelspiel treiben mit
double-decker [dʌbl'dɛkə^r] *n* Doppeldecker *m*
double glazing [-'gleɪzɪŋ] (*Brit*) *n* Doppelverglasung *f*
double room *n* Doppelzimmer *nt*
doubles ['dʌblz] *n* (*Tennis*) Doppel *nt*
doubly ['dʌblɪ] *adv* (ganz) besonders
doubt [daut] *n* Zweifel *m* ▷ *vt* bezweifeln; **without (a) ~** ohne Zweifel; **to ~ sb** jdm nicht glauben; **I ~ it (very much)** das bezweifle ich (sehr), das möchte ich (stark) bezweifeln; **to ~ if** *or* **whether ...** bezweifeln, dass ...; **I don't ~ that ...** ich bezweifle nicht, dass ...
doubtful ['dautful] *adj* zweifelhaft; **to be ~ about sth** an etw *dat* zweifeln; **to be ~ about doing sth** Bedenken haben, ob man etw tun soll; **I'm a bit ~** ich bin nicht ganz sicher
doubtless ['dautlɪs] *adv* ohne Zweifel, sicherlich
dough [dəu] *n* Teig *m*; (*inf: money*) Kohle *f*, Knete *f*
doughnut, (*US*) **donut** ['dəunʌt] *n* ≈ Berliner (Pfannkuchen) *m*
dove [dʌv] *n* Taube *f*
Dover ['dəuvə^r] *n* Dover *nt*
dovetail ['dʌvteɪl] *vi* übereinstimmen ▷ *n* (*also*: **dovetail joint**) Schwalbenschwanzverbindung *f*
dowdy ['daudɪ] *adj* ohne jeden Schick; (*clothes*) unmodern
down [daun] *n* Daunen *pl* ▷ *adv* hinunter, herunter; (*on the ground*) unten ▷ *prep* hinunter, herunter; (*movement along*) entlang ▷ *vt* (*inf: drink*) runterkippen; **~ there/here** da/hier unten; **the price of meat is ~** die Fleischpreise sind gefallen; **I've got it ~ in my diary** ich habe es in meinem Kalender notiert; **to pay £2 ~** £2 anzahlen; **England is two goals ~** England liegt mit zwei Toren zurück; **to ~ tools** (*Brit*) die Arbeit niederlegen; **~ with ...!** nieder mit ...!
down-and-out ['daunəndaut] *n* Penner(in) *m(f)* (*inf*)
down-at-heel ['daunət'hi:l] *adj* (*appearance, person*) schäbig, heruntergekommen; (*shoes*) abgetreten
downcast ['daunkɑ:st] *adj* niedergeschlagen
downfall ['daunfɔ:l] *n* Ruin *m*; (*of dictator etc*) Sturz *m*, Fall *m*
downhearted ['daun'hɑ:tɪd] *adj* niedergeschlagen, entmutigt
downhill ['daun'hɪl] *adv* bergab ▷ *n* (*Ski: also*: **downhill race**) Abfahrtslauf *m*; **to go ~** (*road*) bergab führen; (*person*) hinuntergehen, heruntergehen; (*car*) hinunterfahren, herunterfahren; (*fig*) auf dem absteigenden Ast sein
download ['daunləud] *vt* (*Comput*) herunterladen, downloaden ▷ *n* Download *m*
down payment *n* Anzahlung *f*
downpour ['daunpɔ:^r] *n* Wolkenbruch *m*
downright ['daunraɪt] *adj* (*liar etc*) ausgesprochen; (*refusal, lie*) glatt
downsize ['daun'saɪz] *vi* (*Econ: company*) sich verkleinern
Down's syndrome *n* (*Med*) Downsyndrom *nt*
downstairs ['daun'stɛəz] *adv* unten; (*downwards*) nach unten
downstream ['daunstri:m] *adv* flussabwärts, stromabwärts
down-to-earth ['dauntu'ə:θ] *adj* (*person*) nüchtern; (*solution*) praktisch
downtown ['daun'taun] (*esp US*) *adv* im Zentrum, in der (Innen)stadt; (*go*) ins Zentrum, in die (Innen)stadt ▷ *adj*: **~ Chicago** das Zentrum von Chicago
down under *adv* (*be*) in Australien/

Neuseeland; (*go*) nach Australien/ Neuseeland
downward ['daunwəd] *adj, adv* nach unten; **a ~ trend** ein Abwärtstrend *m*
downwards ['daunwədz] *adv* = **downward**
dowry ['daurɪ] *n* Mitgift *f*
doz. *abbr* = **dozen**
doze [dəuz] *vi* ein Nickerchen *nt* machen
▸ **doze off** *vi* einschlafen, einnicken
dozen ['dʌzn] *n* Dutzend *nt*; **a ~ books** ein Dutzend Bücher; **80p a ~** 80 Pence das Dutzend; **~s of** Dutzende von
drab [dræb] *adj* trist
draft [drɑ:ft] *n* Entwurf *m*; (*also*: **bank draft**) Tratte *f*; (*US*: *call-up*) Einberufung *f* ▹ *vt* entwerfen; *see also* **draught**
drag [dræg] *vt* schleifen, schleppen; (*river*) absuchen ▹ *vi* sich hinziehen ▹ *n* (*Aviat*) Luftwiderstand *m*; (*Naut*) Wasserwiderstand *m*; (*inf*): **to be a ~** (*boring*) langweilig sein; (*a nuisance*) lästig sein; (*women's clothing*): **in ~** in Frauenkleidung
▸ **drag away** *vt*: **to ~ away (from)** wegschleppen *or* wegziehen (von)
▸ **drag on** *vi* sich hinziehen
dragon ['drægn] *n* Drache *m*
dragonfly ['drægənflaɪ] *n* Libelle *f*
drain [dreɪn] *n* Belastung *f*; (*in street*) Gully *m* ▹ *vt* entwässern; (*pond*) trockenlegen; (*vegetables*) abgießen; (*glass, cup*) leeren ▹ *vi* ablaufen; **to feel ~ed (of energy/emotion)** sich ausgelaugt fühlen
drainage ['dreɪnɪdʒ] *n* Entwässerungssystem *nt*; (*process*) Entwässerung *f*
draining board ['dreɪnɪŋ-], (*US*) **drainboard** ['dreɪnbɔ:d] *n* Ablaufbrett *nt*
drainpipe ['dreɪnpaɪp] *n* Abflussrohr *nt*
drama ['drɑ:mə] *n* Drama *nt*
dramatic [drə'mætɪk] *adj* dramatisch; (*theatrical*) theatralisch
dramatist ['dræmətɪst] *n* Dramatiker(in) *m(f)*
dramatize ['dræmətaɪz] *vt* dramatisieren; (*for TV/cinema*) für das Fernsehen/den Film bearbeiten
drank [dræŋk] *pt of* **drink**
drape [dreɪp] *vt* drapieren
drastic ['dræstɪk] *adj* drastisch
draught, (*US*) **draft** [drɑ:ft] *n* (Luft)zug *m*; (*Naut*) Tiefgang *m*; (*of chimney*) Zug *m*; **on ~** vom Fass
draught beer *n* Bier *nt* vom Fass
draughtboard ['drɑ:ftbɔ:d] (*Brit*) *n* Damebrett *nt*
draughts [drɑ:fts] (*Brit*) *n* Damespiel *nt*
draughtsman, (*US*) **draftsman** ['drɑ:ftsmən] (*irreg*: *like* **man**) *n* Zeichner(in) *m(f)*; (*as job*) technischer Zeichner *m*, technische Zeichnerin *f*
draw [drɔ:] (*pt* **drew**, *pp* **~n**) *vt* zeichnen; (*cart, gun, tooth, conclusion*) ziehen; (*curtain*: *open*) aufziehen; (: *close*) zuziehen; (*admiration, attention*) erregen; (*money*) abheben; (*wages*) bekommen ▹ *vi* (*Sport*) unentschieden spielen ▹ *n* (*Sport*) Unentschieden *nt*; (*lottery*) Lotterie *f*; (: *picking of ticket*) Ziehung *f*; **to ~ a comparison/distinction (between)** einen Vergleich ziehen/Unterschied machen (zwischen +*dat*); **to ~ near** näher kommen; (*event*) nahen; **to ~ to a close** zu Ende gehen
▸ **draw back** *vi*: **to ~ back (from)** zurückweichen (von)
▸ **draw in** *vi* (*Brit*: *car*) anhalten; (: *train*) einfahren; (*nights*) länger werden
▸ **draw on** *vt* (*resources*) zurückgreifen auf +*acc*; (*imagination*) zu Hilfe nehmen; (*person*) einsetzen
▸ **draw out** *vi* länger werden ▹ *vt* (*money*) abheben
▸ **draw up** *vi* (an)halten ▹ *vt* (*chair etc*) heranziehen; (*document*) aufsetzen
drawback ['drɔ:bæk] *n* Nachteil *m*
drawbridge ['drɔ:brɪdʒ] *n* Zugbrücke *f*
drawer [drɔ:ʳ] *n* Schublade *f*
drawing ['drɔ:ɪŋ] *n* Zeichnung *f*; (*skill, discipline*) Zeichnen *nt*
drawing board *n* Reißbrett *nt*; **back to the ~** (*fig*) das muss noch einmal neu überdacht werden
drawing pin (*Brit*) *n* Reißzwecke *f*
drawing room *n* Salon *m*
drawl [drɔ:l] *n* schleppende Sprechweise *f* ▹ *vi* schleppend sprechen
drawn [drɔ:n] *pp of* **draw** ▹ *adj* abgespannt
dread [drɛd] *n* Angst *f*, Furcht *f* ▹ *vt* große Angst haben vor +*dat*
dreadful ['drɛdful] *adj* schrecklich, furchtbar; **I feel ~!** (*ill*) ich fühle mich schrecklich; (*ashamed*) es ist mir schrecklich peinlich
dream [dri:m] (*pt, pp* **dreamed** *or* **~t**) *n* Traum *m* ▹ *vt, vi* träumen; **to have a ~ about sb/sth** von jdm/etw träumen; **sweet ~s!** träume süß!
▸ **dream up** *vt* sich *dat* einfallen lassen, sich *dat* ausdenken
dreamer ['dri:məʳ] *n* Träumer(in) *m(f)*
dreamt [drɛmt] *pt, pp of* **dream**
dreamy ['dri:mɪ] *adj* verträumt; (*music*) zum Träumen
dreary ['drɪərɪ] *adj* langweilig; (*weather*) trüb
dredge [drɛdʒ] *vt* ausbaggern
▸ **dredge up** *vt* ausbaggern; (*fig*: *unpleasant facts*) ausgraben
dregs [drɛgz] *npl* Bodensatz *m*; (*of humanity*) Abschaum *m*
drench [drɛntʃ] *vt* durchnässen; **~ed to the skin** nass bis auf die Haut
dress [drɛs] *n* Kleid *nt*; (*no pl*: *clothing*) Kleidung *f* ▹ *vt* anziehen; (*wound*) verbinden ▹ *vi* sich anziehen; **she ~es very well** sie kleidet sich sehr gut; **to ~ a shop window** ein Schaufenster dekorieren; **to get ~ed** sich anziehen
▸ **dress up** *vi* sich fein machen; (*in fancy dress*) sich verkleiden
dress circle (*Brit*) *n* (*Theat*) erster Rang *m*
dresser ['drɛsəʳ] *n* (*Brit*) Anrichte *f*; (*US*)

Kommode *f*; (*also*: **window dresser**) Dekorateur(in) *m(f)*
dressing ['drɛsɪŋ] *n* Verband *m*; (*Culin*) (Salat)soße *f*
dressing gown (*Brit*) *n* Morgenrock *m*
dressing room *n* Umkleidekabine *f*; (*Theat*) (Künstler)garderobe *f*
dressing table *n* Frisierkommode *f*
dressmaker ['drɛsmeɪkəʳ] *n* (Damen)schneider(in) *m(f)*
dress rehearsal *n* Generalprobe *f*
drew [druː] *pt of* **draw**
dribble ['drɪbl] *vi* tropfen; (*baby*) sabbern; (*Football*) dribbeln ▷ *vt* (*ball*) dribbeln mit
dried [draɪd] *adj* (*fruit*) getrocknet, Dörr-; **~ egg** Trockenei *nt*, Eipulver *nt*; **~ milk** Trockenmilch *f*, Milchpulver *nt*
drier ['draɪəʳ] *n* = **dryer**
drift [drɪft] *n* Strömung *f*; (*of snow*) Schneewehe *f*; (*of questions*) Richtung *f* ▷ *vi* treiben; (*sand*) wehen; **to let things ~** die Dinge treiben lassen; **to ~ apart** sich auseinanderleben; **I get** *or* **catch your ~** ich verstehe, worauf Sie hinauswollen
driftwood ['drɪftwud] *n* Treibholz *nt*
drill [drɪl] *n* Bohrer *m*; (*machine*) Bohrmaschine *f*; (*Mil*) Drill *m* ▷ *vt* bohren; (*troops*) drillen ▷ *vi*: **to ~ (for)** bohren (nach); **to ~ pupils in grammar** mit den Schülern Grammatik pauken
drink [drɪŋk] (*pt* **drank**, *pp* **drunk**) *n* Getränk *nt*; (*alcoholic*) Glas *nt*, Drink *m*; (*sip*) Schluck *m* ▷ *vt, vi* trinken; **to have a ~** etwas trinken; **a ~ of water** etwas Wasser; **we had ~s before lunch** vor dem Mittagessen gab es einen Drink; **would you like something to ~?** möchten Sie etwas trinken?
▸ **drink in** *vt* (*fresh air*) einatmen, einsaugen; (*story, sight*) (begierig) in sich aufnehmen
drink-driving ['drɪŋk'draɪvɪŋ] *n* Trunkenheit *f* am Steuer
drinker ['drɪŋkəʳ] *n* Trinker(in) *m(f)*
drinking water *n* Trinkwasser *nt*
drip [drɪp] *n* Tropfen *nt*; (*one drip*) Tropfen *m*; (*Med*) Tropf *m* ▷ *vi* tropfen; (*wall*) triefnass sein
drip-dry ['drɪp'draɪ] *adj* bügelfrei
dripping ['drɪpɪŋ] *n* Bratenfett *nt* ▷ *adj* triefend; **I'm ~** ich bin klatschnass (*inf*); **~ wet** triefnass
drive [draɪv] (*pt* **drove**, *pp* **~n**) *n* Fahrt *f*; (*also*: **driveway**) Einfahrt *f*; (*: longer*) Auffahrt *f*; (*energy*) Schwung *m*, Elan *m*; (*campaign*) Aktion *f*; (*Sport*) Treibschlag *m*; (*Comput*: *also*: **disk drive**) Laufwerk *nt* ▷ *vt* fahren; (*Tech*) antreiben ▷ *vi* fahren; **to go for a ~** ein bisschen (raus)fahren; **it's 3 hours' ~ from London** es ist drei Stunden Fahrt von London (entfernt); **left-/right-hand ~** Links-/Rechtssteuerung *f*; **front-/rear-wheel ~** Vorderrad-/Hinterradantrieb *m*; **he ~s a taxi** er ist Taxifahrer; **to ~ sth into sth** (*nail, stake etc*) etw in etw schlagen *acc*; (*animal*) treiben; (*ball*) weit schlagen; (*incite, encourage*: *also*: **drive on**) antreiben; **to ~ sb home/to the airport** jdn nach Hause/zum Flughafen fahren; **to ~ sb mad** jdn verrückt machen; **to ~ sb to (do) sth** jdn dazu treiben, etw zu tun; **to ~ at 50 km an hour** mit (einer Geschwindigkeit von) 50 Stundenkilometern fahren; **what are you driving at?** worauf wollen Sie hinaus?
▸ **drive off** *vt* vertreiben
▸ **drive out** *vt* (*evil spirit*) austreiben; (*person*) verdrängen
drive-in ['draɪvɪn] (*esp US*) *adj, n*: **~ (cinema)** Autokino *nt*; **~ (restaurant)** Autorestaurant *nt*
drivel ['drɪvl] (*inf*) *n* Blödsinn *m*
driven ['drɪvn] *pp of* **drive**
driver ['draɪvəʳ] *n* Fahrer(in) *m(f)*; (*Rail*) Führer(in) *m(f)*
driver's license ['draɪvəz-] (*US*) *n* Führerschein *m*
driveway ['draɪvweɪ] *n* Einfahrt *f*; (*longer*) Auffahrt *f*
driving ['draɪvɪŋ] *n* Fahren *nt* ▷ *adj*: **~ rain** strömender Regen *m*; **~ snow** Schneetreiben *nt*
driving instructor *n* Fahrlehrer(in) *m(f)*
driving lesson *n* Fahrstunde *f*
driving licence (*Brit*) *n* Führerschein *m*
driving school *n* Fahrschule *f*
driving test *n* Fahrprüfung *f*
drizzle ['drɪzl] *n* Nieselregen *m* ▷ *vi* nieseln
drool [druːl] *vi* sabbern; **to ~ over sth/sb** etw/jdn sehnsüchtig anstarren
droop [druːp] *vi* (*flower*) den Kopf hängen lassen; **his shoulders/head ~ed** er ließ die Schultern/den Kopf herabhängen
drop [drɔp] *n* Tropfen *m*; (*lessening*) Rückgang *m*; (*distance*) Höhenunterschied *m*; (*in salary*) Verschlechterung *f*; (*also*: **parachute drop**) (Ab)sprung *m* ▷ *vt* fallen lassen; (*voice, eyes, price*) senken; (*set down from car*) absetzen; (*omit*) weglassen ▷ *vi* (herunter)fallen; (*wind*) sich legen; **drops** *npl* Tropfen *pl*; **a 300 ft ~** ein Höhenunterschied von 300 Fuß; **a ~ of 10%** ein Rückgang um 10%; **cough ~s** Hustentropfen *pl*; **to ~ anchor** ankern, vor Anker gehen; **to ~ sb a line** jdm ein paar Zeilen schreiben
▸ **drop in** (*inf*) *vi*: **to ~ in (on sb)** (bei jdm) vorbeikommen
▸ **drop off** *vi* einschlafen ▷ *vt* (*passenger*) absetzen
▸ **drop out** *vi* (*withdraw*) ausscheiden; (*student*) sein Studium abbrechen
dropout ['drɔpaut] *n* Aussteiger(in) *m(f)*; (*Scol*) Studienabbrecher(in) *m(f)*
dropper ['drɔpəʳ] *n* Pipette *f*
droppings ['drɔpɪŋz] *npl* Kot *m*
drought [draut] *n* Dürre *f*
drove [drəuv] *pt of* **drive** ▷ *n*: **~s of people** Scharen *pl* von Menschen
drown [draun] *vt* ertränken; (*fig*: *also*: **drown**

out) übertönen ▷ *vi* ertrinken
drowsy ['drauzɪ] *adj* schläfrig
drug [drʌg] *n* Medikament *nt*, Arzneimittel *nt*; (*narcotic*) Droge *f*, Rauschgift *nt* ▷ *vt* betäuben; **to be on ~s** drogensüchtig sein; **hard/soft ~s** harte/weiche Drogen *pl*
drug addict *n* Drogensüchtige(r) *f(m)*, Rauschgiftsüchtige(r) *f(m)*
druggist ['drʌgɪst] (*US*) *n* Drogist(in) *m(f)*
drugstore ['drʌgstɔːʳ] (*US*) *n* Drogerie *f*
drum [drʌm] *n* Trommel *f*; (*for oil, petrol*) Fass *nt* ▷ *vi* trommeln; **drums** *npl* (*kit*) Schlagzeug *nt*
▸ **drum up** *vt* (*enthusiasm*) erwecken; (*support*) auftreiben
drummer ['drʌməʳ] *n* Trommler(in) *m(f)*; (*in band, pop group*) Schlagzeuger(in) *m(f)*
drunk [drʌŋk] *pp of* **drink** ▷ *adj* betrunken ▷ *n* (*also*: **drunkard**) Trinker(in) *m(f)*; **to get ~** sich betrinken; **a ~ driving offence** Trunkenheit *f* am Steuer
drunken ['drʌŋkən] *adj* betrunken; (*party*) feucht-fröhlich; **~ driving** Trunkenheit *f* am Steuer
dry [draɪ] *adj* trocken ▷ *vt, vi* trocknen; **on ~ land** auf festem Boden; **to ~ one's hands/hair/eyes** sich *dat* die Hände (ab)trocknen/die Haare trocknen/die Tränen abwischen; **to ~ the dishes** (das Geschirr) abtrocknen
▸ **dry up** *vi* austrocknen; (*in speech*) den Faden verlieren
dry-cleaning ['draɪ'kliːnɪŋ] *n* (*process*) chemische Reinigung *f*
dryer ['draɪəʳ] *n* Wäschetrockner *m*; (*US: spin-dryer*) Wäscheschleuder *f*
dryness ['draɪnɪs] *n* Trockenheit *f*
dry rot *n* (Haus)schwamm *m*, (Holz)schwamm *m*
DSS (*Brit*) *n abbr* (= *Department of Social Security*) *Ministerium für Sozialfürsorge*
DTP *n abbr* (= *desktop publishing*) DTP *nt*; *see also* **desktop publishing**; (= *diphtheria, tetanus, pertussis*) Diphtherie, Tetanus und Keuchhusten
dual ['djuəl] *adj* doppelt; (*personality*) gespalten
dual carriageway (*Brit*) *n* ≈ Schnellstraße *f*
dual-purpose ['djuəl'pəːpəs] *adj* zweifach verwendbar
dubbed [dʌbd] *adj* synchronisiert; (*nicknamed*) getauft
dubious ['djuːbɪəs] *adj* zweifelhaft; **I'm very ~ about it** ich habe da (doch) starke Zweifel
duchess ['dʌtʃɪs] *n* Herzogin *f*
duck [dʌk] *n* Ente *f* ▷ *vi* (*also*: **duck down**) sich ducken ▷ *vt* (*blow*) ausweichen *+dat*; (*duty, responsibility*) aus dem Weg gehen *+dat*
duckling ['dʌklɪŋ] *n* Entenküken *nt*; (*Culin*) (junge) Ente *f*
duct [dʌkt] *n* Rohr *nt*; (*Anat*) Röhre *f*; **tear ~** Tränenkanal *m*
dud [dʌd] *n* Niete *f* (*inf*); (*note*) Blüte *f* (*inf*) ▷ *adj*: **~ cheque** (*Brit*) ungedeckter Scheck *m*
due [djuː] *adj* fällig; (*attention etc*) gebührend; (*consideration*) reiflich ▷ *n*: **to give sb his/her ~** jdn gerecht behandeln ▷ *adv*: **~ north** direkt nach Norden; **dues** *npl* Beitrag *m*; (*in harbour*) Gebühren *pl*; **in ~ course** zu gegebener Zeit; (*eventually*) im Laufe der Zeit; **~ to** (*owing to*) wegen *+gen*, aufgrund *+gen*; **to be ~ to do sth** etw tun sollen; **the rent is ~ on the 30th** die Miete ist am 30. fällig; **the train is ~ at 8** der Zug soll (laut Fahrplan) um 8 ankommen; **she is ~ back tomorrow** sie müsste morgen zurück sein; **I am ~ 6 days' leave** mir stehen 6 Tage Urlaub zu
duel ['djuəl] *n* Duell *nt*
duet [djuː'ɛt] *n* Duett *nt*
duffel bag ['dʌfl-] *n* Matchbeutel *m*
duffel coat *n* Dufflecoat *m*
dug [dʌg] *pt, pp of* **dig**
duke [djuːk] *n* Herzog *m*
dull [dʌl] *adj* trüb; (*intelligence, wit*) schwerfällig, langsam; (*event*) langweilig; (*sound, pain*) dumpf ▷ *vt* (*pain, grief*) betäuben; (*mind, senses*) abstumpfen
duly ['djuːlɪ] *adv* (*properly*) gebührend; (*on time*) pünktlich
dumb [dʌm] *adj* stumm; (*pej: stupid*) dumm, doof (*inf*); **he was struck ~** es verschlug ihm die Sprache
▸ **dumb down** *vi* an Niveau *or* Qualität verlieren, verflachen ▷ *vt fus* verdummen, dumm machen
dumbfounded [dʌm'faundɪd] *adj* verblüfft
dummy ['dʌmɪ] *n* (Schneider)puppe *f*; (*mock-up*) Attrappe *f*; (*Sport*) Finte *f*; (*Brit: for baby*) Schnuller *m* ▷ *adj* (*firm*) fiktiv; **~ bullets** Übungsmunition *f*
dump [dʌmp] *n* (*also*: **rubbish dump**) Abfallhaufen *m*; (*inf: place*) Müllkippe *f*; (*Mil*) Depot *nt* ▷ *vt* fallen lassen; (*get rid of*) abladen; (*car*) abstellen; (*Comput: data*) ausgeben; **to be down in the ~s** (*inf*) deprimiert *or* down sein; **"no ~ing"** "Schuttabladen verboten"
dumpling ['dʌmplɪŋ] *n* Kloß *m*, Knödel *m*
dumpy ['dʌmpɪ] *adj* pummelig
dunce [dʌns] *n* Niete *f*
dune [djuːn] *n* Düne *f*
dung [dʌŋ] *n* (*Agr*) Dünger *m*, Mist *m*; (*Zool*) Dung *m*
dungarees [dʌŋgə'riːz] *npl* Latzhose *f*
dungeon ['dʌndʒən] *n* Kerker *m*, Verlies *nt*
duplex ['djuːplɛks] (*US*) *n* Zweifamilienhaus *nt*; (*apartment*) zweistöckige Wohnung *f*
duplicate [*n, adj* 'djuːplɪkət, *vt* 'djuːplɪkeɪt] *n* (*also*: **duplicate copy**) Duplikat *nt*, Kopie *f*; (*also*: **duplicate key**) Zweitschlüssel *m* ▷ *adj* doppelt ▷ *vt* kopieren; (*repeat*) wiederholen; **in ~** in doppelter Ausfertigung
durable ['djuərəbl] *adj* haltbar
duration [djuə'reɪʃən] *n* Dauer *f*
during ['djuərɪŋ] *prep* während *+gen*
dusk [dʌsk] *n* (Abend)dämmerung *f*
dust [dʌst] *n* Staub *m* ▷ *vt* abstauben; (*cake etc*): **to ~ with** bestäuben mit
▸ **dust off** *vt* abwischen, wegwischen; (*fig*)

hervorkramen
dustbin ['dʌstbɪn] (*Brit*) *n* Mülltonne *f*
duster ['dʌstəʳ] *n* Staubtuch *nt*
dustman ['dʌstmən] (*Brit irreg: like* **man**) *n* Müllmann *m*
dustpan ['dʌstpæn] *n* Kehrschaufel *f*, Müllschaufel *f*
dusty ['dʌstɪ] *adj* staubig
Dutch [dʌtʃ] *adj* holländisch, niederländisch ▷ *n* Holländisch *nt*, Niederländisch *nt* ▷ *adv*: **to go ~** (*inf*) getrennte Kasse machen; **the Dutch** *npl* die Holländer *pl*, die Niederländer *pl*
Dutchman ['dʌtʃmən] (*irreg: like* **man**) *n* Holländer *m*, Niederländer *m*
Dutchwoman ['dʌtʃwumən] (*irreg: like* **woman**) *n* Holländerin *f*, Niederländerin *f*
duty ['dju:tɪ] *n* Pflicht *f*; (*tax*) Zoll *m*; **duties** *npl* (*functions*) Aufgaben *pl*; **to make it one's ~ to do sth** es sich *dat* zur Pflicht machen, etw zu tun; **to pay ~ on sth** Zoll auf etw *acc* zahlen; **on/off ~** im/nicht im Dienst
duty-free ['dju:tɪ'fri:] *adj* zollfrei; **~ shop** Dutyfreeshop *m*, Duty-free-Shop *m*
duvet ['du:veɪ] (*Brit*) *n* Federbett *nt*
DVD *n abbr* (= *digital versatile or video disc*) DVD *f*
dwarf [dwɔ:f] (*pl* **dwarves**) *n* Zwerg(in) *m(f)* ▷ *vt*: **to be ~ed by sth** neben etw *dat* klein erscheinen
dwell [dwɛl] (*pt, pp* **dwelt**) *vi* wohnen, leben ▶ **dwell on** *vt fus* (in Gedanken) verweilen bei
dwelt [dwɛlt] *pt, pp of* **dwell**
dwindle ['dwɪndl] *vi* abnehmen; (*interest*) schwinden; (*attendance*) zurückgehen
dye [daɪ] *n* Farbstoff *m*; (*for hair*) Färbemittel *nt* ▷ *vt* färben
dying ['daɪɪŋ] *adj* sterbend; (*moments, words*) letzte(r, s)
dyke [daɪk] *n* (*Brit: wall*) Deich *m*, Damm *m*; (*channel*) (Entwässerungs)graben *m*; (*causeway*) Fahrdamm *m*
dynamic [daɪ'næmɪk] *adj* dynamisch
dynamite ['daɪnəmaɪt] *n* Dynamit *nt* ▷ *vt* sprengen
dynamo ['daɪnəməu] *n* Dynamo *m*; (*Aut*) Lichtmaschine *f*
dyslexia [dɪs'lɛksɪə] *n* Legasthenie *f*
dyslexic [dɪs'lɛksɪk] *adj* legasthenisch ▷ *n* Legastheniker(in) *m(f)*

Ee

E¹, e [iː] *n* (*letter*) E *nt*, e *nt*; **E for Edward, E for Easy** (*US*) E wie Emil

E² [iː] *n* (*Mus*) E *nt*, e *nt*

E³ [iː] *abbr* (= *east*) O ▷ *n abbr* (*drug*: = *Ecstasy*) Ecstasy *nt*

each [iːtʃ] *adj, pron* jede(r, s); **~ other** sich, einander; **they hate ~ other** sie hassen sich *or* einander; **you are jealous of ~ other** ihr seid eifersüchtig aufeinander; **~ day** jeden Tag; **they have 2 books ~** sie haben je 2 Bücher; **they cost £5 ~** sie kosten 5 Pfund das Stück; **~ of us** jede(r, s) von uns

eager [ˈiːgəʳ] *adj* eifrig; **to be ~ to do sth** etw unbedingt tun wollen; **to be ~ for sth** auf etw *acc* erpicht *or* aus (*inf*) sein

eagle [ˈiːgl] *n* Adler *m*

ear [ɪəʳ] *n* Ohr *nt*; (*of corn*) Ähre *f*; **to be up to one's ~s in debt/work** bis über beide Ohren in Schulden/Arbeit stecken; **to be up to one's ~s in paint/baking** mitten im Anstreichen/Backen stecken; **to give sb a thick ~** jdm ein paar hinter die Ohren geben; **we'll play it by ~** (*fig*) wir werden es auf uns zukommen lassen

earache [ˈɪəreɪk] *n* Ohrenschmerzen *pl*

eardrum [ˈɪədrʌm] *n* Trommelfell *nt*

earl [əːl] (*Brit*) *n* Graf *m*

earlier [ˈəːlɪəʳ] *adj, adv* früher; **I can't come any ~** ich kann nicht früher *or* eher kommen

early [ˈəːlɪ] *adv* früh; (*ahead of time*) zu früh ▷ *adj* früh; (*Christians*) Ur-; (*death, departure*) vorzeitig; (*reply*) baldig; **~ in the morning** früh am Morgen; **to have an ~ night** früh ins Bett gehen; **in the ~ hours** in den frühen Morgenstunden; **in the ~** *or* **~ in the spring/19th century** Anfang des Frühjahrs/des 19. Jahrhunderts; **take the ~ train** nimm den früheren Zug; **you're ~!** Sie sind früh dran!; **she's in her ~ forties** sie ist Anfang Vierzig; **at your earliest convenience** so bald wie möglich

early retirement *n*: **to take ~** vorzeitig in den Ruhestand gehen

earmark [ˈɪəmɑːk] *vt*: **to ~ (for)** bestimmen (für), vorsehen (für)

earn [əːn] *vt* verdienen; (*interest*) bringen; **to ~ one's living** seinen Lebensunterhalt verdienen; **this ~ed him much praise, he ~ed much praise for this** das trug ihm viel Lob ein; **he's ~ed his rest/reward** er hat sich seine Pause/Belohnung verdient

earnest [ˈəːnɪst] *adj* ernsthaft; (*wish, desire*) innig ▷ *n* (*also*: **earnest money**) Angeld *nt*; **in ~** (*adv*) richtig; (*adj*): **to be in ~** es ernst meinen; **work on the tunnel soon began in ~** die Tunnelarbeiten begannen bald richtig; **is the Minister in ~ about these proposals?** meint der Minister diese Vorschläge ernst?

earnings [ˈəːnɪŋz] *npl* Verdienst *m*; (*of company etc*) Ertrag *m*

earphones [ˈɪəfəunz] *npl* Kopfhörer *pl*

earplugs [ˈɪəplʌgz] *npl* Ohropax® *nt*

earring [ˈɪərɪŋ] *n* Ohrring *m*

earshot [ˈɪəʃɔt] *n*: **within/out of ~** in/außer Hörweite

earth [əːθ] *n* Erde *f*; (*of fox*) Bau *m* ▷ *vt* (*Brit*: *Elec*) erden

earthenware [ˈəːθnwɛəʳ] *n* Tongeschirr *nt* ▷ *adj* Ton-

earthquake [ˈəːθkweɪk] *n* Erdbeben *nt*

earthy [ˈəːθɪ] *adj* (*humour*) derb

ease [iːz] *n* Leichtigkeit *f*; (*comfort*) Behagen *nt* ▷ *vt* (*problem*) vereinfachen; (*pain*) lindern; (*tension*) verringern; (*loosen*) lockern ▷ *vi* nachlassen; (*situation*) sich entspannen; **to ~ sth in/out** (*push/pull*) etw behutsam hineinschieben/herausziehen; **at ~!** (*Mil*) rührt euch!; **with ~** mit Leichtigkeit; **life of ~** Leben *nt* der Muße; **to ~ in the clutch** die Kupplung behutsam kommen lassen

▸ **ease off** *vi* nachlassen; (*slow down*) langsamer werden

▸ **ease up** *vi* = **ease off**

easel [ˈiːzl] *n* Staffelei *f*

easily [ˈiːzɪlɪ] *adv* (*see adj*) leicht; ungezwungen; bequem

east [iːst] *n* Osten *m* ▷ *adj* (*coast, Asia etc*) Ost- ▷ *adv* ostwärts, nach Osten; **the E~** der Osten

Easter [ˈiːstəʳ] *n* Ostern *nt* ▷ *adj* (*holidays etc*) Oster-

Easter egg *n* Osterei *nt*

easterly [ˈiːstəlɪ] *adj* östlich; (*wind*) Ost-

eastern [ˈiːstən] *adj* östlich; **E~ Europe** Osteuropa *nt*; **the E~ bloc** (*formerly*) der Ostblock

Easter Sunday *n* Ostersonntag *m*

eastward ['i:stwəd], **eastwards** ['i:stwədz] *adv* ostwärts, nach Osten
easy ['i:zɪ] *adj* leicht; (*relaxed*) ungezwungen; (*comfortable*) bequem ▷ *adv*: **to take it/things ~** (*go slowly*) sich *dat* Zeit lassen; (*not worry*) es nicht so schwernehmen; (*rest*) sich schonen; **payment on ~ terms** Zahlung zu günstigen Bedingungen; **that's easier said than done** das ist leichter gesagt als getan; **I'm ~** (*inf*) mir ist alles recht
easy chair *n* Sessel *m*
easy-going ['i:zɪ'gəuɪŋ] *adj* gelassen
eat [i:t] (*pt* **ate**, *pp* **~en**) *vt*, *vi* essen; (*animal*) fressen
▸ **eat away** *vt* (*subj*: *sea*) auswaschen; (: *acid*) zerfressen
▸ **eat away at** *vt fus* (*metal*) anfressen; (*savings*) angreifen
▸ **eat into** *vt fus* = **eat away at**
▸ **eat out** *vi* essen gehen
▸ **eat up** *vt* aufessen; **it ~s up electricity** es verbraucht viel Strom
eaves [i:vz] *npl* Dachvorsprung *m*
eavesdrop ['i:vzdrɔp] *vi* lauschen; **to ~ on** belauschen *+acc*
ebb [ɛb] *n* Ebbe *f* ▷ *vi* ebben; (*fig*: *also*: **ebb away**) dahinschwinden; (: *feeling*) abebben; **the ~ and flow** (*fig*) das Auf und Ab; **to be at a low ~** (*fig*) auf einem Tiefpunkt angelangt sein
ebony ['ɛbənɪ] *n* Ebenholz *nt*
ECB *n abbr* (= *European Central Bank*) EZB *f*
eccentric [ɪk'sɛntrɪk] *adj* exzentrisch ▷ *n* Exzentriker(in) *m(f)*
echo ['ɛkəu] (*pl* **~es**) *n* Echo *nt* ▷ *vt* wiederholen ▷ *vi* widerhallen; (*place*) hallen
eclipse [ɪ'klɪps] *n* Finsternis *f* ▷ *vt* in den Schatten stellen
ecological [i:kə'lɔdʒɪkəl] *adj* ökologisch; (*damage*, *disaster*) Umwelt-
ecology [ɪ'kɔlədʒɪ] *n* Ökologie *f*
e-commerce [i:'kɔmə:s] *n* E-Commerce *nt*, elektronischer Handel
economic [i:kə'nɔmɪk] *adj* (*system*, *policy etc*) Wirtschafts-; (*profitable*) wirtschaftlich
economical [i:kə'nɔmɪkl] *adj* wirtschaftlich; (*person*) sparsam
economics [i:kə'nɔmɪks] *n* Wirtschaftswissenschaften *pl* ▷ *npl* Wirtschaftlichkeit *f*; (*of situation*) wirtschaftliche Seite *f*
economist [ɪ'kɔnəmɪst] *n* Wirtschaftswissen schaftler(in) *m(f)*
economize [ɪ'kɔnəmaɪz] *vi* sparen
economy [ɪ'kɔnəmɪ] *n* Wirtschaft *f*; (*financial prudence*) Sparsamkeit *f*; **economies of scale** (*Comm*) Einsparungen *pl* durch erhöhte Produktion
economy class *n* Touristenklasse *f*
economy size *n* Sparpackung *f*
ecstasy ['ɛkstəsɪ] *n* Ekstase *f*; (*drug*) Ecstasy *nt*; **to go into ecstasies over** in Verzückung geraten über *+acc*; **in ~** verzückt
ecstatic [ɛks'tætɪk] *adj* ekstatisch
eczema ['ɛksɪmə] *n* Ekzem *nt*
edge [ɛdʒ] *n* Rand *m*; (*of table*, *chair*) Kante *f*; (*of lake*) Ufer *nt*; (*of knife etc*) Schneide *f* ▷ *vt* einfassen ▷ *vi*: **to ~ forward** sich nach vorne schieben; **on ~** (*fig*) = **edgy**; **to have the ~ on** überlegen sein *+dat*; **to ~ away from** sich allmählich entfernen von; **to ~ past** sich vorbeischieben, sich vorbeidrücken
edgeways ['ɛdʒweɪz] *adv*: **he couldn't get a word in ~** er kam überhaupt nicht zu Wort
edgy ['ɛdʒɪ] *adj* nervös
edible ['ɛdɪbl] *adj* essbar, genießbar
Edinburgh ['ɛdɪnbərə] *n* Edinburg(h) *nt*
edit ['ɛdɪt] *vt* (*text*) redigieren; (*book*) lektorieren; (*film*, *broadcast*) schneiden, cutten; (*newspaper*, *magazine*) herausgeben; (*Comput*) editieren
edition [ɪ'dɪʃən] *n* Ausgabe *f*
editor ['ɛdɪtə^r] *n* Redakteur(in) *m(f)*; (*of newspaper*, *magazine*) Herausgeber(in) *m(f)*; (*of book*) Lektor(in) *m(f)*; (*Cine*, *Radio*, *TV*) Cutter(in) *m(f)*
editorial [ɛdɪ'tɔ:rɪəl] *adj* redaktionell; (*staff*) Redaktions- ▷ *n* Leitartikel *m*
educate ['ɛdjukeɪt] *vt* erziehen; **~d at ...** zur Schule/Universität gegangen in ...
educated ['ɛdjukeɪtɪd] *adj* gebildet
education [ɛdju'keɪʃən] *n* Erziehung *f*; (*schooling*) Ausbildung *f*; (*knowledge*, *culture*) Bildung *f*; **primary ~**, **elementary ~** (*US*) Grundschul(aus)bildung *f*; **secondary ~** höhere Schul(aus)bildung *f*
educational [ɛdju'keɪʃənl] *adj* pädagogisch; (*experience*) lehrreich; (*toy*) pädagogisch wertvoll; **~ technology** Unterrichtstechnologie *f*
eel [i:l] *n* Aal *m*
eerie ['ɪərɪ] *adj* unheimlich
effect [ɪ'fɛkt] *n* Wirkung *f*, Effekt *m* ▷ *vt* bewirken; (*repairs*) durchführen; **effects** *npl* Effekten *pl*; (*Theat*, *Cine etc*) Effekte *pl*; **to take ~** (*law*) in Kraft treten; (*drug*) wirken; **to put into ~** in Kraft setzen; **to have an ~ on sb/sth** eine Wirkung auf jdn/etw haben; **in ~** eigentlich, praktisch; **his letter is to the ~ that ...** sein Brief hat zum Inhalt, dass ...
effective [ɪ'fɛktɪv] *adj* effektiv, wirksam; (*actual*) eigentlich, wirklich; **to become ~** in Kraft treten; **~ date** Zeitpunkt *m* des Inkrafttretens
effectively [ɪ'fɛktɪvlɪ] *adv* effektiv
effectiveness [ɪ'fɛktɪvnɪs] *n* Wirksamkeit *f*, Effektivität *f*
effeminate [ɪ'fɛmɪnɪt] *adj* feminin, effeminiert
effervescent [ɛfə'vɛsnt] *adj* sprudelnd
efficiency [ɪ'fɪʃənsɪ] *n* (*see adj*) Fähigkeit *f*, Tüchtigkeit *f*; Rationalität *f*; Leistungsfähigkeit *f*
efficient [ɪ'fɪʃənt] *adj* fähig, tüchtig; (*organization*) rationell; (*machine*) leistungsfähig

efficiently [ɪ'fɪʃəntlɪ] *adv* gut, effizient
effort ['ɛfət] *n* Anstrengung *f*; (*attempt*) Versuch *m*; **to make an ~ to do sth** sich bemühen, etw zu tun
effortless ['ɛfətlɪs] *adj* mühelos; (*style*) flüssig
effusive [ɪ'fju:sɪv] *adj* überschwänglich
e.g. *adv abbr* (*= exempli gratia*) z. B.
egg [ɛg] *n* Ei *nt*; **hard-boiled/soft-boiled ~** hart/weich gekochtes Ei *nt*
▸ **egg on** *vt* anstacheln
eggshell ['ɛgʃɛl] *n* Eierschale *f* ▹ *adj* eierschalenfarben
egg white *n* Eiweiß *nt*
egg yolk *n* Eigelb *nt*
ego ['i:gəu] *n* (*self-esteem*) Selbstbewusstsein *nt*
egotism ['ɛgəutɪzəm] *n* Ichbezogenheit *f*, Egotismus *m*
egotist ['ɛgəutɪst] *n* ichbezogener Mensch *m*, Egotist(in) *m(f)*
Egypt ['i:dʒɪpt] *n* Ägypten *nt*
Egyptian [ɪ'dʒɪpʃən] *adj* ägyptisch ▹ *n* Ägypter(in) *m(f)*
eiderdown ['aɪdədaun] *n* Federbett *nt*, Daunendecke *f*
eight [eɪt] *num* acht
eighteen [eɪ'ti:n] *num* achtzehn
eighteenth [eɪ'ti:nθ] *num* achtzehnte(r, s)
eighth [eɪtθ] *num* achte(r, s) ▹ *n* Achtel *nt*
eighty ['eɪtɪ] *num* achtzig
Eire ['ɛərə] *n* (Republik *f*) Irland *nt*
either ['aɪðəʳ] *adj* (*one or other*) eine(r, s) (von beiden); (*both, each*) beide *pl*, jede(r, s) ▹ *pron*: **~ (of them)** eine(r, s) (davon) ▹ *adv* auch nicht ▹ *conj*: **~ yes or no** entweder ja oder nein; **on ~ side** (*on both sides*) auf beiden Seiten; (*on one or other side*) auf einer der beiden Seiten; **I don't like ~** ich mag beide nicht *or* keinen von beiden; **no, I don't ~** nein, ich auch nicht; **I haven't seen ~ one or the other** ich habe weder den einen noch den anderen gesehen
eject [ɪ'dʒɛkt] *vt* ausstoßen; (*tenant, gatecrasher*) hinauswerfen ▹ *vi* den Schleudersitz betätigen
elaborate [*adj* ɪ'læbərɪt, *vb* ɪ'læbəreɪt] *adj* kompliziert; (*plan*) ausgefeilt ▹ *vt* näher ausführen; (*refine*) ausarbeiten ▹ *vi* mehr ins Detail gehen; **to ~ on** näher ausführen
elastic [ɪ'læstɪk] *n* Gummi *nt* ▹ *adj* elastisch
elastic band (*Brit*) *n* Gummiband *nt*
elated [ɪ'leɪtɪd] *adj*: **to be ~** hocherfreut *or* in Hochstimmung sein
elation [ɪ'leɪʃən] *n* große Freude *f*, Hochstimmung *f*
elbow ['ɛlbəu] *n* Ell(en)bogen *m* ▹ *vt*: **to ~ one's way through the crowd** sich durch die Menge boxen
elder ['ɛldəʳ] *adj* älter ▹ *n* (*Bot*) Holunder *m*; (*older person: gen pl*) Ältere(r) *f(m)*
elderly ['ɛldəlɪ] *adj* ältere(r, s) ▹ *npl*: **the ~** ältere Leute *pl*
eldest ['ɛldɪst] *adj* älteste(r, s) ▹ *n* Älteste(r) *f(m)*
elect [ɪ'lɛkt] *vt* wählen ▹ *adj*: **the president ~** der designierte *or* künftige Präsident; **to ~ to do sth** sich dafür entscheiden, etw zu tun
election [ɪ'lɛkʃən] *n* Wahl *f*; **to hold an ~** eine Wahl abhalten
electioneering [ɪlɛkʃə'nɪərɪŋ] *n* Wahlkampf *m*
elector [ɪ'lɛktəʳ] *n* Wähler(in) *m(f)*
electoral [ɪ'lɛktərəl] *adj* Wähler-
electorate [ɪ'lɛktərɪt] *n* Wähler *pl*, Wählerschaft *f*
electric [ɪ'lɛktrɪk] *adj* elektrisch
electrical [ɪ'lɛktrɪkl] *adj* elektrisch; (*appliance*) Elektro-; (*failure*) Strom-
electric blanket *n* Heizdecke *f*
electric fire (*Brit*) *n* elektrisches Heizgerät *nt*
electrician [ɪlɛk'trɪʃən] *n* Elektriker(in) *m(f)*
electricity [ɪlɛk'trɪsɪtɪ] *n* Elektrizität *f*; (*supply*) (elektrischer) Strom *m* ▹ *cpd* Strom-; **to switch on/off the ~** den Strom an-/abschalten
electric shock *n* elektrischer Schlag *m*, Stromschlag *m*
electrify [ɪ'lɛktrɪfaɪ] *vt* (*fence*) unter Strom setzen; (*rail network*) elektrifizieren; (*audience*) elektrisieren
electronic [ɪlɛk'trɔnɪk] *adj* elektronisch
electronic mail *n* elektronische Post *f*
electronics [ɪlɛk'trɔnɪks] *n* Elektronik *f*
elegance ['ɛlɪgəns] *n* Eleganz *f*
elegant ['ɛlɪgənt] *adj* elegant
element ['ɛlɪmənt] *n* Element *nt*; (*of heater, kettle etc*) Heizelement *nt*
elementary [ɛlɪ'mɛntərɪ] *adj* grundlegend; **~ school** Grundschule *f*; **~ education** Elementarunterricht *m*; **~ maths/French** Grundbegriffe *pl* der Mathematik/des Französischen
elephant ['ɛlɪfənt] *n* Elefant *m*
elevate ['ɛlɪveɪt] *vt* erheben; (*physically*) heben
elevation [ɛlɪ'veɪʃən] *n* Erhebung *f*; (*height*) Höhe *f* über dem Meeresspiegel; (*Archit*) Aufriss *m*
elevator ['ɛlɪveɪtəʳ] *n* (*US*) Aufzug *m*, Fahrstuhl *m*; (*in warehouse etc*) Lastenaufzug *m*
eleven [ɪ'lɛvn] *num* elf
elevenses [ɪ'lɛvnzɪz] (*Brit*) *npl* zweites Frühstück *nt*
eleventh [ɪ'lɛvnθ] *num* elfte(r, s); **at the ~ hour** (*fig*) in letzter Minute
elicit [ɪ'lɪsɪt] *vt*: **to ~ (from sb)** (*information*) (aus jdm) herausbekommen; (*reaction, response*) (von jdm) bekommen
eligible ['ɛlɪdʒəbl] *adj* (*marriage partner*) begehrt; **to be ~ for sth** für etw infrage kommen; **to be ~ for a pension** pensionsberechtigt sein
eliminate [ɪ'lɪmɪneɪt] *vt* beseitigen; (*candidate etc*) ausschließen; (*team, contestant*) aus dem Wettbewerb werfen
elm [ɛlm] *n* Ulme *f*
elongated ['i:lɔŋgeɪtɪd] *adj* lang gestreckt; (*shadow*) verlängert

elope [ɪ'ləup] *vi* weglaufen
eloquent ['ɛləkwənt] *adj* beredt, wortgewandt; (*speech, description*) ausdrucksvoll
else [ɛls] *adv* andere(r, s); **something ~** etwas anderes; **somewhere ~** woanders, anderswo; **everywhere ~** sonst überall; **where ~?** wo sonst?; **is there anything ~ I can do?** kann ich sonst noch etwas tun?; **there was little ~ to do** es gab nicht viel anderes zu tun; **everyone ~** alle anderen; **nobody ~ spoke** niemand anders sagte etwas, sonst sagte niemand etwas
elsewhere [ɛls'wɛəʳ] *adv* woanders, anderswo; (*go*) woandershin, anderswohin
elude [ɪ'lu:d] *vt* (*captor*) entkommen *+dat*; (*capture*) sich entziehen *+dat*; **this fact/idea ~d him** diese Tatsache/Idee entging ihm
elusive [ɪ'lu:sɪv] *adj* schwer zu fangen; (*quality*) unerreichbar; **he's very ~** er ist sehr schwer zu erreichen
emaciated [ɪ'meɪsɪeɪtɪd] *adj* abgezehrt, ausgezehrt
emancipate [ɪ'mænsɪpeɪt] *vt* (*women*) emanzipieren; (*poor*) befreien; (*slave*) freilassen
embankment [ɪm'bæŋkmənt] *n* Böschung *f*; (*of railway*) Bahndamm *m*; (*of river*) Damm *m*
embargo [ɪm'bɑ:gəu] (*pl* **~es**) *n* Embargo *nt* ▷ *vt* mit einem Embargo belegen; **to put** *or* **impose** *or* **place an ~ on sth** ein Embargo über etw *acc* verhängen; **to lift an ~** ein Embargo aufheben
embark [ɪm'bɑ:k] *vt* einschiffen ▷ *vi*: **to ~ (on)** sich einschiffen (auf); **to ~ on** (*journey*) beginnen; (*task*) in Angriff nehmen; (*course of action*) einschlagen
embarkation [ɛmbɑ:'keɪʃən] *n* Einschiffung *f*
embarrass [ɪm'bærəs] *vt* in Verlegenheit bringen
embarrassed [ɪm'bærəst] *adj* verlegen
embarrassing [ɪm'bærəsɪŋ] *adj* peinlich
embarrassment [ɪm'bærəsmənt] *n* Verlegenheit *f*; (*embarrassing problem*) Peinlichkeit *f*
embassy ['ɛmbəsɪ] *n* Botschaft *f*; **the Swiss E~** die Schweizer Botschaft
embellish [ɪm'bɛlɪʃ] *vt* (*account*) ausschmücken; **to be ~ed with** geschmückt sein mit
embers ['ɛmbəz] *npl* Glut *f*
embezzle [ɪm'bɛzl] *vt* unterschlagen
embezzlement [ɪm'bɛzlmənt] *n* Unterschlagung *f*
embitter [ɪm'bɪtəʳ] *vt* verbittern
embody [ɪm'bɔdɪ] *vt* verkörpern; (*include, contain*) enthalten
embossed [ɪm'bɔst] *adj* geprägt; **~ with a logo** mit geprägtem Logo
embrace [ɪm'breɪs] *vt* umarmen; (*include*) umfassen ▷ *vi* sich umarmen ▷ *n* Umarmung *f*
embroider [ɪm'brɔɪdəʳ] *vt* (*cloth*) besticken; (*fig: story*) ausschmücken
embroidery [ɪm'brɔɪdərɪ] *n* Stickerei *f*; (*activity*) Sticken *nt*
embryo ['ɛmbrɪəu] *n* Embryo *m*; (*fig*) Keim *m*
emerald ['ɛmərəld] *n* Smaragd *m*
emerge [ɪ'mə:dʒ] *vi*: **to ~ (from)** auftauchen (aus); (*from sleep*) erwachen (aus); (*from imprisonment*) entlassen werden (aus); (*from discussion etc*) sich herausstellen (bei); (*new idea, industry, society*) entstehen (aus); **it ~s that** (*Brit*) es stellt sich heraus, dass
emergency [ɪ'mə:dʒənsɪ] *n* Notfall *m* ▷ *cpd* Not-; (*repair*) notdürftig; **in an ~** im Notfall; **state of ~** Notstand *m*
emergency exit *n* Notausgang *m*
emergency landing *n* Notlandung *f*
emergency services *npl*: **the ~** der Notdienst
emery board ['ɛmərɪ-] *n* Papiernagelfeile *f*
emigrate ['ɛmɪgreɪt] *vi* auswandern, emigrieren
emigration [ɛmɪ'greɪʃən] *n* Auswanderung *f*, Emigration *f*
eminent ['ɛmɪnənt] *adj* bedeutend
emissions [ɪ'mɪʃənz] *npl* Emissionen *pl*
emit [ɪ'mɪt] *vt* abgeben; (*smell*) ausströmen; (*light, heat*) ausstrahlen
emotion [ɪ'məuʃən] *n* Gefühl *nt*
emotional [ɪ'məuʃənl] *adj* emotional; (*exhaustion*) seelisch; (*scene*) ergreifend; (*speech*) gefühlsbetont
emotive [ɪ'məutɪv] *adj* emotional
emperor ['ɛmpərəʳ] *n* Kaiser *m*
emphasis ['ɛmfəsɪs] (*pl* **emphases**) *n* Betonung *f*; (*importance*) (Schwer)gewicht *nt*; **to lay** *or* **place ~ on sth** etw betonen; **the ~ is on reading** das Schwergewicht liegt auf dem Lesen
emphasize ['ɛmfəsaɪz] *vt* betonen; (*feature*) hervorheben; **I must ~ that ...** ich möchte betonen, dass ...
emphatic [ɛm'fætɪk] *adj* nachdrücklich; (*denial*) energisch; (*person, manner*) bestimmt, entschieden
empire ['ɛmpaɪəʳ] *n* Reich *nt*
employ [ɪm'plɔɪ] *vt* beschäftigen; (*tool, weapon*) verwenden; **he's ~ed in a bank** er ist bei einer Bank angestellt
employee [ɪmplɔɪ'i:] *n* Angestellte(r) *f(m)*
employer [ɪm'plɔɪəʳ] *n* Arbeitgeber(in) *m(f)*
employment [ɪm'plɔɪmənt] *n* Arbeit *f*; **to find ~** Arbeit *or* eine (An)stellung finden; **without ~** stellungslos; **your place of ~** Ihre Arbeitsstätte *f*
employment agency *n* Stellenvermittlung *f*
empower [ɪm'pauəʳ] *vt*: **to ~ sb to do sth** jdn ermächtigen, etw zu tun
empress ['ɛmprɪs] *n* Kaiserin *f*
emptiness ['ɛmptɪnɪs] *n* Leere *f*
empty ['ɛmptɪ] *adj* leer; (*house, room*) leer stehend; (*space*) frei ▷ *vt* leeren; (*place, house etc*) räumen ▷ *vi* sich leeren; (*liquid*) abfließen; (*river*) münden; **on an ~ stomach** auf nüchternen Magen; **to ~ into** (*river*)

münden *or* sich ergießen in *+acc*

empty-handed ['ɛmptɪ'hændɪd] *adj* mit leeren Händen; **he returned ~** er kehrte unverrichteter Dinge zurück

EMU *n abbr* (*= Economic and Monetary Union*) EWU *f*

emulate ['ɛmjuleɪt] *vt* nacheifern *+dat*

emulsion [ɪ'mʌlʃən] *n* Emulsion *f*; (*also*: **emulsion paint**) Emulsionsfarbe *f*

enable [ɪ'neɪbl] *vt*: **to ~ sb to do sth** (*permit*) es jdm erlauben, etw zu tun; (*make possible*) es jdm ermöglichen, etw zu tun

enamel [ɪ'næməl] *n* Email *nt*, Emaille *f*; (*also*: **enamel paint**) Email(le)lack *m*; (*of tooth*) Zahnschmelz *m*

enchant [ɪn'tʃɑ:nt] *vt* bezaubern

enchanting [ɪn'tʃɑ:ntɪŋ] *adj* bezaubernd

encl. *abbr* (*on letters etc: = enclosed, enclosure*) Anl.

enclose [ɪn'kləuz] *vt* umgeben; (*land, space*) begrenzen; (*with fence*) einzäunen; (*letter etc*): **to ~ (with)** beilegen (*+dat*); **please find ~d** als Anlage übersenden wir Ihnen

enclosure [ɪn'kləuʒə^r] *n* eingefriedeter Bereich *m*; (*in letter etc*) Anlage *f*

encompass [ɪn'kʌmpəs] *vt* umfassen

encore [ɔŋ'kɔ:^r] *excl* Zugabe! ▷ *n* Zugabe *f*

encounter [ɪn'kauntə^r] *n* Begegnung *f* ▷ *vt* begegnen *+dat*; (*problem*) stoßen auf *+acc*

encourage [ɪn'kʌrɪdʒ] *vt* (*activity, attitude*) unterstützen; (*growth, industry*) fördern; **to ~ sb (to do sth)** jdn ermutigen(, etw zu tun)

encouragement [ɪn'kʌrɪdʒmənt] *n* (*see vb*) Unterstützung *f*; Förderung *f*; Ermutigung *f*

encouraging [ɪn'kʌrɪdʒɪŋ] *adj* ermutigend

encroach [ɪn'krəutʃ] *vi*: **to ~ (up)on** (*rights*) eingreifen in *+acc*; (*property*) eindringen in *+acc*; (*time*) in Anspruch nehmen

encyclopaedia, **encyclopedia** [ɛnsaɪkləu'pi:dɪə] *n* Lexikon *nt*, Enzyklopädie *f*

end [ɛnd] *n* Ende *nt*; (*of film, book*) Schluss *m*, Ende *nt*; (*of table*) Schmalseite *f*; (*of pointed object*) Spitze *f*; (*aim*) Zweck *m*, Ziel *nt* ▷ *vt* (*also*: **bring to an end, put an end to**) beenden ▷ *vi* enden; **from ~ to end** von einem Ende zum anderen; **to come to an ~** zu Ende gehen; **to be at an ~** zu Ende sein; **in the ~** schließlich; **on ~** hochkant; **to stand on ~** (*hair*) zu Berge stehen; **for hours on ~** stundenlang ununterbrochen; **for 5 hours on ~** 5 Stunden ununterbrochen; **at the ~ of the street** am Ende der Straße; **at the ~ of the day** (*Brit: fig*) letztlich; **to this end, with this ~ in view** mit diesem Ziel vor Augen

▸ **end up** *vi*: **to ~ up in** (*place*) landen in *+dat*; **to ~ up in trouble** Ärger bekommen; **to ~ up doing sth** etw schließlich tun

endanger [ɪn'deɪndʒə^r] *vt* gefährden; **an ~ed species** eine vom Aussterben bedrohte Art

endearing [ɪn'dɪərɪŋ] *adj* gewinnend

endeavour, (*US*) **endeavor** [ɪn'dɛvə^r] *n* Anstrengung *f*, Bemühung *f*; (*effort*) Bestrebung *f* ▷ *vi*: **to ~ to do sth** (*attempt*) sich anstrengen *or* bemühen, etw zu tun; (*strive*) bestrebt sein, etw zu tun

ending ['ɛndɪŋ] *n* Ende *nt*, Schluss *m*; (*Ling*) Endung *f*

endive ['ɛndaɪv] *n* Endivie *f*; (*chicory*) Chicorée *f or m*

endless ['ɛndlɪs] *adj* endlos; (*patience, resources, possibilities*) unbegrenzt

endorse [ɪn'dɔ:s] *vt* (*cheque*) indossieren, auf der Rückseite unterzeichnen; (*proposal, plan*) billigen; (*candidate*) unterstützen

endorsement [ɪn'dɔ:smənt] *n* Billigung *f*; (*of candidate*) Unterstützung *f*; (*Brit: on driving licence*) Strafvermerk *m*

endurance [ɪn'djuərəns] *n* Durchhaltevermögen *nt*; (*patience*) Geduld *f*

endure [ɪn'djuə^r] *vt* ertragen ▷ *vi* Bestand haben

enemy ['ɛnəmɪ] *adj* feindlich; (*strategy*) des Feindes ▷ *n* Feind(in) *m(f)*; **to make an ~ of sb** sich *dat* jdn zum Feind machen

energetic [ɛnə'dʒɛtɪk] *adj* aktiv

energy ['ɛnədʒɪ] *n* Energie *f*; **Department of E~** Energieministerium *nt*

enforce [ɪn'fɔ:s] *vt* (*law, rule, decision*) Geltung verschaffen *+dat*

engage [ɪn'geɪdʒ] *vt* in Anspruch nehmen; (*employ*) einstellen; (*lawyer*) sich *dat* nehmen; (*Mil*) angreifen ▷ *vi* (*Tech*) einrasten; **to ~ the clutch** einkuppeln; **to ~ sb in conversation** jdn in ein Gespräch verwickeln; **to ~ in** sich beteiligen an *+dat*; **to ~ in commerce** kaufmännisch tätig sein; **to ~ in study** studieren

engaged [ɪn'geɪdʒd] *adj* verlobt; (*Brit: busy, in use*) besetzt; **to get ~** sich verloben; **he is ~ in research/a survey** er ist mit Forschungsarbeit/einer Umfrage beschäftigt

engaged tone (*Brit*) *n* Besetztzeichen *nt*

engagement [ɪn'geɪdʒmənt] *n* Verabredung *f*; (*booking*) Engagement *nt*; (*to marry*) Verlobung *f*; (*Mil*) Gefecht *nt*, Kampf *m*; **I have a previous ~** ich habe schon eine Verabredung

engagement ring *n* Verlobungsring *m*

engaging [ɪn'geɪdʒɪŋ] *adj* einnehmend

engine ['ɛndʒɪn] *n* Motor *m*; (*Rail*) Lok(omotive) *f*

engine driver *n* (*Rail*) Lok(omotiv)führer(in) *m(f)*

engineer [ɛndʒɪ'nɪə^r] *n* Ingenieur(in) *m(f)*; (*Brit: for repairs*) Techniker(in) *m(f)*; (*US: Rail*) Lok(omotiv)führer(in) *m(f)*; (*on ship*) Maschinist(in) *m(f)*; **civil/mechanical ~** Bau-/Maschinenbauingenieur(in) *m(f)*

engineering [ɛndʒɪ'nɪərɪŋ] *n* Technik *f*; (*design, construction*) Konstruktion *f* ▷ *cpd*: **~ works** *or* **factory** Maschinenfabrik *f*

England ['ɪŋglənd] *n* England *nt*

English ['ɪŋglɪʃ] *adj* englisch ▷ *n* Englisch *nt*; **the English** *npl* die Engländer *pl*; **an ~ speaker** *jd, der Englisch spricht*

English Channel *n*: **the ~** der Ärmelkanal
Englishman ['ɪŋglɪʃmən] (*irreg: like* **man**) *n* Engländer *m*
Englishwoman ['ɪŋglɪʃwumən] (*irreg: like* **woman**) *n* Engländerin *f*
engrave [ɪn'greɪv] *vt* gravieren; (*name etc*) eingravieren; (*fig*) einprägen
engraving [ɪn'greɪvɪŋ] *n* Stich *m*
engrossed [ɪn'grəust] *adj*: **~ in** vertieft in *+acc*
engulf [ɪn'gʌlf] *vt* verschlingen; (*subj: panic, fear*) überkommen
enhance [ɪn'hɑ:ns] *vt* verbessern; (*enjoyment, beauty*) erhöhen
enjoy [ɪn'dʒɔɪ] *vt* genießen; (*health, fortune*) sich erfreuen *+gen*; (*success*) haben; **to ~ o.s.** sich amüsieren; **I ~ dancing** ich tanze gerne
enjoyable [ɪn'dʒɔɪəbl] *adj* nett, angenehm
enjoyment [ɪn'dʒɔɪmənt] *n* Vergnügen *nt*; (*activity*) Freude *f*
enlarge [ɪn'lɑ:dʒ] *vt* vergrößern; (*scope*) erweitern ▷ *vi*: **to ~ on** weiter ausführen
enlargement [ɪn'lɑ:dʒmənt] *n* Vergrößerung *f*
enlighten [ɪn'laɪtn] *vt* aufklären
enlightened [ɪn'laɪtnd] *adj* aufgeklärt
enlightenment [ɪn'laɪtnmənt] *n* (*also Hist: Enlightenment*) Aufklärung *f*
enlist [ɪn'lɪst] *vt* anwerben; (*support, help*) gewinnen ▷ *vi*: **to ~ in** eintreten in *+acc*; **~ed man** (*US: Mil*) gemeiner Soldat *m*; (*US: in navy*) Matrose *m*
enmity ['ɛnmɪtɪ] *n* Feindschaft *f*
enormous [ɪ'nɔ:məs] *adj* gewaltig, ungeheuer; (*pleasure, success etc*) riesig
enough [ɪ'nʌf] *adj* genug, genügend ▷ *pron* genug ▷ *adv*: **big ~** groß genug; **he has not worked ~** er hat nicht genug *or* genügend gearbeitet; **have you got ~?** haben Sie genug?; **~ to eat** genug zu essen; **will 5 be ~?** reichen 5?; **I've had ~!** jetzt reichts mir aber!; **it's hot ~ (as it is)** es ist heiß genug; **he was kind ~ to lend me the money** er war so gut und hat mir das Geld geliehen; **~!** es reicht!; **that's ~, thanks** danke, das reicht *or* ist genug; **I've had ~ of him** ich habe genug von ihm; **funnily/oddly ~ ...** komischerweise ...
enquire [ɪn'kwaɪə^r] *vt, vi* = **inquire**
enrage [ɪn'reɪdʒ] *vt* wütend machen
enrich [ɪn'rɪtʃ] *vt* bereichern
enrol, (*US*) **enroll** [ɪn'rəul] *vt* anmelden; (*at university*) einschreiben, immatrikulieren ▷ *vi* (*see vt*) sich anmelden; sich einschreiben, sich immatrikulieren
enrolment, (*US*) **enrollment** [ɪn'rəulmənt] *n* (*v vb*) Anmeldung *f*; Einschreibung *f*, Immatrikulation *f*
en route [ɔn'ru:t] *adv* unterwegs; **~ for** auf dem Weg nach; **~ from London to Berlin** auf dem Weg von London nach Berlin
ensure [ɪn'ʃuə^r] *vt* garantieren; **to ~ that** sicherstellen, dass
entail [ɪn'teɪl] *vt* mit sich bringen
enter ['ɛntə^r] *vt* betreten; (*club*) beitreten *+dat*; (*army*) gehen zu; (*profession*) ergreifen; (*race, contest*) sich beteiligen an *+dat*; (*sb for a competition*) anmelden; (*write down*) eintragen; (*Comput: data*) eingeben ▷ *vi* (*come in*) hereinkommen; (*go in*) hineingehen
▸ **enter for** *vt fus* anmelden für
▸ **enter into** *vt fus* (*discussion, negotiations*) aufnehmen; (*correspondence*) treten in *+acc*; (*agreement*) schließen
▸ **enter up** *vt* eintragen
▸ **enter (up)on** *vt fus* (*career, policy*) einschlagen
enterprise ['ɛntəpraɪz] *n* Unternehmen *nt*; (*initiative*) Initiative *f*; **free ~** freies Unternehmertum *nt*; **private ~** Privatunternehmertum *nt*
enterprising ['ɛntəpraɪzɪŋ] *adj* einfallsreich
entertain [ɛntə'teɪn] *vt* unterhalten; (*invite*) einladen; (*idea, plan*) erwägen
entertainer [ɛntə'teɪnə^r] *n* Unterhalter(in) *m(f)*, Entertainer(in) *m(f)*
entertaining [ɛntə'teɪnɪŋ] *adj* amüsant ▷ *n*: **to do a lot of ~** sehr oft Gäste haben
entertainment [ɛntə'teɪnmənt] *n* Unterhaltung *f*; (*show*) Darbietung *f*
enthralled [ɪn'θrɔ:ld] *adj* gefesselt; **he was ~ by** *or* **with the book** das Buch fesselte ihn
enthusiasm [ɪn'θu:zɪæzəm] *n* Begeisterung *f*
enthusiast [ɪn'θu:zɪæst] *n* Enthusiast(in) *m(f)*; **he's a jazz/sports ~** er begeistert sich für Jazz/Sport
enthusiastic [ɪnθu:zɪ'æstɪk] *adj* begeistert; (*response, reception*) enthusiastisch; **to be ~ about** begeistert sein von
entire [ɪn'taɪə^r] *adj* ganz
entirely [ɪn'taɪəlɪ] *adv* völlig
entirety [ɪn'taɪərətɪ] *n*: **in its ~** in seiner Gesamtheit
entitle [ɪn'taɪtl] *vt*: **to ~ sb to sth** jdn zu etw berechtigen; **to ~ sb to do sth** jdn dazu berechtigen, etw zu tun
entitled [ɪn'taɪtld] *adj*: **a book/film** *etc* **~ ...** ein Buch/Film *etc* mit dem Titel ...; **to be ~ to do sth** das Recht haben, etw zu tun
entrance [*n* 'ɛntrns, *vt* ɪn'trɑ:ns] *n* Eingang *m*; (*arrival*) Ankunft *f*; (*on stage*) Auftritt *m* ▷ *vt* bezaubern; **to gain ~ to** (*building etc*) sich *dat* Zutritt verschaffen zu; (*university*) die Zulassung erhalten zu; (*profession etc*) Zugang erhalten zu
entrance examination *n* Aufnahmeprüfung *f*
entrance fee *n* Eintrittsgeld *nt*
entrance ramp (*US*) *n* Auffahrt *f*
entrant ['ɛntrnt] *n* Teilnehmer(in) *m(f)*; (*Brit: in exam*) Prüfling *m*
entrenched [ɛn'trɛntʃt] *adj* verankert; (*ideas*) festgesetzt
entrepreneur ['ɔntrəprə'nə:^{r}] *n* Unternehmer(in) *m(f)*
entrust [ɪn'trʌst] *vt*: **to ~ sth to sb** jdm etw anvertrauen; **to ~ sb with sth** (*task*) jdn

mit etw betrauen; (*secret, valuables*) jdm etw anvertrauen

entry ['ɛntrɪ] *n* Eingang *m*; (*in competition*) Meldung *f*; (*in register, account book, reference book*) Eintrag *m*; (*arrival*) Eintritt *m*; (*to country*) Einreise *f*; **"no ~"** "Zutritt verboten"; (*Aut*) "Einfahrt verboten"; **single/double ~ bookkeeping** einfache/doppelte Buchführung *f*

entry form *n* Anmeldeformular *nt*

entry phone (*Brit*) *n* Türsprechanlage *f*

envelop [ɪn'vɛləp] *vt* einhüllen

envelope ['ɛnvələup] *n* Umschlag *m*

envious ['ɛnvɪəs] *adj* neidisch; **to be ~ of sth/sb** auf etw/jdn neidisch sein

environment [ɪn'vaɪərnmənt] *n* Umwelt *f*; **Department of the E~** (*Brit*) Umweltministerium *nt*

environmental [ɪnvaɪərn'mɛntl] *adj* (*problems, pollution etc*) Umwelt-; **~ expert** Umweltexperte *m*, Umweltexpertin *f*; **~ studies** Umweltkunde *f*

envisage [ɪn'vɪzɪdʒ] *vt* sich *dat* vorstellen; **I ~ that ...** ich stelle mir vor, dass ...

envoy ['ɛnvɔɪ] *n* Gesandte(r) *f(m)*

envy ['ɛnvɪ] *n* Neid *m* ▷ *vt* beneiden; **to ~ sb sth** jdn um etw beneiden

epic ['ɛpɪk] *n* Epos *nt* ▷ *adj* (*journey*) lang und abenteuerlich

epidemic [ɛpɪ'dɛmɪk] *n* Epidemie *f*

epilepsy ['ɛpɪlɛpsɪ] *n* Epilepsie *f*

epileptic [ɛpɪ'lɛptɪk] *adj* epileptisch ▷ *n* Epileptiker(in) *m(f)*

episode ['ɛpɪsəud] *n* Episode *f*; (TV, *Radio*) Folge *f*

epitome [ɪ'pɪtəmɪ] *n* Inbegriff *m*

epitomize [ɪ'pɪtəmaɪz] *vt* verkörpern

equal ['i:kwl] *adj* gleich ▷ *n* Gleichgestellte(r) *f(m)* ▷ *vt* gleichkommen *+dat*; (*number*) gleich sein *+dat*; **they are roughly ~ in size** sie sind ungefähr gleich groß; **the number of exports should be ~ to imports** Export- und Importzahlen sollten gleich sein; **~ opportunities** Chancengleichheit *f*; **to be ~ to** (*task*) gewachsen sein *+dat*; **two times two ~s four** zwei mal zwei ist (gleich) vier

equality [i:'kwɔlɪtɪ] *n* Gleichheit *f*; **~ of opportunity** Chancengleichheit *f*

equalize ['i:kwəlaɪz] *vt* angleichen ▷ *vi* (*Sport*) ausgleichen

equally ['i:kwəlɪ] *adv* gleichmäßig; (*good, bad etc*) gleich; **they are ~ clever** sie sind beide gleich klug

equanimity [ɛkwə'nɪmɪtɪ] *n* Gleichmut *m*, Gelassenheit *f*

equate [ɪ'kweɪt] *vt*: **to ~ sth with** etw gleichsetzen mit ▷ *vt* (*compare*) auf die gleiche Stufe stellen; **to ~ A to B** A und B auf die gleiche Stufe stellen

equation [ɪ'kweɪʃən] *n* Gleichung *f*

equator [ɪ'kweɪtə^r] *n* Äquator *m*

equilibrium [i:kwɪ'lɪbrɪəm] *n* Gleichgewicht *nt*

equip [ɪ'kwɪp] *vt*: **to ~ (with)** (*person, army*) ausrüsten (mit); (*room, car etc*) ausstatten (mit); **to ~ sb for** jdn vorbereiten auf *+acc*; **to be well ~ped** gut ausgerüstet sein

equipment [ɪ'kwɪpmənt] *n* Ausrüstung *f*

equities ['ɛkwɪtɪz] (*Brit*) *npl* Stammaktien *pl*

equivalent [ɪ'kwɪvələnt] *adj* gleich, gleichwertig ▷ *n* Gegenstück *nt*; **to be ~ to** *or* **the ~ of** entsprechen *+dat*

ER (*Brit*) *abbr* (*= Elizabeth Regina*) *offizieller Namenszug der Königin*

era ['ɪərə] *n* Ära *f*, Epoche *f*

eradicate [ɪ'rædɪkeɪt] *vt* ausrotten

erase [ɪ'reɪz] *vt* (*tape, Comput*) löschen; (*writing*) ausradieren; (*thought, feeling*) auslöschen

eraser [ɪ'reɪzə^r] *n* Radiergummi *m*

erect [ɪ'rɛkt] *adj* aufrecht; (*tail*) hoch erhoben; (*ears*) gespitzt ▷ *vt* bauen; (*assemble*) aufstellen

erection [ɪ'rɛkʃən] *n* Bauen *nt*; (*of statue*) Errichten *nt*; (*of tent, machinery etc*) Aufstellen *nt*; (*Physiol*) Erektion *f*

ERM *n abbr* (*= Exchange Rate Mechanism*) Wechselkursmechanismus *m*

erode [ɪ'rəud] *vt* erodieren, auswaschen; (*metal*) zerfressen; (*confidence, power*) untergraben

erosion [ɪ'rəuʒən] *n* (*see vb*) Erosion *f*, Auswaschen *nt*; Zerfressen *nt*; Untergraben *nt*

erotic [ɪ'rɔtɪk] *adj* erotisch

errand ['ɛrənd] *n* Besorgung *f*; (*to give a message etc*) Botengang *m*; **to run ~s** Besorgungen/Botengänge machen; **~ of mercy** Rettungsaktion *f*

erratic [ɪ'rætɪk] *adj* unberechenbar; (*attempts*) unkoordiniert; (*noise*) unregelmäßig

error ['ɛrə^r] *n* Fehler *m*; **typing/spelling ~** Tipp-/Rechtschreibfehler *m*; **in ~** irrtümlicherweise; **~s and omissions excepted** Irrtum vorbehalten

erupt [ɪ'rʌpt] *vi* ausbrechen

eruption [ɪ'rʌpʃən] *n* Ausbruch *m*

escalate ['ɛskəleɪt] *vi* eskalieren, sich ausweiten

escalator ['ɛskəleɪtə^r] *n* Rolltreppe *f*

escapade [ɛskə'peɪd] *n* Eskapade *f*

escape [ɪs'keɪp] *n* Flucht *f*; (*Tech: of liquid*) Ausfließen *nt*; (*of gas*) Ausströmen *nt*; (*of air, heat*) Entweichen *nt* ▷ *vi* entkommen; (*from prison*) ausbrechen; (*liquid*) ausfließen; (*gas*) ausströmen; (*air, heat*) entweichen ▷ *vt* (*pursuers etc*) entkommen *+dat*; (*punishment etc*) entgehen *+dat*; **his name ~s me** sein Name ist mir entfallen; **to ~ from** flüchten aus; (*prison*) ausbrechen aus; (*person*) entkommen *+dat*; **to ~ to Peru** nach Peru fliehen; **to ~ to safety** sich in Sicherheit bringen; **to ~ notice** unbemerkt bleiben

escapism [ɪs'keɪpɪzəm] *n* Wirklichkeitsflucht *f*, Eskapismus *m*

escort [*n* 'ɛskɔ:t, *vt* ɪs'kɔ:t] *n* Eskorte *f*; (*companion*) Begleiter(in) *m(f)* ▷ *vt* begleiten; **his ~** seine Begleiterin; **her ~** ihr Begleiter

Eskimo ['ɛskɪməu] *n* Eskimo(frau) *m(f)*
especially [ɪs'pɛʃlɪ] *adv* besonders
espionage ['ɛspɪənɑːʒ] *n* Spionage *f*
Esquire [ɪs'kwaɪəʳ] *n (abbr Esq.)*: **J. Brown, ~** Herrn J. Brown
essay ['ɛseɪ] *n* Aufsatz *m*; *(Liter)* Essay *m or nt*
essence ['ɛsns] *n* Wesen *nt*; *(Culin)* Essenz *f*; **in ~** im Wesentlichen; **speed is of the ~** Geschwindigkeit ist von entscheidender Bedeutung
essential [ɪ'sɛnʃl] *adj* notwendig; *(basic)* wesentlich ▷ *n (see adj)* Notwendigste(s) *nt*; Wesentliche(s) *nt*; **it is ~ that** es ist unbedingt *or* absolut erforderlich, dass
essentially [ɪ'sɛnʃəlɪ] *adv* im Grunde genommen
establish [ɪs'tæblɪʃ] *vt* gründen; *(facts)* feststellen; *(proof)* erstellen; *(relations, contact)* aufnehmen; *(reputation)* sich *dat* verschaffen
established [ɪs'tæblɪʃt] *adj* üblich; *(business)* eingeführt
establishment [ɪs'tæblɪʃmənt] *n (see vb)* Gründung *f*; Feststellung *f*; Erstellung *f*; Aufnahme *f*; *(of reputation)* Begründung *f*; *(shop etc)* Unternehmen *nt*; **the E~** das Establishment
estate [ɪs'teɪt] *n* Gut *nt*; *(Brit: also:* **housing estate**) Siedlung *f*; *(Law)* Nachlass *m*
estate agent *(Brit) n* Immobilienmakler(in) *m(f)*
estate car *(Brit) n* Kombiwagen *m*
esteem [ɪs'tiːm] *n*: **to hold sb in high ~** eine hohe Meinung von jdm haben
esthetic [ɪs'θɛtɪk] *(US) adj* = **aesthetic**
estimate ['ɛstɪmət] *n* Schätzung *f*; *(assessment)* Einschätzung *f*; *(Comm)* (Kosten)voranschlag *m* ▷ *vt* schätzen ▷ *vi (Brit: Comm)*: **to ~ for** einen Kostenvoranschlag machen für; **to give sb an ~ of sth** jdm eine Vorstellung von etw geben; **to ~ for** einen Kostenvoranschlag machen für; **at a rough ~** grob geschätzt, über den Daumen gepeilt *(inf)*; **I ~ that** ich schätze, dass
estimation [ɛstɪ'meɪʃən] *n* Schätzung *f*; *(opinion)* Einschätzung *f*; **in my ~** meiner Einschätzung nach
estranged [ɪs'treɪndʒd] *adj* entfremdet; *(from spouse)* getrennt; *(couple)* getrennt lebend
eternal [ɪ'təːnl] *adj* ewig
eternity [ɪ'təːnɪtɪ] *n* Ewigkeit *f*
ethical ['ɛθɪkl] *adj* ethisch
ethics ['ɛθɪks] *n* Ethik *f* ▷ *npl (morality)* Moral *f*
Ethiopia [iːθɪ'əupɪə] *n* Äthiopien *nt*
ethnic ['ɛθnɪk] *adj* ethnisch; *(music)* folkloristisch; *(culture etc)* urwüchsig
ethnic minority *n* ethnische Minderheit *f*
ethos ['iːθɔs] *n* Ethos *nt*
e-ticket ['iːtɪkɪt] *n abbr (= electronic ticket)* E-Ticket *nt, elektronische Eintrittskarte/Fahrkarte etc*
etiquette ['ɛtɪkɛt] *n* Etikette *f*
EU *n abbr (= European Union)* EU *f*
euro ['juərəu] *n (Fin)* Euro *m*
Euroland ['juərəulænd] *n (Fin)* Eurozone *f*
Europe ['juərəp] *n* Europa *nt*
European [juərə'piːən] *adj* europäisch ▷ *n* Europäer(in) *m(f)*
European Community *n*: **the ~** die Europäische Gemeinschaft
evacuate [ɪ'vækjueɪt] *vt* evakuieren; *(place)* räumen
evade [ɪ'veɪd] *vt (person, question)* ausweichen *+dat*; *(tax)* hinterziehen; *(duty, responsibility)* sich entziehen *+dat*
evaluate [ɪ'væljueɪt] *vt* bewerten; *(situation)* einschätzen
evaporate [ɪ'væpəreɪt] *vi* verdampfen; *(feeling, attitude)* dahinschwinden
evaporated milk [ɪ'væpəreɪtɪd-] *n* Kondensmilch *f*, Büchsenmilch *f*
evasion [ɪ'veɪʒən] *n* Ausweichen *nt*; *(of tax)* Hinterziehung *f*
eve [iːv] *n*: **on the ~ of** am Tag vor *+dat*; **Christmas E~** Heiligabend *m*; **New Year's E~** Silvester *m or nt*
even ['iːvn] *adj (level)* eben; *(smooth)* glatt; *(equal)* gleich; *(number)* gerade ▷ *adv* sogar, selbst; *(introducing a comparison)* sogar noch; **~ if, ~ though** selbst wenn; **~ more** sogar noch mehr; **he loves her ~ more** er liebt sie umso mehr; **it's going ~ faster now** es fährt jetzt sogar noch schneller; **~ so** (aber) trotzdem; **not ~** nicht einmal; **~ he was there** sogar er war da; **to break ~** die Kosten decken; **to get ~ with sb** es jdm heimzahlen
▸ **even out** *vi* sich ausgleichen ▷ *vt* ausgleichen
evening ['iːvnɪŋ] *n* Abend *m*; **in the ~** abends, am Abend; **this ~** heute Abend; **tomorrow/yesterday ~** morgen/gestern Abend
evening class *n* Abendkurs *m*
evening dress *n (no pl)* Abendkleidung *f*; *(woman's)* Abendkleid *nt*
event [ɪ'vɛnt] *n* Ereignis *nt*; *(Sport)* Wettkampf *m*; **in the normal course of ~s** normalerweise; **in the ~ of** im Falle *+gen*; **in the ~** schließlich; **at all ~s** *(Brit)*: **in any ~** auf jeden Fall
eventful [ɪ'vɛntful] *adj* ereignisreich
eventual [ɪ'vɛntʃuəl] *adj* schließlich; *(goal)* letztlich
eventuality [ɪvɛntʃu'ælɪtɪ] *n* Eventualität *f*
eventually [ɪ'vɛntʃuəlɪ] *adv* endlich; *(in time)* schließlich
ever ['ɛvəʳ] *adv* immer; *(at any time)* je(mals); **why ~ not?** warum denn bloß nicht?; **the best ~** der/die/das Allerbeste; **have you ~ seen it?** haben Sie es schon einmal gesehen?; **for ~** für immer; **hardly ~** kaum je(mals); **better than ~** besser als je zuvor; **~ since** *adv* seitdem ▷ *conj* seit, seitdem; **~ so pretty** unheimlich hübsch *(inf)*; **thank you ~ so much** ganz herzlichen Dank; **yours ~** *(Brit: in letters)* alles Liebe
evergreen ['ɛvəgriːn] *n (tree/bush)* immergrüner Baum/Strauch *m*

everlasting [ɛvə'lɑ:stɪŋ] *adj* ewig
every ['ɛvrɪ] *adj* **1** jede(r, s); **every one of them** (*persons*) jede(r) (Einzelne) von ihnen; (*objects*) jedes einzelne Stück; **every day** jeden Tag; **every week** jede Woche; **every other car** jedes zweite Auto; **every other/third day** alle zwei/drei Tage; **every shop in the town was closed** alle Geschäfte der Stadt waren geschlossen; **every now and then** ab und zu, hin und wieder
2 (*all possible*): **I have every confidence in him** ich habe volles Vertrauen in ihn; **we wish you every success** wir wünschen Ihnen alles Gute
everybody ['ɛvrɪbɔdɪ] *pron* jeder, alle *pl*; **~ knows about it** alle wissen es; **~ else** alle anderen *pl*
everyday ['ɛvrɪdeɪ] *adj* täglich; (*usual, common*) alltäglich; (*life, language*) Alltags-
everyone ['ɛvrɪwʌn] *pron* = **everybody**
everything ['ɛvrɪθɪŋ] *pron* alles; **he did ~ possible** er hat sein Möglichstes getan
everywhere ['ɛvrɪwɛəʳ] *adv* überall; (*wherever*) wo auch *or* immer; **~ you go you meet ...** wo man auch *or* wo immer man hingeht, trifft man ...
evict [ɪ'vɪkt] *vt* zur Räumung zwingen
eviction [ɪ'vɪkʃən] *n* Ausweisung *f*
evidence ['ɛvɪdns] *n* Beweis *m*; (*of witness*) Aussage *f*; (*sign, indication*) Zeichen *nt*, Spur *f*; **to give ~** (als Zeuge) aussagen; **to show ~ of** zeigen; **in ~** sichtbar
evident ['ɛvɪdnt] *adj* offensichtlich
evidently ['ɛvɪdntlɪ] *adv* offensichtlich
evil ['i:vl] *adj* böse; (*influence*) schlecht ▷ *n* Böse(s) *nt*; (*unpleasant situation or activity*) Übel *nt*
evoke [ɪ'vəuk] *vt* hervorrufen; (*memory*) wecken
evolution [i:və'lu:ʃən] *n* Evolution *f*; (*development*) Entwicklung *f*
evolve [ɪ'vɔlv] *vt* entwickeln ▷ *vi* sich entwickeln
ewe [ju:] *n* Mutterschaf *nt*
ex- [ɛks] *pref* Ex-, frühere(r, s); **the price ex works** der Preis ab Werk
exact [ɪg'zækt] *adj* genau; (*word*) richtig ▷ *vt*: **to ~ sth (from)** etw verlangen (von); (*payment*) etw eintreiben (von)
exacting [ɪg'zæktɪŋ] *adj* anspruchsvoll
exactly [ɪg'zæktlɪ] *adv* genau; **~!** (ganz) genau!; **not ~** (*hardly*) nicht gerade
exaggerate [ɪg'zædʒəreɪt] *vt, vi* übertreiben
exaggeration [ɪgzædʒə'reɪʃən] *n* Übertreibung *f*
exalted [ɪg'zɔ:ltɪd] *adj* hoch; (*elated*) exaltiert
exam [ɪg'zæm] *n abbr* = **examination**
examination [ɪgzæmɪ'neɪʃən] *n* (*see vb*) Untersuchung *f*; Prüfung *f*; Verhör *nt*; **to take an ~, to sit an ~** (*Brit*) eine Prüfung machen; **the matter is under ~** die Angelegenheit wird geprüft *or* untersucht
examine [ɪg'zæmɪn] *vt* untersuchen; (*accounts, candidate*) prüfen; (*witness*) verhören
examiner [ɪg'zæmɪnəʳ] *n* Prüfer(in) *m(f)*
example [ɪg'zɑ:mpl] *n* Beispiel *nt*; **for ~** zum Beispiel; **to set a good/bad ~** ein gutes/schlechtes Beispiel geben
exasperate [ɪg'zɑ:spəreɪt] *vt* (*annoy*) verärgern; (*frustrate*) zur Verzweiflung bringen; **~d by** *or* **with** verärgert/verzweifelt über *+acc*
exasperation [ɪgzɑ:spə'reɪʃən] *n* Verzweiflung *f*; **in ~** verzweifelt
excavate ['ɛkskəveɪt] *vt* ausgraben; (*hole*) graben ▷ *vi* Ausgrabungen machen
excavation [ɛkskə'veɪʃən] *n* Ausgrabung *f*
exceed [ɪk'si:d] *vt* übersteigen; (*hopes*) übertreffen; (*limit, budget, powers*) überschreiten
exceedingly [ɪk'si:dɪŋlɪ] *adv* äußerst
excel [ɪk'sɛl] *vt* übertreffen ▷ *vi*: **to ~ (in** *or* **at)** sich auszeichnen (in *+dat*); **to ~ o.s.** (*Brit*) sich selbst übertreffen
excellence ['ɛksələns] *n* hervorragende Leistung *f*
excellent ['ɛksələnt] *adj* ausgezeichnet, hervorragend
except [ɪk'sɛpt] *prep* (*also*: **except for**) außer *+dat* ▷ *vt*: **to ~ sb (from)** jdn ausnehmen (bei); **~ if, ~ when** außer wenn; **~ that** nur dass
exception [ɪk'sɛpʃən] *n* Ausnahme *f*; **to take ~ to** Anstoß nehmen an *+dat*; **with the ~ of** mit Ausnahme von
exceptional [ɪk'sɛpʃənl] *adj* außergewöhnlich
excerpt ['ɛksə:pt] *n* Auszug *m*
excess [ɪk'sɛs] *n* Übermaß *nt*; (*Insurance*) Selbstbeteiligung *f*; **excesses** *npl* Exzesse *pl*; **an ~ of £15, a £15 excess** eine Selbstbeteiligung von £15; **in ~ of** über *+dat*
excess baggage *n* Übergepäck *nt*
excess fare (*Brit*) *n* Nachlösegebühr *f*
excessive [ɪk'sɛsɪv] *adj* übermäßig
exchange [ɪks'tʃeɪndʒ] *n* Austausch *m*; (*conversation*) Wortwechsel *m*; (*also*: **telephone exchange**) Fernsprechamt *nt* ▷ *vt*: **to ~ (for)** tauschen (gegen); (*in shop*) umtauschen (gegen); **in ~ for** für; **foreign ~** Devisenhandel *m*; (*money*) Devisen *pl*
exchange rate *n* Wechselkurs *m*
excise ['ɛksaɪz] *n* Verbrauchssteuer *f* ▷ *vt* entfernen
excite [ɪk'saɪt] *vt* aufregen; (*arouse*) erregen; **to get ~d** sich aufregen
excitement [ɪk'saɪtmənt] *n* Aufregung *f*; (*exhilaration*) Hochgefühl *nt*
exciting [ɪk'saɪtɪŋ] *adj* aufregend
exclaim [ɪks'kleɪm] *vi* aufschreien
exclamation [ɛksklə'meɪʃən] *n* Ausruf *m*; **~ of joy** Freudenschrei *m*
exclamation mark *n* Ausrufezeichen *nt*
exclude [ɪks'klu:d] *vt* ausschließen
excluding [ɪks'klu:dɪŋ] *prep*: **~ VAT** ohne Mehrwertsteuer

exclusion [ɪks'klu:ʒən] *n* Ausschluss *m*; **to concentrate on sth to the ~ of everything else** sich ausschließlich auf etw *dat* konzentrieren
exclusion zone *n* Sperrzone *f*
exclusive [ɪks'klu:sɪv] *adj* exklusiv; (*story, interview*) Exklusiv-; (*use*) ausschließlich ▷ *n* Exklusivbericht *m* ▷ *adv*: **from 1st to 15th March ~** vom 1. bis zum 15. März ausschließlich; **~ of postage** ohne *or* exklusive Porto; **~ of tax** ausschließlich *or* exklusive Steuern; **to be mutually ~** sich *or* einander ausschließen
exclusively [ɪks'klu:sɪvlɪ] *adv* ausschließlich
excruciating [ɪks'kru:ʃɪeɪtɪŋ] *adj* grässlich, fürchterlich; (*noise, embarrassment*) unerträglich
excursion [ɪks'kə:ʃən] *n* Ausflug *m*
excuse [ɪks'kju:s] *n* Entschuldigung *f* ▷ *vt* entschuldigen; (*forgive*) verzeihen; **to ~ sb from sth** jdm etw erlassen; **to ~ sb from doing sth** jdn davon befreien, etw zu tum; **~ me!** entschuldigen Sie!, Entschuldigung!; **if you will ~ me ...** entschuldigen Sie mich bitte ...; **to ~ o.s. for sth** sich für *or* wegen etw entschuldigen; **to ~ o.s. for doing sth** sich entschuldigen, dass man etw tut; **to make ~s for sb** jdn entschuldigen; **that's no ~!** das ist keine Ausrede!
ex-directory ['ɛksdɪ'rɛktərɪ] (*Brit*) *adj* (*number*) geheim; **she's ~** sie steht nicht im Telefonbuch
execute ['ɛksɪkju:t] *vt* ausführen; (*person*) hinrichten
execution [ɛksɪ'kju:ʃən] *n* (*see vb*) Ausführung *f*; Hinrichtung *f*
executive [ɪg'zɛkjutɪv] *n* leitende(r) Angestellte(r) *f(m)*; (*committee*) Vorstand *m* ▷ *adj* geschäftsführend; (*role*) führend; (*secretary*) Chef-; (*car, chair*) für gehobene Ansprüche; (*toys*) Manager-; (*plane*) ≈ Privat-
exemplify [ɪg'zɛmplɪfaɪ] *vt* verkörpern; (*illustrate*) veranschaulichen
exempt [ɪg'zɛmpt] *adj*: **~ from** befreit von ▷ *vt*: **to ~ sb from** jdn befreien von
exercise ['ɛksəsaɪz] *n* Übung *f*; (*no pl: keep-fit*) Gymnastik *f*; (*: energetic movement*) Bewegung *f*; (*: of authority etc*) Ausübung *f* ▷ *vt* (*patience*) üben; (*right*) ausüben; (*dog*) ausführen; (*mind*) beschäftigen ▷ *vi* (*also*: **to take exercise**) Sport treiben
exercise book *n* (Schul)heft *nt*
exert [ɪg'zə:t] *vt* (*influence*) ausüben; (*authority*) einsetzen; **to ~ o.s.** sich anstrengen
exertion [ɪg'zə:ʃən] *n* Anstrengung *f*
exhale [ɛks'heɪl] *vt, vi* ausatmen
exhaust [ɪg'zɔ:st] *n* (*also*: **exhaust pipe**) Auspuff *m*; (*fumes*) Auspuffgase *pl* ▷ *vt* erschöpfen; (*money*) aufbrauchen; (*topic*) erschöpfend behandeln; **to ~ o.s.** sich verausgaben
exhausted [ɪg'zɔ:stɪd] *adj* erschöpft
exhaustion [ɪg'zɔ:stʃən] *n* Erschöpfung *f*; **nervous ~** nervöse Erschöpfung
exhaustive [ɪg'zɔ:stɪv] *adj* erschöpfend
exhibit [ɪg'zɪbɪt] *n* Ausstellungsstück *nt*; (*Law*) Beweisstück *nt* ▷ *vt* zeigen, an den Tag legen; (*paintings*) ausstellen
exhibition [ɛksɪ'bɪʃən] *n* Ausstellung *f*; **to make an ~ of o.s.** sich unmöglich aufführen; **an ~ of bad manners** schlechte Manieren *pl*; **an ~ of draughtsmanship** zeichnerisches Können *nt*
exhilarating [ɪg'zɪləreɪtɪŋ] *adj* erregend, berauschend; (*news*) aufregend
exile ['ɛksaɪl] *n* Exil *nt*; (*person*) Verbannte(r) *f(m)* ▷ *vt* verbannen; **in ~** im Exil
exist [ɪg'zɪst] *vi* existieren
existence [ɪg'zɪstəns] *n* Existenz *f*; **to be in ~** existieren
existing [ɪg'zɪstɪŋ] *adj* bestehend
exit ['ɛksɪt] *n* Ausgang *m*; (*from motorway*) Ausfahrt *f*; (*departure*) Abgang *m* ▷ *vi* (*Theat*) abgehen; (*Comput: from program/file etc*) das Programm/die Datei *etc* verlassen; **to ~ from** hinausgehen aus; (*motorway etc*) abfahren von
exit poll *n bei Wählern unmittelbar nach Verlassen der Wahllokale durchgeführte Umfrage*
exit ramp (*US*) *n* Ausfahrt *f*
exodus ['ɛksədəs] *n* Auszug *m*; **the ~ to the cities** die Abwanderung in die Städte
exonerate [ɪg'zɔnəreɪt] *vt*: **to ~ from** entlasten von
exotic [ɪg'zɔtɪk] *adj* exotisch
expand [ɪks'pænd] *vt* erweitern; (*staff, numbers etc*) vergrößern; (*influence*) ausdehnen ▷ *vi* expandieren; (*population*) wachsen; (*gas, metal*) sich ausdehnen; **to ~ on** weiter ausführen
expanse [ɪks'pæns] *n* Weite *f*
expansion [ɪks'pænʃən] *n* Expansion *f*; (*of population*) Wachstum *nt*; (*of gas, metal*) Ausdehnung *f*
expect [ɪks'pɛkt] *vt* erwarten; (*suppose*) denken, glauben; (*count on*) rechnen mit ▷ *vi*: **to be ~ing** ein Kind erwarten; **to ~ sb to do sth** erwarten, dass jd etw tut; **to ~ to do sth** vorhaben, etw zu tun; **as ~ed** wie erwartet; **I ~ so** ich glaube schon
expectancy [ɪks'pɛktənsɪ] *n* Erwartung *f*; **life ~** Lebenserwartung *f*
expectant [ɪks'pɛktənt] *adj* erwartungsvoll
expectation [ɛkspɛk'teɪʃən] *n* Erwartung *f*; (*hope*) Hoffnung *f*; **in ~ of** in Erwartung *+gen*; **against** *or* **contrary to all ~(s)** wider Erwarten; **to come** *or* **live up to sb's ~s** jds Erwartungen *dat* entsprechen
expedient [ɪks'pi:dɪənt] *adj* zweckmäßig ▷ *n* Hilfsmittel *nt*
expedition [ɛkspə'dɪʃən] *n* Expedition *f*; (*for shopping etc*) Tour *f*
expel [ɪks'pɛl] *vt* (*from school*) verweisen; (*from organization*) ausschließen; (*from place*) vertreiben; (*gas, liquid*) ausstoßen
expend [ɪks'pɛnd] *vt* ausgeben; (*time, energy*)

aufwenden
expenditure [ɪks'pɛndɪtʃə^r] *n* Ausgaben *pl*; (*of energy, time*) Aufwand *m*
expense [ɪks'pɛns] *n* Kosten *pl*; (*expenditure*) Ausgabe *f*; **expenses** *npl* Spesen *pl*; **at the ~ of** auf Kosten *+gen*; **to go to the ~ of buying a new car** (viel) Geld für ein neues Auto anlegen; **at great/little ~** mit hohen/geringen Kosten
expense account *n* Spesenkonto *nt*
expensive [ɪks'pɛnsɪv] *adj* teuer; **to have ~ tastes** einen teuren Geschmack haben
experience [ɪks'pɪərɪəns] *n* Erfahrung *f*; (*event, activity*) Erlebnis *nt* ▷ *vt* erleben; **by** *or* **from ~** aus Erfahrung; **to learn by ~** durch eigene Erfahrung lernen
experienced [ɪks'pɪərɪənst] *adj* erfahren
experiment [ɪks'pɛrɪmənt] *n* Experiment *nt*, Versuch *m* ▷ *vi*: **to ~ (with/on)** experimentieren (mit/an *+dat*); **to perform** *or* **carry out an ~** einen Versuch *or* ein Experiment durchführen; **as an ~** versuchsweise
experimental [ɪkspɛrɪ'mɛntl] *adj* experimentell; **at the ~ stage** im Versuchsstadium
expert ['ɛkspə:t] *adj* ausgezeichnet, geschickt; (*opinion, help etc*) eines Fachmanns ▷ *n* Fachmann *m*, Fachfrau *f*, Experte *m*, Expertin *f*; **to be ~ in** *or* **at doing sth** etw ausgezeichnet können; **an ~ on sth/on the subject of sth** ein Experte für etw/auf dem Gebiet einer Sache *gen*; **~ witness** (*Law*) sachverständiger Zeuge *m*
expertise [ɛkspə:'ti:z] *n* Sachkenntnis *f*
expire [ɪks'paɪə^r] *vi* ablaufen
expiry [ɪks'paɪərɪ] *n* Ablauf *m*
expiry date *n* Ablauftermin *m*; (*of voucher, special offer etc*) Verfallsdatum *nt*
explain [ɪks'pleɪn] *vt* erklären
▸ **explain away** *vt* eine Erklärung finden für
explanation [ɛksplə'neɪʃən] *n* Erklärung *f*; **to find an ~ for sth** eine Erklärung für etw finden
explanatory [ɪks'plænətrɪ] *adj* erklärend
explicit [ɪks'plɪsɪt] *adj* ausdrücklich; (*sex, violence*) deutlich, unverhüllt; **to be ~** (*frank*) sich deutlich ausdrücken
explode [ɪks'pləud] *vi* explodieren; (*population*) sprunghaft ansteigen ▷ *vt* zur Explosion bringen; (*myth, theory*) zu Fall bringen
exploit ['ɛksplɔɪt] *n* Heldentat *f* ▷ *vt* ausnutzen; (*workers etc*) ausbeuten; (*resources*) nutzen
exploitation [ɛksplɔɪ'teɪʃən] *n* (*see vb*) Ausnutzung *f*; Ausbeutung *f*; Nutzung *f*
exploratory [ɪks'plɔrətrɪ] *adj* exploratorisch; (*expedition*) Forschungs-; **~ operation** (*Med*) Explorationsoperation *f*; **~ talks** Sondierungsgespräche *pl*
explore [ɪks'plɔ:^r] *vt* erforschen; (*with hands etc, idea*) untersuchen
explorer [ɪks'plɔ:rə^r] *n* Forschungsreisende(r) *f(m)*; (*of place*) Erforscher(in) *m(f)*
explosion [ɪks'pləuʒən] *n* Explosion *f*; (*outburst*) Ausbruch *m*
explosive [ɪks'pləusɪv] *adj* explosiv; (*device*) Spreng-; (*temper*) aufbrausend ▷ *n* Sprengstoff *m*; (*device*) Sprengkörper *m*
exponent [ɪks'pəunənt] *n* Vertreter(in) *m(f)*, Exponent(in) *m(f)*; (*Math*) Exponent *m*
export [ɛks'pɔ:t] *vt* exportieren, ausführen; (*ideas, values*) verbreiten ▷ *n* Export *m*, Ausfuhr *f*; (*product*) Exportgut *nt* ▷ *cpd* Export-, Ausfuhr-
exporter [ɛks'pɔ:tə^r] *n* Exporteur *m*
expose [ɪks'pəuz] *vt* freilegen; (*to heat, radiation*) aussetzen; (*unmask*) entlarven; **to ~ o.s.** sich entblößen
exposed [ɪks'pəuzd] *adj* ungeschützt; (*wire*) bloßliegend; **to be ~ to** (*radiation, heat etc*) ausgesetzt sein *+dat*
exposure [ɪks'pəuʒə^r] *n* (*to heat, radiation*) Aussetzung *f*; (*publicity*) Publicity *f*; (*of person*) Entlarvung *f*; (*Phot*) Belichtung *f*; (*: shot*) Aufnahme *f*; **to be suffering from ~** an Unterkühlung leiden; **to die from ~** erfrieren
exposure meter *n* Belichtungsmesser *m*
express [ɪks'prɛs] *adj* ausdrücklich; (*intention*) bestimmt; (*Brit: letter etc*) Express-, Eil- ▷ *n* (*train*) Schnellzug *m*; (*bus*) Schnellbus *m* ▷ *adv* (*send*) per Express ▷ *vt* ausdrücken; (*view, emotion*) zum Ausdruck bringen; **to ~ o.s.** sich ausdrücken
expression [ɪks'prɛʃən] *n* Ausdruck *m*; (*on face*) (Gesichts)ausdruck *m*
expressly [ɪks'prɛslɪ] *adv* ausdrücklich; (*intentionally*) absichtlich
expressway [ɪks'prɛsweɪ] (*US*) *n* Schnellstraße *f*
exquisite [ɛks'kwɪzɪt] *adj* exquisit, erlesen; (*keenly felt*) köstlich
extend [ɪks'tɛnd] *vt* verlängern; (*building*) anbauen an *+acc*; (*offer, invitation*) aussprechen; (*arm, hand*) ausstrecken; (*deadline*) verschieben ▷ *vi* sich erstrecken; (*period*) dauern
extension [ɪks'tɛnʃən] *n* Verlängerung *f*; (*of building*) Anbau *m*; (*of time*) Aufschub *m*; (*of campaign, rights*) Erweiterung *f*; (*Tel*) (Neben)anschluss *m*; **~ 3718** (*Tel*) Apparat 3718
extension cable *n* Verlängerungskabel *nt*
extensive [ɪks'tɛnsɪv] *adj* ausgedehnt; (*effect*) weitreichend; (*damage*) beträchtlich; (*coverage, discussion*) ausführlich; (*inquiries*) umfangreich; (*use*) häufig
extensively [ɪks'tɛnsɪvlɪ] *adv*: **he's travelled ~** er ist viel gereist
extent [ɪks'tɛnt] *n* Ausdehnung *f*; (*of problem, damage, loss etc*) Ausmaß *nt*; **to some ~** bis zu einem gewissen Grade; **to a certain ~** in gewissem Maße; **to a large ~** in hohem

Maße; **to the ~ of ...** (*debts*) in Höhe von ...; **to go to the ~ of doing sth** so weit gehen, etw zu tun; **to such an ~ that ...** dermaßen, dass ...; **to what ~?** inwieweit?

extenuating [ɪks'tɛnjueɪtɪŋ] *adj*: **~ circumstances** mildernde Umstände *pl*

exterior [ɛks'tɪərɪə^r] *adj* (*surface, angle, world*) Außen- ▷ *n* Außenseite *f*; (*appearance*) Äußere(s) *nt*

external [ɛks'tə:nl] *adj* (*wall etc*) Außen-; (*use*) äußerlich; (*evidence*) unabhängig; (*examiner, auditor*) extern ▷ *n*: **the ~s** die Äußerlichkeiten *pl*; **for ~ use only** nur äußerlich (anzuwenden); **~ affairs** (*Pol*) auswärtige Angelegenheiten *pl*

extinct [ɪks'tɪŋkt] *adj* ausgestorben; (*volcano*) erloschen

extinction [ɪks'tɪŋkʃən] *n* Aussterben *nt*

extinguish [ɪks'tɪŋgwɪʃ] *vt* löschen; (*hope*) zerstören

extort [ɪks'tɔ:t] *vt* erpressen; (*confession*) erzwingen

extortionate [ɪks'tɔ:ʃnɪt] *adj* überhöht; (*price*) Wucher-

extra ['ɛkstrə] *adj* zusätzlich ▷ *adv* extra ▷ *n* Extra *nt*; (*surcharge*) zusätzliche Kosten *pl*; (*Cine, Theat*) Statist(in) *m(f)*; **wine will cost ~** Wein wird extra berechnet

extract [*vt* ɪks'trækt, *n* 'ekstrækt] *vt* (*tooth*) ziehen; (*mineral*) gewinnen ▷ *n* Auszug *m*; (*also*: **malt extract, vanilla extract** *etc*) Extrakt *m*; **to ~ (from)** (*object*) herausziehen (aus); (*money*) herausholen (aus); (*promise*) abringen *+dat*

extracurricular ['ɛkstrəkə'rɪkjulə^r] *adj* außerhalb des Lehrplans

extradite ['ɛkstrədaɪt] *vt* ausliefern

extramarital ['ɛkstrə'mærɪtl] *adj* außerehelich

extramural ['ɛkstrə'mjuərl] *adj* außerhalb der Universität; **~ classes** von der Universität veranstaltete Teilzeitkurse *pl*

extraordinary [ɪks'trɔ:dnrɪ] *adj* ungewöhnlich; (*special*) außerordentlich; **the ~ thing is that ...** das Merkwürdige ist, dass ...

extravagance [ɪks'trævəgəns] *n* (*no pl*) Verschwendungssucht *f*; (*example of spending*) Luxus *m*

extravagant [ɪks'trævəgənt] *adj* extravagant; (*tastes, gift*) teuer; (*wasteful*) verschwenderisch; (*praise*) übertrieben; (*ideas*) ausgefallen

extreme [ɪks'tri:m] *adj* extrem; (*point, edge, poverty*) äußerste(r, s) ▷ *n* Extrem *nt*; **the ~ right/left** (*Pol*) die äußerste *or* extreme Rechte/Linke; **~s of temperature** extreme Temperaturen *pl*

extremely [ɪks'tri:mlɪ] *adv* äußerst, extrem

extremist [ɪks'tri:mɪst] *n* Extremist(in) *m(f)* ▷ *adj* extremistisch

extricate ['ɛkstrɪkeɪt] *vt*: **to ~ sb/sth (from)** jdn/etw befreien (aus)

extrovert ['ɛkstrəvə:t] *n* extravertierter Mensch *m*

eye [aɪ] *n* Auge *nt*; (*of needle*) Öhr *nt* ▷ *vt* betrachten; **to keep an ~ on** aufpassen auf *+acc*; **as far as the ~ can see** so weit das Auge reicht; **in the public ~** im Blickpunkt der Öffentlichkeit; **to have an ~ for sth** einen Blick für etw haben; **with an ~ to doing sth** (*Brit*) mit der Absicht, etw zu tun; **there's more to this than meets the ~** da steckt mehr dahinter(, als man auf den ersten Blick meint)

eyeball ['aɪbɔ:l] *n* Augapfel *m*

eyebrow ['aɪbrau] *n* Augenbraue *f*

eye drops *npl* Augentropfen *pl*

eyelash ['aɪlæʃ] *n* Augenwimper *f*

eyelid ['aɪlɪd] *n* Augenlid *nt*

eyeliner ['aɪlaɪnə^r] *n* Eyeliner *m*

eye-opener ['aɪəupnə^r] *n* Überraschung *f*; **to be an ~ to sb** jdm die Augen öffnen

eye shadow *n* Lidschatten *m*

eyesight ['aɪsaɪt] *n* Sehvermögen *nt*

eyesore ['aɪsɔ:^r] *n* Schandfleck *m*

Ff

F[1], **f** [ɛf] *n* (*letter*) F *nt*, f *nt*; **F for Frederick, F for Fox** (US) ≈ F wie Friedrich
F[2] [ɛf] *n* (*Mus*) F *nt*, f *nt*
F[3] [ɛf] *abbr* (= *Fahrenheit*) F
fable ['feɪbl] *n* Fabel *f*
fabric ['fæbrɪk] *n* Stoff *m*; (*of society*) Gefüge *nt*; (*of building*) Bausubstanz *f*
fabulous ['fæbjuləs] *adj* fabelhaft, toll (*inf*); (*extraordinary*) sagenhaft; (*mythical*) legendär
face [feɪs] *n* Gesicht *nt*; (*expression*) Gesichtsausdruck *m*; (*grimace*) Grimasse *f*; (*of clock*) Zifferblatt *nt*; (*of mountain, cliff*) (Steil)wand *f*; (*of building*) Fassade *f*; (*side, surface*) Seite *f* ▷ *vt* (*subj: person*) gegenübersitzen/-stehen *+dat etc*; (*: building, street etc*) liegen zu; (*: north, south etc*) liegen nach; (*unpleasant situation*) sich gegenübersehen *+dat*; (*facts*) ins Auge sehen *+dat*; **~ down** mit dem Gesicht nach unten; (*card*) mit der Bildseite nach unten; (*object*) mit der Vorderseite nach unten; **to lose/save ~** das Gesicht verlieren/wahren; **to make** *or* **pull a ~** das Gesicht verziehen; **in the ~ of** trotz *+gen*; **on the ~ of it** so, wie es aussieht; **to come ~ to ~ with sb** jdn treffen; **to come ~ to ~ with a problem** einem Problem gegenüberstehen; **to ~ each other** einander gegenüberstehen/-liegen/-sitzen *etc*; **to ~ the fact that ...** der Tatsache ins Auge sehen, dass ...; **the man facing me** der Mann mir gegenüber
▸ **face up to** *vt fus* (*obligations, difficulty*) auf sich *acc* nehmen; (*situation, possibility*) sich abfinden mit; (*danger, fact*) ins Auge sehen *+dat*
face cloth (*Brit*) *n* Waschlappen *m*
face cream *n* Gesichtscreme *f*
face powder *n* Gesichtspuder *m*
face value *n* Nennwert *m*; **to take sth at ~** (*fig*) etw für bare Münze nehmen
facial ['feɪʃl] *adj* (*expression, massage etc*) Gesichts- ▷ *n* kosmetische Gesichtsbehandlung *f*
facilitate [fə'sɪlɪteɪt] *vt* erleichtern
facilities [fə'sɪlɪtɪz] *npl* Einrichtungen *pl*; **cooking ~** Kochgelegenheit *f*; **credit ~** Kreditmöglichkeiten *pl*
facility [fə'sɪlɪtɪ] *n* Einrichtung *f*; **to have a ~ for** (*skill, aptitude*) eine Begabung haben für
facing ['feɪsɪŋ] *prep* gegenüber *+dat* ▷ *n* (*Sewing*) Besatz *m*
facsimile [fæk'sɪmɪlɪ] *n* Faksimile *nt*; (*also:* **facsimile machine**) Fernkopierer *m*, (Tele)faxgerät *nt*; (*transmitted document*) Fernkopie *f*, (Tele)fax *nt*
fact [fækt] *n* Tatsache *f*; (*truth*) Wirklichkeit *f*; **in ~** eigentlich; (*in reality*) tatsächlich, in Wirklichkeit; **to know for a ~ that ...** ganz genau wissen, dass ...; **the ~ (of the matter) is that ...** die Sache ist die, dass ...; **it's a ~ of life that ...** es ist eine Tatsache, dass ...; **to tell sb the ~s of life** (*sex*) jdn aufklären
faction ['fækʃən] *n* Fraktion *f*
factor ['fæktə^r] *n* Faktor *m*; (*Comm*) Kommissionär *m*; (*: agent*) Makler *m*; **safety ~** Sicherheitsfaktor *m*; **human ~** menschlicher Faktor
factory ['fæktərɪ] *n* Fabrik *f*
factual ['fæktjuəl] *adj* sachlich; (*information*) Sach-
faculty ['fækəltɪ] *n* Vermögen *nt*, Kraft *f*; (*ability*) Talent *nt*; (*of university*) Fakultät *f*; (*US: teaching staff*) Lehrkörper *m*
fad [fæd] *n* Fimmel *m*, Tick *m*
fade [feɪd] *vi* verblassen; (*light*) nachlassen; (*sound*) schwächer werden; (*flower*) verblühen; (*hope*) zerrinnen; (*smile*) verschwinden
▸ **fade in** *vt sep* allmählich einblenden
▸ **fade out** *vt sep* ausblenden
fag [fæg] *n* (*Brit: inf: cigarette*) Glimmstängel *m*; (*: chore*) Schinderei *f* (*inf*), Plackerei *f* (*inf*); (*US: inf: homosexual*) Schwule(r) *m*
fail [feɪl] *vt* (*exam*) nicht bestehen; (*candidate*) durchfallen lassen; (*subj: courage*) verlassen; (*: leader, memory*) im Stich lassen ▷ *vi* (*candidate*) durchfallen; (*attempt*) fehlschlagen; (*brakes*) versagen; (*also:* **be failing**: *health*) sich verschlechtern; (*: eyesight, light*) nachlassen; **to ~ to do sth** etw nicht tun; (*neglect*) (es) versäumen, etw zu tun; **without ~** ganz bestimmt
failing ['feɪlɪŋ] *n* Schwäche *f*, Fehler *m* ▷ *prep* in Ermangelung *+gen*; **~ that** (oder) sonst, und wenn das nicht möglich ist
failure ['feɪljə^r] *n* Misserfolg *m*; (*person*) Versager(in) *m(f)*; (*of brakes, heart*) Versagen *nt*; (*of engine, power*) Ausfall *m*; (*of crops*) Missernte

f; (*in exam*) Durchfall *m*; **his ~ to turn up meant that we had to ...** weil er nicht kam, mussten wir ...; **it was a complete ~** es war ein totaler Fehlschlag

faint [feɪnt] *adj* schwach; (*breeze, trace*) leicht ▷ *n* Ohnmacht *f* ▷ *vi* ohnmächtig werden, in Ohnmacht fallen; **she felt ~** ihr wurde schwach

faintest ['feɪntɪst] *adj, n*: **I haven't the ~ (idea)** ich habe keinen blassen Schimmer

faintly ['feɪntlɪ] *adv* schwach

fair [fɛəʳ] *adj* gerecht, fair; (*size, number*) ansehnlich; (*chance, guess*) recht gut; (*hair*) blond; (*skin, complexion*) hell; (*weather*) schön ▷ *adv*: **to play ~** fair spielen ▷ *n* (*also*: **trade fair**) Messe *f*; (*Brit: funfair*) Jahrmarkt *m*, Rummel *m*; **it's not ~!** das ist nicht fair!; **a ~ amount of** ziemlich viel

fairground ['fɛəgraund] *n* Rummelplatz *m*

fair-haired [fɛə'hɛəd] *adj* blond

fairly ['fɛəlɪ] *adv* gerecht; (*quite*) ziemlich; **I'm ~ sure** ich bin (mir) ziemlich sicher

fairness ['fɛənɪs] *n* Gerechtigkeit *f*; **in all ~** gerechterweise, fairerweise

fairway ['fɛəweɪ] *n* (*Golf*): **the ~** das Fairway

fairy ['fɛərɪ] *n* Fee *f*

fairy tale *n* Märchen *nt*

faith [feɪθ] *n* Glaube *m*; (*trust*) Vertrauen *nt*; **to have ~ in sb** jdm vertrauen; **to have ~ in sth** Vertrauen in etw *acc* haben

faithful ['feɪθful] *adj* (*account*) genau; **~ (to)** (*person*) treu +*dat*

faithfully ['feɪθfəlɪ] *adv* (*see adj*) genau; treu

fake [feɪk] *n* Fälschung *f*; (*person*) Schwindler(in) *m(f)* ▷ *adj* gefälscht ▷ *vt* fälschen; (*illness, emotion*) vortäuschen; **his illness is a ~** er simuliert seine Krankheit nur

falcon ['fɔːlkən] *n* Falke *m*

fall [fɔːl] (*pt* **fell**, *pp* **~en**) *n* Fall *m*; (*of price, temperature*) Sinken *nt*; (*: sudden*) Sturz *m*; (*US: autumn*) Herbst *m* ▷ *vi* fallen; (*night, darkness*) hereinbrechen; (*silence*) eintreten; **falls** *npl* (*waterfall*) Wasserfall *m*; **a ~ of snow** ein Schneefall *m*; **a ~ of earth** ein Erdrutsch *m*; **to ~ flat** auf die Nase fallen; (*plan*) ins Wasser fallen; (*joke*) nicht ankommen; **to ~ in love (with sb/sth)** sich (in jdn/etw) verlieben; **to ~ short of sb's expectations** jds Erwartungen nicht erfüllen

▸ **fall apart** *vi* auseinanderfallen, kaputtgehen; (*inf: emotionally*) durchdrehen

▸ **fall back** *vi* zurückweichen

▸ **fall back on** *vi* zurückgreifen auf +*acc*; **to have sth to ~ back on** auf etw *acc* zurückgreifen können

▸ **fall behind** *vi* zurückbleiben; (*fig: with payment*) in Rückstand geraten

▸ **fall down** *vi* hinfallen; (*building*) einstürzen

▸ **fall for** *vt fus* (*trick, story*) hereinfallen auf +*acc*; (*person*) sich verlieben in +*acc*

▸ **fall in** *vi* einstürzen; (*Mil*) antreten

▸ **fall in with** *vt fus* eingehen auf +*acc*

▸ **fall off** *vi* herunterfallen; (*takings, attendance*) zurückgehen

▸ **fall out** *vi* (*hair, teeth*) ausfallen; **to ~ out with sb** sich mit jdm zerstreiten

▸ **fall over** *vi* hinfallen; (*object*) umfallen ▷ *vt*: **to ~ over o.s. to do sth** sich *dat* die größte Mühe geben, etw zu tun

▸ **fall through** *vi* (*plan, project*) ins Wasser fallen

fallacy ['fæləsɪ] *n* Irrtum *m*

fallen ['fɔːlən] *pp of* **fall**

fallout ['fɔːlaut] *n* radioaktiver Niederschlag *m*

fallow ['fæləu] *adj* brach(liegend)

false [fɔːls] *adj* falsch; (*imprisonment*) widerrechtlich

false alarm *n* falscher *or* blinder Alarm *m*

false teeth (*Brit*) *npl* Gebiss *nt*

falter ['fɔːltəʳ] *vi* stocken; (*hesitate*) zögern

fame [feɪm] *n* Ruhm *m*

familiar [fə'mɪlɪəʳ] *adj* vertraut; (*intimate*) vertraulich; **to be ~ with** vertraut sein mit; **to make o.s. ~ with sth** sich mit etw vertraut machen; **to be on ~ terms with sb** mit jdm auf vertrautem Fuß stehen

familiarize [fə'mɪlɪəraɪz] *vt*: **to ~ o.s. with sth** sich mit etw vertraut machen

family ['fæmɪlɪ] *n* Familie *f*; (*relations*) Verwandtschaft *f*

family doctor *n* Hausarzt *m*, Hausärztin *f*

family planning *n* Familienplanung *f*; **~ clinic** ≈ Familienberatungsstelle *f*

famine ['fæmɪn] *n* Hungersnot *f*

famished ['fæmɪʃt] (*inf*) *adj* ausgehungert; **I'm ~** ich sterbe vor Hunger

famous ['feɪməs] *adj* berühmt

famously ['feɪməslɪ] *adv* (*get on*) prächtig

fan [fæn] *n* (*person*) Fan *m*; (*object: folding*) Fächer *m*; (*: Elec*) Ventilator *m* ▷ *vt* fächeln; (*fire*) anfachen; (*quarrel*) schüren

▸ **fan out** *vi* ausschwärmen; (*unfurl*) sich fächerförmig ausbreiten

fanatic [fə'nætɪk] *n* Fanatiker(in) *m(f)*; (*enthusiast*) Fan *m*

fan belt *n* (*Aut*) Keilriemen *m*

fan club *n* Fanklub *m*

fancy ['fænsɪ] *n* Laune *f*; (*imagination*) Fantasie *f*; (*fantasy*) Fantasievorstellung *f* ▷ *adj* (*clothes, hat*) toll, chic *inv*; (*hotel*) fein, vornehm; (*food*) ausgefallen ▷ *vt* mögen; (*imagine*) sich *dat* einbilden; (*think*) glauben; **to take a ~ to sth** Lust auf etw *acc* bekommen; **when the ~ takes him** wenn ihm gerade danach ist; **it took** *or* **caught my ~** es gefiel mir; **to ~ that ...** meinen, dass ...; **~ that!** (nein) so was!; **he fancies her** (*inf*) sie gefällt ihm

fancy dress *n* Verkleidung *f*, (Masken)kostüm *nt*

fancy-dress ball ['fænsɪdrɛs-] *n* Maskenball *m*

fang [fæŋ] *n* (*tooth*) Fang *m*; (*: of snake*) Giftzahn *m*

fan heater (*Brit*) *n* Heizlüfter *m*

fantasize ['fæntəsaɪz] *vi* fantasieren
fantastic [fæn'tæstɪk] *adj* fantastisch
fantasy ['fæntəsɪ] *n* Fantasie *f*; (*dream*) Traum *m*
fanzine ['fænzi:n] *n* Fanmagazin *nt*
FAQ *abbr* (*Comput: = frequently-asked questions*) FAQ *pl*
far [fɑ:ʳ] *adj*: **at the ~ side** auf der anderen Seite ▷ *adv* weit; **at the ~ end** am anderen Ende; **the ~ left/right** die extreme Linke/Rechte; **~ away, ~ off** weit entfernt *or* weg; **her thoughts were ~ away** sie war mit ihren Gedanken weit weg; **~ from** (*fig*) alles andere als; **by ~** bei Weitem; **is it ~ to London?** ist es weit bis nach London?; **it's not ~ from here** es ist nicht weit von hier; **go as ~ as the church** gehen/fahren Sie bis zur Kirche; **as ~ back as the 13th century** schon im 13. Jahrhundert; **as ~ as I know** soweit ich weiß; **as ~ as possible** so weit wie möglich; **how ~?** wie weit?; **how ~ have you got with your work?** wie weit sind Sie mit Ihrer Arbeit (gekommen)?
faraway ['fɑ:rəweɪ] *adj* weit entfernt; (*look, voice*) abwesend
farce [fɑ:s] *n* Farce *f*
fare [fɛəʳ] *n* Fahrpreis *m*; (*money*) Fahrgeld *nt*; (*passenger*) Fahrgast *m*; (*food*) Kost *f* ▷ *vi*: **he ~d well/badly** es ging ihm gut/schlecht; **half/full ~** halber/voller Fahrpreis; **how did you ~?** wie ist es Ihnen ergangen?; **they ~d badly in the recent elections** sie haben bei den letzten Wahlen schlecht abgeschnitten
Far East *n*: **the ~** der Ferne Osten
farewell [fɛə'wɛl] *excl* lebe/lebt *etc* wohl! ▷ *n* Abschied *m* ▷ *cpd* Abschieds-
farm [fɑ:m] *n* Bauernhof *m* ▷ *vt* bebauen
▸ **farm out** *vt* (*work etc*) vergeben
farmer ['fɑ:məʳ] *n* Bauer *m*, Bäu(e)rin *f*, Landwirt(in) *m(f)*
farmhouse ['fɑ:mhaus] *n* Bauernhaus *nt*
farming ['fɑ:mɪŋ] *n* Landwirtschaft *f*; (*of crops*) Ackerbau *m*; (*of animals*) Viehzucht *f*; **sheep ~** Schafzucht *f*; **intensive ~** (*of crops*) Intensivanbau *m*; (*of animals*) Intensivhaltung *f*
farmland ['fɑ:mlænd] *n* Ackerland *nt*
farm worker *n* = **farm hand**
farmyard ['fɑ:mjɑ:d] *n* Hof *m*
far-reaching ['fɑ:'ri:tʃɪŋ] *adj* weitreichend
fart [fɑ:t] *vi* furzen (*inf!*) ▷ *n* Furz *m* (*inf!*)
farther ['fɑ:ðəʳ] *adv* weiter ▷ *adj* weiter entfernt
farthest ['fɑ:ðɪst] *superl of* **far**
fascinate ['fæsɪneɪt] *vt* faszinieren
fascinating ['fæsɪneɪtɪŋ] *adj* faszinierend
fascination [fæsɪ'neɪʃən] *n* Faszination *f*
fascism ['fæʃɪzəm] *n* Faschismus *m*
fascist ['fæʃɪst] *adj* faschistisch ▷ *n* Faschist(in) *m(f)*
fashion ['fæʃən] *n* Mode *f*; (*manner*) Art *f* ▷ *vt* formen; **in ~** modern; **out of ~** unmodern; **after a ~** recht und schlecht; **in the Greek ~** im griechischen Stil
fashionable ['fæʃnəbl] *adj* modisch, modern; (*subject*) Mode-; (*club, writer*) in Mode
fashion show *n* Modenschau *f*
fast [fɑ:st] *adj* schnell; (*dye, colour*) farbecht ▷ *adv* schnell; (*stuck, held*) fest ▷ *n* Fasten *nt*; (*period of fasting*) Fastenzeit *f* ▷ *vi* fasten; **my watch is (5 minutes) ~** meine Uhr geht (5 Minuten) vor; **to be ~ asleep** tief *or* fest schlafen; **as ~ as I can** so schnell ich kann; **to make a boat ~** (*Brit*) ein Boot festmachen
fasten ['fɑ:sn] *vt* festmachen; (*coat, belt etc*) zumachen ▷ *vi* (*see vt*) festgemacht werden; zugemacht werden
▸ **fasten (up)on** *vt fus* sich *dat* in den Kopf setzen
fastener ['fɑ:snəʳ] *n* Verschluss *m*
fast food *n* Fast Food *nt*, Schnellgerichte *pl*
fastidious [fæs'tɪdɪəs] *adj* penibel
fat [fæt] *adj* dick; (*person*) dick, fett (*pej*); (*animal*) fett; (*profit*) üppig ▷ *n* Fett *nt*; **that's a ~ lot of use** (*inf*) das hilft herzlich wenig; **to live off the ~ of the land** wie Gott in Frankreich *or* wie die Made im Speck leben
fatal ['feɪtl] *adj* tödlich; (*mistake*) verhängnisvoll
fatality [fə'tælɪtɪ] *n* Todesopfer *nt*
fatally ['feɪtəlɪ] *adv* (*see adj*) tödlich; verhängnisvoll
fate [feɪt] *n* Schicksal *nt*; **to meet one's ~** vom Schicksal ereilt werden
fateful ['feɪtful] *adj* schicksalhaft
father ['fɑ:ðəʳ] *n* Vater *m*
Father Christmas *n* der Weihnachtsmann
father-in-law ['fɑ:ðərənlɔ:] *n* Schwiegervater *m*
fatherly ['fɑ:ðəlɪ] *adj* väterlich
fathom ['fæðəm] *n* (*Naut*) Faden *m* ▷ *vt* (*also*: **fathom out**) verstehen
fatigue [fə'ti:g] *n* Erschöpfung *f*; **fatigues** *npl* (*Mil*) Arbeitsanzug *m*; **metal ~** Metallermüdung *f*
fatten ['fætn] *vt* mästen ▷ *vi* (*person*) dick werden; (*animal*) fett werden; **chocolate is ~ing** Schokolade macht dick
fatty ['fætɪ] *adj* fett ▷ *n* (*inf*) Dickerchen *nt*
fatuous ['fætjuəs] *adj* albern, töricht
faucet ['fɔ:sɪt] (*US*) *n* (Wasser)hahn *m*
fault [fɔ:lt] *n* Fehler *m*; (*blame*) Schuld *f*; (*in machine*) Defekt *m*; (*Geog*) Verwerfung *f* ▷ *vt* (*also*: **find fault with**) etwas auszusetzen haben an *+dat*; **it's my ~** es ist meine Schuld; **at ~** im Unrecht; **generous to a ~** übermäßig großzügig
faulty ['fɔ:ltɪ] *adj* defekt
fauna ['fɔ:nə] *n* Fauna *f*
favour, (*US*) **favor** ['feɪvəʳ] *n* (*approval*) Wohlwollen *nt*; (*help*) Gefallen *m* ▷ *vt* bevorzugen; (*be favourable for*) begünstigen; **to ask a ~ of sb** jdn um einen Gefallen bitten; **to do sb a ~** jdm einen Gefallen tun; **to find ~ with sb** bei jdm Anklang finden; **in ~ of** (*biased*) zugunsten von; (*rejected*) zugunsten

+*gen*; **to be in ~ of sth** für etw sein; **to be in ~ of doing sth** dafür sein, etw zu tun

favourable ['feɪvrəbl] *adj* günstig; (*reaction*) positiv; (*comparison*) vorteilhaft

favourite ['feɪvrɪt] *adj* Lieblings- ▷ *n* Liebling *m*; (*in race*) Favorit(in) *m(f)*

fawn [fɔ:n] *n* Rehkitz *nt* ▷ *adj* (*also*: **fawn-coloured**) hellbraun ▷ *vi*: **to ~ (up)on** sich einschmeicheln bei

fax [fæks] *n* Fax *nt*; (*machine*) Fax(gerät) *nt* ▷ *vt* faxen

FBI (US) *n abbr* (= *Federal Bureau of Investigation*) FBI *nt*

fear [fɪəʳ] *n* Furcht *f*, Angst *f* ▷ *vt* fürchten, Angst haben vor +*dat*; (*be worried about*) befürchten ▷ *vi* sich fürchten; **~ of heights** Höhenangst *f*; **for ~ of doing sth** aus Angst, etw zu tun; **to ~ for** fürchten um; **to ~ that ...** befürchten, dass ...

fearful ['fɪəful] *adj* (*frightening*) furchtbar, schrecklich; (*apprehensive*) ängstlich; **to be ~ of** Angst haben vor +*dat*

fearless ['fɪəlɪs] *adj* furchtlos

feasible ['fi:zəbl] *adj* machbar; (*proposal, plan*) durchführbar

feast [fi:st] *n* Festmahl *nt*; (*Rel*: *also*: **feast day**) Festtag *m*, Feiertag *m* ▷ *vi* schlemmen; **to ~ on** sich gütlich tun an +*dat*

feat [fi:t] *n* Leistung *f*

feather ['fɛðəʳ] *n* Feder *f* ▷ *cpd* Feder-; (*mattress*) Federkern- ▷ *vt*: **to ~ one's nest** (*fig*) sein Schäfchen ins Trockene bringen

feature ['fi:tʃəʳ] *n* Merkmal *nt*; (*Press, TV*) Feature *nt* ▷ *vt*: **the film ~s Marlon Brando** Marlon Brando spielt in dem Film mit ▷ *vi*: **to ~ in** vorkommen in +*dat*; (*film*) mitspielen in +*dat*; **features** *npl* (*of face*) (Gesichts)züge *pl*; **it ~d prominently in** es spielte eine große Rolle in +*dat*; **a special ~ on sth/sb** ein Sonderbeitrag *m* über etw/jdn

feature film *n* Spielfilm *m*

Feb. *abbr* (= *February*) Feb.

February ['fɛbruərɪ] *n* Februar *m*; *see also* **July**

fed [fɛd] *pt, pp of* **feed**

federal ['fɛdərəl] *adj* föderalistisch

federation [fɛdə'reɪʃən] *n* Föderation *f*, Bund *m*

fed up *adj*: **to be ~ with** die Nase vollhaben von

fee [fi:] *n* Gebühr *f*; (*of doctor, lawyer*) Honorar *nt*; **school ~s** Schulgeld *nt*; **entrance ~** Eintrittsgebühr *f*; **membership ~** Mitgliedsbeitrag *m*; **for a small ~** gegen eine geringe Gebühr

feeble ['fi:bl] *adj* schwach; (*joke*) lahm

feed [fi:d] (*pt, pp* **fed**) *n* Mahlzeit *f*; (*of animal*) Fütterung *f*; (*on printer*) Papiervorschub *m* ▷ *vt* füttern; (*family etc*) ernähren; (*machine*) versorgen; **to ~ sth into sth** etw in etw *acc* einfüllen *or* eingeben; (*data, information*) etw in etw *acc* eingeben; **to ~ material into sth** Material in etw *acc* eingeben

▸ **feed back** *vt* zurückleiten

▸ **feed on** *vt fus* sich nähren von

feedback ['fi:dbæk] *n* Feedback *nt*, Rückmeldung *f*; (*from person*) Reaktion *f*

feel [fi:l] (*pt, pp* **felt**) *n* (*sensation, touch*) Gefühl *nt*; (*impression*) Atmosphäre *f* ▷ *vt* (*object*) fühlen; (*desire, anger, grief*) empfinden; (*pain*) spüren; (*cold*) leiden unter +*dat*; (*think, believe*): **I ~ that you ought to do it** ich meine *or* ich bin der Meinung, dass Sie es tun sollten; **it has a soft ~** es fühlt sich weich an; **I ~ hungry** ich habe Hunger; **I ~ cold** mir ist kalt; **to ~ lonely/better** sich einsam/besser fühlen; **I don't ~ well** mir geht es nicht gut; **I ~ sorry for him** er tut mir leid; **it ~s soft** es fühlt sich weich an; **it ~s colder here** es kommt mir hier kälter vor; **it ~s like velvet** es fühlt sich wie Samt an; **to ~ like** (*desire*) Lust haben auf +*acc*; **to ~ like doing sth** Lust haben, etw zu tun; **to get the ~ of sth** ein Gefühl für etw bekommen; **I'm still ~ing my way** ich versuche noch, mich zu orientieren

▸ **feel about** *vi* umhertasten; **to ~ about** *or* **around in one's pocket for** in seiner Tasche herumsuchen nach

▸ **feel around** *vi* = **feel about**

feeler ['fi:ləʳ] *n* Fühler *m*; **to put out a ~** *or* **feelers** (*fig*) seine Fühler ausstrecken

feeling ['fi:lɪŋ] *n* Gefühl *nt*; (*impression*) Eindruck *m*; **~s ran high about it** man ereiferte sich sehr darüber; **what are your ~s about the matter?** was meinen Sie dazu?; **I have a ~ that ...** ich habe das Gefühl, dass ...; **my ~ is that ...** meine Meinung ist, dass ...; **to hurt sb's ~s** jdn verletzen

feet [fi:t] *npl of* **foot**

feign [feɪn] *vt* vortäuschen

fell [fɛl] *pt of* **fall** ▷ *vt* fällen; (*opponent*) niederstrecken ▷ *n* (*Brit*: *mountain*) Berg *m*; (: *moorland*): **the ~s** das Moor(land) ▷ *adj*: **in one ~ swoop** auf einen Schlag

fellow ['fɛləu] *n* Mann *m*, Typ *m* (*inf*); (*comrade*) Kamerad *m*; (*of learned society*) Mitglied *nt*; (*of university*) Fellow *m*; **their ~ prisoners/students** ihre Mitgefangenen/Kommilitonen (und Kommilitoninnen); **his ~ workers** seine Kollegen (und Kolleginnen)

fellow citizen *n* Mitbürger(in) *m(f)*

fellow countryman (*irreg*: *like* **man**) *n* Landsmann *m*, Landsmännin *f*

fellow men *npl* Mitmenschen *pl*

fellowship ['fɛləuʃɪp] *n* Kameradschaft *f*; (*society*) Gemeinschaft *f*; (*Scol*) Forschungsstipendium *nt*

felony ['fɛlənɪ] *n* (*Law*) (schweres) Verbrechen *nt*

felt [fɛlt] *pt, pp of* **feel** ▷ *n* Filz *m*

female ['fi:meɪl] *n* Weibchen *nt*; (*pej*: *woman*) Frau *f*, Weib *nt* (*pej*) ▷ *adj* weiblich; (*vote etc*) Frauen-; (*Elec*: *connector, plug*) Mutter-, Innen-; **male and ~ students** Studenten und Studentinnen

feminine ['fɛmɪnɪn] *adj* weiblich, feminin ▷ *n* Femininum *nt*
feminist ['fɛmɪnɪst] *n* Feminist(in) *m(f)*
fence [fɛns] *n* Zaun *m*; (*Sport*) Hindernis *nt* ▷ *vt* (*also*: **fence in**) einzäunen ▷ *vi* (*Sport*) fechten; **to sit on the ~** (*fig*) neutral bleiben, nicht Partei ergreifen
fencing ['fɛnsɪŋ] *n* (*Sport*) Fechten *nt*
fend [fɛnd] *vi*: **to ~ for o.s.** für sich (selbst) sorgen, sich allein durchbringen
▸ **fend off** *vt* abwehren
fender ['fɛndəʳ] *n* Kamingitter *nt*; (*on boat*) Fender *m*; (*US*: *of car*) Kotflügel *m*
fennel ['fɛnl] *n* Fenchel *m*
ferment [*vi* fə'mɛnt, *n* 'fə:mɛnt] *vi* gären ▷ *n* (*fig*: *unrest*) Unruhe *f*
fern [fə:n] *n* Farn *m*
ferocious [fə'rəuʃəs] *adj* wild; (*behaviour*) heftig; (*competition*) scharf
ferret ['fɛrɪt] *n* Frettchen *nt*
▸ **ferret about** *vi* herumstöbern
▸ **ferret around** *vi* = **ferret about**
▸ **ferret out** *vt* aufspüren
ferry ['fɛrɪ] *n* (*also*: **ferryboat**) Fähre *f* ▷ *vt* transportieren; **to ~ sth/sb across** *or* **over** jdn/etw übersetzen
fertile ['fə:taɪl] *adj* fruchtbar; **~ period** fruchtbare Tage *pl*
fertilize ['fə:tɪlaɪz] *vt* düngen; (*Biol*) befruchten
fertilizer ['fə:tɪlaɪzəʳ] *n* Dünger *m*
fester ['fɛstəʳ] *vi* (*wound*) eitern; (*insult*) nagen; (*row*) sich verschlimmern
festival ['fɛstɪvəl] *n* Fest *nt*; (*Art, Mus*) Festival *nt*, Festspiele *pl*
festive ['fɛstɪv] *adj* festlich; **the ~ season** (*Brit*: *Christmas and New Year*) die Festzeit *f*
festivities [fɛs'tɪvɪtɪz] *npl* Feierlichkeiten *pl*
festoon [fɛs'tu:n] *vt*: **to ~ with** schmücken mit
fetch [fɛtʃ] *vt* holen; (*sell for*) (ein)bringen; **would you ~ me a glass of water please?** kannst du mir bitte ein Glas Wasser bringen?; **how much did it ~?** wie viel hat es eingebracht?
▸ **fetch up** (*inf*) *vi* landen (*inf*)
fête [feɪt] *n* Fest *nt*
fetus ['fi:təs] (*US*) *n* = **foetus**
feud [fju:d] *n* Streit *m* ▷ *vi* im Streit liegen; **a family ~** ein Familienstreit *m*
fever ['fi:vəʳ] *n* Fieber *nt*; **he has a ~** er hat Fieber
feverish ['fi:vərɪʃ] *adj* fiebrig; (*activity, emotion*) fieberhaft
few [fju:] *adj* wenige; **a ~** (*adj*) ein paar, einige; (*pron*) ein paar; **a ~ more (days)** noch ein paar (Tage); **they were ~** sie waren nur wenige; **~ succeed** nur wenigen gelingt es; **very ~ survive** nur sehr wenige überleben; **I know a ~** ich kenne einige; **a good ~, quite a ~** ziemlich viele; **in the next/past ~ days** in den nächsten/letzten paar Tagen; **every ~ days/months** alle paar Tage/Monate
fewer ['fju:əʳ] *adj* weniger; **there are ~ buses on Sundays** Sonntags fahren weniger Busse
fewest ['fju:ɪst] *adj* die wenigsten
fiancé [fɪ'ɑ̃:ŋseɪ] *n* Verlobte(r) *m*
fiancée [fɪ'ɑ̃:ŋseɪ] *n* Verlobte *f*
fiasco [fɪ'æskəu] *n* Fiasko *nt*
fib [fɪb] *n* Flunkerei *f* (*inf*)
fibre, (*US*) **fiber** ['faɪbəʳ] *n* Faser *f*; (*cloth*) (Faser)stoff *m*; (*roughage*) Ballaststoffe *pl*; (*Anat*: *tissue*) Gewebe *nt*
fibreglass, (*US*) **fiberglass** ['faɪbəglɑ:s] *n* Fiberglas *nt*
fickle ['fɪkl] *adj* unbeständig; (*weather*) wechselhaft
fiction ['fɪkʃən] *n* Erfindung *f*; (*Liter*) Erzählliteratur *f*, Prosaliteratur *f*
fictional ['fɪkʃənl] *adj* erfunden
fictitious [fɪk'tɪʃəs] *adj* (*false*) falsch; (*invented*) fiktiv, frei erfunden
fiddle ['fɪdl] *n* Fiedel *f* (*inf*), Geige *f*; (*fraud, swindle*) Schwindelei *f* ▷ *vt* (*Brit*: *accounts*) frisieren (*inf*); **tax ~** Steuermanipulation *f*; **to work a ~** ein krummes Ding drehen (*inf*)
▸ **fiddle with** *vt fus* herumspielen mit
fidelity [fɪ'dɛlɪtɪ] *n* Treue *f*; (*accuracy*) Genauigkeit *f*
fidget ['fɪdʒɪt] *vi* zappeln
field [fi:ld] *n* Feld *nt*; (*Sport*: *ground*) Platz *m*; (*subject, area of interest*) Gebiet *nt*; (*Comput*) Datenfeld *nt* ▷ *cpd* Feld-; **to lead the ~** das Feld anführen; **~ trip** Exkursion *f*
field marshal *n* Feldmarschall *m*
fiend [fi:nd] *n* Teufel *m*
fierce [fɪəs] *adj* wild; (*look*) böse; (*fighting, wind*) heftig; (*loyalty*) leidenschaftlich; (*enemy*) erbittert; (*heat*) glühend
fiery ['faɪərɪ] *adj* glühend; (*temperament*) feurig, hitzig
fifteen [fɪf'ti:n] *num* fünfzehn
fifteenth [fɪf'ti:nθ] *num* fünfzehnte(r, s)
fifth [fɪfθ] *num* fünfte(r, s) ▷ *n* Fünftel *nt*
fiftieth ['fɪftɪɪθ] *num* fünfzigste(r, s)
fifty ['fɪftɪ] *num* fünfzig
fifty-fifty ['fɪftɪ'fɪftɪ] *adj, adv* halbe-halbe, fifty-fifty; **to go/share ~ with sb** mit jdm halbe-halbe *or* fifty-fifty machen; **we have a ~ chance (of success)** unsere Chancen stehen fifty-fifty
fig [fɪg] *n* Feige *f*
fight [faɪt] (*pt, pp* **fought**) *n* Kampf *m*; (*quarrel*) Streit *m*; (*punch-up*) Schlägerei *f* ▷ *vt* kämpfen mit *or* gegen; (*prejudice etc*) bekämpfen; (*election*) kandidieren bei; (*emotion*) ankämpfen gegen; (*Law*: *case*) durchkämpfen, durchfechten ▷ *vi* kämpfen; (*quarrel*) sich streiten; (*punch-up*) sich schlagen; **to put up a ~** sich zur Wehr setzen; **to ~ one's way through a crowd/the undergrowth** sich *dat* einen Weg durch die Menge/das Unterholz bahnen; **to ~ against** bekämpfen; **to ~ for one's rights** für seine Rechte kämpfen
▸ **fight back** *vi* zurückschlagen; (*Sport*)

zurückkämpfen; (*after illness*) zu Kräften kommen ▷ *vt fus* unterdrücken
▸ **fight down** *vt* unterdrücken
▸ **fight off** *vt* abwehren; (*sleep, urge*) ankämpfen gegen
▸ **fight out** *vt*: **to ~ it out** es untereinander ausfechten
fighter ['faɪtəʳ] *n* Kämpfer(in) *m(f)*; (*plane*) Jagdflugzeug *nt*; (*fig*) Kämpfernatur *f*
fighting ['faɪtɪŋ] *n* Kämpfe *pl*; (*brawl*) Schlägereien *pl*
figment ['fɪgmənt] *n*: **a ~ of the imagination** ein Hirngespinst *nt*, pure Einbildung *f*
figurative ['fɪgjurətɪv] *adj* bildlich, übertragen; (*style*) gegenständlich
figure ['fɪgəʳ] *n* Figur *f*; (*illustration*) Abbildung *f*; (*number, statistic, cipher*) Zahl *f*; (*person*) Gestalt *f*; (*personality*) Persönlichkeit *f* ▷ *vt* (*esp US*) glauben, schätzen ▷ *vi* eine Rolle spielen; **to put a ~ on sth** eine Zahl für etw angeben; **public ~** Persönlichkeit *f* des öffentlichen Lebens
▸ **figure out** *vt* ausrechnen
figurehead ['fɪgəhɛd] *n* Galionsfigur *f*
file [faɪl] *n* Akte *f*; (*folder*) (Akten)ordner *m*; (*for loose leaf*) (Akten)mappe *f*; (*Comput*) Datei *f*; (*row*) Reihe *f*; (*tool*) Feile *f* ▷ *vt* ablegen, abheften; (*claim*) einreichen; (*wood, metal, fingernails*) feilen ▷ *vi*: **to ~ in/out** nacheinander hereinkommen/hinausgehen; **to ~ a suit against sb** eine Klage gegen jdn erheben; **to ~ past** in einer Reihe vorbeigehen; **to ~ for divorce** die Scheidung einreichen
filing cabinet *n* Aktenschrank *m*
Filipino [fɪlɪ'pi:nəu] *n* Filipino *m*, Filipina *f*; (*Ling*) Philippinisch *nt*
fill [fɪl] *vt* füllen; (*space, area*) ausfüllen; (*tooth*) plombieren; (*need*) erfüllen ▷ *vi* sich füllen ▷ *n*: **to eat one's ~** sich satt essen; **we've already ~ed that vacancy** wir haben diese Stelle schon besetzt
▸ **fill in** *vt* füllen; (*time*) überbrücken; (*form*) ausfüllen ▷ *vi*: **to ~ in for sb** für jdn einspringen; **to ~ sb in on sth** (*inf*) jdn über etw *acc* ins Bild setzen
▸ **fill out** *vt* ausfüllen
▸ **fill up** *vt* füllen ▷ *vi* (*Aut*) tanken; **~ it up, please** (*Aut*) bitte volltanken
fillet ['fɪlɪt] *n* Filet *nt* ▷ *vt* filetieren
fillet steak *n* Filetsteak *nt*
filling ['fɪlɪŋ] *n* Füllung *f*; (*for tooth*) Plombe *f*
filling station *n* Tankstelle *f*
film [fɪlm] *n* Film *m*; (*of powder etc*) Schicht *f*; (*for wrapping*) Plastikfolie *f* ▷ *vt, vi* filmen
film star *n* Filmstar *m*
filter ['fɪltəʳ] *n* Filter *m* ▷ *vt* filtern
▸ **filter in** *vi* durchsickern
▸ **filter through** *vi* = **filter in**
filter lane (*Brit*) *n* Abbiegespur *f*
filter tip *n* Filter *m*
filth [fɪlθ] *n* Dreck *m*, Schmutz *m*
filthy ['fɪlθɪ] *adj* dreckig, schmutzig; (*language*) unflätig
fin [fɪn] *n* Flosse *f*; (*Tech*) Seitenflosse *f*
final ['faɪnl] *adj* letzte(r, s); (*ultimate*) letztendlich; (*definitive*) endgültig ▷ *n* Finale *nt*, Endspiel *nt*; **finals** *npl* (*Univ*) Abschlussprüfung *f*
finale [fɪ'nɑ:lɪ] *n* Finale *nt*; (*Theat*) Schlussszene *f*
finalist ['faɪnəlɪst] *n* Endrundenteilnehmer(in) *m(f)*, Finalist(in) *m(f)*
finalize ['faɪnəlaɪz] *vt* endgültig festlegen
finally ['faɪnəlɪ] *adv* endlich, schließlich; (*lastly*) schließlich, zum Schluss; (*irrevocably*) endgültig
finance [faɪ'næns] *n* Geldmittel *pl*; (*money management*) Finanzwesen *nt* ▷ *vt* finanzieren; **finances** *npl* (*personal*) Finanzen *pl*, Finanzlage *f*
financial [faɪ'nænʃəl] *adj* finanziell; **~ statement** Bilanz *f*
financial year *n* Geschäftsjahr *nt*
find [faɪnd] (*pt, pp* **found**) *vt* finden; (*discover*) entdecken ▷ *n* Fund *m*; **to ~ sb guilty** jdn für schuldig befinden; **to ~ (some) difficulty in doing sth** (einige) Schwierigkeiten haben, etw zu tun
▸ **find out** *vt* herausfinden; (*person*) erwischen ▷ *vi*: **to ~ out about** etwas herausfinden über *+acc*; (*by chance*) etwas erfahren über *+acc*
findings ['faɪndɪŋz] *npl* (*Law*) Urteil *nt*; (*of report*) Ergebnis *nt*
fine [faɪn] *adj* fein; (*excellent*) gut; (*thin*) dünn ▷ *adv* gut; (*small*) fein ▷ *n* Geldstrafe *f* ▷ *vt* mit einer Geldstrafe belegen; **he's ~** es geht ihm gut; **the weather is ~** das Wetter ist schön; **that's cutting it (a bit) ~** das ist aber (ein bisschen) knapp; **you're doing ~** das machen Sie gut
fine arts *npl* schöne Künste *pl*
finery ['faɪnərɪ] *n* (*of dress*) Staat *m*
finger ['fɪŋgəʳ] *n* Finger *m* ▷ *vt* befühlen; **little ~** kleiner Finger; **index ~** Zeigefinger *m*
fingernail ['fɪŋgəneɪl] *n* Fingernagel *m*
fingerprint ['fɪŋgəprɪnt] *n* Fingerabdruck *m* ▷ *vt* Fingerabdrücke abnehmen *+dat*
fingertip ['fɪŋgətɪp] *n* Fingerspitze *f*; **to have sth at one's ~s** (*to hand*) etw parat haben; (*know well*) etw aus dem Effeff kennen (*inf*)
finish ['fɪnɪʃ] *n* Schluss *m*, Ende *nt*; (*Sport*) Finish *nt*; (*polish etc*) Verarbeitung *f* ▷ *vt* fertig sein mit; (*work*) erledigen; (*book*) auslesen; (*use up*) aufbrauchen ▷ *vi* enden; (*person*) fertig sein; **to ~ doing sth** mit etw fertig werden; **to ~ third** als Dritter durchs Ziel gehen; **to have ~ed with sth** mit etw fertig sein; **she's ~ed with him** sie hat mit ihm Schluss gemacht
▸ **finish off** *vt* fertig machen; (*kill*) den Gnadenstoß geben
▸ **finish up** *vt* (*food*) aufessen; (*drink*) austrinken ▷ *vi* (*end up*) landen

finishing line ['fɪnɪʃɪŋ-] *n* Ziellinie *f*
finite ['faɪnaɪt] *adj* begrenzt; (*verb*) finit
Finland ['fɪnlənd] *n* Finnland *nt*
Finn [fɪn] *n* Finne *m*, Finnin *f*
Finnish ['fɪnɪʃ] *adj* finnisch ▷ *n* (*Ling*) Finnisch *nt*
fir [fəːʳ] *n* Tanne *f*
fire ['faɪəʳ] *n* Feuer *nt*; (*in hearth*) (Kamin)feuer *nt*; (*accidental fire*) Brand *m* ▷ *vt* abschießen; (*imagination*) beflügeln; (*enthusiasm*) befeuern; (*inf: dismiss*) feuern ▷ *vi* feuern, schießen; **to ~ a gun** ein Gewehr abschießen; **to be on ~** brennen; **to set ~ to sth, set sth on fire** etw anzünden; **insured against ~** feuerversichert; **electric/gas ~** Elektro-/Gasofen *m*; **to come/be under ~ (from)** unter Beschuss (von) geraten/stehen
fire alarm *n* Feuermelder *m*
firearm ['faɪərɑːm] *n* Feuerwaffe *f*, Schusswaffe *f*
fire brigade *n* Feuerwehr *f*
fire department (*US*) *n* Feuerwehr *f*
fire engine *n* Feuerwehrauto *nt*
fire escape *n* Feuertreppe *f*
fireman ['faɪəmən] (*irreg: like* **man**) *n* Feuerwehrmann *m*
fireplace ['faɪəpleɪs] *n* Kamin *m*
fireside ['faɪəsaɪd] *n*: **by the ~** am Kamin
fire station *n* Feuerwache *f*
firewood ['faɪəwud] *n* Brennholz *nt*
fireworks ['faɪəwəːks] *npl* Feuerwerkskörper *pl*; (*display*) Feuerwerk *nt*
firing squad *n* Exekutionskommando *nt*
firm [fəːm] *adj* fest; (*mattress*) hart; (*measures*) durchgreifend ▷ *n* Firma *f*; **to be a ~ believer in sth** fest von etw überzeugt sein
firmly ['fəːmlɪ] *adv* (*see adj*) fest; hart; (*definitely*) entschlossen
first [fəːst] *adj* erste(r, s) ▷ *adv* als Erste(r, s); (*before other things*) zuerst; (*when listing reasons etc*) erstens; (*for the first time*) zum ersten Mal ▷ *n* Erste(r, s); (*Aut: also*: **first gear**) der erste Gang; (*Brit: Scol*) ≈ Eins *f*; **the ~ of January** der erste Januar; **at ~** zuerst, zunächst; **~ of all** vor allem; **in the ~ instance** zuerst *or* zunächst einmal; **I'll do it ~ thing (tomorrow)** ich werde es (morgen) als Erstes tun; **from the very ~** gleich von Anfang an
first aid *n* erste Hilfe *f*
first-aid kit [fəːst'eɪd-] *n* Erste-Hilfe-Ausrüstung *f*
first-class ['fəːst'klɑːs] *adj* erstklassig; (*carriage, ticket*) Erste(r)-Klasse-; (*post*) bevorzugt befördert ▷ *adv* (*travel, send*) erster Klasse
first-hand ['fəːst'hænd] *adj* aus erster Hand
first lady (*US*) *n* First Lady *f*; **the ~ of jazz** die Königin des Jazz
firstly ['fəːstlɪ] *adv* erstens, zunächst einmal
first name *n* Vorname *m*
first-rate ['fəːst'reɪt] *adj* erstklassig
fiscal ['fɪskl] *adj* (*year*) Steuer-; (*policies*) Finanz-
fish [fɪʃ] *n inv* Fisch *m* ▷ *vt* (*area*) fischen in *+dat*; (*river*) angeln in *+dat* ▷ *vi* fischen; (*as sport, hobby*) angeln; **to go ~ing** fischen/angeln gehen
▸ **fish out** *vt* herausfischen
fisherman ['fɪʃəmən] (*irreg: like* **man**) *n* Fischer *m*
fish farm *n* Fischzucht(anlage) *f*
fishing boat ['fɪʃɪŋ-] *n* Fischerboot *nt*
fishing line *n* Angelschnur *f*
fishing rod *n* Angelrute *f*
fishing tackle *n* Angelgeräte *pl*
fishmonger ['fɪʃmʌŋgəʳ] (*esp Brit*) *n* Fischhändler(in) *m(f)*
fishmonger's ['fɪʃmʌŋgəz], **fishmonger's shop** (*esp Brit*) *n* Fischgeschäft *nt*
fish slice (*Brit*) *n* Fischvorlegemesser *nt*
fish sticks (*US*) *npl* = **fishfingers**
fishy ['fɪʃɪ] (*inf*) *adj* verdächtig, faul
fist [fɪst] *n* Faust *f*
fit [fɪt] *adj* geeignet; (*healthy*) gesund; (*Sport*) fit ▷ *vt* passen *+dat*; (*adjust*) anpassen; (*match*) entsprechen *+dat*; (*be suitable for*) passen auf *+acc*; (*put in*) einbauen; (*attach*) anbringen; (*equip*) ausstatten ▷ *vi* passen; (*parts*) zusammenpassen; (*in space, gap*) hineinpassen ▷ *n* (*Med*) Anfall *m*; **to ~ the description** der Beschreibung entsprechen; **~ to** bereit zu; **~ to eat** essbar; **~ to drink** trinkbar; **to be ~ to keep** es wert sein, aufbewahrt zu werden; **~ for** geeignet für; **~ for work** arbeitsfähig; **to keep ~** sich fit halten; **do as you think** *or* **see ~** tun Sie, was Sie für richtig halten; **a ~ of anger** ein Wutanfall *m*; **a ~ of pride** eine Anwandlung von Stolz; **to have a ~** einen Anfall haben; (*inf: fig*) einen Anfall kriegen; **this dress is a good ~** dieses Kleid sitzt *or* passt gut; **by ~s and starts** unregelmäßig
▸ **fit in** *vi* (*person*) sich einfügen; (*object*) hineinpassen ▷ *vt* (*fig: appointment*) unterbringen, einschieben; (*visitor*) Zeit finden für; **to ~ in with sb's plans** sich mit jds Plänen vereinbaren lassen
fitful ['fɪtful] *adj* unruhig
fitment ['fɪtmənt] *n* Einrichtungsgegenstand *m*
fitness ['fɪtnɪs] *n* Gesundheit *f*; (*Sport*) Fitness *f*
fitted carpet ['fɪtɪd-] *n* Teppichboden *m*
fitted kitchen (*Brit*) *n* Einbauküche *f*
fitter ['fɪtəʳ] *n* Monteur *m*; (*for machines*) (Maschinen)schlosser *m*
fitting ['fɪtɪŋ] *adj* passend; (*thanks*) gebührend ▷ *n* (*of dress*) Anprobe *f*; (*of piece of equipment*) Installation *f*; **fittings** *npl* Ausstattung *f*
fitting room *n* Anprobe(kabine) *f*
five [faɪv] *num* fünf
fiver ['faɪvəʳ] (*inf*) *n* (*Brit*) Fünfpfundschein *m*; (*US*) Fünfdollarschein *m*
fix [fɪks] *vt* (*attach*) befestigen; (*arrange*) festsetzen, festlegen; (*mend*) reparieren; (*meal, drink*) machen; (*inf*) manipulieren ▷ *n*: **to be in a ~** in der Patsche *or* Klemme

sitzen; **to ~ sth to/on sth** etw an/auf etw *dat* befestigen; **to ~ one's eyes/attention on** seinen Blick/seine Aufmerksamkeit richten auf *+acc*; **the fight was a ~** (*inf*) der Kampf war eine abgekartete Sache

▸ **fix up** *vt* arrangieren; **to ~ sb up with sth** jdm etw besorgen

fixation [fɪk'seɪʃən] *n* Fixierung *f*

fixed [fɪkst] *adj* fest; (*ideas*) fix; (*smile*) starr; **~ charge** Pauschale *f*; **how are you ~ for money?** wie sieht es bei dir mit dem Geld aus?

fixture ['fɪkstʃəʳ] *n* Ausstattungsgegenstand *m*; (*Football etc*) Spiel *nt*; (*Athletics etc*) Veranstaltung *f*

fizzy ['fɪzɪ] *adj* sprudelnd

flabbergasted ['flæbəgɑːstɪd] *adj* verblüfft

flabby ['flæbɪ] *adj* schwammig, wabbelig (*inf*)

flag [flæg] *n* Fahne *f*; (*of country*) Flagge *f*; (*for signalling*) Signalflagge *f*; (*also*: **flagstone**) (Stein)platte *f* ▹ *vi* erlahmen; **~ of convenience** Billigflagge *f*; **to ~ down** anhalten

flagpole ['flægpəul] *n* Fahnenstange *f*

flagship ['flægʃɪp] *n* Flaggschiff *nt*

flair [flɛəʳ] *n* Talent *nt*; (*style*) Flair *nt*

flak [flæk] *n* Flakfeuer *nt*; **to get a lot of ~ (for sth)** (*inf*: *criticism*) (wegen etw) unter Beschuss geraten

flake [fleɪk] *n* Splitter *m*; (*of snow, soap powder*) Flocke *f* ▹ *vi* (*also*: **flake off**) abblättern, absplittern

▸ **flake out** (*inf*) *vi* aus den Latschen kippen; (*go to sleep*) einschlafen

flamboyant [flæm'bɔɪənt] *adj* extravagant

flame [fleɪm] *n* Flamme *f*; **to burst into ~s** in Flammen aufgehen; **an old ~** (*inf*) eine alte Flamme

flamingo [flə'mɪŋgəu] *n* Flamingo *m*

flammable ['flæməbl] *adj* leicht entzündbar

flan [flæn] *n* Kuchen *m*; **~ case** Tortenboden *m*

flank [flæŋk] *n* Flanke *f* ▹ *vt* flankieren

flannel ['flænl] *n* Flanell *m*; (*Brit*: *also*: **face flannel**) Waschlappen *m*; (: *inf*) Geschwafel *nt*; **flannels** *npl* (*trousers*) Flanellhose *f*

flap [flæp] *n* Klappe *f*; (*of envelope*) Lasche *f* ▹ *vt* schlagen mit ▹ *vi* flattern; (*inf*: *also*: **be in a flap**) in heller Aufregung sein

flare [flɛəʳ] *n* Leuchtsignal *nt*; (*in skirt etc*) Weite *f*

▸ **flare up** *vi* auflodern; (*person*) aufbrausen; (*fighting, violence, trouble*) ausbrechen; *see also* **flared**

flash [flæʃ] *n* Aufblinken *nt*; (*also*: **newsflash**) Eilmeldung *f*; (*Phot*) Blitz *m*, Blitzlicht *nt*; (*US*: *torch*) Taschenlampe *f* ▹ *vt* aufleuchten lassen; (*news, message*) durchgeben; (*look, smile*) zuwerfen ▹ *vi* aufblinken; (*light on ambulance*) blinken; (*eyes*) blitzen; **in a ~** im Nu; **quick as a ~** blitzschnell; **~ of inspiration** Geistesblitz *m*; **to ~ one's headlights** die Lichthupe betätigen; **the thought ~ed through his mind** der Gedanke schoss ihm durch den Kopf; **to ~ by** *or* **past** vorbeiflitzen (*inf*)

flashback ['flæʃbæk] *n* Rückblende *f*

flashbulb ['flæʃbʌlb] *n* Blitzbirne *f*

flashcube ['flæʃkjuːb] *n* Blitzwürfel *m*

flashlight ['flæʃlaɪt] *n* Blitzlicht *nt*

flashy ['flæʃɪ] (*pej*) *adj* auffällig, protzig

flask [flɑːsk] *n* Flakon *m*; (*Chem*) Glaskolben *m*; (*also*: **vacuum flask**) Thermosflasche® *f*

flat [flæt] *adj* flach; (*surface*) eben; (*tyre*) platt; (*battery*) leer; (*beer*) schal; (*refusal, denial*) glatt; (*note, voice*) zu tief; (*rate, fee*) Pauschal- ▹ *n* (*Brit*: *apartment*) Wohnung *f*; (*Aut*) (Reifen)panne *f*; (*Mus*) Erniedrigungszeichen *nt*; **to work ~ out** auf Hochtouren arbeiten; **~ rate of pay** Pauschallohn *m*

flatly ['flætlɪ] *adv* (*refuse, deny*) glatt, kategorisch

flatten ['flætn] *vt* (*also*: **flatten out**) (ein)ebnen; (*paper, fabric etc*) glätten; (*building, city*) dem Erdboden gleichmachen; (*crop*) zu Boden drücken; (*inf*: *person*) umhauen; **to ~ o.s. against a wall/door** *etc* sich platt gegen *or* an eine Wand/Tür *etc* drücken

flatter ['flætəʳ] *vt* schmeicheln *+dat*

flattering ['flætərɪŋ] *adj* schmeichelhaft; (*dress etc*) vorteilhaft

flattery ['flætərɪ] *n* Schmeichelei *f*

flaunt [flɔːnt] *vt* zur Schau stellen, protzen mit

flavour, (US) **flavor** ['fleɪvəʳ] *n* Geschmack *m*; (*of ice-cream etc*) Geschmacksrichtung *f* ▹ *vt* Geschmack verleihen *+dat*; **to give** *or* **add ~ to** Geschmack verleihen *+dat*; **music with an African ~** (*fig*) Musik mit einer afrikanischen Note; **strawberry-~ed** mit Erdbeergeschmack

flavouring ['fleɪvərɪŋ] *n* Aroma *nt*

flaw [flɔː] *n* Fehler *m*

flawless ['flɔːlɪs] *adj* (*performance*) fehlerlos; (*complexion*) makellos

flax [flæks] *n* Flachs *m*

flea [fliː] *n* Floh *m*

flea market *n* Flohmarkt *m*

fleck [flɛk] *n* Tupfen *m*, Punkt *m*; (*of dust*) Flöckchen *nt*; (*of mud, paint, colour*) Fleck(en) *m* ▹ *vt* bespritzen; **brown ~ed with white** braun mit weißen Punkten

fled [flɛd] *pt, pp of* **flee**

flee [fliː] (*pt, pp* **fled**) *vt* fliehen *or* flüchten vor *+dat*; (*country*) fliehen *or* flüchten aus ▹ *vi* fliehen, flüchten

fleece [fliːs] *n* Schafwolle *f*; (*sheep's coat*) Schaffell *nt*, Vlies *nt* ▹ *vt* (*inf*: *cheat*) schröpfen

fleet [fliːt] *n* Flotte *f*; (*of lorries, cars*) Fuhrpark *m*

fleeting ['fliːtɪŋ] *adj* flüchtig

Flemish ['flɛmɪʃ] *adj* flämisch ▹ *n* (*Ling*) Flämisch *nt*; **the Flemish** *npl* die Flamen

flesh [flɛʃ] *n* Fleisch *nt*; (*of fruit*) Fruchtfleisch *nt*

▸ **flesh out** *vt* ausgestalten

flesh wound [-wuːnd] *n* Fleischwunde *f*

flew [fluː] *pt of* **fly**

flex [flɛks] *n* Kabel *nt* ▷ *vt* beugen; (*muscles*) spielen lassen
flexibility [flɛksɪ'bɪlɪtɪ] *n* (*see adj*) Flexibilität *f*; Biegsamkeit *f*
flexible ['flɛksəbl] *adj* flexibel; (*material*) biegsam
flexitime ['flɛksɪtaɪm] *n* gleitende Arbeitszeit *f*, Gleitzeit *f*
flick [flɪk] *n* (*of finger*) Schnipsen *nt*; (*of hand*) Wischen *nt*; (*of whip*) Schnalzen *nt*; (*of towel etc*) Schlagen *nt*; (*of switch*) Knipsen *nt* ▷ *vt* schnipsen; (*with hand*) wischen; (*whip*) knallen mit; (*switch*) knipsen; **flicks** (*inf*) *npl* Kino *nt*; **to ~ a towel at sb** mit einem Handtuch nach jdm schlagen
▸ **flick through** *vt fus* durchblättern
flicker ['flɪkə^r^] *vi* flackern; (*eyelids*) zucken ▷ *n* Flackern *nt*; (*of pain, fear*) Aufflackern *nt*; (*of smile*) Anflug *m*; (*of eyelid*) Zucken *nt*
flier ['flaɪə^r^] *n* Flieger(in) *m(f)*
flight [flaɪt] *n* Flug *m*; (*escape*) Flucht *f*; (*also*: **flight of steps**) Treppe *f*; **to take ~** die Flucht ergreifen; **to put to ~** in die Flucht schlagen
flight attendant (*US*) *n* Flugbegleiter(in) *m(f)*
flight deck *n* (*Aviat*) Cockpit *nt*; (*Naut*) Flugdeck *nt*
flimsy ['flɪmzɪ] *adj* leicht, dünn; (*building*) leicht gebaut; (*excuse*) fadenscheinig; (*evidence*) nicht stichhaltig
flinch [flɪntʃ] *vi* zusammenzucken; **to ~ from** zurückschrecken vor *+dat*
fling [flɪŋ] (*pt, pp* **flung**) *vt* schleudern; (*arms*) werfen; (*oneself*) stürzen ▷ *n* (flüchtige) Affäre *f*
flint [flɪnt] *n* Feuerstein *m*
flip [flɪp] *vt* (*switch*) knipsen; (*coin*) werfen; (*US*: *pancake*) umdrehen ▷ *vi*: **to ~ for sth** (*US*) um etw mit einer Münze knobeln
▸ **flip through** *vt fus* durchblättern; (*records etc*) durchgehen
flippant ['flɪpənt] *adj* leichtfertig
flipper ['flɪpə^r^] *n* Flosse *f*; (*for swimming*) (Schwimm)flosse *f*
flirt [flə:t] *vi* flirten; (*with idea*) liebäugeln ▷ *n*: **he/she is a ~** er/sie flirtet gern
float [fləut] *n* Schwimmkork *m*; (*for fishing*) Schwimmer *m*; (*lorry*) Festwagen *m*; (*money*) Wechselgeld *nt* ▷ *vi* schwimmen; (*swimmer*) treiben; (*through air*) schweben; (*currency*) floaten ▷ *vt* (*currency*) freigeben, floaten lassen; (*company*) gründen; (*idea, plan*) in den Raum stellen
▸ **float around** *vi* im Umlauf sein; (*person*) herumschweben (*inf*); (*object*) herumfliegen (*inf*)
flock [flɔk] *n* Herde *f*; (*of birds*) Schwarm *m* ▷ *vi*: **to ~ to** (*place*) strömen nach; (*event*) in Scharen kommen zu
flog [flɔg] *vt* auspeitschen; (*inf*: *sell*) verscherbeln
flood [flʌd] *n* Überschwemmung *f*; (*of letters, imports etc*) Flut *f* ▷ *vt* überschwemmen; (*Aut*) absaufen lassen (*inf*) ▷ *vi* überschwemmt werden; **to be in ~** Hochwasser führen; **to ~ the market** den Markt überschwemmen; **to ~ into Hungary/the square/the palace** nach Ungarn/auf den Platz/in den Palast strömen
flooding ['flʌdɪŋ] *n* Überschwemmung *f*
floodlight ['flʌdlaɪt] *n* Flutlicht *nt* ▷ *vt* (mit Flutlicht) beleuchten; (*building*) anstrahlen
floor [flɔ:^r^] *n* (Fuß)boden *m*; (*storey*) Stock *nt*; (*of sea, valley*) Boden *m* ▷ *vt* (*subj*: *blow*) zu Boden werfen; (: *question, remark*) die Sprache verschlagen *+dat*; **on the ~** auf dem Boden; **ground ~** (*Brit*): **first ~** (*US*) Erdgeschoss *nt*, Erdgeschoß *nt* (*Österr*); **first ~** (*Brit*): **second ~** (*US*) erster Stock *m*; **top ~** oberstes Stockwerk *nt*; **to have the ~** (*speaker*: *at meeting*) das Wort haben
floorboard ['flɔ:bɔ:d] *n* Diele *f*
flooring ['flɔ:rɪŋ] *n* (Fuß)boden *m*; (*covering*) Fußbodenbelag *m*
floor show *n* Show *f*, Vorstellung *f*
flop [flɔp] *n* Reinfall *m* ▷ *vi* (*play, book*) durchfallen; (*fall*) sich fallen lassen; (*scheme*) ein Reinfall sein
floppy ['flɔpɪ] *adj* schlaff, schlapp ▷ *n* (*also*: **floppy disk**) Diskette *f*, Floppy Disk *f*; **~ hat** Schlapphut *m*
flora ['flɔ:rə] *n* Flora *f*
floral ['flɔ:rl] *adj* geblümt
florid ['flɔrɪd] *adj* (*style*) blumig; (*complexion*) kräftig
florist ['flɔrɪst] *n* Blumenhändler(in) *m(f)*
florist's ['flɔrɪsts], **florist's shop** *n* Blumengeschäft *nt*
flotation [fləu'teɪʃən] *n* (*of shares*) Auflegung *f*; (*of company*) Umwandlung *f* in eine Aktiengesellschaft
flounder ['flaundə^r^] *vi* sich abstrampeln; (*fig*: *speaker*) ins Schwimmen kommen; (*economy*) in Schwierigkeiten geraten ▷ *n* Flunder *f*
flour ['flauə^r^] *n* Mehl *nt*
flourish ['flʌrɪʃ] *vi* gedeihen; (*business*) blühen, florieren ▷ *vt* schwenken ▷ *n* (*in writing*) Schnörkel *m*; (*bold gesture*): **with a ~** mit einer schwungvollen Bewegung
flout [flaut] *vt* sich hinwegsetzen über *+acc*
flow [fləu] *n* Fluss *m*; (*of sea*) Flut *f* ▷ *vi* fließen; (*clothes, hair*) wallen
flow chart *n* Flussdiagramm *nt*
flower ['flauə^r^] *n* Blume *f*; (*blossom*) Blüte *f* ▷ *vi* blühen; **to be in ~** blühen
flowerpot ['flauəpɔt] *n* Blumentopf *m*
flowery ['flauərɪ] *adj* blumig; (*pattern*) Blumen-
flown [fləun] *pp of* **fly**
flu [flu:] *n* Grippe *f*
fluctuate ['flʌktjueɪt] *vi* schwanken; (*opinions, attitudes*) sich ändern
fluent ['flu:ənt] *adj* flüssig; **he speaks ~ German, he's ~ in German** er spricht fließend Deutsch

fluff [flʌf] *n* Fussel *m*; (*fur*) Flaum *m* ▷ *vt* (*inf: do badly*) verpatzen; (*also*: **fluff out**) aufplustern
fluffy ['flʌfɪ] *adj* flaumig; (*jacket etc*) weich, kuschelig; ~ **toy** Kuscheltier *nt*
fluid ['flu:ɪd] *adj* fließend; (*situation, arrangement*) unklar ▷ *n* Flüssigkeit *f*
fluid ounce (*Brit*) *n* flüssige Unze *f* (*= 28 ml*)
fluke [flu:k] (*inf*) *n* Glücksfall *m*; **by a ~** durch einen glücklichen Zufall
flung [flʌŋ] *pt, pp of* **fling**
fluorescent [fluə'rɛsnt] *adj* fluoreszierend; (*paint*) Leucht-; (*light*) Neon-
fluoride ['fluəraɪd] *n* Fluorid *nt*
flurry ['flʌrɪ] *n* (*of snow*) Gestöber *nt*; **a ~ of activity/excitement** hektische Aktivität/Aufregung
flush [flʌʃ] *n* Röte *f*; (*fig: of beauty etc*) Blüte *f* ▷ *vt* (durch)spülen, (aus)spülen ▷ *vi* erröten ▷ *adj*: **~ with** auf gleicher Ebene mit; **~ against** direkt an *+dat*; **in the first ~ of youth** in der ersten Jugendblüte; **in the first ~ of freedom** im ersten Freiheitstaumel; **hot ~es** (*Brit*) Hitzewallungen *pl*; **to ~ the toilet** spülen, die Wasserspülung betätigen
▸ **flush out** *vt* aufstöbern
flushed [flʌʃt] *adj* rot
flustered ['flʌstəd] *adj* nervös; (*confused*) durcheinander
flute [flu:t] *n* Querflöte *f*
flutter ['flʌtəʳ] *n* Flattern *nt*; (*of panic, nerves*) kurzer Anfall *m*; (*of excitement*) Beben *nt* ▷ *vi* flattern; (*person*) tänzeln; **to have a ~** (*Brit: inf: gamble*) sein Glück (beim Wetten) versuchen
flux [flʌks] *n*: **in a state of ~** im Fluss
fly [flaɪ] (*pt* **flew**, *pp* **flown**) *n* Fliege *f*; (*on trousers: also*: **flies**) (Hosen)schlitz *m* ▷ *vt* fliegen; (*kite*) steigen lassen ▷ *vi* fliegen; (*escape*) fliehen; (*flag*) wehen; **to ~ open** auffliegen; **to ~ off the handle** an die Decke gehen (*inf*); **pieces of metal went ~ing everywhere** überall flogen Metallteile herum; **she came ~ing into the room** sie kam ins Zimmer gesaust; **her glasses flew off** die Brille flog ihr aus dem Gesicht
▸ **fly away** *vi* wegfliegen
▸ **fly in** *vi* einfliegen; **he flew in yesterday** er ist gestern mit dem Flugzeug gekommen
▸ **fly off** *vi* = **fly away**
▸ **fly out** *vi* ausfliegen; **he flew out yesterday** er ist gestern hingeflogen
flying ['flaɪɪŋ] *n* Fliegen *nt* ▷ *adj*: **a ~ visit** ein Blitzbesuch *m*; **he doesn't like ~** er fliegt nicht gerne; **with ~ colours** mit fliegenden Fahnen
flying saucer *n* fliegende Untertasse *f*
flying start *n*: **to get off to a ~** (*Sport*) hervorragend wegkommen; (*fig*) einen glänzenden Start haben
flyover ['flaɪəuvəʳ] *n* (*Brit*) Überführung *f*; (*US*) Luftparade *f*
flysheet ['flaɪʃi:t] *n* (*for tent*) Überzelt *nt*
FM *abbr* (*Brit: Mil*) = **field marshal** (*Radio*: = *frequency modulation*) FM, ≈ UKW
foal [fəul] *n* Fohlen *nt*
foam [fəum] *n* Schaum *m*; (*also*: **foam rubber**) Schaumgummi *m* ▷ *vi* schäumen
fob [fɔb] *vt*: **to ~ sb off** jdn abspeisen ▷ *n* (*also*: **watch fob**) Uhrkette *f*
focal point ['fəukl-] *n* Mittelpunkt *m*; (*of camera, telescope etc*) Brennpunkt *m*
focus ['fəukəs] (*pl* **~es**) *n* Brennpunkt *m*; (*of storm*) Zentrum *nt* ▷ *vt* einstellen; (*light rays*) bündeln ▷ *vi*: **to ~ (on)** (*with camera*) klar *or* scharf einstellen *+acc*; (*person*) sich konzentrieren (auf *+acc*); **in/out of ~** (*camera etc*) scharf/unscharf eingestellt; (*photograph*) scharf/unscharf
fodder ['fɔdəʳ] *n* Futter *nt*
foe [fəu] *n* Feind(in) *m(f)*
foetus, (*US*) **fetus** ['fi:təs] *n* Fötus *m*, Fetus *m*
fog [fɔg] *n* Nebel *m*
foggy ['fɔgɪ] *adj* neb(e)lig
fog lamp, (*US*) **fog light** *n* (*Aut*) Nebelscheinwerfer *m*
foil [fɔɪl] *vt* vereiteln ▷ *n* Folie *f*; (*complement*) Kontrast *m*; (*Fencing*) Florett *nt*; **to act as a ~ to** einen Kontrast darstellen zu
fold [fəuld] *n* Falte *f*; (*Agr*) Pferch *m*; (*fig*) Schoß *m* ▷ *vt* (zusammen)falten; (*arms*) verschränken ▷ *vi* (*business*) eingehen (*inf*)
▸ **fold up** *vi* sich zusammenfalten lassen; (*bed, table*) sich zusammenklappen lassen; (*business*) eingehen (*inf*) ▷ *vt* zusammenfalten
folder ['fəuldəʳ] *n* Aktenmappe *f*; (*binder*) Hefter *m*; (*brochure*) Informationsblatt *nt*
folding ['fəuldɪŋ] *adj* (*chair, bed*) Klapp-
foliage ['fəulɪɪdʒ] *n* Laubwerk *nt*
folk [fəuk] *npl* Leute *pl* ▷ *cpd* Volks-; **my ~s** (*parents*) meine alten Herrschaften
folklore ['fəuklɔ:ʳ] *n* Folklore *f*
folk music *n* Volksmusik *f*; (*contemporary*) Folk *m*
folk song *n* Volkslied *nt*; (*contemporary*) Folksong *m*
follow ['fɔləu] *vt* folgen *+dat*; (*with eyes*) verfolgen; (*advice, instructions*) befolgen ▷ *vi* folgen; **to ~ in sb's footsteps** in jds Fußstapfen *acc* treten; **I don't quite ~ you** ich kann Ihnen nicht ganz folgen; **it ~s that** daraus folgt, dass; **to ~ suit** (*fig*) jds Beispiel *dat* folgen
▸ **follow on** *vi* (*continue*): **to ~ on from** aufbauen auf *+dat*
▸ **follow out** *vt* (*idea, plan*) zu Ende verfolgen
▸ **follow through** *vt* = **follow out**
▸ **follow up** *vt* nachgehen *+dat*; (*offer*) aufgreifen; (*case*) weiterverfolgen
follower ['fɔləuəʳ] *n* Anhänger(in) *m(f)*
following ['fɔləuɪŋ] *adj* folgend ▷ *n* Anhängerschaft *f*
follow-up ['fɔləuʌp] *n* Weiterführung *f* ▷ *adj*: **~ treatment** Nachbehandlung *f*
folly ['fɔlɪ] *n* Torheit *f*; (*building*) exzentrisches Bauwerk *nt*

fond [fɔnd] *adj* liebevoll; (*memory*) lieb; (*hopes, dreams*) töricht; **to be ~ of** mögen; **she's ~ of swimming** sie schwimmt gerne
fondle ['fɔndl] *vt* streicheln
font [fɔnt] *n* Taufbecken *nt*; (*Typ*) Schrift *f*
food [fu:d] *n* Essen *nt*; (*for animals*) Futter *nt*; (*nourishment*) Nahrung *f*; (*groceries*) Lebensmittel *pl*
food mixer *n* Küchenmixer *m*
food poisoning *n* Lebensmittelvergiftung *f*
food processor *n* Küchenmaschine *f*
food stamp *n* Lebensmittelmarke *f*
foodstuffs ['fu:dstʌfs] *npl* Lebensmittel *pl*
fool [fu:l] *n* Dummkopf *m*; (*Culin*) *Sahnespeise aus Obstpüree* ▹ *vt* hereinlegen, täuschen ▹ *vi* herumalbern; **to make a ~ of sb** jdn lächerlich machen; (*trick*) jdn hereinlegen; **to make a ~ of o.s.** sich blamieren; **you can't ~ me** du kannst mich nicht zum Narren halten
▸ **fool about** (*pej*) *vi* herumtrödeln; (*behave foolishly*) herumalbern
▸ **fool around** *vi* = **fool about**
foolhardy ['fu:lhɑ:dɪ] *adj* tollkühn
foolish ['fu:lɪʃ] *adj* dumm
foolproof ['fu:lpru:f] *adj* idiotensicher
foot [fut] (*pl* **feet**) *n* Fuß *m*; (*of animal*) Pfote *f* ▹ *vt* (*bill*) bezahlen; **on ~** zu Fuß; **to find one's feet** sich eingewöhnen; **to put one's ~ down** (*Aut*) Gas geben; (*say no*) ein Machtwort sprechen
footage ['futɪdʒ] *n* Filmmaterial *nt*
foot-and-mouth [futənd'mauθ], **foot-and-mouth disease** *n* Maul- und Klauenseuche *f*
football ['futbɔ:l] *n* Fußball *m*; (*US*) Football *m*, amerikanischer Fußball *m*
footballer ['futbɔ:ləʳ] (*Brit*) *n* Fußballspieler(in) *m(f)*
football match (*Brit*) *n* Fußballspiel *nt*
football player *n* (*Brit*) Fußballspieler(in) *m(f)*; (*US*) Footballspieler(in) *m(f)*
footbridge ['futbrɪdʒ] *n* Fußgängerbrücke *f*
foothills ['futhɪlz] *npl* (Gebirgs)ausläufer *pl*
foothold ['futhəuld] *n* Halt *m*; **to get a ~** Fuß fassen
footing ['futɪŋ] *n* Stellung *f*; (*relationship*) Verhältnis *nt*; **to lose one's ~** den Halt verlieren; **on an equal ~** auf gleicher Basis
footlights ['futlaɪts] *npl* Rampenlicht *nt*
footnote ['futnəut] *n* Fußnote *f*
footpath ['futpɑ:θ] *n* Fußweg *m*; (*in street*) Bürgersteig *m*
footprint ['futprɪnt] *n* Fußabdruck *m*; (*of animal*) Spur *f*
footstep ['futstɛp] *n* Schritt *m*; (*footprint*) Fußabdruck *m*; **to follow in sb's ~s** in jds Fußstapfen *acc* treten
footwear ['futwɛəʳ] *n* Schuhe *pl*, Schuhwerk *nt*
for [fɔ:ʳ] *prep* **1** für *+acc*; **is this for me?** ist das für mich?; **the train for London** der Zug nach London; **it's time for lunch** es ist Zeit zum Mittagessen; **what's it for?** wofür ist das?; **he works for the government/a local firm** er arbeitet für die Regierung/eine Firma am Ort; **he's mature for his age** er ist reif für sein Alter; **I sold it for £20** ich habe es für £20 verkauft; **I'm all for it** ich bin ganz dafür; **G for George** ≈ G wie Gustav
2 (*because of*): **for this reason** aus diesem Grund; **for fear of being criticised** aus Angst, kritisiert zu werden
3 (*referring to distance*): **there are roadworks for 5 km** die Straßenbauarbeiten erstrecken sich über 5 km; **we walked for miles** wir sind meilenweit gelaufen
4 (*referring to time*): **he was away for 2 years** er war 2 Jahre lang weg; **I have known her for years** ich kenne sie bereits seit Jahren
5 (*with infinitive clause*): **it is not for me to decide** es liegt nicht an mir, das zu entscheiden; **for this to be possible ...** um dies möglich zu machen, ...
6 (*in spite of*) trotz *+gen or dat*; **for all his complaints, he is very fond of her** trotz seiner vielen Klagen mag er sie sehr
▹ *conj* (*form: since, as*) denn; **she was very angry, for he was late again** sie war sehr böse, denn er kam wieder zu spät
forage ['fɔrɪdʒ] *n* Futter *nt* ▹ *vi* herumstöbern; **to ~ (for food)** nach Futter suchen
foray ['fɔreɪ] *n* (Raub)überfall *m*
forbid [fə'bɪd] (*pt* **forbade**, *pp* **~den**) *vt* verbieten; **to ~ sb to do sth** jdm verbieten, etw zu tun
forbidden [fə'bɪdn] *pp of* **forbid** ▹ *adj* verboten
forbidding [fə'bɪdɪŋ] *adj* (*look*) streng; (*prospect*) grauenhaft
force [fɔ:s] *n* Kraft *f*; (*violence*) Gewalt *f*; (*of blow, impact*) Wucht *f*; (*influence*) Macht *f* ▹ *vt* zwingen; (*push*) drücken; (*: person*) drängen; (*lock, door*) aufbrechen; **the Forces** (*Brit*) *npl* die Streitkräfte *pl*; **in ~** (*law etc*) geltend; (*people: arrive etc*) zahlreich; **to come into ~** in Kraft treten; **to join ~s** sich zusammentun; **a ~ 5 wind** Windstärke 5; **the sales ~** das Verkaufspersonal; **to ~ o.s./sb to do sth** sich/jdn zwingen, etw zu tun
▸ **force back** *vt* zurückdrängen; (*tears*) unterdrücken
▸ **force down** *vt* (*food*) hinunterwürgen (*inf*)
forced [fɔ:st] *adj* gezwungen; **~ labour** Zwangsarbeit *f*; **~ landing** Notlandung *f*
force-feed ['fɔ:sfi:d] *vt* zwangsernähren; (*animal*) stopfen
forceful ['fɔ:sful] *adj* energisch; (*attack*) wirkungsvoll; (*point*) überzeugend
forcibly ['fɔ:səblɪ] *adv* mit Gewalt; (*express*) eindringlich
ford [fɔ:d] *n* Furt *f* ▹ *vt* durchqueren; (*on foot*) durchwaten
fore [fɔ:ʳ] *n*: **to come to the ~** ins Blickfeld geraten
forearm ['fɔ:rɑ:m] *n* Unterarm *m*
foreboding [fɔ:'bəudɪŋ] *n* Vorahnung *f*
forecast ['fɔ:kɑ:st] (*irreg: like* **cast**) *n* Prognose

f; (*of weather*) (Wetter)vorhersage *f* ▷ *vt* voraussagen
forecourt ['fɔːkɔːt] *n* Vorplatz *m*
forefinger ['fɔːfɪŋgəʳ] *n* Zeigefinger *m*
forefront ['fɔːfrʌnt] *n*: **in the ~ of** an der Spitze *+gen*
foregone ['fɔːgɔn] *pp of* **forego** ▷ *adj*: **it's a ~ conclusion** es steht von vornherein fest
foreground ['fɔːgraund] *n* Vordergrund *m*
forehead ['fɔrɪd] *n* Stirn *f*
foreign ['fɔrɪn] *adj* ausländisch; (*holiday*) im Ausland; (*customs, appearance*) fremdartig; (*trade, policy*) Außen-; (*correspondent*) Auslands-; (*object, matter*) fremd; **goods from ~ countries/a ~ country** Waren aus dem Ausland
foreign currency *n* Devisen *pl*
foreigner ['fɔrɪnəʳ] *n* Ausländer(in) *m(f)*
foreign exchange *n* Devisenhandel *m*; (*money*) Devisen *pl*
Foreign Office (*Brit*) *n* Außenministerium *nt*
Foreign Secretary (*Brit*) *n* Außenminister(in) *m(f)*
foreleg ['fɔːlɛg] *n* Vorderbein *nt*
foreman ['fɔːmən] (*irreg: like* **man**) *n* Vorarbeiter *m*; (*of jury*) Obmann *m*
foremost ['fɔːməust] *adj* führend ▷ *adv*: **first and ~** zunächst, vor allem
forename ['fɔːneɪm] *n* Vorname *m*
forensic [fə'rɛnsɪk] *adj* (*test*) forensisch; (*medicine*) Gerichts-; (*expert*) Spurensicherungs-
forerunner ['fɔːrʌnəʳ] *n* Vorläufer *m*
foresee [fɔː'siː] (*irreg: like* **see**) *vt* vorhersehen
foreseeable [fɔː'siːəbl] *adj* vorhersehbar; **in the ~ future** in absehbarer Zeit
foreseen [fɔː'siːn] *pp of* **foresee**
foreshadow [fɔː'ʃædəu] *vt* andeuten
foresight ['fɔːsaɪt] *n* Voraussicht *f*, Weitblick *m*
forest ['fɔrɪst] *n* Wald *m*
forestry ['fɔrɪstrɪ] *n* Forstwirtschaft *f*
foretaste ['fɔːteɪst] *n*: **a ~ of** ein Vorgeschmack von
foretell [fɔː'tɛl] (*irreg: like* **tell**) *vt* vorhersagen
foretold [fɔː'təuld] *pt, pp of* **foretell**
forever [fə'rɛvəʳ] *adv* für immer; (*endlessly*) ewig; (*consistently*) dauernd, ständig; **you're ~ finding difficulties** du findest ständig *or* dauernd neue Schwierigkeiten
foreword ['fɔːwəːd] *n* Vorwort *nt*
forfeit ['fɔːfɪtʳ] *n* Strafe *f*, Buße *f* ▷ *vt* (*right*) verwirken; (*friendship etc*) verlieren; (*one's happiness, health*) einbüßen
forgave [fə'geɪv] *pt of* **forgive**
forge [fɔːdʒ] *n* Schmiede *f* ▷ *vt* fälschen; (*wrought iron*) schmieden
▸ **forge ahead** *vi* große *or* schnelle Fortschritte machen
forger ['fɔːdʒəʳ] *n* Fälscher(in) *m(f)*
forgery ['fɔːdʒərɪ] *n* Fälschung *f*
forget [fə'gɛt] (*pt* **forgot**, *pp* **forgotten**) *vt* vergessen ▷ *vi* es vergessen; **to ~ o.s.** sich vergessen
forgetful [fə'gɛtful] *adj* vergesslich; **~ of sth** (*of duties etc*) nachlässig gegenüber etw
forget-me-not [fə'gɛtmɪnɔt] *n* Vergissmeinnicht *nt*
forgive [fə'gɪv] (*pt* **forgave**, *pp* **~n**) *vt* verzeihen *+dat*, vergeben *+dat*; **to ~ sb for sth** jdm etw verzeihen *or* vergeben; **to ~ sb for doing sth** jdm verzeihen *or* vergeben, dass er etw getan hat; **~ me, but ...** entschuldigen Sie, aber ...; **they could be ~n for thinking that ...** es ist verständlich, wenn sie denken, dass ...
forgiveness [fə'gɪvnɪs] *n* Verzeihung *f*
forgo [fɔː'gəu] (*pt* **forwent**, *pp* **~ne**) *vt* = **forego**
forgot [fə'gɔt] *pt of* **forget**
forgotten [fə'gɔtn] *pp of* **forget**
fork [fɔːk] *n* Gabel *f*; (*in road, river, railway*) Gabelung *f* ▷ *vi* (*road*) sich gabeln
▸ **fork out** (*inf*) *vt, vi* (*pay*) blechen
fork-lift truck ['fɔːklɪft-] *n* Gabelstapler *m*
forlorn [fə'lɔːn] *adj* verlassen; (*person*) einsam und verlassen; (*attempt*) verzweifelt; (*hope*) schwach
form [fɔːm] *n* Form *f*; (*Scol*) Klasse *f*; (*questionnaire*) Formular *nt* ▷ *vt* formen, gestalten; (*queue, organization, group*) bilden; (*idea, habit*) entwickeln; **in the ~ of** in Form von *or* *+gen*; **in the ~ of Peter** in Gestalt von Peter; **to be in good ~** gut in Form sein; **in top ~** in Hochform; **on ~** in Form; **to ~ part of sth** Teil von etw sein
formal ['fɔːməl] *adj* offiziell; (*person, behaviour*) förmlich, formell; (*occasion, dinner*) feierlich; (*clothes*) Gesellschafts-; (*garden*) formell angelegt; (*Art, Philosophy*) formal; **~ dress** Gesellschaftskleidung *f*
formality [fɔː'mælɪtɪ] *n* Förmlichkeit *f*; (*procedure*) Formalität *f*
formally ['fɔːməlɪ] *adv* (*see adj*) offiziell; förmlich, formell; feierlich; **to be ~ invited** ausdrücklich eingeladen sein
format ['fɔːmæt] *n* Format *nt*; (*form, style*) Aufmachung *f* ▷ *vt* (*Comput*) formatieren
formation [fɔː'meɪʃən] *n* Bildung *f*; (*of theory*) Entstehung *f*; (*of business*) Gründung *f*; (*pattern: of rocks, clouds*) Formation *f*
formative ['fɔːmətɪv] *adj* (*influence*) prägend; (*years*) entscheidend
former ['fɔːməʳ] *adj* früher; **the ~ ... the latter ...** Erstere(r, s) ... Letztere(r, s); **the ~ president** der ehemalige Präsident; **the ~ East Germany** die ehemalige DDR
formerly ['fɔːməlɪ] *adv* früher
formidable ['fɔːmɪdəbl] *adj* (*task*) gewaltig, enorm; (*opponent*) furchterregend
formula ['fɔːmjulə] (*pl* **formulae** *or* **~s**) *n* Formel *f*; **F~ One** (*Aut*) Formel Eins
forsake [fə'seɪk] (*pt* **forsook**, *pp* **~n**) *vt* im Stich lassen; (*belief*) aufgeben
fort [fɔːt] *n* Fort *nt*; **to hold the ~** die Stellung halten
forte ['fɔːtɪ] *n* Stärke *f*, starke Seite *f*
forth [fɔːθ] *adv* aus; **back and ~** hin und her;

to go back and ~ auf und ab gehen; **to bring ~** hervorbringen; **and so ~** und so weiter
forthcoming [fɔ:θ'kʌmɪŋ] *adj* (*event*) bevorstehend; (*person*) mitteilsam; **to be ~** (*help*) erfolgen; (*evidence*) geliefert werden
forthright ['fɔ:θraɪt] *adj* offen
forthwith ['fɔ:θ'wɪθ] *adv* umgehend
fortieth ['fɔ:tɪɪθ] *num* vierzigste(r, s)
fortify ['fɔ:tɪfaɪ] *vt* (*city*) befestigen; (*person*) bestärken; (: *subj*: *food, drink*) stärken
fortitude ['fɔ:tɪtju:d] *n* innere Kraft *or* Stärke *f*
fortnight ['fɔ:tnaɪt] (*Brit*) *n* vierzehn Tage *pl*, zwei Wochen *pl*; **it's a ~ since ...** es ist vierzehn Tage *or* zwei Wochen her, dass ...
fortnightly ['fɔ:tnaɪtlɪ] *adj* vierzehntägig, zweiwöchentlich ▷ *adv* alle vierzehn Tage, alle zwei Wochen
fortress ['fɔ:trɪs] *n* Festung *f*
fortunate ['fɔ:tʃənɪt] *adj* glücklich; **to be ~** Glück haben; **he is ~ to have ...** er kann sich glücklich schätzen, ... zu haben; **it is ~ that ...** es ist ein Glück, dass ...
fortunately ['fɔ:tʃənɪtlɪ] *adv* glücklicherweise, zum Glück
fortune ['fɔ:tʃən] *n* Glück *nt*; (*wealth*) Vermögen *nt*; **to make a ~** ein Vermögen machen; **to tell sb's ~** jdm wahrsagen
fortune-teller ['fɔ:tʃəntɛlə^r] *n* Wahrsager(in) *m(f)*
forty ['fɔ:tɪ] *num* vierzig
forum ['fɔ:rəm] *n* Forum *nt*
forward ['fɔ:wəd] *adj* vordere(r, s); (*movement*) Vorwärts-; (*not shy*) dreist; (*Comm*: *buying, price*) Termin- ▷ *adv* nach vorn; (*movement*) vorwärts; (*in time*) voraus ▷ *n* (*Sport*) Stürmer *m* ▷ *vt* (*letter etc*) nachsenden; (*career, plans*) voranbringen; **~ planning** Vorausplanung *f*; **to move ~** vorwärtskommen; **"please ~"** "bitte nachsenden"
fossil ['fɔsl] *n* Fossil *nt*
foster ['fɔstə^r] *vt* (*child*) in Pflege nehmen; (*idea, activity*) fördern
foster child *n* Pflegekind *nt*
fought [fɔ:t] *pt, pp of* **fight**
foul [faul] *adj* abscheulich; (*taste, smell, temper*) übel; (*water*) faulig; (*air*) schlecht; (*language*) unflätig ▷ *n* (*Sport*) Foul *nt* ▷ *vt* beschmutzen; (*Sport*) foulen; (*entangle*) sich verheddern in *+dat*
foul play *n* unnatürlicher *or* gewaltsamer Tod *m*; **~ is not suspected** es besteht kein Verdacht auf ein Verbrechen
found [faund] *pt, pp of* **find** ▷ *vt* gründen
foundation [faun'deɪʃən] *n* Gründung *f*; (*base*: *also fig*) Grundlage *f*; (*organization*) Stiftung *f*; (*also*: **foundation cream**) Grundierungscreme *f*; **foundations** *npl* (*of building*) Fundament *nt*; **the rumours are without ~** die Gerüchte entbehren jeder Grundlage; **to lay the ~s** (*fig*) die Grundlagen schaffen
founder ['faundə^r] *n* Gründer(in) *m(f)* ▷ *vi* (*ship*) sinken
foundry ['faundrɪ] *n* Gießerei *f*
fountain ['fauntɪn] *n* Brunnen *m*
fountain pen *n* Füllfederhalter *m*, Füller *m*
four [fɔ:^{r}] *num* vier; **on all ~s** auf allen vieren
four-letter word ['fɔ:lɛtə-] *n* Vulgärausdruck *m*
four-poster ['fɔ:'pəustə^r] *n* (*also*: **four-poster bed**) Himmelbett *nt*
fourteen ['fɔ:'ti:n] *num* vierzehn
fourteenth ['fɔ:'ti:nθ] *num* vierzehnte(r, s)
fourth [fɔ:θ] *num* vierte(r, s) ▷ *n* (*Aut*: *also*: **fourth gear**) der vierte (Gang)
four-wheel drive ['fɔ:wi:l-] *n* (*Aut*): **with ~** mit Vierradantrieb *m*
fowl [faul] *n* Vogel *m* (*besonders Huhn, Gans, Ente etc*)
fox [fɔks] *n* Fuchs *m* ▷ *vt* verblüffen
foyer ['fɔɪeɪ] *n* Foyer *nt*
fraction ['frækʃən] *n* Bruchteil *m*; (*Math*) Bruch *m*
fracture ['fræktʃə^r] *n* Bruch *m* ▷ *vt* brechen
fragile ['frædʒaɪl] *adj* zerbrechlich; (*economy*) schwach; (*health*) zart; (*person*) angeschlagen
fragment [*n* 'frægmənt, *vb* fræg'mɛnt] *n* Stück *nt* ▷ *vt* aufsplittern ▷ *vi* sich aufsplittern
fragrance ['freɪgrəns] *n* Duft *m*
fragrant ['freɪgrənt] *adj* duftend
frail [freɪl] *adj* schwach, gebrechlich; (*structure*) zerbrechlich
frame [freɪm] *n* Rahmen *m*; (*of building*) (Grund)gerippe *nt*; (*of human, animal*) Gestalt *f*; (*of spectacles*: *also*: **frames**) Gestell *nt* ▷ *vt* (*picture*) rahmen; (*reply*) formulieren; (*law, theory*) entwerfen; **~ of mind** Stimmung *f*, Laune *f*; **to ~ sb** (*inf*) jdm etwas anhängen
framework ['freɪmwə:k] *n* Rahmen *m*
France [frɑ:ns] *n* Frankreich *nt*
franchise ['fræntʃaɪz] *n* Wahlrecht *nt*; (*Comm*) Konzession *f*, Franchise *f*
frank [fræŋk] *adj* offen ▷ *vt* (*letter*) frankieren
frankly ['fræŋklɪ] *adv* ehrlich gesagt; (*candidly*) offen
frantic ['fræntɪk] *adj* verzweifelt; (*hectic*) hektisch; (*desperate*) übersteigert
fraternity [frə'tə:nɪtɪ] *n* Brüderlichkeit *f*; (*US*: *Univ*) Verbindung *f*; **the legal/medical/golfing ~** die Juristen/Mediziner/Golfer *pl*
fraud [frɔ:d] *n* Betrug *m*; (*person*) Betrüger(in) *m(f)*
fraught [frɔ:t] *adj* (*person*) nervös; **to be ~ with danger/problems** voller Gefahren/Probleme sein
fray [freɪ] *n*: **the ~** der Kampf ▷ *vi* (*cloth*) ausfransen; (*rope*) sich durchscheuern; **to return to the ~** sich wieder ins Getümmel stürzen; **tempers were ~ed** die Gemüter erhitzten sich; **her nerves were ~ed** sie war mit den Nerven am Ende
freak [fri:k] *n* Irre(r) *f(m)*; (*in appearance*) Missgeburt *f*; (*event, accident*) außergewöhnlicher Zufall *m*; (*pej*: *fanatic*): **health ~** Gesundheitsapostel *m*

▸ **freak out** (*inf*) *vi* aussteigen; (*on drugs*) ausflippen
freckle ['frɛkl] *n* Sommersprosse *f*
free [fri:] *adj* frei; (*costing nothing*) kostenlos, gratis ▷ *vt* freilassen, frei lassen; (*jammed object*) lösen; **to give sb a ~ hand** jdm freie Hand lassen; **~ and easy** ungezwungen; **admission ~** Eintritt frei; **~ (of charge), for free** umsonst, gratis
freedom ['fri:dəm] *n* Freiheit *f*
Freefone® ['fri:fəun] *n*: **call ~ 0800** rufen Sie gebührenfrei 0800 an
free-for-all ['fri:fərɔ:l] *n* Gerangel *nt*; **the fight turned into a ~** schließlich beteiligten sich alle an der Schlägerei
free gift *n* Werbegeschenk *nt*
freehold ['fri:həuld] *n* (*of property*) Besitzrecht *nt*
free kick *n* Freistoß *m*
freelance ['fri:lɑ:ns] *adj* (*journalist etc*) frei(schaffend), freiberuflich tätig
freely ['fri:lɪ] *adv* frei; (*spend*) mit vollen Händen; (*liberally*) großzügig; **drugs are ~ available in the city** Drogen sind in der Stadt frei erhältlich
Freepost® ['fri:pəust] *n* ≈ "Gebühr zahlt Empfänger"
free-range ['fri:'reɪndʒ] *adj* (*eggs*) von frei laufenden Hühnern
free trade *n* Freihandel *m*
freeway ['fri:weɪ] (*US*) *n* Autobahn *f*
free will *n* freier Wille *m*; **of one's own ~** aus freien Stücken
freeze [fri:z] (*pt* **froze**, *pp* **frozen**) *vi* frieren; (*liquid*) gefrieren; (*pipe*) einfrieren; (*person: stop moving*) erstarren ▷ *vt* einfrieren; (*water, lake*) gefrieren ▷ *n* Frost *m*; (*on arms, wages*) Stopp *m*
▸ **freeze over** *vi* (*river*) überfrieren; (*windscreen, windows*) vereisen
▸ **freeze up** *vi* zufrieren
freeze-dried ['fri:zdraɪd] *adj* gefriergetrocknet
freezer ['fri:zəʳ] *n* Tiefkühltruhe *f*; (*upright*) Gefrierschrank *m*; (*in fridge: also*: **freezer compartment**) Gefrierfach *nt*
freezing ['fri:zɪŋ] *adj*: **~ (cold)** eiskalt ▷ *n*: **3 degrees below ~** 3 Grad unter null; **I'm ~** mir ist eiskalt
freezing point *n* Gefrierpunkt *m*
freight [freɪt] *n* Fracht *f*; (*money charged*) Frachtkosten *pl*; **~ forward** Fracht gegen Nachnahme; **~ inward** Eingangsfracht *f*
freight train (*US*) *n* Güterzug *m*
French [frɛntʃ] *adj* französisch ▷ *n* (*Ling*) Französisch *nt*; **the French** *npl* die Franzosen *pl*
French bean (*Brit*) *n* grüne Bohne *f*
French dressing *n* Vinaigrette *f*
French fried potatoes *npl* Pommes frites *pl*
Frenchman ['frɛntʃmən] (*irreg: like* **man**) *n* Franzose *m*
French stick *n* Stangenbrot *nt*
French window *n* Verandatür *f*
Frenchwoman ['frɛntʃwumən] (*irreg: like* **woman**) *n* Französin *f*
frenzy ['frɛnzɪ] *n* Raserei *f*; (*of joy, excitement*) Taumel *m*; **to drive sb into a ~** jdn zum Rasen bringen; **to be in a ~** in wilder Aufregung sein
frequency ['fri:kwənsɪ] *n* Häufigkeit *f*; (*Radio*) Frequenz *f*
frequent [*adj* 'fri:kwənt, *vt* frɪ'kwɛnt] *adj* häufig ▷ *vt* (*pub, restaurant*) oft *or* häufig besuchen
frequently ['fri:kwəntlɪ] *adv* oft, häufig
fresh [frɛʃ] *adj* frisch; (*instructions, approach, start*) neu; (*cheeky*) frech; **to make a ~ start** einen neuen Anfang machen
freshen ['frɛʃən] *vi* (*wind*) auffrischen; (*air*) frisch werden
▸ **freshen up** *vi* sich frisch machen
fresher ['frɛʃəʳ] (*Brit: inf*) *n* Erstsemester(in) *m(f)*
freshly ['frɛʃlɪ] *adv* frisch
freshman ['frɛʃmən] (*US irreg: like* **man**) *n* = **fresher**
freshness ['frɛʃnɪs] *n* Frische *f*
freshwater ['frɛʃwɔ:təʳ] *adj* (*fish etc*) Süßwasser-
fret [frɛt] *vi* sich *dat* Sorgen machen
friar ['fraɪəʳ] *n* Mönch *m*, (Ordens)bruder *m*
friction ['frɪkʃən] *n* Reibung *f*; (*between people*) Reibereien *pl*
Friday ['fraɪdɪ] *n* Freitag *m*; *see also* **Tuesday**
fridge [frɪdʒ] (*Brit*) *n* Kühlschrank *m*
fried [fraɪd] *pt, pp of* **fry** ▷ *adj* gebraten; **~ egg** Spiegelei *nt*; **~ fish** Bratfisch *m*
friend [frɛnd] *n* Freund(in) *m(f)*; (*less intimate*) Bekannte(r) *f(m)*; **to make ~s with** sich anfreunden mit
friendly ['frɛndlɪ] *adj* freundlich; (*government*) befreundet; (*game, match*) Freundschafts- ▷ *n* (*also*: **friendly match**) Freundschaftsspiel *nt*; **to be ~ with** befreundet sein mit; **to be ~ to** freundlich *or* nett sein zu
friendship ['frɛndʃɪp] *n* Freundschaft *f*
frieze [fri:z] *n* Fries *m*
frigate ['frɪgɪt] *n* Fregatte *f*
fright [fraɪt] *n* Schreck(en) *m*; **to take ~** es mit der Angst zu tun bekommen; **she looks a ~** sie sieht verboten *or* zum Fürchten aus (*inf*)
frighten ['fraɪtn] *vt* erschrecken
▸ **frighten away** *or* **off** *vt* verscheuchen
frightened ['fraɪtnd] *adj* ängstlich; **to be ~ (of)** Angst haben (vor +*dat*)
frightening ['fraɪtnɪŋ] *adj* furchterregend
frightful ['fraɪtful] *adj* schrecklich, furchtbar
frigid ['frɪdʒɪd] *adj* frigide
frill [frɪl] *n* Rüsche *f*; **without ~s** (*fig*) schlicht
fringe [frɪndʒ] *n* (*Brit: of hair*) Pony *m*; (*decoration*) Fransen *pl*; (*edge: also fig*) Rand *m*
fringe benefits *npl* zusätzliche Leistungen *pl*
Frisbee® ['frɪzbɪ] *n* Frisbee® *nt*
frisk [frɪsk] *vt* durchsuchen, filzen (*inf*) ▷ *vi* umhertollen
fritter ['frɪtəʳ] *n* Schmalzgebackenes *nt no pl*

mit Füllung
▸ **fritter away** *vt* vergeuden
frivolous ['frɪvələs] *adj* frivol; (*activity*) leichtfertig
frizzy ['frɪzɪ] *adj* kraus
fro [frəu] *adv*: **to and ~** hin und her; (*walk*) auf und ab
frock [frɔk] *n* Kleid *nt*
frog [frɔg] *n* Frosch *m*; **to have a ~ in one's throat** einen Frosch im Hals haben
frogman ['frɔgmən] (*irreg: like* **man**) *n* Froschmann *m*
frolic ['frɔlɪk] *vi* umhertollen ▹ *n* Ausgelassenheit *f*; (*fun*) Spaß *m*
from [frɔm] *prep* **1** (*indicating starting place, origin*) von *+dat*; **where do you come from?** woher kommen Sie?; **from London to Glasgow** von London nach Glasgow; **a letter/telephone call from my sister** ein Brief/Anruf von meiner Schwester; **to drink from the bottle** aus der Flasche trinken
2 (*indicating time*) von (... an); **from one o'clock to** *or* **until** *or* **till now** von ein Uhr bis jetzt; **from January (on)** von Januar an, ab Januar
3 (*indicating distance*) von ... entfernt; **the hotel is 1 km from the beach** das Hotel ist 1 km vom Strand entfernt
4 (*indicating price, number etc*): **trousers from £20** Hosen ab £20; **prices range from £10 to £50** die Preise liegen zwischen £10 und £50
5 (*indicating difference*): **he can't tell red from green** er kann Rot und Grün nicht unterscheiden; **to be different from sb/sth** anders sein als jd/etw
6 (*because of, on the basis of*): **from what he says** nach dem, was er sagt; **to act from conviction** aus Überzeugung handeln; **weak from hunger** schwach vor Hunger
front [frʌnt] *n* Vorderseite *f*; (*of dress*) Vorderteil *nt*; (*promenade: also*: **sea front**) Strandpromenade *f*; (*Mil, Met*) Front *f*; (*fig: appearances*) Fassade *f* ▹ *adj* vorderste(r, s); (*wheel, tooth, view*) Vorder- ▹ *vi*: **to ~ onto sth** (*house*) auf etw *acc* hinausliegen; (*window*) auf etw *acc* hinausgehen; **in ~** vorne; **in ~ of** vor; **at the ~ of the coach/train/car** vorne im Bus/Zug/Auto; **on the political ~, little progress has been made** an der politischen Front sind kaum Fortschritte gemacht worden
frontage ['frʌntɪdʒ] *n* Vorderseite *f*, Front *f*; (*of shop*) Front
front door *n* Haustür *f*
frontier ['frʌntɪə^r^] *n* Grenze *f*
front page *n* erste Seite *f*, Titelseite *f*
front room (*Brit*) *n* Wohnzimmer *nt*
front-wheel drive ['frʌntwi:l-] *n* (*Aut*) Vorderradantrieb *m*
frost [frɔst] *n* Frost *m*; (*also*: **hoarfrost**) Raureif *m*
frostbite ['frɔstbaɪt] *n* Erfrierungen *pl*
frosted ['frɔstɪd] *adj* (*glass*) Milch-; (*esp US*) glasiert, mit Zuckerguss überzogen
frosting ['frɔstɪŋ] (*esp US*) *n* Zuckerguss *m*
frosty ['frɔstɪ] *adj* frostig; (*look*) eisig; (*window*) bereift
froth [frɔθ] *n* Schaum *m*
frown [fraun] *n* Stirnrunzeln *nt* ▹ *vi* die Stirn runzeln
▸ **frown on** *vt fus* missbilligen
froze [frəuz] *pt of* **freeze**
frozen ['frəuzn] *pp of* **freeze** ▹ *adj* tiefgekühlt; (*food*) Tiefkühl-; (*Comm*) eingefroren
fruit [fru:t] *n inv* Frucht *f*; (*collectively*) Obst *nt*; (*fig: results*) Früchte *pl*
fruiterer ['fru:tərə^r^] (*esp Brit*) *n* Obsthändler(in) *m(f)*
fruitful ['fru:tful] *adj* fruchtbar
fruition [fru:'ɪʃən] *n*: **to come to ~** (*plan*) Wirklichkeit werden; (*efforts*) Früchte tragen; (*hope*) in Erfüllung gehen
fruit juice *n* Fruchtsaft *m*
fruit machine (*Brit*) *n* Spielautomat *m*
fruit salad *n* Obstsalat *m*
frustrate [frʌs'treɪt] *vt* frustrieren; (*attempt*) vereiteln; (*plan*) durchkreuzen
frustrated [frʌs'treɪtɪd] *adj* frustriert
fry [fraɪ] (*pt, pp* **fried**) *vt* braten; *see also* **small**
frying pan ['fraɪɪŋ-] *n* Bratpfanne *f*
ft. *abbr* = **foot; feet**
fudge [fʌdʒ] *n* Fondant *m* ▹ *vt* (*issue, problem*) ausweichen *+dat*, aus dem Weg gehen *+dat*
fuel ['fjuəl] *n* Brennstoff *m*; (*for vehicle*) Kraftstoff *m*; (*: petrol*) Benzin *nt*; (*for aircraft, rocket*) Treibstoff *m* ▹ *vt* (*furnace etc*) betreiben; (*aircraft, ship etc*) antreiben
fuel oil *n* Gasöl *nt*
fuel tank *n* Öltank *m*; (*in vehicle*) (Benzin)tank *m*
fugitive ['fju:dʒɪtɪv] *n* Flüchtling *m*
fulfil, (*US*) **fulfill** [ful'fɪl] *vt* erfüllen; (*order*) ausführen
fulfilment, (*US*) **fulfillment** [ful'fɪlmənt] *n* Erfüllung *f*
full [ful] *adj* voll; (*complete*) vollständig; (*skirt*) weit; (*life*) ausgefüllt ▹ *adv*: **to know ~ well that ...** sehr wohl wissen, dass ...; **~ up** (*hotel etc*) ausgebucht; **I'm ~ (up)** ich bin satt; **a ~ two hours** volle zwei Stunden; **~ marks** die beste Note, ≈ eine Eins; (*fig*) höchstes Lob *nt*; **at ~ speed** in voller Fahrt; **in ~** ganz, vollständig; **to pay in ~** den vollen Betrag bezahlen; **to write one's name** *etc* **in ~** seinen Namen *etc* ausschreiben
full-length ['ful'lɛŋθ] *adj* (*film*) abendfüllend; (*coat*) lang; (*portrait*) lebensgroß; (*mirror*) groß; **~ novel** Roman *m*
full moon *n* Vollmond *m*
full-scale ['fulskeɪl] *adj* (*war*) richtig; (*attack*) Groß-; (*model*) in Originalgröße; (*search*) groß angelegt
full stop *n* Punkt *m*
full-time ['ful'taɪm] *adj* (*work*) Ganztags-; (*study*) Voll- ▹ *adv* ganztags
fully ['fulɪ] *adv* völlig; **~ as big as** mindestens

so groß wie

fumble ['fʌmbl] *vi*: **to ~ with** herumfummeln an +*dat* ▷ *vt* (*ball*) nicht sicher fangen

fume [fju:m] *vi* wütend sein, kochen (*inf*)

fumes [fju:mz] *npl* (*of fire*) Rauch *m*; (*of fuel*) Dämpfe *pl*; (*of car*) Abgase *pl*

fun [fʌn] *n* Spaß *m*; **he's good ~ (to be with)** es macht viel Spaß, mit ihm zusammen zu sein; **for ~** aus *or* zum Spaß; **it's not much ~** es macht keinen Spaß; **to make ~ of, to poke ~ at** sich lustig machen über +*acc*

function ['fʌŋkʃən] *n* Funktion *f*; (*social occasion*) Veranstaltung *f*, Feier *f* ▷ *vi* funktionieren; **to ~ as** (*thing*) dienen als; (*person*) fungieren als

functional ['fʌŋkʃənl] *adj* (*operational*) funktionsfähig; (*practical*) funktionell, zweckmäßig

fund [fʌnd] *n* (*of money*) Fonds *m*; (*source, store*) Schatz *m*, Vorrat *m*; **funds** *npl* (*money*) Mittel *pl*, Gelder *pl*

fundamental [fʌndə'mɛntl] *adj* fundamental, grundlegend

funeral ['fju:nərəl] *n* Beerdigung *f*

funeral director *n* Beerdigungsunternehmer(in) *m(f)*

funeral parlour *n* Leichenhalle *f*

funeral service *n* Trauergottesdienst *m*

funfair ['fʌnfɛəʳ] (*Brit*) *n* Jahrmarkt *m*

fungus ['fʌŋgəs] (*pl* **fungi**) *n* Pilz *m*; (*mould*) Schimmel(pilz) *m*

funnel ['fʌnl] *n* Trichter *m*; (*of ship*) Schornstein *m*

funny ['fʌnɪ] *adj* komisch; (*strange*) seltsam, komisch

fur [fə:ʳ] *n* Fell *nt*, Pelz *m*; (*Brit: in kettle etc*) Kesselstein *m*

fur coat *n* Pelzmantel *m*

furious ['fjuərɪəs] *adj* wütend; (*exchange, argument*) heftig; (*effort*) riesig; (*speed*) rasend; **to be ~ with sb** wütend auf jdn sein

furlong ['fə:lɔŋ] *n* Achtelmeile *f* (= *201,17 m*)

furnace ['fə:nɪs] *n* (*in foundry*) Schmelzofen *m*; (*in power plant*) Hochofen *m*

furnish ['fə:nɪʃ] *vt* einrichten; (*room*) möblieren; **to ~ sb with sth** jdm etw liefern; **~ed flat, ~ed apartment** (US) möblierte Wohnung *f*

furnishings ['fə:nɪʃɪŋz] *npl* Einrichtung *f*

furniture ['fə:nɪtʃəʳ] *n* Möbel *pl*; **piece of ~** Möbelstück *nt*

furrow ['fʌrəu] *n* Furche *f*; (*in skin*) Runzel *f* ▷ *vt* (*brow*) runzeln

furry ['fə:rɪ] *adj* (*coat, tail*) flauschig; (*animal*) Pelz-; (*toy*) Plüsch-

further ['fə:ðəʳ] *adj* weitere(r, s) ▷ *adv* weiter; (*moreover*) darüber hinaus ▷ *vt* fördern; **until ~ notice** bis auf Weiteres; **how much ~ is it?** wie weit ist es noch?; **~ to your letter of ...** (*Comm*) Bezug nehmend auf Ihr Schreiben vom ...

further education (*Brit*) *n* Weiterbildung *f*, Fortbildung *f*

furthermore [fə:ðə'mɔ:ʳ] *adv* außerdem

furthest ['fə:ðɪst] *superl of* **far**

fury ['fjuərɪ] *n* Wut *f*; **to be in a ~** in Rage sein

fuse, (US) **fuze** [fju:z] *n* (*Elec*) Sicherung *f*; (*for bomb etc*) Zündschnur *f* ▷ *vt* (*pieces of metal*) verschmelzen; (*fig*) vereinigen ▷ *vi* (*pieces of metal*) sich verbinden; (*fig*) sich vereinigen; **to ~ the lights** (*Brit*) die Sicherung durchbrennen lassen; **a ~ has blown** eine Sicherung ist durchgebrannt

fuse box *n* Sicherungskasten *m*

fusion ['fju:ʒən] *n* Verschmelzung *f*; (*also*: **nuclear fusion**) Kernfusion *f*

fuss [fʌs] *n* Theater *nt* (*inf*) ▷ *vi* sich (unnötig) aufregen ▷ *vt* keine Ruhe lassen +*dat*; **to make a ~** Krach schlagen (*inf*); **to make a ~ of sb** viel Getue um jdn machen (*inf*)
▸ **fuss over** *vt fus* bemuttern

fussy ['fʌsɪ] *adj* kleinlich, pingelig (*inf*); (*clothes, room etc*) verspielt; **I'm not ~** es ist mir egal

future ['fju:tʃəʳ] *adj* zukünftig ▷ *n* Zukunft *f*; (*Ling*) Futur *nt*; **futures** *npl* (*Comm*) Termingeschäfte *pl*; **in (the) ~** in Zukunft; **in the near ~** in der nahen Zukunft; **in the immediate ~** sehr bald

fuze [fju:z] (US) *n, vt, vi* = **fuse**

fuzzy ['fʌzɪ] *adj* verschwommen; (*hair*) kraus; (*thoughts*) verworren

FYI *abbr* (= *for your information*) zu Ihrer Information

Gg

G¹, g¹ [dʒiː] *n (letter)* G *nt*, g *nt*; **G for George** ≈ G wie Gustav
G² [dʒiː] *n (Mus)* G *nt*, g *nt*
G³ [dʒiː] *n abbr (Brit: Scol)* = **good**; (*US: Cine:* = *general (audience)) Klassifikation für jugendfreie Filme*; (*Phys*): **G-force** g-Druck *m*
g² *abbr (= gram(me))* g; *(Phys)* = **gravity**
gabble ['gæbl] *vi* brabbeln *(inf)*
gable ['geɪbl] *n* Giebel *m*
gadget ['gædʒɪt] *n* Gerät *nt*
Gaelic ['geɪlɪk] *adj* gälisch ▷ *n (Ling)* Gälisch *nt*
gag [gæg] *n* Knebel *m*; *(joke)* Gag *m* ▷ *vt* knebeln ▷ *vi* würgen
gaiety ['geɪɪtɪ] *n* Fröhlichkeit *f*
gain [geɪn] *n* Gewinn *m* ▷ *vt* gewinnen ▷ *vi (clock, watch)* vorgehen; **to do sth for ~** etw aus Berechnung tun; *(for money)* etw des Geldes wegen tun; **~ (in)** *(increase)* Zunahme *f* (an *+dat*); *(in rights, conditions)* Verbesserung *f +gen*; **to ~ ground** (an) Boden gewinnen; **to ~ speed** schneller werden; **to ~ weight** zunehmen; **to ~ 3lbs (in weight)** 3 Pfund zunehmen; **to ~ (in) confidence** sicherer werden; **to ~ from sth** von etw profitieren; **to ~ in strength** stärker werden; **to ~ by doing sth** davon profitieren, etw zu tun; **to ~ on sb** jdn einholen
gal. *abbr* = **gallon**
gala ['gɑːlə] *n* Galaveranstaltung *f*; **swimming ~** großes Schwimmfest *nt*
galaxy ['gæləksɪ] *n* Galaxis *f*, Sternsystem *nt*
gale [geɪl] *n* Sturm *m*; **~ force 10** Sturmstärke 10
gallant ['gælənt] *adj* tapfer; *(polite)* galant
gall bladder *n* Gallenblase *f*
gallery ['gælərɪ] *n (also:* **art gallery***)* Galerie *f*, Museum *nt*; *(private)* (Privat)galerie *f*; *(in hall, church)* Galerie *f*; *(in theatre)* oberster Rang *m*, Balkon *m*
gallon ['gæln] *n* Gallone *f (Brit = 4,5 l, US = 3,8 l)*
gallop ['gæləp] *n* Galopp *m* ▷ *vi* galoppieren; **~ing inflation** galoppierende Inflation *f*
gallows ['gæləuz] *n* Galgen *m*
gallstone ['gɔːlstəun] *n* Gallenstein *m*
galore [gə'lɔːʳ] *adv* in Hülle und Fülle
Gambia ['gæmbɪə] *n* Gambia *nt*
gambit ['gæmbɪt] *n*: **(opening) ~** (einleitender) Schachzug *m*; *(in conversation)* (einleitende) Bemerkung *f*
gamble ['gæmbl] *n* Risiko *nt* ▷ *vt* einsetzen ▷ *vi* ein Risiko eingehen; *(bet)* spielen; *(on horses etc)* wetten; **to ~ on the Stock Exchange** an der Börse spekulieren; **to ~ on sth** *(horses, race)* auf etw *acc* wetten; *(success, outcome etc)* sich auf etw *acc* verlassen
gambler ['gæmbləʳ] *n* Spieler(in) *m(f)*
gambling ['gæmblɪŋ] *n* Spielen *nt*; *(on horses etc)* Wetten *nt*
game [geɪm] *n* Spiel *nt*; *(sport)* Sport *m*; *(strategy, scheme)* Vorhaben *nt*; *(Culin, Hunting)* Wild *nt* ▷ *adj*: **to be ~ (for)** mitmachen (bei); **games** *npl (Scol)* Sport *m*; **to play a ~ of football/tennis** Fußball/(eine Partie) Tennis spielen; **big ~** Großwild *nt*
gamekeeper ['geɪmkiːpəʳ] *n* Wildhüter(in) *m(f)*
games console ['geɪmz-] *n (Comput)* Gameboy® *m*, Konsole *f*
game show *n (TV)* Spielshow *f*
gammon ['gæmən] *n* Schinken *m*
gamut ['gæmət] *n* Skala *f*; **to run the ~ of** die ganze Skala *+gen* durchlaufen
gang [gæŋ] *n* Bande *f*; *(of friends)* Haufen *m*; *(of workmen)* Kolonne *f*
▸ **gang up** *vi*: **to ~ up on sb** sich gegen jdn zusammentun
gangster ['gæŋstəʳ] *n* Gangster *m*
gangway ['gæŋweɪ] *n* Laufplanke *f*, Gangway *f*; *(in cinema, bus, plane etc)* Gang *m*
gaol [dʒeɪl] *(Brit) n, vt* = **jail**
gap [gæp] *n* Lücke *f*; *(in time)* Pause *f*; *(difference)*: **~ (between)** Kluft *f* (zwischen *+dat*)
gape [geɪp] *vi* starren, gaffen; *(hole)* gähnen; *(shirt)* offen stehen
gaping ['geɪpɪŋ] *adj (hole)* gähnend; *(shirt)* offen
garage ['gærɑːʒ] *n* Garage *f*; *(for car repairs)* (Reparatur)werkstatt *f*; *(petrol station)* Tankstelle *f*
garbage ['gɑːbɪdʒ] *n (US: rubbish)* Abfall *m*, Müll *m*; *(inf: nonsense)* Blödsinn *m*, Quatsch *m*; *(fig: film, book)* Schund *m*
garbage can *(US) n* Mülleimer *m*, Abfalleimer *m*
garbage collector *(US) n* Müllmann *m*
garbled ['gɑːbld] *adj (account)* wirr; *(message)* unverständlich

garden ['gɑːdn] *n* Garten *m* ▷ *vi* gärtnern; **gardens** *npl* (*public park*) Park *m*; (*private*) Gartenanlagen *pl*; **she was ~ing** sie arbeitete im Garten

garden centre *n* Gartencenter *nt*

gardener ['gɑːdnəʳ] *n* Gärtner(in) *m(f)*

gardening ['gɑːdnɪŋ] *n* Gartenarbeit *f*

gargle ['gɑːgl] *vi* gurgeln ▷ *n* Gurgelwasser *nt*

garish ['gɛərɪʃ] *adj* grell

garland ['gɑːlənd] *n* Kranz *m*

garlic ['gɑːlɪk] *n* Knoblauch *m*

garment ['gɑːmənt] *n* Kleidungsstück *nt*

garnish ['gɑːnɪʃ] *vt* garnieren

garrison ['gærɪsn] *n* Garnison *f*

garter ['gɑːtəʳ] *n* Strumpfband *nt*; (*US: suspender*) Strumpfhalter *m*

gas [gæs] *n* Gas *nt*; (*US: gasoline*) Benzin *nt* ▷ *vt* mit Gas vergiften; (*Mil*) vergasen; **to be given ~** (*as anaesthetic*) Lachgas bekommen

gas cooker (*Brit*) *n* Gasherd *m*

gas cylinder *n* Gasflasche *f*

gas fire (*Brit*) *n* Gasofen *m*

gash [gæʃ] *n* klaffende Wunde *f*; (*tear*) tiefer Schlitz *m* ▷ *vt* aufschlitzen

gasket ['gæskɪt] *n* Dichtung *f*

gas mask *n* Gasmaske *f*

gas meter *n* Gaszähler *m*

gasoline ['gæsəliːn] (*US*) *n* Benzin *nt*

gasp [gɑːsp] *n* tiefer Atemzug *m* ▷ *vi* keuchen; (*in surprise*) nach Luft schnappen; **to give a ~ (of shock/horror)** (vor Schreck/Entsetzen) die Luft anhalten; **to be ~ing for** sich sehnen nach +*dat*
▸ **gasp out** *vt* hervorstoßen

gas ring *n* Gasbrenner *m*

gas station (*US*) *n* Tankstelle *f*

gas tank *n* Benzintank *m*

gastric ['gæstrɪk] *adj* (*upset, ulcer etc*) Magen-

gate [geɪt] *n* (*of garden*) Pforte *f*; (*of field*) Gatter *nt*; (*of building*) Tor *nt*; (*at airport*) Flugsteig *m*; (*of level crossing*) Schranke *f*; (*of lock*) Tor *nt*

gateau ['gætəu] (*pl* **~x**) *n* Torte *f*

gateway ['geɪtweɪ] *n* (*also fig*) Tor *nt*

gather ['gæðəʳ] *vt* sammeln; (*flowers, fruit*) pflücken; (*understand*) schließen; (*Sewing*) kräuseln ▷ *vi* (*assemble*) sich versammeln; (*dust*) sich ansammeln; (*clouds*) sich zusammenziehen; **to ~ (from)** schließen (aus); **to ~ (that)** annehmen(, dass); **as far as I can ~** so wie ich es sehe; **to ~ speed** schneller werden

gathering ['gæðərɪŋ] *n* Versammlung *f*

gaudy ['gɔːdɪ] *adj* knallig

gauge, (*US*) **gage** [geɪdʒ] *n* Messgerät *nt*, Messinstrument *nt*; (*Rail*) Spurweite *f* ▷ *vt* messen; (*fig*) beurteilen; **petrol ~, fuel ~, gas gage** (*US*) Benzinuhr *f*; **to ~ the right moment** den richtigen Moment abwägen

gaunt [gɔːnt] *adj* (*haggard*) hager; (*bare, stark*) öde

gauntlet ['gɔːntlɪt] *n* (Stulpen)handschuh *m*; (*fig*): **to run the ~** Spießruten laufen; **to throw down the ~** den Fehdehandschuh hinwerfen

gauze [gɔːz] *n* Gaze *f*

gave [geɪv] *pt of* **give**

gay [geɪ] *adj* (*homosexual*) schwul; (*cheerful*) fröhlich; (*dress*) bunt

gaze [geɪz] *n* Blick *m* ▷ *vi*: **to ~ at sth** etw anstarren

gazump [gə'zʌmp] (*Brit*) *vt*: **to be ~ed** *ein mündlich zugesagtes Haus an einen Höherbietenden verlieren*

GB *abbr* (= *Great Britain*) GB

GCE (*Brit*) *n abbr* (= *General Certificate of Education*) *Schulabschlusszeugnis*, ≈ Abitur *nt*

GCSE (*Brit*) *n abbr* (= *General Certificate of Secondary Education*) *Schulabschlusszeugnis*, ≈ mittlere Reife *f*

gear [gɪəʳ] *n* (*equipment*) Ausrüstung *f*; (*belongings*) Sachen *pl*; (*Tech*) Getriebe *nt*; (*Aut*) Gang *m*; (*on bicycle*) Gangschaltung *f* ▷ *vt* (*fig: adapt*): **to ~ sth to** etw ausrichten auf +*acc*; **top/low/bottom ~, high/low/bottom ~** (*US*) hoher/niedriger/erster Gang; **to put a car into ~** einen Gang einlegen; **to leave the car in ~** den Gang eingelegt lassen; **to leave out of ~** im Leerlauf lassen; **our service is ~ed to meet the needs of the disabled** unser Betrieb ist auf die Bedürfnisse von Behinderten eingerichtet
▸ **gear up** *vt, vi*: **to ~ (o.s.) up (to)** sich vorbereiten (auf +*acc*) ▷ *vt*: **to ~ o.s. up to do sth** sich darauf vorbereiten, etw zu tun

gear lever, (*US*) **gear shift** *n* Schalthebel *m*

geese [giːs] *npl of* **goose**

gel [dʒɛl] *n* Gel *nt*

gem [dʒɛm] *n* Edelstein *m*; **she/the house is a ~** (*fig*) sie/das Haus ist ein Juwel; **a ~ of an idea** eine ausgezeichnete Idee

Gemini ['dʒɛmɪnaɪ] *n* (*Astrol*) Zwillinge *pl*; **to be ~** (ein) Zwilling sein

gender ['dʒɛndəʳ] *n* Geschlecht *nt*

gene [dʒiːn] *n* Gen *nt*

general ['dʒɛnərl] *n* General *m* ▷ *adj* allgemein; (*widespread*) weitverbreitet; (*non-specific*) generell; **in ~** im Allgemeinen; **the ~ public** die Öffentlichkeit, die Allgemeinheit; **~ audit** (*Comm*) Jahresabschlussprüfung *f*

general anaesthetic *n* Vollnarkose *f*

general delivery (*US*) *n*: **to send sth ~** etw postlagernd schicken

general election *n* Parlamentswahlen *pl*

generalize ['dʒɛnrəlaɪz] *vi* verallgemeinern

generally ['dʒɛnrəlɪ] *adv* im Allgemeinen

general practitioner *n* praktischer Arzt *m*, praktische Ärztin *f*

generate ['dʒɛnəreɪt] *vt* erzeugen; (*jobs*) schaffen; (*profits*) einbringen

generation [dʒɛnə'reɪʃən] *n* Generation *f*; (*of electricity etc*) Erzeugung *f*

generator ['dʒɛnəreɪtəʳ] *n* Generator *m*

generosity [dʒɛnə'rɔsɪtɪ] *n* Großzügigkeit *f*

generous ['dʒɛnərəs] *adj* großzügig; (*measure, remuneration*) reichlich

genetic [dʒɪ'nɛtɪk] *adj* genetisch
genetics [dʒɪ'nɛtɪks] *n* Genetik *f*
Geneva [dʒɪ'ni:və] *n* Genf *nt*
genial ['dʒi:nɪəl] *adj* freundlich; (*climate*) angenehm
genitals ['dʒɛnɪtlz] *npl* Genitalien *pl*, Geschlechtsteile *pl*
genius ['dʒi:nɪəs] *n* Talent *nt*; (*person*) Genie *nt*
gent [dʒɛnt] (*Brit: inf*) *n abbr* = **gentleman**
genteel [dʒɛn'ti:l] *adj* vornehm, fein
gentle ['dʒɛntl] *adj* sanft; (*movement, breeze*) leicht; **a ~ hint** ein zarter Hinweis
gentleman ['dʒɛntlmən] (*irreg: like* **man**) *n* Herr *m*; (*referring to social position or good manners*) Gentleman *m*; **~'s agreement** Vereinbarung *f* auf Treu und Glauben
gently ['dʒɛntlɪ] *adv* (*see adj*) sanft; leicht; zart
gentry ['dʒɛntrɪ] *n inv*: **the ~** die Gentry, der niedere Adel
gents [dʒɛnts] *n*: **the ~** die Herrentoilette
genuine ['dʒɛnjuɪn] *adj* echt; (*person*) natürlich, aufrichtig
genuinely ['dʒɛnjuɪnlɪ] *adv* wirklich
geographic [dʒɪə'græfɪk], **geographical** [dʒɪə'græfɪkl] *adj* geografisch
geography [dʒɪ'ɔgrəfɪ] *n* Geografie *f*; (*Scol*) Erdkunde *f*
geology [dʒɪ'ɔlədʒɪ] *n* Geologie *f*
geometric [dʒɪə'mɛtrɪk], **geometrical** [dʒɪə'mɛtrɪkl] *adj* geometrisch
geometry [dʒɪ'ɔmətrɪ] *n* Geometrie *f*
geranium [dʒɪ'reɪnɪəm] *n* Geranie *f*
geriatric [dʒɛrɪ'ætrɪk] *adj* geriatrisch ▷ *n* Greis(in) *m(f)*
germ [dʒə:m] *n* Bazillus *m*; (*Biol, fig*) Keim *m*
German ['dʒə:mən] *adj* deutsch ▷ *n* Deutsche(r) *f(m)*; (*Ling*) Deutsch *nt*
German measles (*Brit*) *n* Röteln *pl*
Germany ['dʒə:mənɪ] *n* Deutschland *nt*
gesture ['dʒɛstjə^r] *n* Geste *f*; **as a ~ of friendship** als Zeichen der Freundschaft
get [gɛt] (*pt, pp* **got**, *US pp* **gotten**) *vi* **1** (*become, be*) werden; **to get old/tired/cold** alt/müde/kalt werden; **to get dirty** sich schmutzig machen; **to get killed** getötet werden; **to get married** heiraten
2 (*go*): **to get (from ...) to ...** (von ...) nach ... kommen; **how did you get here?** wie sind Sie hierhin gekommen?
3 (*begin*): **to get to know sb** jdn kennenlernen; **let's get going** *or* **started** fangen wir an!
▷ *modal aux vb*: **you've got to do it** du musst es tun
▷ *vt* **1: to get sth done** (*do oneself*) etw gemacht bekommen; (*have done*) etw machen lassen; **to get one's hair cut** sich *dat* die Haare schneiden lassen; **to get the car going** *or* **to go** das Auto in Gang bringen; **to get sb to do sth** etw von jdm machen lassen; (*persuade*) jdn dazu bringen, etw zu tun
2 (*obtain: money, permission, results*) erhalten; (*find: job, flat*) finden; (*fetch: person, doctor, object*) holen; **to get sth for sb** jdm etw besorgen; **can I get you a drink?** kann ich Ihnen etwas zu trinken anbieten?
3 (*receive, acquire: present, prize*) bekommen; **how much did you get for the painting?** wie viel haben Sie für das Bild bekommen?
4 (*catch*) bekommen, kriegen (*inf*); (*hit: target etc*) treffen; **to get sb by the arm/throat** jdn am Arm/Hals packen; **the bullet got him in the leg** die Kugel traf ihn ins Bein
5 (*take, move*) bringen; **to get sth to sb** jdm etw zukommen lassen
6 (*plane, bus etc: take*) nehmen; (*: catch*) bekommen
7 (*understand: joke etc*) verstehen; **I get it** ich verstehe
8 (*have, possess*): **to have got** haben; **how many have you got?** wie viele hast du?
▸ **get about** *vi* (*person*) herumkommen; (*news, rumour*) sich verbreiten
▸ **get across** *vt* (*message, meaning*) klarmachen
▸ **get along** *vi* (*be friends*) (miteinander) auskommen; (*depart*) sich auf den Weg machen
▸ **get around** *vt fus* = **get round**
▸ **get at** *vt fus* (*attack, criticize*) angreifen; (*reach*) herankommen an *+acc*; **what are you getting at?** worauf willst du hinaus?
▸ **get away** *vi* (*leave*) wegkommen; (*on holiday*) verreisen; (*escape*) entkommen
▸ **get away with** *vt fus* (*stolen goods*) entkommen mit; **he'll never get away with it!** damit kommt er nicht durch
▸ **get back** *vi* (*return*) zurückkommen ▷ *vt* (*regain*) zurückbekommen; **get back!** zurück!
▸ **get back at** (*inf*) *vt fus*: **to get back at sb for sth** jdm etw heimzahlen
▸ **get back to** *vt fus* (*return to*) zurückkehren zu; (*contact again*) zurückkommen auf *+acc*; **to get back to sleep** wieder einschlafen
▸ **get by** *vi* (*pass*) vorbeikommen; (*manage*) zurechtkommen; **I can get by in German** ich kann mich auf Deutsch verständlich machen
▸ **get down** *vi* (*from tree, ladder etc*) heruntersteigen; (*from horse*) absteigen; (*leave table*) aufstehen; (*bend down*) sich bücken; (*duck*) sich ducken
▷ *vt* (*depress: person*) fertigmachen; (*write*) aufschreiben
▸ **get down to** *vt fus*: **to get down to sth** (*work*) etw in Angriff nehmen; (*find time*) zu etw kommen; **to get down to business** (*fig*) zur Sache kommen
▸ **get in** *vi* (*be elected: candidate, party*) gewählt werden; (*arrive*) ankommen
▷ *vt* (*bring in: harvest*) einbringen; (*: shopping, supplies*) (herein)holen
▸ **get into** *vt fus* (*conversation, argument, fight*) geraten in *+acc*; (*vehicle*) einsteigen in *+acc*; (*clothes*) hineinkommen in *+acc*; **to get into**

bed ins Bett gehen; **to get into the habit of doing sth** sich *dat* angewöhnen, etw zu tun
▶ **get off** *vi* (*from train etc*) aussteigen; (*escape punishment*) davonkommen
▷ *vt* (*remove: clothes*) ausziehen; (*: stain*) herausbekommen
▷ *vt fus* (*leave: train, bus*) aussteigen aus; **we get 3 days off at Christmas** zu Weihnachten bekommen wir 3 Tage frei; **to get off to a good start** (*fig*) einen guten Anfang machen
▶ **get on** *vi* (*be friends*) (miteinander) auskommen
▷ *vt fus* (*bus, train*) einsteigen in *+acc*; **how are you getting on?** wie kommst du zurecht?; **time is getting on** es wird langsam spät
▶ **get on to** (*Brit*) *vt fus* (*subject, topic*) übergehen zu; (*contact: person*) sich in Verbindung setzen mit
▶ **get on with** *vt fus* (*person*) auskommen mit; (*meeting, work etc*) weitermachen mit
▶ **get out** *vi* (*leave: on foot*) hinausgehen; (*of vehicle*) aussteigen; (*news etc*) herauskommen
▷ *vt* (*take out: book etc*) herausholen; (*remove: stain*) herausbekommen
▶ **get out of** *vt fus* (*money: bank etc*) abheben von; (*avoid: duty etc*) herumkommen um
▷ *vt* (*extract: confession etc*) herausbekommen aus; (*derive: pleasure*) haben an *+dat*; (*: benefit*) haben von
▶ **get over** *vt fus* (*overcome*) überwinden; (*: illness*) sich erholen von; (*communicate: idea etc*) verständlich machen
▷ *vt*: **to get it over with** (*finish*) es hinter sich *acc* bringen
▶ **get round** *vt fus* (*law, rule*) umgehen; (*person*) herumkriegen
▶ **get round to** *vt fus*: **to get round to doing sth** dazu kommen, etw zu tun
▶ **get through** *vi* (*Tel*) durchkommen
▷ *vt fus* (*finish: work*) schaffen; (*: book*) lesen
▶ **get through to** *vt fus* (*Tel*) durchkommen zu; (*make o.s. understood*) durchdringen zu
▶ **get together** *vi* (*people*) zusammenkommen
▷ *vt* (*people*) zusammenbringen; (*project, plan etc*) zusammenstellen
▶ **get up** *vi* (*rise*) aufstehen
▷ *vt*: **to get up enthusiasm for sth** Begeisterung für etw aufbringen
▶ **get up to** *vt fus* (*prank etc*) anstellen

getaway ['gɛtəweɪ] *n*: **to make a/one's ~** sich davonmachen
geyser ['gi:zəʳ] *n* Geiser *m*; (*Brit: water heater*) Durchlauferhitzer *m*
Ghana ['gɑ:nə] *n* Ghana *nt*
ghastly ['gɑ:stlɪ] *adj* grässlich; (*complexion*) totenblass; **you look ~!** (*ill*) du siehst grässlich aus!
gherkin ['gə:kɪn] *n* Gewürzgurke *f*
ghetto ['gɛtəu] *n* G(h)etto *nt*
ghetto blaster [-'blɑ:stəʳ] (*inf*) *n* Gettoblaster *m*
ghost [gəust] *n* Geist *m*, Gespenst *nt* ▷ *vt* für jdn (als Ghostwriter) schreiben; **to give up the ~** den Geist aufgeben
giant ['dʒaɪənt] *n* (*also fig*) Riese *m* ▷ *adj* riesig, riesenhaft; **~ (size) packet** Riesenpackung *f*
gibberish ['dʒɪbərɪʃ] *n* Quatsch *m*
giblets ['dʒɪblɪts] *npl* Geflügelinnereien *pl*
Gibraltar [dʒɪ'brɔ:ltəʳ] *n* Gibraltar *nt*
giddy ['gɪdɪ] *adj*: **I am/feel ~** mir ist schwind(e)lig; (*height*) schwindelerregend; **~ with excitement** vor Aufregung ganz ausgelassen
gift [gɪft] *n* Geschenk *nt*; (*donation*) Spende *f*; (*Comm: also*: **free gift**) (Werbe)geschenk *nt*; (*ability*) Gabe *f*; **to have a ~ for sth** ein Talent für etw haben
gifted ['gɪftɪd] *adj* begabt
gift token *n* Geschenkgutschein *m*
gig [gɪg] (*inf*) *n* Konzert *nt*
gigabyte ['dʒɪgəbaɪt] *n* Gigabyte *nt*
gigantic [dʒaɪ'gæntɪk] *adj* riesig, riesengroß
giggle ['gɪgl] *vi* kichern ▷ *n* Spaß *m*; **to do sth for a ~** etw aus Spaß tun
gill [dʒɪl] *n* Gill *nt* (*Brit* = 15 cl, *US* = 12 cl)
gills [gɪlz] *npl* Kiemen *pl*
gilt [gɪlt] *adj* vergoldet ▷ *n* Vergoldung *f*; **gilts** *npl* (*Comm*) mündelsichere Wertpapiere *pl*
gilt-edged ['gɪltɛdʒd] *adj* (*stocks, securities*) mündelsicher
gimmick ['gɪmɪk] *n* Gag *m*; **sales ~** Verkaufsmasche *f*, Verkaufstrick *m*
gin [dʒɪn] *n* Gin *m*
ginger ['dʒɪndʒəʳ] *n* Ingwer *m* ▷ *adj* (*hair*) rötlich; (*cat*) rötlich gelb
ginger ale *n* Gingerale *nt*
gingerbread ['dʒɪndʒəbrɛd] *n* (*cake*) Ingwerkuchen *m*; (*biscuit*) ≈ Pfefferkuchen *m*
gingerly ['dʒɪndʒəlɪ] *adv* vorsichtig
gipsy ['dʒɪpsɪ] *n* Zigeuner(in) *m(f)*
giraffe [dʒɪ'rɑ:f] *n* Giraffe *f*
girder ['gə:dəʳ] *n* Träger *m*
girl [gə:l] *n* Mädchen *nt*; (*young unmarried woman*) (junges) Mädchen *nt*; (*daughter*) Tochter *f*; **this is my little ~** das ist mein Töchterchen; **an English ~** eine Engländerin
girlfriend ['gə:lfrɛnd] *n* Freundin *f*
Girl Guide *n* Pfadfinderin *f*
girlish ['gə:lɪʃ] *adj* mädchenhaft
Girl Scout (*US*) *n* Pfadfinderin *f*
giro ['dʒaɪrəu] *n* Giro *nt*, Giroverkehr *m*; (*post office giro*) Postscheckverkehr *m*; (*Brit: welfare cheque*) Sozialhilfescheck *m*
gist [dʒɪst] *n* Wesentliche(s) *nt*
give [gɪv] (*pt* **gave**, *pp* **given**) *vt* **1** (*hand over*): **to give sb sth, give sth to sb** jdm etw geben; **I'll give you £5 for it** ich gebe dir £5 dafür
2 (*used with noun to replace a verb*): **to give a sigh/cry/laugh** *etc* seufzen/schreien/lachen *etc*; **to give a speech/a lecture** eine Rede/einen Vortrag halten; **to give three cheers** ein dreifaches Hoch ausbringen
3 (*tell, deliver: news, message etc*) mitteilen;

(: *advice, answer*) geben
4 (*supply, provide: opportunity, job etc*) geben; (: *surprise*) bereiten; (*bestow: title, honour, right*) geben, verleihen; **that's given me an idea** dabei kommt mir eine Idee
5 (*devote: time, one's life*) geben; (: *attention*) schenken
6 (*organize: party, dinner etc*) geben
▷ *vi* **1** (*also*: **give way**: *break, collapse*) nachgeben
2 (*stretch: fabric*) sich dehnen
▶ **give away** *vt* (*money, opportunity*) verschenken; (*secret, information*) verraten; (*bride*) zum Altar führen; **that immediately gave him away** dadurch verriet er sich sofort
▶ **give back** *vt* (*money, book etc*) zurückgeben
▶ **give in** *vi* (*yield*) nachgeben
▷ *vt* (*essay etc*) abgeben
▶ **give off** *vt* (*heat, smoke*) abgeben
▶ **give out** *vt* (*prizes, books, drinks etc*) austeilen
▷ *vi* (*be exhausted: supplies*) zu Ende gehen; (*fail*) versagen
▶ **give up** *vt, vi* aufgeben; **to give up smoking** das Rauchen aufgeben; **to give o.s. up** sich stellen; (*after siege etc*) sich ergeben
▶ **give way** *vi* (*yield, collapse*) nachgeben; (*Brit: Aut*) die Vorfahrt achten

given ['gɪvn] *pp of* **give** ▷ *adj* (*time, amount*) bestimmt ▷ *conj*: **~ the circumstances ...** unter den Umständen ...; **~ that ...** angesichts der Tatsache, dass ...

glacier ['glæsɪəʳ] *n* Gletscher *m*

glad [glæd] *adj* froh; **to be ~ about sth** sich über etw *acc* freuen; **to be ~ that** sich freuen, dass; **I was ~ of his help** ich war froh über seine Hilfe

gladly ['glædlɪ] *adv* gern(e)

glamorous ['glæmərəs] *adj* reizvoll; (*model etc*) glamourös

glamour ['glæməʳ] *n* Glanz *m*, Reiz *m*

glance [glɑ:ns] *n* Blick *m* ▷ *vi*: **to ~ at** einen Blick werfen auf *+acc*
▶ **glance off** *vt fus* abprallen von

glancing ['glɑ:nsɪŋ] *adj*: **to strike sth a ~ blow** etw streifen

gland [glænd] *n* Drüse *f*

glare [glɛəʳ] *n* wütender Blick *m*; (*of light*) greller Schein *m*; (*of publicity*) grelles Licht *nt* ▷ *vi* (*light*) grell scheinen; **to ~ at** (wütend) anstarren

glaring ['glɛərɪŋ] *adj* eklatant

glass [glɑ:s] *n* Glas *nt*; **glasses** *npl* (*spectacles*) Brille *f*

glasshouse ['glɑ:shaus] *n* Gewächshaus *nt*

glassware ['glɑ:swɛəʳ] *n* Glaswaren *pl*

glaze [gleɪz] *vt* (*door, window*) verglasen; (*pottery*) glasieren ▷ *n* Glasur *f*

glazed [gleɪzd] *adj* (*eyes*) glasig; (*pottery, tiles*) glasiert

glazier ['gleɪzɪəʳ] *n* Glaser(in) *m(f)*

gleam [gli:m] *vi* (*light*) schimmern; (*polished surface, eyes*) glänzen ▷ *n*: **a ~ of hope** ein Hoffnungsschimmer *m*

glean [gli:n] *vt* (*information*) herausbekommen, ausfindig machen

glee [gli:] *n* Freude *f*

glen [glɛn] *n* Tal *nt*

glib [glɪb] *adj* (*person*) glatt; (*promise, response*) leichthin gemacht

glide [glaɪd] *vi* gleiten ▷ *n* Gleiten *nt*

glider ['glaɪdəʳ] *n* Segelflugzeug *nt*

gliding ['glaɪdɪŋ] *n* Segelfliegen *nt*

glimmer ['glɪməʳ] *n* Schimmer *m*; (*of interest, hope*) Funke *m* ▷ *vi* schimmern

glimpse [glɪmps] *n* Blick *m* ▷ *vt* einen Blick werfen auf *+acc*; **to catch a ~ (of)** einen flüchtigen Blick erhaschen (von *+dat*)

glint [glɪnt] *vi* glitzern; (*eyes*) funkeln ▷ *n* (*see vb*) Glitzern *nt*; Funkeln *nt*

glisten ['glɪsn] *vi* glänzen

glitter ['glɪtəʳ] *vi* glitzern; (*eyes*) funkeln ▷ *n* (*see vb*) Glitzern *nt*; Funkeln *nt*

gloat [gləut] *vi*: **to ~ (over)** (*own success*) sich brüsten (mit); (*sb's failure*) sich hämisch freuen (über *+acc*)

global ['gləubl] *adj* global

globalization [gləublaɪ'zeɪʃn] *n* (*Pol, Econ*) Globalisierung *f*

global warming [-'wɔ:mɪŋ] *n* Erwärmung *f* der Erdatmosphäre

globe [gləub] *n* Erdball *m*; (*model*) Globus *m*; (*shape*) Kugel *f*

gloom [glu:m] *n* Düsterkeit *f*; (*sadness*) düstere *or* gedrückte Stimmung *f*

gloomy ['glu:mɪ] *adj* düster; (*person*) bedrückt; (*situation*) bedrückend

glorious ['glɔ:rɪəs] *adj* herrlich; (*victory*) ruhmreich; (*future*) glanzvoll

glory ['glɔ:rɪ] *n* Ruhm *m*; (*splendour*) Herrlichkeit *f* ▷ *vi*: **to ~ in** sich sonnen in *+dat*

gloss [glɔs] *n* Glanz *m*; (*also*: **gloss paint**) Lack *m*, Lackfarbe *f*
▶ **gloss over** *vt fus* vom Tisch wischen

glossary ['glɔsərɪ] *n* Glossar *nt*

glossy ['glɔsɪ] *adj* glänzend; (*photograph, magazine*) Hochglanz- ▷ *n* (*also*: **glossy magazine**) (Hochglanz)magazin *nt*

glove [glʌv] *n* Handschuh *m*

glove compartment *n* Handschuhfach *nt*

glow [gləu] *vi* glühen; (*stars, eyes*) leuchten ▷ *n* (*see vb*) Glühen *nt*; Leuchten *nt*

glower ['glauəʳ] *vi*: **to ~ at sb** jdn finster ansehen

glucose ['glu:kəus] *n* Traubenzucker *m*

glue [glu:] *n* Klebstoff *m* ▷ *vt*: **to ~ sth onto sth** etw an etw *acc* kleben; **to ~ sth into place** etw festkleben

glum [glʌm] *adj* bedrückt, niedergeschlagen

glut [glʌt] *n*: **~ (of)** Überangebot *nt* (an *+dat*) ▷ *vt*: **to be ~ted (with)** überschwemmt sein (mit); **a ~ of pears** eine Birnenschwemme

glutton ['glʌtn] *n* Vielfraß *m*; **a ~ for work** ein Arbeitstier *nt*; **a ~ for punishment** ein Masochist *m*

GM *abbr* = **genetically modified**

gm *abbr* (= *gram(me)*) g
GMT *abbr* (= *Greenwich Mean Time*) WEZ *f*
gnat [næt] *n* (Stech)mücke *f*
gnaw [nɔː] *vt* nagen an *+dat* ▷ *vi* (*fig*): **to ~ at** quälen
go [gəu] (*pt* **went**, *pp* **gone**) *vi* **1** gehen; (*travel*) fahren; **a car went by** ein Auto fuhr vorbei
2 (*depart*) gehen; **"I must go," she said** „ich muss gehen", sagte sie; **she has gone to Sheffield/Australia** (*permanently*) sie ist nach Sheffield/Australien gegangen
3 (*attend, take part in activity*) gehen; **she went to university in Oxford** sie ist in Oxford zur Universität gegangen; **to go for a walk** spazieren gehen; **to go dancing** tanzen gehen
4 (*work*) funktionieren; **the tape recorder was still going** das Tonband lief noch
5 (*become*): **to go pale/mouldy** blass/schimmelig werden
6 (*be sold*): **to go for £100** für £100 weggehen *or* verkauft werden
7 (*be about to, intend to*): **we're going to stop in an hour** wir hören in einer Stunde auf; **are you going to come?** kommst du?, wirst du kommen?
8 (*time*) vergehen
9 (*event, activity*) ablaufen; **how did it go?** wie wars?
10 (*be given*): **the job is to go to someone else** die Stelle geht an jemand anders
11 (*break etc*) kaputtgehen; **the fuse went** die Sicherung ist durchgebrannt
12 (*be placed*) hingehören; **the milk goes in the fridge** die Milch kommt in den Kühlschrank
▷ *n* **1** (*try*): **to have a go at sth** etw versuchen; **I'll have a go at mending it** ich will versuchen, es zu reparieren; **to have a go** es versuchen
2 (*turn*): **whose go is it?** wer ist dran *or* an der Reihe?
3 (*move*): **to be on the go** auf Trab sein
▸ **go about** *vi* (*also*: **go around**: *rumour*) herumgehen
▷ *vt fus*: **how do I go about this?** wie soll ich vorgehen?; **to go about one's business** seinen eigenen Geschäften nachgehen
▸ **go after** *vt fus* (*pursue*: *person*) nachgehen *+dat*; (: *job etc*) sich bemühen um; (: *record*) erreichen wollen
▸ **go against** *vt fus* (*be unfavourable to*) ungünstig verlaufen für; (*disregard*: *advice, wishes etc*) handeln gegen
▸ **go ahead** *vi* (*proceed*) weitergehen; **to go ahead with** weitermachen mit
▸ **go along** *vi* gehen
▸ **go along with** *vt fus* (*agree with*) zustimmen *+dat*; (*accompany*) mitgehen mit
▸ **go away** *vi* (*leave*) weggehen
▸ **go back** *vi* zurückgehen
▸ **go back on** *vt fus* (*promise*) zurücknehmen
▸ **go by** *vi* (*years, time*) vergehen
▷ *vt fus* (*rule etc*) sich richten nach
▸ **go down** *vi* (*descend*) hinuntergehen; (*ship, sun*) untergehen; (*price, level*) sinken
▷ *vt fus* (*stairs, ladder*) hinuntergehen; **his speech went down well** seine Rede kam gut an
▸ **go for** *vt fus* (*fetch*) holen (gehen); (*like*) mögen; (*attack*) losgehen auf *+acc*; (*apply to*) gelten für
▸ **go in** *vi* (*enter*) hineingehen
▸ **go in for** *vt fus* (*competition*) teilnehmen an *+dat*; (*favour*) stehen auf *+acc*
▸ **go into** *vt fus* (*enter*) hineingehen in *+acc*; (*investigate*) sich befassen mit; (*career*) gehen in *+acc*
▸ **go off** *vi* (*leave*) weggehen; (*food*) schlecht werden; (*bomb, gun*) losgehen; (*event*) verlaufen; (*lights etc*) ausgehen
▷ *vt fus* (*inf*): **I've gone off it/him** ich mache mir nichts mehr daraus/aus ihm; **the gun went off** das Gewehr ging los; **to go off to sleep** einschlafen; **the party went off well** die Party verlief gut
▸ **go on** *vi* (*continue*) weitergehen; (*happen*) vor sich gehen; (*lights*) angehen
▷ *vt fus* (*be guided by*) sich stützen auf *+acc*; **to go on doing sth** mit etw weitermachen; **what's going on here?** was geht hier vor?, was ist hier los?
▸ **go on at** (*inf*) *vt fus* (*nag*) herumnörgeln an *+dat*
▸ **go on with** *vt fus* weitermachen mit
▸ **go out** *vt fus* (*leave*) hinausgehen
▷ *vi* (*for entertainment*) ausgehen; (*fire, light*) ausgehen; (*couple*): **they went out for 3 years** sie gingen 3 Jahre lang miteinander
▸ **go over** *vi* hinübergehen
▷ *vt* (*check*) durchgehen; **to go over sth in one's mind** etw überdenken
▸ **go round** *vi* (*circulate*: *news, rumour*) umgehen; (*revolve*) sich drehen; (*suffice*) ausreichen; (*visit*): **to go round (to sb's)** (bei jdm) vorbeigehen; **there's not enough to go round** es reicht nicht (für alle)
▸ **go through** *vt fus* (*place*) gehen durch; (*by car*) fahren durch; (*undergo*) durchmachen; (*search through*: *files, papers*) durchsuchen; (*describe*: *list, book, story*) durchgehen; (*perform*) durchgehen
▸ **go through with** *vt fus* (*plan, crime*) durchziehen; **I couldn't go through with it** ich brachte es nicht fertig
▸ **go under** *vi* (*sink*: *person*) untergehen; (*fig*: *business, project*) scheitern
▸ **go up** *vi* (*ascend*) hinaufgehen; (*price, level*) steigen; **to go up in flames** in Flammen aufgehen
▸ **go with** *vt fus* (*suit*) passen zu
▸ **go without** *vt fus* (*food, treats*) verzichten auf *+acc*
goad [gəud] *vt* aufreizen
▸ **goad on** *vt* anstacheln
go-ahead ['gəuəhɛd] *adj* zielstrebig; (*firm*)

fortschrittlich ▷ *n* grünes Licht *nt*; **to give sb the ~** jdm grünes Licht geben
goal [gəul] *n* Tor *nt*; (*aim*) Ziel *nt*; **to score a ~** ein Tor schießen *or* erzielen
goalkeeper ['gəulki:pəʳ] *n* Torwart *m*
goat [gəut] *n* Ziege *f*
gobble ['gɔbl] *vt* (*also*: **gobble down, gobble up**) verschlingen
go-between ['gəubıtwi:n] *n* Vermittler(in) *m(f)*
god [gɔd] *n* Gott *m*
godchild ['gɔdtʃaıld] *n* Patenkind *nt*
goddaughter ['gɔddɔ:təʳ] *n* Patentochter *f*
goddess ['gɔdıs] *n* Göttin *f*
godfather ['gɔdfɑ:ðəʳ] *n* Pate *m*
godmother ['gɔdmʌðəʳ] *n* Patin *f*
godsend ['gɔdsɛnd] *n* Geschenk *nt* des Himmels
godson ['gɔdsʌn] *n* Patensohn *m*
goggles ['gɔglz] *npl* Schutzbrille *f*
going ['gəuıŋʳ] *n*: **it was slow/hard ~** (*fig*) es ging nur langsam/schwer voran ▷ *adj*: **the ~ rate** der gängige Preis; **when the ~ gets tough** wenn es schwierig wird; **a ~ concern** ein gut gehendes Unternehmen
gold [gəuld] *n* Gold *nt*; (*also*: **gold medal**) Gold *nt*, Goldmedaille *f* ▷ *adj* golden; (*reserves, jewellery, tooth*) Gold-
golden ['gəuldən] *adj* (*also fig*) golden
goldfish ['gəuldfıʃ] *n* Goldfisch *m*
gold-plated ['gəuld'pleıtıd] *adj* vergoldet
goldsmith ['gəuldsmıθ] *n* Goldschmied(in) *m(f)*
golf [gɔlf] *n* Golf *nt*
golf ball *n* (*for game*) Golfball *m*; (*on typewriter*) Kugelkopf *m*
golf club *n* Golfklub *m*; (*stick*) Golfschläger *m*
golf course *n* Golfplatz *m*
golfer ['gɔlfəʳ] *n* Golfspieler(in) *m(f)*, Golfer(in) *m(f)*
gone [gɔn] *pp of* **go** ▷ *adj* weg; (*days*) vorbei
gong [gɔŋ] *n* Gong *m*
good [gud] *adj* gut; (*well-behaved*) brav, lieb ▷ *n* (*virtue, morality*) Gute(s) *nt*; (*benefit*) Wohl *nt*; **goods** *npl* (*Comm*) Güter *pl*; **to have a ~ time** sich (gut) amüsieren; **to be ~ at sth** (*swimming, talking etc*) etw gut können; (*science, sports etc*) gut in etw *dat* sein; **to be ~ for sb/sth** gut für jdn/zu etw *dat* sein; **it's ~ for you** das tut dir gut; **it's a ~ thing you were there** gut, dass Sie da waren; **she is ~ with children** sie kann gut mit Kindern umgehen; **she is ~ with her hands** sie ist geschickt; **to feel ~** sich wohlfühlen; **it's ~ to see you** (es ist) schön, Sie zu sehen; **would you be ~ enough to ...?** könnten Sie bitte ...?; **that's very ~ of you** das ist wirklich nett von Ihnen; **a ~ deal (of)** ziemlich viel; **a ~ many** ziemlich viele; **take a ~ look** sieh dir das genau *or* gut an; **a ~ while ago** vor einiger Zeit; **to make ~** (*damage*) wiedergutmachen; (*loss*) ersetzen; **it's no ~ complaining** es ist sinnlos *or* es nützt nichts, sich zu beklagen; **~ morning/afternoon/evening!** guten Morgen/Tag/Abend!; **~ night!** gute Nacht!; **he's up to no ~** er führt nichts Gutes im Schilde; **for the common ~** zum Wohle aller; **is this any ~?** (*will it help you?*) können Sie das gebrauchen?; (*is it good enough?*) reicht das?; **is the book/film any ~?** was halten Sie von dem Buch/Film?; **for ~** für immer; **~s and chattels** Hab und Gut *nt*
goodbye [gud'baı] *excl* auf Wiedersehen!; **to say ~** sich verabschieden
Good Friday *n* Karfreitag *m*
good-looking ['gud'lukıŋ] *adj* gut aussehend
good-natured ['gud'neıtʃəd] *adj* gutmütig; (*discussion*) freundlich
goodness ['gudnıs] *n* Güte *f*; **for ~ sake!** um Himmels willen!; **~ gracious!** ach du liebe *or* meine Güte!
goods train (*Brit*) *n* Güterzug *m*
goodwill [gud'wıl] *n* Wohlwollen *nt*; (*Comm*) Goodwill *m*
goose [gu:s] (*pl* **geese**) *n* Gans *f*
gooseberry ['guzbərı] *n* Stachelbeere *f*; **to play ~** (*Brit*) das fünfte Rad am Wagen sein
gore [gɔ:ʳ] *vt* aufspießen ▷ *n* Blut *nt*
gorge [gɔ:dʒ] *n* Schlucht *f* ▷ *vt*: **to ~ o.s. (on)** sich vollstopfen (mit)
gorgeous ['gɔ:dʒəs] *adj* herrlich; (*person*) hinreißend
gorilla [gə'rılə] *n* Gorilla *m*
gorse [gɔ:s] *n* Stechginster *m*
gory ['gɔ:rı] *adj* blutig
go-slow ['gəu'sləu] (*Brit*) *n* Bummelstreik *m*
gospel ['gɔspl] *n* Evangelium *nt*; (*doctrine*) Lehre *f*
gossip ['gɔsıp] *n* (*rumours*) Klatsch *m*, Tratsch *m*; (*chat*) Schwatz *m*; (*person*) Klatschbase *f* ▷ *vi* schwatzen; **a piece of ~** eine Neuigkeit
gossip column *n* Klatschkolumne *f*, Klatschspalte *f*
got [gɔt] *pt, pp of* **get**
gotten ['gɔtn] (*US*) *pp of* **get**
gourmet ['guəmeı] *n* Feinschmecker(in) *m(f)*, Gourmet *m*
gout [gaut] *n* Gicht *f*
govern ['gʌvən] *vt* (*also Ling*) regieren; (*event, conduct*) bestimmen
governess ['gʌvənıs] *n* Gouvernante *f*
government ['gʌvnmənt] *n* Regierung *f* ▷ *cpd* Regierungs-; **local ~** Kommunalverwaltung *f*, Gemeindeverwaltung *f*
governor ['gʌvənəʳ] *n* Gouverneur(in) *m(f)*; (*of bank, hospital, Brit: of prison*) Direktor(in) *m(f)*; (*of school*) ≈ Mitglied *nt* des Schulbeirats
gown [gaun] *n* (Abend)kleid *nt*; (*of teacher, Brit: of judge*) Robe *f*
GP *n abbr* = **general practitioner**
grab [græb] *vt* packen; (*chance, opportunity*) (beim Schopf) ergreifen ▷ *vi*: **to ~ at** greifen *or* grapschen nach +*dat*; **to ~ some food** schnell etwas essen; **to ~ a few hours sleep** ein paar Stunden schlafen

grace [greɪs] *n* Gnade *f*; (*gracefulness*) Anmut *f* ▷ *vt* (*honour*) beehren; (*adorn*) zieren; **5 days' ~** 5 Tage Aufschub; **with (a) good ~** anstandslos; **with (a) bad ~** widerwillig; **his sense of humour is his saving ~** was einen mit ihm versöhnt, ist sein Sinn für Humor; **to say ~** das Tischgebet sprechen
graceful ['greɪsful] *adj* anmutig; (*style, shape*) gefällig; (*refusal, behaviour*) charmant
gracious ['greɪʃəs] *adj* (*kind, courteous*) liebenswürdig; (*compassionate*) gnädig; (*smile*) freundlich; (*house, mansion etc*) stilvoll; (*living etc*) kultiviert ▷ *excl*: **(good) ~!** (ach) du meine Güte!, (ach du) lieber Himmel!
grade [greɪd] *n* (*Comm*) (Güte)klasse *f*; (*in hierarchy*) Rang *m*; (*Scol: mark*) Note *f*; (*US: school class*) Klasse *f*; (*: gradient: upward*) Neigung *f*, Steigung *f*; ((*: downward*) Neigung *f*, Gefälle *nt* ▷ *vt* klassifizieren; (*work, student*) einstufen; **to make the ~** (*fig*) es schaffen
grade crossing (*US*) *n* Bahnübergang *m*
grade school (*US*) *n* Grundschule *f*
gradient ['greɪdɪənt] *n* (*upward*) Neigung *f*, Steigung *f*; (*downward*) Neigung, Gefälle *nt*; (*Geom*) Gradient *m*
gradual ['grædjuəl] *adj* allmählich
gradually ['grædjuəlɪ] *adv* allmählich
graduate [*n* 'grædjuɪt, *vi* 'grædjueɪt] *n* (*of university*) Hochschulabsolvent(in) *m(f)*; (*US: of high school*) Schulabgänger(in) *m(f)* ▷ *vi* (*from university*) graduieren; (*US*) die (Schul)abschlussprüfung bestehen
graduation [grædju'eɪʃən] *n* (Ab)schlussfeier *f*
graffiti [grə'fi:tɪ] *n, npl* Graffiti *pl*
graft [grɑ:ft] *n* (*Agr*) (Pfropf)reis *nt*; (*Med*) Transplantat *nt*; (*Brit: inf: hard work*) Schufterei *f*; (*bribery*) Schiebung *f* ▷ *vt*: **to ~ (onto)** (*Agr*) (auf)pfropfen (auf *+acc*); (*Med*) übertragen (auf *+acc*), einpflanzen (in *+acc*); (*fig*) aufpfropfen *+dat*
grain [greɪn] *n* Korn *nt*; (*no pl: cereals*) Getreide *nt*; (*US: corn*) Getreide *nt*, Korn; (*of wood*) Maserung *f*; **it goes against the ~** (*fig*) es geht einem gegen den Strich
gram [græm] *n* Gramm *nt*
grammar ['græmə^r] *n* Grammatik *f*, Sprachlehre *f*
grammar school (*Brit*) *n* ≈ Gymnasium *nt*
grammatical [grə'mætɪkl] *adj* grammat(ikal)isch
gramme [græm] *n* = **gram**
grand [grænd] *adj* großartig; (*inf: wonderful*) fantastisch ▷ *n* (*inf*) ≈ Riese *m* (*1000 Pfund/Dollar*)
grandchild ['græntʃaɪld] (*irreg: like* **child**) *n* Enkelkind *nt*, Enkel(in) *m(f)*
granddad ['grændæd] (*inf*) *n* Opa *m*
granddaughter ['grændɔ:tə^r] *n* Enkelin *f*
grandfather ['grændfɑ:ðə^r] *n* Großvater *m*
grandma ['grænmɑ:] (*inf*) *n* Oma *f*
grandmother ['grænmʌðə^r] *n* Großmutter *f*
grandpa ['grænpɑ:] (*inf*) *n* Opa *m*
grandparents ['grændpɛərənts] *npl* Großeltern *pl*
grand piano *n* Flügel *m*
Grand Prix ['grɑ̃:'pri:] *n* (*Aut*) Grand Prix *m*
grandson ['grænsʌn] *n* Enkel *m*
grandstand ['grændstænd] *n* Haupttribüne *f*
granite ['grænɪt] *n* Granit *m*
granny ['grænɪ] (*inf*) *n* Oma *f*
grant [grɑ:nt] *vt* (*money*) bewilligen; (*request etc*) gewähren; (*visa*) erteilen; (*admit*) zugeben ▷ *n* Stipendium *nt*; (*subsidy*) Subvention *f*; **to take sth for ~ed** etw für selbstverständlich halten; **to take sb for ~ed** jdn als selbstverständlich hinnehmen; **to ~ that** zugeben, dass
grape [greɪp] *n* (Wein)traube *f*; **a bunch of ~s** eine (ganze) Weintraube
grapefruit ['greɪpfru:t] (*pl* **~** *or* **grapefruits**) *n* Pampelmuse *f*, Grapefruit *f*
graph [grɑ:f] *n* (*diagram*) grafische Darstellung *f*, Schaubild *nt*
graphic ['græfɪk] *adj* plastisch, anschaulich; (*art, design*) grafisch; *see also* **graphics**
graphics ['græfɪks] *n* Grafik *f* ▷ *npl* (*drawings*) Zeichnungen *pl*, grafische Darstellungen *pl*
grapple ['græpl] *vi*: **to ~ with sb/sth** mit jdm/etw kämpfen; **to ~ with a problem** sich mit einem Problem herumschlagen
grasp [grɑ:sp] *vt* (*seize*) ergreifen; (*hold*) festhalten; (*understand*) begreifen ▷ *n* Griff *m*; (*understanding*) Verständnis *nt*; **it slipped from my ~** es entglitt mir; **to have sth within one's ~** etw in greifbarer Nähe haben; **to have a good ~ of sth** (*fig*) etw gut beherrschen
▸ **grasp at** *vt fus* greifen nach; (*fig: opportunity*) ergreifen
grasping ['grɑ:spɪŋ] *adj* habgierig
grass [grɑ:s] *n* Gras *nt*; (*lawn*) Rasen *m*; (*Brit: inf: informer*) (Polizei)spitzel *m*
grasshopper ['grɑ:shɔpə^r] *n* Grashüpfer *m*, Heuschrecke *f*
grate [greɪt] *n* (Feuer)rost *m* ▷ *vt* reiben; (*carrots etc*) raspeln ▷ *vi*: **to ~ (on)** kratzen (auf *+dat*)
grateful ['greɪtful] *adj* dankbar; (*thanks*) aufrichtig
grater ['greɪtə^r] *n* Reibe *f*
gratifying ['grætɪfaɪɪŋ] *adj* (*see vt*) erfreulich; befriedigend
grating ['greɪtɪŋ] *n* Gitter *nt* ▷ *adj* (*noise*) knirschend; (*voice*) schrill
gratitude ['grætɪtju:d] *n* Dankbarkeit *f*
gratuity [grə'tju:ɪtɪ] *n* Trinkgeld *nt*
grave [greɪv] *n* Grab *nt* ▷ *adj* (*decision, mistake*) schwer (wiegend), schwerwiegend; (*expression, person*) ernst
gravel ['grævl] *n* Kies *m*
gravestone ['greɪvstəun] *n* Grabstein *m*
graveyard ['greɪvjɑ:d] *n* Friedhof *m*
gravity ['grævɪtɪ] *n* Schwerkraft *f*; (*seriousness*) Ernst *m*, Schwere *f*
gravy ['greɪvɪ] *n* (*juice*) (Braten)saft *m*; (*sauce*)

(Braten)soße *f*
gray [greɪ] (US) *adj* = **grey**
graze [greɪz] *vi* grasen, weiden ▷ *vt* streifen; (*scrape*) aufschürfen ▷ *n* (*Med*) Abschürfung *f*
grease [gri:s] *n* (*lubricant*) Schmiere *f*; (*fat*) Fett *nt* ▷ *vt* (*see n*) schmieren; fetten; **to ~ the skids** (US: *fig*) die Maschinerie in Gang halten
greaseproof paper ['gri:spru:f-] (*Brit*) *n* Pergamentpapier *nt*
greasy ['gri:sɪ] *adj* fettig; (*food: containing grease*) fett; (*tools*) schmierig, ölig; (*clothes*) speckig; (*Brit: road, surface*) glitschig, schlüpfrig
great [greɪt] *adj* groß; (*city*) bedeutend; (*inf: terrific*) prima, toll; **they're ~ friends** sie sind gute Freunde; **we had a ~ time** wir haben uns glänzend amüsiert; **it was ~!** es war toll!; **the ~ thing is that ...** das Wichtigste ist, dass ...
Great Britain *n* Großbritannien *nt*
great-grandfather [greɪt'grænfɑ:ðəʳ] *n* Urgroßvater *m*
great-grandmother [greɪt'grænmʌðəʳ] *n* Urgroßmutter *f*
greatly ['greɪtlɪ] *adv* sehr; (*influenced*) stark
greatness ['greɪtnɪs] *n* Bedeutung *f*
Greece [gri:s] *n* Griechenland *nt*
greed [gri:d] *n* (*also*: **greediness**): **~ for** Gier *f* nach; **~ for power** Machtgier *f*; **~ for money** Geldgier *f*
greedy ['gri:dɪ] *adj* gierig
Greek [gri:k] *adj* griechisch ▷ *n* Grieche *m*, Griechin *f*; (*Ling*) Griechisch *nt*; **ancient/ modern ~** Alt-/Neugriechisch *nt*
green [gri:n] *adj* (*also ecological*) grün ▷ *n* (*also Golf*) Grün *nt*; (*stretch of grass*) Rasen *m*, Grünfläche *f*; (*also*: **village green**) Dorfwiese *f*, Anger *m*; **greens** *npl* (*vegetables*) Grüngemüse *nt*; (*Pol*): **the G~s** die Grünen *pl*; **to have ~ fingers, to have a ~ thumb** (US) eine Hand für Pflanzen haben; **to give sb the ~ light** jdm grünes Licht geben
green belt *n* Grüngürtel *m*
green card *n* (*Aut*) grüne (Versicherungs)karte *f*; (US) ≈ Aufenthaltserlaubnis *f*
greenery ['gri:nərɪ] *n* Grün *nt*
greengage ['gri:ngeɪdʒ] *n* Reneklode *f*
greengrocer ['gri:ngrəusəʳ] (*Brit*) *n* Obst- und Gemüsehändler(in) *m(f)*
greenhouse ['gri:nhaus] *n* Gewächshaus *nt*, Treibhaus *nt*; **~ effect** Treibhauseffekt *m*; **~ gas** Treibhausgas *nt*
greenish ['gri:nɪʃ] *adj* grünlich
Greenland ['gri:nlənd] *n* Grönland *nt*
greet [gri:t] *vt* begrüßen; (*news*) aufnehmen
greeting ['gri:tɪŋ] *n* Gruß *m*; (*welcome*) Begrüßung *f*; **Christmas ~s** Weihnachtsgrüße *pl*; **birthday ~s** Geburtstagsglückwünsche *pl*; **Season's ~s** frohe Weihnachten und ein glückliches neues Jahr
greeting card, greetings card *n* Grußkarte *f*; (*congratulating*) Glückwunschkarte *f*
gregarious [grə'gɛərɪəs] *adj* gesellig
grenade [grə'neɪd] *n* (*also*: **hand grenade**) (Hand)granate *f*
grew [gru:] *pt of* **grow**
grey, (US) **gray** [greɪ] *adj* grau; (*dismal*) trüb, grau; **to go ~** grau werden
grey-haired [greɪ'hɛəd] *adj* grauhaarig
greyhound ['greɪhaund] *n* Windhund *m*
grid [grɪd] *n* Gitter *nt*; (*Elec*) (Verteiler)netz *nt*; (*US: Aut: intersection*) Kreuzung *f*
gridlock ['grɪdlɔk] *n* (*esp US: on road*) totaler Stau *m*; (*stalemate*) Patt *nt* ▷ *vt*: **to be ~ed** (*roads*) total verstopft sein; (*talks etc*) festgefahren sein
grief [gri:f] *n* Kummer *m*, Trauer *f*; **to come to ~** (*plan*) scheitern; (*person*) zu Schaden kommen; **good ~!** ach du liebe Gute!
grievance ['gri:vəns] *n* Beschwerde *f*; (*feeling of resentment*) Groll *m*
grieve [gri:v] *vi* trauern ▷ *vt* Kummer bereiten *+dat*, betrüben; **to ~ for** trauern um
grievous ['gri:vəs] *adj* (*mistake*) schwer; (*situation*) betrüblich; **~ bodily harm** (*Law*) schwere Körperverletzung *f*
grill [grɪl] *n* Grill *m*; (*grilled food: also*: **mixed grill**) Grillgericht *nt*; (*restaurant*) = **grillroom** ▷ *vt* (*Brit*) grillen; (*inf: question*) in die Zange nehmen, ausquetschen
grille [grɪl] *n* (*screen*) Gitter *nt*; (*Aut*) Kühlergrill *m*
grillroom ['grɪlrum] *n* Grillrestaurant *nt*
grim [grɪm] *adj* trostlos; (*serious, stern*) grimmig
grimace [grɪ'meɪs] *n* Grimasse *f* ▷ *vi* Grimassen schneiden
grime [graɪm] *n* Dreck *m*, Schmutz *m*
grin [grɪn] *n* Grinsen *nt* ▷ *vi* grinsen; **to ~ at sb** jdn angrinsen
grind [graɪnd] (*pt, pp* **ground**) *vt* zerkleinern; (*coffee, pepper etc*) mahlen; (*US: meat*) hacken, durch den Fleischwolf drehen; (*knife*) schleifen, wetzen; (*gem, lens*) schleifen ▷ *vi* (*car gears*) knirschen ▷ *n* (*work*) Schufterei *f*; **to ~ one's teeth** mit den Zähnen knirschen; **to ~ to a halt** (*vehicle*) quietschend zum Stehen kommen; (*fig: talks, scheme*) sich festfahren; (*work*) stocken; (*production*) zum Erliegen kommen; **the daily ~** (*inf*) der tägliche Trott
grip [grɪp] *n* Griff *m*; (*of tyre, shoe*) Halt *m*; (*holdall*) Reisetasche *f* ▷ *vt* packen; (*audience, attention*) fesseln; **to come to ~s with sth** etw in den Griff bekommen; **to lose one's ~** den Halt verlieren; (*fig*) nachlassen; **to ~ the road** (*car*) gut auf der Straße liegen
gripping ['grɪpɪŋ] *adj* fesselnd, packend
grisly ['grɪzlɪ] *adj* grässlich, grausig
gristle ['grɪsl] *n* Knorpel *m*
grit [grɪt] *n* (*for icy roads: sand*) Sand *m*; (*crushed stone*) Splitt *m*; (*determination, courage*) Mut *m* ▷ *vt* (*road*) streuen; **grits** *npl* (US) Grütze *f*; **I've got a piece of ~ in my eye** ich habe ein

Staubkorn im Auge; **to ~ one's teeth** die Zähne zusammenbeißen

groan [grəun] *n* Stöhnen *nt* ▷ *vi* stöhnen; (*tree, floorboard etc*) ächzen, knarren

grocer ['grəusəʳ] *n* Lebensmittelhändler(in) *m(f)*

groceries ['grəusərız] *npl* Lebensmittel *pl*

grocer's, **grocer's shop** *n* Lebensmittelgeschäft *nt*

groin [grɔın] *n* Leistengegend *f*

groom [gru:m] *n* Stallbursche *m*; (*also*: **bridegroom**) Bräutigam *m* ▷ *vt* (*horse*) striegeln; (*fig*): **to ~ sb for** (*job*) jdn aufbauen für; **well-~ed** gepflegt

groove [gru:v] *n* Rille *f*

grope [grəup] *vi*: **to ~ for** tasten nach; (*fig: try to think of*) suchen nach

gross [grəus] *adj* (*neglect*) grob; (*injustice*) krass; (*behaviour, speech*) grob, derb; (*Comm: income, weight*) Brutto- ▷ *n inv* Gros *nt* ▷ *vt*: **to ~ £500,000** £500 000 brutto einnehmen

grossly ['grəuslı] *adv* äußerst; (*exaggerated*) grob

grotesque [grə'tɛsk] *adj* grotesk

grotto ['grɔtəu] *n* Grotte *f*

grotty ['grɔtı] (*inf*) *adj* mies

ground [graund] *pt, pp of* **grind** ▷ *n* Boden *m*, Erde *f*; (*land*) Land *nt*; (*Sport*) Platz *m*, Feld *nt*; (*US: Elec: also*: **ground wire**) Erde *f*; (*reason: gen pl*) Grund *m* ▷ *vt* (*plane*) aus dem Verkehr ziehen; (*US: Elec*) erden ▷ *adj* (*coffee etc*) gemahlen ▷ *vi* (*ship*) auflaufen; **grounds** *npl* (*of coffee etc*) Satz *m*; (*gardens etc*) Anlagen *pl*; **below ~** unter der Erde; **to gain/lose ~** Boden gewinnen/verlieren; **common ~** Gemeinsame(s) *nt*; **on the ~s that** mit der Begründung, dass

ground cloth (*US*) *n* = **groundsheet**

ground floor *n* Erdgeschoss *nt*, Erdgeschoß *nt* (*Österr*)

grounding ['graundıŋ] *n* (*in education*) Grundwissen *nt*

groundless ['graundlıs] *adj* grundlos, unbegründet

groundsheet ['graundʃi:t] (*Brit*) *n* Zeltboden *m*

ground staff *n* (*Aviat*) Bodenpersonal *nt*

groundwork ['graundwə:k] *n* Vorarbeit *f*

group [gru:p] *n* Gruppe *f*; (*Comm*) Konzern *m* ▷ *vt* (*also*: **group together**: *in one group*) zusammentun; (*: in several groups*) in Gruppen einteilen ▷ *vi* (*also*: **group together**) sich zusammentun

grouse [graus] *n inv* schottisches Moorhuhn *nt* ▷ *vi* (*complain*) schimpfen

grove [grəuv] *n* Hain *m*, Wäldchen *nt*

grovel ['grɔvl] *vi* (*crawl*) kriechen; (*fig*): **to ~ (before)** kriechen (vor *+dat*)

grow [grəu] (*pt* **grew**, *pp* **~n**) *vi* wachsen; (*increase*) zunehmen; (*become*) werden ▷ *vt* (*roses*) züchten; (*vegetables*) anbauen, ziehen; (*beard*) sich *dat* wachsen lassen; **to ~ tired of waiting** das Warten leid sein; **to ~ (out of** *or* **from)** (*develop*) entstehen (aus)

▸ **grow apart** *vi* (*fig*) sich auseinanderentwickeln

▸ **grow away from** *vt fus* (*fig*) sich entfremden *+dat*

▸ **grow on** *vt fus*: **that painting is ~ing on me** allmählich finde ich Gefallen an dem Bild

▸ **grow out of** *vt fus* (*clothes*) herauswachsen aus; (*habit*) ablegen; **he'll ~ out of it** diese Phase geht auch vorbei

▸ **grow up** *vi* aufwachsen; (*mature*) erwachsen werden; (*idea, friendship*) entstehen

grower ['grəuəʳ] *n* (*Bot*) Züchter(in) *m(f)*; (*Agr*) Pflanzer(in) *m(f)*

growing ['grəuıŋ] *adj* wachsend; (*number*) zunehmend; **~ pains** Wachstumsschmerzen *pl*; (*fig*) Kinderkrankheiten *pl*, Anfangsschwierigkeiten *pl*

growl [graul] *vi* knurren

grown [grəun] *pp of* **grow**

grown-up [grəun'ʌp] *n* Erwachsene(r) *f(m)*

growth [grəuθ] *n* Wachstum *nt*; (*what has grown: of weeds, beard etc*) Wuchs *m*; (*of person, character*) Entwicklung *f*; (*Med*) Gewächs *nt*, Wucherung *f*

grub [grʌb] *n* (*larva*) Larve *f*; (*inf: food*) Fressalien *pl*, Futter *nt* ▷ *vi*: **to ~ about** *or* **around (for)** (herum)wühlen (nach)

grubby ['grʌbı] *adj* (*dirty*) schmuddelig; (*fig*) schmutzig

grudge [grʌdʒ] *n* Groll *m* ▷ *vt*: **to ~ sb sth** jdm etw nicht gönnen; **to bear sb a ~** jdm böse sein, einen Groll gegen jdn hegen

gruelling, (*US*) **grueling** ['gruəlıŋ] *adj* (*encounter*) aufreibend; (*trip, journey*) äußerst strapaziös

gruesome ['gru:səm] *adj* grauenhaft

gruff [grʌf] *adj* barsch, schroff

grumble ['grʌmbl] *vi* murren, schimpfen

grumpy ['grʌmpı] *adj* mürrisch, brummig

grunt [grʌnt] *vi* grunzen ▷ *n* Grunzen *nt*

G-string ['dʒi:strıŋ] *n* Minislip *m*, Tangaslip *m*

guarantee [gærən'ti:] *n* Garantie *f* ▷ *vt* garantieren; **he can't ~ (that) he'll come** er kann nicht dafür garantieren, dass er kommt

guard [gɑ:d] *n* Wache *f*; (*Boxing, Fencing*) Deckung *f*; (*Brit: Rail*) Schaffner(in) *m(f)*; (*on machine*) Schutz *m*, Schutzvorrichtung *f*; (*also*: **fireguard**) (Schutz)gitter *nt* ▷ *vt* (*prisoner*) bewachen; (*protect*): **to ~ (against)** (be)schützen (vor *+dat*); (*secret*) hüten (vor *+dat*); **to be on one's ~** auf der Hut sein

▸ **guard against** *vt fus* (*disease*) vorbeugen *+dat*; (*damage, accident*) verhüten

guarded ['gɑ:dıd] *adj* vorsichtig, zurückhaltend

guardian ['gɑ:dıən] *n* Vormund *m*; (*defender*) Hüter *m*

guard's van (*Brit*) *n* (*Rail*) Schaffnerabteil *nt*, Dienstwagen *m*

guerrilla [gəˈrɪlə] *n* Guerilla *m*, Guerillakämpfer(in) *m(f)*
guess [gɛs] *vt* schätzen; (*answer*) (er)raten; (*US: think*) schätzen (*inf*) ▷ *vi* (*see vt*) schätzen; raten ▷ *n* Vermutung *f*; **I ~ you're right** da haben Sie wohl recht; **to keep sb ~ing** jdn im Ungewissen lassen; **to take** *or* **have a ~** raten; (*estimate*) schätzen; **my ~ is that ...** ich schätze *or* vermute, dass ...
guesswork [ˈgɛswəːk] *n* Vermutungen *pl*; **I got the answer by ~** ich habe die Antwort nur geraten
guest [gɛst] *n* Gast *m*; **be my ~** (*inf*) nur zu!
guest room *n* Gästezimmer *nt*
guffaw [gʌˈfɔː] *vi* schallend lachen ▷ *n* schallendes Lachen *nt*
guidance [ˈgaɪdəns] *n* Rat *m*, Beratung *f*; **under the ~ of** unter der Leitung von; **vocational ~** Berufsberatung *f*; **marriage ~** Eheberatung *f*
guide [gaɪd] *n* (*person*) Führer(in) *m(f)*; (*book*) Führer *m*; (*Brit: also:* **girl guide**) Pfadfinderin *f* ▷ *vt* führen; (*direct*) lenken; **to be ~d by sb/sth** sich von jdm/etw leiten lassen
guidebook [ˈgaɪdbuk] *n* Führer *m*
guide dog *n* Blindenhund *m*
guidelines [ˈgaɪdlaɪnz] *npl* Richtlinien *pl*
guild [gɪld] *n* Verein *m*
guillotine [ˈgɪlətiːn] *n* Guillotine *f*, Fallbeil *nt*; (*for paper*) (Papier)schneidemaschine *f*
guilt [gɪlt] *n* Schuld *f*; (*remorse*) Schuldgefühl *nt*
guilty [ˈgɪltɪ] *adj* schuldig; (*expression*) schuldbewusst; (*secret*) dunkel; **to plead ~/not ~** sich schuldig/nicht schuldig bekennen; **to feel ~ about doing sth** ein schlechtes Gewissen haben, etw zu tun
guinea pig *n* Meerschweinchen *nt*; (*fig: person*) Versuchskaninchen *nt*
guise [gaɪz] *n*: **in** *or* **under the ~ of** in der Form *+gen*, in Gestalt *+gen*
guitar [gɪˈtɑːʳ] *n* Gitarre *f*
guitarist [gɪˈtɑːrɪst] *n* Gitarrist(in) *m(f)*
gulf [gʌlf] *n* Golf *m*; (*abyss*) Abgrund *m*; (*fig: difference*) Kluft *f*; **the (Persian) G~** der (Persische) Golf
gull [gʌl] *n* Möwe *f*
gullible [ˈgʌlɪbl] *adj* leichtgläubig
gully [ˈgʌlɪ] *n* Schlucht *f*
gulp [gʌlp] *vi* schlucken ▷ *vt* (*also:* **gulp down**) hinunterschlucken ▷ *n*: **at one ~** mit einem Schluck
gum [gʌm] *n* (*Anat*) Zahnfleisch *nt*; (*glue*) Klebstoff *m*; (*also:* **gumdrop**) Weingummi *nt*; (*also:* **chewing-gum**) Kaugummi *m* ▷ *vt*: **to ~ (together)** (zusammen)kleben
▶ **gum up** *vt*: **to ~ up the works** (*inf*) alles vermasseln
gumboots [ˈgʌmbuːts] (*Brit*) *npl* Gummistiefel *pl*
gun [gʌn] *n* (*small*) Pistole *f*; (*medium-sized*) Gewehr *nt*; (*large*) Kanone *f* ▷ *vt* (*also:* **gun down**) erschießen; **to stick to one's ~s** (*fig*) nicht nachgeben, festbleiben
gunboat [ˈgʌnbəut] *n* Kanonenboot *nt*
gunfire [ˈgʌnfaɪəʳ] *n* Geschützfeuer *nt*
gunman [ˈgʌnmən] (*irreg: like* **man**) *n* bewaffneter Verbrecher *m*
gunpoint [ˈgʌnpɔɪnt] *n*: **at ~** mit vorgehaltener Pistole; mit vorgehaltenem Gewehr
gunpowder [ˈgʌnpaudəʳ] *n* Schießpulver *nt*
gunshot [ˈgʌnʃɔt] *n* Schuss *m*
gurgle [ˈgəːgl] *vi* (*baby*) glucksen; (*water*) gluckern
gush [gʌʃ] *vi* hervorquellen, hervorströmen; (*person*) schwärmen ▷ *n* Strahl *m*
gust [gʌst] *n* Windstoß *m*, Bö(e) *f*; (*of smoke*) Wolke *f*
gusto [ˈgʌstəu] *n*: **with ~** mit Genuss, mit Schwung
gut [gʌt] *n* (*Anat*) Darm *m*; (*for violin, racket*) Darmsaiten *pl* ▷ *vt* (*poultry, fish*) ausnehmen; (*building*) ausräumen; (*by fire*) ausbrennen;
guts *npl* (*Anat*) Eingeweide *pl*; (*inf: courage*) Mumm *m*; **to hate sb's ~s** jdn auf den Tod nicht ausstehen können
gutter [ˈgʌtəʳ] *n* (*in street*) Gosse *f*, Rinnstein *m*; (*of roof*) Dachrinne *f*
guy [gaɪ] *n* (*inf: man*) Typ *m*, Kerl *m*; (*also:* **guyrope**) Haltetau *nt*, Halteseil *nt*; (*for Guy Fawkes' night*) (Guy-Fawkes-)Puppe *f*
guzzle [ˈgʌzl] *vt* (*food*) futtern; (*drink*) saufen (*inf*)
gym [dʒɪm] *n* (*also:* **gymnasium**) Turnhalle *f*; (*also:* **gymnastics**) Gymnastik *f*, Turnen *nt*
gymnasium [dʒɪmˈneɪzɪəm] *n* Turnhalle *f*
gymnast [ˈdʒɪmnæst] *n* Turner(in) *m(f)*
gymnastics [dʒɪmˈnæstɪks] *n* Gymnastik *f*, Turnen *nt*
gym shoes *npl* Turnschuhe *pl*
gynaecologist, (*US*) **gynecologist** [gaɪnɪˈkɔlədʒɪst] *n* Gynäkologe *m*, Gynäkologin *f*, Frauenarzt *m*, Frauenärztin *f*
gypsy [ˈdʒɪpsɪ] *n* = **gipsy**

haberdashery [hæbə'dæʃərɪ] *(Brit) n* Kurzwaren *pl*
habit ['hæbɪt] *n* Gewohnheit *f*; *(esp undesirable)* Angewohnheit *f*; *(addiction)* Sucht *f*; *(Rel)* Habit *m or nt*; **to get out of/into the ~ of doing sth** sich abgewöhnen/angewöhnen, etw zu tun; **to be in the ~ of doing sth** die (An)gewohnheit haben, etw zu tun
habitat ['hæbɪtæt] *n* Heimat *f*; *(of animals)* Lebensraum *m*, Heimat *f*
habitual [hə'bɪtjuəl] *adj (action)* gewohnt; *(drinker)* Gewohnheits-; *(liar)* gewohnheitsmäßig
hack [hækʳ] *vt, vi (also Comput)* hacken ▷ *n (pej: writer)* Schreiberling *m*; *(horse)* Mietpferd *nt*
hacker ['hækəʳ] *n (Comput)* Hacker *m*
hackneyed ['hæknɪd] *adj* abgedroschen
had [hæd] *pt, pp of* **have**
haddock ['hædək] *(pl ~ or* **haddocks**) *n* Schellfisch *m*
hadn't ['hædnt] = **had not**
haemorrhage, *(US)* **hemorrhage** ['hɛmərɪdʒ] *n* Blutung *f*
haemorrhoids, *(US)* **hemorrhoids** ['hɛmərɔɪdz] *npl* Hämorr(ho)iden *pl*
haggle ['hægl] *vi*: **to ~ (over)** feilschen (um)
Hague [heɪg] *n*: **The ~** Den Haag *m*
hail [heɪl] *n* Hagel *m* ▷ *vt (person)* zurufen *+dat*; *(taxi)* herbeiwinken, anhalten; *(acclaim: person)* zujubeln *+dat*; *(: event etc)* bejubeln ▷ *vi* hageln; **he ~s from Scotland** er kommt *or* stammt aus Schottland
hailstone ['heɪlstəun] *n* Hagelkorn *nt*
hair [hɛəʳ] *n (collectively: of person)* Haar *nt*, Haare *pl*; *(: of animal)* Fell *nt*; *(single hair)* Haar *nt*; **to do one's ~** sich frisieren; **by a ~'s breadth** um Haaresbreite
hairbrush ['hɛəbrʌʃ] *n* Haarbürste *f*
haircut ['hɛəkʌt] *n* Haarschnitt *m*; *(style)* Frisur *f*
hairdo ['hɛədu:] *n* Frisur *f*
hairdresser ['hɛədrɛsəʳ] *n* Friseur *m*, Friseuse *f*
hairdresser's ['hɛədrɛsəz] *n* Friseursalon *m*
hair dryer *n* Haartrockner *m*, Föhn *f*, Fön® *m*
hairgrip ['hɛəgrɪp] *n* Haarklemme *f*
hairnet ['hɛənɛt] *n* Haarnetz *nt*
hairpiece ['hɛəpi:s] *n* Haarteil *nt*; *(for men)* Toupet *nt*
hairpin ['hɛəpɪn] *n* Haarnadel *f*
hairpin bend, *(US)* **hairpin curve** *n* Haarnadelkurve *f*
hair-raising ['hɛəreɪzɪŋ] *adj* haarsträubend
hair spray *n* Haarspray *nt*
hairstyle ['hɛəstaɪl] *n* Frisur *f*
hairy ['hɛərɪ] *adj* behaart; *(inf: situation)* brenzlig, haarig
hake [heɪk] *(pl ~ or* **hakes**) *n* Seehecht *m*
half [hɑ:f] *(pl* **halves**) *n* Hälfte *f*; *(of beer etc)* kleines Bier *nt etc*; *(Rail, bus)* Fahrkarte *f* zum halben Preis ▷ *adj, adv* halb; **first/second ~** *(Sport)* erste/zweite Halbzeit *f*; **two and a ~** zweieinhalb; **~-an-hour** eine halbe Stunde; **~ a dozen/pound** ein halbes Dutzend/Pfund; **a week and a ~** eineinhalb *or* anderthalb Wochen; **~ (of it)** die Hälfte; **~ (of)** die Hälfte (von *or +gen*); **~ the amount of** die halbe Menge an *+dat*; **to cut sth in ~** etw halbieren; **~ past three** halb vier; **to go halves (with sb)** (mit jdm) halbe-halbe machen; **she never does things by halves** sie macht keine halben Sachen; **he's too clever by ~** er ist ein richtiger Schlaumeier; **~ empty** halb leer; **~ closed** halb geschlossen
half board *n* Halbpension *f*
half-brother ['hɑ:fbrʌðəʳ] *n* Halbbruder *m*
half-caste ['hɑ:fkɑ:st] *n* Mischling *m*
half-hearted ['hɑ:f'hɑ:tɪd] *adj* halbherzig, lustlos
half-hour [hɑ:f'auəʳ] *n* halbe Stunde *f*
half-mast ['hɑ:f'mɑ:st]: **at ~** *adv* (auf) halbmast
halfpenny ['heɪpnɪ] *(Brit) n* halber Penny *m*
half-price ['hɑ:f'praɪs] *adj, adv* zum halben Preis
half term *(Brit) n* kleine Ferien *pl (in der Mitte des Trimesters)*
half-time [hɑ:f'taɪm] *n (Sport)* Halbzeit *f*
halfway ['hɑ:f'weɪ] *adv*: **~ to** auf halbem Wege nach; **~ through** mitten in *+dat*; **to meet sb ~** *(fig)* jdm auf halbem Wege entgegenkommen
hall [hɔ:l] *n* Diele *f*, (Haus)flur *m*; *(corridor)* Korridor *m*, Flur *m*; *(mansion)* Herrensitz *m*, Herrenhaus *nt*; *(for concerts etc)* Halle *f*; **to live in ~** *(Brit)* im Wohnheim wohnen
hallmark ['hɔ:lmɑ:k] *n (on gold, silver)*

(Feingehalts)stempel *m*; (*of writer, artist etc*) Kennzeichen *nt*

hallo [hə'ləu] *excl* = **hello**

hall of residence (*pl* **halls of residence**) (*Brit*) *n* Studentenwohnheim *nt*

Hallowe'en ['hæləu'i:n] *n* der Tag vor Allerheiligen

hallucination [həlu:sɪ'neɪʃən] *n* Halluzination *f*

hallway ['hɔ:lweɪ] *n* Diele *f*, (Haus)flur *m*

halo ['heɪləu] *n* Heiligenschein *m*; (*circle of light*) Hof *m*

halt [hɔ:lt] *vt* anhalten; (*progress etc*) zum Stillstand bringen ▷ *vi* anhalten, zum Stillstand kommen ▷ *n*: **to come to a ~** zum Stillstand kommen; **to call a ~ to sth** (*fig*) einer Sache *dat* ein Ende machen

halve [hɑ:v] *vt* halbieren

halves [hɑ:vz] *pl of* **half**

ham [hæm] *n* Schinken *m*; (*inf*: *also*: **radio ham**) Funkamateur *m*; (: *actor*) Schmierenkomödiant(in) *m(f)*

hamburger ['hæmbə:gə^r] *n* Hamburger *m*

hamlet ['hæmlɪt] *n* Weiler *m*, kleines Dorf *nt*

hammer ['hæmə^r] *n* Hammer *m* ▷ *vt* hämmern; (*fig*: *criticize*) vernichtend kritisieren; (: *defeat*) vernichtend schlagen ▷ *vi* hämmern; **to ~ sth into sb, to ~ sth across to sb** jdm etw einhämmern *or* einbläuen

▸ **hammer out** *vt* hämmern; (*solution, agreement*) ausarbeiten

hammock ['hæmək] *n* Hängematte *f*

hamper ['hæmpə^r] *vt* behindern ▷ *n* Korb *m*

hamster ['hæmstə^r] *n* Hamster *m*

hamstring ['hæmstrɪŋ] *n* Kniesehne *f* ▷ *vt* einengen

hand [hænd] *n* Hand *f*; (*of clock*) Zeiger *m*; (*handwriting*) Hand(schrift) *f*; (*worker*) Arbeiter(in) *m(f)*; (*of cards*) Blatt *nt*; (*measurement*: *of horse*) ≈ 10 cm ▷ *vt* geben, reichen; **to give** *or* **lend sb a ~** jdm helfen; **at ~** (*place*) in der Nähe; (*time*) unmittelbar bevorstehend; **by ~** von Hand; **in ~** (*time*) zur Verfügung; (*job*) anstehend; (*situation*) unter Kontrolle; **we have the matter in ~** wir haben die Sache im Griff; **on ~** zur Verfügung; **out of ~** *adj* außer Kontrolle ▷ *adv* (*reject etc*) rundweg; **to ~** zur Hand; **on the one ~ ..., on the other ~ ...** einerseits ... andererseits ...; **to force sb's ~** jdn zwingen; **to have a free ~** freie Hand haben; **to change ~s** den Besitzer wechseln; **to have in one's ~** (*also fig*) in der Hand halten; **"~s off!"** "Hände weg!"

▸ **hand down** *vt* (*knowledge*) weitergeben; (*possessions*) vererben; (*Law*: *judgement, sentence*) fällen

▸ **hand in** *vt* abgeben, einreichen

▸ **hand out** *vt* verteilen; (*information*) austeilen; (*punishment*) verhängen

▸ **hand over** *vt* übergeben

▸ **hand round** *vt* (*Brit*) verteilen; (*chocolates etc*) herumreichen

handbag ['hændbæg] *n* Handtasche *f*

hand baggage *n* Handgepäck *nt*

handbook ['hændbuk] *n* Handbuch *nt*

handbrake ['hændbreɪk] *n* Handbremse *f*

handcuffs ['hændkʌfs] *npl* Handschellen *pl*

handful ['hændful] *n* Handvoll *f*

handicap ['hændɪkæp] *n* Behinderung *f*; (*disadvantage*) Nachteil *m*; (*Sport*) Handicap *nt* ▷ *vt* benachteiligen; **mentally/physically ~ped** geistig/körperlich behindert

handicraft ['hændɪkrɑ:ft] *n* Kunsthandwerk *nt*; (*object*) Kunsthandwerksarbeit *f*

handiwork ['hændɪwə:k] *n* Arbeit *f*; **this looks like his ~** (*pej*) das sieht nach seiner Arbeit aus

handkerchief ['hæŋkətʃɪf] *n* Taschentuch *nt*

handle ['hændl] *n* Griff *m*; (*of door*) Klinke *f*; (*of cup*) Henkel *m*; (*of broom, brush etc*) Stiel *m*; (*for winding*) Kurbel *f*; (*CB Radio*: *name*) Sendezeichen *nt* ▷ *vt* anfassen, berühren; (*problem etc*) sich befassen mit; (: *successfully*) fertig werden mit; (*people*) umgehen mit; **"~ with care"** "Vorsicht – zerbrechlich"; **to fly off the ~** an die Decke gehen; **to get a ~ on a problem** (*inf*) ein Problem in den Griff bekommen

handlebar ['hændlbɑ:^r] *n*, **handlebars** ['hændlbɑ:z] *npl* Lenkstange *f*

hand luggage *n* Handgepäck *nt*

handmade ['hænd'meɪd] *adj* handgearbeitet

handrail ['hændreɪl] *n* Geländer *nt*

handset ['hændsɛt] *n* (*Tel*) Hörer *m*

hands-free ['hændzfri:] *adj* (*telephone, microphone*) Freisprech-

handshake ['hændʃeɪk] *n* Händedruck *m*

handsome ['hænsəm] *adj* gut aussehend; (*building*) schön; (*gift*) großzügig; (*profit, return*) ansehnlich

handwriting ['hændraɪtɪŋ] *n* Handschrift *f*

handy ['hændɪ] *adj* praktisch; (*skilful*) geschickt; (*close at hand*) in der Nähe; **to come in ~** sich als nützlich erweisen

hang [hæŋ] (*pt, pp* **hung**) *vt* aufhängen; (*criminal*) (*pt, pp* **~ed**) hängen; (*head*) hängen lassen ▷ *vi* hängen; (*hair, drapery*) fallen ▷ *n*: **to get the ~ of sth** (*inf*) den richtigen Dreh (bei etw) herauskriegen

▸ **hang about** *vi* herumlungern

▸ **hang around** *vi* = **hang about**

▸ **hang back** *vi*: **to ~ back (from doing sth)** zögern(, etw zu tun)

▸ **hang on** *vi* warten ▷ *vt fus* (*depend on*) abhängen von; **to ~ on to** festhalten; (*for protection, support*) sich festhalten an *+dat*; (*hope, position*) sich klammern an *+acc*; (*ideas*) festhalten an *+dat*; (*keep*) behalten

▸ **hang out** *vt* draußen aufhängen ▷ *vi* heraushängen; (*inf*: *live*) wohnen

▸ **hang together** *vi* (*argument*) folgerichtig *or* zusammenhängend sein; (*story, explanation*) zusammenhängend sein; (*statements*) zusammenpassen

▶ **hang up** *vt* aufhängen ▷ *vi* (*Tel*): **to ~ up (on sb)** einfach auflegen
hangar ['hæŋəʳ] *n* Hangar *m*, Flugzeughalle *f*
hanger ['hæŋəʳ] *n* Bügel *m*
hanger-on [hæŋər'ɔn] *n* (*parasite*) Trabant *m* (*inf*); **the hangers-on** der Anhang
hang-gliding ['hæŋglaɪdɪŋ] *n* Drachenfliegen *nt*
hangover ['hæŋəuvəʳ] *n* Kater *m*; (*from past*) Überbleibsel *nt*
hang-up ['hæŋʌp] *n* Komplex *m*
hanker ['hæŋkəʳ] *vi*: **to ~ after** sich sehnen nach
hankie, hanky ['hæŋkɪ] (*pl* **~s**) *n* = **handkerchief**
haphazard [hæp'hæzəd] *adj* planlos, wahllos
happen ['hæpən] *vi* geschehen; **to ~ to do sth** zufällig(erweise) etw tun; **as it ~s** zufälligerweise; **what's ~ing?** was ist los?; **she ~ed to be free** sie hatte zufällig(erweise) gerade Zeit; **if anything ~ed to him** wenn ihm etwas zustoßen *or* passieren sollte
▶ **happen (up)on** *vt fus* zufällig stoßen auf *+acc*; (*person*) zufällig treffen
happening ['hæpnɪŋ] *n* Ereignis *nt*, Vorfall *m*
happily ['hæpɪlɪ] *adv* (*luckily*) glücklicherweise; (*cheerfully*) fröhlich
happiness ['hæpɪnɪs] *n* Glück *nt*
happy ['hæpɪ] *adj* glücklich; (*cheerful*) fröhlich; **to be ~ (with)** zufrieden sein (mit); **to be ~ to do sth** etw gerne tun; **~ birthday!** herzlichen Glückwunsch zum Geburtstag!
happy-go-lucky ['hæpɪgəu'lʌkɪ] *adj* unbekümmert
happy hour *n Zeit, in der Bars, Pubs usw Getränke zu ermäßigten Preisen anbieten*
harass ['hærəs] *vt* schikanieren
harassment ['hærəsmənt] *n* Schikanierung *f*; **sexual ~** sexuelle Belästigung *f*
harbour, (*US*) **harbor** ['hɑːbəʳ] *n* Hafen *m* ▷ *vt* (*hope, fear, grudge etc*) hegen; (*criminal, fugitive*) Unterschlupf gewähren *+dat*
hard [hɑːd] *adj* hart; (*question, problem*) schwierig; (*evidence*) gesichert ▷ *adv* (*work*) hart, schwer; (*think*) scharf; (*try*) sehr; **~ luck!** Pech!; **no ~ feelings!** ich nehme es dir nicht übel; **to be ~ of hearing** schwerhörig sein; **to be ~ done by** ungerecht behandelt werden; **I find it ~ to believe that ...** ich kann es kaum glauben, dass ...; **to look ~ at sth** (*object*) sich *+dat* etw genau ansehen; (*idea*) etw gründlich prüfen
hardback ['hɑːdbæk] *n* gebundene Ausgabe *f*
hardboard ['hɑːdbɔːd] *n* Hartfaserplatte *f*
hard cash *n* Bargeld *nt*
hard disk *n* (*Comput*) Festplatte *f*
harden ['hɑːdn] *vt* härten; (*attitude, person*) verhärten ▷ *vi* hart werden, sich verhärten
hard-headed ['hɑːd'hɛdɪd] *adj* nüchtern
hard labour *n* Zwangsarbeit *f*
hardly ['hɑːdlɪ] *adv* kaum; (*harshly*) hart, streng; **it's ~ the case** (*ironic*) das ist wohl kaum der Fall; **I can ~ believe it** ich kann es kaum glauben
hardship ['hɑːdʃɪp] *n* Not *f*
hard shoulder (*Brit*) *n* (*Aut*) Seitenstreifen *m*
hardware ['hɑːdwɛəʳ] *n* Eisenwaren *pl*; (*household goods*) Haushaltswaren *pl*; (*Comput*) Hardware *f*; (*Mil*) Waffen *pl*
hardware shop *n* Eisenwarenhandlung *f*
hard-wearing [hɑːd'wɛərɪŋ] *adj* strapazierfähig
hard-working [hɑːd'wəːkɪŋ] *adj* fleißig
hardy ['hɑːdɪ] *adj* (*animals*) zäh; (*people*) abgehärtet; (*plant*) winterhart
hare [hɛəʳ] *n* Hase *m*
harm [hɑːm] *n* Schaden *m*; (*injury*) Verletzung *f* ▷ *vt* schaden *+dat*; (*person: physically*) verletzen; **to mean no ~** es nicht böse meinen; **out of ~'s way** in Sicherheit; **there's no ~ in trying** es kann nicht schaden, es zu versuchen
harmful ['hɑːmful] *adj* schädlich
harmless ['hɑːmlɪs] *adj* harmlos
harmony ['hɑːmənɪ] *n* Einklang *m*; (*Mus*) Harmonie *f*
harness ['hɑːnɪs] *n* (*for horse*) Geschirr *nt*; (*for child*) Laufgurt *m*; (*also*: **safety harness**) Sicherheitsgurt *m* ▷ *vt* (*resources, energy etc*) nutzbar machen; (*horse, dog*) anschirren
harp [hɑːp] *n* Harfe *f* ▷ *vi*: **to ~ on about** (*pej*) herumreiten auf *+dat*
harrowing ['hærəuɪŋ] *adj* (*film*) erschütternd; (*experience*) grauenhaft
harsh [hɑːʃ] *adj* (*sound, light*) grell; (*judge, winter*) streng; (*criticism, life*) hart
harvest ['hɑːvɪst] *n* Ernte *f* ▷ *vt* ernten
has [hæz] *vb see* **have**
hash [hæʃ] *n* (*Culin*) Haschee *nt*; (*fig*): **to make a ~ of sth** etw verpfuschen (*inf*); (*inf*) ▷ *n abbr* (= *hashish*) Hasch *nt*
hasn't ['hæznt] = **has not**
hassle ['hæsl] (*inf*) *n* (*bother*) Theater *nt* ▷ *vt* schikanieren
haste [heɪst] *n* Hast *f*; (*speed*) Eile *f*; **in ~** in Eile; **to make ~ (to do sth)** sich beeilen(, etw zu tun)
hasten ['heɪsn] *vt* beschleunigen ▷ *vi*: **to ~ to do sth** sich beeilen, etw zu tun; **I ~ to add ...** ich muss allerdings hinzufügen, ...; **she ~ed back to the house** sie eilte zum Haus zurück
hastily ['heɪstɪlɪ] *adv* (*see adj*) hastig, eilig; vorschnell
hasty ['heɪstɪ] *adj* hastig, eilig; (*rash*) vorschnell
hat [hæt] *n* Hut *m*; **to keep sth under one's ~** etw für sich behalten
hatch [hætʃ] *n* (*Naut*: *also*: **hatchway**) Luke *f*; (*also*: **service hatch**) Durchreiche *f* ▷ *vi* (*bird*) ausschlüpfen ▷ *vt* ausbrüten; **the eggs ~ed after 10 days** nach 10 Tagen schlüpften die Jungen aus
hatchback ['hætʃbæk] *n* (*Aut*: *car*) Heckklappenmodell *nt*

hatchet ['hætʃɪt] *n* Beil *nt*; **to bury the ~** das Kriegsbeil begraben
hate [heɪt] *vt* hassen ▷ *n* Hass *m*; **I ~ him/ milk** ich kann ihn/ Milch nicht ausstehen; **to ~ to do/doing sth** es hassen, etw zu tun; (*weaker*) etw ungern tun; **I ~ to trouble you, but ...** es ist mir sehr unangenehm, dass ich Sie belästigen muss, aber ...
hateful ['heɪtful] *adj* abscheulich
hatred ['heɪtrɪd] *n* Hass *m*; (*dislike*) Abneigung *f*
haughty ['hɔ:tɪ] *adj* überheblich
haul [hɔ:l] *vt* ziehen; (*by lorry*) transportieren; (*Naut*) den Kurs ändern *+gen* ▷ *n* Beute *f*; (*of fish*) Fang *m*; **he ~ed himself out of the pool** er stemmte sich aus dem Schwimmbecken
haulage ['hɔ:lɪdʒ] *n* (*cost*) Transportkosten *pl*; (*business*) Transport *m*
haulier ['hɔ:lɪəʳ] (*Brit*) *n* Transportunternehmer(in) *m(f)*, Spediteur *m*
haunch [hɔ:ntʃ] *n* Hüftpartie *f*; (*of meat*) Keule *f*
haunt [hɔ:nt] *vt* (*place*) spuken in *+dat*, umgehen in *+dat*; (*person, fig*) verfolgen ▷ *n* Lieblingsplatz *m*; (*of crooks etc*) Treffpunkt *m*
haunted ['hɔ:ntɪd] *adj* (*expression*) gehetzt, gequält; **this building/room is ~** in diesem Gebäude/Zimmer spukt es
have [hæv] (*pt, pp* **had**) *aux vb* **1** haben; (*with verbs of motion*) sein; **to have arrived/gone** angekommen/gegangen sein; **to have eaten/slept** gegessen/geschlafen haben; **he has been promoted** er ist befördert worden; **having eaten** *or* **when he had eaten, he left** nachdem er gegessen hatte, ging er
2 (*in tag questions*): **you've done it, haven't you?** du hast es gemacht, nicht wahr?; **he hasn't done it, has he?** er hat es nicht gemacht, oder?
3 (*in short answers and questions*): **you've made a mistake — no I haven't/so I have** du hast einen Fehler gemacht — nein(, das habe ich nicht)/ja, stimmt; **we haven't paid — yes we have!** wir haben nicht bezahlt — doch!; **I've been there before — have you?** ich war schon einmal da — wirklich *or* tatsächlich?
▷ *modal aux vb* (*be obliged*): **to have (got) to do sth** etw tun müssen; **this has (got) to be a mistake** das muss ein Fehler sein
▷ *vt* **1** (*possess*) haben; **she has (got) blue eyes/dark hair** sie hat blaue Augen/dunkle Haare; **I have (got) an idea** ich habe eine Idee
2 (*referring to meals etc*): **to have breakfast** frühstücken; **to have lunch/dinner** zu Mittag/Abend essen; **to have a drink** etwas trinken; **to have a cigarette** eine Zigarette rauchen
3 (*receive, obtain etc*) haben; **may I have your address?** kann ich Ihre Adresse haben *or* bekommen?; **to have a baby** ein Kind bekommen
4 (*allow*): **I won't have this nonsense** dieser Unsinn kommt nicht infrage!; **we can't have that** das kommt nicht infrage
5: **to have sth done** etw machen lassen; **to have one's hair cut** sich *dat* die Haare schneiden lassen; **to have sb do sth** (*order*) jdn etw tun lassen; **he soon had them all laughing/working** bald hatte er alle zum Lachen/Arbeiten gebracht
6 (*experience, suffer*): **to have a cold/flu** eine Erkältung/die Grippe haben; **she had her bag stolen** ihr *dat* wurde die Tasche gestohlen
7 (*+ noun: take, hold etc*): **to have a swim** schwimmen gehen; **to have a walk** spazieren gehen; **to have a rest** sich ausruhen; **to have a meeting** eine Besprechung haben; **to have a party** eine Party geben
8 (*inf: dupe*): **you've been had** man hat dich hereingelegt
▸ **have in** (*inf*) *vt*: **to have it in for sb** jdn auf dem Kieker haben
▸ **have on** *vt* (*wear*) anhaben; (*Brit: inf: tease*) auf den Arm nehmen; **I don't have any money on me** ich habe kein Geld bei mir; **do you have** *or* **have you anything on tomorrow?** haben Sie morgen etwas vor?
▸ **have out** *vt*: **to have it out with sb** (*settle a problem etc*) ein Wort mit jdm reden
haven ['heɪvn] *n* Hafen *m*; (*safe place*) Zufluchtsort *m*
haven't ['hævnt] = **have not**
havoc ['hævək] *n* Verwüstung *f*; (*confusion*) Chaos *nt*; **to play ~ with sth** (*disrupt*) etw völlig durcheinanderbringen
Hawaii [hə'waɪi:] *n* Hawaii *nt*
hawk [hɔ:k] *n* Habicht *m*
hawthorn ['hɔ:θɔ:n] *n* Weißdorn *m*, Rotdorn *m*
hay [heɪ] *n* Heu *nt*
hay fever *n* Heuschnupfen *m*
haystack ['heɪstæk] *n* Heuhaufen *m*; **like looking for a needle in a ~** als ob man eine Stecknadel im Heuhaufen suchte
haywire ['heɪwaɪəʳ] (*inf*) *adj*: **to go ~** (*machine*) verrücktspielen; (*plans etc*) über den Haufen geworfen werden
hazard ['hæzəd] *n* Gefahr *f* ▷ *vt* riskieren; **to be a health/fire ~** eine Gefahr für die Gesundheit/feuergefährlich sein; **to ~ a guess** (es) wagen, eine Vermutung anzustellen
hazardous ['hæzədəs] *adj* gefährlich
haze [heɪz] *n* Dunst *m*
hazel ['heɪzl] *n* Hasel(nuss)strauch *m*, Haselbusch *m* ▷ *adj* haselnussbraun
hazelnut ['heɪzlnʌt] *n* Haselnuss *f*
hazy ['heɪzɪ] *adj* dunstig, diesig; (*idea, memory*) unklar, verschwommen; **I'm rather ~ about the details** an die Einzelheiten kann ich mich nur vage *or* verschwommen erinnern; (*ignorant*) die genauen Einzelheiten

sind mir nicht bekannt

he [hi:] *pron* er ▷ *pref* männlich; **he who ...** wer ...

head [hɛd] *n* Kopf *m*; (*of table*) Kopfende *nt*; (*of queue*) Spitze *f*; (*of company, organization*) Leiter(in) *m(f)*; (*of school*) Schulleiter(in) *m(f)*; (*on coin*) Kopfseite *f*; (*on tape recorder*) Tonkopf *m* ▷ *vt* anführen, an der Spitze stehen von; (*group, company*) leiten; (*Football: ball*) köpfen; **~s (or tails)** Kopf (oder Zahl); **~ over heels** Hals über Kopf; (*in love*) bis über beide Ohren; **£10 a** *or* **per ~** 10 Pfund pro Kopf; **at the ~ of the list** oben auf der Liste; **to have a ~ for business** einen guten Geschäftssinn haben; **to have no ~ for heights** nicht schwindelfrei sein; **to come to a ~** sich zuspitzen; **they put their ~s together** sie haben sich zusammengesetzt; **off the top of my** *etc* **~** ohne lange zu überlegen; **on your own ~ be it!** auf Ihre eigene Verantwortung *or* Kappe (*inf*)!; **to bite** *or* **snap sb's ~ off** jdn grob anfahren; **he won't bite your ~ off** er wird dir schon nicht den Kopf abreißen; **it went to my ~** es ist mir in den Kopf *or* zu Kopf gestiegen; **to lose/keep one's ~** den Kopf verlieren/nicht verlieren; **I can't make ~ nor tail of this** hieraus werde ich nicht schlau; **he's off his ~!** (*inf*) er ist nicht (ganz) bei Trost!

▸ **head for** *vt fus* (*on foot*) zusteuern auf *+acc*; (*by car*) in Richtung ... fahren; (*plane, ship*) Kurs nehmen auf *+acc*; **you are ~ing for trouble** du wirst Ärger bekommen

▸ **head off** *vt* abwenden

headache ['hɛdeɪk] *n* Kopfschmerzen *pl*, Kopfweh *nt*; (*fig*) Problem *nt*; **to have a ~** Kopfschmerzen *or* Kopfweh haben

headdress ['hɛddrɛs] (*Brit*) *n* Kopfschmuck *m*

heading ['hɛdɪŋ] *n* Überschrift *f*

headlamp ['hɛdlæmp] (*Brit*) *n* = **headlight**

headland ['hɛdlənd] *n* Landspitze *f*

headlight ['hɛdlaɪt] *n* Scheinwerfer *m*

headline ['hɛdlaɪn] *n* Schlagzeile *f*; (*Radio, TV*): **(news) ~s** Nachrichtenüberblick *m*

headlong ['hɛdlɔŋ] *adv* kopfüber; (*rush*) Hals über Kopf

headmaster [hɛd'mɑ:stəʳ] *n* Schulleiter *m*

headmistress [hɛd'mɪstrɪs] *n* Schulleiterin *f*

head office *n* Zentrale *f*

head-on ['hɛd'ɔn] *adj* (*collision*) frontal; (*confrontation*) direkt

headphones ['hɛdfəunz] *npl* Kopfhörer *pl*

headquarters ['hɛdkwɔ:təz] *npl* Zentrale *f*; (*Mil*) Hauptquartier *nt*

headrest ['hɛdrɛst] *n* (*Aut*) Kopfstütze *f*

headroom ['hɛdrum] *n* (*in car*) Kopfraum *m*; (*under bridge*) lichte Höhe *f*

headscarf ['hɛdskɑ:f] *n* Kopftuch *nt*

headset ['hɛdsɛt] *n* = **headphones**

headstrong ['hɛdstrɔŋ] *adj* eigensinnig

head waiter *n* Oberkellner *m*

headway ['hɛdweɪ] *n*: **to make ~** vorankommen

headwind ['hɛdwɪnd] *n* Gegenwind *m*

heady ['hɛdɪ] *adj* (*experience etc*) aufregend; (*drink, atmosphere*) berauschend

heal [hi:l] *vt, vi* heilen

health [hɛlθ] *n* Gesundheit *f*

health care *n* Gesundheitsfürsorge *f*

health centre (*Brit*) *n* Ärztezentrum *nt*

health food *n* Reformkost *f*, Naturkost *f*

health food shop *n* Reformhaus *nt*, Naturkostladen *m*

healthy ['hɛlθɪ] *adj* gesund; (*profit*) ansehnlich

heap [hi:p] *n* Haufen *m* ▷ *vt*: **to ~ (up)** (auf)häufen; **~s of** (*inf*) jede Menge; **to ~ sth with** etw beladen mit; **to ~ sth on** etw häufen auf *+acc*; **to ~ favours/gifts** *etc* **on sb** jdn mit Gefälligkeiten/Geschenken *etc* überhäufen; **to ~ praises on sb** jdn mit Lob überschütten

hear [hɪəʳ] (*pt, pp* **~d**) *vt* hören; (*Law: case*) verhandeln; (*: witness*) vernehmen; **to ~ about** hören von; **to ~ from sb** von jdm hören; **I've never ~d of that book** von dem Buch habe ich noch nie etwas gehört; **I wouldn't ~ of it!** davon will ich nichts hören

▸ **hear out** *vt* ausreden lassen

heard [hə:d] *pt, pp of* **hear**

hearing ['hɪərɪŋ] *n* Gehör *nt*; (*of facts, by committee*) Anhörung *f*; (*of witnesses*) Vernehmung *f*; (*of a case*) Verhandlung *f*; **to give sb a ~** (*Brit*) jdn anhören

hearing aid *n* Hörgerät *nt*

hearsay ['hɪəseɪ] *n* Gerüchte *pl*; **by ~** vom Hörensagen

hearse [hə:s] *n* Leichenwagen *m*

heart [hɑ:t] *n* Herz *nt*; (*of problem*) Kern *m*; **hearts** *npl* (*Cards*) Herz *nt*; **to lose ~** den Mut verlieren; **to take ~** Mut fassen; **at ~** im Grunde; **by ~** auswendig; **to set one's ~ on sth** sein Herz an etw *acc* hängen; **to set one's ~ on doing sth** alles daransetzen, etw zu tun; **the ~ of the matter** der Kern der Sache

heart attack *n* Herzanfall *m*

heartbeat ['hɑ:tbi:t] *n* Herzschlag *m*

heartbreaking ['hɑ:tbreɪkɪŋ] *adj* herzzerreißend

heartbroken ['hɑ:tbrəukən] *adj*: **to be ~** todunglücklich sein

heartburn ['hɑ:tbə:n] *n* Sodbrennen *nt*

heart failure *n* Herzversagen *nt*

heartfelt ['hɑ:tfɛlt] *adj* tief empfunden

hearth [hɑ:θ] *n* ≈ Kamin *m*

heartily ['hɑ:tɪlɪ] *adv* (*see adj*) (laut und) herzlich; herzhaft; tief; ungeteilt

heartless ['hɑ:tlɪs] *adj* herzlos

hearty ['hɑ:tɪ] *adj* (*person*) laut und herzlich; (*laugh, appetite*) herzhaft; (*welcome*) herzlich; (*dislike*) tief; (*support*) ungeteilt

heat [hi:t] *n* Hitze *f*; (*warmth*) Wärme *f*; (*temperature*) Temperatur *f*; (*Sport: also:* **qualifying heat**) Vorrunde *f* ▷ *vt* erhitzen, heiß machen; (*room, house*) heizen; **in ~, on ~**

(*Brit: Zool*) brünstig, läufig
▸ **heat up** *vi* sich erwärmen, warm werden ▹ *vt* aufwärmen; (*water, room*) erwärmen

heated ['hi:tɪd] *adj* geheizt; (*pool*) beheizt; (*argument*) hitzig

heater ['hi:təʳ] *n* (Heiz)ofen *m*; (*in car*) Heizung *f*

heath [hi:θ] (*Brit*) *n* Heide *f*

heather ['hɛðəʳ] *n* Heidekraut *nt*, Erika *f*

heating ['hi:tɪŋ] *n* Heizung *f*

heatstroke ['hi:tstrəuk] *n* Hitzschlag *m*

heave [hi:v] *vt* (*pull*) ziehen; (*push*) schieben; (*lift*) (hoch)heben ▹ *vi* sich heben und senken; (*retch*) sich übergeben ▹ *n* (*see vt*) Zug *m*; Stoß *m*; Heben *nt*; **to ~ a sigh** einen Seufzer ausstoßen
▸ **heave to** (*pt, pp* **hove**) *vi* (*Naut*) beidrehen

heaven ['hɛvn] *n* Himmel *m*; **thank ~!** Gott sei Dank!; **~ forbid!** bloß nicht!; **for ~'s sake!** um Himmels *or* Gottes willen!

heavenly ['hɛvnlɪ] *adj* himmlisch

heavily ['hɛvɪlɪ] *adv* schwer; (*drink, smoke, depend, rely*) stark; (*sleep, sigh*) tief; (*say*) mit schwerer Stimme

heavy ['hɛvɪ] *adj* schwer; (*clothes*) dick; (*rain, snow, drinker, smoker*) stark; (*build, frame*) kräftig; (*breathing, sleep*) tief; (*schedule, week*) anstrengend; (*weather*) drückend, schwül; **the conversation was ~ going** die Unterhaltung war mühsam; **the book was ~ going** das Buch las sich schwer

heavy goods vehicle *n* Lastkraftwagen *m*

heavyweight ['hɛvɪweɪt] *n* (*Sport*) Schwergewicht *nt*

Hebrew ['hi:bru:] *adj* hebräisch ▹ *n* (*Ling*) Hebräisch *nt*

Hebrides ['hɛbrɪdi:z] *npl*: **the ~** die Hebriden *pl*

heckle ['hɛkl] *vt* durch Zwischenrufe stören

hectare ['hɛktɑ:ʳ] (*Brit*) *n* Hektar *nt or m*

hectic ['hɛktɪk] *adj* hektisch

he'd [hi:d] = **he would; he had**

hedge [hɛdʒ] *n* Hecke *f* ▹ *vi* ausweichen, sich nicht festlegen ▹ *vt*: **to ~ one's bets** (*fig*) sich absichern; **as a ~ against inflation** als Absicherung *or* Schutz gegen die Inflation
▸ **hedge in** *vt* (*person*) (in seiner Freiheit) einschränken; (*proposals etc*) behindern

hedgehog ['hɛdʒhɔg] *n* Igel *m*

heed [hi:d] *vt* (*also*: **take heed of**) beachten ▹ *n*: **to pay (no) ~ to, take (no) ~ of** (nicht) beachten

heedless ['hi:dlɪs] *adj* achtlos; **~ of sb/sth** ohne auf jdn/etw zu achten

heel [hi:l] *n* Ferse *f*; (*of shoe*) Absatz *m* ▹ *vt* (*shoe*) mit einem neuen Absatz versehen; **to bring to ~** (*dog*) bei Fuß gehen lassen; (*fig: person*) an die Kandare nehmen; **to take to one's ~s** (*inf*) sich aus dem Staub machen

hefty ['hɛftɪ] *adj* kräftig; (*parcel etc*) schwer; (*profit*) ansehnlich

heifer ['hɛfəʳ] *n* Färse *f*

height [haɪt] *n* Höhe *f*; (*of person*) Größe *f*; (*fig: of luxury, good taste etc*) Gipfel *m*; **what ~ are you?** wie groß bist du?; **of average ~** durchschnittlich groß; **to be afraid of ~s** nicht schwindelfrei sein; **it's the ~ of fashion** das ist die neueste Mode; **at the ~ of the tourist season** in der Hauptsaison

heighten ['haɪtn] *vt* erhöhen

heir [ɛəʳ] *n* Erbe *m*; **the ~ to the throne** der Thronfolger

heiress ['ɛərɛs] *n* Erbin *f*

heirloom ['ɛəlu:m] *n* Erbstück *nt*

held [hɛld] *pt, pp of* **hold**

helicopter ['hɛlɪkɔptəʳ] *n* Hubschrauber *m*

hell [hɛl] *n* Hölle *f*; **~!** (*inf!*) verdammt! (*inf!*); **a ~ of a lot** (*inf*) verdammt viel (*inf*); **a ~ of a mess** (*inf*) ein wahnsinniges Chaos (*inf*); **a ~ of a noise** (*inf*) ein Höllenlärm *m*; **a ~ of a nice guy** ein wahnsinnig netter Typ

he'll [hi:l] = **he will; he shall**

hellish ['hɛlɪʃ] (*inf*) *adj* höllisch

hello [hə'ləu] *excl* hallo; (*expressing surprise*) nanu, he

helm [hɛlm] *n* Ruder *nt*, Steuer *nt*; **at the ~** am Ruder

helmet ['hɛlmɪt] *n* Helm *m*

help [hɛlp] *n* Hilfe *f*; (*charwoman*) (Haushalts)hilfe *f* ▹ *vt* helfen *+dat*; **with the ~ of** (*person*) mit (der) Hilfe *+gen*; (*tool etc*) mithilfe *+gen*; **to be of ~ to sb** jdm behilflich sein, jdm helfen; **can I ~ you?** (*in shop*) womit kann ich Ihnen dienen?; **~ yourself** bedienen Sie sich; **he can't ~ it** er kann nichts dafür; **I can't ~ thinking that ...** ich kann mir nicht helfen, ich glaube, dass ...

helper ['hɛlpəʳ] *n* Helfer(in) *m(f)*

helpful ['hɛlpful] *adj* hilfsbereit; (*advice, suggestion*) nützlich, hilfreich

helping ['hɛlpɪŋ] *n* Portion *f*

helpless ['hɛlplɪs] *adj* hilflos

helpline ['hɛlplaɪn] *n* (*for emergencies*) Notruf *m*; (*for information*) Informationsdienst *m*

hem [hɛm] *n* Saum *m* ▹ *vt* säumen
▸ **hem in** *vt* einschließen, umgeben; **to feel ~med in** (*fig*) sich eingeengt fühlen

hemisphere ['hɛmɪsfɪəʳ] *n* Hemisphäre *f*; (*of sphere*) Halbkugel *f*

hemorrhage ['hɛmərɪdʒ] (*US*) *n* = **haemorrhage**

hemorrhoids ['hɛmərɔɪdz] (*US*) *npl* = **haemorrhoids**

hen [hɛn] *n* Henne *f*, Huhn *nt*; (*female bird*) Weibchen *nt*

hence [hɛns] *adv* daher; **2 years ~** in zwei Jahren

henceforth [hɛns'fɔ:θ] *adv* von nun an; (*from that time on*) von da an

hen night, hen party (*inf*) *n* Damenkränzchen *nt*

hepatitis [hɛpə'taɪtɪs] *n* Hepatitis *f*

her [hə:ʳ] *pron* sie; (*indirect*) ihr ▹ *adj* ihr; **I see ~** ich sehe sie; **give ~ a book** gib ihr ein Buch; **after ~** nach ihr; *see also* **me; my**

herald ['hɛrəld] *n* (Vor)bote *m* ▹ *vt*

ankündigen

heraldry ['hɛrəldrɪ] *n* Wappenkunde *f*, Heraldik *f*; (*coats of arms*) Wappen *pl*

herb [hə:b] *n* Kraut *nt*

herbal ['hə:bl] *adj* (*tea, medicine*) Kräuter-

herd [hə:d] *n* Herde *f*; (*of wild animals*) Rudel *nt* ▷ *vt* treiben; (*gather*) zusammentreiben; **~ed together** zusammengetrieben

here [hɪəʳ] *adv* hier; **she left ~ yesterday** sie ist gestern von hier abgereist; **~ is/are ...** hier ist/sind ...; **~ you are** (*giving*) (hier,) bitte; **~ we are!** (*finding sth*) da ist es ja!; **~ she is!** da ist sie ja!; **~ she comes** da kommt sie ja; **come ~!** komm hierher *or* hierhin!; **~ and there** hier und da; **"~'s to ..."** "auf ... *acc*"

hereafter [hɪər'ɑ:ftəʳ] *adv* künftig

hereby [hɪə'baɪ] *adv* hiermit

hereditary [hɪ'rɛdɪtrɪ] *adj* erblich, Erb-

heresy ['hɛrəsɪ] *n* Ketzerei *f*

heritage ['hɛrɪtɪdʒ] *n* Erbe *nt*; **our national ~** unser nationales Erbe

hermit ['hə:mɪt] *n* Einsiedler(in) *m(f)*

hernia ['hə:nɪə] *n* Bruch *m*

hero ['hɪərəu] (*pl* **~es**) *n* Held *m*; (*idol*) Idol *nt*

heroic [hɪ'rəuɪk] *adj* heroisch; (*figure, person*) heldenhaft

heroin ['hɛrəuɪn] *n* Heroin *nt*

heroine ['hɛrəuɪn] *n* Heldin *f*; (*idol*) Idol *nt*

heron ['hɛrən] *n* Reiher *m*

herring ['hɛrɪŋ] *n* Hering *m*

hers [hə:z] *pron* ihre(r, s); **a friend of ~** ein Freund von ihr; **this is ~** das gehört ihr; *see also* **mine**

herself [hə:'sɛlf] *pron* sich; (*emphatic*) (sie) selbst; *see also* **oneself**

he's [hi:z] = **he is**; = **he has**

hesitant ['hɛzɪtənt] *adj* zögernd; **to be ~ about doing sth** zögern, etw zu tun

hesitate ['hɛzɪteɪt] *vi* zögern; (*be unwilling*) Bedenken haben; **to ~ about** Bedenken haben wegen; **don't ~ to see a doctor if you are worried** gehen Sie ruhig zum Arzt, wenn Sie sich Sorgen machen

hesitation [hɛzɪ'teɪʃən] *n* Zögern *nt*; Bedenken *pl*; **to have no ~ in saying sth** etw ohne Weiteres sagen können

heterosexual ['hɛtərəu'sɛksjuəl] *adj* heterosexuell ▷ *n* Heterosexuelle(r) *f(m)*

hexagon ['hɛksəgən] *n* Sechseck *nt*

hey [heɪ] *excl* he; (*to attract attention*) he du/Sie

heyday ['heɪdeɪ] *n*: **the ~ of** (*person*) die Glanzzeit *+gen*; (*nation, group etc*) die Blütezeit *+gen*

HGV (*Brit*) *n abbr* (*Hist*: = *heavy goods vehicle*) Lkw *m*

hi [haɪ] *excl* hallo

hiatus [haɪ'eɪtəs] *n* Unterbrechung *f*

hibernate ['haɪbəneɪt] *vi* Winterschlaf halten *or* machen

hiccough ['hɪkʌp] *vi* hicksen

hid [hɪd] *pt of* **hide**

hidden ['hɪdn] *pp of* **hide** ▷ *adj* (*advantage, danger*) unsichtbar; (*place*) versteckt; **there are no ~ extras** es gibt keine versteckten Extrakosten

hide [haɪd] (*pt* **hid**, *pp* **hidden**) *n* Haut *f*, Fell *nt*; (*of birdwatcher etc*) Versteck *nt* ▷ *vt* verstecken; (*feeling, information*) verbergen; (*obscure*) verdecken ▷ *vi*: **to ~ (from sb)** sich (vor jdm) verstecken; **to ~ sth (from sb)** etw (vor jdm) verstecken

hide-and-seek ['haɪdən'si:k] *n* Versteckspiel *nt*; **to play ~** Verstecken spielen

hideous ['hɪdɪəs] *adj* scheußlich; (*conditions*) furchtbar

hiding ['haɪdɪŋ] *n* Tracht *f* Prügel; **to be in ~** (*concealed*) sich versteckt halten

hierarchy ['haɪərɑ:kɪ] *n* Hierarchie *f*

hi-fi ['haɪfaɪ] *n abbr* (= *high fidelity*) Hi-Fi *nt* ▷ *adj* (*equipment etc*) Hi-Fi-

high [haɪ] *adj* hoch; (*wind*) stark; (*risk*) groß; (*quality*) gut; (*inf*: *on drugs*) high; (: *on drink*) blau; (*Brit*: *food*) schlecht; (: *game*) anbrüchig ▷ *adv* hoch ▷ *n*: **exports have reached a new ~** der Export hat einen neuen Höchststand erreicht; **to pay a ~ price for sth** etw teuer bezahlen; **it's ~ time you did it** es ist *or* wird höchste Zeit, dass du es machst; **~ in the air** hoch oben in der Luft

highbrow ['haɪbrau] *adj* intellektuell; (*book, discussion etc*) anspruchsvoll

highchair ['haɪtʃɛəʳ] *n* Hochstuhl *m*

high-class ['haɪ'klɑ:s] *adj* erstklassig; (*neighbourhood*) vornehm

higher education *n* Hochschulbildung *f*

high-handed [haɪ'hændɪd] *adj* eigenmächtig

high-heeled [haɪ'hi:ld] *adj* hochhackig

high heels *npl* hochhackige Schuhe *pl*

high jump *n* Hochsprung *m*

highlight ['haɪlaɪt] *n* (*of event*) Höhepunkt *m*; (*in hair*) Strähnchen *nt* ▷ *vt* (*problem, need*) ein Schlaglicht werfen auf *+acc*

highlighter ['haɪlaɪtəʳ] *n* Textmarker *m*

highly ['haɪlɪ] *adv* hoch-; **to speak ~ of** sich sehr positiv äußern über *+acc*; **to think ~ of** eine hohe Meinung haben von

highly strung *adj* nervös

highness ['haɪnɪs] *n*: **Her/His/Your H~** Ihre/Seine/Eure Hoheit *f*

high-pitched [haɪ'pɪtʃt] *adj* hoch

high-rise ['haɪraɪz] *adj* (*apartment, block*) Hochhaus-; **~ building/flats** Hochhaus *nt*

high school *n* ≈ Oberschule *f*

high season (*Brit*) *n* Hochsaison *f*

high street (*Brit*) *n* Hauptstraße *f*

highway ['haɪweɪ] (*US*) *n* Straße *f*; (*between towns, states*) Landstraße *f*; **information ~** Datenautobahn *f*

Highway Code (*Brit*) *n* Straßenverkehrsordnung *f*

hijack ['haɪdʒæk] *vt* entführen ▷ *n* (*also*: **hijacking**) Entführung *f*

hijacker ['haɪdʒækəʳ] *n* Entführer(in) *m(f)*

hike [haɪk] *vi* wandern ▷ *n* Wanderung *f*; (*inf*: *in prices etc*) Erhöhung *f* ▷ *vt* (*inf*) erhöhen

hiker ['haɪkəʳ] *n* Wanderer *m*, Wanderin *f*

hiking ['haɪkɪŋ] *n* Wandern *nt*
hilarious [hɪ'lɛərɪəs] *adj* urkomisch
hill [hɪl] *n* Hügel *m*; (*fairly high*) Berg *m*; (*slope*) Hang *m*; (*on road*) Steigung *f*
hillside ['hɪlsaɪd] *n* Hang *m*
hill walking *n* Bergwandern *nt*
hilly ['hɪlɪ] *adj* hügelig
hilt [hɪlt] *n* (*of sword, knife*) Heft *nt*; **to the ~** voll und ganz
him [hɪm] *pron* ihn; (*indirect*) ihm; *see also* **me**
himself [hɪm'sɛlf] *pron* sich; (*emphatic*) (er) selbst; *see also* **oneself**
hind [haɪnd] *adj* (*legs*) Hinter- ▷ *n* (*female deer*) Hirschkuh *f*
hinder ['hɪndəʳ] *vt* behindern; **to ~ sb from doing sth** jdn daran hindern, etw zu tun
hindrance ['hɪndrəns] *n* Behinderung *f*
hindsight ['haɪndsaɪt] *n*: **with ~** im Nachhinein
Hindu ['hɪndu:] *adj* hinduistisch, Hindu-
hinge [hɪndʒ] *n* (*on door*) Angel *f* ▷ *vi*: **to ~ on** anhängen von
hint [hɪnt] *n* Andeutung *f*; (*advice*) Tipp *m*; (*sign, glimmer*) Spur *f* ▷ *vt*: **to ~ that** andeuten, dass ▷ *vi*: **to ~ at** andeuten; **to drop a ~** eine Andeutung machen; **give me a ~** geben Sie mir einen Hinweis; **white with a ~ of pink** weiß mit einem Hauch von Rosa
hip [hɪp] *n* Hüfte *f*
hippie ['hɪpɪ] *n* Hippie *m*
hippo ['hɪpəu] *n* Nilpferd *nt*
hippopotamus [hɪpə'pɔtəməs] (*pl* **~es** *or* **hippopotami**) *n* Nilpferd *nt*
hippy ['hɪpɪ] *n* = **hippie**
hire ['haɪəʳ] *vt* (*Brit*) mieten; (*worker*) einstellen ▷ *n* (*Brit*) Mieten *nt*; **for ~** (*taxi*) frei; (*boat*) zu vermieten; **on ~** gemietet
▸ **hire out** *vt* vermieten
hire car, **hired car** (*Brit*) *n* Mietwagen *m*, Leihwagen *m*
his [hɪz] *pron* seine(r, s) ▷ *adj* sein; *see also* **my; mine²**
hiss [hɪs] *vi* zischen; (*cat*) fauchen ▷ *n* Zischen *nt*; (*of cat*) Fauchen *nt*
historian [hɪ'stɔ:rɪən] *n* Historiker(in) *m(f)*
historic [hɪ'stɔrɪk] *adj* historisch
history ['hɪstərɪ] *n* Geschichte *f*; **there's a ~ of heart disease in his family** Herzleiden liegen bei ihm in der Familie; **medical ~** Krankengeschichte *f*
hit [hɪt] (*pt, pp* **~**) *vt* schlagen; (*reach, affect*) treffen; (*vehicle: another vehicle*) zusammenstoßen mit; (*: wall, tree*) fahren gegen; (*: more violently*) prallen gegen; (*: person*) anfahren ▷ *n* Schlag *m*; (*success*) Erfolg *m*; (*song*) Hit *m*; **to ~ it off with sb** sich gut mit jdm verstehen; **to ~ the headlines** Schlagzeilen machen; **to ~ the road** (*inf*) sich auf den Weg *or* die Socken (*inf*) machen; **to ~ the roof** (*inf*) an die Decke *or* in die Luft gehen
▸ **hit back** *vi*: **to ~ back at sb** jdn zurückschlagen; (*fig*) jdm Kontra geben
▸ **hit out at** *vt fus* auf jdn losschlagen; (*fig*) jdn scharf angreifen
▸ **hit (up)on** *vt fus* stoßen auf *+acc*, finden
hit-and-run driver ['hɪtən'rʌn-] *n* unfallflüchtiger Fahrer *m*, unfallflüchtige Fahrerin *f*
hitch [hɪtʃ] *vt* festmachen, anbinden; (*also*: **hitch up**: *trousers, skirt*) hochziehen ▷ *n* Schwierigkeit *f*, Problem *nt*; **to ~ a lift** trampen, per Anhalter fahren; **technical ~** technische Panne *f*
▸ **hitch up** *vt* anspannen; *see also* **hitch**
hi-tech ['haɪ'tɛk] *adj* Hightech-, hoch technisiert ▷ *n* Hightech *nt*, Hochtechnologie *f*
hitherto [hɪðə'tu:] *adv* bisher, bis jetzt
HIV *n abbr* (= *human immunodeficiency virus*) HIV; **~-negative** HIV-negativ; **~-positive** HIV-positiv
hive [haɪv] *n* Bienenkorb *m*; **to be a ~ of activity** einem Bienenhaus gleichen
▸ **hive off** (*inf*) *vt* ausgliedern, abspalten
HMS (*Brit*) *abbr* (= *His* (*or Her*) *Majesty's Ship*) *Namensteil von Schiffen der Kriegsmarine*
hoard [hɔ:d] *n* (*of food*) Vorrat *m*; (*of money, treasure*) Schatz *m* ▷ *vt* (*food*) hamstern; (*money*) horten
hoarding ['hɔ:dɪŋ] (*Brit*) *n* Plakatwand *f*
hoarse [hɔ:s] *adj* heiser
hoax [həuks] *n* (*false alarm*) blinder Alarm *m*
hob [hɔb] *n* Kochmulde *f*
hobble ['hɔbl] *vi* humpeln
hobby ['hɔbɪ] *n* Hobby *nt*, Steckenpferd *nt*
hobo ['həubəu] (*US*) *n* Penner *m* (*inf*)
hockey ['hɔkɪ] *n* Hockey *nt*
hog [hɔg] *n* (Mast)schwein *nt* ▷ *vt* (*road*) für sich beanspruchen; (*telephone etc*) in Beschlag nehmen; **to go the whole ~** Nägel mit Köpfen machen
Hogmanay [hɔgmə'neɪ] (*Scot*) *n* Silvester *nt*
hoist [hɔɪst] *n* Hebevorrichtung *f* ▷ *vt* hochheben; (*flag, sail*) hissen
hold [həuld] (*pt, pp* **held**) *vt* halten; (*contain*) enthalten; (*power, qualification*) haben; (*opinion*) vertreten; (*meeting*) abhalten; (*conversation*) führen; (*prisoner, hostage*) festhalten ▷ *vi* halten; (*be valid*) gelten; (*weather*) sich halten ▷ *n* (*grasp*) Griff *m*; (*of ship, plane*) Laderaum *m*; **to ~ one's head up** den Kopf hochhalten; **to ~ sb responsible/liable** *etc* jdn verantwortlich/haftbar *etc* machen; **~ the line!** (*Tel*) bleiben Sie am Apparat!; **~ it!** Moment mal!; **to ~ one's own** sich behaupten; **he ~s the view that ...** er ist der Meinung *or* er vertritt die Ansicht, dass ...; **to ~ firm** *or* **fast** halten; **~ still!**, **~ steady!** stillhalten!; **his luck held** das Glück blieb ihm treu; **I don't ~ with ...** ich bin gegen ...; **to catch** *or* **get (a) ~ of** sich festhalten an *+dat*; **to get ~ of** (*fig*) finden, auftreiben; **to get ~ of o.s.** sich in den Griff bekommen; **to have a ~ over** in der Hand haben

▸ **hold back** *vt* zurückhalten; (*tears, laughter*) unterdrücken; (*secret*) verbergen; (*information*) geheim halten
▸ **hold down** *vt* niederhalten; (*job*) sich halten in *+dat*
▸ **hold forth** *vi*: **to ~ forth (about)** sich ergehen *or* sich auslassen (über *+acc*)
▸ **hold off** *vt* abwehren ▹ *vi*: **if the rain ~s off** wenn es nicht regnet
▸ **hold on** *vi* sich festhalten; (*wait*) warten; **~ on!** (*Tel*) einen Moment bitte!
▸ **hold on to** *vt fus* sich festhalten an; (*keep*) behalten
▸ **hold out** *vt* (*hand*) ausstrecken; (*hope*) haben; (*prospect*) bieten ▹ *vi* nicht nachgeben
▸ **hold over** *vt* vertagen
▸ **hold up** *vt* hochheben; (*support*) stützen; (*delay*) aufhalten; (*rob*) überfallen

holdall ['həuldɔ:l] (*Brit*) *n* Tasche *f*; (*for clothes*) Reisetasche *f*

holder ['həuldəʳ] *n* Halter *m*; (*of ticket, record, office, title etc*) Inhaber(in) *m(f)*

holding ['həuldɪŋ] *n* (*share*) Anteil *m*; (*small farm*) Gut *nt* ▹ *adj* (*operation, tactic*) zur Schadensbegrenzung

hold-up ['həuldʌp] *n* bewaffneter Raubüberfall *m*; (*delay*) Verzögerung *f*; (*Brit: in traffic*) Stockung *f*

hole [həul] *n* Loch *nt*; (*unpleasant town*) Kaff *nt* (*inf*) ▹ *vt* (*ship*) leckschlagen; (*building etc*) durchlöchern; **~ in the heart** Loch im Herz(en); **to pick ~s** (*fig*) (über)kritisch sein; **to pick ~s in sth** (*fig*) an etw *dat* herumkritisieren
▸ **hole up** *vi* sich verkriechen

holiday ['hɔlɪdeɪ] *n* (*Brit*) Urlaub *m*; (*Scol*) Ferien *pl*; (*day off*) freier Tag *m*; (*also*: **public holiday**) Feiertag *m*; **on ~** im Urlaub, in den Ferien

holiday camp (*Brit*) *n* (*also*: **holiday centre**) Feriendorf *nt*

holiday-maker ['hɔlɪdɪmeɪkəʳ] (*Brit*) *n* Urlauber(in) *m(f)*

holiday resort *n* Ferienort *m*

Holland ['hɔlənd] *n* Holland *nt*

hollow ['hɔləu] *adj* hohl; (*eyes*) tief liegend; (*laugh*) unecht; (*sound*) dumpf; (*fig*) leer; (*: victory, opinion*) wertlos ▹ *n* Vertiefung *f* ▹ *vt*: **to ~ out** aushöhlen

holly ['hɔlɪ] *n* Stechpalme *f*, Ilex *m*; (*leaves*) Stechpalmenzweige *pl*

holocaust ['hɔləkɔ:st] *n* Inferno *nt*; (*in Third Reich*) Holocaust *m*

holster ['həulstəʳ] *n* Pistolenhalfter *m or nt*

holy ['həulɪ] *adj* heilig

Holy Ghost *n* Heiliger Geist *m*

homage ['hɔmɪdʒ] *n* Huldigung *f*; **to pay ~ to** huldigen *+dat*

home [həum] *n* Heim *nt*; (*house, flat*) Zuhause *nt*; (*area, country*) Heimat *f*; (*institution*) Anstalt *f* ▹ *cpd* Heim-; (*Econ, Pol*) Innen- ▹ *adv* (*go etc*) nach Hause, heim; **at ~** zu Hause (*Österr, Schweiz*); (*in country*) im Inland; **to be** *or* **feel at ~** (*fig*) sich wohlfühlen; **make yourself at ~** machen Sie es sich *dat* gemütlich *or* bequem; **to make one's ~ somewhere** sich irgendwo niederlassen; **the ~ of free enterprise/jazz** *etc* die Heimat des freien Unternehmertums/Jazz *etc*; **when will you be ~?** wann bist du wieder zu Hause?; **a ~ from home** ein zweites Zuhause *nt*; **~ and dry** aus dem Schneider; **to drive a nail ~** einen Nagel einschlagen; **to bring sth ~ to sb** jdm etw klarmachen
▸ **home in on** *vt fus* (*missiles*) sich ausrichten auf *+acc*

home address *n* Heimatanschrift *f*

homeland ['həumlænd] *n* Heimat *f*, Heimatland *nt*

homeless ['həumlɪs] *adj* obdachlos; (*refugee*) heimatlos

homely ['həumlɪ] *adj* einfach; (*US: plain*) unscheinbar

home-made [həum'meɪd] *adj* selbst gemacht

Home Office (*Brit*) *n* Innenministerium *nt*

home page *n* (*Comput*) Homepage *f*

home rule *n* Selbstbestimmung *f*, Selbstverwaltung *f*

Home Secretary (*Brit*) *n* Innenminister(in) *m(f)*

homesick ['həumsɪk] *adj* heimwehkrank; **to be ~** Heimweh haben

home town *n* Heimatstadt *f*

homeward ['həumwəd] *adj* (*journey*) Heim- ▹ *adv* = **homewards**

homework ['həumwə:k] *n* Hausaufgaben *pl*

homicide ['hɔmɪsaɪd] (*US*) *n* Mord *m*

homoeopathy, (*US*) **homeopathy** [həumɪ'ɔpəθɪ] *n* Homöopathie *f*

homogeneous [hɔməu'dʒi:nɪəs] *adj* homogen

homosexual [hɔməu'sɛksjuəl] *adj* homosexuell ▹ *n* Homosexuelle(r) *f(m)*

honest ['ɔnɪst] *adj* ehrlich; (*trustworthy*) redlich; (*sincere*) aufrichtig; **to be quite ~ with you ...** um ehrlich zu sein, ...

honestly ['ɔnɪstlɪ] *adv* (*see adj*) ehrlich; redlich; aufrichtig

honesty ['ɔnɪstɪ] *n* (*see adj*) Ehrlichkeit *f*; Redlichkeit *f*; Aufrichtigkeit *f*

honey ['hʌnɪ] *n* Honig *m*; (*US: inf*) Schätzchen *nt*

honeycomb ['hʌnɪkəum] *n* Bienenwabe *f*; (*pattern*) Wabe *f* ▹ *vt*: **to ~ with** durchlöchern mit

honeymoon ['hʌnɪmu:n] *n* Flitterwochen *pl*; (*trip*) Hochzeitsreise *f*

honeysuckle ['hʌnɪsʌkl] *n* Geißblatt *nt*

Hong Kong ['hɔŋ'kɔŋ] *n* Hongkong *nt*

honk [hɔŋk] *vi* (*Aut*) hupen

honorary ['ɔnərərɪ] *adj* ehrenamtlich; (*title, degree*) Ehren-

honour, (*US*) **honor** ['ɔnəʳ] *vt* ehren; (*commitment, promise*) stehen zu ▹ *n* Ehre *f*; (*tribute*) Auszeichnung *f*; **in ~ of** zu Ehren von *or +gen*

honourable ['ɔnərəbl] *adj* (*person*) ehrenwert; (*action, defeat*) ehrenvoll
honours degree ['ɔnəz-] *n akademischer Grad mit Prüfung im Spezialfach*
hood [hud] *n* (*of coat etc*) Kapuze *f*; (*of cooker*) Abzugshaube *f*; (*Aut: Brit: folding roof*) Verdeck *nt*; (: *US: bonnet*) (Motor)haube *f*
hoof [hu:f] (*pl* **hooves**) *n* Huf *m*
hook [huk] *n* Haken *m* ▷ *vt* festhaken; (*fish*) an die Angel bekommen; **by ~ or by crook** auf Biegen und Brechen; **to be ~ed on** (*inf: film, exhibition, etc*) fasziniert sein von; (: *drugs*) abhängig sein von; (: *person*) stehen auf *+acc*
▸ **hook up** *vt* (*Radio, TV etc*) anschließen
hooligan ['hu:lɪgən] *n* Rowdy *m*
hoop [hu:p] *n* Reifen *m*; (*for croquet: arch*) Tor *nt*
hoot [hu:t] *vi* hupen; (*siren*) heulen; (*owl*) schreien, rufen; (*person*) johlen ▷ *vt* (*horn*) drücken auf *+acc* ▷ *n* (*see vi*) Hupen *nt*; Heulen *nt*; Schreien *nt*, Rufen *nt*; Johlen *nt*; **to ~ with laughter** in johlendes Gelächter ausbrechen
hooter ['hu:təʳ] *n* (*Brit: Aut*) Hupe *f*; (*Naut, of factory*) Sirene *f*
Hoover® ['hu:vəʳ] (*Brit*) *n* Staubsauger *m* ▷ *vt*: **hoover** (*carpet*) saugen
hooves [hu:vz] *npl of* **hoof**
hop [hɔp] *vi* hüpfen ▷ *n* Hüpfer *m*; *see also* **hops**
hope [həup] *vi* hoffen ▷ *n* Hoffnung *f* ▷ *vt*: **to ~ that** hoffen, dass; **I ~ so** ich hoffe es, hoffentlich; **I ~ not** ich hoffe nicht, hoffentlich nicht; **to ~ for the best** das Beste hoffen; **to have no ~ of sth/doing sth** keine Hoffnung auf etw *+acc* haben/darauf haben, etw zu tun; **in the ~ of/that** in der Hoffnung auf/, dass; **to ~ to do sth** hoffen, etw zu tun
hopeful ['həupful] *adj* hoffnungsvoll; (*situation*) vielversprechend; **I'm ~ that she'll manage** ich hoffe, dass sie es schafft
hopefully ['həupfulɪ] *adv* hoffnungsvoll; (*one hopes*) hoffentlich; **~, he'll come back** hoffentlich kommt er wieder
hopeless ['həuplɪs] *adj* hoffnungslos; (*situation*) aussichtslos; (*useless*): **to be ~ at sth** etw überhaupt nicht können
hops [hɔps] *npl* Hopfen *m*
horizon [hə'raɪzn] *n* Horizont *m*
horizontal [hɔrɪ'zɔntl] *adj* horizontal
hormone ['hɔ:məun] *n* Hormon *nt*
horn [hɔ:n] *n* Horn *nt*; (*Aut*) Hupe *f*
hornet ['hɔ:nɪt] *n* Hornisse *f*
horoscope ['hɔrəskəup] *n* Horoskop *nt*
horrendous [hə'rɛndəs] *adj* abscheulich, entsetzlich
horrible ['hɔrɪbl] *adj* fürchterlich, schrecklich; (*scream, dream*) furchtbar
horrid ['hɔrɪd] *adj* entsetzlich, schrecklich
horrific [hɔ'rɪfɪk] *adj* entsetzlich, schrecklich
horrify ['hɔrɪfaɪ] *vt* entsetzen
horrifying ['hɔrɪfaɪɪŋ] *adj* schrecklich, fürchterlich, entsetzlich
horror ['hɔrəʳ] *n* Entsetzen *nt*, Grauen *nt*; **~ (of sth)** (*abhorrence*) Abscheu *m* (vor etw *dat*); **the ~s of war** die Schrecken *pl* des Krieges
horror film *n* Horrorfilm *m*
horse [hɔ:s] *n* Pferd *nt*
horseback ['hɔ:sbæk]: **on ~** *adj, adv* zu Pferd
horse chestnut *n* Rosskastanie *f*
horseman ['hɔ:smən] (*irreg: like* **man**) *n* Reiter *m*
horsepower ['hɔ:spauəʳ] *n* Pferdestärke *f*
horseradish ['hɔ:srædɪʃ] *n* Meerrettich *m*
horseshoe ['hɔ:sʃu:] *n* Hufeisen *nt*
hose [həuz] *n* (*also*: **hose pipe**) Schlauch *m*
▸ **hose down** *vt* abspritzen
hospitable ['hɔspɪtəbl] *adj* gastfreundlich; (*climate*) freundlich
hospital ['hɔspɪtl] *n* Krankenhaus *nt*; **in ~, in the ~** (*US*) im Krankenhaus
hospitality [hɔspɪ'tælɪtɪ] *n* Gastfreundschaft *f*
host [həust] *n* Gastgeber *m*; (*Rel*) Hostie *f* ▷ *adj* Gast- ▷ *vt* Gastgeber sein bei; **a ~ of** eine Menge
hostage ['hɔstɪdʒ] *n* Geisel *f*; **to be taken/held ~** als Geisel genommen/festgehalten werden
hostel ['hɔstl] *n* (Wohn)heim *nt*; (*also*: **youth hostel**) Jugendherberge *f*
hostess ['həustɪs] *n* Gastgeberin *f*; (*Brit: also*: **air hostess**) Stewardess *f*; (*in night-club*) Hostess *f*
hostile ['hɔstaɪl] *adj* (*conditions*) ungünstig; (*environment*) unwirtlich; (*person*): **~ (to** *or* **towards)** feindselig (gegenüber *+dat*)
hostility [hɔ'stɪlɪtɪ] *n* Feindseligkeit *f*; **hostilities** *npl* (*fighting*) Feindseligkeiten *pl*
hot [hɔt] *adj* heiß; (*moderately hot*) warm; (*spicy*) scharf; (*temper*) hitzig; **I am** *or* **feel ~** mir ist heiß; **to be ~ on sth** (*knowledgeable etc*) sich gut mit etw auskennen; (*strict*) sehr auf etw *acc* achten
▸ **hot up** (*Brit: inf*) *vi* (*situation*) sich verschärfen *or* zuspitzen; (*party*) in Schwung kommen ▷ *vt* (*pace*) steigern; (*engine*) frisieren
hotbed ['hɔtbɛd] *n* (*fig*) Brutstätte *f*
hot dog *n* Hotdog *m or nt*
hotel [həu'tɛl] *n* Hotel *nt*
hothouse ['hɔthaus] *n* Treibhaus *nt*
hotly ['hɔtlɪ] *adv* (*contest*) heiß; (*speak, deny*) heftig
hotplate ['hɔtpleɪt] *n* Kochplatte *f*
hotpot ['hɔtpɔt] (*Brit*) *n* Fleischeintopf *m*
hot-water bottle [hɔt'wɔ:təʳ-] *n* Wärmflasche *f*
hound [haund] *vt* hetzen, jagen ▷ *n* Jagdhund *m*; **the ~s** die Meute
hour ['auəʳ] *n* Stunde *f*; (*time*) Zeit *f*; **at 60 miles an ~** mit 60 Meilen in der Stunde; **lunch ~** Mittagspause *f*; **to pay sb by the ~** jdn stundenweise bezahlen
hourly ['auəlɪ] *adj* stündlich; (*rate*) Stunden- ▷ *adv* stündlich, jede Stunde; (*soon*) jederzeit

house [haus] *n* Haus *nt*; (*household*) Haushalt *m*; (*dynasty*) Geschlecht *nt*, Haus *nt*; (*Theat*: *performance*) Vorstellung *f* ▷ *vt* unterbringen; **at my ~** bei mir (zu Hause); **to my ~** zu mir (nach Hause); **on the ~** (*fig*) auf Kosten des Hauses; **the H~ (of Commons)** (*Brit*) das Unterhaus; **the H~ (of Lords)** (*Brit*) das Oberhaus; **the H~ (of Representatives)** (*US*) das Repräsentantenhaus
house arrest *n* Hausarrest *m*
houseboat ['hausbəut] *n* Hausboot *nt*
housebound ['hausbaund] *adj* ans Haus gefesselt
housebreaking ['hausbreɪkɪŋ] *n* Einbruch *m*
household ['haushəuld] *n* Haushalt *m*; **to be a ~ name** ein Begriff sein
householder ['haushəuldəʳ] *n* Hausinhaber(in) *m(f)*; (*of flat*) Wohnungsinhaber(in) *m(f)*
housekeeper ['hauski:pəʳ] *n* Haushälterin *f*
housekeeping ['hauski:pɪŋ] *n* Hauswirtschaft *f*; (*money*) Haushaltsgeld *nt*, Wirtschaftsgeld *nt*
house-warming ['hauswɔ:mɪŋ], **house-warming party** *n* Einzugsparty *f*
housewife ['hauswaɪf] (*irreg*: *like* **wife**) *n* Hausfrau *f*
housework ['hauswə:k] *n* Hausarbeit *f*
housing ['hauzɪŋ] *n* Wohnungen *pl*; (*provision*) Wohnungsbeschaffung *f* ▷ *cpd* Wohnungs-
housing development *n* (Wohn)siedlung *f*
hovel ['hɔvl] *n* (armselige) Hütte *f*
hover ['hɔvəʳ] *vi* schweben; (*person*) herumstehen; **to ~ round sb** jdm nicht von der Seite weichen
hovercraft ['hɔvəkrɑ:ft] *n* Hovercraft *nt*, Luftkissenfahrzeug *nt*
how [hau] *adv* **1** (*in what way*) wie; **how was the film?** wie war der Film?; **how is school?** was macht die Schule?; **how are you?** wie geht es Ihnen?
2 (*to what degree*): **how much milk?** wie viel Milch?; **how many people?** wie viele Leute?; **how long have you been here?** wie lange sind Sie schon hier?; **how old are you?** wie alt bist du?; **how lovely/awful!** wie schön/furchtbar!
however [hau'ɛvəʳ] *conj* jedoch, aber ▷ *adv* wie ... auch; (*in questions*) wie ... bloß *or* nur
howl [haul] *vi* heulen; (*animal*) jaulen; (*baby, person*) schreien ▷ *n* (*see vb*) Heulen *nt*; Jaulen *nt*; Schreien *nt*
h.p. *abbr* (*Aut*: = *horsepower*) PS
HQ *abbr* = **headquarters**
hr *abbr* (= *hour*) Std.
hrs *abbr* (= *hours*) Std.
HTML (*Comput*) *abbr* (= *hypertext markup language*) HTML *f*
hub [hʌb] *n* (Rad)nabe *f*; (*fig*: *centre*) Mittelpunkt *m*, Zentrum *nt*
hubcap ['hʌbkæp] *n* Radkappe *f*
huddle ['hʌdl] *vi*: **to ~ together** sich zusammendrängen ▷ *n*: **in a ~** dicht zusammengedrängt
hue [hju:] *n* Farbton *m*
huff [hʌf] *n*: **in a ~** beleidigt, eingeschnappt ▷ *vi*: **to ~ and puff** sich aufregen
hug [hʌg] *vt* umarmen; (*thing*) umklammern ▷ *n* Umarmung *f*; **to give sb a ~** jdn umarmen
huge [hju:dʒ] *adj* riesig
hulk [hʌlk] *n* (*wrecked ship*) Wrack *nt*; (*person, building etc*) Klotz *m*
hull [hʌl] *n* Schiffsrumpf *m*; (*of nuts*) Schale *f*; (*of fruit*) Blättchen *nt* ▷ *vt* (*fruit*) entstielen
hullo [hə'ləu] *excl* = **hello**
hum [hʌm] *vt* summen ▷ *vi* summen; (*machine*) brummen ▷ *n* Summen *nt*; (*of traffic*) Brausen *nt*; (*of machines*) Brummen *nt*; (*of voices*) Gemurmel *nt*
human ['hju:mən] *adj* menschlich ▷ *n* (*also*: **human being**) Mensch *m*
humane [hju:'meɪn] *adj* human
humanitarian [hju:mænɪ'tɛərɪən] *adj* humanitär
humanity [hju:'mænɪtɪ] *n* Menschlichkeit *f*; (*mankind*) Menschheit *f*; (*humaneness*) Humanität *f*; **humanities** *npl* (*Scol*): **the humanities** die Geisteswissenschaften *pl*
human rights *npl* Menschenrechte *pl*
humble ['hʌmbl] *adj* bescheiden ▷ *vt* demütigen
humdrum ['hʌmdrʌm] *adj* eintönig, langweilig
humid ['hju:mɪd] *adj* feucht
humidity [hju:'mɪdɪtɪ] *n* Feuchtigkeit *f*
humiliate [hju:'mɪlɪeɪt] *vt* demütigen
humiliating [hju:'mɪlɪeɪtɪŋ] *adj* demütigend
humiliation [hju:mɪlɪ'eɪʃən] *n* Demütigung *f*
humorous ['hju:mərəs] *adj* (*remark*) witzig; (*book*) lustig; (*person*) humorvoll
humour, (*US*) **humor** ['hju:məʳ] *n* Humor *m*; (*mood*) Stimmung *f* ▷ *vt* seinen Willen lassen *+dat*; **sense of ~** (Sinn *m* für) Humor; **to be in good/bad ~** gute/schlechte Laune haben
hump [hʌmp] *n* Hügel *m*; (*of camel*) Höcker *m*; (*deformity*) Buckel *m*
hunch [hʌntʃ] *n* Gefühl *nt*, Ahnung *f*; **I have a ~ that ...** ich habe den (leisen) Verdacht, dass ...
hunchback ['hʌntʃbæk] *n* Bucklige(r) *f(m)*
hunched [hʌntʃt] *adj* gebeugt; (*shoulders*) hochgezogen; (*back*) krumm
hundred ['hʌndrəd] *num* hundert; **a** *or* **one ~ books/people/dollars** (ein)hundert Bücher/Personen/Dollar; **~s of** Hunderte von; **I'm a ~ per cent sure** ich bin absolut sicher
hundredth ['hʌndrədθ] *num* hundertste(r, s)
hundredweight ['hʌndrɪdweɪt] *n* *Gewichtseinheit* (*Brit* = *50,8 kg*; *US* = *45,3 kg*), ≈ Zentner *m*
hung [hʌŋ] *pt, pp of* **hang**
Hungarian [hʌŋ'gɛərɪən] *adj* ungarisch ▷ *n* Ungar(in) *m(f)*; (*Ling*) Ungarisch *nt*
Hungary ['hʌŋgərɪ] *n* Ungarn *nt*

hunger ['hʌŋgəʳ] *n* Hunger *m* ▷ *vi*: **to ~ for** hungern nach
hungry ['hʌŋgrɪ] *adj* hungrig; **to be ~** Hunger haben; **to be ~ for** hungern nach; (*news*) sehnsüchtig warten auf; **to go ~** hungern
hunk [hʌŋk] *n* großes Stück *nt*; (*inf: man*) (großer, gut aussehender) Mann *m*
hunt [hʌnt] *vt* jagen; (*criminal, fugitive*) fahnden nach ▷ *vi* (*Sport*) jagen ▷ *n* (*see vb*) Jagd *f*; Fahndung *f*; (*search*) Suche *f*; **to ~ for** (*search*) suchen (nach)
▸ **hunt down** *vt* Jagd machen auf +*acc*
hunter ['hʌntəʳ] *n* Jäger(in) *m(f)*
hunting ['hʌntɪŋ] *n* Jagd *f*, Jagen *nt*
hurdle ['hə:dl] *n* Hürde *f*
hurl [hə:l] *vt* schleudern; **to ~ sth at sb** (*also fig*) jdm etw entgegenschleudern
hurrah [hu'rɑ:] *n* Hurra *nt* ▷ *excl* hurra
hurricane ['hʌrɪkən] *n* Orkan *m*
hurried ['hʌrɪd] *adj* eilig; (*departure*) überstürzt
hurriedly ['hʌrɪdlɪ] *adv* eilig
hurry ['hʌrɪ] *n* Eile *f* ▷ *vi* eilen; (*to do sth*) sich beeilen ▷ *vt* (zur Eile) antreiben; (*work*) beschleunigen; **to be in a ~** es eilig haben; **to do sth in a ~** etw schnell tun; **there's no ~** es eilt nicht; **what's the ~?** warum so eilig?; **they hurried to help him** sie eilten ihm zu Hilfe; **to ~ home** nach Hause eilen
▸ **hurry along** *vi* sich beeilen
▸ **hurry away** *vi* schnell weggehen, forteilen
▸ **hurry off** *vi* = **hurry away**
▸ **hurry up** *vt* (zur Eile) antreiben ▷ *vi* sich beeilen
hurt [hə:t] (*pt, pp* **~**) *vt* wehtun +*dat*; (*injure, fig*) verletzen ▷ *vi* wehtun ▷ *adj* verletzt; **I've ~ my arm** ich habe mir am Arm wehgetan; (*injured*) ich habe mir den Arm verletzt; **where does it ~?** wo tut es weh?
hurtful ['hə:tful] *adj* verletzend
hurtle ['hə:tl] *vi*: **to ~ past** vorbeisausen; **to ~ down** (*fall*) hinunterfallen
husband ['hʌzbənd] *n* (Ehe)mann *m*
hush [hʌʃ] *n* Stille *f* ▷ *vt* zum Schweigen bringen; **~!** pst!
▸ **hush up** *vt* vertuschen
husk [hʌsk] *n* Schale *f*; (*of wheat*) Spelze *f*; (*of maize*) Hüllblatt *nt*
husky ['hʌskɪ] *adj* (*voice*) rau ▷ *n* Schlittenhund *m*
hustle ['hʌsl] *vt* drängen ▷ *n*: **~ and bustle** Geschäftigkeit *f*
hut [hʌt] *n* Hütte *f*
hutch [hʌtʃ] *n* (Kaninchen)stall *m*
hyacinth ['haɪəsɪnθ] *n* Hyazinthe *f*
hydrant ['haɪdrənt] *n* (*also*: **fire hydrant**) Hydrant *m*
hydraulic [haɪ'drɔ:lɪk] *adj* hydraulisch
hydroelectric ['haɪdrəuɪ'lɛktrɪk] *adj* hydroelektrisch
hydrofoil ['haɪdrəfɔɪl] *n* Tragflächenboot *nt*, Tragflügelboot *nt*
hydrogen ['haɪdrədʒən] *n* Wasserstoff *m*
hyena [haɪ'i:nə] *n* Hyäne *f*
hygiene ['haɪdʒi:n] *n* Hygiene *f*
hygienic [haɪ'dʒi:nɪk] *adj* hygienisch
hymn [hɪm] *n* Kirchenlied *nt*
hype [haɪp] (*inf*) *n* Rummel *m*
hypermarket ['haɪpəmɑ:kɪt] (*Brit*) *n* Verbrauchermarkt *m*
hypertext ['haɪpətɛkst] *n* (*Comput*) Hypertext *m*
hyphen ['haɪfn] *n* Bindestrich *m*; (*at end of line*) Trennungsstrich *m*
hypnotize ['hɪpnətaɪz] *vt* hypnotisieren
hypocrisy [hɪ'pɔkrɪsɪ] *n* Heuchelei *f*
hypocrite ['hɪpəkrɪt] *n* Heuchler(in) *m(f)*
hypocritical [hɪpə'krɪtɪkl] *adj* heuchlerisch
hypothesis [haɪ'pɔθɪsɪs] (*pl* **hypotheses**) *n* Hypothese *f*
hysterical [hɪ'stɛrɪkl] *adj* hysterisch; (*situation*) wahnsinnig komisch; **to become ~** hysterisch werden
hysterics [hɪ'stɛrɪks] *npl*: **to be in** *or* **to have ~** einen hysterischen Anfall haben; (*laughter*) einen Lachanfall haben

Ii

I¹, i [aɪ] *n (letter)* I *nt*, i *nt*; **I for Isaac, I for Item** *(US)* ≈ I wie Ida
I² [aɪ] *pron* ich
ice [aɪs] *n* Eis *nt*; *(on road)* Glatteis *nt* ▷ *vt (cake)* mit Zuckerguss überziehen, glasieren ▷ *vi (also:* **ice over, ice up***)* vereisen; *(puddle etc)* zufrieren; **to put sth on ~** *(fig)* etw auf Eis legen
iceberg ['aɪsbəːg] *n* Eisberg *m*; **the tip of the ~** *(fig)* die Spitze des Eisbergs
icebox ['aɪsbɔks] *n (US: fridge)* Kühlschrank *m*; *(Brit: compartment)* Eisfach *nt*; *(insulated box)* Kühltasche *f*
ice cream *n* Eis *nt*
ice cube *n* Eiswürfel *m*
iced [aɪst] *adj (cake)* mit Zuckerguss überzogen, glasiert; *(beer etc)* eisgekühlt; *(tea, coffee)* Eis-
ice hockey *n* Eishockey *nt*
Iceland ['aɪslənd] *n* Island *nt*
Icelander ['aɪsləndəʳ] *n* Isländer(in) *m(f)*
Icelandic [aɪs'lændɪk] *adj* isländisch ▷ *n (Ling)* Isländisch *nt*
ice lolly *(Brit) n* Eis *nt* am Stiel
ice rink *n* (Kunst)eisbahn *f*, Schlittschuhbahn *f*
icicle ['aɪsɪkl] *n* Eiszapfen *m*
icing ['aɪsɪŋ] *n (Culin)* Zuckerguss *m*; *(Aviat etc)* Vereisung *f*
icing sugar *(Brit) n* Puderzucker *m*
icon ['aɪkɔn] *n* Ikone *f*; *(Comput)* Ikon *nt*
ICT *(Brit) n abbr (Scol)* = **information and communication technology**
icy ['aɪsɪ] *adj* eisig; *(road)* vereist
I'd [aɪd] = **I would**; = **I had**
ID card *n* = **identity card**
idea [aɪ'dɪə] *n* Idee *f*; *(opinion)* Ansicht *f*; *(notion)* Vorstellung *f*; *(objective)* Ziel *nt*; **good ~!** gute Idee!; **to have a good ~ that** sich *dat* ziemlich sicher sein, dass; **I haven't the least ~** ich habe nicht die leiseste Ahnung
ideal [aɪ'dɪəl] *n* Ideal *nt* ▷ *adj* ideal
ideally [aɪ'dɪəlɪ] *adv* ideal; **~ the book should ...** idealerweise *or* im Idealfall sollte das Buch ...; **she's ~ suited for ...** sie eignet sich hervorragend für ...
identical [aɪ'dɛntɪkl] *adj* identisch; *(twins)* eineiig
identification [aɪdɛntɪfɪ'keɪʃən] *n* Identifizierung *f*; **(means of) ~** Ausweispapiere *pl*
identify [aɪ'dɛntɪfaɪ] *vt (recognize)* erkennen; *(distinguish)* identifizieren; **to ~ sb/sth with** jdn/etw identifizieren mit
Identikit® [aɪ'dɛntɪkɪt] *n*: **~ (picture)** Phantombild *nt*
identity [aɪ'dɛntɪtɪ] *n* Identität *f*
identity card *n* (Personal)ausweis *m*
ideology [aɪdɪ'ɔlədʒɪ] *n* Ideologie *f*, Weltanschauung *f*
idiom ['ɪdɪəm] *n (style)* Ausdrucksweise *f*; *(phrase)* Redewendung *f*
idiosyncrasy [ɪdɪəu'sɪŋkrəsɪ] *n* Eigenheit *f*, Eigenart *f*
idiot ['ɪdɪət] *n* Idiot(in) *m(f)*, Dummkopf *m*
idiotic [ɪdɪ'ɔtɪk] *adj* idiotisch, blöd(sinnig)
idle ['aɪdl] *adj* untätig; *(lazy)* faul; *(unemployed)* unbeschäftigt; *(machinery, factory)* stillstehend; *(question)* müßig; *(conversation, pleasure)* leer ▷ *vi* leerlaufen, im Leerlauf sein; **to lie ~** *(machinery)* außer Betrieb sein; *(factory)* die Arbeit eingestellt haben
▶ **idle away** *vt (time)* vertrödeln, verbummeln
idol ['aɪdl] *n* Idol *nt*; *(Rel)* Götzenbild *nt*
idolize ['aɪdəlaɪz] *vt* vergöttern
idyllic [ɪ'dɪlɪk] *adj* idyllisch
i.e. *abbr (= id est)* d. h.
if [ɪf] *conj* **1** *(given that, providing that etc)* wenn, falls; **if anyone comes in** wenn *or* falls jemand hereinkommt; **if necessary** wenn *or* falls nötig; **if I were you** wenn ich Sie wäre, an Ihrer Stelle
2 *(whenever)* wenn
3 *(although)*: **(even) if** auch *or* selbst wenn; **I like it, (even) if you don't** mir gefällt es, auch wenn du es nicht magst
4 *(whether)* ob; **ask him if he can come** frag ihn, ob er kommen kann
5: if so/not falls ja/nein; **if only** wenn nur; *see also* **as**
ignite [ɪg'naɪt] *vt* entzünden ▷ *vi* sich entzünden
ignition [ɪg'nɪʃən] *n (Aut)* Zündung *f*
ignition key *n (Aut)* Zündschlüssel *m*
ignorance ['ɪgnərəns] *n* Unwissenheit *f*, Ignoranz *f*; **to keep sb in ~ of sth** jdn in Unkenntnis über etw *acc* lassen
ignorant ['ɪgnərənt] *adj* unwissend,

ignorant; **to be ~ of** (*subject*) sich nicht auskennen in *+dat*; (*events*) nicht informiert sein über *+acc*
ignore [ɪg'nɔːʳ] *vt* ignorieren; (*fact*) außer Acht lassen
I'll [aɪl] = **I will**; = **I shall**
ill [ɪl] *adj* krank; (*effects*) schädlich ▷ *n* Übel *nt*; (*trouble*) Schlechte(s) *nt* ▷ *adv*: **to speak ~ of sb** Schlechtes über jdn sagen; **to be taken ~** krank werden; **to think ~ of sb** schlecht von jdm denken
ill-advised [ɪləd'vaɪzd] *adj* unklug; (*person*) schlecht beraten
illegal [ɪ'liːgl] *adj* illegal
illegible [ɪ'lɛdʒɪbl] *adj* unleserlich
illegitimate [ɪlɪ'dʒɪtɪmət] *adj* (*child*) unehelich; (*activity, treaty*) unzulässig
ill-fated [ɪl'feɪtɪd] *adj* unglückselig
ill feeling *n* Verstimmung *f*
ill health *n* schlechter Gesundheitszustand *m*
illiterate [ɪ'lɪtərət] *adj* (*person*) des Lesens und Schreibens unkundig; (*letter*) voller Fehler
ill-mannered [ɪl'mænəd] *adj* unhöflich
illness ['ɪlnɪs] *n* Krankheit *f*
ill-treat [ɪl'triːt] *vt* misshandeln
illuminate [ɪ'luːmɪneɪt] *vt* beleuchten
illumination [ɪluːmɪ'neɪʃən] *n* Beleuchtung *f*; **illuminations** *npl* (*decorative lights*) festliche Beleuchtung *f*, Illumination *f*
illusion [ɪ'luːʒən] *n* Illusion *f*; (*trick*) (Zauber)trick *m*; **to be under the ~ that ...** sich *dat* einbilden, dass ...
illustrate ['ɪləstreɪt] *vt* veranschaulichen; (*book*) illustrieren
illustration [ɪlə'streɪʃən] *n* Illustration *f*; (*example*) Veranschaulichung *f*
ill will *n* böses Blut *nt*
I'm [aɪm] = **I am**
image ['ɪmɪdʒ] *n* Bild *nt*; (*public face*) Image *nt*; (*reflection*) Abbild *nt*
imagery ['ɪmɪdʒərɪ] *n* (*in writing*) Metaphorik *f*; (*in painting etc*) Symbolik *f*
imaginary [ɪ'mædʒɪnərɪ] *adj* erfunden; (*being*) Fantasie-; (*danger*) eingebildet
imagination [ɪmædʒɪ'neɪʃən] *n* Fantasie *f*; (*illusion*) Einbildung *f*; **it's just your ~** das bildest du dir nur ein
imaginative [ɪ'mædʒɪnətɪv] *adj* fantasievoll; (*solution*) einfallsreich
imagine [ɪ'mædʒɪn] *vt* sich *dat* vorstellen; (*dream*) sich *dat* träumen lassen; (*suppose*) vermuten
imbalance [ɪm'bæləns] *n* Unausgeglichenheit *f*
imitate ['ɪmɪteɪt] *vt* imitieren; (*mimic*) nachahmen
imitation [ɪmɪ'teɪʃən] *n* Imitation *f*, Nachahmung *f*
immaculate [ɪ'mækjulət] *adj* makellos; (*appearance, piece of work*) tadellos; (*Rel*) unbefleckt
immaterial [ɪmə'tɪərɪəl] *adj* unwichtig, unwesentlich
immature [ɪmə'tjuəʳ] *adj* unreif; (*organism*) noch nicht voll entwickelt
immediate [ɪ'miːdɪət] *adj* sofortig; (*need*) dringend; (*neighbourhood, family*) nächste(r, s)
immediately [ɪ'miːdɪətlɪ] *adv* sofort; (*directly*) unmittelbar; **~ next to** direkt neben
immense [ɪ'mɛns] *adj* riesig, enorm
immerse [ɪ'məːs] *vt* eintauchen; **to ~ sth in** etw tauchen in *+acc*; **to be ~d in** (*fig*) vertieft sein in *+acc*
immersion heater [ɪ'məːʃən-] (*Brit*) *n* elektrischer Heißwasserboiler *m*
immigrant ['ɪmɪgrənt] *n* Einwanderer *m*, Einwanderin *f*
immigration [ɪmɪ'greɪʃən] *n* Einwanderung *f*; (*at airport etc*) Einwanderungsstelle *f* ▷ *cpd* Einwanderungs-
imminent ['ɪmɪnənt] *adj* bevorstehend
immoral [ɪ'mɔrl] *adj* unmoralisch; (*behaviour*) unsittlich
immortal [ɪ'mɔːtl] *adj* unsterblich
immune [ɪ'mjuːn] *adj*: **~ (to)** (*disease*) immun (gegen); (*flattery*) unempfänglich (für); (*criticism*) unempfindlich (gegen); (*attack*) sicher (vor *+dat*)
immune system *n* Immunsystem *nt*
immunity [ɪ'mjuːnɪtɪ] *n* (*see adj*) Immunität *f*; Unempfänglichkeit *f*; Unempfindlichkeit *f*; Sicherheit *f*; (*of diplomat, from prosecution*) Immunität *f*
immunize ['ɪmjunaɪz] *vt*: **to ~ (against)** immunisieren (gegen)
impact ['ɪmpækt] *n* Aufprall *m*; (*of crash*) Wucht *f*; (*of law, measure*) (Aus)wirkung *f*
impair [ɪm'pɛəʳ] *vt* beeinträchtigen
impart [ɪm'pɑːt] *vt*: **to ~ (to)** (*information*) mitteilen *+dat*; (*flavour*) verleihen *+dat*
impartial [ɪm'pɑːʃl] *adj* unparteiisch
impassable [ɪm'pɑːsəbl] *adj* unpassierbar
impassive [ɪm'pæsɪv] *adj* gelassen
impatience [ɪm'peɪʃəns] *n* Ungeduld *f*
impatient [ɪm'peɪʃənt] *adj* ungeduldig; **to get** *or* **grow ~** ungeduldig werden; **to be ~ to do sth** es nicht erwarten können, etw zu tun
impatiently [ɪm'peɪʃəntlɪ] *adv* ungeduldig
impeccable [ɪm'pɛkəbl] *adj* (*dress*) untadelig; (*manners*) tadellos
impede [ɪm'piːd] *vt* behindern
impediment [ɪm'pɛdɪmənt] *n* Hindernis *nt*; (*also*: **speech impediment**) Sprachfehler *m*
impending [ɪm'pɛndɪŋ] *adj* bevorstehend; (*catastrophe*) drohend
imperative [ɪm'pɛrətɪv] *adj* dringend; (*tone*) Befehls- ▷ *n* (*Ling*) Imperativ *m*, Befehlsform *f*
imperfect [ɪm'pəːfɪkt] *adj* mangelhaft; (*goods*) fehlerhaft ▷ *n* (*Ling*: *also*: **imperfect tense**) Imperfekt *nt*, Vergangenheit *f*
imperial [ɪm'pɪərɪəl] *adj* kaiserlich; (*Brit*: *measure*) britisch
impersonal [ɪm'pəːsənl] *adj* unpersönlich
impersonate [ɪm'pəːsəneɪt] *vt* sich ausgeben als; (*Theat*) imitieren
impertinent [ɪm'pəːtɪnənt] *adj* unverschämt

impervious [ɪm'pə:vɪəs] *adj*: **~ to** (*criticism, pressure*) unberührt von; (*charm, influence*) unempfänglich für
impetuous [ɪm'pɛtjuəs] *adj* ungestüm, stürmisch; (*act*) impulsiv
impetus ['ɪmpətəs] *n* Schwung *m*; (*fig: driving force*) treibende Kraft *f*
impinge [ɪm'pɪndʒ]: **to ~ on** *vt fus* sich auswirken auf *+acc*; (*rights*) einschränken
implant [ɪm'plɑ:nt] *vt* (*Med*) einpflanzen; (*fig: idea, principle*) einimpfen
implement [*n* 'ɪmplɪmənt, *vt* 'ɪmplɪmɛnt] *n* Gerät *nt*, Werkzeug *nt* ▷ *vt* durchführen
implicate ['ɪmplɪkeɪt] *vt* verwickeln
implication [ɪmplɪ'keɪʃən] *n* Auswirkung *f*; (*involvement*) Verwicklung *f*; **by ~** implizit
implicit [ɪm'plɪsɪt] *adj* (*inferred*) implizit, unausgesprochen; (*unquestioning*) absolut
imply [ɪm'plaɪ] *vt* andeuten; (*mean*) bedeuten
impolite [ɪmpə'laɪt] *adj* unhöflich
import [*vt* ɪm'pɔ:t, *n* 'ɪmpɔ:t] *vt* importieren, einführen ▷ *n* Import *m*, Einfuhr *f*; (*article*) Importgut *nt* ▷ *cpd* Import-, Einfuhr-
importance [ɪm'pɔ:tns] *n* (*see adj*) Wichtigkeit *f*; Bedeutung *f*; **to be of little/great ~** nicht besonders wichtig/sehr wichtig sein
important [ɪm'pɔ:tənt] *adj* wichtig; (*influential*) bedeutend; **it's not ~** es ist unwichtig
importer [ɪm'pɔ:tər] *n* Importeur *m*
impose [ɪm'pəuz] *vt* auferlegen; (*sanctions*) verhängen ▷ *vi*: **to ~ on sb** jdm zur Last fallen
imposing [ɪm'pəuzɪŋ] *adj* eindrucksvoll
imposition [ɪmpə'zɪʃən] *n* (*of tax etc*) Auferlegung *f*; **to be an ~ on** eine Zumutung sein für
impossible [ɪm'pɔsɪbl] *adj* unmöglich; **it's ~ for me to leave now** ich kann jetzt unmöglich gehen
impotent ['ɪmpətnt] *adj* machtlos; (*Med*) impotent
impound [ɪm'paund] *vt* beschlagnahmen
impoverished [ɪm'pɔvərɪʃt] *adj* verarmt
impractical [ɪm'præktɪkl] *adj* (*plan*) undurchführbar; (*person*) unpraktisch
impregnable [ɪm'prɛgnəbl] *adj* uneinnehmbar; (*fig*) unerschütterlich
impress [ɪm'prɛs] *vt* beeindrucken; (*mark*) aufdrücken; **to ~ sth on sb** jdm etw einschärfen
impression [ɪm'prɛʃən] *n* Eindruck *m*; (*of stamp, seal*) Abdruck *m*; (*imitation*) Nachahmung *f*, Imitation *f*; **to make a good/bad ~ on sb** einen guten/schlechten Eindruck auf jdn machen; **to be under the ~ that ...** den Eindruck haben, dass ...
impressionist [ɪm'prɛʃənɪst] *n* Impressionist(in) *m(f)*; (*entertainer*) Imitator(in) *m(f)*
impressive [ɪm'prɛsɪv] *adj* beeindruckend
imprint ['ɪmprɪnt] *n* (*of hand etc*) Abdruck *m*; (*Publishing*) Impressum *nt*
imprison [ɪm'prɪzn] *vt* inhaftieren, einsperren
imprisonment [ɪm'prɪznmənt] *n* Gefangenschaft *f*; **three years' ~** drei Jahre Gefängnis *or* Freiheitsstrafe
improbable [ɪm'prɔbəbl] *adj* unwahrscheinlich
improper [ɪm'prɔpər] *adj* ungehörig; (*procedure*) unrichtig; (*dishonest*) unlauter
improve [ɪm'pru:v] *vt* verbessern ▷ *vi* sich bessern; **the patient is improving** dem Patienten geht es besser
▸ **improve (up)on** *vt fus* verbessern
improvement [ɪm'pru:vmənt] *n*: **~ (in)** Verbesserung *f* (*+gen*); **to make ~s to** Verbesserungen durchführen an *+dat*
improvise ['ɪmprəvaɪz] *vt, vi* improvisieren
impudent ['ɪmpjudnt] *adj* unverschämt
impulse ['ɪmpʌls] *n* Impuls *m*; (*urge*) Drang *m*; **to act on ~** aus einem Impuls heraus handeln
impulsive [ɪm'pʌlsɪv] *adj* impulsiv, spontan; (*purchase*) Impulsiv-
in [ɪn] *prep* **1** (*indicating place, position*) in *+dat*; (*with motion*) in *+acc*; **in the house/garden** im Haus/Garten; **in town** in der Stadt; **in the country** auf dem Land; **in here** hierin; **in there** darin
2 (*with place names: of town, region, country*) in *+dat*; **in London/Bavaria** in London/Bayern
3 (*indicating time*) in *+dat*; **in spring/summer/May** im Frühling/Sommer/Mai; **in 1994** 1994; **in the afternoon** am Nachmittag; **at 4 o'clock in the afternoon** um 4 Uhr nachmittags; **I did it in 3 hours/days** ich habe es in 3 Stunden/Tagen gemacht; **in 2 weeks** *or* **2 weeks' time** in 2 Wochen
4 (*indicating manner, circumstances, state*) in *+dat*; **in a loud/soft voice** mit lauter/weicher Stimme; **in English/German** auf Englisch/Deutsch; **in the sun** in der Sonne; **in the rain** im Regen; **in good condition** in guter Verfassung
5 (*with ratios, numbers*): **1 in 10** eine(r, s) von 10; **20 pence in the pound** 20 Pence pro Pfund; **they lined up in twos** sie stellten sich in Zweierreihen auf
6 (*referring to people, works*): **the disease is common in children** die Krankheit ist bei Kindern verbreitet; **in (the works of) Dickens** bei Dickens; **they have a good leader in him** in ihm haben sie einen guten Führer
7 (*indicating profession etc*): **to be in teaching/the army** Lehrer(in)/beim Militär sein
8 (*with present participle*): **in saying this, I ...** wenn ich das sage, ...
▷ *adv*: **to be in** (*person: at home, work*) da sein; (*train, ship, plane*) angekommen sein; (*in fashion*) in sein; **to ask sb in** jdn hereinbitten; **to run/limp** *etc* **in** hereinlaufen/-humpeln *etc*
▷ *n*: **the ins and outs** (*of proposal, situation etc*)

die Einzelheiten *pl*
in. *abbr* = **inch**
inability [ɪnə'bɪlɪtɪ] *n* Unfähigkeit *f*
inaccurate [ɪn'ækjurət] *adj* ungenau; (*not correct*) unrichtig
inadequate [ɪn'ædɪkwət] *adj* unzulänglich
inadvertently [ɪnəd'və:tntlɪ] *adv* ungewollt
inadvisable [ɪnəd'vaɪzəbl] *adj* unratsam; **it is ~ to ...** es ist nicht ratsam, zu ...
inane [ɪ'neɪn] *adj* dumm
inanimate [ɪn'ænɪmət] *adj* unbelebt
inappropriate [ɪnə'prəuprɪət] *adj* unpassend; (*word, expression*) unangebracht
inarticulate [ɪnɑ:'tɪkjulət] *adj* (*speech*) unverständlich; **he is ~** er kann sich nur schlecht ausdrücken
inaugurate [ɪ'nɔ:gjureɪt] *vt* einführen; (*president, official*) (feierlich) in sein/ihr Amt einführen
inauguration [ɪnɔ:gju'reɪʃən] *n* (*see vb*) Einführung *f*; (feierliche) Amtseinführung *f*
inborn [ɪn'bɔ:n] *adj* angeboren
inbred [ɪn'brɛd] *adj* angeboren; **an ~ family** eine Familie, in der Inzucht herrscht
Inc. *abbr* = **incorporated company**
incapable [ɪn'keɪpəbl] *adj* hilflos; **to be ~ of sth** unfähig zu etw sein; **to be ~ of doing sth** unfähig sein, etw zu tun
incapacitate [ɪnkə'pæsɪteɪt] *vt*: **to ~ sb** jdn unfähig machen
incense [*n* 'ɪnsɛns, *vt* ɪn'sɛns] *n* Weihrauch *m*; (*perfume*) Duft *m* ▷ *vt* wütend machen
incentive [ɪn'sɛntɪv] *n* Anreiz *m*
incessant [ɪn'sɛsnt] *adj* unablässig
incessantly [ɪn'sɛsntlɪ] *adv* unablässig
inch [ɪntʃ] *n* Zoll *m*; **to be within an ~ of sth** kurz vor etw *dat* stehen; **he didn't give an ~** (*fig*) er gab keinen Fingerbreit nach
▸ **inch forward** *vi* sich millimeterweise vorwärtsschieben
incidence ['ɪnsɪdns] *n* Häufigkeit *f*
incident ['ɪnsɪdnt] *n* Vorfall *m*; (*diplomatic etc*) Zwischenfall *m*
incidental [ɪnsɪ'dɛntl] *adj* zusätzlich; (*unimportant*) nebensächlich; **~ to** verbunden mit; **~ expenses** Nebenkosten *pl*
incidentally [ɪnsɪ'dɛntəlɪ] *adv* übrigens
inclination [ɪnklɪ'neɪʃən] *n* Neigung *f*
incline [*n* 'ɪnklaɪn, *vb* ɪn'klaɪn] *n* Abhang *m* ▷ *vt* neigen ▷ *vi* sich neigen; **to be ~d to** neigen zu; **to be well ~d towards sb** jdm geneigt *or* gewogen sein
include [ɪn'klu:d] *vt* einbeziehen; (*in price*) einschließen; **the tip is not ~d in the price** Trinkgeld ist im Preis nicht inbegriffen
including [ɪn'klu:dɪŋ] *prep* einschließlich; **~ service charge** inklusive Bedienung
inclusion [ɪn'klu:ʒən] *n* (*see vb*) Einbeziehung *f*; Einschluss *m*
inclusive [ɪn'klu:sɪv] *adj* (*terms*) inklusive; (*price*) Inklusiv-, Pauschal-; **~ of** einschließlich *+gen*
income ['ɪnkʌm] *n* Einkommen *nt*; (*from property, investment, pension*) Einkünfte *pl*; **gross/net ~** Brutto-/Nettoeinkommen *nt*; **~ and expenditure account** Gewinn- und Verlustrechnung *f*; **~ bracket** Einkommensklasse *f*
income support *n* ≈ Sozialhilfe *f*
income tax *n* Einkommenssteuer *f* ▷ *cpd* Steuer-
incoming ['ɪnkʌmɪŋ] *adj* (*passenger*) ankommend; (*flight*) landend; (*call, mail*) eingehend; (*government, official*) neu; (*wave*) hereinbrechend; **~ tide** Flut *f*
incompatible [ɪnkəm'pætɪbl] *adj* unvereinbar
incompetence [ɪn'kɔmpɪtns] *n* Unfähigkeit *f*
incompetent [ɪn'kɔmpɪtnt] *adj* unfähig; (*job*) unzulänglich
incomplete [ɪnkəm'pli:t] *adj* unfertig; (*partial*) unvollständig
incongruous [ɪn'kɔŋgruəs] *adj* (*strange*) absurd; (*inappropriate*) unpassend
inconsiderate [ɪnkən'sɪdərət] *adj* rücksichtslos
inconsistency [ɪnkən'sɪstənsɪ] *n* (*see adj*) Widersprüchlichkeit *f*; Inkonsequenz *f*; Unbeständigkeit *f*
inconsistent [ɪnkən'sɪstnt] *adj* widersprüchlich; (*person*) inkonsequent; (*work*) unbeständig; **to be ~ with** im Widerspruch stehen zu
inconspicuous [ɪnkən'spɪkjuəs] *adj* unauffällig; **to make o.s. ~** sich unauffällig benehmen
inconvenience [ɪnkən'vi:njəns] *n* Unannehmlichkeit *f*; (*trouble*) Umstände *pl* ▷ *vt* Umstände bereiten *+dat*; **don't ~ yourself** machen Sie sich keine Umstände
inconvenient [ɪnkən'vi:njənt] *adj* (*time, place*) ungünstig; (*house*) unbequem, unpraktisch; (*visitor*) ungelegen
incorporate [ɪn'kɔ:pəreɪt] *vt* aufnehmen; (*contain*) enthalten; **safety features have been ~d in the design** in der Konstruktion sind auch Sicherheitsvorkehrungen enthalten
incorrect [ɪnkə'rɛkt] *adj* falsch
increase [*vb* ɪn'kri:s, *n* 'ɪnkri:s] *vi* (*level etc*) zunehmen; (*price*) steigen; (*in size*) sich vergrößern; (*in number, quantity*) sich vermehren ▷ *vt* vergrößern; (*price*) erhöhen ▷ *n*: **~ (in)** Zunahme *f* (*+gen*); (*in wages, spending etc*) Erhöhung *f* (*+gen*); **an ~ of 5%** eine Erhöhung von 5%, eine Zunahme um 5%; **to be on the ~** zunehmen
increasing [ɪn'kri:sɪŋ] *adj* zunehmend
increasingly [ɪn'kri:sɪŋlɪ] *adv* zunehmend
incredible [ɪn'krɛdɪbl] *adj* unglaublich; (*amazing, wonderful*) unwahrscheinlich (*inf*), sagenhaft (*inf*)
incubator ['ɪnkjubeɪtə^r] *n* (*for babies*) Brutkasten *m*, Inkubator *m*
incumbent [ɪn'kʌmbənt] *n* Amtsinhaber(in) *m(f)* ▷ *adj*: **it is ~ on him to ...** es obliegt ihm

or es ist seine Pflicht, zu ...
incur [ɪn'kəːʳ] *vt* (*expenses, debt*) machen; (*loss*) erleiden; (*disapproval, anger*) sich *dat* zuziehen
indebted [ɪn'dɛtɪd] *adj*: **to be ~ to sb** jdm (zu Dank) verpflichtet sein
indecent [ɪn'diːsnt] *adj* unanständig, anstößig; (*haste*) ungebührlich
indecent assault (*Brit*) *n* Sexualverbrechen *nt*
indecent exposure *n* Erregung *f* öffentlichen Ärgernisses
indecisive [ɪndɪ'saɪsɪv] *adj* unentschlossen
indeed [ɪn'diːd] *adv* aber sicher; (*in fact*) tatsächlich, in der Tat; (*furthermore*) sogar; **yes ~!** oh ja!, das kann man wohl sagen!
indefinitely [ɪn'dɛfɪnɪtlɪ] *adv* (*continue*) endlos; (*wait*) unbegrenzt (lange); (*postpone*) auf unbestimmte Zeit
indemnity [ɪn'dɛmnɪtɪ] *n* (*insurance*) Versicherung *f*; (*compensation*) Entschädigung *f*
independence [ɪndɪ'pɛndns] *n* Unabhängigkeit *f*
independent [ɪndɪ'pɛndnt] *adj* unabhängig
index ['ɪndɛks] (*pl* **~es**) *n* (*in book*) Register *nt*; (*in library etc*) Katalog *m*; (*also*: **card index**) Kartei *f* (*pl* **indices**) (*ratio*) Index *m*; (: *sign*) (An)zeichen *nt*
index card *n* Karteikarte *f*
index finger *n* Zeigefinger *m*
index-linked ['ɪndɛks'lɪŋkt] *adj* der Inflationsrate *dat* angeglichen
India ['ɪndɪə] *n* Indien *nt*
Indian ['ɪndɪən] *adj* indisch; (*American Indian*) indianisch ▷ *n* Inder(in) *m(f)*; **American ~** Indianer(in) *m(f)*
Indian Ocean *n*: **the ~** der Indische Ozean
indicate ['ɪndɪkeɪt] *vt* (an)zeigen; (*point to*) deuten auf *+acc*; (*mention*) andeuten ▷ *vi* (*Brit*: *Aut*): **to ~ left/right** links/rechts blinken
indication [ɪndɪ'keɪʃən] *n* (An)zeichen *nt*
indicative [ɪn'dɪkətɪv] *n* (*Ling*) Indikativ *m*, Wirklichkeitsform *f* ▷ *adj*: **to be ~ of sth** auf etw *acc* schließen lassen
indicator ['ɪndɪkeɪtəʳ] *n* (*instrument, gauge*) Anzeiger *m*; (*fig*) (An)zeichen *nt*; (*Aut*) Richtungsanzeiger *m*, Blinker *m*
indices ['ɪndɪsiːz] *npl of* **index**
indict [ɪn'daɪt] *vt* anklagen
indictment [ɪn'daɪtmənt] *n* Anklage *f*; **to be an ~ of sth** (*fig*) ein Armutszeugnis *nt* für etw sein
indifference [ɪn'dɪfrəns] *n* Gleichgültigkeit *f*
indifferent [ɪn'dɪfrənt] *adj* gleichgültig; (*mediocre*) mittelmäßig
indigenous [ɪn'dɪdʒɪnəs] *adj* einheimisch
indigestion [ɪndɪ'dʒɛstʃən] *n* Magenverstimmung *f*
indignant [ɪn'dɪgnənt] *adj*: **to be ~ at sth/ with sb** entrüstet über etw/jdn sein
indignity [ɪn'dɪgnɪtɪ] *n* Demütigung *f*
indirect [ɪndɪ'rɛkt] *adj* indirekt; **~ way** *or* **route** Umweg *m*
indiscreet [ɪndɪs'kriːt] *adj* indiskret
indiscriminate [ɪndɪs'krɪmɪnət] *adj* wahllos; (*taste*) unkritisch
indispensable [ɪndɪs'pɛnsəbl] *adj* unentbehrlich
indisputable [ɪndɪs'pjuːtəbl] *adj* unbestreitbar
individual [ɪndɪ'vɪdjuəl] *n* Individuum *nt*, Einzelne(r) *f(m)* ▷ *adj* eigen; (*single*) einzeln; (*case, portion*) Einzel-; (*particular*) individuell
individually [ɪndɪ'vɪdjuəlɪ] *adv* einzeln, individuell
indoctrination [ɪndɔktrɪ'neɪʃən] *n* Indoktrination *f*
Indonesia [ɪndə'niːzɪə] *n* Indonesien *nt*
indoor ['ɪndɔːʳ] *adj* (*plant, aerial*) Zimmer-; (*clothes, shoes*) Haus-; (*swimming pool, sport*) Hallen-; (*games*) im Haus
indoors [ɪn'dɔːz] *adv* drinnen; **to go ~** hineingehen
induce [ɪn'djuːs] *vt* herbeiführen; (*persuade*) dazu bringen; (*Med: birth*) einleiten; **to ~ sb to do sth** jdn dazu bewegen *or* bringen, etw zu tun
inducement [ɪn'djuːsmənt] *n* Anreiz *m*; (*pej: bribe*) Bestechung *f*
indulge [ɪn'dʌldʒ] *vt* nachgeben *+dat*; (*person, child*) verwöhnen ▷ *vi*: **to ~ in** sich hingeben *+dat*
indulgence [ɪn'dʌldʒəns] *n* (*pleasure*) Luxus *m*; (*leniency*) Nachgiebigkeit *f*
indulgent [ɪn'dʌldʒənt] *adj* nachsichtig
industrial [ɪn'dʌstrɪəl] *adj* industriell; (*accident*) Arbeits-; (*city*) Industrie-
industrial action *n* Arbeitskampfmaßnahmen *pl*
industrial estate (*Brit*) *n* Industriegebiet *nt*
industrialist [ɪn'dʌstrɪəlɪst] *n* Industrielle(r) *f(m)*
industrial park (*US*) *n* = **industrial estate**
industrious [ɪn'dʌstrɪəs] *adj* fleißig
industry ['ɪndəstrɪ] *n* Industrie *f*; (*diligence*) Fleiß *m*
inebriated [ɪ'niːbrɪeɪtɪd] *adj* betrunken
inedible [ɪn'ɛdɪbl] *adj* ungenießbar
ineffective [ɪnɪ'fɛktɪv] *adj* wirkungslos; (*government*) unfähig
inefficient [ɪnɪ'fɪʃənt] *adj* ineffizient; (*machine*) leistungsunfähig
inequality [ɪnɪ'kwɔlɪtɪ] *n* Ungleichheit *f*
inescapable [ɪnɪ'skeɪpəbl] *adj* unvermeidlich; (*conclusion*) zwangsläufig
inevitable [ɪn'ɛvɪtəbl] *adj* unvermeidlich; (*result*) zwangsläufig
inevitably [ɪn'ɛvɪtəblɪ] *adv* zwangsläufig; **~, he was late** es konnte ja nicht ausbleiben, dass er zu spät kam; **as ~ happens ...** wie es immer so ist ...
inexpensive [ɪnɪk'spɛnsɪv] *adj* preisgünstig
inexperienced [ɪnɪk'spɪərɪənst] *adj* unerfahren; (*swimmer etc*) ungeübt; **to be ~ in sth** wenig Erfahrung mit etw haben
inexplicable [ɪnɪk'splɪkəbl] *adj* unerklärlich

infallible [ɪn'fælɪbl] *adj* unfehlbar
infamous ['ɪnfəməs] *adj* niederträchtig
infancy ['ɪnfənsɪ] *n* frühe Kindheit *f*; (*of movement, firm*) Anfangsstadium *nt*
infant ['ɪnfənt] *n* Säugling *m*; (*young child*) Kleinkind *nt* ▷ *cpd* Säuglings-
infantry ['ɪnfəntrɪ] *n* Infanterie *f*
infant school (*Brit*) *n* Grundschule *f* (*für die ersten beiden Jahrgänge*)
infatuated [ɪn'fætjueɪtɪd] *adj*: **~ with** vernarrt in *+acc*; **to become ~ with** sich vernarren in *+acc*
infatuation [ɪnfætju'eɪʃən] *n* Vernarrtheit *f*
infect [ɪn'fɛkt] *vt* anstecken (*also fig*), infizieren; (*food*) verseuchen; **to become ~ed** (*wound*) sich entzünden
infection [ɪn'fɛkʃən] *n* Infektion *f*, Entzündung *f*; (*contagion*) Ansteckung *f*
infectious [ɪn'fɛkʃəs] *adj* ansteckend
infer [ɪn'fəːʳ] *vt* schließen; (*imply*) andeuten
inferior [ɪn'fɪərɪəʳ] *adj* (*in rank*) untergeordnet, niedriger; (*in quality*) minderwertig; (*in quantity, number*) geringer ▷ *n* Untergebene(r) *f(m)*; **to feel ~ (to sb)** sich (jdm) unterlegen fühlen
inferiority [ɪnfɪərɪ'ɔrətɪ] *n* (*see adj*) untergeordnete Stellung *f*, niedriger Rang *m*; Minderwertigkeit *f*; geringere Zahl *f*
infertile [ɪn'fəːtaɪl] *adj* unfruchtbar
infertility [ɪnfəː'tɪlɪtɪ] *n* Unfruchtbarkeit *f*
infested [ɪn'fɛstɪd] *adj*: **~ (with)** verseucht (mit)
infinite ['ɪnfɪnɪt] *adj* unendlich; (*time, money*) unendlich viel
infinitely ['ɪnfɪnɪtlɪ] *adv* unendlich viel
infinitive [ɪn'fɪnɪtɪv] *n* (*Ling*) Infinitiv *m*, Grundform *f*
infinity [ɪn'fɪnɪtɪ] *n* Unendlichkeit *f*; (*Math, Phot*) Unendliche *nt*; **an ~ of ...** unendlich viel(e) ...
infirmary [ɪn'fəːmərɪ] *n* Krankenhaus *nt*
inflamed [ɪn'fleɪmd] *adj* entzündet
inflammable [ɪn'flæməbl] *adj* feuergefährlich
inflammation [ɪnflə'meɪʃən] *n* Entzündung *f*
inflatable [ɪn'fleɪtəbl] *adj* aufblasbar; (*dinghy*) Schlauch-
inflate [ɪn'fleɪt] *vt* aufpumpen; (*balloon*) aufblasen; (*price*) hochtreiben; (*expectation*) steigern; (*position, ideas etc*) hochspielen
inflation [ɪn'fleɪʃən] *n* Inflation *f*
inflationary [ɪn'fleɪʃənərɪ] *adj* inflationär; (*spiral*) Inflations-
inflexible [ɪn'flɛksɪbl] *adj* inflexibel; (*rule*) starr
inflict [ɪn'flɪkt] *vt*: **to ~ sth on sb** (*damage, suffering, wound*) jdm etw zufügen; (*punishment*) jdm etw auferlegen; (*fig: problems*) jdn mit etw belasten
influence ['ɪnfluəns] *n* Einfluss *m* ▷ *vt* beeinflussen; **under the ~ of alcohol** unter Alkoholeinfluss
influential [ɪnflu'ɛnʃl] *adj* einflussreich
influenza [ɪnflu'ɛnzə] *n* (*Med*) Grippe *f*
influx ['ɪnflʌks] *n* (*of refugees*) Zustrom *m*; (*of funds*) Zufuhr *f*
inform [ɪn'fɔːm] *vt*: **to ~ sb of sth** jdn von etw unterrichten, jdn über etw *acc* informieren ▷ *vi*: **to ~ on sb** jdn denunzieren
informal [ɪn'fɔːml] *adj* ungezwungen; (*manner, clothes*) leger; (*unofficial*) inoffiziell; (*announcement, invitation*) informell
informality [ɪnfɔː'mælɪtɪ] *n* (*see adj*) Ungezwungenheit *f*; legere Art *f*; inoffizieller Charakter *m*; informeller Charakter *m*
informant [ɪn'fɔːmənt] *n* Informant(in) *m(f)*
information [ɪnfə'meɪʃən] *n* Informationen *pl*, Auskunft *f*; (*knowledge*) Wissen *nt*; **to get ~ on** sich informieren über *+acc*; **a piece of ~** eine Auskunft *or* Information; **for your ~** zu Ihrer Information
information desk *n* Auskunftsschalter *m*
information office *n* Auskunftsbüro *nt*
information technology *n* Informationstechnik *f*
informative [ɪn'fɔːmətɪv] *adj* aufschlussreich
informer [ɪn'fɔːməʳ] *n* Informant(in) *m(f)*; (*also*: **police informer**) Polizeispitzel *m*
infrastructure ['ɪnfrəstrʌktʃəʳ] *n* Infrastruktur *f*
infrequent [ɪn'friːkwənt] *adj* selten
infringe [ɪn'frɪndʒ] *vt* (*law*) verstoßen gegen, übertreten ▷ *vi*: **to ~ on** (*rights*) verletzen
infringement [ɪn'frɪndʒmənt] *n* (*see vb*) Verstoß *m*, Übertretung *f*; Verletzung *f*
infuriate [ɪn'fjuərɪeɪt] *vt* wütend machen
infuriating [ɪn'fjuərɪeɪtɪŋ] *adj* äußerst ärgerlich
ingenious [ɪn'dʒiːnjəs] *adj* genial
ingenuity [ɪndʒɪ'njuːɪtɪ] *n* Einfallsreichtum *m*; (*skill*) Geschicklichkeit *f*
ingenuous [ɪn'dʒɛnjuəs] *adj* offen, aufrichtig; (*innocent*) naiv
ingot ['ɪŋgət] *n* Barren *m*
ingrained [ɪn'greɪnd] *adj* (*habit*) fest; (*belief*) unerschütterlich
ingratiate [ɪn'greɪʃɪeɪt] *vt*: **to ~ o.s. with sb** sich bei jdm einschmeicheln
ingredient [ɪn'griːdɪənt] *n* (*of cake etc*) Zutat *f*; (*of situation*) Bestandteil *m*
inhabit [ɪn'hæbɪt] *vt* bewohnen, wohnen in *+dat*
inhabitant [ɪn'hæbɪtnt] *n* Einwohner(in) *m(f)*; (*of street, house*) Bewohner(in) *m(f)*
inhale [ɪn'heɪl] *vt* einatmen ▷ *vi* einatmen; (*when smoking*) inhalieren
inhaler [ɪn'heɪləʳ] *n* Inhalationsapparat *m*
inherent [ɪn'hɪərənt] *adj*: **~ in** *or* **to** eigen *+dat*
inherit [ɪn'hɛrɪt] *vt* erben
inheritance [ɪn'hɛrɪtəns] *n* Erbe *nt*
inhibit [ɪn'hɪbɪt] *vt* hemmen
inhibition [ɪnhɪ'bɪʃən] *n* Hemmung *f*
inhuman [ɪn'hjuːmən] *adj* (*behaviour*) unmenschlich; (*appearance*) nicht menschlich
initial [ɪ'nɪʃl] *adj* anfänglich; (*stage*) Anfangs-

▷ *n* Initiale *f*, Anfangsbuchstabe *m* ▷ *vt* (*document*) abzeichnen; **initials** *npl* Initialen *pl*; (*as signature*) Namenszeichen *nt*
initially [ɪˈnɪʃəlɪ] *adv* zu Anfang; (*first*) zuerst
initiate [ɪˈnɪʃɪeɪt] *vt* (*talks*) eröffnen; (*process*) einleiten; (*new member*) feierlich aufnehmen; **to ~ sb into a secret** jdn in ein Geheimnis einweihen; **to ~ proceedings against sb** (*Law*) einen Prozess gegen jdn anstrengen
initiative [ɪˈnɪʃətɪv] *n* Initiative *f*; **to take the ~** die Initiative ergreifen
inject [ɪnˈdʒɛkt] *vt* (ein)spritzen; (*fig*: *funds*) hineinpumpen; **to ~ sb with sth** jdm etw spritzen *or* injizieren; **to ~ money into sth** (*fig*) Geld in etw *acc* pumpen
injection [ɪnˈdʒɛkʃən] *n* Spritze *f*, Injektion *f*; **to give/have an ~** eine Spritze *or* Injektion geben/bekommen; **an ~ of money/funds** (*fig*) eine Finanzspritze
injure [ˈɪndʒəʳ] *vt* verletzen; (*reputation*) schaden *+dat*; **to ~ o.s.** sich verletzen
injured [ˈɪndʒəd] *adj* verletzt; (*tone*) gekränkt; **~ party** (*Law*) Geschädigte(r) *f(m)*
injury [ˈɪndʒərɪ] *n* Verletzung *f*; **to escape without ~** unverletzt davonkommen
injury time *n* (*Sport*) Nachspielzeit *f*; **to play ~** nachspielen
injustice [ɪnˈdʒʌstɪs] *n* Ungerechtigkeit *f*; **you do me an ~** Sie tun mir unrecht
ink [ɪŋk] *n* Tinte *f*; (*in printing*) Druckfarbe *f*
ink-jet printer [ˈɪŋkdʒɛt-] *n* Tintenstrahldrucker *m*
inkling [ˈɪŋklɪŋ] *n* (dunkle) Ahnung *f*; **to have an ~ of** ahnen
inlaid [ˈɪnleɪd] *adj* eingelegt
inland [ˈɪnlənd] *adj* (*port, sea, waterway*) Binnen- ▷ *adv* (*travel*) landeinwärts
Inland Revenue (*Brit*) *n* ≈ Finanzamt *nt*
in-laws [ˈɪnlɔːz] *npl* (*parents-in-law*) Schwiegereltern *pl*; (*other relatives*) angeheiratete Verwandte *pl*
inlet [ˈɪnlɛt] *n* (schmale) Bucht *f*
inmate [ˈɪnmeɪt] *n* Insasse *m*, Insassin *f*
inn [ɪn] *n* Gasthaus *nt*
innate [ɪˈneɪt] *adj* angeboren
inner [ˈɪnəʳ] *adj* innere(r, s); (*courtyard*) Innen-
inner city *n* Innenstadt *f*
inner tube *n* (*of tyre*) Schlauch *m*
innocence [ˈɪnəsns] *n* Unschuld *f*
innocent [ˈɪnəsnt] *adj* unschuldig
innocuous [ɪˈnɔkjuəs] *adj* harmlos
innovation [ɪnəuˈveɪʃən] *n* Neuerung *f*
innuendo [ɪnjuˈɛndəu] (*pl* **~es**) *n* versteckte Andeutung *f*
innumerable [ɪˈnjuːmrəbl] *adj* unzählig
input [ˈɪnput] *n* (*of capital, manpower*) Investition *f*; (*of energy*) Zufuhr *f*; (*Comput*) Eingabe *f*, Input *m or nt* ▷ *vt* (*Comput*) eingeben
inquest [ˈɪnkwɛst] *n* gerichtliche Untersuchung *f* der Todesursache
inquire [ɪnˈkwaɪəʳ] *vi*: **to ~ about** sich erkundigen nach, fragen nach ▷ *vt* sich erkundigen nach, fragen nach; **to ~ when/where/whether** fragen *or* sich erkundigen, wann/wo/ob
▸ **inquire after** *vt fus* sich erkundigen nach
▸ **inquire into** *vt fus* untersuchen
inquiry [ɪnˈkwaɪərɪ] *n* Untersuchung *f*; (*question*) Anfrage *f*; **to hold an ~ into sth** eine Untersuchung *+gen* durchführen
inquisitive [ɪnˈkwɪzɪtɪv] *adj* neugierig
insane [ɪnˈseɪn] *adj* wahnsinnig; (*Med*) geisteskrank
insanity [ɪnˈsænɪtɪ] *n* Wahnsinn *m*; (*Med*) Geisteskrankheit *f*
inscription [ɪnˈskrɪpʃən] *n* Inschrift *f*; (*in book*) Widmung *f*
inscrutable [ɪnˈskruːtəbl] *adj* (*comment*) unergründlich; (*expression*) undurchdringlich
insect [ˈɪnsɛkt] *n* Insekt *nt*
insecticide [ɪnˈsɛktɪsaɪd] *n* Insektizid *nt*, Insektengift *nt*
insect repellent *n* Insektenbekämpfungsmittel *nt*
insecure [ɪnsɪˈkjuəʳ] *adj* unsicher
insecurity [ɪnsɪˈkjuərɪtɪ] *n* Unsicherheit *f*
insensitive [ɪnˈsɛnsɪtɪv] *adj* gefühllos
insert [*vt* ɪnˈsəːt, *n* ˈɪnsəːt] *vt* einfügen; (*into sth*) hineinstecken ▷ *n* (*in newspaper etc*) Beilage *f*; (*in shoe*) Einlage *f*
insertion [ɪnˈsəːʃən] *n* Hineinstecken *nt*; (*of needle*) Einstechen *nt*; (*of comment*) Einfügen *nt*
in-service [ˈɪnˈsəːvɪs] *adj*: **~ training** (berufsbegleitende) Fortbildung *f*; **~ course** Fortbildungslehrgang *m*
inshore [ˈɪnˈʃɔːʳ] *adj* (*fishing, waters*) Küsten- ▷ *adv* in Küstennähe; (*move*) auf die Küste zu
inside [ˈɪnˈsaɪd] *n* Innere(s) *nt*, Innenseite *f*; (*of road*: *in Britain*) linke Spur *f*; (: *in US, Europe etc*) rechte Spur *f* ▷ *adj* innere(r, s); (*pocket, cabin, light*) Innen- ▷ *adv* (*go*) nach innen, hinein; (*be*) drinnen ▷ *prep* (*location*) in *+dat*; (*motion*) in *+acc*; **~ 10 minutes** innerhalb von 10 Minuten; **insides** *npl* (*inf*) Bauch *m*; (*innards*) Eingeweide *pl*
inside lane *n* (*Brit*) linke Spur *f*; (*in US, Europe etc*) rechte Spur *f*
inside out *adv* (*know*) in- und auswendig; (*piece of clothing*: *be*) links *or* verkehrt herum; (: *turn*) nach links
insider dealing, **insider trading** *n* (*Stock Exchange*) Insiderhandel *m or* -geschäfte *pl*
insight [ˈɪnsaɪt] *n* Verständnis *nt*; **to gain (an) ~ into** einen Einblick gewinnen in *+acc*
insignificant [ɪnsɪgˈnɪfɪknt] *adj* belanglos
insincere [ɪnsɪnˈsɪəʳ] *adj* unaufrichtig, falsch
insinuate [ɪnˈsɪnjueɪt] *vt* anspielen auf *+acc*
insist [ɪnˈsɪst] *vi* bestehen; **to ~ on** bestehen auf *+dat*; **to ~ that** darauf bestehen, dass; (*claim*) behaupten, dass
insistent [ɪnˈsɪstənt] *adj* (*determined*) hartnäckig; (*continual*) andauernd, penetrant (*pej*)
insole [ˈɪnsəul] *n* Einlegesohle *f*
insolent [ˈɪnsələnt] *adj* frech, unverschämt
insolvent [ɪnˈsɔlvənt] *adj* zahlungsunfähig

insomnia [ɪn'sɔmnɪə] *n* Schlaflosigkeit *f*
inspect [ɪn'spɛkt] *vt* kontrollieren; (*examine*) prüfen; (*troops*) inspizieren
inspection [ɪn'spɛkʃən] *n* (*see vb*) Kontrolle *f*; Prüfung *f*; Inspektion *f*
inspector [ɪn'spɛktə^r] *n* Inspektor(in) *m(f)*; (*Brit: on buses, trains*) Kontrolleur(in) *m(f)*; (*: Police*) Kommissar(in) *m(f)*
inspiration [ɪnspə'reɪʃən] *n* Inspiration *f*; (*idea*) Eingebung *f*
inspire [ɪn'spaɪə^r] *vt* inspirieren; (*confidence, hope etc*) (er)wecken
inspiring [ɪn'spaɪərɪŋ] *adj* inspirierend
instability [ɪnstə'bɪlɪtɪ] *n* Instabilität *f*; (*of person*) Labilität *f*
install [ɪn'stɔ:l] *vt* installieren; (*telephone*) anschließen; (*official*) einsetzen; **to ~ o.s.** sich niederlassen
installation [ɪnstə'leɪʃən] *n* Installation *f*; (*of telephone*) Anschluss *m*; (*Industry, Mil: plant*) Anlage *f*
instalment, (US) **installment** [ɪn'stɔ:lmənt] *n* Rate *f*; (*of story*) Fortsetzung *f*; (*of TV serial etc*) (Sende)folge *f*; **in ~s** in Raten
instance ['ɪnstəns] *n* Beispiel *nt*; **for ~** zum Beispiel; **in that ~** in diesem Fall; **in many ~s** in vielen Fällen; **in the first ~** zuerst *or* zunächst (einmal)
instant ['ɪnstənt] *n* Augenblick *m* ▷ *adj* (*reaction*) unmittelbar; (*success*) sofortig; **~ food** Schnellgerichte *pl*; **~ coffee** Instantkaffee *m*; **the 10th ~** (*Comm, Admin*) der 10. dieses Monats
instantly ['ɪnstəntlɪ] *adv* sofort
instead [ɪn'stɛd] *adv* stattdessen; **~ of** statt *+gen*; **~ of sb** an jds Stelle *dat*; **~ of doing sth** anstatt *or* anstelle etw zu tun
instep ['ɪnstɛp] *n* (*of foot*) Spann *m*; (*of shoe*) Blatt *nt*
instigate ['ɪnstɪgeɪt] *vt* anstiften, anzetteln; (*talks etc*) initiieren
instil [ɪn'stɪl] *vt*: **to ~ sth into sb** (*confidence, fear etc*) jdm etw einflößen
instinct ['ɪnstɪŋkt] *n* Instinkt *m*; (*reaction, inclination*) instinktive Reaktion *f*
instinctive [ɪn'stɪŋktɪv] *adj* instinktiv
institute ['ɪnstɪtju:t] *n* Institut *nt*; (*for teaching*) Hochschule *f*; (*professional body*) Bund *m*, Verband *m* ▷ *vt* einführen; (*inquiry, course of action*) einleiten; (*proceedings*) anstrengen
institution [ɪnstɪ'tju:ʃən] *n* Einführung *f*; (*organization*) Institution *f*, Einrichtung *f*; (*hospital, mental home*) Anstalt *f*, Heim *nt*
instruct [ɪn'strʌkt] *vt*: **to ~ sb in sth** jdn in etw *dat* unterrichten; **to ~ sb to do sth** jdn anweisen, etw zu tun
instruction [ɪn'strʌkʃən] *n* Unterricht *m*; **instructions** *npl* (*orders*) Anweisungen *pl*; **~s (for use)** Gebrauchsanweisung *f*, Gebrauchsanleitung *f*; **~ book/manual/leaflet** *etc* Bedienungsanleitung *f*
instructor [ɪn'strʌktə^r] *n* Lehrer(in) *m(f)*
instrument ['ɪnstrumənt] *n* Instrument *nt*; (*Mus*) (Musik)instrument *nt*
instrumental [ɪnstru'mɛntl] *adj* (*Mus: music, accompaniment*) Instrumental-; **to be ~ in** eine bedeutende Rolle spielen bei
instrument panel *n* Armaturenbrett *nt*
insufficient [ɪnsə'fɪʃənt] *adj* unzureichend
insular ['ɪnsjulə^r] *adj* engstirnig
insulate ['ɪnsjuleɪt] *vt* isolieren; (*person, group*) abschirmen
insulation [ɪnsju'leɪʃən] *n* (*see vb*) Isolierung *f*; Abschirmung *f*
insulin ['ɪnsjulɪn] *n* Insulin *nt*
insult [*n* 'ɪnsʌlt, *vt* ɪn'sʌlt] *n* Beleidigung *f* ▷ *vt* beleidigen
insulting [ɪn'sʌltɪŋ] *adj* beleidigend
insurance [ɪn'ʃuərəns] *n* Versicherung *f*; **fire/life ~** Brand-/Lebensversicherung *f*; **to take out ~ (against)** eine Versicherung abschließen (gegen)
insurance policy *n* Versicherungspolice *f*
insure [ɪn'ʃuə^r] *vt* versichern; **to ~ o.s./sth against sth** sich/etw gegen etw versichern; **to ~ o.s.** *or* **one's life** eine Lebensversicherung abschließen; **to ~ (o.s.) against sth** (*fig*) sich gegen etw absichern; **to be ~d for £5,000** für £5000 versichert sein
intact [ɪn'tækt] *adj* intakt; (*whole*) ganz; (*unharmed*) unversehrt
intake ['ɪnteɪk] *n* (*of food*) Aufnahme *f*; (*of air*) Zufuhr *f*; (*Brit: Scol*): **an ~ of 200 a year** 200 neue Schüler pro Jahr
integral ['ɪntɪgrəl] *adj* wesentlich
integrate ['ɪntɪgreɪt] *vt* integrieren ▷ *vi* sich integrieren
integrity [ɪn'tɛgrɪtɪ] *n* Integrität *f*; (*of group*) Einheit *f*; (*of culture, text*) Unversehrtheit *f*
intellect ['ɪntəlɛkt] *n* Intellekt *m*
intellectual [ɪntə'lɛktjuəl] *adj* intellektuell, geistig ▷ *n* Intellektuelle(r) *f(m)*
intelligence [ɪn'tɛlɪdʒəns] *n* Intelligenz *f*; (*information*) Informationen *pl*
intelligent [ɪn'tɛlɪdʒənt] *adj* intelligent; (*decision*) klug
intend [ɪn'tɛnd] *vt*: **to be ~ed for sb** für jdn gedacht sein; **to ~ to do sth** beabsichtigen, etw zu tun
intense [ɪn'tɛns] *adj* intensiv; (*anger, joy*) äußerst groß; (*person*) ernsthaft
intensely [ɪn'tɛnslɪ] *adv* äußerst; **I dislike him ~** ich verabscheue ihn
intensify [ɪn'tɛnsɪfaɪ] *vt* intensivieren, verstärken
intensity [ɪn'tɛnsɪtɪ] *n* Intensität *f*; (*of anger*) Heftigkeit *f*
intensive [ɪn'tɛnsɪv] *adj* intensiv
intensive care *n*: **to be in ~** auf der Intensivstation sein
intensive care unit *n* Intensivstation *f*
intent [ɪn'tɛnt] *n* Absicht *f* ▷ *adj* (*attentive*) aufmerksam; (*absorbed*): **~ (on)** versunken (in *+acc*); **to all ~s and purposes** im Grunde; **to be ~ on doing sth** entschlossen sein, etw

zu tun
intention [ɪn'tɛnʃən] *n* Absicht *f*
intentional [ɪn'tɛnʃənl] *adj* absichtlich
intently [ɪn'tɛntlɪ] *adv* konzentriert
interact [ɪntər'ækt] *vi* (*people*) interagieren; (*things*) aufeinander einwirken; (*ideas*) sich gegenseitig beeinflussen; **to ~ with** interagieren mit; einwirken auf *+acc*; beeinflussen
interaction [ɪntər'ækʃən] *n* (*see vb*) Interaktion *f*; gegenseitige Einwirkung *f*; gegenseitige Beeinflussung *f*
interactive [ɪntər'æktɪv] *adj* (*also Comput*) interaktiv
intercept [ɪntə'sɛpt] *vt* abfangen
interchange ['ɪntətʃeɪndʒ] *n* Austausch *m*; (*on motorway*) (Autobahn)kreuz *nt*
interchangeable [ɪntə'tʃeɪndʒəbl] *adj* austauschbar
intercom ['ɪntəkɔm] *n* (Gegen)sprechanlage *f*
intercourse ['ɪntəkɔ:s] *n* (*sexual*) (Geschlechts)verkehr *m*; (*social, verbal*) Verkehr *m*
interest ['ɪntrɪst] *n* Interesse *nt*; (*Comm: in company*) Anteil *m*; (*: sum of money*) Zinsen *pl* ▷ *vt* interessieren; **compound ~** Zinseszins *m*; **simple ~** einfache Zinsen; **British ~s in the Middle East** britische Interessen im Nahen Osten; **his main ~ is ...** er interessiert sich hauptsächlich für ...
interested ['ɪntrɪstɪd] *adj* interessiert; (*party, body etc*) beteiligt; **to be ~ in sth** sich für etw interessieren; **to be ~ in doing sth** daran interessiert sein, etw zu tun
interesting ['ɪntrɪstɪŋ] *adj* interessant
interest rate *n* Zinssatz *m*
interface ['ɪntəfeɪs] *n* Verbindung *f*; (*Comput*) Schnittstelle *f*
interfere [ɪntə'fɪə^r] *vi*: **to ~ in** sich einmischen in *+acc*; **to ~ with** (*object*) sich zu schaffen machen an *+dat*; (*plans*) durchkreuzen; (*career, duty, decision*) beeinträchtigen; **don't ~** misch dich nicht ein
interference [ɪntə'fɪərəns] *n* Einmischung *f*; (*Radio, TV*) Störung *f*
interim ['ɪntərɪm] *adj* (*agreement, government etc*) Übergangs- ▷ *n*: **in the ~** in der Zwischenzeit
interior [ɪn'tɪərɪə^r] *n* Innere(s) *nt*; (*decor etc*) Innenausstattung *f* ▷ *adj* Innen-
interior decorator *n* Innenausstatter(in) *m(f)*
interjection [ɪntə'dʒɛkʃən] *n* Einwurf *m*; (*Ling*) Interjektion *f*
interlock [ɪntə'lɔk] *vi* ineinandergreifen
interlude ['ɪntəlu:d] *n* Unterbrechung *f*, Pause *f*; (*Theat*) Zwischenspiel *nt*
intermediate [ɪntə'mi:dɪət] *adj* (*stage*) Zwischen-; **an ~ student** ein fortgeschrittener Anfänger
intermission [ɪntə'mɪʃən] *n* Pause *f*
intern [*vt* ɪn'tə:n, *n* 'ɪntə:n] *vt* internieren ▷ *n* (*US*) Assistenzarzt *m*, Assistenzärztin *f*
internal [ɪn'tə:nl] *adj* innere(r, s); (*pipes*) im Haus; (*politics*) Innen-; (*dispute, reform, memo, structure etc*) intern
internally [ɪn'tə:nəlɪ] *adv*: **"not to be taken ~"** "nicht zum Einnehmen"
Internal Revenue Service (*US*) *n* ≈ Finanzamt *nt*
international [ɪntə'næʃənl] *adj* international ▷ *n* (*Brit: Sport*) Länderspiel *nt*
Internet ['ɪntənɛt] *n* Internet *nt*
Internet café *n* Internetcafé *nt*
interplay ['ɪntəpleɪ] *n*: **~ (of** *or* **between)** Zusammenspiel *nt* (von)
interpret [ɪn'tə:prɪt] *vt* auslegen, interpretieren; (*translate*) dolmetschen ▷ *vi* dolmetschen
interpretation [ɪntə:prɪ'teɪʃən] *n* (*see vb*) Auslegung *f*, Interpretation *f*; Dolmetschen *nt*
interpreter [ɪn'tə:prɪtə^r] *n* Dolmetscher(in) *m(f)*
interrelated [ɪntərɪ'leɪtɪd] *adj* zusammenhängend
interrogate [ɪn'tɛrəugeɪt] *vt* verhören; (*witness*) vernehmen
interrogation [ɪntɛrəu'geɪʃən] *n* (*see vb*) Verhör *nt*; Vernehmung *f*
interrogative [ɪntə'rɔgətɪv] *adj* (*Ling: pronoun*) Interrogativ-, Frage-
interrupt [ɪntə'rʌpt] *vt, vi* unterbrechen
interruption [ɪntə'rʌpʃən] *n* Unterbrechung *f*
intersect [ɪntə'sɛkt] *vi* sich kreuzen ▷ *vt* durchziehen; (*Math*) schneiden
intersection [ɪntə'sɛkʃən] *n* Kreuzung *f*; (*Math*) Schnittpunkt *m*
intersperse [ɪntə'spə:s] *vt*: **to be ~d with** durchsetzt sein mit; **he ~d his lecture with ...** er spickte seine Rede mit ...
intertwine [ɪntə'twaɪn] *vi* sich ineinander verschlingen
interval ['ɪntəvl] *n* Pause *f*; (*Mus*) Intervall *nt*; **bright ~s** (*in weather*) Aufheiterungen *pl*; **at ~s** in Abständen
intervene [ɪntə'vi:n] *vi* eingreifen; (*event*) dazwischenkommen; (*time*) dazwischenliegen
intervention [ɪntə'vɛnʃən] *n* Eingreifen *nt*
interview ['ɪntəvju:] *n* (*for job*) Vorstellungsgespräch *nt*; (*for place at college etc*) Auswahlgespräch *nt*; (*Radio, TV etc*) Interview *nt* ▷ *vt* (*see n*) ein Vorstellungsgespräch/Auswahlgespräch führen mit; interviewen
interviewer ['ɪntəvjuə^r] *n* Leiter(in) *m(f)* des Vorstellungsgesprächs/Auswahlgesprächs; (*Radio, TV etc*) Interviewer(in) *m(f)*
intestine [ɪn'tɛstɪn] *n* Darm *m*
intimacy ['ɪntɪməsɪ] *n* Vertrautheit *f*
intimate [*adj* 'ɪntɪmət, *vt* 'ɪntɪmeɪt] *adj* eng; (*sexual, also restaurant, dinner, atmosphere*) intim; (*conversation, matter, detail*) vertraulich; (*knowledge*) gründlich ▷ *vt* andeuten; (*make*

known) zu verstehen geben
intimidate [ɪn'tɪmɪdeɪt] *vt* einschüchtern
into ['ɪntu] *prep* **1** (*indicating motion or direction*) in *+acc*; **to go into town** in die Stadt gehen; **he worked late into the night** er arbeitete bis spät in die Nacht; **the car bumped into the wall** der Wagen fuhr gegen die Mauer **2** (*indicating change of condition, result*): **it broke into pieces** es zerbrach in Stücke; **she translated into English** sie übersetzte ins Englische; **to change pounds into dollars** Pfund in Dollar wechseln; **5 into 25** 25 durch 5
intolerant [ɪn'tɔlərnt] *adj*: **~ (of)** intolerant (gegenüber)
intoxicated [ɪn'tɔksɪkeɪtɪd] *adj* betrunken; (*fig*) berauscht
intractable [ɪn'træktəbl] *adj* hartnäckig; (*child*) widerspenstig; (*temper*) unbeugsam
intranet ['ɪntrənɛt] *n* (*Comput*) Intranet *nt*
intransitive [ɪn'trænsɪtɪv] *adj* (*Ling*) intransitiv
intravenous [ɪntrə'vi:nəs] *adj* intravenös
in-tray ['ɪntreɪ] *n* Ablage *f* für Eingänge
intricate ['ɪntrɪkət] *adj* kompliziert
intrigue [ɪn'tri:g] *n* Intrigen *pl* ▷ *vt* faszinieren
intriguing [ɪn'tri:gɪŋ] *adj* faszinierend
intrinsic [ɪn'trɪnsɪk] *adj* wesentlich
introduce [ɪntrə'dju:s] *vt* (*sth new*) einführen; (*speaker, TV show etc*) ankündigen; **to ~ sb (to sb)** jdn (jdm) vorstellen; **to ~ sb to** (*pastime, technique*) jdn einführen in *+acc*; **may I ~ ...?** darf ich ... vorstellen?
introduction [ɪntrə'dʌkʃən] *n* Einführung *f*; (*of person*) Vorstellung *f*; (*to book*) Einleitung *f*; **a letter of ~** ein Einführungsschreiben *nt*
introductory [ɪntrə'dʌktərɪ] *adj* Einführungs-; **~ remarks** einführende Bemerkungen *pl*; **~ offer** Einführungsangebot *nt*
intrude [ɪn'tru:d] *vi* eindringen; **to ~ on** stören; (*conversation*) sich einmischen in *+acc*; **am I intruding?** störe ich?
intruder [ɪn'tru:dəʳ] *n* Eindringling *m*
intuition [ɪntju:'ɪʃən] *n* Intuition *f*
inundate ['ɪnʌndeɪt] *vt*: **to ~ with** überschwemmen mit
invade [ɪn'veɪd] *vt* einfallen in *+acc*; (*fig*) heimsuchen
invalid [*n* 'ɪnvəlɪd, *adj* ɪn'vælɪd] *n* Kranke(r) *f(m)*; (*disabled*) Invalide *m* ▷ *adj* ungültig
invaluable [ɪn'væljuəbl] *adj* unschätzbar
invariably [ɪn'vɛərɪəblɪ] *adv* ständig, unweigerlich; **she is ~ late** sie kommt immer zu spät
invasion [ɪn'veɪʒən] *n* Invasion *f*; **an ~ of privacy** ein Eingriff *m* in die Privatsphäre
invent [ɪn'vɛnt] *vt* erfinden
invention [ɪn'vɛnʃən] *n* Erfindung *f*
inventive [ɪn'vɛntɪv] *adj* erfinderisch
inventor [ɪn'vɛntəʳ] *n* Erfinder(in) *m(f)*
inventory ['ɪnvəntrɪ] *n* Inventar *nt*
invert [ɪn'və:t] *vt* umdrehen
inverted commas [ɪn'və:tɪd-] (*Brit*) *npl* Anführungszeichen *pl*
invest [ɪn'vɛst] *vt* investieren ▷ *vi*: **~ in** investieren in *+acc*; (*fig*) sich *dat* anschaffen; **to ~ sb with sth** jdm etw verleihen
investigate [ɪn'vɛstɪgeɪt] *vt* untersuchen
investigation [ɪnvɛstɪ'geɪʃən] *n* Untersuchung *f*
investigator [ɪn'vɛstɪgeɪtəʳ] *n* Ermittler(in) *m(f)*; **private ~** Privatdetektiv(in) *m(f)*
investment [ɪn'vɛstmənt] *n* Investition *f*
investor [ɪn'vɛstəʳ] *n* (Kapital)anleger(in) *m(f)*
invigilator [ɪn'vɪdʒɪleɪtəʳ] *n* Aufsicht *f*
invigorating [ɪn'vɪgəreɪtɪŋ] *adj* belebend; (*experience etc*) anregend
invisible [ɪn'vɪzɪbl] *adj* unsichtbar
invitation [ɪnvɪ'teɪʃən] *n* Einladung *f*; **by ~ only** nur auf Einladung; **at sb's ~** auf jds Aufforderung *acc* (hin)
invite [ɪn'vaɪt] *vt* einladen; (*discussion*) auffordern zu; (*criticism*) herausfordern; **to ~ sb to do sth** jdn auffordern, etw zu tun; **to ~ sb to dinner** jdn zum Abendessen einladen
▸ **invite out** *vt* einladen
inviting [ɪn'vaɪtɪŋ] *adj* einladend; (*desirable*) verlockend
invoice ['ɪnvɔɪs] *n* Rechnung *f* ▷ *vt* in Rechnung stellen; **to ~ sb for goods** jdm für Waren eine Rechnung ausstellen
involuntary [ɪn'vɔləntrɪ] *adj* unbeabsichtigt; (*reflex*) unwillkürlich
involve [ɪn'vɔlv] *vt* (*person*) beteiligen; (*thing*) verbunden sein mit; (*concern, affect*) betreffen; **to ~ sb in sth** jdn in etw *acc* verwickeln
involved [ɪn'vɔlvd] *adj* kompliziert; **the work/problems ~** die damit verbundene Arbeit/verbundenen Schwierigkeiten; **to be ~ in** beteiligt sein an *+dat*; (*be engrossed*) engagiert sein in *+dat*; **to become ~ with sb** Umgang mit jdm haben; (*emotionally*) mit jdm eine Beziehung anfangen
involvement [ɪn'vɔlvmənt] *n* Engagement *nt*; (*participation*) Beteiligung *f*
inward ['ɪnwəd] *adj* innerste(r, s); (*movement*) nach innen ▷ *adv* nach innen
inwards ['ɪnwədz] *adv* nach innen
I/O *abbr* (*Comput*: = *input/output*) E/A
iodine ['aɪəudi:n] *n* Jod *nt*
IOM (*Brit*) *abbr* (*Post*: = *Isle of Man*)
iota [aɪ'əutə] *n* Jota *nt*
IOU *n abbr* (= *I owe you*) Schuldschein *m*
IQ *n abbr* (= *intelligence quotient*) IQ *m*
IRA *n abbr* (= *Irish Republican Army*) IRA *f*; (*US*: = *individual retirement account*) *privates Rentensparkonto*
Iran [ɪ'rɑ:n] *n* (der) Iran
Iranian [ɪ'reɪnɪən] *adj* iranisch ▷ *n* Iraner(in) *m(f)*; (*Ling*) Iranisch *nt*
Iraq [ɪ'rɑ:k] *n* (der) Irak
Iraqi [ɪ'rɑ:kɪ] *adj* irakisch ▷ *n* Iraker(in) *m(f)*
irate [aɪ'reɪt] *adj* zornig
Ireland ['aɪələnd] *n* Irland *nt*; **the Republic**

of ~ die Republik Irland
iris ['aɪrɪs] (*pl* **~es**) *n* (*Anat*) Iris *f*, Regenbogenhaut *f*; (*Bot*) Iris, Schwertlilie *f*
Irish ['aɪrɪʃ] *adj* irisch ▷ *npl*: **the ~** die Iren *pl*, die Irländer *pl*
Irishman ['aɪrɪʃmən] (*irreg: like* **man**) *n* Ire *m*, Irländer *m*
Irish Sea *n*: **the ~** die Irische See
Irishwoman ['aɪrɪʃwumən] (*irreg: like* **woman**) *n* Irin *f*, Irländerin *f*
iron ['aɪən] *n* Eisen *nt*; (*for clothes*) Bügeleisen *nt* ▷ *cpd* Eisen-; (*will, discipline etc*) eisern ▷ *vt* bügeln
▶ **iron out** *vt* (*fig*) aus dem Weg räumen
ironic [aɪ'rɔnɪk], **ironical** [aɪ'rɔnɪkl] *adj* ironisch; (*situation*) paradox, witzig
ironically [aɪ'rɔnɪklɪ] *adv* ironisch; **~, the intelligence chief was the last to find out** witzigerweise war der Geheimdienstchef der Letzte, der es erfuhr
ironing ['aɪənɪŋ] *n* Bügeln *nt*; (*clothes*) Bügelwäsche *f*
ironing board *n* Bügelbrett *nt*
ironmonger ['aɪənmʌŋgə^r] (*Brit*) *n* Eisen- und Haushaltswarenhändler(in) *m(f)*
irony ['aɪrənɪ] *n* Ironie *f*; **the ~ of it is that ...** das Ironische daran ist, dass ...
irrational [ɪ'ræʃənl] *adj* irrational
irregular [ɪ'rɛgjulə^r] *adj* unregelmäßig; (*surface*) uneben; (*behaviour*) ungehörig
irrelevant [ɪ'rɛləvənt] *adj* unwesentlich, irrelevant
irresistible [ɪrɪ'zɪstɪbl] *adj* unwiderstehlich
irrespective [ɪrɪ'spɛktɪv]: **~ of** *prep* ungeachtet *+gen*
irresponsible [ɪrɪ'spɔnsɪbl] *adj* verantwortungslos; (*action*) unverantwortlich
irrigate ['ɪrɪgeɪt] *vt* bewässern
irrigation [ɪrɪ'geɪʃən] *n* Bewässerung *f*
irritable ['ɪrɪtəbl] *adj* reizbar
irritate ['ɪrɪteɪt] *vt* ärgern, irritieren; (*Med*) reizen
irritating ['ɪrɪteɪtɪŋ] *adj* ärgerlich, irritierend; **he is ~** er kann einem auf die Nerven gehen
irritation [ɪrɪ'teɪʃən] *n* Ärger *m*; (*Med*) Reizung *f*; (*annoying thing*) Ärgernis *nt*
IRS (*US*) *n abbr* (= *Internal Revenue Service*) *Steuereinzugsbehörde*
is [ɪz] *vb see* **be**
ISDN *n abbr* (= *Integrated Services Digital Network*) ISDN *nt*
Islam ['ɪzlɑːm] *n* der Islam; (*Islamic countries*) die islamischen Länder *pl*
Islamic [ɪz'læmɪk] *adj* islamisch
island ['aɪlənd] *n* Insel *f*; (*also:* **traffic island**) Verkehrsinsel *f*
islander ['aɪləndə^r] *n* Inselbewohner(in) *m(f)*
isle [aɪl] *n* Insel *f*
isn't ['ɪznt] = **is not**
isolate ['aɪsəleɪt] *vt* isolieren
isolated ['aɪsəleɪtɪd] *adj* isoliert; (*place*) abgelegen; **~ incident** Einzelfall *m*
isolation [aɪsə'leɪʃən] *n* Isolierung *f*
ISP (*Comput*) *n abbr* (= *Internet Service Provider*) Provider *m*
Israel ['ɪzreɪl] *n* Israel *nt*
Israeli [ɪz'reɪlɪ] *adj* israelisch ▷ *n* Israeli *mf*
issue ['ɪʃjuː] *n* Frage *f*; (*subject*) Thema *nt*; (*problem*) Problem *nt*; (*of book, stamps etc*) Ausgabe *f*; (*offspring*) Nachkommenschaft *f* ▷ *vt* ausgeben; (*statement*) herausgeben; (*documents*) ausstellen ▷ *vi*: **to ~ (from)** dringen (aus); (*liquid*) austreten (aus); **the point at ~** der Punkt, um den es geht; **to avoid the ~** ausweichen; **to confuse** *or* **obscure the ~** es unnötig kompliziert machen; **to ~ sth to sb** *or* **~ sb with sth** jdm etw geben; (*documents*) jdm etw ausstellen; (*gun etc*) jdn mit etw ausstatten; **to take ~ with sb (over)** jdm widersprechen (in *+dat*); **to make an ~ of sth** etw aufbauschen
IT *n abbr* = **information technology**
it [ɪt] *pron* **1** (*specific: subject*) er/sie/es; (*: direct object*) ihn/sie/es; (*: indirect object*) ihm/ihr/ihm; **it's on the table** es ist auf dem Tisch; **I can't find it** ich kann es nicht finden; **give it to me** gib es mir; **about it** darüber; **from it** davon; **in it** darin; **of it** davon; **what did you learn from it?** was hast du daraus gelernt?; **I'm proud of it** ich bin stolz darauf **2** (*impersonal*) es; **it's raining** es regnet; **it's Friday tomorrow** morgen ist Freitag; **who is it? — it's me** wer ist da? — ich bins
Italian [ɪ'tæljən] *adj* italienisch ▷ *n* Italiener(in) *m(f)*; (*Ling*) Italienisch *nt*; **the ~s** die Italiener *pl*
italics [ɪ'tælɪks] *npl* Kursivschrift *f*
Italy ['ɪtəlɪ] *n* Italien *nt*
itch [ɪtʃ] *n* Juckreiz *m* ▷ *vi* jucken; **I am ~ing all over** mich juckt es überall; **to ~ to do sth** darauf brennen, etw zu tun
itchy ['ɪtʃɪ] *adj* juckend; **my back is ~** mein Rücken juckt
it'd ['ɪtd] = **it would; it had**
item ['aɪtəm] *n* Punkt *m*; (*of collection*) Stück *nt*; (*also:* **news item**) Meldung *f*; (*: in newspaper*) Zeitungsnotiz *f*; **~s of clothing** Kleidungsstücke *pl*
itemize ['aɪtəmaɪz] *vt* einzeln aufführen
itinerary [aɪ'tɪnərərɪ] *n* Reiseroute *f*
it'll ['ɪtl] = **it will; it shall**
its [ɪts] *adj* sein(e), ihr(e) ▷ *pron* seine(r, s), ihre(r, s)
it's [ɪts] = **it is; it has**
itself [ɪt'sɛlf] *pron* sich; (*emphatic*) selbst
ITV (*Brit*) *n abbr* (*TV*: = *Independent Television*) *kommerzieller Fernsehsender*
IUD *n abbr* = **intrauterine device**
I've [aɪv] = **I have**
ivory ['aɪvərɪ] *n* Elfenbein *nt*
ivy ['aɪvɪ] *n* Efeu *m*

jab [dʒæb] *vt* stoßen; (*with finger, needle*) stechen ▷ *n* (*inf*) Spritze *f* ▷ *vi*: **to ~ at** einstechen auf *+acc*; **to ~ sth into sth** etw in etw *acc* stoßen/stechen
jack [dʒæk] *n* (*Aut*) Wagenheber *m*; (*Bowls*) Zielkugel *f*; (*Cards*) Bube *m*
▸ **jack in** (*inf*) *vt* aufgeben
▸ **jack up** *vt* (*Aut*) aufbocken
jackal ['dʒækl] *n* Schakal *m*
jacket ['dʒækɪt] *n* Jackett *nt*; (*of book*) Schutzumschlag *m*; **potatoes in their jackets, ~ potatoes** in der Schale gebackene Kartoffeln *pl*
jack plug *n* Bananenstecker *m*
jackpot ['dʒækpɔt] *n* Hauptgewinn *m*; **to hit the ~** (*fig*) das große Los ziehen
Jacuzzi® [dʒə'ku:zɪ] *n* Whirlpool *m*
jaded ['dʒeɪdɪd] *adj* abgespannt; **to get ~** die Nase vollhaben
jagged ['dʒægɪd] *adj* gezackt
jail [dʒeɪl] *n* Gefängnis *nt* ▷ *vt* einsperren
jam [dʒæm] *n* Marmelade *f*, Konfitüre *f*; (*also*: **traffic jam**) Stau *m*; (*inf*: *difficulty*) Klemme *f* ▷ *vt* blockieren; (*mechanism, drawer etc*) verklemmen; (*Radio*) stören ▷ *vi* klemmen; (*gun*) Ladehemmung haben; **I'm in a real ~** (*inf*) ich stecke wirklich in der Klemme; **to get sb out of a ~** (*inf*) jdm aus der Klemme helfen; **to ~ sth into sth** etw in etw *acc* stopfen; **the telephone lines are ~med** die Leitungen sind belegt
Jamaica [dʒə'meɪkə] *n* Jamaika *nt*
jam-packed [dʒæm'pækt] *adj*: **~ (with)** vollgestopft (mit)
jangle ['dʒæŋgl] *vi* klimpern
janitor ['dʒænɪtə^r] *n* Hausmeister(in) *m(f)*
January ['dʒænjuərɪ] *n* Januar *m*; *see also* **July**
Japan [dʒə'pæn] *n* Japan *nt*
Japanese [dʒæpə'ni:z] *adj* japanisch ▷ *n inv* Japaner(in) *m(f)*; (*Ling*) Japanisch *nt*
jar [dʒɑ:^r] *n* Topf *m*, Gefäß *nt*; (*glass*) Glas *nt* ▷ *vi* (*sound*) gellen; (*colours*) nicht harmonieren, sich beißen ▷ *vt* erschüttern; **to ~ on sb** jdm auf die Nerven gehen
jargon ['dʒɑ:gən] *n* Jargon *m*
jaundice ['dʒɔ:ndɪs] *n* Gelbsucht *f*
javelin ['dʒævlɪn] *n* Speer *m*
jaw [dʒɔ:] *n* Kiefer *m*
jay [dʒeɪ] *n* Eichelhäher *m*
jaywalker ['dʒeɪwɔ:kə^r] *n* unachtsamer Fußgänger *m*, unachtsame Fußgängerin *f*
jazz [dʒæz] *n* Jazz *m*
▸ **jazz up** *vt* aufpeppen (*inf*)
jealous ['dʒɛləs] *adj* eifersüchtig; (*envious*) neidisch
jealousy ['dʒɛləsɪ] *n* Eifersucht *f*; (*envy*) Neid *m*
jeans [dʒi:nz] *npl* Jeans *pl*
jeer [dʒɪə^r] *vi* höhnische Bemerkungen machen; **to ~ at** verhöhnen
jelly ['dʒɛlɪ] *n* Götterspeise *f*; (*jam*) Gelee *m or nt*
jellyfish ['dʒɛlɪfɪʃ] *n* Qualle *f*
jeopardize ['dʒɛpədaɪz] *vt* gefährden
jeopardy ['dʒɛpədɪ] *n*: **to be in ~** gefährdet sein
jerk [dʒə:k] *n* Ruck *m*; (*inf*: *idiot*) Trottel *m* ▷ *vt* reißen ▷ *vi* (*vehicle*) ruckeln
jersey ['dʒə:zɪ] *n* Pullover *m*; (*fabric*) Jersey *m*
Jesus ['dʒi:zəs] *n* Jesus *m*; **~ Christ** Jesus Christus *m*
jet [dʒɛt] *n* Strahl *m*; (*Aviat*) Düsenflugzeug *nt*; (*Mineralogy, Jewellery*) Jett *m or nt*, Gagat *m*
jet-black ['dʒɛt'blæk] *adj* pechschwarz
jet engine *n* Düsentriebwerk *nt*
jet lag *n* Jetlag *nt*
jettison ['dʒɛtɪsn] *vt* abwerfen; (*from ship*) über Bord werfen
jetty ['dʒɛtɪ] *n* Landesteg *m*, Pier *m*
Jew [dʒu:] *n* Jude *m*, Jüdin *f*
jewel ['dʒu:əl] *n* Edelstein *m*, Juwel *nt* (*also fig*); (*in watch*) Stein *m*
jeweller, (*US*) **jeweler** ['dʒu:ələ^r] *n* Juwelier *m*
jeweller's, jeweller's shop *n* Juwelier *m*, Juweliergeschäft *nt*
jewellery, (*US*) **jewelry** ['dʒu:əlrɪ] *n* Schmuck *m*
Jewess ['dʒu:ɪs] *n* Jüdin *f*
Jewish ['dʒu:ɪʃ] *adj* jüdisch
jibe [dʒaɪb] *n* = **gibe**
jiffy ['dʒɪfɪ] (*inf*) *n*: **in a ~** sofort
jigsaw ['dʒɪgsɔ:] *n* (*also*: **jigsaw puzzle**) Puzzle(spiel) *nt*; (*tool*) Stichsäge *f*
jilt [dʒɪlt] *vt* sitzen lassen
jingle ['dʒɪŋgl] *n* (*tune*) Jingle *m* ▷ *vi* (*bracelets*) klimpern; (*bells*) bimmeln
jinx [dʒɪŋks] (*inf*) *n* Fluch *m*; **there's a ~ on it** es ist verhext
jitters ['dʒɪtəz] (*inf*) *npl*: **to get the ~** das

große Zittern bekommen

job [dʒɔb] *n* Arbeit *f*; (*post, employment*) Stelle *f*, Job *m*; **it's not my ~** es ist nicht meine Aufgabe; **a part-time ~** eine Teilzeitbeschäftigung; **a full-time ~** eine Ganztagsstelle; **he's only doing his ~** er tut nur seine Pflicht; **it's a good ~ that ...** nur gut, dass ...; **just the ~!** genau das Richtige!

job centre (*Brit*) *n* Arbeitsamt *nt*

jobless ['dʒɔblɪs] *adj* arbeitslos ▷ *npl*: **the ~** die Arbeitslosen *pl*

jockey ['dʒɔkɪ] *n* Jockey *m* ▷ *vi*: **to ~ for position** um eine gute Position rangeln

jog [dʒɔg] *vt* (an)stoßen ▷ *vi* joggen, Dauerlauf machen; **to ~ sb's memory** jds Gedächtnis *dat* nachhelfen

▶**jog along** *vi* entlangzuckeln (*inf*)

jogging ['dʒɔgɪŋ] *n* Jogging *nt*, Joggen *nt*

join [dʒɔɪn] *vt* (*club, party*) beitreten +*dat*; (*queue*) sich stellen in +*acc*; (*things, places*) verbinden; (*group of people*) sich anschließen +*dat* ▷ *vi* (*roads*) sich treffen; (*rivers*) zusammenfließen ▷ *n* Verbindungsstelle *f*; **to ~ forces (with)** (*fig*) sich zusammentun (mit); **will you ~ us for dinner?** wollen Sie mit uns zu Abend essen?; **I'll ~ you later** ich komme später

▶**join in** *vi* mitmachen ▷ *vt fus* sich beteiligen an +*dat*

▶**join up** *vi* sich treffen; (*Mil*) zum Militär gehen

joiner ['dʒɔɪnəʳ] (*Brit*) *n* Schreiner(in) *m(f)*

joint [dʒɔɪnt] *n* (*in woodwork*) Fuge *f*; (*in pipe etc*) Verbindungsstelle *f*; (*Anat*) Gelenk *nt*; (*Brit: Culin*) Braten *m*; (*inf: place*) Laden *m*; (*: of cannabis*) Joint *m* ▷ *adj* gemeinsam; (*combined*) vereint

joint account *n* gemeinsames Konto *nt*

jointly ['dʒɔɪntlɪ] *adv* gemeinsam

joke [dʒəuk] *n* Witz *m*; (*also*: **practical joke**) Streich *m* ▷ *vi* Witze machen; **to play a ~ on sb** jdm einen Streich spielen

joker ['dʒəukəʳ] *n* (*Cards*) Joker *m*

jolly ['dʒɔlɪ] *adj* fröhlich; (*enjoyable*) lustig ▷ *adv* (*Brit: inf: very*) ganz (schön) ▷ *vt* (*Brit*): **to ~ sb along** jdm aufmunternd zureden; **~ good!** prima!

jolt [dʒəult] *n* Ruck *m*; (*shock*) Schock *m* ▷ *vt* schütteln; (*subj: bus etc*) durchschütteln; (*emotionally*) aufrütteln

Jordan ['dʒɔ:dən] *n* Jordanien *nt*; (*river*) Jordan *m*

jostle ['dʒɔsl] *vt* anrempeln ▷ *vi* drängeln

jot [dʒɔt] *n*: **not one ~** kein bisschen

▶**jot down** *vt* notieren

jotter ['dʒɔtəʳ] (*Brit*) *n* Notizbuch *nt*; (*pad*) Notizblock *m*

journal ['dʒə:nl] *n* Zeitschrift *f*; (*diary*) Tagebuch *nt*

journalism ['dʒə:nəlɪzəm] *n* Journalismus *m*

journalist ['dʒə:nəlɪst] *n* Journalist(in) *m(f)*

journey ['dʒə:nɪ] *n* Reise *f* ▷ *vi* reisen; **a 5-hour ~** eine Fahrt von 5 Stunden; **return ~** Rückreise *f*; (*both ways*) Hin- und Rückreise *f*

joy [dʒɔɪ] *n* Freude *f*

joyful ['dʒɔɪful] *adj* freudig

joyrider ['dʒɔɪraɪdəʳ] *n* *Autodieb, der den Wagen nur für eine Spritztour benutzt*

JP *n abbr* = **Justice of the Peace**

Jr *abbr* (*in names: = junior*) jun.

jubilant ['dʒu:bɪlnt] *adj* überglücklich

judge [dʒʌdʒ] *n* Richter(in) *m(f)*; (*in competition*) Preisrichter(in) *m(f)*; (*fig: expert*) Kenner(in) *m(f)* ▷ *vt* (*Law: person*) die Verhandlung führen über +*acc*; (*: case*) verhandeln; (*competition*) Preisrichter(in) sein bei; (*person etc*) beurteilen; (*consider*) halten für; (*estimate*) einschätzen ▷ *vi*: **judging by** *or* **to ~ by his expression** seinem Gesichtsausdruck nach zu urteilen; **she's a good ~ of character** sie ist ein guter Menschenkenner; **I'll be the ~ of that** das müssen Sie mich schon selbst beurteilen lassen; **as far as I can ~** soweit ich es beurteilen kann; **I ~d it necessary to inform him** ich hielt es für nötig, ihn zu informieren

judgment, **judgement** ['dʒʌdʒmənt] *n* Urteil *nt*; (*Rel*) Gericht *nt*; (*view, opinion*) Meinung *f*; (*discernment*) Urteilsvermögen *nt*; **in my judg(e)ment** meiner Meinung nach; **to pass judg(e)ment (on)** (*Law*) das Urteil sprechen (über +*acc*); (*fig*) ein Urteil fällen (über +*acc*)

judicial [dʒu:'dɪʃl] *adj* gerichtlich, Justiz-; (*fig*) kritisch; **~ review** gerichtliche Überprüfung *f*

judiciary [dʒu:'dɪʃɪərɪ] *n*: **the ~** die Gerichtsbehörden *pl*

judo ['dʒu:dəu] *n* Judo *nt*

jug [dʒʌg] *n* Krug *m*

juggernaut ['dʒʌgənɔ:t] (*Brit*) *n* Fernlastwagen *m*

juggle ['dʒʌgl] *vi* jonglieren

juggler ['dʒʌgləʳ] *n* Jongleur *m*

juice [dʒu:s] *n* Saft *m*; (*inf: petrol*): **we've run out of ~** wir haben keinen Sprit mehr

juicy ['dʒu:sɪ] *adj* saftig

jukebox ['dʒu:kbɔks] *n* Musikbox *f*

July [dʒu:'laɪ] *n* Juli *m*; **the first of ~** der erste Juli; **on the eleventh of ~** am elften Juli; **in the month of ~** im (Monat) Juli; **at the beginning/end of ~** Anfang/Ende Juli; **in the middle of ~** Mitte Juli; **during ~** im Juli; **in ~ of next year** im Juli nächsten Jahres; **each** *or* **every ~** jedes Jahr im Juli; **~ was wet this year** der Juli war dieses Jahr ein nasser Monat

jumble ['dʒʌmbl] *n* Durcheinander *nt*; (*items for sale*) gebrauchte Sachen *pl* ▷ *vt* (*also*: **jumble up**) durcheinanderbringen

jumbo ['dʒʌmbəu]

jumbo jet *n* Jumbo(jet) *m*

jump [dʒʌmp] *vi* springen; (*with fear, surprise*) zusammenzucken; (*increase*) sprunghaft ansteigen ▷ *vt* springen über +*acc* ▷ *n* (*see vb*) Sprung *m*; Zusammenzucken *nt*;

sprunghafter Anstieg *m*; **to ~ the queue** (*Brit*) sich vordrängeln
▸**jump about** *vi* herumspringen
▸**jump at** *vt fus* (*idea*) sofort aufgreifen; (*chance*) sofort ergreifen; **he ~ed at the offer** er griff bei dem Angebot sofort zu
▸**jump down** *vi* herunterspringen
▸**jump up** *vi* hochspringen; (*from seat*) aufspringen

jumper ['dʒʌmpəʳ] *n* (*Brit*) Pullover *m*; (*US: dress*) Trägerkleid *nt*; (*Sport*) Springer(in) *m(f)*

jump leads (*Brit*) *npl* Starthilfekabel *nt*

jumpy ['dʒʌmpɪ] *adj* nervös

Jun. *abbr* = **June**

junction ['dʒʌŋkʃən] (*Brit*) *n* Kreuzung *f*; (*Rail*) Gleisanschluss *m*

juncture ['dʒʌŋktʃəʳ] *n*: **at this ~** zu diesem Zeitpunkt

June [dʒu:n] *n* Juni *m*; *see also* **July**

jungle ['dʒʌŋgl] *n* Urwald *m*, Dschungel *m* (*also fig*)

junior ['dʒu:nɪəʳ] *adj* jünger; (*subordinate*) untergeordnet ▹*n* Jüngere(r) *f(m)*; (*young person*) Junior *m*; **he's ~ to me (by 2 years), he's my ~ (by 2 years)** (*younger*) er ist (2 Jahre) jünger als ich; **he's ~ to me** (*subordinate*) er steht unter mir

junior high school (*US*) *n* ≈ Mittelschule *f*

junior school (*Brit*) *n* ≈ Grundschule *f*

junk [dʒʌŋk] *n* (*rubbish*) Gerümpel *nt*; (*cheap goods*) Ramsch *m*; (*ship*) Dschunke *f* ▹*vt* (*inf*) ausrangieren

junk food *n* ungesundes Essen *nt*

junkie ['dʒʌŋkɪ] (*inf*) *n* Fixer(in) *m(f)*

junk mail *n* (Post)wurfsendungen *pl*

junk shop *n* Trödelladen *m*

Junr *abbr* (*in names: = junior*) jun.

Jupiter ['dʒu:pɪtəʳ] *n* Jupiter *m*

jurisdiction [dʒuərɪs'dɪkʃən] *n* Gerichtsbarkeit *f*; (*Admin*) Zuständigkeit *f*, Zuständigkeitsbereich *m*; **it falls** *or* **comes within/outside my ~** dafür bin ich zuständig/nicht zuständig

juror ['dʒuərəʳ] *n* Schöffe *m*, Schöffin *f*; (*for capital crimes*) Geschworene(r) *f(m)*; (*in competition*) Preisrichter(in) *m(f)*

jury ['dʒuərɪ] *n*: **the ~** die Schöffen *pl*; (*for capital crimes*) die Geschworenen *pl*; (*for competition*) die Jury, das Preisgericht

just [dʒʌst] *adj* gerecht ▹*adv* (*exactly*) genau; (*only*) nur; **he's ~ done it/left** er hat es gerade getan/ist gerade gegangen; **~ as I expected** genau wie ich erwartet habe; **~ right** genau richtig; **~ two o'clock** erst zwei Uhr; **we were ~ going** wir wollten gerade gehen; **I was ~ about to phone** ich wollte gerade anrufen; **she's ~ as clever as you** sie ist genauso klug wie du; **it's ~ as well (that ...)** nur gut, dass ...; **~ as he was leaving** gerade als er gehen wollte; **~ before** gerade noch; **~ enough** gerade genug; **~ here** genau hier, genau an dieser Stelle; **he ~ missed** er hat genau danebengetroffen; **it's ~ me** ich bins nur; **it's ~ a mistake** es ist nur ein Fehler; **~ listen** hör mal; **~ ask someone the way** frage doch einfach jemanden nach dem Weg; **not ~ now** nicht gerade jetzt; **~ a minute!, ~ one moment!** einen Moment, bitte!

justice ['dʒʌstɪs] *n* Justiz *f*; (*of cause, complaint*) Berechtigung *f*; (*fairness*) Gerechtigkeit *f*; (*US: judge*) Richter(in) *m(f)*; **Lord Chief J~** (*Brit*) *oberster Richter in Großbritannien*; **to do ~ to** (*fig*) gerecht werden +*dat*

Justice of the Peace *n* Friedensrichter(in) *m(f)*

justification [dʒʌstɪfɪ'keɪʃən] *n* Rechtfertigung *f*; (*Typ*) Justierung *f*

justify ['dʒʌstɪfaɪ] *vt* rechtfertigen; (*text*) justieren; **to be justified in doing sth** etw zu *or* mit Recht tun

jut [dʒʌt] *vi* (*also*: **jut out**) vorstehen

juvenile ['dʒu:vənaɪl] *adj* (*crime, offenders*) Jugend-; (*humour, mentality*) kindisch, unreif ▹*n* Jugendliche(r) *f(m)*

K¹, k [keɪ] *n* (*letter*) K *nt*, k *nt*; **K for King** ≈ K wie Kaufmann
K² [keɪ] *abbr* (= *one thousand*) K; (*Comput*: = *kilobyte*) KB; (*Brit*: *in titles*) = **knight**
kangaroo [kæŋgəˈruː] *n* Känguru *nt*
karaoke [kɑːrəˈəukɪ] *n* Karaoke *nt*
karate [kəˈrɑːtɪ] *n* Karate *nt*
kebab [kəˈbæb] *n* Kebab *m*
keel [kiːl] *n* Kiel *m*; **on an even ~** (*fig*) stabil
▸ **keel over** *vi* kentern; (*person*) umkippen
keen [kiːn] *adj* begeistert, eifrig; (*interest*) groß; (*desire*) heftig; (*eye, intelligence, competition, edge*) scharf; **to be ~ to do** *or* **on doing sth** scharf darauf sein, etw zu tun (*inf*); **to be ~ on sth** an etw *dat* sehr interessiert sein; **to be ~ on sb** von jdm sehr angetan sein; **I'm not ~ on going** ich brenne nicht gerade darauf, zu gehen
keep [kiːp] (*pt, pp* **kept**) *vt* behalten; (*preserve, store*) aufbewahren; (*house, shop, accounts, diary*) führen; (*garden etc*) pflegen; (*chickens, bees, promise*) halten; (*family etc*) versorgen, unterhalten; (*detain*) aufhalten; (*prevent*) abhalten ▹ *vi* (*remain*) bleiben; (*food*) sich halten ▹ *n* (*food etc*) Unterhalt *m*; (*of castle*) Bergfried *m*; **to ~ doing sth** etw immer wieder tun; **to ~ sb happy** jdn zufriedenstellen; **to ~ a room tidy** ein Zimmer in Ordnung halten; **to ~ sb waiting** jdn warten lassen; **to ~ an appointment** eine Verabredung einhalten; **to ~ a record of sth** über etw *acc* Buch führen; **to ~ sth to o.s.** etw für sich behalten; **to ~ sth (back) from sb** etw vor jdm geheim halten; **to ~ sb from doing sth** jdn davon abhalten, etw zu tun; **to ~ sth from happening** etw verhindern; **to ~ time** (*clock*) genau gehen; **enough for his ~** genug für seinen Unterhalt
▸ **keep away** *vt* fernhalten ▹ *vi*: **to ~ away (from)** wegbleiben (von)
▸ **keep back** *vt* zurückhalten; (*tears*) unterdrücken; (*money*) einbehalten ▹ *vi* zurückbleiben
▸ **keep down** *vt* (*prices*) niedrig halten; (*spending*) einschränken; (*food*) bei sich behalten ▹ *vi* unten bleiben
▸ **keep in** *vt* im Haus behalten; (*at school*) nachsitzen lassen ▹ *vi* (*inf*): **to ~ in with sb** sich mit jdm gut stellen
▸ **keep off** *vt* fernhalten ▹ *vi* wegbleiben; **"~ off the grass"** "Betreten des Rasens verboten"; **~ your hands off** Hände weg
▸ **keep on** *vi*: **to ~ on doing sth** (*continue*) etw weiter tun; **to ~ on (about sth)** unaufhörlich (von etw) reden
▸ **keep out** *vt* fernhalten; **"~ out"** "Zutritt verboten"
▸ **keep up** *vt* (*payments*) weiterbezahlen; (*standards etc*) aufrechterhalten ▹ *vi*: **to ~ up (with)** mithalten können (mit)
keeper [ˈkiːpəʳ] *n* Wärter(in) *m(f)*
keeping [ˈkiːpɪŋ] *n* (*care*) Obhut *f*; **in ~ with** in Übereinstimmung mit; **out of ~ with** nicht im Einklang mit; **I'll leave this in your ~** ich vertraue dies deiner Obhut an
keepsake [ˈkiːpseɪk] *n* Andenken *nt*
kennel [ˈkɛnl] *n* Hundehütte *f*
Kenya [ˈkɛnjə] *n* Kenia *nt*
kept [kɛpt] *pt, pp of* **keep**
kerb [kəːb] (*Brit*) *n* Bordstein *m*
kernel [ˈkəːnl] *n* Kern *m*
kerosene [ˈkɛrəsiːn] *n* Kerosin *nt*
ketchup [ˈkɛtʃəp] *n* Ket(s)chup *m or nt*
kettle [ˈkɛtl] *n* Kessel *m*
key [kiː] *n* Schlüssel *m*; (*Mus*) Tonart *f*; (*of piano, computer, typewriter*) Taste *f* ▹ *cpd* (*issue etc*) Schlüssel- ▹ *vt* (*also*: **key in**) eingeben
keyboard [ˈkiːbɔːd] *n* Tastatur *f*
keyed up [kiːd-] *adj*: **to be (all) ~** (ganz) aufgedreht sein (*inf*)
keyhole [ˈkiːhəul] *n* Schlüsselloch *nt*
keyhole surgery *n* Schlüssellochchirurgie *f*, minimal invasive Chirurgie *f*
keynote [ˈkiːnəut] *n* Grundton *m*; (*of speech*) Leitgedanke *m*
kg *abbr* (= *kilogram*) kg
khaki [ˈkɑːkɪ] *n* K(h)aki *nt*
kick [kɪk] *vt* treten; (*table, ball*) treten gegen +*acc*; (*inf*: *habit*) ablegen; (: *addiction*) wegkommen von ▹ *vi* (*horse*) ausschlagen ▹ *n* Tritt *m*; (*to ball*) Schuss *m*; (*of rifle*) Rückstoß *m*; (*thrill*): **he does it for ~s** er macht es zum Spaß
▸ **kick around** (*inf*) *vi* (*person*) rumhängen; (*thing*) rumliegen
▸ **kick off** *vi* (*Sport*) anstoßen
kid [kɪd] *n* (*inf*: *child*) Kind *nt*; (*animal*) Kitz *nt*;

(*leather*) Ziegenleder *nt*, Glacéleder *nt* ▷ *vi* (*inf*) Witze machen; **~ brother** kleiner Bruder *m*; **~ sister** kleine Schwester *f*
kidnap ['kɪdnæp] *vt* entführen, kidnappen
kidnapper ['kɪdnæpəʳ] *n* Entführer(in) *m(f)*, Kidnapper(in) *m(f)*
kidnapping ['kɪdnæpɪŋ] *n* Entführung *f*, Kidnapping *nt*
kidney ['kɪdnɪ] *n* Niere *f*
kidney bean *n* Gartenbohne *f*
kill [kɪl] *vt* töten; (*murder*) ermorden, umbringen; (*plant*) eingehen lassen; (*proposal*) zu Fall bringen; (*rumour*) ein Ende machen *+dat* ▷ *n* Abschuss *m*; **to ~ time** die Zeit totschlagen; **to ~ o.s. to do sth** (*fig*) sich fast umbringen, um etw zu tun; **to ~ o.s. (laughing)** (*fig*) sich totlachen
▸ **kill off** *vt* abtöten; (*fig: romance*) beenden
killer ['kɪləʳ] *n* Mörder(in) *m(f)*
killing ['kɪlɪŋ] *n* Töten *nt*; (*instance*) Mord *m*; **to make a ~** (*inf*) einen Riesengewinn machen
killjoy ['kɪldʒɔɪ] *n* Spielverderber(in) *m(f)*
kiln [kɪln] *n* Brennofen *m*
kilo ['ki:ləu] *n* Kilo *nt*
kilobyte ['ki:ləubaɪt] *n* Kilobyte *nt*
kilogram, **kilogramme** ['kɪləugræm] *n* Kilogramm *nt*
kilometre, (*US*) **kilometer** ['kɪləmi:təʳ] *n* Kilometer *m*
kilowatt ['kɪləuwɔt] *n* Kilowatt *nt*
kilt [kɪlt] *n* Kilt *m*, Schottenrock *m*
kin [kɪn] *n* *see* **kith** *see* **next**
kind [kaɪnd] *adj* freundlich ▷ *n* Art *f*; (*sort*) Sorte *f*; **would you be ~ enough to ...?, would you be so ~ as to ...?** wären Sie (vielleicht) so nett und ...?; **it's very ~ of you (to do ...)** es ist wirklich nett von Ihnen(, ... zu tun); **in ~** (*Comm*) in Naturalien; **a ~ of ...** eine Art ...; **they are two of a ~** sie sind beide von der gleichen Art; (*people*) sie sind vom gleichen Schlag
kindergarten ['kɪndəgɑ:tn] *n* Kindergarten *m*
kind-hearted [kaɪnd'hɑ:tɪd] *adj* gutherzig
kindle ['kɪndl] *vt* anzünden; (*emotion*) wecken
kindly ['kaɪndlɪ] *adj, adv* freundlich, nett; **will you ~ ...** würden Sie bitte ...; **he didn't take it ~** er konnte sich damit nicht anfreunden
kindness ['kaɪndnɪs] *n* Freundlichkeit *f*
king [kɪŋ] *n* (*also fig*) König *m*
kingdom ['kɪŋdəm] *n* Königreich *nt*
kingfisher ['kɪŋfɪʃəʳ] *n* Eisvogel *m*
king-size ['kɪŋsaɪz], **king-sized** ['kɪŋsaɪzd] *adj* extragroß; (*cigarette*) Kingsize-
kiosk ['ki:ɔsk] *n* Kiosk *m*; (*Brit*) (Telefon)zelle *f*; (*also*: **newspaper kiosk**) (Zeitungs)kiosk *m*
kipper ['kɪpəʳ] *n* Räucherhering *m*
kiss [kɪs] *n* Kuß *m* ▷ *vt* küssen ▷ *vi* sich küssen; **to ~ (each other)** sich küssen; **to ~ sb goodbye** jdm einen Abschiedskuss geben
kiss of life (*Brit*) *n*: **the ~** Mund-zu-Mund-Beatmung *f*
kit [kɪt] *n* Zeug *nt*, Sachen *pl*; (*equipment: also Mil*) Ausrüstung *f*; (*set of tools*) Werkzeug *nt*; (*for assembly*) Bausatz *m*
▸ **kit out** (*Brit*) *vt* ausrüsten, ausstatten
kitchen ['kɪtʃɪn] *n* Küche *f*
kitchen sink *n* Spüle *f*
kite [kaɪt] *n* Drachen *m*; (*Zool*) Milan *m*
kitten ['kɪtn] *n* Kätzchen *nt*
kitty ['kɪtɪ] *n* (gemeinsame) Kasse *f*
kiwi ['ki:wi:], **kiwi fruit** *n* Kiwi(frucht) *f*
km *abbr* (= *kilometre*) km
km/h *abbr* (= *kilometres per hour*) km/h
knack [næk] *n*: **to have the ~ of doing sth** es heraushaben, wie man etw macht; **there's a ~ to doing this** da ist ein Trick *or* Kniff dabei
knapsack ['næpsæk] *n* Rucksack *m*
knead [ni:d] *vt* kneten
knee [ni:] *n* Knie *nt*
kneecap ['ni:kæp] *n* Kniescheibe *f*
kneel [ni:l] (*pt, pp* **knelt**) *vi* knien; (*also*: **kneel down**) niederknien
knelt [nɛlt] *pt, pp of* **kneel**
knew [nju:] *pt of* **know**
knickers ['nɪkəz] (*Brit*) *npl* Schlüpfer *m*
knife [naɪf] (*pl* **knives**) *n* Messer *nt* ▷ *vt* (*injure, attack*) einstechen auf *+acc*; **~, fork and spoon** Messer, Gabel und Löffel
knight [naɪt] *n* (*Brit*) Ritter *m*; (*Chess*) Springer *m*, Pferd *nt*
knighthood ['naɪthud] (*Brit*) *n*: **to get a ~** in den Adelsstand erhoben werden
knit [nɪt] *vt* stricken ▷ *vi* stricken; (*bones*) zusammenwachsen; **to ~ one's brows** die Stirn runzeln
knitting ['nɪtɪŋ] *n* Stricken *nt*; (*garment being made*) Strickzeug *nt*
knitting needle *n* Stricknadel *f*
knitwear ['nɪtwɛəʳ] *n* Strickwaren *pl*
knives [naɪvz] *npl of* **knife**
knob [nɔb] *n* Griff *m*; (*of stick*) Knauf *m*; (*on radio, TV etc*) Knopf *m*; **a ~ of butter** (*Brit*) ein Stückchen *nt* Butter
knock [nɔk] *vt* schlagen; (*bump into*) stoßen gegen *+acc*; (*inf: criticize*) runtermachen ▷ *vi* klopfen ▷ *n* Schlag *m*; (*bump*) Stoß *m*; (*on door*) Klopfen *nt*; **to ~ a nail into sth** einen Nagel in etw *acc* schlagen; **to ~ some sense into sb** jdn zur Vernunft bringen; **to ~ at/on** klopfen an/auf *+acc*; **he ~ed at the door** er klopfte an, er klopfte an die Tür
▸ **knock about** (*inf*) *vt* schlagen, verprügeln ▷ *vi* rumziehen; **~ about with** sich rumtreiben mit
▸ **knock around** *vt, vi* = **knock about**
▸ **knock back** (*inf*) *vt* (*drink*) sich *dat* hinter die Binde kippen
▸ **knock down** *vt* anfahren; (*fatally*) überfahren; (*building etc*) abreißen; (*price: buyer*) herunterhandeln; (*: seller*) heruntergehen mit
▸ **knock off** *vi* (*inf*) Feierabend machen ▷ *vt* (*from price*) nachlassen; (*inf: steal*) klauen; **to ~ off £10** £10 nachlassen
▸ **knock out** *vt* bewusstlos schlagen;

(*subj: drug*) bewusstlos werden lassen; (*Boxing*) k. o. schlagen; (*in game, competition*) besiegen
▸ **knock over** *vt* umstoßen; (*with car*) anfahren

knocker ['nɔkə^r] *n* Türklopfer *m*

knockout ['nɔkaut] *n* (*Boxing*) K.-o.-Schlag *m*, Ko.-Schlag *m* ▹ *cpd* (*competition etc*) Ausscheidungs-

knot [nɔt] *n* Knoten *m*; (*in wood*) Ast *m* ▹ *vt* einen Knoten machen in *+acc*; (*knot together*) verknoten; **to tie a ~** einen Knoten machen

know [nəu] (*pt* **knew**, *pp* **~n**) *vt* kennen; (*facts*) wissen; (*language*) können ▹ *vi*: **to ~ about** *or* **of sth/sb** von etw/jdm gehört haben; **to ~ how to swim** schwimmen können; **to get to ~ sth** etw erfahren; (*place*) etw kennenlernen; **I don't ~ him** ich kenne ihn nicht; **to ~ right from wrong** Gut und Böse unterscheiden können; **as far as I ~** soviel ich weiß; **yes, I ~** ja, ich weiß; **I don't ~** ich weiß (es) nicht

know-all ['nəuɔːl] (*Brit: pej*) *n* Alleswisser *m*

know-how ['nəuhau] *n* Know-how *nt*, Sachkenntnis *f*

knowing ['nəuɪŋ] *adj* wissend

knowingly ['nəuɪŋlɪ] *adv* (*purposely*) bewusst; (*smile, look*) wissend

know-it-all ['nəuɪtɔːl] (*US*) *n* = **know-all**

knowledge ['nɔlɪdʒ] *n* Wissen *nt*, Kenntnis *f*; (*learning, things learnt*) Kenntnisse *pl*; **to have no ~ of** nichts wissen von; **not to my ~** nicht, dass ich wüsste; **without my ~** ohne mein Wissen; **it is common ~ that ...** es ist allgemein bekannt, dass ...; **it has come to my ~ that ...** ich habe erfahren, dass ...; **to have a working ~ of French** Grundkenntnisse in Französisch haben

knowledgeable ['nɔlɪdʒəbl] *adj* informiert

known [nəun] *pp of* **know** ▹ *adj* bekannt; (*expert*) anerkannt

knuckle ['nʌkl] *n* (Finger)knöchel *m*
▸ **knuckle down** (*inf*) *vi* sich dahinter klemmen; **to ~ down to work** sich an die Arbeit machen
▸ **knuckle under** (*inf*) *vi* sich fügen, spuren

koala [kəu'ɑːlə] *n* (*also*: **koala bear**) Koala(bär) *m*

Koran [kɔ'rɑːn] *n*: **the ~** der Koran

Korea [kə'rɪə] *n* Korea *nt*; **North ~** Nordkorea *nt*; **South ~** Südkorea *nt*

Korean [kə'rɪən] *adj* koreanisch ▹ *n* Koreaner(in) *m(f)*

kosher ['kəuʃə^r] *adj* koscher

Kuwait [ku'weɪt] *n* Kuwait *nt*

L¹, **l¹** [ɛl] *n* (*letter*) L *nt*, l *nt*; **L for Lucy, L for Love** (*US*) ≈ L wie Ludwig
L² [ɛl] *abbr* (*Brit: Aut: = learner*) *am Auto angebrachtes Kennzeichen für Fahrschüler*; = **lake**; (= *large*) gr.; (= *left*) l.
l² *abbr* (= *litre*) l
lab [læb] *n abbr* = **laboratory**
label ['leɪbl] *n* Etikett *nt*; (*brand: of record*) Label *nt* ▷ *vt* etikettieren; (*fig: person*) abstempeln
laboratory [lə'bɔrətərɪ] *n* Labor *nt*
labor union (*US*) *n* Gewerkschaft *f*
labour, (*US*) **labor** ['leɪbəʳ] *n* Arbeit *f*; (*work force*) Arbeitskräfte *pl*; (*Med*): **to be in ~** in den Wehen liegen ▷ *vi*: **to ~ (at sth)** sich (mit etw) abmühen ▷ *vt*: **to ~ a point** auf einem Thema herumreiten; **L~, the Labour Party** (*Brit*) die Labour Party; **hard ~** Zwangsarbeit *f*
laboured ['leɪbəd] *adj* (*breathing*) schwer; (*movement, style*) schwerfällig
labourer ['leɪbərəʳ] *n* Arbeiter(in) *m(f)*; **farm ~** Landarbeiter(in) *m(f)*
lace [leɪs] *n* (*fabric*) Spitze *f*; (*of shoe etc*) (Schuh)band *nt*, Schnürsenkel *m* ▷ *vt* (*also*: **lace up**) (zu)schnüren; **to ~ a drink** einen Schuss Alkohol in ein Getränk geben
lack [læk] *n* Mangel *m* ▷ *vt*, *vi*: **sb ~s sth, sb is ~ing in sth** jdm fehlt es an etw *dat*; **through** *or* **for ~ of** aus Mangel an +*dat*; **to be ~ing** fehlen
lacquer ['lækəʳ] *n* Lack *m*; (*also*: **hair lacquer**) Haarspray *nt*
lacy ['leɪsɪ] *adj* Spitzen-; (*like lace*) spitzenartig
lad [læd] *n* Junge *m*
ladder ['lædəʳ] *n* (*also fig*) Leiter *f*; (*Brit: in tights*) Laufmasche *f* ▷ *vt* (*Brit*) Laufmaschen bekommen in +*dat* ▷ *vi* (*Brit*) Laufmaschen bekommen
laden ['leɪdn] *adj*: **~ (with)** beladen (mit); **fully ~** vollbeladen
ladle ['leɪdl] *n* Schöpflöffel *m*, (Schöpf)kelle *f* ▷ *vt* schöpfen
▸ **ladle out** *vt* (*fig*) austeilen
lady ['leɪdɪ] *n* (*woman*) Frau *f*; (*: dignified, graceful etc*) Dame *f*; (*Brit: title*) Lady *f*; **ladies and gentlemen ...** meine Damen und Herren ...; **young ~** junge Dame; **the ladies' (room)** die Damentoilette
ladybird ['leɪdɪbə:d], (*US*) **ladybug** *n* Marienkäfer *m*
ladylike ['leɪdɪlaɪk] *adj* damenhaft
ladyship ['leɪdɪʃɪp] *n*: **your L~** Ihre Ladyschaft
lag [læg] *n* (*period of time*) Zeitabstand *m* ▷ *vi* (*also*: **lag behind**) zurückbleiben; (*trade, investment etc*) zurückgehen ▷ *vt* (*pipes etc*) isolieren; **old ~** (*inf: prisoner*) (ehemaliger) Knacki *m*
lager ['lɑ:gəʳ] *n* helles Bier *nt*
lagoon [lə'gu:n] *n* Lagune *f*
laid [leɪd] *pt*, *pp of* **lay**
laid up *adj*: **to be ~ (with)** im Bett liegen (mit)
lain [leɪn] *pp of* **lie**
lake [leɪk] *n* See *m*
lamb [læm] *n* Lamm *nt*; (*meat*) Lammfleisch *nt*
lamb chop *n* Lammkotelett *nt*
lame [leɪm] *adj* lahm; (*argument, answer*) schwach
lament [lə'mɛnt] *n* Klage *f* ▷ *vt* beklagen
laminated ['læmɪneɪtɪd] *adj* laminiert; (*metal*) geschichtet; **~ glass** Verbundglas *nt*; **~ wood** Sperrholz *nt*
lamp [læmp] *n* Lampe *f*
lamppost ['læmppəust] (*Brit*) *n* Laternenpfahl *m*
lampshade ['læmpʃeɪd] *n* Lampenschirm *m*
lance [lɑ:ns] *n* Lanze *f* ▷ *vt* (*Med*) aufschneiden
land [lænd] *n* Land *nt*; (*as property*) Grund und Boden *m* ▷ *vi* (*Aviat, fig*) landen; (*from ship*) an Land gehen ▷ *vt* (*passengers*) absetzen; (*goods*) an Land bringen; **to own ~** Land besitzen; **to go** *or* **travel by ~** auf dem Landweg reisen; **to ~ on one's feet** (*fig*) auf die Füße fallen; **to ~ sb with sth** (*inf*) jdm etw aufhalsen
▸ **land up** *vi*: **to ~ up in/at** landen in +*dat*
landfill site ['lændfɪl-] *n* ≈ Mülldeponie *f*
landing ['lændɪŋ] *n* (*of house*) Flur *m*; (*outside flat door*) Treppenabsatz *m*; (*Aviat*) Landung *f*
landing card *n* Einreisekarte *f*
landing strip *n* Landebahn *f*
landlady ['lændleɪdɪ] *n* Vermieterin *f*; (*of pub*) Wirtin *f*
landlocked ['lændlɔkt] *adj* von Land eingeschlossen; **~ country** Binnenstaat *m*
landlord ['lændlɔ:d] *n* Vermieter *m*; (*of pub*) Wirt *m*
landmark ['lændmɑ:k] *n* Orientierungspunkt *m*; (*famous building*) Wahrzeichen *nt*; (*fig*)

Meilenstein *m*
landowner ['lændəunəʳ] *n* Grundbesitzer(in) *m(f)*
landscape ['lændskeɪp] *n* Landschaft *f* ▷ *vt* landschaftlich *or* gärtnerisch gestalten
landscape architect *n* Landschaftsarchitekt(in) *m(f)*
landslide ['lændslaɪd] *n* Erdrutsch *m*; (*fig: electoral*) Erdrutschsieg *m*
lane [leɪn] *n* (*in country*) Weg *m*; (*in town*) Gasse *f*; (*of carriageway*) Spur *f*; (*of race course, swimming pool*) Bahn *f*; **shipping ~** Schifffahrtsweg *m*
language ['læŋgwɪdʒ] *n* Sprache *f*; **bad ~** Kraftausdrücke *pl*
language laboratory *n* Sprachlabor *nt*
lank [læŋk] *adj* (*hair*) strähnig
lanky ['læŋkɪ] *adj* schlaksig
lantern ['læntən] *n* Laterne *f*
lap [læp] *n* Schoß *m*; (*in race*) Runde *f* ▷ *vt* (*also*: **lap up**) aufschlecken ▷ *vi* (*water*) plätschern
▸ **lap up** *vt* (*fig*) genießen
lapel [lə'pɛl] *n* Aufschlag *m*, Revers *nt or m*
Lapland ['læplænd] *n* Lappland *nt*
lapse [læps] *n* (*bad behaviour*) Fehltritt *m*; (*of memory etc*) Schwäche *f*; (*of time*) Zeitspanne *f* ▷ *vi* ablaufen; (*law*) ungültig werden; **to ~ into bad habits** in schlechte Gewohnheiten verfallen
laptop ['læptɔp] (*Comput*) *n* Laptop *m* ▷ *cpd* Laptop-
larceny ['lɑːsənɪ] *n* Diebstahl *m*
larch [lɑːtʃ] *n* Lärche *f*
lard [lɑːd] *n* Schweineschmalz *nt*
larder ['lɑːdəʳ] *n* Speisekammer *f*; (*cupboard*) Speiseschrank *m*
large [lɑːdʒ] *adj* groß; (*person*) korpulent; **to make ~r** vergrößern; **a ~ number of people** eine große Anzahl von Menschen; **on a ~ scale** im großen Rahmen; (*extensive*) weitreichend; **at ~** (*as a whole*) im Allgemeinen; (*at liberty*) auf freiem Fuß; **by and ~** im Großen und Ganzen
largely ['lɑːdʒlɪ] *adv* (*mostly*) zum größten Teil; (*mainly*) hauptsächlich
large-scale ['lɑːdʒ'skeɪl] *adj* im großen Rahmen; (*extensive*) weitreichend; (*map, diagram*) in einem großen Maßstab
lark [lɑːk] *n* (*bird*) Lerche *f*; (*joke*) Spaß *m*, Jux *m*
▸ **lark about** *vi* herumalbern
laryngitis [lærɪn'dʒaɪtɪs] *n* Kehlkopfentzündung *f*
lasagne [lə'zænjə] *n* Lasagne *pl*
laser ['leɪzəʳ] *n* Laser *m*
laser printer *n* Laserdrucker *m*
lash [læʃ] *n* (*also*: **eyelash**) Wimper *f*; (*blow with whip*) Peitschenhieb *m* ▷ *vt* peitschen; (*rain, wind*) peitschen gegen; (*tie*): **to ~ to** festbinden an *+dat*; **to ~ together** zusammenbinden
▸ **lash down** *vt* festbinden ▷ *vi* (*rain*) niederprasseln
▸ **lash out** *vi* um sich schlagen; **to ~ out at sb** auf jdn losschlagen; **to ~ out at** *or* **against sb** (*criticize*) gegen jdn wettern
lass [læs] (*Brit*) *n* Mädchen *nt*
lasso [læ'suː] *n* Lasso *nt* ▷ *vt* mit dem Lasso einfangen
last [lɑːst] *adj* letzte(r, s) ▷ *adv* (*most recently*) zuletzt, das letzte Mal; (*finally*) als Letztes ▷ *vi* (*continue*) dauern; (*: in good condition*) sich halten; (*money, commodity*) reichen; **~ week** letzte Woche; **~ night** gestern Abend; **~ but one** vorletzte(r, s); **the ~ time** das letzte Mal; **at ~** endlich; **it ~s (for) 2 hours** es dauert 2 Stunden
last-ditch ['lɑːst'dɪtʃ] *adj* (*attempt*) allerletzte(r, s)
lasting ['lɑːstɪŋ] *adj* dauerhaft
lastly ['lɑːstlɪ] *adv* (*finally*) schließlich; (*last of all*) zum Schluss
last-minute ['lɑːstmɪnɪt] *adj* in letzter Minute
latch [lætʃ] *n* Riegel *m*; **to be on the ~** nur eingeklinkt sein
▸ **latch on to** *vt fus* (*person*) sich anschließen *+dat*; (*idea*) abfahren auf *+acc* (*inf*)
late [leɪt] *adj* spät; (*not on time*) verspätet ▷ *adv* spät; (*behind time*) zu spät; (*recently*): **~ of Glasgow** bis vor Kurzem in Glasgow wohnhaft; **the ~ Mr X** (*deceased*) der verstorbene Herr X; **in ~ May** Ende Mai; **to be (10 minutes) ~** (10 Minuten) zu spät kommen; (*train etc*) (10 Minuten) Verspätung haben; **to work ~** länger arbeiten; **~ in life** relativ spät (im Leben); **of ~** in letzter Zeit
latecomer ['leɪtkʌməʳ] *n* Nachzügler(in) *m(f)*
lately ['leɪtlɪ] *adv* in letzter Zeit
later ['leɪtəʳ] *adj, adv* später; **~ on** nachher
latest ['leɪtɪst] *adj* neueste(r, s) ▷ *n*: **at the ~** spätestens
lathe [leɪð] *n* Drehbank *f*
lather ['lɑːðəʳ] *n* (Seifen)schaum *m* ▷ *vt* einschäumen
Latin ['lætɪn] *n* Latein *nt*; (*person*) Südländer(in) *m(f)* ▷ *adj* lateinisch; (*temperament etc*) südländisch
Latin America *n* Lateinamerika *nt*
Latin American *adj* lateinamerikanisch ▷ *n* Lateinamerikaner(in) *m(f)*
latitude ['lætɪtjuːd] *n* (*Geog*) Breite *f*; (*fig: freedom*) Freiheit *f*
latter ['lætəʳ] *adj* (*of two*) letztere(r, s); (*later*) spätere(r, s); (*second part of period*) zweite(r, s); (*recent*) letzte(r, s) ▷ *n*: **the ~** der/die/das Letztere, die Letzteren
latterly ['lætəlɪ] *adv* in letzter Zeit
laudable ['lɔːdəbl] *adj* lobenswert
laugh [lɑːf] *n* Lachen *nt* ▷ *vi* lachen; **(to do sth) for a ~** (etw) aus Spaß (tun)
▸ **laugh at** *vt fus* lachen über *+acc*
▸ **laugh off** *vt* mit einem Lachen abtun
laughable ['lɑːfəbl] *adj* lächerlich, lachhaft
laughing stock *n*: **to be the ~ of** zum Gespött *+gen* werden
laughter ['lɑːftəʳ] *n* Lachen *nt*, Gelächter *nt*

launch [lɔːntʃ] *n* (*of rocket, missile*) Abschuss *m*; (*of satellite*) Start *m*; (*Comm: of product*) Einführung *f*; (*: with publicity*) Lancierung *f*; (*motorboat*) Barkasse *f* ▷ *vt* (*ship*) vom Stapel lassen; (*rocket, missile*) abschießen; (*satellite*) starten; (*fig: start*) beginnen mit; (*Comm*) auf den Markt bringen; (*: with publicity*) lancieren
▶ **launch into** *vt fus* (*speech*) vom Stapel lassen; (*activity*) in Angriff nehmen
▶ **launch out** *vi*: **to ~ out (into)** beginnen (mit)
launder [ˈlɔːndəʳ] *vt* waschen und bügeln; (*pej: money*) waschen
laundry [ˈlɔːndrɪ] *n* Wäsche *f*; (*dirty*) (schmutzige) Wäsche; (*business*) Wäscherei *f*; (*room*) Waschküche *f*; **to do the ~** (Wäsche) waschen
laurel [ˈlɔrl] *n* (*tree*) Lorbeer(baum) *m*; **to rest on one's ~s** sich auf seinen Lorbeeren ausruhen
lava [ˈlɑːvə] *n* Lava *f*
lavatory [ˈlævətərɪ] *n* Toilette *f*
lavender [ˈlævəndəʳ] *n* Lavendel *m*
lavish [ˈlævɪʃ] *adj* großzügig; (*meal*) üppig; (*surroundings*) feudal; (*wasteful*) verschwenderisch ▷ *vt*: **to ~ sth on sb** jdn mit etw überhäufen
law [lɔː] *n* Recht *nt*; (*a rule: also of nature, science*) Gesetz *nt*; (*professions connected with law*) Rechtswesen *nt*; (*Scol*) Jura *no art*; **against the ~** rechtswidrig; **to study ~** Jura *or* Recht(swissenschaft) studieren; **to go to ~** vor Gericht gehen; **to break the ~** gegen das Gesetz verstoßen
law-abiding [ˈlɔːəbaɪdɪŋ] *adj* gesetzestreu
law court *n* Gerichtshof *m*, Gericht *nt*
lawful [ˈlɔːful] *adj* rechtmäßig
lawless [ˈlɔːlɪs] *adj* gesetzwidrig
lawn [lɔːn] *n* Rasen *m*
lawn tennis *n* Rasentennis *nt*
law school (*US*) *n* juristische Hochschule *f*
lawsuit [ˈlɔːsuːt] *n* Prozess *m*
lawyer [ˈlɔːjəʳ] *n* (Rechts)anwalt *m*, (Rechts)anwältin *f*
lax [læks] *adj* lax
laxative [ˈlæksətɪv] *n* Abführmittel *nt*
lay [leɪ] (*pt, pp* **laid**) *pt of* **lie** ▷ *adj* (*Rel: preacher etc*) Laien- ▷ *vt* legen; (*table*) decken; (*carpet, cable etc*) verlegen; (*plans*) schmieden; (*trap*) stellen; **the ~ person** (*not expert*) der Laie; **to ~ facts/proposals before sb** jdm Tatsachen vorlegen/Vorschläge unterbreiten; **to ~ one's hands on sth** (*fig*) etw in die Finger bekommen; **to get laid** (*inf!*) bumsen (*!*)
▶ **lay aside** *vt* weglegen, zur Seite legen
▶ **lay by** *vt* beiseitelegen, auf die Seite legen
▶ **lay down** *vt* hinlegen; (*rules, laws etc*) festlegen; **to ~ down the law** Vorschriften machen; **to ~ down one's life** sein Leben geben
▶ **lay in** *vt* (*supply*) anlegen
▶ **lay into** *vt fus* losgehen auf *+acc*; (*criticize*) herunterputzen
▶ **lay off** *vt* (*workers*) entlassen
▶ **lay on** *vt* (*meal*) auftischen; (*entertainment etc*) sorgen für; (*water, gas*) anschließen; (*paint*) auftragen
▶ **lay out** *vt* ausbreiten; (*inf: spend*) ausgeben
▶ **lay up** *vt* (*illness*) außer Gefecht setzen; *see also* **lay by**
layabout [ˈleɪəbaut] (*inf: pej*) *n* Faulenzer *m*
lay-by [ˈleɪbaɪ] (*Brit*) *n* Parkbucht *f*
layer [ˈleɪəʳ] *n* Schicht *f*
layman [ˈleɪmən] (*irreg: like* **man**) *n* Laie *m*
layout [ˈleɪaut] *n* (*of garden*) Anlage *f*; (*of building*) Aufteilung *f*; (*Typ*) Layout *nt*
laze [leɪz] *vi* (*also*: **laze about**) (herum)faulenzen
lazy [ˈleɪzɪ] *adj* faul; (*movement, action*) langsam, träge
lead¹ [liːd] (*pt, pp* **led**) *n* (*Sport, fig*) Führung *f*; (*clue*) Spur *f*; (*in play, film*) Hauptrolle *f*; (*for dog*) Leine *f*; (*Elec*) Kabel *nt* ▷ *vt* anführen; (*guide*) führen; (*organization, orchestra*) leiten ▷ *vi* führen; **to be in the ~** (*Sport, fig*) in Führung liegen; **to take the ~** (*Sport*) in Führung gehen; **to ~ the way** vorangehen; **to ~ sb astray** jdn vom rechten Weg abführen; (*mislead*) jdn irreführen; **to ~ sb to believe that ...** jdm den Eindruck vermitteln, dass ...; **to ~ sb to do sth** jdn dazu bringen, etw zu tun
▶ **lead away** *vt* wegführen; (*prisoner etc*) abführen
▶ **lead back** *vt* zurückführen
▶ **lead off** *vi* (*in conversation etc*) den Anfang machen; (*room, road*) abgehen ▷ *vt fus* abgehen von
▶ **lead on** *vt* (*tease*) aufziehen
▶ **lead to** *vt fus* führen zu
▶ **lead up to** *vt fus* (*events*) vorangehen *+dat*; (*in conversation*) hinauswollen auf *+acc*
lead² [lɛd] *n* Blei *nt*; (*in pencil*) Mine *f*
leaden [ˈlɛdn] *adj* (*sky, sea*) bleiern; (*movements*) bleischwer
leader [ˈliːdəʳ] *n* Führer(in) *m(f)*; (*Sport*) Erste(r) *f(m)*; (*in newspaper*) Leitartikel *m*; **the L~ of the House (of Commons/of Lords)** (*Brit*) der Führer des Unterhauses/des Oberhauses
leadership [ˈliːdəʃɪp] *n* Führung *f*; (*position*) Vorsitz *m*; (*quality*) Führungsqualitäten *pl*
lead-free [ˈlɛdfriː] (*old*) *adj* bleifrei
leading [ˈliːdɪŋ] *adj* führend; (*role*) Haupt-; (*first, front*) vorderste(r, s)
leading lady *n* (*Theat*) Hauptdarstellerin *f*
leading light *n* führende Persönlichkeit *f*
leading man *n* (*Theat*) Hauptdarsteller *m*
lead singer [liːd-] *n* Leadsänger(in) *m(f)*
leaf [liːf] (*pl* **leaves**) *n* Blatt *nt*; (*of table*) Ausziehplatte *f*; **to turn over a new ~** einen neuen Anfang machen; **to take a ~ out of sb's book** sich *dat* von jdm eine Scheibe abschneiden
▶ **leaf through** *vt fus* durchblättern
leaflet [ˈliːflɪt] *n* Informationsblatt *nt*

league [li:g] *n* (*of people, clubs*) Verband *m*; (*of countries*) Bund *m*; (*Football*) Liga *f*; **to be in ~ with sb** mit jdm gemeinsame Sache machen

leak [li:k] *n* Leck *nt*; (*in roof, pipe etc*) undichte Stelle *f*; (*piece of information*) zugespielte Information *f* ▷ *vi* (*shoes, roof, pipe*) undicht sein; (*ship*) lecken; (*liquid*) auslaufen; (*gas*) ausströmen ▷ *vt* (*information*) durchsickern lassen; **to ~ sth to sb** jdm etw zuspielen

▶ **leak out** *vi* (*liquid*) auslaufen; (*news, information*) durchsickern

lean [li:n] (*pt, pp* **leaned** *or* **~t**) *adj* (*person*) schlank; (*meat, time*) mager ▷ *vt*: **to ~ sth on sth** etw an etw *acc* lehnen; (*rest*) etw auf etw *acc* stützen ▷ *vi* (*slope*) sich neigen; **to ~ against** sich lehnen gegen; **to ~ on** sich stützen auf *+acc*; **to ~ forward/back** sich vorbeugen/zurücklehnen; **to ~ towards** tendieren zu

▶ **lean out** *vi* sich hinauslehnen

▶ **lean over** *vi* sich vorbeugen

leaning ['li:nɪŋ] *n* Hang *m*, Neigung *f*

leant [lɛnt] *pt, pp of* **lean**

leap [li:p] (*pt, pp* **leaped** *or* **~t**) *n* Sprung *m*; (*in price, number etc*) sprunghafter Anstieg *m* ▷ *vi* springen; (*price, number etc*) sprunghaft (an)steigen

▶ **leap at** *vt fus* (*offer*) sich stürzen auf *+acc*; (*opportunity*) beim Schopf ergreifen

▶ **leap up** *vi* aufspringen

leapfrog ['li:pfrɔg] *n* Bockspringen *nt*

leapt [lɛpt] *pt, pp of* **leap**

leap year *n* Schaltjahr *nt*

learn [lə:n] (*pt, pp* **learned** *or* **~t**) *vt* lernen; (*facts*) erfahren ▷ *vi* lernen; **to ~ about** *or* **of sth** von etw erfahren; **to ~ about sth** (*study*) etw lernen; **to ~ that ...** (*hear, read*) erfahren, dass ...; **to ~ to do sth** etw lernen

learned ['lə:nɪd] *adj* gelehrt; (*book, paper*) wissenschaftlich

learner ['lə:nəʳ] (*Brit*) *n* (*also*: **learner driver**) Fahrschüler(in) *m(f)*

learning ['lə:nɪŋ] *n* Gelehrsamkeit *f*

learnt [lə:nt] *pt, pp of* **learn**

lease [li:s] *n* Pachtvertrag *m* ▷ *vt*: **to ~ sth (to sb)** etw (an jdn) verpachten; **on ~ (to)** verpachtet (an *+acc*); **to ~ sth (from sb)** etw (von jdm) pachten

▶ **lease back** *vt* rückmieten

leash [li:ʃ] *n* Leine *f*

least [li:st] *adv* am wenigsten ▷ *adj*: **the ~** (*+ noun*) der/die/das wenigste; (*: slightest*) der/die/das geringste; **the ~ expensive car** das billigste Auto; **at ~** mindestens; (*still, rather*) wenigstens; **you could at ~ have written** du hättest wenigstens schreiben können; **not in the ~** nicht im Geringsten; **it was the ~ I could do** das war das wenigste, was ich tun konnte

leather ['lɛðəʳ] *n* Leder *nt*

leave [li:v] (*pt, pp* **left**) *vt* verlassen; (*leave behind*) zurücklassen; (*mark, stain*) hinterlassen; (*object: accidentally*) liegen lassen, stehen lassen; (*food*) übrig lassen; (*space, time etc*) lassen ▷ *vi* (*go away*) (weg)gehen; (*bus, train*) abfahren ▷ *n* Urlaub *m*; **to ~ sth to sb** (*money etc*) jdm etw hinterlassen; **to ~ sb with sth** (*impose*) jdm etw aufhalsen; (*possession*) jdm etw lassen; **they were left with nothing** ihnen blieb nichts; **to be left** übrig sein; **to be left over** (*remain*) übrig (geblieben) sein; **to ~ for** gehen/fahren nach; **to take one's ~ of sb** sich von jdm verabschieden; **on ~** auf Urlaub

▶ **leave behind** *vt* zurücklassen; (*object: accidentally*) liegen lassen, stehen lassen

▶ **leave off** *vt* (*cover, lid*) ablassen; (*heating, light*) auslassen ▷ *vi* (*inf: stop*) aufhören

▶ **leave on** *vt* (*light, heating*) anlassen

▶ **leave out** *vt* auslassen

leaves [li:vz] *npl of* **leaf**

Lebanon ['lɛbənən] *n* Libanon *m*

lecherous ['lɛtʃərəs] (*pej*) *adj* lüstern

lecture ['lɛktʃəʳ] *n* Vortrag *m*; (*Univ*) Vorlesung *f* ▷ *vi* Vorträge/Vorlesungen halten ▷ *vt* (*scold*): **to ~ sb on** *or* **about sth** jdm wegen etw eine Strafpredigt halten; **to give a ~ on** einen Vortrag/eine Vorlesung halten über *+acc*

lecture hall *n* Hörsaal *m*

lecturer ['lɛktʃərəʳ] (*Brit*) *n* Dozent(in) *m(f)*; (*speaker*) Redner(in) *m(f)*

led [lɛd] *pt, pp of* **lead¹**

ledge [lɛdʒ] *n* (*of mountain*) (Fels)vorsprung *m*; (*of window*) Fensterbrett *nt*; (*on wall*) Leiste *f*

ledger ['lɛdʒəʳ] *n* (*Comm*) Hauptbuch *nt*

leech [li:tʃ] *n* Blutegel *m*; (*fig*) Blutsauger *m*

leek [li:k] *n* Porree *m*, Lauch *m*

leer [lɪəʳ] *vi*: **to ~ at sb** jdm lüsterne Blicke zuwerfen

leeway ['li:weɪ] *n* (*fig*): **to have some ~** etwas Spielraum haben; **there's a lot of ~ to make up** ein großer Rückstand muss aufgeholt werden

left [lɛft] *pt, pp of* **leave** ▷ *adj* (*remaining*) übrig; (*of position*) links; (*of direction*) nach links ▷ *n* linke Seite *f* ▷ *adv* links; nach links; **on the ~, to the ~** links; **the L~** (*Pol*) die Linke

left-hand drive ['lɛfthænd-] *adj* mit Linkssteuerung

left-handed [lɛft'hændɪd] *adj* linkshändig

left-luggage [lɛft'lʌgɪdʒ], **left-luggage office** (*Brit*) *n* Gepäckaufbewahrung *f*

left-wing ['lɛft'wɪŋ] *adj* (*Pol*) linke(r, s)

leg [lɛg] *n* Bein *nt*; (*Culin*) Keule *f*; (*Sport*) Runde *f*; (*: of relay race*) Teilstrecke *f*; (*of journey etc*) Etappe *f*; **to stretch one's ~s** sich *dat* die Beine vertreten; **to get one's ~ over** (*inf*) bumsen

legacy ['lɛgəsɪ] *n* Erbschaft *f*; (*fig*) Erbe *nt*

legal ['li:gl] *adj* (*requirement*) rechtlich, gesetzlich; (*system*) Rechts-; (*allowed by law*) legal, rechtlich zulässig; **to take ~ action** *or* **proceedings against sb** jdn verklagen

legal holiday (*US*) *n* gesetzlicher Feiertag *m*

legalize ['li:gəlaɪz] *vt* legalisieren
legally ['li:gəlɪ] *adv* rechtlich, gesetzlich; (*in accordance with the law*) rechtmäßig; **~ binding** rechtsverbindlich
legal tender *n* gesetzliches Zahlungsmittel *nt*
legend ['lɛdʒənd] *n* Legende *f*, Sage *f*; (*fig: person*) Legende *f*
legendary ['lɛdʒəndərɪ] *adj* legendär; (*very famous*) berühmt
leggings ['lɛgɪŋz] *npl* Leggings *pl*, Leggins *pl*
legible ['lɛdʒəbl] *adj* leserlich
legislation [lɛdʒɪs'leɪʃən] *n* Gesetzgebung *f*; (*laws*) Gesetze *pl*
legislative ['lɛdʒɪslətɪv] *adj* gesetzgebend; **~ reforms** Gesetzesreformen *pl*
legislature ['lɛdʒɪslətʃə^r] *n* Legislative *f*
legitimate [lɪ'dʒɪtɪmət] *adj* (*reasonable*) berechtigt; (*excuse*) begründet; (*legal*) rechtmäßig
leisure ['lɛʒə^r] *n* Freizeit *f*; **at ~** in Ruhe
leisure centre *n* Freizeitzentrum *nt*
leisurely ['lɛʒəlɪ] *adj* geruhsam
lemon ['lɛmən] *n* Zitrone *f*; (*colour*) Zitronengelb *nt*
lemonade [lɛmə'neɪd] *n* Limonade *f*
lemon tea *n* Zitronentee *m*
lend [lɛnd] (*pt, pp* **lent**) *vt*: **to ~ sth to sb** jdm etw leihen; **to ~ sb a hand (with sth)** jdm (bei etw) helfen; **it ~s itself to ...** es eignet sich für ...
length [lɛŋθ] *n* Länge *f*; (*piece*) Stück *nt*; (*amount of time*) Dauer *f*; **the ~ of the island** (*all along*) die ganze Insel entlang; **2 metres in ~** 2 Meter lang; **at ~** (*at last*) schließlich; (*for a long time*) lange; **to go to great ~s to do sth** sich *dat* sehr viel Mühe geben, etw zu tun; **to fall full-~** lang hinfallen; **to lie full-~** in voller Länge daliegen
lengthen ['lɛŋθn] *vt* verlängern ▷ *vi* länger werden
lengthways ['lɛŋθweɪz] *adv* der Länge nach
lengthy ['lɛŋθɪ] *adj* lang
lenient ['li:nɪənt] *adj* nachsichtig
lens [lɛnz] *n* (*of spectacles*) Glas *nt*; (*of camera*) Objektiv *nt*; (*of telescope*) Linse *f*
Lent [lɛnt] *n* Fastenzeit *f*
lent [lɛnt] *pt, pp of* **lend**
lentil ['lɛntɪl] *n* Linse *f*
Leo ['li:əu] *n* Löwe *m*; **to be ~** Löwe sein
leopard ['lɛpəd] *n* Leopard *m*
leotard ['li:ətɑ:d] *n* Gymnastikanzug *m*
leprosy ['lɛprəsɪ] *n* Lepra *f*
lesbian ['lɛzbɪən] *adj* lesbisch ▷ *n* Lesbierin *f*
less [lɛs] *adj, pron, adv* weniger ▷ *prep*: **~ tax/10% discount** abzüglich Steuer/10% Rabatt; **~ than half** weniger als die Hälfte; **~ than ever** weniger denn je; **~ and less** immer weniger; **the ~ he works ...** je weniger er arbeitet ...; **the Prime Minister, no ~** kein Geringerer als der Premierminister
lessen ['lɛsn] *vi* nachlassen, abnehmen ▷ *vt* verringern
lesser ['lɛsə^r] *adj* geringer; **to a ~ extent** in geringerem Maße
lesson ['lɛsn] *n* (*class*) Stunde *f*; (*example, warning*) Lehre *f*; **to teach sb a ~** (*fig*) jdm eine Lektion erteilen
let [lɛt] (*pt, pp* **~**) *vt* (*allow*) lassen; (*Brit: lease*) vermieten; **to ~ sb do sth** jdn etw tun lassen, jdm erlauben, etw zu tun; **to ~ sb know sth** jdn etw wissen lassen; **~'s go** gehen wir!; **~ him come** lassen Sie ihn kommen; **"to ~"** "zu vermieten"
▶ **let down** *vt* (*tyre etc*) die Luft herauslassen aus; (*person*) im Stich lassen; (*dress etc*) länger machen; (*hem*) auslassen; **to ~ one's hair down** (*fig*) aus sich herausgehen
▶ **let go** *vi* loslassen ▷ *vt* (*release*) freilassen; **to ~ go of** loslassen; **to ~ o.s. go** aus sich herausgehen; (*neglect o.s.*) sich gehen lassen
▶ **let in** *vt* hereinlassen; (*water*) durchlassen
▶ **let off** *vt* (*culprit*) laufen lassen; (*firework, bomb*) hochgehen lassen; (*gun*) abfeuern; **to ~ sb off sth** (*excuse*) jdm etw erlassen; **to ~ off steam** (*inf: fig*) sich abreagieren
▶ **let on** *vi* verraten
▶ **let out** *vt* herauslassen; (*sound*) ausstoßen; (*house, room*) vermieten
▶ **let up** *vi* (*cease*) aufhören; (*diminish*) nachlassen
lethal ['li:θl] *adj* tödlich
letter ['lɛtə^r] *n* Brief *m*; (*of alphabet*) Buchstabe *m*; **small/capital ~** Klein-/Großbuchstabe *m*
letter bomb *n* Briefbombe *f*
lettering ['lɛtərɪŋ] *n* Beschriftung *f*
lettuce ['lɛtɪs] *n* Kopfsalat *m*
let-up ['lɛtʌp] *n* Nachlassen *nt*; **there was no ~** es ließ nicht nach
leukaemia, (*US*) **leukemia** [lu:'ki:mɪə] *n* Leukämie *f*
level ['lɛvl] *adj* eben ▷ *n* (*on scale, of liquid*) Stand *m*; (*of lake, river*) Wasserstand *m*; (*height*) Höhe *f*; (*fig: standard*) Niveau *nt*; (*also*: **spirit level**) Wasserwaage *f* ▷ *vt* (*building*) abreißen; (*forest etc*) einebnen ▷ *vi*: **to ~ with sb** (*inf*) ehrlich mit jdm sein ▷ *adv*: **to draw ~ with** einholen; **to be ~ with** auf gleicher Höhe sein mit; **to do one's ~ best** sein Möglichstes tun; **"A" ~s** (*Brit*) ≈ Abitur *nt*; **"O" ~s** (*Brit*) ≈ mittlere Reife *f*; **on the ~** (*fig: honest*) ehrlich, reell; **to ~ a gun at sb** ein Gewehr auf jdn richten; **to ~ an accusation at** *or* **against sb** eine Anschuldigung gegen jdn erheben; **to ~ a criticism at** *or* **against sb** Kritik an jdm üben
▶ **level off** *vi* (*prices etc*) sich beruhigen
▶ **level out** *vi* = **level off**
level crossing (*Brit*) *n* (beschrankter) Bahnübergang *m*
level-headed [lɛvl'hɛdɪd] *adj* (*calm*) ausgeglichen
lever ['li:və^r] *n* Hebel *m*; (*bar*) Brechstange *f*; (*fig*) Druckmittel *nt* ▷ *vt*: **to ~ up** hochhieven; **to ~ out** heraushieven
leverage ['li:vərɪdʒ] *n* Hebelkraft *f*;

(*fig: influence*) Einfluss *m*
levy ['lɛvɪ] *n* (*tax*) Steuer *f*; (*charge*) Gebühr *f* ▷ *vt* erheben
lewd [lu:d] *adj* (*look etc*) lüstern; (*remark*) anzüglich
liability [laɪə'bɪlətɪ] *n* Belastung *f*; (*Law*) Haftung *f*; **liabilities** *npl* (*Comm*) Verbindlichkeiten *pl*
liable ['laɪəbl] *adj*: **to be ~ to** (*subject to*) unterliegen *+dat*; (*prone to*) anfällig sein für; **~ for** (*responsible*) haftbar für; **to be ~ to do sth** dazu neigen, etw zu tun
liaise [li:'eɪz] *vi*: **to ~ (with)** sich in Verbindung setzen (mit)
liaison [li:'eɪzɔn] *n* Zusammenarbeit *f*; (*sexual relationship*) Liaison *f*
liar ['laɪə^r] *n* Lügner(in) *m(f)*
libel ['laɪbl] *n* Verleumdung *f* ▷ *vt* verleumden
liberal ['lɪbərl] *adj* (*Pol*) liberal; (*tolerant*) aufgeschlossen; (*generous: offer*) großzügig; (*: amount etc*) reichlich ▷ *n* (*tolerant person*) liberal eingestellter Mensch *m*; (*Pol*): **L~** Liberale(r) *f(m)*; **~ with** großzügig mit
Liberal Democrat *n* Liberaldemokrat(in) *m(f)*
liberate ['lɪbəreɪt] *vt* befreien
liberation [lɪbə'reɪʃən] *n* Befreiung *f*
liberty ['lɪbətɪ] *n* Freiheit *f*; **to be at ~** (*criminal*) auf freiem Fuß sein; **to be at ~ to do sth** etw tun dürfen; **to take the ~ of doing sth** sich *dat* erlauben, etw zu tun
Libra ['li:brə] *n* Waage *f*; **to be ~** Waage sein
librarian [laɪ'brɛərɪən] *n* Bibliothekar(in) *m(f)*
library ['laɪbrərɪ] *n* Bibliothek *f*; (*institution*) Bücherei *f*
libretto [lɪ'brɛtəu] *n* Libretto *nt*
Libya ['lɪbɪə] *n* Libyen *nt*
lice [laɪs] *npl of* **louse**
licence, (US) **license** ['laɪsns] *n* (*document*) Genehmigung *f*; (*also:* **driving licence**) Führerschein *m*; (*Comm*) Lizenz *f*; (*excessive freedom*) Zügellosigkeit *f*; **to get a TV ~** ≈ Fernsehgebühren bezahlen; **under ~** (*Comm*) in Lizenz
license ['laɪsns] *n* (*US*) = **licence** ▷ *vt* (*person, organization*) eine Lizenz vergeben an *+acc*; (*activity*) eine Genehmigung erteilen für
licensed ['laɪsnst] *adj*: **the car is ~** die Kfz-Steuer für das Auto ist bezahlt; **~ hotel/restaurant** Hotel/Restaurant mit Schankerlaubnis
license plate (*US*) *n* Nummernschild *nt*
licensing hours ['laɪsnsɪŋ-] (*Brit*) *npl* Ausschankzeiten *pl*
lick [lɪk] *vt* lecken; (*stamp etc*) lecken an *+dat*; (*inf: defeat*) in die Pfanne hauen ▷ *n* Lecken *nt*; **to ~ one's lips** sich *dat* die Lippen lecken; (*fig*) sich *dat* die Finger lecken; **a ~ of paint** ein Anstrich *m*
licorice ['lɪkərɪs] (*US*) *n* = **liquorice**
lid [lɪd] *n* Deckel *m*; (*eyelid*) Lid *nt*; **to take the ~ off sth** (*fig*) etw enthüllen *or* aufdecken
lie¹ [laɪ] (*pt, pp* **~d**) *vi* lügen ▷ *n* Lüge *f*; **to tell ~s** lügen
lie² [laɪ] (*pt* **lay**, *pp* **lain**) *vi* (*lit, fig*) liegen; **to ~ low** (*fig*) untertauchen
▸ **lie about** *vi* herumliegen
▸ **lie around** *vi* = **lie about**
▸ **lie back** *vi* sich zurücklehnen; (*fig: accept the inevitable*) sich fügen
▸ **lie down** *vi* sich hinlegen
▸ **lie up** *vi* (*hide*) untertauchen; (*rest*) im Bett bleiben
Liechtenstein ['lɪktənstaɪn] *n* Liechtenstein *nt*
lie-down ['laɪdaun] (*Brit*) *n*: **to have a ~** ein Schläfchen machen
lie-in ['laɪɪn] (*Brit*) *n*: **to have a ~** (sich) ausschlafen
lieutenant [lɛf'tɛnənt, (US) lu:'tɛnənt] *n* Leutnant *m*
life [laɪf] (*pl* **lives**) *n* Leben *nt*; (*of machine etc*) Lebensdauer *f*; **true to ~** lebensecht; **painted from ~** aus dem Leben gegriffen; **to be sent to prison for ~** zu einer lebenslänglichen Freiheitsstrafe verurteilt werden; **such is ~** so ist das Leben; **to come to ~** (*fig: person*) munter werden; (*: party etc*) in Schwung kommen
life assurance (*Brit*) *n* = **life insurance**
lifeboat ['laɪfbəut] *n* Rettungsboot *nt*
lifeguard ['laɪfgɑ:d] *n* (*at beach*) Rettungsschwimmer(in) *m(f)*; (*at swimming pool*) Bademeister(in) *m(f)*
life insurance *n* Lebensversicherung *f*
life jacket *n* Schwimmweste *f*
lifeless ['laɪflɪs] *adj* leblos; (*fig: person, party etc*) langweilig
lifelike ['laɪflaɪk] *adj* lebensecht; (*painting*) naturgetreu
lifelong ['laɪflɔŋ] *adj* lebenslang
life preserver (*US*) *n* = **life belt; life jacket**
life sentence *n* lebenslängliche Freiheitsstrafe *f*
life-size ['laɪfsaɪz], **life-sized** ['laɪfsaɪzd] *adj* in Lebensgröße
life span *n* Lebensdauer *f*; (*of person*) Lebenszeit *f*
life-support system ['laɪfsəpɔ:t-] *n* (*Med*) Lebenserhaltungssystem *nt*
lifetime ['laɪftaɪm] *n* Lebenszeit *f*; (*of thing*) Lebensdauer *f*; (*of parliament*) Legislaturperiode *f*; **in my ~** während meines Lebens; **the chance of a ~** eine einmalige Chance
lift [lɪft] *vt* (*raise*) heben; (*end: ban etc*) aufheben; (*plagiarize*) abschreiben; (*inf: steal*) mitgehen lassen, klauen ▷ *vi* (*fog*) sich auflösen ▷ *n* (*Brit*) Aufzug *m*, Fahrstuhl *m*; **to take the ~** mit dem Aufzug *or* Fahrstuhl fahren; **to give sb a ~** (*Brit*) jdn (im Auto) mitnehmen
▸ **lift off** *vi* abheben
▸ **lift up** *vt* hochheben
light [laɪt] (*pt, pp* **lit**) *n* Licht *nt* ▷ *vt* (*candle, cigarette, fire*) anzünden; (*room*) beleuchten ▷ *adj* leicht; (*pale, bright*) hell; (*traffic etc*)

gering; (*music*) Unterhaltungs- ▷ *adv*: **to travel ~** mit leichtem Gepäck reisen; **lights** *npl* (*Aut*: *also*: **traffic lights**) Ampel *f*; **the ~s** (*of car*) die Beleuchtung; **have you got a ~?** haben Sie Feuer?; **to turn the ~ on/off** das Licht an-/ausmachen; **to come to ~** ans Tageslicht kommen; **to cast** *or* **shed** *or* **throw ~ on** (*fig*) Licht bringen in *+acc*; **in the ~ of** angesichts *+gen*; **to make ~ of sth** (*fig*) etw auf die leichte Schulter nehmen; **~ blue/green** *etc* hellblau/-grün *etc*
▸ **light up** *vi* (*face*) sich erhellen ▷ *vt* (*illuminate*) beleuchten, erhellen
light bulb *n* Glühbirne *f*
lighten ['laɪtn] *vt* (*make less heavy*) leichter machen ▷ *vi* (*become less dark*) sich aufhellen
lighter ['laɪtə^r] *n* (*also*: **cigarette lighter**) Feuerzeug *nt*
light-headed [laɪt'hɛdɪd] *adj* (*dizzy*) benommen; (*excited*) ausgelassen
light-hearted [laɪt'hɑːtɪd] *adj* unbeschwert; (*question, remark etc*) scherzhaft
lighthouse ['laɪthaus] *n* Leuchtturm *m*
lighting ['laɪtɪŋ] *n* Beleuchtung *f*
lightly ['laɪtlɪ] *adv* leicht; (*not seriously*) leichthin; **to get off ~** glimpflich davonkommen
lightness ['laɪtnɪs] *n* (*in weight*) Leichtigkeit *f*
lightning ['laɪtnɪŋ] *n* Blitz *m* ▷ *adj* (*attack etc*) Blitz-; **with ~ speed** blitzschnell
lightning conductor *n* Blitzableiter *m*
light pen *n* Lichtstift *m*, Lichtgriffel *m*
lightweight ['laɪtweɪt] *adj* leicht ▷ *n* (*Boxing*) Leichtgewichtler *m*
like [laɪk] *vt* mögen ▷ *prep* wie; (*such as*) wie (zum Beispiel) ▷ *n*: **and the ~** und dergleichen; **I would ~, I'd ~** ich hätte *or* möchte gern; **would you ~ a coffee?** möchten Sie einen Kaffee?; **if you ~** wenn Sie wollen; **to be/look ~ sb/sth** jdm/etw ähnlich sein/sehen; **something ~ that** so etwas Ähnliches; **what does it look/taste/sound ~?** wie sieht es aus/schmeckt es/hört es sich an?; **what's he/the weather ~?** wie ist er/das Wetter?; **I feel ~ a drink** ich möchte gerne etwas trinken; **there's nothing ~ …** es geht nichts über *+acc*; **that's just ~ him** das sieht ihm ähnlich; **do it ~ this** mach es so; **it is nothing ~** (*+noun*) es ist ganz anders als; (*+adj*) es ist alles andere als; **it is nothing ~ as …** es ist bei Weitem nicht so …; **his ~s and dislikes** seine Vorlieben und Abneigungen
likeable ['laɪkəbl] *adj* sympathisch
likelihood ['laɪklɪhud] *n* Wahrscheinlichkeit *f*; **there is every ~ that …** es ist sehr wahrscheinlich, dass …; **in all ~** aller Wahrscheinlichkeit nach
likely ['laɪklɪ] *adj* wahrscheinlich; **to be ~ to do sth** wahrscheinlich etw tun; **not ~!** (*inf*) wohl kaum!
likeness ['laɪknɪs] *n* Ähnlichkeit *f*; **that's a good ~** (*photo, portrait*) das ist ein gutes Bild von ihm/ihr *etc*
likewise ['laɪkwaɪz] *adv* ebenso; **to do ~** das Gleiche tun
liking ['laɪkɪŋ] *n*: **~ (for)** (*person*) Zuneigung *f* (zu); (*thing*) Vorliebe *f* (für); **to be to sb's ~** nach jds Geschmack sein; **to take a ~ to sb** an jdm Gefallen finden
lilac ['laɪlək] *n* (*Bot*) Flieder *m* ▷ *adj* fliederfarben, (zart)lila
Lilo® ['laɪləu] *n* Luftmatratze *f*
lily ['lɪlɪ] *n* Lilie *f*
limb [lɪm] *n* Glied *nt*; (*of tree*) Ast *m*; **to be out on a ~** (*fig*) (ganz) allein (da)stehen
limbo ['lɪmbəu] *n*: **to be in ~** (*fig: plans etc*) in der Schwebe sein; (*: person*) in der Luft hängen (*inf*)
lime [laɪm] *n* (*fruit*) Limone *f*; (*tree*) Linde *f*; (*also*: **lime juice**) Limonensaft *m*; (*for soil*) Kalk *m*; (*rock*) Kalkstein *m*
limelight ['laɪmlaɪt] *n*: **to be in the ~** im Rampenlicht stehen
limerick ['lɪmərɪk] *n* Limerick *m*
limestone ['laɪmstəun] *n* Kalkstein *m*
limit ['lɪmɪt] *n* Grenze *f*; (*restriction*) Beschränkung *f* ▷ *vt* begrenzen, einschränken; **within ~s** innerhalb gewisser Grenzen
limited ['lɪmɪtɪd] *adj* begrenzt, beschränkt; **to be ~ to** beschränkt sein auf *+acc*
limited liability company (*Brit*) *n* ≈ Gesellschaft *f* mit beschränkter Haftung
limousine ['lɪməziːn] *n* Limousine *f*
limp [lɪmp] *adj* schlaff; (*material etc*) weich ▷ *vi* hinken ▷ *n*: **to have a ~** hinken
limpet ['lɪmpɪt] *n* Napfschnecke *f*
line [laɪn] *n* Linie *f*; (*written, printed*) Zeile *f*; (*wrinkle*) Falte *f*; (*row: of people*) Schlange *f*; (*: of things*) Reihe *f*; (*for fishing, washing*) Leine *f*; (*wire, Tel*) Leitung *f*; (*railway track*) Gleise *pl*; (*fig: attitude*) Standpunkt *m*; (*: business*) Branche *f*; (*Comm: of product(s)*) Art *f* ▷ *vt* (*road*) säumen; (*container*) auskleiden; (*clothing*) füttern; **hold the ~ please!** (*Tel*) bleiben Sie am Apparat!; **to cut in ~** (*US*) sich vordrängeln; **in ~** in einer Reihe; **in ~ with** im Einklang mit, in Übereinstimmung mit; **to be in ~ for sth** mit etw an der Reihe sein; **to bring sth into ~ with sth** etw auf die gleiche Linie wie etw *acc* bringen; **on the right ~s** auf dem richtigen Weg; **I draw the ~ at that** da mache ich nicht mehr mit; **to ~ sth with sth** etw mit etw auskleiden; (*drawers etc*) etw mit etw auslegen; **to ~ the streets** die Straßen säumen
▸ **line up** *vi* sich aufstellen ▷ *vt* (*in a row*) aufstellen; (*engage*) verpflichten; (*prepare*) arrangieren; **to have sb ~d up** jdn verpflichtet haben; **to have sth ~d up** etw geplant haben
linear ['lɪnɪə^r] *adj* linear; (*shape, form*) gerade
lined [laɪnd] *adj* (*face*) faltig; (*paper*) liniert; (*skirt, jacket*) gefüttert
linen ['lɪnɪn] *n* (*cloth*) Leinen *nt*; (*tablecloths,*

sheets etc) Wäsche *f*
liner ['laɪnə^r] *n* (*ship*) Passagierschiff *nt*; (*also*: **bin liner**) Müllbeutel *m*
linesman ['laɪnzmən] (*irreg*: *like* **man**) *n* (*Sport*) Linienrichter *m*
line-up ['laɪnʌp] *n* (*US*: *queue*) Schlange *f*; (*Sport*) Aufstellung *f*; (*at concert etc*) Künstleraufgebot *nt*; (*identity parade*) Gegenüberstellung *f*
linger ['lɪŋgə^r] *vi* (*smell*) sich halten; (*tradition etc*) fortbestehen; (*person*) sich aufhalten
lingerie ['lænʒəriː] *n* (Damen)unterwäsche *f*
linguist ['lɪŋgwɪst] *n* (*person who speaks several languages*) Sprachkundige(r) *f(m)*
linguistic [lɪŋ'gwɪstɪk] *adj* sprachlich
linguistics [lɪŋ'gwɪstɪks] *n* Sprachwissenschaft *f*
lining ['laɪnɪŋ] *n* (*cloth*) Futter *nt*; (*Anat*: *of stomach*) Magenschleimhaut *f*; (*Tech*) Auskleidung *f*; (*of brakes*) (Brems)belag *m*
link [lɪŋk] *n* Verbindung *f*, Beziehung *f*; (*communications link*) Verbindung; (*of a chain*) Glied *nt*; (*Comput*) Link *m* ▷ *vi* (*Comput*): **to ~ to a site** einen Link zu einer Website haben ▷ *vt* (*join*) verbinden; (*Comput*) per Link verbinden; **links** *npl* (*Golf*) Golfplatz *m*; **rail ~** Bahnverbindung *f*
▸ **link up** *vt* verbinden ▷ *vi* verbunden werden
lino ['laɪnəu] *n* = **linoleum**
linoleum [lɪ'nəulɪəm] *n* Linoleum *nt*
lion ['laɪən] *n* Löwe *m*
lioness ['laɪənɪs] *n* Löwin *f*
lip [lɪp] *n* (*Anat*) Lippe *f*; (*of cup etc*) Rand *m*; (*inf*: *insolence*) Frechheiten *pl*
liposuction ['lɪpəusʌkʃən] *n* Liposuktion *f*
lip salve *n* Fettstift *m*
lip service (*pej*) *n*: **to pay ~ to sth** ein Lippenbekenntnis *nt* zu etw ablegen
lipstick ['lɪpstɪk] *n* Lippenstift *m*
liqueur [lɪ'kjuə^r] *n* Likör *m*
liquid ['lɪkwɪd] *adj* flüssig ▷ *n* Flüssigkeit *f*
liquidize ['lɪkwɪdaɪz] *vt* (im Mixer) pürieren
liquidizer ['lɪkwɪdaɪzə^r] *n* Mixer *m*
liquor ['lɪkə^r] *n* Spirituosen *pl*, Alkohol *m*; **hard ~** harte Drinks *pl*
liquorice ['lɪkərɪs] (*Brit*) *n* Lakritze *f*
liquor store (*US*) *n* Spirituosengeschäft *nt*
Lisbon ['lɪzbən] *n* Lissabon *nt*
lisp [lɪsp] *n* Lispeln *nt* ▷ *vi* lispeln
list [lɪst] *n* Liste *f* ▷ *vt* aufführen; (*Comput*) auflisten; (*write down*) aufschreiben ▷ *vi* (*ship*) Schlagseite haben
listed building ['lɪstɪd-] (*Brit*) *n* unter Denkmalschutz stehendes Gebäude *nt*
listen ['lɪsn] *vi* hören; **to ~ (out) for** horchen auf *+acc*; **to ~ to sb** jdm zuhören; **to ~ to sth** etw hören; **~!** hör zu!
listener ['lɪsnə^r] *n* Zuhörer(in) *m(f)*; (*Radio*) Hörer(in) *m(f)*
listless ['lɪstlɪs] *adj* lustlos
lit [lɪt] *pt*, *pp of* **light**
liter ['liːtə^r] (*US*) *n* = **litre**
literacy ['lɪtərəsɪ] *n* die Fähigkeit, lesen und schreiben zu können
literal ['lɪtərəl] *adj* wörtlich, eigentlich; (*translation*) (wort)wörtlich
literally ['lɪtrəlɪ] *adv* buchstäblich
literary ['lɪtərərɪ] *adj* literarisch
literate ['lɪtərət] *adj* (*educated*) gebildet; **to be ~** lesen und schreiben können
literature ['lɪtrɪtʃə^r] *n* Literatur *f*; (*printed information*) Informationsmaterial *nt*
lithe [laɪð] *adj* gelenkig; (*animal*) geschmeidig
litigation [lɪtɪ'geɪʃən] *n* Prozess *m*
litre, (*US*) **liter** ['liːtə^r] *n* Liter *m or nt*
litter ['lɪtə^r] *n* (*rubbish*) Abfall *m*; (*young animals*) Wurf *m*
litter bin (*Brit*) *n* Abfalleimer *m*
little ['lɪtl] *adj* klein; (*short*) kurz ▷ *adv* wenig; **a ~** ein wenig, ein bisschen; **a ~ bit** ein kleines bisschen; **to have ~ time/money** wenig Zeit/Geld haben; **~ by little** nach und nach
little finger *n* kleiner Finger *m*
live [*vi* lɪv, *adj* laɪv] *vi* leben; (*in house, town*) wohnen ▷ *adj* lebend; (*TV, Radio*) live; (*performance, pictures etc*) Live-; (*Elec*) Strom führend; (*bullet, bomb etc*) scharf; **to ~ with sb** mit jdm zusammenleben
▸ **live down** *vt* hinwegkommen über *+acc*
▸ **live for** *vt* leben für
▸ **live in** *vi* (*student/servant*) im Wohnheim/Haus wohnen
▸ **live off** *vt fus* leben von; (*parents etc*) auf Kosten *+gen* leben
▸ **live on** *vt fus* leben von
▸ **live out** *vi* (*Brit*: *student/servant*) außerhalb (des Wohnheims/Hauses) wohnen ▷ *vt*: **to ~ out one's days** *or* **life** sein Leben verbringen
▸ **live together** *vi* zusammenleben
▸ **live up** *vt*: **to ~ it up** einen draufmachen (*inf*)
▸ **live up to** *vt fus* erfüllen, entsprechen *+dat*
livelihood ['laɪvlɪhud] *n* Lebensunterhalt *m*
lively ['laɪvlɪ] *adj* lebhaft; (*place, event, book etc*) lebendig
liven up ['laɪvn-] *vt* beleben, Leben bringen in *+acc*; (*person*) aufmuntern ▷ *vi* (*person*) aufleben; (*discussion, evening etc*) in Schwung kommen
liver ['lɪvə^r] *n* (*Anat, Culin*) Leber *f*
lives [laɪvz] *npl of* **life**
livestock ['laɪvstɔk] *n* Vieh *nt*
livid ['lɪvɪd] *adj* (*colour*) bleifarben; (*inf*: *furious*) fuchsteufelswild
living ['lɪvɪŋ] *adj* lebend ▷ *n*: **to earn** *or* **make a ~** sich *dat* seinen Lebensunterhalt verdienen; **within ~ memory** seit Menschengedenken; **the cost of ~** die Lebenshaltungskosten *pl*
living conditions *npl* Wohnverhältnisse *pl*
living room *n* Wohnzimmer *nt*
living standards *npl* Lebensstandard *m*
living wage *n* ausreichender Lohn *m*
lizard ['lɪzəd] *n* Eidechse *f*

load [ləud] *n* Last *f*; (*of vehicle*) Ladung *f*; (*weight, Elec*) Belastung *f* ▷ *vt* (*also*: **load up**) beladen; (*gun, program, data*) laden; **that's a ~ of rubbish** (*inf*) das ist alles Blödsinn; **loads of, a ~ of** (*fig*) jede Menge; **to ~ a camera** einen Film einlegen
loaded ['ləudɪd] *adj* (*inf: rich*) steinreich; (*dice*) präpariert; (*vehicle*): **to be ~ with** beladen sein mit; **a ~ question** eine Fangfrage
loaf [ləuf] (*pl* **loaves**) *n* Brot *nt*, Laib *m* ▷ *vi* (*also*: **loaf about, loaf around**) faulenzen; **use your ~!** (*inf*) streng deinen Grips an!
loan [ləun] *n* Darlehen *nt* ▷ *vt*: **to ~ sth to sb** jdm etw leihen; **on ~** geliehen
loath [ləuθ] *adj*: **to be ~ to do sth** etw ungern tun
loathe [ləuð] *vt* verabscheuen
loaves [ləuvz] *npl of* **loaf**
lobby ['lɔbɪ] *n* (*of building*) Eingangshalle *f*; (*Pol: pressure group*) Interessenverband *m* ▷ *vt* Einfluss nehmen auf *+acc*
lobster ['lɔbstəʳ] *n* Hummer *m*
local ['ləukl] *adj* örtlich; (*council*) Stadt-, Gemeinde-; (*paper*) Lokal- ▷ *n* (*pub*) Stammkneipe *f*; **the locals** *npl* (*local inhabitants*) die Einheimischen *pl*
local anaesthetic *n* örtliche Betäubung *f*
local authority *n* Gemeindeverwaltung *f*, Stadtverwaltung *f*
local call *n* Ortsgespräch *nt*
local government *n* Kommunalverwaltung *f*
locality [ləu'kælɪtɪ] *n* Gegend *f*
locally ['ləukəlɪ] *adv* am Ort
locate [ləu'keɪt] *vt* (*find*) ausfindig machen; **to be ~d in** sich befinden in *+dat*
location [ləu'keɪʃən] *n* Ort *m*; (*position*) Lage *f*; (*Cine*) Drehort *m*; **he's on ~ in Mexico** er ist bei Außenaufnahmen in Mexiko; **to be filmed on ~** als Außenaufnahme gedreht werden
loch [lɔx] (*Scot*) *n* See *m*
lock [lɔk] *n* (*of door etc*) Schloss *nt*; (*on canal*) Schleuse *f*; (*also*: **lock of hair**) Locke *f* ▷ *vt* (*door etc*) abschließen; (*steering wheel*) sperren; (*Comput: keyboard*) verriegeln ▷ *vi* (*door etc*) sich abschließen lassen; (*wheels, mechanism etc*) blockieren; **on full ~** (*Aut*) voll eingeschlagen; **~, stock and barrel** mit allem Drum und Dran; **his jaw ~ed** er hatte Mundsperre
▸ **lock away** *vt* wegschließen; (*criminal*) einsperren
▸ **lock in** *vt* einschließen
▸ **lock out** *vt* aussperren
▸ **lock up** *vt* (*criminal etc*) einsperren; (*house*) abschließen ▷ *vi* abschließen
locker ['lɔkəʳ] *n* Schließfach *nt*
locket ['lɔkɪt] *n* Medaillon *nt*
locksmith ['lɔksmɪθ] *n* Schlosser *m*
locomotive [ləukə'məutɪv] *n* Lokomotive *f*
locum ['ləukəm] *n* (*Med*) Vertreter(in) *m(f)*
lodge [lɔdʒ] *n* Pförtnerhaus *nt*; (*also*: **hunting lodge**) Hütte *f*; (*Freemasonry*) Loge *f* ▷ *vt* (*complaint, protest etc*) einlegen ▷ *vi* (*bullet*) stecken bleiben; (*person*): **to ~ (with)** zur Untermiete wohnen (bei)
lodger ['lɔdʒəʳ] *n* Untermieter(in) *m(f)*
lodging ['lɔdʒɪŋ] *n* Unterkunft *f*
lodgings ['lɔdʒɪŋz] *npl* möbliertes Zimmer *nt*; (*several rooms*) Wohnung *f*
loft [lɔft] *n* Boden *m*, Speicher *m*
lofty ['lɔftɪ] *adj* (*noble*) hoch(fliegend); (*self-important*) hochmütig; (*high*) hoch
log [lɔg] *n* (*of wood*) Holzblock *m*, Holzklotz *m*; (*written account*) Log *nt* ▷ *n abbr* (*Math*: = *logarithm*) log ▷ *vt* (ins Logbuch) eintragen
▸ **log in** *vi* (*Comput*) sich anmelden
▸ **log into** *vt fus* (*Comput*) sich anmelden bei
▸ **log off** *vi* (*Comput*) sich abmelden
▸ **log on** *vi* (*Comput*) = **log in**
▸ **log out** *vi* (*Comput*) = **log off**
logbook ['lɔgbuk] *n* (*Naut*) Logbuch *nt*; (*Aviat*) Bordbuch *nt*; (*of car*) Kraftfahrzeugbrief *m*; (*of lorry driver*) Fahrtenbuch *nt*; (*of events*) Tagebuch *nt*; (*of movement of goods etc*) Dienstbuch *nt*
loggerheads ['lɔgəhɛdz] *npl*: **to be at ~** Streit haben
logic ['lɔdʒɪk] *n* Logik *f*
logical ['lɔdʒɪkl] *adj* logisch
logo ['ləugəu] *n* Logo *nt*
loin [lɔɪn] *n* Lende *f*
loiter ['lɔɪtəʳ] *vi* sich aufhalten
loll [lɔl] *vi* (*also*: **loll about**: *person*) herumhängen; (*head*) herunterhängen; (*tongue*) heraushängen
lollipop ['lɔlɪpɔp] *n* Lutscher *m*
lolly ['lɔlɪ] (*inf*) *n* (*lollipop*) Lutscher *m*; (*money*) Mäuse *pl*
London ['lʌndən] *n* London *nt*
Londoner ['lʌndənəʳ] *n* Londoner(in) *m(f)*
lone [ləun] *adj* einzeln, einsam; (*only*) einzig
loneliness ['ləunlɪnɪs] *n* Einsamkeit *f*
lonely ['ləunlɪ] *adj* einsam
long [lɔŋ] *adj* lang ▷ *adv* lang(e) ▷ *vi*: **to ~ for sth** sich nach etw sehnen; **in the ~ run** auf die Dauer; **how ~ is the lesson?** wie lange dauert die Stunde?; **6 metres/months ~** 6 Meter/Monate lang; **so** *or* **as ~ as** (*on condition that*) solange; (*while*) während; **don't be ~!** bleib nicht so lange!; **all night ~** die ganze Nacht; **he no ~er comes** er kommt nicht mehr; **~ ago** vor langer Zeit; **~ before/after** lange vorher/danach; **before ~** bald; **at ~ last** schließlich und endlich; **the ~ and the short of it is that ...** kurz gesagt, ...
long-distance [lɔŋ'dɪstəns] *adj* (*travel, phone call*) Fern-; (*race*) Langstrecken-
longhand ['lɔŋhænd] *n* Langschrift *f*
longing ['lɔŋɪŋ] *n* Sehnsucht *f*
longitude ['lɔŋgɪtju:d] *n* Länge *f*
long jump *n* Weitsprung *m*
long-life ['lɔŋlaɪf] *adj* (*batteries etc*) mit langer Lebensdauer; **~ milk** H-Milch *f*
long-lost ['lɔŋlɔst] *adj* verloren geglaubt

long-range ['lɔŋ'reɪndʒ] *adj* (*plan, forecast*) langfristig; (*missile, plane etc*) Langstrecken-
long-sighted ['lɔŋ'saɪtɪd] *adj* weitsichtig
long-standing ['lɔŋ'stændɪŋ] *adj* langjährig
long-suffering [lɔŋ'sʌfərɪŋ] *adj* schwer geprüft
long-term ['lɔŋtə:m] *adj* langfristig
long wave *n* Langwelle *f*
long-winded [lɔŋ'wɪndɪd] *adj* umständlich, langatmig
loo [lu:] (*Brit: inf*) *n* Klo *nt*
look [luk] *vi* sehen, schauen, gucken (*inf*); (*seem, appear*) aussehen ▷ *n* (*glance*) Blick *m*; (*appearance*) Aussehen *nt*; (*expression*) Miene *f*; (*Fashion*) Look *m*; **looks** *npl* (*good looks*) (gutes) Aussehen; **to ~ (out) onto the sea/south** (*building etc*) Blick aufs Meer/nach Süden haben; **~ (here)!** (*expressing annoyance*) hör (mal) zu!; **~!** (*expressing surprise*) sieh mal!; **to ~ like sb/sth** wie jd/etw aussehen; **it ~s like him** es sieht ihm ähnlich; **it ~s about 4 metres long** es scheint etwa 4 Meter lang zu sein; **it ~s all right to me** es scheint mir in Ordnung zu sein; **to ~ ahead** vorausschauen; **to have a ~ at sth** sich *dat* etw ansehen; **let me have a ~** lass mich mal sehen; **to have a ~ for sth** nach etw suchen
▸ **look after** *vt fus* sich kümmern um
▸ **look at** *vt fus* ansehen; (*read quickly*) durchsehen; (*study, consider*) betrachten
▸ **look back** *vi*: **to ~ back (on)** zurückblicken (auf *+acc*); **to ~ back at sth/sb** sich nach jdm/etw umsehen
▸ **look down on** *vt fus* (*fig*) herabsehen auf *+acc*
▸ **look for** *vt fus* suchen
▸ **look forward to** *vt fus* sich freuen auf *+acc*; **we ~ forward to hearing from you** (*in letters*) wir hoffen, bald von Ihnen zu hören
▸ **look in** *vi*: **to ~ in on sb** bei jdm vorbeikommen
▸ **look into** *vt fus* (*investigate*) untersuchen
▸ **look on** *vi* (*watch*) zusehen
▸ **look out** *vi* (*beware*) aufpassen
▸ **look out for** *vt fus* Ausschau halten nach
▸ **look over** *vt* (*essay etc*) durchsehen; (*house, town etc*) sich *dat* ansehen; (*person*) mustern
▸ **look round** *vi* sich umsehen
▸ **look through** *vt fus* durchsehen
▸ **look to** *vt fus* (*rely on*) sich verlassen auf *+acc*
▸ **look up** *vi* aufsehen; (*situation*) sich bessern ▷ *vt* (*word etc*) nachschlagen; **things are ~ing up** es geht bergauf
▸ **look up to** *vt fus* aufsehen zu
lookout ['lukaut] *n* (*tower etc*) Ausguck *m*; (*person*) Wachtposten *m*; **to be on the ~ for sth** nach etw Ausschau halten
loom [lu:m] *vi* (*also*: **loom up**: *object, shape*) sich abzeichnen; (*event*) näher rücken ▷ *n* Webstuhl *m*
loony ['lu:nɪ] (*inf*) *adj* verrückt ▷ *n* Verrückte(r) *f*(*m*)
loop [lu:p] *n* Schlaufe *f*; (*Comput*) Schleife *f* ▷ *vt*: **to ~ sth around sth** etw um etw schlingen
loophole ['lu:phəul] *n* Hintertürchen *nt*; **a ~ in the law** eine Lücke im Gesetz
loose [lu:s] *adj* lose, locker; (*clothes etc*) weit; (*long hair*) offen; (*not strictly controlled, promiscuous*) locker; (*definition*) ungenau; (*translation*) frei ▷ *vt* (*animal*) loslassen; (*prisoner*) freilassen; (*set off, unleash*) entfesseln ▷ *n*: **to be on the ~** frei herumlaufen
loose change *n* Kleingeld *nt*
loose chippings *npl* Schotter *m*
loosely ['lu:slɪ] *adv* lose, locker
loosen ['lu:sn] *vt* lösen, losmachen; (*clothing, belt etc*) lockern
loot [lu:t] *n* (*inf*) Beute *f* ▷ *vt* plündern
lord [lɔ:d] *n* (*Brit*) Lord *m*; **L~ Smith** Lord Smith; **the L~** (*Rel*) der Herr; **my ~** (*to bishop*) Exzellenz; (*to noble*) Mylord; (*to judge*) Euer Ehren; **good L~!** ach, du lieber Himmel!; **the (House of) L~s** (*Brit*) das Oberhaus
lordship ['lɔ:dʃɪp] *n*: **your L~** Eure Lordschaft
lore [lɔ:ʳ] *n* Überlieferungen *pl*
lorry ['lɔrɪ] (*Brit*) *n* Lastwagen *m*, Lkw *m*
lorry driver (*Brit*) *n* Lastwagenfahrer *m*
lose [lu:z] (*pt, pp* **lost**) *vt* verlieren; (*opportunity*) verpassen; (*pursuers*) abschütteln ▷ *vi* verlieren; **to ~ (time)** (*clock*) nachgehen; **to ~ weight** abnehmen; **to ~ 5 pounds** 5 Pfund abnehmen; **to ~ sight of sth** (*also fig*) etw aus den Augen verlieren
loser ['lu:zəʳ] *n* Verlierer(in) *m*(*f*); (*inf: failure*) Versager *m*; **to be a good/bad ~** ein guter/schlechter Verlierer sein
loss [lɔs] *n* Verlust *m*; **to make a ~ (of £1,000)** (1000 Pfund) Verlust machen; **to sell sth at a ~** etw mit Verlust verkaufen; **heavy ~es** schwere Verluste *pl*; **to cut one's ~es** aufgeben, bevor es noch schlimmer wird; **to be at a ~** nicht mehr weiterwissen
lost [lɔst] *pt, pp of* **lose** ▷ *adj* (*person, animal*) vermisst; (*object*) verloren; **to be ~** sich verlaufen/verfahren haben; **to get ~** sich verlaufen/verfahren; **get ~!** (*inf*) verschwinde!; **~ in thought** in Gedanken verloren
lost property (*Brit*) *n* Fundsachen *pl*; (*also*: **lost property office**) Fundbüro *nt*
lot [lɔt] *n* (*kind*) Art *f*; (*group*) Gruppe *f*; (*at auctions, destiny*) Los *nt*; **to draw ~s** losen, Lose ziehen; **the ~** alles; **a ~ (of)** (*a large number (of)*) viele; (*a great deal (of)*) viel; **~s of** viele; **I read a ~** ich lese viel; **this happens a ~** das kommt oft vor
lotion ['ləuʃən] *n* Lotion *f*
lottery ['lɔtərɪ] *n* Lotterie *f*
loud [laud] *adj* laut; (*clothes*) schreiend ▷ *adv* laut; **to be ~ in one's support of sb/sth** jdn/etw lautstark unterstützen; **out ~** (*read, laugh etc*) laut
loud-hailer [laud'heɪləʳ] (*Brit*) *n* Megafon *nt*
loudly ['laudlɪ] *adv* laut
loudspeaker [laud'spi:kəʳ] *n* Lautsprecher *m*

lounge [laundʒ] *n* (*in house*) Wohnzimmer *nt*; (*in hotel*) Lounge *f*; (*at airport, station*) Wartehalle *f*; (*Brit*: *also*: **lounge bar**) Salon *m* ▹ *vi* faulenzen
▸ **lounge about** *vi* herumliegen, herumsitzen, herumstehen
▸ **lounge around** *vi* = **lounge about**
lounge suit (*Brit*) *n* Straßenanzug *m*
louse [laus] (*pl* **lice**) *n* Laus *f*
▸ **louse up** (*inf*) *vt* vermasseln
lousy ['lauzɪ] (*inf*) *adj* (*bad-quality*) lausig, mies; (*despicable*) fies, gemein; (*ill*): **to feel ~** sich miserabel *or* elend fühlen
lout [laut] *n* Lümmel *m*, Flegel *m*
lovable ['lʌvəbl] *adj* liebenswert
love [lʌv] *n* Liebe *f* ▹ *vt* lieben; (*thing, activity etc*) gern mögen; **"~ (from) Anne"** (*on letter*) "mit herzlichen Grüßen, Anne"; **to be in ~ with** verliebt sein in *+acc*; **to fall in ~ with** sich verlieben in *+acc*; **to make ~** sich lieben; **~ at first sight** Liebe auf den ersten Blick; **to send one's ~ to sb** jdn grüßen lassen; **"fifteen ~"** (*Tennis*) "fünfzehn null"; **to ~ doing sth** etw gern tun; **I'd ~ to come** ich würde sehr gerne kommen; **I ~ chocolate** ich esse Schokolade liebend gern
love affair *n* Verhältnis *nt*, Liebschaft *f*
love life *n* Liebesleben *nt*
lovely ['lʌvlɪ] *adj* (*beautiful*) schön; (*delightful*) herrlich; (*person*) sehr nett
lover ['lʌvə^r] *n* Geliebte(r) *f(m)*; (*person in love*) Liebende(r) *f(m)*; **~ of art/music** Kunst-/Musikliebhaber(in) *m(f)*; **to be ~s** ein Liebespaar sein
loving ['lʌvɪŋ] *adj* liebend; (*actions*) liebevoll
low [ləu] *adj* niedrig; (*bow, curtsey*) tief; (*quality*) schlecht; (*sound: deep*) tief; (*: quiet*) leise; (*depressed*) niedergeschlagen, bedrückt ▹ *adv* (*sing*) leise; (*fly*) tief ▹ *n* (*Met*) Tief *nt*; **to be/run ~** knapp sein/werden; **sb is running ~ on sth** jdm wird etw knapp; **to reach a new** *or* **an all-time ~** einen neuen Tiefstand erreichen
low-alcohol ['ləu'ælkəhɔl] *adj* alkoholarm
low-calorie ['ləu'kælərɪ] *adj* kalorienarm
low-cut ['ləukʌt] *adj* (*dress*) tief ausgeschnitten
lower ['ləuə^r] *adj* untere(r, s); (*lip, jaw, arm*) Unter- ▹ *vt* senken
low-fat ['ləu'fæt] *adj* fettarm
lowly ['ləulɪ] *adj* (*position*) niedrig; (*origin*) bescheiden
loyal ['lɔɪəl] *adj* treu; (*support*) loyal
loyalty ['lɔɪəltɪ] *n* (*see adj*) Treue *f*; Loyalität *f*
loyalty card (*Brit*) *n* (*Comm*) Paybackkarte *f*
lozenge ['lɔzɪndʒ] *n* Pastille *f*; (*shape*) Raute *f*
Lt *abbr* (*Mil*: = *lieutenant*) Lt.
Ltd *abbr* (*Comm*: = *limited (liability)*) ≈ GmbH *f*
lubricant ['lu:brɪkənt] *n* Schmiermittel *nt*
lubricate ['lu:brɪkeɪt] *vt* schmieren, ölen
luck [lʌk] *n* (*esp good luck*) Glück *nt*; **bad ~** Unglück *nt*; **good ~!** viel Glück!; **bad** *or* **hard** *or* **tough ~!** so ein Pech!; **hard** *or* **tough ~!** (*showing no sympathy*) Pech gehabt!; **to be in ~** Glück haben; **to be out of ~** kein Glück haben
luckily ['lʌkɪlɪ] *adv* glücklicherweise
lucky ['lʌkɪ] *adj* (*situation, event*) glücklich; (*object*) Glück bringend; (*person*): **to be ~** Glück haben; **to have a ~ escape** noch einmal davonkommen; **~ charm** Glücksbringer *m*
lucrative ['lu:krətɪv] *adj* einträglich
ludicrous ['lu:dɪkrəs] *adj* grotesk
lug [lʌg] (*inf*) *vt* schleppen
luggage ['lʌgɪdʒ] *n* Gepäck *nt*
luggage rack *n* Gepäckträger *m*; (*in train*) Gepäckablage *f*
lukewarm ['lu:kwɔ:m] *adj* lauwarm; (*fig: person, reaction etc*) lau
lull [lʌl] *n* Pause *f* ▹ *vt*: **to ~ sb to sleep** jdn einlullen *or* einschläfern; **to be ~ed into a false sense of security** in trügerische Sicherheit gewiegt werden
lullaby ['lʌləbaɪ] *n* Schlaflied *nt*
lumbago [lʌm'beɪgəu] *n* Hexenschuss *m*
lumber ['lʌmbə^r] *n* (*wood*) Holz *nt*; (*junk*) Gerümpel *nt* ▹ *vi*: **to ~ about/along** herum-/entlangtapsen
▸ **lumber with** *vt*: **to be/get ~ed with sth** etw am Hals haben/aufgehalst bekommen
lumberjack ['lʌmbədʒæk] *n* Holzfäller *m*
luminous ['lu:mɪnəs] *adj* leuchtend, Leucht-
lump [lʌmp] *n* Klumpen *m*; (*on body*) Beule *f*; (*in breast*) Knoten *m*; (*also*: **sugar lump**) Stück *nt* (Zucker) ▹ *vt*: **to ~ together** in einen Topf werfen; **a ~ sum** eine Pauschalsumme
lumpy ['lʌmpɪ] *adj* klumpig
lunar ['lu:nə^r] *adj* Mond-
lunatic ['lu:nətɪk] *adj* wahnsinnig ▹ *n* Wahnsinnige(r) *f(m)*, Irre(r) *f(m)*
lunch [lʌntʃ] *n* Mittagessen *nt*; (*time*) Mittagszeit *f* ▹ *vi* zu Mittag essen
lunch break *n* Mittagspause *f*
luncheon ['lʌntʃən] *n* Mittagessen *nt*
luncheon meat *n* Frühstücksfleisch *nt*
luncheon voucher (*Brit*) *n* Essensmarke *f*
lung [lʌŋ] *n* Lunge *f*
lunge [lʌndʒ] *vi* (*also*: **lunge forward**) sich nach vorne stürzen; **to ~ at** sich stürzen auf *+acc*
lurch [lə:tʃ] *vi* ruckeln; (*person*) taumeln ▹ *n* Ruck *m*; (*of person*) Taumeln *nt*; **to leave sb in the ~** jdn im Stich lassen
lure [luə^r] *n* Verlockung *f* ▹ *vt* locken
lurid ['luərɪd] *adj* (*story etc*) reißerisch; (*pej: brightly coloured*) grell, in grellen Farben
lurk [lə:k] *vi* (*also fig*) lauern
luscious ['lʌʃəs] *adj* (*attractive*) fantastisch; (*food*) köstlich, lecker
lush [lʌʃ] *adj* (*fields*) saftig; (*gardens*) üppig; (*luxurious*) luxuriös
lust [lʌst] (*pej*) *n* (*sexual*) (sinnliche) Begierde *f*; (*for money, power etc*) Gier *f*
▸ **lust after** *vt fus* (*sexually*) begehren; (*crave*) gieren nach
▸ **lust for** *vt fus* = **lust after**

lusty ['lʌstɪ] *adj* gesund und munter
Luxembourg ['lʌksəmbə:g] *n* Luxemburg *nt*
luxurious [lʌg'zjuərɪəs] *adj* luxuriös
luxury ['lʌkʃərɪ] *n* Luxus *m* (*no pl*) ▷ *cpd* (*hotel, car etc*) Luxus-; **little luxuries** kleine Genüsse
Lycra® ['laɪkrə] *n* Lycra *nt*
lying ['laɪɪŋ] *n* Lügen *nt* ▷ *adj* verlogen
lyric ['lɪrɪk] *adj* lyrisch
lyrical ['lɪrɪkl] *adj* lyrisch; (*fig: praise etc*) schwärmerisch
lyrics ['lɪrɪks] *npl* (*of song*) Text *m*

Mm

M¹, m¹ [ɛm] *n (letter)* M *nt*, m *nt*; **M for Mary, M for Mike** *(US)* ≈ M wie Martha
M² [ɛm] *n abbr (Brit: = motorway)*: **the M8** ≈ die A8 ▷ *abbr* = **medium**
m² *abbr* (= *metre*) m; = **mile**; (= *million*) Mio.
mac [mæk] *(Brit) n* Regenmantel *m*
macaroni [mækəˈrəunɪ] *n* Makkaroni *pl*
Macedonia [mæsɪˈdəunɪə] *n* Makedonien *nt*
Macedonian [mæsɪˈdəunɪən] *adj* makedonisch ▷ *n* Makedonier(in) *m(f)*; *(Ling)* Makedonisch *nt*
machine [məˈʃi:n] *n* Maschine *f*; *(fig: party machine etc)* Apparat *m* ▷ *vt (Tech)* maschinell herstellen *or* bearbeiten; *(dress etc)* mit der Maschine nähen
machine gun *n* Maschinengewehr *nt*
machine language *n* Maschinensprache *f*
machinery [məˈʃi:nərɪ] *n* Maschinen *pl*; *(fig: of government)* Apparat *m*
machine washable *adj* waschmaschinenfest
macho [ˈmætʃəu] *adj* Macho-; **a ~ man** ein Macho *m*
mackerel [ˈmækrl] *n inv* Makrele *f*
mackintosh [ˈmækɪntɔʃ] *(Brit) n* Regenmantel *m*
mad [mæd] *adj* wahnsinnig, verrückt; *(angry)* böse, sauer *(inf)*; **to be ~ about** verrückt sein auf *+acc*; **to be ~ at sb** böse *or* sauer auf jdn sein; **to go ~** *(insane)* verrückt *or* wahnsinnig werden; *(angry)* böse *or* sauer werden
madam [ˈmædəm] *n* gnädige Frau *f*; **yes, ~** ja(wohl); **M~ Chairman** Frau Vorsitzende
mad cow disease *n* Rinderwahn *m*
madden [ˈmædn] *vt* ärgern, fuchsen *(inf)*
made [meɪd] *pt, pp of* **make**
Madeira [məˈdɪərə] *n* Madeira *nt*; *(wine)* Madeira *m*
made-to-measure [ˈmeɪdtəˈmɛʒəʳ] *(Brit) adj* maßgeschneidert
madly [ˈmædlɪ] *adv* wie verrückt; **~ in love** bis über beide Ohren verliebt
madman [ˈmædmən] *(irreg: like* **man***) n* Verrückte(r) *m*, Irre(r) *m*
madness [ˈmædnɪs] *n* Wahnsinn *m*
Madrid [məˈdrɪd] *n* Madrid *nt*
Mafia [ˈmæfɪə] *n* Mafia *f*
mag [mæg] *(Brit: inf) n* = **magazine**
magazine [mægəˈzi:n] *n* Zeitschrift *f*; *(Radio, TV)* Magazin *nt*; *(Radio, TV, of firearm)* Magazin *nt*; *(Mil: store)* Depot *nt*
maggot [ˈmægət] *n* Made *f*
magic [ˈmædʒɪk] *n* Magie *f*; *(conjuring)* Zauberei *f* ▷ *adj* magisch; *(formula)* Zauber-; *(fig: place, moment etc)* zauberhaft
magical [ˈmædʒɪkl] *adj* magisch; *(experience, evening)* zauberhaft
magician [məˈdʒɪʃən] *n (wizard)* Magier *m*; *(conjurer)* Zauberer *m*
magistrate [ˈmædʒɪstreɪt] *n* Friedensrichter(in) *m(f)*
magnet [ˈmægnɪt] *n* Magnet *m*
magnetic [mægˈnɛtɪk] *adj* magnetisch; *(field, compass, pole etc)* Magnet-; *(personality)* anziehend
magnificent [mægˈnɪfɪsnt] *adj* großartig; *(robes)* prachtvoll
magnify [ˈmægnɪfaɪ] *vt* vergrößern; *(sound)* verstärken; *(fig: exaggerate)* aufbauschen
magnifying glass [ˈmægnɪfaɪɪŋ-] *n* Vergrößerungsglas *nt*, Lupe *f*
magnitude [ˈmægnɪtju:d] *n (size)* Ausmaß *nt*, Größe *f*; *(importance)* Bedeutung *f*
magpie [ˈmægpaɪ] *n* Elster *f*
mahogany [məˈhɔgənɪ] *n* Mahagoni *nt* ▷ *cpd* Mahagoni-
maid [meɪd] *n* Dienstmädchen *nt*; **old ~** *(pej)* alte Jungfer
maiden [ˈmeɪdn] *n (liter)* Mädchen *nt* ▷ *adj* unverheiratet; *(speech, voyage)* Jungfern-
maiden name *n* Mädchenname *m*
mail [meɪl] *n* Post *f* ▷ *vt* aufgeben; **by ~** mit der Post
mailbox [ˈmeɪlbɔks] *n (US)* Briefkasten *m*; *(Comput)* Mailbox *f*, elektronischer Briefkasten *m*
mailing list [ˈmeɪlɪŋ-] *n* Anschriftenliste *f*
mailman [ˈmeɪlmæn] *(US irreg: like* **man***) n* Briefträger *m*, Postbote *m*
maim [meɪm] *vt* verstümmeln
main [meɪn] *adj* Haupt-, wichtigste(r, s); *(door, entrance, meal)* Haupt- ▷ *n* Hauptleitung *f*; **the mains** *npl (Elec)* das Stromnetz; *(gas, water)* die Hauptleitung; **in the ~** im Großen und Ganzen
main course *n (Culin)* Hauptgericht *nt*
mainframe [ˈmeɪnfreɪm] *n (Comput)* Großrechner *m*
mainland [ˈmeɪnlənd] *n* Festland *nt*

mainly ['meɪnlɪ] *adv* hauptsächlich
main road *n* Hauptstraße *f*
mainstay ['meɪnsteɪ] *n* (*foundation*) (wichtigste) Stütze *f*; (*chief constituent*) Hauptbestandteil *m*
mainstream ['meɪnstriːm] *n* Hauptrichtung *f* ▷ *adj* (*cinema etc*) populär; (*politics*) der Mitte
maintain [meɪn'teɪn] *vt* (*preserve*) aufrechterhalten; (*keep up*) beibehalten; (*provide for*) unterhalten; (*look after: building*) instand halten; (*: equipment*) warten; (*affirm: opinion*) vertreten; (*: innocence*) beteuern; **to ~ that ...** behaupten, dass ...
maintenance ['meɪntənəns] *n* (*of building*) Instandhaltung *f*; (*of equipment*) Wartung *f*; (*preservation*) Aufrechterhaltung *f*; (*Law: alimony*) Unterhalt *m*
maisonette [meɪzə'nɛt] (*Brit*) *n* Maisonettewohnung *f*
maize [meɪz] *n* Mais *m*
majestic [mə'dʒɛstɪk] *adj* erhaben
majesty ['mædʒɪstɪ] *n* (*title*): **Your M~** Eure Majestät; (*splendour*) Erhabenheit *f*
major ['meɪdʒəʳ] *n* Major *m* ▷ *adj* bedeutend; (*Mus*) Dur ▷ *vi* (*US*): **to ~ in French** Französisch als Hauptfach belegen; **a ~ operation** eine größere Operation
Majorca [mə'jɔːkə] *n* Mallorca *nt*
majority [mə'dʒɔrɪtɪ] *n* Mehrheit *f* ▷ *cpd* (*verdict, holding*) Mehrheits-
make [meɪk] (*pt, pp* **made**) *vt* machen; (*clothes*) nähen; (*cake*) backen; (*speech*) halten; (*manufacture*) herstellen; (*earn*) verdienen; (*cause to be*): **to ~ sb sad** jdn traurig machen; (*force*): **to ~ sb do sth** jdn zwingen, etw zu tun; (*cause*) jdn dazu bringen, etw zu tun; (*equal*): **2 and 2 ~ 4** 2 und 2 ist *or* macht 4 ▷ *n* Marke *f*, Fabrikat *nt*; **to ~ a fool of sb** jdn lächerlich machen; **to ~ a profit/loss** Gewinn/Verlust machen; **to ~ it** (*arrive*) es schaffen; (*succeed*) Erfolg haben; **what time do you ~ it?** wie spät hast du?; **to ~ good** erfolgreich sein; (*threat*) wahr machen; (*promise*) einlösen; (*damage*) wiedergutmachen; (*loss*) ersetzen; **to ~ do with** auskommen mit
▸ **make for** *vt fus* (*place*) zuhalten auf *+acc*
▸ **make off** *vi* sich davonmachen
▸ **make out** *vt* (*decipher*) entziffern; (*understand*) verstehen; (*see*) ausmachen; (*write: cheque*) ausstellen; (*claim, imply*) behaupten; (*pretend*) so tun, als ob; **to ~ out a case for sth** für etw argumentieren
▸ **make over** *vt*: **to ~ over (to)** überschreiben (*+dat*)
▸ **make up** *vt* (*constitute*) bilden; (*invent*) erfinden; (*prepare: bed*) zurechtmachen; (*: parcel*) zusammenpacken ▷ *vi* (*after quarrel*) sich versöhnen; (*with cosmetics*) sich schminken; **to ~ up one's mind** sich entscheiden; **to be made up of** bestehen aus
▸ **make up for** *vt fus* (*loss*) ersetzen; (*disappointment etc*) ausgleichen
make-believe ['meɪkbɪliːv] *n* Fantasie *f*; **a world of ~** eine Fantasiewelt; **it's just ~** es ist nicht wirklich
maker ['meɪkəʳ] *n* Hersteller *m*; **film ~** Filmemacher(in) *m(f)*
makeshift ['meɪkʃɪft] *adj* behelfsmäßig
make-up ['meɪkʌp] *n* Make-up *nt*, Schminke *f*
making ['meɪkɪŋ] *n* (*fig*): **in the ~** im Entstehen; **to have the ~s of** das Zeug haben zu
malaria [mə'lɛərɪə] *n* Malaria *f*
Malaysia [mə'leɪzɪə] *n* Malaysia *nt*
male [meɪl] *n* (*animal*) Männchen *nt*; (*man*) Mann *m* ▷ *adj* männlich; (*Elec*): **~ plug** Stecker *m*; **because he is ~** weil er ein Mann/Junge ist; **~ and female students** Studenten und Studentinnen; **a ~ child** ein Junge
malevolent [mə'lɛvələnt] *adj* boshaft; (*intention*) böswillig
malfunction [mæl'fʌŋkʃən] *n* (*of computer*) Funktionsstörung *f*; (*of machine*) Defekt *m* ▷ *vi* (*computer*) eine Funktionsstörung haben; (*machine*) defekt sein
malice ['mælɪs] *n* Bosheit *f*
malicious [mə'lɪʃəs] *adj* boshaft; (*Law*) böswillig
malignant [mə'lɪgnənt] *adj* bösartig; (*intention*) böswillig
mall [mɔːl] *n* (*also*: **shopping mall**) Einkaufszentrum *nt*
mallet ['mælɪt] *n* Holzhammer *m*
malnutrition [mælnjuː'trɪʃən] *n* Unterernährung *f*
malpractice [mæl'præktɪs] *n* Berufsvergehen *nt*
malt [mɔːlt] *n* Malz *nt*; (*also*: **malt whisky**) Malt Whisky *m*
Malta ['mɔːltə] *n* Malta *nt*
Maltese [mɔːl'tiːz] *adj* maltesisch ▷ *n inv* Malteser(in) *m(f)*; (*Ling*) Maltesisch *nt*
mammal ['mæml] *n* Säugetier *nt*
mammoth ['mæməθ] *n* Mammut *nt* ▷ *adj* (*task*) Mammut-
man [mæn] (*pl* **men**) *n* Mann *m*; (*mankind*) der Mensch, die Menschen *pl*; (*Chess*) Figur *f* ▷ *vt* (*ship*) bemannen; (*gun, machine*) bedienen; (*post*) besetzen; **~ and wife** Mann und Frau
manage ['mænɪdʒ] *vi*: **to ~ to do sth** es schaffen, etw zu tun; (*get by financially*) zurechtkommen ▷ *vt* (*business, organization*) leiten; (*control*) zurechtkommen mit; **to ~ without sb/sth** ohne jdn/etw auskommen; **well ~d** (*business, shop etc*) gut geführt
manageable ['mænɪdʒəbl] *adj* (*task*) zu bewältigen; (*number*) überschaubar
management ['mænɪdʒmənt] *n* Leitung *f*, Führung *f*; (*persons*) Unternehmensleitung *f*; **"under new ~"** "unter neuer Leitung"
manager ['mænɪdʒəʳ] *n* (*of business*) Geschäftsführer(in) *m(f)*; (*of institution etc*) Direktor(in) *m(f)*; (*of department*) Leiter(in) *m(f)*; (*of pop star*) Manager(in) *m(f)*; (*Sport*)

Trainer(in) *m(f)*; **sales ~** Verkaufsleiter(in) *m(f)*

manageress [mænɪdʒəˈrɛs] *n (of shop, business)* Geschäftsführerin *f*; *(of office, department etc)* Leiterin *f*

managerial [mænɪˈdʒɪərɪəl] *adj (role, post)* leitend; *(decisions)* geschäftlich; **~ staff/skills** Führungskräfte *pl*/-qualitäten *pl*

managing director [ˈmænɪdʒɪŋ-] *n* Geschäftsführer(in) *m(f)*

mandarin [ˈmændərɪn] *n (also:* **mandarin orange***)* Mandarine *f*; *(official: Chinese)* Mandarin *m*; *(: gen)* Funktionär *m*

mandate [ˈmændeɪt] *n* Mandat *nt*; *(task)* Auftrag *m*

mandatory [ˈmændətərɪ] *adj* obligatorisch

mane [meɪn] *n* Mähne *f*

maneuver *etc* [məˈnuːvəʳ] *(US)* = **manoeuvre** *etc*

manfully [ˈmænfəlɪ] *adv* mannhaft, beherzt

mangetout [ˈmɔnʒˈtuː] *(Brit) n* Zuckererbse *f*

mangle [ˈmæŋgl] *vt* (übel) zurichten ▷ *n* Mangel *f*

mango [ˈmæŋgəu] *(pl* **~es***) n* Mango *f*

mangy [ˈmeɪndʒɪ] *adj (animal)* räudig

manhandle [ˈmænhændl] *vt (mistreat)* grob behandeln; *(move by hand)* (von Hand) befördern

manhole [ˈmænhəul] *n* Kanalschacht *m*

manhood [ˈmænhud] *n* Mannesalter *nt*

man-hour [ˈmænauəʳ] *n* Arbeitsstunde *f*

manhunt [ˈmænhʌnt] *n* Fahndung *f*

mania [ˈmeɪnɪə] *n* Manie *f*; *(craze)* Sucht *f*; **persecution ~** Verfolgungswahn *m*

maniac [ˈmeɪnɪæk] *n* Wahnsinnige(r) *f(m)*, Verrückte(r) *f(m)*; *(fig)* Fanatiker(in) *m(f)*

manic [ˈmænɪk] *adj (behaviour)* manisch; *(activity)* rasend

manicure [ˈmænɪkjuəʳ] *n* Maniküre *f* ▷ *vt* maniküren

manifest [ˈmænɪfɛst] *vt* zeigen, bekunden ▷ *adj* offenkundig ▷ *n* Manifest *nt*

manifesto [mænɪˈfɛstəu] *n* Manifest *nt*

manipulate [məˈnɪpjuleɪt] *vt* manipulieren

mankind [mænˈkaɪnd] *n* Menschheit *f*

manly [ˈmænlɪ] *adj* männlich

man-made [ˈmænˈmeɪd] *adj* künstlich; *(fibre)* synthetisch

manner [ˈmænəʳ] *n (way)* Art *f*, Weise *f*; *(behaviour)* Art *f*; *(type, sort)*: **all ~ of things** die verschiedensten Dinge; **manners** *npl (conduct)* Manieren *pl*, Umgangsformen *pl*; **bad ~s** schlechte Manieren; **that's bad ~s** das gehört sich nicht

mannerism [ˈmænərɪzəm] *n* Eigenheit *f*

manoeuvre, *(US)* **maneuver** [məˈnuːvəʳ] *vt* manövrieren; *(situation)* manipulieren ▷ *vi* manövrieren ▷ *n (skilful move)* Manöver *nt*; **manoeuvres** *npl (Mil)* Manöver *nt*, Truppenübungen *pl*; **to ~ sb into doing sth** jdn dazu bringen, etw zu tun

manor [ˈmænəʳ] *n (also:* **manor house***)* Herrenhaus *nt*

manpower [ˈmænpauəʳ] *n* Personal *nt*, Arbeitskräfte *pl*

mansion [ˈmænʃən] *n* Villa *f*

manslaughter [ˈmænslɔːtəʳ] *n* Totschlag *m*

mantelpiece [ˈmæntlpiːs] *n* Kaminsims *nt or m*

manual [ˈmænjuəl] *adj* manuell, Hand-; *(controls)* von Hand ▷ *n* Handbuch *nt*

manufacture [mænjuˈfæktʃəʳ] *vt* herstellen ▷ *n* Herstellung *f*

manufacturer [mænjuˈfæktʃərəʳ] *n* Hersteller *m*

manure [məˈnjuəʳ] *n* Dung *m*

manuscript [ˈmænjuskrɪpt] *n* Manuskript *nt*; *(old document)* Handschrift *f*

many [ˈmɛnɪ] *adj, pron* viele; **a great ~** eine ganze Reihe; **how ~?** wie viele?; **too ~ difficulties** zu viele Schwierigkeiten; **twice as ~** doppelt so viele; **~ a time** so manches Mal

map [mæp] *n* (Land)karte *f*; *(of town)* Stadtplan *m* ▷ *vt* eine Karte anfertigen von

▶ **map out** *vt* planen; *(plan)* entwerfen; *(essay)* anlegen

maple [ˈmeɪpl] *n (tree, wood)* Ahorn *m*

mar [mɑːʳ] *vt (appearance)* verunstalten; *(day)* verderben; *(event)* stören

marathon [ˈmærəθən] *n* Marathon *m* ▷ *adj*: **a ~ session** eine Marathonsitzung

marble [ˈmɑːbl] *n* Marmor *m*; *(toy)* Murmel *f*

March [mɑːtʃ] *n* März *m*; *see also* **July**

march [mɑːtʃ] *vi* marschieren; *(protesters)* ziehen ▷ *n* Marsch *m*; *(demonstration)* Demonstration *f*; **to ~ out of/into** (heraus)marschieren aus *+dat*/ (herein)marschieren in *+acc*

mare [mɛəʳ] *n* Stute *f*

margarine [mɑːdʒəˈriːn] *n* Margarine *f*

margin [ˈmɑːdʒɪn] *n* Rand *m*; *(of votes)* Mehrheit *f*; *(for safety, error etc)* Spielraum *m*; *(Comm)* Gewinnspanne *f*

marginal [ˈmɑːdʒɪnl] *adj* geringfügig; *(note)* Rand-

marginally [ˈmɑːdʒɪnəlɪ] *adv* nur wenig, geringfügig

marigold [ˈmærɪgəuld] *n* Ringelblume *f*

marijuana [mærɪˈwɑːnə] *n* Marihuana *nt*

marina [məˈriːnə] *n* Jachthafen *m*

marinade [mærɪˈneɪd] *n* Marinade *f* ▷ *vt* = **marinate**

marinate [ˈmærɪneɪt] *vt* marinieren

marine [məˈriːn] *adj (plant, biology)* Meeres- ▷ *n (Brit: soldier)* Marineinfanterist *m*; *(US: sailor)* Marinesoldat *m*; **~ engineer** Schiff(s)bauingenieur *m*; **~ engineering** Schiff(s)bau *m*

marital [ˈmærɪtl] *adj* ehelich; *(problem)* Ehe-; **~ status** Familienstand *m*

maritime [ˈmærɪtaɪm] *adj (nation)* Seefahrer-; *(museum)* Seefahrts-; *(law)* See-

marjoram [ˈmɑːdʒərəm] *n* Majoran *m*

mark [mɑːk] *n* Zeichen *nt*; *(stain)* Fleck *m*; *(in snow, mud etc)* Spur *f*; *(Brit: Scol)* Note *f*; *(level,*

point): **the halfway ~** die Hälfte *f*; (*currency*) Mark *f*; (*Brit: Tech*): **M~ 2/3** Version *f* 2/3 ▷ *vt* (*with pen*) beschriften; (*with shoes etc*) schmutzig machen; (*with tyres etc*) Spuren hinterlassen auf *+dat*; (*damage*) beschädigen; (*stain*) Flecken machen auf *+dat*; (*indicate*) markieren; (*: price*) auszeichnen; (*commemorate*) begehen; (*characterize*) kennzeichnen; (*Brit: Scol*) korrigieren (und benoten); (*Sport: player*) decken; **punctuation ~s** Satzzeichen *pl*; **to be quick off the ~ (in doing sth)** (*fig*) blitzschnell reagieren (und etw tun); **to be up to the ~** den Anforderungen entsprechen; **to ~ time** auf der Stelle treten
▶ **mark down** *vt* (*prices, goods*) herabsetzen, heruntersetzen
▶ **mark off** *vt* (*tick off*) abhaken
▶ **mark out** *vt* markieren; (*person*) auszeichnen
▶ **mark up** *vt* (*price*) heraufsetzen
marked [mɑːkt] *adj* deutlich
marker ['mɑːkəʳ] *n* Markierung *f*; (*bookmark*) Lesezeichen *nt*
market ['mɑːkɪt] *n* Markt *m* ▷ *vt* (*sell*) vertreiben; (*new product*) auf den Markt bringen; **to be on the ~** auf dem Markt sein; **on the open ~** auf dem freien Markt; **to play the ~** (*Stock Exchange*) an der Börse spekulieren
market garden (*Brit*) *n* Gemüseanbaubetrieb *m*
marketing ['mɑːkɪtɪŋ] *n* Marketing *nt*
marketplace ['mɑːkɪtpleɪs] *n* Marktplatz *m*; (*Comm*) Markt *m*
market research *n* Marktforschung *f*
marksman ['mɑːksmən] (*irreg: like* **man**) *n* Scharfschütze *m*
marmalade ['mɑːməleɪd] *n* Orangenmarmelade *f*
maroon [mə'ruːn] *vt*: **to be ~ed** festsitzen ▷ *adj* kastanienbraun
marquee [mɑː'kiː] *n* Festzelt *nt*
marriage ['mærɪdʒ] *n* Ehe *f*; (*institution*) die Ehe; (*wedding*) Hochzeit *f*; **~ of convenience** Vernunftehe *f*
marriage certificate *n* Heiratsurkunde *f*
married ['mærɪd] *adj* verheiratet; (*life*) Ehe-; (*love*) ehelich; **to get ~** heiraten
marrow ['mærəu] *n* (*vegetable*) Kürbis *m*; (*also*: **bone marrow**) (Knochen)mark *nt*
marry ['mærɪ] *vt* heiraten; (*father*) verheiraten; (*priest*) trauen ▷ *vi* heiraten
Mars [mɑːz] *n* Mars *m*
Marseilles [mɑː'seɪlz] *n* Marseilles *nt*
marsh [mɑːʃ] *n* Sumpf *m*; (*also*: **salt marsh**) Salzsumpf *m*
marshal ['mɑːʃl] *n* (*Mil: also*: **field marshal**) (Feld)marschall *m*; (*official*) Ordner *m*; (*US: of police*) Bezirkspolizeichef *m* ▷ *vt* (*thoughts*) ordnen; (*support*) auftreiben; (*soldiers*) aufstellen
marshy ['mɑːʃɪ] *adj* sumpfig
martyr ['mɑːtəʳ] *n* Märtyrer(in) *m(f)* ▷ *vt* martern
martyrdom ['mɑːtədəm] *n* Martyrium *nt*
marvel ['mɑːvl] *n* Wunder *nt* ▷ *vi*: **to ~ (at)** staunen (über *+acc*)
marvellous, (*US*) **marvelous** ['mɑːvləs] *adj* wunderbar
Marxism ['mɑːksɪzəm] *n* Marxismus *m*
Marxist ['mɑːksɪst] *adj* marxistisch ▷ *n* Marxist(in) *m(f)*
marzipan ['mɑːzɪpæn] *n* Marzipan *nt*
mascara [mæs'kɑːrə] *n* Wimperntusche *f*
mascot ['mæskət] *n* Maskottchen *nt*
masculine ['mæskjulɪn] *adj* männlich; (*atmosphere, woman*) maskulin; (*Ling*) männlich, maskulin
mash [mæʃ] *vt* zerstampfen
mask [mɑːsk] *n* Maske *f* ▷ *vt* (*cover*) verdecken; (*hide*) verbergen; **surgical ~** Mundschutz *m*
mason ['meɪsn] *n* (*also*: **stone mason**) Steinmetz *m*; (*also*: **freemason**) Freimaurer *m*
masonry ['meɪsnrɪ] *n* Mauerwerk *nt*
masquerade [mæskə'reɪd] *vi*: **to ~ as** sich ausgeben als ▷ *n* Maskerade *f*
mass [mæs] *n* Masse *f*; (*of people*) Menge *f*; (*large amount*) Fülle *f*; (*Rel*): **M~** Messe *f* ▷ *cpd* Massen- ▷ *vi* (*troops*) sich massieren; (*protesters*) sich versammeln; **the masses** *npl* (*ordinary people*) die Masse, die Massen *pl*; **to go to M~** zur Messe gehen; **~es of** (*inf*) massenhaft, jede Menge
massacre ['mæsəkəʳ] *n* Massaker *nt* ▷ *vt* massakrieren
massage ['mæsɑːʒ] *n* Massage *f* ▷ *vt* massieren
massive ['mæsɪv] *adj* (*furniture, person*) wuchtig; (*support*) massiv; (*changes, increase*) enorm
mass media *npl* Massenmedien *pl*
mass-produce ['mæsprə'djuːs] *vt* in Massenproduktion herstellen
mast [mɑːst] *n* (*Naut*) Mast *m*; (*Radio etc*) Sendeturm *m*
master ['mɑːstəʳ] *n* Herr *m*; (*teacher*) Lehrer *m*; (*title*): **M~ X** (der junge) Herr X; (*Art, Mus, of craft etc*) Meister *m* ▷ *cpd*: **~ baker/plumber** *etc* Bäcker-/Klempnermeister *etc m* ▷ *vt* meistern; (*feeling*) unter Kontrolle bringen; (*skill, language*) beherrschen
masterly ['mɑːstəlɪ] *adj* meisterhaft
mastermind ['mɑːstəmaɪnd] *n* (führender) Kopf *m* ▷ *vt* planen und ausführen
masterpiece ['mɑːstəpiːs] *n* Meisterwerk *nt*
master plan *n* kluger Plan *m*
mastery ['mɑːstərɪ] *n* (*of language etc*) Beherrschung *f*; (*skill*) (meisterhaftes) Können *nt*
masturbate ['mæstəbeɪt] *vi* masturbieren, onanieren
mat [mæt] *n* Matte *f*; (*also*: **doormat**) Fußmatte *f*; (*also*: **table mat**) Untersetzer *m*; (*: of cloth*) Deckchen *nt* ▷ *adj* = **matt**
match [mætʃ] *n* Wettkampf *m*; (*team game*)

Spiel *nt*; (*Tennis*) Match *nt*; (*for lighting fire etc*) Streichholz *nt*; (*equivalent*): **to be a good/ perfect ~** gut/perfekt zusammenpassen ▷ *vt* (*go well with*) passen zu; (*equal*) gleichkommen *+dat*; (*correspond to*) entsprechen *+dat*; (*suit*) sich anpassen *+dat*; (*also*: **match up**: *pair*) passend zusammenbringen ▷ *vi* zusammenpassen; **to be a good ~** gut zusammenpassen; **to be no ~ for** sich nicht messen können mit; **with shoes to ~** mit (dazu) passenden Schuhen

▸ **match up** *vi* zusammenpassen

matchbox ['mætʃbɔks] *n* Streichholzschachtel *f*

matching ['mætʃɪŋ] *adj* (dazu) passend

mate [meɪt] *n* (*inf*: *friend*) Freund(in) *m(f)*, Kumpel *m*; (*animal*) Männchen *nt*, Weibchen *nt*; (*assistant*) Gehilfe *m*, Gehilfin *f*; (*in merchant navy*) Maat *m* ▷ *vi* (*animals*) sich paaren

material [mə'tɪərɪəl] *n* Material *nt*; (*cloth*) Stoff *m* ▷ *adj* (*possessions, existence*) materiell; (*relevant*) wesentlich; **materials** *npl* (*equipment*) Material *nt*

materialize [mə'tɪərɪəlaɪz] *vi* (*event*) zustande kommen; (*plan*) verwirklicht werden; (*hope*) sich verwirklichen; (*problem*) auftreten; (*crisis, difficulty*) eintreten

maternal [mə'təːnl] *adj* mütterlich, Mutter-

maternity [mə'təːnɪtɪ] *n* Mutterschaft *f* ▷ *cpd* (*ward etc*) Entbindungs-; (*care*) für werdende und junge Mütter

maternity dress *n* Umstandskleid *nt*

maternity hospital *n* Entbindungsheim *nt*

maternity leave *n* Mutterschaftsurlaub *m*

math [mæθ] (*US*) *n* = **maths**

mathematical [mæθə'mætɪkl] *adj* mathematisch

mathematician [mæθəmə'tɪʃən] *n* Mathematiker(in) *m(f)*

mathematics [mæθə'mætɪks] *n* Mathematik *f*

maths [mæθs], (*US*) **math** [mæθ] *n* Mathe *f*

matinée ['mætɪneɪ] *n* Nachmittagsvorstellung *f*

mating call *n* Lockruf *m*

matrices ['meɪtrɪsiːz] *npl of* **matrix**

matriculation [mətrɪkju'leɪʃən] *n* Immatrikulation *f*

matrimonial [mætrɪ'məunɪəl] *adj* Ehe-

matrimony ['mætrɪmənɪ] *n* Ehe *f*

matrix ['meɪtrɪks] (*pl* **matrices**) *n* (*Math*) Matrix *f*; (*framework*) Gefüge *nt*

matron ['meɪtrən] *n* (*in hospital*) Oberschwester *f*; (*in school*) Schwester *f*

matt [mæt] *adj* matt; (*paint*) Matt-

matted ['mætɪd] *adj* verfilzt

matter ['mætə[r]] *n* (*event, situation*) Sache *f*, Angelegenheit *f*; (*Phys*) Materie *f*; (*substance, material*) Stoff *m*; (*Med*: *pus*) Eiter *m* ▷ *vi* (*be important*) wichtig sein; **matters** *npl* (*affairs*) Angelegenheiten *pl*, Dinge *pl*; (*situation*) Lage *f*; **what's the ~?** was ist los?; **no ~ what** egal was (passiert); **that's another ~** das ist etwas anderes; **as a ~ of course** selbstverständlich; **as a ~ of fact** eigentlich; **it's a ~ of habit** es ist eine Gewohnheitssache; **vegetable ~** pflanzliche Stoffe *pl*; **printed ~** Drucksachen *pl*; **reading ~** (*Brit*) Lesestoff *m*; **it doesn't ~** es macht nichts

matter-of-fact ['mætərəv'fækt] *adj* sachlich

mattress ['mætrɪs] *n* Matratze *f*

mature [mə'tjuə[r]] *adj* reif; (*wine*) ausgereift ▷ *vi* reifen; (*Comm*) fällig werden

mature student *n* älterer Student *m*, ältere Studentin *f*

maturity [mə'tjuərɪtɪ] *n* Reife *f*; **to have reached ~** (*person*) erwachsen sein; (*animal*) ausgewachsen sein

maul [mɔːl] *vt* (anfallen und) übel zurichten

mauve [məuv] *adj* mauve

maximize ['mæksɪmaɪz] *vt* maximieren

maximum ['mæksɪməm] (*pl* **maxima** *or* **~s**) *adj* (*amount, speed etc*) Höchst-; (*efficiency*) maximal ▷ *n* Maximum *nt*

May [meɪ] *n* Mai *m*; *see also* **July**

may [meɪ] (*conditional* **might**) *vi* (*be possible*) können; (*have permission*) dürfen; **he ~ come** vielleicht kommt er; **~ I smoke?** darf ich rauchen?; **~ God bless you!** (*wish*) Gott segne dich!; **~ I sit here?** kann ich mich hier hinsetzen?; **he might be there** er könnte da sein; **you might like to try** vielleicht möchten Sie es mal versuchen; **you ~ as well go** Sie können ruhig gehen

maybe ['meɪbiː] *adv* vielleicht; **~ he'll ...** es kann sein, dass er ...; **~ not** vielleicht nicht

May Day *n* der 1. Mai

mayhem ['meɪhɛm] *n* Chaos *nt*

mayonnaise [meɪə'neɪz] *n* Mayonnaise *f*

mayor [mɛə[r]] *n* Bürgermeister *m*

mayoress ['mɛərɛs] *n* Bürgermeisterin *f*; (*partner*) Frau *f* des Bürgermeisters

maze [meɪz] *n* Irrgarten *m*; (*fig*) Wirrwarr *m*

MD *n abbr* (= *Doctor of Medicine*) ≈ Dr. med.; (*Comm*) = **managing director** ▷ *abbr* (*US*: *Post*: = *Maryland*)

me [miː] *pron* **1** (*direct*) mich; **can you hear me?** können Sie mich hören?; **it's me** ich bins

2 (*indirect*) mir; **he gave me the money, he gave the money to me** er gab mir das Geld

3 (*after prep*): **it's for me** es ist für mich; **with me** mit mir; **give them to me** gib sie mir; **without me** ohne mich

meadow ['mɛdəu] *n* Wiese *f*

meagre, (*US*) **meager** ['miːgə[r]] *adj* (*amount*) kläglich; (*meal*) dürftig

meal [miːl] *n* Mahlzeit *f*; (*food*) Essen *nt*; (*flour*) Schrotmehl *nt*; **to go out for a ~** essen gehen; **to make a ~ of sth** (*fig*) etw auf sehr umständliche Art machen

mealtime ['miːltaɪm] *n* Essenszeit *f*

mean [miːn] (*pt, pp* **~t**) *adj* (*with money*) geizig; (*unkind*) gemein; (*US*: *inf*: *animal*) bösartig; (*shabby*) schäbig; (*average*) Durchschnitts-, mittlere(r, s) ▷ *vt* (*signify*) bedeuten; (*refer to*) meinen; (*intend*) beabsichtigen ▷ *n* (*average*) Durchschnitt *m*; **means** *npl* (*way*) Möglichkeit *f*; (*money*) Mittel *pl*; **by ~s of** durch; **by all ~s!** aber natürlich *or* selbstverständlich!; **do you ~ it?** meinst du das ernst?; **what do you ~?** was willst du damit sagen?; **to be ~t for sb/sth** für jdn/etw bestimmt sein; **to ~ to do sth** etw tun wollen

meander [mɪ'ændəʳ] *vi* (*river*) sich schlängeln; (*person: walking*) schlendern; (*: talking*) abschweifen

meaning ['mi:nɪŋ] *n* Sinn *m*; (*of word, gesture*) Bedeutung *f*

meaningful ['mi:nɪŋful] *adj* sinnvoll; (*glance, remark*) vielsagend, bedeutsam; (*relationship*) tiefer gehend

meaningless ['mi:nɪŋlɪs] *adj* sinnlos; (*word, song*) bedeutungslos

meanness ['mi:nnɪs] *n* (*with money*) Geiz *m*; (*unkindness*) Gemeinheit *f*; (*shabbiness*) Schäbigkeit *f*

meant [mɛnt] *pt, pp of* **mean**

meantime ['mi:ntaɪm] *adv* (*also*: **in the meantime**) inzwischen

meanwhile ['mi:nwaɪl] *adv* = **meantime**

measles ['mi:zlz] *n* Masern *pl*

measure ['mɛʒəʳ] *vt, vi* messen ▷ *n* (*amount*) Menge *f*; (*ruler*) Messstab *m*; (*of achievement*) Maßstab *m*; (*action*) Maßnahme *f*; **a litre ~** ein Messbecher *m*, der einen Liter fasst; **a/some ~ of** ein gewisses Maß an *+dat*; **to take ~s to do sth** Maßnahmen ergreifen, um etw zu tun

▸ **measure up** *vi*: **to ~ up to** herankommen an *+acc*

measurements ['mɛʒəmənts] *npl* Maße *pl*; **to take sb's ~** bei jdm Maß nehmen

meat [mi:t] *n* Fleisch *nt*; **cold ~s** (*Brit*) Aufschnitt *m*; **crab ~** Krabbenfleisch *nt*

meatball ['mi:tbɔ:l] *n* Fleischkloß *m*

Mecca ['mɛkə] *n* (*Geog, fig*) Mekka *nt*

mechanic [mɪ'kænɪk] *n* Mechaniker(in) *m(f)*

mechanical [mɪ'kænɪkl] *adj* mechanisch

mechanics [mɪ'kænɪks] *n* (*Phys*) Mechanik *f* ▷ *npl* (*of reading etc*) Technik *f*; (*of government etc*) Mechanismus *m*

mechanism ['mɛkənɪzəm] *n* Mechanismus *m*

medal ['mɛdl] *n* Medaille *f*; (*decoration*) Orden *m*

medallion [mɪ'dælɪən] *n* Medaillon *nt*

medallist, (*US*) **medalist** ['mɛdlɪst] *n* Medaillengewinner(in) *m(f)*

meddle ['mɛdl] *vi*: **to ~ (in)** sich einmischen (in *+acc*); **to ~ with sb** sich mit jdm einlassen; **to ~ with sth** (*tamper*) sich *dat* an etw *dat* zu schaffen machen

media ['mi:dɪə] *npl* Medien *pl*

mediaeval [mɛdɪ'i:vl] *adj* = **medieval**

median ['mi:dɪən] (*US*) *n* (*also*: **median strip**) Mittelstreifen *m*

mediate ['mi:dɪeɪt] *vi* vermitteln

Medicaid ['mɛdɪkeɪd] (*US*) *n staatliche Krankenversicherung und Gesundheitsfürsorge für Einkommensschwache*

medical ['mɛdɪkl] *adj* (*care*) medizinisch; (*treatment*) ärztlich ▷ *n* (ärztliche) Untersuchung *f*

medical certificate *n* (*confirming health*) ärztliches Gesundheitszeugnis *nt*; (*confirming illness*) ärztliches Attest *nt*

Medicare ['mɛdɪkɛəʳ] (*US*) *n staatliche Krankenversicherung und Gesundheitsfürsorge für ältere Bürger*

medicated ['mɛdɪkeɪtɪd] *adj* medizinisch

medication [mɛdɪ'keɪʃən] *n* Medikamente *pl*

medicine ['mɛdsɪn] *n* Medizin *f*; (*drug*) Arznei *f*

medieval [mɛdɪ'i:vl] *adj* mittelalterlich

mediocre [mi:dɪ'əukəʳ] *adj* mittelmäßig

meditate ['mɛdɪteɪt] *vi* nachdenken; (*Rel*) meditieren

meditation [mɛdɪ'teɪʃən] *n* Nachdenken *nt*; (*Rel*) Meditation *f*

Mediterranean [mɛdɪtə'reɪnɪən] *adj* (*country, climate etc*) Mittelmeer-; **the ~ (Sea)** das Mittelmeer

medium ['mi:dɪəm] (*pl* **media** *or* **~s**) *adj* mittlere(r, s) ▷ *n* (*means*) Mittel *nt*; (*substance, material*) Medium *nt* (*pl* **~s**) (*person*) Medium *nt*; **of ~ height** mittelgroß; **to strike a happy ~** den goldenen Mittelweg finden

medium-sized ['mi:dɪəm'saɪzd] *adj* mittelgroß

medium wave *n* (*Radio*) Mittelwelle *f*

medley ['mɛdlɪ] *n* Gemisch *nt*; (*Mus*) Medley *nt*

meek [mi:k] *adj* sanft(mütig), duldsam

meet [mi:t] (*pt, pp* **met**) *vt* (*encounter*) treffen; (*by arrangement*) sich treffen mit; (*for the first time*) kennenlernen; (*go and fetch*) abholen; (*opponent*) treffen auf *+acc*; (*condition, standard*) erfüllen; (*need, expenses*) decken; (*problem*) stoßen auf *+acc*; (*challenge*) begegnen *+dat*; (*bill*) begleichen; (*join: line*) sich schneiden mit; (*: road etc*) treffen auf *+acc* ▷ *vi* (*encounter*) sich begegnen; (*by arrangement*) sich treffen; (*for the first time*) sich kennenlernen; (*for talks etc*) zusammenkommen; (*committee*) tagen; (*join: lines*) sich schneiden; (*: roads etc*) aufeinandertreffen ▷ *n* (*Brit: Hunting*) Jagd *f*; (*US: Sport*) Sportfest *nt*; **pleased to ~ you!** (sehr) angenehm!

▸ **meet up** *vi*: **to ~ up with sb** sich mit jdm treffen

▸ **meet with** *vt fus* (*difficulty, success*) haben

meeting ['mi:tɪŋ] *n* (*assembly, people assembling*) Versammlung *f*; (*Comm, of committee etc*) Sitzung *f*; (*also*: **business meeting**) Besprechung *f*; (*encounter*) Begegnung *f*; (*: arranged*) Treffen *nt*; (*Pol*) Gespräch *nt*; (*Sport*) Veranstaltung *f*; **she's at** *or* **in a ~** (*Comm*) sie ist bei einer Besprechung; **to call a ~** eine Sitzung/Versammlung einberufen

megabyte ['mɛgəbaɪt] *n* Megabyte *nt*

megaphone ['mɛgəfəun] *n* Megafon *nt*
melancholy ['mɛlənkəlı] *n* Melancholie *f*, Schwermut *f* ▷ *adj* melancholisch, schwermütig
mellow ['mɛləu] *adj* (*sound*) voll, weich; (*light, colour, stone*) warm; (*weathered*) verwittert; (*person*) gesetzt; (*wine*) ausgereift ▷ *vi* (*person*) gesetzter werden
melody ['mɛlədı] *n* Melodie *f*
melon ['mɛlən] *n* Melone *f*
melt [mɛlt] *vi* (*lit, fig*) schmelzen ▷ *vt* schmelzen; (*butter*) zerlassen
▸ **melt down** *vt* einschmelzen
meltdown ['mɛltdaun] *n* (*in nuclear reactor*) Kernschmelze *f*
melting pot *n* (*lit, fig*) Schmelztiegel *m*; **to be in the ~** in der Schwebe sein
member ['mɛmbə^r] *n* Mitglied *nt*; (*Anat*) Glied *nt* ▷ *cpd*: **~ country** Mitgliedsland *nt*; **~ state** Mitgliedsstaat *m*; **M~ of Parliament** (*Brit*) Abgeordnete(r) *f(m)* (des Unterhauses); **M~ of the European Parliament** (*Brit*) Abgeordnete(r) *f(m)* des Europaparlaments
membership ['mɛmbəʃıp] *n* Mitgliedschaft *f*; (*members*) Mitglieder *pl*; (*number of members*) Mitgliederzahl *f*
membership card *n* Mitgliedsausweis *m*
memento [mə'mɛntəu] *n* Andenken *nt*
memo ['mɛməu] *n* Memo *nt*, Mitteilung *f*
memoir ['mɛmwɑː^r] *n* Kurzbiografie *f*
memorable ['mɛmərəbl] *adj* denkwürdig; (*unforgettable*) unvergesslich
memorandum [mɛmə'rændəm] (*pl* **memoranda**) *n* Mitteilung *f*
memorial [mı'mɔːrıəl] *n* Denkmal *nt* ▷ *adj* (*service, prize*) Gedenk-
memorize ['mɛməraız] *vt* sich *dat* einprägen
memory ['mɛmərı] *n* Gedächtnis *nt*; (*sth remembered*) Erinnerung *f*; (*Comput*) Speicher *m*; **in ~ of** zur Erinnerung an *+acc*; **to have a good/bad ~** ein gutes/schlechtes Gedächtnis haben; **loss of ~** Gedächtnisschwund *m*
men [mɛn] *npl of* **man**
menace ['mɛnıs] *n* Bedrohung *f*; (*nuisance*) (Land)plage *f* ▷ *vt* bedrohen; **a public ~** eine Gefahr für die Öffentlichkeit
menacing ['mɛnısıŋ] *adj* drohend
mend [mɛnd] *vt* reparieren; (*darn*) flicken ▷ *n*: **to be on the ~** auf dem Wege der Besserung sein; **to ~ one's ways** sich bessern
mending ['mɛndıŋ] *n* Reparaturen *pl*; (*clothes*) Flickarbeiten *pl*
menial ['miːnıəl] (*often pej*) *adj* niedrig, untergeordnet
meningitis [mɛnın'dʒaıtıs] *n* Hirnhautentzündung *f*
menopause ['mɛnəupɔːz] *n*: **the ~** die Wechseljahre *pl*
men's room (*US*) *n* Herrentoilette *f*
menstruation [mɛnstru'eıʃən] *n* Menstruation *f*
menswear ['mɛnzwɛə^r] *n* Herren(be)kleidung *f*
mental ['mɛntl] *adj* geistig; (*illness*) Geistes-; **~ arithmetic** Kopfrechnen *nt*
mental hospital *n* psychiatrische Klinik *f*
mentality [mɛn'tælıtı] *n* Mentalität *f*
mentally ['mɛntlı] *adv*: **to be ~ handicapped** geistig behindert sein
menthol ['mɛnθɔl] *n* Menthol *nt*
mention ['mɛnʃən] *n* Erwähnung *f* ▷ *vt* erwähnen; **don't ~ it!** (bitte,) gern geschehen!; **not to ~ ...** von ... ganz zu schweigen
menu ['mɛnjuː] *n* Menü *nt*; (*printed*) Speisekarte *f*
MEP (*Brit*) *n abbr* (*= Member of the European Parliament*) Abgeordnete(r) *f(m)* des Europaparlaments
mercenary ['məːsınərı] *adj* (*person*) geldgierig ▷ *n* Söldner *m*
merchandise ['məːtʃəndaız] *n* Ware *f*
merchant ['məːtʃənt] *n* Kaufmann *m*; **timber/wine ~** Holz-/Weinhändler *m*
merchant bank (*Brit*) *n* Handelsbank *f*
merchant navy, (*US*) **merchant marine** *n* Handelsmarine *f*
merciful ['məːsıful] *adj* gnädig; **a ~ release** eine Erlösung
merciless ['məːsılıs] *adj* erbarmungslos
mercury ['məːkjurı] *n* Quecksilber *nt*
mercy ['məːsı] *n* Gnade *f*; **to have ~ on sb** Erbarmen mit jdm haben; **at the ~ of** ausgeliefert *+dat*
mere [mıə^r] *adj* bloß; **his ~ presence irritates her** schon *or* allein seine Anwesenheit ärgert sie; **she is a ~ child** sie ist noch ein Kind; **it's a ~ trifle** es ist eine Lappalie; **by ~ chance** rein durch Zufall
merely ['mıəlı] *adv* lediglich, bloß
merge [məːdʒ] *vt* (*combine*) vereinen; (*Comput: files*) mischen ▷ *vi* (*Comm*) fusionieren; (*colours, sounds, shapes*) ineinander übergehen; (*roads*) zusammenlaufen
merger ['məːdʒə^r] *n* (*Comm*) Fusion *f*
meringue [mə'ræŋ] *n* Baiser *nt*
merit ['mɛrıt] *n* (*worth, value*) Wert *m*; (*advantage*) Vorzug *m*; (*achievement*) Verdienst *nt* ▷ *vt* verdienen
mermaid ['məːmeıd] *n* Seejungfrau *f*, Meerjungfrau *f*
merry ['mɛrı] *adj* vergnügt; (*music*) fröhlich; **M~ Christmas!** fröhliche *or* frohe Weihnachten!
merry-go-round ['mɛrıgəuraund] *n* Karussell *nt*
mesh [mɛʃ] *n* Geflecht *nt*; **wire ~** Maschendraht *m*
mesmerize ['mɛzməraız] *vt* (*fig*) faszinieren
mess [mɛs] *n* Durcheinander *nt*; (*dirt*) Dreck *m*; (*Mil*) Kasino *nt*; **to be in a ~** (*untidy*) unordentlich sein; (*in difficulty*) in Schwierigkeiten stecken; **to be a ~** (*fig: life*) verkorkst sein; **to get o.s. in a ~** in

Schwierigkeiten geraten
▸ **mess about** (*inf*) *vi* (*fool around*) herumalbern
▸ **mess about with** (*inf*) *vt fus* (*play around with*) herumfummeln an +*dat*
▸ **mess around** (*inf*) *vi* = **mess about**
▸ **mess around with** (*inf*) *vt fus* = **mess about with**
▸ **mess up** *vt* durcheinanderbringen; (*dirty*) verdrecken

message ['mɛsɪdʒ] *n* Mitteilung *f*, Nachricht *f*; (*meaning*) Aussage *f*; **to get the ~** (*inf: fig*) kapieren
messenger ['mɛsɪndʒəʳ] *n* Bote *m*
Messrs ['mɛsəz] *abbr* (*on letters:* = *messieurs*) An (die Herren)
messy ['mɛsɪ] *adj* (*dirty*) dreckig; (*untidy*) unordentlich
met [mɛt] *pt, pp of* **meet**
metabolism [mɛ'tæbəlɪzəm] *n* Stoffwechsel *m*
metal ['mɛtl] *n* Metall *nt*
metallic [mɪ'tælɪk] *adj* metallisch; (*made of metal*) aus Metall
metaphor ['mɛtəfəʳ] *n* Metapher *f*
meteor ['mi:tɪəʳ] *n* Meteor *m*
meteorite ['mi:tɪəraɪt] *n* Meteorit *m*
meteorology [mi:tɪə'rɔlədʒɪ] *n* Wetterkunde *f*, Meteorologie *f*
meter ['mi:təʳ] *n* Zähler *m*; (*also:* **water meter**) Wasseruhr *f*; (*also:* **parking meter**) Parkuhr *f*; (*US: unit*) = **metre**
method ['mɛθəd] *n* Methode *f*; **~ of payment** Zahlungsweise *f*
methodical [mɪ'θɔdɪkl] *adj* methodisch
Methodist ['mɛθədɪst] *n* Methodist(in) *m(f)*
methylated spirit ['mɛθɪleɪtɪd-] (*Brit*) *n* (Brenn)spiritus *m*
meticulous [mɪ'tɪkjuləs] *adj* sorgfältig; (*detail*) genau
metre, (*US*) **meter** ['mi:təʳ] *n* Meter *m or nt*
metric ['mɛtrɪk] *adj* metrisch; **to go ~** auf das metrische Maßsystem umstellen
metropolitan [mɛtrə'pɔlɪtn] *adj* großstädtisch
mettle ['mɛtl] *n*: **to be on one's ~** auf dem Posten sein
mew [mju:] *vi* miauen
mews [mju:z] (*Brit*) *n* Gasse *f* mit ehemaligen Kutscherhäuschen
Mexican ['mɛksɪkən] *adj* mexikanisch ▹ *n* Mexikaner(in) *m(f)*
Mexico ['mɛksɪkəu] *n* Mexiko *nt*
mg *abbr* (= *milligram(me)*) mg
miaow [mi:'au] *vi* miauen
mice [maɪs] *npl of* **mouse**
micro ['maɪkrəu] *n* = **microcomputer**
micro ... ['maɪkrəu] *pref* mikro-, Mikro-
microchip ['maɪkrəutʃɪp] *n* Mikrochip *m*
microcomputer ['maɪkrəukəm'pju:təʳ] *n* Mikrocomputer *m*
microphone ['maɪkrəfəun] *n* Mikrofon *nt*
microscope ['maɪkrəskəup] *n* Mikroskop *nt*; **under the ~** unter dem Mikroskop
midday [mɪd'deɪ] *n* Mittag *m*
middle ['mɪdl] *n* Mitte *f* ▹ *adj* mittlere(r, s); **in the ~ of the night** mitten in der Nacht; **I'm in the ~ of reading it** ich bin mittendrin; **a ~ course** ein Mittelweg *m*
middle-aged [mɪdl'eɪdʒd] *adj* mittleren Alters
Middle Ages *npl* Mittelalter *nt*
middle-class [mɪdl'klɑ:s] *adj* mittelständisch
middle classes *npl* Mittelstand *m*
Middle East *n* Naher Osten *m*
middleman ['mɪdlmæn] (*irreg: like* **man**) *n* Zwischenhändler *m*
middle name *n* zweiter Vorname *m*
middle-of-the-road ['mɪdləvðə'rəud] *adj* gemäßigt; (*politician*) der Mitte; (*Mus*) leicht
middleweight ['mɪdlweɪt] *n* (*Boxing*) Mittelgewicht *nt*
middling ['mɪdlɪŋ] *adj* mittelmäßig
midge [mɪdʒ] *n* Mücke *f*
midget ['mɪdʒɪt] *n* Liliputaner(in) *m(f)*
Midlands ['mɪdləndz] (*Brit*) *npl*: **the ~** Mittelengland *nt*
midnight ['mɪdnaɪt] *n* Mitternacht *f* ▹ *cpd* Mitternachts-; **at ~** um Mitternacht
midriff ['mɪdrɪf] *n* Taille *f*
midst [mɪdst] *n*: **in the ~ of** mitten in +*dat*; **to be in the ~ of doing sth** mitten dabei sein, etw zu tun
midsummer [mɪd'sʌməʳ] *n* Hochsommer *m*; **M~('s) Day** Sommersonnenwende *f*
midway [mɪd'weɪ] *adj*: **we have reached the ~ point** wir haben die Hälfte hinter uns *dat* ▹ *adv* auf halbem Weg; **~ between** (*in space*) auf halbem Weg zwischen; **~ through** (*in time*) mitten in +*dat*
midweek [mɪd'wi:k] *adv* mitten in der Woche ▹ *adj* Mitte der Woche
midwife ['mɪdwaɪf] (*pl* **midwives**) *n* Hebamme *f*
midwinter [mɪd'wɪntəʳ] *n*: **in ~** im tiefsten Winter
might [maɪt] *vb see* **may** ▹ *n* Macht *f*; **with all one's ~** mit aller Kraft
mighty ['maɪtɪ] *adj* mächtig
migraine ['mi:greɪn] *n* Migräne *f*
migrant ['maɪgrənt] *adj* (*bird*) Zug-; (*worker*) Wander- ▹ *n* (*bird*) Zugvogel *m*; (*worker*) Wanderarbeiter(in) *m(f)*
migrate [maɪ'greɪt] *vi* (*bird*) ziehen; (*person*) abwandern
migration [maɪ'greɪʃən] *n* Wanderung *f*; (*to cities*) Abwanderung *f*; (*of birds*) (Vogel)zug *m*
mike [maɪk] *n* = **microphone**
mild [maɪld] *adj* mild; (*gentle*) sanft; (*slight: infection etc*) leicht; (*: interest*) gering
mildly ['maɪldlɪ] *adv* (*say*) sanft; (*slight*) leicht; **to put it ~** gelinde gesagt
mile [maɪl] *n* Meile *f*; **to do 30 ~s per gallon** ≈ 9 Liter auf 100 km verbrauchen
mileage ['maɪlɪdʒ] *n* Meilenzahl *f*; (*fig*) Nutzen *m*; **to get a lot of ~ out of sth** etw

gründlich ausnutzen; **there is a lot of ~ in the idea** aus der Idee lässt sich viel machen
mileometer [maɪ'lɔmɪtə^r] *n* ≈ Kilometerzähler *m*
milestone ['maɪlstəun] *n* (*lit, fig*) Meilenstein *m*
militant ['mɪlɪtnt] *adj* militant ▷ *n* Militante(r) *f(m)*
military ['mɪlɪtərɪ] *adj* (*history, leader etc*) Militär- ▷ *n*: **the ~** das Militär
militia [mɪ'lɪʃə] *n* Miliz *f*
milk [mɪlk] *n* Milch *f* ▷ *vt* (*lit, fig*) melken
milk chocolate *n* Vollmilchschokolade *f*
milkman ['mɪlkmən] (*irreg: like* **man**) *n* Milchmann *m*
milk shake *n* Milchmixgetränk *nt*
milky ['mɪlkɪ] *adj* milchig; (*drink*) mit viel Milch; **~ coffee** Milchkaffee *m*
Milky Way *n* Milchstraße *f*
mill [mɪl] *n* Mühle *f*; (*factory*) Fabrik *f*; (*woollen mill*) Spinnerei *f* ▷ *vt* mahlen ▷ *vi* (*also*: **mill about**) umherlaufen
millennium [mɪ'lɛnɪəm] (*pl* **~s** *or* **millennia**) *n* Jahrtausend *nt*
millennium bug *n* (*Comput*) Jahrtausendfehler *m*
miller ['mɪlə^r] *n* Müller *m*
milli ... ['mɪlɪ] *pref* Milli-
milligram, milligramme ['mɪlɪgræm] *n* Milligramm *nt*
millilitre, (*US*) **milliliter** ['mɪlɪli:tə^r] *n* Milliliter *m or nt*
millimetre, (*US*) **millimeter** ['mɪlɪmi:tə^r] *n* Millimeter *m or nt*
million ['mɪljən] *n* Million *f*; **a ~ times** (*fig*) tausend Mal, x-mal
millionaire [mɪljə'nɛə^r] *n* Millionär *m*
milometer [maɪ'lɔmɪtə^r] *n* = **mileometer**
mime [maɪm] *n* Pantomime *f*; (*actor*) Pantomime *m* ▷ *vt* pantomimisch darstellen
mimic ['mɪmɪk] *n* Imitator *m* ▷ *vt* (*for amusement*) parodieren; (*animal, person*) imitieren, nachahmen
min. *abbr* (*= minute*) Min.; = **minimum**
mince [mɪns] *vt* (*meat*) durch den Fleischwolf drehen ▷ *vi* (*in walking*) trippeln ▷ *n* (*Brit: meat*) Hackfleisch *nt*; **he does not ~ (his) words** er nimmt kein Blatt vor den Mund
mincemeat ['mɪnsmi:t] *n süße Gebäckfüllung aus Dörrobst und Sirup*; (*US: meat*) Hackfleisch *nt*; **to make ~ of sb** (*inf*) Hackfleisch aus jdm machen
mince pie *n mit Mincemeat gefülltes Gebäck*
mincer ['mɪnsə^r] *n* Fleischwolf *m*
mind [maɪnd] *n* Geist *m*, Verstand *m*; (*thoughts*) Gedanken *pl*; (*memory*) Gedächtnis *nt* ▷ *vt* aufpassen auf *+acc*; (*office etc*) nach dem Rechten sehen in *+dat*; (*object to*) etwas haben gegen; **to my ~** meiner Meinung nach; **to be out of one's ~** verrückt sein; **it is on my ~** es beschäftigt mich; **to keep** *or* **bear sth in ~** etw nicht vergessen, an etw denken; **to make up one's ~** sich entscheiden; **to change one's ~** es sich *dat* anders überlegen; **to be in two ~s about sth** sich *dat* über etw *acc* nicht im Klaren sein; **to have it in ~ to do sth** die Absicht haben, etw zu tun; **to have sb/sth in ~** an jdn/etw denken; **it slipped my ~** ich habe es vergessen; **to bring** *or* **call sth to ~** etw in Erinnerung rufen; **I can't get it out of my ~** es geht mir nicht aus dem Kopf; **his ~ was on other things** er war mit den Gedanken woanders; **"~ the step"** "Vorsicht Stufe"; **do you ~ if ...?** macht es Ihnen etwas aus, wenn ...?; **I don't ~** es ist mir egal; **~ you, ...** allerdings ...; **never ~!** (*it makes no odds*) ist doch egal!; (*don't worry*) macht nichts!
minder ['maɪndə^r] *n* Betreuer(in) *m(f)*; (*inf: bodyguard*) Aufpasser(in) *m(f)*
mindful ['maɪndful] *adj*: **~ of** unter Berücksichtigung *+gen*
mindless ['maɪndlɪs] *adj* (*violence*) sinnlos; (*work*) geistlos
mine[1] [maɪn] *n* (*also*: **coal mine, gold mine**) Bergwerk *nt*; (*bomb*) Mine *f* ▷ *vt* (*coal*) abbauen; (*beach etc*) verminen; (*ship*) eine Mine befestigen an *+dat*
mine[2] [maɪn] *pron* meine(r, s); **that book is ~** das Buch ist mein(e)s, das Buch gehört mir; **this is ~** das ist meins; **a friend of ~** ein Freund/eine Freundin von mir
minefield ['maɪnfi:ld] *n* Minenfeld *nt*; (*fig*) brisante Situation *f*
miner ['maɪnə^r] *n* Bergmann *m*, Bergarbeiter *m*
mineral ['mɪnərəl] *adj* (*deposit, resources*) Mineral- ▷ *n* Mineral *nt*; **minerals** *npl* (*Brit: soft drinks*) Erfrischungsgetränke *pl*
mineral water *n* Mineralwasser *nt*
mingle ['mɪŋgl] *vi*: **to ~ (with)** sich vermischen (mit); **to ~ with** (*people*) Umgang haben mit; (*at party etc*) sich unterhalten mit; **you should ~ a bit** du solltest dich unter die Leute mischen
miniature ['mɪnətʃə^r] *adj* winzig; (*version etc*) Miniatur- ▷ *n* Miniatur *f*; **in ~** im Kleinen, im Kleinformat
minibus ['mɪnɪbʌs] *n* Kleinbus *m*
minicab ['mɪnɪkæb] *n* Kleintaxi *nt*
minimal ['mɪnɪml] *adj* minimal
minimize ['mɪnɪmaɪz] *vt* auf ein Minimum reduzieren; (*play down*) herunterspielen
minimum ['mɪnɪməm] (*pl* **minima**) *n* Minimum *nt* ▷ *adj* (*income, speed*) Mindest-; **to reduce to a ~** auf ein Mindestmaß reduzieren; **~ wage** Mindestlohn *m*
mining ['maɪnɪŋ] *n* Bergbau *m* ▷ *cpd* Bergbau-
miniskirt ['mɪnɪskə:t] *n* Minirock *m*
minister ['mɪnɪstə^r] *n* (*Brit: Pol*) Minister(in) *m(f)*; (*Rel*) Pfarrer *m* ▷ *vi*: **to ~ to** sich kümmern um; (*needs*) befriedigen
ministerial [mɪnɪs'tɪərɪəl] (*Brit*) *adj* (*Pol*) ministeriell
ministry ['mɪnɪstrɪ] *n* (*Brit: Pol*) Ministerium *nt*; **to join the ~** (*Rel*) Geistliche(r) werden

mink [mɪŋk] (*pl* **minks** *or* **~**) *n* Nerz *m*
minor ['maɪnəʳ] *adj* kleinere(r, s); (*poet*) unbedeutend; (*planet*) klein; (*Mus*) Moll ▷ *n* Minderjährige(r) *f(m)*
minority [maɪ'nɔrɪtɪ] *n* Minderheit *f*; **to be in a ~** in der Minderheit sein
mint [mɪnt] *n* Minze *f*; (*sweet*) Pfefferminz(bonbon) *nt*; (*place*): **the M~** die Münzanstalt ▷ *vt* (*coins*) prägen; **in ~ condition** neuwertig
minus ['maɪnəs] *n* (*also*: **minus sign**) Minuszeichen *nt* ▷ *prep* minus, weniger; **~ 24°C** 24 Grad unter null
minute¹ [maɪ'nju:t] *adj* winzig; (*search*) peinlich genau; (*detail*) kleinste(r, s); **in ~ detail** in allen Einzelheiten
minute² ['mɪnɪt] *n* Minute *f*; (*fig*) Augenblick *m*, Moment *m*; **minutes** *npl* (*of meeting*) Protokoll *nt*; **it is 5 ~s past 3** es ist 5 Minuten nach 3; **wait a ~!** einen Augenblick *or* Moment!; **up-to-the-~** (*news*) hochaktuell; (*technology*) allerneueste(r, s); **at the last ~** in letzter Minute
miracle ['mɪrəkl] *n* (*Rel, fig*) Wunder *nt*
miraculous [mɪ'rækjuləs] *adj* wunderbar; (*powers, effect, cure*) Wunder-; (*success, change*) unglaublich; **to have a ~ escape** wie durch ein Wunder entkommen
mirage ['mɪrɑ:ʒ] *n* Fata Morgana *f*; (*fig*) Trugbild *nt*
mirror ['mɪrəʳ] *n* Spiegel *m* ▷ *vt* (*lit, fig*) widerspiegeln
mirth [mə:θ] *n* Heiterkeit *f*
misadventure [mɪsəd'vɛntʃəʳ] *n* Missgeschick *nt*; **death by ~** (*Brit*) Tod *m* durch Unfall
misapprehension ['mɪsæprɪ'hɛnʃən] *n* Missverständnis *nt*; **you are under a ~** Sie befinden sich im Irrtum
misappropriate [mɪsə'prəuprɪeɪt] *vt* veruntreuen
misbehave [mɪsbɪ'heɪv] *vi* sich schlecht benehmen
misc. *abbr* = **miscellaneous**
miscalculate [mɪs'kælkjuleɪt] *vt* falsch berechnen; (*misjudge*) falsch einschätzen
miscarriage ['mɪskærɪdʒ] *n* (*Med*) Fehlgeburt *f*; **~ of justice** (*Law*) Justizirrtum *m*
miscellaneous [mɪsɪ'leɪnɪəs] *adj* verschieden; (*subjects, items*) divers; **~ expenses** sonstige Unkosten *pl*
mischief ['mɪstʃɪf] *n* (*bad behaviour*) Unfug *m*; (*playfulness*) Verschmitztheit *f*; (*harm*) Schaden *m*; (*pranks*) Streiche *pl*; **to get into ~** etwas anstellen; **to do sb a ~** jdm etwas antun
mischievous ['mɪstʃɪvəs] *adj* (*naughty*) ungezogen; (*playful*) verschmitzt
misconception ['mɪskən'sɛpʃən] *n* fälschliche Annahme *f*
misconduct [mɪs'kɔndʌkt] *n* Fehlverhalten *nt*; **professional ~** Berufsvergehen *nt*
misdemeanour, (*US*) **misdemeanor** [mɪsdɪ'mi:nəʳ] *n* Vergehen *nt*
miser ['maɪzəʳ] *n* Geizhals *m*
miserable ['mɪzərəbl] *adj* (*unhappy*) unglücklich; (*wretched*) erbärmlich, elend; (*unpleasant*: *weather*) trostlos; (: *person*) gemein; (*contemptible*: *offer, donation*) armselig; (: *failure*) kläglich; **to feel ~** sich elend fühlen
miserly ['maɪzəlɪ] *adj* geizig; (*amount*) armselig
misery ['mɪzərɪ] *n* (*unhappiness*) Kummer *m*; (*wretchedness*) Elend *nt*; (*inf*: *person*) Miesepeter *m*
misfire [mɪs'faɪəʳ] *vi* (*plan*) fehlschlagen; (*car engine*) fehlzünden
misfit ['mɪsfɪt] *n* Außenseiter(in) *m(f)*
misfortune [mɪs'fɔ:tʃən] *n* Pech *nt*, Unglück *nt*
misgiving [mɪs'gɪvɪŋ] *n* Bedenken *pl*; **to have ~s about sth** sich bei etw nicht wohlfühlen
misguided [mɪs'gaɪdɪd] *adj* töricht; (*opinion, view*) irrig; (*misplaced*) unangebracht
mishandle [mɪs'hændl] *vt* falsch handhaben
mishap ['mɪshæp] *n* Missgeschick *nt*
misinform [mɪsɪn'fɔ:m] *vt* falsch informieren
misinterpret [mɪsɪn'tə:prɪt] *vt* (*gesture, situation*) falsch auslegen; (*comment*) falsch auffassen
misjudge [mɪs'dʒʌdʒ] *vt* falsch einschätzen
mislay [mɪs'leɪ] (*irreg*: *like* **lay**) *vt* verlegen
mislead [mɪs'li:d] (*irreg*: *like* **lead**) *vt* irreführen
misleading [mɪs'li:dɪŋ] *adj* irreführend
mismanage [mɪs'mænɪdʒ] *vt* (*business*) herunterwirtschaften; (*institution*) schlecht führen
misprint ['mɪsprɪnt] *n* Druckfehler *m*
misrepresent [mɪsrɛprɪ'zɛnt] *vt* falsch darstellen; **he was ~ed** seine Worte wurden verfälscht wiedergegeben
Miss [mɪs] *n* Fräulein *nt*; **Dear ~ Smith** Liebe Frau Smith
miss [mɪs] *vt* (*train etc, chance, opportunity*) verpassen; (*target*) verfehlen; (*notice loss of, regret absence of*) vermissen; (*class, meeting*) fehlen bei ▷ *vi* danebentreffen; (*missile, object*) danebengehen ▷ *n* Fehltreffer *m*; **you can't ~ it** du kannst es nicht verfehlen; **the bus just ~ed the wall** der Bus wäre um ein Haar gegen die Mauer gefahren; **you're ~ing the point** das geht an der Sache vorbei
▸ **miss out** (*Brit*) *vt* auslassen
▸ **miss out on** *vt fus* (*party*) verpassen; (*fun*) zu kurz kommen bei
misshapen [mɪs'ʃeɪpən] *adj* missgebildet
missile ['mɪsaɪl] *n* (*Mil*) Rakete *f*; (*object thrown*) (Wurf)geschoss *nt*, (Wurf)geschoß *nt* (*Österr*)
missing ['mɪsɪŋ] *adj* (*lost*: *person*) vermisst; (: *object*) verschwunden; (*absent, removed*) fehlend; **to be ~** fehlen; **to go ~** verschwinden; **~ person** Vermisste(r) *f(m)*
mission ['mɪʃən] *n* (*task*) Mission *f*, Auftrag *m*; (*representatives*) Gesandtschaft *f*; (*Mil*) Einsatz *m*; (*Rel*) Mission *f*; **on a ~ to ...** (*to place/people*) im Einsatz in *+dat*/bei ...

missionary ['mɪʃənrɪ] *n* Missionar(in) *m(f)*
misspell ['mɪs'spɛl] (*irreg: like* **spell**) *vt* falsch schreiben
mist [mɪst] *n* Nebel *m*; (*light*) Dunst *m* ▷ *vi* (*also*: **mist over**: *eyes*) sich verschleiern; (*Brit*: *also*: **mist over, mist up**: *windows*) beschlagen
mistake [mɪs'teɪk] (*irreg: like* **take**) *n* Fehler *m* ▷ *vt* sich irren in +*dat*; (*intentions*) falsch verstehen; **by ~** aus Versehen; **to make a ~** (*in writing, calculation*) sich vertun; **to make a ~ (about sb/sth)** sich (in jdm/etw) irren; **to ~ A for B** A mit B verwechseln
mistaken [mɪs'teɪkən] *pp of* **mistake** ▷ *adj* falsch; **to be ~** sich irren
mister ['mɪstəʳ] (*inf*) *n* (*sir*) *not translated see* **Mr**
mistletoe ['mɪsltəu] *n* Mistel *f*
mistook [mɪs'tuk] *pt of* **mistake**
mistress ['mɪstrɪs] *n* (*lover*) Geliebte *f*; (*of house, servant, situation*) Herrin *f*; (*Brit: teacher*) Lehrerin *f*
mistrust [mɪs'trʌst] *vt* misstrauen +*dat* ▷ *n*: **~ (of)** Misstrauen *nt* (gegenüber)
misty ['mɪstɪ] *adj* (*day etc*) neblig; (*glasses, windows*) beschlagen
misunderstand [mɪsʌndə'stænd] (*irreg: like* **understand**) *vt* missverstehen, falsch verstehen ▷ *vi* es falsch verstehen
misunderstanding ['mɪsʌndə'stændɪŋ] *n* Missverständnis *nt*; (*disagreement*) Meinungsverschiedenheit *f*
misunderstood [mɪsʌndə'stud] *pt, pp of* **misunderstand**
misuse [*n* mɪs'ju:s, *vt* mɪs'ju:z] *n* Missbrauch *m* ▷ *vt* missbrauchen; (*word*) falsch gebrauchen
mitigate ['mɪtɪgeɪt] *vt* mildern; **mitigating circumstances** mildernde Umstände *pl*
mitt ['mɪt], **mitten** ['mɪtn] *n* Fausthandschuh *m*
mix [mɪks] *vt* mischen; (*drink*) mixen; (*sauce, cake*) zubereiten; (*ingredients*) verrühren ▷ *vi*: **to ~ (with)** verkehren (mit) ▷ *n* Mischung *f*; **to ~ sth with sth** etw mit etw vermischen; **to ~ business with pleasure** das Angenehme mit dem Nützlichen verbinden; **cake ~** Backmischung *f*
▸ **mix in** *vt* (*eggs etc*) unterrühren
▸ **mix up** *vt* (*people*) verwechseln; (*things*) durcheinanderbringen; **to be ~ed up in sth** in etw *acc* verwickelt sein
mixed [mɪkst] *adj* gemischt; **~ marriage** Mischehe *f*
mixed grill (*Brit*) *n* Grillteller *m*
mixed-up [mɪkst'ʌp] *adj* durcheinander
mixer ['mɪksəʳ] *n* (*for food*) Mixer *m*; (*drink*) Tonic *etc zum Auffüllen von alkoholischen Mixgetränken*; **to be a good ~** (*sociable person*) kontaktfreudig sein
mixture ['mɪkstʃəʳ] *n* Mischung *f*; (*Culin*) Gemisch *nt*; (*: for cake*) Teig *m*; (*Med*) Mixtur *f*
mix-up ['mɪksʌp] *n* Durcheinander *nt*
mm *abbr* (= *millimetre*) mm
moan [məun] *n* Stöhnen *nt* ▷ *vi* stöhnen; (*inf: complain*): **to ~ (about)** meckern (über +*acc*)
moat [məut] *n* Wassergraben *m*
mob [mɔb] *n* Mob *m*; (*organized*) Bande *f* ▷ *vt* herfallen über +*acc*
mobile ['məubaɪl] *adj* beweglich; (*workforce, society*) mobil ▷ *n* (*decoration*) Mobile *nt*; **applicants must be ~** Bewerber müssen motorisiert sein
mobile home *n* Wohnwagen *m*
mobility [məu'bɪlɪtɪ] *n* Beweglichkeit *f*; (*of workforce etc*) Mobilität *f*
mobilize ['məubɪlaɪz] *vt* mobilisieren; (*Mil*) mobil machen ▷ *vi* (*Mil*) mobil machen
mock [mɔk] *vt* sich lustig machen über +*acc* ▷ *adj* (*fake: Elizabethan etc*) Pseudo-; (*exam*) Probe-; (*battle*) Schein-
mockery ['mɔkərɪ] *n* Spott *m*; **to make a ~ of sb** jdn zum Gespött machen; **to make a ~ of sth** etw zur Farce machen
mock-up ['mɔkʌp] *n* Modell *nt*
mod cons ['mɔd'kɔnz] (*Brit*) *npl* (= *modern conveniences*) Komfort *m*
mode [məud] *n* Form *f*; (*Comput, Tech*) Betriebsart *f*; **~ of life** Lebensweise *f*; **~ of transport** Transportmittel *nt*
model ['mɔdl] *n* Modell *nt*; (*also*: **fashion model**) Mannequin *nt*; (*example*) Muster *nt* ▷ *adj* (*excellent*) vorbildlich; (*small scale: railway etc*) Modell- ▷ *vt* (*clothes*) vorführen; (*with clay etc*) modellieren, formen ▷ *vi* (*for designer, photographer etc*) als Modell arbeiten; **to ~ o.s. on sb** sich *dat* jdn zum Vorbild nehmen
modem ['məudɛm] *n* Modem *nt*
moderate [*adj* 'mɔdərət, *vb* 'mɔdəreɪt] *adj* gemäßigt; (*amount*) nicht allzu groß; (*change*) leicht ▷ *n* Gemäßigte(r) *f(m)* ▷ *vi* (*storm, wind etc*) nachlassen ▷ *vt* (*tone, demands*) mäßigen
moderation [mɔdə'reɪʃən] *n* Mäßigung *f*; **in ~** in *or* mit Maßen
modern ['mɔdən] *adj* modern; **~ languages** moderne Fremdsprachen *pl*
modernize ['mɔdənaɪz] *vt* modernisieren
modest ['mɔdɪst] *adj* bescheiden; (*chaste*) schamhaft
modesty ['mɔdɪstɪ] *n* Bescheidenheit *f*; (*chastity*) Schamgefühl *nt*
modification [mɔdɪfɪ'keɪʃən] *n* Änderung *f*; (*to policy etc*) Modifizierung *f*; **to make ~s to** (Ver)änderungen vornehmen an +*dat*, modifizieren
modify ['mɔdɪfaɪ] *vt* (ver)ändern; (*policy etc*) modifizieren
module ['mɔdju:l] *n* (Bau)element *nt*; (*Space*) Raumkapsel *f*; (*Scol*) Kurs *m*
mogul ['məugl] *n* (*fig*) Mogul *m*
mohair ['məuhɛəʳ] *n* Mohair *m*
Mohammed [mə'hæmɛd] *n* Mohammed *m*
moist [mɔɪst] *adj* feucht
moisten ['mɔɪsn] *vt* anfeuchten
moisture ['mɔɪstʃəʳ] *n* Feuchtigkeit *f*
moisturizer ['mɔɪstʃəraɪzəʳ] *n*

Feuchtigkeitscreme *f*
molar ['məuləʳ] *n* Backenzahn *m*
molasses [mə'læsɪz] *n* Melasse *f*
mole [məul] *n* (*on skin*) Leberfleck *m*; (*Zool*) Maulwurf *m*; (*fig: spy*) Spion(in) *m(f)*
molecule ['mɔlɪkju:l] *n* Molekül *nt*
molest [mə'lɛst] *vt* (*assault sexually*) sich vergehen an +*dat*; (*harass*) belästigen
mollycoddle ['mɔlɪkɔdl] *vt* verhätscheln
molt [məult] (*US*) *vi* = **moult**
molten ['məultən] *adj* geschmolzen, flüssig
mom [mɔm] (*US*) *n* = **mum**
moment ['məumənt] *n* Moment *m*, Augenblick *m*; (*importance*) Bedeutung *f*; **for a ~** (für) einen Moment *or* Augenblick; **at that ~** in diesem Moment *or* Augenblick; **at the ~** momentan; **for the ~** vorläufig; **in a ~** gleich; **"one ~ please"** (*Tel*) "bleiben Sie am Apparat"
momentarily ['məuməntrɪlɪ] *adv* für einen Augenblick *or* Moment; (*US: very soon*) jeden Augenblick *or* Moment
momentary ['məuməntərɪ] *adj* (*brief*) kurz
momentous [məu'mɛntəs] *adj* (*occasion*) bedeutsam; (*decision*) von großer Tragweite
momentum [məu'mɛntəm] *n* (*Phys*) Impuls *m*; (*fig: of movement*) Schwung *m*; (*: of events, change*) Dynamik *f*; **to gather ~** schneller werden; (*fig*) richtig in Gang kommen
mommy ['mɔmɪ] (*US*) *n* = **mummy**
Monaco ['mɔnəkəu] *n* Monaco *nt*
monarch ['mɔnək] *n* Monarch(in) *m(f)*
monarchy ['mɔnəkɪ] *n* Monarchie *f*; **the M~** (*royal family*) die königliche Familie
monastery ['mɔnəstərɪ] *n* Kloster *nt*
Monday ['mʌndɪ] *n* Montag *m*; *see also* **Tuesday**
monetary ['mʌnɪtərɪ] *adj* (*system, union*) Währungs-
money ['mʌnɪ] *n* Geld *nt*; **to make ~** (*person*) Geld verdienen; (*business*) etwas einbringen; **danger ~** (*Brit*) Gefahrenzulage *f*; **I've got no ~ left** ich habe kein Geld mehr
money order *n* Zahlungsanweisung *f*
money-spinner ['mʌnɪspɪnəʳ] (*inf*) *n* Verkaufsschlager *m*; (*person, business*) Goldgrube *f*
mongrel ['mʌŋgrəl] *n* Promenadenmischung *f*
monitor ['mɔnɪtəʳ] *n* Monitor *m* ▷ *vt* überwachen; (*broadcasts*) mithören
monk [mʌŋk] *n* Mönch *m*
monkey ['mʌŋkɪ] *n* Affe *m*
monkey nut (*Brit*) *n* Erdnuss *f*
monologue ['mɔnəlɔg] *n* Monolog *m*
monopoly [mə'nɔpəlɪ] *n* Monopol *nt*; **to have a ~ on** *or* **of sth** (*fig: domination*) etw für sich gepachtet haben; **Monopolies and Mergers Commission** (*Brit*) ≈ Kartellamt *nt*
monosodium glutamate [mɔnə'səudɪəm'glu:təmeɪt] *n* Glutamat *nt*
monotone ['mɔnətəun] *n*: **in a ~** monoton
monotonous [mə'nɔtənəs] *adj* monoton, eintönig
monsoon [mɔn'su:n] *n* Monsun *m*
monster ['mɔnstəʳ] *n* Ungetüm *nt*, Monstrum *nt*; (*imaginary creature*) Ungeheuer *nt*, Monster *nt*; (*person*) Unmensch *m*
monstrous ['mɔnstrəs] *adj* (*huge*) riesig; (*ugly*) abscheulich; (*atrocious*) ungeheuerlich
month [mʌnθ] *n* Monat *m*; **every ~** jeden Monat; **300 dollars a ~** 300 Dollar im Monat
monthly ['mʌnθlɪ] *adj* monatlich; (*ticket, magazine*) Monats- ▷ *adv* monatlich; **twice ~** zweimal im Monat
Montreal [mɔntrɪ'ɔ:l] *n* Montreal *nt*
monument ['mɔnjumənt] *n* Denkmal *nt*
moo [mu:] *vi* muhen
mood [mu:d] *n* Stimmung *f*; (*of person*) Laune *f*, Stimmung *f*; **to be in a good/bad ~** gut/schlecht gelaunt sein; **to be in the ~ for** aufgelegt sein zu
moody ['mu:dɪ] *adj* launisch; (*sullen*) schlecht gelaunt
moon [mu:n] *n* Mond *m*
moonlight ['mu:nlaɪt] *n* Mondschein *m* ▷ *vi* (*inf*) schwarzarbeiten
moonlighting ['mu:nlaɪtɪŋ] (*inf*) *n* Schwarzarbeit *f*
moonlit ['mu:nlɪt] *adj* (*night*) mondhell
moor [muəʳ] *n* (Hoch)moor *nt*, Heide *f* ▷ *vt* vertäuen ▷ *vi* anlegen
moorland ['muələnd] *n* Moorlandschaft *f*, Heidelandschaft *f*
moose [mu:s] *n inv* Elch *m*
mop [mɔp] *n* (*for floor*) Mop *m*; (*for dishes*) Spülbürste *f*; (*of hair*) Mähne *f* ▷ *vt* (*floor*) wischen; (*face*) abwischen; (*eyes*) sich *dat* wischen; **to ~ the sweat from one's brow** sich *dat* den Schweiß von der Stirn wischen
▸ **mop up** *vt* aufwischen
mope [məup] *vi* Trübsal blasen
▸ **mope about** *vi* mit einer Jammermiene herumlaufen
▸ **mope around** *vi* = **mope about**
moped ['məupɛd] *n* Moped *nt*
moral ['mɔrl] *adj* moralisch; (*welfare, values*) sittlich; (*behaviour*) moralisch einwandfrei ▷ *n* Moral *f*; **morals** *npl* (*principles, values*) Moralvorstellungen *pl*; **~ support** moralische Unterstützung *f*
morale [mɔ'rɑ:l] *n* Moral *f*
morality [mə'rælɪtɪ] *n* Sittlichkeit *f*; (*system of morals*) Moral *f*, Ethik *f*; (*correctness*) moralische Richtigkeit *f*
morass [mə'ræs] *n* Morast *m*, Sumpf *m*, Sumpf *m* (*also fig*)
morbid ['mɔ:bɪd] *adj* (*imagination*) krankhaft; (*interest*) unnatürlich; (*comments, behaviour*) makaber
more [mɔ:ʳ] *adj* **1** (*greater in number etc*) mehr; **more people/work/letters than we expected** mehr Leute/Arbeit/Briefe, als wir erwarteten; **I have more wine/money than you** ich habe mehr Wein/Geld als du
2 (*additional*): **do you want (some) more**

tea? möchten Sie noch mehr Tee?; **is there any more wine?** ist noch Wein da?; **I have no more money, I don't have any more money** ich habe kein Geld mehr
▷ *pron* **1** (*greater amount*) mehr; **more than 10** mehr als 10; **it cost more than we expected** es kostete mehr, als wir erwarteten **2** (*further or additional amount*): **is there any more?** gibt es noch mehr?; **there's no more** es ist nichts mehr da; **many/much more** viel mehr
▷ *adv* mehr; **more dangerous/difficult/ easily** *etc* **(than)** gefährlicher/schwerer/ leichter *etc* (als); **more and more** mehr und mehr, immer mehr; **more and more excited/expensive** immer aufgeregter/ teurer; **more or less** mehr oder weniger; **more than ever** mehr denn je, mehr als jemals zuvor; **more beautiful than ever** schöner denn je; **no more, not any more** nicht mehr

moreover [mɔː'rəuvəʳ] *adv* außerdem, zudem

morgue [mɔːg] *n* Leichenschauhaus *nt*

morning ['mɔːnɪŋ] *n* Morgen *m*; (*as opposed to afternoon*) Vormittag *m* ▷ *cpd* Morgen-; **in the ~** morgens; vormittags; (*tomorrow*) morgen früh; **7 o'clock in the ~** 7 Uhr morgens; **this ~** heute Morgen

morning sickness *n* (Schwangerschafts)-übelkeit *f*

Moroccan [mə'rɔkən] *adj* marokkanisch ▷ *n* Marokkaner(in) *m(f)*

Morocco [mə'rɔkəu] *n* Marokko *nt*

moron ['mɔːrɔn] (*inf*) *n* Schwachkopf *m*

morphine ['mɔːfiːn] *n* Morphium *nt*

morris dancing ['mɔrɪs-] *n* Moriskentanz *m*, *alter englischer Volkstanz*

Morse [mɔːs] *n* (*also*: **Morse code**) Morsealphabet *nt*

morsel ['mɔːsl] *n* Stückchen *nt*

mortal ['mɔːtl] *adj* sterblich; (*wound, combat*) tödlich; (*danger*) Todes-; (*sin, enemy*) Tod- ▷ *n* (*human being*) Sterbliche(r) *f(m)*

mortar ['mɔːtəʳ] *n* (*Mil*) Minenwerfer *m*; (*Constr*) Mörtel *m*; (*Culin*) Mörser *m*

mortgage ['mɔːgɪdʒ] *n* Hypothek *f* ▷ *vt* mit einer Hypothek belasten; **to take out a ~** eine Hypothek aufnehmen

mortgage company (*US*) *n* Hypothekenbank *f*

mortician [mɔː'tɪʃən] (*US*) *n* Bestattungsunternehmer *m*

mortified ['mɔːtɪfaɪd] *adj*: **he was ~** er empfand das als beschämend; (*embarrassed*) es war ihm schrecklich peinlich

mortuary ['mɔːtjuərɪ] *n* Leichenhalle *f*

mosaic [məu'zeɪɪk] *n* Mosaik *nt*

Moscow ['mɔskəu] *n* Moskau *nt*

Moslem ['mɔzləm] *adj, n* = **Muslim**

mosque [mɔsk] *n* Moschee *f*

mosquito [mɔs'kiːtəu] (*pl* **~es**) *n* Stechmücke *f*; (*in tropics*) Moskito *m*

moss [mɔs] *n* Moos *nt*

most [məust] *adj* **1** (*almost all: people, things etc*) meiste(r, s); **most people** die meisten Leute **2** (*largest, greatest: interest, money etc*) meiste(r, s); **who has (the) most money?** wer hat das meiste Geld?
▷ *pron* (*greatest quantity, number*) der/die/das meiste; **most of it** das meiste (davon); **most of them** die meisten von ihnen; **most of the time/work** die meiste Zeit/Arbeit; **most of the time he's very helpful** er ist meistens sehr hilfsbereit; **to make the most of sth** das Beste aus etw machen; **at the (very) most** (aller)höchstens
▷ *adv* (*+ vb: spend, eat, work etc*) am meisten; (*+ adv: carefully, easily etc*) äußerst; (*very: polite, interesting etc*) höchst; (*+ adj*): **the most intelligent/expensive** *etc* der/die/das intelligenteste/teuerste *etc*; **a most interesting book** ein höchst interessantes Buch

mostly ['məustlɪ] *adv* (*chiefly*) hauptsächlich; (*usually*) meistens

MOT (*Brit*) *n abbr* (= *Ministry of Transport*): **~ (test)** ≈ TÜV *m*; **the car failed its ~** das Auto ist nicht durch den TÜV gekommen

motel [məu'tɛl] *n* Motel *nt*

moth [mɔθ] *n* Nachtfalter *m*; (*also*: **clothes moth**) Motte *f*

mother ['mʌðəʳ] *n* Mutter *f* ▷ *adj* (*country*) Heimat-; (*company*) Mutter- ▷ *vt* großziehen; (*pamper, protect*) bemuttern

motherhood ['mʌðəhud] *n* Mutterschaft *f*

mother-in-law ['mʌðərɪnlɔː] *n* Schwiegermutter *f*

motherly ['mʌðəlɪ] *adj* mütterlich

mother-of-pearl ['mʌðərəv'pəːl] *n* Perlmutt *nt*

mother-to-be ['mʌðətə'biː] *n* werdende Mutter *f*

mother tongue *n* Muttersprache *f*

motif [məu'tiːf] *n* Motiv *nt*

motion ['məuʃən] *n* Bewegung *f*; (*proposal*) Antrag *m*; (*Brit: also*: **bowel motion**) Stuhlgang *m* ▷ *vt, vi*: **to ~ (to) sb to do sth** jdm ein Zeichen geben, dass er/sie etw tun solle; **to be in ~** (*vehicle*) fahren; **to set in ~** in Gang bringen; **to go through the ~s (of doing sth)** (*fig*) etw der Form halber tun; (*pretend*) so tun, als ob (man etw täte)

motionless ['məuʃənlɪs] *adj* reg(ungs)los

motion picture *n* Film *m*

motivate ['məutɪveɪt] *vt* motivieren

motivated ['məutɪveɪtɪd] *adj* motiviert; **~ by** getrieben von

motivation [məutɪ'veɪʃən] *n* Motivation *f*

motive ['məutɪv] *n* Motiv *nt*, Beweggrund *m* ▷ *adj* (*power, force*) Antriebs-; **from the best (of) ~s** mit den besten Absichten

motley ['mɔtlɪ] *adj* bunt (gemischt)

motor ['məutəʳ] *n* Motor *m*; (*Brit: inf: car*) Auto *nt* ▷ *cpd* (*industry, trade*) Auto(mobil)-

motorbike ['məutəbaɪk] *n* Motorrad *nt*

motorboat ['məutəbəut] *n* Motorboot *nt*

motorcar ['məutəkɑː] *(Brit) n* (Personenkraft)wagen *m*
motorcycle ['məutəsaɪkl] *n* Motorrad *nt*
motorcycle racing *n* Motorradrennen *nt*
motorcyclist ['məutəsaɪklɪst] *n* Motorradfahrer(in) *m(f)*
motoring ['məutərɪŋ] *(Brit) n* Autofahren *nt* ▷ *cpd* Auto-; *(offence, accident)* Verkehrs-
motorist ['məutərɪst] *n* Autofahrer(in) *m(f)*
motor racing *(Brit) n* Autorennen *nt*
motorway ['məutəweɪ] *(Brit) n* Autobahn *f*
mottled ['mɔtld] *adj* gesprenkelt
motto ['mɔtəu] *(pl* **~es**) *n* Motto *nt*
mould, *(US)* **mold** [məuld] *n (cast)* Form *f*; *(: for metal)* Gussform *f*; *(mildew)* Schimmel *m* ▷ *vt (lit, fig)* formen
mouldy ['məuldɪ] *adj* schimmelig; *(smell)* moderig
moult, *(US)* **molt** [məult] *vi (animal)* sich haaren; *(bird)* sich mausern
mound [maund] *n (of earth)* Hügel *m*; *(heap)* Haufen *m*
mount [maunt] *n (in proper names)*: **M~ Carmel** der Berg Karmel; *(horse)* Pferd *nt*; *(for picture)* Passepartout *nt* ▷ *vt (horse)* besteigen; *(exhibition etc)* vorbereiten; *(jewel)* (ein)fassen; *(picture)* mit einem Passepartout versehen; *(staircase)* hochgehen; *(stamp)* aufkleben; *(attack, campaign)* organisieren ▷ *vi (increase)* steigen; *(: problems)* sich häufen; *(on horse)* aufsitzen
▸ **mount up** *vi (costs, savings)* sich summieren, sich zusammenläppern *(inf)*
mountain ['mauntɪn] *n* Berg *m* ▷ *cpd (road, stream)* Gebirgs-; **to make a ~ out of a molehill** aus einer Mücke einen Elefanten machen
mountain bike *n* Mountainbike *nt*
mountaineer [mauntɪ'nɪə^r] *n* Bergsteiger(in) *m(f)*
mountaineering [mauntɪ'nɪərɪŋ] *n* Bergsteigen *nt*; **to go ~** bergsteigen gehen
mountainous ['mauntɪnəs] *adj* gebirgig
mountain range *n* Gebirgskette *f*
mountain rescue team *n* Bergwacht *f*
mountainside ['mauntɪnsaɪd] *n* (Berg)hang *m*
mourn [mɔːn] *vt* betrauern ▷ *vi*: **to ~ (for)** trauern (um)
mourner ['mɔːnə^r] *n* Trauernde(r) *f(m)*
mourning ['mɔːnɪŋ] *n* Trauer *f*; **to be in ~** trauern; *(wear special clothes)* Trauer tragen
mouse [maus] *(pl* **mice**) *n (Zool, Comput)* Maus *f*; *(fig: person)* schüchternes Mäuschen *nt*
mousetrap ['maustræp] *n* Mausefalle *f*
moussaka [mu'sɑːkə] *n* Moussaka *f*
mousse [muːs] *n (Culin)* Mousse *f*; *(cosmetic)* Schaumfestiger *m*
moustache, *(US)* **mustache** [məs'tɑːʃ] *n* Schnurrbart *m*
mousy ['mausɪ] *adj (hair)* mausgrau
mouth [mauθ] *(pl* **~s**) *n* Mund *m*; *(of cave, hole, bottle)* Öffnung *f*; *(of river)* Mündung *f*
mouthful ['mauθful] *n (of food)* Bissen *m*; *(of drink)* Schluck *m*
mouth organ *n* Mundharmonika *f*
mouthpiece ['mauθpiːs] *n* Mundstück *nt*; *(spokesman)* Sprachrohr *nt*
mouthwash ['mauθwɔʃ] *n* Mundwasser *nt*
mouth-watering ['mauθwɔːtərɪŋ] *adj* appetitlich
movable ['muːvəbl] *adj* beweglich; **~ feast** beweglicher Feiertag *m*
move [muːv] *n (movement)* Bewegung *f*; *(in game)* Zug *m*; *(change: of house)* Umzug *m*; *(: of job)* Stellenwechsel *m* ▷ *vt* bewegen; *(furniture)* (ver)rücken; *(car)* umstellen; *(in game)* ziehen mit; *(emotionally)* bewegen, ergreifen; *(Pol: resolution etc)* beantragen ▷ *vi* sich bewegen; *(traffic)* vorankommen; *(in game)* ziehen; *(also:* **move house**) umziehen; *(develop)* sich entwickeln; **it's my ~** ich bin am Zug; **to get a ~ on** sich beeilen; **to ~ sb to do sth** jdn (dazu) veranlassen, etw zu tun; **to ~ towards** sich nähern *+dat*
▸ **move about** *vi* sich (hin- und her)bewegen; *(travel)* unterwegs sein; *(from place to place)* umherziehen; *(change residence)* umziehen; *(change job)* die Stelle wechseln; **I can hear him moving about** ich höre ihn herumlaufen
▸ **move along** *vi* weitergehen
▸ **move around** *vi* = **move about**
▸ **move away** *vi (from town, area)* wegziehen
▸ **move back** *vi (return)* zurückkommen
▸ **move forward** *vi (advance)* vorrücken
▸ **move in** *vi (to house)* einziehen; *(police, soldiers)* anrücken
▸ **move off** *vi (car)* abfahren
▸ **move on** *vi (leave)* weitergehen; *(travel)* weiterfahren ▷ *vt (onlookers)* zum Weitergehen auffordern
▸ **move out** *vi (of house)* ausziehen
▸ **move over** *vi (to make room)* (zur Seite) rücken
▸ **move up** *vi (employee)* befördert werden; *(pupil)* versetzt werden; *(deputy)* aufrücken
moveable ['muːvəbl] *adj* = **movable**
movement ['muːvmənt] *n (action, group)* Bewegung *f*; *(freedom to move)* Bewegungsfreiheit *f*; *(transportation)* Beförderung *f*; *(shift)* Trend *m*; *(Mus)* Satz *m*; *(Med: also:* **bowel movement**) Stuhlgang *m*
movie ['muːvɪ] *n* Film *m*; **to go to the ~s** ins Kino gehen
moving ['muːvɪŋ] *adj* beweglich; *(emotional)* ergreifend; *(instigating)*: **the ~ spirit/force** die treibende Kraft
mow [məu] *(pt* **~ed**, *pp* **mowed** *or* **~n**) *vt* mähen
▸ **mow down** *vt (kill)* niedermähen
mower ['məuə^r] *n (also:* **lawnmower**) Rasenmäher *m*
Mozambique [məuzəm'biːk] *n* Mosambik *nt*
MP *n abbr (= Member of Parliament)* ≈ MdB; = **military police**; *(Canada: = Mounted Police)* berittene Polizei *f*

MP3 *abbr (Comput)* MP3
MP3 player *n (Comput)* MP3-Spieler *m*
mpg *n abbr (= miles per gallon) see* **mile**
Mr, *(US)* **Mr.** ['mɪstəʳ] *n*: **Mr Smith** Herr Smith
Mrs, *(US)* **Mrs.** ['mɪsɪz] *n*: **~ Smith** Frau Smith
Ms, *(US)* **Ms.** [mɪz] *n (= Miss or Mrs)*: **Ms Smith** Frau Smith
MSc *n abbr (= Master of Science) akademischer Grad in Naturwissenschaften*
MSP *(Brit) n abbr (Pol: = Member of the Scottish Parliament)* Abgeordnete *f(m)* des schottisches Parlaments
Mt *abbr (Geog)* = **mount**
much [mʌtʃ] *adj (time, money, effort)* viel; **how much money/time do you need?** wie viel Geld/Zeit brauchen Sie?; **he's done so much work for us** er hat so viel für uns gearbeitet; **as much as** so viel wie; **I have as much money/intelligence as you** ich besitze genauso viel Geld/Intelligenz wie du ▷ *pron* viel; **how much is it?** was kostet es? ▷ *adv* **1** *(greatly, a great deal)* sehr; **thank you very much** vielen Dank, danke sehr; **I read as much as I can** ich lese so viel wie ich kann
2 *(by far)* viel; **I'm much better now** mir geht es jetzt viel besser
3 *(almost)* fast; **how are you feeling? — much the same** wie fühlst du dich? — fast genauso; **the two books are much the same** die zwei Bücher sind sich sehr ähnlich
muck [mʌk] *n (dirt)* Dreck *m*
▸ **muck about** *(inf) vi (fool about)* herumalbern ▷ *vt*: **to ~ sb about** mit jdm beliebig umspringen
▸ **muck around** *vi* = **muck about**
▸ **muck in** *(Brit: inf) vi* mit anpacken
▸ **muck out** *vt (stable)* ausmisten
▸ **muck up** *(inf) vt (exam etc)* verpfuschen
mucky ['mʌkɪ] *adj (dirty)* dreckig; *(field)* matschig
mucus ['mju:kəs] *n* Schleim *m*
mud [mʌd] *n* Schlamm *m*
muddle ['mʌdl] *n (mess)* Durcheinander *nt*; *(confusion)* Verwirrung *f* ▷ *vt (person)* verwirren; *(also:* **muddle up***)* durcheinanderbringen; **to be in a ~** völlig durcheinander sein; **to get in a ~** *(person)* konfus werden; *(things)* durcheinandergeraten
▸ **muddle along** *vi* vor sich *acc* hin wursteln
▸ **muddle through** *vi (get by)* sich durchschlagen
muddy ['mʌdɪ] *adj (floor)* schmutzig; *(field)* schlammig
mudguard ['mʌdgɑ:d] *(Brit) n* Schutzblech *nt*
muesli ['mju:zlɪ] *n* Müsli *nt*
muffin ['mʌfɪn] *n (Brit) weiches, flaches Milchbrötchen, meist warm gegessen*; *(US) kleiner runder Rührkuchen*
muffle ['mʌfl] *vt (sound)* dämpfen; *(against cold)* einmummeln
muffled ['mʌfld] *adj (see vt)* gedämpft; eingemummelt
muffler ['mʌfləʳ] *n (US: Aut)* Auspufftopf *m*; *(scarf)* dicker Schal *m*
mug [mʌg] *n (cup)* Becher *m*; *(for beer)* Krug *m*; *(inf: face)* Visage *f*; *(: fool)* Trottel *m* ▷ *vt* (auf der Straße) überfallen; **it's a ~'s game** *(Brit)* das ist doch Schwachsinn
▸ **mug up** *(Brit: inf) vt (also:* **mug up on***)* pauken
mugger ['mʌgəʳ] *n* Straßenräuber *m*
mugging ['mʌgɪŋ] *n* Straßenraub *m*
muggy ['mʌgɪ] *adj (weather, day)* schwül
mule [mju:l] *n* Maultier *nt*
multicoloured, *(US)* **multicolored** ['mʌltɪkʌləd] *adj* mehrfarbig
multi-level ['mʌltɪlɛvl] *(US) adj* = **multistorey**
multinational [mʌltɪ'næʃənl] *adj* multinational ▷ *n* multinationaler Konzern *m*, Multi *m (inf)*
multiple ['mʌltɪpl] *adj (injuries)* mehrfach; *(interests, causes)* vielfältig ▷ *n* Vielfache(s) *nt*; **~ collision** Massenkarambolage *f*
multiple sclerosis *n* multiple Sklerose *f*
multiplex ['mʌltɪplɛks] *n*: **~ transmitter** Multiplexsender *m*; **~ (cinema)** Multiplexkino *nt* ▷ *adj (Tech)* Mehrfach- ▷ *vt (Tel)* gleichzeitig senden
multiplication [mʌltɪplɪ'keɪʃən] *n* Multiplikation *f*; *(increase)* Vervielfachung *f*
multiply ['mʌltɪplaɪ] *vt* multiplizieren ▷ *vi (increase: problems)* stark zunehmen; *(: number)* sich vervielfachen; *(breed)* sich vermehren
multistorey [mʌltɪ'stɔ:rɪ] *(Brit) adj (building, car park)* mehrstöckig
mum [mʌm] *(Brit: inf) n* Mutti *f*, Mama *f* ▷ *adj*: **to keep ~** den Mund halten; **~'s the word** nichts verraten!
mumble ['mʌmbl] *vt, vi (indistinctly)* nuscheln; *(quietly)* murmeln
mummy ['mʌmɪ] *n (Brit: mother)* Mami *f*; *(embalmed body)* Mumie *f*
mumps [mʌmps] *n* Mumps *m or f*
munch [mʌntʃ] *vt, vi* mampfen
mundane [mʌn'deɪn] *adj (life)* banal; *(task)* stumpfsinnig
municipal [mju:'nɪsɪpl] *adj* städtisch, Stadt-; *(elections, administration)* Kommunal-
mural ['mjuərl] *n* Wandgemälde *nt*
murder ['mə:dəʳ] *n* Mord *m* ▷ *vt* ermorden; *(spoil: piece of music, language)* verhunzen; **to commit ~** einen Mord begehen
murderer ['mə:dərəʳ] *n* Mörder *m*
murderous ['mə:dərəs] *adj* blutrünstig; *(attack)* Mord-; *(fig: look, attack)* vernichtend; *(: pace, heat)* mörderisch
murky ['mə:kɪ] *adj* düster; *(water)* trübe
murmur ['mə:məʳ] *n (of voices)* Murmeln *nt*; *(of wind, waves)* Rauschen *nt* ▷ *vt, vi* murmeln; **heart ~** Herzgeräusche *pl*
muscle ['mʌsl] *n* Muskel *m*; *(fig: strength)* Macht *f*

▸**muscle in** *vi*: **to ~ in (on sth)** (bei etw) mitmischen
muscular ['mʌskjulə[r]] *adj* (*pain, dystrophy*) Muskel-; (*person, build*) muskulös
muse [mju:z] *vi* nachgrübeln ▹*n* Muse *f*
museum [mju:'zɪəm] *n* Museum *nt*
mushroom ['mʌʃrum] *n* (*edible*) (essbarer) Pilz *m*; (*poisonous*) Giftpilz *m*; (*button mushroom*) Champignon *m* ▹*vi* (*fig: buildings etc*) aus dem Boden schießen; (*: town, organization*) explosionsartig wachsen
music ['mju:zɪk] *n* Musik *f*; (*written music, score*) Noten *pl*
musical ['mju:zɪkl] *adj* musikalisch; (*sound, tune*) melodisch ▹*n* Musical *nt*
musical instrument *n* Musikinstrument *nt*
music centre *n* Musikcenter *nt*
musician [mju:'zɪʃən] *n* Musiker(in) *m(f)*
Muslim ['mʌzlɪm] *adj* moslemisch ▹*n* Moslem *m*, Moslime *f*
muslin ['mʌzlɪn] *n* Musselin *m*
mussel ['mʌsl] *n* (Mies)muschel *f*
must [mʌst] *aux vb* müssen; (*in negative*) dürfen ▹*n* Muss *nt*; **I ~ do it** ich muss es tun; **you ~ not do that** das darfst du nicht tun; **he ~ be there by now** jetzt müsste er schon dort sein; **you ~ come and see me soon** Sie müssen mich bald besuchen; **why ~ he behave so badly?** warum muss er sich so schlecht benehmen?; **I ~ have made a mistake** ich muss mich geirrt haben; **the film is a ~** den Film muss man unbedingt gesehen haben
mustache ['mʌstæʃ] (*US*) *n* = **moustache**
mustard ['mʌstəd] *n* Senf *m*
muster ['mʌstə[r]] *vt* (*support*) zusammenbekommen; (*also*: **muster up**: *energy, strength, courage*) aufbringen; (*troops, members*) antreten lassen ▹*n*: **to pass ~** den Anforderungen genügen
mustn't ['mʌsnt] = **must not**
mute [mju:t] *adj* stumm
muted ['mju:tɪd] *adj* (*colour*) gedeckt; (*reaction, criticism*) verhalten; (*sound, trumpet, Mus*) gedämpft
mutilate ['mju:tɪleɪt] *vt* verstümmeln
mutiny ['mju:tɪnɪ] *n* Meuterei *f* ▹*vi* meutern
mutter ['mʌtə[r]] *vt, vi* murmeln
mutton ['mʌtn] *n* Hammelfleisch *nt*
mutual ['mju:tʃuəl] *adj* (*feeling, attraction*) gegenseitig; (*benefit*) beiderseitig; (*interest, friend*) gemeinsam; **the feeling was ~** das beruhte auf Gegenseitigkeit
mutually ['mju:tʃuəlɪ] *adv* (*beneficial, satisfactory*) für beide Seiten; (*accepted*) von beiden Seiten; **to be ~ exclusive** einander ausschließen; **~ incompatible** nicht miteinander vereinbar
muzzle ['mʌzl] *n* (*of dog*) Maul *nt*; (*of gun*) Mündung *f*; (*guard: for dog*) Maulkorb *m* ▹*vt* (*dog*) einen Maulkorb anlegen *+dat*; (*fig: press, person*) mundtot machen
my [maɪ] *adj* mein(e); **this is my brother/sister/house** das ist mein Bruder/meine Schwester/mein Haus; **I've washed my hair/cut my finger** ich habe mir die Haare gewaschen/mir *or* mich in den Finger geschnitten; **is this my pen or yours?** ist das mein Stift oder deiner?
myself [maɪ'sɛlf] *pron* (*acc*) mich; (*dat*) mir; (*emphatic*) selbst; *see also* **oneself**
mysterious [mɪs'tɪərɪəs] *adj* geheimnisvoll, mysteriös
mystery ['mɪstərɪ] *n* (*puzzle*) Rätsel *nt*; (*strangeness*) Rätselhaftigkeit *f* ▹*cpd* (*guest, voice*) mysteriös; **~ tour** Fahrt *f* ins Blaue
mystical ['mɪstɪkl] *adj* mystisch
mystify ['mɪstɪfaɪ] *vt* vor ein Rätsel stellen
myth [mɪθ] *n* Mythos *m*; (*fallacy*) Märchen *nt*
mythology [mɪ'θɔlədʒɪ] *n* Mythologie *f*

Nn

N¹, n [ɛn] *n* (*letter*) N *nt*, n *nt*; **N for Nellie, N for Nan** (*US*) ≈ N wie Nordpol
N² [ɛn] *abbr* (= *north*) N
n/a *abbr* (= *not applicable*) entf.
nag [næg] *vt* herumnörgeln an +*dat* ▷ *vi* nörgeln ▷ *n* (*pej: horse*) Gaul *m*; (: *person*) Nörgler(in) *m(f)*; **to ~ at sb** jdn plagen, jdm keine Ruhe lassen
nagging ['nægɪŋ] *adj* (*doubt, suspicion*) quälend; (*pain*) dumpf
nail [neɪl] *n* Nagel *m* ▷ *vt* (*inf: thief etc*) drankriegen; (: *fraud*) aufdecken; **to ~ sth to sth** etw an etw *acc* nageln; **to ~ sb down (to sth)** jdn (auf etw *acc*) festnageln
nailbrush ['neɪlbrʌʃ] *n* Nagelbürste *f*
nailfile ['neɪlfaɪl] *n* Nagelfeile *f*
nail polish *n* Nagellack *m*
nail polish remover *n* Nagellackentferner *m*
nail scissors *npl* Nagelschere *f*
nail varnish (*Brit*) *n* = **nail polish**
naked ['neɪkɪd] *adj* nackt; (*flame, light*) offen; **with the ~ eye** mit bloßem Auge; **to the ~ eye** für das bloße Auge
name [neɪm] *n* Name *m* ▷ *vt* nennen; (*ship*) taufen; (*identify*) (beim Namen) nennen; (*date etc*) bestimmen, festlegen; **what's your ~?** wie heißen Sie?; **my ~ is Peter** ich heiße Peter; **by ~** mit Namen; **in the ~ of** im Namen +*gen*; **to give one's ~ and address** Namen und Adresse angeben; **to make a ~ for o.s.** sich *dat* einen Namen machen; **to give sb a bad ~** jdn in Verruf bringen; **to call sb ~s** jdn beschimpfen; **to be ~d after sb/sth** nach jdm/etw benannt werden
nameless ['neɪmlɪs] *adj* namenlos; **who/which shall remain ~** der/die/das ungenannt bleiben soll
namely ['neɪmlɪ] *adv* nämlich
namesake ['neɪmseɪk] *n* Namensvetter(in) *m(f)*
nanny ['nænɪ] *n* Kindermädchen *nt*
nap [næp] *n* Schläfchen *nt*; (*of fabric*) Strich *m* ▷ *vi*: **to be caught ~ping** (*fig*) überrumpelt werden; **to have a ~** ein Schläfchen *or* ein Nickerchen (*inf*) machen
nape [neɪp] *n*: **the ~ of the neck** der Nacken
napkin ['næpkɪn] *n* (*also*: **table napkin**) Serviette *f*
nappy ['næpɪ] (*Brit*) *n* Windel *f*
nappy rash *n* Wundsein *nt*
narcissus [nɑː'sɪsəs] (*pl* **narcissi**) *n* Narzisse *f*
narcotic [nɑː'kɔtɪk] *adj* narkotisch ▷ *n* Narkotikum *nt*; **narcotics** *npl* (*drugs*) Drogen *pl*; **~ drug** Rauschgift *nt*
narrative ['nærətɪv] *n* Erzählung *f*; (*of journey etc*) Schilderung *f*
narrator [nə'reɪtə^r] *n* Erzähler(in) *m(f)*; (*in film etc*) Kommentator(in) *m(f)*
narrow ['nærəu] *adj* eng; (*ledge etc*) schmal; (*majority, advantage, victory, defeat*) knapp; (*ideas, view*) engstirnig ▷ *vi* sich verengen; (*gap, difference*) sich verringern ▷ *vt* (*gap, difference*) verringern; (*eyes*) zusammenkneifen; **to have a ~ escape** mit knapper Not davonkommen; **to ~ sth down (to sth)** etw (auf etw *acc*) beschränken
narrowly ['nærəulɪ] *adv* knapp; (*escape*) mit knapper Not
narrow-minded [nærəu'maɪndɪd] *adj* engstirnig
nasal ['neɪzl] *adj* Nasen-; (*voice*) näselnd
nasty ['nɑːstɪ] *adj* (*remark*) gehässig; (*person*) gemein; (*taste, smell*) ekelhaft; (*wound, disease, accident, shock*) schlimm; (*problem, question*) schwierig; (*weather, temper*) abscheulich; **to turn ~** unangenehm werden; **it's a ~ business** es ist schrecklich; **he's got a ~ temper** mit ihm ist nicht gut Kirschen essen
nation ['neɪʃən] *n* Nation *f*; (*people*) Volk *nt*
national ['næʃənl] *adj* (*character, flag*) National-; (*interests*) Staats-; (*newspaper*) überregional ▷ *n* Staatsbürger(in) *m(f)*; **foreign ~** Ausländer(in) *m(f)*
national anthem *n* Nationalhymne *f*
national dress *n* Nationaltracht *f*
National Health Service (*Brit*) *n* Staatlicher Gesundheitsdienst *m*
National Insurance (*Brit*) *n* Sozialversicherung *f*
nationalism ['næʃnəlɪzəm] *n* Nationalismus *m*
nationalist ['næʃnəlɪst] *adj* nationalistisch ▷ *n* Nationalist(in) *m(f)*
nationality [næʃə'nælɪtɪ] *n* Staatsangehörigkeit *f*, Nationalität *f*
nationalize ['næʃnəlaɪz] *vt* verstaatlichen
nationally ['næʃnəlɪ] *adv* landesweit
national park *n* Nationalpark *m*

National Trust (*Brit*) *n Organisation zum Schutz historischer Bauten und Denkmäler sowie zum Landschaftsschutz*
nationwide ['neɪʃənwaɪd] *adj, adv* landesweit
native ['neɪtɪv] *n* Einheimische(r) *f(m)* ▷ *adj* einheimisch; (*country*) Heimat-; (*language*) Mutter-; (*innate*) angeboren; **a ~ of Germany, a ~ German** ein gebürtiger Deutscher, eine gebürtige Deutsche; **~ to** beheimatet in *+dat*
Native American *adj* indianisch, der Ureinwohner Amerikas ▷ *n* Ureinwohner(in) *m(f)* Amerikas
native speaker *n* Muttersprachler(in) *m(f)*
NATO ['neɪtəu] *n abbr* (= *North Atlantic Treaty Organization*) NATO *f*
natural ['nætʃrəl] *adj* natürlich; (*disaster*) Natur-; (*innate*) angeboren; (*born*) geboren; (*Mus*) ohne Vorzeichen; **to die of ~ causes** eines natürlichen Todes sterben; **~ foods** Naturkost *f*; **she played F ~ not F sharp** sie spielte f statt fis
natural gas *n* Erdgas *nt*
natural history *n* Naturkunde *f*; **the ~ of England** die Naturgeschichte Englands
naturalist ['nætʃrəlɪst] *n* Naturforscher(in) *m(f)*
naturally ['nætʃrəlɪ] *adv* natürlich; (*happen*) auf natürlichem Wege; (*die*) eines natürlichen Todes; (*occur*: cheerful, talented, blonde) von Natur aus
natural resources *npl* Naturschätze *pl*
nature ['neɪtʃə^r] *n* (Nature) Natur *f*; (*kind, sort*) Art *f*; (*character*) Wesen *nt*; **by ~** von Natur aus; **by its (very) ~** naturgemäß; **documents of a confidential ~** Unterlagen vertraulicher Art
nature reserve (*Brit*) *n* Naturschutzgebiet *nt*
naught [nɔ:t] *n* = **nought**
naughty ['nɔ:tɪ] *adj* (*child*) unartig, ungezogen; (*story, film, words*) unanständig
nausea ['nɔ:sɪə] *n* Übelkeit *f*
naval ['neɪvl] *adj* Marine-; (*battle, forces*) See-
naval officer *n* Marineoffizier *m*
nave [neɪv] *n* Hauptschiff *nt*, Mittelschiff *nt*
navel ['neɪvl] *n* Nabel *m*
navigate ['nævɪgeɪt] *vt* (*river*) befahren; (*path*) begehen ▷ *vi* navigieren; (*Aut*) den Fahrer dirigieren
navigation [nævɪ'geɪʃən] *n* Navigation *f*
navvy ['nævɪ] (*Brit*) *n* Straßenarbeiter *m*
navy ['neɪvɪ] *n* (Kriegs)marine *f*; (*ships*) (Kriegs)flotte *f* ▷ *adj* marineblau; **Department of the N~** (*US*) Marineministerium *nt*
navy-blue ['neɪvɪ'blu:] *adj* marineblau
Nazi ['nɑ:tsɪ] *n* Nazi *m*
NB *abbr* (= *nota bene*) NB; (*Canada*: = *New Brunswick*)
near [nɪə^r] *adj* nahe ▷ *adv* nahe; (*almost*) fast, beinahe ▷ *prep* (*also*: **near to**: *in space*) nahe an *+dat*; (: *in time*) um *acc* ... herum; (: *in situation, in intimacy*) nahe *+dat* ▷ *vt* sich nähern *+dat*; (*state, situation*) kurz vor *+dat* stehen; **Christmas is ~** bald ist Weihnachten; **£25,000 or ~est offer** (*Brit*) £25.000 oder das nächstbeste Angebot; **in the ~ future** in naher Zukunft, bald; **in ~ darkness** fast im Dunkeln; **a ~ tragedy** beinahe eine Tragödie; **~ here/there** hier/dort in der Nähe; **to be ~ (to) doing sth** nahe daran sein, etw zu tun; **the building is ~ing completion** der Bau steht kurz vor dem Abschluss
nearby [nɪə'baɪ] *adj* nahe gelegen ▷ *adv* in der Nähe
nearly ['nɪəlɪ] *adv* fast; **I ~ fell** ich wäre beinahe gefallen; **it's not ~ big enough** es ist bei Weitem nicht groß genug; **she was ~ crying** sie war den Tränen nahe
near miss *n* Beinahezusammenstoß *m*; **that was a ~** (*shot*) das war knapp daneben
nearside ['nɪəsaɪd] (*Aut*) *adj* (*when driving on left*) linksseitig; (*when driving on right*) rechtsseitig ▷ *n*: **the ~** (*when driving on left*) die linke Seite; (*when driving on right*) die rechte Seite
near-sighted [nɪə'saɪtɪd] *adj* kurzsichtig
neat [ni:t] *adj* ordentlich; (*handwriting*) sauber; (*plan, solution*) elegant; (*description*) prägnant; (*spirits*) pur; **I drink it ~** ich trinke es pur
neatly ['ni:tlɪ] *adv* ordentlich; (*conveniently*) sauber
necessarily ['nɛsɪsrɪlɪ] *adv* notwendigerweise; **not ~** nicht unbedingt
necessary ['nɛsɪsrɪ] *adj* notwendig, nötig; (*inevitable*) unausweichlich; **if ~** wenn nötig, nötigenfalls; **it is ~ to ...** man muss ...
necessity [nɪ'sɛsɪtɪ] *n* Notwendigkeit *f*; **of ~** notgedrungen; **out of ~** aus Not; **the necessities (of life)** das Notwendigste (zum Leben)
neck [nɛk] *n* Hals *m*; (*of shirt, dress, jumper*) Ausschnitt *m* ▷ *vi* (*inf*) knutschen; **~ and neck** Kopf an Kopf; **to stick one's ~ out** (*inf*) seinen Kopf riskieren
necklace ['nɛklɪs] *n* (Hals)kette *f*
neckline ['nɛklaɪn] *n* Ausschnitt *m*
necktie ['nɛktaɪ] (*esp US*) *n* Krawatte *f*
nectarine ['nɛktərɪn] *n* Nektarine *f*
need [ni:d] *n* Bedarf *m*; (*necessity*) Notwendigkeit *f*; (*requirement*) Bedürfnis *nt*; (*poverty*) Not *f* ▷ *vt* brauchen; (*could do with*) nötig haben; **in ~** bedürftig; **to be in ~ of sth** etw nötig haben; **£10 will meet my immediate ~s** mit £ 10 komme ich erst einmal aus; **(there's) no ~** (das ist) nicht nötig; **there's no ~ to get so worked up about it** du brauchst dich darüber nicht so aufzuregen; **he had no ~ to work** er hatte es nicht nötig zu arbeiten; **I ~ to do it** ich muss es tun; **you don't ~ to go, you needn't go** du brauchst nicht zu gehen; **a signature is ~ed** das bedarf einer Unterschrift *gen*
needle ['ni:dl] *n* Nadel *f* ▷ *vt* (*fig: inf: goad*) ärgern, piesacken
needless ['ni:dlɪs] *adj* unnötig; **~ to say**

natürlich
needlework ['ni:dlwə:k] *n* Handarbeit *f*
needn't ['ni:dnt] = **need not**
needy ['ni:dɪ] *adj* bedürftig ▷ *npl*: **the ~** die Bedürftigen *pl*
negative ['nɛgətɪv] *adj* negativ; (*answer*) abschlägig ▷ *n* (*Phot*) Negativ *nt*; (*Ling*) Verneinungswort *nt*, Negation *f*; **to answer in the ~** eine verneinende Antwort geben
neglect [nɪ'glɛkt] *vt* vernachlässigen; (*writer, artist*) unterschätzen ▷ *n* Vernachlässigung *f*
neglected [nɪ'glɛktɪd] *adj* vernachlässigt; (*writer, artist*) unterschätzt
negligee ['nɛglɪʒeɪ] *n* Negligee *nt*, Negligé *nt*
negotiate [nɪ'gəuʃɪeɪt] *vi* verhandeln ▷ *vt* aushandeln; (*obstacle, hill*) überwinden; (*bend*) nehmen; **to ~ with sb (for sth)** mit jdm (über etw *acc*) verhandeln
negotiation [nɪgəuʃɪ'eɪʃən] *n* Verhandlung *f*; **the matter is still under ~** über die Sache wird noch verhandelt
negotiator [nɪ'gəuʃɪeɪtə^r] *n* Unterhändler(in) *m(f)*
neigh [neɪ] *vi* wiehern
neighbour, (US) **neighbor** ['neɪbə^r] *n* Nachbar(in) *m(f)*
neighbourhood ['neɪbəhud] *n* (*place*) Gegend *f*; (*people*) Nachbarschaft *f*; **in the ~ of ...** in der Nähe von ...; (*sum of money*) so um die ...
neighbouring ['neɪbərɪŋ] *adj* benachbart, Nachbar-
neighbourly ['neɪbəlɪ] *adj* nachbarlich
neither ['naɪðə^r] *conj*: **I didn't move and ~ did John** ich bewegte mich nicht und John auch nicht ▷ *pron* keine(r, s) (von beiden) ▷ *adv*: **~ ... nor ...** weder ... noch ...; **~ story is true** keine der beiden Geschichten stimmt; **~ is true** beides stimmt nicht; **~ do I/have I** ich auch nicht
neon ['ni:ɔn] *n* Neon *nt*
neon light *n* Neonlampe *f*
Nepal [nɪ'pɔ:l] *n* Nepal *nt*
nephew ['nɛvju:] *n* Neffe *m*
nerve [nə:v] *n* (*Anat*) Nerv *m*; (*courage*) Mut *m*; (*impudence*) Frechheit *f*; **nerves** *npl* (*anxiety*) Nervosität *f*; (*emotional strength*) Nerven *pl*; **he gets on my ~s** er geht mir auf die Nerven; **to lose one's ~** die Nerven verlieren
nerve-racking ['nə:vrækɪŋ] *adj* nervenaufreibend
nervous ['nə:vəs] *adj* Nerven-, nervlich; (*anxious*) nervös; **to be ~ of/about** Angst haben vor *+dat*
nervous breakdown *n* Nervenzusammenbruch *m*
nest [nɛst] *n* Nest *nt* ▷ *vi* nisten; **a ~ of tables** ein Satz Tische *or* von Tischen
nest egg *n* Notgroschen *m*
nestle ['nɛsl] *vi* sich kuscheln; (*house*) eingebettet sein
Net [nɛt] *n*: **the ~** (*Comput*) das Internet
net [nɛt] *n* Netz *nt*; (*fabric*) Tüll *m* ▷ *adj* (*Comm*) Netto-; (*final: result, effect*) End- ▷ *vt* (mit einem Netz) fangen; (*profit*) einbringen; (*deal, sale, fortune*) an Land ziehen; **~ of tax** steuerfrei; **he earns £10,000 ~ per year** er verdient £ 10.000 netto im Jahr; **it weighs 250g ~** es wiegt 250 g netto
netball ['nɛtbɔ:l] *n* Netzball *m*
Netherlands ['nɛðələndz] *npl*: **the ~** die Niederlande *pl*
nett [nɛt] *adj* = **net**
netting ['nɛtɪŋ] *n* (*for fence etc*) Maschendraht *m*; (*fabric*) Netzgewebe *nt*, Tüll *m*
nettle ['nɛtl] *n* Nessel *f*; **to grasp the ~** (*fig*) in den sauren Apfel beißen
network ['nɛtwə:k] *n* Netz *nt*; (*TV, Radio*) Sendenetz *nt* ▷ *vt* (*Radio, TV*) im ganzen Netzbereich ausstrahlen; (*computers*) in einem Netzwerk zusammenschließen
neurotic [njuə'rɔtɪk] *adj* neurotisch ▷ *n* Neurotiker(in) *m(f)*
neuter ['nju:tə^r] *adj* (*Ling*) sächlich ▷ *vt* kastrieren; (*female*) sterilisieren
neutral ['nju:trəl] *adj* neutral ▷ *n* (*Aut*) Leerlauf *m*
neutralize ['nju:trəlaɪz] *vt* neutralisieren, aufheben
never ['nɛvə^r] *adv* nie; (*not*) nicht; **~ in my life** noch nie; **~ again** nie wieder; **well I ~!** nein, so was!; *see also* **mind**
never-ending [nɛvər'ɛndɪŋ] *adj* endlos
nevertheless [nɛvəðə'lɛs] *adv* trotzdem, dennoch
new [nju:] *adj* neu; (*mother*) jung; **as good as ~** so gut wie neu; **to be ~ to sb** jdm neu sein
New Age *n* New Age *nt*
newborn ['nju:bɔ:n] *adj* neugeboren
newcomer ['nju:kʌmə^r] *n* Neuankömmling *m*; (*in job*) Neuling *m*
new-fangled ['nju:'fæŋgld] (*pej*) *adj* neumodisch
new-found ['nju:faund] *adj* neu entdeckt; (*confidence*) neu geschöpft
newly ['nju:lɪ] *adv* neu
newly-weds ['nju:lɪwɛdz] *npl* Neuvermählte *pl*, Frischvermählte *pl*
news [nju:z] *n* Nachricht *f*; **a piece of ~** eine Neuigkeit; **the ~** (*Radio, TV*) die Nachrichten *pl*; **good/bad ~** gute/schlechte Nachrichten
news agency *n* Nachrichtenagentur *f*
newsagent ['nju:zeɪdʒənt] (*Brit*) *n* Zeitungshändler(in) *m(f)*
newscaster ['nju:zkɑ:stə^r] *n* Nachrichtensprecher(in) *m(f)*
newsletter ['nju:zlɛtə^r] *n* Rundschreiben *nt*, Mitteilungsblatt *nt*
newspaper ['nju:zpeɪpə^r] *n* Zeitung *f*; **daily/weekly ~** Tages-/Wochenzeitung *f*
newsprint ['nju:zprɪnt] *n* Zeitungspapier *nt*
newsreader ['nju:zri:də^r] *n* = **newscaster**
newsreel ['nju:zri:l] *n* Wochenschau *f*
newt [nju:t] *n* Wassermolch *m*
New Year *n* neues Jahr *nt*; (*New Year's Day*) Neujahr *nt*; **Happy ~!** (ein) glückliches *or* frohes neues Jahr!

New Year's Day *n* Neujahr *nt*, Neujahrstag *m*
New Year's Eve *n* Silvester *nt*
New York [-'jɔ:k] *n* New York *nt*; (*also*: **New York State**) der Staat New York
New Zealand [-'zi:lənd] *n* Neuseeland *nt* ▷ *adj* neuseeländisch
New Zealander [-'zi:ləndəʳ] *n* Neuseeländer(in) *m(f)*
next [nɛkst] *adj* nächste(r, s); (*room*) Neben- ▷ *adv* dann; (*do, happen*) als Nächstes; (*afterwards*) danach; **the ~ day** am nächsten *or* folgenden Tag; **~ time** das nächste Mal; **~ year** nächstes Jahr; **~ please!** der Nächste bitte!; **who's ~?** wer ist der Nächste?; **"turn to the ~ page"** "bitte umblättern"; **the week after ~** übernächste Woche; **the ~ on the right/left** der/die/das Nächste rechts/links; **the ~ thing I knew** das Nächste, woran ich mich erinnern konnte; **~ to** neben +*dat*; **~ to nothing** so gut wie nichts; **when do we meet ~?** wann treffen wir uns wieder *or* das nächste Mal?; **the ~ best** der/die/das Nächstbeste
next door *adv* nebenan ▷ *adj*: **next-door** nebenan; **the house ~** das Nebenhaus; **to go ~** nach nebenan gehen; **my next-door neighbour** mein direkter Nachbar
next-of-kin ['nɛkstəv'kɪn] *n* nächster Verwandter *m*, nächste Verwandte *f*
NHS (*Brit*) *n abbr* = **National Health Service**
nib [nɪb] *n* Feder *f*
nibble ['nɪbl] *vt* knabbern; (*bite*) knabbern an +*dat* ▷ *vi*: **to ~ at** knabbern an +*dat*
nice [naɪs] *adj* nett; (*holiday, weather, picture etc*) schön; (*taste*) gut; (*person, clothes etc*) hübsch
nicely ['naɪslɪ] *adv* (*attractively*) hübsch; (*politely*) nett; (*satisfactorily*) gut; **that will do ~** das reicht (vollauf)
niceties ['naɪsɪtɪz] *npl*: **the ~** die Feinheiten *pl*
niche [ni:ʃ] *n* Nische *f*; (*job, position*) Plätzchen *nt*
nick [nɪk] *n* Kratzer *m*; (*in metal, wood etc*) Kerbe *f* ▷ *vt* (*Brit*: *inf*: *steal*) klauen; (: *arrest*) einsperren, einlochen; (*cut*): **to ~ o.s.** sich schneiden; **in good ~** (*Brit*: *inf*) gut in Schuss; **in the ~** (*Brit*: *inf*: *in prison*) im Knast; **in the ~ of time** gerade noch rechtzeitig
nickel ['nɪkl] *n* Nickel *nt*; (*US*) Fünfcentstück *nt*
nickname ['nɪkneɪm] *n* Spitzname *m* ▷ *vt* betiteln, taufen (*inf*)
nicotine ['nɪkəti:n] *n* Nikotin *nt*
nicotine patch *n* Nikotinpflaster *nt*
niece [ni:s] *n* Nichte *f*
Nigeria [naɪ'dʒɪərɪə] *n* Nigeria *nt*
niggling ['nɪglɪŋ] *adj* quälend; (*pain, ache*) bohrend
night [naɪt] *n* Nacht *f*; (*evening*) Abend *m*; **the ~ before last** vorletzte Nacht, vorgestern Abend; **at ~, by ~** nachts, abends; **nine o'clock at ~** neun Uhr abends; **in the ~, during the ~** in der Nacht; **~ and day** Tag und Nacht
nightcap ['naɪtkæp] *n* Schlaftrunk *m*
nightdress ['naɪtdrɛs] *n* Nachthemd *nt*
nightfall ['naɪtfɔ:l] *n* Einbruch *m* der Dunkelheit
nightie ['naɪtɪ] *n* = **nightdress**
nightingale ['naɪtɪŋgeɪl] *n* Nachtigall *f*
nightlife ['naɪtlaɪf] *n* Nachtleben *nt*
nightly ['naɪtlɪ] *adj* (all)nächtlich, Nacht-; (*every evening*) (all)abendlich, Abend- ▷ *adv* jede Nacht; (*every evening*) jeden Abend
nightmare ['naɪtmɛəʳ] *n* Albtraum *m*
night porter *n* Nachtportier *m*
night school *n* Abendschule *f*
night shift *n* Nachtschicht *f*
night-time ['naɪttaɪm] *n* Nacht *f*
night watchman *n* Nachtwächter *m*
nil [nɪl] *n* Nichts *nt*; (*Brit*: *Sport*) Null *f*
Nile [naɪl] *n*: **the ~** der Nil
nimble ['nɪmbl] *adj* flink; (*mind*) beweglich
nine [naɪn] *num* neun
nineteen ['naɪn'ti:n] *num* neunzehn
nineteenth [naɪn'ti:nθ] *num* neunzehnte(r, s)
ninety ['naɪntɪ] *num* neunzig
ninth [naɪnθ] *num* neunte(r, s) ▷ *n* Neuntel *nt*
nip [nɪp] *vt* zwicken ▷ *n* Biss *m*; (*drink*) Schlückchen *nt* ▷ *vi* (*Brit*: *inf*): **to ~ out/down/up** kurz raus-/runter-/raufgehen; **to ~ into a shop** (*Brit*: *inf*) kurz in einen Laden gehen
nipple ['nɪpl] *n* (*Anat*) Brustwarze *f*
nitrogen ['naɪtrədʒən] *n* Stickstoff *m*
no [nəu] (*pl* **noes**) *adv* (*opposite of "yes"*) nein; **no thank you** nein danke
▷ *adj* (*not any*) kein(e); **I have no money/time/books** ich habe kein Geld/keine Zeit/keine Bücher; **"no entry"** "kein Zutritt"; **"no smoking"** "Rauchen verboten"
▷ *n* Nein *nt*; **there were 20 noes and one abstention** es gab 20 Neinstimmen und eine Enthaltung; **I won't take no for an answer** ich bestehe darauf
nobility [nəu'bɪlɪtɪ] *n* Adel *m*; (*quality*) Edelmut *m*
noble ['nəubl] *adj* edel, nobel; (*aristocratic*) ad(e)lig; (*impressive*) prächtig
nobody ['nəubədɪ] *pron* niemand, keiner ▷ *n*: **he's a ~** er ist ein Niemand *m*
nod [nɔd] *vi* nicken; (*fig*: *flowers etc*) wippen ▷ *vt*: **to ~ one's head** mit dem Kopf nicken ▷ *n* Nicken *nt*; **they ~ded their agreement** sie nickten zustimmend
▸ **nod off** *vi* einnicken
noise [nɔɪz] *n* Geräusch *nt*; (*din*) Lärm *m*
noisy ['nɔɪzɪ] *adj* laut
nominal ['nɔmɪnl] *adj* nominell
nominate ['nɔmɪneɪt] *vt* nominieren; (*appoint*) ernennen
nomination [nɔmɪ'neɪʃən] *n* Nominierung *f*; (*appointment*) Ernennung *f*
nominee [nɔmɪ'ni:] *n* Kandidat(in) *m(f)*
non- [nɔn] *pref* nicht-, Nicht-
nondescript ['nɔndɪskrɪpt] *adj* unauffällig; (*colour*) unbestimmbar

none [nʌn] *pron* (*not one*) kein(e, er, es); (*not any*) nichts; **~ of us** keiner von uns; **I've ~ left** (*not any*) ich habe nichts übrig; (*not one*) ich habe kein(e, en, es) übrig; **~ at all** (*not any*) überhaupt nicht; (*not one*) überhaupt kein(e, er, es); **I was ~ the wiser** ich war auch nicht klüger; **she would have ~ of it** sie wollte nichts davon hören; **it was ~ other than X** es war kein anderer als X
nonentity [nɔ'nɛntɪtɪ] *n* (*person*) Nichts *nt*, unbedeutende Figur *f*
nonetheless ['nʌnðə'lɛs] *adv* nichtsdestoweniger, trotzdem
non-fiction [nɔn'fɪkʃən] *n* Sachbücher *pl* ▷ *adj* (*book*) Sach-; (*prize*) Sachbuch-
nonplussed [nɔn'plʌst] *adj* verdutzt, verblüfft
nonsense ['nɔnsəns] *n* Unsinn *m*; **~!** Unsinn!, Quatsch!; **it is ~ to say that ...** es ist dummes Gerede zu sagen, dass ...; **to make (a) ~ of sth** etw ad absurdum führen
non-smoker ['nɔn'sməukə^r] *n* Nichtraucher(in) *m(f)*
non-stick ['nɔn'stɪk] *adj* kunststoffbeschichtet, Teflon-®
noodles ['nu:dlz] *npl* Nudeln *pl*
nook [nuk] *n*: **every ~ and cranny** jeder Winkel
noon [nu:n] *n* Mittag *m*
no-one ['nəuwʌn] *pron* = **nobody**
noose [nu:s] *n* Schlinge *f*
nor [nɔ:^r] *conj, adv* = **neither**
norm [nɔ:m] *n* Norm *f*
normal ['nɔ:məl] *adj* normal ▷ *n*: **to return to ~** sich wieder normalisieren
normally ['nɔ:məlɪ] *adv* normalerweise; (*act, behave*) normal
Normandy ['nɔ:məndɪ] *n* Normandie *f*
north [nɔ:θ] *n* Norden *m* ▷ *adj* nördlich, Nord- ▷ *adv* nach Norden; **~ of** nördlich von
North Africa *n* Nordafrika *nt*
North African *adj* nordafrikanisch ▷ *n* Nordafrikaner(in) *m(f)*
North America *n* Nordamerika *nt*
North American *adj* nordamerikanisch ▷ *n* Nordamerikaner(in) *m(f)*
northbound ['nɔ:θbaund] *adj* in Richtung Norden; (*carriageway*) nach Norden (führend)
north-east [nɔ:θ'i:st] *n* Nordosten *m* ▷ *adj* nordöstlich, Nordost- ▷ *adv* nach Nordosten; **~ of** nordöstlich von
northerly ['nɔ:ðəlɪ] *adj* nördlich
northern ['nɔ:ðən] *adj* nördlich, Nord-
Northern Ireland *n* Nordirland *nt*
North Korea *n* Nordkorea *nt*
North Pole *n*: **the ~** der Nordpol
North Sea *n*: **the ~** die Nordsee *f*
northward ['nɔ:θwəd], **northwards** ['nɔ:θwədz] *adv* nach Norden, nordwärts
north-west [nɔ:θ'wɛst] *n* Nordwesten *m* ▷ *adj* nordwestlich, Nordwest- ▷ *adv* nach Nordwesten; **~ of** nordwestlich von
Norway ['nɔ:weɪ] *n* Norwegen *nt*
Norwegian [nɔ:'wi:dʒən] *adj* norwegisch ▷ *n* Norweger(in) *m(f)*; (*Ling*) Norwegisch *nt*
nose [nəuz] *n* Nase *f*; (*of car*) Schnauze *f* ▷ *vi* (*also*: **nose one's way**) sich schieben; **to follow one's ~** immer der Nase nach gehen; **to get up one's ~** (*inf*) auf die Nerven gehen *+dat*; **to have a (good) ~ for sth** eine (gute) Nase für etw haben; **to keep one's ~ clean** (*inf*) eine saubere Weste behalten; **to look down one's ~ at sb/sth** (*inf*) auf jdn/etw herabsehen; **to pay through the ~ (for sth)** (*inf*) (für etw) viel blechen; **to rub sb's ~ in sth** (*inf*) jdm etw unter die Nase reiben; **to turn one's ~ up at sth** (*inf*) die Nase über etw *acc* rümpfen; **under sb's ~** vor jds Augen
▸ **nose about** *vi* herumschnüffeln
▸ **nose around** *vi* = **nose about**
nosebleed ['nəuzbli:d] *n* Nasenbluten *nt*
nose-dive ['nəuzdaɪv] *n* (*of plane*) Sturzflug *m* ▷ *vi* (*plane*) im Sturzflug herabgehen
nosey ['nəuzɪ] (*inf*) *adj* = **nosy**
nostalgia [nɔs'tældʒɪə] *n* Nostalgie *f*
nostalgic [nɔs'tældʒɪk] *adj* nostalgisch
nostril ['nɔstrɪl] *n* Nasenloch *nt*; (*of animal*) Nüster *f*
nosy ['nəuzɪ] (*inf*) *adj* neugierig
not [nɔt] *adv* nicht; **he is not** *or* **isn't here** er ist nicht hier; **you must not** *or* **you mustn't do that** das darfst du nicht tun; **it's too late, isn't it?** es ist zu spät, nicht wahr?; **not that I don't like him** nicht, dass ich ihn nicht mag; **not yet** noch nicht; **not now** nicht jetzt; *see also* **all; only**
notable ['nəutəbl] *adj* bemerkenswert
notably ['nəutəblɪ] *adv* hauptsächlich; (*markedly*) bemerkenswert
notary ['nəutərɪ] *n* (*also*: **notary public**) Notar(in) *m(f)*
notch [nɔtʃ] *n* Kerbe *f*; (*in blade, saw*) Scharte *f*; (*fig*) Klasse *f*
▸ **notch up** *vt* erzielen; (*victory*) erringen
note [nəut] *n* Notiz *f*; (*of lecturer*) Manuskript *nt*; (*of student etc*) Aufzeichnung *f*; (*in book etc*) Anmerkung *f*; (*letter*) paar Zeilen *pl*; (*banknote*) Note *f*, Schein *m*; (*Mus: sound*) Ton *m*; (*: symbol*) Note *f*; (*tone*) Ton *m*, Klang *m* ▷ *vt* beachten; (*point out*) anmerken; (*also*: **note down**) notieren; **of ~** bedeutend; **to make a ~ of sth** sich *dat* etw notieren; **to take ~s** Notizen machen, mitschreiben; **to take ~ of sth** etw zur Kenntnis nehmen
notebook ['nəutbuk] *n* Notizbuch *nt*; (*for shorthand*) Stenoblock *m*
noted ['nəutɪd] *adj* bekannt
notepad ['nəutpæd] *n* Notizblock *m*
notepaper ['nəutpeɪpə^r] *n* Briefpapier *nt*
nothing ['nʌθɪŋ] *n* nichts; **~ new/worse** *etc* nichts Neues/Schlimmeres *etc*; **~ much** nicht viel; **~ else** sonst nichts; **for ~** umsonst; **~ at all** überhaupt nichts
notice ['nəutɪs] *n* Bekanntmachung *f*; (*sign*) Schild *nt*; (*warning*) Ankündigung *f*; (*dismissal*) Kündigung *f*; (*Brit: review*) Kritik *f*, Rezension

f ▷ *vt* bemerken; **to bring sth to sb's ~** jdn auf etw *acc* aufmerksam machen; **to take no ~ of** ignorieren, nicht beachten; **to escape sb's ~** jdm entgehen; **it has come to my ~ that ...** es ist mir zu Ohren gekommen, dass ...; **to give sb ~ of sth** jdm von etw Bescheid geben; **without ~** ohne Ankündigung; **advance ~** Vorankündigung *f*; **at short/a moment's ~** kurzfristig/ innerhalb kürzester Zeit; **until further ~** bis auf Weiteres; **to hand in one's ~** kündigen; **to be given one's ~** gekündigt werden *+dat*

noticeable ['nəutɪsəbl] *adj* deutlich

notify ['nəutɪfaɪ] *vt*: **to ~ sb (of sth)** jdn (von etw) benachrichtigen

notion ['nəuʃən] *n* Vorstellung *f*; **notions** (*US*) *npl* (*haberdashery*) Kurzwaren *pl*

notorious [nəu'tɔːrɪəs] *adj* berüchtigt

notwithstanding [nɔtwɪθ'stændɪŋ] *adv* trotzdem ▷ *prep* trotz *+dat*

nought [nɔːt] *n* Null *f*

noun [naun] *n* Hauptwort *nt*, Substantiv *nt*

nourish ['nʌrɪʃ] *vt* nähren

nourishing ['nʌrɪʃɪŋ] *adj* nahrhaft

nourishment ['nʌrɪʃmənt] *n* Nahrung *f*

Nov. *abbr* (= *November*) Nov.

novel ['nɔvl] *n* Roman *m* ▷ *adj* neu(artig)

novelist ['nɔvəlɪst] *n* Romanschriftsteller(in) *m(f)*

novelty ['nɔvəltɪ] *n* Neuheit *f*; (*object*) Kleinigkeit *f*

November [nəu'vɛmbəʳ] *n* November *m*; *see also* **July**

novice ['nɔvɪs] *n* Neuling *m*, Anfänger(in) *m(f)*; (*Rel*) Novize *m*, Novizin *f*

now [nau] *adv* jetzt; (*these days*) heute ▷ *conj*: **~ (that)** jetzt, wo; **right ~** gleich, sofort; **by ~** inzwischen, mittlerweile; **that's the fashion just ~** das ist gerade modern; **I saw her just ~** ich habe sie gerade gesehen; **(every) ~ and then, (every) ~ and again** ab und zu, gelegentlich; **from ~ on** von nun an; **in 3 days from ~** (heute) in 3 Tagen; **between ~ and Monday** bis Montag; **that's all for ~** das ist erst einmal alles; **any day ~** jederzeit; **~ then** also

nowadays ['nauədeɪz] *adv* heute

nowhere ['nəuwɛəʳ] *adv* (*be*) nirgends, nirgendwo; (*go*) nirgendwohin; **~ else** nirgendwo anders

nozzle ['nɔzl] *n* Düse *f*

nuclear ['njuːklɪəʳ] *adj* (*bomb, industry etc*) Atom-; **~ physics** Kernphysik *f*; **~ war** Atomkrieg *m*

nucleus ['njuːklɪəs] (*pl* **nuclei**) *n* Kern *m*

nude [njuːd] *adj* nackt ▷ *n* (*Art*) Akt *m*; **in the ~** nackt

nudge [nʌdʒ] *vt* anstoßen

nudist ['njuːdɪst] *n* Nudist(in) *m(f)*

nudity ['njuːdɪtɪ] *n* Nacktheit *f*

nuisance ['njuːsns] *n*: **to be a ~** lästig sein; (*situation*) ärgerlich sein; **he's a ~** er geht einem auf die Nerven; **what a ~!** wie ärgerlich/lästig!

null [nʌl] *adj*: **~ and void** null und nichtig

numb [nʌm] *adj* taub, gefühllos; (*fig: with fear etc*) wie betäubt ▷ *vt* taub *or* gefühllos machen; (*pain, mind*) betäuben

number ['nʌmbəʳ] *n* Zahl *f*; (*quantity*) (An)zahl *f*; (*of house, bank account, bus etc*) Nummer *f* ▷ *vt* (*pages etc*) nummerieren; (*amount to*) zählen; **a ~ of** einige; **any ~ of** beliebig viele; (*reasons*) alle möglichen; **wrong ~** (*Tel*) falsch verbunden; **to be ~ed among** zählen zu

number plate (*Brit*) *n* (*Aut*) Nummernschild *nt*

Number Ten (*Brit*) *n* (*Pol*: = *10 Downing Street*) Nummer zehn *f* (Downing Street)

numeral ['njuːmərəl] *n* Ziffer *f*

numerate ['njuːmərɪt] (*Brit*) *adj*: **to be ~** rechnen können

numerical [njuː'mɛrɪkl] *adj* numerisch

numerous ['njuːmərəs] *adj* zahlreich

nun [nʌn] *n* Nonne *f*

nurse [nəːs] *n* Krankenschwester *f*; (*also*: **nursemaid**) Kindermädchen *nt* ▷ *vt* pflegen; (*cold, toothache etc*) auskurieren; (*baby*) stillen; (*fig: desire, grudge*) hegen

nursery ['nəːsərɪ] *n* Kindergarten *m*; (*room*) Kinderzimmer *nt*; (*for plants*) Gärtnerei *f*

nursery rhyme *n* Kinderreim *m*

nursery school *n* Kindergarten *m*

nursery slope (*Brit*) *n* (*Ski*) Anfängerhügel *m*

nursing ['nəːsɪŋ] *n* Krankenpflege *f*; (*care*) Pflege *f*

nursing home *n* Pflegeheim *nt*

nurture ['nəːtʃəʳ] *vt* hegen und pflegen; (*fig: ideas, creativity*) fördern

nut [nʌt] *n* (*Tech*) (Schrauben)mutter *f*; (*Bot*) Nuss *f*; (*inf: lunatic*) Spinner(in) *m(f)*

nutcrackers ['nʌtkrækəz] *npl* Nussknacker *m*

nutmeg ['nʌtmɛg] *n* Muskat *m*, Muskatnuss *f*

nutrient ['njuːtrɪənt] *n* Nährstoff *m*

nutrition [njuː'trɪʃən] *n* Ernährung *f*; (*nourishment*) Nahrung *f*

nutritious [njuː'trɪʃəs] *adj* nahrhaft

nuts [nʌts] (*inf*) *adj* verrückt; **he's ~** er spinnt

nutshell ['nʌtʃɛl] *n* Nussschale *f*; **in a ~** (*fig*) kurz gesagt

NVQ *n abbr* (= *National Vocational Qualification*) *Qualifikation für berufsbegleitende Ausbildungsinhalte*

nylon ['naɪlɔn] *n* Nylon *nt* ▷ *adj* Nylon-; **nylons** *npl* (*stockings*) Nylonstrümpfe *pl*

Oo

oak [əuk] *n* (*tree, wood*) Eiche *f* ▷ *adj* (*furniture, door*) Eichen-
oar [ɔ:ʳ] *n* Ruder *nt*; **to put** *or* **shove one's ~ in** (*inf: fig*) mitmischen, sich einmischen
oasis [əu'eɪsɪs] (*pl* **oases**) *n* (*lit, fig*) Oase *f*
oath [əuθ] *n* (*promise*) Eid *m*, Schwur *m*; (*swear word*) Fluch *m*; **on ~** (*Brit*): **under ~** unter Eid; **to take the ~** (*Law*) vereidigt werden
oatmeal ['əutmi:l] *n* Haferschrot *m*; (*colour*) Hellbeige *nt*
oats [əuts] *npl* Hafer *m*; **he's getting his ~** (*Brit: inf: fig*) er kommt im Bett auf seine Kosten
obedience [ə'bi:dɪəns] *n* Gehorsam *m*; **in ~ to** gemäß *+dat*
obedient [ə'bi:dɪənt] *adj* gehorsam; **to be ~ to sb** jdm gehorchen
obese [əu'bi:s] *adj* fettleibig
obesity [əu'bi:sɪtɪ] *n* Fettleibigkeit *f*
obey [ə'beɪ] *vt* (*person*) gehorchen *+dat*, folgen *+dat*; (*orders, law*) befolgen ▷ *vi* gehorchen
obituary [ə'bɪtjuərɪ] *n* Nachruf *m*
object [*n* 'ɔbdʒɪkt, *vi* əb'dʒɛkt] *n* (*also Ling*) Objekt *nt*; (*aim, purpose*) Ziel *nt*, Zweck *m* ▷ *vi* dagegen sein; **to be an ~ of ridicule** (*person*) sich lächerlich machen; (*thing*) lächerlich wirken; **money is no ~** Geld spielt keine Rolle; **he ~ed that ...** er wandte ein, dass ...; **I ~!** ich protestiere!; **do you ~ to my smoking?** haben Sie etwas dagegen, wenn ich rauche?
objection [əb'dʒɛkʃən] *n* (*argument*) Einwand *m*; **I have no ~ to ...** ich habe nichts dagegen, dass ...; **if you have no ~** wenn Sie nichts dagegen haben; **to raise** *or* **voice an ~** einen Einwand erheben *or* vorbringen
objectionable [əb'dʒɛkʃənəbl] *adj* (*language, conduct*) anstößig; (*person*) unausstehlich
objective [əb'dʒɛktɪv] *adj* objektiv ▷ *n* Ziel *nt*
obligation [ɔblɪ'geɪʃən] *n* Pflicht *f*; **to be under an ~ to do sth** verpflichtet sein, etw zu tun; **to be under an ~ to sb** jdm verpflichtet sein; **"no ~ to buy"** (*Comm*) "kein Kaufzwang"
obligatory [ə'blɪgətərɪ] *adj* obligatorisch
oblige [ə'blaɪdʒ] *vt* (*compel*) zwingen; (*do a favour for*) einen Gefallen tun *+dat*; **I felt ~d to invite him in** ich fühlte mich verpflichtet, ihn hereinzubitten; **to be ~d to sb for sth** (*grateful*) jdm für etw dankbar sein; **anything to ~!** (*inf*) stets zu Diensten!
obliging [ə'blaɪdʒɪŋ] *adj* entgegenkommend
oblique [ə'bli:k] *adj* (*line, angle*) schief; (*reference, compliment*) indirekt, versteckt ▷ *n* (*Brit: also:* **oblique stroke**) Schrägstrich *m*
obliterate [ə'blɪtəreɪt] *vt* (*village etc*) vernichten; (*fig: memory, error*) auslöschen
oblivion [ə'blɪvɪən] *n* (*unconsciousness*) Bewusstlosigkeit *f*; (*being forgotten*) Vergessenheit *f*; **to sink into ~** (*event etc*) in Vergessenheit geraten
oblivious [ə'blɪvɪəs] *adj*: **he was ~ of** *or* **to it** er war sich dessen nicht bewusst
oblong ['ɔblɔŋ] *adj* rechteckig ▷ *n* Rechteck *nt*
obnoxious [əb'nɔkʃəs] *adj* widerwärtig, widerlich
oboe ['əubəu] *n* Oboe *f*
obscene [əb'si:n] *adj* obszön; (*fig: wealth*) unanständig; (*income etc*) unverschämt
obscure [əb'skjuəʳ] *adj* (*little known*) unbekannt, obskur; (*difficult to understand*) unklar ▷ *vt* (*obstruct, conceal*) verdecken
observant [əb'zə:vənt] *adj* aufmerksam
observation [ɔbzə'veɪʃən] *n* (*remark*) Bemerkung *f*; (*act of observing, Med*) Beobachtung *f*; **she's in hospital under ~** sie ist zur Beobachtung im Krankenhaus
observatory [əb'zə:vətrɪ] *n* Observatorium *nt*
observe [əb'zə:v] *vt* (*watch*) beobachten; (*notice, comment*) bemerken; (*abide by: rule etc*) einhalten
observer [əb'zə:vəʳ] *n* Beobachter(in) *m(f)*
obsess [əb'sɛs] *vt* verfolgen; **to be ~ed by** *or* **with sb/sth** von jdm/etw besessen sein
obsession [əb'sɛʃən] *n* Besessenheit *f*
obsessive [əb'sɛsɪv] *adj* (*person*) zwanghaft; (*interest, hatred, tidiness*) krankhaft; **to be ~ about cleaning/tidying up** einen Putz-/Ordnungsfimmel haben (*inf*)
obsolete ['ɔbsəli:t] *adj* veraltet
obstacle ['ɔbstəkl] *n* (*lit, fig*) Hindernis *nt*
obstacle race *n* Hindernisrennen *nt*
obstinate ['ɔbstɪnɪt] *adj* (*person*) starrsinnig, stur; (*refusal, cough etc*) hartnäckig
obstruct [əb'strʌkt] *vt* (*road, path*) blockieren; (*traffic, fig*) behindern
obstruction [əb'strʌkʃən] *n* (*object*) Hindernis *nt*; (*of plan, law*) Behinderung *f*

obtain [əb'teɪn] *vt* erhalten, bekommen ▷ *vi* (*form: exist, be the case*) gelten

obvious ['ɔbvɪəs] *adj* offensichtlich; (*lie*) klar; (*predictable*) naheliegend

obviously ['ɔbvɪəslɪ] *adv* (*clearly*) offensichtlich; (*of course*) natürlich; **~!** selbstverständlich!; **~ not** offensichtlich nicht; **he was ~ not drunk** er war natürlich nicht betrunken; **he was not ~ drunk** offenbar war er nicht betrunken

occasion [ə'keɪʒən] *n* Gelegenheit *f*; (*celebration etc*) Ereignis *nt* ▷ *vt* (*form: cause*) verursachen; **on ~** (*sometimes*) gelegentlich; **on that ~** bei der Gelegenheit; **to rise to the ~** sich der Lage gewachsen zeigen

occasional [ə'keɪʒənl] *adj* gelegentlich; **he likes the ~ cigar** er raucht gelegentlich gern eine Zigarre

occasionally [ə'keɪʒənəlɪ] *adv* gelegentlich; **very ~** sehr selten

occult [ɔ'kʌlt] *n*: **the ~** der Okkultismus ▷ *adj* okkult

occupant ['ɔkjupənt] *n* (*of house etc*) Bewohner(in) *m(f)*; (*temporary: of car*) Insasse *m*, Insassin *f*; **the ~ of this table/office** derjenige, der an diesem Tisch sitzt/in diesem Büro arbeitet

occupation [ɔkju'peɪʃən] *n* (*job*) Beruf *m*; (*pastime*) Beschäftigung *f*; (*of building, country etc*) Besetzung *f*

occupational hazard *n* Berufsrisiko *nt*

occupier ['ɔkjupaɪə^r] *n* Bewohner(in) *m(f)*

occupy ['ɔkjupaɪ] *vt* (*house, office*) bewohnen; (*place etc*) belegen; (*building, country etc*) besetzen; (*time, attention*) beanspruchen; (*position, space*) einnehmen; **to ~ o.s. (in** *or* **with sth)** sich (mit etw) beschäftigen; **to ~ o.s. in** *or* **with doing sth** sich damit beschäftigen, etw zu tun; **to be occupied in** *or* **with sth** mit etw beschäftigt sein; **to be occupied in** *or* **with doing sth** damit beschäftigt sein, etw zu tun

occur [ə'kəː^r] *vi* (*take place*) geschehen, sich ereignen; (*exist*) vorkommen; **to ~ to sb** jdm einfallen

occurrence [ə'kʌrəns] *n* (*event*) Ereignis *nt*; (*incidence*) Auftreten *nt*

ocean ['əuʃən] *n* Ozean *m*, Meer *nt*; **~s of** (*inf*) jede Menge

o'clock [ə'klɔk] *adv*: **it is 5 ~** es ist 5 Uhr

OCR *n abbr* (*Comput*) = **optical character reader; optical character recogniton**

Oct. *abbr* (= *October*) Okt.

October [ɔk'təubə^r] *n* Oktober *m*; *see also* **July**

octopus ['ɔktəpəs] *n* Tintenfisch *m*

odd [ɔd] *adj* (*person*) sonderbar, komisch; (*behaviour, shape*) seltsam; (*number*) ungerade; (*sock, shoe etc*) einzeln; (*occasional*) gelegentlich; **60-~** etwa 60; **at ~ times** ab und zu; **to be the ~ one out** der Außenseiter/die Außenseiterin sein; **add meat or the ~ vegetable to the soup** fügen Sie der Suppe Fleisch oder auch etwas Gemüse bei

oddity ['ɔdɪtɪ] *n* (*person*) Sonderling *m*; (*thing*) Merkwürdigkeit *f*

odd-job man [ɔd'dʒɔb-] *n* Mädchen *nt* für alles

odd jobs *npl* Gelegenheitsarbeiten *pl*

oddly ['ɔdlɪ] *adv* (*behave, dress*) seltsam; *see also* **enough**

oddments ['ɔdmənts] *npl* (*Comm*) Restposten *m*

odds [ɔdz] *npl* (*in betting*) Gewinnquote *f*; (*fig*) Chancen *pl*; **the ~ are in favour of/against his coming** es sieht so aus, als ob er kommt/nicht kommt; **to succeed against all the ~** allen Erwartungen zum Trotz erfolgreich sein; **it makes no ~** es spielt keine Rolle; **to be at ~ (with)** (*in disagreement*) uneinig sein (mit); (*at variance*) sich nicht vertragen (mit)

odometer [ɔ'dɔmɪtə^r] (*US*) *n* Tacho(meter) *m*

odour, (*US*) **odor** ['əudə^r] *n* Geruch *m*

of [ɔv] *prep* **1** von; **the history of Germany** die Geschichte Deutschlands; **a friend of ours** ein Freund von uns; **a boy of ten** ein Junge von zehn Jahren, ein zehnjähriger Junge; **that was kind of you** das war nett von Ihnen; **the city of New York** die Stadt New York

2 (*expressing quantity, amount, dates etc*): **a kilo of flour** ein Kilo Mehl; **how much of this do you need?** wie viel brauchen Sie davon?; **3 of them** (*people*) 3 von ihnen; (*objects*) 3 davon; **a cup of tea** eine Tasse Tee; **a vase of flowers** eine Vase mit Blumen; **the 5th of July** der 5. Juli

3 (*from, out of*) aus; **a bracelet of solid gold** ein Armband aus massivem Gold; **made of wood** aus Holz (gemacht)

off [ɔf] *adv* **1** (*referring to distance, time*): **it's a long way off** es ist sehr weit weg; **the game is 3 days off** es sind noch 3 Tage bis zum Spiel

2 (*departure*): **to go off to Paris/Italy** nach Paris/Italien fahren; **I must be off** ich muss gehen

3 (*removal*): **to take off one's coat/clothes** seinen Mantel/sich ausziehen; **the button came off** der Knopf ging ab; **10 % off** (*Comm*) 10% Nachlass

4: to be off (*on holiday*) im Urlaub sein; (*due to sickness*) krank sein; **I'm off on Fridays** freitags habe ich frei; **he was off on Friday** Freitag war er nicht da; **to have a day off** (*from work*) einen Tag freihaben; **to be off sick** wegen Krankheit fehlen

▷ *adj* **1** (*not turned on: machine, light, engine etc*) aus; (*: water, gas*) abgedreht; (*: tap*) zu

2: to be off (*meeting, match*) ausfallen; (*agreement*) nicht mehr gelten

3 (*Brit: not fresh*) verdorben, schlecht

4: on the off chance that ... für den Fall, dass ...; **to have an off day** (*not as good as usual*) nicht in Form sein; **to be badly off** sich schlecht stehen

▷ *prep* **1** (*indicating motion, removal etc*) von +*dat*; **to fall off a cliff** von einer Klippe fallen; **to take a picture off the wall** ein Bild von der Wand nehmen
2 (*distant from*): **5 km off the main road** 5 km von der Hauptstraße entfernt; **an island off the coast** eine Insel vor der Küste
3: I'm off meat/beer (*no longer eat/drink it*) ich esse kein Fleisch/trinke kein Bier mehr; (*no longer like it*) ich kann kein Fleisch/Bier *etc* mehr sehen

offal ['ɔfl] *n* (*Culin*) Innereien *pl*

off-colour ['ɔf'kʌləʳ] (*Brit*) *adj* (*ill*) unpässlich; **to feel ~** sich unwohl fühlen

offence, (*US*) **offense** [ə'fɛns] *n* (*crime*) Vergehen *nt*; (*insult*) Beleidigung *f*, Kränkung *f*; **to commit an ~** eine Straftat begehen; **to take ~ (at)** Anstoß nehmen (an +*dat*); **to give ~ (to)** Anstoß erregen (bei); **"no ~"** "nichts für ungut"

offend [ə'fɛnd] *vt* (*upset*) kränken; **to ~ against** (*law, rule*) verstoßen gegen

offender [ə'fɛndəʳ] *n* Straftäter(in) *m(f)*

offense [ə'fɛns] (*US*) *n* = **offence**

offensive [ə'fɛnsɪv] *adj* (*remark, behaviour*) verletzend; (*smell etc*) übel; (*weapon*) Angriffs- ▷ *n* (*Mil*) Offensive *f*

offer ['ɔfəʳ] *n* Angebot *nt* ▷ *vt* anbieten; (*money, opportunity, service*) bieten; (*reward*) aussetzen; **to make an ~ for sth** ein Angebot für etw machen; **on ~** (*Comm: available*) erhältlich; (*: cheaper*) im Angebot; **to ~ sth to sb** jdm etw anbieten; **to ~ to do sth** anbieten, etw zu tun

offering ['ɔfərɪŋ] *n* Darbietung *f*; (*Rel*) Opfergabe *f*

office ['ɔfɪs] *n* Büro *nt*; (*position*) Amt *nt*; **doctor's ~** (*US*) Praxis *f*; **to take ~** das Amt antreten; **in ~** (*minister etc*) im Amt; **through his good ~s** durch seine guten Dienste; **O~ of Fair Trading** (*Brit*) Behörde *f* gegen unlauteren Wettbewerb

office block, (*US*) **office building** *n* Bürogebäude *nt*

office hours *npl* (*Comm*) Bürostunden *pl*; (*US: Med*) Sprechstunde *f*

officer ['ɔfɪsəʳ] *n* (*Mil etc*) Offizier *m*; (*also*: **police officer**) Polizeibeamte(r) *m*, Polizeibeamtin *f*; (*of organization*) Funktionär *m*

office worker *n* Büroangestellte(r) *f(m)*

official [ə'fɪʃl] *adj* offiziell ▷ *n* (*in government*) Beamte(r) *m*, Beamtin *f*; (*in trade union etc*) Funktionär *m*

officiate [ə'fɪʃɪeɪt] *vi* amtieren; **to ~ at a marriage** eine Trauung vornehmen

officious [ə'fɪʃəs] *adj* übereifrig

offing ['ɔfɪŋ] *n*: **in the ~** in Sicht

off-licence ['ɔflaɪsns] (*Brit*) *n* ≈ Wein- und Spirituosenhandlung *f*

off-line [ɔf'laɪn] (*Comput*) *adj* Offline- ▷ *adv* offline; (*switched off*) abgetrennt

off-peak ['ɔf'pi:k] *adj* (*heating*) Nachtspeicher-; (*electricity*) Nacht-; (*train*) außerhalb der Stoßzeit; **~ ticket** Fahrkarte *f* zur Fahrt außerhalb der Stoßzeit

off-putting ['ɔfputɪŋ] (*Brit*) *adj* (*remark, behaviour*) abstoßend

off-season ['ɔf'si:zn] *adj, adv* außerhalb der Saison

offset ['ɔfsɛt] (*irreg: like* **set**) *vt* (*counteract*) ausgleichen

offshoot ['ɔfʃu:t] *n* (*Bot, fig*) Ableger *m*

offshore [ɔf'ʃɔ:ʳ] *adj* (*breeze*) ablandig; (*oil rig, fishing*) küstennah

offside ['ɔf'saɪd] *adj* (*Sport*) im Abseits; (*Aut: when driving on left*) rechtsseitig; (*: when driving on right*) linksseitig ▷ *n*: **the ~** (*Aut: when driving on left*) die rechte Seite; (*: when driving on right*) die linke Seite

offspring ['ɔfsprɪŋ] *n inv* Nachwuchs *m*

offstage [ɔf'steɪdʒ] *adv* hinter den Kulissen

off-the-peg ['ɔfðə'pɛg], (*US*) **off-the-rack** ['ɔfðə'ræk] *adv* von der Stange

off-white ['ɔfwaɪt] *adj* gebrochen weiß

often ['ɔfn] *adv* oft; **how ~?** wie oft?; **more ~ than not** meistens; **as ~ as not** ziemlich oft; **every so ~** ab und zu

Ofwat ['ɔfwɔt] *n Überwachungsgremium zum Verbraucherschutz nach Privatisierung der Wasserindustrie*

oh [əu] *excl* oh

oil [ɔɪl] *n* Öl *nt*; (*petroleum*) (Erd)öl *nt* ▷ *vt* ölen

oilcan ['ɔɪlkæn] *n* Ölkanne *f*

oilfield ['ɔɪlfi:ld] *n* Ölfeld *nt*

oil filter *n* Ölfilter *m*

oil painting *n* Ölgemälde *nt*

oil refinery *n* Ölraffinerie *f*

oil rig *n* Ölförderturm *m*; (*at sea*) Bohrinsel *f*

oil slick *n* Ölteppich *m*

oil tanker *n* (*ship*) (Öl)tanker *m*; (*truck*) Tankwagen *m*

oil well *n* Ölquelle *f*

oily ['ɔɪlɪ] *adj* (*substance*) ölig; (*rag*) öldurchtränkt; (*food*) fettig

ointment ['ɔɪntmənt] *n* Salbe *f*

O.K. ['əu'keɪ] (*inf*) *excl* okay; (*granted*) gut ▷ *adj* (*average*) einigermaßen; (*acceptable*) in Ordnung ▷ *vt* genehmigen ▷ *n*: **to give sb/sth the ~** jdm/etw seine Zustimmung geben; **is it ~?** ist es in Ordnung?; **are you ~?** bist du in Ordnung?; **are you ~ for money?** hast du (noch) genug Geld?; **it's ~ with** *or* **by me** mir ist es recht

old [əuld] *adj* alt; **how ~ are you?** wie alt bist du?; **he's 10 years ~** er ist 10 Jahre alt; **~er brother** ältere(r) Bruder; **any ~ thing will do for him** ihm ist alles recht

old age *n* Alter *nt*

old-fashioned ['əuld'fæʃnd] *adj* altmodisch

old people's home *n* Altersheim *nt*

olive ['ɔlɪv] *n* Olive *f*; (*tree*) Olivenbaum *m* ▷ *adj* (*also*: **olive-green**) olivgrün; **to offer an ~ branch to sb** (*fig*) jdm ein Friedensangebot machen

olive oil *n* Olivenöl *nt*

Olympic [əu'lɪmpɪk] *adj* olympisch

omelette, (US) **omelet** ['ɔmlɪt] *n* Omelett *nt*; **ham/cheese omelet(te)** Schinken-/Käseomelett *nt*

omen ['əumən] *n* Omen *nt*

ominous ['ɔmɪnəs] *adj* (*silence, warning*) ominös; (*clouds, smoke*) bedrohlich

omit [əu'mɪt] *vt* (*deliberately*) unterlassen; (*by mistake*) auslassen ▷ *vi*: **to ~ to do sth** es unterlassen, etw zu tun

on [ɔn] *prep* **1** (*indicating position*) auf *+dat*; (*with vb of motion*) auf *+acc*; **it's on the table** es ist auf dem Tisch; **she put the book on the table** sie legte das Buch auf den Tisch; **on the left** links; **on the right** rechts; **the house is on the main road** das Haus liegt an der Hauptstraße
2 (*indicating means, method, condition etc*): **on foot** (*go, be*) zu Fuß; **to be on the train/plane** im Zug/Flugzeug sein; **to go on the train/plane** mit dem Zug/Flugzeug reisen; **(to be wanted) on the telephone** am Telefon (verlangt werden); **on the radio/television** im Radio/Fernsehen; **to be on drugs** Drogen nehmen; **to be on holiday** im Urlaub sein; **I'm here on business** ich bin geschäftlich hier
3 (*referring to time*): **on Friday** am Freitag; **on Fridays** freitags; **on June 20th** am 20. Juni; **on Friday, June 20th** am Freitag, dem 20. Juni; **a week on Friday** Freitag in einer Woche; **on (his) arrival he went straight to his hotel** bei seiner Ankunft ging er direkt in sein Hotel; **on seeing this he ...** als er das sah, ... er ...
4 (*about, concerning*) über *+acc*; **a book on physics** ein Buch über Physik
▷ *adv* **1** (*referring to dress*): **to have one's coat on** seinen Mantel anhaben; **what's she got on?** was hat sie an?
2 (*referring to covering*): **screw the lid on tightly** dreh den Deckel fest zu
3 (*further, continuously*): **to walk/drive/read on** weitergehen/-fahren/-lesen
▷ *adj* **1** (*functioning, in operation: machine, radio, TV, light*) an; (*: tap*) auf; (*: handbrake*) angezogen; **there's a good film on at the cinema** im Kino läuft ein guter Film
2: that's not on! (*inf: of behaviour*) das ist nicht drin!

once [wʌns] *adv* (*on one occasion*) einmal; (*formerly*) früher; (*a long time ago*) früher einmal ▷ *conj* (*as soon as*) sobald; **at ~** (*immediately*) sofort; (*simultaneously*) gleichzeitig; **~ a week** einmal pro Woche; **~ more** *or* **again** noch einmal; **~ and for all** ein für alle Mal; **~ upon a time** es war einmal; **~ in a while** ab und zu; **all at ~** (*suddenly*) plötzlich; **for ~** ausnahmsweise (einmal); **~ or twice** ein paarmal; **~ he had left** sobald er gegangen war; **~ it was done** nachdem es getan war

oncoming ['ɔnkʌmɪŋ] *adj* (*traffic etc*) entgegenkommend

one [wʌn] *num* ein(e); (*counting*) eins; **one hundred and fifty** (ein)hundert(und)fünfzig; **one day there was a sudden knock at the door** eines Tages klopfte es plötzlich an der Tür; **one by one** einzeln
▷ *adj* **1** (*sole*) einzige(r, s); **the one book which ...** das einzige Buch, das ...
2 (*same*): **they came in the one car** sie kamen in demselben Wagen; **they all belong to the one family** sie alle gehören zu ein und derselben Familie
▷ *pron* **1: this one** diese(r, s); **that one** der/die/das (da); **which one?** welcher/welche/welches?; **he is one of us** er ist einer von uns; **I've already got one/a red one** ich habe schon eins/ein rotes
2: one another einander; **do you two ever see one another?** seht ihr zwei euch jemals?
3 (*impersonal*) man; **one never knows** man weiß nie; **to cut one's finger** sich *dat* in den Finger schneiden

one-day excursion ['wʌndeɪ-] (US) *n* (*day return*) Tagesrückfahrkarte *f*

one-man ['wʌn'mæn] *adj* (*business, show*) Einmann-

one-man band *n* Einmannkapelle *f*

one-off [wʌn'ɔf] (*Brit: inf*) *n* einmaliges Ereignis *nt*

oneself [wʌn'sɛlf] *pron* (*reflexive: after prep*) sich; (*emphatic*) selbst; **to hurt oneself** sich *dat* wehtun; **to keep sth for oneself** etw für sich behalten; **to talk to oneself** Selbstgespräche führen

one-shot ['wʌnʃɔt] (US) *n* = **one-off**

one-sided [wʌn'saɪdɪd] *adj* einseitig

one-to-one ['wʌntəwʌn] *adj* (*relationship, tuition*) Einzel-

one-way ['wʌnweɪ] *adj* (*street, traffic*) Einbahn-; (*ticket*) Einzel-

ongoing ['ɔngəuɪŋ] *adj* (*project*) laufend; (*situation etc*) andauernd

onion ['ʌnjən] *n* Zwiebel *f*

on-line ['ɔnlaɪn] (*Comput*) *adj* (*printer, database*) Online-; (*switched on*) gekoppelt ▷ *adv* online

onlooker ['ɔnlukə[r]] *n* Zuschauer(in) *m(f)*

only ['əunlɪ] *adv* nur ▷ *adj* einzige(r, s) ▷ *conj* nur, bloß; **I ~ took one** ich nahm nur eins; **I saw her ~ yesterday** ich habe sie erst gestern gesehen; **I'd be ~ too pleased to help** ich würde allzu gern helfen; **not ~ ... but (also) ...** nicht nur ..., sondern auch ...; **an ~ child** ein Einzelkind *nt*; **I would come, ~ I'm too busy** ich würde kommen, wenn ich nicht so viel zu tun hätte

onset ['ɔnsɛt] *n* Beginn *m*

onshore ['ɔnʃɔː[r]] *adj* (*wind*) auflandig, See-

onslaught ['ɔnslɔːt] *n* Attacke *f*

onto ['ɔntu] *prep* = **on to**

onward ['ɔnwəd], **onwards** ['ɔnwədz] *adv* weiter; **from that time ~(s)** von der Zeit an ▷ *adj* fortschreitend

ooze [uːz] *vi* (*mud, water etc*) triefen

opaque [əu'peɪk] *adj* *(substance)* undurchsichtig, trüb
OPEC ['əupɛk] *n abbr* *(= Organization of Petroleum-Exporting Countries)* OPEC *f*
open ['əupn] *adj* offen; *(packet, shop, museum)* geöffnet; *(view)* frei; *(meeting, debate)* öffentlich; *(ticket, return)* unbeschränkt; *(vacancy)* verfügbar ▷ *vt* öffnen, aufmachen; *(book, paper etc)* aufschlagen; *(account)* eröffnen; *(blocked road)* frei machen ▷ *vi* *(door, eyes, mouth)* sich öffnen; *(shop, bank etc)* aufmachen; *(commence)* beginnen; *(film, play)* Premiere haben; *(flower)* aufgehen; **in the ~ (air)** im Freien; **the ~ sea** das offene Meer; **to have an ~ mind on sth** etw *dat* aufgeschlossen gegenüberstehen; **to be ~ to** *(ideas etc)* offen sein für; **to be ~ to criticism** der Kritik *dat* ausgesetzt sein; **to be ~ to the public** für die Öffentlichkeit zugänglich sein; **to ~ one's mouth** *(speak)* den Mund aufmachen
▸ **open on to** *vt fus* *(room, door)* führen auf *+acc*
▸ **open up** *vi* *(unlock)* aufmachen; *(confide)* sich äußern
open-air [əupn'ɛər] *adj* im Freien; **~ concert** Open-Air-Konzert *nt*; **~ swimming pool** Freibad *nt*
opening ['əupnɪŋ] *adj* *(commencing: stages, scene)* erste(r, s); *(remarks, ceremony etc)* Eröffnungs- ▷ *n* *(gap, hole)* Öffnung *f*; *(of play etc)* Anfang *m*; *(of new building etc)* Eröffnung *f*; *(opportunity)* Gelegenheit *f*
opening hours *npl* Öffnungszeiten *pl*
open learning *n* *Weiterbildungssystem auf Teilzeitbasis*
openly ['əupnlɪ] *adv* offen
open-minded [əupn'maɪndɪd] *adj* aufgeschlossen
open-necked ['əupnnɛkt] *adj* *(shirt)* mit offenem Kragen
open-plan ['əupn'plæn] *adj* *(office)* Großraum-
Open University *(Brit)* *n* ≈ Fernuniversität *f*
opera ['ɔpərə] *n* Oper *f*
opera house *n* Opernhaus *nt*
opera singer *n* Opernsänger(in) *m(f)*
operate ['ɔpəreɪt] *vt* *(machine etc)* bedienen ▷ *vi* *(machine etc)* funktionieren; *(company)* arbeiten; *(laws, forces)* wirken; *(Med)* operieren; **to ~ on sb** jdn operieren
operatic [ɔpə'rætɪk] *adj* *(singer etc)* Opern-
operating room ['ɔpəreɪtɪŋ-] *(US)* *n* Operationssaal *m*
operating theatre *n* *(Med)* Operationssaal *m*
operation [ɔpə'reɪʃən] *n* *(activity)* Unternehmung *f*; *(of machine etc)* Betrieb *m*; *(Mil, Med)* Operation *f*; *(Comm)* Geschäft *nt*; **to be in ~** *(law, scheme)* in Kraft sein; **to have an ~** *(Med)* operiert werden; **to perform an ~** *(Med)* eine Operation vornehmen
operational [ɔpə'reɪʃənl] *adj* *(machine etc)* einsatzfähig
operative ['ɔpərətɪv] *adj* *(measure, system)* wirksam; *(law)* gültig ▷ *n* *(in factory)* Maschinenarbeiter(in) *m(f)*; **the ~ word** das entscheidende Wort
operator ['ɔpəreɪtər] *n* *(Tel)* Vermittlung *f*; *(of machine)* Bediener(in) *m(f)*
opinion [ə'pɪnjən] *n* Meinung *f*; **in my ~** meiner Meinung nach; **to have a good/high ~ of sb/o.s.** eine gute/hohe Meinung von jdm/sich haben; **to be of the ~ that ...** der Ansicht *or* Meinung sein, dass ...; **to get a second ~** *(Med etc)* ein zweites Gutachten einholen
opinionated [ə'pɪnjəneɪtɪd] *(pej)* *adj* rechthaberisch
opinion poll *n* Meinungsumfrage *f*
opponent [ə'pəunənt] *n* Gegner(in) *m(f)*
opportunity [ɔpə'tju:nɪtɪ] *n* Gelegenheit *f*, Möglichkeit *f*; *(prospects)* Chance *f*; **to take the ~ of doing sth** die Gelegenheit ergreifen, etw zu tun
oppose [ə'pəuz] *vt* *(opinion, plan)* ablehnen; **to be ~d to sth** gegen etw sein; **as ~d to** im Gegensatz zu
opposing [ə'pəuzɪŋ] *adj* *(side, team)* gegnerisch; *(ideas, tendencies)* entgegengesetzt
opposite ['ɔpəzɪt] *adj* *(house, door)* gegenüberliegend; *(end, direction)* entgegengesetzt; *(point of view, effect)* gegenteilig ▷ *adv* gegenüber ▷ *prep* *(in front of)* gegenüber; *(next to: on list, form etc)* neben ▷ *n*: **the ~** das Gegenteil; **the ~ sex** das andere Geschlecht; **"see ~ page"** "siehe gegenüber"
opposition [ɔpə'zɪʃən] *n* *(resistance)* Widerstand *m*; *(Sport)* Gegner *pl*; **the O~** *(Pol)* die Opposition
oppress [ə'prɛs] *vt* unterdrücken
oppressive [ə'prɛsɪv] *adj* *(weather, heat)* bedrückend; *(political regime)* repressiv
opt [ɔpt] *vi*: **to ~ for** sich entscheiden für; **to ~ to do sth** sich entscheiden, etw zu tun
▸ **opt out (of)** *vi* *(not participate)* sich nicht beteiligen (an *+dat*); *(of insurance scheme etc)* kündigen; **to ~ out (of local authority control)** *(Pol: hospital, school)* aus der Kontrolle der Gemeindeverwaltung austreten
optical ['ɔptɪkl] *adj* optisch
optical character reader *n* optischer Klarschriftleser *m*
optical character recognition *n* optische Zeichenerkennung *f*
optician [ɔp'tɪʃən] *n* Optiker(in) *m(f)*
optimism ['ɔptɪmɪzəm] *n* Optimismus *m*
optimist ['ɔptɪmɪst] *n* Optimist(in) *m(f)*
optimistic [ɔptɪ'mɪstɪk] *adj* optimistisch
optimum ['ɔptɪməm] *adj* optimal
option ['ɔpʃən] *n* *(choice)* Möglichkeit *f*; *(Scol)* Wahlfach *nt*; *(Comm)* Option *f*; **to keep one's ~s open** sich *dat* alle Möglichkeiten offenhalten; **to have no ~** keine (andere) Wahl haben
optional ['ɔpʃənl] *adj* freiwillig; **~ extras** *(Comm)* Extras *pl*
or [ɔ:r] *conj* oder; **he hasn't seen or heard**

anything er hat weder etwas gesehen noch gehört; **or else** (*otherwise*) sonst; **fifty or sixty people** fünfzig bis sechzig Leute

oral ['ɔ:rəl] *adj* (*test, report*) mündlich; (*Med: vaccine, contraceptive*) zum Einnehmen ▷ *n* (*exam*) mündliche Prüfung *f*

orange ['ɔrɪndʒ] *n* Orange *f*, Apfelsine *f* ▷ *adj* (*colour*) orange

orbit ['ɔ:bɪt] *n* (*of planet etc*) Umlaufbahn *f* ▷ *vt* umkreisen

orchard ['ɔ:tʃəd] *n* Obstgarten *m*; **apple ~** Obstgarten mit Apfelbäumen

orchestra ['ɔ:kɪstrə] *n* Orchester *nt*; (*US: stalls*) Parkett *nt*

orchid ['ɔ:kɪd] *n* Orchidee *f*

ordain [ɔ:'deɪn] *vt* (*Rel*) ordinieren; (*decree*) verfügen

ordeal [ɔ:'di:l] *n* Qual *f*

order ['ɔ:dəʳ] *n* (*command*) Befehl *m*; (*Comm, in restaurant*) Bestellung *f*; (*sequence*) Reihenfolge *f*; (*discipline, organization*) Ordnung *f*; (*Rel*) Orden *m* ▷ *vt* (*command*) befehlen; (*Comm, in restaurant*) bestellen; (*also*: **put in order**) ordnen; **in ~** (*permitted*) in Ordnung; **in (working) ~** betriebsfähig; **in ~ to do sth** um etw zu tun; **in ~ of size** nach Größe (geordnet); **on ~** (*Comm*) bestellt; **out of ~** (*not working*) außer Betrieb; (*in the wrong sequence*) durcheinander; (*motion, proposal*) nicht zulässig; **to place an ~ for sth with sb** eine Bestellung für etw bei jdm aufgeben; **made to ~** (*Comm*) auf Bestellung (gemacht); **to be under ~s to do sth** die Anweisung haben, etw zu tun; **to take ~s** Befehle entgegennehmen; **a point of ~** (*in debate etc*) eine Verfahrensfrage; **"pay to the ~ of ..."** "zahlbar an *+dat* ..."; **of** *or* **in the ~ of** in der Größenordnung von; **to ~ sb to do sth** jdn anweisen, etw zu tun

▸ **order around** *vt* (*also*: **order about**) herumkommandieren

order form *n* Bestellschein *m*

orderly ['ɔ:dəlɪ] *n* (*Mil*) Offiziersbursche *m*; (*Med*) Pfleger(in) *m(f)* ▷ *adj* (*manner*) ordentlich; (*sequence, system*) geordnet

ordinary ['ɔ:dnrɪ] *adj* (*everyday*) gewöhnlich, normal; (*pej: mediocre*) mittelmäßig; **out of the ~** außergewöhnlich

ore [ɔ:ʳ] *n* Erz *nt*

organ ['ɔ:gən] *n* (*Anat*) Organ *nt*; (*Mus*) Orgel *f*

organic [ɔ:'gænɪk] *adj* organisch

organism ['ɔ:gənɪzəm] *n* Organismus *m*

organization [ɔ:gənaɪ'zeɪʃən] *n* Organisation *f*

organize ['ɔ:gənaɪz] *vt* organisieren; **to get ~d** sich fertig machen

organizer ['ɔ:gənaɪzəʳ] *n* (*of conference etc*) Organisator *m*, Veranstalter *m*

orgasm ['ɔ:gæzəm] *n* Orgasmus *m*

orgy ['ɔ:dʒɪ] *n* Orgie *f*; **an ~ of destruction** eine Zerstörungsorgie

Orient ['ɔ:rɪənt] *n*: **the ~** der Orient

oriental [ɔ:rɪ'ɛntl] *adj* orientalisch

origin ['ɔrɪdʒɪn] *n* Ursprung *m*; (*of person*) Herkunft *f*; **country of ~** Herkunftsland *nt*

original [ə'rɪdʒɪnl] *adj* (*first*) ursprünglich; (*genuine*) original; (*imaginative*) originell ▷ *n* Original *nt*

originally [ə'rɪdʒɪnəlɪ] *adv* (*at first*) ursprünglich

originate [ə'rɪdʒɪneɪt] *vi*: **to ~ in** (*idea, custom etc*) entstanden sein in *+dat*; **to ~ with** *or* **from** stammen von

ornament ['ɔ:nəmənt] *n* (*object*) Ziergegenstand *m*; (*decoration*) Verzierungen *pl*

ornamental [ɔ:nə'mɛntl] *adj* (*garden, pond*) Zier-

ornate [ɔ:'neɪt] *adj* (*necklace, design*) kunstvoll

orphan ['ɔ:fn] *n* Waise *f*, Waisenkind *nt* ▷ *vt*: **to be ~ed** zur Waise werden

orthodox ['ɔ:θədɔks] *adj* orthodox; **~ medicine** die konventionelle Medizin

orthopaedic, (*US*) **orthopedic** [ɔ:θə'pi:dɪk] *adj* orthopädisch

ostensibly [ɔs'tɛnsɪblɪ] *adv* angeblich

ostentatious [ɔstɛn'teɪʃəs] *adj* (*building, car etc*) pompös; (*person*) protzig

osteopath ['ɔstɪəpæθ] *n* Osteopath(in) *m(f)*

ostracize ['ɔstrəsaɪz] *vt* ächten

ostrich ['ɔstrɪtʃ] *n* Strauß *m*

other ['ʌðəʳ] *adj* andere(r, s) ▷ *pron*: **the ~ (one)** der/die/das andere; **~s** andere *pl*; **the ~s** die anderen *pl*; **~ than** (*apart from*) außer; **the ~ day** (*recently*) neulich; **some actor or ~** irgendein Schauspieler; **somebody or ~** irgendjemand; **the car was none ~ than Robert's** das Auto gehörte keinem anderen als Robert

otherwise ['ʌðəwaɪz] *adv* (*differently*) anders; (*apart from that, if not*) sonst, ansonsten; **an ~ good piece of work** eine im Übrigen gute Arbeit

otter ['ɔtəʳ] *n* Otter *m*

ouch [autʃ] *excl* autsch

ought [ɔ:t] (*pt* **~**) *aux vb*: **I ~ to do it** ich sollte es tun; **this ~ to have been corrected** das hätte korrigiert werden müssen; **he ~ to win** (*he probably will win*) er dürfte wohl gewinnen; **you ~ to go and see it** das solltest du dir ansehen

ounce [auns] *n* Unze *f*; (*fig: small amount*) bisschen *nt*

our ['auəʳ] *adj* unsere(r, s); *see also* **my**

ours [auəz] *pron* unsere(r, s); *see also* **mine**[1]

ourselves [auə'sɛlvz] *pron pl* uns (selbst); (*emphatic*) selbst; **we did it (all) by ~** wir haben alles selbst gemacht; *see also* **oneself**

oust [aust] *vt* (*forcibly remove*) verdrängen

out[1] [aut] *adv* **1** (*not in*) draußen; **out in the rain/snow** draußen im Regen/Schnee; **out here** hier; **out there** dort; **to go/come** *etc* **out** hinausgehen/-kommen *etc*; **to speak out loud** laut sprechen

2 (*not at home, absent*) nicht da

3 (*indicating distance*): **the boat was 10 km**

out das Schiff war 10 km weit draußen; **3 days out from Plymouth** 3 Tage nach dem Auslaufen von Plymouth
4 (*Sport*) aus; **the ball is out/has gone out** der Ball ist aus
▷ *adj* **1: to be out** (*person: unconscious*) bewusstlos sein; (*: out of game*) ausgeschieden sein; (*out of fashion: style, singer*) out sein
2 (*have appeared: flowers*) da; (*: news, secret*) heraus
3 (*extinguished, finished: fire, light, gas*) aus; **before the week was out** ehe die Woche zu Ende war
4: to be out to do sth (*intend*) etw tun wollen
5 (*wrong*): **to be out in one's calculations** sich in seinen Berechnungen irren
out² [aut] *vt* (*inf: expose as homosexual*) outen
out-and-out ['autəndaut] *adj* (*liar, thief etc*) ausgemacht
outback ['autbæk] *n* (*in Australia*): **the ~** das Hinterland
outboard ['autbɔ:d] *n* (*also:* **outboard motor**) Außenbordmotor *m*
outbound ['autbaund] *adj* (*ship*) auslaufend
outbreak ['autbreɪk] *n* (*of war, disease etc*) Ausbruch *m*
outburst ['autbə:st] *n* (*of anger etc*) Gefühlsausbruch *m*
outcast ['autkɑ:st] *n* Ausgestoßene(r) *f(m)*
outcome ['autkʌm] *n* Ergebnis *nt*, Resultat *nt*
outcrop ['autkrɔp] *n* (*of rock*) Block *m*
outcry ['autkraɪ] *n* Aufschrei *m*
outdated [aut'deɪtɪd] *adj* (*custom, idea*) veraltet
outdo [aut'du:] (*irreg: like* **do**) *vt* übertreffen
outdoor [aut'dɔ:ʳ] *adj* (*activities*) im Freien; (*clothes*) für draußen; **~ swimming pool** Freibad *nt*; **she's an ~ person** sie liebt die freie Natur
outdoors [aut'dɔ:z] *adv* (*play, sleep*) draußen, im Freien
outer ['autəʳ] *adj* äußere(r, s); **~ suburbs** (äußere) Vorstädte *pl*; **the ~ office** das Vorzimmer
outer space *n* der Weltraum
outfit ['autfɪt] *n* (*clothes*) Kleidung *f*; (*inf: team*) Verein *m*
outgoing ['autgəuɪŋ] *adj* (*extrovert*) kontaktfreudig; (*retiring: president etc*) scheidend; (*mail etc*) ausgehend
outgoings ['autgəuɪŋz] (*Brit*) *npl* Ausgaben *pl*
outgrow [aut'grəu] (*irreg: like* **grow**) *vt* (*clothes*) herauswachsen aus; (*habits etc*) ablegen
outhouse ['authaus] *n* Nebengebäude *nt*
outing ['autɪŋ] *n* Ausflug *m*
outlaw ['autlɔ:] *n* Geächtete(r) *f(m)* ▷ *vt* verbieten
outlay ['autleɪ] *n* Auslagen *pl*
outlet ['autlɛt] *n* (*hole, pipe*) Abfluss *m*; (*US: Elec*) Steckdose *f*; (*Comm: also:* **retail outlet**) Verkaufsstelle *f*; (*fig: for grief, anger etc*) Ventil *nt*
outline ['autlaɪn] *n* (*shape*) Umriss *m*; (*brief explanation*) Abriss *m*; (*rough sketch*) Skizze *f* ▷ *vt* (*fig: theory, plan etc*) umreißen, skizzieren
outlive [aut'lɪv] *vt* (*survive*) überleben
outlook ['autluk] *n* (*attitude*) Einstellung *f*; (*prospects*) Aussichten *pl*; (*for weather*) Vorhersage *f*
outlying ['autlaɪɪŋ] *adj* (*area, town etc*) entlegen
outmoded [aut'məudɪd] *adj* veraltet
outnumber [aut'nʌmbəʳ] *vt* zahlenmäßig überlegen sein *+dat*; **to be ~ed (by) 5 to 1** im Verhältnis 5 zu 1 in der Minderheit sein
out of *prep* **1** (*outside, beyond: position*) nicht in *+dat*; (*: motion*) aus *+dat*; **to look out of the window** aus dem Fenster blicken; **to be out of danger** außer Gefahr sein
2 (*cause, origin*) aus *+dat*; **out of curiosity/fear/greed** aus Neugier/Angst/Habgier; **to drink sth out of a cup** etw aus einer Tasse trinken
3 (*from among*) von *+dat*; **one out of every three smokers** einer von drei Rauchern
4 (*without*): **to be out of sugar/milk/petrol** *etc* keinen Zucker/keine Milch/kein Benzin *etc* mehr haben
out-of-date [autəv'deɪt] *adj* (*passport, ticket etc*) abgelaufen; (*clothes, idea*) veraltet
out-of-doors [autəv'dɔ:z] *adv* (*play, stay etc*) im Freien
out-of-the-way ['autəvðə'weɪ] *adj* (*place*) entlegen; (*pub, restaurant etc*) kaum bekannt
outpatient ['autpeɪʃənt] *n* ambulanter Patient *m*, ambulante Patientin *f*
outpost ['autpəust] *n* (*Mil, Comm*) Vorposten *m*
output ['autput] *n* (*production: of factory, writer etc*) Produktion *f*; (*Comput*) Output *m*, Ausgabe *f* ▷ *vt* (*Comput*) ausgeben
outrage ['autreɪdʒ] *n* (*scandal*) Skandal *m*; (*atrocity*) Verbrechen *nt*, Ausschreitung *f*; (*anger*) Empörung *f* ▷ *vt* (*shock, anger*) empören
outrageous [aut'reɪdʒəs] *adj* (*remark etc*) empörend; (*clothes*) unmöglich; (*scandalous*) skandalös
outright [aut'raɪt] *adv* (*kill*) auf der Stelle; (*win*) überlegen; (*buy*) auf einen Schlag; (*ask, refuse*) ohne Umschweife ▷ *adj* (*winner, victory*) unbestritten; (*refusal, hostility*) total
outset ['autsɛt] *n* Anfang *m*, Beginn *m*; **from the ~** von Anfang an; **at the ~** am Anfang
outside [aut'saɪd] *n* (*of building etc*) Außenseite *f* ▷ *adj* (*wall, lavatory*) Außen- ▷ *adv* (*be, wait*) draußen; (*go*) nach draußen ▷ *prep* außerhalb *+gen*; (*door etc*) vor *+dat*; **at the ~** (*at the most*) höchstens; (*at the latest*) spätestens; **an ~ chance** eine geringe Chance
outside lane *n* Überholspur *f*
outside line *n* (*Tel*) Amtsanschluss *m*
outsider [aut'saɪdəʳ] *n* (*stranger*) Außenstehende(r) *f(m)*; (*odd one out, in race etc*) Außenseiter(in) *m(f)*
outsize ['autsaɪz] *adj* (*clothes*) übergroß
outskirts ['autskə:ts] *npl* (*of town*) Stadtrand *m*
outspoken [aut'spəukən] *adj* offen
outstanding [aut'stændɪŋ] *adj* (*exceptional*)

hervorragend; (*remaining*) ausstehend; **your account is still ~** Ihr Konto weist noch Außenstände auf
outstay [aut'steɪ] *vt*: **to ~ one's welcome** länger bleiben als erwünscht
outstretched [aut'strɛtʃt] *adj* ausgestreckt
outstrip [aut'strɪp] *vt* (*competitors, supply*): **to ~ (in)** übertreffen (an *+dat*)
outward ['autwəd] *adj* (*sign, appearances*) äußere(r, s) ▷ *adv* (*move, face*) nach außen; **~ journey** Hinreise *f*
outwards ['autwədz] *adv* (*move, face*) nach außen
outweigh [aut'weɪ] *vt* schwerer wiegen als
outwit [aut'wɪt] *vt* überlisten
oval ['əuvl] *adj* oval ▷ *n* Oval *nt*
ovary ['əuvərɪ] *n* (*Anat, Med*) Eierstock *m*
oven ['ʌvn] *n* (*Culin*) Backofen *m*
ovenproof ['ʌvnpru:f] *adj* (*dish etc*) feuerfest
oven-ready ['ʌvnrɛdɪ] *adj* backfertig
over ['əuvə[r]] *adv* **1** (*across: walk, jump, fly etc*) hinüber; **over here** hier; **over there** dort (drüben); **to ask sb over** (*to one's house*) jdn zu sich einladen
2 (*indicating movement*): **to fall over** (*person*) hinfallen; (*object*) umfallen; **to knock sth over** etw umstoßen; **to turn over** (*in bed*) sich umdrehen; **to bend over** sich bücken
3 (*finished*): **to be over** (*game, life, relationship etc*) vorbei sein, zu Ende sein
4 (*excessively: clever, rich, fat etc*) übermäßig
5 (*remaining: money, food etc*) übrig; **is there any cake (left) over?** ist noch Kuchen übrig?
6: all over (*everywhere*) überall
7 (*repeatedly*): **over and over (again)** immer (und immer) wieder; **five times over** fünfmal
▷ *prep* **1** (*on top of, above*) über *+dat*; (*with vb of motion*) über *+acc*; **to spread a sheet over sth** ein Laken über etw *acc* breiten
2 (*on the other side of*): **the pub over the road** die Kneipe gegenüber; **he jumped over the wall** er sprang über die Mauer
3 (*more than*) über *+acc*; **over 200 people** über 200 Leute; **over and above my normal duties** über meine normalen Pflichten hinaus; **over and above that** darüber hinaus
4 (*during*) während; **let's discuss it over dinner** wir sollten es beim Abendessen besprechen
overall ['əuvərɔ:l] *adj* (*length, cost etc*) Gesamt-; (*impression, view*) allgemein ▷ *adv* (*measure, cost*) insgesamt; (*generally*) im Allgemeinen ▷ *n* (*Brit*) Kittel *m*; **overalls** *npl* Overall *m*
overawe [əuvər'ɔ:] *vt*: **to be ~d (by)** überwältigt sein (von)
overbalance [əuvə'bæləns] *vi* das Gleichgewicht verlieren
overboard ['əuvəbɔ:d] *adv* (*Naut*) über Bord; **to go ~** (*fig*) es übertreiben, zu weit gehen
overbook [əuvə'buk] *vt* überbuchen
overcame [əuvə'keɪm] *pt of* **overcome**
overcast ['əuvəka:st] *adj* (*day, sky*) bedeckt
overcharge [əuvə'tʃa:dʒ] *vt* zu viel berechnen *+dat*
overcoat ['əuvəkəut] *n* Mantel *m*
overcome [əuvə'kʌm] (*irreg: like* **come**) *vt* (*problem, fear*) überwinden ▷ *adj* überwältigt; **she was ~ with grief** der Schmerz übermannte sie
overcrowded [əuvə'kraudɪd] *adj* überfüllt
overdo [əuvə'du:] (*irreg: like* **do**) *vt* übertreiben; **to ~ it** es übertreiben
overdose ['əuvədəus] *n* Überdosis *f*
overdraft ['əuvədra:ft] *n* Kontoüberziehung *f*; **to have an ~** sein Konto überziehen
overdrawn [əuvə'drɔ:n] *adj* (*account*) überzogen; **I am ~** ich habe mein Konto überzogen
overdue [əuvə'dju:] *adj* überfällig; **that change was long ~** diese Änderung war schon lange fällig
overestimate [əuvər'ɛstɪmeɪt] *vt* überschätzen
overflow [əuvə'fləu] *vi* (*river*) über die Ufer treten; (*bath, jar etc*) überlaufen ▷ *n* (*also*: **overflow pipe**) Überlaufrohr *nt*
overgrown [əuvə'grəun] *adj* (*garden*) verwildert; **he's just an ~ schoolboy** er ist nur ein großes Kind
overhaul [əuvə'hɔ:l] *vt* (*equipment, car etc*) überholen ▷ *n* Überholung *f*
overhead [əuvə'hɛd] *adv* (*above*) oben; (*in the sky*) in der Luft ▷ *adj* (*lighting*) Decken-; (*cables, wires*) Überland- ▷ *n* (*US*) = **overheads**
overheads *npl* allgemeine Unkosten *pl*
overhear [əuvə'hɪə[r]] (*irreg: like* **hear**) *vt* (zufällig) mit anhören
overheat [əuvə'hi:t] *vi* (*engine*) heißlaufen
overjoyed [əuvə'dʒɔɪd] *adj* überglücklich; **to be ~ (at)** überglücklich sein (über *+acc*)
overland ['əuvəlænd] *adj* (*journey*) Überland- ▷ *adv* (*travel*) über Land
overlap [əuvə'læp] *vi* (*figures, ideas etc*) sich überschneiden
overleaf [əuvə'li:f] *adv* umseitig, auf der Rückseite
overload [əuvə'ləud] *vt* (*vehicle*) überladen; (*Elec*) überbelasten; (*fig: with work etc*) überlasten
overlook [əuvə'luk] *vt* (*have view over*) überblicken; (*fail to notice*) übersehen; (*excuse, forgive*) hinwegsehen über *+acc*
overnight [əuvə'naɪt] *adv* über Nacht ▷ *adj* (*bag, clothes*) Reise-; (*accommodation, stop*) für die Nacht; **to travel ~** nachts reisen; **he'll be away ~** (*tonight*) er kommt erst morgen zurück; **to stay ~** über Nacht bleiben; **~ stay** Übernachtung *f*
overpass ['əuvəpa:s] (*esp US*) *n* Überführung *f*
overpower [əuvə'pauə[r]] *vt* überwältigen
overpowering [əuvə'pauərɪŋ] *adj* (*heat*) unerträglich; (*stench*) durchdringend; (*feeling, desire*) überwältigend
overrate [əuvə'reɪt] *vt* überschätzen

overreact [əuvəri:'ækt] *vi* übertrieben reagieren
override [əuvə'raɪd] (*irreg: like* **ride**) *vt* (*order etc*) sich hinwegsetzen über *+acc*
overriding [əuvə'raɪdɪŋ] *adj* vorrangig
overrule [əuvə'ru:l] *vt* (*claim, person*) zurückweisen; (*decision*) aufheben
overrun [əuvə'rʌn] (*irreg: like* **run**) *vt* (*country, continent*) einfallen in *+acc* ▷ *vi* (*meeting etc*) zu lange dauern; **the town is ~ with tourists** die Stadt ist von Touristen überlaufen
overseas [əuvə'si:z] *adv* (*live, work*) im Ausland; (*travel*) ins Ausland ▷ *adj* (*market, trade*) Übersee-; (*student, visitor*) aus dem Ausland
oversee [əuvə'si:] *vt* (*supervise*) beaufsichtigen, überwachen
overshadow [əuvə'ʃædəu] *vt* (*place, building etc*) überschatten; (*fig*) in den Schatten stellen
oversight ['əuvəsaɪt] *n* Versehen *nt*; **due to an ~** aus Versehen
oversleep [əuvə'sli:p] (*irreg: like* **sleep**) *vi* verschlafen
overspend [əuvə'spɛnd] (*irreg: like* **spend**) *vi* zu viel ausgeben; **we have overspent by 5,000 dollars** wir haben 5000 Dollar zu viel ausgegeben
overstep [əuvə'stɛp] *vt*: **to ~ the mark** zu weit gehen
overt [əu'və:t] *adj* offen
overtake [əuvə'teɪk] (*irreg: like* **take**) *vt* (*Aut*) überholen; (*event, change*) hereinbrechen über *+acc*; (*emotion*) befallen ▷ *vi* (*Aut*) überholen
overthrow [əuvə'θrəu] (*irreg: like* **throw**) *vt* (*government etc*) stürzen
overtime ['əuvətaɪm] *n* Überstunden *pl*; **to do** *or* **work ~** Überstunden machen
overtone ['əuvətəun] *n* (*fig: also:* **overtones**): **~s of** Untertöne *pl* von
overture ['əuvətʃuəʳ] *n* (*Mus*) Ouvertüre *f*; (*fig*) Annäherungsversuch *m*
overturn [əuvə'tə:n] *vt* (*car, chair*) umkippen; (*fig: decision*) aufheben; (*: government*) stürzen ▷ *vi* (*train etc*) umkippen; (*car*) sich überschlagen; (*boat*) kentern
overweight [əuvə'weɪt] *adj* (*person*) übergewichtig
overwhelm [əuvə'wɛlm] *vt* überwältigen
overwhelming [əuvə'wɛlmɪŋ] *adj* überwältigend; **one's ~ impression is of heat/noise** man bemerkt vor allem die Hitze/den Lärm
overwrought [əuvə'rɔ:t] *adj* (*person*) überreizt
owe [əu] *vt*: **to ~ sb sth, to ~ sth to sb** (*lit, fig*) jdm etw schulden; (*life, talent, good looks etc*) jdm etw verdanken
owing to ['əuɪŋ-] *prep* (*because of*) wegen *+gen*, aufgrund *+gen*
owl [aul] *n* Eule *f*
own [əun] *vt* (*possess*) besitzen ▷ *vi* (*Brit: form*): **to ~ up to sth** etw zugeben ▷ *adj* eigen; **a room of my ~** mein eigenes Zimmer; **to get one's ~ back** (*take revenge*) sich rächen; **on one's ~** allein; **to come into one's ~** sich entfalten
▸ **own up** *vi* gestehen, es zugeben
owner ['əunəʳ] *n* Besitzer(in) *m(f)*, Eigentümer(in) *m(f)*
ownership ['əunəʃɪp] *n* Besitz *m*; **under new ~** (*shop etc*) unter neuer Leitung
ox [ɔks] (*pl* **oxen**) *n* Ochse *m*
oxtail ['ɔksteɪl] *n*: **~ soup** Ochsenschwanzsuppe *f*
oxygen ['ɔksɪdʒən] *n* Sauerstoff *m*
oyster ['ɔɪstəʳ] *n* Auster *f*
ozone ['əuzəun] *n* Ozon *nt*
ozone hole *n* Ozonloch *nt*
ozone layer *n*: **the ~** die Ozonschicht

Pp

P, **p**[1] [piː] *n* (*letter*) P *nt*, p *nt*; **P for Peter** ≈ P wie Paula
p[2] (*Brit*) *abbr* = **penny; pence**
pa [pɑː] (*inf*) *n* Papa *m*
p.a. *abbr* (= *per annum*) p.a.
pace [peɪs] *n* (*step*) Schritt *m*; (*speed*) Tempo *nt* ▷ *vi*: **to ~ up and down** auf und ab gehen; **to keep ~ with** Schritt halten mit; **to set the ~** das Tempo angeben; **to put sb through his/her ~s** (*fig*) jdn auf Herz und Nieren prüfen
pacemaker ['peɪsmeɪkəʳ] *n* (*Med*) (Herz)schrittmacher *m*; (*Sport*: *pacesetter*) Schrittmacher *m*
Pacific [pə'sɪfɪk] *n* (*Geog*): **the ~ (Ocean)** der Pazifik, der Pazifische Ozean
pacifier ['pæsɪfaɪəʳ] (*US*) *n* (*dummy*) Schnuller *m*
pack [pæk] *n* (*packet*) Packung *f*; (*US*: *of cigarettes*) Schachtel *f*; (*of people, hounds*) Meute *f*; (*also*: **back pack**) Rucksack *m*; (*of cards*) (Karten)spiel *nt* ▷ *vt* (*clothes etc*) einpacken; (*suitcase etc, Comput*) packen; (*press down*) pressen ▷ *vi* packen; **to ~ one's bags** (*fig*) die Koffer packen; **to ~ into** (*cram*: *people, objects*) hineinstopfen in +*acc*; **to send sb ~ing** (*inf*) jdn kurz abfertigen
▸ **pack in** (*Brit*: *inf*) *vt* (*job*) hinschmeißen; **~ it in!** hör auf!
▸ **pack off** *vt* schicken
▸ **pack up** *vi* (*Brit*: *inf*: *machine*) den Geist aufgeben; (: *person*) Feierabend machen ▷ *vt* (*belongings*) zusammenpacken
package ['pækɪdʒ] *n* (*parcel, Comput*) Paket *nt*; (*also*: **package deal**) Pauschalangebot *nt* ▷ *vt* verpacken
package holiday (*Brit*), **package tour** (*US*) *n* Pauschalreise *f*
packaging ['pækɪdʒɪŋ] *n* Verpackung *f*
packed [pækt] *adj* (*crowded*) randvoll
packed lunch (*Brit*) *n* Lunchpaket *nt*
packet ['pækɪt] *n* Packung *f*; (*of cigarettes*) Schachtel *m*; **to make a ~** (*Brit*: *inf*) einen Haufen Geld verdienen
packing ['pækɪŋ] *n* (*act*) Packen *nt*; (*material*) Verpackung *f*
packing case *n* Kiste *f*
pact [pækt] *n* Pakt *m*
pad [pæd] *n* (*paper*) Block *m*; (*to prevent damage*) Polster *nt*; (*inf*: *home*) Bude *f* ▷ *vt* (*upholstery etc*) polstern ▷ *vi*: **to ~ about/in** herum-/hereintrotten
padding ['pædɪŋ] *n* (*material*) Polsterung *f*; (*fig*) Füllwerk *nt*
paddle ['pædl] *n* (*oar*) Paddel *nt*; (*US*: *for table tennis*) Schläger *m* ▷ *vt* paddeln ▷ *vi* (*at seaside*) plan(t)schen
paddling pool ['pædlɪŋ-] (*Brit*) *n* Plan(t)schbecken *nt*
paddock ['pædək] *n* (*small field*) Koppel *f*; (*at race course*) Sattelplatz *m*
padlock ['pædlɔk] *n* Vorhängeschloss *nt* ▷ *vt* (mit einem Vorhängeschloss) verschließen
paediatrics, (*US*) **pediatrics** [piːdɪ'ætrɪks] *n* Kinderheilkunde *f*, Pädiatrie *f*
paedophile ['piːdəufaɪl] *n* Pädophile(r) *f(m)* ▷ *adj* pädophil
pagan ['peɪgən] *adj* heidnisch ▷ *n* Heide *m*, Heidin *f*
page [peɪdʒ] *n* (*of book etc*) Seite *f*; (*also*: **pageboy**: *in hotel*) Page *m* ▷ *vt* (*in hotel etc*) ausrufen lassen
pageant ['pædʒənt] *n* (*historical procession*) Festzug *m*; (*show*) Historienspiel *nt*
pageantry ['pædʒəntrɪ] *n* Prunk *m*
pager ['peɪdʒəʳ] *n* Funkrufempfänger *m*, Piepser *m* (*inf*)
paid [peɪd] *pt, pp of* **pay** ▷ *adj* bezahlt; **to put ~ to** (*Brit*) zunichtemachen
pail [peɪl] *n* Eimer *m*
pain [peɪn] *n* Schmerz *m*; (*also*: **pain in the neck**: *inf*: *nuisance*) Plage *f*; **to have a ~ in the chest/arm** Schmerzen in der Brust/im Arm haben; **to be in ~** Schmerzen haben; **to take ~s to do sth** (*make an effort*) sich *dat* Mühe geben, etw zu tun; **on ~ of death** bei Todesstrafe; **he is/it is a right ~ (in the neck)** (*inf*) er/das geht einem auf den Wecker
pained [peɪnd] *adj* (*expression*) gequält
painful ['peɪnful] *adj* (*back, injury etc*) schmerzhaft; (*sight, decision etc*) schmerzlich; (*laborious*) mühsam; (*embarrassing*) peinlich
painfully ['peɪnfəlɪ] *adv* (*fig*: *extremely*) furchtbar
painkiller ['peɪnkɪləʳ] *n* schmerzstillendes Mittel *nt*
painless ['peɪnlɪs] *adj* schmerzlos

painstaking ['peɪnzteɪkɪŋ] *adj* (*work, person*) gewissenhaft
paint [peɪnt] *n* Farbe *f* ▷ *vt* (*door, house etc*) anstreichen; (*person, picture*) malen; (*fig*) zeichnen; **a tin of ~** eine Dose Farbe; **to ~ the door blue** die Tür blau streichen; **to ~ in oils** in Öl malen
paintbrush ['peɪntbrʌʃ] *n* Pinsel *m*
painter ['peɪntəʳ] *n* (*artist*) Maler(in) *m(f)*; (*decorator*) Anstreicher(in) *m(f)*
painting ['peɪntɪŋ] *n* (*activity: of artist*) Malerei *f*; (*: of decorator*) Anstreichen *nt*; (*picture*) Bild *nt*, Gemälde *nt*
paintwork ['peɪntwəːk] *n* (*of wall etc*) Anstrich *m*; (*of car*) Lack *m*
pair [pɛəʳ] *n* Paar *nt*; **a ~ of scissors** eine Schere; **a ~ of trousers** eine Hose
▸ **pair off** *vi*: **to ~ off with sb** sich jdm anschließen
pajamas [pə'dʒɑːməz] (*US*) *npl* Schlafanzug *m*, Pyjama *m*
Pakistan [pɑːkɪ'stɑːn] *n* Pakistan *nt*
Pakistani [pɑːkɪ'stɑːnɪ] *adj* pakistanisch ▷ *n* Pakistani *m*, Pakistaner(in) *m(f)*
pal [pæl] (*inf*) *n* (*friend*) Kumpel *m*, Freund(in) *m(f)*
palace ['pæləs] *n* Palast *m*
palatable ['pælɪtəbl] *adj* (*food, drink*) genießbar; (*fig: idea, fact etc*) angenehm
palate ['pælɪt] *n* (*Anat*) Gaumen *m*; (*sense of taste*) Geschmackssinn *m*
pale [peɪl] *adj* blass; (*light*) fahl ▷ *vi* erblassen ▷ *n*: **beyond the ~** (*unacceptable: behaviour*) indiskutabel; **to grow** *or* **turn ~** erblassen, blass werden; **~ blue** zartblau; **to ~ into insignificance (beside)** zur Bedeutungslosigkeit herabsinken (gegenüber *+dat*)
Palestine ['pælɪstaɪn] *n* Palästina *nt*
Palestinian [pælɪs'tɪnɪən] *adj* palästinensisch ▷ *n* Palästinenser(in) *m(f)*
palette ['pælɪt] *n* Palette *f*
pall [pɔːl] *n* (*cloud of smoke*) (Rauch)wolke *f* ▷ *vi* an Reiz verlieren
pallet ['pælɪt] *n* (*for goods*) Palette *f*
pallid ['pælɪd] *adj* bleich
palm [pɑːm] *n* (*also*: **palm tree**) Palme *f*; (*of hand*) Handteller *m* ▷ *vt*: **to ~ sth off on sb** (*inf*) jdm etw andrehen
Palm Sunday *n* Palmsonntag *m*
paltry ['pɔːltrɪ] *adj* (*amount, wage*) armselig
pamper ['pæmpəʳ] *vt* verwöhnen
pamphlet ['pæmflət] *n* Broschüre *f*; (*political*) Flugschrift *f*
pan [pæn] *n* (*also*: **saucepan**) Topf *m*; (*also*: **frying pan**) Pfanne *f* ▷ *vi* (*Cine, TV*) schwenken ▷ *vt* (*inf: book, film*) verreißen; **to ~ for gold** Gold waschen
pancake ['pænkeɪk] *n* Pfannkuchen *m*
panda ['pændə] *n* Panda *m*
pandemonium [pændɪ'məunɪəm] *n* Chaos *nt*
pander ['pændəʳ] *vi*: **to ~ to** (*person, desire etc*) sich richten nach, entgegenkommen *+dat*
pane [peɪn] *n* (*of glass*) Scheibe *f*
panel ['pænl] *n* (*wood, metal, glass etc*) Platte *f*, Tafel *f*; (*group of experts etc*) Diskussionsrunde *f*; **~ of judges** Jury *f*
panelling, (*US*) **paneling** ['pænəlɪŋ] *n* Täfelung *f*
pang [pæŋ] *n*: **to have** *or* **feel a ~ of regret** Reue empfinden; **hunger ~s** quälender Hunger *m*; **~s of conscience** Gewissensbisse *pl*
panhandler ['pænhændləʳ] (*US: inf*) *n* Bettler(in) *m(f)*
panic ['pænɪk] *n* Panik *f* ▷ *vi* in Panik geraten
panicky ['pænɪkɪ] *adj* (*person*) überängstlich; (*feeling*) Angst-; (*reaction*) Kurzschluss-
panic-stricken ['pænɪkstrɪkən] *adj* (*person, face*) von Panik erfasst
panorama [pænə'rɑːmə] *n* (*view*) Panorama *nt*
pansy ['pænzɪ] *n* (*Bot*) Stiefmütterchen *nt*; (*inf: pej: sissy*) Tunte *f*
pant [pænt] *vi* (*person*) keuchen; (*animal*) hecheln
panther ['pænθəʳ] *n* Pant(h)er *m*
panties ['pæntɪz] *npl* Höschen *nt*
pantry ['pæntrɪ] *n* (*cupboard*) Vorratsschrank *m*; (*room*) Speisekammer *f*
pants [pænts] *npl* (*Brit: woman's*) Höschen *nt*; (*: man's*) Unterhose *f*; (*US: trousers*) Hose *f*
paper ['peɪpəʳ] *n* Papier *nt*; (*also*: **newspaper**) Zeitung *f*; (*exam*) Arbeit *f*; (*academic essay*) Referat *nt*; (*document*) Dokument *nt*, Papier; (*wallpaper*) Tapete *f* ▷ *adj* (*made from paper: hat, plane etc*) Papier-, aus Papier ▷ *vt* (*room*) tapezieren; **papers** *npl* (*also*: **identity papers**) Papiere *pl*; **a piece of ~** (*odd bit*) ein Stück *nt* Papier, ein Zettel *m*; (*sheet*) ein Blatt *nt* Papier; **to put sth down on ~** etw schriftlich festhalten
paperback ['peɪpəbæk] *n* Taschenbuch *nt*, Paperback *nt* ▷ *adj*: **~ edition** Taschenbuchausgabe *f*
paper bag *n* Tüte *f*
paper shop *n* Zeitungsladen *m*
paperweight ['peɪpəweɪt] *n* Briefbeschwerer *m*
paperwork ['peɪpəwəːk] *n* Schreibarbeit *f*
paprika ['pæprɪkə] *n* Paprika *m*
par [pɑːʳ] *n* (*Golf*) Par *nt*; **to be on a ~ with** sich messen können mit; **at ~** (*Comm*) zum Nennwert; **above/below ~** (*Comm*) über/unter dem Nennwert; **above** *or* **over ~** (*Golf*) über dem Par; **below** *or* **under ~** (*Golf*) unter dem Par; **to feel below** *or* **under ~** sich nicht auf der Höhe fühlen; **to be ~ for the course** (*fig*) zu erwarten sein
parachute ['pærəʃuːt] *n* Fallschirm *m*
parade [pə'reɪd] *n* (*procession*) Parade *f*; (*ceremony*) Zeremonie *f* ▷ *vt* (*people*) aufmarschieren lassen; (*wealth, knowledge etc*) zur Schau stellen ▷ *vi* (*Mil*) aufmarschieren; **fashion ~** Modenschau *f*
paradise ['pærədaɪs] *n* (*also fig*) Paradies *nt*
paradox ['pærədɔks] *n* Paradox *nt*

paradoxically [pærə'dɔksɪklɪ] *adv* paradoxerweise
paraffin ['pærəfɪn] *(Brit)* *n* *(also:* **paraffin oil***)* Petroleum *nt*; **liquid ~** Paraffinöl *nt*
paragon ['pærəgən] *n*: **a ~ of** *(honesty, virtue etc)* ein Muster *nt* an *+dat*
paragraph ['pærəgrɑ:f] *n* Absatz *m*, Paragraf *m*; **to begin a new ~** einen neuen Absatz beginnen
parallel ['pærəlɛl] *adj* *(also Comput)* parallel; *(fig: similar)* vergleichbar ▷ *n* Parallele *f*; *(Geog)* Breitenkreis *m*; **to run ~ (with** *or* **to)** *(lit, fig)* parallel verlaufen (zu); **to draw ~s between/with** Parallelen ziehen zwischen/mit; **in ~** *(Elec)* parallel
paralysis [pə'rælɪsɪs] *(pl* **paralyses***)* *n* Lähmung *f*
paralyze ['pærəlaɪz] *(US)* *vt* = **paralyse**
paramedic [pærə'mɛdɪk] *n* Sanitäter(in) *m(f)*; *(in hospital)* medizinisch-technischer Assistent *m*, medizinisch-technische Assistentin *f*
paramount ['pærəmaunt] *adj* vorherrschend; **of ~ importance** von höchster *or* größter Wichtigkeit
paranoid ['pærənɔɪd] *adj* paranoid
paraphernalia [pærəfə'neɪlɪə] *n* Utensilien *pl*
parasite ['pærəsaɪt] *n* *(also fig)* Parasit *m*
parasol ['pærəsɔl] *n* Sonnenschirm *m*
paratrooper ['pærətru:pə^r] *n* Fallschirmjäger *m*
parcel ['pɑ:sl] *n* Paket *nt* ▷ *vt* *(also:* **parcel up***)* verpacken
▸ **parcel out** *vt* aufteilen
parchment ['pɑ:tʃmənt] *n* Pergament *nt*
pardon ['pɑ:dn] *n* *(Law)* Begnadigung *f* ▷ *vt* *(forgive)* verzeihen *+dat*, vergeben *+dat*; *(Law)* begnadigen; **~ me!, I beg your pardon!** *(I'm sorry!)* verzeihen Sie bitte!; **(I beg your) ~?, ~ me?** *(US: what did you say?)* bitte?
parent ['pɛərənt] *n* *(mother)* Mutter *f*; *(father)* Vater *m*; **parents** *npl* *(mother and father)* Eltern *pl*
parental [pə'rɛntl] *adj* *(love, control etc)* elterlich
Paris ['pærɪs] *n* Paris *nt*
parish ['pærɪʃ] *n* Gemeinde *f*
Parisian [pə'rɪzɪən] *adj* Pariser *inv*, paris(er)isch ▷ *n* Pariser(in) *m(f)*
park [pɑ:k] *n* Park *m* ▷ *vt, vi* *(Aut)* parken
parking ['pɑ:kɪŋ] *n* Parken *nt*; **"no ~"** "Parken verboten"
parking lot *(US)* *n* Parkplatz *m*
parking meter *n* Parkuhr *f*
parking ticket *n* Strafzettel *m*
parkway ['pɑ:kweɪ] *(US)* *n* Allee *f*
parliament ['pɑ:ləmənt] *n* Parlament *nt*
parliamentary [pɑ:lə'mɛntərɪ] *adj* parlamentarisch
parlour, *(US)* **parlor** ['pɑ:lə^r] *n* Salon *m*
Parmesan [pɑ:mɪ'zæn] *n* *(also:* **Parmesan cheese***)* Parmesan(käse) *m*
parochial [pə'rəukɪəl] *(pej)* *adj* *(person, attitude)* engstirnig
parole [pə'rəul] *n* *(Law)* Bewährung *f*; **on ~** auf Bewährung
parrot ['pærət] *n* Papagei *m*
parry ['pærɪ] *vt* *(blow, argument)* parieren, abwehren
parsley ['pɑ:slɪ] *n* Petersilie *f*
parsnip ['pɑ:snɪp] *n* Pastinake *f*
parson ['pɑ:sn] *n* Pfarrer *m*
part [pɑ:t] *n* Teil *m*; *(Tech)* Teil *nt*; *(Theat, Cine etc: role)* Rolle *f*; *(US: in hair)* Scheitel *m*; *(Mus)* Stimme *f* ▷ *adv* = **partly** ▷ *vt* *(separate)* trennen; *(hair)* scheiteln ▷ *vi* *(roads, people)* sich trennen; *(crowd)* sich teilen; **to take ~ in** teilnehmen an *+dat*; **to take sth in good ~** etw nicht übel nehmen; **to take sb's ~** *(support)* sich auf jds Seite *acc* stellen; **on his ~** seinerseits; **for my ~** für meinen Teil; **for the most ~** *(generally)* zumeist; **for the better** *or* **best ~ of the day** die meiste Zeit des Tages; **to be ~ and parcel of** dazugehören zu; **~ of speech** *(Ling)* Wortart *f*
▸ **part with** *vt fus* sich trennen von
part exchange *(Brit)* *n*: **to give/take sth in ~** etw in Zahlung geben/nehmen
partial ['pɑ:ʃl] *adj* *(victory, solution)* Teil-; *(support)* teilweise; *(biassed)* parteiisch; **to be ~ to** *(person, drink etc)* eine Vorliebe haben für
participant [pɑ:'tɪsɪpənt] *n* Teilnehmer(in) *m(f)*
participate [pɑ:'tɪsɪpeɪt] *vi* sich beteiligen; **to ~ in** teilnehmen an *+dat*
participation [pɑ:tɪsɪ'peɪʃən] *n* Teilnahme *f*
participle ['pɑ:tɪsɪpl] *n* Partizip *nt*
particle ['pɑ:tɪkl] *n* Teilchen *nt*, Partikel *f*
particular [pə'tɪkjulə^r] *adj* *(distinct: person, time, place etc)* bestimmt, speziell; *(special)* speziell, besondere(r, s) ▷ *n*: **in ~** im Besonderen, besonders; **particulars** *npl* Einzelheiten *pl*; *(name, address etc)* Personalien *pl*; **to be very ~ about sth** *(fussy)* in Bezug auf etw *acc* sehr eigen sein
particularly [pə'tɪkjuləlɪ] *adv* besonders
parting ['pɑ:tɪŋ] *n* *(action)* Teilung *f*; *(farewell)* Abschied *m*; *(Brit: in hair)* Scheitel *m* ▷ *adj* *(words, gift etc)* Abschieds-; **his ~ shot was ...** *(fig)* seine Bemerkung zum Abschied war ...
partisan [pɑ:tɪ'zæn] *adj* *(politics, views)* voreingenommen ▷ *n* *(supporter)* Anhänger(in) *m(f)*; *(fighter)* Partisan *m*
partition [pɑ:'tɪʃən] *n* *(wall, screen)* Trennwand *f*; *(of country)* Teilung *f* ▷ *vt* *(room, office)* aufteilen; *(country)* teilen
partly ['pɑ:tlɪ] *adv* teilweise, zum Teil
partner ['pɑ:tnə^r] *n* Partner(in) *m(f)*; *(Comm)* Partner(in), Teilhaber(in) *m(f)* ▷ *vt* *(at dance, cards etc)* als Partner(in) haben
partnership ['pɑ:tnəʃɪp] *n* *(Pol etc)* Partnerschaft *f*; *(Comm)* Teilhaberschaft *f*; **to go into ~ (with sb), form a ~ (with sb)** (mit jdm) eine Partnerschaft eingehen
partridge ['pɑ:trɪdʒ] *n* Rebhuhn *nt*
part-time ['pɑ:t'taɪm] *adj* *(work, staff)* Teilzeit-,

Halbtags- ▷ *adv*: **to work ~** Teilzeit arbeiten; **to study ~** Teilzeitstudent(in) *m(f)* sein

party ['pɑ:tɪ] *n* (*Pol, Law*) Partei *f*; (*celebration, social event*) Party *f*, Fete *f*; (*group of people*) Gruppe *f*, Gesellschaft *f* ▷ *cpd* (*Pol*) Partei-; **dinner ~** Abendgesellschaft *f*; **to give** *or* **throw a ~** eine Party geben, eine Fete machen; **we're having a ~ next Saturday** bei uns ist nächsten Samstag eine Party; **our son's birthday ~** die Geburtstagsfeier unseres Sohnes; **to be a ~ to a crime** an einem Verbrechen beteiligt sein

party dress *n* Partykleid *nt*

pass [pɑ:s] *vt* (*spend: time*) verbringen; (*hand over*) reichen, geben; (*go past*) vorbeikommen an *+dat*; (*: in car*) vorbeifahren an *+dat*; (*overtake*) überholen; (*fig: exceed*) übersteigen; (*exam*) bestehen; (*law, proposal*) genehmigen ▷ *vi* (*go past*) vorbeigehen; (*: in car*) vorbeifahren; (*in exam*) bestehen ▷ *n* (*permit*) Ausweis *m*; (*in mountains, Sport*) Pass *m*; **to ~ sth through sth** etw durch etw führen; **to ~ the ball to** den Ball zuspielen *+dat*; **could you ~ the vegetables round?** könnten Sie das Gemüse herumreichen?; **to get a ~ in ...** (*Scol*) die Prüfung in ... bestehen; **things have come to a pretty ~ when ...** (*Brit: inf*) so weit ist es schon gekommen, dass ...; **to make a ~ at sb** (*inf*) jdn anmachen

▸ **pass away** *vi* (*die*) dahinscheiden

▸ **pass by** *vi* (*go past*) vorbeigehen; (*: in car*) vorbeifahren ▷ *vt* (*ignore*) vorbeigehen an *+dat*

▸ **pass down** *vt* (*customs, inheritance*) weitergeben

▸ **pass for** *vt*: **she could ~ for 25** sie könnte für 25 durchgehen

▸ **pass on** *vi* (*die*) verscheiden ▷ *vt*: **to ~ on (to)** weitergeben (an *+acc*)

▸ **pass out** *vi* (*faint*) ohnmächtig werden; (*Brit: Mil*) die Ausbildung beenden

▸ **pass over** *vt* (*ignore*) übergehen ▷ *vi* (*die*) entschlafen

▸ **pass up** *vt* (*opportunity*) sich *dat* entgehen lassen

passable ['pɑ:səbl] *adj* (*road*) passierbar; (*acceptable*) passabel

passage ['pæsɪdʒ] *n* Gang *m*; (*in book*) Passage *f*; (*way through crowd etc, Anat*) Weg *m*; (*act of passing: of train etc*) Durchfahrt *f*; (*journey: on boat*) Überfahrt *f*

passenger ['pæsɪndʒə^r] *n* (*in boat, plane*) Passagier *m*; (*in car*) Fahrgast *m*

passer-by [pɑ:sə'baɪ] (*pl* **passers-by**) *n* Passant(in) *m(f)*

passing ['pɑ:sɪŋ] *adj* (*moment, thought etc*) flüchtig; **in ~** (*incidentally*) beiläufig, nebenbei; **to mention sth in ~** etw beiläufig *or* nebenbei erwähnen

passing place *n* (*Aut*) Ausweichstelle *f*

passion ['pæʃən] *n* Leidenschaft *f*; **to have a ~ for sth** eine Leidenschaft für etw haben

passionate ['pæʃənɪt] *adj* leidenschaftlich

passion fruit *n* Passionsfrucht *f*, Maracuja *f*

passive ['pæsɪv] *adj* passiv; (*Ling*) Passiv- ▷ *n* (*Ling*) Passiv *nt*

passive smoking *n* passives Rauchen, Passivrauchen *nt*

Passover ['pɑ:səuvə^r] *n* Passah(fest) *nt*

passport ['pɑ:spɔ:t] *n* Pass *m*; (*fig: to success etc*) Schlüssel *m*

passport control *n* Passkontrolle *f*

passport office *n* Passamt *nt*

password ['pɑ:swə:d] *n* Kennwort *nt*; (*Comput*) Passwort *nt*

past [pɑ:st] *prep* (*in front of*) vorbei an *+dat*; (*beyond*) hinter *+dat*; (*later than*) nach ▷ *adj* (*government etc*) früher, ehemalig; (*week, month etc*) vergangen ▷ *n* Vergangenheit *f* ▷ *adv*: **to run ~** vorbeilaufen; **he's ~ 40** er ist über 40; **it's ~ midnight** es ist nach Mitternacht; **ten/quarter ~ eight** zehn/Viertel nach acht; **he ran ~ me** er lief an mir vorbei; **I'm ~ caring** es kümmert mich nicht mehr; **to be ~ it** (*Brit: inf: person*) es nicht mehr bringen; **for the ~ few/3 days** während der letzten Tage/3 Tage; **in the ~** (*also Ling*) in der Vergangenheit

pasta ['pæstə] *n* Nudeln *pl*

paste [peɪst] *n* (*wet mixture*) Teig *m*; (*glue*) Kleister *m*; (*jewellery*) Strass *m*; (*fish, tomato paste*) Paste *f* ▷ *vt* (*stick*) kleben

pastel ['pæstl] *adj* (*colour*) Pastell-

pasteurized ['pæstʃəraɪzd] *adj* pasteurisiert

pastille ['pæstɪl] *n* Pastille *f*

pastime ['pɑ:staɪm] *n* Zeitvertreib *m*, Hobby *nt*

pastor ['pɑ:stə^r] *n* Pastor(in) *m(f)*

pastry ['peɪstrɪ] *n* (*dough*) Teig *m*; (*cake*) Gebäckstück *nt*

pasture ['pɑ:stʃə^r] *n* Weide *f*

pasty [*n* 'pæstɪ, *adj* 'peɪstɪ] *n* (*pie*) Pastete *f* ▷ *adj* (*complexion*) bläßlich

pat [pæt] *vt* (*with hand*) tätscheln ▷ *adj* (*answer, remark*) glatt ▷ *n*: **to give sb/o.s. a ~ on the back** (*fig*) jdm/sich auf die Schulter klopfen; **he knows it off ~, he has it down ~** (*US*) er kennt das in- und auswendig

patch [pætʃ] *n* (*piece of material*) Flicken *m*; (*also*: **eye patch**) Augenklappe *f*; (*damp, bald etc*) Fleck *m*; (*of land*) Stück *nt*; (*: for growing vegetables etc*) Beet *nt* ▷ *vt* (*clothes*) flicken; **(to go through) a bad ~** eine schwierige Zeit (durchmachen)

▸ **patch up** *vt* (*clothes etc*) flicken; (*quarrel*) beilegen

patchy ['pætʃɪ] *adj* (*colour*) ungleichmäßig; (*information, knowledge etc*) lückenhaft

pâté ['pæteɪ] *n* Pastete *f*

patent ['peɪtnt] *n* Patent *nt* ▷ *vt* patentieren lassen ▷ *adj* (*obvious*) offensichtlich

patent leather *n* Lackleder *nt*

paternal [pə'tə:nl] *adj* väterlich; **my ~ grandmother** meine Großmutter väterlicherseits

paternity leave *n* Vaterschaftsurlaub *m*

path [pɑ:θ] *n* (*also fig*) Weg *m*; (*trail, track*) Pfad

m; (*trajectory: of bullet, aircraft, planet*) Bahn *f*
pathetic [pə'θɛtɪk] *adj* (*pitiful*) mitleiderregend; (*very bad*) erbärmlich
pathological [pæθə'lɔdʒɪkl] *adj* (*liar, hatred*) krankhaft; (*Med*) pathologisch
pathway ['pɑːθweɪ] *n* Pfad *m*, Weg *m*; (*fig*) Weg
patience ['peɪʃns] *n* Geduld *f*; (*Brit: Cards*) Patience *f*; **to lose (one's) ~** die Geduld verlieren
patient ['peɪʃnt] *n* Patient(in) *m(f)* ▷ *adj* geduldig; **to be ~ with sb** Geduld mit jdm haben
patio ['pætɪəu] *n* Terrasse *f*
patriotic [pætrɪ'ɔtɪk] *adj* patriotisch
patrol [pə'trəul] *n* (*Mil*) Patrouille *f*; (*Police*) Streife *f* ▷ *vt* (*Mil, Police: city, streets etc*) patrouillieren; **to be on ~** (*Mil*) auf Patrouille sein; (*Police*) auf Streife sein
patrol car *n* Streifenwagen *m*
patrolman [pə'trəulmən] (*US irreg: like* **man**) *n* (*Police*) (Streifen)polizist *m*
patron ['peɪtrən] *n* (*customer*) Kunde *m*, Kundin *f*; (*benefactor*) Förderer *m*; **~ of the arts** Kunstmäzen *m*
patronize ['pætrənaɪz] *vt* (*pej: look down on*) von oben herab behandeln; (*artist etc*) fördern; (*shop, club*) besuchen
patronizing ['pætrənaɪzɪŋ] *adj* herablassend
patter ['pætəʳ] *n* (*of feet*) Trappeln *nt*; (*of rain*) Prasseln *nt*; (*sales talk etc*) Sprüche *pl* ▷ *vi* (*footsteps*) trappeln; (*rain*) prasseln
pattern ['pætən] *n* Muster *nt*; (*Sewing*) Schnittmuster *nt*; **behaviour ~s** Verhaltensmuster *pl*
patterned ['pætənd] *adj* gemustert; **~ with flowers** mit Blumenmuster
pauper ['pɔːpəʳ] *n* Arme(r) *f(m)*; **~'s grave** Armengrab *nt*
pause [pɔːz] *n* Pause *f* ▷ *vi* eine Pause machen; (*hesitate*) innehalten; **to ~ for breath** eine Verschnaufpause einlegen
pave [peɪv] *vt* (*street, yard etc*) pflastern; **to ~ the way for** (*fig*) den Weg bereiten *or* bahnen für
pavement ['peɪvmənt] *n* (*Brit*) Bürgersteig *m*; (*US: roadway*) Straße *f*
pavilion [pə'vɪlɪən] *n* (*Sport*) Klubhaus *nt*
paving ['peɪvɪŋ] *n* (*material*) Straßenbelag *m*
paving stone *n* Pflasterstein *m*
paw [pɔː] *n* (*of cat, dog etc*) Pfote *f*; (*of lion, bear etc*) Tatze *f*, Pranke *f* ▷ *vt* (*pej: touch*) betatschen; **to ~ the ground** (*animal*) scharren
pawn [pɔːn] *n* (*Chess*) Bauer *m*; (*fig*) Schachfigur *f* ▷ *vt* versetzen
pawnbroker ['pɔːnbrəukəʳ] *n* Pfandleiher *m*
pawnshop ['pɔːnʃɔp] *n* Pfandhaus *nt*
pay [peɪ] (*pt, pp* **paid**) *n* (*wage*) Lohn *m*; (*salary*) Gehalt *nt* ▷ *vt* (*sum of money, wage*) zahlen; (*bill, person*) bezahlen ▷ *vi* (*be profitable*) sich bezahlt machen; (*fig*) sich lohnen; **how much did you ~ for it?** wie viel hast du dafür bezahlt?; **I paid 10 pounds for that book** ich habe 10 Pfund für das Buch bezahlt, das Buch hat mich 10 Pfund gekostet; **to ~ one's way** seinen Beitrag leisten; **to ~ dividends** (*fig*) sich bezahlt machen; **to ~ the price/penalty for sth** (*fig*) den Preis/die Strafe für etw zahlen; **to ~ sb a compliment** jdm ein Kompliment machen; **to ~ attention (to)** achtgeben (auf +*acc*); **to ~ sb a visit** jdn besuchen; **to ~ one's respects to sb** jdm seine Aufwartung machen
▸ **pay back** *vt* zurückzahlen; **I'll ~ you back next week** ich gebe dir das Geld nächste Woche zurück
▸ **pay for** *vt fus* (*also fig*) (be)zahlen für
▸ **pay in** *vt* einzahlen
▸ **pay off** *vt* (*debt*) abbezahlen; (*person*) auszahlen; (*creditor*) befriedigen; (*mortgage*) tilgen ▷ *vi* sich auszahlen; **to ~ sth off in instalments** etw in Raten (ab)zahlen
▸ **pay out** *vt* (*money*) ausgeben; (*rope*) ablaufen lassen
▸ **pay up** *vi* zahlen
payable ['peɪəbl] *adj* zahlbar; **to make a cheque ~ to sb** einen Scheck auf jdn ausstellen
payee [peɪ'iː] *n* Zahlungsempfänger *m*
pay envelope (*US*) *n* = **pay packet**
payment ['peɪmənt] *n* (*act*) Zahlung *f*, Bezahlung *f*; (*of bill*) Begleichung *f*; (*sum of money*) Zahlung *f*; **advance ~** (*part sum*) Anzahlung *f*; (*total sum*) Vorauszahlung *f*; **deferred payment, ~ by instalments** Ratenzahlung *f*; **monthly ~** (*sum of money*) Monatsrate *f*; **on ~ of** gegen Zahlung von
pay packet (*Brit*) *n* Lohntüte *f*
payroll ['peɪrəul] *n* Lohnliste *f*; **to be on a firm's ~** bei einer Firma beschäftigt sein
pay slip (*Brit*) *n see* **pay** Lohnstreifen *m*; Gehaltsstreifen *m*
PC *n abbr* (*= personal computer*) PC *m*; (*Brit*) = **police constable** ▷ *adj abbr* = **politically correct** ▷ *abbr* (*Brit*) = **Privy Councillor**
pcm *abbr* (*= per calendar month*) pro Monat
PDA *abbr* (*Comput*) *of* **personal digital assistant** PDA *m*
PE *n abbr* (*Scol*) = **physical education**
pea [piː] *n* Erbse *f*
peace [piːs] *n* Frieden *m*; **to be at ~ with sb/sth** mit jdm/etw in Frieden leben; **to keep the ~** (*policeman*) die öffentliche Ordnung aufrechterhalten; (*citizen*) den Frieden wahren
peaceful ['piːsful] *adj* friedlich
peach [piːtʃ] *n* Pfirsich *m*
peacock ['piːkɔk] *n* Pfau *m*
peak [piːk] *n* (*of mountain*) Spitze *f*, Gipfel *m*; (*of cap*) Schirm *m*; (*fig*) Höhepunkt *m*
peak hours *npl* Stoßzeit *f*
peal [piːl] *n* (*of bells*) Läuten *nt*; **~s of laughter** schallendes Gelächter *nt*
peanut ['piːnʌt] *n* Erdnuss *f*
peanut butter *n* Erdnussbutter *f*

pear [pɛəʳ] *n* Birne *f*
pearl [pə:l] *n* Perle *f*
peasant ['pɛznt] *n* Bauer *m*
peat [pi:t] *n* Torf *m*
pebble ['pɛbl] *n* Kieselstein *m*
peck [pɛk] *vt* (*bird*) picken; (*also*: **peck at**) picken an *+dat* ▷ *n* (*of bird*) Schnabelhieb *m*; (*kiss*) Küsschen *nt*
pecking order ['pɛkɪŋ-] *n* (*fig*) Hackordnung *f*
peckish ['pɛkɪʃ] (*Brit*: *inf*) *adj* (*hungry*) leicht hungrig; **I'm feeling ~** ich könnte was zu essen gebrauchen
peculiar [pɪ'kju:lɪəʳ] *adj* (*strange*) seltsam; **~ to** (*exclusive to*) charakteristisch für
pedal ['pɛdl] *n* Pedal *nt* ▷ *vi* in die Pedale treten
pedantic [pɪ'dæntɪk] *adj* pedantisch
peddler ['pɛdləʳ] *n* (*also*: **drug peddler**) Pusher *m*
pedestal ['pɛdəstl] *n* Sockel *m*
pedestrian [pɪ'dɛstrɪən] *n* Fußgänger(in) *m(f)* ▷ *adj* Fußgänger-; (*fig*) langweilig
pedestrian crossing (*Brit*) *n* Fußgängerüberweg *m*
pedestrian precinct (*Brit*) *n* Fußgängerzone *f*
pediatrics [pi:dɪ'ætrɪks] (*US*) *n* = **paediatrics**
pedigree ['pɛdɪgri:] *n* (*of animal*) Stammbaum *m*; (*fig*: *background*) Vorgeschichte *f* ▷ *cpd* (*dog*) Rasse-, reinrassig
pee [pi:] (*inf*) *vi* pinkeln
peek [pi:k] *vi*: **to ~ at/over/into** *etc* gucken nach/über *+acc*/in *+acc etc* ▷ *n*: **to have** *or* **take a ~ (at)** einen (kurzen) Blick werfen (auf *+acc*)
peel [pi:l] *n* Schale *f* ▷ *vt* schälen ▷ *vi* (*paint*) abblättern; (*wallpaper*) sich lösen; (*skin, back etc*) sich schälen
▸ **peel back** *vt* abziehen
peep [pi:p] *n* (*look*) kurzer Blick *m*; (*sound*) Pieps *m* ▷ *vi* (*look*) gucken; **to have** *or* **take a ~ (at)** einen kurzen Blick werfen (auf *+acc*)
▸ **peep out** *vi* (*be visible*) hervorgucken
peephole ['pi:phəul] *n* Guckloch *nt*
peer [pɪəʳ] *n* (*noble*) Peer *m*; (*equal*) Gleichrangige(r) *f(m)*; (*contemporary*) Gleichaltrige(r) *f(m)* ▷ *vi*: **to ~ at** starren auf *+acc*
peerage ['pɪərɪdʒ] *n* (*title*) Adelswürde *f*; (*position*) Adelsstand *m*; **the ~** (*all the peers*) der Adel
peeved [pi:vd] *adj* verärgert, sauer (*inf*)
peg [pɛg] *n* (*hook, knob*) Haken *m*; (*Brit*: *also*: **clothes peg**) Wäscheklammer *f*; (*also*: **tent peg**) Zeltpflock *m*, Hering *m* ▷ *vt* (*washing*) festklammern; (*prices*) festsetzen; **off the ~** von der Stange
Pekinese [pi:kɪ'ni:z] *n* = **Pekingese**
pelican ['pɛlɪkən] *n* Pelikan *m*
pelican crossing (*Brit*) *n* (*Aut*) Fußgängerüberweg *m* mit Ampel
pellet ['pɛlɪt] *n* (*of paper etc*) Kügelchen *nt*; (*of mud etc*) Klümpchen *nt*; (*for shotgun*) Schrotkugel *f*
pelt [pɛlt] *vi* (*rain*: *also*: **pelt down**) niederprasseln; (*inf*: *run*) rasen ▷ *n* (*animal skin*) Pelz *m*, Fell *nt* ▷ *vt*: **to ~ sb with sth** jdn mit etw bewerfen
pelvis ['pɛlvɪs] *n* Becken *nt*
pen [pɛn] *n* (*also*: **fountain pen**) Füller *m*; (*also*: **ballpoint pen**) Kugelschreiber *m*; (*also*: **felt-tip pen**) Filzstift *m*; (*enclosure*: *for sheep, pigs etc*) Pferch *m*; (*US*: *inf*: *prison*) Knast *m*; **to put ~ to paper** zur Feder greifen
penal ['pi:nl] *adj* (*Law*: *colony, institution*) Straf-; (: *system, reform*) Strafrechts-; **~ code** Strafgesetzbuch *nt*
penalize ['pi:nəlaɪz] *vt* (*punish*) bestrafen; (*fig*) benachteiligen
penalty ['pɛnltɪ] *n* Strafe *f*; (*Sport*) Strafstoß *m*; (: *Football*) Elfmeter *m*
penance ['pɛnəns] *n* (*Rel*): **to do ~ for one's sins** für seine Sünden Buße tun
pence [pɛns] *npl of* **penny**
pencil ['pɛnsl] *n* Bleistift *m* ▷ *vt*: **to ~ sb/sth in** jdn/etw vormerken
pencil case *n* Federmäppchen *nt*
pencil sharpener *n* Bleistiftspitzer *m*
pendant ['pɛndnt] *n* Anhänger *m*
pending ['pɛndɪŋ] *adj* anstehend ▷ *prep*: **~ his return** bis zu seiner Rückkehr; **~ a decision** bis eine Entscheidung getroffen ist
pendulum ['pɛndjuləm] *n* Pendel *nt*
penetrate ['pɛnɪtreɪt] *vt* (*person*: *territory etc*) durchdringen; (*light, water, sound*) eindringen in *+acc*
penguin ['pɛŋgwɪn] *n* Pinguin *m*
penicillin [pɛnɪ'sɪlɪn] *n* Penizillin *nt*
peninsula [pə'nɪnsjulə] *n* Halbinsel *f*
penis ['pi:nɪs] *n* Penis *m*
penitentiary [pɛnɪ'tɛnʃərɪ] (*US*) *n* Gefängnis *nt*
penknife ['pɛnnaɪf] *n* Taschenmesser *nt*
pen name *n* Pseudonym *nt*
penniless ['pɛnɪlɪs] *adj* mittellos
penny ['pɛnɪ] (*Brit*) (*pl* **pence**) *n* Penny *m*; (*US*) Cent *m*; **it was worth every ~** es war jeden Pfennig wert; **it won't cost you a ~** es kostet dich keinen Pfennig
pension ['pɛnʃən] *n* Rente *f*
▸ **pension off** *vt* (vorzeitig) pensionieren
pensioner ['pɛnʃənəʳ] (*Brit*) *n* Rentner(in) *m(f)*
pentagon ['pɛntəgən] (*US*) *n*: **the P~** das Pentagon
Pentecost ['pɛntɪkɔst] *n* (*in Judaism*) Erntefest *nt*; (*in Christianity*) Pfingsten *nt*
penthouse ['pɛnthaus] *n* Penthouse *nt*
pent-up ['pɛntʌp] *adj* (*feelings*) aufgestaut
penultimate [pɛ'nʌltɪmət] *adj* vorletzte(r, s)
people ['pi:pl] *npl* (*persons*) Leute *pl*; (*inhabitants*) Bevölkerung *f* ▷ *n* (*nation, race*) Volk *nt*; **old ~** alte Menschen *or* Leute; **young ~** junge Leute; **the room was full of ~** das Zimmer war voller Leute *or* Menschen; **several ~ came** mehrere (Leute) kamen; **~ say that ...** man sagt, dass ...; **the ~** (*Pol*) das Volk; **a man of the ~** ein Mann des Volkes

pepper ['pɛpəʳ] *n* (*spice*) Pfeffer *m*; (*vegetable*) Paprika *m* ▷ *vt*: **to ~ with** (*fig*) übersäen mit; **two ~s** zwei Paprikaschoten
pepper mill *n* Pfeffermühle *f*
peppermint ['pɛpəmɪnt] *n* (*sweet*) Pfefferminz *nt*; (*plant*) Pfefferminze *f*
pep talk (*inf*) *n* aufmunternde Worte *pl*
per [pəːʳ] *prep* (*for each*) pro; **~ day/person/kilo** pro Tag/Person/Kilo; **~ annum** pro Jahr; **as ~ your instructions** gemäß Ihren Anweisungen
perceive [pə'siːv] *vt* (*see*) wahrnehmen; (*view, understand*) verstehen
per cent *n* Prozent *nt*; **a 20 ~ discount** 20 Prozent Rabatt
percentage [pə'sɛntɪdʒ] *n* Prozentsatz *m*; **on a ~ basis** auf Prozentbasis
perception [pə'sɛpʃən] *n* (*insight*) Einsicht *f*; (*opinion, understanding*) Erkenntnis *f*; (*faculty*) Wahrnehmung *f*
perceptive [pə'sɛptɪv] *adj* (*person*) aufmerksam; (*analysis etc*) erkenntnisreich
perch [pəːtʃ] *n* (*for bird*) Stange *f*; (*fish*) Flussbarsch *m* ▷ *vi*: **to ~ (on)** (*bird*) sitzen (auf +*dat*); (*person*) hocken (auf +*dat*)
percolator ['pəːkəleɪtəʳ] *n* (*also*: **coffee percolator**) Kaffeemaschine *f*
percussion [pə'kʌʃən] *n* (*Mus*) Schlagzeug *nt*
perennial [pə'rɛnɪəl] *adj* (*plant*) mehrjährig; (*fig: problem, feature etc*) immer wiederkehrend ▷ *n* (*Bot*) mehrjährige Pflanze *f*
perfect [*adj, n* 'pəːfɪkt, *vt* pə'fɛkt] *adj* perfekt; (*nonsense, idiot etc*) ausgemacht ▷ *vt* (*technique*) perfektionieren ▷ *n*: **the ~** (*also*: **the perfect tense**) das Perfekt; **he's a ~ stranger to me** er ist mir vollkommen fremd
perfection [pə'fɛkʃən] *n* Perfektion *f*, Vollkommenheit *f*
perfectly ['pəːfɪktlɪ] *adv* vollkommen; (*faultlessly*) perfekt; **I'm ~ happy with the situation** ich bin mit der Lage vollkommen zufrieden; **you know ~ well that ...** Sie wissen ganz genau, dass ...
perforate ['pəːfəreɪt] *vt* perforieren
perforation [pəːfə'reɪʃən] *n* (*small hole*) Loch *nt*; (*line of holes*) Perforation *f*
perform [pə'fɔːm] *vt* (*operation, ceremony etc*) durchführen; (*task*) erfüllen; (*piece of music, play etc*) aufführen ▷ *vi* auftreten; **to ~ well/badly** eine gute/schlechte Leistung zeigen
performance [pə'fɔːməns] *n* Leistung *f*; (*of play, show*) Vorstellung *f*; **the team put up a good ~** die Mannschaft zeigte eine gute Leistung
performer [pə'fɔːməʳ] *n* Künstler(in) *m(f)*
perfume ['pəːfjuːm] *n* Parfüm *nt*; (*fragrance*) Duft *m* ▷ *vt* parfümieren
perhaps [pə'hæps] *adv* vielleicht; **~ he'll come** er kommt vielleicht; **~ not** vielleicht nicht
peril ['pɛrɪl] *n* Gefahr *f*
perimeter [pə'rɪmɪtəʳ] *n* Umfang *m*
period ['pɪərɪəd] *n* (*length of time*) Zeitraum *m*, Periode *f*; (*era*) Zeitalter *nt*; (*Scol*) Stunde *f*; (*esp US: full stop*) Punkt *m*; (*Med: also*: **menstrual period**) Periode ▷ *adj* (*costume etc*) zeitgenössisch; **for a ~ of 3 weeks** für eine Dauer *or* einen Zeitraum von 3 Wochen; **the holiday ~** (*Brit*) die Urlaubszeit; **I won't do it. P~.** ich mache das nicht, und damit basta!
periodical [pɪərɪ'ɔdɪkl] *n* Zeitschrift *f* ▷ *adj* periodisch
periodically [pɪərɪ'ɔdɪklɪ] *adv* periodisch
peripheral [pə'rɪfərəl] *adj* (*feature, issue*) Rand-, nebensächlich; (*vision*) peripher ▷ *n* (*Comput*) Peripheriegerät *nt*
perish ['pɛrɪʃ] *vi* (*die*) umkommen; (*rubber, leather etc*) verschleißen
perishable ['pɛrɪʃəbl] *adj* (*food*) leicht verderblich
perjury ['pəːdʒərɪ] *n* (*in court*) Meineid *m*; (*breach of oath*) Eidesverletzung *f*
perky ['pəːkɪ] *adj* (*cheerful*) munter
perm [pəːm] *n* Dauerwelle *f* ▷ *vt*: **to have one's hair ~ed** sich *dat* eine Dauerwelle machen lassen
permanent ['pəːmənənt] *adj* dauerhaft; (*job, position*) fest; **~ address** ständiger Wohnsitz *m*; **I'm not ~ here** ich bin hier nicht fest angestellt
permanently ['pəːmənəntlɪ] *adv* (*damage*) dauerhaft; (*stay, live*) ständig; (*locked, open, frozen etc*) dauernd
permeate ['pəːmɪeɪt] *vt* durchdringen ▷ *vi*: **to ~ through** dringen durch
permissible [pə'mɪsɪbl] *adj* zulässig
permission [pə'mɪʃən] *n* Erlaubnis *f*, Genehmigung *f*; **to give sb ~ to do sth** jdm die Erlaubnis geben, etw zu tun
permissive [pə'mɪsɪv] *adj* permissiv
permit [*n* 'pəːmɪt, *vt* pə'mɪt] *n* Genehmigung *f* ▷ *vt* (*allow*) erlauben; (*make possible*) gestatten; **fishing ~** Angelschein *m*; **to ~ sb to do sth** jdm erlauben, etw zu tun; **weather ~ting** wenn das Wetter es zulässt
perpendicular [pəːpən'dɪkjuləʳ] *adj* senkrecht ▷ *n*: **the ~** die Senkrechte; **~ to** senkrecht zu
perplex [pə'plɛks] *vt* verblüffen
persecute ['pəːsɪkjuːt] *vt* verfolgen
persecution [pəːsɪ'kjuːʃən] *n* Verfolgung *f*
persevere [pəːsɪ'vɪəʳ] *vi* durchhalten, beharren
Persian ['pəːʃən] *adj* persisch ▷ *n* (*Ling*) Persisch *nt*; **the (persian) Gulf** der (Persische) Golf
persist [pə'sɪst] *vi*: **to ~ (with** *or* **in)** beharren (auf +*dat*), festhalten (an +*dat*); **to ~ in doing sth** darauf beharren, etw zu tun
persistent [pə'sɪstənt] *adj* (*person, noise*) beharrlich; (*smell, cough etc*) hartnäckig; (*lateness, rain*) andauernd; **~ offender** Wiederholungstäter(in) *m(f)*
person ['pəːsn] *n* Person *f*, Mensch *m*; **in ~** persönlich; **on** *or* **about one's ~** bei sich; **~ to ~ call** (*Tel*) Gespräch *nt* mit Voranmeldung
personal ['pəːsnl] *adj* persönlich; (*life*) Privat-;

nothing ~! nehmen Sie es nicht persönlich!
personal assistant *n* persönlicher Referent *m*, persönliche Referentin *f*
personal column *n* private Kleinanzeigen *pl*
personal computer *n* Personal Computer *m*
personality [pə:sə'nælɪtɪ] *n* (*character, person*) Persönlichkeit *f*
personally ['pə:snəlɪ] *adv* persönlich; **to take sth ~** etw persönlich nehmen
personal organizer *n* Terminplaner *m*
personal stereo *n* Walkman® *m*
personnel [pə:sə'nɛl] *n* Personal *nt*
perspective [pə'spɛktɪv] *n* (*also fig*) Perspektive *f*; **to get sth into ~** (*fig*) etw in Relation zu anderen Dingen sehen
perspiration [pə:spɪ'reɪʃən] *n* Transpiration *f*
persuade [pə'sweɪd] *vt*: **to ~ sb to do sth** jdn dazu überreden, etw zu tun; **to ~ sb that** jdn davon überzeugen, dass; **to be ~d of sth** von etw überzeugt sein
persuasion [pə'sweɪʒən] *n* (*act*) Überredung *f*; (*creed*) Überzeugung *f*
persuasive [pə'sweɪsɪv] *adj* (*person, argument*) überzeugend
perverse [pə'və:s] *adj* (*person*) borniert; (*behaviour*) widernatürlich, pervers
pervert [*n* 'pə:və:t, *vt* pə'və:t] *n* (*sexual deviant*) perverser Mensch *m* ▷ *vt* (*person, mind*) verderben; (*distort: truth, custom*) verfälschen
pessimism ['pɛsɪmɪzəm] *n* Pessimismus *m*
pessimist ['pɛsɪmɪst] *n* Pessimist(in) *m(f)*
pessimistic [pɛsɪ'mɪstɪk] *adj* pessimistisch
pest [pɛst] *n* (*insect*) Schädling *m*; (*fig: nuisance*) Plage *f*
pester ['pɛstə^r] *vt* belästigen
pesticide ['pɛstɪsaɪd] *n* Schädlingsbekämpfungsmittel *nt*, Pestizid *nt*
pet [pɛt] *n* (*animal*) Haustier *nt* ▷ *adj* (*theory etc*) Lieblings- ▷ *vt* (*stroke*) streicheln ▷ *vi* (*inf: sexually*) herumknutschen; **teacher's ~** (*favourite*) Lehrers Liebling *m*; **a ~ rabbit/snake** *etc* ein Kaninchen/eine Schlange *etc* (als Haustier); **that's my ~ hate** das hasse ich besonders
petal ['pɛtl] *n* Blütenblatt *nt*
petite [pə'ti:t] *adj* (*woman*) zierlich
petition [pə'tɪʃən] *n* (*signed document*) Petition *f*; (*Law*) Klage *f* ▷ *vt* ersuchen ▷ *vi*: **to ~ for divorce** die Scheidung einreichen
petrified ['pɛtrɪfaɪd] *adj* (*fig: terrified*) starr vor Angst
petrol ['pɛtrəl] (*Brit*) *n* Benzin *nt*; **two-star ~** Normalbenzin *nt*; **four-star ~** Super(benzin) *nt*; **unleaded ~** bleifreies *or* unverbleites Benzin
petrol can (*Brit*) *n* Benzinkanister *m*
petroleum [pə'trəulɪəm] *n* Petroleum *nt*
petrol pump (*Brit*) *n* (*in garage*) Zapfsäule *f*; (*in engine*) Benzinpumpe *f*
petrol station (*Brit*) *n* Tankstelle *f*
petrol tank (*Brit*) *n* Benzintank *m*
petticoat ['pɛtɪkəut] *n* (*underskirt: full-length*) Unterkleid *nt*; (*: waist*) Unterrock *m*
petty ['pɛtɪ] *adj* (*trivial*) unbedeutend; (*small-minded*) kleinlich; (*crime*) geringfügig; (*official*) untergeordnetent; (*excuse*) billig; (*remark*) spitz
petty cash *n* (*in office*) Portokasse *f*
petty officer *n* Maat *m*
petulant ['pɛtjulənt] *adj* (*person, expression*) gereizt
pew [pju:] *n* (*in church*) Kirchenbank *f*
pewter ['pju:tə^r] *n* Zinn *nt*
phantom ['fæntəm] *n* Phantom *nt* ▷ *adj* (*fig*) Phantom-
pharmacist ['fɑ:məsɪst] *n* Apotheker(in) *m(f)*
pharmacy ['fɑ:məsɪ] *n* (*shop*) Apotheke *f*; (*science*) Pharmazie *f*
phase [feɪz] *n* Phase *f* ▷ *vt*: **to ~ sth in/out** etw stufenweise einführen/abschaffen
pheasant ['fɛznt] *n* Fasan *m*
phenomena [fə'nɔmɪnə] *npl of* **phenomenon**
phenomenal [fə'nɔmɪnl] *adj* phänomenal
phenomenon [fə'nɔmɪnən] (*pl* **phenomena**) *n* Phänomen *nt*
Philippines ['fɪlɪpi:nz] *npl*: **the ~** die Philippinen *pl*
philosopher [fɪ'lɔsəfə^r] *n* Philosoph(in) *m(f)*
philosophical [fɪlə'sɔfɪkl] *adj* philosophisch; (*fig: calm, resigned*) gelassen
philosophy [fɪ'lɔsəfɪ] *n* Philosophie *f*
phlegm [flɛm] *n* (*Med*) Schleim *m*
phobia ['fəubjə] *n* Phobie *f*
phone [fəun] *n* Telefon *nt* ▷ *vt* anrufen ▷ *vi* anrufen, telefonieren; **to be on the ~** (*possess a phone*) Telefon haben; (*be calling*) telefonieren
▸ **phone back** *vt, vi* zurückrufen
▸ **phone up** *vt, vi* anrufen
phone book *n* Telefonbuch *nt*
phone box (*Brit*) *n* Telefonzelle *f*
phone call *n* Anruf *m*
phonecard ['fəunkɑ:d] *n* Telefonkarte *f*
phone-in ['fəunɪn] (*Brit*) *n* (*Radio, TV*) *Radio-/Fernsehsendung mit Hörer-/Zuschauerbeteiligung per Telefon*, Phone-in *nt* ▷ *adj* mit Hörer-/Zuschaueranrufen
phonetics [fə'nɛtɪks] *n* Phonetik *f*
phoney ['fəunɪ] *adj* (*address*) falsch; (*accent*) unecht; (*person*) unaufrichtig
photo ['fəutəu] *n* Foto *nt*
photocopier ['fəutəukɔpɪə^r] *n* Fotokopierer *m*
photocopy ['fəutəukɔpɪ] *n* Fotokopie *f* ▷ *vt* fotokopieren
photograph ['fəutəgræf] *n* Fotografie *f* ▷ *vt* fotografieren; **to take a ~ of sb** jdn fotografieren
photographer [fə'tɔgrəfə^r] *n* Fotograf(in) *m(f)*
photography [fə'tɔgrəfɪ] *n* Fotografie *f*
phrase [freɪz] *n* Satz *m*; (*Ling*) Redewendung *f*; (*Mus*) Phrase *f* ▷ *vt* ausdrücken; (*letter*) formulieren
phrase book *n* Sprachführer *m*
physical ['fɪzɪkl] *adj* (*bodily*) körperlich; (*geography, properties*) physikalisch; (*law, explanation*) natürlich; **~ examination**

ärztliche Untersuchung *f*; **the ~ sciences** die Naturwissenschaften
physical education *n* Sportunterricht *m*
physically ['fɪzɪklɪ] *adv* (*fit, attractive*) körperlich
physician [fɪ'zɪʃən] *n* Arzt *m*, Ärztin *f*
physicist ['fɪzɪsɪst] *n* Physiker(in) *m(f)*
physics ['fɪzɪks] *n* Physik *f*
physiotherapist [fɪzɪəu'θɛrəpɪst] *n* Physiotherapeut(in) *m(f)*
physiotherapy [fɪzɪəu'θɛrəpɪ] *n* Physiotherapie *f*
physique [fɪ'zi:k] *n* Körperbau *m*
pianist ['pi:ənɪst] *n* Pianist(in) *m(f)*
piano [pɪ'ænəu] *n* Klavier *nt*, Piano *nt*
pick [pɪk] *n* (*also*: **pickaxe**) Spitzhacke *f* ▷ *vt* (*select*) aussuchen; (*gather: fruit, mushrooms*) sammeln; (*: flowers*) pflücken; (*remove, take out*) herausnehmen; (*lock*) knacken; (*scab, spot*) kratzen an *+dat*; **take your ~** (*choose*) Sie haben die Wahl; **the ~ of** (*best*) das Beste *+gen*; **to ~ one's nose** in der Nase bohren; **to ~ one's teeth** in den Zähnen stochern; **to ~ sb's brains** jdn als Informationsquelle nutzen; **to ~ sb's pocket** jdn bestehlen; **to ~ a quarrel (with sb)** einen Streit (mit jdm) anfangen
▸ **pick at** *vt fus* (*food*) herumstochern in *+dat*
▸ **pick off** *vt* (*shoot*) abschießen
▸ **pick on** *vt fus* (*criticize*) herumhacken auf *+dat*
▸ **pick out** *vt* (*distinguish*) ausmachen; (*select*) aussuchen
▸ **pick up** *vi* (*health*) sich verbessern; (*economy*) sich erholen ▷ *vt* (*from floor etc*) aufheben; (*arrest*) festnehmen; (*collect: person, parcel etc*) abholen; (*hitchhiker*) mitnehmen; (*for sexual encounter*) aufreißen; (*learn: skill etc*) mitbekommen; (*Radio*) empfangen; **to ~ up where one left off** da weitermachen, wo man aufgehört hat; **to ~ up speed** schneller werden; **to ~ o.s. up** (*after falling etc*) sich aufrappeln
picket ['pɪkɪt] *n* (*in strike*) Streikposten *m* ▷ *vt* (*factory etc*) Streikposten aufstellen vor *+dat*
pickle ['pɪkl] *n* (*also*: **pickles**: *as condiment*) Pickles *pl* ▷ *vt* einlegen; **to be in a ~** in der Klemme sitzen; **to get in a ~** in eine Klemme geraten
pickpocket ['pɪkpɔkɪt] *n* Taschendieb(in) *m(f)*
pick-up ['pɪkʌp] *n* (*also*: **pick-up truck**) offener Kleintransporter *m*; (*Brit: on record player*) Tonabnehmer *m*
picnic ['pɪknɪk] *n* Picknick *nt* ▷ *vi* picknicken
picture ['pɪktʃə^r] *n* Bild *nt*; (*film*) Film *m* ▷ *vt* (*imagine*) sich *dat* vorstellen; **the ~s** (*Brit: inf: the cinema*) das Kino; **to take a ~ of sb** ein Bild von jdm machen; **to put sb in the ~** jdn ins Bild setzen
picture book *n* Bilderbuch *nt*
picture messaging *n* Picture Messaging *nt*
picturesque [pɪktʃə'rɛsk] *adj* malerisch
pie [paɪ] *n* (*vegetable, meat*) Pastete *f*; (*fruit*) Torte *f*
piece [pi:s] *n* Stück *nt*; (*Draughts etc*) Stein *m*; (*Chess*) Figur *f*; **in ~s** (*broken*) kaputt; (*taken apart*) auseinandergenommen, in Einzelteilen; **a ~ of clothing/furniture/music** ein Kleidungs-/Möbel-/Musikstück *nt*; **a ~ of machinery** eine Maschine; **a ~ of research** eine Forschungsarbeit; **a ~ of advice** ein Rat *m*; **to take sth to ~s** etw auseinandernehmen; **in one ~** (*object*) unbeschädigt; (*person*) wohlbehalten; **a 10p ~** (*Brit*) ein 10-Pence-Stück *nt*; **~ by piece** Stück für Stück; **a six-~ band** eine sechsköpfige Band; **let her say her ~** lass sie ausreden
▸ **piece together** *vt* zusammenfügen
piecemeal ['pi:smi:l] *adv* stückweise, Stück für Stück
piecework ['pi:swə:k] *n* Akkordarbeit *f*
pie chart *n* Tortendiagramm *nt*
pier [pɪə^r] *n* Pier *m*
pierce [pɪəs] *vt* durchstechen; **to have one's ears ~d** sich *dat* die Ohrläppchen durchstechen lassen
pig [pɪg] *n* (*also pej*) Schwein *nt*; (*greedy person*) Vielfraß *m*
pigeon ['pɪdʒən] *n* Taube *f*
pigeonhole ['pɪdʒənhəul] *n* (*for letters etc*) Fach *nt*; (*fig*) Schublade *f* ▷ *vt* (*fig: person*) in eine Schublade stecken
piggy bank ['pɪgɪ-] *n* Sparschwein *nt*
piglet ['pɪglɪt] *n* Schweinchen *nt*, Ferkel *nt*
pigskin ['pɪgskɪn] *n* Schweinsleder *nt*
pigsty ['pɪgstaɪ] *n* (*also fig*) Schweinestall *m*
pigtail ['pɪgteɪl] *n* Zopf *m*
pike [paɪk] *n* (*fish*) Hecht *m*; (*spear*) Spieß *m*
pilchard ['pɪltʃəd] *n* Sardine *f*
pile [paɪl] *n* (*heap*) Haufen *m*; (*stack*) Stapel *m*; (*of carpet, velvet*) Flor *m*; (*pillar*) Pfahl *m* ▷ *vt* (*also*: **pile up**) (auf)stapeln; **in a ~** in einem Haufen; **to ~ into/out of** (*vehicle*) sich drängen in *+acc*/aus
▸ **pile on** *vt*: **to ~ it on** (*inf*) zu dick auftragen
▸ **pile up** *vi* sich stapeln
piles [paɪlz] *npl* (*Med*) Hämorr(ho)iden *pl*
pile-up ['paɪlʌp] *n* (*Aut*) Massenkarambolage *f*
pilfering ['pɪlfərɪŋ] *n* Diebstahl *m*
pilgrim ['pɪlgrɪm] *n* Pilger(in) *m(f)*
pilgrimage ['pɪlgrɪmɪdʒ] *n* Pilgerfahrt *f*, Wallfahrt *f*
pill [pɪl] *n* Tablette *f*, Pille *f*; **the ~** (*contraceptive*) die Pille; **to be on the ~** die Pille nehmen
pillage ['pɪlɪdʒ] *n* Plünderung *f* ▷ *vt* plündern
pillar ['pɪlə^r] *n* Säule *f*; **a ~ of society** (*fig*) eine Säule *or* Stütze der Gesellschaft
pillar box (*Brit*) *n* Briefkasten *m*
pillion ['pɪljən] *n*: **to ride ~** (*on motorcycle*) auf dem Soziussitz mitfahren; (*on horse*) hinten auf dem Pferd mitreiten
pillow ['pɪləu] *n* (Kopf)kissen *nt*
pillowcase ['pɪləukeɪs] *n* (Kopf)kissenbezug *m*

pilot ['paɪlət] *n* (*Aviat*) Pilot(in) *m*(*f*); (*Naut*) Lotse *m* ▷ *adj* (*scheme, study etc*) Pilot- ▷ *vt* (*aircraft*) steuern; (*fig: new law, scheme*) sich zum Fürsprecher machen +*gen*
pilot light *n* (*on cooker, boiler*) Zündflamme *f*
pimp [pɪmp] *n* Zuhälter *m*
pimple ['pɪmpl] *n* Pickel *m*
PIN *n abbr* (= *personal identification number*) PIN; ~ **number** PIN-Nummer *f*
pin [pɪn] *n* (*metal: for clothes, papers*) Stecknadel *f*; (*Tech*) Stift *m*; (*Brit: also:* **drawing pin**) Heftzwecke *f*; (*in grenade*) Sicherungsstift *m*; (*Brit: Elec*) Pol *m* ▷ *vt* (*fasten with pin*) feststecken; **~s and needles** (*in arms, legs etc*) Kribbeln *nt*; **to ~ sb against/to sth** jdn gegen/an etw *acc* pressen; **to ~ sth on sb** (*fig*) jdm etw anhängen
▸ **pin down** *vt* (*fig: person*) festnageln; **there's something strange here but I can't quite ~ it down** hier stimmt etwas nicht, aber ich weiß nicht genau was
pinafore ['pɪnəfɔːʳ] (*Brit*) *n* (*also:* **pinafore dress**) Trägerkleid *nt*
pinball ['pɪnbɔːl] *n* (*game*) Flippern *nt*; (*machine*) Flipper *m*
pincers ['pɪnsəz] *npl* (*tool*) Kneifzange *f*; (*of crab, lobster etc*) Schere *f*
pinch [pɪntʃ] *n* (*of salt etc*) Prise *f* ▷ *vt* (*with finger and thumb*) zwicken, kneifen; (*inf: steal*) klauen ▷ *vi* (*shoe*) drücken; **at a ~** zur Not; **to feel the ~** (*fig*) die schlechte Lage zu spüren bekommen
pincushion ['pɪnkuʃən] *n* Nadelkissen *nt*
pine [paɪn] *n* (*also:* **pine tree**) Kiefer *f*; (*wood*) Kiefernholz *nt* ▷ *vi*: **to ~ for** sich sehnen nach
▸ **pine away** *vi* sich (vor Kummer) verzehren
pineapple ['paɪnæpl] *n* Ananas *f*
ping [pɪŋ] *n* (*noise*) Klingeln *nt*
pink [pɪŋk] *adj* rosa *inv* ▷ *n* (*colour*) Rosa *nt*; (*Bot*) Gartennelke *f*
pinpoint ['pɪnpɔɪnt] *vt* (*identify*) genau festlegen, identifizieren; (*position of sth*) genau aufzeigen
pint [paɪnt] *n* (*Brit:* = *568 cc*) (britisches) Pint *nt*; (*US:* = *473 cc*) (amerikanisches) Pint; **a ~** (*Brit: inf: of beer*) ≈ eine Halbe
pioneer [paɪə'nɪəʳ] *n* (*lit, fig*) Pionier *m* ▷ *vt* (*invention etc*) Pionierarbeit leisten für
pious ['paɪəs] *adj* fromm
pip [pɪp] *n* (*of apple, orange*) Kern *m* ▷ *vt*: **to be ~ped at the post** (*Brit: fig*) um Haaresbreite geschlagen werden; **the pips** *npl* (*Brit: Radio*) das Zeitzeichen
pipe [paɪp] *n* (*for water, gas*) Rohr *nt*; (*for smoking*) Pfeife *f*; (*Mus*) Flöte *f* ▷ *vt* (*water, gas, oil*) (durch Rohre) leiten; **pipes** *npl* (*also:* **bagpipes**) Dudelsack *m*
▸ **pipe down** (*inf*) *vi* (*be quiet*) ruhig sein
pipe cleaner *n* Pfeifenreiniger *m*
pipe dream *n* Hirngespinst *nt*
pipeline ['paɪplaɪn] *n* Pipeline *f*; **it's in the ~** (*fig*) es ist in Vorbereitung
piper ['paɪpəʳ] *n* (*bagpipe player*) Dudelsackspieler(in) *m*(*f*)
piping ['paɪpɪŋ] *adv*: **~ hot** kochend heiß
pique ['piːk] *n*: **in a fit of ~** eingeschnappt, pikiert
pirate ['paɪərət] *n* Pirat *m*, Seeräuber *m* ▷ *vt* (*Comm: video tape, cassette etc*) illegal herstellen
Pisces ['paɪsiːz] *n* Fische *pl*; **to be ~** Fische *or* (ein) Fisch sein
piss [pɪs] (*inf!*) *vi* pissen ▷ *n* Pisse *f*; **~ off!** verpiss dich!; **to be ~ed off (with sb/sth)** (von jdm/etw) die Schnauze vollhaben; **it's ~ing down** (*Brit: raining*) es schifft; **to take the ~ out of sb** (*Brit*) jdn verarschen
pissed [pɪst] (*inf!*) *adj* (*drunk*) besoffen
pistol ['pɪstl] *n* Pistole *f*
piston ['pɪstən] *n* Kolben *m*
pit [pɪt] *n* Grube *f*; (*in surface of road*) Schlagloch *nt*; (*coal mine*) Zeche *f*; (*also:* **orchestra pit**) Orchestergraben *m* ▷ *vt*: **to ~ one's wits against sb** seinen Verstand mit jdm messen; **the pits** *npl* (*Aut*) die Box; **to ~ o.s. against sth** den Kampf gegen etw aufnehmen; **to ~ sb against sb** jdn gegen jdn antreten lassen; **the ~ of one's stomach** die Magengrube
pitch [pɪtʃ] *n* (*Brit: Sport: field*) Spielfeld *nt*; (*Mus*) Tonhöhe *f*; (*fig: level, degree*) Grad *m*; (*tar*) Pech *nt*; (*also:* **sales pitch**) Verkaufsmasche *f*; (*Naut*) Stampfen *nt* ▷ *vt* (*throw*) werfen, schleudern; (*set: price, message*) ansetzen ▷ *vi* (*fall forwards*) hinschlagen; (*Naut*) stampfen; **to ~ a tent** ein Zelt aufschlagen; **to be ~ed forward** vornüber geworfen werden
pitch-black ['pɪtʃ'blæk] *adj* pechschwarz
pitched battle [pɪtʃt-] *n* offene Schlacht *f*
pitfall ['pɪtfɔːl] *n* Falle *f*
pith [pɪθ] *n* (*of orange etc*) weiße Haut *f*; (*of plant*) Mark *nt*; (*fig*) Kern *m*
pithy ['pɪθɪ] *adj* (*comment etc*) prägnant
pitiful ['pɪtɪful] *adj* (*sight etc*) mitleiderregend; (*excuse, attempt*) jämmerlich, kläglich
pitiless ['pɪtɪlɪs] *adj* mitleidlos
pittance ['pɪtns] *n* Hungerlohn *m*
pity ['pɪtɪ] *n* Mitleid *nt* ▷ *vt* bemitleiden, bedauern; **what a ~!** wie schade!; **it is a ~ that you can't come** schade, dass du nicht kommen kannst; **to take ~ on sb** Mitleid mit jdm haben
pizza ['piːtsə] *n* Pizza *f*
placard ['plækɑːd] *n* Plakat *nt*, Aushang *m*; (*in march etc*) Transparent *nt*
placate [plə'keɪt] *vt* beschwichtigen, besänftigen
place [pleɪs] *n* Platz *m*; (*position*) Stelle *f*, Ort *m*; (*seat: on committee etc*) Sitz *m*; (*home*) Wohnung *f*; (*in street names*) ≈ Straße *f* ▷ *vt* (*put: object*) stellen, legen; (*identify: person*) unterbringen; **~ of birth** Geburtsort *m*; **to take ~** (*happen*) geschehen, passieren; **at/to his ~** (*home*) bei/zu ihm; **from ~ to place** von Ort zu Ort; **all over the ~** überall; **in ~s** stellenweise; **in sb's/sth's ~** anstelle von jdm/etw; **to take sb's/sth's ~** an die Stelle von jdm/etw treten, jdn/etw ersetzen; **out**

of ~ (*inappropriate*) unangebracht; **I feel out of ~ here** ich fühle mich hier fehl am Platze; **in the first ~** (*first of all*) erstens; **to change ~s with sb** mit jdm den Platz tauschen; **to put sb in his ~** (*fig*) jdn in seine Schranken weisen; **he's going ~s** er bringt es noch mal weit; **it's not my ~ to do it** es ist nicht an mir, das zu tun; **to be ~d** (*in race, exam*) platziert sein; **to be ~d third** den dritten Platz belegen; **to ~ an order with sb (for sth)** eine Bestellung bei jdm (für etw) aufgeben; **how are you ~d next week?** wie sieht es bei Ihnen nächste Woche aus?

place mat *n* Set *nt or m*

placement ['pleɪsmənt] *n* Platzierung *f*

placid ['plæsɪd] *adj* (*person*) ruhig, gelassen; (*place, river etc*) friedvoll

plague [pleɪg] *n* (*Med*) Seuche *f*; (*fig: of locusts etc*) Plage *f* ▷ *vt* (*fig: problems etc*) plagen; **to ~ sb with questions** jdn mit Fragen quälen

plaice [pleɪs] *n inv* Scholle *f*

plaid [plæd] *n* Plaid *nt*

plain [pleɪn] *adj* (*unpatterned*) einfarbig; (*simple*) einfach, schlicht; (*clear, easily understood*) klar; (*not beautiful*) unattraktiv; (*frank*) offen ▷ *adv* (*wrong, stupid etc*) einfach ▷ *n* (*area of land*) Ebene *f*; (*Knitting*) rechte Masche *f*; **to make sth ~ to sb** jdm etw klarmachen

plain chocolate *n* Bitterschokolade *f*

plainly ['pleɪnlɪ] *adv* (*obviously*) eindeutig; (*clearly*) deutlich, klar

plaintiff ['pleɪntɪf] *n* Kläger(in) *m(f)*

plait [plæt] *n* (*of hair*) Zopf *m*; (*of rope, leather*) Geflecht *nt* ▷ *vt* flechten

plan [plæn] *n* Plan *m* ▷ *vt* planen; (*building, schedule*) entwerfen ▷ *vi* planen; **to ~ to do sth** planen *or* vorhaben, etw zu tun; **how long do you ~ to stay?** wie lange haben Sie vor, zu bleiben?; **to ~ for** *or* **on** (*expect*) sich einstellen auf *+acc*; **to ~ on doing sth** vorhaben, etw zu tun

plane [pleɪn] *n* (*Aviat*) Flugzeug *nt*; (*Math*) Ebene *f*; (*fig: level*) Niveau *nt*; (*tool*) Hobel *m*; (*also*: **plane tree**) Platane *f* ▷ *vt* (*wood*) hobeln ▷ *vi* (*Naut, Aut*) gleiten

planet ['plænɪt] *n* Planet *m*

plank [plæŋk] *n* (*of wood*) Brett *nt*; (*fig: of policy etc*) Schwerpunkt *m*

planner ['plænəʳ] *n* Planer(in) *m(f)*

planning ['plænɪŋ] *n* Planung *f*

planning permission (*Brit*) *n* Baugenehmigung *f*

plant [plɑːnt] *n* (*Bot*) Pflanze *f*; (*machinery*) Maschinen *pl*; (*factory*) Anlage *f* ▷ *vt* (*seed, plant, crops*) pflanzen; (*field, garden*) bepflanzen; (*microphone, bomb etc*) anbringen; (*incriminating evidence*) schleusen; (*fig: object*) stellen; (*: kiss*) drücken

plantation [plæn'teɪʃən] *n* Plantage *f*; (*wood*) Anpflanzung *f*

plaque [plæk] *n* (*on building etc*) Tafel *f*, Plakette *f*; (*on teeth*) Zahnbelag *m*

plaster ['plɑːstəʳ] *n* (*for walls*) Putz *m*; (*also*: **plaster of Paris**) Gips *m*; (*Brit*: *also*: **sticking plaster**) Pflaster *nt* ▷ *vt* (*wall, ceiling*) verputzen; **in ~** (*Brit*) in Gips; **to ~ with** (*cover*) bepflastern mit

plaster cast *n* (*Med*) Gipsverband *m*; (*model, statue*) Gipsform *f*

plastered ['plɑːstəd] (*inf*) *adj* (*drunk*) sturzbesoffen

plastic ['plæstɪk] *n* Plastik *nt* ▷ *adj* (*bucket, cup etc*) Plastik-; (*flexible*) formbar; **the ~ arts** die bildende Kunst

plastic bag *n* Plastiktüte *f*

plastic surgery *n* plastische Chirurgie *f*

plate [pleɪt] *n* Teller *m*; (*metal cover*) Platte *f*; (*Typ*) Druckplatte *f*; (*Aut*) Nummernschild *nt*; (*in book: picture*) Tafel *f*; (*also*: **dental plate**) Gaumenplatte *f*; (*on door*) Schild *nt*; **gold/silver ~** vergoldeter/versilberter Artikel *m*; **that necklace is just ~** die Halskette ist nur vergoldet/versilbert

plateau ['plætəu] (*pl* **plateaus** *or* **~x**) *n* (*Geog*) Plateau *nt*, Hochebene *f*; (*fig*) stabiler Zustand *m*

plate glass *n* Tafelglas *nt*

platform ['plætfɔːm] *n* (*stage*) Podium *nt*; (*for landing, loading on etc, Brit: of bus*) Plattform *f*; (*Rail*) Bahnsteig *m*; (*Pol*) Programm *nt*; **the train leaves from ~ 7** der Zug fährt von Gleis 7 ab

platinum ['plætɪnəm] *n* Platin *nt*

platoon [plə'tuːn] *n* Zug *m*

platter ['plætəʳ] *n* Platte *f*

plausible ['plɔːzɪbl] *adj* (*theory, excuse*) plausibel; (*liar etc*) glaubwürdig

play [pleɪ] *n* (*Theat*) (Theater)stück *nt*; (*TV*) Fernsehspiel *nt*; (*Radio*) Hörspiel *nt*; (*activity*) Spiel *nt* ▷ *vt* spielen; (*team, opponent*) spielen gegen ▷ *vi* spielen; **to bring into ~** ins Spiel bringen; **a ~ on words** ein Wortspiel *nt*; **to ~ a trick on sb** jdn hereinlegen; **to ~ a part** *or* **role in sth** (*fig*) eine Rolle bei etw spielen; **to ~ for time** (*fig*) auf Zeit spielen, Zeit gewinnen wollen; **to ~ safe** auf Nummer sicher gehen; **to ~ into sb's hands** jdm in die Hände spielen

▸ **play about with** *vt fus* = **play around with**

▸ **play along with** *vt fus* (*person*) sich richten nach; (*plan, idea*) eingehen auf *+acc*

▸ **play around with** *vt fus* (*fiddle with*) herumspielen mit

▸ **play at** *vt fus* (*do casually*) spielen mit; **to ~ at being sb/sth** jdn/etw spielen

▸ **play back** *vt* (*recording*) abspielen

▸ **play down** *vt* herunterspielen

▸ **play on** *vt fus* (*sb's feelings etc*) ausnutzen; **to ~ on sb's mind** jdm im Kopf herumgehen

▸ **play up** *vi* (*machine, knee etc*) Schwierigkeiten machen; (*children*) frech werden

playboy ['pleɪbɔɪ] *n* Playboy *m*

player ['pleɪəʳ] *n* (*Sport, Mus*) Spieler(in) *m(f)*; (*Theat*) Schauspieler(in) *m(f)*

playful ['pleɪful] *adj* (*person, gesture*)

spielerisch; (*animal*) verspielt
playground ['pleɪgraund] *n* (*in park*) Spielplatz *m*; (*in school*) Schulhof *m*
playgroup ['pleɪgru:p] *n* Spielgruppe *f*
playing card ['pleɪɪŋ-] *n* Spielkarte *f*
playing field *n* Sportplatz *m*
playmate ['pleɪmeɪt] *n* Spielkamerad(in) *m(f)*
play-off ['pleɪɔf] *n* Ausscheidungsspiel *nt*, Play-off *nt*
playpen ['pleɪpɛn] *n* Laufstall *m*
playschool ['pleɪsku:l] *n* = **playgroup**
plaything ['pleɪθɪŋ] *n* (*also fig*) Spielzeug *nt*
playtime ['pleɪtaɪm] *n* (kleine) Pause *f*
playwright ['pleɪraɪt] *n* Dramatiker(in) *m(f)*
plc (*Brit*) *n abbr* (= *public limited company*) ≈ AG *f*
plea [pli:] *n* (*request*) Bitte *f*; (*Law*): **to enter a ~ of guilty/not guilty** sich schuldig/unschuldig erklären; (*excuse*) Vorwand *m*
plead [pli:d] *vi* (*Law*) *vor Gericht eine Schuld-/Unschuldserklärung abgeben* ▷ *vt* (*Law*): **to ~ sb's case** jdn vertreten; (*give as excuse: ignorance, ill health etc*) vorgeben, sich berufen auf *+acc*; **to ~ with sb** (*beg*) jdn inständig bitten; **to ~ for sth** um etw nachsuchen; **to ~ guilty/not guilty** sich schuldig/nicht schuldig bekennen
pleasant ['plɛznt] *adj* angenehm; (*smile*) freundlich
please [pli:z] *excl* bitte ▷ *vt* (*satisfy*) zufriedenstellen ▷ *vi* (*give pleasure*) gefällig sein; **~ Miss/Sir!** (*to attract teacher's attention*) ≈ Frau/Herr X!; **yes, ~** ja, bitte; **my bill, ~** die Rechnung, bitte; **~ don't cry!** bitte wein doch nicht!; **~ yourself!** (*inf*) wie du willst!; **do as you ~** machen Sie, was Sie für richtig halten
pleased [pli:zd] *adj* (*happy*) erfreut; (*satisfied*) zufrieden; **~ to meet you** freut mich(, Sie kennenzulernen); **~ with** zufrieden mit; **we are ~ to inform you that ...** wir freuen uns, Ihnen mitzuteilen, dass ...
pleasing ['pli:zɪŋ] *adj* (*remark, picture etc*) erfreulich; (*person*) sympathisch
pleasure ['plɛʒəʳ] *n* (*happiness, satisfaction*) Freude *f*; (*fun, enjoyable experience*) Vergnügen *nt*; **it's a ~, my ~** gern geschehen; **with ~** gern, mit Vergnügen; **is this trip for business or ~?** ist diese Reise geschäftlich oder zum Vergnügen?
pleat [pli:t] *n* Falte *f*
pledge [plɛdʒ] *n* (*promise*) Versprechen *nt* ▷ *vt* (*promise*) versprechen; **to ~ sb to secrecy** jdn zum Schweigen verpflichten
plentiful ['plɛntɪful] *adj* reichlich
plenty ['plɛntɪ] *n* (*lots*) eine Menge; (*sufficient*) reichlich; **~ of** eine Menge; **we've got ~ of time to get there** wir haben jede Menge Zeit, dorthin zu kommen
pliable ['plaɪəbl] *adj* (*material*) biegsam; (*fig: person*) leicht beeinflussbar
pliers ['plaɪəz] *npl* Zange *f*
plight [plaɪt] *n* (*of person, country*) Not *f*
plimsolls ['plɪmsəlz] (*Brit*) *npl* Turnschuhe *pl*
plinth [plɪnθ] *n* Sockel *m*
PLO *n abbr* (= *Palestine Liberation Organization*) PLO *f*
plod [plɔd] *vi* (*walk*) trotten; (*fig*) sich abplagen
plonk [plɔŋk] (*inf*) *n* (*Brit: wine*) (billiger) Wein *m* ▷ *vt*: **to ~ sth down** etw hinknallen
plot [plɔt] *n* (*secret plan*) Komplott *nt*, Verschwörung *f*; (*of story, play, film*) Handlung *f* ▷ *vt* (*sb's downfall etc*) planen; (*on chart, graph*) markieren ▷ *vi* (*conspire*) sich verschwören; **a ~ of land** ein Grundstück *nt*; **a vegetable ~** (*Brit*) ein Gemüsebeet *nt*
plough, (*US*) **plow** [plau] *n* Pflug *m* ▷ *vt* pflügen; **to ~ money into sth** (*project etc*) Geld in etw *acc* stecken
▸ **plough back** *vt* (*Comm*) reinvestieren
▸ **plough into** *vt fus* (*crowd*) rasen in *+acc*
ploughman, (*US*) **plowman** ['plaumən] (*irreg: like* **man**) *n* Pflüger *m*
plow *etc* (*US*) = **plough** *etc*
ploy [plɔɪ] *n* Trick *m*
pls *abbr* (= *please*) b
pluck [plʌk] *vt* (*fruit, flower, leaf*) pflücken; (*musical instrument, eyebrows*) zupfen; (*bird*) rupfen ▷ *n* (*courage*) Mut *m*; **to ~ up courage** allen Mut zusammennehmen
plug [plʌg] *n* (*Elec*) Stecker *m*; (*stopper*) Stöpsel *m*; (*Aut: also*: **spark(ing) plug**) Zündkerze *f* ▷ *vt* (*hole*) zustopfen; (*inf: advertise*) Reklame machen für; **to give sb/sth a ~** für jdn/etw Reklame machen
▸ **plug in** *vt* (*Elec*) einstöpseln, anschließen ▷ *vi* angeschlossen werden
plughole ['plʌghəul] (*Brit*) *n* Abfluss *m*
plum [plʌm] *n* (*fruit*) Pflaume *f* ▷ *adj* (*inf*): **a ~ job** ein Traumjob *m*
plumb [plʌm] *vt*: **to ~ the depths of despair/humiliation** die tiefste Verzweiflung/Erniedrigung erleben
▸ **plumb in** *vt* anschließen, installieren
plumber ['plʌməʳ] *n* Installateur *m*, Klempner *m*
plumbing ['plʌmɪŋ] *n* (*piping*) Installationen *pl*, Rohrleitungen *pl*; (*trade*) Klempnerei *f*; (*work*) Installationsarbeiten *pl*
plummet ['plʌmɪt] *vi* (*bird, aircraft*) (hinunter)stürzen; (*price, rate*) rapide absacken
plump [plʌmp] *adj* (*person*) füllig, mollig
▸ **plump for** (*inf*) *vt fus* sich entscheiden für
▸ **plump up** *vt* (*cushion*) aufschütteln
plunder ['plʌndəʳ] *n* (*activity*) Plünderung *f*; (*stolen things*) Beute *f* ▷ *vt* (*city, tomb*) plündern
plunge [plʌndʒ] *n* (*of bird, person*) Sprung *m*; (*fig: of prices, rates etc*) Sturz *m* ▷ *vt* (*hand, knife*) stoßen ▷ *vi* (*thing*) stürzen; (*bird, person*) sich stürzen; (*fig: prices, rates etc*) abfallen, stürzen; **to take the ~** (*fig*) den Sprung wagen; **the room was ~d into darkness** das Zimmer war in Dunkelheit getaucht
plunging ['plʌndʒɪŋ] *adj*: **~ neckline** tiefer Ausschnitt *m*
pluperfect [plu:'pə:fɪkt] *n*: **the ~** das

Plusquamperfekt

plural ['pluərl] *adj* Plural- ▷ *n* Plural *m*, Mehrzahl *f*

plus [plʌs] *n* (*also*: **plus sign**) Pluszeichen *nt* ▷ *prep, adj* plus; **it's a ~** (*fig*) es ist ein Vorteil *or* ein Pluspunkt; **ten/twenty ~** (*more than*) über zehn/zwanzig; **B ~** (*Scol*) ≈ Zwei plus

plush [plʌʃ] *adj* (*car, hotel etc*) feudal ▷ *n* (*fabric*) Plüsch *m*

ply [plaɪ] *vt* (*a trade*) ausüben, nachgehen *+dat*; (*tool*) gebrauchen, anwenden ▷ *vi* (*ship*) verkehren ▷ *n* (*of wool, rope*) Stärke *f*; (*also*: **plywood**) Sperrholz *nt*; **to ~ sb with drink** jdn ausgiebig bewirten; **to ~ sb with questions** jdm viele Fragen stellen; **two-/three-~ wool** zwei-/dreifädige Wolle

plywood ['plaɪwud] *n* Sperrholz *nt*

p.m. *adv abbr* (= *post meridiem*) nachmittags; (*later*) abends

PMT *abbr* = **premenstrual tension**

pneumatic [nju:'mætɪk] *adj* pneumatisch

pneumatic drill *n* Presslufbohrer *m*

pneumonia [nju:'məunɪə] *n* Lungenentzündung *f*

poach [pəutʃ] *vt* (*steal: fish, animals, birds*) illegal erbeuten, wildern; (*Culin: egg*) pochieren; (*: fish*) dünsten ▷ *vi* (*steal*) wildern

poached [pəutʃt] *adj*: **~ eggs** verlorene Eier

poacher ['pəutʃəʳ] *n* Wilderer *m*

pocket ['pɔkɪt] *n* Tasche *f*; (*fig: small area*) vereinzelter Bereich *m* ▷ *vt* (*put in one's pocket, steal*) einstecken; **to be out of ~** (*Brit*) Verlust machen; **~ of resistance** Widerstandsnest *nt*

pocketbook ['pɔkɪtbuk] *n* (*notebook*) Notizbuch *nt*; (*US: wallet*) Brieftasche *f*; (*: handbag*) Handtasche *f*

pocket money *n* Taschengeld *nt*

pod [pɔd] *n* Hülse *f*

podgy ['pɔdʒɪ] (*inf*) *adj* rundlich, pummelig

podiatrist [pɔ'di:ətrɪst] (*US*) *n* Fußspezialist(in) *m(f)*

podium ['pəudɪəm] *n* Podium *nt*

poem ['pəuɪm] *n* Gedicht *nt*

poet ['pəuɪt] *n* Dichter(in) *m(f)*

poetic [pəu'ɛtɪk] *adj* poetisch, dichterisch; (*fig*) malerisch

poetry ['pəuɪtrɪ] *n* (*poems*) Gedichte *pl*; (*writing*) Poesie *f*

poignant ['pɔɪnjənt] *adj* ergreifend; (*situation*) herzzerreißend

point [pɔɪnt] *n* Punkt *m*; (*of needle, knife etc*) Spitze *f*; (*purpose*) Sinn *m*, Zweck *m*; (*significant part*) Entscheidende(s) *nt*; (*moment*) Zeitpunkt *m*; (*Elec: also*: **power point**) Steckdose *f*; (*also*: **decimal point**) ≈ Komma *nt* ▷ *vt* (*show, mark*) deuten auf *+acc* ▷ *vi* (*with finger, stick etc*) zeigen, deuten; **points** *npl* (*Aut*) (Unterbrecher)kontakte *pl*; (*Rail*) Weichen *pl*; **two ~ five** (= *2.5*) zwei Komma fünf; **good/bad ~s** (*of person*) gute/schlechte Seiten *or* Eigenschaften; **the train stops at Carlisle and all ~s south** der Zug hält in Carlisle und allen Orten weiter südlich; **to be on the ~ of doing sth** im Begriff sein, etw zu tun; **to make a ~ of doing sth** besonders darauf achten, etw zu tun; (*make a habit of*) Wert darauf legen, etw zu tun; **to get/miss the ~** verstehen/nicht verstehen, worum es geht; **to come** *or* **get to the ~** zur Sache kommen; **to make one's ~** seinen Standpunkt klarmachen; **that's the whole ~!** darum geht es ja gerade!; **what's the ~?** was solls?; **to be beside the ~** unwichtig *or* irrelevant sein; **there's no ~ talking to you** es ist sinnlos, mit dir zu reden; **you've got a ~ there!** da könnten Sie recht haben!; **in ~ of fact** in Wirklichkeit; **~ of sale** (*Comm*) Verkaufsstelle *f*; **to ~ sth at sb** (*gun etc*) etw auf jdn richten; (*finger*) mit etw auf jdn *acc* zeigen; **to ~ at** zeigen auf *+acc*; **to ~ to** zeigen auf *+acc*; (*fig*) hinweisen auf *+acc*

▸ **point out** *vt* hinweisen auf *+acc*

▸ **point to** *vt fus* hindeuten auf *+acc*

point-blank ['pɔɪnt'blæŋk] *adv* (*say, ask*) direkt; (*refuse*) glatt; (*also*: **at point-blank range**) aus unmittelbarer Entfernung

pointed ['pɔɪntɪd] *adj* spitz; (*fig: remark*) spitz, scharf

pointer ['pɔɪntəʳ] *n* (*on chart, machine*) Zeiger *m*; (*fig: piece of information or advice*) Hinweis *m*; (*stick*) Zeigestock *m*; (*dog*) Pointer *m*

pointless ['pɔɪntlɪs] *adj* sinnlos, zwecklos

point of view *n* Ansicht *f*, Standpunkt *m*; **from a practical ~** von einem praktischen Standpunkt aus

poise [pɔɪz] *n* (*composure*) Selbstsicherheit *f*; (*balance*) Haltung *f* ▷ *vt*: **to be ~d for sth** (*fig*) bereit zu etw sein

poison ['pɔɪzn] *n* Gift *nt* ▷ *vt* vergiften

poisonous ['pɔɪznəs] *adj* (*animal, plant*) Gift-; (*fumes, chemicals etc*) giftig; (*fig: rumours etc*) zersetzend

poke [pəuk] *vt* (*with finger, stick etc*) stoßen; (*fire*) schüren ▷ *n* (*jab*) Stoß *m*, Schubs *m* (*inf*); **to ~ sth in(to)** (*put*) etw stecken in *+acc*; **to ~ one's head out of the window** seinen Kopf aus dem Fenster strecken; **to ~ fun at sb** sich über jdn lustig machen

▸ **poke about** *vi* (*search*) herumstochern

▸ **poke out** *vi* (*stick out*) vorstehen

poker ['pəukəʳ] *n* (*metal bar*) Schürhaken *m*; (*Cards*) Poker *nt*

poky ['pəukɪ] (*pej*) *adj* (*room, house*) winzig

Poland ['pəulənd] *n* Polen *nt*

polar ['pəuləʳ] *adj* (*icecap*) polar; (*region*) Polar-

polar bear *n* Eisbär *m*

Pole [pəul] *n* Pole *m*, Polin *f*

pole [pəul] *n* (*post, stick*) Stange *f*; (*flag pole, telegraph pole etc*) Mast *m*; (*Geog, Elec*) Pol *m*; **to be ~s apart** (*fig*) durch Welten (voneinander) getrennt sein

pole bean (*US*) *n* (*runner bean*) Stangenbohne *f*

pole vault ['pəulvɔ:lt] *n* Stabhochsprung *m*

police [pə'li:s] *npl* (*organization*) Polizei *f*; (*members*) Polizisten *pl*, Polizeikräfte *pl* ▷ *vt* (*street, area, town*) kontrollieren; **a large**

number of ~ were hurt viele Polizeikräfte wurden verletzt
police car *n* Polizeiauto *nt*
police constable *(Brit) n* Polizist(in) *m(f)*, Polizeibeamte(r) *m*, Polizeibeamtin *f*
police force *n* Polizei *f*
policeman [pə'li:smən] *(irreg: like* **man***) n* Polizist *m*
police officer *n* = **police constable**
police station *n* Polizeiwache *f*
policewoman [pə'li:swumən] *(irreg: like* **woman***) n* Polizistin *f*
policy ['pɔlɪsɪ] *n (Pol, Econ)* Politik *f*; *(also:* **insurance policy***)* (Versicherungs)police *f*; *(of newspaper)* Grundsatz *m*; **to take out a ~** *(Insurance)* eine Versicherung abschließen
polio ['pəulɪəu] *n* Kinderlähmung *f*, Polio *f*
Polish ['pəulɪʃ] *adj* polnisch ▷ *n (Ling)* Polnisch *nt*
polish ['pɔlɪʃ] *n (for shoes)* Creme *f*; *(for furniture)* Politur *f*; *(for floors)* Bohnerwachs *nt*; *(shine: on shoes, floor etc)* Glanz *m*; *(fig: refinement)* Schliff *m* ▷ *vt (shoes)* putzen; *(floor, furniture etc)* polieren
▶ **polish off** *vt (work)* erledigen; *(food)* verputzen
polished ['pɔlɪʃt] *adj (fig: person)* mit Schliff; *(: style)* geschliffen
polite [pə'laɪt] *adj* höflich; *(company, society)* fein; **it's not ~ to do that** es gehört sich nicht, das zu tun
politely [pə'laɪtlɪ] *adv* höflich
politeness [pə'laɪtnɪs] *n* Höflichkeit *f*
political [pə'lɪtɪkl] *adj* politisch
politically [pə'lɪtɪklɪ] *adv* politisch; **~ correct** politisch korrekt
politician [pɔlɪ'tɪʃən] *n* Politiker(in) *m(f)*
politics ['pɔlɪtɪks] *n* Politik *f* ▷ *npl (beliefs, opinions)* politische Ansichten *pl*
poll [pəul] *n (also:* **opinion poll***)* (Meinungs)umfrage *f*; *(election)* Wahl *f* ▷ *vt (in opinion poll)* befragen; *(number of votes)* erhalten; **to go to the ~s** *(voters)* zur Wahl gehen; *(government)* sich den Wählern stellen
pollen ['pɔlən] *n* Pollen *m*, Blütenstaub *m*
polling day *(Brit) n* Wahltag *m*
polling station *(Brit) n* Wahllokal *nt*
pollute [pə'lu:t] *vt* verschmutzen
pollution [pə'lu:ʃən] *n (process)* Verschmutzung *f*; *(substances)* Schmutz *m*
polo ['pəuləu] *n* Polo *nt*
polyester [pɔlɪ'ɛstəʳ] *n* Polyester *m*
polystyrene [pɔlɪ'staɪri:n] *n* ≈ Styropor® *nt*
polythene ['pɔlɪθi:n] *n* Polyäthylen *nt*
polythene bag *n* Plastiktüte *f*
pomegranate ['pɔmɪgrænɪt] *n* Granatapfel *m*
pomp [pɔmp] *n* Pomp *m*, Prunk *m*
pompous ['pɔmpəs] *(pej) adj (person)* aufgeblasen; *(piece of writing)* geschwollen
pond [pɔnd] *n* Teich *m*
ponder ['pɔndəʳ] *vt* nachdenken über *+acc* ▷ *vi* nachdenken
ponderous ['pɔndərəs] *adj (style, language)* schwerfällig
pong [pɔŋ] *(Brit: inf) n* Gestank *m* ▷ *vi* stinken
pony ['pəunɪ] *n* Pony *nt*
ponytail ['pəunɪteɪl] *n* Pferdeschwanz *m*; **to have one's hair in a ~** einen Pferdeschwanz tragen
pony trekking *(Brit) n* Ponytrecken *nt*
poodle ['pu:dl] *n* Pudel *m*
pool [pu:l] *n (pond)* Teich *m*; *(also:* **swimming pool***)* Schwimmbad *nt*; *(of blood)* Lache *f*; *(Sport)* Poolbillard *nt*; *(of cash, workers)* Bestand *m*; *(Cards: kitty)* Kasse *f*; *(Comm: consortium)* Interessengemeinschaft *f* ▷ *vt (money)* zusammenlegen; *(knowledge, resources)* vereinigen; **pools** *npl (also:* **football pools***)* ≈ Fußballtoto *nt*; **a ~ of sunlight/shade** eine sonnige/schattige Stelle; **car ~** Fahrgemeinschaft *f*; **typing ~, secretary ~** *(US)* Schreibzentrale *f*; **to do the (football) ~s** ≈ im Fußballtoto spielen
poor [puəʳ] *adj* arm; *(bad)* schlecht ▷ *npl*: **the ~** die Armen *pl*; **~ in** *(resources etc)* arm an *+dat*; **~ Bob** der arme Bob
poorly ['puəlɪ] *adj (ill)* elend, krank ▷ *adv (badly: designed, paid, furnished)* schlecht
pop [pɔp] *n (Mus)* Pop *m*; *(fizzy drink)* Limonade *f*; *(US: inf: father)* Papa *m*; *(sound)* Knall *m* ▷ *vi (balloon)* platzen; *(cork)* knallen ▷ *vt*: **to ~ sth into/onto sth** etw schnell in etw *acc* stecken/auf etw *acc* legen; **his eyes ~ped out of his head** *(inf)* ihm fielen fast die Augen aus dem Kopf; **she ~ped her head out of the window** sie streckte den Kopf aus dem Fenster
▶ **pop in** *vi* vorbeikommen
▶ **pop out** *vi* kurz weggehen
▶ **pop up** *vi* auftauchen; *(Comput: window)* aufpoppen
popcorn ['pɔpkɔ:n] *n* Popcorn *nt*
pope [pəup] *n* Papst *m*
poplar ['pɔpləʳ] *n* Pappel *f*
popper ['pɔpəʳ] *(Brit: inf) n (for fastening)* Druckknopf *m*
poppy ['pɔpɪ] *n* Mohn *m*
Popsicle® ['pɔpsɪkl] *(US) n* Eis *nt* am Stiel
pop star *n* Popstar *m*
popular ['pɔpjuləʳ] *adj (well-liked, fashionable)* beliebt, populär; *(general, non-specialist)* allgemein; *(idea)* weitverbreitet; *(Pol: movement)* Volks-; *(: cause)* des Volkes; **to be ~ with** beliebt sein bei; **the ~ press** die Boulevardpresse
popularity [pɔpju'lærɪtɪ] *n* Beliebtheit *f*, Popularität *f*
population [pɔpju'leɪʃən] *n* Bevölkerung *f*; *(of a species)* Zahl *f*, Population *f*; **a prison ~ of 44,000** (eine Zahl von) 44.000 Gefängnisinsassen; **the civilian ~** die Zivilbevölkerung
porcelain ['pɔ:slɪn] *n* Porzellan *nt*
porch [pɔ:tʃ] *n (entrance)* Vorbau *m*; *(US)* Veranda *f*
porcupine ['pɔ:kjupaɪn] *n* Stachelschwein *nt*

pore [pɔː[r]] *n* Pore *f* ▷ *vi*: **to ~ over** (*book etc*) gründlich studieren
pork [pɔːk] *n* Schweinefleisch *nt*
pork chop *n* Schweinekotelett *nt*
porn [pɔːn] (*inf*) *n* Porno *m*; **~ channel/magazine/shop** Pornokanal *m*/-magazin *nt*/-laden *m*
pornographic [pɔːnə'græfɪk] *adj* pornografisch
pornography [pɔː'nɔgrəfɪ] *n* Pornografie *f*
porpoise ['pɔːpəs] *n* Tümmler *m*
porridge ['pɔrɪdʒ] *n* Haferbrei *m*, Porridge *nt*
port [pɔːt] *n* (*harbour*) Hafen *m*; (*Naut: left side*) Backbord *nt*; (*wine*) Portwein *m*; (*Comput*) Port *m* ▷ *adj* (*Naut*) Backbord-; **to ~** (*Naut*) an Backbord; **~ of call** (*Naut*) Anlaufhafen *nt*
portable ['pɔːtəbl] *adj* (*television, typewriter etc*) tragbar, portabel
porter ['pɔːtə[r]] *n* (*for luggage*) Gepäckträger *m*; (*doorkeeper*) Pförtner *m*; (*US: Rail*) Schlafwagenschaffner(in) *m(f)*
portfolio [pɔːt'fəulɪəu] *n* (*case*) Aktenmappe *f*; (*Pol*) Geschäftsbereich *m*; (*Fin*) Portefeuille *nt*; (*of artist*) Kollektion *f*
porthole ['pɔːthəul] *n* Bullauge *nt*
portion ['pɔːʃən] *n* (*part*) Teil *m*; (*helping of food*) Portion *f*
portrait ['pɔːtreɪt] *n* Porträt *nt*
portray [pɔː'treɪ] *vt* darstellen
Portugal ['pɔːtjugl] *n* Portugal *nt*
Portuguese [pɔːtju'giːz] *adj* portugiesisch ▷ *n inv* (*person*) Portugiese *m*, Portugiesin *f*; (*Ling*) Portugiesisch *nt*
pose [pəuz] *n* Pose *f* ▷ *vt* (*question, problem*) aufwerfen; (*danger*) mit sich bringen ▷ *vi*: **to ~ as** (*pretend*) sich ausgeben als; **to strike a ~** sich in Positur werfen; **to ~ for** (*painting etc*) Modell sitzen für, posieren für
posh [pɔʃ] (*inf*) *adj* vornehm; **to talk ~** vornehm daherreden
position [pə'zɪʃən] *n* (*place: of thing, person*) Position *f*, Lage *f*; (*of person's body*) Stellung *f*; (*job*) Stelle *f*; (*in race etc*) Platz *m*; (*attitude*) Haltung *f*, Standpunkt *m*; (*situation*) Lage ▷ *vt* (*person, thing*) stellen; **to be in a ~ to do sth** in der Lage sein, etw zu tun
positive ['pɔzɪtɪv] *adj* positiv; (*certain*) sicher; (*decisive: action, policy*) konstruktiv
positively ['pɔzɪtɪvlɪ] *adv* (*emphatic: rude, stupid etc*) eindeutig; (*encouragingly, Elec*) positiv; **the body has been ~ identified** die Leiche ist eindeutig identifiziert worden
possess [pə'zɛs] *vt* besitzen; (*subj: feeling, belief*) Besitz ergreifen von; **like a man ~ed** wie besessen; **whatever ~ed you to do it?** was ist in dich gefahren, das zu tun?
possession [pə'zɛʃən] *n* Besitz *m*; **possessions** *npl* (*belongings*) Besitz *m*; **to take ~ of** Besitz ergreifen von
possessive [pə'zɛsɪv] *adj* (*nature etc*) besitzergreifend; (*Ling: pronoun*) Possessiv-; (*: adjective*) besitzanzeigend; **to be ~ about sb/sth** Besitzansprüche an jdn/etw *acc* stellen
possibility [pɔsɪ'bɪlɪtɪ] *n* Möglichkeit *f*
possible ['pɔsɪbl] *adj* möglich; **it's ~** (*may be true*) es ist möglich, es kann sein; **it's ~ to do it** es ist machbar *or* zu machen; **as far as ~** so weit wie möglich; **if ~** falls *or* wenn möglich; **as soon as ~** so bald wie möglich
possibly ['pɔsɪblɪ] *adv* (*perhaps*) möglicherweise, vielleicht; (*conceivably*) überhaupt; **if you ~ can** falls überhaupt möglich; **what could they ~ want?** was um alles in der Welt wollen sie?; **I cannot ~ come** ich kann auf keinen Fall kommen
post [pəust] *n* (*Brit*) Post *f*; (*pole, goal post*) Pfosten *m*; (*job*) Stelle *f*; (*Mil*) Posten *m*; (*also*: **trading post**) Handelsniederlassung *f* ▷ *vt* (*Brit: letter*) aufgeben; (*Mil*) aufstellen; **by ~** (*Brit*) per Post; **by return of ~** (*Brit*) postwendend, umgehend; **to keep sb ~ed** (*informed*) jdn auf dem Laufenden halten; **to ~ sb to** (*town, country*) jdn versetzen nach; (*embassy, office*) jdn versetzen zu; (*Mil*) jdn abkommandieren nach
▸ **post up** *vt* anschlagen
postage ['pəustɪdʒ] *n* Porto *nt*
postal ['pəustl] *adj* (*charges, service*) Post-
postal order (*Brit*) *n* Postanweisung *f*
postbox ['pəustbɔks] *n* Briefkasten *m*
postcard ['pəustkaːd] *n* Postkarte *f*
postcode ['pəustkəud] (*Brit*) *n* Postleitzahl *f*
poster ['pəustə[r]] *n* Poster *nt*, Plakat *nt*
poste restante [pəust'rɛstɑ̃ːnt] (*Brit*) *n* Stelle *f* für postlagernde Sendungen ▷ *adv* postlagernd
postgraduate ['pəust'grædjuət] *n* Graduierte(r) *f(m)* (*im Weiterstudium*)
posthumous ['pɔstjuməs] *adj* posthum
postman ['pəustmən] (*irreg: like* **man**) *n* Briefträger *m*, Postbote *m*
postmark ['pəustmaːk] *n* Poststempel *m*
post office *n* (*building*) Post *f*, Postamt *nt*; **the Post Office** (*organization*) die Post
postpone [pəus'pəun] *vt* verschieben
posture ['pɔstʃə[r]] *n* (*also fig*) Haltung *f* ▷ *vi* (*pej*) posieren
postwar [pəust'wɔː[r]] *adj* Nachkriegs-
posy ['pəuzɪ] *n* Blumensträußchen *nt*
pot [pɔt] *n* Topf *m*; (*teapot, coffee pot, potful*) Kanne *f*; (*inf: marijuana*) Pot *nt* ▷ *vt* (*plant*) eintopfen; **to go to ~** (*inf*) auf den Hund kommen; **~s of** (*Brit: inf*) jede Menge
potato [pə'teɪtəu] (*pl* **~es**) *n* Kartoffel *f*
potato peeler *n* Kartoffelschäler *m*
potent ['pəutnt] *adj* (*powerful*) stark; (*sexually*) potent
potential [pə'tɛnʃl] *adj* potenziell ▷ *n* Potenzial *nt*; **to have ~** (*person, machine*) Fähigkeiten *or* Potenzial haben; (*idea, plan*) ausbaufähig sein
pothole ['pɔthəul] *n* (*in road*) Schlagloch *nt*; (*cave*) Höhle *f*
potholing ['pɔthəulɪŋ] (*Brit*) *n*: **to go ~** Höhlenforschung betreiben

potluck [pɔt'lʌk] *n*: **to take ~** sich überraschen lassen
potted ['pɔtɪd] *adj* (*food*) eingemacht; (*plant*) Topf-; (*abbreviated: history etc*) Kurz-, kurz gefasst
potter ['pɔtə^r] *n* Töpfer(in) *m(f)* ▷ *vi*: **to ~ around, ~ about** (*Brit*) herumhantieren; **to ~ around the house** im Haus herumwerkeln
pottery ['pɔtərɪ] *n* (*pots, dishes etc*) Keramik *f*, Töpferwaren *pl*; (*work, hobby*) Töpfern *nt*; (*factory, workshop*) Töpferei *f*; **a piece of ~** ein Töpferstück *nt*
potty ['pɔtɪ] *adj* (*inf: mad*) verrückt ▷ *n* (*for child*) Töpfchen *nt*
pouch [pautʃ] *n* Beutel *m* (*also Zool*)
poultry ['pəultrɪ] *n* Geflügel *nt*
pounce [pauns] *vi*: **to ~ on** (*also fig*) sich stürzen auf *+acc*
pound [paund] *n* (*unit of money*) Pfund *nt*; (*unit of weight*) (britisches) Pfund (*= 453,6g*); (*for dogs*) Zwinger *m*; (*for cars*) Abholstelle *f* (*für abgeschleppte Fahrzeuge*) ▷ *vt* (*beat: table, wall etc*) herumhämmern auf *+dat*; (*crush: grain, spice etc*) zerstoßen; (*bombard*) beschießen ▷ *vi* (*heart*) klopfen, pochen; (*head*) dröhnen; **half a ~ of butter** ein halbes Pfund Butter; **a five-~ note** ein Fünfpfundschein *m*
pound sterling *n* Pfund *nt* Sterling
pour [pɔː^r] *vt* (*tea, wine etc*) gießen; (*cereal etc*) schütten ▷ *vi* strömen; **to ~ sb a glass of wine/a cup of tea** jdm ein Glas Wein/eine Tasse Tee einschenken; **to ~ with rain** in Strömen gießen
▸ **pour away** *vt* wegschütten
▸ **pour in** *vi* (*people*) hereinströmen; (*letters etc*) massenweise eintreffen
▸ **pour out** *vi* (*people*) herausströmen ▷ *vt* (*tea, wine etc*) eingießen; (*fig: thoughts, feelings, etc*) freien Lauf lassen *+dat*
pouring ['pɔːrɪŋ] *adj*: **~ rain** strömender Regen *m*
pout [paut] *vi* einen Schmollmund ziehen
poverty ['pɔvətɪ] *n* Armut *f*
poverty-stricken ['pɔvətɪstrɪkn] *adj* verarmt, Not leidend
powder ['paudə^r] *n* Pulver *nt* ▷ *vt*: **to ~ one's face** sich *dat* das Gesicht pudern; **to ~ one's nose** (*euph*) kurz mal verschwinden
powder compact *n* Puderdose *f*
powdered milk ['paudəd-] *n* Milchpulver *nt*
powder room (*euph*) *n* Damentoilette *f*
power ['pauə^r] *n* (*control, legal right*) Macht *f*; (*ability*) Fähigkeit *f*; (*of muscles, ideas, words*) Kraft *f*; (*of explosion, engine*) Gewalt *f*; (*electricity*) Strom *m*; **2 to the ~ (of) 3** (*Math*) 2 hoch 3; **to do everything in one's ~ to help** alles in seiner Macht Stehende tun, um zu helfen; **a world ~** eine Weltmacht; **the ~s that be** (*authority*) diejenigen, die das Sagen haben; **~ of attorney** Vollmacht *f*; **to be in ~** (*Pol etc*) an der Macht sein
power cut *n* Stromausfall *m*
powered ['pauəd] *adj*: **~ by** angetrieben von; **nuclear-~ submarine** atomgetriebenes U-Boot
power failure *n* Stromausfall *m*
powerful ['pauəful] *adj* (*person, organization*) mächtig; (*body, voice, blow etc*) kräftig; (*engine*) stark; (*unpleasant: smell*) streng; (*emotion*) überwältigend; (*argument, evidence*) massiv
powerless ['pauəlɪs] *adj* machtlos; **to be ~ to do sth** nicht die Macht haben, etw zu tun
power point (*Brit*) *n* Steckdose *f*
power station *n* Kraftwerk *nt*
PR *n abbr* = **public relations** (*Pol*) = **proportional representation** ▷ *abbr* (*US: Post: = Puerto Rico*)
practical ['præktɪkl] *adj* praktisch; (*person: good with hands*) praktisch veranlagt; (*ideas, methods*) praktikabel
practicality [præktɪ'kælɪtɪ] *n* (*of person*) praktische Veranlagung *f*; **practicalities** *npl* (*of situation etc*) praktische Einzelheiten *pl*
practical joke *n* Streich *m*
practically ['præktɪklɪ] *adv* praktisch
practice ['præktɪs] *n* (*also Med, Law*) Praxis *f*; (*custom*) Brauch *m*; (*exercise*) Übung *f* ▷ *vt, vi* (*US*) = **practise**; **in ~** in der Praxis; **out of ~** aus der Übung; **2 hours' piano ~** 2 Stunden Klavierübungen; **it's common** *or* **standard ~** es ist allgemein üblich; **to put sth into ~** etw in die Praxis umsetzen; **target ~** Zielschießen *nt*
practise, (*US*) **practice** ['præktɪs] *vt* (*train at*) üben; (*carry out: custom*) pflegen; (*: activity etc*) ausüben; (*profession*) praktizieren ▷ *vi* (*train*) üben; (*lawyer, doctor etc*) praktizieren
practising ['præktɪsɪŋ] *adj* praktizierend
practitioner [præk'tɪʃənə^r] *n*: **medical ~** praktischer Arzt *m*, praktische Ärztin *f*; **legal ~** Rechtsanwalt *m*, Rechtsanwältin *f*
pragmatic [præg'mætɪk] *adj* pragmatisch
prairie ['prɛərɪ] *n* (Gras)steppe *f*; **the ~s** (*US*) die Prärien
praise [preɪz] *n* Lob *nt* ▷ *vt* loben; (*Rel*) loben, preisen
praiseworthy ['preɪzwəːðɪ] *adj* lobenswert
pram [præm] (*Brit*) *n* Kinderwagen *m*
prance [prɑːns] *vi* (*horse*) tänzeln; **to ~ about/in/out** (*person*) herum-/hinein-/hinausstolzieren
prank [præŋk] *n* Streich *m*
prawn [prɔːn] *n* (*Culin, Zool*) Garnele *f*, Krabbe *f*; **~ cocktail** Krabbencocktail *m*
pray [preɪ] *vi* beten; **to ~ for sb/sth** (*Rel, fig*) für jdn/um etw beten
prayer [prɛə^r] *n* Gebet *nt*; **to say one's ~s** beten
preach [priːtʃ] *vi* (*Rel*) predigen; (*pej: moralize*) Predigten halten ▷ *vt* (*sermon*) direkt halten; (*fig: advocate*) predigen, verkünden; **to ~ at sb** (*fig*) jdm Moralpredigten halten; **to ~ to the converted** (*fig*) offene Türen einrennen
preacher ['priːtʃə^r] *n* Prediger(in) *m(f)*
precarious [prɪ'kɛərɪəs] *adj* prekär

precaution [prɪ'kɔːʃən] *n* Vorsichtsmaßnahme *f*; **to take ~s** Vorsichtsmaßnahmen treffen

precede [prɪ'siːd] *vt* (*event*) vorausgehen *+dat*; (*person*) vorangehen *+dat*; (*words, sentences*) vorangestellt sein *+dat*

precedent ['prɛsɪdənt] *n* (*Law*) Präzedenzfall *m*; **without ~** noch nie da gewesen; **to establish** *or* **set a ~** einen Präzedenzfall schaffen

preceding [prɪ'siːdɪŋ] *adj* vorhergehend

precinct ['priːsɪŋkt] *n* (*US: part of city*) Bezirk *m*; **precincts** *npl* (*of cathedral, palace*) Gelände *nt*; **shopping ~** (*Brit*) Einkaufsviertel *nt*; (*under cover*) Einkaufscenter *nt*

precious ['prɛʃəs] *adj* wertvoll, kostbar; (*pej: person, writing*) geziert; (*ironic: damned*) heiß geliebt, wundervoll ▷ *adv* (*inf*): **~ little/few** herzlich wenig/wenige

precipitate [*vt* prɪ'sɪpɪteɪt, *adj* prɪ'sɪpɪtɪt] *vt* (*event*) heraufbeschwören ▷ *adj* (*hasty*) überstürzt, übereilt

precise [prɪ'saɪs] *adj* genau, präzise; **at 4 o'clock to be ~** um 4 Uhr, um genau zu sein

precisely [prɪ'saɪslɪ] *adv* genau, exakt; (*emphatic*) ganz genau; **~!** genau!

precision [prɪ'sɪʒən] *n* Genauigkeit *f*, Präzision *f*

precocious [prɪ'kəuʃəs] *adj* (*child, behaviour*) frühreif

precondition ['priːkən'dɪʃən] *n* Vorbedingung *f*

predator ['prɛdətəʳ] *n* (*Zool*) Raubtier *nt*; (*fig*) Eindringling *m*

predecessor ['priːdɪsɛsəʳ] *n* Vorgänger(in) *m(f)*

predicament [prɪ'dɪkəmənt] *n* Notlage *f*, Dilemma *nt*; **to be in a ~** in einer Notlage *or* einem Dilemma stecken

predict [prɪ'dɪkt] *vt* vorhersagen

predictable [prɪ'dɪktəbl] *adj* vorhersagbar

prediction [prɪ'dɪkʃən] *n* Voraussage *f*

predominantly [prɪ'dɔmɪnəntlɪ] *adv* überwiegend

pre-empt [priː'ɛmt] *vt* zuvorkommen *+dat*

preen [priːn] *vt*: **to ~ itself** (*bird*) sich putzen; **to ~ o.s.** sich herausputzen

prefab ['priːfæb] *n* Fertighaus *nt*

preface ['prɛfəs] *n* Vorwort *nt* ▷ *vt*: **to ~ with/by** (*speech, action*) einleiten mit/durch

prefect ['priːfɛkt] (*Brit*) *n* (*in school*) Aufsichtsschüler(in) *m(f)*

prefer [prɪ'fəːʳ] *vt* (*like better*) vorziehen; **to ~ charges** (*Law*) Anklage erheben; **to ~ doing** *or* **to do sth** (es) vorziehen, etw zu tun; **I ~ tea to coffee** ich mag lieber Tee als Kaffee

preferable ['prɛfrəbl] *adj*: **to be ~ (to)** vorzuziehen sein (*+dat*)

preferably ['prɛfrəblɪ] *adv* vorzugsweise, am besten

preference ['prɛfrəns] *n*: **to have a ~ for** (*liking*) eine Vorliebe haben für; **I drink beer in ~ to wine** ich trinke lieber Bier als Wein; **to give ~ to** (*priority*) vorziehen, Vorrang einräumen *+dat*

preferential [prɛfə'rɛnʃəl] *adj*: **~ treatment** bevorzugte Behandlung *f*; **to give sb ~ treatment** jdn bevorzugt behandeln

prefix ['priːfɪks] *n* (*Ling*) Präfix *nt*

pregnancy ['prɛgnənsɪ] *n* (*of woman*) Schwangerschaft *f*; (*of female animal*) Trächtigkeit *f*

pregnant ['prɛgnənt] *adj* (*woman*) schwanger; (*female animal*) trächtig; (*fig: pause, remark*) bedeutungsschwer; **3 months ~** im vierten Monat (schwanger)

prehistoric ['priːhɪs'tɔrɪk] *adj* prähistorisch, vorgeschichtlich

prejudice ['prɛdʒudɪs] *n* (*bias against*) Vorurteil *nt*; (*bias in favour*) Voreingenommenheit *f* ▷ *vt* beeinträchtigen; **without ~ to** (*form*) unbeschadet *+gen*, ohne Beeinträchtigung *+gen*; **to ~ sb in favour of/against sth** jdn für/gegen etw einnehmen

prejudiced ['prɛdʒudɪst] *adj* (*person, view*) voreingenommen

preliminary [prɪ'lɪmɪnərɪ] *adj* (*step, arrangements*) vorbereitend; (*remarks*) einleitend

prelude ['prɛljuːd] *n* (*Mus*) Präludium *nt*; (*: as introduction*) Vorspiel *nt*; **a ~ to** (*fig*) ein Vorspiel *or* ein Auftakt zu

premarital ['priː'mærɪtl] *adj* vorehelich

premature ['prɛmətʃuəʳ] *adj* (*earlier than expected*) vorzeitig; (*too early*) verfrüht; **you are being a little ~** Sie sind etwas voreilig; **~ baby** Frühgeburt *f*

premier ['prɛmɪəʳ] *adj* (*best*) beste(r, s), bedeutendste(r, s) ▷ *n* (*Pol*) Premierminister(in) *m(f)*

premiere ['prɛmɪɛəʳ] *n* Premiere *f*

premise ['prɛmɪs] *n* (*of argument*) Voraussetzung *f*; **premises** *npl* (*of business etc*) Räumlichkeiten *pl*; **on the ~s** im Hause

premium ['priːmɪəm] *n* (*Comm, Insurance*) Prämie *f*; **to be at a ~** (*expensive*) zum Höchstpreis gehandelt werden; (*hard to get*) Mangelware sein

premium bond (*Brit*) *n* Prämienanleihe *f*

premonition [prɛmə'nɪʃən] *n* Vorahnung *f*

preoccupied [priː'ɔkjupaɪd] *adj* (*thoughtful*) gedankenverloren; (*with work, family*) beschäftigt

prep [prɛp] (*Scol*) *adj* (*= preparatory*) *see* **preparatory school** ▷ *n* (*= preparation*) Hausaufgaben *pl*

prepaid [priː'peɪd] *adj* (*paid in advance*) im Voraus bezahlt; (*envelope*) frankiert

preparation [prɛpə'reɪʃən] *n* Vorbereitung *f*; (*food, medicine, cosmetic*) Zubereitung *f*; **preparations** *npl* Vorbereitungen *pl*; **in ~ for sth** als Vorbereitung für etw

preparatory [prɪ'pærətərɪ] *adj* vorbereitend; **~ to sth/to doing sth** als Vorbereitung für etw/, um etw zu tun

prepare [prɪ'pɛəʳ] *vt* vorbereiten; (*food, meal*)

zubereiten ▷ *vi*: **to ~ for** sich vorbereiten auf *+acc*

prepared [prɪ'pɛəd] *adj*: **to be ~ to do sth** (*willing*) bereit sein, etw zu tun; **to be ~ for sth** (*ready*) auf etw *acc* vorbereitet sein

preposition [prɛpə'zɪʃən] *n* Präposition *f*

preposterous [prɪ'pɔstərəs] *adj* grotesk, widersinnig

prep school *n* = **preparatory school**

prerequisite [pri:'rɛkwɪzɪt] *n* Vorbedingung *f*, Grundvoraussetzung *f*

preschool ['pri:'sku:l] *adj* (*age, child, education*) Vorschul-

prescribe [prɪ'skraɪb] *vt* (*Med*) verschreiben; (*demand*) anordnen, vorschreiben

prescription [prɪ'skrɪpʃən] *n* (*Med: slip of paper*) Rezept *nt*; (*: medicine*) Medikament *nt*; **to make up a ~, to fill a ~** (US) ein Medikament zubereiten; **"only available on ~"** "rezeptpflichtig"

presence ['prɛzns] *n* Gegenwart *f*, Anwesenheit *f*; (*fig: personality*) Ausstrahlung *f*; (*spirit, invisible influence*) Erscheinung *f*; **in sb's ~** in jds *dat* Gegenwart *or* Beisein; **~ of mind** Geistesgegenwart *f*

present [*adj, n* 'prɛznt, *vt* prɪ'zɛnt] *adj* (*current*) gegenwärtig, derzeitig; (*in attendance*) anwesend ▷ *n* (*gift*) Geschenk *nt*; (*Ling: also:* **present tense**) Präsens *nt*, Gegenwart *f* ▷ *vt* (*give: prize etc*) überreichen; (*plan, report*) vorlegen; (*cause, provide, portray*) darstellen; (*information, view*) darlegen; (*Radio, TV*) leiten; **to be ~ at** anwesend *or* zugegen sein bei; **those ~** die Anwesenden; **to give sb a ~** jdm ein Geschenk geben; **the ~** (*actuality*) die Gegenwart; **at ~** gegenwärtig, im Augenblick; **to ~ sth to sb, ~ sb with sth** jdm etw übergeben *or* überreichen; **to ~ sb (to)** (*formally: introduce*) jdn vorstellen *+dat*; **to ~ itself** (*opportunity*) sich bieten

presentable [prɪ'zɛntəbl] *adj* (*person*) präsentabel, ansehnlich

presentation [prɛzn'teɪʃən] *n* (*of prize*) Überreichung *f*; (*of plan, report etc*) Vorlage *f*; (*appearance*) Erscheinungsbild *nt*; (*talk*) Vortrag *m*; **on ~ of** (*voucher etc*) gegen Vorlage *+gen*

present-day ['prɛzntdeɪ] *adj* heutig, gegenwärtig

presenter [prɪ'zɛntə^r] *n* (*on radio, TV*) Moderator(in) *m(f)*

presently ['prɛzntlɪ] *adv* (*soon after*) gleich darauf; (*soon*) bald, in Kürze; (*currently*) derzeit, gegenwärtig

preservation [prɛzə'veɪʃən] *n* (*of peace, standards etc*) Erhaltung *f*; (*of furniture, building*) Konservierung *f*

preservative [prɪ'zə:vətɪv] *n* Konservierungsmittel *nt*

preserve [prɪ'zə:v] *vt* erhalten; (*peace*) wahren; (*wood*) schützen; (*food*) konservieren ▷ *n* (*often pl: jam, chutney etc*) Eingemachte(s) *nt*; (*for game, fish*) Revier *nt*; **a male ~** (*fig*) eine männliche Domäne; **a working class ~** (*fig*) eine Domäne der Arbeiterklasse

preside [prɪ'zaɪd] *vi*: **to ~ over** (*meeting etc*) vorsitzen *+dat*, den Vorsitz haben bei

president ['prɛzɪdənt] *n* (*Pol*) Präsident(in) *m(f)*; (*of organization*) Vorsitzende(r) *f(m)*

presidential [prɛzɪ'dɛnʃl] *adj* (*election, campaign etc*) Präsidentschafts-; (*adviser, representative etc*) des Präsidenten

press [prɛs] *n* (*also:* **printing press**) Presse *f*; (*of switch, bell*) Druck *m*; (*for wine*) Kelter *f* ▷ *vt* drücken, pressen; (*button, sb's hand etc*) drücken; (*iron: clothes*) bügeln; (*put pressure on: person*) drängen; (*pursue: idea, claim*) vertreten ▷ *vi* (*squeeze*) drücken, pressen; **the P~** (*newspapers, journalists*) die Presse; **to go to ~** (*newspaper*) in Druck gehen; **to be in ~** (*at the printer's*) im Druck sein; **to be in the ~** (*in the newspapers*) in der Zeitung stehen; **at the ~ of a button** auf Knopfdruck; **to ~ sth (up)on sb** (*force*) jdm etw aufdrängen; **we are ~ed for time/money** wir sind in Geldnot/Zeitnot; **to ~ sb for an answer** auf jds *acc* Antwort drängen; **to ~ sb to do** *or* **into doing sth** jdn drängen, etw zu tun; **to ~ charges (against sb)** (*Law*) Klage (gegen jdn) erheben; **to ~ for** (*changes etc*) drängen auf *+acc*

▸ **press ahead** *vi* weitermachen; **to ~ ahead with sth** etw durchziehen

▸ **press on** *vi* weitermachen

press conference *n* Pressekonferenz *f*

pressing ['prɛsɪŋ] *adj* (*urgent*) dringend

press stud (*Brit*) *n* Druckknopf *m*

press-up ['prɛsʌp] (*Brit*) *n* Liegestütz *m*

pressure ['prɛʃə^r] *n* (*also fig*) Druck *m* ▷ *vt*: **to ~ sb to do sth** jdn dazu drängen, etw zu tun; **to put ~ on sb (to do sth)** Druck auf jdn ausüben(, etw zu tun); **high/low ~** (*Tech, Met*) Hoch-/Tiefdruck *m*

pressure cooker *n* Schnellkochtopf *m*

pressure gauge *n* Druckmesser *m*, Manometer *nt*

pressure group *n* Interessenverband *m*, Pressuregroup *f*

prestige [prɛs'ti:ʒ] *n* Prestige *nt*

prestigious [prɛs'tɪdʒəs] *adj* (*institution, appointment*) mit hohem Prestigewert

presumably [prɪ'zju:məblɪ] *adv* vermutlich; **~ he did it** vermutlich *or* wahrscheinlich hat er es getan

presume [prɪ'zju:m] *vt*: **to ~ (that)** (*assume*) annehmen(, dass); **to ~ to do sth** (*dare*) sich anmaßen, etw zu tun; **I ~ so** das nehme ich an

pretence, (US) **pretense** [prɪ'tɛns] *n* (*false appearance*) Vortäuschung *f*; **under false ~s** unter Vorspiegelung falscher Tatsachen; **she is devoid of all ~** sie ist völlig natürlich; **to make a ~ of doing sth** vortäuschen, etw zu tun

pretend [prɪ'tɛnd] *vt* (*feign*) vorgeben ▷ *vi* (*feign*) sich verstellen, so tun, als ob; **I don't**

~ to understand it (*claim*) ich erhebe nicht den Anspruch, es zu verstehen
pretense [prɪ'tɛns] (*US*) *n* = **pretence**
pretentious [prɪ'tɛnʃəs] *adj* anmaßend
pretext ['pri:tɛkst] *n* Vorwand *m*; **on** *or* **under the ~ of doing sth** unter dem Vorwand, etw zu tun
pretty ['prɪtɪ] *adj* hübsch, nett ▷ *adv*: **~ clever** ganz schön schlau; **~ good** ganz gut
prevail [prɪ'veɪl] *vi* (*be current*) vorherrschen; (*triumph*) siegen; **to ~ (up)on sb to do sth** (*persuade*) jdn dazu bewegen *or* überreden, etw zu tun
prevailing [prɪ'veɪlɪŋ] *adj* (*wind, fashion etc*) vorherrschend
prevalent ['prɛvələnt] *adj* (*belief, custom*) vorherrschend
prevent [prɪ'vɛnt] *vt* verhindern; **to ~ sb from doing sth** jdn daran hindern, etw zu tun; **to ~ sth from happening** verhindern, dass etw geschieht
preventative [prɪ'vɛntətɪv] *adj* = **preventive**
prevention [prɪ'vɛnʃən] *n* Verhütung *f*
preventive [prɪ'vɛntɪv] *adj* (*measures, medicine*) vorbeugend
preview ['pri:vju:] *n* (*of film*) Vorpremiere *f*; (*of exhibition*) Vernissage *f*
previous ['pri:vɪəs] *adj* (*earlier*) früher; (*preceding*) vorhergehend; **~ to** vor *+dat*
previously ['pri:vɪəslɪ] *adv* (*before*) zuvor; (*formerly*) früher
prewar [pri:'wɔ:[r]] *adj* (*period*) Vorkriegs-
prey [preɪ] *n* Beute *f*; **to fall ~ to** (*fig*) zum Opfer fallen *+dat*
▶ **prey on** *vt fus* (*animal*) Jagd machen auf *+acc*; **it was ~ing on his mind** es ließ ihn nicht los
price [praɪs] *n* (*also fig*) Preis *m* ▷ *vt* (*goods*) auszeichnen; **what is the ~ of ...?** was kostet ...?; **to go up** *or* **rise in ~** im Preis steigen, teurer werden; **to put a ~ on sth** (*also fig*) einen Preis für etw festsetzen; **what ~ his promises now?** wie steht es jetzt mit seinen Versprechungen?; **he regained his freedom, but at a ~** er hat seine Freiheit wieder, aber zu welchem Preis!; **to be ~d at £30** £30 kosten; **to ~ o.s. out of the market** durch zu hohe Preise konkurrenzunfähig werden
priceless ['praɪslɪs] *adj* (*diamond, painting*) von unschätzbarem Wert; (*inf: amusing*) unbezahlbar, köstlich
price list *n* Preisliste *f*
prick [prɪk] *n* (*sting*) Stich *m*; (*inf!: penis*) Schwanz *m*; (*: idiot*) Arsch *m* ▷ *vt* stechen; (*sausage, balloon*) einstechen; **to ~ up one's ears** die Ohren spitzen
prickle ['prɪkl] *n* (*of plant*) Dorn *m*, Stachel *m*; (*sensation*) Prickeln *nt*
prickly ['prɪklɪ] *adj* (*plant*) stachelig; (*fabric*) kratzig
prickly heat *n* Hitzebläschen *pl*
pride [praɪd] *n* Stolz *m*; (*pej: arrogance*) Hochmut *m* ▷ *vt*: **to ~ o.s. on** sich rühmen *+gen*; **to take (a) ~ in** stolz sein auf *+acc*; **to take a ~ in doing sth** etw mit Stolz tun; **to have** *or* **take ~ of place** (*Brit*) die Krönung sein
priest [pri:st] *n* Priester *m*
priesthood ['pri:sthud] *n* Priestertum *nt*
prim [prɪm] (*pej*) *adj* (*person*) etepetete
primarily ['praɪmərɪlɪ] *adv* in erster Linie, hauptsächlich
primary ['praɪmərɪ] *adj* (*principal*) Haupt-, hauptsächlich; (*education, teacher*) Grundschul- ▷ *n* (*US: election*) Vorwahl *f*
primary school (*Brit*) *n* Grundschule *f*
prime [praɪm] *adj* (*most important*) oberste(r, s); (*best quality*) erstklassig ▷ *n* (*of person's life*) die besten Jahre *pl* ▷ *vt* (*wood*) grundieren; (*fig: person*) informieren; (*gun*) schussbereit machen; (*pump*) auffüllen; **~ example** erstklassiges Beispiel; **in the ~ of life** im besten Alter
Prime Minister *n* Premierminister(in) *m(f)*
primeval [praɪ'mi:vl] *adj* (*beast*) urzeitlich; (*fig: feelings*) instinktiv; **~ forest** Urwald *m*
primitive ['prɪmɪtɪv] *adj* (*tribe, tool, conditions etc*) primitiv; (*life form, machine etc*) frühzeitlich; (*man*) der Urzeit
primrose ['prɪmrəuz] *n* Primel *f*, gelbe Schlüsselblume *f*
prince [prɪns] *n* Prinz *m*
princess [prɪn'sɛs] *n* Prinzessin *f*
principal ['prɪnsɪpl] *adj* (*most important*) Haupt-, wichtigste(r, s) ▷ *n* (*of school, college*) Rektor(in) *m(f)*; (*Theat*) Hauptdarsteller(in) *m(f)*; (*Fin*) Kapitalsumme *f*
principally ['prɪnsɪplɪ] *adv* vornehmlich
principle ['prɪnsɪpl] *n* Prinzip *nt*; **in ~** im Prinzip, prinzipiell; **on ~** aus Prinzip
print [prɪnt] *n* (*Art*) Druck *m*; (*Phot*) Abzug *m*; (*fabric*) bedruckter Stoff *m* ▷ *vt* (*produce*) drucken; (*publish*) veröffentlichen; (*cloth, pattern*) bedrucken; (*write in capitals*) in Druckschrift schreiben; **prints** *npl* (*fingerprints etc*) Abdrücke *pl*; **out of ~** vergriffen; **in ~** erhältlich; **the fine** *or* **small ~** das Kleingedruckte
▶ **print out** *vt* (*Comput*) ausdrucken
printed matter *n* Drucksache *f*
printer ['prɪntə[r]] *n* (*person*) Drucker(in) *m(f)*; (*firm*) Druckerei *f*; (*machine*) Drucker *m*
printing ['prɪntɪŋ] *n* (*activity*) Drucken *nt*
prior ['praɪə[r]] *adj* (*previous: knowledge, warning*) vorherig; (*: engagement*) früher; (*more important: claim, duty*) vorrangig ▷ *n* (*Rel*) Prior *m*; **without ~ notice** ohne vorherige Ankündigung; **to have a ~ claim on sth** ein Vorrecht auf etw *acc* haben; **~ to** vor *+dat*
priority [praɪ'ɔrɪtɪ] *n* vorrangige Angelegenheit *f*; **priorities** *npl* Prioritäten *pl*; **to take** *or* **have ~ (over sth)** Vorrang (vor etw *dat*) haben; **to give ~ to sb/sth** jdm/etw Vorrang einräumen
prise [praɪz] (*Brit*) *vt*: **to ~ open** aufbrechen
prison ['prɪzn] *n* Gefängnis *nt* ▷ *cpd* (*officer,*

food, cell etc) Gefängnis-
prisoner ['prɪznəʳ] *n* Gefangene(r) *f(m)*; **the ~ at the bar** (*Law*) der/die Angeklagte; **to take sb ~** jdn gefangen nehmen
prisoner of war *n* Kriegsgefangene(r) *f(m)*
pristine ['prɪsti:n] *adj* makellos; **in ~ condition** in makellosem Zustand
privacy ['prɪvəsɪ] *n* Privatsphäre *f*
private ['praɪvɪt] *adj* privat; (*life*) Privat-; (*thoughts, plans etc*) persönlich; (*place*) abgelegen; (*secretive: person*) verschlossen ▷ *n* (*Mil*) Gefreite(r) *m*; **"~"** (*on envelope*) "vertraulich"; (*on door*) "privat"; **in ~** privat; **in (his) ~ life** in seinem Privatleben; **to be in ~ practice** (*Med*) Privatpatienten haben; **~ hearing** (*Law*) nicht öffentliche Verhandlung *f*
private enterprise *n* Privatunternehmen *nt*
privately ['praɪvɪtlɪ] *adv* privat; (*secretly*) insgeheim; **a ~ owned company** eine Firma im Privatbesitz
private property *n* Privatbesitz *m*
private school *n* (*fee-paying*) Privatschule *f*
privatize ['praɪvɪtaɪz] *vt* privatisieren
privet ['prɪvɪt] *n* Liguster *m*
privilege ['prɪvɪlɪdʒ] *n* (*advantage*) Privileg *nt*; (*honour*) Ehre *f*
privy ['prɪvɪ] *adj*: **to be ~ to** eingeweiht sein in *+acc*
prize [praɪz] *n* Preis *m* ▷ *adj* (*prize-winning*) preisgekrönt; (*classic: example*) erstklassig ▷ *vt* schätzen; **~ idiot** (*inf*) Vollidiot *m*
prizewinner ['praɪzwɪnəʳ] *n* Preisträger(in) *m(f)*
pro [prəu] *n* (*Sport*) Profi *m* ▷ *prep* (*in favour of*) pro *+acc*, für *+acc*; **the ~s and cons** das Für und Wider
probability [prɔbə'bɪlɪtɪ] *n* Wahrscheinlichkeit *f*; **in all ~** aller Wahrscheinlichkeit nach
probable ['prɔbəbl] *adj* wahrscheinlich; **it seems ~ that ...** es ist wahrscheinlich, dass ...
probably ['prɔbəblɪ] *adv* wahrscheinlich
probation [prə'beɪʃən] *n*: **on ~** (*lawbreaker*) auf Bewährung; (*employee*) auf Probe
probe [prəub] *n* (*Med, Space*) Sonde *f*; (*enquiry*) Untersuchung *f* ▷ *vt* (*investigate*) untersuchen; (*poke*) bohren in *+dat*
problem ['prɔbləm] *n* Problem *nt*; **to have ~s with the car** Probleme *or* Schwierigkeiten mit dem Auto haben; **what's the ~?** wo fehlts?; **I had no ~ finding her** ich habe sie ohne Schwierigkeiten gefunden; **no ~!** kein Problem!
procedure [prə'si:dʒəʳ] *n* Verfahren *nt*
proceed [prə'si:d] *vi* (*carry on*) fortfahren; (*person: go*) sich bewegen; **to ~ to do sth** etw tun; **to ~ with** fortfahren mit; **I am not sure how to ~** ich bin nicht sicher über die weitere Vorgehensweise; **to ~ against sb** (*Law*) gegen jdn gerichtlich vorgehen
proceedings [prə'si:dɪŋz] *npl* (*organized events*) Vorgänge *pl*; (*Law*) Verfahren *nt*; (*records*) Protokoll *nt*
proceeds ['prəusi:dz] *npl* Erlös *m*
process ['prəusɛs] *n* (*series of actions*) Verfahren *nt*; (*Biol, Chem*) Prozess *m* ▷ *vt* (*raw materials, food, Comput: data*) verarbeiten; (*application*) bearbeiten; (*Phot*) entwickeln; **in the ~** dabei; **to be in the ~ of doing sth** (gerade) dabei sein, etw zu tun
processing ['prəusɛsɪŋ] *n* (*Phot*) Entwickeln *nt*
procession [prə'sɛʃən] *n* Umzug *m*, Prozession *f*; **wedding/funeral ~** Hochzeits-/Trauerzug *m*
proclaim [prə'kleɪm] *vt* verkünden, proklamieren
procrastinate [prəu'kræstɪneɪt] *vi* zögern, zaudern
procure [prə'kjuəʳ] *vt* (*obtain*) beschaffen
prod [prɔd] *vt* (*push: with finger, stick etc*) stoßen, stupsen (*inf*); (*fig: urge*) anspornen ▷ *n* (*with finger, stick etc*) Stoß *m*, Stups *m* (*inf*); (*fig: reminder*) mahnender Hinweis *m*
prodigal ['prɔdɪgl] *adj*: **~ son** verlorener Sohn *m*
prodigy ['prɔdɪdʒɪ] *n* (*person*) Naturtalent *nt*; **child ~** Wunderkind *nt*
produce [*n* 'prɔdju:s, *vt* prə'dju:s] *n* (*Agr*) (Boden)produkte *pl* ▷ *vt* (*result etc*) hervorbringen; (*goods, commodity*) produzieren, herstellen; (*Biol, Chem*) erzeugen; (*fig: evidence etc*) liefern; (*: passport etc*) vorlegen; (*play, film, programme*) produzieren
producer [prə'dju:səʳ] *n* (*person*) Produzent(in) *m(f)*; (*country, company*) Produzent *m*, Hersteller *m*
product ['prɔdʌkt] *n* Produkt *nt*
production [prə'dʌkʃən] *n* Produktion *f*; (*Theat*) Inszenierung *f*; **to go into ~** (*goods*) in Produktion gehen; **on ~ of** gegen Vorlage *+gen*
production line *n* Fließband *nt*, Fertigungsstraße *f*
productive [prə'dʌktɪv] *adj* produktiv
productivity [prɔdʌk'tɪvɪtɪ] *n* Produktivität *f*
Prof. *n abbr* (= *professor*) Prof.
profession [prə'fɛʃən] *n* Beruf *m*; (*people*) Berufsstand *m*; **the ~s** die gehobenen Berufe
professional [prə'fɛʃənl] *adj* (*organization, musician etc*) Berufs-; (*misconduct, advice*) beruflich; (*skilful*) professionell ▷ *n* (*doctor, lawyer, teacher etc*) Fachmann *m*, Fachfrau *f*; (*Sport*) Profi *m*; (*skilled person*) Experte *m*, Expertin *f*; **to seek ~ advice** fachmännischen Rat einholen
professionally [prə'fɛʃnəlɪ] *adv* beruflich; (*for a living*) berufsmäßig; **I only know him ~** ich kenne ihn nur beruflich
professor [prə'fɛsəʳ] *n* (*Brit*) Professor(in) *m(f)*; (*US, Canada*) Dozent(in) *m(f)*
proficiency [prə'fɪʃənsɪ] *n* Können *nt*, Fertigkeiten *pl*
profile ['prəufaɪl] *n* (*of person's face*) Profil *nt*;

(*fig: biography*) Porträt *nt*; **to keep a low ~** (*fig*) sich zurückhalten; **to have a high ~** (*fig*) eine große Rolle spielen

profit ['prɔfɪt] *n* (*Comm*) Gewinn *m*, Profit *m* ▹ *vi*: **to ~ by** *or* **from** (*fig*) profitieren von; **~ and loss account** Gewinn-und-Verlust-Rechnung; **to make a ~** einen Gewinn machen; **to sell (sth) at a ~** (etw) mit Gewinn verkaufen

profitable ['prɔfɪtəbl] *adj* (*business, deal*) rentabel, einträglich; (*fig: useful*) nützlich

profound [prə'faund] *adj* (*shock*) schwer, tief; (*effect, differences*) weitreichend; (*idea, book*) tief schürfend

profusely [prə'fjuːslɪ] *adv* (*apologise, thank*) vielmals; (*sweat, bleed*) stark

prognosis [prɔg'nəusɪs] (*pl* **prognoses**) *n* (*Med, fig*) Prognose *f*

programme, (*US*) **program** ['prəugræm] *n* Programm *nt* ▹ *vt* (*machine, system*) programmieren

programmer ['prəugræmə^r] *n* Programmierer(in) *m(f)*

programming, (US) **programing** ['prəugræmɪŋ] *n* Programmierung *f*

progress [*n* 'prəugrɛs, *vi* prə'grɛs] *n* Fortschritt *m*; (*improvement*) Fortschritte *pl* ▹ *vi* (*advance*) vorankommen; (*become higher in rank*) aufsteigen; (*continue*) sich fortsetzen; **in ~** (*meeting, battle, match*) im Gange; **to make ~** Fortschritte machen

progressive [prə'grɛsɪv] *adj* (*enlightened*) progressiv, fortschrittlich; (*gradual*) fortschreitend

prohibit [prə'hɪbɪt] *vt* (*ban*) verbieten; **to ~ sb from doing sth** jdm verbieten *or* untersagen, etw zu tun; **"smoking ~ed"** "Rauchen verboten"

project [*n* 'prɔdʒɛkt, *vt, vi* prə'dʒɛkt] *n* (*plan, scheme*) Projekt *nt*; (*Scol*) Referat *nt* ▹ *vt* (*plan*) planen; (*estimate*) schätzen, voraussagen; (*light, film, picture*) projizieren ▹ *vi* (*stick out*) hervorragen

projection [prə'dʒɛkʃən] *n* (*estimate*) Schätzung *f*, Voraussage *f*; (*overhang*) Vorsprung *m*; (*Cine*) Projektion *f*

projector [prə'dʒɛktə^r] *n* Projektor *m*

prolific [prə'lɪfɪk] *adj* (*artist, writer*) produktiv

prolong [prə'lɔŋ] *vt* verlängern

prom [prɔm] *n abbr* = **promenade**; (*Mus*) = **promenade concert**; (*US: college ball*) Studentenball *m*

promenade [prɔmə'nɑːd] *n* Promenade *f*

promenade concert (*Brit*) *n* Promenadenkonzert *nt*

prominent ['prɔmɪnənt] *adj* (*person*) prominent; (*thing*) bedeutend; (*very noticeable*) herausragend; **he is ~ in the field of science** er ist eine führende Persönlichkeit im naturwissenschaftlichen Bereich

promiscuous [prə'mɪskjuəs] *adj* promisk

promise ['prɔmɪs] *n* (*vow*) Versprechen *nt*; (*potential, hope*) Hoffnung *f* ▹ *vi* versprechen ▹ *vt*: **to ~ sb sth, ~ sth to sb** jdm etw versprechen; **to make/break/keep a ~** ein Versprechen geben/brechen/halten; **a young man of ~** ein vielversprechender junger Mann; **she shows ~** sie gibt zu Hoffnungen Anlass; **it ~s to be lively** es verspricht lebhaft zu werden; **to ~ (sb) to do sth** (jdm) versprechen, etw zu tun

promising ['prɔmɪsɪŋ] *adj* vielversprechend

promote [prə'məut] *vt* (*employee*) befördern; (*advertise*) werben für; (*encourage: peace etc*) fördern; **the team was ~d to the first division** (*Brit: Football*) die Mannschaft stieg in die erste Division auf

promoter [prə'məutə^r] *n* (*of concert, event*) Veranstalter(in) *m(f)*; (*of cause, idea*) Förderer *m*, Förderin *f*

promotion [prə'məuʃən] *n* (*at work*) Beförderung *f*; (*of product, event*) Werbung *f*; (*of idea*) Förderung *f*; (*publicity campaign*) Werbekampagne *f*

prompt [prɔmpt] *adj* prompt, sofortig ▹ *adv* (*exactly*) pünktlich ▹ *n* (*Comput*) Prompt *m* ▹ *vt* (*cause*) veranlassen; (*when talking*) auf die Sprünge helfen *+dat*; (*Theat*) soufflieren *+dat*; **they're very ~** (*punctual*) sie sind sehr pünktlich; **he was ~ to accept** er nahm unverzüglich an; **at 8 o'clock ~** (um) Punkt 8 Uhr; **to ~ sb to do sth** jdn dazu veranlassen, etw zu tun

promptly ['prɔmptlɪ] *adv* (*immediately*) sofort; (*exactly*) pünktlich

prone [prəun] *adj* (*face down*) in Bauchlage; **to be ~ to sth** zu etw neigen; **she is ~ to burst into tears if ...** sie neigt dazu, in Tränen auszubrechen, wenn ...

prong [prɔŋ] *n* (*of fork*) Zinke *f*

pronoun ['prəunaun] *n* Pronomen *nt*, Fürwort *nt*

pronounce [prə'nauns] *vt* (*word*) aussprechen; (*give verdict, opinion*) erklären ▹ *vi*: **to ~ (up)on** sich äußern zu; **they ~d him dead/unfit to drive** sie erklärten ihn für tot/fahruntüchtig

pronunciation [prənʌnsɪ'eɪʃən] *n* Aussprache *f*

proof [pruːf] *n* (*evidence*) Beweis *m*; (*Typ*) (Korrektur)fahne *f* ▹ *adj*: **~ against** sicher vor *+dat*; **to be 70 % ~** (*alcohol*) ≈ einen Alkoholgehalt von 40% haben

prop [prɔp] *n* (*support*) Stütze *f* ▹ *vt* (*lean*): **to ~ sth against sth** etw an etw *acc* lehnen
▸ **prop up** *vt sep* (*thing*) (ab)stützen; (*fig: government, industry*) unterstützen

propaganda [prɔpə'gændə] *n* Propaganda *f*

propel [prə'pɛl] *vt* (*vehicle, machine*) antreiben; (*person*) schubsen; (*fig: person*) treiben

propeller [prə'pɛlə^r] *n* Propeller *m*

propensity [prə'pɛnsɪtɪ] *n*: **a ~ for** *or* **to sth** ein Hang *m or* eine Neigung zu etw; **to have a ~ to do sth** dazu neigen, etw zu tun

proper ['prɔpə^r] *adj* (*genuine, correct*) richtig; (*socially acceptable*) schicklich; (*inf: real*) echt;

the town/city ~ die Stadt selbst; **to go through the ~ channels** den Dienstweg einhalten

properly ['prɔpəlɪ] *adv* (*eat, work*) richtig; (*behave*) anständig

proper noun *n* Eigenname *m*

property ['prɔpətɪ] *n* (*possessions*) Eigentum *nt*; (*building and its land*) Grundstück *nt*; (*quality*) Eigenschaft *f*; **it's their ~** es gehört ihnen

prophecy ['prɔfɪsɪ] *n* Prophezeiung *f*

prophesy ['prɔfɪsaɪ] *vt* prophezeien ▷ *vi* Prophezeiungen machen

prophet ['prɔfɪt] *n* Prophet *m*; **~ of doom** Unheilsprophet(in) *m(f)*

proportion [prə'pɔːʃən] *n* (*part*) Teil *m*; (*number: of people, things*) Anteil *m*; (*ratio*) Verhältnis *nt*; **in ~ to** im Verhältnis zu; **to be out of all ~ to sth** in keinem Verhältnis zu etw stehen; **to get sth in/out of ~** etw im richtigen/falschen Verhältnis sehen; **a sense of ~** (*fig*) ein Sinn für das Wesentliche

proportional [prə'pɔːʃənl] *adj*: **~ to** proportional zu

proposal [prə'pəuzl] *n* (*plan*) Vorschlag *m*; **~ (of marriage)** Heiratsantrag *m*

propose [prə'pəuz] *vt* (*plan, idea*) vorschlagen; (*motion*) einbringen; (*toast*) ausbringen ▷ *vi* (*offer marriage*) einen Heiratsantrag machen; **to ~ to do sth** *or* **doing sth** (*intend*) die Absicht haben, etw zu tun

proposition [prɔpə'zɪʃən] *n* (*statement*) These *f*; (*offer*) Angebot *nt*; **to make sb a ~** jdm ein Angebot machen

proprietor [prə'praɪətəʳ] *n* (*of hotel, shop etc*) Inhaber(in) *m(f)*; (*of newspaper*) Besitzer(in) *m(f)*

propriety [prə'praɪətɪ] *n* (*seemliness*) Schicklichkeit *f*

prose [prəuz] *n* (*not poetry*) Prosa *f*; (*Brit: Scol: translation*) Übersetzung *f* in die Fremdsprache

prosecute ['prɔsɪkjuːt] *vt* (*Law: person*) strafrechtlich verfolgen; (*: case*) die Anklage vertreten in *+dat*

prosecution [prɔsɪ'kjuːʃən] *n* (*Law: action*) strafrechtliche Verfolgung *f*; (*: accusing side*) Anklage(vertretung) *f*

prosecutor ['prɔsɪkjuːtəʳ] *n* Anklagevertreter(in) *m(f)*; (*also*: **public prosecutor**) Staatsanwalt *m*, Staatsanwältin *f*

prospect [*n* 'prɔspɛkt, *vi* prə'spɛkt] *n* Aussicht *f* ▷ *vi*: **to ~ (for)** suchen (nach); **prospects** *npl* (*for work etc*) Aussichten *pl*, Chancen *pl*; **we are faced with the ~ of higher unemployment** wir müssen mit der Möglichkeit rechnen, dass die Arbeitslosigkeit steigt

prospecting ['prɔspɛktɪŋ] *n* (*for gold, oil etc*) Suche *f*

prospective [prə'spɛktɪv] *adj* (*son-in-law*) zukünftig; (*customer, candidate*) voraussichtlich

prospectus [prə'spɛktəs] *n* (*of college, company*) Prospekt *m*

prosper ['prɔspəʳ] *vi* (*person*) Erfolg haben; (*business, city etc*) gedeihen, florieren

prosperity [prɔ'spɛrɪtɪ] *n* Wohlstand *m*

prosperous ['prɔspərəs] *adj* (*person*) wohlhabend; (*business, city etc*) blühend

prostitute ['prɔstɪtjuːt] *n* (*female*) Prostituierte *f*; (*male*) männliche(r) Prostituierte(r) *m*, Strichjunge *m* (*inf*) ▷ *vt*: **to ~ o.s.** (*fig*) sich prostituieren, sich unter Wert verkaufen

protect [prə'tɛkt] *vt* schützen

protection [prə'tɛkʃən] *n* Schutz *m*; **police ~** Polizeischutz *m*

protective [prə'tɛktɪv] *adj* (*clothing, layer etc*) Schutz-; (*person*) fürsorglich; **~ custody** Schutzhaft *f*

protein ['prəutiːn] *n* Protein *nt*, Eiweiß *nt*

protest [*n* 'prəutɛst, *vi, vt* prə'tɛst] *n* Protest *m* ▷ *vi*: **to ~ about** *or* **against** *or* **at sth** gegen etw protestieren ▷ *vt*: **to ~ (that)** (*insist*) beteuern(, dass)

Protestant ['prɔtɪstənt] *adj* protestantisch ▷ *n* Protestant(in) *m(f)*

protester [prə'tɛstəʳ] *n* (*in demonstration*) Demonstrant(in) *m(f)*

protracted [prə'træktɪd] *adj* (*meeting etc*) langwierig, sich hinziehend; (*absence*) länger

protractor [prə'træktəʳ] *n* (*Geom*) Winkelmesser *m*

protrude [prə'truːd] *vi* (*rock, ledge, teeth*) vorstehen

proud [praud] *adj* stolz; (*arrogant*) hochmütig; **~ of sb/sth** stolz auf jdn/etw; **to be ~ to do sth** stolz (darauf) sein, etw zu tun; **to do sb/o.s. ~** (*inf*) jdn/sich verwöhnen

prove [pruːv] *vt* beweisen ▷ *vi*: **to ~ (to be) correct** sich als richtig herausstellen *or* erweisen; **to ~ (o.s./itself) (to be) useful** sich als nützlich erweisen; **he was ~d right in the end** er hat schließlich recht behalten

proverb ['prɔvəːb] *n* Sprichwort *nt*

provide [prə'vaɪd] *vt* (*food, money, shelter etc*) zur Verfügung stellen; (*answer, example etc*) liefern; **to ~ sb with sth** jdm etw zur Verfügung stellen

▸ **provide for** *vt fus* (*person*) sorgen für; (*future event*) vorsorgen für

provided [prə'vaɪdɪd] *conj*: **~ (that)** vorausgesetzt(, dass)

providing [prə'vaɪdɪŋ] *conj*: **~ (that)** vorausgesetzt(, dass)

province ['prɔvɪns] *n* (*of country*) Provinz *f*; (*responsibility etc*) Bereich *m*, Gebiet *nt*; **provinces** *npl*: **the ~s** *außerhalb der Hauptstadt liegende Landesteile*, Provinz *f*

provincial [prə'vɪnʃəl] *adj* (*town, newspaper etc*) Provinz-; (*pej: parochial*) provinziell

provision [prə'vɪʒən] *n* (*supplying*) Bereitstellung *f*; (*preparation*) Vorsorge *f*, Vorkehrungen *pl*; (*stipulation, clause*) Bestimmung *f*; **provisions** *npl* (*food*)

Proviant *m*; **to make ~ for** vorsorgen für; (*for people*) sorgen für; **there's no ~ for this in the contract** dies ist im Vertrag nicht vorgesehen

provisional [prə'vɪʒənl] *adj* vorläufig, provisorisch ▷ *n*: **P~** (*Irish: Pol*) *Mitglied der provisorischen Irisch-Republikanischen Armee*

proviso [prə'vaɪzəu] *n* Vorbehalt *m*; **with the ~ that ...** unter dem Vorbehalt, dass ...

provocative [prə'vɔkətɪv] *adj* provozierend, herausfordernd; (*sexually stimulating*) aufreizend

provoke [prə'vəuk] *vt* (*person*) provozieren, herausfordern; (*fight*) herbeiführen; (*reaction etc*) hervorrufen; **to ~ sb to do** *or* **into doing sth** jdn dazu provozieren, etw zu tun

prowess ['prauɪs] *n* Können *nt*, Fähigkeiten *pl*; **his ~ as a footballer** sein fußballerisches Können

prowl [praul] *vi* (*also*: **prowl about, prowl around**) schleichen ▷ *n*: **on the ~** auf Streifzug

prowler ['praulə^r] *n* Herumtreiber *m*

proximity [prɔk'sɪmɪtɪ] *n* Nähe *f*

proxy ['prɔksɪ] *n*: **by ~** durch einen Stellvertreter

prudent ['pru:dnt] *adj* (*sensible*) klug

prune [pru:n] *n* Backpflaume *f* ▷ *vt* (*plant*) stutzen, beschneiden

pry [praɪ] *vi*: **to ~ (into)** seine Nase hineinstecken (in *+acc*), herumschnüffeln (in *+dat*)

PS *abbr* (*= postscript*) PS

psalm [sɑ:m] *n* Psalm *m*

pseudonym ['sju:dənɪm] *n* Pseudonym *nt*

PSHE (*Brit*) *n abbr* (*Scol*) = **personal, social and health education**

psyche ['saɪkɪ] *n* Psyche *f*

psychiatric [saɪkɪ'ætrɪk] *adj* psychiatrisch

psychiatrist [saɪ'kaɪətrɪst] *n* Psychiater(in) *m(f)*

psychic ['saɪkɪk] *adj* (*person*) übersinnlich begabt; (*damage, disorder*) psychisch ▷ *n* Mensch *m* mit übersinnlichen Fähigkeiten

psychoanalysis [saɪkəuə'nælɪsɪs] *n* Psychoanalyse *f*

psychoanalyst [saɪkəu'ænəlɪst] *n* Psychoanalytiker(in) *m(f)*

psychological [saɪkə'lɔdʒɪkl] *adj* psychologisch

psychologist [saɪ'kɔlədʒɪst] *n* Psychologe *m*, Psychologin *f*

psychology [saɪ'kɔlədʒɪ] *n* (*science*) Psychologie *f*; (*character*) Psyche *f*

psychotherapy [saɪkəu'θɛrəpɪ] *n* Psychotherapie *f*

pt *abbr* = **pint; point**

PTO *abbr* (*= please turn over*) b. w.

PTV (*US*) *n abbr* (*= pay television*) Pay-TV *nt*; (*= public television*) öffentliches Fernsehen *nt*

pub [pʌb] *n* = **public house**

puberty ['pju:bətɪ] *n* Pubertät *f*

public ['pʌblɪk] *adj* öffentlich ▷ *n*: **the ~** (*in general*) die Öffentlichkeit; (*particular set of people*) das Publikum; **to be ~ knowledge** allgemein bekannt sein; **to make sth ~** etw bekannt machen; **to go ~** (*Comm*) in eine Aktiengesellschaft umgewandelt werden; **in ~** in aller Öffentlichkeit; **the general ~** die Allgemeinheit

publican ['pʌblɪkən] *n* Gastwirt(in) *m(f)*

publication [pʌblɪ'keɪʃən] *n* Veröffentlichung *f*

public company *n* Aktiengesellschaft *f*

public convenience (*Brit*) *n* öffentliche Toilette *f*

public holiday *n* gesetzlicher Feiertag *m*

public house (*Brit*) *n* Gaststätte *f*

publicity [pʌb'lɪsɪtɪ] *n* (*information*) Werbung *f*; (*attention*) Publicity *f*

publicize ['pʌblɪsaɪz] *vt* (*fact*) bekannt machen; (*event*) Publicity machen für

public limited company *n* ≈ Aktiengesellschaft *f*

publicly ['pʌblɪklɪ] *adv* öffentlich; **to be ~ owned** (*Comm*) in Staatsbesitz sein

public opinion *n* die öffentliche Meinung

public relations *n* Public Relations *pl*, Öffentlichkeitsarbeit *f*

public school *n* (*Brit*) Privatschule *f*; (*US*) staatliche Schule *f*

public-spirited [pʌblɪk'spɪrɪtɪd] *adj* gemeinsinnig

public transport *n* öffentliche Verkehrsmittel *pl*

publish ['pʌblɪʃ] *vt* veröffentlichen

publisher ['pʌblɪʃə^r] *n* (*person*) Verleger(in) *m(f)*; (*company*) Verlag *m*

publishing ['pʌblɪʃɪŋ] *n* (*profession*) das Verlagswesen

pub lunch *n in Pubs servierter Imbiss*

pucker ['pʌkə^r] *vi* (*lips, face*) sich verziehen; (*fabric etc*) Falten werfen ▷ *vt* (*lips, face*) verziehen; (*fabric etc*) Falten machen in *+acc*

pudding ['pudɪŋ] *n* (*cooked sweet food*) Süßspeise *f*; (*Brit: dessert*) Nachtisch *m*; **rice ~** Milchreis *m*; **black ~, blood ~** (*US*) ≈ Blutwurst *f*

puddle ['pʌdl] *n* (*of rain*) Pfütze *f*; (*of blood*) Lache *f*

puff [pʌf] *n* (*of cigarette, pipe*) Zug *m*; (*gasp*) Schnaufer *m*; (*of air*) Stoß *m*; (*of smoke*) Wolke *f* ▷ *vt* (*also*: **puff on, puff at**: *cigarette, pipe*) ziehen an *+dat* ▷ *vi* (*gasp*) keuchen, schnaufen

▸ **puff out** *vt* (*one's chest*) herausdrücken; (*one's cheeks*) aufblasen

puff pastry, (*US*) **puff paste** *n* Blätterteig *m*

puffy ['pʌfɪ] *adj* (*eye*) geschwollen; (*face*) aufgedunsen

pull [pul] *vt* (*rope, handle etc*) ziehen an *+dat*; (*cart etc*) ziehen; (*close: curtain*) zuziehen; (*: blind*) herunterlassen; (*inf: attract: people*) anlocken; (*: sexual partner*) aufreißen; (*pint of beer*) zapfen ▷ *vi* ziehen ▷ *n* (*also fig: attraction*) Anziehungskraft *f*; **to ~ the trigger** abdrücken; **to ~ a face** ein Gesicht schneiden; **to ~ a muscle** sich *dat* einen Muskel zerren; **not to ~ one's** *or* **any punches** (*fig*) sich *dat* keine Zurückhaltung auferlegen; **to ~ to pieces** (*fig*) zerreißen; **to ~ one's weight** (*fig*) sich ins Zeug legen; **to ~ o.s. together** sich zusammenreißen; **to ~ sb's leg** (*fig*) jdn auf den Arm nehmen; **to ~ strings (for sb)** seine Beziehungen (für jdn) spielen lassen; **to give sth a ~** an etw *dat* ziehen

▸ **pull apart** *vt* (*separate*) trennen

▸ **pull away** *vi* (*Aut*) losfahren

▸ **pull back** *vi* (*retreat*) sich zurückziehen; (*fig*) einen Rückzieher machen (*inf*)

▸ **pull down** *vt* (*building*) abreißen

▸ **pull in** *vi* (*Aut: at kerb*) anhalten; (*Rail*) einfahren ▹ *vt* (*inf: money*) einsacken; (*crowds, people*) anlocken; (*police: suspect*) sich *dat* schnappen (*inf*)

▸ **pull off** *vt* (*clothes etc*) ausziehen; (*fig: difficult thing*) schaffen, bringen (*inf*)

▸ **pull out** *vi* (*Aut: from kerb*) losfahren; (*: when overtaking*) ausscheren; (*Rail*) ausfahren; (*withdraw*) sich zurückziehen ▹ *vt* (*extract*) herausziehen

▸ **pull over** *vi* (*Aut*) an den Straßenrand fahren

▸ **pull through** *vi* (*Med*) durchkommen

▸ **pull up** *vi* (*Aut, Rail: stop*) anhalten ▹ *vt* (*raise*) hochziehen; (*uproot*) herausreißen; (*chair*) heranrücken

pulley ['pulɪ] *n* Flaschenzug *m*

pullover ['puləuvəʳ] *n* Pullover *m*

pulp [pʌlp] *n* (*of fruit*) Fruchtfleisch *nt*; (*for paper*) (Papier)brei *m*; (*Liter: pej*) Schund *m* ▹ *adj* (*pej: magazine, novel*) Schund-; **to reduce sth to a ~** etw zu Brei machen

pulpit ['pulpɪt] *n* Kanzel *f*

pulsate [pʌl'seɪt] *vi* (*heart*) klopfen; (*music*) pulsieren

pulse [pʌls] *n* (*Anat*) Puls *m*; (*rhythm*) Rhythmus *m*; **pulses** *npl* (*Bot*) Hülsenfrüchte *pl*; (*Tech*) Impuls *m* ▹ *vi* pulsieren; **to take** *or* **feel sb's ~** jdm den Puls fühlen; **to have one's finger on the ~ (of sth)** (*fig*) den Finger am Puls (einer Sache *gen*) haben

puma ['pju:mə] *n* Puma *m*

pump [pʌmp] *n* Pumpe *f*; (*also*: **petrol pump**) Zapfsäule *f*; (*shoe*) Turnschuh *m* ▹ *vt* pumpen; **to ~ sb for information** jdn aushorchen; **she had her stomach ~ed** ihr wurde der Magen ausgepumpt

▸ **pump up** *vt* (*inflate*) aufpumpen

pumpkin ['pʌmpkɪn] *n* Kürbis *m*

pun [pʌn] *n* Wortspiel *nt*

punch [pʌntʃ] *n* (*blow*) Schlag *m*; (*fig: force*) Schlagkraft *f*; (*tool*) Locher *m*; (*drink*) Bowle *f*, Punsch *m* ▹ *vt* (*hit*) schlagen; (*make a hole in*) lochen; **to ~ a hole in sth** ein Loch in etw *acc* stanzen

▸ **punch in** (*US*) *vi* (bei Arbeitsbeginn) stempeln

▸ **punch out** (*US*) *vi* (bei Arbeitsende) stempeln

punch line *n* Pointe *f*

punch-up ['pʌntʃʌp] (*Brit: inf*) *n* Schlägerei *f*

punctual ['pʌŋktjuəl] *adj* pünktlich

punctuation [pʌŋktju'eɪʃən] *n* Zeichensetzung *f*

puncture ['pʌŋktʃəʳ] *n* (*Aut*) Reifenpanne *f* ▹ *vt* durchbohren; **I have a ~** ich habe eine Reifenpanne

pundit ['pʌndɪt] *n* Experte *m*, Expertin *f*

pungent ['pʌndʒənt] *adj* (*smell, taste*) scharf; (*fig: speech, article etc*) spitz, scharf

punish ['pʌnɪʃ] *vt* bestrafen; **to ~ sb for sth** jdn für etw bestrafen; **to ~ sb for doing sth** jdn dafür bestrafen, dass er etw getan hat

punishment ['pʌnɪʃmənt] *n* (*act*) Bestrafung *f*; (*way of punishing*) Strafe *f*; **to take a lot of ~** (*fig: car, person etc*) viel abbekommen

punk [pʌŋk] *n* (*also*: **punk rocker**) Punker(in) *m(f)*; (*also*: **punk rock**) Punk *m*; (*US: inf: hoodlum*) Gangster *m*

punt[1] [pʌnt] *n* (*boat*) Stechkahn *m* ▹ *vi* mit dem Stechkahn fahren

punt[2] [pʌnt] (*Irish*) *n* (*currency*) irisches Pfund *nt*

punter ['pʌntəʳ] (*Brit*) *n* (*gambler*) Wetter(in) *m(f)*; **the ~s** (*inf: customers*) die Leute; **the average ~** (*inf*) Otto Normalverbraucher

puny ['pju:nɪ] *adj* (*person, arms etc*) schwächlich; (*efforts*) kläglich, kümmerlich

pup [pʌp] *n* (*young dog*) Welpe *m*, junger Hund *m*; **seal ~** Welpenjunge(s) *nt*

pupil ['pju:pl] *n* (*Scol*) Schüler(in) *m(f)*; (*of eye*) Pupille *f*

puppet ['pʌpɪt] *n* Handpuppe *f*; (*with strings, fig: person*) Marionette *f*

puppy ['pʌpɪ] *n* (*young dog*) Welpe *m*, junger Hund *m*

purchase ['pə:tʃɪs] *n* Kauf *m*; (*grip*) Halt *m* ▹ *vt* kaufen; **to get** *or* **gain (a) ~ on** (*grip*) Halt finden an *+dat*

purchaser ['pə:tʃɪsəʳ] *n* Käufer(in) *m(f)*

pure [pjuəʳ] *adj* rein; **a ~ wool jumper** ein Pullover aus reiner Wolle; **it's laziness ~ and simple** es ist nichts als reine Faulheit

purely ['pjuəlɪ] *adv* rein

purge [pə:dʒ] *n* (*Pol*) Säuberung *f* ▹ *vt* (*Pol: organization*) säubern; (*: extremists etc*) entfernen; (*fig: thoughts, mind etc*) befreien

purify ['pjuərɪfaɪ] *vt* reinigen

purity ['pjuərɪtɪ] *n* Reinheit *f*

purple ['pə:pl] *adj* violett

purpose ['pə:pəs] *n* (*reason*) Zweck *m*; (*aim*) Ziel *nt*, Absicht *f*; **on ~** absichtlich; **for illustrative ~s** zu Illustrationszwecken; **for all practical ~s** praktisch (gesehen); **for the ~s of this meeting** zum Zweck dieses Treffens; **to little ~** mit wenig Erfolg; **to no ~** ohne Erfolg; **a sense of ~** ein Zielbewusstsein *nt*

purposeful ['pə:pəsful] *adj* entschlossen

purr [pə:ʳ] *vi* (*cat*) schnurren

purse [pə:s] *n* (*Brit: for money*) Geldbörse *f*,

Portemonnaie *nt*; (*US: handbag*) Handtasche *f* ▷ *vt* (*lips*) kräuseln

purser ['pəːsə^r] *n* (*Naut*) Zahlmeister *m*

pursue [pə'sjuː] *vt* (*person, vehicle, plan, aim*) verfolgen; (*fig: interest etc*) nachgehen *+dat*

pursuit [pə'sjuːt] *n* (*chase*) Verfolgung *f*; (*pastime*) Beschäftigung *f*; (*fig*): **~ of** (*of happiness etc*) Streben *nt* nach; **in ~ of** (*person, car etc*) auf der Jagd nach; (*fig: happiness etc*) im Streben nach

pus [pʌs] *n* Eiter *m*

push [puʃ] *n* Stoß *m*, Schub *m* ▷ *vt* (*press*) drücken; (*shove*) schieben; (*fig: put pressure on: person*) bedrängen; (*: promote: product*) werben für; (*inf: sell: drugs*) pushen ▷ *vi* (*press*) drücken; (*shove*) schieben; **at the ~ of a button** auf Knopfdruck; **at a ~** (*Brit: inf*) notfalls; **to ~ a door open/shut** eine Tür auf-/zudrücken; **"~"** (*on door*) "drücken"; (*on bell*) "klingeln"; **to be ~ed for time/money** (*inf*) in Zeitnot/Geldnot sein; **she is ~ing fifty** (*inf*) sie geht auf die fünfzig zu; **to ~ for** (*demand*) drängen auf *+acc*

▸ **push around** *vt* (*bully*) herumschubsen

▸ **push aside** *vt* beiseiteschieben

▸ **push in** *vi* sich dazwischendrängeln

▸ **push off** (*inf*) *vi* abhauen

▸ **push on** *vi* (*continue*) weitermachen

▸ **push over** *vt* umstoßen

▸ **push through** *vt* (*measure etc*) durchdrücken

▸ **push up** *vt* (*total, prices*) hochtreiben

pushchair ['puʃtʃɛə^r] (*Brit*) *n* Sportwagen *m*

pusher ['puʃə^r] *n* (*drug dealer*) Pusher *m*

pushover ['puʃəuvə^r] (*inf*) *n*: **it's a ~** das ist ein Kinderspiel

push-up ['puʃʌp] (*US*) *n* Liegestütz *m*

pushy ['puʃɪ] (*pej*) *adj* aufdringlich

pussy ['pusɪ], **pussycat** ['pusɪkæt] (*inf*) *n* Mieze(katze) *f*

put [put] (*pt, pp* **~**) *vt* (*thing*) tun; (*: upright*) stellen; (*: flat*) legen; (*person: in room, institution etc*) stecken; (*: in state, situation*) versetzen; (*express: idea etc*) ausdrücken; (*present: case, view*) vorbringen; (*ask: question*) stellen; (*classify*) einschätzen; (*write, type*) schreiben; **to ~ sb in a good/bad mood** jdn gut/schlecht stimmen; **to ~ sb to bed** jdn ins Bett bringen; **to ~ sb to a lot of trouble** jdm viele Umstände machen; **how shall I ~ it?** wie soll ich es sagen *or* ausdrücken?; **to ~ a lot of time into sth** viel Zeit auf etw *acc* verwenden; **to ~ money on a horse** Geld auf ein Pferd setzen; **the cost is now ~ at 2 million pounds** die Kosten werden jetzt auf 2 Millionen Pfund geschätzt; **I ~ it to you that ...** (*Brit*) ich behaupte, dass ...; **to stay ~** (an Ort und Stelle) bleiben

▸ **put about** *vi* (*Naut*) den Kurs ändern ▷ *vt* (*rumour*) verbreiten

▸ **put across** *vt* (*ideas etc*) verständlich machen

▸ **put around** *vt* = **put about**

▸ **put aside** *vt* (*work*) zur Seite legen; (*idea, problem*) unbeachtet lassen; (*sum of money*) zurücklegen

▸ **put away** *vt* (*store*) wegräumen; (*inf: consume*) verdrücken; (*save: money*) zurücklegen; (*imprison*) einsperren

▸ **put back** *vt* (*replace*) zurücktun; (*: upright*) zurückstellen; (*: flat*) zurücklegen; (*postpone*) verschieben; (*delay*) zurückwerfen

▸ **put by** *vt* (*money, supplies etc*) zurücklegen

▸ **put down** *vt* (*upright*) hinstellen; (*flat*) hinlegen; (*cup, glass*) absetzen; (*in writing*) aufschreiben; (*riot, rebellion*) niederschlagen; (*humiliate*) demütigen; (*kill*) töten

▸ **put down to** *vt* (*attribute*) zurückführen auf *+acc*

▸ **put forward** *vt* (*ideas etc*) vorbringen; (*watch, clock*) vorstellen; (*date, meeting*) vorverlegen

▸ **put in** *vt* (*application, complaint*) einreichen; (*time, effort*) investieren; (*gas, electricity etc*) installieren ▷ *vi* (*Naut*) einlaufen

▸ **put in for** *vt fus* (*promotion*) sich bewerben um; (*leave*) beantragen

▸ **put off** *vt* (*delay*) verschieben; (*distract*) ablenken; **to ~ sb off sth** (*discourage*) jdn von etw abbringen

▸ **put on** *vt* (*clothes, brake*) anziehen; (*glasses, kettle*) aufsetzen; (*make-up, ointment etc*) auftragen; (*light, TV*) anmachen; (*play etc*) aufführen; (*record, tape, video*) auflegen; (*dinner etc*) aufsetzen; (*assume: look, behaviour etc*) annehmen; (*inf: tease*) auf den Arm nehmen; (*extra bus, train etc*) einsetzen; **to ~ on airs** sich zieren; **to ~ on weight** zunehmen

▸ **put on to** *vt* (*tell about*) vermitteln

▸ **put out** *vt* (*fire, light*) ausmachen; (*take out: rubbish*) herausbringen; (*: cat etc*) vor die Tür setzen; (*one's hand*) ausstrecken; (*story, announcement*) verbreiten; (*Brit: dislocate: shoulder etc*) verrenken; (*inf: inconvenience*) Umstände machen *+dat* ▷ *vi* (*Naut*): **to ~ out to sea** in See stechen; **to ~ out from Plymouth** von Plymouth auslaufen

▸ **put through** *vt* (*Tel: person*) verbinden; (*: call*) durchstellen; (*plan, agreement*) durchbringen; **~ me through to Ms Blair** verbinden Sie mich mit Frau Blair

▸ **put together** *vt* (*furniture etc*) zusammenbauen; (*plan, campaign*) ausarbeiten; **more than the rest of them ~ together** mehr als alle anderen zusammen

▸ **put up** *vt* (*fence, building*) errichten; (*tent*) aufstellen; (*umbrella*) aufspannen; (*hood*) hochschlagen; (*poster, sign etc*) anbringen; (*price, cost*) erhöhen; (*accommodate*) unterbringen; **to ~ up resistance** Widerstand leisten; **to ~ up a fight** sich zur Wehr setzen; **to ~ sb up to sth** jdn zu etw anstiften; **to ~ sb up to doing sth** jdn dazu anstiften, etw zu tun; **to ~ sth up for sale** etw zum Verkauf anbieten

▸ **put upon** *vt fus*: **to be ~ upon** (*imposed on*)

ausgenutzt werden

▸ **put up with** *vt fus* sich abfinden mit

putt [pʌt] *n* Putt *m*

putting green ['pʌtɪŋ-] *n* kleiner Golfplatz *m* zum Putten

putty ['pʌtɪ] *n* Kitt *m*

put-up ['putʌp] *adj*: **a ~ job** ein abgekartetes Spiel *nt*

puzzle ['pʌzl] *n* (*game, toy*) Geschicklichkeitsspiel *nt*; (*mystery*) Rätsel *nt* ▹ *vt* verwirren ▹ *vi*: **to ~ over sth** sich *dat* über etw *acc* den Kopf zerbrechen; **to be ~d as to why ...** vor einem Rätsel stehen, warum ...

puzzling ['pʌzlɪŋ] *adj* verwirrend; (*mysterious*) rätselhaft

pyjamas, (US) **pajamas** [pə'dʒɑ:məz] *npl* Pyjama *m*, Schlafanzug *m*; **a pair of ~** ein Schlafanzug

pylon ['paɪlən] *n* Mast *m*

pyramid ['pɪrəmɪd] *n* Pyramide *f*

Pyrenees [pɪrə'ni:z] *npl*: **the ~** die Pyrenäen *pl*

Qq

quack [kwæk] *n* (*of duck*) Schnattern *nt*, Quaken *nt*; (*inf*: *pej*: *doctor*) Quacksalber *m* ▷ *vi* schnattern, quaken
quad [kwɔd] *abbr* = **quadrangle**; (= *quadruplet*) Vierling *m*
quadrangle ['kwɔdræŋgl] *n* (*courtyard*) Innenhof *m*
quadruple [kwɔ'dru:pl] *vt* vervierfachen ▷ *vi* sich vervierfachen
quail [kweɪl] *n* Wachtel *f* ▷ *vi*: **he ~ed at the thought/before her anger** ihm schauderte bei dem Gedanken/vor ihrem Zorn
quaint [kweɪnt] *adj* (*house, village*) malerisch; (*ideas, customs*) urig, kurios
quake [kweɪk] *vi* beben, zittern ▷ *n* = **earthquake**
qualification [kwɔlɪfɪ'keɪʃən] *n* (*often pl*: *degree etc*) Qualifikation *f*; (*attribute*) Voraussetzung *f*; (*reservation*) Vorbehalt *m*; **what are your ~s?** welche Qualifikationen haben Sie?
qualified ['kwɔlɪfaɪd] *adj* (*trained*: *doctor etc*) qualifiziert, ausgebildet; (*limited*: *agreement, praise*) bedingt; **to be/feel ~ to do sth** (*fit, competent*) qualifiziert sein/sich qualifiziert fühlen, etw zu tun; **it was a ~ success** es war kein voller Erfolg; **he's not ~ for the job** ihm fehlen die Qualifikationen für die Stelle
qualify ['kwɔlɪfaɪ] *vt* (*entitle*) qualifizieren; (*modify*: *statement*) einschränken ▷ *vi* (*pass examination*) sich qualifizieren; **to ~ for** (*be eligible*) die Berechtigung erlangen für; (*in competition*) sich qualifizieren für; **to ~ as an engineer** die Ausbildung zum Ingenieur abschließen
quality ['kwɔlɪtɪ] *n* Qualität *f*; (*characteristic*) Eigenschaft *f* ▷ *cpd* Qualitäts-; **of good/poor ~** von guter/schlechter Qualität; **~ of life** Lebensqualität *f*
qualm [kwɑ:m] *n* Bedenken *pl*; **to have ~s about sth** Bedenken wegen etw haben
quandary ['kwɔndrɪ] *n*: **to be in a ~** in einem Dilemma sein
quantity ['kwɔntɪtɪ] *n* (*amount*) Menge *f*; **in large/small quantities** in großen/kleinen Mengen; **in ~** (*in bulk*) in großen Mengen; **an unknown ~** (*fig*) eine unbekannte Größe
quantity surveyor *n* Baukostenkalkulator(in) *m(f)*
quarantine ['kwɔrnti:n] *n* Quarantäne *f*; **in ~** in Quarantäne
quarrel ['kwɔrl] *n* (*argument*) Streit *m* ▷ *vi* sich streiten; **to have a ~ with sb** sich mit jdm streiten; **I've no ~ with him** ich habe nichts gegen ihn; **I can't ~ with that** dagegen kann ich nichts einwenden
quarry ['kwɔrɪ] *n* (*for stone*) Steinbruch *m*; (*prey*) Beute *f* ▷ *vt* (*marble etc*) brechen
quart [kwɔ:t] *n* Quart *nt*
quarter ['kwɔ:tə^r] *n* Viertel *nt*; (*US*: *coin*) 25-Cent-Stück *nt*; (*of year*) Quartal *nt*; (*district*) Viertel *nt* ▷ *vt* (*divide*) vierteln; (*Mil*: *lodge*) einquartieren; **quarters** *npl* (*Mil*) Quartier *nt*; (*also*: **living quarters**) Unterkünfte *pl*; **a ~ of an hour** eine viertel Stunde; **it's a ~ to three, it's a ~ of three** (*US*) es ist Viertel vor drei; **it's a ~ past three, it's a ~ after three** (*US*) es ist Viertel nach drei; **from all ~s** aus allen Richtungen; **at close ~s** aus unmittelbarer Nähe
quarterly ['kwɔ:təlɪ] *adj, adv* vierteljährlich ▷ *n* Vierteljahresschrift *f*
quartet [kwɔ:'tɛt] *n* (*Mus*) Quartett *nt*
quartz [kwɔ:ts] *n* Quarz *m* ▷ *cpd* (*watch, clock*) Quarz-
quash [kwɔʃ] *vt* (*verdict*) aufheben
quaver ['kweɪvə^r] *n* (*Brit*: *Mus*) Achtelnote *f* ▷ *vi* (*voice*) beben, zittern
quay [ki:] *n* Kai *m*
queasy ['kwi:zɪ] *adj* (*nauseous*) übel; **I feel ~** mir ist übel *or* schlecht
Quebec [kwɪ'bɛk] *n* Quebec *nt*
queen [kwi:n] *n* (*also Zool*) Königin *f*; (*Cards, Chess*) Dame *f*
queen mother *n* Königinmutter *f*
queer [kwɪə^r] *adj* (*odd*) sonderbar, seltsam ▷ *n* (*inf!*: *pej*: *male homosexual*) Schwule(r) *m*; **I feel ~** (*Brit*: *unwell*) mir ist ganz komisch
quell [kwɛl] *vt* (*riot*) niederschlagen; (*fears*) überwinden
quench [kwɛntʃ] *vt*: **to ~ one's thirst** seinen Durst stillen
query ['kwɪərɪ] *n* Anfrage *f* ▷ *vt* (*check*) nachfragen bezüglich +*gen*; (*express doubt about*) bezweifeln
quest [kwɛst] *n* Suche *f*
question ['kwɛstʃən] *n* Frage *f* ▷ *vt* (*interrogate*) befragen; (*doubt*) bezweifeln; **to ask sb a**

question, put a ~ to sb jdm eine Frage stellen; **to bring** *or* **call sth into ~** etw infrage stellen; **the ~ is ...** die Frage ist ...; **there's no ~ of him playing for England** es ist ausgeschlossen, dass er für England spielt; **the person/night in ~** die fragliche Person/Nacht; **to be beyond ~** außer Frage stehen; **to be out of the ~** nicht infrage kommen

questionable ['kwɛstʃənəbl] *adj* fraglich

question mark *n* Fragezeichen *nt*

questionnaire [kwɛstʃə'nɛəʳ] *n* Fragebogen *m*

queue [kju:] (*Brit*) *n* Schlange *f* ▷ *vi* (*also*: **queue up**) Schlange stehen

quibble ['kwɪbl] *vi*: **to ~ about** *or* **over** sich streiten über *+acc*; **to ~ with** herumnörgeln an *+dat* ▷ *n* Krittelei *f*

quiche [ki:ʃ] *n* Quiche *f*

quick [kwɪk] *adj* schnell; (*mind, wit*) wach; (*look, visit*) flüchtig ▷ *adv* schnell ▷ *n*: **to cut sb to the ~** (*fig*) jdn tief verletzen; **be ~!** mach schnell!; **to be ~ to act** schnell handeln; **she was ~ to see that ...** sie begriff schnell, dass ...; **she has a ~ temper** sie wird leicht hitzig

quicken ['kwɪkən] *vt* beschleunigen ▷ *vi* schneller werden, sich beschleunigen

quickly ['kwɪklɪ] *adv* schnell

quicksand ['kwɪksænd] *n* Treibsand *m*

quick-witted [kwɪk'wɪtɪd] *adj* schlagfertig

quid [kwɪd] (*Brit: inf*) *n inv* Pfund *nt*

quiet ['kwaɪət] *adj* leise; (*place*) ruhig, still; (*silent, reserved*) still; (*business, day*) ruhig; (*without fuss etc: wedding*) in kleinem Rahmen ▷ *n* (*peacefulness*) Stille *f*, Ruhe *f*; (*silence*) Ruhe *f* ▷ *vt, vi* (*US*) = **quieten**; **keep** *or* **be ~!** sei still!; **I'll have a ~ word with him** ich werde mal unter vier Augen mit ihm reden; **on the ~** (*in secret*) heimlich

quieten ['kwaɪətn] (*Brit: also*: **quieten down**) *vi* ruhiger werden ▷ *vt* (*person, animal*) beruhigen

quietly ['kwaɪətlɪ] *adv* leise; (*silently*) still; (*calmly*) ruhig; **~ confident** insgeheim sicher

quietness ['kwaɪətnɪs] *n* (*peacefulness*) Ruhe *f*; (*silence*) Stille *f*

quilt [kwɪlt] *n* Decke *f*; (*also*: **continental quilt**) Federbett *nt*

quin [kwɪn] (*Brit*) *n abbr* (= *quintuplet*) Fünfling *m*

quip [kwɪp] *n* witzige *or* geistreiche Bemerkung *f* ▷ *vt* witzeln

quirk [kwə:k] *n* Marotte *f*; **a ~ of fate** eine Laune des Schicksals

quit [kwɪt] (*pt, pp* **~** *or* **quitted**) *vt* (*smoking*) aufgeben; (*job*) kündigen; (*premises*) verlassen ▷ *vi* (*give up*) aufgeben; (*resign*) kündigen; **to ~ doing sth** aufhören, etw zu tun; **~ stalling!** (*US: inf*) weichen Sie nicht ständig aus!; **notice to ~** (*Brit*) Kündigung *f*

quite [kwaɪt] *adv* (*rather*) ziemlich; (*entirely*) ganz; **not ~** nicht ganz; **I ~ like it** ich mag es ganz gern; **I ~ understand** ich verstehe; **I don't ~ remember** ich erinnere mich nicht genau; **not ~ as many as the last time** nicht ganz so viele wie das letzte Mal; **that meal was ~ something!** das Essen konnte sich sehen lassen!; **it was ~ a sight** das war vielleicht ein Anblick; **~ a few of them** eine ganze Reihe von Ihnen; **~ (so)!** ganz recht!

quits [kwɪts] *adj*: **we're ~** wir sind quitt; **let's call it ~** lassen wirs dabei

quiver ['kwɪvəʳ] *vi* zittern

quiz [kwɪz] *n* (*game*) Quiz *nt* ▷ *vt* (*question*) befragen

quizzical ['kwɪzɪkl] *adj* (*look, smile*) wissend

quota ['kwəutə] *n* (*allowance*) Quote *f*

quotation [kwəu'teɪʃən] *n* (*from book etc*) Zitat *nt*; (*estimate*) Preisangabe *f*; (*Comm*) Kostenvoranschlag *m*

quotation marks *npl* Anführungszeichen *pl*

quote [kwəut] *n* (*from book etc*) Zitat *nt*; (*estimate*) Kostenvoranschlag *m* ▷ *vt* zitieren; (*fact, example*) anführen; (*price*) nennen; **quotes** *npl* (*quotation marks*) Anführungszeichen *pl*; **in ~s** in Anführungszeichen; **the figure ~d for the repairs** die für die Reparatur genannte Summe; **~ ... unquote** Zitat Anfang ... Zitat Ende

Rr

R¹, r [ɑːʳ] *n* (*letter*) R *nt*, r *nt*; **R for Robert, R for Roger** (US) ≈ R wie Richard
R² [ɑːʳ] *abbr* (= *Réaumur (scale)*) R; (*US: Cine: = restricted*) *Klassifikation für nicht jugendfreie Filme*
Rabat [rəˈbɑːt] *n* Rabat *nt*
rabbi [ˈræbaɪ] *n* Rabbi *m*
rabbit [ˈræbɪt] *n* Kaninchen *nt* ▷ *vi* (*Brit: inf: also*: **to rabbit on**) quatschen, schwafeln
rabbit hutch *n* Kaninchenstall *m*
rabble [ˈræbl] (*pej*) *n* Pöbel *m*
rabies [ˈreɪbiːz] *n* Tollwut *f*
RAC (*Brit*) *n abbr* (= *Royal Automobile Club*) *Autofahrerorganisation*, ≈ ADAC *m*
raccoon [rəˈkuːn] *n* Waschbär *m*
race [reɪs] *n* (*species*) Rasse *f*; (*competition*) Rennen *nt*; (*for power, control*) Wettlauf *m* ▷ *vt* (*horse, pigeon*) an Wettbewerben teilnehmen lassen; (*car etc*) ins Rennen schicken; (*person*) um die Wette laufen mit ▷ *vi* (*compete*) antreten; (*hurry*) rennen; (*pulse, heart*) rasen; (*engine*) durchdrehen; **the human ~** die Menschheit; **a ~ against time** ein Wettlauf mit der Zeit; **he ~d across the road** er raste über die Straße; **to ~ in/out** hinein-/hinausstürzen
race car (US) *n* = **racing car**
race car driver (US) *n* = **racing driver**
racecourse [ˈreɪskɔːs] *n* Rennbahn *f*
racehorse [ˈreɪshɔːs] *n* Rennpferd *nt*
racetrack [ˈreɪstræk] *n* Rennbahn *f*; (US) = **racecourse**
racial [ˈreɪʃl] *adj* Rassen-
racing [ˈreɪsɪŋ] *n* (*also*: **horse racing**) Pferderennen *nt*; (*also*: **motor racing**) Rennsport *m*
racing car (*Brit*) *n* Rennwagen *m*
racing driver (*Brit*) *n* Rennfahrer(in) *m(f)*
racism [ˈreɪsɪzəm] *n* Rassismus *m*
racist [ˈreɪsɪst] *adj* rassistisch ▷ *n* (*pej*) Rassist(in) *m(f)*
rack [ræk] *n* (*also*: **luggage rack**) Gepäckablage *f*; (*also*: **roof rack**) Dachgepäckträger *m*; (*for dresses etc*) Ständer *m*; (*for dishes*) Gestell *nt* ▷ *vt*: **~ed by** (*pain etc*) gemartert von; **magazine/toast ~** Zeitungs-/Toastständer *m*; **to ~ one's brains** sich *dat* den Kopf zerbrechen; **to go to ~ and ruin** (*building*) zerfallen; (*business, country*) herunterkommen
racket [ˈrækɪt] *n* (*for tennis etc*) Schläger *m*; (*noise*) Krach *m*, Radau *m*; (*swindle*) Schwindel *m*
racquet [ˈrækɪt] *n* (*for tennis etc*) Schläger *m*
racy [ˈreɪsɪ] *adj* (*book, story*) rasant
radar [ˈreɪdɑːʳ] *n* Radar *m or nt* ▷ *cpd* Radar-
radial [ˈreɪdɪəl] *adj* (*roads*) strahlenförmig verlaufend; (*pattern*) strahlenförmig ▷ *n* (*also*: **radial tyre**) Gürtelreifen *m*
radiant [ˈreɪdɪənt] *adj* strahlend; (*Phys: heat*) Strahlungs-
radiate [ˈreɪdɪeɪt] *vt* (*lit, fig*) ausstrahlen ▷ *vi* (*lines, roads*) strahlenförmig verlaufen
radiation [reɪdɪˈeɪʃən] *n* (*radioactivity*) radioaktive Strahlung *f*; (*from sun etc*) Strahlung *f*
radiator [ˈreɪdɪeɪtəʳ] *n* (*heater*) Heizkörper *m*; (*Aut*) Kühler *m*
radical [ˈrædɪkl] *adj* radikal ▷ *n* (*person*) Radikale(r) *f(m)*
radii [ˈreɪdɪaɪ] *npl of* **radius**
radio [ˈreɪdɪəu] *n* (*broadcasting*) Radio *nt*, Rundfunk *m*; (*device: for receiving broadcasts*) Radio *nt*; (*: for transmitting and receiving*) Funkgerät *nt* ▷ *vi*: **to ~ to sb** mit jdm per Funk sprechen ▷ *vt* (*person*) per Funk verständigen; (*message, position*) per Funk durchgeben; **on the ~** im Radio
radioactive [ˈreɪdɪəuˈæktɪv] *adj* radioaktiv
radio-controlled [ˈreɪdɪəukənˈtrəuld] *adj* ferngesteuert
radio station *n* Radiosender *m*
radish [ˈrædɪʃ] *n* Radieschen *nt*; (*long white variety*) Rettich *m*
radius [ˈreɪdɪəs] (*pl* **radii**) *n* Radius *m*; (*area*) Umkreis *m*; **within a ~ of 50 miles** in einem Umkreis von 50 Meilen
RAF (*Brit*) *n abbr* = **Royal Air Force**
raffle [ˈræfl] *n* Verlosung *f*, Tombola *f* ▷ *vt* (*prize*) verlosen; **~ ticket** Los *nt*
raft [rɑːft] *n* Floß *nt*; (*also*: **life raft**) Rettungsfloß *nt*
rafter [ˈrɑːftəʳ] *n* Dachsparren *m*
rag [ræg] *n* (*piece of cloth*) Lappen *m*; (*torn cloth*) Fetzen *m*; (*pej: newspaper*) Käseblatt *nt*; (*Brit: Univ*) *studentische Wohltätigkeitsveranstaltung* ▷ *vt* (*Brit: tease*)

aufziehen; **rags** *npl* (*torn clothes*) Lumpen *pl*; **in ~s** (*person*) zerlumpt; **his was a ~s-to-riches story** er brachte es vom Tellerwäscher zum Millionär
rag doll *n* Stoffpuppe *f*
rage [reɪdʒ] *n* (*fury*) Wut *f*, Zorn *m* ▷ *vi* toben, wüten; **it's all the ~** (*fashionable*) es ist der letzte Schrei; **to fly into a ~** einen Wutanfall bekommen
ragged ['rægɪd] *adj* (*jagged*) zackig; (*clothes, person*) zerlumpt; (*beard*) ausgefranst
raid [reɪd] *n* (*Mil*) Angriff *m*, Überfall *m*; (*by police*) Razzia *f*; (*by criminal: forcefully*) Überfall *m*; (*: secretly*) Einbruch *m* ▷ *vt* (*Mil*) angreifen, überfallen; (*police*) stürmen; (*criminal: forcefully*) überfallen; (*: secretly*) einbrechen in *+acc*
rail [reɪl] *n* Geländer *nt*; (*on deck of ship*) Reling *f*; **rails** *npl* (*for train*) Schienen *pl*; **by ~** mit der Bahn
railcard ['reɪlkɑːd] (*Brit*) *n* (*for young people*) ≈ Juniorenpass *m*; (*for pensioners*) ≈ Seniorenpass *m*
railing ['reɪlɪŋ] *n*, **railings** ['reɪlɪŋz] *npl* (*fence*) Zaun *m*
railway ['reɪlweɪ] (*Brit*) *n* Eisenbahn *f*; (*track*) Gleis *nt*; (*company*) Bahn *f*
railway line (*Brit*) *n* Bahnlinie *f*; (*track*) Gleis *nt*
railwayman ['reɪlweɪmən] (*irreg: like* **man**) (*Brit*) *n* Eisenbahner *m*
railway station (*Brit*) *n* Bahnhof *m*
rain [reɪn] *n* Regen *m* ▷ *vi* regnen; **in the ~** im Regen; **as right as ~** voll auf der Höhe; **it's ~ing** es regnet; **it's ~ing cats and dogs** es regnet in Strömen
rainbow ['reɪnbəu] *n* Regenbogen *m*
raincoat ['reɪnkəut] *n* Regenmantel *m*
raindrop ['reɪndrɔp] *n* Regentropfen *m*
rainfall ['reɪnfɔːl] *n* Niederschlag *m*
rainforest ['reɪnfɔrɪst] *n* Regenwald *m*
rainy ['reɪnɪ] *adj* (*day*) regnerisch, verregnet; (*area*) regenreich; **~ season** Regenzeit *f*; **to save sth for a ~ day** etw für schlechte Zeiten aufheben
raise [reɪz] *n* (*pay rise*) Gehaltserhöhung *f* ▷ *vt* (*lift: hand*) hochheben; (*: window*) hochziehen; (*siege*) beenden; (*embargo*) aufheben; (*increase*) erhöhen; (*improve*) verbessern; (*question etc*) zur Sprache bringen; (*doubts etc*) vorbringen; (*child, cattle*) aufziehen; (*crop*) anbauen; (*army*) aufstellen; (*funds*) aufbringen; (*loan*) aufnehmen; **to ~ a glass to sb/sth** das Glas auf jdn/etw erheben; **to ~ one's voice** die Stimme erheben; **to ~ sb's hopes** jdm Hoffnungen machen; **to ~ a laugh/smile** Gelächter/ein Lächeln hervorrufen; **this ~s the question ...** das wirft die Frage auf ...
raisin ['reɪzn] *n* Rosine *f*
rake [reɪk] *n* Harke *f*; (*old: person*) Schwerenöter *m* ▷ *vt* harken; (*light, gun: area*) bestreichen; **he's raking it in** (*inf*) er scheffelt das Geld nur so
rally ['rælɪ] *n* (*Pol etc*) Kundgebung *f*; (*Aut*) Rallye *f*; (*Tennis etc*) Ballwechsel *m* ▷ *vt* (*support*) sammeln ▷ *vi* (*sick person, Stock Exchange*) sich erholen
▸ **rally round** *vi* sich zusammentun ▷ *vt fus* zu Hilfe kommen *+dat*
RAM [ræm] *n abbr* (*Comput: = random access memory*) RAM
ram [ræm] *n* Widder *m* ▷ *vt* rammen
ramble ['ræmbl] *n* Wanderung *f* ▷ *vi* wandern; (*also:* **ramble on**: *talk*) schwafeln
rambler ['ræmbləʳ] *n* Wanderer *m*, Wanderin *f*; (*Bot*) Kletterrose *f*
rambling ['ræmblɪŋ] *adj* (*speech, letter*) weitschweifig; (*house*) weitläufig; (*Bot*) rankend, Kletter-
ramp [ræmp] *n* Rampe *f*; (*in garage*) Hebebühne *f*; **on ~** (*US: Aut*) Auffahrt *f*; **off ~** (*US: Aut*) Ausfahrt *f*
rampage [ræm'peɪdʒ] *n*: **to be/go on the ~** randalieren ▷ *vi*: **they went rampaging through the town** sie zogen randalierend durch die Stadt
rampant ['ræmpənt] *adj*: **to be ~** (*crime, disease etc*) wild wuchern
ram raiding [-reɪdɪŋ] *n Einbruchdiebstahl, wobei die Diebe mit einem Wagen in die Schaufensterfront eines Ladens eindringen*
ramshackle ['ræmʃækl] *adj* (*house*) baufällig; (*cart*) klapprig; (*table*) altersschwach
ran [ræn] *pt of* **run**
ranch [rɑːntʃ] *n* Ranch *f*
rancher ['rɑːntʃəʳ] *n* Rancher(in) *m(f)*; (*worker*) Farmhelfer(in) *m(f)*
rancid ['rænsɪd] *adj* ranzig
rancour, (*US*) **rancor** ['ræŋkəʳ] *n* Verbitterung *f*
random ['rændəm] *adj* (*arrangement*) willkürlich; (*selection*) zufällig; (*Comput*) wahlfrei; (*Math*) Zufalls- ▷ *n*: **at ~** aufs Geratewohl
random access memory *n* (*Comput*) Schreib-Lese-Speicher *m*
randy ['rændɪ] (*Brit: inf*) *adj* geil, scharf
rang [ræŋ] *pt of* **ring**
range [reɪndʒ] *n* (*of mountains*) Kette *f*; (*of missile*) Reichweite *f*; (*of voice*) Umfang *m*; (*series*) Reihe *f*; (*of products*) Auswahl *f*; (*Mil: also:* **rifle range**) Schießstand *m*; (*also:* **kitchen range**) Herd *m* ▷ *vt* (*place in a line*) anordnen ▷ *vi*: **to ~ over** (*extend*) sich erstrecken über *+acc*; **price ~** Preisspanne *f*; **do you have anything else in this price ~?** haben Sie noch etwas anderes in dieser Preisklasse?; **within (firing) ~** in Schussweite; **at close ~** aus unmittelbarer Entfernung; **~d left/right** (*text*) links-/rechtsbündig; **to ~ from ... to ...** sich zwischen ... und ... bewegen
ranger ['reɪndʒəʳ] *n* Förster(in) *m(f)*
rank [ræŋk] *n* (*row*) Reihe *f*; (*Mil*) Rang *m*; (*social class*) Schicht *f*; (*Brit: also:* **taxi rank**) Taxistand *m* ▷ *vi*: **to ~ as/among** zählen zu

▷ *vt*: **he is ~ed third in the world** er steht weltweit an dritter Stelle ▷ *adj* (*stinking*) stinkend; (*sheer: hypocrisy etc*) rein; **the ranks** *npl* (*Mil*) die Mannschaften *pl*; **the ~ and file** (*ordinary members*) die Basis *f*; **to close ~s** (*Mil, fig*) die Reihen schließen

ransack ['rænsæk] *vt* (*search*) durchwühlen; (*plunder*) plündern

ransom ['rænsəm] *n* (*money*) Lösegeld *nt*; **to hold sb to ~** (*hostage*) jdn als Geisel halten; (*fig*) jdn erpressen

rant [rænt] *vi* schimpfen, wettern; **to ~ and rave** herumwettern

rap [ræp] *vi* klopfen ▷ *vt*: **to ~ sb's knuckles** jdm auf die Finger klopfen ▷ *n* (*at door*) Klopfen *nt*; (*also*: **rap music**) Rap *m*

rape [reɪp] *n* Vergewaltigung *f*; (*Bot*) Raps *m* ▷ *vt* vergewaltigen

rape oil, rapeseed oil ['reɪpsi:d-] *n* Rapsöl *nt*

rapid ['ræpɪd] *adj* schnell; (*growth, change*) schnell, rapide

rapidly ['ræpɪdlɪ] *adv* schnell; (*grow, change*) schnell, rapide

rapids ['ræpɪdz] *npl* Stromschnellen *pl*

rapist ['reɪpɪst] *n* Vergewaltiger *m*

rapport [ræ'pɔ:ʳ] *n* enges Verhältnis *nt*

rapturous ['ræptʃərəs] *adj* (*applause, welcome*) stürmisch

rare [rɛəʳ] *adj* selten; (*steak*) nur angebraten, englisch (gebraten); **it is ~ to find that ...** es kommt nur selten vor, dass ...

rarely ['rɛəlɪ] *adv* selten

raring ['rɛərɪŋ] *adj*: **~ to go** (*inf*) in den Startlöchern

rascal ['rɑ:skl] *n* (*child*) Frechdachs *m*; (*rogue*) Schurke *m*

rash [ræʃ] *adj* (*person*) unbesonnen; (*promise, act*) übereilt ▷ *n* (*Med*) Ausschlag *m*; (*of events etc*) Flut *f*; **to come out in a ~** einen Ausschlag bekommen

rasher ['ræʃəʳ] *n* (*of bacon*) Scheibe *f*

raspberry ['rɑ:zbərɪ] *n* Himbeere *f*; **~ bush** Himbeerstrauch *m*; **to blow a ~** (*inf*) verächtlich schnauben

rasping ['rɑ:spɪŋ] *adj*: **a ~ noise** ein kratzendes Geräusch

rat [ræt] *n* Ratte *f*

rate [reɪt] *n* (*speed: of change etc*) Tempo *nt*; (*of inflation, unemployment etc*) Rate *f*; (*of interest, taxation*) Satz *m*; (*price*) Preis *m* ▷ *vt* einschätzen; **rates** *npl* (*Brit: property tax*) Kommunalabgaben *pl*; **at a ~ of 60 kph** mit einem Tempo von 60 km/h; **~ of growth** (*Econ*) Wachstumsrate *f*; **~ of return** (*Fin*) Rendite *f*; **pulse ~** Pulszahl *f*; **at this/that ~** wenn es so weitergeht; **at any ~** auf jeden Fall; **to ~ sb/sth as** jdn/etw einschätzen als; **to ~ sb/sth among** jdn/etw zählen zu; **to ~ sb/sth highly** jdn/etw hoch einschätzen

ratepayer ['reɪtpeɪəʳ] (*Brit*) *n* Steuerzahler(in) *m(f)*

rather ['rɑ:ðəʳ] *adv* (*somewhat*) etwas; (*very*) ziemlich; **~ a lot** ziemlich *or* recht viel; **I would ~ go** ich würde lieber gehen; **~ than** (*instead of*) anstelle von; **or ~** (*more accurately*) oder vielmehr; **I'd ~ not say** das möchte ich lieber nicht sagen; **I ~ think he won't come** ich glaube eher, dass er nicht kommt

rating ['reɪtɪŋ] *n* (*score*) Rate *f*; (*assessment*) Beurteilung *f*; (*Naut: Brit: sailor*) Matrose *m*; **ratings** *npl* (*Radio, TV*) Einschaltquote *f*; **~s hit** Quotenhit *m*

ratio ['reɪʃɪəu] *n* Verhältnis *nt*; **a ~ of 5 to 1** ein Verhältnis von 5 zu 1

ration ['ræʃən] *n* Ration *f* ▷ *vt* rationieren; **rations** *npl* (*Mil*) Rationen *pl*

rational ['ræʃənl] *adj* rational, vernünftig

rationale [ræʃə'nɑ:l] *n* Grundlage *f*

rationalize ['ræʃnəlaɪz] *vt* (*see n*) rechtfertigen, rationalisieren

rat race *n*: **the ~** der ständige *or* tägliche Konkurrenzkampf *m*

rattle ['rætl] *n* (*of door, window, snake*) Klappern *nt*; (*of train, car etc*) Rattern *nt*; (*of chain*) Rasseln *nt*; (*toy*) Rassel *f* ▷ *vi* (*chains*) rasseln; (*windows*) klappern; (*bottles*) klirren ▷ *vt* (*shake noisily*) rütteln an +*dat*; (*fig: unsettle*) nervös machen; **to ~ along** (*car, bus*) dahinrattern

rattlesnake ['rætlsneɪk] *n* Klapperschlange *f*

raucous ['rɔ:kəs] *adj* (*voice etc*) rau

rave [reɪv] *vi* (*in anger*) toben ▷ *adj* (*inf: review*) glänzend; (*scene, culture*) Rave- ▷ *n* (*Brit: inf: party*) Rave *m*, Fete *f*
▸ **rave about** schwärmen von

raven ['reɪvən] *n* Rabe *m*

ravenous ['rævənəs] *adj* (*person*) ausgehungert; (*appetite*) unersättlich

ravine [rə'vi:n] *n* Schlucht *f*

raving ['reɪvɪŋ] *adj*: **a ~ lunatic** ein total verrückter Typ

ravishing ['rævɪʃɪŋ] *adj* hinreißend

raw [rɔ:] *adj* roh; (*sore*) wund; (*inexperienced*) unerfahren; (*weather, day*) rau; **to get a ~ deal** ungerecht behandelt werden

raw material *n* Rohmaterial *nt*

ray [reɪ] *n* Strahl *m*; **~ of hope** Hoffnungsschimmer *m*

raze [reɪz] *vt* (*also*: **to raze to the ground**) dem Erdboden gleichmachen

razor ['reɪzəʳ] *n* Rasierapparat *m*; (*open razor*) Rasiermesser *nt*

razor blade *n* Rasierklinge *f*

Rd *abbr* (*= road*) Str.

RE (*Brit*) *n abbr* (*Scol*) = **religious education** (*Mil: = Royal Engineers*) *Königliches Pionierkorps*

re [ri:] *prep* (*with regard to*) bezüglich +*gen*

reach [ri:tʃ] *n* (*range*) Reichweite *f* ▷ *vt* erreichen; (*conclusion, decision*) kommen zu; (*be able to touch*) kommen an +*acc* ▷ *vi* (*stretch out one's arm*) langen; **reaches** *npl* (*of river*) Gebiete *pl*; **within/out of ~** in/außer Reichweite; **within easy ~ of the supermarket/station** ganz in der Nähe des Supermarkts/Bahnhofs; **beyond the ~ of sb/sth** außerhalb der Reichweite von jdm/etw; **"keep out of the ~ of children"**

"von Kindern fernhalten"; **can I ~ you at your hotel?** kann ich Sie in Ihrem Hotel erreichen?

▸ **reach out** *vt* (*hand*) ausstrecken ▹ *vi* die Hand ausstrecken; **to ~ out for sth** nach etw greifen

react [ri:'ækt] *vi*: **to ~ (to)** (*also Med*) reagieren (auf *+acc*); (*Chem*): **to ~ (with)** reagieren (mit); **to ~ (against)** (*rebel*) sich wehren (gegen)

reaction [ri:'ækʃən] *n* Reaktion *f*; **reactions** *npl* (*reflexes*) Reaktionen *pl*; **a ~ against sth** Widerstand gegen etw

reactor [ri:'æktə^r] *n* (*also*: **nuclear reactor**) Kernreaktor *m*

read [ri:d] (*pt, pp* **~** [rɛd]) *vi* lesen; (*piece of writing etc*) sich lesen ▹ *vt* lesen; (*meter, thermometer etc*) ablesen; (*understand: mood, thoughts*) sich versetzen in *+acc*; (*meter, thermometer etc: measurement*) anzeigen; (*study*) studieren; **to ~ sb's lips** jdm von den Lippen ablesen; **to ~ sb's mind** jds Gedanken lesen; **to ~ between the lines** zwischen den Zeilen lesen; **to take sth as ~** (*self-evident*) etw für selbstverständlich halten; **you can take it as ~ that ...** Sie können davon ausgehen, dass ...; **do you ~ me?** (*Tel*) verstehen Sie mich?; **to ~ sth into sb's remarks** etw in jds Bemerkungen hineininterpretieren

▸ **read out** *vt* vorlesen

▸ **read over** *vt* durchlesen

▸ **read through** *vt* durchlesen

▸ **read up on** *vt fus* sich informieren über *+acc*

readable ['ri:dəbl] *adj* (*legible*) lesbar; (*book, author etc*) lesenswert

reader ['ri:də^r] *n* (*person*) Leser(in) *m(f)*; (*book*) Lesebuch *nt*; (*Brit: at university*) ≈ Dozent(in) *m(f)*; **to be an avid/slow ~** eifrig/langsam lesen

readership ['ri:dəʃɪp] *n* (*of newspaper etc*) Leserschaft *f*

readily ['rɛdɪlɪ] *adv* (*without hesitation*) bereitwillig; (*easily*) ohne Weiteres

readiness ['rɛdɪnɪs] *n* Bereitschaft *f*; **in ~ for** bereit für

reading ['ri:dɪŋ] *n* Lesen *nt*; (*understanding*) Verständnis *nt*; (*from bible, of poetry etc*) Lesung *f*; (*on meter, thermometer etc*) Anzeige *f*

ready ['rɛdɪ] *adj* (*prepared*) bereit, fertig; (*willing*) bereit; (*easy*) leicht; (*available*) fertig ▹ *n*: **at the ~** (*Mil*) einsatzbereit; (*fig*) griffbereit; **~ for use** gebrauchsfertig; **to be ~ to do sth** bereit sein, etw zu tun; **to get ~** sich fertig machen; **to get sth ~** etw bereitmachen

ready-cooked ['rɛdɪkukt] *adj* vorgekocht

ready-made ['rɛdɪ'meɪd] *adj* (*clothes*) von der Stange, Konfektions-; **~ meal** Fertiggericht *nt*

ready-to-wear ['rɛdɪtə'wɛə^r] *adj* (*clothes*) von der Stange, Konfektions-

real [rɪəl] *adj* (*reason, result etc*) wirklich; (*leather, gold etc*) echt; (*life, feeling*) wahr; (*for emphasis*) echt ▹ *adv* (*US: inf: very*) echt; **in ~ life** im wahren *or* wirklichen Leben; **in ~ terms** effektiv

real ale *n* Real Ale *nt*

real estate *n* Immobilien *pl* ▹ *cpd* (*US: agent, business etc*) Immobilien-

realistic [rɪə'lɪstɪk] *adj* realistisch

reality [ri:'ælɪtɪ] *n* Wirklichkeit *f*, Realität *f*; **in ~** in Wirklichkeit

realization [rɪəlaɪ'zeɪʃən] *n* (*understanding*) Erkenntnis *f*; (*fulfilment*) Verwirklichung *f*, Realisierung *f*; (*Fin: of asset*) Realisation *f*

realize ['rɪəlaɪz] *vt* (*understand*) verstehen; (*fulfil*) verwirklichen, realisieren; (*Fin: amount, profit*) realisieren; **I ~ that ...** es ist mir klar, dass ...

really ['rɪəlɪ] *adv* wirklich; **what ~ happened** was wirklich geschah; **~?** wirklich?; **~!** (*indicating annoyance*) also wirklich!

realm [rɛlm] *n* (*fig: field*) Bereich *m*; (*kingdom*) Reich *nt*

reap [ri:p] *vt* (*crop*) einbringen, ernten; (*fig: benefits*) ernten; (*: rewards*) bekommen

reappear [ri:ə'pɪə^r] *vi* wieder auftauchen

rear [rɪə^r] *adj* hintere(r, s); (*wheel etc*) Hinter- ▹ *n* Rückseite *f*; (*buttocks*) Hinterteil *nt* ▹ *vt* (*family, animals*) aufziehen ▹ *vi* (*also*: **rear up**: *horse*) sich aufbäumen

rearguard ['rɪəgɑ:d] *n* (*Mil*) Nachhut *f*; **to fight a ~ action** (*fig*) sich erbittert wehren

rearrange [ri:ə'reɪndʒ] *vt* (*furniture*) umstellen; (*meeting*) den Termin ändern *+gen*

rear-view mirror ['rɪəvju:-] *n* Rückspiegel *m*

reason ['ri:zn] *n* (*cause*) Grund *m*; (*rationality*) Verstand *m*; (*common sense*) Vernunft *f* ▹ *vi*: **to ~ with sb** vernünftig mit jdm reden; **the ~ for/why** der Grund für/, warum; **we have ~ to believe that ...** wir haben Grund zu der Annahme, dass ...; **it stands to ~ that ...** es ist zu erwarten, dass ...; **she claims with good ~ that ...** sie behauptet mit gutem Grund *or* mit Recht, dass ...; **all the more ~ why ...** ein Grund mehr, warum ...; **yes, but within ~** ja, solange es sich im Rahmen hält

reasonable ['ri:znəbl] *adj* vernünftig; (*number, amount*) angemessen; (*not bad*) ganz ordentlich; **be ~!** sei doch vernünftig!

reasonably ['ri:znəblɪ] *adv* (*fairly*) ziemlich; (*sensibly*) vernünftig; **one could ~ assume that ...** man könnte durchaus annehmen, dass ...

reasoning ['ri:znɪŋ] *n* Argumentation *f*

reassurance [ri:ə'ʃuərəns] *n* (*comfort*) Beruhigung *f*; (*guarantee*) Bestätigung *f*

reassure [ri:ə'ʃuə^r] *vt* beruhigen

rebate ['ri:beɪt] *n* (*on tax etc*) Rückerstattung *f*; (*discount*) Ermäßigung *f*

rebel ['rɛbl] *n* Rebell(in) *m(f)* ▹ *vi* rebellieren

rebellion [rɪ'bɛljən] *n* Rebellion *f*

rebellious [rɪ'bɛljəs] *adj* rebellisch

rebound [rɪ'baund] *vi* (*ball*) zurückprallen ▹ *n*: **on the ~** (*fig*) als Tröstung

rebuff [rɪ'bʌf] *n* Abfuhr *f* ▹ *vt* zurückweisen

rebuild [ri:'bɪld] (*irreg: like* **build**)

vt wiederaufbauen; (*confidence*) wiederherstellen

rebuke [rɪ'bjuːk] *vt* zurechtweisen, tadeln ▷ *n* Zurechtweisung *f*, Tadel *m*

rebut [rɪ'bʌt] (*form*) *vt* widerlegen

recall [rɪ'kɔːl] *vt* (*remember*) sich erinnern an *+acc*; (*ambassador*) abberufen; (*product*) zurückrufen ▷ *n* (*of memories*) Erinnerung *f*; (*of ambassador*) Abberufung *f*; (*of product*) Rückruf *m*; **beyond ~** unwiederbringlich

recant [rɪ'kænt] *vi* widerrufen

recap ['riːkæp] *vt, vi* zusammenfassen ▷ *n* Zusammenfassung *f*

recede [rɪ'siːd] *vi* (*tide*) zurückgehen; (*lights etc*) verschwinden; (*memory, hope*) schwinden; **his hair is beginning to ~** er bekommt eine Stirnglatze

receding [rɪ'siːdɪŋ] *adj* (*hairline*) zurückweichend; (*chin*) fliehend

receipt [rɪ'siːt] *n* (*document*) Quittung *f*; (*act of receiving*) Erhalt *m*; **receipts** *npl* (*Comm*) Einnahmen *pl*; **on ~ of** bei Erhalt *+gen*; **to be in ~ of sth** etw erhalten

receive [rɪ'siːv] *vt* erhalten, bekommen; (*injury*) erleiden; (*treatment*) erhalten; (*visitor, guest*) empfangen; **to be on the receiving end of sth** der/die Leidtragende von etw sein; **"~d with thanks"** (*Comm*) "dankend erhalten"

receiver [rɪ'siːvəʳ] *n* (*Tel*) Hörer *m*; (*Radio, TV*) Empfänger *m*; (*of stolen goods*) Hehler(in) *m(f)*; (*Comm*) Empfänger(in) *m(f)*

recent ['riːsnt] *adj* (*event*) kürzlich; (*times*) letzte(r, s); **in ~ years** in den letzten Jahren

recently ['riːsntlɪ] *adv* (*not long ago*) kürzlich; (*lately*) in letzter Zeit; **as ~ as** erst; **until ~** bis vor Kurzem

receptacle [rɪ'sɛptɪkl] *n* Behälter *m*

reception [rɪ'sɛpʃən] *n* (*in hotel, office etc*) Rezeption *f*; (*party, Radio, TV*) Empfang *m*; (*welcome*) Aufnahme *f*

reception desk *n* Rezeption *f*

receptionist [rɪ'sɛpʃənɪst] *n* (*in hotel*) Empfangschef *m*, Empfangsdame *f*; (*in doctor's surgery*) Sprechstundenhilfe *f*

recess [rɪ'sɛs] *n* (*in room*) Nische *f*; (*secret place*) Winkel *m*; (*Pol etc: holiday*) Ferien *pl*; (*US: Law: short break*) Pause *f*; (*esp US: Scol*) Pause *f*

recession [rɪ'sɛʃən] *n* (*Econ*) Rezession *f*

recharge [riː'tʃɑːdʒ] *vt* (*battery*) aufladen

recipe ['rɛsɪpɪ] *n* Rezept *nt*; **a ~ for success** ein Erfolgsrezept *nt*; **to be a ~ for disaster** in die Katastrophe führen

recipient [rɪ'sɪpɪənt] *n* Empfänger(in) *m(f)*

recital [rɪ'saɪtl] *n* (*concert*) Konzert *nt*

recite [rɪ'saɪt] *vt* (*poem*) vortragen; (*complaints etc*) aufzählen

reckless ['rɛkləs] *adj* (*driving, driver*) rücksichtslos; (*spending*) leichtsinnig

reckon ['rɛkən] *vt* (*consider*) halten für; (*calculate*) berechnen ▷ *vi*: **he is somebody to be ~ed with** mit ihm muss man rechnen; **I ~ that ...** (*think*) ich schätze, dass ...; **to ~ without sb/sth** nicht mit jdm/etw rechnen
▸ **reckon on** *vt fus* rechnen mit

reckoning ['rɛknɪŋ] *n* (*calculation*) Berechnung *f*; **the day of ~** der Tag der Abrechnung

reclaim [rɪ'kleɪm] *vt* (*luggage*) abholen; (*tax etc*) zurückfordern; (*land*) gewinnen; (*waste materials*) zur Wiederverwertung sammeln

recline [rɪ'klaɪn] *vi* (*sit or lie back*) zurückgelehnt sitzen

reclining [rɪ'klaɪnɪŋ] *adj* (*seat*) Liege-

recluse [rɪ'kluːs] *n* Einsiedler(in) *m(f)*

recognition [rɛkəg'nɪʃən] *n* (*of person, place*) Erkennen *nt*; (*of problem, fact*) Erkenntnis *f*; (*of achievement*) Anerkennung *f*; **in ~ of** in Anerkennung *+gen*; **to gain ~** Anerkennung finden; **she had changed beyond ~** sie war nicht wieder zu erkennen

recognizable ['rɛkəgnaɪzəbl] *adj* erkennbar

recognize ['rɛkəgnaɪz] *vt* (*person, place, voice*) wiedererkennen; (*sign, problem*) erkennen; (*qualifications, government, achievement*) anerkennen; **to ~ sb by/as** jdn erkennen an *+dat*/als

recoil [rɪ'kɔɪl] *vi* (*person*): **to ~ from** zurückweichen vor *+dat*; (*fig*) zurückschrecken vor *+dat* ▷ *n* (*of gun*) Rückstoß *m*

recollect [rɛkə'lɛkt] *vt* (*remember*) sich erinnern an *+acc*

recollection [rɛkə'lɛkʃən] *n* Erinnerung *f*; **to the best of my ~** soweit ich mich erinnern *or* entsinnen kann

recommend [rɛkə'mɛnd] *vt* empfehlen; **she has a lot to ~ her** es spricht sehr viel für sie

recommendation [rɛkəmɛn'deɪʃən] *n* Empfehlung *f*; **on the ~ of** auf Empfehlung *+gen*

reconcile ['rɛkənsaɪl] *vt* (*people*) versöhnen; (*facts, beliefs*) (miteinander) vereinbaren, in Einklang bringen; **to ~ o.s. to sth** sich mit etw abfinden

recondition [riːkən'dɪʃən] *vt* (*machine*) überholen

reconnoitre, (US) **reconnoiter** [rɛkə'nɔɪtəʳ] *vt* (*Mil*) erkunden

reconsider [riːkən'sɪdəʳ] *vt* (noch einmal) überdenken ▷ *vi* es sich *dat* noch einmal überlegen

reconstruct [riːkən'strʌkt] *vt* (*building*) wiederaufbauen; (*policy, system*) neu organisieren; (*event, crime*) rekonstruieren

record ['rɛkɔːd] *n* (*written account*) Aufzeichnung *f*; (*of meeting*) Protokoll *nt*; (*of decision*) Beleg *m*; (*Comput*) Datensatz *m*; (*file*) Akte *f*; (*Mus: disc*) Schallplatte *f*; (*history*) Vorgeschichte *f*; (*also*: **criminal record**) Vorstrafen *pl*; (*Sport*) Rekord *m* ▷ *vt* aufzeichnen; (*song etc*) aufnehmen; (*temperature, speed etc*) registrieren ▷ *adj* (*sales, profits*) Rekord-; **~ of attendance** Anwesenheitsliste *f*; **public ~s** Urkunden *pl* des Nationalarchivs; **to keep a ~ of sth** etw schriftlich festhalten; **to have a good/poor ~** gute/schlechte Leistungen vorzuweisen haben; **to have a (criminal) ~** vorbestraft sein; **to set** *or* **put the ~ straight** *(fig)* Klarheit schaffen; **he is on ~ as saying that ...** er hat nachweislich gesagt, dass ...; **off the ~** *(remark)* inoffiziell ▷ *adv* *(speak)* im Vertrauen; **in ~ time** in Rekordzeit

recorded delivery [rɪ'kɔːdɪd-] *(Brit)* *n* *(Post)* Einschreiben *nt*; **to send sth (by) ~** etw per Einschreiben senden

recorder [rɪ'kɔːdəʳ] *n* *(Mus)* Blockflöte *f*; *(Law)* *nebenamtlich als Richter tätiger Rechtsanwalt*

record holder *n* *(Sport)* Rekordinhaber(in) *m(f)*

recording [rɪ'kɔːdɪŋ] *n* Aufnahme *f*

record player *n* Plattenspieler *m*

recount [rɪ'kaunt] *vt* *(story etc)* erzählen

re-count ['riːkaunt] *n* *(of votes)* Nachzählung *f* ▷ *vt* *(votes)* nachzählen

recoup [rɪ'kuːp] *vt*: **to ~ one's losses** seine Verluste ausgleichen

recourse [rɪ'kɔːs] *n*: **to have ~ to sth** Zuflucht zu etw nehmen

recover [rɪ'kʌvəʳ] *vt* *(get back)* zurückbekommen; *(stolen goods)* sicherstellen; *(wreck, body)* bergen; *(financial loss)* ausgleichen ▷ *vi* sich erholen

recovery [rɪ'kʌvərɪ] *n* *(from illness etc)* Erholung *f*; *(in economy)* Aufschwung *m*; *(of lost items)* Wiederfinden *nt*; *(of stolen goods)* Sicherstellung *f*; *(of wreck, body)* Bergung *f*; *(of financial loss)* Ausgleich *m*

recreation [rɛkrɪ'eɪʃən] *n* *(leisure)* Erholung *f*, Entspannung *f*

recreational [rɛkrɪ'eɪʃənl] *adj* *(facilities etc)* Freizeit-

recreational drug *n* Freizeitdroge *f*

recreational vehicle *(US)* *n* Caravan *m*

recruit [rɪ'kruːt] *n* *(Mil)* Rekrut *m*; *(in company)* neuer Mitarbeiter *m*, neue Mitarbeiterin *f* ▷ *vt* *(Mil)* rekrutieren; *(staff, new members)* anwerben

recruitment [rɪ'kruːtmənt] *n* *(of staff)* Anwerbung *f*

rectangle ['rɛktæŋgl] *n* Rechteck *nt*

rectangular [rɛk'tæŋgjuləʳ] *adj* *(shape)* rechteckig

rectify ['rɛktɪfaɪ] *vt* *(mistake etc)* korrigieren

rector ['rɛktəʳ] *n* *(Rel)* Pfarrer(in) *m(f)*

recuperate [rɪ'kjuːpəreɪt] *vi* *(recover)* sich erholen

recur [rɪ'kəːʳ] *vi* *(error, event)* sich wiederholen; *(pain etc)* wiederholt auftreten

recurrence [rɪ'kəːrns] *n* *(see vi)* Wiederholung *f*; wiederholtes Auftreten *nt*

recurrent [rɪ'kəːrnt] *adj* *(see vi)* sich wiederholend; wiederholt auftretend

recurring [rɪ'kəːrɪŋ] *adj* *(problem, dream)* sich wiederholend; *(Math)*: **six point five four ~** sechs Komma fünf Periode vier

recycle [riː'saɪkl] *vt* *(waste, paper etc)* recyceln, wiederverwerten

recycling [riː'saɪklɪŋ] *n* Recycling *nt*; **~ site** Recycling- *or* Wertstoffhof *m*

red [rɛd] *n* Rot *nt*; *(pej: Pol)* Rote(r) *f(m)* ▷ *adj* rot; **to be in the ~** *(business etc)* in den roten Zahlen sein

red carpet treatment *n*: **to give sb the ~** den roten Teppich für jdn ausrollen

Red Cross *n* Rotes Kreuz *nt*

redcurrant ['rɛdkʌrənt] *n* Rote Johannisbeere *f*

redden ['rɛdn] *vt* röten ▷ *vi* *(blush)* erröten

redecorate [riː'dɛkəreɪt] *vt, vi* renovieren

redeem [rɪ'diːm] *vt* *(situation etc)* retten; *(voucher, sth in pawn)* einlösen; *(loan)* abzahlen; *(Rel)* erlösen; **to ~ oneself for sth** etw wiedergutmachen

redeeming [rɪ'diːmɪŋ] *adj* *(feature, quality)* versöhnend

redeploy [riːdɪ'plɔɪ] *vt* *(resources, staff)* umverteilen; *(Mil)* verlegen

red-handed [rɛd'hændɪd] *adj*: **to be caught ~** auf frischer Tat ertappt werden

redhead ['rɛdhɛd] *n* Rotschopf *m*

red herring *n* *(fig)* falsche Spur *f*

red-hot [rɛd'hɔt] *adj* *(metal)* rot glühend

redirect [riːdaɪ'rɛkt] *vt* *(mail)* nachsenden; *(traffic)* umleiten

red light *n* *(Aut)*: **to go through a ~** eine Ampel bei Rot überfahren

red-light district ['rɛdlaɪt-] *n* Rotlichtviertel *nt*

red meat *n* *Rind- und Lammfleisch*

redo [riː'duː] *(irreg: like* **do***)* *vt* noch einmal machen

redress [rɪ'drɛs] *n* *(compensation)* Wiedergutmachung *f* ▷ *vt* *(error etc)* wiedergutmachen; **to ~ the balance** das Gleichgewicht wiederherstellen

Red Sea *n*: **the ~** das Rote Meer

redskin ['rɛdskɪn] *(old: offensive)* *n* Rothaut *f*

red tape *n* *(fig)* Bürokratie *f*

reduce [rɪ'djuːs] *vt* *(spending, numbers, risk etc)* vermindern, reduzieren; **to ~ sth by/to 5%** etw um/auf 5% *acc* reduzieren; **to ~ sb to tears/silence** jdn zum Weinen/Schweigen bringen; **to ~ sb to begging/stealing** jdn zur Bettelei/zum Diebstahl zwingen; **"~ speed now"** *(Aut)* "langsam fahren"

reduced [rɪ'djuːst] *adj* *(goods, ticket etc)* ermäßigt; **"greatly ~ prices"** "Preise stark reduziert"

reduction [rɪ'dʌkʃən] *n* *(in price etc)* Ermäßigung, Reduzierung *f*; *(in numbers)* Verminderung *f*

redundancy [rɪ'dʌndənsɪ] *(Brit)* *n* *(dismissal)* Entlassung *f*; *(unemployment)* Arbeitslosigkeit *f*; **compulsory ~** Entlassung *f*; **voluntary ~** freiwilliger Verzicht *m* auf den Arbeitsplatz

redundant [rɪ'dʌndnt] *adj* *(Brit: worker)* arbeitslos; *(word, object)* überflüssig; **to be made ~** *(worker)* den Arbeitsplatz verlieren

reed [riːd] *n* *(Bot)* Schilf *nt*; *(Mus: of clarinet etc)* Rohrblatt *nt*

reef [riːf] *n* (*at sea*) Riff *nt*
reek [riːk] *vi*: **to ~ (of)** (*lit, fig*) stinken (nach)
reel [riːl] *n* (*of thread etc, on fishing-rod*) Rolle *f*; (*Cine: scene*) Szene *f*; (*of film, tape*) Spule *f*; (*dance*) Reel *m* ▷ *vi* (*sway*) taumeln; **my head is ~ing** mir dreht sich der Kopf
▸ **reel in** *vt* (*fish, line*) einholen
▸ **reel off** *vt* (*say*) herunterrasseln
ref [rɛf] (*inf*) *n abbr* (*Sport*) = **referee**
refectory [rɪ'fɛktərɪ] *n* (*in university*) Mensa *f*
refer [rɪ'fəːʳ] *vt*: **to ~ sb to** (*book etc*) jdn verweisen auf *+acc*; (*doctor, hospital*) jdn überweisen zu; **to ~ sth to** (*task, problem*) etw übergeben an *+acc*; **he ~red me to the manager** er verwies mich an den Geschäftsführer
▸ **refer to** *vt fus* (*mention*) erwähnen; (*relate to*) sich beziehen auf *+acc*; (*consult*) hinzuziehen
referee [rɛfə'riː] *n* (*Sport*) Schiedsrichter(in) *m(f)*; (*Brit: for job application*) Referenz *f* ▷ *vt* als Schiedsrichter(in) leiten
reference ['rɛfrəns] *n* (*mention*) Hinweis *m*; (*in book, article*) Quellenangabe *f*; (*for job application, person*) Referenz *f*; **with ~ to** mit Bezug auf *+acc*; **"please quote this ~"** (*Comm*) "bitte dieses Zeichen angeben"
reference book *n* Nachschlagewerk *nt*
reference number *n* Aktenzeichen *nt*
refill [riː'fɪl] *vt* nachfüllen ▷ *n* (*for pen etc*) Nachfüllmine *f*; (*drink*) Nachfüllung *f*
refine [rɪ'faɪn] *vt* (*sugar, oil*) raffinieren; (*theory, idea*) verfeinern
refined [rɪ'faɪnd] *adj* (*person*) kultiviert; (*taste*) fein, vornehm; (*sugar, oil*) raffiniert
refinery [rɪ'faɪnərɪ] *n* (*for oil etc*) Raffinerie *f*
reflect [rɪ'flɛkt] *vt* reflektieren; (*fig*) widerspiegeln ▷ *vi* (*think*) nachdenken
▸ **reflect on** *vt fus* (*discredit*) ein schlechtes Licht werfen auf *+acc*
reflection [rɪ'flɛkʃən] *n* (*image*) Spiegelbild *nt*; (*of light, heat*) Reflexion *f*; (*fig*) Widerspiegelung *f*; (*: thought*) Gedanke *m*; **on ~** nach genauerer Überlegung; **this is a ~ on ...** (*criticism*) das sagt einiges über ...
reflex ['riːflɛks] *adj* Reflex-; **reflexes** *npl* (*Physiol, Psych*) Reflexe *pl*
reflexive [rɪ'flɛksɪv] *adj* (*Ling*) reflexiv
reform [rɪ'fɔːm] *n* Reform *f* ▷ *vt* reformieren ▷ *vi* (*criminal etc*) sich bessern
reformatory [rɪ'fɔːmətərɪ] (*US*) *n* Besserungsanstalt *f*
refrain [rɪ'freɪn] *vi*: **to ~ from doing sth** etw unterlassen ▷ *n* (*of song*) Refrain *m*
refresh [rɪ'frɛʃ] *vt* erfrischen; **to ~ one's memory** sein Gedächtnis auffrischen
refresher course [rɪ'frɛʃə-] *n* Auffrischungskurs *m*
refreshing [rɪ'frɛʃɪŋ] *adj* erfrischend; (*sleep*) wohltuend; (*idea etc*) angenehm
refreshment [rɪ'frɛʃmənt] *n* Erfrischung *f*
refreshments [rɪ'frɛʃmənts] *npl* (*food and drink*) Erfrischungen *pl*
refrigerator [rɪ'frɪdʒəreɪtəʳ] *n* Kühlschrank *m*
refuel [riː'fjuəl] *vt, vi* auftanken
refuge ['rɛfjuːdʒ] *n* Zuflucht *f*; **to seek/take ~ in** Zuflucht suchen/nehmen in *+dat*
refugee [rɛfju'dʒiː] *n* Flüchtling *m*; **a political ~** ein politischer Flüchtling
refund ['riːfʌnd] *n* Rückerstattung *f* ▷ *vt* (*money*) zurückerstatten
refurbish [riː'fəːbɪʃ] *vt* (*shop etc*) renovieren
refusal [rɪ'fjuːzəl] *n* Ablehnung *f*; **a ~ to do sth** eine Weigerung, etw zu tun; **to give sb first ~ on sth** jdm etw zuerst anbieten
refuse[1] [rɪ'fjuːz] *vt* (*request, offer etc*) ablehnen; (*gift*) zurückweisen; (*permission*) verweigern ▷ *vi* ablehnen; (*horse*) verweigern; **to ~ to do sth** sich weigern, etw zu tun
refuse[2] ['rɛfjuːs] *n* (*rubbish*) Abfall *m*, Müll *m*
refuse collection *n* Müllabfuhr *f*
regain [rɪ'geɪn] *vt* wiedererlangen
regal ['riːgl] *adj* königlich
regard [rɪ'gɑːd] *n* (*esteem*) Achtung *f* ▷ *vt* (*consider*) ansehen, betrachten; (*view*) betrachten; **to give one's ~s to sb** jdm Grüße bestellen; **"with kindest ~s"** "mit freundlichen Grüßen"; **as regards, with ~ to** bezüglich *+gen*
regarding [rɪ'gɑːdɪŋ] *prep* bezüglich *+gen*
regardless [rɪ'gɑːdlɪs] *adv* trotzdem ▷ *adj*: **~ of** ohne Rücksicht auf *+acc*
regenerate [rɪ'dʒɛnəreɪt] *vt* (*inner cities, arts*) erneuern; (*person, feelings*) beleben ▷ *vi* (*Biol*) sich regenerieren
reggae ['rɛgeɪ] *n* Reggae *m*
regiment ['rɛdʒɪmənt] *n* (*Mil*) Regiment *nt* ▷ *vt* reglementieren
regimental [rɛdʒɪ'mɛntl] *adj* Regiments-
region ['riːdʒən] *n* (*of land*) Gebiet *nt*; (*of body*) Bereich *m*; (*administrative division of country*) Region *f*; **in the ~ of** (*approximately*) im Bereich von
regional ['riːdʒənl] *adj* regional
register ['rɛdʒɪstəʳ] *n* (*list, Mus*) Register *nt*; (*also*: **electoral register**) Wählerverzeichnis *nt*; (*Scol*) Klassenbuch *nt* ▷ *vt* registrieren; (*car*) anmelden; (*letter*) als Einschreiben senden; (*amount, measurement*) verzeichnen ▷ *vi* (*person*) sich anmelden; (*: at doctor's*) sich (als Patient) eintragen; (*amount etc*) registriert werden; (*make impression*) (einen) Eindruck machen; **to ~ a protest** Protest anmelden
registered ['rɛdʒɪstəd] *adj* (*letter, parcel*) eingeschrieben; (*drug addict, childminder etc*) (offiziell) eingetragen
registered trademark *n* eingetragenes Warenzeichen *nt*
registrar ['rɛdʒɪstrɑːʳ] *n* (*in registry office*) Standesbeamte(r) *m*, Standesbeamtin *f*; (*in college etc*) Kanzler *m*; (*Brit: in hospital*) Krankenhausarzt *m*, Krankenhausärztin *f*
registration [rɛdʒɪs'treɪʃən] *n* Registrierung *f*; (*of students, unemployed etc*) Anmeldung *f*
registry ['rɛdʒɪstrɪ] *n* Registratur *f*
registry office (*Brit*) *n* Standesamt *nt*; **to get**

married in a ~ standesamtlich heiraten
regret [rɪ'grɛt] *n* Bedauern *nt* ▷ *vt* bedauern; **with ~** mit Bedauern; **to have no ~s** nichts bereuen; **we ~ to inform you that ...** wir müssen Ihnen leider mitteilen, dass ...
regretfully [rɪ'grɛtfəlɪ] *adv* mit Bedauern
regrettable [rɪ'grɛtəbl] *adj* bedauerlich
regular ['rɛgjuləʳ] *adj* (*also Ling*) regelmäßig; (*usual: time, doctor*) üblich; (*: customer*) Stamm-; (*soldier*) Berufs-; (*Comm: size*) normal ▷ *n* (*client*) Stammkunde *m*, Stammkundin *f*
regularly ['rɛgjuləlɪ] *adv* regelmäßig; (*breathe, beat: evenly*) gleichmäßig
regulate ['rɛgjuleɪt] *vt* regulieren
regulation [rɛgju'leɪʃən] *n* Regulierung *f*; (*rule*) Vorschrift *f*
rehabilitation ['ri:əbɪlɪ'teɪʃən] *n* (*see vt*) Wiedereingliederung *f* (in die Gesellschaft); Rehabilitation *f*
rehearsal [rɪ'hə:səl] *n* (*Theat*) Probe *f*; **dress ~** Generalprobe *f*
rehearse [rɪ'hə:s] *vt* (*play, speech etc*) proben
reign [reɪn] *n* (*lit, fig*) Herrschaft *f* ▷ *vi* (*lit, fig*) herrschen
reimburse [ri:ɪm'bə:s] *vt* die Kosten erstatten *+dat*
rein [reɪn] *n* Zügel *m*; **to give sb free ~** (*fig*) jdm freie Hand lassen; **to keep a tight ~ on sth** (*fig*) bei etw die Zügel kurz halten
reincarnation [ri:ɪnkɑ:'neɪʃən] *n* (*belief*) die Wiedergeburt *f*; (*person*) Reinkarnation *f*
reindeer ['reɪndɪəʳ] *n inv* Ren(tier) *nt*
reinforce [ri:ɪn'fɔ:s] *vt* (*strengthen*) verstärken; (*support: idea etc*) stützen; (*: prejudice*) stärken
reinforced concrete *n* Stahlbeton *m*
reinforcement [ri:ɪn'fɔ:smənt] *n* (*strengthening*) Verstärkung *f*; (*of attitude etc*) Stärkung *f*; **reinforcements** *npl* (*Mil*) Verstärkung *f*
reinstate [ri:ɪn'steɪt] *vt* (*employee*) wiedereinstellen; (*tax, law*) wiedereinführen; (*text*) wiedereinfügen
reject ['ri:dʒɛkt] *n* (*Comm*) Ausschuss *m no pl* ▷ *vt* ablehnen; (*admirer*) abweisen; (*goods*) zurückweisen; (*machine: coin*) nicht annehmen; (*Med: heart, kidney*) abstoßen
rejection [rɪ'dʒɛkʃən] *n* Ablehnung *f*; (*of admirer*) Abweisung *f*; (*Med*) Abstoßung *f*
rejoice [rɪ'dʒɔɪs] *vi*: **to ~ at** *or* **over** jubeln über *+acc*
rejuvenate [rɪ'dʒu:vəneɪt] *vt* (*person*) verjüngen; (*organization etc*) beleben
relapse [rɪ'læps] *n* (*Med*) Rückfall *m* ▷ *vi*: **to ~ into** zurückfallen in *+acc*
relate [rɪ'leɪt] *vt* (*tell*) berichten; (*connect*) in Verbindung bringen ▷ *vi*: **to ~ to** (*empathize with: person, subject*) eine Beziehung finden zu; (*connect with*) zusammenhängen mit
related [rɪ'leɪtɪd] *adj*: **to be ~** (miteinander) verwandt sein; (*issues etc*) zusammenhängen
relating to [rɪ'leɪtɪŋ-] *prep* bezüglich *+gen*, mit Bezug auf *+acc*
relation [rɪ'leɪʃən] *n* (*member of family*) Verwandte(r) *f(m)*; (*connection*) Beziehung *f*; **relations** *npl* (*contact*) Beziehungen *pl*; **diplomatic/international ~s** diplomatische/internationale Beziehungen; **in ~ to** im Verhältnis zu; **to bear no ~ to** in keinem Verhältnis stehen zu
relationship [rɪ'leɪʃənʃɪp] *n* Beziehung *f*; (*between countries*) Beziehungen *pl*; (*affair*) Verhältnis *nt*; **they have a good ~** sie haben ein gutes Verhältnis zueinander
relative ['rɛlətɪv] *n* Verwandte(r) *f(m)* ▷ *adj* relativ; **all her ~s** ihre ganze Verwandtschaft; **~ to** im Vergleich zu; **it's all ~** es ist alles relativ
relatively ['rɛlətɪvlɪ] *adv* relativ
relax [rɪ'læks] *vi* (*person, muscle*) sich entspannen; (*calm down*) sich beruhigen ▷ *vt* (*one's grip*) lockern; (*mind, person*) entspannen; (*control etc*) lockern
relaxation [ri:læk'seɪʃən] *n* Entspannung *f*; (*of control etc*) Lockern *nt*
relaxed [rɪ'lækst] *adj* (*person, atmosphere*) entspannt; (*discussion*) locker
relaxing [rɪ'læksɪŋ] *adj* entspannend
relay ['ri:leɪ] *n* (*race*) Staffel *f*, Staffellauf *m* ▷ *vt* (*message etc*) übermitteln; (*broadcast*) übertragen
release [rɪ'li:s] *n* (*from prison*) Entlassung *f*; (*from obligation, situation*) Befreiung *f*; (*of documents, funds etc*) Freigabe *f*; (*of gas etc*) Freisetzung *f*; (*of film, book, record*) Herausgabe *f*; (*record, film*) Veröffentlichung *f*; (*Tech: device*) Auslöser *m* ▷ *vt* (*from prison*) entlassen; (*person: from obligation, from wreckage*) befreien; (*gas etc*) freisetzen; (*Tech, Aut: catch, brake etc*) lösen; (*record, film*) herausbringen; (*news, figures*) bekannt geben; **on general ~** (*film*) überall in den Kinos; *see also* **press release**
relegate ['rɛləgeɪt] *vt* (*downgrade*) herunterstufen; (*Brit: Sport*): **to be ~d** absteigen
relent [rɪ'lɛnt] *vi* (*give in*) nachgeben
relentless [rɪ'lɛntlɪs] *adj* (*heat, noise*) erbarmungslos; (*enemy etc*) unerbittlich
relevant ['rɛləvənt] *adj* relevant; (*chapter, area*) entsprechend; **~ to** relevant für
reliable [rɪ'laɪəbl] *adj* zuverlässig
reliably [rɪ'laɪəblɪ] *adv*: **to be ~ informed that ...** zuverlässige Informationen darüber haben, dass ...
reliance [rɪ'laɪəns] *n*: **~ (on)** (*person*) Angewiesenheit *f* (auf *+acc*); (*drugs, financial support*) Abhängigkeit *f* (von)
relic ['rɛlɪk] *n* (*Rel*) Reliquie *f*; (*of the past*) Relikt *nt*
relief [rɪ'li:f] *n* (*from pain etc*) Erleichterung *f*; (*aid*) Hilfe *f*; (*Art, Geog*) Relief *nt* ▷ *cpd* (*bus*) Entlastungs-; (*driver*) zur Ablösung; **light ~** leichte Abwechslung *f*
relieve [rɪ'li:v] *vt* (*pain*) lindern; (*fear, worry*) mildern; (*take over from*) ablösen; **to ~ sb of sth** (*load*) jdm etw abnehmen; (*duties, post*) jdn einer Sache *gen* entheben; **to ~ o.s.**

(*euphemism*) sich erleichtern
relieved [rɪ'li:vd] *adj* erleichtert; **I'm ~ to hear it** es erleichtert mich, das zu hören
religion [rɪ'lɪdʒən] *n* Religion *f*
religious [rɪ'lɪdʒəs] *adj* religiös
religious education *n* Religionsunterricht *m*
relinquish [rɪ'lɪŋkwɪʃ] *vt* (*control etc*) aufgeben; (*claim*) verzichten auf *+acc*
relish ['rɛlɪʃ] *n* (*Culin*) würzige Soße *f*, Relish *nt*; (*enjoyment*) Genuss *m* ▷ *vt* (*enjoy*) genießen; **to ~ doing sth** etw mit Genuss tun
relocate [ri:ləu'keɪt] *vt* verlegen ▷ *vi* den Standort wechseln; **to ~ in** seinen Standort verlegen nach
reluctance [rɪ'lʌktəns] *n* Widerwille *m*
reluctant [rɪ'lʌktənt] *adj* unwillig, widerwillig; **I'm ~ to do that** es widerstrebt mir, das zu tun
reluctantly [rɪ'lʌktəntlɪ] *adv* widerwillig, nur ungern
rely on [rɪ'laɪ-] *vt fus* (*be dependent on*) abhängen von; (*trust*) sich verlassen auf *+acc*
remain [rɪ'meɪn] *vi* bleiben; (*survive*) übrig bleiben; **to ~ silent** weiterhin schweigen; **to ~ in control** die Kontrolle behalten; **much ~s to be done** es ist noch viel zu tun; **the fact ~s that ...** Tatsache ist und bleibt, dass ...; **it ~s to be seen whether ...** es bleibt abzuwarten, ob ...
remainder [rɪ'meɪndə^r] *n* Rest *m* ▷ *vt* (*Comm*) zu ermäßigtem Preis anbieten
remaining [rɪ'meɪnɪŋ] *adj* übrig
remains [rɪ'meɪnz] *npl* (*of meal*) Überreste *pl*; (*of building etc*) Ruinen *pl*; (*of body*) sterbliche Überreste *pl*
remand [rɪ'mɑ:nd] *n*: **to be on ~** in Untersuchungshaft sein ▷ *vt*: **to be ~ed in custody** in Untersuchungshaft bleiben müssen
remark [rɪ'mɑ:k] *n* Bemerkung *f* ▷ *vt* bemerken ▷ *vi*: **to ~ on sth** Bemerkungen über etw *acc* machen; **to ~ that** die Bemerkung machen, dass
remarkable [rɪ'mɑ:kəbl] *adj* bemerkenswert
remarry [ri:'mærɪ] *vi* wieder heiraten
remedial [rɪ'mi:dɪəl] *adj* (*tuition, classes*) Förder-; **~ exercise** Heilgymnastik *f*
remedy ['rɛmədɪ] *n* (*lit, fig*) (Heil)mittel *nt* ▷ *vt* (*mistake, situation*) abhelfen *+dat*
remember [rɪ'mɛmbə^r] *vt* (*call back to mind*) sich erinnern an *+acc*; (*bear in mind*) denken an *+acc*; **~ me to him** (*send greetings*) grüße ihn von mir; **I ~ seeing it, I ~ having seen it** ich erinnere mich (daran), es gesehen zu haben; **she ~ed to do it** sie hat daran gedacht, es zu tun
remembrance [rɪ'mɛmbrəns] *n* Erinnerung *f*; **in ~ of sb/sth** im Gedenken an *+acc*
remind [rɪ'maɪnd] *vt*: **to ~ sb to do sth** jdn daran erinnern, etw zu tun; **to ~ sb of sth** jdn an etw *acc* erinnern; **to ~ sb that ...** jdn daran erinnern, dass ...; **she ~s me of her mother** sie erinnert mich an ihre Mutter; **that ~s me!** dabei fällt mir etwas ein!
reminder [rɪ'maɪndə^r] *n* (*of person, place etc*) Erinnerung *f*; (*letter*) Mahnung *f*
reminisce [rɛmɪ'nɪs] *vi*: **to ~ (about)** sich in Erinnerungen ergehen (über *+acc*)
reminiscent [rɛmɪ'nɪsnt] *adj*: **to be ~ of sth** an etw *acc* erinnern
remiss [rɪ'mɪs] *adj* nachlässig; **it was ~ of him** es war nachlässig von ihm
remission [rɪ'mɪʃən] *n* (*of sentence*) Straferlass *m*; (*Med*) Remission *f*; (*Rel*) Erlass *m*
remit [rɪ'mɪt] *vt* (*money*) überweisen ▷ *n* (*of official etc*) Aufgabenbereich *m*
remittance [rɪ'mɪtns] *n* Überweisung *f*
remnant ['rɛmnənt] *n* Überrest *m*; (*Comm: of cloth*) Rest *m*
remorse [rɪ'mɔ:s] *n* Reue *f*
remorseful [rɪ'mɔ:sful] *adj* reumütig
remorseless [rɪ'mɔ:slɪs] *adj* (*noise, pain*) unbarmherzig
remote [rɪ'məut] *adj* (*distant: place, time*) weit entfernt; (*aloof*) distanziert; (*slight: chance etc*) entfernt; **there is a ~ possibility that ...** es besteht eventuell die Möglichkeit, dass ...
remote control *n* Fernsteuerung *f*; (*TV etc*) Fernbedienung *f*
remotely [rɪ'məutlɪ] *adv* (*slightly*) entfernt
remould ['ri:məuld] (*Brit*) *n* (*Aut*) runderneuerter Reifen *m*
removable [rɪ'mu:vəbl] *adj* (*detachable*) abnehmbar
removal [rɪ'mu:vəl] *n* (*of object etc*) Entfernung *f*; (*of threat etc*) Beseitigung *f*; (*Brit: from house*) Umzug *m*; (*dismissal*) Entlassung *f*; (*Med: of kidney etc*) Entfernung *f*
removal man (*Brit*) *n* Möbelpacker *m*
removal van (*Brit*) *n* Möbelwagen *m*
remove [rɪ'mu:v] *vt* entfernen; (*clothing*) ausziehen; (*bandage etc*) abnehmen; (*employee*) entlassen; (*name: from list*) streichen; (*doubt, threat, obstacle*) beseitigen; **my first cousin once ~d** mein Vetter ersten Grades
Renaissance [rɪ'neɪsɑ̃:s] *n*: **the ~** die Renaissance
rename [ri:'neɪm] *vt* umbenennen
render ['rɛndə^r] *vt* (*give: assistance, aid*) leisten; (*cause to become: unconscious, harmless, useless*) machen; (*submit*) vorlegen
rendering ['rɛndərɪŋ] (*Brit*) *n* = **rendition**
rendezvous ['rɔndɪvu:] *n* (*meeting*) Rendezvous *nt*; (*place*) Treffpunkt *m* ▷ *vi* (*people*) sich treffen; (*spacecraft*) ein Rendezvousmanöver durchführen; **to ~ with sb** sich mit jdm treffen
renew [rɪ'nju:] *vt* erneuern; (*attack, negotiations*) wiederaufnehmen; (*loan, contract etc*) verlängern; (*relationship etc*) wiederaufleben lassen
renewal [rɪ'nju:əl] *n* Erneuerung *f*; (*of conflict*) Wiederaufnahme *f*; (*of contract etc*) Verlängerung *f*
renounce [rɪ'nauns] *vt* verzichten auf *+acc*; (*belief*) aufgeben

renovate ['rɛnəveɪt] *vt* (*building*) restaurieren; (*machine*) überholen
renown [rɪ'naun] *n* Ruf *m*
renowned [rɪ'naund] *adj* berühmt
rent [rɛnt] *pt, pp of* **rend** ▷ *n* (*for house*) Miete *f* ▷ *vt* mieten; (*also*: **rent out**) vermieten
rental ['rɛntl] *n* (*for television, car*) Mietgebühr *f*
reorganize [riː'ɔːgənaɪz] *vt* umorganisieren
rep [rɛp] *n abbr* (*Comm*) = **representative**; (*Theat*) = **repertory**
repair [rɪ'pɛə^r] *n* Reparatur *f* ▷ *vt* reparieren; (*clothes, road*) ausbessern; **in good/bad ~** in gutem/schlechtem Zustand; **beyond ~** nicht mehr zu reparieren; **to be under ~** (*road*) ausgebessert werden
repair kit *n* (*for bicycle*) Flickzeug *nt*
repatriate [riː'pætrɪeɪt] *vt* repatriieren
repay [riː'peɪ] (*irreg*: *like* **pay**) *vt* zurückzahlen; (*sb's efforts, attention*) belohnen; (*favour*) erwidern; **I'll ~ you next week** ich zahle es dir nächste Woche zurück
repayment [riː'peɪmənt] *n* Rückzahlung *f*
repeal [rɪ'piːl] *n* (*of law*) Aufhebung *f* ▷ *vt* (*law*) aufheben
repeat [rɪ'piːt] *n* (*Radio, TV*) Wiederholung *f* ▷ *vt, vi* wiederholen ▷ *cpd* (*performance*) Wiederholungs-; (*order*) Nach-; **to ~ o.s./itself** sich wiederholen; **to ~ an order for sth** etw nachbestellen
repeatedly [rɪ'piːtɪdlɪ] *adv* wiederholt
repel [rɪ'pɛl] *vt* (*drive away*) zurückschlagen; (*disgust*) abstoßen
repellent [rɪ'pɛlənt] *adj* abstoßend ▷ *n*: **insect ~** Insekten(schutz)mittel *nt*
repent [rɪ'pɛnt] *vi*: **to ~ of sth** etw bereuen
repentance [rɪ'pɛntəns] *n* Reue *f*
repercussions [riːpə'kʌʃənz] *npl* Auswirkungen *pl*
repertory ['rɛpətərɪ] *n* (*also*: **repertory theatre**) Repertoiretheater *nt*
repetition [rɛpɪ'tɪʃən] *n* (*repeat*) Wiederholung *f*
repetitive [rɪ'pɛtɪtɪv] *adj* eintönig, monoton
replace [rɪ'pleɪs] *vt* (*put back*: *upright*) zurückstellen; (*: flat*) zurücklegen; (*take the place of*) ersetzen; **to ~ X with Y** X durch Y ersetzen; **"~ the receiver"** (*Tel*) "Hörer auflegen"
replacement [rɪ'pleɪsmənt] *n* Ersatz *m*
replay ['riːpleɪ] *n* (*of match*) Wiederholungsspiel *nt* ▷ *vt* (*match*) wiederholen; (*track, song*: *on tape*) nochmals abspielen
replenish [rɪ'plɛnɪʃ] *vt* (*glass, stock etc*) auffüllen
replica ['rɛplɪkə] *n* (*of object*) Nachbildung *f*
reply [rɪ'plaɪ] *n* Antwort *f* ▷ *vi*: **to ~ (to sb/sth)** (jdm/auf etw *acc*) antworten; **in ~ to** als Antwort auf *+acc*; **there's no ~** (*Tel*) es meldet sich niemand
report [rɪ'pɔːt] *n* Bericht *m*; (*Brit*: *also*: **school report**) Zeugnis *nt*; (*of gun*) Knall *m* ▷ *vt* berichten; (*casualties, damage, theft etc*) melden; (*person*: *to police*) anzeigen ▷ *vi* (*make a report*) Bericht erstatten; **to ~ to sb** (*present o.s. to*) sich bei jdm melden; (*be responsible to*) jdm unterstellt sein; **to ~ on sth** über etw *acc* Bericht erstatten; **to ~ sick** sich krankmelden; **it is ~ed that** es wird berichtet *or* gemeldet, dass ...
report card (*US, Scot*) *n* Zeugnis *nt*
reportedly [rɪ'pɔːtɪdlɪ] *adv*: **she is ~ living in Spain** sie lebt angeblich in Spanien
reporter [rɪ'pɔːtə^r] *n* Reporter(in) *m(f)*
repose [rɪ'pəuz] *n*: **in ~** in Ruhestellung
represent [rɛprɪ'zɛnt] *vt* (*person, nation*) vertreten; (*show*: *view, opinion*) darstellen; (*symbolize*: *idea*) symbolisieren, verkörpern; **to ~ sth as** (*describe*) etw darstellen als
representation [rɛprɪzɛn'teɪʃən] *n* (*state of being represented*) Vertretung *f*; (*picture etc*) Darstellung *f*; **representations** *npl* (*protest*) Proteste *pl*
representative [rɛprɪ'zɛntətɪv] *n* (*also Comm*) Vertreter(in) *m(f)*; (*US*: *Pol*) Abgeordnete(r) *f(m)* des Repräsentantenhauses ▷ *adj* repräsentativ; **~ of** repräsentativ für
repress [rɪ'prɛs] *vt* unterdrücken
repression [rɪ'prɛʃən] *n* Unterdrückung *f*
reprieve [rɪ'priːv] *n* (*cancellation*) Begnadigung *f*; (*postponement*) Strafaufschub *m*; (*fig*) Gnadenfrist *f* ▷ *vt*: **he was ~d** (*see n*) er wurde begnadigt; ihm wurde Strafaufschub gewährt
reprimand ['rɛprɪmɑːnd] *n* Tadel *m* ▷ *vt* tadeln
reprisal [rɪ'praɪzl] *n* Vergeltung *f*; **reprisals** *npl* Repressalien *pl*; (*in war*) Vergeltungsaktionen *pl*; **to take ~s** zu Repressalien greifen; (*in war*) Vergeltungsaktionen durchführen
reproach [rɪ'prəutʃ] *n* (*rebuke*) Vorwurf *m* ▷ *vt*: **to ~ sb for sth** jdm etw zum Vorwurf machen; **beyond ~** über jeden Vorwurf erhaben; **to ~ sb with sth** jdm etw vorwerfen
reproachful [rɪ'prəutʃful] *adj* vorwurfsvoll
reproduce [riːprə'djuːs] *vt* reproduzieren ▷ *vi* (*Biol*) sich vermehren
reproduction [riːprə'dʌkʃən] *n* Reproduktion *f*; (*Biol*) Fortpflanzung *f*
reproof [rɪ'pruːf] *n* (*rebuke*) Tadel *m*; **with ~** tadelnd
reptile ['rɛptaɪl] *n* Reptil *nt*
republic [rɪ'pʌblɪk] *n* Republik *f*
republican [rɪ'pʌblɪkən] *adj* republikanisch ▷ *n* Republikaner(in) *m(f)*; **the R~s** (*US*: *Pol*) die Republikaner
repudiate [rɪ'pjuːdɪeɪt] *vt* (*accusation*) zurückweisen; (*violence*) ablehnen; (*old*: *friend, wife etc*) verstoßen
repulsive [rɪ'pʌlsɪv] *adj* widerwärtig, abstoßend
reputable ['rɛpjutəbl] *adj* (*make, company etc*) angesehen
reputation [rɛpju'teɪʃən] *n* Ruf *m*; **to have**

a ~ for einen Ruf haben für; **he has a ~ for being awkward** er gilt als schwierig
reputed [rɪ'pju:tɪd] *adj* angeblich; **he is ~ to be rich** er ist angeblich reich
reputedly [rɪ'pju:tɪdlɪ] *adv* angeblich
request [rɪ'kwɛst] *n* (*polite*) Bitte *f*; (*formal*) Ersuchen *nt*; (*Radio*) Musikwunsch *m* ▷ *vt* (*politely*) bitten um; (*formally*) ersuchen; **at the ~ of** auf Wunsch von; **"you are ~ed not to smoke"** "bitte nicht rauchen"
request stop (*Brit*) *n* Bedarfshaltestelle *f*
require [rɪ'kwaɪə^r] *vt* (*need*) benötigen; (*: situation*) erfordern; (*demand*) verlangen; **to ~ sb to do sth** von jdm verlangen, etw zu tun; **if ~d** falls nötig; **what qualifications are ~d?** welche Qualifikationen werden verlangt?; **~d by law** gesetzlich vorgeschrieben
requirement [rɪ'kwaɪəmənt] *n* (*need*) Bedarf *m*; (*condition*) Anforderung *f*; **to meet sb's ~s** jds Anforderungen erfüllen
requisition [rɛkwɪ'zɪʃən] *n*: **~ (for)** (*demand*) Anforderung *f* (von) ▷ *vt* (*Mil*) beschlagnahmen
rescue ['rɛskju:] *n* Rettung *f* ▷ *vt* retten; **to come to sb's ~** jdm zu Hilfe kommen
rescue party *n* Rettungsmannschaft *f*
rescuer ['rɛskjuə^r] *n* Retter(in) *m(f)*
research [rɪ'sə:tʃ] *n* Forschung *f* ▷ *vt* erforschen ▷ *vi*: **to ~ into sth** etw erforschen; **to do ~** Forschung betreiben; **a piece of ~** eine Forschungsarbeit; **~ and development** Forschung und Entwicklung
resemblance [rɪ'zɛmbləns] *n* Ähnlichkeit *f*; **to bear a strong ~ to** starke Ähnlichkeit haben mit; **it bears no ~ to ...** es hat keine Ähnlichkeit mit ...
resemble [rɪ'zɛmbl] *vt* ähneln *+dat*, gleichen *+dat*
resent [rɪ'zɛnt] *vt* (*attitude, treatment*) missbilligen; (*person*) ablehnen
resentful [rɪ'zɛntful] *adj* (*person*) gekränkt; (*attitude*) missbilligend
resentment [rɪ'zɛntmənt] *n* Verbitterung *f*
reservation [rɛzə'veɪʃən] *n* (*booking*) Reservierung *f*; (*doubt*) Vorbehalt *m*; (*land*) Reservat *nt*; **to make a ~** (*in hotel etc*) eine Reservierung vornehmen; **with ~(s)** (*doubts*) unter Vorbehalt
reservation desk *n* Reservierungsschalter *m*
reserve [rɪ'zə:v] *n* Reserve *f*, Vorrat *m*; (*fig: of talent etc*) Reserve *f*; (*Sport*) Reservespieler(in) *m(f)*; (*also*: **nature reserve**) Naturschutzgebiet *nt*; (*restraint*) Zurückhaltung *f* ▷ *vt* reservieren; (*table, ticket*) reservieren lassen; **reserves** *npl* (*Mil*) Reserve *f*; **in ~** in Reserve
reserved [rɪ'zə:vd] *adj* (*restrained*) zurückhaltend; (*seat*) reserviert
reservoir ['rɛzəvwɑ:^r] *n* (*lit, fig*) Reservoir *nt*
reshuffle [ri:'ʃʌfl] *n*: **cabinet ~** Kabinettsumbildung *f*
residence ['rɛzɪdəns] *n* (*form: home*) Wohnsitz *m*; (*length of stay*) Aufenthalt *m*; **to take up ~** sich niederlassen; **in ~** (*queen etc*) anwesend; **writer/artist in ~** *Schriftsteller/Künstler, der in einer Ausbildungsstätte bei freier Unterkunft lehrt und arbeitet*
residence permit (*Brit*) *n* Aufenthaltserlaubnis *f*
resident ['rɛzɪdənt] *n* (*of country, town*) Einwohner(in) *m(f)*; (*in hotel*) Gast *m* ▷ *adj* (*in country, town*) wohnhaft; (*population*) ansässig; (*doctor*) hauseigen; (*landlord*) im Hause wohnend
residential [rɛzɪ'dɛnʃəl] *adj* (*area*) Wohn-; (*course*) mit Wohnung am Ort; (*staff*) im Hause wohnend
residue ['rɛzɪdju:] *n* (*Chem*) Rückstand *m*; (*fig*) Überrest *m*
resign [rɪ'zaɪn] *vt* (*one's post*) zurücktreten von ▷ *vi* (*from post*) zurücktreten; **to ~ o.s. to** (*situation etc*) sich abfinden mit
resignation [rɛzɪg'neɪʃən] *n* (*from post*) Rücktritt *m*; (*state of mind*) Resignation *f*; **to tender one's ~** seine Kündigung einreichen
resigned [rɪ'zaɪnd] *adj*: **to be ~ to sth** sich mit etw abgefunden haben
resilient [rɪ'zɪlɪənt] *adj* (*see n*) widerstandsfähig; unverwüstlich
resin ['rɛzɪn] *n* Harz *nt*
resist [rɪ'zɪst] *vt* (*change, demand*) sich widersetzen *+dat*; (*attack etc*) Widerstand leisten *+dat*; (*urge etc*) widerstehen *+dat*; **I couldn't ~ (doing) it** ich konnte nicht widerstehen(, es zu tun)
resistance [rɪ'zɪstəns] *n* (*also Elec*) Widerstand *m*; (*to illness*) Widerstandsfähigkeit *f*
resolution [rɛzə'lu:ʃən] *n* (*decision*) Beschluss *m*; (*determination*) Entschlossenheit *f*; (*of problem*) Lösung *f*; **to make a ~** einen Entschluss fassen
resolve [rɪ'zɔlv] *n* (*determination*) Entschlossenheit *f* ▷ *vt* (*problem*) lösen; (*difficulty*) beseitigen ▷ *vi*: **to ~ to do sth** beschließen, etw zu tun
resort [rɪ'zɔ:t] *n* (*town*) Urlaubsort *m*; (*recourse*) Zuflucht *f* ▷ *vi*: **to ~ to** Zuflucht nehmen zu; **seaside ~** Seebad *nt*; **winter sports ~** Wintersportort *m*; **as a last ~** als letzter Ausweg; **in the last ~** schlimmstenfalls
resounding [rɪ'zaundɪŋ] *adj* (*noise*) widerhallend; (*voice*) schallend; (*fig: success*) durchschlagend; (*: victory*) überlegen
resource [rɪ'sɔ:s] *n* (*raw material*) Bodenschatz *m*; **resources** *npl* (*coal, oil etc*) Energiequellen *pl*; (*money*) Mittel *pl*, Ressourcen *pl*; **natural ~s** Naturschätze *pl*
resourceful [rɪ'sɔ:sful] *adj* einfallsreich
respect [rɪs'pɛkt] *n* (*consideration, esteem*) Respekt *m* ▷ *vt* respektieren; **respects** *npl* (*greetings*) Grüße *pl*; **to have ~ for sb/sth** Respekt vor jdm/etw haben; **to show sb/sth ~** Respekt vor jdm/etw zeigen; **out of ~ for** aus Rücksicht auf *+acc*; **with ~ to, in ~ of** in Bezug auf *+acc*; **in this ~** in dieser

Hinsicht; **in some/many ~s** in gewisser/ vielfacher Hinsicht; **with (all due) ~** bei allem Respekt

respectable [rɪs'pɛktəbl] *adj* anständig; (*amount, income*) ansehnlich; (*standard, mark etc*) ordentlich

respectful [rɪs'pɛktful] *adj* respektvoll

respective [rɪs'pɛktɪv] *adj* jeweilig

respectively [rɪs'pɛktɪvlɪ] *adv* beziehungsweise; **Germany and Britain were 3rd and 4th ~** Deutschland und Großbritannien belegten den 3. beziehungsweise 4. Platz

respite ['rɛspaɪt] *n* (*rest*) Ruhepause *f*

respond [rɪs'pɔnd] *vi* (*answer*) antworten; (*react*) reagieren

response [rɪs'pɔns] *n* (*to question*) Antwort *f*; (*to event etc*) Reaktion *f*; **in ~ to** als Antwort/ Reaktion auf *+acc*

responsibility [rɪspɔnsɪ'bɪlɪtɪ] *n* Verantwortung *f*; **to take ~ for sth/sb** die Verantwortung für etw/jdn übernehmen

responsible [rɪs'pɔnsɪbl] *adj* verantwortlich; (*reliable, important*) verantwortungsvoll; **to be ~ for sth** für etw verantwortlich sein; **to be ~ for doing sth** dafür verantwortlich sein, etw zu tun; **to be ~ to sb** jdm gegenüber verantwortlich sein

responsibly [rɪs'pɔnsɪblɪ] *adv* verantwortungsvoll

responsive [rɪs'pɔnsɪv] *adj* (*person*) ansprechbar

rest [rɛst] *n* (*relaxation*) Ruhe *f*; (*pause*) Ruhepause *f*; (*remainder*) Rest *m*; (*support*) Stütze *f*; (*Mus*) Pause *f* ▷ *vi* (*relax*) sich ausruhen ▷ *vt* (*eyes, legs etc*) ausruhen; **the ~ of them** die Übrigen; **to put** *or* **set sb's mind at ~** jdn beruhigen; **to come to ~** (*object*) zum Stillstand kommen; **to lay sb to ~** jdn zur letzten Ruhe betten; **to ~ on sth** (*lit, fig*) sich auf etw *acc* stützen; **to let the matter ~** die Sache auf sich beruhen lassen; **~ assured that ...** seien Sie versichert, dass ...; **I won't ~ until ...** ich werde nicht ruhen, bis ...; **may he/she ~ in peace** möge er/sie in Frieden ruhen; **to ~ sth on/against sth** (*lean*) etw an *acc*/gegen etw lehnen; **to ~ one's eyes** *or* **gaze on sth** den Blick auf etw heften; **I ~ my case** mehr brauche ich dazu wohl nicht zu sagen

restaurant ['rɛstərɔŋ] *n* Restaurant *nt*

restaurant car (*Brit*) *n* (*Rail*) Speisewagen *m*

restful ['rɛstful] *adj* (*music*) ruhig; (*lighting*) beruhigend; (*atmosphere*) friedlich

restive ['rɛstɪv] *adj* (*person, crew*) unruhig; (*horse*) störrisch

restless ['rɛstlɪs] *adj* rastlos; (*audience*) unruhig; **to get ~** unruhig werden

restoration [rɛstə'reɪʃən] *n* (*of painting etc*) Restauration *f*; (*of law and order, health, sight etc*) Wiederherstellung *f*; (*of land, rights*) Rückgabe *f*; (*Hist*): **the R~** die Restauration

restore [rɪ'stɔːʳ] *vt* (*painting etc*) restaurieren; (*law and order, faith, health etc*) wiederherstellen; (*property*) zurückgeben; **to ~ sth to** (*to former state*) etw zurückverwandeln in *+acc*; **to ~ sb to power** jdn wieder an die Macht bringen

restrain [rɪs'treɪn] *vt* (*person*) zurückhalten; (*feeling*) unterdrücken; (*growth, inflation*) dämpfen; **to ~ sb from doing sth** jdn davon abhalten, etw zu tun; **to ~ o.s. from doing sth** sich beherrschen, etw nicht zu tun

restrained [rɪs'treɪnd] *adj* (*person*) beherrscht; (*style etc*) zurückhaltend

restraint [rɪs'treɪnt] *n* (*restriction*) Einschränkung *f*; (*moderation*) Zurückhaltung *f*; **wage ~** Zurückhaltung *f* bei Lohnforderungen

restrict [rɪs'trɪkt] *vt* beschränken

restriction [rɪs'trɪkʃən] *n* Beschränkung *f*

rest room (*US*) *n* Toilette *f*

restructure [riː'strʌktʃəʳ] *vt* umstrukturieren

result [rɪ'zʌlt] *n* Resultat *nt*; (*of match, election, exam etc*) Ergebnis *nt* ▷ *vi*: **to ~ in** führen zu; **as a ~ of the accident** als Folge des Unfalls; **he missed the train as a ~ of sleeping in** er verpasste den Zug, weil er verschlafen hatte; **to ~ from** resultieren *or* sich ergeben aus; **as a ~ it is too expensive** folglich ist es zu teuer

resume [rɪ'zjuːm] *vt* (*work, journey*) wiederaufnehmen; (*seat*) wieder einnehmen ▷ *vi* (*start again*) von Neuem beginnen

résumé ['reɪsjuːmeɪ] *n* Zusammenfassung *f*; (*US: curriculum vitae*) Lebenslauf *m*

resumption [rɪ'zʌmpʃən] *n* (*of work etc*) Wiederaufnahme *f*

resurgence [rɪ'səːdʒəns] *n* Wiederaufleben *nt*

resurrection [rɛzə'rɛkʃən] *n* (*of hopes, fears*) Wiederaufleben *nt*; (*of custom etc*) Wiederbelebung *f*; (*Rel*): **the R~** die Auferstehung *f*

resuscitate [rɪ'sʌsɪteɪt] *vt* (*Med, fig*) wiederbeleben

retail ['riːteɪl] *adj* (*trade, department*) Verkaufs-; (*shop, goods*) Einzelhandels- ▷ *adv* im Einzelhandel ▷ *vt* (*sell*) (im Einzelhandel) verkaufen ▷ *vi*: **to ~ at** (im Einzelhandel) kosten; **this product ~s at £25** dieses Produkt kostet im Laden £25

retailer ['riːteɪləʳ] *n* Einzelhändler(in) *m(f)*

retail price *n* Einzelhandelspreis *m*

retain [rɪ'teɪn] *vt* (*keep*) behalten; (*: heat, moisture*) zurückhalten

retainer [rɪ'teɪnəʳ] *n* (*fee*) Vorauszahlung *f*

retaliate [rɪ'tælɪeɪt] *vi* Vergeltung üben

retaliation [rɪtælɪ'eɪʃən] *n* Vergeltung *f*; **in ~ for** als Vergeltung für

retarded [rɪ'tɑːdɪd] *adj* zurückgeblieben; **mentally ~** geistig zurückgeblieben

retch [rɛtʃ] *vi* würgen

retentive [rɪ'tɛntɪv] *adj* (*memory*) merkfähig

retina ['rɛtɪnə] *n* Netzhaut *f*

retire [rɪ'taɪəʳ] *vi* (*give up work*) in den Ruhestand treten; (*withdraw, go to bed*) sich

zurückziehen
retired [rɪ'taɪəd] *adj (person)* im Ruhestand
retirement [rɪ'taɪəmənt] *n (state)* Ruhestand *m*; *(act)* Pensionierung *f*
retiring [rɪ'taɪərɪŋ] *adj (leaving)* ausscheidend; *(shy)* zurückhaltend
retort [rɪ'tɔ:t] *vi* erwidern ▷ *n (reply)* Erwiderung *f*
retrace [ri:'treɪs] *vt*: **to ~ one's steps** *(lit, fig)* seine Schritte zurückverfolgen
retract [rɪ'trækt] *vt (promise)* zurücknehmen; *(confession)* zurückziehen; *(claws, undercarriage)* einziehen
retrain [ri:'treɪn] *vt* umschulen ▷ *vi* umgeschult werden
retread ['ri:trɛd] *n (tyre)* runderneuerter Reifen *m*
retreat [rɪ'tri:t] *n (place)* Zufluchtsort *m*; *(withdrawal: also Mil)* Rückzug *m* ▷ *vi* sich zurückziehen; **to beat a hasty ~** schleunigst den Rückzug antreten
retribution [rɛtrɪ'bju:ʃən] *n* Strafe *f*
retrieval [rɪ'tri:vəl] *n (of object)* Zurückholen *nt*; *(Comput)* Abruf *m*
retrieve [rɪ'tri:v] *vt (object)* zurückholen; *(situation)* retten; *(error)* wiedergutmachen; *(dog)* apportieren; *(Comput)* abrufen
retriever [rɪ'tri:vəʳ] *n (dog)* Apportierhund *m*
retrospect ['rɛtrəspɛkt] *n*: **in ~** rückblickend, im Rückblick
retrospective [rɛtrə'spɛktɪv] *adj (opinion etc)* im Nachhinein; *(law, tax)* rückwirkend ▷ *n (Art)* Retrospektive *f*
return [rɪ'tə:n] *n (going or coming back)* Rückkehr *f*; *(of sth stolen etc)* Rückgabe *f*; *(also*: **return ticket**: *Brit)* Rückfahrkarte *f*; *(Fin: from investment etc)* Ertrag *m*; *(of merchandise)* Rücksendung *f*; *(official report)* Erklärung *f* ▷ *cpd (journey)* Rück- ▷ *vi (person etc: come or go back)* zurückkehren; *(feelings, symptoms etc)* wiederkehren ▷ *vt (favour, greetings etc)* erwidern; *(sth stolen etc)* zurückgeben; *(Law: verdict)* fällen; *(Pol: candidate)* wählen; *(ball)* zurückspielen; **returns** *npl (Comm)* Gewinne *pl*; **in ~ (for)** als Gegenleistung (für); **by ~ of post** postwendend; **many happy ~s (of the day)!** herzlichen Glückwunsch zum Geburtstag!; **~ match** Rückspiel *nt*
▶ **return to** *vt fus (regain: consciousness, power)* wiedererlangen
reunion [ri:'ju:nɪən] *n* Treffen *nt*; *(after long separation)* Wiedervereinigung *f*
reunite [ri:ju:'naɪt] *vt* wiedervereinigen
rev [rɛv] *n abbr (Aut: = revolution per minute)* Umdrehung *f* pro Minute, U/min. ▷ *vt (also*: **rev up**: *engine)* aufheulen lassen
revamp [ri:'væmp] *vt (company, system)* auf Vordermann bringen
reveal [rɪ'vi:l] *vt (make known)* enthüllen; *(make visible)* zum Vorschein bringen
revealing [rɪ'vi:lɪŋ] *adj (comment, action)* aufschlussreich; *(dress)* tief ausgeschnitten
revel ['rɛvl] *vi*: **to ~ in sth** in etw schwelgen; **to ~ in doing sth** es genießen, etw zu tun
revelation [rɛvə'leɪʃən] *n (disclosure)* Enthüllung *f*
revenge [rɪ'vɛndʒ] *n (for insult etc)* Rache *f* ▷ *vt* rächen; **to get one's ~ (for sth)** seine Rache (für etw) bekommen; **to ~ o.s.** *or* **take one's ~ (on sb)** sich (an jdm) rächen
revenue ['rɛvənju:] *n (of person, company)* Einnahmen *pl*; *(of government)* Staatseinkünfte *pl*
reverberate [rɪ'və:bəreɪt] *vi (sound etc)* widerhallen; *(fig: shock etc)* Nachwirkungen haben
reverence ['rɛvərəns] *n* Ehrfurcht *f*
Reverend ['rɛvərənd] *adj (in titles)* Pfarrer; **the ~ John Smith** Pfarrer John Smith
reversal [rɪ'və:sl] *n (of policy, trend)* Umkehr *f*; **a ~ of roles** ein Rollentausch *m*
reverse [rɪ'və:s] *n (opposite)* Gegenteil *nt*; *(back: of cloth)* linke Seite *f*; *(: of coin, paper)* Rückseite *f*; *(Aut: also*: **reverse gear**) Rückwärtsgang *m*; *(setback)* Rückschlag *m* ▷ *adj (side)* Rück-; *(process)* umgekehrt ▷ *vt (position, trend etc)* umkehren; *(Law: verdict)* revidieren; *(roles)* vertauschen; *(car)* zurücksetzen ▷ *vi (Brit: Aut)* zurücksetzen; **in ~** umgekehrt; **to go into ~** den Rückwärtsgang einlegen; **in ~ order** in umgekehrter Reihenfolge; **to ~ direction** sich um 180 Grad drehen
reversing lights [rɪ'və:sɪŋ-] *(Brit) npl* Rückfahrscheinwerfer *m*
revert [rɪ'və:t] *vi*: **to ~ to** *(former state)* zurückkehren zu, zurückfallen in *+acc*; *(Law: money, property)* zurückfallen an *+acc*
review [rɪ'vju:] *n (magazine)* Zeitschrift *f*; *(Mil)* Inspektion *f*; *(of book, film etc)* Kritik *f*, Besprechung *f*, Rezension *f*; *(of policy etc)* Überprüfung *f* ▷ *vt (Mil: troops)* inspizieren; *(book, film etc)* besprechen, rezensieren; *(policy etc)* überprüfen; **to be/come under ~** überprüft werden
reviewer [rɪ'vju:əʳ] *n* Kritiker(in) *m(f)*, Rezensent(in) *m(f)*
revise [rɪ'vaɪz] *vt (manuscript)* überarbeiten, revidieren; *(opinion etc)* ändern; *(price, procedure)* revidieren ▷ *vi (study)* wiederholen; **~d edition** überarbeitete Ausgabe
revision [rɪ'vɪʒən] *n (of manuscript, law etc)* Überarbeitung *f*, Revision *f*; *(for exam)* Wiederholung *f*
revival [rɪ'vaɪvəl] *n (recovery)* Aufschwung *m*; *(of interest, faith)* Wiederaufleben *nt*; *(Theat)* Wiederaufnahme *f*
revive [rɪ'vaɪv] *vt (person)* wiederbeleben; *(economy etc)* Auftrieb geben *+dat*; *(custom)* wiederaufleben lassen; *(hope, interest etc)* neu beleben; *(play)* wiederaufnehmen ▷ *vi (person)* wieder zu sich kommen; *(activity, economy etc)* wieder aufblühen; *(hope, interest etc)* wiedererweckt werden
revoke [rɪ'vəuk] *vt (law etc)* aufheben; *(title,*

licence) entziehen *+dat*; (*promise, decision*) widerrufen
revolt [rɪ'vəult] *n* Revolte *f*, Aufstand *m* ▷ *vi* rebellieren ▷ *vt* abstoßen; **to ~ against sb/sth** gegen jdn/etw rebellieren
revolting [rɪ'vəultɪŋ] *adj* (*disgusting*) abscheulich, ekelhaft
revolution [rɛvə'lu:ʃən] *n* (*Pol etc*) Revolution *f*; (*rotation*) Umdrehung *f*
revolutionary [rɛvə'lu:ʃənrɪ] *adj* revolutionär; (*leader, army*) Revolutions- ▷ *n* Revolutionär(in) *m(f)*
revolve [rɪ'vɔlv] *vi* sich drehen; **to ~ (a)round** sich drehen um
revolver [rɪ'vɔlvə^r] *n* Revolver *m*
revolving [rɪ'vɔlvɪŋ] *adj* (*chair*) Dreh-; (*sprinkler etc*) drehbar
revolving door *n* Drehtür *f*
revulsion [rɪ'vʌlʃən] *n* (*disgust*) Abscheu *m*, Ekel *m*
reward [rɪ'wɔ:d] *n* Belohnung *f*; (*satisfaction*) Befriedigung *f* ▷ *vt* belohnen
rewarding [rɪ'wɔ:dɪŋ] *adj* lohnend; **financially ~** einträglich
rewind [ri:'waɪnd] (*irreg: like* **wind**) *vt* (*tape etc*) zurückspulen
rewire [ri:'waɪə^r] *vt* neu verkabeln
rewrite [ri:'raɪt] (*irreg: like* **write**) *vt* neu schreiben
rheumatism ['ru:mətɪzəm] *n* Rheuma *nt*, Rheumatismus *m*
Rhine [raɪn] *n*: **the ~** der Rhein
rhinoceros [raɪ'nɔsərəs] *n* Rhinozeros *nt*
rhubarb ['ru:bɑ:b] *n* Rhabarber *m*
rhyme [raɪm] *n* Reim *m*; (*verse*) Verse *pl* ▷ *vi*: **to ~ (with)** sich reimen (mit); **without ~ or reason** ohne Sinn und Verstand
rhythm ['rɪðm] *n* Rhythmus *m*
rib [rɪb] *n* Rippe *f* ▷ *vt* (*mock*) aufziehen
ribbon ['rɪbən] *n* (*for hair, decoration*) Band *nt*; (*of typewriter*) Farbband *nt*; **in ~s** (*torn*) in Fetzen
rice [raɪs] *n* Reis *m*
rice pudding *n* Milchreis *m*
rich [rɪtʃ] *adj* reich; (*soil*) fruchtbar; (*food*) schwer; (*diet*) reichhaltig; (*colour*) satt; (*voice*) volltönend; (*tapestries, silks*) prächtig ▷ *npl*: **the ~** die Reichen; **~ in** reich an *+dat*
richly ['rɪtʃlɪ] *adv* (*decorated, carved*) reich; (*reward, benefit*) reichlich; **~ deserved/earned** wohlverdient
rickets ['rɪkɪts] *n* Rachitis *f*
rid [rɪd] (*pt, pp* **~**) *vt*: **to ~ sb/sth of** jdn/etw befreien von; **to get ~ of** loswerden; (*inhibitions, illusions etc*) sich befreien von
riddle ['rɪdl] *n* Rätsel *nt* ▷ *vt*: **to be ~d with** (*guilt, doubts*) geplagt sein von; (*holes, corruption*) durchsetzt sein von
ride [raɪd] (*pt* **rode**, *pp* **ridden**) *n* (*in car, on bicycle*) Fahrt *f*; (*on horse*) Ritt *m*; (*path*) Reitweg *m* ▷ *vi* (*on horse*) reiten; (*on bicycle, bus etc*) fahren ▷ *vt* (*see vi*) reiten; fahren; **car ~** Autofahrt *f*; **to go for a ~** eine Fahrt/einen Ausritt machen; **to take sb for a ~** (*fig*) jdn hereinlegen; **we rode all day/all the way** wir sind den ganzen Tag/den ganzen Weg geritten/gefahren; **to ~ at anchor** (*Naut*) vor Anker liegen; **can you ~ a bike?** kannst du Fahrrad fahren?
▸ **ride out** *vt*: **to ~ out the storm** (*fig*) den Sturm überstehen
rider ['raɪdə^r] *n* (*on horse*) Reiter(in) *m(f)*; (*on bicycle etc*) Fahrer(in) *m(f)*; (*in document etc*) Zusatz *m*
ridge [rɪdʒ] *n* (*of hill*) Grat *m*; (*of roof*) First *m*; (*in sand etc*) Rippelmarke *f*
ridicule ['rɪdɪkju:l] *n* Spott *m* ▷ *vt* (*person*) verspotten; (*proposal, system etc*) lächerlich machen; **she was the object of ~** alle machten sich über sie lustig
ridiculous [rɪ'dɪkjuləs] *adj* lächerlich
riding ['raɪdɪŋ] *n* Reiten *nt*
riding school *n* Reitschule *f*
rife [raɪf] *adj*: **to be ~** (*corruption, disease etc*) grassieren; **to be ~ with** (*rumours etc*) durchsetzt sein von
riffraff ['rɪfræf] *n* Gesindel *nt*
rifle ['raɪfl] *n* (*gun*) Gewehr *nt* ▷ *vt* (*wallet etc*) plündern
▸ **rifle through** *vt fus* (*papers etc*) durchwühlen
rifle range *n* Schießstand *m*
rift [rɪft] *n* Spalt *m*; (*fig*) Kluft *f*
rig [rɪg] *n* (*also*: **oil rig**: *at sea*) Bohrinsel *f*; (*: on land*) Bohrturm *m* ▷ *vt* (*election, game etc*) manipulieren
▸ **rig out** (*Brit*) *vt*: **to ~ sb out as/in** jdn ausstaffieren als/in *+dat*
▸ **rig up** *vt* (*device*) montieren
rigging ['rɪgɪŋ] *n* (*Naut*) Takelage *f*
right [raɪt] *adj* (*correct*) richtig; (*not left*) rechte(r, s) ▷ *n* Recht *nt* ▷ *adv* (*correctly, properly*) richtig; (*directly, exactly*) genau; (*not on the left*) rechts ▷ *vt* (*ship, car etc*) aufrichten; (*fault, situation*) korrigieren, berichtigen ▷ *excl* okay; **the ~ time** (*exact*) die genaue Zeit; (*most suitable*) die richtige Zeit; **to be ~** (*person*) recht haben; (*answer, fact*) richtig sein; (*clock*) genau gehen; (*reading etc*) korrekt sein; **to get sth ~** etw richtig machen; **let's get it ~ this time!** diesmal machen wir es richtig!; **you did the ~ thing** du hast das Richtige getan; **to put sth ~** (*mistake etc*) etw berichtigen; **on/to the ~** rechts; **the R~** (*Pol*) die Rechte; **by ~s** richtig genommen; **to be in the ~** im Recht sein; **you're within your ~s (to do that)** es ist dein gutes Recht(, das zu tun); **he is a well-known author in his own ~** er ist selbst auch ein bekannter Autor; **film ~s** Filmrechte *pl*; **~ now** im Moment; **~ before/after the party** gleich vor/nach der Party; **~ against the wall** unmittelbar an der Wand; **~ ahead** geradeaus; **~ away** (*immediately*) sofort; **~ in the middle** genau in der Mitte; **he went ~ to the end of the road** er ging bis ganz ans Ende der Straße
right angle *n* rechter Winkel *m*
righteous ['raɪtʃəs] *adj* (*person*) rechtschaffen;

(*indignation*) gerecht
rightful ['raɪtful] *adj* rechtmäßig
right-hand drive *adj* (*vehicle*) mit Rechtssteuerung
right-handed [raɪt'hændɪd] *adj* rechtshändig
right-hand man *n* rechte Hand *f*
rightly ['raɪtlɪ] *adv* (*with reason*) zu Recht; **if I remember ~** (*Brit*) wenn ich mich recht entsinne
right of way *n* (*on path etc*) Durchgangsrecht *f*; (*Aut*) Vorfahrt *f*
right wing *n* (*Pol, Sport*) rechter Flügel *m*
right-wing [raɪt'wɪŋ] *adj* (*Pol*) rechtsgerichtet
rigid ['rɪdʒɪd] *adj* (*structure, views*) starr; (*principle, control etc*) streng
rigmarole ['rɪgmərəul] *n* Gedöns *nt* (*inf*)
rigorous ['rɪgərəs] *adj* (*control etc*) streng; (*training*) gründlich
rile [raɪl] *vt* ärgern
rim [rɪm] *n* (*of glass, spectacles*) Rand *m*; (*of wheel*) Felge *f*, Radkranz *m*
rind [raɪnd] *n* (*of bacon*) Schwarte *f*; (*of lemon, melon*) Schale *f*; (*of cheese*) Rinde *f*
ring [rɪŋ] (*pt* **rang**, *pp* **rung**) *n* Ring *m*; (*of people, objects*) Kreis *m*; (*of circus*) Manege *f*; (*bullring*) Arena *f*; (*sound of telephone*) Klingeln *nt*; (*sound of bell*) Läuten *nt*; (*on cooker*) Kochstelle *m* ▷ *vi* (*Tel: person*) anrufen; (*telephone, doorbell*) klingeln; (*bell*) läuten; (*also*: **ring out**) ertönen ▷ *vt* (*Brit: Tel*) anrufen; (*bell etc*) läuten; (*encircle*) einen Kreis machen um; **to give sb a ~** (*Brit: Tel*) jdn anrufen; **that has a ~ of truth about it** das könnte stimmen; **to run ~s round sb** (*inf: fig*) jdn in die Tasche stecken; **to ~ true/false** wahr/falsch klingen; **my ears are ~ing** mir klingen die Ohren; **to ~ the doorbell** klingeln; **the name doesn't ~ a bell (with me)** der Name sagt mir nichts
▸ **ring back** (*Brit*) *vt, vi* (*Tel*) zurückrufen
▸ **ring off** (*Brit*) *vi* (*Tel*) (den Hörer) auflegen
▸ **ring up** (*Brit*) *vt* (*Tel*) anrufen
ring binder *n* Ringbuch *nt*
ringing ['rɪŋɪŋ] *n* (*of telephone*) Klingeln *nt*; (*of bell*) Läuten *nt*; (*in ears*) Klingen *nt*
ringing tone (*Brit*) *n* (*Tel*) Rufzeichen *nt*
ringleader ['rɪŋliːdə^r] *n* Rädelsführer(in) *m(f)*
ringlets ['rɪŋlɪts] *npl* Ringellocken *pl*; **in ~** in Ringellocken
ring road (*Brit*) *n* Ringstraße *f*
rink [rɪŋk] *n* (*also*: **ice rink**) Eisbahn *f*; (*also*: **roller skating rink**) Rollschuhbahn *f*
rinse [rɪns] *n* Spülen *nt*; (*of hands*) Abspülen *nt*; (*hair dye*) Tönung *f* ▷ *vt* spülen; (*hands*) abspülen; (*also*: **rinse out**: *clothes*) auswaschen; (*: mouth*) ausspülen; **to give sth a ~** etw spülen; (*dishes*) etw abspülen
riot ['raɪət] *n* (*disturbance*) Aufruhr *m* ▷ *vi* randalieren; **a ~ of colours** ein Farbenmeer *nt*; **to run ~** randalieren
riotous ['raɪətəs] *adj* (*crowd*) randalierend; (*nights, party*) ausschweifend; (*welcome etc*) tumultartig
rip [rɪp] *n* (*tear*) Riss *m* ▷ *vt* zerreißen ▷ *vi* reißen
▸ **rip off** *vt* (*clothes*) herunterreißen; (*inf: swindle*) übers Ohr hauen
▸ **rip up** *vt* zerreißen
ripcord ['rɪpkɔːd] *n* Reißleine *f*
ripe [raɪp] *adj* reif; **to be ~ for sth** (*fig*) reif für etw sein; **he lived to a ~ old age** er erreichte ein stolzes Alter
ripen ['raɪpn] *vt* reifen lassen ▷ *vi* reifen
rip-off ['rɪpɔf] (*inf*) *n*: **it's a ~!** das ist Wucher!
ripple ['rɪpl] *n* (*wave*) kleine Welle *f*; (*of laughter, applause*) Welle *f* ▷ *vi* (*water*) sich kräuseln; (*muscles*) spielen ▷ *vt* (*surface*) kräuseln
rise [raɪz] (*pt* **rose**, *pp* **~n**) *n* (*incline*) Steigung *f*; (*Brit: salary increase*) Gehaltserhöhung *f*; (*in prices, temperature etc*) Anstieg *m*; (*fig: to fame etc*) Aufstieg *m* ▷ *vi* (*prices, water*) steigen; (*sun, moon*) aufgehen; (*wind*) aufkommen; (*from bed, chair*) aufstehen; (*sound, voice*) ansteigen; (*also*: **rise up**: *tower, rebel*) sich erheben; (*in rank*) aufsteigen; **to give ~ to** Anlass geben zu; **to ~ to power** an die Macht kommen
risen [rɪzn] *pp of* **rise**
rising ['raɪzɪŋ] *adj* (*increasing*) steigend; (*up-and-coming*) aufstrebend
risk [rɪsk] *n* (*danger, chance*) Gefahr *f*; (*deliberate*) Risiko *nt* ▷ *vt* riskieren; **to take a ~** ein Risiko eingehen; **to run the ~ of sth** etw zu fürchten haben; **to run the ~ of doing sth** Gefahr laufen, etw zu tun; **at ~** in Gefahr; **at one's own ~** auf eigene Gefahr; **at the ~ of sounding rude ...** auf die Gefahr hin, unhöflich zu klingen, ...; **it's a fire/health ~** es ist ein Feuer-/Gesundheitsrisiko; **I'll ~ it** ich riskiere es
risky ['rɪskɪ] *adj* riskant
rissole ['rɪsəul] *n* (*of meat, fish etc*) Frikadelle *f*
rite [raɪt] *n* Ritus *m*; **last ~s** (*Rel*) Letzte Ölung *f*
ritual ['rɪtjuəl] *adj* (*law, murder*) Ritual-; (*dance*) rituell ▷ *n* Ritual *nt*
rival ['raɪvl] *n* Rivale *m*, Rivalin *f* ▷ *adj* (*firm, newspaper etc*) Konkurrenz-; (*teams, groups etc*) rivalisierend ▷ *vt* (*match*) sich messen können mit; **to ~ sth/sb in sth** sich mit etw/jdm in Bezug auf etw messen können
rivalry ['raɪvlrɪ] *n* Rivalität *f*
river ['rɪvə^r] *n* Fluss *m*; (*fig: of blood etc*) Strom *m* ▷ *cpd* (*port, traffic*) Fluss-; **up/down ~** flussaufwärts/-abwärts
rivet ['rɪvɪt] *n* Niete *f* ▷ *vt* (*fig: attention*) fesseln; (*: eyes*) heften
Riviera [rɪvɪ'ɛərə] *n*: **the (French) ~** die (französische) Riviera; **the Italian ~** die italienische Riviera
road [rəud] *n* Straße *f*; (*fig*) Weg *m* ▷ *cpd* (*accident, sense*) Verkehrs-; **main ~** Hauptstraße *f*; **it takes four hours by ~** man braucht vier Stunden mit dem Auto; **let's hit the ~** machen wir uns auf den Weg!; **to be on the ~** (*salesman etc*)

unterwegs sein; *(pop group etc)* auf Tournee sein; **on the ~ to success** auf dem Weg zum Erfolg; **major/minor ~** Haupt-/ Nebenstraße *f*

road accident *n* Verkehrsunfall *m*

roadblock ['rəudblɔk] *n* Straßensperre *f*

roadhog ['rəudhɔg] *n* Verkehrsrowdy *m*

road map *n* Straßenkarte *f*

road rage *n* Aggressivität *f* im Straßenverkehr

road safety *n* Verkehrssicherheit *f*

roadside ['rəudsaɪd] *n* Straßenrand *m* ▷ *cpd* *(building, sign etc)* am Straßenrand; **by the ~** am Straßenrand

road sign *n* Verkehrszeichen *nt*

roadway ['rəudweɪ] *n* Fahrbahn *f*

roadworthy ['rəudwəːðɪ] *adj* verkehrstüchtig

roam [rəum] *vi* wandern, streifen ▷ *vt* *(streets, countryside)* durchstreifen

roar [rɔːʳ] *n* *(of animal, crowd)* Brüllen *nt*; *(of vehicle)* Getöse *nt*; *(of storm)* Heulen *nt* ▷ *vi* *(animal, person)* brüllen; *(engine, wind etc)* heulen; **~s of laughter** brüllendes Gelächter; **to ~ with laughter** vor Lachen brüllen

roast [rəust] *n* Braten *m* ▷ *vt* *(meat, potatoes)* braten; *(coffee)* rösten

roast beef *n* Roastbeef *nt*

rob [rɔb] *vt* *(person)* bestehlen; *(house, bank)* ausrauben; **to ~ sb of sth** jdm etw rauben; *(fig: deprive)* jdm etw vorenthalten

robber ['rɔbəʳ] *n* Räuber(in) *m(f)*

robbery ['rɔbərɪ] *n* Raub *m*

robe [rəub] *n* *(for ceremony etc)* Gewand *nt*; *(also:* **bath robe***)* Bademantel *m*; (US) Morgenrock *m* ▷ *vt*: **to be ~d in** *(form)* (festlich) in etw *acc* gekleidet sein

robin ['rɔbɪn] *n* Rotkehlchen *nt*

robot ['rəubɔt] *n* Roboter *m*

robust [rəu'bʌst] *adj* robust; *(appetite)* gesund

rock [rɔk] *n* *(substance)* Stein *m*; *(boulder)* Felsen *m*; (US: *small stone*) Stein *m*; (Brit: *sweet*) ≈ Zuckerstange *f*; *(Mus: also:* **rock music***)* Rock *m*, Rockmusik *f* ▷ *vt* *(swing gently: cradle)* schaukeln; *(: child)* wiegen; *(shake: also fig)* erschüttern ▷ *vi* *(object)* schwanken; *(person)* schaukeln; **on the ~s** *(drink)* mit Eis; *(ship)* (auf Felsen) aufgelaufen; *(marriage etc)* gescheitert; **to ~ the boat** *(fig)* Unruhe stiften

rock and roll *n* Rock and Roll *m*

rock climbing *n* Felsenklettern *nt*

rockery ['rɔkərɪ] *n* Steingarten *m*

rocket ['rɔkɪt] *n* Rakete *f* ▷ *vi* *(prices)* in die Höhe schießen

rocking chair ['rɔkɪŋ-] *n* Schaukelstuhl *m*

rocking horse *n* Schaukelpferd *nt*

rocky ['rɔkɪ] *adj* *(path, ground)* felsig; *(fig: business, marriage)* wackelig

rod [rɔd] *n* *(also Tech)* Stange *f*; *(also:* **fishing rod***)* Angelrute *f*

rode [rəud] *pt of* **ride**

rodent ['rəudnt] *n* Nagetier *nt*

rodeo ['rəudɪəu] (US) *n* Rodeo *nt*

roe [rəu] *n* *(Culin)*: **hard ~** Rogen *m*; **soft ~** Milch *f*

rogue [rəug] *n* Gauner *m*

role [rəul] *n* Rolle *f*

roll [rəul] *n* *(of paper)* Rolle *f*; *(of cloth)* Ballen *m*; *(of banknotes)* Bündel *nt*; *(also:* **bread roll***)* Brötchen *nt*; *(register, list)* Verzeichnis *nt*; *(of drums etc)* Wirbel *m* ▷ *vt* rollen; *(also:* **roll up***: string)* aufrollen; *(: sleeves)* aufkrempeln; *(cigarette)* drehen; *(also:* **roll out***: pastry)* ausrollen; *(flatten: lawn, road)* walzen ▷ *vi* rollen; *(drum)* wirbeln; *(thunder)* grollen; *(ship)* schlingern; *(tears, sweat)* fließen; *(camera, printing press)* laufen; **cheese/ham ~** Käse-/Schinkenbrötchen *nt*; **he's ~ing in it** *(inf: rich)* er schwimmt im Geld

▸ **roll about** *vi* sich wälzen

▸ **roll around** *vi* = **roll about**

▸ **roll in** *vi* *(money, invitations)* hereinströmen

▸ **roll over** *vi* sich umdrehen

▸ **roll up** *vi* *(inf: arrive)* aufkreuzen ▷ *vt* *(carpet, umbrella etc)* aufrollen; **to ~ o.s. up into a ball** sich zusammenrollen

roll call *n* namentlicher Aufruf *m*

roller ['rəuləʳ] *n* Rolle *f*; *(for lawn, road)* Walze *f*; *(for hair)* Lockenwickler *m*

Rollerblades® *npl* Rollerblades *pl*

roller coaster *n* Achterbahn *f*

roller skates *npl* Rollschuhe *pl*

rolling ['rəulɪŋ] *adj* *(hills)* wellig

rolling pin *n* Nudelholz *nt*

rolling stock *n* *(Rail)* Fahrzeuge *pl*

ROM [rɔm] *n abbr* (Comput: = *read only memory*) ROM

Roman ['rəumən] *adj* römisch ▷ *n* *(person)* Römer(in) *m(f)*

Roman Catholic *adj* römisch-katholisch ▷ *n* Katholik(in) *m(f)*

romance [rə'mæns] *n* *(love affair)* Romanze *f*; *(romanticism)* Romantik *f*; *(novel)* fantastische Erzählung *f*

Romania [rəu'meɪnɪə] *n* Rumänien *nt*

Romanian [rəu'meɪnɪən] *adj* rumänisch ▷ *n* *(person)* Rumäne *m*, Rumänin *f*; *(Ling)* Rumänisch *nt*

Roman numeral *n* römische Ziffer *f*

romantic [rə'mæntɪk] *adj* romantisch

Rome [rəum] *n* Rom *nt*

romp [rɔmp] *n* Klamauk *m* ▷ *vi* *(also:* **romp about***)* herumtollen; **to ~ home** *(horse)* spielend gewinnen

rompers ['rɔmpəz] *npl* *(clothing)* *einteiliger Spielanzug für Babys*

roof [ruːf] *(pl* **~s***)* *n* Dach *nt* ▷ *vt* *(house etc)* überdachen; **the ~ of the mouth** der Gaumen

roofing ['ruːfɪŋ] *n* Deckung *f*; **~ felt** Dachpappe *f*

roof rack *n* Dachgepäckträger *m*

rook [ruk] *n* *(bird)* Saatkrähe *f*; *(Chess)* Turm *m*

room [ruːm] *n* *(in house, hotel)* Zimmer *nt*; *(space)* Raum *m*, Platz *m*; *(scope: for change* *etc*) Raum *m* ▷ *vi*: **to ~ with sb** (*esp US*) ein Zimmer mit jdm teilen; **rooms** *npl* (*lodging*) Zimmer *pl*; **"~s to let", "~s for rent"** (US) "Zimmer zu vermieten"; **single/double ~** Einzel-/Doppelzimmer *nt*; **is there ~ for this?** ist dafür Platz vorhanden?; **to make ~ for sb** für jdn Platz machen; **there is ~ for improvement** es gibt Möglichkeiten zur Verbesserung

rooming house ['ru:mɪŋ-] (*US*) *n* Mietshaus *nt*

roommate ['ru:mmeɪt] *n* Zimmergenosse *m*, Zimmergenossin *f*

room service *n* Zimmerservice *m*

roomy ['ru:mɪ] *adj* (*building, car*) geräumig

roost [ru:st] *vi* (*birds*) sich niederlassen

rooster ['ru:stə^r] (*esp US*) *n* Hahn *m*

root [ru:t] *n* (*also Math*) Wurzel *f* ▷ *vi* (*plant*) Wurzeln schlagen ▷ *vt*: **to be ~ed in** verwurzelt sein in *+dat*; **roots** *npl* (*family origins*) Wurzeln *pl*; **to take ~** (*plant, idea*) Wurzeln schlagen; **the ~ cause of the problem** die Wurzel des Problems

▸ **root about** *vi* (*search*) herumwühlen

▸ **root for** *vt fus* (*support*) anfeuern

▸ **root out** *vt* ausrotten

rope [rəup] *n* Seil *nt*; (*Naut*) Tau *nt* ▷ *vt* (*tie*) festbinden; (*also*: **rope together**) zusammenbinden; **to know the ~s** (*fig*) sich auskennen

▸ **rope in** *vt* (*fig: person*) einspannen

▸ **rope off** *vt* (*area*) mit einem Seil absperren

rosary ['rəuzərɪ] *n* Rosenkranz *m*

rose [rəuz] *pt of* **rise** ▷ *n* (*flower*) Rose *f*; (*also*: **rosebush**) Rosenstrauch *m*; (*on watering can*) Brause *f* ▷ *adj* rosarot

rosé ['rəuzeɪ] *n* (*wine*) Rosé *m*

rosebud ['rəuzbʌd] *n* Rosenknospe *f*

rosemary ['rəuzmərɪ] *n* Rosmarin *m*

roster ['rɔstə^r] *n*: **duty ~** Dienstplan *m*

rostrum ['rɔstrəm] *n* Rednerpult *nt*

rosy ['rəuzɪ] *adj* (*colour*) rosarot; (*face, situation*) rosig; **a ~ future** eine rosige Zukunft

rot [rɔt] *n* (*decay*) Fäulnis *f*; (*fig: rubbish*) Quatsch *m* ▷ *vt* verfaulen lassen ▷ *vi* (*teeth, wood, fruit etc*) verfaulen; **to stop the ~** (*Brit: fig*) den Verfall stoppen; **dry ~** Holzschwamm *m*; **wet ~** Nassfäule *f*

rota ['rəutə] *n* Dienstplan *m*; **on a ~ basis** reihum nach Plan

rotary ['rəutərɪ] *adj* (*cutter*) rotierend; (*motion*) Dreh-

rotate [rəu'teɪt] *vt* (*spin*) drehen, rotieren lassen; (*crops*) im Wechsel anbauen; (*jobs*) turnusmäßig wechseln ▷ *vi* (*revolve*) rotieren, sich drehen

rotating [rəu'teɪtɪŋ] *adj* (*revolving*) rotierend; (*drum, mirror*) Dreh-

rotten ['rɔtn] *adj* (*decayed*) faul, verfault; (*inf: person, situation*) gemein; (*: film, weather, driver etc*) mies; **to feel ~** sich elend fühlen

rotund [rəu'tʌnd] *adj* (*person*) rundlich

rough [rʌf] *adj* rau; (*terrain, road*) uneben; (*person, plan, drawing, guess*) grob; (*life, conditions, journey*) hart; (*sea, crossing*) stürmisch ▷ *n* (*Golf*): **in the ~** im Rough ▷ *vt*: **to ~ it** primitiv *or* ohne Komfort leben; **the sea is ~ today** die See ist heute stürmisch; **to have a ~ time** eine harte Zeit durchmachen; **can you give me a ~ idea of the cost?** können Sie mir eine ungefähre Vorstellung von den Kosten geben?; **to feel ~** (*Brit*) sich elend fühlen; **to sleep ~** (*Brit*) im Freien übernachten; **to play ~** (*fig*) auf die grobe Tour kommen

▸ **rough out** *vt* (*drawing, idea etc*) skizzieren

roughage ['rʌfɪdʒ] *n* Ballaststoffe *pl*

rough-and-ready ['rʌfən'rɛdɪ] *adj* provisorisch

rough copy *n* Entwurf *m*

roughly ['rʌflɪ] *adv* grob; (*approximately*) ungefähr; **~ speaking** grob gesagt

roulette [ru:'lɛt] *n* Roulette *nt*

round [raund] *adj* rund ▷ *n* Runde *f*; (*of ammunition*) Ladung *f* ▷ *vt* (*corner*) biegen um; (*cape*) umrunden ▷ *prep* um ▷ *adv*: **all ~** rundherum; **in ~ figures** rund gerechnet; **the daily ~** (*fig*) der tägliche Trott; **a ~ of applause** Beifall *m*; **a ~ (of drinks)** eine Runde; **a ~ of sandwiches** ein Butterbrot; **a ~ of toast** (*Brit*) eine Scheibe Toast; **it's just ~ the corner** (*fig*) es steht vor der Tür; **to go ~ the back** hinten herum gehen; **to go ~ (an obstacle)** (um ein Hindernis) herumgehen; **~ the clock** rund um die Uhr; **~ his neck/the table** um seinen Hals/den Tisch; **to sail ~ the world** die Welt umsegeln; **to walk ~ the room/park** im Zimmer/Park herumgehen; **~ about 300** (*approximately*) ungefähr 300; **the long way ~** auf Umwegen; **all (the) year ~** das ganze Jahr über; **the wrong way ~** falsch herum; **to ask sb ~** jdn zu sich einladen; **I'll be ~ at 6 o'clock** ich komme um 6 Uhr; **to go ~** (*rotate*) sich drehen; **to go ~ to sb's (house)** jdn (zu Hause) besuchen; **enough to go ~** genug für alle

▸ **round off** *vt* abrunden

▸ **round up** *vt* (*cattle etc*) zusammentreiben; (*people*) versammeln; (*figure*) aufrunden

roundabout ['raundəbaut] (*Brit*) *n* (*Aut*) Kreisverkehr *m*; (*at fair*) Karussell *nt* ▷ *adj*: **by a ~ route** auf Umwegen; **in a ~ way** auf Umwegen

rounders ['raundəz] *n* ≈ Schlagball *m*

roundly ['raundlɪ] *adv* (*fig: criticize etc*) nachdrücklich

round trip *n* Rundreise *f*

roundup ['raundʌp] *n* (*of news etc*) Zusammenfassung *f*; (*of animals*) Zusammentreiben *nt*; (*of criminals*) Aufgreifen *nt*; **a ~ of the latest news** ein Nachrichtenüberblick *m*

rouse [rauz] *vt* (*wake up*) aufwecken; (*stir up*) reizen

rousing ['rauzɪŋ] *adj* (*speech*) mitreißend;

(*welcome*) stürmisch
route [ru:t] *n* Strecke *f*; (*of bus, train, shipping*) Linie *f*; (*of procession, fig*) Weg *m*; **"all ~s"** (*Aut*) "alle Richtungen"; **the best ~ to London** der beste Weg nach London
routine [ru:'ti:n] *adj* (*work, check etc*) Routine- ▷ *n* (*habits*) Routine *f*; (*drudgery*) Stumpfsinn *m*; (*Theat*) Nummer *f*; **~ procedure** Routinesache *f*
row[1] [rəu] *n* (*line*) Reihe *f* ▷ *vi* (*in boat*) rudern ▷ *vt* (*boat*) rudern; **three times in a ~** dreimal hintereinander
row[2] [rau] *n* (*din*) Krach *m*, Lärm *m*; (*dispute*) Streit *m* ▷ *vi* (*argue*) sich streiten; **to have a ~** sich streiten
rowboat ['rəubəut] (US) *n* = **rowing boat**
rowdy ['raudɪ] *adj* (*person*) rüpelhaft; (*party etc*) lärmend
rowing ['rəuɪŋ] *n* (*sport*) Rudern *nt*
rowing boat (*Brit*) *n* Ruderboot *nt*
royal ['rɔɪəl] *adj* königlich; **the ~ family** die königliche Familie
Royal Air Force (*Brit*) *n*: **the ~** die Königliche Luftwaffe
royalty ['rɔɪəltɪ] *n* (*royal persons*) die königliche Familie; **royalties** *npl* (*to author*) Tantiemen *pl*; (*to inventor*) Honorar *nt*
rpm *abbr* (*= revolutions per minute*) U/min.
rub [rʌb] *vt* reiben ▷ *n*: **to give sth a ~** (*polish*) etw polieren; **he ~bed his hands together** er rieb sich *dat* die Hände; **to ~ sb up the wrong way, to ~ sb the wrong way** (US) bei jdm anecken
▸ **rub down** *vt* (*body, horse*) abreiben
▸ **rub in** *vt* (*ointment*) einreiben; **don't ~ it in!** (*fig*) reite nicht so darauf herum!
▸ **rub off** *vi* (*paint*) abfärben
▸ **rub off on** *vt fus* abfärben auf *+acc*
▸ **rub out** *vt* (*with eraser*) ausradieren
rubber ['rʌbə[r]] *n* (*also inf: condom*) Gummi *nt or m*; (*Brit: eraser*) Radiergummi *m*
rubber band *n* Gummiband *nt*
rubber plant *n* Gummibaum *m*
rubbish ['rʌbɪʃ] (*Brit*) *n* (*waste*) Abfall *m*; (*fig: junk*) Schrott *m*; (*: pej: nonsense*) Quatsch *m* ▷ *vt* (*inf*) heruntermachen; **~!** Quatsch!
rubbish bin (*Brit*) *n* Abfalleimer *m*
rubbish dump (*Brit*) *n* Müllabladeplatz *m*
rubble ['rʌbl] *n* (*debris*) Trümmer *pl*; (*Constr*) Schutt *m*
ruby ['ru:bɪ] *n* (*gem*) Rubin *m* ▷ *adj* (*red*) rubinrot
rucksack ['rʌksæk] *n* Rucksack *m*
rudder ['rʌdə[r]] *n* (*of ship, plane*) Ruder *nt*
ruddy ['rʌdɪ] *adj* (*complexion etc*) rötlich; (*inf: damned*) verdammt
rude [ru:d] *adj* (*impolite*) unhöflich; (*naughty*) unanständig; (*unexpected: shock etc*) böse; (*crude: table, shelter etc*) primitiv; **to be ~ to sb** unhöflich zu jdm sein; **a ~ awakening** ein böses Erwachen
ruffle ['rʌfl] *vt* (*hair, feathers*) zerzausen; (*water*) kräuseln; (*fig: person*) aus der Fassung bringen
rug [rʌg] *n* (*on floor*) Läufer *m*; (*Brit: blanket*) Decke *f*
rugby ['rʌgbɪ] *n* (*also*: **rugby football**) Rugby *nt*
rugged ['rʌgɪd] *adj* (*landscape*) rau; (*man*) robust; (*features, face*) markig; (*determination, independence*) wild
ruin ['ru:ɪn] *n* (*destruction, downfall*) Ruin *m*; (*remains*) Ruine *f* ▷ *vt* ruinieren; (*building*) zerstören; (*clothes, carpet etc*) verderben; **ruins** *npl* (*of castle*) Ruinen *pl*; (*of building*) Trümmer *pl*; **in ~s** (*lit, fig*) in Trümmern
rule [ru:l] *n* (*norm*) Regel *f*; (*regulation*) Vorschrift *f*; (*government*) Herrschaft *f*; (*ruler*) Lineal *nt* ▷ *vt* (*country, people*) herrschen über *+acc* ▷ *vi* (*monarch etc*) herrschen; **it's against the ~s** das ist nicht gestattet; **as a ~ of thumb** als Faustregel; **under British ~** unter britischer Herrschaft; **as a ~** in der Regel; **to ~ in favour of/against/on sth** (*Law*) für/gegen/über etw *acc* entscheiden; **to ~ that ...** (*umpire, judge etc*) entscheiden, dass ...
▸ **rule out** *vt* (*possibility etc*) ausschließen; **murder cannot be ~d out** Mord ist nicht auszuschließen
ruled [ru:ld] *adj* (*paper*) liniert
ruler ['ru:lə[r]] *n* (*sovereign*) Herrscher(in) *m(f)*; (*for measuring*) Lineal *nt*
ruling ['ru:lɪŋ] *adj* (*party*) Regierungs-; (*body*) maßgebend ▷ *n* (*Law*) Entscheidung *f*; **the ~ class** die herrschende Klasse
rum [rʌm] *n* Rum *m* ▷ *adj* (*Brit: inf: peculiar*) komisch
Rumania *etc n* = **Romania** *etc*
rumble ['rʌmbl] *n* (*of thunder*) Grollen *nt*; (*of traffic*) Rumpeln *nt*; (*of guns*) Donnern *nt*; (*of voices*) Gemurmel *nt* ▷ *vi* (*stomach*) knurren; (*thunder*) grollen; (*traffic*) rumpeln; (*guns*) donnern
rummage ['rʌmɪdʒ] *vi* herumstöbern
rumour, (US) **rumor** ['ru:mə[r]] *n* Gerücht *nt* ▷ *vt*: **it is ~ed that ...** man sagt, dass ...
rump [rʌmp] *n* (*of animal*) Hinterteil *nt*; (*of group etc*) Rumpf *m*
rump steak *n* Rumpsteak *nt*
rumpus ['rʌmpəs] *n* Krach *m*; **to kick up a ~** Krach schlagen
run [rʌn] (*pt* **ran**, *pp* **~**) *n* (*as exercise, sport*) Lauf *m*; (*in car, train etc*) Fahrt *f*; (*series*) Serie *f*; (*Ski*) Abfahrt *f*; (*Cricket, Baseball*) Run *m*; (*Theat*) Spielzeit *f*; (*in tights etc*) Laufmasche *f* ▷ *vt* (*race, distance*) laufen, rennen; (*operate: business*) leiten; (*: hotel, shop*) führen; (*: competition, course*) durchführen; (*Comput: program*) laufen lassen; (*hand, fingers*) streichen mit; (*water, bath*) einlaufen lassen; (*Press: feature, article*) bringen ▷ *vi* laufen, rennen; (*flee*) weglaufen; (*bus, train*) fahren; (*river, tears*) fließen; (*colours*) auslaufen; (*jumper*) färben; (*in election*) antreten; (*road, railway etc*) verlaufen; **to go for a ~** (*as exercise*) einen Dauerlauf machen; **to break into a ~** zu laufen *or* rennen beginnen; **a ~ of**

good/bad luck eine Glücks-/Pechsträhne; **to have the ~ of sb's house** jds Haus zur freien Verfügung haben; **there was a ~ on ...** (*meat, tickets*) es gab einen Ansturm auf *+acc*; **in the long ~** langfristig; **in the short ~** kurzfristig; **to make a ~ for it** die Beine in die Hand nehmen; **on the ~** (*fugitive*) auf der Flucht; **I'll ~ you to the station** ich fahre dich zum Bahnhof; **to ~ the risk of doing sth** Gefahr laufen, etw zu tun; **she ran her finger down the list** sie ging die Liste mit dem Finger durch; **it's very cheap to ~** (*car, machine*) es ist sehr billig im Verbrauch; **to ~ a bath** das Badewasser einlaufen lassen; **to be ~ off one's feet** (*Brit*) ständig auf Trab sein; **the baby's nose was ~ning** dem Baby lief die Nase; **the train ~s between Gatwick and Victoria** der Zug verkehrt zwischen Gatwick und Victoria; **the bus ~s every 20 minutes** der Bus fährt alle 20 Minuten; **to ~ on petrol/off batteries** mit Benzin/auf Batterie laufen; **to ~ for president** für das Amt des Präsidenten kandidieren; **to ~ dry** (*well etc*) austrocknen; **tempers were ~ning high** alle waren sehr erregt; **unemployment is ~ning at 20 per cent** die Arbeitslosigkeit beträgt 20 Prozent; **blonde hair ~s in the family** blonde Haare liegen in der Familie

▸ **run across** *vt fus* (*find*) stoßen auf *+acc*

▸ **run after** *vt fus* nachlaufen *+dat*

▸ **run away** *vi* weglaufen

▸ **run down** *vt* (*production*) verringern; (*factory*) allmählich stilllegen; (*Aut: person*) überfahren; (*criticize*) schlechtmachen ▹ *vi* (*battery*) leer werden

▸ **run in** (*Brit*) *vt* (*car*) einfahren

▸ **run into** *vt fus* (*meet: person*) begegnen *+dat*; (*: trouble etc*) bekommen; (*collide with*) laufen/fahren gegen; **to ~ into debt** in Schulden geraten; **their losses ran into millions** ihre Schulden gingen in die Millionen

▸ **run off** *vt* (*liquid*) ablassen; (*copies*) machen ▹ *vi* weglaufen

▸ **run out** *vi* (*time, passport*) ablaufen; (*money*) ausgehen; (*luck*) zu Ende gehen

▸ **run out of** *vt fus*: **we're ~ning out of money/petrol** uns geht das Geld/das Benzin aus; **we're ~ning out of time** wir haben keine Zeit mehr

▸ **run over** *vt* (*Aut*) überfahren ▹ *vt fus* (*repeat*) durchgehen ▹ *vi* (*bath, water*) überlaufen

▸ **run through** *vt fus* (*instructions, lines*) durchgehen

▸ **run up** *vt* (*debt*) anhäufen

▸ **run up against** *vt fus* (*difficulties*) stoßen auf *+acc*

runaway ['rʌnəweɪ] *adj* (*horse*) ausgerissen; (*truck, train*) außer Kontrolle geraten; (*child, slave*) entlaufen; (*fig: inflation*) unkontrollierbar; (*: success*) überwältigend

rung [rʌŋ] *pp of* **ring** ▹ *n* (*also fig*) Sprosse *f*

runner ['rʌnə^r] *n* Läufer(in) *m(f)*; (*horse*) Rennpferd *nt*; (*on sledge, drawer etc*) Kufe *f*

runner bean (*Brit*) *n* Stangenbohne *f*

runner-up [rʌnər'ʌp] *n* Zweitplatzierte(r) *f(m)*

running ['rʌnɪŋ] *n* (*sport*) Laufen *nt*; (*of business etc*) Leitung *f*; (*of machine etc*) Betrieb *m* ▹ *adj* (*water, stream*) laufend; **to be in/out of the ~ for sth** bei etw im Rennen liegen/aus dem Rennen sein; **to make the ~** (*in race, fig*) das Rennen machen; **6 days ~** 6 Tage hintereinander; **to have a ~ battle with sb** ständig im Streit mit jdm liegen; **to give a ~ commentary on sth** etw fortlaufend kommentieren; **a ~ sore** eine nässende Wunde

running costs *npl* (*of car, machine*) Unterhaltskosten *pl*

runny ['rʌnɪ] *adj* (*egg, butter*) dünnflüssig; (*nose, eyes*) triefend

run-of-the-mill ['rʌnəvðə'mɪl] *adj* gewöhnlich

runt [rʌnt] *n* (*animal*) *kleinstes und schwächstes Tier eines Wurfs*; (*pej: person*) Zwerg *m*

run-up ['rʌnʌp] *n*: **the ~ to** (*election etc*) die Zeit vor *+dat*

runway ['rʌnweɪ] *n* (*Aviat*) Start- und Landebahn *f*

rupture ['rʌptʃə^r] *n* (*Med*) Bruch *m*; (*conflict*) Spaltung *f* ▹ *vt*: **to ~ o.s.** (*Med*) sich *dat* einen Bruch zuziehen

rural ['ruərl] *adj* ländlich; (*crime*) auf dem Lande

rush [rʌʃ] *n* (*hurry*) Eile *f*, Hetze *f*; (*Comm: sudden demand*) starke Nachfrage *f*; (*of water, air*) Stoß *m*; (*of feeling*) Woge *f* ▹ *vt* (*lunch, job etc*) sich beeilen bei; (*person, supplies etc*) schnellstens bringen ▹ *vi* (*person*) sich beeilen; (*air, water*) strömen; **rushes** *npl* (*Bot*) Schilf *nt*; (*for chair, basket etc*) Binsen *pl*; **is there any ~ for this?** eilt das?; **we've had a ~ of orders** wir hatten einen Zustrom von Bestellungen; **I'm in a ~ (to do sth)** ich habe es eilig (, etw zu tun); **gold ~** Goldrausch *m*; **don't ~ me!** drängen Sie mich nicht!; **to ~ sth off** (*send*) etw schnellstens abschicken; **to ~ sb into doing sth** jdn dazu drängen, etw zu tun

▸ **rush through** *vt* (*order, application*) schnellstens erledigen

rush hour *n* Hauptverkehrszeit *f*, Rushhour *f*

rusk [rʌsk] *n* Zwieback *m*

Russia ['rʌʃə] *n* Russland *nt*

Russian ['rʌʃən] *adj* russisch ▹ *n* (*person*) Russe *m*, Russin *f*; (*Ling*) Russisch *nt*

rust [rʌst] *n* Rost *m* ▹ *vi* rosten

rustic ['rʌstɪk] *adj* (*style, furniture*) rustikal ▹ *n* (*pej: person*) Bauer *m*

rustle ['rʌsl] *vi* (*paper, leaves*) rascheln ▹ *vt* (*paper*) rascheln mit; (*US: cattle*) stehlen

rustproof ['rʌstpru:f] *adj* nicht rostend

rusty ['rʌstɪ] *adj* (*car*) rostig; (*fig: skill etc*) eingerostet

rut [rʌt] *n* (*in path etc*) Furche *f*; (*Zool: season*) Brunft *f*, Brunst *f*; **to be in a ~** (*fig*) im Trott stecken

ruthless ['ru:θlɪs] *adj* rücksichtslos

RV *abbr (Bible: = revised version) englische Bibelübersetzung von 1885* ▷ *n abbr* (*US*) = **recreational vehicle**

rye [raɪ] *n* (*cereal*) Roggen *m*

Ss

S¹, **s** [ɛs] *n* (*letter*) S *nt*, s *nt*; (*US*: *Scol*: *satisfactory*) ≈ 3; **S for sugar** ≈ S wie Samuel

S² [ɛs] *abbr* (= *saint*) St.; (= *small*) kl.; (= *south*) S

Sabbath [ˈsæbəθ] *n* (*Jewish*) Sabbat *m*; (*Christian*) Sonntag *m*

sabotage [ˈsæbətɑːʒ] *n* Sabotage *f* ▹ *vt* einen Sabotageakt verüben auf +*acc*; (*plan, meeting*) sabotieren

saccharin, **saccharine** [ˈsækərɪn] *n* Sa(c)charin *nt* ▹ *adj* (*fig*) zuckersüß

sachet [ˈsæʃeɪ] *n* (*of shampoo*) Beutel *m*; (*of sugar etc*) Tütchen *nt*

sack [sæk] *n* Sack *m* ▹ *vt* (*dismiss*) entlassen; (*plunder*) plündern; **to get the ~** rausfliegen (*inf*); **to give sb the ~** jdn rausschmeißen (*inf*)

sacking [ˈsækɪŋ] *n* (*dismissal*) Entlassung *f*; (*material*) Sackleinen *nt*

sacrament [ˈsækrəmənt] *n* Sakrament *nt*

sacred [ˈseɪkrɪd] *adj* heilig; (*music, history*) geistlich; (*memory*) geheiligt; (*building*) sakral

sacrifice [ˈsækrɪfaɪs] *n* Opfer *nt* ▹ *vt* opfern; **to make ~s (for sb)** (für jdn) Opfer bringen

sad [sæd] *adj* traurig; **he was ~ to see her go** er war traurig (darüber), dass sie wegging

saddle [ˈsædl] *n* Sattel *m* ▹ *vt* (*horse*) satteln; **to be ~d with sb/sth** (*inf*) jdn/etw am Hals haben

saddlebag [ˈsædlbæg] *n* Satteltasche *f*

sadistic [səˈdɪstɪk] *adj* sadistisch

sadly [ˈsædlɪ] *adv* traurig, betrübt; (*unfortunately*) leider, bedauerlicherweise; (*seriously*) schwer; **he is ~ lacking in humour** ihm fehlt leider jeglicher Humor

sadness [ˈsædnɪs] *n* Traurigkeit *f*

s.a.e. (*Brit*) *abbr* (= *stamped addressed envelope*) *see* **stamp**

safari [səˈfɑːrɪ] *n* Safari *f*; **to go on ~** auf Safari gehen

safe [seɪf] *adj* sicher; (*out of danger*) in Sicherheit ▹ *n* Safe *m or nt*, Tresor *m*; **~ from** sicher vor +*dat*; **~ and sound** gesund und wohlbehalten; **(just) to be on the ~ side** (nur) um sicherzugehen; **to play ~** auf Nummer sicher gehen (*inf*); **it is ~ to say that ...** man kann wohl sagen, dass ...; **~ journey!** gute Fahrt *or* Reise!

safe-conduct [seɪfˈkɒndʌkt] *n* freies *or* sicheres Geleit *nt*

safe-deposit [ˈseɪfdɪpɒzɪt] *n* (*vault*) Tresorraum *m*; (*also*: **safe-deposit box**) Banksafe *m*

safeguard [ˈseɪfgɑːd] *n* Schutz *m* ▹ *vt* schützen; (*interests*) wahren; (*future*) sichern; **as a ~ against** zum Schutz gegen

safekeeping [ˈseɪfˈkiːpɪŋ] *n* sichere Aufbewahrung *f*

safely [ˈseɪflɪ] *adv* sicher; (*assume, say*) wohl, ruhig; (*arrive*) wohlbehalten; **I can ~ say ...** ich kann wohl sagen ...

safe sex *n* Safer Sex *m*

safety [ˈseɪftɪ] *n* Sicherheit *f*; **~ first!** Sicherheit geht vor!

safety belt *n* Sicherheitsgurt *m*

safety pin *n* Sicherheitsnadel *f*

safety valve *n* Sicherheitsventil *nt*

saffron [ˈsæfrən] *n* Safran *m*

sag [sæg] *vi* durchhängen; (*breasts*) hängen; (*fig*: *spirits, demand*) sinken

sage [seɪdʒ] *n* (*herb*) Salbei *m*; (*wise man*) Weise(r) *m*

Sagittarius [sædʒɪˈtɛərɪəs] *n* Schütze *m*; **to be ~** Schütze sein

Sahara [səˈhɑːrə] *n*: **the ~ (Desert)** die (Wüste) Sahara

said [sɛd] *pt, pp of* **say**

sail [seɪl] *n* Segel *nt* ▹ *vt* segeln ▹ *vi* fahren; (*Sport*) segeln; (*begin voyage*: *ship*) auslaufen; (: *passenger*) abfahren; (*fig*: *ball etc*) fliegen, segeln; **to go for a ~** segeln gehen; **to set ~** losfahren, abfahren

▸ **sail through** *vt fus* (*fig*: *exam etc*) spielend schaffen

sailboat [ˈseɪlbəut] (*US*) *n* = **sailing boat**

sailing [ˈseɪlɪŋ] *n* (*Sport*) Segeln *nt*; (*voyage*) Überfahrt *f*; **to go ~** segeln gehen

sailing boat *n* Segelboot *nt*

sailing ship *n* Segelschiff *nt*

sailor [ˈseɪlə^r] *n* Seemann *m*, Matrose *m*

saint [seɪnt] *n* (*lit, fig*) Heilige(r) *f*(*m*)

sake [seɪk] *n*: **for the ~ of sb/sth, for sb's/sth's sake** um jds/einer Sache *gen* willen; (*out of consideration for*) jdm/etw zuliebe; **he enjoys talking for talking's ~** er redet gerne, nur damit etwas gesagt wird; **for the ~ of argument** rein theoretisch; **art for art's ~** Kunst um der Kunst willen; **for heaven's ~!** um Gottes willen!

salad ['sæləd] *n* Salat *m*; **tomato ~** Tomatensalat *m*; **green ~** grüner Salat *m*
salad bowl *n* Salatschüssel *f*
salad cream (*Brit*) *n* ≈ Mayonnaise *f*
salad dressing *n* Salatsoße *f*
salami [sə'lɑːmɪ] *n* Salami *f*
salary ['sælərɪ] *n* Gehalt *nt*
sale [seɪl] *n* Verkauf *m*; (*at reduced prices*) Ausverkauf *m*; (*auction*) Auktion *f*; **sales** *npl* (*total amount sold*) Absatz *m* ▷ *cpd* (*campaign*) Verkaufs-; (*conference*) Vertreter-; (*figures*) Absatz-; **"for ~"** "zu verkaufen"; **on ~** im Handel; **on ~ or return** auf Kommissionsbasis; **closing-down ~, liquidation ~** (*US*) Räumungsverkauf *m*
saleroom ['seɪlruːm] *n* Auktionsraum *m*
sales assistant, (*US*) **sales clerk** [seɪlz-] *n* Verkäufer(in) *m(f)*
salesman ['seɪlzmən] (*irreg: like* **man**) *n* Verkäufer *m*; (*representative*) Vertreter *m*
saleswoman ['seɪlzwumən] (*irreg: like* **woman**) *n* Verkäuferin *f*; (*representative*) Vertreterin *f*
saline ['seɪlaɪn] *adj* (*solution etc*) Salz-
saliva [sə'laɪvə] *n* Speichel *m*
salmon ['sæmən] *n inv* Lachs *m*
salon ['sælɔn] *n* Salon *m*
saloon [sə'luːn] *n* (*US: bar*) Saloon *m*; (*Brit: Aut*) Limousine *f*; (*ship's lounge*) Salon *m*
salt [sɔːlt] *n* Salz *nt* ▷ *vt* (*preserve*) einsalzen; (*put salt on*) salzen; (*road*) mit Salz streuen ▷ *cpd* Salz-; (*pork, beef*) gepökelt; **the ~ of the earth** (*fig*) das Salz der Erde; **to take sth with a pinch** *or* **grain of ~** (*fig*) etw nicht ganz so ernst nehmen
salt cellar *n* Salzstreuer *m*
saltwater ['sɔːlt'wɔːtə^r] *adj* (*fish, plant*) Meeres-
salty ['sɔːltɪ] *adj* salzig
salute [sə'luːt] *n* (*Mil, greeting*) Gruß *m*; (*Mil: with guns*) Salut *m* ▷ *vt* (*Mil*) grüßen, salutieren vor +*dat*; (*fig*) begrüßen
salvage ['sælvɪdʒ] *n* Bergung *f*; (*things saved*) Bergungsgut *nt* ▷ *vt* bergen; (*fig*) retten
salvation [sæl'veɪʃən] *n* (*Rel*) Heil *nt*; (*economic etc*) Rettung *f*
Salvation Army *n* Heilsarmee *f*
same [seɪm] *adj* (*similar*) gleiche(r, s); (*identical*) selbe(r, s) ▷ *pron*: **the ~** (*similar*) der/die/das Gleiche; (*identical*) derselbe/dieselbe/dasselbe; **the ~ book as** das gleiche Buch wie; **they are the ~ age** sie sind gleichaltrig; **they are exactly the ~** sie sind genau gleich; **on the ~ day** am gleichen *or* selben Tag; **at the ~ time** (*simultaneously*) gleichzeitig, zur gleichen Zeit; (*yet*) doch; **they're one and the ~** (*person*) das ist doch ein und derselbe/dieselbe; (*thing*) das ist doch dasselbe; **~ again** (*in bar etc*) das Gleiche noch mal; **all** *or* **just the ~** trotzdem; **to do the ~ (as sb)** das Gleiche (wie jd) tun; **the ~ to you!** (danke) gleichfalls!; **~ here!** ich/wir *etc* auch!; **thanks all the ~** trotzdem vielen Dank; **it's all the ~ to me** es ist mir egal
sample ['sɑːmpl] *n* Probe *f*; (*of merchandise*) Probe *f*, Muster *nt* ▷ *vt* probieren; **to take a ~** eine Stichprobe machen; **free ~** kostenlose Probe
sanction ['sæŋkʃən] *n* Zustimmung *f* ▷ *vt* sanktionieren; **sanctions** *npl* (*Pol*) Sanktionen *pl*; **to impose economic ~s on** *or* **against** Wirtschaftssanktionen verhängen gegen
sanctity ['sæŋktɪtɪ] *n* (*holiness*) Heiligkeit *f*; (*inviolability*) Unantastbarkeit *f*
sanctuary ['sæŋktjuərɪ] *n* (*for birds/animals*) Schutzgebiet *nt*; (*place of refuge*) Zuflucht *f*; (*Rel: in church*) Altarraum *m*
sand [sænd] *n* Sand *m* ▷ *vt* (*also*: **sand down**) abschmirgeln; *see also* **sands**
sandal ['sændl] *n* Sandale *f*
sandbox ['sændbɔks] (*US*) *n* Sandkasten *m*; (*Comput: antivirus software*) Sandbox *f*
sand dune *n* Sanddüne *f*
sandpaper ['sændpeɪpə^r] *n* Schmirgelpapier *nt*
sandpit ['sændpɪt] *n* Sandkasten *m*; (*Comput: antivirus software*) Sandbox *f*
sands [sændz] *npl* (*beach*) Sandstrand *m*
sandstone ['sændstəun] *n* Sandstein *m*
sandwich ['sændwɪtʃ] *n* Sandwich *nt* ▷ *vt*: **~ed between** eingequetscht zwischen; **cheese/ham ~** Käse-/Schinkenbrot *nt*
sandwich course (*Brit*) *n Ausbildungsgang, bei dem sich Theorie und Praxis abwechseln*
sandy ['sændɪ] *adj* sandig; (*beach*) Sand-; (*hair*) rotblond
sane [seɪn] *adj* geistig gesund; (*sensible*) vernünftig
sang [sæŋ] *pt of* **sing**
sanitary ['sænɪtərɪ] *adj* hygienisch; (*facilities*) sanitär; (*inspector*) Gesundheits-
sanitary towel, (*US*) **sanitary napkin** *n* Damenbinde *f*
sanitation [sænɪ'teɪʃən] *n* Hygiene *f*; (*toilets etc*) sanitäre Anlagen *pl*; (*drainage*) Kanalisation *f*
sanitation department (*US*) *n* Stadtreinigung *f*
sanity ['sænɪtɪ] *n* geistige Gesundheit *f*; (*common sense*) Vernunft *f*
sank [sæŋk] *pt of* **sink**
Santa Claus [sæntə'klɔːz] *n* ≈ der Weihnachtsmann
sap [sæp] *n* Saft *m* ▷ *vt* (*strength*) zehren an +*dat*; (*confidence*) untergraben
sapling ['sæplɪŋ] *n* junger Baum *m*
sapphire ['sæfaɪə^r] *n* Saphir *m*
sarcasm ['sɑːkæzm] *n* Sarkasmus *m*
sarcastic [sɑː'kæstɪk] *adj* sarkastisch
sardine [sɑː'diːn] *n* Sardine *f*
Sardinia [sɑː'dɪnɪə] *n* Sardinien *nt*
SASE (*US*) *n abbr* (= *self-addressed stamped envelope*) frankierter Rückumschlag *m*
sash [sæʃ] *n* Schärpe *f*; (*of window*) Fensterrahmen *m*
sat [sæt] *pt, pp of* **sit**
Sat. *abbr* (= *Saturday*) Sa.

satchel ['sætʃl] *n* (*child's*) Schultasche *f*
satellite ['sætəlaɪt] *n* Satellit *m*; (*also*: **satellite state**) Satellitenstaat *m*
satellite dish *n* Satellitenantenne *f*, Parabolantenne *f*
satellite television *n* Satellitenfernsehen *nt*
satin ['sætɪn] *n* Satin *m* ▷ *adj* (*dress etc*) Satin-; **with a ~ finish** mit Seidenglanz
satire ['sætaɪəʳ] *n* Satire *f*
satisfaction [sætɪs'fækʃən] *n* Befriedigung *f*; **to get ~ from sb** (*refund, apology etc*) Genugtuung von jdm erhalten; **has it been done to your ~?** sind Sie damit zufrieden?
satisfactory [sætɪs'fæktərɪ] *adj* zufriedenstellend
satisfied ['sætɪsfaɪd] *adj* zufrieden
satisfy ['sætɪsfaɪ] *vt* zufriedenstellen; (*needs, demand*) befriedigen; (*requirements, conditions*) erfüllen; **to ~ sb/o.s. that ...** jdn/sich davon überzeugen, dass ...
satisfying ['sætɪsfaɪɪŋ] *adj* befriedigend; (*meal*) sättigend
Saturday ['sætədɪ] *n* Samstag *m*; *see also* **Tuesday**
sauce [sɔːs] *n* Soße *f*
saucepan ['sɔːspən] *n* Kochtopf *m*
saucer ['sɔːsəʳ] *n* Untertasse *f*
Saudi Arabia ['saudɪ-] *n* Saudi-Arabien *nt*
sauna ['sɔːnə] *n* Sauna *f*
saunter ['sɔːntəʳ] *vi* schlendern
sausage ['sɔsɪdʒ] *n* Wurst *f*
sausage roll *n* Wurst *f* im Schlafrock
savage ['sævɪdʒ] *adj* (*attack etc*) brutal; (*dog*) gefährlich; (*criticism*) schonungslos ▷ *n* (*old: pej*) Wilde(r) *f*(*m*) ▷ *vt* (*maul*) zerfleischen; (*fig: criticize*) verreißen
save [seɪv] *vt* (*rescue*) retten; (*money, time*) sparen; (*food etc*) aufheben; (*work, trouble*) (er)sparen; (*keep: receipts etc*) aufbewahren; (*: seat etc*) frei halten; (*Comput: file*) abspeichern; (*Sport: shot, ball*) halten ▷ *vi* (*also*: **save up**) sparen ▷ *n* (*Sport*) (Ball)abwehr *f* ▷ *prep* (*form*) außer +*dat*; **it will ~ me an hour** dadurch spare ich eine Stunde; **to ~ face** das Gesicht wahren; **God ~ the Queen!** Gott schütze die Königin!
saving ['seɪvɪŋ] *n* (*on price etc*) Ersparnis *f* ▷ *adj*: **the ~ grace of sth** das einzig Gute an etw *dat*; **savings** *npl* (*money*) Ersparnisse *pl*; **to make ~s** sparen
savings account *n* Sparkonto *nt*
savings bank *n* Sparkasse *f*
saviour, (US) **savior** ['seɪvjəʳ] *n* Retter(in) *m*(*f*); (*Rel*) Erlöser *m*
savour, (US) **savor** ['seɪvəʳ] *vt* genießen ▷ *n* (*of food*) Geschmack *m*
savoury, (US) **savory** ['seɪvərɪ] *adj* pikant
saw [sɔː] (*pt* **~ed**, *pp* **sawed** *or* **~n**) *vt* sägen ▷ *n* Säge *f* ▷ *pt of* **see**; **to ~ sth up** etw zersägen
sawdust ['sɔːdʌst] *n* Sägemehl *nt*
sawmill ['sɔːmɪl] *n* Sägewerk *nt*
sawn [sɔːn] *pp of* **saw**
sawn-off ['sɔːnɔf], (US) **sawed-off** ['sɔːdɔf] *adj*: **~ shotgun** Gewehr *nt* mit abgesägtem Lauf
saxophone ['sæksəfəun] *n* Saxofon *nt*
say [seɪ] (*pt, pp* **said**) *vt* sagen ▷ *n*: **to have one's ~** seine Meinung äußern; **could you ~ that again?** können Sie das wiederholen?; **my watch ~s 3 o'clock** auf meiner Uhr ist es 3 Uhr; **it ~s on the sign "No Smoking"** auf dem Schild steht "Rauchen verboten"; **shall we ~ Tuesday?** sagen wir Dienstag?; **come for dinner at, ~, 8 o'clock** kommt um, sagen wir mal 8 Uhr, zum Essen; **that doesn't ~ much for him** das spricht nicht gerade für ihn; **when all is said and done** letzten Endes; **there is something/a lot to be said for it** es spricht einiges/vieles dafür; **you can ~ that again!** das kann man wohl sagen!; **that is to ~** das heißt; **that goes without ~ing** das versteht sich von selbst; **to ~ nothing of ...** von ... ganz zu schweigen; **~ (that) ...** angenommen, (dass) ...; **to have a** *or* **some ~ in sth** ein Mitspracherecht bei etw haben
saying ['seɪɪŋ] *n* Redensart *f*
scab [skæb] *n* (*on wound*) Schorf *m*; (*pej*) Streikbrecher(in) *m*(*f*)
scaffold ['skæfəld] *n* (*for execution*) Schafott *nt*
scaffolding ['skæfəldɪŋ] *n* Gerüst *nt*
scald [skɔːld] *n* Verbrühung *f* ▷ *vt* (*burn*) verbrühen
scale [skeɪl] *n* Skala *f*; (*of fish*) Schuppe *f*; (*Mus*) Tonleiter *f*; (*size, extent*) Ausmaß *nt*, Umfang *m*; (*of map, model*) Maßstab *m* ▷ *vt* (*cliff, tree*) erklettern; **(pair of) scales** *npl* (*for weighing*) Waage *f*; **pay ~** Lohnskala *f*; **to draw sth to ~** etw maßstabgetreu zeichnen; **a small-~ model** ein Modell in verkleinertem Maßstab; **on a large ~** im großen Rahmen; **~ of charges** Gebührenordnung *f*
▸ **scale down** *vt* verkleinern; (*fig*) verringern
scallion ['skæljən] *n* Frühlingszwiebel *f*; (*US: shallot*) Schalotte *f*; (*: leek*) Lauch *m*
scallop ['skɔləp] *n* (*Zool*) Kammmuschel *f*; (*Sewing*) Bogenkante *f*
scalp [skælp] *n* Kopfhaut *f* ▷ *vt* skalpieren
scalpel ['skælpl] *n* Skalpell *nt*
scam [skæm] (*inf*) *n* Betrug *m*
scampi ['skæmpɪ] (*Brit*) *npl* Scampi *pl*
scan [skæn] *vt* (*horizon*) absuchen; (*newspaper etc*) überfliegen; (*TV, Radar*) abtasten ▷ *vi* (*poetry*) das richtige Versmaß haben ▷ *n* (*Med*) Scan *m*
scandal ['skændl] *n* Skandal *m*; (*gossip*) Skandalgeschichten *pl*
Scandinavia [skændɪ'neɪvɪə] *n* Skandinavien *nt*
Scandinavian [skændɪ'neɪvɪən] *adj* skandinavisch ▷ *n* Skandinavier(in) *m*(*f*)
scanner ['skænəʳ] *n* (*Med*) Scanner *m*; (*Radar*) Richtantenne *f*
scant [skænt] *adj* wenig
scanty ['skæntɪ] *adj* (*information*) dürftig; (*meal*) kärglich; (*bikini*) knapp

scapegoat ['skeɪpgəut] *n* Sündenbock *m*
scar [skɑ:] *n* Narbe *f*; (*fig*) Wunde *f* ▷ *vt* eine Narbe hinterlassen auf *+dat*; (*fig*) zeichnen
scarce [skɛəs] *adj* knapp; **to make o.s. ~** (*inf*) verschwinden
scarcely ['skɛəslɪ] *adv* kaum; (*certainly not*) wohl kaum; **~ anybody** kaum jemand; **I can ~ believe it** ich kann es kaum glauben
scarcity ['skɛəsɪtɪ] *n* Knappheit *f*; **~ value** Seltenheitswert *m*
scare [skɛə^r] *n* (*fright*) Schreck(en) *m*; (*public fear*) Panik *f* ▷ *vt* (*frighten*) erschrecken; (*worry*) Angst machen *+dat*; **to give sb a ~** jdm einen Schrecken einjagen; **bomb ~** Bombendrohung *f*
▸ **scare away** *vt* (*animal*) verscheuchen; (*investor, buyer*) abschrecken
▸ **scare off** *vt* = **scare away**
scarecrow ['skɛəkrəu] *n* Vogelscheuche *f*
scared ['skɛəd] *adj*: **to be ~** Angst haben; **to be ~ stiff** fürchterliche Angst haben
scarf [skɑ:f] (*pl* **~s** *or* **scarves**) *n* Schal *m*; (*headscarf*) Kopftuch *nt*
scarlet ['skɑ:lɪt] *adj* (scharlach)rot
scarlet fever *n* Scharlach *m*
scarves [skɑ:vz] *npl of* **scarf**
scary ['skɛərɪ] (*inf*) *adj* unheimlich; (*film*) gruselig
scathing ['skeɪðɪŋ] *adj* (*comments*) bissig; (*attack*) scharf; **to be ~ about sth** bissige Bemerkungen über etw *acc* machen
scatter ['skætə^r] *vt* verstreuen; (*flock of birds*) aufscheuchen; (*crowd*) zerstreuen ▷ *vi* (*crowd*) sich zerstreuen
scatterbrained ['skætəbreɪnd] (*inf*) *adj* schusselig
scavenger ['skævəndʒə^r] *n* (*person*) Aasgeier *m* (*inf*); (*animal, bird*) Aasfresser *m*
scenario [sɪ'nɑ:rɪəu] *n* (*Theat, Cine*) Szenarium *nt*; (*fig*) Szenario *nt*
scene [si:n] *n* (*lit, fig*) Szene *f*; (*of crime*) Schauplatz *m*; (*of accident*) Ort *m*; (*sight*) Anblick *m*; **behind the ~s** (*fig*) hinter den Kulissen; **to make a ~** (*inf: fuss*) eine Szene machen; **to appear on the ~** (*fig*) auftauchen, auf der Bildfläche erscheinen; **the political ~** die politische Landschaft
scenery ['si:nərɪ] *n* (*Theat*) Bühnenbild *nt*; (*landscape*) Landschaft *f*
scenic ['si:nɪk] *adj* malerisch, landschaftlich schön
scent [sɛnt] *n* (*fragrance*) Duft *m*; (*track*) Fährte *f*; (*fig*) Spur *f*; (*liquid perfume*) Parfüm *nt*; **to put** *or* **throw sb off the ~** (*fig*) jdn von der Spur abbringen
sceptical, (US) **skeptical** ['skɛptɪkl] *adj* skeptisch
schedule ['ʃɛdju:l, (US) 'skɛdju:l] *n* (*of trains, buses*) Fahrplan *m*; (*of events*) Programm *nt*; (*of prices, details etc*) Liste *f* ▷ *vt* planen; (*visit, meeting etc*) ansetzen; **on ~** wie geplant, pünktlich; **we are working to a very tight ~** wir arbeiten nach einem sehr knappen Zeitplan; **everything went according to ~** alles ist planmäßig verlaufen; **to be ahead of/behind ~** dem Zeitplan voraus sein/im Rückstand sein; **he was ~d to leave yesterday** laut Zeitplan hätte er gestern abfahren sollen
scheduled flight *n* Linienflug *m*
scheme [ski:m] *n* (*personal plan*) Plan *m*; (*plot*) raffinierter Plan *m*, Komplott *nt*; (*formal plan*) Programm *nt* ▷ *vi* Pläne schmieden, intrigieren; **colour ~** Farbzusammenstellung *f*; **pension ~** Rentenversicherung *f*
scheming ['ski:mɪŋ] *adj* intrigierend ▷ *n* Machenschaften *pl*
schizophrenic [skɪtsə'frɛnɪk] *adj* schizophren ▷ *n* Schizophrene(r) *f(m)*
scholar ['skɔlə^r] *n* Gelehrte(r) *f(m)*; (*pupil*) Student(in) *m(f)*, Schüler(in) *m(f)*; (*scholarship holder*) Stipendiat(in) *m(f)*
scholarship ['skɔləʃɪp] *n* Gelehrsamkeit *f*; (*grant*) Stipendium *nt*
school [sku:l] *n* Schule *f*; (*US: inf: university*) Universität *f*; (*of whales, porpoises etc*) Schule *f*, Schwarm *m* ▷ *cpd* Schul-
schoolbook ['sku:lbuk] *n* Schulbuch *nt*
schoolboy ['sku:lbɔɪ] *n* Schuljunge *m*, Schüler *m*
schoolchildren ['sku:ltʃɪldrən] *npl* Schulkinder *pl*, Schüler *pl*
schoolgirl ['sku:lgə:l] *n* Schulmädchen *nt*, Schülerin *f*
schooling ['sku:lɪŋ] *n* Schulbildung *f*
schoolmaster ['sku:lmɑ:stə^r] *n* Lehrer *m*
schoolmistress ['sku:lmɪstrɪs] *n* Lehrerin *f*
schoolteacher ['sku:lti:tʃə^r] *n* Lehrer(in) *m(f)*
science ['saɪəns] *n* Naturwissenschaft *f*; (*branch of knowledge*) Wissenschaft *f*; **the ~s** Naturwissenschaften *pl*
science fiction *n* Science-Fiction *f*
scientific [saɪən'tɪfɪk] *adj* wissenschaftlich
scientist ['saɪəntɪst] *n* Wissenschaftler(in) *m(f)*
sci-fi ['saɪfaɪ] (*inf*) *n abbr* (= *science fiction*) SF
scissors ['sɪzəz] *npl* Schere *f*; **a pair of ~** eine Schere
scoff [skɔf] *vt* (*Brit: inf: eat*) futtern, verputzen ▷ *vi*: **to ~ (at)** (*mock*) spotten (über *+acc*), sich lustig machen (über *+acc*)
scold [skəuld] *vt* ausschimpfen
scone [skɔn] *n* *brötchenartiges Teegebäck*
scoop [sku:p] *n* (*for flour etc*) Schaufel *f*; (*for ice cream etc*) Portionierer *m*; (*amount*) Kugel *f*; (*Press*) Knüller *m*
▸ **scoop out** *vt* aushöhlen
▸ **scoop up** *vt* aufschaufeln; (*liquid*) aufschöpfen
scooter ['sku:tə^r] *n* (*also*: **motor scooter**) Motorroller *m*; (*toy*) (Tret)roller *m*
scope [skəup] *n* (*opportunity*) Möglichkeiten *pl*; (*range*) Ausmaß *nt*, Umfang *m*; (*freedom*) Freiheit *f*; **within the ~ of** im Rahmen *+gen*; **there is plenty of ~ for improvement** (*Brit*)

es könnte noch viel verbessert werden

scorch [skɔ:tʃ] *vt* versengen; (*earth, grass*) verbrennen

scorching ['skɔ:tʃɪŋ] *adj* (*day, weather*) brütend heiß

score [skɔ:ʳ] *n* (*number of points*) (Punkte)stand *m*; (*of game*) Spielstand *m*; (*Mus*) Partitur *f*; (*twenty*) zwanzig ▹ *vt* (*goal*) schießen; (*point, success*) erzielen; (*mark*) einkerben; (*cut*) einritzen ▹ *vi* (*in game*) einen Punkt/Punkte erzielen; (*Football etc*) ein Tor schießen; (*keep score*) (Punkte) zählen; **to settle an old ~ with sb** (*fig*) eine alte Rechnung mit jdm begleichen; **what's the ~?** (*Sport*) wie stehts?; **~s of** Hunderte von; **on that ~** in dieser Hinsicht; **to ~ well** gut abschneiden; **to ~ 6 out of 10** 6 von 10 Punkten erzielen; **to ~ (a point) over sb** (*fig*) jdn ausstechen

▸ **score out** *vt* ausstreichen

scoreboard ['skɔ:bɔ:d] *n* Anzeigetafel *f*

scorer ['skɔ:rəʳ] *n* (*Football etc*) Torschütze *m*, Torschützin *f*; (*person keeping score*) Anschreiber(in) *m(f)*

scorn [skɔ:n] *n* Verachtung *f* ▹ *vt* verachten; (*reject*) verschmähen

Scorpio ['skɔ:pɪəu] *n* Skorpion *m*; **to be ~** Skorpion sein

scorpion ['skɔ:pɪən] *n* Skorpion *m*

Scot [skɔt] *n* Schotte *m*, Schottin *f*

Scotch [skɔtʃ] *n* Scotch *m*

scotch [skɔtʃ] *vt* (*rumour*) aus der Welt schaffen; (*plan, idea*) unterbinden

Scotch tape® *n* ≈ Tesafilm® *m*

scot-free ['skɔt'fri:] *adv*: **to get off ~** ungeschoren davonkommen

Scotland ['skɔtlənd] *n* Schottland *nt*

Scots [skɔts] *adj* schottisch

Scotsman ['skɔtsmən] (*irreg: like* **man**) *n* Schotte *m*

Scotswoman ['skɔtswumən] (*irreg: like* **woman**) *n* Schottin *f*

Scottish ['skɔtɪʃ] *adj* schottisch

scoundrel ['skaundrl] *n* Schurke *m*

scour ['skauəʳ] *vt* (*search*) absuchen; (*clean*) scheuern

scout [skaut] *n* (*Mil*) Kundschafter *m*, Späher *m*; (*also*: **boy scout**) Pfadfinder *m*; **girl ~** (US) Pfadfinderin *f*

▸ **scout around** *vi* sich umsehen

scowl [skaul] *vi* ein böses Gesicht machen ▹ *n* böses Gesicht *nt*; **to ~ at sb** jdn böse ansehen

scrabble ['skræbl] *vi* (*also*: **scrabble around**) herumtasten ▹ *n*: **S~®** Scrabble® *nt*; **to ~ at sth** nach etw krallen; **to ~ about** *or* **around for sth** nach etw herumsuchen

scram [skræm] (*inf*) *vi* abhauen, verschwinden

scramble ['skræmbl] *n* (*climb*) Kletterpartie *f*; (*rush*) Hetze *f*; (*struggle*) Gerangel *nt* ▹ *vi*: **to ~ up/over** klettern auf/über *+acc*; **to ~ for** sich drängeln um; **to go scrambling** (*Sport*) Querfeldeinrennen fahren

scrambled eggs ['skræmbld-] *n* Rührei *nt*

scrap [skræp] *n* (*bit*) Stückchen *nt*; (*fig: of truth, evidence*) Spur *f*; (*fight*) Balgerei *f*; (*also*: **scrap metal**) Altmetall *nt*, Schrott *m* ▹ *vt* (*machines etc*) verschrotten; (*fig: plans etc*) fallen lassen ▹ *vi* (*fight*) sich balgen; **scraps** *npl* (*leftovers*) Reste *pl*; **to sell sth for ~** etw als Schrott *or* zum Verschrotten verkaufen

scrapbook ['skræpbuk] *n* Sammelalbum *nt*

scrap dealer *n* Schrotthändler(in) *m(f)*

scrape [skreɪp] *vt* abkratzen; (*hand etc*) abschürfen; (*car*) verschrammen ▹ *n*: **to get into a ~** (*difficult situation*) in Schwulitäten *pl* kommen (*inf*)

▸ **scrape through** *vt* (*exam etc*) durchrutschen durch (*inf*)

▸ **scrape together** *vt* (*money*) zusammenkratzen

scrap heap *n*: **to be on the ~** (*fig*) zum alten Eisen gehören

scrap merchant (*Brit*) *n* Schrotthändler(in) *m(f)*

scrap paper *n* Schmierpapier *nt*

scratch [skrætʃ] *n* Kratzer *m* ▹ *vt* kratzen; (*one's nose etc*) sich kratzen an *+dat*; (*paint, car, record*) verkratzen; (*Comput*) löschen ▹ *vi* sich kratzen ▹ *cpd* (*team, side*) zusammengewürfelt; **to start from ~** ganz von vorne anfangen; **to be up to ~** den Anforderungen entsprechen; **to ~ the surface** (*fig*) an der Oberfläche bleiben

scrawl [skrɔ:l] *n* Gekritzel *nt*; (*handwriting*) Klaue *f* (*inf*) ▹ *vt* hinkritzeln

scrawny ['skrɔ:nɪ] *adj* dürr

scream [skri:m] *n* Schrei *m* ▹ *vi* schreien; **to be a ~** (*inf*) zum Schreien sein; **to ~ at sb (to do sth)** jdn anschreien(, etw zu tun)

screech [skri:tʃ] *vi* kreischen; (*tyres, brakes*) quietschen ▹ *n* Kreischen *nt*; (*of tyres, brakes*) Quietschen *nt*

screen [skri:n] *n* (*Cine*) Leinwand *f*; (TV, *Comput*) Bildschirm *m*; (*movable barrier*) Wandschirm *m*; (*fig: cover*) Tarnung *f*; (*also*: **windscreen**) Windschutzscheibe *f* ▹ *vt* (*protect*) abschirmen; (*from the wind etc*) schützen; (*conceal*) verdecken; (*film*) zeigen, vorführen; (*programme*) senden; (*candidates etc*) überprüfen; (*for illness*): **to ~ sb for sth** jdn auf etw *acc* (hin) untersuchen

screening ['skri:nɪŋ] *n* (*Med*) Untersuchung *f*; (*of film*) Vorführung *f*; (TV) Sendung *f*; (*for security*) Überprüfung *f*

screenplay ['skri:npleɪ] *n* Drehbuch *nt*

screen saver *n* (*Comput*) Bildschirmschoner *m*

screw [skru:] *n* Schraube *f* ▹ *vt* schrauben; (*inf!*) bumsen (*!*); **to ~ sth in** etw einschrauben; **to ~ sth to the wall** etw an der Wand festschrauben; **to have one's head ~ed on** (*fig*) ein vernünftiger Mensch sein

▸ **screw up** *vt* (*paper etc*) zusammenknüllen; (*inf: ruin*) vermasseln; **to ~ up one's eyes** die Augen zusammenkneifen

screwdriver ['skru:draɪvəʳ] *n*

Schraubenzieher *m*
scribble ['skrɪbl] *n* Gekritzel *nt* ▷ *vt, vi* kritzeln; **to ~ sth down** etw hinkritzeln
script [skrɪpt] *n* (*Cine*) Drehbuch *nt*; (*of speech, play etc*) Text *m*; (*alphabet*) Schrift *f*; (*in exam*) schriftliche Arbeit *f*
scroll [skrəul] *n* Schriftrolle *f* ▷ *vi* (*Comput*) scrollen
scrounge [skraundʒ] (*inf*) *vt*: **to ~ sth off sb** etw bei jdm schnorren ▷ *vi* schnorren ▷ *n*: **on the ~** am Schnorren
scrounger ['skraundʒəʳ] (*inf*) *n* Schnorrer(in) *m(f)*
scrub [skrʌb] *n* Gestrüpp *nt* ▷ *vt* (*floor etc*) schrubben; (*inf: idea, plan*) fallen lassen
scruff [skrʌf] *n*: **by the ~ of the neck** am Genick
scruffy ['skrʌfɪ] *adj* gammelig, verwahrlost
scrum ['skrʌm], **scrummage** ['skrʌmɪdʒ] *n* (*Rugby*) Gedränge *nt*
scruple ['skru:pl] *n* (*gen pl*) Skrupel *m*, Bedenken *nt*; **to have no ~s about doing sth** keine Skrupel *or* Bedenken haben, etw zu tun
scrutiny ['skru:tɪnɪ] *n* genaue Untersuchung *f*; **under the ~ of sb** unter jds prüfendem Blick
scuba diving *n* Sporttauchen *nt*
scuff [skʌf] *vt* (*shoes, floor*) abwetzen
scuffle ['skʌfl] *n* Handgemenge *nt*
sculptor ['skʌlptəʳ] *n* Bildhauer(in) *m(f)*
sculpture ['skʌlptʃəʳ] *n* (*art*) Bildhauerei *f*; (*object*) Skulptur *f*
scum [skʌm] *n* (*on liquid*) Schmutzschicht *f*; (*pej*) Abschaum *m*
scurry ['skʌrɪ] *vi* huschen
▸ **scurry off** *vi* forthasten
scuttle ['skʌtl] *n* (*also*: **coal scuttle**) Kohleneimer *m* ▷ *vt* (*ship*) versenken ▷ *vi*: **to ~ away** *or* **off** verschwinden
scythe [saɪð] *n* Sense *f*
sea [si:] *n* Meer *nt*, See *f*; (*fig*) Meer *nt* ▷ *cpd* See-; **by ~** (*travel*) mit dem Schiff; **beside** *or* **by the ~** (*holiday*) am Meer, an der See; (*village*) am Meer; **on the ~** (*boat*) auf See; **at ~** auf See; **to be all at ~** (*fig*) nicht durchblicken (*inf*); **out to ~** aufs Meer (hinaus); **to look out to ~** aufs Meer hinausblicken; **heavy/rough ~(s)** schwere/raue See *f*
seaboard ['si:bɔ:d] *n* Küste *f*
seafood ['si:fu:d] *n* Meeresfrüchte *pl*
seagoing ['si:gəuɪŋ] *adj* hochseetüchtig
seagull ['si:gʌl] *n* Möwe *f*
seal [si:l] *n* (*animal*) Seehund *m*; (*official stamp*) Siegel *nt*; (*in machine etc*) Dichtung *f*; (*on bottle etc*) Verschluss *m* ▷ *vt* (*envelope*) zukleben; (*crack, opening*) abdichten; (*with seal*) versiegeln; (*agreement, sb's fate*) besiegeln; **to give sth one's ~ of approval** einer Sache *dat* seine offizielle Zustimmung geben
▸ **seal off** *vt* (*place*) abriegeln
sea level *n* Meeresspiegel *m*; **2,000 ft above/below ~** 2000 Fuß über/unter dem Meeresspiegel
sea lion *n* Seelöwe *m*
seam [si:m] *n* Naht *f*; (*lit, fig: where edges join*) Übergang *m*; (*of coal etc*) Flöz *nt*; **the hall was bursting at the ~s** der Saal platzte aus allen Nähten
seaman ['si:mən] (*irreg: like* **man**) *n* Seemann *m*
seaplane ['si:pleɪn] *n* Wasserflugzeug *nt*
search [sə:tʃ] *n* Suche *f*; (*inspection*) Durchsuchung *f*; (*Comput*) Suchlauf *m* ▷ *vt* durchsuchen; (*mind, memory*) durchforschen ▷ *vi*: **to ~ for** suchen nach; **"~ and replace"** (*Comput*) "suchen und ersetzen"; **in ~ of** auf der Suche nach
▸ **search through** *vt fus* durchsuchen
searching ['sə:tʃɪŋ] *adj* (*question*) bohrend; (*look*) prüfend; (*examination*) eingehend
searchlight ['sə:tʃlaɪt] *n* Suchscheinwerfer *m*
search party *n* Suchtrupp *m*; **to send out a ~** einen Suchtrupp ausschicken
search warrant *n* Durchsuchungsbefehl *m*
seashore ['si:ʃɔ:ʳ] *n* Strand *m*; **on the ~** am Strand
seasick ['si:sɪk] *adj* seekrank
seaside ['si:saɪd] *n* Meer *nt*, See *f*; **to go to the ~** ans Meer *or* an die See fahren; **at the ~** am Meer, an der See
seaside resort *n* Badeort *m*
season ['si:zn] *n* Jahreszeit *f*; (*Agr*) Zeit *f*; (*Sport, of films etc*) Saison *f*; (*Theat*) Spielzeit *f* ▷ *vt* (*food*) würzen; **strawberries are in ~/out of ~** für Erdbeeren ist jetzt die richtige Zeit/nicht die richtige Zeit; **the busy ~** die Hochsaison *f*; **the open ~** (*Hunting*) die Jagdzeit *f*
seasonal ['si:znl] *adj* (*work*) Saison-
seasoned ['si:znd] *adj* (*fig: traveller*) erfahren; (*wood*) abgelagert; **she's a ~ campaigner** sie ist eine alte Kämpferin
seasoning ['si:znɪŋ] *n* Gewürz *nt*
season ticket *n* (*Rail*) Zeitkarte *f*; (*Sport*) Dauerkarte *f*; (*Theat*) Abonnement *nt*
seat [si:t] *n* (*chair, of government, Pol*) Sitz *m*; (*place*) Platz *m*; (*buttocks*) Gesäß *nt*; (*of trousers*) Hosenboden *m*; (*of learning*) Stätte *f* ▷ *vt* setzen; (*have room for*) Sitzplätze bieten für; **are there any ~s left?** sind noch Plätze frei?; **to take one's ~** sich setzen; **please be ~ed** bitte nehmen Sie Platz; **to be ~ed** sitzen
seat belt *n* Sicherheitsgurt *m*
sea water *n* Meerwasser *nt*
seaweed ['si:wi:d] *n* Seetang *m*
seaworthy ['si:wə:ðɪ] *adj* seetüchtig
sec. *abbr* (= *second*) Sek.
secluded [sɪ'klu:dɪd] *adj* (*place*) abgelegen; (*life*) zurückgezogen
seclusion [sɪ'klu:ʒən] *n* Abgeschiedenheit *f*; **in ~** zurückgezogen
second[1] [sɪ'kɔnd] (*Brit*) *vt* (*employee*) abordnen
second[2] ['sɛkənd] *adj* zweite(r, s) ▷ *adv* (*come, be placed*) Zweite(r, s); (*when listing*) zweitens

▷ *n* (*time*) Sekunde *f*; (*Aut: also*: **second gear**) der zweite Gang; (*person*) Zweite(r) *f(m)*; (*Comm: imperfect*) zweite Wahl *f* ▷ *vt* (*motion*) unterstützen; **upper/lower ~** (*Brit: Univ*) ≈ Zwei plus/minus; **Charles the S~** Karl der Zweite; **just a ~!** einen Augenblick!; **~ floor** (*Brit*) zweiter Stock *m*; (*US*) erster Stock *m*; **to ask for a ~ opinion** ein zweites Gutachten einholen

secondary ['sɛkəndərɪ] *adj* weniger wichtig

secondary school *n* höhere Schule *f*

second-class ['sɛkənd'klɑ:s] *adj* zweitklassig; (*citizen*) zweiter Klasse; (*Rail, Post*) Zweite-Klasse- ▷ *adv* (*Rail, Post*) zweiter Klasse; **to send sth ~** etw zweiter Klasse schicken; **to travel ~** zweiter Klasse reisen

second hand *n* (*on clock*) Sekundenzeiger *m*

secondly ['sɛkəndlɪ] *adv* zweitens

secondment [sɪ'kɔndmənt] (*Brit*) *n* Abordnung *f*; **to be on ~** abgeordnet sein

second-rate ['sɛkənd'reɪt] *adj* zweitklassig

second thoughts *npl*: **on ~, on second thought** (*US*) wenn ich es mir (recht) überlege; **to have ~ (about doing sth)** es sich *dat* anders überlegen (und etw doch nicht tun)

secrecy ['si:krəsɪ] *n* Geheimhaltung *f*; (*of person*) Verschwiegenheit *f*; **in ~** heimlich

secret ['si:krɪt] *adj* geheim; (*admirer*) heimlich ▷ *n* Geheimnis *nt*; **in ~** heimlich; **~ passage** Geheimgang *m*; **to keep sth ~ from sb** etw vor jdm geheim halten; **can you keep a ~?** kannst du schweigen?; **to make no ~ of sth** kein Geheimnis *or* keinen Hehl aus etw machen

secretary ['sɛkrətərɪ] *n* (*Comm*) Sekretär(in) *m(f)*; (*of club*) Schriftführer(in) *m(f)*; **S~ of State (for)** (*Brit: Pol*) Minister(in) *m(f)* (für); **S~ of State** (*US: Pol*) Außenminister(in) *m(f)*

secretive ['si:krətɪv] *adj* verschlossen; (*pej*) geheimnistuerisch

secretly ['si:krɪtlɪ] *adv* heimlich; (*hope*) insgeheim

secret service *n* Geheimdienst *m*

sect [sɛkt] *n* Sekte *f*

sectarian [sɛk'tɛərɪən] *adj* (*killing etc*) konfessionell motiviert; **~ violence** gewalttätige Konfessionsstreitigkeiten *pl*

section ['sɛkʃən] *n* (*part*) Teil *m*; (*department*) Abteilung *f*; (*of document*) Absatz *m*; (*cross-section*) Schnitt *m* ▷ *vt* (*divide*) teilen; **the business/sport ~** (*Press*) der Wirtschafts-/Sportteil

sector ['sɛktə^r] *n* Sektor *m*

secular ['sɛkjulə^r] *adj* weltlich

secure [sɪ'kjuə^r] *adj* sicher; (*firmly fixed*) fest ▷ *vt* (*fix*) festmachen; (*votes etc*) erhalten; (*contract etc*) (sich *dat*) sichern; (*Comm: loan*) (ab)sichern; **to make sth ~** etw sichern; **to ~ sth for sb** jdm etw sichern

security [sɪ'kjuərɪtɪ] *n* Sicherheit *f*; (*freedom from anxiety*) Geborgenheit *f*; **securities** *npl* (*Stock Exchange*) Effekten *pl*, Wertpapiere *pl*; **securities market** Wertpapiermarkt *m*; **to increase/tighten ~** die Sicherheitsvorkehrungen verschärfen; **~ of tenure** Kündigungsschutz *m*

security guard *n* Sicherheitsbeamte(r) *m*; (*transporting money*) Wachmann *m*

sedan [sə'dæn] (*US*) *n* (*Aut*) Limousine *f*

sedate [sɪ'deɪt] *adj* (*person*) ruhig, gesetzt; (*life*) geruhsam; (*pace*) gemächlich ▷ *vt* (*Med*) Beruhigungsmittel geben *+dat*

sedative ['sɛdɪtɪv] *n* (*Med*) Beruhigungsmittel *nt*

seduce [sɪ'dju:s] *vt* verführen; **to ~ sb into doing sth** jdn dazu verleiten, etw zu tun

seduction [sɪ'dʌkʃən] *n* (*attraction*) Verlockung *f*; (*act of seducing*) Verführung *f*

seductive [sɪ'dʌktɪv] *adj* verführerisch; (*fig: offer*) verlockend

see [si:] (*pt* **saw**, *pp* **~n**) *vt* sehen; (*look at*) sich *dat* ansehen; (*understand*) verstehen, (ein)sehen; (*doctor etc*) aufsuchen ▷ *vi* sehen ▷ *n* (*Rel*) Bistum *nt*; **to ~ that** (*ensure*) dafür sorgen, dass; **to ~ sb to the door** jdn zur Tür bringen; **there was nobody to be ~n** es war niemand zu sehen; **to go and ~ sb** jdn besuchen (gehen); **to ~ a doctor** zum Arzt gehen; **~ you!** tschüss! (*inf*); **~ you soon!** bis bald!; **let me ~** (*show me*) lass mich mal sehen; (*let me think*) lass mich mal überlegen; **I ~** ich verstehe, aha; (*annoyed*) ach so; **you ~** weißt du, siehst du; **~ for yourself** überzeug dich doch selbst; **I don't know what she ~s in him** ich weiß nicht, was sie an ihm findet; **as far as I can ~** so wie ich das sehe

▸ **see about** *vt fus* sich kümmern um *+acc*

▸ **see off** *vt* verabschieden

▸ **see through** *vt fus* durchschauen ▷ *vt*: **to ~ sb through sth** jdm in etw *dat* beistehen; **to ~ sth through to the end** etw zu Ende bringen; **this should ~ you through** das müsste dir reichen

▸ **see to** *vt fus* sich kümmern um *+acc*

seed [si:d] *n* Samen *m*; (*of fruit*) Kern *m*; (*fig: usu pl*) Keim *m*; (*Tennis*) gesetzter Spieler *m*, gesetzte Spielerin *f*; **to go to ~** (*plant*) Samen bilden; (*lettuce etc*) schießen; (*fig: person*) herunterkommen

seedling ['si:dlɪŋ] *n* (*Bot*) Sämling *m*

seedy ['si:dɪ] *adj* (*person, place*) zwielichtig, zweifelhaft

seeing ['si:ɪŋ] *conj*: **~ as** *or* **that** da

seek [si:k] (*pt, pp* **sought**) *vt* suchen; **to ~ advice from sb** jdn um Rat fragen; **to ~ help from sb** jdn um Hilfe bitten

▸ **seek out** *vt* ausfindig machen

seem [si:m] *vi* scheinen; **there ~s to be a mistake** da scheint ein Fehler zu sein; **it ~s (that)** es scheint(, dass); **it ~s to me that ...** mir scheint, dass ...; **what ~s to be the trouble?** worum geht es denn?; (*doctor*) was fehlt Ihnen denn?

seemingly ['si:mɪŋlɪ] *adv* anscheinend

seen [si:n] *pp of* **see**

seep [si:p] *vi* sickern
seesaw ['si:sɔ:] *n* Wippe *f*
seethe [si:ð] *vi*: **to ~ with** *(place)* wimmeln von; **to ~ with anger** vor Wut kochen
see-through ['si:θru:] *adj* durchsichtig
segment ['sɛgmənt] *n* Teil *m*; *(of orange)* Stück *nt*
segregate ['sɛgrɪgeɪt] *vt* trennen, absondern
Seine [seɪn] *n*: **the ~** die Seine *f*
seize [si:z] *vt* packen, ergreifen; *(fig: opportunity)* ergreifen; *(power, control)* an sich *acc* reißen; *(territory, airfield)* besetzen; *(hostage)* nehmen; *(Law)* beschlagnahmen
▸ **seize up** *vi (engine)* sich festfressen
▸ **seize (up)on** *vt fus* sich stürzen auf *+acc*
seizure ['si:ʒə^r] *n (Med)* Anfall *m*; *(of power)* Ergreifung *f*; *(Law)* Beschlagnahmung *f*
seldom ['sɛldəm] *adv* selten
select [sɪ'lɛkt] *adj* exklusiv ▷ *vt* (aus)wählen; *(Sport)* aufstellen; **a ~ few** wenige Auserwählte *pl*
selection [sɪ'lɛkʃən] *n (being chosen)* Wahl *f*; *(range)* Auswahl *f*
selective [sɪ'lɛktɪv] *adj* wählerisch; *(not general)* selektiv
self [sɛlf] *(pl* **selves**) *n* Selbst *nt*, Ich *nt*; **she was her normal ~ again** sie war wieder ganz die Alte
self-assured [sɛlfə'ʃuəd] *adj* selbstsicher
self-catering [sɛlf'keɪtərɪŋ] *(Brit) adj (holiday, flat)* für Selbstversorger
self-centred, *(US)* **self-centered** [sɛlf'sɛntəd] *adj* egozentrisch, ichbezogen
self-confidence [sɛlf'kɔnfɪdns] *n* Selbstbewusstsein *nt*, Selbstvertrauen *nt*
self-confident [sɛlf'kɔnfɪdənt] *adj* selbstbewusst, selbstsicher
self-conscious [sɛlf'kɔnʃəs] *adj* befangen, gehemmt
self-contained [sɛlfkən'teɪnd] *(Brit) adj (flat)* abgeschlossen; *(person)* selb(st)ständig
self-control [sɛlfkən'trəul] *n* Selbstbeherrschung *f*
self-defence, *(US)* **self-defense** [sɛlfdɪ'fɛns] *n* Selbstverteidigung *f*; *(Law)* Notwehr *f*; **in ~** zu seiner/ihrer *etc* Verteidigung; *(Law)* in Notwehr
self-discipline [sɛlf'dɪsɪplɪn] *n* Selbstdisziplin *f*
self-employed [sɛlfɪm'plɔɪd] *adj* selbstständig
self-esteem [sɛlfɪs'ti:m] *n* Selbstachtung *f*
self-evident [sɛlf'ɛvɪdnt] *adj* offensichtlich
self-governing [sɛlf'gʌvənɪŋ] *adj* selbst verwaltet
self-indulgent [sɛlfɪn'dʌldʒənt] *adj* genießerisch; **to be ~** sich verwöhnen
self-interest [sɛlf'ɪntrɪst] *n* Eigennutz *m*
selfish ['sɛlfɪʃ] *adj* egoistisch, selbstsüchtig
selfishness ['sɛlfɪʃnɪs] *n* Egoismus *m*, Selbstsucht *f*
selfless ['sɛlflɪs] *adj* selbstlos
self-pity [sɛlf'pɪtɪ] *n* Selbstmitleid *nt*
self-possessed [sɛlfpə'zɛst] *adj* selbstbeherrscht
self-preservation ['sɛlfprɛzə'veɪʃən] *n* Selbsterhaltung *f*
self-raising ['sɛlf'reɪzɪŋ], *(US)* **self-rising** ['sɛlf'raɪzɪŋ] *adj*: **~ flour** *Mehl mit bereits beigemischtem Backpulver*
self-respect [sɛlfrɪs'pɛkt] *n* Selbstachtung *f*
self-righteous [sɛlf'raɪtʃəs] *adj* selbstgerecht
self-sacrifice [sɛlf'sækrɪfaɪs] *n* Selbstaufopferung *f*
self-satisfied [sɛlf'sætɪsfaɪd] *adj* selbstzufrieden
self-service [sɛlf'sə:vɪs] *adj (shop, restaurant etc)* Selbstbedienungs-
self-sufficient [sɛlfsə'fɪʃənt] *adj (country)* autark; *(person)* selb(st)ständig, unabhängig; **to be ~ in coal** seinen Kohlebedarf selbst decken können
self-taught [sɛlf'tɔ:t] *adj*: **to be ~** Autodidakt sein; **he is a ~ pianist** er hat sich das Klavierspielen selbst beigebracht
sell [sɛl] *(pt, pp* **sold**) *vt* verkaufen; *(shop: goods)* führen, haben *(inf)*; *(fig: idea)* schmackhaft machen *+dat*, verkaufen *(inf)* ▷ *vi* sich verkaufen (lassen); **to ~ at** *or* **for 10 pounds** für 10 Pfund verkauft werden; **to ~ sb sth** jdm etw verkaufen; **to ~ o.s.** sich verkaufen
▸ **sell off** *vt* verkaufen
▸ **sell out** *vi*: **we/the tickets are sold out** wir/die Karten sind ausverkauft; **we have sold out of ...** wir haben kein ... mehr, ... ist ausverkauft
▸ **sell up** *vi* sein Haus/seine Firma *etc* verkaufen
sell-by date ['sɛlbaɪ-] *n* ≈ Haltbarkeitsdatum *nt*
seller ['sɛlə^r] *n* Verkäufer(in) *m(f)*; **~'s market** Verkäufermarkt *m*
selling price ['sɛlɪŋ-] *n* Verkaufspreis *m*
selves [sɛlvz] *pl of* **self**
semblance ['sɛmblns] *n* Anschein *m*
semen ['si:mən] *n* Samenflüssigkeit *f*, Sperma *nt*
semester [sɪ'mɛstə^r] *(esp US) n* Semester *nt*
semi ... ['sɛmɪ] *pref* halb-, Halb-
semicircle ['sɛmɪsə:kl] *n* Halbkreis *m*
semicolon [sɛmɪ'kəulən] *n* Strichpunkt *m*, Semikolon *nt*
semidetached house *(Brit) n* Doppelhaushälfte *f*
seminar ['sɛmɪnɑ:^r] *n* Seminar *nt*
seminary ['sɛmɪnərɪ] *n (Rel)* Priesterseminar *nt*
semiskilled [sɛmɪ'skɪld] *adj (work)* Anlern-; *(worker)* angelernt
semi-skimmed [sɛmɪ'skɪmd] *adj (milk)* teilentrahmt, Halbfett-
senate ['sɛnɪt] *n* Senat *m*
senator ['sɛnɪtə^r] *n* Senator(in) *m(f)*
send [sɛnd] *(pt, pp* **sent**) *vt* schicken; *(transmit)* senden; **to ~ sth by post, to ~ sth by mail** *(US)* etw mit der Post schicken; **to ~ sb for**

sth (*for check-up etc*) jdn zu etw schicken; **to ~ word that ...** Nachricht geben, dass ...; **she ~s (you) her love** sie lässt dich grüßen; **to ~ sb to Coventry** (*Brit*) jdn schneiden (*inf*); **to ~ sb to sleep** jdn einschläfern; **to ~ sth flying** etw umwerfen
▸ **send away** *vt* wegschicken
▸ **send away for** *vt fus* (per Post) anfordern
▸ **send back** *vt* zurückschicken
▸ **send for** *vt fus* (per Post) anfordern; (*doctor, police*) rufen
▸ **send in** *vt* einsenden, einschicken
▸ **send off** *vt* abschicken; (*Brit: player*) vom Platz weisen
▸ **send on** *vt* (*Brit: letter*) nachsenden; (*luggage etc*) vorausschicken
▸ **send out** *vt* verschicken; (*light, heat*) abgeben; (*signal*) aussenden
▸ **send round** *vt* schicken; (*circulate*) zirkulieren lassen
▸ **send up** *vt* (*astronaut*) hochschießen; (*price, blood pressure*) hochtreiben; (*Brit: parody*) verulken (*inf*)

sender ['sɛndəʳ] *n* Absender(in) *m(f)*
send-off ['sɛndɔf] *n*: **a good ~** eine große Verabschiedung
senile ['siːnaɪl] *adj* senil
senior ['siːnɪəʳ] *adj* (*staff, manager*) leitend; (*officer*) höher; (*post, position*) leitend ▹ *n* (*Scol*): **the ~s** die Oberstufenschüler *pl*; **to be ~ to sb** jdm übergeordnet sein; **she is 15 years his ~** sie ist 15 Jahre älter als er; **P. Jones ~** P. Jones senior
senior citizen *n* Senior(in) *m(f)*
senior high school (*US*) *n* Oberstufe *f*
seniority [siːnɪ'ɔrɪtɪ] *n* (*in service*) (längere) Betriebszugehörigkeit *f*; (*in rank*) (höhere) Position *f*
sensation [sɛn'seɪʃən] *n* (*feeling*) Gefühl *nt*; (*great success*) Sensation *f*; **to cause a ~** großes Aufsehen erregen
sensational [sɛn'seɪʃənl] *adj* (*wonderful*) wunderbar; (*result*) sensationell; (*headlines etc*) reißerisch
sense [sɛns] *n* Sinn *m*; (*feeling*) Gefühl *nt*; (*good sense*) Verstand *m*, gesunder Menschenverstand *m*; (*meaning*) Bedeutung *f*, Sinn *m* ▹ *vt* spüren; **~ of smell** Geruchssinn *m*; **it makes ~** (*can be understood*) es ergibt einen Sinn; (*is sensible*) es ist vernünftig *or* sinnvoll; **there's no ~ in that** das hat keinen Sinn; **there is no ~ in doing that** es hat keinen Sinn, das zu tun; **to come to one's ~s** Vernunft annehmen; **to take leave of one's ~s** den Verstand verlieren
senseless ['sɛnslɪs] *adj* (*pointless*) sinnlos; (*unconscious*) besinnungslos, bewusstlos
sense of humour *n* Sinn *m* für Humor
sensible ['sɛnsɪbl] *adj* vernünftig; (*shoes, clothes*) praktisch
sensitive ['sɛnsɪtɪv] *adj* empfindlich; (*understanding*) einfühlsam; (*touchy: person*) sensibel; (*: issue*) heikel; **to be ~ to sth** in Bezug auf etw *acc* empfindlich sein; **he is very ~ about it/to criticism** er reagiert sehr empfindlich darauf/auf Kritik
sensual ['sɛnsjuəl] *adj* sinnlich; (*person, life*) sinnenfroh
sensuous ['sɛnsjuəs] *adj* sinnlich
sent [sɛnt] *pt, pp of* **send**
sentence ['sɛntns] *n* (*Ling*) Satz *m*; (*Law: judgement*) Urteil *nt*; (*: punishment*) Strafe *f* ▹ *vt*: **to ~ sb to death/to 5 years in prison** jdn zum Tode/zu 5 Jahren Haft verurteilen; **to pass ~ on sb** das Urteil über jdn verkünden; (*fig*) jdn verurteilen; **to serve a life ~** eine lebenslängliche Freiheitsstrafe verbüßen
sentiment ['sɛntɪmənt] *n* Sentimentalität *f*; (*also pl: opinion*) Ansicht *f*
sentimental [sɛntɪ'mɛntl] *adj* sentimental
sentry ['sɛntrɪ] *n* Wachtposten *m*
separate ['sɛprɪt] *adj* getrennt; (*occasions*) verschieden; (*rooms*) separat ▹ *vt* trennen ▹ *vi* sich trennen; **~ from** getrennt von; **to go ~ ways** getrennte Wege gehen; **under ~ cover** (*Comm*) mit getrennter Post; **to ~ into** aufteilen in *+acc*; *see also* **separates**
separately ['sɛprɪtlɪ] *adv* getrennt
separates ['sɛprɪts] *npl* (*clothes*) kombinierbare Einzelteile *pl*
separation [sɛpə'reɪʃən] *n* Trennung *f*
September [sɛp'tɛmbəʳ] *n* September *m*; *see also* **July**
septic ['sɛptɪk] *adj* vereitert, septisch; **to go ~** eitern
septic tank *n* Faulbehälter *m*
sequel ['siːkwl] *n* (*follow-up*) Nachspiel *nt*; (*of film, story*) Fortsetzung *f*
sequence ['siːkwəns] *n* Folge *f*; (*dance/film sequence*) Sequenz *f*; **in ~** der Reihe nach
sequin ['siːkwɪn] *n* Paillette *f*
Serbia ['səːbɪə] *n* Serbien *nt*
Serbian ['səːbɪən] *adj* serbisch ▹ *n* Serbier(in) *m(f)*; (*Ling*) Serbisch *nt*
serene [sɪ'riːn] *adj* (*landscape etc*) friedlich; (*expression*) heiter; (*person*) gelassen
sergeant ['sɑːdʒənt] *n* (*Mil etc*) Feldwebel *m*; (*Police*) Polizeimeister *m*
serial ['sɪərɪəl] *n* (*TV*) Serie *f*; (*Radio*) Sendereihe *f*; (*in magazine*) Fortsetzungsroman *m* ▹ *adj* (*Comput*) seriell
serial killer *n* Serienmörder(in) *m(f)*
serial number *n* Seriennummer *f*
series ['sɪərɪz] *n inv* (*group*) Serie *f*, Reihe *f*; (*of books*) Reihe *f*; (*TV*) Serie *f*
serious ['sɪərɪəs] *adj* ernst; (*important*) wichtig; (*: illness*) schwer; (*: condition*) bedenklich; **are you ~ (about it)?** meinst du das ernst?
seriously ['sɪərɪəslɪ] *adv* ernst; (*talk, interested*) ernsthaft; (*ill, hurt, damaged*) schwer; (*not jokingly*) im Ernst; **to take sb/sth ~** jdn/etw ernst nehmen; **do you ~ believe that ...** glauben Sie ernsthaft *or* im Ernst, dass ...
sermon ['səːmən] *n* Predigt *f*; (*fig*) Moralpredigt *f*

serrated [sɪ'reɪtɪd] *adj* gezackt; **~ knife** Sägemesser *nt*
servant ['sə:vənt] *n* (*lit, fig*) Diener(in) *m(f)*; (*domestic*) Hausangestellte(r) *f(m)*
serve [sə:v] *vt* dienen *+dat*; (*in shop, with food/drink*) bedienen; (*food, meal*) servieren; (*purpose*) haben; (*apprenticeship*) durchmachen; (*prison term*) verbüßen ▷ *vi* (*at table*) auftragen, servieren; (*Tennis*) aufschlagen; (*soldier*) dienen; (*be useful*): **to ~ as/for** dienen als ▷ *n* (*Tennis*) Aufschlag *m*; **are you being ~d?** werden Sie schon bedient?; **to ~ its purpose** seinen Zweck erfüllen; **to ~ sb's purpose** jds Zwecken dienen; **it ~s him right** das geschieht ihm recht; **to ~ on a committee** einem Ausschuss angehören; **to ~ on a jury** Geschworene(r) *f(m)* sein; **it's my turn to ~** (*Tennis*) ich habe Aufschlag; **it ~s to show/explain ...** das zeigt/erklärt ...
▸ **serve out** *vt* (*food*) auftragen, servieren
▸ **serve up** *vt* = **serve out**
service ['sə:vɪs] *n* Dienst *m*; (*commercial*) Dienstleistung *f*; (*in hotel, restaurant*) Bedienung *f*, Service *m*; (*also*: **train service**) Bahnverbindung *f*; (*: generally*) Zugverkehr *m*; (*Rel*) Gottesdienst *m*; (*Aut*) Inspektion *f*; (*Tennis*) Aufschlag *m*; (*plates etc*) Service *nt* ▷ *vt* (*car, machine*) warten; **the Services** *npl* (*army, navy etc*) die Streitkräfte *pl*; **military/national ~** Militärdienst *m*; **to be of ~ to sb** jdm nützen; **to do sb a ~** jdm einen Dienst erweisen; **to put one's car in for a ~** sein Auto zur Inspektion geben; **dinner ~** Essservice *nt*
serviceable ['sə:vɪsəbl] *adj* zweckmäßig
service area *n* (*on motorway*) Raststätte *f*
service charge (*Brit*) *n* Bedienungsgeld *nt*
serviceman ['sə:vɪsmən] (*irreg: like* **man**) *n* Militärangehörige(r) *m*
service station *n* Tankstelle *f*
serviette [sə:vɪ'ɛt] (*Brit*) *n* Serviette *f*
session ['sɛʃən] *n* Sitzung *f*; (*US, Scot: Scol*) Studienjahr *nt*; (*: term*) Semester *nt*; **recording ~** Aufnahme *f*; **to be in ~** tagen
set [sɛt] (*pt, pp* **~**) *n* (*of saucepans, books, keys etc*) Satz *m*; (*group*) Reihe *f*; (*of cutlery*) Garnitur *f*; (*also*: **radio set**) Radio(gerät) *nt*; (*also*: **TV set**) Fernsehgerät *nt*; (*Tennis*) Satz *m*; (*group of people*) Kreis *m*; (*Math*) Menge *f*; (*Theat: stage*) Bühne *f*; (*: scenery*) Bühnenbild *nt*; (*Cine*) Drehort *m*; (*Hairdressing*) (Ein)legen *nt* ▷ *adj* (*fixed*) fest; (*ready*) fertig, bereit ▷ *vt* (*table*) decken; (*place*) auflegen; (*time, price, rules etc*) festsetzen; (*record*) aufstellen; (*alarm, watch, task*) stellen; (*exam*) zusammenstellen; (*Typ*) setzen ▷ *vi* (*sun*) untergehen; (*jam, jelly, concrete*) fest werden; (*bone*) zusammenwachsen; **a ~ of false teeth** ein Gebiss *nt*; **a ~ of dining-room furniture** eine Esszimmergarnitur; **a chess ~** ein Schachspiel *nt*; **to be ~ on doing sth** etw unbedingt tun wollen; **to be all ~ to do sth** bereit sein, etw zu tun; **he's ~ in his ways** er ist in seinen Gewohnheiten festgefahren; **a ~ phrase** eine feste Redewendung; **a novel ~ in Rome** ein Roman, der in Rom spielt; **to ~ to music** vertonen; **to ~ on fire** anstecken; **to ~ free** freilassen; **to ~ sail** losfahren
▸ **set about** *vt fus* (*task*) anpacken; **to ~ about doing sth** sich daranmachen, etw zu tun
▸ **set aside** *vt* (*money etc*) beiseitelegen; (*time*) einplanen
▸ **set back** *vt*: **to ~ sb back 5 pounds** jdn 5 Pfund kosten; **to ~ sb back (by)** (*in time*) jdn zurückwerfen (um); **a house ~ back from the road** ein Haus, das etwas von der Straße abliegt
▸ **set in** *vi* (*bad weather*) einsetzen; (*infection*) sich einstellen; **the rain has ~ in for the day** es hat sich für heute eingeregnet
▸ **set off** *vi* (*depart*) aufbrechen ▷ *vt* (*bomb*) losgehen lassen; (*alarm, chain of events*) auslösen; (*show up well*) hervorheben
▸ **set out** *vi* (*depart*) aufbrechen ▷ *vt* (*goods etc*) ausbreiten; (*chairs etc*) aufstellen; (*arguments*) darlegen; **to ~ out to do sth** sich *dat* vornehmen, etw zu tun; **to ~ out from home** zu Hause aufbrechen
▸ **set up** *vt* (*organization*) gründen; (*monument*) errichten; **to ~ up shop** ein Geschäft eröffnen; (*fig*) sich selb(st)ständig machen
setback ['sɛtbæk] *n* Rückschlag *m*
set menu *n* Menü *nt*
settee [sɛ'ti:] *n* Sofa *nt*
setting ['sɛtɪŋ] *n* (*background*) Rahmen *m*; (*position*) Einstellung *f*; (*of jewel*) Fassung *f*
settle ['sɛtl] *vt* (*matter*) regeln; (*argument*) beilegen; (*accounts*) begleichen; (*affairs, business*) in Ordnung bringen; (*colonize: land*) besiedeln ▷ *vi* (*also*: **settle down**) sich niederlassen; (*sand, dust etc*) sich legen; (*sediment*) sich setzen; (*calm down*) sich beruhigen; **to ~ one's stomach** den Magen beruhigen; **that's ~d then!** das ist also abgemacht!; **to ~ down to work** sich an die Arbeit setzen; **to ~ down to watch TV** es sich *dat* vor dem Fernseher gemütlich machen
▸ **settle for** *vt fus* sich zufriedengeben mit
▸ **settle in** *vi* sich einleben; (*in job etc*) sich eingewöhnen
▸ **settle on** *vt fus* sich entscheiden für
▸ **settle up** *vi*: **to ~ up with sb** mit jdm abrechnen
settlement ['sɛtlmənt] *n* (*payment*) Begleichung *f*; (*Law*) Vergleich *m*; (*agreement*) Übereinkunft *f*; (*of conflict*) Beilegung *f*; (*village etc*) Siedlung *f*, Niederlassung *f*; (*colonization*) Besiedelung *f*; **in ~ of our account** (*Comm*) zum Ausgleich unseres Kontos
settler ['sɛtlə^r] *n* Siedler(in) *m(f)*
setup, set-up ['sɛtʌp] *n* (*organization*) Organisation *f*; (*system*) System *nt*; (*Comput*) Setup *nt*
seven ['sɛvn] *num* sieben

seventeen [sɛvn'ti:n] *num* siebzehn
seventh ['sɛvnθ] *num* siebte(r, s)
seventy ['sɛvntɪ] *num* siebzig
sever ['sɛvə^r] *vt* durchtrennen; (*fig: relations*) abbrechen; (*: ties*) lösen
several ['sɛvərl] *adj* einige, mehrere ▷ *pron* einige; **~ of us** einige von uns; **~ times** einige Male, mehrmals
severance ['sɛvərəns] *n* (*of relations*) Abbruch *m*
severance pay *n* Abfindung *f*
severe [sɪ'vɪə^r] *adj* (*damage, shortage*) schwer; (*pain*) stark; (*person, expression, dress, winter*) streng; (*punishment*) hart; (*climate*) rau
severity [sɪ'vɛrɪtɪ] *n* (*gravity: of punishment*) Härte *f*; (*: of manner, voice, winter*) Strenge *f*; (*: of weather*) Rauheit *f*; (*austerity*) Strenge *f*
sew [səu] (*pt* **~ed**, *pp* **~n**) *vt, vi* nähen
▸ **sew up** *vt* (zusammen)nähen; **it is all ~n up** (*fig*) es ist unter Dach und Fach
sewage ['su:ɪdʒ] *n* Abwasser *nt*
sewer ['su:ə^r] *n* Abwasserkanal *m*
sewing ['səuɪŋ] *n* Nähen *nt*; (*items*) Näharbeit *f*
sewing machine *n* Nähmaschine *f*
sewn [səun] *pp of* **sew**
sex [sɛks] *n* (*gender*) Geschlecht *nt*; (*lovemaking*) Sex *m*; **to have ~ with sb** (Geschlechts)verkehr mit jdm haben
sexism ['sɛksɪzəm] *n* Sexismus *m*
sexist ['sɛksɪst] *adj* sexistisch
sexual ['sɛksjuəl] *adj* sexuell; (*reproduction*) geschlechtlich; (*equality*) der Geschlechter
sexual intercourse *n* Geschlechtsverkehr *m*
sexy ['sɛksɪ] *adj* sexy; (*pictures, underwear*) sexy, aufreizend
shabby ['ʃæbɪ] *adj* schäbig
shack [ʃæk] *n* Hütte *f*
▸ **shack up** (*inf*) *vi*: **to ~ up (with sb)** (mit jdm) zusammenziehen
shackles ['ʃæklz] *npl* Ketten *pl*; (*fig*) Fesseln *pl*
shade [ʃeɪd] *n* Schatten *m*; (*for lamp*) (Lampen)schirm *m*; (*of colour*) (Farb)ton *m*; (*US: also*: **window shade**) Jalousie *f*, Rollo *nt* ▷ *vt* beschatten; (*eyes*) abschirmen; **shades** *npl* (*inf: sunglasses*) Sonnenbrille *f*; **in the ~** im Schatten; **a ~ of blue** ein Blauton; **a ~ (more/too large)** (*small quantity*) etwas *or* eine Spur (mehr/zu groß)
shadow ['ʃædəu] *n* Schatten *m* ▷ *vt* (*follow*) beschatten; **without** *or* **beyond a ~ of a doubt** ohne den geringsten Zweifel
shadow cabinet (*Brit*) *n* Schattenkabinett *nt*
shadowy ['ʃædəuɪ] *adj* schattig; (*figure, shape*) schattenhaft
shady ['ʃeɪdɪ] *adj* schattig; (*fig: dishonest*) zwielichtig; **~ deals** dunkle Geschäfte
shaft [ʃɑ:ft] *n* (*of arrow, spear*) Schaft *m*; (*Aut, Tech*) Welle *f*; (*of mine, lift*) Schacht *m*; (*of light*) Strahl *m*; **ventilation ~** Luftschacht *m*
shaggy ['ʃægɪ] *adj* zottelig; (*dog, sheep*) struppig
shake [ʃeɪk] (*pt* **shook**, *pp* **~n**) *vt* schütteln; (*weaken, upset, surprise*) erschüttern; (*weaken: resolve*) ins Wanken bringen ▷ *vi* zittern, beben; (*building, table*) wackeln; (*earth*) beben ▷ *n* Schütteln *nt*; **to ~ one's head** den Kopf schütteln; **to ~ hands with sb** jdm die Hand schütteln; **to ~ one's fist (at sb)** (jdm) mit der Faust drohen; **give it a good ~** schütteln Sie es gut durch; **a ~ of the head** ein Kopfschütteln
▸ **shake off** *vt* (*lit, fig*) abschütteln
▸ **shake up** *vt* schütteln; (*fig: upset*) erschüttern
shaky ['ʃeɪkɪ] *adj* (*hand, voice*) zittrig; (*memory*) schwach; (*knowledge, prospects, future, start*) unsicher
shall [ʃæl] *aux vb*: **I ~ go** ich werde gehen; **~ I open the door?** soll ich die Tür öffnen?; **I'll go, ~ I?** soll ich gehen?
shallow ['ʃæləu] *adj* flach; (*fig*) oberflächlich; **the shallows** *npl* die Untiefen *pl*
sham [ʃæm] *n* Heuchelei *f*; (*person*) Heuchler(in) *m(f)*; (*object*) Attrappe *f* ▷ *adj* unecht; (*fight*) Schein- ▷ *vt* vortäuschen
shambles ['ʃæmblz] *n* heilloses Durcheinander *nt*; **the economy is (in) a complete ~** die Wirtschaft befindet sich in einem totalen Chaos
shame [ʃeɪm] *n* Scham *f*; (*disgrace*) Schande *f* ▷ *vt* beschämen; **it is a ~ that ...** es ist eine Schande, dass ...; **what a ~!** wie schade!; **to bring ~ on** Schande bringen über *+acc*; **to put sb/sth to ~** jdn/etw in den Schatten stellen
shameful ['ʃeɪmful] *adj* schändlich
shameless ['ʃeɪmlɪs] *adj* schamlos
shampoo [ʃæm'pu:] *n* Shampoo(n) *nt* ▷ *vt* waschen
shamrock ['ʃæmrɔk] *n* (*plant*) Klee *m*; (*leaf*) Kleeblatt *nt*
shandy ['ʃændɪ] *n* Bier *nt* mit Limonade, Radler *m*
shan't [ʃɑ:nt] = **shall not**
shantytown ['ʃæntɪtaun] *n* Elendsviertel *nt*
shape [ʃeɪp] *n* Form *f* ▷ *vt* gestalten; (*form*) formen; (*sb's ideas*) prägen; (*sb's life*) bestimmen; **to take ~** Gestalt annehmen; **in the ~ of a heart** in Herzform; **I can't bear gardening in any ~ or form** ich kann Gartenarbeit absolut nicht ausstehen; **to get (o.s.) into ~** in Form kommen
▸ **shape up** *vi* sich entwickeln
-shaped [ʃeɪpt] *suff*: **heart-~** herzförmig
shapeless ['ʃeɪplɪs] *adj* formlos
shapely ['ʃeɪplɪ] *adj* (*woman*) wohlproportioniert; (*legs*) wohlgeformt
share [ʃɛə^r] *n* (*part*) Anteil *m*; (*contribution*) Teil *m*; (*Comm*) Aktie *f* ▷ *vt* teilen; (*room, bed, taxi*) sich *dat* teilen; (*have in common*) gemeinsam haben; **to ~ in** (*joy, sorrow*) teilen; (*profits*) beteiligt sein an *+dat*; (*work*) sich beteiligen an *+dat*
▸ **share out** *vt* aufteilen
shareholder ['ʃɛəhəuldə^r] *n* Aktionär(in) *m(f)*

shark [ʃɑːk] *n* Hai(fisch) *m*
sharp [ʃɑːp] *adj* scharf; (*point, nose, chin*) spitz; (*pain*) heftig; (*cold*) schneidend; (*Mus*) zu hoch; (*increase*) stark; (*person: quick-witted*) clever; (*: dishonest*) gerissen ▷ *n* (*Mus*) Kreuz *nt* ▷ *adv*: **at 2 o'clock ~** um Punkt 2 Uhr; **turn ~ left** biegen Sie scharf nach links ab; **to be ~ with sb** schroff mit jdm sein; **~ practices** (*Comm*) unsaubere Geschäfte *pl*; **C ~** (*Mus*) Cis *nt*; **look ~!** (ein bisschen) dalli! (*inf*)
sharpen [ˈʃɑːpn] *vt* schleifen, schärfen; (*pencil, stick etc*) (an)spitzen; (*fig: appetite*) anregen
sharpener [ˈʃɑːpnəʳ] *n* (*also*: **pencil sharpener**) (Bleistift)spitzer *m*; (*also*: **knife sharpener**) Schleifgerät *nt*
sharp-eyed [ʃɑːpˈaɪd] *adj* scharfsichtig
sharply [ˈʃɑːplɪ] *adv* scharf; (*stop*) plötzlich; (*retort*) schroff
shatter [ˈʃætəʳ] *vt* zertrümmern; (*fig: hopes, dreams*) zunichtemachen; (*: confidence*) zerstören ▷ *vi* zerbrechen, zerspringen
shattered [ˈʃætəd] *adj* erschüttert; (*inf: exhausted*) fertig, kaputt
shave [ʃeɪv] *vt* rasieren ▷ *vi* sich rasieren ▷ *n*: **to have a ~** sich rasieren
shaver [ˈʃeɪvəʳ] *n* (*also*: **electric shaver**) Rasierapparat *m*
shaving [ˈʃeɪvɪŋ] *n* Rasieren *nt*; **shavings** *npl* (*of wood etc*) Späne *pl*
shaving brush *n* Rasierpinsel *m*
shaving cream *n* Rasiercreme *f*
shaving foam *n* Rasierschaum *m*
shawl [ʃɔːl] *n* (Woll)tuch *nt*
she [ʃiː] *pron* sie ▷ *pref* weiblich; **~-bear** Bärin *f*; **there ~ is** da ist sie
sheaf [ʃiːf] (*pl* **sheaves**) *n* (*of corn*) Garbe *f*; (*of papers*) Bündel *nt*
shear [ʃɪəʳ] (*pt* **~ed**, *pp* **shorn**) *vt* scheren
▸ **shear off** *vi* abbrechen
shears [ˈʃɪəz] *npl* (*for hedge*) Heckenschere *f*
sheath [ʃiːθ] *n* (*of knife*) Scheide *f*; (*contraceptive*) Kondom *nt*
shed [ʃɛd] (*pt, pp* **~**) *n* Schuppen *m*; (*Industry, Rail*) Halle *f* ▷ *vt* (*tears, blood*) vergießen; (*load*) verlieren; (*workers*) entlassen; **to ~ its skin** sich häuten; **to ~ light on** (*problem*) erhellen
she'd [ʃiːd] = **she had; she would**
sheen [ʃiːn] *n* Glanz *m*
sheep [ʃiːp] *n inv* Schaf *nt*
sheepdog [ˈʃiːpdɔg] *n* Hütehund *m*
sheepskin [ˈʃiːpskɪn] *n* Schaffell *nt* ▷ *cpd* Schaffell-
sheer [ʃɪəʳ] *adj* (*utter*) rein; (*steep*) steil; (*almost transparent*) (hauch)dünn ▷ *adv* (*straight up*) senkrecht; **by ~ chance** rein zufällig
sheet [ʃiːt] *n* (*on bed*) (Bett)laken *nt*; (*of paper*) Blatt *nt*; (*of glass, metal*) Platte *f*; (*of ice*) Fläche *f*
sheik, sheikh [ʃeɪk] *n* Scheich *m*
shelf [ʃɛlf] (*pl* **shelves**) *n* Brett *nt*, Bord *nt*; **set of shelves** Regal *nt*
shell [ʃɛl] *n* (*on beach*) Muschel *f*; (*of egg, nut etc*) Schale *f*; (*explosive*) Granate *f*; (*of building*) Mauern *pl* ▷ *vt* (*peas*) enthülsen; (*Mil: fire on*) (mit Granaten) beschießen
▸ **shell out** (*inf*) *vt*: **to ~ out (for)** blechen (für)
she'll [ʃiːl] = **she will; she shall**
shellfish [ˈʃɛlfɪʃ] *n inv* Schalentier *nt*; (*scallop etc*) Muschel *f*; (*as food*) Meeresfrüchte *pl*
shelter [ˈʃɛltəʳ] *n* (*building*) Unterstand *m*; (*refuge*) Schutz *m*; (*also*: **bus shelter**) Wartehäuschen *nt*; (*also*: **night shelter**) Obdachlosenasyl *nt* ▷ *vt* (*protect*) schützen; (*homeless, refugees*) aufnehmen; (*wanted man*) Unterschlupf gewähren *+dat* ▷ *vi* sich unterstellen; (*from storm*) Schutz suchen; **to take ~ (from)** (*from danger*) sich in Sicherheit bringen (vor *+dat*); (*from storm etc*) Schutz suchen (vor *+dat*)
sheltered [ˈʃɛltəd] *adj* (*life*) behütet; (*spot*) geschützt; **~ housing** (*for old people*) Altenwohnungen *pl*; (*for handicapped people*) Behindertenwohnungen *pl*
shelve [ʃɛlv] *vt* (*fig: plan*) ad acta legen
shelves [ʃɛlvz] *npl of* **shelf**
shelving [ˈʃɛlvɪŋ] *n* Regale *pl*
shepherd [ˈʃɛpəd] *n* Schäfer *m* ▷ *vt* (*guide*) führen
shepherd's pie (*Brit*) *n* *Auflauf aus Hackfleisch und Kartoffelbrei*
sheriff [ˈʃɛrɪf] (US) *n* Sheriff *m*
sherry [ˈʃɛrɪ] *n* Sherry *m*
she's [ʃiːz] = **she is; she has**
Shetland [ˈʃɛtlənd] *n* (*also*: **the Shetland Islands**) die Shetlandinseln *pl*
shield [ʃiːld] *n* (*Mil*) Schild *m*; (*trophy*) Trophäe *f*; (*fig: protection*) Schutz *m* ▷ *vt*: **to ~ (from)** schützen (vor *+dat*)
shift [ʃɪft] *n* (*change*) Änderung *f*; (*work-period, workers*) Schicht *f* ▷ *vt* (*move*) bewegen; (*furniture*) (ver)rücken; (*stain*) herausbekommen ▷ *vi* (*move*) sich bewegen; (*wind*) drehen; **a ~ in demand** (*Comm*) eine Nachfrageverschiebung
shift work *n* Schichtarbeit *f*; **to do ~** Schicht arbeiten
shifty [ˈʃɪftɪ] *adj* verschlagen
shimmer [ˈʃɪməʳ] *vi* schimmern
shin [ʃɪn] *n* Schienbein *nt* ▷ *vi*: **to ~ up a tree** einen Baum hinaufklettern
shine [ʃaɪn] (*pt, pp* **shone**) *n* Glanz *m* ▷ *vi* (*sun, light*) scheinen; (*eyes*) leuchten; (*hair: fig: person*) glänzen ▷ *vt* (*polish: pt, pp shined*) polieren; **to ~ a torch on sth** etw mit einer Taschenlampe anleuchten
shingle [ˈʃɪŋgl] *n* (*on beach*) Kiesel(steine) *pl*; (*on roof*) Schindel *f*
shingles [ˈʃɪŋglz] *npl* (*Med*) Gürtelrose *f*
shiny [ˈʃaɪnɪ] *adj* glänzend
ship [ʃɪp] *n* Schiff *nt* ▷ *vt* verschiffen; (*send*) versenden; (*water*) übernehmen; **on board ~** an Bord
shipbuilding [ˈʃɪpbɪldɪŋ] *n* Schiffbau *m*
shipment [ˈʃɪpmənt] *n* (*of goods*) Versand *m*; (*amount*) Sendung *f*

shipping [ˈʃɪpɪŋ] *n* (*transport*) Versand *m*; (*ships*) Schiffe *pl*
shipwreck [ˈʃɪprɛk] *n* Schiffbruch *m*; (*ship*) Wrack *nt* ▷ *vt*: **to be ~ed** schiffbrüchig sein
shipyard [ˈʃɪpjɑːd] *n* Werft *f*
shire [ˈʃaɪəʳ] (*Brit*) *n* Grafschaft *f*
shirt [ʃəːt] *n* (Ober)hemd *nt*; (*woman's*) (Hemd)bluse *f*; **in (one's) ~ sleeves** in Hemdsärmeln
shit [ʃɪt] (*inf!*) *excl* Scheiße (*!*)
shiver [ˈʃɪvəʳ] *n* Schauer *m* ▷ *vi* zittern; **to ~ with cold** vor Kälte zittern
shoal [ʃəul] *n* (*of fish*) Schwarm *m*; (*also*: **shoals**: *fig*) Scharen *pl*
shock [ʃɔk] *n* Schock *m*; (*impact*) Erschütterung *f*; (*also*: **electric shock**) Schlag *m* ▷ *vt* (*upset*) erschüttern; (*offend*) schockieren; **to be suffering from ~** (*Med*) einen Schock haben; **to be in ~** unter Schock stehen; **it gave us a ~** es hat uns erschreckt; **it came as a ~ to hear that ...** wir hörten mit Bestürzung, dass ...
shock absorber *n* (*Aut*) Stoßdämpfer *m*
shocking [ˈʃɔkɪŋ] *adj* schrecklich, fürchterlich; (*outrageous*) schockierend
shoddy [ˈʃɔdɪ] *adj* minderwertig
shoe [ʃuː] (*pt, pp* **shod**) *n* Schuh *m*; (*for horse*) Hufeisen *nt*; (*also*: **brake shoe**) Bremsbacke *f* ▷ *vt* (*horse*) beschlagen
shoelace [ˈʃuːleɪs] *n* Schnürsenkel *m*
shoe polish *n* Schuhcreme *f*
shoestring [ˈʃuːstrɪŋ] *n* (*fig*): **on a ~** mit ganz wenig Geld
shone [ʃɔn] *pt, pp of* **shine**
shook [ʃuk] *pt of* **shake**
shoot [ʃuːt] (*pt, pp* **shot**) *n* (*on branch*) Trieb *m*; (*seedling*) Sämling *m*; (*Sport*) Jagd *f* ▷ *vt* (*gun*) abfeuern; (*arrow, goal*) schießen; (*kill, execute*) erschießen; (*wound*) anschießen; (*Brit*: *game birds*) schießen; (*film*) drehen ▷ *vi*: **to ~ (at)** schießen (auf *+acc*); **to ~ past (sb/sth)** (an jdm/etw) vorbeischießen
▸ **shoot down** *vt* abschießen
▸ **shoot in** *vi* hereingeschossen kommen
▸ **shoot out (of)** *vi* herausgeschossen kommen (aus *+dat*)
▸ **shoot up** *vi* (*fig*: *increase*) in die Höhe schnellen
shooting [ˈʃuːtɪŋ] *n* Schießen *nt*, Schüsse *pl*; (*attack*) Schießerei *f*; (*murder*) Erschießung *f*; (*Cine*) Drehen *nt*; (*Hunting*) Jagen *nt*
shooting star *n* Sternschnuppe *f*
shop [ʃɔp] *n* Geschäft *nt*, Laden *m*; (*workshop*) Werkstatt *f* ▷ *vi* (*also*: **go shopping**) einkaufen (gehen); **repair ~** Reparaturwerkstatt *f*; **to talk ~** (*fig*) über die Arbeit reden
▸ **shop around** *vi* Preise vergleichen; (*fig*) sich umsehen
shop assistant (*Brit*) *n* Verkäufer(in) *m(f)*
shop floor (*Brit*) *n* (*workers*) Arbeiter *pl*; **on the ~** bei *or* unter den Arbeitern
shopkeeper [ˈʃɔpkiːpəʳ] *n* Geschäftsinhaber(in) *m(f)*, Ladenbesitzer(in) *m(f)*
shoplifting [ˈʃɔplɪftɪŋ] *n* Ladendiebstahl *m*
shopper [ˈʃɔpəʳ] *n* Käufer(in) *m(f)*
shopping [ˈʃɔpɪŋ] *n* (*goods*) Einkäufe *pl*
shopping bag *n* Einkaufstasche *f*
shopping centre, (*US*) **shopping center** *n* Einkaufszentrum *nt*
shopping mall *n* Shoppingcenter *nt*
shop-soiled [ˈʃɔpsɔɪld] *adj* angeschmutzt
shop window *n* Schaufenster *nt*
shore [ʃɔːʳ] *n* Ufer *nt*; (*beach*) Strand *m* ▷ *vt*: **to ~ (up)** abstützen; **on ~** an Land
shorn [ʃɔːn] *pp of* **shear**; **to be ~ of** (*power etc*) entkleidet sein *+gen*
short [ʃɔːt] *adj* kurz; (*person*) klein; (*curt*) schroff, kurz angebunden (*inf*); (*scarce*) knapp ▷ *n* (*also*: **short film**) Kurzfilm *m*; **to be ~ of ...** zu wenig ... haben; **I'm 3 ~** ich habe 3 zu wenig, mir fehlen 3; **in ~** kurz gesagt; **to be in ~ supply** knapp sein; **it is ~ for ...** es ist die Kurzform von ...; **a ~ time ago** vor Kurzem; **in the ~ term** auf kurze Sicht; **~ of doing sth** außer etw zu tun; **to cut ~** abbrechen; **everything ~ of ...** alles außer ... *+dat*; **to fall ~ of sth** etw nicht erreichen; (*expectations*) etw nicht erfüllen; **to run ~ of ...** nicht mehr viel ... haben; **to stop ~** plötzlich innehalten; **to stop ~ of** haltmachen vor *+dat*; *see also* **shorts**
shortage [ˈʃɔːtɪdʒ] *n*: **a ~ of** ein Mangel *m* an *+dat*
shortbread [ˈʃɔːtbrɛd] *n* Mürbegebäck *nt*
short-change [ʃɔːtˈtʃeɪndʒ] *vt*: **to ~ sb** jdm zu wenig Wechselgeld geben
shortcoming [ˈʃɔːtkʌmɪŋ] *n* Fehler *m*, Mangel *m*
shortcrust pastry (*Brit*) *n* Mürbeteig *m*
shorten [ˈʃɔːtn] *vt* verkürzen
shortfall [ˈʃɔːtfɔːl] *n* Defizit *nt*
shorthand [ˈʃɔːthænd] *n* Kurzschrift *f*, Stenografie *f*; (*fig*) Kurzform *f*; **to take sth down in ~** etw stenografieren
shorthand typist (*Brit*) *n* Stenotypist(in) *m(f)*
short-lived [ˈʃɔːtˈlɪvd] *adj* kurzlebig; **to be ~** nicht von Dauer sein
shortly [ˈʃɔːtlɪ] *adv* bald
shorts [ʃɔːts] *npl*: **(a pair of) ~** Shorts *pl*
short-sighted [ʃɔːtˈsaɪtɪd] (*Brit*) *adj* (*lit, fig*) kurzsichtig
short-staffed [ʃɔːtˈstɑːft] *adj*: **to be ~** zu wenig Personal haben
short story *n* Kurzgeschichte *f*
short-tempered [ʃɔːtˈtɛmpəd] *adj* gereizt
short-term [ˈʃɔːttəːm] *adj* kurzfristig
shot [ʃɔt] *pt, pp of* **shoot** ▷ *n* Schuss *m*; (*shotgun pellets*) Schrot *m*; (*injection*) Spritze *f*; (*Phot*) Aufnahme *f*; **to fire a ~ at sb/sth** einen Schuss auf jdn/etw abgeben; **to have a ~ at (doing) sth** etw mal versuchen; **to get ~ of sb/sth** (*inf*) jdn/etw loswerden; **a big ~** (*inf*) ein hohes Tier; **a good/poor ~** (*person*) ein guter/schlechter Schütze; **like a ~** sofort
shotgun [ˈʃɔtgʌn] *n* Schrotflinte *f*

should [ʃud] *aux vb*: **I ~ go now** ich sollte jetzt gehen; **he ~ be there now** er müsste eigentlich schon da sein; **I ~ go if I were you** an deiner Stelle würde ich gehen; **I ~ like to** ich möchte gerne, ich würde gerne; **~ he phone ...** falls er anruft ...

shoulder ['ʃəuldəʳ] *n* Schulter *f* ▷ *vt* (*fig*) auf sich *acc* nehmen; **to rub ~s with sb** (*fig*) mit jdm in Berührung kommen; **to give sb the cold ~** (*fig*) jdm die kalte Schulter zeigen

shoulder bag *n* Umhängetasche *f*

shoulder blade *n* Schulterblatt *nt*

shouldn't ['ʃudnt] = **should not**

shout [ʃaut] *n* Schrei *m*, Ruf *m* ▷ *vt* schreien, rufen ▷ *vi* (*also*: **shout out**) aufschreien; **to give sb a ~** jdn rufen

▸ **shout down** *vt* niederbrüllen

shouting ['ʃautɪŋ] *n* Geschrei *nt*

shove [ʃʌv] *vt* schieben; (*with one push*) stoßen, schubsen (*inf*) ▷ *n*: **to give sb a ~** jdn stoßen *or* schubsen (*inf*); **to give sth a ~** etw verrücken; (*door*) gegen etw stoßen; **to ~ sth in sth** (*inf: put*) etw in etw *acc* stecken; **he ~d me out of the way** er stieß mich zur Seite

▸ **shove off** (*inf*) *vi* abschieben

shovel ['ʃʌvl] *n* Schaufel *f*; (*mechanical*) Bagger *m* ▷ *vt* schaufeln

show [ʃəu] (*pt* **~ed**, *pp* **~n**) *n* (*exhibition*) Ausstellung *f*, Schau *f*; (*Theat*) Aufführung *f*; (*TV*) Show *f*; (*Cine*) Vorstellung *f* ▷ *vt* zeigen; (*exhibit*) ausstellen ▷ *vi*: **it ~s** man sieht es; (*is evident*) man merkt es; **to ask for a ~ of hands** um Handzeichen bitten; **without any ~ of emotion** ohne jede Gefühlsregung; **it's just for ~** es ist nur zur Schau; **on ~** ausgestellt, zu sehen; **who's running the ~ here?** (*inf*) wer ist hier verantwortlich?; **to ~ sb to his seat/to the door** jdn an seinen Platz/zur Tür bringen; **to ~ a profit/loss** Gewinn/Verlust aufweisen; **it just goes to ~ that ...** da sieht mans mal wieder, dass

▸ **show in** *vt* hereinführen

▸ **show off** (*pej*) *vi* angeben ▷ *vt* vorführen

▸ **show out** *vt* hinausbegleiten

▸ **show up** *vi* (*stand out*) sich abheben; (*inf: turn up*) auftauchen ▷ *vt* (*uncover*) deutlich erkennen lassen; (*shame*) blamieren

show business *n* Showgeschäft *nt*

showdown ['ʃəudaun] *n* Kraftprobe *f*

shower ['ʃauəʳ] *n* (*of rain*) Schauer *m*; (*of stones etc*) Hagel *m*; (*for bathing in*) Dusche *f*; (*US: party*) *Party, bei der jeder ein Geschenk für den Ehrengast mitbringt* ▷ *vi* duschen ▷ *vt*: **to ~ sb with** (*gifts etc*) jdn überschütten mit; (*missiles, abuse etc*) auf jdn niederhageln lassen; **to have** *or* **take a ~** duschen; **a ~ of sparks** ein Funkenregen *m*

showerproof ['ʃauəpru:f] *adj* regenfest

showing ['ʃəuɪŋ] *n* (*of film*) Vorführung *f*

show jumping *n* Springreiten *nt*

shown [ʃəun] *pp of* **show**

show-off ['ʃəuɔf] (*inf*) *n* Angeber(in) *m(f)*

showpiece ['ʃəupi:s] *n* (*of exhibition etc*) Schaustück *nt*; (*best example*) Paradestück *nt*; (*prime example*) Musterbeispiel *nt*

showroom ['ʃəurum] *n* Ausstellungsraum *m*

shrank [ʃræŋk] *pt of* **shrink**

shrapnel ['ʃræpnl] *n* Schrapnell *nt*

shred [ʃrɛd] *n* (*gen pl*) Fetzen *m*; (*fig*): **not a ~ of truth** kein Fünkchen Wahrheit; **not a ~ of evidence** keine Spur eines Beweises ▷ *vt* zerfetzen; (*Culin*) raspeln

shredder ['ʃrɛdəʳ] *n* (*also*: **vegetable shredder**) Raspel *f*; (*also*: **document shredder**) Reißwolf *m*; (*also*: **garden shredder**) Häcksler *m*

shrewd [ʃru:d] *adj* klug

shriek [ʃri:k] *n* schriller Schrei *m* ▷ *vi* schreien; **to ~ with laughter** vor Lachen quietschen

shrill [ʃrɪl] *adj* schrill

shrimp [ʃrɪmp] *n* Garnele *f*

shrine [ʃraɪn] *n* Schrein *m*; (*fig*) Gedenkstätte *f*

shrink [ʃrɪŋk] (*pt* **shrank**, *pp* **shrunk**) *vi* (*cloth*) einlaufen; (*profits, audiences*) schrumpfen; (*forests*) schwinden; (*also*: **shrink away**) zurückweichen ▷ *vt* (*cloth*) einlaufen lassen ▷ *n* (*inf: pej*) Klapsdoktor *m*; **to ~ from sth** vor etw *dat* zurückschrecken; **to ~ from doing sth** davor zurückschrecken, etw zu tun

shrink-wrap ['ʃrɪŋkræp] *vt* einschweißen

shrivel ['ʃrɪvl] (*also*: **shrivel up**) *vt* austrocknen ▷ *vi* austrocknen, verschrumpeln

shroud [ʃraud] *n* Leichentuch *nt* ▷ *vt*: **~ed in mystery** von einem Geheimnis umgeben

Shrove Tuesday ['ʃrəuv-] *n* Fastnachtsdienstag *m*

shrub [ʃrʌb] *n* Strauch *m*, Busch *m*

shrubbery ['ʃrʌbərɪ] *n* Gebüsch *nt*

shrug [ʃrʌg] *n*: **~ (of the shoulders)** Achselzucken *nt* ▷ *vi*, *vt*: **to ~ (one's shoulders)** mit den Achseln zucken

▸ **shrug off** *vt* (*criticism*) auf die leichte Schulter nehmen; (*illness*) abschütteln

shrunk [ʃrʌŋk] *pp of* **shrink**

shudder ['ʃʌdəʳ] *n* Schauder *m* ▷ *vi* schaudern; **I ~ to think of it** (*fig*) mir graut, wenn ich nur daran denke

shuffle ['ʃʌfl] *vt* (*cards*) mischen ▷ *vi* schlurfen; **to ~ (one's feet)** mit den Füßen scharren

shun [ʃʌn] *vt* meiden; (*publicity*) scheuen

shunt [ʃʌnt] *vt* rangieren

shut [ʃʌt] (*pt*, *pp* **~**) *vt* schließen, zumachen (*inf*) ▷ *vi* sich schließen, zugehen; (*shop*) schließen, zumachen (*inf*)

▸ **shut down** *vt* (*factory etc*) schließen; (*machine*) abschalten ▷ *vi* schließen, zumachen (*inf*)

▸ **shut off** *vt* (*gas, electricity*) abstellen; (*oil supplies etc*) abschneiden

▸ **shut out** *vt* (*person*) aussperren; (*cold, noise*) nicht hereinlassen; (*view*) versperren; (*memory, thought*) verdrängen

▸ **shut up** *vi* (*inf: keep quiet*) den Mund halten ▷ *vt* (*silence*) zum Schweigen bringen

shutter ['ʃʌtəʳ] *n* Fensterladen *m*; (*Phot*) Verschluss *m*

shuttle ['ʃʌtl] *n* (*plane*) Pendelflugzeug *nt*; (*train*) Pendelzug *m*; (*also*: **space shuttle**) Raumtransporter *m*; (*also*: **shuttle service**) Pendelverkehr *m*; (*for weaving*) Schiffchen *nt* ▷ *vi*: **to ~ to and fro** pendeln; **to ~ between** pendeln zwischen ▷ *vt* (*passengers*) transportieren

shuttlecock ['ʃʌtlkɔk] *n* Federball *m*

shuttle diplomacy *n* Reisediplomatie *f*

shy [ʃaɪ] *adj* schüchtern; (*animal*) scheu ▷ *vi*: **to ~ away from doing sth** (*fig*) davor zurückschrecken, etw zu tun; **to fight ~ of** aus dem Weg gehen *+dat*; **to be ~ of doing sth** Hemmungen haben, etw zu tun

Siberia [saɪ'bɪərɪə] *n* Sibirien *nt*

Sicily ['sɪsɪlɪ] *n* Sizilien *nt*

sick [sɪk] *adj* krank; (*humour, joke*) makaber; **to be ~** (*vomit*) brechen, sich übergeben; **I feel ~** mir ist schlecht; **to fall ~** krank werden; **to be (off) ~** wegen Krankheit fehlen; **a ~ person** ein Kranker, eine Kranke; **to be ~ of** (*fig*) satthaben *+acc*

sicken ['sɪkn] *vt* (*disgust*) anwidern ▷ *vi*: **to be ~ing for a cold/flu** eine Erkältung/Grippe bekommen

sickening ['sɪknɪŋ] *adj* (*fig*) widerlich, ekelhaft

sickle ['sɪkl] *n* Sichel *f*

sick leave *n*: **to be on ~** krankgeschrieben sein

sickly ['sɪklɪ] *adj* kränklich; (*causing nausea*) widerlich, ekelhaft

sickness ['sɪknɪs] *n* Krankheit *f*; (*vomiting*) Erbrechen *nt*

sick note *n* Krankmeldung *f*

sick pay *n* Lohnfortzahlung *f* im Krankheitsfall; (*paid by insurance*) Krankengeld *nt*

side [saɪd] *n* Seite *f*; (*team*) Mannschaft *f*; (*in conflict etc*) Partei *f*, Seite *f*; (*of hill*) Hang *m* ▷ *adj* (*door, entrance*) Seiten-, Neben- ▷ *vi*: **to ~ with sb** jds Partei ergreifen; **by the ~ of** neben *+dat*; **~ by side** Seite an Seite; **the right/wrong ~** (*of cloth*) die rechte/linke Seite; **they are on our ~** sie stehen auf unserer Seite; **she never left my ~** sie wich mir nicht von der Seite; **to put sth to one ~** etw beiseitelegen; **from ~ to side** von einer Seite zur anderen; **to take ~s (with)** Partei ergreifen (für); **a ~ of beef** ein halbes Rind; **a ~ of bacon** eine Speckseite

sideboard ['saɪdbɔːd] *n* Sideboard *nt*; **sideboards** (*Brit*) *npl* = **sideburns**

side drum *n* kleine Trommel *f*

side effect *n* (*Med, fig*) Nebenwirkung *f*

sidelight ['saɪdlaɪt] *n* (*Aut*) Begrenzungsleuchte *f*

sideline ['saɪdlaɪn] *n* (*Sport*) Seitenlinie *f*; (*fig: job*) Nebenerwerb *m*; **to stand on the ~s** (*fig*) unbeteiligter Zuschauer sein; **to wait on the ~s** (*fig*) in den Kulissen warten

sidelong ['saɪdlɔŋ] *adj* (*glance*) Seiten-; (*: surreptitious*) verstohlen; **to give sb a ~ glance** jdn kurz aus den Augenwinkeln ansehen

side road *n* Nebenstraße *f*

sideshow ['saɪdʃəu] *n* Nebenattraktion *f*

sidestep ['saɪdstɛp] *vt* (*problem*) umgehen; (*question*) ausweichen *+dat* ▷ *vi* (*Boxing etc*) seitwärts ausweichen

side street *n* Seitenstraße *f*

sidetrack ['saɪdtræk] *vt* (*fig*) ablenken

sidewalk ['saɪdwɔːk] (*US*) *n* Bürgersteig *m*

sideways ['saɪdweɪz] *adv* seitwärts; (*lean, look*) zur Seite

siding ['saɪdɪŋ] *n* Abstellgleis *nt*

siege [siːdʒ] *n* Belagerung *f*; **to be under ~** belagert sein; **to lay ~ to** belagern

sieve [sɪv] *n* Sieb *nt* ▷ *vt* sieben

sift [sɪft] *vt* sieben; (*also*: **sift through**) durchgehen

sigh [saɪ] *n* Seufzer *m* ▷ *vi* seufzen; **to breathe a ~ of relief** erleichtert aufseufzen

sight [saɪt] *n* (*faculty*) Sehvermögen *nt*, Augenlicht *nt*; (*spectacle*) Anblick *m*; (*on gun*) Visier *nt* ▷ *vt* sichten; **in ~** in Sicht; **on ~** (*shoot*) sofort; **out of ~** außer Sicht; **at ~** (*Comm*) bei Sicht; **at first ~** auf den ersten Blick; **I know her by ~** ich kenne sie vom Sehen; **to catch ~ of sb/sth** jdn/etw sehen; **to lose ~ of sth** (*fig*) etw aus den Augen verlieren; **to set one's ~s on sth** ein Auge auf etw werfen

sightseeing ['saɪtsiːɪŋ] *n* Besichtigungen *pl*; **to go ~** auf Besichtigungstour gehen

sign [saɪn] *n* Zeichen *nt*; (*notice*) Schild *nt*; (*evidence*) Anzeichen *nt*; (*also*: **road sign**) Verkehrsschild *nt* ▷ *vt* unterschreiben; (*player*) verpflichten; **a ~ of the times** ein Zeichen unserer Zeit; **it's a good/bad ~** es ist ein gutes/schlechtes Zeichen; **plus/minus ~** Plus-/Minuszeichen *nt*; **there's no ~ of her changing her mind** nichts deutet darauf hin, dass sie es sich anders überlegen wird; **he was showing ~s of improvement** er ließ Anzeichen einer Verbesserung erkennen; **to ~ one's name** unterschreiben; **to ~ sth over to sb** jdm etw überschreiben

▸ **sign away** *vt* (*rights etc*) verzichten auf *+acc*

▸ **sign in** *vi* sich eintragen

▸ **sign off** *vi* (*Radio, TV*) sich verabschieden; (*in letter*) Schluss machen

▸ **sign on** *vi* (*Mil*) sich verpflichten; (*Brit: as unemployed*) sich arbeitslos melden; (*for course*) sich einschreiben ▷ *vt* (*Mil*) verpflichten; (*employee*) anstellen

▸ **sign out** *vi* (*from hotel etc*) sich (aus dem Hotelgästebuch *etc*) austragen

▸ **sign up** *vi* (*Mil*) sich verpflichten; (*for course*) sich einschreiben ▷ *vt* (*player, recruit*) verpflichten

signal ['sɪgnl] *n* Zeichen *nt*; (*Rail*) Signal *nt* ▷ *vi* (*Aut*) Zeichen/ein Zeichen geben ▷ *vt* ein Zeichen geben *+dat*; **to ~ a right/left turn** (*Aut*) rechts/links blinken

signalman ['sɪgnlmən] (*irreg: like* **man**) *n*

Stellwerkswärter *m*
signature ['sɪgnətʃəʳ] *n* Unterschrift *f*; (*Zool, Biol*) Kennzeichen *nt*
signature tune *n* Erkennungsmelodie *f*
signet ring ['sɪgnət-] *n* Siegelring *m*
significance [sɪg'nɪfɪkəns] *n* Bedeutung *f*; **that is of no ~** das ist belanglos *or* bedeutungslos
significant [sɪg'nɪfɪkənt] *adj* bedeutend, wichtig; (*look, smile*) vielsagend, bedeutsam; **it is ~ that ...** es ist bezeichnend, dass ...
signify ['sɪgnɪfaɪ] *vt* bedeuten; (*person*) zu erkennen geben
sign language *n* Zeichensprache *f*
signpost ['saɪnpəust] *n* (*lit, fig*) Wegweiser *m*
Sikh [si:k] *n* Sikh *mf* ▷ *adj* (*province etc*) Sikh-
silence ['saɪləns] *n* Stille *f*; (*of person*) Schweigen *nt* ▷ *vt* zum Schweigen bringen; **in ~** still; (*not talking*) schweigend
silencer ['saɪlənsəʳ] *n* (*on gun*) Schalldämpfer *m*; (*Brit: Aut*) Auspufftopf *m*
silent ['saɪlənt] *adj* still; (*machine*) ruhig; **~ film** Stummfilm *m*; **to remain ~** still bleiben; (*about sth*) sich nicht äußern
silent partner *n* stiller Teilhaber *m*
silhouette [sɪlu:'ɛt] *n* Sihouette *f*, Umriss *m* ▷ *vt*: **to be ~d against sth** sich als Silhouette gegen etw abheben
silicon chip *n* Silikonchip *m*
silk [sɪlk] *n* Seide *f* ▷ *adj* (*dress etc*) Seiden-
silky ['sɪlkɪ] *adj* seidig
silly ['sɪlɪ] *adj* (*person*) dumm; **to do something ~** etwas Dummes tun
silt [sɪlt] *n* Schlamm *m*, Schlick *m*
▸ **silt up** *vi* verschlammen ▷ *vt* verschlämmen
silver ['sɪlvəʳ] *n* Silber *nt*; (*coins*) Silbergeld *nt* ▷ *adj* silbern
silver-plated [sɪlvə'pleɪtɪd] *adj* versilbert
silversmith ['sɪlvəsmɪθ] *n* Silberschmied(in) *m(f)*
silvery ['sɪlvrɪ] *adj* silbern; (*sound*) silberhell
similar ['sɪmɪləʳ] *adj*: **~ (to)** ähnlich (wie *or* +*dat*)
similarity [sɪmɪ'lærɪtɪ] *n* Ähnlichkeit *f*
similarly ['sɪmɪləlɪ] *adv* ähnlich; (*likewise*) genauso
simmer ['sɪməʳ] *vi* auf kleiner Flamme kochen
▸ **simmer down** (*inf*) *vi* (*fig*) sich abregen
simple ['sɪmpl] *adj* einfach; (*dress*) einfach, schlicht; (*foolish*) einfältig; **the ~ truth is that ...** es ist einfach so, dass ...
simplicity [sɪm'plɪsɪtɪ] *n* Einfachheit *f*; (*of dress*) Schlichtheit *f*
simplify ['sɪmplɪfaɪ] *vt* vereinfachen
simply ['sɪmplɪ] *adv* (*just, merely*) nur, bloß; (*in a simple way*) einfach
simulate ['sɪmjuleɪt] *vt* vortäuschen, spielen; (*illness*) simulieren
simultaneous [sɪməl'teɪnɪəs] *adj* gleichzeitig; (*translation, interpreting*) Simultan-
simultaneously [sɪməl'teɪnɪəslɪ] *adv* gleichzeitig
sin [sɪn] *n* Sünde *f* ▷ *vi* sündigen
since [sɪns] *adv* inzwischen, seitdem ▷ *prep* seit ▷ *conj* (*time*) seit(dem); (*because*) da; **~ then, ever since** seitdem
sincere [sɪn'sɪəʳ] *adj* aufrichtig, offen; (*apology, belief*) aufrichtig
sincerely [sɪn'sɪəlɪ] *adv* aufrichtig, offen; **yours ~** (*in letter*) mit freundlichen Grüßen
sincerity [sɪn'sɛrɪtɪ] *n* Aufrichtigkeit *f*
sinew ['sɪnju:] *n* Sehne *f*
sing [sɪŋ] (*pt* **sang**, *pp* **sung**) *vt, vi* singen
Singapore [sɪŋgə'pɔ:ʳ] *n* Singapur *nt*
singe [sɪndʒ] *vt* versengen; (*lightly*) ansengen
singer ['sɪŋəʳ] *n* Sänger(in) *m(f)*
singing ['sɪŋɪŋ] *n* Singen *nt*, Gesang *m*; **a ~ in the ears** ein Dröhnen in den Ohren
single ['sɪŋgl] *adj* (*solitary*) einzige(r, s); (*individual*) einzeln; (*unmarried*) ledig, unverheiratet; (*not double*) einfach ▷ *n* (*Brit: also*: **single ticket**) Einzelfahrschein *m*; (*record*) Single *f*; **not a ~ one was left** es war kein Einziges mehr übrig; **every ~ day** jeden Tag; **~ spacing** einfacher Zeilenabstand *m*
▸ **single out** *vt* auswählen; **to ~ out for praise** lobend erwähnen
single bed *n* Einzelbett *nt*
single-breasted ['sɪŋglbrɛstɪd] *adj* einreihig
single file *n*: **in ~** im Gänsemarsch
single-handed [sɪŋgl'hændɪd] *adv* ganz allein
single-minded [sɪŋgl'maɪndɪd] *adj* zielstrebig
single parent *n* Alleinerziehende(r) *f(m)*
single room *n* Einzelzimmer *nt*
singly ['sɪŋglɪ] *adv* einzeln
singular ['sɪŋgjuləʳ] *adj* (*odd*) eigenartig; (*outstanding*) einzigartig; (*Ling: form etc*) Singular- ▷ *n* (*Ling*) Singular *m*, Einzahl *f*; **in the ~** im Singular
sinister ['sɪnɪstəʳ] *adj* unheimlich
sink [sɪŋk] (*pt* **sank**, *pp* **sunk**) *n* Spülbecken *nt* ▷ *vt* (*ship*) versenken; (*well*) bohren; (*foundations*) absenken ▷ *vi* (*ship*) sinken, untergehen; (*ground*) sich senken; (*person*) sinken; **to ~ one's teeth/claws into sth** die Zähne/seine Klauen in etw *acc* schlagen; **his heart/spirits sank at the thought** bei dem Gedanken verließ ihn der Mut; **he sank into the mud/a chair** er sank in den Schlamm ein/in einen Sessel
▸ **sink back** *vi* (zurück)sinken
▸ **sink down** *vi* (nieder)sinken
▸ **sink in** *vi* (*fig*) verstanden werden; **it's only just sunk in** ich begreife es erst jetzt
sinner ['sɪnəʳ] *n* Sünder(in) *m(f)*
sinus ['saɪnəs] *n* (Nasen)nebenhöhle *f*
sip [sɪp] *n* Schlückchen *nt* ▷ *vt* nippen an +*dat*
siphon ['saɪfən] *n* Heber *m*; (*also*: **soda siphon**) Siphon *m*
▸ **siphon off** *vt* absaugen; (*petrol*) abzapfen
sir [səʳ] *n* mein Herr, Herr X; **S~ John Smith**

Sir John Smith; **yes, ~** ja(, Herr X); **Dear S~ (or Madam)** (*in letter*) Sehr geehrte (Damen und) Herren!
siren ['saɪərn] *n* Sirene *f*
sirloin ['sə:lɔɪn] *n* (*also*: **sirloin steak**) Filetsteak *nt*
sissy ['sɪsɪ] (*inf*: *pej*) *n* Waschlappen *m* ▷ *adj* weichlich
sister ['sɪstəʳ] *n* Schwester *f*; (*nun*) (Ordens)schwester *f*; (*Brit*: *nurse*) Oberschwester *f* ▷ *cpd*: **~ organization** Schwesterorganisation *f*; **~ ship** Schwesterschiff *nt*
sister-in-law ['sɪstərɪnlɔ:] *n* Schwägerin *f*
sit [sɪt] (*pt, pp* **sat**) *vi* (*sit down*) sich setzen; (*be sitting*) sitzen; (*assembly*) tagen; (*for painter*) Modell sitzen ▷ *vt* (*exam*) machen; **to ~ on a committee** in einem Ausschuss sitzen; **to ~ tight** abwarten
▸ **sit about** *vi* herumsitzen
▸ **sit around** *vi* = **sit about**
▸ **sit back** *vi* sich zurücklehnen
▸ **sit down** *vi* sich (hin)setzen; **to be ~ting down** sitzen
▸ **sit in on** *vt fus* dabei sein bei
▸ **sit up** *vi* sich aufsetzen; (*straight*) sich gerade hinsetzen; (*not go to bed*) aufbleiben
sitcom ['sɪtkɔm] *n abbr* (TV) = **situation comedy**
site [saɪt] *n* (*place*) Platz *m*; (*of crime*) Ort *m*; (*also*: **building site**) Baustelle *f*; (*Comput*) Site *f* ▷ *vt* (*factory*) legen; (*missiles*) stationieren
sit-in ['sɪtɪn] *n* Sit-in *nt*
sitting ['sɪtɪŋ] *n* Sitzung *f*; **we have two ~s for lunch** bei uns wird das Mittagessen in zwei Schüben serviert; **at a single ~** auf einmal
sitting room *n* Wohnzimmer *nt*
situated ['sɪtjueɪtɪd] *adj* gelegen; **to be ~** liegen
situation [sɪtju'eɪʃən] *n* Situation *f*, Lage *f*; (*job*) Stelle *f*; (*location*) Lage *f*; **"~s vacant** *or* **wanted"** "Stellenangebote"
six [sɪks] *num* sechs
sixteen [sɪks'ti:n] *num* sechzehn
sixth [sɪksθ] *num* sechste(r, s); **the upper/lower ~** (*Brit*: *Scol*) ≈ die Ober-/Unterprima
sixty ['sɪkstɪ] *num* sechzig
size [saɪz] *n* Größe *f*; (*extent*) Ausmaß *nt*; **I take ~ 14** ich habe Größe 14; **the small/large ~** (*of soap powder etc*) die kleine/große Packung; **it's the ~ of ...** es ist so groß wie ...; **cut to ~** auf die richtige Größe zurechtgeschnitten
▸ **size up** *vt* einschätzen
sizeable ['saɪzəbl] *adj* ziemlich groß; (*income etc*) ansehnlich
sizzle ['sɪzl] *vi* brutzeln
skate [skeɪt] *n* (*also*: **ice skate**) Schlittschuh *m*; (*also*: **roller skate**) Rollschuh *m*; (*fish*: *pl inv*) Rochen *m* ▷ *vi* Schlittschuh laufen
▸ **skate around** *vt fus* (*problem, issue*) einfach übergehen
▸ **skate over** *vt fus* = **skate around**
skateboard ['skeɪtbɔ:d] *n* Skateboard *nt*
skater ['skeɪtəʳ] *n* Schlittschuhläufer(in) *m(f)*
skating ['skeɪtɪŋ] *n* Eislauf *m*
skating rink *n* Eisbahn *f*
skeleton ['skɛlɪtn] *n* Skelett *nt* ▷ *attrib* (*plan, outline*) skizzenhaft
skeleton staff *n* Minimalbesetzung *f*
sketch [skɛtʃ] *n* Skizze *f*; (*Theat, TV*) Sketch *m* ▷ *vt* skizzieren; (*also*: **sketch out**: *ideas*) umreißen
sketchy ['skɛtʃɪ] *adj* (*coverage*) oberflächlich; (*notes etc*) bruchstückhaft
skewer ['skju:əʳ] *n* Spieß *m*
ski [ski:] *n* Ski *m* ▷ *vi* Ski laufen *or* fahren
ski boot *n* Skistiefel *m*
skid [skɪd] *n* (*Aut*) Schleudern *nt* ▷ *vi* rutschen; (*Aut*) schleudern; **to go into a ~** ins Schleudern geraten *or* kommen
skier ['ski:əʳ] *n* Skiläufer(in) *m(f)*, Skifahrer(in) *m(f)*
skiing ['ski:ɪŋ] *n* Skilaufen *nt*, Skifahren *nt*; **to go ~** Ski laufen *or* Ski fahren gehen
ski jump *n* (*event*) Skispringen *nt*; (*ramp*) Sprungschanze *f*
skilful, (US) **skillful** ['skɪlful] *adj* geschickt
ski lift *n* Skilift *m*
skill [skɪl] *n* (*ability*) Können *nt*; (*dexterity*) Geschicklichkeit *f*; **skills** (*acquired abilities*) Fähigkeiten *pl*; **computer/language ~s** Computer-/Sprachkenntnisse *pl*; **to learn a new ~** etwas Neues lernen
skilled [skɪld] *adj* (*skilful*) geschickt; (*trained*) ausgebildet; (*work*) qualifiziert
skim [skɪm] *vt* (*also*: **skim off**: *cream, fat*) abschöpfen; (*glide over*) gleiten über *+acc* ▷ *vi*: **to ~ through** (*book etc*) überfliegen
skimmed milk [skɪmd-] *n* Magermilch *f*
skimp [skɪmp] (*also*: **skimp on**) *vt* (*work etc*) nachlässig machen; (*cloth etc*) sparen an *+dat*
skimpy ['skɪmpɪ] *adj* (*meagre*) dürftig; (*too small*) knapp
skin [skɪn] *n* Haut *f*; (*fur*) Fell *nt*; (*of fruit*) Schale *f* ▷ *vt* (*animal*) häuten; **wet** *or* **soaked to the ~** nass bis auf die Haut
skin cancer *n* Hautkrebs *m*
skin-deep ['skɪn'di:p] *adj* oberflächlich
skin diving *n* Sporttauchen *nt*
skinhead ['skɪnhɛd] *n* Skinhead *m*
skinny ['skɪnɪ] *adj* dünn
skintight ['skɪntaɪt] *adj* hauteng
skip [skɪp] *n* Sprung *m*, Hüpfer *m*; (*Brit*: *container*) (Müll)container *m* ▷ *vi* springen, hüpfen; (*with rope*) seilspringen ▷ *vt* überspringen; (*miss*: *lunch, lecture*) ausfallen lassen; **to ~ school** (*esp US*) die Schule schwänzen
ski pass *n* Skipass *nt*
ski pole *n* Skistock *m*
skipper ['skɪpəʳ] *n* (*Naut*) Kapitän *m*; (*inf*: *Sport*) Mannschaftskapitän *m* ▷ *vt*: **to ~ a boat/team** Kapitän eines Schiffes/einer Mannschaft sein

skipping rope ['skɪpɪŋ-] *(Brit) n* Sprungseil *nt*
skirmish ['skəːmɪʃ] *n (Mil)* Geplänkel *nt*; *(political etc)* Zusammenstoß *m*
skirt [skəːt] *n* Rock *m* ▷ *vt (fig)* umgehen
skirting board ['skəːtɪŋ-] *(Brit) n* Fußleiste *f*
ski slope *n* Skipiste *f*
ski suit *n* Skianzug *m*
ski tow *n* Schlepplift *m*
skittle ['skɪtl] *n* Kegel *m*
skive [skaɪv] *(Brit: inf) vi* blaumachen; *(from school)* schwänzen
skull [skʌl] *n* Schädel *m*
skunk [skʌŋk] *n* Skunk *m*, Stinktier *nt*; *(fur)* Skunk *m*
sky [skaɪ] *n* Himmel *m*; **to praise sb to the skies** jdn in den Himmel heben
skylight ['skaɪlaɪt] *n* Dachfenster *nt*
skyscraper ['skaɪskreɪpəʳ] *n* Wolkenkratzer *m*
slab [slæb] *n (stone)* Platte *f*; *(of wood)* Tafel *f*; *(of cake, cheese)* großes Stück *nt*
slack [slæk] *adj (loose)* locker; *(rope)* durchhängend; *(skin)* schlaff; *(careless)* nachlässig; *(Comm: market)* flau; *(: demand)* schwach; *(period)* ruhig ▷ *n (in rope etc)* durchhängendes Teil *nt*; **slacks** *npl (trousers)* Hose *f*; **business is ~** das Geschäft geht schlecht
slacken ['slækn] *vi (also:* **slacken off***: speed, rain)* nachlassen; *(: pace)* langsamer werden; *(: demand)* zurückgehen ▷ *vt (grip)* lockern; *(speed)* verringern; *(pace)* verlangsamen
slag heap [slæg-] *n* Schlackenhalde *f*
slag off *(Brit: inf) vt (criticize)* (he)runtermachen
slain [sleɪn] *pp of* **slay**
slam [slæm] *vt (door)* zuschlagen, zuknallen *(inf)*; *(throw)* knallen *(inf)*; *(criticize)* verreißen ▷ *vi (door)* zuschlagen, zuknallen *(inf)*; **to ~ on the brakes** *(Aut)* auf die Bremse steigen *(inf)*
slander ['slɑːndəʳ] *n (Law)* Verleumdung *f*; *(insult)* Beleidigung *f* ▷ *vt* verleumden
slang [slæŋ] *n* Slang *m*; *(jargon)* Jargon *m*
slant [slɑːnt] *n* Neigung *f*, Schräge *f*; *(fig: approach)* Perspektive *f* ▷ *vi (floor)* sich neigen; *(ceiling)* schräg sein
slanted ['slɑːntɪd] *adj (roof)* schräg; *(eyes)* schräg gestellt
slanting ['slɑːntɪŋ] *adj* = **slanted**
slap [slæp] *n* Schlag *m*, Klaps *m* ▷ *vt* schlagen ▷ *adv (inf: directly)* direkt; **to ~ sth on sth** etw auf etw *acc* klatschen; **it fell ~(-bang) in the middle** es fiel genau in die Mitte
slapdash ['slæpdæʃ] *adj* nachlässig, schludrig *(inf)*
slapstick ['slæpstɪk] *n* Klamauk *m*
slap-up ['slæpʌp] *adj*: **a ~ meal** *(Brit)* ein Essen mit allem Drum und Dran
slash [slæʃ] *vt* aufschlitzen; *(fig: prices)* radikal senken; **to ~ one's wrists** sich *dat* die Pulsadern aufschneiden
slat [slæt] *n* Leiste *f*, Latte *f*
slate [sleɪt] *n* Schiefer *m*; *(piece)* Schieferplatte *f* ▷ *vt (criticize)* verreißen
slaughter ['slɔːtəʳ] *n (of animals)* Schlachten *nt*; *(of people)* Gemetzel *nt* ▷ *vt (animals)* schlachten; *(people)* abschlachten
slaughterhouse ['slɔːtəhaus] *n* Schlachthof *m*
Slav [slɑːv] *adj* slawisch ▷ *n* Slawe *m*, Slawin *f*
slave [sleɪv] *n* Sklave *m*, Sklavin *f* ▷ *vi (also:* **slave away***)* sich abplagen, schuften *(inf)*; **to ~ (away) at sth** sich mit etw herumschlagen
slavery ['sleɪvərɪ] *n* Sklaverei *f*
slay [sleɪ] *(pt* **slew**, *pp* **slain***) vt (liter)* erschlagen
sleazy ['sliːzɪ] *adj* schäbig
sledge [slɛdʒ] *n* Schlitten *m*
sledgehammer ['slɛdʒhæməʳ] *n* Vorschlaghammer *m*
sleek [sliːk] *adj* glatt, glänzend; *(car, boat etc)* schnittig
sleep [sliːp] *(pt, pp* **slept***) n* Schlaf *m* ▷ *vi* schlafen ▷ *vt*: **we can ~ 4** bei uns können 4 Leute schlafen; **to go to ~** einschlafen; **to have a good night's ~** sich richtig ausschlafen; **to put to ~** *(euph: kill)* einschläfern; **to ~ lightly** einen leichten Schlaf haben; **to ~ with sb** *(euph: have sex)* mit jdm schlafen
▸ **sleep around** *vi* mit jedem/jeder schlafen
▸ **sleep in** *vi (oversleep)* verschlafen; *(rise late)* lange schlafen
sleeper ['sliːpəʳ] *n (train)* Schlafwagenzug *m*; *(berth)* Platz *m* im Schlafwagen; *(Brit: on track)* Schwelle *f*; *(person)* Schläfer(in) *m(f)*
sleeping bag *n* Schlafsack *m*
sleeping car *n* Schlafwagen *m*
sleeping partner *(Brit)* = **silent partner**
sleeping pill *n* Schlaftablette *f*
sleepless ['sliːplɪs] *adj (night)* schlaflos
sleepwalk ['sliːpwɔːk] *vi* schlafwandeln
sleepwalker ['sliːpwɔːkəʳ] *n* Schlafwandler(in) *m(f)*
sleepy ['sliːpɪ] *adj* müde, schläfrig; *(fig: village etc)* verschlafen; **to be** *or* **feel ~** müde sein
sleet [sliːt] *n* Schneeregen *m*
sleeve [sliːv] *n* Ärmel *m*; *(of record)* Hülle *f*; **to have sth up one's ~** *(fig)* etw in petto haben
sleeveless ['sliːvlɪs] *adj (garment)* ärmellos
sleigh [sleɪ] *n* (Pferde)schlitten *m*
sleight [slaɪt] *n*: **~ of hand** Fingerfertigkeit *f*
slender ['slɛndəʳ] *adj* schlank, schmal; *(small)* knapp
slept [slɛpt] *pt, pp of* **sleep**
slew [sluː] *vi (Brit: also:* **slew round***)* herumschwenken; **the bus ~ed across the road** der Bus rutschte über die Straße ▷ *pt of* **slay**
slice [slaɪs] *n* Scheibe *f*; *(utensil)* Wender *m* ▷ *vt* (in Scheiben) schneiden; **~d bread** aufgeschnittenes Brot *nt*; **the best thing since ~d bread** der/die/das Allerbeste
slick [slɪk] *adj* professionell; *(pej)* glatt ▷ *n (also:* **oil slick***)* Ölteppich *m*
slide [slaɪd] *(pt, pp* **slid***) n (on ice etc)* Rutschen *nt*; *(fig: to ruin etc)* Abgleiten *nt*; *(in playground)*

Rutschbahn *f*; (*Phot*) Dia *nt*; (*Brit*: *also*: **hair slide**) Spange *f*; (*microscope slide*) Objektträger *m*; (*in prices*) Preisrutsch *m* ▷ *vt* schieben ▷ *vi* (*slip*) rutschen; (*glide*) gleiten; **to let things ~** (*fig*) die Dinge schleifen lassen

sliding ['slaɪdɪŋ] *adj* (*door, window etc*) Schiebe-

sliding scale *n* gleitende Skala *f*

slight [slaɪt] *adj* zierlich; (*small*) gering; (*error, accent, pain etc*) leicht; (*trivial*) leicht ▷ *n*: **a ~ (on sb/sth)** ein Affront *m* (gegen jdn/etw); **the ~est noise** der geringste Lärm; **the ~est problem** das kleinste Problem; **I haven't the ~est idea** ich habe nicht die geringste Ahnung; **not in the ~est** nicht im Geringsten

slightly ['slaɪtlɪ] *adv* etwas, ein bisschen; **~ built** zierlich

slim [slɪm] *adj* schlank; (*chance*) gering ▷ *vi* eine Schlankheitskur machen, abnehmen

slime [slaɪm] *n* Schleim *m*

slimming ['slɪmɪŋ] *n* Abnehmen *nt*

slimy ['slaɪmɪ] *adj* (*lit, fig*) schleimig

sling [slɪŋ] (*pt, pp* **slung**) *n* Schlinge *f*; (*for baby*) Tragetuch *nt*; (*weapon*) Schleuder *f* ▷ *vt* schleudern; **to have one's arm in a ~** den Arm in der Schlinge tragen

slip [slɪp] *n* (*fall*) Ausrutschen *nt*; (*mistake*) Fehler *m*, Schnitzer *m*; (*underskirt*) Unterrock *m*; (*also*: **slip of paper**) Zettel *m* ▷ *vt* (*slide*) stecken ▷ *vi* ausrutschen; (*decline*) fallen; **he had a nasty ~** er ist ausgerutscht und böse gefallen; **to give sb the ~** jdm entwischen; **a ~ of the tongue** ein Versprecher *m*; **to ~ into/out of sth, to ~ sth on/off** in etw *acc*/aus etw schlüpfen; **to let a chance ~ by** eine Gelegenheit ungenutzt lassen; **it ~ped from her hand** es rutschte ihr aus der Hand

▸ **slip away** *vi* sich davonschleichen

▸ **slip in** *vt* stecken in *+acc*

▸ **slip out** *vi* kurz weggehen

▸ **slip up** *vi* sich vertun (*inf*)

slipped disc [slɪpt-] *n* Bandscheibenschaden *m*

slipper ['slɪpə^r] *n* Pantoffel *m*, Hausschuh *m*

slippery ['slɪpərɪ] *adj* (*lit, fig*) glatt; (*fish etc*) schlüpfrig

slip road (*Brit*) *n* (*to motorway etc*) Auffahrt *f*; (*from motorway etc*) Ausfahrt *f*

slip-up ['slɪpʌp] *n* Fehler *m*, Schnitzer *m*

slipway ['slɪpweɪ] *n* (*Naut*) Ablaufbahn *f*

slit [slɪt] (*pt, pp* **~**) *n* Schlitz *m*; (*tear*) Riss *m* ▷ *vt* aufschlitzen; **to ~ sb's throat** jdm die Kehle aufschlitzen

slither ['slɪðə^r] *vi* rutschen; (*snake etc*) gleiten

sliver ['slɪvə^r] *n* (*of glass, wood*) Splitter *m*; (*of cheese etc*) Scheibchen *nt*

slob [slɔb] (*inf*) *n* Drecksau *f* (*!*)

slog [slɔg] (*Brit*) *vi* (*work hard*) schuften ▷ *n*: **it was a hard ~** es war eine ganz schöne Schufterei; **to ~ away at sth** sich mit etw abrackern

slogan ['sləugən] *n* Slogan *m*

slope [sləup] *n* Hügel *m*; (*side of mountain*) Hang *m*; (*ski slope*) Piste *f*; (*slant*) Neigung *f* ▷ *vi*: **to ~ down** abfallen; **to ~ up** ansteigen

sloping ['sləupɪŋ] *adj* (*upwards*) ansteigend; (*downwards*) abfallend; (*roof, handwriting*) schräg

sloppy ['slɔpɪ] *adj* (*work*) nachlässig; (*appearance*) schlampig; (*sentimental*) rührselig

slot [slɔt] *n* Schlitz *m*; (*fig*: *in timetable*) Termin *m*; (: *Radio, TV*) Sendezeit *f* ▷ *vt*: **to ~ sth in** etw hineinstecken ▷ *vi*: **to ~ into** sich einfügen lassen in *+acc*

sloth [sləuθ] *n* (*laziness*) Trägheit *f*, Faulheit *f*; (*Zool*) Faultier *nt*

slot machine *n* (*Brit*) Münzautomat *m*; (*for gambling*) Spielautomat *m*

slouch [slautʃ] *vi* eine krumme Haltung haben; (*when walking*) krumm gehen ▷ *n*: **he's no ~** er hat etwas los (*inf*); **she was ~ed in a chair** sie hing auf einem Stuhl

Slovakia [sləu'vækɪə] *n* die Slowakei

Slovene ['sləuvi:n] *n* Slowene *m*, Slowenin *f*; (*Ling*) Slowenisch *nt* ▷ *adj* slowenisch

Slovenia [sləu'vi:nɪə] *n* Slowenien *nt*

Slovenian [sləu'vi:nɪən] *adj*, *n* = **Slovene**

slovenly ['slʌvənlɪ] *adj* schlampig; (*careless*) nachlässig, schludrig (*inf*)

slow [sləu] *adj* langsam; (*not clever*) langsam, begriffsstutzig ▷ *adv* langsam ▷ *vt* (*also*: **slow down, slow up**) verlangsamen; (*business*) verschlechtern ▷ *vi* (*also*: **slow down, slow up**) sich verlangsamen; (*business*) schlechter gehen; **to be ~** (*watch, clock*) nachgehen; **"~"** "langsam fahren"; **at a ~ speed** langsam; **to be ~ to act** sich *dat* Zeit lassen; **to be ~ to decide** lange brauchen, um sich zu entscheiden; **my watch is 20 minutes ~** meine Uhr geht 20 Minuten nach; **business is ~** das Geschäft geht schlecht; **to go ~** (*driver*) langsam fahren; (*Brit*: *in industrial dispute*) einen Bummelstreik machen

slowly ['sləulɪ] *adv* langsam

slow motion *n*: **in ~** in Zeitlupe

sludge [slʌdʒ] *n* Schlamm *m*

slug [slʌg] *n* Nacktschnecke *f*; (*US*: *inf*: *bullet*) Kugel *f*

sluggish ['slʌgɪʃ] *adj* träge; (*engine*) lahm; (*Comm*) flau

sluice [slu:s] *n* Schleuse *f*; (*channel*) (Wasch)rinne *f* ▷ *vt*: **to ~ down** *or* **out** abspritzen

slum [slʌm] *n* Slum *m*, Elendsviertel *nt*

slump [slʌmp] *n* Rezession *f* ▷ *vi* fallen; **~ in sales** Absatzflaute *f*; **~ in prices** Preissturz *m*; **he was ~ed over the wheel** er war über dem Steuer zusammengesackt

slung [slʌŋ] *pt, pp of* **sling**

slur [slə:^r] *n* (*fig*): **~ (on)** Beleidigung *f* (für) ▷ *vt* (*words*) undeutlich aussprechen; **to cast a ~ on** verunglimpfen

slush [slʌʃ] *n* (*melted snow*) Schneematsch *m*

slut [slʌt] (*pej*) *n* Schlampe *f*

sly [slaɪ] *adj* (*smile, expression*) wissend; (*remark*) vielsagend; (*person*) schlau, gerissen; **on the**

~ heimlich

smack [smæk] *n* Klaps *m*; (*on face*) Ohrfeige *f* ▷ *vt* (*hit*) schlagen; (: *child*) einen Klaps geben +*dat*; (: *on face*) ohrfeigen ▷ *vi*: **to ~ of** riechen nach ▷ *adv*: **it fell ~ in the middle** (*inf*) es fiel genau in die Mitte; **to ~ one's lips** schmatzen

small [smɔːl] *adj* klein ▷ *n*: **the ~ of the back** das Kreuz; **to get** *or* **grow ~er** (*thing*) kleiner werden; (*numbers*) zurückgehen; **to make ~er** (*amount, income*) kürzen; (*object, garment*) kleiner machen; **a ~ shopkeeper** der Inhaber eines kleinen Geschäfts; **a ~ business** ein Kleinunternehmen *nt*

small ads (*Brit*) *npl* Kleinanzeigen *pl*

small change *n* Kleingeld *nt*

smallholder ['smɔːlhəuldəʳ] (*Brit*) *n* Kleinbauer *m*

small hours *npl*: **in the ~** in den frühen Morgenstunden

smallpox ['smɔːlpɔks] *n* Pocken *pl*

small talk *n* (oberflächliche) Konversation *f*

smart [smɑːt] *adj* (*neat*) ordentlich, gepflegt; (*fashionable*) chic *inv*, elegant; (*clever*) intelligent, clever (*inf*); (*quick*) schnell ▷ *vi* (*sting*) brennen; (*suffer*) leiden; **the ~ set** die Schickeria (*inf*); **and look ~ (about it)!** und zwar ein bisschen plötzlich! (*inf*)

smart card *n* Chipkarte *f*

smarten up ['smɑːtn-] *vi* sich fein machen ▷ *vt* verschönern

smash [smæʃ] *n* (*also*: **smash-up**) Unfall *m*; (*sound*) Krachen *nt*; (*song, play, film*) Superhit *m*; (*Tennis*) Schmetterball *m* ▷ *vt* (*break*) zerbrechen; (*car etc*) kaputt fahren; (*hopes*) zerschlagen; (*Sport*: *record*) haushoch schlagen ▷ *vi* (*break*) zerbrechen; (*against wall, into sth etc*) krachen

▸ **smash up** *vt* (*car*) kaputt fahren; (*room*) kurz und klein schlagen (*inf*)

smashing ['smæʃɪŋ] (*inf*) *adj* super, toll

smattering ['smætərɪŋ] *n*: **a ~ of Greek** *etc* ein paar Brocken Griechisch *etc*

smear [smɪəʳ] *n* (*trace*) verschmierter Fleck *m*; (*insult*) Verleumdung *f*; (*Med*) Abstrich *m* ▷ *vt* (*spread*) verschmieren; (*make dirty*) beschmieren; **his hands were ~ed with oil/ink** seine Hände waren mit Öl/Tinte beschmiert

smear campaign *n* Verleumdungskampagne *f*

smear test *n* Abstrich *m*

smell [smɛl] (*pt, pp* **smelt** *or* **~ed**) *n* Geruch *m*; (*sense*) Geruchssinn *m* ▷ *vt* riechen ▷ *vi* riechen; (*pej*) stinken; (*pleasantly*) duften; **to ~ of** riechen nach

smelly ['smɛlɪ] (*pej*) *adj* stinkend

smelt [smɛlt] *pt, pp of* **smell** ▷ *vt* schmelzen

smile [smaɪl] *n* Lächeln *nt* ▷ *vi* lächeln

smirk [smɔːk] (*pej*) *n* Grinsen *nt*

smock [smɔk] *n* Kittel *m*; (*US*: *overall*) Overall *m*

smog [smɔg] *n* Smog *m*

smoke [sməuk] *n* Rauch *m* ▷ *vi, vt* rauchen; **to have a ~** eine rauchen; **to go up in ~** in Rauch (und Flammen) aufgehen; (*fig*) sich in Rauch auflösen; **do you ~?** rauchen Sie?

smoked [sməukt] *adj* geräuchert, Räucher-; **~ glass** Rauchglas *nt*

smoker ['sməukəʳ] *n* Raucher(in) *m(f)*; (*Rail*) Raucherabteil *nt*

smoke screen *n* Rauchvorhang *m*; (*fig*) Deckmantel *m*

smoking ['sməukɪŋ] *n* Rauchen *nt*; **"no ~"** "Rauchen verboten"

smoking compartment, (US) **smoking car** *n* Raucherabteil *nt*

smoky ['sməukɪ] *adj* verraucht; (*taste*) rauchig

smolder ['sməuldəʳ] (US) *vi* = **smoulder**

smooth [smuːð] *adj* (*lit, fig*: *pej*) glatt; (*flavour, whisky*) weich; (*movement*) geschmeidig; (*flight*) ruhig

▸ **smooth out** *vt* glätten; (*fig*: *difficulties*) aus dem Weg räumen

▸ **smooth over** *vt*: **to ~ things over** (*fig*) die Sache bereinigen

smother ['smʌðəʳ] *vt* (*fire, person*) ersticken; (*repress*) unterdrücken

smoulder, (US) **smolder** ['sməuldəʳ] *vi* (*lit, fig*) glimmen, schwelen

SMS *n abbr* (= *Short Message Service*) SMS *m*

smudge [smʌdʒ] *n* Schmutzfleck *m* ▷ *vt* verwischen

smug [smʌg] (*pej*) *adj* selbstgefällig

smuggle ['smʌgl] *vt* schmuggeln; **to ~ in/out** einschmuggeln/herausschmuggeln

smuggler ['smʌgləʳ] *n* Schmuggler(in) *m(f)*

smuggling ['smʌglɪŋ] *n* Schmuggel *m*

smutty ['smʌtɪ] *adj* (*fig*: *joke, book*) schmutzig

snack [snæk] *n* Kleinigkeit *f* (zu essen); **to have a ~** eine Kleinigkeit essen

snack bar *n* Imbissstube *f*

snag [snæg] *n* Haken *m*, Schwierigkeit *f*

snail [sneɪl] *n* Schnecke *f*

snake [sneɪk] *n* Schlange *f*

snap [snæp] *n* Knacken *nt*; (*photograph*) Schnappschuss *m*; (*card game*) ≈ Schnippschnapp *nt* ▷ *adj* (*decision*) plötzlich, spontan ▷ *vt* (*break*) (zer)brechen ▷ *vi* (*break*) (zer)brechen; (*rope, thread etc*) reißen; **a cold ~** ein Kälteeinbruch *m*; **his patience ~ped** ihm riss der Geduldsfaden; **his temper ~ped** er verlor die Beherrschung; **to ~ one's fingers** mit den Fingern schnipsen *or* schnalzen; **to ~ open/shut** auf-/zuschnappen

▸ **snap at** *vt fus* (*dog*) schnappen nach; (*fig*: *person*) anschnauzen (*inf*)

▸ **snap off** *vt* (*break*) abbrechen

▸ **snap up** *vt* (*bargains*) wegschnappen

snappy ['snæpɪ] (*inf*) *adj* (*answer*) kurz und treffend; (*slogan*) zündend; **make it ~** ein bisschen dalli!; **he is a ~ dresser** er zieht sich flott an

snapshot ['snæpʃɔt] *n* Schnappschuss *m*

snare [snɛəʳ] *n* Falle *f* ▷ *vt* (*lit, fig*) fangen

snarl [snɑːl] *vi* knurren ▷ *vt*: **to get ~ed up**

(*plans*) durcheinanderkommen; (*traffic*) stocken
snatch [snætʃ] *n* (*of conversation*) Fetzen *m*; (*of song*) paar Takte *pl* ▷ *vt* (*grab*) greifen; (*steal*) stehlen, klauen (*inf*); (*child*) entführen; (*fig: opportunity*) ergreifen; (*: look*) werfen ▷ *vi*: **don't ~!** nicht grapschen!; **to ~ a sandwich** schnell ein Butterbrot essen; **to ~ some sleep** etwas Schlaf ergattern
▸ **snatch up** *vt* schnappen
sneak [sni:k] (*pt* **snuck**) (US) *vi*: **to ~ in/out** sich einschleichen/sich hinausschleichen ▷ *vt*: **to ~ a look at sth** heimlich auf etw *acc* schielen ▷ *n* (*inf: pej*) Petze *f*
▸ **sneak up** *vi*: **to ~ up on sb** sich an jdn heranschleichen
sneakers ['sni:kəz] *npl* Freizeitschuhe *pl*
sneer [snɪə[r]] *vi* (*smile nastily*) spöttisch lächeln; (*mock*): **to ~ at** verspotten ▷ *n* (*smile*) spöttisches Lächeln *nt*; (*remark*) spöttische Bemerkung *f*
sneeze [sni:z] *n* Niesen *nt* ▷ *vi* niesen
▸ **sneeze at** *vt fus*: **it's not to be ~d at** es ist nicht zu verachten
sniff [snɪf] *n* Schniefen *nt*; (*smell*) Schnüffeln *nt* ▷ *vi* schniefen ▷ *vt* riechen, schnuppern an *+dat*; (*glue*) schnüffeln
snigger ['snɪgə[r]] *vi* kichern
snip [snɪp] *n* Schnitt *m*; (*Brit: inf: bargain*) Schnäppchen *nt* ▷ *vt* schnippeln; **to ~ sth off/through sth** etw abschnippeln/durchschnippeln
sniper ['snaɪpə[r]] *n* Heckenschütze *m*
snippet ['snɪpɪt] *n* (*of information*) Bruchstück *nt*; (*of conversation*) Fetzen *m*
snob [snɔb] *n* Snob *m*
snobbish ['snɔbɪʃ] *adj* snobistisch, versnobt (*inf*)
snooker ['snu:kə[r]] *n* Snooker *nt* ▷ *vt* (*Brit: inf*): **to be ~ed** festsitzen
snoop [snu:p] *vi*: **to ~ about** herumschnüffeln; **to ~ on sb** jdm nachschnüffeln
snooze [snu:z] *n* Schläfchen *nt* ▷ *vi* ein Schläfchen machen
snore [snɔ:[r]] *n* Schnarchen *nt* ▷ *vi* schnarchen
snorkel ['snɔ:kl] *n* Schnorchel *m*
snort [snɔ:t] *n* Schnauben *nt* ▷ *vi* (*animal*) schnauben; (*person*) prusten ▷ *vt* (*inf: cocaine*) schnüffeln
snout [snaut] *n* Schnauze *f*
snow [snəu] *n* Schnee *m* ▷ *vi* schneien ▷ *vt*: **to be ~ed under with work** mit Arbeit reichlich eingedeckt sein; **it's ~ing** es schneit
snowball ['snəubɔ:l] *n* Schneeball *m* ▷ *vi* (*fig: problem*) eskalieren; (*: campaign*) ins Rollen kommen
snowbound ['snəubaund] *adj* eingeschneit
snowdrift ['snəudrɪft] *n* Schneewehe *f*
snowdrop ['snəudrɔp] *n* Schneeglöckchen *nt*
snowfall ['snəufɔ:l] *n* Schneefall *m*
snowflake ['snəufleɪk] *n* Schneeflocke *f*
snowman ['snəumæn] (*irreg: like* **man**) *n* Schneemann *m*
snowplough, (US) **snowplow** ['snəuplau] *n* Schneepflug *m*
snowshoe ['snəuʃu:] *n* Schneeschuh *m*
snowstorm ['snəustɔ:m] *n* Schneesturm *m*
snub [snʌb] *vt* (*person*) vor den Kopf stoßen ▷ *n* Abfuhr *f*
snub-nosed [snʌb'nəuzd] *adj* stupsnasig
snuff [snʌf] *n* Schnupftabak *m* ▷ *vt* (*also*: **snuff out**: *candle*) auslöschen
snug [snʌg] *adj* behaglich, gemütlich; (*well-fitting*) gut sitzend; **it's a ~ fit** es passt genau
snuggle ['snʌgl] *vi*: **to ~ up to sb** sich an jdn kuscheln; **to ~ down in bed** sich ins Bett kuscheln
so [səu] *adv* **1** (*thus, likewise*) so; **so saying he walked away** mit diesen Worten ging er weg; **if so** falls ja; **I didn't do it — you did so!** ich hab es nicht getan — hast du wohl!; **so do I, so am I** *etc* ich auch; **it's 5 o'clock — so it is!** es ist 5 Uhr — tatsächlich!; **I hope/think so** ich hoffe/glaube ja; **so far** bis jetzt
2 (*in comparisons etc: to such a degree*) so; **so big/quickly (that)** so groß/schnell(, dass); **I'm so glad to see you** ich bin ja so froh, dich zu sehen
3: **so much** so viel; **I've got so much work** ich habe so viel Arbeit; **I love you so much** ich liebe dich so sehr; **so many** so viele
4 (*phrases*): **10 or so** 10 oder so; **so long!** (*inf: goodbye*) tschüss!
▷ *conj* **1** (*expressing purpose*): **so as to do sth** um etw zu tun; **so (that)** damit
2 (*expressing result*) also; **so I was right after all** ich hatte also doch Recht; **so you see, I could have gone** wie Sie sehen, hätte ich gehen können; **so (what)?** na und?
soak [səuk] *vt* (*drench*) durchnässen; (*steep*) einweichen ▷ *vi* einweichen; **to be ~ed through** völlig durchnässt sein
▸ **soak in** *vi* einziehen
▸ **soak up** *vt* aufsaugen
soaking ['səukɪŋ] *adj* (*also*: **soaking wet**) patschnass
so-and-so ['səuənsəu] *n* (*somebody*) Soundso *no art*; **Mr/Mrs ~** Herr/Frau Soundso; **the little ~!** (*pej*) das Biest!
soap [səup] *n* Seife *f*; (TV: *also*: **soap opera**) Fernsehserie *f*, Seifenoper *f* (*inf*)
soapflakes ['səupfleɪks] *npl* Seifenflocken *pl*
soap opera *n* (TV) Fernsehserie *f*, Seifenoper *f* (*inf*)
soap powder *n* Seifenpulver *nt*
soapy ['səupɪ] *adj* seifig; **~ water** Seifenwasser *nt*
soar [sɔ:[r]] *vi* aufsteigen; (*price, temperature*) hochschnellen; (*building etc*) aufragen
sob [sɔb] *n* Schluchzer *m* ▷ *vi* schluchzen
sober ['səubə[r]] *adj* nüchtern; (*serious*) ernst; (*colour*) gedeckt; (*style*) schlicht
▸ **sober up** *vt* nüchtern machen ▷ *vi*

nüchtern werden
so-called ['səu'kɔ:ld] *adj* sogenannt
soccer ['sɔkə^r] *n* Fußball *m*
sociable ['səuʃəbl] *adj* gesellig
social ['səuʃl] *adj* sozial; (*history*) Sozial-; (*structure*) Gesellschafts-; (*event, contact*) gesellschaftlich; (*person*) gesellig; (*animal*) gesellig lebend ▷ *n* (*party*) geselliger Abend *m*; **~ life** gesellschaftliches Leben *nt*; **to have no ~ life** nicht mit anderen Leuten zusammenkommen
social club *n* Klub *m* für geselliges Beisammensein
socialism ['səuʃəlɪzəm] *n* Sozialismus *m*
socialist ['səuʃəlɪst] *adj* sozialistisch ▷ *n* Sozialist(in) *m(f)*
socialize ['səuʃəlaɪz] *vi* unter die Leute kommen; **to ~ with** (*meet socially*) gesellschaftlich verkehren mit; (*chat to*) sich unterhalten mit
socially ['səuʃəlɪ] *adv* (*visit*) privat; (*acceptable*) in Gesellschaft
social security (*Brit*) *n* Sozialhilfe *f*; **Department of Social Security** Ministerium *nt* für Soziales
social services *npl* soziale Einrichtungen *pl*
social work *n* Sozialarbeit *f*
social worker *n* Sozialarbeiter(in) *m(f)*
society [sə'saɪətɪ] *n* Gesellschaft *f*; (*people, their lifestyle*) die Gesellschaft; (*club*) Verein *m*; (*also*: **high society**) High Society *f* ▷ *cpd* (*party, lady*) Gesellschafts-
sociology [səusɪ'ɔlədʒɪ] *n* Soziologie *f*
sock [sɔk] *n* Socke *f* ▷ *vt* (*inf: hit*) hauen; **to pull one's ~s up** (*fig*) sich am Riemen reißen
socket ['sɔkɪt] *n* (*of eye*) Augenhöhle *f*; (*of joint*) Gelenkpfanne *f*; (*Brit: Elec: also*: **wall socket**) Steckdose *f*; (*: for light bulb*) Fassung *f*
sod [sɔd] *n* (*earth*) Sode *f*; (*Brit: inf!*) Sau *f* (*!*); **the poor ~** das arme Schwein
▸ **sod off** (*Brit: inf!*) *vi*: **~ off!** verpiss dich!
soda ['səudə] *n* Soda *nt*; (*also*: **soda water**) Soda(wasser) *nt*; (*US: also*: **soda pop**) Brause *f*
sodium ['səudɪəm] *n* Natrium *nt*
sofa ['səufə] *n* Sofa *nt*
soft [sɔft] *adj* weich; (*not rough*) zart; (*voice, music, light, colour*) gedämpft; (*lenient*) nachsichtig; **~ in the head** (*inf*) nicht ganz richtig im Kopf
soft drink *n* alkoholfreies Getränk *nt*
soft drugs *npl* weiche Drogen *pl*
soften ['sɔfn] *vt* weich machen; (*effect, blow*) mildern ▷ *vi* weich werden; (*voice, expression*) sanfter werden
softly ['sɔftlɪ] *adv* (*gently*) sanft; (*quietly*) leise
softness ['sɔftnɪs] *n* Weichheit *f*; (*gentleness*) Sanftheit *f*
software ['sɔftwɛə^r] *n* (*Comput*) Software *f*
soggy ['sɔgɪ] *adj* (*ground*) durchweicht; (*sandwiches etc*) matschig
soil [sɔɪl] *n* Erde *f*, Boden *m* ▷ *vt* beschmutzen
solar ['səulə^r] *adj* (*eclipse, power station etc*) Sonnen-
solar panel *n* Sonnenkollektor *m*
solar power *n* Sonnenenergie *f*
solar system *n* Sonnensystem *nt*
sold [səuld] *pt, pp of* **sell**
solder ['səuldə^r] *vt* löten ▷ *n* Lötmittel *nt*
soldier ['səuldʒə^r] *n* Soldat *m* ▷ *vi*: **to ~ on** unermüdlich weitermachen; **toy ~** Spielzeugsoldat *m*
sold out *adj* ausverkauft
sole [səul] *n* Sohle *f*; (*fish: pl inv*) Seezunge *f* ▷ *adj* einzig, Allein-; (*exclusive*) alleinig; **the ~ reason** der einzige Grund
solely ['səullɪ] *adv* nur, ausschließlich; **I will hold you ~ responsible** ich mache Sie allein dafür verantwortlich
solemn ['sɔləm] *adj* feierlich; (*person*) ernst
sole trader *n* (*Comm*) Einzelunternehmer *m*
solicit [sə'lɪsɪt] *vt* (*request*) erbitten, bitten um ▷ *vi* (*prostitute*) Kunden anwerben
solicitor [sə'lɪsɪtə^r] (*Brit*) *n* Rechtsanwalt *m*, Rechtsanwältin *f*
solid ['sɔlɪd] *adj* (*not hollow, pure*) massiv; (*not liquid*) fest; (*reliable*) zuverlässig; (*strong: structure*) stabil; (*: foundations*) solide; (*substantial: advice*) gut; (*: experience*) solide; (*unbroken*) ununterbrochen ▷ *n* (*solid object*) Festkörper *m*; **solids** *npl* (*food*) feste Nahrung *f*; **to be on ~ ground** (*fig*) sich auf festem Boden befinden; **I read for 2 hours ~** ich habe 2 Stunden ununterbrochen gelesen
solidarity [sɔlɪ'dærɪtɪ] *n* Solidarität *f*
solitary ['sɔlɪtərɪ] *adj* einsam; (*single*) einzeln
solitary confinement *n* Einzelhaft *f*
solitude ['sɔlɪtju:d] *n* Einsamkeit *f*; **to live in ~** einsam leben
solo ['səuləu] *n* Solo *nt* ▷ *adv* (*fly*) allein; (*play, perform*) solo; **~ flight** Alleinflug *m*
soloist ['səuləuɪst] *n* Solist(in) *m(f)*
soluble ['sɔljubl] *adj* löslich
solution [sə'lu:ʃən] *n* (*answer, liquid*) Lösung *f*; (*to crossword*) Auflösung *f*
solve [sɔlv] *vt* lösen; (*mystery*) enträtseln
solvent ['sɔlvənt] *adj* (*Comm*) zahlungsfähig ▷ *n* (*Chem*) Lösungsmittel *nt*
sombre, (*US*) **somber** ['sɔmbə^r] *adj* (*dark*) dunkel, düster; (*serious*) finster
some [sʌm] *adj* **1** (*a certain amount or number of*) einige; **some tea/water/money** etwas Tee/Wasser/Geld; **some biscuits** ein paar Plätzchen; **some children came** einige Kinder kamen; **he asked me some questions** er stellte mir ein paar Fragen
2 (*certain: in contrasts*) manche(r, s); **some people say that ...** manche Leute sagen, dass ...; **some films were excellent** einige *or* manche Filme waren ausgezeichnet
3 (*unspecified*) irgendein(e); **some woman was asking for you** eine Frau hat nach Ihnen gefragt; **some day** eines Tages; **some day next week** irgendwann nächste Woche; **that's some house!** das ist vielleicht ein Haus!
▷ *pron* **1** (*a certain number*) einige; **I've got**

some (*books etc*) ich habe welche
2 (*a certain amount*) etwas; **I've got some** (*money, milk*) ich habe welche(s); **I've read some of the book** ich habe das Buch teilweise gelesen
▷ *adv*: **some 10 people** etwa 10 Leute

somebody ['sʌmbədɪ] *pron* = **someone**

somehow ['sʌmhau] *adv* irgendwie

someone ['sʌmwʌn] *pron* (irgend)jemand; **there's ~ coming** es kommt jemand; **I saw ~ in the garden** ich habe jemanden im Garten gesehen

someplace ['sʌmpleɪs] (*US*) *adv* = **somewhere**

somersault ['sʌməsɔːlt] *n* Salto *m* ▷ *vi* einen Salto machen; (*vehicle*) sich überschlagen

something ['sʌmθɪŋ] *pron* etwas; **~ nice** etwas Schönes; **there's ~ wrong** da stimmt etwas nicht; **would you like ~ to eat/drink?** möchten Sie etwas zu essen/trinken?

sometime ['sʌmtaɪm] *adv* irgendwann; **~ last month** irgendwann letzten Monat; **I'll finish it ~** ich werde es irgendwann fertig machen

sometimes ['sʌmtaɪmz] *adv* manchmal

somewhat ['sʌmwɔt] *adv* etwas, ein wenig; **~ to my surprise** ziemlich zu meiner Überraschung

somewhere ['sʌmwɛəʳ] *adv* (*be*) irgendwo; (*go*) irgendwohin; **~ (or other) in Scotland** irgendwo in Schottland; **~ else** (*be*) woanders; (*go*) woandershin

son [sʌn] *n* Sohn *m*

song [sɔŋ] *n* Lied *nt*; (*of bird*) Gesang *m*

son-in-law ['sʌnɪnlɔː] *n* Schwiegersohn *m*

soon [suːn] *adv* bald; (*a short time after*) bald, schnell; (*early*) früh; **~ afterwards** kurz *or* bald danach; **quite ~** ziemlich bald; **how ~ can you finish it?** bis wann haben Sie es fertig?; **how ~ can you come back?** wann können Sie frühestens wiederkommen?; **see you ~!** bis bald!; *see also* **as**

sooner ['suːnəʳ] *adv* (*time*) früher, eher; (*preference*) lieber; **I would ~ do that** das würde ich lieber tun; **~ or later** früher oder später; **the ~ the better** je eher, desto besser; **no ~ said than done** gesagt, getan; **no ~ had we left than ...** wir waren gerade gegangen, da ...

soot [sut] *n* Ruß *m*

soothe [suːð] *vt* beruhigen; (*pain*) lindern

sophisticated [sə'fɪstɪkeɪtɪd] *adj* (*woman, lifestyle*) kultiviert; (*audience*) anspruchsvoll; (*machinery*) hoch entwickelt; (*arguments*) differenziert

sophomore ['sɔfəmɔːʳ] (*US*) *n* *Student(in) im 2. Studienjahr*

sopping ['sɔpɪŋ] *adj*: **~ (wet)** völlig durchnässt

soppy ['sɔpɪ] (*pej*) *adj* (*person*) sentimental; (*film*) schmalzig

soprano [sə'prɑːnəu] *n* Sopranist(in) *m(f)*

sorbet ['sɔːbeɪ] *n* Sorbet *nt or m*, Fruchteis *nt*

sorcerer ['sɔːsərəʳ] *n* Hexenmeister *m*

sordid ['sɔːdɪd] *adj* (*dirty*) verkommen; (*wretched*) elend

sore [sɔːʳ] *adj* wund; (*esp US: offended*) verärgert, sauer (*inf*) ▷ *n* wunde Stelle *f*; **to have a ~ throat** Halsschmerzen haben; **it's a ~ point** (*fig*) es ist ein wunder Punkt

sorely ['sɔːlɪ] *adv*: **I am ~ tempted (to)** ich bin sehr in Versuchung(, zu)

sorrow ['sɔrəu] *n* Trauer *f*; **sorrows** *npl* (*troubles*) Sorgen und Nöte *pl*

sorry ['sɔrɪ] *adj* traurig; (*excuse*) faul; (*sight*) jämmerlich; **~!** Entschuldigung!, Verzeihung!; **~?** wie bitte?; **I feel ~ for him** er tut mir leid; **I'm ~ to hear that ...** es tut mir leid, dass ...; **I'm ~ about ...** es tut mir leid wegen ...

sort [sɔːt] *n* Sorte *f*; (*make: of car etc*) Marke *f* ▷ *vt* (*also*: **sort out**) sortieren; (*: problems*) ins Reine bringen; (*Comput*) sortieren; **all ~s of reasons** alle möglichen Gründe; **what ~ do you want?** welche Sorte möchten Sie?; **what ~ of car?** was für ein Auto?; **I'll do nothing of the ~!** das kommt überhaupt nicht infrage!; **it's ~ of awkward** (*inf*) es ist irgendwie schwierig; **to ~ sth out** etw in Ordnung bringen

sorting office ['sɔːtɪŋ-] *n* Postverteilstelle *f*

SOS *n abbr* (*= save our souls*) SOS *nt*

so-so ['səusəu] *adv, adj* so lala

sought [sɔːt] *pt, pp of* **seek**

soul [səul] *n* Seele *f*; (*Mus*) Soul *m*; **the poor ~ had nowhere to sleep** der Ärmste hatte keine Unterkunft; **I didn't see a ~** ich habe keine Menschenseele gesehen

soulful ['səulful] *adj* (*eyes*) seelenvoll; (*music*) gefühlvoll

sound [saund] *adj* (*healthy*) gesund; (*safe, secure*) sicher; (*not damaged*) einwandfrei; (*reliable*) solide; (*thorough*) gründlich; (*sensible, valid*) vernünftig ▷ *adv*: **to be ~ asleep** tief und fest schlafen ▷ *n* Geräusch *nt*; (*Mus*) Klang *m*; (*on TV etc*) Ton *m*; (*Geog*) Meerenge *f*, Sund *m* ▷ *vt*: **to ~ the alarm** Alarm schlagen ▷ *vi* (*alarm, horn*) ertönen; (*fig: seem*) sich anhören, klingen; **to be of ~ mind** bei klarem Verstand sein; **I don't like the ~ of it** das klingt gar nicht gut; **to ~ one's horn** (*Aut*) hupen; **to ~ like** sich anhören wie; **that ~s like them arriving** das hört sich so an, als ob sie ankommen; **it ~s as if ...** es klingt *or* es hört sich so an, als ob ...
▸ **sound off** (*inf*) *vi*: **to ~ off (about)** sich auslassen (über +*acc*)
▸ **sound out** *vt* (*person*) aushorchen; (*opinion*) herausbekommen

sound barrier *n* Schallmauer *f*

sound bite *n* prägnantes Zitat *nt*

sound effects *npl* Toneffekte *pl*

soundly ['saundlɪ] *adv* (*sleep*) tief und fest; (*beat*) tüchtig

soundproof ['saundpruːf] *adj* schalldicht ▷ *vt* schalldicht machen

soundtrack ['saundtræk] *n* Filmmusik *f*

soup [suːp] *n* Suppe *f*; **to be in the ~** (*fig*) in

der Tinte sitzen
soup plate *n* Suppenteller *m*
soupspoon ['su:pspu:n] *n* Suppenlöffel *m*
sour ['sauə[r]] *adj* sauer; (*fig: bad-tempered*) säuerlich; **to go** *or* **turn ~** (*milk, wine*) sauer werden; (*fig: relationship*) sich trüben; **it's ~ grapes** (*fig*) die Trauben hängen zu hoch
source [sɔ:s] *n* Quelle *f*; (*fig: of problem, anxiety*) Ursache *f*; **I have it from a reliable ~ that ...** ich habe es aus sicherer Quelle, dass ...
south [sauθ] *n* Süden *m* ▷ *adj* südlich, Süd- ▷ *adv* nach Süden; **(to the) ~ of** im Süden *or* südlich von; **to travel ~** nach Süden fahren; **the S~ of France** Südfrankreich *nt*
South Africa *n* Südafrika *nt*
South African *adj* südafrikanisch ▷ *n* Südafrikaner(in) *m(f)*
South America *n* Südamerika *nt*
South American *adj* südamerikanisch ▷ *n* Südamerikaner(in) *m(f)*
southbound ['sauθbaund] *adj* in Richtung Süden; (*carriageway*) Richtung Süden
south-east [sauθ'i:st] *n* Südosten *m*
southerly ['sʌðəlɪ] *adj* südlich; (*wind*) aus südlicher Richtung
southern ['sʌðən] *adj* südlich, Süd-; **the ~ hemisphere** die südliche Halbkugel *or* Hemisphäre
South Korea *n* Südkorea *nt*
South Pole *n* Südpol *m*
southward ['sauθwəd], **southwards** ['sauθwədz] *adv* nach Süden, in Richtung Süden
south-west [sauθ'wɛst] *n* Südwesten *m*
souvenir [su:və'nɪə[r]] *n* Andenken *nt*, Souvenir *nt*
sovereign ['sɔvrɪn] *n* Herrscher(in) *m(f)*
soviet ['səuvɪət] (*formerly*) *adj* sowjetisch ▷ *n* Sowjetbürger(in) *m(f)*; **the S~ Union** die Sowjetunion *f*
sow[1] [sau] *n* Sau *f*
sow[2] [səu] (*pt* **~ed**, *pp* **~n**) *vt* (*lit, fig*) säen
soya ['sɔɪə], **soy** [sɔɪ] (*US*) *n*: **~ bean** Sojabohne *f*; **~ sauce** Sojasoße *f*
spa [spɑ:] *n* (*town*) Heilbad *nt*; (*US: also*: **health spa**) Fitnesszentrum *nt*
space [speɪs] *n* Platz *m*, Raum *m*; (*gap*) Lücke *f*; (*beyond Earth*) der Weltraum; (*interval, period*) Zeitraum *m* ▷ *cpd* Raum- ▷ *vt* (*also*: **space out**) verteilen; **to clear a ~ for sth** für etw Platz schaffen; **in a confined ~** auf engem Raum; **in a short ~ of time** in kurzer Zeit; **(with)in the ~ of an hour** innerhalb einer Stunde
spacecraft ['speɪskrɑ:ft] *n* Raumfahrzeug *nt*
spaceman ['speɪsmæn] (*irreg: like* **man**) *n* Raumfahrer *m*
spaceship ['speɪsʃɪp] *n* Raumschiff *nt*
spacing ['speɪsɪŋ] *n* Abstand *m*; **single/double ~** einfacher/doppelter Zeilenabstand
spacious ['speɪʃəs] *adj* geräumig
spade [speɪd] *n* Spaten *m*; (*child's*) Schaufel *f*; **spades** *npl* (*Cards*) Pik *nt*
spaghetti [spə'gɛtɪ] *n* Spag(h)etti *pl*
Spain [speɪn] *n* Spanien *nt*
spam [spæm] (*Comput*) *n* Spam *m* ▷ *vt* wit Werbung bombardieren
span [spæn] *n* (*of bird, plane, arch*) Spannweite *f*; (*in time*) Zeitspanne *f* ▷ *vt* überspannen; (*fig: time*) sich erstrecken über *+acc*
Spaniard ['spænjəd] *n* Spanier(in) *m(f)*
spaniel ['spænjəl] *n* Spaniel *m*
Spanish ['spænɪʃ] *adj* spanisch ▷ *n* (*Ling*) Spanisch *nt*; **the Spanish** *npl* die Spanier *pl*; **~ omelette** *Omelett mit Paprikaschoten, Zwiebeln, Tomaten etc*
spank [spæŋk] *vt*: **to ~ sb's bottom** jdm den Hintern versohlen (*inf*)
spanner ['spænə[r]] (*Brit*) *n* Schraubenschlüssel *m*
spare [spɛə[r]] *adj* (*free*) frei; (*extra: part, fuse etc*) Ersatz- ▷ *n* = **spare part** ▷ *vt* (*save: trouble etc*) (er)sparen; (*make available*) erübrigen; (*afford to give*) (übrig) haben; (*refrain from hurting*) verschonen; **these 2 are going ~** diese beiden sind noch übrig; **to ~** (*surplus*) übrig; **to ~ no expense** keine Kosten scheuen, an nichts sparen; **can you ~ the time?** haben Sie Zeit?; **I've a few minutes to ~** ich habe ein paar Minuten Zeit; **there is no time to ~** es ist keine Zeit; **~ me the details** verschone mich mit den Einzelheiten
spare part *n* Ersatzteil *nt*
spare room *n* Gästezimmer *nt*
spare time *n* Freizeit *f*
spare tyre *n* Reservereifen *m*
spare wheel *n* Reserverad *nt*
sparingly ['spɛərɪŋlɪ] *adv* sparsam
spark [spɑ:k] *n* (*lit, fig*) Funke *m*
sparkle ['spɑ:kl] *n* Funkeln *nt*, Glitzern *nt* ▷ *vi* funkeln, glitzern
sparkling ['spɑ:klɪŋ] *adj* (*water*) mit Kohlensäure; (*conversation*) vor Geist sprühend; (*performance*) glänzend; **~ wine** Schaumwein *m*
spark plug *n* Zündkerze *f*
sparrow ['spærəu] *n* Spatz *m*
sparse [spɑ:s] *adj* spärlich; (*population*) dünn
spartan ['spɑ:tən] *adj* (*fig*) spartanisch
spasm ['spæzəm] *n* (*Med*) Krampf *m*; (*fig: of anger etc*) Anfall *m*
spasmodic [spæz'mɔdɪk] *adj* (*fig*) sporadisch
spastic ['spæstɪk] (*old*) *n* Spastiker(in) *m(f)* ▷ *adj* spastisch
spat [spæt] *pt, pp of* **spit** ▷ *n* (*US: quarrel*) Krach *m*
spate [speɪt] *n* (*fig*): **a ~ of** eine Flut von; **to be in full ~** (*river*) Hochwasser führen
spatula ['spætjulə] *n* (*Culin*) Spachtel *m*; (*Med*) Spatel *m*
spawn [spɔ:n] *vi* laichen ▷ *vt* hervorbringen, erzeugen ▷ *n* Laich *m*
speak [spi:k] (*pt* **spoke**, *pp* **spoken**) *vt* (*say*) sagen; (*language*) sprechen ▷ *vi* sprechen, reden; (*make a speech*) sprechen; **to ~ one's mind** seine Meinung sagen; **to ~ to sb/of**

or **about sth** mit jdm/über etw *acc* sprechen *or* reden; **~ up!** sprich lauter!; **to ~ at a conference** bei einer Tagung einen Vortrag halten; **to ~ in a debate** in einer Debatte sprechen; **he has no money to ~ of** er hat so gut wie kein Geld; **so to ~** sozusagen
▸ **speak for** *vt fus*: **to ~ for sb** (*on behalf of*) in jds Namen *dat or* für jdn sprechen; **that picture is already spoken for** (*in shop*) das Bild ist schon verkauft *or* vergeben; **~ for yourself!** das meinst auch nur du!

speaker ['spi:kəʳ] *n* (*in public*) Redner(in) *m(f)*; (*also*: **loudspeaker**) Lautsprecher *m*; (*Pol*): **the S~** (*Brit, US*) der Sprecher, die Sprecherin; **are you a Welsh ~?** sprechen Sie Walisisch?

spear [spɪəʳ] *n* Speer *m* ▹ *vt* aufspießen

spearhead ['spɪəhɛd] *vt* (*Mil, fig*) anführen

spec [spɛk] (*inf*) *n*: **on ~** auf Verdacht, auf gut Glück; **to buy/go on ~** auf gut Glück kaufen/hingehen

special ['spɛʃl] *adj* besondere(r, s); (*service, performance, adviser, permission, school*) Sonder- ▹ *n* (*train*) Sonderzug *m*; **take ~ care** pass besonders gut auf; **nothing ~** nichts Besonderes; **today's ~** (*at restaurant*) Tagesgericht *nt*

special delivery *n* (*Post*): **by ~** durch Eilzustellung

special effects *npl* Spezialeffekte *pl*

specialist ['spɛʃəlɪst] *n* Spezialist(in) *m(f)*; (*Med*) Facharzt *m*, Fachärztin *f*; **heart ~** Facharzt *m*/Fachärztin *f* für Herzkrankheiten

speciality [spɛʃɪ'ælɪtɪ] *n* Spezialität *f*; (*study*) Spezialgebiet *nt*

specialize ['spɛʃəlaɪz] *vi*: **to ~ (in)** sich spezialisieren (auf *+acc*)

specially ['spɛʃlɪ] *adv* besonders, extra

special offer *n* Sonderangebot *nt*

specialty ['spɛʃəltɪ] (*esp US*) = **speciality**

species ['spi:ʃi:z] *n inv* Art *f*

specific [spə'sɪfɪk] *adj* (*fixed*) bestimmt; (*exact*) genau; **to be ~ to** eigentümlich sein für

specifically [spə'sɪfɪklɪ] *adv* (*specially*) speziell; (*exactly*) genau; **more ~** und zwar

specification [spɛsɪfɪ'keɪʃən] *n* genaue Angabe *f*; (*requirement*) Bedingung *f*; **specifications** *npl* (*Tech*) technische Daten *pl*

specify ['spɛsɪfaɪ] *vt* angeben; **unless otherwise specified** wenn nicht anders angegeben

specimen ['spɛsɪmən] *n* Exemplar *nt*; (*Med*) Probe *f*

speck [spɛk] *n* Fleckchen *nt*; (*of dust*) Körnchen *nt*

speckled ['spɛkld] *adj* gesprenkelt

specs [spɛks] (*inf*) *npl* Brille *f*

spectacle ['spɛktəkl] *n* (*scene*) Schauspiel *nt*; (*sight*) Anblick *m*; (*grand event*) Spektakel *nt*; **spectacles** *npl* (*glasses*) Brille *f*

spectacular [spɛk'tækjuləʳ] *adj* sensationell; (*success*) spektakulär ▹ *n* (*Theat etc*) Show *f*

spectator [spɛk'teɪtəʳ] *n* Zuschauer(in) *m(f)*; **~ sport** Publikumssport *m*

spectrum ['spɛktrəm] (*pl* **spectra**) *n* (*lit, fig*) Spektrum *nt*

speculate ['spɛkjuleɪt] *vi* (*Fin*) spekulieren; **to ~ about** spekulieren *or* Vermutungen anstellen über *+acc*

speculation [spɛkju'leɪʃən] *n* Spekulation *f*

sped [spɛd] *pt, pp of* **speed**

speech [spi:tʃ] *n* Sprache *f*; (*manner of speaking*) Sprechweise *f*; (*enunciation*) (Aus)sprache *f*; (*formal talk: Theat*) Rede *f*

speechless ['spi:tʃlɪs] *adj* sprachlos

speed [spi:d] (*pt, pp* **sped**) *n* Geschwindigkeit *f*, Schnelligkeit *f* ▹ *vi* (*exceed speed limit*) zu schnell fahren; **to ~ along** dahinsausen; **to ~ by** (*car etc*) vorbeischießen; (*years*) verfliegen; **at ~** (*Brit*) mit hoher Geschwindigkeit; **at full** *or* **top ~** mit Höchstgeschwindigkeit; **at a ~ of 70km/h** mit (einer Geschwindigkeit *or* einem Tempo von) 70 km/h; **shorthand/typing ~s** Silben/Anschläge pro Minute; **a five-~ gearbox** ein Fünfganggetriebe *nt*
▸ **speed up** (*pt, pp* **~ed up**) *vi* beschleunigen; (*fig*) sich beschleunigen ▹ *vt* beschleunigen

speedboat ['spi:dbəut] *n* Rennboot *nt*

speedily ['spi:dɪlɪ] *adv* schnell

speeding ['spi:dɪŋ] *n* Geschwindigkeitsüberschreitung *f*

speed limit *n* Tempolimit *nt*, Geschwindigkeitsbegrenzung *f*

speedometer [spɪ'dɔmɪtəʳ] *n* Tachometer *m*

speedway ['spi:dweɪ] *n* (*also*: **speedway racing**) Speedway-Rennen *nt*

speedy ['spi:dɪ] *adj* schnell; (*reply, settlement*) prompt

spell [spɛl] (*Brit*) (*pt, pp* **~ed**) *n* (*also*: **magic spell**) Zauber *m*; (*incantation*) Zauberspruch *m*; (*period of time*) Zeit *f*, Weile *f* ▹ *vt* schreiben; (*also*: **spell out**: *aloud*) buchstabieren; (*signify*) bedeuten; **to cast a ~ on sb** jdn verzaubern; **cold ~** Kältewelle *f*; **how do you ~ your name?** wie schreibt sich Ihr Name?; **can you ~ it for me?** können Sie das bitte buchstabieren?; **he can't ~** er kann keine Rechtschreibung

spellbound ['spɛlbaund] *adj* gebannt

spelling ['spɛlɪŋ] *n* Schreibweise *f*; (*ability*) Rechtschreibung *f*; **~ mistake** Rechtschreibfehler *m*

spelt [spɛlt] *pt, pp of* **spell**

spend [spɛnd] (*pt, pp* **spent**) *vt* (*money*) ausgeben; (*time, life*) verbringen; **to ~ time/money/effort on sth** Zeit/Geld/Mühe für etw aufbringen

spending ['spɛndɪŋ] *n* Ausgaben *pl*; **government ~** öffentliche Ausgaben *pl*

spendthrift ['spɛndθrɪft] *n* Verschwender(in) *m(f)*

spent [spɛnt] *pt, pp of* **spend** ▹ *adj* (*patience*) erschöpft; (*cartridge, bullets*) verbraucht; (*match*) abgebrannt

sperm [spə:m] *n* Samenzelle *f*, Spermium *nt*

sphere [sfɪəʳ] *n* Kugel *f*; (*area*) Gebiet *nt*, Bereich *m*
spice [spaɪs] *n* Gewürz *nt* ▷ *vt* würzen
spicy ['spaɪsɪ] *adj* stark gewürzt
spider ['spaɪdəʳ] *n* Spinne *f*; **~'s web** Spinnengewebe *nt*, Spinnennetz *nt*
spike [spaɪk] *n* (*point*) Spitze *f*; (*Bot*) Ähre *f*; (*Elec*) Spannungsspitze *f*; **spikes** *npl* (*Sport*) Spikes *pl*
spill [spɪl] (*pt, pp* **spilt** *or* **~ed**) *vt* verschütten ▷ *vi* verschüttet werden; **to ~ the beans** (*inf: fig*) alles ausplaudern
▸ **spill out** *vi* (*people*) herausströmen
▸ **spill over** *vi* überlaufen; (*fig: spread*) sich ausbreiten; **to ~ over into** sich auswirken auf +*acc*
spin [spɪn] (*pt* **spun, span**, *pp* **spun**) *n* (*trip*) Spritztour *f*; (*revolution*) Drehung *f*; (*Aviat*) Trudeln *nt*; (*on ball*) Drall *m* ▷ *vt* (*wool etc*) spinnen; (*ball, coin*) (hoch)werfen; (*wheel*) drehen; (*Brit: also:* **spin-dry**) schleudern ▷ *vi* (*make thread*) spinnen; (*person*) sich drehen; (*car etc*) schleudern; **to ~ a yarn** Seemannsgarn spinnen; **to ~ a coin** (*Brit*) eine Münze werfen; **my head is ~ning** mir dreht sich alles
▸ **spin out** *vt* (*talk*) ausspinnen; (*job, holiday*) in die Länge ziehen; (*money*) strecken
spinach ['spɪnɪtʃ] *n* Spinat *m*
spinal ['spaɪnl] *adj* (*injury etc*) Rückgrat-
spinal cord *n* Rückenmark *nt*
spin doctor *n* PR-Fachmann *m*, PR-Fachfrau *f*
spin-dryer [spɪn'draɪəʳ] (*Brit*) *n* (Wäsche)schleuder *f*
spine [spaɪn] *n* (*Anat*) Rückgrat *nt*; (*thorn*) Stachel *m*
spineless ['spaɪnlɪs] *adj* (*fig*) rückgratlos
spinning ['spɪnɪŋ] *n* (*art*) Spinnen *nt*
spinning top *n* Kreisel *m*
spin-off ['spɪnɔf] *n* (*fig*) Nebenprodukt *nt*
spinster ['spɪnstəʳ] *n* unverheiratete Frau; (*pej*) alte Jungfer
spiral ['spaɪərl] *n* Spirale *f* ▷ *vi* (*fig: prices etc*) in die Höhe klettern; **the inflationary ~** die Inflationsspirale
spiral staircase *n* Wendeltreppe *f*
spire ['spaɪəʳ] *n* Turmspitze *f*
spirit ['spɪrɪt] *n* Geist *m*; (*soul*) Seele *f*; (*energy*) Elan *m*, Schwung *m*; (*courage*) Mut *m*; (*sense*) Geist *m*, Sinn *m*; (*frame of mind*) Stimmung *f*; **spirits** *npl* (*drink*) Spirituosen *pl*; **in good ~s** guter Laune; **community ~** Gemeinschaftssinn *m*
spirited ['spɪrɪtɪd] *adj* (*resistance, defence*) mutig; (*performance*) lebendig
spiritual ['spɪrɪtjuəl] *adj* geistig, seelisch; (*religious*) geistlich ▷ *n* (*also:* **Negro spiritual**) Spiritual *nt*
spit [spɪt] (*pt, pp* **spat**) *n* (*for roasting*) Spieß *m*; (*saliva*) Spucke *f* ▷ *vi* spucken; (*fire*) Funken sprühen; (*cooking*) spritzen; (*inf: rain*) tröpfeln
spite [spaɪt] *n* Boshaftigkeit *f* ▷ *vt* ärgern; **in ~ of** trotz +*gen*
spiteful ['spaɪtful] *adj* boshaft, gemein
spittle ['spɪtl] *n* Speichel *m*, Spucke *f*
splash [splæʃ] *n* (*sound*) Platschen *nt*; (*of colour*) Tupfer *m* ▷ *excl* platsch! ▷ *vt* bespritzen ▷ *vi* (*also:* **splash about**) herumplan(t)schen; (*water, rain*) spritzen; **to ~ paint on the floor** den Fußboden mit Farbe bespritzen
spleen [spli:n] *n* Milz *f*
splendid ['splɛndɪd] *adj* hervorragend, ausgezeichnet; (*impressive*) prächtig
splint [splɪnt] *n* Schiene *f*
splinter ['splɪntəʳ] *n* Splitter *m* ▷ *vi* (zer)splittern
split [splɪt] (*pt, pp* **~**) *n* (*tear*) Riss *m*; (*fig: division*) Aufteilung *f*; (*: difference*) Kluft *f*; (*Pol*) Spaltung *f* ▷ *vt* (*divide*) aufteilen; (*party*) spalten; (*share equally*) teilen ▷ *vi* (*divide*) sich aufteilen; (*tear*) reißen; **to do the ~s** (einen) Spagat machen; **let's ~ the difference** teilen wir uns die Differenz
▸ **split up** *vi* sich trennen; (*meeting*) sich auflösen
spoil [spɔɪl] (*pt, pp* **spoilt** *or* **~ed**) *vt* verderben; (*child*) verwöhnen; (*ballot paper, vote*) ungültig machen ▷ *vi*: **to be ~ing for a fight** Streit suchen
spoils [spɔɪlz] *npl* Beute *f*; (*fig*) Gewinn *m*
spoilsport ['spɔɪlspɔ:t] (*pej*) *n* Spielverderber *m*
spoilt [spɔɪlt] *pt, pp of* **spoil** ▷ *adj* (*child*) verwöhnt; (*ballot paper*) ungültig
spoke [spəuk] *pt of* **speak** ▷ *n* Speiche *f*
spoken ['spəukn] *pp of* **speak**
spokesman ['spəuksmən] (*irreg: like* **man**) *n* Sprecher *m*
spokesperson ['spəukspə:sn] *n* Sprecher(in) *m(f)*
spokeswoman ['spəukswumən] (*irreg: like* **woman**) *n* Sprecherin *f*
sponge [spʌndʒ] *n* Schwamm *m*; (*also:* **sponge cake**) Biskuit(kuchen) *m* ▷ *vt* mit einem Schwamm waschen ▷ *vi*: **to ~ off** *or* **on sb** jdm auf der Tasche liegen
sponge bag (*Brit*) *n* Waschbeutel *m*, Kulturbeutel *m*
sponsor ['spɔnsəʳ] *n* Sponsor(in) *m(f)*, Geldgeber(in) *m(f)*; (*Brit: for charitable event*) Sponsor(in) *m(f)*; (*for application, bill etc*) Befürworter(in) *m(f)* ▷ *vt* sponsern, finanziell unterstützen; (*fund-raiser*) sponsern; (*applicant*) unterstützen; (*proposal, bill etc*) befürworten; **I ~ed him at 3p a mile** (*in fund-raising race*) ich habe mich verpflichtet, ihm 3 Pence pro Meile zu geben
sponsorship ['spɔnsəʃɪp] *n* finanzielle Unterstützung *f*
spontaneous [spɔn'teɪnɪəs] *adj* spontan; **~ combustion** Selbstentzündung *f*
spooky ['spu:kɪ] (*inf*) *adj* gruselig
spool [spu:l] *n* Spule *f*
spoon [spu:n] *n* Löffel *m*
spoon-feed ['spu:nfi:d] *vt* (mit dem Löffel) füttern; (*fig*) gängeln

spoonful ['spu:nful] *n* Löffel *m*
sport [spɔ:t] *n* Sport *m*; (*type*) Sportart *f*; (*also*: **good sport**: *person*) feiner Kerl *m* ▷ *vt* (*wear*) tragen; **indoor ~s** Hallensport *m*; **outdoor ~s** Sport *m* im Freien
sporting ['spɔ:tɪŋ] *adj* (*event etc*) Sport-; (*generous*) großzügig; **to give sb a ~ chance** jdm eine faire Chance geben
sport jacket (*US*) *n* = **sports jacket**
sports car *n* Sportwagen *m*
sports centre *n* Sportzentrum *nt*
sports jacket (*Brit*) *n* Sakko *m*
sportsman ['spɔ:tsmən] (*irreg*: *like* **man**) *n* Sportler *m*
sportsmanship ['spɔ:tsmənʃɪp] *n* Sportlichkeit *f*
sportswear ['spɔ:tswɛəʳ] *n* Sportkleidung *f*
sportswoman ['spɔ:tswumən] (*irreg*: *like* **woman**) *n* Sportlerin *f*
sporty ['spɔ:tɪ] *adj* sportlich
spot [spɔt] *n* (*mark*) Fleck *m*; (*dot*) Punkt *m*; (*on skin*) Pickel *m*; (*place*) Stelle *f*, Platz *m*; (*Radio, TV*) Nummer *f*, Auftritt *m*; (*also*: **spot advertisement**) Werbespot *m*; (*small amount*): **a ~ of** ein bisschen ▷ *vt* entdecken; **on the ~** (*in that place*) an Ort und Stelle; (*immediately*) auf der Stelle; **to be in a ~** in der Klemme sitzen; **to put sb on the ~** jdn in Verlegenheit bringen; **to come out in ~s** Pickel bekommen
spot check *n* Stichprobe *f*
spotless ['spɔtlɪs] *adj* makellos sauber
spotlight ['spɔtlaɪt] *n* Scheinwerfer *m*; (*in room*) Strahler *m*
spotted ['spɔtɪd] *adj* gepunktet
spotty ['spɔtɪ] *adj* pickelig
spouse [spaus] *n* (*male*) Gatte *m*; (*female*) Gattin *f*
spout [spaut] *n* (*of jug, teapot*) Tülle *f*; (*of pipe*) Ausfluss *m*; (*of liquid*) Strahl *m* ▷ *vi* spritzen; (*flames*) sprühen
sprain [spreɪn] *n* Verstauchung *f* ▷ *vt*: **to ~ one's ankle/wrist** sich *dat* den Knöchel/das Handgelenk verstauchen
sprang [spræŋ] *pt of* **spring**
sprawl [sprɔ:l] *vi* (*person*) sich ausstrecken; (*place*) wild wuchern ▷ *n*: **urban ~** wild wuchernde Ausbreitung des Stadtgebietes; **to send sb ~ing** jdn zu Boden werfen
spray [spreɪ] *n* (*small drops*) Sprühnebel *m*; (*sea spray*) Gischt *m or f*; (*container*) Sprühdose *f*; (*garden spray*) Sprühgerät *nt*; (*of flowers*) Strauß *m* ▷ *vt* sprühen, spritzen; (*crops*) spritzen ▷ *cpd* (*deodorant*) Sprüh-; **~ can** Sprühdose *f*
spread [sprɛd] (*pt, pp* **~**) *n* (*range*) Spektrum *nt*; (*selection*) Auswahl *f*; (*distribution*) Verteilung *f*; (*for bread*) (Brot)aufstrich *m*; (*inf*: *food*) Festessen *nt*; (*Press, Typ*: *two pages*) Doppelseite *f* ▷ *vt* ausbreiten; (*butter*) streichen; (*workload, wealth, repayments etc*) verteilen; (*scatter*) verstreuen; (*rumour, disease*) verbreiten ▷ *vi* (*disease, news*) sich verbreiten; (*also*: **spread out**: *stain*) sich ausbreiten; **to get a middle-age ~** in den mittleren Jahren Speck ansetzen
▸ **spread out** *vi* (*move apart*) sich verteilen
spread-eagled ['sprɛdi:gld] *adj* mit ausgestreckten Armen und Beinen; **to be** *or* **lie ~** mit ausgestreckten Armen und Beinen daliegen
spreadsheet ['sprɛdʃi:t] *n* (*Comput*) Tabellenkalkulation *f*
spree [spri:] *n*: **to go on a ~** (*drinking*) eine Zechtour machen; (*spending*) groß einkaufen gehen
sprightly ['spraɪtlɪ] *adj* rüstig
spring [sprɪŋ] (*pt* **sprang**, *pp* **sprung**) *n* (*coiled metal*) Sprungfeder *f*; (*season*) Frühling *m*, Frühjahr *nt*; (*of water*) Quelle *f* ▷ *vi* (*leap*) springen ▷ *vt*: **to ~ a leak** (*pipe etc*) undicht werden; **in ~** im Frühling *or* Frühjahr; **to walk with a ~ in one's step** mit federnden Schritten gehen; **to ~ from** (*result*) herrühren von; **to ~ into action** aktiv werden; **he sprang the news on me** er hat mich mit der Nachricht überrascht
▸ **spring up** *vi* (*building, plant*) aus dem Boden schießen
springboard ['sprɪŋbɔ:d] *n* (*Sport, fig*) Sprungbrett *nt*
spring-clean [sprɪŋ'kli:n], **spring-cleaning** [sprɪŋ'kli:nɪŋ] *n* Frühjahrsputz *m*
spring onion (*Brit*) *n* Frühlingszwiebel *f*
springtime ['sprɪŋtaɪm] *n* Frühling *m*
sprinkle ['sprɪŋkl] *vt* (*liquid*) sprenkeln; (*salt, sugar*) streuen; **to ~ water on, ~ with water** mit Wasser besprengen; **to ~ sugar** *etc* **on, ~ with sugar** *etc* mit Zucker *etc* bestreuen
sprinkler ['sprɪŋkləʳ] *n* (*for lawn*) Rasensprenger *m*; (*to put out fire*) Sprinkler *m*
sprint [sprɪnt] *n* Sprint *m* ▷ *vi* rennen; (*Sport*) sprinten; **the 200 metres ~** der 200-Meter-Lauf
sprinter ['sprɪntəʳ] *n* Sprinter(in) *m(f)*
sprout [spraut] *vi* sprießen; (*vegetable*) keimen
sprouts [sprauts] *npl* (*also*: **Brussels sprouts**) Rosenkohl *m*
spruce [spru:s] *n inv* Fichte *f* ▷ *adj* gepflegt, adrett
▸ **spruce up** *vt* auf Vordermann bringen (*inf*); **to ~ o.s. up** sein Äußeres pflegen
sprung [sprʌŋ] *pp of* **spring**
spun [spʌn] *pt, pp of* **spin**
spur [spə:ʳ] *n* Sporn *m*; (*fig*) Ansporn *m* ▷ *vt* (*also*: **spur on**: *fig*) anspornen; **on the ~ of the moment** ganz spontan
spurious ['spjuərɪəs] *adj* falsch
spurn [spə:n] *vt* verschmähen
spurt [spə:t] *n* (*of blood etc*) Strahl *m*; (*of energy*) Anwandlung *f* ▷ *vi* (*blood*) (heraus)spritzen; **to put on a ~** (*lit, fig*) einen Spurt einlegen
spy [spaɪ] *n* Spion(in) *m(f)* ▷ *vi*: **to ~ on** nachspionieren +*dat* ▷ *vt* sehen ▷ *cpd* (*film, story*) Spionage-
spying ['spaɪɪŋ] *n* Spionage *f*
sq. *abbr* = **square**

squabble ['skwɔbl] *vi* (sich) zanken ▷ *n* Streit *m*
squad [skwɔd] *n* (*Mil*) Trupp *m*; (*Police*) Kommando *nt*; (: *drug/fraud squad*) Dezernat *nt*; (*Sport*) Mannschaft *f*; **flying ~** (*Police*) Überfallkommando *nt*
squadron ['skwɔdrn] *n* (*Mil*) Schwadron *f*; (*Aviat*) Staffel *f*; (*Naut*) Geschwader *nt*
squalid ['skwɔlɪd] *adj* verkommen; (*conditions*) elend; (*sordid*) erbärmlich
squall [skwɔ:l] *n* Bö(e) *f*
squalor ['skwɔlə^r] *n* Elend *nt*
squander ['skwɔndə^r] *vt* verschwenden; (*chances*) vertun
square [skwɛə^r] *n* Quadrat *nt*; (*in town*) Platz *m*; (*US: block of houses*) Block *m*; (*also*: **set square**) Zeichendreieck *nt*; (*inf: person*) Spießer *m* ▷ *adj* quadratisch; (*inf: ideas, person*) spießig ▷ *vt* (*arrange*) ausrichten; (*Math*) quadrieren; (*reconcile*) in Einklang bringen ▷ *vi* (*accord*) übereinstimmen; **we're back to ~ one** jetzt sind wir wieder da, wo wir angefangen haben; **all ~** (*Sport*) unentschieden; (*fig*) quitt; **a ~ meal** eine ordentliche Mahlzeit; **2 metres ~** 2 Meter im Quadrat; **2 ~ metres** 2 Quadratmeter; **I'll ~ it with him** (*inf*) ich mache das mit ihm ab; **can you ~ it with your conscience?** können Sie das mit Ihrem Gewissen vereinbaren?
▸ **square up** (*Brit*) *vi* abrechnen
squarely ['skwɛəlɪ] *adv* (*directly*) direkt, genau; (*firmly*) fest; (*honestly*) ehrlich; (*fairly*) gerecht, fair
square root *n* Quadratwurzel *f*
squash [skwɔʃ] *n* (*Brit*): **lemon/orange ~** Zitronen-/Orangensaftgetränk *nt*; (*US: marrow etc*) Kürbis *m*; (*Sport*) Squash *nt* ▷ *vt* zerquetschen
squat [skwɔt] *adj* gedrungen ▷ *vi* (*also*: **squat down**) sich (hin)hocken; (*on property*): **to ~ (in a house)** ein Haus besetzen
squatter ['skwɔtə^r] *n* Hausbesetzer(in) *m(f)*
squeak [skwi:k] *vi* quietschen; (*mouse etc*) piepsen ▷ *n* Quietschen *nt*; (*of mouse etc*) Piepsen *nt*
squeal [skwi:l] *vi* quietschen
squeamish ['skwi:mɪʃ] *adj* empfindlich
squeeze [skwi:z] *n* Drücken *nt*; (*Econ*) Beschränkung *f*; (*also*: **credit squeeze**) Kreditbeschränkung *f* ▷ *vt* drücken; (*lemon etc*) auspressen ▷ *vi*: **to ~ past sth** sich an etw *dat* vorbeidrücken; **to ~ under sth** sich unter etw *dat* durchzwängen; **to give sth a ~** etw drücken; **a ~ of lemon** ein Spritzer *m* Zitronensaft
▸ **squeeze out** *vt* (*juice etc*) (her)auspressen; (*fig: exclude*) hinausdrängen
squelch [skwɛltʃ] *vi* (*mud etc*) quatschen
squid [skwɪd] *n* Tintenfisch *m*
squiggle ['skwɪgl] *n* Schnörkel *m*
squint [skwɪnt] *vi* (*in the sunlight*) blinzeln ▷ *n* (*Med*) Schielen *nt*; **he has a ~** er schielt
squirm [skwə:m] *vi* (*lit, fig*) sich winden
squirrel ['skwɪrəl] *n* Eichhörnchen *nt*
squirt [skwə:t] *vi, vt* spritzen
Sr *abbr* (*in names: = senior*) sen.; (*Rel*) = **sister**
Sri Lanka [srɪ'læŋkə] *n* Sri Lanka *nt*
St *abbr* (= *saint*) St.; (= *street*) Str.
stab [stæb] *n* Stich *m*, Stoß *m*; (*inf: try*): **to have a ~ at sth** etw probieren ▷ *vt* (*person*) niederstechen; (*body*) einstechen auf +*acc*; **a ~ of pain** ein stechender Schmerz; **to ~ sb to death** jdn erstechen
stability [stə'bɪlɪtɪ] *n* Stabilität *f*
stable ['steɪbl] *adj* stabil; (*marriage*) dauerhaft ▷ *n* Stall *m*; **riding ~s** Reitstall *m*
stack [stæk] *n* Stapel *m*; (*of books etc*) Stoß *m* ▷ *vt* (*also*: **stack up**) aufstapeln; **~s of time** (*Brit: inf*) jede Menge Zeit; **to ~ with** vollstapeln mit
stadium ['steɪdɪəm] (*pl* **stadia** *or* **~s**) *n* Stadion *nt*
staff [stɑ:f] *n* (*workforce, servants*) Personal *nt*; (*Brit: also*: **teaching staff**) (Lehrer)kollegium *nt*; (*stick: Mil*) Stab *m* ▷ *vt* (mit Personal) besetzen; **one of his ~** einer seiner Mitarbeiter; **a member of ~** ein(e) Mitarbeiter(in) *m(f)*; (*Scol*) ein(e) Lehrer(in) *m(f)*
stag [stæg] *n* Hirsch *m*; (*Brit: Stock Exchange*) Spekulant *m* (*der junge Aktien aufkauft*); **~ market** (*Brit: Stock Exchange*) Spekulantenmarkt *m*
stage [steɪdʒ] *n* Bühne *f*; (*platform*) Podium *nt*; (*point, period*) Stadium *nt* ▷ *vt* (*play*) aufführen; (*demonstration*) organisieren; (*perform: recovery etc*) schaffen; **the ~** das Theater, die Bühne; **in ~s** etappenweise; **to go through a difficult ~** eine schwierige Phase durchmachen; **in the early/final ~s** im Anfangs-/Endstadium
stagecoach ['steɪdʒkəutʃ] *n* Postkutsche *f*
stage manager *n* Inspizient(in) *m(f)*
stagger ['stægə^r] *vi* schwanken, taumeln ▷ *vt* (*amaze*) die Sprache verschlagen +*dat*; (*hours, holidays*) staffeln
staggering ['stægərɪŋ] *adj* (*amazing*) atemberaubend
stagnant ['stægnənt] *adj* (*water*) stehend; (*economy etc*) stagnierend
stagnate [stæg'neɪt] *vi* (*economy etc*) stagnieren; (*person*) verdummen
stag night, **stag party** *n* Herrenabend *m*
staid [steɪd] *adj* gesetzt
stain [steɪn] *n* Fleck *m*; (*colouring*) Beize *f* ▷ *vt* beflecken; (*wood*) beizen
stainless steel ['steɪnlɪs-] *n* (rostfreier) Edelstahl *m*
stain remover *n* Fleckentferner *m*
stair [stɛə^r] *n* (*step*) Stufe *f*; **stairs** *npl* (*flight of steps*) Treppe *f*; **on the ~s** auf der Treppe
staircase ['stɛəkeɪs] *n* Treppe *f*
stairway ['stɛəweɪ] *n* = **staircase**
stake [steɪk] *n* (*post*) Pfahl *m*, Pfosten *m*; (*Comm*) Anteil *m*; (*Betting: gen pl*) Einsatz *m* ▷ *vt* (*money*) setzen; (*also*: **stake out**: *area*)

abstecken; **to be at ~** auf dem Spiel stehen; **to have a ~ in sth** einen Anteil an etw *dat* haben; **to ~ a claim (to sth)** sich *dat* ein Anrecht (auf etw *acc*) sichern; **to ~ one's life on sth** seinen Kopf auf etw *acc* wetten; **to ~ one's reputation on sth** sich für etw verbürgen

stale [steɪl] *adj* (*bread*) altbacken; (*food*) alt; (*smell*) muffig; (*air*) verbraucht; (*beer*) schal

stalemate ['steɪlmeɪt] *n* (*Chess*) Patt *nt*; (*fig*) Sackgasse *f*

stalk [stɔːk] *n* Stiel *m* ▷ *vt* sich heranpirschen an *+acc* ▷ *vi*: **to ~ out/off** hinaus-/davonstolzieren

stall [stɔːl] *n* (*Brit: in market etc*) Stand *m*; (*in stable*) Box *f* ▷ *vt* (*engine, car*) abwürgen; (*fig: person*) hinhalten; (*: decision etc*) hinauszögern ▷ *vi* (*engine*) absterben; (*car*) stehen bleiben; (*fig: person*) ausweichen; **stalls** *npl* (*Brit: in cinema, theatre*) Parkett *nt*; **a seat in the ~s** ein Platz im Parkett; **a clothes/flower ~** ein Kleidungs-/Blumenstand; **to ~ for time** versuchen, Zeit zu gewinnen

stallion ['stæljən] *n* Hengst *m*

stamina ['stæmɪnə] *n* Ausdauer *f*

stammer ['stæmə^r] *n* Stottern *nt* ▷ *vi* stottern; **to have a ~** stottern

stamp [stæmp] *n* (*lit, fig*) Stempel *m*; (*also*: **postage stamp**) Briefmarke *f* ▷ *vi* stampfen; (*also*: **stamp one's foot**) (mit dem Fuß) aufstampfen ▷ *vt* stempeln; (*with postage stamp*) frankieren; **~ed addressed envelope** frankierter Rückumschlag
▸ **stamp out** *vt* (*fire*) austreten; (*fig: crime*) ausrotten; (*: opposition*) unterdrücken

stamp album *n* Briefmarkenalbum *nt*

stamp collecting *n* Briefmarkensammeln *nt*

stampede [stæm'piːd] *n* (*of animals*) wilde Flucht *f*; (*fig*) Massenandrang *m*

stance [stæns] *n* Haltung *f*; (*fig*) Einstellung *f*

stand [stænd] (*pt, pp* **stood**) *n* (*Comm*) Stand *m*; (*Sport*) Tribüne *f*; (*piece of furniture*) Ständer *m* ▷ *vi* stehen; (*rise*) aufstehen; (*remain*) bestehen bleiben; (*in election etc*) kandidieren ▷ *vt* stellen; (*tolerate, withstand*) ertragen; **to make a ~ against sth** Widerstand gegen etw leisten; **to take a ~ on sth** einen Standpunkt zu etw vertreten; **to take the ~** (*US: Law*) in den Zeugenstand treten; **to ~ at** (*value, score etc*) betragen; (*level*) liegen bei; **to ~ for parliament** (*Brit*) in den Parlamentswahlen kandidieren; **to ~ to gain/lose sth** etw gewinnen/verlieren können; **it ~s to reason** es ist einleuchtend; **as things ~** nach Lage der Dinge; **to ~ sb a drink/meal** jdm einen Drink/ein Essen spendieren; **I can't ~ him** ich kann ihn nicht leiden *or* ausstehen; **we don't ~ a chance** wir haben keine Chance; **to ~ trial** vor Gericht stehen
▸ **stand by** *vi* (*be ready*) sich bereithalten; (*fail to help*) (unbeteiligt) danebenstehen ▷ *vt fus* (*opinion, decision*) stehen zu; (*person*) halten zu
▸ **stand down** *vi* zurücktreten
▸ **stand for** *vt fus* (*signify*) bedeuten; (*represent*) stehen für; (*tolerate*) sich *dat* gefallen lassen
▸ **stand in for** *vt fus* vertreten
▸ **stand out** *vi* hervorstechen
▸ **stand up** *vi* aufstehen
▸ **stand up for** *vt fus* eintreten für
▸ **stand up to** *vt fus* standhalten *+dat*; (*person*) sich behaupten gegenüber *+dat*

standard ['stændəd] *n* (*level*) Niveau *nt*; (*norm*) Norm *f*; (*criterion*) Maßstab *m*; (*flag*) Standarte *f* ▷ *adj* (*size, model, value etc*) Standard-; (*normal*) normal; **standards** *npl* (*morals*) (sittliche) Maßstäbe *pl*; **to be** *or* **to come up to ~** den Anforderungen genügen; **to apply a double ~** mit zweierlei Maß messen

standard lamp (*Brit*) *n* Stehlampe *f*

standard of living *n* Lebensstandard *m*

stand-by, standby ['stændbaɪ] *n* Reserve *f*; (*also*: **standby ticket**) Stand-by-Ticket *nt* ▷ *adj* (*generator*) Reserve-, Ersatz-; **to be on ~** (*doctor*) Bereitschaftsdienst haben; (*crew, firemen etc*) in Bereitschaft sein, einsatzbereit sein

stand-by ticket *n* Stand-by-Ticket *nt*

stand-in ['stændɪn] *n* Ersatz *m*

standing ['stændɪŋ] *adj* (*permanent*) ständig; (*army*) stehend ▷ *n* (*status*) Rang *m*, Stellung *f*; **a ~ ovation** stürmischer Beifall; **of many years' ~** von langjähriger Dauer; **a relationship of 6 months' ~** eine seit 6 Monaten bestehende Beziehung; **a man of some ~** ein angesehener Mann

standing order (*Brit*) *n* (*at bank*) Dauerauftrag *m*

standing room *n* Stehplätze *pl*

standpoint ['stændpɔɪnt] *n* Standpunkt *m*

standstill ['stændstɪl] *n*: **to be at a ~** stillstehen; (*fig: negotiations*) in eine Sackgasse geraten sein; **to come to a ~** (*traffic*) zum Stillstand kommen

stank [stæŋk] *pt of* **stink**

staple ['steɪpl] *n* (*for papers*) Heftklammer *f*; (*chief product*) Hauptartikel *m* ▷ *adj* (*food, diet*) Grund-, Haupt- ▷ *vt* heften

stapler ['steɪplə^r] *n* Hefter *m*

star [stɑː^r] *n* Stern *m*; (*celebrity*) Star *m* ▷ *vt* (*Theat, Cine*) in der Hauptrolle zeigen ▷ *vi*: **to ~ in** die Hauptrolle haben in; **the stars** *npl* (*horoscope*) das Horoskop; **4-~ hotel** 4-Sterne-Hotel *nt*; **2-~ petrol** (*Brit*) Normal(benzin) *nt*; **4-~ petrol** (*Brit*) Super(benzin) *nt*

starboard ['stɑːbɔːd] *adj* (*side*) Steuerbord-; **to ~** (nach) Steuerbord

starch [stɑːtʃ] *n* Stärke *f*

stardom ['stɑːdəm] *n* Berühmtheit *f*

stare [stɛə^r] *n* starrer Blick *m* ▷ *vi*: **to ~ at** anstarren

starfish ['stɑːfɪʃ] *n* Seestern *m*

stark [stɑːk] *adj* (*bleak*) kahl; (*simplicity*) schlicht; (*colour*) eintönig; (*reality, poverty*) nackt ▷ *adv*: **~ naked** splitternackt

starling ['stɑːlɪŋ] *n* Star *m*
starry ['stɑːrɪ] *adj* sternklar; **~ sky** Sternenhimmel *m*
starry-eyed [stɑːrɪ'aɪd] *adj* (*innocent*) arglos, blauäugig; (*from wonder*) verzückt
start [stɑːt] *n* Beginn *m*, Anfang *m*; (*departure*) Aufbruch *m*; (*advantage*) Vorsprung *m* ▷ *vt* anfangen mit; (*panic*) auslösen; (*fire*) anzünden; (*found*) gründen; (: *restaurant etc*) eröffnen; (*engine*) anlassen; (*car*) starten ▷ *vi* anfangen; (*with fright*) zusammenfahren; (*engine etc*) anspringen; **at the ~** am Anfang, zu Beginn; **for a ~** erstens; **to make an early ~** frühzeitig aufbrechen; **to give a ~** zusammenfahren; **to wake up with a ~** aus dem Schlaf hochschrecken; **to ~ doing** *or* **to do sth** anfangen, etw zu tun; **to ~ (off) with ...** (*firstly*) erstens; (*at the beginning*) zunächst
▸ **start off** *vi* (*begin*) anfangen; (*begin moving*) losgehen/-fahren
▸ **start out** *vi* (*leave*) sich aufmachen
▸ **start over** (*US*) *vi* noch einmal von vorn anfangen
▸ **start up** *vt* (*business*) gründen; (*restaurant etc*) eröffnen; (*car*) starten; (*engine*) anlassen
starter ['stɑːtəʳ] *n* (*Aut*) Anlasser *m*; (*Sport: official, runner, horse*) Starter *m*; (*Brit: Culin*) Vorspeise *f*; **for ~s** (*inf*) für den Anfang
starting point ['stɑːtɪŋ-] *n* (*lit, fig*) Ausgangspunkt *m*
startle ['stɑːtl] *vt* erschrecken
startling ['stɑːtlɪŋ] *adj* (*news etc*) überraschend
starvation [stɑː'veɪʃən] *n* Hunger *m*; **to die of/from ~** verhungern
starve [stɑːv] *vi* hungern; (*to death*) verhungern ▷ *vt* hungern lassen; (*fig: deprive*): **to ~ sb of sth** jdm etw vorenthalten; **I'm starving** ich sterbe vor Hunger
state [steɪt] *n* (*condition*) Zustand *m*; (*Pol*) Staat *m* ▷ *vt* (*say*) feststellen; (*declare*) erklären; **the States** *npl* (*Geog*) die (Vereinigten) Staaten *pl*; **to be in a ~** aufgeregt sein; (*on edge*) nervös sein; (*in a mess*) in einem schrecklichen Zustand sein; **to get into a ~** durchdrehen (*inf*); **in ~** feierlich; **to lie in ~** (feierlich) aufgebahrt sein; **~ of emergency** Notstand *m*; **~ of mind** Verfassung *f*
stately ['steɪtlɪ] *adj* würdevoll; (*walk*) gemessen; **~ home** Schloss *nt*
statement ['steɪtmənt] *n* (*thing said*) Feststellung *f*; (*declaration*) Erklärung *f*; (*Fin*) (Konto)auszug *m*; **official ~** (amtliche) Erklärung *f*; **bank ~** Kontoauszug *m*
state school *n* öffentliche Schule *f*
statesman ['steɪtsmən] (*irreg: like* **man**) *n* Staatsmann *m*
static ['stætɪk] *n* (*Radio, TV*) atmosphärische Störungen *pl* ▷ *adj* (*not moving*) konstant
station ['steɪʃən] *n* (*Rail*) Bahnhof *m*; (*also*: **bus station**) Busbahnhof *m*; (*also*: **police station**) (Polizei)wache *f*; (*Radio*) Sender *m* ▷ *vt* (*guards etc*) postieren; (*soldiers etc*) stationieren; **action ~s** (*Mil*) Stellung *f*; **above one's ~** über seinem Stand
stationary ['steɪʃnərɪ] *adj* (*vehicle*) haltend; **to be ~** stehen
stationer ['steɪʃənəʳ] *n* Schreibwarenhändler(in) *m(f)*
stationer's, **stationer's shop** *n* Schreibwarenhandlung *f*
stationery ['steɪʃnərɪ] *n* Schreibwaren *pl*; (*writing paper*) Briefpapier *nt*
station wagon (*US*) *n* Kombi(wagen) *m*
statistic [stə'tɪstɪk] *n* Statistik *f*
statistics [stə'tɪstɪks] *n* (*science*) Statistik *f*
statue ['stætjuː] *n* Statue *f*
stature ['stætʃəʳ] *n* Wuchs *m*, Statur *f*; (*fig: reputation*) Format *nt*
status ['steɪtəs] *n* Status *m*; (*position*) Stellung *f*; **the ~ quo** der Status quo
status symbol *n* Statussymbol *nt*
statute ['stætjuːt] *n* Gesetz *nt*; **statutes** *npl* (*of club etc*) Satzung *f*
statutory ['stætjutrɪ] *adj* gesetzlich; **~ declaration** eidesstattliche Erklärung *f*
staunch [stɔːntʃ] *adj* treu ▷ *vt* (*flow*) stauen; (*blood*) stillen
stay [steɪ] *n* Aufenthalt *m* ▷ *vi* bleiben; (*with sb, as guest*) wohnen; (*in hotel*) übernachten; **~ of execution** (*Law*) Aussetzung *f*; **to ~ put** bleiben; **to ~ with friends** bei Freunden untergebracht sein; **to ~ the night** übernachten
▸ **stay behind** *vi* zurückbleiben
▸ **stay in** *vi* (*at home*) zu Hause bleiben
▸ **stay on** *vi* bleiben
▸ **stay out** *vi* (*of house*) wegbleiben; (*remain on strike*) weiterstreiken
▸ **stay up** *vi* (*at night*) aufbleiben
staying power ['steɪɪŋ-] *n* Stehvermögen *nt*, Durchhaltevermögen *nt*
stead [stɛd] *n*: **in sb's ~** an jds Stelle; **to stand sb in good ~** jdm zugute- *or* zustattenkommen
steadfast ['stɛdfɑːst] *adj* standhaft
steadily ['stɛdɪlɪ] *adv* (*regularly*) regelmäßig; (*constantly*) stetig; (*fixedly*) fest, unverwandt
steady ['stɛdɪ] *adj* (*job, boyfriend, girlfriend, look*) fest; (*income*) regelmäßig; (*speed*) gleichmäßig; (*rise*) stetig; (*person, character*) zuverlässig, solide; (*voice, hand etc*) ruhig ▷ *vt* (*stabilize*) ruhig halten; (*nerves*) beruhigen; **to ~ o.s. on sth** sich auf etw *acc* stützen; **to ~ o.s. against sth** sich an etw *dat* abstützen
steak [steɪk] *n* Steak *nt*; (*fish*) Filet *nt*
steal [stiːl] (*pt* **stole**, *pp* **stolen**) *vt* stehlen ▷ *vi* stehlen; (*move secretly*) sich stehlen, schleichen
▸ **steal away** *vi* sich davonschleichen
stealth [stɛlθ] *n*: **by ~** heimlich
steam [stiːm] *n* Dampf *m* ▷ *vt* (*Culin*) dämpfen, dünsten ▷ *vi* dampfen; **covered with ~** (*window etc*) beschlagen; **under one's**

own ~ (*fig*) allein, ohne Hilfe; **to run out of ~** (*fig*) den Schwung verlieren; **to let off ~** (*inf: fig*) Dampf ablassen
▸**steam up** *vi* (*window*) beschlagen; **to get ~ed up about sth** (*inf: fig*) sich über etw *acc* aufregen
steam engine *n* (*Rail*) Dampflok(omotive) *f*
steamer ['sti:mə^r] *n* Dampfer *m*; (*Culin*) Dämpfer *m*
steamship ['sti:mʃɪp] *n* = **steamer**
steamy ['sti:mɪ] *adj* (*room*) dampfig; (*window*) beschlagen; (*book, film*) heiß
steel [sti:l] *n* Stahl *m* ▹*adj* (*girder, wool etc*) Stahl-
steelworks ['sti:lwə:ks] *n* Stahlwerk *nt*
steep [sti:p] *adj* steil; (*increase, rise*) stark; (*price, fees*) gepfeffert ▹*vt* einweichen; **to be ~ed in history** geschichtsträchtig sein
steeple ['sti:pl] *n* Kirchturm *m*
steer [stɪə^r] *vt* steuern; (*car etc*) lenken; (*person*) lotsen ▹*vi* steuern; (*in car etc*) lenken; **to ~ for** zusteuern auf *+acc*; **to ~ clear of sb** (*fig*) jdm aus dem Weg gehen; **to ~ clear of sth** (*fig*) etw meiden
steering ['stɪərɪŋ] *n* (*Aut*) Lenkung *f*
steering wheel *n* (*Aut*) Lenkrad *nt*, Steuer *nt*
stem [stɛm] *n* Stiel *m*; (*of pipe*) Hals *m* ▹*vt* aufhalten; (*flow*) eindämmen; (*bleeding*) zum Stillstand bringen
▸**stem from** *vt fus* zurückgehen auf *+acc*
stench [stɛntʃ] (*pej*) *n* Gestank *m*
stencil ['stɛnsl] *n* Schablone *f* ▹*vt* mit Schablone zeichnen
stenographer [stɛ'nɔgrəfə^r] (*US*) *n* Stenograf(in) *m(f)*
step [stɛp] *n* (*lit, fig*) Schritt *m*; (*of stairs*) Stufe *f* ▹*vi*: **to ~ forward/back** vor-/zurücktreten; **steps** *npl* (*Brit*) = **stepladder**; **~ by step** (*fig*) Schritt für Schritt; **in/out of ~ (with)** im/nicht im Tritt (mit); (*fig*) im/nicht im Gleichklang (mit)
▸**step down** *vi* (*fig: resign*) zurücktreten
▸**step in** *vi* (*fig*) eingreifen
▸**step off** *vt fus* aussteigen aus *+dat*
▸**step on** *vt fus* treten auf *+acc*
▸**step over** *vt fus* steigen über *+acc*
▸**step up** *vt* (*efforts*) steigern; (*pace etc*) beschleunigen
stepbrother ['stɛpbrʌðə^r] *n* Stiefbruder *m*
stepchild ['stɛptʃaɪld] *n* Stiefkind *nt*
stepdaughter ['stɛpdɔ:tə^r] *n* Stieftochter *f*
stepfather ['stɛpfɑ:ðə^r] *n* Stiefvater *m*
stepladder ['stɛplædə^r] (*Brit*) *n* Trittleiter *f*
stepmother ['stɛpmʌðə^r] *n* Stiefmutter *f*
stepping stone ['stɛpɪŋ-] *n* Trittstein *m*; (*fig*) Sprungbrett *nt*
stepsister ['stɛpsɪstə^r] *n* Stiefschwester *f*
stepson ['stɛpsʌn] *n* Stiefsohn *m*
stereo ['stɛrɪəu] *n* (*system*) Stereoanlage *f* ▹*adj* (*sound etc*) Stereo-; **in ~** in Stereo
stereotype ['stɪərɪətaɪp] *n* Klischee *nt*, Klischeevorstellung *f* ▹*vt* in ein Klischee zwängen; **~d** stereotyp
sterile ['stɛraɪl] *adj* steril, keimfrei; (*barren*) unfruchtbar; (*fig: debate*) fruchtlos
sterilize ['stɛrɪlaɪz] *vt* sterilisieren
sterling ['stə:lɪŋ] *adj* (*silver*) Sterling-; (*fig*) gediegen ▹*n* (*Econ*) das Pfund Sterling, das englische Pfund; **one pound ~** ein Pfund Sterling
stern [stə:n] *adj* streng ▹*n* Heck *nt*
steroid ['stɪərɔɪd] *n* Steroid *nt*
stew [stju:] *n* Eintopf *m* ▹*vt* schmoren; (*fruit, vegetables*) dünsten ▹*vi* schmoren; **~ed tea** bitterer Tee *m*; **~ed fruit** (Obst)kompott *nt*
steward ['stju:əd] *n* Steward *m*; (*at public event*) Ordner(in) *m(f)*; (*also*: **shop steward**) gewerkschaftliche Vertrauensperson *f*
stewardess ['stjuədɛs] *n* Stewardess *f*
stick [stɪk] (*pt, pp* **stuck**) *n* Zweig *m*; (*of dynamite*) Stange *f*; (*of chalk etc*) Stück *nt*; (*as weapon*) Stock *m*; (*also*: **walking stick**) (Spazier)stock *m* ▹*vt* (*with glue etc*) kleben; (*inf: put*) tun, stecken; (*: tolerate*) aushalten; (*thrust*) stoßen ▹*vi*: **to ~ (to)** kleben (an *+dat*); (*remain*) (hängen) bleiben; (*door etc*) klemmen; (*lift*) stecken bleiben; **to get hold of the wrong end of the ~** (*Brit: fig*) es falsch verstehen; **to ~ in sb's mind** jdm im Gedächtnis (haften) bleiben
▸**stick around** (*inf*) *vi* hier-/dableiben
▸**stick out** *vi* (*ears etc*) abstehen ▹*vt*: **to ~ it out** (*inf*) durchhalten
▸**stick to** *vt fus* (*one's word, promise*) halten; (*agreement, rules*) sich halten an *+acc*; (*the truth, facts*) bleiben bei
▸**stick up** *vi* hochstehen
▸**stick up for** *vt fus* eintreten für
sticker ['stɪkə^r] *n* Aufkleber *m*
sticking plaster ['stɪkɪŋ-] *n* Heftpflaster *nt*
stick shift (*US*) *n* Schaltknüppel *m*; (*car*) Wagen *m* mit Handschaltung
stick-up ['stɪkʌp] (*inf*) *n* Überfall *m*
sticky ['stɪkɪ] *adj* klebrig; (*label, tape*) Klebe-; (*weather, day*) schwül
stiff [stɪf] *adj* steif; (*hard, firm*) hart; (*paste, egg-white*) fest; (*door, zip etc*) schwer gehend; (*competition*) hart; (*sentence*) schwer; (*drink*) stark ▹*adv* (*bored, worried, scared*) zu Tode; **to be** *or* **feel ~** steif sein; **to have a ~ neck** einen steifen Hals haben; **to keep a ~ upper lip** (*Brit: fig*) die Haltung bewahren
stiffen ['stɪfn] *vi* steif werden; (*body*) erstarren
stifle ['staɪfl] *vt* unterdrücken; (*heat*) erdrücken
stifling ['staɪflɪŋ] *adj* (*heat*) drückend
stigma ['stɪgmə] *n* Stigma *nt*; (*Bot*) Narbe *f*, Stigma *nt*; **stigmata** *npl* (*Med*) Wundmal *nt*
stile [staɪl] *n* Zaunübertritt *m*
stiletto [stɪ'lɛtəu] (*Brit*) *n* (*also*: **stiletto heel**) Bleistiftabsatz *m*
still [stɪl] *adj* (*motionless*) bewegungslos; (*tranquil*) ruhig; (*air, water*) still; (*Brit: drink*) ohne Kohlensäure ▹*adv* (immer) noch; (*yet, even*) noch; (*nonetheless*) trotzdem ▹*n* (*Cine*) Standfoto *nt*; **to stand ~** (*machine, motor*)

stillstehen; (*motionless*) still stehen; **keep ~!** halte still!; **he ~ hasn't arrived** er ist immer noch nicht angekommen

stillborn ['stɪlbɔ:n] *adj* tot geboren

still life *n* Stillleben *nt*

stilt [stɪlt] *n* (*pile*) Pfahl *m*; (*for walking on*) Stelze *f*

stilted ['stɪltɪd] *adj* gestelzt

stimulate ['stɪmjuleɪt] *vt* anregen, stimulieren; (*demand*) ankurbeln

stimulus ['stɪmjuləs] (*pl* **stimuli**) *n* (*incentive*) Anreiz *m*; (*Biol*) Reiz *m*; (*Psych*) Stimulus *m*

sting [stɪŋ] (*pt, pp* **stung**) *n* Stich *m*; (*pain*) Stechen *nt*; (*organ: of insect*) Stachel *m*; (*inf: confidence trick*) Ding *nt* ▷ *vt* stechen; (*fig*) treffen, verletzen ▷ *vi* stechen; (*eyes, ointment, plant etc*) brennen; **my eyes are ~ing** mir brennen die Augen

stingy ['stɪndʒɪ] (*pej*) *adj* geizig, knauserig

stink [stɪŋk] (*pt* **stank**, *pp* **stunk**) *n* Gestank *m* ▷ *vi* stinken

stinking ['stɪŋkɪŋ] (*inf*) *adj* (*fig*) beschissen (!); **a ~ cold** eine scheußliche Erkältung; **~ rich** stinkreich

stint [stɪnt] *n* (*period*) Zeit *f*; (*batch of work*) Pensum *nt*; (*share*) Teil *m* ▷ *vi*: **to ~ on** sparen mit

stir [stə:ʳ] *n* (*fig*) Aufsehen *nt* ▷ *vt* umrühren; (*fig: emotions*) aufwühlen; (*: person*) bewegen ▷ *vi* sich bewegen; **to give sth a ~** etw umrühren; **to cause a ~** Aufsehen erregen

▸ **stir up** *vt*: **to ~ up trouble** Unruhe stiften; **to ~ things up** stänkern

stir-fry ['stə:'fraɪ] *vt* unter Rühren kurz anbraten ▷ *n* Pfannengericht *nt* (*das unter Rühren kurz angebraten wurde*)

stirrup ['stɪrəp] *n* Steigbügel *m*

stitch [stɪtʃ] *n* (*Sewing*) Stich *m*; (*Knitting*) Masche *f*; (*Med*) Faden *m*; (*pain*) Seitenstiche *pl* ▷ *vt* nähen; **he had to have ~es** er musste genäht werden

stoat [stəut] *n* Wiesel *nt*

stock [stɔk] *n* Vorrat *m*; (*Comm*) Bestand *m*; (*Agr*) Vieh *nt*; (*Culin*) Brühe *f*; (*descent, origin*) Abstammung *f*, Herkunft *f*; (*Fin*) Wertpapiere *pl*; (*Rail: also:* **rolling stock**) rollendes Material *nt* ▷ *adj* (*reply, excuse etc*) Standard- ▷ *vt* (*in shop*) führen; **in/out of ~** vorrätig/nicht vorrätig; **~s and shares** (Aktien und) Wertpapiere *pl*; **government ~** Staatsanleihe *f*; **to take ~ of** (*fig*) Bilanz ziehen über *+acc*; **well-~ed** (*shop*) mit gutem Sortiment

▸ **stock up** *vi*: **to ~ up (with)** sich eindecken (mit)

stockbroker ['stɔkbrəukəʳ] *n* Börsenmakler *m*

stock cube (*Brit*) *n* Brühwürfel *m*

stock exchange *n* Börse *f*

stockholder ['stɔkhəuldəʳ] (*esp US*) *n* Aktionär(in) *m(f)*

stocking ['stɔkɪŋ] *n* Strumpf *m*

stock market (*Brit*) *n* Börse *f*

stockpile ['stɔkpaɪl] *n* Vorrat *m*; (*of weapons*) Lager *nt* ▷ *vt* horten

stocktaking ['stɔkteɪkɪŋ] (*Brit*) *n* Inventur *f*

stocky ['stɔkɪ] *adj* stämmig

stodgy ['stɔdʒɪ] *adj* (*food*) pampig (*inf*), schwer

stoke [stəuk] *vt* (*fire*) schüren; (*furnace, boiler*) heizen

stole [stəul] *pt of* **steal** ▷ *n* Stola *f*

stolen ['stəuln] *pp of* **steal**

stomach ['stʌmək] *n* Magen *m*; (*belly*) Bauch *m* ▷ *vt* (*fig*) vertragen

stone [stəun] *n* Stein *m*; (*Brit: weight*) *Gewichtseinheit* (*= 6,35 kg*) ▷ *adj* (*wall, jar etc*) Stein-, steinern ▷ *vt* (*person*) mit Steinen bewerfen; (*fruit*) entkernen, entsteinen; **within a ~'s throw of the station** nur einen Katzensprung vom Bahnhof entfernt

stone-cold ['stəun'kəuld] *adj* eiskalt

stone-deaf ['stəun'dɛf] *adj* stocktaub

stonework ['stəunwə:k] *n* Mauerwerk *nt*

stood [stud] *pt, pp of* **stand**

stool [stu:l] *n* Hocker *m*

stoop [stu:p] *vi* (*also:* **stoop down**) sich bücken; (*walk*) gebeugt gehen; **to ~ to sth** (*fig*) sich zu etw herablassen; **to ~ to doing sth** sich dazu herablassen, etw zu tun

stop [stɔp] *n* Halt *m*; (*short stay*) Aufenthalt *m*; (*in punctuation: also:* **full stop**) Punkt *m*; (*bus stop etc*) Haltestelle *f* ▷ *vt* stoppen; (*car etc*) anhalten; (*block*) sperren; (*prevent*) verhindern ▷ *vi* (*car etc*) anhalten; (*train*) halten; (*pedestrian, watch, clock*) stehen bleiben; (*end*) aufhören; **to come to a ~** anhalten; **to put a ~ to** einen Riegel vorschieben *+dat*; **to ~ doing sth** aufhören, etw zu tun; **to ~ sb (from) doing sth** jdn davon abhalten, etw zu tun; **~ it!** lass das!, hör auf!

▸ **stop by** *vi* kurz vorbeikommen

▸ **stop off** *vi* kurz haltmachen, Zwischenstation machen

▸ **stop up** *vt* (*hole*) zustopfen

stopgap ['stɔpgæp] *n* (*person*) Lückenbüßer *m*; (*thing*) Notbehelf *m*; **~ measure** Überbrückungsmaßnahme *f*

stopover ['stɔpəuvəʳ] *n* Zwischenaufenthalt *m*; (*Aviat*) Zwischenlandung *f*

stoppage ['stɔpɪdʒ] *n* (*strike*) Streik *m*; (*blockage*) Unterbrechung *f*; (*of pay, cheque*) Sperrung *f*; (*deduction*) Abzug *m*

stopper ['stɔpəʳ] *n* Stöpsel *m*

stop press *n* letzte Meldungen *pl*

stopwatch ['stɔpwɔtʃ] *n* Stoppuhr *f*

storage ['stɔ:rɪdʒ] *n* Lagerung *f*; (*also:* **storage space**) Stauraum *m*; (*Comput*) Speicherung *f*

storage heater (*Brit*) *n* (Nacht)speicherofen *m*

store [stɔ:ʳ] *n* Vorrat *m*; (*depot*) Lager *nt*; (*Brit: large shop*) Geschäft *nt*, Kaufhaus *nt*; (*US: shop*) Laden *m*; (*fig*): **a ~ of** eine Fülle an *+dat* ▷ *vt* lagern; (*information etc, Comput*) speichern; (*food, medicines etc*) aufbewahren; (*in filing system*) ablegen; **stores** *npl* (*provisions*) Vorräte *pl*; **in ~** eingelagert; **who knows what's in ~ for us?** wer weiß, was uns bevorsteht?; **to set great/little ~ by sth** viel/wenig von etw halten

▸ **store up** *vt* einen Vorrat anlegen von; (*memories*) im Gedächtnis bewahren

storekeeper ['stɔ:ki:pəʳ] (*US*) *n* Ladenbesitzer(in) *m(f)*

storeroom ['stɔ:ru:m] *n* Lagerraum *m*

storey, (*US*) **story** ['stɔ:rɪ] *n* Stock *m*, Stockwerk *nt*

stork [stɔ:k] *n* Storch *m*

storm [stɔ:m] *n* (*lit, fig*) Sturm *m*; (*bad weather*) Unwetter *nt*; (*also*: **electrical storm**) Gewitter *nt* ▹ *vi* (*fig*) toben ▹ *vt* (*attack*) stürmen

stormy ['stɔ:mɪ] *adj* (*lit, fig*) stürmisch

story ['stɔ:rɪ] *n* Geschichte *f*; (*Press*) Artikel *m*; (*lie*) Märchen *nt*; (*US*) = **storey**

storybook ['stɔ:rɪbuk] *n* Geschichtenbuch *nt*

stout [staut] *adj* (*strong*) stark; (*fat*) untersetzt; (*resolute*) energisch ▹ *n* Starkbier *nt*

stove [stəuv] *n* Herd *m*; (*small*) Kocher *m*; (*for heating*) (Heiz)ofen *m*; **gas ~** Gasherd *m*

stow [stəu] *vt* (*also*: **stow away**) verstauen

stowaway ['stəuəweɪ] *n* blinder Passagier *m*

straddle ['strædl] *vt* (*sitting*) rittlings sitzen auf *+dat*; (*standing*) breitbeinig stehen über *+dat*; (*jumping*) grätschen über *+acc*; (*fig*) überspannen

straggle ['strægl] *vi* (*houses etc*) verstreut liegen; (*people etc*) zurückbleiben

straight [streɪt] *adj* gerade; (*hair*) glatt; (*honest*) offen, direkt; (*simple*) einfach; (*: fight*) direkt; (*Theat*) ernst; (*inf: heterosexual*) hetero; (*whisky etc*) pur ▹ *adv* (*in time*) sofort; (*in direction*) direkt; (*drink*) pur ▹ *n* (*Sport*) Gerade *f*; **to put** *or* **get sth ~** (*make clear*) etw klären; (*make tidy*) etw in Ordnung bringen; **let's get this ~** das wollen wir mal klarstellen; **10 ~ wins** 10 Siege hintereinander; **to win in ~ sets** (*Tennis*) ohne Satzverlust gewinnen; **to go ~ home** direkt nach Hause gehen; **~ out** rundheraus; **~ away, ~ off** sofort, gleich

straighten ['streɪtn] *vt* (*skirt, sheet etc*) gerade ziehen

▸ **straighten out** *vt* (*fig*) klären

straight-faced [streɪt'feɪst] *adj*: **to be/ remain ~** ernst bleiben ▹ *adv* ohne zu lachen

straightforward [streɪt'fɔ:wəd] *adj* (*simple*) einfach; (*honest*) offen

strain [streɪn] *n* Belastung *f*; (*Med: also*: **back strain**) überanstrengter Rücken *m*; (*: tension*) Überlastung *f*; (*of virus*) Art *f*; (*breed*) Sorte *f* ▹ *vt* (*back etc*) überanstrengen; (*resources*) belasten; (*Culin*) abgießen ▹ *vi*: **to ~ to do sth** sich anstrengen, etw zu tun; **strains** *npl* (*Mus*) Klänge *pl*; **he's been under a lot of ~** er hat unter großem Stress gestanden

strained [streɪnd] *adj* (*back*) überanstrengt; (*muscle*) gezerrt; (*forced*) gezwungen; (*relations*) gespannt

strainer ['streɪnəʳ] *n* Sieb *nt*

strait [streɪt] *n* Meerenge *f*, Straße *f*; **straits** *npl* (*fig*): **to be in dire ~s** in großen Nöten sein

straitjacket ['streɪtdʒækɪt] *n* Zwangsjacke *f*

strait-laced [streɪt'leɪst] *adj* prüde, puritanisch

strand [strænd] *n* (*lit, fig*) Faden *m*; (*of wire*) Litze *f*; (*of hair*) Strähne *f*

stranded ['strændɪd] *adj*: **to be ~** (*traveller*) festsitzen; (*ship, sea creature*) gestrandet

strange [streɪndʒ] *adj* fremd; (*odd*) seltsam, merkwürdig

strangely ['streɪndʒlɪ] *adv* seltsam, merkwürdig; *see also* **enough**

stranger ['streɪndʒəʳ] *n* Fremde(r) *f(m)*; **I'm a ~ here** ich bin hier fremd

strangle ['stræŋgl] *vt* erwürgen, erdrosseln; (*fig: economy etc*) ersticken

stranglehold ['stræŋglhəuld] *n* (*fig*) absolute Machtposition *f*

strap [stræp] *n* Riemen *m*; (*of dress etc*) Träger *m* ▹ *vt* (*also*: **strap in**) anschnallen; (*also*: **strap on**) umschnallen

strategic [strə'ti:dʒɪk] *adj* strategisch; (*error*) taktisch

strategy ['strætɪdʒɪ] *n* Strategie *f*

straw [strɔ:] *n* Stroh *nt*; (*also*: **drinking straw**) Strohhalm *m*; **that's the last ~!** das ist der Gipfel!

strawberry ['strɔ:bərɪ] *n* Erdbeere *f*

stray [streɪ] *adj* (*animal*) streunend; (*bullet*) verirrt; (*scattered*) einzeln, vereinzelt ▹ *vi* (*children*) sich verirren; (*animals*) streunen; (*thoughts*) abschweifen

streak [stri:k] *n* Streifen *m*; (*in hair*) Strähne *f*; (*fig: of madness etc*) Zug *m* ▹ *vt* streifen ▹ *vi*: **to ~ past** vorbeiflitzen; **a winning/losing ~** eine Glücks-/Pechsträhne

stream [stri:m] *n* (*small river*) Bach *m*; (*current*) Strömung *f*; (*of people, vehicles*) Strom *m*; (*of questions, insults etc*) Flut *f*, Schwall *m*; (*of smoke*) Schwaden *m*; (*Scol*) Leistungsgruppe *f* ▹ *vt* (*Scol*) in Leistungsgruppen einteilen ▹ *vi* strömen; **against the ~** gegen den Strom; **to come on ~** (*new power plant etc*) in Betrieb genommen werden

streamer ['stri:məʳ] *n* Luftschlange *f*

streamlined ['stri:mlaɪnd] *adj* stromlinienförmig; (*Aviat, Aut*) windschlüpfrig; (*fig*) rationalisiert

street [stri:t] *n* Straße *f*; **the back ~s** die Seitensträßchen *pl*; **to be on the ~s** (*homeless*) obdachlos sein; (*as prostitute*) auf den Strich gehen

streetcar ['stri:tkɑ:ʳ] (*US*) *n* Straßenbahn *f*

street lamp *n* Straßenlaterne *f*

street map *n* Stadtplan *m*

streetwise ['stri:twaɪz] (*inf*) *adj*: **to be ~** wissen, wos langgeht

strength [strɛŋθ] *n* (*lit, fig*) Stärke *f*; (*physical*) Kraft *f*, Stärke *f*; (*of girder etc*) Stabilität *f*; (*of knot etc*) Festigkeit *f*; (*of chemical solution*) Konzentration *f*; (*of wine*) Schwere *f*; **on the ~ of** aufgrund *+gen*; **at full ~** vollzählig; **to be below ~** nicht die volle Stärke haben

strengthen ['strɛŋθn] *vt* (*lit, fig*) verstärken; (*muscle*) kräftigen; (*economy, currency,*

relationship) festigen
strenuous ['strɛnjuəs] *adj* anstrengend; (*determined*) unermüdlich
stress [strɛs] *n* Druck *m*; (*mental*) Belastung *f*, Stress *m*; (*Ling*) Betonung *f*; (*emphasis*) Akzent *m*, Gewicht *nt* ▷ *vt* betonen; **to lay great ~ on sth** großen Wert auf etw *acc* legen; **to be under ~** großen Belastungen ausgesetzt sein, unter Stress stehen
stressful ['strɛsful] *adj* anstrengend, stressig; (*situation*) angespannt
stretch [strɛtʃ] *n* (*of sand, water etc*) Stück *nt*; (*of time*) Zeit *f* ▷ *vi* (*person, animal*) sich strecken; (*land, area*) sich erstrecken ▷ *vt* (*pull*) spannen; (*fig: job, task*) fordern; **at a ~** an einem Stück, ohne Unterbrechung; **by no ~ of the imagination** beim besten Willen nicht; **to ~ to** *or* **as far as the frontier** (*extend*) sich bis zur Grenze erstrecken; **to ~ one's legs** sich *dat* die Beine vertreten
▸ **stretch out** *vi* sich ausstrecken ▷ *vt* ausstrecken
▸ **stretch to** *vt fus* (*be enough*) reichen für
stretcher ['strɛtʃə^r] *n* (Trag)bahre *f*
strewn [stru:n] *adj*: **~ with** übersät mit
stricken ['strɪkən] *adj* (*person*) leidend; (*city, industry etc*) Not leidend; **~ with** (*disease*) geschlagen mit; (*fear etc*) erfüllt von
strict [strɪkt] *adj* streng; (*precise*) genau; **in the ~est confidence** streng vertraulich; **in the ~ sense of the word** streng genommen
strictly ['strɪktlɪ] *adv* streng; (*exactly*) genau; (*solely*) ausschließlich; **~ confidential** streng vertraulich; **~ speaking** genau genommen; **not ~ true** nicht ganz richtig; **~ between ourselves** ganz unter uns
stride [straɪd] (*pt* **strode**, *pp* **stridden**) *n* Schritt *m* ▷ *vi* schreiten; **to take sth in one's ~** (*fig*) mit etw spielend fertig werden
strife [straɪf] *n* Streit *m*, Zwietracht *f*
strike [straɪk] (*pt, pp* **struck**) *n* Streik *m*, Ausstand *m*; (*Mil*) Angriff *m* ▷ *vt* (*hit*) schlagen; (*fig: idea, thought*) in den Sinn kommen *+dat*; (*oil etc*) finden, stoßen auf *+acc*; (*bargain, deal*) aushandeln; (*coin, medal*) prägen ▷ *vi* streiken; (*illness, killer*) zuschlagen; (*disaster*) hereinbrechen; (*clock*) schlagen; **on ~** streikend; **to be on ~** streiken; **to ~ a balance** einen Mittelweg finden; **to be struck by lightning** vom Blitz getroffen werden; **to ~ a match** ein Streichholz anzünden
▸ **strike back** *vi* (*Mil*) zurückschlagen; (*fig*) sich wehren
▸ **strike down** *vt* niederschlagen
▸ **strike off** *vt* (*from list*) (aus)streichen; (*doctor etc*) die Zulassung entziehen *+dat*
▸ **strike out** *vi* losziehen, sich aufmachen ▷ *vt* (*word, sentence*) (aus)streichen
▸ **strike up** *vt* (*Mus*) anstimmen; (*conversation*) anknüpfen; (*friendship*) schließen
striker ['straɪkə^r] *n* Streikende(r) *f(m)*; (*Sport*) Stürmer *m*
striking ['straɪkɪŋ] *adj* auffallend; (*attractive*) attraktiv
string [strɪŋ] (*pt, pp* **strung**) *n* Schnur *f*; (*of islands*) Kette *f*; (*of people, cars*) Schlange *f*; (*series*) Serie *f*; (*Comput*) Zeichenfolge *f*; (*Mus*) Saite *f* ▷ *vt*: **to ~ together** aneinanderreihen; **the strings** *npl* (*Mus*) die Streichinstrumente *pl*; **to pull ~s** (*fig*) Beziehungen spielen lassen; **with no ~s attached** (*fig*) ohne Bedingungen; **to ~ sth out** etw verteilen
stringed instrument *n* Saiteninstrument *nt*
stringent ['strɪndʒənt] *adj* streng; (*measures*) drastisch
strip [strɪp] *n* Streifen *m*; (*of metal*) Band *nt*; (*Sport*) Trikot *nt*, Dress *m* ▷ *vt* (*undress*) ausziehen; (*paint*) abbeizen; (*also*: **strip down**: *machine etc*) auseinandernehmen ▷ *vi* (*undress*) sich ausziehen
strip cartoon *n* Comic(strip) *m*
stripe [straɪp] *n* Streifen *m*; **stripes** *npl* (*Mil, Police*) (Ärmel)streifen *pl*
striped [straɪpt] *adj* gestreift
stripper ['strɪpə^r] *n* Stripper(in) *m(f)*, Stripteasetänzer(in) *m(f)*
strip-search ['strɪpsɛtʃ] *n* Leibesvisitation *f* (*bei der man sich ausziehen muss*) ▷ *vt*: **to be ~ed** sich ausziehen müssen und durchsucht werden
strive [straɪv] (*pt* **strove**, *pp* **~n**) *vi*: **to ~ for sth** nach etw streben; **to ~ to do sth** danach streben, etw zu tun
strode [strəud] *pt of* **stride**
stroke [strəuk] *n* Schlag *m*, Hieb *m*; (*Swimming: style*) Stil *m*; (*Med*) Schlaganfall *m*; (*of clock*) Schlag *m*; (*of paintbrush*) Strich *m* ▷ *vt* (*caress*) streicheln; **at a ~** mit einem Schlag; **on the ~ of 5** Punkt 5 (Uhr); **a ~ of luck** ein Glücksfall *m*; **a 2-~ engine** ein Zweitaktmotor *m*
stroll [strəul] *n* Spaziergang *m* ▷ *vi* spazieren; **to go for a ~, have** *or* **take a ~** einen Spaziergang machen
stroller ['strəulə^r] (US) *n* (*pushchair*) Sportwagen *m*
strong [strɔŋ] *adj* stark; (*person, arms, grip*) stark, kräftig; (*healthy*) kräftig; (*object, material*) solide, stabil; (*letter*) geharnischt; (*measure*) drastisch; (*language*) derb; (*nerves*) gut; (*taste, smell*) streng ▷ *adv*: **to be going ~** (*company*) sehr erfolgreich sein; (*person*) gut in Schuss sein; **I have no ~ feelings about it** es ist mir ziemlich egal; **they are 50 ~** sie sind insgesamt 50
stronghold ['strɔŋhəuld] *n* Festung *f*; (*fig*) Hochburg *f*
strongly ['strɔŋlɪ] *adv* (*solidly*) stabil; (*forcefully*) entschieden; (*deeply*) fest; **to feel ~ that ...** fest davon überzeugt sein, dass ...; **I feel ~ about it** mir liegt sehr viel daran; (*negatively*) ich bin sehr dagegen
strongroom ['strɔŋru:m] *n* Tresorraum *m*
strove [strəuv] *pt of* **strive**
struck [strʌk] *pt, pp of* **strike**

structural ['strʌktʃrəl] *adj* strukturell; (*damage*) baulich; (*defect*) Konstruktions-
structure ['strʌktʃə^r] *n* Struktur *f*, Aufbau *m*; (*building*) Gebäude *nt*
struggle ['strʌgl] *n* Kampf *m*; (*difficulty*) Anstrengung *f* ▷ *vi* (*try hard*) sich abmühen; (*fight*) kämpfen; (*in self-defence*) sich wehren; **to have a ~ to do sth** Mühe haben, etw zu tun; **to be a ~ for sb** jdm große Schwierigkeiten bereiten
strum [strʌm] *vt* (*guitar*) klimpern auf *+dat*
strung [strʌŋ] *pt, pp of* **string**
strut [strʌt] *n* Strebe *f*, Stütze *f* ▷ *vi* stolzieren
stub [stʌb] *n* (*of cheque, ticket etc*) Abschnitt *m*; (*of cigarette*) Kippe *f* ▷ *vt*: **to ~ one's toe** sich *dat* den Zeh stoßen
▸**stub out** *vt* (*cigarette*) ausdrücken
stubble ['stʌbl] *n* Stoppeln *pl*
stubborn ['stʌbən] *adj* hartnäckig; (*child*) störrisch
stuck [stʌk] *pt, pp of* **stick** ▷ *adj*: **to be ~** (*jammed*) klemmen; (*unable to answer*) nicht klarkommen; **to get ~** stecken bleiben; (*fig*) nicht weiterkommen
stuck-up [stʌk'ʌp] (*inf*) *adj* hochnäsig
stud [stʌd] *n* (*on clothing etc*) Niete *f*; (*on collar*) Kragenknopf *m*; (*earring*) Ohrstecker *m*; (*on boot*) Stollen *m*; (*also*: **stud farm**) Gestüt *nt*; (*also*: **stud horse**) Zuchthengst *m* ▷ *vt* (*fig*): **~ded with** übersät mit; (*with jewels*) dicht besetzt mit
student ['stju:dənt] *n* Student(in) *m(f)*; (*at school*) Schüler(in) *m(f)* ▷ *cpd* Studenten-; **law/medical ~** Jura-/Medizinstudent(in) *m(f)*; **~ nurse** Krankenpflegeschüler(in) *m(f)*; **~ teacher** Referendar(in) *m(f)*
student driver (US) *n* Fahrschüler(in) *m(f)*
students' union ['stju:dənts-] (*Brit*) *n* Studentenvereinigung *f*, ≈ AStA *m*; (*building*) Gebäude *nt* der Studentenvereinigung
studio ['stju:dɪəu] *n* Studio *nt*; (*sculptor's etc*) Atelier *nt*
studio flat, (US) **studio apartment** *n* Einzimmerwohnung *f*
studious ['stju:dɪəs] *adj* lernbegierig
studiously ['stju:dɪəslɪ] *adv* (*carefully*) sorgsam
study ['stʌdɪ] *n* Studium *nt*, Lernen *nt*; (*room*) Arbeitszimmer *nt* ▷ *vt* studieren; (*face*) prüfend ansehen; (*evidence*) prüfen ▷ *vi* studieren, lernen; **studies** *npl* (*studying*) Studien *pl*; **to make a ~ of sth** etw untersuchen; (*academic*) etw studieren; **to ~ for an exam** sich auf eine Prüfung vorbereiten
stuff [stʌf] *n* Zeug *nt* ▷ *vt* ausstopfen; (*Culin*) füllen; (*inf*: *push*) stopfen; **my nose is ~ed up** ich habe eine verstopfte Nase; **get ~ed!** (*inf!*) du kannst mich mal!
stuffing ['stʌfɪŋ] *n* Füllung *f*; (*in sofa etc*) Polstermaterial *nt*
stuffy ['stʌfɪ] *adj* (*room*) stickig; (*person, ideas*) spießig
stumble ['stʌmbl] *vi* stolpern; **to ~ across** *or* **on** (*fig*) (zufällig) stoßen auf *+acc*
stumbling block ['stʌmblɪŋ-] *n* Hürde *f*, Hindernis *nt*
stump [stʌmp] *n* Stumpf *m* ▷ *vt*: **to be ~ed** überfragt sein
stun [stʌn] *vt* betäuben; (*news*) fassungslos machen
stung [stʌŋ] *pt, pp of* **sting**
stunk [stʌŋk] *pp of* **stink**
stunning ['stʌnɪŋ] *adj* (*news, event*) sensationell; (*girl, dress*) hinreißend
stunt [stʌnt] *n* (*in film*) Stunt *m*; (*publicity stunt*) (Werbe)gag *m*
stuntman ['stʌntmæn] (*irreg*: *like* **man**) *n* Stuntman *m*
stupendous [stju:'pɛndəs] *adj* enorm
stupid ['stju:pɪd] *adj* dumm
stupidity [stju:'pɪdɪtɪ] *n* Dummheit *f*
sturdy ['stə:dɪ] *adj* (*person*) kräftig; (*thing*) stabil
stutter ['stʌtə^r] *n* Stottern *nt* ▷ *vi* stottern; **to have a ~** stottern
sty [staɪ] *n* Schweinestall *m*
stye [staɪ] *n* Gerstenkorn *nt*
style [staɪl] *n* Stil *m*; (*design*) Modell *nt*; **in the latest ~** nach der neuesten Mode; **hair ~** Frisur *f*
stylish ['staɪlɪʃ] *adj* elegant
stylist ['staɪlɪst] *n* (*hair stylist*) Friseur *m*, Friseuse *f*; (*literary stylist*) Stilist(in) *m(f)*
stylus ['staɪləs] (*pl* **styli** *or* **~es**) *n* Nadel *f*
suave [swɑ:v] *adj* zuvorkommend
sub... [sʌb] *pref* Unter-, unter-
subconscious [sʌb'kɔnʃəs] *adj* unterbewusst
subcontract [*vt* 'sʌbkən'trækt, *n* 'sʌb'kɔntrækt] *vt* (vertraglich) weitervergeben ▷ *n* Nebenvertrag *m*
subdue [səb'dju:] *vt* unterwerfen; (*emotions*) dämpfen
subdued [səb'dju:d] *adj* (*light*) gedämpft; (*person*) bedrückt
subject [*n* 'sʌbdʒɪkt, *vt* səb'dʒɛkt] *n* (*matter*) Thema *nt*; (*Scol*) Fach *nt*; (*of country*) Staatsbürger(in) *m(f)*; (*Gram*) Subjekt *nt* ▷ *vt*: **to ~ sb to sth** jdn einer Sache *dat* unterziehen; (*expose*) jdn einer Sache *dat* aussetzen; **to change the ~** das Thema wechseln; **to be ~ to** (*law, tax*) unterworfen sein *+dat*; (*heart attacks etc*) anfällig sein für; **~ to confirmation in writing** vorausgesetzt, es wird schriftlich bestätigt
subjective [səb'dʒɛktɪv] *adj* subjektiv
subject matter *n* Stoff *m*; (*content*) Inhalt *m*
subjunctive [səb'dʒʌŋktɪv] *n* Konjunktiv *m*; **in the ~** im Konjunktiv
sublet [sʌb'lɛt] *vt* untervermieten
submarine [sʌbmə'ri:n] *n* Unterseeboot *nt*, U-Boot *nt*
submerge [səb'mə:dʒ] *vt* untertauchen; (*flood*) überschwemmen ▷ *vi* tauchen; **~d** unter Wasser
submission [səb'mɪʃən] *n* (*subjection*) Unterwerfung *f*; (*of plan, application etc*)

Einreichung *f*; (*proposal*) Vorlage *f*
submissive [səb'mɪsɪv] *adj* gehorsam; (*gesture*) demütig
submit [səb'mɪt] *vt* (*proposal*) vorlegen; (*application etc*) einreichen ▷ *vi*: **to ~ to sth** sich einer Sache *dat* unterwerfen
subnormal [sʌb'nɔ:ml] *adj* (*below average*) unterdurchschnittlich; (*old: child etc*) minderbegabt; **educationally ~** lernbehindert
subordinate [sə'bɔ:dɪnət] *n* Untergebene(r) *f(m)*; (*Ling*): **~ clause** Nebensatz *m* ▷ *adj* untergeordnet; **to be ~ to sb** jdm untergeordnet sein
subpoena [səb'pi:nə] *n* (*Law*) Vorladung *f* ▷ *vt* vorladen
subscribe [səb'skraɪb] *vi* spenden; **to ~ to** (*opinion, theory*) sich anschließen *+dat*; (*fund, charity*) regelmäßig spenden an *+acc*; (*magazine etc*) abonnieren
subscriber [səb'skraɪbəʳ] *n* (*to magazine*) Abonnent(in) *m(f)*; (*Tel*) Teilnehmer(in) *m(f)*
subscription [səb'skrɪpʃən] *n* (*to magazine etc*) Abonnement *nt*; (*membership dues*) (Mitglieds)beitrag *m*; **to take out a ~ to** (*magazine etc*) abonnieren
subsequent ['sʌbsɪkwənt] *adj* später, nachfolgend; (*further*) weiter; **~ to** im Anschluss an *+acc*
subsequently ['sʌbsɪkwəntlɪ] *adv* später
subside [səb'saɪd] *vi* (*feeling, pain*) nachlassen; (*flood*) sinken; (*earth*) sich senken
subsidence [səb'saɪdns] *n* Senkung *f*
subsidiary [səb'sɪdɪərɪ] *adj* (*question, role, Brit: Scol: subject*) Neben- ▷ *n* (*also*: **subsidiary company**) Tochtergesellschaft *f*
subsidize ['sʌbsɪdaɪz] *vt* subventionieren
subsidy ['sʌbsɪdɪ] *n* Subvention *f*
substance ['sʌbstəns] *n* Substanz *f*, Stoff *m*; (*fig: essence*) Kern *m*; **a man of ~** ein vermögender Mann; **to lack ~** (*book*) keine Substanz haben; (*argument*) keine Durchschlagskraft haben
substantial [səb'stænʃl] *adj* (*solid*) solide; (*considerable*) beträchtlich, größere(r, s); (*meal*) kräftig
substantially [səb'stænʃəlɪ] *adv* erheblich; (*in essence*) im Wesentlichen
substantiate [səb'stænʃɪeɪt] *vt* erhärten, untermauern
substitute ['sʌbstɪtju:t] *n* Ersatz *m* ▷ *vt*: **to ~ A for B** B durch A ersetzen
substitution [sʌbstɪ'tju:ʃən] *n* Ersetzen *nt*; (*Football*) Auswechseln *nt*
subterranean [sʌbtə'reɪnɪən] *adj* unterirdisch
subtle ['sʌtl] *adj* fein; (*indirect*) raffiniert
subtotal [sʌb'təutl] *n* Zwischensumme *f*
subtract [səb'trækt] *vt* abziehen, subtrahieren
subtraction [səb'trækʃən] *n* Abziehen *nt*, Subtraktion *f*
suburb ['sʌbə:b] *n* Vorort *m*
suburban [sə'bə:bən] *adj* (*train etc*) Vorort-; (*lifestyle etc*) spießig, kleinbürgerlich
suburbia [sə'bə:bɪə] *n* die Vororte *pl*
subway ['sʌbweɪ] *n* (*US*) Untergrundbahn *f*, U-Bahn *f*; (*Brit: underpass*) Unterführung *f*
succeed [sək'si:d] *vi* (*plan etc*) gelingen, erfolgreich sein; (*person*) erfolgreich sein, Erfolg haben ▷ *vt* (*in job*) Nachfolger werden *+gen*; (*in order*) folgen *+dat*; **sb ~s in doing sth** es gelingt jdm, etw zu tun
succeeding [sək'si:dɪŋ] *adj* folgend; **~ generations** spätere *or* nachfolgende Generationen *pl*
success [sək'sɛs] *n* Erfolg *m*; **without ~** ohne Erfolg, erfolglos
successful [sək'sɛsful] *adj* erfolgreich; **to be ~** erfolgreich sein, Erfolg haben; **sb is ~ in doing sth** es gelingt jdm, etw zu tun
successfully [sək'sɛsfəlɪ] *adv* erfolgreich, mit Erfolg
succession [sək'sɛʃən] *n* Folge *f*, Serie *f*; (*to throne etc*) Nachfolge *f*; **3 years in ~** 3 Jahre nacheinander *or* hintereinander
successive [sək'sɛsɪv] *adj* aufeinanderfolgend; **on 3 ~ days** 3 Tage nacheinander *or* hintereinander
successor [sək'sɛsəʳ] *n* Nachfolger(in) *m(f)*
succumb [sə'kʌm] *vi*: **to ~ to** (*temptation*) erliegen *+dat*; (*illness: become affected by*) bekommen; (*: die of*) erliegen *+dat*
such [sʌtʃ] *adj* (*of that kind*): **~ a book** so ein Buch; (*so much*): **~ courage** so viel Mut; (*emphasizing similarity*): **or some ~ place/name** *etc* oder so ähnlich ▷ *adv* so; **~ books** solche Bücher; **~ a lot of** so viel; **she made ~ a noise that ...** sie machte so einen Lärm, dass ...; **~ books as I have** was ich an Büchern habe; **I said no ~ thing** das habe ich nie gesagt; **~ a long trip** so eine lange Reise; **~ as** wie (zum Beispiel); **as ~** an sich
such-and-such ['sʌtʃənsʌtʃ] *adj* die und die, der und der, das und das
suck [sʌk] *vt* (*sweet etc*) lutschen; (*ice-lolly*) lutschen an *+dat*; (*baby*) saugen an *+dat*; (*pump, machine*) saugen
sucker ['sʌkəʳ] *n* (*Zool*) Saugnapf *m*; (*Tech*) Saugfuß *m*; (*Bot*) unterirdischer Ausläufer *m*; (*inf*) Dummkopf *m*
suction ['sʌkʃən] *n* Saugwirkung *f*
Sudan [su'dɑ:n] *n* der Sudan
sudden ['sʌdn] *adj* plötzlich; **all of a ~** ganz plötzlich
suddenly ['sʌdnlɪ] *adv* plötzlich
suds [sʌdz] *npl* Seifenschaum *m*
sue [su:] *vt* verklagen ▷ *vi* klagen, vor Gericht gehen; **to ~ sb for damages** jdn auf Schadenersatz verklagen; **to ~ for divorce** die Scheidung einreichen
suede [sweɪd] *n* Wildleder *nt* ▷ *cpd* Wildleder-
suet ['sʊɪt] *n* Nierenfett *nt*
suffer ['sʌfəʳ] *vt* erleiden; (*rudeness etc*) ertragen ▷ *vi* leiden; **to ~ from** leiden an *+dat*; **to ~ the effects of sth** an den Folgen

von etw leiden
sufferer ['sʌfərəʳ] *n* Leidende(r) *f(m)*
suffering ['sʌfərɪŋ] *n* Leid *nt*
suffice [sə'faɪs] *vi* genügen
sufficient [sə'fɪʃənt] *adj* ausreichend; **~ money** genug Geld
sufficiently [sə'fɪʃəntlɪ] *adv* genug, ausreichend; **~ powerful/enthusiastic** mächtig/begeistert genug
suffocate ['sʌfəkeɪt] *vi* (*lit, fig*) ersticken
sugar ['ʃugəʳ] *n* Zucker *m* ▷ *vt* zuckern
sugar beet *n* Zuckerrübe *f*
sugar cane *n* Zuckerrohr *nt*
suggest [sə'dʒɛst] *vt* vorschlagen; (*indicate*) andeuten, hindeuten auf *+acc*; **what do you ~ I do?** was schlagen Sie vor?
suggestion [sə'dʒɛstʃən] *n* Vorschlag *m*; (*indication*) Anflug *m*; (*trace*) Spur *f*
suicide ['suɪsaɪd] *n* (*lit, fig*) Selbstmord *m*; (*person*) Selbstmörder(in) *m(f)*; *see also* **commit**
suicide bomber *n* Selbstmordattentäter(in) *m(f)*
suit [su:t] *n* (*man's*) Anzug *m*; (*woman's*) Kostüm *nt*; (*Law*) Prozess *m*, Verfahren *nt*; (*Cards*) Farbe *f* ▷ *vt* passen *+dat*; (*colour, clothes*) stehen *+dat*; **to bring a ~ against sb** (*Law*) gegen jdn Klage erheben *or* einen Prozess anstrengen; **to follow ~** (*fig*) das Gleiche tun; **to ~ sth to** etw anpassen an *+acc*; **to be ~ed to do sth** sich dafür eignen, etw zu tun; **~ yourself!** wie du willst!; **well ~ed** (*couple*) gut zusammenpassend
suitable ['su:təbl] *adj* (*convenient*) passend; (*appropriate*) geeignet; **would tomorrow be ~?** würde Ihnen morgen passen?; **Monday isn't ~** Montag passt nicht; **we found somebody ~** wir haben jemand Passenden gefunden
suitably ['su:təblɪ] *adv* passend; (*impressed*) gebührend
suitcase ['su:tkeɪs] *n* Koffer *m*
suite [swi:t] *n* (*of rooms*) Suite *f*, Zimmerflucht *f*; (*Mus*) Suite *f*; **bedroom/dining room ~** Schlafzimmer-/Esszimmereinrichtung *f*; **a three-piece ~** eine dreiteilige Polstergarnitur
suitor ['su:təʳ] *n* Kläger(in) *m(f)*
sulfur ['sʌlfəʳ] (*US*) *n* = **sulphur**
sulk [sʌlk] *vi* schmollen
sulky ['sʌlkɪ] *adj* schmollend
sullen ['sʌlən] *adj* mürrisch, verdrossen
sulphur, (*US*) **sulfur** ['sʌlfəʳ] *n* Schwefel *m*
sultana [sʌl'tɑ:nə] *n* Sultanine *f*
sultry ['sʌltrɪ] *adj* schwül
sum [sʌm] *n* (*calculation*) Rechenaufgabe *f*; (*amount*) Summe *f*, Betrag *m*
▸ **sum up** *vt* zusammenfassen; (*evaluate rapidly*) einschätzen ▷ *vi* zusammenfassen
summarize ['sʌməraɪz] *vt* zusammenfassen
summary ['sʌmərɪ] *n* Zusammenfassung *f* ▷ *adj* (*justice, executions*) im Schnellverfahren
summer ['sʌməʳ] *n* Sommer *m* ▷ *cpd* Sommer-; **in ~** im Sommer
summer holidays *npl* Sommerferien *pl*
summerhouse ['sʌməhaus] *n* (*in garden*) Gartenhaus *nt*, Gartenlaube *f*
summertime ['sʌmətaɪm] *n* Sommer *m*, Sommerszeit *f*
summer time *n* Sommerzeit *f*
summit ['sʌmɪt] *n* Gipfel *m*; (*also:* **summit conference/meeting**) Gipfelkonferenz *f*/-treffen *nt*
summon ['sʌmən] *vt* rufen, kommen lassen; (*help*) holen; (*meeting*) einberufen; (*Law: witness*) vorladen
▸ **summon up** *vt* aufbringen
summons ['sʌmənz] *n* (*Law*) Vorladung *f*; (*fig*) Aufruf *m* ▷ *vt* (*Law*) vorladen; **to serve a ~ on sb** jdn vor Gericht laden
Sun. *abbr* (= *Sunday*) So.
sun [sʌn] *n* Sonne *f*; **to catch the ~** einen Sonnenbrand bekommen; **everything under the ~** alles Mögliche
sunbathe ['sʌnbeɪð] *vi* sich sonnen
sunbed ['sʌnbɛd] *n* (*with sun lamp*) Sonnenbank *f*
sunblock *n* Sonnenschutzcreme *f*
sunburn ['sʌnbə:n] *n* Sonnenbrand *m*
sunburned ['sʌnbə:nd] *adj* = **sunburnt**
Sunday ['sʌndɪ] *n* Sonntag *m*; *see also* **Tuesday**
Sunday school *n* Sonntagsschule *f*
sundial ['sʌndaɪəl] *n* Sonnenuhr *f*
sundown ['sʌndaun] (*esp US*) *n* Sonnenuntergang *m*
sundries ['sʌndrɪz] *npl* Verschiedenes *nt*
sundry ['sʌndrɪ] *adj* verschiedene; **all and ~** jedermann
sunflower ['sʌnflauəʳ] *n* Sonnenblume *f*
sung [sʌŋ] *pp of* **sing**
sunglasses ['sʌnglɑ:sɪz] *npl* Sonnenbrille *f*
sunk [sʌŋk] *pp of* **sink**
sunlight ['sʌnlaɪt] *n* Sonnenlicht *nt*
sunlit ['sʌnlɪt] *adj* sonnig, sonnenbeschienen
sunny ['sʌnɪ] *adj* sonnig; (*fig*) heiter
sunrise ['sʌnraɪz] *n* Sonnenaufgang *m*
sun roof *n* (*Aut*) Schiebedach *nt*; (*on building*) Sonnenterrasse *f*
sunset ['sʌnsɛt] *n* Sonnenuntergang *m*
sunshade ['sʌnʃeɪd] *n* Sonnenschirm *m*
sunshine ['sʌnʃaɪn] *n* Sonnenschein *m*
sunstroke ['sʌnstrəuk] *n* Sonnenstich *m*
suntan ['sʌntæn] *n* (Sonnen)bräune *f*; **to get a ~** braun werden
suntan lotion *n* Sonnenmilch *f*
suntan oil *n* Sonnenöl *nt*
super ['su:pəʳ] (*inf*) *adj* fantastisch, toll
superannuation [su:pərænju'eɪʃən] *n* Beitrag *m* zur Rentenversicherung
superb [su:'pə:b] *adj* ausgezeichnet, großartig; (*meal*) vorzüglich
supercilious [su:pə'sɪlɪəs] *adj* herablassend
superficial [su:pə'fɪʃəl] *adj* oberflächlich
superimpose ['su:pərɪm'pəuz] *vt* (*two things*) übereinanderlegen; **to ~ on** legen auf *+acc*; **to ~ with** überlagern mit
superintendent [su:pərɪn'tɛndənt] *n*

Aufseher(in) *m(f)*; (*Police*) Kommissar(in) *m(f)*
superior [su'pɪərɪə^r] *adj* besser, überlegen +*dat*; (*more senior*) höhergestellt; (*smug*) überheblich; (*: smile*) überlegen ▷ *n* Vorgesetzte(r) *f(m)*; **Mother S~** (*Rel*) Mutter Oberin
superiority [supɪərɪ'ɔrɪtɪ] *n* Überlegenheit *f*
superlative [su'pə:lətɪv] *n* Superlativ *m* ▷ *adj* überragend
superman ['su:pəmæn] (*irreg: like* **man**) *n* Übermensch *m*
supermarket ['su:pəmɑ:kɪt] *n* Supermarkt *m*
supernatural [su:pə'nætʃərəl] *adj* übernatürlich ▷ *n*: **the ~** das Übernatürliche
superpower ['su:pəpauə^r] *n* Supermacht *f*
supersede [su:pə'si:d] *vt* ablösen, ersetzen
superstition [su:pə'stɪʃən] *n* Aberglaube *m*
superstitious [su:pə'stɪʃəs] *adj* abergläubisch
superstore ['su:pəstɔ:^r] (*Brit*) *n* Großmarkt *m*
supervise ['su:pəvaɪz] *vt* beaufsichtigen
supervision [su:pə'vɪʒən] *n* Beaufsichtigung *f*; **under medical ~** unter ärztlicher Aufsicht
supervisor ['su:pəvaɪzə^r] *n* Aufseher(in) *m(f)*; (*of students*) Tutor(in) *m(f)*
supper ['sʌpə^r] *n* Abendessen *nt*; **to have ~** zu Abend essen
supple ['sʌpl] *adj* geschmeidig; (*person*) gelenkig
supplement ['sʌplɪmənt] *n* Zusatz *m*; (*of book*) Ergänzungsband *m*; (*of newspaper etc*) Beilage *f* ▷ *vt* ergänzen
supplementary [sʌplɪ'mɛntərɪ] *adj* zusätzlich, ergänzend
supplementary benefit (*Brit: old*) *n* ≈ Sozialhilfe *f*
supplier [sə'plaɪə^r] *n* Lieferant(in) *m(f)*
supply [sə'plaɪ] *vt* liefern; (*provide*) sorgen für; (*a need*) befriedigen ▷ *n* Vorrat *m*; (*supplying*) Lieferung *f*; **supplies** *npl* (*food*) Vorräte *pl*; (*Mil*) Nachschub *m*; **to ~ sth to sb** jdm etw liefern; **to ~ sth with sth** etw mit etw versorgen; **it comes supplied with an adaptor** es wird mit einem Adapter geliefert; **office supplies** Bürobedarf *m*; **to be in short ~** knapp sein; **the electricity/water/gas ~** die Strom-/Wasser-/Gasversorgung *f*; **~ and demand** Angebot *nt* und Nachfrage
supply teacher (*Brit*) *n* Vertretung *f*
support [sə'pɔ:t] *n* Unterstützung *f*; (*Tech*) Stütze *f* ▷ *vt* unterstützen, eintreten für; (*financially: family etc*) unterhalten; (*: party etc*) finanziell unterstützen; (*Tech*) (ab)stützen; (*theory etc*) untermauern; **they stopped work in ~ of ...** sie sind in den Streik getreten, um für ... einzutreten; **to ~ o.s.** (*financially*) finanziell unabhängig sein; **to ~ Arsenal** Arsenal-Fan sein
supporter [sə'pɔ:tə^r] *n* (*Pol etc*) Anhänger(in) *m(f)*; (*Sport*) Fan *m*
suppose [sə'pəuz] *vt* annehmen, glauben; (*imagine*) sich *dat* vorstellen; **to be ~d to do sth** etw tun sollen; **it was worse than she'd ~d** es war schlimmer, als sie es sich vorgestellt hatte; **I don't ~ she'll come** ich glaube kaum, dass sie kommt; **he's about sixty, I ~** er muss wohl so um die Sechzig sein; **he's ~d to be an expert** er ist angeblich ein Experte; **I ~ so/not** ich glaube schon/nicht
supposedly [sə'pəuzɪdlɪ] *adv* angeblich
supposing [sə'pəuzɪŋ] *conj* angenommen
suppress [sə'prɛs] *vt* unterdrücken; (*publication*) verbieten
supreme [su'pri:m] *adj* Ober-, oberste(r, s); (*effort*) äußerste(r, s); (*achievement*) höchste(r, s)
surcharge ['sə:tʃɑ:dʒ] *n* Zuschlag *m*
sure [ʃuə^r] *adj* sicher; (*reliable*) zuverlässig, sicher ▷ *adv* (*inf: esp US*): **that ~ is pretty, that's ~ pretty** das ist aber schön; **to make ~ of sth** sich einer Sache *gen* vergewissern; **to make ~ that** sich vergewissern, dass; **I'm ~ of it** ich bin mir da sicher; **I'm not ~ how/why/when** ich bin mir nicht sicher *or* ich weiß nicht genau, wie/warum/wann; **to be ~ of o.s.** selbstsicher sein; **~!** klar!; **~ enough** tatsächlich
surely ['ʃuəlɪ] *adv* sicherlich, bestimmt; **~ you don't mean that!** das meinen Sie doch bestimmt *or* sicher nicht (so)!
surf [sə:f] *n* Brandung *f*
surface ['sə:fɪs] *n* Oberfläche *f* ▷ *vt* (*road*) mit einem Belag versehen ▷ *vi* (*lit, fig*) auftauchen; (*feeling*) hochkommen; (*rise from bed*) hochkommen; **on the ~** (*fig*) oberflächlich betrachtet
surface mail *n* Post *f* auf dem Land-/Seeweg
surfboard ['sə:fbɔ:d] *n* Surfbrett *nt*
surfeit ['sə:fɪt] *n*: **a ~ of** ein Übermaß an +*dat*
surfer ['sə:fə^r] *n* Surfer(in) *m(f)*
surfing ['sə:fɪŋ] *n* Surfen *nt*; **to go ~** surfen gehen
surge [sə:dʒ] *n* Anstieg *m*; (*fig: of emotion*) Woge *f*; (*Elec*) Spannungsstoß *m* ▷ *vi* (*water*) branden; (*people*) sich drängen; (*vehicles*) sich wälzen; (*emotion*) aufwallen; (*Elec: power*) ansteigen; **to ~ forward** nach vorne drängen
surgeon ['sə:dʒən] *n* Chirurg(in) *m(f)*
surgery ['sə:dʒərɪ] *n* Chirurgie *f*; (*Brit: room*) Sprechzimmer *nt*; (*: building*) Praxis *f*; (*also*: **surgery hours**: *of doctor, MP etc*) Sprechstunde *f*; **to have ~** operiert werden; **to need ~** operiert werden müssen
surgical ['sə:dʒɪkl] *adj* chirurgisch; (*treatment*) operativ
surgical spirit (*Brit*) *n* Wundbenzin *nt*
surname ['sə:neɪm] *n* Nachname *m*
surpass [sə:'pɑ:s] *vt* übertreffen
surplus ['sə:pləs] *n* Überschuss *m* ▷ *adj* überschüssig; **it is ~ to our requirements** das benötigen wir nicht
surprise [sə'praɪz] *n* Überraschung *f* ▷ *vt* überraschen; (*astonish*) erstaunen; (*army*) überrumpeln; (*thief*) ertappen; **to take sb by ~** jdn überraschen
surprising [sə'praɪzɪŋ] *adj* überraschend;

(*situation*) erstaunlich; **it is ~ how/that** es ist erstaunlich, wie/dass
surprisingly [sə'praɪzɪŋlɪ] *adv* überraschend, erstaunlich; **(somewhat) ~, he agreed** erstaunlicherweise war er damit einverstanden
surrender [sə'rɛndəʳ] *n* Kapitulation *f* ▷ *vi* sich ergeben ▷ *vt* aufgeben
surreptitious [sʌrəp'tɪʃəs] *adj* heimlich, verstohlen
surrogate ['sʌrəgɪt] *n* Ersatz *m* ▷ *adj* (*parents*) Ersatz-
surrogate mother *n* Leihmutter *f*
surround [sə'raund] *vt* umgeben; (*Mil, Police etc*) umstellen
surrounding [sə'raundɪŋ] *adj* umliegend; **the ~ area** die Umgebung
surroundings [sə'raundɪŋz] *npl* Umgebung *f*
surveillance [səː'veɪləns] *n* Überwachung *f*; **to be under ~** überwacht werden
survey ['səːveɪ] *n* (*of land*) Vermessung *f*; (*of house*) Begutachtung *f*; (*investigation*) Untersuchung *f*; (*report*) Gutachten *nt*; (*comprehensive view*) Überblick *m* ▷ *vt* (*land*) vermessen; (*house*) inspizieren; (*look at*) betrachten
surveyor [sə'veɪəʳ] *n* (*of land*) Landvermesser(in) *m(f)*; (*of house*) Baugutachter(in) *m(f)*
survival [sə'vaɪvl] *n* Überleben *nt*; (*relic*) Überbleibsel *nt*; **~ course/kit** Überlebenstraining *nt*/-ausrüstung *f*; **~ bag** Expeditionsschlafsack *m*
survive [sə'vaɪv] *vi* überleben; (*custom etc*) weiter bestehen ▷ *vt* überleben
survivor [sə'vaɪvəʳ] *n* Überlebende(r) *f(m)*
susceptible [sə'sɛptəbl] *adj*: **~ (to)** anfällig (für); (*influenced by*) empfänglich (für)
suspect ['sʌspɛkt] *adj* verdächtig ▷ *n* Verdächtige(r) *f(m)* ▷ *vt*: **to ~ sb of** jdn verdächtigen *+gen*; (*think*) vermuten; (*doubt*) bezweifeln
suspend [səs'pɛnd] *vt* (*hang*) (auf)hängen; (*delay, stop*) einstellen; (*from employment*) suspendieren; **to be ~ed (from)** (*hang*) hängen (an *+dat*)
suspended sentence *n* (*Law*) zur Bewährung ausgesetzte Strafe *f*
suspender belt [səs'pɛndəʳ-] *n* Strumpfhaltergürtel *m*
suspenders [səs'pɛndəz] *npl* (*Brit*) Strumpfhalter *pl*; (*US*) Hosenträger *pl*
suspense [səs'pɛns] *n* Spannung *f*; (*uncertainty*) Ungewissheit *f*; **to keep sb in ~** jdn auf die Folter spannen
suspension [səs'pɛnʃən] *n* (*from job*) Suspendierung *f*; (*from team*) Sperrung *f*; (*Aut*) Federung *f*; (*of driving licence*) zeitweiliger Entzug *m*; (*of payment*) zeitweilige Einstellung *f*
suspension bridge *n* Hängebrücke *f*
suspicion [səs'pɪʃən] *n* Verdacht *m*; (*distrust*) Misstrauen *nt*; (*trace*) Spur *f*; **to be under ~** unter Verdacht stehen; **arrested on ~ of murder** wegen Mordverdacht(s) festgenommen
suspicious [səs'pɪʃəs] *adj* (*suspecting*) misstrauisch; (*causing suspicion*) verdächtig; **to be ~ of** *or* **about sb/sth** jdn/etw mit Misstrauen betrachten
sustain [səs'teɪn] *vt* (*continue*) aufrechterhalten; (*food, drink*) bei Kräften halten; (*suffer: injury*) erleiden
sustainable [səs'teɪnəbl] *adj*: **to be ~** aufrechtzuerhalten sein; **~ growth** stetiges Wachstum *nt*
sustained [səs'teɪnd] *adj* (*effort*) ausdauernd; (*attack*) anhaltend
sustenance ['sʌstɪnəns] *n* Nahrung *f*
swab [swɔb] *n* (*Med*) Tupfer *m* ▷ *vt* (*Naut: also:* **swab down**) wischen
swagger ['swægəʳ] *vi* stolzieren
swallow ['swɔləu] *n* (*bird*) Schwalbe *f*; (*of food, drink etc*) Schluck *m* ▷ *vt* (herunter)schlucken; (*fig: story, insult, one's pride*) schlucken; **to ~ one's words** (*speak indistinctly*) seine Worte verschlucken; (*retract*) alles zurücknehmen
▸ **swallow up** *vt* verschlingen
swam [swæm] *pt of* **swim**
swamp [swɔmp] *n* Sumpf *m* ▷ *vt* (*lit, fig*) überschwemmen
swan [swɔn] *n* Schwan *m*
swap [swɔp] *n* Tausch *m* ▷ *vt*: **to ~ (for)** (ein)tauschen (gegen)
swarm [swɔːm] *n* Schwarm *m*; (*of people*) Schar *f* ▷ *vi* (*bees, people*) schwärmen; **to be ~ing with** wimmeln von
swastika ['swɔstɪkə] *n* Hakenkreuz *nt*
swat [swɔt] *vt* totschlagen ▷ *n* (*Brit: also:* **fly swat**) Fliegenklatsche *f*
sway [sweɪ] *vi* schwanken ▷ *vt* (*influence*) beeinflussen ▷ *n*: **to hold ~** herrschen; **to hold ~ over sb** jdn beherrschen *or* in seiner Macht haben
swear [swɛəʳ] (*pt* **swore**, *pp* **sworn**) *vi* (*curse*) fluchen ▷ *vt* (*promise*) schwören; **to ~ an oath** einen Eid ablegen
▸ **swear in** *vt* vereidigen
swearword ['swɛəwəːd] *n* Fluch *m*, Kraftausdruck *m*
sweat [swɛt] *n* Schweiß *m* ▷ *vi* schwitzen; **to be in a ~** schwitzen
sweater ['swɛtəʳ] *n* Pullover *m*
sweatshirt ['swɛtʃəːt] *n* Sweatshirt *nt*
sweaty ['swɛtɪ] *adj* verschwitzt; (*hands*) schweißig
Swede [swiːd] *n* Schwede *m*, Schwedin *f*
swede [swiːd] (*Brit*) *n* Steckrübe *f*
Sweden ['swiːdn] *n* Schweden *nt*
Swedish ['swiːdɪʃ] *adj* schwedisch ▷ *n* Schwedisch *nt*
sweep [swiːp] (*pt, pp* **swept**) *n*: **to give sth a ~** etw fegen *or* kehren; (*curve*) Bogen *m*; (*range*) Bereich *m*; (*also:* **chimney sweep**) Kaminkehrer *m*, Schornsteinfeger *m* ▷ *vt* fegen, kehren; (*current*) reißen ▷ *vi* (*through*

air) gleiten; *(wind)* fegen
▸ **sweep away** *vt* hinwegfegen
▸ **sweep past** *vi* vorbeirauschen
▸ **sweep up** *vi* zusammenfegen, zusammenkehren

sweeping ['swi:pɪŋ] *adj (gesture)* weit ausholend; *(changes, reforms)* weitreichend; *(statement)* verallgemeinernd

sweet [swi:t] *n (candy)* Bonbon *nt or m*; *(Brit: Culin)* Nachtisch *m* ▷ *adj* süß; *(air, water)* frisch; *(kind)* lieb ▷ *adv*: **to smell/taste ~** süß duften/schmecken; **~ and sour** süß-sauer

sweetcorn ['swi:tkɔ:n] *n* Mais *m*

sweeten ['swi:tn] *vt* süßen; *(temper)* bessern; *(person)* gnädig stimmen

sweetener ['swi:tnə^r] *n* Süßstoff *m*; *(fig)* Anreiz *m*

sweetheart ['swi:thɑ:t] *n* Freund(in) *m(f)*; *(in speech, writing)* Schatz *m*, Liebling *m*

sweetness ['swi:tnɪs] *n* Süße *f*; *(kindness)* Liebenswürdigkeit *f*

sweet pea *n* (Garten)wicke *f*

swell [swɛl] *(pt* **~ed**, *pp* **swollen** *or* **~ed**) *n* Seegang *m* ▷ *adj (US: inf)* toll, prima ▷ *vi (increase)* anwachsen; *(sound)* anschwellen; *(feeling)* stärker werden; *(also:* **swell up**) anschwellen

swelling ['swɛlɪŋ] *n* Schwellung *f*

sweltering ['swɛltərɪŋ] *adj (heat)* glühend; *(weather, day)* glühend heiß

swept [swɛpt] *pt, pp of* **sweep**

swerve [swə:v] *vi (animal)* ausbrechen; *(driver, vehicle)* ausschwenken; **to ~ off the road** ausschwenken und von der Straße abkommen

swift [swɪft] *n* Mauersegler *m* ▷ *adj* schnell

swig [swɪg] *(inf) n* Schluck *m* ▷ *vt* herunterkippen

swill [swɪl] *vt (also:* **swill out**) ausspülen; *(also:* **swill down**) abspülen ▷ *n (for pigs)* Schweinefutter *nt*

swim [swɪm] *(pt* **swam**, *pp* **swum**) *vi* schwimmen; *(before one's eyes)* verschwimmen ▷ *vt (the Channel etc)* durchschwimmen; *(a length)* schwimmen ▷ *n*: **to go for a ~** schwimmen gehen; **to go ~ming** schwimmen gehen; **my head is ~ming** mir dreht sich der Kopf

swimmer ['swɪmə^r] *n* Schwimmer(in) *m(f)*

swimming ['swɪmɪŋ] *n* Schwimmen *nt*

swimming cap *n* Badekappe *f*, Bademütze *f*

swimming costume *(Brit) n* Badeanzug *m*

swimming pool *n* Schwimmbad *nt*

swimming trunks *npl* Badehose *f*

swimsuit ['swɪmsu:t] *n* Badeanzug *m*

swindle ['swɪndl] *n* Schwindel *m*, Betrug *m* ▷ *vt*: **to ~ sb (out of sth)** jdn (um etw) betrügen *or* beschwindeln

swine [swaɪn] *(inf!) n* Schwein *nt*

swing [swɪŋ] *(pt, pp* **swung**) *n (in playground)* Schaukel *f*; *(movement)* Schwung *m*; *(change)* Umschwung *m*; *(Mus)* Swing *m* ▷ *vt (arms, legs)* schwingen (mit); *(also:* **swing round**) herumschwenken ▷ *vi* schwingen; *(also:* **swing round**) sich umdrehen; *(vehicle)* herumschwenken; **a ~ to the left** *(Pol)* ein Linksruck *m*; **to get into the ~ of things** richtig reinkommen; **to be in full ~** *(party etc)* in vollem Gang sein

swing bridge *n* Drehbrücke *f*

swing door, *(US)* **swinging door** *n* Pendeltür *f*

swingeing ['swɪndʒɪŋ] *(Brit) adj (blow)* hart; *(attack)* scharf; *(cuts, increases)* extrem

swipe [swaɪp] *vt (also:* **swipe at**) schlagen nach; *(inf: steal)* klauen ▷ *n* Schlag *m*

swirl [swə:l] *vi* wirbeln ▷ *n* Wirbeln *nt*

Swiss [swɪs] *adj* schweizerisch, Schweizer ▷ *n inv* Schweizer(in) *m(f)*

switch [swɪtʃ] *n* Schalter *m*; *(change)* Änderung *f* ▷ *vt (change)* ändern; *(exchange)* tauschen, wechseln; **to ~ (round** *or* **over)** vertauschen
▸ **switch off** *vt* abschalten; *(light)* ausschalten ▷ *vi (fig)* abschalten
▸ **switch on** *vt* einschalten; *(radio)* anstellen; *(engine)* anlassen

switchboard ['swɪtʃbɔ:d] *n* Vermittlung *f*, Zentrale *f*

Switzerland ['swɪtsələnd] *n* die Schweiz *f*

swivel ['swɪvl] *vi (also:* **swivel round**) sich (herum)drehen

swollen ['swəulən] *pp of* **swell** ▷ *adj* geschwollen; *(lake etc)* angeschwollen

swoon [swu:n] *vi* beinahe ohnmächtig werden ▷ *n* Ohnmacht *f*

swoop [swu:p] *n (by police etc)* Razzia *f*; *(of bird etc)* Sturzflug *m* ▷ *vi (also:* **swoop down**: *bird)* herabstoßen; *(plane)* einen Sturzflug machen

swop [swɔp] = **swap**

sword [sɔ:d] *n* Schwert *nt*

swordfish ['sɔ:dfɪʃ] *n* Schwertfisch *m*

swore [swɔ:^r] *pt of* **swear**

sworn [swɔ:n] *pp of* **swear** ▷ *adj (statement)* eidlich; *(evidence)* unter Eid; *(enemy)* geschworen

swot [swɔt] *vi* pauken ▷ *n (pej)* Streber(in) *m(f)*
▸ **swot up** *vt*: **to ~ up (on)** pauken *(+acc)*

swum [swʌm] *pp of* **swim**

swung [swʌŋ] *pt, pp of* **swing**

syllable ['sɪləbl] *n* Silbe *f*

syllabus ['sɪləbəs] *n* Lehrplan *m*; **on the ~** im Lehrplan

symbol ['sɪmbl] *n* Symbol *nt*

symbolic [sɪm'bɔlɪk], **symbolical** [sɪm'bɔlɪkl] *adj* symbolisch; **to be ~(al) of sth** etw symbolisieren, ein Symbol für etw sein

symmetrical [sɪ'mɛtrɪkl] *adj* symmetrisch

symmetry ['sɪmɪtrɪ] *n* Symmetrie *f*

sympathetic [sɪmpə'θɛtɪk] *adj (understanding)* verständnisvoll; *(showing pity)* mitfühlend; *(likeable)* sympathisch; *(supportive)* wohlwollend; **to be ~ to a cause** *(well-disposed)* einer Sache wohlwollend gegenüberstehen

sympathize ['sɪmpəθaɪz] *vi*: **to ~ with** (*person*) Mitleid haben mit; (*feelings*) Verständnis haben für; (*cause*) sympathisieren mit

sympathizer ['sɪmpəθaɪzə^r] *n* (*Pol*) Sympathisant(in) *m(f)*

sympathy ['sɪmpəθɪ] *n* Mitgefühl *nt*; **sympathies** *npl* (*support, tendencies*) Sympathien *pl*; **with our deepest ~** mit aufrichtigem *or* herzlichem Beileid; **to come out in ~** (*workers*) in einen Sympathiestreik treten

symphony ['sɪmfənɪ] *n* Sinfonie *f*

symptom ['sɪmptəm] *n* (*Med, fig*) Symptom *nt*, Anzeichen *nt*

synagogue ['sɪnəgɔg] *n* Synagoge *f*

syndicate ['sɪndɪkɪt] *n* Interessengemeinschaft *f*; (*of businesses*) Verband *m*; (*of newspapers*) Pressezentrale *f*

syndrome ['sɪndrəum] *n* Syndrom *nt*; (*fig*) Phänomen *nt*

synonym ['sɪnənɪm] *n* Synonym *nt*

synopsis [sɪ'nɔpsɪs] (*pl* **synopses**) *n* Abriss *m*, Zusammenfassung *f*

synthetic [sɪn'θɛtɪk] *adj* synthetisch; (*speech*) künstlich; **synthetics** *npl* (*man-made fabrics*) Synthetik *f*

syphon ['saɪfən] = **siphon**

Syria ['sɪrɪə] *n* Syrien *nt*

syringe [sɪ'rɪndʒ] *n* Spritze *f*

syrup ['sɪrəp] *n* Sirup *m*; (*also*: **golden syrup**) (gelber) Sirup *m*

system ['sɪstəm] *n* System *nt*; (*body*) Körper *m*; (*Anat*) Apparat *m*, System *nt*; **it was a shock to his ~** er hatte schwer damit zu schaffen

systematic [sɪstə'mætɪk] *adj* systematisch

system disk *n* (*Comput*) Systemdiskette *f*

systems analyst ['sɪstəmz-] *n* (*Comput*) Systemanalytiker(in) *m(f)*

Tt

ta [tɑː] (*Brit: inf*) *interj* danke
tab [tæb] *n* (*on drinks can*) Ring *m*; (*on garment*) Etikett *nt*; **to keep ~s on sb/sth** (*fig*) jdn/ etw im Auge behalten
tabby ['tæbɪ] *n* (*also*: **tabby cat**) getigerte Katze *f*
table ['teɪbl] *n* Tisch *m*; (*Math, Chem etc*) Tabelle *f* ▹ *vt* (*Brit: Parl: motion etc*) einbringen; **to lay** *or* **set the ~** den Tisch decken; **to clear the ~** den Tisch abräumen; **league ~** (*Brit: Sport*) Tabelle *f*
tablecloth ['teɪblklɔθ] *n* Tischdecke *f*
table d'hôte [tɑːbl'dəut] *adj* (*menu, meal*) Tagesmenü *nt*
table lamp *n* Tischlampe *f*
tablemat ['teɪblmæt] *n* (*of cloth*) Set *nt or m*; (*for hot dish*) Untersatz *m*
tablespoon ['teɪblspuːn] *n* Esslöffel *m*; (*also*: **tablespoonful**) Esslöffel(voll) *m*
tablet ['tæblɪt] *n* (*Med*) Tablette *f*; (*Hist: for writing*) Tafel *f*; (*plaque*) Plakette *f*; **~ of soap** (*Brit*) Stück *nt* Seife
table tennis *n* Tischtennis *nt*
table wine *n* Tafelwein *m*
tabloid ['tæblɔɪd] *n* (*newspaper*) Boulevardzeitung *f*; **the ~s** die Boulevardpresse
taboo [tə'buː] *n* Tabu *nt* ▹ *adj* tabu; **a ~ subject/word** ein Tabuthema/Tabuwort
tack [tæk] *n* (*nail*) Stift *m* ▹ *vt* (*nail*) anheften; (*stitch*) heften ▹ *vi* (*Naut*) kreuzen; **to change ~** (*fig*) den Kurs ändern; **to ~ sth on to (the end of) sth** etw (hinten) an etw *acc* anheften
tackle ['tækl] *n* (*for fishing*) Ausrüstung *f*; (*for lifting*) Flaschenzug *m*; (*Football, Rugby*) Angriff *m* ▹ *vt* (*deal with: difficulty*) in Angriff nehmen; (*challenge: person*) zur Rede stellen; (*physically, also Sport*) angreifen
tacky ['tækɪ] *adj* (*sticky*) klebrig; (*pej: cheap-looking*) schäbig
tact [tækt] *n* Takt *m*
tactful ['tæktful] *adj* taktvoll; **to be ~** taktvoll sein
tactical ['tæktɪkl] *adj* taktisch; **~ error** taktischer Fehler; **~ voting** taktische Stimmabgabe
tactics ['tæktɪks] *npl* Taktik *f*
tactless ['tæktlɪs] *adj* taktlos
tadpole ['tædpəul] *n* Kaulquappe *f*
taffy ['tæfɪ] (*US*) *n* (*toffee*) Toffee *nt*, Sahnebonbon *nt*
tag [tæg] *n* (*label*) Anhänger *m*; **price/name ~** Preis-/Namensschild *nt*; **(electronic) ~** (elektronische) Fußfessel *f*
▸ **tag along** *vi* sich anschließen
tail [teɪl] *n* (*of animal*) Schwanz *m*; (*of plane*) Heck *nt*; (*of shirt, coat*) Schoß *m* ▹ *vt* (*follow*) folgen +*dat*; **tails** *npl* (*formal suit*) Frack *m*; **to turn ~** die Flucht ergreifen; *see also* **head**
▸ **tail off** *vi* (*in size etc*) abnehmen; (*voice*) schwächer werden
tailback ['teɪlbæk] (*Brit*) *n* (*Aut*) Stau *m*
tail end *n* Ende *nt*
tailgate ['teɪlgeɪt] *n* (*Aut*) Heckklappe *f*
tailor ['teɪlə[r]] *n* Schneider(in) *m(f)* ▹ *vt*: **to ~ sth (to)** etw abstimmen (auf +*acc*); **~'s shop** Schneiderei *f*
tailoring ['teɪlərɪŋ] *n* (*craft*) Schneiderei *f*; (*cut*) Verarbeitung *f*
tailor-made ['teɪlə'meɪd] *adj* (*also fig*) maßgeschneidert
tailwind ['teɪlwɪnd] *n* Rückenwind *m*
tainted ['teɪntɪd] *adj* (*food, water, air*) verdorben; (*fig: profits, reputation etc*): **~ with** behaftet mit
Taiwan ['taɪ'wɑːn] *n* Taiwan *nt*
take [teɪk] (*pt* **took**, *pp* **~n**) *vt* nehmen; (*photo, notes*) machen; (*decision*) fällen; (*require: courage, time*) erfordern; (*tolerate: pain etc*) ertragen; (*hold: passengers etc*) fassen; (*accompany: person*) begleiten; (*carry, bring*) mitnehmen; (*exam, test*) machen; (*conduct: meeting*) leiten; (*: class*) unterrichten ▹ *vi* (*have effect: drug*) wirken; (*: dye*) angenommen werden ▹ *n* (*Cine*) Aufnahme *f*; **to ~ sth from** (*drawer etc*) etw nehmen aus +*dat*; **I ~ it (that)** ich nehme an(, dass); **I took him for a doctor** (*mistake*) ich hielt ihn für einen Arzt; **to ~ sb's hand** jds Hand nehmen; **to ~ sb for a walk** mit jdm spazieren gehen; **to be ~n ill** krank werden; **to ~ it upon o.s. to do sth** es auf sich nehmen, etw zu tun; **~ the first (street) on the left** nehmen Sie die erste Straße links; **to ~ Russian at university** Russisch studieren; **it won't ~ long** es dauert nicht lange; **I was quite ~n with her/it** (*attracted to*) ich war von ihr/davon recht angetan

▸**take after** *vt fus* (*resemble*) ähneln *+dat*, ähnlich sein *+dat*
▸**take apart** *vt* auseinandernehmen
▸**take away** *vt* wegnehmen; (*carry off*) wegbringen; (*Math*) abziehen ▹*vi*: **to ~ away from** (*detract from*) schmälern, beeinträchtigen
▸**take back** *vt* (*return*) zurückbringen; (*one's words*) zurücknehmen
▸**take down** *vt* (*write down*) aufschreiben; (*dismantle*) abreißen
▸**take in** *vt* (*deceive*: *person*) hereinlegen, täuschen; (*understand*) begreifen; (*include*) einschließen; (*lodger*) aufnehmen; (*orphan, stray dog*) zu sich nehmen; (*dress, waistband*) enger machen
▸**take off** *vi* (*Aviat*) starten; (*go away*) sich absetzen ▹*vt* (*clothes*) ausziehen; (*glasses*) abnehmen; (*make-up*) entfernen; (*time*) freinehmen; (*imitate*: *person*) nachmachen
▸**take on** *vt* (*work, responsibility*) übernehmen; (*employee*) einstellen; (*compete against*) antreten gegen
▸**take out** *vt* (*invite*) ausgehen mit; (*remove*: *tooth*) herausnehmen; (*licence*) erwerben; **to ~ sth out of sth** (*drawer, pocket etc*) etw aus etw nehmen; **don't ~ it out on me!** lass es nicht an mir aus!
▸**take over** *vt* (*business*) übernehmen; (*country*) Besitz ergreifen von ▹*vi* (*replace*): **to ~ over from sb** jdn ablösen
▸**take to** *vt fus* (*person, thing*) mögen; (*activity*) Gefallen finden an *+dat*; (*form habit of*): **to ~ to doing sth** sich *dat* angewöhnen, etw zu tun
▸**take up** *vt* (*hobby, sport*) anfangen mit; (*job*) antreten; (*idea etc*) annehmen; (*time, space*) beanspruchen; (*continue*: *task, story*) fortfahren mit; (*shorten*: *hem, garment*) kürzer machen ▹*vi* (*befriend*): **to ~ up with sb** sich mit jdm anfreunden; **to ~ sb up on an offer/a suggestion** auf jds Angebot/Vorschlag eingehen

takeaway ['teɪkəweɪ] (*Brit*) *n* (*shop, restaurant*) ≈ Schnellimbiss *m*; (*food*) Imbiss *m* (*zum Mitnehmen*)
taken ['teɪkən] *pp of* **take**
takeoff ['teɪkɔf] *n* (*Aviat*) Start *m*
takeout ['teɪkaut] (*US*) *n* = **takeaway**
takeover ['teɪkəuvə^r] *n* (*Comm*) Übernahme *f*; (*of country*) Inbesitznahme *f*
takings ['teɪkɪŋz] *npl* Einnahmen *pl*
talc [tælk] *n* (*also*: **talcum powder**) Talkumpuder *nt*
tale [teɪl] *n* Geschichte *f*; **to tell ~s (to sb)** (*child*) (jdm) Geschichten erzählen
talent ['tælnt] *n* Talent *nt*
talented ['tæləntɪd] *adj* talentiert, begabt
talk [tɔ:k] *n* (*speech*) Vortrag *m*; (*conversation, discussion*) Gespräch *nt*; (*gossip*) Gerede *nt* ▹*vi* (*speak*) sprechen; (*chat*) reden; (*gossip*) klatschen; **talks** *npl* (*Pol etc*) Gespräche *pl*; **to give a ~** einen Vortrag halten; **to ~ about** (*discuss*) sprechen *or* reden über; **~ing of films, have you seen ...?** da wir gerade von Filmen sprechen: hast du ... gesehen?; **to ~ sb into doing sth** jdn zu etw überreden; **to ~ sb out of doing sth** jdm etw ausreden
▸**talk over** *vt* (*problem etc*) besprechen, bereden

talkative ['tɔ:kətɪv] *adj* gesprächig
talk show *n* Talkshow *f*
tall [tɔ:l] *adj* (*person*) groß; (*glass, bookcase, tree, building*) hoch; (*ladder*) lang; **to be 6 feet ~** (*person*) ≈ 1,80m groß sein; **how ~ are you?** wie groß bist du?
tall story *n* unglaubliche Geschichte *f*
tally ['tælɪ] *n* (*of marks, amounts etc*) aktueller Stand *m* ▹*vi*: **to ~ (with)** (*figures, stories etc*) übereinstimmen mit; **to keep a ~ of sth** über etw *acc* Buch führen
talon ['tælən] *n* Kralle *f*
tambourine [tæmbə'ri:n] *n* Tamburin *nt*
tame [teɪm] *adj* (*animal, bird*) zahm; (*fig*: *story, party, performance*) lustlos, lahm (*inf*)
tamper ['tæmpə^r] *vi*: **to ~ with sth** an etw *dat* herumpfuschen (*inf*)
tampon ['tæmpɔn] *n* Tampon *m*
tan [tæn] *n* (*also*: **suntan**) (Sonnen)bräune *f* ▹*vi* (*person, skin*) braun werden ▹*vt* (*hide*) gerben; (*skin*) bräunen ▹*adj* (*colour*) hellbraun; **to get a ~** braun werden
tandem ['tændəm] *n* Tandem *nt*; (*together*): **in ~** (*fig*) zusammen
tang [tæŋ] *n* (*smell*) Geruch *m*; (*taste*) Geschmack *m*
tangent ['tændʒənt] *n* (*Math*) Tangente *f*; **to go off at a ~** (*fig*) vom Thema abschweifen
tangerine [tændʒə'ri:n] *n* (*fruit*) Mandarine *f*; (*colour*) Orangerot *nt*
tangle ['tæŋgl] *n* (*of branches, wire etc*) Gewirr *nt*; **to be in a ~** verheddert sein; (*fig*) durcheinander sein; **to get in a ~** sich verheddern; (*fig*) durcheinandergeraten
tank [tæŋk] *n* Tank *m*; (*for photographic processing*) Wanne *f*; (*also*: **fish tank**) Aquarium *nt*; (*Mil*) Panzer *m*
tanker ['tæŋkə^r] *n* (*ship*) Tanker *m*; (*truck*) Tankwagen *m*
tanned [tænd] *adj* (*person*) braun gebrannt; (*hide*) gegerbt
tantalizing ['tæntəlaɪzɪŋ] *adj* (*smell*) verführerisch; (*possibility*) verlockend
tantamount ['tæntəmaunt] *adj*: **~ to** gleichbedeutend mit
tantrum ['tæntrəm] *n* Wutanfall *m*; **to throw a ~** einen Wutanfall bekommen
Tanzania [tænzə'nɪə] *n* Tansania *nt*
tap [tæp] *n* (*on sink, gas tap*) Hahn *m*; (*gentle blow*) leichter Schlag *m*, Klaps *m* ▹*vt* (*hit gently*) klopfen; (*exploit*: *resources, energy*) nutzen; (*telephone*) abhören, anzapfen; **on ~** (*fig*: *resources, information*) zur Verfügung; (*beer*) vom Fass
tape [teɪp] *n* (*also*: **magnetic tape**) Tonband *nt*; (*cassette*) Kassette *f*; (*also*: **sticky tape**) Klebeband *nt*; (*for tying*) Band *nt* ▹*vt* (*record,*

conversation) aufnehmen, aufzeichnen; (*stick with tape*) mit Klebeband befestigen; **on ~** (*song etc*) auf Band

tape deck *n* Tapedeck *nt*

tape measure *n* Bandmaß *nt*

taper ['teɪpər] *n* (*candle*) lange, dünne Kerze ▷ *vi* sich verjüngen

tape recorder *n* Tonband(gerät) *nt*

tapestry ['tæpɪstrɪ] *n* (*on wall*) Wandteppich *m*; (*fig*) Kaleidoskop *nt*

tar [tɑː] *n* Teer *m*; **low/middle ~ cigarettes** Zigaretten mit niedrigem/mittlerem Teergehalt

target ['tɑːgɪt] *n* Ziel *nt*; (*fig: of joke, criticism etc*) Zielscheibe *f*; **to be on ~** (*project, work*) nach Plan verlaufen

tariff ['tærɪf] *n* (*tax on goods*) Zoll *m*; (*Brit: in hotels etc*) Preisliste *f*

tarnish ['tɑːnɪʃ] *vt* (*silver, brass etc*) stumpf werden lassen; (*fig: reputation etc*) beflecken, in Mitleidenschaft ziehen

tarpaulin [tɑː'pɔːlɪn] *n* Plane *f*

tarragon ['tærəgən] *n* Estragon *m*

tart [tɑːt] *n* (*Culin*) Torte *f*; (*: small*) Törtchen *nt*; (*Brit: inf: prostitute*) Nutte *f* ▷ *adj* (*apple, grapefruit etc*) säuerlich

▸ **tart up** (*Brit: inf*) *vt* (*room, building*) aufmotzen; **to ~ o.s. up** sich fein machen; (*pej*) sich auftakeln

tartan ['tɑːtn] *n* Tartan *m*, Schottenstoff *m* ▷ *adj* (*scarf etc*) mit Schottenmuster

tartar ['tɑːtər] *n* (*on teeth*) Zahnstein *m*; (*pej: person*) Tyrann(in) *m(f)*

tartar sauce, tartare sauce ['tɑːtə-] *n* Remouladensoße *f*

task [tɑːsk] *n* Aufgabe *f*; **to take sb to ~** jdn ins Gebet nehmen

task force *n* (*Mil*) Sonderkommando *nt*; (*Police*) Spezialeinheit *f*

tassel ['tæsl] *n* Quaste *f*

taste [teɪst] *n* Geschmack *m*; (*sample*) Kostprobe *f*; (*fig: of suffering, freedom etc*) Vorgeschmack *m* ▷ *vt* (*get flavour of*) schmecken; (*test*) probieren, versuchen ▷ *vi*: **to ~ of/like sth** nach/wie etw schmecken; **sense of ~** Geschmackssinn *m*; **to have a ~ of sth** (*sample*) etw probieren; **to acquire a ~ for sth** (*liking*) Geschmack an etw *dat* finden; **to be in good/bad ~** (*joke etc*) geschmackvoll/geschmacklos sein; **you can ~ the garlic (in it)** (*detect*) man schmeckt den Knoblauch durch; **what does it ~ like?** wie schmeckt es?

tasteful ['teɪstful] *adj* geschmackvoll

tasteless ['teɪstlɪs] *adj* geschmacklos

tasty ['teɪstɪ] *adj* schmackhaft

tatters ['tætəz] *npl*: **to be in ~** (*clothes*) in Fetzen sein

tattoo [tə'tuː] *n* (*on skin*) Tätowierung *f*; (*spectacle*) Zapfenstreich *m* ▷ *vt*: **to ~ sth on sth** etw auf etw *acc* tätowieren

tatty ['tætɪ] (*Brit: inf*) *adj* schäbig

taught [tɔːt] *pt, pp of* **teach**

taunt [tɔːnt] *n* höhnische Bemerkung *f* ▷ *vt* (*person*) verhöhnen

Taurus ['tɔːrəs] *n* Stier *m*; **to be ~** (ein) Stier sein

taut [tɔːt] *adj* (*skin, thread etc*) straff

tax [tæks] *n* Steuer *f* ▷ *vt* (*earnings, goods etc*) besteuern; (*fig: memory, knowledge*) strapazieren; (*: patience etc*) auf die Probe stellen; **before/after ~** vor/nach Abzug der Steuern; **free of ~** steuerfrei

taxable ['tæksəbl] *adj* steuerpflichtig; (*income*) steuerbar

taxation [tæk'seɪʃən] *n* (*system*) Besteuerung *f*; (*money paid*) Steuern *pl*

tax avoidance *n* Steuerumgehung *f*

tax disc (*Brit*) *n* (*Aut*) Steuerplakette *f*

tax evasion *n* Steuerhinterziehung *f*

tax-free ['tæksfriː] *adj* steuerfrei

taxi ['tæksɪ] *n* Taxi *nt* ▷ *vi* (*Aviat: plane*) rollen

taxi driver *n* Taxifahrer(in) *m(f)*

taxi rank (*Brit*) *n* Taxistand *m*

tax relief *n* Steuernachlass *m*

tax return *n* Steuererklärung *f*

TB *n abbr* (*= tuberculosis*) Tb *f*, Tbc *f*

tbc *abbr* (*= to be confirmed*) noch zu bestätigen

tea [tiː] *n* (*drink*) Tee *m*; (*Brit: evening meal*) Abendessen *nt*; **afternoon ~** (*Brit*) Nachmittagstee *m*

tea bag *n* Teebeutel *m*

tea break (*Brit*) *n* Teepause *f*

teach [tiːtʃ] (*pt, pp* **taught**) *vt*: **to ~ sb sth, ~ sth to sb** (*instruct*) jdm etw beibringen; (*in school*) jdn in etw *dat* unterrichten ▷ *vi* unterrichten; **it taught him a lesson** (*fig*) er hat seine Lektion gelernt

teacher ['tiːtʃər] *n* Lehrer(in) *m(f)*; **German ~** Deutschlehrer(in) *m(f)*

teaching ['tiːtʃɪŋ] *n* (*work of teacher*) Unterricht *m*

tea cosy *n* Teewärmer *m*

teacup ['tiːkʌp] *n* Teetasse *f*

teak [tiːk] *n* Teak *nt*

tea leaves *npl* Teeblätter *pl*

team [tiːm] *n* (*of experts etc*) Team *nt*; (*Sport*) Mannschaft *f*, Team *nt*; (*of horses, oxen*) Gespann *nt*

▸ **team up** *vi*: **to ~ up (with)** sich zusammentun (mit)

teamwork ['tiːmwəːk] *n* Teamwork *nt*, Teamarbeit *f*

teapot ['tiːpɔt] *n* Teekanne *f*

tear[1] [tɛər] (*pt* **tore**, *pp* **torn**) *n* (*hole*) Riss *m* ▷ *vt* (*rip*) zerreißen ▷ *vi* (*become torn*) reißen; **to ~ sth to pieces** *or* **bits** *or* **shreds** (*lit, fig*) etw in Stücke reißen; **to ~ sb to pieces** jdn fertigmachen

▸ **tear along** *vi* (*rush: driver, car*) entlangrasen

▸ **tear apart** *vt* (*book, clothes, people*) auseinanderreißen; (*upset: person*) hin- und herreißen

▸ **tear away** *vt*: **to ~ o.s. away (from sth)** (*fig*) sich (von etw) losreißen

▸ **tear out** *vt* (*sheet of paper etc*) herausreißen

▸ **tear up** *vt* (*sheet of paper etc*) zerreißen
tear² [tɪəʳ] *n* (*in eye*) Träne *f*; **in ~s** in Tränen; **to burst into ~s** in Tränen ausbrechen
tearful ['tɪəful] *adj* (*person*) weinend; (*face*) tränenüberströmt
tear gas *n* Tränengas *nt*
tearoom ['ti:ru:m] *n* = **teashop**
tease [ti:z] *vt* necken; (*unkindly*) aufziehen ▹ *n*: **she's a real ~** sie zieht einen ständig auf
tea set *n* Teeservice *nt*
teaspoon ['ti:spu:n] *n* Teelöffel *m*; (*also*: **teaspoonful**: *measure*) Teelöffel(voll) *m*
teat [ti:t] *n* (*on bottle*) Sauger *m*
teatime ['ti:taɪm] *n* Teestunde *f*
tea towel (*Brit*) *n* Geschirrtuch *nt*
technical ['tɛknɪkl] *adj* technisch; (*terms, language*) Fach-
technicality [tɛknɪ'kælɪtɪ] *n* (*point of law*) Formalität *f*; (*detail*) technische Einzelheit *f*; **on a (legal) ~** aufgrund einer (juristischen) Formalität
technically ['tɛknɪklɪ] *adv* (*strictly speaking*) genau genommen; (*regarding technique*) technisch (gesehen)
technician [tɛk'nɪʃən] *n* Techniker(in) *m(f)*
technique [tɛk'ni:k] *n* Technik *f*
techno ['tɛknəu] *n* (*Mus*) Techno *nt*
technological [tɛknə'lɔdʒɪkl] *adj* technologisch
technology [tɛk'nɔlədʒɪ] *n* Technologie *f*
teddy ['tɛdɪ], **teddy bear** *n* Teddy(bär) *m*
tedious ['ti:dɪəs] *adj* langweilig
tee [ti:] *n* (*Golf*) Tee *nt*
▸ **tee off** *vi* (vom Tee) abschlagen
teem [ti:m] *vi*: **to ~ with** (*tourists etc*) wimmeln von; **it is ~ing down** es gießt in Strömen
teenage ['ti:neɪdʒ] *adj* (*fashions etc*) Jugend-; (*children*) im Teenageralter
teenager ['ti:neɪdʒəʳ] *n* Teenager *m*, Jugendliche(r) *f(m)*
teens [ti:nz] *npl*: **to be in one's ~** im Teenageralter sein
teeter ['ti:təʳ] *vi* (*also fig*) schwanken, taumeln
teeth [ti:θ] *npl of* **tooth**
teethe [ti:ð] *vi* Zähne bekommen, zahnen
teething troubles *npl* (*fig*) Kinderkrankheiten *pl*
teetotal ['ti:'təutl] *adj* (*person*) abstinent
telecommunications ['tɛlɪkəmju:nɪ'keɪʃənz] *n* Nachrichtentechnik *f*
teleconferencing [tɛlɪ'kɔnfərənsɪŋ] *n* Telekonferenzen *pl*
telegram ['tɛlɪgræm] *n* Telegramm *nt*
telegraph ['tɛlɪgrɑ:f] *n* (*system*) Telegraf *m*
telegraph pole *n* Telegrafenmast *m*
telephone ['tɛlɪfəun] *n* Telefon *nt* ▹ *vt* (*person*) anrufen ▹ *vi* anrufen, telefonieren; **to be on the ~** (*talking*) telefonieren; (*possessing phone*) ein Telefon haben
telephone call *n* Anruf *m*
telephone directory *n* Telefonbuch *nt*
telephone number *n* Telefonnummer *f*
telephonist [tə'lɛfənɪst] (*Brit*) *n* Telefonist(in) *m(f)*
telesales ['tɛlɪseɪlz] *n* Verkauf *m* per Telefon
telescope ['tɛlɪskəup] *n* Teleskop *nt* ▹ *vi* (*fig*: *bus, lorry*) sich ineinanderschieben ▹ *vt* (*make shorter*) zusammenschieben
televise ['tɛlɪvaɪz] *vt* (im Fernsehen) übertragen
television ['tɛlɪvɪʒən] *n* Fernsehen *nt*; (*set*) Fernseher *m*, Fernsehapparat *m*; **to be on ~** im Fernsehen sein
television programme *n* Fernsehprogramm *nt*
television set *n* Fernseher *m*, Fernsehapparat *m*
telex ['tɛlɛks] *n* (*system, machine, message*) Telex *nt* ▹ *vt* (*message*) telexen; (*person*) ein Telex schicken *+dat* ▹ *vi* telexen
tell [tɛl] (*pt, pp* **told**) *vt* (*say*) sagen; (*relate*: *story*) erzählen; (*distinguish*): **to ~ sth from** etw unterscheiden von; (*be sure*) wissen ▹ *vi* (*have an effect*) sich auswirken; **to ~ sb to do sth** jdm sagen, etw zu tun; **to ~ sb of** *or* **about sth** jdm von etw erzählen; **to be able to ~ the time** (*know how to*) die Uhr kennen; **can you ~ me the time?** können Sie mir sagen, wie spät es ist?; **(I) ~ you what, let's go to the cinema** weißt du was? Lass uns ins Kino gehen!; **I can't ~ them apart** ich kann sie nicht unterscheiden
▸ **tell off** *vt*: **to ~ sb off** jdn ausschimpfen
▸ **tell on** *vt fus* (*inform against*) verpetzen
teller ['tɛləʳ] *n* (*in bank*) Kassierer(in) *m(f)*
telling ['tɛlɪŋ] *adj* (*remark etc*) verräterisch
telltale ['tɛlteɪl] *adj* verräterisch ▹ *n* (*pej*) Petzer *m*, Petze *f*
telly ['tɛlɪ] (*Brit*: *inf*) *n abbr* = **television**
temp [tɛmp] (*Brit*: *inf*) *n abbr* (= *temporary office worker*) Zeitarbeitskraft *f* ▹ *vi* als Zeitarbeitskraft arbeiten
temper ['tɛmpəʳ] *n* (*nature*) Naturell *nt*; (*mood*) Laune *f* ▹ *vt* (*moderate*) mildern; **a (fit of) ~** ein Wutanfall *m*; **to be in a ~** gereizt sein; **to lose one's ~** die Beherrschung verlieren
temperament ['tɛmprəmənt] *n* Temperament *nt*
temperamental [tɛmprə'mɛntl] *adj* (*person, car*) launisch
temperate ['tɛmprət] *adj* gemäßigt
temperature ['tɛmprətʃəʳ] *n* Temperatur *f*; **to have** *or* **run a ~** Fieber haben; **to take sb's ~** bei jdm Fieber messen
temple ['tɛmpl] *n* (*building*) Tempel *m*; (*Anat*) Schläfe *f*
temporary ['tɛmpərərɪ] *adj* (*arrangement*) provisorisch; (*worker, job*) Aushilfs-; **~ refugee** Flüchtling *m* mit zeitlich begrenzter Aufenthaltserlaubnis; **~ secretary** Sekretärin zur Aushilfe; **~ teacher** Aushilfslehrer(in) *m(f)*
tempt [tɛmpt] *vt* in Versuchung führen; **to ~ sb into doing sth** jdn dazu verleiten, etw zu tun; **to be ~ed to do sth** versucht sein,

etw zu tun

temptation [tɛmp'teɪʃən] *n* Versuchung *f*

tempting ['tɛmptɪŋ] *adj* (*offer*) verlockend; (*food*) verführerisch

ten [tɛn] *num* zehn ▷ *n*: **~s of thousands** Zehntausende *pl*

tenacity [tə'næsɪtɪ] *n* Zähigkeit *f*, Hartnäckigkeit *f*

tenancy ['tɛnənsɪ] *n* (*of room*) Mietverhältnis *nt*; (*of land*) Pachtverhältnis *nt*

tenant ['tɛnənt] *n* (*of room*) Mieter(in) *m(f)*; (*of land*) Pächter(in) *m(f)*

tend [tɛnd] *vt* (*crops, sick person*) sich kümmern um ▷ *vi*: **to ~ to do sth** dazu neigen *or* tendieren, etw zu tun

tendency ['tɛndənsɪ] *n* (*of person*) Neigung *f*; (*of thing*) Tendenz *f*

tender ['tɛndə^r] *adj* (*person, care*) zärtlich; (*heart*) gut; (*sore*) empfindlich; (*meat, age*) zart ▷ *n* (*Comm*) Angebot *nt*; (*money*): **legal ~** gesetzliches Zahlungsmittel *nt* ▷ *vt* (*offer*) vorlegen; (*resignation*) einreichen; (*apology*) anbieten; **to put in a ~ (for)** ein Angebot vorlegen (für); **to put work out to ~** (*Brit*) Arbeiten ausschreiben

tendon ['tɛndən] *n* Sehne *f*

tenement ['tɛnəmənt] *n* Mietshaus *nt*

tenner ['tɛnə^r] (*Brit: inf*) *n* Zehner *m*

tennis ['tɛnɪs] *n* Tennis *nt*

tennis ball *n* Tennisball *m*

tennis court *n* Tennisplatz *m*

tennis match *n* Tennismatch *nt*

tennis player *n* Tennisspieler(in) *m(f)*

tennis racket *n* Tennisschläger *m*

tennis shoes *npl* Tennisschuhe *pl*

tenor ['tɛnə^r] *n* (*Mus*) Tenor *m*; (*of speech etc*) wesentlicher Gehalt *m*

tenpin bowling ['tɛnpɪn-] (*Brit*) *n* Bowling *nt*

tense [tɛns] *adj* (*person, muscle*) angespannt; (*smile*) verkrampft; (*period, situation*) gespannt ▷ *n* (*Ling*) Zeit *f*, Tempus *nt* ▷ *vt* (*muscles*) anspannen

tension ['tɛnʃən] *n* (*nervousness*) Angespanntheit *f*; (*between ropes etc*) Spannung *f*

tent [tɛnt] *n* Zelt *nt*

tentative ['tɛntətɪv] *adj* (*person, smile*) zögernd; (*step*) unsicher; (*conclusion, plans*) vorläufig

tenterhooks ['tɛntəhuks] *npl*: **to be on ~** wie auf glühenden Kohlen sitzen

tenth [tɛnθ] *num* zehnte(r, s) ▷ *n* Zehntel *nt*

tent peg *n* Hering *m*

tent pole *n* Zeltstange *f*

tenuous ['tɛnjuəs] *adj* (*hold, links etc*) schwach

tenure ['tɛnjuə^r] *n* (*of land etc*) Nutzungsrecht *nt*; (*of office*) Amtszeit *f*; (*Univ*): **to have ~** eine Dauerstellung haben

tepid ['tɛpɪd] *adj* (*also fig*) lauwarm

term [tə:m] *n* (*word*) Ausdruck *m*; (*period in power etc*) Amtszeit *f*; (*Scol: three per year*) Trimester *nt* ▷ *vt* (*call*) nennen; **terms** *npl* (*also Comm*) Bedingungen *pl*; **in economic/political ~s** wirtschaftlich/politisch gesehen; **in ~s of business** was das Geschäft angeht *or* betrifft; **~ of imprisonment** Gefängnisstrafe *f*; **"easy ~s"** (*Comm*) "günstige Bedingungen"; **in the short/long ~** auf kurze/lange Sicht; **to be on good ~s with sb** sich mit jdm gut verstehen; **to come to ~s with** (*problem*) sich abfinden mit

terminal ['tə:mɪnl] *adj* (*disease, patient*) unheilbar ▷ *n* (*Aviat, Comm, Comput*) Terminal *nt*; (*Elec*) Anschluss *m*; (*Brit: also:* **bus terminal**) Endstation *f*

terminate ['tə:mɪneɪt] *vt* beenden ▷ *vi*: **to ~ in** enden in *+dat*

termini ['tə:mɪnaɪ] *npl of* **terminus**

terminology [tə:mɪ'nɔlədʒɪ] *n* Terminologie *f*

terminus ['tə:mɪnəs] (*pl* **termini**) *n* (*for buses, trains*) Endstation *f*

terrace ['tɛrəs] *n* (*Brit: row of houses*) Häuserreihe *f*; (*Agr, patio*) Terrasse *f*; **the terraces** *npl* (*Brit: Sport*) die Ränge *pl*

terraced ['tɛrəst] *adj* (*house*) Reihen-; (*garden*) terrassenförmig angelegt

terracotta ['tɛrə'kɔtə] *n* (*clay*) Terrakotta *f*; (*colour*) Braunrot *nt* ▷ *adj* (*pot, roof etc*) Terrakotta-

terrain [tɛ'reɪn] *n* Gelände *nt*, Terrain *nt*

terrible ['tɛrɪbl] *adj* schrecklich, furchtbar

terribly ['tɛrɪblɪ] *adv* (*very*) furchtbar; (*very badly*) entsetzlich

terrier ['tɛrɪə^r] *n* Terrier *m*

terrific [tə'rɪfɪk] *adj* (*very great: thunderstorm, speed*) unheimlich; (*time, party*) sagenhaft

terrify ['tɛrɪfaɪ] *vt* erschrecken; **to be terrified** schreckliche Angst haben

terrifying ['tɛrɪfaɪɪŋ] *adj* entsetzlich, grauenvoll

territorial [tɛrɪ'tɔ:rɪəl] *adj* (*boundaries, dispute*) territorial, Gebiets-; (*waters*) Hoheits- ▷ *n* (*Mil*) Soldat *m* der Territorialarmee

territory ['tɛrɪtərɪ] *n* (*also fig*) Gebiet *nt*

terror ['tɛrə^r] *n* (*great fear*) panische Angst *f*

terrorism ['tɛrərɪzəm] *n* Terrorismus *m*

terrorist ['tɛrərɪst] *n* Terrorist(in) *m(f)*

test [tɛst] *n* Test *m*; (*of courage etc*) Probe *f*; (*Scol*) Prüfung *f*; (*also:* **driving test**) Fahrprüfung *f* ▷ *vt* testen; (*check:, Scol*) prüfen; **to put sth to the ~** etw auf die Probe stellen; **to ~ sth for sth** etw auf etw *acc* prüfen

testament ['tɛstəmənt] *n* Zeugnis *nt*; **the Old/New T~** das Alte/Neue Testament; **last will and ~** Testament *nt*

testicle ['tɛstɪkl] *n* Hoden *m*

testify ['tɛstɪfaɪ] *vi* (*Law*) aussagen; **to ~ to sth** (*Law, fig*) etw bezeugen

testimony ['tɛstɪmənɪ] *n* (*statement*) Aussage *f*; (*clear proof*): **to be (a) ~ to** ein Zeugnis *nt* sein für

test match *n* (*Cricket, Rugby*) Testmatch *nt*, Test Match *nt*, Länderspiel *nt*

test tube *n* Reagenzglas *nt*

tetanus ['tɛtənəs] *n* Tetanus *m*

tether ['tɛðə^r] *vt* (*animal*) festbinden ▷ *n*: **to be at the end of one's ~** völlig am Ende sein

text [tɛkst] *n* Text *m* ▷ *vt* (*on mobile phone*) eine SMS schreiben *+dat*
textbook ['tɛkstbuk] *n* Lehrbuch *nt*
text message *n* (*Tel*) SMS *f*
text messaging *n* (*Tel*) Textnachrichten *pl*
texture ['tɛkstʃəʳ] *n* Beschaffenheit *f*, Struktur *f*
Thai [taɪ] *adj* thailändisch ▷ *n* Thailänder(in) *m(f)*
Thailand ['taɪlænd] *n* Thailand *nt*
Thames [tɛmz] *n*: **the ~** die Themse
than [ðæn] *conj* (*in comparisons*) als; **more ~ 10** mehr als 10; **she is older ~ you think** sie ist älter, als Sie denken; **more ~ once** mehr als einmal
thank [θæŋk] *vt* danken *+dat*; **~ you** danke; **~ you very much** vielen Dank; **~ God!** Gott sei Dank!
thankful ['θæŋkful] *adj*: **~ (for/that)** dankbar (für/, dass)
thankfully ['θæŋkfəlɪ] *adv* dankbar; **~ there were few victims** zum Glück gab es nur wenige Opfer
thankless ['θæŋklɪs] *adj* undankbar
Thanksgiving ['θæŋksgɪvɪŋ], **Thanksgiving Day** (*US*) *n* Thanksgiving Day *m*
that [ðæt, ðət] (*pl* **those**) *adj* (*demonstrative*) der/die/das; **that man** der Mann; **that woman** die Frau; **that book** das Buch; **that one** der/die/das da; **I want this one, not that one** ich will dieses (hier), nicht das (da) ▷ *pron* **1** (*demonstrative*) das; **who's/what's that?** wer/was ist das?; **is that you?** bist du das?; **will you eat all that?** isst du das alles?; **that's what he said** das hat er gesagt; **what happened after that?** was geschah danach?; **that is (to say)** das heißt; **and that's that!** und damit Schluss!
2 (*relative: subject*) der/die/das; (*pl*) die; (*: direct object*) den/die/das; (*pl*) die; (*: indirect object*) dem/der/dem; (*pl*) denen; **the man that I saw** der Mann, den ich gesehen habe; **all that I have** alles was ich habe; **the people that I spoke to** die Leute, mit denen ich geredet habe
3 (*relative: of time*): **the day that he came** der Tag, an dem er kam; **the winter that he came to see us** der Winter, in dem er uns besuchte
▷ *conj* dass; **he thought that I was ill** er dachte, dass ich krank sei, er dachte, ich sei krank
▷ *adv* (*demonstrative*) so; **I can't work that much** ich kann nicht so viel arbeiten; **that high** so hoch
thatched [θætʃt] *adj* strohgedeckt
thaw [θɔː] *n* Tauwetter *nt* ▷ *vi* (*ice*) tauen; (*food*) auftauen ▷ *vt* (*also*: **thaw out**) auftauen; **it's ~ing** es taut
the [ðiː, ðə] *def art* **1** (*before masculine noun*) der; (*before feminine noun*) die; (*before neuter noun*) das; (*before plural noun*) die; **to play the piano/violin** Klavier/Geige spielen; **I'm going to the butcher's/the cinema** ich gehe zum Metzger/ins Kino
2 (*+ adj to form noun*): **the rich and the poor** die Reichen und die Armen; **to attempt the impossible** das Unmögliche versuchen
3 (*in titles*): **Elizabeth the First** Elisabeth die Erste; **Peter the Great** Peter der Große
4 (*in comparisons*): **the more he works the more he earns** je mehr er arbeitet, desto mehr verdient er; **the sooner the better** je eher, desto besser
theatre, (*US*) **theater** ['θɪətəʳ] *n* Theater *nt*; (*also*: **lecture theatre**) Hörsaal *m*; (*also*: **operating theatre**) Operationsaal *m*
theatre-goer ['θɪətəgəuəʳ] *n* Theaterbesucher(in) *m(f)*
theatrical [θɪ'ætrɪkl] *adj* (*event, production*) Theater-; (*gestures etc*) theatralisch
theft [θɛft] *n* Diebstahl *m*
their [ðɛəʳ] *adj* ihr
theirs [ðɛəz] *pron* ihre(r, s); **it is ~** es gehört ihnen; **a friend of ~** ein Freund/eine Freundin von ihnen; *see also* **my; mine¹**
them [ðɛm] *pron* (*direct*) sie; (*indirect*) ihnen; **I see ~** ich sehe sie; **give ~ the book** gib ihnen das Buch; **give me a few of ~** geben Sie mir ein paar davon; **with ~** mit ihnen; **without ~** ohne sie; *see also* **me**
theme [θiːm] *n* (*also Mus*) Thema *nt*
theme park *n* Themenpark *m*
theme song *n* Titelmusik *f*
themselves [ðəm'sɛlvz] *pl pron* (*reflexive, after prep*) sich; (*emphatic, alone*) selbst; **between ~** unter sich
then [ðɛn] *adv* (*at that time*) damals; (*next, later*) dann ▷ *conj* (*therefore*) also ▷ *adj*: **the ~ president** der damalige Präsident; **by ~** (*past*) bis dahin; (*future*) bis dann; **from ~ on** von da an; **before ~** davor; **until ~** bis dann; **and ~ what?** und was dann?; **what do you want me to do ~?** was soll ich dann machen?; **... but ~ (again) he's the boss** ... aber er ist ja der Chef
theology [θɪ'ɔlədʒɪ] *n* Theologie *f*
theoretical [θɪə'rɛtɪkl] *adj* theoretisch
theory ['θɪərɪ] *n* Theorie *f*; **in ~** theoretisch
therapist ['θɛrəpɪst] *n* Therapeut(in) *m(f)*
therapy ['θɛrəpɪ] *n* Therapie *f*
there [ðɛəʳ] *adv* **1: there is/are** da ist/sind; (*there exist(s)*) es gibt; **there are 3 of them** es gibt 3 davon; **there has been an accident** da war ein Unfall; **there will be a meeting tomorrow** morgen findet ein Treffen statt
2 (*referring to place*) da, dort; **down/over there** da unten/drüben; **put it in/on there** leg es dorthinein/-hinauf; **I want that book there** ich möchte das Buch da; **there he is!** da ist er ja!
3: there, there (*esp to child*) ist ja gut
thereabouts ['ðɛərə'bauts] *adv*: **or ~** (*place*) oder dortherum; (*amount, time*) oder so
thereafter [ðɛər'ɑːftəʳ] *adv* danach
thereby ['ðɛəbaɪ] *adv* dadurch

therefore ['ðɛəfɔːʳ] *adv* daher, deshalb
there's ['ðɛəz] = **there is; there has**
thermal ['θəːml] *adj (springs)* Thermal-; *(underwear, paper, printer)* Thermo-
thermometer [θə'mɔmɪtəʳ] *n* Thermometer *nt*
Thermos® ['θəːməs] *n (also:* **Thermos flask***)* Thermosflasche® *f*
thermostat ['θəːməustæt] *n* Thermostat *m*
thesaurus [θɪ'sɔːrəs] *n* Synonymwörterbuch *nt*
these [ðiːz] *pl adj, pl pron* diese
thesis ['θiːsɪs] *(pl* **theses***) n* These *f*; *(for doctorate etc)* Dissertation *f*, Doktorarbeit *f*
they [ðeɪ] *pl pron* sie; **~ say that …** *(it is said that)* man sagt, dass …
they'd [ðeɪd] = **they had; they would**
they'll [ðeɪl] = **they shall; they will**
they're [ðɛəʳ] = **they are**
they've [ðeɪv] = **they have**
thick [θɪk] *adj* dick; *(sauce etc)* dickflüssig; *(fog, forest, hair etc)* dicht; *(inf: stupid)* blöd ▷ *n*: **in the ~ of the battle** mitten im Gefecht; **it's 20 cm ~** es ist 20 cm dick
thicken ['θɪkn] *vi (fog etc)* sich verdichten ▷ *vt (sauce etc)* eindicken; **the plot ~s** die Sache wird immer verwickelter
thickness ['θɪknɪs] *n (of rope, wire)* Dicke *f*; *(layer)* Lage *f*
thickset [θɪk'sɛt] *adj (person, body)* gedrungen
thief [θiːf] *(pl* **thieves***) n* Dieb(in) *m(f)*
thigh [θaɪ] *n* Oberschenkel *m*
thimble ['θɪmbl] *n* Fingerhut *m*
thin [θɪn] *adj* dünn; *(fog)* leicht; *(hair, crowd)* spärlich ▷ *vt*: **to ~ (down)** *(sauce, paint)* verdünnen ▷ *vi (fog, crowd)* sich lichten; **his hair is ~ning** sein Haar lichtet sich
thing [θɪŋ] *n* Ding *nt*; *(matter)* Sache *f*; *(inf)*: **to have a ~ about sth** *(be fascinated by)* wie besessen sein von etw; *(hate)* etw nicht ausstehen können; **things** *npl (belongings)* Sachen *pl*; **to do sth first ~ (every morning/tomorrow morning)** etw (morgens/morgen früh) als Erstes tun; **I look awful first ~ in the morning** ich sehe frühmorgens immer furchtbar aus; **to do sth last ~ (at night)** etw als Letztes (am Abend) tun; **the ~ is …** die Sache ist die: …; **for one ~** zunächst mal; **don't worry about a ~** du brauchst dir überhaupt keine Sorgen zu machen; **you'll do no such ~!** das lässt du schön bleiben!; **poor ~** armes Ding; **the best ~ would be to …** das Beste wäre, zu …; **how are ~s?** wie gehts?
think [θɪŋk] *(pt, pp* **thought***) vi (reflect)* nachdenken; *(reason)* denken ▷ *vt (be of the opinion)* denken; *(believe)* glauben; **to ~ of** denken an *+acc*; *(recall)* sich erinnern an *+acc*; **what did you ~ of them?** was hielten Sie von ihnen?; **to ~ about sth/sb** *(ponder)* über etw/jdn nachdenken; **I'll ~ about it** ich werde es mir überlegen; **to ~ of doing sth** daran denken, etw zu tun; **to ~ highly of sb** viel von jdm halten; **to ~ aloud** laut nachdenken; **~ again!** denk noch mal nach!; **I ~ so/not** ich glaube ja/nein
▸ **think over** *vt (offer, suggestion)* überdenken; **I'd like to ~ things over** ich möchte mir die Sache noch einmal überlegen
▸ **think through** *vt* durchdenken
▸ **think up** *vt* sich *dat* ausdenken
thinly ['θɪnlɪ] *adv* dünn; *(disguised, veiled)* kaum
third [θəːd] *num* dritte(r, s) ▷ *n (fraction)* Drittel *nt*; *(Aut: also:* **third gear***)* dritter Gang *m*; *(Brit: Scol: degree)* ≈ Ausreichend *nt*; **a ~ of** ein Drittel *+gen*
thirdly ['θəːdlɪ] *adv* drittens
third party insurance *(Brit) n* ≈ Haftpflichtversicherung *f*
third-rate ['θəː'dreɪt] *(pej) adj* drittklassig
Third World *n*: **the ~** die Dritte Welt ▷ *adj* der Dritten Welt
thirst [θəːst] *n* Durst *m*
thirsty ['θəːstɪ] *adj* durstig; **to be ~** Durst haben; **gardening is ~ work** Gartenarbeit macht durstig
thirteen [θəː'tiːn] *num* dreizehn
thirteenth ['θəː'tiːnθ] *num* dreizehnte(r, s)
thirtieth ['θəːtɪɪθ] *num* dreißigste(r, s)
thirty ['θəːtɪ] *num* dreißig
this [ðɪs] *(pl* **these***) adj (demonstrative)* diese(r, s); **this man** dieser Mann; **this woman** diese Frau; **this book** dieses Buch; **this one** diese(r, s) (hier)
▷ *pron (demonstrative)* dies, das; **who/what is this?** wer/was ist das?; **this is where I live** hier wohne ich; **this is what he said** das hat er gesagt; **this is Mr Brown** *(in introductions, photo)* das ist Herr Brown; *(on telephone)* hier ist Herr Brown
▷ *adv (demonstrative)*: **this high/long** *etc* so hoch/lang *etc*
thistle ['θɪsl] *n* Distel *f*
thorn [θɔːn] *n* Dorn *m*
thorough ['θʌrə] *adj* gründlich
thoroughbred ['θʌrəbrɛd] *n (horse)* Vollblüter *m*
thoroughfare ['θʌrəfɛəʳ] *n (road)* Durchgangsstraße *f*; **"no ~"** *(Brit)* "Durchfahrt verboten"
thoroughly ['θʌrəlɪ] *adv* gründlich; *(very)* äußerst; **I ~ agree** ich stimme vollkommen zu
those [ðəuz] *pl adj, pl pron* die (da); **~ (of you) who …** diejenigen (von Ihnen), die …
though [ðəu] *conj* obwohl ▷ *adv* aber; **even ~** obwohl; **it's not easy, ~** es ist aber nicht einfach
thought [θɔːt] *pt, pp of* **think** ▷ *n* Gedanke *m*; **thoughts** *npl (opinion)* Gedanken *pl*; **after much ~** nach langer Überlegung; **I've just had a ~** mir ist gerade etwas eingefallen; **to give sth some ~** sich *dat* Gedanken über etw *acc* machen
thoughtful ['θɔːtful] *adj (deep in thought)* nachdenklich; *(considerate)* aufmerksam

thoughtless ['θɔ:tlɪs] *adj* gedankenlos
thousand ['θauzənd] *num* (ein)tausend; **two ~** zweitausend; **~s of** Tausende von
thousandth ['θauzəntθ] *num* tausendste(r, s)
thrash [θræʃ] *vt* (*beat*) verprügeln; (*defeat*) (vernichtend) schlagen
▸ **thrash about** *vi* um sich schlagen
▸ **thrash around** *vi* = **thrash about**
▸ **thrash out** *vt* (*problem*) ausdiskutieren
thread [θrɛd] *n* (*yarn*) Faden *m*; (*of screw*) Gewinde *nt* ▷ *vt* (*needle*) einfädeln; **to ~ one's way between** sich hindurchschlängeln zwischen
threadbare ['θrɛdbɛə^r] *adj* (*clothes*) abgetragen; (*carpet*) abgelaufen
threat [θrɛt] *n* Drohung *f*; (*fig*): **~ (to)** Gefahr *f* (für); **to be under ~ of** (*closure etc*) bedroht sein von
threaten ['θrɛtn] *vi* bedrohen ▷ *vt*: **to ~ sb with sth** jdm mit etw drohen; **to ~ to do sth** (damit) drohen, etw zu tun
threatening ['θrɛtnɪŋ] *adj* drohend, bedrohlich
three [θri:] *num* drei
three-dimensional [θri:dɪ'mɛnʃənl] *adj* dreidimensional
three-piece suit ['θri:pi:s-] *n* dreiteiliger Anzug *m*
three-piece suite *n* dreiteilige Polstergarnitur *f*
three-ply [θri:'plaɪ] *adj* (*wool*) dreifädig; (*wood*) dreilagig
three-quarters [θri:'kwɔ:təz] *npl* drei Viertel *pl*; **~ full** drei viertel voll
threshold ['θrɛʃhəuld] *n* Schwelle *f*; **to be on the ~ of sth** (*fig*) an der Schwelle zu etw sein *or* stehen
threw [θru:] *pt of* **throw**
thrifty ['θrɪftɪ] *adj* sparsam
thrill [θrɪl] *n* (*excitement*) Aufregung *f*; (*shudder*) Erregung *f* ▷ *vi* zittern ▷ *vt* (*person, audience*) erregen; **to be ~ed** (*with gift etc*) sich riesig freuen
thriller ['θrɪlə^r] *n* Thriller *m*
thrilling ['θrɪlɪŋ] *adj* (*ride, performance etc*) erregend; (*news*) aufregend
thrive [θraɪv] (*pt* **~d** *or* **throve**, *pp* **~d**) *vi* gedeihen; **to ~ on sth** von etw leben
thriving ['θraɪvɪŋ] *adj* (*business, community*) blühend, florierend
throat [θrəut] *n* Kehle *f*; **to have a sore ~** Halsschmerzen haben
throb [θrɔb] *n* (*of heart*) Klopfen *nt*; (*pain*) Pochen *nt*; (*of engine*) Dröhnen *nt* ▷ *vi* (*heart*) klopfen; (*pain*) pochen; (*machine*) dröhnen; **my head is ~bing** ich habe rasende Kopfschmerzen
throes [θrəuz] *npl*: **in the ~ of** (*war, moving house etc*) mitten in *+dat*; **death ~** Todeskampf *m*
throne [θrəun] *n* Thron *m*; **on the ~** auf dem Thron
throng ['θrɔŋ] *n* Masse *f* ▷ *vt* (*streets etc*) sich drängen in *+dat* ▷ *vi*: **to ~ to** strömen zu; **a ~ of people** eine Menschenmenge; **to be ~ed with** wimmeln von
throttle ['θrɔtl] *n* (*in car*) Gaspedal *nt*; (*on motorcycle*) Gashebel *m* ▷ *vt* (*strangle*) erdrosseln
through [θru:] *prep* durch; (*time*) während; (*owing to*) infolge *+gen* ▷ *adj* (*ticket, train*) durchgehend ▷ *adv* durch; **(from) Monday ~ Friday** (*US*) von Montag bis Freitag; **to be ~** (*Tel*) verbunden sein; **to be ~ with sb/sth** mit jdm/etw fertig sein; **we're ~!** es ist aus zwischen uns!; **"no ~ road"**, **"no ~ traffic"** (*US*) "keine Durchfahrt"; **to let sb ~** jdn durchlassen; **to put sb ~ to sb** (*Tel*) jdn mit jdm verbinden
throughout [θru:'aut] *adv* (*everywhere*) überall; (*the whole time*) die ganze Zeit über ▷ *prep* (*place*) überall in *+dat*; (*time*): **~ the morning/afternoon** während des ganzen Morgens/Nachmittags; **~ her life** ihr ganzes Leben lang
throw [θrəu] (*pt* **threw**, *pp* **~n**) *n* Wurf *m* ▷ *vt* werfen; (*rider*) abwerfen; (*fig: confuse*) aus der Fassung bringen; (*pottery*) töpfern; **to ~ a party** eine Party geben; **to ~ open** (*doors, windows*) aufreißen; (*debate*) öffnen
▸ **throw about** *vt* (*money*) herumwerfen mit
▸ **throw around** *vt* = **throw about**
▸ **throw away** *vt* wegwerfen; (*waste*) verschwenden
▸ **throw off** *vt* (*get rid of: burden*) abwerfen
▸ **throw out** *vt* (*rubbish*) wegwerfen; (*idea*) verwerfen; (*person*) hinauswerfen
▸ **throw together** *vt* (*meal*) hinhauen; (*clothes*) zusammenpacken
▸ **throw up** *vi* (*vomit*) sich übergeben
throwaway ['θrəuəweɪ] *adj* (*cutlery etc*) Einweg-; (*line, remark*) beiläufig
throw-in ['θrəuɪn] *n* (*Football*) Einwurf *m*
thrown [θrəun] *pp of* **throw**
thru [θru:] (*US*) *prep, adj, adv* = **through**
thrush [θrʌʃ] *n* (*bird*) Drossel *f*; (*Med: esp in children*) Soor *m*; (*: Brit: in women*) vaginale Pilzerkrankung *f*
thrust [θrʌst] (*pt, pp* **~**) *n* (*Tech*) Schubkraft *f*; (*push*) Stoß *m*; (*fig: impetus*) Stoßkraft *f* ▷ *vt* stoßen
thud [θʌd] *n* dumpfes Geräusch *nt*
thug [θʌg] *n* Schlägertyp *m*
thumb [θʌm] *n* Daumen *m* ▷ *vt*: **to ~ a lift** per Anhalter fahren; **to give sb/sth the ~s up** (*approve*) jdm/etw *dat* grünes Licht geben; **to give sb/sth the ~s down** (*disapprove*) jdn/etw ablehnen
▸ **thumb through** *vt fus* (*book*) durchblättern
thumbtack ['θʌmtæk] (*US*) *n* Heftzwecke *f*
thump [θʌmp] *n* (*blow*) Schlag *m*; (*sound*) dumpfer Schlag *m* ▷ *vt* schlagen auf *+acc* ▷ *vi* (*heart etc*) heftig pochen
thunder ['θʌndə^r] *n* Donner *m* ▷ *vi* donnern; (*shout angrily*) brüllen; **to ~ past** (*train etc*) vorbeidonnern

thunderbolt ['θʌndəbəult] *n* Blitzschlag *m*
thunderclap ['θʌndəklæp] *n* Donnerschlag *m*
thunderstorm ['θʌndəstɔ:m] *n* Gewitter *nt*
thundery ['θʌndərɪ] *adj* (*weather*) gewitterig
Thursday ['θə:zdɪ] *n* Donnerstag *m*; *see also* **Tuesday**
thus [ðʌs] *adv* (*in this way*) so; (*consequently*) somit
thwart [θwɔ:t] *vt* (*person*) einen Strich durch die Rechnung machen *+dat*; (*plans*) vereiteln
thyme [taɪm] *n* Thymian *m*
tiara [tɪ'ɑ:rə] *n* Diadem *nt*
Tibet [tɪ'bɛt] *n* Tibet *nt*
tick [tɪk] *n* (*sound*) Ticken *nt*; (*mark*) Häkchen *nt*; (*Zool*) Zecke *f*; (*Brit*: *inf*: *moment*) Augenblick *m*; (: *credit*): **to buy sth on ~** etw auf Pump kaufen ▷ *vi* (*clock, watch*) ticken ▷ *vt* (*item on list*) abhaken; **to put a ~ against sth** etw abhaken; **what makes him ~?** was ist er für ein Mensch?
▸ **tick off** *vt* (*item on list*) abhaken; (*person*) rüffeln
▸ **tick over** *vi* (*engine*) im Leerlauf sein; (*fig*: *business etc*) sich über Wasser halten
ticket ['tɪkɪt] *n* (*for public transport*) Fahrkarte *f*; (*for theatre etc*) Eintrittskarte *f*; (*in shop*: *on goods*) Preisschild *nt*; (: *from cash register*) Kassenbon *m*; (*for raffle*) Los *nt*; (*for library*) Ausweis *m*; (*also*: **parking ticket**: *fine*) Strafzettel *m*; (*US*: *Pol*) Wahlliste *f*; **to get a (parking) ~** (*Aut*) einen Strafzettel bekommen
ticket collector *n* (*Rail*: *at station*) Fahrkarten kontrolleur(in) *m(f)*; (*on train*) Schaffner(in) *m(f)*
ticket inspector *n* Fahrkartenkontrolleur(in) *m(f)*
ticket office *n* (*Rail*) Fahrkartenschalter *m*; (*Theat*) Theaterkasse *f*
tickle ['tɪkl] *vt* kitzeln; (*fig*: *amuse*) amüsieren ▷ *vi* kitzeln; **it ~s!** das kitzelt!
ticklish ['tɪklɪʃ] *adj* (*person, situation*) kitzlig
tidal ['taɪdl] *adj* (*force*) Gezeiten-, der Gezeiten; (*river*) Tide-
tidal wave *n* Flutwelle *f*
tidbit ['tɪdbɪt] (*US*) *n* = **titbit**
tiddlywinks ['tɪdlɪwɪŋks] *n* Flohhüpfen *nt*
tide [taɪd] *n* (*in sea*) Gezeiten *pl*; (*fig*: *of events, opinion etc*) Trend *m*; **high ~** Flut *f*; **low ~** Ebbe *f*; **the ~ is in/out** es ist Flut/Ebbe; **the ~ is coming in** die Flut kommt
▸ **tide over** *vt* über die Runden helfen *+dat*
tidy ['taɪdɪ] *adj* (*room, desk*) ordentlich, aufgeräumt; (*person*) ordnungsliebend; (*sum, income*) ordentlich ▷ *vt* (*also*: **tidy up**) aufräumen
tie [taɪ] *n* (*Brit*: *also*: **necktie**) Krawatte *f*; (*string etc*) Band *nt*; (*fig*: *link*) Verbindung *f*; (*Sport*: *match*) Spiel *nt*; (*in competition*: *draw*) Unentschieden *nt* ▷ *vt* (*parcel*) verschnüren; (*shoelaces*) zubinden; (*ribbon*) binden ▷ *vi* (*Sport etc*): **to ~ with sb for first place** sich mit jdm den ersten Platz teilen; **"black ~"** "Abendanzug"; **"white ~"** "Frackzwang"; **family ~s** familiäre Bindungen; **to ~ sth in a bow** etw zu einer Schleife binden; **to ~ a knot in sth** einen Knoten in etw *acc* machen
▸ **tie down** *vt* (*fig*: *restrict*) binden; (: *to date, price etc*) festlegen
▸ **tie in** *vi*: **to ~ in with** zusammenpassen mit
▸ **tie on** *vt* (*Brit*) anbinden
▸ **tie up** *vt* (*parcel*) verschnüren; (*dog*) anbinden; (*boat*) festmachen; (*person*) fesseln; (*arrangements*) unter Dach und Fach bringen; **to be ~d up** (*busy*) zu tun haben, beschäftigt sein
tier [tɪə^r] *n* (*of stadium etc*) Rang *m*; (*of cake*) Lage *f*
tiger ['taɪgə^r] *n* Tiger *m*
tight [taɪt] *adj* (*screw, knot, grip*) fest; (*shoes, clothes, bend*) eng; (*security*) streng; (*budget, money*) knapp; (*schedule*) gedrängt; (*inf*: *drunk*) voll; (: *stingy*) knickerig ▷ *adv* fest; **to be packed ~** (*suitcase*) prallvoll sein; (*room*) gerammelt voll sein; **everybody hold ~!** alle festhalten!
tighten ['taɪtn] *vt* (*rope, strap*) straffen; (*screw, bolt*) anziehen; (*grip*) festigen; (*security*) verschärfen ▷ *vi* (*grip*) sich festigen; (*rope etc*) sich spannen
tightfisted [taɪt'fɪstɪd] *adj* knickerig (*inf*)
tightly ['taɪtlɪ] *adv* fest
tightrope ['taɪtrəup] *n* Seil *nt*; **to be on** *or* **walking a ~** (*fig*) einen Balanceakt vollführen
tights [taɪts] (*Brit*) *npl* Strumpfhose *f*
tile [taɪl] *n* (*on roof*) Ziegel *m*; (*on floor*) Fliese *f*; (*on wall*) Kachel *f* ▷ *vt* (*floor*) mit Fliesen auslegen; (*bathroom*) kacheln
tiled [taɪld] *adj* (*floor*) mit Fliesen ausgelegt; (*wall*) gekachelt
till [tɪl] *n* (*in shop etc*) Kasse *f* ▷ *vt* (*land*) bestellen ▷ *prep, conj* = **until**
tiller ['tɪlə^r] *n* (*Naut*) Ruderpinne *f*
tilt [tɪlt] *vt* neigen ▷ *vi* sich neigen ▷ *n* (*slope*) Neigung *f*; **to wear one's hat at a ~** den Hut schief aufhaben; **(at) full ~** mit Volldampf
timber ['tɪmbə^r] *n* (*material*) Holz *nt*; (*trees*) Nutzholz *nt*
time [taɪm] *n* Zeit *f*; (*occasion*) Gelegenheit *f*, Mal *nt*; (*Mus*) Takt *m* ▷ *vt* (*measure time of*) die Zeit messen bei; (*runner*) stoppen; (*fix moment for*: *visit etc*) den Zeitpunkt festlegen für; **a long ~** eine lange Zeit; **for the ~ being** vorläufig; **4 at a ~** 4 auf einmal; **from ~ to time** von Zeit zu Zeit; **~ after time, ~ and again** immer (und immer) wieder; **at ~s** manchmal, zuweilen; **in ~** (*soon enough*) rechtzeitig; (*eventually*) mit der Zeit; (*Mus*) im Takt; **in a week's ~** in einer Woche; **in no ~** im Handumdrehen; **any ~** jederzeit; **on ~** rechtzeitig; **to be 30 minutes behind/ahead of ~** 30 Minuten zurück/voraus sein; **by the ~ he arrived** als er ankam; **5 ~s 5** 5 mal 5; **what ~ is it?** wie spät ist es?; **to have**

a good ~ sich amüsieren; **we/they** *etc* **had a hard ~** wir/sie *etc* hatten es schwer; **~'s up!** die Zeit ist um!; **I've no ~ for it** *(fig)* dafür habe ich nichts übrig; **he'll do it in his own (good) ~** *(without being hurried)* er macht es, ohne sich hetzen zu lassen; **he'll do it in his own ~, he'll do it on his own ~** *(US: out of working hours)* er macht es in seiner Freizeit; **to be behind the ~s** rückständig sein; **to ~ sth well/badly** den richtigen/falschen Zeitpunkt für etw wählen; **the bomb was ~d to go off 5 minutes later** die Bombe war so eingestellt, dass sie 5 Minuten später explodieren sollte

time bomb *n (also fig)* Zeitbombe *f*

timeless ['taɪmlɪs] *adj* zeitlos

time limit *n* zeitliche Grenze *f*

timely ['taɪmlɪ] *adj (arrival)* rechtzeitig; *(reminder)* zur rechten Zeit

time off *n*: **to take ~** sich *dat* freinehmen

timer ['taɪməʳ] *n (time switch)* Schaltuhr *f*; *(on cooker)* Zeitmesser *m*; *(on video)* Timer *m*

timescale ['taɪmskeɪl] *(Brit) n* Zeitspanne *f*

time-share ['taɪmʃɛəʳ] *n* Ferienwohnung *f* auf Timesharingbasis

time switch *n* Zeitschalter *m*

timetable ['taɪmteɪbl] *n (Rail etc)* Fahrplan *m*; *(Scol)* Stundenplan *m*; *(programme of events)* Programm *nt*

time zone *n* Zeitzone *f*

timid ['tɪmɪd] *adj (person)* schüchtern; *(animal)* scheu

timing ['taɪmɪŋ] *n (Sport)* Timing *nt*; **the ~ of his resignation** der Zeitpunkt seines Rücktritts

timpani ['tɪmpənɪ] *npl* Kesselpauken *pl*

tin [tɪn] *n (metal)* Blech *nt*; *(container)* Dose *f*; *(: for baking)* Form *f*; *(: Brit: can)* Büchse *f*, Dose *f*; **two ~s of paint** zwei Dosen Farbe

tinfoil ['tɪnfɔɪl] *n* Alufolie *f*

tinge [tɪndʒ] *n (of colour)* Färbung *f*; *(fig: of emotion etc)* Anflug *m*, Anstrich *m* ▷ *vt*: **~d with blue/red** leicht blau/rot gefärbt; **to be ~d with sth** *(fig: emotion etc)* einen Anstrich von etw haben

tingle ['tɪŋgl] *vi* prickeln; *(from cold)* kribbeln; **I was tingling with excitement** ich zitterte vor Aufregung

tinker ['tɪŋkəʳ] *n (gipsy)* Kesselflicker *m*

▸ **tinker with** *vt fus* herumbasteln an *+dat*

tinkle ['tɪŋkl] *vi* klingeln ▷ *n (inf)*: **to give sb a ~** *(Tel)* bei jdm anklingeln

tinned [tɪnd] *(Brit) adj (food, peas)* Dosen-, in Dosen

tinsel ['tɪnsl] *n* Rauschgoldgirlanden *pl*

tint [tɪnt] *n (colour)* Ton *m*; *(for hair)* Tönung *f* ▷ *vt (hair)* tönen

tinted ['tɪntɪd] *adj* getönt

tiny ['taɪnɪ] *adj* winzig

tip [tɪp] *n (end)* Spitze *f*; *(gratuity)* Trinkgeld *nt*; *(Brit: for rubbish)* Müllkippe *f*; *(: for coal)* Halde *f*; *(advice)* Tipp *m*, Hinweis *m* ▷ *vt (waiter)* ein Trinkgeld geben *+dat*; *(tilt)* kippen; *(also*: **tip over**: *overturn)* umkippen; *(also*: **tip out**: *empty)* leeren; *(predict: winner etc)* tippen *or* setzen auf *+acc*; **he ~ped out the contents of the box** er kippte den Inhalt der Kiste aus

▸ **tip off** *vt* einen Tipp *or* Hinweis geben *+dat*

tip-off ['tɪpɔf] *n* Hinweis *m*

tipped ['tɪpt] *adj (Brit: cigarette)* Filter-; **steel-~** mit Stahlspitze

tipsy ['tɪpsɪ] *(inf) adj* beschwipst

tiptoe ['tɪptəu] *n*: **on ~** auf Zehenspitzen

tire ['taɪəʳ] *n (US)* = **tyre** ▷ *vt* müde machen, ermüden ▷ *vi (become tired)* müde werden; **to ~ of sth** genug von etw haben

▸ **tire out** *vt* erschöpfen

tired ['taɪəd] *adj* müde; **to be/look ~** müde sein/aussehen; **to feel ~** sich müde fühlen; **to be ~ of sth** etw satthaben; **to be ~ of doing sth** es satthaben, etw zu tun

tireless ['taɪəlɪs] *adj* unermüdlich

tiresome ['taɪəsəm] *adj* lästig

tiring ['taɪərɪŋ] *adj* ermüdend, anstrengend

tissue ['tɪʃu:] *n (Anat, Biol)* Gewebe *nt*; *(paper handkerchief)* Papiertaschentuch *nt*

tissue paper *n* Seidenpapier *nt*

tit [tɪt] *n (bird)* Meise *f*; *(inf: breast)* Titte *f*; **~ for tat** wie du mir, so ich dir

titbit, (US) **tidbit** ['tɪtbɪt] *n (food, news)* Leckerbissen *m*

title ['taɪtl] *n* Titel *m*; *(Law)*: **~ to** Anspruch auf *+acc*

title deed *n* Eigentumsurkunde *f*

title role *n* Titelrolle *f*

T-junction ['ti:'dʒʌŋkʃən] *n* T-Kreuzung *f*

TM *abbr (= trademark)* Wz; = **transcendental meditation**

to [tu:] *prep* **1** *(direction)* nach *+dat*, zu *+dat*; **to go to France/London/school/the station** nach Frankreich/nach London/zur Schule/zum Bahnhof gehen; **to the left/right** nach links/rechts; **I have never been to Germany** ich war noch nie in Deutschland

2 *(as far as)* bis; **to count to 10** bis 10 zählen

3 *(with expressions of time)* vor *+dat*; **a quarter to 5** *(Brit)* Viertel vor 5

4 *(for, of)*: **the key to the front door** der Schlüssel für die Haustür; **a letter to his wife** ein Brief an seine Frau

5 *(expressing indirect object)*: **to give sth to sb** jdm etw geben; **to talk to sb** mit jdm sprechen; **I sold it to a friend** ich habe es an einen Freund verkauft; **you've done something to your hair** du hast etwas mit deinem Haar gemacht

6 *(in relation to)* zu; **A is to B as C is to D** A verhält sich zu B wie C zu D; **3 goals to 2** 3 zu 2 Tore; **40 miles to the gallon** 40 Meilen pro Gallone

7 *(purpose, result)* zu; **to sentence sb to death** jdn zum Tode verurteilen; **to my surprise** zu meiner Überraschung

▷ *with vb* **1** *(simple infinitive)*: **to go** gehen; **to eat** essen

2 *(following another vb)*: **to want to do sth**

etw tun wollen; **to try/start to do sth** versuchen/anfangen, etw zu tun
3 (*with vb omitted*): **I don't want to** ich will nicht; **you ought to** du solltest es tun
4 (*purpose, result*) (um ...) zu; **I did it to help you** ich habe es getan, um dir zu helfen
5 (*equivalent to relative clause*) zu; **he has a lot to lose** er hat viel zu verlieren; **the main thing is to try** die Hauptsache ist, es zu versuchen
6 (*after adjective etc*): **ready to use** gebrauchsfertig; **too old/young to ...** zu alt/jung, um zu ...; **it's too heavy to lift** es ist zu schwer zu heben
▷ *adv*: **to push/pull the door to** die Tür zudrücken/zuziehen; **to and fro** hin und her

toad [təud] *n* Kröte *f*
toadstool ['təudstu:l] *n* Giftpilz *m*
toast [təust] *n* (*bread, drink*) Toast *m* ▷ *vt* (*bread etc*) toasten; (*drink to*) einen Toast *or* Trinkspruch ausbringen auf *+acc*; **a piece** *or* **slice of ~** eine Scheibe Toast
toaster ['təustə^r] *n* Toaster *m*
tobacco [tə'bækəu] *n* Tabak *m*; **pipe ~** Pfeifentabak *m*
tobacconist [tə'bækənɪst] *n* Tabakhändler(in) *m(f)*
toboggan [tə'bɔgən] *n* Schlitten *m*
today [tə'deɪ] *adv, n* heute; **what day is it ~?** welcher Tag ist heute?; **what date is it ~?** der Wievielte ist heute?; **~ is the 4th of March** heute ist der 4. März; **a week ago ~** heute vor einer Woche; **~'s paper** die Zeitung von heute
toddler ['tɔdlə^r] *n* Kleinkind *nt*
toe [təu] *n* Zehe *f*, Zeh *m*; (*of shoe, sock*) Spitze *f*; **to ~ the line** (*fig*) auf Linie bleiben; **big/little ~** großer/kleiner Zeh
toenail ['təuneɪl] *n* Zehennagel *m*
toffee ['tɔfɪ] *n* Toffee *m*
toffee apple (*Brit*) *n* ≈ kandierter Apfel *m*
together [tə'gɛðə^r] *adv* zusammen; (*at the same time*) gleichzeitig; **~ with** gemeinsam mit
toil [tɔɪl] *n* Mühe *f* ▷ *vi* sich abmühen
toilet ['tɔɪlət] *n* Toilette *f* ▷ *cpd* (*kit, accessories etc*) Toiletten-; **to go to the ~** auf die Toilette gehen
toilet bag (*Brit*) *n* Kulturbeutel *m*
toilet paper *n* Toilettenpapier *nt*
toiletries ['tɔɪlətrɪz] *npl* Toilettenartikel *pl*
toilet roll *n* Rolle *f* Toilettenpapier
token ['təukən] *n* (*sign, souvenir*) Zeichen *nt*; (*substitute coin*) Wertmarke *f* ▷ *adj* (*strike, payment etc*) symbolisch; **by the same ~** (*fig*) in gleicher Weise; **book/record/gift ~** (*Brit*) Bücher-/Platten-/Geschenkgutschein *m*
Tokyo ['təukjəu] *n* Tokio *nt*
told [təuld] *pt, pp of* **tell**
tolerable ['tɔlərəbl] *adj* (*bearable*) erträglich; (*fairly good*) passabel
tolerant ['tɔlərnt] *adj* tolerant; **to be ~ of sth** tolerant gegenüber etw sein
tolerate ['tɔləreɪt] *vt* (*pain, noise*) erdulden, ertragen; (*injustice*) tolerieren
toll [təul] *n* (*of casualties, deaths*) (Gesamt)zahl *f*; (*tax, charge*) Gebühr *f* ▷ *vi* (*bell*) läuten; **the work took its ~ on us** die Arbeit blieb nicht ohne Auswirkungen auf uns
toll call (*US*) *n* Ferngespräch *nt*
toll-free ['təulfri:] (*US*) *adj* gebührenfrei
tomato [tə'mɑ:təu] (*pl* **~es**) *n* Tomate *f*
tomb [tu:m] *n* Grab *nt*
tomboy ['tɔmbɔɪ] *n* Wildfang *m*
tombstone ['tu:mstəun] *n* Grabstein *m*
tomcat ['tɔmkæt] *n* Kater *m*
tomorrow [tə'mɔrəu] *adv* morgen ▷ *n* morgen; (*future*) Zukunft *f*; **the day after ~** übermorgen; **a week ~** morgen in einer Woche; **~ morning** morgen früh
ton [tʌn] *n* (*Brit*) (britische) Tonne *f*; (*US*: *also*: **short ton**) (US-)Tonne *f* (*ca. 907 kg*); (*also*: **metric ton**) (metrische) Tonne *f*; **~s of** (*inf*) Unmengen von
tone [təun] *n* Ton *m* ▷ *vi* (*also*: **tone in**: *colours*) (farblich) passen
▸ **tone down** *vt* (*also fig*) abschwächen
▸ **tone up** *vt* (*muscles*) kräftigen
tone-deaf [təun'dɛf] *adj* ohne Gefühl für Tonhöhen
tongs [tɔŋz] *npl* Zange *f*; (*also*: **curling tongs**) Lockenstab *m*
tongue [tʌŋ] *n* Zunge *f*; (*form*: *language*) Sprache *f*; **~-in-cheek** (*speak, say*) ironisch
tongue-tied ['tʌŋtaɪd] *adj* (*fig*) sprachlos
tonic ['tɔnɪk] *n* (*Med*) Tonikum *nt*; (*fig*) Wohltat *f*; (*also*: **tonic water**) Tonic *nt*; (*Mus*) Tonika *f*, Grundton *m*
tonight [tə'naɪt] *adv* (*this evening*) heute Abend; (*this night*) heute Nacht ▷ *n* (*this evening*) der heutige Abend; (*this night*) die kommende Nacht; **(I'll) see you ~!** bis heute Abend!
tonne [tʌn] (*Brit*) *n* (*metric ton*) Tonne *f*
tonsil ['tɔnsl] *n* Mandel *f*; **to have one's ~s out** sich *dat* die Mandeln herausnehmen lassen
tonsillitis [tɔnsɪ'laɪtɪs] *n* Mandelentzündung *f*
too [tu:] *adv* (*excessively*) zu; (*also*) auch; **it's ~ sweet** es ist zu süß; **I went ~** ich bin auch mitgegangen; **~ much** (*adj*) zu viel; (*adv*) zu sehr; **~ many** zu viele; **~ bad!** das ist eben Pech!
took [tuk] *pt of* **take**
tool [tu:l] *n* (*also fig*) Werkzeug *nt*
tool box *n* Werkzeugkasten *m*
tool kit *n* Werkzeugsatz *m*
toot [tu:t] *n* (*of horn*) Hupton *m*; (*of whistle*) Pfeifton *m* ▷ *vi* (*with car-horn*) hupen
tooth [tu:θ] (*pl* **teeth**) *n* (*also Tech*) Zahn *m*; **to have a ~ out, to have a ~ pulled** (*US*) sich *dat* einen Zahn ziehen lassen; **to brush one's teeth** sich *dat* die Zähne putzen; **by the skin of one's teeth** (*fig*) mit knapper

Not
toothache ['tu:θeɪk] *n* Zahnschmerzen *pl*; **to have ~** Zahnschmerzen haben
toothbrush ['tu:θbrʌʃ] *n* Zahnbürste *f*
toothpaste ['tu:θpeɪst] *n* Zahnpasta *f*
toothpick ['tu:θpɪk] *n* Zahnstocher *m*
top [tɔp] *n* (*of mountain, tree, ladder*) Spitze *f*; (*of cupboard, table, box*) Oberseite *f*; (*of street*) Ende *nt*; (*lid*) Verschluss *m*; (*Aut: also*: **top gear**) höchster Gang *m*; (*also*: **spinning top**: *toy*) Kreisel *m*; (*blouse etc*) Oberteil *nt*; (*of pyjamas*) Jacke *f* ▷ *adj* höchste(r, s); (*highest in rank*) oberste(r, s); (: *golfer etc*) Top- ▷ *vt* (*poll, vote, list*) anführen; (*estimate etc*) übersteigen; **at the ~ of the stairs/page** oben auf der Treppe/Seite; **at the ~ of the street** am Ende der Straße; **on ~ of** (*above*) auf +*dat*; (*in addition to*) zusätzlich zu; **from ~ to bottom** von oben bis unten; **from ~ to toe** (*Brit*) von Kopf bis Fuß; **at the ~ of the list** oben auf der Liste; **at the ~ of his voice** so laut er konnte; **over the ~** (*inf: behaviour etc*) übertrieben; **to go over the ~** (*inf*) übertreiben; **at ~ speed** bei Höchstgeschwindigkeit
▸**top up**, (*US*) **top off** *vt* (*drink*) nachfüllen; (*salary*) aufbessern
top floor *n* oberster Stock *m*
top hat *n* Zylinder *m*
top-heavy [tɔp'hɛvɪ] *adj* (*also fig*) kopflastig
topic ['tɔpɪk] *n* Thema *nt*
topical ['tɔpɪkl] *adj* (*issue etc*) aktuell
topless ['tɔplɪs] *adj* (*waitress*) Oben-ohne-; (*bather*) barbusig ▷ *adv* oben ohne
top-level ['tɔplɛvl] *adj* auf höchster Ebene
topmost ['tɔpməust] *adj* oberste(r, s)
topping ['tɔpɪŋ] *n* (*Culin*) Überzug *m*
topple ['tɔpl] *vt* (*government etc*) stürzen ▷ *vi* (*person*) stürzen; (*object*) fallen
top-secret ['tɔp'si:krɪt] *adj* streng geheim
topsy-turvy ['tɔpsɪ'tə:vɪ] *adj* auf den Kopf gestellt ▷ *adv* durcheinander; (*fall, land*) verkehrt herum
top-up ['tɔpʌp] *n*: **would you like a ~?** darf ich Ihnen nachschenken?
torch [tɔ:tʃ] *n* Fackel *f*; (*Brit: electric*) Taschenlampe *f*
tore [tɔ:ʳ] *pt of* **tear**
torment [*n* 'tɔ:mɛnt, *vt* tɔ:'mɛnt] *n* Qual *f* ▷ *vt* quälen; (*annoy*) ärgern
torn [tɔ:n] *pp of* **tear¹** ▷ *adj*: **~ between** (*fig*) hin- und hergerissen zwischen
tornado [tɔ:'neɪdəu] (*pl* **~es**) *n* (*storm*) Tornado *m*
torpedo [tɔ:'pi:dəu] (*pl* **~es**) *n* Torpedo *m*
torrent ['tɔrnt] *n* (*flood*) Strom *m*; (*fig*) Flut *f*
torrential [tɔ'rɛnʃl] *adj* (*rain*) wolkenbruchartig
tortoise ['tɔ:təs] *n* Schildkröte *f*
tortoiseshell ['tɔ:təʃɛl] *adj* (*jewellery, ornaments*) aus Schildpatt; (*cat*) braungelbschwarz, braun-gelb-schwarz
torture ['tɔ:tʃəʳ] *n* Folter *f*; (*fig*) Qual *f* ▷ *vt* foltern; (*fig: torment*) quälen; **it was ~** (*fig*) es war eine Qual
Tory ['tɔ:rɪ] (*Brit: Pol*) *adj* konservativ ▷ *n* Tory *m*, Konservative(r) *f(m)*
toss [tɔs] *vt* (*throw*) werfen; (*one's head*) zurückwerfen; (*salad*) anmachen; (*pancake*) wenden ▷ *n*: **with a ~ of her head** mit einer Kopfbewegung; **to ~ a coin** eine Münze werfen; **to win/lose the ~** die Entscheidung per Münzwurf gewinnen/verlieren; **to ~ up for sth** etw per Münzwurf entscheiden; **to ~ and turn** (*in bed*) sich hin und her wälzen
tot [tɔt] *n* (*Brit: drink*) Schluck *m*; (*child*) Knirps *m*
▸**tot up** (*Brit*) *vt* (*figures*) zusammenzählen
total ['təutl] *adj* (*number etc*) gesamt; (*failure, wreck etc*) völlig, total ▷ *n* Gesamtzahl *f* ▷ *vt* (*add up*) zusammenzählen; (*add up to*) sich belaufen auf; **in ~** insgesamt
totalitarian [təutælɪ'tɛərɪən] *adj* totalitär
totally ['təutəlɪ] *adv* völlig
totter ['tɔtəʳ] *vi* (*person*) wanken, taumeln; (*fig: government*) im Wanken sein
touch [tʌtʃ] *n* (*sense of touch*) Gefühl *nt*; (*contact*) Berührung *f*; (*skill: of pianist etc*) Hand *f* ▷ *vt* berühren; (*tamper with*) anrühren; (*emotionally*) rühren ▷ *vi* (*make contact*) sich berühren; **the personal ~** die persönliche Note; **to put the finishing ~es to sth** letzte Hand an etw *acc* legen; **a ~ of** (*fig: frost etc*) etwas, ein Hauch von; **in ~ with** (*person, group*) in Verbindung mit; **to get in ~ with sb** mit jdm in Verbindung treten; **I'll be in ~** ich melde mich; **to lose ~** (*friends*) den Kontakt verlieren; **to be out of ~ with sb** keine Verbindung mehr zu jdm haben; **to be out of ~ with events** nicht auf dem Laufenden sein; **~ wood!** hoffen wir das Beste!
▸**touch on** *vt fus* (*topic*) berühren
▸**touch up** *vt* (*car etc*) ausbessern
touch-and-go ['tʌtʃən'gəu] *adj* (*situation*) auf der Kippe; **it was ~ whether we'd succeed** es war völlig offen, ob wir Erfolg haben würden
touchdown ['tʌtʃdaun] *n* (*of rocket, plane*) Landung *f*; (*US: Football*) Touchdown *m*
touched [tʌtʃt] *adj* (*moved*) gerührt; (*inf: mad*) plemplem
touching ['tʌtʃɪŋ] *adj* rührend
touchline ['tʌtʃlaɪn] *n* (*Sport*) Seitenlinie *f*
touch-sensitive ['tʌtʃ'sɛnsɪtɪv] *adj* berührungsempfindlich; (*switch*) Kontakt-
touchy ['tʌtʃɪ] *adj* (*person, subject*) empfindlich
tough [tʌf] *adj* (*strong, firm, difficult*) hart; (*resistant*) widerstandsfähig; (*meat, animal, person*) zäh; (*rough*) rau; **~ luck!** Pech!
toughen ['tʌfn] *vt* (*sb's character*) hart machen; (*glass etc*) härten
toupee ['tu:peɪ] *n* Toupet *nt*
tour ['tuəʳ] *n* (*journey*) Reise *f*, Tour *f*; (*of factory, museum etc*) Rundgang *m*; (: *also*: **guided tour**) Führung *f*; (*by pop group etc*) Tournee

f ▷ *vt* (*country, factory etc: on foot*) ziehen durch; (*: in car*) fahren durch; **to go on a ~ of a museum/castle** an einer Museums-/Schlossführung teilnehmen; **to go on a ~ of the Highlands** die Highlands bereisen; **to go/be on ~** (*pop group, theatre company etc*) auf Tournee gehen/sein

tour guide *n* Reiseleiter(in) *m(f)*

tourism ['tuərɪzm] *n* Tourismus *m*

tourist ['tuərɪst] *n* Tourist(in) *m(f)* ▷ *cpd* (*attractions, season*) Touristen-; **the ~ trade** die Tourismusbranche

tourist office *n* Verkehrsamt *nt*

tournament ['tuənəmənt] *n* Turnier *nt*

tour operator (*Brit*) *n* Reiseveranstalter *m*

tousled ['tauzld] *adj* (*hair*) zerzaust

tout [taut] *vi*: **to ~ for business** die Reklametrommel schlagen; **to ~ for custom** auf Kundenfang gehen ▷ *n* (*also*: **ticket tout**) *Schwarzhändler, der Eintrittskarten zu überhöhten Preisen verkauft*

tow [təu] *vt* (*vehicle*) abschleppen; (*caravan, trailer*) ziehen ▷ *n*: **to give sb a ~** (*Aut*) jdn abschleppen; **"on ~", "in ~"** (*US*) "Fahrzeug wird abgeschleppt"

▸ **tow away** *vt* (*vehicle*) abschleppen

toward [tə'wɔːd], **towards** [tə'wɔːdz] *prep* (*direction*) zu; (*attitude*) gegenüber *+dat*; (*purpose*) für; (*in time*) gegen; **~(s) noon/the end of the year** gegen Mittag/Ende des Jahres; **to feel friendly ~(s) sb** jdm freundlich gesinnt sein

towel ['tauəl] *n* Handtuch *nt*; **to throw in the ~** (*fig*) das Handtuch werfen

towelling ['tauəlɪŋ] *n* Frottee *nt or m*

towel rail, (*US*) **towel rack** *n* Handtuchstange *f*

tower ['tauə^r] *n* Turm *m* ▷ *vi* aufragen; **to ~ above** *or* **over sb/sth** über jdm/etw aufragen

tower block (*Brit*) *n* Hochhaus *nt*

towering ['tauərɪŋ] *adj* hoch aufragend

town [taun] *n* Stadt *f*; **to go (in)to ~** in die Stadt gehen; **to go to ~ on sth** (*fig*) sich bei etw ins Zeug legen; **in ~** in der Stadt; **to be out of ~** (*person*) nicht in der Stadt sein

town centre *n* Stadtzentrum *nt*

town council *n* Stadtrat *m*

town hall *n* Rathaus *nt*

town plan *n* Stadtplan *m*

town planning *n* Stadtplanung *f*

towrope ['təurəup] *n* Abschleppseil *nt*

tow truck (*US*) *n* Abschleppwagen *m*

toxic ['tɔksɪk] *adj* giftig, toxisch

toy [tɔɪ] *n* Spielzeug *nt*

▸ **toy with** *vt fus* (*object, idea*) spielen mit

toyshop ['tɔɪʃɔp] *n* Spielzeugladen *m*

trace [treɪs] *n* (*sign, small amount*) Spur *f* ▷ *vt* (*draw*) nachzeichnen; (*follow*) verfolgen; (*locate*) aufspüren; **without ~** (*disappear*) spurlos; **there was no ~ of it** es war spurlos verschwunden

tracing paper ['treɪsɪŋ-] *n* Pauspapier *nt*

track [træk] *n* Weg *m*; (*of comet, Sport*) Bahn *f*; (*of suspect, animal*) Spur *f*; (*Rail*) Gleis *nt*; (*on tape, record*) Stück *nt*, Track *m* ▷ *vt* (*follow*) verfolgen; **to keep ~ of sb/sth** (*fig*) jdn/etw im Auge behalten; **to be on the right ~** (*fig*) auf der richtigen Spur sein

▸ **track down** *vt* aufspüren

tracksuit ['træksuːt] *n* Trainingsanzug *m*

tract [trækt] *n* (*Geog*) Gebiet *nt*; (*pamphlet*) Traktat *m or nt*; **respiratory ~** Atemwege *pl*

traction ['trækʃən] *n* (*power*) Zugkraft *f*; (*Aut: grip*) Bodenhaftung *f*; (*Med*): **in ~** im Streckverband

tractor ['træktə^r] *n* Traktor *m*

trade [treɪd] *n* (*activity*) Handel *m*; (*skill, job*) Handwerk *nt* ▷ *vi* (*do business*) handeln ▷ *vt*: **to ~ sth (for sth)** etw (gegen etw) eintauschen; **foreign ~** Außenhandel *m*; **Department of T~ and Industry** (*Brit*) ≈ Wirtschaftsministerium *nt*; **to ~ with** Handel treiben mit; **to ~ in** (*merchandise*) handeln in *+dat*

▸ **trade in** *vt* in Zahlung geben

trade fair *n* Handelsmesse *f*

trademark ['treɪdmɑːk] *n* Warenzeichen *nt*

trade name *n* Handelsname *m*

trader ['treɪdə^r] *n* Händler(in) *m(f)*

tradesman ['treɪdzmən] (*irreg: like* **man**) *n* (*shopkeeper*) Händler *m*

trade union *n* Gewerkschaft *f*

trade unionist [-'juːnjənɪst] *n* Gewerkschaftler(in) *m(f)*

trading ['treɪdɪŋ] *n* Handel *m*

tradition [trə'dɪʃən] *n* Tradition *f*

traditional [trə'dɪʃənl] *adj* traditionell

traffic ['træfɪk] *n* Verkehr *m*; (*in drugs etc*) Handel *m* ▷ *vi*: **to ~ in** handeln mit

traffic calming *n* Verkehrsberuhigung *f*

traffic circle (*US*) *n* Kreisverkehr *m*

traffic island *n* Verkehrsinsel *f*

traffic jam *n* Verkehrsstauung *f*, Stau *m*

traffic lights *npl* Ampel *f*

traffic warden *n* *Verkehrspolizist für Parkvergehen*; (*woman*) ≈ Politesse *f*

tragedy ['trædʒədɪ] *n* Tragödie *f*

tragic ['trædʒɪk] *adj* tragisch

trail [treɪl] *n* (*path*) Weg *m*; (*track*) Spur *f*; (*of smoke, dust*) Wolke *f* ▷ *vt* (*drag*) schleifen; (*follow*) folgen *+dat* ▷ *vi* (*hang loosely*) schleifen; (*in game, contest*) zurückliegen; **to be on sb's ~** jdm auf der Spur sein

▸ **trail away** *vi* (*sound, voice*) sich verlieren

▸ **trail behind** *vi* hinterhertrotten

▸ **trail off** *vi* = **trail away**

trailer ['treɪlə^r] *n* (*Aut*) Anhänger *m*; (*US: caravan*) Caravan *m*, Wohnwagen *m*; (*Cine, TV*) Trailer *m*

trailer truck (*US*) *n* Sattelschlepper *m*

train [treɪn] *n* (*Rail*) Zug *m*; (*of dress*) Schleppe *f* ▷ *vt* (*apprentice etc*) ausbilden; (*dog*) abrichten; (*athlete*) trainieren; (*mind*) schulen; (*plant*) ziehen; (*point: camera, gun etc*): **to ~ on** richten auf *+acc* ▷ *vi* (*learn a skill*) ausgebildet

werden; (*Sport*) trainieren; **~ of thought** Gedankengang *m*; **to go by ~** mit dem Zug fahren; **~ of events** Ereignisfolge *f*; **to ~ sb to do sth** jdn dazu ausbilden, etw zu tun
trained [treɪnd] *adj* (*worker*) gelernt; (*teacher*) ausgebildet; (*animal*) dressiert; (*eye*) geschult
trainee [treɪ'ni:] *n* Auszubildende(r) *f(m)*
trainer ['treɪnəʳ] *n* (*Sport: coach*) Trainer(in) *m(f)*; (*: shoe*) Trainingsschuh *m*; (*of animals*) Dresseur(in) *m(f)*
training ['treɪnɪŋ] *n* (*for occupation*) Ausbildung *f*; (*Sport*) Training *nt*; **in ~** (*Sport*) im Training
training college *n* (*for teachers*) ≈ pädagogische Hochschule *f*
training course *n* Ausbildungskurs *m*
trait [treɪt] *n* Zug *m*, Eigenschaft *f*
traitor ['treɪtəʳ] *n* Verräter(in) *m(f)*
tram [træm] (*Brit*) *n* (*also*: **tramcar**) Straßenbahn *f*
tramp [træmp] *n* Landstreicher *m*; (*pej: woman*) Flittchen *nt* ▷ *vi* stapfen ▷ *vt* (*walk through: town, streets*) latschen durch
trample ['træmpl] *vt*: **to ~ (underfoot)** niedertrampeln ▷ *vi* (*also fig*): **to ~ on** herumtrampeln auf *+dat*
trampoline ['træmpəli:n] *n* Trampolin *nt*
tranquil ['træŋkwɪl] *adj* ruhig, friedlich
tranquillizer, (*US*) **tranquilizer** ['træŋkwɪlaɪzəʳ] *n* Beruhigungsmittel *nt*
transact [træn'zækt] *vt* (*business*) abwickeln
transaction [træn'zækʃən] *n* Geschäft *nt*; **cash ~** Bargeldtransaktion *f*
transatlantic ['trænzət'læntɪk] *adj* transatlantisch; (*phone-call*) über den Atlantik
transcript ['trænskrɪpt] *n* Niederschrift *f*, Transkription *f*
transfer ['trænsfəʳ] *n* (*of employees*) Versetzung *f*; (*of money*) Überweisung *f*; (*of power*) Übertragung *f*; (*Sport*) Transfer *m*; (*picture, design*) Abziehbild *nt* ▷ *vt* (*employees*) versetzen; (*money*) überweisen; (*power, ownership*) übertragen; **by bank ~** per Banküberweisung; **to ~ the charges** (*Brit: Tel*) ein R-Gespräch führen
transform [træns'fɔ:m] *vt* umwandeln
transformation [trænsfə'meɪʃən] *n* Umwandlung *f*
transfusion [træns'fju:ʒən] *n* (*also*: **blood transfusion**) Bluttransfusion *f*
transient ['trænzɪənt] *adj* vorübergehend
transistor [træn'zɪstəʳ] *n* (*Elec*) Transistor *m*; (*also*: **transistor radio**) Transistorradio *nt*
transit ['trænzɪt] *n*: **in ~** unterwegs
transition [træn'zɪʃən] *n* Übergang *m*
transitive ['trænzɪtɪv] *adj* (*verb*) transitiv
transit lounge *n* Transithalle *f*
translate [trænz'leɪt] *vt* übersetzen; **to ~ (from/into)** übersetzen (aus/in *+acc*)
translation [trænz'leɪʃən] *n* Übersetzung *f*; **in ~** als Übersetzung
translator [trænz'leɪtəʳ] *n* Übersetzer(in) *m(f)*
transmission [trænz'mɪʃən] *n* (*also TV*) Übertragung *f*; (*of information*) Übermittlung *f*; (*Aut*) Getriebe *nt*
transmit [trænz'mɪt] *vt* (*also TV*) übertragen; (*message, signal*) übermitteln
transmitter [trænz'mɪtəʳ] *n* (*TV, Radio*) Sender *m*
transparency [træns'pɛərnsɪ] *n* (*of glass etc*) Durchsichtigkeit *f*; (*Brit: Phot*) Dia *nt*
transparent [træns'pærnt] *adj* durchsichtig; (*fig: obvious*) offensichtlich
transpire [træns'paɪəʳ] *vi* (*turn out*) bekannt werden; (*happen*) passieren; **it finally ~d that ...** schließlich sickerte durch, dass ...
transplant [*vt* træns'plɑ:nt, *n* 'trɑ:nsplɑ:nt] *vt* (*organ, seedlings*) verpflanzen ▷ *n* (*Med*) Transplantation *f*; **to have a heart ~** sich einer Herztransplantation unterziehen
transport ['trænspɔ:t] *n* Transport *m*, Beförderung *f* ▷ *vt* transportieren; **do you have your own ~?** haben Sie ein Auto?; **public ~** öffentliche Verkehrsmittel *pl*; **Department of T~** (*Brit*) Verkehrsministerium *nt*
transportation ['trænspɔ:'teɪʃən] *n* Transport *m*, Beförderung *f*; (*means of transport*) Beförderungsmittel *nt*; **Department of T~** (*US*) Verkehrsministerium *nt*
transport café (*Brit*) *n* Fernfahrerlokal *nt*
transvestite [trænz'vɛstaɪt] *n* Transvestit *m*
trap [træp] *n* (*also fig*) Falle *f*; (*carriage*) zweirädriger Pferdewagen *m* ▷ *vt* (*animal*) (mit einer Falle) fangen; (*person: trick*) in die Falle locken; (*: confine*) gefangen halten; (*immobilize*) festsetzen; (*capture: energy*) stauen; **to set** *or* **lay a ~ (for sb)** (jdm) eine Falle stellen; **to shut one's ~** (*inf*) die Klappe halten; **to ~ one's finger in the door** sich *dat* den Finger in der Tür einklemmen
trap door *n* Falltür *f*
trapeze [trə'pi:z] *n* Trapez *nt*
trappings ['træpɪŋz] *npl* äußere Zeichen *pl*; (*of power*) Insignien *pl*
trash [træʃ] *n* (*rubbish*) Abfall *m*, Müll *m*; (*pej: nonsense*) Schund *m*, Mist *m*
trash can (*US*) *n* Mülleimer *m*
trashy ['træʃɪ] *adj* (*goods*) minderwertig, wertlos; (*novel etc*) Schund-
trauma ['trɔ:mə] *n* Trauma *nt*
traumatic [trɔ:'mætɪk] *adj* traumatisch
travel ['trævl] *n* (*travelling*) Reisen *nt* ▷ *vi* reisen; (*short distance*) fahren; (*move: car, aeroplane*) sich bewegen; (*sound etc*) sich fortpflanzen; (*news*) sich verbreiten ▷ *vt* (*distance*) zurücklegen; **travels** *npl* (*journeys*) Reisen *pl*; **this wine doesn't ~ well** dieser Wein verträgt den Transport nicht
travel agency *n* Reisebüro *nt*
travel agent *n* Reisebürokaufmann *m*, Reisebürokauffrau *f*
traveller, (*US*) **traveler** ['trævləʳ] *n* Reisende(r) *f(m)*; (*Comm*) Vertreter(in) *m(f)*
traveller's cheque, (*US*) **traveler's check** *n* Reisescheck *m*

travelling, (US) **traveling** ['trævlɪŋ] *n* Reisen *nt* ▷ *cpd* *(circus, exhibition)* Wander-; *(bag, clock)* Reise-; **~ expenses** Reisespesen *pl*
travel sickness *n* Reisekrankheit *f*
trawler ['trɔːləʳ] *n* Fischdampfer *m*
tray [treɪ] *n* *(for carrying)* Tablett *nt*; *(also:* **in-tray/out-tray***: on desk)* Ablage *f* für Eingänge/Ausgänge
treacherous ['trɛtʃərəs] *adj* *(person, look)* verräterisch; *(ground, tide)* tückisch; **road conditions are ~** die Straßen sind in gefährlichem Zustand
treacle ['triːkl] *n* Sirup *m*
tread [trɛd] *(pt* **trod**, *pp* **trodden***)* *n* *(of tyre)* Profil *nt*; *(footstep)* Schritt *m*; *(of stair)* Stufe *f* ▷ *vi* gehen
▸ **tread on** *vt fus* treten auf *+acc*
treason ['triːzn] *n* Verrat *m*
treasure ['trɛʒəʳ] *n* *(also fig)* Schatz *m* ▷ *vt* schätzen; **treasures** *npl* *(art treasures etc)* Schätze *pl*, Kostbarkeiten *pl*
treasurer ['trɛʒərəʳ] *n* Schatzmeister(in) *m(f)*
treasury ['trɛʒərɪ] *n*: **the T~, the T~ Department** (US) das Finanzministerium
treat [triːt] *n* *(present)* (besonderes) Vergnügen *nt* ▷ *vt* *(also Med, Tech)* behandeln; **it came as a ~** es war eine besondere Freude; **to ~ sth as a joke** etw als Witz ansehen; **to ~ sb to sth** jdm etw spendieren
treatment ['triːtmənt] *n* Behandlung *f*; **to have ~ for sth** wegen etw in Behandlung sein
treaty ['triːtɪ] *n* Vertrag *m*
treble ['trɛbl] *adj* *(triple)* dreifach; *(Mus: voice, part)* (Knaben)sopran-; *(instrument)* Diskant- ▷ *n* *(singer)* (Knaben)sopran *m*; *(on hi-fi, radio etc)* Höhen *pl* ▷ *vt* verdreifachen ▷ *vi* sich verdreifachen; **to be ~ the amount/size of sth** dreimal so viel/so groß wie etw sein
treble clef *n* Violinschlüssel *m*
tree [triː] *n* Baum *m*
trek [trɛk] *n* Treck *m*; *(tiring walk)* Marsch *m* ▷ *vi* trecken
tremble ['trɛmbl] *vi* *(voice, body, trees)* zittern; *(ground)* beben
tremendous [trɪ'mɛndəs] *adj* *(amount, success etc)* gewaltig, enorm; *(holiday, view etc)* fantastisch
tremor ['trɛməʳ] *n* Zittern *nt*; *(also:* **earth tremor***)* Beben *nt*, Erschütterung *f*
trench [trɛntʃ] *n* Graben *m*
trend [trɛnd] *n* Tendenz *f*; *(fashion)* Trend *m*; **a ~ towards/away from sth** eine Tendenz zu/weg von etw; **to set a/the ~** richtungsweisend sein
trendy ['trɛndɪ] *adj* modisch
trespass ['trɛspəs] *vi*: **to ~ on** *(private property)* unbefugt betreten; **"no ~ing"** "Betreten verboten"
trestle ['trɛsl] *n* Bock *m*
trial ['traɪəl] *n* *(Law)* Prozess *m*; *(test: of machine, drug etc)* Versuch *m*; *(worry)* Plage *f*; **trials** *npl* *(unpleasant experiences)* Schwierigkeiten *pl*; **~ by jury** Schwurgerichtsverfahren *nt*; **to be sent for ~** vor Gericht gestellt werden; **to be/go on ~** *(Law)* angeklagt sein/werden; **by ~ and error** durch Ausprobieren
trial period *n* Probezeit *f*
triangle ['traɪæŋgl] *n* Dreieck *nt*; *(US: set square)* (Zeichen)dreieck *nt*; *(Mus)* Triangel *f*
triangular [traɪ'æŋgjuləʳ] *adj* dreieckig
tribe [traɪb] *n* Stamm *m*
tribesman ['traɪbzmən] *(irreg: like* **man***)* *n* Stammesangehörige(r) *m*
tribunal [traɪ'bjuːnl] *n* Gericht *nt*
tributary ['trɪbjutərɪ] *n* *(of river)* Nebenfluss *m*
tribute ['trɪbjuːt] *n* Tribut *m*; **to pay ~ to** Tribut zollen *+dat*
trick [trɪk] *n* Trick *m*; *(Cards)* Stich *m* ▷ *vt* hereinlegen; **to play a ~ on sb** jdm einen Streich spielen; **it's a ~ of the light** das Licht täuscht; **that should do the ~** das müsste hinhauen; **to ~ sb into doing sth** jdn (mit einem Trick) dazu bringen, etw zu tun; **to ~ sb out of sth** jdn um etw prellen
trickery ['trɪkərɪ] *n* Tricks *pl*, Betrügerei *f*
trickle ['trɪkl] *n* *(of water etc)* Rinnsal *nt* ▷ *vi* *(water, rain etc)* rinnen; *(people)* sich langsam bewegen
tricky ['trɪkɪ] *adj* *(job, problem)* schwierig
tricycle ['traɪsɪkl] *n* Dreirad *nt*
trifle ['traɪfl] *n* *(detail)* Kleinigkeit *f*; *(Culin)* Trifle *nt* ▷ *adv*: **a ~ long** ein bisschen lang ▷ *vi*: **to ~ with sb/sth** jdn/etw nicht ernst nehmen; **he is not (someone) to be ~d with** mit ihm ist nicht zu spaßen
trifling ['traɪflɪŋ] *adj* *(detail)* unbedeutend
trigger ['trɪgəʳ] *n* Abzug *m*
▸ **trigger off** *vt fus* auslösen
trim [trɪm] *adj* *(house, garden)* gepflegt; *(figure, person)* schlank ▷ *n* *(haircut etc)*: **to have a ~** sich *dat* die Haare nachschneiden lassen; *(on clothes, car)* Besatz *m* ▷ *vt* *(hair, beard)* nachschneiden; *(decorate)*: **to ~ (with)** besetzen (mit); *(Naut: a sail)* trimmen mit; **to keep o.s. in (good) ~** (gut) in Form bleiben
trimmings ['trɪmɪŋz] *npl* *(Culin)*: **with all the ~** mit allem Drum und Dran; *(cuttings: of pastry etc)* Reste *pl*
trinket ['trɪŋkɪt] *n* *(ornament)* Schmuckgegenstand *m*; *(piece of jewellery)* Schmuckstück *nt*
trio ['triːəu] *n* Trio *nt*
trip [trɪp] *n* *(journey)* Reise *f*; *(outing)* Ausflug *m* ▷ *vi* *(stumble)* stolpern; *(go lightly)* trippeln; **on a ~** auf Reisen
▸ **trip over** *vt fus* stolpern über *+acc*
▸ **trip up** *vi* stolpern ▷ *vt* *(person)* zu Fall bringen
tripe [traɪp] *n* *(Culin)* Kaldaunen *pl*; *(pej: rubbish)* Stuss *m*
triple ['trɪpl] *adj* dreifach ▷ *adv*: **~ the distance/the speed** dreimal so weit/schnell; **~ the amount** dreimal so viel
triplets ['trɪplɪts] *npl* Drillinge *pl*
triplicate ['trɪplɪkət] *n*: **in ~** in dreifacher

Ausfertigung
tripod ['traɪpɔd] *n (Phot)* Stativ *nt*
trite [traɪt] *(pej) adj (comment, idea etc)* banal
triumph ['traɪʌmf] *n* Triumph *m* ▷ *vi*: **to ~ (over)** triumphieren (über *+acc*)
triumphant [traɪ'ʌmfənt] *adj* triumphal; *(victorious)* siegreich
trivia ['trɪvɪə] *(pej) npl* Trivialitäten *pl*
trivial ['trɪvɪəl] *adj* trivial
trod [trɔd] *pt of* **tread**
trodden [trɔdn] *pp of* **tread**
trolley ['trɔlɪ] *n (for luggage)* Kofferkuli *m*; *(for shopping)* Einkaufswagen *m*; *(table on wheels)* Teewagen *m*; *(also:* **trolley bus***)* Oberleitungsomnibus *m*, Obus *m*
trombone [trɔm'bəun] *n* Posaune *f*
troop [tru:p] *n (of people, monkeys etc)* Gruppe *f* ▷ *vi*: **to ~ in/out** hinein-/hinausströmen; **troops** *npl (Mil)* Truppen *pl*
trophy ['trəufɪ] *n* Trophäe *f*
tropic ['trɔpɪk] *n* Wendekreis *m*; **the tropics** *npl* die Tropen *pl*; **T~ of Cancer/Capricorn** Wendekreis des Krebses/Steinbocks
tropical ['trɔpɪkl] *adj* tropisch
trot [trɔt] *n (fast pace)* Trott *m*; *(of horse)* Trab *m* ▷ *vi (horse)* traben; *(person)* trotten; **on the ~** *(Brit: fig)* hintereinander
▸ **trot out** *vt (facts, excuse etc)* vorbringen
trouble ['trʌbl] *n* Schwierigkeiten *pl*; *(bother, effort)* Umstände *pl*; *(unrest)* Unruhen *pl* ▷ *vt (worry)* beunruhigen; *(disturb: person)* belästigen ▷ *vi*: **to ~ to do sth** sich *dat* die Mühe machen, etw zu tun; **troubles** *npl (personal)* Probleme *pl*; *(Pol etc)* Unruhen *pl*; **to be in ~** in Schwierigkeiten sein; **to have ~ doing sth** Schwierigkeiten *or* Probleme haben, etw zu tun; **to go to the ~ of doing sth** sich *dat* die Mühe machen, etw zu tun; **it's no ~!** das macht mir nichts aus!; **the ~ is ...** das Problem ist ...; **what's the ~?** wo fehlts?; **stomach** *etc* **~** Probleme mit dem Magen *etc*; **please don't ~ yourself** bitte bemühen Sie sich nicht
troubled [trʌbld] *adj (person)* besorgt; *(country, life, era)* von Problemen geschüttelt
troublemaker ['trʌblmeɪkə^r] *n* Unruhestifter(in) *m(f)*
troubleshooter ['trʌblʃu:tə^r] *n* Vermittler(in) *m(f)*
troublesome ['trʌblsəm] *adj (child)* schwierig; *(cough etc)* lästig
trough [trɔf] *n (also:* **drinking trough***)* Wassertrog *m*; *(also:* **feeding trough***)* Futtertrog *m*; *(channel)* Rinne *f*; *(low point)* Tief *nt*; **a ~ of low pressure** ein Tiefdruckkeil *m*
trousers ['trauzəz] *npl* Hose *f*; **short ~** kurze Hose; **a pair of ~** eine Hose
trout [traut] *n inv* Forelle *f*
trowel ['trauəl] *n (garden tool)* Pflanzkelle *f*; *(builder's tool)* (Maurer)kelle *f*
truant ['truənt] *(Brit) n*: **to play ~** die Schule schwänzen
truce [tru:s] *n* Waffenstillstand *m*
truck [trʌk] *n (lorry)* Lastwagen *m*; *(Rail)* Güterwagen *m*; *(for luggage)* Gepäckwagen *m*; **to have no ~ with sb** nichts mit jdm zu tun haben
truck driver *n* Lkw-Fahrer(in) *m(f)*
truck farm *(US) n* Gemüsefarm *f*
true [tru:] *adj* wahr; *(accurate)* genau; *(genuine)* echt; *(faithful: friend)* treu; *(wall, beam)* gerade; *(circle)* rund; **to come ~** wahr werden; **~ to life** lebensecht
truffle ['trʌfl] *n (fungus, sweet)* Trüffel *f*
truly ['tru:lɪ] *adv* wahrhaft, wirklich; *(truthfully)* wirklich; **yours ~** *(in letter)* mit freundlichen Grüßen
trump [trʌmp] *n (also:* **trump card***: also fig)* Trumpf *m*; **to turn up ~s** *(fig)* sich als Retter in der Not erweisen
trumpet ['trʌmpɪt] *n* Trompete *f*
truncheon ['trʌntʃən] *(Brit) n* Gummiknüppel *m*
trundle ['trʌndl] *vt (trolley etc)* rollen ▷ *vi*: **to ~ along** *(person)* dahinschlendern; *(vehicle)* dahinrollen
trunk [trʌŋk] *n (of tree)* Stamm *m*; *(of person)* Rumpf *m*; *(of elephant)* Rüssel *m*; *(case)* Schrankkoffer *m*; *(US: Aut)* Kofferraum *m*; **trunks** *npl (also:* **swimming trunks***)* Badehose *f*
truss [trʌs] *n (Med)* Bruchband *nt*
▸ **truss (up)** *vt (Culin)* dressieren; *(person)* fesseln
trust [trʌst] *n* Vertrauen *nt*; *(Comm: for charity etc)* Stiftung *f* ▷ *vt* vertrauen *+dat*; **to take sth on ~** *(advice etc)* etw einfach glauben; **to be in ~** *(Law)* treuhänderisch verwaltet werden; **to ~ (that)** *(hope)* hoffen(, dass)
trusted ['trʌstɪd] *adj (friend, servant)* treu
trustee [trʌs'ti:] *n (Law)* Treuhänder(in) *m(f)*; *(of school etc)* Aufsichtsratsmitglied *nt*
trustful ['trʌstful] *adj* vertrauensvoll
trustworthy ['trʌstwə:ðɪ] *adj (person)* vertrauenswürdig
truth [tru:θ] *(pl* **~s***) n*: **the ~** die Wahrheit *f*
truthful ['tru:θful] *adj (person)* ehrlich; *(answer etc)* wahrheitsgemäß
try [traɪ] *n (also Rugby)* Versuch *m* ▷ *vt (attempt)* versuchen; *(test)* probieren; *(Law)* vor Gericht stellen; *(strain: patience)* auf die Probe stellen ▷ *vi* es versuchen; **to have a ~** es versuchen, einen Versuch machen; **to ~ to do sth** versuchen, etw zu tun; **to ~ one's (very) best** *or* **hardest** sein Bestes versuchen *or* tun
▸ **try on** *vt (clothes)* anprobieren; **she's ~ing it on** *(fig)* sie probiert, wie weit sie gehen kann
▸ **try out** *vt* ausprobieren
trying ['traɪɪŋ] *adj (person)* schwierig; *(experience)* schwer
T-shirt ['ti:ʃə:t] *n* T-Shirt *nt*
T-square ['ti:skwɛə^r] *n (Tech)* Reißschiene *f*
tub [tʌb] *n (container)* Kübel *m*; *(bath)* Wanne *f*
tubby ['tʌbɪ] *adj* rundlich
tube [tju:b] *n (pipe)* Rohr *nt*; *(container)* Tube

f; (*Brit: underground*) U-Bahn *f*; (*US: inf*): **the ~** (*television*) die Röhre
tuberculosis [tjubəːkju'ləusɪs] *n* Tuberkulose *f*
tube station (*Brit*) *n* U-Bahn-Station *f*
TUC (*Brit*) *n abbr* (= *Trades Union Congress*) *britischer Gewerkschafts-Dachverband*
tuck [tʌk] *vt* (*put*) stecken ▷ *n* (*Sewing*) Biese *f*
▸ **tuck away** *vt* (*money*) wegstecken; **to be ~ed away** (*building*) versteckt liegen
▸ **tuck in** *vt* (*clothing*) feststecken; (*child*) zudecken ▷ *vi* (*eat*) zulangen
▸ **tuck up** *vt* (*invalid, child*) zudecken
tuck shop *n* Süßwarenladen *m*
Tuesday ['tjuːzdɪ] *n* Dienstag *m*; **it is ~ 23rd March** heute ist Dienstag, der 23. März; **on ~** am Dienstag; **on ~s** dienstags; **every ~** jeden Dienstag; **every other ~** jeden zweiten Dienstag; **last/next ~** letzten/nächsten Dienstag; **the following ~** am Dienstag darauf; **~'s newspaper** die Zeitung von Dienstag; **a week/fortnight on ~** Dienstag in einer Woche/in vierzehn Tagen; **the ~ before last** der vorletzte Dienstag; **the ~ after next** der übernächste Dienstag; **~ morning/lunchtime/afternoon/evening** Dienstag Morgen/Mittag/Nachmittag/Abend; **~ night** (*overnight*) Dienstag Nacht
tuft [tʌft] *n* Büschel *nt*
tug [tʌg] *n* (*ship*) Schlepper *m* ▷ *vt* zerren
tug-of-war [tʌgəv'wɔːʳ] *n* (*also fig*) Tauziehen *nt*
tuition [tjuː'ɪʃən] *n* (*Brit*) Unterricht *m*; (*US: school fees*) Schulgeld *nt*
tulip ['tjuːlɪp] *n* Tulpe *f*
tumble ['tʌmbl] *n* (*fall*) Sturz *m* ▷ *vi* (*fall*) stürzen
▸ **tumble to** (*inf*) *vt fus* kapieren
tumbledown ['tʌmbldaun] *adj* (*building*) baufällig
tumble dryer (*Brit*) *n* Wäschetrockner *m*
tumbler ['tʌmbləʳ] *n* (*glass*) Trinkglas *nt*
tummy ['tʌmɪ] (*inf*) *n* Bauch *m*
tumour, (*US*) **tumor** ['tjuːməʳ] *n* (*Med*) Tumor *m*, Geschwulst *f*
tuna ['tjuːnə] *n inv* (*also:* **tuna fish**) T(h)unfisch *m*
tune [tjuːn] *n* (*melody*) Melodie *f* ▷ *vt* (*Mus*) stimmen; (*Radio, TV, Aut*) einstellen; **to be in/out of ~** (*instrument*) richtig gestimmt/verstimmt sein; (*singer*) richtig/falsch singen; **to be in/out of ~ with** (*fig*) in Einklang/nicht in Einklang stehen mit; **she was robbed to the ~ of 10,000 pounds** sie wurde um einen Betrag in Höhe von 10.000 Pfund beraubt
▸ **tune in** *vi* (*Radio, TV*) einschalten; **to ~ in to BBC1** BBC1 einschalten
▸ **tune up** *vi* (*Mus*) (das Instrument/die Instrumente) stimmen
tuneful ['tjuːnful] *adj* melodisch
tuner ['tjuːnəʳ] *n*: **piano ~** Klavierstimmer(in) *m(f)*; (*radio set*) Tuner *m*
tunic ['tjuːnɪk] *n* Hemdbluse *f*
Tunis ['tjuːnɪs] *n* Tunis *nt*
Tunisia [tjuː'nɪzɪə] *n* Tunesien *nt*
Tunisian [tjuː'nɪzɪən] *adj* tunesisch ▷ *n* (*person*) Tunesier(in) *m(f)*
tunnel ['tʌnl] *n* Tunnel *m*; (*in mine*) Stollen *m* ▷ *vi* einen Tunnel bauen
turbulence ['təːbjuləns] *n* (*Aviat*) Turbulenz *f*
tureen [tə'riːn] *n* Terrine *f*
turf [təːf] *n* (*grass*) Rasen *m*; (*clod*) Sode *f* ▷ *vt* (*area*) mit Grassoden bedecken; **the T~** (*horse-racing*) der Pferderennsport
▸ **turf out** (*inf*) *vt* (*person*) rausschmeißen
Turk [təːk] *n* Türke *m*, Türkin *f*
Turkey ['təːkɪ] *n* die Türkei *f*
turkey ['təːkɪ] *n* (*bird*) Truthahn *m*, Truthenne *f*; (*meat*) Puter *m*
Turkish ['təːkɪʃ] *adj* türkisch ▷ *n* (*Ling*) Türkisch *nt*
turmoil ['təːmɔɪl] *n* Aufruhr *m*; **in ~** in Aufruhr
turn [təːn] *n* (*change*) Wende *f*; (*in road*) Kurve *f*; (*rotation*) Drehung *f*; (*performance*) Nummer *f*; (*inf: Med*) Anfall *m* ▷ *vt* (*handle, key*) drehen; (*collar, steak*) wenden; (*page*) umblättern; (*shape: wood*) drechseln; (*: metal*) drehen ▷ *vi* (*object*) sich drehen; (*person*) sich umdrehen; (*change direction*) abbiegen; (*milk*) sauer werden; **to do sb a good ~** jdm einen guten Dienst erweisen; **a ~ of events** eine Wendung der Dinge; **it gave me quite a ~** (*inf*) das hat mir einen schönen Schrecken eingejagt; **"no left ~"** (*Aut*) "Linksabbiegen verboten"; **it's your ~** du bist dran; **in ~** der Reihe nach; **to take ~s (at)** sich abwechseln (bei); **at the ~ of the century/year** zur Jahrhundertwende/Jahreswende; **to take a ~ for the worse** (*events*) sich zum Schlechten wenden; **his health** *or* **he has taken a ~ for the worse** sein Befinden hat sich verschlechtert; **to ~ nasty/forty/grey** unangenehm/vierzig/grau werden
▸ **turn against** *vt fus* sich wenden gegen
▸ **turn around** *vi* sich umdrehen; (*in car*) wenden
▸ **turn away** *vi* sich abwenden ▷ *vt* (*applicants*) abweisen; (*business*) zurückweisen
▸ **turn back** *vi* umkehren ▷ *vt* (*person, vehicle*) zurückweisen
▸ **turn down** *vt* (*request*) ablehnen; (*heating*) kleiner stellen; (*radio etc*) leiser stellen; (*bedclothes*) aufschlagen
▸ **turn in** *vi* (*inf: go to bed*) sich hinhauen ▷ *vt* (*to police*) anzeigen; **to ~ o.s. in** sich stellen
▸ **turn into** *vt fus* (*change*) sich verwandeln in +*acc* ▷ *vt* machen zu
▸ **turn off** *vi* (*from road*) abbiegen ▷ *vt* (*light, radio etc*) ausmachen; (*tap*) zudrehen; (*engine*) abstellen
▸ **turn on** *vt* (*light, radio etc*) anmachen; (*tap*) aufdrehen; (*engine*) anstellen
▸ **turn out** *vt* (*light*) ausmachen; (*gas*) abstellen ▷ *vi* (*appear, attend*) erscheinen; **to**

~ out to be (*prove to be*) sich erweisen als; **to ~ out well/badly** (*situation*) gut/schlecht enden
▸ **turn over** *vi* (*person*) sich umdrehen ▹ *vt* (*object*) umdrehen, wenden; (*page*) umblättern; **to ~ sth over to** (*to sb*) etw übertragen *+dat*; (*to sth*) etw verlagern zu
▸ **turn round** *vi* sich umdrehen; (*vehicle*) wenden
▸ **turn up** *vi* (*person*) erscheinen; (*lost object*) wieder auftauchen ▹ *vt* (*collar*) hochklappen; (*heater*) höher stellen; (*radio etc*) lauter stellen

turning [ˈtəːnɪŋ] *n* (*in road*) Abzweigung *f*; **the first ~ on the right** die erste Straße rechts
turning point *n* (*fig*) Wendepunkt *m*
turnip [ˈtəːnɪp] *n* Rübe *f*
turnout [ˈtəːnaut] *n* (*of voters etc*) Beteiligung *f*
turnover [ˈtəːnəuvəʳ] *n* (*Comm: amount of money*) Umsatz *m*; (*: of staff*) Fluktuation *f*; (*Culin*): **apple ~** Apfeltasche *f*; **there is a rapid ~ in staff** der Personalbestand wechselt ständig
turnpike [ˈtəːnpaɪk] (*US*) *n* gebührenpflichtige Autobahn *f*
turnstile [ˈtəːnstaɪl] *n* Drehkreuz *nt*
turntable [ˈtəːnteɪbl] *n* (*on record player*) Plattenteller *m*
turn-up [ˈtəːnʌp] (*Brit*) *n* (*on trousers*) Aufschlag *m*; **that's a ~ for the books!** (*inf*) das ist eine echte Überraschung!
turpentine [ˈtəːpəntaɪn] *n* (*also*: **turps**) Terpentin *nt*
turquoise [ˈtəːkwɔɪz] *n* (*stone*) Türkis *m* ▹ *adj* (*colour*) türkis
turret [ˈtʌrɪt] *n* Turm *m*
turtle [ˈtəːtl] *n* Schildkröte *f*
turtleneck [ˈtəːtlnɛk], **turtleneck sweater** *n* Pullover *m* mit rundem Kragen
tusk [tʌsk] *n* (*of elephant*) Stoßzahn *m*
tutor [ˈtjuːtəʳ] *n* Tutor(in) *m(f)*; (*private tutor*) Privatlehrer(in) *m(f)*
tutorial [tjuːˈtɔːrɪəl] *n* Kolloquium *nt*
tuxedo [tʌkˈsiːdəu] (*US*) *n* Smoking *m*
TV [tiːˈviː] *n abbr* (*= television*) TV *nt*
twang [twæŋ] *n* (*of instrument*) singender Ton *m*; (*of voice*) näselnder Ton *m* ▹ *vi* einen singenden Ton von sich geben ▹ *vt* (*guitar*) zupfen
tweed [twiːd] *n* Tweed *m* ▹ *adj* (*jacket, skirt*) Tweed-
tweezers [ˈtwiːzəz] *npl* Pinzette *f*
twelfth [twɛlfθ] *num* zwölfte(r, s) ▹ *n* Zwölftel *nt*
twelve [twɛlv] *num* zwölf; **at ~ (o'clock)** (*midday*) um zwölf Uhr (mittags); (*midnight*) um zwölf Uhr nachts
twentieth [ˈtwɛntɪɪθ] *num* zwanzigste(r, s)
twenty [ˈtwɛntɪ] *num* zwanzig
twice [twaɪs] *adv* zweimal; **~ as much** zweimal so viel; **~ a week** zweimal die Woche; **she is ~ your age** sie ist doppelt so alt wie du
twiddle [ˈtwɪdl] *vt* drehen an *+dat* ▹ *vi*: **to ~ (with)** herumdrehen (an *+dat*); **to ~ one's thumbs** (*fig*) Däumchen drehen
twig [twɪg] *n* Zweig *m* ▹ *vi, vt* (*Brit: inf: realize*) kapieren
twilight [ˈtwaɪlaɪt] *n* Dämmerung *f*; **in the ~** in der Dämmerung
twin [twɪn] *adj* (*sister, brother*) Zwillings-; (*towers*) Doppel- ▹ *n* Zwilling *m*; (*room in hotel etc*) Zweibettzimmer *nt* ▹ *vt* (*towns etc*): **to be ~ned with ...** ... als Partnerstadt haben
twin-bedded room [ˈtwɪnˈbɛdɪd-] *n* Zweibettzimmer *nt*
twin beds *npl* zwei (gleiche) Einzelbetten *pl*
twine [twaɪn] *n* Bindfaden *m* ▹ *vi* sich winden
twinge [twɪndʒ] *n* (*of pain*) Stechen *nt*; **a ~ of conscience** Gewissensbisse *pl*; **a ~ of fear/guilt** ein Angst-/Schuldgefühl *nt*
twinkle [ˈtwɪŋkl] *vi* funkeln ▹ *n* Funkeln *nt*
twirl [twəːl] *vt* herumwirbeln ▹ *vi* wirbeln ▹ *n* Wirbel *m*
twist [twɪst] *n* (*action*) Drehung *f*; (*in road*) Kurve; (*in coil, flex*) Biegung *f*; (*in story*) Wendung *f* ▹ *vt* (*turn*) drehen; (*injure: ankle etc*) verrenken; (*twine*) wickeln; (*fig: meaning etc*) verdrehen ▹ *vi* (*road, river*) sich winden; **~ my arm!** (*inf*) überreden Sie mich einfach!
twit [twɪt] (*inf*) *n* Trottel *m*
twitch [twɪtʃ] *n* (*jerky movement*) Zucken *nt* ▹ *vi* zucken
two [tuː] *num* zwei; **~ by two, in twos** zu zweit; **to put ~ and ~ together** (*fig*) zwei und zwei zusammenzählen
two-door [tuːˈdɔːʳ] *adj* zweitürig
two-faced [tuːˈfeɪst] (*pej*) *adj* scheinheilig
twofold [ˈtuːfəuld] *adv*: **to increase ~** um das Doppelte ansteigen ▹ *adj* (*increase*) um das Doppelte; (*aim, value etc*) zweifach
two-piece [ˈtuːpiːs] *n* (*also*: **two-piece suit**) Zweiteiler *m*; (*also*: **two-piece swimsuit**) zweiteiliger Badeanzug *m*
twosome [ˈtuːsəm] *n* (*people*) Paar *nt*
two-way [ˈtuːweɪ] *adj*: **~ traffic** Verkehr *m* in beiden Richtungen; **~ radio** Funksprechgerät *nt*
tycoon [taɪˈkuːn] *n* Magnat *m*
type [taɪp] *n* (*category, model, example*) Typ *m*; (*Typ*) Schrift *f* ▹ *vt* (*letter etc*) tippen, (mit der) Maschine schreiben; **a ~ of** eine Art von; **what ~ do you want?** welche Sorte möchten Sie?; **in bold/italic ~** in Fett-/Kursivdruck
typecast [ˈtaɪpkɑːst] (*irreg: like* **cast**) *vt* (*actor*) (auf eine Rolle) festlegen
typeface [ˈtaɪpfeɪs] *n* Schrift *f*, Schriftbild *nt*
typescript [ˈtaɪpskrɪpt] *n* (maschinengeschriebenes) Manuskript *nt*
typewriter [ˈtaɪpraɪtəʳ] *n* Schreibmaschine *f*
typewritten [ˈtaɪprɪtn] *adj* maschine(n)geschrieben
typhoid [ˈtaɪfɔɪd] *n* Typhus *m*
typhoon [taɪˈfuːn] *n* Taifun *m*
typical [ˈtɪpɪkl] *adj* typisch; **~ (of)** typisch (für); **that's ~!** das ist typisch!

typing ['taɪpɪŋ] *n* Maschine(n)schreiben *nt*
typist ['taɪpɪst] *n* Schreibkraft *f*
tyrant ['taɪərnt] *n* Tyrann(in) *m(f)*
tyre, (*US*) **tire** ['taɪə[r]] *n* Reifen *m*
tyre pressure *n* Reifendruck *m*

Uu

U¹, u [juː] *n* (*letter*) U *nt*, u *nt*; **U for Uncle** ≈ U wie Ulrich
U² [juː] (*Brit*) *n abbr* (*Cine*: = *universal*) *Klassifikation für jugendfreie Filme*
U-bend [ˈjuːbɛnd] *n* (*in pipe*) U-Krümmung *f*
ubiquitous [juːˈbɪkwɪtəs] *adj* allgegenwärtig
udder [ˈʌdəʳ] *n* Euter *nt*
UFO [ˈjuːfəu] *n abbr* (= *unidentified flying object*) UFO *nt*
Uganda [juːˈgændə] *n* Uganda *nt*
ugh [əːh] *excl* igitt
ugly [ˈʌglɪ] *adj* hässlich; (*nasty*) schlimm
UHT *abbr* (= *ultra heat treated*): **~ milk** H-Milch *f*
UK *n abbr* = **United Kingdom**
ulcer [ˈʌlsəʳ] *n* (*stomach ulcer etc*) Geschwür *nt*; (*also*: **mouth ulcer**) Abszess *m* im Mund
Ulster [ˈʌlstəʳ] *n* Ulster *nt*
ulterior [ʌlˈtɪərɪəʳ] *adj*: **~ motive** Hintergedanke *m*
ultimate [ˈʌltɪmət] *adj* (*final*) letztendlich; (*greatest*) größte(r, s); (*: deterrent*) äußerste(r, s); (*: authority*) höchste(r, s) ▷ *n*: **the ~ in luxury** das Äußerste *or* Höchste an Luxus
ultimately [ˈʌltɪmətlɪ] *adv* (*in the end*) schließlich, letzten Endes; (*basically*) im Grunde (genommen)
ultimatum [ʌltɪˈmeɪtəm] (*pl* **~s** *or* **ultimata**) *n* Ultimatum *nt*
ultrasound [ˈʌltrəsaund] *n* Ultraschall *m*
ultraviolet [ˈʌltrəˈvaɪəlɪt] *adj* ultraviolett
umbrella [ʌmˈbrɛlə] *n* (*for rain*) (Regen)schirm *m*; (*for sun*) Sonnenschirm *m*; (*fig*): **under the ~ of** unter der Leitung von
umpire [ˈʌmpaɪəʳ] *n* Schiedsrichter(in) *m(f)* ▷ *vt* (*game*) als Schiedsrichter leiten
umpteen [ʌmpˈtiːn] *adj* zig
UN *n abbr* (= *United Nations*) UNO *f*
unable [ʌnˈeɪbl] *adj*: **to be ~ to do sth** etw nicht tun können
unacceptable [ʌnəkˈsɛptəbl] *adj* unannehmbar, nicht akzeptabel
unaccompanied [ʌnəˈkʌmpənɪd] *adj* (*child, song*) ohne Begleitung; (*luggage*) unbegleitet
unaccustomed [ʌnəˈkʌstəmd] *adj*: **to be ~ to** nicht gewöhnt sein an *+acc*
unanimous [juːˈnænɪməs] *adj* einstimmig
unanimously [juːˈnænɪməslɪ] *adv* einstimmig
unarmed [ʌnˈɑːmd] *adj* unbewaffnet; **~ combat** Nahkampf *m* ohne Waffen
unattached [ʌnəˈtætʃt] *adj* (*single: person*) ungebunden; (*unconnected*) ohne Verbindung
unattended [ʌnəˈtɛndɪd] *adj* (*car, luggage, child*) unbeaufsichtigt
unattractive [ʌnəˈtræktɪv] *adj* unattraktiv
unauthorized [ʌnˈɔːθəraɪzd] *adj* (*visit, use*) unbefugt; (*version*) nicht unautorisiert
unavailable [ʌnəˈveɪləbl] *adj* (*article, room*) nicht verfügbar; (*person*) nicht zu erreichen; **~ for comment** nicht zu sprechen
unavoidable [ʌnəˈvɔɪdəbl] *adj* unvermeidlich
unaware [ʌnəˈwɛəʳ] *adj*: **he was ~ of it** er war sich *dat* dessen nicht bewusst
unawares [ʌnəˈwɛəz] *adv* (*catch, take*) unerwartet
unbalanced [ʌnˈbælənst] *adj* (*report*) unausgewogen; **(mentally) ~** geistig gestört
unbearable [ʌnˈbɛərəbl] *adj* unerträglich
unbeatable [ʌnˈbiːtəbl] *adj* unschlagbar
unbeknown [ʌnbɪˈnəun], **unbeknownst** [ʌnbɪˈnəunst] *adv*: **~(st) to me/Peter** ohne mein/Peters Wissen
unbelievable [ʌnbɪˈliːvəbl] *adj* unglaublich
unbend [ʌnˈbɛnd] (*irreg: like* **bend**) *vi* (*relax*) aus sich herausgehen ▷ *vt* (*wire etc*) gerade biegen
unbiased, unbiassed [ʌnˈbaɪəst] *adj* unvoreingenommen
unborn [ʌnˈbɔːn] *adj* ungeboren
unbreakable [ʌnˈbreɪkəbl] *adj* (*object*) unzerbrechlich
unbroken [ʌnˈbrəukən] *adj* (*seal*) unversehrt; (*silence*) ununterbrochen; (*record, series*) ungebrochen
unbutton [ʌnˈbʌtn] *vt* aufknöpfen
uncalled-for [ʌnˈkɔːldfɔːʳ] *adj* (*remark etc*) unnötig
uncanny [ʌnˈkænɪ] *adj* unheimlich
unceremonious [ʌnsɛrɪˈməunɪəs] *adj* (*abrupt, rude*) brüsk, barsch
uncertain [ʌnˈsəːtn] *adj* (*person*) unsicher; (*future, outcome*) ungewiss; **to be ~ about sth** unsicher über etw *acc* sein; **in no ~ terms** unzweideutig
uncertainty [ʌnˈsəːtntɪ] *n* Ungewissheit *f*; **uncertainties** *npl* (*doubts*) Unsicherheiten *pl*
unchanged [ʌnˈtʃeɪndʒd] *adj* unverändert
uncivilized [ʌnˈsɪvɪlaɪzd] *adj* unzivilisiert
uncle [ˈʌŋkl] *n* Onkel *m*

unclear [ʌnˈklɪəʳ] *adj* unklar; **I'm still ~ about what I'm supposed to do** mir ist immer noch nicht klar, was ich tun soll
uncomfortable [ʌnˈkʌmfətəbl] *adj* (*person, chair*) unbequem; (*room*) ungemütlich; (*nervous*) unbehaglich; (*unpleasant*: *situation, fact*) unerfreulich
uncommon [ʌnˈkɔmən] *adj* ungewöhnlich
uncompromising [ʌnˈkɔmprəmaɪzɪŋ] *adj* (*person, belief*) kompromisslos
unconcerned [ʌnkənˈsə:nd] *adj* (*person*) unbekümmert; **to be ~ about sth** sich nicht um etw kümmern
unconditional [ʌnkənˈdɪʃənl] *adj* bedingungslos; (*acceptance*) vorbehaltlos
unconscious [ʌnˈkɔnʃəs] *adj* (*in faint*) bewusstlos; (*unaware*): **~ of** nicht bewusst *+gen* ▷ *n*: **the** ~ das Unbewusste; **to knock sb ~** jdn bewusstlos schlagen
unconsciously [ʌnˈkɔnʃəslɪ] *adv* unbewusst
uncontrollable [ʌnkənˈtrəuləbl] *adj* unkontrollierbar; (*laughter*) unbändig
unconventional [ʌnkənˈvɛnʃənl] *adj* unkonventionell
uncouth [ʌnˈku:θ] *adj* (*person, behaviour*) ungehobelt
uncover [ʌnˈkʌvəʳ] *vt* aufdecken
undecided [ʌndɪˈsaɪdɪd] *adj* (*person*) unentschlossen; (*question*) unentschieden
undeniable [ʌndɪˈnaɪəbl] *adj* unbestreitbar
under [ˈʌndəʳ] *prep* (*position*) unter *+dat*; (*motion*) unter *+acc*; (*according to*: *law etc*) nach, gemäß *+dat* ▷ *adv* (*go, fly etc*) darunter; **to come from ~ sth** unter etw *dat* hervorkommen; **~ there** darunter; **in ~ 2 hours** in weniger als 2 Stunden; **~ anaesthetic** unter Narkose; **to be ~ discussion** diskutiert werden; **~ repair** in Reparatur; **~ the circumstances** unter den Umständen
underage [ʌndərˈeɪdʒ] *adj* (*person*) minderjährig; **~ drinking** Alkoholgenuss *m* von Minderjährigen
undercarriage [ˈʌndəkærɪdʒ] *n* (*Aviat*) Fahrgestell *nt*
undercharge [ʌndəˈtʃɑ:dʒ] *vt* zu wenig berechnen *+dat*
undercoat [ˈʌndəkəut] *n* (*paint*) Grundierung *f*
undercover [ʌndəˈkʌvəʳ] *adj* (*duty, agent*) Geheim- ▷ *adv* (*work*) insgeheim
undercurrent [ˈʌndəkʌrnt] *n* (*also fig*) Unterströmung *f*
undercut [ʌndəˈkʌt] (*irreg*: *like* **cut**) *vt* (*person, prices*) unterbieten
underdog [ˈʌndədɔg] *n*: **the** ~ der/die Benachteiligte
underdone [ʌndəˈdʌn] *adj* (*food*) nicht gar; (: *meat*) nicht durchgebraten
underestimate [ˈʌndərˈɛstɪmeɪt] *vt* unterschätzen
underfed [ʌndəˈfɛd] *adj* unterernährt
underfoot [ʌndəˈfut] *adv*: **to crush sth ~** etw am Boden zerdrücken; **to trample sth ~** auf etw *dat* herumtrampeln
undergo [ʌndəˈgəu] (*irreg*: *like* **go**) *vt* (*change*) durchmachen; (*test, operation*) sich unterziehen; **the car is ~ing repairs** das Auto wird gerade repariert
undergraduate [ʌndəˈgrædjuɪt] *n* Student(in) *m(f)* ▷ *cpd*: **~ courses** Kurse *pl* für nicht graduierte Studenten
underground [ˈʌndəgraund] *adj* unterirdisch; (*Pol*: *newspaper, activities*) Untergrund- ▷ *adv* (*work*) unterirdisch; (: *miners*) unter Tage; (*Pol*): **to go ~** untertauchen ▷ *n*: **the ~** (*Brit*) die U-Bahn; (*Pol*) die Untergrundbewegung; **~ car park** Tiefgarage *f*
undergrowth [ˈʌndəgrəuθ] *n* Unterholz *nt*
underhand [ʌndəˈhænd], **underhanded** [ʌndəˈhændɪd] *adj* (*fig*: *behaviour, person*) hinterhältig
underlie [ʌndəˈlaɪ] (*irreg*: *like* **lie**) *vt* (*fig*: *be basis of*) zugrunde liegen *+dat*; **the underlying cause** der eigentliche Grund
underline [ʌndəˈlaɪn] *vt* unterstreichen; (*fig*: *emphasize*) betonen
undermine [ʌndəˈmaɪn] *vt* unterminieren, unterhöhlen
underneath [ʌndəˈni:θ] *adv* darunter ▷ *prep* (*position*) unter *+dat*; (*motion*) unter *+acc*
underpaid [ʌndəˈpeɪd] *adj* unterbezahlt
underpants [ˈʌndəpænts] *npl* Unterhose *f*
underpass [ˈʌndəpɑ:s] (*Brit*) *n* Unterführung *f*
underprivileged [ʌndəˈprɪvɪlɪdʒd] *adj* unterprivilegiert
underrate [ʌndəˈreɪt] *vt* unterschätzen
underscore [ʌndəˈskɔ:ʳ] *vt* unterstreichen
undershirt [ˈʌndəʃə:t] (*US*) *n* Unterhemd *nt*
undershorts [ˈʌndəʃɔ:ts] (*US*) *npl* Unterhose *f*
underside [ˈʌndəsaɪd] *n* Unterseite *f*
underskirt [ˈʌndəskə:t] (*Brit*) *n* Unterrock *m*
understand [ʌndəˈstænd] (*irreg*: *like* **stand**) *vt, vi* verstehen; **I ~ (that) you have ...** (*believe*) soweit ich weiß, haben Sie ...; **to make o.s. understood** sich verständlich machen
understandable [ʌndəˈstændəbl] *adj* verständlich
understanding [ʌndəˈstændɪŋ] *adj* verständnisvoll ▷ *n* Verständnis *nt*; **to come to an ~ with sb** mit jdm übereinkommen; **on the ~ that ...** unter der Voraussetzung, dass ...
understatement [ˈʌndəsteɪtmənt] *n* Understatement *nt*, Untertreibung *f*; **that's an ~!** das ist untertrieben!
understood [ʌndəˈstud] *pt, pp of* **understand** ▷ *adj* (*agreed*) abgemacht; (*implied*) impliziert
understudy [ˈʌndəstʌdɪ] *n* zweite Besetzung *f*
undertake [ʌndəˈteɪk] (*irreg*: *like* **take**) *vt* (*task*) übernehmen ▷ *vi*: **to ~ to do sth** es übernehmen, etw zu tun
undertaker [ˈʌndəteɪkəʳ] *n* (Leichen)bestatter *m*
undertaking [ˈʌndəteɪkɪŋ] *n* (*job*)

Unternehmen *nt*; (*promise*) Zusicherung *f*
undertone ['ʌndətəun] *n* (*of criticism etc*) Unterton *m*; **in an ~** mit gedämpfter Stimme
underwater ['ʌndə'wɔːtəʳ] *adv* (*swim etc*) unter Wasser ▷ *adj* (*exploration, camera etc*) Unterwasser-
underwear ['ʌndəwɛəʳ] *n* Unterwäsche *f*
underworld ['ʌndəwəːld] *n* Unterwelt *f*
underwrite [ʌndə'raɪt] *vt* (*Fin*) garantieren; (*Insurance*) versichern
undesirable [ʌndɪ'zaɪərəbl] *adj* unerwünscht
undies ['ʌndɪz] (*inf*) *npl* Unterwäsche *f*
undiplomatic ['ʌndɪplə'mætɪk] *adj* undiplomatisch
undisputed ['ʌndɪs'pjuːtɪd] *adj* unbestritten
undo [ʌn'duː] (*irreg: like* **do**) *vt* (*unfasten*) aufmachen; (*spoil*) zunichtemachen
undoing [ʌn'duːɪŋ] *n* Verderben *nt*
undone [ʌn'dʌn] *pp of* **undo** ▷ *adj*: **to come ~** (*shoelaces etc*) aufgehen
undoubted [ʌn'dautɪd] *adj* unzweifelhaft
undoubtedly [ʌn'dautɪdlɪ] *adv* zweifellos
undress [ʌn'drɛs] *vi* sich ausziehen ▷ *vt* ausziehen
undue [ʌn'djuː] *adj* (*excessive*) übertrieben
undulating ['ʌndjuleɪtɪŋ] *adj* (*movement*) Wellen-; (*hills*) sanft
unduly [ʌn'djuːlɪ] *adv* (*excessively*) übermäßig
unearth [ʌn'əːθ] *vt* (*skeleton etc*) ausgraben; (*fig: secrets etc*) ausfindig machen
unearthly [ʌn'əːθlɪ] *adj* (*eerie*) unheimlich; **at some ~ hour** zu nachtschlafender Zeit
uneasy [ʌn'iːzɪ] *adj* (*person*) unruhig; (*feeling*) unbehaglich; (*peace, truce*) unsicher; **to feel ~ about doing sth** ein ungutes Gefühl dabei haben, etw zu tun
uneconomic ['ʌniːkə'nɔmɪk] *adj* unwirtschaftlich
uneducated [ʌn'ɛdjukeɪtɪd] *adj* ungebildet
unemployed [ʌnɪm'plɔɪd] *adj* arbeitslos ▷ *npl*: **the ~** die Arbeitslosen *pl*
unemployment [ʌnɪm'plɔɪmənt] *n* Arbeitslosigkeit *f*
unemployment benefit (*Brit*) *n* Arbeitslosenunterstützung *f*
unending [ʌn'ɛndɪŋ] *adj* endlos
unequal [ʌn'iːkwəl] *adj* ungleich; **to feel ~ to** sich nicht gewachsen fühlen *+dat*
unerring [ʌn'əːrɪŋ] *adj* unfehlbar
uneven [ʌn'iːvn] *adj* (*teeth, road etc*) uneben; (*performance*) ungleichmäßig
unexpected [ʌnɪks'pɛktɪd] *adj* unerwartet
unexpectedly [ʌnɪks'pɛktɪdlɪ] *adv* unerwartet
unfailing [ʌn'feɪlɪŋ] *adj* (*support, energy*) unerschöpflich
unfair [ʌn'fɛəʳ] *adj* unfair, ungerecht; (*advantage*) ungerechtfertigt; **~ to** unfair *or* ungerecht zu
unfaithful [ʌn'feɪθful] *adj* (*lover, spouse*) untreu
unfamiliar [ʌnfə'mɪlɪəʳ] *adj* ungewohnt; (*person*) fremd; **to be ~ with sth** mit etw nicht vertraut sein
unfashionable [ʌn'fæʃnəbl] *adj* (*clothes, ideas*) unmodern; (*place*) unbeliebt
unfasten [ʌn'fɑːsn] *vt* (*seat belt, strap*) lösen
unfavourable, (US) **unfavorable** [ʌn'feɪvrəbl] *adj* (*circumstances, weather*) ungünstig; (*opinion, report*) negativ
unfeeling [ʌn'fiːlɪŋ] *adj* gefühllos
unfinished [ʌn'fɪnɪʃt] *adj* unvollendet
unfit [ʌn'fɪt] *adj* (*physically*) nicht fit; (*incompetent*) unfähig; **~ for work** arbeitsunfähig; **~ for human consumption** zum Verzehr ungeeignet
unfold [ʌn'fəuld] *vt* (*sheets, map*) auseinanderfalten ▷ *vi* (*situation, story*) sich entfalten
unforeseen ['ʌnfɔː'siːn] *adj* unvorhergesehen
unforgettable [ʌnfə'gɛtəbl] *adj* unvergesslich
unfortunate [ʌn'fɔːtʃənət] *adj* (*unlucky*) unglücklich; (*regrettable*) bedauerlich; **it is ~ that ...** es ist bedauerlich, dass ...
unfortunately [ʌn'fɔːtʃənətlɪ] *adv* leider
unfounded [ʌn'faundɪd] *adj* (*allegations, fears*) unbegründet
unfriendly [ʌn'frɛndlɪ] *adj* unfreundlich
unfurnished [ʌn'fəːnɪʃt] *adj* unmöbliert
ungainly [ʌn'geɪnlɪ] *adj* (*person*) unbeholfen
ungodly [ʌn'gɔdlɪ] *adj* (*annoying*) heillos; **at some ~ hour** zu nachtschlafender Zeit
ungrateful [ʌn'greɪtful] *adj* undankbar
unhappiness [ʌn'hæpɪnɪs] *n* Traurigkeit *f*
unhappy [ʌn'hæpɪ] *adj* unglücklich; **~ about/with** (*dissatisfied*) unzufrieden über *+acc*/mit
unharmed [ʌn'hɑːmd] *adj* (*person, animal*) unversehrt
UNHCR *n abbr* (*= United Nations High Commission for Refugees*) *Flüchtlingskommission der Vereinten Nationen*
unhealthy [ʌn'hɛlθɪ] *adj* (*person*) nicht gesund; (*place*) ungesund; (*fig: interest*) krankhaft
unheard-of [ʌn'həːdɔv] *adj* (*unknown*) unbekannt; (*outrageous*) unerhört
unhelpful [ʌn'hɛlpful] *adj* (*person*) nicht hilfreich; (*advice*) nutzlos
unhurt [ʌn'həːt] *adj* unverletzt
unidentified [ʌnaɪ'dɛntɪfaɪd] *adj* (*unknown*) unbekannt; (*unnamed*) ungenannt; *see also* **UFO**
uniform ['juːnɪfɔːm] *n* Uniform *f* ▷ *adj* (*length, width etc*) einheitlich
unify ['juːnɪfaɪ] *vt* vereinigen
unimportant [ʌnɪm'pɔːtənt] *adj* unwichtig
uninhabited [ʌnɪn'hæbɪtɪd] *adj* unbewohnt
unintentional [ʌnɪn'tɛnʃənəl] *adj* unbeabsichtigt
union ['juːnjən] *n* (*unification*) Vereinigung *f*; (*also:* **trade union**) Gewerkschaft *f* ▷ *cpd* (*activities, leader etc*) Gewerkschafts-; **the U~** (*US*) die Vereinigten Staaten
Union Jack *n* Union Jack *m*
unique [juː'niːk] *adj* (*object etc*) einmalig;

(*ability, skill*) einzigartig; **to be ~ to** charakteristisch sein für
unisex ['ju:nɪsɛks] *adj* (*clothes*) Unisex-; (*hairdresser*) für Damen und Herren
unison ['ju:nɪsn] *n*: **in ~** (*say, sing*) einstimmig; (*act*) in Übereinstimmung
unit ['ju:nɪt] *n* Einheit *f*; **production ~** Produktionsabteilung *f*; **kitchen ~** Küchen-Einbauelement *nt*
unite [ju:'naɪt] *vt* vereinigen ▷ *vi* sich zusammenschließen
united [ju:'naɪtɪd] *adj* (*agreed*) einig; (*country, party*) vereinigt
United Kingdom *n*: **the ~** das Vereinigte Königreich
United Nations *npl*: **the ~** die Vereinten Nationen *pl*
United States, United States of America *n*: **the ~ (of America)** die Vereinigten Staaten *pl* (von Amerika)
unit trust (*Brit*) *n* (*Comm*) Investmenttrust *m*
unity ['ju:nɪtɪ] *n* Einheit *f*
universal [ju:nɪ'və:sl] *adj* allgemein
universe ['ju:nɪvə:s] *n* Universum *nt*
university [ju:nɪ'və:sɪtɪ] *n* Universität *f* ▷ *cpd* (*student, professor*) Universitäts-; (*education, year*) akademisch
unjust [ʌn'dʒʌst] *adj* ungerecht; (*society*) unfair
unkempt [ʌn'kɛmpt] *adj* ungepflegt
unkind [ʌn'kaɪnd] *adj* (*person, comment etc*) unfreundlich
unknown [ʌn'nəun] *adj* unbekannt; **~ to me, ...** ohne dass ich es wusste, ...; **~ quantity** (*fig*) unbekannte Größe
unlawful [ʌn'lɔ:ful] *adj* gesetzwidrig
unleaded ['ʌn'lɛdɪd] *adj* (*petrol*) bleifrei, unverbleit; **I use ~** ich fahre bleifrei
unleash [ʌn'li:ʃ] *vt* (*fig: feeling, forces etc*) entfesseln
unless [ʌn'lɛs] *conj* es sei denn; **~ he comes** wenn er nicht kommt; **~ otherwise stated** wenn nicht anders angegeben; **~ I am mistaken** wenn ich mich nicht irre; **there will be a strike ~ ...** es wird zum Streik kommen, es sei denn, ...
unlike [ʌn'laɪk] *adj* (*not alike*) unähnlich ▷ *prep* (*different from*) verschieden von; **~ me, she is very tidy** im Gegensatz zu mir ist sie sehr ordentlich
unlikely [ʌn'laɪklɪ] *adj* unwahrscheinlich; (*combination etc*) merkwürdig; **in the ~ event of/that ...** im unwahrscheinlichen Fall *+gen*/dass ...
unlimited [ʌn'lɪmɪtɪd] *adj* unbeschränkt
unlisted ['ʌn'lɪstɪd] *adj* (*Stock Exchange*) nicht notiert; (*US: Tel*): **to be ~** nicht im Telefonbuch stehen
unload [ʌn'ləud] *vt* (*box etc*) ausladen; (*car etc*) entladen
unlock [ʌn'lɔk] *vt* aufschließen
unlucky [ʌn'lʌkɪ] *adj* (*object*) Unglück bringend; (*number*) Unglücks-; **to be ~** (*person*) Pech haben
unmarried [ʌn'mærɪd] *adj* unverheiratet
unmistakable, unmistakeable [ʌnmɪs'teɪkəbl] *adj* unverkennbar
unmitigated [ʌn'mɪtɪgeɪtɪd] *adj* (*disaster etc*) total
unnatural [ʌn'nætʃrəl] *adj* unnatürlich; (*against nature: habit*) widernatürlich
unnecessary [ʌn'nɛsəsərɪ] *adj* unnötig
unnoticed [ʌn'nəutɪst] *adj*: **to go** *or* **pass ~** unbemerkt bleiben
UNO ['ju:nəu] *n abbr* (= *United Nations Organization*) UNO *f*
unobtainable [ʌnəb'teɪnəbl] *adj* (*item*) nicht erhältlich; **this number is ~** (*Tel*) kein Anschluss unter dieser Nummer
unobtrusive [ʌnəb'tru:sɪv] *adj* unauffällig
unofficial [ʌnə'fɪʃl] *adj* inoffiziell
unorthodox [ʌn'ɔ:θədɔks] *adj* (*also Rel*) unorthodox
unpack [ʌn'pæk] *vt, vi* auspacken
unpaid [ʌn'peɪd] *adj* unbezahlt
unpalatable [ʌn'pælətəbl] *adj* (*meal*) ungenießbar; (*truth*) bitter
unparalleled [ʌn'pærəlɛld] *adj* beispiellos
unpleasant [ʌn'plɛznt] *adj* unangenehm; (*person, manner*) unfreundlich
unplug [ʌn'plʌg] *vt* (*iron, record player etc*) den Stecker herausziehen *+gen*
unpopular [ʌn'pɔpjuləʳ] *adj* unpopulär; **to make o.s. ~ (with)** sich unbeliebt machen (bei)
unprecedented [ʌn'prɛsɪdɛntɪd] *adj* noch nie da gewesen; (*decision*) einmalig
unpredictable [ʌnprɪ'dɪktəbl] *adj* (*person, weather*) unberechenbar; (*reaction*) unvorhersehbar
unprofessional [ʌnprə'fɛʃənl] *adj* unprofessionell
UNPROFOR *n abbr* (= *United Nations Protection Force*) UNPROFOR *f*; **~ troops** UNPROFOR-Truppen, UNO-Schutztruppen
unprotected ['ʌnprə'tɛktɪd] *adj* ungeschützt
unqualified [ʌn'kwɔlɪfaɪd] *adj* unqualifiziert; (*disaster, success*) vollkommen
unquestionably [ʌn'kwɛstʃənəblɪ] *adv* fraglos
unravel [ʌn'rævl] *vt* (*also fig*) entwirren
unreal [ʌn'rɪəl] *adj* (*artificial*) unecht; (*peculiar*) unwirklich
unrealistic ['ʌnrɪə'lɪstɪk] *adj* unrealistisch
unreasonable [ʌn'ri:znəbl] *adj* (*person, attitude*) unvernünftig; (*demand, length of time*) unzumutbar
unrelated [ʌnrɪ'leɪtɪd] *adj* (*incidents*) ohne Beziehung; (*people*) nicht verwandt
unreliable [ʌnrɪ'laɪəbl] *adj* unzuverlässig
unremitting [ʌnrɪ'mɪtɪŋ] *adj* (*efforts, attempts*) unermüdlich
unreservedly [ʌnrɪ'zə:vɪdlɪ] *adv* ohne Vorbehalt
unrest [ʌn'rɛst] *n* Unruhen *pl*
unroll [ʌn'rəul] *vt* entrollen ▷ *vi* sich

entrollen
unruly [ʌn'ru:lɪ] *adj* (*child, behaviour*) ungebärdig; (*hair*) widerspenstig
unsafe [ʌn'seɪf] *adj* unsicher; (*machine, bridge, car etc*) gefährlich; **~ to eat/drink** ungenießbar
unsaid [ʌn'sɛd] *adj*: **to leave sth ~** etw ungesagt lassen
unsatisfactory ['ʌnsætɪs'fæktərɪ] *adj* unbefriedigend
unsavoury, (US) **unsavory** [ʌn'seɪvərɪ] *adj* (*fig: person, place*) widerwärtig
unscathed [ʌn'skeɪðd] *adj* unversehrt
unscrew [ʌn'skru:] *vt* losschrauben
unscrupulous [ʌn'skru:pjuləs] *adj* skrupellos
unsettled [ʌn'sɛtld] *adj* (*person*) unruhig; (*future*) unsicher; (*question*) ungeklärt; (*weather*) unbeständig
unsettling [ʌn'sɛtlɪŋ] *adj* beunruhigend
unshaven [ʌn'ʃeɪvn] *adj* unrasiert
unsightly [ʌn'saɪtlɪ] *adj* unansehnlich
unskilled [ʌn'skɪld] *adj* (*work, worker*) ungelernt
unspeakable [ʌn'spi:kəbl] *adj* (*indescribable*) unsagbar; (*awful*) abscheulich
unstable [ʌn'steɪbl] *adj* (*piece of furniture*) nicht stabil; (*government*) instabil; (*person: mentally*) labil
unsteady [ʌn'stɛdɪ] *adj* (*step, voice, legs*) unsicher; (*ladder*) wack(e)lig
unstuck [ʌn'stʌk] *adj*: **to come ~** (*label etc*) sich lösen; (*fig: plan, idea etc*) versagen
unsuccessful [ʌnsək'sɛsful] *adj* erfolglos; (*marriage*) gescheitert; **to be ~** keinen Erfolg haben
unsuitable [ʌn'su:təbl] *adj* (*time*) unpassend; (*clothes, person*) ungeeignet
unsure [ʌn'ʃuə^r] *adj* unsicher; **to be ~ of o.s.** unsicher sein
unsuspecting [ʌnsəs'pɛktɪŋ] *adj* ahnungslos
unsympathetic ['ʌnsɪmpə'θɛtɪk] *adj* (*showing little understanding*) abweisend; (*unlikeable*) unsympathisch; **to be ~ to(wards) sth** einer Sache *dat* ablehnend gegenüberstehen
untapped [ʌn'tæpt] *adj* (*resources*) ungenutzt
unthinkable [ʌn'θɪŋkəbl] *adj* undenkbar
untidy [ʌn'taɪdɪ] *adj* unordentlich
untie [ʌn'taɪ] *vt* (*knot, parcel*) aufschnüren; (*prisoner, dog*) losbinden
until [ən'tɪl] *prep* bis *+acc*; (*after negative*) vor *+dat* ▹ *conj* bis; (*after negative*) bevor; **~ now** bis jetzt; **~ then** bis dann; **from morning ~ night** von morgens bis abends; **~ he comes** bis er kommt
untimely [ʌn'taɪmlɪ] *adj* (*moment*) unpassend; (*arrival*) ungelegen; (*death*) vorzeitig
untold [ʌn'təuld] *adj* (*joy, suffering, wealth*) unermesslich; **the ~ story** die Hintergründe
untoward [ʌntə'wɔ:d] *adj* (*events, effects etc*) ungünstig
untrue [ʌn'tru:] *adj* unwahr
unused¹ [ʌn'ju:zd] *adj* (*new*) unbenutzt
unused² [ʌn'ju:st] *adj*: **to be ~ to sth** an etw *acc* nicht gewöhnt sein; **to be ~ to doing sth** nicht daran gewöhnt sein, etw zu tun
unusual [ʌn'ju:ʒuəl] *adj* ungewöhnlich; (*exceptional*) außergewöhnlich
unusually [ʌn'ju:ʒuəlɪ] *adv* (*large, high etc*) ungewöhnlich
unveil [ʌn'veɪl] *vt* (*also fig*) enthüllen
unwanted [ʌn'wɔntɪd] *adj* unerwünscht
unwelcome [ʌn'wɛlkəm] *adj* (*guest*) unwillkommen; (*news*) unerfreulich; **to feel ~** sich nicht willkommen fühlen
unwell [ʌn'wɛl] *adj*: **to be ~, to feel ~** sich nicht wohlfühlen
unwieldy [ʌn'wi:ldɪ] *adj* (*object*) unhandlich; (*system*) schwerfällig
unwilling [ʌn'wɪlɪŋ] *adj*: **to be ~ to do sth** etw nicht tun wollen
unwillingly [ʌn'wɪlɪŋlɪ] *adv* widerwillig
unwind [ʌn'waɪnd] (*irreg: like* **wind**) *vt* abwickeln ▹ *vi* sich abwickeln; (*relax*) sich entspannen
unwise [ʌn'waɪz] *adj* unklug
unwitting [ʌn'wɪtɪŋ] *adj* (*accomplice*) unwissentlich; (*victim*) ahnungslos
unworkable [ʌn'wə:kəbl] *adj* (*plan*) undurchführbar
unworthy [ʌn'wə:ðɪ] *adj* unwürdig; **to be ~ of sth** einer Sache *gen* nicht wert *or* würdig sein; **to be ~ to do sth** es nicht wert sein, etw zu tun; **that remark is ~ of you** diese Bemerkung ist unter deiner Würde
unwrap [ʌn'ræp] *vt* auspacken
unwritten [ʌn'rɪtn] *adj* (*law*) ungeschrieben; (*agreement*) stillschweigend
unzip [ʌn'zɪp] *vt* aufmachen
up [ʌp] *prep*: **to be up sth** (oben) auf etw *dat* sein; **to go up sth** (auf) etw *acc* hinaufgehen; **go up that road and turn left** gehen Sie die Straße hinauf und biegen Sie links ab
▹ *adv* **1** (*upwards, higher*) oben; **put it a bit higher up** stelle es etwas höher; **up there** dort oben; **up above** hoch oben
2: **to be up** (*out of bed*) auf sein; (*prices, level*) gestiegen sein; (*building, tent*) stehen; **time's up** die Zeit ist um *or* vorbei
3: **up to** (*as far as*) bis; **up to now** bis jetzt
4: **to be up to** (*depending on*) abhängen von; **it's up to you** das hängt von dir ab; **it's not up to me to decide** es liegt nicht bei mir, das zu entscheiden
5: **to be up to** (*equal to*) gewachsen sein *+dat*; **he's not up to it** (*job, task etc*) er ist dem nicht gewachsen; **his work is not up to the required standard** seine Arbeit entspricht nicht dem gewünschten Niveau
6: **to be up to** (*inf: be doing*) vorhaben; **what is he up to?** (*showing disapproval, suspicion*) was führt er im Schilde?
▹ *n*: **ups and downs** (*in life, career*) Höhen und Tiefen *pl*
▹ *vi* (*inf*): **she upped and left** sie sprang auf und rannte davon

▷ *vt* (*inf: price*) heraufsetzen
up-and-coming [ʌpənd'kʌmɪŋ] *adj* (*actor, company etc*) kommend
upbringing ['ʌpbrɪŋɪŋ] *n* Erziehung *f*
update [ʌp'deɪt] *vt* aktualisieren
upfront [ʌp'frʌnt] *adj* (*person*) offen ▷ *adv*: **20% ~** 20% (als) Vorschuss, 20% im Voraus
upgrade [ʌp'greɪd] *vt* (*house*) Verbesserungen durchführen in *+dat*; (*job*) verbessern; (*employee*) befördern; (*Comput*) nachrüsten
upheaval [ʌp'hi:vl] *n* Unruhe *f*
uphill ['ʌp'hɪl] *adj* bergaufwärts (führend); (*fig: task*) mühsam ▷ *adv* (*push, move*) bergaufwärts; (*go*) bergauf
uphold [ʌp'həuld] (*irreg: like* **hold**) *vt* (*law, principle*) wahren; (*decision*) unterstützen
upholstery [ʌp'həulstərɪ] *n* Polsterung *f*
upkeep ['ʌpki:p] *n* (*maintenance*) Instandhaltung *f*
upon [ə'pɔn] *prep* (*position*) auf *+dat*; (*motion*) auf *+acc*
upper ['ʌpə^r] *adj* obere(r, s) ▷ *n* (*of shoe*) Oberleder *nt*
upper class *n*: **the ~** die Oberschicht
upper-class ['ʌpə'klɑ:s] *adj* vornehm
upper hand *n*: **to have the ~** die Oberhand haben
uppermost ['ʌpəməust] *adj* oberste(r, s); **what was ~ in my mind** woran ich in erster Linie dachte
upright ['ʌpraɪt] *adj* (*vertical*) vertikal; (*fig: honest*) rechtschaffen ▷ *adv* (*sit, stand*) aufrecht ▷ *n* (*Constr*) Pfosten *m*
uprising ['ʌpraɪzɪŋ] *n* Aufstand *m*
uproar ['ʌprɔ:^r] *n* Aufruhr *m*
uproot [ʌp'ru:t] *vt* (*tree*) entwurzeln; (*fig: people*) aus der gewohnten Umgebung reißen; (*: in war etc*) entwurzeln
upset [*vt, adj* ʌp'sɛt, *n* 'ʌpsɛt] (*irreg: like* **set**) *vt* (*knock over*) umstoßen; (*person: offend, make unhappy*) verletzen; (*routine, plan*) durcheinanderbringen ▷ *adj* (*unhappy*) aufgebracht; (*stomach*) verstimmt ▷ *n*: **to have/get a stomach ~** (*Brit*) eine Magenverstimmung haben/bekommen; **to get ~** sich aufregen
upshot ['ʌpʃɔt] *n* Ergebnis *nt*; **the ~ of it all was that ...** es lief schließlich darauf hinaus, dass ...
upside down ['ʌpsaɪd-] *adv* verkehrt herum; **to turn a room ~** (*fig*) ein Zimmer auf den Kopf stellen
upstairs [ʌp'stɛəz] *adv* (*be*) oben; (*go*) nach oben ▷ *adj* (*room*) obere(r, s); (*window*) im oberen Stock ▷ *n* oberes Stockwerk *nt*; **there's no ~** das Haus hat kein Obergeschoss
upstart ['ʌpstɑ:t] (*pej*) *n* Emporkömmling *m*
upstream [ʌp'stri:m] *adv, adj* flussaufwärts
uptake ['ʌpteɪk] *n*: **to be quick on the ~** schnell kapieren; **to be slow on the ~** schwer von Begriff sein
uptight [ʌp'taɪt] (*inf*) *adj* nervös
up-to-date ['ʌptə'deɪt] *adj* (*modern*) modern; (*person*) up to date
upturn ['ʌptə:n] *n* (*in economy*) Aufschwung *m*
upward ['ʌpwəd] *adj* (*movement*) Aufwärts-; (*glance*) nach oben gerichtet
upwards ['ʌpwədz] *adv* (*move*) aufwärts; (*glance*) nach oben; **upward(s) of** (*more than*) über *+acc*
uranium [juə'reɪnɪəm] *n* Uran *nt*
Uranus [juə'reɪnəs] *n* Uranus *m*
urban ['ə:bən] *adj* städtisch; (*unemployment*) in den Städten
urbane [ə:'beɪn] *adj* weltgewandt
urchin ['ə:tʃɪn] (*pej*) *n* Gassenkind *nt*
urge [ə:dʒ] *n* (*need, desire*) Verlangen *nt* ▷ *vt*: **to ~ sb to do sth** jdn eindringlich bitten, etw zu tun; **to ~ caution** zur Vorsicht mahnen
▸ **urge on** *vt* antreiben
urgency ['ə:dʒənsɪ] *n* Dringlichkeit *f*
urgent ['ə:dʒənt] *adj* dringend; (*voice*) eindringend
urinal ['juərɪnl] *n* (*building*) Pissoir *nt*; (*vessel*) Urinal *nt*
urinate ['juərɪneɪt] *vi* urinieren
urine ['juərɪn] *n* Urin *m*
urn [ə:n] *n* Urne *f*; (*also*: **tea urn**) Teekessel *m*
US *n abbr* (*= United States*) USA *pl*
us [ʌs] *pl pron* uns; (*emphatic*) wir; *see also* **me**
USA *n abbr* (*= United States of America*) USA *f*; (*Mil: = United States Army*) US-Armee *f*
use [*n* ju:s, *vt* ju:z] *n* (*using*) Gebrauch *m*, Verwendung *f*; (*usefulness, purpose*) Nutzen *m* ▷ *vt* benutzen, gebrauchen; (*phrase*) verwenden; **in ~** in Gebrauch; **out of ~** außer Gebrauch; **to be of ~** nützlich *or* von Nutzen sein; **to make ~ of sth** Gebrauch von etw machen; **it's no ~** es hat keinen Zweck; **to have the ~ of sth** über etw *acc* verfügen können; **what's this ~d for?** wofür wird das gebraucht?; **to be ~d to sth** etw gewohnt sein; **to get ~d to sth** sich an etw *acc* gewöhnen; **she ~d to do it** sie hat es früher gemacht
▸ **use up** *vt* (*food, leftovers*) aufbrauchen; (*money*) verbrauchen
used [ju:zd] *adj* gebraucht; (*car*) Gebraucht-
useful ['ju:sful] *adj* nützlich; **to come in ~** sich als nützlich erweisen
usefulness ['ju:sfəlnɪs] *n* Nützlichkeit *f*
useless ['ju:slɪs] *adj* nutzlos; (*person: hopeless*) hoffnungslos
user ['ju:zə^r] *n* Benutzer(in) *m(f)*; (*of petrol, gas etc*) Verbraucher(in) *m(f)*
user-friendly ['ju:zə'frɛndlɪ] *adj* benutzerfreundlich
usher ['ʌʃə^r] *n* (*at wedding*) Platzanweiser *m* ▷ *vt*: **to ~ sb in** jdn hineinführen
usherette [ʌʃə'rɛt] *n* Platzanweiserin *f*
usual ['ju:ʒuəl] *adj* üblich, gewöhnlich; **as ~** wie gewöhnlich
usually ['ju:ʒuəlɪ] *adv* gewöhnlich
utensil [ju:'tɛnsl] *n* Gerät *nt*; **kitchen ~s** Küchengeräte *pl*
uterus ['ju:tərəs] *n* Gebärmutter *f*, Uterus *m*

utility [juːˈtɪlɪtɪ] *n* (*usefulness*) Nützlichkeit *f*; (*public utility*) Versorgungsbetrieb *m*
utility room *n* ≈ Hauswirtschaftsraum *m*
utilize [ˈjuːtɪlaɪz] *vt* verwenden
utmost [ˈʌtməust] *adj* äußerste(r, s) ▷ *n*: **to do one's ~** sein Möglichstes tun; **of the ~ importance** von äußerster Wichtigkeit
utter [ˈʌtəʳ] *adj* (*amazement*) äußerste(r, s); (*rubbish, fool*) total ▷ *vt* (*sounds, words*) äußern
utterance [ˈʌtərəns] *n* Äußerung *f*
utterly [ˈʌtəlɪ] *adv* (*totally*) vollkommen
U-turn [ˈjuːˈtəːn] *n* (*also fig*) Kehrtwendung *f*

Vv

V¹, **v** [viː] *n* (*letter*) V *nt*, v *nt*; **V for Victor** ≈ V wie Viktor
V² *abbr* (= *volt*) V
v. *abbr* = **verse**; (= *versus*) vs.; (= *vide*) s.
vacancy ['veɪkənsɪ] *n* (*Brit: job*) freie Stelle *f*; (*room in hotel etc*) freies Zimmer *nt*; **"no vacancies"** "belegt"; **have you any vacancies?** (*hotel*) haben Sie Zimmer frei?; (*office*) haben Sie freie Stellen?
vacant ['veɪkənt] *adj* (*room, seat, job*) frei; (*look*) leer
vacate [və'keɪt] *vt* (*house*) räumen; (*one's seat*) frei machen; (*job*) aufgeben
vacation [və'keɪʃən] (*esp US*) *n* (*holiday*) Urlaub *m*; (*Scol*) Ferien *pl*; **to take a ~** Urlaub machen; **on ~** im Urlaub
vaccinate ['væksɪneɪt] *vt*: **to ~ sb (against sth)** jdn (gegen etw) impfen
vaccination [væksɪ'neɪʃən] *n* Impfung *f*
vaccine ['væksiːn] *n* Impfstoff *m*
vacuum ['vækjum] *n* (*empty space*) Vakuum *nt*
vacuum cleaner *n* Staubsauger *m*
vacuum-packed ['vækjum'pækt] *adj* vakuumverpackt
vagina [və'dʒaɪnə] *n* Scheide *f*, Vagina *f*
vagrant ['veɪgrənt] *n* Landstreicher(in) *m(f)*; (*in town, city*) Stadtstreicher(in) *m(f)*
vague [veɪg] *adj* (*memory*) vage; (*outline*) undeutlich; (*look, idea, instructions*) unbestimmt; (*person: not precise*) unsicher; (*: evasive*) unbestimmt; **to look ~** (*absent-minded*) zerstreut aussehen; **I haven't the ~st idea** ich habe nicht die leiseste Ahnung
vaguely ['veɪglɪ] *adv* (*unclearly*) vage, unbestimmt; (*slightly*) in etwa
vain [veɪn] *adj* (*person*) eitel; (*attempt, action*) vergeblich; **in ~** vergebens; **to die in ~** umsonst sterben
valentine ['væləntaɪn] *n* (*also*: **valentine card**) Valentinsgruß *m*; (*person*) *Freund/Freundin, dem/der man am Valentinstag einen Gruß schickt*
valiant ['vælɪənt] *adj* (*effort*) tapfer
valid ['vælɪd] *adj* (*ticket, document*) gültig; (*argument, reason*) stichhaltig
valley ['vælɪ] *n* Tal *nt*
valour, (*US*) **valor** ['væləʳ] *n* Tapferkeit *f*
valuable ['væljuəbl] *adj* wertvoll; (*time*) kostbar
valuables ['væljuəblz] *npl* Wertsachen *pl*
valuation [vælju'eɪʃən] *n* (*of house etc*) Schätzung *f*; (*judgement of quality*) Einschätzung *f*
value ['væljuː] *n* Wert *m*; (*usefulness*) Nutzen *m* ▷ *vt* schätzen; **values** *npl* (*principles, beliefs*) Werte *pl*; **you get good ~ (for money) in that shop** in dem Laden bekommt man etwas für sein Geld; **to lose (in) ~** an Wert verlieren; **to gain (in) ~** im Wert steigen; **to be of great ~ (to sb)** (*fig*) von großem Wert (für jdn) sein
valued ['væljuːd] *adj* (*customer, advice*) geschätzt
valve [vælv] *n* Ventil *nt*; (*Med*) Klappe *f*
vampire ['væmpaɪəʳ] *n* Vampir *m*
van [væn] *n* (*Aut*) Lieferwagen *m*; (*Brit: Rail*) Wa(g)gon *m*
vandal ['vændl] *n* Rowdy *m*
vandalism ['vændəlɪzəm] *n* Vandalismus *m*
vandalize ['vændəlaɪz] *vt* mutwillig zerstören
vanguard ['vængɑːd] *n* (*fig*): **in the ~ of** an der Spitze *+gen*
vanilla [və'nɪlə] *n* Vanille *f*
vanish ['vænɪʃ] *vi* verschwinden
vanity ['vænɪtɪ] *n* (*of person*) Eitelkeit *f*
vapour, (*US*) **vapor** ['veɪpəʳ] *n* (*gas, steam*) Dampf *m*; (*mist*) Dunst *m*
variable ['vɛərɪəbl] *adj* (*likely to change: mood, quality, weather*) veränderlich, wechselhaft; (*able to be changed: temperature, height, speed*) variabel ▷ *n* veränderlicher Faktor *m*; (*Math*) Variable *f*
variance ['vɛərɪəns] *n*: **to be at ~ (with)** nicht übereinstimmen (mit)
variant ['vɛərɪənt] *n* Variante *f*
variation [vɛərɪ'eɪʃən] *n* (*change*) Veränderung *f*; (*different form: of plot, theme etc*) Variation *f*
varicose ['værɪkəus] *adj*: **~ veins** Krampfadern *pl*
varied ['vɛərɪd] *adj* (*diverse*) unterschiedlich; (*full of changes*) abwechslungsreich
variety [və'raɪətɪ] *n* (*diversity*) Vielfalt *f*; (*varied collection*) Auswahl *f*; (*type*) Sorte *f*; **a wide ~ of ...** eine Vielfalt an *+acc* ...; **for a ~ of reasons** aus verschiedenen Gründen
variety show *n* Varietévorführung *f*
various ['vɛərɪəs] *adj* (*reasons, people*) verschiedene; **at ~ times** (*different*) zu

verschiedenen Zeiten; (*several*) mehrmals, mehrfach
varnish ['vɑːnɪʃ] *n* Lack *m* ▷ *vt* (*wood, one's nails*) lackieren
vary ['vɛərɪ] *vt* verändern ▷ *vi* (*be different*) variieren; **to ~ with** (*weather, season etc*) sich ändern mit
vase [vɑːz] *n* Vase *f*
Vaseline® ['væsɪliːn] *n* Vaseline *f*
vast [vɑːst] *adj* (*knowledge*) enorm; (*expense, area*) riesig
VAT [væt] (*Brit*) *n abbr* (= *value-added tax*) MwSt *f*
vat [væt] *n* Fass *nt*
vault [vɔːlt] *n* (*of roof*) Gewölbe *nt*; (*tomb*) Gruft *f*; (*in bank*) Tresorraum *m*; (*jump*) Sprung *m* ▷ *vt* (*also*: **vault over**) überspringen
vaunted ['vɔːntɪd] *adj*: **much-~** viel gepriesen
VCR *n abbr* = **video cassette recorder**
VD *n abbr* = **venereal disease**
VDU *n abbr* (*Comput*) = **visual display unit**
veal [viːl] *n* Kalbfleisch *nt*
veer [vɪəʳ] *vi* (*wind*) sich drehen; (*vehicle*) ausscheren
vegan ['viːgən] *n* Veganer(in) *m(f)* ▷ *adj* radikal vegetarisch
vegeburger ['vɛdʒɪbəːgəʳ] *n* vegetarischer Hamburger *m*
vegetable ['vɛdʒtəbl] *n* (*plant*) Gemüse *nt*; (*plant life*) Pflanzen *pl* ▷ *cpd* (*oil etc*) Pflanzen-; (*garden, plot*) Gemüse-
vegetarian [vɛdʒɪ'tɛərɪən] *n* Vegetarier(in) *m(f)* ▷ *adj* vegetarisch
vegetation [vɛdʒɪ'teɪʃən] *n* (*plants*) Vegetation *f*
vehement ['viːɪmənt] *adj* heftig
vehicle ['viːɪkl] *n* (*machine*) Fahrzeug *nt*; (*fig*: *means*) Mittel *nt*
veil [veɪl] *n* Schleier *m* ▷ *vt* (*also fig*) verschleiern; **under a ~ of secrecy** unter einem Schleier von Geheimnissen
vein [veɪn] *n* Ader *f*; (*fig*: *mood, style*) Stimmung *f*
Velcro® ['vɛlkrəu] *n* (*also*: **Velcro fastener** *or* **fastening**) Klettverschluss *m*
velocity [vɪ'lɔsɪtɪ] *n* Geschwindigkeit *f*
velvet ['vɛlvɪt] *n* Samt *m* ▷ *adj* (*skirt, jacket*) Samt-
vending machine ['vɛndɪŋ-] *n* Automat *m*
vendor ['vɛndəʳ] *n* Verkäufer(in) *m(f)*; **street ~** Straßenhändler(in) *m(f)*
veneer [və'nɪəʳ] *n* (*on furniture*) Furnier *nt*; (*fig*) Anstrich *m*
venereal [vɪ'nɪərɪəl] *adj*: **~ disease** Geschlechtskrankheit *f*
Venetian blind *n* Jalousie *f*
vengeance ['vɛndʒəns] *n* Rache *f*; **with a ~** (*fig*: *fiercely*) gewaltig; **he broke the rules with a ~** er verstieß die Regeln – und nicht zu knapp
venison ['vɛnɪsn] *n* Rehfleisch *nt*
venom ['vɛnəm] *n* (*poison*) Gift *nt*; (*bitterness, anger*) Gehässigkeit *f*
vent [vɛnt] *n* (*also*: **air vent**) Abzug *m*; (*in jacket*) Schlitz *m* ▷ *vt* (*fig*: *feelings*) abreagieren
ventilation [vɛntɪ'leɪʃən] *n* Belüftung *f*
ventilator ['vɛntɪleɪtəʳ] *n* (*Tech*) Ventilator *m*; (*Med*) Beatmungsgerät *nt*
ventriloquist [vɛn'trɪləkwɪst] *n* Bauchredner(in) *m(f)*
venture ['vɛntʃəʳ] *n* Unternehmung *f* ▷ *vt* (*opinion*) zu äußern wagen ▷ *vi* (*dare to go*) sich wagen; **a business ~** ein geschäftliches Unternehmen; **to ~ to do sth** es wagen, etw zu tun
venue ['vɛnjuː] *n* (*for meeting*) Treffpunkt *m*; (*for big events*) Austragungsort *m*
Venus ['viːnəs] *n* Venus *f*
verb [vəːb] *n* Verb *nt*
verbal ['vəːbl] *adj* verbal; (*skills*) sprachlich; (*translation*) wörtlich
verbatim [vəː'beɪtɪm] *adj* wörtlich ▷ *adv* Wort für Wort
verdict ['vəːdɪkt] *n* (*Law, fig*) Urteil *nt*; **~ of guilty/not guilty** Schuld-/Freispruch *m*
verge [vəːdʒ] (*Brit*) *n* (*of road*) Rand *m*, Bankett *nt*; **"soft ~s"** (*Brit*: *Aut*) "Seitenstreifen nicht befahrbar"; **to be on the ~ of doing sth** im Begriff sein, etw zu tun
▶ **verge on** *vt fus* grenzen an +*acc*
verify ['vɛrɪfaɪ] *vt* (*confirm*) bestätigen; (*check*) überprüfen
vermin ['vəːmɪn] *npl* Ungeziefer *nt*
vermouth ['vəːməθ] *n* Wermut *m*
versatile ['vəːsətaɪl] *adj* vielseitig
verse [vəːs] *n* (*poetry*) Poesie *f*; (*stanza*) Strophe *f*; (*in bible*) Vers *m*; **in ~** in Versform
version ['vəːʃən] *n* Version *f*
versus ['vəːsəs] *prep* gegen
vertical ['vəːtɪkl] *adj* vertikal, senkrecht ▷ *n* Vertikale *f*
vertigo ['vəːtɪgəu] *n* Schwindelgefühle *pl*; **to suffer from ~** leicht schwindlig werden
verve [vəːv] *n* Schwung *m*
very ['vɛrɪ] *adv* sehr ▷ *adj*: **the ~ book which ...** genau das Buch, das ...; **the ~ last** der/die/das Allerletzte; **at the ~ least** allerwenigstens; **~ well/little** sehr gut/wenig; **~ much** sehr viel; (*like, hope*) sehr; **the ~ thought (of it) alarms me** der bloße Gedanke (daran) beunruhigt mich; **at the ~ end** ganz am Ende
vessel ['vɛsl] *n* Gefäß *nt*; (*Naut*) Schiff *nt* *see* **blood**
vest [vɛst] *n* (*Brit*: *underwear*) Unterhemd *nt*; (*US*: *waistcoat*) Weste *f* ▷ *vt*: **to ~ sb with sth, ~ sth in sb** jdm etw verleihen
vested interest ['vɛstɪd-] *n* (*Comm*) finanzielles Interesse *nt*; **to have a ~ in doing sth** ein besonderes Interesse daran haben, etw zu tun
vet [vɛt] (*Brit*) *n* = **veterinary surgeon**; (*US*) = **veteran** ▷ *vt* (*examine*) überprüfen
veteran ['vɛtərn] *n* Veteran(in) *m(f)* ▷ *adj*: **she's a ~ campaigner for ...** sie ist eine altgediente Kämpferin für ...
veterinary surgeon (*Brit*) *n* Tierarzt *m*,

Tierärztin *f*
veto ['vi:təu] (*pl* **~es**) *n* Veto *nt* ▷ *vt* ein Veto einlegen gegen; **to put a ~ on sth** gegen etw ein Veto einlegen
vex [vɛks] *vt* (*irritate, upset*) ärgern
vexed [vɛkst] *adj* (*upset*) verärgert; (*question*) umstritten
via ['vaɪə] *prep* über *+acc*
viable ['vaɪəbl] *adj* (*project*) durchführbar; (*company*) rentabel
vibrate [vaɪ'breɪt] *vi* (*house*) zittern, beben; (*machine, sound etc*) vibrieren
vibration [vaɪ'breɪʃən] *n* (*act of vibrating*) Vibrieren *nt*; (*instance*) Vibration *f*
vicar ['vɪkə^r] *n* Pfarrer *m*
vicarage ['vɪkərɪdʒ] *n* Pfarrhaus *nt*
vicarious [vɪ'kɛərɪəs] *adj* (*pleasure, experience*) indirekt
vice [vaɪs] *n* (*moral fault*) Laster *nt*; (*Tech*) Schraubstock *m*
vice- [vaɪs] *pref* Vize-
vice-chairman [vaɪs'tʃɛəmən] *n* stellvertretender Vorsitzender *m*
vice squad *n* (*Police*) Sittendezernat *nt*
vice versa ['vaɪsɪ'və:sə] *adv* umgekehrt
vicinity [vɪ'sɪnɪtɪ] *n*: **in the ~ (of)** in der Nähe *or* Umgebung (*+gen*)
vicious ['vɪʃəs] *adj* (*attack, blow*) brutal; (*words, look*) gemein; (*horse, dog*) bösartig
victim ['vɪktɪm] *n* Opfer *nt*; **to be the ~ of an attack** einem Angriff zum Opfer fallen
victor ['vɪktə^r] *n* Sieger(in) *m(f)*
Victorian [vɪk'tɔ:rɪən] *adj* viktorianisch
victorious [vɪk'tɔ:rɪəs] *adj* (*team*) siegreich; (*shout*) triumphierend
victory ['vɪktərɪ] *n* Sieg *m*; **to win a ~ over sb** einen Sieg über jdn erringen
video ['vɪdɪəu] *n* (*film, cassette, recorder*) Video *nt* ▷ *vt* auf Video aufnehmen ▷ *cpd* Video-
video camera *n* Videokamera *f*
video cassette recorder *n* Videorekorder *m*
video game *n* Videospiel *nt*, Telespiel *nt*
video recorder *n* Videorekorder *m*
video tape *n* Videoband *nt*
vie [vaɪ] *vi*: **to ~ with sb/for sth** mit jdm/um etw wetteifern
Vienna [vɪ'ɛnə] *n* Wien *nt*
Vietnam ['vjɛt'næm] *n* Vietnam *nt*
Vietnamese [vjɛtnə'mi:z] *adj* vietnamesisch ▷ *n inv* (*person*) Vietnamese *m*, Vietnamesin *f*; (*Ling*) Vietnamesisch *nt*
view [vju:] *n* (*from window etc*) Aussicht *f*; (*sight*) Blick *m*; (*outlook*) Sicht *f*; (*opinion*) Ansicht *f* ▷ *vt* betrachten; (*house*) besichtigen; **to be on ~** (*in museum etc*) ausgestellt sein; **in full ~ of** vor den Augen *+gen*; **to take the ~ that ...** der Ansicht sein, dass ...; **in ~ of the weather/the fact that** in Anbetracht des Wetters/der Tatsache, dass ...; **in my ~** meiner Ansicht nach; **an overall ~ of the situation** ein allgemeiner Überblick über die Lage; **with a ~ to doing sth** mit der Absicht, etw zu tun
viewer ['vju:ə^r] *n* (*person*) Zuschauer(in) *m(f)*; (*viewfinder*) Sucher *m*
viewfinder ['vju:faɪndə^r] *n* Sucher *m*
viewpoint ['vju:pɔɪnt] *n* (*attitude*) Standpunkt *m*; (*place*) Aussichtspunkt *m*
vigilant ['vɪdʒɪlənt] *adj* wachsam
vigorous ['vɪgərəs] *adj* (*action, campaign*) energisch, dynamisch; (*plant*) kräftig
vile [vaɪl] *adj* abscheulich
villa ['vɪlə] *n* Villa *f*
village ['vɪlɪdʒ] *n* Dorf *nt*
villager ['vɪlɪdʒə^r] *n* Dorfbewohner(in) *m(f)*
villain ['vɪlən] *n* (*scoundrel*) Schurke *m*; (*in novel etc*) Bösewicht *m*; (*Brit: criminal*) Verbrecher(in) *m(f)*
vinaigrette [vɪneɪ'grɛt] *n* Vinaigrette *f*
vindicate ['vɪndɪkeɪt] *vt* (*person*) rehabilitieren; (*action*) rechtfertigen
vindictive [vɪn'dɪktɪv] *adj* (*person*) nachtragend; (*action*) aus Rache
vine [vaɪn] *n* (*Bot: producing grapes*) Weinrebe *f*; (*: in jungle*) Rebengewächs *nt*
vinegar ['vɪnɪgə^r] *n* Essig *m*
vineyard ['vɪnjɑ:d] *n* Weinberg *m*
vintage ['vɪntɪdʒ] *n* (*of wine*) Jahrgang *m* ▷ *cpd* (*classic*) klassisch; **the 1980 ~** (*of wine*) der Jahrgang 1980
vinyl ['vaɪnl] *n* Vinyl *nt*; (*records*) Schallplatten *pl*
viola [vɪ'əulə] *n* Bratsche *f*
violate ['vaɪəleɪt] *vt* (*agreement*) verletzen; (*peace*) stören; (*graveyard*) schänden
violation [vaɪə'leɪʃən] *n* (*of agreement etc*) Verletzung *f*; **in ~ of** (*rule, law*) unter Verletzung *+gen*
violence ['vaɪələns] *n* Gewalt *f*; (*strength*) Heftigkeit *f*
violent ['vaɪələnt] *adj* (*behaviour*) gewalttätig; (*death*) gewaltsam; (*explosion, criticism, emotion*) heftig; **a ~ dislike of sb/sth** eine heftige Abneigung gegen jdn/etw
violet ['vaɪələt] *adj* violett ▷ *n* (*colour*) Violett *nt*; (*plant*) Veilchen *nt*
violin [vaɪə'lɪn] *n* Geige *f*, Violine *f*
violinist [vaɪə'lɪnɪst] *n* Violinist(in) *m(f)*, Geiger(in) *m(f)*
VIP *n abbr* (*= very important person*) VIP *m*
virgin ['və:dʒɪn] *n* Jungfrau *f* ▷ *adj* (*snow, forest etc*) unberührt; **she is a ~** sie ist Jungfrau; **the Blessed V~** die Heilige Jungfrau
Virgo ['və:gəu] *n* (*sign*) Jungfrau *f*; **to be ~** Jungfrau sein
virile ['vɪraɪl] *adj* (*person*) männlich
virtual ['və:tjuəl] *adj* (*Comput, Phys*) virtuell; **it's a ~ impossibility** es ist so gut wie unmöglich; **to be the ~ leader** eigentlich *or* praktisch der Führer sein
virtually ['və:tjuəlɪ] *adv* praktisch, nahezu; **it is ~ impossible** es ist so gut wie unmöglich
virtual reality *n* virtuelle Realität *f*
virtue ['və:tju:] *n* Tugend *f*; (*advantage*) Vorzug *m*; **by ~ of** aufgrund *+gen*
virtuous ['və:tjuəs] *adj* tugendhaft

virus ['vaɪərəs] *n* (*Med, Comput*) Virus *m or nt*
visa ['vi:zə] *n* Visum *nt*
vise [vaɪs] (US) *n* (*Tech*) = **vice**
visibility [vɪzɪ'bɪlɪtɪ] *n* (*range of vision*) Sicht(weite) *f*
visible ['vɪzəbl] *adj* sichtbar; **~ exports/imports** sichtbare Ausfuhren/Einfuhren
vision ['vɪʒən] *n* (*sight*) Sicht *f*; (*foresight*) Weitblick *m*; (*in dream*) Vision *f*
visit ['vɪzɪt] *n* Besuch *m* ▷ *vt* besuchen; **a private/official ~** ein privater/offizieller Besuch
visiting hours *npl* Besuchszeiten *pl*
visitor ['vɪzɪtə^r] *n* Besucher(in) *m(f)*
visor ['vaɪzə^r] *n* (*of helmet etc*) Visier *nt*
vista ['vɪstə] *n* Aussicht *f*
visual ['vɪzjuəl] *adj* (*image etc*) visuell; **the ~ arts** die darstellenden Künste
visual aid *n* Anschauungsmaterial *nt*
visual display unit *n* (Daten)sichtgerät *nt*
visualize ['vɪzjuəlaɪz] *vt* sich *dat* vorstellen
vital ['vaɪtl] *adj* (*essential*) unerlässlich; (*organ*) lebenswichtig; (*full of life*) vital; **of ~ importance (to sb/sth)** von größter Wichtigkeit (für jdn/etw)
vitality [vaɪ'tælɪtɪ] *n* (*liveliness*) Vitalität *f*
vitally ['vaɪtəlɪ] *adv*: **~ important** äußerst wichtig
vital statistics *npl* (*fig: of woman*) Körpermaße *pl*; (*of population*) Bevölkerungsstatistik *f*
vitamin ['vɪtəmɪn] *n* Vitamin *nt* ▷ *cpd* (*pill, deficiencies*) Vitamin-
vivacious [vɪ'veɪʃəs] *adj* lebhaft
vivid ['vɪvɪd] *adj* (*description*) lebendig; (*memory, imagination*) lebhaft; (*colour*) leuchtend; (*light*) hell
vividly ['vɪvɪdlɪ] *adv* (*describe*) lebendig; (*remember*) lebhaft
V-neck ['vi:nɛk] *n* (*also:* **V-neck jumper** *or* **pullover**) Pullover *m* mit V-Ausschnitt
vocabulary [vəu'kæbjulərɪ] *n* (*words known*) Vokabular *nt*, Wortschatz *m*
vocal ['vəukl] *adj* (*of the voice*) stimmlich; (*articulate*) lautstark
vocal cords *npl* Stimmbänder *pl*
vocation [vəu'keɪʃən] *n* (*calling*) Berufung *f*; (*profession*) Beruf *m*
vocational [vəu'keɪʃənl] *adj* (*training, guidance etc*) Berufs-
vociferous [və'sɪfərəs] *adj* (*protesters, demands*) lautstark
vodka ['vɔdkə] *n* Wodka *m*
vogue [vəug] *n* (*fashion*) Mode *f*; (*popularity*) Popularität *f*; **in ~** in Mode
voice [vɔɪs] *n* (*also fig*) Stimme *f* ▷ *vt* (*opinion*) zum Ausdruck bringen; **in a loud/soft ~** mit lauter/leiser Stimme; **to give ~ to** Ausdruck verleihen *+dat*
voice mail *n* (*Comput*) Voicemail *f*
void [vɔɪd] *n* (*hole*) Loch *nt*; (*fig: emptiness*) Leere *f* ▷ *adj* (*invalid*) ungültig; **~ of** (*empty*) ohne
volatile ['vɔlətaɪl] *adj* (*person*) impulsiv; (*situation*) unsicher; (*liquid etc*) flüchtig
volcano [vɔl'keɪnəu] (*pl* **~es**) *n* Vulkan *m*
volition [və'lɪʃən] *n*: **of one's own ~** aus freiem Willen
volley ['vɔlɪ] *n* (*of gunfire*) Salve *f*; (*of stones, questions*) Hagel *m*; (*Tennis etc*) Volley *m*
volleyball ['vɔlɪbɔ:l] *n* Volleyball *m*
volt [vəult] *n* Volt *nt*
voltage ['vəultɪdʒ] *n* Spannung *f*; **high/low ~** Hoch-/Niederspannung *f*
volume ['vɔlju:m] *n* (*space*) Volumen *nt*; (*amount*) Umfang *m*, Ausmaß *nt*; (*book*) Band *m*; (*sound level*) Lautstärke *f*; **~ one/two** (*of book*) Band eins/zwei; **his expression spoke ~s** sein Gesichtsausdruck sprach Bände
voluntarily ['vɔləntrɪlɪ] *adv* freiwillig
voluntary ['vɔləntərɪ] *adj* freiwillig
volunteer [vɔlən'tɪə^r] *n* Freiwillige(r) *f(m)* ▷ *vt* (*information*) vorbringen ▷ *vi* (*for army etc*) sich freiwillig melden; **to ~ to do sth** sich anbieten, etw zu tun
vomit ['vɔmɪt] *n* Erbrochene(s) *nt* ▷ *vt* erbrechen ▷ *vi* sich übergeben
vote [vəut] *n* Stimme *f*; (*votes cast*) Stimmen *pl*; (*right to vote*) Wahlrecht *nt*; (*ballot*) Abstimmung *f* ▷ *vt* (*elect*): **to be ~d chairman** *etc* zum Vorsitzenden *etc* gewählt werden; (*propose*): **to ~ that** vorschlagen, dass ▷ *vi* (*in election etc*) wählen; **to put sth to the vote, (take a) ~ on sth** über etw *acc* abstimmen; **~ of censure** Tadelsantrag *m*; **to pass a ~ of confidence/no confidence** ein Vertrauens-/Misstrauensvotum annehmen; **to ~ to do sth** dafür stimmen, etw zu tun; **to ~ yes/no** mit Ja/Nein stimmen; **to ~ Labour/Green** *etc* Labour/die Grünen *etc* wählen; **to ~ for** *or* **in favour of sth/against sth** für/gegen etw stimmen
voter ['vəutə^r] *n* Wähler(in) *m(f)*
voting ['vəutɪŋ] *n* Wahl *f*
vouch [vautʃ]: **~ for** *vt fus* bürgen für
voucher ['vautʃə^r] *n* Gutschein *m*; (*receipt*) Beleg *m*; **gift ~** Geschenkgutschein *m*; **luncheon ~** Essensmarke *f*; **travel ~** Reisegutschein *m*
vow [vau] *n* Versprechen *nt* ▷ *vt*: **to ~ to do sth/that** geloben, etw zu tun/dass; **to take** *or* **make a ~ to do sth** geloben, etw zu tun
vowel ['vauəl] *n* Vokal *m*
voyage ['vɔɪɪdʒ] *n* Reise *f*
vulgar ['vʌlgə^r] *adj* (*remarks, gestures*) vulgär; (*decor, ostentation*) geschmacklos
vulnerable ['vʌlnərəbl] *adj* (*person, position*) verletzlich
vulture ['vʌltʃə^r] *n* (*also fig*) Geier *m*

W[1], **w** ['dʌblju:] *n* (*letter*) W *nt*, w *nt*; **W for William** ≈ W wie Wilhelm
W[2] ['dʌblju:] *abbr* (*Elec*: = *watt*) W; (= *west*) W
wad [wɔd] *n* (*of cotton wool*) Bausch *m*; (*of paper, banknotes*) Bündel *nt*
waddle ['wɔdl] *vi* watscheln
wade [weɪd] *vi*: **to ~ across** (*a river, stream*) waten durch; **to ~ through** (*fig*: *a book*) sich durchkämpfen durch
wafer ['weɪfəʳ] *n* (*biscuit*) Waffel *f*
waffle ['wɔfl] *n* (*Culin*) Waffel *f*; (*inf*: *empty talk*) Geschwafel *nt* ▷ *vi* (*in speech etc*) schwafeln
waft [wɔft] *vt, vi* wehen
wag [wæg] *vt* (*tail*) wedeln mit; (*finger*) drohen mit ▷ *vi* (*tail*) wedeln; **the dog ~ged its tail** der Hund wedelte mit dem Schwanz
wage [weɪdʒ] *n* (*also*: **wages**) Lohn *m* ▷ *vt*: **to ~ war** Krieg führen; **a day's ~s** ein Tageslohn
wage earner [-ə:nəʳ] *n* Lohnempfänger(in) *m(f)*
wage packet *n* Lohntüte *f*
wager ['weɪdʒəʳ] *n* Wette *f* ▷ *vt* wetten
wagon, **waggon** ['wægən] *n* (*horse-drawn*) Fuhrwerk *nt*; (*Brit*: *Rail*) Wa(g)gon *m*
wail [weɪl] *n* (*of person*) Jammern *nt*; (*of siren*) Heulen *nt* ▷ *vi* (*person*) jammern; (*siren*) heulen
waist [weɪst] *n* (*Anat, of clothing*) Taille *f*
waistcoat ['weɪskəut] (*Brit*) *n* Weste *f*
waistline ['weɪstlaɪn] *n* Taille *f*
wait [weɪt] *n* Wartezeit *f* ▷ *vi* warten; **to lie in ~ for sb** jdm auflauern; **to keep sb ~ing** jdn warten lassen; **I can't ~ to ...** (*fig*) ich kann es kaum erwarten, zu ...; **to ~ for sb/sth** auf jdn/etw warten; **~ a minute!** Moment mal!; **"repairs while you ~"** "Reparaturen sofort"
▸ **wait behind** *vi* zurückbleiben
▸ **wait on** *vt fus* (*serve*) bedienen
▸ **wait up** *vi* aufbleiben; **don't ~ up for me** warte nicht auf mich
waiter ['weɪtəʳ] *n* Kellner *m*
waiting ['weɪtɪŋ] *n*: **"no ~"** (*Brit*: *Aut*) "Halten verboten"
waiting list *n* Warteliste *f*
waiting room *n* (*in surgery*) Wartezimmer *nt*; (*in railway station*) Wartesaal *m*
waitress ['weɪtrɪs] *n* Kellnerin *f*
waive [weɪv] *vt* (*rule*) verzichten auf *+acc*
wake [weɪk] (*pt* **woke, ~d**, *pp* **woken, ~d**) *vt* (*also*: **wake up**) wecken ▷ *vi* (*also*: **wake up**) aufwachen ▷ *n* (*for dead person*) Totenwache *f*; (*Naut*) Kielwasser *nt*; **to ~ up to** (*fig*) sich *dat* bewusst werden *+gen*; **in the ~ of** (*fig*) unmittelbar nach, im Gefolge *+gen*; **to follow in sb's ~** (*fig*) hinter jdm herziehen
Wales [weɪlz] *n* Wales *nt*; **the Prince of ~** der Prinz von Wales
walk [wɔ:k] *n* (*hike*) Wanderung *f*; (*shorter*) Spaziergang *m*; (*gait*) Gang *m*; (*path*) Weg *m*; (*in park, along coast etc*) (Spazier)weg *m* ▷ *vi* gehen; (*instead of driving*) zu Fuß gehen; (*for pleasure, exercise*) spazieren gehen ▷ *vt* (*distance*) gehen, laufen; (*dog*) ausführen; **it's 10 minutes' ~ from here** es ist 10 Minuten zu Fuß von hier; **to go for a ~** spazieren gehen; **to slow to a ~** im Schritttempo weitergehen; **people from all ~s of life** Leute aus allen Gesellschaftsschichten; **to ~ in one's sleep** schlafwandeln; **I'd rather ~ than take the bus** ich gehe lieber zu Fuß als mit dem Bus zu fahren; **I'll ~ you home** ich bringe dich nach Hause
▸ **walk out** *vi* (*audience*) den Saal verlassen; (*workers*) in Streik treten
▸ **walk out on** (*inf*) *vt fus* (*family etc*) verlassen
walker ['wɔ:kəʳ] *n* (*person*) Spaziergänger(in) *m(f)*
walkie-talkie ['wɔ:kɪ'tɔ:kɪ] *n* Walkie-Talkie *nt*
walking ['wɔ:kɪŋ] *n* Wandern *nt*; **it's within ~ distance** es ist zu Fuß erreichbar
walking shoes *npl* Wanderschuhe *pl*
walking stick *n* Spazierstock *m*
Walkman® ['wɔ:kmən] *n* Walkman® *m*
walkout ['wɔ:kaut] *n* (*of workers*) Streik *m*
walkover ['wɔ:kəuvəʳ] (*inf*) *n* (*competition, exam etc*) Kinderspiel *nt*
walkway ['wɔ:kweɪ] *n* Fußweg *m*
wall [wɔ:l] *n* Wand *f*; (*exterior, city wall etc*) Mauer *f*; **to go to the ~** (*fig*: *firm etc*) kaputtgehen
▸ **wall in** *vt* (*enclose*) ummauern
walled [wɔ:ld] *adj* von Mauern umgeben
wallet ['wɔlɪt] *n* Brieftasche *f*
wallflower ['wɔ:lflauəʳ] *n* (*Bot*) Goldlack *m*; **to be a ~** (*fig*) ein Mauerblümchen sein
wallow ['wɔləu] *vi* (*in mud, water*) sich wälzen; (*in guilt, grief*) schwelgen

wallpaper ['wɔːlpeɪpəʳ] *n* Tapete *f* ▷ *vt* tapezieren
walnut ['wɔːlnʌt] *n* (*nut*) Walnuss *f*; (*tree*) Walnussbaum *m*; (*wood*) Nussbaumholz *nt*
walrus ['wɔːlrəs] (*pl* **~** *or* **walruses**) *n* Walross *nt*
waltz [wɔːlts] *n* Walzer *m* ▷ *vi* Walzer tanzen
wand [wɔnd] *n* (*also*: **magic wand**) Zauberstab *m*
wander ['wɔndəʳ] *vi* (*person*) herumlaufen; (*mind, thoughts*) wandern ▷ *vt* (*the streets, the hills etc*) durchstreifen
wane [weɪn] *vi* (*moon*) abnehmen; (*influence etc*) schwinden
wangle ['wæŋgl] (*Brit*: *inf*) *vt* sich *dat* verschaffen
want [wɔnt] *vt* (*wish for*) wollen; (*need*) brauchen ▷ *n* (*lack*): **for ~ of** aus Mangel an +*dat*; **wants** *npl* (*needs*) Bedürfnisse *pl*; **to ~ to do sth** etw tun wollen; **to ~ sb to do sth** wollen, dass jd etw tut; **to ~ in/out** herein-/hinauswollen; **you're ~ed on the phone** Sie werden am Telefon verlangt; **he is ~ed by the police** er wird von der Polizei gesucht; **a ~ of foresight** ein Mangel *m* an Voraussicht
wanted ['wɔntɪd] *adj* (*criminal etc*) gesucht; **"cook ~"** "Koch/Köchin gesucht"
wanting ['wɔntɪŋ] *adj*: **to be found ~** sich als unzulänglich erweisen
war [wɔːʳ] *n* Krieg *m*; **to go to ~** (*start*) einen Krieg anfangen; **to be at ~ (with)** sich im Kriegszustand befinden (mit); **to make ~ (on)** Krieg führen (gegen); **a ~ on drugs/crime** ein Feldzug gegen Drogen/das Verbrechen
ward [wɔːd] *n* (*in hospital*) Station *f*; (*Pol*) Wahlbezirk *m*; (*Law*: *also*: **ward of court**) Mündel *nt* unter Amtsvormundschaft
▸ **ward off** *vt* (*attack, enemy, illness*) abwehren
warden ['wɔːdn] *n* (*of park etc*) Aufseher(in) *m(f)*; (*of jail*) Wärter(in) *m(f)*; (*Brit*: *of youth hostel*) Herbergsvater *m*, Herbergsmutter *f*; (: *in university*) Wohnheimleiter(in) *m(f)*; (: *also*: **traffic warden**) Verkehrspolizist(in) *m(f)*
warder ['wɔːdəʳ] (*Brit*) *n* Gefängniswärter(in) *m(f)*
wardrobe ['wɔːdrəub] *n* (*for clothes*) Kleiderschrank *m*; (*collection of clothes*) Garderobe *f*; (*Cine, Theat*) Kostüme *pl*
warehouse ['wɛəhaus] *n* Lager *nt*
wares [wɛəz] *npl* Waren *pl*
warfare ['wɔːfɛəʳ] *n* Krieg *m*
warhead ['wɔːhɛd] *n* Sprengkopf *m*
warily ['wɛərɪlɪ] *adv* vorsichtig
warm [wɔːm] *adj* warm; (*thanks, applause, welcome, person*) herzlich; **it's ~** es ist warm; **I'm ~** mir ist warm; **to keep sth ~** etw warm halten; **with my ~est thanks/congratulations** mit meinem herzlichsten Dank/meinen herzlichsten Glückwünschen
▸ **warm up** *vi* warm werden; (*athlete*) sich aufwärmen ▷ *vt* aufwärmen
warm-hearted [wɔːm'hɑːtɪd] *adj* warmherzig
warmly ['wɔːmlɪ] *adv* (*applaud, welcome*) herzlich; (*dress*) warm
warmth [wɔːmθ] *n* Wärme *f*; (*friendliness*) Herzlichkeit *f*
warn [wɔːn] *vt*: **to ~ sb that ...** jdn warnen, dass ...; **to ~ sb of sth** jdn vor etw *dat* warnen; **to ~ sb not to do sth** *or* **against doing sth** jdn davor warnen, etw zu tun
warning ['wɔːnɪŋ] *n* Warnung *f*; **without (any) ~** (*suddenly*) unerwartet; (*without notifying*) ohne Vorwarnung; **gale ~** Sturmwarnung *f*
warning light *n* Warnlicht *nt*
warning triangle *n* (*Aut*) Warndreieck *nt*
warp [wɔːp] *vi* (*wood etc*) sich verziehen ▷ *vt* (*fig*: *character*) entstellen ▷ *n* (*Textiles*) Kette *f*
warrant ['wɔrnt] *n* (*Law*: *for arrest*) Haftbefehl *m*; (: *also*: **search warrant**) Durchsuchungsbefehl *m* ▷ *vt* (*justify, merit*) rechtfertigen
warranty ['wɔrəntɪ] *n* Garantie *f*; **under ~** (*Comm*) unter Garantie
warren ['wɔrən] *n* (*of rabbits*) Bau *m*; (*fig*: *of passages, streets*) Labyrinth *nt*
warrior ['wɔrɪəʳ] *n* Krieger *m*
Warsaw ['wɔːsɔː] *n* Warschau *nt*
warship ['wɔːʃɪp] *n* Kriegsschiff *nt*
wart [wɔːt] *n* Warze *f*
wartime ['wɔːtaɪm] *n*: **in ~** im Krieg
wary ['wɛərɪ] *adj* (*person*) vorsichtig; **to be ~ about** *or* **of doing sth** Bedenken haben, etw zu tun
was [wɔz] *pt of* **be**
wash [wɔʃ] *vt* waschen; (*dishes*) spülen, abwaschen; (*remove grease, paint etc*) ausspülen ▷ *vi* (*person*) sich waschen ▷ *n* (*clothes etc*) Wäsche *f*; (*washing programme*) Waschgang *m*; (*of ship*) Kielwasser *nt*; **he was ~ed overboard** er wurde über Bord gespült; **to ~ over/against sth** (*sea etc*) über/gegen etw *acc* spülen; **to have a ~** sich waschen; **to give sth a ~** etw waschen
▸ **wash away** *vt* wegspülen
▸ **wash down** *vt* (*wall, car*) abwaschen; (*food*: *with wine etc*) hinunterspülen
▸ **wash off** *vi* sich herauswaschen ▷ *vt* abwaschen
▸ **wash out** *vt* (*stain*) herauswaschen
▸ **wash up** *vi* (*Brit*: *wash dishes*) spülen, abwaschen; (*US*: *have a wash*) sich waschen
washable ['wɔʃəbl] *adj* (*fabric*) waschbar; (*wallpaper*) abwaschbar
washbasin ['wɔʃbeɪsn], (*US*) **washbowl** ['wɔʃbəul] *n* Waschbecken *nt*
washer ['wɔʃəʳ] *n* (*on tap etc*) Dichtungsring *m*
washing ['wɔʃɪŋ] *n* Wäsche *f*
washing line (*Brit*) *n* Wäscheleine *f*
washing machine *n* Waschmaschine *f*
washing powder (*Brit*) *n* Waschpulver *nt*
Washington ['wɔʃɪŋtən] *n* Washington *nt*
washing-up [wɔʃɪŋ'ʌp] *n* Abwasch *m*; **to do**

the ~ spülen, abwaschen
washing-up liquid *(Brit) n* (Geschirr)spülmittel *nt*
wash-out ['wɔʃaut] *(inf) n (failed event)* Reinfall *m*
washroom ['wɔʃrum] *(US) n* Waschraum *m*
wasn't ['wɔznt] = **was not**
wasp [wɔsp] *n* Wespe *f*
wastage ['weɪstɪdʒ] *n* Verlust *m*; **natural ~** natürliche Personalreduzierung
waste [weɪst] *n* Verschwendung *f*; *(rubbish)* Abfall *m* ▷ *adj (material)* Abfall-; *(left over: paper etc)* ungenutzt ▷ *vt* verschwenden; *(opportunity)* vertun; **wastes** *npl (area of land)* Wildnis *f*; **it's a ~ of money** das ist Geldverschwendung; **to go to ~** umkommen; **to lay ~** *(area, town)* verwüsten
▸ **waste away** *vi* verkümmern
wasteful ['weɪstful] *adj (person)* verschwenderisch; *(process)* aufwendig
waste ground *(Brit) n* unbebautes Grundstück *nt*
wastepaper basket ['weɪstpeɪpə-] *(Brit) n* Papierkorb *m*
watch [wɔtʃ] *n (also:* **wristwatch***)* (Armband)uhr *f*; *(surveillance)* Bewachung *f*; *(Mil, Naut: group of guards)* Wachmannschaft *f*; *(Naut: spell of duty)* Wache *f* ▷ *vt (look at)* betrachten; *(: match, programme)* sich *dat* ansehen; *(spy on, guard)* beobachten; *(be careful of)* aufpassen auf *+acc* ▷ *vi (look)* zusehen; **to be on ~** Wache halten; **to keep a close ~ on sb/sth** jdn/etw genau im Auge behalten; **to ~ TV** fernsehen; **~ what you're doing!** pass auf!; **~ how you drive!** fahr vorsichtig!
▸ **watch out** *vi* aufpassen; **~ out!** Vorsicht!
watchdog ['wɔtʃdɔg] *n (dog)* Wachhund *m*; *(fig)* Aufpasser(in) *m(f)*
watchful ['wɔtʃful] *adj* wachsam
watchmaker ['wɔtʃmeɪkəʳ] *n* Uhrmacher(in) *m(f)*
watchman ['wɔtʃmən] *(irreg: like* **man***) n see* **night watchman**
water ['wɔːtəʳ] *n* Wasser *nt* ▷ *vt (plant)* gießen; *(garden)* bewässern ▷ *vi (eyes)* tränen; **a drink of ~** ein Schluck Wasser; **in British ~s** in britischen (Hoheits)gewässern; **to pass ~** *(urinate)* Wasser lassen; **my mouth is ~ing** mir läuft das Wasser im Mund zusammen; **to make sb's mouth ~** jdm den Mund wässrig machen
▸ **water down** *vt (also fig)* verwässern
watercolour, (US) **watercolor** ['wɔːtəkʌləʳ] *n (picture)* Aquarell *nt*; **watercolours** *npl (paints)* Wasserfarben *pl*
watercress ['wɔːtəkrɛs] *n* Brunnenkresse *f*
waterfall ['wɔːtəfɔːl] *n* Wasserfall *m*
water heater *n* Heißwassergerät *nt*
watering can ['wɔːtərɪŋ-] *n* Gießkanne *f*
water lily *n* Seerose *f*
waterlogged ['wɔːtəlɔgd] *adj (ground)* unter Wasser
water main *n* Hauptwasserleitung *f*
watermelon ['wɔːtəmɛlən] *n* Wassermelone *f*
waterproof ['wɔːtəpruːf] *adj (trousers, jacket etc)* wasserdicht
watershed ['wɔːtəʃɛd] *n (Geog)* Wasserscheide *f*; *(fig)* Wendepunkt *m*
water-skiing ['wɔːtəskiːɪŋ] *n* Wasserski *nt*
watertight ['wɔːtətaɪt] *adj* wasserdicht; *(fig: excuse, case, agreement etc)* hieb- und stichfest
waterway ['wɔːtəweɪ] *n* Wasserstraße *f*
waterworks ['wɔːtəwəːks] *n* Wasserwerk *nt*; *(inf: fig: bladder)* Blase *f*
watery ['wɔːtərɪ] *adj (coffee, soup etc)* wässrig; *(eyes)* tränend
watt [wɔt] *n* Watt *nt*
wave [weɪv] *n (also fig)* Welle *f*; *(of hand)* Winken *nt* ▷ *vi (signal)* winken; *(branches)* sich hin und her bewegen; *(grass)* wogen; *(flag)* wehen ▷ *vt (hand, flag etc)* winken mit; *(gun, stick)* schwenken; *(hair)* wellen; **short/medium/long ~** *(Radio)* Kurz-/Mittel-/Langwelle *f*; **the new ~** *(Cine, Mus)* die neue Welle *f*; **he ~d us over to his table** er winkte uns zu seinem Tisch hinüber; **to ~ goodbye to sb** jdm zum Abschied winken
▸ **wave aside** *vt (fig: suggestion etc)* zurückweisen
wavelength ['weɪvlɛŋθ] *n (Radio)* Wellenlänge *f*; **on the same ~** *(fig)* auf derselben Wellenlänge
waver ['weɪvəʳ] *vi (voice)* schwanken; *(eyes)* zucken; *(love, person)* wanken
wavy ['weɪvɪ] *adj (line)* wellenförmig; *(hair)* wellig
wax [wæks] *n* Wachs *nt*; *(for sealing)* Siegellack *m*; *(in ear)* Ohrenschmalz *nt* ▷ *vt (floor)* bohnern; *(car, skis)* wachsen ▷ *vi (moon)* zunehmen
waxworks ['wækswəːks] *npl (models)* Wachsfiguren *pl* ▷ *n (place)* Wachsfigurenkabinett *nt*
way [weɪ] *n* Weg *m*; *(distance)* Strecke *f*; *(direction)* Richtung *f*; *(manner)* Art *f*; *(method)* Art und Weise *f*; *(habit)* Gewohnheit *f*; **which ~ to ...?** wo geht es zu ...?; **this ~, please** hier entlang, bitte; **on the ~** *(en route)* auf dem Weg, unterwegs; **to be on one's ~** auf dem Weg sein; **to fight one's ~ through a crowd** sich *acc* durch die Menge kämpfen; **to lie one's ~ out of sth** sich aus etw herauslügen; **to keep out of sb's ~** jdm aus dem Weg gehen; **it's a long ~ away** es ist weit entfernt; *(event)* das ist noch lange hin; **the village is rather out of the ~** das Dorf ist recht abgelegen; **to go out of one's ~ to do sth** sich sehr bemühen, etw zu tun; **to be in the ~** im Weg sein; **to lose one's ~** sich verirren; **under ~** *(project etc)* im Gang; **the ~ back** der Rückweg; **to make ~ (for sb/sth)** (für jdn/etw) Platz machen; **to get one's own ~** seinen Willen bekommen; **put it the right ~ up** *(Brit)* stell es richtig herum hin; **to be the wrong ~ round** verkehrt herum

sein; **he's in a bad ~** ihm geht es schlecht; **in a ~** in gewisser Weise; **in some ~s** in mancher Hinsicht; **no ~!** (*inf*) kommt nicht infrage!; **by the ~ ...** übrigens ...; **"~ in"** (*Brit*) "Eingang"; **"~ out"** (*Brit*) "Ausgang"; **"give ~"** (*Brit: Aut*) "Vorfahrt beachten"; **~ of life** Lebensstil *m*

waylay [weɪ'leɪ] (*irreg: like* **lay**) *vt* auflauern *+dat*; **to get waylaid** (*fig*) abgefangen werden

wayward ['weɪwəd] *adj* (*behaviour*) eigenwillig; (*child*) eigensinnig

we [wi:] *pl pron* wir; **here we are** (*arriving*) da sind wir; (*finding sth*) na bitte

weak [wi:k] *adj* schwach; (*tea, coffee*) dünn; **to grow ~(er)** schwächer werden

weaken ['wi:kn] *vi* (*resolve, person*) schwächer werden; (*influence, power*) nachlassen ▷ *vt* schwächen

weakling ['wi:klɪŋ] *n* Schwächling *m*

weakness ['wi:knɪs] *n* Schwäche *f*; **to have a ~ for** eine Schwäche haben für

wealth [wɛlθ] *n* Reichtum *m*; (*of details, knowledge etc*) Fülle *f*

wealthy ['wɛlθɪ] *adj* wohlhabend, reich

wean [wi:n] *vt* (*also fig*) entwöhnen

weapon ['wɛpən] *n* Waffe *f*; **~s of mass destruction** Massenvernichtungswaffen *pl*

wear [wɛəʳ] (*pt* **wore**, *pp* **worn**) *vt* (*clothes, shoes, beard*) tragen; (*put on*) anziehen ▷ *vi* (*last*) halten; (*become old: carpet, jeans*) sich abnutzen ▷ *n* (*damage*) Verschleiß *m*; (*use*): **I got a lot of/very little ~ out of the coat** der Mantel hat lange/nicht sehr lange gehalten; **baby~** Babykleidung *f*; **sports~** Sportkleidung *f*; **evening ~** Kleidung für den Abend; **to ~ a hole in sth** (*coat etc*) etw durchwetzen

▸ **wear away** *vt* verschleißen ▷ *vi* (*inscription etc*) verwittern

▸ **wear down** *vt* (*heels*) abnutzen; (*person, strength*) zermürben

▸ **wear off** *vi* (*pain etc*) nachlassen

▸ **wear on** *vi* sich hinziehen

▸ **wear out** *vt* (*shoes, clothing*) verschleißen; (*person, strength*) erschöpfen

weary ['wɪərɪ] *adj* (*tired*) müde; (*dispirited*) lustlos ▷ *vi*: **to ~ of sb/sth** jds/etw *gen* überdrüssig werden

weasel ['wi:zl] *n* Wiesel *nt*

weather ['wɛðəʳ] *n* Wetter *nt* ▷ *vt* (*storm, crisis*) überstehen; (*rock, wood*) verwittern; **what's the ~ like?** wie ist das Wetter?; **under the ~** (*fig: ill*) angeschlagen

weather-beaten ['wɛðəbi:tn] *adj* (*face*) vom Wetter gegerbt; (*building, stone*) verwittert

weather forecast *n* Wettervorhersage *f*

weatherman ['wɛðəmæn] (*irreg: like* **man**) *n* Mann *m* vom Wetteramt, Wetterfrosch *m* (*hum inf*)

weather vane [-veɪn] *n* = **weathercock**

weave [wi:v] (*pt* **wove**, *pp* **woven**) *vt* (*cloth*) weben; (*basket*) flechten ▷ *vi* (*fig: pt, pp weaved: move in and out*) sich schlängeln

weaver ['wi:vəʳ] *n* Weber(in) *m(f)*

web [wɛb] *n* (*also fig*) Netz *nt*; (*on duck's foot*) Schwimmhaut *f*

website ['wɛbsaɪt] *n* (*Comput*) Website *f*, Webseite *f*

wed [wɛd] (*pt, pp* **~ded**) *vt, vi* heiraten ▷ *n*: **the newly-~s** die Jungvermählten *pl*

we'd [wi:d] = **we had**; = **we would**

wedding [wɛdɪŋ] *n* Hochzeit *f*; **silver/golden ~** silberne/goldene Hochzeit

wedding day *n* Hochzeitstag *m*

wedding dress *n* Hochzeitskleid *nt*

wedding ring *n* Trauring *m*

wedge [wɛdʒ] *n* Keil *m*; (*of cake*) Stück *nt* ▷ *vt* (*fasten*) festklemmen; (*pack tightly*) einkeilen

Wednesday ['wɛdnzdɪ] *n* Mittwoch *m*; *see also* **Tuesday**

wee [wi:] (*Scot*) *adj* klein

weed [wi:d] *n* (*Bot*) Unkraut *nt*; (*pej: person*) Schwächling *m* ▷ *vt* (*garden*) jäten

▸ **weed out** *vt* (*fig*) aussondern

weedkiller ['wi:dkɪləʳ] *n* Unkrautvertilger *m*

weedy ['wi:dɪ] *adj* (*person*) schwächlich

week [wi:k] *n* Woche *f*; **once/twice a ~** einmal/zweimal die Woche; **in two ~s' time** in zwei Wochen; **a ~ today/on Friday** heute/Freitag in einer Woche

weekday ['wi:kdeɪ] *n* Wochentag *m*; (*Comm: Monday to Saturday*) Werktag *m*; **on ~s** an Wochentagen/Werktagen

weekend [wi:k'ɛnd] *n* Wochenende *nt*; **this/next/last ~** an diesem/am nächsten/am letzten Wochenende; **what are you doing at the ~?** was machen Sie am Wochenende?; **open at ~s** an Wochenenden geöffnet

weekly ['wi:klɪ] *adv* wöchentlich ▷ *adj* (*newspaper*) Wochen- ▷ *n* (*newspaper*) Wochenzeitung *f*; (*magazine*) Wochenzeitschrift *f*

weep [wi:p] (*pt, pp* **wept**) *vi* (*person*) weinen; (*wound*) nässen

weeping willow ['wi:pɪŋ-] *n* (*tree*) Trauerweide *f*

weigh [weɪ] *vt* wiegen; (*fig: evidence, risks*) abwägen ▷ *vi* wiegen; **to ~ anchor** den Anker lichten

▸ **weigh down** *vt* niederdrücken

▸ **weigh out** *vt* (*goods*) auswiegen

▸ **weigh up** *vt* (*person, offer, risk*) abschätzen

weight [weɪt] *n* Gewicht *nt* ▷ *vt* (*fig*): **to be ~ed in favour of sb/sth** jdn/etw begünstigen; **to be sold by ~** nach Gewicht verkauft werden; **to lose ~** abnehmen; **to put on ~** zunehmen; **~s and measures** Maße und Gewichte

weighting ['weɪtɪŋ] *n* (*allowance*) Zulage *f*

weightlifter ['weɪtlɪftəʳ] *n* Gewichtheber *m*

weighty ['weɪtɪ] *adj* schwer; (*fig: important*) gewichtig

weir [wɪəʳ] *n* (*in river*) Wehr *nt*

weird [wɪəd] *adj* (*object, situation, effect*) komisch; (*person*) seltsam

welcome ['wɛlkəm] *adj* willkommen ▷ *n*

Willkommen *nt* ▷ *vt* begrüßen, willkommen heißen; **~ to London!** willkommen in London!; **to make sb ~** jdn freundlich aufnehmen; **you're ~ to try** du kannst es gern versuchen; **thank you — you're ~!** danke — nichts zu danken!

weld [wɛld] *n* Schweißnaht *f* ▷ *vt* schweißen

welder ['wɛldəʳ] *n (person)* Schweißer(in) *m(f)*

welfare ['wɛlfɛəʳ] *n (well-being)* Wohl *nt*; *(social aid)* Sozialhilfe *f*

welfare state *n* Wohlfahrtsstaat *m*

well [wɛl] *n (for water)* Brunnen *m*; *(oil well)* Quelle *f* ▷ *adv* gut; *(for emphasis with adj)* durchaus ▷ *adj*: **to be ~** *(person)* gesund sein ▷ *excl* nun!, na!; **as ~** *(in addition)* ebenfalls; **you might as ~ tell me** sag es mir ruhig; **he did as ~ as he could** er machte es so gut er konnte; **pretty as ~ as rich** sowohl hübsch als auch reich; **~ done!** gut gemacht!; **to do ~** *(person)* gut vorankommen; *(business)* gut gehen; **~ before dawn** lange vor Tagesanbruch; **~ over 40** weit über 40; **I don't feel ~** ich fühle mich nicht gut *or* wohl; **get ~ soon!** gute Besserung!; **~, as I was saying ...** also, wie ich bereits sagte, ...
▸ **well up** *vi (tears, emotions)* aufsteigen

we'll [wi:l] = **we will; we shall**

well-behaved ['wɛlbɪ'heɪvd] *adj* wohlerzogen

well-being ['wɛl'bi:ɪŋ] *n* Wohl(ergehen) *nt*

well-built ['wɛl'bɪlt] *adj* gut gebaut

well-deserved ['wɛldɪ'zə:vd] *adj* wohlverdient

well-dressed ['wɛl'drɛst] *adj* gut gekleidet

well-groomed ['wɛl'gru:md] *adj* gepflegt

well-heeled ['wɛl'hi:ld] *(inf) adj* betucht

wellingtons ['wɛlɪŋtənz] *npl (also:* **wellington boots***)* Gummistiefel *pl*

well-known ['wɛl'nəun] *adj* wohlbekannt

well-mannered ['wɛl'mænəd] *adj* wohlerzogen

well-meaning ['wɛl'mi:nɪŋ] *adj (person)* wohlmeinend; *(offer etc)* gut gemeint

well-off ['wɛl'ɔf] *adj (rich)* begütert

well-read ['wɛl'rɛd] *adj* belesen

well-to-do ['wɛltə'du:] *adj* wohlhabend

well-wisher ['wɛlwɪʃəʳ] *n (friend, admirer)* wohlmeinender Mensch *m*; **scores of ~s had gathered** eine große Gefolgschaft hatte sich versammelt; **letters from ~s** Briefe von Leuten, die es gut meinen

Welsh [wɛlʃ] *adj* walisisch ▷ *n (Ling)* Walisisch *nt*; **the Welsh** *npl* die Waliser *pl*

Welshman ['wɛlʃmən] *(irreg: like* **man***) n* Waliser *m*

Welshwoman ['wɛlʃwumən] *(irreg: like* **woman***) n* Waliserin *f*

went [wɛnt] *pt of* **go**

wept [wɛpt] *pt, pp of* **weep**

were [wə:ʳ] *pt of* **be**

we're [wɪəʳ] = **we are**

weren't [wə:nt] = **were not**

west [wɛst] *n* Westen *m* ▷ *adj (wind, side, coast)* West-, westlich ▷ *adv (to or towards the west)* westwärts; **the W~** *(Pol)* der Westen

westbound ['wɛstbaund] *adj (traffic, carriageway)* in Richtung Westen

westerly ['wɛstəlɪ] *adj* westlich

western ['wɛstən] *adj* westlich ▷ *n (Cine)* Western *m*

West Indian *adj* westindisch ▷ *n (person)* Westinder(in) *m(f)*

West Indies [-'ɪndɪz] *npl*: **the ~** Westindien *nt*

westward ['wɛstwəd], **westwards** ['wɛstwədz] *adv* westwärts

wet [wɛt] *adj* nass ▷ *n (Brit: Pol)* Gemäßigte(r) *f(m)*, Waschlappen *m (pej)*; **to get ~** nass werden; **"~ paint"** "frisch gestrichen"; **to be a ~ blanket** *(fig: pej: person)* ein(e) Spielverderber(in) *m(f)* sein; **to ~ one's pants/o.s.** sich *dat* in die Hosen machen

we've [wi:v] = **we have**

whack [wæk] *vt* schlagen

whale [weɪl] *n* Wal *m*

wharf [wɔ:f] *(pl* **wharves***) n* Kai *m*

what [wɔt] *adj* **1** *(in direct/indirect questions)* welche(r, s); **what colour/shape is it?** welche Farbe/Form hat es?; **for what reason?** aus welchem Grund?
2 *(in exclamations)* was für ein(e); **what a mess!** was für ein Durcheinander!; **what a fool I am!** was bin ich doch (für) ein Idiot!
▷ *pron (interrogative, relative)* was; **what are you doing?** was machst du?; **what are you talking about?** wovon redest du?; **what is it called?** wie heißt das?; **what about me?** und ich?; **what about a cup of tea?** wie wärs mit einer Tasse Tee?; **what about going to the cinema?** sollen wir ins Kino gehen?; **I saw what you did/what was on the table** ich habe gesehen, was du getan hast/was auf dem Tisch war; **tell me what you're thinking about** sag mir, woran du denkst
▷ *excl (disbelieving)* was, wie; **what, no coffee!** was *or* wie, kein Kaffee?

whatever [wɔt'ɛvəʳ] *adj*: **~ book** welches Buch auch immer ▷ *pron*: **do ~ is necessary/you want** tun Sie, was nötig ist/was immer Sie wollen; **~ happens** was auch passiert; **no reason ~** *or* **whatsoever** überhaupt kein Grund; **nothing ~** *or* **whatsoever** überhaupt nichts

whatsoever [wɔtsəu'ɛvəʳ] *adj* = **whatever**

wheat [wi:t] *n* Weizen *m*

wheedle ['wi:dl] *vt*: **to ~ sb into doing sth** jdn beschwatzen, etw zu tun; **to ~ sth out of sb** jdm etw abluchsen

wheel [wi:l] *n* Rad *nt*; *(also:* **steering wheel***)* Lenkrad *nt*; *(Naut)* Steuer *nt* ▷ *vt (pram etc)* schieben ▷ *vi (birds)* kreisen; *(also:* **wheel round***: person)* sich herumdrehen

wheelbarrow ['wi:lbærəu] *n* Schubkarre *f*

wheelchair ['wi:ltʃɛəʳ] *n* Rollstuhl *m*

wheel clamp *n* Parkkralle *f*

wheeze [wi:z] *vi (person)* keuchen ▷ *n (idea, joke etc)* Scherz *m*

when [wɛn] *adv* wann
▷ *conj* **1** *(at, during, after the time that)* wenn; **she was reading when I came in** als ich hereinkam, las sie gerade; **be careful when you cross the road** sei vorsichtig, wenn du die Straße überquerst
2 *(on, at which)* als; **on the day when I met him** am Tag, als ich ihn traf
3 *(whereas)* wo ... doch, obwohl; **why did you buy that when you can't afford it?** warum hast du das gekauft, obwohl du es dir nicht leisten kannst?
whenever [wɛn'ɛvəʳ] *adv, conj* *(any time that)* wann immer; *(every time that)* (jedes Mal,) wenn; **I go ~ I can** ich gehe, wann immer ich kann
where [wɛəʳ] *adv, conj* wo; **this is ~ ...** hier ...; **~ possible** so weit möglich; **~ are you from?** woher kommen Sie?
whereabouts [wɛərə'bauts] *adv* wo ▷ *n*: **nobody knows his ~** keiner weiß, wo er ist
whereas [wɛər'æz] *conj* während
whereby [wɛə'baɪ] *(form) adv* wonach
wherever [wɛər'ɛvəʳ] *conj* *(position)* wo (auch) immer; *(motion)* wohin (auch) immer ▷ *adv* *(surprise)* wo (um alles in der Welt); **sit ~ you like** nehmen Sie Platz, wo immer Sie wollen
wherewithal ['wɛəwɪðɔːl] *n*: **the ~ (to do sth)** *(money)* das nötige Kleingeld(, um etw zu tun)
whether ['wɛðəʳ] *conj* ob; **I don't know ~ to accept or not** ich weiß nicht, ob ich annehmen soll oder nicht; **~ you go or not** ob du gehst oder nicht; **it's doubtful ~ ...** es ist zweifelhaft, ob ...
which [wɪtʃ] *adj* **1** *(interrogative: direct, indirect)* welche(r, s); **which picture?** welches Bild?; **which books?** welche Bücher?; **which one?** welche(r, s) ?
2: in which case in diesem Fall; **by which time** zu dieser Zeit
▷ *pron* **1** *(interrogative)* welche(r, s); **which of you are coming?** wer von Ihnen kommt?; **I don't mind which** mir ist gleich, welche(r, s)
2 *(relative)* der/die/das; **the apple which you ate/which is on the table** der Apfel, den du gegessen hast/der auf dem Tisch liegt; **the chair on which you are sitting** der Stuhl, auf dem Sie sitzen; **the book of which you spoke** das Buch, wovon *or* von dem Sie sprachen; **he said he saw her, which is true** er sagte, er habe sie gesehen, was auch stimmt; **after which** wonach
whichever [wɪtʃ'ɛvəʳ] *adj*: **take ~ book you want** nehmen Sie irgendein *or* ein beliebiges Buch; **~ book you take** welches Buch Sie auch nehmen
while [waɪl] *n* Weile *f* ▷ *conj* während; **for a ~** eine Weile (lang); **in a ~** gleich; **all the ~** die ganze Zeit (über); **I'll/we'll** *etc* **make it worth your ~** es wird sich für Sie lohnen
▶ **while away** *vt* *(time)* sich *dat* vertreiben
whilst [waɪlst] *conj* = **while**
whim [wɪm] *n* Laune *f*
whimper ['wɪmpəʳ] *n* *(cry, moan)* Wimmern *nt* ▷ *vi* wimmern
whimsical ['wɪmzɪkəl] *adj* wunderlich, seltsam; *(story)* kurios
whine [waɪn] *n* *(of pain)* Jammern *nt*; *(of engine, siren)* Heulen *nt* ▷ *vi* *(person)* jammern; *(dog)* jaulen; *(engine, siren)* heulen
whip [wɪp] *n* Peitsche *f*; *(Pol)* ≈ Fraktionsführer *m* ▷ *vt* *(person, animal)* peitschen; *(cream, eggs)* schlagen; *(move quickly)*: **to ~ sth out/off** etw blitzschnell hervorholen/wegbringen
▶ **whip up** *vt* *(cream)* schlagen; *(inf: meal)* hinzaubern; *(arouse: support)* anheizen; *(: people)* mitreißen
whipped cream [wɪpt-] *n* Schlagsahne *f*
whip-round ['wɪpraund] *(Brit: inf) n* (Geld)sammlung *f*
whirl [wəːl] *vt* *(arms, sword etc)* herumwirbeln ▷ *vi* wirbeln ▷ *n* *(of activity, pleasure)* Wirbel *m*; **to be in a ~** *(mind, person)* völlig verwirrt sein
whirlpool ['wəːlpuːl] *n* *(lit)* Strudel *m*
whirlwind ['wəːlwɪnd] *n* *(lit)* Wirbelwind *m*
whirr [wəːʳ] *vi* *(motor etc)* surren
whisk [wɪsk] *n* *(Culin)* Schneebesen *m* ▷ *vt* *(cream, eggs)* schlagen; **to ~ sb away** *or* **off** jdn in Windeseile wegbringen
whiskers ['wɪskəz] *npl* *(of animal)* Barthaare *pl*; *(of man)* Backenbart *m*
whisky, *(US, Ireland)* **whiskey** ['wɪskɪ] *n* Whisky *m*
whisper ['wɪspəʳ] *n* Flüstern *nt*; *(fig: of wind)* Wispern *nt* ▷ *vt, vi* flüstern; **to ~ sth to sb** jdm etw zuflüstern
whistle ['wɪsl] *n* *(sound)* Pfiff *m*; *(object)* Pfeife *f* ▷ *vi* pfeifen ▷ *vt*: **to ~ a tune** eine Melodie pfeifen
white [waɪt] *adj* weiß ▷ *n* *(colour)* Weiß *nt*; *(person)* Weiße(r) *f(m)*; *(of egg, eye)* Weiße(s) *nt*; **to turn** *or* **go ~** *(person: with fear)* weiß *or* bleich werden; *(: with age)* weiße Haare bekommen; *(hair)* weiß werden; **the ~s** *(washing)* die Weißwäsche *f*; **tennis/cricket ~s** weiße Tennis-/Krickettrikots
white coffee *(Brit) n* Kaffee *m* mit Milch
white-collar worker ['waɪtkɔlə-] *n* Schreibtischarbeiter(in) *m(f)*
white elephant *n* *(fig: venture)* Fehlinvestition *f*
white lie *n* Notlüge *f*
white paper *n* *(Pol)* Weißbuch *nt*
whitewash ['waɪtwɔʃ] *n* *(paint)* Tünche *f*; *(inf: Sport)* totale Niederlage *f* ▷ *vt* *(building)* tünchen; *(fig: incident, reputation)* reinwaschen
whiting ['waɪtɪŋ] *n inv* *(fish)* Weißling *m*
Whitsun ['wɪtsn] *n* Pfingsten *nt*
whittle ['wɪtl] *vt*: **to ~ away** *or* **down** *(costs etc)* verringern
whizz [wɪz] *vi*: **to ~ past** *or* **by** vorbeisausen
whizz kid *(inf) n* Senkrechtstarter(in) *m(f)*

who [hu:] *pron* **1** (*interrogative*) wer; (: *acc*) wen; (: *dat*) wem; **who is it?, who's there?** wer ist da?; **who did you give it to?** wem hast du es gegeben?
2 (*relative*) der/die/das; **the man/woman who spoke to me** der Mann, der/die Frau, die mit mir gesprochen hat

whodunit, whodunnit [hu:'dʌnɪt] (*inf*) *n* Krimi *m*

whoever [hu:'ɛvə^r] *pron*: **~ finds it** wer (auch immer) es findet; **ask ~ you like** fragen Sie, wen Sie wollen; **~ he marries** ganz gleich *or* egal, wen er heiratet; **~ told you that?** wer um alles in der Welt hat dir das erzählt?

whole [həul] *adj* (*entire*) ganz; (*not broken*) heil ▷ *n* Ganze(s) *nt*; **the ~ lot (of it)** alles; **the ~ lot (of them)** alle; **the ~ (of the) time** die ganze Zeit; **~ villages were destroyed** ganze Dörfer wurden zerstört; **the ~ of** der/die/das ganze; **the ~ of Glasgow/Europe** ganz Glasgow/Europa; **the ~ of the town** die ganze Stadt; **on the ~** im Ganzen (gesehen)

wholefood ['həulfu:d] *n*, **wholefoods** ['həulfu:dz] *npl* Vollwertkost *f*

wholehearted [həul'hɑ:tɪd] *adj* (*agreement etc*) rückhaltlos

wholeheartedly [həul'hɑ:tɪdlɪ] *adv* (*agree etc*) rückhaltlos

wholemeal ['həulmi:l] (*Brit*) *adj* (*bread, flour*) Vollkorn-

wholesale ['həulseɪl] *n* (*business*) Großhandel *m* ▷ *adj* (*price*) Großhandels-; (*destruction etc*) umfassend ▷ *adv* (*buy, sell*) im Großhandel

wholesaler ['həulseɪlə^r] *n* Großhändler *m*

wholesome ['həulsəm] *adj* (*food*) gesund; (*effect*) zuträglich; (*attitude*) positiv

wholewheat ['həulwi:t] *adj* = **wholemeal**

wholly ['həulɪ] *adv* ganz und gar

whom [hu:m] *pron* **1** (*interrogative*: *acc*) wen; (: *dat*) wem; **whom did you see?** wen hast du gesehen?; **to whom did you give it?** wem hast du es gegeben?
2 (*relative*: *acc*) den/die/das; (: *dat*) dem/der/dem; **the man whom I saw/to whom I spoke** der Mann, den ich gesehen habe/mit dem ich gesprochen habe

whooping cough ['hu:pɪŋ-] *n* Keuchhusten *m*

whore [hɔ:^r] (*inf*: *pej*) *n* Hure *f*

whose [hu:z] *adj* **1** (*possessive*: *interrogative*) wessen; **whose book is this?, whose is this book?** wessen Buch ist das?, wem gehört das Buch?; **I don't know whose it is** ich weiß nicht, wem es gehört
2 (*possessive*: *relative*) dessen/deren/dessen; **the man whose son you rescued** der Mann, dessen Sohn du gerettet hast; **the woman whose car was stolen** die Frau, deren Auto gestohlen worden war
▷ *pron*: **whose is this?** wem gehört das?; **I know whose it is** ich weiß, wem es gehört

why [waɪ] *adv* warum; **why not?** warum nicht?
▷ *conj* warum; **I wonder why he said that** ich frage mich, warum er das gesagt hat; **that's not why I'm here** ich bin nicht deswegen hier; **the reason why** der Grund, warum *or* weshalb
▷ *excl* (*expressing surprise, shock*) na so was; (*expressing annoyance*) ach; **why, yes (of course)** aber ja doch; **why, it's you!** na so was, du bists!

wicked ['wɪkɪd] *adj* (*crime, person*) böse; (*smile, wit*) frech; (*inf*: *prices*) unverschämt; (: *weather*) schrecklich

wicket ['wɪkɪt] *n* (*Cricket*: *stumps*) Tor *nt*, Wicket *nt*; (: *grass area*) Spielbahn *f*

wide [waɪd] *adj* breit; (*area*) weit; (*publicity*) umfassend ▷ *adv*: **to open sth ~** etw weit öffnen; **it is 3 metres ~** es ist 3 Meter breit; **to go ~** vorbeigehen

wide-awake [waɪdə'weɪk] *adj* hellwach

widely ['waɪdlɪ] *adv* (*differ, vary*) erheblich; (*travel*) ausgiebig, viel; (*spaced*) weit; (*believed, known*) allgemein; **to be ~ read** (*reader*) sehr belesen sein

widen ['waɪdn] *vt* (*road, river*) verbreitern; (*one's experience*) erweitern ▷ *vi* sich verbreitern

wide open *adj* (*window, eyes, mouth*) weit geöffnet

widespread ['waɪdsprɛd] *adj* weitverbreitet

widow ['wɪdəu] *n* Witwe *f*

widowed ['wɪdəud] *adj* verwitwet

widower ['wɪdəuə^r] *n* Witwer *m*

width [wɪdθ] *n* Breite *f*; (*in swimming pool*) (Quer)bahn *f*; **it's 7 metres in ~** es ist 7 Meter breit

wield [wi:ld] *vt* (*sword*) schwingen; (*power*) ausüben

wife [waɪf] (*pl* **wives**) *n* Frau *f*

wig [wɪg] *n* Perücke *f*

wiggle ['wɪgl] *vt* wackeln mit

wild [waɪld] *adj* wild; (*weather*) rau, stürmisch; (*person, behaviour*) ungestüm; (*idea*) weit hergeholt; (*applause*) stürmisch ▷ *n*: **the ~** (*natural surroundings*) die freie Natur *f*; **the wilds** *npl* die Wildnis; **I'm not ~ about it** ich bin nicht versessen *or* scharf darauf

wild card *n* (*Comput*) Wildcard *f*, Ersatzzeichen *nt*

wilderness ['wɪldənɪs] *n* Wildnis *f*

wildlife ['waɪldlaɪf] *n* (*animals*) die Tierwelt *f*

wildly ['waɪldlɪ] *adv* wild; (*very*: *romantic*) wild-; (: *inefficient*) furchtbar

wilful, (*US*) **willful** ['wɪlful] *adj* (*obstinate*) eigensinnig; (*deliberate*) vorsätzlich

will [wɪl] *aux vb* **1** (*forming future tense*): **I will finish it tomorrow** ich werde es morgen fertig machen, ich mache es morgen fertig; **will you do it? — yes I will/no I won't** machst du es? — ja/nein
2 (*in conjectures, predictions*): **that will be the postman** das ist bestimmt der Briefträger
3 (*in commands, requests, offers*): **will you sit down** (*politely*) bitte nehmen Sie Platz;

(*angrily*) nun setz dich doch; **will you be quiet!** seid jetzt still!; **will you help me?** hilfst du mir?; **will you have a cup of tea?** möchten Sie eine Tasse Tee?; **I won't put up with it!** das lasse ich mir nicht gefallen!
▷ *vt* (*pt, pp* **willed**) **to will sb to do sth** jdn durch Willenskraft dazu bewegen, etw zu tun; **he willed himself to go on** er zwang sich dazu, weiterzumachen
▷ *n* (*volition*) Wille *m*; (*testament*) Testament *nt*; **he did it against his will** er tat es gegen seinen Willen

willing ['wɪlɪŋ] *adj* (*having no objection*) gewillt; (*enthusiastic*) bereitwillig; **he's ~ to do it** er ist bereit, es zu tun; **to show ~** guten Willen zeigen

willingly ['wɪlɪŋlɪ] *adv* bereitwillig

willingness ['wɪlɪŋnɪs] *n* (*readiness*) Bereitschaft *f*; (*enthusiasm*) Bereitwilligkeit *f*

willow ['wɪləu] *n* (*tree*) Weide *f*; (*wood*) Weidenholz *nt*

willpower ['wɪl'pauəʳ] *n* Willenskraft *f*

willy-nilly ['wɪlɪ'nɪlɪ] *adv* (*willingly or not*) wohl oder übel

wilt [wɪlt] *vi* (*plant*) welken

win [wɪn] (*pt, pp* **won**) *n* Sieg *m* ▷ *vt* gewinnen ▷ *vi* siegen, gewinnen
▸ **win over** *vt* (*persuade*) gewinnen
▸ **win round** (*Brit*) *vt* = **win over**

wince [wɪns] *vi* zusammenzucken

winch [wɪntʃ] *n* Winde *f*

wind¹ [wɪnd] *n* (*air*) Wind *m*; (*Med*) Blähungen *pl*; (*breath*) Atem *m* ▷ *vt* (*take breath away from*) den Atem nehmen *+dat*; **the winds** *npl* (*Mus*) die Bläser *pl*; **into** *or* **against the ~** gegen den Wind; **to get ~ of sth** (*fig*) von etw Wind bekommen; **to break ~** Darmwind entweichen lassen

wind² [waɪnd] (*pt, pp* **wound**) *vt* (*thread, rope, bandage*) wickeln; (*clock, toy*) aufziehen ▷ *vi* (*road, river*) sich winden
▸ **wind down** *vt* (*car window*) herunterdrehen; (*fig: production*) zurückschrauben
▸ **wind up** *vt* (*clock, toy*) aufziehen; (*debate*) abschließen

windfall ['wɪndfɔ:l] *n* (*money*) unverhoffter Glücksfall *m*; (*apple*) Fallobst *nt*

winding ['waɪndɪŋ] *adj* gewunden

wind instrument ['wɪnd-] *n* Blasinstrument *nt*

windmill ['wɪndmɪl] *n* Windmühle *f*

window ['wɪndəu] *n* (*also Comput*) Fenster *nt*; (*in shop*) Schaufenster *nt*

window box *n* Blumenkasten *m*

window cleaner *n* Fensterputzer(in) *m(f)*

window ledge *n* Fenstersims *m*

window pane *n* Fensterscheibe *f*

window-shopping ['wɪndəuʃɔpɪŋ] *n* Schaufensterbummel *m*; **to go ~** einen Schaufensterbummel machen

windowsill ['wɪndəusɪl] *n* Fensterbank *f*

windpipe ['wɪndpaɪp] *n* Luftröhre *f*

wind power ['wɪnd-] *n* Windkraft *f*, Windenergie *f*

windscreen ['wɪndskri:n] *n* Windschutzscheibe *f*

windscreen washer *n* Scheibenwaschanlage *f*

windscreen wiper [-waɪpəʳ] *n* Scheibenwischer *m*

windshield ['wɪndʃi:ld] (*US*) *n* = **windscreen**

windsurfing ['wɪndsə:fɪŋ] *n* Windsurfen *nt*

windswept ['wɪndswɛpt] *adj* (*place*) vom Wind gepeitscht; (*person*) vom Wind zerzaust

windy ['wɪndɪ] *adj* windig; **it's ~** es ist windig

wine [waɪn] *n* Wein *m* ▷ *vt*: **to ~ and dine sb** jdm zu einem guten Essen ausführen

wine bar *n* Weinlokal *nt*

wine cellar *n* Weinkeller *m*

wine glass *n* Weinglas *nt*

wine list *n* Weinkarte *f*

wine tasting [-teɪstɪŋ] *n* Weinprobe *f*

wine waiter *n* Weinkellner *m*

wing [wɪŋ] *n* (*of bird, insect, plane*) Flügel *m*; (*of building*) Trakt *m*; (*of car*) Kotflügel *m*; **the wings** *npl* (*Theat*) die Kulissen *pl*

winger ['wɪŋəʳ] *n* (*Sport*) Flügelspieler(in) *m(f)*

wing mirror (*Brit*) *n* Seitenspiegel *m*

wink [wɪŋk] *n* (*of eye*) Zwinkern *m* ▷ *vi* (*with eye*) zwinkern; (*light etc*) blinken

winner ['wɪnəʳ] *n* (*of race, competition*) Sieger(in) *m(f)*; (*of prize*) Gewinner(in) *m(f)*

winning ['wɪnɪŋ] *adj* (*team, entry*) siegreich; (*shot, goal*) entscheidend; (*smile*) einnehmend; *see also* **winnings**

winnings ['wɪnɪŋz] *npl* Gewinn *m*

winter ['wɪntəʳ] *n* Winter *m* ▷ *vi* (*birds*) überwintern; **in ~** im Winter

winter sports *npl* Wintersport *m*

wintry ['wɪntrɪ] *adj* (*weather, day*) winterlich, Winter-

wipe [waɪp] *vt* wischen; (*dry*) abtrocknen; (*clean*) abwischen; (*erase: tape*) löschen; **to ~ one's nose** sich *dat* die Nase putzen ▷ *n*: **to give sth a ~** etw abwischen
▸ **wipe off** *vt* abwischen
▸ **wipe out** *vt* (*destroy: city etc*) auslöschen
▸ **wipe up** *vt* (*mess*) aufwischen

wire ['waɪəʳ] *n* Draht *m*; (*US: telegram*) Telegramm *nt* ▷ *vt* (*US*): **to ~ sb** jdm telegrafieren; (*also*: **wire up**: *electrical fitting*) anschließen

wireless ['waɪəlɪs] (*Brit: old*) *n* Funk *m*; (*set*) Rundfunkgerät *nt*

wiring ['waɪərɪŋ] *n* elektrische Leitungen *pl*

wiry ['waɪərɪ] *adj* (*person*) drahtig; (*hair*) borstig

wisdom ['wɪzdəm] *n* (*of person*) Weisheit *f*; (*of action, remark*) Klugheit *f*

wisdom tooth *n* Weisheitszahn *m*

wise *adj* (*person*) weise; (*action, remark*) klug; **I'm none the ~r** ich bin genauso klug wie vorher
▸ **wise up** (*inf*) *vi*: **to ~ up to sth** hinter etw *acc* kommen

wish [wɪʃ] *n* Wunsch *m* ▷ *vt* wünschen; **best ~es** (*for birthday etc*) herzliche Grüße, alle guten Wünsche; **with best ~es** (*in letter*) mit den besten Wünschen *or* Grüßen; **give her my best ~es** grüßen Sie sie herzlich von mir; **to make a ~** sich *dat* etw wünschen; **to ~ sb goodbye** jdm Auf Wiedersehen sagen; **he ~ed me well** er wünschte mir alles Gute; **to ~ to do sth** etw tun wollen; **to ~ sth on sb** jdm etw wünschen; **to ~ for sth** sich *dat* etw wünschen

wishful ['wɪʃful] *adj*: **it's ~ thinking** das ist reines Wunschdenken

wistful ['wɪstful] *adj* wehmütig

wit [wɪt] *n* (*wittiness*) geistreiche Art *f*; (*person*) geistreicher Mensch *m*; (*presence of mind*) Verstand *m*; **wits** *npl* (*intelligence*) Verstand *m*; **to be at one's ~s' end** mit seinem Latein am Ende sein; **to have one's ~s about one** einen klaren Kopf haben; **to ~** (*namely*) und zwar

witch [wɪtʃ] *n* Hexe *f*

witchcraft ['wɪtʃkrɑːft] *n* Hexerei *f*

with [wɪð] *prep* **1** (*accompanying, in the company of*) mit; **we stayed with friends** wir wohnten bei Freunden; **I'll be with you in a minute** einen Augenblick, ich bin sofort da; **I'm with you** (*I understand*) ich verstehe; **to be with it** (*inf: up-to-date*) auf dem Laufenden sein; (*: alert*) da sein

2 (*descriptive, indicating manner*) mit; **the man with the grey hat/blue eyes** der Mann mit dem grauen Hut/den blauen Augen; **with tears in her eyes** mit Tränen in den Augen; **red with anger** rot vor Wut

withdraw [wɪθ'drɔː] (*irreg: like* **draw**) *vt* (*object, offer*) zurückziehen; (*remark*) zurücknehmen ▷ *vi* (*troops*) abziehen; (*person*) sich zurückziehen; **to ~ money** (*from bank*) Geld abheben; **to ~ into o.s.** sich in sich *acc* selbst zurückziehen

withdrawal [wɪθ'drɔːəl] *n* (*of offer, remark*) Zurücknahme *f*; (*of troops*) Abzug *m*; (*of participation*) Ausstieg *m*; (*of services*) Streichung *f*; (*of money*) Abhebung *f*

withdrawal symptoms *npl* Entzugserscheinungen *pl*

withdrawn [wɪθ'drɔːn] *pp of* **withdraw** ▷ *adj* (*person*) verschlossen

wither ['wɪðəʳ] *vi* (*plant*) verwelken

withhold [wɪθ'həuld] (*irreg: like* **hold**) *vt* vorenthalten

within [wɪð'ɪn] *prep* (*place*) innerhalb *+gen*; (*time, distance*) innerhalb von ▷ *adv* innen; **~ reach** in Reichweite; **~ sight (of)** in Sichtweite (*+gen*); **~ the week** vor Ende der Woche; **~ a mile of** weniger als eine Meile entfernt von; **~ an hour** innerhalb einer Stunde; **~ the law** im Rahmen des Gesetzes

without [wɪð'aut] *prep* ohne; **~ a coat** ohne Mantel; **~ speaking** ohne zu sprechen; **it goes ~ saying** das versteht sich von selbst; **~ anyone knowing** ohne dass jemand davon wusste

withstand [wɪθ'stænd] (*irreg: like* **stand**) *vt* widerstehen *+dat*

witness ['wɪtnɪs] *n* Zeuge *m*, Zeugin *f* ▷ *vt* (*event*) sehen, Zeuge/Zeugin sein *+gen*; (*fig*) miterleben; **to bear ~ to sth** Zeugnis für etw ablegen; **~ for the prosecution/defence** Zeuge/Zeugin der Anklage/Verteidigung; **to ~ to sth** etw bezeugen; **to ~ having seen sth** bezeugen, etw gesehen zu haben

witness box *n* Zeugenstand *m*

witty ['wɪtɪ] *adj* geistreich

wives [waɪvz] *npl of* **wife**

wizard ['wɪzəd] *n* Zauberer *m*

wk *abbr* = **week**

wobble ['wɔbl] *vi* wackeln; (*legs*) zittern

woe [wəu] *n* (*sorrow*) Jammer *m*; (*misfortune*) Kummer *m*

woke [wəuk] *pt of* **wake**

woken ['wəukn] *pp of* **wake**

wolf [wulf] (*pl* **wolves**) *n* Wolf *m*

woman ['wumən] (*pl* **women**) *n* Frau *f*; **~ friend** Freundin *f*; **~ teacher** Lehrerin *f*; **young ~** junge Frau; **women's page** Frauenseite *f*

womanly ['wumənlɪ] *adj* (*virtues etc*) weiblich

womb [wuːm] *n* Mutterleib *m*; (*Med*) Gebärmutter *f*

women ['wɪmɪn] *npl of* **woman**

won [wʌn] *pt, pp of* **win**

wonder ['wʌndəʳ] *n* (*miracle*) Wunder *nt*; (*awe*) Verwunderung *f* ▷ *vi*: **to ~ whether/why** *etc* sich fragen, ob/warum *etc*; **it's no ~ (that)** es ist kein Wunder(, dass); **to ~ at** (*marvel at*) staunen über *+acc*; **to ~ about** sich *dat* Gedanken machen über *+acc*; **I ~ if you could help me** könnten Sie mir vielleicht helfen

wonderful ['wʌndəful] *adj* wunderbar

won't [wəunt] = **will not**

wood [wud] *n* (*timber*) Holz *nt*; (*forest*) Wald *m* ▷ *cpd* Holz-

wooded ['wudɪd] *adj* bewaldet

wooden ['wudn] *adj* (*also fig*) hölzern

woodpecker ['wudpɛkəʳ] *n* Specht *m*

woodwind ['wudwɪnd] *adj* (*instrument*) Holzblasinstrument *nt*; **the ~** die Holzbläser *pl*

woodwork ['wudwəːk] *n* (*skill*) Holzarbeiten *pl*

woodworm ['wudwəːm] *n* Holzwurm *m*

wool [wul] *n* Wolle *f*; **to pull the ~ over sb's eyes** (*fig*) jdn hinters Licht führen

woollen, (US) **woolen** ['wulən] *adj* (*hat*) Woll-, wollen

woolly, (US) **wooly** ['wulɪ] *adj* (*socks, hat etc*) Woll-; (*fig: ideas*) schwammig; (*person*) verworren ▷ *n* (*pullover*) Wollpullover *m*

word [wəːd] *n* Wort *nt*; (*news*) Nachricht *f* ▷ *vt* (*letter, message*) formulieren; **~ for word** Wort für Wort, (wort)wörtlich; **what's the ~ for "pen" in German?** was heißt "pen" auf Deutsch?; **to put sth into ~s** etw in Worte fassen; **in other ~s** mit anderen Worten; **to break/keep one's ~** sein Wort brechen/halten; **to have ~s with sb** eine

Auseinandersetzung mit jdm haben; **to have a ~ with sb** mit jdm sprechen; **I'll take your ~ for it** ich verlasse mich auf Sie; **to send ~ of sth** etw verlauten lassen; **to leave ~ (with sb/for sb) that ...** (bei jdm/für jdn) die Nachricht hinterlassen, dass ...; **by ~ of mouth** durch mündliche Überlieferung

wording ['wəːdɪŋ] *n* (*of message, contract etc*) Wortlaut *m*, Formulierung *f*

word processing *n* Textverarbeitung *f*

word processor [-prəusɛsəʳ] *n* Textverarbeitungssystem *nt*

wore [wɔːʳ] *pt of* **wear**

work [wəːk] *n* Arbeit *f*; (*Art, Liter*) Werk *nt* ▷ *vi* arbeiten; (*mechanism*) funktionieren; (*be successful: medicine etc*) wirken ▷ *vt* (*clay, wood, land*) bearbeiten; (*mine*) arbeiten in; (*machine*) bedienen; (*create: effect, miracle*) bewirken; **to go to ~** zur Arbeit gehen; **to set to ~, to start ~** sich an die Arbeit machen; **to be at ~ (on sth)** (an etw *dat*) arbeiten; **to be out of ~** arbeitslos sein; **to be in ~** eine Stelle haben; **to ~ hard** hart arbeiten; **to ~ loose** (*part, knot*) sich lösen; **to ~ on the assumption that ...** von der Annahme ausgehen, dass ...
▸ **work on** *vt fus* (*task*) arbeiten an *+dat*; (*person: influence*) bearbeiten; **he's ~ing on his car** er arbeitet an seinem Auto
▸ **work out** *vi* (*plans etc*) klappen; (*Sport*) trainieren ▷ *vt* (*problem*) lösen; (*plan*) ausarbeiten; **it ~s out at 100 pounds** es ergibt 100 Pfund
▸ **work up** *vt*: **to get ~ed up** sich aufregen

workable ['wəːkəbl] *adj* (*system*) durchführbar; (*solution*) brauchbar

workaholic [wəːkə'hɔlɪk] *n* Arbeitstier *nt*

worker ['wəːkəʳ] *n* Arbeiter(in) *m(f)*; **office ~** Büroarbeiter(in) *m(f)*

workforce ['wəːkfɔːs] *n* Arbeiterschaft *f*

working ['wəːkɪŋ] *adj* (*day, conditions*) Arbeits-; (*population*) arbeitend; (*mother*) berufstätig; **a ~ knowledge of English** (*adequate*) Grundkenntnisse in Englisch

working class *n* Arbeiterklasse *f*

working week *n* Arbeitswoche *f*

workman ['wəːkmən] (*irreg: like* **man**) *n* Arbeiter *m*

workmanship ['wəːkmənʃɪp] *n* Arbeitsqualität *f*

workout ['wəːkaut] *n* Fitnesstraining *nt*

work permit *n* Arbeitserlaubnis *f*

workshop ['wəːkʃɔp] *n* (*building*) Werkstatt *f*; (*practical session*) Workshop *nt*

work station *n* Arbeitsplatz *m*; (*Comput*) Workstation *f*

worktop ['wəːktɔp] *n* Arbeitsfläche *f*

work-to-rule ['wəːktə'ruːl] (*Brit*) *n* Dienst *m* nach Vorschrift

world [wəːld] *n* Welt *f* ▷ *cpd* (*champion, power, war*) Welt-; **all over the ~** auf der ganzen Welt; **to think the ~ of sb** große Stücke auf jdn halten; **what in the ~ is he doing?** was um alles in der Welt macht er?; **to do sb a** *or* **the ~ of good** jdm unwahrscheinlich guttun; **W~ War One/Two** der Erste/Zweite Weltkrieg; **out of this ~** fantastisch

World Cup *n*: **the ~** (*Football*) die Fußballweltmeisterschaft *f*

worldly ['wəːldlɪ] *adj* weltlich; (*knowledgeable*) weltgewandt

worm [wəːm] *n* Wurm *m*
▸ **worm out** *vt*: **to ~ sth out of sb** jdm etw entlocken

worn [wɔːn] *pp of* **wear** ▷ *adj* (*carpet*) abgenutzt; (*shoe*) abgetragen

worn-out ['wɔːnaut] *adj* (*object*) abgenutzt; (*person*) erschöpft

worried ['wʌrɪd] *adj* besorgt; **to be ~ about sth** sich wegen etw Sorgen machen

worry ['wʌrɪ] *n* Sorge *f* ▷ *vt* beunruhigen ▷ *vi* sich *dat* Sorgen machen; **to ~ about** *or* **over sth/sb** sich um etw/jdn Sorgen machen

worrying ['wʌrɪɪŋ] *adj* beunruhigend

worse [wəːs] *adj* schlechter, schlimmer ▷ *adv* schlechter ▷ *n* Schlechtere(s) *nt*, Schlimmere(s) *nt*; **to get ~** (*situation etc*) sich verschlechtern *or* verschlimmern; **he is none the ~ for it** er hat keinen Schaden dabei erlitten; **so much the ~ for you!** um so schlimmer für dich!; **a change for the ~** eine Wendung zum Schlechten

worsen ['wəːsn] *vt* verschlimmern ▷ *vi* sich verschlechtern

worse off *adj* (*also fig*) schlechter dran; **he is now ~ than before** er ist jetzt schlechter dran als zuvor

worship ['wəːʃɪp] *n* (*act*) Verehrung *f* ▷ *vt* (*god*) anbeten; (*person, thing*) verehren; **Your W~** (*Brit: to mayor*) verehrter Herr Bürgermeister; (*: to judge*) Euer Ehren

worst [wəːst] *adj* schlechteste(r, s), schlimmste(r, s) ▷ *adv* am schlimmsten ▷ *n* Schlimmste(s) *nt*; **at ~** schlimmstenfalls; **if the ~ comes to the worst** wenn alle Stricke reißen

worth [wəːθ] *n* Wert *m* ▷ *adj*: **to be ~** wert sein; **£2 ~ of apples** Äpfel für £ 2; **how much is it ~?** was *or* wie viel ist es wert?; **it's ~ it** (*effort, time*) es lohnt sich; **it's ~ every penny** es ist sein Geld wert

worthless ['wəːθlɪs] *adj* wertlos

worthwhile ['wəːθ'waɪl] *adj* lohnend

worthy [wəːðɪ] *adj* (*person*) würdig; (*motive*) ehrenwert; **~ of** wert *+gen*

would [wud] *aux vb* **1** (*conditional tense*): **if you asked him he would do it** wenn du ihn fragtest, würde er es tun; **if you had asked him he would have done it** wenn du ihn gefragt hättest, hätte er es getan
2 (*in offers, invitations, requests*): **would you like a biscuit?** möchten Sie ein Plätzchen?; **would you ask him to come in?** würden Sie ihn bitten hereinzukommen?
3 (*in indirect speech*): **I said I would do it** ich sagte, ich würde es tun
4 (*emphatic*): **it WOULD have to snow today!**

ausgerechnet heute musste es schneien! **5** (*insistence*): **she wouldn't behave** sie wollte sich partout nicht benehmen **6** (*conjecture*): **it would have been midnight** es mochte etwa Mitternacht gewesen sein; **it would seem so** so scheint es wohl **7** (*indicating habit*): **he would go there on Mondays** er ging montags immer dorthin; **he would spend every day on the beach** er verbrachte jeden Tag am Strand

would-be ['wudbi:] *adj* (*singer, writer*) Möchtegern-

wouldn't ['wudnt] = **would not**

wound¹ [waund] *pt, pp of* **wind²**

wound² [wu:nd] *n* Wunde *f* ▷ *vt* verwunden; **~ed in the leg** am Bein verletzt

wove [wəuv] *pt of* **weave**

woven ['wəuvn] *pp of* **weave**

wrap [ræp] *n* (*shawl*) Umhang *m*; (*cape*) Cape *nt* ▷ *vt* einwickeln; (*also*: **wrap up**: *pack*) einpacken; (*wind*: *tape etc*) wickeln; **under ~s** (*fig*: *plan*) geheim

wrapper ['ræpəʳ] *n* (*on chocolate*) Papier *nt*; (*Brit*: *of book*) Umschlag *m*

wrapping paper ['ræpɪŋ-] *n* (*brown*) Packpapier *nt*; (*fancy*) Geschenkpapier *nt*

wreak [ri:k] *vt*: **to ~ havoc (on)** verheerenden Schaden anrichten (bei); **to ~ vengeance** *or* **revenge on sb** Rache an jdm üben

wreath [ri:θ] (*pl* **~s**) *n* Kranz *m*

wreck [rɛk] *n* Wrack *nt*; (*vehicle*) Schrotthaufen *m* ▷ *vt* kaputt machen; (*car*) zu Schrott fahren; (*chances*) zerstören

wreckage ['rɛkɪdʒ] *n* (*of car, plane, building*) Trümmer *pl*; (*of ship*) Wrackteile *pl*

wren [rɛn] *n* (*Zool*) Zaunkönig *m*

wrench [rɛntʃ] *n* (*Tech*) Schraubenschlüssel *m*; (*tug*) Ruck *m*; (*fig*) schmerzhaftes Erlebnis *nt* ▷ *vt* (*pull*) reißen; (*injure*: *arm, back*) verrenken; **to ~ sth from sb** jdm etw entreißen

wrestle ['rɛsl] *vi*: **to ~ (with sb)** (mit jdm) ringen; **to ~ with a problem** mit einem Problem kämpfen

wrestler ['rɛsləʳ] *n* Ringer(in) *m(f)*

wrestling ['rɛslɪŋ] *n* Ringen *nt*; (*also*: **all-in wrestling**) Freistilringen *nt*

wretched ['rɛtʃɪd] *adj* (*poor*) erbärmlich; (*unhappy*) unglücklich; (*inf*: *damned*) elend

wriggle ['rɪgl] *vi* (*also*: **wriggle about**: *person*) zappeln; (*fish*) sich winden; (*snake etc*) sich schlängeln ▷ *n* Zappeln *nt*

wring [rɪŋ] (*pt, pp* **wrung**) *vt* (*wet clothes*) auswringen; (*hands*) wringen; (*neck*) umdrehen; **to ~ sth out of sth/sb** (*fig*) etw/jdm etw abringen

wrinkle ['rɪŋkl] *n* Falte *f* ▷ *vt* (*nose, forehead etc*) runzeln ▷ *vi* (*skin, paint etc*) sich runzeln

wrinkled ['rɪŋkld] *adj* (*fabric, paper*) zerknittert; (*surface*) gekräuselt; (*skin*) runzlig

wrist [rɪst] *n* Handgelenk *nt*

writ [rɪt] *n* (*Law*) (gerichtliche) Verfügung *f*; **to issue a ~ against sb, serve a ~ on sb** eine Verfügung gegen jdn erlassen

write [raɪt] (*pt* **wrote**, *pp* **written**) *vt* schreiben; (*cheque*) ausstellen ▷ *vi* schreiben; **to ~ to sb** jdm schreiben

▸ **write away** *vi*: **to ~ away for sth** etw anfordern

▸ **write down** *vt* aufschreiben

▸ **write off** *vt* (*debt, project*) abschreiben; (*wreck*: *car etc*) zu Schrott fahren ▷ *vi* = **write away**

▸ **write out** *vt* (*put in writing*) schreiben; (*cheque, receipt etc*) ausstellen

▸ **write up** *vt* (*report etc*) schreiben

write-off ['raɪtɔf] *n* (*Aut*) Totalschaden *m*

writer ['raɪtəʳ] *n* (*author*) Schriftsteller(in) *m(f)*; (*of report, document etc*) Verfasser(in) *m(f)*

writhe [raɪð] *vi* sich krümmen

writing ['raɪtɪŋ] *n* Schrift *f*; (*of author*) Arbeiten *pl*; (*activity*) Schreiben *nt*; **in ~** schriftlich; **in my own ~** in meiner eigenen Handschrift

writing paper *n* Schreibpapier *nt*

written ['rɪtn] *pp of* **write**

wrong [rɔŋ] *adj* falsch; (*morally bad*) unrecht; (*unfair*) ungerecht ▷ *adv* falsch ▷ *n* (*injustice*) Unrecht *nt*; (*evil*): **right and ~** Gut und Böse ▷ *vt* (*treat unfairly*) unrecht *or* ein Unrecht tun *+dat*; **to be ~** (*answer*) falsch sein; (*in doing, saying sth*) unrecht haben; **you are ~ to do it** es ist ein Fehler von dir, das zu tun; **it's ~ to steal, stealing is wrong** Stehlen ist unrecht; **you are ~ about that, you've got it wrong** da hast du unrecht; **what's ~?** wo fehlts?; **there's nothing ~** es ist alles in Ordnung; **to go ~** (*person*) einen Fehler machen; (*plan*) schiefgehen; (*machine*) versagen; **to be in the ~** im Unrecht sein

wrongful ['rɔŋful] *adj* unrechtmäßig

wrongly ['rɔŋlɪ] *adv* falsch; (*unjustly*) zu Unrecht

wrong number *n* (*Tel*): **you've got the ~** Sie sind falsch verbunden

wrong side *n*: **the ~** (*of material*) die linke Seite

wrote [rəut] *pt of* **write**

wrought [rɔ:t] *adj*: **~ iron** Schmiedeeisen *nt*

wrung [rʌŋ] *pt, pp of* **wring**

wt. *abbr* = **weight**

WWW *n abbr* (= *World Wide Web*) WWW *nt*

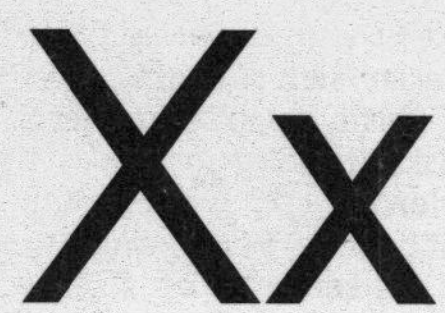

XL *abbr* (= *extra large*) XL
Xmas ['ɛksməs] *n abbr* = **Christmas**
X-ray ['ɛksreɪ] *n* Röntgenstrahl *m*; (*photo*) Röntgenbild *nt* ▷ *vt* röntgen; **to have an ~** sich röntgen lassen
xylophone ['zaɪləfəun] *n* Xylofon *nt*

yacht [jɔt] *n* Jacht *f*
yachting ['jɔtɪŋ] *n* Segeln *nt*
yachtsman ['jɔtsmən] (*irreg: like* **man**) *n* Segler *m*
Yank [jæŋk] (*pej*) *n* Ami *m*
yank [jæŋk] *vt* reißen ▷ *n* Ruck *m*; **to give sth a ~** mit einem Ruck an etw *dat* ziehen
yap [jæp] *vi* (*dog*) kläffen
yard [jɑːd] *n* (*of house etc*) Hof *m*; (*US: garden*) Garten *m*; (*measure*) Yard *nt* (= 0,91 m); **builder's ~** Bauhof *m*
yardstick ['jɑːdstɪk] *n* (*fig*) Maßstab *m*
yarn [jɑːn] *n* (*thread*) Garn *nt*; (*tale*) Geschichte *f*
yawn [jɔːn] *n* Gähnen *nt* ▷ *vi* gähnen
yawning ['jɔːnɪŋ] *adj* (*gap*) gähnend
yeah [jɛə] (*inf*) *adv* ja
year [jɪə^r] *n* Jahr *nt*; (*referring to wine*) Jahrgang *m*; **every ~** jedes Jahr; **this ~** dieses Jahr; **a** *or* **per ~** pro Jahr; **~ in, ~ out** jahrein, jahraus; **to be 8 ~s old** 8 Jahre alt sein; **an eight-~-old child** ein achtjähriges Kind
yearly ['jɪəlɪ] *adj, adv* (*once a year*) jährlich; **twice ~** zweimal jährlich *or* im Jahr
yearn [jəːn] *vi*: **to ~ for sth** sich nach etwas sehnen; **to ~ to do sth** sich danach sehnen, etw zu tun
yeast [jiːst] *n* Hefe *f*
yell [jɛl] *n* Schrei *m* ▷ *vi* schreien
yellow ['jɛləu] *adj* gelb ▷ *n* Gelb *nt*
Yellow Pages® *npl*: **the Yellow Pages** die gelben Seiten *pl*, das Branchenverzeichnis
yelp [jɛlp] *n* Jaulen *nt* ▷ *vi* jaulen
yes [jɛs] *adv* ja; (*in reply to negative*) doch ▷ *n* Ja *nt*; **to say ~** Ja sagen; **to answer ~** mit Ja antworten
yesterday ['jɛstədɪ] *adv* gestern ▷ *n* Gestern *nt*; **~ morning/evening** gestern Morgen/Abend; **~'s paper** die Zeitung von gestern; **the day before ~** vorgestern; **all day ~** gestern den ganzen Tag (lang)
yet [jɛt] *adv* noch ▷ *conj* jedoch; **it is not finished ~** es ist noch nicht fertig; **must you go just ~?** musst du schon gehen?; **the best ~** der/die/das bisher Beste; **as ~** bisher; **it'll be a few days ~** es wird noch ein paar Tage dauern; **not for a few days ~** nicht in den nächsten paar Tagen; **~ again** wiederum
yew [juː] *n* (*tree*) Eibe *f*; (*wood*) Eibenholz *nt*
Yiddish ['jɪdɪʃ] *n* Jiddisch *nt*
yield [jiːld] *n* (*Agr*) Ertrag *m*; (*Comm*) Gewinn *m* ▷ *vt* (*surrender: control etc*) abtreten; (*produce: results, profit*) hervorbringen ▷ *vi* (*surrender, give way*) nachgeben; (*US: Aut*) die Vorfahrt achten; **a ~ of 5%** ein Ertrag *or* Gewinn von 5%
YMCA *n abbr* (*organization*): = *Young Men's Christian Association*) CVJM *m*
yob ['jɔb], **yobbo** ['jɔbəu] (*Brit: inf: pej*) *n* Rowdy *m*
yoga ['jəugə] *n* Yoga *m or nt*
yoghurt, yogurt ['jəugət] *n* Joghurt *m or nt*
yoke [jəuk] *n* (*also fig*) Joch *nt* ▷ *vt* (*also*: **yoke together**: *oxen*) einspannen
yolk [jəuk] *n* (*of egg*) Dotter *m*, Eigelb *nt*
you [juː] *pron* **1** (*subject: familiar: singular*) du; (*: plural*) ihr; (*: polite*) Sie; **you Germans enjoy your food** ihr Deutschen esst gern gut
2 (*object: direct: familiar: singular*) dich; (*: plural*) euch; (*: polite*) Sie; (*: indirect: familiar: singular*) dir; (*: plural*) euch; (*: polite*) Ihnen; **I know you** ich kenne dich/euch/Sie; **I gave it to you** ich habe es dir/euch/Ihnen gegeben; **if I were you I would ...** an deiner/eurer/Ihrer Stelle würde ich ...
3 (*after prep, in comparisons*): **it's for you** es ist für dich/euch/Sie; **she's younger than you** sie ist jünger als du/ihr/Sie
4 (*impersonal: one*) man; **you never know** man weiß nie
you'd [juːd] = **you had; you would**
you'll [juːl] = **you will; you shall**
young [jʌŋ] *adj* jung; **the young** *npl* (*of animal*) die Jungen *pl*; (*people*) die jungen Leute *pl*; **a ~ man** ein junger Mann; **a ~ lady** eine junge Dame
younger [jʌŋgə^r] *adj* jünger; **the ~ generation** die jüngere Generation
youngster ['jʌŋstə^r] *n* Kind *nt*
your [jɔː^r] *adj* (*familiar: sing*) dein/deine/dein; (*: pl*) euer/eure/euer; (*polite*) Ihr/Ihre/Ihr; (*one's*) sein; **you mustn't eat with ~ fingers** man darf nicht mit den Fingern essen; *see also* **my**
you're [juə^r] = **you are**
yours [jɔːz] *pron* (*familiar: sing*) deiner/deine/dein(e)s; (*: pl*) eurer/eure/eures; (*polite*) Ihrer/Ihre/Ihres; **a friend of ~** ein Freund

von dir/Ihnen; **is it ~?** gehört es dir/Ihnen?; **~ sincerely/faithfully** mit freundlichen Grüßen; *see also* **mine[1]**

yourself [jɔː'sɛlf] *pron* (*reflexive*: *familiar*: *sing*: *ac*) dich; (*dat*) dir; (*pl*) euch; (: *polite*) sich; (*emphatic*) selbst; **you ~ told me** das haben Sie mir selbst gesagt

yourselves [jɔː'sɛlvz] *pl pron* (*reflexive*: *familiar*) euch; (: *polite*) sich; (*emphatic*) selbst; *see also* **oneself**

youth [juːθ] *n* Jugend *f*; (*young man*: *pl youths*) Jugendliche(r) *m*; **in my ~** in meiner Jugend

youth club *n* Jugendklub *m*

youthful ['juːθful] *adj* jugendlich

youth hostel *n* Jugendherberge *f*

you've [juːv] = **you have**

Yugoslav ['juːgəuslaːv] (*formerly*) *adj* jugoslawisch ▷ *n* Jugoslawe *m*, Jugoslawin *f*

Yugoslavia ['juːgəu'slaːvɪə] (*formerly*) *n* Jugoslawien *nt*

yuppie ['jʌpɪ] (*inf*) *n* Yuppie *m* ▷ *adj* yuppiehaft; (*job*, *car*) Yuppie-

YWCA *n abbr* (*organization*): = *Young Women's Christian Association*) CVJF *m*

Zz

zany ['zeɪnɪ] *adj* verrückt
zap [zæp] *vt* (*Comput: delete*) löschen
zeal [zi:l] *n* Eifer *m*
zebra ['zi:brə] *n* Zebra *nt*
zebra crossing (*Brit*) *n* Zebrastreifen *m*
zero ['zɪərəu] *n* (*number*) Null *f* ▷ *vi*: **to ~ in on sth** (*target*) etw einkreisen; **5 degrees below ~** 5 Grad unter null
zest [zɛst] *n* (*for life*) Begeisterung *f*; (*of orange*) Orangenschale *f*
zigzag ['zɪgzæg] *n* Zickzack *m* ▷ *vi* sich im Zickzack bewegen
Zimbabwe [zɪm'bɑ:bwɪ] *n* Zimbabwe *nt*
zinc [zɪŋk] *n* Zink *nt*
zip [zɪp] *n* (*also*: **zip fastener**) Reißverschluss *m* ▷ *vt* (*also*: **zip up**: *dress etc*) den Reißverschluss zumachen an *+dat*
zip code (*US*) *n* Postleitzahl *f*
zipper ['zɪpə^{r}] (*US*) *n* = **zip**
zodiac ['zəudɪæk] *n* Tierkreis *m*
zone [zəun] *n* (*also Mil*) Zone *f*, Gebiet *nt*; (*in town*) Bezirk *m*
zoo [zu:] *n* Zoo *m*
zoology [zu:'ɔlədʒɪ] *n* Zoologie *f*
zoom [zu:m] *vi*: **to ~ past** vorbeisausen; **to ~ in (on sth/sb)** (*Phot, Cine*) (etw/jdn) näher heranholen
zoom lens *n* Zoomobjektiv *nt*
zucchini [zu:'ki:nɪ] (*US*) *n(pl)* Zucchini *pl*